FANNIN

ILLUSTRATED G

OF THE

UNITED STATES,

GIVING

THE LOCATION, PHYSICAL ASPECT, MOUNTAINS, RIVERS, LAKES, CLIMATE,
PRODUCTIVE AND MANUFACTURING RESOURCES, COMMERCE,
GOVERNMENT, EDUCATION, GENERAL HISTORY, ETC.

OF THE

STATES, TERRITORIES, COUNTIES, CITIES, TOWNS, AND POST-OFFICES IN THE AMERICAN UNION,

WITH THE

POPULATION AND OTHER STATISTICS FROM THE CENSUS OF 1850,

ILLUSTRATED WITH SEALS AND

THIRTY-ONE STATE MAPS

IN COUNTIES, AND FOURTEEN MAPS OF CITIES.

NEW YORK:
PUBLISHED BY ENSIGN, BRIDGMAN, & FANNING,
156 WILLIAM ST.

1855.

- Notice -

The foxing, or discoloration with age,
characteristic of old books, sometimes
shows through to some extent in
reprints such as this, especially when
the foxing is very severe in the original book. We feel that the contents of
this book warrant its reissue despite
these blemishes, and hope you will
agree and read it with pleasure.

Facsimile Reprint

Published 1990 By

HERITAGE BOOKS, INC.
1540-E Pointer Ridge Place, Bowie, Maryland 20716
(301) 390-7709

ISBN 1-55613-371-5

PREFACE.

The Publishers, in issuing the present work, desire to briefly state some of the causes which have induced them to present it for public patronage.

First, *the Reasons that demand a New Gazetteer of the United States.*
1. Since the census taken in 1840, such extensive and essential changes have taken place in our vast republic, that one would scarcely recognise the present, by the most faithful picture of that ten years ago.

Within that time there have been added to the territory of the republic, by annexation, conquest, and purchase, 833,970 square miles; and our title to a region covering 341,463 square miles, which before properly belonged to us, but was claimed and partially occupied by a foreign power, has been established by negotiation and been brought within our acknowledged boundaries. By such means the area of the United States has been extended during the past ten years, from 2,055,163 to 3,230,572 square miles, without including the great lakes which lie upon our northern border or the bays which indent our Atlantic and Pacific shores. Five new states have been admitted to the Union, and five new territories organized within the same period. Of course old Gazetteers can not faithfully give the present condition of the country.

2. Another reason for a new work is, that existing ones are inaccessible to the masses, by reason of their size and extravagant price, or are small, imperfect in their details and range of subjects, and entirely local in their interest. While the publishers do not claim entire perfection, in the present work, they yet have endeavored most earnestly, in all of these respects, to meet the demands for a new Gazetteer.

Second, *the Plan of this Work.*
The plan is simple; indeed, the design of such a work suggests the plan to be pursued in its compilation. It is not a work of biography, nor of history, nor of science, nor of art, but one descriptive of the country as it is, especially of its geographical and statistical facts; also, with such reference to the commercial and political relations of the principal places named, as may be desirable or practically useful.

PREFACE.

Concise and comprehensive in its plan and composition, the publishers believe it is just such a book as the people desire in a Gazetteer of the United States.

THIRD, *the Reasons that especially commend this Book to the Favor of the Public.*

1. The returns of the late census giving the population of towns, have been procured at considerable cost, from the department at Washington in advance of the publication of the official reports, and are accessible in this work before they can be had through any other source.

2. It contains *Thirty-one State Maps*, executed at great expense, and which, for the first time, are introduced into a Gazetteer. The maps are divided into counties, and will be of invaluable service to persons desirous of correct information of every part of the country.

3. Another new feature of this work is the presentation of beautifully engraved and very expensive *Maps of Fourteen of the principal Cities* of the Union. These must prove a rare acquisition, to those desirous of becoming familiar with the topography of our great and most important cities.

4. The *price* of the present volume being only *one half* that of works of a similar character, places it within the means of the multitude; and the publishers are confident they will cheerfully respond to efforts to meet their wants, by extending to this Gazetteer a liberal patronage. Indeed, the Maps of States and Cities alone would cost, by ordinary purchase, more than the price of the whole book.

NEW YORK, *June* 1, 1853.

LIST OF MAPS.

EXPLANATIONS AND REFERENCES.

For the purpose of economizing room, the names of the states, the character of the places, direction from the state capital, &c., have been uniformly abbreviated. A few moments' attention will however enable the reader to understand them all. These contractions, with their explanations, will be found in the following list.

Contractions.	Explanations.	Contractions.	Explanations.
Me.................	Maine.	Ind..................	Indiana.
N. H...............	New Hampshire.	Ill...................	Illinois.
Vt..................	Vermont.	Wis.................	Wisconsin.
Mass...............	Massachusetts.	Ia..................	Iowa.
R. I...............	Rhode Island.	Mo..................	Missouri.
Ct. or Conn.........	Connecticut.	Cal..................	California.
N. Y...............	New York.	Ter..................	Territory.
N. J........	New Jersey.		
Pa.................	Pennsylvania.	co...................	county.
Del...............	Delaware.	dis..................	district.
Md.................	Maryland.	c....................	city.
Va.................	Virginia.	t....................	town or township.
D. C...............	District of Columbia.	p. t.................	post-town.
N. C...............	North Carolina.	p. v.................	post-village.
S. C...............	South Carolina.	p. b.................	post-borough.
Ga.................	Georgia.	p. o.................	post-office.
Fa.................	Florida.	c. h.................	court-house.
Ala................	Alabama.	pop..................	population.
La.................	Louisiana.	ms...................	miles.
Tex................	Texas.	sq. ms...............	square miles.
Ark................	Arkansas.	W...................	Washington.
Miss...............	Mississippi.	N. E. S. W...........	north, east, south,
Tenn...............	Tennessee.		west, indicating the
Ky.................	Kentucky.		point of direction
O..................	Ohio.		from the place re-
Mich...............	Michigan.		ferred to.

NOTE.—There are generally several villages and post-offices in a town in New England, and in a township in New York and the Western States, these villages and post-offices are known by distinct names, for the purposes of convenience. While there may be a number of townships of the same name in a state in different counties, it is a general rule to avoid having more than one post-office of the same designation in a state.

Counties are called districts in South Carolina, and parishes in Louisiana. There are no such marked sub-division of counties in the southern, as exist in the northern states, the dwellings being more scattered; the centre of a district is generally the court-house.

The population is only made out by towns and townships at the census office, so that it is impossible to give the population of each village in their bounds separately. Where no year is stated before the population, it is that of 1850.

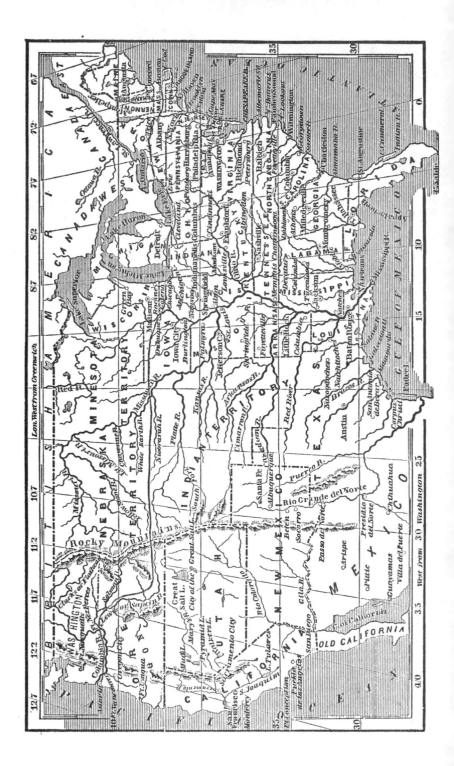

DESCRIPTION OF THE UNITED STATES.

The "United States of America" is the most interesting and important division of the western hemisphere. Comprising a territory equal in extent to that of half of the kingdoms and principalities of Europe combined, with a population exceeded by but three or perhaps four of the European states, and numbering scarce three fourths of a century since it broke loose from the leading-strings of the mother-country, the American republic stands unparalelled in the history of the rise and growth of nations. The territory of the United States lies between the meridians of 67° and 125° longitude west from Greenwich, and the parallels 24° and 49° of north latitude. It is bounded by the Atlantic ocean on the east, and the Pacific on the west; by the British possessions on the north, and the republic of Mexico and the great gulf of that name on the south. It comprises an area of over 3,200,000 square miles. The frontier line has a length of about 10,000 miles, and about 5,000 miles of sea and lake coast.

PHYSICAL ASPECT.—A territory of such vast extent must of course comprise a great variety of surface, soil, and climate. A large proportion of it is not only susceptible of cultivation, but has a fertile soil capable of supporting a dense population. There are but few barrens, and no great deserts, except one in the territory of Utah. It is numerously threaded by navigable streams, besides immense lakes, which not only give fertility to their borders, but are available in bearing the gifts of the soil to domestic and foreign markets, and in bringing back to the inhabitants the products and luxuries of other climes.

MOUNTAINS.—The territory of the United States is traversed by several chains of mountains. The Allegany, or Appalachian range, on the Atlantic side, runs in a northeasterly direction, from the northern part of Georgia to the gulf and river of St. Lawrence, stretching along in uniform ridges, at the distance of from 250 to 80 miles from the seacoast, and following its general directions. It occupies in breadth a space of from 60 to 120 miles, and separates the waters which run into the Atlantic ocean, from those which flow into the Mississippi and its tributaries. The highest elevation in this range, and the most prominent in the Atlantic states, is Black Mountain, in the western part of North Carolina; it is 6,476 feet in height. The general elevation is from 2,000 to 3,000 feet above the level of the sea. The Rocky mountains, situated about 800 miles from the Pacific coast, are on a much grander scale than the Alleganies. Their base is about 300 miles in breadth, and their loftiest summits, covered with everlasting snow, rise to the height of from 12,000 to 18,000 feet above the level of the sea. These vast chains may be considered as a continuation of the Cordilleras in Mexico. The Sierra Nevada is a range of mountains extending through California, and from these branch off to the northwest the Cascade range, which traverses Oregon into the British territories. Both these ranges become more elevated as they extend farther north, where some of their peaks enter the regions of perpetual snow. Still farther west is the Coast range, running almost parallel to, and at a short distance from the Pacific coast. Other minor ranges will be found described in the states in which they are situated.

BAYS.—The principal bays and sounds on the Atlantic border are—Passamaquoddy bay, which lies between the state of Maine and the British province of New Brunswick; Massachusetts bay, between Capes Ann and Cod; Long Island sound, between Long Island and the coast of Connecticut; Delaware bay, which sets up between Cape May and Cape Henlopen, separating the states of New Jersey and Delaware; Chesapeake bay, which communicates with the ocean between Cape Charles and Cape Henry, extending in a northern direction for 200 miles, through the states of Virginia and Maryland; Albermarle sound and Pamlico sound, on the coast of North Carolina. There are no large bays or sounds on the coast of the gulf of Mexico. On the Pacific coast, however, there are several excellent bays, but the principal, and only one necessary to mention, is the bay of San Francisco, in the newly-acquired domain of California.

LAKES.—The chain of inland seas, on the northern boundary, are unsurpassed in any country for size and utility. Their dimensions are as follows :—

Names.	Length in miles.	Breadth in miles.	Circumference. in miles.	Average depth in feet.	Elevation above the sea.
Superior	420	140	1,500	1,000	627
Huron	250	220	1,200	860	594
Michigan	300	80	800	780	
Erie	265	63	700	250	565
Ontario	180	60	500	500	234
Champlain	105	12	235		

Lakes Michigan and Champlain are the only two of these lying wholly within the United States. Lakes Superior, Huron, Erie, and Ontario, have the boundary between the United States and the British provinces, running directly through their centre. The other lakes of any magnitude in the United States are Lakes George, Oneida, Otsego, Skaneateles, Owasco, Cayuga, Seneca, Crooked, Canandaigua, Honeoye, Chautauque, and Canesis, all in New York; Moosehead, Chesuncook, Pemadumcook, Moosetogmaguntie, Sebago, and Schoodic, in Maine; Winnipiseogee, in New Hampshire, and Memphremagog, between Canada and Vermont. In Louisiana, are the great lakes of Pontchartrain, Borgne, Ouacha, Grand, and others formed by the waters of the Mississippi; Bodeau, Cadoe, Bistinoe, Caunisnia, Bayou-Pierre, Spanish, Black, and others formed by the Red river and its branches. In Wisconsin, is Lake Winnebago, formed by Fox river. There are several extensive lakes and everglades also in Florida, of which Okeechobee is the principal. In California are the Tulare lakes, and the Pyramid lake, in the centre of which stands a natural granite pyramid. There is also the Great Salt lake in the territory of Utah.

RIVERS.—The rivers of the United States are numerous, and some of them among the most important, and affording facilities for inland navigation and trade unparalleled in any section of the globe. They may be divided into four great classes: 1st. The streams which rise on the east side of the Allegany mountains, and flow into the Atlantic ocean; 2d. Those south of the Allegany range, which discharge themselves into the gulf of Mexico; 3d. The Mississippi and its wide tributaries, which drain the waters of the vast valley included between the Rocky and Allegany ranges; and 4th. The rivers which, rising on the western declivity of the Rocky mountains, direct their course to the Pacific ocean. The Mississippi is the largest river in the United States, and one of the noblest in the world. Its course, in conjunction with its great auxiliary, the Missouri, is about 4,200 miles. The Mississippi rises west of Lake Superior, in latitude 47° 47′ north, amid lakes and swamps, in a dreary and desolate region, and after a course southeast for about 500 miles, reaches the falls of the St. Anthony. Thence it flows in a southeasterly and then a southerly direction, and discharges its waters into the gulf of Mexico. The principal tributaries of the Mississippi from the east are the Wisconsin, the Illinois, and the Ohio, which is itself formed by the junction of the Allegany and Monongahela, at Pittsburgh. The chief tributaries of the Ohio are the Wabash, the Cumberland, and the Tennessee. The principal tributaries of the Mississippi from the west, are the St. Peter's, the Des Moines, the Missouri, the Arkansas, and the Red rivers. The Missouri enters the Mississippi river about eighteen miles above St. Louis, after a course of 3,217 miles, and being much the longer and larger stream of the two, should properly carry its name to the gulf of Mexico, but the Mississippi, having been first discovered and explored, has retained its name through its whole length. The Missouri is formed of numerous branches, which rise among the Rocky mountains, between the parallels of 42° and 48° north latitude, the principal of which are the Yellow Stone, the Nebraska or Platte, and the Kansas. The most remote are the Jefferson, Madison, and Gallatin rivers. The only obstruction that occurs to its navigation is at the Great Falls, a distance of 2,000 miles from the Mississippi. The principal rivers east of the Alleganies, emptying into the Atlantic, are the Penobscot, Connecticut, Hudson, Delaware, Susquehannah, Potomac, James, Roanoke, Great Pedee, Santee, Savannah, and Altamaha. The principal rivers which rise south of the Alleganies, and fall into the gulf of Mexico, are the Appalachicola, which is formed by the junction of the Chattahoochee and Flint rivers; the Mobile, which is formed of the Alabama and Tombigbee, which unite near latitude 31°, after a separate course of several hundred miles, and the Colorado, Brazos, and Rio Grande del Norte, in Texas. The latter stream, and the Gila which empties into the gulf of California, nearly form the boundary line between the United States and Mexico. The rivers flowing from the Rocky mountains to the Pacific are, the Columbia, in Oregon, which rises near latitude 55° north, and falls into the Pacific ocean, after a course of 1,500 miles. Its principal tributaries are Carke, Lewis, Colville, and Willamette rivers. The Colorado, in California, after a course of 1,000 miles, empties in the gulf of California. The other rivers in California are the Sacramento and San Joaquin, which empty into the bay of San Francisco, and the Buena-ventura, which empties into the bay of Monterey.

CLIMATE.—The United States, though lying within the temperate zone, embraces almost every variety of climate. In the northern parts, the winters are long and severe; snow often falls to the depth of three or four feet, and the cold is so piercing as to oblige the inhabitants to make very diligent provision against it. Spring returns here in April, and the heat is great in summer. In the southern parts of the country, snow is seldom seen, ice is rarely formed in the rivers, and those fruits which shrink from a northern climate, and flourish only in warm regions, are scattered over the soil. In Georgia, the inhabitants may load their tables with oranges, lemons, and other exquisite fruits that grow in their gardens and groves, while in parts of Maine, New Hampshire, and Vermont, even peaches will not flourish. Between these extremities, as in Virginia, Kentucky, Missouri, Illinois, and California, there is a region adapted to the wine-grape, which thrives best in places removed from both the torrid and frigid zones.

PUBLIC LANDS.—The public lands form a very important feature of the national wealth. The property of the soil within the limits of the United States, not owned by the several states, or by individuals, is vested in the general government. They are principally located in the western and southwestern states and territories, and in California and Oregon. The following table exhibits the number of acres of the public domain that have been sold, and remaining unsold and unappropriated, to the first of July, 1852:—

	Acres sold.	Acres unsold.		Acres sold.	Acres unsold.
Ohio	12,646,858	385,264	Utah Territory		113,589,013
Indiana	15,960,902	503,417	Northwest Territory		338,384,000
Illinois	16,008,331	7,271,975	Nebraska Territory		87,488,000
Missouri	10,800,723	24,309,606	Indian Territory		119,789,440
Alabama	11,662,608	15,069,977			
Mississippi	9,869,714	8,807,112	Total	102,113,864	1,387,584,002
Louisiana	3,536,656	9,931,070			
Michigan	9,372,907	19,679,811			
Arkansas	3,328,986	22,069,493			
Florida	1,035,416	30,454,518			
Iowa	2,810,044	24,065,513			
Wisconsin	4,995,023	24,100,106			
California		120,447,840			
Minnesota Territory	19,695	87,365,474			
Oregon Territory		206,349,333			
New Mexico Territ'y		127,383,040			

Congress has granted during the same period, for

	Acres.
Schools and universities	40,588,978
Deaf and dumb asylums	44,691
Internal improvements	10,007,677
Individuals and companies	279,792
Military services	18,709,220
Swamp lands to states	28,156,671

MINERALS.—Minerals abound in the United States in great variety and profusion. It has all the useful, as well as all the precious metals. Iron is very generally diffused, and is very abundant. Coal, both bituminous and anthracite, is found in great quantities, especially in Pennsylvania, Virginia, Ohio, Indiana, Illinois, and Tennessee. Rich copper mines exist in Michigan and some other states, and lead mines in Missouri and Illinois. The gold mines of California seem inexhaustible; quicksilver mines have also been profitably worked there. Granite, marble, and other building stones, are found in every section of the country. Salt springs abound in many parts of the Union, and large quantities of salt are manufactured in New York, Western Pennsylvania, Western Virginia, Ohio, and Illinois; it is also made from sea-water in some parts of New England.

FISHERIES.—The fisheries of the United States are extensive and valuable. About 250 vessels and about 12,000 seamen and landsmen are employed in the whale-fishery. The products of this fishery amount to from 400,000 to 500,000 barrels of oil annually. The cod-fishery is pursued off the coasts of New England, and as far north as Labrador, and about 100,000 tons of shipping are thus employed. The mackerel fishery employs about 60,000 tons of shipping.

COMMERCE.—In the extent and prosperity of its commerce, the United States is second only to Great Britain. There is no part of the globe to which American merchantmen do not find their way; and the coasting and inland trade is carried on to a far greater extent. The foreign exports are confined principally to agricultural products, with naval stores, timber, and other productions of the forest. The imports are European manufactures, principally of the finer descriptions, and the productions of the tropics, as sugar, coffee, spices, wines, &c. The table of imports, exports, revenue from customs, public lands, &c., with the tonnage employed in foreign commerce, and the public debt of the United States, from 1791 to 1852, will be found on the succeeding page, exhibiting the rapid progress of the country.

THE UNITED STATES.

IMPORTS, EXPORTS, REVENUES, TONNAGE, DEBT, &c., OF THE U. STATES, FROM 1791 TO 185$.

Year.	Imports.	Exports.	Excess of Imports.	Excess of Exports.	Tot. Receipts Customs, Lands, &c.	Tonnage.	Debt.
1791....	$52,000,000	$19,012,041	$32,987.959	....	$4,399,473	502,146	$75,463,476
1792....	31,500,000	20,753,098	10,746,902	....	3,652,014	564,437	77,227,924
1793....	31,100,000	25,109,572	4,990,428	....	4,593,012	491,780	80,352,634
1794....	34,600,000	33,026,233	1,573,767	....	5,075,155	628,817	78,427,405
1795....	69,756,268	47,989,472	21,766,796	....	5,926,216	747,964	80,747,587
1796....	81,436,164	67,064,097	14,372,067	....	7,048,114	831,900	83,762,172
1797....	75,379,406	56,850,206	18,529,200	....	8,208,682	876,913	82,064,479
1798....	68,551,700	61,527,097	7,024,603	....	7,762,383	898,328	79,228,529
1799....	79,068,148	78,665,522	402,626	....	7,389,585	946,408	78,408,670
1800....	91,252,768	70,971,780	280,988	....	10,624,997	972,492	82,976,294
1801....	111,363,511	94,115,225	17,247,586	....	12,500,882	1,033,219	87,038,051
1802....	76,333,333	72,483,160	3,850,173	....	13,455,328	892,101	80,712,632
1803....	64,666,666	55,800,033	8,866,633	....	10,932,153	949,147	77,054,686
1804....	85,000,000	77,699,074	7,300,926	....	11,687,231	1,042,404	86,427,121
1805....	120,000,000	95,566,021	24,433,979	....	13,520,312	1,140,369	82,312,150
1806 ...	129,000,000	101,536,963	27,463,037	....	15,508,809	1,208.735	75,723,271
1807....	138,000,000	108,343,150	29,656,850	....	16,359,469	1,268,548	69,218,399
1808....	56,990,000	22,430,960	34,559,040	....	17,038,859	1,242,595	65,196,318
1809....	59,400,000	52,203,231	7,196 769	....	7,749,835	1,350,287	57,023,192
1810....	85,400,000	66,757,974	18,642,026	....	9,299,737	1,424,783	53,173,217
1811....	53,400,000	61,316,831	....	7,916,831	14,363,423	1,232,502	48,005,588
1812....	77,030,000	38,527,236	38,502,764	....	9,674,968	1,269,997	45,209,738
1813....	22,005,000	27,855,997	....	5,859,997	14,068,632	1,666,628	55,962,828
1814....	12,965,000	6,927,441	6,037,553	....	11,017,225	1,159,209	81,487,846
1815....	113,041,274	52,557,753	60,483,521	....	15,411,634	1,368,127	99,833,660
1816....	147,103,000	81,920,452	65,182,548	....	47,403.204	1,372,218	127,334,934
1817....	99,250,000	87,671,569	11,578,431	....	32,786,862	1,399,911	123,491,965
1818....	121,750,000	93,281,133	28,468,867	....	21,002,563	1,225,184	103,466,634
1819....	87,125,000	70,142,521	16,982,479	....	23,871,276	1,260,751	95,529,648
1820....	74,450,000	69,691,669	4,758,331	....	16,779,331	1,280,166	91,015,566
1821....	62,585,724	64,974,382	....	2,389,658	14,315,790	1,298,958	89,987,428
1822....	82,241,541	72,160,281	10,081,260	....	19,481,961	1,324,699	93,546,677
1823....	77,579,267	74,699,030	2,880,237	....	20,049,536	1,336,565	90,875.877
1824....	80,549,007	75,986,657	4,562,350	....	18,903,609	1,389,163	90,269,778
1825....	96,340,075	99,535,388	....	3,195,313	21,342,906	1,423,112	83,788,433
1826....	84,974,477	77,595,322	7,379,155	....	24,763,345	1,534,190	81,054,060
1827....	79,484,068	82,324,827	....	2,840,759	21,230,641	1,620,608	73,987,357
1828....	88,509,824	72,264,686	16,245,138	....	24,243,504	1,741,392	67,475,044
1829....	74,492,227	72,358,671	2,133,856	....	24,224,979	1,260,978	58,421,414
1830....	70,876,920	73,849,508	....	2,972,588	24,280,888	1,191,776	48,565,406
1831....	103,191,124	81,310,583	21,880,541	....	27,452,697	1,267,846	39,123,192
1832....	101,029,266	87,176,943	3,852,323	....	31,107,040	1,439,450	24,322,235
1833....	108,181,311	90,140,433	18,040,878	....	33,003,344	1,601,150	7,001,699
1834....	126,521,332	104,336,972	22,184,360	....	21,076,774	1,758,907	4,760,082
1835....	149,895,742	121,693,577	28,202,165	....	34,163,635	1,824,940	37,733
1836....	189,980,035	128,663,040	61,316,995	....	48,288,219	1,892,102	37,513
1837....	140,989,217	117,419,376	23,469,841	....	18,032,846	1,896,685	1,878,224
1838....	113,717,404	108,486,616	5,230,788	....	19,372,984	1,995,639	4,857,660
1839....	162,092,132	121,028,416	41,063,716	....	30,399,043	2,096,478	11,983,738
1840....	107,141,519	132,085,946	....	24,944,427	16,993,858	2,180,764	5,125,078
1841....	127,946,477	121,851,803	6,094,674	....	15,957,512	2,130,744	6,737,398
1842....	100,162,087	104,691,534	....	4,529,447	19,643,967	2,092,390	15,028,486
1843‡....	*64,763,799	*84,346,480	....	19,582,681	†8,065,326	2,158,602	26,898,953
1844‡....	108,435,035	111,200,046	....	2,715,001	28,504,519	2,280,095	26,143,996
1845‡....	117,254,564	114,646,606	....	2,607,958	29,769,134	2,417,002	16,801,647
1846‡....	121,691,797	113,488,516	8,203,281	....	29,499,247	2,562,085	24,256,495
1847‡....	146,545,638	158,648,622	....	12,102,984	26.346,790	2,839,046	45,659,659
1848‡....	154,998,928	154,032,131	966,797	....	35,436,750	3,154,042	65,804,450
1849‡....	147,857,439	145,755,820	2,101,619	....	31,074,347	3,334,015	64,704,693
1850‡....	178,138,318	151,898,720	26,239,598	....	43,375,798	3,535,454	64,228,238
1851‡..	216,224,932	218,388,011	....	2,163,079	52,312,979	3,772,439	62.560,395
1852‡..	212,613,282	209,641,625	2,971,557	....	49,728,387	4,138,441	65,131,692

* For nine months.　　　　† For six months.　　　　‡ Year ending June 30.

MANUFACTURES.—The manufactures of the United States are various, comprising almost every article known to commerce. From the great variety of soil and climate, producing in abundance every species of raw material, the cheap and inexhaustible supply of moving power furnished by innumerable running streams, combined with the improvements which are every day taking place in machinery, the United States is destined eventually to distance all other countries in its progress in this branch of industry. The entire capital invested in manufactures in the United States on the first day of June, 1850, was $530,000,000; amount paid for labor, year ending as above, $240,000,000; value of raw materials, $550,000,000; value of manufactured articles, $1,020,300,000; persons employed, 1,050,000. For *cotton goods*, there were 1,094 establishments, with $74,501,031 capital invested, using 256,496,000 pounds of cotton, and 121,099 tons of coal; value of all raw materials, $34,835,056; number of persons employed, 92,286, producing 763,678,407 yards of sheeting, &c., valued at $61,869,184. For *woollen goods*, there were 1,559 establishments, with $28,118,650 capital invested, using 70,862,829 pounds of wool, and 46,370 tons of coal; value of all raw materials, $25,755,988; number of persons employed, 39,252, producing 82,206,652 yards of cloth, valued at $43,207,555. For the production and manufacture of *iron*, there were 1,190 establishments, with $49,258,006 capital invested, employing 57,294 persons, producing 564,755 tons of pig iron, and manufacturing 322,745 tons of castings and 278,044 tons of wrought iron; using 1,374,196 tons of mineral coal and 71,089,814 bushels of coke and charcoal; value of raw material, fuel, &c., used, $27,049,753; value of entire products, $54,604,006. For the production of *malt and spirituous liquors*, there were $8,334,254 capital invested, employing 5,487 persons, consuming 17,582,240 bushels of grain, &c., producing 1,177,924 barrels of ale, &c., 42,133,955 gallons of whiskey and high wines, and 6,500,500 gallons of rum.

POPULATION.—The first census was taken in 1790, since which period there have been six decennial enumerations. Their results are as follows:—

Census Year.	White Persons.	Colored Persons. Free.	Slave.	Total. Population.	Ratio of Increase per cent.
1790	3,172,464	59,466	697,897	3,929,827	
1800	4,304,489	108,395	893,041	5,305,925	35.01
1810	5,862,004	186,446	1,191,364	7,239,814	36.45
1820	7,872,711	238,197	1,543,688	9,654,596	33.12
1830	10,537,178	319,599	2,009,043	12,866,020	33.48
1840	14,189,705	386,295	2,487,355	17,063,355	32.67
1850	19,467,537	426,762	3,204,089	23,263,488	36.25

The following table contains some of the more important details of the population from the census of 1850, classified by states and territories:—

STATES.	Dwellings.	Families.	White Males.	White Females.	Colored Males.	Colored Females.	Total Free Population.	Slaves.	Deaths in 1850.	Farms in Cultivation.	Manufacturing Establishments.*	Rep. in Cong.†
Alabama	73,070	73,786	219,728	106,770	1,047	1,225	428,779	342,892	9,084	41,964	1,022	7
Arkansas	29,252	28,416	85,699	76,369	318	271	162,657	46,982	2,987	17,758	271	2
California	No returns.				Estimated at		165,000					2
Connecticut	64,013	73,448	180,001	183,304	3,749	3,737	370,791		5,781	22,445	3,918	4
Delaware	15,290	15,439	35,771	35,518	8,989	8,968	89,246	2,289	1,209	6,063	513	1
Florida	9,022	9,117	25,674	21,493	420	505	48,092	39,309	933	4,304	121	1
Georgia	91,011	91,471	266,096	255,342	1,368	1,512	524,318	381,681	9,920	51,759	1,407	8
Illinois	146,544	149,153	445,644	400,460	2,756	2,610	851,470		11,619	76,208	3,099	9
Indiana	170,178	171,564	506,408	471,220	5,472	5,316	988,416		12,728	93,896	4,326	11
Iowa	32,962	35,517	100,885	90,994	168	167	192,214		2,044	14,805	482	2
Kentucky	130,769	132,920	392,840	368,848	4,771	4,965	771,424	210,981	15,206	74,777	3,471	10
Louisiana	49,101	54,112	141,059	114,357	7,598	9,939	272,953	244,786	11,948	18,422	1,021	4
Maine	95,797	103,787	296,788	285,404	705	620	583,188		7,545	46,760	3,682	6
Maryland	81,708	87,384	211,493	207,005	34,914	39,163	492,667	90,368	9,594	21,860	3,863	6
Massachusetts	152,835	192,679	484,284	501,420	4,314	4,481	994,499		19,414	34,235	9,637	11
Michigan	71,616	72,611	208,471	186,626	1,412	1,145	397,654		4,520	34,089	1,979	4
Mississippi	51,691	52,107	156,260	139,498	473	426	296,657	309,898	8,711	33,960	866	5
Missouri	96,849	100,890	312,986	279,091	1,338	1,206	594,621	87,422	12,211	54,458	3,030	7
New Hampshire	57,339	62,287	155,954	161,535	243	232	317,964		4,268	29,229	3,301	3
New Jersey	81,064	89,080	233,746	232,494	11,542	11,521	489,333	222	4,339	23,905	4,374	5
New York	478,936	566,369	1,545,052	1,564,405	22,978	24,959	3,097,394		44,639	170,621	23,823	33
North Carolina	105,542	106,023	272,789	280,596	13,226	13,970	580,491	288,412	10,207	56,916	2,523	8
Ohio	336,098	348,523	1,004,111	951,997	12,289	12,061	1,980,408		28,949	143,807	10,550	21
Pennsylvania	386,216	408,497	1,142,863	1,115,600	25,057	23,266	2,311,786		28,318	127,577	22,036	25
Rhode Island	22,379	28,216	70,417	78,583	1,660	1,884	147,544		2,241	5,385	1,144	2
South Carolina	52,642	52,937	137,773	136,850	4,110	4,790	283,523	384,984	7,907	29,969	1,473	6
Tennessee	129,420	130,005	382,270	374,623	3,072	3,199	763,164	239,461	11,759	72,710	2,789	10
Texas	27,988	28,377	84,863	69,237	171	160	154,431	58,161	3,046	12,198	307	2
Vermont	56,642	59,753	159,678	153,752	367	343	314,120		3,132	29,885	1,839	3
Virginia	165,815	167,530	451,552	443,752	25,843	27,986	949,133	472,528	19,053	77,013	4,433	13
Wisconsin	56,316	57,608	164,221	140,844	365	261	305,191		2,884	20,177	1,273	3
Ter. Minnesota	1,002	1,016	3,695	2,343	21	18	6,077		30	157	5	
Ter. N. Mexico	13,453	13,502	31,730	29,800	14	3	61,547		1,157	3,750	20	
Ter. Oregon	2,374	2,374	8,142	4,945	119	87	13,293		47	1,164	51	
Ter. Utah	2,922	2,622	6,022	5,308	12	12	11,354	26	239	926	16	
Dist. Columbia	7,917	8,292	18,543	19,479	4,210	5,763	48,000	3,687	846	264	427	
Totals	3,339,163	3,575,602	9,943,415	9,524,122	204,961	221,301	20,059,399	3,204,089	318,305	1,448,495	123,087	234

* Producing each $500 and upward per annum.   † Number of representatives in Congress under the census of 1850.

The annexed table is designed to show the comparative aggregate population of the states and territories according to the census of 1840 and 1850, with the value of the real and personal estate in each in 1850, and the state capitals.

States.	Seats of Government.	Aggregate Population.		Real and Personal Estate.	
		1840.	1850.	Assessed value.	True or estimated value.
Maine	Augusta........	501,793	583,169	$96,765,868	$122,777,571
New Hampshire...	Concord	284,574	317,976	92,177,959	103,652,835
Vermont.........	Montpelier.....	291,948	314,120	71,671,651	92,205,049
Massachusetts.....	Boston.........	737,699	994,499	546,003,057	573,342,286
Rhode Island......	Prov. & Newport	108,830	147,544	77,758,974	80,508,794
Connecticut.......	Hartf'd & N.Hav.	309,678	370,791	119,088,672	155,707,980
New York........	Albany........	2,428,921	3,097,394	715,369,028	1,080,309,216
New Jersey.......	Trenton........	373,306	489,561	190,000,000	200,000,000
Pennsylvania......	Harrisburgh....	1,724,033	2,311,786	497,039,649	722,486,120
Delaware.........	Dover	78,085	91,532	16,406,884	21,062,556
Maryland.........	Annapolis......	470,019	583,034	208,563,566	219,217,364
Virginia..........	Richmond	1,239,797	1,421,661	381,376,660	430,701,082
North Carolina....	Raleigh........	753,419	868,903	212,071,413	226,800,472
South Carolina....	Columbia.......	594,398	668,507	283,867,709	288,257,694
Georgia	Milledgeville ...	691,392	905,999	335,110,225	335,425,714
Florida	Tallahassee	54,477	87,401	22,784,837	22,862,270
Alabama	Montgomery....	590,756	771,671	219,476,150	228,904,332
Mississippi.......	Jackson	375,651	606,555	208,422,167	228,951,130
Louisiana	Baton Rouge...	352,411	517,839	220,165,172	233,998,764
Texas............	Austin	....	212,592	51,027,456	52,740,473
Arkansas...	Little Rock.....	97,574	209,639	36,428,675	39,841,025
Tennessee........	Nashville......	829,210	1,002,625	189,435,623	201,246,686
Kentucky........	Frankfort......	779,828	982,405	291,387,554	301,628,456
Ohio............	Columbus......	1,519,467	1,980,408	433,872,632	504,726,120
Indiana	Indianapolis....	685,866	988,416	152,870,399	202,650,264
Illinois..........	Springfield.....	476,183	851,470	114,782,645	156,265,006
Missouri.........	Jefferson City...	383,702	682,043	98,595,463	137,247,707
Michigan.........	Lansing	212,267	397,654	30,877,223	59,787,255
Iowa	Iowa City......	43,112	192,214	21,690,642	23,714,638
Wisconsin	Madison........	30,945	305,191	26,715,525	42,056,595
District of Columbia	Washington City	43,712	51,687	14,018,874	14,018,874
California........	Benicia ?......	....	165,000	22,123,173	22,161,872
Minnesota Territory	St. Paul's......	....	6,077	....	....
Utah Territory....	Salt Lake City..	....	11,380	986,083	986,083
Oregon	Salem	....	13,293	5,063,474	5,063,474
New Mexico......	Santa Fé.......	....	61,547	5,174,471	5,174,471
Total.........	....	17,063,353	23,263,488	$6,009,171,553	$7,135,780,228

Nativity of the Population.—One of the most interesting results of the census of 1850, is the classification of inhabitants according to the countries of their birth. The investigations under this head have resulted in showing that, of the free inhabitants of the United States, 17,737,505 are natives of its soil, and that 2,210,828 were born in foreign countries; while the nativity of 39,014 could not be determined. It is shown that 1,965,518 of the whole number of foreign-born inhabitants were residents of the free states, and 245,310 of the slave states. It is found that the persons of foreign birth form 11.06 per cent. of the whole free population. The countries whence have been derived the largest portions of these additions to our population, and their relative proportion to each other, appear in the following statement:—

Natives of Ireland in the United States in 1850		....	961,719	43.04 per cent.
Natives of Germany	do.	do.................	573,225	25.09 do.
Natives of England	do.	do.................	278,675	12.06 do.
Natives of British America	do.	do.................	147,700	6.68 do.
Natives of Scotland	do.	do.................	70,550	3.17 do.
Natives of France	do.	do	54,069	2.44 do.
Natives of Wales	do.	do.................	29,868	1.34 do.
All other countries	do.	do.................	95,022	4.47 do.
			2,210,828	

Another interesting branch of this inquiry is that which concerns the inter-migration of our native citizens among the states. The facts developed show how far one section has impressed its own characteristics and peculiar customs on others. It is found that out of 17,736,792 free inhabitants, 4,112,433 have migrated and settled beyond the states of their birth. Three hundred and thirty-five thousand natives of Virginia, equal to 26 per cent. of the whole, have found homes outside of her own borders. South Carolina has sent forth 163,000, which is 36 per cent. of all native citizens of that state living in the United States at the date of the census, and the very remarkable proportion of 59 per cent. of the number remaining in the state of their nativity. North Carolina has lost 261,575 free inhabitants, equal to 31 per cent. by emigration. Among the northern states, Vermont and Connecticut have contributed most largely to the settlement of other parts of the country. Their proportion, about 25 per cent. of their native citizens, would exceed, perhaps, that of either of the southern states already mentioned, were the number of slaves in the latter admitted as an element of the calculation.

Persons subject to Misfortune.—There were in 1850, 5,027 white males, 4,058 females, and 632 colored, *deaf and dumb* in the United States, being an average of one to each 2,151 persons among the whites, and of one to each 3,005 of the free colored, and one to each 6,552 among the slaves. Of *blind*, there were 4,519 males, 3,478 females, and 1,705 colored, averaging one to each 2,445 among the white population, one to 870 of the free colored, and one to 2,645 of slaves. Of *insane*, there were 7,697 males, 7,459 females, and 612 colored, averaging one to each 1,290 among the whites, one to 1,338 of free colored, and one to 11,010 of slaves. Of *idiots*, there were 8,276 males, 5,954 females, and 1,476 colored, averaging among the whites one in each 1,374, of free colored one in 985, and of slave one in 3,080.

Pauperism.—The whole number of persons who had received the benefit of the public funds of the different states for the benefit of indigent persons, for the year ending June 30, 1850, amounted to 134,972. Of this number there were 68,538 of foreign birth, and 66,434 Americans; while of the whole number receiving support on the first day of June, there were 36,916 natives and 13,437 foreigners, making a total of 50,353 persons. Of those termed Americans, many are free persons of color. The entire cost of the support of these individuals during the year, amounted to $2,954,806.

Crime.—The whole number of persons convicted of crime in the United States, for the year ending the first day of June, 1850, was about 27,000; of these, 13,000 were native and 14,000 foreign born. The whole number in prison on the first day of June, was about 6,700, of whom 4,300 were native 2,460 foreign.

AGRICULTURAL PRODUCTS, &c.—The agricultural products, live stock, &c., of the United States, according to the census statistics, were, for the year ending June 1, 1850—

Wheat......100,503,899 bus.	Flax,.. . 7,715,961 lbs.		Number of
Rye....... 14,180,039 "	Maple Sugar, 34,249,886 "	Horses.......... 4,335,388	
Indian Corn.592,326,612 "	Cane Sugar..247,581,000 "	Asses and Mules... 559,220	
Oats.........116,507,879 "	Beeswax & ⎰ 14,853,857 "	Milch cows....... 6,392,044	
Peas & Beans. 9,219,975 "	Honey .. ⎱	Working oxen.... 1,699,241	
Potatoes,Irish 65,796,793 "	Silk .... 10,843 "	Other cattle......10,268,856	
Potatoes,sw't. 38,259,196 "	Molasses.... 12,700,606 gals	Sheep 21,721,814	
Barley ..... 5,167,016 "	Wine....... 221,240 "	Swine 30,316,608	
Buckwheat .. 8,956,916 "	Hay........ 13,838,579 tons	Value of live ⎰ $543,969,420	
Flaxseed ... 562,312 "	Hemp...... 35,093 "	stock..... ⎱	
Grass seeds.. 885,790 "	In value.	Acres imp'd. land.118,457,622	
Rice ....215,312,710 lbs.	Orchard products. $7,723,326	Unimpro'd land ⎰ 184,621,348	
Tobacco.....199,752,646 "	Garden products. $5,269,930	in farms..... ⎱	
Cotton ......987,449,000 "	Homemade ⎰ $27,481,399	Their total ⎰ $3,270,733,093	
Wool....... 52,789,174 "	manufactures ⎱	cash value ⎱	
Butter......313,266,962 "	Slaughtered ⎰ ..$109,485,757	Farming im- ⎰ $151,569,675	
Cheese......105,535,219 "	Animals.. ⎱ ..	plements, &c. ⎱	

RAILROADS, &c.—About fourteen thousand miles of railroad are in successful operation in the various sections of the United States, and the same number in progress of construction. They are nearly equal, in the aggregate, to the railroads of all the rest of the world; and if extended in one line, would reach more than halfway round the globe. There are about 5,000 miles of canals in the United States, forming valuable artificial means of navigation for transporting the heavy products of the country; but since the rapid increase of railroad communication, few canals have been commenced. It is within ten years that the first line of telegraph was erected in the United States, and there are now more than 18,000 miles in operation, connecting the most important points of the country with each other, for the instantaneous transmission of intelligence.

EDUCATION.—There is great attention paid to education in most of the states. Common and primary schools are widely distributed, and high schools are numerous. The common schools are supported either by a fund accumulated from various sources, or by taxation; and in the new states and territories 640 acres of the public lands in every township is specially reserved for purposes of education. There are in the United States 130 colleges and universities, 50 theological seminaries, 16 law schools, and 40 medical schools. Nearly 4,000,000 youth were receiving instruction in the various educational institutions of the country in 1850, distributed in about 100,000 schools and colleges, and employing more than 115,000 teachers. At the same period, there were 2,800 newspapers and periodicals published in the Union, with a circulation of 5,000,000, and an annual aggregate issue of 422,600,000 copies.

RELIGION.—There is no established or national church in the United States, religion being left to the voluntary choice of the people. No special privileges or immunities are granted to one denomination beyond another, it being an essential principle in the national and state governments, that legislation may of right interfere in the concerns of public worship, only so far as to protect every individual in the exercise, without molestation, of that of his choice. The following table gives the number of churches, their aggregate accommodation, average accommodation, and total value of church property of the several denominations in the United States in 1850:—

Denominations.	No. of churc's.	Agg. accommodations.	Ave. ac'n.	Value of ch'h property.	Denominations.	No. of churc's.	Agg. accommodations.	Ave. ac'n.	Value of ch'h property.
Baptist	8,791	3,130,878	356	$10,931,382	Moravian	331	112,185	338	$443,347
Christian	812	296,050	365	845,810	Presbyterian	4,584	2,040,316	445	14,369,889
Congregational	1,674	795,177	475	7,973,962	Roman Catholic	1,112	620,950	558	8,973,838
Dutch Reformed	324	181,986	561	4,096,730	Swedenborgian	15	5,070	338	108,100
Episcopal	1,422	625,213	440	11,261,970	Tunker	52	35,075	674	46,025
Free	361	108,605	300	252,255	Union	619	213,552	345	690,065
Friends	714	282,823	396	1,709,867	Unitarian	243	137,367	565	3,268,122
Germ'n Reformed	327	156,932	479	965,880	Universalist	494	205,462	415	1,767,015
Jewish	31	16,575	534	371,600	Minor Sects	325	115,347	354	741,980
Lutheran	1,203	531,100	441	2,867,886					
Mennonite	110	29,900	272	94,245	Total	36,011	13,849,896	384	$86,416,639
Methodist	12,467	4,209,333	337	14,636,671					

GOVERNMENT.—The government of the United States is a confederated republic, each state being independent, and having the exclusive control of all concerns merely local, with its own executive, legislature, judiciary, &c. But the regulation of commerce, the defence of the country, and all the general concerns of the confederacy, are committed, by the constitution, to a general government. The legislative power is vested in a Congress, consisting of a senate and house of representatives. The senate is composed of two members from each state, chosen for a period of six years, and so arranged that one third of the senate is renewed biennially. The members of the house of representatives are chosen every two years. Their number is proportioned to the number of inhabitants, two fifths of the slaves being omitted in the enumeration. The house of representatives represents the people; the senate represents the states. The executive power is vested in a president, who, together with the vice-president, is chosen for four years, by electors from all the states. The principal subordinate officers of the executive department are the secretaries of state, of the treasury, of the interior, of war, and of the navy, the postmaster-general, and the attorney-general. The president must be a native-born citizen, and 35 years of age. The judiciary is composed of a supreme court, of one chief and eight associate judges, of forty-six district courts, held respectively by a district judge alone, and of nine circuit courts, composed of the judge of the district and one of the judges of the supreme court. There are, besides, territorial courts, which are temporary, and lose that character when the territory becomes a state. The present constitution of the United States was adopted in 1789, and has since been amended. It secures to the people the grand principles of freedom, liberty of conscience in matters of religion, liberty of the press, trial by jury, and the right of suffrage in elections.

COLONIAL HISTORY.—The original thirteen states, it is well known, were formerly colonies of Great Britain. The English made the first settlement at Jamestown, in Virginia, in 1607; New York was settled by the Dutch in 1614, and afterward ceded to the English; and at Plymouth, in Massachusetts, in 1620, the first settlement was made by the English in New England. The remaining colonies were principally offshoots from these parent-stems. The dates of their settlements are as follows: New Hampshire in 1623; New Jersey in 1623; Maryland and Delaware in 1627; Connecticut in 1633; Rhode Island in 1636; Pennsylvania in 1640; North Carolina in 1665; South Carolina in 1670; and Georgia in 1732. Among the earliest settlers in North America were many who emigrated from Great Britain on account of civil or religious persecution; men who, being of republican principles, naturally instilled those principles into the minds of their children, and thus laid the foundation of that spirit of resistance to arbitrary acts of power, which kindled the flames of war between the mother-country and the colonies, and ended in the establishment of a powerful republic.

In 1765, a stamp-duty on various articles was imposed by the British parliament on the colonies; but on their remonstrating, this was soon after repealed. But it was subsequently followed by several oppressive acts, against which the colonists remonstrated and petitioned in vain. At length, despairing of redress, a general congress of delegates was called to consult upon the public good. The Congress assembled at Philadelphia, September 4, 1774, and various measures were adopted to obtain justice from the British government. But their petitions were answered by new aggressions, and their remonstrances were replied to by sending arms to intimidate them, and to coerce them into submission to arbitrary power. The alternate presented was, WAR or SLAVERY. The colonists chose the former, and made vigorous preparations for the coming storm. The first martyr-blood of the Revolution flowed at Concord and Lexington, Massachusetts, April 19, 1775. The church-bells rang throughout the neighboring region, and the people seized arms and flocked to Boston by hundreds. On the 17th of June following, the battle of Bunker's Hill occurred between 1,500 Americans and about 3,000 British regulars. The enemy was three times repulsed, but at length the Americans were compelled to retreat across Charlestown Neck. Among the Americans slain was the brave General Warren. The loss of the Americans was 450; that of the British upward of 1,000. About the time of the battle of Bunker's Hill, Washington was appointed commander-in-chief, and Congress adopted the army collected at Boston, under the name of the "continental army." He took the command about the first of July, and proceeded to invest Boston. In March following, the British under General Howe evacuated the town, and New England became freed from foreign soldiery. The battles at Lexington and Bunker's Hill had aroused the minds of the colonists to a more determined resistance; and when, in the spring of 1776, intelligence was received of the intention of the king to subdue them at all hazards, public opinion soon became decidedly in favor of union and independence. A resolution was adopted by Congress, on the 9th of June, that "the united colonies are, and ought to be, free and independent states; that they are absolved from all allegiance to the British crown; and that all political connection between them and the state of Great Britain is, and ought to be, totally dissolved." This bold proposition was soon after followed by the appointment of a committee to draft a declaration of independence. This committee consisted of Thomas Jefferson, John Adams, Benjamin Franklin, Roger Sherman, and Robert R. Livingston. The draft was made by Jefferson, and after a few verbal alterations by Dr. Franklin and Mr. Adams, it was submitted to Congress on the 28th of June. It was laid upon the table until the 1st of July, when it was taken up in committee of the whole, and after several amendments were made, nine states voted for independence. The assemblies of Maryland and Pennsylvania refused their concurrence; but conventions of the people having been called, majorities were obtained, and on the 4th of July, votes from all the colonies were procured in its favor, and the thirteen united colonies were declared free and independent states. The contest thus auspiciously commenced, was continued with varied success—victory sometimes perching upon the banner of the patriots, and sometimes rout and disaster—till the defeat and surrender of Cornwallis, with his whole army, at Yorktown, October 19, 1781, proved the death-blow to British power in the United States, and a cessation of hostilities was soon after proclaimed. A preliminary treaty of peace between the United States and Great Britain, was signed on the 20th of January, 1783, and on the 3d of September following, a definite treaty was signed, and speedily ratified, and the United States declared to be "a free and independent nation."

FEDERAL HISTORY.—The year subsequent to the declaration of independence, the united colonies had entered into a compact for the general good, and adopted articles of confederation as organic law for the whole. But when peace returned, and commerce and the arts began to revive, they were found too defective for sound and efficient government, and accordingly, in May, 1787, delegates from the several states met at Philadelphia, and adopted the present federal constitution on the 17th of September following. The government was organized under it, and George Washington, who had commanded the American army through the trying times of the Revolution, was elected the first president. He was inaugurated in the city of New York, on the 30th of April, 1789. Washington filled the presidential chair eight consecutive years, and within that time established a wise financial and foreign policy for the government—the chief features of which were, an economical expenditure, a judicious tariff for revenue, and strict neutrality in relation to the wars of nations in the eastern hemisphere. Vermont, Kentucky, and Tennessee, were admitted into the Union during Washington's administration. Our neutral policy irritated the French, and they not only committed aggressions upon our commerce, but threatened us with invasion. John Adams succeeded Washington in 1797, and in view of the threats of the French, he raised an army and increased the navy. Washington was appointed to the command of the former, but he died soon after. Happily for humanity, the services of the army were not needed. Thomas Jefferson succeeded John Adams as president of the United States in 1801. During his administration a treaty was effected with France (then ruled by Napoleon as first-consul) for the cession of Louisiana to the United States, for which our government paid fifteen millions of dollars. The energetic measures of President Jefferson, made the commercial and political influence of the United States seriously felt in Europe. The scar which England received, in her contest with America during the Revolution, still mortified her pride, and the growing commercial importance of the new republic excited her fiercest jealousy. In her impotent wrath, she committed aggression after aggression, until at length they could no longer be borne with honor; and during the fourth year of Mr. Madison's administration (which succeeded Mr. Jefferson's, in 1809), war was formally declared against Great Britain. This war was continued until February, 1815, when peace was restored, a treaty having been agreed to at Ghent, by commissioners appointed by both powers. During Mr. Madison's administration, Ohio, Louisiana, and Indiana, were admitted into the Union. The total expenditures of the United States government during the war, may be stated in round numbers at $100,000,000, and the loss of lives at about 30,000 persons. The war with England had scarcely closed, when the depredations upon our commerce by the Algerine corsairs, rendered it necessary to declare war against that power. A squadron under Commodore Decatur sailed for the Mediterranean in May, 1815, and in a very short time he obtained payment for property destroyed, and treaties highly advantageous to the United States from the dey of Algiers, and the beys of Tunis and Tripoli. James Monroe succeeded Mr. Madison in the presidential chair in 1817. His administration (which lasted eight years) was a quiet one, and no foreign war disturbed the repose of our people. A brief war with the Seminole Indians occurred in 1818; and in 1819 Spain ceded to the United States the whole of East and West Florida, and the adjacent islands. During Mr. Monroe's administration, Mississippi, Illinois, Alabama, Maine, and Missouri, were admitted into the Union. On the admission of the latter state, in 1820, the slavery question first arrayed the North and South as antagonists upon sectional grounds. In 1822, Congress, by an almost unanimous vote, acknowledged the independence of the South American republics. John Quincy Adams succeeded Mr. Monroe, in 1825, and his administration was one of almost unbroken peace and prosperity. Andrew Jackson succeeded Mr. Adams as president in 1829. A tariff law, passed in 1828, caused much discontent at the south, and a threatened rebellion, called *Nullification*, was manifested in South Carolina in 1831–'32. During Jackson's administration, the Indian "Black Hawk war," occurred, and a second war with the Seminoles commenced in 1835; and Arkansas and Michigan came into the Union. Martin Van Buren succeeded Jackson in the presidential chair, in 1837. It was during his administration that the troubles on our Canada frontier took place, when the sympathizing aid which our people lent to the revolted Canadians, came very near involving us in hostilities with Great Britain. Van Buren was succeeded by General Harrison in 1841, but death terminated his earthly career just one month after he was inaugurated, and John Tyler, the vice-president, succeeded him. During Mr. Tyler's administration a new tariff was instituted; Texas, an independent republic, and Florida, were annexed to our confederacy. James K. Polk succeeded Mr. Tyler in 1845, and war soon after followed between this government and that of Mexico, in consequence of the annexation of Texas. General Taylor, with a small force, was sent to the Mexican frontier of Texas to oppose a threatened invasion; and two severe battles were fought between the Americans, under Taylor, and the Mexicans, at Palo Alto and Resaca de la Palma, on the 8th and 9th of May, 1846. General Scott was also sent to Mexico, and there took the chief command. Taylor captured Matamoras and Monterey, and defeated a Mexican army of four times the number of his own forces, at Buena Vista; while Scott, after securing Vera Cruz, pushing on toward the capital. After several successful battles, he hoisted the American flag over "the halls of the Montezumas." A treaty was finally concluded between our government and that of Mexico, by which California and New Mexico became the property of the United States. Iowa and Wisconsin were admitted into the Union, and the Oregon boundary question settled, during Mr. Polk's administration. General Zachary Taylor was elected the twelfth president in 1848. The discovery of gold in California, and the colonization and founding of a new state on the Pacific coast, were the chief events of Taylor's administration. President Taylor died quite suddenly, on the 9th of July, 1850, and was succeeded in office by the vice-president, Millard Fillmore, whose administration was signalized by the admission of California into the Union, and the passage of the compromise measure. On the 4th of March, 1853, Franklin Pierce entered on the discharge of the duties of the executive office, as the fourteenth president of the United States.

PRESIDENTS OF THE UNITED STATES.

No.	NAME.	RESIDENCE.	BORN.	Installed into office.	Age at that time	Years in the office.	DIED.	Age at his death.
1	George Washington	Virginia	Feb. 22, 1732	1789	57	8	Dec. 14, 1799	68
2	John Adams	Massachusetts	Oct. 30, 1735	1797	61	4	July 4, 1826	91
3	Thomas Jefferson	Virginia	April 13, 1743	1801	58	8	July 4, 1826	83
4	James Madison	Virginia	March 16, 1751	1809	58	8	June 28, 1836	85
5	James Monroe	Virginia	April 2, 1759	1817	58	8	July 4, 1831	72
6	John Quincy Adams	Massachusetts	July 11, 1767	1825	58	4	Feb. 23, 1848	80
7	Andrew Jackson	Tennessee	March 15, 1767	1829	62	8	June 8, 1845	78
8	Martin Van Buren	New York	Dec. 5, 1782	1837	54	4		
9	William Henry Harrison	Ohio	Feb. 9, 1773	1841	68	–	April 4, 1841	68
10	John Tyler	Virginia	March 29, 1790	1841	51	4		
11	James Knox Polk	Tennessee	Nov. 2, 1795	1845	49	4	June 15, 1849	54
12	Zachary Taylor	Louisiana	Nov. 24, 1784	1849	64	1	July 9, 1850	66
13	Millard Fillmore	New York	Jan. 7, 1800	1850	50	3		
14	Franklin Pierce	New Hampshire	Nov. 23, 1804	1853	48			

ILLUSTRATED GAZETTEER

OF THE

UNITED STATES.

AARONSBURGH, p. v, Haines' township, Centre co., Pa., 89 ms. N. W. of Harrisburgh; from W. 181 ms.

AARON'S RUN, p. o., Montgomery co., Ky., 65 ms. E. of Frankfort; from W.

ABBERVILLE, p. o., Lafayette co., Miss.

ABBEVILLE DISTRICT, west part of South Carolina, bordering on the Savannah river. It is about 31 miles square, with an area of 1,000 square miles. The surface is agreeably diversified by hill and dale, the soil generally rich and well watered, and susceptible of profitable cultivation. Courts are held at Abbeville, the chief town. Pop., in 1820, 22,189; in 1830, 28,149; in 1840, 29,351; in 1850, 32,318.

ABBEVILLE, c. h., p. v., seat of justice of Abbeville district, S. C., 97 ms. W. of Columbia; from W. 259 ms. Pop. 371.

ABBEVILLE, c. h., p. v., seat of justice of Henry co., Ala., 211 ms. S. E. of Tuscaloosa; from W. 837 ms. Watered by Yattayaba creek.

ABBEVILLE, p. o., Vermilion parish, La,

ABBEYVILLE, p. v., Medina co., O., 123 ms. N. E. of Columbus; from W. 357 ms.

ABBOT, p. t., Piscataquis co., Me., 70 ms. N. by E. of Augusta; from W. 674 ms. Watered by Piscataquis river. Pop. 747.

ABBOTT'S CREEK, p. o., Davidson co., N. C.

ABBOTSFORD, p. o., Westchester co., N. Y.

ABBOTSTOWN, p. v., Berwick township, Adams co., Pa., 29 ms. s. of Harrisburgh; from W. 88 ms. Watered by Beaver creek.

ABERDEEN, p. v., Monroe co., Miss., 170 ms. N. of Jackson. Watered by Tombigbee river.

ABERDEEN, p. t., Brown co., O., 123 ms. s. w. of Columbus; from W. 460 ms. Situated on the Ohio river. Pop. 807.

ABERDEEN, p. o., Monroe co., Ark.

ABERFOIL, p. o., Macon co., Ala., 158 ms. s. E. of Tuscaloosa; from W. 460 ms.

ABINGDON, p. o., Jefferson co., Iowa.

ABINGDON, p. v. seat of justice of Washington co., Va., 304 ms. s. w. of Richmond; from W. 372 ms. Watered by Holston river.

ABINGDON, p. v., Harford co., Md., 52 ms. N. E. of Annapolis; from W. 62 ms.

ABINGDON, p. o., Lake co., Ill., 243 ms. N. by E. of Springfield; from W. 749 ms.

ABINGTON, p. t., Plymouth co., Mass., 20 ms. s. s. E. of Boston; from W. 438 ms. Pop 5,269.

ABINGTON, p. v., Pomfret township, Windham co., Ct., 39 ms. E. by N. of Hartford; from W 394 ms.

ABINGTON, p. t., Montgomery co., Pa., 109 ms. E. of Harrisburgh; from W., 149 ms. Pop. 1,836.

ABINGTON. p. t., Wayne co., Ind., 72 ms. E. of Indianapolis; from W. 505 ms. Watered by White Water river. Pop. 206.

ABINGTON CENTRE, p. v. Luzerne co., Pa. (now Waverly.)

ABOITE, p. t., Allen co., Ind., 120 ms. N. N. E. of Indianapolis; from W. 555 ms.

ABRAM'S PLAINS, p. o., Granville co., N. C. Pop. 1,767.

ABSCOTA, p. o., Calhoun co., Mich., 120 ms. w. of Detroit; from W. 578 ms.

ABSECUM, or ABSECON, v., Galloway township, Atlantic co., N. J., 95 ms. s. of Trenton; from W. 105 ms. Watered by Absecum creek.

ACADEMIA, p. o., Knox co., Tenn., 193 ms. E. of Nashville; from W. 488 ms.

ACADEMIA, p. o., Juniata co., Pa.

ACADEMY, p. o., Ontario co., N. Y.

ACASTO, p. o., Kane co., Ill., 187 ms. N. by E. of Springfield; from W. 764 ms.

ACCATINK, p. o., Fairfax co., Va.

ACCIDENT, p. o., Alleghany co., Md

ACCOMAC COUNTY, on the eastern shore of Virginia, between Chesapeake bay and the ocean. It is about 20 miles long, and 10 miles wide, with an area of 240 square miles. The surface is generally sandy and flat. Courts are held at Drummond town, Pop., in 1820, 15,969; in 1830, 19,656; in 1840, 17,096; in 1850, 17,890.

ACCOMAC, c. h., p. v., seat of justice of Accomac co., Va., 193 ms. E. by N. of Richmond; from W. 197 ms.

ACCOMAN, p. o. Accomac co., Va., 212 ms. E. by N. of Richmond; from W. 178 ms.

ACCORD, p. o., Ulster co., N. Y., 76 ms. s. of Albany; from W. 306 ms.

ACHOR, p. o., Columbiana co., O., 172 ms. N. E. of Columbus; from W. 278 ms.

ACHORSTOWN, v., Achor township, Columbiana co., O.

ACQUACKANONCK, p. t., Passaic co., N J., 79 ms. N. E. of Trenton; from W. 236 ms. Situated on Passaic river, at the head of sloop navigation. Pop. 2,925.

ACQUINTON, p. o., King William co., Va.

ACRA, p. v., Greene co., N. Y., 47 ms. s. s. w. of Albany; from W. 349 ms.

ACTON, p. t., York co., Me., 91 ms. s. w. of Augusta; from W. 520 ms., near the head waters of Salmon Fall river. Pop. 1,359.

ACTON, t. Windham co., Vt., 90 ms. s. Montpelier.

ACTON, p. t., Middlesex co., Mass., 22 ms. N. w. of Boston; from W. 426 ms. Watered by Assabet river. Pop. 1,605.

ACTON CORNER, p. o., York co., Me., 91 ms. s. w. of Augusta; from W. 520 ms.

ACWORTH, p. t., Sullivan co., N. H., 46 ms. w. of Concord; from W. 460 ms. Watered by Cold river. Pop. 1,251.

ACWORTH, p. o., Cobb co., Ga.

ADA, p. t. Kent co., Mich., 158 ms. N. w. of Detroit; from W. 639 ms. Watered by Grand river. Pop. 593.

ADAIR COUNTY, southern part of Kentucky, having a mean length of about 28 miles, and an area of 800 square miles. The face of the country is generally broken, with a diversity of soil. Courts are held at Columbia, the chief town. Pop., in 1820, 8,765; in 1830, 9220; in 1840, 8,460; in 1850, 9,898.

ADAIR COUNTY, in the northern part of Missouri, and traversed by Chariton river. Area —— square miles. Courts are held at Kirksville. Pop., in 1850, 2,342.

ADAIR'S, p. o. Natchitoches parish, La.

ADAIRSVILLE, p. o., Cass., co., Ga., 156 ms. N. w. of Milledgeville; from W. 633 ms.

ADAIRSVILLE, p. v., Logan co., Ky., 182 ms. s. w. of Frankfort; from W. 706 ms.

ADALINE, p. o., Marshall co., Va.

ADAMS COUNTY, in the south part of Ohio, situated along the Ohio river. It is about 25 miles square, with an area of 550 square miles. The face of the country is very hilly, sloping toward the Ohio; and the soil varying from the poorest to the best, but generally inclining to the former. Courts are held at Adamsville, and West Union. Pop., in 1830, 12,278; 1840, 13,183; in 1850, 18,883.

ADAMS COUNTY, in the westernmost part of Illinois, bordering the Mississippi river. It is 32 miles in length, with a mean breadth of 24, and contains an area of 768 square miles. The western and most extensive slope declines toward the Mississippi, while that of the east gives rise to the streams running into the Illinois river. Courts are held at Quincy. Pop., in 1830, 2,186; in 1840, 14,476; in 1850, 26,508.

ADAMS COUNTY, south part of Pennsylvania, about 20 miles in length, 18 in width, and contains 360 square miles. The surface is extremely diversified by hill and dale, and the soil varying in quality from the poorest to the best, but generally well-watered. Courts are held at Gettysburgh, the chief town. Pop., in 1820, 19,681; in 1830, 21,379; in 1840, 23,044; in 1850, 25,981.

ADAMS COUNTY, in the southwest part of Mississippi, bordering on the Mississippi and Homochitto rivers. It is 40 miles in length, with a mean breadth of about 15, and an area of about 600 square miles. The surface is by hill and dale, the soil fertile and well-watered. Courts are held at Natchez. Pop., in 1820, 12,073; in 1830, 14,919; in 1840, 19,434; in 1850, 18,069.

ADAMS COUNTY, on the east side of Indiana. Watered by Wabash and St. Mary's rivers, and contains 336 square miles. Courts are held at Decatur. Pop., in 1840, 2,264; in 1850, 5,797.

ADAMS, p. t., Berkshire co., Mass., 132 ms. w. n. w. of Boston; from W. 390 ms. Watered by Hoosack river. Pop. 6,172.

ADAMS, p. t., Jefferson co., N. Y., 162 ms. n. w. of Albany; from W. 403 ms. Watered by Sandy creek. Pop. 3,106.

ADAMS, t. Coshocton, co.,O. Watered by Tuscarawas river. Pop 1,419.

ADAMS, t., Guernsey co., O. Pop. 860.

ADAMS, t., Monroe co., O. Pop. 1,092.

ADAMS, t., Seneca co., O., 99 ms. N. of Columbus; from W. 417 ms. Watered by Green creek. Pop. 1,416.

ADAMS, t., Washington co., O. Watered by Muskingum river. Pop. 1,293.

ADAMS, t., Muskingum co., O. Watered by Wills creek, and Muskingum river. Pop. 998.

ADAMS, t., Darke co., O. Watered by Greenville and Panther creeks. Pop. 414.

ADAMS, t., Champaign co., O. Watered by Stony and Tawawa creeks. Pop. 1,123.

ADAMS, p. t.. Hillsdale co., Mich., 93 ms. s. w. of Detroit; from W. 533 ms. Pop. 1,129.

ADAMS, p. t., Decatur co., Ind., 54 ms. s. E. by E. of Indianapolis; from W. 557 ms. Pop. 1,593.

ADAMS, t., Hamilton co.. Ind. Pop. 861.

ADAMS, p. o., Irwin co., Ga., 97 ms. s. of Milledgeville; from W. 761 ms.

ADAMS, p. o., Walworth co., Wis.

ADAMS BASIN, p. v., Monroe co., N. Y., 230 ms. w. of Albany; from W. 379 ms. Situated on the Erie canal.

ADAMSBURGH, p. v. Hempfield township, Westmoreland co., Pa., 183 ms. w. of Harrisburgh; from W. 209 ms. Pop. 263.

ADAMS CENTRE, p. o., Jefferson co., N. Y., 162 ms. N. w. of Albany; from W. 403 ms.

ADAMS' MILLS, p. v., Muskingum co., O., 61 ms. E. of Columbus; from W. 346 ms. Situated on the Ohio canal.

ADAMS' MILLS, p. o., Pulaski co., Ky., 76 ms. s. by E. of Frankfort; from W. 587.

ADAMS' RUN, p. o., Colleton district, S. C.

ADAMSTOWN, p. v., Cocalico township, Lancaster co., Pa., 47 ms. s. E. of Harrisburgh; from W. 136 ms.

ADAMSTOWN, p. o., Frederick co., Md.

ADAMSVILLE, p. o., Kingsbury township, Washington co., N. Y., 58 ms. N. of Albany; from W. 430 ms.

ADAMSVILLE, p. o. Newport co., R. I.

ADAMSVILLE, p. o., Crawford co., Pa., 252 ms. N. w. of Harrisburgh; from W. 302 ms.

ADAMSVILLE. p. o., Muskingum co. O.

ADAMSVILLE, p. v., Ontwa township, Cass co., Mich., 175 ms. w. by s. of Detroit; from W. 717 ms. Watered by Christiana river.

ADAMSVILLE, p. o., Franklin co., Mass.

ADAMSVILLE, p. v., McNairy co., Tenn. 139 ms. s. w. of Nashville; from W. 815 ms.

ADAMSVILLE, p. o., Harrison co., Va.

ADAMSVILLE, v., Marlborough district, S. C., 114 ms. E. N. E. of Columbia; from W. 402 ms.

ADAMSVILLE, p. o., Morgan co., Ky.

ADARIO, p. o., Richland co., O.

ADARIO CREEK, p. o., Wemkesha co., Wis.

ADDISON COUNTY, in the west part of Vermont, lying along Lake Champlain. It has a mean length of 25 miles, and an average breadth of 20, and containing 500 square miles. The surface, although not mountainous, is agreeably diversified by hill and dale, the soil fertile, generally well-cultivated, and suitable for grazing and staple crops. Otter river flows obliquely through this county, which, by its numerous tributaries, affords several excellent mill-sites. Courts are held at Maddlebury. Pop., in 1820, 20,620; in 1830, 24,940; in 1840, 23,583; in 1850, 26,549.

ADDISON, p. t., Addison co., Vt., 72 ms. s. w. of Montpelier; from W. 483 ms. Situated on Lake Champlain. Pop. 1,279.

ADDISON, p. t. Washington co., Me., 138 ms. E. by N. of Augusta; from W. 720 ms. Pop. 1,152.

ADDISON POINT, p. o., Addison townships, Washington co., Me.

ADDISON, p. t., Steuben co., N. Y., 227 ms. w. by s. of Albany; from W. 292 ms. Watered by Canisteo and Tuscarora creeks. Pop. 3,721.

ADDISON, p. t., Somerset co., Pa., 153 ms. s. w. of Harrisburgh; from W. 354 ms. Watered by the Youghio-geny river. Pop. 1,665.

ADDISON, p. v., Dupage co., Ill.

ADDISON, t., Oakland co., Mich. Pop. 924.

ADDISON, p. t., Shelby co., Ind. Pop. 1,917

ADDISON, p. t., Gallia co., O. Pop. 924.

ADELINE, p. o., Ogle co., Ill.

ADELL, p. o., Dallas co., Iowa.

ADELPHI, p. o., Ross co., O.

ADELPHIA, p. v. Colraine township, Ross co., O., 67 ms. s. w. of Columbus; from W. 412 ms. Watered by Salt creek. Pop. 412.

ADIRONDACK, p. o., Essex co., N. Y.

ADOLPH, p. o., Chatham co., N. C.

ADRIAN, p. t., seat of justice of Lenawee co., Mich., 67 ms. s. w. of Detroit; from W. 501 ms. Watered by Beaver creek and Raisin river. Pop. 3,006.

ADRIANCE, p. o., Fishkill township, Dutchess co., N. Y., 98 ms. s. of Albany; from W. 358 ms.

ADVENTURE, p. o., Ontonagon co., Mich.

AGAWAM, p. v., West Springfield township, Hampden co., Mass., 98 ms. w. of Boston; from W. 358 ms. Watered by Connecticut river.

AGENCY CITY, p. t, Wapello co., Iowa.

AGNEW'S MILLS, p. o., Venango co., Pa., 220 ms. N. w. of Harrisburgh; from W. 274 ms.

AGUA TRIO, p. o., Mariposa co., Cal.

AI, p. o., Grant co., Ind., 60 ms. N. by E. of Indianapolis; from W. 568 ms.

AID, t. Lawrence co., O., 15 ms. from Burlington, the seat of justice of the county. Pop. 884.

AIKEN, p. v., Barnwell district, S. C., 77 ms. s. by w. of Columbia; from W. 590 ms.

AIKEN'S STORE, p. o., Montgomery co., Ark.

AIR, t., Bedford co., P.

AIR MOUNT, p. o., Clarke co., Ala., 118 ms. s. of Tuscaloosa; from W. 930 ms.

AIRY GROVE, p. v., Lenoir co., N. C., 88 ms. w. of Raleigh; from W. 310 ms.

AKRON, p. v., Erie co., N. Y., 268 ms. w. of Albany; from W. 388 ms. Watered by Muddy creek.

AKRON, c. h., p. o., Portage township, seat of justice of Summit co., O., 123 ms. N. E. of Columbus; from W. 321 ms. Situated on the Ohio and Pennsylvania canals. Pop. 3,266.

ALABAMA, one of the United States, lies between 30° 17, and 35° N. latitude, and 84° 58' and 88° 26' longitude w. from Greenwich; and is bounded N. by Tennessee, E. by Georgia, S. by Florida and the Mexican gulf, and w. by Mississippi. Its superficial area is 50,722 square miles.

Physical Aspect.—The face of Alabama is somewhat varied. Near the gulf of Mexico the country is low and level, embracing numerous swamps and savannas. A large portion of the upland, toward the centre, consists of pine-barrens, thinly wooded, or covered with coarse grass. The soil here is generally sandy and thin. The central part of the state consists of a table-land, with a deep, rich, productive soil. Toward the north, the surface becomes mountainous and hilly, beyond which lies the valley of the Tennessee, where the soil is highly fertile.

Mountains.—The Cumberland or Appalachian range extends into this state from the northeast, and is believed to abound in mineral wealth.

Rivers and Bays.—The principal rivers are, the Alabama, Tombigbee, Black, Warrior, Coosa, Tallapoosa, Tennessee, Chattahoochee, Perdido, Cahawba, and the Mobile. The chief bays are, Mobile, and Bon Secour, which are situated in the southwest part of the state.

Islands.—At the mouth of Mobile bay is a chain of low islands, the three principal of which are, Dauphine, Hurricane, and Horn.

Climate.—The climate of the uplands is generally salubrious, with mild winters, and pleasant summers; but in the southern parts, and along the borders of the streams, it is unhealthy. The extremes of the seasons greatly vary. Those portions of the state lying along the gulf may be regarded as sub-tropical, while those situated in the more elevated and northerly parts, are more or less subject to excessive frosts, and abiding snows. Although the navigation of the rivers is sometimes impeded by ice, it is more frequently the case that it is suspended by excessive droughts.

Productive Resources.—No part of this state will admit of the profitable cultivation of the sugar-cane, unless we except a narrow strip along its extreme border on the southwest. The staple products are cotton, rice, tobacco, wheat, oats, potatoes, and Indian corn. Indigo was formerly ranked among the staple crops, but its cultivation has long since ceased. The farms under cultivation, in 1850, were 41,964. Mines of gold, silver, and iron, are successfully worked in the county of Randolph. Gold also occurs in Tallapoosa, Coosa, Talladega, and Chambers. Silver is found in Tallapoosa; iron in Benton, Clarke, and Talladega; nitre in Blount; and lead in the bed of the Tennessee, on Muscle shoal. Coal abounds in Tuscaloosa, and on the Cahawba, and Black Warrior; marble, granite, limestone, &c., in Clarke, which also produces salt.

Manufactures.—There are upward of 1,000 manufacturing establishments in this state, producing $500 and more each annually. There are several cotton factories established, though they produce only the more common fabrics required for domestic use. Tanneries, flouring, and saw mills, are numerous; and the products of individual industry in the mechanic arts are considerable.

Railroads and Canals.—There are as yet but about 150 miles of railroad completed in Alabama. But new lines are projected, and some of them will be carried through at an early day. The principal canals are, the Muscle Shoal canal, thirty six miles long, and the Huntsville canal, sixteen miles.

Commerce.—The foreign trade of Alabama (mostly exports of domestic produce) amounts to about $12,000,000 annually. The shipping engaged in the foreign trade is about 100,000 tons, and about as much more in the coasting-trade, principally with the northern Atlantic ports.

Education.—Of the educational institutions in Alabama, the university at Tuscaloosa, founded in 1828, is is the principal; besides this are, La Grange college, founded in 1831; Spring-Hill college, founded in 1830; and Howard college, at Marion, founded in 1841. A law-school is attached to the university, and theological seminaries to Spring-Hill and Howard colleges. There are in the state about 200 academies and grammar-schools, and about 1,000 primary and common schools.

Population.—In 1800, estimated at 2,000; in 1810, at 20,845; in 1820, it was 127,901; in 1830, 309,527; in 1840, 590,756; in 1850, 771,672. Number of slaves. in 1820, 41,879; in 1830, 117,549; in 1840, 253,532; in 1850, 342,892.

Government.—The legislative power is vested in two branches, a senate, and house of representatives. The house of representatives consists of 100 members, elected for two years; the senate consists of 33 members, elected for four years, one half retiring every two years. The executive power is vested in a governor, who is elected by the people for two years; and is eligible four years out of six. State election first Monday in August. The legislature meets biennially at Montgomery. The judical power is vested in a supreme court, of three justices; in a court of chancery, of three chancellors, the state being divided into three chancery districts; in circuit courts, each held by one judge, the state being divided into eight circuits, and such inferior courts as the legislature may establish. The judges of the supreme and circuit courts, and the chancellors, are elected by a joint vote of the two houses of the general assembly, for six years. The right of suffrage is possessed by every white male citizen, of twenty-one years of age, who has resided within the state one year preceding an election, and the last three months within the district in which he offers his vote.

History.—The territory of Alabama was formerly held by France, as a part of Louisiana, its first permanent settlement by Europeans having been established by D'Iberville, in 1702, on Mobile bay. Subsequently, four degrees of latitude, of its most northerly part, fell into the possession of the English, and was embraced within the grant to the Georgia colony, in 1732. After the treaty of Paris, in 1763, when Florida was ceded to Great Britain, and the French restricted to the western side of the Mississippi, the southern part of the present state of Alabama was attached to the western division of Florida, the northern division being claimed by Georgia, as a part of the original grant, which embraced the region between the rivers Savannah and Altamaha, extending from their head waters westward to the "South sea." In 1781, Governor Galvez, of Louisiana, invaded and conquered West Florida, which, together with a part of East Florida, then held by the British, once more fell into the hands of Spain, in 1783, who held it until 1798, at which time, all that portion of Georgia south of the Altamaha was ceded to the United States. By act of Congress, subsequent to the adjustment of the boundary between Louisiana and Florida, and our then newly-acquired territory, north of the thirty-first degree of latitude, provision was made for a territorial government, in what is now comprised Mississippi and Alabama, called the "Mississippi Territory." In 1802, cession was made, by Georgia, to the United States, of all her territory on the west, between Chattahoochee and Mississippi rivers, as far up the former as near the thirty-third parallel of latitude, and then to latitude thirty-five degrees by the existing line between Georgia and Alabama. In this condition the Mississippi territory remained until 1817, when it was organized by act of Congress into two states, Mississippi and Alabama. In 1819, the inhabitants of the latter formed its constitution, and in 1820 it was admitted into the Union as an independent state.

ALABAMA, p. t., Genesee co., N. Y., 263 ms. w. by N. of Albany; from W. 388 ms. Watered by Tonawanda creek. Pop. 2,054.

ALACHUA COUNTY, in the northern part of Florida, situated along the east margin of Suwannee river. Although its surface is generally flat and marshy toward the gulf, this county in other parts is undulating, and contains much good land. It is drained by Wakassassee and Withlacoochee rivers, and contains 2,500 square miles. Courts are held at Newmansville. Pop. in 1840, 2,282; in 1850, 2,524.

ALAMO, p. t., Kalamazoo co., Mich. Pop. 420.

ALAMO, p. o., Montgomery co., Ind.

ALAMODE, p. o., Reynolds co., Mo.

ALAMUTCHA, p. o., Lauderdale co , Miss.

ALANTHUS GROVE, p. o., Gentry co., Mo.

ALAQUA, p. v., Walton co., Flor., 161 ms. w. by N. of

Tallahassee ; from W. 1,011 ms. Watered by Alaqua river.

ALAPAHA, p. o., Lowndes co., Ga., 262 ms. s. of Milledgeville ; from W. 861 ms.

ALBA. p. v., Bradford co., Pa., 143 ms. N. by E. of Harrisburgh ; from W. 250 ms.

ALBANY COUNTY, New York, on the west side of Hudson river, and bounded by the Mohawk on the northeast. Its length is about 22 miles, and its breadth 21 miles, containing about 462 square miles. The face of the country is generally hilly, the soil sandy and light, though much of it well cultivated and fertile, particularly along the Hudson. Courts are held at Albany, the capital of the state. Pop. in 1820. 38,116 ; in 1830. 53,560 ; in 1840, 68,593 ; in 1850, 93,279.

ALBANY, city, capital of the state of New York, and seat of justice of Albany county, situated on the west side of Hudson river. 145 ms. N. of New York. and 164 ms. w. of Boston. Rising by a bold ascent from the water, and crowned with the glittering domes of the capitol and city-hall, it presents an interesting appearance from the river, and creates anticipations which are rarely realized on entering its streets ; many of these retain their early irregularity and narrowness, but the more modern avenues and buildings are generally spacious and elegant. The capitol, at the head of State street, a broad avenue. ascending steeply from the river, stands on the east side of a beautiful public square. In the north part of this square, which is divided by a street running from east to west, stands the city-hall and the state-hall, both of white marble, the former adorned with a beautiful gilded dome. The other public buildings are : churches, over thirty in number, the Albany academy, and the Female academy. Few inland cities combine so many natural advantages for trade, improved by such extensive and costly public works, as Albany. It is the terminus of the Erie canal, and the great chain of railroads which connects the central counties of New York, the great lakes, and their shores. The Green Mountain state sends its productions to Albany through Lake Champlain and the Champlain canal. Some of the products brought through these channels, pass through Massachusetts to Boston by railroad ; more are whirled in a few hours to New York, by the gigantic Hudson River railroad, which now sweeps majestically through the solid mountains and rocky headlands which skirt that mighty stream. Steamboats, schooners, and sloops, also convey large cargoes to and from the towns along the route. Pop. in 1790. 3,498 ; in 1800, 5,349; in 1810, 9,356 ; in 1820, 12,630, In 1830, 24,238 ; in 1840. 33,721 ; in 1850, 50,763.

ALBANY, t., Bradford co., Pa. Watered by Towanda and west branch of Mahoopeny creeks. Pop. 1,043.

ALBANY, p. t., Bedford co., Pa.

ALBANY, p. t., Berks co.. Pa., 64 ms. E. of Harrisburgh ; from W. 164 ms. Pop. 1,406.

ALBANY, p. t., Oxford co., Me., 62 ms. w. of Augusta; from W. 597 ms. Pop. 747.

ALBANY, p. t.. Orleans co., Vt., 39 ms. N. of Montpelier ; from W. 555 ms. Watered by Black river. Pop. 1,052.

ALBANY, p. v., Carroll co., N. H. Pop. 455.

ALBANY, t., Strafford co., N. H., 6 ms. N. by E. of Concord ; from W. 486 ms.

ALBANY, p. o., Delaware co., Ind.

ALBANY, p. v., seat of justice of Clinton co., Ky., 126 ms. s. by w. of Frankfort ; from W. 620 ms. Watered by Spring creek.

ALBANY, p. v., Henry co., Tenn., 106 ms. w. of Nashville; from W. 792 ms.

ALBANY, p. v., Baker co., Ga.. 128 ms. s. s. w. of Milledgeville ; from W. 785 ms. Watered by Flint river.

ALBANY, p. o., Whitesides co , Ill.

ALBANY, p. o., Greene co., Wis.

ALBANY, p. o., Tuscarawas co., O.

ALBEMARLE COUNTY, in the central part of Virginia, situated on the northerly side of James river. Length. about 35 ms. ; mean width about 20, with an area of 700 square miles. The chief part of this county is drained by the tributaries of Rivanna and Hardware rivers, the general surface sloping toward James river ; and the face of the country is beautifully diversified by mountain, hill, and dale, the Blue Ridge forming the northwestern border. The soil, of course, varies from productive river alluvion to the most mountainous and sterile. The productive, however, predominates.

Courts are held at Charlottesville. Pop. in 1820, 19,750; in 1830, 22,618 ; in 1840, 22,924 ; in 1850, 25,800.

ALBEMARLE, c. h., p. v., seat of justice of Stanley district. N. C., 146 ms. s. w. of Raleigh ; from W. 383 ms.

ALBEMARLE, p. o., Carroll co., Miss.

ALBEMARLE, p. o., Assumption parish, La.

ALBERTSON'S, p. o., Dauphin co., N. C.. 79 ms. s. E. of Raleigh ; from W. 309 ms.

ALBIA, p. o., Monroe co., Iowa.

ALBION, p. t., Kennebec co., Me., 26 ms. N. E. of Augusta ; from W. 621 ms. Pop. 1,604.

ALBION, p. v., Barre township, seat of justice of Orleans co., N. Y., 250 ms. w. by N. of Albany ; from W. 392 ms. Situated on the Erie canal. Pop. 2,251.

ALBION, p. t., Oswego co., N. Y., 147 ms. w. N. w. of Albany ; from W. 369 ms. Pop. 2,010.

ALBION, p. o., Erie co., Pa.

ALBION, p. o., Providence co., R. I.

ALBION, p. v., Fairfield district, S. C., 34 ms. E. by N. of Columbia ; from W. 475 ms.

ALBION, c. h., p. t., seat of justice of Ashland co., O.

ALBION, c. h., p. v., seat of justice of Edwards co., Ill., 165 ms. s. E. of Springfield ; from W. 731 ms. Pop. 365.

ALBION, c. h., p. v., seat of justice of Noble co., Ind.

ALBION, p. t., Calhoun co., Mich. Pop. 1,665.

ALBION. p. o., Dane co., Wis.

ALBRIGHT'S, p. o., Des Moines co., Iowa.

ALBRIGHTSVILLE, p. o., Carbon co., Pa.

ALBURGH, p. t., Grand Isle co., Vt., 83 ms. N. w. of Montpelier ; from W. 557 ms. Situated on Lake Champlain. Pop.

ALLBURGH SPRINGS, p. v., Allburgh township, Grand Isle co.. Vt., 87 ms. N. w. of Montpelier ; from W. 561 ms. Pop. 1,568.

ALCOVE, p. o.. Fond du Lac co., Wis.

ALDEN. p. t.. Erie co., N. Y., 270 ms. w. of Albany ; from W. 380 ms. Pop. 2,520.

ALDEN. p. o., McHenry co., Ill.

ALDENVILLE, p. o., Wayne co.. Pa.

ALDER BRANCH, p. o., Bradley co., Tenn., 168 ms. s. E. of Nashville ; from W. 593 ms.

ALDER BROOK, p. o., Independence co,, Ark

ALDER CREEK, p. o., Booneville township, Oneida co., N. Y., 107 ms. w. N. w. of Albany ; from W. 412 ms.

ALDER CREEK, p. o., Dubois co., Ind.

ALDIE, p. o., Loudoun co., Va., 139 ms. N. of Richmond ; from W. 42 ms.

ALFDON, t., Ingham co., Mich., 92 ms. w. of Detroit ; from W. 578 ms.

ALEPPO, t., Greene co., Pa. Pop. 1,176.

ALERT, p. o., Butler co., O.

ALEXANDER, p. t., Washington co., Me., 202 ms. E. N. E. of Augusta ; from W. 788 ms. Pop. 544.

ALEXANDER COUNTY, in the extreme south part of Illinois, situated at the junction of Ohio and Mississippi rivers. Length 23 miles ; mean breadth about 17, with an area of 390 square miles. The surface along the borders of the rivers is flat and low, so much so that considerable tracts are annually overflowed. The general character of the soil is fertile, producing excellent crops. Courts are held at Unity. Pop. in 1830, 1,390 ; in 1840, 3,313 ; in 1850, 2,484.

ALEXANDER COUNTY, towards the westerly part of North Carolina. Area, —— square miles. Courts are held at   . Pop. in 1850, 5,220.

ALEXANDER, t., Licking co., O.

ALEXANDER. p. t., Genesee co., N. Y., 258 ms. w. by N. of Albany ; from W. 382 ms. Watered by Tonawanda creek. Pop. 1,927.

ALEXANDER, p. o., Putnam co., Va.

ALEXANDER, p. t., Athens co., O., 78 ms. s. E. of Columbus ; from W. 345 ms. Pop. 1,735.

ALEXANDER. p. o., Burke co.. Ga.

ALEXANDERSVILLE, p. v., Montgomery co., O., 74 ms. w. s. w. of Columbus ; from W. 409 ms. Situated on Miami canal.

ALEXANDRIA COUNTY, situated on the east boundary of Virginia, and formerly comprised that part of the District of Columbia west of Potomac river. Length 10 miles, increasing in width below the city of Alexandria, where it is a mere point to 4 miles opposite the Little falls, in the Potomac. Area, 36 square miles. The surface is somewhat hilly, and the soil thin and poor. Seat of justice, the city of Alexandria. Pop. in 1830, 9,608, including the city ; in 1840, 9,967 ; in 1850, 10,008.

ALEXANDRIA, p. t., Grafton co., N. H., 34 ms. N. W. of Concord; from W. 515 ms. Pop. 1,273.

ALEXANDRIA, p. t., Jefferson co., N. Y., 195 ms. N. W. of Albany; from W. 447 ms. Watered by the St. Lawrence river. Pop. 2,178.

ALEXANDRIA CENTRE, p. o., Alexandria township, Jefferson co., N. Y.

ALEXANDRIA, city, and seat of justice of Alexandria co.. D. C., 7 ms. s. of W. Watered by Potomac river. Seat of Alexandria P. E. Theological Seminary. Pop. 8,734.

ALEXANDRIA, p. b., Porter township, Huntington co., Pa., 98 ms. w. of Harrisburgh; from W. 157 ms.

ALEXANDRIA, t., Hunterdon co., N. J. Pop. 3,811.

ALEXANDRIA, p. o., St. Albans township, Licking co., O., 40 ms. E. by N. of Columbus; from W. 379 ms.

ALEXANDRIA, p. v., Campbell co., Ky., 85 ms. N. N. E. of Frankfort; from W. 506 ms. Watered by the Ohio river.

ALEXANDRIA, p. v., De Kalb co., Tenn., 50 ms. E. of Nashville; from W. 640 ms. Watered by Lickneus creek.

ALEXANDRIA, p. o., Madison co., Ind., 48 miles N. N. E. of Indianapolis; from W. 556 ms.

ALEXANDRIA, p. o., Clarke co., Mo.

ALEXANDRIA, p. o., Benton co., Ala., 129 ms. N. E. of Tuscaloosa; from W. 727 ms.

ALEXANDRIA, c. h., p. v., seat of justice of Rapides parish, La., 291 ms. N. W. of New Orleans; from W. 1,210 ms.

ALEXANDRIANA, p. v., Mecklenburgh co., N. C., 161 ms. s. w. by w. of Raleigh; from W. 398 ms.

ALFONT, p. o., Madison co., Ind.

ALFORD. p. t., Berkshire co., Mass., 145 w. of Boston; from W. 361 ms. Pop. 502.

ALFORDSVILLE, p. v. Robeson co., N. C., 107 ms. s. s. w. of Raleigh; from W. 398 ms.

ALFRED. p. t., York co., Me., seat of justice, together with York, 78 ms. s. w. of Augusta; from W. 517 ms. Pop. 1,319.

ALFRED, p. t., Alleghany co., N. Y.. 249 ms. w. s. w. of Albany; from W. 321 ms. Pop. 2,679.

ALFRED, p. o., Meigs co., O., 101 ms. s. E. by s. of Columbus; from W. 328 ms.

ALFRED CENTRE, p. o., Alfred township, Alleghany co., N. Y.

ALGANSI, c. h., p. t., Branch co., Mich. Pop. 609.

ALGOMA. p. o., Winnebago co., Wis.

ALGOMAC, p. o., St. Clair co., Mich.

ALGONQUIN, p. o., Carroll co.. O.

ALGONQUIN, p. o., McHenry co., Ill.

ALGOOD, Spartanburgh district, S. C.

ALIDA, p. o., Stephenson co., Ill.

ALHAMBRA, p. o., Madison co., Ill.

ALLEGAN COUNTY, situated in the southwestern part of Michigan, on Lake Michigan. Length about 35 miles; breadth, 20, with an area of about 700 square miles. The soil is generally rich alluvion. It is drained by Kalamazoo, Black, and Rabbit rivers. Courts are held at Allegan, the chief town. Pop. in 1840, 1,783; in 1850, 5,125.

ALLAMUCHY, p. o., Warren co., N. J., 66 ms. N. by w. of Trenton; from W. 227 ms.

ALLANDALE, p. o., Habersham co., Ga.

ALLATOONA, p. o., Cass Co., Ga., 130 ms. N. w. of Milledgeville; from W. 659 ms.

ALLEGAN, c. h., p. t., seat of justice of Allegan co., Mich., 161 ms. w. by N. of Detroit; from W. 626 ms. Watered by Kalamazoo river. Pop. 752.

ALLEGHANY COUNTY, situated in the southwestern part of New York. Length, 40 miles; mean breadth, 28, with an area of 1,120 square miles. It is traversed by Alleghany river, along the borders of which there are considerable tracts of alluvion. The surface of the residue of this county is diversified by hill and dale, and is generally well adapted for grazing. Courts are held at Angelica. Pop. in 1820, 9,330; in 1830, 26,218; in 1840, 40,975; in 1850, 37,812.

ALLEGHANY COUNTY, in the southwestern part of Pennsylvania. Watered by Alleghany, Youghiogheny, Monongahela, and Ohio rivers. Length of this county, 32 miles; mean breadth, 18, with an area of 575 square miles. The face of the country is peculiarly diversified by depressed vales, lying within large swelling hills, which are productive to their summits. In the bosom of these hills there exist inexhaustible beds of fine bituminous coal. Excellent lime and building stone also abounds. Courts are held at Pittsburgh. Pop. in 1820,

34,921: in 1830, 50,552; in 1840, 81,235; in 1850, 138,-300.

ALLEGHANY COUNTY, in the central part of Virginia, and drained by branches of James river. Length, 28 miles; mean breadth, 18, with an area of about 500 square miles. This county occupies a high mountain valley, exceeding in some places 1,000 feet above the level of the sea. Consequently, the climate is influenced by mountain exposure and increased elevation. Much of the soil is fertile, particularly along the streams, while in other parts it is barren. Courts are held at Covington. Pop. in 1830, 2,816; in 1840, 2,740; in 1850, 3,515.

ALLEGHANY COUNTY, in the extreme western part of Maryland, bordering on the north side of Potomac river. Entire length, 65 miles; breadth very unequal, averaging about 12½, with an area of about 800 square miles. This county is traversed by the main chain of the Alleghany mountains, which discharge the upper branches of the Youghiogheny into the Potomac. The face of the country is excessively broken and rocky, notwithstanding there is much excellent arable land in the valleys, and some even on the mountain plains. The mountains contain extensive beds of bituminous coal, that of Frostburgh being of superior quality. Courts are held at Cumberland. Pop. in 1820, 8,654; in 1830, 10,609; in 1840, 15,686: in 1850, 22,769.

ALLEGHANY, city, Ross township, Alleghany co., Pa., 200 ms. w. N. w. of Harrisburgh; from W. 226 m. Watered by the Alleghany river. Pop. in 1840, 10,089; in 1850, 21,262.

ALLEGHANY, t., Armstrong co., Pa., Pop. 2,506.

ALLEGHANY, t., Huntingdon co., Pa.

ALLEGHANY, t., Somerset co., Pa. Watered by Rush and Willis' creeks. Pop. 948.

ALLEGHANY, t., Potter co., Pa. Pop. 381.

ALLEGHANY, t., Venango co., Pa. Pop. 1,174.

ALLEGHANY, t., Westmoreland co., Pa. Watered by Alleghany river. Pop. 3,329.

ALLEGHANY, t., Cambria co., Pa., Pop. 1,488.

ALLEGHANY, p. t., Cattaraugus co., N. Y., 297 ms. w. of Albany; from W. 397 ms. Watered by head waters of Alleghany river.

ALLEGHANY BRIDGE, p. o., McKean co., Pa., 206 ms. N. w. of Harrisbugh; from W. 303 ms.

ALLEMANCE COUNTY, situated in the northern part of North Carolina. Area, —— square miles. Seat of justice, Allemance. Pop. in 1850, 11,444.

ALLEMANCE, p. v., Guilford co., N. C., 69 ms. w. N. w. of Raleigh; from W. 341 ms.

ALLEN COUNTY, situated in the northwestern part of Ohio, drained by the tributaries of Auglaize, St. Mary's, and Miami rivers, and the Miami canal. This county is about 24 miles square, and contains 554 square miles. The face of the country is flat, comprising a portion of a vast table-land, generally fertile and productive. Courts are held at Lima. Pop. in 1830, 578; in 1840, 9,079; in 1850, 12,109.

ALLEN COUNTY, in the northeast part of Indiana, along the state of Ohio, watered by St. Joseph and St. Mary's rivers, which unite and form the Maumee, and the Wabash and Erie canal. Area, about 650 square miles. Courts are held at Fort Wayne. Pop. in 1830, 996; in 1840, 3,654; in 1850, 16,920.

ALLEN COUNTY, in the south part of Kentucky, adjoining Tennessee, drained by Big Barren branch of Green river. Length, 23 miles; breadth, 17, with an area of about 400 square miles. Courts are held at Scottsville. Pop. in 1820, 5,327; in 1830, 6,485; in 1840, 7,329; in 1850, 8,909.

ALLEN, p. t., Alleghany co., N. Y., 268 ms. w. by s. of Albany; from W. 341 ms. Pop. 955.

ALLEN CENTRE, p. o., Allen township, Alleghany co., N. Y.

ALLEN CENTRE, p. o., Union co., O.

ALLEN, t., Dark co., O. Pop. 290.

ALLEN, t., Noble co., Ind. Pop. 933.

ALLEN, t., Northampton co., Pa. Pop. 1,156.

ALLEN, t., Union co., O. Pop. 979.

ALLEN, t., Hillsdale co., Mich. Pop. 1,033.

ALLENDALE, p. o., Greene co., Ky.

ALLENDALE, p. o., Barnwell district, S. C.

ALLENS, p. o., Miami co., O., 62 ms. w. of Columbus; from W. 456 ms.

ALLEN'S BRIDGE, p. o., Marion district, S. C., 148 ms. N. E. of Columbia; from W. 437 ms.

ALLENSBURGH, p. o., Highland co., O.

ALLEN'S FRESH, p. o., Charles co., Md., 81 ms. s. s. w. of Annapolis ; from W. 41 ms.

ALLEN'S GROVE, p. o., Lee co., Ill.

ALLEN'S GROVE, p. o., Walworth co., Wis.

ALLEN'S HILL, p. o., Richmond township, Ontario co., N. Y., 217 ms. w. of Albany ; from W. 354 ms.

ALLEN'S SETTLEMENT, p. o., Claiborne parish, La., 396 ms. N. w. of New Orleans ; from W. 1,266 ms.

ALLENSTOWN, p. t., Merrimac co., N. H., 8 ms. s. E. of Concord ; from W. 480 ms. Watered by Suncook river. Pop. 526.

ALLENSVILLE, p. o., Mifflin co., Pa., 76 ms. N. w. of Harrisburgh ; from w. 157 ms.

ALLENSVILLE, p. o., Vinton co., O.

ALLENSVILLE, p. o., Alleghany co., N. Y.

ALLENSVILLE, p. o., Todd co., Ky., 186 ms. s. w. of Frankfort ; from W. 710 ms.

ALLENSVILLE, p. o., Switzerland co., Ind., 102 ms. s. s. E. of Indianapolis ; from W. 534 ms.

ALLENTON, p. o., Washington co., R. I.

ALLENTON, p. v., Wilcox co., Ala., 111 ms. s. of Tuscaloosa ; from W. 903 ms.

ALLENTOWN, p. v., Upper Freehold township, Monmouth co., N. J., 12 ms. E. by N. of Trenton ; from W. 178 ms.

ALLENTOWN, p. o., Allen co., O.

ALLENTOWN, or NORTHAMPTON, p. b., seat of justice of Lehigh co., Pa., 87 ms. N. N. E. of Harrisburgh ; from W. 180 ms. Pop. 3,779.

ALLIGATOR, p. o., St. Mary's parish, La.

ALLIGATOR, p. o., Columbia co., Flor., 110 ms. s. E. by E. of Tallahassee ; from W. 851 ms.

ALLISONVILLE, p. o., Marion co., Ind.

ALLINSONVILLE, p. o., Marion co., Ind., 19 ms. N. by E. of Indianapolis ; from W. 571 ms.

ALLISON, t. Clinton co., Pa., Pop. 411.

ALLISON, p. o., Logan co., Ky.

ALLAMAKEE COUNTY, situated at the extreme northeast angle of Iowa, on the west side of the Mississippi, and traversed by upper Iowa river. Area, —— square miles. Courts are held at Lansing. Pop. in 1850, 777.

ALLOWAY, p. v., Lyons township, Wayne co., N. Y., 183 ms. w. N. w. of Albany ; from W. 354 ms. Situated on Canandaigua outlet.

ALLOWAYSTOWN, p. v., Salem co., N. J., 60 ms. s. s. w. of Trenton ; from W. 171 ms.

ALLSBOROUGH, p. o., Franklin co., Ala.

ALMIRANTE, p. o., Walton co., Flor., 199 ms. w. of Tallahassee.

ALMOND, p. t., Alleghany co., N. Y., 240 ms. w. by s. of Albany ; from W. 314 ms. Watered by Canisteo river. Pop. 1,914.

ALMOND, p. o., Portage co., Wis.

ALMOND GROVE, p. o., Red River co., Tex.

ALMONT, p. o., Lapeer co., Mich.

ALNA, p. t., Lincoln co., Me., 20 ms. s. by E. of Augusta ; from W. 598 ms. Watered by Sheepscot river. Pop. 916.

ALPHA, p. o., Greene co., O.

ALPINE, p. o., Chattooga co., Ga.

ALPINE, p. o., Clark co., Ark.

ALPINE DEPOT, p. o., Morgan co., Va.

ALPS, p. v., Nassau township, Rensselaer co., N. Y., 24 ms. E. by s. of Albany ; from W. 384 ms.

ALQUINA, p. o., Fayette co., Ind., 65 ms. E. s. E. of Indianapolis ; from W. 521 ms.

ALSACE, t., Berks co., Pa., watered by Schuylkill river. Pop. 2,697.

ALSTEAD, p. t., Cheshire co., N. H., 66 ms. w. by s. of Concord : from W. 450 ms. Pop. 1,425.

ALSTON, p. o., Fairfield co., S. C.

ALTAMONT, p. o., Grundy co., Tenn.

ALTA SPRINGS, p. o., Limeston co., Tex.

ALTAY, p. o., Steuben co., N. Y.

ALTO, p. o., Howard co., Ind.

ALTO, p. o., Fond du Lac co., Wis.

ALTO, p. o., Kent co., Mich.

ALTO, p. o., Louisa co., Va.

ALTON, city, p. t., Madison co., Ill., 82 ms. w. by s. of Springfield ; from W. 808 ms. Watered by the Mississippi river. Pop. in 1840, 2,304 ; in 1850, .

ALTON, p. t., Belknap co., N. H., 28 ms. N. E. of Concord ; from W. 509 ms. Situated on Lake Winnipiseogee. Pop. 1,795.

ALTON, p. v., Sodus township, Wayne co., N. Y., 219 ms. N. w. of Albany ; from W. 509 ms.

ALTON, p. o., Penobscot co., Me.

ALTON, p. o., Franklin co., O., 9 ms. N. of Columbus from W. 402 ms.

ALTON, p. o., Denton co., Tex.

ALTON, p. o., Kent co., Mich.

ALTON HILL, p. o., Macon co., Tenn.

ALTOONA, p. o., Blair co., Pa.

ALUM BANK, p. o., Bedford co., Pa., 117 ms. w. s. w of Harrisburgh ; from W. 143 ms.

ALUM CREEK, p. o., Delaware county, O., 31 ms. N of Columbus ; from W. 401 ms.

ALUM CREEK, p. o., Bastrop co., Texas

ALUM ROCK, p. o., Alleghany co., Va.

ALUM RUN, p. o., Monroe co., O.

ALUM SPRINGS, p. o., Rockbridge co., Va.

ALVAN, p. o., Jefferson co., Pa.

ALVIRA, p. o., Lycoming co., Pa.

AMACETTA, p. o., Wayne co., Va.

AMAGANSETT, p. v., East Hampton township, Suffolk co., L. I., N. Y., 270 ms. s. of Albany ; from W. 353 ms.

AMANDA, p. o., Greenup co., Ky., 156 ms. E. N. E. of Frankfort ; from W. 419 ms.

AMANDA, p. t. Fairfield co., O., 38 ms. s. s. E. of Columbus ; from W. 348 ms. Watered by Clear creek. Pop. 1,368.

AMANDA, t., Allen co., O. Pop. 607.

AMANDA, t., Hancock co., O. Pop. 1,162.

AMANDAVILLE, p. o., Elbert co., Ga., 108 ms. N. by E. of Milledgeville ; from W. 582 ms.

AMBER, p. v., Otisco township, Onondago co., N. Y., 142 ms. w. N. w. of Albany ; from W. 336 ms.

AMBERSON'S VALLEY, p. o., Franklin co., Pa.

AMBLER'S MILLS, p. o., Louisa co., Va.

AMBOY, p. o., Ashtabula co., O., 217 ms. N. E. of Columbus ; from W. 344 ms.

AMBOY, p. o., Lapeer co., Mich , 49 ms. N. by w. of Detroit ; from W. 574 ms.

AMBOY, p. o., Washington co., Iowa.

AMBOY, t., Lucas co., O.

AMBOY, p. t., Oswego co., N. Y., now CARTERSVILLE. Pop. 1,132.

AMELIA, p. o., Clermont co., O., 123 ms. s. s. w. of Columbus ; from W. 494 ms.

AMELIA COUNTY, situated in the southeast part of Virginia, along the southerly side of Appomattox river. Length, 30 miles ; mean breadth, about 10 miles, with an area of 300 square miles. Courts are held at Amelia. Pop. in 1820, 11,106 : in 1830, 11,031 ; in 1840, 10,-320 ; in 1850, 9,768.

AMELIA, p. o., p. v., seat of justice of Amelia co., Va., 45 ms. s. w. by w. of Richmond : from W. 162 ms.

AMENIA, p. t., Dutchess co., N. Y., 70 ms. s. by E. of Albany ; from W. 324 ms. Pop. 2,229.

AMENIA UNION, p. v., Amenia township, Dutchess co., N. Y.

AMENIAVILLE, v., Amenia township, Dutchess co., N. Y.

AMERICA, p. v., Wabash co., Ind., 81 ms. N. by E. of Indianapolis ; from W. 570 ms.

AMERICUS, c. h., p. v., seat of justice of Sumpter co., Ga., 104 ms. s. s. w. of Milledgeville ; from W. 760 ms.

AMERICUS, p. o., Tippecanoe co., Ind., 73 ms. N. w. of Indianapolis ; from W. 631 ms.

AMES, p. v., Canajoharie township, Montgomery co., N. Y., 56 ms. N. w. of Albany ; from W. 395 ms.

AMES, t., Athens co., O., 84 ms. s. E. of Columbus ; from W. 327 ms. Pop. 1,482.

AMESBURY, p. t., Essex co., Mass., 44 ms. N. E. of Boston ; from W. 475 ms. Watered by Merrimac and Powow rivers, on the latter of which is situated the village of Salisbury and Amesbury, known also by the name of Amesbury Mills. Pop. in 1840, 2,471 ; in 1850, 3,143.

AMESVILLE, p. v., Ames township, Athens co., O.

AMESVILLE, p. o., Boone co., Ill., 224 ms. N. by E. of Springfield ; from W. 783 ms.

AMESVILLE, p. o., Ulster co., N. Y.

AMICALOLA, p. o., Lumpkin co , Ga.

AMHERST, p. t., Hancock co., Me., 113 ms. N. E. of Augusta ; from W. 695 ms. Pop. 323.

AMHERST, c. h., p. t., seat of justice of Hillsborough co., N. H., 30 ms. s. of Concord ; from W. 495 ms. Watered by Souhegan river. Pop. 1,613.

AMHERST, p. t., Hampshire co., Mass., 82 ms. w. of Boston ; from W. 385 ms. Seat of Amherst college. Pop. 3,057.

AMHERST, p. t., Lorain co., O., 121 ms. N. N. E. of Columbus ; from W. 382 ms. Pop. 1,399.

AMHERST, t., Erie co., N. Y., 283 ms. w. of Albany ;

watered by Tonawanda and Ellicott's creeks. Pop. 4,153.

AMHERST COUNTY, situated in the central part of Virginia, on the northerly side of James river. Length 22 miles; breadth, 19, with an area of 418 square miles. The face of the country is agreeably diversified by hill and dale, and the soil, though widely varied in many localities, is very productive. Courts are held at Amherst. Pop. in 1820, 10,426; in 1830, 12,072; in 1840, 12,576: in 1850, 12,699.

AMHERST, c. h., p. v., seat of justice of Amherst co., Va., 115 ms. w. of Richmond; from W. 176 m.

AMISSVILLE, p. o., Rappahannock co., Va., 116 ms. N. N. w. of Richmond; from W. 65 ms.

AMITTSVILLE, p. o., Monongalia co., Va.

AMITE COUNTY, situated in the southwest part of Mississippi, on the north line of Louisiana. Length, 30 miles; breadth, 24, with an area of 720 square miles. The face of the country is moderately hilly, but contains a considerable alluvion or "bottom land," and much of the surface is covered by pine forests. Courts are held at Liberty. Pop. in 1820, 6,859; in 1830, 7,943; in 1840, 9,511; in 1850, 9,694. .

AMITY, p. v., Aroostook co., Me., 210 ms. N. E. of Augusta; from W. 805 ms. Pop. 256.

AMITY, t., Alleghany co., N. Y., 255 ms. w. s. w. of Albany; watered by Tennessee river. Pop. 1,792.

AMITY, p. v., Orange co., N. Y., 122 ms. s. of Albany; from W. 268 ms.

AMITY, t., Berks co., Pa. Watered by Manatawny and Manokesy creeks, Pop. 1,566.

AMITY, t., Erie co., Pa. Pop. 739.

AMITY, p. v., Washington co., Pa., 225 ms. w. by s. of Harrisburgh; from W. 244 ms.

AMITY, p. o., Scott co., Iowa.

AMITY, p. o., Clark co., Ark.

AMITY, p. o., Johnson co., Ind.

AMITY HILL, p. o., Iredell co., N. C.

AMITYVILLE, p. o., Suffolk co., N. Y.

AMMONIA, p. o., Shelby co., Tenn.

AMOSKEAG, p. v., Goffstown township, Hillsborough co., N. H., 17 ms. s. by E. of Concord; from W. 464 ms.

AMSTERDAM, p. v., Botetourt co., Va., 181 ms. w. by s. of Richmond; from W. 231 ms.

AMSTERDAM, p. v., Carroll township, Jefferson co., O., 131 ms. E. by N. of Columbus; from W. 284 ms.

AMSTERDAM, p. o., Cass co., Ind., 79 ms. N. by w. of Indianapolis; from W. 617 ms.

AMSTERDAM, t., Montgomery co., N. Y., 32 ms. w. of Albany; from W. 400 ms. Watered by Mohawk river. Pop. 4,128.

AMSTERDAM, p. v., Amsterdam township, Montgomery co., N. Y.

AMWELL, t., Hunterdon co., N. J. Watered by Raritan river. Pop. in 1840, 3,071.

AMWELL, t., Washington co., Pa. Watered by Ten-Mile creek. Pop. 1,754.

ANACOSTIA, p. o., Washington co., D. C.

ANADARCO, p. o., Rusk co., Tex.

ANAHUAC, p. o., Liberty co., Tex.

ANAMOSA, p. o., Jones co., Iowa.

ANALOMINK, p. o., Cherokee co., Tex.

ANANDALE, p. o., Butler co., Pa.

ANANDALE, p. o., Fairfax co., Va.

ANAQUASCOOK, p. o., Washington co., N. Y., 40 ms. N. by E. of Albany; from W. 410 ms.

ANCIENT, p. o., Dane co., Wis.

ANCRAM, p. t., Columbia co., N. Y., 45 ms. s. s. E. of Albany; from W. 340 ms. Watered by Ancram and Punch creeks. Pop. 1,569.

ANCRAM LEAD MINES, p. v., Ancram township, 50 ms. s. s. E. of Albany; from W. 345 ms.

ANDALUSIA, p. o., Bucks co., Pa., 113 ms. E. of Harrisburgh; from W. 153 ms.

ANDALUSIA, p. o., Covington co. Ala.

ANDERSON COUNTY, situated in the central part of Kentucky, along the westerly side of Kentucky river. Area 170 square miles. Drained by Salt river and its branches. Courts are held at Lawrenceburgh. Pop. in 1830, 4,520; in 1840, 5,452; in 1850, 6,260.

ANDERSON COUNTY, in the northeasterly part of Tennessee, and watered by Clinch river. Length, about 30 miles; mean breadth, 25, extending over 750 square miles. This county is traversed by Cumberland mountains, from which protrude several spurs; therefore, its surface is mountainous, broken, and

rocky, though possessing much good soil. Courts are held at Clinton. Pop. in 1820, 4,674; in 1830, 5,310; in 1840, 5,658; in 1850, 6,938.

ANDERSON COUNTY, situated toward the eastern part of Texas, between Neches and Trinity rivers. Area, —— square miles. Courts are held at —— Pop. in 1850, 2,884.

ANDERSON DISTRICT, situated in the western part of South Carolina, between Savannah and Saluda rivers, by branches of which it is drained. It is of a rhomboidal shape, about 28 miles on each side, extending over an area of about 800 square miles. Courts are held at Anderson. Pop. in 1830, 17,169; in 1840, 18,493; in 1850, 21,475.

ANDERSON, p. o., Warren co., N. J., 51 ms. N. of Trenton; from W. 212 ms.

ANDERSON, t., Warrick co., Ind. Pop. 392.

ANDERSON, ch., p., seat of justice of Anderson district, S. C., 127 ms. N. w. of Columbia; from W. 546 ms.

ANDERSON, t., Hamilton, co., O. Watered by the Ohio river.

ANDERSON, t. Rush co., Ind.

ANDERSON, p. o., Walker co., Ga.

ANDERSON, p. o., Grimes co., Tex.

ANDERSON, p. o., Clark co., Ill.

ANDERSONBURGH, p. o., Perry co., Pa., 40 ms. N. w. of Harrisburgh; from W. 128 ms.

ANDERSON RIVER, p. o., Spencer co., Ind.

ANDERSON'S MILLS, p. o., Butler co., Pa.

ANDERSON'S STORE, p. o., Caswell co., N. C., 81 ms. N. N. w. of Raleigh; from W. 277 ms.

ANDERSON'S STORE, p. o., McNairy co., Tenn.

ANDERSON'S STORE, p. o., Morgan co., O., 83 ms. s. E. of Columbus; from W. 325 ms.

ANDERSONTOWN, c. h., p. v., seat of justice of Madison co., Ind., 39 ms. N. E. of Indianapolis; from W. 548 ms. Watered by White river.

ANDERSONVILLE, v., Pickens district, S. C., 145 ms. N. w. of Columbia; from W. 547 ms.

ANDERSONVILLE, p. v., Anderson district, S. C.

ANDERSONVILLE. p. v., Franklin co., Ind., 53 ms. s. E. of Indianapolis; from W. 537 ms.

ANDERSONVILLE p. o., Saline co., Ill.

ANDES, p. t., Delaware co., N, Y., 87 ms. s. w, of Albany; from W. 344 ms. Watered by the Papacton, branch of Delaware river. Pop. in 1840, 2,176; in 1850, 2,672.

ANDESVILLE, p. o., Perry co., Pa., 33 ms., w. by N. of Harrisburgh; from W. 121 ms.

ANDORA, p. o., Philadelphia co., Pa.

ANDOVER, p. t., Oxford co., Me., 62 ms., w. s. w. of Augusta; from W. 524 ms. Watered by Ellis' river. Pop. 710.

ANDOVER, p. t., Merrimack co., N. H., 22 ms. N. w. of Concord; from W. 497 ms. Watered by Blackwater river. Pop. 1,220.

ANDOVER, p. t. Windsor co., Vt., 91 ms. s. of Montpelier; from W. 453 ms. Watered by sources of Williams river. Pop. 725.

ANDOVER, p. t., Essex co., Mass., 21 ms. N. of Boston, from W. 454 ms. Watered by Merrimac and Shawsheen rivers. Seat of Andover Theological Seminary. Pop., in 1840, 5,207; in 1850, 6,945.

ANDOVER, p. v., Sussex co., N. J., 64 ms. N. of Trenton; from W. 236 ms.

ANDOVER, p. v., Tolland co., Ct., 19 ms. E. of Hartford; from W. 350 ms. Pop. 500.

ANDOVER, p. t. Alleghany co., N. Y., 257 ms. w. by s. of Albany; from W. 317 ms. Pop. 1,476.

ANDOVER, v. Calhoun co., Mich., 142 ms. w. of Detroit; from W. 577 ms.

ANDOVER, p. v. Henry co., Ill., 130 ms. N. w. of Springfield; from W. 859 ms.

ANDOVER, p. t., Ashtabula co., O. Pop. 963.

ANDREW COUNTY, situated in the northwest part of Missouri, with Nodaway and Missouri rivers on the west. Area —— square miles. Courts are held at Savannah. Pop., in 1850, 9,433.

ANDREW, p. o., Jackson co., Iowa.

ANDREW CHAPEL, p. o., Madison co., Tenn.

ANDREWS, p. v., Marrow co., O.

ANDREWS, p. o., Spottsylvania co., Va.

ANDREWS' BRIDGE, p. o., Lancaster co., Pa., 61 ms. s. E. of Harrisburgh; from W. 106 ms.

ANGELICA, c. h., p. v., seat of justice of Alleghany co., N, Y., 262 ms. w. of Albany; from W. 335 ms. Pop. 1,592.

ANGELINA COUNTY, in the easterly part of Texas, between Neches and Angelina rivers. Area —— square miles. Courts are held at ————. Pop., in 1850, 1,165.

ANGLEY'S BRANCH, p. o., Barnwell district S. C., 97 ms. s. by w. of Columbia ; from W. 603 ms.

ANGOLA, p. o., Collins township, Erie co., N. Y., 306 ms. w. of Albany ; from w. 358 ms.

ANGOLA, p. o., Sussex co., Del.

ANGOLA, p. o. Onslow co., N. C.

ANGOLA, p. o., Lake co., Ill.

ANGOLA, c. h., p. v., seat of justice of Steuben co., Ind., 174 ms. N. N. E. of Indianapolis ; from W. 549 ms.

ANGOSTURA, p. o., Pike co., Ind.

ANGUILLA, p. o., Clay co., Ind.

ANNAPOLIS, p. v., Salem township, Jefferson co., O., 128 ms. E. by N. of Columbus ; from W. 281 ms.

ANNAPOLIS, p. o., Park co., Ind., 68 ms. w. of Indianapolis ; from W. 637 ms.

ANNAPOLIS JUNCTION, p. o., Anne Arundel co., Md.

ANNAPOLIS, CITY, capital of Maryland, and seat of justice of Anne Arundel county, is situated on the southwest bank of Severn river, three miles from its entrance into Chesapeake bay, 20 miles southeast of Baltimore, and 40 miles from Washington. Though located favorably enough for commerce, on a good harbor, the tide of trade and prosperity is drawn too strongly toward Baltimore to allow it to flourish as vigorously as it otherwise might. The site and plan of the city are pleasant and agreeable. The statehouse is venerable and interesting from its Revolutionary associations. Here, in 1783, Washington resigned his commission to the continental congress, one month after the departure of the enemy from the American shores. The walls of the senate-chamber are honored with the portraits of Carroll, Chase, Paca, and Stone, signers of the Declaration of Independence, and of other distinguished contemporaries. In the hall of the house of delegates, is a picture of the surrender of Cornwallis at Yorktown. Aside from these attractions, the capitol is beautiful for its situation and architecture, as well as for the magnificent prospect viewed from its dome. Besides several churches, banks, &c., Annapolis contains St. John's college.

The population, in 1810, was about 2,000 ; in 1820, 2,260 ; in 1830, 2,623 ; in 1840, 2,792 ; in 1850, 3,011.

ANN ARBOR, c. h., p v., seat of justice of Washtenaw co., Mich., 42 ms. w. of Detroit ; from W. 535 ms. Watered by Huron river. Pop. 4,869.

ANNE ARUNDEL COUNTY, situated on the westerly side of Patapsco river and Chesapeake bay, in Maryland, with Patuxent river on the west. Length, 60 miles ; mean breadth, 12, extending over an area of 720 square miles. The face of the country, in general, is agreeably undulating, with a varied soil, mostly of a secondary quality. Courts are held at the city of Annapolis. Pop., in 1830, 28,295 ; in 1840, 29,532 ; in 1850, 32,393.

ANNAWAIKA, p. o., De Kalb co., Ala.

ANNISQUAM, p. o., Essex co., Mass., 39 ms. N. by E. of Boston ; from W. 479 ms.

ANNIN CREEK, p. o., McKean co., Pa.

ANNSVILLE. t., Oneida co., N. Y., 118 ms. N. w. of Albany ; from W. 412 ms. Watered by Fish creek. Pop. 2,688.

ANNSBURGH, t., Washington co., Me., 110 ms. A. of Augusta ; from W. 708 ms. Pop.

ANNSVILLE, v., Dinwiddie co., Va., 57 ms. s. w. of Richmond.

ANNVILLE, p. t., Lebanon co., Pa., 19 ms. E. of Harrisburgh ; from W. 129 ms. Watered by Quitapahilla creek.

ANSELM, p. o., Gallia co., O.

ANSON COUNTY, situated in the south part of North Carolina. on the westerly side of the river Yadkin. Length, about 33 miles ; mean width, 23, covering an area of about 760 square miles. The face of the country is mountainous and rather broken, the river lands fertile, but the uplands thin and unproductive. Courts are held at Wadesborough. Pop., in 1820, 12,534 ; in 1830, 14,085 ; 1840, 15,077 : in 1850, 13,489.

ANSON, p. t., Somerset co., Me., 44 ms. N. E. of Augusta ; from W. 639 ms. Watered by Kennebec river. Pop. 848.

ANSONIA, p. v., New Haven co., Ct.

ANTESTOWN, p. o., Blair co., Pa.

ANTESTOWN, v., Huntingdon co., Pa, 124 ms. w. of Harrisburgh.

ANTES', p. t., Huntingdon co., Pa., 116 ms. w. of Harrisburgh ; from W. 172 ms.

ANTHONY, p. o., Delaware co., Ind.

ANTHONY'S CREEK, p. o., Greenbrier co., Va., 220 ms. w. by N. of Richmond ; from W. 257 ms.

ANTHONY SHOALS, p. o., Elbert co., Ga.

ANTHONY, p. o., Kent co., R. I.

ANTI-BANK, p. o., Hinds co., Miss.

ANTIOCH, p. o., Pickens co., Ala.

ANTIOCH, p. o., Monroe co., O., 274 ms. E. by s. of Columbus ; from W. 126 ms.

ANTIOCH, p. o., Barren co., Ky.

ANTIOCH, p. o., Lake co., Ill.

ANTIOCH, p. o., Gibson co., Tenn.

ANTIOCH, p. o., York co., S. C.

ANTIOCH, p. o., Contra Costa., co., Cal.

ANTOINE, p. t., Clark co., Ark., 86 ms. s. w. Little Rock ; from W. 1,151 ms. Pop. 269.

ANTRIM, p. t., Hillsborough co., N. H., 28 ms. w. by s. of Concord, from W. 460 ms. Watered by Contocook and North Branch rivers. Pop. 1,143.

ANTRIM, p. v., Guernsey co., O., 91 ms. E. of Columbus ; from W. 307 ms.

ANTRIM, t., Crawford co., O., 62 ms. N. of Columbus ; from W. 430 ms.

ANTRIM, t., Franklin co., Pa. Watered by Conecheague creek. Pop., in 1840, 4,061 ; in 1850, 3,005.

ANTRIM, p. o., Alleghany county., Pa., 209 ms. w. of Harrisburgh ; from W. 229 ms.

ANTRIM, p. t., Shiawasse co., Mich.

ANTWERP, p. t., Jefferson co., N. Y., 169 ms. N. w. of Albany ; from W. 438 ms. Watered by Oswegatchie and Indian rivers. Pop. 3,665.

ANTWERP, p. o., Paulding co., O.

ANTWERP, t., Van Buren co., Mich. Pop. 614.

ANVIL, p. o., Clark co., Ark.

AONIA, p. o., Wilkes co., Ga.

APALACHIN, p. o., Tioga co., N. Y., 169 ms. s. w. of Albany ; from W. 283 ms.

APALACHIN, p. o., Tioga co., N. Y.

APOLLO, p. v., Armstrong co., Pa., 193 ms. w. of Harrisburgh ; from W. 216 ms. Pop. 331.

APPALACHICOLA, c. h., p. v., seat of justice of Franklin co., Flor., 135 ms. s. w. of Tallahassee ; from W. 976 ms.

APPANOOSE COUNTY, situated on the south boundary of Iowa. Area —— square miles. Courts are held at Centreville Pop., in 1850, 3,131.

APANOOS, p. o., Hancock co., Ill., 122 ms w. N. w. of Springfield ; from W. 883 ms.

APPERSON'S, p. o., Charles City co., Va.

APPLE CREEK, p. o., Wayne co., O., 99 ms. N. E. of Columbus ; from W. 341 ms.

APPLE CREEK, p. o., Cape Girardeau co., Mo., 212 ms. s. E. of Jefferson city ; from W. 880 ms.

APPLE CREEK, p. o., Morgan co., Ill., 37 ms. w. by s. of Springfield ; from W. 809 ms.

APPLE GROVE, p. o., York co., Pa.

APPLE GROVE, p. o., Morgan co., Ala.

APPLE GROVE, p. o., Polk co., Iowa.

APPLE GROVE, p. o., Meigs co., O.

APPLETON, p. o., Bennington township, Licking co., O., 52 ms. E. by N. of Columbus ; from W. 389 ms.

APPLETON, t., Waldo, co., Me., 35 ms. E. by s. of Augusta ; from W. 625 ms. Watered by the sources of St. George's and Muscongus rivers. Pop. 1,727.

APPLETON, p. o., Perry co., Ill.

APPLETON, p. o., Winnebago co. Wis.

APPLING COUNTY, situated in the southeast part of Georgia, on the southerly side of Ocmulgee and Altamaha rivers. The northern part of this county is drained by Saltilla, and the southern by Suwanee rivers. The face of the country is generally level, with swamps in the southeasterly part. Courts are held at Holmesville. Pop., in 1820, 1,264 ; in 1830. 1,468 ; in 1840, 2,052 ; in 1850, 2,949.

APPLING, p, o., Jefferson co., N. Y., 169 ms. N. w. of Albany ; from W. 410 ms.

APPLING, c. h., p. v., seat of justice of Columbia co., Ga., 111 ms. s. s. E. of Milledgeville ; from W. 597 ms. Watered by Great Kiokee creek.

APPOMATTOX COUNTY, situated on James river, southeast of the central part of Virginia. Area —— square miles. Courts held at Clover Hill. Pop., in 1850, 9,193.

APPOMATTOX DEPOT, p. o., Amelia co., Va., 32 ms. s. w. of Richmond ; from W. 149 ms.

APPOQUIMIMINK, hundred, Newcastle co., Delaware,

16 ms. from Dover; from W. 106 ms. Pop., in 1840, 3,075; in 1850,

APULIA, p. o., Fabius township, Onondaga co., N. Y., 124 ms. w. of Albany; from W. 331 ms.

AQUACKANOCK, p. o., Passaic co., N. J.

AQUASCO, p. o., Prince George's co., Md., 51 ms. s. w. of Annapolis; from W. 44 ms.

AQUEBOGUE, p. v. Riverhead township, Suffolk co., (L. I.) N. Y., 229 ms. s. s. e. of Albany; from W. 309 ms.

AQUEDUCT, p. o., Westmoreland co., Va.

AQUIA, p. o.. Stafford co., Va., 42 ms. s. s. w. of W. Watered by Aquia creek.

AQUILLA, p. o., Franklin co., Ga., 120 ms. N. by E. of Milledgeville; from W. 576 ms.

AQUONE, p. o., Macon co., N. C.

ARANSAS, p. o., Refugio co., Tex.

ARARAT, p. o., Washington co., Ala., 122 ms. s. s. w. of Tuscaloosa; from W. 940 ms.

ARARAT, p. o., Patrick co., Va.

ARATOR, p. o., Pettis co., Mo., 58 ms. w. by N. of Jefferson city; from W. 994 ms.

ARBA, p. o., Randolph co., Ind.

ARBACOOCHEE, p. o., Randolph co., Ala.

ARBUCKLE, p. o., Mason co., Va., 354 ms. w. by N. of Richmond; from W. 367 ms.

ARCADIA, p. o., Washington co., R. I.

ARCADIA, p. t., Wayne co., N. Y., 190 ms. w. N. w. of Albany; from W. 344 ms. Watered by Meed creek. Pop. 5,145.

ARCADIA, v., Arcadia township, Wayne co., N. Y., situated on the Erie canal.

ARCADIA, p. o., Sullivan co., Tenn.

ARCADIA, p. o., Madison co., Mo.

ARCADIA, p. o., Morgan co., Ill., 40 ms. s. w. of Springfield; from W. 820.

ARCADIA, t., Kalamazoo co., Mich., 144 ms. w. of Detroit; from W. 640 ms.

ARCADIA, p. o., Bienville parish, La.

ARCHER, p. t., Harrison co., O., 122 ms., E. by N. of Columbus; from W. 202 ms. Pop. 875.

ARCHIBALD, p. o., Luzerne co., Pa.

ARCOLA p. o., Loudoun co., Va., 144 ms. N. of Richmond; from W. 36 ms.

ARCOLA, p. o., Warren co., N. C.

ARDEN, p. o., Berkley co., Va.

ARENA, p. o., Iowa co., Wis.

ARENDTSVILLE, p. o., Adams co., Pa.

ARENOSA, p. o., Victoria co., Tex

ARENZVILLE, p. o., Morgan co., Ill., 52 ms. s. w. of Springfield; from W. 832 ms.

ARGENTINE, p. o., Genesee co., Mich.

ARGO, p. o., Hall co., Ga.

ARGO, p. o., Crawford co., Mo.

ARGO, p. o., Carroll co., Ill.

ARGOSVILLE, p. o., Schoharie co., N. Y., 46 ms. w. of Albany; from W. 395 ms.

ARGUS, p. o. Montgomery co., Ala., 141 ms. s. e. of Tuscaloosa; from W. 870 ms.

ARGYLE, p. t., Penobscot co., Me., 89 ms. N. e. of Augusta; from W. 684 ms.

ARGYLE, t., Cumberland co., N. C., 74 ms. s. s. w. of Raleigh; from W. 361 ms.

ARGYLE, p. t., Washington co., N. Y., 36 ms. N. of Albany; from W, 416 ms. Pop. 3,274.

ARGYLE, p. o., Jefferson co., Ohio.

ARGYLE, p. o.. McDonough co., Ill., 92 ms. N. w. of Springfield; from W. 865 ms.

ARGYLE, p. o., Lafayette co., Wis.

ARIEL, p. o., Marion district, S. C.

ARIEL, p. o., Wayne co., Pa.

ARIETTA, t., Hamilton co., N. Y., 72 ms. N. w. of Albany. Watered by Canada and Sacondaga rivers.

ARISPE, p. o., Bureau co., Ill.

ARK, p. o., De Kalb co., Ga.

ARK, p. o., Lafayette co., Ark.

ARKADELPHIA, c. h., p. v., seat of justice of Clark co., Arkansas.

ARKANSAS COUNTY, situated in the southeast part of the state of Arkansas, and watered by Arkansas, White, and Bœuf rivers, and Bayou Barthelany. The face of the country is generally level, except the westerly part which rises into eminences. Length, 60 miles; mean width, 40, extending over an area of 2,400 square miles. Courts are held at Arkansas. Pop., in 1830, 1,426; in 1840, 1,346; in 1850, 3,246.

ARKANSAS, t., Arkansas co., Ark. Pop. 584.

ARKANSAS POST, c. h., p. v., seat of justice of Arkan-

sas co., Ark. 117 ms. s. E. of Little Rock; from W. 1,087 ms. Watered by Arkansas river.

ARKANSAS, one of the United States, lies between 33° and 36° 30′ north lat., and 89° 30′ and 94° 30′ west long. from Greenwich: and is bounded north and northeast by Missouri, east by Mississippi river, which separates it from Mississippi and Tennessee, south by Louisiana, southwest by Texas, and west by the Indian territory. Its superficial area is 52,198 square miles.

Physical Aspect.—In the eastern part of the state, say a distance of 100 miles from the Mississippi, the country is low and wet, and much of the land, except along the borders of the streams, is subject to inundation. With the exception of some prairie, the eastern portion is covered with dense forests. The soil here, where arable, is of the most productive kind. In the middle of the state, the surface is uneven and broken, and in the western parts it is mountainous and hilly, interspersed by timber lands, prairies, and barren plains. In some respects, Arkansas may be regarded as a barren country, although along the margins of the streams the soil is generally fertile, but remote from these it is sterile and poor.

Mountains.—The chief mountains in this state are the Ozark, which lie at its northwest corner, rising to a height of some 2,000 feet. A range of hills, called the Black mountains, runs between the Arkansas and White rivers, extending from the latter to the western border of the state.

Rivers and Springs.—The principal rivers that traverse this state, are the Arkansas, Wachita, White, and St. Francis. The Mississippi waters its almost entire boundary on the east. Toward the source of the Wachita, there are hot springs, which are much resorted to by invalids. Their waters are pure and limpid, possessing little or no mineral properties, and, though varying considerably in the range of their temperature, sometimes rise nearly to the boiling point.

Climate.—The climate of the easterly part, particularly on the borders of the rivers, is generally moist and unhealthy; but in the middle and westerly portions it is regarded by the settlers as salubrious. The climate of the southerly part, resembles that of Louisiana, while that at the north is similar to Missouri.

Productive Resources.—The staple products are, cotton, wool, lumber, peltry, wheat, oats, potatoes, tobacco, Indian corn, cattle, horses, and mules. The southern portion of the state is well adapted to the cultivation of cotton. Its mineral productions consists of iron ore, lead, gypsum, salt, and coal.

Manufactures.—The manufactures of Arkansas are confined principally to supplying the immediate wants of the people. The number of manufacturing establishments in the state, in 1850, producing $500 and upward each annually, was 271.

Commerce.—Arkansas has no direct foreign commerce, its staples being shipped principally at New Orleans; but its river trade is considerable.

Education.—There is no collegiate institution in Arkansas. It has about 15 academies and 200 common schools.

Population.—In 1820, 14,273; in 1830, 30,388; in 1840, 97,574; in 1850, 209,639. Number of slaves, in 1820, 1,617; in 1830, 4,576; in 1840, 19,935; in 1850, 46,982.

Government.—The legislative power is vested in a general assembly. consisting of a senate and house of representatives. The senators are elected by the people, by districts, for the term of four years; the representatives, by counties, for two years. The senate consists of not less than 17, nor more than 33 members; the house of representatives of not less than 54, nor more than 100 members. The general elections are holden every two years, on the first Monday in October, and the legislature meets biennially, on the first Monday in November, at Little Rock. The executive power is vested in a governor, elected by the people once in four years; but he is not eligible for more than eight years

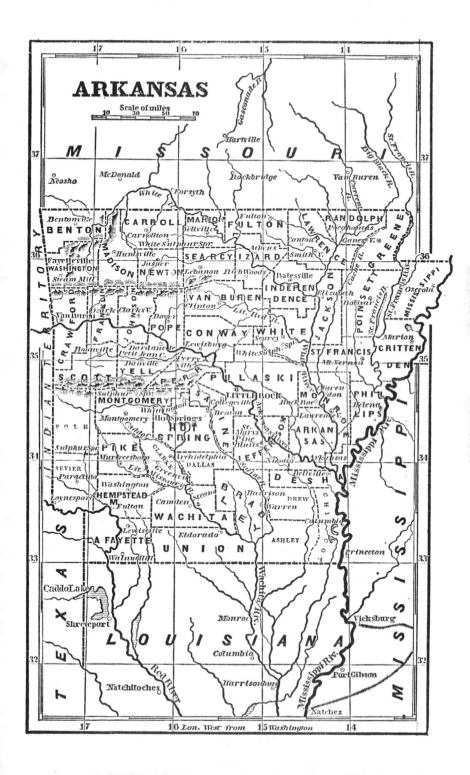

In any term of twelve years. The judicial power is vested in a supreme court, of three justices, in circuit courts, in county courts, and justices of the peace. The judges of the supreme and circuit courts are chosen by the general assembly, of the former for eight, of the latter for four years. Justices of the peace are elected by the people for two years. Judges of the county courts are chosen by the justices of the peace. Every white male citizen of the United States (excepting soldiers and seamen of the army and navy), a resident of the state six months, is entitled to vote at elections.

History.—Arkansas was originally a part of the province of Louisiana, and constituted a portion of that undefined region lying west of the Mississippi, which received not the tread of the white man until the present century, unless visited by De Soto, who explored the valley of the Mississippi in 1541. In the arrangement of territories it was separated from Louisiana and attached to Missouri. It remained in this connection till 1819, when it was erected into a distinct territory, under its present name. The Rocky mountains were its western limits; but by congressional acts in 1824, and by subsequent treaties with the Cherokee Indians, its area was curtailed. In 1836, a convention of the representatives of the people assembled at Little Rock, and adopted a state constitution; and the same year Arkansas was admitted into the Union as an independent state.

ARKPORT, p. v., Hornellsville township, Steuben co., N. Y., 246 ms. w. by s. of Albany; from W. 322 ms. Watered by Canisteo river.

ARSENAL, p. o., Alleghany co., Pa.

ARKVILLE, p. o., Middletown township, Delaware co., N. Y., 83 ms. s. w. of Albany; from W. 393 ms.

ARKWRIGHT, p. t., Chautauque co., N. Y. 328 ms. w. by s. of Albany; from W. 356 ms. Pop. 1,283.

ARLINGTON, p. t., Bennington co., 103 ms. s. w. of Montpelier; from W. 420 ms. Watered by Green river. Pop. 1,084.

ARLINGTON, p. o., Hancock co., O.

ARLINGTON, p. o., Bureau co., Ill.

ARMADA, p. t., Macomb co., Mich. Pop. 1,146.

ARMAGH, p. b. Indiana co., Pa., 158 ms. w. by N. of Harrisburgh; from W. 201 ms.

ARMAGH, t., Mifflin co., Pa., 65 ms. N. w. of Harrisburgh; from W. 172 ms. Pop. 1,742.

ARMENIA, p. o. Scriven co., Ga., 122 ms. E. s. E. of Milledge♦lle; from W. 661 ms.

ARMIESBURGH, p. o., Parke co., Ind.

ARMINGTON, p. o., Tazewell co., Ill.

ARMSTRONG COUNTY, situated in the westerly part of Pennsylvania, and is watered by Alleghany river. Length, 35 miles; mean width, 20, with an area of about 700 square miles. The face of the country is hilly, rocky, and broken, though much of the soil consists of a fertile loam, particularly along the Alleghany river. Courts are held at Kittaning. Pop., in 1820, 10,324; in 1830, 17,695; in 1840, 28,365; in 1850, 29,560.

ARMSTRONG, t., Indiana co., Pa., 167 ms. w. by N. of Harrisburgh; from W. 199 ms. Pop. 1,185.

ARMSTRONG, p. o., Wabash co., Ill., 176 ms. s. E. of Springfield; from W. 708 ms.

ARMSTRONG, p. t., Vanderburgh co., Ind. Pop. 849.

ARMSTRONG'S MILLS, p. o., Belmont co., O., 131 ms. E. of Columbus; from W. 292 ms.

ARMUCHEE, p. o., Floyd co., Ga., 174 ms. N. w. of Milledgeville; from W. 659 ms.

ARNEYTOWN, p. v., Hanover township, Burlington co., N. J., 15 ms. s. E. of Trenton; from W. 176 ms.

ARNHEIM, p. o., Brown co., O., 97 ms. s. s. w. of Columbus; from W. 464 ms.

ARNOLDSBURGH, t., Gilmer co., Va., 352 ms. w. N. w. of Richmond; from W. 320 ms.

ARNOLDTON, p. v., Campbell co., Va., 138 ms. w. by s. of Richmond; from W. 213 ms.

ARNOLDTOM, p. o., Ulster co., N. Y.

ARNON, p. o., Will co., Ill.

AROOSTOOK COUNTY, situated in the northeast part of Maine, adjoining the British provinces on the north and east, on the westerly side of St. John's river. It is traversed by Aroostook and Matawamkeg rivers. The northern part is unsettled, being principally covered by extensive pine forests. Courts are held at Conway. Pop. in 1840, 9,413; in 1850, 12,529.

AROOSTOOK, p. o., Aroostook co., Me.

ARRINGTON, p. o., Williamson co., Tenn.

ARROWOOD, p. o., Spartanburgh district, S. C.

ARROW ROCK, p. v., Saline co., Mo., 72 ms. N. w. of Jefferson city; from W. 986 ms. Situated on Missouri river.

ARROWSMITH'S, p o., Defiance co., O.

ARTHURSBURGH, p. o., La Grange township. Dutchess co., N. Y., 83 ms. s. of Albany; from W. 310 ms.

ARTHURTON, p. o., McHenry co., Ill.

ARTIC, p. o., De Kalb co., Ind.

ASBURY, p. o., Perry co., O., 46 ms. E. S. E. of Columbus; from W. 357 ms.

ASBURY, p. v., Mansfield township, Warren co., N. J., 42 ms. N. of Trenton; from W. 202 ms.

ASBURY, p. o., Fayette co., Ala., 52 ms. N. w. of Tuscaloosa; from W. 854 ms.

ASBURY, p. o., Montgomery co., Tenn.

ASBURY, p. o., La Salle co., Ill.

ASBURY, p. o., Troup co., Ga.

ASCENSION PARISH, La., situated toward the southeast part of the state. and traversed by Mississippi river. Area ———. The surface is level, and annually overflowed; the soil fertile and well-suited for cotton and sugar-cane. Courts are held at Donaldsonville. Pop. in 1840. 6,951; in 1850, 10,752.

ASH. t., Monroe co., Mich. Pop. 1,229.

ASHAPOO FERRY, p. o., Colleton district, S. C.

ASHBURNHAM, p. t., Worcester co., Mass., 53 ms. N. w. of Boston; from W. 426 ms. Watered by Miller's river. Pop., in 1840, 1,652; in 1850, 1,875.

ASHBURNHAM DEPOT, p. o., Worcester co., Mass.

ASHBY, p. t., Middlesex co., Mass., 47 ms. N. N. w. of Boston; from W. 426 ms. Pop. 1,208.

ASHBY, p. o., Coles co., Ill.

ASHBYSBURGH, p. o., Hopkins co., Ky.

Ash CREEK, p. o., Oktibbeha co., Miss.

ASHE COUNTY, situated in the northwest part of North Carolina, and drained by branches of the Great Kanawha and Holston rivers. Length, 64 miles; mean breadth, 120, covering an area of 768 square miles. The face of the country is generally hilly and mountainous, the air pure and healthy, and the soil in many parts productive. Courts are held at Jefferson. Pop., in 1820, 4,335; in 1830, 6,987; in 1840, 7,467; in 1850, 8,777.

ASHERY, p. o., Hancock co., O.

ASHE'S CREEK, p. o., Spencer co., Ky.

ASHFIELD, p. t., Franklin co., Mass., 108 ms. w. of Boston; from W. 403 ms. Watered by Deerfield and Westfield rivers. Pop. 1,394.

ASHFORD, p. t., Windham co., Ct., 32 ms. E. of Hartford; from W. 368 ms. Pop., in 1840, 2,651; in 1850, 1,295.

ASHFORD, p. t., Cattaraugus co., N. Y., 295 ms. w. by s. of Albany; from W. 345 ms. Watered by Cattarau gus creek. Pop. 1,658.

ASH GROVE, p. o., Greene co., Mo.

ASH GROVE, p. o., Iroquois co., Ill.

ASHIPUM, p. o., Washington co., Wis.

ASHLAND COUNTY, situated in the northern part of Ohio. Area, ——— square miles. Courts are held at Ashland. Pop., in 1850, 23,811.

ASHLAND, p. o., Bertie co., N. C.

ASHLAND, p. o., Union co., Ky., 224 ms. w. s. w. of Frankfort; from W. 765 ms.

ASHLAND, p. v., Ashland co., O., 79 ms. N. w. of Columbus; from W. 368 ms. Pop. 1,344.

ASHLAND, p. o., Forsyth co., Ga.

ASHLAND, p. o., Wayne co., Tenn., 88 ms. s. w. of Nashville; from W. 765 ms.

ASHLAND, p. t., Greene co., N. Y. Pop. 1,290.

ASHLAND, p. t., Middlesex co., Mass. Pop. 1,304.

ASHLAND, p. o., Wapello co., Iowa.

ASHLAND, p. o., De Soto co., La.

ASHLAND, p. o., Henry co., Ind.

ASHLAND, p. o., Wayne co., Pa.

ASHLAND FURNACE, p. o. Cambria co., Pa.

ASHLEY COUNTY, situated in the southeast part of Arkansas, drained by Bayou Bartholomew and Saline river. Area, ——— square miles. Courts are held at Hamburgh. Pop., in 1850, 2,058.

ASHLEY, p. o., Pike co., Mo., 69 ms. N. E. of Jefferson city; from W. 887 ms.

ASHLEY, p. o., Delaware co., O.

ASHLEY, p. o., Carroll co., Ark.

ASHLEYSVILLE, p. o., Hampden co., Mass., 97 ms. w. of Boston; from W. 367 ms.

ASHLEY FALLS, p. o., Berkshire co., Mass.

ASHPORT, v., Landerdale co., Tenn. Watered by Mississippi river.

ASH RIDGE, p. o., Brown co., O.

ASH RIDGE, p. o., Pulaski co., Ill.

ASH RUN, p. o., Pendleton co., Ky.

ASH SPRING, p. o., Harrison co., Tex.

ASHTABULA COUNTY, situated in the northeast part of Ohio, on Lake Erie, and watered by Grand and Ashtabula rivers. Length, 28 miles ; breadth, 25. with an area of about 700 square miles. The face of the country is undulating, having a soil generally fertile, well-watered and wooded. Courts are held at Jefferson. Pop., in 1820, 7,382; in 1830, 14,584; in 1840, 23,724 ; in 1850, 28,766.

ASHTABULA, p. t., Ashtabula co., O., 194 ms. N. E. of Columbus ; from W. 341 ms. Pop. 1,356.

ASHTON, p. o., Carlisle parish, La.

ASHTON, p. o., Clark co., Mo.

ASHTON, p. o., Dane co., Wis.

ASHTON, p. o., Carroll co., La.

ASHTON'S, Shelby co., Tex.

ASHTON'S MILLS. p. o., Frederick co., Va.

ASHVILLE. p. o., Pickaway co., O.

ASHVILLE, c. h., p. v., seat of justice of St. Clair co., Ala., 90 ms. N. E. of Tuscaloosa. Watered by Canoe creek.

ASHVILLE, c. h., p. v., seat of justice of Buncombe co., N. C., 256 ms. w. of Raleigh ; from W. 486 ms. Watered by French Broad river. Pop. 420.

ASHWOOD, p. o., Maury co., Tenn.

ASKLEYVILLE, p. o., Macomb co., Mich.

ASPALAGA, v., Gadsden co., Flor., 35 ms. w. of Talahassee.

ASPEN GROVE, p. o., Pittsylvania co., Va., 148 ms. s. w. of Richmond ; from W. 235 ms.

ASPEN GROVE, p. o., Calhoun co., Flor.

ASPEN WALL, p. o., Charlotte co., Va.

ASSABET, p. o., Middlesex co., Mass.

ASSUMPTION PARISH, La., situated toward the southeast part of the state, and watered by the Mississippi and Bayou La Fourche. Area, —— square miles. Courts are held at Assumption. Pop., 1840, 7,141 ; in 1850, 10,538.

ASSUMPTION, c. h., p. v., Assumption parish La., 89 ms. w. of New Orleans ; from W. 1,261 ms.

ASSYRIA, p. o., Barry co., Mich.

ASTON, t., Delaware co., Pa.

ASTORIA, p. v., Newtown township, Queens co., N. Y., 6 ms. N. E. of New York city,

ASTORIA, p. o., Butler co., O.

ASTORIA, p. o., Fulton co., Ill., 72 ms. N. N. W. of Springfield ; from W. 850 ms.

ASTORIA, p. o., Clatsop co., Oregon.

ASTORIA, p. o., Wright co., Mo.

ASSYLUM. p. t., Bradford co., Pa., 145 ms. N. of Harrisburgh ; from W. 255 ms. Watered by Susquehanna, river. Pop. 820.

ATCHAFALAYA. p. o., Point Coupee parish. La.

ATCHISON COUNTY, situated in the extreme northwest angle of Missouri, between Missouri and Nodaway rivers. Area —— square miles. Courts are held at ————. Pop., in 1850, 1,687.

ATHENS COUNTY, situated in the southeast part of Ohio, adjoining the Ohio and traversed by Hockhocking rivers. Length, about 40 miles ; mean breadth, 23, extending over an area of about 900 square miles. The face of the country is undulating or hilly, but well-wooded and watered, with an extremely fertile soil. Courts are held at Athens. Pop., in 1820, 6,338 ; in 1830, 9,787; in 1840, 19,109 ; in 1850, 18,215.

ATHENS, p. b., Bradford co., Pa., 152 ms. N. by E. of Harrisburgh ; from W. 262 ms. Watered by Susquehanna and Chemung rivers. Pop. 2,127.

ATHENS, p. o., Henderson co., Tex.

ATHENS, t., Crawford co., Pa., 237 ms. N. W. of Harrisburgh ; from W. 304 ms. Pop. 928.

ATHENS, c. h., p. v., seat of justice of Athens co., O., 72 ms. s. E. of Columbus ; from W. 339 ms., situated on Hockhocking river. Pop. 1,462.

ATHENS, p. t., Greene co., N. Y., 29 ms. s. of Albany; from W. 341 ms. Watered by Hudson river. Pop. 2,986.

ATHENS. p. t., Somerset co., Me., 49 ms. N. of Augusta ; from W. 644 ms. Pop. 1,460.

ATHENS, p. t., Windham co., Vt., 109 ms. s. of Montpelier ; from W. 447 ms. Pop. 359.

ATHENS, p. t., Calhoun co., Mich., 126 ms. w. of Detroit ; from W. 584 ms. Pop. 533.

ATHENS, t., Harrison co., O., 130 ms. E. by N. of Columbus ; from W. 284 ms. Pop. 1,085.

ATHENS, p. o., Caroline co., Va.

ATHENS, c. h., p. v., Clarke co., Ga., 75 ms. N. by w. of Milledgeville ; from W. 610 ms. Watered by Oconee river. Pop. 3,795.

ATHENS, c. h., p. v., seat of justice of Limestone co., Ala., 154 ms. N. by E. of Tuscaloosa; from W. 733 ms.

ATHENS, p. v., Monroe co., Miss., 175 ms. N. w. of Jackson ; from W. 906 ms. Watered by Tombigbee river.

ATHENS, c. h., p. v., seat of justice of McMinn co., Tenn., 154 ms. s. E. of Nashville; from W. 555 ms. Watered by Eastanalla creek.

ATHENS, p. o., Claiborne parish, La.

ATHENS, p. o., Henderson co., Tex.

ATHENS, p. o., Fayette co., Ky., 34 ms. s. E. of Frankfort ; from W. 532 ms. Watered by Kentucky river.

ATHENS. p. v., Menard co., Ill., 14 ms. N. of Springfield ; from W. 794 ms. Watered by Sangamon river.

ATHENS, p. o., Clark co., Mo.

ATHENS, p. v., seat of justice of Izard co., Ark. Watered by White river.

ATHENS, p. o., Dodge co., Wis.

ATHENSVILLE, p. o., Greene co., Ill., 52 ms. s. w. of Springfield ; from W. 833 ms.

ATHOL, p t., Worcester co., Mass., 69 ms. w. N. w. of Boston ; from W. 410 ms. Watered by Miller's river. Pop. 2,034.

ATHOL, p. t., Warren co., N. Y., 74 ms. N. by w. of Albany ; from W. 443 ms. Watered by Hudson river. Pop. 1,590.

ATHOL DEPOT, p. o., Worcester co., Mass.

ATKINSON, p. t., Piscataquis co., Me., 90 ms. N. E. of Augusta ; from W. 687 ms. Pop. 895.

ATKINSON, p. t., Rockingham co., N. H., 33 ms. s. E. of Concord ; from W. 466 ms. Pop. 600.

ATKINSON'S MILLS, p. o., Mifflin co., Pa., 73 ms. N. w. of Harrisburgh ; from W. 149 ms.

ATLANTA CITY, p. o., De Kalb co., Ga., Pop. 2,572.

ATLANTIC COUNTY, situated in the southeast part of New Jersey, on the Atlantic ocean, and watered by Great and Little Egg-Harbor rivers. Area, 550 square miles. The surface is generally level, with numerous marshes, bays, and islands on the southeast, and a light sandy soil, which is productive only from cultivation. Courts are held at May's Landing. Pop., in 1840, 8,726; in 1850, 8,962.

ATLAS. p v., Pike co., Ill., 81 ms. w. by s. of Springfield ; from W. 861 ms. Watered by Mississippi river.

ATLAS, t., Lapeer co., Mich. Pop. 1,207.

ATSION, p. v., Galloway township, Burlington co., N. J., 43 ms. s. of Trenton; from W. 167 ms. Watered by Atsion river.

ATTALA COUNTY, situated in the central part of Mississippi, and drained by Black river and the head branches of Pearl river. Area, 720 square miles. Face of the country level ; soil moderately fertile. Courts are held at Kosciusko. Pop., in 1840, 4,303 ; in 1850, 10,999.

ATTALAVILLE, p. o., Attala co., Miss.

ATTAPULGUS, p. o., Decatur co., Ga., 200 ms. s. s. w. of Milledgeville ; from W. 858 ms.

ATTICA, p. t., Wyoming co., N. Y., 257 ms. w. of Albany ; from W. 375 ms. Watered by Tonawanda creek. Pop. 2,363.

ATTICA CENTRE, p. v., Attica township, Wyoming co., N. Y., 261 ms. w. of Albany ; from W. 371 ms.

ATTICA, p. t., Venice township, Seneca co., O., 80 ms. N. of Columbus ; from W. 405 ms.

ATTICA, p. o., Greene co., Wis.

ATTICA, p. o., Fountain co., Ind., 73 ms. w. N. w. of Indianapolis ; from W. 644 ms. Watered by Wabash river.

- ATTICA, p. o., Lenawee co., Mich. *

ATTLEBOROUGH, p. t., Bristol co., Mass., 30 ms. s. of Boston ; from W. 412 ms. Watered by Pautucket river. Pop. 4,200.

ATTLEBOROUGH, p v., Bucks co., Pa., 120 ms. E. of Harrisburgh ; from W. 162 ms.

ATTLEBURY, p. o., Sandford township, Dutchess co., N. Y., 71 ms. s. of Albany ; from W. 322 ms.

ATWATER, p. t., Portage co., O., 144 ms. N. E. of Columbus ; from W. 310 ms. Pop. 1,119.

ATWOOD, p. o., De Kalb co., Ala.

AUBBEENAUBEE, p. o., Fulton co., Ind.

AUBURN, p. t., Worcester co., Mass., 47 ms. w. s. w. of Boston ; from W. 395 ms. Watered by French river.

AUBURN, c. h., p. v., seat of justice of Cayuga co., N. Y., 173 ms. w. of Albany ; from W. 333 ms. Watered by Owasco outlet. Pop., in 1840, 5,626; in 1850, 9,548.

AUBURN, c. h., p. v., seat of justice of Placer co., Cal.

AUBURN; p. o., Fauquier co., Va., 109 ms. N. by w. of Richmond; from W. 58 ms.

AUBURN, p. t., Geauga, co., O., 156 ms. N. E. of Columbus; from W. 330 ms. Pop. 1,184.

AUBURN, p. t., Richland co., O.

AUBURN, p. v., Pontiac township, Oakland co., Mich., 27 ms. N. w. of Detroit; from W. 549 ms. Watered by Clinton river.

AUBURN, p. t., De Kalb co., Ind., 153 ms. N. N. E. of Indianapolis; from W. 566 ms. Pop. 260.

AUBURN, p. v., Sangamon co., Ill., 15 ms. s. by w. of Springfield; from W. 795 ms. Watered by Sugar creek.

AUBURN, p. v., Lincoln co., Mo., 84 ms. E. N. E. of Jefferson City; from W. 872 ms.

AUBURN, p. o., Hinds co., Miss., 32 ms. w. of Jackson; from W. 1,042 ms.

AUBURN, p. o., Chester co., Pa., 79 ms. s. E. of Harrisburgh; from W. 103 ms.

AUBURN, p. o., Gwinnett co., Ga., 94 ms. N. N. w. of Milledgeville; from W. 655 ms.

AUBURN, p. v., Macon co., Ala., 172 ms. s. E. of Tuscaloosa; from W. 786 ms.

AUBURN, p. o., Mahaska co., Iowa.

AUBURN, p. o., Wake co., N. C.

AUBURN, p. o., Fond du Lac co., Wis.

AUBURN, p. o. t., Cumberland co., Me. Pop. 2,840.

AUBURN, p. t., Rockingham co., N. H. Pop. 810.

AUBURN, p. o., Schuylkill co., Pa.

AUBURN (FOUR-CORNERS), p. v., Susquehanna co., Pa., 185 ms. N. by E. of Harrisburg; from W. 285 ms.

AUBURN, p. o., Cannon co., Tenn.

AUCILLA. p. o., Jefferson co., Flo.

AUDRAIN COUNTY, situated toward the northeast part of Missouri, drained by the south fork of Salt river. Area, 435 square miles. Courts are held at Mexico. Pop. in 1840, 1,949; in 1850, 3,506.

AUDUBON, p. o., Hardiman co., Tenn., 172 ms. s. w. of Nashville; from W. 887 miles. Watered by Cat creek.

AUDUBON, p. o., Montgomery co., Ill.

AUGERONA, p. o., Jackson co., Va.

AUGLAIZE COUNTY, situated in the western part of Ohio. Area, —— square miles. Courts are held at Wapaukonetta. Pop. in 1850, 11,338.

AUGLAIZE, t., Allen co., O. Pop. 1,344.

AUGLAIZE, t., Paulding co., O.

AUGLAIZE, p. o., Van Wert co., O.

AUGUSTA COUNTY, situated in the central part of Virginia, and drained by the tributaries of James and Shenandoah rivers. Superficial extent, 930 miles square, or 900 square miles, The face of the country undulating and somewhat hilly; the soil varied, but generally productive. Courts are held at Staunton. Pop. in 1820, 16,742; in 1830, 19,926; in 1840, 19,628; in 1850, 24,610.

AUGUSTA, the capital of the state of Maine, and seat of justice of Kennebec county, is situated on both sides of Kennebec river, at the head of sloop navigation, 42 miles from the ocean, 163 northeast of Boston, and 595 miles from Washington. In 1831 the seat of government was removed from Portland to this place. The statehouse is situated a little south of the town, on the west side of the river, and is constructed of granite, after the plan of the Massachusetts statehouse, in Boston. Length of the central part, 84 feet; depth, 56 feet, with a wing on each side 34 by 54 feet. It is entered by a Doric portico of eight granite columns, 21 feet high. The central part of the building is surmounted by a handsome cupola and dome, and the whole is embosomed in a spacious park of ornamental trees. An elegant and costly stone bridge of two arches, each of 180 feet span, connects the two parts of the village. Among other public structures are the United States arsenal, which is on the east side of the river, the state lunatic asylum, and the Augusta high school. The growth of the place has been rapid since it became the capital of the state. Pop. in 1810, 1,805; in 1820, 2,475; in 1830, 3,800; in 1840, 5,314; in 1850, 8,255.

AUGUSTA, p. o., Benton co., Flo.

AUGUSTA, p. t., Oneida co., N. Y., 100 ms. w. N. w. of Albany; from W. 370 ms. Watered by Skanandoah creek. Pop. 2,271.

AUGUSTA, p. v, Frankford township, Sussex co., N. J., 75 ms. N. of Trenton; from W. 244 ms.

AUGUSTA, p. t., Northumberland co., Pa., 65 ms. N. of Harrisburgh; from W. 165 ms. Watered by Shamokin creek.

AUGUSTA, p. t., Carroll co., O., 135 miles E. of Columbus; from W. 304 ms. Watered by Sandy creek. Pop. 1,297.

AUGUSTA, p. v., Des Moines co., Iowa. Watered by Skunk river. Pop. 496.

AUGUSTA, c. h., p. v., seat of justice of Bracken co., Ky., 73 ms. N. E. of Frankfort; from W. 487 ms.

AUGUSTA CITY, seat of justice of Richmond co., Ga., is situated on the west side of the Savannah river, 98 miles east-northeast of Milledgeville, and 125 from Savannah. The streets cross each other at right angles, and are lined with beautiful shade-trees, giving the city a fine appearance. The public and many of the private buildings are costly and elegant. It is connected with Charleston, Savannah, and the interior of the states of Georgia, Alabama, and Tennessee, by railroads, and is a place of much commercial enterprise. Pop. in 1830 was 4,634; in 1840, 6,436; in 1850, ——.

AUGUSTA, c. h., p. v., seat of justice of Perry co., Miss., 173 ms. s. E. of Jackson; from W. 1,051 ms. Watered by Leaf river.

AUGUSTA, p. v., Marion co., Ind., nine miles N. of Indianapolis; from W. 580 ms. Watered by White river.

AUGUSTA, p. v., Hancock co., Ill., 87 ms. w. by s. of Springfield; from W. 865 ms.

AUGUSTA, t., Kalamazoo co., Mich., 129 ms. w. of Detroit. Watered by Kalamazoo river.

AUGUSTA, p. o., St. Charles co., Mo.

AUGUSTA, t., Washtenaw co., Mich.

AUGUSTA, p. o., Jackson co., Ark.

AUMAN'S HILL, p. o., Montgomery co., N. C.

AURARIA, p. v., Lumpkin co., Ga., 135 ms. N. N. w. of Milledgeville; from W. 625 ms. Watered by Chestatee and Etowah rivers.

AURELIA, p. o., Washington co., O.

AURELIUS, p. t., Cayuga co., N. Y., 158 ms. w. by N. of Albany; from W. 337 ms. Watered by Owasco outlet. Pop. 2,831.

AURELIUS, t., Washington co., O., 113 ms. s. E. of Columbus; from W. 315 ms. Watered by Duck creek. Pop. 1,251.

AURELIUS, t., Ingham co., Mich. Pop. 501.

AURIESVILLE, p. o., Glen township, Montgomery co., N. Y., 40 ms. N. w. of Albany; from W. 408 ms.

AURORA, p. t., Erie co., N. Y., 276 ms. W. of Albany; 383 ms. Watered by Seneca and Cazenovia creeks. Pop. 3,435.

AURORA, p. v., Ledyard township, Cayuga co., N. Y., 170 ms. W. of Albany; from W. 323 ms. Situated on Cayuga lake.

AURORA. Hancock co., Me., 116 ms. E. of Augusta; from W. 698 ms. Pop. 217.

AURORA. p. t., Portage co., O.; 144 ms. N. E. of Columbus; from W. 335 ms. Pop. 828.

AURORA, v., Racine co., Wis., 110 ms. s. E. of Madison; from W. 776 ms.

AURORA, p. t., Dearborn co., Ind. Pop. 2,616.

AURORA, p. v., Kane co., Ill., 117 ms. N. N. E. of Springfield; from W. 754 ms. Watered by Fox river. Pop. 1,895.

AURORA, p. v., Marshall co., Ky., 243 ms. s. w. of Frankfort; from W. 770 ms.

AURORA, p. o., Marshall co., Ala., 122 ms. N. N. E. of Tuscaloosa; from W. 715 ms.

AURORA, p. o., Clark co., Ark.

AU SABLE, t., Clinton co., N. Y., 140 ms. N. of Albany; from W. 510 ms. Watered by Great and Little Au Sable rivers. Pop. 4,492.

AU SABLE, p. o., Jay township, Essex co., N. Y., 144 ms. N. of Albany; from W. 519 ms.

AU SABLE, p. o., Kendall co., Ill.

AU SABLE FORKS, p. v., Jay township, Essex co., N. Y., 154 ms. N. of Albany; from W. 529 ms.

AUSTERLITZ, p. t., Columbia co., N. Y., 31 ms. s. s. w. of Albany; from W. 363 ms. Watered by Green river.

AUSTERLITZ, p. v., Kent co., Mich., 178 ms. w. N. w. of Detroit; from W. 659 ms. Pop. 1,873.

AUSTIN COUNTY, situated in the southern part of Texas, and traversed by Brazos river. Area, —— square miles. Courts are held at ——. Pop. in 1850, 3,841.

AUSTIN, the capital of Texas, and seat of justice of Travis county, is situated on the northeasterly side of Colorado river, 200 miles northwest of Galveston.

The site is salubrious, being removed from the unhealthy atmosphere of the seaboard. The city is laid out on an extensive scale, with regular streets and avenues, which, when lined with the contemplated rows of buildings, will present an imposing spectacle. At present the buildings are not remarkable for elegance or number. In 1845 a convention met at this place, and organized a state government and constitution, which were ratified by the popular vote in the same year. In 1846 the first state legislature met at Austin, where it has since held biennial sessions. The population in 1840 was about 400 ; in 1850, 4,346.

AUSTIN, p. o., Ross co., O.

AUSTIN, c. h., p. v., seat of justice of Tunica co., Miss.

AUSTINBURGH, p. t., Ashtabula co., O., 201 ms. N. E. of Columbus; from W. 334 ms. Pop. 1,285.

AUSTINTOWN, t., Trumbull co., O., 160 ms. N. E. of Columbus; from W. 297 ms.

AUSTINVILLE, p. o., Wythe co., Va., 247 ms. s. w. of Richmond; from W. 315 ms.

AUSTINVILLE, p. o., Livingston co., Mo., 173 ms. N. w. of Jefferson city, from W. 1,067 ms.

AUTAUGA COUNTY, situated in the central part of Alabama, on the northerly and westerly side of Coosa river. Length, about 43 miles ; breadth, 18; with an area of 774 square miles. The face of the country is undulating and hilly ; the soil varied in its quality, from the productive alluvion to extremely sterile. Courts are held at Kingston. Pop. in 1820, 3,853; in 1830, 11,784 ; in 1840, 14,342; in 1850, 15,023.

AUTAUGAVILLE, p. o., Autauga co., Ala.

AUVASE, p. t., Callaway co., Mo.

AVA, p. o., Boonville township, Oneida county, N. Y., 124 ms. w. N. w. of Albany ; from W. 408 ms.

AVA, p. v., Winnebago co., Ill.

AVERILL, t., Essex co., Vt., 100 ms. N. E. of Montpelier; from W. 616 ms. Watered by Nulhegan river.

AVENT'S CROSS ROADS, p. o., Greenville co., Va., 99 ms. s. of Richmond; from W. 215 ms.

AVERY, p. o., Monroe co., Iowa.

AVERY, p. o., Jo-Daviess co., Ill.

AVERYSBOROUGH, p. v., Cumberland co., N. C., 35 ms. s. of Raleigh; fm. W. 323 ms. Watered by Cape Fear river.

AVERY'S CREEK, p. o., Buncombe co., N. C,

AVERY'S GORE, t., Addison co., Vt., 43 ms. s. w. of Montpelier; from W. 497 ms.

AVERY'S GORE, t., Franklin co., Vt., 57 ms. w. by N. of Montpelier; from W. 567 ms. Pop. 48.

AVILLA, p. o., Noble co., Ind.

AVISTON, p. t., Clinton co., Ill., 102 ms. s. of Spring field ; from W. 786 ms.

AVO, p. o., Patrick co., Va.

AVOCA, p. v., Bath township, Steuben co., N. Y., 22 ms. w. by s. of Albany ; from W. 307 ms. Pop. 1,574.

AVOCA, Livingston co., Ill.

AVOCA, p. o., Fond du Lac co., Wis.

AVOCA, p. o., Jefferson co, Mo., 159 ms. E. by s. of Jefferson city ; from W. 921 ms.

AVOCA, p. o., Lawrence co., Ala.

AVON, p. t., Franklin co., Me., 49 ms. N. w. of Augusta ; from W. 635 ms. Pop. 778.

AVON, p. t., Hartford co., Ct., 10 ms. w. N. w. of Hartford; from W. 336 ms. Pop. 995.

AVON, p. v., Livingston co., N. Y., 222 ms. w. by N. of Albany; from W. 355 ms. Watered by Genesee river. Pop. 2,809.

AVON, p. t., Lorain co., O. 135 ms. N. N. E. of Columbus ; from W. 377 ms. Pop. 1,782.

AVON, v., Kane co., Ill., 198 ms. N. N. E. of Springfield ; from W. 769 ms.

AVON, p., St. Genevieve co., Mo.

AVON, t., Oakland co., Mich. Pop. 1,456.

AVON, p., Rock co., Wis.

AVON, p. o., Ionia co., Mich.

AVONDALE, p. o., Chester co., Pa., 71 ms. s. E. of Harrisburgh; from W. 101 ms.

AVON LAKE, p. o., Lorain co., O.

AVOYELLES PARISH, La., situated on the west side of the Mississippi, and watered by Atchafalaya and Red rivers. Area, 1,080 square miles. The portion bordering on the streams is subject to inundation, but the westerly part is a slightly-elevated table-land, which is dry and fertile. Courts are held at Marksville. Pop. in 1830, 3,484 ; in 1840, 6,616 ; in 1850, 9,326.

AXEVILLE, p. o., Connewango township, Cattaraugus co., N. Y., 312 ms. w. by s. of Albany; from W. 342 ms.

AYERSVILLE, p. o., Stokes co., N. C., 122 ms. w. N. w. of Raleigh ; from W. 302 ms.

AYERSVILLE, p. o., Defiance co., O.

AYLETT'S, p. o., King William co., Va., 28 ms. N. E. of Richmond; from W. 110 ms.

AZALIA, p. v., Bartholomew co., Ind., 60 ms. s. s. E. of Indianapolis ; from W. 596 ms.

AZTALAN, p. t., Jefferson co., Wis., 30 ms. E. by s. of Madison ; from W. 840 ms.

B.

BABCOCK HILL, p. o., Oneida co., N. Y.

BABCOCK'S GROVE, p. o., Dupage co., Ill.

BABYLON, p. v., Huntington township, Suffolk co., Long Island, N. Y., 185 ms. s. E. of Albany ; from W. 265 ms.

BACHELOR'S GROVE, p. o., Rock co., Va.

BACHELOR'S HALL, p. o., Pittsylvania co., Va.

BACHELOR'S RETREAT, p. o., Pickens district, S. C., 167 ms. N. w. of Columbia ; from W. 572 ms.

BACHMAN'S MILLS, p. o., Carroll co., Md., 65 ms. N. of Annapolis : from W. 75 ms.

BACK CREEK, p. o., Somerset co., Md., 117 ms. s. E. of Annapolis ; from W. 157 ms.

BACK CREEK VALLEY, p. o., Frederick co., Va., 159 ms. N. of Richmond; from W. 87 ms.

BACON CASTLE, p. o., Surry co., Va., 63 ms. s. E. of Richmond ; from W. 186 ms.

BAD-AXE, p. o., Crawford co., Wis.

BADGER, p. o., Fond du Lac co., Wis.

BAGDAD, p. o., Smith co., Tenn., 64 ms. E. N. E. of Nashville; from W. 643 ms.

BAGDAD, p. o., Lafayette co., Mo.

BAILEY CREEK, p. o., Tioga co., Pa.

BAILEYSBURGH, p. o., Perry co., Pa.

BAILEYSBURGH, p. v., Surry co., Va., 66 ms. s. E. of Richmond; from W. 185 ms.

BAILEY'S CREEK, p. o., Osage co., Mo.

BAILEY'S FOUR CORNERS, p. o., Greene co., N. Y.,

BAILEY'S LANDING, p. o., Lincoln co., Mo., 96 ms. N. E. of Jefferson City ; from W. 865 ms.

BAILEY'S MILLS, p. o., Jefferson co., Flor.

BAILEYVILLE, p. t., Washington co., Me., 209 ms. E. of Augusta ; from W. 795 ms. Watered by St. Croix river. Pop. 431.

BAILEYVILLE, p. o., Centre co., Pa., 98 ms. N. w. of Harrisburgh; from W. 170 ms.

BAINBRIDGE, p. t., Chenango co., N. Y., 104 ms. w. by s. of Albany ; from W. 320 ms. Watered by Susquehanna river. Pop. 3,338.

BAINBRIDGE, p. v., West Donnegal township, Lancaster co., Pa., 20 ms. s. E. of Harrisburgh; from W. 112 ms. Watered by Susquehanna river. Pop. 503.

BAINBRIDGE, p. o., Christian co., Ky.

BAINBRIDGE, p. v., Ross co., O., 69 ms. s. of Columbus ; from W. 424 ms. Watered by Paint creek. Pop. 626.

BAINBRIDGE, t., Geauga co., O., 136 ms. N. E. of Columbus ; from W. 333 ms. Watered by Chagrus river Pop. 1,014.

BAINBRIDGE, t., Berrien co., Mich.

BAINBRIDGE, c. h., p. v., seat of justice of Decatur co., Ga., 188 ms. s. s. w. of Milledgeville; from W. 845 ms. Watered by Flint river.

BAINBRIDGE, p. v., Putnam co., Ind., 38 ms. w. of Indianapolis; from W. 609 ms. Watered by Walnut fork of Eel river.

BAINBRIDGE, p. v., Williamson co., Ill., 176 ms. s. by E. of Springfield ; from W. 827 ms. Watered by Big Muddy creek.

BAINBRIDGE, v., Cape Girardeau co., Mo. Watered by Mississippi river.

BAINBRIDGE, p. o., Robertson co., Tenn.

BAINBRIDGE CENTRE, p. o., Bainbridge township, Chenango co., N. Y., 107 ms. w. by s. of Albany; from W. 311 ms.

BAIRDSTOWN, c. h., p. t., seat of justice of Nelson co., Ky., 40 ms. s. w. of Frankfort; from W. 615 ms. Watered by Beech Fork of Salt river.

BAITING HOLLOW, p. v., Riverhead township, Suffolk co., Long Island, N. Y., 221 ms. s. e. of Albany; from W. 301 ms.

BAKER COUNTY, situated in the southwest part of Georgia, and watered by Flint river, and branches. Area, 1,350 square miles. Courts are held at Newton. Pop., in 1830, 1,253; in 1840, 4,226; in 1850, 8,120.

BAKER'S, p. o., Jackson township, Champaign co., O., 56 ms. w. of Columbus; from W. 450 ms.

BAKER'S, p. o., Lenawee co., Mich., 82 ms. s. w. of Detroit; from W. 497 ms.

BAKER'S CORNERS, p. o., Walworth co., Wis.

BAKERSFIELD, p. t., Franklin co., Vt., 49 ms. n. n. w. of Montpelier; from W. 551 ms. Watered by Mississque river. Pop. 1,523.

BAKER'S GAP, p. o., Johnson co., Tenn.

BAKER'S RUN, p. o., Hardy co., Va.

BAKERSVILLE, p. o., Litchfield co., Ct.

BAKERSVILLE, p. o., Coshocton co., O.

BAKERSVILLE, p. o., Washington co., Md.

BAKERSVILLE, p. o., Somerset co., Pa.

BAKERSTOWN, p. v., Alleghany co., Pa., 217 ms. w. of Harrisburgh; from W. 243 ms.

BAKERSVILLE, p. v., Yancey co., N. C., 247 ms. w. of Raleigh; from W. 473 ms.

BALCONY FALLS, p. o., Rockbridge co., Va., 147 ms. w. of Richmond; from W. 210 ms. Watered by James river.

BALD CREEK, p. o., Yancey co., N. C., 251 ms. w. of Raleigh; from W. 481 ms.

BALD EAGLE, p. o., Bath co., Ky.

BALD EAGLE, t., Clinton co., Pa. Pop. 683.

BALD EAGLE, p. o., York co., Pa.

BALD HILL, p. o., Norfolk co., Mass.

BALD HILL, p. o., Muscogee co., Ga.

BALD MOUNT, p. o., Luzerne co., Pa., 147 ms. n. n. e. of Harrisburgh; from w. 251 ms.

BALDWIN COUNTY, situated in the central part of Georgia, and traversed by the river Oconee. Length, 30 miles; breadth, 27, extending over an area of 810 square miles. The face of the country is rolling, and the soil, in general, of middling quality. Courts are held at Milledgeville, the capital of the state. Pop., in 1820, 5,665; in 1830, 7,295; in 1840, 7,250; in 1850, 8,148.

BALDWIN COUNTY, in the southwest part of Alabama, on the gulf of Mexico, with Tensaw and Alabama rivers on the west, and Perdido river on the east. Area, 200 square miles. The face of the country is hilly, and the soil generally thin, covered with pine forests, except along the streams, where it is highly fertile. Courts are held at Blakeley. Pop. in 1820, 1,713; in 1830, 2,334 ; in 1840, 2,951; in 1850, 4,414.

BALDWIN, p. o., Butler co., Pa., 207 ms. w. n. w. of Harrisburgh; from W. 259 ms.

BALDWIN, t., Cumberland co., Me., 80 ms. s. w. of Augusta; from W. 551 ms. Watered by Saco river. Pop. 1,100.

BALDWIN, p., Chemung co., N. Y.

BALDWIN, p., Butler co., Pa.

BALDWIN, v., Hinds co., Miss., 43 ms. from Jackson; from W. 1,053. Watered by Big Black river.

BALDWINSVILLE, p. v., Templeton township, Worcester co., Mass., 64 ms. w. by n. of Boston; from W. 414 ms.

BALDWINSVILLE, p. v., Lysander township, Onondaga co., N. Y., 145 ms. w. by n. of Albany; from W. 262 ms. Watered by Seneca river.

BALDWINSVILLE, p. v., Scott co., Mo., 260 ms. s. e. of Jefferson City; from W. 838 ms.

BALDWINSVILLE, p. o., Edgar co., Ill.

BALE'S BRANCH, p. o., Green co., Tenn., 262 ms. e. by n. of Nashville; from W. 424 ms.

BALEY, t., Benton co., Ark.

BALIZE, v., Plaquemine parish, La., 175 ms. n. e. of Pass, below New Orleans, near the mouth of Mississippi river.

BALLARD COUNTY, Ky., situated in the westernmost part of the state, on the southerly side of the Ohio, and on the easterly side of the Mississippi river. It is traversed by Mayfield creek. Area, 375 square miles. Courts are held at Columbus. Pop. in 1850, 5,496.

BALLARD'S BRIDGE, p. o., Chowan co., N. C., 195 ms. e. n. e. of Raleigh; from W. 275 ms.

BALLARDSVILLE, v., Logan co., Va., 346 ms. w. of Richmond; from W. 383 ms.

BALLARDSVILLE, p. v., Oldham co., Ky., 29 ms. n. w. of Frankfort; from W. 571 ms.

BALLARDSVILLE, p. o., Boone co., Va.

BALLARD VALE, p. o., Essex co., Mass.

BALLEW'S FERRY, p. o., St. Landre parish, La.

BALL GROUND, p. o., Cherokee co., Ga.

BALL MOUNTAIN, p. o., Oakland co., Mich.

BALL PLAY, p. o., Monroe co., Tenn.

BALL'S POND, p. o., Fairfield co., Ct.

BALLSVILLE, p. o., Powhattan co., Va., 48 ms. w. of Richmond; from W. 151 ms.

BALLSTON, p. t., Saratoga co., N. Y., 26 ms. n. w. of Albany; from W. 395 ms. Watered by Ballston, or Long lake. Pop. 2,269.

BALLSTON CENTRE, p. v., Ballston township, Saratoga co., N. Y.

BALLSTON SPA, p. v., Milton township, seat of justice of Saratoga co., N. Y. Watered by Kayaderosseras creek.

BALLSTOWN, p. o., Ripley co., Ind.

BALLVILLE, t., Sandusky co., O., 98 ms. n. of Columbus; from W. 423 ms. Watered by Sandusky river. Pop. 1,556.

BALTIMORE COUNTY, situated in the northerly part of Maryland, on the north side of Patapsco river, and the westerly side of Chesapeake bay. Length, about 30 miles; mean breadth, 25, with an area of 750 square miles. The face of the country is agreeably diversified by hill and dale, abundantly wooded and watered, and generally well cultivated, the soil being good for grazing, orchards, and the production of grain. Courts are held at Baltimore. Pop., in 1820, exclusive of that of the city and its precincts, 33,352; in 1830, including that of Baltimore, 120,870; in 1840, 134,379; in 1850, 203,928.

BALTIMORE, the principal city of the state, and the third city of the United States in population, is situated on the north side of Patapsco river, 14 miles from its entrance into Chesapeake bay, 100 miles southwest of Philadelphia, and 40 miles from Washington. It is built on uneven ground, bending around the innermost of three harbors, which successively diminish in space and depth. The outer one is 22 feet deep, one mile and a quarter long, from its entrance into the second, which is fifteen feet deep, half a mile wide, and one mile long. Vessels of about 600 tons enter this harbor, while the third, which enters the city, is deep enough for vessels of 200 tons. The outer entrance is defended by fortifications, which repulsed a British fleet of sixteen ships in 1814.

The appearance of the city, when viewed from the water, is imposing. The most conspicuous and fashionable part is built on a bold, but not steep elevation; and the steeples, monuments, and domes with which it is crowned, greatly relieve and beautify the scene. Within the town the streets and buildings exhibit various degrees of beauty and regularity when viewed from different points. In the construction of the houses, convenience and solidity appear to have been studied, rather than magnificence; but the abodes of wealthy citizens exhibit the same elegance here as in other great cities of the Union. Many of the public structures are also splendid and costly. Baltimore has been named the "Monumental city," chiefly from the two great monuments it contains. Washington monument is a Doric column, of white marble, 180 feet high, resting on a base of the same material, 20 feet high, and surmounted by a statue of the man it commemorates. Ascending by a winding staircase within the column, the visiter beholds a wide prospect of the city and its varied environs. Battle monument, also of white marble, is 52 feet high, and was erected in memory of the patriots who fell in defence of this city against the British in 1814. Many of the churches are remarkable for architectural beauty. The courthouse, state penitentiary, customhouse, St. Mary's college, and the halls of numerous literary and scientific institutions, are among the other important public buildings. The exchange is 225 feet wide, 141 feet deep, and 115 feet to the top of the dome. Colonnades of the Ionic order, made of Italian marble, extend across its east and west fronts. Water is supplied in abundance from fountains in the city, and from Jones's fall, in the vicinity, by an aqueduct and pipes. In manufactures, as in commerce, Baltimore ranks with the great cities of America. Jones's fall (a small creek dividing the city, and spanned by several beautiful bridges) and the Patapsco afford numerous excellent seats for mills and manufactories of various kinds. The population in 1775 was 5,936; in 1790, 13,503; in 1800, 26,614; in 1810, 46,555; in 1820,

BALTIMORE

½ Mile Circles from Post Office

Green Mt. Cemetery

CITY DOCK

62,738; in 1830, 80,625; in 1840, 102,313; in 1850, 166,303.

BALTIMORE, p. v., Liberty township, Fairfield co., O., 32 ms. s. w. of Columbus; from W. 378 ms. Situated on the Ohio canal. Pop. 492.

BALTIMORE, t., Windsor co., Vt., 65 ms. S. of Montpelier; from W. 448 ms. Pop. 124.

BALTIMORE, hundred, Sussex co., Del. Pop. 2,748.

BALTIMORE, p. o., Barry co., Mich.

BALTIMORE, p. v., Warren co., Ind., 77 miles N. w. of Indianapolis; from W. 648 ms. Watered by Wabash river.

BALTIMORE, p. o., Jo-Daviess co., Ill.

BANCROFT, p. o., Hampshire co., Mass.

BANGALL, p. o., Dutchess co., N. Y.

BANGOR, p. t., Franklin co., N. Y., 219 ms. N. N. w. of Albany; from W. 530 ms. Watered by Salmon river. Pop. 2,160.

BANGOR CITY, the seat of justice of Penobscot co., Me., situated on the west side of Penobscot river, at the head of tidewater, 58 miles from the Atlantic, 68 northeast from Augusta, 230 northeast of Boston. Vast quantities of lumber are annually floated down the river to this place, whence it is shipped to the West Indies and various parts of the Union. This city is built on elevated ground, affording a fine view of the surrounding country, and is tastefully laid out, and adorned with trees. The public as well as the private buildings are, many of them, neat and elegant. The harbor is inaccessible for four months in the winter, but will admit, at other times, vessels of 300 or 400 tons, the tide alone rising to the height of 17 feet. Lines of steamboats connect the city with Portland, and a railroad extends 12 miles up the river to Oldtown. The Bangor Theological seminary was incorporated in 1834, and is in prosperous condition. Population in 1790, 169; in 1800, 277; in 1810, 850; in 1820, 1,221; in 1830, 2,867; in 1840, 8,627; in 1850, 14,432.

BANGOR, p. o., Richland co., O., 65 ms. N. by E. of Columbus; from W. 390 ms.

BANK LICK, p. o., Kenton co., Ky.

BANKSVILLE, p. o., Fairfield co., Ct.

BANKSTON, p. o., Choctaw co., Miss.

BANKTON, p. o., Saline co., Ill.

BANNER, p. o., Kane co., Ill.

BANNER, p. o., Lafayette co., Miss.

BANNERMAN, p. o., New Hanover co., N. C.

BANTAM, p. o., Clermont co., O., 108 ms. s. w. of Columbus; from W. 479 ms.

BANTAM FALLS, p. o., Litchfield co., Ct., 36 ms. w. of Hartford; from W. 328 ms.

BAPTIST MISSION, p. o., Cherokee Nation co., Ark.

BAPTISTOWN, p. v., Kingwood township, Hunterdon co., N. J., 33 ms. N. N. w. of Trenton; from W. 190 ms.

BAPTIST VALLEY, p. o., Tazewell co., Va.

BARABOO, p. o., Sauk co., Wis.

BARBER'S, p. o., Columbia co., Flo.

BARBER'S CORNERS, p. o., Will co., Ill.

BARBER'S CREEK, p. o., Jackson co., Ga.

BARBER'S CROSS ROADS, p. o., Isle of Wight co., Va.

BARBERSVILLE, p. o., Jefferson co., Ind.

BARBOUR, p. o., Choctaw co., Ala.

BARBOUR COUNTY, situated in the southeasterly part of Alabama, on the west side of Chattahoochee river. Area, 1,200 square miles. Courts are held at Clayton. Pop. in 1840, 12,024; in 1850, 23,632.

BARBOUR COUNTY, Va., situated in the northwestern part of the state. Area, —— square miles. Courts are held at Philippi. Pop. in 1850, 9,005.

BARBOUR'S MILLS, p. o., Lycoming co., Pa., 113 ms. N. by w. of Harrisburg; from W. 223 ms.

BARBOURVILLE, p. o., Tompkins township, Delaware co., N. Y., 117 ms. w. by s. of Albany; from W. 300 ms.

BARBOURSVILLE, p. v., Orange co., Va., 80 ms. N. w. of Richmond; from W. 107 ms.

BARBOURSVILLE, c. h., p. v., seat of justice of Knox co., Ky., 119 ms. s. E. by s. of Frankfort; from W. 519 ms. Watered by Cumberland river. Pop. 184.

BARBOURSVILLE, c. h. v., seat of justice of Cabell co., Va., 352 ms. w. N. w. of Richmond; from W. 399 ms. Watered by Great Guyandot river.

BARCELONA, p. v., Westfield township, Chautauque co., N. Y., 343 ms. w. of Albany; from W. 346 ms. Situated on Lake Erie.

BARCELONA, p. o., Bloomfield township, Richland co., O., 60 ms. N. N. E. of Columbus; from W. 393 ms.

BARCLAY, p. o., Whitesides co., Ill.

BARCLAYSVILLE, p. o., Cumberland co., N. C.

BARDSTOWN, p. t., Nelson co., Ky. (See Bairdstown.)

BARESVILLE, p. o., Monroe co., O., 144 ms. E. of Columbus; from W. 278 ms.

BAREVILLE, p. o., Lancaster co., N. C.

BARGAINTOWN, p. v., Egg Harbor township, Atlantic co., N. J., 87 ms. s. by E. of Trenton; from W. 197 ms.

BARGES, p. o., Wilcox co., Ala., 122 ms. s. by E. of Tuscaloosa; from W. 903 ms.

BARHAMSVILLE, p. o., New Kent co., Va., 40 ms. E. of Richmond; from W. 157 ms.

BAR HARBOR, p. o., Hancock co., Me., 109 ms. w. of Augusta; from W. 691 ms.

BARING, p. t., Washington co., Me., 201 ms. E. N. E. of Augusta; from W. 871 ms. Watered by St. Croix river. Pop. 380.

BARK CAMP, p. o., Burke co., Ga., 68 ms. E. of Milledgeville; from W. 642 ms.

BARKER, t., Broome co., N. Y., 135 ms. s. w. of Albany; from W. 307 ms. Watered by Tioughnioga creek. Pop. 1,456.

BARKER'S, p. o., Greene co., Pa., 219 ms. w. s. w. of Harrisburg; from W. 235 ms.

BARKERSVILLE, p. o., Saratoga co., N. Y.

BARKERSVILLE, p. o., Marion co., Iowa.

BARKER'S SETTLEMENT, p. o., Randolph co., Va., 221 ms. N. w. of Richmond; from W. 248 ms.

BARKHAMSTEAD, p. t., Litchfield co.. Ct., 24 ms. N. w. of Hartford; from W. 360 ms. Watered by Farmington river. Pop. 1,524.

BARK RIVER, p. t., Jefferson co., Wis.

BARKSDALE, p. o., Halifax co., Va., 132 ms. s. w. of Richmond; from W. 219 ms.

BARLOW, p. t., Washington co., O. Pop. 1,662.

BARNARD, t., Piscataquis co., Me. Pop. 181.

BARNARD, p. t., Windsor co., Vt., 42 ms. S. of Montpelier; from W. 491 ms. Watered by White and Queechee river. Pop. 1,647.

BARNARDSVILLE, p. v., Roane co., Tenn., 151 ms. E. by s. of Nashville; from W. 546 ms.

BARLOW, p. t., Washington co., O., 98 ms. s. by E. of Columbus; from W. 310 ms.

BARNEGAT, v., Poughkeepsie township, Dutchess co., N. Y. Watered by Hudson river.

BARNEGAT, p. v., Stafford township, Ocean co., N. J., 55 ms. s. E. of Trenton; from W. 205 ms.

BARNERVILLE, p. o., Schoharie co., N. Y.

BARNES, p. o., Richland co., O., 67 ms. N. of Columbus; from W. 379 ms.

BARNES, p. o., Dallas co., Ala, 97 ms. s. by E. of Tuscaloosa; from W. 858 ms.

BARNES' BRIDGE, p. o., Richmond co., N. C., 100 ms s. w. of Raleigh, from W. 396 ms.

BARNES' CORNERS, p. o., Lewis co., N. Y.

BARNES' CROSS ROADS, p. o., Dale co., Ala.

BARNESVILLE, v., Pike co., Ga., 65 ms. W. of Milledgeville; from W. 687 ms.

BARNESVILLE, p. o., Montgomery co., Ind., 79 ms. w. by N. of Annapolis; from W. 39 ms.

BARNESVILLE, v., Warren township, Belmont co., O., 101 ms. E. of Columbus; from W. 299 ms. Pop. 823.

BARNESVIEW, v., Clark co., Mo. Watered by Wisconda river.

BARNET, p. t., Caledonia co., Vt., 48 ms. E. of Montpelier; from W. 535 ms. Watered by Connecticut river. Pop. 2,521.

BARNETT'S CREEK, p. o., Ohio co., Ky., 162 ms. s. by w. of Frankfort; from W. 706 ms.

BARNETT'S MILLS, p. o., Fauquier co., Va., 91 ms. N. by w. of Richmond; from W. 79 ms.

BARNEY'S, p. o., Phillips co., Ark.

BARNHART'S MILLS, p. o., Butler co., Pa., 212 ms. w. by N. of Harrisburgh; from W. 254 ms.

BARNSBOROUGH, p. o., Gloucester co., N. J.

BARNSTABLE, p. t., seat of justice of Barnstable co., Mass., 74 ms. s. E. of Boston; from W. 475 ms.; extending across Cape Cod. The principal village is situated on the south side of Barnstable bay, is nearly built, flourishing, and has some commerce, fishing business, &c. This township also contains another village called Hyannis, situated near the southeasterly side, on a good harbor. Pop. in 1810, 3,646; in 1820, 3,824; in 1830, 3,975; in 1840, 4,301; in 1850, 4,901.

BARNSTABLE COUNTY, situated at the extreme easterly part of Massachusetts, comprising the whole of the peninsula of Cape Cod and the Elizabeth island, with the Atlantic ocean on the south and east, Cape Cod bay on the north, and Buzzard bay on the west. Length, 65 miles; mean width, 5; with an area of 325 square miles. The surface is generally flat, the soil naturally sandy and barren, but covered in some places with forests of oak and pine. Courts are held at Barnstable. Pop. in 1820, 24,046; in 1830, 15,310; in 1840, 32,548; in 1850, 35,276.

BARNSTEAD, p. t., Belknap co., N. H., 18 ms. N. E. of Concord; from W. 499 ms. Pop. 1,848.

BARNWELL DISTRICT, situated in the southwest part of South Carolina, between Edisto and Savannah rivers. Length, 50 miles; mean breadth, 35; with an area of 1,680 square miles. The face of the country is hilly, and the soil of fair quality, suitable for growing cotton and grain. Courts are held at Barnwell. Pop. in 1820, 14,750; in 1830, 19,236; in 1840, 21,471; in 1850, 26,608.

BARNWELL, c. h., p. v., seat of justice of Barnwell district, S. C., 100 ms. s. by w. of Columbia; from W. 604 ms. Watered by Turkey creek and Great Salkahatchie river.

BARRACKSVILLE, p. o., Marion co., Va.

BARRE, p. t., Washington co., Vt., 7 ms. s. of Montpelier; from W. 520 ms. Watered by Onion river. Pop. 1,845.

BARRE, t., Huntingdon co., Pa., 93 ms. w. by N. of Harrisburgh; from W. 170 miles. Pop. 1,271.

BARRE, p. t., Worcester co., Mass., 65 ms. w. of Boston; from W. 409 ms. Watered by Ware river. Pop. 2,976.

BARRE FORGE, p. o., Huntingdon co., Pa.

BARRE, p. t., Orleans co., N. Y., 252 ms. w. of Albany; from W. 390 ms. Situated on the Erie canal. Pop. in 1840, 5,539; in 1850, 4,186.

BARRE CENTRE, p. v., Barre township, Orleans co., N. Y.

BARRE PLAINS, p. o., Worcester co., Mass.

BARREN, p. o., Harrison co., Ind., 118 ms. s. of Indianapolis; from W. 622 ms.

BARREN COUNTY, situated in the southerly part of Kentucky. Length, 45 miles; mean width, 20; extending over an area of 900 square miles. The face of the country is generally level, and the soil of middling quality. Courts are held at Glasgow. Pop. in 1820, 10,328; in 1830, 15,079; in 1840, 17,288; and in 1850, 20,240.

BARREN, p. o., Williamson co., Tenn., 25 ms. s. of Nashville; from W. 709 ms.

BARREN CREEK SPRINGS, p. o., Somerset co., Ind., 84 ms. s. E. of Annapolis; from W. 124 ms.

BARREN GROVE, p. o., Bureau co., Ill.

BARREN HILL, p. o., Montgomery co., Pa., 96 ms. E. by s. of Harrisburgh; from W. 149 ms.

BARREN HILL, p. o., Henry co., Tenn., 32 ms. N. w. of Nashville; from W. 791 ms.

BARREN PLAIN, p. o., Robertson co., Tenn., 32 ms. N. of Nashville; from W. 714 ms.

BARREN RIDGE, p. o., Vanzant co., Tex.

BARRETTSVILLE, p. v., Lumpkin co., Ga., 124 ms. N. N. w. of Milledgeville; from W. 645 ms. Watered by Etowah river.

BARREVILLE, p. o., McHenry co., Ill.

BARRINGTON, p. t., Strafford co., N. H., 35 ms. E. of Concord; from W. 505 ms. Pop. 1,752.

BARRINGTON. p. t., Bristol co., R. I., 8 ms. E. s. E. of Providence; from W. 408 ms. Pop. 795.

BARRINGTON, p. t., Yates co., N. Y., 201 ms. w. of Albany : from W. 322 ms. Watered by Crooked lake. Pop. 1,550.

BARRINGTON, p. t., Cook co., Ill. Pop. 676.

BARROWDALE, p. v., Fairfield district, S. C., 26 ms. N. of Columbia; from W. 479 ms.

BARRY COUNTY, situated toward the southwest part of Michigan, and drained by Thornapple river. Area, 576 square miles. Courts are held at Hastings. Pop. in 1840. 1,078; in 1850, 5,072.

BARRY COUNTY, in the southwest of Missouri, and drained by White river and branches of the Osage. Area, 830 miles. Courts are held at McDonald. Pop. in 1836, 2,504; in 1840, 4,795; in 1850, 3,467.

BARRY, p. o., Frederick co., Md., 91 ms. N. w. of Annapolis; from W. 59 ms.

BARRY, p. t., Schuylkill co., Pa., 76 ms. N. E. of Harrisburgh; from W. 186 ms. Watered by Deep creek.

BARRY, p. o., Cuyahoga co., O., 158 ms. N. E. of Columbus; from W. 346 ms.

BARRY, p. o., Lawrence co., Ark.

BARRY, p. v., Sandstone township, Jackson co., Mich., 85 ms. w. of Detroit; from W. 555 ms. Watered by Sandstone creek.

BARRY, p. o., Pike co., Ill., 78 ms. w. s. w. of Springfield; from W. 858 ms.

BARRY, p. o., Clay co., Mo., 169 ms. w. by N. of Jefferson city; from W. 1,082 ms.

BARRY, t., Barry co., Mich. Pop. 478.

BARRY'S BRIDGE, p. o., Lunenburgh co., Va., 119 ms. s. w. of Richmond; from W. 235 ms.

BARRYTON, c. h., p. o., seat of justice of Washington co., Ala., 133 ms. s. s. w. of Tuscaloosa; from W. 951 ms.

BARRYTON, p. o., Choctaw co., Ala.

BARRYTOWN, p. o., Redhook township, Dutchess co., N. Y., 53 ms. s. of Albany; from W. 325 ms. Watered by Hudson river.

BARRYVILLE, p. o., Forreetburgh township, Sullivan co., N. Y., 137 ms. s. s. w. of Albany; from W. 295 ms.

BARRYVILLE, p. o., Stark co., O., 131 ms. N. E. of Columbus; from W. 310 ms.

BARRYVILLE, p. o., Fayette co., Ga., 93 ms. w. N. w. of Milledgeville; from W. 697 ms.

BART, p. t,, Lancaster co., Pa., 55 ms. E. of Harrisburgh; from W. 112 ms. Watered by Octarara creek. Pop. 2,337.

BARTER-BROOK, p. o., Augusta co., Va., 114 ms. N. E. by E. of Richmond; from W. 156 ms.

BARTHOLOMEW COUNTY, Ind., situated toward the southeasterly part of the state, and traversed by Driftwood fork of White river and its branches. Area, 480 square miles. Courts are held at Columbus. Pop. in 1830, 5,476; in 1840. 10,042; in 1850, 5,763.

BARTHOLOMEW COUNTY, in Arkansas. Area, —— square miles. Courts are held at ————.

BARTHOLOMEW, t., Jefferson co., Ark. Pop. 247.

BARTHOLEMEW, p. o., Chicot co., Ark., 116 ms. s. E. of Little Rock; from W. 1,154 ms.

BARTLETT, t., Jefferson co., Pa.

BARTLETT, p. t., Coos co., N. H., 80 ms. N. N. E. of Concord; from W. 566 ms. Watered by Saco river. Pop. 761.

BARTLETT, p. o., Wesley township, Washington co., O., 90 ms. E. of Columbus; from W. 319 ms.

BARTON, p. t., Orleans co., Vt., 42 ms. N. E. of Montpelier; from W. 558 ms. Watered by Barton river. Pop. 987.

BARTON, p. t., Lowndes co., Miss.

BARTON, p. t., Tioga co., N. Y., 174 ms. s. w. of Albany; from W. 269 ms. Watered by Susquehannah and Chemung rivers, and Cayuga creek. Pop. 3,522.

BARTON, p. o., Washington co., Wis.

BARTON HILL, p. o., Schoharie co., N. Y.

BARTON'S, p. o., Lauderdale co., Ala., 150 ms. N. by w. of Tuscaloosa; from W. 795 ms.

BARTON'S CREEK, p. o., Dickson co., Tenn.

BARTON'S LANDING, p. o., Orleans co., Vt.

BARTONSVILLE, p. o., Windham co., Vt.

BARTONSVILLE, p. o., Monroe co., Pa., 121 ms. N. E. of Harrisburgh; from W. 214 ms.

BASCODEL, p. v., Jackson co., Ga., 83 ms. N. by w. of Milledgeville; from W. 618 ms.

BASCOM, p. o., Seneca co., O.

BASE LAKE, p. o., Washtenaw co., Mich.

BASHAM'S GAP, p. o., Morgan co., Ala.

BASHAM'S MILLS, p. o., Johnson co., Ark.

BASHAM, p. o., Meigs co., O.

BASHI, p. o., Clark co., Ala.

BASIN HARBOR, v., Ferrisburgh township, Addison co., Vt., situated on Lake Champlain.

BASIN KNOB, p. o., Johnson co., Mo.

BASKINGRIDGE, p. v., Somerset co., N. J. 46 ms. N. by E. of Trenton; from W. 216 ms.

BASSNETTSVILLE, p. o., Marion co., Va.

BASS RIVER HOTEL, p. o., Little Egg Harbor township, Burlington co., N. J., 63 ms. s. E. of Trenton; from W. 187 ms.

BASTROP, p. o., Morehouse parish, La.

BASTROP, p. o., Bastrop co., Tex.

BASSVILLE, p. o., Madison co., Miss., 11 ms. N. of Jackson; from W. 999 ms.

BATAVIA, p. v., Genesee co., N. Y., 249 ms. w. of Albany; from W. 374 ms. Watered by Tonawanda creek. Pop. in 1840, 4,219; in 1850, 4,461.

BATAVIA, c. h., p. v., Batavia township, seat of justice of Genesee co., N. Y.

BATAVIA, p. t., O., 103 ms. s. w. of Columbus; from W. 474 ms. Watered by Little Miami river. Pop. 2,791.

BATAVIA, t., Geauga co., O. Watered by Cuyahoga and Grand rivers.

BATAVIA. p. t. Kane co., Ill., 184 ms. N. of Springfield; from W. 755 ms. Pop. 892.

BATAVIA, p. t., Branch co., Mich., 117 ms. s. w. of Detroit; from W. 565 ms. Pop. 724.

BATAVIA KILL, p. o., Westchester co., N. Y., 77 ms. s. of Albany; from W. 350 ms.

BATEMAN'S STORE, p. o., Houston co., Ga., 49 ms. s. s. w. of Milledgeville; from W. 705 ms.

BATES COUNTY, situated on the westerly boundary of Missouri, and traversed by Osage river and tributaries. Area, 1,160 square miles. Seat of justice, Batesville. Pop. in 1850, 3,669.

BASTROP COUNTY, situated toward the southerly part of Texas, and traversed by Colorado river. Area, —— square miles. Seat of justice, Bastrop. Pop. in 1850, 3,099.

BATH COUNTY, Ky., situated in the northeast part of the state, on the westerly side of Licking river. Length, 34 miles; mean breadth, 10; with an area of 340 square miles. Seat of justice, Owingsville. Pop. in 1810, 7,961; in 1820, 8,799; in 1840, 9,763; in 1850, 12,115.

BATH COUNTY, in the central part of Virginia, and watered by the head branches of James, Cowpasture, and Jackson rivers. Length, 45 miles; mean breadth, 20, extending over an area of 900 square miles. The face of the country is mountainous, being situated on the Appalachian ridges. The air is pure and healthy; the soil generally sterile, though productive along the streams. Seat of justice, Bath. Pop. in 1820, 5,237; in 1830, 4,002; in 1840, 4,300; in 1850, 3,426.

BATESVILLE, p. o., Habersham co., Ga., 163 ms. N. by w. of Milledgeville; from W. 603 ms.

BATESVILLE, p. v., Guernsey co., O., 111 ms. E. of Columbus; from W. 314 ms.

BATESVILLE, c. h., p. v., seat of justice of Independence co., Ark., 90 ms. N. N. E. of Little Rock; from W. 1,086 ms. Pop. 848.

BATH p. t., Lincoln co., Me., situated on the west bank of Kennebec river, at the head of winter navigation, 12 miles from the ocean, 37 miles south of Augusta, 153 northeast of Boston. It occupies a gentle slope, about a mile and a half along the river, and extends back about three quarters of a mile. The harbor is safe and commodious, admitting vessels drawing sixteen feet of water. A large amount of capital is employed in manufactures and ship-building. The village is connected with Portland, Portsmouth, and Boston, by both railroad and steamboat lines. Pop. in 1810, 2,491; in 1820, 3,056; in 1830, 3,773; in 1840, 5,148; in 1850, 8,020.

BATH, p. t., Grafton co., N. H., 83 ms. N. w. of Concord; from W. 528 ms. Watered by Connecticut and Ammonoosuck rivers. Pop. 1,574.

BATH, c. h., p. t., seat of justice of Steuben co., N. Y., 219 ms. w. s. w. of Albany; from W. 299 ms. Watered by Coshocton river. Pop. 6,185.

BATH, v., Bath township, Steuben co., N. Y., 216 ms. w. of Albany.

BATH, v., Greenbush township, Rensselaer co., N. Y., opposite Albany, on the Hudson river; from W. 370 ms.

BATH, p. v., Northampton co., Pa., 100 ms. N. E. of Harrisburgh; from W. 193 ms.

BATH, p. t., Summit co., O., 129 ms. N. E. of Columbus; from W. 342 ms. Pop. 1,400.

BATH, c. h., p. v., seat of justice of Bath co., Va., 164 ms. w. N. w. of Richmond; from W. 201 ms.

BATH, p. v., Beaufort co., N. C., 143 ms. E. by s. of Raleigh; from W. 329 ms.

BATH, p. v., Mason co., Ill., 48 ms. w. by N. of Springfield; from W. 828 ms.

BATH, t., Allen co., O. Pop. 1,509.

BATH, t., Greene co., O. Watered by Mad river. Pop. 1,647.

BATH, v., Richmond co., Ga., 80 ms. N. E. of Milledgeville; from W. 560 ms.

BATH, p. o., Mason co., Ill.

BATH ALUM, p. o., Bath co., Va.

BATHES, v., Jefferson co., Ga. Watered by Reedy creek.

BATH SPRING, p. o., Decatur co., Tenn.

BATON ROUGE, p. o., Chester district, S. C., 67 ms. N. of Columbia; from W. 462 ms.

BATON ROUGE, seat of justice of East Baton Rouge parish, and capital of La. It occupies a pleasant slope on the east bank of the Mississippi river, 117 miles N. w. of New Orleans, and 1,237 miles from Washington. Upon the elevation east of the city stand the United States barracks; it also contains Baton Rouge college, and other prominent public buildings. This place is not otherwise particularly remarkable, except in being the seat of the state government, having succeeded New Orleans in that relation in December, 1849. Opposite is the village of West Baton Rouge. The town is pleasantly located, with good facilities for business, being nearly equally distant from Natchez and from New Orleans, from which places, and other points on the Mississippi, come steamboats to its wharves. The population in 1830 was about 1,000; in 1840, 2,269; in 1850, 3,905.

BATSON'S, p. o., Humphreys co., Tenn., 48 ms. w. of Nashville; from W. 732 ms.

BATTENVILLE, p. v., Greenwich township, Washington co., N. Y., 38 ms. N. by E. of Albany; fm. W. 408 ms.

BATTLEBOROUGH, p. v., Edgecomb co., N. C., 66 ms. E. by N. of Raleigh; from W. 232 ms.

BATTLE CREEK, p. o., Battle Creek township, Calhoun co., Mich., 117 ms. w. of Detroit; from W. 582 ms. Watered by Battle Creek and Kalamazoo rivers. Pop. 1,897.

BATTLE CREEK, p. o., Marion co., Tenn., 110 ms. s. E. of Nashville; from W. 638 ms.

BATTLEFIELD, p. o., Lauderdale co., Miss.

BATTLE GROUND, p. o., Tippecanoe co., Ind., 77 ms. N. w. of Indianapolis; from W. 635 ms.

BAUGHMAN, t., Wayne co., O. Watered by Newman's creek. Pop. 1,727.

BAUMSTOWN. p. v., Berks co., Pa., 60 ms. E. by N. of Harrisburgh; from W. 153 ms.

BAVINGTON, p. o., Washington co., Pa., 223 ms. w. of Harrisburgh; from W. 248 ms.

BAXTER'S, p. o., Muskingum co., O.

BAY, t., Ottowa co., O. Watered by Sandusky river and Mud Creek bay.

BAY CREEK, p. o., Laurens district, S. C.

BAY HUNDRED, p. o., Talbot co., Md.

BAYARD, p. o.. Shelby co., Ky., 31 ms. w. of Frankfort; from W. 573 ms.

BAY MOUNT, p. o., Greene co., Tenn.

BAYOU CHICOT, p. v., Calcasieu parish, La., 250 ms. w. N. w. of New Orleans; from W. 1,251 ms.

BAYOU GOULD, p. v., Iberville parish, La.

BAYOU MASON, t., Chicot co., Ark.

BAYOU PIERRE, p. o., De Soto parish, La.

BAYOU ROUGE, p. o., Avoyelles parish, La.

BAY RIVER, p. o., Craven co., N. C.

BAZETTA, p. t., Trumbull co., O. Pop. 1,302.

BEACH BRANCH, p. o., Beaufort district, S. C., 113 ms. s. of Columbia; from W. 619 ms.

BEACH GROVE, p. o., Salem township, Luzerne co., Pa., 104 ms. N. N. E. of Harrisburgh; from W. 208 ms. Watered by Susquehanna river.

BEACH HAVEN, p. o., Luzerne co., Pa.

BEACHLAND, p. o., Chattooga co., Ga.

BEACHWOOD, p. o., Sheboygan co., Wis.

BEALE'S MILLS, p. v., Washington co., Pa., 200 ms. w. of Harrisburgh; from W. 216 ms.

BEALLSVILLE, p. v., Sunbury township, Monroe co., O., 127 ms. E. s. E. of Columbus; from W. 293 ms. Pop. 276.

BEALLSVILLE, p. o., Washington co., Pa.

BEAMSVILLE, p. o., Darke co., O., 98 ms. w. of Columbus; from W. 490 ms.

BEAN'S STATION, p. o., Granger co., Tenn., 225 ms. E. by N. of Nashville; from W. 457 ms.

BEAN BLOSSOM, p. o., Browne co., Ind.

BEANTOWN, p. o., Charles co., Md.

BEAR BRANCH, p. o., Duplin co., N. C.

BEAR BRANCH, p. o., Ohio co., Ind.

BEAR CREEK, p. o., Pickens co., Ala.

BEAR CREEK, p. o., Sabine co., Tex.

BEAR CREEK, p. o., Poweshiek co., Iowa.

BEAR CREEK, p. o., Sauk co., Wis.

BEAR CREEK, t., Columbia co., Pa.

BEAR CREEK, p. o., Luzerne co., Pa.

BEAR CREEK, p. o., Cedar co., Mo.

BEAR CREEK, p. o., Montgomery co., Ill.

BEAR CREEK, p. o., Hamilton co., Ill., 166 ms. s. by E. of Springfield; from W. 786 ms.

BEAR CREEK, t., Montgomery co., O.

BEARDEN, p. o., La Vaca co., Tex.

BEARD'S BLUFF, p. o., Marshall co., Ala.

BEARDSTOWN, p. o., Perry co., Tenn., 79 ms. s. w. of Nashville; from W. 763 ms.

BEARDSTOWN, p. v., Cass co., Ill. Watered by Illinois river.

BEARFIELD, t., Perry co., O. Pop. 1,710.

BEAR GAP, p. o., Northumberland co., Pa., 76 ms. N. of Harrisburgh; from W. 186 ms.

BEARMONT, p. o., Schuylkill co., Pa.

BEAR RANGE, p. o., Autauga co., Ala.

BEARSVILLE, p. o., Ulster co., N. Y.

BEAR TOWN, p. o., Lancaster co., Pa., 51 ms. s. E. of Harrisburgh; from W. 129 ms.

BEAR WALLOW, p. o., Barren co., Ky.

BEASELEY, p. o., Jefferson co., Flo.

BEATTIE'S BLUFF, p. o., Madison co., Miss., 35 ms. N. by E. of Jackson; from W. 1,010 ms.

BEATTIE'S BRIDGE, p. o., Bladen co., N. C.

BEATTIE'S FORD, p. o., Lincoln co., N. C., 154 ms. w. by s. of Raleigh; from W. 391 ms.

BEATTIE'S PRAIRIE, p. o., Benton co., Ark.

BEATTYSTOWN, p. v., Mansfield township, Warren co., N. J., 58 ms. N. of Trenton; from W. 219 miles. Watered by Musconetcong creek.

BEAUCOUP, v., Washington co., Ill., 126 ms. s. of Springfield; from W. 801 ms.

BEAUFORT COUNTY, situated in the easterly part of North Carolina, on Pamlico sound, and traversed by Pamlico river. Length, 40 miles; mean breadth, 17; with an area of 670 square miles. The face of the country is generally level. Seat of justice, Washington. Pop. in 1820, 9,900; in 1830, 10,969; in 1840, 12,225; in 1850, 13,816.

BEAUFORT DISTRICT, situated at the southeast extremity of South Carolina, with Savannah river on the southwest, and Combahee river on the northeast. Length, 60 miles; mean breadth, 30; with an area of 1,800 square miles. The face of the country is generally level, and a considerable portion of the soil sandy and light. Much of it, however, is well adapted for cotton, rice, and Indian corn. Seat of justice, Coosawhatchee. Pop. in 1820, 32,199; in 1830, 37,032; in 1840, 35,794; in 1850, 38,805.

BEAUFORT, c. h., p. t., seat of justice of Carteret co., N. C., 168 ms. s. E. of Raleigh; from W. 369 ms.

BEAUFORT, p. t., Beaufort district, S. C., 146 ms. s. of Columbia; from W. 695 ms. Watered by Port Royal river. Pop. 1,108.

BEAUFORT, p. o., Kenton co., Ky.

BEAUFORT, p. o., Franklin co., Mo.

BEAUMONT, p. o., Luzerne co., Pa.

BEAUMONT, p. o., Dane co., Wis.; from W. 872 ms.

BEAUMONT, p. o., Chatham co., N. C.

BEAUVAIS, p. o., St. Genevieve co., Mo.

BEAVER COUNTY, situated in the western boundary of Pennsylvania, and traversed by Ohio and Beaver rivers. Length, about 40 miles; mean breadth, 15; with an area of 600 square miles. The face of the country is broken and hilly; the soil generally fertile, well wooded and watered. Seat of justice, Beaver. Pop. in 1820, 13,340; in 1830, 24,183; in 1840, 29,368; in 1850, 26,689.

BEAVER, t., Crawford co., Pa. Pop. 672.

BEAVER, c. h., p. b., seat of justice of Beaver co., Pa., 27 ms. N. by w. of Harrisburgh; from W. 253 ms. Pop. 2,054.

BEAVER, t., Venango co., Pa.

BEAVER, c. h., p. t., seat of justice of Beaver co., Pa., 232 ms. w. by N. of Harrisburgh; from W. 260 ms.

BEAVER, p. t., Pike co., O., 73 ms. s. of Columbus; from W. 389 ms. Pop. 530.

BEAVER, p. t., Union co., Pa. Pop. 1,659.

BEAVER, p. t., Guernsey co., O. Pop. 1,991.

BEAVER, t., Columbiana co., O.

BEAVER, p. o., Anderson co., Tex.

BEAVER, p. o., Pike co., O.

BEAVER, t., Boone co., Ill.

BEAVER BROOK, p. o., Sullivan co., N. Y., 132 ms. s. s. w. of Albany; from W. 292 ms.

BEAVER CREEK, t., Greene co., O. Watered by Little Miami river. Pop. 2,063.

BEAVER CREEK, p. o., Washington co., Md., 103 ms. N. w. of Annapolis; from W. 71 ms.

BEAVER CREEK, p. o., Dale co., Ala.

BEAVER CREEK, p. o., Henry co., O., 139 ms. N. w. of Columbus; from W. 484 ms.

BEAVER CREEK, p. o., Surry co., N. C., 155 ms. w. N. w. of Raleigh; from W. 343 ms.

BEAVER CREEK, p. o., Anderson co., Ky., 27 ms. s. w. of Frankfort; from W. 569 ms.

BEAVER CREEK, p. o., Pulaski co., Ind.

BEAVER CREEK, p. o., Bond co., Ill., 84 ms. s. of Springfield; from W. 768 ms.

BEAVER CREEK, p. o., Campbell co., Va.

BEAVER CREEK, p. o., Pulaski co., Ind.

BEAVER DAM, p. o., Anne Arundel co., Md., 18 ms. from Annapolis; from W. 35 ms.

BEAVER DAM, p. o., Goochland co., Va., 24 ms. w. of Richmond; from W. 136 ms.

BEAVER DAM, p. o., Anson co., N. C., 161 ms. s. w. of Raleigh; from W. 430 ms.

BEAVER DAM, t., Erie co., Pa.

BEAVER DAM, p. o., Union co., N. C.

BEAVER DAM, p. o., Middleburgh co., S. C.

BEAVER DAM, p. o., Randolph co., Ala., 172 ms. E. of Tuscaloosa; from W. 770 ms.

BEAVER DAM, p. o., Kosciusko co., Ind.

BEAVER DAM, p. o., Allen co., O.

BEAVER DAM DEPOT, p. o., Hanover co., Va., 36 ms. N. of Richmond; from W. 105 ms.

BEAVER DAM, p. o., Clark co., Miss.

BEAVER DAM, p. o., Dodge co., Wis.

BEAVER DAM FORKS, p. o., Tipton co., Tenn., 176 ms. w. s. w. of Nashville; from W. 879 ms.

BEAVER DAMS, p. o., Chemung co., N. Y.

BEAVER DAM SPRINGS, p. o., Hickman, Tenn.

BEAVER ISLAND, Michilimackinac co., Mich.

BEAVER KILL, p. o., Rockland township, Sullivan co., N. Y., 97 ms. s. s. w. of Albany; from W. 326 ms.

BEAVER MEADOW, p. o., Chenango co., N. Y.

BEAVER MEADOW, p. o., Lausanne township, Northampton co., Pa., 102 ms. N. E. of Harrisburgh; from W. 210 ms.

BEAVER MEADOWS, p. o., Carbon co., Pa.

BEAVER RIDGE, p. o., Knox co., Tenn., 176 ms. E. by s. of Nashville; from W. 521 ms.

BEAVER RUIN, p. o., Union co., Ark.

BEAVER PONDS, p. o., Montgomery co., Ky.

BEAVERTOWN, p. v., Union co., Pa., 83 ms. N. w. of Harrisburgh; from W. 174 ms.

BECCARIA, t., Clearfield co., Pa. Pop. 687.

BECKAMSVILLE, p. o., Chester district, S. C., 52 ms. N. by w. of Columbia; from W. 455 ms.

BECKET, p. t., Berkshire co., Mass., 118 ms. w. of Boston; from W. 377 ms.

BECKETTSVILLE, p. o., Tallapoosa co., Ala.

BECKETT'S STORE, p. o. Pickaway co., O.

BECKLEY, p. o., Fayette co., Va., 288 ms. w. by N. of Richmond; from W. 325 ms.

BECKVILLE, p. o., Raleigh co., Va.

BEBBINGTON, t., Washington co., Me. Pop. 147.

BEDDINGTON, p. o., Berkley co., Va. (Now Haines-ville.)

BEDFORD COUNTY, situated in the southern boundary of Pennsylvania, and drained by branches of Juniata and Potomac rivers. Length, 52 miles; mean breadth, 31; with an area of 1,600 square miles. The face of the country is extremely diversified by mountains, hills, and valleys, with an equally varied soil—barren and rocky in the mountains, and fertile and well watered in the valleys. Seat of justice, Bedford. Pop. in 1820, 20,248; in 1830, 24,502; in 1840, 29,335; in 1850, 23,052.

BEDFORD COUNTY, in the southerly part of Virginia, between James and Staunton rivers. Length, 30 miles; mean breadth, 22; with an area of 660 square miles. The face of the country is generally hilly, and in some parts mountainous. The soil is moderately fertile. Seat of justice, Liberty. Pop. in 1820, 19,305; in 1830, 20,253; in 1840, 20,203; in 1850, 24,081.

BEDFORD COUNTY, in the central part of Tennessee. Length, 35 miles; mean breadth, 25; with an area of 875 square miles. The face of the country is rolling, and the soil moderately fertile. Seat of justice, Shelbyville. Pop. in 1820, 16,006; in 1830, 30,444; in 1840, 10,546; in 1850, 21,512.

BEDFORD, p. t., Hillsborough co., N. H., 21 ms. s. by E. of Concord; from W. 460 ms. Watered by Merrimack and Piscataquog rivers. Pop. 1,905.

BEDFORD, p. t., Middlesex co., Mass., 15 ms. N. w. of Boston; from W. 455 ms. Watered by Shawsheen river. Pop. 975.

BEDFORD, c. h., p. v., seat of justice, together with White Plains, of Westchester co., N. Y., 125 ms. s. of Albany; from W. 270 ms. Pop. 3,270.

BEDFORD, p. t., Cuyahoga co., O., 149 ms. N. w. of Columbus; from W. 347 ms. Watered by Tinker's creek. Pop. 1,853.

BEDFORD, p. t., Calhoun co., Mich., 124 ms. w. of Detroit; from W. 589 ms. Watered by Kalamazoo river. Pop. 747.

BEDFORD, c. h., p. b., Bedford township, seat of justice of Bedford co., Pa., 103 ms. s. w. by w. of Harrisburgh; from W. 129 ms. Pop. 1,203.

BEDFORD, t., Bedford co., Pa. Watered by Roystown river. Pop. 1,831.

BEDFORD, c. h., p. v., seat of justice of Trimble co., Ky., 41 ms. s. w. by w. of Frankfort; from W. 572 ms. Pop. 285.

BEDFORD, c. h., p. v., seat of justice of Lawrence co., Ind., 71 ms. s. w. of Indianapolis; from W. 621 ms.

BEDFORD, p. o., Warren co., Ill., 103 ms. N. w. of Springfield; from W. 860 ms.

BEDFORD, p. o., Assumption parish, La., 98 ms. w. of New Orleans; from W. 1,270 ms.

BEDFORD, t., Monroe co., Mich. Pop. 888.

BEDFORD, t., Coshocton co.. O., 60 ms. N. E. of Columbus.

BEDFORD, t., Meigs co., O. Watered by Shade river. Pop. 917.

BEDFORD STATION, p. o., Westchester co., N. Y.

BEDI, p. o., Grimes co., Tex.

BEDMINSTER, t., Somerset co., N. J. Pop. 1,814.

BEDMINSTER, p. t., Bucks co., Pa. Watered by Tohicton creek. Pop. 1,911.

BEE BRANCH, p. o., Pettis co., Mo.

BEECH BLUFF, p. o., Marion co., Ill., 166 ms. s. by E. of Springfield; from W. 772 ms.

BEECH BLUFF, p. o., Dallas co., Ark.

BEECH CREEK, p. o., Clinton co., Pa.

BEECH FORK, p. o., Washington co., Ky.

BEECH GROVE, p. o., Marshall co., Ala., 137 ms. N. E. of Tuscaloosa; from W. 711 ms.

BEECH GROVE, p. o., Rush co., Ind., 33 ms. s. E. of Indianapolis; from W. 545 ms.

BEECH GROVE, p. o., Coffee co., Tenn., 55 ms. s. E. of Nashville; from W. 665 ms.

BEECH GROVE, p. o., Phillips co., Ark.

BEECH HILL, p. o., Livingston parish, La., 87 ms. N. w. of New Orleans; from W. 1,174 ms.

BEECH ISLAND, p. o., Edgefield district, S. C.

BEECH LAND, p. o., Union co., Ark.

BEECH PARK, p. o., Gallatin co., Ky., 44 ms. N. of Frankfort; from W. 542 ms.

BEECH POINT, p. o., Gibson co., Tenn.

BEECH RIVER, p. o., Perry co., Tenn., 103 ms. s. w. of Nashville; from W. 787 ms.

BEECH WOODS, p. o., Warren co., Pa.

BEECHY MIRE, p. o., Preble co., O., 107 ms. w. by s. of Columbus; from W. 500 ms.

BEE CREEK MILLS, p. o., Platte co., Mo.

BEE HIVE, p. o., Clinton co., Mo.

BEEKMAN, p. t., Dutchess co., N. Y., 87 ms. s. of Albany, from W. 307 ms. Watered by Fishkill river. Pop. 1,386.

BEEKMAN'S MILLS, p. o., Somerset co., N. J., 26 ms. N. by E. of Trenton; from W. 196 ms.

BEEKMANTOWN, p. t., Clinton co., N. Y., 169 ms. N. of Albany; from W. 544 ms. Watered by Chazy and Chateaugay lakes and rivers. Pop. 3,384.

BEELERSVILLE, v., Carroll co., Ark. Watered by Crooked creek.

BEELER'S STATION, p. o., Marshall co., Va., 351 ms. N. w. by w. of Richmond; from W. 256 ms.

BEEMERVILLE, p. o., Sussex co., N. J., 84 ms. N. of Trenton; from W. 253 ms.

BEESLEY'S POINT, p. o., Cape May co., N. J.

BEESON's STORE, p. o., Highland co., O., 69 ms. s. w. of Columbus; from W. 442 ms.

BEETOWN, p. o., Grant co., Wis.

BEETREE, p. o., Kershaw district, S. C.

BEGLEY'S, p. o., Perry co., Ky.

BEL AIR, c. h., p. v., seat of justice of Harford co., Md., 53 ms. N. by E. of Annapolis; from W. 63 ms.

BELAIR, p. v., Lancaster district, S. C., 90 ms. N. by E. of Columbia; from W. 416 ms.

BELAIR, p. o., Richmond co., Ga., 85 ms. E. by N. of Milledgeville; from W. 586 ms.

BELCHER, p. o., Washington co., N. Y.

BELCHERTOWN, p. t., Hampshire co., Mass., 78 ms. w. of Boston; from W. 382 ms. Pop. 2,680.

BELDEN, p. o., McHenry co., Ill.

BELEW's CREEK, p. o., Stokes co., N. C., 102 ms. N. w. of Raleigh; from W. 305 ms.

BELFAST, p. t., port of entry and seat of justice of Waldo co., Me., situated at the head of Belfast bay, on the west side of Penobscot river, and 30 miles from the ocean; 43 ms. E. of Augusta, and 636 ms. from W. It has a spacious harbor. safe for vessels of the largest class, and is extensively engaged in the coasting and foreign trade, fisheries, and ship-building; principal exports, lumber and fish. Pop. in 1810, 1,259; in 1820, 2,026; in 1830, 3,077; in 1840, 4,186; in 1850, 5,051.

BELFAST, t., Bedford co., Pa., 78 ms. s. w. of Harrisburgh; from W. 98 ms.

BELFAST, p. t., Alleghany co., N. Y., 268 ms. w. of Albany; from W. 341 ms. Watered by Genesee river. Pop. 1,679.

BELFAST, p. o., Northampton co., Pa., 112 ms. N. E. of Harrisburgh; from W. 205 ms.

BELFAST, p. o., Clermont co., O., 105 ms. E. of Columbus; from W. 476 ms.

BELFAST, p. o., Marshall co., Tenn., 61 ms. s. of Nashville; from W. 703 ms.

BELFORD, p. v., Nash co., N. C., 51 ms. E. of Raleigh; from W. 247 ms.

BELFORT, p. o., Crogan township, Lewis co., N. Y., 150 ms. N. w. of Albany; from W. 449 ms.

BELGRADE, p. t., Kennebec co., Me., 11 ms. N. of Augusta; from W. 606 ms. Pop. 1,722.

BELGRADE MILLS, p. v., Kennebec co., Me., 17 ms. N. of Augusta; from W. 610 ms. Pop.

BELHAM, p. o., Goochland co., Va., 35 ms. w. by N. of Richmond; from W. 125 ms.

BELKNAP COUNTY, situated in the easterly part of New Hampshire, with Lake Winnipisiogee on the northeast, and Pemigewasset river on the west. Winnipisiogee river intersects this county, which forms a portion of its southeast boundary. Area, 288 square miles. The face of the country is mountainous and hilly, and much of the soil highly fertile. Seat of justice, Gilford. Pop. in 1850, 17,721.

BELL COUNTY, situated in Texas. Area, ―― square miles. Seat of justice, Nolansville.

BELL, t., Clearfield co., Pa.

BELL AIR, p. o., Belmont co., O.

BELL AIR, p. o., Cooper co., Mo.

BELL AIR, p. o., Crawford co., Ill.

BELL BROOK, p. o., Greene co., O., 70 ms. s. w. of Columbus; from W. 463 ms.

BELL CENTRE, p. o., Logan co., O.

BELLEFONTAINE, c. h., p. v., Lake township, seat of justice of Logan co., O., 69 ms. N. w. of Columbus; from W. 456 ms.

BELLEFONTAINE, v., St. Louis co., Mo. Watered by Missouri and Mississippi rivers.

BELLEFONTAINE, p. o., Choctaw co., Miss., 120 ms. N. N. E. of Jackson; from W. 935 ms.

BELLEFONTE, c. h., p. b., seat of justice of Centre co., Pa., 85 ms. N. w. of Harrisburg; from W. 117 ms. Watered by Spring creek. Pop. 1,179.

BELLEFONTE, c. h., p. v., seat of justice of Jackson co., Ala., 166 ms. N. E. of Tuscaloosa; from W. 667 ms. Watered by Paint Rock river.

BELLEFONTE, p. o., Pulaski co., Mo., 81 ms. s. of Jefferson city; from W. 996 ms.

BELLEFOUNTAIN, p. o., Columbia co., Wis.

BELLEFOUNTAIN, p. o., Mahaska co., Iowa.

BELLE HAVEN, p. o., Accomac co., Va., 175 ms. E. by N. of Richmond; from W. 215 ms.

BELLE ISLE, p. v., Camillus township, Onondaga co., N. Y., 137 ms. w. by N. of Albany; from W. 354 ms.

BELLEMONT, p. o., Lancaster co., Pa.

BELLEMONTE, p. o., St. Louis co., Mo.

BELLE OMBRE, p. o., Ballard co., Ky.

BELLEPOINT, p. o., Delaware co., O., 32 ms. N. of Columbus; from W. 416 ms.

BELLEPOINT, p. o., Boone co., Iowa.

BELLE PRAIRIE, p. o., Hamilton co., Ill.

BELLERICA, t., Washington co., Mo.

BELLE RIVER, p. o., St. Clair co., Mich., 55 ms. N. by E. of Detroit; from W. 579 ms.

BELLE VERNON, p. o., Wyandott co., O.

BELLE VERNON, p. o., Fayette co., Pa., 197 ms. w. s. w. of Harrisburgh; from W. 219 ms.

BELLEVIEW, p. o., Talbot co., Ga., 97 ms. w. s. w. of Milledgeville; from W. 719 ms.

BELLEVIEW, p. o., Christian co., Ky., 214 ms. s. w. of Frankfort; from W. 741 ms.

BELLEVIEW, p. v., Calhoun co., Ill., 85 ms. s. w. of Springfield; from W. 859 ms.

BELLEVIEW, t., Washington co., Mo.

BELLEVIEW, c. h., p. t., seat of justice of Jackson co., Pop. 714.

BELLEVIEW, p. o., Rusk co., Tex.

BELLEVIEW, p. o., Bossier parish, La.

BELLEVIEW, p. o., Lebanon co., Pa.

BELLEVILLE, p. v., Ellisburgh township, Jefferson co., N. Y., 173 ms. N, w. of Albany; from W. 403 ms.

BELLEVILLE, p. v., Belleville township, Essex co., N. J., 69 ms. N. E. of Trenton; from W. 234 ms. Watered by Passaic river. Pop. 3,513.

BELLEVILLE, p. o, Mifflin co., Pa., 70 ms. N. w. of Harrisburgh; from W. 162 ms.

BELLEVILLE, p. o., Wood co., Va., 351 ms. N. w. of Richmond; from W. 319 ms.

BELLEVILLE, p. v., Richland co., O., 68 ms. N. N. E. of Columbus; from W. 387 ms.

BELLEVILLE, p. o., Hendricks co., Ind., 20 ms. w. of Indianapolis; from W. 591 ms.

BELLEVILLE, c. h., p. v., seat of justice of St. Clair co., Ill., 100 ms. s. by w. of Springfield; from W. 809 ms.

BELLEVILLE, c. h., p. v., seat of justice of Desha co., Ark. Watered by Arkansas river.

BELLEVILLE, p. v., Conecuh co., Ala., 154 ms. s. by E. of Tuscaloosa; from W. 935 ms.

BELLEVILLE, p. o., Wayne co., Mich.

BELLEVILLE, p. o., Roane co., Tenn., 131 ms. E. by s. of Nashville; from W. 550 ms.

BELLEVILLE PORT, p. v., Essex co., Mass., 40 ms. N. by E. of Boston; from W. 476 ms. Watered by Merrimack river.

BELLEVUE, p. v., Huron co., O., 96 ms. N. by E. of Columbus; from W. 405 ms.

BELLEVUE, p. t., Eaton co., Mich., 119 ms. w. N. w. of Detroit; from W. 584 ms. Pop. 767.

BELLEVUE, v., Bellevue township, Eaton co., Mich. Watered by Battle creek. Pop.

BELLFAIR MILLS, p. o., Stafford co., Va.

BELLINGHAM, p. t., Norfolk co., Mass., 36 ms. s. w. of Boston; from W. 419 ms. Watered by Charles river. Pop. 1,281.

BELL MOUNT, p. o., Somerset co., Md.

BELLONA ARSENAL, v., Chesterfield co., Va., 12 ms. N. w of Richmond; from W. 129 ms. Watered by James river.

BELLOWS FALLS, p. v., Rockingham township, Windham co., Vt., 98 ms. s. by E. of Montpelier; from W. 445 ms. Watered by Connecticut river.

BELL PLAIN, p. o., Marshall co., Ill., 97 ms. N. of Springfield; from W. 780 ms.

BELL POINT, p. o., Giles co., Va.

BELLPORT, p. v., Brookhaven township, Suffolk co., N. Y., 209 ms. s. e. m. of Albany; from W. 200 ms. Situated on Fireplace bay, L. I.

BELLSBURGH, p. o., Dickson co., Tenn.

BELL'S CROSS ROADS, p. o., Louisa co., Va.

BELL'S LANDING, p. v., Monroe co., Ala., 117 ms. s. of Tuscaloosa; from W. 909 ms. Watered by Alabama river.

BELL'S MINES, p. o., Crittenden co., Ky.

BELL'S RIDGE, p. o., Madison co., Iowa.

BELL'S STORE, p. o., Fairfield district, S. C., 37 ms. N. of Columbia; from W. 491 ms.

BELL'S VALLEY, p. o., Rockbridge co., Va., 163 ms. w. by N. of Richmond; from W. 205 ms.

BELLVALE, p. o., Orange co., N. Y.

BELLVILLE, c. h., p. t., seat of justice of Austin co., Texas.

BELLVILLE, p. o., Hamilton co., Flo.

BELMONT COUNTY, situated in the east part of Ohio, on the westerly side of Ohio river. Length, 25 miles; mean breadth, 20; with an area of 500 square miles. The face of the country is hilly; the soil generally very productive. Seat of justice, St. Clairsville. Pop. in 1820, 2,329; in 1830, 28,627; in 1840, 30,901; in 1850, 34,600.

BELMONT, p. t., Waldo co., Me., 34 ms. E. by N. of Augusta; from W. 635 ms. Pop. 1,486.

BELMONT, t., Franklin co., N. Y., 202 ms. N. of Albany; from W. 572 ms. Watered by Chateaugy and Trout rivers. Pop. 660.

BELMONT, p. o., Sabine co., La.

BELMONT, p. v., Goshen township, Belmont co., O., 109 ms. E. of Columbus; from W. 292 ms.

BELMONT, p. o., Newberry district, S. C., 51 ms. N. w. of Columbia; from W. 515 ms.

BELMONT, p. v., Panola co., Miss., 169 ms. N. of Jackson; from W. 937 ms.

BELMONT, p. v., Fayette co., Tenn., 195 ms. s. w. of Nashville; from W. 884 ms.

BELMONT, p. o., Sumter co., Ala., 72 ms. s. w. of Tuscaloosa; from W. 884 ms.

BELMONT, p. o., Loudoun co., Va., 148 ms. N. of Richmond; from W. 29 ms.

BELMONT, p. o., Pike co., Ill., 69 ms. w. by s. of Springfield; from W. 849 ms.

BELMONT, p. v., Lafayette co., Wis., 64 ms. s. w. of Madison; from W. 896 ms.

BELMONT, p. o., Crawford co., Ark.

BELMONT, p. o., Gonzales co., Tex.

BELOIT, p. o., Rock co., Wis., 55 ms. s. s. E. of Madison; from W. 820 ms.

BELPRE, p. t., Washington co., O., 116 ms. s. E. of Columbus; from W. 304 ms. Watered by Ohio river. Pop. 1,622.

BELSARNE, p. o., Cambria co., Pa.

BELTON, p. o., Anderson co., S. C.

BELTSVILLE, p. o., Prince George's co., Md., 28 ms. w. s. w. of Annapolis; from W. 13 ms.

BELVIDERE, t., Lamoille co., Vt., 47 ms. N. by w, of Montpelier; from W. 557 ms. Watered by Lamoille river. Pop. 256.

BELVIDERE, c. h., p. v., Oxford township, seat of justice of Warren co., N. J., 57 ms. N. N. w. of Trenton; from W. 212 ms. Watered by Delaware river and Pequest creek. Pop. 1,001.

BELVIDERE, p. o., Sumner co., Tenn., 55 ms. N. E. of Nashville; from W. 696 ms.

BELVIDERE, t., Boone co., Ill.

BELVIDERE, p. o., Alleghany co., N. Y., 267 ms. w. of Albany; from W. 330 ms.

BELVIDERE, p. v., Winnebago co., Ill., 219 ms. N. by E. of Springfield; from W. 788 ms.

BEM, p. o., Greene co., Wis.

BEMAN'S CROSS-ROADS, p. o., Sampson co., N. C.

BEMUS'S HEIGHTS, p. o., Stillwater township, Saratoga co., N. Y., 26 ms. N. of Albany; from W. 396 ms.

BENBROOK'S MILLS, p. o., Izard co., Ark.

BENDERSVILLE, p. o., Adams co., Pa.

BENDY'S LANDING, p. o., Tyler co., Tex.

BENEDICT, p. v., Charles co., Md., 59 ms. s. s. E. of Annapolis; from W. 54 ms. Watered by Patuxent river.

BENEDICTA, t., Aroostook co., Me. Pop. 325.

BENELA, p. o., Chickasaw co., Miss.

BENEVOLA, p. o., Pickens co., Ala., 34 ms. w. of Tuscaloosa; from W. 852 ms.

BENEVOLA, p. o., Washington co., Md.

BENEZETTE, p. o., Elk co., Pa.

BENFORD'S STORE, p. o., Somerset co., Pa.

BENGAL, p. o., Clinton co., Mich.

BENHADEN, p. o., Wakulla co., Flo.

BENICIA, c. h., p. v., seat of justice of Solans co., Cal.

BENJAMINTOWN, p. o., Bradford co., Pa., 142 ms. N. of Harrisburgh; from W. 252 ms.

BENNET'S BAYOU, t., Benton co., Ark.

BENNETT'S CORNERS, p. o., Lenox township, Madison co., N. Y.

BENNETT'S CREEK, p. o., Steuben co., N. Y.

BENNETT'S FERRY, p. o., Jackson co., Tenn.

BENNETT'S MILLS, p. o., Lewis co., Va.

BENNETT'S RIVER, p. o., Fulton co., Ark.

BENNETTSVILLE, p. o., Chenango co., N. Y.

BENNETTSVILLE, c. h., p. v., seat of justice of Marlborough district, S. C., 107 ms. N. E. of Columbia; from W. 409 ms.

BENNETTSVILLE, p. o., St. Clair co., Ala., 112 ms. N. E. of Tuscaloosa; from W. 705 ms.

BENNETTSVILLE, p. o., Clark co., Ind.

BENNINGTON COUNTY, situated at the southwest corner of Vermont. Length, 40 miles; mean width, 17; with an area of 680 square miles. The face of the country is mountainous and hilly; the soil generally productive, and particularly suited for grazing and fruit. Seats of justice at Bennington and Manchester. Pop. in 1820, 16,125; in 1830, 17,470; in 1840, 16,872; in 1850, 18,589.

BENNINGTON, p. v., seat of justice, together with Manchester, of Bennington co., Vt., 130 ms. N. w. of Boston, 117 ms. s. of Montpelier, and 407 ms. from W. It was named from Benning Wentworth, who, in 1749, was the royal governor of New Hampshire. It is drained by branches of Hoosick river, which afford good water-power. Marble, iron ore, and yellow ochre, are found here. The principal village is on elevated ground, and makes a good appearance. A little to the east is a considerable manufacturing village. In 1777, General Stark, with 800 Americans, defeated a superior British force, on the west border of this town. Pop. in 1850, 3,923.

BENNINGTON, p. t., Wyoming co., N. Y., 264 ms. w. of Albany; from W. 370 ms. Watered by Cayuga and Tonawanda creeks. Pop. 2,406.

BENNINGTON, p. t., Shiawassee co., Mich. Watered by Looking-Glass river. Pop. 601.

BENNINGTON, p. t., Morrow co., O., 40 ms. N. E. of Columbus; from W. 409 ms. Pop. 1,265.

BENNINGTON, p. t., Hillsborough co., N. H. Pop. 541.

BENNINGTON, p. o., Switzerland co., Ind.

BENNINGTON, p. o , Marion co., Iowa.

BENNINGTON CENTRE. p. o., Bennington co., Vt.

BENSALEM, t., Bucks co., Pa. Pop. 2,239.

BENSON, p. t., Rutland co., Vt., 85 ms. s. w. of Montpelier; from W. 457 ms. Situated on Lake Champlain. Pop. 1,305.

BENSON, p. o., Hope township, Hamilton co., N. Y., 65 ms. N. by w. of Albany; from W. 434 ms.

BENT CREEK, p. o., Appomattox, Va., 106 ms. w. of Richmond; from W. 192 ms.

BENTIVOGLIO, p. o., Albemarle co., Va., 80 ms. w. of Richmond; from W. 110 ms.

BENTLEY'S CORNERS, p. o., Jefferson co., N. Y.

BENTLEYVILLE, p. v., Washington co., Pa., 198 ms. w. of Harrisburg; from W. 220 ms. Watered by Pigeon creek.

BENTLEYVILLE, p. o., Halifax co., Va., 115 ms. s. w. of Richmond; from W. 213 ms.

BENTLEY CREEK, p. o., Bradford co., Pa.

BENTON COUNTY, situated on the easterly boundary of Alabama, and watered by the Tallapoosa and a branch of Coosa river. Area, 1,060 square miles. Seat of justice, Jacksonville. Pop. in 1840, 14,260; in 1850, 17,163.

BENTON COUNTY, situated toward the westerly part of Missouri, and traversed by Osage river. Area, 1,050 square miles. Face of the country generally uneven, and the soil fertile. Seat of justice, Warsaw. Pop. in 1836, 1,512; in 1840, 4,205; in 1850, 5,015.

BENTON COUNTY, Tenn., situated in the westerly part of the state, between Tennessee and Big-Sandy rivers. Area, 375 square miles. Seat of justice, Camden. Pop. in 1840, 4,772; in 1850, 6,305.

BENTON COUNTY, situated at the northwest corner of Arkansas, and watered by White river and branches of the Neosho. Area, 1,050 square miles. Seat of justice, Bentonville. Pop. in 1840, 2,228; in 1850, 3,710.

BENTON COUNTY, situated on the western boundary of Indiana. Area, 520 square miles. Seat of justice, Oxford. Pop. in 1850, 1,144.

BENTON COUNTY, situated on the western boundary of Florida, between Withlacoochee river and the gulf of Mexico. Area, 120 square miles. Seat of justice, Melendez. Pop. in 1850, 926.

BENTON COUNTY, situated toward the easterly part of Iowa, and traversed by Cedar river. Area, 660 square miles. Seat of justice, Vinton. Pop. in 1850, 672.

BENTON COUNTY, situated toward the easterly part of Minnesota, on the easterly side of the Mississippi river. Area, —— square miles. Seat of justice, Sauk Rapids.

BENTON COUNTY, Oregon, on St. Mary's river. Area, —— square miles. Seat of justice, ——. Pop. in 1850, 418.

BENTON, p. t., Yates co., N. Y., 184 ms. w. of Albany; from W. 337 ms. Watered by Crooked Lane outlet and Cashong creek. Pop. 3,456.

BENTON CENTRE, p. v., Benton township, Yates co., N. Y.

BENTON, p. o., Columbia co., Pa., 110 ms. N. by E. of Harrisburg; from W. 221 ms.

BENTON, v., Lumpkin co., Ga., 125 ms. N. N. w. of Milledgeville; from W. 635 ms. Watered by Chestatee and Etowah rivers.

BENTON, p. o., Lowndes co., Ala., 98 ms. s. s. E. of Tuscaloosa; from W. 859 ms.

BENTON, t., Hocking co., O. Pop. 933.

BENTON, c. h., p. v., seat of justice of Saline co., Ark., 24 ms. s. w. of Little Rock; from W. 1,089 ms.

BENTON, p. o., Marshall co., Tenn., 57 ms. s. of Nashville; from W. 708 ms.

BENTON, p. v., Salt-Creek township, Holmes co., O., 92 ms. N. E. of Columbus; from W. 344 ms. Watered by Martin's creek.

BENTON, c. h., p. v., seat of justice of Franklin co., Ill., 151 ms. s. s. E. of Springfield; from W. 816 ms.

BENTON, p. o., Washtenaw co., Mich., 45 ms. w. of Detroit; from W. 522 ms.

BENTON, c. h., p. v., seat of justice of Yazoo co., Miss 50 ms. N. w. of Jackson; from W. 1,019 ms.

BENTON, c. h., p. v., seat of justice of Scott co., M. 222 ms. s. E. of Jefferson city; from W. 870 ms

BENTON, p. o., Hamilton co., Flo.

BENTON, t., Macon co., Mo.

BENTON, p. o. Iowa co., Wis.

BENTON, t., Linn co., Mo.

BENTON, t., Newton co., Mo.

BENTON, t., Polk co., Mo.

BENTON, t., Taney co., Mo.

BENTON, t., Wayne co., Mo.

BENTON, p. o., Grafton co., N. H.

BENTON, p. t., Elkhart co., Ind. Pop. 1,193.

BENTON, p. o., Franklin co., Ill.

BENTON, p. o., Iowa co., Wis.

BENTON, p. o., Marshall co., Ky.

BENTON, c. h., p. v., seat of justice of Polk co., Tenn.

BENTON CENTRE, p. o., Yates co., N. Y.

BENTON RIDGE, p. o., Hancock co., O., 99 ms. N. W. of Columbus, from W. 464 ms. Pop.

BENTON'S PORT, p. v., Van Buren co., Iowa.

BENTONSVILLE, p. o.. Johnson co., N. C.

BENTONVILLE, p. o., Fayette co., Ind., 50 ms. E. s. E. of Indianapolis; from W. 574 ms.

BENTONVILLE, p. o., Adams co., O.

BENTONVILLE, p. o., Warren co., Va.

BENTONVILLE, c. h., p. v., seat of justice of Benton co., Ark.

BENTONVILLE, p. o., Coffee co., Ala.

BENVENUE, p. o., Dauphin co., Pa., 15 ms. N. of Harrisburgh; from W. 125 ms.

BEREA, p. v., Middleburgh township, Cuyahoga co., O., 136 ms. N. N. E. of Columbus; from W. 366 ms. Watered by East Rocky river.

BEREA, p. o., Granville co., N. C.

BEREA, p. o., Cuyahoga co., O.

BERGEN, p. t., Genesee co., N. Y., 237 ms. w. of Albany. Watered by Black creek. Pop. 1,897.

BERGEN, c. h., p. t., seat of justice of Hudson co., N. J., 56 ms. N. E. of Trenton. Pop. 2,758.

BERGEN IRON WORKS. p. o., Ocean co., N. J.

BERGEN POINT, p. o., Hudson co., N. J.

BERGER'S STORE, p. o., Pittsylvania co., Va., 163 ms. s. w. of Richmond; from W. 238 ms.

BERKLEY, p. t., Bristol co., Mass., 37 ms. s. of Boston; from W. 424 ms. Watered by Taunton river. Pop. 908.

BERKLEY SPRINGS, c. h., p. o., seat of justice of Morgan co., Va., 180 ms, N. N. w. of Richmond.

BERKS COUNTY, situated in the southeastern part of Pennsylvania. Area, 1,020 square miles. Seat of justice, Reading. Pop. in 1840, 64,569; in 1850, 77,129.

BERKSHIRE COUNTY situated on the western border of Massachusetts. Area, 1,400 square miles. Seat of justice, Lenox. Pop. in 1840, 41,745; in 1850, 49,591.

BERKSHIRE, p. t., Franklin co., Vt., 65 ms. N. by w. of Montpelier; from W. 562 ms. Watered by Missisque river and its branches. Pop. 1,955.

BERKSHIRE, p. t., Tioga co., N. Y., 148 ms. w. s. w. of Albany; from W. 291 ms. Pop. 1,049.

BERKSHIRE, p. v., Berkshire township, Tioga co., N. Y. Watered by East Oswego creek.

BERKSHIRE, p. t., Delaware co., O., 28 ms. N. of Columbus; from W. 398 ms. Pop. 1,557.

BERKSHIRE, p. o., Kane co., Ill.

BERKSHIRE, p o., Gwinnet co., Ga.

BERKSHIRE VALLEY, p. v., Jefferson township, Morris co., N. J., 67 ms. N. of Trenton; from W. 238 ms. Watered by Rockaway river.

BERLIN, p. t., Coos co., N. H., 111 ms. N. of Concord; from W. 594 ms. Watered by Androscoggin and Amonoosuck rivers. Pop. 1,763.

BERLIN, t., Oxford co., Me., 45 ms. N. w. of Augusta.

BERLIN, p. t., Washington co., Vt., 4 ms. s. of Montpelier; from W. 517 ms. Watered by Onion river. Pop. 1,507.

BERLIN, p. t., Worcester co., Mass., 34 ms. w. by N. of Boston; from W. 413 ms. Watered by Assabet river. Pop. 866.

BERLIN, p. t., Hartford co., Ct., 10 ms. s. by w. of Hartford; from W. 327 ms. Pop. 1,868.

BERLIN, p. t., Rensselaer co., N. Y., 26 ms. E. of Albany; from W. 387 ms. Pop. 2,005.

BERLIN, v., Berlin township, Rensselaer co., N. Y. Watered by Little Hoosic creek.

BERLIN, t., Wayne co., Pa. Watered by Masthope and Lackawana creeks.

BERLIN, p. b., Brothers's Valley township, Somerset co., Pa., 143 ms. w. by s. of Harrisburgh; from W. 160 ms. Watered by Stony creek. Pop. 665.

BERLIN, p. v., Worcester co., Md., 123 ms. s. e. of Annapolis; from W. 163 ms. Pop. 494.

BERLIN, p. t., Holmes co., O., 95 ms. N. E. of Columbus; from W. 163 ms. Pop. 1,452.

BERLIN, p. v., Scott co., Iowa. Pop.

BERLIN, t., Erie co., O. Pop. 1,582.

BERLIN, p. t., Delaware co., O. Pop. 1,151.

BERLIN, t., Knox co., O. Pop. 1,156.

BERLIN, p. t., Mahoning co., O., 156 ms. N. E. of Columbus; from W. 303 ms. Watered by Mahoning creek. Pop. 1,376.

BERLIN, t., Milwaukie co., Wis.

BERLIN, p. o., Marquette co., Wis.

BERLIN, p. o., Southampton co., Va., 70 ms. s. of Richmond; from W. 189 ms.

BERLIN, p. v., Marshall co., Tenn., 48 ms. s. of Nashville; from W. 705 ms.

BELLIN, t., St. Clair co., Mich. Pop. 533.

BERLIN, p. o., Holmes co., O.

BERLIN, p. o., Clinton co., Ind.

BERLIN, p. o., Marshall co., Tenn.

BERLIN, p. v., Sangamon co., Ill., 14 ms. s. by w. of Springfield; from W. 794 ms.

BERLIN, p. v., Sumter co., Ala., 86 ms. s. w. of Tuscaloosa; from W. 904 ms.

BERLIN CENTRE, p. o., Mahoning co., O.

BERLIN CROSS-ROADS, p. o., Jackson co,, O.

BERLIN FALLS, p. o., Coos co., N. H.

BERLINVILLE, p. o., Berlin township, Huron co., O., 108 ms. N. N. E. of Columbus; from W. 395 ms.

BERMUDIAN, p. v., Adams co., Pa., 19 ms. s. by w. of Harrisburgh; from W. 96 ms.

BERNADOTTE, p. v., Fulton co,, Ill., 35 ms. N. w. of Springfield; from W. 143 ms. Pop. 787.

BERNALILLO COUNTY, situated toward the easterly part of New Mexico. Area, —— square miles. Chief town, Albuquerque. Pop. in 1850, 7,751.

BERNARDSTOWN, p. t., Franklin co., Mass., 99 ms. w. by N. of Boston; from W. 409 ms.

BERNARD, t., Somerset co., N. J. Pop. 2,263.

BERNARDSVILLE, v., Mercer co., N. J.

BERNE, p. t., Albany co., N. Y., 23 ms. w. of Albany; from W. 393 miles. Watered by Fox's creek. Pop. 3,441.

BERNE, t., Athens co., O Watered by Federal creek. Pop. 819.

BERNE, t., Fairfield co., O. Pop. 2,656.

BERNE, t., Berks co., Pa. Watered by Schuylkill river. Pop. 1,724.

BERNE, p. o., Monroe co,, O., 108 ms. E. o. E. of Columbus; from W. 297 ms.

BERNHARD'S BAY, p. o., Oswego co., N. Y.

BERNVILLE, p. v., Lower Berne township, Berks co., Pa., 63 ms. E. by N. of Harrisburgh; from W. 158 ms.

BERRIEN COUNTY, situated at the southwest corner of Michigan, with Lake Michigan on the west, and watered by St. Joseph and Gallon rivers. Area, 576 square miles. Seat of justice, Berrien Spring. Pop. in 1830, 325; in 1840, 5,011; in 1850, 11,417.

BERRIEN SPRINGS, p. v., Berrien township, Berrien co., Mich., 192 ms. s. w. of Detroit; from W. 637 ms. Watered by St. Joseph's river.

BERRY, p. o., Dane co., Wis.

BERRYSBURGH, p. v., Mifflin township, Dauphin co., Pa., 39 ms. N. of Harrisburgh; from W. 149 ms.

BERRY'S FENNY, p. o., Clark co., Va., 133 ms. N. N. w. of Richmond; from W. 64 ms.

BERRY'S LICK, p. o., Butler co., Ky.

BERRY'S MILL, p. o., Union co., Ky.

BERRYSVILLE, p. v., Knox co., Ind., 113 ms. s. w. of Indianapolis; from W. 675 ms.

BERRYSVILLE, p. o., Clark co., Va., 158 ms. N. N. w. of Richmond; from W. 62 ms.

BERRYTON, p. o., Cass co., Ill.

BERRYTOWN, p. o., Kent co., Del., 14 ms. s. by w. of Dover; from W. 122 ms.

BERRYVILLE, p. o., Highland co., O.

BERRYVILLE, p. o., Clarke co., Va.

BERRYVILLE, v., Scott co., Miss., 40 ms. E. of Jackson; from W. 1,000 ms.

BERSHEBA, p. o., Henry co., Ga.

BERTRAND, p. t., Berrien co., Mich., 186 ms. w. by s. of Detroit; from W. 631 ms. Watered by St. Joseph's river.

BERTIE COUNTY, situated in the northeast part of North Carolina, on the northerly side of Roanoke river. Watered also by Cashie and Chowan rivers. Length,

28 miles; mean width, 25; with an area of 700 square miles. The face of the country is generally level, in some parts low and marshy; the soil moderately fertile. Seat of justice, Windsor. Pop. in 1820, 10,805; in 1830, 12,262; in 1840, 12,175; in 1850, 12,851.

BERWICK, p. v., Brier Creek township, Columbia co., Pa., 97 ms. N. by E. of Harrisburgh; from W. 207 ms. Watered by Susquehannah river. Pop. 486.

BERWICK, p. o., Seneca co., O.

BERWICK, p. o., Warren co., Ill.

BERWICK, t., York co., Me., 103 ms. s. w. of Augusta; from W. 501 ms. Watered by South Berwick river. Pop. 2,121.

BERWICK, t., Adams co., Pa., 41 ms. s. w. of Harrisburgh; from W. 87 ms. Watered by Conewago and Beaver creeks. Pop. 811.

BERZELIA, p. o., Columbia co., Ga., 74 ms. N. E. of Milledgeville; from W. 597 ms.

BESTLAND, p. o., Essex co., Va.

BETHABARA, v., Stokes co., N. C., 118 ms. N. w. by w. of Raleigh; from W. 344 ms.

BETHANIA, p. v., Forsyth co., N. C., 118 ms. N. w. by w. of Raleigh; from W. 339 ms.

BETHANY, p. t., New Haven co., Ct., 46 ms. s. w. of Hartford; from W. 316 ms. Pop. 914.

BETHANY, p. o. York district, S. C.

BETHANY, p. v., Bethany township, Genesee co., N. Y., 252 ms. w. of Albany; from W. 370 ms. Watered by Little Tonawanda and Black creeks. Pop. 1,904.

BETHANY, c. h., p. b., Dyberry township, seat of justice of Wayne co., Pa., 165 ms. N. E. of Harrisburgh; from W. 272 ms. Pop. 295.

BETHANY, c. h., p. v., Harrison co., Mo.

BETHANY, p. o., Butler co., O.

BETHANY, p. o., Panola co., Tex.

BETHANY, p. v., Brooke co., Va., 352 ms. N. w. of Richmond; from W. 259 ms.

BETHANY CHURCH, p. o., Iredell co., N. C., 152 ms. w. of Raleigh; from W. 379 ms.

BETH EDEN, p. o., Newberry district, S. C.

BETHEL, p. t., Oxford co., Me., 63 ms. w. of Augusta; from W. 603 ms. Watered by Androscoggin river. Pop. 2,233.

BETHEL, p. t., Windsor co., Vt., 34 ms. s. by w. of Montpelier; from W. 483 ms. Watered by White river. Pop. 1,730.

BETHEL, p. v., Danbury township, Fairfield co., Ct., 71 ms. s. w. of Hartford; from W. 289 ms.

BETHEL, p. t., Sullivan co., N. Y., 121 ms. s. w. of Albany; from W. 303 ms. Watered by Delaware river. Pop. 2,087.

BETHEL, p. t., Berks co., Pa., 52 ms. E. of Harrisburgh; from W. 162 ms. Pop. 1,871.

BETHEL, p. o., York co., S. C.

BETHEL, t., Bedford co., Pa. Watered by Great Conoloway creek.

BETHEL, t., Delaware co., Pa. Watered by Naaman's creek. Pop. 426.

BETHEL, t., Clark co., O. Watered by Mad creek. Pop. 1,747.

BETHEL, p. o., Mercer co., Va.

BETHEL, p. o., Morgan co., Ill., 45 ms. w. of Springfield; from W. 825 ms.

BETHEL, p. o., Shelby co., Mo.

BETHEL, p. o., Bath co., Ky.

BETHEL, p. o., Giles co., Tenn.

BETHEL, p. v., Hertford co., N. C., 169 ms. N. E. of Raleigh; from W. 241 ms.

BETHEL, p. v., Glynn co., Ga., 238 ms. s. E. of Milledgeville; from W. 747 ms.

BETHEL, t., Posey co., Ind. Pop. 382.

BETHEL, t., Branch co., Mich. Pop. 679.

BETHEL, p. v., Clermont co., O., 110 ms. s. w. of Columbus; from W. 477 ms.

BETHEL, p. o., Wayne co., Ind.

BETHEL, t., Monroe co., O. Pop. 1,028.

BETHEL, t., Miami co., O. Watered by Miami river. Pop. 1,755.

BETHEL, v., Wayne co., Ga. Watered by Turtle river.

BETHEL, p. o., Wilcox co., Ala.

BETHEL, t., Lebanon co., Pa. Watered by Swatara creek. Pop. 1,894.

BETHESDA, p. o., Williamson co., Tenn.

BETHLEHEM, p. t., Grafton co., N. H., 88 ms. N. w. of Concord; from W. 549 ms. Watered by Great Amonoosuck river. Pop. 950.

BETHLEHEM, p. t., Litchfield co., Ct., 43 ms. w. s. w. of Hartford; from W. 315 ms. Watered by Pomperang river. Pop. 815.

BETHLEHEM, t., Albany co., N. Y., 5 ms. s. of Albany. Watered by Normanskill, Vlamanskill, and Coeyman's creeks. Pop. 4,102.

BETHLEHEM, p. t., Hunterdon co., N. J., 40 ms. N. by w. of Trenton; from W. 202 ms. Pop. 2,746.

BETHLEHEM, p. b., Northampton co., Pa., 93 ms. E. of Harrisburgh; from W. 186 ms. Watered by Lehigh river and Manokicy creek. Pop. 1,516.

BETHLEHEM, p. o., Gilmer co., Va.

BETHLEHEM, t., Stark co., O. Watered by Tuscarawas river. Pop. 2,398.

BETHLEHEM, t., Coshocton co., O. Watered by Walhonding river. Pop. 822.

BETHLEHEM, p. v., Clark co., Ind. Watered by Ohio river. 104 ms. E. of Indianapolis; from W. 585 ms. Pop. 872.

BETHLEHEM, p. o., Sumter district, S. C.

BETHLEHEM, v., Oglethorpe co., Ga., 65 ms. N. N. E. of Milledgeville.

BETHLEHEM, p. o., Marshall co., Miss.

BETHLEHEM CENTRE, p. o., Albany co., N. Y.

BETHLEHEM CROSS-ROADS, p. o., Southampton co., Va., 80 ms. s. by E. of Richmond; from W. 199 ms.

BETHMONT, p. o., Orange co., N. C.

BETHSAIDA, p. o., Cole co., Ill., 88 ms. E. s. E. of Springfield; from W. 696 ms.

BETTSVILLE, p. o., Seneca co., O., 101 ms. N. of Columbus; from W. 433 ms.

BEULAH, p. o., Johnson co., N. C.

BEVENS, p. o., Sussex co., N. J., 96 ms. N. of Trenton; from W. 253 ms.

BEVANSVILLE, p. o., Alleghany co., Md., 144 ms. N.W. by w. of Annapolis; from W. 112 ms.

BEVERLY, p. t., Essex co., Mass., 16 ms. N. E. of Boston; from W. 456 ms. Pop. 5,376.

BEVERLY, p. o., Burlington co., N. J.

BEVERLY, c. h., p. v., seat of justice of Randolph co., Va., 205 ms. N. W. of Richmond; from W. 232 ms. Watered by Monongahela river.

BEVERLY, p. v., Anson co., N. C., 149 ms. s. w. of Raleigh; from W. 406 ms.

BEVERLY, p. t., Washington co., O., 87 ms. s. E. of Columbus; from W. 321 ms.

BEVERLY, p. o., Adams co., Ill., 78 ms. w. of Springfield; from W. 858 ms.

BEVERLY FARMS, p. o., Essex co., Mass.

BEVIS TAVERN, p. o., Hamilton co., O., 114 ms. s. w. of Columbus; from W. 504 ms.

BEWLEYVILLE, p. o., Breckenridge co., Ky.

BEXAR. p. o., Coweta co., Ga., 100 ms. w. by N. of Milledgeville.

BEXAR, p. o., Marion co., Ala.

BIBB COUNTY, situated in the central part of Georgia, and traversed by Ocmulgee river. Area, 450 square miles. Seat of justice, Macon. Pop. in 1830, 7,143; in 1840, 9,802; in 1850, 12,699.

BIBB COUNTY, in the central part of Alabama, and traversed by Cahawba river, with Coosa river on the east. Length, 45 ms.; mean width, 25; extending over an area of 1,100 square miles. Seat of justice, Centreville. Pop. in 1820, 3,676; in 1830, 6,305; in 1840, 8,284; in 1850, 9,969.

BICKLEY'S MILLS, p. o., Russell co., Va., 338 ms. w. by s. of Richmond; from W. 397 ms.

BIDDEFORD, t., York co., Me. Watered by Saco river. Pop. 6,095.

BIDWELL'S BAR, p. o., Butte co., Cal.

BIENVILLE PARISH, situated in the northwest part of Louisiana, on the easterly side of Lake Bisteneau. Area, —— square miles. Seat of justice ——. Pop. in 1850, 5,539.

BIG BAR, p. o., Trinity co., Cal.

BIG BARREN, p. o., Claiborne co., Tenn.

BIG BEAVER, t., Beaver co., Pa. Pop. 922.

BIG BEAVER, p. t., Oakland co., Mich.

BIG BEND, p. o., Venango co., Pa.

BIG BEND, p. o., Gilmer co., Va.

BIG BEND, p. o., Waukesha co., Wis.

BIG BEND, p. o., Avoyelles parish, La.

BIG BLUE, p. o., Jackson co., Mo., 153 ms. w. N. w. of Jefferson city; from W. 1,079 ms.

BIG BROOK, p. o., Western township, Oneida co., N. Y., 104 ms. w. by N. of Albany; from W. 404 ms.

BIGBY FORK, p. o., Monroe co., Miss.

BIGBYVILLE, p. o., Maury co., Tenn., 60 ms. s. by w. of Nashville; from W. 732 ms.

FIG CANE, p. o., St. Landry parish, La.

BIG CEDAR, p. o., Jackson co., Mo.

BIG CLEAR CREEK, p. o., Greenbrier co., Pa.

BIG CLIFTY, p. o., Hardin co., Ky.

BIG COAL, p. o., Kanawha co., Va.

BIG COLE, p. o., Boone co., Va.

BIG CREEK, p. o., Edgefield district, S. C.

BIG CREEK, p. o., Stokes co., N. C., 142 ms. N. w. of Raleigh; from W. 313 ms.

BIG CREEK, p. o., Forsyth co., Ga.

BIG CREEK, p.t., Phillips co., Ark., 103 ms. E. of Little Rock; from W. 1,030 ms. Pop. 677.

BIG CREEK, p. o., Fort Bend co., Tex.

BIG CREEK, p. o., Johnson co., Mo., 118 ms. w. by N. of Jefferson city; from W. 1,050 ms.

BIG CREEK, p. o., Rapides parish, La.

BIG CREEK, t., Van Buren co., Mo.

BIG CREEK, p. o., Steuben co., N. Y.

BIG CREEK, p. o., Yallabusha co., Miss.

BIG CREEK, t., Crawford co., Ark. Pop. 395.

BIG CREEK, p. o., Dale co., Ala.

BIG CREEK, p. o., Shelby co., Tenn.

BIG CREEK, t., Rives co., Mo.

BIGELOW'S MILLS, p. o., La Porte co., Ind., 140 ms. N. by w. of Indianapolis; from W. 674 ms.

BIG EQUINUNCK, p. o., Wayne co., Pa., 95 ms. N. E. of Harrisburgh; from W. 291 ms.

BIG FALLS, p. o., Orange co., N. C.

BIG FLATS, p. t., Chemung co., N. Y., 204 ms. s. w. of Albany; from W. 284 ms. Watered by Chemung river. Pop. 1,709.

BIG FOOT PRAIRIE, p. o., Walworth co., Wis.

BIG GLADES, p. o., Russell co., Va.

BIG HILL, p. o., Madison co., Ky.

BIG HOLLOW, p. o., Windham township, Greene co., N. Y., 54 ms. s. by w. of Albany; from W. 361 ms.

BIG ISLAND, p. o., Bedford co., Va.

BIG ISLAND, p. t., Marion co., O., 47 ms. w. by N. of Columbus; from W. 421 ms. Pop. 600.

BIG ISLAND, v., Big Island township, Marion co., O.

BIG LAUREL, p. o., Yancey co., N. C.

BIG LICK, p. t., Hancock co., O. Pop. 1,008.

BIG LICK, p. o., Roanoke co., Va., 172 ms. w. of Richmond; from W. 241 ms.

BIG MEADOW, p. o., Grayson co., Va.

BIG MILLS, p. o., Dorchester co., Md., 75 ms. s. E. of Annapolis; from W. 115 ms.

BIG NECK, p. o., Adams co., Ill.

BIG OAK, p. o., Kemper co., Miss.

BIG OTTER, p. o., Braxton co., Va.

BIG PLAIN, p. o., Madison co., O.

BIG POND, p. o., Fayette co., Ala.

BIG PRAIRIE, t., New Madrid co., Mo.

BIG PRAIRIE, p. o., Clinton township, Wayne co., O., 84 ms. N. E. of Columbus; from W. 353 ms.

BIG READY, p. o., Edmonson co., Ky.

BIG RIVER MILLS, p. o., St. Francis co., Mo., 149 ms. s. E. of Jefferson city; from W. 911 miles.

BIG RIVER, t., Jefferson co., Mo.

BIG ROCK, p. o., Sumter co., Ala., 121 ms. s. w. of Tuscaloosa; from W. 939 ms.

BIG ROCK, p. t., Kane co., Ill. Pop. 496.

BIG SKIN CREEK, p. o., Lewis co., Va.

BIG SPRING, p. o., Wilson co., Tenn., 39 ms. E. of Nashville; from W. 645 ms.

BIG SPRING, p. o., Breckenridge co., Ky.

BIG SPRING, p. o., Montgomery co., Mo., 50 ms. N. E. of Jefferson city; from W. 900 ms.

BIG SPRINGS, t., Seneca co., O. Pop. 1,932.

BIG SPRINGS, p. o., Laporte co., Ind., 151 ms. N. by W. of Indianapolis; from W. 654 ms.

BIG SPRING, p. o., Marshall co., Ala.

BIG SPRING, p. o., Pocahontas co., Va.

BIG SPRING, p. o., Cumberland co., Pa.

BIG SPRING, p. o., Ottawa co., Mich.

BIG SPRING, p. o., Shelby co., Ill.

BIG STREAM POINT, p. v., Starkey township, Yates co., N. Y., 192 ms. w. of Albany; from W. 311 ms.

BIG SWAMP, p. o., Bladen co., N. C., 120 ms. s. of Raleigh; from W. 408 ms.

BIG TREE CORNERS, p. o., Erie co., N. Y.

BIG VALLEY, p. o., Anderson co., Tenn., 184 ms. E. by N. of Nashville; from W. 510 ms.

BIG WANHOO, p. o., Hall co., Ga.

BIG WOODS, p. o., Dupage co., Ill.

BILLERICA, p. t., Middlesex co., Mass., 18 ms. N. w. of Boston; from W. 450 ms. Watered by Concord and Shawshee rivers. Pop. 1,646.

BILLING'S GROVE, p. o., Livingston co., Ill.

BILLINGSVILLE, p. o., Union co., Ind., 74 ms. E. by S. of Indianapolis; from W. 512 ms.

BILOXI, p. v., Harrison co. Miss., 227 ms. S. E. of Jackson; from W. 1,155 ms. Situated on Biloxi bay.

BILOXI, p. o., Newton co., Tex.

BILTON, p. o., Logan co., Va., 376 ms. w. of Richmond; from W. 413 ms.

BINGHAM, p. t., Somerset co., Me., 60 ms. N. of Augusta: from W. 655 ms. Watered by Kennebec river. Pop. 752.

BINGHAM, p. t., Potter co., Pa., 181 ms. N. w. of Harrisburgh; from W. 295 ms. Pop. 584.

BINGHAM, p. t., Clinton co., Mich.

BINGHAMPTON, p. o., Lee co., Ill.

BINGHAMTON, c. h., p. v., Chenango township, seat of justice of Broome co., N. Y., 138 ms. s. w. of Albany; from W. 296 ms. Watered by Chenango and Susquehanna rivers.

BIRCHARDVILLE, p. o. Susquehanna co., Pa.

BIRCHETTSVILLE, p. o., Cleveland co., N. C.

BIRCH POND, p. o., Fayette co., Tenn., 199 ms. s. w. by w. of Nashville; from W. 884 ms.

BIRCH POND, p. o., Crawford co., Miss.

BIRCH RIVER, p. o., Nicholas co., Va., 330 ms. N. w. by w. of Richmond; from W. 302 ms.

BIRD, p. o., Hillsdale co., Mich.

BIRDSALL, p. t., Alleghany co., N. Y., 225 ms. w. by s. of Albany; from W. 336 ms. Watered by Black creek.

BIRDSBOROUH, p. o., Berks co., Pa.

BIRDSVILLE, p. v., Burke co., Ga., 74 ms. E. of Milledgeville; from W. 636 ms.

BIRD'S RUN, p. o., Guernsey co., O.

BIRDSVILLE, p. o., Tarrant co., Tex.

BIRMINGHAM, p. b., Warrior Mark township, Huntingdon co., Pa., 107 ms. N. w. by w. of Harrisburgh; from W. 166 ms. Watered by Little Juniata river. Pop. 200.

BIRMINGHAM, t., Delaware co., Pa. Pop. 566.

BIRMINGHAM, t., Chester co., Pa. Pop. 328.

BIRMINGHAM, p. v., Florence township, Erie co., O., 115 ms. N. by E. of Columbus; from W. 388 ms. Watered by Vermilion river.

BIRMINGHAM, p. v., Oakland co., Mich., 19 ms. N. w. of Detroit; from W. 542 ms. Watered by Rouge river.

BIRMINGHAM, b., St. Clair township, Alleghany co., Pa. Pop. 3,742.

BIRMINGHAM, p. o., Jackson co., Ala.

BIRMINGHAM, p. o., Pontotoc co., Miss.

BIRMINGHAM, p. o., Marshall co., Ky.

BIRMINGHAM, p. o., Schuyler co., Ill.

BIRMINGHAM, p. o., Van Buren co., Iowa.

BISHOP HILL, p. o., Henry co., Ill.

BISHOPSVILLE, p. v., Sumter district, S. C., 87 ms. N. E. by E. of Columbia; from W. 495 ms.

BISSELL, p. o., Calhoun co., Ill.

BISSELL, p. o., Grant co., Ind. (Now Trask.)

BISSELL'S, p. o., Geauga co., O., 149 ms. N. E. of Columbus; from W. 337 ms.

BIVINGSVILLE, p. o., Spartanburgh district, S. C., 101 ms. N. w. of Columbia; from W. 469 ms.

BLACK, t., Posey co., Ind. Pop. 2,376.

BLACKFORD COUNTY, situated toward the northeast of Indiana, and watered by Salamanic river, a branch of the Wabash. Area, 182 square miles. Seat of justice, Blackford. Pop. in 1840, 1,226; in 1850, 2,860.

BLACKLYSVILLE, p. o., Wayne co., O.

BLACKBERRY, p. o., Kane co., Ill.

BLACK BIRD, p. o., New Castle co., Del., 18 ms. N. of Dover; from W. 138 ms.

BLACK BROOK, p. t., Clinton co., N. Y., 158 ms. N. of Albany; from W. 533 ms. Watered by Saranac and Au Sable rivers, and Black brook. Pop. 2,525.

BLACK CREEK, p. v., New Hudson township, Alleghany co., N. Y., 275 ms. w. by s. of Albany; from W. 325 ms.

BLACK CREEK, p. o., Wayne co., N. C., 73 ms. S. E. of Raleigh; from W. 281 ms.

BLACK CREEK, p. o., Luzerne co., Pa.

BLACK CREEK, p. o., Holmes co., O.

BLACK CREEK, p. o., Scriven co., Ga., 128 ms. E. by S. of Milledgeville; from W. 650 ms.

BLACK CREEK, t., Mercer co., O.

BLACK CREEK, p. o., Sullivan co., Ind., 96 ms. s. w. of Indianapolis; from W. 663 ms.

BLACK CREEK, p. o., Marquette co., Wis.

BLACK FACE, p. o., Nottaway co., Va.

BLACKFORD, c. h., p. v., Hartford township, seat of justice of Blackford co., Ind., 81 ms. N. E. of Indianapolis; from W. 552 ms.

BLACKFORD, p. o., Hancock co., Ky.

BLACK HAWK COUNTY, situated toward the northeast part of Iowa, and traversed by Cedar and Black Hawk rivers. Area, 625 square miles. Cedar Falls is the chief town. Pop. in 1850, 135.

BLACK HAWK, p. o., Beaver co., Pa.

BLACK HAWK, p. o., Carroll co., Miss., 77 ms. N. of Jackson; from W. 994 ms.

BLACK HAWK, p. o., Holt co., Mo.

BLACK HAWK, t., Shelby co., Ind., 34 ms. s. E. of Indianapolis; from W. 577 ms.

BLACKHEATH, p. o., Chesterfield co., Va., 14 ms. N. w. of Richmond; from W. 131 ms.

BLACK HILL, p. o., Kaufman co., Tex.

BLACK HOLE, p. o., Lycoming co., Pa., 87 ms. N. by w. of Harrisburgh; from W. 197 ms.

BLACK HORSE, p. o., Middlesex co., N. J.

BLACK HORSE, p. o., Chester township, Chester co., Pa., 57 ms. S. E. of Harrisburgh; from W. 127 ms.

BLACK HORSE, p. o., Middlesex co., N. J.

BLACK HORSE, p. o., Harford co., Md., 57 ms. N. by E. of Annapolis; from W. 67 ms.

BLACK JACK, p. o., Scott co., Ark.

BLACK JACK, p. o., De Soto parish, La.

BLACK JACK GROVE, p. o., Hopkins co., Tex.

BLACK JACK VALLEY, p. o., Spartanburgh dis., S. C.

BLACK LAKE, p. o., St. Lawrence co., N. Y.

BLACK LAND, p. o., Tishamingo co., Miss.

BLACK LEGS, p. o., Indiana co., Pa., 175 ms. w. by N. of Harrisburgh; from W. 215 ms.

BLACKLEYSVILLE, p. v., Plain township, Wayne co., O., 94 ms. N. E. of Columbus; from W. 353 ms.

BLACK LICK, p. t., Indiana co., Pa.

BLACK MINGO, p. o., Williamsburgh district, S. C.

BLACK OAK, p. o., Charleston district, S. C., 139 ms. s. E. by s. of Columbia; from W. 527 ms.

BLACK OAK, p. o., Tallahatchie co., Miss., 128 ms. N. of Jackson; from W. 975 ms.

BLACK OAK GROVE, p. o., Hardeman co., Tenn.

BLACK OAK POINT, p. o., Hickory co., Mo.

BLACK RIVER, p. t., Lorain co., O., 130 ms. N. N. E. of Columbus; from W. 387 ms. Watered by Black river and Lake Erie.

BLACK RIVER, v., Black river township, Lorain co., O.

BLACK RIVER, t., St. Francis co., Mo.

BLACK RIVER, t., Wayne co., Mo.

BLACK RIVER, t., Washington co., Mo.

BLACK RIVER, t., Independence co., Ark.

BLACK RIVER, t., Lawrence co., Ark.

BLACK RIVER, p. o., Jefferson co., N. Y.

BLACK RIVER, p. o., Ottawa co., Mich. (Now Holland.)

BLACK RIVER CHAPEL, p. o., New Hanover co., N. C., 126 ms. s. by E. of Raleigh; from W. 356 ms.

BLACK RIVER FALLS, p. o., Crawford co., Wis.

BLACK ROCK, p. t., Erie co., N. Y., 300 ms. w. of Albany; from W. 383 ms. Watered by Lake Erie and Niagara river. Pop. 7,508.

BLACK ROCK, p. v., Black Rock township, Erie co., N. Y.

BLACK ROCK, p. o., Rappahannock co., Va., 131 ms. N. N. w. of Richmond; from W. 83 ms.

BLACKS, p. o., Waldo co., Me., 53 ms. E. of Augusta; from W. 647 ms.

BLACKS AND WHITES, p. o., Nottaway co., Va., 60 ms. s. w. of Richmond; from W. 179 ms.

BLACK'S BLUFF, p. o., Wilcox co., Ala., 109 ms. s. by E. of Tuscaloosa; from W. 901 ms.

BLACKSBURGH, p. o., Montgomery co., Va., 212 ms. s. w. of Richmond; from W. 278 ms.

BLACKSNAKE HILLS, p. o., Buchanan co., Mo.

BLACKSHIRES, p. o., Marion co., Va.

BLACKSTOCKS, p. o., Chester district, S. C., 46 ms. N. by w. of Columbia; from W. 463 ms.

BLACK'S STORE, p. o., Tippah co., Miss., 224 ms. N. N. E. of Jackson; from W. 858 ms.

BLACKSTONE, p. o., Worcester co., Mass., 40 ms. s. w. of Boston; from W. 418 ms.

BLACKSVILLE, p. v., Monongalia co., Va., 300 ms. N. w. of Richmond; from W. 233 ms. Watered by Robert's run and Drunkard's creek.

BLACK SWAMP, p. o., Sandusky co., O., 113 ms. N. of Columbus ; from W. 431 ms.

BLACKVILLE, p. o., Barnwell district, S. C., 90 ms. s. s. w. of Columbia ; from W. 594 ms.

BLACK WALNUT, p. o., Halifax co., Va., 138 ms. s. w. of Richmond ; from W. 225 ms.

BLACKWATER, p. o., Sussex co., Va.

BLACKWATER, t., Pettis co., Mo.

BLACKWATER, p. t., Morgan co., Ky.

BLACKWATER, p. o., Kemper co., Miss., 224 ms. w. n. w. of Jackson ; from W. 858 ms.

BLACKWATER, p. o., Johnson co., Mo., 110 ms. w. by N. of Jefferson city ; from W. 1,046 ms.

BLACKWELL'S, p. o., Caswell co., N. C., 94 ms. N. w. of Raleigh ; from W. 270 ms.

BLACK WOLF, p o., Winnebago co., Wis.

BLACKWOODTOWN, p. o., Camden co., N. J.

BLADEN COUNTY, situated toward the southeast part of North Carolina, and traversed by Cape Fear river. Length, 50 miles ; mean width, 30 ; with an area of 1,500 square miles. The face of the country is generally level ; soil of moderate fertility. Seat of justice, Elizabethtown. Pop. in 1820, 7,276 ; in 1830, 7,814 ; in 1840, 8,022 ; in 1850, 9,767.

BLADENSBURGH, p. o., Knox co., O., 61 ms. N. E. of Columbus ; from W. 362 ms.

BLADENSBURGH, p. v., Prince George's co., Md., 34 ms. w. of Annapolis ; from W. 6 ms. Pop. 1,412.

BLADEN SPRINGS, p. o., Choctaw co., Ala.

BLANDFORD, t., Hampden co., Mass., 114 ms. w. of Boston ; from W. 363 ms. Watered by Westfield river.

BLAIN, p. o., Perry co., Pa.

BLAINE, p. o., Lawrence co., Ky., 139 ms. E. of Frankfort ; from W. 455 ms.

BLAINE'S CROSS ROADS, p. o., Grainger co., Tenn., 202 ms. E. of Nashville ; from W. 480 ms.

BLAIR COUNTY, situated in the central part of Pennsylvania, and traversed by the Frankstown branch of Juniata river. Area, 700 square miles. Seat of justice, Hollidaysburgh. Pop. in 1850, 21,777.

BLAIR, p. t., Huntingdon co., Pa.

BLAIR FURNACE, p. o., Blair co., Pa.

BLAIRSPORT, p. o., Roane co., Tenn., 165 ms. E. of Nashville ; from W. 582 ms.

BLAIRSTOWN, p. t., Warren co., N. J., 74 ms. N. by w. of Trenton ; from W. 229 ms. Pop. 1,405.

BLAIRSVILLE, p. b., Indiana co., Pa., 171 ms. w. by N. of Harrisburgh ; from W. 199 ms. Watered by Kiskiminitas river, and Black Lick creek. Pop. 1,135.

BLAIRSVILLE, p. o., York district, S. C., 88 ms. N. of Columbia ; from W. 440 ms.

BLAIRSVILLE, c. h., p. v., seat of justice of Union co., Ga., 118 ms. N. N. w. of Milledgeville ; from W. 617 ms.

BLAIRSVILLE, p. v., Posey co., Ind., 183 ms. s. w. of Indianapolis ; from W. 741 ms.

BLAKELEY, p. t., Luzerne co., Pa., 150 ms. N. E. of Harrisburgh ; from W. 254 ms. Watered by Lackawanock river. Pop. 1,703.

BLAKELY, p. o., Stokes co., N. C., 127 ms. N. w. of Raleigh ; from W. 307 ms.

BLAKELY, c. h., p. v., seat of justice of Early co., Ga., 203 ms. s. w. of Milledgeville ; from W. 850 ms.

BLAKELY, c. h., p. v., seat of justice of Baldwin co., Ala. Watered by Tensaw river.

BLAKESBURGH, p. o., Wapello co., Iowa.

BLAKESVILLE, p. o., Harrison co., Ind.

BLANC, p. o., Lucas co., O.

BLANCHARD, p. t., Piscataquis co., Me., 73 ms. N. by E. of Augusta ; from W. 668 ms. Pop. 192.

BLANCHARD BRIDGE, p. v., Blanchard township, Hancock co., O., 80 ms. N. by w. of Columbus ; from W. 451 ms.

BLANCHARD, t., Hardin co., O. Watered by Blanchard's Fork of Auglaize river.

BLANCHARD, t., Hancock co., O. Pop. 1,151.

BLANCHARD, t., Putnam co., O. Pop. 1,395.

BLANCHESTER, p. o., Marion township, Clinton co., O., 80 ms. s. w. of Columbus ; from W. 668 ms.

BLANCHE, p. o., Lafayette co., Mo.

BLANDINSVILLE, p. o., McDonough co., Ill.

BLANDVILLE, c. h., p. v., Ballard co., Ky.

BLANFORD, p. t., Hampden co., Mass., 110 ms. w. by s. of Boston ; from W. 370 ms. Watered by Westfield river. Pop. 1,418.

BLANKET HILL, p. o., Armstrong co., Pa.

BLAUVELTVILLE, p. v., Orangetown township, Rockland co., N. Y., 131 ms. s. of Albany ; from W. 259 ms.

BLAWENBURGH, p. o., Somerset co., N. J., 15 ms. N. by E. of Trenton ; from W. 187 ms.

BLEDSOE COUNTY, situated toward the south east part of Tennessee, and traversed by Sequatchie river. Length, 35 ms. ; mean width, 13, with an area of 455 square miles. The face of the country is generally mountainous or hilly ; soil varied, in many situations highly productive. Seat of justice, Pikeville. Pop. in 1820, 4,005 ; in 1830, 4,688 ; in 1840, 5,676 ; in 1850, 5,959.

BLEEKER, p. t., Fulton co., N. Y. Watered by Caroga creek, and Sacondaga river. Pop. 510.

BLENDON, p. t., Franklin co., O., 11 ms. N. of Columbus ; from W. 404 ms. Watered by Alum and Big Walnut creeks. Pop. 1,303.

BLENDON INSTITUTE, v., Franklin co., O.

BLENHEIM, t., Schoharie co., N. Y. Pop. 1,314, (p. o., now called South Gilboa.)

BLINK BONNY, p. o., St. Lawrence co., N. Y.

BLISH'S MILLS, p. o., Franklin co., O.

BLISSFIELD, p. v., Blissfield township, Lenawee co., Mich., 71 ms. s. w. of Detroit ; from W. 489 ms. Watered by Raisin river. Pop. 924.

BLISSVILLE, p. o., Jefferson co., Ill.

BLISSVILLE, p. o., Marshall co., Ind.

BLIVEN MILLS, p. o., McHenry co., Ill.

BLOCKER'S, p. o., Cumberland co., S. C.

BLOCK HOUSE, p. o., Scott co., Va.

BLOCKLEY, t., Philadelphia co., Pa. Watered by Mill and Cobb creeks, and Schuylkill river. Pop. 5,916.

BLOCKVILLE, p. o., Chautauque co., N. Y.

BLODGET MILLS, p. o., Cortland co., N. Y.

BLOOD'S POINT, p. o., De Kalb co., Ill.

BLOODY RUN, p. v., Providence township, Bedford co., Pa., 95 ms. w. by s. of Harrisburgh ; from W. 121 ms. Watered by Roystown branch of Juniata river.

BLOOM, p. t., Seneca co., O., 86 ms. N. of Columbus ; from W. 420 ms. Watered by Honey creek. Pop. 1,742.

BLOOM, t., Columbia co., Pa. Watered by Susquehanna river, and Fishing creek. Pop. 3,122.

BLOOM, v., Bloom township, Columbia co., Pa.

BLOOM, p. t., Morgan co., O. Watered by Muskingum river.

BLOOM, t., Sciota co., O. Pop. 1,648.

BLOOM, t., Fairfield co., O.

BLOOM, t., Wood co., O. Pop. 658.

BLOOM, p. o., Rush co., Ind.

BLOOM, p. o., Cook co., Ill.

BLOOMER, p. o., Sebastian co., Ark.

BLOOMFIELD, p. t., Somerset co., Me., 35 ms. N. of Augusta ; from W. 630 ms. Watered by Kennebec river. Pop. 1,301.

BLOOMFIELD, p. t., Essex co., Vt., 90 ms. N. E. of Montpelier ; from W. 587 ms. Watered by Connecticut and Nulhegan rivers. Pop. 244.

BLOOMFIELD, p. t., Hartford co., Ct., 7 ms. N. w. of Hartford ; from W. 343 ms. Watered by Wood river. Pop. 1,412.

BLOOMFIELD, p. t., Essex co., N. J., 54 ms. N. E. of Trenton ; from W. 224 ms. Pop. 3,385.

BLOOMFIELD, p. v., Bloomfield township, Crawford co., Pa., 243 ms. N. w. of Harrisburgh ; from W. 324 ms. Pop. 838.

BLOOMFIELD, c. h., v., Juniata township, seat of justice of Perry co., Pa.

BLOOMFIELD, p. v., Loudoun co., Va., 135 ms. N. of Richmond ; from W. 54 ms.

BLOOMFIELD, p. v., Nelson co., Ky., 43 ms. s. w. of Frankfort ; from W. 585 ms.

BLOOMFIELD, p. o., Knox co., O., 46 ms. N. N. E. of Columbus ; from W. 391 ms.

BLOOMFIELD, t., La Grange co., Ind. Pop. 934.

BLOOMFIELD, c. h., p. v., seat of justice of Greene co., Ind., 74 ms. s. w. of Indianapolis ; from W. 641 ms. Watered by White river.

BLOOMFIELD, p. v., Edgar co., Ill., 128 ms. E. by s of Springfield ; from W. 662 ms.

BLOOMFIELD, t., Oakland co., Mich. Watered by Rouge river. Pop. 1,003.

BLOOMFIELD, t., Trumbull co., O., 175 ms. N. E. of Columbus ; from W. 313 ms. Pop. 1,451.

BLOOMFIELD, t., Richland co., O., 60 ms. N. E. of Columbus ; from W. 390 ms. Pop. 1,430.

BLOOMFIELD, t., Logan co., O. Pop. 671.

BLOOMFIELD, t., Jackson co., O. Watered by branch of Raccoon creek. Pop. 1,402.

BLOOMFIELD, p. o., Kemper co., Miss.

BLOOMFIELD, c. h., p. o., Davis co., Iowa. Pop. 792.

BLOOMFIELD, p. o., Walworth co., Wis.
BLOOMFIELD, c. h., p. v., seat of justice of Stoddard co., Mo., 233 ms. s. E. of Jefferson city; fm. W. 957 ms.
BLOOMINGBURGH, p. v., Mamakating township, Sullivan co., N. Y., 100 ms. s. w. by s. of Albany; from W. 285 ms.
BLOOMINGBURGH, p. v., Paint township, Fayette co., O., 45 ms. s. s. w. of Columbus; from W. 246 ms.
BLOOMINGDALE, p. o., Cabell co., Va.
BLOOMINGDALE, p. o., Jefferson co., O., 124 ms. E. N. E. of Columbus; from W. 279 ms.
BLOOMINGDALE, p. o., Du Page co., Ill., 211 ms. N. E. of Springfield; from W. 740 ms.
BLOOMINGDALE, v., county of New York. Watered by Hudson river.
BLOOMING GROVE, p. t., Orange co., N. Y., 94 ms. s. of Albany; from W. 285 ms. Watered by Murderer's creek.
BLOOMING GROVE, p. t., Richland co., O.
BLOOMING GROVE, p. o., Montgomery co., Tenn.
BLOOMING GROVE, p. o., Franklin co., Ind., 79 ms. s. E. of Indianapolis; from W. 525 ms.
BLOOMINGSBURGH, p. o., Fulton co., Ind.
BLOOMINGSPORT, p. o., Randolph co., Ind.
BLOOMINGTON, c. h., p. v., seat of justice of Monroe co., Ind., 49 ms. s. w. of Indianapolis; from W. 616 ms. Pop. 879.
BLOOMINGTON, p. v., McLean co., Ill., 73 ms. N. N. E. of Springfield; from W. 744 ms. Pop. 1,594.
BLOOMINGTON, c. h., p. v., seat of justice of Muscatine co., Iowa. Watered by Mississippi river. Pop. 200.
BLOOMINGTON, p. o., Clinton co., O.
BLOOMINGTON, c. h., p. v., seat of justice of Macon co., Mo., 106 ms. N. of Jefferson city, from W. 989 ms. Pop. 194.
BLOOMINGTON, p. o., Morgan co., Ky.
BLOOMINGTON, p. o., Van Buren co., Ark., 110 ms. N. of Little Rock; from W. 1,100 ms.
BLOOMINGTON, p. o., Tipton co., Tenn.
BLOOMINGTON, t., Buchanan co., Mo. Pop. 2,197.
BLOOMING VALLEY, p. o., Crawford co., Pa., 240 ms. N. w. of Harrisburgh; from W. 313 ms.
BLOOMINGVILLE, p. v., Oxford township, Erie co., O., 121 ms. N. by E. of Columbus; from W. 431 ms.
BLOOMSBURGH, p. v., Columbia co., Pa., 87 ms. N. by E. of Harrisburgh; from W. 197 ms. Watered by Susquehanna river.
BLOOMSBURGH, p. v., Halifax co., Va., 140 ms. s. w. by w. of Richmond; from W. 227 ms.
BLOOMSBURY, p. v., Warren co., N. J., 43 ms. N N W of Trenton; from W. 202 ms. Watered by Musconetcong creek.
BLOOMVILLE, p. v., Delaware co., N. Y., 74 ms. s. w. of Albany; from W. 344 ms. Watered by Delaware river.
BLOOMVILLE, p. o., Seneca co., O., 86 ms. N. of Columbus; from W. 412 ms.
BLOOMVILLE, p. o., Will co., Ill.
BLOSSBURGH, p. v., Tioga co., Pa., 133 ms. N. N. W. of Harrisburgh; from W. 243 ms. Pop. 850.
BLOSSOM HILL, p. o., Caddo parish, La.
BLOUNT COUNTY, situated in the northern part of Alabama. Length, 32 miles; breadth, 30; with an area of 960 square miles. The face of the country is generally hilly. Seat of justice, Blountsville. Pop. in 1820, 2,415; in 1830, 4,233; in 1840, 5,570; in 1850, 7,367.
BLOUNT COUNTY, on the southeast boundary of Tennessee, with Tennessee river on the northwest. Area, 900 square miles. The face of the country is hilly, and the soil varied. Seat of justice, Maryville. Pop. in 1820, 11,258; in 1830, 11,028; in 1840, 11,745; in 1850, 12,382.
BLOUNT'S CREEK, p. o., Beaufort co., N. C.
BLOUNT'S FERRY, p. o., Columbia co.
BLOUNT SPRINGS, p. o., Blount co., Ala., 88 ms. N. E. of Tuscaloosa; from W. 704 ms.
BLOUNTSTOWN, p. o., Calhoun co., Flor.
BLOUNTSVILLE, p. o., Jones co., Ga., 16 ms. w. of Milledgeville; from W. 661 ms.
BLOUNTSVILLE, c. h., p. v., seat of justice of Blount co., Ala., 104 ms. N. E. of Tuscaloosa; from W. 734 ms. Watered by Locust fork of Black Warrior river.
BLOUNTSVILLE, c. h., p. v., seat of justice of Sullivan co., Tenn., 288 ms. E. by N. of Nashville; from W. 394 ms.
BLOUNTSVILLE, p. v., Henry co., Ind., 72 ms. E. by N. of Indianapolis; from W. 535 ms.

BLUE SPRING GROVE, p. o., Barren co., Ky., 110 ms. s. s. w. of Frankfort; from W. 633 ms.
BLUE BALL, p. o., Lancaster co., Pa., 47 ms. s. E. of Harrisburgh; from W. 125 ms.
BLUE BALL, p. o., Cecil co., Md., 81 ms. N. E. of Annapolis; from W. 91 ms.
BLUE BALL, p. o., Butler co., O.
BLUE BELL, p. o., Montgomery co., Pa., 95 ms. E. of Harrisburgh; from W. 158 ms.
BLUE GRASS, p. o., Scott co., Iowa.
BLUE CREEK, p. o., Adams co., O.
BLUE CREEK, p. o., Habersham co., Ga.
BLUE CREEK, p. o., Pike co., Ala.
BLUE CREEK, p. o., Franklin co., Ind.
BLUE CREEK, t., Adams co., Ind. Pop. 425.
BLUE EYE, p. o., Benton co., Ala.
BLUE HILL, p. t., Hancock co., Me., 75 ms. E. of Augusta; from W. 671 ms. Pop. 1,939.
BLUE HILL, p., Williamson co., Tex.
BLUE HOUSE, p. o., Colleton district, S. C., 111 ms. s. by E. of Columbia; from W. 600 ms.
BLUE ISLAND, p. o., Cook co., Ill., 200 ms. N. N. E. of Springfield; from W. 735 ms.
BLUE GRASS, p. o., Fulton co., Ind.
BLUE LICK, p. o., Clark co., Ind., 112 ms. s. by E. of Indianapolis; from W. 613 ms.
BLUE LICK, p. o., Franklin co., Ala.
BLUE LICK SPRINGS, p. o., Nicholas co., Ky.
BLUE MOUND, p. o., Dane co., Wis.
BLUE MOUNTAIN, t., Izard co., Ark. Pop. 337.
BLUE PLUM, p. o., Washington co., Tenn.
BLUE POND, p. o., Cherokee co., Ala.
BLUE RIDGE, p. o., Botetourt co., Va.
BLUE RIDGE, p. o., Yancy co., N. C.
BLUE RIDGE, p. o., Gilmer co., Ga.
BLUE RIDGE, p. o., Shelby co., Ind.
BLUE RIVER, t., Hancock co., Ind. Pop. 941.
BLUE RIVER, p. o., Iowa co., Wis., 72 ms. s. s. w. of Madison; from W. 904 ms.
BLUE RIVER, t., Johnson co., Ind. Pop. 964.
BLUE ROCK, p. t., Muskingum co., O., 65 ms. E. of Columbus; from W. 346 ms. Watered by Muskingum river. Pop. 1,476.
BLUE SPRING, p. o., Stewart co., Tenn., 61 ms. w. N. w. of Nashville; from W. 746 ms.
BLUE SPRING, p. o., Morgan co., Ala.
BLUE SPRING, p. o., Smyth co., Va.
BLUE SPRING GROVE, p. o., Barren co., Ky.
BLUE SPRINGS, p. o., Jackson co., Mo.
BLUE STORM, p. o., Tazewell co., Va., 279 ms. w. by s. of Richmond; from W. 325 ms.
BLUE SULPHUR SPRINGS, p. o., Green Brier co., Va., 227 ms. N. by w. of Richmond; from W. 264 ms.
BLUE WING, p. o., Granville co., N. C., 69 ms. N. of Raleigh; from W. 246 ms.
BLUFF, p. o., Mercer co., Ill., (now POPE'S MILLS.)
BLUFF, p. o. Sauk co., Wis.
BLUFF DALE, p. o., Greene co., Ill., 78 ms. s. w. of Springfield; from W. 842 ms.
BLUFF DALE, p. o., Des Moines co., Iowa.
BLUFF GROVE, p. o., Grundy co., Mo.
BLUFF POINT, p. o., Yates co., N. Y.
BLUFF PORT, p. o., Sumter co., Ala., 76 ms. s. w. of Tuscaloosa; from W. 891 ms.
BLUFF SPRING, p. o., Johnson co., Mo.
BLUFF SPRING, p. o., Attila co., Miss.
BLUFF SPRING, p. o., Talladega co., Ala.
BLUFF SPRING, p. o., Talbot co., Ga., 104 ms. E. S. E. of Milledgeville; from W. 726 ms.
BLUFF SPRINGS, p. o., Gibson co., Tenn.
BLUFFTON, c. h., p. v., seat of justice of Wells co., Ind., 107 ms. N. N. E. of Indianapolis; from W. 549 ms. Pop. 477.
BLUFFTON, p. o., Marquette co., Wis.
BLUFFTON, p. o., Beaufort co., S. C.
BLUFFVILLE, p. v., Carroll co., Ill.
BLYTHE, t., Marion co., Ark.
BLYTHE, t., Caldwell co., Mo.
BLYTHEVILLE, p. o., Jasper co., Ill.
BOALSBURGH, p. v., Ferguson township, Centre co., Pa., 84 ms. N. w. of Harrisburgh; from W. 176 ms. Watered by Spring creek.
BOARDMAN, p. t., Mahoning co., O., 170 ms. N. E. of Columbus; from W. 287 ms. Watered by Mill, Indian and Yellow creeks. Pop. 1,026.
BOARDTREE, p. v., Cherokee co., Ga.
BODENHAM, p. v., Giles co., Tenn., 82 ms. s. by w. of Nashville; from W. 742 ms.

BOETIA, p. o., Mercer co., O.
BŒUFF PRAIRIE, t., Franklin co., Mo.
BOGANSVILLE, p. o., Union co., S. C.
BOGARD, p. o., Daviess co., Ind.
BOGGESS CROSS ROADS, p. o., Meigs co., Tenn., 158 ms. s. E. of Nashville ; from W. 550 ms.
BOGGS, p. t., Centre co., Pa. Pop. 1,923.
BOGGS, t., Clearfield co., Pa. Pop. 464.
BOGGY DEPOT, p. o., Choctaw Nation co., Ark.
BOGLES, p. o., Iredell co., N. C., 165 ms. w. of Raleigh ; from W. 403 ms.
BOGHT, p. o., Albany co., N. Y.
BOGUE CHITTO, p. o., Dallas co., Ala., 89 ms. s. s. E. of Tuscaloosa ; from W. 872 ms.
BOGUS RUN, p. o., Stark co., Ind.
BOILING SPRING, p. o., Fentress co., Tenn., 133 ms. E. N. E. of Nashville ; from W. 571 ms.
BOILING SPRINGS, p. o., Benton co., Ala.
BOILING SPRINGS, p. o., Cumberland co., Pa.
BOILSTON, p. o., Henderson co., N. C.
BOIS D'ARC, t., Hempstead co., Ark.
BOKE'S CREEK, p. t., Union co., O.
BOLAND'S, p. o., Itawamba co., Miss.
BOLEN'S MILLS, p. o., Vinton co., O., 83 ms. s. E. of Columbus ; from W. 353 ms.
BOLIGEE, p. o., Greene co., Ala., 52 ms. s. s. w. of Tuscaloosa ; from W. 870 ms.
BOLINGTON, p. o., Loudoun co., Va., 163 ms. N. of Richmond ; from W. 44 ms.
BOLIVAR COUNTY, situated on the westerly boundary of Mississippi, on the east side of Mississippi river. Area, 1,700 square miles. Seat of justice, Bolivar. Pop. in 1840, 1,356 ; in 1850, 2.577.
BOLIVAR, p. t., Alleghany co., N. Y., 285 ms. w. s. w. of Albany ; from W. 312 ms. Pop. 708.
BOLIVAR, t., Westmoreland co., Pa., 165 m. w. of Harrisburgh ; from W. 191 ms. Watered by Conemaugh river.
BOLIVAR, p. v., Lawrence township, Tuscarawas co., O., 118 ms. N. E. of Columbus ; from W. 321 ms. Watered by Tuscarawas river.
BOLIVAR, p. o., Frederick co., Md.
BOLIVAR, v., Robeson co., N. C., 112 ms. s. by w. of Raleigh ; from W. 400 ms.
BOLIVAR, c. h., p. v., seat of justice of Hardeman co., Tenn., 162 ms. s. w. of Nashville ; from W. 847 ms. Watered by Big Hatchee river.
BOLIVAR, p. o., Jackson co. Ala.
BOLIVAR, c. h., p. v., seat of justice of Polk co., Mo., 132 ms. s. w. of Jefferson city ; from W. 1,068 ms.
BOLIVAR, c. h., p. v., seat of justice of Bolivar co., Miss. Watered by Mississippi river, and Lake Bolivar.
BOLIVAR, p. t., Poinsett co., Ark., 147 ms. E. N. E. of Little Rock ; from W. 902 ms. Pop. 581.
BOLIVIA, t., Gasconade co., Mo.
BOLIVIA, t., Jefferson co., Ark. Pop. 686.
BOLSTER'S MILLS, p. v., Cumberland co., Me., 68 ms. s. w. of Augusta ; from W. 578 ms.
BOLTON, p. t., Chittenden co., Vt., 19 ms. N. N. w. of Montpelier ; from W. 521 ms. Watered by Onion river: Pop. 602.
BOLTON, p. t., Worcester co., Mass., 33 ms. W. of Boston ; from W. 419 ms. Watered by Concord and Nashua rivers. Pop. 1,263.
BOLTON, p. t., Tolland co., Ct. Watered by Hop river. Pop. 600.
BOLTON, p. t., Warren co., N. Y., 73 ms. N. of Albany ; from W. 446 ms. Watered by Schroon river and Lake George. Pop. 1,147.
BOLTON, p. o., Williamson co., Ill.
BOLTON DEPOT, p. o., Hinds co., Miss.
BOLTONVILLE, p. o., Orange co., Vt., 35 ms. s. E. of Montpelier ; from W. 527 ms.
BOLT'S FORK, p. o., Lawrence co., Ky.
BOMBAY, p. t., Franklin co., N. Y., 232 ms. N. of Albany ; from W. 552 ms. Watered by Little Salmon and St. Regis rivers. Pop. 1,963.
BONAPARTE, p. o., Van Buren co., Iowa.
BONAPARTE, p. o., Du Page co.. Ill.
BON AIR SPRINGS, p. o., White co., Tenn., 88 ms. E. s. E. of Nashville ; from W 592 ms.
BON AQUA, p. o., Hickman co., Tenn.
BOND'S POINT, p. o., Christian co., Ill.
BOND'S VILLAGE, p. o., Hampden co., Mass.
BONDVILLE, p. o., Bennington co., Vt.
BONDVILLE, p. o., Columbia co., Pa., 76 ms. N. of Harrisburgh ; from W. 186 ms.
BONE CREEK, p. o., Ritchie co., Va.

BONE YARD, p. o., Tishamingo co., Miss.
BONHAM, p. o., Fannin co., Tex.
BONN, p. o., Washington co.
BONNE FEMME, t., Howard co., Mo.
BON HOMME, t., St. Genevieve co., Mo.
BON HOMME, t., St. Louis co., Mo.
BONNET CARRE, c. h., p. v., seat of justice of St. John Baptist parish, La., 38 ms. w. of New Orleans ; from W. 1,210 ms. Watered by Mississippi river.
BONNY DOON, p. o., Jefferson co., Ga.
BONO, p. t., Lawrence co., Ind., 89 ms. s. by w. of Indianapolis ; from W. 620 ms. Pop. 1,001.
BON PAS, p. o., Richland co., Ill.
BONNS, p. o., Boone co., Ill.
BOONE COUNTY, situated at the extreme north part of Kentucky, on the south side of Ohio river. Length, 25 miles ; mean width. 12 ; with an area of 300 square miles. The face of the country is generally hilly, and the soil productive. Seat of justice, Burlington. Pop. in 1820, 6,582 ; in 1830, 9,075 ; in 1840, 10,034 ; in 1850, 11,125.
BOONE COUNTY, in the central part of Indiana. Area, 408 square miles. Seat of justice, Lebanon. Pop. 1830, 621 ; in 1840. 8,121 ; in 1850, 11,631.
BOONE COUNTY, in the central part of Missouri, on the northeasterly side of Missouri river. Area, 600 square miles. Face of the country undulating. Soil, generally good. Seat of justice, Columbia. Pop. in 1830, 8,859 ; in 1840, 13.561 ; in 1850, 14,979.
BOONE COUNTY, in the north boundary of Illinois, and drained by Kishwaukee river. Area, 400 square miles. Seat of justice, Belvidere. Pop. in 1840, 1,705, in 1850. 7,626.
BOONE COUNTY, in the westerly part of Virginia Area, —— square miles. Seat of justice, Ballardsville. Pop. in 1850, 3,237.
BOONE COUNTY, in the central part of Iowa, and traversed by Des Moines river. Area, 600 square miles. Seat of justice, Booneville. Pop. in 1850, 735
BOONE, t., Warrick co., Ind. Pop. 2,207.
BOONE, t., Harrison co., Ind.
BOONE, p. o., Ashe co., N. C.
BOONE, p. t., Franklin co., Mo.
BOONE, t., Van Buren co., Mo.
BOONESBOROUGH, p. v., Madison co., Ky., 53 ms. s. w. of Frankfort ; from W. 534 ms. Watered by Kentucky river.
BOONESBOROUGH, p. o., Washington co., Ark.
BOONESBOROUGH, p. v., Washington co., Md., 91 ms. s. s. w. of Annapolis ; from W. 51 ms. Pop. 854.
BOONESBOROUGH, o., Boone co., Mo.
BOONE'S CREEK, p. o., Washington co., Tenn.
BOONE'S HILL, p. o., Lincoln co. Tenn.
BOON'S LICK, p. t., Howard co., Mo.
BOON'S MILLS, p. o., Franklin co., Va., 175 ms. s. w. by w. of Richmond ; from W. 250 ms.
BOONVILLE, p. t., Oneida co., N. Y., 114 ms. w. N. w. of Albany ; from W. 419 ms. Watered by Black and Mohawk rivers. Pop. 3,306.
BOONVILLE, p. o., Warwick co., Ind.
BOONVILLE, c. h., p. v., seat of justice of Scott co., Ark., 120 ms. w. by N. of Little Rock ; from W. 1,185 ms.
BOONVILLE, c. h., p. v., seat of justice of Cooper co., Mo., 50 ms. N. w. of Jefferson city ; from W. 964 ms. Watered by Missouri river. Pop. 1,657.
BOONVILLE, p. o., Brazos co., Tex.
BOONHILL, p. o.. Johnson co., N. C., 37 ms. s. E. of Raleigh ; from W. 295 ms.
BOONSBOROUGH, p. o., Ogle co., Ill., 182 ms. N. of Springfield ; from W. 842 ms.
BOON'S GROVE, p. o., Washington co., Ark.
BOOTHBAY, p. t., Lincoln co., Me., 40 ms. s. by E. of Augusta ; from W. 601 ms. Watered by Sheepscot and Damariscotta rivers. Pop. 2,504.
BOOTHSVILLE, p. o., Marion co., Va., 270 ms. N. w. of Richmond ; from W. 218 ms.
BOOTON, v., Genesee co., Mich., 67 ms. N. N. w. of Detroit ; from W. 589 ms.
BOOTON'S TAN-YARD, p. o., Madison co., Va., 92 ms. N. w. of Richmond ; from W. 104 ms.
BORDEAUX, p. o., Abbeville district, S. C., 105 ms. N. by w. of Columbia ; from W. 553 ms.
BORDEAUX, p. o., Avoyelles parish, La.
BORDENTOWN, p. b., Chesterfield township, Burlington co., N. J., 7 ms. s. E. of Trenton ; from W. 168 ms. Watered by Delaware river.
BORDER SPRING, p. o., Lowndes co., Miss., 158 ms, N. E., of Jackson ; from W. 873 ms.

BORDLEY, p. v., Union co.. Ky., 224 ms. w. by s. of Frankfort; from W. 765 ms.

BORLAND, p. o., Newton co., Ark.

BORODINO. p. o., Wayne co., Mich., 29 ms. s. of Detroit; from W. 533 ms.

BORODINO. p. o., Spafford township, Onondaga co., N. Y., 150 ms. w. by N. of Albany; from W. 339 ms.

BORODINO. p. o., Avoyelles parish, La.

BOSCAWEN, p. t., Merrimac co., N. H., 8 ms. N. w. of Concord; from W. 490 ms. Watered by Merrimac and Blackwater rivers. Pop. 2,063.

BOSSARDSVILLE, p. o., Monroe co., Pa.

BOSSERMAN'S MILLS. p. o., Perry co., Pa.

BOSSIER PARISH, situated near the northwest corner of Louisiana, between Red river and Lake Bistencau, containing also Lake Bodeau. Area, 880 square miles. Seat of justice, Belleview. Pop., in 1850, 6,962.

BOSSIER POINT, p. o., Bossier parish, La.

BOSTWICK'S MILLS, p. o., Richmond co., N. C., 122 s. w. by w. of Raleigh; from W. 396 ms.

BOSTON CITY, the capital of Massachusetts, and seat of justice of Suffolk co., occupies a peninsula and other adjacent points, at the head of Massachusetts bay. The original town was confined to the peninsula, but this, although enlarged by artificial means, has long since proved too narrow for the growing city, which, passing the barriers thrown around it by nature, now embraces, independently of the populous towns and villages that are its offspring, the triple division of "Old Boston," "South Boston," and "East Boston." The "Neck" was formerly the only avenue from the town to the main land, but it is now united by bridges, and other avenues, to Charlestown, Cambridge, South Boston, and other surrounding points. From the west side of the city, Western avenue is continued to Brookline, on the opposite side of Charles river bay, by a costly dam one mile and a half in length, and 100 feet broad. Proceeding from the middle of this, on which are several tidemills, a second dam divides the bay into two spacious basins. Several of the Boston railroads also enter the city, by bridges built expressly for that purpose.

The harbor extends from Nantasket to the city, and spreads from Chelsea and Nahant to Hingham, containing about seventy-five square miles. It is studded with upward of fifty islands, or rocks, and receives the waters from the Mystic, Charles, Neponset, and Manatticut rivers, with several other smaller streams. One of the most remarkable features connected with the harbor, is the costly and splendid wharves. These marks of commercial enterprise and prosperity are about one hundred in number, and of various dimensions. Long wharf is 1,650 feet long, and 200 feet wide; Central wharf, 1,397 feet long, and 150 feet wide; India wharf, 980 feet long, and from 246 to 280 feet wide; and Commercial wharf is 1,100 feet long, and 160 feet wide. These, like most of the others, are lined with extensive and magnificent warehouses, constructed of the most substantial materials.

Another valuable acquisition is Boston Common, a pleasant park of about fifty acres, situated at the southwesterly slope of Beacon hill. It is pleasantly diversified with knolls, avenues, fountains, a small lake, or pond, and trees, some of the latter being interesting relics of colonial and revolutionary times. The common is surrounded by an iron fence, over one mile in extent. Between the common and Charles river bay, lies the Botanic Garden, a beautiful and tasteful enclosure. On the north side of the common, and at the summit of the hill, stands the statehouse, an elegant structure, 173 feet in length. 61 feet in depth, and 120 feet in height. The top of the dome is 230 feet above tide-water. The view from the top of the statehouse is very extensive and variegated; perhaps nothing in the country is superior to it. To the east appears the bay and harbor, interspersed with beautiful islands; and in the distance beyond, the wide ocean. To the north the eye is met by Charlestown, with its interesting and memorable heights, of Bunker Hill, crowned with the monument, 220 feet in height, and the navy-yard of the United States; the towns of Chelsea, Malden, and Medford, and other villages, and the natural forests mingling in the distant horizon. To the west, is a fine view of the Charles river and bay, the city of Cambridge, rendered venerable for the university, now about two hundred years old; of the highly-cultivated towns of Brighton, Brookline, and Newton; and to the south is the city of Roxbury, which seems to be only a con-tinuation of Boston, and which is rapidly increasing Dorchester, a rich, agricultural town, with Milton and Quincy beyond; and farther south, the Blue hills, at the distance of eight miles, which seem to bound the prospect.

Faneuil Hall, which is justly styled the "cradle of American liberty," was originally built in 1740, for a town-hall and market-house. It has been enlarged and beautified on several occasions, and will always be a place of historical interest to the lovers of liberty. Adjoining it on the east is Quincy Market, one of the most splendid and commodious edifices of the kind in the country. It is constructed of granite, or sienite, 540 feet in length, 50 feet wide, and two stories high. The courthouse, merchants' exchange, postoffice, customhouse, Massachusetts general hospital, the old south meetinghouse, Park-street, Brattle-street, and Trinity churches, the Tremont house, Revere house, the Athenæum, the jail, Society of Natural History, the houses of industry, correction, and reformation, are among other objects of interest. The water-works may be regarded as one of the most important of the recent improvements. By a series of pipes and reservoirs, water is conveyed to all parts of the city proper, and East and South Boston, from Long Pond, or Lake Cochituate, a distance of nearly 20 miles. It will supply 10,000,000 gallons of water daily, and cost about $5,000,000.

Railroads diverge from this city in various directions, connecting it with Plymouth, New Bedford, Fall River, Providence, Stonington, New York (via Worcester, Springfield. Hartford, New-Haven); with Albany, via Worcester and Springfield; with Vermont, via Fitchburgh; also, with Lake Winnipisiogee and the White Mountains, in New Hampshire, via Nashua, Concord, and Meredith Bridge; also, via Haverhill, Exeter, and Dover; with Lawrence, via Lowell and Manchester; with Augusta, Me., via Salem, Newburyport, Portsmouth, Portland, and Bath.

Boston is pre-eminently distinguished for its efforts in behalf of education. Its public schools are unrivalled in excellence, and it numbers among its citizens some of the most munificent patrons of learning, literature, and science; which, with its many eminent literary and philosophical societies, has led to its being honored with the title of the "Athens of America."

Mount Auburn, a beautiful cemetery, belonging principally to Boston, is picturesquely situated near Cambridge, about five miles distance. Within this interesting "city of the dead" rest the remains of many of the illustrious sons of New England.

The population of Boston in 1700, was 7,000; in 1722, 10,567; in 1765, 15,520; in 1790, 18,033; in 1800, 24,937; in 1810, 33,250; in 1820, 43,298; in 1830, 61,392; in 1840, 93,383; in 1850, 136,657.

BOSTON, p. t., Erie co., N. Y., 299 ms. w. of Albany; from W. 362 ms. Watered by Cauquaga creek. Pop. 1,872.

BOSTON, v., Boston township, Erie co., N. Y.

BOSTON, p. t., Wayne co., Ind. Pop. 959.

BOSTON, p. t., Summit co., O., 139 ms. N. E. of Columbus; from W. 343 ms. Watered by Cuyahoga river. Pop. 1,180.

BOSTON, p. o., Williamson co., Tenn.

BOSTON, p. o., Ionia co., Mich., 146 ms. N. w. of Detroit; from W. 621 ms. Watered by Grand river.

BOSTON, p. o., Culpeper co., Va.

BOSTON, p. o., Thomas co., Ga.

BOSTON, p. o., Northampton, Pa.

BOSTON, p. t., Nelson co., Ky., 66 ms. s. w., of Frankfort; from W. 608 ms.

BOSTON, p. t., Bowie co., Tex.

BOSTON, p. v., Marengo co., Ala., 70 ms. s. by w. of Tuscaloosa; from W. 882 ms.

BOSTON, t., Franklin co., Ark. Pop. 338.

BOSTON, p. o., Andrew co., Mo.

BOSTON CORNER, p. o., Berkshire co., Mass., 160 ms. w. of Boston; from W. 338 ms.

BOST'S MILLS, p. o., Cabarras co., N. C., 153 ms w. s. w. of Raleigh; from W. 392 ms.

BOTANIC HILL, p. o., Nash co., N. C.

BOTANIC GARDEN, p. o., Perry co., Tenn.

BOTETOURT COUNTY, situated in the central part of Virginia, on the sources of James and Roanoke rivers. Length, 40 miles; mean width, 28; with an area of 1,120 square miles. This county embraces a part of the great limestone and slate valley at the north-west of the Blue Ridge, and contains much excellent

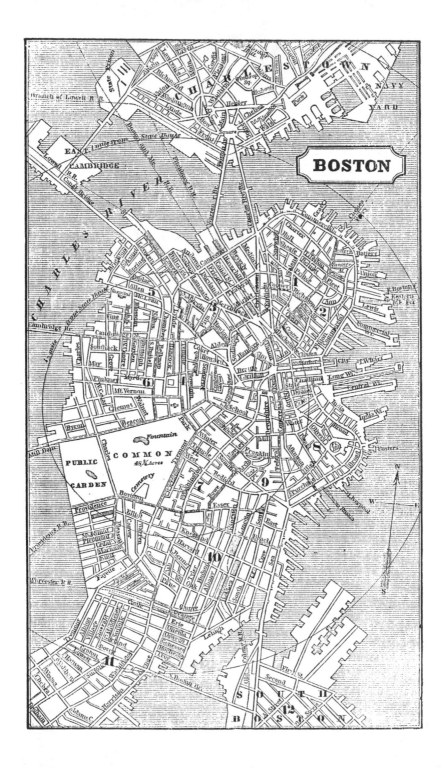

land. The surface, however, is considerably broken, and even mountainous. Seat of justice, Fincastle. Pop. in 1820, 13,590; in 1830, 16,354; in 1840, 11,679; in 1850, 14,908.

BOTETOURT SPRINGS, p. v., Roanoke co., Va., 186 ms. w. by s. of Richmond ; from W. 238 ms.

BOTHELLE, p. o., Fond du Lac c., Wis.

BOTTLE HILL, v., Chatham township, Morris co. N J., 57 ms. N. by E. of Trenton ; from W. 223 ms.

BOUCHE SALINE, p. o., Cole co., Mo., 48 ms. w. of Jefferson city; from W. 984 ms.

BOUCKVILLE, p. o., Madison township, Madison co., N. Y., 97 ms. w. of Albany ; from W. 363 ms.

BOUND BROOK, p. v., Bridgewater township, Somerset co., N. J., 33 ms. N. by E. of Trenton ; from W. 200 ms.

BOUNTY LAND, p. o., Pickens district, S. C.

BOURBON COUNTY, situated in the northern part of Kentucky, between Kentucky and Licking rivers. Length, 16 miles ; mean breadth, 11 ; with an area of 176 square miles. The face of the country is somewhat hilly, and the soil fertile and well cultivated. Seat of justice, Paris. Pop. in 1830, 18,434 ; in 1840, 14,478 ; In 1850, 14,466.

BOURBONTON, p. t., Boone cp., Mo.

BOURNEVILLE, p. v., Twin township, Ross co., O., 63 ms. s. of Columbus ; from W. 413 ms.

BOURNSBURGH, p. v., Randolph co., Mo., 75 ms. N. by w. of Jefferson city ; from W. 964 ms.

BOVEY, t., St. Genevieve co., Mo.

BOVINA, p. t., Delaware co., N. Y., 76 ms. s. s. w. of Albany ; from W. 350 ms. Watered by Little Delaware river. Pop. 1,316.

BOVINA, p. o., Warren co., Miss., 34 ms. w. of Jackson ; from W. 1,044 ms.

BOVINA CENTRE, p. o., Bovina township, Delaware co., N. Y., 76 ms. s. s. w. of Albany ; from W. 350 ms.

Bow, p. t., Merrimac co., N. H., 7 ms. s. of Concord ; from W. 477 ms. Watered by Turkey and Merrimac rivers. Pop. 1,055.

BOWDARK, p. o., Greene co., Mo.

BOWDOIN, p. t., Lincoln co., Me., 18 ms. s. s. w. of Augusta, from W. 579 ms. Pop. 1,857.

BOWDOIN CENTRE, p. o., Bowdoin township, Lincoln co., Me.

BOWDOINHAM, p. t., Lincoln co., Me., 21 ms. s. by w. of Augusta ; from W. 759 ms. Watered by Kennebec river. Pop. 2,382.

BOWDON, p. o., Carroll co., Ga.

BOWDON, p. o., Talladega co., Ala.

BOWEN, t., Madison co., Ark.

BOWEN'S PRAIRIE, p. o., Jones co., Iowa.

BOWENVILLE, p. o., Carroll co., Ga.

BOWER, p. o., Clearfield co., Pa.

BOWERBANK, p. t., Piscataquis co., Me. Pop. 173.

BOWER HILL, p. o., Washington co., Pa.

BOWERS, p. o., Southampton co., Va., 78 ms. s. by E. of Richmond ; from W. 197 ms.

BOWER'S MILLS, p. o., Lawrence co., Mo.

BOWERS' STORE, p. o., Ashe co., N. C.

BOWERSVILLE, p. v., Franklin co., Ga., 124 ms. N. of Milledgeville ; from W. 595 ms.

BOWERSVILLE, p. o., Greene co., O.

BOWLESVILLE, p. o., Fluvanna co., Va.

BOWIE COUNTY, situated at the northeast corner of Texas, between Red River and the Sulphur Fork of the same. Area, —— square miles. Seat of justice, Boston. Pop. in 1850, 2,912.

BOWLES, t., Franklin co., Mo.

BOWLING GREEN, p. o., Stewart co., Tenn.

BOWLING GREEN, p. o., Plain township, Wood co., O., 115 ms. N. N. W. of Columbus ; from W. 469 ms.

BOWLING GREEN, c. h., p. v., seat of justice of Caroline co., Va., 40 ms. N. of Richmond ; from W. 80 ms. Pop. 218.

BOWLING GREEN, t., Licking co., O. Pop. 1,538.

BOWLING GREEN, c. h., p. v., seat of justice of Clay co., Ind., 60 ms. s. by w. of Indianapolis ; from W. 631 ms. Watered by Eel river.

BOWLING GREEN, t., Fayette co., Ill., 80 ms. s. s. E. of Springfield ; from W. 742 ms.

BOWLING GREEN, t., Pettis co., Mo.

BOWLING GREEN, p. o., Pike co., Mo., 76 ms. N. E. of Jefferson city ; from W. 880 ms.

BOWLING GREEN, p. o., Oglethorpe co., Ga., 63 ms. N. N. E. of Milledgeville ; from W. 595 ms.

BOWLING GREEN, p. v., seat of justice of Warren co.,

Ky., 144 ms. s. w. of Frankfort; from W. 668 ms. Watered by Big Barren river.

BOWLING GREEN, t., Marion co., O. Watered by Scioto river.

BOWLINGSVILLE, p. v., Union district, S. C.

BOWMAN'S CREEK, p. o., Wyoming co., Pa., 139 ms. N. N. E. of Harrisburgh; from W. 248 ms.

BOWMAN'S MILLS, p. o., Rockingham co., Va.

BOWSHERVILLE, p. o., Crawford co., O., 61 ms. N. of Columbus ; from W. 424 ms.

BOWYER'S KNOB, p. o., Fayette co., Pa.

BOWMANSVILLE, p. o., Lancaster co., Pa.

BOWNE, p. o., Kent co., Mich.

BOXBOROUGH, p. t., Middlesex co., Mass., 28 ms. N. W. by w. of Boston; from W. 476 ms. Pop. 395.

BOX CREEK, p. o., Cherokee co., Tex.

BOXFORD, p. t., Essex co., Mass., 29 ms. N. by E. of Boston ; from W. 469 ms. Pop. 982.

BOXLEY, p. o.. Hamilton co., Ind., 40 ms. N. by E. of Indianapolis ; from W. 578 ms.

BOXVILLE, p. v., Montgomery co., Ga., 129 ms. s. s. E. of Milledgeville ; from W. 740 ms.

BOYD'S, p. o., Columbiana co., O., 150 ms. N. E. of Columbus ; from W. 294 ms.

BOYD'S CREEK, p. o., Sevier co., Tenn., 225 ms. E. by s. of Nashville ; from W. 502 ms.

BOYD'S STORE, p. o., Polk co., Mo., 145 ms. s. w. of Jefferson city ; from W. 1,081 ms.

BOYD'S TAVERN, p. o., Albemarle co., Va., 74 ms. w. N. w. of Richmond ; from W. 123 ms.

BOYDSTOWN, p. t., Penobscot co., Me., 101 ms. N. E. of Augusta ; from W. 696 ms.

BOYDSVILLE, p. o., Weakley co., Tenn., 118 ms. w. by N. of Nashville ; from W. 804 ms.

BOYDTON, c. h., p. v., seat of justice of Mecklenburgh co., Va., 109 ms. s. s. w. of Richmond ; from W. 222 ms.

BOYER'S SETTLEMENT, p. o., Buchanan co., Mo.

BOYERSTOWN, p. o., Berks co., Pa., 69 ms. E. by N. of Harrisburgh ; from W. 162 ms.

BOYKIN'S DEPOT, p. o., Southampton co., Va., 84 ms. s. by E. of Richmond ; from W. 203 ms.

BOYKIN'S DEPOT, p. o., Kershaw district, S. C.

BOYLE COUNTY, situated in the central part of Kentucky, on the southwest side of Dick's river. Area, 175 square miles. Soil fertile. Seat of justice, Danville. Pop. in 1850, 9,116.

BOYLSTON, p. t., Worcester co., Mass., 39 ms. w. of Boston, from W. 408 ms. Watered by Nashua river. Pop. 918.

BOYLSTON, t., Oswego co., N. Y., 140 ms. N. w. of Albany. from W. 441 ms. Watered by Little Sandy and Trout creeks. Pop. 661.

BOYLE'S STORE, p. o., Stokes co., N. C., 142 ms. w. N. w. of Raleigh ; from W. 313 ms.

BOYLSTON CENTRE, p. o., Worcester co., Mass.

BOZRAH, p. t., New London co., Ct., 33 ms. E. s. E. of Hartford ; from W. 359 ms. Watered by Yantic river. Pop. 867.

BOZRAHVILLE, p. v., Bozrah township, New London co., Ct., 31 ms. E. s. E. of Hartford ; from W. 359 ms.

BRACEVILLE, p. t., Trumbull co., O., 164 ms. N. E. of Columbus ; from W. 310 ms. Pop. 956.

BRACKEN COUNTY, situated on the northern boundary of Kentucky, between Ohio and Licken rivers. Area, 220 square miles. Seat of justice, Augusta. Pop. in 1820, 5,280 ; in 1830, 6,518 ; in 1840, 7,053 ; in 1850, 8,903.

BRACKNEY, p. o., Susquehanna co., Pa.

BRADENVILLE, p. o., Westmoreland co., Pa.

BRADFORD COUNTY, situated on the north boundary of Pennsylvania, and traversed by Susquehanna river. Length, 38 miles ; and mean width, 35 ; with an area of 1,330 square miles. The face of the country rocky and hilly, and the soil varied, but not very fertile. Seat of justice, Towanda. Pop. in 1820, 11,554 ; in 1830, 19,609; in 1840, 32,769; in 1850, 42,839.

BRADFORD, p. t., Steuben co., N. Y., 204 ms. w. s. w. of Albany. Pop. 2,010.

BRADFORD, p. t., Penobscot co., Me., 94 ms. N. E. of Augusta ; from W. 689 ms. Pop. 1,296.

BRADFORD, p. t., Merrimac co., N. H., 25 ms. w. of Concord ; from W. 472 ms. Pop. 1,341.

BRADFORD, p. t., Orange co., Vt., 32 ms. s. E. of Montpelier, from W. 512 ms. Watered by Connecticut river. Pop. 1,723.

BRADFORD, p. t., Essex co., Mass., 35 ms. N. of Boston ; from W. 466 ms. Watered by Merrimac river. Pop. 1,328.

BRADFORD, p. o., Washington township, Scioto co., O., 92 ms. s. of Columbus ; from W. 426 ms.

BRADFORD, t., McKean co., Pa. Pop. 990.

BRADFORD, p. o., Coosa co., Ala.

BRADFORD, t., Lincoln co., Mo.

BRADFORD, p. o., Harrison co., Ind.

BRADFORD CENTRE. p. o., Orange co., Vt.

BRADFORD INSTITUTE, p. o., Sumter district, S. C

BRADFORD SPRINGS, p. o., Sumter district, S. C., 48 ms. E. of Columbia ; from W. 488 ms.

BRADFORDVILLE, p. v., Marion co., Ky., 68 ms. from Frankfort ; from W. 590 ms.

BRADLEY COUNTY, situated in the south part of Arkansas, north of the junction of Wachita and Saline rivers. Area, —— square miles. Seat of justice, Warren. Pop., in 1850. 3,829.

BRADLEY COUNTY, in the southeast part of Tennessee, and drained by Hiawassee river. Area, —— square miles. The face of the county is uneven. Seat of justice, Cleveland. Pop., in 1840, 7,385 ; in 1850, 12,259.

BRADLEY, Penobscot co., Me. Pop. 796.

BRADLEY, p. o., Jackson co., Ill.

BRADLEY, p. o., Allegan co., Mich.

BRADLEYVALE, Caledonia co., Vt.

BRADLEYVILLE, p. o., Sumter district, S. C., 77 ms. E. of Columbia ; from W. 513 ms.

BRADSHAW, p. o., Giles co., Tenn. 84 ms. s. w. of Nashville ; from W. 744 ms.

BRADY, t., Clearfield co., Pa. Pop. 1,083.

BRADY, t., Williams co., O. Watered by Tiffins river. Pop. 1,128.

BRADY, p. t. Kalamazoo co., Mich., 146 ms. w. of Detroit ; from W. 608 ms. Watered by Portage river. Pop. 578.

BRADY'S BEND, p. o., Armstrong co., Pa.

BRADYVILLE. p. v., Cannon co., Tenn., 56 ms. s. E. of Nashville ; from W. 661 ms.

BRADYVILLE, p. o., Adams co., O.

BRAGG'S, p. o., Lowndes co., Ala., 120 ms. s. E. of Tuscalóosa ; from W. 877 ms.

BRAGGVILLE, p. o., Middlesex co., Mass.

BRAINARD'S BRIDGE, p. v., Nassau township, Rensslaer co., N. Y., 16 ms. N. E. of Albany ; from W. 369 ms.

BRAINTREE, p. t., Orange co., Vt., 23 ms. s. of Montpelier ; from W. 494 ms. Watered by White river. Pop. 1,228.

BRAINTREE, p. t., Norfolk co., Mass., 14 ms. s of Boston ; from W. 442 ms. Watered by Mantiquot river. Pop. 2,969.

BRAINTREM, p. t., Wyoming co., Pa., 163 ms. N. N. w. of Harrisburg ; from W. 273 ms. Pop. 836.

BRALSVILLE. v., Monroe co., O.

BRAMAN'S CORNERS, p. o., Duanesburgh township, Schenectady co., N. Y., 35 ms. w. N. w. of Albany ; from W. 402 ms.

BRAKELEYVILLE, p. o., Monroe co., Pa.

BRAKES' RUN. p. o., Hardy co., Va.

BRANCH COUNTY, situated on the south boundary of Michigan, and drained by St. Joseph's river. Area, 528 square miles. Seat of justice, Branch Court House. Pop., in 1840, 5,715 ; in 1850, 18,472.

BRANCH, c. h., p. v., Coldwater township. Seat of justice of Branch co., Mich., 113 w. s. w. of Detroit ; from W. 561 ms. Watered by Coldwater river.

BRANCH, Schuylkill co., Pa. Pop. 2,653.

BRANCH HILL. p. o., Clermont co., O.

BRANCH DALE, p. o., Schuylkill co., Pa.

BRANCH ISLAND, p. o., Pickens district, S. C.

BRANCH PORT, p. v., Jerusalem township, Yates co., N. Y., 201 ms. w. of Albany ; from W. 327 ms. Watered by Crooked lake.

BRANCHTOWN, p. o., Cherokee co., Tex. (now Analo-mink).

BRANCHVILLE, p. v., Frankford township, Sussex co., N. J., 77 ms. N. of Trenton ; from W. 246 ms. Watered by Paulin's Kill.

BRANCHVILLE, p. o., Orangeburgh district, S. C., 62 ms. s. of Columbia ; from W. 568 ms.

BRANCHVILLE, p. o.. St. Clair co., Ala., 108 ms. N. E. of Tuscaloosa ; from W. 736 ms.

BRANDENBURGH, c. h., p. v., seat of justice of Meade co., Ky., 94 ms. w. by s. of Frankfort ; from W. 634 ms.

BRANDON, p. t., Rutland co., Vt., 14 ms. s. w. of Mont-

pelier ; from W. 472 ms. Watered by Otter creek and Mill river. Pop. 2,835.

BRANDON, c. h., p. v.. seat of justice of Rankin co., Miss., 13 ms. E. of Jackson ; from W. 1,003 ms.

BRANDON t., Oakland co., Mich. Watered by Flint river. Pop. 893.

BRANDON, p., Knox Co., O.

BRANDON, t., Franklin co.. N. Y., 215 N. by w. of Albany ; from W. 511 ms. Watered by Saranac and St. Regis rivers. Pop. 590.

BRANDONVILLE. p. v., Preston co., Va., 267 ms. N. w. of Richmond ; from W. 189 ms.

BRAND'S IRON WORKS, p. o., Washington co., R. I., 28 ms. s. by w, of Providence ; from W. 380 ms.

BRANDT, t., Erie co., N. Y., 20 ms. s. w. of Buffalo ; from W. 300 ms. Situated on Lake Erie.

BRANDY, t., Williams co., O.

BRANDYWINE, p. o., Prince George's co., Md., 40 ms. s. w. of Annapolis ; from W. 94 ms.

BRANDYWINE, t., Hancock co. Ind.

BRANDYWINE, hundred, New Castle co., Del.

BRANDYWINE, p. o., Shelby co., Ind., 20 ms. s. E. of Indianapolis ; from W. 570 ms.

BRANDYWINE, t., Chester co., Pa., 63 ms. N. w. from Harrisburgh ; from W. 129 ms. Pop.

BRANDYWINE MANOR, p. o., Chester co., Pa., 60 ms. s. E. of Harrisburgh ; from W. 131 ms.

BRANDYWINE MILLS, p. v., Northfield township, Summit co., O., 141 ms. N. E. of Columbus ; from W. 341 ms.

BRANDYWINE SPRINGS, p. o., New Castle co., Del.

BRANFORD, p. t., New Haven co., Ct, 43 ms. s. by w. of Hartford ; from W. 307 ms. Watered by Branford river. Pop. 1,423.

BRANT, p. o., Erie co., N. Y.

BRANTINGHAM, p. o., Greig township. Lewis co., N. Y., 136 ms. N. w. of Albany ; from W. 435 ms.

BRASHERVILLE, p. o., Perry co., Ky., 166 ms. s. E. by E. of Frankfort ; from W. 515 ms.

BRASHER FALLS, p. v., Brasher township, St. Lawrence co., N. Y. Watered by Deer river. Pop. 2,582.

BRASHER IRON WORKS, p. o., St. Lawrence co., N. Y.

BRASS BELL, p. o., Pendleton co., Ky.

BRASSTOWN, p. o., Union co., Ga.

BRATTLEBOROUGH, p.t., Windham co., Vt., 121 ms. s. of Montpelier ; frrom W. 422 ms. Pop. 3,816.

BRATTON'S, p. o., Smith co., Tenn., 54 ms. N. E. of Nashville ; from W. 663 ms.

BRATTONSVILLE, p. o., York district, S. C., 96 ms. N. N. w. of Columbia ; from W. 440 ms.

BRAUNFELS, p. o., Manitouwoc co., Wis.

BRAXTON, c. h., p. v., seat of justice of Braxton co., Va., 321 ms. w. N. w. of Richmond ; from W. 289 ms. Watered by Elk river.

BRAZIL. p. o., Clay co., Ind.

BRAZORIA COUNTY, situated on the southeast boundary of Texas, on the gulf of Mexico, and watered by Brazos and San Bernard rivers. Area. —— square miles. Seat of justice, Brazoria. Pop., in 1850, 4,841.

BRAZORIA, p. t., Brazoria co., Tex.

BRAZOS COUNTY, situated toward the southwest part of Texas, between Brazos and Navasoto rivers. Area, ——square miles. Seat of justice, Booneville. Pop., in 1850, 614.

BRAZOS SANTIAGO, p. o., Cameron co., Tex.

BREAKABEEN, p. v., Fulton township, Schoharie co., N. Y., 45 ms. W. of Albany ; from W. 381 ms.

BREAKNECK, p. o., Butler co., Pa., 219 ms. w. by N. of Harrisburgh ; from W. 257 ms.

BREAN'S BRIDGE, p. o., St. Martin's parish, La., 188 ms. W. of New Orleans ; from W. 1,271 ms.

BREATHITT COUNTY, situated in the east part of Kentucky, and traversed by the north fork of Kentucky river. Area, 700 square miles. Seat of justice, Breathitt. Pop., in 1840, 2,195 ; in 1850, 3,785.

BREATHITT, p. t., Breathitt co., Ky., 121 ms. E. s. E. of Frankfort ; from W. 530 ms. Watered by Kentucky river.

BRECKENRIDGE COUNTY, situated on the northerly boundary of Kentucky, on the southerly side of Ohio river. Length, 38 miles ; mean breadth 20, with an area of 760 square miles. The face of the country is broken, and the soil generally fertile. Seat of justice, Hardensburgh. Pop.. in 1820, 7,485 ; in 1830, 7,345 ; in 1840, 8,994 ; in 1850, 10,593.

BRECKNOCK, t., Lancaster co., Pa. Watered by Marshy creek.

BRECKNOCK, t., Berks co., Pa. Watered by Big and Little Muddy creeks. Pop. 875.

BRECKVILLE, p. o., Madison co., Cal.

BREEDING'S, p. o., Adair co., Ky., 132 ms. s. by w. of Frankfort ; from W. 626 ms.

BREESE, p. o., Green co., Ill.

BREESVILLE, Jackson co., Ill., 177 ms. s. by E. of Springfield ; from W. 853 ms.

BREGENZ, p. o., Choctaw co., Ala.

BREININGSVILLE, p. o., Lehigh co., Pa., 77 ms. E. N. E. of Harrisburgh ; from W. 170 ms.

BREMEN, p. t., Lincoln co., Me., 40 ms. s. E. of Augusta ; from W. 610 ms. Pop. 891.

BREMEN, p. v., Rush creek township, Fairfield co., O., 39 ms. s. E. of Columbus; from W. 364 ms.

BREMEN, p. o., Muhlenburgh co., Ky., 182 ms. w. s. w. of Frankfort; from W. 724 ms.

BREMEN, p t., Cook co., Ill. Pop. 250.

BREMEN, p. v., Marshall co., Ind.

BREMEN, p. v., St. Louis co., Mo.

BREMO, p. o., Callaway co., Ky., 36 ms. N. w. of Frankfort ; from W. 790 ms.

BRENNERSVILLE. p. o., Preble co., O.

BRENHAM, p. o., Washington co., Tex.

BRENT'S, p. o., Henry co., Ky., 263 ms. s. w. of Frankfort ; from W. 578 ms.

BRENTSVILLE, c. h., p. v., seat of justice of Prince William co., Va., 101 ms. N. of Richmond ; from W. 45 ms.

BRENTWOOD, p. t., Rockingham co., N. H., 35 ms. s. E. of Concord ; from W. 485 ms. Watered by Exeter river. Pop. 923.

BREST, p. v., Frenchtown township, Monroe co., Mich., 38 ms. s. by w. of Detroit, from W. 491 ms. Watered by Stony creek.

BREWER, p. t., Penobscot co., Me., 70 ms. E. N. E. of Augusta; from W. 665 ms. Watered by Penobscot river. Pop. 2,628.

BREWER, t., Pike co., Ark.

BREWER CENTRE, p. o., Penobscot co., Me.

BREWERSVILLE, p. o., Sumter co., Ala.

BREWERSVILLE, p. o., Jennings co., Ind.

BREWERTON, p v., Cicero township, Onondaga co., N. Y., 144 ms. w. N. w. of Albany ; from W. 362 ms. Watered by Oneida river.

BREWERTON, p. o., Laurens district, S. C., 95 ms. N. w. of Columbia ; from W. 523 ms.

BREWER VILLAGE, p. o., Brewer township, Penobscot co., Me., 72 ms. E. N. E. of Augusta ; from W. 667 ms.

BREWINGTON, p. o., Sumter district, S. C., 81 ms. E. by s. of Columbus ; from W. 517 ms.

BREWSTER, p. t., Barnstable co., Mass., 90 ms. s. E. of Boston ; from W. 499 ms. Situated on Cape Cod Bay. Pop. 1,525.

BREWSTER'S FERRY, p. o., Stephenson co., Ill., 216 ms. N. of Springfield ; from W. 848 ms.

BREWSTER'S STATION, p. o., Putnam co., N. Y.

BRICKERVILLE, p. o., Lancaster co., 30 ms. E. s. E. of Harrisburgh ; from W. 124 ms.

BRICK CHURCH, p. o., Giles co., Tenn.

BRICKLAND, p. o., Lunenburgh co., Va., 95 ms. s. s. w. of Richmond ; from W. 211 m.

BRICK MEETING HOUSE, p. o., Cecil co., Md., 78 ms. N. E. of Annapolis ; from W. 88 ms.

BRICK STORE, p. o., Newton co., Ga.

BRICKSVILLE, p. t., Cuyahoga co., O., 140 ms. N. E. of Columbus ; from W. 353 ms. Watered by Cuyahoga river and Ohio canal. Pop. 1,116.

BRICKVILLE, p. o., Lawrence co., Ala., 141 ms. E. by N. of Tuscaloosa ; from W. 781 ms.

BRIDESBURGH, p. v., Philadelphia co., Pa., 153 ms. E. by s. of Harrisburgh ; from W. 333 ms. Pop. 915.

BRIDGE, p. o., St. Francis co., Ark.

BRIDGEBOROUGH, p. o., Burlington co., N. J.

BRIDGE CREEK, p. o., Geauga co., O., 256 ms. N. E. of Columbus ; from W. 336 ms.

BRIDGEFORTHS, p. o., Limestone co., Ala.

BRIDGEHAMPTON, p. v., Southampton township, Suffolk co., N. Y., 154 ms. s. s. E. of Albany ; from W. 283 ms.

BRIDGEPORT CITY, Fairfield co., Ct., 75 ms. s. w. of Hartford ; 17 ms. from New Haven ; 62 ms. N. E. of New York ; from W. 270 ms. Watered by Pequinock river, and Long Island sound. The city is built on a plain, which, as it retreats from the water, rises into an elevation that affords a fine prospect of the surrounding country, and thence spreads away into undulations and hills. It is well laid out with handsome houses. In the

last few years especially, a large number of substantial brick stores and dwellings, have added much to the appearance and wealth of the place. The Housatonic railroad, traversing the valley of Housatonic river, meets the West Stockbridge railroad in Massachusetts, which is the connecting link between Albany and Boston. Several vessels sail from this port, and it would probably carry on a more extensive foreign commerce, if the harbor was not obstructed by a sand-bar, 13 feet below high-water mark. A bridge 1,236 feet long extends across the harbor, admitting vessels through a draw. The population in 1810, was 572 ; in 1820, —— ; in 1830, 2,803 ; in 1840, 4,570 ; in 1850. 7,560.

BRIDGEPORT, p. o., Frederick co., Md.

BRIDGEPORT, p. v., Pease township, Belmont co., O., 126 ms. E. of Columbus ; from W. 267 ms. Watered by Ohio river.

BRIDGEPORT, p. o., Gloucester co., N. J.

BRIDGEPORT, b., Fayette co., Pa. Watered by Monongahela river and Dunlap's creek. 199 ms. s. w. by w. of Harrisburgh ; from W. 206 ms. Pop. 1,292.

BRIDGEPORT, p. t., Saginaw co., Mich., 85 ms. N. w. of Detroit ; from W. 609 ms. Pop. 374.

BRIDGEPORT, p. o., Franklin co., Ky., 5 ms. from Frankfort ; from W. 547 ms.

BRIDGEPORT, p. v., Harrison co., Va., 257 ms. N. w. of Richmond ; from W. 215 ms. Watered by Simpson's creek, a tributary of Monongahela river.

BRIDGEPORT, p. v., Marion co., Ind., 9 ms. from Indianapolis ; from W. 580 ms.

BRIDGEPORT, p. o., Warren co., Mo., 49 ms. N. N. E. of Jefferson city ; from W. 897 ms.

BRIDGEPORT, p. v., Brown co., Wis., 143 ms. N. E. of Madison ; from W. 953 ms.

BRIDGEPORT, p. o., Madison co., N. Y.

BRIDGEPORT, v., Seneca Falls township, Seneca co., N. Y., 132 ms. w. by N. of Albany ; from W. 363 ms. Situated on Cayuga lake.

BRIDGEPORT, p. o., Jackson co., Iowa.

BRIDGEPORT CENTRE, p. o., Saginaw co., Mich.

BRIDGEPORT MILLS. p. o., Franklin co., Pa., 58 ms. s. w. of Harrisburgh ; from W. 89 ms.

BRIDGETON, p. t., Cumberland co., Me., 63 ms. s. w. of Augusta ; from W. 577 ms. Situated on Long Pond. Pop. 2,710.

BRIDGE'S TAN-YARD, p. o., Jackson co., Ala., 183 ms. N. N. E. of Tuscaloosa ; from W. 694 ms.

BRIDGETON, p. o., Park co., Ind.

BRIDGETON, p. o., St. Louis co., Mo.

BRIDGETON, p o., Shelby co., Ala.

BRIDGETON, c. h., p. v., seat of justice of Cumberland co., N. J., 68 ms. s. by w. of Trenton ; from W. 179 ms. Watered by Cohansey creek. Pop. 2,446.

BRIDGETOWN, p. o., Caroline co., Md.

BRIDGETOWN, p. o., Northampton co., Va., 163 ms. E. by s. of Richmond ; from W. 227 ms.

BRIDGE VALLEY, p. o., Bucks co., Pa.

BRIDGEVILLE, p. v., Thompson township, Sullivan co., N. Y., 106 ms. s. s. w. of Albany ; from W. 289 ms. Watered by Navesink river.

BRIDGEVILLE, p. v., Oxford township, Warren co., N. J., 60 ms. N. by w. of Trenton ; from W. 215 ms.

BRIDGEVILLE, p. v., Sussex co., Del., 38 ms. w. by s. of Dover ; from W. 115 ms. Watered by Nanticoke river.

BRIDGEVILLE. p. v., Berry township, Muskingum co., O., 62 ms. E. of Columbus ; from W. 331 ms.

BRIDGEVILLE, p. o., Dale co., Ala., 216 ms. s. E. of Tuscaloosa ; from W. 896 ms.

BRIDGEWATER, p. o., Aroostook co., Me.

BRIDGEWATER, p. o., Grafton co., N. H., 37 ms. N. N. w. of Concord ; from W. 516 ms. Watered by Pemigewasset river and Newfound pond. Pop. 667.

BRIDGEWATER, p. t., Plymouth co., Mass., 25 ms. s. by E. of Boston ; from W. 433 ms. Watered by branches of Taunton river. Pop. 2,790.

BRIDGEWATER, p. t., Windsor co., Vt., 78 ms. s. of Montpelier ; from W. 458 ms. Watered by Queechy river. Pop. 1,311.

BRIDGEWATER, p. o., Litchfield co., Ct., 56 ms. w. of Hartford ; from W. 315 ms.

BRIDGEWATER, p. t., Williams co., O. Pop. 493.

BRIDGEWATER, p. t., Oneida co., N. Y., 81 ms. w. by N. of Albany ; from W. 370 ms. Watered by Unadilla river. Pop. 1,315.

BRIDGEWATER, t., Somerset co., N. J. Pop. 4,070.

BRIDGEWATER, p. v., Bucks co., Pa., 113 ms. E. by N. of Harrisburgh ; from W. 153 ms

BRIDGEWATER, b., Beaver co., Pa. Watered by Beaver river.

BRIDGEWATER, p. t., Susquehanna co., Pa. Pop. 1,548.

BRIDGEWATER, p. t., Washtenaw co., Mich. Watered by Raisin river.

BRIDGEWATER, p. v., Rockingham co., Va., 139 ms. N. w. of Richmond ; from W. 139 ms.

BRIDGES, t., Taney co., Mo.

BRIDLE CREEK, p. o., Grayson co., Va.

BRIDGEPORT, p. t., Addison co., Vt., 79 ms. s. w. of Montpelier ; from W. 475 ms. Situated on Lake Champlain.

BRIER CREEK, p. t., Columbia co., Pa., 94 ms. N. of Harrisburgh ; from W. 205 ms. Pop. 1,091.

BRIER CREEK, p. o., Wilkes co., N. C., 17 ms. w.N.w. of Raleigh ; from W. 376 ms.

BRIER HILL, p. o., St. Lawrence co., N. Y.

BRIGGS' MILLS, p. o., Ohio co., Ky.

BRIGHT, p. o., Dearborn co., Ind.

BRIGHTON, p. t., Somerset co., Me., 57 ms. N. of Augusta ; from W. 652 ms. Pop. 748.

BRIGHTON, p. t., Middlesex co., Mass., 5 ms. w. of Boston ; from W. 433 ms. Watered by Charles river. Pop. 2,356.

BRIGHTON, p. t., Essex co., Vt. Pop. 193.

BRIGHTON, p. t., Monroe co., N. Y., 217 ms. w. by N. of Albany ; from W. 366 ms. Watered by Genesee river. Pop. 3,117.

BRIGHTON, p. t., Beaver co., Pa., 231 ms. w. by N. of Harrisburgh ; from W. 257 ms. Watered by Big Beaver river. Pop. 1,111.

BRIGHTON, p. t., Lorain co., O., 105 ms. N. by E. of Columbus ; from W. 374 ms. Pop. 669.

BRIGHTON, p. o., Beaufort district, S. C.

BRIGHTON, p. o., Livingston co., Mich., 42 ms. N. w. of Detroit ; from W. 551 ms. Watered by branches of Huron river. Pop. 1,015.

BRIGHTON, p. o., Lagrange co., Ind., 181 ms. N. by E. of Indianapolis ; from W. 571 ms.

BRIGHTON, p. v., Macoupin co., Ill., 71 ms. s. by w. of Springfield ; from W. 814 ms.

BRIGHTON, p. v., Washington co., Iowa, 37 ms. s.s.w. of Iowa city. Pop. 472.

BRIGHTON, p. o., Racine co., Wis.

BRIGHTON CENTRE, p. v., Clark co., O., 33 ms. w. of Columbus ; from W. 426 ms.

BRIGHT SEAT, p. o., Anne Arundel co., Md.

BRIGHTSVILLE, p. v., Marlborough district. S. C., 117 ms. N. E. of Columbia ; from W. 419 ms.

BRIMFIELD, p. t., Hampden co., Mass., 68 ms. w. by s. of Boston ; from W. 378 ms. Watered by Chicopee and Quinnebaug rivers.

BRIMFIELD, p. t., Portage co., O., 150 ms. N. E. of Columbus ; from W. 324 ms. Pop. 1,015.

BRIMFIELD, p. o., Peoria co., Ill.

BRIMMERSVILLE, p. o., Steuben co., N. Y., 235 ms. w. s. w. of Albany ; from W. 290 ms.

BRINDLETOWN, p. t., Burke co., N. C., 211 ms. w. of Raleigh ; from W. 441 ms.

BRINTON, p. o., Champaign co., O.

BRINGHAM'S GROVE, p. o., Tippecanoe co., Ind.

BRINGIERS, c. h., p. v., St. James parish, La., 58 ms w. by N. of New Orleans ; from W. 1,230 ms. Watered by Mississippi river.

BRINKLEYVILLE, p. v., Halifax co., N. C., 90 ms. N. E. of Raleigh ; from W. 236 ms.

BRINSONVILLE, p. o., Burke co., Ga., 78 ms. E. by s. of Milledgeville ; from W. 627 ms.

BRISCOE RUN, p. o., Wood co., Va.

BRISTERBURGH, p. o., Fauquier co., Va.

BRISTOL COUNTY, situated in the southeast part of Massachusetts, on Buzzard's bay and Rhode Island line. Length, 35 miles ; mean breadth 17, with an area of 600 square miles. The face of the county is generally level, though hilly in some parts. The soil is naturally of a fair quality, but somewhat worn. Seats of justice New Bedford and Taunton. Pop., in 1820, 40,908 ; in 1830, 49,592 ; in 1840, 60,164 ; in 1850, 74,577.

BRISTOL COUNTY, on the easterly boundary of. Rhode Island between Narragansct and Mount Hope bays. Length, 10 miles ; mean width 4, with an area of 40 square miles. The face of the country is pleasantly diversified, and the soil generally stony, but productive. Seat of justice, Bristol. Pop., in 1820, 5,637 ; in 1830, 5,446 ; in 1840, 6,476 ; in 1850, 8,514.

BRISTOL, p. t., Lincoln co., Me., 39 s. s. E. of Augusta ; from W. 607 ms. Watered by the Atlantic ocean. Damariscotta and Pemaquid rivers. Pop. 2,931.

BRISTOL, p. t., Grafton co., N. H., 30 ms. N. of Concord ; from W. 511 ms. Watered by Newfound lake outlet. Pop. 1,103.

BRISTOL, p. t., Addison co., Vt., 50 ms. s. w. of Montpelier ; from W. 490 ms. Watered by New Haven river, and Baldwin and Lewis creeks. Pop. 1,344.

BRISTOL, c. h., p. t. seat of justice of Bristol co., R. I., 18 ms. s. by E. of Providence ; from W. 418 ms. Situated on Narraganset bay. Pop. 4,616.

BRISTOL, p. t., Hartford co., Ct., 17 ms. s. w. of Hartford ; from W. 338 ms. Watered by Farmington river. Pop. 2,884.

BRISTOL, t., Philadelphia co., Pa., Watered by Taconey creek. Pop. 2,230.

BRISTOL, p. t., Ontario co., N. Y., 212 ms. w. of Albany ; from W. 349 ms. Watered by Mudd creek. Pop. 1,733.

BRISTOL, p. o., Anne Arundel co., Md., 31 ms. N. N. w. of Annapolis ; from W. 51 ms.

BRISTOL, p. b., Bristol township, Bucks co., Pa., 115 ms. E. by s. of Harrisburgh ; from W. 155 ms. Watered by Delaware river. Pop. 2,570.

BRISTOL, t., Morgan co., O. Watered by Meigs creek. Pop. 1,724.

BRISTOL, t., Bucks co., Pa.

BRISTOL, p. t., Morgan co., O., 67 ms. E. s. E. of Columbus ; from W. 336 ms.

BRISTOL, p. t., Lapeer co., Mich., 43 ms. N. of Detroit ; from W. 568 ms. Watered by Bell and Clinton rivers.

BRISTOL, p. v., Elkhart co., Ind., 162 ms. N. of Indianapolis ; from W. 601 ms.

BRISTOL, p. o., Kendall co., Ill.

BRISTOL, p. o., Racine co., Wis. 99 ms. s. E. of Madison ; from W. 780 ms.

BRISTOL CENTRE, p. o., Bristol township, Ontario co., N. Y., 202 ms., w. of Albany ; from W. 344 ms.

BRISTOL MILLS, p. o., Lincoln co., Me., 42 ms. s. s. w. of Augusta ; from W. 610 ms.

BRISTOLVILLE, p. o., Bristol township, Trumbull co., O., 173 ms., N. E., of Columbus ; from W. 314 ms

BRISTOLVILLE, p. o., Barry co., Mich.

BRITTON'S NECK, p. o., Marion district, S. C.

BRITTON'S STORE, p. o., Bertie co., N. C., 141 ms. E. N. E. of Raleigh ; from W. 234 ms.

BRIXTON, p. o., Alexandria co., Va.

BROADALBIN, p. t., Fulton co., N. Y., 42 ms., N. w. of Albany ; from W. 423 ms. Pop. 2,474.

BROAD BROOK, p. o., Hartford co., Ct., 15 ms. from Hartford ; from W. 351 ms.

BROAD CREEK, hundred. Sussex co., Del.

BROAD CREEK, p. o., Queen Anne co., Md., 12 ms. E. of Annapolis ; from W. 52 ms.

BROADFORD, p. o., Smyth co., Va., 281 ms. w. s. w. of Richmond ; from W. 349 ms.

BROAD KILL, hundred. Sussex co., Del. Pop. 3,468.

BROAD MOUNTAIN, p. o., Schuylkill co., Pa.

BROAD OAKS, p. o., Pope co., Ill.

BROAD RIPPLE, p. o., Marion co., Ind.

BROAD RIVER, p. o., Elbert co., Ga.

BROAD TOP, t., Bedford co., Pa. Pop. 632.

BROAD TOP., p. o., Huntingdon co., Pa., 92 ms. w. of Harrisburgh ; from W. 118 ms.

BROADWAY, p. o., Warren co., N. J.

BROADWELL, p. o., Harrison co., Ky.

BROCK, p. o., Darke co., O.

BROCKETTS' p. o., Effingham co., Ill., 97 ms. s. E. of Springfield ; from W. 726 ms.

BROCKETT'S BRIDGE, p. o., Oppenheim township, Fulton co., N. Y.. 68 ms. N. w. of Albany ; from W. 398 ms.

BROCKPORT, p. v., Sweden township, Monroe co., N. Y., 45 ms. w. N. w. of Albany ; from W. 384 ms. Situated on the Erie Canal.

BROCK'S CROSSING, p. o., St. Croix co., Wis.

BROCK'S GAP, p. o., Rockingham co., Va., 148 ms. N. w. of Richmond ; from W. 123 ms.

BROCKT, p. o., Pike co., Ark.

BROCKVILLE, p. v., Steuben co., Ind., 188 ms. N. N. E of Indianapolis ; from W. 547 ms.

BROCKWAYVILLE, p. o., Jefferson co., Va.

BROKEN ARROW, p. o., St. Clair co., Ala., 109 ms. N. E. of Tuscaloosa ; from W. 732 ms.

BROKEN STRAW, t., Warren co., Pa. Pop. 634.

BROKEN SWORD, p. o., Crawford co., O., 70 ms. N. of Columbus ; from W. 414 ms. Watered by Broken Sword creek.

BRONSON, p. t., Huron co., O., 102 ms. N. by E. of Columbus ; from W. 395 ms. Watered by Huron river Pop. 1,220.

BRONSON'S PRAIRIE, p, o., Bronson township, Branch co., Mich., 121 ms. w. s. w. of Detroit ; from W. 570 ms.

BRONX, p. o., Westchester co., N. Y., 137 ms. s. of Albany ; from W. 246 ms. Situated near Bronx river.

BROOK, p. o., Jasper co., Ind., 116 ms. N. w. of Indianapolis ; from W. 675 ms.

BROOKDALE, p. o., McHenry co., Ill.

BROOKE COUNTY, situated at the extreme north part of Virginia, between Ohio river and Pennsylvania line. Length, 30 miles ; mean width, 5 ; with an area of 150 square miles. The surface is extremely hilly, and the soil fertile. Seat of justice, Willsburgh. Pop. in 1820, 6,611 ; in 1830, 7,041 ; in 1840, 7.948 ; in 1850, 5,054.

BROOKFIELD, p. t., Carroll co., N. H., 46 ms. N. E. of Concord ; from W. 527 ms. Pop. 552.

BROOKFIELD, p. t., Worcester co., Mass., 60 ms. w. of Boston ; from W. 388 ms. Pop. 3,018.

BROOKFIELD, p. t., Orange co., Vt., 17 ms. s. of Montpelier ; from. W, 504 ms. Pop. 1,672.

BROOKFIELD, t., Morgan co.. O. Pop. 1,482.

BROOKFIELD, v., Tuscarawas township, Stark co., O.

BROOKFIELD, p. o., Lee co., Ill.

BROOKFIELD, p. o., Jackson co., Iowa.

BROOKFIELD, t., Eaton co., Mich. Pop. 255.

BROOKFIELD, p. o., Waukesha co., Wis.

BROOKFIELD, p. t., Fairfield co., Ct., 60 ms. s. w. of Hartford ; from W. 299 ms. Watered by Housatonic river. Pop. 1,359.

BROOKFIELD, p. t., Madison co., N. Y., 88 ms. w. by N. of Albany ; from W. 363 ms. Watered by Unadilla river. Pop. 3,585.

BROOKFIELD, b., Jefferson co., Pa.

BROOKFIELD, p. t., Tioga co., Pa., 174 ms. N. by w. of Harrisburgh ; from W. 288 ms. Pop. 741.

BROOKFIELD, t., Stark co., O.

BROOKFIELD, p. t., Trumbull co., O.,183 ms. N. E. of Columbus ; from W. 295 ms. Pop. 1,451.

BROOKHAVEN, t., Suffolk co., N. Y. Watered by Connecticut brook, South bay, and Ronkonkoma lake. Pop. 8,595.

BROOKHAVEN, p. v., Lawrence co., Miss.

BROOKLANDVILLE, p. o., Baltimore co., Md.

BROOKLIN. p. o., Hancock co., Me.

BROOKLIN, p. o., Clarke co., Mo.

BROOKLINE, p. t., Windham co., Vt., 110 ms. s. of Montpelier ; from W. 439 ms. Watered by Grassy brook. Pop. 285.

BROOKLINE, p. t., Hillsborough co., N. H.. 50 ms. s. by w. of Concord ; from W. 445 ms. Watered by Nissitissot river. Pop. 118.

BROOKLINE, p. t., Norfolk co., Mass., 4 ms. w. by s. of Boston ; from W. 440 ms. Watered by Charles river. Pop. 2,516.

BROOKLINE, p. v., Madison co., Ga., 85 ms. N. of Milledgeville ; from W. 608 ms.

BROOKLINE, p. o., Jackson co., La.

BROOKLYN, city, seat of justice of King's co., N. Y., the second in population in the state, is situated at the west end of Long Island. on the easterly side of East river, opposite the city of New York. Its surface was originally rough and broken, but has since been graded sufficiently low to be passed with ease. From the top of the " Heights," the city spreads over a gentle, or undulating slope, for several miles, toward Gowanus bay on the south and Williamsburgh on the northeast. It is destined, like each in the constellation of cities which cluster around New York, to attain inconceivable greatness. Its ample limits, and fine situation close to the business part of the great commercial emporium, with which it is connected by six steam-ferries—two of them, the Fulton and the South ferry, probably unsurpassed for elegance and despatch by any in the world—render it a favorite residence for merchants and others who do business in New York, and to these causes it is indebted for its rapid growth in population and wealth. Most of the streets are broad and pleasant, lined with handsome shade-trees, and substantial and often princely dwellings, which are lighted in the night with gas, The new avenues toward the east part of the city, are arranged with great regularity and taste, with open, airy gardens attached to the dwellings. The city-hall, in a central situation, at the union of several of the principal streets, is a fine edifice of white marble. The United States Naval hospital, on a gentle swell near Wallabout bay, seen with its white marble walls through groups of trees, makes an agreeable picture. On this bay, at the north side of the city, appear also the large buildings of the navy-yard. which includes an area of 45 acres, enclosed by a substantial brick wall. Here, too, is the U. S. dry-dock, a structure of almost unequalled vastness. The foundation is 406 feet long, and 120 feet wide. The main chamber is 286 feet long, and 30 feet wide at the bottom ; at the top 307 feet long, and 98 feet wide. The iron folding-gates weigh 150 tons. Pumps discharge 40,000 gallons of water per minute. Ships-of-war of the largest class, here enter and are repaired. Sixteen years were occupied in the construction of this dock. The churches, which in proportion to the population of the place, are equalled in number and beauty by no other city, except, perhaps, by those of New York, are of all orders of architecture, from the chaste and simple Grecian, to the pure Gothic, with lofty walls, richly-sculptured columns, and tinted windows. The literary advantages of Brooklyn are also numerous and valuable. Libraries. lectures, scientific, and literary societies; and schools of various grades, are flourishing and well supported. The harbor of Brooklyn is deep, spacious, and sufficient for any number of vessels. Along the southwest front, opposite Governor's Island, extends the Atlantic dock, a deep and spacious basin, of 42 acres, which is surrounded by piers and bulkheads, containing a large number of substantial warehouses, built of stone. Other warehouses and factories of various kinds line the wharves along East river, from the Atlantic dock to Wallabout bay. A few miles south of the city, beyond Gowanus bay, lies the beautiful and enchanting Greenwood cemetery, which, for combination of romantic nature with splendid art, is probably surpassed by no necropolis in the world. The Long Island railroad terminates in Brooklyn, at the South ferry. The population in 1800, was 3,298 ; in 1810, 4,402 ; in 1820, 7,175 ; in 1830, 12,042 ; in 1840, 36,233 ; in 1850, 96,850.

BROOKLYN, c. h., p. t., seat of justice of Windham co., Ct., 44 ms. E. by N. of Hartford ; from W. 371 ms. Watered by Quinnebaug and Blackwell's rivers. Pop. 1,514.

BROOKLYN, p. t., Susquehanna co., Pa., 171 ms. N.N.E. of Harrisburgh ; from W. 278 ms. Watered by Martin's creek. Pop. 1,082.

BROOKLYN, p. t., Cuyahoga co., O., 145 ms. N. N. E. of Columbus ; from W. 360 ms. Pop. 6,375.

BROOKLYN, p. o., Halifax co., Va., 145 ms. s. w. of Richmond ; from W. 232 ms.

BROOKLYN, p. o., Campbell co., Ky.

BROOKLYN, p. o., Schuyler co., Ill., 77 ms. w. N. w. of Springfield ; from W. 857 ms.

BROOKLYN, p. o., Conecuh co., Ala., 180 ms. s. by E. of Tuscaloosa ; from W. 932 ms.

BROOKLYN, p. o., Jackson co., Mich.

BROOKLYN, p. o., Noxubee co., Miss., 126 ms. N. E. of Jackson ; from W. 89 ms.

BROOKLYN, p. o., Greene co., Wis.

BROOKNEAL, p. v., Campbell co., Va., 122 ms, w. s. w. of Richmond ; from W. 209 ms. Watered by Staunton river.

BROOKS, p. t., Waldo co., Me., 45 ms. N. E. of Augusta ; from W. 644 ms. Pop. 1,021.

BROOK'S GROVE, p. o., Mount Morris township, Livingston co., N. Y., 249 ms. W. of Albany ; from W. 360 ms.

BROOKSVILLE, p. t., Hancock co., Me., 79 ms. E. of Augusta ; from W. 675 ms. Situated on Penobscot bay. Pop. 1,333.

BROOKVILLE, p. o., Montgomery co., Md., 64 ms. N. N. w. of Annapolis ; from W. 24 ms.

BROOKVILLE, p. o., Alexander township, Genesee county, N. Y., 255 ms. w. of Albany ; from W. 385 ms

BROOKVILLE, p. o., Jackson co., Mich.

BROOKVILLE, p. v., Jefferson co., Pa., 167 ms. N. w. of Harrisburgh ; from W. 256 ms.

BROOKVILLE, p. t., seat of justice of Franklin co., Ind., 69 ms. s. E. of Indianapolis ; from W. 519 ms. Watered by Whitewater river. Pop. 3,466.

BROOKVILLE, p. v., Brecken co., Ky., 65 ms. N. E. of Frankfort; from W. 495 ms.

BROOKVILLE, p. v., Marion co., Mo., 119 ms. N. N. E of Jefferson City ; from W. 933 ms.

BROOKVILLE, p. o., Jefferson co., Iowa.

BROOKSVILLE, p. o., Albemarle co, Va., 98 ms. N w. of Richmond ; from W. 140 ms.

BROOKSVILLE, p. o., Randolph co., Ga., 151 ms. s. w. of Milledgeville ; from W. 807 ms.

BROOKSVILLE, p. o., Blount co., Ala., 114 ms. N. N. E. of Tuscaloosa ; from W. 724 ms.

BROOKVILLE, p. o., Noxubee co., Miss.

BROOKVILLE, p. o., Granville co., N. C.

BROOKVILLE, p. o., Ogle co., Ill.
BROOKVILLE, p. o.. Ogden co., Utah.
BROOME COUNTY, situated on the south boundary of New York, and traversed by Susquehanna river. Length, 43 miles ; mean breadth, 20, with an area of 860 square miles. The face of the country is hilly, and the soil generally productive. Seat of justice, Binghamton, which is connected with Utica by the Chenango canal. Pop. in 1820, 14,343 ; in 1830, 17,749 ; in 1840, 22,338 ; in 1850, 30,660.
BROOME, t., Schoharie co., N. Y., 38 ms. w. of Albany ; from W., 367 ms. Watered by Schoharie creek. Pop. 2,268.
BROOME CENTRE, p. o., Schoharie co., N. Y.
BROTHERS' VALLEY, t., Somerset co., Pa. Watered by Castleman's river. Pop. 1,430.
BROTHERTON, p. o., Anne Arundel co., Md., 10 ms. N. by w. of Annapolis ; from W. 50 ms.
BROTZMANSVILLE, p. o., Warren co., N. J., 78 ms. N. N. w. of Trenton ; from W. 226 ms.
BROWER, p. o., Berks co., Pa., 66 ms. N. E. of Harrisburgh ; from W. 159 miles.
BROWER'S MILLS, p. o., Randolph co., N. C., 73 ms. w. by s. of Raleigh ; from W. 347 ms.
BROWN COUNTY, situated on the south boundary of Ohio, on the north side of Ohio river. Length, 30 miles ; mean width, 17, with an area of about 470 square miles. The face of the country is hilly, and the soil generally fertile. Seat of justice, Georgetown. Pop. in 1830, 17,857 ; in 1840, 22,715 ; in 1850, 27,332.
BROWN COUNTY, situated towards the southerly part of Indiana. Area, 310 square miles. Seat of justice, Nashville. Pop. in 1840, 2,364 ; in 1850, 4,846.
BROWN COUNTY, in the western part of Illinois, with Illinois river on the east, and Crooked river on the northeast. Area, 300 square miles. Seat of justice, Mount Sterling. Pop. in, 1840, 4,183 ; in 1850, 7,198.
BROWN COUNTY, in the northeast part of Wisconsin, intersected by Depere. Area, 1,150 square miles. Seat of justice, Green Bay. Pop. 1840, 2,107 ; in 1850, 6,215.
BROWN, t., Lycoming co., Pa. Watered by Pine creek. Pop. 552.
BROWN, t., Mifflin co., Pa. Pop. 1,015.
BROWN, t., Montgomery co., Ind. Pop. 1,957.
BROWN, t., Hancock co., Ind. Pop. 1,322.
BROWN, t.. Washington co., Ind. Pop. 1,636.
BROWN, t., Athens co., O. Watered by Racoon creek.
BROWN, t., Carroll co., O. Watered by Sandy creek. Pop. 2,099.
BROWN, t., Darke co., O. Watered by Stillwater creek. Pop. 684.
BROWN, t., Delaware co., O. Pop. 1,176.
BROWN, t, Franklin co., O. Pop. 681.
BROWN, t., Knox co., O. Watered by Yellow creek. Pop. 1,525.
BROWN, t., Miami co., O. Watered by Miami river. Pop. 1,046.
BROWN, t., Paulding co., O.
BROWNILL'S MILLS, p. o., Lenawee co.. Mich., 83 ms. s. w. of Detroit ; from W. 523 ms.
BROWNFIELD, p. t., Oxford co., Me.. 78 ms. s. w. of Augusta ; from W. 563 ms. Watered by Saco river. Pop. 1,320.
BROWNHELM, p. t., Lorain co.. O., 124 ms. N. E. of Columbus ; from W. 348 ms. Watered by Vermilion river. Pop. 1,080.
BROWNING, p. o., Schuyler co., Ill.
BROWNINGTON, p. t., Orleans co., Vt., 49 ms. N. N. E. of Montpelier ; from W. 565 ms. Watered by Willoughby river. Pop. 613.
BROWNINGTON, p. v., Butler co., Pa., 215 ms. w. N. w. of Harrisburgh ; from W. 257 ms.
BROWNINGTON CENTRE, p. o., Orleans co., Vt.
BROWN'S, p. o., Fairfield district, S. C., 24 ms. N. of Columbia ; from W. 504 ms.
BROWNSBOROUGH, p. v., Oldham co., Ky., 42 ms. N. w. of Frankfort ; from W. 584 ms.
BROWNSBURGH, p. v., Makefield township, Bucks co., Pa., 114 ms. E. of Harrisburgh ; from W. 170 ms. Watered by Delaware river.
BROWNSBURGH, p. v., Rockbridge co., Va., 139 ms. w. by N. of Richmond ; from W. 180 ms. Watered by Maffit's creek.
BROWNSBURGH, p. o., Hendricks co., Ind., 14 ms. w. of Indianapolis ; from W. 585 ms.
BROWN'S CORNER, p. o., Kennebec co., Me., 6 ms. from Augusta ; from W. 601 ms.

BROWN'S COVE, p. o., Albemarle co., Va., 112 ms. N. w. of Richmond ; from W. 136 ms.
BROWN'S GROVE, p. o., Hamilton co., O.
BROWN'S MILLS, p. o., Roxbury township, Washington co., O., 87 ms. s. E. of Columbus ; from W. 317 ms.
BROWN'S MILLS, p. o., Brown township, Mifflin co., Pa., 62 ms. N. w. of Harrisburgh ; from W. 154 ms.
BROWN'S MILLS, p. o., Burlington co., N. J.
BROWN'S PORT, p. v., Perry co., Tenn., 101 ms. s. w. of Nashville ; from W. 785 ms.
BROWN'S STORE, p. o., Warren co., O.
BROWN'S STORE, p. o., Caswell co., N. C., 96 ms. N. w. of Raleigh ; from W. 272 ms.
BROWNSTOWN, p. t., Wayne co., Mich., 25 ms. s. s. w. of Detroit ; from W. 504 ms. Watered by Huron river and Lake Erie. Pop. 1,025.
BROWNSTOWN, p. o., Sevier co,, Ark.
BROWNSTOWN, c. h., p. v., seat of justice of Jackson co.. Ind., 71 ms. s. E of Indianapolis ; from W. 597 ms. Watered by east fork of White river. Pop. 1,732.
BROWN'S VALLEY, p. o., Montgomery co., Ind.
BROWNSVILLE, p. t., Piscataquis co., Me., 102 ms. N. N. E. of Augusta ; from W. 699 ms. Watered by Piscataquis river. Pop. 787.
BROWNSVILLE, p. o., Windsor co., Vt., 63 ms. s. of Montpelier ; from W. 474 ms.
BROWNSVILLE, p. v., Brownville township, Jefferson co., N. Y., 168 ms. N. w. of Albany ; from W. 420 ms Watered by Black and Perch rivers.
BROWNSVILLE, p. t., Jefferson co., N. Y. Pop. 4,282.
BROWNSVILLE, p. v., Fayette co., Pa., 191 ms E. by s of Harrisburgh ; from W. 207 ms. Watered by Monongahela river and Redstone creek. Pop. 2,369.
BROWNSVILLE, p. v., Washington co., Md., 95 ms. N w. of Annapolis ; from W. 63 ms.
BROWNSVILLE, p. v., Licking township, Licking co., O., 40 ms. E. of Columbus ; from W. 353 ms.
BROWNSVILLE, c. h., p. v., seat of justice of Edmonson co., Ky., 132 ms. s. w. of Frankfort ; from W. 663 ms. Watered by Green river.
BROWNSVILLE, p. v., Granville co., N. C., 64 ms. N. of Raleigh ; from W. 267 ms.
BROWNSVILLE, p. o., Marlborough district, S. C., 131 ms. N. E. of Columbia ; from W. 423 ms.
BROWNSVILLE, p. v., Talladega co., Ala., 141 ms. E. by N. of Tuscaloosa ; from W. 791 ms.
BROWNSVILLE, p. t., Union co., Ind.. 68 ms. E. by s. of Indianapolis ; from W. 511 ms. Pop. 1,443.
BROWNSVILLE, c. h., p. v., seat of justice of Jackson co., Ill., 177 ms. s. of Springfield ; from W. 842 ms. Watered by Big Muddy river.
BROWNSVILLE, p. o., Haywood co., Tenn., 164 w. s. w. of Nashville ; from W. 847 ms.
BROWNSVILLE, p. o., Saline co., Mo., 100 ms. N. w. of Jefferson city ; from W. 1,016 ms.
BROWNSVILLE, p. v., Hinds co., Miss., 20 ms. N. w. of Jackson ; from W. 1,030 ms.
BROWNSVILLE, p. o., Prairie co., Ark.
BROWNSVILLE, p. v., Johnson co., Ark. (now Enterprise).
BROWNSVILLE, p. v., Cameron co., Tex.
BROWNSVILLE, v., Monroe co., Ga. Watered by Ocmulgee river.
BROWNTOWN, p. v., Bradford co., Pa., 153 ms. N. of Harrisburgh ; from W. 263 ms.
BRUCE, p. t., Macomb co., Mich., 58 ms. N. of Detroit ; from W. 563 ms. Pop. 1,555.
BRUCE, p. o., Hamilton co., Tenn., 147 ms. s. E. of Nashville ; from W. 603 ms.
BRUCE'S VALLEY, p. o., Susquehanna co., Pa., 164 ms. N. by E. of Harrisburgh ; from W. 274 ms.
BRUCEVILLE, p. v., Carroll co., Md., 79 ms. N. w. of Annapolis ; from W. 62 ms.
BRUCETOWN, p. o., Frederick co., Va., 154 ms. N. N. w.. of Richmond ; from W. 78 ms.
BRUCEVILLE, p. o., Pike co., Ala.
BRUCEVILLE, p. o., Knox co., Ind., 119 ms. s. w. of Indianapolis ; from W. 686 ms.
BRUCKVILLE, p. o., Morgan co., Ill.
BRUIN, p. o., Carter co., Ky.
BRUIN, p. o., Butler co., Pa.
BRUINGTON, p. v., King and Queen co., Va., 42 ms. N. E. of Richmond ; from W. 127 ms.
BRUIN'S CROSS ROADS, p. o., Park co., Ind., 58 ms w. of Indianapolis ; from W. 629 ms.
BRULY LANDING, p. o., West Baton Rouge parish, La.
BRUMFIELDVILLE, p. v., Berks co., Pa., 63 ms. E. N. E. of Harrisburgh ; from W 155 ms.

BRUMMELS, p. o., Davidson co., N. C., 103 ms. w. of Raleigh ; from W. 324 ms.

BRUNERSBURGH, p. o., Defiance co., O., 156 ms. N. w. of Columbus ; from W. 508 ms.

BRUNERSTOWN, p. o., Putnam co., Ind., 55 ms. from Indianapolis ; from W. 620 ms.

BRUNNETT'S CREEK, p. o.. White co., Ind., 83 ms. N. by w. of Indianapolis ; from W. 622 ms.

BRUNSWICK COUNTY, situated on the south boundary of Virginia, with Nottoway river on the northeast. Area, 676 square miles. The face of the country is generally undulating, and the soil of a middling quality. Seat of justice, Lawrenceville. Pop., in 1820, 16,687 ; in 1830, 15,767 ; in 1840, 14,346; in 1850, 13,994.

BRUNSWICK COUNTY, on the southern boundary of North Carolina, with Cape Fear river on the east, and the Atlantic ocean on the south. Area, 1,344 square miles. The surface is level, abounding in marshes, and the soil is generally poor and thin. Seat of justice, Smithville. Pop., in 1820, 5,480 ; in 1830, 6,523 ; in 1840, 5.265 ; in 1850, 7.272.

BRUNSWICK. p. t., Essex co., Vt., 86 ms. N. of Montpelier ; from W. 583 ms. Watered by Connecticut, Nulhegan, and Paul's rivers. Pop. 119.

BRUNSWICK, p. t., Cumberland co., Me., 30 ms. s. by w. of Augusta ; from W. 570 ms. Watered by Androscoggin river. Seat of Bowdoin college. Pop., in 1840, 4,259 ; in 1850, 4,977.

BRUNSWICK, t., Rensselaer co., N. Y., 10 ms. N. E. of Albany ; from W. 318 ms. Watered by Poestenkill river. Pop. 3,146.

BRUNSWICK, c. h., p. v., seat of justice of Glynn co., Ga., 233 ms. s. E. of Milledgeville ; from W. 742 ms. Watered by Turtle river.

BRUNSWICK. p. t., Medina co., O., 120 ms. N. E. of Columbus; from W. 355 ms. Pop. 1,417.

BRUNSWICK, p. o., Peoria co., Ill.

BRUNSWICK, p v., Chariton co., Mo., 102 ms. N. w. of Jefferson city; from W. 996 ms. Watered by Missouri river. Pop. 1,595

BRUSH CREEK, p. o., Green co., Ky.

BRUSH CREEK, t., Highland co., O. Watered by Brush creek. Pop. 1,515

BRUSH CREEK, p. o., Randolph co., N. C.

BRUSH CREEK, p. o., Perry co., Ala.

BRUSH CREEK, p. o., Knox co., Ill.

BRUSH CREEK, t., Jefferson co,, O, Pop. 1,121

BRUSH CREEK, t., Muskingum co., O. Pop. 1,392.

BRUSH CREEK, t., Scioto co., O. Pop. 660.

BRUSH CREEK, t., Washington co., Ark. Pop. 589.

BRUSH HILL, p. v., Dupage co., Ill, 188 ms. N. E. of Springfield ; from W. 735 ms.

BRUSHLAND, p. o., Delaware co., N. Y.

BRUSH RUN, p. o., Washington co., Pa.

BRUSH'S MILLS, p. o., Franklin co., N. Y.

BRUSH VALLEY, p. o., Indiana co., Pa.

BRUSHVILLE, p. o., Queen's co., N. Y.

BRUSHY CREEK, p. o., Cleveland co., N. C., 200 ms. w. by s. of Raleigh ; from W. 437 ms.

BRUSHY CREEK, p. o., Anderson district, S. C., 216 ms. w. s. w. of Columbia ; from W. 519 ms.

BRUSHY FLAT, p. o., Watauga co., N. C.

BRUSHY FORK, p. o., Breckenridge co., Ky., 106 ms. w. s. w. of Frankfort ; from W. 646 ms.

BRUSHY FORK, p. o., Coles co., Ill.

BRUSHY PRAIRIE, p. o., La Grange co., Ind.

BRUYNSWICK, p. o., Ulster co., N. Y., 85 ms. s. s. w. of Albany ; from W. 300 ms.

BRUTUS, t., Cayuga co., N. Y., 153 ms. w. by N. of Albany ; from W. 349 ms. Watered by Branch creek and Cold Spring stream. Pop. 3,046.

BRUTUS, t., Ingham co., Mich.

BRYAN COUNTY, situated on the southeast boundary of Georgia, with Ocmulgee river on the northeast, and the Atlantic ocean on the southeast. Drained by Connouchee river. Area, 480 square miles. Surface level, containing marshes, and the soil generally poor and thin. Seat of justice, Bryan courthouse. Pop. in 1830, 3,139 ; in 1840, 3,182 ; in 1850, 3,424.

BRYAN, c. h., p. v., Pulaski township, seat of justice of Williams co., O.

BRYAN, p. o., Saline co., Mo.

BRYANSBURGH, p. v., Jefferson co., Ind., 83 ms. s. E. of Indianapolis ; from W. 563 ms.

BRYANSVILLE, p. o., York co., Pa.

BRYANTOWN, p. v., Charles co., Md., 69 ms. s. w. of Annapolis ; from W. 44 ms.

BRYANT'S CREEK. p. o., Monroe co., Ind.

BRYANT'S STATION, p. o., Milan co., Tex.

BRYANTSVILLE, p. o., Lawrence co., Ind.

BRYANTSVILLE, p. o., Garrard co., Ky.

BRYDEE'S STORE, p. o., Lunenburgh co., Va., 88 ms. s. w. of Richmond ; from W. 202 ms.

BUCHANAN COUNTY, situated on the westerly boundary of Missouri, on the east side of Missouri river. Area, 800 square miles. Seat of justice, Sparta. Pop. in 1840, 6,237; in 1850, 12.975.

BUCHANAN COUNTY, in the easterly part of Iowa. Area, — square miles. Seat of justice, Independence. Pop. in 1850, 517.

BUCHANAN, p. o., Birmingham borough, Alleghany co., Pa., 201 ms. w. of Harrisburgh ; from W. 227 ms.

BUCHANAN, v., Botetourt co., Va. Watered by James river.

BUCHANAN, p. t., Berrien co., Mich. Watered by St. Joseph's river.

BUCHANAN'S FERRY, p. o., Calcasieu parish, La., 307 ms. w. of New Orleans ; from W. 1,332 ms.

BUCHANAN'S STATION, p. o., Ripley co., Ind., 80 ms. s. E. of Indianapolis ; from W. 556 ms.

BUCHANANSVILLE, p. v., Rutherford co., Tenn., 12 ms. s. E. of Nashville ; from W. 678 ms.

BUCK, p. o., Lancaster co., Pa., 50 ms. s. E. of Harrisburgh ; from W. 99 ms.

BUCK, t., Luzerne co., Pa. Pop. 539.

BUCK BRANCH, p. o., De Kalb co., Ill.

BUCK's BRIDGE, p. v., Potsdam township, St. Lawrence co., N. Y., 231 ms. N. w. of Albany ; from W. 503 ms.

BUCK CREEK, p. o., Spartansburgh district, S. C., 114 ms. N. w. of Columbia ; from W. 475 ms.

BUCK CREEK, t., Hancock co., Ind. Pop. 420.

BUCK CREEK, p. o., Scriven co., Ga.

BUCK CREEK, p. o., Tuscaloosa co., Ala., 20 ms. from Tuscaloosa ; from W. 838 ms.

BUCK EYE, p. o., Putnam co., O., 119 ms. N. w. of Columbus; from W. 484 ms.

BUCK EYE, p. o., Garrard co., Ky.

BUCK EYE, p. o., Laurens co., Ga., 50 ms. N. by w. of Milledgeville ; from W. 678 ms.

BUCK EYE COTTAGE, p. o., Perry co., O.

BUCKEYE FURNACE, p, o., Jackson co., O.

BUCKEYESTOWN, p. v., Frederick co., Md., 81 ms, N w. of Annapolis, from W. 49 ms. Pop. 2,829.

BUCKFIELD, p. t., Oxford co., Me., 32 ms w hy s. of Augusta; from W. 591 ms. Watered by Androscoggin river. Pop. 1,657.

BUCK GROVE, p. o., Rush co., Ind.

BUCKHANNON. p. o., Lewis co., Va.

BUCKHEAD, p. o., Morgan co., Ga., 48 ms. N. N. w. of Milledgeville ; from W, 618 ms.

BUCKHEAD, p. o., Fairfield district, S. C., 44 ms. N. w. of Columbia ; from W. 484 ms.

BUCKHEAD, p. o., Pike co., Ala.

BUCKHEAD CAUSEWAY, p. o., Colleton district, S. C., 113 ms. s. by E. of Columbia ; from W. 619 ms.

BUCK HILL, p. o.. Yallabusha co., Miss.

BUCK HILL, p. o., De Kalb co., Ala.

BUCK HOLLOW, p. o., Franklin co., Vt.

BUCKHORN, p. o., Columbia co., Pa.

BUCKHORN, p. o., Carroll co., Ga.

BUCKHORN, p. o., Bienville parish, La.

BUCKHORN, p. o., Winston co., Miss.

BUCKHORN, p. o., Brown co., Ill.

BUCKINGHAM COUNTY, situated toward the southeast part of Virginia, on the southerly side of James river. Length, 34 ms. ; mean width, 20 ; with an area of 680 square miles. The face of the country is rocky and hilly, soil generally good. Seat of justice, Maysville. Pop. in 1820, 17,582; in 1830, 18,351 ; in 1840, 18,786 ; in 1850, 13,837.

BUCKINGHAM, p. o., Baltimore co., Md.

BUCKINGHAM, t., Wayne co., Pa. Watered by Delaware river. Pop. 592.

BUCKINGHAM, p. t., Bucks co., Pa., 104 ms. E. by N. of Harrisburgh ; from W. 166 ms. Pop. 2,766.

BUCKINGHAM, c. h., p. o., Maysville v., Buckingham co., Va., 79 ms. w. of Richmond ; from W. 158 ms.

BUCKLAND, p. t., Franklin co., Mass., 104 ms. w. N. w. of Boston ; from W. 412 ms. Watered by Deerfield river. Pop. 1,056.

BUCKLAND, p. v., Prince William co., Va., 111 ms. N. of Richmond ; from W. 42 ms. Watered by Broad Run.

BUCKLAND, p. o., Gates co., Va.

BUCKLAND. p. o., Hartford co., Ct., 6 ms. from Hartford ; from W. 342 ms.

BUCKLEY, p. o., Gates co., N. C.

BUCK POINT, p. o., Jackson co., Tenn.

BUCKRAM, p. v., Queen's co., N. Y., 179 ms. s. of Albany; from W. 259 ms. Watered by Beaver-dam creek.

BUCK PRAIRIE, p. o., Barry co., Mo.

BUCK RUN, p. o., Union co., O., 46 ms. N. by w. of Columbus ; from W. 436 ms.

BUCKS COUNTY, situated on the easterly boundary of Pennsylvania, on the westerly side of Delaware river. Length, 37 miles ; mean breadth, 16 ; with an area of about 600 square miles. The face of the country is somewhat hilly and rolling, and the soil generally good and well cultivated. Seat of justice, Doylestown. Pop. in 1820, 37,842 ; in 1830, 45,740 ; in 1840, 48,107 ; in 1850, 56,091.

BUCKS, t., Tuscarawas co., O.

BUCKS, p. o., Columbiana co., O., 153 ms. N. E. of Columbus ; from W. 285 ms.

BUCKS, t., St, Joseph's co., Mich. Watered by St. Joseph's river.

BUCKSKIN, p. o., Gibson co.. Ind.

BUCKSPORT, p. t., Hancock co., Me., 58 ms. N. E. by E. of Augusta ; from W. 654 ms. Watered by Penobscot river. Pop. 3,381.

BUCKSPORT CENTRE, p. o., Hancock co., Me.

BUCKSTOWN, p. o., Somerset co., Pa.

BUCKSVILLE, p. o., Bucks co. Pa.

BUCK'S SHOALS, p. o., Rutherford co., N. C., 216 ms. w. by s. of Raleigh ; from W. 453 ms.

BUCKSVILLE, p. o., Horrey district, S. C., 187 ms. E. of Columbia ; from W. 477 ms.

BUCK TOOTH, p. o., Little Valley township, Cattaraugus co., N. Y.

BUCYRUS, c. h. p. t., seat of justice of Crawford co., O., 62 ms. N. of Columbus ; from W. 406 ms. Watered by Sandusky river. Pop. 2,315.

BUEL, p. o., Montgomery co., N. Y., 62 ms. N. w. by w. of Albany'; from W. 387 ms.

BUEL'S LOWELL, t., Washington co., O.

BUENA VISTA, p. o., Alleghany co., Pa.

BUENA VISTA, p. o., Prince George's co., Md.

BUENA VISTA, p, o., Carroll co., Tenn.

BUENA VISTA, p. o., Duplin co., N. C.

BUENA VISTA, p. o., Jefferson co., Ind.

BUENA VISTA, p. o., Washita co.. Ark.

BUENA VISTA, p. o., Harrison co., Ky.

BUENA VISTA, p. o., Monroe co., Ala.

BUENA VISTA, p. o., Stephenson co., Ill.

BUENA VISTA, p. o., Platte co., Mo.

BUENA VISTA, p. o., Chickasaw co., Miss.

BUENA VISTA, p. o., Clinton co., Iowa.

BUENA VISTA, p. o., Shelby co., Tex.

BUENA VISTA, p. o., Greenville district, S. C.

BUENA VISTA, p. o., Marion co., Ga.

BUENA VISTA, p. o., Holmes co., O.

BUENA VISTA, p. o., Portage co., Wis.

BUENA VISTA FURNACE, p. o., Rockbridge co., Va.

BUENA VISTA SPRINGS, p. o., Logan co., Ky.

BUFFALO, city, and seat of justice of Erie co., N. Y., is situated at the confluence of Buffalo creek with the east end of Lake Erie. and at the western terminus of the Erie canal, by which route it is 363 miles distant from Albany. It occupies a slope, chiefly on the north side of the creek, which is here deep enough for vessels drawing eight feet of water. The streets are generally regular, the buildings substantial, and many of them imposing. The longest and broadest is Main street, the Broadway of Buffalo, on each side of which, for more than two miles, extend lines of stores and other buildings. From the top of the elevation above the city, appears a wide panorama of the lake, Black Rock basin, Niagara river, the Erie canal, and the surrounding country.

Buffalo is the offspring of the Erie canal, and ever since the completion of that stupendous work, has continued to increase in population, wealth, and importance. It is the gate through which the vast commerce of the great lakes and the western states passes on its way to New York and the east. A great chain of railroads binds Buffalo to New York, Boston, Albany, and the richest portion of the Empire state along the course of the Erie canal ; and another, traversing the valleys of the Susquehanna and Delaware, links it with New Jersey, New York city, and Philadelphia. By either of

these routes, the passenger may reach Buffalo from New York, a distance of about 500 miles, in less than 20 hours. The Lake-shore railroad connects it with the vast network of railroads in the western states.

The harbor of Buffalo was formerly impeded by sands which the winds and storms of Lake Erie deposited at its entrance. By the construction of a mole and pier, 1,500 feet long, this obstacle is removed, and vessels drawing eight feet of water, now enter the creek. Here, in the winter season, a large number of vessels, steamboats, ships, schooners, and canal-boats, are congregated and protected from ice and storms. Several hundred schooners, and a number of steamboats. navigate Lake Erie from Buffalo to the different ports on its shores. A large amount of capital is invested in manufactures.

The population in 1810, was 1,508 ; in 1820, 2,095 ; in 1830, 8,653 ; in 1840, 18,213 ; in 1850, 42,261.

BUFFALO, t., Armstrong co., Pa. Pop. 2,182.

BUFFALO, p. t., Union co., Pa. Pop. 1,346.

BUFFALO, p. t., Washington co., Pa., 217 ms. w. of Harrisburgh ; from W. 243 ms. Pop. 1,210.

BUFFALO, p. t., Guernsey co., O., 87 ms. E. of Columbus ; from W. 319 ms.

BUFFALO. v., Mason co., Va., 347 ms. N. N. W. of Richmond ; from W. 384 ms. Watered by the Great Kanawha river.

BUFFALO, v.. Cleveland co., N. C., 190 ms. w. by s. of Raleigh ; from W. 427 ms.

BUFFALO, p. o., Dallas co., Mo.

BUFFALO, t., Pike co., Mo.

BUFFALO, t., Morgan co., Mo.

BUFFALO, t., Marian co., Ark.

BUFFALO, c. h. v., seat of justice of Niangua co , Mo.

BUFFALO, t., Butler co., Pa. Watered by Thorn, Great and Little Buffalo Creeks. Pop. 275.

BUFFALO, t., Perry co., Pa. Watered by Susquehanna river. Pop. 618.

BUFFALO, b., Perry co., Pa. Watered by Susquehanna river. Pop. 164.

BUFFALO, p. o., Perry co., Tenn., 92 ms. s. w. of Nashville ; from W. 769 ms.

BUFFALO, p. o., White co., Ind.

BUFFALO, p. o., Washita co., Ark.

BUFFALO, p. o., Dallas co., Mo.

BUFFALO, p. o., Washington co., Pa.

BUFFALO, p. o., Putnam co., Va.

BUFFALO, p. o., Henderson co., Tex.

BUFFALO CITY, p. o., Marion co., Ark.

BUFFALO CREEK, p. o., Campbell co., Tenn.

BUFFALO CROSS ROADS, p. o., Union co., Pa., 75 ms. N. by w. of Harrisburgh ; from W. 185 ms.

BUFFALO FORD, p. o., Randolph co., N. C.

BUFFALO FORD, p. o., Wythe co., Va., 266 ms. w. s. w. of Richmond ; from W. 333 ms.

BUFFALO FORGE, p. o., Rockbridge co., Va., 152 ms w. by N. of Richmond ; from W. 196 ms.

BUFFALO GROVE, p. o., Ogle co., Ill.

BUEFALO HEART, p. o., Sangamon co., Ill.

BUFFALO HILL, p. o., Orange co., N. C. (Now DIAL'S CREEK.)

BUFFALO PLAINS, p. o., Erie co., N. Y.

BUFFALO PRAIRIE, p. o., Rock Island co., Ill.

BUFFALO RUN, p. o., Monroe co., Va. (Now MOUTH OF INDIAN.)

BUFFALO RUN, p. o., Centre co., Pa., 91 ms. N. w. of Harrisburgh ; from W. 183 ms.

BUFFALO SPRINGS, p. o., Amherst co., Va.

BUFORD, p. o., Ohio co.. Ky.

BUFORD, p. o., Highland co., O., 90 ms. s. s. w. of Columbus ; from W. 183 ms.

BUFORD'S, p. o., Bedford co., Va., 156 ms. w. by s. of Richmond ; from W. 230 ms.

BUFORD'S BRIDGE, p. o., Barnwell district, S. C., 88 ms. s. s. w. of Columbia ; from W. 594 ms.

BUGGABO, p. o., Wilkes co., N. C.

BUG HALL, p. o., Macon co., Ala.

BULAH, p, o., Obion co., Tenn.

BULGER, p. o., Washington co., Pa., 223 ms. w. of Harrisburgh ; from W. 247 ms.

BULGER'S MILLS, p. o., Coosa co., Ala.

BULL CREEK, p. o., Wood co., Va., 324 ms. N. w. of Richmond ; from W. 292 ms.

BULLBONUS GROVE, p. o., Will co,, Ill., 168 ms. N. N. E. of Springfield ; from W. 710 ms.

BULLITT COUNTY, situated in the northern part of Kentucky, on the northeasterly side of Salt river. Length, 30 miles ; mean breadth, 10, with an area of 300

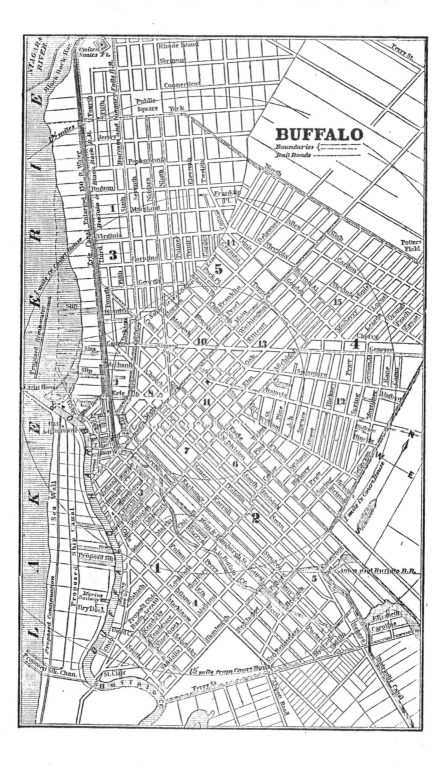

square miles. The face of the country is hilly ; the soil varied, but generally productive. Seat of justice Shepnerdsville, Pop. in 1820, 5,381 ; in 1830, 5,642 ; in 1840, 6,334 ; in 1850, 6,774.

BULLION, p. o., Waukesha co., Wis.

BULL MILLS, p. o., Taney co., Mo.

BULLOCK COUNTY, situated in the easterly part of Georgia, between Ogechee and Cannouchee rivers. Length, 45 miles ; mean breadth, 12, with an area of 540 square miles. The face of the country is generally undulating and hilly ; soil of a middling quality. Seat of justice, Statesborough. Pop. in 1820, 2,578 ; in 1830, 2,287 ; in 1840, 3,102 ; in 1850, 4,300.

BULLOCK'S, p, o., Granville co., N. C.. 56 ms. N. of Raleigh ; from W. 272 ms.

BULLOCK'S CREEK, p. o., York co., S. C.

BULLOCKTOWN. p. v., Queen Anne co., Md., 64 ms. E. of Annapolis ; from W. 104 ms.

BULL PASTURE, p. o., Bath co., Va., 161 ms. w. N. w. of Richmond ; from W. 188 ms.

BULL RUN, p. o., Grainger co., Tenn., 213 ms. E. of Nashville ; from W. 492 ms.

BULL'S HEAD, p, o., Dutchess co., N. Y.

BULL SKIN, p. o., Gallia co., O., 111 ms. s. s. E. of Columbus ; from W. 369 ms.

BULL SKIN, p. t., Fayette co., Pa. Pop. 1,428.

BULL SWAMP, p. o., Orangeburgh district, S. C.

BULL TOWN, p. o., Braxton co., Va. 306 ms. w. N. w. of Richmond ; from W. 274 ms.

BULLUCTAH, p. o., Leake co., Miss.

BULLVILLE, p. o., Crawford township, Orange co.. N. Y., 103 ms. s. by w. of Albany ; from W. 288 ms.

BUNCOMB, p. o., Pontotoc co., Miss.

BUNGER'S MILL, p. o., Greenbrier co., Va.

BUNKER'S HILL, p. o., Giles co., Tenn.

BUNKER'S HILL, p. o., Catawba co., N. C.

BUNDYSBURGH, p. v., Parkman township, Geauga co., O., 166 N. E. of Columbus ; from W. 325 ms.

BUNCOMBE COUNTY, situated on the northwest boundary of North Carolina. Length, 65 ms. ; mean width, 22 ; with an area of 1,430 square miles. The surface is generally hilly and mountainous ; the soil rocky, though fertile. Seat of justice, Ashville. Pop. in 1830, 16,281 ; in 1840, 10,084 ; in 1850, 13,425.

BUNKER HILL, p.o., Bucks co., Pa., 102 ms. E. by N. of Harrisburgh ; from W. 171 ms.

BUNKER HILL, p.o., Macoupin co., Ill.

BUNKER HILL, p. o., Bedford co., Va., 148 ms. w. by s. of Richmond ; from W. 223 ms.

BUNKER HILL, p. o., Jefferson co., Flor.

BUNKER HILL, p. t., Ingham co., Mich. Pop. 374.

BURNS' LEVEL, p. o., Cumberland co., N. C.

BURBANK, Wayne co., O., 109 ms. N. E. of Columbus ; from W. 360 ms.

BURBOISE, p. v., Franklin co., Mo. Pop. 504.

BURCHVILLE. p. o., St. Clair co., Mich.

BURDETT, p. v., Hector township, Tompkins co., N. Y., 184 ms. w. by s. of Albany ; from W. 307 ms.

BURDSFIELD, p. o., Bedford co., Pa., 117 w. s. w. of Harrisburgh ; from W. 144 ms.

BUREAU COUNTY, situated toward the north part of Illinois, on the northwesterly side of Illinois river. Area, 648 square miles. Watered by Bureau creek and Winnebago lake. Seat of justice, Princeton. Pop. in 1840, 3,067 ; in 1850, 8,841.

BURGERSVILLE, p. o., Johnson co., Ark.

BURGESS' STORE, p. o., Northumberland co., Va., 107 ms. N. N. E. of Richmond ; from W. 166 ms.

BURGESSVILLE, p.o., Johnson co., Ind.

BURGETTSTOWN, p. o., Washington co., Pa., 227 ms. w. of Harrisburgh ; from W. 250 ms.

BURKE COUNTY, situated on the northeast boundary of Georgia, on the southwest side of Savannah river. Length, 40 miles ; mean breadth, 24, with an area of 960 square miles. The face of the country is generally undulating, and the soil of middling quality. Seat of justice, Waynesborough. Pop. in 1820, 11,576 ; in 1830, 17,888 ; in 1840, 13,176 ; in 1850, 16,100.

BURKE COUNTY, in the western part of North Carolina, and traversed by Catawba river. Length, 60 miles ; mean width, 22, with an area of 1,320 square miles. The surface is mountainous and hilly ; soil varied. Seat of justice, Morgantown. Pop. in 1820, 13,411 ; in 1830, 17,727 ; in 1840, 15,799 ; in 1850, 7,772.

BURKE, p. o., Franklin co.. N. Y.

BURKE'S GARDEN, p. o., Tazewell co., Va., 274 ms. w. by s. of Richmond ; from W. 340 ms.

BURKE, p. t., Caledonia co., Vt., 51 ms. N. E. of Montpelier ; from W. 561 ms. Pop. 1,103.

BURKESVILLE. p. v., Prince Edward co., Va., 81 ms. » w. by w. of Richmond ; fcom W. 176 ms.

BURKESVILLE, c. h., p. v., seat of justice of Cumberland co., Ky., 124 ms. w. by s. of Frankfort ; from W. 637 ms. Watered by Cumberland river.

BURKEVILLE, p. o., Newton co., Tex.

BURKITTSVILLE. p. v., Frederick co., Md., 92 ms. N. w. of Annapolis ; from W. 60 ms.

BURKITTSVILLE, p. o., Attila co., Miss.

BURLESON COUNTY, situated toward the southwest part of Texas, between Brazos and Yegua rivers. Area, —— square miles. Seat of justice, Caldwell. Pop., in 1850, 2,613.

BURLESCN, p. o., Franklin co., Ala.

BURLINGHAM, p. v., Mamakating township., Sullivan co., N. Y.

BURLINGHAM, p. v. Bedford township, Meigs co., O., 86 ms. s. E. of Columbus, from W. 341 ms.

BURLINGTON COUNTY, situated toward the southern part of New Jersey, between the river Delaware and the Atlantic ocean. Length, 40 miles ; mean width, 12½ ; with an area of 500 square miles. The face of the country is generally level ; the soil sandy, but productive. Seat of justice, Mount Holly. Pop. in 1830, 31,066 ; in 1840, 32,831 ; in 1850, 43,203.

BURLINGTON, p. t. Penobscot co., Me., 120 ms. N. E. of Augusta ; from W. 713 ms. Pop. 481.

BURLINGTON, c. h., p. t., seat of justice of Chittenden co., Vt., 40 ms. w. N. w. of Montpelier ; from W. 513 ms. Situated on Lake Champlain. Pop., in 1840, 4,271 ; in 1850, 6,110.

BURLINGTON, p. t. Kane co., Ill. Pop. 664.

BURLINGTON, p. t., Hartford co., Ct., 19 ms. w. of Hartford ; from W. 339 ms. Watered by Farmington river. Pop. 1,161.

BURLINGTON, p. t., Middlesex co., Mass., 13 ms. N. w. by N. of Boston ; from W. 453 ms. Watered by Shawsheen river. Pop. 545.

BURLINGTON. p. t., Otsego co., N. Y., 79 ms. w. of Albany ; from W. 356 ms. Pop. 1,835.

BURLINGTON, city and p. t., Burlington co., N. J., 12 ms. s. of Trenton ; from W. 156 ms. Watered by Delaware river. Pop., in 1840, 3,403 ; in 1850, 4,536.

BURLINGTON, p. t., Bradford co., Pa., 144 ms. N. of Harrisburgh ; from W. 254 ms. Watered by Sugar creek. Pop. 1,927.

BURLINGTON, p. v., Fayette township, seat of justice of Lawrence co., O. Watered by Ohio river.

BURLINGTON, p. t., Calhoun co., Mich., 111 ms. w. of Detroit ; from W. 572 ms. Pop. 811.

BURLINGTON, v., Hampshire co., Va., 198 ms. N. w. of Richmond ; from W. 126 ms.

BURLINGTON. p. t., seat of justice of Chittenden county, and the chief port of entry of Vermont. It is pleasantly situated on a beautiful bay of Champlain, and commands the principal trade of the county and of the lake. To this point flow a large portion of the products of the Green Mountain state, and thence they are conveyed by railroad, steamboats, or other vessels, to Troy, Albany, New York, St. John, and other places. Rising from the water by a gentle acclivity, and laid out in regular streets, adorned with gardens and dwellings, Burlington is as conspicuous for its pleasant and healthful location, as for its commercial advantages. The dome of the University of Vermont, which stands on an eminence 250 feet above the lake, commands a most varied, extensive, and delightful prospect. A light-house on Juniper island marks the entrance of the harbor, and a breakwater, erected by the general government, protects it from the west winds of the lake. This village communicates by railroad with Montpelier, Boston, and the intermediate places. Population, in 1810, 1,690 ; in 1820, —— ; in 1830, 3,525 ; in 1840, 4,271 ; in 1850, 5,211.

BURLINGTON. p. v., Carroll co., Ind., 53 ms. N. N. W. of Indianapolis ; from W. 611 ms.

BURLINGTON, p. o., Racine co., Wis., 82 ms. s. E. of Madison ; from W. 791 ms.

BURLINGTON, p. v., formerly the capital, and the largest town in Iowa, and the seat of justice of Des Moines county, occupies a pleasant slope on the west bank of the Mississippi, 75 miles southeast of Iowa city, 248 ms. N. of St. Louis, 1,429 ms. N. of New Orleans, and 871 ms. from W. Pleasant hills and woody slopes rise behind the city, and enhance the effect of its other advantages. It is the centre of an active, extended, and increasing commerce with the rich interior of the state, together with that of Illinois, and the valley of the Mississippi. Possessing a combination of so many favorable circumstances, it has already received a vigorous impulse, and will undoubtedly advance with accelerated growth. Its broad and delightful streets, either along the water, or on higher ground, are admirably suited for business, as well as for residence, and the number of public buildings, elegant stores, and dwellings, is already large, and receives almost daily accessions. A steam-ferry connects the town with the opposite side of the river. Pop. in 1840, 1,300 ; in 1850, 4,081.

BURLINGTON, t., Licking co., O. Pop. 1,388.

BURLINGTON, p. o., East Baton Rouge parish, La.

BURLINGTON, c. h., p. v., seat of justice of Boone co., Ky., 83 ms. N. by E. of Frankfort ; from W. 508 ms.

BURLINGTON FLATS, p. o., Burlington township, Otsego co., N. Y., 83 ms. w. of Albany ; from W. 360 ms.

BURNINGTON, t., Shiawassee co., Mich.

BURNERSVILLE, p. o., Barbour co., Va., 231 ms. N. W. of Richmond ; from W. 243 ms.

BURNES, t., Alleghany co., N. Y., 237 ms. w. by s. of Albany ; from W. 318 ms. Watered by Canasarega creek. Pop. 948.

BURNETT, p. o., Dodge co., Wis.

BURNETT'S CREEK, p. o., White co., Ind.

BURNETTSTON, t., Franklin co., Mass.

BURNHAM, p. t., Waldo co., Me., 34 ms. E. of Augusta ; from W. 630 ms. Pop. 784.

BURNHAM VILLAGE, p. o., Waldo co., Me., 34 ms. E. of Augusta ; from W. 629 ms.

BURNING SPRING, p. o., Wirt co., Va.

BURNS, p. o., Alleghany co., N. Y.

BURNS, p. t., Shiawassee co., Mich.

BURNS, p. o., Henry co., Ill.

BURNSIDE, p. t., Clearfield co., Pa., 156 ms. N. w. of Harrisburgh ; from W. 234 ms. Pop. 1,046.

BURNSVILLE, p. o., Yancey co., N. C., 245 ms. w. by N. of Raleigh ; from W. 475 ms.

BURNSVILLE, p. o., Dallas co., Ala.

BURNSVILLE, p. o., McDonough co., Ill.

BURNT CAIRNS, p. o., Bedford co., Pa., 67 ms. w. s. w. of Harrisburgh. from W. 111 ms.

BURNT CORN, p. o.. Monroe co., Ala., 142 ms. s. of Tuscaloosa ; from W. 934 ms.

BURNT HILLS, p. o., Ballston township, Saratoga co., N. Y., 25 ms. N. of Albany ; from W. 393 ms.

BURNT ORDINARY, p. o., James City co., Va., 46 ms. E. by s. of Richmond ; from W. 163 ms.

BURNT PRAIRIE, p. v., White co., Ill., 155 ms. s. s. E. of Springfield ; from W. 761 ms.

BURNT QUARTER, p. o., Dinwiddie co., Va., 44 ms. s. by w. of Richmond ; from W. 163 ms.

BURNT STAND, p. o., Carroll co., Ga.

BURNT TAVERN, p. o., Monmouth co., N. J., 27 ms. E. by s. of Trenton ; from W. 193 ms.

BURNT TAVERN, p. o., Garrard co., Ky., 49 ms. s. by E. of Frankfort ; from W. 547 ms.

BURNTVILLE, p. o., Brunswick co., Va.

BURRILLVILLE, p. t., Providence co., R. I., 19 ms. N.W. of Providence ; from W. 398 ms. Watered by Branch river. Pop. 3,838.

BURRITT, p. o., Winnebago co., Ill.

BURR OAK GROVE, p. o., Stephenson co., Ill., 215 ms. N. of Springfield ; from W. 847 ms.

BURR OAK, p. o., Mercer co., Mo.

BURR OAK, p. t., St. Joseph's co., Mich., 128 ms. s. w. of Detroit ; from W. 576 ms.

BURR'S FERRY, p. o., Sabine co., La.

BURR'S MILLS, p. o., Jefferson co., N. Y., 166 ms. N.W. of Albany ; from W. 411 ms.

BURRSVILLE. p. v., Caroline co.. Md., 71 ms. E of Annapolis ; from W. 111 ms.

BURSHLEY CREEK, p. o., Catahoula parish, La., 251 ms. N. w. of New Orleans ; from W 1,165 ms.

BURRSVILLE, p. o., Russell co., Ala.

BURRVILLE, p. o., Litchfield co., Ct.

BURSONVILLE, p. o., Bucks co., Pa., 119 ms. E. of Harrisburgh ; from W. 184 ms.

BURTON, t., Pike co., O. Pop. 639.

BURTON, t., Luzerne co., Pa. Pop. 1,063.

BURTON, p. o., Parke co., Ind., 78 ms. w. of Indianapolis ; from W. 649 ms.

BURTON. p. o., Adams co., Ill.

BURTON'S, p. o., Tishamingo co., Miss.

BURTON'S CORNERS, p. o., Boone co., Ill.

BURTONSVILLE, p. o., Charleston township, Montgomery co., N. Y.

BURTONSVILLE, p. o., Greene co., Va., 89 ms. N. w. of Richmond ; from W. 109 ms.

BURTONSVILLE, p. o.. Daviess co., Ky.

BURTONTON, p. o., Copiah co., Miss., 59 ms. s. by w. of Jackson ; from W. 1,076 ms.

BURTVILLE, p. o., McKean co., Pa.

BURWELL'S BAY, p. o., Isle of Wight co., Va., 69 ms. s. E. of Richmond ; from W. 192 ms.

BUSBAYVILLE, p. o., Houston co., Ga., 47 ms. s. s. w. of Milledgeville ; from W. 703 ms.

BUSBEE'S STORE, p. o., Wake co., N. C., 9 ms. from Raleigh ; from W. 397 ms.

BUSH CREEK, p. o., Bureau co., Ill., 131 ms. N. of Springfield ; from W. 802 ms.

BUSH CREEK, t., Washington co., Ark.

BUSH CREEK, t.. Scioto co., O. Pop. 650.

BUSHKILL, p. o., Pike co., Pa., 142 ms. N. E. of Harrisburgh ; from W. 232 ms.

BUSHKILL, t., Northampton co., Pa. Watered by Bushkill creek. Pop. 1,839.

BUSHNELL'S BASIN, p. v., Perrinton township, Monroe co., N. Y., 217 ms. w. by N. of Albany ; from W. 366 ms. Situated on the Erie canal.

BUSHNELLSVILLE, p. o., Greene co., N. Y.

BUSH'S MILLS, p. o., Lewis co., Va., 291 ms. N. w. of Richmond ; from W. 259 ms.

BUSH'S STORE, p. o., Laurel co., Ky., 107 ms. s. s. E. of Frankfort ; from W. 552 ms.

BUSHVILLE, p. o., Franklin co., Ga., 109 ms. N. by E. of Milledgeville ; from W. 618 ms.

BUSHWICK, t., King's co., Long Island, N. Y. Watered by Bushwick creek. Pop. 3,739.

BUSHY CREEK, p. o., Williamson co., Tex.

BUSINESS CORNER, p. o., Van Buren co., Iowa.

BUSKIRK'S BRIDGE. p. v., Cambridge township, Washington co., N. Y., 29 ms. N. by E. of Albany ; from W. 399 ms. Watered by Hoosick river.

BUSKOEN MILLS, p. o., Sullivan co., Ind., 88 ms, s.w. of Indianapolis , from W. 659 ms.

BUSTI, p. t., Chautauque co., N. Y., 323 ms. w. by s, of Albany ; from W. 336 ms. Pop. 1,990.

BUSTOM, t., Luzerne co., Pa.

BUSTLETON, p. v., Philadelphia co., Pa., 110 ms. E. by s. of Harrisburgh ; from W. 150 ms.

BUTCHER'S STORE, p. o.. Randolph co., Va.

BUTEVILLE, p. o., Marion co., Oregon.

BUTLER COUNTY, situated in the western part of Pennsylvania. Length, 35 miles ; mean width, 24, with an area of 840 square miles. The face of the country is generally hilly ; soil fertile and well watered Seat of justice, Butler. Pop. in 1820, 10,251 ; in 1830, 14,683 ; in 1840, 22,378 ; in 1850, 30,346.

BUTLER COUNTY, situated toward the southern part of Alabama. Area, 1,000 square miles. Seat of justice, Greenville. Pop. in 1830, 5,650 ; in 1840, 8,685 ; in 1850, 10,836.

BUTLER COUNTY, situated toward the southwest part of Kentucky, and traversed by Green river. Area, 570 square miles. Seat of justice. Morgantown. Pop. in 1830, 3,058 ; in 1840, 3,898 ; in 1850, 5,754.

BUTLER COUNTY, in the southwest part of Ohio, and traversed by Miami river, and the Miami canal. Area, 480 square miles. Seat of justice, Hamilton. Pop. in 1830, 27,144 ; in 1840. 28,173 ; in 1850, 30,789.

BUTLER COUNTY, situated on the south boundary of Missouri, and traversed by Big Black river. Area, —— square miles. Seat of justice, Cane creek. Pop. in 1850, 1,616.

BUTLER, p. t., Wayne co., N. Y., 178 ms. w. N. w. of Albany ; from W. 358 ms. Pop. 2,272.

BUTLER, c. h., p. b., seat of justice of Butler co., Pa., 203 ms. N. N. w. of Harrisburgh ; from W. 245 ms. Watered by Connequenessing creek. Pop. 1,148.

BUTLER, t., Luzerne co., Pa.. Pop. 725.

BUTLER, p. o., Baltimore co., Md.

BUTLER, p. t., De Kalb co., Ind., 145 ms. N. N. E. of Indianapolis ; from W. 558 ms. Pop. 651.

BUTLER, c. h., p. o., seat of justice of Choctaw co., Ala.

BUTLER, t., Branch co., Mich. Watered by Hog river. Pop. 611.

BUTLER, t., Columbiana co., O. Pop. 1,692.

BUTLER, p. o., Richland co., O.

BUTLER, t., Darke co., O. Pop. 1,446.

BUTLER, t., Knox co., O. Pop. 763.

BUTLER, t., Mercer co., O. Pop. 221.

BUTLER, p. o., Franklin co., Pa.

BUTLER, p. o., Milwaukee co., Wis.

BUTLER, p. o., Fulton co., Ky.

BUTLER, t., Montgomery co., O.

BUTLER, p. o., Keokuk co., Iowa.

BUTLER'S LANDING, p. v., Jackson co., Tenn., 85 ms. N. E. of Nashville ; from W. 636 ms. Watered by Cumberland river.

BUTLER'S MILLS, p. o., Montgomery co., N. C., 106 ms. s. w. of Raleigh ; from W. 380 ms.

BUTLER SPRING, p. o., Butler co., Ala.

BUTLERVILLE, p. o., Warren co., O., 94 ms. N. E. of Columbus ; from W. 466 ms.

BUTLERVILLE, p. o., Butler co., Ala.

BUTLERVILLE, p. o., Jennings co., Ind.

BUTLERSVILLE, p. o., Anderson district, S. C.

BUTTAHATCHY. p. o., Monroe co., Miss.

BUTTE COUNTY, situated in the central part of California, on the eastern side of Sacramento river. Area, —— square miles. Seat of justice, Butte. Pop. in 1850, 2,016.

BUTTE DES MORTS, p. o., Winnebago co., Wis.

BUTTERFLY. p. o., New Haven township, Oswego co., N. Y., 161 ms. N. w. of Albany ; from W. 386 ms.

BUTTERNUTS, p. t., Otsego co., N. Y., 94 ms. w. by s. of Albany ; from W. 341 ms. Watered by Butternut creek and Unadilla river. Pop. 1,928.

BUTTERNUT RIDGE, p. o., Sandusky co., O.

BUTTERMILK FALLS, p. o., Orange co., N. Y.

BUTTS COUNTY, situated in the central part of Georgia, on the westerly side of Ocmulgee river. Area, 420 square miles. Seat of justice, Jackson. Pop. in 1830, 4,944 ; in 1840, 5,308 ; in 1850, 6,488.

BUTZTOWN, p. o., Northampton co., Pa., 97 ms. N. E. of Harrisburgh ; from W. 190 ms.

BUYCKSVILLE, p. o., Coosa co., Ala.

BUXTON, p. t., York co., Me., 65 ms. s. w. of Augusta ; from W. 532 ms. Watered by Saco river. Pop. 2,995.

BUXTON CENTRE, p. o., Buxton township, York co., Me., 66 ms. s. w. of Augusta ; from W. 535 ms.

BUZZARD ROOST, p. o., Franklin co., Ala., 147 ms. N. by w. of Tuscaloosa ; from W. 800 ms.

BYBERRY, p. t., Philadelphia co., Pa., 113 ms. E. by s of Harrisburgh ; from W. 155 ms. Watered by Poquessing creek. Pop. 1,130.

BYERSVILLE, p. o., Sparta township, Livingston co., N. Y., 249 ms. w. of Albany ; from W. 339 ms.

BYESVILLE, p. o., Guernsey co., O., 82 ms. E. of Columbus ; from W. 322 ms.

BYFIELD, p. v., Newbury and Rowley townships, Essex co., Mass. Watered by Parker river.

BYHALIA, p. o., Marshall co., Miss.

BYINGTON, p. o., Pike co., O.

BYRAM, p. t., Sussex co., N. J. Watered by Musconetcong river. Pop. 1,340.

BYRD, p. t., Brown co., O. Pop. 2,642.

BYRD, t., Cape Girardeau co., Miss.

BYRNEVILLE, p. o., Harrison co., Ind.

BYRNEVILLE, p. v. Fulton township, Schoharie co., N. Y., 46 ms. w. by s. of Albany ; from W. 384 ms.

BYRON, p. o., Oxford co., Me., 56 ms. s. w. of Augusta ; from W. 633 ms.

BYRON, p. t., Genesee co., N. Y., 243 ms. w. by N. of Albany ; from W. 384 ms. Watered by Black creek. Pop. 1,566.

BYRON, p. v., Shiawassee co., Mich., 72 ms. N. w. of Detroit ; from W. 589 ms.

BYRON, p. o., Greene co., O.

BYRON, p. o., Laporte co., Ind.

BYRON, p. o., Fond du Lac co., Wis.

BYRON, p. t., Ogle co., Ill., 187 ms. N. of Springfield ; from W. 820 ms. Pop. 644.

BYRON FORGE, p. o., Stewart co., Tenn., 65 ms. N. w. of Nashville ; from W. 749 ms.

C.

CABARRAS COUNTY, situated in the southern part of North Carolina. Area, 300 square miles. The face of the country is mountainous and broken, with a soil of middling quality. Seat of justice, Concord. Pop. in 1820, 7,228 ; in 1830, 8,796 ; in 1840, 9,259 ; in 1850, 9,747.

CABELL COUNTY, situated on the northwest boundary of Virginia, on the southerly side of the Ohio river, and traversed by Guyandott river. Area, 100 square miles. The face of the country is mountainous, hilly, and rocky, well watered, wooded, and generally fertile. Seat of justice, Barboursville. Pop. in 1840, 8,163 ; in 1850, 6,299.

CABELL, c. h., p. o., Cabell co., Va.

CABELLO, p. o., Carroll co., O.

CABIN CREEK, p. o., Lewis co., Ky., 92 ms. N. E. of Frankfort : from W. 471 ms.

CABIN HILL, p. o., Andes township, Delaware co., N. Y., 85 ms. s. w. of Albany ; from W. 345 ms.

CABIN HILL, p. o., Elkhart co., Ind.

CABIN POINT, p. v., Surry co., Va., 45 ms. s. E. of Richmond ; from W. 166 ms. Watered by Chipoak creek.

CABLE, p. o., Guernsey co., O.

CABOT, p. t., Caledonia co., Vt., 20 ms. N. E. of Montpelier ; from W. 535 ms. Watered by Onion river. Pop. 1,356.

CABOTVILLE, p. v., Springfield township, Hampden co., Mass., 95 ms. w. by s. of Boston ; from W. 367 ms. Watered by Chickapee and Connecticut rivers.

CACAPONVILLE, p. o., Hampshire co., Va.

CACHE, t., Greene co., Ark.

CACHE, t., Monroe co., Ark. Pop. 449.

CACHEMASSO, p. o., Dallas co., Ark.

CADIS COVE, p. o., Blount co., Tenn., 199 ms. E. by s. of Nashville ; from W. 527 m.

CADDO PARISH, situated at the northwest corner of Louisiana, on the westerly side of Red river, and watered by Caddo lake. Area, 2,500 square miles. Seat of justice, Shrewsport. Pop. in 1840, 5,282 ; in 1850, 8,884.

CADDO, t., Clark co., Ark. Pop. 1,001.

CADDO COVE, t., Hot Springs co., Ark. Pop. 489.

CADIZ. p. o., Cattaraugus co., N. Y.

CADIZ, c. h., p. t. Seat of justice of Harrison co., O., 114 E. N. E. of Columbus ; from W. 284 ms. Pop. 2,453.

CADIZ, p. v., Trigg co., Ky. Watered by Little river.

CADIZ, p. v., Henry co., Ind., 45 ms. E. N. E. of Indianapolis ; from W. 455 ms.

CADIZ, p. o., Greene co., Wis.

CADRON, t., Conway co., Ark.

CADWALLADER, p. o., Perry township, Tuscarawas co., O., 95 ms. E. by N. of Columbus ; from W. 308 ms.

CADDYVILLE, p. v., Plattsburgh township, Clinton co., N. Y., 173 N. of Albany ; from W. 548 ms. Watered by Saranac river. Pop. ——.

CÆSAR'S CREEK, t., Greene co., O. Watered by Cæsar's creek. Pop, 1,870.

CAERNARROON, t., Lancaster co., Pa. Pop. 1,551.

CAERNARROON, t., Berks co., Pa. Pop. 977.

CAGEVILLE, p. o., Haywood co., Tenn.

CAHABA, c. h., p. v., seat of justice of Dallas co., Ala., 92 ms. s. s. E. of Tuscaloosa ; from W. 853 ms. Watered by Alabama and Cahaba rivers.

CAHOKIA, p. v., St. Clair co., Ill., 98 ms. s. by w. of Springfield ; from W. 811 ms. Watered by Mississippi river.

CAIN, t., Fountain co., Ind. Pop. 1,008.

CAIN's, p. o., Lancaster co., Pa. Pop. 1,135.

CAIN's. p. o., Gwinnett co., Ga. 100 ms. N. N. w. of Milledgeville ; from W. 639 ms.

CAINSVILLE. p. o., Wilson co., Tenn., 31 ms. E. by N. of Nashville ; from W. 650 ms.

CA IRA, p. v., Cumberland co., Va., 57 ms. w. by s. of Richmond ; from W. 147 ms. Watered by Willis river.

CAIRO, p. t., Greene co., N. Y,, 44 ms. s. s. w. of Albany ; from W. 346 ms. Watered by Catskill creek. Pop. 2,831.

CAIRO, p. o., Edgefield district, S. C., 115 E. s. E. of Columbia ; from W. 563 ms.

CAIRO, p. v., Henderson co., Ky., 209 ms. w. by s. of Frankfort ; from W. 736 ms.

CAIRO, p. v., Decatur co., Ga., 209 s. s. w. of Milledgeville ; from W. 866 ms. Watered by Little river.

CAIRO, p. o., Stark co., O.

CAIRO, p. o., Sumner co., Tenn., 31 ms. N. N. E. of Nashville ; from W. 662 ms. Watered by Cumberland river.

CAIRO, p. v., Alexander co., Ill., 233 ms. s. by E. of Springfield ; from W. 867 ms. Watered by Mississippi and Ohio rivers.

CALABEE, p. o.. Macon co., Ala.

CALAIS, p. t., Washington co., Me., 200 ms. E. N. E. of Augusta; from W. 786 ms. Watered by St. Croix or Schoodic river. Pop. 4,749.

CALAIS, p. t., Washington co., Vt., 10 ms. N. E. of Montpelier; from W. 526 ms. Watered by Onion river. Pop. 1,410.

CALAIS, p. o., Monroe co., O.

CALAPOOIA, p. o., Linn co., Oregon.

CALANBRIA, p. o., Rowan co., N. C.

CALCASIEU PARISH, situated on the southwest corner of Louisiana, on the east side of Sabine river, with the Gulf of Mexico on the south. Area, 5,000 square miles. Seat of justice, Lisbon. Pop. in 1840, 2,057; in 1850, 3,914.

CALAVERAS COUNTY, California. Area, — square miles. Seat of justice, ——. Pop. in 1850, 16,884.

CALCUTTA, p. v.. St. Clair township, Columbiana co., O., 163 ms. N. E. of Columbus; from W. 270 ms. Pop. 147.

CALDWELL COUNTY, situated in the southwest part of Kentucky, on the easterly side of Tennessee river, and traversed by the Cumberland. Area, 600 square miles. Face of the country generally level; soil fertile. Seat of justice, Princeton. Pop. in 1820, 9,022; in 1830, 5,332; in 1840, 10,365; in 1850, 13,048.

CALDWELL COUNTY, situated toward the northeast part of North Carolina, on the north side of Catawba river. Area, — square miles. Seat of justice, Lenoir. Pop. in 1850, 6,317.

CALDWELL COUNTY, situated toward the northwest part of Missouri. Area, — square miles. Seat of justice, Kingston. Pop. in 1840, 1,458; in 1850, 2,316.

CALDWELL COUNTY, Texas. Area, — square miles. Seat of justice. Lockhart. Pop. in 1850, 1,329.

CALDWELL PARISH, situated toward the north part of Louisiana, and traversed by Wachita river. Area, — square miles. Seat of justice, Columbia. Pop. in 1840, 2,017; in 1850, 2,815.

CALDWELL, c. h , p. t., seat of justice of Warren co.. N. Y., 63 ms. N. of Albany; from W. 436 ms. Situated on Lake George. Pop. 752.

CALDWELL, p. t., Essex co., N. J., 60 ms. N. N. E. of Trenton; from W. 230 ms. Watered by Deep and Green brooks. Pop. 2,376.

CALDWELL, p. o., Greenville district, S. C., 124 ms. N. w. of Columbia; from W. 486 ms.

CALDWELL, p o., Orange co., N. C.

CALDWELL. p. o. Burleson co., Tex.

CALDWELL, p. o., Pulaski co., Ark., 24 ms. from Little Rock; from W. 1,089 ms

CALDWELLS. p. v., Wachita parish, La., 288 ms N. w. of New Orleans; from W. 1,197 ms. Watered by Wachita river.

CALDWELL'S PRAIRIE, p. o.. Racine co., Wis.

CALEDONIA COUNTY. situated toward the northeast part of Vermont, on the westerly side of Connecticut river. and traversed by Passumpsic river. Area, 700 square miles. Face of the county mountainous and hilly; soil generally productive. Seat of justice, Danville. Pop.. in 1820, 16,670; in 1830, 20,967; in 1840, 21,891; in 1850, 23,086.

CALEDONIA, p. t., Livingston co., N. Y., 229 ms. w. of Albany; from W. 363 ms. Watered by Genesee river. Pop. 1,804.

CALEDONIA, p. o., Elk co., Pa., 138 ms. N. w. of Harrisburgh; from W. 230 ms.

CALEDONIA, p. v., Moore co., N. C., 85 ms. s. w. of Raleigh; from W. 359 ms.

CALEDONIA, p. v., Claridon township, Marion co., O., 52 ms. N. of Columbus; from W. 408 ms. Watered by Olentagy, or Whetstone river.

CALEDONIA, p. v.. Lowndes co., Miss., 157 ms. N. E. of Jackson; from W. 888 ms.

CALEDONIA, p. v., Henry co.. Tenn., 124 ms. w. by N. of Nashville; from W. 814 ms.

CALEDONIA, p. v.. Pulaski co., Ill,. 229 ms. s. of Springfield; from W. 846 ms. Watered by Ohio river.

CALEDONIA, p. v., Washington co., Mo., 117 ms. s. E. of Jefferson city; from W. 891 ms. Watered by Big river.

CALEDONIA, p. o., Kent co., Mich.

CALEDONIA, t., Shiawassee co., Mich. Pop. 500.

CALEDONIA, p. o., Rusk co., Texas.

CALHOUN COUNTY. situated in the southern part of Michigan, and drained by Kalamazoo and St. Joseph's rivers. Area, 720 square miles. Seat of justice, Marshall. Pop., in 1834, 3,280; in 1840, 10,599; in 1850, 19,162.

CALHOUN COUNTY, situated on the westerly boundary of Illinois, between Illinois and Mississippi rivers. Area, 240 square miles, containing a rich table land 37 miles long, and from 3 to 10 miles wide. Seat of justice, Gilead. Pop., in 1830, 1,092; in 1840, 1,741 · in 1850, 3,231.

CALHOUN COUNTY, situated on the southwesterly boundary of Florida, between Apalachicola river and the gulf of Mexico. Area, 1,100 square miles. Seat of justice, St. Joseph. Pop., 1840, 1,142; in 1850, 1,377.

CALHOUN, p. o., Autauga co., Ala.

CALHOUN, p. v., Anderson district, S. C., 115 ms. w. N. w. of Columbia; from W. 525 ms.

CALHOUN, p. v.. Lumpkin co., Ga., 130 ms. N. N. w. of Milledgeville; from W. 639 ms.

CALHOUN, p. o., Daviess co., Ky.

CALHOUN, p. v., McMinn co., Tenn., 168 ms. s. w. of Knoxville; from W. 569 ms. Watered by Hiawassee river.

CALHOUN. p. v., Henry co., Mo., 117 ms. w. by s. of Jefferson City; from W. 1,053 ms.

CALHOUN, p. o., Lafayette co., Ark.

CALHOUN'S MILLS, p. o., Abbeville district. S. C., 94 ms. w. by N. of Columbia; from W. 541 ms.

CALICO ROCK, p. o., Izard co., Ark.

CALIFORNIA, one of the United States, lies between 42° and 32° 40′ N. latitude, and 120° and 124° 30′ longitude w. from Greenwich; and is bounded N. by Oregon. E. by Utah and New Mexico, from which it is separated in part by Rio Colorado, s. by Sonora and Lower California, in Mexico, and w. by the Pacific. Its superficial area is 190,000 square miles.

Physical Aspect.—The general features of this state are mountainous and hilly, with the exception of the great valley of the Sacramento and San Joaquin, which covers an area of 500 miles in length, and 50 or 60 miles in width. Here the surface is level, and the soil fertile along the borders of the streams; but further back it is either arid and unproductive, or consists of extensive, low, alluvial marshes (*tulares*), thickly covered with rushes, which are traversed by numerous navigable creeks, or streams. This valley is bounded on the east by the Sierra Nevada, the most prominent range in the state, which run nearly parallel with the coast, at a distance of 100 to 200 miles. On the west of this valley lies another range of lesser mountains called the Coast range, some of them rising to the height of 3,000 feet, which also run parallel with the coast, at a distance of 30 to 60 miles. Among these hills are numerous valleys, some of which are highly fertile, and are surrounded by scenery of great beauty and picturesque effect. The soil which appears to be best adapted to the purposes of tillage, is that embraced within the above-named valleys, and those adjacent to Eel river, Humboldt harbor, and San Francisco bay.

Mountains.—The most prominent range of mountains in this state is the Sierra Nevada, along the western slope of which lie the far-famed gold regions, extending over an area 400 or 500 miles in length, and 30 to 60 in breadth. This slope is intersected by numerous gorges, or ravines, which afford egress to the tributaries of the Sacramento and San Joaquin, and presents to the landscape an aspect extremely picturesque, ragged, and rough. In the coast range the most prominent are Carnero, Diablo, and Santa Cruz mountains.

Rivers, Bays, Harbors, and Lakes.—The principal streams are, the Sacramento, San Joaquin, Klamath, Trinity, Feather, Yuba, Eel, Nappa, Calaveras, Salinas, Guadalupe, Tuolumne, Moquelumne, Pajaro, Merced, Mariposa. Stanislaus, Fall, and American rivers. The bays worthy of note are, San Francisco, San Pablo, and the Suisun, all entered through the Golden-Gate, which together form a harbor sufficient for the collected fleets of the whole world. They afford good anchorage, and are completely land-locked, and consequently are safe at all seasons. Humboldt and St. Diego harbors, and Trinidad bay, are well protected from the ocean winds, and afford a safe anchorage. The harbor of Monterey

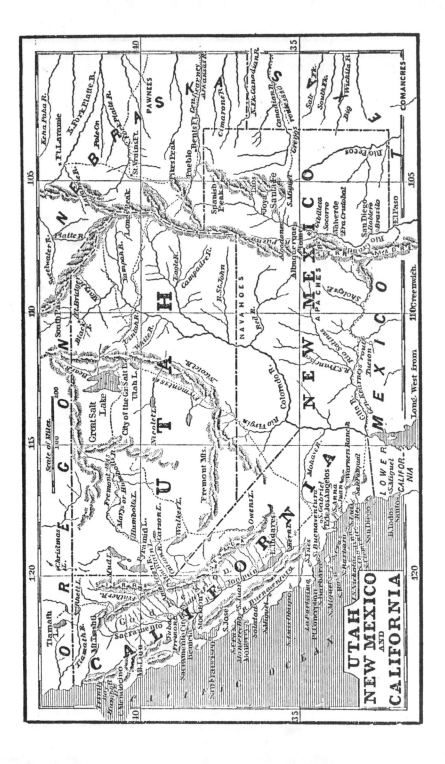

UTAH
NEW MEXICO
AND
CALIFORNIA

is good, but is subject to the swell of the Pacific at all times. This country has some lakes, the most noted of which are, the Tulares, Owen's, Clear, and Rhett.

Climate.—The climate of California, with the exception of that in the valley of Sacramento, and San Joaquin, from June to October, may be regarded as salubrious. The dry season, in which little or no rain falls, lasts generally from April to November. The rainy months occur from November to May, during which period it is estimated that nearly one third of the days are stormy. In the region near the coast, snow rarely falls to remain in the valleys, but occasionally caps the mountains and larger hills; but further inland it is more frequent, and the Sierra Nevada is often capped with snow till snow falls again. The annual inundations of the valley of Sacramento and San Joaquin occur in the winter and spring, and the streams are frequently at great height in April and May, in consequence of the melting of the mountain snows. The temperature of the coast, particularly in the northwestern part of the state, is mild during the year; but the climate of the coast at the south is much warmer, and in summer it often is exceedingly hot. A few miles from the coast the breezes from the ocean become tempered to mildness, and the climate is pleasant and healthy. Still further inland, beyond the reach of the ocean breeze, particularly in the great valley, the summer temperature is often intensely hot. The nights, however, are usually cool. The winter temperature in the valley of Sacramento and San Joaquin, and on the coast, is usually remarkably mild. ice seldom forming over an eighth of an inch thick, and the morning frosts commonly disappear under the midday sun.

Productive Resources.—Although California is not generally adapted to the purposes of profitable agriculture, yet there is land enough of the finest quality to supply a large population with their ordinary vegetable wants. The valleys are exceedingly fertile, and will produce all of our common grain crops, without irrigation, with the exception of Indian corn. Most of the ordinary vegetables require irrigation, and when properly cultivated, their yield and size are truly enormous. The lands, however, in the vicinity of Humboldt harbor, are represented to be highly fertile, and in consequence of occasional showers, which occur in the course of the dry season, they need no artificial watering to produce the finest crops. The rich alluvial soil of the Tulares, it reclaimed by dikes, so as to afford the requisite inundation, doubtless would prove well adapted to the cultivation of rice. The vine flourishes in different parts of the state, and wine has long been made at Los Angelos, and in other places. Many of the recent settlers have commenced the cultivation of our northern fruits. In the southern counties the orange, castor-bean, and some other tropical productions, are cultivated with success. This country seems by nature to be peculiarly well adapted for grazing. The valleys, in spring and summer, are covered with luxuriant vegetation, consisting of various wild grasses, and the hills generally afford excellent pasturage during a large portion of the year, but less so than valleys, in consequence of droughts. The cattle of the country are generally owned by the native Californians, who often have herds of many thousands. These, though quite small, afford excellent flesh, and were formerly slaughtered in immense numbers for their tallow and hides, being the chief source of wealth of the inhabitants. This state is not well timbered, except on the mountains. On the range along the coast are extensive forests of cedar, which grow to an immense size, and furnishes a durable material for building. Toward the north and east, at the base of the Sierra Nevada, are immense forests of gigantic pines, cedars, firs, and other valuable timber trees, some of which are said to exceed 15 feet in diameter, and 200 feet in height. Omitting the lead, copper, and silver mines, which have been discovered, but not worked, in California, its gold, and cinnabar, or quicksilver mines, may be said to constitute its principal resources. The latter, though not much worked as yet, are regarded by many as the most valuable mining property in the state. That at New Almaden, a few miles south of San José, is one of the richest veins in the world, yielding from 40 to 75 per cent. of pure quicksilver. It is the opinion of good judges that, if properly worked, this mine would yield full $1,000,000 per annum. Although the existence of gold in this country had long been known, it never attracted general attention before 1848, when it was discovered near Sutter's Mill, on the south fork

of American river. Since that time it has been found on all of the principal eastern branches of the Sacramento and San Joaquin, as well as among the coast range on the tributaries of the Trinity and Klamath, in the northern part of the state. In the spring of 1850 a new impulse was given to the enterprise, from the discovery of numerous veins of auriferous quartz in Mariposa county, since which others, richly impregnated with the precious metal, have been successfully worked in various parts of the golden belt. The discovery of quartz veins in Mariposa, led to a more careful examination of other parts of the state, when gold-bearing quartz was found in almost every county along the foot hills of the Sierra Nevada, as far north as the northern branches of the Feather river; and the county of Nevada has probably more quartz mills now in operation than all the state besides; while El Dorado county has produced the richest quartz yet discovered, with perhaps the exception of the Carson creek vein. The product of the gold mines in 1852 is estimated at $70,000,000. The gold is found under two general forms—interspersed in irregular veins of quartz in the mountain rocks, and in lumps and scales, of all sizes down to "golden pebbles," metallic gravel, and sand, mingled with the alluvion, or drift, which occurs in the bottoms of valleys and ravines, and in the beds of the streams. In general, the loose gold, or *placers*, is found at no great distance from the parent veins, from which it has been disintegrated, and washed down the slopes by mountain torrents or rills. The scale or lump gold is found in the greatest abundance in the bottoms of the "gulches," or ravines, and in the banks and beds of the streams, particularly in the bars of sand and gravel, formed by the eddies, or counter currents. Most of the gold hitherto dug has been taken from such localities, the river banks and beds yielding the most abundantly at the lowest stage of the water, which usually occurs during the first two months of fall. Sometimes the courses of the streams are diverted into new channels, by the erection of dams, in order to obtain the gold deposited in their beds. This is termed " wet digging," and can best be performed during summer and fall. The "gulches," or ravines, are usually free from water in the dry season, and hence the operations carried on in them, during spring and summer, are called "dry-diggings," which may be divided into three classes: 1st, the sand or earth in which the gold exists is collected in the dry ravines, or plains, and conveyed to some lake or stream, for washing; 2d, where lumps and scales are obtained, by means of shovels, picks, &c., from the sides of mountains, distant from water; 3d, the old Spanish method, by winnowing, from a large wooden bowl, the fine earthy particles, after the ore has been dried and pulverized, leaving the gold in the bottom. The modes of washing, or separating the gold from the earth, are various. The simplest method is the use of the wooden bowl. Some employ small wooden cradles, three or four feet long, with cleats, or rockers, on the bottom, and a riddle at one end; others are made of sheet iron, with rounded bottoms and wooden rockers. Some use the "Long Tom," a structure eight or ten feet long, while others use the "Virginia rocker," amalgamating the gold with quicksilver. A great variety of other apparatus and expensive machines have been invented for separating the gold, some of which answer an admirable purpose: but the "Burke" and the "Long Tom" are the general favorites, wherever an abundance of water is at command. In cases, however, where the gold occurs in fine particles, blended with black sand or alluvion, it can not be separated to advantage without the use of Mercury.

Railroads.—California has no railroad in operation as yet, though one has been projected from San José, the recent capital, to San Francisco.

Commerce.—San Francisco is the principal commercial port of California. Its commercial resources are at present based upon its metallic wealth. Gold supplies the medium of domestic exchange, and of foreign commerce. San Francisco, therefore, is a mart for the competing trade of the whole world. The number of arrivals and departures of vessels at this port are more numerous than those at any other port in the United States, New York alone excepted. There are now about twenty ocean-steamers traversing the Pacific and connecting with ports on the Atlantic, about sixty engaged in the river trade, and some four hundred other craft of various kinds navigating the rivers and bay. It has also considerable direct trade with the

South American states, China, and the East Indies.

Education.—The constitution of California makes the following provision for the support of common schools throughout the state : " The legislature shall encourage, by all suitable means, the promotion of intellectual, scientific, moral, and agricultural improvement. The proceeds of all land that may be granted by the United States to this state for the support of schools, which may be sold or disposed of, and the 500,000 acres of land granted to the new states, under an act of Congress distributing the proceeds of the public lands among the several states of the Union, approved A. D. 1841 ; and all estates of deceased persons who may have died without leaving a will, or heir, and also such per cent. as may be granted by Congress on the sale of lands in this state, shall be and remain a perpetual fund, the interest of which, together with all the rents of the unsold lands, and such other means as the legislature may provide, shall be inviolably appropriated to the support of common schools throughout the state. The legislature shall provide for a system of common schools, by which a school shall be kept up and supported in each district at least three months in every year." The legislature is also required to provide for the election of a superintendent of public instruction ; and to take measures for the improvement and permanent security of any funds arising from the sale of lands, or from any other source, for the endowment and support of a university.

Population.—The population of Upper California, in 1802, was estimated at 17,000 ; in 1831, 23,025 ; and in the state of California, in 1851, estimated at 165,000.

Government.—The legislative power is vested in a senate and assembly. Senators not less in number than one third, nor more than one half the number of members of assembly, are elected by the people in districts, for a term of two years, so classified that one half may be chosen annually at the general election, on the Tuesday after the first Monday in November. Members of the assembly are elected by the people annually in districts. There shall never be more than eighty, nor less than thirty. The executive power is vested in a governor and lieutenant-governor, elected by the people for a term of two years. They must be over twenty-five years of age, citizens of the United States, and residents of the state two years next before the election. A secretary of state is appointed by the governor. A comptroller, treasurer, attorney, and surveyor-general, are to be elected by the people at the same time, and for the same term, as the governor. In elections by the legislature, the members vote *viva voce*—by the people by ballot. The judicial power is vested in a supreme, district, and county courts, the judges of all of which are elected by the people. Every white male citizen of the United States, and every citizen of Mexico under the treaty of Queretaro, twenty-one years of age, resident in the state six months, and of the district where he offers to vote thirty days preceding the election, is entitled to vote.

History.—California was first settled by the Spaniards, in 1602, but prior to the year 1697, the colonists were all expelled by the ill-used natives, when Charles II., of Spain, granted the country to the Jesuits, with the view of converting the Indians to Christianity. Under their guidance, and the protection afforded by military posts in the vicinity of their missions, by the end of the last century, numerous flourishing towns had sprung up, around which gathered thousands of the natives, by whose labor in rearing herds, and cultivating the most fertile parts of the soil, the wealth and prosperity of the Jesuits became immensely great. In 1824, California constituted one of the provinces of the new republic of Mexico, by whose acts the missions were virtually broken up, the reclaimed Indians dispersed, many of them joining the wild mountain tribes, and in the course of time, from the superior knowledge and bad habits they had acquired from the whites, they became notorious for their thievish and marauding character. In this state the country remained until 1846, when it was subjugated by the United States under the joint efforts of Stockton, Kearney, and Fremont. In 1848, it was ceded to our government by Mexico. In September of the year following its constitution was formed, by a convention of delegates at Monterey, and ratified by the people in November following ; and in 1850 it was admitted into the Union as an independent state. The following is an explanation of the design on the state

seal :—Around the bevel of the ring are represented thirty-one stars, being the number of the states of the Union, on the admission of California. The foreground figure represents the goddess Minerva, having sprung full-grown from the brain of Jupiter. She is introduced as a type of the political birth of California, without having gone through the probation of a territory. At her feet crouches a grisly bear, feeding upon clusters from a grape-vine, which, with a sheaf of wheat, are emblematic of the peculiar characteristics of the country. A miner is engaged at work, with a rocker and bowl at his side ; illustrating the golden wealth of the Sacramento, upon whose waters are seen shipping, typical of commercial greatness ; and the snow-clad peaks of the Sierra Nevada make up the background. Above is the Greek motto, *Eureka* (I have found it), applying either to the principle involved in the admission of the state or to the success of the miners at work.

CALIFORNIA, p. o., Moniteau co., Mo., 25 ms. s. w. of Jefferson City ; from W. 961 ms.

CALIFORNIA, p. o., Branch co., Mich.

CALIFORNIA, p. o., Yallobusha co., Miss.

CALIFORNIA, p o., Clermont co., O.

CALIFORNIA, p. o., Floyd co., Ga.

CALLAND'S, p. o., Pittsylvania co., Va., 174 ms. w. s. w. of Richmond ; from W. 257 ms.

CALLAWAY COUNTY, situated on the southerly boundary of Kentucky, on the westerly side of Tennessee river. Area, 600 square miles. Seat of justice, Wadesborough. Pop. in 1840, 9,794 ; in 1850, 8,096.

CALLAWAY COUNTY, situated in the central part of Missouri, on the northerly side of Missouri river. Area, 760 square miles. Seat of justice, Fulton. Pop in 1840, 11,765 ; in 1850, 13,827.

CALLAWAY'S MILLS, p. o., Franklin co., Va., 182 ms. w. s. w. of Richmond ; from W. 257 ms.

CALLENSBURGH, p. v., Toby township, Clarion co., Pa., 190 ms. w. n. w. of Harrisburgh ; from W. 276 ms.

CALLENSVILLE, p. o., Pendleton co., Ky.

CALLICOON, p. o., Sullivan co., N. Y.

CALLICOON DEPOT, p. o., Sullivan co., N. Y.

CALN, p. o., Chester co., Pa.

CALNO, p. o., Warren co., N. J.

CALUMET COUNTY, situated in the easterly part of Wisconsin, on the east side of Lake Winnebago. Area, 300 square miles. Seat of justice, Pequot. Pop. in 1840, 275 ; in 1850, 1,743.

CALUMET VILLAGE, p. v., Calumet co., Wis., 110 ms. n. e. of Madison ; from W. 957 ms. Situated on Lake Winnebago.

CALUMET, t., Pike co., Mo.

CALVARY, t., Franklin co., Mo.

CALVARY, p. o., Athens co., O., 82 ms. s. e. of Columbus ; from W. 348 ms.

CALVERT COUNTY, situated in the south part of Maryland, between Patuxent river and Chesapeake bay. Area, 264 square miles. Seat of justice, Prince Frederick. Pop. in 1840, 9,229 ; in 1850, 9,646.

CALVIN, p. o., Huntingdon co., Pa.

CALVIN, t., Cass co., Mich. Pop. 624.

CAMAK, p. o., Warren co., Ga., 48 ms. n. e. of Milledgeville ; from W. 662 ms.

CAMANCHE, c. h., p. v., seat of justice of Clinton co., Iowa, 60 ms. e. of Iowa city ; from W. 912 ms. Watered by the Mississippi river. Pop. 454.

CAMARGO, p. o., Lancaster co., Pa.

CAMARGO, p. o., Lincoln co., Tenn.

CAMARGO, p. o., Monroe co., Miss.

CAMARGO, p. o., Jefferson co., Ind.

CAMARGO, p. o., Montgomery co., Ky.

CAMBRA, p. o., Luzerne co., Pa., 104 ms. n. n. e. of Harrisburgh ; from W. 215 ms.

CAMBRIA COUNTY, situated in the central part of Pennsylvania, and drained by Connemaugh river. Area, 720 square miles. Face of the country hilly and rocky , soil generally of fair quality. Seat of justice, Ebensburgh. Pop. in 1820, 3,287 ; in 1830, 7,079 ; in 1840, 11,250 ; in 1850, 17,773.

CAMBRIA, p. o., Wayne co., Iowa.

CAMBRIA, p. t., Niagara co., N. Y., 283 ms. w. by n. of Albany ; from W. 406 ms. Pop. 2,366.

CAMBRIA, t., Cambria co., Pa. Watered by Black Lick creek and Little Connemaugh river. Pop. 1,400.

CAMBRIA, p. o., Hillsdale co., Mich.

CAMBRIDGE, p. t., Somerset co., Me., 63 ms. n. of Augusta ; from W. 658 ms. Pop. 487.

CAMBRIDGE, p. t., Lamoille co., Vt., 48 ms. N. W. of Montpelier. Watered by Lamoille river. Pop. 1,849.

CAMBRIDGE, city, seat of justice, together with Concord and Lowell, of Middlesex co., Mass., 3 ms. N. W. of Boston; from W. 537 m. Watered by Charles river. In the old part of the city, stands Harvard university. the most ancient and wealthy collegiate institution in America. This includes a theological, medical, and law school, and has a library of about 100,000 volumes, the largest in the Union. Merchants and others doing business in Boston, reside in this city, and some of the dwellings are costly and splendid. At Cambridge, were the entrenchments of the American army when besieging Boston under Washington. Glass and other manufactures are extensively produced. From its proximity to Boston, the railroads and other lines of travel are common to both places. One mile west of the college is Mount Auburn cemetery, consecrated by nature and by art to the holy purpose to which it is devoted. The population in 1810, was 2,323; in 1820, ——; in 1830, 6,071; in 1840, 8,409; in 1850, 17,417.

CAMBRIDGE, p. t., Washington co., N. Y., 34 ms. N. by E. of Albany; from W. 404 ms. Watered by Hoosick river. Pop. 2,593.

CAMBRIDGE, p. o., Lancaster co., Pa.

CAMBRIDGE, t., Coos co., N. H. Watered by Androscoggin river.

CAMBRIDGE, c. h., p. v. Seat of justice of Dorchester co., Md., 61 ms. S. E. of Annapolis; from W. 101 ms. Watered by Choptank river.

CAMBRIDGE, p. o., Henry co., Ill.

CAMBRIDGE, p. t., Lenawee co., Mich., 66 ms. s. W. of Detroit; from W. 526 ms. Pop. 973.

CAMBRIDGE, p. o., Dane co., Wis.

CAMBRIDGE, c. h., p. t. Seat of justice of Guernsey co., O., 77 ms. E. of Columbus; from W. 316 ms. Watered by Wills creek. Pop. 2,488.

CAMBRIDGE, p. o., Saline co., Mo.

CAMBRIDGE, p. v.. Abbeville district, S. C., 79 ms. W. by N. of Columbia; from W. 525 ms.

CAMBRIDGE, p. v., Wayne co.. Ind., 52 ms. E. of Indianapolis; from W. 519 ms. Watered by the west branch of White Water river.

CAMBRIDGE, p. v., Dallas co., Ala., 84 ms. s. by E. of Tuscaloosa; from W. 867 ms.

CAMBRIDGEPORT, p. o., Windham co., Vt.. 101 ms. s. of Montpelier; from W. 448 ms.

CAMBRIDGEPORT, p. o., Cambridge city, Middlesex co., Mass., 3 ms. W. of Boston; from W. 438 ms.

CAMDEN COUNTY, situated on the westerly boundary of New Jersey, on the northeasterly side of Delaware river. Area, —— square miles. Face of the country level; soil of fair quality. Seat of justice, Camden. Pop. in 1850, 25,422.

CAMDEN COUNTY, situated in the northeast part of North Carolina, on the northeast side of Pasquotauk river. Area, 228 square miles. Face of the country level; soil thin and generally sterile. Seat of justice, Jonesburgh. Pop. in 1820, 6,305; in 1830, 6,721; in 1840, 5.663; in 1850, 6,049.

CAMDEN COUNTY, situated at the southeast part of Georgia, on the northerly side of St. Mary's river, and separated from the ocean by Cumberland island. Area, 700 square miles. Face of the country flat; soil sandy, and in some places marshy. Seat of justice, Jeffersonton. Pop. in 1820, 3,402; in 1830, 4,578; in 1840, 6,075; in 1850, 6,319.

CAMDEN COUNTY, situated in the central part of Missouri, on the south side of Osage river. Area, —— square miles. Seat of justice, Erie. Pop. in 1850, 2,338.

CAMDEN, p. t., Waldo co., Me., 42 ms. E. s. E. of Augusta; from W. 632 ms. Situated on Penobscot bay. Pop. 4,005.

CAMDEN, p. t., Oneida co.. N. Y., 128 ms. N. W. of Albany; from W. 397 ms. Watered by Fish creek. Pop. 2,820.

CAMDEN CITY, seat of justice of Camden co., N. J., 29 ms. s. s. W. of Trenton; from W. 139 ms. Watered by Delaware river. Pop. 9,479.

CAMDEN, p. v., Kent co., Del., 3 ms. s. of Dover; from W. 121 ms. Watered by Jones' creek.

CAMDEN, p. v., Somers township, Preble co.. O., 102 ms. w. s. W. of Columbus; from W. 495 ms. Watered by Seven-mile creek.

CAMDEN, p. t.. Hillsdale co., Mich., 120 ms. s. E. of Detroit; from W. 537 ms. Pop. 594.

CAMDEN, p. v., Shelby co., Ky., 31 ms. w. of Frankfort; from W. 573 ms.

CAMDEN, c. h., p, v., seat of justice of Benton co., Tenn., 79 ms. w. of Nashville; from W. 763 ms. Pop. 175.

CAMDEN, p. v., Carroll co., Ind., 74 ms. N. of Indianapolis; from W. 632 ms. Watered by Passianong creek. Pop. 168.

CAMDEN, p. v., Madison co.. Miss., 39 ms. N. by E. of Jackson; from W. 1,007 ms.

CAMDEN. c. h., p. v., seat of justice of Kirshaw district, S. C., 33 ms. N. E. of Columbia; from W. 473 ms. Watered by Wateree river.

CAMDEN, p. o., Wilcox co., Ala.

CAMDEN, p. o., Camden co., Ga.

CAMDEN, p. v., Schuyler co., Ill., 79 ms. w. N. w. of Springfield; from W. 850 ms. Pop. 420.

CAMDEN, p. v., Ray co., Mo., 149 ms. w. N. w. of Jefferson city; from W. 1,052 ms. Watered by Missouri river.

CAMDEN, c. h., p. v., seat of justice of Camden co., N. C., 219 ms. E. N. E. of Raleigh; from W. 287 ms. Watered by Pasquotank river.

CAMDEN, t., Lorain co., O. Pop. 1,025.

CAMDEN, p. o., Wachita co., Ark.

CAMDEN POINT, p. o., Platte co., Mo.

CAMDEN MILLS, p. o., Rock Island co., Ill.

CAMDENVILLE, p. o., Anderson co., Ky.

CAMERON COUNTY, Tex. Area, —— square miles. Seat of justice, Brownsville.

CAMERON, p. o., Clinton co.. Pa.

CAMERON, p. o., Milan co., Tex.

CAMERON, p. t.. Steuben co., N. Y.. 225 ms. w. s. w. of Albany; from W. 304 ms. Watered by Canisteo river. Pop. 1,701.

CAMERON MILLS, p. o., Steuben co., N. Y.

CAMILLUS, p. t., Onondaga co., N. Y., 130 ms. w. N. w. of Albany; from W. 347 ms. Situated on the Erie canal and Nine mile creek. Pop. 3,016.

CAMPBELL COUNTY, situated in the southern part of Virginia, between James and Roanoke rivers. Area, 576 square miles. Face of the country hilly; soil varied. Seat of justice, Campbell courthouse. Pop. in 1820, 16,570; in 1830, 15,704; in 1840, 21,030; in 1850, 23,245.

CAMPBELL COUNTY, situated in the western part of Georgia, and traversed by Chattahoochee river. Area, 300 square miles. Seat of justice, Campbellton. Pop. in 1830, 3,323; in 1840, 5,370; in 1850, 7,232.

CAMPBELL COUNTY, situated on the north boundary on the northwest side of Clinch river. Area, 672 square miles. Face of the country hilly and mountainous; soil fertile in the valleys and along the streams. Seat of justice, Jacksborough. Pop. in 1820, 4,244; in 1830, 5,110; in 1840, 6,149; in 1850, 6,068.

CAMPBELL COUNTY, situated on the northerly boundary of Kentucky, on the southerly side of Ohio river. Area, 260 square miles. Face of the country hilly; soil fertile. Seat of justice, Newport. Pop. in 1820; 9,022; in 1830, 9,893; in 1840, 5,214; in 1850, 13,127.

CAMPBELL, c. h., p. v., seat of justice of Campbell co., Va., 125 ms. w. s. w. of Richmond; from W. 203 ms.

CAMPBELL, t., Warwick co., Ind. Pop. 1,157.

CAMPBELL, p. o., Coles co., Ill.

CAMPBELL, p. o., Lawrence co., O.

CAMPBELL, p. t., Steuben co., N. Y., 209 ms. w. s. w. of Albany. Watered by Conhocton river. Pop. 1,175.

CAMPBELL CREEK, p. o., Bath township, Steuben co., N. Y., 224 ms. w. by s. of Albany; from W. 304 ms.

CAMPBELL'S BRIDGE, p. o., Marion district, S. C., 139 ms. E. by N. of Columbia; from W. 441 ms.

CAMPBELLSBURGH, p. v., Henry co., Ky., 31 ms. N. w. of Frankfort; from W. 573 ms.

CAMPBELL'S CORNERS, p. o., Oakland co., Mich.

CAMPBELL'S MILLS, p. o., Windham co., Ct.

CAMPBELL'S PORT, p. o., Portage co., O.

CAMPBELL'S STATION, p. o., Knox co., Tenn., 168 ms. E. of Nashville; from W. 513 ms.

CAMPBELL'S STORE, p. o., Pendleton co., Va.

CAMPBELL'S REST, p. o., Sullivan co., Tenn.

CAMPBELLSVILLE, p. v., Giles co., Tenn., 67 ms. s. by w. of Nashville; from W. 731 ms.

CAMPBELLSVILLE, p. v., Greene co., Ky., 77 ms. s. s. w. of Frankfort; from W. 599 ms.

CAMPBELLTON, c. h., p. v., seat of justice of Campbell co., Ga., 102 ms. N. w. of Milledgeville; from W. 699 ms. Watered by Chattahoochee river.

CAMPBELLTON, p. o., Jackson co., Flor.

CAMPBELLTON, p. o., Itawamba co., Miss.

CAMPBELLTOWN, p. o., Campbell township, Steuben co., N. Y., 223 ms. w. by s. of Albany; from W. 288 ms.

CAMPBELLTOWN, p. v., Lebanon co., Pa., 15 ms. E. of Harrisburgh; from W. 125 ms.

CAMPBELLVILLE, p. o., Sullivan co., Pa.

CAMPBELLVILLE, p. o., Dutchess co., N. Y.

CAMP BRANCH, t., Warren co., Mo.

CAMP CALL, p. o., Cleveland co., N. C.

CAMP CHARLOTTE, p. o., Pickaway co., O.

CAMP CREEK, p. o., Livingston co., Ky., 240 ms. w. s. w. of Frankfort; from W. 767 ms.

CAMP CREEK, p. o., Greene co., Tenn.. 264 ms. E. of Nashville; from W. 440 ms.

CAMP CREEK, t., Pike co., O.

CAMP CREEK, p. o., Kosciusko co., Ind.

CAMP CREEK, p. o., Hancock co., Ill. 113 ms. N. w. of Springfield; from W. 874 ms.

CAMP CREEK, p. o., Jefferson co., Ark.

CAMPELLO, p. o., Plymouth co., Mass.

CAMP GROUND, p. o., Pickens district, S. C.

CAMP GROUND, p. o, Appling co., Ga.

CAMP HILL, p. o., Tallapoosa co., Ala.

CAMP IZARD, p. o., Marion co., Flor.

CAMPOBELLA. p. o., Spartanburgh district, S. C.

CAMP POINT, p. o., Adams co., Ill.

CAMP RIDGE, p. o., Williamsburgh district, S. C., 114 ms. s. E. of Columbia; from W. 492 ms.

CAMP SPRING, p. o., Lawrence co., Ala., 93 ms. N. by E. of Tuscaloosa; from W. 778 ms.

CAMPTI, p. o., Natchitotches parish, La.

CAMPTON, p. t., Grafton co., N. H., 47 ms. N. by w. of Concord; from.W. 528 ms. Watered by Pemigewasset river. Pop. 1,439.

CAMPTON, p. o., Kane co., Ill.

CAMPTON VILLAGE, p. o., Grafton co., N. H.

CAMPTOWN, p. v., Orange township. Essex co., N. J., 52 ms. N. E. of Trenton; from W. 218 ms. Watered by Elizabeth river.

CAMPTOWN, p. o., Bradford co., Pa.

CAMPVILLE, p. o., Owego township, Tioga co., N. Y., 154 ms. s. w. of Albany; from W. 282 ms.

CAMPVILLE, p. o., Litchfield co., Ct.

CAMPVILLE, p. o., Coles co., Ill., 103 ms. E. s. E. of Springfield; from W. 695 ms.

CANA, p. o., Jennings co., Ind.

CANAAN, p. t., Somerset co., Me., 36 ms. N. by E. of Augusta; from W. 631 ms. Watered by Kennebec river. Pop. 1,696.

CANAAN, p. t., Grafton co., N. H., 41 ms. N. w. of Concord; from W. 496 ms. Watered by Masconry river. Pop. 1,682.

CANAAN, p. t.. Essex co., Vt., 106 ms. N. E. of Montpelier; from W. 603 ms. Watered by Connecticut river. Pop. 471.

CANAAN, p. t., Litchfield co., Ct., 42 ms. N. w. of Hartford; from W. 343 ms. Watered by Housatonic river. Pop. 2,627.

CANAAN, p. t. Columbia co., N. Y., 24 ms. s. E. of Albany; from W. 362 ms. Watered by Kinderhook creek. Pop. 1,941.

CANAAN, p. t., Wayne co., Pa., 159 ms. N. E. of Harrisburgh; from W. 253 ms. Watered by Lackawaxen creek. Pop. 1,938.

CANAAN, p. t., Wayne co., O., 107 ms. N. E. of Columbus; from W. 350 ms. Pop. 1,923.

CANAAN, p. v., Jefferson co., Ind., 84 ms. s. s. E. of Indianapolis; from W. 560 ms.

CANAAN, t., Hillsdale co., Mich. Pop. 594.

CANAAN, t., Wayne co., O. Pop. 1,922.

CANAAN, t., Madison co., O. Pop. 565.

CANAAN, t., Marion co., O. Pop. 982.

CANAAN, t., Athens co., O. Watered by Hockhocking river. Pop. 1,142.

CANAAN, p. o., Marion co., Ala.

CANAAN CENTRE, p. v., Canaan township, Columbia co., N. Y., 26 ms. s. E. of Albany; from W. 364 ms.

CANAAN FOUR CORNERS, p. v., Canaan township, Columbia co., N. Y., 25 ms. s. E. of Albany; from W. 363 ms.

CANAANVILLE, p. o., Athens co., O., 80 ms. s. E. of Columbus; from W. 341 ms.

CANADIAN, p. o., Mississippi co., Ark.

CANADICE, p. t., Ontario co., N. Y., 218 ms. w. of Albany; from W. 334 ms. Pop. 1,071.

CANAJOHARIE, p. t., Montgomery co., N. Y., 50 ms. w. N. w. of Albany; from W. 395 ms. Watered by Mohawk river, and Bowman's and Otsquake creek. Pop. 4,097.

CANAL, p. o., Van Buren township, Onondaga co., N. Y., 147 ms. w. N. w. of Albany; from W. 354 ms.

CANAL, p. o., Warwick co., Ind. Watered by Big Pigeon creek.

CANAL, p. t., Venango co., Pa., 218 ms. N. w. of Harrisburgh; from W. 292 ms. Pop. 870.

CANAL DOVER, p. o., Dover township, Tuscarawas co., O., 116 ms. N. E. of Columbus; from W. 316 ms.

CANAL PORT, p. o., Allen co., Ind.

CANAL FULTON, p. v., Lawrence township, Tuscarawas co., O., 125 ms. N. E. of Columbus; from W. 330 ms. Watered by Tuscarawas river.

CANAL LEWISVILLE, p. o., Coshocton co., O.

CANAL WINCHESTER, p. o., Fairfield co., O.

CANANDAIGUA, c. h., p. t., seat of justice of Ontario co., N. Y., 195 ms. w. by N. of Albany; from W. 341 ms. Situated on Canandaigua lake. Pop. 6,143.

CANANDAIGUA, p. v., Lenawee co., Mich., 82 ms. s. w. of Detroit. Watered by Bean creek.

CANASAUGA, p. v., Bradley co., Tenn., 174 ms. s. E. by E. of Nashville; from W. 586 ms.

CANASTOTA, p. v., Lenox township, Madison co., N. Y., 119 ms. w. N. w. of Albany; from W. 364 ms. Situated on the Erie canal.

CANDIA, p. t., Rockingham co., N. H., 118 ms. s. E. of Concord; from W. 470 ms. Pop. 1,482.

CANDLEVILLE, p. o., Coffee co., Ala.

CANDOR, p. t., Tioga co., N. Y., 171 ms. s. w. of Albany; from W. 285 ms. Watered by Cottotong and West Owego creeks. Pop. 3,433.

CANDOR CENTRE, p. o., Tioga co., N. Y.

CANDOR, p. v., Washington co., Pa., 227 ms. w. of Harrisburgh; from W. 254 ms.

CANEADEA, p. t., Alleghany co., N. Y., 271 ms. w. by s. of Albany; from W. 347 ms. Watered by Genesee river. Pop. 1,477.

CANE BOTTOM, p. o., Lauderdale co., Tenn.

CANE CREEK, p. o., Chatham co., N. C., 50 ms. w. of Raleigh; from W. 324 ms.

CANE CREEK, p. o., Lincoln co., Tenn. 75 ms. s. of Nashville; from W. 720 ms.

CANE CREEK, p. o., Butler co., Mo.

CANE CREEK, p. o., White co., Ill., 196 ms. s. E. of Springfield; from W. 766 ms.

CANE CREEK, p. o., Benton co., Ala., 162 ms. N. E. by E. of Tuscaloosa; from W. 740 ms.

CANE CREEK, p. o., Wayne co., Mo., 216 ms. s. E. of Jefferson City; from W. 940 ms.

CANE CREEK, p. o., Franklin co., Ala.

CANE HILL, p t., Washington co., Ark., 192 ms. N. w. of Little Rock; from W. 1,201 ms. Pop. 1,082.

CANE POINT, p. o., Troup co., Ga.

CANE RIDGE, p. o., Claiborne parish La.

CANE SPRING, p. o., Bullitt co., Ky., 62 ms. w. by s. of Frankfort; from W. 606 ms.

CANEY, p. o., Matagorda co., Tex.

CANEY BRANCH, p. o., Greene co., Tenn.

CANEY BRIDGE, p. o., Chicot co., Ark.

CANEY FORK, p. o., Warren co., Tenn.

CANEY SPRING, p. o., Marshall co., Tenn., 42 ms. s. of Nashville; from W. 705 ms.

CANEYVILLE, p. v., Grayson co., Ky., 173 ms. s. w. of Frankfort; from W. 661 ms.

CANFIELD, p. t., Mahoning co., O., 164 ms. N. E. by E. of Columbus; from W. 293 ms. Pop. 1,463.

CANFIELD'S CORNER, p. o., Nichols township, Tioga co., N. Y., 166 ms. s. w. by w. of Albany; from W. 272 ms.

CANICELLO, p. o., Rockbridge co., Va.

CANISTEO, p. t., Steuben co., N. Y., 243 ms. w. s. w. of Albany; from W. 711 ms. Watered by Canisteo river. Pop. 2,030.

CANNADAY GAP, p. o., Floyd co., Va.

CANNELTON, p. o., Perry co., Ind.

CANNON COUNTY, situated in the central part of Tennessee. Area, 100 square miles. Seat of justice, Woodbury. Pop. in 1840, 7,193; in 1850, 8,982.

CANNONSBURGH, p. o., Kent co., Mich.

CANNONSBURGH, p. o., Greenup co., Ky.

CANNONSBURGH, p. o., Hancock co., O.

CANNONSBURGH, p. b., Washington co., Pa., 216 ms. w. of Harrisburgh; from W. 243 ms. Watered by Chartier's creek. Seat of Jefferson college. Pop. 627.

CANNON'S FERRY, p. o., Sussex co., Del. 51 ms. s. of Dover; from W. 115 ms.

CANNON'S MILL, p. o., Columbiana co., O.

CANNON STORE, p. o., Sevier co., Ark.

CANNON'S STORE, p. o., Spartanburgh district, S. C., 121 ms. N. N. w. of Columbia; from W. 479 ms.

CANNONSVILLE, p. o., Tompkins township, Delaware co., N. Y., 111 ms. w. by s. of Albany; from W. 307 ms.

CANOE CREEK, p. o., Burke co., N. C.

CANOGA, p. v., Fayette township, Seneca co., N. Y., 173 ms. w. of Albany; from W. 339 ms.

CANTATOE, p. o., Bedford township, Westchester co., N. Y., 125 ms. s. of Albany; from W. 273 ms.

CANTOCHEE, p. o., Emanuel co., Ga.

CANTERBURY, p. t., Merrimack co., N. H., 8 ms. N. of Concord; from W. 482 ms. Watered by Merrimack river. Pop. 1,614.

CANTERBURY. p. t., Windham co., Ct., 41 ms. E. of Hartford; from W. 368 ms. Watered by Quinnebaug river. Pop. 1,668.

CANTERBURY, p. v., Cornwall township, Orange co., N. Y., 89 ms. s. of Albany; from W. 289 ms.

CANTERBURY, p. v., Kent co., Del., 8 ms. s. by w. of Dover; from W. 116 ms. Watered by Motherkill creek.

CANTON, p. t., Oxford co., Me., 30 ms. w. N. w. of Augusta; from W. 602 ms. Watered by Androscoggin river. Pop. 926.

CANTON, p. t., Norfolk co., Mass., 16 ms. s. by w. of Boston; from W. 426 ms. Watered by Neponset river. Pop. 2,598.

CANTON, p. t., Hartford co., Ct., 13 ms. N. w. by w. of Hartford; from W. 339 ms. Watered by Farmington river. Pop. 1,986.

CANTON, c. h., p. t., seat of justice of St. Lawrence co., N. Y., 223 ms. N. N. w. of Albany; from W. 495 ms. Watered by Grass and Oswegatchie rivers. Pop. 4,685.

CANTON, p. v., Salem co., N. J., 69 ms. s. s. w. of Trenton; from W. 184 ms.

CANTON, p. t., Bradford co., Pa., 136 ms. N. of Harrisburgh; from W. 246 ms. Watered by Towanda creek. Pop. 1,746.

CANTON, t., Washington co., Pa. Watered by Charticr's creek. Pop. 1,281.

CANTON, c. h., p. t., seat of justice of Stark co., O., 124 ms. N. E. of Columbus; from W. 313 ms. Watered by Nimishillon creek. Pop. 4,322.

CANTON, p. v., Washington co., Ind., 97 ms. s. of Indianapolis; from W. 600 ms.

CANTON, p. v., Fulton co., Ill., 69 ms. N. N. w. of Springfield; from W. 819 ms. Pop. 1,568.

CANTON, p. o., Jackson co., Iowa.

CANTON, c. h., p. v., seat of justice of Cherokee co., Ga. Watered by Etowah river.

CANTON, p. v., Wilcox co., Ala., 91 ms. s. by E. of Tuscaloosa; from W. 883 ms.

CANTON, p. v., Trigg co., Ky., 235 ms. s. w. by w. of Frankfort; from W. 762 ms. Watered by Cumberland river.

CANTON, c. h., p. v., seat of justice of Madison co., Miss., 23 ms. N. by E. of Jackson; from W. 998 ms.

CANTON, p. v., Lawrence co., Ark., 164 ms. N. N. E. of Little Rock; from W. 1,021 ms.

CANTON, p. o., Lewis co., Mo.

CANTON, t., Wayne co., Mich. Watered by Rouge river. Pop. 1,333.

CANTON, p. o., Smith co., Tex.

CANTON CENTRE, p. v., Canton township, Hartford co., Ct.

CANTON MILLS, p. o., Oxford co., Me.

CANTRELL'S CROSS ROADS, p. o., McMinn co., Tenn.

CANTWELL's BRIDGE, p. v., New Castle co., Del., 24 ms. N. by w. of Dover; from W. 133 ms. Watered by Appoquinimink creek. Pop. 505.

CAP AU GREY, p. o., Lincoln co., Mo.

CAPE ELIZABETH, t., 6 ms. s. of Portland, Me.

CAPE FARE, p. o., Taney co., Mo.

CAPE GIRARDEAU COUNTY, situated in the southeast part of Missouri, on the westerly side of Mississippi river. Area, 864 square miles. The face of the country is generally level, a part of which is subject to annual inundation. Soil fertile. Seat of justice, Jackson. Pop. in 1820, 5,968; in 1830, 7,430; in 1840, 9,359; in 1850, 13,912.

CAPE GIRARDEAU, p. v., Cape Girardeau co., Mo., 207 ms. s. E. of Jefferson city; from W. 850 ms. Watered by Mississippi river.

CAPE ISLAND, p. v., Cape May co., N. J., 108 ms. s. of Trenton; from W. 218 ms.

CAPE MAY COUNTY, situated in the extreme southeast part of New Jersey, with Tuckahoe river on the north, Delaware bay on the west, and the Atlantic ocean on the east. Area, 252 square miles. Face of the country level. Soil sandy; in some parts marshy. Seat of justice, Cape May Court House. Pop. in 1820, 4,265; in 1830, 4,945; in 1840, 5,324; in 1850, 6,433.

CAPE MAY. c. h., p. v., Middle township, seat of justice of Cape May co., N. J., 93 ms. s. of Trenton; from W. 203 ms. Watered by Atlantic ocean.

CAPE NEDDICK, p. o., York co., Me.

CAPE's CREEK, p. o., Newton co., Mo.

CAPEVILLE, p. o., Northampton co., Va., 170 ms. E. by s. of Richmond; from W. 246 ms.

CAPE VINCENT, p. v., Lyme township, Jefferson co., N. Y., 190 ms. N. w. of Albany; from W. 442 ms. Watered by St. Lawrence river.

CAPTINO, p. o., York township, Belmont co., O., 134 ms. E. of Columbus; from W. 295 ms.

CAPON BRIDGE, p. o., Hampshire co., Va.

CAPON SPRINGS, p. o., Hampshire co., Va.

CARAWAY, p. o., Randolph co., N. C.

CARBONDALE, p. v., Luzerne co., Pa., 160 ms. N. N. E. of Harrisburgh; from W. 264 ms. Watered by Lackawana creek.

CARBON COUNTY, situated in the eastern part of Pennsylvania, and traversed by Lehigh river. Area, ——— square miles. Seat of justice, Mauch Chunk. Pop. in 1850, 15,686.

CARDIFF, p. v., Lafayette township, Onondaga co., N. Y.; 132 ms. w. N. w. of Albany; from W. 335 ms.

CARDIFF, p. o., Warren co., Miss.

CARDINGTON, p. v., Morven township, Morrow co., O., 36 ms. N. of Columbus; from W. 405 ms. Pop. 1,398.

CARREY, p. o., Wyandott co., O.

CARLILE'S MILLS, p. o., Perry co., Miss., 173 ms. s. E. of Jackson; from W. 1,051 ms.

CARLINVILLE, c. h., p. v., seat of justice of Macoupin co., Ill., 39 ms. s. s. w. of Springfield; from W. 811 ms. Watered by Lake Fork of Macoupin river.

CARLISLE, p. t., Middlesex co., Mass., 19 ms. N. w. of Boston; from W. 456 ms. Watered by Concord river. Pop. 632.

CARLISLE, p. t., Schoharie co., N. Y., 36 ms. w. by N. of Albany; from W. 394 ms. Pop. 1,817.

CARLISLE, c. h., p. v., seat of justice of Cumberland co., Pa., 15 ms. w. by s. of Harrisburgh; from W. 103 ms. Seat of Dickinson college. Pop. 4,581.

CARLISLE, c. h., p. v., seat of justice of Troup co., Ga., 133 ms. w. of Milledgeville; from W. 751 ms. Watered by Flat Shoal creek.

CARLISLE, c. h., p. v., seat of justice of Nicholas co., Ky., 53 ms. E. N. E. of Frankfort; from W. 496 ms. Watered by a branch of Licking river.

CARLISLE, t., Lorain co., O. Watered by Black river. Pop. 1,512.

CARLISLE, p. v., Sullivan co., Ind., 100 ms. s. w. of Indianapolis; from W. 671 ms.

CARLISLE, p. o., Eaton co., Mich.

CARLISLE SPRINGS, p. o., Cumberland co., Pa., 19 ms. w. by s. of Harrisburgh; from W. 107 ms.

CARLO, p. o., Hopkins co., Ky., 216 ms. w. s. w. of Frankfort; from W. 749 ms.

CARLOCKVILLE, p. o., Rutherford co., Tenn.

CARLOWSVILLE, p. o., Dallas co., Ala.

CARLTON, p. t., Orleans co., N. Y., 258 ms. w. by N. of Albany; from W. 401 ms. Watered by Oak Orchard creek and Lake Ontario. Pop. 2,809.

CARLTON, p. o., Barry co., Mich.

CARLTON'S STORE, p. o., King and Queen co., Va., 58 ms. N. E. by E. of Richmond; from W. 104 ms.

CARLYLE, c. h., p. v., seat of justice of Clinton co., Ill., 96 ms. s. by E. of Springfield; from W. 771 ms. Watered by Kaskaskia river.

CARMEL, p. t., Penobscot co., Me., 65 ms. N. E. of Augusta; from W. 660 ms. Watered by Sowadabscook river. Pop. 1,255.

CARMEL, c. h., p. v., seat of justice of Putnam co., N. Y., 100 ms. s. of Albany; from W. 287 ms. Pop. 2,442.

CARMEL, v., St. Joseph co., Ind., 129 ms. N. of Indianapolis; from W. 648 ms.

CARMEL, p. v., Hamilton co., Ind.

CARMEL, t., Eaton co., Mich. Pop. 567.

CARMEL HILL, p. o., Chester district, S. C., 71 ms. N. of Columbia; from W. 460 ms.

CARMI, c. h., p. v., seat of justice of White co., Ill., 181 ms. s. E. of Springfield; from W. 751 ms. Watered by Little Wabash river.

CARMICHAELS, p. o., Greene co., Pa., 190 ms. w. by s. of Harrisburgh; from W. 214 ms.

CARNENT PRAIRIE, p. o., Perry co., Ill.

CARNESVILLE, c. h., p. v., seat of justice of Franklin co., Ga., 111 ms. N. of Milledgeville; from W. 585 ms. Watered by Stephen's creek.

CAROLINA, p. o., Haywood co., Tenn., 174 ms. w. s. w. of Nashville; from W. 857 m.

CAROLINA FEMALE COLLEGE, p. o., Anson co., N. C.

CAROLINE COUNTY, situated on the easterly boundary of Maryland, on the eastern side of Choptank river. Area, 240 square miles. Face of the country level; soil sandy. Seat of justice, Denton. Pop. in 1820, 10,108; in 1830, 9,070; in 1840, 7,806; in 1850, 9,692.

CAROLINE COUNTY, situated in the eastern part of Virginia, between Rappahannock and North Anna rivers. Area, 600 square miles. Face of the country hilly; soil varied. Seat of justice, Bowling Green. Pop. in 1820, 18,008; in 1830, 17,760; in 1840, 17,813; in 1850, 18,456.

CAROLINE, p. t., Tompkins co., N. Y., 150 ms. w. by s. of Albany; from W. 331 ms. Watered by West Oswego and Six Mile creeks. Pop. 2,537.

CAROLINE CENTRE, p. o., Caroline township, Tompkins co., N. Y., 173 ms. w. by s. of Albany; from W. 330 ms.

CAROLINE FURNACE, p. o., Perry co., Pa., 23 ms. w. of Harrisburgh; from W. 133 ms.

CAROLINE MILLS, p. o., Washington co., R. I.

CARONDELET, p. v., St. Louis co., Mo., 134 ms. E. of Jefferson City; from W. 814 ms. Watered by the Mississippi river.

CARPENTER'S CREEK, p. o., Jasper co., Ind.

CARPENTER'S MILLS, p. o., Allen co., Ky., 155 ms. s. w. of Frankfort; from W. 678 ms.

CARPENTER'S LANDING, p. v., Greenwich township, Gloucester co., N. J., 40 ms. s. w. of Trenton; from W. 151 m. Watered by Mantua creek.

CARP RIVER, p. o., Marquette co., Mich.

CARR, p. o., Jasper co., Iowa.

CARRIBOU, p. o., Aroostook co., Me.

CARRICK, p. o., Franklin co., Pa., 63 ms. w. s. w. of Harrisburgh; from W. 111 ms.

CARRITUNK, p. v., Somerset co., Me.

CARROLL COUNTY, situated on the westerly boundary of Georgia, on the northwest side of Chattahoochee river. Area, 800 square miles. Face of the country generally hilly; soil varied. Seat of justice, Carrolton. Pop. in 1830, 3,419; in 1840, 5,252; in 1850, 9,357.

CARROLL COUNTY, situated in the western part of Tennessee, and drained by Big Sandy river. Area, 960 square miles. Seat of justice, Huntingdon. Pop. in 1830, 9,378; in 1840, 12,362; in 1850, 15,967.

CARROLL COUNTY, situated in the eastern part of Ohio. Area, 400 square miles. Seat of justice, Carrollton. Pop. in 1840, 18,108; in 1850, 17,685.

CARROLL COUNTY, situated near the southern boundary of Virginia. Area, —— square miles. Face of the country mountainous and hilly. Seat of justice, Hillsville. Pop. in 1850, 5,909.

CARROLL COUNTY, situated on the easterly boundary of New Hampshire, with Squam and Winnipisiogee lakes on the west and southwest. Area, 550 square miles. Face of the country generally mountainous and hilly; soil varied, much of which is highly fertile. Seat of justice, Ossipee. Pop. in 1850, 20,157.

CARROLL COUNTY, situated on the north boundary of Maryland, on the northwest side of Patapsco river. Area, 500 square miles. Seat of justice, Westminster. Pop. in 1840, 17,241; in 1850, 20,616.

CARROLL COUNTY, situated toward the northwest part of Indiana, and traversed by the Wabash river. Area, 380 square miles. Seat of justice, Delphi. Pop. in 1830, 1,614; in 1840, 7,819; in 1850, 11,015.

CARROLL COUNTY, situated toward the westerly part of Missouri, on the north side of the Missouri river. Area, 700 square miles. Seat of justice, Carrollton. Pop. in 1840, 2,423; in 1850, 5,441.

CARROLL COUNTY, situated on the north boundary of Arkansas. Area, 1,650 square miles. Seat of justice, Carrollton. Pop. in 1840, 2,844; in 1850, 4,614.

CARROLL COUNTY, situated toward the northwestern part of Mississippi, on the east side of Yazoo river. Area, 950 square miles. Seat of justice, Carrollton, Pop. in 1840. 10.481; in 1850, 18,495.

CARROLL COUNTY, situated on the northerly boundary of Kentucky, on the south side of the Ohio river, and traversed by Kentucky river. Area, 140 square miles. Seat of justice, Carrollton. Pop. in 1840, 3,966; in 1850, 5,526.

CARROLL COUNTY, situated on the westerly boundary of Illinois, on the east side of Mississippi river. Area, 445 square miles. Seat of justice, Mount Carroll. Pop. in 1840, 1,023; in 1850, 4,586.

CARROLL PARISH, situated in the northeast corner of Louisiana, on the west side of Mississippi river. Area, 1,100 square miles. Seat of justice, Providence. Pop. in 1840, 4,237; in 1850, 8,789.

CARROLL, p. o., Penobscot co., Me.

CARROLL, p. t., Coos co., N. H.

CARROLL, p. t., Chautauque co., N. Y., 336 ms. w. by s. of Albany; from W. 313 ms. Watered by Conewango and Stillwater creeks. Pop. 1,833.

CARROLL, t., York co., Pa. Pop. 807.

CARROLL, t., Washington co., Pa. Pop. 1,469.

CARROLL, t., Cambria co., Pa. Pop. 1,129.

CARROLL, t., Perry co., Pa.

CARROLL, p. o., Fairfield co., O.

CARROLL, t., Ottawa co., O. Pop. 403.

CARROLL, p. o., Calhoun co., Mich., 121 ms. w. by s. of Detroit; from W. 586 ms.

CARROLL, p. v., Carroll co., Ind., 59 ms. N. of Indianapolis; from W. 616 ms. Watered by Wabash river. Pop. 665.

CARROLL HOUSE, p. o., Coos co., N. H.

CARROLLSVILLE, p. v., Tishamingo co., Miss., 208 ms. N. E. by N. of Jackson; from W, 855 ms.

CARROLLTON, c. h., p. v., Centre township, seat of justice of Carroll co., O., 125 ms. N. E. of Columbia; from W. 296 ms. Pop. 865.

CARROLLTON, c. h., p. v., seat of justice of Carroll co., Ky., 46 ms. N. N. w. of Frankfort; from W. 588 ms. Watered by Ohio and Kentucky rivers. Pop.

CARROLLTON, c. h., p. v., seat of justice of Carroll co., Ga., 131 ms. w. N. w. of Milledgeville; from W. 719 ms. Watered by south fork of Tallapoosa river.

CARROLLTON, c. h., p. v., seat of justice of Pickens co., Ala., 42 ms. w. of Tuscaloosa; from W. 860 ms. Watered by Lubbub creek.

CARROLLTON, c. h., p. v., seat of justice of Carroll co., Miss., 92 ms. N. by E. of Jackson; from W. 997 ms. Watered by Big Sandy creek.

CARROLLTON, p. o., Jefferson parish, La.

CARROLLTON, c. h., p. v., seat of justice of Carroll co., Ark., 212 ms. N. N. w. of Little Rock; from W. 1,146 ms. Watered by Crooked creek.

CARROLLTON, c. h., p. v., seat of justice of Greene co., Ill., 69 ms. s. w. of Springfield; from W. 834 ms. Pop. 787.

CARROLLTON, c. h., p. v., seat of justice of Carroll co., Mo., 124 ms. N. w. of Jefferson city; from W. 1,018 ms. Watered by Waconda creek.

CARROLLTON, c. h., p. v., Centre township, seat of justice of Carroll co., O.

CARROLLTON, p. o., Cambria co., Pa.

CARROLLVILLE, p. v., Wayne co., Tenn., 113 ms. s. w. of Nashville; from W. 790 ms.

CARRSVILLE, p. o., Isle of Wight co., Va.

CARRSVILLE, p. o., Cooper co., Mo.

CARRYALL, t., Paulding co., O. Pop. 387.

CARSON'S CREEK, p. o., Calaveras co., Cal.

CARSONVILLE, p. v., Talbot co., Ga., 75 ms. w. s. w. of Milledgeville; from W. 731 ms.

CARTER CAMP, p. o., Potter co., Pa.

CARTER COUNTY, situated on the northeast boundary of Kentucky, on the west side of Big Sandy river. Area, 800 square miles. Seat of justice, Grayson. Pop. in 1840, 2,905; in 1850, 6,241.

CARTER COUNTY, situated near the northeast corner of Tennessee. Area, 540 square miles. Face of the country mountainous and hilly; soil generally sterile, but in some places good. Seat of justice, Elizabethtown. Pop. in 1820, 4,835; in 1830, 6,418; in 1840, 5,237; in 1850, 6,296.

CARTERET COUNTY, situated on the southeast boundary of North Carolina, on the Atlantic ocean. Area, 600 square miles. Face of the country level; soil generally sandy, but in part marshy. Seat of justice, Beaufort. Pop. in 1820, 5,609; in 1830, 6,607; in 1840, 6.591; in 1850, 6,853.

CARTER'S BRIDGE, p. o., Albemarle co., Va., 83 ms. w. N. w. of Richmond; from W. 140 ms.

CARTER'S CREEK, p. o., Williamson co., Tenn., 30 ms. s. of Nashville; from W. 707 ms.

CARTER'S HILL, p. o., Montgomery co., Ala., 130 ms. s. E. of Tuscaloosa; from W. 841 ms.

CARTER'S STATION, p. o., Greene co., Tenn., 255 ms. E. of Nashville ; from W. 441 ms.

CARTER'S STORE, p. o., Nicholas co., Ky., 62 ms. E. by N. of Frankfort ; from W. 506 ms.

CARTERSVILLE, p. t., Oswego co., N. Y., 137 ms. N. W. by W. of Albany ; from W. 386 ms. Watered by Salmon and Scriba creeks.

CARTERSVILLE, p. v., Cumberland co., Va., 46 ms. w. by N. of Richmond ; from W. 124 ms. Watered by James river.

CARTERSVILLE, p. o., Cass co.. Ga.

CARTERSVILLE, p. o., Tishamingo co., Miss., 248 ms. N. N. E. of Jackson ; from W. 815 ms.

CARTERSVILLE, p. o., Darlington co., S. C.

CARTHAGE, p. t., Franklin co., Me., 41 ms. N. w. of Augusta ; from W. 619 ms. Watered by Webb's river. Pop. 420.

CARTHAGE, p. v., Wilna township, Jefferson co., N. Y., 152 ms. N. w. of Albany ; from W. 431 ms. Watered by Black river.

CARTHAGE, p. v., Mill Creek township, Hamilton co., O., 116 ms. s. w. of Columbus ; from W. 502 ms.

CARTHAGE, p. o., Campbell co., Ky.

CARTHAGE, c. h., p. v., seat of justice of Moore co., N. C., 79 ms. s. w. of Raleigh ; from W. 367 ms. Watered by McLennon's creek.

CARTHAGE, p. v., Tuscaloosa co., Ala., 17 ms. s. of Tuscaloosa ; from W. 835 ms.

CARTHAGE, c. h., p. v., seat of justice of Leake co., Miss., 57 ms. N. E. of Jackson ; from W. 961 ms.

CARTHAGE, c. h., p. v., seat of justice of Smith co., Tenn., 52 ms. E. of Nashville ; from W. 632 ms. Watered by Cumberland river.

CARTHAGE, t., Athens co., O., 88 ms. s. E. of Columbus ; from W. 338 ms. Pop. 1,087.

CARTHAGE, p. v., Rush co., Ind., 32 ms. E. S. E. of Indianapolis ; from W. 547 ms.

CARTHAGE, v., Brighton township, Monroe co., N. Y. Watered by Genesee river.

CARTHAGE, p. o., Franklin co., Me.

CARTHAGE, c. h., p. v., seat of justice of Smith co., Tenn.

CARTHAGE, c. h., p. v., seat of justice of Hancock co., Ill., 106 ms. w. N. w. of Springfield ; from W. 880 ms. Watered by Mississippi river.

CARTHAGE, c. h., p. v., seat of justice of Jasper co., Mo.

CARTHAGE, c, h,, p, v,, seat of justice of Panola co., Tex.

CARTHAGE LANDING, p. o., Dutchess co., N. Y.

CARTICAY, p. o., Gilmer co., Ga.

CARVER, p. t., Plymouth co., Mass., 47 ms. s. E. of Boston ; from W. 447 ms. Pop. 1,186.

CARVER'S HARBOR, p. o., Waldo co., Me.

CARVERSVILLE, p. o., Bucks co., Pa., 108 ms. E. of Harrisburgh ; from W. 170 ms.

CARVERTON, p. o., Luzerne co., Pa.

CARYSVILLE, p. o., Champaign co., O., 60 ms. w. N. w. of Columbus ; from W. 454 ms.

CASCADE, p. o., Clark co., Oregon.

CASCADE, p. o., Pittsylvania co., Pa., 192 ms. w. s. w. of Richmond ; from W. 275 ms.

CASCADE, p. o., Sheboygan co., Wis.

CASCADE, p. o., Dubuque co., Iowa.

CASCO, p. o., Cumberland co., Me.

CASEY COUNTY, situated in the central part of Kentucky. Area, 448 square miles. Surface hilly, soil productive. Seat of justice, Liberty. Pop. in 1830, 4,342 ; in 1840, 4,939 ; in 1850, 6,556.

CASEVILLE, p. v., Olive township, Ulster co., N. Y., 76 ms. s. s. w. of Albany ; from W. 330 ms.

CASEY, p. o., Clark co., Ill., 121 ms. E. s. E. of Springfield ; from W. 679 ms.

CASEYVILLE, p. o., Union co., Ky.

CASHER'S VALLEY, p. o., Macon co., N. C., 337 ms. w. by s. of Raleigh ; from W. 567 ms.

CASH'S NOB, p. o., Montgomery co., Ky.

CASHTOWN, p. v., Adams co., Pa., 43 ms. s. w. of Harrisburgh ; from W. 83 ms.

CASHVILLE, p. v., Spartanburg district, S. C., 102 ms. N. w. of Columbia ; from W. 488 ms.

CASNOVIA, p. o., Ottawa co., Mich.

CASS, p. t.. Hancock co., O.. 100 ms. N. w. of Columbus ; from W. 446 ms. Pop. 621.

CASS, t., Ionia co., Mich., 133 ms. w. N. w. of Detroit ; from W. 620 ms.

CASS, p. o., Tippecanoe co., Ind.

CASS, p. o., Venango co., Pa.

CASS, p. o., Du Page co., Ill.

CASS, p. o., Hillsdale co., Mich.

CASS, p. o., Franklin co., Ark.

CASS, p. o., Lawrence co., Tenn.

CASS COUNTY, situated on the east boundary of Texas, on the northeast side of Cypress river. Area, —— square miles. Seat of justice, Linden. Pop. 3,089.

CASS COUNTY, situated toward the northwest corner of Georgia, and traversed by Etowah and Oostanaula rivers. Area, 600 square miles. Seat of justice, Cassville. Pop. in 1840, 9,390 ; in 1850, 13,300.

CASS COUNTY, situated on the south boundary of Michigan. Area, 528 square miles. Seat of justice. Cassopolis. Pop. in 1840, 5,710 ; in 1850, 10,907.

CASS COUNTY, situated toward the north part of Indiana, and traversed by Wabash river. Area, 415 square miles. Seat of justice, Logansport. Pop. in 1840, 5,840 ; in 1850, 10,998.

CASS COUNTY, situated toward the western part of Illinois, on the southeast side of Illinois river. Area, 256 square miles. Seat of justice, Virginia. Pop. in 1840, 2,981 ; in 1850, 3,253.

CASS COUNTY, situated on the west boundary of Missouri. Area, —— square miles. Seat of justice. Harrisonville. Pop. in 1850, 6,090.

CASSADAGA, p. o., Pomfret township, Chautauque co., N. Y., 331 ms. w. by s. of Albany ; from W. 337 ms.

CASSAPOLIS, c. h., p. v., seat of justice of Cass co., Mich., 167 ms. s. w. of Detroit ; from W. 615 ms.

CASSITY'S MILLS, p. o., Morgan co., Ky.

CASSTOWN, p. o., Miami co., O.

CASSVILLE, p. o., Harrison co., O.

CASSVILLE, p. o., Barry co., Mo.

CASSVILLE, p. o., Huntingdon co., Pa.

CASSVILLE, p. o., Monongalia co., Va.

CASSVILLE, p. v., Paris township, Oneida co., N. Y., 86 ms. N. N. w. of Albany ; from W. 375 ms. Watered by Sanquoit creek.

CASSVILLE, p. o., Monmouth co. N. J., 25 ms. E. of Trenton ; from W. 188 ms.

CASSVILLE, c. h., p. v., seat of justice of Cass co., Ga., 144 ms. N. w. of Milledgeville ; from W. 645 ms.

CASSVILLE, p. v., Grant co., Wis., 126 ms. w. s. w. of Madison ; from W. 928 ms. Watered by Mississippi river.

CASTALIA, p. o., Erie co., O.

CASTALIAN SPRINGS, p. o., Sumner co., Tenn., 31 ms. N. E. of Nashville ; from W. 675 ms.

CASTILE, p t., Wyoming co., N. Y., 249 ms. w. of Albany ; from W. 355 ms. Watered by Genesee river and Silver Lake. Pop. 2,446.

CASTILE, p. o., Greene co., Pa.

CASTILE, p. o., Clinton co., Mo.

CASTINE, c. h., p. t., seat of justice of Hancock co., Me., 75 ms. E. of Augusta ; from W. 671 ms. Watered by Penobscot bay. Pop. 1,260.

CASTINE, p. o., Darke co., O.

CASTLE CRAIG, p. o., Campbell co., Va., 136 ms. w. by s. of Richmond ; from W. 214 ms.

CASTLE CREEK, p. o., Broome co., N. Y.

CASTLEFIN. p. o., York co., Pa., 55 ms. s. of Harrisburgh ; from W. 85 ms.

CASTLEFIN, p. o., Jefferson co., Ill.

CASTLE GROVE, p. o., Jones co., Iowa.

CASTLEMAN'S FERRY, p. o., Clarke co., Va.

CASTLETON. p. t., Rutland co., Vt., 74 ms. s. s. w. of Montpelier ; from W. 450 ms. Watered by Castleton river. Pop. 3,016.

CASTLETON, p. v., Schodack township. Rennselaer co., N. Y., 8 ms. s. by E. of Albany ; from W. 362 ms. Watered by Hudson river.

CASTLETON, t., Richmond co., Staten Island, N. Y. Pop. 5,389.

CASTLETON, p. o., Barry co., Mich.

CASTOR, t., Madison co., Mo.

CASTOR, p. o., Caldwell co., La.

CASWELL COUNTY, situated in the north boundary of North Carolina. Area, 400 square miles. Seat of justice, Yanceyville. Pop. in 1830, 15,499 ; in 1840, 14,639 ; in 1850, 15,269.

CASWELL, p. o., Lafayette co., Mo.

CATAHOOLA PARISH, situated toward the easterly part of Louisiana, and watered by Catahoola lake, and Catahoola and Washita rivers. Area, 2,100 square miles. Face of the country generally flat, and partially subject to annual inundation. Seat of justice, Harrisonburgh. Pop. in 1830, 2,581 ; in 1840, 4,955 ; in 1850, 6,982.

CATALPA GROVE, p. o., Greene co., Ky.
CATALPA GROVE, p. o., Marshall co., Tenn.
CATALPA GROVE, p. o., Benton co., Ind.
CATALAMET, p. o., Lewis co., Oregon.
CATARACT, p. o.. Owen co., Ind.
CATASAUQUA, p. o., Lehigh co., Pa.
CATATONK, p. o., Tioga co., N. Y.
CATAULA, p. o., Harris co., Ga.
CATAWBA COUNTY, situated toward the wester-ly part of North Carolina, on the southwest side of Ca-tawba river. Area, —— square miles. Seat of justice, Newtown. Pop. in 1850, 8,862.
CATAWBA. p. o., Chester district, S. C., 62 ms. N. of Columbia; from W. 456 ms.
CATAWBA, p. o. Bottetourt co., Va.
CATAWBA, p. o., Clark co., O., 34 ms. w. of Colum-bus; from w. 437 ms.
CATAWBA CREEK, p. o., Gaston co., N. C., 188 ms. w. by s. of Raleigh; from W. 427 ms.
CATAWBA SPRINGS, p. v., Lincoln co., N. C., 158 ms. w. by s. of Raleigh; from W. 395 ms.
CATAWBA VIEW, p. o., Caldwell co., N. C., 173 ms. w. by s. of Raleigh; from W. 410 ms. Watered by Ca-tawba river.
CATAWISSA, p. t., Columbia co., Pa., 81 ms. N. E. of Harrisburgh; from W. 191 ms. Watered by Susque-hanna river. Pop. 1,143.
CATAWISSA FORGE, v., Catawissa township, Columbia co., Pa., 87 ms. N. N. E. of Harrisburgh; from W. 197 ms.
CATAWISSA VALLEY, p. o., Schuylkill co., Pa., 87 ms. N. E. of Harrisburgh; from W. 197 ms.
CATFISH, p. o., Marion district, S. C., 138 E. of Co-lumbia; from W. 431 ms.
CATFISH FURNACE, p. o., Clarion co., Pa.
CATHARINE, p. t., Chemung co., N. Y., 182 ms. w. by s. of Albany; from W. 295 ms. Watered by Catharine's creek. Pop. 3,070.
CATHARINE LAKE, p. o., Onslow co., N. Y.
CATHCART, p. o., White co., Ind.
CATHEY'S CREEK, p. o., Buncombe co., N. C., 294 ms. w. of Raleigh; from W. 524 ms.
CATLETTSBURGH, p. v., Greenup co., Ky., 150 ms. E. N. E. of Frankfort; from W. 410 ms. Watered by Ohio river.
CATLIN, t., Chemung co., N. Y., 190 ms. w. s. w. of Albany; from W. 291 ms. Watered by Catharine's creek. Pop. 1,474.
CATO, p. t., Cayuga co., N. Y., 163 ms. w. by N. of Albany; from W. 349 ms. Watered by Seneca river and Cross' lake. Pop. 2,247.
CATO, p. o., Clay co., Ill., 126 ms. s. E. of Springfield; from W. 752 ms.
CATOCTIN FURNACE, p. o., Frederick co., Me.
CATO FOUR CORNERS. p. o., Cato township, Cayuga co., N. Y., 165 ms. w. by N. of Albany; from W. 351 ms.
CATON, t., Steuben co., N. Y., 216 ms. w. s. w. of Al-bany; watered by tributaries of Chemung river. Pop. 1,214.
CATONSVILLE, p. v., Baltimore co., Md., 36 ms. N. of Annapolis; from W. 46 ms.
CATO SPRINGS, p. o., Rankin co , Miss.
CATRON, p. o., Lawrence co., Tenn., 73 ms. s. s. w. of Nashville; from W. 750 ms.
CATSKILL, c. h., p. t., seat of justice of Greene co., N. Y., 34 ms. s. of Albany; from W. 336 ms. Watered by Hudson river and Catskill creek. Pop. 5,454.
CATTARAUGUS COUNTY, situated on the south boundary of New York. Area, 1,232 square miles. Face of the country hilly; soil productive. Seat of justice, Ellicottville. Pop. in 1820, 4,090; in 1830, 16,726; in 1840, 28,872; in 1850, 38,950.
CATTARAUGUS, p. o., Cattaraugus co., N. Y.
CAUGHDENOY, p. o., Oswego co. N. Y.
CAUGHNAWAGA, v., Mohawk township, Montgomery co., N. Y. Watered by Mohawk river.
CAULEYSVILLE. v., Covington co., Ala., 199 ms. s. s. E. of Tuscaloosa; from W. 895 ms.
CAVE, p. o., Franklin co., Ill.
CAVE, p. o., White co., Tenn.
CAVE IN ROCK, p. o., Hardin co., Ill.
CAVE HILL, p. t., Washington co., Ark. Pop. 1,082.
CAVEHILL, p. o., Greene co., Tenn., 271 ms. E. of Nashville; from W. 450 ms.
CAVENDISH, p. t., Windsor co., Vt., 74 ms. s. of Mont-pelier; from W. 466 ms. Watered by Black river and Twenty Mile stream. Pop. 1,576.

CAVE SPRING, p. o., Floyd co., Ga., 178 ms. N. w. of Milledgeville; from W. 689 ms.
CAVE SPRING, p. o., Maury co., Tenn., 54 ms. s. s. w. of Nashville; from W. 730 ms.
CAVE SPRING, p. o., Wright co., Me., 115 ms. s. of Jef-ferson city; from W. 1,030 ms.
CAVE SPRING, p. o., Roanoke co., Va.
CAVETOWN, p. v., Washington co., Md., 107 ms. N. w. of Annapolis; from W. 77 ms. Pop. 167.
CAYUGA COUNTY, situated toward the western part of New York, with Cayuga lake on the west, Skane-ateles lake on the east, and Lake Ontario on the north; watered, also, by Seneca river, Owasco lake, and the Erie canal. Area, 648 square miles. Face of the coun-try somewhat hilly, with a very productive soil. Seat of justice, Auburn. Pop. in 1820, 38,897; in 1830, 47,947; in 1840, 50,338; in 1850, 55,460.
CAYUGA, p. v., Aurelius township, Cayuga co., N. Y., 162 ms. w. by N. of Albany; from W. 339 ms. Situated on Cayuga lake.
CAYUGA, p. o., Jackson co., Mich., 100 ms. w. of De-troit: from W. 570 ms.
CAYUGA, p. o., Hinds co., Miss., 27 ms. s. w. of Jack-son; from W. 570 ms.
CAYUTA, p. t., Chemung co., N. Y., 188 ms. w. s. w. of Albany; from W. 289 ms. Watered by Cayuta creek. Pop. 1,035.
CAYUTA, p. o., Tompkins co., N. Y.
CAZENOVIA. p. t., Madison co., N. Y., 113 ms. w. by N. of Albany; from W. 348 ms. Watered by Chittenan-go creek and Cazenovia lake. Pop. 4,812.
CAZENOVIA, p. o., Cook's co., Ill., 215 ms. N. E. by N. of Springfield; from W. 728 ms.
CEARCY, t., Phillips co., Ark.
CECIL COUNTY, situated at the northeast corner of Maryland, with Susquehanna river and Chesapeake bay on the west and southwest. Area, 264 square miles. Face of the country generally level; soil varied, with much good land along the streams. Seat of justice, Elkton. Pop. in 1820, 16,048; in 1830, 15,492; in 1840, 17,232; in 1850, 18,939.
CECILTOWN, p. v., Cecil co., Md., 78 ms. N. E. of An-napolis; from W. 112 ms.
CECIL, t., Washington co., Pa. Watered by Miller's branch of Chartier's creek. Pop. 1,008.
CECIL'S TAVERN, p. o., Anne Arundel co., Md., 30 ms. N. w. of Annapolis; from W. 33 ms.
CEDAR COUNTY, situated in the eastern part of Iowa, and traversed by Cedar river. Area, —— square miles. Seat of justice, Tipton. Pop. in 1840, 1,253; in 1850. 3,941.
CEDAR COUNTY, situated toward the southwest part of Missouri. Area. —— square miles. Seat of jus-tice, Fremont. Pop. in 1850, 3,361.
CEDAR, t., Boone co., Mo.
CEDAR, t., Callaway co., Me.
CEDAR, p. o., Allen co., Ind.
CEDAR, p. o., Livingston co., Mich.. 59 ms. w. by N. of Detroit; from W. 562 ms.
CEDAR BAYOU, p. o., Liberty co., Tex.
CEDAR BLUFF. c. h., p. v., seat of justice of Cherokee co., Ala., 152 ms. N. E. of Tuscaloosa; from W. 677 ms.
CEDAR BLUFF, p. o., Oktibbeha co., Miss.
CEDAR BLUFF, p. o., Tazewell co., Va.
CEDARBURGH, p. o., Washington co.. Wis.
CEDAR BRANCH, p. o., Campbell co., Ga.
CEDAR CREEK, t., Cooper co., Mo.
CEDAR CREEK, p. o., Ocean co., N. J., 46 ms. s. E. of Trenton; from W. 207 ms.
CEDAR CREEK, hundred and p. v., Sussex co., Del. Pop, 2,326.
CEDAR CREEK, p. o., Frederick co., Va., 158 ms. N. N. w. of Richmond; from W. 86 ms.
CEDAR CREEK, p. o., Rutherford co., N. C.
CEDAR CREEK, p. o.. Richland district, S. C., 14 ms. E. of Columbia; from W. 514 ms.
CEDAR CREEK, p. o., Dooly co., Ga., 103 ms. s. s. w. of Milledgeville, from W. 760 ms.
CEDAR CREEK, p. o., Owen co., Ky., 17 ms. N. of Frankfort; from W. 559 ms.
CEDAR CREEK, t., Allen co., Ind. Pop. 814.
CEDAR CREEK, p. o., Greene co., Tenn., 253 ms. E. of Nashville; from W. 451 ms.
CEDAR CREEK, p. o., Warren co., Ill., 127 ms. N w. of Springfield; from W. 857 miles.
CEDAR CREEK, p. o., Barry co., Mich.
CEDAR CREEK, p. v., Lowndes co., Miss., 143 ms. w. E. of Jackson; from W. 897 ms.

CEDAR CREEK, p. o., Washington co., Wis.

CEDAR CREEK MILLS, p. o., Stephenson co., Ill., 206 ms. N. of Springfield; from W. 838 ms.

CEDAR FALLS, p. o., Black Hawk co., Iowa.

CEDAR FALLS, p. o., Randolph co., N. C.

CEDAR FALLS, p. o., Greenville district, S. C.

CEDAR FORD, p. o., Grainger co., Tenn.

CEDAR GROVE, p. o., Union district, S. C., 76 ms. N. w. of Columbia; from W. 470 ms.

CEDAR GROVE, p. o., Orange co., N. C., 48 ms. N. W. of Raleigh; from W. 284 ms,

CEDAR GROVE, p. o.. Jefferson co., Ala., 95 ms. N. E. of Tuscaloosa; from W. 749 ms.

CEDAR GROVE, p. o., Franklin co., Ind., 76 ms. E. S. E. of Indianapolis; from W. 521 ms.

CEDAR GROVE, p. o., Kaufman co., Tex.

CEDAR GROVE, p. o., Breckenridge co., Ky.

CEDAR GROVE, p. o., Orange co., N. C.

CEDAR GROVE, p. o., Sheboygan co., Wis.

CEDAR GROVE MILLS, p, o., Rockbridge co., Va., 153 ms. w. of Richmond; from W. 195 ms.

CEDAR HILL, p. o., Bethlehem township, Albany co., N. Y., 8 ms. s. by w. of Albany; from W. 363 ms.

CEDAR HILL, p. o., Augusta co., Va.

CEDAR HILL, p. o., Anson co., N. C., 155 ms. s. w. of Raleigh; from W. 400 ms.

CEDAR HILL, p. o., Albany co., N. Y.

CEDAR KEY, p. o., Levy co., Flor.

CEDAR LAKE, p. o., Herkimer co., N. Y.

CEDAR LAKE, p. o., Calhoun co., Mich., 110 ms. w. of Detroit; from W. 575 ms.

CEDAR LAKE, p. o., Lake co., Ind.

CEDAR LAKE, p. o., Brazoria co., Tex.

CEDAR LAWN, p. o., Lunenburgh co., Va., 104 ms. s. w. of Richmond; from W. 220 ms.

CEDAR PLAINS, p. o., Morgan co., Ala., 124 ms. N. N. E. of Tuscaloosa; from W. 747 ms.

CEDAR POINT, p. o., Page co., Va.

CEDAR RIVER, p. o., Cedar co., Iowa.

CEDAR RAPIDS, p. o., Linn co., Iowa.

CEDAR RIDGE, p. o., Murray co., Ga.

CEDAR SHOAL, p. o., Chester district, S. C., 57 ms. N. of Columbia; from W. 450 ms.

CEDAR SPRING, p. o., Wythe co., Va.

CEDAR SPRING, p, o., Cumberland co., Pa.

CEDAR SPRING. p. o., Benton co., Ark.

CEDAR SPRING ASYLUM, p. o., Spartanburgh district, S. C.

CEDAR SPRINGS, p. o., Spartanburgh district, S. C., 96 ms. N. W. of Columbia; from W. 477 ms.

CEDAR SPRINGS, p. o., Allen co., Ky.

CEDAR SWAMP, p. v., Oyster Bay township, Queens co., N. Y., 173 ms. s. by E. of Albany; from W. 253 ms.

CEDARTOWN, p. v., Paulding co., Ga., 151 ms. N. W. of Milledgeville; from W. 691 ms. Watered by Tallapoosa river.

CEDAR TREE, p. o., Talladega co., Ala.

CEDAR VALLEY, p. o., Wayne co., O.

CEDARVILLE, p. v., Litchfield township, Herkimer co., N. Y., 79 ms. w. by N. of Albany; from W. 383 ms.

CEDARVILLE, p. o., Fairfield township, Cumberland co., N. J., 75 ms. s. by w. of Trenton; from W. 186 ms. Watered by Cedar creek.

CEDARVILLE, p. o., Washington co., Va., 297 ms. w. by s. of Richmond; from W. 365 ms.

CEDARVILLE, p. o., Greene co., O.

CEDRON, p. o., Clermont co., O.

CELESTINE, p. o., Dubois co., Ind.

CELINA, c. h., p. v., seat of justice of Mercer co., O., 127 ms. w. N. w. of Columbus; from W. 507 ms. Situated on the Reservoir of Miami canal. Pop. 222.

CELINA, p. o., Jackson co., Tenn., 91 ms. E. of Nashville; from W. 630 ms.

CENTENARY COLLEGE, p. o., Rankin co., Miss.

CENTRAL, p. o., Columbia co., Pa., 118 ms. N. by E. of Harrisburgh; from W. 236 ms.

CENTRAL, t., St. Louis co., Mo.

CENTRAL BRIDGE, p. o., Schoharie township, Schoharie co., N. Y., 32 ms. w. of Albany; from W. 388 ms.

CENTRAL COLLEGE, p. o., Franklin co., O.

CENTRAL SQUARE, p. o., Hastings township, Oswego co., N. Y., 144 ms. w. of Albany; from W. 365 ms.

CENTRAL PLAINS, p. o., Fluvanna co., Va.

CENTRAL POINT, p. o., Caroline co., Va.

CENTRAL VILLAGE, p. v., Windham co., Ct., 43 ms. E. of Hartford; from W. 374 ms.

CENTRE COUNTY, situated in the central part of Pennsylvania, with the west branch of Susquehanna river on the northwest. Area, 1,560 square miles. Face of the country, mountainous and hilly; soil generally rocky and sterile, but much good land along the streams. Seat of justice, Bellefonte. Pop. in 1820, 13,786; in 1830, 18,765; in 1840, 20,492; in 1850, 23,355.

CENTRE, p. v., Butler co., Pa. Pop. 278.

CENTRE, p. t., Perry co., Pa., 36 ms. N. w. of Harrisburgh; from W. 124 ms. Pop. 944.

CENTRE, t., Greene co., Pa., 228 ms. s. w. by w. of Harrisburgh; from W. 235 ms. Watered by Ten-Mile creek. Pop. 1,733.

CENTRE, t., Indiana co., Pa., 152 ms. w. N. w. of Harrisburgh; from W. 186 ms. Watered by Yellow and Twolick creeks. Pop. 1,193.

CENTRE, t., Union co., Pa., 52 ms. N. by w. of Harrisburgh; from W. 162 ms. Watered by Penns and Little Mahonialy creeks. Pop. 2,171.

CENTER, p. o., Barren co., Ky., 106 ms. s. w. of Frankfort; from W. 629 ms.

CENTRE, p. o., Guilford co., N. C., 88 ms. w. N. w. of Raleigh; from W. 313 ms.

CENTRE, p. o., Cass co., Tex.

CENTRE, p. o., Talbot co., Ga., 87 ms. w. s. w. of Milledgeville; from W. 731 ms.

CENTRE, p. o., Cherokee co., Ala.

CENTRE, p. o., Delaware co., O., 32 ms. N. of Columbus; from W. 402 ms.

CENTRE, p. t., Rush co., O.

CENTRE, t., Wood co., O.

CENTRE, t., Morgan co., O., 80 ms. E. s. E. of Columbus; from W. 330 ms. Pop. 1,439.

CENTRE, p. o., Montgomery co., O.

CENTRE, t., Williams co., O. Pop. 881.

CENTRE, t, Carroll co., O. Pop. 1,190.

CENTRE, t., Columbiana co., O., 152 ms., E. N. E. of Columbus; from W. 282 ms. Watered by Little Beaver river and Sandy and Beaver canal. Pop. 2,818.

CENTRE, t., Monroe co., O. 140 m. E. by s. of Columbus; from W. 294 ms. Pop. 2,454.

CENTRE, t., Mercer co., O.

CENTRE, t., Guernsey co., O., 86 ms. E. of Columbus; from W. 311 ms. Pop. 1,066.

CENTRE, t., Crawford co., O.

CENTRE, t., Delaware co., Ind., 59 ms. N. E. of Indianapolis; from W. 546 ms.

CENTRE, t., Hancock co., Ind., 21 ms. E. of Indianapolis; from W. 552 ms. Pop. 915.

CENTRE, t., Hendricks co., Ind., 20 ms. w. of Indianapolis; from W. 592 ms. Pop. 1,215.

CENTRE, t., Union co., Ind.

CENTRE, p. t., Grant co., Ind., 67 ms. N. N. E. of Indianapolis; from W. 568 ms.

CENTRE, t., Marion co., Ind., from W. 573 ms. Pop. 1,683.

CENTRE, t., Rush co., Ind., 36 ms. s. E. of Indianapolis; from W. 538 ms. Pop. 1,252.

CENTRE, t., Wayne co., Ind., 63 ms. E. of Indianapolis; from W. 510 ms.

CENTRE, p. o., Rock co., Wis.

CENTRE ALMOND, p. o., Almond township, Alleghany co., N. Y., 250 ms. w. by s. of Albany; from W. 325 ms.

CENTRE BARNSTEAD, p. o., Barnstead township, Belknap co., N. H., 21 ms. N. E. of Concord; from W. 502 ms.

CENTRE BELPHRE, p. o., Washington co., O., 110 ms. E. s. E. of Columbus; from W. 311 ms.

CENTRE BERLIN, p. o., Berlin township, Rensselaer co., N. Y., 28 ms. E. of Albany; from W. 385 ms.

CENTRE BRIDGE, p. o., Bucks co., Pa.

CENTRE BROOK, p. o., Middlesex co., Ct.

CENTREBURGH, p. v., Liberty township, Knox co., O., 36 ms. N. E. of Columbus; from W. 391 ms. Watered by North Fork of Licking river.

CENTRE CAMBRIDGE, p. o., Cambridge township, Washington co., N. Y., 39 ms. N. N. E. of Albany; from W. 409 ms.

CENTRE CANISTEO, p. o., Steuben co., N. Y.

CENTRE CONWAY, p. o., Conway township, Carroll co., N. H., 72 ms. N. N. w. of Concord; from W. 556 ms.

CENTRE CREEK, p. o., Iron co., Utah.

CENTRE CROSS, p. o., Essex co., Va.

CENTREDALE, p. o., Providence co., R. I.

CENTRE FARMINGTON, p. o., Farmington township, Trumbull co., O., 109 ms. N. E. of Columbus; from W. 317 ms.

CENTREFIELD, p. v., Canandaigua township, Ontario co., N. Y., 199 ms. w. by N. of Albany; from W. 345 ms.

CENTREFIELD, p. o., Oldham co., Ky.

CENTREFIELD, p. o., Highland co., O.

CENTRE GORHAM, p. o., Gorham township, Ontario co., N. Y., 201 ms. w. by N. of Albany; from W. 335 ms.

CENTRE GROTON, p. o., Groton township, New London co., Ct., 48 ms. s. E. of Hartford; from W. 358 ms.

CENTRE GROVE, p. o., Leake co., Miss., 58 ms. N. E. of Jackson; from W. 973 ms.

CENTRE GUILFORD, p. o., Piscataquis co., Me.

CENTRE HARBOR. p. t. Belknap co., N. H., 41 ms. N. of Concord; from W. 522 ms. Watered by Winnipiseogee and Squam lakes. Pop. 543.

CENTRE HILL, p. o., Washington co., Iowa.

CENTRE HILL, p. v., Bucks co., Pa., 111 ms. E. of Harrisburgh; from W. 173 ms.

CENTRE INDEPENDENCE, p. o., Independence township, Alleghany co., N. Y., 270 ms. w. by s. of Albany; from W. 306 ms.

CENTRE LEBANON, p. o., Lebanon township, York co., Me. 91 ms. s. w. of Augusta; from W. 513 ms.

CENTRE LINCOLNVILLE, p. o., Lincolnville township, Waldo co., Me., 44 ms. E. s. E. of Augusta; from W. 633 ms.

CENTRE LINE, p. o., Centre co., Pa., 105 ms. N. w. of Harrisburgh; from W. 174 ms.

CENTRE LOVELL, p. o., Oxford co., Me.

CENTRE LISLE, p. o., Broome co., N. Y.

CENTRE MINOT, p. o., Minot township, Cumberland co., Me., 41 ms. s. w. of Augusta; from W. 582 ms.

CENTRE MONTVILLE. p. o., Montville township, Waldo co., Me., 32 ms. E. by N. of Augusta; from W. 628 ms.

CENTRE MORELAND, p. v., Luzerne co., Pa. 136 ms. N. N. E. of Harrisburgh; from W. 245 ms.

CENTRE OSSIPEE, p. o., Ossipee township, Carroll co., N. H., 57 ms. N. by E. of Concord; from W. 538 ms.

CENTRE POINT, p. o., Monroe co., Ky., 143 ms. s. s. w. of Frankfort; from W. 656 ms.

CENTRE POINT, p. o., Knox co., Ill.

CENTRE POINT, p. o., Linn co., Ark.

CENTRE POINT, p. o., Sevier co., Ark.

CENTRE PORT, p. v., Huntington township, Suffolk co., N. Y., 192 ms. s. s. E. of Albany; from W. 272 ms. Situated on Great Cow Harbor.

CENTRE PORT, p. o., Wayne co., Mich., 16 ms. s. w. of Detroit; from W. 540 ms.

CENTRE RIDGE, p. o., Kemper co., Miss.

CENTRE RUTLAND, p. o., Rutland co., Vt.

CENTRE SANDWICH, p. o., Sandwich township, Carroll co., N. H., 51 ms. N. of Concord; from W. 532 ms.

CENTRE SHERMAN, p. o., Sherman township, Chautauque co., N. Y., 358 ms. w. by s. of Albany; from W. 342 ms.

CENTRE SIDNEY, p. o., Sidney township, Kennebec co., Me., 12 ms. N. of Augusta; from W. 607 ms.

CENTRE STAR, p. o., Lauderdale co., Ala.

CENTRE STRAFFORD, p. o., Strafford township, Strafford co., N. H., 29 ms. N. E. of Concord; from W. 510 ms.

CENTRETON, p. o., Salem co. N. J.

CENTRETON, p. o., Huron co., O.

CENTRETOWN, p. o., Du Buque co., Iowa.

CENTRETOWN, p. o., Anderson district, S. C.

CENTRETOWN, p. o., Mercer co., Pa., 225 ms. w. N. w. of Harrisburgh; from W. 272 ms.

CENTRE VALLEY, p. o., Lehigh co., Pa.

CENTRE VALLEY, p. o., Otsego co., N. Y.

CENTRE VILLAGE, p. v., Broome co., N. Y.

CENTREVILLAGE, p. v., Camden co., Ga.

CENTREVILLE, p. v., Barnstable township, Barnstable co., Mass., 78 ms. s. E. of Boston; from W. 476 ms.

CENTREVILLE, p. v., Warwick township, Kent co., R. I., 11 ms. s. s. w. of Providence; from W. 397 ms. Watered by Pawtuxet river.

CENTREVILLE, p. t., Alleghany co., N. Y., 265 ms. w. by s. of Albany; from W. 342 ms. Pop. 1,445.

CENTREVILLE, p. o., Hunterdon co., N. J., 32 ms. N. of Trenton; from W. 192 ms.

CENTREVILLE, v., Slippery Rock township, Butler co., Pa. Pop. 278.

CENTREVILLE, p. v., Crawford co., Pa., 237 ms. N. w. of Harrisburgh; from W. 318 ms.

CENTREVILLE, c. h., p. v., seat of justice of St.

Joseph co., Mich., 139 ms. w. s. w. of Detroit; from W. 587 ms. Watered by Prairie river.

CENTREVILLE, p. v., Washington township, Montgomery co., O., 75 ms. w. s. w. of Columbus; from W. 468 ms.

CENTREVILLE, p. v., Newcastle co., Del., 54 ms. N. of Dover; from W. 127 ms.

CENTREVILLE, v., Mt. Pleasant township, Wayne co., Pa.

CENTREVILLE, c. h., p. v., seat of justice of Queen Anne co., Md., 39 ms. E. by N. of Annapolis; from W. 79 ms.

CENTREVILLE, c. h., p. v., Fairfax co., Va., 114 ms. N. of Richmond; from W. 28 ms.

CENTREVILLE, p. o., Moore co., N. C.

CENTREVILLE, p. v., Laurens district, S. C., 91 ms. N. w. of Columbia; from W. 499 ms.

CENTREVILLE, p. v., Wilkes co., Ga., 77 ms. N. N. E of Milledgeville; from W. 582 ms.

CENTREVILLE, c. h., p. v., seat of justice of Bibb co., Ala., 38 ms. s. E. of Tuscaloosa; from W. 806 ms. Watered by Cahawba river.

CENTREVILLE, p. o., Nevada co., Cal.

CENTREVILLE, p. v., Amite co., Miss., 117 ms. s. s. w. of Jackson; from W. 1,117 ms. Watered by Dawson's creek.

CENTREVILLE, p. v., St. Mary's parish, La., 139 ms. w. by s. of New Orleans; from W. 1,111 ms. Watered by Bayou Teche.

CENTREVILLE, p. v., Bourbon co., Ky., 28 ms. E. of Frankfort; from W. 515 ms.

CENTREVILLE, c. h., seat of justice of Hickman co., Tenn., 54 ms. s. w. of Nashville; from W. 378 ms. Watered by Duck creek.

CENTREVILLE, c. h., p. v., seat of justice of Wayne co., Ind., 62 ms. E. of Indianapolis; from W. 509 ms. Watered by Whitewater river. Pop. 920.

CENTREVILLE, p. o., Wabash co.. Ill., 159 ms. s. E. of Springfield; from W. 721 ms.

CENTREVILLE, p. o., Montgomery co., Ark.

CENTREVILLE, p. o., Leon co., Tex.

CENTREVILLE, p. o., Appanoose co., Iowa.

CENTRE WHITE CREEK, p. v., White Creek township, Washington co., N. Y., 39 ms. N. E. of Albany; from W. 409 ms.

CERALVO, p. o., Carroll co., Miss.

CERES, t., McKeon co., Pa., 220 ms. from Harrisburgh; from W. 293 ms. Watered by Tunangwant, Willow, Sugar, and Kenjua creeks.

CERESCO, p. o., Calhoun co., Mich.

CERESCO, p. o., Fond du Lac co., Wis.

CRESTOWN, p. v., Keating township, Alleghany co., N. Y.; from W. 303 ms. Watered by Alleghany river.

CERRO GORDO, p. o., Holmes co., Flor.

CERRO GORDO, p. o., Platt co., Ill.

CERULEAN SPRINGS, p. v., Trigg co., Ky., 223 ms. s. w. by w. of Frankfort; from W. 747 ms. Watered by Muddy fork of Little river.

CESSNA, t., Hardin co.. O.

CHADD'S FORD, p. o., Delaware co.. Pa.

CHAGRIN FALLS, p. v., Orange township, Cuyahoga co., O., 153 ms. N. E. of Columbus; from W. 341 ms. Pop. 1,250.

CHALK BLUFF, p. o., Greene co., Ark.

CHALK LEVEL, p. o., Pittsylvania co., Va., 150 ms. s. w. of Richmond; from W. 233 ms.

CHALK LEVEL, p. o., Cumberland co., N. C.

CHALK LEVEL, p. o., St. Clair co., Mo.

CHALK LEVEL, p. o., Hopkins co., Ky.

CHALK LEVEL, v., Humphreys co., Tenn., 70. ms. w. of Nashville.

CHALKVILLE, p. o., Chester co., S. C.

CHALMERS, p. o., Niagara township, Niagara co., N. Y., 291 ms. w. by N. of Albany; from W. 410 ms.

CHAMBERLAND, v., McNairy co., Tenn., 146 ms. s. w. by w. of Nashville; from W. 823 ms.

CHAMBERSBURGH, c. h., p. b., seat of justice of Franklin co., Pa., 45 ms. s. w. of Harrisburgh; from W. 90 ms. Watered by Conecocheague creek. Pop. 3,335.

CHAMBERSBURGH, p. v., Butler township, Montgomery co., O., 75 ms. s. w. of Columbus; from W. 468 ms.

CHAMBERSBURGH, p. v., Pike co., Ill., 63 ms. w. by s. of Springfield; from W. 843 ms.

CHAMBERSBURGH, p. o., Clark co., Mo.

CHAMBERSBURGH, p. o., Orange co., Ind.

CHAMBERSBURGH, v., West township, Columbiana co., O.

CHAMBERS COUNTY situated on the easterly

boundary of Alabama, with Chattahoochee river on the east, and traversed by Tallapoosa river in the northwest section. Area, 700 square miles. Seat of justice, Lafayette. Pop. in 1840, 17,333; in 1850, 23,960.

CHAMBERS, or LAFAYETTE, c. h., p. v., seat of justice of Chambers co., Ala., 164 ms. E. by S. of Tuscaloosa; from W. 769 ms.

CHAMBERS' CREEK, p. o., Navarro co., Tex.

CHAMBERS' MILLS, p. o., Buckingham co., Va., 81 ms. w. of Richmond; from W. 155 ms.

CHAMBERSVILLE, p. o., Dallas co., Ark.

CHAMBLISSBURGH, p. v., Bradford co., Va., 156 ms. w. by s. of Richmond; from W. 231 ms.

CHAMELEON SPRINGS, p. o., Edmonson co., Ky., 135 ms. s. w. of Frankfort; from W. 658 ms.

CHAMPAGNOLLE, p. o., Union co., Ark.

CHAMPAIGN COUNTY, situated toward the westerly part of Ohio, and traversed by Mad river. Area, 450 square miles. Face of the country level, or gently undulating, with a soil exuberantly fertile. Seat of justice, Urbana. Pop. in 1820, 8,479; in 1830, 12,130; in 1840, 16.721; in 1850, 19,762.

CHAMPAIGN COUNTY, situated in the eastern part of Illinois, and drained by Kaskaskia, Embarrass, Sangamon, and Vermilion rivers. Area, 792 square miles. Face of the country generally level, containing much prairie with fine timber. Seat of justice, Urbana. Pop. in 1840, 1,475; in 1850, 2,649.

CHAMPION, p. t., Jefferson co., N. Y., 152 ms. N. w. of Albany; from W. 428 ms. Watered by Black river and tributaries. Pop. 2,085.

CHAMPION, p. t., Trumbull co., O. Pop. 1,070.

CHAMPION SOUTH ROADS, p. o., Champion township, Jefferson co., N. Y., 152 ms. N. w. of Albany; from W. 420 ms.

CHAMPLAIN, p. t., Clinton co., N. Y., 185 ms. N. by E. of Albany; from W. 560 ms. Watered by Chazy river and Lake Champlain. Pop. 5,067.

CHAMPOAG, p. o., Marion co., Oregon.

CHANANHATCHIE, p. o., Tallapoosa co., Ala.

CHANCE PRAIRIE, p. o., Burleson co., Tex.

CHANCEFORD, p. t., York co., Pa., 47 ms. s. s. E. of Harrisburgh; from W. 97 ms. Pop. 1,614.

CHANCELLORSVILLE, p. o., Spottsylvania co., Va., 72 N. of Richmond; from W. 66 ms.

CHANCERY. p. o., Howard co., Ind.

CHANCEVILLE, p. o., Monmouth co., N. J.

CHANDLERSVILLE, p. o., Muskingum co., O.

CHANDLERVILLE, t., Somerset co., Me., 39 ms w by w. of Augusta, from W. 657 ms. Watered by Sebasticook river.

CHANDLERVILLE, p. o., Chester co., Pa.

CHANEYVILLE, p. o., Morgan co., O., 75 ms. E. by s. of Columbus; from W. 334 ms.

CHANNAHON, p. o., Will co., Iowa, 156 ms. N. E. of Springfield; from W. 751 ms.

CHANNING, t., Lenawell co., Mich.

CHANNINGVILLE, p. o., Du Buque co., Iowa.

CHANTILLY, p. o., Fairfax co., Va., 127 ms. N. of Richmond; from W. 27 ms.

CHAPEL HILL, p. v., Orange co., N. C., 28 ms. N. w. of Raleigh; from W. 286 ms. Watered by New Hope river. Seat of the University of North Carolina.

CHAPEL HILL, p. v., Marshall co., Tenn., 38 ms. s. of Nashville; from W. 701 ms.

CHAPEL HILL, p. o., Perry co., O.

CHAPEL HILL, p. o., Washington co., Tex.

CHAPEL HILL, p. o., Monmouth co., N. J.

CHAPEL HILL, p. o., Lafayette co., Mo.

CHAPELBURGH. p. o., Humphrey township, Cattaraugus co., N. Y., 305 ms. w. by s. of Albany; from W. 320 ms.

CHAPINVILLE, p. o., Hopewell township, Ontario co., N. Y., 198 ms. w. of Albany; from W. 344 ms.

CHAPINVILLE, p. o., Litchfield co., Conn., 56 ms. w. of Hartford; from W. 348 ms.

CHAPLIN, p. t., Windham co., Ct., 37 ms. E. by N. of Hartford; from W. 366 ms. Watered by Natchang river. Pop. 796.

CHAPLIN. p. o., Nelson co., Ky., 37 ms. s. w. of Frankfort; from W. 579 ms.

CHAPMAN, p. t., Union co., Pa., 42 ms. N. by w. of Harrisburgh; from W. 152 ms. Watered by Mahantango creek. Pop. 1,501.

CHAPMAN, t., Clinton co., Pa. Pop. 542.

CHAPMANVILLE, p. o., Logan co., Va., 361 ms. w. of Richmond; from W. 398 ms.

CHAPPAQUA, p. o. Westchester co., N. Y.

CHAPPELL, p. o., Dallas co., Ark.

CHAPPELL'S BRIDGE, p. o., Newberry district, S. C.

CHAPTICO, p. v., St. Mary's co., Md., 75 ms. s. of Annapolis; from W. 52 ms.

CHAPULTEPEC, p. o., Blount co., Ala.

CHAPULTEPEC, p. o., Benton co., Tenn.

CHARDON, c. h., p. t., seat of justice of Geauga co., O., 170 ms. N. E. of Columbus; from W. 338 ms. Pop. 1,621.

CHARENTON, p. o., St. Mary's parish, La.

CHARETTE, t., Warren co., Mo.

CHARITON COUNTY, situated toward the northerly part of Missouri, with Missouri river on the southwest, and Grand river on the west. Area, 832 square miles. Seat of justice, Keytesville. Pop. in 1840, 4,746; in 1850, 7,514.

CHARITON, t., Howard co., Mo.

CHARITON, v., Chariton co., Mo., 75 ms. N. w. of Jefferson city; from W. 980 ms. Watered by Missouri and Chariton rivers. Pop. 564.

CHARITON, t., Macon co., Mo.

CHARITON, c. h. p. v., seat of justice of Lucas co., Iowa.

CHARITON MILLS, p. o., Adair co., Mo.

CHARITY, p. o., Lincoln co., Tenn.

CHARLEMONT, p. t., Franklin co., Mass., 109 ms. w. by N. of Boston; from W. 415 ms. Watered by Deerfield river. Pop. 1,173.

CHARLEMONT, p. o., Bedford co., Va.

CHARLES COUNTY, situated in the southwest part of Maryland, on the northeast side of Potomac river. Area, 450 square miles. Face of the country hilly; soil generally of fair quality, but in some parts sandy. Seat of justice, Port Tobacco. Pop. in 1820. 16,500; in 1830, 17,666; in 1840. 16.023; in 1850, 16.162.

CHARLES CITY COUNTY, situated toward the southeast part of Virginia, between James and Chickahoming rivers. Area, 208 square miles. Face of the country generally hilly or rolling; soil of middling quality. Seat of justice, Charles City Court House. Pop. in 1820, 5,255; in 1830, 5,504; in 1840, 4,774; in 1850, 5,200.

CHARLES CITY, c. h., p. v., seat of justice of Charles City co., Va., 45 ms. s. E. by E. of Richmond; from W. 162 ms.

CHARLES RIVER VILLAGE, p. v., Norfolk co., Mass.

CHARLESTON DISTRICT, situated on the southeast boundary of South Carolina, on the Atlantic ocean, with Santee river on the northeast, and Combahee river on the southwest. Area, 2,244 square miles. Face of the country generally level; soil, in parts highly productive, while in others it is marshy or sandy. Seat of justice, Charleston. Pop, in 1820, 80,212; in 1830, 86,338; in 1840, 82,661; in 1850, 72,805.

CHARLESTON, city, and seat of justice of the district of the same name, occupies a point of land formed by the confluence of Ashley and Cooper rivers, which together enter the ocean by a spacious and deep harbor, extending seven miles below the city. It is 120 miles southeast of Columbia, the state capital, and 540 miles from Washington. Four channels, of different depths, afford an entrance into the harbor through a sand-bar which obstructs it. The deepest of these admits ships with 16 feet draught. The harbor is defended by Fort Moultrie, on Sullivan island, lying at its mouth, and by Forts Pinckney and Johnson.

The city stands on ground somewhat elevated above tide-water, and may be said to resemble New York on a smaller scale. It is constructed with regularity and taste, and many rich and varied trees of southern climes lend their charms. Besides the city proper, there are populous suburbs, which afford fine sites for residences, and are identified with its growth and interests. Charleston may be considered as the metropolis of the southern Atlantic states, as New Orleans is of those on the Mexican gulf and the Mississippi. Into this basin, flow many of the products of North Carolina and Georgia. Its foreign commerce is extensive and valuable, as is also its coasting trade, and packets, as well as splendid steamships, ply to New York and other maritime cities. The Santee canal connects Santee with Cooper river, thus opening a communication from Columbia, the state capital, to Charleston.

The public buildings and institutions of the city, indicate the wealth, intelligence, and liberality of the people. There are a number of banks, churches, and hotels, some of them splendid and costly. Other prominent buildings are the customhouse, guard-house, exchange, city-hall state citadel, almshouse, orphan asy-

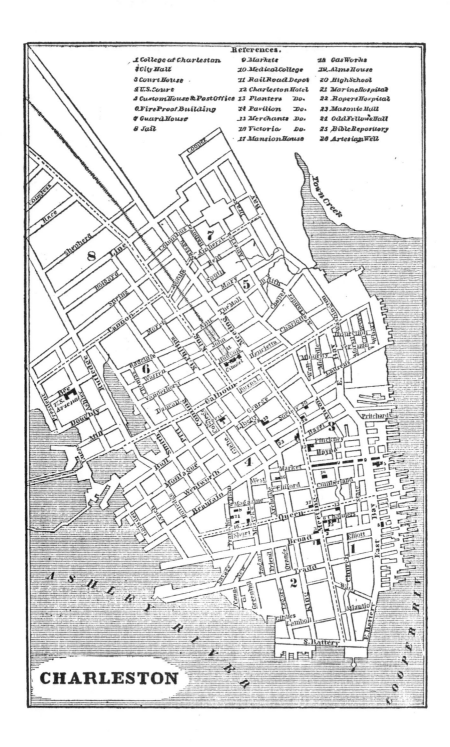

References.

1 College at Charleston
2 City Hall
3 Court House
4 U.S. Court
5 Custom House & Post Office
6 Fire Proof Building
7 Guard House
8 Jail
9 Markets
10 Medical College
11 Rail Road Depot
12 Charleston Hotel
13 Planters   Do.
14 Pavilion   Do.
15 Merchants Do.
16 Victoria   Do.
17 Mansion House
18 Gas Works
19 Alms House
20 High School
21 Marine Hospital
22 Ropers Hospital
23 Masonic Hall
24 Odd Fellows Hall
25 Bible Repository
26 Artesian Well

CHARLESTON

lum, jail, and the College of Charleston. The literary and scientific institutions and libraries, are generally respectable and flourishing. No city is more justly noted for hospitality and refinement, and its climate is more salubrious than that of most southern cities, affording a delightful and safe summer resort for planters from the low country and the West Indies, and a pleasant winter resort for people from the north.

The South Carolina railroad extends to Augusta, on the Savannah, 137 miles, where it communicates with the Georgia railroad. At Branchtown, 62 miles from Charleston, the Columbia branch diverges to Camden and Columbia.

The population in 1790, was 16,359 ; in 1800, 18,712; in 1810, 24,711 ; in 1820, 24,480 ; in 1830, 30,289 ; in 1840, 29,261 ; in 1850, 42,985.

CHARLESTON, p. t., Montgomery co., N. Y., 40 ms. w. N. w. of Albany ; from W. 399 ms. Watered by Schoharie river and branches of the Mohawk. Pop. 2,216.

CHARLESTON, p. t., Tioga co., Pa., 146 ms. N. of Harrisburgh ; from W. 256 ms. Pop. 1,470.

CHARLESTON, p. t., Penobscot co., Me., 98 ms. N. E. of Augusta ; from W. 689 ms. Pop. 1,283.

CHARLESTON, v., Peoria co., Ill., 91 ms. N. of Springfield ; from W. 805 ms.

CHARLESTON, p. t., Coles co., Ill., 78 ms. E. by s. of Springfield ; from W. 707 ms. Pop. 2,262.

CHARLESTON, p. t., Kalamazoo co., Mich., 127 ms. w. of Detroit ; from W. 592 ms. Pop. 846.

CHARLESTON, p. o., Mississippi co., Mo.

CHARLESTON, p. v., Bradley co., Tenn., 167 ms. s. E. of Nashville ; from W. 570 ms.

CHARLESTON, p. v., Tallahatchee co., Miss., 136 ms. N. of Jackson ; from. 967 ms.

CHARLESTON, p. o., Lee co., Iowa.

CHARLESTON, t., Orleans co., Vt., 55 ms. N. N. E. of Montpelier ; from W. 571 ms. Pop. 1,008.

CHARLESTON FOUR CORNERS, p. o., Charleston township, Montgomery co., N. Y., 38 m. w. N. w. of Albany ; from W. 397 ms.

CHARLESTOWN, p. t., Sullivan co.. N. H., 54 ms. w. of Concord ; from W. 453 ms. Watered by Connecticut and Little Sugar rivers. Pop. 1,644.

CHARLESTOWN, city, Middlesex co., Mass., 1 m. N. of Boston ; from W. 441 ms. Watered by Charles and Mystic rivers. It contains one of the U. S. Navy Yards, with a dry dock ; also, the Massachusetts stateprison, and the Bunker Hill Monument. Pop. in 1840, 11,484 ; in 1850, 17,216.

CHARLESTOWN, p. t., Washington co., R. I., 45 ms. s. s. w. of Providence ; from W. 385 ms. Watered by Charles and Pawcatuck rivers. Pop. 994.

CHARLESTOWN, p. v., Cecil co., Md., 70 ms. N. E. of Annapolis ; from W. 80 ms.

CHARLESTOWN, c. h., p. v., seat of justice of Jefferson co., Va., 168 ms. N. of Richmond ; from W. 65 ms. Pop. 1,507.

CHARLESTOWN, p. t., Portage co., O., 145 ms. N. E. of Columbus ; from W. 321 ms. Watered by branches of Mahoning river.

CHARLESTOWN, t., Chester co., Pa., 82 ms. E. of Harrisburgh ; from W. 90 ms. Watered by Susquehanna river. Pop. 979.

CHARLESTOWN, c. h., p. v., seat of justice of Clark co., Ind., 101 ms. s. s. E. of Indianapolis ; from W. 589 ms. Pop. 3,905.

CHARLOE, c. h., p. v., seat of justice of Paulding co., O., 137 ms. N. w. of Columbus ; from W. 506 ms.

CHARLOTTE COUNTY, situated in the southerly part of Virginia, on the northeast side of Staunton river. Area 600 square miles ; surface pleasantly variegated by hill and dale ; soil excellent and well watered. Seat of justice, Marysville, or Charlotte Court House. Pop. in 1820, 13,290 ; in 1830, 15,254 ; in 1840, 14,595 ; in 1850, 13,955.

CHARLOTTE, p. t., Washington co., Me., 186 ms. E. N. E. of Augusta ; from W. 772 ms. Pop. 718.

CHARLOTTE, p. t., Chittenden co., Vt., 54 ms. w. of Montpelier ; from W. 449 ms. Watered by Lake Champlain, Platte river, and Lewis creek. Pop. 1,634.

CHARLOTTE, p. v., Greece township, Monroe co., N. Y., 224 ms, w. N. w. of Albany ; from W. 375 ms. Watered by Genesee river and Lake Ontario.

CHARLOTTE, c. h., p. v., seat of justice of Charlotte co., Va., 98 ms. w. s. w. of Richmond ; from W. 185 ms.

CHARLOTTE, c. h., p. v., seat of justice of Mecklen-

burgh co., N. C., 158 ms. s. w. of Raleigh ; from W. 397 ms. Watered by Sugar creek.

CHARLOTTE, c. h., p. v., seat of justice of Dickson co., Tenn., 38 ms. w. by N. of Nashville ; from W. 722 ms.

CHARLOTTE, p. t., Eaton co., Mich., 116 ms. w. by s. of Detroit ; from W. 586 ms.

CHARLOTTE, t., Chautauque co., N. Y.. 330 ms. w. by s. of Albany ; from W. 349 ms. Watered by Cassadaga creek. Pop. 1,718.

CHARLOTTE CENTRE, p. o., Charlotte township, Chautauque co., N. Y., 333 ms. w. by s. of Albany ; from W. 333 ms.

CHARLOTTE HALL, p. v., containing a seat of learning of the same name, St. Mary's co., Md., 66 ms. s. of Annapolis ; from W. 60 ms.

CHARLOTTESVILLE, p. o., Hancock co., Ind.. 28 ms. E of Indianapolis ; from W. 543 ms.

CHARLOTTESVILLE, c. h., p. t., seat of justice of Albermarle co., Va., 85 ms. N. w. of Richmond ; from W. 121 ms. Watered by Moore's creek.

CHARLOTTEVILLE, p. o., Summit township, Schoharie co., N. Y., 57 ms. w. of Albany ; from W. 373 ms.

CHARLTON, p. t., Worcester co., Mass., 53 ms. s. w. by w. of Boston ; from W. 387 ms.

CHARLTON, p. t., Saratoga co., N. Y., 25 ms. N. N. w. of Albany ; from W. 393 ms. Watered by a branch of Mohawk river. Pop. 1,902.

CHARLTON DEPOT, p. o., Charlton township, Worcester co., Mass., 56 ms. w. s. w. of Boston ; from W. 386 ms.

CHARTIERS, p. t., Washington co., Pa., 223 ms. w. by s. of Harrisburgh ; from W. 240 ms. Watered by. Chartiers creek. Pop. 1,677.

CHASEVILLE, p. o., Murray co., Ga.

CHASEVILLE, p o., Benton co., Tenn.

CHATEAUGAY, p. t., Franklin co., N. Y.. 202 ms. N. by w. of Albany ; from W. 541 ms. Watered by Chateaugay river. Pop. 3,728.

CHATATY, p. o., Bradley co., Tenn.

CHATFIELD, p. t., Crawford co., O., 73 ms N. of Columbus ; from W. 412 ms. Watered by Sycamore creek. Pop. 1,351.

CHATHAM COUNTY, situated in the central part of North Carolina, and traversed by Haw and Deep rivers. Area, 858 square miles. Face of the country generally hilly ; soil varied. Seat of justice, Pittsborough. Pop. in 1820, 12,661 ; in 1830, 15,499 ; in 1840, 16,242 ; in 1850, 18,449

CHATHAM COUNTY, situated at the eastern angle of Georgia, on the Atlantic ocean, between Ogeechee and Savannah rivers. Area, 405 square miles. Face of the country level ; soil in general sandy, or marshy, but in some parts fertile. Seat of justice, Savannah. Pop. in 1820, 14,737 ; in 1830, 14,230 ; in 1840, 18,801 ; in 1850, 23,901.

CHATHAM, p. t., Barnstable co., Mass., 96 ms. s. E. of Boston ; from W. 497 ms. Situated on Pleasant bay. Pop. 2,439.

CHATHAM, p. t., Middlesex co., Ct., 16 ms. s. of Hartford ; from W. 326 ms. Watered by Connecticut and Salmon rivers. Pop. 1,525.

CHATHAM, p. t., Columbia co., N. Y., 18 ms. s. by E. of Albany ; from W. 362 ms. Watered by Kinderhook creek. Pop. 3,839.

CHATHAM, p. t., Morris co., N. J., 56 ms. N. N. E. of Trenton ; from W. 221 ms. Watered by Passaic river. Pop. 2,469.

CHATHAM, t., Carroll co., N. H., 83 ms. N. E. of Concord ; from W. 559 ms. Watered by a head branch of Saco river. Pop. 516.

CHATHAM, t., Tioga co., Pa. Pop. 1,248.

CHATHAM, p. v., Chester co., Pa., 68 ms. E. s. E. of Harrisburgh ; from W. 102 ms.

CHATHAM, t., Medina co., O. Pop. 1,167.

CHATHAM, p. v., Newton township, Licking co., O.

CHATHAM, p. o., Sangamon co., Ill., 10 ms. N. N. w. of Springfield ; from W. 790 ms.

CHATHAM, p. o., Buchanan co., Iowa.

CHATHAM CENTRE, p. o., Chatham township, Columbia co., N. Y., 19 ms. s. by E. of Albany ; from W. 359 ms.

CHATHAM CENTRE, p. o., Chatham township, Medina co., O.

CHATHAM FOUR CORNERS, p. v., Chatham township, Columbia co., N. Y., 23 ms. s. by E. of Albany ; from W. 355 ms.

CHATHAM HILL, p. o., Smyth co., Va., 273 ms. w. by s. of Richmond ; from W. 341 ms.

CHATHAM RUN, p. o., Clinton co., Pa.

CHATHAM VALLEY, p. o., Tioga co., Pa.

CHATTAHOOCHEE, p. v., Gadsden co., Flor., 45 ms. w. of Tallahassee; from W. 886 ms. Watered by Appalachicola river.

CHATTOOGA COUNTY, situated on the westerly boundary of Georgia. Area. 300 square miles. Seat of justice, Summerville. Pop. in 1840, 3,438; in 1850, 6,815.

CHATTANOOGA, p. o., Hamilton co., Ten., 141 ms. s. E. of Nashville; from W. 610 ms.

CHATTOOGAVILLE, p. v., Chattooga co., Ga., 185 ms. N. w. of Milledgeville; from W. 662 ms.

CHAUMONT, p. v., Lyme township, Jefferson co., N. Y., 178 ms. N. w. of Albany; from W. 430 ms. Watered by Chaumont bay and Lake Ontario.

CHAUNCEY, p. o., Athens co., O., 67 ms. s. E. of Columbus; from W. 345 ms.

CHAUNCEYVILLE, p. o., Manitowoc co., Wis.

CHAUTAUQUE COUNTY, situated in the extreme southwest corner of New York, with Lake Erie on the northwest, and also contains Chautauque lake. Area, 1,017 square miles. Face of the country rocky and hilly, with a very productive soil. Seat of justice, Mayville. Pop. in 1820, 12,568; in 1830, 34,057; in 1840, 47,975; in 1850, 50,493.

CHAUTAUQUE, p. t., seat of justice of Chautauque co., N. Y., 336 ms. w. by s. of Albany. Pop. 2,622.

CHAUTAUQUE VALLEY, p. o., Alleghany co., N. Y.

CHAZY, p. t., Clinton co., N. Y., 178 ms. N. of Albany; from W. 553 ms. Watered by Little Chazy river and Lake Champlain. Pop. 4,324.

CHEAP VALLEY, p. o., Henry co., Tenn.

CHEAT BRIDGE, p. o., Preston co., Va.

CHEEKSVILLE, p. o., Marion co., Tenn., 122 ms. s. E. of Nashville; from W. 487 ms.

CHEBOYGAN COUNTY, situated at the north part of the peninsula of Michigan, with the straits of Mackinaw on the north. Area, 300 square miles. Seat of justice, Duncan.

CHEEKTOWAGA, p. o., Erie co., N. Y.

CHEESEQUAKES, p. o., Middlesex co., N. J.

CHEHALEM. p. o., Yam Hill co., Oregon.

CHELMSFORD, p. t., Middlesex co., Mass., 27 ms. N. N. w., of Boston; from W. 442 ms. Watered by Merrimack river. Pop. 2,097.

CHELSEA, p. t., seat of justice of Orange co., Vt., 24 ms. s. E. of Montpelier; from W. 503 ms. Watered by a branch of White river. Pop. 1,958.

CHELSEA, p. t., Suffolk co., Mass., 4 ms. N. E. of Boston; from W. 444 ms. Watered by Charles and Saugus rivers. Pop. 6,701.

CHELSEA, p. o., Will co., Ill.

CHELSEA, p. o., Washtenaw co., Mich.

CHELTENHAM, t., Montgomery co., Pa., 108 ms. E. of Harrisburgh; from W. 145 ms. Pop. 1,292.

CHEMUNG COUNTY, situated on the south boundary of New York, and watered by Chemung river, Cayuta, and Newtown creeks, Seneca lake inlet and Chemung canal. Area, 530 square miles. Seat of justice, Elmira. Pop. in 1840, 20,732; in 1850, 28,795.

CHEMUNG, p. t., Chemung co., N. Y., 198 ms. w. s. w. of Albany; from W. 263 ms. * Watered by Chemung river. Pop. 2,673.

CHEMUNG, p. o., McHenry co., Ill.

CHENANGO COUNTY, situated near the central part of New York, and watered by Chenango canal and the river of the same name. Area, 800 square miles. Face of the country generally hilly, with a productive soil. Seat of justice, Norwich. Pop. in 1820, 31,215; in 1830, 37,406; in 1840, 40,785; in 1850, 55,460.

CHENANGO. t., Broome co., N. Y., 145 ms. s. w. of Albany; from W. 291 ms. Watered by Chenango and Susquehanna rivers. Pop. 8,734.

CHENANGO, p. o., Lawrence co., Pa., 238 ms. w. by N. of Harrisburgh; from W. 269 ms.

CHENANGO FORKS, p. v., Chenango township, Broome co.. N. Y., 127 ms. w. s. w. of Albany; from W. 307 ms. Watered by Tioughnioga and Chenango rivers, and Chenango canal.

CHENEY'S GROVE, p. o., McLean co., Ill.

CHENEYVILLE, v., Rapides parish, La., 265 ms. N. w. of New Orleans; from W. 1,236 ms.

CHENINGO, p. o., Cortland co., N. Y., 135 ms. w. by s. of Albany; from W. 332 ms.

CHENUBA. p. o., Lee co., Ga., 150 ms. s. w. of Milledgeville; from W. 795 ms.

CHEOHEE, p. o., Pickens co., S. C.

CHEPATCHET, p. v., Gloucester township, Providence co., R. I., 16 ms. w. by N. of Providence; from W. 395 ms. Watered by Chepatchet river.

CHEQUIST, p. o., Davis co., Iowa.

CHERAW, p. v., Chesterfield district, S. C., 93 ms. N. E. of Columbia; from W. 423 ms. Watered by Great Pedee river.

CHEROKEE COUNTY, situated at the extreme westerly angle of North Carolina. Area, 1,000 square miles. Face of the country generally mountainous and hilly, with a fertile soil along the stream. Seat of justice, Murphy. Pop. in 1840, 3,427; in 1850, 6,838.

CHEROKEE COUNTY, situated toward the northerly part of Georgia, and traversed by Etowah river. Area, 620 square miles. Seat of justice, Canton. Pop. in 1840, 5,895; in 1850, 12,800.

CHEROKEE COUNTY, situated on the easterly boundary of Alabama, and traversed by Coosa river. Seat of justice, Jefferson. Pop. in 1840, 8,773; in 1850, 13,884.

CHEROKEE COUNTY, situated toward the easterly part of Texas, between Angelina and Neches rivers. Area, —— square miles. Seat of justice, Rusk. Pop. in 1850, 5,057.

CHEROKEE NATION of Indians, who formerly inhabited the north part of Georgia, Alabama, and Mississippi, and a portion of Tennessee, most of whom have been removed to a territory west of Arkansas, provided for them by the United States government. Schools and missionary establishments have been successfully instituted among this people from time to time; but equally or more efficacious means of civilization have been introduced through the agency of agriculture and the mechanic arts. Their numbers in 1826 amounted to about 16,000. Their territory embraces —— square miles, and is traversed by Arkansas, Verdigris, and Neosho rivers. The chief town and military station is Fort Gibson on Neosho river.

CHEROKEE, v., McArthur township, Logan co., O., 75 ms. N. w. of Columbus; from W. 469 ms.

CHEROKEE CORNER, v., Oglethorpe co., Ga., 77 ms. N. of Milledgeville; from W. 602 ms.

CHEROKEE HEIGHTS, p. o., Abbeville district, S. C., 118 ms. w. of Columbia; from W. 555 ms.

CHEROKEE IRON WORKS, p. o., York district, S. C., 104 ms. N. of Columbia; from W. 455 ms.

CHERRY, p. t., Lycoming co., Pa.

CHERRY, p. o., Sullivan co., Pa.. 130 ms. N. of Harrisburgh; from W. 241 ms.

CHERRY, t., Butler co., Pa. Pop. 970.

CHERRY CREEK, p. t., Chautauque co., N. Y., 324 ms. w. by s. of Albany; from W. 340 ms. Watered by Connewango creek and tributaries. Pop. 1,311.

CHERRYFIELD, t., Washington co., Me.. 116 ms. E. by N. of Augusta. from W. 708 ms. Watered by Narragaugus river. Pop. 1,648.

CHERRY CREEK, p. o., Pontotoc co., Miss.

CHERRY FLAT, p. o., Rutherford co., Tenn.

CHERRY FLATS, p. o., Tioga co., Pa.

CHERRY GROVE, p. o., Carroll co., Ill., 190 ms. N. by w. of Springfield; from W. 853 ms.

CHERRY GROVE, p. o., Schuyler co., Mo.

CHERRY GROVE, p. o., Saline co., Ark.

CHERRY GROVE, v., St. Clair co., Ill.

CHERRY HILL, p. o., Brooke co., Va.

CHERRY HILL, p. o., Erie co., Pa.

CHERRY HILL, p. o., Cecil co., Md.

CHERRY HILL, p. o., Chickasaw co., Miss.

CHERRY LAKE, p. o., Madison co., Flor.

CHERRY MILLS, p. o., Sullivan co., Pa.

CHERRY RIDGE, p. v., Dyberry township, Wayne co., Pa., 167 ms. N. E. of Harrisburgh; from W. 304 ms. Pop. 614.

CHERRY RIDGE, p. o., Union parish, La.

CHERRY STORE, p. o., Northampton co., Va.

CHERRY TREE, p. t., Venango co., Pa., 230 ms. N. w. by w. of Harrisburgh; from W. 304 ms. Pop. 930.

CHERRY VALLEY, p. t., Otsego co., N. Y., 55 ms. w. of Albany; from W. 380 ms. Watered by Cherry Valley creek and branches of Canajoharie creek. Pop. 4,186.

CHERRY VALLEY, p. o., Washington co., Pa.

CHERRY VALLEY, p. o., Wilson co., Tenn.

CHERRY VALLEY, p. t., Ashtabula co., O., 202 ms. N. E. of Columbus; from W. 325 ms. Pop. 839.

CHERRY VALLEY, p. o., Boone co., Ill.

CHERRYVILLE, p. v., Northampton co., Pa., 107 ms. E. N. E. of Harrisburgh; from W. 200 ms.

CHERRYVILLE, p. o., Haywood co., Tenn., 154 ms. w. s. w. of Nashville; from W 837 ms.

CHERRYVILLE. p. o., Hunterdon co., N. J.

CHESAPEAKE, p. o., Lawrence co., Mo.

CHESAPEAKE, city, p. v., Cecil co., Md., 84 ms. N. E. of Annapolis ; from W. 96 ms. Watered by Elk river and Chesapeake bay.

CHESHER'S STORE, p. o., Anderson co., Ky.

CHESHIRE COUNTY, situated at the southwest corner of New Hampshire, on the easterly side of Connecticut river. Area, 442 square miles. Face of the country mountainous and hilly ; soil generally rocky, but productive and well watered. Seat of justice, Keene. Pop. in 1820, 45,376 ; in 1830, 27,016 ; in 1840, 26,429 ; in 1850, 28,344.

CHESHIRE, p. t., Berkshire co, Mass., 130 ms. w. by N. of Boston ; from W. 387 ms. Watered by Hoosack river. Pop. 1,298.

CHESHIRE, p. t., New Haven, Ct, 25 ms. s. s. w. of Hartford ; from W. 314 ms. Watered by Quinipiac river. Pop. 1,626.

CHESHIRE, v., Cheshire township, New Haven co., Ct.

CHESHIRE, p. v., Canandaigua township, Ontario co., N. Y., 203 ms. w. by N. of Albany ; from W. 346 ms.

CHESHIRE, p. t., Gallia co., O., 102 ms. s. s. E. of Columbus ; from W. 349 ms.· Watered by Ohio river. Pop. 1,410.

CHESNUT BLUFFS, p. o., Dyer co., Tenn., 157 ms. w. of Nashville ; from W. 840 ms.

CHESNUT CREEK, p. o.. Autauga co.,Ala., — ms. from Montgomery ; from W. 813 ms.

CHESNUT FLAT, p. o., Walker co., Ga.

CHESNUT GROVE, p. o., Lycoming co., Pa.

CHESNUT GROVE, p. o., Pittsylvania, Va., 175 ms. w. s. w. of Richmond ; from W. 258 ms.

CHESNUT GROVE, p. o., Shelby co., Ky., 23 ms. w. of Frankfort ; from W. 565 ms.

CHESNUT GROVE, p. o., Chester district, S. C., 64 ms. N. E. of Columbia ; from W. 445 ms.

CHESNUT GROVE, p. o., Davidson co., Tenn., 20 ms. from Nashville ; from W. 704 ma.

CHESNUT HILL, p. o., Strafford co., N. H., 49 ms. E. of Concord ; from W. 513 ms.

CHESNUT HILL, p. v., Germantown township, Philadelphia co., Pa., 104 ms. E. s. E. of Harrisburgh ; from W. 144 ms.

CHESNUT HILL, p.o., Northumberland co., Va., 95 ms. E. by N. of Richmond ; from W. 156 ms.

CHESNUT HILL, p. v.. Hall co., Ga., 107 ms. N. N. w. of Milledgeville ; from W. 679 ms.

CHESNUT HILL, t., Monroe co., Pa, Watered by Head's creek. Pop. 1,029.

CHESNUT HILL, p. o., Washington co., Ind., 107 ms. s. of Indianapolis ; from W. 618 ms.

CHESNUT HILL, p. o., Walton co., Flor.

CHESNUT LEVEL, p. o., Lancaster co., Pa., 53 ms. s. E. of Harrisburgh ; from W. 95 ms.

CHESNUT RIDGE, p. o., Dover township, Dutchess co., N. Y., 78 ms. s. by E. of Albany ; from W. 315 ms.

CHESNUT RIDGE, p. o., Union co., Pa.

CHESNUT RIDGE, p. o., Lincoln co., Tenn.

CHESS SPRINGS, p. o., Cambria co., Pa.

CHEST, p. t, Clearfield co., Pa., 150 ms. N. w. of Harrisburgh ; from W. 240 ms. Watered by West branch of Susquehanna river.

CHESTER COUNTY, situated at the southeast corner of Pennsylvania, with Schuylkill river on the northeast. Area, 729 square miles. Face of the country extremely diversified by mountains, hills, valleys and plains, with a soil equally varied, changing from rocky to the productive limestone valley, and the fertile loamy plain. Seat of justice, Westchester. Pop. in 1820, 44,455 ; in 1830, 50,910 : in 1840, 57,515 ; in 1850, 66,438.

CHESTER DISTRICT, situated in the northern part of South Carolina, between Broad and Catawba rivers. Area, 600 square miles. Face of the country pleasantly diversified by hill and dale ; soil of fair quality and well watered. Seat of justice, Chesterville. Pop. in 1820, 14,389 ; in 1830, 17,182 ; in 1840, 17,747 ; in 1850, 18,038.

CHESTER, p. t., Rockingham co., N. H., 22 miles s. E. of Concord ; from W. 463 ms. Watered by Exeter river and Massabesick pond. Pop.1,301.

CHESTER, t., Penobscot co., Me. Pop. 340.

CHESTER, p. t., Windsor co., Vt., 83 ms. s. of Montpelier ; from W. 457 ms. Pop. 2,001.

CHESTER, p. t., Eaton co., Mich.

CHESTER, p. t., Hampden co., Mass., 116 ms. w. by s. of Boston ; from W. 380 ms. Watered by tributaries of Westfield river. Pop. 1 521.

CHESTER, p. t., Middlesex co., Ct.. 34 ms. s. by E. of Hartford ; from W. 340 ms. Pop. 992.

CHESTER, p. v., Goshen township. Orange co., N. Y., 102 ms. s. by w. of Albany ; from W. 277 ms.

CHESTER, t., Warren co., N. Y., 80 ms. N. of Albany ; from W. 457 ms. Watered by Hudson river and Schroon lake. Pop. 1,850.

CHESTER, p. t., Morris co., N. J., 50 ms. N. by E. of Trenton ; from W. 224 ms. Watered by Black river and tributaries of the Raritan. Pop. 1,334.

CHESTER, c. h., p. v., seat of justice of Delaware co., Pa.. 94 ms. E. s. E. of Harrisburgh ; from W. 124 ms. Watered by Delaware river. Pop. 1,667.

CHESTER, p. t., Delaware co., Pa. Pop. 3,910.

CHESTER, c. h., p. v., seat of justice of Chester district, S. C., 67 ms. N. by w. of Columbia ; from W. 452 ms.

CHESTER, p. v., Gwinett co., Ga., 82 ms. N. w. of Milledgeville ; from W. 656 ms.

CHESTER, p. t., Meigs co., O., 95 ms. s. s. E. of Columbus ; from W. 334 ms. Watered by Shade river. Pop. 1,598.

CHESTER, t., Burlington co., N. J., 11 ms. s. w. of Trenton ; from W. 177 ms. Watered by Pensauken, Rancocus, and Pompeston creeks, and Swedes branch. Pop. 3,598.

CHESTER, t., Knox co., O., 40 ms. N. N. E. of Columbus ; from W. 386 ms. Watered by a branch of Vernon river.

CHESTER, t., Butler co., O.

CHESTER, t., Clinton co., O. Watered by tributaries of Little Miami river. Pop. 1,600.

CHESTER, t., Geauga co., O., 160 ms. N. E. of Columbus. Pop. 1,103.

CHESTER, p. o., Dodge co., Wis.

CHESTER, p. o., Wayne co., Ind.

CHESTER, p. o., Randolph co., Ill.

CHESTER, p. o., Gibson co., Tenn.

CHESTER CROSS ROADS, p. o., Chester township, Geauga co., O.

CHESTER FACTORIES, p. o., Chester township, Hampden co., Mass.,113 ms. w. by s. of Boston ; from W. 390 ms.

CHESTERFIELD COUNTY, situated toward the southeast part of Virginia, between Appomattox and James rivers. Area, 456 square miles. Face of the country hilly ; soil of fair quality. Seat of justice, Chesterfield Court House. Pop. 1820, 18,003 ; in 1830, 18,637 : in 1840, 17,140 ; in 1850, 17,486.

CHESTERFIELD DISTRICT, situated on the north boundary of South Carolina, Great Pedee river, and Lynch creek. Area, 750 square miles. Face of the country hilly ; soil sandy and generally of fair quality. Seat of justice, Chesterfield Court House. Pop. in 1820, 6,645 ; in 1830, 17,182 ; in 1840, 8,574 ; in 1850, 10,790.

CHESTERFIELD, p. t., Cheshire co.. N. H., 59 ms. s. w. of Concord ; from W. 430 ms. Watered by Catt's Bane and Partridge brooks, Spafford's lake, and Connecticut river. Pop 1 680.

CHESTERFIELD, p. t., Hampshire co., Mass., 106 ms. w. of Boston ; from W. 393 ms. Watered by a branch of Westfield, river. Pop. 1,014.

CHESTERFIELD, p. v., Montville township, New London co., Ct., 36 ms. s. E. of Hartford ; from W. 360 ms.

CHESTERFIELD, p. t., Fulton co., O., 170 ms. N. N. w. of Columbus ; from W. 501 ms. Watered by Bean creek. Pop. 539.

CHESTERFIELD, p. t., Burlington co., N. J. Watered by Black and Crosswick's creeks. Pop. 4,514.

CHESTERFIELD, p. o., Madison co., Ind.

CHESTERFIELD, p. o., Macoupin co., Ill., 49 ms. s. s. w. of Springfield ; from W. 821 ms.

CHESTERFIELD, t., Essex co., N. Y., 150 ms. N. of Albany. Watered by Lake Champlain and Au Sable river. Pop. 4171.

CHESTERFIELD, c. h., p. o., seat of justice of Chesterfield co., Va., 16 ms. s. by w. of Richmond ; from W. 133 ms.

CHESTERFIELD, c. h., p. v., seat of justice of Chesterfield district, S. C., 105 ms. N. N. E. of Columbia ; from W. 435 ms. Watered by Thompson's creek.

CHESTERFIELD, p. o., Madison Parish, La.

CHESTERFIELD FACTORY, p. o., Chesterfield township, Cheshire co., N. H., 56 ms. s. w. of Concord ; from W. 433 ms.

CHESTER HILL, p. o., Morgan co., O., 83 ms. s. E. of Columbus ; from W. 326 ms.

CHESTER SPRINGS, p. o., Pikeland township, Chester co., Pa., 72 ms. s. E. of Harrisburgh ; from W. 150 ms.

* CHESTERTOWN, p. v., Chester township, Warren co., N. Y., 81 ms. N. of Albany ; from W. 456 ms.

CHESTERTOWN, c. h., p. v., seat of justice of Kent co., Md., 54 ms. N. E of Annapolis ; from W. 94 ms. Watered by Chester river.

CHESTER VILLAGE, p. v., Hampden co., Mass. Pop. 1,521.

CHESTERVILLE, p. t., Franklin co., Me., 26 ms. N. w. of Augusta ; from W. 611 ms. Watered by Wilson's stream. Pop. 1,142.

CHESTERVILLE, p. o., Chester co., Pa.

CHESTERVILLE, p. v., Chester township, Morrow co., O., 53 ms. N. N. E. of Columbus ; from W. 389 ms. Pop. 407.

CHESTERVILLE, p. o., Kent co., Md.

CHESTERVILLE. v., Gibson co., Tenn., 148 ms. w. of Nashville ; from W. 830 ms.

CHEVOIT, p. v., Green township, Hamilton co., O., 122 ms. s. w. of Columbus ; from W. 496 ms.

CHEW'S LANDING, p. v., Gloucester township, Gloucester co., N. J., 38 ms. s. s. E. of Trenton ; from W. 148 ms. Watered by Big Timber creek.

CHEWSVILLE, p. v., Washington co., Md. 105 ms. N. w. of Annapolis ; from W. 73 ms.

CHICAGO, city, and seat of justice of Cook co., Ill., is situated on the west side of Lake Michigan, and occupies both sides of the river, from which it takes its name, and is built on the border of a prairie, elevated a little above the level of the lake. Few towns have a more advantageous position. The river, formed by the confluence of two branches, in the upper part of the city, is deep and spacious enough for a vast number of steamboats and vessels of various kinds, which here assemble from different points on the lakes, the St. Lawrence, the Erie, and Welland canals, and thickly line the wharves for some distance up the streams which form the harbor. The shore of the lake, naturally shallow, has been extended into deep water, by means of two piers, which, projecting from both sides of the harbor, protect it from the accumulation of sand. The streets of Chicago are generally broad and pleasant, lined with trees, and leading to the open prairie, or affording fine views of the lake. The buildings have the appearance of unusual comfort and convenience, while many of the public edifices are surpassed by those of few cities in the Union. Large warehouses and stores, five or six stories high, splendid hotels, churches, fine public schools, and dwellings, frequently magnificent, are some of the structures which strike the eye, and excite admiration. Twenty years ago, the lands of the adjacent prairie were the property of the Pottawatomie Indians. In 1833, the tribe removed, by treaty, to lands in Missouri, and gave up their prairie to the settlers of Chicago ; since then, it has continued to increase, and of late with unexampled rapidity. The Illinois and Michigan canal, by connecting the navigation of the lake with that of the great river of the state, has caused the current of trade, which formerly flowed toward Mississippi river, to turn toward the "garden city," making it the market of the rich productions of Illinois, and of vast quantities of goods from New York and other eastern cities. The branches of commerce in which Chicago is most extensively engaged, are lumber, grain, and cattle. It exceeds all other western cities in the quantity of lumber exported ; vast forests of pine and other trees, covering the northern part of Wisconsin, while immense numbers of cattle, from the interior, are here slaughtered and transported eastward, frequently to New York. The canal, which has contributed so largely to the growth of Chicago, is worthy of extended notice. Commencing about 3 miles above the mouth of the river, it traverses the valley of that stream, and of the Des Plains, and terminus at Peru, the head of steamboat navigation on the Illinois. The whole length is 106 miles, width 60 feet, depth 6 feet. A navigable feeder, four miles long, communicates with Fox river, and the canal descends 20 feet by two locks toward the Illinois. It was begun in 1836, and finished in 1849.

The Galena and Chicago Union Railroad, commences at Chicago, and extends to Galena, the head of steamboat navigation on the Mississippi, and the depot of a region rich in lead. The central road will unite it with Mississippi river near the mouth of the Ohio, while the Southern and central Michigan roads connect it with the eastern states.

The population in 1840, was 4,479 ; in 1850, 29,964 ; in 1852, 38,733.

CHICHESTER, p. t., Merrimack co., N. H., 8 ms. E. of Concord ; from W. 489 ms. Watered by Suncook river. Pop. 997.

CHICKAHOMINY, p. o., Hanover co., Va., 13 ms. N. of Richmond ; from W. 122 ms.

CHICKAMAUGAH. p. o., Hamilton co., Tenn.

CHICKASAW COUNTY, situated toward the north erly part of Mississippi. Area, 970 square miles. Seat of justice, Houston. Pop. in 1840, 2,055 ; in 1850, 16,368.

CHICKASAW NATION of Indians, who formerly inhabited the regions along the head branches of Alabama, Tombigbee, and Yazoo rivers, in the northwest part of Georgia and the northerly parts of Alabama and Mississippi, most of whom have emigrated to the territory west of Arkansas on the north side of Red river, appropriated for them by the United States government. Their number in 1830, was about 3,500. Area of their territory, —— square miles. Chief town, Fort Washita. Pop. in 1850

CHICKASAW, p. o., Mercer co., O., 102 ms. w. N. w. of Columbus ; from W. 496 ms.

CHICKASAW, p. o., Franklin co., Ala.

CHICKASAWHATCHIE, p. o., Lee co., Ga.

CHICKTAWAGA, t., Erie co., N. Y., 278 ms. w. of Albany. Watered by Cayuga and Cazenovia creeks.

CHICK'S SPRINGS, p. o., Greenville district, S. C.

CHICOPEE FALLS, p. v., Springfield township, Hampden co., Mass., 87 ms. w. s. w. of Boston ; from W. 368 ms. Watered by Chicopee river.

CHICOPEE, p. o., Hampden co., Mass.

CHICOT COUNTY, situated at the southeast corner of Arkansas, on the westerly side of Mississippi river. Area, 1,800 square miles. Seat of justice, Columbia. Pop. in 1830, 1,165 ; in 1840, 3,806 ; in 1850, 5,115.

CHICOT, p. o., Butte co., Cal.

CHIKALAH, p. o., Yell co., Ark.

CHILDSBURGH, v., Fayette co., Ky., 32 ms. E. of Frankfort ; from W. 530 ms.

CHILDSVILLE, p. o., Yancey co., N. C.

CHILHOWEE, p. o,, Blount co., Tenn., 197 ms. E. by s. of Nashville ; from W. 540 ms.

CHILI, p. t., Monroe co., N. Y., 224 ms. w. by N. of Albany ; from W. 379 ms. Watered by Black creek. Pop. 2,247.

CHILI, p. o., Miami co., Ind.

CHILI, p. o., Hancock co., Ill., 109 ms. w. N. w. of Springfield ; from W. 882 ms.

CHILI, p. o., Coshocton co., O., 92 ms. N. E. of Columbus ; from W. 340 ms.

CHILLICOTHE, p. t., seat of justice of Ross co., O., and formerly capital of the state, is situated on the west bank of the Scioto river, 45 ms. s. of Columbus, and 93 E. N. E. from Cincinnati ; from W. 405 ms. The Scioto washes its northern limit, and Paint creek its southern, here three-fourths of a mile apart. The principal streets follow the course of the river, and these are crossed by others at right angles, extending from the river to the creek. The two main streets, which cross each other at right angles at the centre of the township, are ninety feet wide. Water street, which fronts the river, is eighty-two and a half feet wide ; the other streets are sixty-six feet wide. A number of ancient mounds formerly stood in the town and its vicinity. The Ohio canal passes through the place. Pop. in 1830, 2,846 ; in 1840, 3,977 ; in 1850, 7,100.

CHILLICOTHE, c. h., p. v., seat of justice of Livingston co., Mo., 150 ms. N. w. of Jefferson city ; from W. 1,053 ms.

CHILLICOTHE, p. v., Peoria co., Ill., 88 ms. N. of Springfield ; from W. 802 ms. Watered by Peoria lake.

CHILLISQUAQUE, p. t., Northumberland co., Pa., 65 ms. N. of Harrisburgh ; from W. 482 ms.

CHILLITECAUX, p. o., Dunklin co., Mo.

CHILMARK, p. t., Duke's co., Martha's Vineyard, Mass.. 100 ms. s. s. E. of Boston ; from W. 482 ms. Watered by Atlantic ocean. Pop. 747.

CHILO, p. v., Franklin township. Clermont co., O., 123 ms. w. of Columbus ; from W. 483 ms. Watered by Ohio river.

CHILTON'S MILLS, p. o., Walker co., Ala.

CHILTONVILLE. p. o., Plymouth co., Mass.

CHIMNEY POINT, p. o.. Addison township, Addison co., Vt., 86 ms. s. w. of Montpelier ; from W. 482 ms. Watered by Lake Champlain.

CHIMNEY ROCK, p. o.. Rutherford co., N. C.

CHINA, p. t., Kennebec co., Me., 21 ms E. by N. of

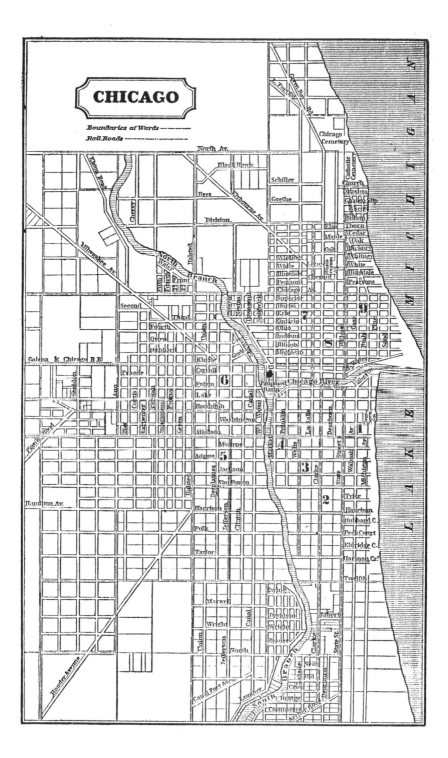

Augusta; from W. 616 ms. Watered by Twelve-Mile pond. Pop. 2,769.

CHINA, p. t., Wyoming co., N. Y., 273 ms. w. of Albany; from W. 348 ms. Watered by Clear creek. Pop. 1,961.

CHINA, p. t., St. Clair co.,Mich., 51 ms. N. N. E. of Detroit; from W. 575 ms. Watered by Belle river and Swan creek. Pop. 1,037.

CHINA, p. o., Lee co., Ill.

CHINA GROVE, p. o., Rowan co., N. C., 128 ms. w. by s. of Raleigh; from W. 365 ms.

CHINA GROVE, p. o., Williamsburgh district, S. C., 131 ms. E. S. E. of Columbia; from W. 476 ms.

CHINA GROVE, p. o., Pike co., Ala.,, 60 ms. S. E. of Montgomery; from W. 860 ms.

CHINA GROVE, p. t., Pike co., Miss., 101 ms. s. of Jackson; from W. 1,081 ms.

CHINA HILL, p. o., Gadsden co., Flor.

CHINCOTEAGUE, p. o., Accomac co., Va.

CHINKAPKIN, p. o., Duplin co., N. C.

CHINKAPKIN GROVE, p. o., Gwinnett co., Ga.

CHINNIBEE, p. o., Talladega co.. Ala.

CHIPMAN'S POINT, p. o., Addison co., Vt.

CHIPPEWAY COUNTY, situated on the northerly boundary of Michigan. Area, 7,200 square miles. Seat of justice, Sault de St. Marie. Pop. in 1840, 534; in 1850, 898.

CHIPPEWA COUNTY, situated toward the northwest part of Wisconsin, on the northeast side of Mississippi river, and traversed by Chippewa river. Area, —— square miles. Pop. in 1850, 615.

CHIPPEWA, p. o., Newcastle co., Del.

CHIPPEWA, p. t., Beaver co., Pa., 237 ms. w. by N. of Harrisburgh; from W. 259 ms. Pop. 908.

CHIPPEWA, p. t., Wayne co., O., 113 ms. N. E. of Columbus; from W. 336 ms. Pop. 2,637.

CHIPPEWA FALLS, p. o., Chippewa co., Wis.

CHITTENANGO, p. v., Sullivan township, Madison co., N. Y., 120 ms. w. N. w. of Albany; from W. 350 ms. Situated on the Erie canal.

CHITTENANGO FALLS, p. o., Madison co., N. Y.

CHITTENDEN COUNTY, situated on the western boundary of Vermont, on the east side of Lake Champlain, and traversed by Onion river. Area, 500 square miles. The face of the country is undulating near the lake, but becomes mountainous and hilly at the east; much of the soil is highly productive. Seat of justice, Burlington. Pop. in 1830, 21,775; in 1840, 22,977; in 1850, 29,036.

CHITTENDEN, p. t., Rutland co., Vt., 40 ms. s. by w. of Montpelier; from W. 472 ms. Watered by Philadelphia and Tweed rivers. Pop. 675.

CHOCCHUMA, v., Tallahatchie co., Miss., 113 ms. N. of Jackson; from W. 994 ms. Watered by Yalla Busha river..

CHOCONUT, p. t., Susquehanna co., Pa., 189 ms. N.N.E. of Harrisburgh; from W. 299 ms. Pop. 709.

CHOCTAW AGENCY, p. o., Choctaw Nation co., Ark., 166 ms. w. by N. of Little Rock; from W. 1,231 ms.

CHOCTAW AGENCY, p. o., Oktibbeha co., Miss., 117 ms. N. E. of Jackson; from W. 909 ms.

CHOCTAW CORNER, p. o., Clark co., Ala.

CHOCTAW COUNTY, situated in the central part of Mississippi. Area, 920 square miles. Seat of justice, Greensborough. Pop. in 1840, 6,010; in 1850, 11,402.

CHOCTAW COUNTY, situated on the westerly boundary of Alabama, on the west side of Tombigbee river. Area, —— square miles. Seat of justice, Butler. Pop. in 1850, 8,384.

CHOCTAW NATION of Indians (Flat Heads), who dwelt in the northwest part of Mississippi, most of whom have emigrated to the territory appropriated for them by the United States government, west of Arkansas, on the south side of Canadian river. Their number in 1840 was estimated to be 22,000. The principal stations are Armstrong, Academy, Boggy Depôt, Choctaw Agency, Doaksville, Eagletown, and Wheelock, where there are postoffices.

CHOESTOE, p. o.. Union co., Ga.

CHOPPEEN, p. o., Wells co., Ind.

CHOWAN COUNTY, situated in the northeast part of North Carolina, on the northeast side of Albemarle sound. Area, 200 square miles. Face of the country flat; soil in general of middling quality, but in some parts swampy. Seat of justice, Edenton. Pop. in 1820, 6,464; in 1830, 6,688; in 1840, 6,690; in 1850, 6,721.

CHRISTIAN COUNTY, situated on the south bound-

ary of Kentucky. Area, 612 square miles. Seat of justice, Hopkinsville. Pop. in 1820, 10,459; in 1830, 12,694; in 1840, 15,587; in 1850, 9,580.

CHRISTIAN COUNTY, situated in the central part of Illinois. Area, 350 square miles. Seat of justice, Edinburgh. Pop. in 1840, 1,878; in 1850, 3,203.

CHRISTIAN, t., Independence co., Ark.

CHRISTIANA, p. b., Newcastle co., Del., 85 ms. N. by w. of Dover; from W, 102 ms. Watered by Christiana creek. Pop. 4,831.

CHRISTIANA, p. o., Lancaster co., Pa.

CHRISTIANA, p. o., Dane co., Wis.

CHRISTIANSBURGH, p. v., Shelby co., Ky., 13 ms. w. by N. of Frankfort; from W. 555 ms.

CHRISTIANSBURGH, p. o., Brown co., Ind.

CHRISTIANSBURGH, p. v., Jackson township, Champaign co., O., 60 ms. w. by N. of Columbus; from W. 454 ms.

CHRISTIANSBURGH, c. h., p. v., seat of justice of Montgomery co., Va., 203 ms. w. s. w. of Richmond; from W. 271 ms.

CHRISTIANSVILLE, p. v., Mecklenburgh co., Va., 97 ms. s. w. of Richmond; from W. 210 ms.

CHRISTMASVILLE, p. v., Carroll co., Tenn., 113 ms. w. of Nashville; from W. 798 ms.

CHRISTY'S FORK, p. o., Morgan co.. Ky.

CHRISTY'S PRAIRIE, p. o., Clay co., Ind., 70 ms. w. s. w. of Indianapolis; from W. 641 ms.

CHUCKATUCK, p. v., Nansemond co., Va., 75 ms. s. E. of Richmond; from W. 208 ms. Watered by Chuckatuck creek.

CHRONICLE, p. o., Lincoln co., N. C.

CHUCKY BEND, p. o., Jefferson co., Tenn., 234 ms. E. of Nashville; from W. 462 ms.

CHULAFINNE, p. o., Randolph co., Ala.

CHULAHOMA, p. o., Marshall co., Miss., 184 ms, N. by E. of Jackson; from W. 907 ms.

CHUNENUGGEE, p. o.,. Macon co., Ala.

CHUNKEYVILLE, p. o., Lauderdale co., Miss.

CHURCH CREEK, p. o., Dorchester co., Md., 69 ms. s. E. of Annapolis; from W. 109 ms.

CHURCH GROVE, p. o., Knox co., Tenn., 195 ms. E. of Nashville; from W. 496 ms.

CHURCH HILL, p. v.,.Queen Anne co., Md., 48 ms. E. of Annapolis; from W. 88 ms. Watered by Chester river.

CHURCH HILL, p. o., Luzerne co., Pa.

CHURCH HILL, p. o., Halifax co., Va., 141 ms. s. w. of Richmond; from W. 228 ms.

CHURCH HILL, p. o., Abbeville district, S. C., 109 ms. w. of Columbia; from W. 546 ms.

CHURCH HILL, p. o., Christian co., Ky.

CHURCHILLSVILLE, v., Dearborn co., Ind., 77 ms. s. E. of Indianapolis; from W. 527 ms.

CHURCH'S STORE, p. o., Wilkes co., N. C.

CHURCHTOWN, p. v., Lancaster co., Pa.. 52 ms. E. by s. of Harrisburgh; from W. 130 ms.

CHURCHTOWN, p. o., Columbia co., N. Y.

CHURCHVILLE, p. v., Riga township, Monroe co., N. Y., 234 ms. w. N. w. of Albany; from W. 381 ms.

CHURCHVILLE, p. v., Harford co., Md., 61 ms. N. of Annapolis; from W. 71 ms.

CHURCHVILLE, p. o., Augusta co., Va.

CHURCHVILLE, v., Clark co., Mo. Watered by Mississippi and Des Moines river.

CHURUBUSCO, p. o., Franklin co., Ala.

CHURUBUSCO, p. o., Anderson district, S. C.

CHURUBUSCO, p. o., Whitley co., Ind.

CICERO, p. t., Onondaga co., N. Y., 140 ms. w. N. w. of Albany; from W. 358 ms. Watered by Oneida lake and Chittenango creek. Pop. 2,980.

CICERO, p. t., Hamilton co., Ind., 32 ms. N. of Indianapolis; from W. 570 ms.

CINCINNATI, p. v., Ralls co., Mo., 101 ms. N. N. E. of Jefferson city; from W. 933 ms. Watered by Salt river.

CINCINNATI, p. o., Appanoose co., Iowa.

CINCINNATI, p. o., Walker co., Tex.

CINCINNATI, city, and seat of justice of Hamilton co., O., is situated on the north bank of Ohio river, 494 miles from its entrance into the Mississippi, 1,447 miles from New Orleans, and 492 miles from Washington. It occupies two terraces, or even surfaces, the higher rising by a regular grade, about 60 feet above the lower Great uniformity characterizes the streets, and the city is more splendid than it appears from the water. The surrounding country is a pleasant, fertile valley, bounded by undulating slopes and hills which command de-

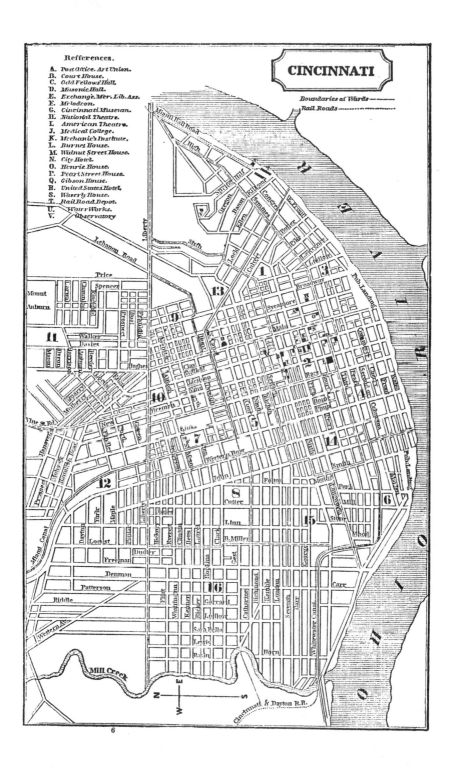

Refferences.

A. Post Office. Art Union.
B. Court House.
C. Odd Fellows' Hall.
D. Masonic Hall.
E. Exchange. Mer. Lib. Ass.
F. Melodeon.
G. Cincinnati Museum.
H. National Theatre.
I. American Theatre.
J. Medical College.
K. Mechanic's Institute.
L. Burnet House.
M. Walnut Street House.
N. City Howl.
O. Henrie House.
P. Pearl Street House.
Q. Gibson House.
R. United States Hotel.
S. Wavery House.
T. Rail Road Depot.
U. Water Works.
V. Observatory

CINCINNATI

Boundaries of Wards ————
Rail Roads ·····················

lightful views of the city, the river, and its banks. Near Cincinnati are several thriving villages and towns, which are connected with it in prosperity and interests. Like most rapidly-increasing American cities, Cincinnati exhibits great diversity in the appearance of its buildings. Some are of wood and cheap material; others are solid, durable, and splendid. Extensive warehouses, stores, and dwellings, adorn the compact central portions; toward the outskirts, the buildings are more scattered and less comely.

The public buildings are numerous and generally elegant, consisting of from seventy to eighty churches; market-houses; a courthouse, 120 feet high to the top of the dome; banks, asylums, and hospitals; large and splendid hotels; public schools; libraries; the Observatory; scientific and literary institutions. Cincinnati, St. Xavier, and Woodward colleges, and Lane seminary, are located in the city, and exhibit the high regard for education which is cherished in the west.

The manufactures of Cincinnati include a great variety of articles of necessity, comfort, and luxury. Nature has supplied no remarkable water privileges; yet enterprise has constructed extensive appliances for the prosecution of manufactures. Several canals, approaching the city from different points, by means of locks and dams, perform the functions of rivers in respect to industry and trade. Cincinnati is the market and emporium of a wide extent of country, exchanging its manufactures for vast numbers of hogs and other agricultural products. This extensive trade is facilitated by the numerous natural and artificial channels of communication from various points. From its position on the Ohio, it commands the commerce of its valley, with that of the Mississippi, while Licking river enters the Ohio opposite the city, after meandering 230 miles in Kentucky. Whitewater and Miami rivers, with their navigation improved by extensive canals, largely contribute to the trade and prosperity of the place.

The water-works of Cincinnati consist of a steam engine and reservoirs on the Ohio, which contain 1,600,000 gallons.

From Cleveland and Sandusky city, 60 miles apart, on Lake Erie, two lines of railroad traverse the state, meet at Xenia, and terminate at Cincinnati.

The population in 1800, was 750; in 1810, 2,540; in 1820, 9,644; in 1830, 24,831; in 1840, 46,338; in 1850, 115,436.

CINCINNATI, p. o., Polk co., Oregon.

CINCINNATUS, p. t., Cortland co., N. Y., 128 ms. w. by s. of Albany; from W. 327 ms. Watered by Ostelic creek and tributaries. Pop. 1,206.

CINNAMINSON, p. o., Burlington co., N. J.

CIRCLEVILLE, p. o., Tazewell co., Ill., 54 ms. N. of Springfield; from W. 787 ms.

CIRCLEVILLE, c. h., p. t., seat of justice of Pickaway co., O., 26 ms. s. of Columbus; from W. 396 ms. Watered by Scioto river and the Ohio canal. Pop. 3,411.

CIRCLEVILLE, p. o., Loudoun co., Va., 145 ms. N. of Richmond; from W. 44 ms.

CITICO, p. o., Monroe co., Tenn.

CITY, p. o., Amenia township, Dutchess co., N. Y., 70 ms. s. by E. of Albany; from W. 323 ms.

CITY POINT, p. v., Prince George co., Va., 33 ms. s. E. of Richmond; from W. 162 ms. Watered by James and Appomattox rivers.

CITY POINT, p. o., Itawamba co., Miss.

CITY WEST, v., Porter co., Ind., 155 ms. N. N. w. of Indianapolis; from W. 680 ms. Watered by Lake Michigan.

CLACKAMAS COUNTY, Nebraska. Area, — square miles. Seat of justice, ———. Pop. in 1850, —.

CLACKAMAS COUNTY, Oregon. Area, — square miles. Seat of justice, ———. Pop. in 1850, 1,162.

CLAIBORNE COUNTY, situated on the western boundary of Mississippi, on the east side of Mississippi river, with Big Black river on the northwest. Area, 500 square miles. Face of the country hilly, except along the stream. Soil varied from rich bottom lands to sterile hills and sandy pine plains. Seat of justice, Port Gibson. Pop. in 1820, 5,963; in 1830, 9,818; in 1840, 13,078; in 1850, 14,899.

CLAIBORNE COUNTY, situated on the north boundary of Tennessee, on the north side of Clinch river, and drained by Powell's river. Area, 580 square miles. Face of the country mountainous and hilly, except along the streams; soil of fair quality. Seat of justice, Tazewell. Pop. in 1820, 5,508; in 1830, 8,470; in 1840, 9,474; in 1850, 9,369.

CLAIBORNE PARISH, situated on the north boundary of Louisiana, on the east side of Bayou Dorcheat. Area, — square miles. Face of the country generally level; soil, along the streams, fertile. Seat of justice, Oveston. Pop. in 1830, 1,764; in 1840, 6,185; in 1850, 7,471.

CLAIBORNE, p. v., Monroe co., Ala., 90 ms. s. w. of Montgomery; from W. 930 ms. Watered by Alabama river.

CLAIBORNE, p. o., Jasper co., Miss.

CLAIBORNE, t., Union co., O. Pop. 919.

CLAIBORNESVILLE, p. v., Yazoo co., Miss., 57 miles N. of Jackson; from W. 1,046 ms.

CLAIRVILLE, p. o., Winnebago co., Wis.

CLAPPS, p. o., Guilford co., N. C., 68 ms. w. N. w. of Raleigh; from W. 311 ms.

CLAPPVILLE, p. v., Leicester township, Worcester co., Mass., 50 ms. w. by s. of Boston; from W. 390 ms Watered by tributaries of Quinebaug river.

CLARA, p. t., Potter co., Pa. Pop. 89.

CLAREMONT, p. t., Sullivan co., N. H., 49 ms. w. by N. of Concord; from W. 464 ms. Watered by Connecticut and Sugar rivers. Pop. 3,606.

CLAREMONT, p. v., Pickens district, S. C., 162 ms. N. w. of Columbia; from W. 560 ms.

CLARENCE, p. t., Erie co., N. Y., 270 ms. w. of Albany; from W. 390 miles. Watered by Ransom's and Tonawanda creeks. Pop. 2,727.

CLARENCE, p. o., Calhoun co., Mich.

CLARENCE CENTRE, p. o., Erie co., N. Y.

CLARENDON, p. t., Rutland co., Vt., 70 ms. s. s. w. of Montpelier; from W. 449 ms. Watered by Otter creek. Pop. 1,477.

CLARENDON, p. t., Orleans co., N. Y., 243 ms. w. by N. of Albany; from W. 392 ms. Watered by Oak Orchard and Sandy creeks. Pop. 1,809.

CLARENDON, p. t., Calhoun co., Mich., 101 ms. w. of Detroit; from W. 562 ms. Pop. 669.

CLARENDON, p. o., Monroe co., Ark., 60 ms. E. of Little Rock; from W. 1,005 ms.

CLARENDON SPRINGS, p. o., Clarendon township, Rutland co., Vt., 70 ms. s. s. w. of Montpelier; from W. 448 ms.

CLARENDON, p. o., Sumter district, S. C.

CLARIDON, p. o., Geauga co., O., 169 ms. N. E. of Columbus; from W. 334 ms. Watered by tributaries of Cuyahoga river.

CLARIDON, t., Marion co., O.

CLARION COUNTY, situated toward the northwest part of Pennsylvania, on the northeast side of Alleghany river, and traversed by Clarion river. Area, 530 square miles. Seat of justice, Clarion. Pop. in 1850, 23,565.

CLARION, c. h., p. t., seat of justice of Clarion co., Pa., 184 ms. w. N. w. of Harrisburgh; from W. 273 ms. Watered by Piney, Licking, and Mill creeks. Pop. 1,343.

CLARION, p. o., Grundy co., Ill.

CLARK COUNTY, situated on the eastern boundary of Illinois, on the west side of Wabash river. Area, 500 square miles. Seat of justice, Marshall. Pop. in 1830. 3,124; in 1840, 7,453; in 1850, 9,532.

CLARK COUNTY, situated toward the northeast part of Georgia, and watered by branches of Oconee river. Area, 414 square miles. Seat of justice, Athens. Pop. in 1820, 8,867; in 1830, 10,176; in 1840, 10,552; in 1850, 11,119.

CLARK COUNTY, situated toward the southwest part of Ohio. Area, 412 square miles. Face of the country beautifully undulating; soil exceedingly fertile. Seat of justice, Springfield. Pop. in 1830, 13,114; in 1840, 16,882; in 1850, 22,178.

CLARK COUNTY, situated toward the southwest part of Arkansas, between Little Missouri and Wachita rivers. Area, 1,500 square miles. Seat of justice, Greenville. Pop. in 1830, 1,369; in 1840, 2,309; in 1850, 4,011.

CLARK COUNTY, situated at the northeast corner of Missouri, with Des Moines river on the northeast, and the Mississippi on the east. Soil generally fertile. Area, 560 square miles. Seat of justice, Waterloo. Pop. in 1840, 2,846; in 1850, 5,527.

CLARK COUNTY, Oregon. Area, — square miles, Seat of justice, Columbia city. Pop. in 1850, 643.

CLARKE COUNTY, situated in the northeast part of Virginia, and traversed by Shenandoah river. Area, 225 square miles. Seat of justice, Berryville. Pop. in 1840, 6,353; in 1850, 7,352.

CLARKE COUNTY, situated in the northwestern part of Alabama, between Alabama and Tombigbee rivers. Area, 1,200 square miles. Face of the country somewhat hilly, except along the streams, where the soil is extremely fertile. Seat of justice, Clarksville. Pop. in 1830, 7,593 ; in 1840, 8,640 ; in 1850, 9,786.

CLARKE COUNTY, situated toward the northeast part of Kentucky, on the north side of Kentucky river. Area, 300 square miles. Face of the country moderately hilly ; soil productive. Seat of justice, Winchester. Pop. in 1820, 11,449 ; in 1830, 13,051 ; in 1840, 10,802 ; in 1850, 12,683.

CLARKE COUNTY, situated on the southeast boundary of Indiana, on the northwest side of Ohio river. Area, 400 square miles. Face of the country hilly ; soil generally productive. Seat of justice, Charleston. Pop. in 1820, 8,079 ; in 1830, 10,686 ; in 1840, 14,595 ; in 1850, 15,828.

CLARKE COUNTY, situated on the east boundary of Mississippi, and watered by Chickasaw river. Area, 650 square miles. Seat of justice, Quitman. Pop. in 1840, 2,986 ; in 1850, 5,477.

CLARKE COUNTY, situated toward the southwest part of Iowa. Area, —— square miles. Seat of justice, ————. Pop. in 1850, 79.

CLARK, p. o., Mercer co., Pa., 245 ms. w. n. w. of Harrisburgh ; from W. 288 ms.

CLARK, t., Lincoln co., Mo.

CLARK, t., Chariton co., Mo. Pop. 720.

CLARK, t., Gasconade co., Mo.,

CLARK, t., Johnson co., Ark. Pop. 574.

CLARK, t., Pope co., Ark.

CLARK, t., Brown co., O. Pop. 1,281.

CLARK, t., Clinton co., O. Pop. 1,654.

CLARK, t., Montgomery co., Ind. Pop, 1,301.

CLARKS, p. t., Coshocton co., 85 ms. n. e. of Columbus ; from W. 351 ms. Pop. 833.

CLARKSBOROUGH, p. v., Greenwich township, Glou cester co., N. J., 41 ms. s. w. of Trenton ; from W. 152 ms.

CLARKSBURGH, p. o., Erie co., N. Y.

CLARKSBURGH, p. v., Upper Freehold township, Monmouth co., N. J., 21 ms. e. of Trenton ; from W. 187 ms.

CLARKSBURGH, p. v., Montgomery co., Md., 68 ms. w. n. w. of Annapolis ; from W. 28 ms.

CLARKSBURGH, c. h., p. v., seat of justice of Lewis co., Ky., 107 ms. e. n. e. of Frankfort ; from W. 469 ms. Watered by Salt Lick creek.

CLARKSBURGH, p. v., Deerfield township, Ross co., O., 41 ms. s. of Columbus ; from W. 411 ms.

CLARKSBURGH, v., Decatur co., Ind., 55 ms s. e. of Indianapolis ; from W. 539 ms.

CLARKSBURGH, t., Berkshire co., Mass., 125 ms. w. by n. of Boston ; from W. 392 ms. Watered by a branch of Hoosack river. Pop. 386.

CLARKSBURGH, p. o., Indiana co., Pa.,

CLARKSBURGH, c. h., p. t., seat of justice of Harrison co., Va., 260 ms. n. w. of Richmond ; from W. 226 ms.

CLARK'S CORNERS, p. o., Ashtabula co., O.

CLARK'S FACTORY, p. o., Delaware co., N. Y.

CLARKSFIELD, p. t., Huron co., O., 102 ms. n. by e. of Columbus ; from W. 380 ms. Watered by Vermilion river. Pop. 1,454.

CLARK'S FORK, p. o., York district, S. C.

CLARK'S FORK, p. o., Cooper co., Mo.

CLARK'S GREEN, p. o., Luzerne, Pa.

CLARK'S MILLS, p. o., Moore co., N. C., 110 ms. s. w. of Raleigh ; from W. 394 ms.

CLARK'S MILLS, p. o., Hempstead co., Ark.

CLARK'S MILLS, p. o., Washington co., Va.

CLARK'S RIVER, p. o., Callaway co., Ky.

CLARKSON, p. t., Monroe co., N. Y., 236 ms. w. by n. of Albany ; from W. 385 ms. Watered by Little Salmon and Sandy creeks, and Lake Ontario. Pop. 4,555.

CLARKSON CENTRE, p. o., Clarkson township, Monroe co., N. Y.

CLARKSON, p. v., Middleton township, Columbiana co., O., 159 ms. n. e. of Columbus ; from W. 271 ms.

CLARKSTON, p. o., Oakland co., Mich., 35 ms. n. w. of Detroit ; from W. 559 ms.

CLARKSTOWN, p. t., seat of justice of Rockland co., N. Y., 122 ms. s. of Albany ; from W. 267 ms. Watered by Hudson river and Rockland lake. Pop. 3,111.

CLARKSVILLE, c. h., p. v., seat of justice of Clarke co., Ala., from W. 935 ms.

CLARKSVILLE, p. o., New Scotland township, Albany co., N. Y., 14 ms. s. w. of Albany ; from W. 376 ms.

CLARKSVILLE, t., Coos co., N. H. Watered by Connecticut river. Pop. 187.

CLARKSVILLE, p. v., Lebanon township, Hunterdon co., N. J., 45 ms. n. by w. of Trenton ; from W. 202 ms. Watered by Spruce run.

CLARKSVILLE, t., Alleghany co., N. Y. Pop. 668.

CLARKSVILLE, p. o., Anne Arundel co., Md., 50 ms. w. by n. of Annapolis ; from W. 35 ms.

CLARKSVILLE, p. v., Greene co., Pa., 203 ms. w. s. w. of Harrisburgh ; from W. 219 ms. Watered by Ten Mile creek.

CLARKSVILLE, p. v., Mecklenburgh co., Va., 121 ms. s. w. of Richmond ; from W. 226 ms.

CLARKSVILLE, p. v., seat of justice of Habersham co., Ga., 138 ms. n. of Milledgeville ; from W. 549 ms.

CLARKSVILLE, c. h., p. v., seat of justice of Montgomery co., Tenn., 45 ms. n. w. of Nashville ; from W. 730 ms. Watered by Red and Cumberland rivers.

CLARKSVILLE, p. v., Vernon township, Clinton co., O., 82 ms. s. w. of Columbus ; from W. 455 ms.

CLARKSVILLE, p. v., Pike co., Mo., 99 ms. n. e. of Jefferson city ; from W. 871 ms. Watered by Mississippi river.

CLARKSVILLE, c. h., p. v., seat of justice of Johnson co., Ark.

CLARKSVILLE, p. o., Spartanburgh district, S. C.

CLARKSVILLE, p. o., Red River co., Tex.

CLARKSVILLE, p. o., Hamilton co., Ind.

CLARYVILLE, p. o., Sullivan co., N. Y.

CLATSOP COUNTY, situated on the western boundary of Oregon. and Watered by Columbia river. Area, —— square miles. Seat of justice, Astoria. Pop. in 1850, ————.

CLAUSELVILLE, p. o., Monroe co., Ala.

CLAUSSVILLE, p. o., Lehigh co., Pa

CLAVERACK, p. t., Columbia co., N. Y., 34 ms. s. of Albany ; from W. 348 ms. Watered by Claverack creek. Pop. 3,208.

CLAY COUNTY, situated toward the southeast part of Kentucky. Area, 880 square miles. Face of the country hilly ; soil very rocky, but in some parts productive. Seat of justice, Manchester. Pop. in 1820, 4,393 ; in 1830, 3,549 ; in 1840, 4,607 ; in 1850, 5,421.

CLAY COUNTY, situated in the western part of Indiana. Area, 360 square miles. Seat of justice, Bowling Green. Pop. in 1830, 1,616 ; in 1840, 5,567 ; in 1850, 7,947.

CLAY COUNTY, situated toward the southeast part of Illinois. Area, 475 square miles. Seat of justice, Lewisville. Pop. in 1830, 755 ; in 1840, 3,228 ; in 1850, 4,009.

CLAY COUNTY, situated in the westerly part of Missouri, on the north side of Missouri river. Area, 432 square miles. Seat of justice, Liberty. Pop. in 1830, 5,338 ; in 1840, 8,282 ; in 1850, 10,332.

CLAY, p. t., Onondaga co., N. Y., 142 ms. w. n. w. of Albany ; from W. 359 ms. Watered by Oneida, Seneca and Oswego rivers. Pop. 3,402.

CLAY, p. t., St. Clair co., Mich., 62 ms. n. n. e. of Detroit ; from W. 586 ms. Pop. 691.

CLAY, t., Lafayette co., Mo. Pop. 1,716.

CLAY, t., Ralls co., Mo.

CLAY, t., Tuscarawas co., O. Watered by Muskingum river and Ohio canal. Pop. 1,270.

CLAY, t., Scioto co., O. Watered by Scioto river. Pop. 882.

CLAY, t., Ottawa co., O. Watered by Portage.

CLAY, t., Montgomery co., O., 80 ms. w. by s. of Columbus ; from W. 476 ms. Pop. 1,905.

CLAY, t., Highland co., O. Pop. 1,108.

CLAY, t., Hamilton co., Ind. Pop. 1,107.

CLAY, t., Allen co., O.

CLAY, t., Gallia co., O. Pop. 949.

CLAY, t., Knox co., O., 55 ms. n. e. of Columbus ; from W. 365 ms. Pop, 1,140.

CLAY, t., La Grange co., Ind. Pop. 464.

CLAY, t., Owen co., Ind.

CLAY, t., Wayne co., Ind. Pop. 769.

CLAY, p. o., Dunklin co., Ill. Pop. 510.

CLAY, p. o., Yancey co., N. C.

CLAY HILL, p. o., Marengo co., Ala.

CLAY HILL, p. o., York district, S. C.

CLAYPOOL, p. o., Kosciusko co., Ind.

CLAY'S POINT, p. o., Lewis co., Va.

CLAYSVILLE, p. v., Westland township, Guernsey co., O., 87 ms. e. of Columbus ; from W. 320 ms.

CLAYSVILLE, p. v., Washington co., Pa., 219 ms. w. of Harrisburgh ; from W. 246 ms. Pop. 275.

CLAYSVILLE, p. v., Marshall co., Ala.; from W. 700 ms. Watered by Tennessee river.

CLAYSVILLE, p. v., Harrison co., Ky., 49 ms. E. N. E. of Frankfort; from W. 493 ms.

CLAYSVILLE, p. v., Washington co., Ind., 96 ms. s. of Indianapolis; from W. 615 ms.

CLAYSVILLE, p. o., Wood co., Va.

CLAYSVILLE, p. o., Boone co., Mo.

CLAYTON COUNTY, situated on the northeast boundary of Iowa, on the westerly side of Mississippi river. Area, 720 square miles. Seat of justice, Gottenburgh. Pop. in 1840, 1,101; in 1850, 4,053.

CLAYTON, p. t., Jefferson co., N. Y., 186 ms. N. w. of Albany; from W. 431 ms. Watered by St. Lawrence and Chaumont rivers, and French creek. Pop. 4,195.

CLAYTON, p. o., Montgomery co., O.

CLAYTON, c. h., p. v., seat of justice of Rabun co., Ga., 181 ms. N. of Milledgeville; from W. 585 ms.

CLAYTON, c. h., p. v., seat of justice of Barbour co., Ala.; from W. 827 ms.

CLAYTON, p. v., Adams co., Ill., 89 ms. w. of Springfield; from W. 866 ms. Pop. 781.

CLAYTON, t., Perry co., O., 51 ms. s. E. of Columbus; from W. 359 ms. Pop. 1,594.

CLAYTON, p. o., Berks co., Pa.

CLAYTON, p. o., Lenawee co., Mich.

CLAYTON, p. o., Clayton co., Iowa.

CLAYTONA, p. o., Morgan co., O.

CLAYTON'S MILLS, p. o., Pickens district, S. C.

CLAYTONVILLE, c. h., p. v., seat of justice of Henderson co., N. C., 284 ms. w. by s. of Raleigh; from W. 514 ms. Watered by French Broad river.

CLAY VILLAGE, p. v., Shelby so., Ky., 17 ms. w. of Frankfort; from W. 559 ms.

CLAYVILLE, p. o., Oneida co., N. Y.

CLAYVILLE, p. o., Providence co., R. I.

CLEAR BRANCH. p. o.. Washington co., Va., 314 ms. w. by s. of Richmond; from W. 382 ms.

CLEAR CREEK, p. v., Ellington township, Chautauque co., N. Y., 319 ms. w. by s. of Albany; from W. 335 ms.

CLEAR CREEK, p. o., Mecklenburg co., N. C., 160 ms. w. s. w. of Raleigh; from W. 397 ms.

CLEAR CREEK, p. o., Daviess co., Mo.

CLEAR CREEK, p. o., Greene co., Tenn.

CLEAR CREEK, p. t., Fairfield co., O. Pop. 1,606.

CLEAR CREEK LANDING, p. v., Alexander co., Ill., 215 ms. s. of Springfield; from W. 849 ms.

CLEAR CREEK, t., Warren co., O. Pop. 2,770.

CLEAR CREEK, t., Richland co., O.

CLEARFIELD COUNTY, situated toward the westerly part of Pennsylvania, and traversed by the west branch of Susquehanna river. Area, 1,425 square miles. Although much of the soil of this county is excellent, it is truly an Alpine region, rich in the most varied scenery, the surface being generally broken, and much of it mountainous. It is well watered, and has a salubrious climate. Seat of justice, Clearfield. Pop. in 1820, 2,342; in 1830, 4,803; in 1840. 7,834; in 1850, 12,586.

CLEARFIELD, c. h., p. v., seat of justice of Clearfield co., Pa., 126 ms. N. w. of Harrisburgh; from W. 218 ms. Watered by the west branch of Susquehanna river. Pop. 503.

CLEARFIELD, t., Butler co., Pa. Pop. 1,924.

CLEARFIELD, t., Cambria co., Pa., 141 ms. w. of Harrisburgh; from W. 188 ms. Pop. 802.

CLEARFIELD BRIDGE, p. o., Clearfield co., Pa.

CLEAR FORK, p. o., Whitley co., Ky., 137 ms. s. s. E. of Frankfort; from W. 538 ms.

CLEAR FORK, p. o., Tazewell co., Va.

CLEAR FORK MILLS, p. o., Johnson co., Mo.

CLEAR LAKE, p. o., Sangamon co., Ill.

CLEARMONT, p. o., Warren co., Tenn.

CLEARPOINT, p. o., Hart co., Ky.

CLEAR SPRING, p. v., Washington co., Ind., 112 ms. N. w. of Annapolis; from W. 80 ms.

CLEAR SPRING, t. Lagrange co., Ind. Pop. 674.

CLEAR SPRING, p. o., Kosciusko co., Ind.

CLEAR SPRING, p. o., Greenville district, S. C.

CLEAR SPRING, p. o.. Chickasaw co., Miss.

CLEAR SPRING, p. o., Grainger co., Tenn.

CLEARSVILLE, p. o., Bedford co., Pa.

CLEAR WATER, p. o., Chippewa co., Wis.

CLEAVELAND, p. o., Oswego co., N. Y.

CLEAVELAND, c. h., p. v., seat of justice of Bradley co., Tenn., 156 ms. s. E. by E. of Nashville; from W. 581 ms.

CLEMENT, p. o., Hancock co., O.

CLEMENTSVILLE, p. o., Jackson co., Tenn.

CLEMMONSVILLE, p. v., Davidson co., N. C., 130 ms. w. of Raleigh; from W. 331 ms.

CLENDENIN, p. o., Kanawha co., Va., 333 ms. w. by N. of Richmond; from W. 338 ms.

CLERMONT COUNTY, situated on the south boundary of Ohio, on the north side of Ohio river. Area, 450 square miles. Much of the soil of this county is of an excellent quality. Seat of justice, Batavia. Pop. in 1820, 15,820; in 1830, 20,466; in 1840, 23,106; in 1850, 30,455.

CLERMONT, p. t., Columbia co., N. Y., 41 ms. s. of Albany; from W. 329 ms. Watered by Hudson river, and Ancram creek. Pop. 1,130.

CLERMONT, p. o., Marion co., Ind.

CLERMONT, p. o., Richland co., Ill.

CLERMONT, p. o., Fayette co., Iowa.

CLERMONT MILLS, p. o., Harford co., Md.

CLERMONTVILLE, p. o., McKean co., Pa.

CLEVELAND COUNTY, situated on the southern boundary of North Carolina. Area, 550 square miles. Seat of justice, Shelby. Pop. in 1850, 10,396.

CLEVELAND, p. v., Constantia township, Oswego co., N. Y. Watered by Oneida lake.

CLEVELAND, city, and seat of justice of Cuyahoga co., O., is finely situated on the south shore of Lake Erie, at the mouth of Cuyahoga river. It is 200 miles east of Columbus, and 359 miles from W. The shore of Lake Erie here is a bold bluff, about 80 feet high, upon the level top of which the largest and best part of the city is built. Here the streets are straight and spacious, the buildings neat and pleasant, and an open park, shaded with trees, occupies the centre. Fronting this square, are the courthouse, a church, and other prominent buildings. Hitherto, the rapid growth of Cleveland, has caused it to want that aspect of permanence which is the result of slower increase; but solid stores, hotels, and dwellings, are now rising in every quarter, making it as substantial as it is flourishing. Toward Cuyahoga river, the ground descends steeply, affording a convenient locality for stores, warehouses, and places of business. Here, the plan of the town is less regular, and not so attractive. The mouth of the river constitutes the harbor, which is deep, spacious, and accessible. Two piers of solid masonry project 1,200 feet into the lake, and mark the entrance. At the end of one of these piers stands a lighthouse; another occupies the brow of the hill on the lake. Vessels of the largest class enter the harbor, and proceed some distance up the river, but the Ohio and Erie canal, along the stream and through its bed, is the principal channel of inland navigation. This great canal connects Portsmouth, 307 miles distant, on the Ohio river, with Cleveland, and traverses the rich interior of the state. It meets the Ohio and Pennsylvania canal at Akron, in Summit county, and thus communicates with Pittsburgh and the east. By these channels, and the facilities of intercourse with New York, Canada, and Michigan, which Lakes Erie, Ontario, and Huron afford, Cleveland maintains a commerce as varied as it is extensive. Here congregate steamboats and other vessels, from every point on the vast shores of the great lakes, exchanging many foreign articles for the grain and other agricultural products of Ohio. Here, also, terminate the Cleveland and Pittsburgh, and the Cincinnati, Columbus, and Cleveland railroads. The Lake-shore railroad connects it with the Erie at Dunkirk, the Central at Buffalo, and the Southern Michigan at Toledo. The manufacturing facilities of this city are not equal to its commercial advantages. The only water-power is afforded by the Cuyahoga river and the Ohio canal, which serve to keep several establishments in operation. Such articles as are necessary to supply the demand for domestic manufacture, existing in every flourishing city, are produced by the aid of steam and other mechanical powers. The population in 1802, was about 200; in 1810, 547; in 1820, 606; in 1830, 1,076; in 1840, 6,071; in 1850, 17,034; in 1852, 25,670.

CLEVELAND, v., Merriwether co., Ga., 107 ms. w. of Milledgeville; from W. 726 ms.

CLEVES, p. v., Miami township, Hamilton co., O., 128 ms. w. of Columbus; from W. 504 ms. Watered by Big Miami river. Pop. 251.

CLIFFORD, p. t., Susquehanna co., Pa. Pop. 1,353.

CLIFT MILLS, p. o., Fauquier co., Va.

CLIFTON, p. v., Miami township, Greene co., O., 52 ms. w. s. w. of Columbus; from W, 445 ms. Watered by Little Miami river.

CLIFTON, p. o., Luzerne co., Pa., 142 ms. N. E. of Harrisburgh; from W. 236 ms.

CLIFTON, v.. Russell co., Va., 309 ms. s. w. of Richmond; from W. 364 ms. Watered by Maiden Spring fork.

CLIFTON, p. o., Penobscot co., Me.

CLIFTON, p. o., King George co., Va.

CLIFTON, Monroe co., N. Y.

CLIFTON, p. o., Wayne co., Tenn.

CLIFTON FACTORY, v., St. Mary's co., Md., 99 ms. s. of Annapolis; from W. 76 ms.

CLIFTON FORGE, p. o., Alleghany co., Va., 182 ms. w. by N. of Richmond; from W. 229 ms.

CLIFTON MILLS, p. o., Breckenridge co., Ky.

CLIFTON PARK, p. t., Saratoga co., N. Y., 17 ms. N. by w. of Albany; from W. 387 ms. Watered by Mohawk river. Pop. 2,868.

CLIFTON SPRINGS, p. o., Ontario co., N. Y.

CLIFTY, p. o., Decatur co., Ind., 55 ms. s. E. of Indianapolis; from W. 558 ms.

CLIFTY, t., Bartholomew co., Ind., 42 ms. s. E. of Indianapolis; from W. 576 ms. Pop. 946.

CLIFTY, p. o., Todd co., Ky.

CLIMAX PRAIRIE, p. o., Kalamazoo co., Mich., 131 ms. w. of Detroit; from W. 593 ms.

CLINCH, t., Van Buren co., Mich.

CLINE'S MILL, p. o., Augusta co., Va.

CLINGMAN, p. o., Cleveland co., N. C.

CLINTON COUNTY, situated at the northeast part of New York, on the west side of Lake Champlain. Area, 932 square miles. Face of the county mountainous and hilly; soil generally inferior. Seat of justice, Plattsburgh. Pop. in 1820, 12,070; in 1830, 19,344; in 1840, 28,157; in 1850, 40,048.

CLINTON COUNTY, situated toward the southwest corner of Ohio, and drained by tributaries of Little Miami river. Area, 400 square miles. Face of the country generally level, but sufficiently undulated for cultivating. The soil in general is rich and easily cultivated or reclaimed. Seat of justice, Wilmington, Pop. in 1820, 8,085; in 1830, 11,430; in 1840, 15,719; in 1850, 18,838.

CLINTON COUNTY, situated in the central part of Indiana. Area, 432 square miles. Seat of justice, Frankfort. Pop. in 1830, 1,423; in 1840, 7,508; in 1850, 11,869.

CLINTON COUNTY, situated in the southern part of Illinois, and traversed by Kaskaskia river. Area, 480 square miles. This county is well-watered, and contains both timber and prairie lands. Seat of justice, Carlyle. Pop., in 1830, 2,330; in 1840, 3,718; in 1850, 5,139.

CLINTON COUNTY, situated toward the northwestern part of Missouri. Area, 425 square miles. Soil fertile, and generally prairie. Seat of justice, Plattsburgh. Pop. in 1836, 1,890; in 1840, 2,724; in 1850, 3,786.

CLINTON COUNTY, situated on the south boundary of Kentucky. Area, 200 square miles. Seat of justice, Albany. Pop. in 1840, 3,863; in 1850, 4,889.

CLINTON COUNTY, situated toward the south part of Michigan, and watered by Grand, Maple, and Lookinglass rivers. Area, 576 square miles. Seat of justice, De Witt. Pop. in 1840, 1,614; in 1850, 5,102.

CLINTON COUNTY, situated on the east boundary of Iowa, on the west side of Mississippi river, with Wabesipinica river on the south. Area, 1,012 square miles. Seat of justice, Camanche. Pop. in 1840, 821; in 1850, 2,922.

CLINTON COUNTY, situated toward the north part of Pennsylvania, and traversed by the west branch of Susquehanna river. Area, 840 square miles. Face of the county mountainous and hilly. Soil varied. Seat of justice, Lock Haven. Pop. in 1840, 8,323; in 1850, 11,207.

CLINTON, p. t., Kennebec co., Me., 25 ms. N. N. E. of Augusta; from W. 620 ms. Watered by Kennebec and Sebasticook rivers. Pop. 1,743.

CLINTON, p. t., Middlesex co., Ct., 51 ms. s. by E. of Hartford; from W. 325 ms. Pop. 1,314.

CLINTON, t., Dutchess co., N. Y., 75 ms. s. of Albany; from W. 316 ms. Pop. 1,795.

CLINTON, p., v., Kirkland township, Oneida co., N. Y., 99 ms. w. N. w. of Albany; from W. 380 ms. Watered by Oriskany creek.

CLINTON, p. v., Hunterdon co., N. J., 37 ms. N. by w. of Trenton; from W. 197 ms. Watered by Raritan river. Pop. 2,368.

CLINTON, t., Essex co., N. J. Pop. 2,508.

CLINTON, p. v.. Alleghany co., Pa., 226 ms. w. of Harrisburgh; from W. 251 ms.

CLINTON, t., Wayne co., Pa. Pop. 840.

CLINTON, t., Lycoming co., Pa., 79 ms. N. of Harrisburgh; from W. 186 ms. Watered by west branch of Susquehannah river. Pop. 850.

CLINTON, p. t., Summit co., O., 118 ms. N. w. of Columbus; from W. 334 ms. Watered by Indian creek.

CLINTON. p. v., Tecumseh township, Lenawee co.. Mich., 52 ms. s. w. of Detroit; from W. 516 ms. Watered by north branch of Raisin river.

CLINTON, c. h., p. v., seat of justice of Jones co., Ga., 26 ms. w. of Milledgeville; from W. 671 ms.

CLINTON, p. v., Hickman co., Ky., 298 ms. w. s. w. of Frankfort; from W. 825 ms. Watered by Bayou Desha.

CLINTON, c. h., p. v., seat of justice of Sampson co., N. C., 94 ms. s. s. E. of Raleigh; from W. 324 ms. Watered by Black river.

CLINTON, p. v., Greene co., Ala., from W. 859 ms.

CLINTON, p. v., Hinds co., Miss., 10 ms. w. by N. of Jackson; from W. 1,020 ms. Seat of Mississippi college.

CLINTON, p. v., East Feliciana parish, La., 112 ms. N. w. of New Orleans; from W. 1,130.

CLINTON, p. v., Van Buren co., Ark., 90 ms. N. of Little Rock; from W. 1,096 ms. Watered by Little Red river.

CLINTON, c. h., p. v., seat of justice of Anderson co., Tenn., 175 ms., E. of Nashville; from W. 514 ms. Watered by Clinch river.

CLINTON, p. t., Vermilion co., Ind., 82 ms. w. of Indianapolis; from W. 659 ms. Watered by Wabash river. Pop. 1,509.

CLINTON, p. v., Dewitt co., Ill., 64 ms. E. N. E. of Springfield; from W. 739 ms. Watered by Salt creek.

CLINTON, t., Macomb co., Mich., 15 ms. N. E. of Detroit; from W. 541 ms. Watered by Lake St. Clair and Red river. Pop. 2,130.

CLINTON, t., Franklin co., O., 6 ms. from Columbus; from W. 402 ms. Pop. 1,186.

CLINTON, t., Putnam co., Ind., 46 ms. w. of Indianapolis; from W. 624 ms.

CLINTON, t., Lucas co., O.

CLINTON, p. v., t., seat of justice of Rives co., Mo. Watered by Grand river.

CLINTON, p. t. Jackson co., O., 62 ms. s. E. by s. of Columbus. from W. 371 ms.

CLINTON, t., Seneca co., O. Pop. 1,680.

CLINTON t., Shelby co., O.. 85 ms. N. w. of Columbus; from W. 431 ms. Pop. 764

CLINTON, t., Wayne co., O., 76 ms. N. E. of Columbus; from W. 352 ms. Pop. 1,121.

CLINTON, p. t., Knox co., O., 45 ms. N. E. of Columbus; from W. 375 ms. Pop. 802.

CLINTON, p. o., Worcester co., Mass.

CLINTON, p. o., Henry co., Mo.

CLINTON, p. o., Dewitt co., Tex.

CLINTON COLLEGE, p. v., Smith co., Tenn., 53 ms. E. N. E. of Nashville; from W. 644 ms.

CLINTON CORNERS, p. o., Dutchess co., N. Y.

CLINTONDALE, p. o., Ulster co., N. Y.

CLINTON FURNACE, p. o., Clarion co., Pa.

CLINTON GORE, p. o., Kennebec co., Me.

CLINTON HOLLOW, p. o., Clinton township, Dutchess co., N. Y., 63 ms. s. of Albany; from W. 316 ms.

CLINTONVILLE, p. v., Au Sable township, Clinton co., N. Y., 153 ms., N. of Albany; from W. 528 ms. Watered by Au Sable river and Lake Champlain.

CLINTONVILLE, p. v., Venango co., Pa., 214 w. N. w. of Harrisburgh; from W. 269 ms.

CLINTONVILLE, p. v., Greenbrier co., Va., 224 ms. w. by N. of Richmond; from W. 261 ms.

CLINTONVILLE, p. v., Bourbon co., Ky., 45 ms. E. of Frankfort; from W. 516 ms.

CLINTONVILLE, p. o., Franklin co., O.

CLINTONVILLE, p. o., Kane co., Ill.

CLIO, p. v., Marlborough district, S. C., 117 ms. N. B. of Columbia; from W. 419 ms.

CLIO, p. o., Wayne co., Ky., 94 ms. s. s. of Frankfort; from W. 600 ms.

CLIO, p. o., Greene co., O.

CLOCKVILLE, p. v., Lenox township, Madison co., N. Y., 120 ms. w by N. of Albany; from W. 360 ms.

CLOKEY, p. o., Washington co., Pa.

CLOPTON'S MILLS, p. o., Putnam co., Ga., 16 ms. N w. of Milledgeville; from W. 637 ms.

CLOUTIERVILLE, p. v., Natchitoches parish, La., 337 ms. N. w. by w. of New Orleans; from W. 1 256 ms.

CLOVE, p. o., Unionvale township, Dutchess co., N. Y., 78 ms. s. by E. of Albany; from W. 317 ms.

CLOVE, p. o., Wantage township, Sussex co., N. J.

CLOVER, p. o., Clermont co., O.

CLOVER, p. o., Blair co., Pa.

CLOVER BEND, p. o., Lawrence co., Ark.

CLOVER BOTTOM, p. o., Sullivan co., Tenn.

CLOVER CREEK, p. o., Highland co., Va.

CLOVER DALE, p. o., Botetourt co., Va., 184 ms. w. of Richmond; from W. 234 ms.

CLOVER DALE, p. o., Putnam co., Ind., 49 ms. w. of Indianapolis; from W. 614 ms.

CLOVERDALE HOTEL, p. o., Bath co., Va., 142 ms. w. N. w. of Richmond; from W. 180 ms.

CLOVER GARDEN, p. o., Orange co., N. C., 41 ms. N. w. of Raleigh; from W. 299 ms.

CLOVER GREEN, p. o., Spottsylvania co., Va.

CLOVER HILL, p. o., Hunterdon co., N. J., 30 ms. N. of Trenton; from W. 190 ms.

CLOVER HILL, p. o., Blount co., Tenn.

CLOVER HILL, c. h., p. v., seat of justice of Appomattox co., Va.

CLOVER HILL, p. o., Green co., Ky.

CLOVERLAND, p. o., Clay co., Ind.

CLOVER ORCHARD, p. o., Orange co., N. C.

CLOVERPORT, p. v., Breckenridge co., Ky., 125 ms. w. by s. of Frankfort; from W. 668 ms. Watered by Ohio and Clover rivers.

CLOVERPORT, p. o., Hardeman co., Tenn

CLOVES DEPOT, p. o., Oldham co., Ky.

CLOYD'S CREEK, p. o., Blount co., Tenn., 182 ms. w. by s. of Nashville; from W. 527 ms.

CLYATTSVILLE, p. o., Lowndes co., Ga.

CLYDE, p. v., Galen township, Wayne co., N. Y., 174 ms. w. by N. of Albany; from W. 354 ms. Watered by Clyde river and Erie canal.

CLYDE, p. o., Whitesides co., Ill.

CLYDE MILLS, p. o., Clyde township, St. Clair co., Mich., 67 ms. N. E. of Detroit; from W. 590 ms. Watered by Black river.

CLYMAN, p. o., Dodge co., Wis.

CLYMER, p. t., Chautauque co., N. Y., 355 ms. w. by s. of Albany; from W. 334 ms. Watered by Broken Straw creek. Pop. 1,127.

CLYMER CENTRE, p. o., Clymer township, Chautauque co., N. Y., 350 ms. w. by s. of Albany; from W. 329 ms.

COAHOMA COUNTY, situated on the western boundary of Mississippi river, and watered by Sunflower river. Area, 680 square miles. Seat of justice, Coahoma Court-House. Pop. in 1840, 1,290; in 1850, 2,724.

COAL, t., Northumberland co., Pa. Pop. 146.

COAL BROOK, t., Clinton co., Pa. Pop. 326.

COAL GROVE, p. o., Lawrence co., O.

COAL HILL, p. o., Goochland co., Va., 14 ms. N. w. of Richmond; from W. 131 ms.

COAL MOUNTAIN, p. o., Forsyth co., Ga., 115 ms. N. w. of Milledgeville; from W. 638 ms.

COAL PORT, p. o., Indiana co., Pa.

COAL RIVER MARSHES, p. o., Fayette co., Va., 300 ms. w. of Richmond; from W. 337 ms.

COAL RUN, p. o., Washington co., O., 92 ms. s. E. of Columbus; from W. 316 ms.

COALSMOUTH, p. o., Kanawha co., Va. Watered by Kanawha and Coal rivers.

COAL VALLEY, p. o., Alleghany co., Pa.

COATES' TAVERN, p. o., York district, S. C., 76 ms. N. of Columbia; from W. 452 ms.

COATESVILLE, p. o., Hendricks co., Ind.

COATSVILLE, p. v., Chester co., Pa., 62 ms. E. s. E. of Harrisburgh; from W. 130 ms. Watered by the West Branch of Brandywine creek.

COBALT, p. o., Middlesex co., Ct.

COBB COUNTY, situated toward the northwest part of Georgia, on the northwest side of Chattahoochie river. Area, 480 square miles. Seat of justice, Marietta. Pop. in 1840, 7,539; in 1850, 13,843.

COBB, p. o., Jackson co., Iowa.

COBLESKILL CENTRE, p. o., Schoharie co., N. Y.

COBB'S FORK, p. o., Decatur co., Ind., 62 ms. s. E. of Indianapolis; from W. 556 ms.

COBB'S MILLS, p. o., Cherokee co., Ala.

COBBSVILLE, p. o., Telfair co., Ga.

COBERLY'S, p. o., Allen township, Union co., O., 51 ms. N. w. of Columbus; from W. 441 ms.

COBHAM, p. o., Albermarle co., Va.

COBLESKILL, p. t., Schoharie co., N. Y., 42 ms. w. of

Albany; from W. 386 ms. Watered by Cobbeskill creek. Pop. 2,229.

COBURN'S STORE, p..o., Mecklenburgh co., N. C,, 167 ms. w. s. w. of Raleigh; from W. 404 ms.

COCALICO, p. o., Lancaster co., Pa., 37 ms. E. by s. of Harrisburgh; from W. 135 ms.

COCHECTON, p. t., Sullivan co., N. Y., 131 ms. s. w. of Albany; from W. 293 ms. Watered by Delaware river, Callicoon, and Ten mile creeks. Pop. 1,671.

COCHESETT, p. o., Plymouth co., Mass.

COCHITUATE, p. o., Middlesex co., Mass.

COCHRAN, t., Macon co., Mo.

COCHRAN'S CROSS ROADS, p. o., Harris co., Ga.

COCHRAN'S GROVE, p. v., Shelby co., Ill., 72 ms. s. E. of Springfield; from W. 716 ms.

COCHRAN'S LANDING, p. o., Monroe co., O.

COCHRAN'S MILLS, p. o., Pickens co., Ala.; from W. 857 ms.

COCHRANSVILLE, p. v., Chester co., Pa., 62 ms. E. s. E. of Harrisburgh; from W. 106 ms.

COCHRANSVILLE, p. o., Marshall co., Tenn.

COCHRANTON, p. o., Salt Rock township, Marion co., O.

COCKE COUNTY, situated on the southeast boundary of Tennessee, with Nolachucky river on the north. Area, 374 square miles. Seat of justice, Newport. Pop. in 1820, 4,892; in 1830, 6,048; in 1840, 6,992; in 1850, 8,200.

COCKEYSVILLE, p. o., Baltimore co., Md.

COCKRUM, p. o., De Soto co., Miss.

CODDINGVILLE, p. o., Medina co., O.

CODORUS, p. v., Old Codorus township, York co., Pa., 37 ms. s. of Harrisburgh; from W. 83 ms. Watered by Codorus creek.

COELK, p. o., Livingston parish, La.

COE RIDGE, p. o., Cuyahoga co., O.

COESSE, p. o., Whitley co.. Ind.

COEYMAN's. p. t., Albany co., N. Y., 13 ms. s. of Albany; from W. 356 ms. Watered by Coeyman's creek. Pop. 3,050.

COEYMAN'S HOLLOW, p. o., Coeyman's township, Albany co., N. Y., 19 ms. s. of Albany; from W. 362 ms.

COFER, p. o., Hardin co., Ky.

COFFADELIAH p. o., Neshoba co., Miss.

COFFEE COUNTY, situated in the central part of Tennessee. Area, 170 square miles. Seat of justice, Manchester. Pop. in 1840, 8,184; in 1850, 8,350.

COFFEE COUNTY, situated on the south boundary of Alabama, and traversed by Pea river. Seat of justice, Wellborn. Pop. in 1850, 5,940.

COFFEE, p. o., Clay co.. Ind.

COFFEE CORNER, p. o.. Coffee co., Ala.

COFFEE CREEK, p. o., Porter, co., Ind., 148 ms. N. N. w. of Indianapolis; from W. 692 ms.

COFFEE LANDING, p. o., Hardin co., Tenn.

COFFEE RUN, p. o., Huntingdon co., Pa., 103 ms. w. of Harrisburgh; from W. 107 ms.

COFFEEVILLE, p. v., Clark co., Ala., from W. 944 ms. Watered by Tombigbee river.

COFFEEVILLE, c. h., p. v., seat of justice of Yallabusha co., Miss., 130 ms. N. by E. of Jackson; from W. 941 ms. Watered by Turkey creek.

COFFIN'S GROVE, p. o., Delaware co., Iowa.

COGHILL, p. o., McMinn co., Tenn.

COGSWELL, p. o., McHenry co., Ill.

COHASSET, p. t., Norfolk co., Mass., 20 ms. s. E. of Boston; from W. 460 ms. Watered by Atlantic ocean. Pop. 1,775.

COHOCTON, p. o., Steuben co., N. Y., 230 ms. w. by s. of Albany; from W. 315 ms.

COHOES, p. v., Watervliet township, Albany co., N. Y., 8 ms. N. of Albany; from W. 378 ms. Watered by Mohawk river. Pop. 4,229.

COHUTTAH SPRINGS, p. o., Murray co., Ga.

COILA, p. o., Carroll co., Miss.

COILA, p. o., Washington co., N. Y.

COINJOCK, p. o., Currituck co., N. C.

COITSVILLE, p. t., Trumbull co., O., 182 ms. N. E. of Columbus; from W. 289 ms. Watered by Beaver river and Beaver canal.

COKER CREEK, p. o., Monroe co., Tenn.

COKESBURGH, Hunterdon co., N. J.

COKESBURY, p. v., Abbeville district, S. C., 93 ms. w. of Columbia; from W. 523 ms.

COLAPARCHEE, p. o., Monroe co., Ga.

COLBERT, v., Lowndes co., Miss., 155 ms. N. E. of Jackson; from W. 899 ms. Watered by Tombigbee river.

COLBYVILLE, p. v., Clarke co., Ky., 39 ms. E. S. E. of Frankfort; from W. 530 ms.

COLCHESTER, p. t., Chittenden co., Vt., 46 ms. w. s. w. of Montpelier; from W. 519 ms. Watered by Lake Champlain and Onion river. Pop. 2,577.

COLCHESTER, p. t, New London co., Ct., 24 ms. s. s. E. of Hartford ; from W. 384 ms. Watered by Salmon river. Pop. 2,468.

COLCHESTER, p. t., Delaware co., N. Y., 98 ms. s. w. by w. of Albany; from W. 316 ms. Watered by Papacton branch of Delaware river. Pop. 2,184.

COLD BROOK, v. Worcester co., Mass., 61 ms. w. of Boston ; from W. 413 ms. Watered by Cold brook.

COLD BROOK, p. v., Russia township, Herkimer co., N. Y., 86 ms. N. w. of Albany ; from W. 410 ms. Watered by Cold brook.

COLD BROOK, p. o., Warren co., Ill., 115 ms. N. w. of Springfield ; from W. 844 ms.

COLDEN, p. t., Erie co., N. Y., 286 ms. w. of Albany ; from W. 365 ms. Watered by Cazenovia creek. Pop. 1,344.

COLDENHAM, p. o., Newburgh township, Orange co., N. Y., 90 ms. s. by w. of Albany ; from W. 292 ms.

COLD RUN, p. o., Cass co., Ga.

COLD SPRING, p. o., Fairfield co., Ct.

COLD SPRING, p. v., Philipstown township, Putnam co., N. Y., 100 ms. s. of Albany ; from W. 278 ms. Watered by Hudson river.

COLD SPRING, t., Cattaraugus co., N. Y., 308 ms. w. of Albany. Watered by Alleghany river and Cold Spring creek. Pop. 591.

COLD SPRING, p. v., Lower township, Cape May co., N. J., 105 ms. s. of Trenton ; from W. 215 ms.

COLD SPRING, p. o., Edgefield district S. C.

COLD SPRING, p. o., Wilkinson co., Miss., 120 ms. s. w. of Jackson ; from W. 1,130 ms.

COLD SPRING, p. o., Campbell co., Ky., 91 ms. N. N. E. of Frankfort; from W. 501 ms.

COLD SPRING, p. o., Shelby co., Ill., 72 ms. s. E. of Springfield ; from W. 736 ms.

COLD SPRING, p. o., Pottawatomie co., Iowa.

COLD SPRING, p. o., Harrison co., O.

COLD SPRING, p. o., Polk co., Tex.

COLD SPRING, p. o., Jefferson co., Wis.

COLD SPRING HARBOR, p. v., Oyster Bay and Huntington townships, Queens and Suffolk cos., N. Y., 186 ms. s. by E. of Albany ; from W. 266 ms. Watered by Cold Spring Harbor.

COLD STREAM, p. v., Hampshire co. Va. 167 ms. N. w. w. of Richmond ; from W. 595 ms. Watered by Great Cacapon river.

COLD WATER, c. h., p. t., seat of justice of Branch co., Mich., 110 ms. w. s. w. of Detroit; from W. 558 ms. Watered by Coldwater river and tributaries. Pop. 2,166.

COLD WATER, p. o., Elbert co., Ga., 121 ms. N. N. E. of Milledgeville; from W. 575 ms.

COLD WATER, p. o., Marshall co., Miss.

COLD WATER, p. o., Wayne co., Mo.

COLD WATER, p. o., Mercer co., O.

COLD WATER, p. o., Delaware co., Iowa.

COLD WELL, p. o., White co., Ark.

COLE COUNTY, situated in the central part of Missouri, on the southerly side of Missouri river, with Osage river on the southeast. Area, 650 square miles. Seat of justice, Jefferson City. Pop. in 1830, 3,023 ; in 1840, 9,286 ; in 1850, 6,696.

COLE, t., Benton co., Mo.

COLEBATH, t., Clarke co., Ark. Pop. 297.

COLEBROOK, p. t., Litchfield co., Ct., 32 ms. N. w. of Hartford ; from W. 356 ms. Watered by Colebrook river. Pop. 1,317.

COLEBROOK, p. t., Coos co., N. H., 135 ms. N. of Concord ; from W. 596 ms. Watered by Connecticut and Mohawk rivers, and Beaver brook. Pop. 908.

COLEBROOK, t., Ashtabula co., O., 181 ms. N. E. of Columbus ; from W. 312 ms. Watered by Rock and Mosquito creeks. Pop. 688.

COLEBROOK DALE, p. t., Berks co., Pa., 73 ms. E. of Harrisburgh ; from W. 166 ms. Pop. 1,108.

COLEBROOK RIVER, p. o., Colebrook township, Litchfield co., Ct., 31 ms. N. w. of Hartford ; from W. 355 ms.

COLD CAMP, p. o., Benton co., Mo., 65 ms. s. w. of Jefferson City; from W. 1,001 ms.

COLE CREEK, p. o., Fountain co., Ind., 66 ms. w. s. w. of Indianapolis ; from W. 637 ms.

COLE CREEK, t., Montgomery co., Ind. Pop. 1,517.

COLEMAN'S CROSS ROADS, p. o., Edgefield district, S. C., 51 ms. w. of Columbia ; from W. 537 ms.

COLEMANSVILLE, p. o., Harrison co., Ky., 53 ms. N. E. of Frankfort; from W. 521 ms.

COLERAIN, p. t., Franklin co., Mass., 101 ms. w. by N. of Boston ; from W. 411 ms. Watered by a tributary of Deerfield river. Pop. 1,785.

COLERAIN, t., Ross co., O., 48 ms. s. E. of Columbus ; from W. 391 ms. Pop. 986.

COLERAIN, p. t., Lancaster co., Pa., 69 ms. s. E. of Harrisburgh; from W. 104 ms. Pop. 1,602.

COLERAIN, t., Bedford co., Pa., 100 ms. s. w. of Harrisburgh; from W. 122 ms. Pop. 1,281.

COLERAIN, p. t., Hamilton co., O., 113 ms. s. w. of Columbus: from W. 513 ms. Watered by Great Miami river. Pop. 3,125.

COLERAIN, p. t., Belmont co., O., 126 ms. E. of Columbus ; from W. 272 ms. Pop 1,366.

COLERAIN, p. v., Bertie co., N. C., 176 ms E. by N. of Raleigh ; from W. 248 ms. Watered by Chowan river.

COLERAIN, p. o., Jackson co., Ark.

COLERAIN FORGE, p. v., Huntingdon co., Pa., 106 ms. W. of Harrisburgh; from W. 165 ms. Watered by Spruce creek.

COLES COUNTY, situated in the eastern part of Illinois. Area, 1,248 square miles. Seat of justice, Charleston. Pop. in 1840, 9,616 ; in 1850, 9,335.

COLESBURGH, p. o., Potter co., Pa.

COLESBURGH, p. o., Delaware co., Iowa.

COLE'S CREEK, p. o., Columbia co., Pa., 113 ms. N. E. of Harrisburgh ; from W. 224 ms.

COLE'S FERRY, p. o., Wilson co., Tenn.

COLE'S MILLS, p. o., Delaware co., O.

COLESVILLE, p. t., Broome co., N. Y., 124 ms., w. s. w. of Albany ; from W. 306 ms. Watered by Susquehanna river. Pop. 3,061.

COLESVILLE, p. o., Sussex co., N. J.

COLESVILLE, p. o., Montgomery co., Md.

COLESVILLE, p. o., Stokes co., N. C.

COLETA, p. o., Talladega co., Ala.

COLEVILLE, t., Ashtabula co., O. Pop. 688.

COLLAMER, p. o., Copiah co., Miss.

COLLAMER, p. o., Chester co., Pa.

COLLAMER, p. o., Windham co., Ct.

COLLAMER, p. o., Cuyahoga co., O.

COLLAMER, p. o., Kane co., Ill.

COLLAMER, p. o., Onondaga co., N. Y.

COLLAMER, p. o., Whitley co., Ind.

COLLAMER, p. o., Sauk co., Wis.

COLLEGE, t., Knox co., O. Pop.

COLLEGE CORNER, p. v., Butler co., O., 110 ms. s. w. of Columbus ; from W. 507 ms.

COLLEGE GREEN, p. o., Cecil co., Md.

COLLEGE HILL, p. o., Lafayette co., Miss., 166 ms. N. N. E. of Jackson ; from W. 919 ms.

COLLEGE HILL, p o., Hamilton co., O.

COLLEGE MOUND, p. o., Kaufman co., Tex.

COLLEGE OF ST. JAMES, p. o., Washington co., Md.

COLLEGEVILLE, p. v., Saline co., Ark., 15 ms. s. w. of Little Rock ; from W. 1,080 ms.

COLLETON DISTRICT, situated in the southeast part of South Carolina, with St. Helena sound and Cambahee river on the southwest. Area, 2,100 square miles. Seat of justice, Waterborough. Pop. in 1820, 26,373 ; in 1830, 27,256 ; in 1840, 25,548 ; in 1850, 39,508.

COLLETTSVILLE, p. v., Caldwell co., N. C., 213 ms. w. of Raleigh ; from W. 419 ms.

COLLIERS, p. o., Edgefield district, S. C., 91 ms. w. of Columbia ; from W. 569 ms.

COLLIERSTOWN, p. v., Rockbridge co., Va., 155 ms. w. by N. of Richmond ; from W. 195 ms. Watered by Collier Creek.

COLLIERSVILLE, p. o., Shelby co., Tenn.

COLLIN COUNTY, situated in the northern part of Texas. Area, —— square miles. Seat of justice, McKinney. Pop. in 1850, 1,973.

COLLINS, p. t., Erie co., N. Y., 312 ms. w. of Albany ; from W. 364 ms. Watered by Cattaraugus creek. Pop. 4,001.

COLLINS, p. o., Columbia co., Flor.

COLLINS CENTRE, p. o., Collins township, Erie co., N. Y.

COLLINS' DEPOT, p. o., Hampden co., Mass.

COLLINS' SETTLEMENT, p. o., Lewis co. Va., 296 ms. w. N. w. of Richmond ; from W. 264 ms.

COLLINSVILLE, p. v., Canton township, Hartford co.,

Ct., 15 ms. w. by N. of Hartford; from W. 338 ms. Watered by Farmington river.

COLLINSVILLE, p. v., West Turin township, Lewis co.. N. Y., 123 ms. N. w. of Albany; from W. 424 ms.

COLLINSVILLE, v., Huntingdon co., Pa., 122 ms. w. by N. of Harrisburgh; from W. 165 ms.

COLLINSVILLE, p. v., Milford township, Butler co., O., 105 ms. s. w. of Columbus; from W. 498 ms.

COLLINSVILLE, p. v., Addison co., Ill., 86 ms. s. by w. of Springfield; from W. 792 ms.

COLLIRENE, p. o., Lowndes co., Ala.

COLOMO, c. h., p. v., seat of justice of El Dorado co., Cal.

COLLOMSVILLE, p. o., Lycoming co., Pa.

COLLY SWAMP, p. o., Bladen co., N. C.

COLÒNNA, p. o., Cherokee co., Ala.

COLON, p. t., St. Joseph co., Mich., 135 ms. w. s. w. of Detroit; from W. 583 ms. Pop. 846.

COLONEL'S FORK, p. o., Pickens district, S. C.

COLONY, p. o., Knox co., Mo.

COLORADO COUNTY, situated in the southern part of Texas, and traversed by Colorado river. Area, —— square miles. Seat of justice, Columbus. Pop. in 1850, 2,257.

COLOSSE, p. v., Mexico township, Oswego co., N. Y., 149 ms. w. N. w. of Albany; from W. 374 ms.

COLQUITT, p. o., Montgomery co., Ga.

COLTON, p. o., St. Lawrence co., N. Y.

COLT'S NECK, p. v., Shrewsbury township, Monmouth co., N. J., 40 ms. E. of Trenton; from W. 206 ms.

COLUMBIA, DISTRICT OF, was ceded to the United States by Maryland and Virginia, in 1790, and became the seat of the national government in 1800. It was originally ten miles square, lying on both sides of the Potomac, thirty-six square miles having been taken from Virginia, which constituted the city and county of Alexandria, and sixty-four square miles from Maryland, embracing the county of Washington. By an act of Congress, in 1846, which was subsequently accepted by the people of Alexandria, that county was retroceded to the state of Virginia, and the District of Columbia is now restricted to the Maryland side of the Potomac, embracing the cities of Washington and Georgetown. This district was the theatre of disgraceful scenes, in our last war with England, in 1814. In August of that year Washington was left in a defenceless condition, when invaded by the British, and was deserted by the President, the heads of the departments, and by most of the citizens. The enemy entered the city, burned the capitol, including the library of Congress, the mansion of the president, the navy-yard, with its contents, and most of the public-offices, except the patent-office. The whole world regarded this act as a violation of the rules of modern warfare. The surface of this territory is gently undulating, with some low marshes, but there are several eminences which afford fine seats for the cities within its limits. The soil, with little exception, is sterile in its natural state, but has of late been rendered productive by superior cultivation. The climate is similar to that of the contiguous states. The population in 1800 was 14,093; in 1810, 24,023; in 1820, 33,039; in 1830, 39,834; in 1840, 43,712; in 1850, 51,687. Number of slaves in 1800, 3,244; in 1810, 5,395; in 1820, 6,377; in 1830, 6,119; in 1840, 4,694; in 1850, 3,687. The civil government of this district is under the immediate authority of the United States, and the municipal power is exercised by a mayor and corporation. It has never been represented in Congress.

COLUMBIA COUNTY, situated on the east boundary of New York, with Hudson river on the west. Area, 624 square miles. Face of the country mountainous and hilly; soil generally favorable to agriculture. Seat of justice, Hudson. Pop. in 1830, 39,952; in 1840, 43,252; in 1850, 43,092.

COLUMBIA COUNTY, situated in the central part of Pennsylvania, and traversed by the east branch of Susquehanna river. Area, 700 square miles. Face of the country mountainous and hilly, with much excellent soil. Seat of justice, Danville. Pop. in 1830, 20,049; in 1840, 24,267; in 1850, 17,710.

COLUMBIA COUNTY, situated on the northeast boundary of Georgia, on the southwest side of Savannah river. Area, 600 square miles. Seat of justice, Applington. Pop. in 1830, 12,606; in 1840, 11,356; in 1850, 11,961.

COLUMBIA COUNTY, situated on the north boundary of Florida, with Suwanne river on the west. Area,

4,320 square miles. Face of the country generally flat, containing extensive pine forests and numerous small lakes. Seat of justice, Lancaster. Pop. in 1840, 2,102; in 1850, 4,808.

COLUMBIA COUNTY, situated toward the south part of Wisconsin, and traversed by Wisconsin river. Area, —— square miles. Seat of justice, De Korra. Pop. in 1850, 9,565.

COLUMBIA, p. t., Washington co., Me., 120 ms. E. by N. of Augusta; from W. 757· ms. Watered by Pleasant river.

COLUMBIA, p. t., Coos co., N. H., 126 ms. N. of Concord; from W. 587 ms. Watered by Connecticut river. Pop. 762.

COLUMBIA, p. t., Tolland co., Ct., 24 ms. E. by s. of Hartford; from W. 355 ms. Watered by a tributary of Willimantic river. Pop. 876.

COLUMBIA, p. t., Herkimer co., N. Y., 75 ms. w by N. of Albany; from W. 379 ms. Watered by tributaries of Unadilla and Susquehanna rivers. Pop. 2,081.

COLUMBIA, p. b., West Hampfield township, Lancaster co., Pa., 30 ms. s. E. of Harrisburgh; from W. 102 ms. Watered by Susquehanna river and Susquehanna canal. Pop. 4,140.

COLUMBIA, p. v., Warren co., N. J., 71 ms. N. by w. of Trenton; from W. 219 ms.

COLUMBIA, t., Bradford co., Pa. Pop. 1,383.

COLUMBIA, p. t., Jackson co., Mich., 74 ms. w. of Detroit; from W. 534 ms. Pop. 1,142.

COLUMBIA, c. h., p. v., seat of justice of Fluvanna co.. Va., 50 ms. w. N. w. of Richmond; from W. 124 ms. Watered by James and Rivanna rivers.

COLUMBIA, c. h, p. v., seat of justice of Tyrrell co., N. C., 200 ms. E. of Raleigh; from W. 324 ms. Watered by Scoupernong creek.

COLUMBIA, p. v., Henry co., Ala.; from W. 847 ms.

COLUMBIA, c. h., p., v., seat of justice of Marion co., Miss., 113 ms. s. s. E. of Jackson; from W. 1,063 ms. Watered by Pearl river.

COLUMBIA, c. h., p. v., Chicot co., Ark., 142 ms. s. E. of Little Rock; from W. 1,152 ms. Watered by Mississippi river.

COLUMBIA, c. h., p. v., seat of justice of Maury co., Tenn., 42 ms. s. s. w. of Nashville; from W. 719 ms. Watered by Duck river. Seat of Jackson college.

COLUMBIA, v.; late seat of justice of Whitley co., Ind. Watered by Blue river.

COLUMBIA, c. h., p. v., seat of justice of Adair co., Ky., 98 ms. s. by w. of Frankfort; from W. 612 ms. Watered by Russell's creek.

COLUMBIA, p. v., Fayette co., Ind., 55 ms. E. of Indianapolis; from W. 529 ms. Pop. 889.

COLUMBIA, p. t., Fayette co., Ind.

COLUMBIA, p. v., Monroe co., Ill., 107 ms. w. by s. of Springfield; from W. 820 ms.

COLUMBIA, c. h., p. v., seat of justice of Caldwell parish, La., 273 ms. N. w. of New Orleans; from W. 1,187 ms. Watered by Wachita river.

COLUMBIA, p. t., Hamilton co., O. Watered by Little Miami and Ohio rivers. Pop. 2,413.

COLUMBIA, t., Lorain co., O. Watered by Rocky river. Pop. 1,236.

COLUMBIA, t., Gibson co., O.

COLUMBIA, t., Meigs co., O. Watered by tributaries of Leading creek. Pop. 895.

COLUMBIA, t., Randolph co., Ark.

COLUMBIA, v., West Hampfield township, Lancaster co., Pa. Pop. 4,140. ♦

COLUMBIA, p. v., seat of justice of Richland district, and capital of S. C., a pleasant village, situated on the east side of Congaree river, below the confluence of its constituents, the Broad and the Saluda, 120 miles northwest of Charleston, and 506 miles from Washington. The bank of the river gradually ascends to an elevation of about 200 feet, from which the town overlooks an extensive and interesting prospect. The streets are remarkable for breadth and regularity, and the houses for their neat and tasteful appearance. Here is located the College of South Carolina, a flourishing institution, which is liberally supported by the state. A substantial and well-built bridge extends on eight stone piers across the Congaree, and the Saluda canal, making a circuit of six and a quarter miles around the falls, passes through the town. The river affords steamboat communication with the ocean and with Charleston. The Columbia branch railroad meets the South Carolina railroad from Charleston, at Branchville.

Water from springs 1 mile from the town, is forced

by steam to an elevated point, whence it is conveyed to all sections of the village.

The population in 1830, was 3,400 ; in 1840, 4,340 ; in 1850, 6.060.

COLUMBIA CENTRE, p. o., Licking co., O.

COLUMBIA, city, c. h., p. o., seat of justice of Clark co., Oregon. Watered by Columbia river.

COLUMBIA CROSS ROADS, p. o., Bradford co., Pa., 153 ms. N.,by E. of Harrisburgh ; from W. 260 ms.

COLUMBIA FURNACE, p. v., Shenandoah co., Va., 157 ms. N. w. of Richmond ; from W. 111 ms.

COLUMBIANA COUNTY, situated on the east boundary of Ohio, with Ohio river on the southeast. Area, 750 square miles. Face of the country generally rolling and hilly, except along the streams, where it is level, and the soil is highly productive. Seat of justice, New Lisbon. Pop. in 1820, 22,033 ; in 1830, 35,508 ; in 1840, 40,378 ; in 1850, 33,621.

COLUMBIANA, c. h., p. v., seat of justice of Shelby co., Ala. ; from W. 781 ms.

COLUMBIANA, p. o., Columbiana co., O., 110 ms. E. N. E. of Columbus ; from W. 641 ms.

COLUMBIA GROVE. p. o., Lunenburgh co., Va., 101 ms. from Richmond ; from W. 218 ms.

COLUMBIAVILLE, v., Stockport township, Columbia co., N. Y. Watered by Claverack and Kinderhook creeks.

COLUMBUS COUNTY, situated on the southern boundary of North Carolina. Area, 600 square miles. Face of the country generally flat: soil of middling quality. Seat of justice, Whitesville. Pop. in 1820, 3,912 ; in 1830, 4,141 ; in 1840, 3,941 ; in 1850, 5,909.

COLUMBUS, city, seat of justice of Franklin co., and capital of O., occupies a gentle slope on the east side of the Scioto river, 110 miles northeast of Cincinnati, and 363 miles from Washington. A large public square of 10 acres, in the centre of the city, is formed by the intersection of rectangular streets, and contains the statehouse, an imposing edifice of brick, with a cupola 106 feet above the ground,which displays an interesting view of a wide surface of country. Fronting this square, are also the federal courthouse, and a building for state purposes. The penitentiary is a solid and extensive structure of limestone. There are also asylums for the insane, and for the blind, deaf, and dumb ; banks, churches, and numerous other prominent buildings. Columbus owes much of its prosperity to the circumstance of its being the seat of state government ; but manufactures and trade are increasing with the facilities of communication The Columbus Branch canal extends 10 miles, to the Ohio and Erie canal, which traverses the state from Portsmouth, on the Ohio, to Cleveland, on Lake Erie, a distance of 307 miles. The Cincinnati, Cleveland, and Columbus railroad communicates with this place.

The population in 1820, was 1,400 ; in 1830, 2,435 ; in 1840, 6,048 ; in 1850, 16,893.

COLUMBUS, p. t., Chenango co., N. Y., 98 ms. w. of Albany ; from W. 353 ms. Watered by Unadilla river and tributaries. Pop 1,381.

COLUMBUS, p. v., Mansfield township, Burlington co., N. J., 12 ms. s. by E. of Trenton ; from W. 163 ms.

COLUMBUS, p. o., Warren co., Pa.

COLUMBUS, p. t., St. Clair co., Md., 37 ms. N. E. of Detroit ; from W. 561 ms. Pop. 377.

COLUMBUS CITY, p. o., seat of justice of Muscogee co., Ga., 124 ms. w. s. w. of Milledgeville ; from W. 757 ms. Watered by Chattahoochee river.

COLUMBUS, city, seat of justice of Lowndes co., Miss., 141 ms. N. E. of Jackson ; from W. 855 ms. ; situated at the head of steamboat navigation, on the east bank of Tombigbee river, is an important and growing city. Like the other flourishing towns of Mississippi, it is an extensive market for cotton, which finds its way from this point down the Tombigbee to Mobile, and thence to various foreign and domestic ports. The city is well laid out, on an elevation, about 120 feet above the level of the Tombigbee. An elegant bridge spans this stream, and some of the public buildings are beautiful and imposing. The population in 1840, was 4,000 ; in 1850, 9,611.

COLUMBUS, p. v., Hempstead co., Ark., 119 ms. s. w. of Little Rock ; from W. 1,184 ms.

COLUMBUS, p. v., Polk co., Tenn., 170 ms. E. s. E. of Nashville ; from W. 570 ms. Watered by Hiawasee river.

COLUMBUS. p. v., Adams co., Ill., 101 ms. w. of Springfield ; from W. 878 ms. Pop. 1,541.

COLUMBUS, c. h., p. v., seat of justice of Hickman co., Ky., 110 ms. s. w. by w. of Frankfort ; from W. 837 ms. Watered by Mississippi river.

COLUMBUS, c. h., p. v., seat of justice of Bartholomew co., Ind., 41 ms. s. E. of Indianapolis ; from W. 579 ms. Watered by East Fork of White river. Pop. 1,008.

COLUMBUS, p. t., Warren co., Pa., 225 ms. N. w. of Harrisburgh ; from W. 292 ms. Pop. 1,278.

COLUMBUS, p. o., Columbia co., Flor.

COLUMBUS, p. o., Jackson co., Mo.

COLUMBUS, p. o., Colorado co., Tex.

COLUMBUS, p. o., Columbia co., Wis.,

COLUMBUS CITY. p. o., Louisa co., Iowa.

COLVIN'S TAVERN, p. o., Culpeper co., Va., 100 ms. N. N. w. of Richmond ; from W. 86 ms.

COLUSI, p. o., Colusi co., Cal.

COMAL COUNTY, Texas. Area, —— square miles. Chief town, New Braunfels. Pop. in 1850. 1,723.

COMAN'S WELL, p. o., Sussex co., Va., 48 ms. s. s. E. of Richmond ; from W. 167 ms.

COMMACK, p. v., Smithtown township, Suffolk co., Long Island, N. Y., 187 ms. s. by E. of Albany ; from W. 267 ms.

COMMERCE, p. t., Oakland co., Mich., 35 ms. N. w. of Detroit ; from W. 559 ms. Pop. 1,428.

COMMERCE, v., Wilson co., Tenn., 48 ms. E. N. E. of Nashville ; from W. 649 ms.

COMMERCE, p. v., Tunica co., Miss., 211 ms. N. of Jackson ; from W. 950 ms. Watered by Mississippi river.

COMMERCE, p. v., Scott co., Mo., 230 ms. s. E. of Jefferson city ; from W. 863 ms. Watered by Mississippi river.

COMMETTSBURG, p. o., Washington co., Pa.

COMO, p. o., Whitesides co., Ill., 180 ms. N. of Springfield ; from W. 843 ms.

COMO, p. o., Henry co., Tenn.

COMO, p. o., De Soto co., Miss.

COMPETINE, p. o., Wapello co., Iowa.

COMSTOCK, p. v., Kalamazoo co., Mich , 137 ms. w. of Detroit ; from W. 601 ms. Watered by Kalamazoo river.

COMSTOCK'S LANDING, p. o., Fort Ann township, Washington co., N. Y., 66 ms. N. of Albany ; from W. 436 ms.

CONCHARDEE, p. o., Talladega co., Ala.

CONCORD, city, seat of justice of Merrimac co., and capital of N H is situated on both sides of Merrimac river, 65 ms. N. w. of Boston ; from W. 475 ms. Four substantial bridges connect the principal part of the town with the east side of the river, and the Contoocook, flowing through its northwest corner, at its confluence with the Merrimac, forms Dustan island, so named after Mrs. Dustan, famed in heroic Indian history. Its central position, the well-cultivated and productive surrounding region, and the communication by railroad with Boston, Portsmouth, and the interior, contribute to Concord a steady growth and prosperity. The statehouse, built of white granite, taken from the neighboring quarries, is a fine structure in the centre of the town, 126 feet long, 49 feet wide, with projections of four feet on each front, surmounted by a fine cupola. Here also is the stateprison, constructed of the same kind of material. The population in 1775, was 1,052 ; in 1790, 1,747 ; in 1800, 2,052 ; in 1810, 2,393 ; in 1820, 2,838 ; in 1830, 3,727 ; in 1840, 4,897 ; in 1850, 8,576.

CONCORD, p. t., Somerset co., Me., 54 ms. N. of Augusta ; from W. 648 ms. Watered by Kennebec river. Pop. 554.

CONCORD, p. t., Essex co., Vt., 47 ms. N. E. of Montpelier ; from W. 556 ms. Watered by Connecticut and Passumpsic rivers. Pop. 1,153.

CONCORD, c. h., p. t., seat of justice, together with Cambridge and Lowell, of Middlesex co., Mass., 17 ms. N. w. of Boston ; from W. 445 ms. Watered by Concord river. Pop. 2,249.

CONCORD, t., Erie co., N. Y., 282 ms. w. of Albany ; from W. 346 ms. Watered by Cattaraugus creek. Pop. 3,242.

CONCORD, t., Delaware co., Pa., 83 ms. s. E. of Harrisburgh ; from W. 122 ms. Watered by Painter's creek. Pop. 1,049.

CONCORD, p. v., Sussex co., Del., 46 ms. s. of Dover ; from W. 123 ms. Watered by Broad creek.

CONCORD, p. v., Franklin co.. Pa., 72 ms. w. of Harrisburgh ; from W. 122 ms. Watered by Tuscarora creek. Pop. 882.

CONCORD, p. t., Lake co., O., 177 ms. N. E. of Columbus ; from W. 345 ms. Pop. 1,031.

CONCORD, t., Erie co., Pa., 257 ms. N. W. of Harrisburgh ; from W. 318 ms. Watered by tributaries of Broken Straw and French creeks.

CONCORD, p. t., Appomattox co., Va., 102 ms. w. by S. of Richmond ; from W. 188 ms.

CONCORD, c. h., p. v., seat of justice of Cabarrus co., N. C., 139 ms. w. s. w. of Raleigh ; from W. 376 ms. Watered by Big Cold Water creek.

CONCORD, p. v., Tippecanoe co., Ind., 63 ms. N. W. of Indianapolis ; from W. 621 ms.

CONCORD, p. v., Baker co., Ga., 154 ms. s. s. w. of Milledgeville ; from W. 811 ms.

CONCORD, p. v., Lewis co., Ky., 104 ms. E. N. E. of Frankfort ; from W. 483 ms. Watered by Ohio river.

CONCORD, p. t., Jackson co., Mich., 84 ms. w. by s. of Detroit ; from W. 556 ms. Watered by Kalamazoo river. Pop. 893.

CONCORD, v., Lincoln co., Tenn., 78 ms. s. of Nashville ; from W. 713 ms.

CONCORD, p. v., Callaway co., Mo., 35 ms. N. E. of Jefferson city ; from W. 920 ms.

CONCORD, t., Washington co., Mo. Pop. 815.

CONCORD, t., Green co., Ark.

CONCORD, t., Ross co., O., 41 ms. s. of Columbus ; from W. 419 ms. Watered by Paint creek. Pop. 2,672.

CONCORD, t., Champaign co., O., 59 ms. w. by N. of Columbus ; from W. 456 ms. Pop. 1,010.

CONCORD, t., Delaware co., O., 19 ms. N. of Columbus ; from W. 415 ms. Pop. 1,369.

CONCORD, t., Fayette co., O., 52 ms. s. w. of Columbus ; from W. 429 ms. Pop. 836.

CONCORD, t., Highland co., O., 84 ms. s. w. of Columbus ; from W. 445 ms. Pop. 1,500.

CONCORD, t., Miami co., O. Watered by Miami river and Miami canal. Pop 1,353.

CONCORD, p. o., Morgan co., Ill.

CONCORD, p. o., Jefferson co., Wis.

CONCORD, p. o., Louisa co., Iowa.

CONCORD, p. o., Harrison co., Tex.

CONCORDIA PARISH, situated on the east boundary of Louisiana, between Tensas and Mississippi rivers. Area, 1,300 square miles. Face of the country a universal alluvial flat, partially subject to annual inundation. Seat of justice, Vidalia. Pop. in 1820, 2,626 ; in 1830, 4,662 ; in 1840, 9,414 ; in 1850, 7,758.

CONCORDIA, p. v., Fayette co., Tenn., 199 ms. s. w. by w. of Nashville ; from W. 888 ms.

CONCORDIA, p. o., Bolivar co., Miss.

CONCORDIA, p. o., Harrison township, Darke co., O., 105 ms. w. by N. of Columbus ; from W. 501 ms.

CONCORDVILLE, p. t., Delaware co., Pa., 83 ms. E. S. E. of Harrisburgh ; from W. 117 ms. Pop. 1,049.

CONECUH COUNTY, situated on the south boundary of Alabama, and traversed by Conecuh river. Area, 1,531 square miles. Face of the country undulating rather than hilly ; soil sterile, except along the streams. Seat of justice, Sparta. Pop. in 1820, 5,713 ; in 1830, 7,444 ; in 1840, 8,197 ; in 1850, 9,322.

CONEMAUGH, t., Cambria co., Pa., 138 ms. w. of Harrisburgh ; from W. 160 ms. Watered by Stone creek, Little Conemaugh, and Conemaugh rivers. Pop. 3,027.

CONEMAUGH, t., Indiana co., Pa., 164 ms. w. by N. of Harrisburgh ; from W. 196 ms. Watered by Blacklegs creek and Conemaugh river. Pop. 1,748.

CONEMAUGH, p. t., Somerset co., Pa. Pop. 1,434.

CONERLY'S, p. o., Pike co., Miss.

CONESTOGA, p. t., Lancaster co., Pa., 43 ms. s. E. of Harrisburgh ; from W. 107 ms. Pop. 2,723.

CONEQUENESSING, t., Butler co., Pa., 218 ms. w. N. w. of Harrisburgh ; from W. 249 ms. Watered by Conequenessing, Break Neck, and Yellow creeks.

CONESUS, p. t., Livingston co., N. Y., 221 ms. w. from Albany ; from W. 350 ms. Pop. 1,418.

CONESVILLE. p. t., Schoharie co., N. Y., 42 ms. s. w. of Albany ; from W. 370 ms. Watered by Manor Kill. Pop. 1,582.

CONEWAGO, t., York co., Pa. Pop. 1,270.

CONEWAGO, t., Adams co., Pa. Pop. 569.

CONEWANGO, p. t., Cattaraugus co., N. Y., 316 ms. w. by s. of Albany ; from W. 338 ms. Watered by Conewango and Little Conewango creeks. Pop. 1,408.

CONEWANGO, t., Warren co., Pa. Watered by Conewango creek and Alleghany river. Pop. 884.

CONEWINGO, v., Cecil co., Md., 73 ms. N. E. of Annapolis ; from W. 83 ms. Watered by Conewingo creek.

CONGRESS, p. t., Wayne co., O., 105 ms. N. E. of Columbus ; from W. 356 ms. Watered by Killibuck creek. Pop. 2,336.

CONGRESS, t., Richland co., O., 54 ms. N. E., of Columbus ; from W. 394 ms. Watered by tributaries of Whetstone river.

CONHOCTON, t., Steuben co., N. Y., 215 ms. w. s. w. of Albany ; from W. 315 ms. Watered by Conhocton creek. Pop. 1,993.

CONINE, p. o., Licking co., O.

CONKLIN, p. t., Broome co., N. Y,, 145 ms. w. s w. of Albany ; from W. 304 ms. Watered by Susquehanna river. Pop. 2,232.

CONKLIN CENTRE, p. o., Conklin township, Broome co., N. Y.

CONNEAUT, t., Crawford co., Pa. 252 ms. N. w. of Harrisburgh ; from W. 315 ms. Watered by Conneaut lake. Pop. 1,807.

CONNEAUT, t., Erie co., Pa., 265 ms. N. w. of Harrisburgh ; from W. 326 ms. Watered by Conneaut creek. Pop. 1,942.

CONNEAUT, p. t., Ashtabula co., O., 220 ms. N. E. of Columbus ; from W. 341 ms. Watered by Conneaut creek and Lake Erie. Pop. 2,695.

CONNEAUTVILLE, p. v., Beaver township, Crawford co., Pa., 251 ms. N. w. by w. of Harrisburgh ; from W. 324 ms. Pop. 787.

CONNECTICUT, one of the United States, so called from its principal river, lies between 41° and 42° north latitude, and 71° 20′ and 73° 15′ west longitude from Greenwich, and is bounded north by Massachusetts ; east by Rhode Island ; south by Long Island sound : and west by New York, containing 4,674 sq. miles.

Physical Aspect.—The surface is uneven, and greatly diversified by hills and valleys. The soil is generally fertile, particularly so in Fairfield county, and the al luvial meadows in the valley of the Connecticut are uncommonly fine, and well adapted for tillage ; but a large portion of the state is better suited to the purposes of grazing.

Mountains.—Strictly speaking, there are three mountain ranges in this state ; one running a few miles east of the Connecticut, as far south as Chatham, where it is cut off by that river, and reappears again on the western side, and terminates at East Haven. Another range, which extends from Mount Tom, in Massachusetts, runs through the whole state, on the westerly side of the Connecticut, and terminates at New Haven. in a bold bluff called East Rock. A third range, still further west, extends from the Green Mountains, in Vermont, across the state to New Haven, and terminates in a similar bluff called West Rock. The Blue hills, in Southington, belonging to this range, are the most elevated land in the state, being at least 1,000 feet in height. At the westward of Hartford is Talcott mountain, belonging also to this range.

Rivers, Bays, Harbors, &c.—The principal rivers are, the Connecticut, Housatonic, Thames, Farmington, Naugatuck, and the Quinnebaug. The shores of Connecticut are penetrated by numerous bays and creeks, which afford many safe harbors for small vessels. The three best harbors in the state are those of New London, Bridgeport, and New Haven.

Climate.—The climate is generally healthy, though subject to sudden changes of temperature, and extreme degrees of heat and cold. In winter, the northwest winds are piercing and keen, while those which blow from the south are more mild. Near the coast the weather is particularly variable, usually changing with the wind, as it blows from the land or the sea. In the western and northerly parts of the state, the temperature is more uniform and mild.

Productive Resources.—Among the staple products may be enumerated, horses, mules, neat cattle, sheep, swine, poultry, eggs, fish, beef, pork, milk, butter, cheese, silk, wool, tobacco, hemp, flax, hay, straw, wheat, rye, barley, oats, buckwheat, Indian corn, potatoes, garden vegetables, fruits, cider and wine. Iron

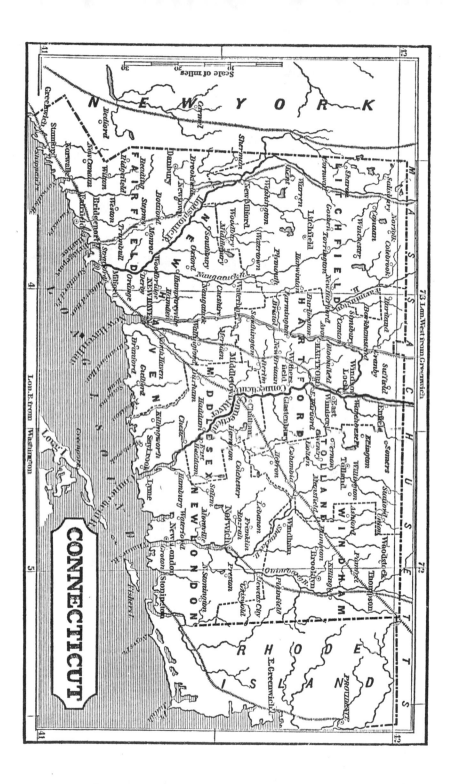

CONNECTICUT

ore, of superior quality, is found in Salisbury and Kent, that of the former being particularly adapted for the manufacture of wire. At Stafford, a bog iron ore is found, from which excellent casting and hollow ware are made. Lead and copper mines exist in different parts of the state, but in general they have not been worked to much extent. A lead mine, near Middletown, was wrought with some success during the revolutionary war. At Simsbury there is also a mine of copper. In Chatham, and Haddam, a reddish-brown freestone is quarried, which is easily wrought, and is highly esteemed in modern architecture, wherever it can economically be obtained. Fine variegated marble is found at Milford, resembling verd-antique.

Manufactures.—A large proportion of the people of Connecticut are engaged in manufactures, more particularly those of cotton and woollens; also, iron, hats, paper, leather, tinware, buttons, cutlery, carriages, ship-building, &c.

Railroads and Canals.—Connecticut has over 600 miles of railroad in operation, and others projected, which will undoubtedly be carried through at an early day. The only canals in the state now in operation are those which have been constructed to facilitate navigation on the Connecticut river.

Commerce.—The commerce of Connecticut is mostly with the southern states and the West Indies. The imports and exports of 1850 amounted to $614,320, one half of which entered and cleared at New Haven, and one fourth at New London. The shipping owned within the state amounts to about 120,000 tons. The foreign commerce of Connecticut has decreased, owing to the facilities afforded by railroad communication for shipping at New York and Boston.

Education.—There are three colleges in Connecticut; Yale college, at New Haven, one of the most flourishing in the Union; Trinity college, at Hartford; and the Wesleyan university, at Middletown. There are in the state 150 academies, and over 2,000 common schools. Connecticut has a large school fund, amounting to about $2,000,000. The asylum for the deaf and dumb at Hartford, is the oldest and most respectable institution of the kind in the United States.

Population.—In 1790, 237,946; in 1800, 251,002; in 1810, 261,942; in 1820, 275,248; in 1830, 297,711; in 1840, 310,015; in 1850, 370,791.

Number of slaves in 1790, 2,759; in 1800, 951; in 1810, 310; in 1820, 97; in 1830, 25, who were not emancipated, on account of advanced age or infirmities.

History.—Connecticut comprises a part of the territory of the Plymouth colony, and was granted to the earl of Warwick, in 1630, extending westward from the Atlantic to the "South sea." The first permanent settlement was made in 1633, by English emigrants from Massachusetts Bay, who located at Windsor, Hartford, and Wethersfield. In 1635, another puritan colony was also established at the mouth of the Connecticut, called the "Saybrook," in honor of Lords Say and Brook, to whom, in 1631, the earl of Warwick had conveyed his title. In 1638, a third puritan colony was formed at New Haven, and remained in force until 1665. In 1639, the inhabitants of Windsor, Hartford, and Wethersfield, formed a separate government for themselves, as one public state, or commonwealth, to which the Saybrook colony was annexed, by purchase, in 1644, and with which the New Haven colony united, under the royal charter, in 1665. In 1662, the royal charter of Connecticut was granted by Charles II., embracing the territory extending westward from Narraganset bay to the Pacific, embracing within its limits the New Haven colony, and most of the present state of Rhode Island. In 1687, Sir Edmund Andros came to Hartford with a body of troops, and, by royal authority, as governor-general of all New England, demanded a surrender of this charter, and a dissolution of the existing government. The Connecticut assembly being in session at the time, were not disposed to make the surrender, and while the subject was under discussion, the lights were extinguished, and the charter secretly conveyed away, and concealed in the cavity of a hollow oak-tree, which is still standing, and bears the name of the "Charter Oak." This charter formed the basis of the government until 1818, when the present constitution was adopted. Within this charter was embraced the "Connecticut Western Reserve," consisting of about 3,300,000 acres of land in the northeast part of Ohio, which, as a compromise, was ceded to the United States, in 1796. It was sold to the Connecticut Land Company, for $1,200,000, and was

the foundation of the state school fund. The constitution of the United States was adopted in 1788. The motto of the state seal is, *Qui transtulit sustinet*—"He who brought us hither still preserves."

Government.—The government is vested in a governor, lieutenant-governor, senate, and house of representatives, all chosen annually by the people, on the first Monday in April. The senate consists of not less than 18, nor more than 24 members. The sessions of the legislature are held annually, alternately, at Hartford and New Haven. The judicial power is vested in a supreme court of errors, superior court, and such inferior courts as the legislature may establish. Judges are chosen by the legislature, and hold office during good behavior, or till seventy years of age. The right of suffrage is enjoyed by every white male citizen of the United States, who has resided in the town six months immediately preceding, and has a freehold of the yearly value of seven dollars, or shall have performed, or been excused from, military duty, or shall have paid a state tax, one year next preceding the election, and who is of good moral character.

CONNELL'S CROSS ROADS, p. o., Bossier parish, La.

CONNELLSVILLE, p. t. and v., Fayette co., Pa., 180 ms. w. by s. of Harrisburgh; from W. 206 ms. Watered by Youghiogany river. Pop. 1,553.

CONNER'S MILLS, p. o., Cooper co., Mo., 45 ms. N. w. of Jefferson City; from W. 960 ms.

CONNERSVILLE, c. h., p. v., seat of justice of Fayette co., Ind., 60 ms. E. s. E. of Indianapolis; from W. 519 ms. Watered by Whitewater river. Pop. 1,396.

CONNERSVILLE, p. o., Harrison co., Ky.

CONN'S CREEK, p. o., Shelby co., Ind., 34 ms. s. E. of Indianapolis; from W. 563 ms.

CONOCOCHEAGUE. p. o., Washington co., Md.

CONOIS, p. o., Calhoun co., Mich.

CONOLTON, p. o. Harrison co., O.

CONOTEN, v., North township, Harrison co., O., 118 ms. N. E. of Columbus; from W. 296 ms.

CONQUEST. p. t., Cayuga co., N. Y., 164 ms. w. by N. of Albany; from W. 347 ms. Watered by Seneca river. Pop. 1,863.

CONRAD'S STORE, p. o., Rockingham co., Va., 109 ms. N. w. of Richmond; from W. 124 ms.

CONSHOHOCKEN, p. o., Montgomery co., Pa.

CONSOLATION, p. o., Shelby co., Ky.

CONSTABLE, t., Franklin co., N. Y., 218 ms. N. by w. of Albany; from W. 536 ms. Watered by Trout river. Pop. 1,447.

CONSTABLEVILLE, p. v., West Turin township, Lewis co., N. Y., 138 ms. N. w. of Albany; from W. 419 ms.

CONSTANTIA, p. t., Oswego co., N. Y., 135 ms. w. N. w. of Albany; from W. 373 ms. Watered by Oneida lake and Scriba creek. Pop. 2,495.

CONSTANTIA CENTRE, p. o., Constantia township, Oswego co., N. Y.

CONSTANTIA, p. o., Delaware co., O.

CONSTANTINE, p. v., St. Joseph co., Mich., 149 ms. w. s. w. of Detroit; from W. 596 ms. Watered by St. Joseph's and Fall rivers. Pop. 1,496.

CONSTITUTION, p. o., Washington co., O.

CONSTITUTION, p. o., Franklin co., Ark.

CONTENT, p. o., Bolivar co., Miss.

CONTENTNIA, p. o., Pitt co., N. C.

CONTOOCOOK VILLAGE, p. o., Hopkinton township, Merrimac co., N. H., 10 ms. w. of Concord; from W. 478 ms. Watered by Contoocook river.

CONTRA COSTA, p. o., Contra Costa co., Cal.

CONTRERAS, p. o., Butler co., O.

CONVENIENCE, p. o., Fayette co., O., 54 ms. s. w. of Columbus; from W. 426 ms.

CONVENIENT, p. o., Smith co., Tenn.

CONVENT, p. o., St. James's parish, La.

CONVIS, t., Calhoun co., Mich., 113 ms. w. of Detroit; from W. 578 ms. Pop. 621.

CONWAY COUNTY, situated in the central part of Arkansas, on the northerly side of Arkansas river. Area, 1,025 square miles. Seat of justice, Lewisburgh. Pop. in 1830, 982; in 1840, 2,892; in 1850, 3,583.

CONWAY, p. o., Aroostook co., Me.

CONWAY, p. t., Carroll co., N. H., 68 ms. N. N. E. of Concord; from W. 552 ms. Watered by Swift and Saco rivers. Pop. 1,767.

CONWAY, p. t., Franklin co., Mass., 102 ms. w. by N. of Boston; from W. 397 ms. Watered by Deerfield river. Pop. 1,831.

CONWAY, p. o., Livingston co., Mich.

CONWAYBOROUGH, c. h., p. v., seat of justice of Horry district, S. C., 196 ms. E. by S. of Columbia; from W. 468 ms. Watered by Waccamaw river.

CONYER'S. p. o., Newton co., Ga.

CONYERSVILLE, p. o., Henry co., Tenn.

CONYNGHAM, p. v., Luzerne co., Pa., 108 ms. N. N. E. of Harrisburgh; from W. 218 ms.

COOCH'S BRIDGE, p o., Newcastle co., Del., 62 ms. w. by N. of Dover; from W. 96 ms.

COOK COUNTY, situated on the easterly boundary of Illinois, on the west side of Lake Michigan, and watered by Des Plaines, Chicago, and Du Page rivers. Area, 864 square miles. Face of the country generally level, containing prairies; soil fertile. Seat of justice, Chicago. Pop. in 1835, 7,500; in 1840, 10,201; in 1850, 43,385.

COOK, p. o., Erie co., Pa.

COOKE'S CORNER, p. o., Erie co., O., 103 ms. N. E. of Columbus; from W. 412 ms.

COOKE'S STORE, p. o., Lafayette co., Mo.

COOKESVILLE, p. o., Cuddo parish, La.

COOKHAM, p. v., Fairfield district, S. C., 20 ms. N. of Columbia; from W. 489 ms.

COOKSBURGH, p, v., Rensselaerville township, Albany co., N. Y.

COOKSEYVILLE, p. o., Crittenden co., Ky.

COOK'S LAW OFFICE, p. o., Elbert co., Ga., 110 ms. N. N. E. of Milledgeville; from W. 566 ms.

COOK'S RUN. p o., Clinton co., Pa., 147 ms. N. N. W. of Harrisburgh; from W. 239 ms.

COOKSTOWN, p. o., Washington township, Fayette co., Pa., 197 ms. w. by S. of Harrisburgh; from W. 219 ms. Watered by Monongahela river.

COOKSTOWN, p. o., Burlington co., N. J.

COOKSVILLE. p. v.. Anne Arundel co., Md., 53 ms. N. w. of Annapolis; from W. 58 ms.

COOKSVILLE, p. v., Noxubee co., Miss., 132 ms. N. E. by E. of Jackson; from W. 885 ms.

COOKSVILLE, p. o., Rock co., Wis.

COOLBAUGH'S, p. t., Monroe co., Pa., 138 ms. N. E. of Harrisburgh; from W. 232 ms. Pop. 246.

COOL SPRING, p. t., Mercer co., Pa., 175 ms. w. N. w. of Harrisburgh; from W. 248 ms. Watered by Cool Spring and Otter creeks. Pop. 2,730.

COOL SPRING, p. o., Wilkinson co., Ga., 50 ms. s. of Milledgeville; from W. 704 ms.

COOL SPRING, p. o., Jefferson co., Pa.

COOLVILLE, p. o., Athens co., O.

COON CREEK, p o, Jasper co., Mo.

COONEWAR, p. o., Pontotoc co., Mich.

COON HILL, p. o., Santa Rosa co., Flor.

COON PRAIRIE, p. o., Crawford co., Wis.

COON'S MILL, p. o., Boone co., Va.

COONSBOROUGH, p. o., Orangeby district, S. C.

COONVILLE, p. o., Pottawatamie co., Iowa.

COOPER COUNTY, situated in the central part of Missouri, on the south side of Missouri river. Area, 400 square miles. Face of the country generally level, with rich and fertile prairies. The alluvial soil along the streams is also of first-rate quality. Seat of justice, Booneville. Pop. in 1820, 6,959; in 1830, 6,019; in 1840, 10,848; in 1850, 12,950.

COOPER, p. t., Washington co., Me., 196 ms. E. N. E. of Augusta; from W. 782 ms. Watered by Cobscook bay. Pop. 562.

COOPER, p. t.. Kalamazoo co., Mich., 131 ms. w. of Detroit; from W. 596 ms. Pop. 733.

COOPER, p. o., Wayne co., O.

COOPER'S, p. o., Franklin co., Va., 169 ms. w. s. w. of Richmond; from W. 244 ms.

COOPERSBURGH, p. o., Lehigh co., Pa., 95 ms. E. N. E. of Harrisburgh; from W. 108 ms.

COOPER'S MILLS, p. o., Lincoln co., Me., 13 ms. s. of Augusta; from W. 605 ms.

COOPERSTOWN, c. h., p. v., Otsego township, seat of justice of Otsego co., N. Y., 69 ms. w. of Albany; from W. 366 ms. Watered by Otsego outlet.

COOPERSTOWN, p. v., Plumb township, Venango co., Pa., 218 ms. w. N. w. of Harrisburgh; from W. 292 ms.

COOPERSTOWN, p. o., Brown co., Wis.

COOPERSVILLE, p. o., Clinton co., N. Y.

COOPERSVILLE. p. v., Lancaster co., Pa., 55 ms. s. E. of Harrisburgh; from W. 113 ms.

COOPERSVILLE, p. o., Dearborn co., Ind.

COOPERSVILLE, p. o., Fentress co., Tenn.

COOPERSVILLE. p. o.. Union district, S. C.

COOPER'S WELL, p. o., Hinds co., Miss.

COOP'S CREEK, p. o., Marion co., Tenn., 107 ms. s. E. of Nashville; from W. 608 ms.

COOS COUNTY, situated at the extreme north part of New Hampshire, on the easterly side of Connecticut river. Area, 1,600 square miles. Face of the country mountainous and generally broken; soil in many parts productive in grain and pasturage. Seat of justice, Lancaster. Pop. in 1820, 5,549; in 1830, 8,390; in 1840. 9,849; in 1850, 11,713.

COOSA COUNTY, situated near the central part of Alabama, on the east side of Coosa river. Area, 870 square miles. Face of the country mountainous and hilly, with extensive forests of pine. Seat of justice, Rockford. Pop. in 1840, 6,995; in 1850, 14,533.

COOSA, p. o., Floyd co., Ga.

COOSAWATTEE, p. o., Murray co., Ga.

COOSAWDA, v., Autauga co., Ala.; from W. 832 ms. Watered by Alabama river.

COOSAWHATCHIE, p. v., Beaufort district, S. C., 134 ms. s. of Columbia; from W. 619 ms. Watered by Coosawhatchie river.

COPAKE, p. t., Columbia co., N. Y., 40 ms. s. by E. of Albany; from W. 342 ms. Watered by Ancram creek. Pop. 1,652.

COPAN, p. o., Haywood co., Tenn.

COPANO, p. o., Refugio co., Tex.

COPELAND, p. o., Telfair co., Ga., 96 ms. s. by E. of Milledgeville; from W. 743 ms.

COPENHAGEN, p. v., Denmark township, Lewis co., N. Y., 149 ms. N. w. of Albany; from W. 423 ms. Watered by Deer river.

COPENHAGEN, p. v., Caldwell co., N. C., 206 ms. w. of Raleigh; from W. 418 ms.

COPENHAGEN, p. v., Caldwell parish, La., 266 ms. N. w. of New Orleans; from W. 1,180 ms.

COPE'S MILLS, p. o., Jefferson co., O., 146 ms. E. by N. of Columbus; from W. 277 ms.

COPLEY, p. t., Summit co., O., 124 ms. N. E. of Columbus; from W. 337 ms. Pop. 1,541.

COPI. p. o., Johnson co., Iowa.

COPIAH COUNTY, situated toward the southwest part of Mississippi, with Pearl river on the northeast. Area, 900 square miles. Seat of justice. Gallatin. Pop. in 1830, 7,001; in 1840, 8,954; in 1850, 11,794

COPIAH CREEK, p. o., Copiah co., Miss., 45 ms. s. of Jackson; from W. 1,049 ms.

COPOPA, p o., Columbia township. Lorain co., O., 135 ms. N. N. E. of Columbus; from W. 365 ms.

COUFFRAS CREEK, p. o., Fulton co., Ill., 77 ms. N. w. of Springfield; from W. 827 ms

COPPER CREEK, p. o., Mercer co., Ill.

COPPER CREEK, p. o., Jackson co., Iowa.

COPPER RIDGE, p. o., Hancock co., Tenn.

CORAL. p. o., McHenry co., Ill., 221 ms. N. N. E. of Springfield; from W. 773 ms.

CORAM, p. v., Brookhaven township, Suffolk co., Long Island, N. Y., 203 ms. s. s. E. of Albany; from W. 283 ms.

CORBEAN, p. v., Champlain township, Clinton co., N. Y.

CORBETTSVILLE, p. o., Conklin township, Broome co., N. Y.

CORDARVILLE, p. o., Worcester co., Mass.

CORDOVA, p. o., Rock Island co., Ill., 166 ms. N. N. w. of Springfield; from W. 884 ms.

CORDOVA, p. o., Grant co., Ky.

COREA FABRE, v., Union co., Ark., 168 ms. s. by w. of Little Rock; from W. 1,213 ms. Watered by Wachita river.

CORFU, p. o., Pembroke township, Genesee co., N. Y., 266 ms. w. by N. of Albany; from W. 380 ms.

CORINNA, p. t., Penobscot co., Me., 64 ms. N. N. w. of Augusta; from W. 659 ms. Watered by head branch of Sebasticook river. Pop. 1,550.

CORINNA CENTRE, p. o., Corinna township, Penobscot co., Me.

CORINTH, p. t., Penobscot co., Me., 85 ms. N. E. of Augusta; from W. 680 ms. Watered by Kenduskeag stream. Pop. 1,600.

CORINTH, p. t., Saratoga co., N. Y., 52 ms. N. by w. of Albany; from W. 421 ms. Watered by Hudson river. Pop. 1,501.

CORINTH, p. v., Heard co., Ga., 120 ms. w. of Milledgeville; from W. 724 ms.

CORINTH, p. o., Orange co., Vt.

CORINTH, p. o., Belmont co., O.

CORK, p. o., Ashtabula co., O., 191 ms. N. E. of Columbus; from W. 342 ms.

CORK, p. o., Dearborn co., Ind.

CORK, p. o., Butts co., Ga.

CORNELIUSVILLE, v., Boone co., Ky., 90 ms. N. by E. of Frankfort; from W. 516 ms.

CORNER GUM, p. o., Currituck co., N. C.

CORNERS, p. o., Windsor co., Vt., 70 ms. s. of Montpelier; from W. 468 ms.

CORNERSBURGH, p. v., Mahoning co., O.

CORNERSVILLE, p. v., Giles co., Tenn., 61 ms. s. of Nashville; from W. 711 ms.

CORNERSVILLE, v., Graves co., Ky., 289 ms. s. w. by w. of Frankfort; from W. 813 ms.

CORNERSVILLE, p. v., Marshall co., Miss., 184 ms. N. w. w. of Jackson; from W. 887 ms.

CORN GROVE, p. o., Benton co., Ala.; from W. 736 ms.

CORNIE, p. o., Union co., Ark.

CORNING, p. v., Painted Post township, Steuben co., N. Y., 213 ms. w. s. w. of Albany; from W. 287 ms. Watered by Chemung river.

CORNISH, p. t., York co., Me., 77 ms. s. w. of Augusta; from W. 547 ms. Watered by Great Ossipee and Saco rivers. Pop. 1,144.

CORNISH, p. t., Sullivan co., N. H., 58 ms. N. w. by w. of Concord; from W. 471 ms. Watered by Connecticut river. Pop. 1,606.

CORNISH FLAT, p. o., Cornish township, Sullivan co., N. H.

CORNISHVILLE, p. o., McHenry co., Ill., 210 ms. N. N. E. of Springfield; from W. 762 ms.

CORNISHVILLE, p. o., Mercer co., Ky.

CORN PLANTER, p. t., Venango co., Pa., 217 ms. w. N. w. of Harrisburgh; from W. 291 ms. Pop. 693.

CORNVILLE, p. t., Somerset co., Me., 42 ms. N. by E. of Augusta; from W. 637 ms. Watered by Wessaransett river. Pop. 1,260.

CORNWALL, p. t., Addison co., Vt., 63 ms. s. w. of Montpelier; from W. 477 ms. Watered by Otter and Lemonfair creeks. Pop. 1,155.

CORNWALL, p. t., Litchfield co., Ct., 39 ms. w. by N. of Hartford; from W. 330 ms. Watered by Housatonic river. Pop. 2,041.

CORNWALL, p. t., Orange co., N. Y., 100 ms. s. of Albany; from W. 270 ms. Watered by Hudson river. Pop. 4,471.

CORNWALL, p. o., Lebanon co., Pa., 42 ms. E. of Harrisburgh; from W. 326 ms.

CORNWALL BRIDGE, p. o., Cornwall township, Litchfield co., Ct., 42 ms. w. by N. of Hartford; from W. 326 ms.

CORNWALL HOLLOW, p. o., Cornwall township, Litchfield co., Ct.

CORNWALL LANDING, v., Cornwall township, Orange co., N. Y. Watered by Hudson river.

CORNWALLVILLE, p. v., Durham township, Greene co., N. Y., 38 ms. s. s. w. of Albany; from W. 361 ms.

CORPUS CHRISTI, p. o., Nueces co., Tex.

CORSICA, p. o., Morrow co., O.

CORSICA, p. o., Jefferson co., Pa.

CORSICANA, p. o., Navarro co., Tex.

CORTLAND COUNTY, situated southwest of the central part of New York, and traversed by Toughnioga river. Area, 500 square miles. Face of the country hilly; soil productive, well-watered and wooded. Seat of justice, Cortland. Pop. in 1820, 16,507; in 1830, 23.791; in 1840, 24,607; in 1850, 25,140.

CORTLAND, p. o., Kent co., Mich., 186 ms. w. N. w. of Detroit; from W. 667 ms.

CORTLAND, p. t., Westchester co., N. Y., 113 ms. s. of Albany; from W. 262 ms. Watered by Croton river. Pop. 7,758.

CORTLAND, p. o., Jackson co., Ind.

CORTLAND, p. o., Newton co., Tex.

CORTLAND VILLAGE, p. v., Cortlandville township, Cortland co., N. Y. Watered by Toughnioga river.

CORTLANDVILLE, p. t., seat of justice of Cortland co., N. Y., 143 ms. w. by s. of Albany; from W. 314 ms. Watered by Toughnioga river. Pop. 4,203.

CORITOISE, p. t., Crawford co., Mo.

CORUNNA, c. h., p. v., seat of justice of Shiawassee co., Mich., 79 ms. N. w. of Detroit; from W. 582 ms. Watered by Shiawassee river.

CORWIN, p. o., Montgomery co., O.

CORYDON, p. t., McKean co., Pa., 233 ms. N. w. of Harrisburgh; from W. 317 ms.

CORYDON, c. h., p. v., seat of justice of Harrison co., Ind., 126 ms. s. of Indianapolis; from W. 623 ms. Watered by Indian creek. Pop. 462.

CORYDON, p. o., Henderson co., Ky.

CORYDON, p. o., Warren co., Pa.

COSGROVE HALL, p. o., Union co., Pa.

COSHOCTON COUNTY, situated near the central part of Ohio. Area, 562 square miles. Face of the county diversified and hilly; soil in the valleys highly fertile. Seat of justice, Coshocton. Pop. in 1820, 7,086; in 1830, 11,161; in 1840, 21,590; in 1850, 25,674.

COSHOCTON, c. h., p. v., seat of justice, Coshocton co., O., 83 ms. E. N. E. of Columbus; from W. 337 ms. Watered by Walhonding, Tuscarawas, and Muskingum rivers. Pop. 850.

COSSAWAGO, t., Crawford co., Pa.

COTE SANS DESSEIN, p. v., Callaway co., Mo., 11 ms. E. by N. of Jefferson City; from W. 935 ms. Watered by Missouri river.

COTILE, p. o., Rapides parish, La., 319 ms. N. w. by w. of New Orleans; from W. 1,238 ms.

COTOMA, p. o., Montgomery co., Ala.

COTOSA, p. o., Walker co., Ga.

COTTAGE, p. o., Cattaraugus co., N. Y.

COTTAGE, p. o., Montgomery co., Md., 48 ms. w. N. w. of Annapolis; from W. 8 ms.

COTTAGE, p. o., Huntingdon co., Pa.

COTTAGE GROVE, p. o., Dane co., Wis., 21 ms. from Madison; from W. 849 ms.

COTTAGE GROVE, p. o., Washington co., Minnesota.

COTTAGE GROVE, p. o., Union co., Ind.

COTTAGE HILL, p. o., Du Page co., Ill.

COTTAGE HILL, p. o., Lauderdale co., Tenn.

COTTAGE HILL, p. o., St. Joseph co., Ind.

COTTAGE HOME, p. o., Harford co., Md.

COTTAGE HOME, p. o., Lincoln co., N. C.

COTTLEVILLE, p. o., St. Charles co., Mo.

COTTON GIN, p. o., Freestone co., Tex.

COTTON GIN PORT, p. v., Monroe co., Miss., 180 ms. N. E. of Jackson; from W. 905 ms. Watered by Tombigbee river.

COTTON GROVE, p. o., Davidson co., N. C., 102 ms. w. of Raleigh; from W. 359 ms.

COTTON GROVE, p. o., Madison co., Tenn., 137 ms. w. s. w. of Nashville; from W. 821 ms.

COTTON GROVE, p. o., Pontotoc co., Miss.

COTTON GROVE, p. o., Wapello co., Iowa.

COTTON HILL, p. o., Randolph co., Ga.

COTTON PLANT, p. o., Tippah co., Mo., 202 ms. N. N. E. of Jackson; from W. 874 ms.

COTTON PLANT, p. o., Rusk co., Tex.

COTTON RIDGE, p. o., Itawamba co., Miss.

COTTON VALLEY, p. o., Macon co., Ala.

COTTONVILLE, p. o., Marshall co., Ala.; from W. 706 ms.

COTTONVILLE, p. o., Jackson co., Iowa.

COTTONWOOD, p. o., Christian co., Ky.

COTTONWOOD GROVE, p. o., Bond co., Ill.

COTTRELVILLE, p. t., St. Clair co., Mich., 50 ms. N. E. of Detroit; from W. 576 ms. Pop. 913.

COTUIT, p. v., Barnstable co., Mass., 68 ms. s. s. E. of Boston; from W. 469 ms.

COTUIT PORT, p. o., Barnstable co., Mass.

COULSON'S MILL, p. o., Linn co., Mo.

COULTER'S STORE, p. o., Macon co., Mo.

COULTERSVILLE, p. o., Butler co., Pa., 213 ms. w. by N. of Harrisburgh; from W. 255 ms.

COUNCIL BEND, p. o., Crittenden co., Ark.

COUNCIL BLUFF, p. o., Pottawatamie co., Iowa.

COUNCIL HILL, p. o., Jo Daviess co., Ill.

COUNTSVILLE, p. o., Lexington district, S. C.

COUNTY LINE, p. o., Tallapoosa co., Ala.; from W. 788 ms.

COUNTY LINE, p. o., Niagara co., N. Y., 272 ms. w. by N. of Albany; from W. 415 ms.

COUNTY LINE, p. o., Davie co., N. C., 146 ms. w. of Raleigh; from W. 364 ms.

COUNTY LINE, p. o., Campbell co., Ga., 117 ms. N. w. of Milledgeville; from W. 712 ms.

COUNTY LINE, p. o., Newton co., Miss., 60 ms. E. of Jackson; from W. 957 ms.

COURSENVILLE, v., Stillwater township, Sussex co., N. J., 83 ms. N. of Trenton; from W. 252 ms.

COURT-HILL, p. o., Talladega co., Ala.

COURT-HOUSE, p. o., Franklin co., Ala.

COURTLAND, p. v., Lawrence co., Ala.; from W. 753 ms.

COURTLAND, p. o., Columbia co., Wis.

COURTWRIGHT, v., Bloom township, Fairfield co., O., 20 ms. s. E. of Columbus; from W. 385 ms.

COURTWRIGHT'S MILLS, p. o., Iroquise co., Ill.

COUSHATTEE CHUTE, p. o., Natchitoches parish, La.

Cove, p. o., Shelby co., Ala.

Cove, p. o., Polk co., Ark.

Cove Creek, p. o., Benton co., Ala., 131 ms. s. e. of Tuscaloosa from W. 724 ms.

Coventry, p. t., Orleans co., Vt., 54 ms. n. of Montpelier; from W. 566 ms. Watered by Barton and Black rivers. Pop. 867.

Coventry, t., Grafton co., N. H., 70 ms. n. w. of Concord; from W. 525 ms. Watered by Wild Amonoosuck river and Oliverian brook.

Coventry, p. t., Tolland co., Ct., 17 ms. e. of Hartford; from W. 353 ms. Watered by Willimantic and Hop rivers. Pop. 1,984.

Coventry. t., Chester co., Pa., 71 ms. s. e. of Harrisburgh; from W. 135 ms. Watered by Tioga river.

Coventry, p. t., Kent co., R. I. 13 ms. s. w. of Providence; from W. 395 ms. Watered by Flat river and South branch of the Pawtuxent. Pop. 3,620.

Coventry, p. t., Chenango co., N. Y., 114 ms. w. of Albany; from W. 320 ms. Watered by Harper's and Kelsey's creeks. Pop. 1,677.

Coventry. Summit co., O., 109 ms. n. e. of Columbus; from W. 330 ms. Pop. 1,299.

Coventryville, p. v., Coventry township, Chenango co., N. Y., 114 ms. w. of Albany; from W. 320 ms.

Covert, p. t., Seneca co., N. Y., 176 ms. w. of Albany; from W. 309 ms. Watered by tributaries of Cayuga lake. Pop. 2,253.

Covesville, p. v., Albemarle co., Va., 92 ms. n. w. of Richmond; from W. 142 ms.

Covesville, p. o., Northumberland township, Saratoga co., N. Y., 33 ms. n. of Albany; from W. 403 ms.

Covesville, p. o., Monroe co., Pa.

COVINGTON COUNTY, situated on the south boundary of Alabama. Area, 1,664 square miles. Seat of justice, Montezuma. Pop. in 1830, 1,522; in 1840, 2,435; in 1850, 3,645.

COVINGTON COUNTY, situated toward the southerly part of Mississippi. Area, 960 square miles. Face of the country, hilly; soil, in some parts, fertile, but generally sterile. Seat of justice, Williamsburgh. Pop. in 1820, 2,230; in 1830, 2,551; in 1840, 2,717; in 1850, 3,358.

Covington, p. t., Wyoming co., N. Y., 241 ms. w. of Albany; from W. 359 ms. Pop. 1,385.

Covington, t., Clearfield co., Pa.

Covington, p. v., Covington township, Tioga co., Pa., 138 ms. n. of Harrisburgh; from W., 248 ms. Watered by tributaries of Tioga creek. Pop. 448.

Covington, t., Luzerne co., Pa., 131 ms. n. e. of Harrisburgh; from W. 239 ms. Watered by Lehigh river. Pop. 650.

Covington, c. h., p. v., seat of justice of Alleghany co., Va., 196 ms. w. of Richmond; from W. 233 ms. Watered by Jackson's river.

Covington, p. v., Richmond co., N. C., 123 ms. s. w. of Raleigh; from W. 397 ms.

Covington, c. h., p. v., seat of justice of Newton co., Ga., 61 ms. n. w. of Milledgeville; from W. 648 ms. Watered by Yellow river.

Covington, c. h., p. v., seat of justice of St. Tammany parish, La., 45 ms. n. of New Orleans; from W. 1,127 ms. Watered by Boug Fallier.

Covington, p. v., Tipton co., Tenn., 185 ms. w. s. w. of Nashville; from W. 868 ms. Watered by a branch of Big Hutchy river.

Covington, city, p. v., Kenton co., Ky., 85 ms. n. e. of Frankfort; from W. 493 ms. Watered by Ohio river and Licking creek.

Covington. p. v., Newbury township, Miami co., O., 77 ms. w. of Columbus; from W. 469 ms. Watered by Stillwater river.

Covington, c. h., p. v., seat of justice of Fountain co., Ind., 74 ms. n. w. of Indianapolis; from W. 645 ms. Watered by Wabash river.

Cowan. t., Wayne co., Mo.

Cowan's Ford, p. o., Mecklenburgh co., N. C.

Cowansville, p. o., Rowan co., N. C., 134 ms. w. of Raleigh; from W. 371 ms.

Cowansville, p. o., Armstrong co., Pa.

Cow Creek, p. o., Saline co., Mo., 72 ms. n. w. of Jefferson city; from W. 997 ms.

Cowdersport, c. h., p. v., seat of justice of Potter co., Pa., 174 ms. n. w. of Harrisburgh; from W. 283 ms. Watered by Alleghany river.

COWETA COUNTY, situated in the western part of Georgia, on the southeast side of Chattahoochee river.

Area, 532 square miles. Seat of justice, Newman. Pop. in 1830, 5,003; in 1840. 10,364; in 1850, 13,635.

Cowikee, p. o., Barbour co., Ala.

Cowlesville, p. o., Bennington township, Wyoming co., N. Y., 268 ms. w. of Albany; from W. 374 ms.

Cowpen Branch, p. o., Barnwell district, S. C.

Cowpens, p. o., Spartanburgh district, S. C., 117 ms. n. w. of Columbia; from W. 458 ms.

Cowper Hill, p. o., Robeson co., N. C., 113 ms. s. w. of Raleigh; from W. 405 ms.

Cowskin, p. o., Ozark co., Mo.

Coxsackie, p. t., Greene co., N. Y., 22 ms. s. of Albany; from W. 347 ms. Watered by Hudson river Pop. 3,741.

Coxes', p. o., Bullitt co., Ky.

Cox's Mills, p. o., Randolph co., N. C.

Cox's Mills. p. o., Gilmer co.. Va.

Cox's Mills, p. o., Wayne co., Ind.

Cox's Store, p. o., Washington co., Tenn.

Coxville, p. o., De Kalb co., Ala.

Coylee, p. o., Monroe co., Tenn.

Coyleyville, p. o., Butler co., Pa.

Cozby, p. o., Hamilton co., Tenn.

Crab Bottom, p. o., Highland co., Va., 173 ms. n. w. of Richmond; from W. 189 ms.

Crab Orchard, p. o., Wythe co., Va.

Crab Orchard, p. v., Lincoln co., Ky., 62 ms. s. s. e. of Frankfort; from W. 575 ms.

Crab Orchard, p. o., Ray co., Mo.

Crab Tree, p. o., Haywood co., N. C.

Cracker's Neck, p. o., Greene co., Ga.

Crafton, v., Pittsylvania co., Va., 167 ms. s. w. of Richmond; from W. 242 ms.

Craftsbury, p. t., Orleans co., Vt., 33 ms. n. of Montpelier; from W. 549 ms. Watered by Black river and a branch of the Lamoille. Pop. 1,223.

Craftsville, p. o., Elbert co., Ga.

Craig, p. t., Switzerland co., Ind.

Craig's Creek, p. o., Botetourt co., Va.

Craigsville, p. o., Blooming Grove township, Orange co., N. Y., 99 ms. w. of Albany; from W. 280 ms.

Crain's Creek, p. o., Moore co., N. C., 76 ms. s. w. of Raleigh; from W. 364 ms.

Crain's Corners, p. o., Warren township, Herkimer co., N. Y., 69 ms. w. n. w. of Albany; from W. 380 ms.

Crainsville, p. o., Hardeman co., Tenn., 165 ms. s. w. of Nashville; from W. 165 ms.

Cranberry, p. o., Middlesex co., N. J., 22 ms. n. e. of Trenton; from W. 188 ms. Watered by Cranberry brook.

Cranberry, t., Butler co., Pa., 213 ms. w. of Harrisburgh; from W. 244 ms. Watered by Glade river, Breakneck, and Brush creeks. Pop. 2,256.

Cranberry, t., Crawford co., O., 79 ms. n. of Columbus; from W. 419 ms. Pop. 1,042.

Cranberry, p. t., Venango co., Pa., 207 ms. w. n. w. of Harrisburgh; from W. 287 ms. Watered by Alleghany river. Pop. 1,317.

Cranberry, p. o., Allen co., O.

Cranberry Creek, p. o., Mayfield township, Fulton co., N. Y.

Cranberry Forge, p. o., Watauga co., N. C.

Cranberry Isles, p. o., Hancock co., Me.

Cranberry Plains, p. o., Carroll co., Va.

Cranberry Prairie, p. o., Mercer co., O.

Crane Creek, p. o., Barry co., Mo.

Crane's Forge, p. o., Assumption parish, La.

Cranesville, p. o., Amsterdam township, Montgomery co., N. Y., 29 ms. w. n. w. of Albany; from W. 397 ms.

Cranesville, p. o., Paulding co., O., 166 ms. n. w. of Columbus; from W. 518 ms.

Cranesville, t., Daviess co., Mo.

Cranesville, p. o., Essex co., N. J.

Cranston, t., Providence co., R. I., 5 ms. s. w. of Providence; from W. 389 ms. Watered by Pawtuxet and Powchasset rivers. Pop. 4,311.

Crary's Mills, p. o., St. Lawrence co., N. Y.

Crater's Mills, p. o., Iredell co., N. C.

CRAVEN COUNTY, situated on the southeast part of North Carolina, and traversed by the river Neuse. Area, 1,100 square miles. Face of the country generally flat; soil in part sandy and marshy. Seat of justice, Newbern. Pop. in 1820, 13,394; in 1830, 13,734; in 1840, 14,438; in 1850, 14,709.

CRAWFORD COUNTY, situated on the west boundary of Pennsylvania. Area, 1,016 square miles. Face of the country moderately hilly; soil generally productive of grain, pasturage, and fruits. Seat of justice, Meadville. Pop. in 1820, 9,397; in 1830, 16,005; in 1840, 31,724: in 1850. 37,849.

CRAWFORD COUNTY, situated toward the west part of Georgia, with Flint river on the southwest. Area, 360 square miles. Seat of justice, Knoxville. Pop. in 1830, 5,313; in 1840, 7.981; in 1850, 8,984.

CRAWFORD COUNTY, situated toward the north part of Ohio, and drained by Sandusky river. Area, 590 square miles. Face of the country generally flat, containing several large prairies or swamps. Seat of justice, Bucyrus. Pop. in 1830, 4,791; in 1840, 13,152; in 1850, 18,177.

CRAWFORD COUNTY, situated on the west boundary of Arkansas, and traversed by Arkansas river. Area, 780 square miles. Seat of justice, Van Buren. Pop. in 1830, 2,440; in 1840, 4,266; in 1850, 7,960.

CRAWFORD COUNTY, situated in the southern part of Indiana. Area, 300 square miles. Face of the country generally hilly; soil productive. Seat of justice, Fredonia. Pop. in 1820, 2,583; in 1830, 3,238; in 1840, 5,282; in 1850, 6,356.

CRAWFORD COUNTY, situated on the eastern boundary of Illinois, with Wabash river on the east, and Embarrass river on the southwest. Area, 426 square miles. Face of the country variegated by hills and plains; soil productive. Seat of justice, Palestine. Pop. in 1820, 3,024; in 1830, 3,117; in 1840, 4.422; in 1850, 7,135.

CRAWFORD COUNTY, situated on the westerly boundary of Wisconsin, between Mississippi and Wisconsin rivers. Area, —— square miles. Seat of justice, Prairie du Chien. Pop. in 1834, 810; in 1840, 1,502; in 1850, 2,498.

CRAWFORD COUNTY, situated toward the southeast part of Missouri, and watered by Marameo river. Area, 1,650 square ms. The face of the country is partly level, and partly hilly; soil generally poor, and abounds in iron. Seat of justice, Steelville. Pop. in 1830, 1,721; in 1840, 3,561; in 1850, 6,397.

CRAWFORD, p. t., Orange co., N. Y., 92 ms. s. by w. of Albany; from W. 294 ms. Watered by Shawangunk river. Pop. 1,912.

CRAWFORD, t., Washington co., Me., 197 ms. N. E. of Augusta; from W. 799 ms. Pop. 324.

CRAWFORD, t., Coshocton co., O. Pop. 1,552.

CRAWFORD, p. t., Wyandott co., O., 84 ms. N. of Columbus; from W. 434 ms. Pop. 1,306.

CRAWFORD, t., Buchanan co., Mo. Pop. 969.

CRAWFORD, v., Estill co., Ky., 98 ms. s. E. of Frankfort; from W. 553 ms. Watered by north fork of Kentucky river.

CRAWFORD, c.h., p.v., seat of justice of Russell co., Ala.

CRAWFORD'S SEMINARY, p. o., Quapaw nation co., Mo.

CRAWFORD'S HOUSE, p., Coos co., N. H.

CRAWFORD'S MILLS, p. o., Westmoreland co., Pa.

CRAWFORD'S COVE, p. o., St. Clair co., Ala.

CRAWFORDSVILLE, c. h., p. v., seat of justice of Tallaferro co., Ga., 62 ms. N. of Milledgeville; from W. 604 ms.

CRAWFORDSVILLE, c. h., p. v., seat of justice of Montgomery, Ind., 45 ms. N. w. of Indianapolis; from W. 616 ms. Watered by Sugar creek.

CRAWFORDSVILLE, p. o., Washington co., Iowa.

CRAWFORDSVILLE, p. o., Spartanburgh district, S. C.

CRAYTONVILLE, p. v., Anderson district, S. C., 114 ms. w. N. w. of Columbia; from W. 542 ms.

CREACHVILLE, p. o., Johnson co., N. C.

CREAGERSTOWN, p. v., Frederick co., Md., 88 ms. N. w. of Annapolis; from W. 56 ms.

CREAGH'S MILLS, p. o., Wilcox co., Ala.

CREEK NATION of Indians (Muscogees), who formerly inhabited the western part of Georgia and eastern portion of Alabama, most of whom have emigrated to the territory west of Arkansas, on Arkansas river, appropriated for them by the United States government. Area of their territory, —— square miles. Chief station, Creek Agency. Pop. 25,000.

CREEK STAND, p. o., Macon co., Ala.

CREESVILLE, p. o., Jefferson co., Iowa.

CREELSBURGH, p. v., Russell co., Ky., 109 ms. s. of Frankfort; from W. 623 ms. Watered by Cumberland river.

CRESCENT, p. o., Lycoming co., Pa.

CRETE, p. o., Will co., Ill., 187 ms. N. E. of Springfield; from W. 720 ms.

CREVE COEUR, p. o., St. Louis, Mo.

CRICHTON'S STORE, p. o., Brunswick co., Va., 91 ms. w. by s. of Richmond; from W. 207 ms.

CRIGLERSVILLE, p. o., Madison co., Va., 106 ms. N. w. of Richmond; from W. 101 ms.

CRIPPLE CREEK, p. o., Greenville district, S. C., 93 ms. N. w. of Columbia; from W. 579 ms.

CRIPPLE DEER, p. o., Tishemingo co., Miss.

CRISP PRAIRIE, p. o., Dade co., Mo.

CRITTENDEN COUNTY, situated on the northwest boundary of Kentucky, on the easterly side of Ohio river. Area, 540 square miles. Surface level; soil fertile. Seat of justice, Marion. Pop. in 1850, 6,351.

CRITTENDEN COUNTY, situated on the eastern boundary of Arkansas, between Mississippi and St. Francis rivers. Area, 2,100 square miles. Face of the country generally level; soil fertile, and in many parts subject to annual inundation. Seat of justice, Marion. Pop. in 1830, 1,272; in 1840, 1,501; in 1850, 2,648.

CRITTENDEN, p. v., Grant co. Ky., 60 ms. N. N. E. of Frankfort; from W. 518 ms.

CRITTENDEN, v., Clarke co., Ark., 82 ms. s. w. of Little Rock; from W. 1,145 ms.

CRITTENDEN, p. o., Erie co., N. Y.

CRITTENDEN, p. o., Howard co., Ind.

CRITTENDEN, p. o., Franklin co., Ill.

CRITTENDEN, p. o., Daviess co., Miss.

CROCKERSVILLE, p. o., Genesee co., Mich.

CROCKERY CREEK, p. o., Ottawa co., Mich.

CROCKETT, p. o., Houston co., Tex.

CROCKETT'S BLUFF, p. o., Arkansas co., Ark.

CROCKETTSVILLE, c. h., v., seat of justice of Ruscell co., Ala.; from W. 769 ms.

CROGHAN, p. t., Lewis co., N. Y., 141 ms. N. w. of Albany. Pop. 1,135.

CROGHAN, p. o., Putnam co., O., 110 ms. N. w. of Columbus; from W. 475 ms.

CROGANSVILLE, v., Alleghany co.. Pa., a suburb of Pittsburgh.

CROMWELL, p.v., Middletown township, Middlesex co., Ct., 12 ms. s. of Hartford; from W. 328 ms. Watered by Connecticut river.

CROOKED CREEK, p. o., Tioga co., Pa., 153 ms. N. of Harrisburgh; from W. 263 ms.

CROOKED CREEK, p. o., Stokes co., N. C., 129 ms w. N. w. of Raleigh; from W. 309 ms.

CROOKED CREEK, p. t., Carroll co., Ark., 205 ms, N. w. of Little Rock; from W. 1,131. Pop. 539.

CROOKED CREEK, p. o., Steuben co., Ind., 182 ms N. N. E. of Indianapolis; from W. 553 ms.

CROOKED CREEK, p. o., Clinton co., Ill., 104 ms. s. of Springfield; from W. 779 ms.

CROOKED CREEK, p. o., Monroe co., Miss.

CROOKED CREEK FURNACE, p. o., Bullitt co., Ky.

CROOKED FORK, p. o., Morgan co., Tenn.

CROOKED HILL, p. o., Montgomery co., Pa., 75 ms. E. of Harrisburgh; from W. 168 ms.

CROOKED LAKE, p. o., Marquette co., Wis.

CROOKED RIVER, t., Ray co., Mo.

CROOKE'S STORE, p. o., Lafayette co., Mo.

CROMWELL, p. o., Noble co., Ind.

CROMWELL, t., Huntingdon co., Pa.

CROPPER'S DELIGHT, p. o., Shelby co., Ky.

CROPWELL, p. o., St. Clair co., Ala.; from W. 745 ms.

CROSBY, t., Hamilton co., O.

CROSBYVILLE, p. v., Chester district, S. C., 72 ms. N. of Columbia; from W. 476 ms.

CROSS ANCHOR, p. o., Spartanburgh district, S. C., 84 ms. N. w. of Columbia; from W. 482 ms.

CROSSANVILLE, p. v., Jackson township, Perry co., O.

CROSS CREEK, t., Jefferson co., O. Watered by Great Miami river.

CROSS CREEK VILLAGE, p. o., Washington co., Pa., 229 ms. w. of Harrisburgh; from W. 256 m.

CROSS CUT, p. o., Beaver co., Pa.

CROSS HILL, p. o., Laurens district, S. C., 69 ms. w. N. w. of Columbia; from W. 517 ms.

CROSSINGVILLE, p. v., Crawford co., Pa., 249 ms. N. w. of Harrisburgh; from W. 322 ms.

CROSS KEYS, p. v., Gloucester co., N. J., 46 ms. s. of Trenton; from W. 156 ms.

CROSS KEYS, p. o., Rockingham co., Va., 123 ms. N. w. of Richmond; from W. 113 ms.

CROSS KEYS, p. o., Union district, S. C., 69 ms. R, w. of Columbia; from W. 517 ms.

CROSS KEYS, p. o., De Kalb co., Ga., 100 ms. N. w. of Milledgeville; from W. 674 ms.

CROSS KEYS, p. o., Roane co., Tenn., 147 ms. s. E. of Nashville ; from W. 558 ms.

CROSS KEYS, p. o., Macon co;, Ala. ; from W. 809 ms.

CROSSKILL MILLS, p. o., Berks co., Pa.

CROSS PLAINS, p. o., Benton co., Ala.

CROSS PLAINS, p. o., Ripley co., Ind., 78 ms. s. E. of Indianapolis ; from W. 553 ms.

CROSS PLAINS, p. o., Robertson co., Tenn., 34 ms. N. w. of Nashville ; from W. 696 ms.

CROSS PLAINS, p. o., Dane co., Wis.

CROSS RIDGE, p. o., Tishemingo co., Miss.

CROSS RIVER, p. o., Lewisborough township. Westchester co., N. Y., 172 ms. s. of Albany ; from W. 275 ms.

CROSS ROADS, p. o., York co., Pa., 37 ms. s. of Harrisburgh ; from W. 103 ms.

CROSS ROADS, p. o., Madison co., O., 53 ms. w. of Columbus ; from W. 434 ms.

CROSS ROADS, p. o., Bedford co., Va., 161 ms. w. of Richmond ; from W. 236 ms.

CROSS ROADS, p. o., Johnson co., Ill.

CROSS ROADS, p. o., Franklin co., Ark.

CROSS TIMBERS, p. o., Hickory co., Mo.

CROSSVILLE, p. o., Lumpkin co., Ga., 120 ms. N. w. of Milledgeville ; from W. 640 ms.

CROSSVILLE, p. o., Bledsoe co., Tenn., 111 ms. s. E. of Nashville ; from W. 570 ms.

CROSSWICK'S, p. v., Chesterfield township, Burlington co., N. J., 8 ms. s. E. of Trenton ; from W. 174 ms. Watered by Crosswick's creek.

CROTON, p. o., Hunterdon co., N. J.

CROTON, p. o., Licking co., O.

CROTON, p. o., Delaware co., N. Y.

CROTON, p. o., Neewaygo co., Mich.

CROTON FALLS, p. o., Westchester co., N. Y.

CROTON LANDING, p. o., Westchester co., N. Y.

CROW CREEK, p. o., Pickens district, S. C.

CROW CREEK, p. o., Franklin co., Tenn.

CROWDER'S CREEK, p. o. Gaston co., N. C., 196 ms. w. of Raleigh ; from W. 433 ms.

CROW MEADOWS, p. o. Marshall co., Ill., 92 ms. N. of Springfield ; from W. 785 ms.

CROW CREEK, p. o., Pickens co., S. C.

CROWN POINT, p. t., Essex co., N. Y., 106 ms. N. of Albany ; from W. 478 ms. Watered by Lake Champlain and Putnam's creek. Pop. 2,378.

CROWN POINT, c. h., p. v., seat of justice of Lake co., Ind., 158 ms. N. w. of Indianapolis ; from W. 702 ms.

CROWNSVILLE, p. o., Anne Arundel co., Md.

CROW'S POND, p. o., Daviess co., Ky.

CROXVILLE, p. o., Spartanburgh district, S. C., 87 ms. N. w. of Columbia ; from W. 500 ms.

CROXTON, p. o., Bush Creek township, Jefferson co., O., 138 ms. E. of Columbus ; from W. 285 ms.

CROYDON, p. t., Sullivan co., N. H., 48 ms. N. w. of Concord ; from W. 482 ms. Watered by Sugar river. Pop. 861.

CROYDON FLAT, p. o., Croydon township, Sullivan co., N. Y.

CRUM ELBOW, p. o., Hyde Park township, Dutchess co., N. Y., 69 ms. s. of Albany ; from W. 309 ms.

CRUSO, p. o., Seneca co., N. Y.

CRYSTAL LAKE, p. o., McHenry co., Ill., 206 ms. N. of Springfield ; from W., 768 ms.

CUBA, p. o., Fulton co., Ill., 61 ms. N. w. of Springfield ; from W. 827 ms.

CUBA, p. t., Alleghany co., N. Y., 280 ms. W. of Albany ; from W. 317 ms. Pop. 2,243.

CUBA. v., Washington township, Clinton co., O., 78 s. w. of Columbus ; from W. 451 ms.

CUBA, p. o., Rutherford co., N. C.

CUBA, p. o., Owen co., Ind.

CUBA, p. o., Kent co., Mich.

CUB CREEK, p. o., Charlotte co., Va., 110 ms. s. w. of Richmond ; from W. 197 ms.

CUBEHATCHEE, p. o., Macon co., Ala.

CUB HILL, p. o., Baltimore co., Md.

CUCKOOVILLE, p. v., Louisa co., Va., 47 ms. N. w. of Richmond ; from W. 98 ms.

CUDDEBACKVILLE, p. o., Deerpark township, Orange co., N. Y., 109 ms. s. of Albany ; from W. 272 ms.

CUDDYHUNK, p. o., Yallabusha co., Miss.

CUERO, p. o., De Witt co., Tex.

CUIVRE, t., St. Charles co., Mo.

CUIVRE, t., Audrain co., Mo.

CULCHOTE, p. o., Polk co., Tenn.

CULLODEN, p. v., Monroe co., Ga., 68 ms. w. of Milledgeville ; from W. 723 ms.

CULLOMA, p. o., El Dorado co., Cal.

CULPEPER COUNTY, situated toward the northeast part of Virginia, on the southwest side of Rappahannock river. Area, 672 square miles. Face of the country pleasantly diversified by hills, mountains, and valleys, with much excellent soil. Seat of justice, Culpeper Court House. Pop. in 1820, 20,942 ; in 1830, 24,026 ; in 1840, 11,393 ; in 1850, 12,282.

CULPEPER, c. h., p. v., Culpeper co., Va., 98 ms. N. w. of Richmond ; from W. 82 ms.

CULVER CREEK, p. o., Delaware co., O.

CUMBERLAND COUNTY, situated toward the southwest part of Maine with the Atlantic ocean on the southeast, and watered by Saco, Androscoggin, and Kennebec rivers. Area, 990 square miles. Face of the country somewhat varied, being much indented by bays on the seaboard, and hilly in the interior ; soil productive in pasturage, but generally poor in quality for other purposes. Seat of justice, Portland. Pop. in 1820, 49,445 ; in 1830, 60,113 ; in 1840, 68,658 ; in 1850, 77,549.

CUMBERLAND COUNTY, situated on the southeast boundary of New Jersey on Delaware bay. Area, 524 square miles. Face of the county generally level ; soil sandy. Seat of justice, Bridgetown. Pop. in 1820, 12,668 ; in 1830. 14,091 ; in 1840, 14,374 ; in 1850, 17,189.

CUMBERLAND COUNTY, situated toward the south part of Pennsylvania, with Susquehanna river on the northeast. Area, 544 square miles. This county lies in the fine valley between the north and south range of mountains. The face of the country is generally hilly, and the soil productive of grain, pasturage, and fruit. Seat of justice, Carlisle. Pop. in 1820, 23,606 ; in 1830, 29,218 ; in 1840, 30,953 ; in 1850, 34,327.

CUMBERLAND COUNTY, situated toward the southeast part of Virginia, with James river on the north. Area, 320 square miles. Face of the country hilly ; soil varied. Seat of justice, Cumberland Court House. Pop. in 1820, 11,023 ; in 1830, 11,689 ; in 1840, 10,339 ; in 1850, 9,751.

CUMBERLAND COUNTY, situated near the central part of North Carolina, and traversed by Cape Fear river. Area, 1,300 square miles. The soil in many places is fertile. Seat of justice, Fayetteville. Pop. in 1830, 14,824 ; in 1840, 15,284 ; in 1850, 20,610.

CUMBERLAND COUNTY, situated on the south boundary of Kentucky, and traversed by Cumberland river. Area, 270 square miles. Face of the county undulating and hilly on the east, and not much cultivated. Seat of justice, Burkesville. Pop. in 1830, 8,624 ; in 1840, 6,090 ; in 1850, 7,005.

CUMBERLAND COUNTY, situated near the easterly part of Illinois, Area, —— square miles. Seat of justice, Greenup. Pop. in 1850, 3,720

CUMBERLAND, p. o., Marion co., Ind., 10 ms. E. of Indianapolis ; from W. 561 ms.

CUMBERLAND, p. t., Cumberland co., Me., 42 ms. s. w. of Augusta ; from W. 553 ms. Watered by Casco bay. Pop. 1,654.

CUMBERLAND, c. h., p. v., seat of justice of Alleghany co., Md., 166 ms., N. w. of Annapolis ; from W. 134 ms. Watered by Potomac river and Will's creek. Pop. 6,067.

CUMBERLAND, t., Adams co., Pa., 35 ms. s. of Harrisburgh ; from W. 74 ms. Watered by Rock and Marsh creeks. Pop. 1,408.

CUMBERLAND, p. o., Fayette co., Ill., 87 ms. s. E. of Springfield ; from W. 735 ms.

CUMBERLAND, c. h., p. v., seat of justice, of Cumberland co., Va., 52 ms. from Richmond ; from W. 142 ms.

CUMBERLAND, t., Green co., Pa. Watered by Muddy creek.

CUMBERLAND, t., Providence co., R. I., 10 ms. N. of Providence ; from W. 406 ms. Watered by Abbott's Mill and Peter's rivers. Pop. 6,661.

CUMBERLAND, p. v., Guernsey co., O. 93 ms. E. of Columbus ; from W. 314 ms. Watered by Buffalo fork of Will's creek.

CUMBERLAND, p. o., Grundy co., Tenn.

CUMBERLAND CENTRE, p. o., Cumberland township, Cumberland co., Me.

CUMBERLAND FORD, p. v., Knox co., Ky., 135 ms. s. E. of Frankfort ; from W. 503 ms. Watered by Cumberland river.

CUMBERLAND GAP, p. o., Knox co., Ky.

CUMBERLAND HILL, p. v., Cumberland township, Providence co., R. I., 16 ms. N. of Providence ; from W. 419 ms. Watered by Blackstone river.

CUMBERLAND IRON WORKS, p. v., Stewart co., Tenn.,

69 ms. N. W. of Nashville ; from W. 754 ms. Watered by Cumberland river.

CUMBERLAND VALLEY, p. t., Bedford co., Pa., 113 s. w. of Harrisburgh : from W. 119 ms. Watered by Evits creek. Pop. 1,114.

CUMINSVILLE, p. o., Hamilton co., O., 121 ms. s. w. of Columbus ; from W. 497 ms.

CUMMING, c. h., p. v., seat of justice of Forsyth co., Ga., 109 ms. N. W. of Milledgeville ; from W. 641 ms.

CUMMINGS, t., Lycoming co., Pa., 111 ms. N. of Harrisburgh ; from W. 221 ms. Pop. 505.

CUMMINGSVILLE, p. o., Itawamba co., Miss.

CUMMINGTON, p. t., Hampshire co., Mass., 111 ms. w. of Boston ; from W. 399 ms. Watered by Westfield river. Pop. 1,172.

CUMMINGTON, p. o., Macoupin co., Ill.

CUMMINGTON, WEST VILLAGE, Cummington township, Hampshire co., Mass., 116 ms. w. of Boston ; from W. 404 ms. Watered by Westfield river.

CUMRU, t., Berks co., Pa., 52 ms. from Harrisburgh ; from W. 141 ms. Watered by Tulpehocken and Schuylkill rivers. Pop. 3,489.

CUNNINGHAM'S, p. o., Bastrop co., Texas.

CUNNINGHAM'S STORE, p. o., Person co., N. C., 64 ms. N. W. of Raleigh ; from W. 240 ms.

CURDSVILLE, p. o., Buckingham co., Va., 68 ms. w. of Richmond ; from W. 158 ms.

CURETON'S BRIDGE, p. o., Henry co., Ala.

CURETON'S STORE, p. o., Lancaster district, S. C., 82 ms. N. E. of Columbus ; from W. 424 ms.

CURIA, p. o., Independence co., Ark.

CURLLSVILLE, p. o., Clarion co., Pa.

CURRITUCK COUNTY, situated at the northeast part of North Carolina, divided by Currituck sound, and comprehending Currituck island. Area, 600 square miles. Face of the country level ; soil generally sandy and barren, but much of it is profitably cultivated with rice. Seat of justice, Currituck. Pop. in 1820, 8,090 ; in 1830, 7,654 ; in 1840, 6,703 ; in 1850, 7,236.

CURRITUCK, c. h., p. v., seat of justice of Currituck co., N. C., 242 ms. N. E. of Raleigh ; from W. 270 ms. Watered by Currituck sound.

CURRY'S MILLS, p. o., Washington co., Ga.

CURRY'S RUN, p. o., Harrison co., Ky.

CURTISVILLE, p. v., Stockbridge township, Berkshire co., Mass., 136 ms. w. of Boston ; from W. 366 ms.

CURWINSVILLE, p. v., Clearfield co., Pa., 132 ms. N. w. of Harrisburgh ; from W. 224 ms. Watered by Anderson's creek.

CUSH, p. o., Clearfield co., Pa.

CUSHING, p. t., Lincoln co., Me., 50 ms. s. E. of Augusta ; from W. 627 ms. Watered by St. George's river and the Atlantic ocean. Pop. 807.

CUSHINGVILLE, p. o., Potter co., Pa.

CUSSAWAGO. p. t., Crawford co., Pa., 246 ms. N. W. of Harrisburgh ; from W. 319 ms. Pop. 1,540.

CUSSETA, p. v., Chambers co., Ala. ; from W. 767 ms.

CUSTARDS, p. v., Crawford co., Pa., 240 ms. N. W. of Harrisburgh ; from W. 298 ms.

CUTCHOGUE. p. v., Southold township, Suffolk co., Long Island, N. Y., 238 ms. s. E. of Albany ; from W. 218 ms.

CUTHBERT, c. h., p. v., seat of justice of Randolph co., Ga., 158 ms. s. w. of Milledgeville ; from W. 814 ms.

CUTLER, p. t., Washington co., Me., 155 ms. from Augusta ; from W. 757 ms. Watered by Atlantic ocean and Machias bay. Pop. 820.

CUT OFF, p. o., Walton co., Ga.

CUT OFF, p. o., Drew co., Ark.

CUTTINGSVILLE, p. o., Rutland co., Vt., 72 ms. s. w. of Montpelier ; from W. 466 ms.

CUYAHOGA COUNTY, situated on the north boundary of Ohio, on Lake Erie, and traversed by Cuyahoga river. Area, 475 square miles. Face of the country generally hilly ; soil generally good. Seat of justice, Cleveland. Pop. in 1810, 1,495 ; in 1820, 6,328 ; in 1830, 10,361 ; in 1840, 26,506 ; in 1850, 48,099.

CUYAHOGA FALLS, Summit co.. O., 128 ms. N. E. of Columbus ; from W. 335 ms. Watered by Cuyahoga river.

CUYLER, p. o., Truxton township, Cortland co., N. Y., 125 ms. w. of Albany ; from W. 337 ms.

CUYLERVILLE, p. o., Livingston co., N. Y.

CYNTHIANA, p. v., Perry township, Pike co., O., 75 ms. of Columbus ; from W. 429 ms.

CYNTHIANA, t.. Shelby co., O. Pop. 797.

CYNTHIANA, c. h., p. v., seat of justice of Harrison co., Ky., 37 ms. N. E. of of Frankfort ; from W. 505 ms. Watered by South Fork Licking river.

CYNTHIANA, v. p., Posey co., Ind., 158 ms. s. w. of Indianapolis ; from W. 728 ms.

CYNTHIANA, p. o., Wapello co., Iowa.

CYPRESS, p. o., Yazoo co., Miss.

CYPRESS, p. o., Union co., Ky., 233 ms. s. w. of Frankfort ; from W. 760 ms.

CYPRESS, p. o., Scott co., Mo.

CYPRESS, p. o., Kenosha co., Wis.

CYPRESS CREEK, p. o., Bladen co., N. C.

CYPRESS CREEK, p. o., Johnson co., Ill.

CYPRESS CROSSING, p. o., Newton co., Tex.

CYPRESS GROVE, p. o., New Hanover co., N. C.

CYPRESS INN, p. o., Wayne co., Tenn.

CYPRESS TOP, p. o., Harris co., Tex.

CYRUSTON, p. v., Lincoln co., Tenn., 97 ms. s. of Nashville ; from W. 726 ms.

D.

DACUSVILLE, p. v., Pickens district, S. C., 129 ms. N. w. of Columbia ; from W. 524 ms.

DADE COUNTY, situated in the northwest corner of Georgia. Area, 225 square miles. Face of the country mountainous, with fertile valleys. Seat of justice, Trenton. Pop. in 1840, 1,364 ; in 1850, 2,680.

DADE COUNTY, situated on the southerly boundary of Florida, with the Gulf stream on the south and east, including several islands, or keys, near the adjacent coast. Area, 5,000 square miles. Face of the country flat, a large portion of which consists of "everglades," or a body of savannas, covered with water several feet deep, containing many small islets of fertile land, and cypress swamps. Seat of justice, Key Biscayune. Pop. in 1840, 446 ; in 1850, 159.

DADE COUNTY, situated near the southwest part of Missouri. Area, 960 square miles. Face of the country undulating ; soil fertile. Seat of justice, Greenfield. Pop. in 1850, 4,246.

DADEVILLE, c. h., p. v., seat of justice of Tallapoosa co., Ala., 44 ms. N. E. of Montgomery ; from W. 793 ms.

DADSVILLE, p. o.. Marion co., Tenn.

DAGGER'S SPRING, p. o., Botetourt co., Va.

DAGGETT'S MILLS. p. o., Tioga co., Pa., 157 ms. N. of Harrisburgh ; from W. 267 ms.

DAGSBOROUGH, hundred, p. v., Sussex co., Del., 54 ms. s. E. of Dover ; from W. 141 ms. Watered by Pepper creek. Pop. 2,668.

DAHLONEGA, c. h., p. v., seat of justice of Lumpkin co., Ga., 140 ms. N. w. of Milledgeville ; from W. 620 ms. Pop. 1,277.

DAHLONEGA, p. o., Wapello co., Iowa.

DAHKOTAH COUNTY, situated in the central part of Minnesota. Area, ―― square miles. Seat of justice, ――. Pop. in 1850, 584.

DAILEY'S CROSS ROADS, p. o., Lowndes co., Miss., 131 ms. N. E. of Jackson ; from W. 905 ms.

DAKOTAH, p. o., Washarah co.. Wis.

DAINGERFIELD, p. o.. Titus co., Tex.

DAIRY, p. o., Scotland co., Mo.

DALE, p. o., Berks co., Pa., 75 ms. E. of Harrisburgh ; from W. 168 ms.

DALE COUNTY, situated on the south boundary of Alabama, and drained by tributaries of Choctawhatchie river. Area, 1,064 square miles. Face of the country generally level. The river swamps and hammocks are very productive, but the soil is mostly poor, covered with pines. Seat of justice, Daleville. Pop. in 1830, 2,031 ; in 1840, 7,397 ; in 1850, 6,346.

DALE, p. o., Spencer co., Ind.

DALE, p. o., Wyoming co., N. Y.

DALEVILLE, p. o., Luzerne co., Pa., 147 ms. N. E. of Harrisburgh ; from W. 244 ms.

DALEVILLE, c. h., p. v., seat of justice of Dale co., Ala., 85 ms. s. E. of Montgomery ; from W. 871 ms. Watered by a tributary of Choctaw river.

DALEVILLE, p. o., Lauderdale co., Miss., 104 ms. E. of Jackson ; from W. 918 ms.

DALEYS, p. o., Montgomery co., Tenn.

DALLAS COUNTY, situated toward the southwest part of Alabama, and watered by Alabama and Cahawba rivers. Area, 925 square miles. Soil fertile along the streams. Seat of justice, Cahawba. Pop. in 1830, 14,017; in 1840, 25,199 ; in 1850, 29,727.

DALLAS COUNTY, situated toward the north part of Texas, and watered by Trinity river and tributaries. Area, —— square miles. Seat of justice, Dallas. Pop. in 1850, 2,743.

DALLAS COUNTY, situated toward the southerly part of Arkansas, between Wachita and Saline rivers. Area, —— square miles. Seat of justice, Princeton. Pop. in 1850, 6,877.

DALLAS COUNTY, situated toward the southwest part of Missouri. Area, —— square miles. Seat of justice, Buffalo. Pop. in 1850, 3,648.

DALLAS COUNTY, situated toward the westerly part of Iowa. Area, —— square miles. Seat of Justice, Adell. Pop. in 1850, 854.

DALLAS, p. t., Luzerne co., Pa., 133 N. E. of Harrisburgh ; from W. 242 ms. Watered by Harvey's lake. Pop. 904.

DALLAS, p. o., Pulaski, Ky.

DALLAS, p. o., Madison parish, La.

DALLAS, p. o., Lafayette co., Miss.

DALLAS, p. o., Greene co., Mo.

DALLAS, p. o., Highland co., O.

DALLAS, p. o., Dallas co., Tex.

DALLAS, p. o., Clinton co., Mich.

DALLAS, p. o., Marshall co., Va.

DALLAS, p. o., Gaston co., N. C.

DALLAS, p. o., Abbeville district, S. C.

DALLAS, p. o., Oregon.

DALLASBURGH, p. o., Owen co., Ky.

DALLASBURGH, p. o., Warren co., O.

DALLAS, city, p. o., Hancock co., Ill,

DALLASTOWN, p. o., York co., Pa.

DALLTON, p. o., Sauk co,, Wis.

DALMATIA, p. v., Northumberland co., Pa., 40 ms. N. of Harrisburgh ; from W. 150 ms.

DALTON. p. t., Coos co., N. H., 96 ms. N. of Concord ; from W. 557 ms. Watered by Connecticut and Bt. John's rivers. Pop. 751.

DALTON, p. t., Berkshire co., Mass., 125 ms. w. of Boston ; from W 369 ms. Watered by tributaries of Housatonic river. Pop. 1,020.

DALTON, p. o., Sugar creek township, Wayne co., O., 106 ms. N. E. of Columbus ; from W. 331 ms.

DALTON, p. v. Wayne co., Ind. 80 ms F of Indianapolis ; from W. 527 ms. Pop. 855.

DALTON. p. o., Murray co., Ga.

DAMARISCOTTA MILLS, p. v., Lincoln co., Me., 30 ms. s. E. of Augusta ; from W. 598 ms. Watered by Damariscotta pond.

DAMASCOVILLE, p. v., Columbiana co., O., 174 ms. N. E. of Columbus ; from W. 295 ms.

DAMASCUS, p. t., Wayne co., Pa., 190 ms. N. E. of Harrisburgh ; from W. 293 ms. Watered by Delaware river. Pop. 1,602.

DAMASCUS, p. v., Montgomery co., Md., 70 ms. N. w. of Annapolis ; from W. 40 ms.

DAMASCUS, p. v., Spartanburgh district, S. C., 107 ms. N. w. of Columbia ; from W. 568 ms.

DAMASCUS, v., Columbiana co., O.

DAMASCUS, p. v., Henry co., O., 147 ms. N. w. of Columbus ; from W. 478 ms. Watered by Maumee river. Pop. 223.

DANA, p. t., Worcester co., Mass., 69 ms. w. of Boston ; from W. 397 ms. Watered by a tributary of Swift river. Pop.842.

DANBOROUGH. p. v., Plumstead township, Bucks co., Pa., 103 ms. E. of Harrisburgh ; from W. 165 ms.

DANBURGH, p. v., Wilkes co., Ga., 88 ms. N. E. of Milledgeville ; from W. 560 ms.

DANBURY, p. t., Grafton co., N. H., 28 ms. N. w. of Concord ; from W. 503 ms. Watered by Smith's river. Pop. 934.

DANBURY, t., Ottawa co., O. Pop. 501.

DANBURY, c. h., p. t., sent of justice, together with Fairfield, of Fairfield co., Ct., 68 ms. s. w. of Hartford ; from W. 292 ms. Watered by Still river. Pop. 5,964.

DANBURY, p. t., Washington co., Vt. Pop. 845.

DANBURY, p. o., Stokes co., N. C.

DANBY, p. t., Rutland co., Vt., 80 ms. s. of Montpelier ; from W. 443 ms. Watered by sources of Otter creek. Pop. 1,535.

DANBY, p. o., Ionia co., Mich.

DANBY, p. t., Tompkins co., N. Y., 116 ms. s. w. of Albany ; from W. 289 ms. Watered by Cattatone creek and tributaries. Pop. 2,411.

DANBY FOUR CORNERS, p. o., Danby township, Rutland co , Vt., 82 ms. s. of Montpelier ; from W. 437 ms.

DANEYVILLE, p. o., Haywood co., Tenn., 183 ms. s. w. of Nashville ; from W. 868 ms.

DANDRIDGE, c. h., p. v., seat of justice of Jefferson co., Tenn., 229 ms. E. of Nashville ; from W. 482 ms. Watered by French Broad river.

DANE COUNTY. situated toward the southerly part of Wisconsin, with Wisconsin river on the northwest, and contains the "Four Lakes." Area, 1,234 square miles. Seat of justice, Madison, which is also the capital of the state. Pop. in 1840, 314 ; in 1850, 9,366.

DANE, p. o., Dane co., Wis.

DANIEL's MILLS, p. o., Person co., N. C.

DANIELSVILLE, c. h., p. v., seat of justice of Madison co., Ga., 91 ms. N. of Milledgeville ; from W. 599 ms.

DANIELSVILLE, p. v., Spottsylvania, Va., 85 ms. N. w. of Richmond ; from W. 84 ms.

DANIELSVILLE, p. o., Dickson co., Tenn.

DANIELTON, p. o., Beaufort district, S. C.

DANNEMORA, p. o., Clinton co., N. Y.

DANSVILLE, t., Steuben co., N. Y., 230 ms. w. of Albany ; from W. 327 ms. Watered by tributaries of Canisteo river and Canasarega creek. Pop. 2,545.

DANSVILLE, p. v., Sparta township, Livingston co., N. Y., 238 ms. w. of Albany ; from W. 329 ms. Watered by Canasarega creek. Pop. 4,377.

DANUBE, p. t., Herkimer co., N. Y., 70 ms. w. of Albany ; from W. 393 ms. Watered by Nowadaga creek and Mohawk river. Pop. 1,730.

DANVERS, p. t., Essex co.,Mass., 16 ms. N. of Boston ; from W. 456 ms. Pop. 8,019.

DANVILLE, p. t., Cumberland co., Me., 42 ms. s. w. of Augusta ; from W. 373 ms. Watered by Androscoggin river. Pop. 1,636.

DANVILLE, c. h., p. v., seat of justice of Yell co., Ark., 70 ms. N. w. of Little Rock ; from W. 1,075 ms.

DANVILLE, p. t., Rockingham co., N. H., 30 ms. s. E. of Concord ; from W. 471 ms. Watered by Exeter river and Cub pond. Pop. 614.

DANVILLE, c. h., p. t., seat of justice of Caledonia co., Vt., 30 ms. N. E. of Montpelier ; from W. 543 ms. Watered by tributaries of Passumpsic river. Pop. 2,577.

DANVILLE, p. o., Warren co., N. J., 67 ms. N. of Trenton ; from W. 226 ms.

DANVILLE, c. h., p. v., seat of justice of Montour co., Pa., 71 ms. N. of Harrisburgh , from W. 181 ms. Watered by the north branch of Susquehanna river and Mahoning creek. Pop. 3,302.

DANVILLE, p. v., Pittsylvania co., Va., 164 ms. s. w. of Richmond ; from W. 251 ms. Watered by Dan river. Pop. 1,514.

DANVILLE, p. v.. Union township, Knox co., O., 65 ms. N. E. of Columbus ; from W. 366 ms.

DANVILLE, c. h., p. v., seat of justice of Boyle co., Ky., 41 ms. s. of Frankfort ; from W. 555 ms. Watered by a tributary of Dix river. Seat of Centre college.

DANVILLE, p. v., Sumter co., Ga., 100 ms. s. w. of Milledgeville ; from W. 757 ms. Watered by Flint r.

DANVILLE, c. h., p. v., seat of justice of Hendricks co., Ind., 90 ms. w. of Indianapolis ; from W. 591 ms. Watered by White Lick creek.

DANVILLE, c. h., p. v., seat of justice of Vermilion co., Ill., 130 ms. E. of Springfield ; from W. 657 ms. Watered by Vermilion river.

DANVILLE, c. h., p. v., seat of justice of Montgomery co., Mo., 47 ms. N. E. of Jefferson city ; from W. 892 ms.

DANVILLE, p. o., Tishemingo co., Miss.

DANVILLE, p. o., Montgomery co., Tex.

DANVILLE, p. o., Des Moines co., Iowa.

DAN WEBSTER, p. o., Henry co., Ind.

DARBY, p. t., Delaware co., Pa., 95 ms. s. E. of Harrisburgh ; from W, 132 ms. Watered by Darby creek. Pop. 1,310.

DARBY, p. t., Franklin co., O.

DARBY, p. t., Pickaway co., O., 29 ms. s. of Columbus ; from W. 422 ms. Watered by Darby creek. Pop. 1,166.

DARBY, t., Union co., O. Pop. 881.

DARBY CREEK, p. o., Jerome township, Madison co., O.. 22 ms. N. w. of Columbus ; from W. 415 ms.

DARBY PLAIN, p. o., Union co., O.. 26 ms. N. w. of Columbus ; from W. 415 ms.

DARBY's, p. o., Columbia co., Ga., 109 ms. N. E. of Milledgeville ; from W. 588 ms.

DARBYVILLE, p. v., Muhlenburg township, Pickaway

co., O., 38 ms. s. of Columbus; from W. 408 ms. Watered by Darby creek.

DARDANELLE, p. v., Polk co., Ark., 72 ms. N. w. of Little Rock; from W. 1,137 ms. Watered by Arkansas river.

DARDENNE, v., St. Charles co., Mo., 100 ms. E. of Jefferson city; from W. 846 ms. Watered by Dardenne river.

DARIEN, p. t., Fairfield co., Ct., 74 ms. s. w. of Hartford; from W. 266 ms. Watered by Long Island sound. Pop. 1,454.

DARIEN, p. t., Genesee co., N. Y., 263 ms. w. of Albany; from W. 377 ms. Watered by Ellicott's and Murder creeks. Pop. 2,086.

DARIEN, city, seat of justice of McIntosh co., Ga., 215 ms. s. E. of Milledgeville; from W. 724 ms. Watered by Attamaha river. Pop. 550.

DARIEN, p. t., Walworth co., Wis., 59 ms. s. E. of Madison; from W. 788 ms.

DARIEN CENTRE, p. o., Darien township, Genesee co., N. Y.

DARIEN DEPOT, p. o., Fairfield co., Ct.

DARK CORNER, p. o., Campbell co., Ga., 114 ms. N. w. of Milledgeville; from W. 711 ms.

DARK CORNER, p. o., De Soto co., Miss.

DARKE COUNTY, situated on the west boundary of Ohio. Area, 714 square miles. Face of the country diversified, but generally level; soil productive. Seat of justice, Greenville. Pop. in 1820, 3,717; in 1830, 6,203; in 1840, 13,282; in 1850, 20,274.

DARKE, p. o., Darke co., O.

DARKESVILLE, p. v., Berkley co., Va., 162 ms. N. of Richmond; from W. 84 ms. Watered by Sulphur Springs creek.

DARLINGTON DISTRICT, situated toward the northeast part of South Carolina, between Great Peedee river and Lynch's creek. Area, 1,050 square miles. Face of the country agreeably undulating; soil of middling quality. Seat of justice, Darlington. Pop. in 1820, 10,949; in 1830, 12,000; in 1840, 14,822; in 1850, 16,830.

DARLINGTON, p. b., Little Beaver township, Beaver co., Pa., 239 ms. w. of Harrisburgh; from W. 265 ms. Pop. 1,160.

DARLINGTON, p. v., Harford co., Md., 71 ms. N. of Annapolis; from W. 81 ms.

DARLINGTON, c. h., p. v., seat of justice of Darlington district, S. C., 129 ms, s. E. of Columbia; fm. W. 453 ms.

DARLINGTON, p. v., Montgomery co., Ind., 46 ms. N. w. of Indianapolis; from W. 617 ms.

DARLINGTON, p. o., Lafayette co., Wis.

DARLINGTON, p. v., St. Helena parish, La.

DARLINGTON HEIGHTS, p. o., Prince Edward co., Va.

DARNESTOWN, p. v., Montgomery co., Md., 65 ms. N. w. of Annapolis; from W. 25 ms.

DARRTOWN, p. v., Milford township, Butler co., O., 109 ms. s. w. of Columbus; from W. 498 ms.

DARTMOUTH, p. t., Bristol co., Mass., 65 ms. s. of Boston; from W. 441 ms. Watered by Buzzard's bay and several inlets. Pop. 3,868.

DARTFORD, p. o., Marquette co., Wis.

DARVILLES, p. v., Dinwiddie co., Va., 66 ms. s. of Richmond; from W. 175 ms.

DARYSAW, p. o., Jefferson co., Ark.

DAUPHIN COUNTY, situated toward the southeast part of Pennsylvania, with Susquehanna river on the west. Area, 608 square miles. Face of the country mountainous and hilly; soil generally fertile. Seat of justice, Harrisburgh, which is also the capital of the state. Pop. in 1820, 21,663; in 1830, 25,303; in 1840 30,118; in 1850, 35,754.

DAUPHIN, p. v., Middle Paxton township, Dauphin co., Pa., 8 ms. from Harrisburgh; from W. 118 ms. Watered by Susquehanna river. Pop. 650.

DAVENPORT, p. t., Delaware co., N. Y., 69 ms. s. w. of Albany; from W. 361 ms. Watered by Charlotte river and tributaries. Pop. 2,305.

DAVENPORT, c. h., p. v., seat of justice of Scott co., Iowa, 50 ms. E. of Iowa city; from W. 870 ms. Watered by Mississippi river.

DAVENPORT CENTRE, p. o., Davenport township, Delaware co., N. Y.

DAVIDSBOROUGH, p. o., Washington co., Ga., 41 ms. s. E. of Milledgeville; from W. 645 ms.

DAVIDSON COUNTY, situated in the central part of North Carolina. Area, 790 square miles. Seat of justice, Lexington. Pop. in 1830, 13,389; in 1840, 14,606; in 1850, 15,320.

DAVIDSON COUNTY, situated in the northern part of Tennessee, and traversed by Cumberland river. Area, 640 square miles. Face of the country moderately hilly; soil generally fertile. Seat of justice, Nashville, which is also capital of the state. Pop. in 1820, 20,154; in 1830, 28,122; in 1840, 30,509; in 1850, 38,881.

DAVIDSON, p. o., Harrison co., Ind., 115 ms. s. of Indianapolis; from W. 626 ms.

DAVIDSON, p. t., Sullivan co., Pa., 109 ms. N. of Harrisburgh; from W. 219 ms. Pop. 536.

DAVIDSON CENTRE, p. o., Genesee co., Mich.

DAVIDSON COLLEGE, p. v., Mecklenburgh co., N. C., 150 ms. w. of Raleigh; from W. 387 ms. Seat of Davidson college.

DAVIDSON, t., Randolph co., Ark.

DAVIDSON, t., Genesee co., Mich. Pop. 1,165.

DAVIDSON'S RIVER, p. o., Henderson co., N. C., 289 w. of Raleigh; from W. 519 ms.

DAVIDSONVILLE, p. v., Anne Arundel co., Md., 10 ms. from Annapolis; from W. 30 ms.

DAVIDSONVILLE, p. o., Genesee co., Mich.

DAVIDSVILLE, v., Somerset co., Pa., 142 ms. w. of Harrisburg; from W. 168 ms.

DAVIE COUNTY, situated toward the westerly part of North Carolina. Area, 175 square miles. Face of the country undulating; soil highly fertile. Seat of justice, Mocksville. Pop. in 1840, 5,574; in 1850, 7,866.

DAVIES COUNTY, situated in the southwest part of Indiana, between the forks of White river. Area, 420 square miles. Seat of justice, Washington. Pop. in 1830, 4,512; in 1840, 6,720; in 1850, 10,354.

DAVIESS COUNTY, situated on the northern boundary of Kentucky, Ohio, and Green rivers. Area, 600 square miles. Face of the country hilly, except along the streams; soil generally productive. Seat of justice, Owensborough. Pop. in 1830, 5,218; in 1840, 8,331; in 1850, 12,361.

DAVIESS COUNTY, situated in the northwest part of Missouri, and traversed by long branch of Grand river. Area, 576 square miles. Seat of justice, Gallatin. Pop. in 1840, 2,736; in 1850, 5,298.

DAVIS COUNTY, situated on the south boundary of Iowa, intersected by Des Moines river at the northeast corner. Area, —— square miles. Seat of justice, Bloomfield. Pop. in 1850, 7,264.

DAVIS COUNTY, Utah. Area, —— square miles. Seat of justice, ——. Pop. in 1850, ——.

DAVIS, t., Lafayette co., Mo.

DAVIS, t., Saline co., Ark.

DAVIS, t., Fountain co., Ind., 65 ms. N. w. of Indianapolis; from W. 638 ms. Pop. 568.

DAVIS, p. o., Panola co., Tex.

DAVIS' CREEK, p. o., Washington co., Iowa.

DAVIS' CREEK, p. o., Dubois co., Ind.

DAVIS' CREEK, p. o., Fayette co., Ala.

DAVIS' MILLS, p. o., Bedford co., Va., 153 ms. w. of Richmond; from W. 228 ms.

DAVIS' MILLS, p. o., Barnwell district, S. C., 106 ms. s. w. of Columbia; from W. 611 ms.

DAVIS' STORE, p. o., Bedford co., Va., 141 ms. w. of Richmond; from W. 204 ms.

DAVISTON, p. o., Talbot co., Ga.

DAVISTON, v., Clay co., Ind., 74 ms. s. w. of Indianapolis; from W. 645 ms.

DAVISTOWN, p. o., Greene co., Pa.

DAVISVILLE, p. v., Bucks co., Pa., 111 ms. E. of Harrisburgh; from W. 153 ms.

DAWSVILLE, p. o., Cherokee co., N. C.

DAWKIN'S MILLS, p. o., Jackson co., O., 75 ms. s. E. of Columbus; from W. 368 ms.

DAWSON, p. o., Habersham co., Ga., 138 ms. N. of Milledgeville; from W. 601 ms.

DAWSONBURGH, p. o., Fremont co., Iowa.

DAWSON'S, p. o., Alleghany co., Md., 183 ms. N. w. of Annapolis; from W. 151 ms.

DAY, p. t., Saratoga co., N. Y., 63 ms. N. of Albany; from W. 431 ms. Watered by Sacondaga creek. Pop. 1,045.

DAY'S LANDING, p. o., York co., Pa., 33 ms. s. E. of Harrisburg; from W. 99 ms.

DAY'S STORE, p. o., Hopkins co., Ky.

DAYSVILLE, p. o., Ogle co., Ill.

DAYSVILLE, p. o., Todd co., Ky.

DAYTON, p. t., Cattaraugus co., N. Y., 312 ms. w. of Albany; from W. 350 ms. Watered by Connewango creek and tributaries. Pop. 1,448.

DAYTON, p. o., Rockingham co., Va.

DAYTON, c. h., p. t., seat of justice of Montgomery co.,

O., 68 ms. w. of Columbus; from W. 461 ms. Watered by Great Miami and Mad rivers and Wolf creek. Pop. 10,977.

DAYTON, p. o., La Salle co., Ill. 137 ms. N. E. of Springfield; from W. 777 ms.

DAYTON, p. v., Tippecanoe co., Ind., 63 ms. N. w. of Indianapolis; from W. 621 ms.

DAYTON, p. v., Marengo co., Ala., from W. 887 ms.

DAYTON, p. o., Berrien co., Mich.

DAYTON, p. o., Yamhill co., Oregon.

DEAD FALL, p. o., Abbeville district, S. C., 89 ms. w. of Columbia; from W. 519 ms.

DEAD RIVER, p, o., Somerset co., Me., 78 ms. N. w. of Augusta; from W. 672 ms.

DEAL'S MILLS, p. o, Caldwell co., N. C., 180 ms. w. of Raleigh; from W. 418 ms.

DEAL, v., Shrewsbury township, Monmouth co., N. J. Watered by Poplar Swamp creek.

DEAM, p. o., Owen co., Ind.

DEAN'S CORNERS, p. o., Saratoga township, Saratoga co., N. Y., 33 ms. N. of Albany; from W. 406 ms.

DEANSVILLE. p. v., Marshall township, Oneida co., N. Y., 104 ms. N. w. of Albany; from W. 375 ms. Situated on Chenango canal.

DEARBORN COUNTY, situated on the easterly boundary of Indiana, on the northwesterly side of Ohio river. Area, 380 square miles. Face of the country rough and hilly; soil generally fertile. Seat of justice, Lawrenceville. Pop. in 1820. 11,468; in 1830, 13,974; in 1840, 19,327; in 1850, 20,165.

DEARBORN. t., Kennebec co., Me., 15 ms. N. of Augusta; from W. 610 ms.

DEARBORN, t., Wayne co., Mich. Watered by Rouge river. Pop. 1385.

DEARBORNVILLE, p. v., Dearborn township, Wayne co., Mich., 10 ms. w. of Detroit; from W. 534 ms. Watered by Rouge river.

DEARDORFF'S MILLS, Wayne township, Tuscarawas co., O., 112 ms. N. E. of Columbus; from W. 324 ms.

DEARMANS, p. o., Westchester co., N. Y.

DEATESVILLE, p. o., Nelson co., Ky.

DEATONVILLE, p. o., Amelia co., Va.

DEAVERTOWN, p. v., York township, Morgan co., O., 71 ms. E. of Columbus; from W. 343 ms.

DE BASTROP (now Holly Point), p. t., Drew co., Ark.

DECATUR COUNTY, situated at the southwest corner of Georgia, with Chattahoochee river on the west, and traversed by the main branch of Flint river. Area, 1,013 square miles. Seat of justice, Bainbridge. Pop. in 1830, 3,854; in 1840, 5,870; in 1850, 8,262.

DECATUR COUNTY, situated in the southeast part of Indiana. Area, 340 square miles. Seat of justice, Greensburgh. Pop. in 1830, 5,887; in 1840, 12,171; in 1850, 15,107.

DECATUR COUNTY, situated toward the westerly part of Tennessee, on the west side of Tennessee river. Area, — square miles. Seat of justice, Derryville. Pop. in 1850, 6,003.

DECATUR COUNTY, situated on the south boundary of Iowa. Area, — square miles. Seat of justice, —. Pop. in 1850, 965.

DECATUR, p. t., Otsego co., N. Y., 61 ms. w. of Albany; from W. 375 ms. Watered by Elk creek. Pop. 927.

DECATUR, t., Clearfield co., Pa. Pop. 445.

DECATUR, p. t., Mifflin co., Pa., 55 ms. N. w. of Harrisburgh; from W. 159 ms. Watered by Jack's creek. Pop. 990.

DECATUR, p. v., Byrd township, Brown co., O., 105 ms. s. w. of Columbus; from W. 452 ms.

DECATUR, p. t., Van Buren co., Mich., 158 ms. w. of Detroit; from W. 615 ms. Pop. 386.

DECATUR, c. h., p. v., seat of justice of De Kalb co., Ga., 90 ms. N. w. of Milledgeville; from W. 676 ms. Pop. 744.

DECATUR, t., Marion co., Ind., 10 ms. from Indianapolis; from W. 609 ms.

DECATUR, t., Washington co., O., 92 ms. s. E. of Columbus; from W. 324 ms. Pop. 807.

DECATUR, v., Union district, S. C., 77 ms. N. w. of Columbia; from W. 457 ms.

DECATUR, t., Lawrence co., O., 128 ms. s. E. of Columbus; from W. 382 ms. Pop. 1,052.

DECATUR, p. v., Morgan co., Ala.; from W. 739 ms. Watered by Tennessee river.

DECATUR, c. h., p. v., seat of justice of Adams co., Ind., 132 ms. N. E. of Indianapolis; from W. 522 ms. Watered by Wabash river. Pop. 231.

DECATUR, c. h., p. v., seat of justice of Newton co., Miss., 76 ms. E. of Jackson; from W. 954 ms. Watered by Chickasaw river.

DECATUR, c. h., p. v., seat of justice of Meigs co., Tenn., 140 ms. s. E. of Nashville; from W. 568 ms.

DECATUR, v., Howard co., Mo., 54 ms. N. w. of Jefferson City; from W. 959 ms.

DECATUR, c. h., p. v., seat of justice of Macon co., Ill., 40 ms. E. of Springfield; from W. 749 ms. Watered by north fork of Sangamon river.

DECATUR, p. o., Greene co., Wis.

DECATURVILLE, p. o., Decatur co., Tenn.

DECATURVILLE, p. o., Washington co., O.

DECKER'S CREEK, p. o., Preston co., Va.

DECKERTOWN, p. v., Wantage township, Sussex co., N. J., 87 ms. N. of Trenton; from W. 256 ms.

DECORAH, p. o., Winnesheik co., Iowa.

DEDHAM, c. h., p. t., seat of justice of Norfolk co., Mass., 13 ms. s. w. of Boston; from W. 431 ms. Watered by Charles and Neponset rivers. Pop. 4,447.

DEED'S CREEK, p. o., Kosciusko co., Ind.

DEEDSVILLE. p. o., Jefferson co., Iowa.

DEEP CREEK, p. v., Norfolk co., Va., 114 ms. s. E. of Richmond; from W. 244 ms.

DEEP CUT, p. o., Mercer co., O.

DEEPIKILL, p. o., Rensselaer co., N. Y.

DEEP RIVER, p. v., Saybrook township, Middlesex co., Ct., 33 ms. s. of Hartford; from W. 338 ms. Watered by Connecticut and Deep rivers.

DEEP RIVER, p. o., Guilford co., N. C., 99 ms. N. w. of Raleigh; from W. 320 ms.

DEEP RIVER, p. o., Lake co., Ind., 148 ms. N. E. of Indianapolis; from W. 692 ms.

DEEP RIVER, p. o., Poweshiek co., Iowa.

DEEP WATER, p. o., Henry co., Mo.

DEEP WATER, t., Van Buren co., Mo.

DEEP WATER, p. o., Marshall co., Miss.

DEEP WELL, p. o., Iredell co., N. C., 137 ms. w. of Raleigh; from W 374 ms.

DEER. t., Alleghany co., Pa., 210 ms. of Harrisburgh; from W. 226 ms.

DEER BROOK, p. o., Noxubee co., Miss.

DEER CREEK, p. o., Mercer co., Pa., 236 ms. N. w. of Harrisburgh; from W. 291 ms.

DEER CREEK, t., Madison co., O., 23 ms. w. of Columbus; from W. 419 ms. Pop. 436.

DEER CREEK, p. o., Livingston co., Mich., 61 ms. w. of Detroit; from W. 564 ms.

DEER CREEK, p. o., Carroll co., Ind.

DEER CREEK, p. o., Issaquena co., Miss.

DEER CREEK, t., Pickaway co., O., 36 ms. s. of Columbus; from W. 404 ms. Pop. 1,354.

DEERFIELD, p. t., Rockingham co., N. H., 19 ms. s. E. of Concord; from W. 475 ms. Watered by Lamprey river, Martin and Pleasant ponds. Pop. 2,022.

DEERFIELD, t., Franklin co., Mass., 95 ms. w. of Boston; from W. 399 ms. Watered by Connecticut and Deerfield rivers. Pop. 2,421.

DEERFIELD, t., Oneida co., N. Y., 96 ms. N. w. of Albany; from W. 395 ms. Watered by tributaries of Mohawk river. Pop. 2,287.

DEERFIELD, t., Cumberland co., N. J., 63 ms. s. of Trenton; from W. 169 ms. Watered by Cohansey creek and Muddy run. Pop. 927.

DEERFIELD, t., Tioga co., Pa., 159 ms. N. of Harrisburgh; from W. 165 ms. Watered by Cowanesque and Marsh creeks. Pop. 721.

DEERFIELD, v., Warren co., Pa., 223 ms. N. w. of Harrisburgh; from W. 312 ms. Pop. 1,022.

DEERFIELD, p. t., Portage co., O., 149 ms. N. E. of Columbus; from W. 310 ms. Watered by Mahoning river, and the Pennsylvania and Ohio canal. Pop. 1,371.

DEERFIELD, p. t. Warren co., O., 91 ms. s. w. of Columbus; from W. 474 ms. Pop. 1,863.

DEERFIELD, p. v., Lenawee co., Mich., 65 ms. s. w. of Detroit; from W. 495 ms.

DEERFIELD, t., Morgan co., O., 63 ms. s. E. of Columbus; from W. 347 ms. Pop. 1,325.

DEERFIELD, p. v., Augusta co., Va., 134 ms. N. w. of Richmond; from W. 171 ms.

DEERFIELD, t., Ross co., O., 40 ms. s. of Columbus; from W. 405 ms. Pop. 1,315.

DEERFIELD, p. v., Randolph co., Ind., 88 ms. N. E. of Indianapolis; from W. 511 ms.

DEERFIELD, t., Van Buren co., Mo.

DEERFIELD, t., Livingston co., Mich. Pop. 882.

DEERFIELD, p. o., Lake co., Ill.

DEERFIELD, p. o., Carroll parish, La.

DEERFIELD, p. o., Dane co., Wis.

DEERFIELD STREET, p. v., Deerfield township, Cumberland co., N. J., 62 ms. s. w. of Trenton ; from W. 173 ms. Watered by Cohansey creek.

DEERFIELD VILLAGE, p. v., Union township, Warren co., O., 89 ms. s. E. of Columbus ; from W. 473 ms. Watered by Little Miami river.

DEER GROVE, p. o., Cook co., Ill.

DEERING, p. t., Hillsborough co., N. H., 25 ms. s. w. of Concord ; from W. 469 ms. Watered by Contoocook river. Pop. 890.

DEER ISLE, p. t., and island, Hancock co., Me., 93 ms. E. of Augusta ; from W. 689 ms. Situated in Penobscot bay. Pop. 3,037.

DEERLICK, p. o., Mason co., Va.

DEERPARK, t., Orange co., N. Y., 108 ms. s. w. of Albany ; from W. 266 ms. Watered by Navesink river and Delaware and Hudson canal. Pop. 4032.

DEER PARK, p. o., Huntington township, Suffolk co., Long Island, N. Y.

DEER PARK, p. o., La Salle co., Ill.

DEER PLAIN, p. o., Calhoun co., Ill.

DEER RIVER, p. o., Lewis co., N. Y.

DEERSVILLE, p. v., Stock township, Harrison co., O., 109 ms. E. of Columbus ; from W. 296 ms. Pop. 289.

DEFIANCE COUNTY, situated on the west boundary of Ohio, and traversed by Maumee river. Area, —— square miles. Seat of justice, Defiance. Pop. in 1850, 6.966.

DEFIANCE, c. h., p. v., Defiance township, seat of justice of Defiance co., O., 152 ms. N. w. of Columbus ; from W. 504 ms. Watered by Maumee and Auglaize rivers. Pop. 890.

DEFRIETSVILLE, p. v., Greenbush township, Rensselaer co., N. Y., 4 ms. s. E. of Albany ; from W. 347 ms.

DE GLAIZE, p. o., Morehouse parish, La.

DE KALB COUNTY, situated toward the northwest part of Georgia, with Chattahoochee river on the northwest. Area, 360 square miles. This county consists principally of an elevated table land. Seat of justice, Decatur. Pop. in 1830, 10,047 ; in 1840, 10,467 ; in 1850, 14,328.

DE KALB COUNTY, situated on the east boundary of Indiana, and traversed by St. Joseph's river. Area, 365 square miles. Seat of justice, Auburn. Pop. in 1840, 1,697 ; in 1850. 8,251.

DE KALB COUNTY, situated in the central part of Tennessee, and traversed by Caney fork of Cumberland river. Area, 275 square miles. Seat of justice, Smithville. Pop. in 1840, 5,868 ; in 1850, 8,016.

DE KALB COUNTY, situated in the northeast part of Alabama. Area, 1,500 square miles. Face of the country mountainous and hilly, but level along the streams ; soil varied. Seat of justice, Lebanon. Pop. in 1840. 5,929 ; in 1850. 8,245.

DE KALB COUNTY, situated in the northern part of Illinois. Area, 648 square miles. Seat of justice, Sycamore. Pop. in 1840, 1,697 ; in 1850, 7,450.

DE KALB COUNTY, situated in the northwest part of Missouri. Area, —— square miles. Seat of justice, Maysville. Pop. in 1850, 2.076.

DE KALB, p. t., St. Lawrence co., N. Y., 195 ms. N. w. of Albany ; from W. 464 ms. Watered by Oswegatchie river and tributaries. Pop. 2,389.

DE KALB, p. o., Crawford co., O., 80 ms. N. E. of Columbus ; from W. 406 ms.

DE KALB, v., Hancock co., Ill., 100 ms. w. of Springfield ; from W. 878 ms.

DE KALB, c. h., p. v., seat of justice of Kemper co., Miss., 106 ms. N. E. of Jackson ; from W. 911 ms. Watered by Sacarnochee creek.

DE KALB, p. v., Lewis co., Va., 313 ms. N. w. of Richmond ; from W. 281 ms. Watered by Little Kanawha river.

DE KALB, p. o., Buchanan co.. Mo.

DE KALB, p. o., De Kalb co., Ind.

DE KALB, p. o., Gilmer co., Va.

DE KALB, p. o., Bowie co., Tex.

DE KALB CENTRE, p. o., De Kalb co., Ill.

DEKORRA, p. o., Columbia co., Wis.

DELAFIELD, p. o., Waukesha co., Wis.

DE LANCEY, p. o., Madison co., N. Y.

DE LA PALMA, p. o., Brown co., O.

DELAVAN, p. o., Yorkshire township, Cattaraugus co., N. Y., 282 ms. w. of Albany ; from W. 337 ms.

DELAVAN, p. o., Tazewell co., Ill., 45 ms. N. of Springfield ; from W. 783 ms.

DELAVAN, p. t., Walworth co., Wis., 64 ms. s. E. of Madison ; from W. 811 ms.

DELAWARE, one of the United States, the smallest in the Union in respect to population, and, next to Rhode Island, in territory also, lies between 38° 27' and 39° 50' north lat., and 75° and 75° 40' west lon. from Greenwich. and is bounded north by Pennsylvania, east by the Delaware river and bay ; and south and west by Maryland. Its length from north to south is 90 miles, its greatest breadth 32 miles, and its superficial area 2,120 miles. It derives its name from the bay on which it lies, and which received its name from Lord Delaware (or de la War), governor of Virginia, who died upon its waters.

Physical Aspect.—The general aspect of this state is that of an extended plain, or several inclined plains, favorable for cultivation. Some of the upper portions of the county of Newcastle, however, are irregular and broken ; the heights of Christiana are lofty and commanding ; and the hills of Brandywine are rough and stony ; but in the region toward Delaware river and bay there is very little diversity of surface. On the table land, forming the dividing ridge between the Delaware and Chesapeake, is a chain of swamps, which give rise to various streams, that descend the slopes to either bay. Along the Delaware river, and some ten miles into the interior, the soil generally consists of a rich clay, well adapted to the purposes of agriculture ; but between this tract and the swamps the soil is sandy and light, and of inferior quality. In the county of Newcastle the soil is a strong clay ; in Kent it is mixed with sand ; and in Sussex the sand greatly predominates.

Rivers and Bays.—The principal streams, besides the Delaware river, which forms a part of the eastern boundary, are Brandywine, Jones, Christiana, Duck, and Mispillion creeks, and Choptank, Marshy Hope, and Nanticoke rivers. India river enters the Atlantic by a broad estuary, and Delaware bay washes the state on the east.

Climate.—The climate is generally mild and healthy ; but the two extremes differ in temperature more than might be expected in so little extent of latitude, and in so small a difference in relative height. The winters in the northern part are somewhat cold, but never severe. The summers are hot in those situations not tempered by the breezes from the bays.

Productive Resources.—The principal staple products are horses, mules, neat cattle, sheep, poultry, eggs, swine, beef, pork, silk, wool, hay, butter, cheese, milk, wheat, rye, barley, oats, buckwheat, potatoes, peaches, and Indian corn. The county of Sussex exports large quantities of timber, obtained from Cypress swamps, or Indian river. Delaware contains but few minerals. Among the branches of the Nanticoke there are large quantities of bog iron ore, however, well adapted for castings. Before the Revolution it was worked to some extent, but since that period the business has declined.

Manufactures.—The manufactures of Delaware consist chiefly of woollen and cotton goods, leather, paper, iron, gunpowder, &c. Its flouring-mills are numerous and extensive, and its flour takes a high stand in the market.

Railroads and Canals.—The only railroads within the state are, the Frenchtown, from Newcastle to Frenchtown, 16 miles ; the Philadelphia and Wilmington, and the Wlimington and Baltimore, which form part of the great line of travel from the northern to the southern Atlantic states. The Chesapeake and Delaware sloop canal, 14 miles long, is the only canal in the state. It extends from Delaware city to Back creek, and unites the waters of the two great bays from which it takes its name.

Commerce.—The foreign commerce of Delaware is very small. The amount of shipping owned in the

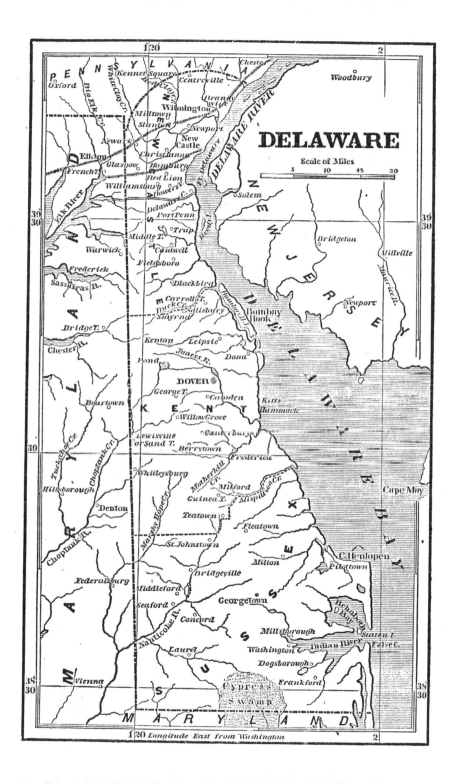

DELAWARE

Scale of Miles

5   10   15   20

PENNSYLVANIA

Oxford
Kennet Square
Centreville
Chester
Woodbury
White Clay Cr.
Big Elk Cr.
Red Clay Cr.
Brandywine
Wilmington
Milltown
Stanton
Newport
Newark
New Castle
Christiana
Hamburg
Ellsdon
Glasgow
French T.
Red Lion
Williamsburg
Flowers V.
Delaware C.
Salem
NEW JERSEY
DELAWARE RIVER
Elk River
Port Penn
Trap
Middle T.
Warwick
Cantwell
Fieldsboro
Bridgeton
Millville
Frederick
Sassafras R.
Blackbird
Carroll T.
Duck Cr.
Salisbury
Bombay Hook
Bridge T.
Smyrna
Newport
Maurice R.
Chester R.
Kenton
Leipsic
Jones R.
Dona
Pond
DOVER
George T.
Camden
Kitts Hammock
Beartown
KENT
Willow Grove
Lewisville or Sand T.
Canterbury
Berrytown
Frederica
Whitleysburg
Motherkill Cr.
Milford
Mispillion Cr.
Hillsborough
Choptank Cr.
Tuckahoe Cr.
Guinea T.
Teatown
Fleatown
Denton
Marshy Hope Cr.
St. Johnstown
Milton
Cape May
C. Henlopen
Filiottown
Federalsburg
Bridgeville
Middleford
Georgetown
Rehoboth Bay
Seaford
Nanticoke R.
Concord
Millsborough
Staten I.
Washington
Indian River
False C.
Laurel
Dogsborough
Frankford
Vienna
CYPRESS SWAMP
MARYLAND

DELAWARE BAY

SUSSEX

MARYLAND

39 30   39 30

30

38 30   38 30

1 20   2

1 20 Longitude East from Washington   2

state is about 17,000 tons, 15,000 of which is engaged in the coasting-trade.

Education.—There is but one college in Delaware, which is located at Newark, and was founded in 1833. There are about 30 academies, and 250 common schools in the state.

Population.—In 1790, 59,094; in 1800, 64,273; in 1810, 72,974; in 1820, 72,749; in 1830, 76,739; in 1840, 78,085; in 1850, 91,535. Number of slaves in 1790, 8,887; in 1800, 6,153; in 1810, 4,177; in 1820, 4,509; in 1830, 3,292; in 1840, 2,605; in 1850, 2,289.

Government.—The legislative power is vested in a senate, of nine members, three from each county, chosen for four years, and a house of representatives, of twenty-one members, seven from each county, chosen for two years. The executive power is vested in a governor, chosen for four years, and ineligible ever after. General election, biennially, second Tuesday in November, and the legislature meets at Dover on the first Tuesday in January. The judicial power is vested in a court of errors, superior court, court of chancery, orphan's court, oyer and terminer, general sessions, register's court, and such other courts as may be established by law. The right of suffrage is granted to every white male citizen, twenty-two years of age, after one year's residence in the state, and one month in the county where he votes, and having within two years paid a tax; also to those persons, qualified as aforesaid, twenty-one years of age, without payment of tax.

History.—Lord Delaware, governor of Virginia, first entered the bay known by his name in 1610. The Dutch from the New Netherlands (New York) soon afterward visited it, and claimed jurisdiction. The first permanent settlement upon the Delaware was made by a colony of Swedes, in 1627, under the auspices of the Swedish West India Company. The Dutch asserted their claim by an appeal to arms, and, with a competent force, took possession of the country, in 1655, and attached it to the New Netherlands. When the latter came into the possession of the Duke of York, in 1681, William Penn, as stated in the history of Pennsylvania, purchased what is now the state of Delaware, and annexed it to Pennsylvania. Delaware had a legislature separate from that of Pennsylvania, but after 1703 one governor ruled both. It remained in this subordinate condition until 1776, when the inhabitants declared it a free and independent state, and organized a government under it. It was the first to ratify the constitution, which it did on the 7th of December, 1787. Its state constitution was adopted in 1792, and revised and amended in 1831. Motto of the state seal, "Liberty and Independence."

DELAWARE COUNTY, situated toward the southeast part of New York, with Delaware river on the southwest. Area, 460 square miles. Face of the country rough and hilly; soil fertile in the valleys. Seat of justice, Delhi. Pop. in 1820, 26,587; in 1830, 32,933; in 1840, 35,396; in 1850, 39,825.

DELAWARE COUNTY, situated in the southeast part of Pennsylvania, with Delaware river on the southeast. Area, 220 square miles. Seat of justice, Chester. Pop. in 1820, 14,810; in 1830, 17,361; in 1840, 19,791; in 1850, 24,679.

DELAWARE COUNTY, situated in the central part of Ohio. Area, 610 square miles. Watered by Scioto and Whetstone rivers. Face of the country flat or rolling; soil generally productive. Seat of justice, Delaware. Pop. in 1820, 7,639; in 1830, 11,523; in 1840, 22,060; in 1850, 21,817.

DELAWARE COUNTY, situated in the eastern part of Indiana. Area, 384 square miles. Seat of justice, Muncietown. Pop. in 1830, 2,372; in 1840, 8,843; in 1850, 10,843.

DELAWARE COUNTY, situated in the eastern part of Iowa. Area, 576 square miles. Seat of justice, Delhi. Pop. in 1840, 168; in 1850, 1,759.

DELAWARE, t., Hunterdon co., N. J. Watered by Delaware river and Wickhecheoke creek. Pop. 2,554.

DELAWARE, p. t., Juniata co., Pa.

DELAWARE, t., Mercer co., Pa., 242 ms. N. w. of Harrisburgh; from W. 272 ms. Watered by Chenango and Lackawanock creeks. Pop. 2,863.

DELAWARE, p. t., Pike co., Pa., 148 ms. N. E. of Harrisburgh; from W. 242 ms. Watered by Dingman's and Bushkill creeks. Pop. 754.

DELAWARE, c. h., p. v., seat of justice of Delaware co., O., 24 ms. N. of Columbus; from W. 408 ms. Watered by Oleatangy or Whetstone river. Pop. 2,074.

DELAWARE, t., Williams co., O., 183 ms. N. w. of Columbus; from W. 517 ms. Watered by Maumee river.

DELAWARE, t., Hancock co., O. Pop. 1,035.

DELAWARE, t., Hamilton co., Ind.

DELAWARE, p. v., Ripley co., Ind., 65 ms. s. E. of Indianapolis; from W. 536 ms.

DELAWARE CITY. p. v., New Castle co., Del., 35 ms. N. of Dover; from W. 130 ms. Watered by Delaware river. Pop. 908.

DELAWARE, p. o., Indian co., Nebraska territory.

DELAWARE BRIDGE, p. o., Sullivan co., N. Y.

DELAWARE GROVE, p. o., Mercer co., Pa., 240 ms. N. w. of Harrisburgh; from W. 283 ms.

DELAY, p. o., Fayette co., Miss.

DELECTABLE HILL, p. o., Pike co., Ind., 139 ms. s. w. of Indianapolis; from W. 670 ms.

DELHI, c. h., p. v., seat of justice of Delaware co., N. Y., 77 ms. s. w. of Albany; from W. 327 ms. Watered by Mohawk branch of Delaware river. Pop. 2,909.

DELHI, t., Hamilton co., O. Watered by Ohio river. Pop. 1,942.

DELHI, p. v., Jersey co., Ill., 78 ms. s. w. of Springfield; from W. 820 ms.

DELHI, c. h., p. v., seat of justice of Delaware co., Iowa, 55 ms s. of Iowa city; from W. 875 ms.

DELHI, p. o., Winnebago co., Wis.

DELHI CENTRE, p. o., Ingham co., Mich.

DELLONA, p. o., Sauk co., Wis.

DEL NORTE, p. o., Davis co., Iowa.

DELPHI, c. h., p. v., seat of justice of Carroll co., Ind., 66 ms. N. w. of Indianapolis; from W. 624 ms. Watered by Wabash river and Deer creek.

DELPHI, p. v., Pompey township, Onondaga co., N. Y., 119 ms. w. of Albany; from W. 342 ms.

DELPHI, v., Marion co., Tenn., 114 ms. s. E. of Nashville; from W. 611 ms. Watered by Sequatchy river.

DELPHI, p. v., Gasconade co., Mo., 53 ms. s. E. of Jefferson City; from W. 917 ms. Watered by Bourbeuse creek.

DELPHOS, p. o., Van Wert co., O.

DELPHTON. v., Fayette co., Ky., 20 ms. E. of Frankfort; from W. 530 ms.

DELRAY, p. o., Upson co., Ga.

DELTA, p. v., Lee township, Oneida co., N. Y., 112 ms. N. w. of Albany; from W. 396 ms.

DELTA, p. o., Fulton co., O., 145 ms. N. of Columbus; from W. 476 ms.

DELTA, p. o., Parke co., Ind., 73 ms. w. of Indianapolis; from W. 644 ms.

DELTA, p. o., Coahoma co., Miss.

DELTA, p. o., Eaton co., Mich.

DELMAR, t., Tioga co., Pa., 141 ms. N. of Harrisburgh, from W. 247 ms. Pop. 1,529.

DEMAND, t., Randolph co., Ark.

DEMOCRACY, p. o., Pike township, Knox co., O., 59 ms. s. of Columbus; from W. 377 ms.

DEMOCRACY, p. o., Pike co., Ky.

DEMOCRAT, p. o., Buncombe co., N. C.

DEMOCRAT, p. o., Iroquois co., Ill.

DEMOPOLIS, p. v., Marengo co., Ala.; from W. 876 ms. Watered by Tombigbee river.

DEMOS, p. o., Belmont co., O., 126 ms. E. of Columbus; from W. 287 ms.

DEMPSEYTOWN, p. o., Venango co., Pa.

DENMARK, p. t., Oxford co., Me., 82 ms. s. w. of Augusta; from W. 569 ms. Watered by Saco river. Pop. 1,203.

DENMARK, p. t., Lewis co., N. Y., 146 ms. N. w. of Albany; from W. 435 ms. Watered by Black river and Deer creek. Pop. 2,824.

DENMARK, p. t., Ashtabula co., O., 208 ms. N. E. of Columbus; from W. 335 ms. Pop. 241.

DENMARK, p. v., Madison co., Tenn., 146 ms. s. w. of Nashville; from W. 831 ms.

DENNING, p. o., Ulster co., N. Y.

DENNIS, p. t., Barnstable co., Mass., 81 ms. s. E. of Boston; from W. 482 ms. Watered by Bass river.

DENNIS, p. t., Cape May co., N. J., 85 ms. s. of Trenton; from W. 195 ms. Watered by Dennis creek. Pop. 1,604.

DENNIS' CREEK, p. o., Dennis township, Cape May co., N. J.

DENNIS' MILLS, p. o., St. Helena co., La.

DENNISON, t., Luzerne co., Pa.

DENNISVILLE, p. o., Amelia co., Va., 53 ms. s. w. of Richmond; from W. 170 ms.

DENNY, p. o., Warren co., Ill.

DENNYSVILLE, p. t., Washington co., Me., 174 ms. N.

E. of Augusta; from W. 760 ms. Watered by Dennis river. Pop. 458.

DENON, p. o., Waukesha co., Wis.

DENSONTOWN, p. o., Rankin co., Pa.

DENT, p. o., Hamilton co., O.

DENTON COUNTY, situated in the northern part of Texas. Area. —— square miles. Seat of justice, Alton. Pop. in 1850, ——.

DENTON, c. h., p. v., seat of justice of Caroline co., Md., 65 ms. E. of Annapolis; from W. 105 ms. Watered by Choptank river.

DENTON CREEK, p. o Denton co., Tex.

DENTONSVILLE, v., Hanover co., Va., 21 ms. N. of Richmond; from W. 138 ms.

DENVILLE, p. o., Morris co., N. J.

DEPAUVILLE, p. v., Clayton township, Jefferson co., N. Y., 178 ms. N. w. of Albany; from W. 428 ms. Watered by Chaumont river.

DE PERE, c. h., p. v., seat of justice of Brown co., Wis., 153 ms.. N. E. of Madison; from W. 943 ms.

DE PEYSTER, p. t., St. Lawrence co., N. Y., 198 ms. N. w. of Albany; from W. 467 ms. Watered by Oswegatchie river and Black lake. Pop. 906.

DEPOSIT, p. v.. Tompkins township, Delaware co., N. Y., 118 ms. s. w. of Albany; from W. 300 ms. Watered by Delaware river.

DEPTFORD, t., Gloucester co., N. J. Watered by Big Timber creek and tributaries of Harbor river. Pop. 3,555.

DERBY, p. t., Orleans co., Vt., 58 ms. N. of Montpelier; from W. 574 ms. Watered by Clyde river and Lake Memphremagog Pop. 1,750.

DERBY, p. t., New Haven co., Ct., 44 ms. s. w. of Hartford; from W. 300 ms. Watered by Housatonic and Naugatuck rivers. Pop. 3,824.

DERBY LINE, p. o., Derby township, Orleans co., Vt., 61 ms. N. E. of Montpelier; from. W. 377 ms.

DERICKSON'S CROSS ROADS, p. o., Worcester co., Md., 107 ms. s. E. of Annapolis; from W. 147 ms.

DERRY, p. t., Westmoreland co., Pa.

DERRY, p. t., Rockingham co., N. H., 28 ms. s. E. of Concord; from W. 457 ms. Watered by Beaver river and Derry pond. Pop. 1,850.

DERRY, t., Mifflin co., Pa., 55 ms. N. w. of Harrisburgh; from W. 162 ms. Watered by Kishkoquilla creek.

DERRY, t., Dauphin co., Pa., 12 ms. s. E. of Harrisburgh; from W. 102 ms Pop 1,649 ms.

DERRY, t,, Columbia co., Pa., 84 ms. N. of Harrisburgh; from W. 104 ms.

DE RUYTER, p. t., Madison co., Y., 122 ms. w. of Albany; from W. 340 ms Watered by Toughnioga river.Pop. 1,931.

DES ARC, p. o., Prairie co., Ark.

DESHA COUNTY, situated in the southeast part of Arkansas, with Mississippi river on the east, and traversed by Arkansas and White rivers. Area, 800 square miles. Face of the country level. Seat of justice, Bellville. Pop. in 1840, 1,598; in 1850, 2,920.

DES MOINES COUNTY, situated in the southeast part of Iowa, with Mississippi river on the east, and Chickahoma river on the southwest. Area, 410 square miles. Seat of justice, Burlington. Pop. in 1840, 6,577; in 1850, 12,987.

DES MOINES, v., Hancock co., Ill., 124 ms. N. w. of Springfield; from W. 899 ms.

DES MOINES, t., Clark co., Mo.

DES MOINES CITY, p. o., Wapello co., Iowa.

DE SOTO PARISH, situated on the westerly boundary of Louisiana, with Sabine river on the west. Area, —— square miles. Seat of justice, Mansfield. Pop. in 1850, 8,019.

DE SOTO COUNTY, situated on the northerly boundary of Mississippi. Area, 925 square miles. Seat of justice, Hernando. Pop. in 1840, 7,002; in 1850, 19,042.

DES PERES, p. o., St. Louis co., Mo.

DESRAYAUXVILLE, p. o., Rapides parish, La.

DETROIT, city, and seat of justice of Wayne co.. Mich., occupies a pleasant and commanding situation, on the west bank of Detroit river, 18 miles from Lake Erie, and 7 miles from Lake St. Clair. Between the two great lakes, Huron and Erie, upon both of which, its vessels carry on an extensive trade, through Lakes Superior and Michigan, and with Canada, Pennsylvania, and New York. It is an important metropolis of the western states, and is destined to a still higher rank than it now holds. The city is agreeably laid out with broad streets, some of which converge at the "Circus," a spacious public ground. Among the other parks, is the "Campus Martius," near the centre of the city. Parallel with the river, at the foot of the eminence upon which the town is built, is a street lined with warehouses and stores. Above this, another street runs in the same direction, and still further to the west, is the principal business street, which is closely built with stores, dwellings, and public buildings. Here, until 1847, when the seat of government was removed to Lansing, stood the statehouse, from the high dome of which appears an enchanting prospect of the river, Lake St. Clair, and their picturesque and romantic shores. Other buildings are the city-hall, bank of Michigan, churches, markets, schools, and various scientific and literary institutions. Several hundred steamboats and other vessels, from various places on the lakes, visit Detroit during the season of navigation, which lasts about two thirds of the year.

The Michigan Central railroad extends 281 miles toward Chicago, on Lake Michigan; and the Detroit and Pontiac railroad is 25 miles long.

The population in 1810, was 770; in 1820, 1,422; in 1830. 2,222; in 1840, 9,102; in 1850, 21,119.

DETROIT, p. o., Somerset co., Me.

DETROIT, p. o., Pike co., Ill.

DETROIT, p. o., Marion co., Ala.

DEVEREAUX, p. o., Herkimer co., N. Y.

DEVEREAUX'S STORE, p. o., Hancock co., Ga., 15 ms. N. E. of Milledgeville; from W. 505 ms.

DEVON, p. o., Henry co., Ind.

DE WITT COUNTY, situated in the southern part of Texas, and traversed by Guadalupe river. Seat of justice, Cuerro. Area, —— square miles. Pop. in 1850, 1,716.

DE WITT COUNTY, situated near the central part of Illinois. Area, —— square miles. Seat of justice, Clinton. Pop. in 1850, 5,002.

DE WITT, p. t., Onondaga co., N. Y., 126 ms. w. of Albany; from W. 351 ms. Pop. 3,302.

DE WITT, c. h., p. v., seat of justice of Clinton co., Mich., 96 ms. N. w. of Detroit; from W. 599 ms. Pop. 706.

DE WITT, p. v., Carroll co., Mo. Watered by Missouri river.

DE WITT, p. o., De Witt co., Ill.

DE WITT, p. o., Clinton co,, Iowa

DE WITTVILLE, p. o., Chautauque township, Chautauque co., N Y, 348 ms. w. of Albany; from W. 335 ms.

DEXTER, p. t., Penobscot co., Me., 71 ms. N. E. of Augusta; from W. 666 ms. Pop. 1,948.

DEXTER, p. v., Brownville township, Jefferson co., N. Y. Watered by Black river.

DEXTER, p. v., Scioto township, Washtenaw co., Mich., 52 ms. w. of Detroit; from W. 538 ms. Watered by Mill creek and Huron river.

DEXTERVILLE, v., Ellicott township, Chautauque co., N. Y. Watered by Chautauque outlet.

DIAL'S CREEK, p. o., Orange co., N. C., 43 ms. N. w. of Raleigh; from W. 269 ms.

DIAMOND GROVE, p. o., Jasper co., Mo.

DIAMOND GROVE, p. v., Brunswick, co., Va., 80 ms. s. w. of Richmond; from W. 196 ms.

DIAMOND GROVE, p. o., Anson co., N. C., 154 ms. s. w. of Raleigh; from W. 423 ms.

DIAMOND HILL, p. o., Providence co., R. I.

DIANA, p. t., Lewis co., N. Y., 154 ms. N. w. of Albany; from W. 453 ms. Watered by Oswegatchie and Indian rivers. Pop. 970.

DIANA MILLS, p. o., Buckingham co., Va., 75 ms. w. of Richmond; from W. 149 ms.

DIAS CREEK, p. o., Cape May co., N. J.

DIBERTSVILLE, p. o., Somerset co., Pa.

DICKENSONVILLE, p. o., Russell co., Va.

DICKENSONVILLE, p. o., Niagara co., N. Y.

DICKEYSVILLE, p. o., Grant co., Wis.

DICKINSON, p. t., Franklin co., N. Y., 222 ms. N. w. of Albany; from W. 523 ms. Watered by tributaries of Packet and St. Regis rivers. Pop. 1,119.

DICKINSON, p. t., Cumberland co., Pa., 24 ms. s. w. of Harrisburgh; from W. 111 ms. Watered by Yellow Breeches creek.

DICKINSON, p. v., Franklin co., Va., 170 ms. s. w. of Richmond; from W. 245 ms.

DICKINSON'S STORE, p. o., Bedford co., Va., 149 ms. w. of Richmond; from W. 401 ms.

DICKINSONVILLE, v., Russell co., Va., 342 ms. w. of Richmond; from W. 401 ms.

DICKSON COUNTY, situated toward the northerly part of Tennessee, with Cumberland river on the northeast. Area, 1,000 square miles. Face of the country level; soil of middling quality. Seat of justice, Charlotte. Pop. in 1810, 4,516; in 1820, 5,190; in 1830, 7,265; in 1840, 7,074; in 1850, 8,404.

DICKSON'S MILLS, p. o., Parke co., Ind., 62 ms. w. of Indianapolis; from W. 627 ms.

DICKSBURGH, v., Knox co., Ind., 130 ms. s. w. of Indianapolis; from W. 700 ms.

DIGHTON, p. t., Bristol co., Mass., 41 ms. s. of Boston; from W. 421 ms. Watered by Taunton river. Pop. 1,641.

DILLE'S BOTTOM, p. o., Mead township, Belmont co., O., 142 ms. E. of Columbus; from W. 269 ms.

DILLINGERSVILLE, p. o., Lehigh co., Pa.

DILLON, p. o., Tazewell co., Ill., 53 ms. N. of Springfield; from W. 775 ms.

DILLON'S RUN, p. o., Hampshire co., Va., 171 ms. N. w. of Richmond; from W. 99 ms.

DILLONSVILLE, v., Mecklenburgh co., N. C., 196 ms. s. w. of Raleigh; from W. 433 ms.

DILLSBOROUGH, p. v., Dearborn co., Ind., 85 ms. s. E. of Indianapolis; from W. 533 ms.

DILLSBURGH, p. v., Carroll township, York co., Pa., 13 ms. s. w. of Harrisburgh; from W. 97 ms.

DILWORTHTOWN, p. v., Birmingham township, Chester co., Pa., 78 ms. s. E. of Harrisburgh; from W. 116 ms.

DIMMICK, p. o., La Salle co., Ill.

DIMOCK, p. t., Susquehanna co., Pa., 176 ms. N. E. of Harrisburgh; from W. 279 ms. Pop. 1,056.

DIMOCKSVILLE, v., Dimock township, Susquehanna co., Pa.

DINGMAN, t., Pike co., Pa. Watered by Pine creek. Pop. 638.

DINGMAN'S FERRY, p. o., Dingman township, Pike co., Pa., 154 ms. N. E. of Harrisburgh; from W. 248 ms.

DINSMORE, p. t., Shelby co., O., 103 ms. N. w. of Columbus: from W. 494 ms. Pop. 701.

DINWIDDIE COUNTY, situated in the southeasterly part of Virginia, with Notaway river on the south, and Appomatox river on the north. Area, 616 square miles. Face of the country undulating; soil varied. Seat of justice, Dinwiddie. Pop. in 1810, 12,524; in 1820, 13,792; in 1830, 18,637; in 1840, 22,558; in 1850, 25,118.

DINWIDDIE c. h., p. v., seat of justice of Dinwiddie co., Va., 37 ms. s. of Richmond; from W. 156 ms. Watered by Stony creek.

DINWIDDIE'S TAN YARD, p. o., Campbell co., Va.

DIRT TOWN, p. o., Chattooga co., Ga.

DISTRICT, t., Berks co.. Pa., 68 ms. E. of Harrisburgh; from W. 159 ms. Pop. 842.

DITNEY HILL, p. o., Dubois co., Ind.

DIVIDING CREEK, p. v., Doune township, Cumberland co., N. J. 81 ms. s. of Trenton; from W. 193 ms. Watered by Dividing creek.

DIX, t., Chemung co., N. Y., 185 ms. s. w. of Albany. Watered by Catharine's creek. Pop. 2,953.

DIXBOROUGH, p. v., Superior township, Washtenaw co., Mich., 36 ms. w. of Detroit; from W. 532 ms.

DIX CREEK, p. o., Chickasaw co., Miss.

DIXFIELD, p. o., Oxford co., Me., 37 ms. N. of Augusta; from W. 609 ms. Watered by Androscoggin river.

DIX HILLS, p. o., Huntingdon township, Suffolk co., N. Y., 183 ms. s. E. of Albany; from W. 263 ms.

DIXMONT, p. t., Penobscot co., Me., 41 ms. N. E. of Augusta; from W. 638 ms. Watered by Penobscot and Kennebec rivers. Pop. 1,605.

DIXMONT MILLS, p. o., Dixmont township, Penobscot co., Me.

DIXON, t., Preble co., O., 97 ms. w. of Columbus; from W. 493 ms. Pop. 1,192.

DIXON, p. v., seat of justice of Ogle co., Ill., 161 ms. N. of Springfield; from W. 824 ms. Watered by Rock river.

DIXON. p. o., Lee co., Ill.

DIXON'S MILLS, p. o., Marengo co., Ala.

DIXON'S SPRINGS, p. o., Smith co., Tenn., 51 ms. E. of Nashville; from W. 642 ms.

DIXONVILLE, p. v., Cole co., Mo., 8 ms. from Jefferson City; from W. 944 ms.

DIXVILLE, t., Coos co., N. H., 152 ms. N. of Concord; from W. 593 ms.

DOAKSVILLE, p. o., Choctaw Nation co., Ark.

DOANSBURGH, p. o., Southeast township, Putnam co., N. Y.

DOBBIN'S RANCHO, p. o., Yuba co., Cal.

DOBBS' FERRY, Greenburgh township, Westchester co., N. Y., 126 ms. s. of Albany; from W. 248 ms.

DOCKERY'S STORE, p. o., Richmond co., N. C., 129 ms. s.,w. of Raleigh; from W. 403 ms.

DODDRIDGE COUNTY, situated in the northwesterly part of Virginia. Area, —— square miles. Face of the country rough and hilly; soil generally fertile. Seat of justice, West Union. Pop. in 1850, 2,750.

DODDSVILLE, p. o., McDonough co., Ill.

DODGE COUNTY, situated toward the easterly part of Wisconsin. Area, 756 square miles. Face of the country level, with prairies and swamps. Pop. in 1840, 67; in 1850, 3,892.

DODGE COUNTY, situated on the northerly boundary of Missouri. Area, —— square miles. Seat of justice. St. John. Pop. in 1850, 353.

DODGEVILLE, p. v., Iowa co., Wis., 44 ms. w. of Madison; from W. 891 ms.

DODGEVILLE. p. o., Des Moines co., Iowa.

DODSONVILLE, p. v., Highland co.. O.

DODSON, t., Highland co., O. Pop. 1,217.

DODSONVILLE. p. v., Jackson co., Ala.; from W. 688 ms.

DOE HILL, p. o., Highland co., Va., 160 ms. N. w. of Richmond; from W. 187 ms.

DOE RUN, p. o., Chester co., Pa., 70 ms. s. E. of Harrisburgh; from W. 114 ms.

DOGWOOD NECK, p. o., Horry district, S. C.

DOLINGTON, p. v., Bucks co., Pa., 119 ms. E. of Harrisburgh; from W. 163 ms.

DOLSENTOWN, v., Minisink township, Orange co., N. Y., 100 ms. s. of Albany; from W. 273 ms.

DOLSON, p. o., Clark co., Ill.

DOMESTIC, p. o., Williams co., O.

DON. p. o., Sullivan co., Ind.

DONALDSON, p. o., Schuylkill co., Pa.

DONALDSONVILLE, p. v., Ascension parish, La., 73 ms. w. of New Orleans; from W. 1,245 ms. Watered by Mississippi river..

DONEGAL, t., Butler co., Pa., 142 ms. w. of Harrisburgh; from W. 304 ms. Watered by Bear creek and tributaries of Conequenessing creek. Pop. 1,177.

DONEGAL, t., Washington co., Pa., 224 ms. w. of Harrisburgh; from W. 245 ms. Watered by Dutch fork of Buffalo creek and Bush and Castleman's runs. Pop. 1,679.

DONEGAL, p. t., Westmoreland co., Pa., 160 ms. w. of Harrisburgh; from W. 186 ms. Watered by Jacob's and Indian creeks, and Four Mile run. Pop. 2,527.

DONGOLA, p. o., Gibson co., Ind.

DONIPHAN, p. o., Ripley co., Mo.

DONNELL'S, p. o., Allen co., O., 98 ms. N. w. of Columbus; from W. 483 ms.

DONNELLSVILLE, p. o., Clarke co., O., 51 ms. w. of Columbus; from W. 444 ms.

DOOLEY COUNTY, situated toward the southwesterly part of Georgia, with Flint river on the west. Area, 1,600 square miles. Seat of justice, Vienna. Pop. in 1830, 2,135; in 1840, 4,427; in 1850, 8,361.

DOOR CREEK, p. o. Dane co., Wis.

DOOR VILLAGE, p. o., La Porte co., Ind., 149 ms. N. of Indianapolis; from W. 664 ms.

DORCHEAT, p. o., Claiborne parish, La.

DORCHESTER COUNTY, situated toward the southeasterly part of Maryland, with Chesapeake bay on the west. Area, 640 square miles. Face of the country level and marshy; soil sandy and of middling quality. Seat of justice, Cambridge. Pop. in 1810, 18,108; in 1820, 17,700; in 1830, 18,686; in 1840, 18,843; in 1850, 18,877.

DORCHESTER, p. t., Norfolk co., Mass., 4 ms s. of Boston; from W. 438 ms. Watered by Neponset river, and Dorchester bay. Pop. in 1840, 4,875; in 1850, 7,969.

DORCHESTER, p. t., Grafton co., N. H., 48 ms. N. w. of Concord; from W. 504 ms. Watered by a branch of Mascomey river. Pop. 711.

DORCHESTER, p. o., Cumberland co.. N. J.

DORMANSVILLE, p. o., Albany co., N. Y.

DORMICKTOWN, p. o., Monongalia co., Va.

DORR, c. h., p. v., seat of justice of McHenry co., Ill., 185 ms. N. E. of Springfield; from W. 650.

DORRANCH, p. o.. Stark co., Ill.

DORRVILLE, p. o., Washington co., R. I.

DORSET, p. o., De Kalb co., Ill.

DORSET, p. o., Ashtabula co., O.

DORSET, p. t., Bennington co., Vt., 95 ms. s. w. of Montpelier; from W. 435 ms. Watered by Battenkill and Paulet creeks.

DORSEY, p. o., Woodford co., Ky.
DOTY'S CORNERS, p. o., Dansville township, Steuben co., N. Y., 245 ms. w. of Albany ; from W. 326 ms.
DOTYVILLE, p. o., Fond du Lac co., Wis.
DOUBLE BRANCHES, p. o., Lincoln co., Ga., 108 ms. N. E. of Milledgeville ; from W. 576 ms.
DOUBLE BRIDGE, p. o., Lunenburgh co., Va., 85 ms. s. w. of Richmond ; from W. 193 ms.
DOUBLE BRIDGES, p. o., Upson co., Ga.
DOUBLE CABINS, p. o., Henry co., Ga., 76 ms. N. w. of Milledgeville.; from W. 680 ms.
DOUBLE OAK. p. o., Camden co., Mo.
DOUBLE PIKE CREEK, p. o., Carroll co., Md., 82 ms. N. w. of Annapolis ; from W. 65 ms.
DOUBLE SHOALS, p. o., Morgan co., Ga.
DOUBLE SPRING, p. o., Benton co., Ark.
DOUBLE SPRINGS, p. v., Cherokee co., Ala. ; from W. 768 ms. Watered by Coosa river.
DOUBLE SPRINGS, p. o., Oktibbeha co., Miss., 128 ms. N. E. of Jackson ; from W. 917 ms.
DOUBLE SPRINGS, p. o.. Calaveras co., Cal.
DOUBLE WELLS, p. o., Warren co., Ga, 58 ms. N. E. of Milledgeville ; from W. 632 ms.
DOUDSVILLE, p. o., Pendleton co., Ky.
DOUGLASS, p. t., Worcester co., Mass., 43 ms. s. w. of Boston ; from W. 396 ms. Watered by Mumford river. Pop. 1,878.
DOUGLASS, p. t., Berks co., Pa., 64 ms. E. of Harrisburgh ; from W. 157 ms. Watered by Manataury creek. Pop. 1,018.
DOUGLASS, p. t., Montgomery co., Pa. Watered by Perkiomen and Swamp creeks. Pop. 1,265.
DOUGLASS, p. o., Fayette co., Iowa.
DOUGLASS, p. o., Nacogdoches co., Tex.
DOUGLASSVILLE,p.v..Douglass township,Berks co.,Pa.
DAUPHIN, p. o., Blount co., Ala.
DOUTHET, p. o., Anderson district, La.
DOVER, c. h., p. t., seat of justice of Piscataquis co., Me., 83 ms. N. E. of Augusta ; from W. 68 ms. Watered by Piscataquis river. Pop. 1,927.
DOVER, c. h., p. t.. seat of justice of Strafford co., N. H., 39 ms. E. of Concord ; from W. 495 ms. Watered by Cocheco and Bettamy bank and rivers. Pop. in 1830, 5,449 ; in 1840, 6 458 ; in 1850 8,186.
DOVER, p. t., Windham co., Vt., 126 ms. s. of Montpelier ; from W. 497 ms. Watered by tributaries of West and Deerfield rivers.
DOVER, p. t., Norfolk co., Mass., 15 ms. s. w. of Boston ; from W. 430 ms. Watered by Charles river. Pop 631
DOVER, p. t., Dutchess co., N. Y., 74 ms. s of Albany ; from W. 313 ms. Watered by a branch of Ten-Mile creek. Pop. 2,146.
DOVER, p. v., Randolph township, Morris co., N. J., 63 ms. N of Trenton ; from W. 234 ms. Watered by Rockaway river and Morris canal.
DOVER, t., Ocean co., N. J. Watered by Tom's and Forked rivers. Pop. 2,385.
DOVER, p. t., York co., Pa., 30 ms. s. of Harrisburgh ; from W. 97 ms. Pop. 2,164.
DOVER, t., Athens co., O. Pop. 1,232.
DOVER, Dover Hundred. the capital of Del., and seat of justice of Kent co., is a borough on Jones' creek, 10 ms. from its entrance into Delaware bay, 50 ms s. of Wilmington ; from W. 120 ms. It is built on four principal streets, which, intersecting, form a square in the centre of the town. Here is an elegant statehouse, and several churches, banks, and other public buildings, are in the vicinity. The buildings are neat, and generally of brick. It contains a monument erected to the memory of Col. John Haslett, who fell at the battle of Princeton, in 1777. The population, in 1810, was about 900 ; in 1820, 600 ; in 1830, 1,300 ; in 1840, 3,790 ; in 1850, 4,207.
DOVER, p. t., Cuyahoga co., O., 127 ms. N. E. of Columbus ; from W. 372 ms. Watered by Lake Erie. Pop. 1,102.
DOVER, t., Union co., O. Pop. 700.
DOVER, c h., p. v., seat of justice of Stewart co., Tenn., 75 ms. N. w. of Nashville ; from W. 755 ms. Watered by Cumberland river.
DOVER, p. t., Lafayette co., Mo. Pop. 857.
DOVER, p. v.. Mason co., Ky., 79 ms. N. E. of Frankfort : from W. 471 ms.
DOVER, p. t., Lenawee co., Mich. Pop. 1,223.
DOVER, p. v., Bureau co., Ill., 130 ms. N. of Springfield ; from W. 813 ms.
DOVER, p. o., Yazoo co., Miss.

DOVER, p. v., Dover township, Lafayette co., Mo.
DOVER, c. h., p. v., seat of justice of Pope co., Ark., 87 ms. N. w. of Little Rock ; from W. 1,152 ms. Watered by Illinois creek.
DOVER, p. v., Russell co., Ala ; from W. 767 ms.
DOVER, t., Tuscarawas co., O. Watered by Tuscarawas river and Ohio canal. Pop. 3,248.
DOVER, p. o., Baltimore co., Md.
DOVER, p. o., Iowa co., Wis.
DOVER HILL, p. o., Martin co., Ind.
DOVER MILLS, p. o., Goochland co., Va.
DOVESVILLE, p. o., Rockingham co., Va.
DOWAGIAC, p. o., Cass co., Mich.
DOWELTOWN, p. v., Surrey co., N. C., 151 ms. N. w. of Raleigh ; from W. 357 ms.
DOWNE, t.. Cumberland co., N. J. Watered by Maurice river, Dividing creek, and Delaware bay. Pop. 2,341.
DOWNER'S GROVE, p. o,. Du Page co., Ill., 184 ms. N. of Springfield ; from W. 739 ms.
DOWNIEVILLE, p. o., Yuba co., Cal.
DOWNING'S MILLS, p. o.. Strafford co., N. H.
DOWNINGSVILLE, p. o., Grant co., Ky.
DOWNINGTON, p. o., Scipio township, Meigs co., O., 83 ms. s. E. of Columbus ; from W. 350 ms.
DOWNINGTOWN. p. v., Chester co., Pa., 67 ms. s. E. of Harrisburgh ; from W. 124 ms. Watered by Brandy wine creek.
DOWNSVILLE, p. o., Ocean co., N. J.
DOWNSVILLE, p. o.. Union parish, La.
DOYLESTOWN, c. h., p. b., seat of justice of Bucks co., Pa.. 100 ms. E. of Harrisburgh ; from W, 162 ms.
DOYLESTOWN, p. o.. Paulding co., O.
DRACUT, p. t.. Middlesex co., Mass., 27 ms. N. w. of Boston ; from W. 446 ms. Watered by Merrimac and Beaver rivers. Pop. 3,503.
DRAKESTOWN, p. v., Morris co., N. J., 59 ms. N. of Trenton ; from W. 224 ms.
DRAKESVILLE, p. o., Morris co., N. J.
DRAKESVILLE, p. o., Davis co., Iowa.
DRANESVILLE, p. v.. Fairfax co., Va., 140 ms. N. of Richmond ; from W. 21 ms.
DRAPER'S VALLEY, p. o., Pulaski co., Va., 232 ms. w of Richmond ; from W. 300 ms.
DRAPERSVILLE, p. o., Mecklenburgh co., Va., 120 ms s. w. of Richmond ; from W. 233 ms.
DRAUGHN'S STORE, p. o., Sampson co., N. C.
DRAWBRIDGE, p. o.. Sussex co., Del.
DRAYTON, p. b., p v. seat of justice of Dooly co., Ga., 98 ms. s. w. of Milledgeville ; from W. 755 ms. Watered by Pennehatchie creek.
DRAYTONSVILLE, p. v., Union district, S. C., 97 ms. N. w. of Columbia ; from W. 454 ms.
DREHERSVILLE, p. o., Schuylkill co., Pa.
DRENNONS. p. o., Henry co., Ky.
DRESDEN, p. t., Lincoln co., Me., 15 ms. s. of Augusta ; from W. 600 ms. Watered by Kennebec river Pop. 1,419.
DRESDEN, p. v., Grundy co., Ill., 153 ms. N. E. of Springfield ; from W. 753 ms. Watered by Kankakee and Des Plains rivers.
DRESDEN, b., Washington co., N. Y., 80 ms. N. of Albany ; from W. 450 ms. Pop. 674.
DRESDEN, p. v.. Jefferson township, Muskingum co., O., 69 ms. E. of Columbus ; from W. 344 ms. Watered by Wakatoma creek. Pop. 1,448.
DRESDEN, p. v., Weakly co., Tenn., 122 ms. w. of Nashville ; from W. 808 ms. Watered by sources of Obion river. Pop. 395.
DRESDEN MILLS, p. o.. Lincoln co., Me., 17 ms. s. of Augusta ; from W. 598 ms.
DRESSERVILLE, p. o., Cayuga co., N. Y.
DREW COUNTY, situated in the southeasterly part of Arkansas, with Sabine river on the west. Area, —— square miles. Seat of justice, Monticello. Pop. in 1850, 3,275.
DREWERSBURGH, p. o., Franklin co., Ind., 85 ms. s. E. of Indianapolis ; from W. 509 ms.
DREWRYSVILLE, p v., Southampton co., Va., 78 ms. s. E. of Richmond ; from W. 197 ms.
DREWSVILLE, p. v., Walpole township, Cheshire co., N. H., 62 ms. w. of Concord ; from W. 450 ms. Watered by Connecticut river.
DRIPPING SPRING, p.o., Edmonson co., Ky., 130 ms. s. w. of Frankfort ; from W. 654 ms.
DRIVER'S HILL, p. o., Clinch co., Ga.
DROMORE, t., Lancaster co., Pa. Watered by Conewingo creek and Susquehanna river. Pop. 2,826.

DROWNING CREEK, p. o., Burke co., N. C., 182 ms. w. of Raleigh ; from W. 419 ms.

DROWNING FORK. p. o., McDonough co., Ill.

DRYBURGH, p. o., Halifax co., Va., 129 ms. N. of Richmond ; from W. 27 ms.

DRY CREEK, p. o., Lancaster district, S. C., 71 ms. N. E. of Columbia ; from W. 466 ms.

DRY CREEK, p. o., Covington co., Miss.

DRY CREEK, p. o., Kenton co., Ky., 79 ms. N. E. of Frankfort; from W. 499 ms.

DRYDEN, p. t., Tompkins co., N. Y., 153 ms. w. of Albany ; from W. 307 ms. Watered by Fall and Virgil creeks. Pop. 5,122.

DRYDEN, p. t., Lapeer co., Mich. Pop. 1,131.

DRY FORK, p. o., Barren co., Ky.

DRY FORK, p. o., Bond co., Ill.

DRY FORK, p. o., Hamilton co., O.

DRY GLAZE, p. o., Camden co., Mo.

DRY HILL. p. o., Lauderdale co., Tenn.

DRY PONDS, p. o., Lincoln co., N. C., 159 ms. w. of Raleigh ; from W. 396 ms.

DRY RIDGE. p. o., Somerset co., Pa.

DRY RIDGE, p. o., Hamilton co., O., 126 ms. s. w. of Columbus ; from W. 500 ms.

DRY RIDGE, p. v., Grant co., Ky., 53 ms. N. E. of Frankfort; from W. 525 ms.

DRY RUN, p. o., Franklin co., Pa., 67 ms. s. w. of Harrisburgh ; from W. 115 ms.

DRY RUN, p. o., Tippah co., Miss.

DRY VALLEY, p. o., White co., Tenn.

DRY WOOD, p. o., Bates co., Mo.

DUANE, p. t., Franklin co., N. Y., 189 ms. N. of Albany ; from W. 538 ms. Watered by tributaries of Salmon river. Pop. 222.

DUANESBURGH, p. t., Schenectady co., N. Y., 23 ms. w. of Albany ; from W. 393 ms. Watered by Schoharie creek. Pop. 3,464.

DUBLIN, p. t., Cheshire co., N. H., 47 ms. s. w. of Concord ; from W. 447 ms. Watered by Goose river. Pop. 1,088.

DUBLIN, p. v., Bucks co., Pa., 106 ms. E. of Harrisburgh ; from W. 168.

DUBLIN, t., Bedford co., Pa., 70 ms. s. w. of Harrisburgh; from W. 100 ms. Watered by sources of Licking creek, and Wooden Bridge, and Little Angwick creeks.

DUBLIN, p. v., Harford co., Md., 68 ms. N. of Annapolis ; from W. 78 ms.

DUBLIN, t., Huntingdon co., Pa., 55 ms. w. of Harrisburgh ; from W. 109 ms. Watered by Shade and Little Augwick creeks. Pop. 908.

DUBLIN, p. v., Washington township, Franklin co., O., 12 ms. N. w. of Columbus ; from W. 405 ms. Watered by Scioto river.

DUBLIN, t., Mercer co., O., 129 ms. N. w. of Columbus ; from W. 526 ms. Pop. 912.

DUBLIN, p. v., Graves co., Ky., 285 ms. s. w. of Frankfort ; from W. 812 ms.

DUBLIN, c. h., p. v., seat of justice of Laurens co., Ga., 79 ms. s. E. of Milledgeville ; from W. 690 ms. Watered by Oconee river.

DUBLIN, p. v., Wayne co., Ind., 50 ms. E. of Indianapolis ; from W. 521 ms. Pop. 713.

DUBLIN, p. o., Fayette co., Ala.

DUBLIN MILLS, p. o., Dublin township, Bedford co., Pa.

DUBOIS COUNTY, situated in the southern part of Indiana, with east fork of White river on the north. Area, 432 square miles. Face of the country undulating and hilly ; soil fertile. Seat of justice, Jasper. Pop. in 1820, 1,168 ; in 1830, 1,774 ; in 1840, 3,632 ; in 1850, 6,321.

DU BUQUE COUNTY, situated in the northeasterly part of Iowa, with Mississippi river on the northeast. Area, —— square miles. Soil fertile. Seat of justice, Du Buque. Pop. in 1840, 3,059 ; in 1850, 10,841.

DU BUQUE, p. v., Du Buque co., Iowa ; from W. 900 ms. Watered by Mississippi river.

DUCHANYET, t., Allen co., O.

DUCK BRANCH, p. o., Beaufort district, S. C., 105 ms. s. of Columbia ; from W. 611 ms.

DUCK CREEK, p. o., Walker co., Ga.

DUCK CREEK, hundred, Kent co., Del., 8 ms. from Dover ; from W. 122 ms.

DUCK CREEK, p. o., Trumbull co., O.

DUCK RIVER, p. o., Hickman co., Tenn.

DUCK SPRING. p. o., De Kalb co., Ala.

DUDLEY, p. t., Worcester co., Mass., 58 ms. s. w. of

Boston ; from W. 391 ms. Watered by Quinnebaug and French rivers. Pop. 1,443.

DUDLEY, p. t., Hardin co., O., 66 ms. N. w. of Columbus ; from W. 437 ms. Pop. 529.

DUDLEY, t., Henry co., Ind., 61 ms. N. E. of Indianapolis ; from W. 537 ms. Pop. 1,279.

DUDLEY, p. o., Polk co., Iowa.

DUDLEYVILLE, p. v., Tallapoosa co., Ala. ; from W. 781 ms.

DUDLYTOWN, p. o., Jackson co., Ind.

DUE WEST CORNER, p. o., Abbeville district, S. C.

DUFFIELD, p. o., Charles co., Md.

DUFFIELDS, p. o., Jefferson co., Va.

DUFF'S FORKS, p. o., Madison township, Fayette co., O., 36 ms. s. w. of Columbus ; from W. 417 ms.

DUGDEMONA, p. o., Jackson parish, La.

DUGGER'S FERRY, p. o., Carter co., Tenn., 314 ms. E. of Nashville ; from W. 410 ms.

DUG SPUR, p. o., Carroll co., Va.

DUGWAY, p. o., Oswego co., N. Y.

DUKEDOM, p. o., Graves co., Ky.

DUKES COUNTY, situated at the southeasterly part of Massachusetts, and comprehends Martha's Vineyard, Chippequiddick, Noman's Land, and Elizabeth islands in the Atlantic ocean. Area, 120 square miles. Face of the country level ; soil generally poor, much of it overgrown with scrub oaks. Seat of justice, Edgarton. Pop. in 1810, 3,290 ; in 1820, 3,292 ; in 1830, 3,518 ; in 1840, 3,958 ; in 1850, 4,540.

DUKES, p. o., Putnam co., O., 106 ms. N. w. of Columbus ; from W. 471 ms.

DUMAS, p. o., Tippah co., Miss.

DUMAS' STORE, p. o., Richmond co., N. C., 131 ms. s. w. of Raleigh ; from W. 405 ms.

DUMFRIES, p. v., Prince William co., Va., 86 ms. N. of Richmond ; from W. 33 ms. Watered by Quantico creek.

DUMMER, p. t., Coos co., N. H., 132 ms. N. of Concord ; from W. 573 ms. Watered by Ammonoosuc and Androscoggin rivers. Pop. 171.

DUMMERSTON, p. t., Windham co., Vt., 115 ms. s. of Montpelier ; from W. 428 ms. Watered by West and Connecticut rivers. Pop. 1,645.

DUMONTVILLE, p. o., Fairfield co., O., 32 ms. s. E. of Columbus ; from W. 380 ms.

DUNBAR, t., Fayette co., Pa., 175 ms. s. w. of Harrisburgh ; from W. 194 ms. Watered by Youghiogeny river. Pop. 2,156.

DUNBARTON, p. t., Merrimac co., N. H., 10 ms. s. of Concord ; from W. 474. Watered by Merrimac river. Pop. 915.

DUNBARTON, p. o., Meigs, township, Adams co., O., 96 ms. s. of Columbus ; from W. 433 ms.

DUNBARTON, p. o., Barnwell district, S. C.

DUNCAN, p. o., Wood co., Va., 331 ms. N. w. of Richmond ; from W. 299 ms.

DUNCAN, t., Linn co., Mo.

DUNCAN, p. o., Cheboygan co., Mich.

DUNCAN, p. o., Mercer co., Ky.

DUNCAMMON, p. o., Perry co., Pa.

DUNCAN'S CREEK, p. o., Cleveland co., N. C., 204 ms. w. of Raleigh ; from W. 441 ms.

DUNCAN'S FALLS, p. v., Muskingum co., O., 62 ms. E. of Columbus ; from W. 347 ms. Watered by Muskingum river.

DUNCAN'S MILLS, p. o., Jasper co., Mo.

DUNCANVILLE, p. o., Blair co., Pa., 120 ms. w. of Harrisburgh ; from W. 163 ms.

DUNCANSVILLE, p. v., Barnwell district, S. C., 80 ms. s. w. of Columbia ; from W. 586 ms.

DUNCANVILLE, p. v., Thomas co., Ga., 227 ms. s. w. of Milledgeville ; from W. 884 ms.

DUNCANTON, p. v., Mantua village, White co., Ill., 172 ms. s. E. of Springfield ; from W. 785 ms.

DUNCARD, t., Greene co., Pa., 224 ms. s. w. of Harrisburgh ; from W. 226 ms. Pop. 1,395.

DUNDAFF, p. b., Susquehanna co., Pa., 166 ms. N. E. of Harrisburgh ; from W. 270 ms. Pop. 293.

DUNDARRACH, p. o., Robeson co., N. C.

DUNDAS, p. o., Calumet co., Wis.

DUNDEE, p. o., Kane co., Ill.

DUNDEE, p. t., Monroe co., Mich., 54 ms. s. w. of Detroit ; from W. 503 ms. Watered by Raisin river. Pop. 1,239.

DUNDEE, p. o., Yates co., N. Y.

DUNDEE, p. o., Tuscarawas co., O.

DUNGANON, p. v., Hanover township, Columbiana co., O., 142 ms. N. E. of Columbus ; from W. 287.

DUNKINSVILLE, p. o., Adams co., O.

DUNKIRK, p. v., Pomfret township, Chautauque co., N. Y., 326 ms. w. of Albany; from W. 348 ms. Watered by Lake Erie. Terminus of New York and Erie railroad.

DUNKIRK, p. o., Calvert co., Md.

DUNKIRK, p. o., Greenville district, S. C.

DUNKIRK, p. o., Dane co., Wis.

DUNKLIN COUNTY, situated at the southeasterly corner of Missouri, with St. Francis river on the west, and Lake Pemisco, and a part of Mississippi river, on the southeast. Area, —— square miles. Seat of justice, Chillitecaux. Pop. in 1850, 1,229.

DUNLAP, p. o., Hamilton co., O., 111 ms. s. w. of Columbus; from W. 499 ms.

DUNLAPSVILLE, p. o., Laurens district, S. C.

DUNLAPSVILLE, p. v., Union co., Ind, 69 ms. E. of Indianapolis; from W. 517 ms. Watered by the east branch of White Water river.

DUNLEVY, p. o., Warren co., O.

DUNMORE, p. o., Luzerne co., Pa.

DUNMORE, p. v., Pocahontas co., Va., 194 ms. N. w. of Richmond: from W. 221 ms.

DUNNINGSVILLE, p. o., Washington co., Pa.

DUNNSBURGH, p. v., Clinton co., Pa., 109 ms. N. w. of Harrisburgh; from W. 201 ms. Watered by the west branch of Susquehanna river. Pop. 356.

DUNN'S CORNERS, p. o., Kennebec co., Me., 10 ms. from Augusta; from W. 605 ms.

DUNNSVILLE, p. o., Albany co., N. Y.

DUNNSVILLE, p. v., Essex co., Va., 56 ms. N. E. of Richmond; from W. 118 ms.

DUNSTABLE, p. t., Middlesex co, Mass., 31 ms. N. w. of Boston; from W. 437 ms. Watered by Nashua and Salmon rivers. Pop. 590.

DUNSTABLE, t., Clinton co., Pa. Watered by the west branch of Susquehanna river. Pop. 356.

DUNTONSVILLE, p. o., Edgefield district, S. C., 65 ms. w. of Columbia; from W. 560 ms.

DUPAGE COUNTY, situated in the northeasterly part of Illinois. Area, 396 square miles. Seat of justice, Napierville. Pop. in 1840, 3,535; in 1850, 9,290.

DUPAGE, p. o., Will co., Ill.

DUPLAIN, p. o., Clinton co., Mich.

DUPLIN COUNTY, situated in the southeasterly part of North Carolina. Area, 640 square miles. Surface level, or moderately hilly; soil, sterile. Seat of justice, Kenansville. Pop. in 1810, 7,863; in 1820, 9,744; in 1830, 11,373; in 1840, 11,182; in 1850, 13,514, DUPONT, p. o., Jefferson co., Ind., 74 ms. s. E. of Indianapolis; from W. 574 ms.

DUPREE'S OLD STORE, p. o., Charlotte co., Va., 102 ms. s. w. of Richmond; from W. 200 ms.

DUQUESNE, p. o., Alleghany co., Pa.

DUQUOIN, p. o., Perry co., Ill.

DURANGO, p. o., Dubuque co., Iowa.

DURAND, p. o., Henry co., O.

DURANT'S NECK, p. o., Perquiman's co., N. C., 215 ms. E. of Raleigh; from W. 305 ms.

DURBIN'S CORNERS, p. o., Williams co., O.

DURELL, p. o., Bradford co., Pa.

DURHAM, p. t., Cumberland co., Me., 39 ms. s. w. of Augusta; from W. 566 ms. Watered by Androscoggin river. Pop. 1,886.

DURHAM, p. o., Hancock co., Ill.

DURHAM, p. t., Strafford co., N. H., 32 ms. E. of Con-

cord; from W. 485 ms. Watered by Lamprey, Piscataqua, and Oyster rivers. Pop. 1,427.

DURHAM, p. t., Middlesex co., Ct., 21 ms. s. of Hartford; from W. 319 ms. Watered by West river. Pop. 1,026.

DURHAM, p. t., Greene co., N. Y., 36 ms. s. w. of Albany; from W. 359 ms. Watered by Catskill river and tributaries. Pop. 2,600.

DURHAM, p. t., Bucks co., Pa., 111 ms. E. of Harrisburgh; from W. 182 ms. Watered by Cook's, or Durham creek, and Delaware river. Pop. 948.

DURHAM CENTRE, p. o., Middlesex co., Ct.

DURHAM'S CREEK, p. o., Beaufort district, S. C.

DURHAMVILLE, p. v., Verona township, Oneida co. N. Y., 125 ms. n. w. of Albany; from W. 368 ms. Watered by Oneida creek.

DURHAMVILLE, p. v., Lauderdale co., Tenn., 181 ms w. of Nashville; from W. 862 ms.

DURHAMVILLE, p. o., Orange co., N. C.

DURLACH, p. o., Lancaster co., Pa., 34 ms. s. E. of Harrisburgh; from W. 128 ms.

DUROC, p. o., Benton co., Mo.

DURRETTSVILLE, p. o., Richmond co., Va., 65 ms N. E. of Richmond; from W. 124 ms.

DUTCH CREEK, p. o., Washington co., Iowa.

DUTCH CREEK. p. o., Brown co., Wis.

DUTCHESS COUNTY, situated on the easterly boundary of New York, with Hudson river on the west. Area, 840 square miles. Face of the country diversified with valleys, hills, and mountains; soil rich and well cultivated. Seat of justice, Poughkeepsie. Pop. in 1810, 41,141; in 1820, 46,615; in 1830, 50,926; in 1840, 52,398; in 1850, 58,992.

DUTCH NECK, p. o., Mercer co., N. Y.

DUTCHVILLE, p. o., Granville co., N C., 40 ms. N. of Raleigh; from W. 274 ms.

DUTOTSBURGH, p. v., Monroe co., Pa., 130 ms. N. E. of Harrisburgh; from W. 223 ms. Watered by Delaware river.

DUVAL COUNTY, situated in the northeasterly part of Florida, with the Atlantic ocean on the east. Area, 720 square miles. Seat of justice, Jacksonville. Pop. in 1830, 1,970; in 1840, 4,156; in 1850, 4,539.

DUVALL'S BLUFF, p. o., Prairie co., Ark.

DUXBURY, p. t., Plymouth co., Mass., 36 ms. s. E. of Boston; from W. 448 ms. Watered by Massachusetts bay. Pop. 2,679.

DUXBURY, t., Washington co., Vt., 13 ms. w, of Montpelier Watered by Mad and Onion rivers. Pop. 845.

DWIGHT, p. v., Pope co., Ark., 77 ms. N. w. of Little Rock, from W. 1,142 ms. Watered by Illinois river Contains a missionary station among the Cherokees, established by the American Board of Foreign Missions, in 1820.

DYBERRY, Wayne co., Pa. Pop. 790.

DYCUSBURGH, p. o., Crittenden co., Ky.

DYER COUNTY, situated on the westerly boundary of Tennessee, with Mississippi river on the west. Area, 840 square miles. Seat of justice, Dyersburgh. Pop. in 1830, 1,904; in 1840, 4,484; in 1850, 6,361.

DYERSBURGH, p. o., Dyer co., Tenn., 161 ms. w. of Nashville; from W. 844 ms. Watered by the north branch of Forked Deer river.

DYKEMAN'S, p. o., Putnam co., N. Y.

DYRE, t., Saline co., Ark.

DYSONS, p. o., Guernsey co., O.

E.

EAGLE, p. t., Wyoming co., N. Y., 264 ms. w. of Albany; from W. 355 ms. Watered by Caneadea and Wiskoy creeks. Pop. 1,381.

EAGLE, p. o., Warren co., Pa., 139 ms. N. w. of Harrisburgh; from W. 320 ms.

EAGLE, p. o., Clinton co., Mich.

EAGLE, p. t., Hancock co., O., 83 ms, N. w. of Columbus, from W. 454 ms. Pop. 954.

EAGLE, t., Brown co., O. Pop. 1,134.

EAGLE, t., Ross co., O.

EAGLE, p. o., La Salle co., Ill.

EAGLE CLIFFS, p. o., Monroe co., Ill.

EAGLE CREEK, p. o., Benton co., Tenn.

EAGLE CREEK, p. o., Bradley co., Ark.

EAGLE EYRY, p. o., Bedford co., Va.

EAGLE FALLS, p. o., Rockingham co. N. Y.

EAGLE FOUNDRY, p. o., Huntingdon co., Pa.

EAGLE FURNACE, p. o., Roane co., Tenn.

EAGLE GROVE, p. o., Elbert co., Ga., 114 ms. N. of Milledgeville; from W. 588 ms.

EAGLE HARBOR, p. v., Gaines township, Orleans co., N. Y., 256 ms. w. of Albany; from W. 398 ms.

EAGLE HARBOR, p. o., Houghton co., Mich.

EAGLE LABE, p. o., Oakland co., Mich.

EAGLE LAKE, p. o., Colorado co., Tex.

EAGLE MILLS, p. o., Rensselaer co., N Y.

EAGLE MILLS, p. o., Iredell, co., N. C.

EAGLE POINT, p. o., Ogle co., Ill.

EAGLE RIVER, p. o., Houghton co., Mich.

EAGLE ROCK, p. v., Wake co., N. C., 12 ms. E. o Raleigh; from W. 286 ms.

EAGLESMERE, p. o., Sullivan co., Pa.

EAGLETOWN, p. o., Hamilton co., Ind.

EAGLETOWN, p. v., Choctaw Nation co., Ark., 177 ms.

w. of Little Rock; from W. 124 ms. Watered by Mountain fork of Little River.

EAGLE VILLAGE, p. v., Boone co., Ind., 15 ms. N. W. of Indianapolis; from W. 586 ms.

EAGLE VILLAGE, p. v., Wyoming co., N. Y.

EAGLEVILLE, v., Centre co., Pa., 102 ms. N. W. of Harrisburgh; from W. 194 ms.

EAGLEVILLE, p. o , Ashtabula co., O., 200 ms. N. E. of Columbus; from W. 340 ms.

EAGLEVILLE, p. v., Williamson co., Tenn., 27 ms. s. of Nashville; from W. 690 ms.

EAGLEVILLE, p. o., Tolland co., Ct.

EAGLEVILLE, p. o., Waukesha co., Wis.

EARL, t., Lancaster co., Pa. Watered by Conestoga and Muddy creeks.

EARL, t., Berks co., Pa. Watered by Manatawny creek. Pop. 1,047.

EARLESVILLE, p. v., Spartanburgh district, S. C., 135 ms N. W. of Columbia; from W. 472 ms.

EARLVILLE, p. v., Hamilton township, Madison co., N. Y., 98 ms. w. of Albany; from W. 352 ms. Watered by Chenango river and Chenango canal.

EARLVILLE, p. o., Earl township, Berks co., Pa., 65 ms. E. of Harrisburgh; from W. 158 ms.

EARLVILLE, p. o., La Salle co., Ill.

EARLY COUNTY, situated in the southwesterly part of Georgia, with Chattahoochee river on the west. Area, 1,280 square miles. Seat of justice, Blakely. Pop. in 1830, 2,081; in 1840, 5,444; in 1850, 7,246.

EARLY GROVE, p. o., Lincoln co., N. C., 180 ms. w. of Raleigh; from W. 417 ms.

EARLY GROVE, p. o., Marshall co., Miss.

EARLYSVILLE, p. o., Albemarle co., Va.

EARPVILLE, p. o., Upshur co., Tex.

EAST, t., Carroll co., O. Pop. 987.

EAST ABINGTON, p. v., Abington township, Plymouth co., Mass., 18 ms. s. E. of Boston; from W. 446 ms. Watered by Pembroke creek.

EAST ALTON, p. v., Alton township, Belknap co., N. H., 33 ms. N. E. of Concord; from W. 514 ms.

EAST ANDOVER, p. o., Merrimack co., N. H.

EAST ASHFORD, p. o., Cattaraugus co., N. Y.

EAST AUBURN, p. o., Cumberland co., Me.

EAST AURORA, p. o., Erie co., N. Y.

EAST AVON, p. v., Avon township, Livingston co., N. Y. 218 ms. w. of Albany; from W. 400 ms.

EAST BALDWIN, p. v., Baldwin township, Cumberland co., Me., 70 ms. s. w. of Augusta; from W. 546 ms.

EAST BARNARD, p. o., Barnard township, Windsor co., Vt., 39 ms. s. of Montpelier; from W. 494 ms.

EAST BARRE, p. o., Huntingdon co., Pa.

EAST BATON ROUGE PARISH, situated toward the southeasterly part of Louisiana, with the Mississippi on the west. Area, —— square miles. Seat of justice. Baton Rouge. Pop. in 1820, 5,220; in 1830, 6,698; in 1840, 8,138; in 1850, 11,977.

EAST BEND, p. o., Hancock co., Ill., 126 ms. N. w. of Springfield; from W. 877 ms.

EAST BERGEN, p. o., Genesee co., N. Y.

EAST BERKSHIRE, p. v., Berkshire township. Franklin co., Vt., 61 ms. N. of Montpelier; from W. 563 ms.

EAST BERLIN, p. v., Adams co., Pa., 25 ms. s. w. of Harrisburgh; from W. 90 ms.

EAST BERLIN, p. o., St. Clair co., Mich.

EAST BERNE, p. v., Berne township, Albany co., N. Y., 19 ms. w. of Albany; from W. 389 ms.

EAST BETHANY, p. o., Bethany township, Genesee co., N. Y., 248 ms. w. of Albany; from W. 367 ms.

EAST BETHEL, p. o., Bethel township, Oxford co., Me., 59 ms. w. of Augusta; from W. 607 ms.

EAST BETHEL, p. v., Bethel township, Windsor co., Vt., 28 ms. s. of Montpelier; from W. 493 ms.

EAST BETHLEHEM, p. t., Washington co., Pa., 197 ms. w. of Harrisburgh; from W. 213 ms. Watered by Monongahela river and Ten Mile creek. Pop. 2,266.

EAST BLOOMFIELD, p. t., Ontario co., N. Y., 203 ms. w. of Albany; from W. 349 ms. Watered by Mud creek. Pop. 2,262.

EAST BOSTON, p. o., Suffolk co., Mass., a part of the city of Boston.

EAST BRADFORD, t., Chester co., Pa. Watered by Brandywine river and Valley creek. Pop. 1,330.

EAST BREWER, p. o., Brewer township. Penobscot co., Me., 76 ms. N. E. of Augusta; from W. 671 ms.

EAST BREWSTER, p. v., Brewster township, Barnstable co., Mass., 93 ms. s. E. of Boston; from W. 494 ms.

EAST BRIDGEWATER, p. t., Plymouth co., Mass., 25 ms. s. E. of Boston; from W. 433 ms. Watered by a branch of Taunton river. Pop. 2,545.

EASTBROOK, t., Hancock co., Me., 96 ms. N. E. of Augusta; from W. 684 ms. Pop. 212.

EAST BROOK, p. o., Lawrence co., Pa., 232 ms. N. w. of Harrisburgh; from W. 274 ms.

EAST BROOKFIELD, p.v., Brookfield township, Orange co., Vt., 22 ms. s. of Montpelier; from W. 504 ms. Watered by a branch of White river.

EAST BROOKFIELD, p. v., Brookfield township, Worcester co., Mass., 56 ms. s. w. of Boston; from W. 392 ms.

EAST BRUNSWICK, p. t., Schuylkill co., Pa. Pop. 1,337.

EAST BUFFALO, t., Union co., Pa. Pop. 970.

EAST BURKE, p. o., Caledonia co., Vt.

EAST BURNHAM, p. o., Waldo co., Me., 40 ms. N. E. of Augusta; from W. 636 ms.

EAST CALAIS, p. o., Calais township, Washington co., Vt., 13 ms. N. E. of Montpelier; from W. 529 ms.

EAST CALN, t., Chester co., Pa., 60 ms. s. E. of Harrisburgh; from W. 114 ms. Pop. 2,292.

EAST CAMBRIDGE, p. v., Cambridge township, Middlesex co., Mass., 1 m. N. w. of Boston; from W. 439 ms. Watered by Charles river.

EAST CANEADEA, p. o., Alleghany co., N. Y.

EAST CANISTEO, p. o., Canisteo township, Steuben co., N. Y., 241 ms. w. of Albany; from W. 308 ms

EAST CAMERON, p. o., Steuben co., N. Y.

EAST CANAAN, p. o., Grafton co., N. H.

EAST CANAAN, p. o., Litchfield co., Ct.

EAST CARLTON, p. o., Carlton township, Orleans co. N. Y., 262 ms. of Albany; from W. 405 ms.

EAST CENTREVILLE, p. o., Indiana co., Pa.

EAST CHARLEMONT, p. o., Franklin co., Mass.

EAST CHARLESTON, p. o. Charleston township, Orleans co., Vt., 68 ms. N. of Montpelier; from W. 578 ms.

EAST CHATHAM, p. o., Columbia co., N. Y.

EAST CHESTER, p. v., Chester township. Rockingham co., N. H., 25 ms. s. E. of Concord; from W. 466 ms.

EAST CHESTER, p. t., Westchester co., N. Y., 142 ms. s. of Albany; from W. 241 ms. Watered by Bronx river, and East Chester and Hutchinson's creeks. Pop. 1,679.

EAST CHINA, p. o., China township, Wyoming co., N. Y., 268 ms. w. of Albany; from W. 351 ms.

EAST CLARENDON, p. o., Clarendon township, Rutland co., Vt., 66 ms. s. of Montpelier; from W. 460 ms.

EAST CLARIDON, p. o., Claridon township, Geauga co., O., 174 ms. N. E. of Columbus; from W. 333 ms.

EAST CLARKSFIELD, p. o., Huron co., O.

EAST CLARKSON, p. o., Monroe co., N. Y.

EAST CLEVELAND, p. o., Cuyahoga co., O.

EAST COBBLESKILL, p. o., Schoharie co., N. Y.

EAST COCALICO, t., Lancaster co., Pa. Watered by Cocalico creek. Pop. 2,117.

EAST CONSTABLE, p. o., Constable township, Franklin co., N. Y., 214 ms. N. of Albany; from W. 553 ms.

EAST CORINTH, p. o., Corinth township, Penobscot co., Me., 88 ms. N. E. of Augusta; from W. 683 ms.

EAST CORINTH, p. o., Corinth township, Orange co., Vt., 23 ms. s. E. of Montpelier; from W. 521 ms.

EAST CRAFTSBURY, p. o., Orleans co., Vt.

EAST CREEK, p. o., Cape May co., N. J.

EAST DEER, t., Alleghany co., Pa. Watered by Alleghany river. Pop. 2,021.

EAST DE KALB, p. o., St., Lawrence co., N. Y.

EAST DENNIS, p. v., Dennis township, Barnstable co., Mass., 83 ms. s. E. of Boston; from W. 484 ms.

EAST DIXFIELD, p. o., Dixfield township, Oxford co., Me., 35 ms. w. of Augusta; from W. 613 ms.

EAST DIXMONT, p. o., Penobscot co., Me.

EAST DONEGAL, t., Lancaster co., Pa. Watered by Little Chicques creek. Pop. 1,997.

EAST DORSET, p. o., Dorset township, Bennington co., Vt., 88 ms. s. w. of Montpelier; from W. 435 ms.

EAST DOUGLASS, p. o., Douglass township, Worcester co., Mass., 41 ms. s. w. of Boston; from W. 398 ms.

EAST DOVER, p. o., Dover township, Piscataquis co., Me., 86 ms. N. E. of Augusta; from W. 683 ms.

EAST DUANESBURGH, p. o., Schenectady co., N. Y.

EAST DURHAM, p. v., Durham township, Greene co., N. Y., 40 ms. s. of Albany; from W. 553 ms.

EAST EDDINGTON, Eddington township, Penobscot co., Me., 79 ms. N. E. of Augusta; from W. 774 ms.

EAST EDEN, p. o., Erie co., N. Y.

EAST ELLIOTT, p. v., Elliott township, York co., Me., 102 ms. s. of Augusta; from W. 502 ms.

EAST EVANS, p. o., Evans township, Erie co., N. Y., 307 ms. w. of Albany; from W. 372 ms.

EAST FAIRFIELD, p. o., Fairfield township, Franklin co., Vt., 52 ms. N. w. of Montpelier; from W. 548 ms.

EAST FAIRFIELD, p. v., Fairfield township, Columbiana co., O., 158 ms. N. E. of Columbus; from W. 276 ms.

EAST FALLOWFIELD, t., Chester co., Pa., 67 ms. s. E. of Harrisburgh; from W. 110 ms. Watered by West branch of Brandywine creek.

EAST FALMOUTH, p. v., Falmouth township, Barnstable co., Mass., 84 ms. s. of Boston; from W. 470 ms.

EAST FARMINGTON, v., Farmington township, Oakland co., Mich., 24 ms. N. w. of Detroit; from W. 546 ms.

EAST FELICIANA PARISH, situated on the northerly boundary of that portion of Louisiana which lies east of Mississippi river. Area, 560 square miles. Soil fertile. Seat of justice, Clinton. Pop in 1830, 8,247; in 1840, 11,893; in 1850, 13,598.

EAST FLORENCE, p. o., Florence township, Oneida co., N. Y., 125 ms. N. w. of Albany; from W. 411 ms.

EAST FINDLAY, t., Washington co., Pa., 251 ms. w. of Harrisburgh; from W. 238 ms. Pop. 1,281.

EASTFORD, p. v., Ashford township, Windham co., Ct., 35 ms. E. of Hartford; from W. 371 ms. Watered by Natchaug river. Pop. 1,127.

EAST FORK, p. o., Montgomery co., Ill.

EAST FORK, p. o., Macon co., Mo.

EAST FOXBOROUGH, p. v., Foxborough township, Norfolk co., Mass., 25 ms. s. of Boston; from W. 417 ms.

EAST FRANKLIN, p. o., Franklin co., Vt.

EAST FREEDOM, p. o., Blair co., Pa.

EAST FREETOWN, p. o., Cortland co., N. Y.

EAST GAINES, p. o., Orleans co., N. Y.

EAST GAINSVILLE, p. o., Wyoming co., N. Y.

EAST GALWAY, p. o., Saratoga co., N. Y.

EAST GENOA, p. o., Genoa township, Cayuga co., N. Y., 164 ms. w. of Albany; from W. 316 ms.

EAST GEORGIA, p. o., Franklin co., Vt.

EAST GERMAN, p. o., Chenango co., N. Y.

EAST GERMANTOWN, p. o., Wayne co., Ind.

EAST GLENVILLE, p. o., Glenville township, Schenectady co., N. Y., 20 ms. N. w. of Albany; from W. 388 ms.

EAST GOSHEN, t., Chester co., Pa., 70 ms. s. E. of Harrisburgh; from W. 119 ms. Watered by Ridley and Chester creeks. Pop. 768.

EAST GRAFTON, p. o., Rensselaer co., N. Y.

EAST GRANBY, p. v., Granby township, Hartford co., Ct. 15 ms. N. of Hartford; from W. 351 ms.

EAST GRANVILLE, p. v., Granville township, Hampden co., Mass., 110 ms. w. of Boston; from W. 362 ms.

EAST GREENBUSH, p. v., Greenbush township, Rensselaer co., N. Y.

EAST GREENE, p. o., Greene township, Chenango co., N. Y., 118 ms. w. of Albany; from W. 318 ms.

EAST GREENVILLE, p. v., Tuscarawas township, Stark co., O., 110 ms. N. E. of Columbus; from W. 327 ms.

EAST GREENWICH, c. h., p. t., Seat of justice of Kent co., R. I., 14 ms. s. of Providence; from W. 397 ms. Watered by an arm of Narraganset bay.

EAST GREENWICH, p. o., Greenwich township, Washington co., N. Y.

EAST GROVE, p. o., Henry co., Iowa.

EAST GROVELAND, p. o., Groveland township, Livingston co., N. Y., 241 ms. w. of Albany; from W. 336 ms.

EAST GUILFORD, p. v., Guildford township, Chenango co., N. Y., 104 ms. w. of Albany; from W. 326 ms.

EAST HADDAM, p. t., Middlesex co., Ct., 30 ms. s. E. of Hartford; from W. 343 ms. Watered by Connecticut river.

EASTHAM, p. t., Barnstable co., Mass., 97 ms. s. E. of Boston; from W. 498 ms. Watered by Barnstable bay. Pop. 845.

EAST HAMBURGH, p. o., Hamburgh township, Erie co., N. Y., 284 ms. w. of Albany; from W. 369 ms.

EAST HAMILTON, p. o., Hamilton town-hip, Madison co., N. Y., 92 ms. w. of Albany from W. 358 ms.

EAST HAMPDEN, p. o., Penobscot co., Me.

EAST HAMPDEN, p. o., Columbia co., Wis.

EAST HAMPTON, p. t., Hampshire co., Mass., 98 ms.

w. of Boston; from W. 376 ms. Watered by Connecticut river, and Hampshire and Hampden canal. Pop. 1,342.

EAST HAMPTON, p. v., Chatham township, Middlesex co., Ct., 16 ms. s. of Hartford; from W. 326 ms. Watered by Pine brook.

EAST HAMPTON, p. t., Suffolk co., Long Island, N. Y., 267 ms. s. E. of Albany; from W. 347 ms. Watered by the Atlantic ocean and Gardener's bay. Pop. 2,122.

EAST HANOVER, p. t., Lebanon co., Pa., 21 ms. E. of Harrisburgh; from W. 131 ms. Pop. 1,815.

EAST HARDWICK, p. o., Caledonia co., Vt.

EAST HARTFORD, p. t., Hartford co., Ct., 1 mile E. of Hartford; from W. 337 ms. Watered by Connecticut river. Pop. 2,497.

EAST HARWICH, p. v., Harwich township, Barnstable co., Mass., 100 ms. s. of Boston; from W. 501 ms.

EAST HAVEN, p. t., New Haven co., Ct., 39 ms. s. w. of Hartford; from W. 303 ms. Watered by Quinnipiack river, and Long Island sound. Pop. 1,670.

EAST HAVEN, p. t., Essex co., Vt., 58 ms. N. E. of Montpelier; from W. 564 ms. Watered by Passumpsic river, and Paul's stream. Pop. 94.

EAST HAVERHILL. p. v., Haverhill township, Essex co., Mass., 38 ms. N. of Boston; from W. 468 ms. Watered by Merrimac river.

EAST HEBRON, p. o., Oxford co., Me., 36 ms. w. of Augusta; from W. 587 ms.

EAST HEMPFIELD, p. t., Lancaster co., Pa., 38 ms. s. E. of Harrisburgh; from W. 118 ms. Watered by Little Conestoga creek. Pop. 2,266.

EAST HERRICK, p. o., Bradford co., Pa., 154 ms. N. of Harrisburgh; from W. 264 ms.

EAST HIGHGATE, p. o., Highgate township, Franklin co., Vt., 71 ms. N w. of Montpelier; from W. 543 ms.

EAST HILL, p. o., Nunda township, Alleghany co., N. Y., 248 ms. w. of Albany; from W. 339 ms.

EAST HOMER. p. o., Homer township, Cortland co., N. Y., 136 ms. w. of Albany; from W. 322 ms.

EAST HOUNDSFIELD, p. o., Jefferson co., N. Y.

EAST HUNTINGDON, t., Westmoreland co., Pa., 176 ms. w. of Harrisburgh; from W. 198 ms. Watered by tributaries of Jacob's creek. Pop. 1,873.

EAST JAFFREY, p. o., Cheshire co., N. H.

EAST JAVA, p. o., Java township, Wyoming co., N. Y., 263 ms. w. of Albany; from W. 356 ms.

EAST KENT, p. o., Kent township, Litchfield co., Ct.

EAST KITT, p. o., Hunter township, Greene co., N. Y., 57 ms. s. w. of Albany; from W. 364 ms.

EAST KILLINGLY, p. v., Killingly township, Windham co., Ct., 49 ms. E. of Hartford; from W. 380 ms.

EAST KINGSTON, p. t., Rockingham co., N. H., 36 ms. s. E. of Concord; from W. 474 ms. Watered by Powow river. Pop. 532.

EAST KNOX, p. o., Knox township, Waldo co., Me., 38 ms. N. E. of Augusta; from. 633 ms.

EAST KOY, p. o., Pike township, Alleghany co., N. Y., 260 ms. w. of Albany; from W. 355 ms.

EAST LANDAFF, p. o., Grafton co., N. H.

EAST LANSING, p. o., Tompkins co., N. Y., 172 ms. w. of Albany; from W. 308 ms.

EAST LA PORTE, p. o., Haywood co., N. C., 317 ms. w. of Raleigh; from W. 547 ms.

EAST LEBANON, p. v., Lebanon township, Grafton co., N. H., 49 ms. N. w. of Concord; from W. 488 ms.

EAST LEBANON, v., Wayne co., O., 108 ms. N. E. of Columbus; from W. 329 ms.

EAST LEE, p. o., Berkshire co., Mass.

EAST LEMPSTER, p. o., Sullivan co., N. H.

EAST LEON, p. o., Cattaraugus co., N. Y.

EAST LEWISTON, p. o., Mahoning co., O.

EAST LEXINGTON, p. o., Middlesex co., Mass., 8 ms. N. w. of Boston; from W. 448 ms.

EAST LIBERTY, p. v., Dunbar township, Fayette co., Pa., 184 ms. w. of Harrisburgh; from W. 209 ms. Watered by Youghiogeny river.

EAST LIBERTY, v., Alleghany co., Pa., 195 ms. w. of Harrisburgh; from W. 217 ms.

EAST LIBERTY, p. v., Allen co., Ind.

EAST LIBERTY, p. v., Perry township, Logan co., O., 59 ms. N. w. of Columbus; from W. 449 ms. Pop. 177.

EAST LIVINGSTON, p. o., York co., Me., 68 ms. s. w. of Augusta; from W. 543 ms.

EAST LINE, p. o., Ballston township, Saratoga co., N. Y.

EAST LIVERMORE, p. o., Livermore township, Kennebec co., Me., 22 ms. w. of Augusta; from W. 602 ms.

EAST LIVERPOOL, p. v., St. Clair township, Columbiana co., O., 156 ms. s. e. of Columbus ; from W. 268 ms. Watered by Ohio river.

East Long Meadow, p. v., Long Meadow township, Hampden co., Mass., 90 ms. s. w. of Boston ; from W. 366 ms.

East Lyman, p. o., Lyman township, Grafton co., N. H., 93 ms. n. w. of Concord ; from W. 538 ms.

East Lyme, p. v., Lyme township, New London co., Ct., 51 ms. s. e. of Hartford ; from W. 346 ms. Pop. 1,382.

East Macdonough, p. o., Macdonough township, Chenango co., N. Y., 114 ms. w. of Albany ; from W. 333 ms.

East Machias, p. o., Washington co., Me., 157 ms. e. of Augusta ; from W. 743 ms.

East Madison, p. o., Somerset co., Me., 42 ms. n. of Augusta ; from W. 437 ms.

East Maine. p. o., Broome co., N. Y.

East Mansville, p. o., Fulton co., N. Y.

East Marion, p. o., Livingston co., Mich.

East Marion. p. o., Suffolk co., Long Island, N. Y.

East Marshfield, p. o., Marshfield township, Plymouth co., Mass.

East Marlborough. t., Chester co., Pa., 70 ms. s. e. of Harrisburgh ; from W. 107 ms. Watered by Pocopsen and Redclay creeks. Pop. 1,425.

East Medway, p. v., Medway township, Norfolk co., Mass., 24 ms. s. w. of Boston ; from W. 422 ms.

East Middleborough, p. v., Plymouth co., Mass., 44 ms. s. of Boston ; from W. 436 ms.

East Middlebury, p. o., Middlebury township, Addison co., Vt., 54 ms. s. w. of Montpelier ; from W. 486 ms.

East Monmouth, p. o., Monmouth township, Kennebec co., Me., 20 ms. s. w., of Augusta ; from W. 596 ms.

East Montpelier, p. o., Montpelier township, Washington co., Vt., 6 ms. e. of Montpelier ; from W. 522 ms.

East Monroe, v. Fairfield township, Highland co., O., 78 ms. s. w. of Columbus ; from W. 433 ms.

East Montville, p. o., Waldo co., Me.

East Moriches, p. o., Suffolk co., Long Island, N. Y.

East Moultonborough, p. o., Moultonborough township, Carroll co., N. H., 49 ms. n. of Concord ; from W. 530 ms.

East Nantmeal, t., Chester co., Pa., 65 ms. s. e. of Harrisburgh ; from W. 143 ms. Watered by north and south branches of French creek. Pop. 921.

East Nassau, p. o., Rensselaer co., N. Y.

East New Market, p. v., Dorchester co., Md., 73 ms. s. e. of Annapolis ; from W. 113 ms.

East Newport. p. o.. Newport township, Penobscot co., Me.

East New Portland, p. o., New Portland township, Somerset co., Me., 52 ms. n. of Augusta ; from W. 646 ms.

East New Sharon, p. o., New Sharon township, Kennebec co., Me., 24 ms. n. w. of Augusta ; from W. 617 ms.

East New Vineyard, p. o., Franklin co., Me.

East New York. p. v., Flatbush township, King's co., Long Island, N. Y., 152 ms. s. of Albany ; from W. 202 ms.

East Northport, p. o., Northport township, Waldo co., 46 ms. e. of Augusta ; from W. 640 ms.

East Northwood, p. v., Northwood township, Rockingham co..N. H., 22 ms. e. of Concord ; from W. 492 ms.

East North Yarmouth, p. o., Cumberland co.. Me.

East Norwich, p. o., Queen's co., Long Island, N. Y.

East Nottingham, t., Chester co., Pa. Watered by Elk and Little Elk creeks. Pop. 2,412.

East Ogden, p. o., Lenawee co., Mich.

Easton. p. t., Bristol co., Mass., 24 ms. s. of Boston ; from W. 429 ms. Watered by tributaries of Taunton river. Pop. 2,337.

Easton, p. t., Washington co., N. Y., 27 ms. n. e. of Albany ; from W. 397 ms. Watered by Batten Kill. Pop. 3,225.

Easton, c. h., p. b., seat of justice of Northampton co., Pa., 106 ms. n. e. of Harrisburgh ; from W. 199 ms. Watered by Delaware and Lehigh rivers, and Bushkill creek, and Delaware, Morris, and Lehigh canals. Seat of Lafayette college. Pop. 4,865.

Easton, c. h., p. v., seat of justice of Talbot co., Md., 45 ms. s. e. of Annapolis ; from W. 85 ms. Watered by Tread Haven creek. Pop. 1,413.

Easton, p. o., Wayne co.,O.

East Orange, p. o., Delaware co., O.

East Orange, p. o., Orange co., Vt.

East Orangeville, p. o., Wyoming co., N. Y.

East Orleans, p. v., Orleans township, Barnstable co., Mass., 98 ms. s. e. of Boston ; from W. 499 ms.

East Orrington, p. o., Penobscot co., Me., 74 ms. n. e. of Augusta : from W. 670 ms.

East Otis, v., Otis township, Berkshire co., Mass., 116 ms. w. of Boston ; from W. 371 ms.

East Otto, p. o., Otto township, Cattaraugus co., N. Y., 298 ms. w. of Albany ; from W. 348 ms.

East Painted Post, p. o., Painted Post township, Steuben co., N. Y., 207 ms. w. of Albany ; from W. 288 ms.

East Palestine, p. v., Columbiana co., O., 167 ms. n. e. of Columbus ; from W. 274 ms.

East Palmyra, p. o., Palmyra township, Wayne co., N. Y., 190 ms. w. of Albany ; from W. 361 ms.

East Parish, p. o., Oswego co., N. Y.

East Parsonsfield, p. o., Parsonsfield township, York co., Me., 80 ms. s. w. of Augusta ; from W. 538 ms.

East Pembroke, p. o., Pembroke township, Genesee co., N. Y., 256 ms. w. of Albany ; from W. 381 ms.

East Penn, p. t., Carbon co., Pa., 91 ms. e. of Harrisburgh. Watered by Mahoning and Lizzard creeks. Pop. 689.

East Pennsborough, t., Cumberland co., Pa. Watered by Susquehanna river and Conedogwinnet creek.

East Pepperell, p. o., Middlesex co., Mass.

East Peru, p. o., Clinton co., N. Y.

East Pharsalia, p. o., Pharsalia township, Chenango co., N. Y., 123 ms. w. of Albany ; from W. 340 ms.

East Pierpont. p. o., Pierpont township, St. Lawrence co., N. Y., 208 ms. n. e. of Albany ; from W. 492 ms.

East Pike, p. o., Pike township. Wyoming co., N.Y., 253 ms. w. of Albany ; from W. 354 ms.

East Pike Run, p. t., Washington co., Pa.

East Pitcairn, p. o., St. Lawrence co., N. Y. Pop. 1,358.

East Pittsfield, p. o., Pittsfield township, Somerset co., Me.

East Pittston, p. o., Pittston township, Kennebec co., Me., 13 ms. s. of Augusta ; from W. 601 ms.

East Plainfield, p. v., Plainfield township, Sullivan co., N. H., 55 ms. n. w. of Concord ; from W. 480 ms.

East Plymouth, p. o., Ashtabula co., O.

East Poestenkill, p. o., Rensselaer co., N. Y., 19 ms. e. of Albany ; from W. 389 ms.

East Poland, p. o., Poland township, Cumberland co.. Me., 43 ms. s. w. of Augusta ; from W. 573 ms.

East Point. p. o., De Kalb co., Ga.

Eastport, p. t., Washington co., Me., 176 ms. n. e. of Augusta ; from W. 769 ms. Watered by Cobscook river.

Eastport, p. v., Tishemingo co., Miss., 256 ms. n. e. of Jackson ; from W. 853 ms. Watered by Tennessee river and Bear creek.

East Portage, t., Jackson co., Mich.

East Poultney, p. o., Poultney township, Rutland co., Vt, 83 ms. s. w. of Montpelier ; from W. 441 ms.

East Princeton, p. o., Worcester co., Mass.

East Providence, p. t., Bedford co., Pa.

East Raisinville, p. o., Raisinville township, Monroe co., Mich., 44 ms. s. w. of Detroit ; from W. 493 ms. Pop. 991.

East Randolph, p. v., Randolph township, Orange co., Vt., 28 ms. s. of Montpelier ; from W. 498 ms.

East Randolph, p. o., Randolph township, Norfolk co., Mass., 14 ms. s. of Boston.

East Randolph, p. o., Cattaraugus co., N. Y.

East Randolph, p. o., Dodge co., Wis.

East Raymond, p. o., Raymond township, Cumberland co., Me., 62 ms. s. w. of Augusta ; from W. 555 ms.

East Readfield, p. o., Readfield township, Kennebec co., Me., 8 ms. w. of Augusta ; from W. 602 ms.

East Richland, p. o., Belmont co., O.

East River, p. o., Mercer co., Va.

East River, p. o., Walton co., Flor.

East Rochester, p. o., Columbiana co., O., 144 ms. n. e. of Columbus ; from W. 296 ms.

East Rodman, p. o., Rodman township, Jefferson co., N. Y., 158 ms. n. w. of Albany ; from W. 414 ms.

East Rockhill, t., Bucks co., Pa.

East Roxbury, p. o., Roxbury township. Washington co., Vt., 15 ms. s. of Montpelier ; from W. 502 ms.

EAST RUMFORD, p. t., Rumford township, Oxford co., Me., 45 ms. N. W. of Augusta ; from W. 617 ms.

EAST RUPERT, p. o., Rupert township. Bennington co., Vt., 93 ms. s. w. of Montpelier ; from W. 437 ms.

EAST SAGANAW, p. o., Saganaw co., Mich.

EAST SALEM, p. o., Salem township, Washington co., N. Y., 47 ms. N. E. of Albany ; from W. 417 ms.

EAST SALISBURY, p. v., Salisbury township, Essex co., Mass., 40 ms. N. E. of Boston ; from W. 480 ms.

EAST SANBORNTON, p. v., Sanbornton township, Belknap co., N. H., 21 ms. N. of Concord ; from W. 502 ms.

EAST SANDWICH, p. v., Sandwich township, Barnstable co., Mass., 64 ms. S. E. of Boston ; from W. 465 ms.

EAST SANDY, p. o., Venango co., Pa.

EAST SANGERVILLE, p. o., Sangerville township, Piscataquis co., Me., 81 ms. N. E. of Augusta ; from W. 676 ms.

EAST SCHUYLER, p. o., Schuyler township, Herkimer co., N. Y., 84 ms. N. W. of Albany ; from W. 396 ms.

EAST SCOTT, p. o., Cortland co., N. Y.

EAST SHEFFIELD, p. o., Sheffield township, Berkshire co., Mass., 144 ms. s. w. of Boston ; from W. 346 ms.

EAST SHARON, p. o., Potter co., Pa.

EAST SHARON, p. o., Norfolk co., Mass.

EAST SHARPSBURGH, p. o., Blair co., Pa.

EAST SHELBY, p. o., Orleans co., N. Y.

EAST SHELBURNE, p. o., Franklin co., Mass.

EAST SHELDON, p. o., Sheldon township, Franklin co., Vt., 63 ms. N. W. of Montpelier ; from W. 551 ms.

EAST SMITHFIELD, p. o., Bradford co., Pa., 151 ms. N. of Harrisburgh ; from W. 261 ms.

EAST SPRINGFIELD, p. o., Springfield township, Otsego co., N. Y., 59 ms. w. of Albany ; from W. 377 ms.

EAST SPRINGFIELD, p. o., Jefferson co., O.

EAST SPRINGHILL, p. o., Bradford co., Pa.

EAST SPRINGWATER, p. o., Livingston co., N. Y.

EAST STANDISH, p. o., Standish township. Cumberland co., Me , 58 ms. s. w. of Augusta ; from W. 542 ms.

EAST STERLING, p. o., Sterling township, Wayne co., Pa., 147 ms. N. E. of Harrisburgh ; from W. 241 ms.

EAST STONEHAM, p. o., Oxford co., Me.

EAST STOUGHTON, p. o., Stoughton township, Norfolk co., Mass., 19 ms. s. of Boston ; from W. 441 ms.

EAST STRONG, p. o., Franklin co., Me.

EAST SUFFIELD, p. o., Hartford co., Ct.

EAST SULLIVAN, p. o., Hancock co., Me.

EAST SULLIVAN, p. o., Cheshire co., N. H.

EAST SUMNER, p. o., Sumner township, Oxford co., Me., 37 ms. w. of Augusta ; from W. 603 ms.

EAST THETFORD, p. o.. Orange co., Vt.

EASTOWN, t., Chester co., Pa., 84 ms. S. E. of Harrisburgh ; from W. 124 ms. Watered by Darby creek. Pop. 710.

EAST TOWNSEND, p. o., Townsend township, Huron co., O., 106 ms. N. of Columbus ; from W. 389 ms.

EAST TRENTON, p. o., Trenton township, Hancock co., O., 98 ms. E. of Augusta ; from W. 680 ms.

EAST TROY, p. v., Walworth co., Wis., 79 ms. S. E. of Madison ; from W. 810 ms.

EAST TROY, p. o., Bradford co., Pa.

EAST TURNER, p. o., Turner township, Oxford co., Me., 26 ms. s. w. of Augusta ; from W. 587 ms.

EAST UNION, p. t., Wayne co., O., 101 ms. N. E. of Columbus ; from W. 336 ms. Pop. 1,940.

EAST UNION, p. o., Lincoln co., Me.

EAST UNITY, p. v., Unity township, Sullivan co., N. H., 44 ms. w. of Concord ; from W. 476 ms.

EAST VASSALBOROUGH, p. o., Vassalborough township. Kennebec co., Me., 15 ms. N. E. of Augusta ; from W. 610 ms.

EAST VARICK, p. o., Seneca co., N. Y.

EASTVILLE, p. v., Randolph co., Ala. ; from W. 741 ms.

EASTVILLE, c. h., p. v., seat of justice of Northampton co., Va., 151 ms. E. of Richmond ; from W. 238 ms. Watered by King's creek.

EASTVILLE, p. o., Bath co., Ky.

EAST VIRGIL, p. o., Virgil township, Cortland co., N. Y., 155 ms. w. of Albany ; from W. 314 ms.

EAST VINCENT, t., Chester co., Pa. Pop. 1,505.

EAST WAKEFIELD, p. o., Carroll co., N. H.

EAST WALLINGFORD, p. o., Rutland co., Vt.

EAST WAREHAM, p v., Wareham township, Plymouth co., Mass., 56 ms. s. of Boston ; from W. 449 ms.

EAST WASHINGTON, p. v., Washington township, Sullivan co., N. H.

EAST WATERFORD, p. v., Lack township, Juniata co., Pa., 54 ms. N. w. of Harrisburgh; from W. 130 ms Watered by Tuscarora creek.

EAST WEARE, p. v., Weare township, Hillsborough co., N. H., 10 ms. s. w. of Concord ; from W. 479 ms.

EAST WESTMORELAND, p. o., Cheshire county, N. H.

EAST WESTVILLE, p. o., Mahoning co., O.

EAST WEYMOUTH, p. v., Weymouth township, Norfolk co., Mass., 15 ms. s. of Boston ; from W. 390 ms.

EAST WHATELY, p. v., Whately township, Franklin co., Mass., 91 ms. w. of Boston ; from W. 390 ms.

EAST WHITELAND, t., Chester co., Pa., 77 ms. S. E. of Harrisburgh ; from W. 131 ms. Pop. 1.194.

EAST WILTON, p. o., Wilton township, Franklin co., Me., 37 ms. N. W. of Augusta ; from W. 615 ms.

EAST WILTON, p. o., Wilton township, Hillsborough co., N. H., 38 ms. s. w. of Concord ; from W. 456 ms.

EAST WINDHAM, p. o., Greene co., N. Y.

EAST WINDSOR, t., Hartford co., Ct., 7 ms. N. E. of Hartford ; from W. 343 ms. Watered by Connecticut and Scantic rivers. Pop. 2,633.

EAST WINDSOR HILL, p. o., East Windsor township, Hartford co., Ct., 11 ms. N. E. of Hartford ; from W. 347 ms.

EAST WINDSOR, t., Mercer co., N. J., 18 ms. from Trenton ; from W. 183 ms. Watered by Millstone river and Assunpink and Miry runs. Pop. 2,596.

EAST WINTHROP, p. o., Winthrop township, Kennebec co., Me., 6 ms. w. of Augusta ; from W. 600 ms.

EAST WOBURN, p. o.. Middlesex co., Mass.

EAST WOLWICH, p. o., Lincoln co., Me.

EAST WORCESTER, p. v., Worcester township, Otsego co., N. Y., 53 ms. from Albany ; from W. 375 ms.

EATON COUNTY, situated near the central part of Michigan. Area, 576 square miles. Soil generally fertile. Seat of Justice, Eaton. Pop. in 1440, 2,379 ; in 1850, 7,058.

EATON, p. t., Carroll co., N. H., 62 ms. N. of Concord ; from W. 546 ms. Pop. 1,743.

EATON, p. t., Madison co., N. Y., 103 ms. w. of Albany ; from W. 359 ms. Watered by sources of Chenango river. Pop. 3,944.

EATON, p.t., Wyoming co., Pa., 143 ms. N. E. of Harrisburgh ; from W. 251 ms. Watered by Bowman's creek and Susquehanna river. Pop. 914.

EATON, c. h., p. v., seat of justice of Preble co., O., 94 ms. w. of Columbus ; from W. 487 ms. Watered by St. Clair's creek. Pop. 1,346.

EATON, p. t., Eaton co., Mich., 110 ms. w. of Detroit ; from W. 580 ms Pop. 539.

EATON, t., Lorain co., O., 125 ms. N. E. of Columbus ; from W. 372 ms. Pop. 111.

EATON, p. v., Gibson co., Tenn., 142 ms. w. of Nashville ; from W. 825 ms. Watered by Forked Deer river.

EATON, p. v., Cedar co., Mo.

EATON CENTRE, p. o., Eaton township, Carroll co., N. H.

EATON RAPIDS, p. o.. Eaton co., Mich., 106 ms. w. of Detroit ; from W. 576 ms.

EATONTON, c. h., p. v., seat of justice of Putnam co., Ga., 22 ms. N. w. of Milledgeville ; from W. 627 ms.

EATONTOWN, p. v., Shrewsbury township, Monmouth co., N. J., 47 ms. E. of Trenton ; from W. 213 ms. Watered by a branch of Swimming river.

EATONVILLE, p. v., Herkimer township, Herkimer co., N. Y., 75 ms. N. W. of Albany ; from W. 394 ms.

EAU PLEINE, p. o., Portage co., O.

EBENEZER, v.. Rutherford co., N. C., 213 ms. w. of Raleigh ; from W. 450 ms.

EBENEZER, p. o., Morgan co., Ga., 51 ms. N. w. of Milledgeville ; from W. 635 ms.

EBENEZER, p. v., Effingham co., Ga., 140 ms. s. E. of Milledgeville ; from W. 661 ms. Watered by Savannah river.

EBENEZER, p. o., Holmes co., Miss.

EBENEZER, p. o., Fayette co., Tenn.

EBENEZERVILLE, p. v., York district, S. C., 84 ms. N. of Columbia ; from W. 442 ms.

EBENSBURGH, c. h., p. v., seat of justice of Cambria co., Pa., 139 ms. w. of Harrisburgh ; from W. 182 ms. Pop. 600.

ECKFORD, p. t., Calhoun co., Mich., 101 ms. w. of Detroit ; from W. 562 ms. Pop. 715.

ECKMANSVILLE, p. v., Adams co., O., 100 ms. s. of Columbus ; from W. 455 ms.

ECLIPSE, p. o., Macon co., Tenn.

ECONOMY, p. t., Beaver co., Pa., 217 ms. w. of Harristurgh; from W. 243 ms. Watered by Ohio river. Pop. 1,390.

ECONOMY. p. o., Wayne co., Ind, 76 ms. E. of Indianapolis; from W. 521 ms.

ECORCE, p. t., Wayne co., Mich. Pop. 653.

ECORE A FABRE, t., Union co., Ark.

EDDINGTON, p. t., Penobscot co., Me.. 73 ms. N. E. of Augusta; from W. 668 ms. Watered by Penobscot river.

EDDYVILLE, c. h., p. v., seat of justice of Caldwell co., Ky., 237 ms. s. w. of Frankfort; from W. 769 ms. Watered by Cumberland river.

EDDYVILLE, v., Kingston township, Ulster co., N. Y. Watered by Rondout creek and Delaware and Hudson canal.

EDDYVILLE. p. o., Cattaraugus co., N. Y.

EDDYVILLE, p. o., Wapello co., Iowa.

EDDYTOWN, v., Starkie township. Yates co., N. Y.

EDEN. p. t., Hancock co., Me., situated on the Port Mount Desert island, 101 ms. E. of Augusta; from W. 683 ms. Watered by Mount Desert sound and Frenchman's bay. Pop. 1,127.

EDEN, p. t., Lamoille co., Vt., 45 ms. N. of Montpelier; from W. 559 ms. Watered by Lamoille river. Pop. 668.

EDEN, p. t., Erie co., N. Y., 306 ms. w. of Albany; from W. 370 ms. Watered by Cauquaga and Big Two Sisters c eeks. Pop. 2,494.

EDEN. p. o.. Trumbull co., O.

EDEN, t., Licking co., O. Pop. 1,307.

EDEN. t., Seneca co., O. Watered by Honey creek. Pop. 1,584.

EDEN. p. o., Laurens district, S. C.

EDEN, p. o.. Bryan co., Ga., 138 ms. s. E. of Milledgeville; from W. 680 ms.

EDEN, p. o., Hancock co., Ind., 28 ms. E. of Indianapolis; from W. 559 ms.

EDEN, p. o., Ingham co., Mich.

EDEN, p. o., Fond du Lac co., Wis.

EDEN, p. o., Randolph co., N. C.

EDEN. p. o., McKean co., Pa., 192 ms. N. w. of Harrisburgh; from W. 281 ms.

EDEN. t., La Grange co., Ind. Pop. 649.

EDENBURGH. p. o., Cameron co., Tex.

EDENBURGH. p. o., Shenandoah co., Va.

EDENFIELD, p. o., Irwin co., Ga.

EDEN'S RIDGE, p. o.. Sullivan co., Tex., 279 ms. E. of Nashville; from W. 403 ms.

EDENTON. c. h., p. v., seat of justice of Chowan co., N. C., 182 ms. E. of Raleigh; from W. 274 ms. Watered by Chowan river and Edenton bay. Pop. 1,607.

EDENTON, p. o., Clermont co., O.

EDENTON, p. o., St. Lawrence co., N. Y.

EDEN VALLEY, p. o., Erie co., N. Y.

EDENVILLE, p. v., Warwick township, Orange co., N. Y., 119 ms., s. of Albany; from W. 267 ms.

EDGAR COUNTY, situated on the easterly boundary of Illinois. Area, 600 square miles. Soil rich. Seat of justice, Paris. Pop. in 1830, 4,076; in 1840, 8,225; in 1850, 10.692.

EDGAR, p. o., St. John Baptist parish, La.

EDGARTOWN, c. h., p. v., seat of justice of Dukes co., Martha's Vineyard, Mass., 97 ms. s. E. of Boston; from W. 979 ms. Pop. 1,990.

EDGECOMBE COUNTY, situated toward the easterly part of North Carolina. Traversed by Tar river. Area, 650 square miles. Face of the country level; soil sandy and of inferior quality. Seat of justice, Tarborough. Pop. in 1810, 12,423; in 1820, 13,276; in 1830, 14.933; in 1840, 15,708; in 1850, 17,189.

EDGECOMB, p. t., Lincoln co., Me., 32 ms. s. E. of Augusta; from W. 593 ms. Watered by Damariscotta and Sheepscot rivers.

EDGEFIELD DISTRICT, situated on the southwesterly boundary of South Carolina, with Savannah river on the southwest. Area, 1,840 square miles. Face of the country uneven. Soil of middling quality. Seat of justice, Edgefield. Pop. in 1810, 23,160; in 1820, 25,179; in 1830, 30,511; in 1840, 32,852; in 1850, 39,262.

EDGEFIELD, c. h., p. v., seat of justice of Edgefield district, S. C., 456 ms. s. w. of Columbia; from W. 554 ms.

EDGEMONT, p. t., Delaware co., Pa., 87 ms. s. E. of Harrisburgh; from W. 129 ms. Watered by Ridley creek. Pop. 623.

EDGE HILL, p. o., Montgomery co., Pa.

EDGE HILL, p. o., King George co., Va.

EDGINGTON, p. o., Rock Island co., Ill.

EDINA, c. h., p. v., seat of justice of Scotland co., Mo., 125 ms. N. of Jefferson City; from W. 700 ms. Wa tered by South Fabius river.

EDINBURGH, p. b., Erie co., Pa., 253 ms. N. w. of Harrisburgh; from W. 326 ms. Pop. 264.

EDINBURGH, p. t., Saratoga co.. N. Y., 52 ms. N. of Albany; from W. 420 ms. Watered by Sacondaga river. Pop. 1,336.

EDINBURGH. p. v., Mahoning township, Mercer co., Pa., 242 ms. N. w. of Harrisburgh; from W. 260 ms.

EDINBURGH. p. t., Portage co., O., 146 ms. N. E. of Columbus; from W. 315. Pop. 1,101.

EDINBURGH, p. v., Johnson co., Ind., 30 ms. s. of Indianapolis; from W. 581 ms. Watered by Blue river and Sugar creek.

EDINBURGH, v., seat of justice of Jones co., Iowa.

EDINBURGH, p. o., Scotland co., Me.

EDINBURGH, p. v., Leake co., Miss., 71 ms. N. E. of Jackson; from W. 947 ms.

EDINBURGH, p. t., Penobscot co., Me. Watered by Penobscot river. Pop. 93.

EDINBURGH, p. o., Garrard co., Ky.

EDINBURGH, p. o., Hillsdale co., Mich.

EDINBURGH, p. c., Lawrence co., Pa.

EDINBURGH CENTRE. p. o., Edinburgh township, Saratoga co., N. Y.

EDISTO. p. o., Lexington district, S. C.

EDISTO MILLS. p. o., Edgefield district, S. C.

EDMESTON. p. t., Otsego co., N. Y., 89 ms. w. of Albany; from W. 355 ms. Watered by Wharton's creek and Unadilla river. Pop. 1,885.

EDMONTON, p. o., Barren co., Ky.

EDMONDS, t., Washington co., Me. Watered by Cobscook bay.

EDMONSON COUNTY, situated toward the central part of Kentucky, and traversed by Green river. Area, 250 square miles. Soil generally fertile. Seat of justice, Brownsville. Pop. in 1830, 2,642; in 1840, 2,914; in 1850, 4,088.

EDMUNDS, p. o., Brunswick co., Va., 88 ms. s. of Richmond; from W. 204 ms.

EDNEYVILLE, p. o., Henderson co., N. C., 257 ms. w. of Raleigh; from W. 499 ms.

EDRAY, p. o., Pocahontas co., Va.

EDSALLVILLE, p. o., Bradford co., Pa., 161 ms. N. of Harrisburgh; from W. 268 ms.

EDWARDS COUNTY. situated in the southeasterly part of Illinois. Area, 200 square miles. Face of the country undulating; soil generally fertile. Seat of justice, Albion. Pop. in 1820, 3,444; in 1830, 1,649; in 1840, 3,070; in 1850, 3,524.

EDWARDS, p. t., St. Lawrence co., N. Y., 184 ms. N. w. of Albany; from W. 468 ms. Watered by Oswegatchie river. Pop. 1,023.

EDWARDSBURGH, p. v., Ontwa township, Cass co., Mich., 172 ms. s. w. of Detroit; from W. 617 ms. Watered by Beardsley's lake.

EDWARD'S DEPOT, p. v., Hinds co., Miss.

EDWARDSPORT. p. v., Knox co., Ind., 105 ms. s. w. of Indianapolis; from W. 672 ms.

EDWARDSVILLE, p. o., Edwards township, St. Lawrence co., N. Y.

EDWARDSVILLE, p. v., Salem township, Warren co., O.

EDWARDSVILLE, c. h., p. v., seat of justice of Madison co., Ill., 74 ms. s. of Springfield; from W. 749 ms.

EEL RIVER, p. o., Plymouth co., Mass., 42 ms. s. E. of Boston; from W. 450 ms.

EFFINGHAM COUNTY, situated on the easterly boundary of Georgia, southwest of Savannah river. Area, 396 square miles. Face of the country level; soil, sandy, but productive in cotton. Seat of justice, Springfield. Pop. in 1810, 2,586; in 1820, 3,018; in 1830, 2,969; in 1840, 3,075; in 1850, 3,864.

EFFINGHAM COUNTY, situated toward the southeasterly part of Illinois. Area, 486 square miles. Soil of middling quality. Seat of justice, Ewington. Pop. in 1840, 1,675; in 1850, 3,799.

EFFINGHAM, p. t., Carroll co.. N. H., 62 ms. N. E. of Concord; from W. 540 ms. Watered by Great Ossipee river, Ossipee lake, and Providence pond. Pop. 1,252.

EFFINGHAM, p. v., Darlington district, S. C., 133 ms. N. E. of Columbia; from W. 473 ms.

EFFINGHAM FALLS, p. o., Carroll co., N. H.

EFFORT. p. o., Monroe co., Pa.

EFIRD'S MILLS, p. o., Stanly co., N. C.

EGREMONT, t, Berkshire co., Mass. Watered by Housatonic river. Pop. 1,013.

EGYPT, p. o., Perrington township, Monroe co., N. Y.

EGYPT, p. o., Monroe co., Va., 261 ms. w. of Richmond; from W. 298 ms.

EGYPT, p. o., Effingham co., Ga.

EGYPT, p. o., Colorado co., Tex.

ELANSVILLE, p. v., Patrick co., Va., 216 ms. s. w. of Richmond; from W. 291 ms.

ELBA, p. t., Genesee co., N. Y., 255 ms. w. of Albany; from W. 380 ms. Watered by Oak Orchard creek. Pop. 1,772.

ELBA, p. o., Washtenaw co., Mich., 59 ms. w. of Detroit; from W. 535 ms.

ELBA, t., Lapeer co., Mich.

ELBA, p. o., Dodge co.. Wis.

ELBERT COUNTY, situated in the northeast part of Georgia, with Savannah river on the northeast. Area, 560 square miles. Face of the country hilly; soil, fertile. Seat of justice, Elberton. Pop. in 1810, 12,156; in 1820, 11,788; in 1830, 12,354; in 1840, 11,125; in 1850, 12,959.

ELBERTON, c. h., p. v., seat of justice of Elbert co., Ga., 111 ms. N. E. of Milledgeville; from W. 568 ms.

ELBRIDGE, p. t., Onondaga co., N. Y., 149 ms. w. of Albany; from W. 347 ms. Watered by Skaneateles lake outlet. and Erie canal. Pop. 3,994.

ELBRIDGE, p. o., Edgar co., Ill., 123 ms. E. of Springfield; from W. 655 ms.

EL DARA, p. o., Pike co., Ill.

ELDEN, p. o., Clark co., O.

ELDERSVILLE, p. v., Cross Creek township, Washington co., Pa., 231 ms. w. of Harrisburgh; from W. 254 ms.

ELDERTON, p. v., Plumb creek township. Armstrong ro., Pa., 168 ms. N. w. of Harrisburgh; from W. 222 ms.

EL DORADO COUNTY, California. Area —— square miles. Seat of justice ——. Pop. 6,842.

EL DORADO, p. o., Clarke co., Mo.

EL DORADO, p. o., Union co., Ark.

EL DORADO, p. o., Culpeper co., Va.

EL DORADO, p. o., Fond du Lac co., Wis.

EL DORADO, p. o., Fayette co., Iowa.

ELDRED, p. o., Wayne co., Pa., 180 ms. N. E. of Harrisburgh; from W. 277 ms.

ELDRED, t., Jefferson co., Pa. Pop. 492.

ELDREDVILLE, p. o., Sullivan co., Pa., 116 ms. N. of Harrisburgh; from W. 296 ms.

ELDRIDGE, p. o., Walker co., Ala.; from W. 819 ms.

ELEVATION, p. o., Johnson co., N. C.

ELGIN, p. o., Lyndon township, Cattaraugus co., N. Y., 285 ms. w. of Albany; from W. 325 ms.

ELGIN, p. v., Kane co., Ill., 199 ms. N. E. of Springfield; from W. 752 ms. Watered by Fox river.

ELIDA, p. o., Winnebago co., Ill.

ELIJAH'S CREEK, p o.. Boone co., Ky.

ELINSPORT, p. o., Lycoming co., Pa., 78 ms. N. of Harrisburgh; from W. 194 ms.

ELIZA p o., Mercer co., Ill., 158 ms. N. w. of Springfield; from W. 888 ms.

ELIZABETH, t., Essex co., N. J., 44 ms. N. E. of Trenton; from W. 213 ms. Watered by Bound and Morss brooks. Pop. 5,583.

ELIZABETH, p. t., Alleghany co., Pa. Watered by Youghiogheny and Monongahela rivers. Pop. 5,090.

ELIZABETH, p. v., Elizabeth township, Alleghany co., Pa., 192 ms. w. of Harrisburgh; from W. 218 ms. Watered by Monongahela river. Pop. 1,120.

ELIZABETH, t., Lancaster co., Pa. Watered by Trout, Hammer, Middle, and Saglock creeks. Pop. 2,309.

ELIZABETH, p. t., Lawrence co., O.

ELIZABETH, t., Miami co., O. Pop. 1,433.

ELIZABETH, v., Wood co., Va., 325 ms. w. of Richmond; from W. 304 ms. Watered by Little Kanawha river.

ELIZABETH, p. v., Harrison co., Ind., 138 ms. s. of Indianapolis; from W. 635 ms.

ELIZABETH, c. h., p. v., seat of justice of Jackson co., Ark., 118 ms. N. E. of Little Rock; from W. 1,008 ms. Watered by White river.

ELIZABETH, p. o., Joe Daviess co., Ill.

ELIZABETH CITY COUNTY, situated toward the southeasterly part of Virginia, with Chesapeake bay on the east, and Hampton Roads on the south. Area, 64 square miles. Seat of justice, Hampton. Pop. in 1810, 3,608; in 1820, 3,789; in 1830, 5,068; in 1840, 3,706; in 1850, 4,568.

ELIZABETH CITY, c. h., p. v., seat of justice of Pasquotank co., N. C., 215 ms. E. of Raleigh; from W. 283 ms. Watered by Pasquotank river.

ELIZABETHPORT. p. v., Elizabeth township. Essex co., N. J., 47 ms. N. E. of Trenton; from W. 214 ms. Watered by Staten Island Kills.

ELIZABETHTOWN, c. h., p. t., seat of justice of Essex co., N. Y., 126 ms. N of Albany; from W. 501 ms. Watered by Boquet river. Pop. 5.583.

ELIZABETHTOWN, p. b.. Elizabeth township, Essex co., N. J., 44 ms. N. E. of Trenton; from W. 213 ms. Watered by Elizabethtown creek.

ELIZABETHTOWN, p. v.. Whitewater township. Hamilton co., O., 132 ms. s. w. of Columbus; from W. 508 ms. Situated on Whitewater canal.

ELIZABETHTOWN, c. h., p. v., seat of justice of Marshall co., Va., 228 ms. N. w. of Richmond; from W. 210 ms. Watered by Grave creek. Pop. 496.

ELIZABETHTOWN, c. h., p. v., seat of justice of Hardin co., Ky., 79 ms. s. w. of Frankfort; from W. 621 ms Watered by Valley creek.

ELIZABETHTOWN, c. h., p. v., seat of justice of Bladen co., N. C., 99 ms. s. of Raleigh; from W. 387 ms. Watered by Cape Fear river.

ELIZABETHTOWN, c. h., p. v., seat of justice of Carter co., Tenn., 301 ms. E. of Nashville; from W. 414 ms. Watered by Watauga river. Pop. 319.

ELIZABETHTOWN, c. h., p. v., seat of justice of Hardin co., Ill., 219 ms. s. E. of Springfield; from W. 786 ms.

ELIZABETHTOWN, p. o., Bartholomew co., Ind.

ELIZABETHVILLE, p. o., Dauphin co., Pa., 39 ms. N. of Harrisburgh; from W. 149 ms.

ELIZAVILLE. p. v., Fleming co., Ky., 99 ms. E. of Frankfort; from W. 492 ms.

ELIZAVILLE, p. o.. Columbia co., N. Y., 44 ms. s. of Albany; from W. 333 ms.

ELK COUNTY, situated toward the northwesterly part o' Pennsylvania. Area, —— square miles. Seat of justice, Ridgeway. Pop. in 1850, 3,498.

ELK, t., Warren co., Pa. Watered by Alleghany river and Conewango creek. Pop. 414.

ELK, t., Athens co., O. Watered by Raccoon creek.

ELK, t., Monroe co., O. Pop. 955.

ELKADER, p. o., Clayton co. Iowa

ELK CREEK, p. t., Erie co., Pa., 256 ms. s. w. of Harrisburgh; from W. 329 ms. Watered by Cussawago creek. Pop. 1,535.

ELK CREEK, p. o., Grayson co., Va., 277 ms. w. of Richmond; from W. 346 ms.

ELK CROSS ROADS, p. o., Ashe co., N. C., 214 ms. w. of Raleigh.

ELK DALE, p. o., Chester co., Pa.

ELK FORK, t., Van Buren co., Mo.

ELK FORK, t., Pettis co., Mo.

ELK FURNACE, p. o., Nelson co., Va.

ELK GARDEN, p. o., Russell co., Va., 320 ms. w. of Richmond; from W. 375 ms.

ELK GROVE, p. o., Iowa co., Wis., 71 ms. s. w. of Madison; from W. 903 ms.

ELK GROVE, p. o., Cook co., Ill., 228 ms. N. E. of Springfield; from W. 741 ms.

ELK GROVE, p. o., Lafayette co., Mo.

ELKHART COUNTY, situated on the northerly boundary of Indiana, and traversed by St. Joseph's river. Area, 460 square miles. Seat of justice. Goshen. Pop. in 1830, 935; in 1840, 6,660; in 1850, 12,690.

ELKHART, p. t., Elkhart co., Ind., 154 ms. N. of Indianapolis; from W. 609 ms. Pop. 1,035.

ELKHART, p. o., Sheboygan co., Wis.

ELKHART, t., Noble co., Ind. Pop. 621.

ELKHEART, p. o., Anderson co., Tex.

ELK HORN, p. v., Franklin co., Ky., 9 ms. N. E. of Frankfort; from W. 551 ms.

ELK HORN, t., Warren co., Mo.

ELK HORN, c. h., p. v., seat of justice of Walworth co., Wis., 68 ms. s. E. of Madison; from W. 797 ms.

ELK HORN, p. o., Washington co., Ill

ELK HORN, p. o., Montgomery co., Mo.

ELK HORN GROVE, p. o., Carroll co., Ill., 179 ms. N. of Springfield; from W. 842 ms.

ELK LAKE, p. o., Susquehanna co., Pa.

ELKLAND, p. t., Tioga co., Pa., 170 ms. N. of Harrisburgh; from W. 280 ms. Watered by Cowanesque and Crooked creeks. Pop. 962.

ELK LICK, p. o., Somerset co., Pa., 145 ms. w. of Harrisburgh; from W. 162 ms.

ELK MILLS, p. o., McDonald co., Mo.

ELK PORT, p. o., Clayton co., Iowa.

ELK RIDGE, p. v., Giles co., Tenn., 65 ms. s. of Nashville; from W. 719 ms. Watered by Robison's fork of Richland creek.

ELK RIDGE LANDING, p. v., Anne Arundel co., Md., 30 ms. N. w. of Annapolis; from W. 30 ms. Watered by Patapsco river.

ELK RIVER, p. o., Clinton co., Iowa.

ELK RIVER, p. o., Benton co., Minnesota.

ELK RIVER, t., Newton co., Mo.

ELK RIVER, p. o., Franklin co., Tenn.

ELK RUN, t., Columbiana co., O., 159 ms. N. E. of Columbus; from W. 275 ms. Pop. 1,447.

ELK RUN, p. o., Fauquier co., Va.

ELK SPRINGS, p. o. Pike co., Mo.

ELK SPUR, p. o., Wilkes co., N. C.

ELKTON, p. v., Elk Run township, Columbiana co., O., 154 ms. N. E. of Columbus; from W. 276 ms. Pop. 111.

ELKTON, p. v., Giles co., Tenn., 90 ms. s. of Nashville; from W. 739 ms. Watered by Elk river.

ELKTON, c. h., p. v., seat of justice of Todd co., Ky., 187 ms. s. w. of Frankfort; from W. 711 ms. Watered by Elk creek.

ELKTON, p. v., Hickory co., Mo., 114 ms. s. w. of Jefferson city; from W. 1,050 ms.

ELKTON, p. o., Crawford co., Ill.

ELKTON, c. h., p. v., seat of justice of Cecil co., Md., 80 ms. N. E. of Annapolis; from W. 90 ms. Watered by Elk river. Pop. 1,880.

ELKTON, p. o., Umpqua co., Oregon.

ELKVILLE, p. v., Caldwell co., N. C., 189 ms. w. of Raleigh; from W. 396 ms. Watered by Yadkin river.

ELLEJAY, c. h., p. v., seat of justice of Gilmer co., Ga., 176 ms. N. W. of Milledgeville; from W. 632 ms. Watered by Ellejay and Cottercay rivers.

ELLEJOY, p. o., Blount co., Tenn., 194 ms. E. of Nashville; from W. 514 ms.

ELLENBOROUGH, p. o., Grant co., Wis.

ELLENBURGH, p. t., Clinton co., N. Y., 189 ms. N. of Albany; from W. 554 ms. Watered by English river, and sources of the Chazy. Pop. 1,504.

ELLENGOWAN, p. o., Baltimore co., Md.

ELLENVILLE, p. v., Wawarsing township, Ulster co., N. Y., 86 ms. s. w. of Albany; from W. 293 ms. Watered by Sand Bar and Good Beerkill creeks, and Delaware and Hudson canal.

ELLEROY, p. o., Stephenson co., Ill.

ELLERSLIE, p. v., Susquehanna co., Pa., 194 ms. N. E. of Harrisburgh; from W. 294 ms.

ELLERSLIE, p. v., Harris co., Ga., 108 ms. s. w. of Milledgeville; from W. 741 ms.

ELLERY, p. t., Chautauque co., N. Y., 343 ms. w. of Albany; from W. 330 ms. Watered by Chautauque lake. Pop. 2,104.

ELL GROVE, p. o., Henry co., Tenn.

ELLICOTT. t., Chautauque co., N. Y., 330 ms. w. of Albany; from W. 334 ms. Watered by Cassadaga creek and Chautauque lake outlet. Pop. 3,523.

ELLICOTT CREEK, p. o., Erie co., N. Y.

ELLICOTT'S MILLS, p. v., Anne Arundel co., Md., 40 ms. N. w. of Annapolis; from W. 45 ms. Watered by Patapsco river. Pop. 1,083.

ELLICOTTSVILLE. c. h., p. t., seat of justice of Cattaraugus co., N. Y., 293 ms. w. of Albany; from W. 335 ms. Watered by Great Valley creek and tributaries. Pop. 1,725.

ELLINGTON, p. t., Tolland co., Ct., 20 ms. N. E. of Hartford; from W. 356 ms. Pop. 1,399.

ELLINGTON, p. t., Chautauque co., N. Y., 324 ms. w. of Albany; from W. 336 ms. Watered by Clear creek. Pop. 2,001.

ELLINGTON, p. o., Outagamie co., Wis.

ELLINGWOOD'S CORNER, p. o., Waldo co., Me.

ELLIOTT, p. t., York co., Me., 102 ms. s. w. of Augusta; from W. 498 ms. Watered by Salmon Fall river. Pop. 1,803.

ELLIOTTSBURGH, p. o., Perry co., Pa., 33 ms. w. of Harrisburgh; from W. 121 ms.

ELLIOTT'S CROSS ROADS, p. o., Morgan co., Pa.

ELLIOTT'S CROSS ROADS, p. o., Clinton co., Ky.

ELLIOTTSVILLE, p. t., Piscataquis co., Me. Pop. 102.

ELLIOTTSVILLE. p. o., Knox township, Jefferson co., O., 145 ms. E. of Columbus; from W. 279 ms.

ELLIS COUNTY, Texas. Area —— square miles. Seat of justice, Waxahachie. Pop. 989.

ELLISBURGH, p. t., Jefferson co., N. Y., 169 ms. N. w. of Albany; from W. 399 ms. Watered by north and south branches of Sandy creek and Lake Ontario. Pop. 5,524.

ELLISBURGH, p. v., La Grange co., Ind., 180 ms. N. of Indianapolis; from W. 581 ms.

ELLISBURGH, p. o., Potter co., Pa.

ELLISON, p. o., Warren co., Ill.

ELLISTON, p. o., Madison co., Ky.

ELLISTON, p. o., Onondaga co., N. Y.

ELLISTOWN, p. o., Pontotoc co., Miss.

ELLISVILLE. p. v., Louisa co., Va., 66 ms. N. w. of Richmond; from W. 108 ms.

ELLISVILLE, c. h., p. v., seat of justice of Jones co., Miss., 144 ms. s. E. of Jackson; from W. 1,022 ms. Watered by Tallahala creek.

ELLISVILLE, p. v., Fulton co., Ill., 75 ms. N. w. of Springfield; from W. 827 ms.

ELLISVILLE, p. o., Columbia co., Flor.

ELLISVILLE, p. o., Bladen co., N. C.

ELLISVILLE, p. o., St. Louis co., Mo.

ELLITTSVILLE, p. v., Monroe co., Ind., 51 ms. s. w. of Indianapolis; from W. 623 ms. Pop. 74.

ELLSWORTH, c. h., p. t., seat of justice of Hancock co., Me., 89 ms. E. of Augusta; from W. 671 ms. Watered by Union river and Orphan lake. Pop. 4,009.

ELLSWORTH, t., Grafton co., N. H., 52 ms. N. of Concord; from W. 528 ms. Watered by a tributary of Pemigewasset river. Pop. 320.

ELLSWORTH, p. v., Sharon township, Litchfield co., Ct., 44 ms. w. of Hartford; from W. 330 ms.

ELLSWORTH, p. t., Mahoning co., O., 160 ms. N. E. of Columbus; from W. 299 ms. Pop. 954.

ELLSWORTH, p. v., Texas co., Tex. Watered by Big Piney fork of Gasconade river.

ELLWOOD, p. o., Muhlenburgh co., Ky.

ELM, p. o., Ballard co., Ky.

ELM BLUFF, p. o., Dallas co., Ala.

ELMER, p. o., Salem co., N. J.

ELM GROVE, p. o., Marion co., Iowa.

ELM GROVE, p. o., De Soto co., Miss., 214 ms. N. of Jackson; from W. 937 ms.

ELM GROVE, p. o., Lewis co., Mo.

ELM GROVE, p. o., Highland co., Ill.

ELM HILL, p. o., Davidson co., Tenn., 71 ms. s. E. of Nashville; from W. 673 ms.

ELMIRA, c. h., p. t., seat of justice of Chemung co., N. Y., 195 ms. s. w. of Albany; from W. 279 ms. Watered by Newton's creek and Chemung river. Pop. 8,166.

ELMIRA, p. o., Fulton co., O., 137 ms. N. w. of Columbus; from W. 468 ms.

ELMIRA, p. o., Stark co., Ill., 113 ms. N. of Springfield; from W. 827 ms.

ELMORE, p. t., Lamoille co., Vt., 20 ms. N. of Montpelier; from W. 536 ms. Watered by Lamoille river. Pop. 504.

ELMORE, p. o., Peoria co., Ill.

ELM POINT, p. o., Bond co., Ill., 65 ms. s. of Springfield; from W. 767 ms.

ELM SPRINGS, p. o., Washington co., Ark.

ELM TREE, p. o., Hancock co., Ill.

ELM WOOD, p. o., Peoria co., Ill.

ELMWOOD, p. o., Saline co., Mo.

ELON, p. o., Amherst co., Va.

ELON, p. o., Ashley co., Ark.

ELROD, p. o., Ripley co., Ind.

ELSINBOROUGH. t., Salem co., N. J., 69 ms. s. of Trenton; from W. 167 ms. Watered by Alloways and Salem creeks. Pop. 655.

ELTON, p. o., Cattaraugus co., N. Y.

ELTON, p. o., Edgefield district, S. C., 64 ms. w. of Columbia; from W. 550 ms.

ELWOOD'S BRIDGE, p. o., Delaware co., N. Y.

ELYRIA, p. t., seat of justice of Lorain co., O., 116 ms. N. E. of Columbus; from W. 374 ms. Watered by Black river. Pop. 2,658.

ELYSBURGH, p. v., Northumberland co., Pa., 79 ms. N. of Harrisburgh; from W. 189 ms.

ELYSIAN FIELDS, p. o., Harrison co., Tex.

ELYSIUM, p. o., McHenry co., Ill.

ELYSVILLE, p. o., Anne Arundel co., Md.

ELYTON, c. h., p. v., seat of justice of Jefferson co., Ala., from W. 764 ms. Watered by Cuttoochee or Valley creek.

EMANUEL COUNTY, situated toward the easterly part of Georgia. Area, 1,100 square miles. Face of the country uneven; soil sandy. Seat of justice,

Swainsborough. Pop. in 1820, 2,928 ; in 1830, 2,681 ; in 1840, 3.129 ; in 1850, 4,577.

EMAUS. p. v.. Salisbury township, Lehigh co., Pa., 87 ms. E. of Harrisburgh ; from W. 180 ms.

EMAUS, p. o., Bedford co., Va.

EMBARRASS POINT, p. o., Edgar co., Ill., 104 ms. E. of Springfield ; from W. 675 ms.

EMBDEN. p. t., Somerset co.. Me., 49 ms. N. w. of Augusta ; from W. 644 ms. Watered by Kennebec river and Seven-Mile brook. Pop. 971.

EMBDEN CENTRE, p. o., Embden township, Somerset co.. Me.

EMBREEVILLE, p. o., Chester co., Pa., 76 ms. E. of Harrisburgh ; from W. 121 ms.

EMERALD GROVE, p. o., Rock co., Wis.

EMERSON's TAN YARD, p. o.. Chatham co., N. C., 50 ms. w. of Raleigh ; from W. 338 ms.

EMERY, p. o., Fulton co., O.

EMERY's MILLS, p. o., York co., Me.

EMIGSVILLE, p. o.. York co., Pa.

EMINENCE. p. o., Logan co., Ill., 67 ms. N. of Springfield ; from W. 763 ms.

EMINENCE, p. o., Henry co., Ky.

EMINENCE, p o., Schoharie co., N. Y.

EMINENCE, c. h., p. v., seat of justice of Shannon co., Mo.

EMINENCE, p. o., Washington co., Oregon.

EMLENTON, p. o., Venango co., Pa.

EMMA, p. o., White co., Ill.

EMMET, p. o., Lake co., Ill.

EMMETT, p. t., Calhoun co., Mich. Pop. 1,582.

EMMETT, p. o., Dodge co., Wis.

EMMETTSVILLE. p. v., Randolph co., Ind.

EMMITT, p. o., Wilkinson co., Ga.

EMMITTSBURGH, p. v., Frederick co., Md., 80 ms. N. w. of Annapolis ; from W. 65 ms. Seat of Mount St. Mary's college. Pop. 812.

EMORY, p. o., Washington co , Va.

EMORY, p.o., Holmes co., Miss.

EMORY IRON WORKS, p. o , Roane co., Tenn., 150 ms. E. of Nashville.

EMPIRE, p. o., Whitesides co., Ill.

EMPIRE IRON WORKS, p. o., Trigg co., Ky.

EMUCKSFAIR, p. o., Tallapoosa co., Ala.

ENDON, p. o., Will co., Ill., 108 ms. N. E. of Springfield ; from W. 712 ms.

ENERGY, p. o., Clark co., Miss.

ENFIELD, p. t., Penobscot co., Me., 104 ms. N. E. of Augusta ; from W. 699 ms. Watered by Penobscot river. Pop. 396.

ENFIELD, p. t., Grafton co., N. H., 42 ms. N. w. of Concord ; from W. 492 ms. Watered by Stony brook and Mascomey pond. Pop. 1,742.

ENFIELD, p. t., Hampshire co., Mass., 75 ms. w. of Boston ; from W. 387 ms. Watered by Swift' river. Pop. 1,026.

ENFIELD, p. t., Hartford co., Ct., 18 ms. N. of Hartford ; from W. 353 ms. Watered by Connecticut river. Pop. 4.460.

ENFIELD, p. t., Tompkins co., N. Y., 168 ms. w. of Albany ; from W. 301 ms. Watered by tributaries of Cayuga inlet. Pop. 2.117.

ENFIELD, p. v., Halifax co., N. C., 76 ms. N, E. of Raleigh ; from W. 222 ms.

ENFIELD. p. v., King William co.. Va., 24 ms. N. E. of Richmond ; from W. 138 ms.

ENFIELD CENTRE, p. o., Enfield township, Tompkins co.. N. Y.

ENGELVILLE, p. o., Schoharie co., N. Y.

ENGLISH NEIGHBORHOOD, p. v., Hackensack township, Bergen co., N. J., 67 ms. N. E. of Trenton ; from W. 233 ms.

ENGLISH PRAIRIE, p. v., McHenry co., Ill.

ENGLISH SETTLEMENT, p. o., Marion co., Iowa.

ENGLISHTOWN, p. v., Freehold township, Monmouth co., N. J., 31 ms. E. of Trenton ; from W. 197 ms. Watered by Matchaponix creek.

ENNISVILLE, p. v., Barre township, Huntingdon co., Pa., 80 ms. w. of Harrisburgh ; from W. 172 ms. Watered by Standingstone creek.

ENOCH. p. t., Monroe co., O. 105 ms. E. of Columbus ; from W. 300 ms. Pop. 1,439.

ENON MILLS, p. o., Orange co., N. C., 45 ms. N. w. of Raleigh ; from W. 279 ms.

ENON, p. o. Bureau co., Ill.

ENON, p. o., Macon co., Ala.

ENON, p. o., Clark co., O., 50 ms. w. of Columbus ; from W. 443 ms.

ENON GROVE, p. o., Heard co., Ga.

ENON VALLEY, p. o., Lawrence co., Pa., 243 ms. w. of Harrisburgh ; from W. 269 ms.

ENOREE, p. o., Spartanburgh district, S. C.

ENOSBURGH. p. t., Franklin co.,Vt., 56 ms. N. of Montpelier ; from W. 558 ms. Watered by Messique river and tributaries. Pop. 2,009.

ENOSBURGH FALLS, p.v., Enosburgh township, Franklin co., Vt.

ENTERPRISE, p. o., Lancaster co., Pa., 45 ms. s. E. of Harrisburgh ; from W. 120 ms.

ENTERPRISE, p. o., Orange co., Flor.

ENTERPRISE, p. o., Wayne co., Ill.

ENTERPRISE, p. o., Shiawassee co., Mich.

ENTERPRISE, p. o., McDonald co., Mo.

ENTERPRISE, p. o., Clark co., Miss.

ENTERPRISE, p. o., Preble co., O.

ENTERPRISE. p. o., Johnson co., Ark.

EOLIA, p. o., Dane co., Wis.

EOLIA, p. o., Tallapoosa co., Ala.

EPHRATA, p. t., Fulton co., N. Y., 58 ms. N. w. of Albany ; from W. 402 ms. Watered by Garoga and Zimmerman's creek. Pop. 2,079.

EPHRATA, p. t., Lancaster co., Pa., 38 ms. E. of Harrisburgh ; from W. 127 ms. Pop. 1,979.

EPPING, p. t., Rockingham co., N. H., 30 ms. E. of Concord ; from W. 477 ms. Watered by Lamprey and North rivers. Pop. 1,663.

EPSOM, p. t., Merrimack co., N. H., 12 ms. E. of Concord ; from W. 482 ms. Watered by Suncook river. Pop. 1,366.

EQUALITY, p. v., Mecklenburgh co., N. C., 166 ms. w. of Raleigh ; from W. 405 ms.

EQUALITY, p. o., Anderson district, S. C., 127 ms. w. of Columbia ; from W. 522 ms.

EQUALITY, t., Miller co., Mo.

EQUALITY, c. h., p. v., seat of justice of Gallatin co., Ill.. 187 ms. s. of Springfield ; from W. 776 ms. Watered by Saline creek. Pop. 794.

EQUALITY, p. o., Coosa co., Ala.

EQUATOR, p. o., Lee co., Ill.

EQUINUNK, p. o., Wayne co., Pa.

ERASMUS, p. o., Lincoln co., N. C.

ERCILDOWN, p. o., Chester co., Pa,

ERIE COUNTY, situated on the westerly boundary of New York, with Lake Erie and Niagara river on the west, Area, 876 square miles. Face of the country, in the easterly part, hilly, in the westerly part, level Soil fertile. Seat of justice, Buffalo. Pop. in 1820, 15,668 ; in 1830, 35,710 ; in 1840, 62,465 ; in 1850, 100,000.

ERIE COUNTY, situated at the northwesterly corner of Pennsylvania, south of Lake Erie. Area, 720 square miles. Face of the country undulating ; soil fertile. Seat of justice, Erie. Pop. in 1810, 3,758 ; in 1820, 8,553 ; in 1830, 16,906 ; in 1840, 31,344 ; in 1850, 38.742.

ERIE COUNTY, situated on the northerly boundary of Ohio, south of Lake Erie. Area, 150 square miles. Soil fertile. Seat of justice, Sandusky City. Pop. in 1840, 12.599 ; in 1850, 18,568.

ERIE, c. h., p. v., seat of justice of Erie co., Pa., 270 ms. N. w. of Harrisburgh ; from W. 343 ms. Watered by Presque Isle bay, Lake Erie. Pop. 5.858.

ERIE, v., Green co., Ala. ; from W. 865 ms. Watered by Black Warrior river.

ERIE, t., Ottawa co., O. Watered by Portage river. Pop. 292.

ERIE. p. t., Monroe co., Mich., 47 ms. s. w. of Detroit; from W. 476 ms. Watered by Vance river and Bay creek. Pop. 1,144.

ERIE, p. o., Whitesides co., Ill.

ERIE, p. o., Roane co., Tenn.

ERIE, p. o., Camden co., Mo.

ERIEVILLE. p. v., Nelson township, Madison co.. N. Y., 110 ms. w. of Albany ; from W. 357 ms.

ERINE, p. t., Chemung co., N. Y., 195 ms. w. of Albany ; from W. 291 ms. Watered by Cayuta creek. Pop. 1,833.

ERINE, p. o., Merriweather co., Ga., 88 ms. w. of Milledgeville ; from W. 708 ms.

ERINE, p. o., McHenry co., Ill.

ERINE, p. o., Chickasaw co., Miss.

ERINE, p. o., Jasper co., Tex.

ERINE SHADES, p. o., Henrico co., Va.

ERROL, p. t., Coos co., N. H., 100 ms. N. of Concord ; from W. 616 ms. Watered by Androscoggin and Mogalloway rivers and Umbagog lake. Pop. 138.

ERWING, p. t., Franklin co., Mass., 79 ms. w. of Boston; from W. 412 ms. Watered by Miller's and Connecticut rivers. Pop. 449.

ERWIN, p. t., Steuben co., N. Y., 217 ms. w. of Albany; from W. 282 ms. Watered by Conhocton, Tioga, and Chemung rivers. Pop. 1,435.

ERWIN CENTRE, p. o., Erwin township, Steuben co., N. Y.

ERWINNA, p. b., Bucks co., Pa., 123 ms. E. of Harrisburgh; from W. 187 ms. Watered by Delaware river.

ERWINSVILLE, p. v., Cleveland co., N. C., 201 ms. w. of Raleigh; from W. 438 ms.

ERWINTON, p. o., Barnwell district, S. C., 237 ms. s. of Columbia; from W. 633 ms.

ESCAMBIA COUNTY, situated at the northwest corner of Florida, with Pensacola bay and the Gulf of Mexico on the south. Area, 600 square miles. Seat of justice, Pensacola. Pop. in 1830, 3,386; in 1840, 3,993; in 1850, 4,351.

ESCOHEAG, p. o., Kent co., R. I.

ESMOND'S CORNERS, p. o., Calhoun co., Mich.

ESON HILL, p. o., Paulding co., O.

ESOPUS, p. t., Ulster co., N. Y., 66 ms. s. of Albany; from W. 307 ms. Watered by Hudson, Wallkill, and Rondout rivers. Pop. 2,900.

ESPERANCE, p. v., Schoharie township, Schoharie co., N. Y., 29 ms. w. of Albany; from W. 396 ms. Pop. 1,428.

ESPY, p. v., Columbia co., Pa., 87 ms. N. of Harrisburgh; from W. 197 ms. Watered by Susquehanna river.

ESPYVILLE, p. v., Crawford co., Pa., 255 ms. N. w. of Harrisburgh; from W. 313 ms.

ESSEX COUNTY, situated at the northeast corner of Vermont, with Connecticut river on the east. Area, 225 square miles. Face of the country hilly and mountainous; soil, on the streams, fertile. Seat of justice, Guildhall. Pop. in 1810, 3,087; in 1820, 3,284; in 1830, 3,981; in 1840, 4,226; in 1850, 4,650.

ESSEX COUNTY, situated at the northeast corner of Massachusetts, with the Atlantic ocean and Massachusetts bay on the east, and traversed by Merrimac river. Face of the country hilly; soil of middling quality. Seats of justice, Ipswich, Salem, and Newburyport. Pop. in 1810, 71,883; in 1820, 74,655; in 1830, 82.887; in 1840, 94,987; in 1850, 131,300.

ESSEX COUNTY, situated in the northeasterly part of New York, on the westerly side of Lake Champlain. Area, 1,779 square miles. Face of the country hilly and mountainous; soil generally sterile. Seat of justice, Elizabethtown. Pop. in 1810, 9,477; in 1820, 12,811; in 1830, 19,387; in 1840, 23,634; in 1850, 30,993.

ESSEX COUNTY, situated toward the northeasterly part of New Jersey. Area, 241 square miles. Face of the country hilly; soil fertile.' Seat of justice, Newark. Pop. in 1810. 25,984; in 1820, 30,793; in 1830, 41,928; in 1840, 44.621; in 1850, 73,944.

ESSEX COUNTY, situated in the easterly part of Virginia, with Rappahannock river on the northeast. Area, 280 square miles. Face of the country moderately hilly; soil of middling quality. Seat of justice, Tappahannock. Pop. in 1810, 9,376; in 1820, 9,909; in 1830, 10,541; in 1840, 11,309; in 1850, 10,206.

ESSEX, p. t., Chittenden co., Vt., 48 ms. N. w. of Montpelier; from W. 523 ms. Watered by Onion, Brown's, and Stevens' rivers. Pop. 2,052.

ESSEX, p. v., Essex co., Mass., 32 ms. N. E. of Boston; from W. 472 ms. Watered by Massachusetts bay. Pop. 1,585.

ESSEX, p. v., Saybrook township, Middlesex co., Ct., 37 ms. s. of Hartford; from W. 334 ms. Watered by Connecticut river. Pop. 950.

ESSEX, p. t., Essex co., N. Y., 138 ms. N. of Albany; from W. 509 ms. Watered by Boquet river and lake Champlain. Pop. 2,351.

ESSEX, p. o., Clinton co., Mich.

ESSEX, p. o., Fulton co., O.

ESTALLINE FURNACE, p. o., Augusta co., Va.

ESTELVILLE, p. o., Atlantic co., N. J.

ESTILL COUNTY, situated toward the easterly part of Kentucky. and traversed by Kentucky river. Area, 864 square miles. Seat of justice, Irvine. Pop. in 1810, 2,082; in 1820, 3,507; in 1830, 4,618; in 1840, 5,535; in 1850, 5,985.

ESTILLVILLE, c. h.. p. v., seat of justice of Scott co., Va., 344 ms. w. of Richmond; from W. 370 ms. Watered by Moccassin creek.

ESTILL'S MILLS, p. o., Platte co., Mo.

ETHERIDGE, p. o., Jones co., Ga.

ETNA, p. t., Penobscot co., Me., 61 ms. N. E. of Au-

gusta; from W. 656 ms. Watered by a branch of Sebasticook river. Pop. 802.

ETNA, p. v., Dryden township, Tompkins co., N. Y., 169 ms. w. of Albany; from W. 302 ms. Watered by Fall creek.

ETNA, p. o., Hanover co., Va.

ETNA, p. o., Paulding co.. Ga.

ETNA, p. o., Lapeer co., Mich.

ETNA, p. v., Lima township, Licking co., O., 17 ms. E. of Columbus; from W. 376 ms. Pop. 1,307.

ETNA, p. o., Whitley co., Ind.

ETNA CENTRE, p. o., Etna township, Penobscot co., Me.

ETOWAH, p. o., Cass co., Ga.

ETTERS, p. o., York co., Pa.

EUBANKS, p. o., Columbia co., Ga., 117 ms. N. E. of Milledgeville; from W. 585 ms.

EUCLID, p. o., Clay township, Onondaga co., N. Y., 142 ms. w. of Albany; from W. 362 ms.

EUCLID, p. t., Cuyahoga co., O., 155 ms. N. E. of Columbus; from W. 367 ms. Watered by Lake Erie. Pop. 1,034.

EUFAULA, p. v., Barbour co., Ala.; from W. 809 ms. Watered by Chattahoochee river.

EUGENE, p. o., Vermilion co., Ind., 85 ms. w. of Indianapolis; from W. 657 ms. Watered by Big Vermilion river.

EUHARLEY, p. o., Cass co., Ga.

EULALIA, t.. Potter co., Pa., 187 ms. N. w. of Harrisburgh; from W. 279 ms. Watered by east branch of Sinnemahony river and tributaries. Pop. 288.

EULOGY, p. o., Holmes co., Miss.

EUPHEMIA, p. o., Preble co., O.

EUREKA, p. o., Winnebago co., Wis.

EUREKA MILLS, p. o., Greene co., O.

EUTAW, c. h., p. v., seat of justice of Greene co., Ala. EUTAW, p. o., De Soto co., Miss., 215 ms. N. of Jackson; from W. 928 ms.

EVANS, p. t., Erie co., N. Y., 311 ms. w. of Albany; from W. 368 ms. Watered by Little and Big Sisters creeks, and Lake Erie. Pop. 2,182.

EVANSBURGH, p. v., Crawford county, Pa., 242 ms. N. w. of Harrisburgh; from W. 312 ms.

EVANSBURGH, p. o., Coshocton co., O.

EVANS' MILLS, v., Le Roy township, Jefferson co., N. Y., 165 ms. N. w. of Albany; from W. 425 ms. Watered by Pleasant creek.

EVANS' MILLS, p. o., Chatham co., N. C.

EVANSPORT, p. v., Defiance co., O., 165 ms. N. w. of Columbus; from W. 517 ms. Pop. 165.

EVANSVILLE, p. v., Preston co., Va., 266 ms. N. w. of Richmond; from W. 190 ms.

EVANSVILLE, c. h., p. v., seat of justice of Vander burgh co., Ind., 172 ms. s. w. of Indianapolis. Watered by Ohio river. Pop. 3,663.

EVANSVILLE, p. o., Washington co., Ark., 189 ms. N. w. of Little Rock; from W. 1,215.

EVANSVILLE, p. o., Randolph co., Ill.

EVANSVILLE, p. o., Rock co., Wis.

EVENING SHADE, p. o., Lawrence co., Ark.

EVERGREEN, p. v., Anderson district, S. C., 131 ms. N. w. of Columbia; from W. 560 ms.

EVERGREEN, p. o., Conecuh co., Ala.

EVERETT'S SPRING, p. o., Floyd co., Ga.

EVERITTSTOWN, p. o., Hunterdon co., N. J.

EVERITTSVILLE, p. o., Wayne co., N. C.

EVERTON, p. v., Fayette co., Ind., 66 ms. E. of Indianapolis; from W. 522 ms.

EVERSHAM, t., Burlington co., N. J., 34 ms. s. of Trenton; from W. 150 ms. Watered by Rancocus and Haines' creeks. Pop. 3,067.

EWING, p. o., Hocking co., O.

EWING, p. o., Franklin co., Ill.

EWING, t., Franklin co., Mass. Pop. 449.

EWING, t., Mercer co., N. J. Pop. 1,480.

EWING'S NECK, p. o., Cumberland co., N. J.

EWINGTON, c. h., p. v., seat of justice of Effingham co., Ill., 85 ms. s. E. of Springfield; from W. 714 ms. Watered by Little Wabash river.

EWINGTON, p. o., Gallia co., O.

EXCHANGE, p. o., Warren co., N. C., 57 ms. N. E. of Raleigh; from W. 237 ms.

EXCHANGEVILLE, p. o.. Mercer co., Pa.

EXETER, p. t., Penobscot co., Me., 79 ms. N. E. of Augusta; from W. 674 ms. Watered by tributaries of Kenduskeag river. Pop. 1,853.

EXETER, t., Washington co., R. I., 24 ms. s. w. of Providence. Watered by Wood river. Pop. 1,620.

EXETER, p. t., Otsego co., N. Y., 77 ms. w. of Albany ; from W. 367 ms. Watered by Butternut and Wharton's creeks. Pop. 1,526.

EXETER, p. t., Luzerne co., Pa., 129 ms. N. E. of Harrisburgh ; from W. 237 ms. Watered by Susquehanna river, Gardner's creek, and Cascade run. Pop. 833.

EXETER, p. t., Monroe co., Mich. Pop. 458.

EXETER, t., Berks co., Pa. Watered by Manokesy and Roush creeks. Pop. 2,074.

EXETER, v., Scott co., Ill., 47 ms. w. of Springfield ; from W. 827 ms. Watered by Mauvaise Terre river.

EXETER, p. o., Greene co., Wis.

EXETER, p. t., Rockingham co., N. H., 27 ms. s. E. of Concord ; from W. 480 ms. Watered by Exeter or Swamscot river. Pop. in 1830, 2,759 ; in 1840, 2,925 ; in 1850, 2,329.

EXETER MILLS, p. o., Penobscot co., Me.

EXPERIMENT MILLS, p. o., Monroe co., Pa., 129 ms. N. E. of Harrisburgh ; from W. 222 ms.

F.

FABER'S MILLS, p. o., Nelson co., Va., 91 ms. w. of Richmond ; from W. 146 ms.

FABIUS, p. t., Onondaga co., N. Y., 120 ms. w. of Albany ; from W. 337 ms. Watered by Toughnioga river. Pop. 2,410.

FABIUS, p. o., Hardy co., Va., 187 ms. N. w. of Richmond ; from W. 115 ms.

FABIUS, t., Marion co., Mo. Pop. 1,455.

FACILITY, p. o., McMinn co., Tenn., 163 ms. s. E. of Nashville ; from W. 544 ms.

FACTOR'S FORK, p. o., Wayne co., Tenn.

FACTORY HILL, p. o., Nansemond co., Va.

FACTORY POINT, p. o., Manchester village, Bennington co., Vt., 93 ms. s. of Montpelier ; from W. 430 ms.

FACTORYVILLE, p. v., Tioga co., N. Y., 178 ms. s. w. of Albany ; from W. 265 ms. Watered by Cayuta creek.

FACTORYVILLE, p. v., Castleton township, Richmond co., Staten Island, N. Y., 153 ms. s. of Albany ; from W. 231 ms. Watered by Kill van Kull.

FACTORYVILLE, p. v., Braintrim township, Wyoming co., Pa., 156 ms. N. E. of Harrisburgh ; from W. 263 ms.

FAIR BLUFF, p. o., Columbus co , N. C., 125 ms. s. of Raleigh ; from W. 415 ms.

FAIRBURN, p. o., Fayette co., Ga.

FAIRDALE, p. v., Rush township, Susquehanna co., Pa., 169 ms. N. E. of Harrisburgh ; from W. 279 ms.

FAIR DEALING, p. o., Calloway co., Ky., 54 ms. s. w. of Frankfort ; from W, 786 ms.

FAIRFAX COUNTY, situated in the northeastern part of Virginia, with Potomac river on the northeast. Area, 450 square miles. Face of the country broken ; soil generally sterile. Seat of justice, Fairfax. Pop. in 1810, 13,111 ; in 1820, 11,404 ; in 1830, 9,206 ; in 1840, 9,370 ; in 1850, 10,682.

FAIRFAX, p. t., Franklin co., Vt., 57 ms. N. w. of Montpelier ; from W. 535 ms. Watered by Lamoille river. Pop. 2,111.

FAIRFAX, c. h., p. v., seat of justice of Fairfax co., Va., 121 ms N. of Richmond ; from W. 21 ms.

FAIRFAX, c. h., v., seat of justice of Culpeper co., Va., 94 ms. N. w. of Richmond ; from W. 76 ms. Watered by Mountain creek.

FAIRFAX, p. o., Highland co., O.

FAIRFAX, p. o., Monroe co., Ind.

FAIRFIELD COUNTY, situated at the southwest corner of Connecticut, with Long Island sound on the south. Area, 630 square miles. Face of the country diversified with hills and valleys ; soil well cultivated and productive. Seats of justice. Fairfield and Danbury. Pop. in 1810, 40,950 ; in 1820, 42,739 ; in 1830, 46950 ; in 1840, 49,917 ; in 1850, 59,775.

FAIRFIELD DISTRICT, situated toward the central part of South Carolina, with Broad river on the west. Area, 796 square miles. Face of the country uneven ; soil fertile. Seat of justice, Winnsborough. Pop. in 1810. 11,857 ; in 1820, 17,174 ; in 1830, 21,546 ; in 1840, 20,165 ; in 1850, 21,404.

FAIRFIELD COUNTY, situated toward the southeast part of Ohio. Area, 540 square miles. Face of the country level, interspersed with broken rocky ranges ; soil varied. In the northern, alluvial part rich ; toward the south, less fertile. Seat of justice, Lancaster. Pop. in 1810, 11,361 ; in 1820, 16,633 ; in 1830, 24,788 ; in 1840, 31,924 ; in 1850, 30,264.

FAIRFIELD, p. t., Somerset co., Me., 22 ms. N. of Augusta ; from W. 617 ms. Watered by Kennebec river. Pop. 2,452.

FAIRFIELD, p. t., Franklin co., Vt., 56 ms. N. w. of Montpelier ; from W. 544 ms. Watered by tributaries of Missisque river. Pop. 2.591.

FAIRFIELD, c. h., p. v., seat of justice, together with

Danbury, of Fairfield co., Ct., 58 ms. s. w. of Hartford ; from W. 279 ms. Pop. 3,614.

FAIRFIELD, p. t., Herkimer co., N. Y., 79 ms. w. of Albany ; from W. 398 ms. Watered by West Canada creek. Pop. 1,646.

FAIRFIELD, t., Cumberland co., N. J., 77 ms. s. of Trenton ; from W. 183 ms. Watered by Cohansey, Nantuxett, and Cedar creeks. Pop. 2.133.

FAIRFIELD, v., Caldwell township, Essex co., N. J., 62 ms. N. E. of Trenton ; from W. 228 ms.

FAIRFIELD, p. v., Hamilton township, Adams co., Pa. 43 ms. s. w. of Harrisburgh ; from W. 82 ms. Watered by Middle creek.

FAIRFIELD, t., Crawford co., Pa., 227 ms. N. w. of Harrisburgh ; from W. 228 ms. Pop 1,224.

FAIRFIELD, t., Westmoreland co., Pa., 148 ms. W. of Harrisburgh : from W. 170 ms. Watered by Conemaugh river. Pop. 3.352.

FAIRFIELD, t., Butler co., O., 101 ms. s. w. of Columbus ; from W. 488 ms. Pop. 5.978.

FAIRFIELD, t., Columbiana co., O., 160 ms. N. E. of Columbus ; from W. 275 ms. Pop. 2,385.

FAIRFIELD, t., Highland co., O., 65 ms. s. w. of Columbus , from W. 445 ms. Pop. 3,174.

FAIRFIELD, t., Tuscarawas co., O., 113 ms. N. E. of Columbus ; from W. 308 ms. Pop. 871.

FAIRFIELD, t., Huron co., O., 108 ms. N. of Columbus ; from W. 388 ms. Pop. 1,594.

FAIRFIELD, p. v., Nelson co., Ky., 47 ms. s. w. of Frankfort ; from W. 589 ms. Watered by a tributary of Salt river.

FAIRFIELD, t., Madison co., O. Pop. 623.

FAIRFIELD, v Rockingham co., Va., 135 ms. N. w. of Richmond ; from W. 177 ms.

FAIRFIELD, p. v., Rockbridge co., Va.

FAIRFIELD, p. v., Bedford co., Tenn., 50 ms. s. of Nashville.

FAIRFIELD, p, v., Pickens co., Ala. ; from W. 873 ms.

FAIRFIELD, p. v., Franklin co., Ind., 73 ms. E. of Indianapolis ; from W. 515 ms. Pop. 910.

FAIRFIELD, c. h., p. v., seat of justice of Wayne co., Ill., 145 ms. s. E. of Springfield ; from W. 751 ms.

FAIRFIELD, p. v., Benton co., Mo., 90 ms. s. w. of Jefferson city ; from W. 1,026 ms.

FAIRFIELD, p. o., Freestone co., Tex.

FAIRFIELD, p. t., Lenawee co., Mich. Pop. 1,327.

FAIRFIELD, p. o., Jefferson co., Iowa.

FAIRFIELD, p. v., Walworth co., Wis., 66 ms. s. E. of Madison ; from W. 810 ms.

FAIRFIELD, p. v., Greene co., O., 56 ms. s. w. of Columbus ; from W. 452 ms. Watered by Mad river.

FAIRFIELD, p. o., Hyde co., N. C.

FAIRFIELD CORNERS, p. o., Fairfield township, Somerset co., Me., 28 ms. N. of Augusta ; from W. 623 ms.

FAIR FOREST, p. o., Union district, S. C.

FAIR FOREST, p. o., Desha co., Ark.

FAIR GARDEN, p. o., Sevier co., Tenn., 224 ms. E. of Nashville ; from W. 484 ms.

FAIR GROVE, p. o., Davidson co., N. C., 96 ms. w. of Raleigh ; from W. 326 ms.

FAIR HAVEN, p. t., Rutland co., Vt., 79 ms. s. w. of Montpelier ; from W. 451 ms. Watered by Castleton and Poultney rivers. Pop. 902.

FAIR HAVEN, p. t. Bristol co., Mass., 59 ms. s. of Boston ; from W. 436 ms. Watered by Accushnet river.

FAIR HAVEN, p. v., New Haven and East Haven townships, New Haven co., Ct., 38 ms. s. of Hartford ; from W. 302 ms. Watered by Quinnipiac river.. Pop. 1,317.

FAIR HAVEN, p. v., Israel township, Preble co., O, 112 ms. w. of Columbus ; from W. 505 ms.

FAIR HAVEN, p. o., Carroll co, Ill.
FAIR HILL, p. o., Cecil co., Md.
FAIR HILL, p. o.! Marshall co., Va., 354 ms. N. w. of Richmond; from W. 261 ms.
FAIR LAND, p. o., Livingston co., Mo.
FAIRLEE, p. t., Orange co., Vt., 38 ms. s. E. of Montpelier; from W. 506 ms. Watered by Connecticut river. Pop. 575.
FAIRMOUNT, t., Luzerne co., Pa. Pop. 958.
FAIRMONT, p. o., Marion co., Va.
FAIRMONT, p o., Clark co.. Mo.
FAIR MOUNT. p. o., Onondaga co., N. Y.
FAIR MOUNT. p. o., Hunterdon co., N. J.
FAIR MOUNT. p. o., Miami co., O.
FAIR MOUNT. p. o., Cass co., Ga.
FAIR MOUNT SPRINGS, p. o., Luzerne co., Pa.
FAIRPLAY, p. o., Hot Springs co., Ark.
FAIRPLAY, p. v., Greene co., Ind., 77 ms. s. w. of Indianapolis; from W. 644 ms. Watered by White river.
FAIRPLAY, p. o., Grant co., Wis., 102 ms. w. of Madison, from W. 892 ms.
FAIRPLAY, p. o., Benton co., Ala.
FAIRPLAY, p. o., Panola co., Tex.
FAIRPLAY, p. o., Morgan co., Ga.
FAIR POINT, p. o., Cooper co., Mo.
FAIRPORT, p. v., Elmira township, Chemung co. N. Y., 192 ms. s. w. of Albany; from W. 285 ms. Situated on the Chemung canal.
FAIRPORT. p. v., Painsville township, Lake co., O., 178 ms. N. E. of Columbus; from W. 352 ms. Watered by Grand river and Lake Erie.
FAIRPORT, t.. Ashtabula co., O.
FAIRTON, p. v., Fairfield township, Cumberland co., N. J., 71 ms. s. of Trenton; from W. 182 ms. Watered by Mill creek and Rattlesnake run.
FAIRVIEW, p. o., Farmersville township, Cattaraugus co., N. Y., 270 ms. w. of Albany; from W. 337 ms.
FAIRVIEW, p. t., York co., Pa., 7 ms. from Harrisburgh; from W. 110 ms. Watered by Yellow Breaches, Fishing, and Newberry creeks. Pop. 2,138.
FAIRVIEW, v., Brooke co., Va., 354 ms. N. w. of Richmond; from W. 267 ms.
FAIRVIEW, p. v., Buncombe co., N. C., 245 ms. w. of Raleigh; from W. 482 ms.
FAIRVIEW, p. v., Greenville district, S. C., 88 ms. N.w. of Columbia; from W. 514 ms.
FAIRVIEW, p. v., Oxford township, Guernsey co., O., 95 ms. E. of Columbus; from W. 298 ms.
FAIRVIEW, p. v., Fulton co., Ill., 83 ms. N. w. of Springfield; from W. 809 ms. Pop. 1,047.
FAIRVIEW, p. o., Pettis co., Mo., 80 ms. w. of Jefferson city; from W. 1,016 ms.
FAIRVIEW, p. o., Washington co., Md.
FAIRVIEW, p. o., Franklin co., Ga.
FAIRVIEW, p. o., Randolph co., Ind.
FAIRVIEW, p. o., Jones co., Iowa.
FAIRVIEW, p. t. Erie co., Pa., 267 ms. N. w. of Harrisburgh; from W. 342 ms. Watered by Walnut and Elk creeks, and Lake Erie. Pop. 1,760.
FAIRVIEW, p. o., Todd co., Ky.
FAIRVIEW, p. o., Marion co., Tenn.
FAIRVIEW, p. o., Hancock co., Va.
FAIRVIEW VILLAGE, p. o., Montgomery co., Pa.
FAIRVILLE, p. v., Arcadia township, Wayne co., N. Y., 192 ms. w. of Albany; from W. 363 ms.
FAIRVILLE, p. o., Chester co., Pa.
FAIR WATER, p. o., Fond du Lac co., Wis.
FAIR WEATHER, p. o., Adams co., Ill.
FAISON'S DEPOT, p. o., Duplin co., N. C., 70 ms. s. E. of Raleigh; from W. 300 ms.
FALKLAND, p. o., Pitt co., N. C., 91 ms. E. of Raleigh; from W. 277 ms.
FALLASBURGH, p. o., Kent co., Mich.
FALL CREEK, p. o., Marion co., Ind.
FALLEN TIMBER, p. o., Cambria co., Pa.
FALLING BRIDGE, p. o., Campbell co., Va., 102 ms. s. w. of Richmond; from W. 202 ms.
FALLING CREEK, p. o., Wayne co., N. C., 61 ms. s. E. of Raleigh; from W. 291 ms.
FALLING MILL. p. o., Moore co., N. C.
FALLING SPRING, p. o., Green Brier co., Va., 232 ms. w. of Richmond; from W. 267 ms.
FALLING SPRING, p. o., Clark co., Miss.
FALLING WATER, p. o., White co., Tenn.
FALLING WATERS, p. v., Berkeley co., Va., 178 ms. N. of Richmond; from W. 80 ms. Watered by Potomac river.
FALLOWFIELD, t., Crawford co., Pa.

FALL RIVER, p. t., Bristol co., Mass., 51 ms. s. of Boston. It lies on the outlet of Watuppa pond, a considerable body of water, which passes through Fall river into the Taunton, affording a good and constant waterpower. Along this stream are numerous mills, and factories of cotton, wool, machinery, &c., which produce articles to a large amount. Having a good harbor at the entrance of Taunton river into Bristol bay, its commerce is considerable. Ships of a large class, engaged in both the whale-fishery and foreign trade, anchor at its wharves. Besides manufactories, the town contains churches, banks, hotels, and schools of a superior order. There is a line of splendid steamboats running daily between this place and New York, and the Fall River railroad connects it with Boston. The population in 1840, was 9,000; in 1850, 11,524.
FALL RIVER, p. o., Columbia co., Wis.
FALLS, p. t. Wyoming co., Pa., 153 ms. s. E. of Harrisburgh; from W. 257 ms. Watered by Susquehanna and Buttermilk Falls creek. Pop. 798.
FALLS, t., Bucks co., Pa. Watered by Delaware river and Penn's and Scott's creeks. Pop. 1,788.
FALLS, t., Hocking co., O. Pop. 1,774.
FALLS, p. o., Lincoln co., N. C., 191 ms. w. of Raleigh; from W. 428 ms.
FALLSBURGH, p. t., Sullivan co., N. Y., 197 ms. s. w. of Albany; from W. 304 ms. Watered by Navesink river, and the head branches of Rondout creek.
FALLSBURGH, p. t. Licking co., O., 65 ms. N. E. of Columbus; from. 363 ms. Pop. 1,206.
FALLS CHURCH, p. o., Fairfax co., Va.
FALLS MILL, p. o., Cabell co., Va.,
FALLSINGTON, p. o., Bucks co., Pa.
FALLS OF BLAINE, p. o., Lawrence co., Ky.
FALLS OF SCHUYLKILL, p. v., Philadelphia co., Pa., 101 ms. s. E. of Harrisburgh; from W. 142 ms.
FALLS OF ST. CROIX, p. o., St. Croix co., Wis.
FALLSTON, p. t., Beaver co., Pa., 229 ms. w. of Harrisburgh; from W. 253 ms. Watered by Big Beaver river. Pop. 571.
FALLSTON, p. o., Harford co., Md.
FALLSTOWN, p. v., Iredell co., N. C., 151 ms. w. of Raleigh; from W. 388 ms.
FALLS VILLAGE, p. v., Canaan township, Litchfield co., Ct., 45 ms. N. w. of Hartford; from W. 337 ms. Watered by Housatonic river.
FALMOUTH, p. t., Cumberland co., Me., 45 ms. s. w. of Augusta; from W. 550 ms. Watered by Presumscut river. Pop. 2,157.
FALMOUTH, p. t., Barnstable co., Mass., 75 ms. s. of Boston; from W. 465 ms. Watered by Buzzard's bay and Vineyard sound. Pop. 2,621.
FALMOUTH, p. v., Donegal township, Lancaster co., Pa., 15 ms. s. E. of Harrisburgh; from W. 117 ms. Watered by Susquehanna river, and Conewago creek.
FALMOUTH, p. v., Stafford co., Va., 64 ms. N. of Richmond; from W. 55 ms. Watered by Rappahannock river.
FALMOUTH, c. h., p. v., seat of justice of Pendleton co., Ky., 60 ms. N. E. of Frankfort; from W 514 ms. Watered by Licking river.
FALMOUTH, p. o., Fayette co., Ind.
FAME, p. o., Choctaw eo., Miss.
FANCY BLUFF, p. o., Glynn co., Ga.
FANCY FARM, p. o., Graves co., Ky.
FANCY GROVE, p. o., Bedford co. Va.
FANCY HILL, p. o., Iredell co., N. C., 151 ms. w. of Raleigh; from W. 388 ms.
FANCY HILL, p. o., Rockbridge co., Va.
FANNET, t., Franklin co., Pa. Watered by Tuscarora creek.
FANNETTSBURGH, p. v., Metal township, Franklin co., Pa., 59 ms. s. of Harrisburgh; from W. 107 ms. Watered by west branch of Conecocheague creek.
FANNIN COUNTY, situated on the northerly boundary of Texas, with Red river on the north Area, —— square miles. Seat of justice, Bonham. Pop. in 1850, ——.
FARLEY, p. o., Culpeper co., Va., 107 ms. N. of Richmond; from W. 91 ms.
FARLOW'S GROVE, p. o., Mercer co., Ill., 148 ms. N. w. of Springfield; from W. 878 ms.
FARMER, p. o., Seneca co., N. Y., 180 ms. w. of Albany; from W. 313 ms.
FARMER, p. t., Defiance co., O. Pop. 894.
FARMERS, p. o., Meriwether co., Ga., 107 ms. w. of Milledgeville; from W. 726 ms.
FARMERS, p. o., York co., Pa.

FARMERS, p. o., Fleming co., Ky.

FARMERS AND MECHANICS' MILLS, p. o., Jackson co., Ga.

FARMERSBURGH, p. o., Clayton co., Iowa.

FARMER'S BRANCH, p. o., Dallas co., Tex.

FARMER'S CREEK, p. o., Lapeer co., Mich., 54 ms. N. of Detroit; from W. 577 ms.

FARMER'S FARM, p. o., Iroquois co., Ill.

FARMER'S GROVE, p. o., South Hampton co., Va., 58 ms. s. of Richmond; from W. 177 ms.

FARMER'S GROVE, p. o., Greene co., Wis.

FARMER'S HALL, p. o., Knox co., Ill.

FARMER'S HILL, p. o., Dutchess co., N. Y.

FARMER'S MILLS, p. o., Kent township, Putnam co. N. Y.

FARMER'S VALLEY, p. o., McKean co., Pa.

FARMERSVILLE, p. o., Crawford co., Pa.

FARMERSVILLE, p. t., Cattaraugas co., N. Y., 279 ms. w. of Albany; from W. 332 ms.

FARMERSVILLE, p. o., Montgomery co., O., 86 ms. w. of Columbus; from W. 479 ms.

FARMERSVILLE, p. o., Lowndes co., Ala.; from W. 875 ms.

FARMERSVILLE, p. v., c. h., seat of justice of Union parish, La., 333 ms. N. w. of New Orleans; from W. 1,223 ms. Watered by Bayou D'Arbonne.

FARMERSVILLE, p. o., Posey co., Ind.

FARMERSVILLE, p. o., Caldwell co., Ky.

FARMERSVILLE, p. o., Dodge co., Wis.

FARMERSVILLE, p. o., Crawford co., Pa.

FARM HILL, p. o., Poinsett co., Ark.

FARMINGDALE, p. o., Kennebec co., Me.

FARMINGDALE, p. o., Queen's co., Long Island, N. Y., 176 ms. s. of Albany; from W. 256 ms.

FARMINGHAM, p o., Barre township, Orleans co., N. Y., 250 ms. w. of Albany; from W. 394 ms.

FARMINGTON, c. h., p. t., seat of justice of Franklin co., Me., 32 ms. N. w. of Augusta; from W. 621 ms. Watered by Sandy and Norridgewock rivers. Pop. 2,725.

FARMINGTON, p. t., Strafford co., N. H., 38 ms. N. E. of Concord; from W. 513 ms. Watered by Cocheco river. Pop. 1,699.

FARMINGTON, p. t., Hartford co., Ct., 9 ms. w. of Hartford; from W. 331 ms. Watered by Farmington river. Pop. 2,630.

FARMINGTON, p. t., Ontario co., N. Y., 205 ms. w. of Albany; from W. 351 ms. Watered by Mud creek. Pop. 1,876.

FARMINGTON, t., Venango co., Pa., 187 ms. N. w. of Harrisburgh; from W. 254 ms.

FARMINGTON, p. o., Fayette co., Pa.

FARMINGTON. t., Tioga co., Pa.

FARMINGTON, p. t., Trumbull co., O., 166 ms. N. E. of Columbus; from W. 317 ms. Watered by Grand river. Pop. 1,283.

FARMINGTON, p. t., Oakland co., Mich., 20 ms. N. w. of Detroit; from W. 542 ms. Watered by north branch of Rouge river and Power's creek. Pop. 1,844.

FARMINGTON. c. h., p. v., seat of justice of Van Buren co., Iowa. Pop. 585.

FARMINGTON, p., Davie co., N. C., 133 ms. w. of Raleigh; from W. 344 ms.

FARMINGTON, p. v., Marshall co., Tenn., 54 ms. s. of Nashville; from W. 698 ms. Watered by a tributary of Duck river.

FARMINGTON, p. o., Clarke co., Ga., 62 ms. N. of Milledgeville; from W. 620 ms. Pop. 659.

FARMINGTON, p. v., Fulton co., Ill., 78 ms. N. w. of Springfield; from W. 809 ms. Pop. 1,420.

FARMINGTON, p. o., Tishemingo co., Miss., 248 ms. N. E. of Jackson; from W. 845 ms.

FARMINGTON, c. h., p. v., seat of justice of St. Francis co., Mo., 139 ms. s. E. of Jefferson City; from W. 901 ms. Watered by Big river.

FARMINGTON, p. o., Rush co., Ind.

FARMINGTON, p. o., Marion co., Va.

FARMINGTON, p. o., Graves co., Ky.

FARMINGTON, p. o., Sevier co., Ark.

FARMINGTON, p. o., Jefferson co., Wis.

FARMINGTON FALLS, p. v., Farmington township, Franklin co., Me., 27 ms. N. w. of Augusta; from W. 618 ms. Watered by Sandy river.

FARM RIDGE, p. o., La Salle co., Ill.

FARMVILLE, p. v., Prince Edward co., Va., 70 ms. s. w. of Richmond; from W. 160 ms. Watered by Appomattox river.

FARNHAM, p. o., Richmond co., Va., 69 ms. s. E. of Richmond; from W. 128 ms.

FARNUMSVILLE. p. v., Northbridge township, Worcester co., Mass., 39 s. w. of Boston; from W. 496 ms.

FARRANDSVILLE, p. v., Clinton co., Pa., 115 ms. N. w. of Harrisburgh; from W. 207 ms. Watered by west branch of Susquehanna river.

FARRELL PLACE, p. o., Clinton co., N. Y., 174 ms. N. of Albany; from W. 549 ms.

FAR ROCKAWAY, v., Hempstead township, Queens co., Long Island, N. Y., 160 ms. s. of Albany; from W. 231 ms. Watered by Jamaica bay and Atlantic ocean.

FARRIORSVILLE, p. o., Pike co., Ala.

FARROWSVILLE, p. o., Fauquier co., Va., 127 ms. N. of Richmond; from W. 70 ms.

FAR WEST, p. o., Johnson co., Ind., 15 ms. s. of Indianapolis; from W. 586 ms.

FAR WEST, c. h., v., seat of justice of Caldwell co., Mo., 169 ms. N w. of Jefferson City; from W. 1,072 ms. Watered by Shoal creek.

FAUQUIER COUNTY, situated toward the northeasterly part of Virginia. Area, 720 square miles. Face of the country diversified with valleys, hills, and mountains; soil varied. Seat of justice, Warrenton. Pop. in 1810, 22,689; in 1820, 23,103; in 1830, 26,379; in 1840, 21,897; in 1850, 20,868.

FAUSSE POINT, p. o., St. Martin's parish, La.

FAUCETT'S STORE, p. o., Orange co., N. C., 70 ms. N. w. of Raleigh; from W. 290 ms.

FAWN GROVE, p. t., York co., Pa., 49 ms. s. E. of Harrisburgh; from W. — ms. Watered by Muddy creek.

FAWN RIVER, p. t., St. Joseph co., Mich.

FAYETTE COUNTY, situated toward the southwesterly part of Pennsylvania, with Monongahela river on the west. Area. 824 square miles. Face of the country broken with hills and mountains; soil fertile. Seat of justice, Union. Pop. in 1810, 24,714; in 1820, 27,285; in 1830, 29,237; in 1840, 33,574; in 1850, 39,312.

FAYETTE COUNTY, situated toward the westerly part of Virginia, and traversed by Great Kanawha river. Area, 1,350 square miles. Face of the country hilly and mountainous. Seat of justice, Fayetteville. Pop. in 1840, 3,924; in 1850, 3,955.

FAYETTE COUNTY, situated toward the westerly part of Georgia. Area, 545 square miles. Seat of justice, Fayetteville. Pop. in 1830, 5,501; in 1840, 6,191; in 1850, 8,709.

FAYETTE COUNTY, situated on the westerly boundary of Alabama. Area. 1,250 square miles. Seat of justice, Fayetteville. Pop. in 1830, 3,547; in 1840, 6,942; in 1850, 9,681.

FAYETTE COUNTY, situated in the southwestern part of Tennessee. Area, 576 square miles. Seat of justice, Somerville. Pop. in 1830, 8,652; in 1840, 21,501; in 1850, 26,719.

FAYETTE COUNTY, situated toward the north part of Kentucky, with Kentucky river on the southeast. Area, 275 square miles. Face of the country level; soil fertile. Seat of justice, Lexington. Pop. in 1810, 21,370; in 1820, 23,250; in 1830, 25,174; in 1840, 22,194; in 1850, 22,735.

FAYETTE COUNTY, situated toward the southerly part of Ohio. Area, 415 square miles. Face of the country level; soil generally fertile. Seat of justice, Washington. Pop. in 1810, 1,854; in 1820, 6,316; in 1830, 8,180; in 1840, 10,984; in 1850, 12,726.

FAYETTE COUNTY, situated in the easterly part of Indiana, and traversed by White Water river. Area, 200 square miles. Seat of justice, Connersville. Pop. in 1830, 9,112; in 1840, 9,837; in 1850, 10,216.

FAYETTE COUNTY, situated toward the central part of Illinois, and traversed by Kaskaskia river. Area, 648 square miles. Seat of justice, Vandalia. Pop. in 1830, 2,704; in 1840, 6,328; in 1850, 8,075.

FAYETTE COUNTY, situated toward the northeasterly part of Iowa. Area, — square miles. Seat of justice, West Union. Pop. in 1850, 825.

FAYETTE COUNTY, situated toward the southerly part of Texas, and traversed by Colorado river. Seat of justice, La Grange. Pop in 1850, —.

FAYETTE, t., Kennebec co., Me., 18 ms. N. w. of Augusta; from W. 600 ms. Watered by a tributary of Sandusky river. Pop. 1,085.

FAYETTE, p. t., Seneca co., N. Y., 178 ms. w. of Albany; from W. 334 ms. Watered by Cayuga and Seneca lakes, and Seneca and Canoga rivers. Pop. 3,786.

FAYETTE, v., Hanover township, Chautauque co., N. Y. Watered by Silver creek and Lake Erie.

FAYETTE, v., Guilford township Chenango co., N. Y.

FAYETTE, p. t., Alleghany co., Pa., 214 ms. w. of Harrisburgh; from W. 239 ms. Watered by tributaries of Chartiers creek.

FAYETTE, p. t., Juniata co., Pa. Pop. 1,550.

FAYETTE, c. h., p. v., seat of justice of Jefferson co., Miss., 88 ms. s. w. of Jackson; from W. 1,091 ms.

FAYETTE, t., Lawrence co., O. Pop. 1,111.

FAYETTE, t., Hillsdale co., Mich. Pop. 895.

FAYETTE, c. h., p. o., seat of justice of Howard co., Mo., 61 ms. N. W. of Jefferson City; from W. 966 ms. Watered by Bonne Femme creek.

FAYETTE, p. v., Green co., Ill., 57 ms. s. w. of Springfield; from W. 829 ms.

FAYETTE, p. o., Lafayette co., Wis.

FAYETTE, c. h., p. v., seat of justice of Fayette co., Ala.; from W. 842 ms.

FAYETTE CORNER, p. o., Fayette co., Tenn., 77 ms. s. of Nashville; from W. 862 ms.

FAYETTE SPRINGS, p. o., Fayette co., Pa.

FAYETTEVILLE, c. h., p. v., Newfane township, seat of justice of Windham co., Vt., 115 ms. s. of Montpelier; from W. 434 ms.

FAYETTEVILLE, p. v., Manlius township, Onondaga co., N. Y., 123 ms. w. of Albany; from W. 348 ms. Situated near the Erie canal.

FAYETTEVILLE, p. v., Greene township, Franklin co., Pa., 52 ms. s. w. of Harrisburgh; from W. 94 ms.

FAYETTEVILLE, c. h., p. v., seat of justice of Cumberland co., N. C., 159 ms. N. E. of Columbia; from W. 348 ms. Watered by Cape Fear river. Pop. in 1830, 2,868; in 1840, 4,285; in 1850, 4,648.

FAYETTEVILLE, c. h., p. v., seat of justice of Fayette co., Ga., 85 ms. N. w. of Milledgeville; from W. 689 ms. Watered by a tributary of Flint river.

FAYETTEVILLE, p. v., Talladega co., Ala.; from W. 780 ms.

FAYETTEVILLE, c. h., p. v., seat of justice of Lincoln co., Tenn., 86 ms. s. of Nashville; from W. 716 ms. Watered by Elk river.

FAYETTEVILLE, c. h., p. v., seat of justice of Washington co., Ark., 196 ms. N. w. of Little Rock; from W. 1,185 ms. Watered by White river. Pop. 598.

FAYETTEVILLE, p. v., Perry township, Brown co., O., 94 ms. s. w. of Columbus; from W. 467 ms. Pop. 317.

FAYETTEVILLE, p. v., St. Clair co., Ill., 100 ms. s. of Springfield; from W. 810 ms. Watered by Kaskaskia river.

FAYETTEVILLE, p. o., Fayette co.. Tex.

FAYETTEVILLE, p. o., Lawrence co., Ind.

FAYSTON, t., Washington co., Vt., 16 ms. s. w. of Montpelier; from W. 510 ms. Watered by Mad river. Pop. 684.

FEARING, p. t., Washington co., O., 109 ms. s. E. of Columbus; from W. 305 ms. Watered by Duck creek. Pop. 1,254.

FEARN'S SPRINGS, p. o., Winston co., Miss., 108 ms. N. E. of Jackson; from W. 906 ms.

FEASTERVILLE, p.o., Bucks co., Pa., 115 ms. E. of Harrisburgh; from W. 155 ms.

FEASTERVILLE, p. o., Fairfield district, S. C.

FEDERALSBURGH, p. v., Caroline co., Md., 65 ms. s. E. of Annapolis; from W. 105 ms. Watered by Marshy Hope creek.

FEDERAL STORE, p. o., Dutchess co., N. Y., 59 ms. s. of Albany; from W. 326 ms.

FEDERALTON, p. v., Rome township, Athens co., O., 92 ms. s. E. of Columbus; from W. 326 ms. Watered by Hocking river and Federal creek.

FEE FEE, p. o., St. Louis co., Mo.

FEEDING HILLS, p. o., Hampden co., Mass., 97 ms. w. of Boston; from W. 359 ms.

FEED SPRING, p. o., Harrison co., O.

FEESBURGH. p. o., Brown co., O., 112 ms. s. of Columbus; from W. 474 ms.

FELICIANA, p. v., Graves co., Ky., 294 ms. w. of Frankfort; from W. 820 ms.

FELCHVILLE, p. o., Windsor co., Vt., 64 ms. s. of Montpelier; from W. 474 ms.

FELICIANA PARISH (see East and West Feliciana).

FELICITY, p. v., Franklin township, Clermont co., O.. 118 ms. s. w. of Columbus; from W. 478 ms.

FELIX, p. o., Wilson co., Tenn.

FELIX. p. o., Morgan co., Mo., 45 ms. w. of Jefferson City; from W. 981 ms.

FELL, p. t., Huntingdon co., Pa.

FELLOWSHIP, p. o., Burlington co., N. J.

FELLOWSVILLE, p. o., Preston co., Va.

FELTONSVILLE, p. v., Middlesex co., Mass., 30 ms from Boston; from W. 417 ms.

FELT'S, p. o., Ingham co., Pa.

FELT'S MILLS, p. v., Rutland township, Jefferson co., N. Y., 162 ms. N. w. of Albany; from W. 424 ms.

FELTVILLE, p. o., Essex co., N. J.

FEMME OSAGE, t., St. Charles co., Mo., 82 ms. E. of Jefferson City; from W. 864 ms. Watered by Missouri river.

FENNER, p. t., Madison co., N. Y., 112 ms. of Albany; from W. 355 ms. Watered by Canaseraga and Chittenango creeks. Pop. 1,690.

FENNERSVILLE, p. o., Monroe co., Pa., 118 ms. N. E. of Harrisburgh; from W. 209 ms.

FENNIMORE, p. o., Grant co., Wis.

FENN'S BRIDGE. p. o., Jefferson co., Ga., 46 ms. E. of Milledgeville; from W. 650 ms.

FENTER, t., Hot Spring co., Ark.

FENTON, p. v., St. Louis co., Mo., 137 ms. E. of Jefferson City; from W. 826 ms. Watered by Marrimec river.

FENTONVILLE, p. v., Fenton township, Genesee co., Mich., 57 ms. N. w. of Detroit; from W. 579 ms.

FENTRESS COUNTY, situated on the northerly boundary of Tennessee. Area, 560 square miles. Seat of justice, Jamestown. Pop. in 1830, 2,748; in 1840, 3,550; in 1850, 4,454.

FENTRISS. p. o., Guilford co., N. C.

FERDINAND, p. o., Mercer co., Ill.

FERDINAND, p. o., Dubois co., Ind.

FERNANDINA, v., Nassau co., Flor., situated on Amelia island, 313 ms. E. of Tallahasse.

FERGUSON, t., Centre co., Pa., 82 ms. N. w of Harrisburgh; from W. 183 ms. Watered by Spring creek and tributaries. Pop. 1,601.

FERGUSON, t., Clearfield co., Pa. Pop. 337.

FERGUSON'S CORNERS, p. o., Yates co., N. Y.

FERMAUGH, p. t., Juniata co., Pa. Pop. 887.

FERONIA, p o., Telfair co., Ind.

FERN CREEK, p. o., Jefferson co., Ky.

FERRISBURGH, p. t., Addison co., Vt., 34 ms. w. of Montpelier; from W. 498 ms. Watered by Otter, Little Otter, and Lewis creeks, and Lake Champlain.

FESSENDEN MILLS, p. o., Rockingham co., N. H.

FETHEROLFFSVILLE, p. o., Berks co., Pa., 78 ms. E. of Harrisburgh; from W. 170 ms.

FELTERMAN, p. o., Taylor co., Va.

FEURA BUSH, p. o., Albany co., N. Y.

FIATT, p o., Fulton co., Ill.

FIDDLE POND, p. o., Barnwell district, S. C.

FIDELITY, p. o., Miami co., O.

FIDELITY, p. o., Jersey co., Ill.

FIELDING, p. o., Jersey co., Ill.

FIFE, p. o., Talladego co., Ala.; from W. 745 ms.

FIFE'S, p. o., Goochland co., Va.. 43 ms. w. of Richmond; from W. 117 ms.

FILLMORE, p. o., Dubuque co., Iowa.

FILLMORE, p. o., Alleghany co., N. Y.

FILLMORE, p. o., Porter co., Ind.

FILLMORE, p. o., Washington co., O.

FILLMORE, p. o., Montgomery co., Ill.

FILLMORE, p. o., Macomb co., Mich.

FILLMORE, p. o., Daviess co., Ky.

FILLMORE, p. o., Washington co., Wis.

FILLMORE, p. o., Randolph co., Va.

FILLMORE, p. o., Monmouth co., N. J.

FILLMORE, p. o., Cleveland co., N. C

FILLMORE, p. o., Centre co., Pa.

FILLMORE, p. o., Bledsoe co., Tenn.

FILLMORE, p. o., Andrew co., Mo.

FINCASTLE, c. h., p. v., seat of justice of Botetourt co., Va., 175 ms. w. of Richmond; from W. 225 ms.

FINCASTLE, p. v., Eagle township, Brown co., O., 100 ms. s. of Columbus; from W. 465 ms.

FINCASTLE, p. t., Campbell co., Tenn., 206 ms. E. of Nashville; from W. 504 ms. Watered by Powel's river.

FINCASTLE, p. o., Putnam co., Ind.

FINCH, t., Jefferson co., Wis.

FINCHVILLE, p. o., New Hope township, Orange co., N. Y., 115 ms. s. of Albany; from W. 273 ms.

FINE FORKS, p. o., Person co., N. C.

FINE'S CREEK, p. o., Haywood co., N. C.

FINGERSVILLE, p. o., Spartanburgh district, S. C.

FINKSBURGH, p. v., Carroll co., Md., 51 ms. N. w. of Annapolis; from W. 61 ms.

FINDLAY, t., Alleghany co., Pa., 221 ms. w. of Harris

burgh; from W. 243 ms. Watered by tributaries of Raccoon creek, and by Monture's run. Pop. 1,318.

FINLEY, c. h., p. t., seat of justice of Hancock co., O.. 90 ms. N. w. of Columbus; from W. 456 ms. Watered by Blanchard's fork of Auglaize river. Pop. 2,032.

FINLEY, p. o., Greene co., Mo.

FINLEYVILLE, p. v., Peters township, Washington co., Pa,, 195 ms. s. w. of Harrisburgh; from W. 222 ms.

FINNEY MILLS, p. o., Amelia co., Va., 51 ms. s. w. of Richmond; from W. 170 ms.

FIREPLACE, p. v., Brookhaven township, Suffolk co., N. Y., 212 ms. s. E. of Albany; from W. 292 ms. Watered by Fireplace bay.

FIRST FORK, p. o., Clinton co., Pa.

FISER'S CROSS ROADS, p. o., Robertson co., Tenn.

FISH CREEK, p. o., Steuben co., Ind.

FISH CREEK, p. o., Marshall co., Va.

FISHDAM, p. v., Wake co., N. C., 22 ms. s. w. of Raleigh; from W. 282 ms.

FISHDAM, p. v., Union district, S. C., 61 ms. N. w. of Columbia; from W. 467 ms. Watered by Broad river.

FISHER'S, p. o., Ontario co., N. Y.

FISHER'S, p. o., Catawba co., N. C., 71 ms. s. w. of Raleigh; from W. 408 ms.

FISHERSBOROUGH, p. v., Franklin co., Va., 175 ms. s. w. of Richmond; from W. 250 ms.

FISHERSVILLE, p. v., Windham co., Ct., 50 ms. E. of Hartford; from W. 386 ms.

FISHERSVILLE, p. o., Augusta co., Va.

FISHERSVILLE, p. v., Merrimac co.. N. H., 5 ms. N.W. of Concord; from W. 486 ms. Watered by Merrimac and Contoocook rivers.

FISHERVILLE, p. o.. Jefferson co., Ky.

FISHERVILLE, p. o., Dauphin co., Pa.

FISHING CREEK, p. o., Cape May co., N, J.

FISHING CREEK, p. t., Columbia co., Pa., 101 ms. N. of Harrisburgh; from W. 212 ms. Watered by Fishing creek. Pop. 1,110.

FISH-HOUSE VILLAGE, v., Northampton township, Fulton co., N. Y. Watered by Sacandaga river.

FISHKILL, p. t. Dutchess co., N. Y.. 88 ms. s. of Albany; from W. 285 ms. Watered by Wappinger's and Fishkill creek. Pop. 9,240.

FISHKILL LANDING, p. v., Fishkill township, Dutchess co., N. Y., 90 ms. s. of Albany; from W. 287 ms.

FISHKILL PLAINS, p. o., Fishkill township, Dutchess co., N. Y.

FISH POND, p. o., Tallapoosa co., Ala

FISH FORT, p. o., Rock Island co., Ill.

FISH TRAP, p. o., Baker co., Ga.

FISKDALE, p. o., Worcester co.. Mass.

FISKEVILLE, p. v., Providence co., R. I., 13 ms. s. w. of Providence; from W. 403 ms.

FISKSBURGH, p. v., Kenton co., Ky, 44 ms. N. E. of Frankfort; from W. 512 ms. Watered by Licking river.

FISK'S CORNERS, p. o., Winnebago co., Wis.

FITCH, p. o., Cass co. Ind.

FITCHBURGH, p. t., Worcester co., Mass., 46 ms. N. w. of Boston; from W. 423 ms. Watered by a branch of Nashua river. Pop. 5,120.

FITCHBURGH, p. o., Dane co., Wis.

FITCHBURGH, p. o., Jasper co., Ind.

FITCHPORT, p. o., Garrard co., Ky., 44 ms. s. E. of Frankfort; from W. 542 ms.

FITCHVILLE, p. t., Huron co., O., 98 ms. N. of Columbus; from W. 389 ms. Pop. 1,178.

FITZ HENRY, p. o., Conway co., Ark.

FITZ HENRY, p. o., Seneca co., O.

FITZ HENRY, p. o., Westmoreland co., Pa.

FITZ HENRY, p. o., Ogle co., Ill.

FITZWILLIAM, p. t., Cheshire co., N. H., 60 ms. s. w. of Concord; from W. 428 ms. Watered by Camp and Priest brooks.

FIVE CORNERS, p. o., Geneva township, Cayuga co., N. Y., 178 ms. w. of Albany; from W. 311 ms

FIVE MILE, p. o., Brown co., O

FIVE MILE, p. o., Pickens district, S. C.

FIVE POINTS, p. o., Venango co., Pa.

FLACKVILLE, p. o., St. Lawrence co.. N. Y.

FLAGG SPRING, p. o., Campbell co., Ky., 90 ms. N. E. of Frankfort; from W. 497 ms.

FLAGGTOWN, p. v., Hillsborough township, Somerset co., N. J., 24 ms. N. E. of Trenton; from W. 196 ms.

FLAG POND, p. o., Washington co.. Tenn.

FLAG STAFF, p. o., Somerset co., Me.

FLANDERS, p. v., South Hampton township, Suffolk

co., N. Y., 229 ms. s. E. of Albany; from W. 309 ms. Watered by Little Peconic.

FLAT, p. o., Pike co., O.

FLATBERG, p. o., Irwin co., Ga.

FLAT BROOK, p. o., Columbia co., N. Y.

FLAT BROOKVILLE, p. o.. Sandystone township, Sussex co., N. J., 85 ms. N. of Trenton; from W. 242 ms.

FLATBUSH, p. t., King's co., N. Y., 151 ms. s. of Albany; from W. 231 ms. Pop. 3,176.

FLAT CREEK, p. o., Montgomery co., N. Y.

FLAT CREEK, p. o., Lowndes co., Ga.

FLAT CREEK, p. o., Bedford co., Tenn., 66 ms. s. E. of Nashville; from W. 689 ms.

FLAT CREEK, p. o., Buncombe co., N. C.

FLAT CREEK, t., Taney co., Mo.

FLAT CREEK, t., Pettis co., Mo.

FLAT CREEK MILLS, p. o.. Campbell co., Va.

FLAT LANDS, p. t., King's co.. N. Y., 153 ms. s. of Albany; from W. 232 ms. Watered by Jamaica bay. Pop. 1,155.

FLAT LICK, p. o., Claiborne parish, La., 401 ms. N.W. of New Orleans; from W. 1,271 ms.

FLAT LICK, p. o., Knox co., Ky.

FLAT RIVER, p. o., Kent co., Mich., 148 ms. N. w. of Detroit; from W. 633 ms.

FLAT ROCK, p. t., Bartholomew co., Ind. Pop. 725.

FLAT ROCK, p. o.. Henry co., Ga., 78 ms. N. w. of Milledgeville; from W. 675 ms.

FLAT ROCK, p. o., Powhattan co., Va., 26 ms. w. of Richmond; from W. 143 ms.

FLAT ROCK, p. o.. Henderson co., N. C., 280 ms. w. of Raleigh; from W. 510 ms.

FLAT ROCK, p. o., Bourbon co.. Ky., 54 ms. E. of Frankfort; from W. 516 ms.

FLAT ROCK, t., Henry co., O. Pop. 406.

FLAT ROCK, p. v.. Shelby co., Ind., 61 ms. s. E. of Indianapolis; from W. 576 ms. Watered by Flat Rock creek.

FLAT ROCK, p. o., Cape Girardeau co.. Mo.

FLAT ROCK, p. o., Seneca co., O.

FLAT ROCK, p. o., Kershaw district, S. C., 49 ms. N. E. of Columbia; from W. 457 ms.

FLAT ROCK, p. o., Crawford co., Ill.

FLAT SHOALS, p. o., Meriwether co., Ga., 89 ms. w. of Milledgeville; from W. 708 ms.

FLAT WOODS, p. o., Baxton co., Va., 311 ms. N. w. of Richmond; from W. 279 ms.

FLAT WOODS, p. o., Fayette co., Pa.

FLAT WOODS, p. o., Izard co., Ark.

FLEETVILLE, p. v., Luzerne co., Pa., 159 ms. N. E. of Harrisburgh; from W. 264 ms.

FLEETWOOD ACADEMY, p. o., King and Queen co., Va., 36 ms. N. E. of Richmond; from W. 124 ms.

FLEMING COUNTY, situated toward the northeasterly part of Kentucky, with Licking river on the southwest. Area, 570 square miles. Face of the country undulating; soil, fertile. Seat of justice, Flemingburgh. Pop. in 1810, 8,947; in 1820, 12,186; in 1830, 13,500; in 1840, 13,268; in 1850, 13,916.

FLEMING, p. t.. Cayuga co., N. Y., 128 ms. w. of Albany; from W. 359 ms. Watered by Crane brook and Owasco lake. Pop. 1,193.

FLEMING, p. o., Livingston co., Mich.

FLEMING, p. o., Centre co., Pa.

FLEMINGS, p. o., Weakly co., Tenn., 121 ms. w. of Nashville; from W. 806 ms.

FLEMINGSBURGH, c. h., p. v., seat of justice of Fleming co., Ky., 95 ms. E. of Frankfort; from W. 488 ms. Watered by Stockton run.

FLEMINGSVILLE, p. o.. Owego township, Tioga co., N. Y., 159 ms. s. w. of Albany; from W. 280 ms.

FLEMINGTON, c. h., p. v., Raritan township, seat of justice of Hunterdon co., N. J., 25 ms. N. of Trenton; from W. 185 ms.

FLEMINGTON, p. v., Wake co., N. C., 15 ms. N. w. of Raleigh; from W. 293 ms.

FLEMINGTON, p. o., Marion co., Flor.

FLETCHER, p. t., Franklin co., Vt. 52 ms. N. w. of Montpelier; from W. 540 ms. Watered by Lamoille and Fairfield rivers, and Stone's brook. Pop. 1,084.

FLETCHER, p. v., Brown township, Miami co., O., 66 ms. w. of Columbus; from W. 460 ms. Pop. 246.

FLEWILLIN'S CROSS ROADS, p. o., De Soto co., Miss.

FLICKSVILLE, p. v., Northampton co., Pa., 117 ms. N. E. of Harrisburgh; from W. 210 ms.

FLINT, p. t., Genesee co., Mich., 61 ms. N. w of Detroit; from W. 585 ms. Pop. 3,304.

FLINT, p. o., Cherokee Nation co., Ark.

FLINT, p. o., Steuben co., Ind.

FLINT CREEK, p. o., Seneca township, Ontario co., N. Y., 184 ms. w. of Albany ; from W. 349 ms.

FLINT CREEK, p. o., Harrison co., Miss.

FLINT CREEK, p. o., Lake co., Ill.

FLINT GAP, p. o., Knox co., Tenn.

FLINT HILL, p. o., Rappahannock co., Va., 125 ms. N. W. of Richmond ; from W. 77 ms.

FLINT HILL, p. o., St. Charles co., Mo., 89 ms. N. E. of Jefferson city ; from W. 850 ms.

FLINT ISLAND," p. o., Mead co., Ky., 112 ms. w. of Frankfort ; from W. 651 ms.

FLINT RIDGE, p. o., Lancaster district, S. C.

FLINT ROCK, p. o., Catawba co., N. C., 165 ms. w. of Raleigh ; from W. 414 ms.

FLINT'S MILLS, p. o., Washington co., O., 129 ms. S. E. of Columbus ; from W. 290 ms.

FLINT SPRING, p. o., Bradley co., Tenn.

FLINTVILLE, p. v., Marion district, S. C., 140 ms. E. of Columbia ; from W. 459 ms.

FLIPPOS, p. o., Caroline co., Va.

FLORA, p. o., Smith co., Tex.

FLORENCE, p. v., Washington co., Pa., 257 ms. w. of Harrisburgh ; from W. 252 ms.

FLORENCE, p. t., St. Joseph co., Mich., 144 ms. s. w. of Detroit ; from W. 592 ms. Pop. 731.

FLORENCE, p. t., Oneida co., N. Y., 129 ms. N. w. of Albany ; from W. 414 ms. Watered by tributaries of Fish creek. Pop. 2,575.

FLORENCE, p. v., Stewart co., Ga., 153 ms. s. w. of Milledgeville ; from W. 794 ms. Watered by Chatta- hoochee river.

FLORENCE, c. h.. p. v., seat of justice of Lauderdale co., Ala. ; from W. 780 ms. Watered by Tennessee river.

FLORENCE, p. t., Boone co., Ky., 76 ms. N. of Frank- fort ; from W. 502 ms.

FLORENCE, p. t., Erie co., O., 112 ms. N. of Columbus ; from W. 391 ms.

FLORENCE, t., Williams co., O. Pop. 669.

FLORENCE, v., Louisa co., Iowa. Watered by Iowa river. Pop. 766.

FLORENCE, p. o., Fremont co., Iowa.

FLORENCE, p. o., Switzerland co., Ind.

FLORENCE, p. v., Morgan co., Mo., 54 ms. w. of Jef- ferson City ; from W. 990 ms. Watered by south fork of La Mine river.

FLORENCE, p. v., Pike co., Ill., 59 ms. w. of Spring- field ; from W. 839 ms.

FLORID, p. o., Putnam co., Ill.

FLORIDA, (so call- ed by Juan Ponce de Leon, in 1812. from having discovered the coast on Pascua Flo- rida, the name, in Spanish, for Easter,) the most southern state in the union, lies between 25° and 31° north latitude, and 80° and 87½° west longitude from Greenwich ; and is bounded north by Alabama and Geor- gia, east by the Atlantic, south by the gulf of Mexico, and west by the gulf of Mexico and Alabama. Its su- perficial area is 59,000 square miles, of which but about one half is yet surveyed and occupied.

Physical Aspect.—The face of the country is generally level, and not much elevated above the sea, though we find along the whole northern boundary considerable diversity of surface. A base of calcareous rock com- mences in the northern part of the state, and probably extends under the whole peninsula. This friable stone outcrops the surface of St. Augustine, and other parts on the main, and reappears again on the southern keys, as well as on the Bahamas, and the northern shores of Cuba, on the opposite side of the gulf. In Florida, this formation is generally overlaid by deep super-strata of clay, shells, and sand. The soil, however, generally is sandy, except in places called "hummocks," where it consists either of reddish-yellow or black clay, mixed with sand. These hummocks, which are nu- merous and much scattered throughout the state, vary from a few acres to several miles in extent, and constitute no small part of the peninsula. Another in-

considerable portion of Florida consists in what is gen- erally known in the south by the name of "pine-bar- rens," much of the soil of which is exceedingly poor ; though there are extensive tracts of hummock, table- land, and swamp, of the richest character, well adapted to cultivation. These barrens, wherever intersected by streams of pure water, however poor they may be, af- ford excellent ranges for grazing. The southern por- tion of the state presents singular alternations of sa- vannas, hummocks, lakes, and grass-ponds, called col- lectively "everglades," which extend from Cape Sable into the heart of the country for several hundred miles. This region, including two large swamps, one named Atsenahooffa, on the western side, and the other Hal- pabeoka, on the northeastern side, embracing the large lake Okeechobee. covers an area of 7,000,000 acres, 4,500,000, of which are usually submerged in water, from two to seven feet deep. The "Pahhayokee," or "grass-water," as the Indians call the everglades com- prises from 1,000,000 to 1,500,000 acres of submerged lands. The basin of the everglades is surrounded by a rim of soft lime-rock, from half a mile to five miles in width, and its bottom is represented to be some 12 to 15 feet above the level of the sea. Deep tide rivers ex- tend from the ocean and gulf quite up to the margin of the river ; and comparatively, at a small outlay, mil- lions of acres of land, now worthless, could be drained by canals, and brought into the highest state of im- provement. Within this basin are thousands of islets, of the richest class of land, and the glades are often filled with tall grass, from six to ten feet in height, the annual decay of which has occasioned a deposite in the water from two to six feet thick. This tract lies south of 27½° of north latitude, where there is seldom or no frost ; and if it were reclaimed, as suggested above, it would be adapted to the cultivation of the orange, the pineapple, rice, sugarcane, and other tropi- cal plants.

Rivers, Lakes, and Bays.—The principal rivers are the St. John's, Appalachicola, Suwanee, St. Mark's, St. Mary's, Ocklocony, Escambia, Withlacoochee, Oscilla, Choctawhatchee, Yellow-Water, Amasura, Anclota, Hillsborough, Charlotte, Gallivan's, Young's, Kissimee, and the Perdido ; the latter of which forms the western boundary between this state and Alabama. The St. John's is an anomaly among the rivers of the Atlantic coast. Its source is rather undefinable, being derived from the flat grassy plains, or savannas, is about lati- tude 28° north, probably not more than 20 miles from the sea. It is exceedingly winding in its course, run- ning in a northerly direction, to a distance of nearly 300 miles. In some places it has more the appearance of a lake, or sound, than a river, swelling out from three to five miles in breadth ; while in other parts it dwindles down to a quarter of a mile wide. Vessels drawing eight feet of water ascend to Lake George, a beautiful expansion of this stream, 150 miles from its mouth. The chief lakes are the Great Okeechobee, George, Dunn's, Cypress, Monroe, Orange, Istopoga, Tobokopoligia, Weeok, Yakapka, Jessup, Harney, Eus- tis, Poinsett, Beresford, Ashey, Winsor, Gardiner, Grif- fin, and Gentry. There are numerous bays on the west- ern side, some of which form good harbors. Among these are, Perdido, Pensacola, Choctawhatchie, St. An- drew's, St. Joseph's, Appalachicola, Appalachee, Tam- pa, Charlotte, and Gallivan's. In front of Pensacola bay is a long, shallow lagoon, called Santa Rosa sound. On the east coast of the state there are but few bays, prop- erly speaking. Fernandina bay forms the mouth of St. Mary's river. Mosquito and Indian river, or St. Lucia sounds, are situated near Cape Canaveral, which are entered by inlets of the same names. Many of the rivers on this side of the peninsula form good harbors for coasting vessels.

Islands and Keys.—Florida is remarkable for the great number of small low islets which lie in the vicini- ty of its shores, called "Keys." The most noted of these are Key West (formerly called Thompson's is- land), Indian, Sand, Pine, and Cedar keys. The most noted islands are, Merit's, and Hutchinson's, near Cape Carnaveral ; Amelia island, near St. Mary's sound ; Sanybel, Pine, Captive, and Gasparilla islands, near Charlotte harbor ; Mullet island, near Tampa bay ; St. George's, and Dog islands, near Appalachicola bay ; Santa Rosa island, near Pensacola bay ; and Drayton island, in Lake George. Cape Sable is the southern- most point in the United States.

Climate.—Florida presents some diversity of seasons ;

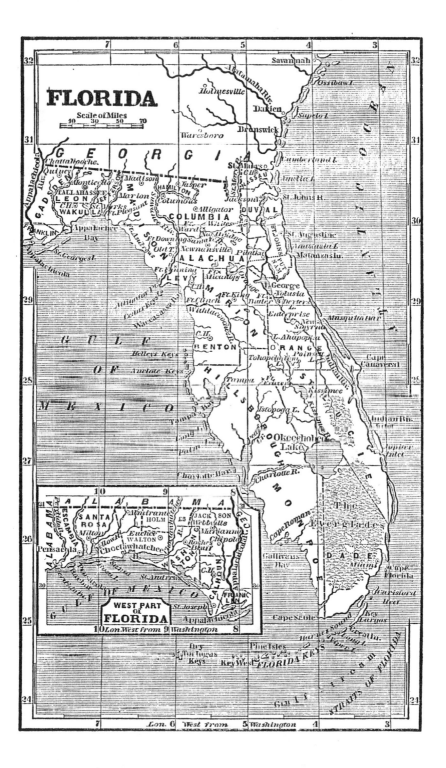

FLORIDA

Scale of Miles
10 30 50 70

but the difference of relative level being small, and surrounded as it is by water on three sides, it enjoys a climate peculiar to itself. On the seaboard it is generally healthy for eight or nine months in the year, and in some parts remarkably so the whole year round. In the interior, it is quite as salubrious as it is in either of the other southern states, unless it be in the vicinity of marshes, or stagnant waters, where fevers and other epidemics invariably prevail. The winters are mild, and usually without frost, though the mercury occasionally sinks to 30° Fahrenheit, and sometimes as low as 26° ; in summer, the temperature seldom exceeds 97°. The climate of the southernmost keys is truly tropical.

Productive Resources.—The staple products consist of horses, mules, neat cattle, sheep, swine, poultry, hay, wool, tobacco, cotton, wheat, oats, potatoes, oranges, sugar, molasses, and Indian corn. The forests produce an abundance of live-oak timber, cedar, and yellow pine. Turtle and other fisheries are carried on somewhat extensively among the keys. Salt is made in small quantities, and granite is quarried to some extent.

Manufactures.—Florida being mostly an agricultural state, but little attention as yet has been paid to manufactures. In 1850 there were but 121 manufacturing establishments, producing to the extent of $500 and upward each annually.

Railroads and Canals.—The legislature of Florida has granted several charters for railroads in this state, but thus far there are neither railroads nor canals within its borders.

Commerce.—The direct foreign commerce of Florida amounts to about $3,000,000 annually. Shipments are also extensively made through New Orleans, and the Atlantic ports. The coasting trade of Florida is also considerable. The shipping in the state amounts to about 12,000 tons.

Education.—The constitution of Florida provides for the establishment of common schools throughout the state, but thus far little progress has been made in affording facilities for elementary education. There are academies and grammar-schools in the more populous towns, but no collegiate institution.

Population.—In 1830, 34,723 ; in 1840, 54,477 ; in 1850, 87,401. Number of slaves in 1830, 15,501 ; in 1840, 25,717 ; in 1850, 39,309.

Government.—The legislative power is vested in a senate and house of representatives. The senate consists of 19 members, elected by the people, in districts, for two years. The representatives are elected by the people, by counties, biennially, their number never to exceed sixty ; present number, thirty. Biennial election, first Monday in October. The executive power is vested in a governor, who is chosen by the people once in four years, and is not eligible the succeeding term. The judicial power is vested in a supreme court, having appellate jurisdiction only ; also in circuit courts, the state being divided into four circuits, in each of which a judge of the supreme court has jurisdiction. The judges are elected by the legislature, at first for five years ; after that term, during good behavior. There are also courts of probate. The right of suffrage may be exercised by every free white male, aged 21 years, or upward, who has resided in the state for two years, and in the county for six months, and who shall be enrolled in the militia, or be by law exempted from serving therein.

History.—The present state of Florida embraces a portion of the ancient Florida, which extended from its southernmost cape to the river Panuco, in Mexico, and westward to the Pacific, and the undefined regions on the north. It was first explored by Juan Ponce de Leon, in 1512, in search of a spring called the "fountain of youth," which was supposed to have the power of renewing the vigor of youth in the aged. In 1526, it was formally taken possession of in the name of the king of Spain, by Pamphilo de Narvaez, who had been sent out as governor. The first permanent settlements were made at St. Augustine, in 1565, and at Pensacola, in 1699 ; though an unsuccessful attempt had been made, by a colony of Huguenots, in 1562–'64, under Ribault. Though often invaded by the English and French, this territory remained a part of the Spanish dominions until 1763, when it was ceded to Great Britain, but restored again to Spain in 1783. From the year 1699 to 1763, the acknowledged boundary between Florida and Louisiana was the river Perdido, but when the

latter came into the possession of the Spaniards, for convenience, West Florida was extended to the Mississippi. From this circumstance arose the difficulties between Spain and the United States, on their purchase of Louisiana of the French, in 1803. In 1781, Governor Galvez, of Louisiana, invaded and conquered West Florida ; but by the treaty of Paris, in 1793, it fell once more to Spain, who held it until 1798, when this portion of Florida, which was claimed as far north as Altamaha river, in Georgia, was relinquished to the United States. By virtue of their claims to that portion of Louisiana lying between the Mississippi and Perdido rivers, as held by France prior to 1763, the United States in 1811, seized Baton Rouge, and all other parts of the disputed territory west of Perdido, except Mobile, which also surrended in 1812. After a protracted and uninterrupted negotiation, Florida was ceded to the United States, in 1819, ratified by Congress as a territory in 1821, and admitted into the Union as an independent state in 1845. Motto of the seal, "Let us alone."

FLORIDA, p. t., Hillsdale co., Mich., 94 ms. s. w. of Detroit ; from W. 526 ms.

FLORIDA, p. t., Berkshire co., Mass. 121 ms. w. of Boston ; from W. 463 ms. Watered by Cold river. Pop. 561.

FLORIDA, p. v., Warwick township, Orange co., N. Y., 111 ms. s. w. of Albany ; from W. 273 ms.

FLORIDA, t., Montgomery co., N. Y., 34 ms. w. of Albany ; from W. 404 ms. Watered by Mohawk river and Schoharie creek. Pop. 3,571.

FLORIDA, p. v., Monroe co., Mo., 83 ms. N. E. of Jefferson City ; from W. 923 ms. Watered by south fork of Salt river.

FLORIDA, p. o., Henry co., O.

FLORIS, p. o., Davis co., Iowa.

FLORISANT, p. o., St. Louis co., Mo., 131 ms. E. of Jefferson City ; from W. 837 ms.

FLOURNOYS, p. o., Nacogdoches co., Tex.

FLOWER CREEK, p. o., Pendleton co., Ky., 79 ms. N. E.. of Frankfort ; from W. 521 ms.

FLOWERFIELD, p. b., St. Joseph co., Mich., 154 ms. s. w. of Detroit ; from W. 603 ms. Pop. 564.

FLOWERY MOUND, p. o., Concordia parish, La.

FLOYD COUNTY, situated in the southern part of Virginia. Area, 525 square miles. Face of the country mountainous ; soil good for pasturage. Seat of justice, Jacksonville. Pop. in 1840, 4,453 ; in 1850, 6,458.

FLOYD COUNTY, situated on the westerly boundary of Georgia, and traversed by Coosa river. Area, 460 square miles. Seat of justice, Rowe. Pop. in 1840, 4,441 ; in 1850, 8,205.

FLOYD COUNTY, situated in the easterly part of Kentucky, and traversed by west fork of Big Sandy river. Area, 1,400 square miles. Face of the country broken with hills and mountains ; soil of middling quality. Seat of justice, Prestonburgh. Pop. in 1810, 3,485 ; in 1820, 8,207 ; in 1830, 4,266 ; in 1840, 6,302 ; in 1850, 5,714.

FLOYD COUNTY, situated in the southerly part of Indiana, with the Ohio river on the southeast. Area, 144 square miles. Face of the country hilly ; soil inferior. Seat of justice, New Albany. Pop. in 1820, 2,776 ; in 1830, 6,363 ; in 1840, 9,444 ; in 1850, 14,875.

FLOYD, p. t., Oneida co., N. Y., 104 ms. N. w. of Albany ; from W. 398 ms. Watered by Mohawk river and Nine Mile creek. Pop. 1,495.

FLOYD, c. h., p. o., Jacksonville village, seat of justice of Floyd co., Va., 215 ms. s. w. of Richmond ; from W. 290 ms.

FLOYD, t., Putnam co., Ind.

FLOYDSBURGH, p. v., Oldham co., Ky., 37 ms. w. of Frankfort ; from W. 580 ms. Watered by Floyd's creek.

FLOYD'S MILLS, p. o., Horry district, S. C.

FLUKE'S, p. o., Botetourt co., Va., 162 w. of Richmond ; from W. 231 ms.

FLUME, p. o., Grafton co., N. H.

FLUSHING, p. t., Queen's co., Long Island, N. Y., 155 ms. s. of Albany ; from W. 235 ms. Watered by Long Island sound, and Flushing and Little Neck bays. Pop. in 1840, 4,124 ; in 1850, 5,376.

FLUSHING, p. t., Belmont co., O., 110 ms. E. of Columbus ; from W. 288 ms. Watered by Stillwater creek. Pop. 1,486.

FLUSHING, p. t., Genesee co., Mich., 67 ms. N. w. of Detroit ; from W. 591 ms. Pop. 708.

FLUVANNA COUNTY, situated toward the central part of Virginia, with James river on the south, and traversad by Rivanna river. Area. 416 square miles. Face of the country beautifully diversified with hills and valleys; soil generally of middling quality. Seat of justice, Palmyra. Pop. in 1810, 4.775; in 1820, 6,704; in 1830, 8,221; in 1840, 8.812; in 1850, 9,487.

FLUVANNA, p. o., Ellicott township, Chautauque co., N. Y., 335 ms. w. of Albany; from W. 322 ms.

FLY CREEK, p. o., La Grange co., Ind.

FLY CREEK, p. o., Otsego co.. N. Y.

FLY MOUNTAIN. p. o., Ulster co., N. Y.

FLYNN'S LICK, p. o., Jackson co., Tenn.

FOCHT'S FORGE, p. o., Schuylkill co., Pa.

FOGLESVILLE, p. o., Macungy township, Lehigh co., Pa., 82 ms. N. E. of Harrisburgh; from W. 175 ms.

FOGO, p. o., Allegan co.. Mich.

FUNDA, c. h., p. v.. Mohawk township, seat of justice of Montgomery co., N. Y., 42 ms. w. of Albany; from W. 404 ms. Watered by Mohawk river. Pop. 3,571.

FOND DU LAC COUNTY, situated toward the easterly part of Wisconsin, with the southern part of Lake Winnebago on the north. Area, 400 square miles. Seat of justice. Fond du Lac. Pop. in 1840. 139; in 1850, 2,024.

FOND DU LAC, c. h., p. v., seat of justice of Fond du Lac co.. Wia., 98 ms. N. E. of Madison; from W. 945 ms. Watered by Lake Winnebago.

FORBUSH, p. o., Surry co., N. C., 136 ms. N. w. of Raleigh; from W. 344 ms.

FORD, p. o., Geauga co., O.

FORDHAM, p. v., Westchester township, Westchester co., N. Y.

FORD'S STORE, p. o., Franklin co., Ga.

FORDSVILLE, p. v., Marion co., Miss., 128 ms. s. E. of Jackson; from W. 407 ms.

FORDSVILLE, p. o., Ohio co., Ky.

FORESTBURGH, p. b., Sullivan co., N. Y., 120 ms. s. w. of Albany; from W. 278 ms. Watered by Navesink river. Pop. 715.

FOREST CITY, p. o., Tompkins co., N. Y.

FOREST DALE, p. o., Rutland co., Vt.

FOREST HILL, p. o., Decatur co., Ind.

FOREST HILL, p. o., Union co., Pa.

FOREST HOME, p. o., Cass co., Tex.

FOREST LAKE, p. t., Susquehannah co.. Pa., 181 ms. N. E. of Harrisburgh; from W. 291 ms. Pop. 780.

FOREST OAK. p. o., Montgomery co., Md.

FOREST RETREAT, p. o., Nicholas co., Ky., 50 ms. N. E. of Frankfort; from W. 493 ms.

FORESTVILLE. p. v., Wake co, N C, 15 ms. w. of Raleigh; from W. 273 ms.

FORESTVILLE, p. o., Hartford co., Ct.

FORESTVILLE, p. o., Otsego co., N. Y.

FORGE VILLAGE, p. v., Middlesex co., Mass., 30 ms. from Boston; from W. 434 ms.

FORKED RIVER, p. o., Monmouth co., N. J.

FORK INN, p. o., Dinwiddie co., Va., 31 ms. s. w. of Richmond; from W. 150 ms.

FORKLAND, p. o., Greene co., Ala.

FORK MEETING-HOUSE, p. o., Baltimore co., Md.

FORK RIDGE, p. o., Marshall co.. Va.

FORKS, t., Lycoming co., Pa., 101 ms. N. of Harrisburgh; from W. 190 ms.

FORKS. t., Northampton co., Pa. Watered by Bushkill creek.

FORKS OF BUFFALO, p. o., Marion co., Va.

FORKS OF ELKHORN, p. o., Franklin co., Ky.

FORKS OF MARY'S RIVER, p. o., Benton co., Oregon.

FORKS OF PIGEON, p. o., Haywood co., N. C.

FORKS OF POTOMAC, p. o., Hampshire co., Va.

FORKSTON, p. o., Wyoming co., Pa., 165 ms. N. E. of Harrisburgh; from W. 270 ms.

FORKSVILLE, p. o., Mecklenburgh co., Va., 87 ms. s. w. of Richmond; from W. 203 ms.

FORKSVILLE, p. o., Lake co., Ill.

FORKSVILLE, p. o., Washita parish, La.

FORKTOWN, p. v., Somerset co., Md., 99 ms. s. E. of Annapolis; from W. 139 ms.

FORK UNION, p. o., Fluvanna co., Va

FORNEY'S, p. o., Lincoln co., N. C.

FORSYTH COUNTY. situated in the northern part of North Carolina. Area, —— square miles. Seat of justice, Winston. Pop. in 1850, 11,168.

FORSYTH COUNTY, situated toward the northerly part of Georgia, with Chattahoochee river on the southeast. Area, 290 square miles. Seat of justice, Cumming. Pop. in 1840, 5,619; in 1850, 8,850.

FORSYTH, c. h., p. v., seat of justice of Monroe co., Ga., 55 ms. w. of Milledgeville; from W. 677 ms. Watered by Towaliggee and Ocmulgee rivers.

FORSYTH, c. h., p. v., seat of justice of Taney co., Mo., 201 ms. s. of Jefferson City; from W. 1,118 ms. Watered by White river and Swan creek.

FORT ADAMS, p. v.. Wilkinson co., Miss., 158 ms. s. w. of Jackson; from W. 1,168 ms.

FORT ANN, p. t., Washington co., N. Y., 68 ms. N. of Albany; from W. 432 ms. Watered by Wood creek, Lake George, and Champlain canal. Pop. 3.383.

FORT ANCIENT, p. o., Warren co., O.

FORT ATKINSON, p. o., Jefferson co., Wis., 43 ms. E. of Madison; from W. 827 ms.

FORT ATKINSON, p. o., Clayton co., Iowa.

FORT ATKINSON, p. o., Nebraska. Tex.

FORT BARRINGTON FERRY, p. o., McIntosh co., Ga.

FORT BEND COUNTY, situated in the southerly part of Texas, and traversed by Brazos river. Area, —— square miles. Seat of justice, Richmond. Pop. in 1850, 2,377.

FORT BLOUNT, p. o.. Jackson co., Tenn., 68 ms. E. of Nashville; from W. 432 ms.

FORT BROWDER, p. o., Barbour co., Ala.

FORT BUFFINGTON, p. o., Benton co., Flor.

FORT BUFFINGTON. p. o., Cherokee co., Ga.

FORT CLARK, p. o., Alachua co., Flor.

FORT COVINGTON, p. t.. Franklin co., N. Y., 266 ms. N. w. of Albany; from W. 546 ms. Watered by Salmon and Little Salmon rivers. Pop. 2.641.

FORT DECATUR, p. o., Macon co., Ala.

FORT DEFIANCE, p. o., Caldwell co., N. C.

FORT DES MOINES, p. o., Polk co., Iowa.

FORT DUNCAN, p. o., Kinney co., Tex.

FORT EDWARD, p. t., Washington co., N. Y., 49 ms. N. of Albany; from W. 419 ms. Watered by Moosekill and Hudson rivers. Pop. 2,328.

FORT EDWARD CENTRE, p. o., Fort Edward township, Washington co., N. Y.

FORT FAIRFIELD, p. o., Aroostook co., Me.

FORT FANNING, p. o., Levy co., Flor.

FORT GAINES, p. o., Early co., Ga., 183 ms. s. w. of Milledgeville; from W. 830 ms.

FORT GIBSON, p. v.. Cherokee Nation co., Ark., 221 ms. N. w. of Little Rock; from W. 1,286 ms. Watered by Neosho river,

FORT GRATIOT, v., St. Clair co., Mich., 60 ms. N. E. of Detroit; from W. 584 ms. Watered by Lake Huron.

FORT HAMILTON, p. v., New Utrecht township, King's co., N. Y. Watered by the Narrows, New York harbor.

FORT HARLEY, p. o., Alachua co., Flor.

FORT HERREE, p. o., Cherokee co., N. C.

FORT HENDERSON, p. o., Macon co., Ala.; from W. 789 ms.

FORT HILL, p. o., Lake co., Ill., 233 ms. N. E. of Springfield, from W. 748 ms.

FORT HUNTER, p. o., Florida township, Montgomery co., N. Y., 38 ms. w. of Albany; from W. 406 ms.

FORT JEFFERSON, p. o., Neave township, Darke co., O., 98 ms. w. of Columbus; from W. 489 ms.

FORT JENNINGS, p. o., Putnam co., O.

FORT JESSUP, p. o., Sabine parish, La., 393 ms. N. w. of New Orleans; from W. 1.312 ms.

FORT KEARNEY, p. o., Indian country, Neb. Ter.

FORT KENT, p. o., Aroostook co., Me.

FORT LACEY, Monroe co., Pa.

FORT LARAMIE, p. o., Clackamas co., Oregon.

FORT LEAVENWORTH, p. v., Clay co., Mo. Watered by Missouri and Flat rivers.

FORT LITTLETON. p. o., Fulton co., Pa, 71 ms. w. of Harrisburgh; from W. 115 ms.

FORT MADISON, p. o., Lee co., Iowa.

FORT MILL, p. o., York district, S. C.

FORT MILLER, p. v., Fort Edward township, Washington co., N. Y., 49 ms. N. of Albany; from W. 419 ms. Watered by Hudson river and Champlain canal.

FORT MITCHELL, p. o., Russell co., Ala.

FORT MONTGOMERY, p. o., Cherokee co., N. C.

FORT MONTPELIER, p. o., Baldwin co., Ala.

FORT MOTTE, p. o., Orangeburgh district, S. C.

FORT OSAGE, p. o., Jackson co., Mo., 158 ms. w. of Jefferson city; from W. 1,074 ms.

FORT PIKE, p. o., Orleans parish, La.

FORT PLAIN, p. v., Minden township, Montgomery co., N. Y., 61 ms. w. of Albany; from W. 396 ms. Watered by Mohawk river and Erie canal.

FORT PRINCE, p. o., Spartanburgh district, S. C.

FORT RECOVERY, p. o., Mercer co., O., 114 ms. w. of Columbus; from W. 508 ms.

FORT RIPLEY, p. o., Wahnahta co., Minn.

FORT SCOTT, p. o., Bates co., Mo.
FORT SENECA. p. o., Seneca co., O., 95 ms. N. of Columbus; from W. 432 ms.
FORT SMITH, p. v., Crawford co., Ark., 161 ms. N. w. of Little Rock; from W. 1,226 ms. Watered by Arkansas and Poteau rivers. Pop. 964.
FORT SNELLING, p. o., Dacotah co.. Min.
FORTSVILLE, p. v., Moreau township, Saratoga co., N. Y., 48 ms. N. of Albany; from W. 418 ms.
FORT TAYLOR, p. o., Benton co., Flor.
FORT TAYLOR, p. o., Cherokee co., Ga.
FORT TOWSON, v., Indian Territory co., Ark., 184 ms. s. w. of Little Rock; from W. 1,289 ms.
FORT UNION, p. o., New Mexico.
FORT VALLEY, p. o., Houston co., Ga.
FORT WASHINGTON, p. o., Prince George's co., Md.
FORT WASHITA, p. o., Chickasaw Nation co.. Ark.
FORT WAYNE, c. h., p. v., seat of justice of Allen co., Ind., 131 ms. N. E. of Indianapolis; from W. 544 ms. Watered by Maumee river.
FORT WILKINS, p. o., Houghton co., Mich.
FORT WINNEBAGO, p. v., Columbia co., Wis.
FORTY FORT, p. o., Luzerne co., Pa.
FORWARDSTOWN, p. o., Somerset co., Pa.
FOSTER, p. t., Providence co., R. I., 19 ms. w. of Providence; from W. 386 ms. Watered by head branches of Pawtuxet river. Pop. 1,932.
FOSTER, p. o., Brachen co., Ky.
FOSTER CENTRE, p. o., Providence co., R. I.
FOSTERDALE, p. o., Cohecton township, Sullivan co., N. Y., 126 ms. s. w. of Albany; from W. 298 ms.
FOSTER'S, p. o., Marion co., Ill., 95 ms. s. E. of Springfield; from W. 755 ms.
FOSTER'S, p. o., Tuscaloosa co,, Ala.; from W. 830 ms.
FOSTER'S BAR, p. o., Yuba co., Cal.
FOSTER'S CROSS ROADS, p. o., Bledsoe co., Tenn., 111 ms. E. of Nashville; from W. 596 ms.
FOSTER'S FORK, p. o., Prince Edward's co., Va.
FOSTER'S MILLS, p. o., Seneca co., O.
FOSTER'S MILLS, p. o., Johnson co., Ind.
FOSTERIA, p. o., Blair co., Pa.
FOSTERVILLE, p. o., Aurelius township, Cayuga co., N. Y., 159 ms. w. of Albany; from W. 338 ms.
FOSTERVILLE, v., Henry co., Ga., 75 ms. N, w. of Milledgeville; from W. 679 ms.
FOSTERVILLE, p. v., Rutherford co., Tenn., 46 ms. s. E. of Nashville; from W. 677 ms.
FOUNDRYVILLE, p. o., Columbia co., Pa., 99 ms. N. E. of Harrisburgh; from W. 209 ms.
FOUNTAIN COUNTY, situated in the westerly part of Indiana, with Wabash river on the west and northwest. Area, 390 square miles. Seat of justice, Covington. Pop. in 1830, 7,619; in 1840, 11,218; in 1850, 13,262.
FOUNTAINDALE, p. o., Adams co., Pa., 47 ms. s. w. of Harrisburgh; from W. 71 ms.
FOUNTAIN GREEN, p. o., Chester co., Pa.
FOUNTAIN GREEN, p. o., Hancock co., Ill., 162 ms. N. w. of Springfield; from W. 875 ms.
FOUNTAIN HEAD, p. o., Sumner co., Tenn., 38 ms. N. E. of Nashville; from W. 682 ms.
FOUNTAIN HILL, p. o., Ashley co., Ark.
FOUNTAIN HILL, p. o., Greene co., N. C.
FOUNTAIN INN, p. o., Greenville district, S. C., 89 ms. N. w. of Columbia; from W. 503 ms.
FOUNTAIN MILLS, p. o., Chester co., Pa.
FOUNTAIN RUN, p. o., Monroe co., Ky.
FOUNTAIN SPRING, p. o., Schuylkill co., Pa., 75 ms. N. E. of Harrisburgh; from W. 185 ms.
FOUNTAIN SPRING, p. o., Wood co., Va.
FOUNTAIN SPRINGS, p. o., Wapello co., Iowa.
FOURCHE A RENAULT, p. v., Washington co., Mo., 103 ms. s. E. of Jefferson city; from W. 887 ms. Watered by Mineral fork of Big river.
FOURCHE DUMAS, p. o., Randolph co., Ark., 154 ms. N. E. of Little Rock; from W. 983 ms.
FOURCHE LA FAVE, t., Conway co., Ark.
FOURCHE LA FAVE, t., Pope co., Ark.
FOUR CORNERS, p. o., Ridgefield township, Huron co., O., 110 ms. N. of Columbus; from W. 386 ms.
FOUR MILE BRANCH, p. o., Barnwell district, S. C., 104 ms. s. of Columbia; from W. 600 ms.
FOUR MILE BRANCH, p. o., Monroe co., Tenn., 178 ms. s. E. of Nashville; from W. 542 ms.
FOUR MILE GROVE, p. o., Lee co., Ill.
FOUR MILE PRAIRIE, p. o., Van Zandt co., Tex.
FOUR MILE PRAIRIE, p. o., Fayette co.. Ill.

FOWLER, p. t., St. Lawrence co., N. Y., 187 ms. N. w. of Albany; from W. 456 ms. Watered by Oswegatchie river and tributaries. Pop. 1,813.
FOWLER, p. t., Trumbull co., O., 183 ms. N. E. of Columbus; from W. 303 ms. Pop. 1,089.
FOWLER'S, p. o., Brooke co., Va.
FOWLER'S KNOB, p. o., Nicholas co., Va.
FOWLER'S MILLS, p. o.. Geauga co., O.
FOWLERSVILLE. p. o., Livingston co., N. Y
Fox, t., Clearfield co., Pa., 143 ms. N. w. of Harrisburgh; from W. 235 ms. Pop. 50.
Fox, t., Carroll co., O. Pop. 1,452.
Fox, p. o., Daviess co., Iowa.
FOXBOROUGH, p. t., Norfolk co., Mass., 27 ms. s. w. of Boston; from W. 418 ms. Watered by Rumford and Cocasset rivers. Pop. 1,880.
Fox CHASE. p. o., Philadelphia co., Pa., 108 ms. E. of Harrisburgh; from W. 148 ms.
Fox CREEK, p. o., St. Louis co., Mo., 94 ms. E. of Jefferson city; from W. 842 ms.
FOXCROFT, p. t., Piscataquis co., Me., 83 ms. N. E. of Augusta; from W. 680 ms. Pop. 1,045.
Fox LAKE, p. o.. Lake co., Ill.
Fox SPRING, p. o., Overton co., Tenn.
FOXVILLE, v., Frederick co., Md., 100 ms. N. w. of Annapolis; from W. 71 ms.
FOXVILLE, p. o., Fauquier co., Va., 116 ms. N. of Richmond; from W. 73 ms. Watered by Rappahanock river.
Foy's STORE, p. o., Onslow co., N. C., 139 ms. s. E. of Raleigh; from W. 369 ms.
FRAMINGHAM, p. t., Middlesex co., Mass., 22 ms. w. of Boston; from W. 418 ms. Watered by Sudbury river. Pop. 4,252.
FRANCESVILLE, p. o., Northampton co., N. C.
FRANCISCO, p. o., Stokes co., N. C.
FRANCISCOVILLE, p. o., Jackson co., Mich.
FRANCIS' CREEK, p. o.. Manitowoc co., Wis.
FRANCISTOWN, p. t., Hillsborough co., N. H. 25 ms. w. of Concord; from W. 460 ms. Watered by branches of Piscataquog river. Pop. 1,114.
FRANCISVILLE, t., Philadelphia co., Pa., 100 ms. E. of Harrisburgh; from W. 140 ms.
FRANCISVILLE, p. v., Crawford co., Ga., 61 ms. s. w. of Milledgeville; from W. 718 ms.
FRANCISVILLE, v., Boon co., Ky., 87 ms. N. of Frankfort; from W. 513 ms.
FRANCONIA, p. t., Grafton co., N. H., 75 ms. N. of Concord; from W. 541 ms. Watered by South branch of Lower Amonoock river.
FRANCONIA, p. t., Montgomery co., Pa., 88 ms. E. of Harrisburgh; from W. 167 ms. Watered by northeast branch of Perkiomen creek, and Indian, Pike, and Shippeack creeks. Pop. 1,270.
FRANCONIA, p. o., Putnam co., O., 129 ms. N. w. of Columbia; from W. 498 ms.
FRANKENMUTH, p. o., Saganaw co., Mich.
FRANKFORD, t., Sussex co., N. J. Watered by Papakating creek. Pop. 1,941.
FRANKFORD, p. b., Oxford township, Philadelphia co., Pa., 104 ms. E. of Harrisburgh; from W. 144 ms Watered by Tacony creek. Pop. 5,346.
FRANKFORD, t., Cumberland co., Pa. Watered by Conedogwiniet creek and branches. Pop. 1,241.
FRANKFORD, p. v.. Greenbrier co., Va., 224 ms. w. of Richmond; from W. 261 ms.
FRANKFORT, c. h., p. v., seat of justice of Clinton co., Ind. Pop. 582.
FRANKFORT, p. t., Waldo co., Me., 64 ms. N. E. of Augusta; from W. 659 ms. Watered by Penobscot and Marsh rivers. Pop..4.233.
FRANKFORT, p. t., Herkimer co., N. Y., 86 ms. N. w. of Albany; from W. 397 ms. Watered by Mohawk river and the Erie canal. Pop. 3,023.
FRANKFORT, p. v., Hampshire co., Va., 203 ms. N. w. of Richmond ;from W. 131 ms. Watered by Patterson's creek.
FRANKFORT, p. v., Concord township, Ross co., O., 59 ms. s. of Columbus; from W. 414 ms. Pop. 640.
FRANKFORT, seat of justice of Franklin co., and capital of the state of Kentucky. Situated on a circular bend, on the north side of Kentucky river, 60 miles from its entrance into the Ohio, and 452 miles from Washington. The river here winds through deep limestone banks, which afford a level site for the town, and for South Frankfort, on the opposite side, with which it is connected by a bridge. Behind the town, the plain rises several hundred feet into a table-land, from which ap-

pears a magnificent prospect of the river, and a wide extent of country. Frankfort is a well-built village, with neat and solid dwellings, of brick or white marble. Of this material, which the limestone region along the river furnishes in great plenty and excellence, the state-house is constructed, a splendid building, with a portico supported by Ionic pillars at the front, and a lighted cupola upon the roof. There are also a penitentiary, courthouse, churches, banks, &c. The citizens of Frankfort display the accustomed intelligent hospitality which is a characteristic of Kentuckians. The manufactures of the town are considerable, and steamboats ascending to this point with high water, carry on a trade with the valleys of the Mississippi and Ohio rivers.

The Lexington and Ohio railroad, between Lexington and Louisville, 92 miles long, communicates with Frankfort.

The population in 1810, was 1,099; in 1820, 1,679; in 1830, 1,680; in 1840, 1,917; in 1850, 4,372.

FRANKFORT, p. v., seat of justice of Clinton co., Ind. 92 ms. N. W. of Indianapolis; from W. 600 ms. Watered by the south fork of Wild Cat creek. Pop. 582.

FRANKFORT, p. v., seat of justice of Franklin co., Ill., 100 ms. S. E. of Springfield; from W. 811 ms.

FRANKFORT HILL, p. o., Herkimer co., N. Y.

FRANKFORT MILLS, p. o., Waldo co., Me.

FRANKFORT SPRINGS, p. o., Beaver co., Pa.

FRANKLIN COUNTY, situated toward the westerly part of Maine. Area, 1,803 square miles. Seat of justice, Farmington. Pop. in 1840, 20,801; in 1850, 20,027.

FRANKLIN COUNTY, situated at the northwest corner of Vermont, with Lake Champlain on the west. Area, 600 square miles. Face of the country hilly and mountainous; soil, on the streams, fertile. Seat of justice, St. Albans. Pop. in 1810, 16,427; in 1820, 17,192; in 1830, 24,525; in 1840, 24,531; in 1850, 28,586.

FRANKLIN COUNTY, situated on the northerly boundary of Massachusetts, and traversed by Connecticut river. Area, 650 square miles. Face of the country agreeably diversified with mountains, hills, and valleys; soil generally fertile, on the streams rich and productive. Seat of justice, Greenfield. Pop. in 1810, 27,201; in 1820, 29,268; in 1830, 29,344; in 1840, 28,812; in 1850, 30,870.

FRANKLIN COUNTY, situated on the northerly boundary of New York. Area, 1,527 square miles. Face of the country, in the southern part, mountainous, toward the north, uneven. Seat of justice, Malone. Pop. in 1810, 2,717; in 1820, 4,439; in 1830, 11,332; in 1840, 16,518; in 1850, 25,109.

FRANKLIN COUNTY, situated on the southerly boundary of Pennsylvania. Area, 734 square miles. Face of the country diversified with mountains, hills, and valleys; soil varied, consisting principally of two formations; one of slate, extending through the northwesterly part; the other, of limestone, which covers the southeasterly part, and is much more of a productive soil. Seat of justice, Chambersburgh. Pop. in 1810, 23,083; in 1820, 31,192; in 1830, 35,103; in 1840, 37,739; in 1850, 39,904.

FRANKLIN COUNTY, situated in the southerly part of Virginia, with Roanoke river on the north. Area, 771 square miles. Face of the country undulating; soil generally fertile. Seat of justice, Rocky Mount. Pop. in 1810, 10,724; in 1820, 12,017; in 1830, 14,911; in 1840, 15,832; in 1850, 17,430.

FRANKLIN COUNTY, situated toward the northerly part of North Carolina, and traversed by Tar river. Area, 540 square miles. Face of the country uneven; soil in the valleys generally fertile. Seat of justice, Louisburgh. Pop. in 1810, 10,166; in 1820, 9,741; in 1830, 10,665; in 1840, 10,980; in 1850, 11,713.

FRANKLIN COUNTY, situated on the northeasterly boundary of Georgia. Area, 680 square miles. Face of the country broken; soil varied. Seat of justice, Carnesville. Pop. in 1820, 9,040; in 1830, 10,135; in 1840, 9,886; in 1850, 11,513.

FRANKLIN COUNTY, situated on the southerly shore of the western section of Florida, on the gulf of Mexico. Area, 700 square miles. Face of the country low and swampy; soil along the Appalachicola river, which bounds it on the west, fertile. Seat of justice, Appalachicola. Pop. in 1840, 1,030; in 1850, 1,561.

FRANKLIN COUNTY, situated on the westerly boundary of Alabama, with Tennessee river on the north. Area, 648 square miles. Face of the country hilly and broken; soil productive. Seat of justice, Rus-

sellville. Pop. in 1820, 4,988; in 1830, 11,078; in 1840, 14,270; in 1850, 19,610.

FRANKLIN COUNTY, situated in the southwesterly part of Mississippi. Area, 720 square miles. Face of the country hilly; soil, on the streams, very productive. Other parts contain open pine woods. Seat of justice, Meadville. Pop. in 1820, 3,881; in 1830, 4,622; in 1840, 4,775; in 1850, 5,904.

FRANKLIN COUNTY, situated on the southerly boundary of Tennessee. Area, 840 square miles. Face of the country mountainous and hilly; soil fertile. Seat of justice, Winchester. Pop. in 1810, 5,730; in 1820, 16,571; in 1830, 15,620; in 1840, 12,033; in 1850, 13,768.

FRANKLIN COUNTY, situated in the northwesterly part of Arkansas, and traversed by Arkansas river. Area, 800 square miles. Seat of justice, Ozark. Pop. in 1840, 2,665; in 1850, 3,500.

FRANKLIN COUNTY, situated toward the northerly part of Kentucky, and traversed by Kentucky river. Area, 200 square miles. Face of the country mountainous and hilly; soil fertile. Seat of justice, Frankfort. Pop. in 1810, 8,013; in 1820, 11,024; in 1830, 9,254; in 1840, 9,420; in 1850, 12,462.

FRANKLIN COUNTY, situated in the central part of Ohio, and traversed by Scioto river. Area, 529 square miles. Face of the country even, inclined to the south; soil mostly alluvial, or mixed sand, pebbles and clay, and in general better suited for grazing than tillage. Seat of justice, Columbus. Pop. in 1810, 3,486; in 1820, 10,300; in 1830, 14,756; in 1840, 25,049; in 1850, 42,910.

FRANKLIN COUNTY, situated in the southerly part of Illinois. Area, 866 square miles. Face of the country generally level; soil productive. Seat of justice, Benton. Pop. in 1820, 1,763; in 1830, 4,083; in 1840, 3,682; in 1850, 5,681.

FRANKLIN COUNTY, situated on the easterly boundary of Indiana, and traversed by White Water river. Area, 540 square miles. Face of the country moderately hilly; soil fertile. Seat of justice, Brookville. Pop. in 1820, 10,763; in 1830, 10,199; in 1840, 13,349; in 1850, 5,768.

FRANKLIN COUNTY, situated toward the easterly part of Missouri, with Missouri river on the north. Area, 850 square miles. Face of the country broken and hilly; soil mostly sterile. Seat of justice, Newport. Pop. in 1820, 2,379; in 1830, 3,484; in 1840, 7,515; in 1850, 11,021.

FRANKLIN PARISH, situated toward the northeasterly part of Louisiana. Area, —— square miles. Seat of justice, Winnsborough. Pop. in 1850, 3,251.

FRANKLIN, p. t., Hancock co., Me., 101 ms. N. E. of Augusta; from W. 683 ms. Watered by Taunton and Frenchman's bays. Pop. 736.

FRANKLIN, p. t., Merrimack co. N. H., 18 ms. N. W. of Concord; from W. 499 ms. Watered by Pemigewasset and Winnipisiogee rivers, where they unite and form the Merrimack. Pop. 1,251.

FRANKLIN, p. t., Franklin co., Vt., 70 ms. N. W. of Montpelier; from W. 550 ms. Watered by Rocher river and branches of the Missisque. Pop. 1,646.

FRANKLIN, p. t., Norfolk co., Mass., 31 ms. s. w. of Boston; from W. 424 ms. Watered by Charles river and its branches. Pop. 1,818.

FRANKLIN, p. t., New London, Ct., 37 ms. s. E. of Hartford; from W. 358 ms. Watered by Shetucket and Susquetonscut rivers, Beaver brook, and a branch of Yantic river. Pop. 895.

FRANKLIN, p. t., Delaware co., N. Y., 84 ms. s. of Albany; from W. 344 ms. Watered by Oleout creek and its branches. Pop. 3,087.

FRANKLIN, t., Franklin co., N. Y., 187 ms. N. of Albany. Watered by Saranac and its tributaries, Salmon river, and several small lakes. Pop. 724.

FRANKLIN, t., Warren co., N. J. Watered by Pohatcong and Musconetcong creeks. Pop. 1,564.

FRANKLIN, t., Somerset co., N. J. Watered by Millstone and Raritan rivers, and Six Mile run. Pop. 3,062.

FRANKLIN, t., Bergen co., N. J. Pop. 1,741.

FRANKLIN, t., Gloucester co., N. J. Watered by Raccoon creek, and branches of Maurice and Great Egg Harbor rivers. Pop. 2,984.

FRANKLIN, t., h. p. b., seat of justice of Venango co., Pa., 210 ms. N. W. of Harrisburgh; from W. 284 ms. Watered by French creek and Alleghany river.

FRANKLIN, t., Fayette co., Pa. Watered by Youghiogheny river and Redstone creek. Pop. 1,422.

FRANKLIN, t., Lycoming co., Pa. Pop. 1,059.

9

FRANKLIN, t., Susquehanna co., Pa. Pop. 703.

FRANKLIN, t., Armstrong co., Pa. Pop. 2,410.

FRANKLIN, t., Adams co., Pa. Watered by Conewago and Conecocheague creeks, and branches of Marsh creek. Pop. 1,806.

FRANKLIN, t., York co., Pa., 4 ms. from Harrisburgh; from W. 100 ms. Watered by a branch of Bermudian creek. Pop. 815.

FRANKLIN, t., Huntingdon co., Pa. Watered by the west branch of Little Juniata river, and Warrior's and Spruce creeks. Pop. 1,401.

FRANKLIN, t., Bradford co., Pa. Pop. 767.

FRANKLIN, t., Westmoreland co., Pa. Pop. 2,560.

FRANKLIN, t., Greene co., Pa. Watered by Ten-Mile creek and its tributaries. Pop. 1,591.

FRANKLIN, t., Alleghany co., Pa. Pop. 1,327.

FRANKLIN, v., Baltimore co., Md., 34 ms. N. of Annapolis; from W. 44 ms. Watered by Patapsco river.

FRANKLIN, c. h., p. v., seat of justice of Pendleton co., Va., 171 ms. N. w. of Richmond; from W. 171 ms. Watered by the south branch of the Potomac.

FRANKLIN, p. v., seat of justice of Macon co., N. C., 33 ms. w. of Raleigh; from W. 561 ms. Watered by a branch of Tennessee river.

FRANKLIN, c. h., p. v., seat of justice of Heard co., Ga., 134 ms. w. of Milledgeville; from W. 738 ms. Watered by Chattahoochee river.

FRANKLIN, p. v., Henry co., Ala.

FRANKLIN, p. v., Holmes co., Miss., 55 ms. N. of Jackson; from W. 1,004 ms. Watered by Big Cypress creek.

FRANKLIN, c. h., p. v., seat of justice of St. Mary's parish, La., 144 ms. w. of New Orleans; from W. 1,315 ms. Watered by Bayou Teche.

FRANKLIN, c. h. p. v., Williamson co., Tenn., 18 ms. s. of Nashville; from W. 695 ms. Watered by Harpeth river.

FRANKLIN, c. h., p. v., seat of justice of Simpson co., Ky., 164 ms. s. w. of Frankfort; from W. 688 ms. Watered by Drake's creek, a branch of Barren river.

FRANKLIN, p. t., Warren co., O., 84 ms. s. w. of Columbus; from W. 474 ms. Watered by Great Miami river, and the Miami canal. Pop. 2,544.

FRANKLIN. t., Adams co., O. Pop. 1,963.

FRANKLIN, p. t., Portage co., O. Pop. 1,749.

FRANKLIN, t., Brown co., O.

FRANKLIN, t., Clermont co., O. Watered by Ohio river. Pop. 3,061.

FRANKLIN, t., Coshocton co., O. Watered by Muskingum river. Pop. 966.

FRANKLIN, t., Columbiana co., O. Pop. 1,164.

FRANKLIN, t., Darke co., O. Pop. 551.

FRANKLIN, t., Franklin co., O. Watered by Scioto river. Pop. 1,253.

FRANKLIN, t., Harrison co., O. Pop. 1,062.

FRANKLIN, t., Knox co., O.

FRANKLIN, t., Licking co., O. Pop. 1,059.

FRANKLIN, t., Monroe co., O. Pop. 1,588.

FRANKLIN, t., Richland co., O. Watered by the head waters of Monhiccan creek. Pop. 1,257.

FRANKLIN, t., Ross co., O. Watered by Scioto river. Pop. 642.

FRANKLIN, t., Shelby co., O. Pop. 788.

FRANKLIN, t., Jackson co., O. Pop. 1,295.

FRANKLIN, t., Wayne co., O. Pop. 1,450.

FRANKLIN, p. t., Summit co., O. Pop. 1,674.

FRANKLIN, t., Lenawee co., Mich. Pop. 1,231.

FRANKLIN, p. v., Southfield township, Oakland co., Mich., 28 ms. N. w. of Detroit; from W. 550 ms.

FRANKLIN, c. h., p. v., seat of justice of Johnson co., Ind., 20 ms. s. of Indianapolis; from W 591 ms. Watered by Young's creek. Pop. 3,166.

FRANKLIN, t., Floyd co., Ind.

FRANKLIN, t., Henry co., Ind. Pop. 1,102.

FRANKLIN, t., Harrison co., Ind.

FRANKLIN, t., Owen co., Ind. Pop. 1,153.

FRANKLIN, t., Putnam co., Ind.

FRANKLIN, t., Marion co., Ind.

FRANKLIN, t., Montgomery co., Ind. Pop. 1,505.

FRANKLIN, t., Washington co., Ind. Pop. 3,032.

FRANKLIN, t., Wayne co., Ind. Pop. 1,362.

FRANKLIN, p. v., Morgan co., Ill.

FRANKLIN, t., Howard co., Mo. Watered by Missouri and Bonne Femme rivers at their junction.

FRANKLIN, t., Livingston co., Mo.

FRANKLIN, v. Walworth co., Wis., 75 ms. s. E. of Madison; from W. 798 ms.

FRANKLIN, p. t., Milwaukee co., Wis.

FRANKLIN, p. t., Fulton co., Ark. Pop. 212.

FRANKLIN, t., Chicot co., Ark. Pop. 561.

FRANKLIN, t., Sevier co., Ark. Pop. 402.

FRANKLIN, t., Union co., Ark. Pop. 1,394.

FRANKLIN CITY, p. v., Franklin township, Norfolk co., Mass., 28 ms. s. w. of Boston; from W. 427 ms. Pop. 1,818.

FRANKLIN CENTRE, p. o., Lee co., Iowa.

FRANKLIN COLLEGE, p. o., Davidson co., Tenn.

FRANKLIN CORNERS, p. o., Erie co., Pa.

FRANKLINDALE, p. o., Bradford co., Pa., 138 ms. N. of Harrisburgh; from W. 258 ms.

FRANKLINDALE, v., Fishkill township, Dutchess co., N. Y.

FRANKLIN DEPOT, p. o., Southampton co., Va.

FRANKLIN FURNACE, p. v., Hardiston township, Sussex co., N. J., 84 ms. N. of Trenton; from W. 252 ms.

FRANKLIN FURNACE, p. v., Green township, Scioto co., O., 105 ms. s. of Columbus; from W. 421 ms.

FRANKLIN FURNACE, p. o., Franklin co., N. Y.

FRANKLIN GROVE, p. o., Lee co., Ill.

FRANKLIN MILLS, p. v., Franklin township, Portage co., O. Watered by Cuyahoga river, and Pennsylvania and Ohio canal.

FRANKLIN SPRINGS, p. o., Franklin co., Ga.

FRANKLIN SQUARE, p. v., Salem township, Columbiana co., O., 155 ms. N. E. of Columbus; from W. 285 ms. Watered by Cherry and middle forks of Little Beaver river at their junction.

FRANKLINTON, c. h., p. o., seat of justice of Washington parish, La., 68 ms. N. of New Orleans; from W. 1,129 ms. Watered by Boguechitto river.

FRANKLINTON, p. v., Franklin co., N. C., 26 ms. N. of Raleigh; from W. 262 ms.

FRANKLINTON, p. o., Middleburgh township, Schoharie co., N. Y.

FRANKLINTON, p. o., Henry co., Ky.

FRANKLINTON, p. v., Franklin township, Franklin co., O.

FRANKLINTON, p. v., York co., Pa., 15 ms. s. E. of Harrisburgh; from W. 100 ms.

FRANKLINVILLE, p. o., Montour co., Pa.

FRANKLINVILLE, p. o., Carroll co., Md.

FRANKLINVILLE, p. v., Randolph co., N. C.

FRANKLINVILLE, p. o., Gloucester co., N. J.

FRANKLINVILLE, p. o., Cattaraugus co., N. Y., 280 ms. w. of Albany; from W. 327 ms. Watered by Ischua and Great Valley creeks.

FRANKS, t., St. Francis co., Ark.

FRANKSTOWN, p. t., Blair co., Pa., 116 ms. w. of Harrisburgh; from W. 164 ms. Watered by a branch of Juniata river. Pop. 1,482.

FRANKSTOWN, p. b., Frankfort township, Blair co., Pa.

FRANKSVILLE, p. o., Claiborne parish, La.

FRANKTOWN, p. o., Northampton co., Va.

FRANTZDALE, p. o., Ulster co., N. Y., 74 ms. s. E. of Harrisburgh; from W. 131 ms.

FRAZER, p. o., Chester co., Pa.

FRAZEYSBURG, p. v., Jackson township, Muskingum co., O., 61 ms. E. of Columbus; from W. 354 ms. Watered by Ohio river and Erie canal.

FRAZIERVILLE, v., Abbeville district, S. C., 88 ms. w. of Columbia; from W. 538 ms.

FREASE'S STORE, p. o., Stark co., O., 108 ms. N. E. of Columbus; from W. 328 ms.

FREDERICA, p. v., Kent co., Del., 13 ms. s. of Dover. Watered by Motherill creek.

FREDERICA, p. v., St. Simon's island, Glynn co., Ga., 229 ms. s. E. of Milledgeville; from W. 378 ms.

FREDERICK COUNTY, situated on the northern boundary of Maryland with Potomac river on the southwest. Area, 750 square miles. Face of the country moderately even, inclined toward the south. Soil. fertile. Seat of justice, Fredericktown. Pop. in 1810, 34,437; in 1820, 40,450; in 1830, 45,793; in 1840, 36,405; in 1850, 40,987.

FREDERICK COUNTY, situated in the northeastern part of Virginia. Area, 660 square miles. Face of the country mountainous and hilly; soil excellent for grain and orchard fruits. Seat of justice, Winchester. Pop. in 1810, 22,574; in 1820, 24,706; in 1830, 26,048; in 1840, 14,242; in 1850, 15,975.

FREDERICK, p. t., Montgomery co., Pa., 77 ms. E. of Harrisburgh; from W. 170 ms. Pop. 1,431.

FREDERICK CITY, c. h., p. v., seat of justice of Frederick co., Md., 75 ms. N. w. of Annapolis; from w. 43 ms. Watered by Carroll's creek. Pop. 6,028.

FREDERICK, p. o., Milton township, Mahoning co., O., 157 ms. N. E. of Columbus ; from W. 305 ms.

FREDERICK, t., Knox co., O. Pop. 712.

FREDERICKSBURGH, p. o., Lebanon co., Pa.

FREDERICKSBURGH, city, Spottsylvania co., Va., 66 ms. N. of Richmond ; from W. 56 ms. Watered by Rappahannock river. Pop. 4,062.

FREDERICKSBURGH, p. v., Salt creek township, Wayne co., O., 98 ms. N. of Columbus ; from W. 353 ms.

FREDERICKSBURGH, t., Muskingum co., O.

FREDERICKSBURGH, v., Ray co., Mo., 154 ms. N. w. of Jefferson City ; from W. 1,059 ms.

FREDERICKSBURGH, p. v., Washington co., Ind., 111 ms. s. of Indianapolis ; from W. 625 ms. Watered by Blue river.

FREDERICKSBURGH, p. o., Osage co., Mo.

FREDERICKSBURGH, p. o., Gillespie co., Tex.

FREDERICKSHALL, p. o., Louisa co., Va., 48 ms. N. w. of Richmond ; from W. 91 ms.

FREDERICKSVILLE, p. o., Schuyler co., Ill.

FREDERICKTOWN, p. o., Washington co., Ky.

FREDERICKTOWN, p. o., Madison co., Mo.

FREDERICKTOWN, p. o., Knox co., O.

FREDERICKTOWN, p. o., Washington co., Pa.

FREDERICKTOWN, p. o., Marion co., Ill.

FREDON, p. o., Stillwater township, Sussex co., N. J., 74 ms. N. of Trenton ; from W. 234 ms.

FREDONIA, p. v., Pomfret township, Chautauque co., N. Y., 323 ms. w. of Albany ; from W. 345 ms.

FREDONIA, p. t., Licking co., O., 40 ms. N. E. of Columbus ; from W. 379 ms.

FREDONIA, p. v., Caldwell co., Ky., 239 ms. s. w. of Frankfort ; from W. 771 ms.

FREDONIA, p. v., Montgomery co., Tenn., 34 ms. N. w. of Nashville ; from W. 791 ms.

FREDONIA, c. h., p. v., seat of justice of Crawford co., Ind., 122 ms. s. of Indianapolis ; from W. 641 ms. Watered by Ohio river.

FREDONIA, p. v., Williamson co., Ill., 175 ms. s. of Springfield ; from W. 826 ms.

FREDONIA, p. v., Chambers co., Ala. ; from W. 758 ms.

FREDONIA, p o., Washtenaw co., Mich.

FREDONIA, t., Calhoun co., Mich. Pop. 623.

FREDONIA, p. o., Rusk co., Tex.

FREDONIA, p. o., Washington co., Wis.

FREDONIA, p. o., Macon co., Ga.

FREE BRIDGE, p. o., Cass co., Ga.

FREEBURGH, p. o., Union co., Pa.

FREEDENSBURGH, P. Y., Schuylkill co., Pa., 52 ms. N. E. of Harrisburgh ; from W. 163 ms.

FREEDOM, p. t., Waldo co., Me., 33 ms. N. E. of Augusta ; from W. 608 ms. Pop. 948.

FREEDOM, p. t., Carroll co., N. H., 61 ms. N. E. of Concord ; from W. 642 ms. Watered by Ossipee lake. Pop. 910.

FREEDOM, p. t., Cattaraugus co., N. Y., 270 ms. w. of Albany ; from W. 346 ms. Watered by Clear creek and tributaries of Cattaraugus creek. Pop. 1,652.

FREEDOM, t., Adams co., Pa. Pop. 473.

FREEDOM, p. b., Beaver co., Pa., 224 ms. w. of Harrisburgh ; from W. 250 ms. Watered by Ohio river. Pop. 534.

FREEDOM, p. v., Carroll co., Md., 50 ms. N. w. of Annapolis ; from W. 60 ms.

FREEDOM, p. t., Portage co., O., 159 ms. N. E. of Columbus ; from W. 315 ms. Pop. 996.

FREEDOM, t., Henry co., O. Pop. 83.

FREEDOM, t., Wood co., Pa.

FREEDOM, t., Washtenaw co., Mich. Pop. 1,215.

FREEDOM, p. v.. Owen co., Ind., 67 ms. s. w. of Indianapolis ; from W. 630 ms.

FREEDOM, p. o., Keokuk co., Iowa.

FREEDOM, p. t., Lafayette co., Mo. Pop. 1,445.

FREEDOM, p. o., Sauk co., Wis.

FREEDOM, p. o., La Salle co., Ill.

FREEDOM PLAINS, p. v., La Grange township, Dutchess co., N. Y., 79 ms. s. of Albany ; from W. 306 ms.

FREEHOLD, p. v., Greenville township, Greene co., N. Y., 42 ms. s. of Albany ; from W. 355 ms.

FREEHOLD, c. h., p. t., seat of justice of Monmouth co., N. J., 35 ms. s. E. of Trenton ; from W. 201 ms. Pop. 2,633.

FREEHOLD, p. t., Warren co., Pa. Pop. 1,162.

FREEL, p. o., Polk co., Iowa.

FREELAND, p. o., Baltimore co., Md.

FREEMAN, p. t., Franklin co., Me., 48 ms. N. w. of Augusta ; from W. 637 ms. Watered by a tributary of Sandy river. Pop. 762.

FREEMANSBURGH, p. v., Northampton co., Pa., 99 ms. N. E. of Harrisburgh ; from W. 192 ms.

FREEMAN'S LANDING, p. o., Hancock co., Va.

FREEMANSVILLE, p. o., Cherokee co., Ga.

FREEMANTON, p. o., Effingham co., Ill., 90 ms. s. E. of Springfield ; from W. 719 ms.

FREEO, p. o., Washita co., Ark.

FREEPORT, p. t., Cumberland co., Me., 34 ms. s. w. of Augusta ; from W. 561 ms. Watered by Casco bay. Pop. 2,629.

FREEPORT, p. b., Buffalo township, Armstrong co., Pa., 196 ms. N. w. of Harrisburgh ; from W. 228 ms. Watered by Buffalo creek. Alleghany river, and Pennsylvania canal. Pop. 1,073.

FREEPORT, p. t., Harrison co., O., 99 ms. N. E. of Columbus ; from W. 304 ms. Watered by Big Stillwater creek. Pop. 1,127.

FREEPORT, p. v., Shelby co., Ind., 29 ms. s. E. of Indianapolis ; from W. 560 ms.

FREEPORT, c. h., p. v., seat of justice of Stephenson co., Ill., 200 ms. N. of Springfield ; from W. 832 ms. Watered by Peekatonica river. Pop. 1,436.

FREEPORT, p. o., Wood co., Va.

FREESHADE, p. o., Middlesex co., Va., 98 ms. E. of Richmond ; from W. 169 ms.

FREESTONE COUNTY, situated in the central part of Texas, with Trinity river on the northeast. Area, —— square miles. Seat of justice, Troy.

FREETOWN, p. t., Bristol co., Mass., 42 ms. s. of Boston ; from W. 427 ms. Watered by Taunton river.

FREETOWN, p. t., Cortland co., N. Y., 139 ms. w. of Albany ; from W. 326 ms. Watered by Tougnioga and Ostelic rivers. Pop. 1,035.

FREETOWN CORNERS, p. v., Freetown township, Cortland co., N. Y.

FREE UNION, p. o., Albemarle co., Va.

FRELSBURGH, p. o., Colorado co., Tex.

FREMONT COUNTY, situated at the southwest corner of Iowa, with Missouri river on the west. Area, —— square miles. Seat of justice, Dawsonburgh. Pop. in 1850, 1,244.

FREMONT, p. o., Pontotoc co., Miss.

FREMONT, p. o., Steuben co., Ind.

FREMONT, p. o., Obion co., Tenn.

FREMONT, p. o., Mahaska co., Iowa.

FREMONT, p. o., Sandusky co., O.

FREMONT, c. h., p. v., seat of justice of Yolo co., Cal.

FREMONT, p. o., Itawanha co., Wis.

FREMONT, p. o., Sullivan co., N. Y.

FREMONT, p. o., Shiawassee co., Mich.

FREMONT, p. o., Brown co., Wis.

FRENCH BROAD, p. v., Buncombe co., N. C., 265 ms. w. of Raleigh ; from W. 488 ms.

FRENCH CAMP, p. o., Choctaw co., Miss.

FRENCH CREEK, p. o., Knox co., Ill.

FRENCH CREEK, p. t., Chautauque co., N. Y., 368 ms. w. of Albany ; from W. 358 ms. Watered by French creek. Pop. 725.

FRENCH CREEK, t., Venango co., Pa. Pop. 962.

FRENCH CREEK, p. t., Mercer co., Pa., 223 ms. w. of Harrisburgh ; from W. 297 ms. Watered by French and Sandy creeks. Pop. 691.

FRENCH CREEK, p. o., Lewis co., Va., 307 ms. w. of Richmond ; from W. 275 ms.

FRENCH GRANT, p. o., Green township, Scioto co., O., 110 ms. s. of Columbus ; from W. 426 ms.

FRENCH GROVE, p. o., Bureau co., Ill. Watered by tributaries of Spoon river.

FRENCH ISLAND, p. o., Spencer co., Ind.

FRENCH LICK, p. o., Orange co., Ind.

FRENCH MOUNTAIN, p. o., Warren co., N. Y.

FRENCH'S CORNER, p. o., Kennebec co., Me.

FRENCH'S MILLS, p. o., Bradford co., Pa.

FRENCHTON, p. v., Lewis co., Va., 311 ms. N. w. of Richmond ; from W. 279 ms.

FRENCHTOWN, p. v., Hunterdon co., N. J., 35 ms. N. of Trenton ; from W. 192 ms.

FRENCHTOWN, v., Lewis co., Va., 311 ms. w. of Richmond ; from W. 279 ms.

FRENCHTOWN, t., Monroe co., Mich. Pop. 1,242.

FRENCH VILLAGE, p. v., St. Clair co., Ill.

FRENCHVILLE, p. v., Clearfield co., Pa.

FREWSBURGH, p. o., Carroll township, Chautauque co., N. Y., 340 ms. w. of Albany ; from W. 317 ms.

FREYSBUSH, p. o., Canajoharie township, Montgomery co., N. Y.

FRIAR'S POINT, p. o., Coahoma co., Miss.

FRICK'S GAP, p. o., Walker co., Ga.

FRIEDENSVILLE, p. o., Lehigh co., Pa.
FRIENDFIELD, p. o., Marion district, S. C
FRIEND'S, p. o., Chautauque co., N. Y.
FRIENDSHIP, p. t., Lincoln co., Me., 54 ms. S. E. of Augusta ; from W. 631 ms. Watered by the Atlantic ocean and Muscongus bay. Pop. 691.
FRIENDSHIP, p. t., Alleghany co., N. Y., 272 ms. W. of Albany ; from W. 325 ms. Watered by Campan's creek, a branch of Genesee river. Pop. 1,675.
FRIENDSHIP, p. v., Anne Arundel co., Md., 31 ms. N. W. of Annapolis ; from W. 61 ms.
FRIENDSHIP, p. o., Guilford co., N. C., 91 ms. N. W. of Raleigh ; from W. 312 ms.
FRIENDSHIP, p. o., Sumter district, S. C., 81 ms. S. E. of Columbia ; from W. 519 ms.
FRIENDSHIP, p. o., Sumter co., Ga., 108 ms. S. W. of Milledgeville ; from W. 764 ms.
FRIENDSHIP, p. o., McDonough co., Ill.
FRIENDSHIP, p. o., Bath co., Ala.
FRIENDSHIP, p. o., Fond du Lac co., Wis.
FRIENDSHIP, p. o., Guilford co., N. C.
FRIENDSHIP, p. o., Franklin co., Miss.
FRIENDSHIP, p. o., Dyer co., Tenn.
FRIENDSHIP, p. o., Scioto co., O.
FRIENDSVILLE, p. v., Middletown township, Susquehanna co., Pa., 175 ms. N. E. of Harrisburgh ; from W. 283 ms. Pop. 185.
FRIENDSVILLE, p. o., Blount co., Tenn.
FRIENDSVILLE, p. o., Wabash co., Ill., 177 ms. S. E. of Springfield ; from W. 715 ms.
FRISBIE'S MILLS, p. o., Warrick co., Ind.
FRONTERO, p. o., Socorro co., Tex.
FRONTIER, p. o., Clinton co., N. Y.
FRONT ROYAL, c. h., p. v., seat of justice of Warren co., Va., 139 ms. N. W. of Richmond ; from W. 85 ms. Watered by Happy creek. Pop. 504.
FROSTBURGH, p. v., Alleghany co., Md.. 176 ms. N. W. of Annapolis ; from W. 144 ms.
FROZEN CREEK, p. o., Breathitt co., Ky.
FRUIT HILL, p. o., Christian co., Ky., 192 ms. S.W. of Frankfort ; from W. 728 ms.
FRUIT HILL, p. v., Clearfield co., Pa., 132 ms. N. W. of Harrisburgh ; from W. 222 ms.
FRUIT HILL, p. o., Vigo co., Ind.
FRUIT HILL, p. o., Edgefield district, S. C.
FRYBURGH, p. o., Auglaize co., O.
FRYEBURGH, p. t., Oxford co., Me., 72 ms. S. W. of Augusta ; from W. 569 ms. Watered by Saco river and Lovell's pond. Pop. 1,523.
FRYER'S BRIDGE, p. o., Pike co., Ala.
FRYER'S PONDS, p. o., Burke co., Ga., 94 ms. E. of Milledgeville ; from W. 617 ms.
FRYREAR'S MILLS, p. o., Miller co., Mo.
FULLER'S POINT, p. o., Coles co., Ill.
FULLERSVILLE IRON WORKS, p. v., Fowler township, St. Lawrence co., N. Y., 190 ms. N. W. of Albany ; from W. 460 ms. Watered by Oswegatchie river.
FULLWOOD'S STORE, p. o., Union co., N. C., 177 ms. S. W. of Raleigh ; from W. 414 ms.
FULTON COUNTY, situated toward the easterly part of New York. Area, 500 square miles. Face of the country hilly ; soil productive. Seat of justice, Johnstown. Pop. in 1840, 18,049 ; in 1850, 20,171.
FULTON COUNTY, situated in the northerly part of Indiana. Area, 350 square miles. Seat of justice, Rochester. Pop. in 1840, 1,993 ; in 1850, 5,981.
FULTON COUNTY, situated toward the westerly part of Illinois, with Illinois river on the southeast.

Area, 874 square miles. Seat of justice, Lewiston. Pop. in 1830, 1,841 : in 1840, 13,142 ; in 1850, 22,508.
FULTON COUNTY, situated at the southwest corner of Kentucky, with Mississippi river on the west. Area, —— square miles. Seat of justice, Hickman. Pop. in 1850, 4,446.
FULTON COUNTY. situated on the northern boundary of Ohio. Area, —— square miles. Seat of justice, Gorham. Pop. in 1850, 7,781.
FULTON COUNTY, situated on the northern boundary of Arkansas. Area, —— square miles. Seat of justice, Pilot Hill. Pop. in 1850, 1,819.
FULTON, p. t., Schoharie co., N. Y., 42 ms. w. of Albany ; from W. 381 ms. Watered by Schoharie creek and tributaries. Pop. 2,566.
FULTON, p. v., Oswego co., N. Y., 190 ms. N. w. of Albany ; from W. 460 ms. Watered by Oswego river. Pop. 2,344.
FULTON, p. o., Westmoreland co., Pa., 183 ms. w. of Harrisburgh ; from W. 209 ms.
FULTON, p. t., Hamilton co., O., 120 ms. s. w. of Columbus ; from W. 496 ms. Watered by Ohio river. Pop. 3,224.
FULTON (CANAL), p. v., Lawrence township, Stark co., O., 125 ms. N. E. of Columbus ; from W. 330 ms. Situated on Ohio canal.
FULTON, p. v., Barry co., Mich., 140 ms. N. W. of Detroit ; from W. 605 ms.
FULTON, p. v., Davie co., N. C., 156 ms. w. of Raleigh ; from W. 364 ms.
FULTON, p. v., Sumter district, S. C., 69 ms. E. of Columbia ; from W. 509 ms.
FULTON, p. v., Hempstead co., Ark., 126 ms. s. w. of Little Rock ; from W. 1,191 miles. Watered by Red river.
FULTON, p. t., Sevier co., Ark. Pop. 481.
FULTON, p. v., Whitesides co., Ill., 185 ms. N. of Springfield ; from W. 865 ms.
FULTON, p. o., Jackson co., Iowa.
FULTON, c. h., p. v., seat of justice of Callaway co., Mo., 22 ms. N. E. of Jefferson city ; from W. 917 ms. Watered by Riviere au Vases.
FULTON, t., Fountain co., Ind. Eop. 1,008.
FULTON, p. v., Lauderdale co., Tenn., 200 ms. w. of Nashville, from W. 882 ms. Watered by Mississippi river.
FULTON, c. h., p. v., seat of justice of Itawamba co., Miss., 210 ms. N. E. of Jackson ; from W. 875 ms. Watered by the east fork of Tombigbee river. Pop. 229.
FULTON, p. o., Dallas co., Ala.
FULTON, p. o., Cobb co., Ga.
FULTON, p. o., Rock co., Wis.
FULTON. p. o., Fulton co., Ill.
FULTON CENTRE, p. o., Schoharie co., N. Y.
FULTONHAM, p. o., Fulton township, Schoharie co., N. Y.
FULTONHAM, p. v., Union township, Muskingum co., O., 57 ms., E. of Columbus ; from W. 348 ms. Watered by Jonathan's creek.
FULTONVILLE, p. v., Glen township, Montgomery co., N. Y., 43 ms. N. w. of Albany ; from W. 407 ms. Watered by Mohawk river, and Erie canal.
FRANKSTOWN, p. v., Washington co., Md., 99 ms. N. w. of Annapolis ; from W. 67 ms. Watered by Antietam creek, a branch of the Potomac. Pop. 915.
FURNACE, p. o., Vermillion township, Erie co., O., 117 ms. N. of Columbus ; from W. 391 ms.
FURNACE, p. o., Berks co., Pa.

G.

GABRIEL'S CREEK, p. o., Yancy, co., N. C.
GADDEYVILLE, p. o., Robeson co., N. C., 122 ms. s. w. of Raleigh ; from W. 400 ms.
GADDISTOWN, p. o., Union co., Ga.
GAD FLY, p. o., Barry co., Mo.
GADSDEN COUNTY, situated on the northern boundary of Florida, with Appalachicola river on the west. Area, 1,800 square miles. Seat of justice, Quincy. Pop. in 1830, 4,855 ; in 1840, 5,992 ; in 1850, 8,783.
GADSDEN, p. o., Cherokee co., Ala.
GADSDEN, p. o., Richland district, S. C.
GAGE'S LAKE, p. o., Lake co., Ill.
GAGE'S POINT, p. o., St. Francis co., Ark.
GAHANNA, p. o., Franklin co., O.
GAILEY'S MILL, p. o., Hall co. Ga.

GAINER'S STORE, p. o., Pike co., Ala.
GAINES, p. t., Orleans co., N. Y., 252 ms. N. w. of Albany ; from W. 395 ms. Watered by branches of Oak Orchard creek. Pop. 2,722.
GAINES, p. t., Tioga co., Pa. Pop. 510.
GAINSBOROUGH, p. v., Frederick co., Va., 154 ms. N. w. of Richmond ; from W. 82 ms.
GAINSBOROUGH, c. h., p. v., seat of justice of Jackson co., Tenn., 73 ms. N. E. of Nashville ; from W. 631 ms. Watered by Cumberland river.
GAINES' CROSS ROADS, p. v., Rappahannock co., Va.. 118 ms. N. w., of Richmond ; from W. 70 ms.
GAINES' LANDING, p. o., Chicot co., Ark.
GAINESTOWN, p. o., Clark co., Ala.
GAINESVILLE, p. t., Wyoming co., N. Y., 252 ms. w.

of Albany; from W. 357 ms. Watered by Allen's creek and another branch of Genesee river. Pop. 1,760.

GAINESVILLE, c. h., p. v., seat of justice of Hall co., Ga., 118 ms. N. W. of Milledgeville; from W. 621 ms.

GAINESVILLE, p. v., Sumter co., Ala.; from W. 872 ms. Watered by Tombigbee river.

GAINESVILLE, p. o., Greene co., Ark.

GAINESVILLE, p. o., Hancock co., Wis.

GAINESVILLE, p. o., Allen co., Ky.

GALEN, t., Wayne co., N. Y., 172 ms. w. of Albany. Watered by Clyde river, and the Erie canal. Pop. 4,609.

GALENA, p. v., Berks township, Delaware co., O., 21 ms. N. of Columbus; from W. 399 ms.

GALENA, a thriving city, the seat of justice of Jo-Daviess co., Ill., is situated on both sides of Fevre, or Bean river, six miles above its entrance into the Mississippi, and the largest boats ascend to this point at all stages of the water. The city is mostly built on the west side of the river, yet it is rapidly extending on the opposite side, with which it is connected by three substantial bridges. This is the centre of the great lead region, which occupies the northwestern portion of Illinois, and the southwestern corner of Wisconsin, together with a strip of a few miles in width on the opposite side of the Mississippi in Iowa, equal to a surface of nearly three thousand square miles. In riding over the country from Galena to the Wisconsin river, the most remarkable feature presented is the numerous "diggings." Its trade with the surrounding country is extensive, embracing a circuit of 30 to 100 ms. The town presents a very metallic appearance, inasmuch as its wharves, for quite a distance, are lined with piles of pig-lead. It is estimated by those whose knowledge and experience render them competent to judge, that if the mines already opened were well worked, they are capable of producing 150,000,000 pounds annually for ages to come. The population of Galena in 1850, was 6,004.

GALENA, t., Franklin co., Mo.

GALENA, p. o., Floyd co., Ind.

GALES, p. o., Sullivan co., N. Y., 103 ms. s. w. of Albany; from W. 286 ms.

GALESBURGH, p. v., Knox co., Ill., 105 ms. N. W. of Springfield; from W. 834 ms.

GALESBURGH, p. v., Kalamazoo co., Mich., 137 ms. w. of Detroit; from W. 596 ms.

GALES' FERRY, p. o., Ledyard township, New London co., Ct., 47 ms. s. E. of Hartford; from W. 360 ms.

GALESVILLE. p. o., Greenwich township, Washington co., N. Y., 39 ms. N. B. of Albany, from W. 409 ms.

GALION, p. o., Sandusky township, Crawford co., O., 68 ms. N. E. of Columbus; from W. 394 ms.

GALLATIA, p. o., Gallatin co., Ill., 177 ms. s. E. of Springfield; from W. 794 ms.

GALLATIN COUNTY, situated on the easterly boundary of Illinois, with Ohio and Wabash rivers on the east. Area, 760 square miles. Face of the country, undulating; soil, productive. Seat of justice, Equality. Pop. in 1820, 3,155; in 1830, 7,405; in 1840, 10,760; in 1850, 5,448.

GALLATIN COUNTY, situated on the northerly boundary of Kentucky, with Ohio river on the northwest. Area, 175 square miles. Face of the country, hilly; soil, generally fertile. Seat of justice, Warsaw. Pop. in 1810, 3,307; in 1820, 6,674; in 1830, 6,680; in 1840, 4,093; in 1850, 5,137.

GALLATIN, v., Allen co., O. 113 ms. N. W. of Columbus; from W. 484 ms.

GALLATIN, c. h., p. v., seat of justice of Sumner co., Tenn., 26 ms. N. E. of Nashville; from W. 667 ms.

GALLATIN, p. v., Parke co., Ind., 78 ms. w. of Indianapolis; from W. 650 ms.

GALLATIN, p. v., Copiah co., Miss., 37 ms. s. of Jackson; from W. 1,047 ms. Watered by Bayou Pierre river.

GALLATIN, c. h., p. v., seat of justice of Daviess co., Mo., 189 ms. N. W. of Jefferson City; from W. 1,092 ms.

GALLATIN, t., Columbia co., N. Y., 44 ms. s. E. of Albany. Watered by Dove creek, and Charlotte lake. Pop. 1,586.

GALLATINVILLE, p. o., Gallatin township, Columbia co., N. Y., 48 ms. s. of Albany; from W. 332 ms.

GALLIA COUNTY, situated on the southeasterly boundary of Ohio, with Ohio river on the east. Area, 500 square miles. Face of the country, uneven; soil, inferior, except along the streams where it is rich. Seat of justice, Gallipolis. Pop. in 1830, 9,773; in 1840, 13,444; in 1850, 17,063.

GALLIA FURNACE, p. o., Gallia co., O.

GALLILEE, p. o., Wayne co., Pa.

GALLIPOLIS, c. h., p. t., seat of justice of Gallia co., O., 100 ms. s. E. of Columbus; from W. 358 ms. Watered by Ohio river. Pop. 2,228.

GALLEY ROCK, t., Pope co., Ark.

GALLOWAY, t., Atlantic co., N. J. Watered by Nacote creek. Pop, 2,307.

GALLOWAY, p. o., La Salle co., Ill.

GALLUPVILLE, p. o., Schoharie township, Schoharie co., N. Y., 27 ms. w. of Albany; from W. 388 ms.

GALLY CREEK, p. o., Pope co., Ark.

GALUM, p. o., Perry co., Ill., 166 ms. s. of Springfield; from W. 848 ms.

GALVESTON COUNTY, situated on the southerly boundary of Texas, with Galveston bay on the east, and the gulf of Mexico on the south. It includes Galveston island. Area, —— square miles. Seat of justice, Galveston. Pop. in 1850, 4,529.

GALVESTON, city, seat of justice of Galveston co., at the northeasterly part of Galveston island, Texas. Between the town and Pelican island, on the northwest, the entrance to the bay is deep and spacious, affording a good harbor and anchorage. Steamboats and other vessels arrive at Galveston from different points on the gulf of Mexico; and it is the chief commercial place in the state. There are a number of stores, dwellings, and other buildings, the white walls of which appear finely from the water, but occasion disappointment when more closely viewed.

The population in 1840, was 5,000 to 7,000; in 1850, 6,000.

GALVESTON, v., Ascension parish, La. Watered by Iberville river.

GALWAY, p. t., Saratoga co., N. Y., 36 ms. N. w. of Albany; from W. 404 ms. Watered by a branch of Kayaderosseras and Chuctenuda creeks.

GAMBIER, p. v., Pleasant township, Knox co., 56 ms. N. E. of Columbus; from W. 371 ms.

GAMBLE, p. o., Jefferson co., Ga.

GAMBLE GROVE, p. o., Fayette co., Iowa.

GAMBLE'S, p. o., Alleghany co., Pa., 156 ms. w. of Harrisburgh; from W. 212 ms.

GAMESVILLE, p. o., Cook co., Tex.

GANGES, p. o., Richland co., O., 75 ms. N. E. of Columbus; from W. 390 ms.

GANSEVOORT, p. o., Northumberland township, Saratoga co., N. Y., 49 ms. N. of Albany; from W. 419 ms.

GAP, p. o., Walker co., Ala.

GAP, p. o., Sadbury township, Lancaster co., Pa., 54 ms. s. E. of Harrisburgh; from W. 114 ms.

GAP CIVIL, p. o., Ashe co., N. C.

GAP CREEK, p. o., Ashe co., N. C.

GAP CREEK, p. o., Knox co., Tenn., 195 ms. E. of Nashville; from W. 510 ms.

GAP GROVE, p. o., Jo-Daviess co., Ill., 167 ms. N. of Springfield; from W. 830 ms.

GAP MILLS, p. o., Monroe co., Va.

GARDEN GROVE, p. o., Decatur co., Iowa.

GARDEN PLAIN, p. o., Whitesides co., Ill.

GARDINER, p. t., Kennebec co., Me., 6 ms. s. of Augusta; from W. 594 ms. Watered by Kennebec and Cobbesseconte rivers. Pop. in 1840, 5,042; in 1850, 6,486.

GARDINER CITY, p. o., Oregon, Ter.

GARDNER, p. t., Worcester co., Mass., 58 ms. N. w. of Boston; from W. 418 ms. Watered by a branch of Miller's river. Pop. 1,533.

GARDNER, p. o., Morgan co., O., 92 ms. E. of Columbus; from W. 314 ms.

GARDNER'S BRIDGE, p. o., Martin co., N. C., 151 ms. E. of Raleigh; from W. 342 ms.

GARDNER'S MILLS, p. o., St. Clair co., Mo.

GARDNERSVILLE, p. o., Seward township, Schoharie co., N. Y., 47 ms. w. of Albany; from W. 392 ms.

GARLAND, p. t., Penobscot co., Me., 98 ms. N. E. of Augusta; from W. 693 ms. Watered by head branches of Kanduskeag stream. Pop. 1,247.

GARLAND'S, p. o., Albemarle co., Va., 85 ms. N. w. of Richmond; from W. 135 ms.

GARLANDVILLE, p. o., Jasper co., Miss., 94 ms. s. E. of Jackson; from W. 972 ms.

GARMON'S MILLS, p. o., Cabarras co., N. C.

GARNAVILLE, p. o., Clayton co., Iowa.

GARNER'S FORD, p. o., Cleveland co., N. C.

GARNETTSVILLE, p. o., Mead co., Ky.

GAROGA, p. o., Ephratah township, Fulton co., N. Y., 54 ms. N. w. of Albany; from W. 400 ms.

GARRARD COUNTY, situated toward the central part of Kentucky, with Kentucky river on the north. Area, 240 square miles. Soil fertile. Seat of justice, Lancaster. Pop, in 1810, 9,186; in 1820, 10,851; in 1830, 11,870; in 1840, 10,480; in 1850, 10,237.

GARRATSVILLE, p. o., New Lisbon township, Otsego co., N. Y., 86 ms. w. of Albany; from W. 349 ms.

GARRETTSBURGH, p. v., Christian co., Ky., 224 ms. s. w. of Frankfort; from W. 748 ms.

GARRETTSVILLE, p. v., Nelson township, Portage co., O., 86 ms. N. E. of Columbus; from W. 349 ms.

GARRETTSVILLE, p. o., Lycoming co., Pa.

GARRISON'S, p. o., Putnam co., N. Y.

GARRISONVILLE, p. o., Stafford co., Va.

GARRY OWEN, p. o., Jackson co., Iowa.

GARYSBURGH, p. v., Northampton co., N. C., 98 ms. N. E. of Raleigh; from W. 201 ms.

GARYSVILLE, p. o., Prince George co., Va., 38 ms. s. E. of Richmond; from W. 157 ms.

GASCONADE COUNTY, situated between the eastern and central parts of Missouri, on the southerly side of Missouri river, and traversed by Gasconade river. Area, 1,260 square miles. Face of the country uneven; soil, on the lowlands, fertile. Seat of justice, Hermann. Pop. in 1830, 1,545; in 1840, 5,330; in 1850, 4,996.

GASCONADE, v., Gasconade co., Mo.

GAS FACTORY, p. o., Lincoln co., Tenn.

GASTON COUNTY, situated on the southern boundary of North Carolina. Area, —— square miles. Seat of justice, Hoylesville. Pop. in 1850, 8,073.

GASTON, p. o., Sumter co., Ala.

GASTON, p. o., Northampton co., N. C.

GASTON, p. o,, Atchison co., Mo.

GASPER, t., Preble co., O. Pop. 908.

GATES, p. t., Monroe co., N. Y., 225 ms. N. w. of Albany; from W. 372 ms. Pop. 2,005.

GATES, p. o., Newton co., Mo.

GATES' MILLS, p. v., Mayfield township, Cuyahoga co., O., 159 ms. N. E. of Columbus; from W. 347 ms. Watered by Chagrin river.

GATESVILLE, p. v., seat of justice of Gates co.. N. C., 214 ms. N. E. of Raleigh; from W. 253 ms. Watered by Bennett's creek.

GAUDALUPE COUNTY, Texas. Area, —— square miles. Seat of justice, Seguin. Pop. in 1850, 1,511.

GAUDALUPE, p. o., Victoria co., Tex.

GAULEY BRIDGE, p. v., Fayette co., Va., 277 ms. w. of Richmond; from W. 314 ms. Situated at the falls of the Great Kanawha river, at the head of navigation.

GAVER'S, p. o., Columbiana co., O.

GAY HEAD, p. o., Greene co., N. Y., 39 ms. s. w. of Albany; from W. 351 ms.

GAY HILL, p. o., Washington co., Tex.

GAYLESVILLE, p. v., Cherokee co., Ala.; from W. 672 ms. Watered by Coosa river.

GAYLORD'S BRIDGE, p. o., Litchfield co., Ct., 58 ms. w. of Hartford; from W. 315 ms.

GAYSVILLE, p. v.. Windsor co., Vt., 39 ms. s. of Montpelier; from W. 478 ms.

GEARSVILLE, p. o.. White co., Tenn.

GEAUGA COUNTY, situated in the northeasterly part of Ohio. Area, 576 square miles. Face of the country hilly; soil fertile. Seat of justice, Chardon. Pop. in 1810, 9,217; in 1820, 7,791; in 1830, 15,813; in 1840, 16,279; in 1850, 17,827.

GEBHART'S, p. o., Somerset co., Pa., 148 ms. w. of Harrisburgh; from W. 174 ms.

GEDDES, p. v., Salina township, Onondaga co., N. Y., 133 ms. N. w. of Albany; from W. 350 ms. Watered by Onondaga lake and the Erie canal. Pop. 2,011.

GEIGER'S MILLS, p. o., Berks co., Pa., 62 ms. E. of Harrisburgh; from W. 140 ms.

GENEGANTSLET, p. o., Greene township, Chenango co., N. Y., 122 ms. w. of Albany; from W. 316 ms.

GENERAL WAYNE, p. o., Montgomery co., Pa.

GENESEE COUNTY, situated toward the westerly part of New York, and traversed by the Erie canal. Area, 473 square miles. Face of the country undulating; soil rich and well cultivated. Seat of justice, Batavia. Pop. in 1810, 12,588; in 1820, 58,693; in 1830, 51,992; in 1840, 59.587; in 1850, 28,490.

GENESEE COUNTY, situated toward the easterly part of Michigan, and traversed by Flint river. Area, 504 square miles. Seat of justice, Flint. Pop. in 1840, 4,268; in 1850, 11,632.

GENESEE, t.. Alleghany co., N. Y., 280 ms. w. of Albany; from W. —— ms. Watered by Little Genesee and Swan creeks. Pop. 672.

GENESEE, t., Potter co., Pa. Pop. 301.

GENESEE, p. t.. Genesee co., Mich., 65 ms. N. w. of Detroit; from W. 589 ms. Watered by Flint river.

GENESEE, t.. Waukesha co., Wis.

GENESEE FORK, p. o., Potter co., Pa., 171 ms. N. w. of Harrisburgh; from W, 287 ms.

GENESEE GROVE, p. o., Whitesides co., Ill.

GENESEO, p. o.. Henry co., Ill., 146 ms. N. w. of Springfield; from W. 875 ms.

GENESEO, c. h., p. t., seat of justice of Livingston co., N. Y., 230 ms. w. of Albany; from W. 347 ms. Watered by Genesee river and small tributaries. Pop. in 1840, 2,892; in 1850, 2,958.

GENEVA, p. v., Seneca township, Ontario co., N. Y., 192 ms. w. of Albany; from W. 345 ms. Watered by the north end of Seneca lake, near the outlet. Seat of Geneva College. Pop. in 1838. 3,400; in 1850, 4,189.

GENEVA, p. t.. Ashtabula co., O., 195 ms. N. E. of Columbus; from W. 350 ms. Watered by Lake Erie.

GENEVA, v., Morgan co., Ill., 41 ms. s. w. of Springfield; from W. 821 ms. Pop. 1,358

GENEVA, p. o., Coffee co., Ala.

GENEVA, p. t., Walworth co., Wis., 75 ms. s. E. of Madison; from W. 790 ms.

GENEVA, p. o., Kane co., Ill.

GENEVA BAY, p. o., Walworth co., Wis.

GENITO, v., Powhatan co., Va.

GENOA, p. t., Cayuga co., N. Y., 161 ms. w. of Albany; from W. 319 ms. Watered by Big Salmon creek. Pop. 2,503.

GENOA, t., Delaware co., O., 23 ms. N. of Columbus; from W. 401 ms. Pop. 1,369.

GENOA, p. t., Livingston co., Mich., 48 ms. N. w. of Detroit; from W. 549 ms. Pop. 754.

GENOA, p. v., De Kalb co., Ill.. 217 ms. N. E. of Springfield; from W. 788 ms. Pop. 605.

GENOA, p. o., Christian co., Ky.

GENOA, p. o., Walworth co., Wis.

GENOA CROSS-ROADS, p. o., Delaware co., O.

GENTRY, c. h., p. v., seat of justice of Gentry co., Mo.

GENTRYVILLE, p. o., Spencer co., Ind.

GENTRYVILLE, p. o., Gentry co., Mo.

GENTSVILLE, p. o., Abbeville district, S. C., 106 ms. w. of Columbia; from W. 534 ms.

GENTSVILLE, p. o., Walton co., Flor.

GEORGE, t., Ottawa co., Mich. Pop. 196.

GEORGE'S, t., Fayette co.. Pa. Pop. 2,536.

GEORGE'S CREEK, p. o., Lawrence co., Ky.

GEORGE'S CREEK, p. o., Massac co., Ill.

GEORGE'S MILLS, p. o., Sullivan co., N. H.

GEORGE'S STORE, p. o., Lincoln co., Tenn.

GEORGESVILLE, p. v., Pleasant township, Franklin co., O.. 13 ms. s. w. of Columbus; from W. 406 ms. Watered by Little Darby creek.

GEORGETOWN DISTRICT, situated on the eastern boundary of South Carolina, with Atlantic ocean on the southeast, and Santee river on the southwest. Area, 1,040 square miles. Face of the country level, and toward the coast, swampy; soil of middling quality. Seat of justice, Georgetown. Pop. in 1810, 15,679; in 1820, 17,603; in 1830, 19,943; in 1840, 18,274; in 1850, 20,647.

GEORGETOWN, p. t., Lincoln co., Me., 50 ms. s. of Augusta; from W. 590 ms.; comprising two small islands at the mouth of the Kennebec river. Watered by Kennebec and Sheepscot rivers and the Atlantic ocean. Pop. 1,121.

GEORGETOWN, p. v., Essex co., Mass., 31 ms. N. of Boston; from W. 464 ms. Watered by a branch of Parker river. Pop. 2,052.

GEORGETOWN, p. t., Madison co., N. Y.. 112 ms. w. of Albany; from W. 348 ms. Watered by head branches of Ostelic river. Pop. 1,411.

GEORGETOWN, p. v., Green township, Beaver co., Pa., 41 ms. w. of Harrisburgh; from W. 267 ms. Watered by Mill creek and Ohio river.

GEORGETOWN, c. h., p.v., seat of justice of Sussex co., Del., 41 ms. E. of Dover; from W. 135 ms.

GEORGETOWN, city, Washington co., D. C.; separated from Washington city by Rock creek, and distant from the Capitol about three miles. It is beautifully located, the ground on which the town stands rising to a considerable height above the Potomac, upon which it fronts. The scenery around is varied and pleasant: and on the west stand the picturesque and rocky hills, which here begin to change the aspect of the river's banks. The public buildings and private

GEO 135 GEO

dwellings have a substantial appearance. The Roman catholic college and the churches are especially magnificent. The Chesapeake and Ohio canal commences at Georgetown. Oak Grove Cemetery is located in this town, and is handsomely laid out. Georgetown was formerly a place of considerable business and manufactures ; but its progress of late years has not kept pace with that of many other towns. Its population has been almost stationary for the last twenty years ; in 1830 it was 7,350 ; in 1840, 7,312 ; and in 1850, 8,366.

GEORGETOWN, c. h., p. v., seat of justice of Georgetown district, S. C., 152 ms. s. e. of Columbia ; from W. 488 ms. Watered by Winyaw bay and Sampit creek. Pop. 915.

GEORGETOWN, p. v., Randolph co., Ga. Watered by Chattahoochee river.

GEORGETOWN, p. v., Copiah co., Miss., 57 ms. s. of Jackson ; from W. 1,037 ms. Watered by Pearl river.

GEORGETOWN, c. h., p. v., seat of justice of Scott co., Ky., 17 ms. e. of Frankfort ; from W. 525 ms. Watered by north branch of Elkhorn river. Seat of Georgetown college.

GEORGETOWN, c. h., p. v., seat of justice of Brown co., O., 107 ms. s. w. of Columbus ; from W. 466 ms. Pop. 618.

GEORGETOWN, c. h., p. v., seat of justice of Pettes co., Mo., 67 ms. w. of Jefferson City ; from W. 1,003 ms. Watered by the south fork of La Mine river.

GEORGETOWN, p. v., Floyd co., Ind., 130 ms. s. of Indianapolis ; from W. 609 ms. Watered by a tributary of Indian creek.

GEORGETOWN, p. v., Vermilion co., Ill., 140 ms. e. of Springfield ; from W. 667 ms. Watered by Little Vermilion river.

GEORGETOWN, c. h., p. v., seat of justice of Sussex co., Del.

GEORGETOWN, p. o., Williamson co., Tex.

GEORGETOWN, p. o., El Dorado co., Cal.

GEORGETOWN, p. o., Burlington co., N. J.

GEORGETOWN, p. o., Lafayette co., Wis.

GEORGETOWN CROSS ROADS, p. o., Kent co., Md., 58 ms. n. e. of Annapolis ; from W. 112 ms.

GEORGIA, so called in honor of its royal grantor, George II. of England, and the most southern of the original thirteen states, lies between 30° 19' and 35° north latitude, and 80° 50' and 85° 40' west longitude from Greenwich ; and is bounded north by North Carolina and Tennessee, northeast by Savannah river, which separates it from South Carolina, southeast by the Atlantic, south by Florida, and west by Alabama. Its superficial area is 61,500 square miles.

Physical Aspect.—This state occupies a large proportion of the great inclined plain, from which the peninsula of Florida protrudes, and down which several rivers flow into the Atlantic and the Mexican gulf. From the Atlantic border of this state, this acclivity gradually rises to an elevation of 1,200 feet above the level of the sea, without estimating the mountain ridges. Like the Carolinas, it may be divided into three zones. First, the flat sea-border, including numerous small islands ; second, the sand-hill zone ; and third, a hilly and partly mountainous tract, beyond the lower falls of the rivers. The soil on the islands, called hummock land, is very rich, producing the celebrated Sea-island cotton. The seacoast on the main land consists of a belt of salt marsh, four or five miles in width. In the rear of this margin commence the "pine barrens," which extend 60 to 90 miles from the ocean. The rivers and creeks are generally bordered with swamps, or marshes, which, at every tide, are either wholly or partially overflowed, for 15 or 20 miles from the coast. These constitute the principal rice plantations. Beyond the pine barrens the country becomes uneven, diversified with hills and mountains, of a strong rich soil. The northwestern part of the state is mountainous, and abounds in beautiful scenery. The soil of Georgia, though varied, is, a large portion of it, productive. At a distance from the sea it changes from gray to red ; in some

places it is gravelly, but fertile : and farther back in the country its color is gradually deepened, till it becomes what is called the "mulatto soil," consisting of black mould and reddish earth. This is succeeded in its turn by a soil that is nearly black, and very rich, In the southwest portion of the state is Okefenokee swamp, about 170 miles in circumference.

Mountains.—This state is traversed on the north by a spur of the Alleghanies, among which are Yonah and Currahee mountains. Pine mountain lies near the western boundary.

Rivers and Sounds.—The principal rivers are, the Savannah, Ogeechee, Altamaha, Satilla, Ocmulgee, Oconee, St. Mary's, Flint, Chattahoochee, Tallapoosa, and Coosa. The coast of Georgia is indented by numerous sounds and inlets, which occur at the mouths of the principal rivers.

Islands.—Along the Atlantic coast there is a chain of islands, which are separated from the main by rivers, creeks, and inlets, forming an inland navigation of more than 100 miles. The principal of these islands are. Tybee, Wassaw, Ossabaw, St. Catherine's, Sapelo, St. Simon's, Jykill, and Cumberland.

Climate.—The climate, from the difference of elevation, is varied, one section producing wheat, and another sugar-cane. The winters are usually mild and pleasant ; snow is seldom seen, nor is vegetation often interrupted by severe frosts. The temperature of winter usually fluctuates from 40° to 60° Fahrenheit, although it occasionally falls as low as 16°. In the low country, in the vicinity of swamps, fevers and bilious attacks are common, owing partly to the badness of the water, but principally to the noxious vapors which arise from stagnant water, and putrid matter in the rice swamps. In the "upper country" the air is pure and salubrious throughout the year, and the water is abundant and good.

Productive Resources.—The staple products of this state consist of horses, mules, neat cattle, sheep, swine, poultry, silk, wool, butter, cheese, cotton, tobacco, rice, sugar, wine, wheat, rye, oats, barley, potatoes, and Indian corn. Among the mineral resources are, copper, iron, and gold. The latter occurs in considerable abundance in the northern part of the state, on both sides of Chattahoochee river, as far north as the Blue Ridge.

Manufactures.—The people of Georgia are more engaged in manufactures than those of any other southern state. It has quite a number of large cotton factories, which are worked by slave labor. It has also extensive tanneries, and mills of various descriptions.

Railroads and Canals.—There are about 1,000 miles of railroad already in successful operation in Georgia, and more in process of construction. The cost of the railroads already completed in this state is over $15,000,000. The principal canals in Georgia are, one from Savannah to the Ogeechee river, 16 miles, and another from Altamaha to Brunswick, 12 miles.

Commerce.—The foreign commerce of Georgia amounts to about $9,000,000 annually. The coasting trade is also important.

Education.—The university of Georgia, founded in 1785, at Athens, is the principal literary institution in the state. There are also, the Oglethorpe university, at Medina, near Milledgeville. The Mercer university, at Penfield, the Georgia Female college, near Macon, and the Georgia medical college, at Augusta. There are about 250 academies scattered through the state, and some 1,500 primary and common schools.

Population.—In 1749, 6,000 ; in 1790, 82,584 ; in 1800, 162,686 ; in 1810, 252,433 ; in 1820, 348,989 ; in 1830, 516,567 ; in 1840, 691,392 ; in 1850, 905,999. Number of slaves in 1790, 29,264 ; in 1800, 59,404 ; in 1810, 105,218 ; in 1820, 149,656 ; in 1830, 217,531 ; in 1840, 280,944 ; in 1850, 381,681.

Government.—The governor is elected by the people, and holds his office two years. The senate consists of 47 members, elected from forty-four districts of two counties each, two districts of three counties each, and one district comprising but a single county. The house of representatives is composed of 130 members : the 35 counties having the largest number of inhabitants are entitled to two members each, and the remainder one each. State election biennially, first Monday in October. The legislature meets biennially, on the first Monday in November (odd years), at Milledgeville. The judges of the superior court are elected for three years by the legislature, and the judges of the inferior courts and justices of the peace are elected quadrennially by the

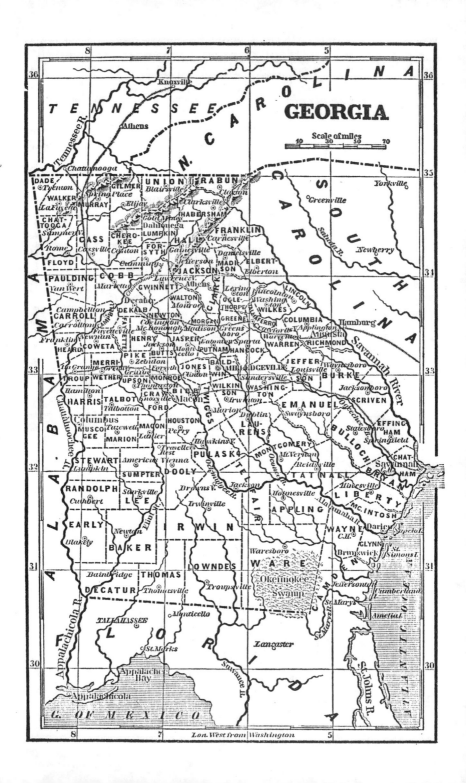

people. All the free white male inhabitants, who shall have resided within the county in which they vote six months preceding the election, and shall have paid taxes in the state for the year previous, have the right of suffrage.

History.—The state of Georgia embraces a part of Virginia, as granted to Sir Walter Raleigh, in 1584; or a portion of South Virginia, as granted by James I., of England, in 1606. A portion of its present territory also embraces a part of the ancient Georgia colony, chartered in 1732, to a corporation "in trust for the poor," for twenty-one years, including the country between the Savannah and Altahama rivers, extending westward from their sources to the "South sea;" also a portion of the northern part of Florida, as claimed at the time by Spain. The first permanent settlement in Georgia, was made under this grant at Savannah, by Oglethorpe, in 1732, who brought out a band of colonists, collected from among the poor and vicious population, as an experimental effort for their reformation, by providing them with the means of self-support. This benevolent design failing of success, the trustees of the colony sent out a better class of emigrants in 1735 from Scotland, Switzerland, and Germany. In the year following Oglethorpe extended his settlements as far south as St. John's river, in Florida, but was repulsed by the Spaniards. He retained his fortification at the mouth of the St. Mary's, and this river afterward became the boundary between Georgia and Florida. In the year 1752, the trustees of the colony surrendered their charter to the king, and their province was forced into a royal government. A general representative assembly was established in 1755; and in 1763, all the territory between the Altamaha and St. Mary's was annexed. In 1775, Georgia acceded to the union of the colonies, and sent deputies to Congress. When military operations were transferred to the southern states, from 1779 to 1781, Georgia became a portion of the bloody arena. It was at the siege of Savannah, Sept. 23, 1779, that Count Pulaski, the brave and patriotic Pole, was killed. In 1777, the first state constitution was adopted, and the parishes then existing were formed into counties. A second constitution was adopted in 1785, and the one now in force in 1798. In 1788, it adopted the constitution of the United States by a unanimous vote. By different conventions, all of the new states, Alabama and Mississippi, lying north of thirty-one degrees, have been yielded to the general government. Motto of the state seal of Georgia, "Constitution" supported by "Wisdom," "Justice," "Moderation," and "Agriculture and Commerce."

GEORGIA, p. t., Franklin co., Vt., 40 ms. N. w. of Montpelier; from W. 535 ms. Watered by Lake Champlain and Lamoille river. Pop. 2,686.

GERMAN, p. t., Chenango co., N. Y., 123 ms. w. of Albany; from W. 326 ms. Pop. 903.

GERMAN, p. t., Darke co., O., 97 ms. w. of Columbus; from W. 491 ms. Pop. 1,501.

GERMAN, t., Allen co., O. Pop. 1,008.

GERMAN. p. t., Harrison co., O. 132 from Columbus; from W. 276 ms. Pop. 1,357.

GERMAN. t., Holmes co., O., 91 ms. from Columbus; from W. 329 ms. Pop. 1,517.

GERMAN, t., Lucas co., O.

GERMAN, p. t., Montgomery co., O. Pop. 2,789.

GERMAN, t., Mercer co., O.

GERMAN, t., Bartholomew co., Ind., 33 ms. from Columbus; from W. 604 ms. Pop. 947.

GERMAN, t., Cape Girardeau co., Mo.

GERMAN, t., Madison co., Mo.

GERMAN FLATS, t., Herkimer co., N. Y., 83 ms. N. w. of Albany; from W. 390 ms. Watered by Mohawk river and Erie canal. Pop. 3,578.

GERMANNA, p. o., Orange co., Va.

GERMANO. p. t., Harrison co., O. Pop. 1,357.

GERMAN SETTLEMENT, p. v., Preston co., Va., 242 ms. N. w. of Richmond; from W. 166 ms.

GERMANTOWN, c. h., p. v., seat of justice of Stokes co., N. C., 123 ms. N. w. of Raleigh; from W. 319 ms. Watered by a branch of Dam river.

GERMANTOWN, p. t., Columbia co., N. Y., 46 ms. s. of Albany; from W. 334 ms. Pop. 903.

GERMANTOWN, t., Fayette co., Pa., 202 ms. from Harrisburgh; from 209 W. ms. Pop. 1,894.

GERMANTOWN, p. t., Philadelphia co., Pa., 104 ms. s. E. of Harrisburgh; from W. 144 ms. Watered by Wissihickon creek and its branches, and Wingohocking creek. Pop. 8,336.

GERMANTOWN, v., Hyde co., N. C., 185 ms. E. of Raleigh; from W. 371 ms. Watered by Tar river and Pamlico sound.

GERMANTOWN, p. v., Shelby co., Tenn., 219 ms. s. w. of Nashville; from W. 902 ms. Pop. 245.

GERMANTOWN, p. v., Marion co., Ind., 16 ms. N. E. of Indianapolis; from W. 573 ms.

GERMANTOWN, p. v., Mason co., Ky., 71 ms. N. E. of Frankfort; from W. 479 ms.

GERMANTOWN, p. v., German township, Montgomery co., O., 82 ms. w. of Columbus; from W. 475 ms. Watered by Big and Little Twin creeks.

GERMANTOWN, p. o., Fauquier co., co., Va.

GERMANTOWN, p. o., Clinton co., Ill.

GERMAN, VALLEY, p. o., Morris co., N. J.

GERMANVILLE, p. v., Edgefield district, S. C., 32 ms. w. of Columbia; from W. 536 ms.

GERMANY, t., Adams co., Pa., 40 ms. from Harrisburgh; from W. 77 ms. Watered by Piney creek and the head waters of Connewago creek. Pop. 720.

GERRARDSTOWN, p.v., Berkeley co., Va., 165 ms. N. of Richmond; from W. 87 ms.

GERRY, p. t., Chautauque co., N. Y., 330 ms. w. of Albany; from W. 330 ms. Watered by Cassadaga creek. Pop. 1,332.

GETTYSBURGH, c. h., p. b., seat of justice of Adams co., Pa., 35 ms. N. E. of Harrisburgh; from 75 ms. Pop. 2,180.

GETTYSBURGH, p. v., Preble co., O., 102 ms. w. of Columbus; from W. 495 ms.

GHENT, p. t., Columbia co., N. Y., 27 ms. s. of Albany; from W. 351 ms. Watered by Claverack creek. Pop. 2,293.

GHENT, p. v., Carroll co., Ky., 59 ms. N. of Frankfort; from W. 543 ms. Watered by Ohio river.

GOSHEN, p. v., Noxubee co., Miss., 113 ms. N. E. of Jackson; from W. 901 ms.

GHOLSONVILLE, p. v., Brunswick co., Va., 85 ms. s. of Richmond; from W. 201 ms. Watered by Meherin river.

GIBBON'S TAVERN, p. o., Delaware co., Pa., 92 ms. s. E. of Harrisburgh; from W. 126 ms.

GIBB'S CROSS ROADS, p. o., Cumberland co., N. C.

GIBBSVILLE, p. o., Sheboygan co., Wis.

GIBSONVILLE, p. o., Hocking co., O.

GIBRALTER, p. v., Brownstown township, Wayne co., Mich., 31 ms. s. of Detroit. Watered by Detroit river and Gibralter and Clinton canals.

GIBSON COUNTY, situated toward the westerly part of Tennessee. Area, 630 square miles. Seat of justice, Trenton. Pop. in 1830, 5,801; in 1010, 10,000, in 1850, 19,548.

GIBSON COUNTY, situated on the westerly boundary of Indiana, with Wabash river on the west. Area, 450 square miles. Seat of justice, Princeton. Pop. in 1830, 5,418; in 1840, 8,977; in 1850, 10,771.

GIBSON, t., Clearfield co., Pa.

GIBSON, p. t., Susquehanna co., Pa., 177 ms. N. E. of Harrisburgh; from W. 281 ms. Watered by Taukhannock and Lackawannoc creeks. Pop, 1,459.

GIBSON, t., Darke co., O.

GIBSON, p. o., Pike co., O.

GIBSON, p. o., Steuben co., N. Y.

GIBSON, t., Washington co., Ind., 80 ms. from Indianapolis; from W. 601 ms. Pop. 1,095.

GIBSON, t., Gasconade co., Mo.

GIBSON'S WELLS, p. o., Gibson co., Tenn.

GIBSONVILLE, p. o., Leicester township, Livingston co., N. Y.

GIDLEY'S STATION, p. o., Jackson co., Mich.

GILBERTSBOROUGH, p. o., Limestone co., Ala.; from W. 749 ms.

GILBERT'S MILLS, p. o., Oswego co., N. Y.

GILBOA, p. v., Broome township, Schoharie co., N.Y., 51 ms. w. of Albany; from W. 367 ms. Watered by Schoharie creek.

GILBOA, p. o., Putnam co., O.

GILCHRIST'S BRIDGE, p. o., Marion district, S. C.

GILDER, p. o., Greenville district, S. C.

GILEAD, p. t., Oxford co., Mo., 71 ms. w. of Augusta; from W. 602 ms. Watered by Androscoggin river. Pop. 1,109.

GILEAD, p. v., Hebron township, Tolland co., Ct., 21 ms. s. E. of Hartford; from W. 349 ms.

GILEAD, t., Marion co., O.

GILEAD, p. v., Weston township, Wood co., O., 136 ms. N. w. of Columbus; from W. 474 ms. Watered by Maumee river.

GILEAD, p. t., Branch co., Mich., 128 ms. s. w. of Detroit; from W. 577 ms. Pop. 503.

GILEAD, p. v., Calhoun co., Ill., 105 ms. s. w. of Springfield ; from W. 855 ms. Pop. 553.

GILEAD, p. o., Upshur co., Tex.

GILEAD, p. o., Miami co., Ind.

GILES COUNTY, situated toward the southwesterly part of Virginia, and traversed by Great Kanawba river. Area, 675 square miles. Face of the country mountainous and broken ; soil generally unproductive. Seat of justice, Parishburgh. Pop. in 1810, 3,745; in 1820, 4,522 ; in 1830, 5,298 ; in 1840, 5,307 ; in 1850, 6,570.

GILES COUNTY, situated on the southern boundary of Tennessee. Area, 625 square miles. Face of the country undulating ; soil fertile. Seat of justice, Pulaski. Pop. in 1810, 4,546 ; in 1820, 12,558 ; in 1830, 18,920; in 1840, 21,494 ; in 1850, 25,949.

GILES, c. h., p. v., seat of justice of Giles co., Va., 240 ms. w. of Richmond ; from W. 298 ms. Watered by New river.

GILFORD, c. h., p. t., seat of justice of Belknap co., N. H., 28 ms. N. of Concord; from W. 509 ms. Watered by Winnipiseogee and Miles rivers and Winnipiseogee lake. Pop. 2,425.

GILFORD VILLAGE, p. v., Gilford township, Belknap co., N. H.. 33 ms. N. of Concord ; from W. 514 ms. Watered by Winnipiseogee lake outlet.

GILL, p. t., Franklin co., Mass., 98 ms. w. of Boston ; from W. 410 ms. Watered by Connecticut and Fall rivers.

GILLELAND CREEK, p. v., Traves co., Tex.

GILLESPIE COUNTY, Texas. Area, —— square ms. Seat of justice, Fredericksburgh. Pop. in 1850, 1,235.

GILLESPIEVILLE, p. o., Ross co., O., 60 ms. s. of Columbus ; from W. 385 ms.

GILL HALL, p. o., Allegany co., Pa.

GILLION'S, p. o., Baker co., Ga., 45 ms. s. w. of Milledgeville ; from W. 802 ms.

GILLISONVILLE, p. o., Beaufort district, S. C., 146 ms. from Columbia ; from W. 613 ms.

GILL'S MILLS, p. o., Bath co., Ky., 87 ms. E. of Frankfort ; from W. 509 ms.

GILL'S STORE, p. o., Lincoln co., Tenn., 84 ms. s. of Nashville ; from W. 707 ms.

GILLSVILLE, p. o., Hall co., Ga., 131 ms. N. w. of Milledgeville ; from W. 630 ms.

GILMAN, p. t., Hamilton co., N. Y., 68 ms. N. w. of Albany. Pop. 1,001.

GILMANTON, p. t., Belknap co., N. H., 20 ms. N. of Concord ; from W. 501 ms. Watered by Suncook and Winnipiseogee rivers. Pop. 3,282. .

GILMANTON IRON WORKS, p. v., Gilmanton township, Belknap co., N. H., 23 ms. N. of Concord ; from W. 504 ms.

GILMER COUNTY, situated toward the northwesterly part of Virginia, and traversed by Little Kanawha river. Area, —— square miles. Face of the country uneven. Seat of justice, Glenville. Pop. in 1850, 3,475.

GILMER COUNTY, situated on the northern boundary of Georgia. Area, 680 square miles. Face of the country mountainous. Seat of justice, Ellijay. Pop. in 1840, 2,536 ; in 1850, 4,933.

GILMER, p. o., Lake co., Ill.

GILMER, p. o., Upshur co., Tex.

GILMER'S STORE, p. o., Guilford co., N. C.

GILOPOLIS, p. o., Robeson co., N. C.

GILROY, p. o., Santa Clara co., Cal.

GILSUM, p. t., Cheshire co., N. H., 56 ms. s. w. of Concord ; from W. 444 ms. Watered by Ashuelot river. Pop. 668.

GINGER HILL, p. o., Washington co., Pa.

GINSENG, p. o., Wyoming co., Va., 326 ms. N. w. of Richmond ; from W. 363 ms.

GIN TOWN, p. o., Irwin co., Ga.

GIRARD, p. t., Branch co., Mich., 110 ms. s. w. of Detroit ; from W. 570 ms. Pop. 934.

GIRARD, p. v., Trumbull co., O., 173 ms. N. E. of Columbus ; from W. 294 ms.

GIRARD, t., Clearfield co., Pa. Pop. 286.

GIRARD, p. t., Erie co., Pa., 264 ms. N. w. of Harrisburgh ; from W. 337 ms. Pop. 2,843.

GIRARD, p. v., Russell co., Ala. ; from 758 ms. Watered by Chattahoochee river.

GIRARD, p. o.. Burke co., Ga.

GLADDEN'S GROVE, p. o., Fairfield district, S. C., 43 ms. N. of Columbia ; from W. 460 ms.

GLADE HILL, p. o., Franklin co., Va.

GLADE MILLS, p. o.. Butler co., Pa., 212 ms. N. w. of Harrisburgh ; from W. 249 ms.

GLADE MINES, p. o., Hall co., Ga.

GLADE RUN, p. o., Armstrong co'., Pa., 184 ms. N. w. of Harrisburgh ; from W. 237 ms.

GLADE SPRING, p. o., Harrison co., Tex.

GLADE SPRING, p. o., Washington co., Va., 292 ms. s. w. of Richmond ; from W. 360 ms.

GLADE'S CROSS ROADS, p. o.. Putnam co., Ga., 31 ms. N. w. of Milledgeville ; from W. 617 ms.

GLADEVILLE, p. o., Preston co., Va.

GLADWIN COUNTY, situated toward the easterly part of Michigan, and traversed by Tittibawasee river. Area, —— square miles. Seat of justice, ——. Pop. in 1850, ——.

GLADY CREEK, p. o., Randolph co., Va., 228 ms. N w. of Richmond ; from W. 254 ms.

GLASCO, p. v., Saugerties township, Ulster co., N. Y. 48 ms. s. of Albany ; from W. 328 ms. Watered by Hudson river.

GLASGOW, p. v., New Castle co., Del. Watered by Christiana creek.

GLASGOW, p. o., Columbiana co., O., 153 ms. N. E. of Columbus ; from W. 276 ms.

GLASGOW, c. h., p. v., seat of justice of Barren co., Ky., 123 ms. s. w. of Frankfort ; from W. 646 ms. Watered by Beaver branch of Green river. Pop. 699.

GLASGOW, p.v., Howard co., Me., 73 ms. N.w. of Jefferson City ; from W. 978 ms. Watered by Missouri river.

GLASGOW, p. o., Scott co., Ill.

GLASGOW, p. o., Jefferson co., Iowa.

GLASSBOROUGH, p. v., Franklin township, Gloucester co., N. J., 47 ms. s. of Trenton ; from W. 158 ms.

GLASS CREEK, p. o., Barry co., Mich.

GLASS LAKE, p. t., Jackson co., Mich. Pop. 1,281.

GLASS VILLAGE, p. o., Conway co., Ark.

GLASTENBURY, p. t., Hartford co., Ct., 6 ms. s. of Hartford ; from W. 338 ms. Watered by Connecticut river and Roaring brook. Pop. 3,390.

GLASTENBURY, t., Bennington co., Vt., 111 ms. from Montpelier ; from W. 423 ms. Pop. 52.

GLAZE, t., Miller co., Mo.

GLEN, p. o., Montgomery co., N. Y.

GLENALTA, p. o., Marion co., Ga.

GLEN BROOK, p. o.. Hart co., Ky., 109 ms. s. w. of Frankfort ; from W. 626 ms.

GLENBURN, p. t., Penobscot co., Me., 77 ms. N. E. of Augusta ; from W. 672 ms. Watered by Kenduskeag stream. Pop. 905.

GLENCOE, p. o., Gallatin co., Ky.

GLENCOE, p. o., Bolivar co., Miss.

GLEN COVE, p. v., Oyster bay township, Queen's co., N. Y., 176 ms. s. of Albany. Watered by Glen Cove.

GLENDALE, p. o., Berkshire co., Mass.

GLENFINLAS, p. o.. Jefferson co., Mo., 122 ms. E. of Jefferson city ; from W. 862 ms.

GLENHAM, p. v., Fishkill township. Dutchess co., N. Y., 88 ms. s. of Albany ; from w. 289 ms. Watered by Fishkill creek and Hudson river.

GLEN HOPE, p. o., Clearfield co., Pa.

GLENMORE, p. o., Oneida co., N. Y.

GLENMORE, p. o., Buckingham co., Va.

GLENN, p. o., McKean co., Pa.

GLENN GROVE, p. o., Fayette co., Ga.

GLENN'S, p. o., Clark co., Iowa.

GLENN'S, p. o., Gloucester co., Va., 87 ms. E. of Richmond ; from W. 155 ms.

GLENN'S FALLS, p. v., Queensbury township. Warren co., N. Y., 54 ms. N. of Albany ; from W. 427 ms. Watered by Hudson river.

GLENN SPRINGS, p. o., Spartanburgh district, S. C., 86 ms. N. w. of Columbia ; from W. 480 ms.

GLENNVILLE, p. o., Barbour co., Ala.

GLEN ROCK, p. o., York co., Pa.

GLENVILLE, p. t., Schenectady co., N. Y., 20 ms. N. w. of Albany ; from W. 388 ms. Watered by Mohawk river and Aelplass creek. Pop. 3,409.

GLENVILLE, p. o., Gilmer co., Va.

GLENVILLE, p. o., Fairfield co., Ct.

GLEN WILD, p. o., Thompson township, Sullivan co., N. Y., 102 ms. s. w. of Albany ; from W. 304 ms.

GLEN WOOD, p. o., Erie co., N. Y.

GLOBE, p. o., Caldwell co., N. C., 220 ms. w. of Raleigh ; from W. 408 ms.

GLOBE, p. o., Johnson co., Mo.

GLOBE VILLAGE, p. o., Worcester co., Mass.

GLOUCESTER COUNTY, situated in the easterly part of Virginia, with Chesapeake bay on the east, and York river on the southwest. Area, 280 square miles. Face of the country level ; soil of middling quality. Seat of justice, Gloucester. Pop. in 1810, 10,427 ; in

1820, 9,678; in 1830, 10,608; in 1840, 10,715; in 1850, 10,527.

GLOUCESTER COUNTY, situated toward the south-westerly part of New Jersey, with Delaware river on the northwest. Area, 580 square miles. Face of the country level; soil generally productive. Seat of justice, Woodbury. Pop. in 1810, 19,744; in 1820, 23,090; in 1830, 28,431; in 1840, 25,438; in 1850, 14,655.

GLOUCESTER, p. t., Essex co., Cape Ann, Mass., 30 ms. N. E. of Boston; from W. 470 ms. Watered by the Atlantic ocean. Pop. in 1830, 7,513; in 1840, 6,350; in 1850, 7,786.

GLOUCESTER, c. h., p. v., seat of justice of Gloucester co., Va., 85 ms. E. of Richmond; from W. 170 ms.

GLOUCESTER, t., Gloucester co., N. J., 47 ms. from Trenton; from W. 151 ms. Watered by Big Timber and Cooper's creeks. Pop. 2,188.

GLOUCESTER, t., Providence co., R. I., 16 ms. s. w. of Providence; from W. 393 ms. Watered by Chepatchet river. Pop. 2,872.

GLOUCESTER, city, p. o., Camden co., N. J.

GLOUCESTER FURNACE. p. v., Mullica township, At-lantic co., N. J., 74 ms. s. of Trenton; from W. 184 ms.

GLOVER, p. t., Orleans co., Vt., 39 ms. N. E. of Mont-pelier; from W. 550 ms. Pop. 1,137.

GLOVERSVILLE, p. v., Johnstown township, Fulton co., N. Y., 40 ms. N. w. of Albany; from W. 413 ms.

GLYMONT, p. o., Charles co., Md.

GLYMPHVILLE. p. o., Newberry district, S. C.

GLYNN COUNTY, situated on the southeasterly boun-dary of Georgia, with the Atlantic ocean on the south-east, and Altamaha river on the northeast. Area, 625 square miles. Face of the country level, and in some parts marshy; soil adapted to cotton and sugar. Seat of justice, Brunswick. Pop. in 1810, 3,417; in 1820, 3,418; in 1830, 4,467; in 1840, 5,302; in 1850, 4,933.

GNADENHUTTEN, p. v., Clay township, Tuscarawas co., O., 105 ms. N. E. of Columbus; from W. 312 ms. Watered by Tuscarawas river.

GODBOLD, p. o., Washita co., Ark.

GODDARD, p. o., Rush co., Ind., 45 ms. s. E. of Indian-apolis; from W. 543 ms.

GODFREY, p. o., Madison co., Ill., 86 ms. s. of Spring-field; from W. 812 ms.

GOFF'S CORNERS, p. o., Cumberland co., Me., 32 ms. s. w. of Augusta; from W. 576 ms.

GOFF'S MILLS, p. o., Howard township, Steuben co., N. Y., 228 ms. w. of Albany; from W. 308 ms.

GOFFSTOWN, p. t., Hillsborough co., N. H., 16 ms s of Concord; from W. 468 ms. Watered by Piscata-quog and Merrimac rivers Pop. 2,270.

GOFFSTOWN CENTRE, p. v., Goffstown township, Hillsborough co., N. H.

GOGGINSVILLE, p. o., Franklin co., Va.

GOLANSVILLE, p. o., Caroline co., Va., 33 ms. N. of Richmond; from W. 90 ms.

GOLCONDA, c. h., p. v., seat of justice of Pope co., Ill., 215 ms. s. E. of Springfield; from W. 706 ms. Watered by Ohio river and Lusk creek.

GOLDEN, p. t., Erie co., N. Y.

GOLDEN BRIDGE, p. o., Lewisborough township, Westchester co., N. Y., 120 ms. s. of Albany; from W. 278 ms.

GOLDEN GROVE, p. o., Greenville district, S. C., 121 ms. N. w. of Columbia; from W. 516 ms.

GOLDEN HILL, p. o., Dorchester co., Md.

GOLDEN LAKE, p. o., Waukesha co., Wis.

GOLDEN POND. p. o., Trigg co., Ky.

GOLDEN SPRINGS, p. o., Anderson district, S. C., 131 ms. N. w. of Columbia; from W. 527 ms.

GOLDEN VALLEY, p. o., Rutherford co., N. C., 217 ms. s. w. of Raleigh; from W. 447 ms.

GOLD HILL, p. o., Meriwether co., Ga., 116 ms. w. of Milledgeville; from W. 734 ms.

GOLD HILL, p. o., Rowan co., N. C.

GOLD MINE, p. o., Chesterfield district, S. C., 99 ms. N. E. of Columbia; from W. 458 ms.

GOLD MINE, p. o., Marion co., Ala.

GOLD REGION, p. o., Moore co., N. C.

GOLDSBOROUGH. p. v., Wayne co., N. C., 51 ms. s. E. of Raleigh; from W. 281 ms.

GOLDSVILLE, p. o., Cherokee co., Ga.

GOLDSVILLE, p. o., Tallapoosa co., Ala.

GOLIAD COUNTY, Texas. Area, —— square miles. Seat of justice, Goliad. Pop. in 1850, 648.

GOLIAD, p. o., Goliad co., Tex.

GONIC, p. o., Strafford co., N. H.

GONZALES COUNTY, situated toward the souther-ly part of Texas, and traversed by Guadalupe river. Area, —— square miles. Seat of justice, Gonzales. Pop. in 1850, 1,492.

GONZALES, c. h., p. v., seat of justice of Gonzales co., Tex.

GOOCHLAND COUNTY, situated toward the east-erly part of Virginia, with James river on the south. Area, 336 square miles. Face of the country mode-rately hilly; soil generally productive. Seat of justice, Goochland. Pop. in 1810, 10,203; in 1820, 10,007; in 1830, 10,348; in 1840, 9,760; in 1850, 10,352.

GOOCHLAND, c. h., p. v., Goochland co., Va., 30 ms. N. w. of Richmond; from W. 130 ms. Situated near James river.

GOOCH'S MILLS, p. o., Cooper co., Mo., 42 ms. N. w. of Jefferson city; from W. 963 ms.

GOOD'S PRECINCT, p. o., Clark co., Ky.

GOODFIELD, p. o., Meigs co., Tenn.

GOOD GROUND, p. o., Southampton township, Suffolk co., Long Island, N. Y., 242 ms. s. of Albany; from W. 322 ms.

GOOD HOPE, p. o., Fayette co., O.

GOOD HOPE, t., Hocking co., O. Pop. 635.

GOOD HOPE, p. o., Walton co., Ga., 75 ms. N. w. of Milledgeville; from W. 629 ms.

GOOD HOPE, p. o., Milwaukee co., Wis.

GOOD HOPE, p. o., Cumberland co., Pa.

GOODING'S GROVE, p. o., Will co., Ill.

GOOD INTENT, p. o., Washington co., Pa., 231 ms. w. of Harrisburgh; from W. 249 ms.

GOOD LUCK, p. o., Prince George's co., Md., 43 ms. s. w. of Annapolis; from W. 15 ms.

GOODRICH, p. o., Genesee co., Mich.

GOOD SPRING, p. o., Williamson co., Tenn., 13 ms. s. of Nashville: from W. 697 ms.

GOOD SPUR, p. o., Carroll co., Va.

GOODVILLE, p. o., Lancaster co., Pa.

GOOD WATER, p. o., Coosa co., Ala.

GOODWIN'S MILLS, p. o., York co., Me., 73 ms. s. w. of Augusta; from W. 524 ms.

GOODWYNSVILLE, p. o., Dinwiddie co., Va., 46 ms. s. of Richmond; from W. 165 ms.

GOODYEAR'S BAR, p. o., Yuba co., Cal.

GOOSE CREEK, p. o., Ritchie co., Va.

GOOSE POND, p. o., Oglethorpe co., Ga., 101 ms. N. of Milledgeville; from W. 593 ms.

GOOSE RIVER. p. o., Waldo co., Me., 44 ms. E. of Augusta; from W. 630 ms.

GORDO p. o., Pickens co., Ala.

GORDON COUNTY, Georgia. Area, —— square miles. Seat of justice, Fair Mount. Pop. in 1850, 5,984.

GORDON, p. o., Wilkinson co., Ga.

GORDON'S SPRINGS, p. o., Walker co., Ga.

GORDONSVILLE, p. v., Orange co., Va., 74 ms. N. w. of Richmond; from W. 104 ms. Watered by the sources of North Anna river.

GORDONSVILLE, p. o., Logan co., Ky.

GORDONSVILLE, p. o., Smith co., Tenn., 58 ms. E. of Nashville; from W. 638 ms.

GORDONSVILLE, p. o., Lancaster co., Pa.

GORDONTON, p. o., Person co., N. C., 64 ms. from Ra-leigh; from W. 268 ms.

GORHAM, p. t., Cumberland co., Me., 60 ms. s. w. of Augusta; from W. 541 ms. Pop. 3,088.

GORHAM, p. t., Coos co., N. H., 197 ms. N. of Con-cord; from W. 586 ms. Pop. 224.

GORHAM, p. t., Ontario co., N. Y., 197 ms. w. of Al-bany; from W. 340 ms. Watered by Flint creek. Pop. 6,143.

GORHAM, p. t., Fulton co., O., 180 ms. N. w. of Co-lumbus; from W. 511 ms. Watered by Tiffiin's river. Pop. 906.

GOSHEN, p. t., Sullivan co., N. H., 40 ms. w. of Con-cord; from W. 480 ms. Watered by branches of Su-gar river. Pop. 659.

GOSHEN, p. t., Hampshire co., Mass., 105 ms. w. of Boston; from W. 393 ms. Pop. 512.

GOSHEN, p. t., Litchfield co., Ct., 33 ms. w. of Hart-ford; from W. 332 ms.

GOSHEN, p. t., Addison co., Vt., 31 ms. s. w. of Mont-pelier. Watered by Leicester river. Pop. 486.

GOSHEN, c. h., p. t., seat of justice together with Newburgh of Orange co., N. Y., 105 ms. s. of Albany; from W. 278 ms. Pop. 3,149.

GOSHEN, p. v., Middle township, Cape May co., N. J., 89 ms. s. of Trenton; from W. 199 ms. Watered by Goshen creek.

GOSHEN, p. v., Lancaster co., Pa., 58 ms. s. e. of Harrisburgh ; from W. 93 ms.

GOSHEN, t., Tuscarawas co., O. Watered by Tuscarawas river. Pop. 3,067.

GOSHEN, p. t., Clermont co , O., 100 ms. s. w. of Columbus ; from W. 472 ms. Pop. 1,937.

GOSHEN, t., Allen co., O. Pop. 1,003.

GOSHEN, t., Belmont co., O. Watered by head branches of Captina and McMahon's creeks. Pop. 1,867.

GOSHEN, t., Champaign co., O. Pop. 1,261.

GOSHEN, t., Columbiana co., O.

GOSHEN, t., Mahoning co., O. Pop. 1,729.

GOSHEN, p. v., Lincoln co., Ga., 58 ms. n. e. of Milledgeville ; from W. 93 ms.

GOSHEN, p. v., Cherokee co., Ga. ; from W. 690 ms.

GOSHEN, c. h., p. v., seat of justice of Elkhart co., Ind., 152 ms. n. of Indianapolis ; from W. 690 ms. Watered by Elkhart river. Pop. 780.

GOSHEN, t., Macon co., Mo.

GOSHEN, p. o., Oldham co., Ky.

GOSHEN GORE, t., Caledonia, Vt. Pop. 215.

GOSHEN HILL, p. o., Union district, S. C., 53 ms. n. w. of Columbia ; from W. 480 ms.

GOSHENVILLE, p. o., Chester co., Pa., 77 ms. s. e. of Harrisburgh ; from W. 122 ms.

GOSPORT, t., Rockingham co., N. H., including the isle of Shoals, 8 ms. from Portsmouth, in the Atlantic ocean. Pop. 102.

GOSPORT, v., Norfolk co., Va. Site of one of the U. S. navy yards. Watered by Elizabeth river.

GOSPORT, p. v., Clark co., Ala. ; from W. 936 ms. Watered by Alabama river.

GOSPORT, p. v., Owen co., Ind., 42 ms. s. w. of Indianapolis ; from W. 613 ms.

GOTT'S CROSS-ROADS, p. o., Sullivan co., Tenn.

GOULDSBOROUGH, p. t., Hancock co., Me., 111 ms. e. of Augusta ; from W. 693 ms. Watered by Gouldsborough, and Frenchman's bays, and the Atlantic ocean. Pop. 1,400.

GOURDVINE, p. o., Union co., N. C.

GOUVERNEUR, p. t., St. Lawrence co., N. Y., 181 ms. n. w. of Albany ; from W. 450 ms. Watered by Oswegatchie river. Pop. 2,143.

GOVANSTOWN, p. v., Baltimore, co., Md., 34 ms. n. of Annapolis ; from W. 44 ms.

GOVERNOR'S BRIDGE, p. o., Anne Arundel co., Md.

GOVERNOR'S ISLAND, p. o., Macon co., N. C.

GOWANDA. p. o., Cattaraugus co., N. Y.

GOWANUS, v., King's co., N. Y., a part of the city of Brooklyn. situated on Gowanus creek, and a bay of the same name.

GOWDEYSVILLE, p. o., Union district, S. C.. 81 ms. n. w of Columbia ; from W. 477 ms.

GOWENSVILLE, p. o., Greenville district, S. C., 133 ms. n. w. of Columbia ; from W. 477 ms.

GOWER'S FERRY, p. o., Cedar co.. Iowa.

GRACEHAM, p. v., Frederick co., Md., 87 ms. n. w. of Annapolis ; from W. 58 ms.

GRADYVILLE, p. o., Adair co., Ky.

GRAFENSBURGH. p. o., Adams co., Pa.

GRAFTON COUNTY, situated on the western boundary of New Hampshire with Connecticut river on the west. Area, 1,740 square miles. Face of the country, mountainous and broken ; soil productive. Seats of justice, Haverhill and Plymouth. Pop. in 1810, 28,462 ; in 1820, 32,989 ; in 1830, 38,691 ; in 1840, 42,311 ; in 1850 41,343.

GRAFTON, p. t., Grafton co., N. H., 33 ms. n. w. of Concord ; from W. 504 ms. Pop. 1,259.

GRAFTON, p. t., Windham co., Vt., 109 ms. s. of Montpelier ; from W. 456. Watered by Williams and Sexton's rivers. Pop. 1,241.

GRAFTON, p. t., Worcester co., Mass., 35 ms. s. w. of Boston ; from W. 406 ms. Watered by Blackstone river. Pop. 3,904.

GRAFTON, p. t., Rensselaer co., N. Y., 20 ms. n e. of Albany ; from W. 390 ms. Watered by Poeson kill and other small streams. Pop. 2,033.

GRAFTON, p. v., Jersey co., Ill., 85 ms. s. of Springfield ; from W. 826 ms. Pop. 222.

GRAFTON, p. o., Lorain co., O.

GRAFTON, p. o., Monroe co., Mich.

GRAFTON, p. o., Washington co., Wis.

GRAHAM, p. o., Jefferson co., Ind.

GRAHAM, p o., Allamance co., N. C.

GRAHAM'S STATION, p. o., Sutton township, Meigs co., O., 103 ms. e. of Columbus ; from W. 338 ms.

GRAHAM'S TURN OUT, p. o., Barnwell district, S. C., 81 ms. s. w. of Columbia ; from W. 587 ms.

GRAHAMSVILLE. p. o., Neversink township, Sullivan co.. N. Y., 96 ms. s. of Albany ; from W. 312 ms.

GRAHAMTON, p. o., Clearfield co., Pa.

GRAHAMTON, p. o., Clearfield co., Pa.

GRAHAMVILLE. p. o., York co., Pa., 45 ms. s. of Harrisburgh ; from W. 95 ms.

GRAHAMVILLE, p. o., Beaufort district co., S. C., 144 ms. s. of Columbia ; from W. 629 ms.

GRANGER COUNTY, situated toward the northeasterly part of Tennessee, with Holston river on the southeast, and Clinch river on the northwest. Area 320 square miles. Face of the country hilly and mountainous; soil, along the streams. fertile ; elsewhere unproductive. Seat of justice, Rutledge. Pop. in 1820, 7,650 ; in 1830, 10,066 ; in 1840, 10,572; in 1850, 12,370.

GRAMPIAN HILLS, p. o., Clearfield co., Pa., 138 ms. n. w. of Harrisburgh ; from W. 230 ms.

GRANBY, p. t., Essex co., Vt. Watered by head branches of Paul's stream and Moose river. Pop. 127.

GRANBY, p. t., Hampshire co., Mass., 85 ms. w. of Boston ; from W. 375 ms. Pop. 1,104.

GRANBY, p. t., Hartford co., Ct., 16 ms. n. w. of Hartford ; from W. 352 ms. Watered by Farmington river and its tributaries. Pop. 2,498.

GRANBY, p. t., Oswego co., N. Y., 158 ms. n. w. of Albany. Watered by Oswego river. Pop. 3,368.

GRANBY CENTRE, p. o., Granby township, Oswego co., N. Y.

GRAND, p. t., Marion co., O., 58 ms. n. of Columbus ; from W. 429 ms. Pop. 553.

GRAND BLANC, p. t., Genesee co., Mich., 53 ms. n. of Detroit ; from W. 577 ms. Pop. 1,165.

GRAND BLUFF, p. o., Panola co., Tex.

GRAND CANE, p. o., De Soto parish. La.

GRAND CANE, p. o., Liberty co., Tex.

GRAND COTEAU, p. o., St. Landry parish, La., 205 ms. w. of New Orleans ; from W. 1,254 ms.

GRAND COTE PRAIRIE, p. o., Perry co., Ill.

GRAND DETOUR, p. o., Ogle co., Ill., 167 ms. n. of Springfield ; from W. 227 ms. Watered by Rock river.

GRAND ECORE, p. o., Natchitoches parish, La.

GRAND FALLS, p. o., Newton co., Mo.

GRAND GLAZE, p. o., Jackson co., Ark.

GRAND GULF, p. v., Claiborne co., Miss., 65 ms. s. of Jackson ; from W. 1,075. Watered by Grand Gulf on the Mississippi river.

GRAND HAVEN, p. v., Ottawa township, seat of justice of Ottawa co., Mich., 213 ms. w. of Detroit ; from W. 694 ms. Watered by Grand river.

GRAND ISLAND. p. v., Tonawanda township, Erie co., N. Y., 299 ms. w. of Albany ; from W. 393 ms. Situated in Niagara river.

GRAND ISLE COUNTY, situated at the northwest corner of Vermont, and comprises Alburg peninsula, and several islands in the northern part of Lake Champlain, the two principal of which are North and South Hero. Area 82 square miles. Face of the country, gently undulating ; soil, rich and well cultivated. Seat, of justice, North Hero. Pop., in 1810, 4.445 ; in 1820, 3,527 ; in 1830, 3,696; in 1840, 3,883 ; in 1850, 4,145.

GRAND ISLE. p, t., Grand Isle co., Vt., 66 ms. n. w. of Montpelier ; from W. 539 ms. Situated on South Hero island in Lake Champlain. Pop. 666.

GRAND LAKE. p. o., Chicot co., Ark., 167 ms. s. of Little Rock; from W. 1,177 ms. Watered by Mississippi river.

GRAND LEDGE, p. o., Eaton co., Mich.

GRAND MARSH, p. o., Columbia co., Wis.

GRAND PRAIRIE. p. t., Marion co., O., 52 ms. from Columbus ; from W. 421 ms. Pop. 474.

GRAND PRAIRIE, p. o., Marquette co., Wis.

GRAND RAPIDS, p. o., Portage co., Wis.

GRAND RAPIDS, p. t.. Kent co., Mich. Pop. 3,147.

GRAND RIVER, p. t., Caldwell co., Mo.

GRAND RIVER, p. o., Wayne co., Iowa.

GRAND RIVER, t., Livingston co., Mo.

GRAND RIVER, t., Van Buren co., Mo.

GRAND RIVER, t., Carroll co., Mo.

GRAND RIVER, t., Henry co., Mo.

GRAND SALINE, p. o., Cherokee Nation co., Ark.

GRAND SPRING, p. o., Dane co., Wis.

GRAND TRAVERSE, p. o., Michilimackinac co.. Mich.

GRAND VIEW, p. t., Washington co., O., 141 ms. s. e of Columbus ; from W. 278 ms. Watered by Ohio river. Pop. 1,154.

GRAND VIEW, p. v., Louisa co., Iowa. Pop. 1,028.
GRAND VIEW, p. v., Edgar co., Ill., 114 ms. E. of Springfield ; from W. 675 ms. Watered by head branches of Big creek. Pop. 1,337.
GRANDVILLE. p. v., Kent co., Mich., 175 ms. w. of Detroit ; from W. 656 ms. Watered by Buck and Rush creeks.
GRANGER, p. t., Alleghany co , N. Y., 250 ms. w. of Albany ; from W, —— ms. Watered by Genesee river and tributaries.
GRANGER, p. t., Medina co., O., 131 ms. N. E. of Columbus ; from W. 1,347.
GRANGERVILLE, p. o., Saratoga township, Saratoga co., N. Y., 37 ms. N. of Albany ; from W. 409.
GRANGERSVILLE, p. o., Macon co., Ga.
GRANITE, p. o., Knox co., Ill.
GRANITEVILLE. p. o., Edgefield district. S. C.
GRANT COUNTY, situated in the northerly part of Kentucky. Area, 184 square miles. Face of the country hilly ; soil of middling quality. Seat of justice, Williamstown. Pop. in 1820, 1,805 ; in 1830, 2,987; in 1840, 4,192 ; in 1850, 6,531.
GRANT COUNTY, situated toward the easterly part of Indiana. Area, 415 square miles. Seat of justice, Marion. Pop. in 1840, 4,875 ; in 1850, 11,092.
GRANT COUNTY, situated at the southwest corner of Wisconsin, with Mississippi river on the southwest, and the Wisconsin on the northwest. Face of the country generally level, or undulating ; soil productive. Seat of justice, Lancaster. Pop. in 1840, 3,926 ; in 1850, 9,107.
GRANT. p. o., Grant co., Ind.
GRANTHAM. p. t., Sullivan co., N. H., 54 ms. N. w. of Concord ; from W. 484 ms. Watered by several ponds. Pop. 784.
GRANTSBOROUGH, p. o., Campbell co., Tenn., 201 ms. from Nashville ; from W. 507 ms.
GRANT'S CREEK, p. o., Switzerland co., Ind., 99 ms. s. E. of Indianapolis ; from W. 530 ms. Watered by Ohio river.
GRANTSVILLE, p. o., Alleghany co., Md.
GRANTVILLE, p. o., Norfolk co., Mass.
GRANVILLE COUNTY, situated on the northern boundary of North Carolina, and traversed by Tar river. Area, 828 square miles. Face of the country hilly ; soil generally productive. Seat of justice, Oxford. Pop. in 1810. 15,576; in 1820, 18,216; in 1830, 19,343; in 1840, 18,817 ; in 1850, 21,249.
GRANVILLE, p. t., Addison co., Vt., 35 ms. s. w. of Montpelier, from W. 490 ms. Watered by head branches of White river. Pop. 603.
GRANVILLE, t., Hampden co , Mass., 120 ms. s. of Boston ; from W. 355 ms. Pop. 1,305.
GRANVILLE, p. t., Washington co., N. Y., 63 ms. N. E. of Albany ; from W. 433 ms. Watered by Pawlet river. Pop. 3,434.
GRANVILLE, p. t., Bradford co. Pa., 147 ms. N. E. of Harrisburgh ; from W. 257 ms. Pop. 1,033.
GRANVILLE, t., Mifflin co., Pa. Pop. 1,052.
GRANVILLE, p. t. Licking co., O., 34 ms. N. E. of Columbus ; from W. 373 ms. Watered by east fork of Licking river. Seat of Granville college. Pop. 2,116.
GRANVILLE, t., Mercer co., O. Pop. 564.
GRANVILLE, t., Muskingum co.. O.
GRANVILLE, p. v., Monongalia co., Va., 298 ms. N. w. of Richmond ; from W. 220 ms. Watered by Duncard creek and Monongalia river.
GRANVILLE, p. v., Delaware co., Ind., 68 ms. N. E. of Indianapolis ; from W. 539 ms. Watered by Missisinewa river.
GRANVILLE, p. v., Jackson co., Tenn., 64 ms. E. of Nashville ; from W. 642 ms. Watered by Cumberland river.
GRANVILLE, v., Platte co., Mo. Watered by Missouri river.
GRANVILLE, p. t., Milwaukee co., Wis.
GRANVILLE, p. o., Putnam co., Ill.
GRAPE GROVE, t., Ray co., Mo., 154 ms. N. w. of Jefferson City ; from W. 1,057 ms.
GRAPE GROVE, p. o., Greene co., O.
GRAPE ISLAND. p. o., Tyler co., Va. 330 ms. N. w. of Richmond ; from W. 286 ms.
GRASS HILLS, p. o., Carroll co., Ky., 50 ms. N. of Frankfort; from W. 548 ms.
GRASS LAKE, p. t., Jackson co., Mich., 67 ms. s. w. of Detroit ; from W. 542 ms. Watered by Grass lake outlet. Pop. 1,281.
GRASS LAND, p. o., Harrison co., Va., 249 ms. N. w. of Richmond ; from W. 238 ms

GRASS LICK, p. o., Jackson co., Va.
GRASSY COVE, p. o., Bledsoe co., Tenn., 120 ms. s. E. of Nashville ; from W. 563 ms.
GRASSY CREEK, p. o., Russell co., Va.
GRASSY CREEK, p. o., Pendleton co.. Ky., 72 ms. s. E. of Frankfort ; from W. 518 ms.
GRASSY CREEK, p. o., Yancey co., N. C.
GRASSY CREEK, p. o., Livingston co., Mo.
GRASSY POINT, v., Rockland co., N. Y., 109 ms. s. of Albany ; from W. 277 ms. Watered by Hudson river.
GRASSY POND, p. o. Spartanburgh district, S. C.
GRASSY VALLEY, p. o., Harrison co., Ind.
GRATIOT COUNTY, situated in the central part of Michigan. Area, 576 square miles. Seat of justice, ——.
GRATIOT, p. v., Hopewell township, Muskingum co., O., 42 ms. E. of Columbus ; from W. 351 ms.
GRATIOT, t. Muskingum co., O.
GRATIOT, p. o., Lafayette co., Wis.
GRATIS, p. t., Preble co., O., 92 ms. w. of Columbus ; from W. 485 ms. Pop. 2,107.
GRATITUDE, p. o., Sussex co., N. J., 74 ms. N. of Trenton ; from W. 231 ms.
GRATTAN, p. o., Kent co., Mich.
GRATZ, p. v., Lykens township, Dauphin co., Pa., 48 ms. N. of Harrisburgh ; from W. 158 ms.
GRATZ, p. o., Owen co., Ky.
GRAVE CREEK, p. o., Marshall co., Va., 352 ms. N. w. of Richmond ; from W. 266 ms.
GRAVEL HILL, p. o., Buckingham co., Va., 67 ms. w. of Richmond ; from W. 249 ms.
GRAVEL HILL, p. o., McNairy co., Tenn.
GRAVELLY HILL, p. o., Bladen co., N. C., 121 ms. s. of Raleigh ; from W. 351 ms.
GRAVELLY SPRING, p. o., Lauderdale co., Ala.
GRAVEL RIDGE, p. o., Bradley co., Ark.
GRAVEL RUN, p. o., Washtenaw co., Mich.
GRAVEL SPRING, p. o., Frederick co., Va., 165 ms. N. w. of Richmond ; from W. 93 ms.
GRAVES, p. o., Hempstead co., Ark.
GRAVES, p. o., Caswell co., N. C.
GRAVESEND, p. t., King's co., Long Island, N. Y., 159 ms. s. of Albany; from W. 227 ms. Watered by Atlantic ocean. Pop. 1,064.
GRAVES' MILL, p. o., Madison co., Va., 105 ms. N. w. of Richmond ; from W. 106 ms.
GRAVESVILLE, p. o., Herkimer co., N. Y.
GRAY'S, p. t., Cumberland co., Me., 47 ms. s. w. of Augusta ; from W. 561 ms. Pop. 1,788.
GRAY, t. Gasconade co , Mo
GRAY ROCK, p. o., Titus co., Tex.
GRAYSBURGH, p. o., Greene co., Tenn.
GRAY'S CREEK, p. o., Cumberland co., N. C.
GRAY'S CREEK, p. o., Monroe co., Iowa.
GRAY'S CROSS-ROADS, p. o., Randolph co., N. C.
GRAYSON COUNTY, situated on the southern boundary of Virginia, and traversed by New river, a main branch of the Great Kanawha. Area, 927 square miles. Face of the country mountainous and broken ; soil generally unproductive. Seat of justice, Greenville. Pop. in 1810, 4,941 ; in 1820, 5,598 ; in 1830, 7,675 ; in 1840, 9,087 ; in 1850, 6,677.
GRAYSON COUNTY, situated toward the westerly part of Kentucky. Area, 800 square miles. Face of the country broken ; soil of middling quality. Seat of justice, Litchfield. Pop. in 1810, 2,301 ; in 1820, 4,055 ; in 1830, 2,504 ; in 1840, 4,461 ; in 1850, 6,837.
GRAYSON COUNTY, situated on the northern boundary of Texas, with Red river on the north. Area, —— square miles. Seat of justice, Sherman. Pop. in 1850, 2,008.
GRAYSON, c. h., p. v., seat of justice of Carter co., Ky., 128 ms. E. of Frankfort ; from W. 432 ms. Watered by Little Sandy river.
GRAYSON, c. h. p. v., seat of justice of Grayson co., Va., 261 ms. s. of Richmond ; from W. 336 ms. Watered by New river.
GRAYSON, p. o., Crittenden co., Ark.
GRAYSON, t., Owen co., Ind.
GRAYSON SPRINGS, p. o., Grayson co., Ky.
GRAYSON'S SULPHUR SPRINGS, p. o., Carroll co., Va.
GRAYSPORT, p. o., Yallabusha co., Miss.
GRAYSPORT, v., Muskingum co., O., 68 ms. E. of Columbus ; from W. 343 ms.
GRAY'S VALLEY, p. o., Tioga co., Pa., 146 ms. N. of Harrisburgh ; from W. 256 ms.
GRAYSVILLE, p. v., Morris township, Huntingdon co., Pa., 101 ms. w. of Harrisburgh ; from W. 170 ms.

GRAYSVILLE, p. o., Herkimer co., N. Y.

GRAYSVILLE, v., Todd co., Ky., 55 ms. from Frankfort; from W. 720 ms.

GRAYSVILLE. p. o., Monroe co., O., 184 ms. E. of Columbus; from W. 281 ms.

GRAYVILLE, p. v., White co., Ill., 61 ms. s. E. of Springfield; from W. 841 ms.

GREASY CREEK, p. o., Floyd co., Va., 230 ms. w. of Richmond; from W. 305 ms.

GREASY CREEK, p. o., Polk co., Tenn.

GREAT BARRINGTON, p. t., Berkshire co., Mass., 134 ms. w. of Boston; from W. 355 ms. Watered by Housatonic river. Pop. 3,264.

GREAT BEND, p. v., Champion township, Jefferson co., N. Y., 159 ms. N. w. of Albany; from W. 428 ms. Watered by Black river.

GREAT BEND, p. t., Susquehanna co., Pa., 191 ms. N. E. of Harrisburg; from W. 295 ms. Watered by Salt Lick creek and Susquehanna river. Pop. 1,150.

GREAT BEND, p. o., Meigs co., O., 112 ms. s. E. of Columbus; from W. 341 ms.

GREAT BRIDGE, p. v., Norfolk co., Va., 115 ms. s. E. of Richmond; from W. 240 ms. Watered by Southern river.

GREAT CROSSINGS, p. v., Scott co., Ky., 15 ms. N. E. of Frankfort; from W. 527 ms. Watered by Elkhorn creek. Seat of the Indian academy.

GREAT EGG HARBOR, t., Atlantic co., N. J. Pop. 2,688.

GREAT FALLS, p. v., Somerworth township, Strafford co., N. H., 34 ms. E. of Concord; from W. 499 ms. Watered by Salmon Fall river.

GREAT MILLS, p. o., St. Mary's co., Md.

GREAT VALLEY, p. t., Cattaraugus co., N. Y., 300 ms. w. of Albany; from W. 328 ms. Watered by Tunianguant and Great Valley creeks.

GREAT WORKS, p. v., Penobscot co., Me., 80 ms. E. of Augusta; from W. 675 ms. Watered by Great Works stream and Penobscot river.

GREECE, p. t., Monroe co., N. Y., 226 ms. w. of Albany; from W. 375 ms. Pop. 4,219.

GREEN, p. o., Wapello co., Iowa.

GREEN BANK, p. o., Burlington co., N. J.

GREEN BANK, p. o., Pocahontas co., Va., 189 ms. N. w. of Richmond; from W. 216. Watered by Deer creek.

GREEN BAY, p. v., Brown co., Wis., 158 ms. N. of Madison; from W. 938 ms. Watered by Fox river and Green bay.

GREENBOROUGH, p. o., Oswego co., N. Y.

GREEN BOTTOM, p. o., Cabell co., Va., 379 ms. w. of Richmond; from W. 384 ms.

GREEN BOTTOM, p. o., Shelby co., Tenn., 213 ms. w. of Nashville; from W. 898 ms.

GREENBRIER COUNTY, situated toward the westerly part of Virginia, and traversed by Greenbrier river. Area, 1,493 square miles. Face of the country hilly, mountainous, and broken; soil stony and sterile. Seat of justice, Lewisburgh. Pop. in 1820, 7,040; in 1830, 9,015; in 1840, 8,695; in 1850, 10.022.

GREENBRIER, p. o., Northumberland co., Pa., 60 ms. N. of Harrisburgh; from W. 170 ms.

GREENBRIER, t., Independence co., Ark.

GREENBRIER RUN, p. o., Doddridge co., Va.

GREEN BUD, p. o., Sussex co., Va.

GREENBUSH, p. v., Warren co., Ill., 92 ms. N. w. of Springfield; from W. 838 ms.

GREENBUSH, p. t., Penobscot co., Me. Pop. 457.

GREENBUSH, p. t., Rensselaer co., N. Y., 1 m. E. of Albany; from W. 370 ms. Watered by Hudson river. Pop. 4,945.

GREENBUSH, p. o., Polk co., Iowa.

GREENBUSH, p. o., Grant co., Ind.

GREENBUSH, p. o., Clinton co., Mich.

GREENBUSH, p. o., Scott co., Miss.

GREENBUSH, p. o., Sheboygan co., Wis.

GREEN CAMP, p. o., Marion co., O. Pop. 407.

GREEN CASTLE, c. h., p. v., seat of justice of Putnam co., Ind., 47 ms. w. of Indianapolis; from W. 612 ms.

GREEN CASTLE, p. b., Franklin co., Pa., 56 ms. from Harrisburgh; from W. 79 ms. Pop. 1,125.

GREEN CASTLE, p. o., Fairfield co., O.

GREEN CREEK, p. o., Sandusky co., O.

GREEN CREEK. p. o., Cape May co., N. J.

GREENE COUNTY, situated toward the southeasterly part of New York, on the west side of Hudson river. Area, 583 square miles. Face of the country beautifully varied, with high mountains and fruitful valleys; soil rich and well cultivated. Seat of justice, Catskill. Pop. in 1810, 19,536; in 1820, 22,996; in 1830, 29,525; in 1840, 30,446; in 1850, 33,126.

GREENE COUNTY, situated at the southwest corner of Pennsylvania, with Monongahela river on the east. Area, 576 square miles. Face of the country hilly; soil fertile. Seat of justice, Waynesburgh. Pop. in 1810, 12.544; in 1820, 15,554; in 1830, 18,028; in 1840, 19.147; in 1850. 22,136.

GREENE COUNTY, situated toward the easterly part of Virginia, with Blue Ridge of the Alleghany mountains on the northwest. Area, 190 square miles. Face of the country mountainous and hilly; soil fertile. Seat of justice, Stannardsville. Pop. in 1840, 4,232; in 1850, 4,400.

GREENE COUNTY, situated toward the northeasterly part of Georgia, with Oconee river on the west. Area, 504 square miles. Face of the country hilly; soil fertile. Seat of justice, Greensborough. Pop. in 1820, 1,445; in 1830, 12,551; in 1840, 11,690; in 1850, 13,068.

GREENE COUNTY, situated toward the easterly part of North Carolina. Face of the country uneven; soil generally productive. Seat of justice, Snow Hill. Pop. in 1820, 4,553; in 1830, 6,313; in 1840, 6,595; in 1850, 6,619.

GREENE COUNTY, situated toward the westerly part of Alabama, traversed by Black Warrior river, and bounded by Tombigbee river on the southwest. Area, 836 square miles. Face of the country generally hilly; soil on the bottom lands rich; in the other parts generally unproductive. Seat of justice, Eutaw. Pop. in 1820, 4,554; in 1830, 15,026; in 1840, 24,024; in 1850, 31,441.

GREENE COUNTY, situated on the eastern boundary of Mississippi, and traversed by Chickasawha river. Area, 864 square miles. Face of the country uneven; soil unproductive, and covered with pine forests. Seat of justice, Leakesville. Pop. in 1820, 1,445; in 1830, 1,854; in 1840, 1.636; in 1850, 2.018.

GREENE COUNTY, situated on the easterly boundary of Tennessee, with Stony mountains on the southeast, and traversed by Nolichucky river. Area, 700 square miles. Face of the country diversified with mountains, hills, and valleys; soil along the streams fertile. Seat of justice. Greenville. Pop. in 1810, 9,713; in 1820, 11,328; in 1830, 14,410; in 1840, 16,076; in 1850, 17.824.

GREENE COUNTY, situated in the central part of Kentucky, and traversed by Greene river. Area, 460 square miles. Face of the country undulating and level; soil fertile. Seat of justice, Greensburgh. Pop. in 1810, 6,735; in 1820, 11,943; in 1830, 13,138; in 1840, 14,212; in 1850, 9,060.

GREENE COUNTY, situated toward the southwesterly part of Ohio, and traversed by Little Miami and Mad rivers. Area, 400 square miles. Face of the country pleasantly diversified; soil fertile, and well cultivated. Seat of justice, Xenia. Pop. in 1830, 14,801; in 1840, 17,528; in 1850, 22,946.

GREENE COUNTY, situated toward the southwesterly part of Indiana, and traversed by west fork of White river. Area, 456 square miles. Seat of justice, Bloomfield. Pop. in 1830, 4,242; in 1840, 8,321; in 1850, 11,424.

GREENE COUNTY, situated toward the westerly part of Illinois, with Illinois river on the west. Area, 912 square miles. Face of the country rolling : soil fertile. Seat of justice, Carrollton. Pop. in 1830, 7,674; in 1840, 11,951; in 1850, 3,658.

GREENE COUNTY, situated toward the southwesterly part of Missouri, and traversed by White river. Area, 1,000 square miles. Face of the country level, and in some parts hilly; soil productive. Seat of justice, Springfield. Pop. in 1840, 5,372; in 1850, 12.785.

GREENE COUNTY, situated at the northeast corner of Arkansas, with St. Francis river on the east, and Cache river on the west. Area, 1,025 square miles. Face of the country level. Seat of justice, Gainesville. Pop. in 1840, 1,586; in 1850, 2,593.

GREENE COUNTY, situated on the southern boundary of Wisconsin. Area, 576 square miles. Seat of justice. Monroe. Pop. in 1840, 933; in 1850, 6,179.

GREENE, t., Kennebec co., Me., 25 ms. s. w. of Augusta; from W. 583 ms. Watered by Androscoggin river Pop. 1,348.

GREENE CORNER, p. o., Kennebec co., Me.

GREENE DEPOT, p. o., Kennebec co., Me.

GREENE, t., Sussex co., N. J. Pop. 823.
GREENE, p. o., Lancaster co., Pa., 56 ms. E. of Harrisburgh ; from W. 93 ms.
GREENE, p. t., Franklin co., Pa. Pop. 3.154.
GREENE, t., Greene co., Pa. Watered by Whitely creek. Pop. 667.
GREENE, t., Pike co., Pa. Pop. 357.
GREENE. t.. Indiana co.. Pa. Watered by Two Lick, Yellow, and Cushion creeks. Pop. 2,281.
GREENE, t., Beaver co., Pa. Watered by Ohio river and Mill creek. Pop. 1,923.
GREENE, t., Franklin co., Pa., 43 ms. s. E. of Harrisburgh. Watered by the east branch of Conecocheague creek. Pop. 3,154.
GREENE, p. t., Hamilton co., O. Pop. 3,948.
GREENE, t., Harrison co., O. Pop. 1,527.
GREENE, t., Adams co., O. Pop. 1,520.
GREENE. t., Brown co., O. Pop. 632.
GREENE, p. t., Clark co., O. Watered by east fork and Todd's fork of Miami river. Pop. 1,230
GREENE, t., Clinton co., O. Pop. 2,026.
GREENE. t., Columbiana co., O.
GREENE, t., Gallia co., O. Pop. 1,276.
GREENE, t. Hocking co., O. Watered by Hockhocking river. Pop. 1,290.
GREENE, t., Fayette co., O. Watered by Rattlesnake fork of Paint creek. Pop. 951.
GREENE, p. t,. Monroe co., O.
GREENE, t., Shelby co., O. Pop. 1,078.
GREENE, p. t., Scioto co., O. Pop. 2,345.
GREENE, t., Ross co., O. Pop. 1,658.
GREENE, t., Richland co., O.
GREENE, p. t., Wayne co., O. Pop. 2,060.
GREENE, p. t., Summit co., O. Pop. 1,928.
GREENE, t., Trumbull co , O. Pop. 958.
GREENE, t., Randolph co , Ind.
GREENE, p. o., Cape Girardeau co., Mo., 214 ms. s. of Jefferson city. Watered by Crooked creek.
GREENE, t., Iowa co., Wis.
GREENE, t., Hancock co., Ind.
GREENE, t., Polk co., Mo.
GREENE, t., Livingston co., Mo.
GREENE GROVE, p. o., Conway co., Ark.
GREENE GARDEN, p. o., Will co.. Ill.
GREENE'S STORE, p. o., Lawrence co., O.
GREENFIELD, p. t., Hancock co., Me. Pop. 694.
GREENFIELD, p. t., Hillsborough co., N. H., 35 ms. s. w. of Concord ; from W. 454 ms. Watered by Contoocook river. Pop, 716.
GREENFIELD. c. h., p. t., seat of justice of Franklin co., Mass.. 92 ms. w. of Boston ; from W. 402 ms. Watered by Connecticut river. Pop. 2,580.
GREENFIELD, p. t., Saratoga co., N. Y., 40 ms. N. of Albany. Watered by Kayaderosseros creek. Pop. 2,890.
GREENFIELD, p. t., Erie co., Pa., 352 ms. N. of Harrisburgh ; from w. 284 ms. Watered by the north branch of French creek. Pop. 731.
GREENFIELD, b., Washington co., Pa. Pop. 380.
GREENFIELD, t., Luzerne co., Pa. Watered by Susquehanna river. Pop. 869.
GREENFIELD, p. v., Madison township, Highland co., O., 72 ms. s.w. of Columbus ; from W. 427 ms. Watered by Paint creek.
GREENFIELD, t., Bedford co., Pa. Watered by Bob's and Dunning's creeks, and by the Frankstown branch of Juniata river.
GREENFIELD, t., Fairfield co., O. Pop. 2,113.
GREENFIELD, t., Gallia co., O. Pop. 952.
GREENFIELD, t., Huron co., O , 106 ms. N. E. of Columbus. Pop. 1,332.
GREENFIELD, p. v., Nelson co., Va., 107 ms. w. of Richmond ; from W. 149 ms.
GREENFIELD, c. h., p. v., seat of justice of Hancock co., Ind., 20 ms. E. of Indianapolis ; from W. 551 ms. Watered by Brandywine creek.
GREENFIELD, t.. La Grange co.. Ind.
GREENFIELD, t., Orange co., Ind. Pop. 725.
GREENFIELD. p. v., Greene co., Ill., 60 ms. s. w. of Springfield ; from W. 832 ms. Pop. 237.
GREENFIELD, p. v., Sullivan co., Tenn., 199 ms. E. of Nashville ; from W. 394 ms.
GREENFIELD, v., Shelby co., Mo. Situated near Fabius river.
GREENFIELD, p. v., seat of justice of Dade co., Mo., 150 ms., s. w. of Jefferson city.
GREENFIELD, t., Wayne co., Mich., 6 ms. N. w. of Detroit ; from W. 530 ms. Pop. 1,674.

GREENFIELD, p. v., Milwaukee co., Wis., 92 ms. E. of Madison ; from W. 814 ms.
GREENFIELD, t., Poinsett co., Ark. Pop. 967.
GREENFIELD. p. t.. Saratoga co., N. Y., 40 ms. N. of Albany ; from W. 410 ms. Pop. 2.890.
GREENFIELD HILL. p. o., Fairfield co., Ct.
GREENFIELD MILLS, p. o., Frederick co., Md., 86 ms. N. w. of Annapolis ; from W. 54 ms.
GREENFORD, p. o., Green township. Mahoning co., O., 158 ms. N. E. of Columbus ; from W. 294 ms.
GREEN GROVE, t., Ray co., Mo.
GREEN GROVE, p. o., Conway co., Ark.
GREEN HILL, p. o., Campbell co., Va., 132 ms. s. w. of Richmond ; from W. 219 ms.
GREEN HILL, p. o., Columbiana co., O., 146 ms. N. E. of Columbus ; from W. 294 ms.
GREEN HILL, p. o., Wilson co., Tenn., 14 ms. E. of Nashville ; from W. 607 ms.
GREEN HILL, p. o., Stewart co., Ga.
GREEN HILL, p. o., Lauderdale co., Ala.
GREEN HILL, p. o., Rutherford co., N. C.
GREEN LAKE, p. o., Marquette co., Wis.
GREENLAND, p. t., Rockingham co., N. H., 45 ms. s. E. of Concord ; from W. 488 ms. Pop. 730.
GREENLAND DEPOT, p. o., Rockingham co., N. H.
GREENLEAF, p. o., De Soto co., Wis.
GREEN LEAD, p. o., Southampton co., Va.
GREEN LEVEL, p. o., Wake co., N. C.
GREEN MEADOW, p. o., Washington co., Tenn.
GREEN MOUNT, p. o., Adams co., Pa.
GREEN OAK, p. o., Livingston co., Mich., 41 ms. w. of Detroit ; from W. 538 ms.
GREEN PLAINS, p. o., Northampton co.. N. C., 90 ms. N. of Raleigh ; from W. 204 ms. Watered by Mississippi river.
GREEN PLAINS, p. o., Et. Francis co., Ark.
GREEN POINT, p. v., King's co., N. Y.
GREEN POND, p. o., Union co., N. C.
GREENPORT, p., Columbia co., N. Y. Watered by Hudson river. Pop, 1,300.
GREENPORT, p. v.. Southold township, Suffolk co., Long Island, N. Y.. 246 ms. s. E. of Albany ; from W. 326. Watered by Peconic bay.
GREENPORT, p. o., Cedar co., Mo.
GREEN RIVER, p. o., Windham co., Vt., 13 ms. s. of Montpelier ; from W. 426 ms.
GREEN RIVER, p. o., Hillsdale township, Columbia co., N. Y., 35 ms. s. E. of Albany ; from W. 363 ms.
GREEN RIVER, p. o., Henry co., Ill., 144 ms. N. w. of Springfield ; from W. 873 ms.
GREEN RIVER, p. o., Rutherford co., N. C
GREEN RIVER, p. o., Hart co., Ky.
GREENE, p. o., Polk co., Tex.
GREEN'S BLUFF, p. o., Jefferson co., Tex.
GREENSBOROUGH, p. t., Orleans co., Vt., 29 ms. N. E. of Montpelier ; from W. 545 ms. Watered by head waters of Lamoille and Caspian lake outlet. Pop. 1,008.
GREENSBOROUGH, p. v., Green co., Pa., 196 ms. w. of Harrisburgh ; from W. 204 ms. Pop. 667.
GREENSBOROUGH, p. v., Caroline co., Md., 59 ms. E. of Annapolis ; from W. 99 ms.
GREENSBOROUGH, c. h., p. v., seat of justice of Greene co., Ky., 89 ms. s. w. of Frankfort ; from W. 611 ms.
GREENSBOROUGH, p. v., seat of justice of Guildford co., N. C., 82 ms. N. w. of Raleigh. Watered by north and south branches of Buckhorn creek.
GREENSBOROUGH, c. h., p. v., seat of justice of Greene co., Ga., 44 ms. N. of Milledgeville ; from W. 604 ms.
GREENSBOROUGH, p. v., Greene co., Ala.; from W. 852 ms.
GREENSBOROUGH, c. h., p. v., seat of justice of Choctaw co., Miss., 110 ms. N. E. of Jackson ; from W. 945 ms. Watered by a head branch of Big Black river.
GREENSBOROUGH, p. t., Henry co., Ind. Pop. 1,190.
GREENSBOROUGH, p. v., Henry co., Ind., 40 ms. E. of Indianapolis ; from W. 541 ms.
GREENSBOROUGH, c. h., p. v., seat of justice of Decatur co., Ind. Pop. 1,202.
GREENSBOROUGH, c. h., p. v., seat of justice of St Helena parish, La.
GREENSBOROUGH, p. o., Greene co., Ark.
GREENSBURGH, p. v., Trumbull co., O., 185 ms. N. E. of Columbus ; from W. 319 ms. Pop. 958.
GREENSBURGH, c. h., p. v., seat of justice of Westmoreland co., Pa., 168 ms. w. of Harrisburgh ; from W. 194 ms.
GREENSBURGH, t., Greene co., Ky.
GREENSBURGH, c. h., p. v., St. Helena parish, La., 75

ns. N. W. of New Orleans; from W. 1,150 ms. Watered by Tickfaw river.

GREENSBURGH, p. v., Green township, seat of justice of Trumbull co., Ind., 47 ms. s. E. of Indianapolis; from W. 550 ms.

GREENSBOROUGH CROSS ROADS, p. o., Sandusky co., O.

GREEN'S FORK. p. o., Washington township, Wayne co., Ind., 68 ms. E. of Indianapolis; from W. 513 ms.

GREEN'S FORK, v., Randolph co., Ind.

GREENSPORT, p. o., St. Clair co., Ala.

GREEN SPRING, p. o., Brown co., Wis.

GREEN SPRING, p. o., Seneca co., O., 101 ms. N. of Columbus; from W. 419 ms.

GREEN SPRING, p. o., Orange co., N. C.

GREEN SPRINGS, p. o., Nevada co.. Cal.

GREEN SPRING RUN, p. o., Hampshire co., Va.

GREEN'S STORE, p. o., Scott co., Ky.

GREENTON, p. v., Lafayette co., Mo., 134 ms. N. W. of Jefferson City; from W. 1,057 ms.

GREEN TOP, p. o., Schuyler co., Mo.

GREENTOWN, p. v., Lake township, Stark co., O.

GREENTOWN, p. o., Howard co., Ind.

GREEN TREE, p. o., Alleghany co., Ind.

GREENUP COUNTY, situated at the northeasterly corner of Kentucky, with Ohio river on the north and northeast, and Sandy river on the southeast. Area, 768 square miles. Face of the country, hilly and broken; soil, inferior. Seat of justice, Greenupsburgh. Pop. in 1820, 4,311; in 1830, 5,853; in 1840, 6,279; in 1850, 9,654.

GREENUP, p. o., Cumberland co., Ill., 111 ms. from Springfield; from W. 689 ms.

GREENUP, c. h., or, GREENUPSBURGH, p. v., seat of justice of Greenup co.. Ky., 146 ms. E. of Frankfort; from W. 429 ms. Watered by Ohio and Little Sandy rivers.

GREENVALE. p. o., Jo-Daviess co., Ill.

GREEN VALLEY, p. o., Bath co., Va.

GREEN VALLEY, p. o., Lafayette co., Miss.

GREEN VALLEY, p. v., Franklin co., Pa.

GREEN VILLAGE, v., Franklin co., Me., 91 ms. N. W. of Augusta; from W. 686 ms.

GREENVILLE COUNTY, situated on the southern boundary of Virginia, with Nottoway river on the north, and traversed by Meherin river. Area, 325 square miles. Face of the country, generally level; soil, of middling quality. Seat of justice, Hicksford. Pop. in 1810, 6,853; in 1820, 6,858; in 1830, 7,117; in 1840, 6.366; in 1850, 5,639.

GREENVILLE DISTRICT, situated on the northerly boundary of South Carolina, with Saluda river on the southwest. Area, 705 square miles. Face of the country, mountainous and diversified; soil, generally fertile and well cultivated. Seat of justice, Greenville. Pop. in 1810, 13,133; in 1820, 14,530; in 1830, 16,476; in 1840, 17,839; in 1850, 20,156.

GREENVILLE, p. o., Brown co., Wis.

GREENVILLE, p. t., Piscataquis co., Me., 91 ms. N. E. of Augusta; from W. 686 ms. Watered by Moosehead lake. Pop. 326.

GREENVILLE, p. v., Providence co., R. I., 9 ms. w. of Providence; from W. 402 ms.

GREENVILLE, p. t., Greene co., N. Y., 29 ms. s. of Albany; from W. 361 ms. Watered by Provost and Catskill creeks. Pop. 2,242.

GREENVILLE, c. h., v., seat of justice of Clark co., Ark., 78 ms. s. w. of Little Rock; from W. 1,143 ms. Pop. 297.

GREENVILLE, v., Green township, Sussex co., N. J., 71 ms. N. of Trenton; from W. 232 ms. Pop. 823.

GREENVILLE, p. t., Erie co., Pa. Pop. 1,542.

GREENVILLE, t., Somerset co., Pa. Pop. 723.

GREENVILLE, p. v., Augusta co., Va., 123 ms. N. W. of Richmond; from W. 165 ms. Watered by South river.

GREENVILLE, c. h., p. v., seat of justice of Pitt co., N. C., 97 ms. E. of Raleigh; from W. 277 ms. Watered by Tar river. Pop. 1,893.

GREENVILLE, c. h., p. v. seat of justice of Merriwether co., Ga., 111 ms. w. of Milledgeville; from W. 753 ms

GREENVILLE, c. h., p. v., seat of justice of Butler co., Ala.; from W. 883 ms. Watered by Sepulgah river.

GREENVILLE, c. h., p. v., seat of justice of Greene co., Tenn., 258 ms. E. of Nashville; from W. 437 ms. Seat of Greenville college. Pop. 580.

GREENVILLE, p. v., Floyd co., Ind., 111 ms. s. of Indianapolis; from W. 612 ms. Pop. 1,815.

GREENVILLE, c. h., p. v., seat of justice of Muhlen burgh co., Ky., 105 ms. s. w. of Frankfort; from W. 717 ms. Watered by a branch of Green river.

GREENVILLE, c. h., p. v., seat of justice of Darke co.. O., 91 ms. w. of Columbus; from W. 485 ms. Watered by Greenville and Mud creeks. Pop. 1,045.

GREENVILLE, c. h., p. v., seat of justice of Bond co.. Ill., 74 ms. s. of Springfield; from W. 758 ms. Watered by east fork of Shoal creek.

GREENVILLE, c. h., p. v., seat of justice of Wayne co., Mo., 113 ms. s. E. of Jefferson City; from W. 917 ms. Watered by St. Francis river.

GREENVILLE, c. h., p. v., seat of justice of Greenville district, S. C., 107 ms. N. w. of Columbia; from W. 502 ms. Pop. 1,305.

GREENVILLE, t., Saline co., Mo.

GREENVILLE, p. o., Hunt co., Tex.

GREENVILLE, p. v., New London co., Ct.

GREENVILLE, p. o., Mount Calm co., Mich.

GREENVILLE, c. h., p. v., seat of justice of Washington co., Miss.

GREENWICH, p. t., Hampshire co., Mass., 75 ms. w. of Boston; from W. 391 ms. Watered by Swift river. Pop. 838.

GREENWICH, p. t., Fairfield co., Ct., 82 ms. s. w. of Hartford; from W. 258 ms. Watered by Byram and Miannus rivers, and Long Island sound. Pop. 5,036.

GREENWICH, p. t., Washington co., N. Y., 35 ms. N. E. of Albany; from W. 410 ms. Watered by Hudson and Battenkill creeks. Pop. 3,803.

GREENWICH, t., Warren co., N. J., 54 ms. from Trenton; from W. 194 ms. Pop. 3,726.

GREENWICH, t., Gloucester co., N. J., 44 ms. from Trenton; from W. 150 ms. Watered by Crab, Mantua, Clonmel, Raccoon and Repaupo creeks. Pop. 3,067.

GREENWICH, t., Cumberland co., N. J., 73 ms. s. w. of Trenton; from W. 184 ms. Watered by Mill, Newport, Stow, Cohansey and Pine Mount creeks. Pop. 1,158.

GREENWICH, t., Berks co., Pa., 64 ms. from Harrisburgh; from W. 159 ms. Watered by Sacony creek and tributaries. Pop. 1,842.

GREENWICH, p. t., Huron co., O., 93 ms. N. of Columbus; from W. 384 ms. Pop. 1,05C.

GREENWICH STATION, p. o., Huron co., O.

GREENWICH VILLAGE, p. v., Greenwich township, Hampshire co., Mass., 73 ms. w. of Boston; from W 393 ms. Pop. 838.

GREENWOOD, p. t., Oxford co., Me., 54 ms. w. of Augusta; from W. 598 ms. Pop. 1,118.

GREENWOOD, p. t., Steuben co., N. Y., 253 ms. w. of Albany; from W. 309 ms. Watered by Bennett's creek. Pop. 1,185.

GREENWOOD, p. t., Columbia co., Pa., 92 ms. N. E. of Harrisburgh; from W. 202 ms. Watered by tributaries of Fishing creek. Pop. 1,260.

GREENWOOD, t., Crawford co., Pa., 236 ms. N. w. of Harrisburgh; from W. 296 ms. Pop. 1,127.

GREENWOOD, t., Perry co., Pa., 29 ms. N. w. of Harrisburgh; from W. 136 ms. Pop. 995.

GREENWOOD, t., Juniata co., Pa., 36 ms. N. w. of Harrisburgh; from W. 143 ms. Watered by Susquehanna river.

GREENWOOD, p. v., Abbeville district, S. C., 81 ms. N. w. of Columbia; from W. 505 ms.

GREENWOOD, p. v., Johnson co., Ind., 10 ms. s. of Indianapolis; from W. 586 ms.

GREENWOOD, p. v., Caddo parish, La., 150 ms. N. w. of New Orleans; from W. 1,300 ms.

GREENWOOD, p. o., Marquette co., Wis.

GREENWOOD, p. o., De Kalb co., Ala.

GREENWOOD, p. o., Doddridge co., Va.

GREENWOOD, p. o., Carroll co., Miss.

GREENWOOD, p. o., McHenry co., Ill.

GREENWOOD, p. o., Sumner co., Tenn.

GREENWOOD, p. o., Jackson co., Flor.

GREENWOOD FURNACE, p. o., Huntingdon co., Pa.

GREERSVILLE, p. o., Knox co., O.

GREGORY'S MILL, p. o., Granville co., N. C.

GREGG, t., Centre co., Pa., 29 ms. N. w. of Harrisburgh; from W. 613 ms. Watered by Sinking creek. Pop. 1,473.

GREIG, p. t., Lewis co., N. Y. Watered by Otter and Fish creeks, and Moose river. Pop. 1,074.

GREIGSVILLE, p. o., York township, Livingston co., N. Y., 234 ms. w. of Albany; from W. 351 ms.

GREIGSVILLE, p. o., Preston co., Va.

GRENADA, p. v., Yallabusha co., Miss., 113 ms. N. of

Jackson ; from W. 958 ms. Watered by Yallabusha river.

GREY ROCK, p. o., Harford co., Md.

GREYSVILLE, p. o., Sullivan co., Ind.

GRIFFIN, p. v., Pike co.. Ga., 80 ms. w. of Milledgeville ; from W. 684 ms. Pop. 2,320.

GRIFFIN'S, p. o., Johnson co., Ark.

GRIFFINSBURGH, p. v., Culpeper co., Va., 106 ms. N. w. of Richmond ; from W. 90 ms.

GRIFFIN'S CORNERS, p. o., Delaware co., N. Y., 70 ms. s. w. of Albany ; from W. 344 ms.

GRIFFIN'S MILLS, p. o., Aurora township, Erie co., N. Y., 283 ms. w. of Albany ; from W. 368 ms. Watered by Cazenove creek.

GRIFFIN'S MILLS, p. o., Lowndes co., Ga.

GRIFFITH'S, p. o., Nicholas co., Ky.

GRIFFITHSVILLE, p. o., Cabell co., Va.

GRIGGSTOWN, p. v., Franklin township, Somerset co., N. J., 20 ms. N. E. of Trenton ; from W. 194 ms. Watered by Millstone river, and the Delaware and Raritan canal.

GRIGGS, t., Van Buren co., Ark.

GRIGGSVILLE. p. v., Pike co., Ill., 61 ms. w. of Springfield ; from W. 841 ms. Watered by Illinois river.

GRIMES COUNTY, situated toward the southerly part of Texas, with Navasoto and Brazos rivers on the west. Area. —— square miles. Seat of justice, Anderson. Pop. in 1850, 4,008.

GRIMESVILLE, p. o., Grimes co., Tex.

GRIMESVILLE, p. o., Berks co., Pa., 77 ms. E. of Harrisburgh ; from W. 169 ms.

GRINDSTONE POINT, p. o., De Kalb co., Mo.

GRISWOLD, p. t., New London co., Ct., 50 ms. s. E. of Hartford ; from W. 368 ms. Watered by Quinebaug river. Pop. 2,065.

GRISWOLD, p. o., Hamilton co., Ill., 167 ms. s. E. of Springfield ; from W 787 ms.

GRISWOLD'S MILLS, p. o.. Fort Ann township, Washington co., N. Y., 61 ms. N. E. of Albany ; from W. 433 ms.

GRISWOLDSVILLE, p. o., Jones, co., Ga.

GRISWOLDVILLE, p. o., Franklin co., Mass.

GROFF'S STORE, p. o., Lancaster co., Pa.

GROGANSVILLE, p. o., Rockingham co., N. C., 127 ms. N w of Raleigh ; from W. 285 ms.

GROOM'S CORNER, p. o., Saratoga co., N. Y.

GROOVERVILLE, p. o., Thomas co., Ga., 279 ms. s. w. of Milledgeville ; from W. 923 ms.

GROSSE ISLE, p. o. Wayne co., Mich.

GROSS TETE, p. o., Iberville parish, La.

GROTON, p. t., Grafton co., N. H., 42 ms. N. w. of Concord ; from W. 510 ms. Watered by Baker's river. Pop. 776.

GROTON, p. t., Caledonia co., Vt., 29 ms. E. of Montpelier ; from W. 531 ms. Watered by Well's river and tributaries. Pop. 895.

GROTON, p. t., Middlesex co., Mass., 33 ms. N. w. of Boston ; from W. 429 ms. Watered by Nashua and Squanecook rivers. Pop. 2,515.

GROTON, p. t., New London co., Ct., 45 ms. s. E. of Hartford ; from W. 354 ms. Watered by Thames, Mystic, and Pequonnuck rivers. Pop. 3,654.

GROTON, p. t., Tompkins co., N. Y., 162 ms. w. of Albany. from W. 312 ms. Watered by Fall creek and Owasco lake inlet. Pop. 3,343.

GROTON, p. t., Erie co., O., 95 ms. N. of Columbus ; from W. 405 ms. Watered by Pipe creek. Pop. 884.

GROTON CENTRE, p. o., Groton township, Erie co., O.

GROTON CITY, p. o., Tompkins co., N. Y.

GROUSE, p. o., Kane co., Ill.

GROUT'S CORNERS, p. o. Franklin co., Mass.

GROVE, p. t., Alleghany co., N. Y., 261 ms. s. w. of Albany ; from W. 347 ms. Watered by Cashaque and Cannaseraga creeks.

GROVE, t., Clinton co., Pa. Pop. 258.

GROVE, p. o., Chatham co., N. C., 20 ms. w. of Raleigh ; from W. 318 ms.

GROVE, p. o., Elbert co., Ga.

GROVE CREEK, p. o., Jones co., Iowa.

GROVE FARM, p. o., Henders n co., Ill.

GROVE HILL, p. o., Warren co., N. C., 73 ms. N. E. of Raleigh ; from W. 219 ms.

GROVE HILL, p. o., Clark co., Ala. ; from W. 928 ms.

GROVE HILL, p. o., Page co., Va.

GROVE HILL, p. o., Jackson parish, La

GROVELAND, p. t., Livingston co., N. Y., 236 ms. w. of Albany ; from W. 338 ms. Watered by Canaseraga creek and Conesus lake. Pop. 1,724.

GROVELAND, p. t., Oakland co., Mich., 44 ms. N. w. of Detroit ; from W. 568 ms. Pop. 988.

GROVELAND, p. v., Tazewell co., Ill., 62 ms. N. of Springfield ; from W. 776 ms.

GROVELAND, p. o., Essex co., Mass.

GROVELAND, p. o., Fulton co., O.

GROVELAND, p. o., Winnebago co., Wis.

GROVELAND CENTRE, p.o., Groveland township, Livingston co., N.Y., 239 ms. w. of Albany; from W. 341 ms.

GROVE LEVEL, p. o., Franklin co., Ga., 105 ms. N. of Milledgeville ; from W. 620 ms.

GROVE MOUNT, p. o., Dyer co., Tenn.

GROVENOR'S CORNER, p. o., Schoharie co., N. Y.

GROVE PORT, p. o., Franklin co., O.

GROVES, p. o., Rush co., Ind., 54 ms. E. of Indianapolis ; from W. 525 ms.

GROVETON, p. o., Prince William co., Va., 107 ms. N. of Richmond ; from W. 35 ms.

GROVEVILLE, p. o.. Mercer co., N. J.

GRUBB'S MILLS, p. o., Putnam co., Ind.

GRUBB SPRINGS, p. o., Monroe co., Miss.

GRUNDY COUNTY, situated toward the southerly part of Tennessee. Area, —— square miles. Seat of justice, Altamont. Pop. in 1850, 2,773.

GRUNDY COUNTY, situated toward the northeasterly part of Illinois, and traversed by Des Plaines river. Area, 324 square miles. Seat of justice, Morris. Pop. in 1850, 3,023.

GRUNDY COUNTY, situated toward the northern part of Missouri, and traversed by numerous branches of Grand river. Seat of justice, Trenton. Pop. in 1850, 3,006.

GRUNDY, p. o., Pulaski co., Ky.

GUERNSEY COUNTY, situated toward the easterly part of Ohio. Area, 676 square miles. Face of the country generally hilly ; soil of middling quality ; along the valley of Wells creek. its principal stream, excellent. Seat of justice. Cambridge. Pop. in 1810, 3,051 ; in 1820, 9,292 ; in 1830, 18,036 ; in 1840, 27,748 ; in 1850, 30,438.

GREAT STATION, p. o., Russell co., Va.

GUILDERLAND, p. t., Albany co., N. Y., 9 ms. w. of Albany ; from W. 379 ms. Watered by Norman's kill. Pop. 3,279.

GUILDERLAND CENTRE, p. o., Guilderland township. Albany co., N. Y.,12 ms. w. of Albany ; from W. 382 ms.

GUILDHALL, c. h., p. t., seat of justice of Essex co., Vt., 71 ms. N. E. of Montpelier ; from W. 568 ms. Watered by Connecticut river. Pop. 501.

GUILFORD COUNTY, situated toward the northerly part of North Carolina. Area, 672 square miles. Face of the country hilly ; soil productive. Seat of justice. Greensborough. Pop. in 1820, 14,511 ; in 1830, 18,735 ; in 1840, 19,175 ; in 1850, 19,754.

GUILFORD, p. t., Piscataquis co., Me., 75 ms. N. E. of Augusta ; from W. 670 ms. Watered by Piscataquis river and tributaries. Pop. 834.

GUILFORD, p. t., New Haven co., Ct., 52 ms. s. of Hartford ; from W. 316 ms. Watered by Long Island sound. Pop. 2,653.

GUILFORD, p. t., Chenango co., N. Y., 102 ms. w. of Albany ; from W. 334 ms. Watered by Unadilla river. Pop. 2,600.

GUILFORD, t., Franklin co., Pa., 46 ms. s. w. of Harrisburgh ; from W. 84 ms. Watered by east branch of Conechocheague creek. Pop. 3,471.

GUILFORD, p. t., Medina co., O., 103 ms. from Columbus ; from W. 352 ms. Pop. 1,800.

GUILFORD, p. t., Hendricks co., Ind., 13 ms. from Indianapolis ; from W. 583 ms. Pop. 1,103.

GUILFORD, v., Hanover township, Columbiana co., O.

GUILFORD, p. o., Accomac co., Va., 207 ms. E. of Richmond ; from W. 188 ms.

GUILFORD, p. t., Windham co., Vt., 124 ms. s. of Montpelier ; from W. 419 ms. Watered by Green river and Broad brook. Pop. 1,389.

GUILFORD, p. o., Dearborn co., Ind.

GUILFORD CENTRE, p. v., Guilford township, Windham co., Vt.

GUILFORD CENTRE, p. o., Guilford township, Chenango co., N. Y.

GUINEY'S, p. o., Caroline co., Va., 49 ms. N. of Richmond ; from W. 68 ms.

GUIONVILLE, p. o., Dearborn co., Ind., 89 ms. s. E. of Indianapolis ; from W. 529 ms.

GULF MILLS, p. o., Montgomery co., Pa., 88 ms. E. of Harrisburgh ; from W. 153 ms.

GULF PRAIRIE, p. o., Brazoria co., Tex.

GULLEY'S STORE, p. o., Johnson co., N. C.

GULLITSVILLE, v., Monroe co., Ga., 60 ms. w. of Milledgeville; from W. 677 ms.

GUMBOROUGH, p. o., Sussex co., Del.

GUM CREEK, p. o., Dooly co., Ga.

GUM BRANCH, p. o., Darlington district, S. C., 100 ms. N. E. of Columbia; from W. 456 ms.

GUM GROVE, p. o., Union co., Ky.

GUM POND, p. o., Baker co., Ga.

GUM SPRING, p. o., Louisa co., Va., 34 ms. N. w. of Richmond; from W. 157 ms.

GUM SPRING, p. o., Smith co., Tex.

GUM SWAMP, p. o., Columbus co., N. C., 145 ms. s. E. of Raleigh; from W, 433 ms.

GUM SWAMP? p. o., Marion district, S. C.

GUM SWAMP, p. o., Pulaski co., Ga.

GUM TREE, p. o., Chester co., Pa., 68 ms. s. E. of Harrisburgh; from W. 112 ms.

GUM LAKE, p. o., Barry co., Mich.

GUM LOG, t., Pope co., Ark.

GUNTER'S LANDING, p. o., Marshall co., Ala.

GUSTAVUS, p. v., Trumbull co., O., 190 ms. N. E. of Columbus; from W. 313 ms. Watered by a branch of Beaver river.

GUSTAVUS, p. o., Greene co., Tenn., 245 ms. E. of Nashville; from W. 448 ms.

GUSTINE, p. o., Adams co., O.

GURTHRIESVILLE, p. o., Chester co., Pa., 63 ms. s. E. of Harrisburgh.

GURTHRIESVILLE, p. o., York district, S. C., 72 ms. N. of Columbia; from W. 437 ms.

GUTTENBURGH, p. o., Clayton co., Iowa.

GUYANDOTTE, p. v., Cabell co., Va., 359 ms. N. w. of Richmond; from W. 396 ms. Watered by Ohio and Guyandotte rivers.

GUY'S MILLS, p. o., Crawford co., Pa., 246 ms. N. w. of Harrisburgh; from W. 319 ms.

GUYSVILLE, p. o., Athens co., O., 86 ms. s. E. of Columbus; from W. 335 ms.

GWINNED, p. t., Montgomery co., Pa., 95 ms. E. of Harrisburgh; from W. 159 ms. Watered by Wissahickon and Towamensing creeks. Pop. 1,571.

GWINNETT COUNTY, situated toward the northerly part of Georgia, with Chattahoochee river on the northwest. Area, 648 square miles. Seat of justice, Lawrenceville. Pop. in 1820, 4,589; in 1830, 12,220; in 1840, 10,804; in 1850, 11,257.

GYPSUM, p. o., Ontario co., N. Y.

H.

HABERSHAM COUNTY, situated on the northeasterly boundary of Georgia, and traversed by Chattahoochee river. Area, 760 square miles. Face of the country hilly, and the eastern part is traversed by the Blue Ridge. Seat of justice, Clarksville. Pop. in 1820, 3,171; in 1830, 10,648; in 1840, 7,961: in 1850, 8,895.

HABOLOCHITTO, p. o., Hancock co., Miss., 168 ms. s. of Jackson; from W. 1,118 ms.

HACKENSACK, t., Bergen co., N. J., 75 ms. N. E. of Trenton; from W. 241 ms. Watered by Hudson and Hackensack rivers. Pop. 3,486.

HACKENSACK, p. v., New Barbadoes township, and seat of justice of Bergen co., N. J., 76 ms. N. E. of Trenton; from Washington 242 ms. Watered by Hackensack river.

HACKETTSTOWN, p. v., Independence township, Warren co., N. J., 61 ms. N. of Trenton; from W. 222 ms. Watered by Musconetcong river and Morris canal.

HACKNEY'S CROSS ROADS, p. o., Chatham co., N. C., 27 ms. w. of Raleigh; from W. 315 ms.

HADDAM, c. h., p. t., seat of justice, together with Middleton, of Middlesex co., Ct., 23 ms. s. of Hartford; from W. 334 ms. Watered by Connecticut river. Pop. 2,279.

HADDONFIELD, p. v., Newton township, Camden co., N. J., 35 ms. s. w. of Trenton; from W. 145 ms. Watered by Cooper creek. Pop. 884.

HADEN'S, p. o., Madison co., Ala.

HADENSVILLE, v., Todd co., Ky., 109 ms. s. w. of Frankfort; from W. 714 ms.

HADENSVILLE, p. o., Goochland co., Va.

HADLEY, p. t., Hampshire co., Mass., 90 ms. w. of Boston; from W. 383 ms. Watered by Connecticut river. Pop. 1.986.

HADLEY, p. t., Saratoga co., N. Y., 58 ms. N. of Albany; from W. 427 ms. Watered by Hudson and Sacandaga rivers. Pop. 1,003.

HADLEY, p. t., Lapeer co., Mich., 58 ms. N. of Detroit; from W. 581 ms. Pop. 847.

HADLEY, p. v., Will co., Ill., 174 ms. N. E. of Springfield; from W. 751 ms.

HADLEY'S MILLS, p. o.. Chatham co., N. C., 45 ms. w. of Raleigh; from W. 329 ms.

HADLYME, p. v., East Haddam township, New London co., Ct., 39 ms. s. of Hartford; from W. 338 ms.

HADNOT'S, p. o., Carteret co., N. C.

HAGAMAN'S MILLS, p. v., Amsterdam township, Montgomery co., N. Y., 36 ms. N. w. of Albany; from W. 404 ms.

HAGER'S GROVE, p. o., Shelby co., Mo.

HAGERSTOWN. c. h., p. v., seat of justice of Washington co., Md., 101 ms. N. w. of Annapolis; from W. 69 ms. Watered by Antietam creek. Pop. 3,696.

HAGERSTOWN, p. v., Monroe township, Preble co., O., 103 ms. w. of Columbus; from W. 496 ms.

HAGERSTOWN, p. v., Wayne co., Ind., 60 ms. E. of Indianapolis; from W. 522 ms. Watered by the west fork of White Water river.

HAGERSVILLE, p. o., Berks co., Pa.

HAGUE, p. t., Warren co., N. Y., 91 ms. N. of Albany; from W. 464 ms. Pop. 771.

HAGUE, p. v., Westmoreland co., Va., 76 ms. N. E. of Richmond; from W. 135 ms.

HAGUE, p. o., Logan co., Ky., 174 ms. s. w. of Frankfort; from W. 688 ms.

HAINS, p. t., Centre co., Pa., containing the villages of Aaronsburg and Millheim. Pop. 1,954.

HAINESBURGH, p. o., Warren co., N. J.

HAINESVILLE, p. o., Sussex co., N. J.

HAINESVILLE, p. o., Lake co., Ill.

HAINESVILLE, p. o., Clinton co., Mo.

HAINESVILLE, p. o., Berkeley co., Va., 175 ms, N. of Richmond; from W. 83 ms.

HALAWAKA, p. o., Chambers co., Ala.

HALCOTTSVILLE, p. o., Delaware co., N. Y.

HALCYONDALE, p. o., Scriven co., Ga.

HALE, p. t., Hardin co., O.

HALE, p. o., Ogle co., Ill.

HALE'S EDDY, p. o., Broome co., N. Y.

HALE'S FORD, p. o., Franklin co., Va., 163 ms. s. w. of Richmond; from W. 238 ms.

HALE'S FORD, p. o., Panola co., Miss.

HALE'S MILLS, p. o., Fentress co., Tenn.

HALE'S POINT, p. o., Andrew co., Mo.

HALE'S POINT, p. o., Lauderdale co., Tenn.

HALEYSBURGH, p. o., Lunenburgh co., Va., 93 ms. s. w. of Richmond; from W. 195 ms.

HALF ACRE, v., Putnam co., Ga.

HALF DAY, p. o., Lake co., Ill., 232 ms. N. E. of Springfield; from W. 738 ms.

HALF MOON, p. t., Saratoga co., N. Y., 13 ms. N. of Albany; from W. 383 ms. Watered by Hudson river, and Champlain canal. Pop. 2,788.

HALF MOON, p. t., Centre co., Pa., 99 ms. N. w. of Harrisburgh; from W. 180 ms. Watered by Bald Eagle creek, and Half Moon run. Pop. 714.

HALF WAY, p. o., Polk co., Mo.

HALF WAY HOUSE, p. o., York co., Va.

HALF WAY PRAIRIE. p. o., Monroe co., Iowa.

HALIFAX COUNTY, situated on the southern boundary of Virginia, with Staunton river on the northeast, and traversed by Dan river. Area, 759 square miles. Face of the country, moderately hilly; soil, fertile. Seat of justice, Banister, or Halifax C. H. Pop. in 1810, 22,133; in 1820, 19,060; in 1830, 28,032; in 1840, 25.936; in 1850, 25,962.

HALIFAX COUNTY, situated toward the northerly part of North Carolina, with Roanoke river on the northeast. Area, 720 square miles. Face of the country, generally level; soil, fertile. Seat of justice, Halifax. Pop. in 1810, 15,620; in 1820, 17,237; in 1830, 17,738; 1840, 16,865; in 1850, 16,589.

HALIFAX, p. t., Plymouth co., Mass., 26 ms. s. E. of Boston; from W. 436 ms. Pop. 784.

HALIFAX, p. t., Windham co., Vt., 136 ms., s. of Montpelier; from W. 421 ms. Watered by Green and north river. Pop. 1,133.

HALIFAX, p. o., Panola co., Miss.

HALIFAX, p. t., Dauphin co., Pa., 23 ms. N. of Harrisburgh; from W. 133 ms. Watered by Susquehanna river and Armstrong creek. Pop. 1,295.

HALIFAX, c. h., p. v., seat of justice of Halifax co., Va., 127 ms. s. w. of Richmond; from W. 214 ms. Watered by Banister river.

HALIFAX, c. h., p. v., seat of justice of Halifax co., N. C., 80 ms. N. E. of Raleigh; from W. 220 ms. Watered by Roanoke river.

HALIFAX, p. v., Wilson co., Tenn., 24 ms. E. of Nashville; from W. 660 ms.

HALIFAX, p. v., Kemper co., Miss., 101 ms. N. E. of Jackson; from W. 913 ms.

HALL COUNTY, situated in the northeasterly part of Georgia, and traversed by Chattahoochee river. Area, 525 square miles. Face of the country mountainous and hilly. Seat of justice, Gainesville. Pop. in 1820, 5,086; in 1830, 11,755; in 1840, 7,875; in 1850, 8,713.

HALL, p. o., York co., Pa.

HALL, p. o., Appling district. S. C.

HALL, p. o., Lawrence co., Mo.

HALL, p. o., Franklin co., Ill.

HALLETSVILLE, p. o., La Vaca co., Tex.

HALLOCA, p. o., Muscogee co., Ga., 140 ms. s. w. of Milledgeville; from W. 773 ms.

HALLOWELL, p. t., Kennebec co., Me., 2 ms. s. of Augusta; from W. 593 ms. Watered by Kennebec river. Pop. in 1830, 3,964; in 1840, 4,654; in 1850, 4,769.

HALLOWELL CROSS-ROADS, p. o., Kennebec co., Me., 4 ms. w. of Augusta; from W. 598 ms.

HALLSA's CREEK, p. o., Nodaway co., Mo.

HALLSBOROUGH, p. o., Powhatan co., Va., 18 ms. s. w. of Richmond; from W. 135 ms.

HALL's CORNERS, p. o., Seneca township, Ontario co., N. Y., 184 ms. w. of Albany; from W. 337 ms.

HALL's CORNERS, p. o., Allen co., Ind.

HALL's CROSS-ROADS, p. o., Harford co., Md., 59 ms. N. of Annapolis; from W. 69 ms.

HALL's CROSS-ROADS, p. o., Franklin co., N. C.

HALL's HILL, p. o., Rutherford co., Tenn.

HALL's MILLS, v., Rensselaerville township, Albany co., N. Y., 31 ms. from Albany; from W. 364 ms.

HALL's RANCHE, p. o., Colusi co., Cal.

HALL's STORE, p. o., Sussex co., Del., 66 ms. s. of Dover; from W. 153 ms.

HALL's VALLEY, p. o., Morgan co., O., 77 ms. E. of Columbus; from W. 336 ms.

HALLSVILLE, p. o., Minden township, Montgomery co., N. Y., 58 ms. N. w. of Albany; from W, 389 ms.

HALLSVILLE, p. v., Duplin co., N. C., 97 ms. s. E. of Raleigh; from W 327 ms

HALLSVILLE, p. o, Coloraino township, Ross co., O., 63 ms. s. of Columbus; from W. 408 ms.

HALLSVILLE, p. o., Boone co., Mo.

HALLTOWN, p. v., Jefferson co., Va., 172 ms. N. of Richmond; from W. 61 ms.

HALSEVILLE, p. o., Chester district, S. C.

HALSEY VALLEY, p. o., Tioga co., N. Y.

HAMBAUGH's, p. o., Warren co., Va., 147 N. w. of Richmond; from W. 93 ms.

HAMBURGH, p. o., St. Charles co., Mo.

HAMBURGH, p. v., Lyme township, New London co., Ct., 34 ms. s. E. of Hartford; from W. 338 ms.

HAMBURGH, p. t., Erie co., N. Y., 300 ms. w. of Albany; from W. 372 ms. Watered by Smoke's, Rush, and Cauquaga creeks, and Lake Erie. Pop. 5,219.

HAMBURGH, p. v., Vernon township, Sussex co., N. J., 86 ms. N. of Trenton; from W. 254 ms. Watered by Wallkill river.

HAMBURGH, p. v., Windsor township, Berks co., Pa., 68 ms. N. E. of Harrisburgh; from W, 161 ms. Pop. 1,034.

HAMBURGH, p. v., Edgefield district, S. C., 79 ms. s. w. of Columbia; from W. 574 ms. Watered by Savannah river.

HAMBURGH, p. v., Macon co., Ga., 88 ms. s. w. of Milledgeville; from W 744 ms.

HAMBURGH, p. v., Calhoun co., Ill., 95 ms. s. w. of Springfield; from W. 865 ms. Watered by Mississippi river. Pop. 374.

HAMBURGH, p. v., Hardin co., Tenn., 140 ms. s. w. of Nashville; from W. 817 ms.

HAMBURGH, p. t., Livingston co., Mich., 51 ms. N. w. of Detroit; from W. 544 ms. Pop. 895.

HAMBURGH, p. v., Clarke co., Ind., 120 ms. s. of Indianapolis; from W. 605 ms.

HAMBURGH, p. o., Franklin co., Wis., 69 ms. s. w. of Jackson; from W. 1,104 ms.

HAMBURGH, p. o., Preble co., O.

HAMBURGH, c. h., p. v., seat of justice of Ashley co., Ark.

HAMBURGH ON THE LAKE, p. v., Hamburgh township, Erie co., N. Y., 300 ms. w. of Albany; from W. 379 ms. Watered by Lake Erie.

HAMDEN, p. t., Delaware co., N. Y., 89 ms. s. w. of Albany; from W. 329 ms. Watered by the west branch of Delaware river. Pop. 1,919.

HAMDEN, p. t., New Haven co., Ct., 33 ms. s. w. of Hartford; from W. 306 ms. Watered by Mill river. Contains the village of Whitneyville. Pop. 2,166.

HAMMERSVILLE. p. o., Clark township, Brown co., O., 115 ms. s. w. of Columbus; from W. 474 ms.

HAMILTON COUNTY, situated toward the northeasterly part of New York. Area, 1,064 square miles. Face of the country, mountainous, broken, and swampy. Soil, generally unproductive. Seat of justice, Lake Pleasant. Pop. in 1820, 1,251; in 1830, 1,324; in 1840, 1,907; in 1850, 2,188.

HAMILTON COUNTY, situated at the southwestcorner of Ohio, with Ohio river on the south, and traversed by Miami, and Little Miami rivers, and the Miami canal. Area, 400 square miles. Face of the country, diversified with hills and vales. Soil, rich and well cultivated. Seat of justice, Cincinnati. Pop. in 1810, 15,258; in 1820, 31,764; in 1830, 52,321; in 1840, 80,145; in 1850, 156,843.

HAMILTON COUNTY, situated on the southern boundary of Tennessee, and traversed by Tennessee river. Area, 464 square miles. Face of the country hilly and partly mountainous. Seat of justice, Harrison. Pop in 1820. 821; in 1830, 2,276; in 1840, 8,175; in 1850, 10,075.

HAMILTON COUNTY, situated on the northern boundary of Florida, bounded on the east and south by Suwanee river, and on the west by the Withlacoochee. Seat of justice, Jasper. Pop. in 1830, 553; in 1840, 1,461; in 1850, 2,469.

HAMILTON COUNTY, situated in the central part of Indiana, and traversed by west fork of White river. Area, 400 square miles. Seat of justice, Noblesville. Pop. in 1830, 1,757; in 1840, 9,855; in 1850, 12,683.

HAMILTON COUNTY, situated in the south easterly part of Illinois. Area, 432 square miles. Seat of justice, McLennsborough. Pop. in 1830, 2,616; in 1840, 3,945; in 1850, 6,362.

HAMILTON, p. t., Essex co., Mass., 22 ms. N. E. of Boston; from W. 462 ms. Watered by a branch of Ipswich river. Pop. 889

HAMILTON, p. t., Madison co., N. Y., 96 ms. w. of Albany; from W. 355 ms. Watered by sources of Chenango river. Pop, 3,599.

HAMILTON, p. t., Atlantic co., N. J., contains the village of May's Landing, the seat of justice of the county. Watered by Great Egg Harbor. Pop. 2,015.

HAMILTON, t., Adams co., Pa., 35 ms. s. w. of Harrisburgh; from W. 83 ms. Watered by Conewago creek and Beaver run. Pop. 2,696.

HAMILTON, p. v., Loudoun co., Va., 159 ms. N. of Richmond; from W. 251 ms.

HAMILTON, p. v., Martin co., N. C., 127 ms. E. of Raleigh; from W. 251 ms.

HAMILTON, c. h., p. v., Fairfield township, seat of justice of Butler co., O., 102 ms. s. w. of Columbus; from W. 490 ms. Watered by Great Miami river. Pop. 1,582.

HAMILTON, v., Blockley township, Philadelphia co., Pa.

HAMILTON, p. t., Franklin co., O., 7 ms. from Columbus; from W. 389 ms. Watered by Scioto river. Pop. 1,485.

HAMILTON, p. t., Jackson co., O., 87 ms. s. E. of Columbus; from W. 392 ms. Pop. 665.

HAMILTON, t., Warren co., O., 88 ms. s. w. of Columbus; from W. 465 ms. Pop. 842.

HAMILTON, p. t., Van Buren co., Mich. Pop. 370.

HAMILTON, c. h., p. v., seat of justice of Harris co., Ga., 130 ms. s. w. of Milledgeville; from W. 776 ms.

HAMILTON, c. h., p. v., seat of justice of Monroe co., Miss., 156 ms. N. E. of Jackson; from W. 897 ms.

HAMILTON, t., McKean co., Pa. Pop. 103.

HAMILTON, t., Franklin co., Pa., 51 ms. s. w. of Harrisburgh; from W. 88 ms. Watered by main branch of Conecocheague creek, and Back creek. Pop. 1,984

HAMILTON, t., Monroe co., Pa. Watered by Cherry Pokons, and McMichael's creeks. Pop. 1,984

HAMILTON, p. o., Marion co., Iowa.

HAMILTON, p. o., Steuben co., Ind.

HAMILTON, p. o., Shelby co., Tex.
HAMILTON, p. o., Boone co., Ky.
HAMILTON, p. o., Union parish, La.
HAMILTON, c. h., p. v., seat of justice of Butte co., Cal.
HAMILTON BAN, t., Adams co., Pa., 42 ms. s. w. of Harrisburgh; from W. 84 ms. Watered by south branch of Marsh creek, Middle and Town's creeks, and Muddy run. Pop. 1,530.
HAMILTON CROSS-ROADS, p. o., McMinn co., Tenn.
HAMILTON LANDING, p. o., Jackson co., Tenn.
HAMILTON SQUARE, p. o., Mercer co., N. Y.
HAMLET, p. o., Chautauque co., N. Y.
HAMLIN, p. o., Cabell co., Va.
HAMLIN's GRANT, t., Oxford co., Me.
HAMLINTON, p. o., Wayne co., Pa., 151 ms. N. E. of Harrisburgh; from W. 245 ms.
HAMMOCK's GROVE, p. o., Crawford co., Ga., 62 ms. s. w. of Milledgeville; from W. 718 ms.
HAMMOND, p. t., St. Lawrence co., N. Y., 189 ms. N. w. of Albany; from W. 459 ms. Watered by St. Lawrence river and Black lake. Pop. 1,819.
HAMMOND's, p. o., St. Joseph co., Ind.
HAMMONDSBURGH, p. o., Warren co., Iowa.
HAMMOND's MILLS, v., Campbell township, Steuben co., N. Y., 214 ms. s. w. of Albany; from W. 285 ms.
HAMMONDSPORT, v., Urbana township, Steuben co., N. Y. Watered by Crooked lake.
HAMMOND's STORE, p. o., Anson co., N. C., 151 ms. s. w. of Raleigh; from W. 430 ms.
HAMMONTON, p. o., Atlantic co., N. J., 60 ms. s. of Trenton; from W. 170 ms.
HAMMONVILLE, p. o., Hart co., Ky.
HAMORTON, p. o., Chester co., Pa., 78 ms. s. E. of Harrisburgh; from W. 109 ms.
HAMPDEN COUNTY situated in the southwest part of Massachusetts, and watered by Connecticut river. Area 585 square miles. Seat of justice, Springfield. Pop. in 1830, 31,639; in 1840, 37,366; in 1850, 51,281.
HAMPDEN, p. t., Penobscot co., Me., 62 ms. N. E. of Augusta; from W. 657 ms. Watered by Penobscot and Sowadabscook rivers. Pop. 3,195.
HAMPDEN, p. t., Geauga co., O., 175 ms. N. E. of Columbus; from W. 338 ms. Pop. 919.
HAMPDEN, p. o., Columbia co., Wis.
HAMPDEN, p. o., Marengo co. Ala.
HAMPDEN SIDNEY COLLEGE, p. o., Prince Edward co., Va.
HAMPSHIRE COUNTY, situated toward the westerly part of Massachusetts, and traversed by Connecticut river. Area 532 square miles. Face of the country greatly diversified; soil fertile. Seat of justice, Northampton. Pop. in 1830, 30,210; in 1840, 30,897; in 1850, 24,084.
HAMPSHIRE COUNTY, situated on the northerly boundary of Virginia, with Potomac river on the north, and traversed by its south branch. Area, 960 square miles. Face of the country mountainous; soil in the river valleys very fertile. Seat of justice, Romney. Pop. in 1810, 9,784; in 1820, 10,889; in 1830, 11,279; in 1840, 12,295; in 1850, 14,036.
HAMPSHIRE, p. o., Kane co., Ill., 215 ms. N. E. of Springfield; from W. 767 ms.
HAMPSHIRE, p. o., Lewis co., Tenn.
HAMPSTEAD, p. t., Rockingham co., N. H., 29 ms. s. E. of Concord; from W. 462 ms. Pop. 789.
HAMPSTEAD, p. v., Carroll co., Md., 56 ms., N. w. of Annapolis; from W. 66 ms.
HAMPSTEAD, p. v., King George co., Va., 89 ms. N. E. of Richmond; from W. 85 ms.
HAMPTON, p. t., Rockingham co., N. H., 47 ms. s. E. of Concord; from W. 484 ms. Watered by the Atlantic ocean. Noted for a promontary called the "Boar's Head." Pop. 1,192.
HAMPTON, p. t., Windham co., Ct., 41 ms. E. of Hartford; from W. 368 ms. Watered by a branch of Shetucket river. Pop. 946.
HAMPTON, p. t., Washington co., N. Y., 73 ms. N. of Albany; from W. 449 ms. Watered by Poultney river. Pop. 899.
HAMPTON, v., Westmoreland township, Oneida co., N. Y. Watered by a branch of Oriskany creek.
HAMPTON, p. v., Reading township, Adams co., Pa., 29 ms. s. w. of Harrisburgh; from W. 86 ms.
HAMPTON, c. h., p. v., seat of justice of Elizabeth City co., Va., 94 ms. s. E. of Richmond; from W. 209 ms. Watered by Hampton river.
HAMPTON, p. v., Rock Island co., Ill., 150 ms. N. w. of Springfield; from W. 880 ms.
HAMPTON, p. o., Hendricks co., Ind.
HAMPTON, p. o., Saganaw co., Mich.

HAMPTONBURGH, p. t., Orange co., N. Y., 99 ms. s. of Albany; from W. 282 ms. Watered by Murderer's and Wallkill creeks. Pop. 1,343.
HAMPTON FALLS, p. t., Rockingham co., N. H. 45 ms. s. E. of Concord; from W. 482 ms. Watered by the Atlantic ocean. Pop. 640.
HAMPTONVILLE, p. v., Surry co., N. C., 146 ms. N. w. of Raleigh; from W. 357 ms.
HAMTRANCK, t., Wayne co., Mich., 13 ms. from Detroit; from W. 539 ms. Pop. 1,628.
HANAUER's STORE, p. o., Randolph co., Ark.
HANCHETTEVILLE, p. o., Dane co., Wis.
HANCOCK COUNTY, situated in the southeasterly part of Maine, on the Atlantic ocean, with Penobscot river and bay on the west. Area, 1,850 square miles. Seat of justice, Cástine. Pop. in 1810, 30,031; in 1820, 31,290; in 1830, 24,347; in 1840, 28,605; in 1850, 34,372.
HANCOCK COUNTY, situated toward the easterly part of Georgia, with Oconee river on the west, and the Ogeechee on the east. Area, 600 square miles. Face of the country undulating; soil fertile. Seat of justice, Sparta. Pop. in 1810, 13,339; in 1820, 12,734; in 1830, 11,822; in 1840, 9,659; in 1850, 11.578.
HANCOCK COUNTY, situated in the southerly part of Mississippi, with Pearl river on the west and Gulf of Mexico on the south. Area, 1,680 square miles. Face of the country diversified; soil generally barren, and covered with pines. Seat of justice, Shieldsborough. Pop. in 1830, 1,961; in 1840, 3,367; in 1850, 3,672.
HANCOCK COUNTY, situated on the northerly boundary of Kentucky, with Ohio river on the northeast and northwest. Area, 200 square miles. Seat of justice, Hawesville. Pop. in 1830, 1,494; in 1840, 2,581; in 1850, 3.853.
HANCOCK COUNTY, situated toward the northwesterly part of Ohio. Area, 576 square miles. Face of the country even; soil productive. Seat of justice, Finley. Pop. in 1830, 813; in 1840, 9,986; in 1850, 11,751.
HANCOCK COUNTY, situated toward the easterly part of Indiana. Area, 310 square miles. Seat of justice, Greenfield. Pop. in 1830, 1 436; in 1840, 7,535; in 1850, 9.698.
HANCOCK COUNTY, situated on the western boundary of Illinois, with Mississippi river on the west. Area, 775 square miles. Face of the country even, consisting of prairie land; soil productive. Seat of justice, Carthage. Pop. in 1830, 483; in 1840, 9,946; in 1850, 14,652.
HANCOCK COUNTY, situated in the northern part of Virginia. Area, —— square miles. Seat of justice, ——. Pop. in 1850. 4.050.
HANCOCK COUNTY, situated in the northeastern part of Tennessee. Area, —— square miles. Seat of justice, ——. Pop. in 1850, 5,660.
HANCOCK, p. t., Hancock co., Me., 95 ms. E. of Augusta; from W. 677 ms. Watered by Frenchman's bay Pop. 960.
HANCOCK, p. t., Hillsborough co., N. H., 34 ms. s. w of Concord; from W. 454 ms. Watered by Contoocook river and Long pond. Pop. 1.012.
HANCOCK, p. t., Addison co., Vt., 39 ms. s. w. of Montpelier; from W. 486 ms. Pop. 430.
HANCOCK, p. t., Berkshire co., Mass., 143 ms. w. of Boston; from W. 379 ms. Watered by sources of Kinderhook creek and Housatonic river. Pop. 789.
HANCOCK, p. t., Delaware co., N. Y., 123 ms. s. w. of Albany; from W. 291 ms. Watered by Delaware river and Papacton branch. Pop. 1,798.
HANCOCK, p. t., Washington co., Md., 125 ms. N. w of Annapolis; from W. 92 ms. Watered by Potomac river.
HANCOCK, p. o., De Soto co., Miss.
HANCOCK's BRIDGE, p. v., Lower Allaway's township, Salem co., N. J., 85 ms. s. w. of Trenton; from W. 180 ms.
HANDY, p. t., Livingston co., Mich. Pop. 484.
HONEYVILLE, p. o., Lycoming co., Pa.
HANFORD's LANDING, p. o., Greece township, Monroe co., N. Y., 223 ms. N. w. of Albany; from W. 373 ms.
HANGING ROCK, p. v., Hampshire co., Va., 175 ms. N. w. of Richmond; from W. 103 ms.
HANGING ROCK, p. o., Kershaw district, S. C.
HANGING ROCK, p. o., Upper township, Lawrence co., O., 118 ms. s. E. of Columbus; from W. 426 ms.
HANNAHATCHIE, p. o., Stewart co., Ga.
HANNA's, p. o., Sumner co., Tenn., 36 ms. N. E. of Nashville; from W. 677 ms.

fiANNA'S MILLS, p. o., Mahoning co., O.

HANNAHSBURGH, v., Butler co., Pa., 207 ms. N. W. of Harrisburgh; from W. 238 ms.

HANNEGAN, p. o., Cherokee co., Ala.

HANNEGAN, p. o., Atchison co., Mo.

HANNEGAN, p. o., Rush co., Ind.

HANNIBAL, p. t., Oswego co., N. Y., 176 ms. N. W. of Albany; from W. 362 ms. Pop. 2,857.

HANNIBAL, p. v., Marion co., Mo., 108 ms. N. E. of Jefferson City; from W. 912 ms. Watered by Mississippi river.

HANNIBAL CENTRE, p. o., Oswego co., N. Y.

HANOVER COUNTY, situated in the eastern part of Virginia, with Pamunky river on the northeast. Area, 630 square miles. Face of the country generally hilly; soil sandy, except along the streams, where it is rich. Seat of justice, Hanover. Pop. in 1810, 15,082; in 1820, 15,267; in 1830, 16,253; in 1840, 14,968; in 1850, 15,153.

HANOVER, p. t., Grafton co., N. H., 54 ms. N. W. of Concord; from W. 488 ms. Watered by Connecticut river. Seat of Dartmouth college. Pop. 2,350.

HANOVER, p. t., Plymouth co., Mass., 24 ms. S. E. of Boston; from W. 443 ms. Watered by Pembroke creek. Pop. 1,592.

HANOVER. p. t., Chautauque co., N. Y., 315 ms. w. of Albany; from W. 353 ms. Watered by Silver creek and Lake Erie. Pop. 5,144.

HANOVER, p. t., Morris co., N. J., 57 ms. N. E. of Trenton; from W. 227 ms. Watered by Whippany, Parsipany, and Rockaway rivers. Pop. 3,608.

HANOVER, p. t., Jefferson co., Ind.

HANOVER, t., Burlington co., N. J., 18 ms. from Trenton; from W. 167 ms. Watered by Black's and Croswick's creeks.

HANOVER, p. b., Heidelberg township, York co., Pa., 35 ms. s. of Harrisburgh; from W. 82 ms. Watered by a branch of Conewago creek. Pop. 1,210.

HANOVER, t., Dauphin co.. Pa., 15 ms. s. E. of Harrisburgh. Watered by Beaver and Manady creeks and Bow run.

HANOVER, t., Lehigh co., Pa., 88 ms. N. E. of Harrisburgh; from W. 181 ms. Watered by Calesoque creek and Lehigh river.

HANOVER, t., Northampton co., Pa., 91 ms. N. F. of Harrisburgh; from W. 184 ms. Watered by Manokesy creek. Pop. 428.

HANOVER, t., Beaver co., Pa., 231 ms. w. of Harrisburgh; from W. 254 ms. Watered by Big and Little Travios creeks. Pop. 1,132.

HANOVER, t., Washington co., Pa., 228 ms. w. of Harrisburgh; from W. 248 ms. Watered by Herman's and Indian creeks. Pop. 1,803.

HANOVER, t., Luzerne co., Pa., 107 ms. N. E. of Harrisburgh; from W. 215 ms. Watered by Susquehanna river and Nanticoke and Solomon's creeks. Pop. 1,506.

HANOVER. p. t., Licking co., O., 48 ms. N. E. of Columbus; from W. 357 ms. Watered by Licking river and Ohio canal.

HANOVER, t., Butler co., O., 106 ms. s. w. of Columbus; from W. 493 ms. Pop 1,493.

HANOVER, p. t, Columbiana co., O., 145 ms. N. E. of Columbus; from W. 292 ms. Pop. 2,858.

HANOVER, p. t., Richland co., O., 62 ms. N. of Columbus; from W. 364 ms. Watered by branches of Mohiccan river.

HANOVER, v., North township. Harrison co., O., 138 ms. E. of Columbus; from W. 283 ms.

HANOVER, t., Shelby co., Ind., 23 ms. s. E. of Indianapolis; from W. 570 ms. Pop. 1,061.

HANOVER. p. t., Jackson co., Mich, 89 ms. w. of Detroit; from W. 549 ms. Pop. 930.

HANOVER, p. o., Jo-Daviess co., Ill., 114 ms. N. of Springfield; from W. 872 ms.

HANOVER, c. h., p. v., seat of justice of Hanover co., Va., 20 ms. N. of Richmond; from W. 103 ms.

HANOVER, p. o., Oxford co., Me.

HANOVER, p. o., Coosa co., Ala.

HANOVER CENTRE, p. o., Hanover township, Grafton co., N. H.

HANOVER NECK, p, o., Hanover township, Morris co.. N. J., 58 ms. N. E. of Trenton; from W. 224 ms.

HANOVERTON, p. v., Hanover township, Columbiana co., O., 149 ms. N. E. of Columbus; from W. 291 ms.

HANSON, p. t., Plymouth co., Mass., 28 ms. s. E. of Boston; from W. 438 ms. Watered by a branch of North river. Pop. 1,217.

HANSON, p. o., Marion co., Mo.

HANSONVILLE, p. o., Russell co., Va., 318 ms. w. of Richmond; from W. 386 ms.

HAP HAZARD, p. o., Catahoula parish, La.

HAPPY VALLEY, p. o., Fairfax co., Va.

HAPPY VALLEY, p. o., Carter co., Tenn.

HARALSON, p. o., Coweta co., Ga.

HARBOR CREEK, p. t., Erie co., Pa., 279 ms. N. w. of Harrisburgh; from W. 352 ms. Watered by Lake Erie. Pop. 2,084.

HARDEMAN COUNTY, situated on the southerly boundary of Tennessee and traversed by Big Hatchee river. Area, 720 square miles. Seat of justice, Bolivar. Pop. in 1830, 11,628; in 1840, 14,563; in 1850, 17.456.

HARDIN COUNTY, situated on the southerly boundary of Tennessee, and traversed by Tennessee river. Area, 700 square miles. Seat of justice, Savannah. Pop. in 1820, 1,462; in 1830, 4,867; in 1840, 8,245; in 1850, 10,328.

HARDIN COUNTY, situated toward the northerly part of Kentucky. Area, 1,200 square miles. Face of the country hilly and broken. Seat of justice, Elizabethtown. Pop. in 1810, 7,581; in 1820, 10,498; in 1830, 13,148; in 1840. 16,357; in 1850, 14,525.

HARDIN COUNTY, situated toward the northwesterly part of Ohio. Area, 482 square miles. Face of the country generally even, consisting of an elevated table land; soil, productive. Seat of justice, Kenton. Pop. in 1830. 500; in 1840, 4,598; in 1850, 8,265.

HARDIN COUNTY, situated in the southeastern part of Illinois, bounded on the east and south by Ohio river. Area, 100 square miles. Seat of justice, Elizabethtown. Pop. in 1840. 1,378; in 1850, 2,887.

HARDIN, c. h., p. v., Turtle Creek township, seat of justice of Shelby co., O., 85 ms. N. w. of Columbus; from W. 479 ms.

HARDIN, c. h., p. v., seat of justice of Calhoun co., Ill. Pop. 596.

HARDIN, t., Conway co., Ark.

HARDIN, p. o., Allemakee co., Iowa.

HARDINGVILLE, p. o., Gloucester co., N. J.

HARDINSBURGH, v., Dearborn co., Ind. Watered by Great Miami river.

HARDINSBURGH, c. h., p. v., seat of justice of Breckenridge co., Ky., 115 ms. s. w. of Frankfort; from W. 657 ms.

HARDINSBURGH, p. v., Washington co., Ind., 106 ms. s. of Indianapolis; from W. 630 ms.

HARDINSBURGH, p. o., Montgomery co., Ill.

HARDIN's TAVERN, p. o., Albermarle co., Va.

HARDINSVILLE, p. v., Shelby co., Ky., 9 ms. w. of Frankfort; from W. 551 ms.

HARD MONEY, p. o., Stewart co., Ga., 144 ms. s. w. of Milledgeville; from W. 799.

HARDWICK, p. t., Worcester co., Mass., 68 ms. w. of Boston; from W. 398 ms. Watered by Ware river. Pop. 1,631.

HARDWICK, p. t., Caledonia co., Vt., 27 ms. N. E. of Montpelier; from W. 543 ms. Watered by Lamoille river. Pop. 1,402.

HARDWICK, t., Warren co., N. J., 82 ms. N. w. of Trenton; from W. 240 ms. Watered by Paulin's kill, Beaver brook, and Bear branch of Pequest creek. Pop. 727.

HARDWICK, v., Bryan co., Ga. Watered by Ogeechee river.

HARDWICKSVILLE, p. o., Nelson co., Va.

HARDY COUNTY, situated in the northern part of Virginia. Area, 1,156 square miles. Face of the country mountainous and rocky; soil, barren. Seat of justice, Moorefield. Pop. in 1810, 5,525; in 1820, 5,700; in 1830, 6,798; in 1840, 7,622; in 1850, 9.543.

HARDYSTON, t., Sussex co., N. J., 78 ms. s. of Trenton; from W. 236 ms. Watered by Wallkill river. Pop. 1,344.

HARDY, t., Holmes co., O., 80 ms. from Columbus; from W. 341 ms. Pop. 2,424.

HARFORD COUNTY, situated on the northern boundary of Maryland, with Susquehanna river on the northeast, and Chesapeake bay on the southeast. Area, 480 square miles. Face of the country undulating; soil, good for grain, pasturage, and fruit. Seat of justice, Belair. Pop. in 1810. 21,258; in 1820, 15,924; in 1830, 16,315; in 1840, 17,120; in 1850, 19,356.

HARFORD, p. t., Susquehanna co., Pa., 175 ms. N. E. of Harrisburgh; from W. 279 ms. Watered by Martin's Partners, and Van Winkle's creeks. Pop. 1,258.

HARFORD, p. o., Virgil township, Cortland co., N. Y., 150 ms. w. of Albany ; from W. 301 ms.

HARGRAVE, p. o., Copiah co., Miss.

HARGROVE'S TAVERN, p. o., Nansemond co., Va.

HAROIS, p. t., Centre co., Pa. Pop. 1,954.

HARLAN, c. h., p. o., Mount Pleasant village ; seat of justice of Harlan co.. Ky., 165 ms. s. E. of Frankfort ; from W. 473 ms. Watered by Clover fork of Cumberland river.

HARLAN COUNTY, situated on the southeastern boundary of Kentucky, traversed by Cumberland river. Area, 480 square miles. Face of the country, mountainous. Cumberland mountains form its southeastern boundary, and Laurel Ridge crosses its northwest part. Seat of justice, Mount Pleasant. Pop. in 1830, 2,929 ; in 1840, 3,015 ; in 1850, 4,268.

HARLAN, p. o., Allen co., Ind.

HARLESSVILLE, p. v., Marion district, S. C., 95 ms. E. of Columbia ; from W. 431 ms. Watered by Little Pedee river.

HARLEM, p. o., Winnebago co., Ill., 211 ms. N. of Springfield ; from W. 812 ms.

HARLEM, t., Delaware co., O., 27 ms. N. of Columbus ; from W. 398 ms. Pop. 1,182.

HARLEM, p. v., city and county of New York, 150 ms. s. of Albany ; from W. 232 ms. Watered by Harlem river.

HARLEM SPRING, p. o., Carroll co., O.

HARLEMVILLE, p. o., Claverack township, Columbia co., N. Y.

HARLENSBURGH, p. o., Lawrence co., Pa.

HARLEYSVILLE, p. o., Montgomery co., Pa.

HARLINGEN, p. v., Montgomery township, Somerset co., N. J., 18 ms. N. of Trenton ; from W. 190 ms.

HARMAR, p. v., Washington co., O., 164 ms. s. E. of Columbus ; from W. 301 ms. Watered by Muskingum river. Pop. 1,010.

HARMERVILLE, p. o., Alleghany co., Pa.

HARMONSBURGH, p. v., Sadsbury township, Crawford co., Pa., 243 ms. N. w. of Harrisburgh ; from W. 316 ms. Watered by Conneaut creek, and Conneaut lake.

HARMONY, p. t., Somerset co., Me., 57 ms. N. E. of Augusta ; from W. 652 ms. Watered by the sources of Sebasticook river. Pop. 1,107.

HARMONY, v., Conequenessing township, Butler co., Pa. Watered by Conequenessing river. Founded and afterward sold by the society of harmonites. Pop. 441.

HARMONY, p. t., Chautauque co., N. Y., 339 ms. w. of Albany ; from W. 326 ms. Watered by Goose, and Little Broken Straw creeks. Pop. 3,749.

HARMONY, p. t., Warren co., N. J., 58 ms. N. of Trenton ; from W. 205 ms. Pop. 1,960.

HARMONY, t., Susquehanna co., Pa. Watered by Susquehanna river. Pop. 1,578.

HARMONY, p. v., Halifax co., Va., 150 ms. s. w. of Richmond ; from W. 237 ms.

HARMONY, p. v., York district, S. C., 102 ms. N. of Columbia ; from W. 459 ms.

HARMONY, p. t., Clark co., O. Pop. 1,804.

HARMONY, t., Delaware co., O., 19 ms. N. E. of Columbus ; from W. 386 ms. Watered by branches of Alum and Big Walnut creeks. Pop. 1,162.

HARMONY, p. o., Clay co., Ind., 54 ms. w. of Indianapolis ; from W. 625 ms.

HARMONY, p. o., Van Buren co., Mo.

HARMONY, p. v., Washington co., Mo., 102 ms. s. E. of Jefferson City ; from W. 896 ms. Watered by Hazel creek.

HARMONY, t., Washington co., Mo. Pop. 700.

HARMONY, p. o., Kent co., Md.

HARMONY, p. t., Perry co., Ind.

HARMONY, p. o., McHenry co., Ill.

HARMONY, p. o., Elbert co., Ga.

HARMONY GROVE, p. o., Jackson co., Ga., 88 ms. N. of Milledgeville ; from W. 623 ms.

HARMONY VALE, p. v., Hardiston township, Sussex co., N. J., 83 ms. N. of Trenton ; from W. 252 ms.

HARNAGEVILLE, p. v., Cherokee co., Ga., 139 ms. N. w. of Milledgeville ; from W. 670 ms.

HARNEDSVILLE, p. o., Somerset co., Pa.

HAROLD, p. o., Montgomery co., Ark.

HARPER'S FERRY, p. o., Abbeville district, co., S. C., 119 ms. w. of Columbia ; from W. 556 ms.

HARPER'S FERRY, p. v., Jefferson co., Va., 173 ms. N. of Richmond ; from W. 57 ms. Watered by Shenandoah and Potomac rivers. Pop. 1,747

HARPERSFIELD, p. t., Delaware co., N. Y., 64 ms. w. of Albany ; from W. 360 ms. Watered by Charlotte and Delaware rivers. Pop. 1,604.

HARPERSFIELD, p. t., Ashtabula co., O., 195 ms. N. E. of Columbus ; from W. 350 ms. Watered by Grand river. Pop. 680 ms.

HARPER'S MILLS, p. o., Pendleton co., Va.

HARPER'S VALLEY, p. o., Raleigh co., Va.

HARPERSVILLE. p. v., Colesville township, Broome co., N. Y., 116 ms. s. w. of Albany ; from W. 310 ms. Watored by Susquehanna river.

HARPERSVILLE, p. v., Shelby co., Ala. ; from W. 763 ms.

HARPETH, p. o., Williamson co., Tenn., 27 ms. s. of Nashville ; from W. 690 ms.

HARPSWELL, t., Cumberland co., Me., 42 ms. s. E. of Augusta ; from W. 576 ms. Watered by Casco bay, and consists of a promontory and islands. Pop. 1,545.

HARRELL'S STORE, p. o., New Hanover co., N. C., 116 ms. s. E. of Raleigh ; from W. 346 ms.

HARRELLSVILLE, p. o., Hertford co., N. C.

HARRIETTSTOWN, p. t., Franklin co., N. Y., 190 ms. N. of Albany ; from W. —— ms. Watered by Lower Saranac lake. Pop. 181.

HARRIETTSVILLE, p. o., Monroe co., O., 121 ms. E. of Columbus ; from W. 295 ms.

HARRINGTON, p. v., Cumberland co., N. C., 59 ms. s. of Raleigh ; from W. 347 ms.

HARRINGTON, p. t., Washington co., Me., 127 ms. E. of Augusta ; from W. 710 ms. Watered by Pleasant and Narragusgus bays and Atlantic ocean. Pop. 1,986.

HARRINGTON, t., Bergen co., N. J., 69 ms. N. E. of Trenton ; from W. 235 ms. Watered by Hudson and Hackensack rivers.

HARRIS COUNTY, situated on the western boundary of Georgia, with Chattahoochee river on the west. Area, 410 square miles. Face of the country, hilly. Seat of justice, Hamilton. Pop. in 1830, 5,105 ; in 1840, 13,933 ; in 1850, 14,721.

HARRIS COUNTY, situated in the southern part of Texas, with Galveston bay on the southeast, and traversed by San Jacinto river. Area —— square miles. Seat of justice, Houston. Pop. in 1850, 4,668.

HARRIS, t., Centre co., Pa. Pop. 1,954.

HARRIS, t., Ottowa co., O., 121 ms. N. of Columbus ; from W. 446 ms. Watered by Portage river. Pop. 407.

HARRIS, p. o., Louisa co., Va., 53 ms. N. w. of Richmond ; from W. 97 ms.

HARRISBURGH, the seat of justice of Dauphin co., and capital of Pa., is situated on the east bank of Susquehanna river, 97 miles northwest of Philadelphia, and 110 miles from Washington. It is a borough, built on rising ground, which subsides toward Paxton creek into a plain. From the elevation upon which the statehouse stands, appears a wide and varied prospect of hills, fertile vales, and winding streams. Across the Susquehanna and the island which here divides it, extends the Harrisburgh bridge, nearly a mile in length, and not far below, the bridge of the Cumberland Valley railroad. The channels of communication, the Pennsylvania lines of railroad and canal, besides opening a way to the remote part of the state, convey to Harrisburgh the products of the neighboring fertile region, of which it is a profitable market. The Susquehanna, with its large volume of water, is not navigable, except for timber rafts, which can only descend with its swift current.

The capitol is an imposing structure, consisting of a main building and two wings, each adorned with a portico and Ionic pillars. The central edifice is 180 feet wide, 80 feet deep, and 108 feet from the ground to the top of the dome. The whole is surrounded by an open space, adorned with trees, walks, and an iron-railing. The other prominent buildings, are a Masonic-hall, two banks, a prison, and a number of churches.

By the Mount Airy water-works, water is elevated from the Susquehanna into a reservoir, on a hill above the borough, and thence is distributed through iron-pipes.

Manufactures, to a considerable extent, are produced in Harrisburgh, and the town is gradually increasing in population and wealth.

The population in 1810, was 2,287 : in 1820, 2,990 ; in 1830, 4,311 ; in 1840. 6.020 ; in 1850. 8,173.

HARRISBURGH, p. o., Lewis co., N. Y., 145 ms. N. w of Albany ; from W. 427 ms. Watered by Deer creek and other branches of Black river. Pop. 1,367.

HARRISBURGH, p. v., Pleasant township, Franklin co., O., 23 ms. s. w. of Columbus; from W. 416 ms. Watered by Darby creek.

HARRISBURGH, p. o., Fayette co., Ind., 56 ms. E. of Indianapolis; from W. 523 ms.

HARRISBURGH, p. o., Pontotoc co., Miss.

HARRISBURGH, p. o., Mecklenburgh co., N. C., 251 ms. s. w. of Raleigh; from W. 390 ms.

HARRISBURGH, p. o., Abbeville district, S. C.

HARRIS' CROSS ROADS, p. o., Franklin co., N. C.

HARRIS' FERRY, p. o., Washington co., Oregon.

HARRIS' HILL, p. o., Erie co., N.Y.

HARRIS' LOT, p. o., Charles co., Md.

HARRISON COUNTY, situated toward the northwesterly part of Virginia, and traversed by west fork of Monongahela river. Area, 110 square miles. Face of the country rugged and hilly; soil generally barren, but fertile on the streams. Seat of justice, Clarksburgh. Pop. in 1810, 9,558; in 1820, 10,932; in 1830, 14,722; in 1840, 17,669; in 1850, 11,728.

HARRISON COUNTY, situated toward the northerly part of Kentucky, and traversed by Licking river. Area, 356 square miles. Soil generally very fertile. Seat of justice, Cynthiana. Pop. in 1810, 7,552; in 1820, 12,271; in 1830, 13,180; in 1840, 12,472; in 1850, 13,064.

HARRISON COUNTY, situated in the eastern part of Ohio. Area, 486 square miles. Face of the country broken and hilly; soil generally productive. Seat of justice, Cadiz. Pop. in 1820. 14,345; in 1830, 20,916; in 1840, 20,099; in 1850. 20,158.

HARRISON COUNTY, situated on the southerly boundary of Indiana, with Ohio river on the south. Area, 470 square miles. Face of the country hilly; soil fertile. Seat of justice, Croydon. Pop. in 1810, 3,595; in 1820, 7,875; in 1830, 10,273; in 1840, 12,459; in 1850, 15,286.

HARRISON COUNTY, situated on the eastern boundary of Texas. Area, —— square miles. Seat of justice, Marshall. Pop. in 1850, 11,882.

HARRISON COUNTY, situated on the southern boundary of Mississippi, with the gulf of Mexico on the south, and Pearl river on the west. Area, —— square miles. Seat of justice, Mississippi city. Pop. in 1850, 4,875.

HARRISON COUNTY, situated on the northern boundary of Missouri. Area, —— square miles. Seat of justice, Bethany. Pop. in 1850, 2,447.

HARRISON, p. t., Cumberland co., Me., 62 ms. s.w. of Augusta; from W. 580 ms. Watered by Long Pond and Crooked river. Pop 1,416

HARRISON, p. t. Westchester co., N. Y., 134 ms. s. of Albany; from W. 259 ms. Watered by Blind brook and Mamaroneck creek. Pop. 1,262.

HARRISON, t., Hudson co., N. J. Watered by Hackensack and Passaic rivers. Pop. 1,344.

HARRISON, t., Potter co., Pa. Pop. 718.

HARRISON, p. v., Crosby township, Hamilton co., O., 126 ms. s. w. of Columbus; from W. 510 ms. Watered by White Water river. Pop. 940.

HARRISON, p. t., Carroll co., O. Pop. 1,268.

HARRISON, t., Champaign co,, O., 62 ms. from Columbus; from W. 459 ms. Watered by Stony creek. Pop. 968.

HARRISON, t., Darke co., O., 102 ms. from Columbus; from W. 499 ms. Pop. 1,705.

HARRISON, t., Gallia co., O., 116 ms. from Columbus; from W. 370 ms. Watered by Raccoon creek.

HARRISON, t., Jackson co., O., 62 ms. from Columbus; from W. 383 ms. Pop. 662.

HARRISON, t., Knox co., O., 55 ms. from Columbus; from W. 365 ms. Watered by Vernon river. Pop. 751.

HARRISON, t., Ross co., O. Pop. 875.

HARRISON, t., Vinton co., O. Pop. 580.

HARRISON, t., Licking co., O., 21 ms. from Columbus; from W. 361 ms. Watered by south fork of Licking river. Pop. 1,150.

HARRISON, t., Logan co., O. Pop. 987.

HARRISON, t., Preble co., O., 90 ms. from Columbus; from W. 486 ms. Pop. 2,100.

HARRISON, t., Scioto co., O. Pop. 1.102.

HARRISON, t., Pickaway co., O., 17 ms. from Columbus; from W. 403 ms. Watered by Scioto river. Pop. 1,176.

HARRISON, t., Blackford co., Ind. Pop. 746.

HARRISON, t,. Harrison co., Ind., 124 ms. from Indianapolis; from W. 614 ms.

HARRISON, p. o., Winnebago co,, Ill.

HARRISON, t., Clay co., Ind., 79 ms from Indianapolis; from W. 644 ms. Pop. 685.

HARRISON, p. t., Fayette co., Ind. Pop. 1,065.

HARRISON, t., Hancock co., Ind., 23 ms. from Indianapolis; from W. 550 ms. Pop. 500.

HARRISON, p. t., Henry co., Ind. Pop. 1,425.

HARRISON, t., Owen co., Ind. Pop. 375.

HARRISON, t., Perry co., O., 64 ms. from Columbus; from W. 351 ms. Pop. 1,078.

HARRISON, t., Macomb co., Mich., 33 ms. from Detroit; from W. 559 ms.

HARRISON, c. h., p. v., seat of justice of Hamilton co., Tenn.

HARRISON, t., Scotland co., Mo. Pop. 419.

HARRISONBURGH, c. h., p. v., seat of justice of Rockingham co, Va., 131 ms. N. w. of Richmond; from W. 131 ms.

HARRISONBURGH, c. h., p. v., seat of justice of Catahoola parish, La., 236 ms. N. w. of New Orleans; from W. 1,150 ms. Watered by Ouchitta river.

HARRISON. city, p. o., Westmoreland co., Pa.

HARRISON CREEK, p. o., Cumberland co., N. C.

HARRISON SQUARE, p. o., Norfolk co., Mass.

HARRISON'S MILLS, p. o., Crawford co., Mo., 88 ms. s. E. of Jefferson city; from W. 902 ms. Watered by Maramec river.

HARRISON VALLEY, p. o., Potter co., Pa., 174 ms. N. w. of Harrisburgh; from W. 288 ms.

HARRISONVILLE, p. o., Gloucester co., N. J.

HARRISONVILLE, c. h., p. v., Shelby co., Ky., 39 ms. w. of Frankfort; from W. 557 ms.

HARRISONVILLE, c. h., p. v., seat of justice of Monroe co.. Ill., 127 ms. s. w. of Springfield; from W. 840 ms. Watered by Mississippi river.

HARRISONVILLE, p. v., Meigs co., O.

HARRISONVILLE, c. h., p. v., seat of justice of Cass co., Mo., 174 ms. w. of Jefferson city; from W. 1,073 ms.

HARRISONVILLE, p. o., Baltimore co., Md.

HARRISONVILLE, p. o., Fulton co., Pa.

HARRISTOWN, p. o., Washington co.. Ind.

HARRISVILLE, p. v., Butler co., Pa., 224 N. w. of Harrisburgh; from W. 204 ms. Pop. 235.

HARRISVILLE, p. v., Short creek township, Harrison co., O.. 123 ms. N. E. of Columbus; from W. 278 ms. Pop. 300.

HARRISVILLE, t., Medina co., O., 112 ms. N. E. of Columbus; from W. 361 ms.

HARRISVILLE, p. o., Montgomery co., N. C., 126 ms. s. w. of Raleigh; from W. 400 ms. Pop. 1,477.

HARRISVILLE, p. o., Cheshire co., N. H.

HARRISVILLE, p. o., Brunswick co., Va.

HARRISVILLE, p o, Marquette co., Wis.

HARRODSBURGH, c. h., p. v., seat of justice of Mercer co., Ky., 31 ms. s. of Frankfort; from W. 553 ms. Watered by Salt river. Seat of Bacon college. Pop. 1,154.

HARRODSBURGH, p. o., Monroe co., Ind.

HARSHMANSVILLE, p. o., Montgomery co., O.

HART COUNTY, situated near the central part of Kentucky, and traversed by Green river. Area, 432 square miles. Face of the country level; soil unproductive, chiefly consisting of barrens. Seat of justice, Munfordsville. Pop. in 1820, 4,184; in 1830, 5,191; in 1840, 7,031; in 1850, 9,093.

HART, t, Warwick co., Ind., 181 ms. from Indianapolis; from W. 722 ms. Pop. 1,434.

HARTFIELD, p. v., Chautauque township, Chautauque co., N. Y.

HARTFORD COUNTY, situated on the northern boundary of Connecticut, and traversed by Connecticut and Farmington rivers. Area, 727 square miles. Face of the country beautifully diversified with mountains and rich valleys; soil fertile, especially on the rivers. Seat of justice, Hartford. Pop. in 1810. 44,733; in 1820, 47,264; in 1830, 51,141; in 1840, 55,629; in 1850, 69,966.

HARTFORD, city, seat of justice of Hartford co.. and state capital, together with New Haven, of Connecticut, is situated on Connecticut river, at the head of sloop navigation, 45 miles from its entrance into Long Island sound, 100 miles southwest of Boston, and 123 northeast of New York. The city is built on the west bank of the river. which rises suddenly into an elevation, and stretches away into an undulating and diversified country. Seated in the centre of the state, and in its richest region, and communicating with the whole valley of the Connecticut, from Vermont to the sound. it enjoys an extensive and valuable trade in all the manufactures and productions peculiar to New England. The plan of the city is not very regular, but many of its buildings are elegant and beautiful for situation. On a public square stands the state-house, a fine structure of the Doric order, 116 feet long, 75 wide, and 54 high. Trinity college, an Episcopal institution, has a fine location near the city. The city-hall in the Doric, and the Athenæum of the Gothic architecture, are conspicuous edifices. But the buildings most honorable to Hartford, are the American Asylum for the education of the Deaf and Dumb, and the Retreat of the Insane. Both of these institutions are widely known, and include persons from all parts of the country. The former is situated on Tower hill, about a mile west of the city, and receives a revenue from grants made by the general government, and from other sources. The buildings of the Insane Asylum are located toward the southwest of the city, upon an eminence, in the midst of picturesque and delightful scenery, well-suited to minister to the injured mind that peace and quietude which nature can best impart. A beautiful freestone bridge spans Mill river, which winds through the city into the Connecticut, by a single arch of 100 feet, and a substantial and costly bridge connects the town with East Hartford. Perhaps the object of most universal interest in the vicinity of Hartford, is the Charter Oak, which still flourishes as in its pristine verdure, though age has robbed it of some of its limbs. It stands on a beautiful elevation south of the city. The New Haven and Hartford, the Hartford and Springfield, and the Connecticut River railroads, traverse the best part of Massachusetts and Connecticut; and sloops and steamboats ply upon the river and Long Island sound. Pop. in 1810, was 3,955; in 1820, 4,726; in 1830, 7,074; in 1840, 12,793; in 1850, 17,966.

HARTFORD, p. t., Oxford co., Me., 34 ms. w. of Augusta; from W. 600 ms. Pop. 1,293.

HARTFORD, p. t., Windsor co., Vt., 52 ms. s. E. of Montpelier; from W. 487 ms. Watered by White, Waterqueechy, and Connecticut rivers. Pop. 2,159.

HARTFORD, t., Susquehanna co., Pa. Pop. 1,258.

HARTFORD, p. t., Washington co., N. Y., 57 ms. N. E. of Albany; from W. 433 ms. Watered by tributaries of Wood creek. Pop. 2,051.

HARTFORD, c. h., p. v., seat of justice of Ohio co., Ky. 154 ms. s. w. of Frankfort; from W. 696 ms. Watered by Rough creek.

HARTFORD, p. t., Trumbull co., O., 187 ms. N. E. of Columbus; from W. 299 ms. Pop. 1,258.

HARTFORD, p. t., Licking co., O., 37 ms. from Columbus; from W. 383 ms. Pop. 1,426.

HARTFORD, v., Pulaski co., Ga., 67 ms. from Milledgeville; from W. 709 ms. Watered by Ocmulgee river.

HARTFORD, p. v., Ohio co., Ind.

HARTFORD, t., Van Buren co., Mich. Pop. 296.

HARTFORD, t., Pike co., Mo.

HARTFORD, p. o., Putnam co., Mo.

HARTFORD, p. v., Knox co., Ill., 93 ms. N. w. of Springfield; from W. 525 ms.

HARTFORD, p. o., Forsyth co., Ga.

HARTFORD, p. o., Putnam co., Mo.

HARTFORD, p, o., Washington co., Wis.

HARTHEGIG, p. o., Mercer co., Pa.

HARTLAND, p. t., Somerset co., Me., 47 ms. N. of Augusta; from W. 642 ms. Pop. 960.

HARTLAND, p. t., Windsor co., Vt., 62 ms. s. E. of Montpelier; from W. 477 ms. Watered by Connecticut and Waterqueechy rivers, and Lull's brook. Pop. 2,063.

HARTLAND, p. t., Hartford co., Ct., 24 ms. N. E. of Hartford; from W. 360 ms. Watered by east branch of Farmington river. Pop. 848.

HARTLAND, p. t., Niagara co., N. Y., 270 ms. w. of Albany; from W. 410 ms. Watered by Johnson's and Eighteen-mile creeks. Pop. 3,028.

HARTLAND. p. t., Huron co., O., 106 ms. N. of Columbus; from W. 384 ms. Pop. 1,024.

HARTLAND, p. t., Livingston co.. Mich., 52 ms. w. of Detroit; from W. 571 ms. Pop. 996.

HARTLAND, p. v., McHenry co., Ill., 226 ms. N. E. of Springfield; from W. 778 ms.

HARTLAND, p. o., Waukesha co., Wis.

HARTLETON, p. v., Hartley township, Union co., Pa., 71 ms. N. of Harrisburgh; from W. 179 ms.

HARTLEY, p. t., Union co., Pa. Pop. 2,142.

HARTLEYVILLE, p. o., Athens co., O.

HART LOT, p. o., Onondaga co., N. Y.

HART's GROVE, p. t., Ashtabula co., O., 181 ms. N. E. of Columbus; from W. 332 ms. Pop. 650.

HARTSHORN, p. o., Orange co., N. C., 61 ms. N. w. of Raleigh; from W. 304 ms.

HART's LOCATION, p. o., Coos co., N. H., 88 ms. N. of Concord; from W. 574 ms. Situated on the southerly part of the White mountains.

HART's MILLS, p. o., Ripley co., Ind., 78 ms. s. E. of Indianapolis; from W. 540 ms.

HARTSTOWN, p. o., Crawford co., Pa.

HART's VILLAGE, p. v., Washington township, Dutchess co., N. Y., 80 ms. s. of Albany; from W. 314 ms.

HARTSVILLE, p. v., Tyringham township, Berkshire co., Mass., 134 ms. w. of Boston; from W. 361 ms.

HARTSVILLE, p. v., Manlius township, Onondaga co., N. Y., 128 ms. N. w. of Albany; from W. 354 ms.

HARTSVILLE, p. v., Bucks co., Pa., 108 ms. E. of Harrisburgh; from W. 157 ms.

HARTSVILLE, p. v., Sumner co., Tenn., 45 ms. N. E. of Nashville; from W. 648 ms. Watered by Cumberland river.

HARTSVILLE, p. v., Bartholomew co., Ind., 54 ms. s of Indianapolis; from W. 566 ms.

HARTSVILLE, p. o., Darlington district, S. C., 105 ms. E. of Columbia; from W. 477 ms.

HARTSVILLE, c. h., p. v., seat of justice of Wright co., Wis. Watered by Wood's fork of Gasconade river.

HARTVILLE, p. o., Stark co., O., 136 ms. N. E. of Columbus; from W. 321 ms.

HARTWELLVILLE, p. o., Shiawassee co., Mich., 83 ms. N. w. of Detroit; from W. 586 ms.

HARTWICK, p. t., Otsego co., N. Y., 74 ms. w. of Albany; from W. 367 ms. Watered by Otsego creek and Susquehanna river. Pop. 2,352.

HARTWICK SEMINARY, p. v., Hartwick township, Otsego co., N. Y. Seat of Hartwick Literary and Theological seminary.

HARTWOOD, p. o., Stafford co., Va., 72 ms. N. of Richmond; from W. 63 ms.

HARTWOOD, p. o., Autauga co., Ala.

HARVARD, p. t., Worcester co., Mass., 32 ms. N. w. of Boston; from W. 472 ms. Watered by Stony and Nashua rivers. Pop. 1,630.

HARVARD, p. o., Delaware co., N. Y.

HARVEY's, p. o., Greene co., Pa., 223 ms. s. w. of Harrisburgh; from W. 239 ms.

HARVEYSBURGH, p. v., Wayne township, Warren co., O., 81 ms. N. E. of Columbus; from W. 455 ms. Pop. 330.

HARVEY's FIVE POINTS, p. o., Westmoreland co., Pa.

HARVEY's POINT, p. o., Polk co., Iowa.

HARVEY's STORE, p. o., Charlotte co., Va., 110 ms. s. w. of Richmond; from W. 197 ms.

HARVEYSVILLE, p. v., Luzerne co., Pa., 108 ms. N. E. of Harrisburgh; from W. 219 ms.

HARWICK, p. t., Barnstable co., Mass., 89 ms. s. E. of Boston; from W. 490 ms. Watered by Herring river, Long pond, and the Atlantic ocean.

HARWICKPORT, p. o., Harwick township, Barnstable co., Mass.

HARWINTON, p. t., Litchfield township, Ct., 24 ms. w. of Hartford; from W. 334 ms. Watered by Naugatuck and Lead Mines rivers.

HASBROUCK, p. o., Sullivan co., N. Y.

HASKELLVILLE, p. o., Lawrence co., O.

HASKENVILLE, p. o., Steuben co., N. Y.

HASKINSVILLE, p. v., Green co., Ky., 97 ms. s. w. of Frankfort; from W. 620 ms.

HASTINGS, p. v., seat of justice of Barry co., Mich., 144 ms. w. of Detroit. Watered by Thorn-Apple river.

HASTINGS, p. t., Oswego co., N. Y., 150 ms. N. w. of Albany.; from W. 371 ms. Watered by Salmon creek and Oneida lake outlet. Pop. 2,920.

HASTINGS-UPON-HUDSON, p. v., Yonkers township, Westchester co., N. Y., 20 ms. N. of New York; from W. 245 ms. Watered by Hudson river.

HASTINGS, p. o., Richland co., 70 ms. N. of Columbus; from W. 376 ms.

HASTINGSVILLE, p. o., Columbiana co., O.

HAT, p. o., Lancaster co., Pa., 50 ms s. E. of Harrisburgh; from W. 125 ms.

HATBOROUGH. p. v., Moreland township, Montgomery co., Pa., 112 ms. E. of Harrisburgh; from W. 153 ms. Pop. 601.

HATCHER's, p. o., Talladega co., Ala.

HATCHY TURNPIKE, p. o., Tippah co., Miss.
HAT CREEK, p. o., Campbell co., Va.
HAT CREEK, t., Taney co., Mo.
HATFIELD, p. t., Hampshire co., Mass., 97 ms. w. of Boston; from W. 384 ms. Watered by Connecticut and Mill rivers. Pop. 1,073.
HATFIELD, t., Montgomery co., Pa., 104 ms. E. of Harrisburgh; from W. 164 ms. Watered by Neshaminy and Towamensing creeks. Pop. 1,135.
HAT GROVE, p. o., Warren co., Ill.
HAUSERTOWN, p. v., Owen co., Ind., 70 ms. s. w. of Indianapolis; from W. 641 ms.
HAVANNA, p. v., Catherine's township, Chemung co., N. Y., 194 ms. s. w. of Albany; from W. 299 ms. Watered by Seneca lake inlet and Chemung canal.
HAVANNA, c. h., p. v., seat of justice of Mason co., Ill., 45 ms. N. W. of Springfield; from W. 825 ms. Watered by Illinois river.
HAVANNA, p. v., Greene co., Ala.; from W. 844 ms.
HAVANNA, p. o., Huron co., O.
HAVANNA, v., Licking co., O.
HAVENSVILLE, p. o., Bradford co., Pa., 157 ms. N. of Harrisburgh; from W. 264 ms.
HAVERFORD, p. t., Delaware co., Pa., 95 ms. s. E. of Harrisburgh; from W. 137 ms. Watered by Darby and Cobb's creeks. Pop. 1,401.
HAVERHILL, p. t., Essex co., Mass., 32 ms. N. w. of Boston; from W. 462 ms. Situated on Merrimack river, at the head of navigation. Pop. in 1840, 4,336; in 1850, 5,877.
HAVERHILL, c. h., p. t., seat of justice, together with Plymouth, of Grafton co., N. H. 70 ms. N. w. of Concord; from W. 515 ms. Watered by Connecticut river and Hazen's and Oliverian brooks. Pop. 2,005.
HAVERHILL CENTRE, p. v, Haverhill township, Grafton co., N. H.
HAVERSTRAW, p. t., Rockland co., N. Y., 115 ms. s. of Albany: from W. 271 ms. Watered by Hudson river. Pop. 5,855.
HAVILAND HOLLOW, p., Patterson township, Putnam co., N. Y., 95 ms. s. of Albany; from W. 298 ms.
HAVILANDSVILLE, p. o., Harrison co., Ky.
HAVRE DE GRACE, p. v., Harford co., Md., 64 ms. N. E. of Annapolis; from W. 74 ms. Watered by Susquehanna river and Chesapeake bay. Pop. 6,105.
HAWESVILLE, c. h., p. v., seat of justice of Hancock co., Ky., 135 ms. w. of Frankfort; from W. 677 ms. Watered by Ohio river and Lead creek.
HAWFIELDS, p. v., Orange co., N. C., 48 ms. N. W. of Raleigh: from W. 282 ms.
HAWKERVILLE, p. o., Franklin co., Tenn.
HAWK EYE, p. o., Des Moines co., Iowa.
HAWKINS COUNTY, situated on the northern boundary of Tennessee, and traversed by Holston and Clinch rivers. Area, 750 square miles. Face of the country broken with hills and mountains; soil generally fertile. Seat of justice, Rogersville. Pop. in 1810, 7,643; in 1820, 10,949; in 1830, 13,683; in 1840, 15,035; in 1850, 13,370.
HAWKINS' LANDING, p. o., Ashley co., Ark.
HAWKINSVILLE, p. o., Sussex co., Va., 43 ms. s. of Richmond; from W. 162 ms.
HAWKINSVILLE, c. h., p. v., seat of justice of Pulaski co., Ga., 71 ms. s. of Milledgeville; from W. 718 ms. Watered by Ocmulgee river.
HAWKINSVILLE, p. v., Oneida co., N. Y
HAWK POINT, p. o., Lincoln co., Mo.
HAWLEY, p. t., Franklin co., Mass., 111 ms. w. of Boston; from W. 405 ms. Watered by branches of Deerfield river. Pop. 881.
HAWLEY, p. o., Wayne co., Pa.
HAWLEY'S STORE, p. o., Sampson co., N. C.
HAWLEYTON, p. o., Broome co., N. Y.
HAWLEYVILLE, p. o., Fairfield co., Ct.
HAW PATCH, p. o., La Grange co., Ind., 157 ms. N. E. of Indianapolis; from W. 596 ms.
HAW CREEK, p. t., Bartholomew co., Ind. Pop. 1,572.
HAW CREEK, t., Morgan co., Mo.
HAWSBURGH, p. v., Rappahannock co., Va., 130 ms. N. w. of Richmond; from W. 87 ms.
HAWTHORN, p. o., Montgomery co., Ala.
HAYCOCK, t., Bucks co. Pa., 100 ms. E. of Harrisburgh; from W. 175 ms. Watered by Tohickon creek and branches. Pop. 1,134.
HAYDENVILLE, p.v., Williamsburgh township, Hampshire co., Mass., 98 ms. w. of Boston: from W. 386 ms. Watered by Mill creek.

HAYE'S STORE, p. o., Gloucester co., Va.
HAYESVILLE, p. v., Vermilion township, Ashland co., O., 78 ms. N. E. of Columbus; from W. 363 ms.
HAYESVILLE, p. o., Chester co., Pa.
HAYFIELD, p t., Crawford co., Pa., 336 ms. N. w. of Harrisburgh; from W. 307 ms. Pop. 1,723.
HAY MARKET, p. v., Prince William co., Va., 114 ms. N. of Richmond; from W. 46 ms.
HAY MEADOW, p. o., Wilkes co., N. C., 184 ms. w. of Raleigh; from W. 388.
HAYNES, p. o., Grainger co., Tenn., 220 ms. E. of Nashville; from W. 485 ms.
HAYNESVILLE, p. o., Aroostook co., Me., 159 ms. N. E. of Augusta; from W. 754 ms.
HAYNEVILLE, c. h., p. v., seat of justice of Lowndes co., Ala.; from W. 859 ms. Watered by Big Swamp creek.
HAYNEVILLE, p. v., Houston co., Ga., 69 ms. s. w of Milledgeville; from W. 725 ms.
HAYS' CREEK, p. o., Carroll co., Miss.
HAY SPRINGS, p. o., Jefferson co., Ky.
HAY STACK, p. o., Surry co., N. C.
HAYS' STORE, p. o., Montgomery co., O
HAYSVILLE, p. o., Dubois co., Ind.
HAYSVILLE, p. o., Marion co., Ky.
HAYTER'S GAP, p. o., Washington co., Va.
HAYWOOD COUNTY, situated on the northwesterly boundary of North Carolina. Area, 1,200 square miles. Face of the country hilly; soil generally sterile, but near the streams, rich. Seat of justice, Waynesville. Pop. in 1810, 2,780; in 1820, 4,073; in 1830, 4,578; in 1840, 4,975; in 1850, 7,074.
HAYWOOD COUNTY, situated in the southwestern part of Tennessee, and traversed by Big Hatchee river. Area, 600 square miles. Seat of justice, Brownsville. Pop. in 1830, 5,334; in 1840, 13,870; in 1850, 17,259.
HAYWOOD, p. v., Chatham co., N. C., 31 ms. w. of Raleigh; from W. 319 ms. Watered by Haw, Deep, and Cape Fear rivers.
HAZARD FORGE, p. o., Hardy co., Va., 188 ms. N. w. of Richmond; from W. 150 ms.
HAZARDVILLE, p. v., Hartford co., Ct.
HAZLE, t., Luzerne co., Pa., 106 ms. N. E. of Harrisburgh; from 214 ms. Pop. 2,080.
HAZLEDELL, p. o., Cumberland co., Ill.
HAZLE BOTTOM, p. o., Barry co., Mo.
HAZLE GREEN, v., Madison co., Ala.; from W. 722 ms.
HAZLE GREEN, p. o., Shelby co., Tenn.
HAZLE GREEN, p. o., Grant co., Wis., 83 ms w of Madison; from W. 891 ms.
HAZLE GREEN, p. o., Morgan co., Ky., 100 ms. E. of Frankfort; from W. 511 ms.
HAZLE GROVE, p. o., Saline co., Mo.
HAZLETON, p. v., Hazle township, Luzerne co., Pa., 106 ms. N. E. of Harrisburgh; from W. 214 ms.
HAZLEWOOD, p. o., Chesire district, S. C., 49 ms. N. of Columbia; from W. 456 ms.
HAZLEWOOD, p. o. Ballard co., Ky.
HAZLEWOOD, p. o., Wright co., Mo.
HEADLEY'S MILLS, p. o., Fountain co., Ind., 85 ms. N. w. of Indianapolis; from W. 656 ms.
HEADS OF BARREN, p. o., Claiborne co., Tenn.
HEAD OF CLINCH, p o., Tazewell co., Va.
HEAD OF HARBOR. v., Smithtown township, Suffolk co. Long Island, N. Y., 50 ms. N. E. of New York. Watered by Stony Brook harbor.
HEAD OF PAINT, p. o., Morgan co., Ky., 125 ms. w. of Frankfort; from W. 469 ms.
HEAD OF SASSAFRAS, p. o., Kent co., Md., 70 ms. N. E. of Annapolis; from W. 110 ms.
HEAD QUARTERS, p. o., Nicholas co., Ky.
HEALING SPRINGS, p. o., Davidson co., N. C., 136 ms. w of Raleigh; from W. 373 ms.
HEARD COUNTY, situated on the western boundary of Georgia, and traversed by Chattahoochee river. Area, 175 square miles. Seat of justice, Franklin. Pop in 1840, 5,329; in 1850, 6,923.
HEARNVILLE, p. o., Putnam co., Ga.
HEART PRAIRIE, p. o., Walworth co., Wis.
HEARTWELLVILLE, p. o., Bennington co., Vt.
HEATH, p. t., Franklin co., Mass., 109 ms. N. w. of Boston; from W. 457 ms. Pop. 803.
HEATH'S CREEK, p. c., Pettis co., Mo.
HEATHSVILLE, c. h., p. t., seat of justice of Northumberland co., Va., 98 ms. E. of Richmond; from W. 157 ms.
HEATHSVILLE, p. v., Halifax co., N. C., 82 ms. N. E. of Raleigh; from W. 228 ms.

HEBBARDSVILLE, p. v., Henderson co., Ky., 183 ms. w. of Frankfort; from W. 710 ms.

HEBBARDSVILLE, p. v., Alexandria township, Athens co., Ga., 78 ms. s. e. of Columbia; from W. 385 ms.

HEBRON, p. t., Oxford co., Me., 45 ms. s. w. of Augusta; from W. 586 ms. Watered by a branch of Androscoggin river. Pop. 839.

HEBRON, p. t., Grafton co., N. H., 40 ms. n. w. of Concord; from W. 512 ms. Pop. 565.

HEBRON, p. t., Tolland co., Ct., 25 ms. s. e. of Hartford; from W. 343 ms. Watered by Hop river, a branch of the Willimantic. Pop 1,864.

HEBRON, p. o., Washington co., Ga.

HEBRON, p. t., Washington co., N. Y., 54 ms. n. of Albany; from W. 424 ms. Watered by Black creek. Pop. 2,548.

HEBRON, p. o., Porter co., Ind.

HEBRON, p. t., Licking co., O., 27 ms. n. e. of Columbus; from W. 366 ms.

HEBRON, p. o., Tyler co., Va.

HEBRON, p. t., Potter co., Pa. Pop. 337.

HEBRON, p. v., McHenry co., Ill., 230 ms. n. e. of Springfield; from W. 765 ms.

HECKTOWN, p. v., Lower Nazareth township, Northampton co., Pa., 99 ms. n. e. of Harrisburgh; from W. 192 ms.

HECLA, p. o., Carroll co., Tenn.

HECLA WORKS. p. o., Oneida co., N. Y.

HECTOR, p. t., Tompkins co., N. Y.. 184 ms. s. w. of Albany; from W. 311 ms. Watered by Seneca lake. Pop. 6.052.

HECTOR, p. t., Potter co., Pa. Pop. 316.

HECTOR, p. o., Jay co., Ind.

HEDGERSVILLE. p. o., Berkeley co., Va., 176 ms. n. of Richmond; from W. 84 ms.

HEIDELBERG, t., Berks co., Pa. Watered by Tulpehocken Spring, and Cacoosing creeks. Pop. 1,034.

HEIDELBERG, t., Lebanon co., Pa. Watered by Mill and Hammer creeks. Pop. 1,467.

HEIDELBERG, t., Lehigh co., Pa. Watered by Lehigh river, and Trout and Jordan's creeks. Pop. 1,385.

HEIDELBERG, t., York co., Pa. Watered by Codorus and Hammer creeks. Pop. 1,616.

HEIDLERSBURGH, Tyrone township, Adams co., Pa., 25 ms. s. e. of Harrisburgh; from W. 85 ms. Pop. 102.

HELENA, p. v., Brasher township, St. Lawrence co., N. Y. 236 ms. n. w. of Albany; from W. 535 ms. Watered by St. Regis river.

HELENA, c. h., p. v., seat of justice of Philips co., Ark., 122 ms. e. of Little Rock; from W. 1,011 ms. Watered by Mississippi river. Pop. 614.

HELENA, p. v., Iowa co., Wis., 59 ms. n. w. of Madison; from W. 906 ms.

HELENA, p. o., Peoria co., Ill.

HELENA, p. o., Mason co., Ky

HELENVILLE, p. o., Jefferson co., Wis.

HELLAM, p. t., York co., Pa., 29 ms. s. of Harrisburgh; from W. 95 ms. Watered by Codorus and Grist creeks, and Susquehanna river. Pop. 1,528.

HELLEN, p. v., Elk co., Pa., 176 ms. n. w. of Harrisburgh; from W. 268 ms.

HELLEN FURNACE, p. o., Clarion co., Pa.

HELLERTOWN. p. v., Northampton co., Pa., 97 ms. n. e. of Harrisburgh; from W. 188 ms.

HELT. t, Vermilion co., Ind. Pop. 2,121.

HELTON, p. o., Ashe co., N. C.

HELTONVILLE, p. o., Lawrence co., Ind.

HEMLO, p. o., Whitesides co., Ill.

HEMLOCK, t., Columbia co., Pa., 70 ms. n. of Harrisburgh; from W. 180 ms. Watered by Hemlock. Mahoning, Great and Little Fishing creeks. Pop. 1,087.

HEMLOCK GROVE, p. o., Meigs co., O.

HEMLOCK LAKE, p. o., Livonia township, Livingston co., N. Y.

HEMPFIELD, p. v., East Hempfield township, Lancaster co., Pa., 40 ms. s. e. of Harrisburgh; from W. 114 ms.

HEMPFIELD, p. t., Westmoreland co., Pa., 170 ms. w. of Harrisburgh; from W. 192 ms. Watered by Bush, and Big and Little Sewickly creeks. Pop. 5,935.

HEMPHILL's STORE, p. o., Mecklenburgh co., N. C., 170 ms. w. of Raleigh; from W. 409 ms.

HEMPSTEAD COUNTY, situated in the southwestern part of Arkansas, with Little Missouri on the northeast, and Red river on the southwest. Area, 1,150 square miles. Soil, generally sterile. Seat of justice, Washington. Pop. in 1820, 2,489; in 1830, 2,512; in 1840, 4,921; in 1850, 7,672.

HEMPSTEAD, p. t., Queen's co., Long Island, N. Y., 170 ms. s. of Albany; from W. 250 ms. Watered by Atlantic ocean. Pop. 8,811.

HEMPSTEAD BRANCH, p. o., Hempstead township, Queen's co., Long Island, N. Y.

HENRY, p. o., Montgomery co., O.

HENDERSON COUNTY, situated toward the western part of Tennessee. Area, 665 square miles. Seat of justice, Lexington. Pop. in 1830, 8,741; in 1840, 11,875; in 1850, 13,164.

HENDERSON COUNTY, situated in the northwesterly part of Kentucky, with Ohio river on the north, and Green river on the east. Area, 725 square miles. Face of the country, hilly; soil, fertile. Seat of justice, Henderson. Pop. in 1810, 4,703; in 1820; 5,714; in 1830, 6,659; in 1840, 9,548; in 1850, 12,171.

HENDERSON COUNTY, situated on the western boundary of Illinois, with Mississippi river on the west. Area, —— square miles. Seat of justice, Oquawka. Pop. in 1850, 4,612.

HENDERSON COUNTY, situated on the southerly boundary of North Carolina. Area, 700 square miles. Face of the country, mountainous, the Blue Ridge traversing the east and south. Seat of justice, Hendersonville. Pop. in 1840, 5,129; in 1850, 6,853.

HENDERSON COUNTY, situated toward the northern part of Texas, with Trinity river on the west. Area, —— square miles. Seat of justice, Centreville. Pop. in 1850, 1,047.

HENDERSON, p. t., Jefferson co., N. Y., 181 ms. n. w. of Albany; from W. 412 ms. Watered by Stony and Little Stony creeks, and Lake Ontario. Pop. 2,239.

HENDERSON, p. o., Mercer co., Pa., 222 ms. n. w. of Harrisburgh; from W. 279 ms.

HENDERSON, t., Huntingdon co., Pa., 90 ms. w. of Harrisburgh; from W. 148 ms. Watered by Juniata river. Pop. 819.

HENDERSON, p. v., Houston co., Ga., 68 ms. s. w. of Milledgeville; from W. 725 ms.

HENDERSON, c. h., p. v., seat of justice of Henderson co., Ky., 197 ms. s. w. of Frankfort; from W. 724 ms. Watered by Ohio river. Pop. 1,765.

HENDERSON, p. v., Granville co., N. C., 44 ms. n. of Raleigh; from W. 244 ms. Pop. 1,629.

HENDERSON, p. v., Knox co., Ill., 110 ms. n. w. of Springfield; from W. 829 ms. Watered by Henderson river.

HENDERSON, p. o., Rusk co., Tex.

HENDERSON'S MILL, p. o., Greene co., Tenn., 264 ms. e. of Nashville; from W. 431 ms.

HENDERSONVILLE. c. h., p. v., seat of justice of N. C. Watered by French Broad river.

HENDERSONVILLE, p. v., Sumner co., Tenn., 16 ms. n. e. of Nashville; from W. 677 ms.

HENDRENSVILLE, p. v., Henry co., Ky., 33 ms. n. w. of Frankfort; from W. 575 ms.

HENDRICKS COUNTY, situated near the centre of Indiana, and watered by Eel river, and White Lick and Mud creeks. The surface of the county is undulating, and soil productive. Area, about 400 square miles. Pop. in 1840, 11,264; in 1850, 14,083.

HENDRICKS. t., Shelby co., Ind., 30 ms. s. e. of Indianapolis; from W. 574 ms. Pop. 1,272.

HENDRICKS' MILLS, p. o., Russell co., Va.

HENDRICKS' STORE, p. o., Bedford co., Va., 158 ms. w. of Richmond; from W. 233 ms.

HENDRICKSVILLE, p. o., De Kalb co., Ala.

HENDRYSBURGH, p. v., Kirkwood township, Belmont co., O., 99 ms. e. of Columbus; from W. 294 ms.

HENLEY's STORE, p. o., Franklin co., Ga.

HENNEPIN, c. h., p. v., seat of justice of Putnam co., Ill., 118 ms. n. of Springfield; from W. 803 ms. Watered by Illinois river. Pop. 430.

HENNIKER, p. t., Merrimack co., N. H., 15 ms. w. of Concord; from W. 467 ms. Watered by Contoocook river, and Long pond. Pop. 1,688.

HENRICO COUNTY, situated in the eastern part of Virginia, with James river on the southwest. Area, 291 square miles. Face of the country, moderately hilly; soil of middling quality. Seat of justice, Richmond. Pop. in 1810, 9,945; in 1820, 22,667; in 1830, 28,798; in 1840, 33,076; in 1850, 43,437.

HENRIE's FORK, p. o., Gilmer co., Va.

HENRIETTA, p. t., Monroe co., N. Y., 223 ms. w. of Albany; from W. 368 ms. Watered by Genesee river. Pop. 2,513.

HENRIETTA, p. t., Lorain co., O., 118 ms. n. e. of Columbus; from W. 385 ms. Pop. 1,042.

HENRIETTA, p. t., Jackson co., Mich. Pop. 830.

HENRIETTA, p. o., Montgomery co., Tenn.

HENRY COUNTY, situated on the southern boundary of Virginia, and traversed by Smith's river. Area, 358 square miles. Face of the country broken; soil generally sterile. Seat of justice, Martinsville. Pop. in 1810, 5.611; in 1820, 5,624; in 1830, 7,100; in 1840, 7,335; in 1850, 8.872.

HENRY COUNTY, situated toward the westerly part of Georgia, with Ocmulgee river on the northeast. Area, 594 square miles. Seat of justice, McDonough. Pop. in 1830, 10.567; in 1840, 11,756; in 1850, 14,726.

HENRY COUNTY, situated at the southeast corner of Alabama, with Chattahoochee river on the east. Area, 975 square miles. Seat of justice, Abbeville. Pop. in 1820, 2,638; in 1830, 3,955; in 1840, 5,787; in 1850, 9,019.

HENRY COUNTY, situated on the north boundary of Tennessee, with Tennessee and Big Sandy rivers on the east. Area, 600 square miles. Seat of justice, Paris. Pop. in 1830. 12,230; in 1840, 14,906; in 1850, 18,233.

HENRY COUNTY, situated in the northern part of Kentucky, with Kentucky river on the northeast. Area, 260 square miles. Face of the country hilly and broken; soil fertile. Seat of justice, Newcastle. Pop. in 1810, 6,777; in 1820, 10,816; in 1830, 11,395; in 1840, 10,015; in 1850, 11,442.

HENRY COUNTY, situated in the northwestern part of Ohio, and traversed by Maumee river. Area, 576 square miles. Seat of justice, Napoleon. Pop. in 1830, 260; in 1840, 2.503; in 1850, 3,435.

HENRY COUNTY, situated toward the easterly part of Indiana. Area, 380 square miles. Seat of justice, Newcastle. Pop. in 1830, 6,498; in 1840, 15,128; in 1850, 17,604.

HENRY COUNTY, situated in the northwesterly part of Illinois, with Rock river on the northwest. Area, 840 square miles. Seat of justice, Cambridge. Pop. in 1840, 1,260; in 1850, 3.807.

HENRY COUNTY, situated in the southeastern part of Iowa, and traversed by Chicagua river. Area, 432 square miles. Seat of justice, Mount Pleasant. Pop. in 1840, 3,772; in 1850, 8,707.

HENRY COUNTY, situated in the western part of Missouri, and traversed by South Grand river. Area, 750 square miles. Seat of justice, Clinton. Pop. in 1840, 4,726; in 1850, 4,052.

HENRY, p. o., Marshall co., Ill.

HENRY, p. o., Spartanburgh district, S. C.

HENRY, p. o., Lawrence co., Tenn.

HENRY, p. t., Henry co., Ind. Pop. 1,270.

HENRY, p. o., Sussex co., Va.

HENRY, t., Wood co., O. Pop. 321.

HENRY CLAY, t., Fayette co., Pa, 168 ms. s. w. of Harrisburgh; from W. 177 ms. Watered by Youghiogheny river. Pop. 1,117.

HENRY CLAY FACTORY, p. o., Newcastle co., Del.

HENRY'S CROSS ROADS, p. o., Sevier co., Tenn., 210 ms. E. of Nashville; from W. 508 ms.

HENRYSVILLE, p. o., Monroe co., Pa.

HEPBURN, t., Lycoming co., Pa. Watered by Plunket's. Loyalsock, and Lycoming creeks. Pop. 1,428.

HERBERT, p. o., Neshoba co., Miss., 86 ms. from Jackson; from W. 931 ms.

HERCULANEUM, p. v., Jefferson co., Mo., 160 ms. w. of Jefferson city; from W. 840 ms. Watered by Mississippi river.

HEREFORD, p. t., Berks co., Pa., 80 ms. E. of Harrisburgh; from W. 170 ms. Watered by tributaries of Perkiomen creek. Pop. 1,244.

HEREFORD, p. v., Baltimore co., Md., 52 ms. from Annapolis; from W. 62 ms.

HEREFORD'S, p. o., Mason co., Va., 386 ms. N. w. of Richmond; from W. 376 ms.

HERKIMER COUNTY, situated in the central part of New York, and traversed by Mohawk river, and the Erie canal. Area, 1,370 square miles. Face of the country mountainous and diversified; soil on the Mohawk and other streams alluvial and rich, in other parts varied. Seat of justice, Herkimer. Pop. in 1810, 22,046; in 1820, 31,017; in 1830, 55,689; in 1840, 37,477; in 1850, 38,244.

HERKIMER, c. h., p. t., seat of justice of Herkimer co., N. Y., 78 ms. N. w. of Albany; from W. 397 ms. Watered by West Canada creek and Mohawk river. Pop. 2,601.

HERMAAN, p. o., Ripley co., Ind.

HERMAN p. o., Dodge co., Wis.

HERMANN, c. h., p. v., seat of justice of Gasconade co., Mo., 77 ms. E. of Jefferson city. Watered by Missouri river. Pop. 943.

HERMITAGE, p. o., Wethersfield township, Wyoming co., N. Y., 255 ms. w. of Albany; from W. 360 ms.

HERMITAGE, p. o., Mercer co., Pa., 243 ms. N. w. of Harrisburgh; from W. 286 ms.

HERMITAGE, p. o., Augusta co., Va.

HERMITAGE, p. o., Coles co., Ill., 77 ms. E. of Springfield; from W. 702 ms.

HERMITAGE, p. o., Floyd co., Ga., 167 ms. N. w. of Milledgeville; from W. 678 ms.

HERMITAGE, p. o., Decatur co., Tenn.

HERMITAGE, p. o., Hickory co., Mo.

HERMITAGE, p. o., Point Coupee parish, La.

HERMON, p. t., Penobscot co. Me., 60 ms. N. E. of Augusta; from W. 655 ms. Watered by Sawodabscook river, and a branch of Kenduskeag river. Pop. 1,174.

HERMON, p. t., St. Lawrence co., N. Y., 201 ms. N. w. of Albany; from W. 470 ms. Watered by tributaries of Grass and Oswegatchie rivers. Pop. 1,819.

HERNANDO, c. h., p. v., seat of justice of De Soto co., Mo., 202 ms. N. of Jackson; from W. 925 ms.

HERNANDO, p. o., Bainbridge township, Macon co., Ala.; from W. 789 ms.

HEROD, p. o., Bartholomew co., Ind.

HERODTOWN, p. o., Randolph co., Ga.

HERRICK, p. t., Bradford co., Pa. Pop. 813.

HERRICK, t., Susquehanna co., Pa., 157 ms. N. E. of Harrisburgh; from W. 265 ms. Watered by sources of Lackawannock river. Pop. 824.

HERRING, p. o., Allen co., O.

HERRIOTTSVILLE, p. o., Alleghany co., Pa., 211 ms. from Harrisburgh; from W. 236 ms.

HERTFORD COUNTY, situated on the northerly boundary of North Carolina, with Chowan river on the northeast, and traversed by Meherrin river. Area, 356 square miles. Face of the country level; soil generally poor. Seat of justice, Winton. Pop. in 1810, 1,052; in 1820, 7,712; in 1830, 8,541; in 1840, 7,484; in 1850. 8,142.

HERTFORD, c. h., p. v., seat of justice of Perquimans co., N. C., 194 ms. N. E. of Raleigh; from W. 286 ms. Watered by Perquimans river.

HESS ROAD, p. o., Niagara co., N. Y.

HESSVILLE, p. o., Montgomery co., N. Y.

HESTER, p. o., Marion co., Mo.

HETRICKS, p. o., York co., Pa., 42 ms. s. w. of Harrisburgh; from W. 78 ms.

HEUVELTON, p. v., Oswegatchie township, St. Lawrence co., N. Y., 203 ms. N. w. of Albany; from W. 479 ms. Watered by Oswegatchie river.

HEVENER'S STORE, p. o., Highland co., Va.

HEVERLYVILLE, p. o., Bradford co., Pa.

HEWIT, p. o., Boone co., Va.

HIBERNIA, p. o., Clarke co., Ind., 102 ms. s. of Indianapolis; from W. 583 ms.

HIBERNIA, p. v., Callaway co., Mo., 1 m. N. of Jefferson city; from W. 937 ms. Watered by Missouri river.

HIBERNIA, p. o., Butler co., Pa.

HIBERNIA, p. o., Duvall co., Flor.

HIBERNIA, p. o., Franklin co., O.

HIBERNIA, p. o., Dutchess co., N. Y.

HICKERSON'S CROSS ROADS, p. o., Morgan co., O.

HICKMAN COUNTY, situated toward the western part of Tennessee. Area, 726 square miles. Face of the country hilly; soil varied. Seat of justice, Centreville. Pop. in 1810, 2.583; in 1820, 6,080; in 1830, 8,132; in 1840, 8,618; in 1850, 9.397.

HICKMAN COUNTY, situated on the western boundary of Kentucky, with Mississippi river on the west. Area, 350 square miles. Seat of justice, Clinton. Pop. in 1830, 5,193; in 1840, 8.968; in 1850, 4,791.

HICKMAN, p. o., Fulton co., Ky.

HICKMAN'S BEND, p. o., Mississippi co., Ark.

HICKORY COUNTY, situated toward the southwesterly part of Missouri. Area, —— square miles. Seat of justice, Hermitage. Pop. in 1850, 2,329.

HICKORY, t., Mercer co., Pa.

HICKORY, p. v., Washington co., Pa., 219 ms. w. of Harrisburgh; from W. 246 ms.

HICKORY, p. o., Carroll co., O., 121 ms. N. E. of Columbus; from W. 292 ms.

HICKORY, p. o., Lake co., Ill.

HICKORY BARREN, p. o., Greene co., Mo.

HICKORY CORNERS, p. o., Barry co., Mich.

HICKORY CORNERS, p. o., Lockport township, Niagara co., N. Y., 280 ms. w. of Albany; from W. 403 ms.

HICKORY CREEK, p. o., Audrain co., Mo., 67 ms. N. E. of Jefferson City; from W. 902 ms.

HICKORY CREEK, p. o., Coffee co., Tenn.

HICKORY CREEK, p. o., Fayette co., Ill.

HICKORY FLAT, p. o., Cherokee co., Ga., 117 ms. N.W. of Milledgeville; from W. 662 ms.

HICKORY FLAT, p. o., Simpson co., Ky., 165 ms. s. w. of Frankfort; from W. 688 ms.

HICKORY FLAT, p. o., Tippah co., Miss., 191 ms. N. E. of Jackson; from W. 880 ms.

HICKORY, p. o., Gloucester co., Va., 78 ms. E. of Richmond; from W. 177 ms.

HICKORY GROUND, p. o., Norfolk co., Va., 124 ms. s. E. of Richmond; from W. 249 ms.

HICKORY GROVE, p. o., York district, S. C. 91 ms. N. of Columbia; from W. 44 ms.

HICKORY GROVE, p. o., Crawford co., Ga., 65 ms. s. w. of Milledgeville; from W. 722 ms.

HICKORY GROVE, p. o., Montgomery co., Ala.; from W. 862 ms.

HICKORY GROVE, p. o., Warren co., Mo., 81 ms. N. E. of Jefferson City; from W. 857 ms.

HICKORY GROVE, p. o., Oktibbeha co., Miss., 149 ms. N. E. of Jackson; from W. 906 ms.

HICKORY GROVE, p. o., Jackson co., Mich., 96 ms. w. of Detroit; from W. 566 ms.

HICKORY GROVE, p. o., Jackson co., Iowa.

HICKORY GROVE, t., Washington co., Mo.

HICKORY HEAD, p. o., Lancaster district, S. C.

HICKORY HILL, p. o., Beaufort district, S. C., 101 ms. s. of Columbia; from W. 601 ms.

HICKORY HILL, p. o., Cole co., Mo., 20 ms. w. of Jefferson City; from W. 956 ms.

HICKORY HILL, p. o., Marion co., Ill.,

HICKORY HILL, p. o., Chester co., Pa.

HICKORY HILL, p. o., Cass co., Tex.

HICKORY LEVEL, p. o., Talladega co., Ala.; from W. 761 ms.

HICKORY LEVEL, p. o., Carroll co., Ga., 130 ms. N. W. of Milledgeville; from W. 710 ms.

HICKORY PLAIN, p. o., Prairie co., Ark.

HICKORY PLAINS, p. o., Tishemingo co., Miss.

HICKORY POINT, p. o., McDonough co., Ill.

HICKORY POINT, p. o., Lake co., Ind.

HICKORY RUN, v., Carbon co., Pa.

HICKORY TAVERN, p. o., Harford co., Md., 58 ms. N. of Annapolis; from W. 68 ms.

HICKORY WITHE, p. o., Fayette co., Tenn.

HICKSBURGH, p. v., Dorchester co., Md.

HICKSFORD, c. h., p. v., seat of justice of Greenville co., Va., 62 ms. s. of Richmond; from W. 181 ms. Watered by Meherrin river.

HICKSHIRVILLE, p. o., Schuylkill co., Pa.

HICK'S MILLS, p. o., De Kalb co., Ill., 221 ms. N. E. of Springfield; from W. 794 ms.

HICK'S RUN, p. o., Elk co., Pa.

HICKSVILLE, p. o., Rutherford co., N. C.

HICKSVILLE, p. v., Defiance co., O., 177 ms. N. w. of Columbus; from W. 529 ms. Pop. 507.

HICKSVILLE, v., Oyster Bay township, Queen's co., Long Island, N. Y., 27 ms. N. E. of New York city; from W. 251 ms.

HICKVILLE, p. o., Oakland co., Mich., 29 ms. N. w. of Detroit; from W. 530 ms.

HICO, p. o., Carroll co., Tenn., 106 ms. w. of Nashville; from W. 791 ms.

HIGGANUM, p. v., Haddam township, Middlesex co., Ct., 21 ms. s. of Hartford; from W. 331 ms. Watered by Connecticut river.

HIGGINS', p. o., Fayette co., Ill.

HIGGINS' FERRY, p. o., Edgefield district, S. C.

HIGGINSPORT, p. v., Lewis township, Brown co., O., 124 ms. s. w. of Columbus; from W. 483 ms. Watered by Ohio river.

HIGGINSVILLE, p. o., Oneida co., N. Y.

HIGGINSVILLE, p. o., Vermilion co., Ill.

HIGGINSPORT, p. o., Jackson co., Iowa.

HIGGINSVILLE, p. o., Hampshire co., Va.

HIGH BLUE, p. o., Jackson co., Mo.

HIGH FALLS, p. v., Marbletown township, Ulster co., N. Y., 49 ms. s. of Albany; from W. 318 ms. Watered by Rondout creek and Delaware and Hudson canal.

HIGHGATE, p. t., Franklin co., Vt., 71 ms. N. w. of Montpelier; from W. 545 ms. Watered by Lake Champlain and Rock and Missisque rivers. Pop. 2,653.

HIGH GROVE, p. o., Nelson co., Ky., 53 ms. s. w. of Frankfort; from W. 595 ms.

HIGH HILL, p. o., Montgomery co., Mo.

HIGH HILL, p. o., Muskingum co., O.

HIGHLAND COUNTY, situated in the central part of Virginia. Area, —— square miles. Face of the country mountainous. Seat of justice, Monterey. Pop. in 1850, 4,227.

HIGHLAND COUNTY, situated in the southern part of Ohio. Area, 555 square miles. Face of the country an elevated, moderately undulated table-land; soil fertile. Seat of justice, Hillsborough. Pop. in 1810, 5,766; in 1820, 12,308; in 1830, 16,347; in 1840, 22,269; in 1850, 25,781.

HIGHLAND COUNTY, Illinois. Area, —— square miles. Seat of justice, Elm Grove. Pop. in 1850, ——.

HIGHLAND, p. o., Bradford co., Pa., 139 ms. N. of Harrisburgh; from W. 249 ms.

HIGHLAND, p. v., Jackson co., Tenn., 69 ms. N. E. of Nashville; from W. 638 ms. Watered by Cumberland river.

HIGHLAND, p. v., Fairfield township, Highland co., O., 50 ms. s. w. of Columbus; from W. —— ms. Watered by Lee's creek.

HIGHLAND, p. t., Muskingum co., O., 72 ms. E. of Columbus; from W. 349 ms. Pop. 556.

HIGHLAND, p. t., Oakland co., Mich., 45 ms. N. w. of Detroit; from W. 569 ms. Pop. 851.

HIGHLAND, p. o., Vermilion co., Ind., 72 ms. w. of Indianapolis; from W. 644 ms.

HIGHLAND, p. o., Tishemingo co., Miss.

HIGHLAND, p. o., Madison co., Ill.

HIGHLAND, p. o., Shelby co., Ala.

HIGHLAND, p. o., Ritchie co. Va

HIGHLAND, p. o., Bath co., Ky.

HIGHLAND, p. o., Iowa co., Wis.

HIGHLAND, p. o., Jackson co., Mo.

HIGHLAND GROVE, p. o., Greenville district, S. C.

HIGHLAND GROVE, p. o., Harford co., Md.

HIGHLAND MILLS, p. v., Monroe township, Orange co., N. Y., 97 ms. s. of Albany; from W. 281 ms.

HIGHLAND MILLS, p. o., Morgan co., Va.

HIGHLAND PRAIRIE, p. o., McHenry co., Ill.

HIGH MARKET, p. o., Lewis co., N. Y.

HIGH PINE, p. o., Randolph co., Ala.

HIGH POINT, p. o., Mercer co., Ill.

HIGH POINT, p. o., Cole co., Mo.

HIGH RIDGE, p. o., Fairfield co., Ct.

HIGH SCHOOL, p. o., Jackson co., Miss.

HIGH SHOALS, p. v., Morgan co., Ga., 70 ms. N. w. of Milledgeville; from W. 624 ms. Situated near High Shoals Rapids, Appalachee river.

HIGH SHOALS, p. o., Rutherford co., N. C., 214 ms. s. w. of Raleigh; from W 451 ms.

HIGH SPIRE, p. o., Dauphin co., Pa., 6 ms. from Harrisburgh; from W. 116 ms.

HIGH TOWER, p. o., Forsyth co., Ga., 119 ms. N. w. of Milledgeville; from W. 650 ms.

HIGH TOWERS, p. o., Caswell co., N. C., 72 ms. N. w. of Raleigh; from W. 268 ms.

HIGHTSTOWN, p. v., East Windsor township, Mercer co., N. J., 19 ms. E. of Trenton; from W. 185 ms.

HIGH VIEW, p. o., Frederick co., Va.

HIGHVILLE, p. o., Lancaster co., Pa.

HIGHWAY, p. o., Greenville district, S. C.

HILBOURNE, t., Madison co., Ark.

HILHAM, p. o., Overton co., Tenn., 88 ms. E. of Nashville; from W. 616 ms.

HILL, p. t., Grafton co., N. H., 24 ms. N. w. of Concord; from W. 499 ms. Watered by Smith's and Pemigewasset rivers. Pop. 954.

HILLABEE, p. o., Talladega co., Ala; from W. 781 ms.

HILLEGASS, p. o., Montgomery co., Pa., 81 ms. E. of Harrisburgh; from W. 174 ms.

HILLERMAN, p. o., Massac co., Ill.

HILL GORE, t., Washington co., Me.

HILL GROVE, p. o., Darke co., O., 100 ms. w. of Columbus; from W. 494 ms.

HILL GROVE, p. o., Pittsylvania co., Va.

HILLHOUSE, p. o., Le Roy township, Lake co., O., 185 ms. N. E. of Columbus; from W. 344 ms.

HILLIAN'S STORE, p. o., Marshall co., Ala.

HILLIAR, t., Knox co., O., 34 ms. N. E. of Columbus; from W. 387 ms. Pop. 1,141.

HILLIARD'S, p. o., Shelby co., Tex.

HILLIARD-TON, p. o., Nash co., N. C., 59 ms. N. E. of Raleigh; from W. 239 ms.

HILLIARDSVILLE, p. o., Henry co., Ala.

HILLSBOROUGH COUNTY, situated on the southern boundary of New Hampshire, and traversed by Merrimack river. Area, 1,245 square miles. Face of the country mountainous and hilly; soil generally fertile. Seat of justice, Amherst. Pop. in 1810, 49,249; in 1820, 35,761; in 1830, 37,762; in 1840, 42,494; in 1850. 57,378.

HILLSBOROUGH COUNTY, situated on the western coast of Florida, with the gulf of Mexico, Tampa bay, and Charlotte harbor, on the west. Area, —— square miles. Seat of justice, Fort Brooke. Pop. in 1840, 452; in 1850, 2,377.

HILLSBOROUGH, p. t., Hillsborough co., N. H., 24 ms. s. w. of Concord; from W. 464 ms. Watered by Contoocook and Hillsborough rivers. Pop. 1,685.

HILLSBOROUGH, t., Somerset co., N. J., 25 ms. N. E. of Trenton; from W. 191 ms. Watered by the south branch of Raritan river and Millstone river. Pop. 3,404.

HILLSBOROUGH, p. v., Bethlehem township, Washington co., Pa., 203 ms. w. of Harrisburgh; from W. 219 ms. Watered by Ohio river.

HILLSBOROUGH, p. v., Caroline co., Md., 59 ms. E. of Annapolis; from W. 99 ms. Watered by Tuckahoe creek.

HILLSBOROUGH, p. v., Loudoun co., Va., 166 ms. N. of Richmond; from W. 47 ms.

HILLSBOROUGH, c. h., p. v., seat of justice of Orange co., N. C., 40 ms. N. w. of Raleigh; from W. 274 ms. Watered by Eno river.

HILLSBOROUGH, p. v., Jasper co., Ga., 28 ms. N. w. of Milledgeville; from W. 651 ms.

HILLSBOROUGH, p. v., Lawrence co., Ala.

HILLSBOROUGH, c. h., p. v., seat of justice of Scott co., Miss., 48 ms. E. of Jackson; from W. 968 ms. Watered by a branch of Pearl river. Pop 630.

HILLSBOROUGH, p. v., Coffee co., Tenn., 76 ms. s. E. of Nashville; from W. 616 ms.

HILLSBOROUGH, p. v., Fleming co., Ky., 91 ms. E. of Frankfort; from W. 498 ms.

HILLSBOROUGH, c. h., p. v., seat of justice of Highland co., O., 75 ms. s.w. of Columbus; from W. 442 ms. Watered by Rocky fork of Paint creek.

HILLSBOROUGH, p. v., Fountain co., Ind., 61 ms. N. w. of Indianapolis; from W. 639 ms.

HILLSBOROUGH, c. h., p. v., seat of justice of Montgomery co., Ill., 64 ms. s. of Springfield; from W 768 ms.

HILLSBOROUGH, c. h., p. v., seat of justice of Jefferson co., Mo., 132 ms. E. of Jefferson city; from W 852 ms Watered by Big river.

HILLSBOROUGH, p. o., Oneida co., N. Y.

HILLSBOROUGH, p. o., Union co., Ark.

HILLSBOROUGH, p. o., Henry co. Iowa.

HILLSBOROUGH, p. o., Washington co., Oregon.

HILLSBOROUGH BRIDGE, p. v., Hillsborough co., N. H., 21 ms. s. w. of Concord; from W. 461 ms.

HILLSBOROUGH CENTRE, p. v., Hillsborough co., N. H., 21 ms. s. w. of Concord; from W. 464 ms.

HILL'S CORNERS, p. o., Penobscot co., Me.

HILLSDALE COUNTY, situated on the southern boundary of Michigan. Area, 576 square miles. Soil rich. Seat of justice, Hillsdale. Pop. in 1840, 7,240; in 1850, 16,159.

HILLSDALE, p. t., Columbia co., N. Y., 45 ms. s. of Albany; from W. 357 ms. Watered by Ancram and Copakake creeks. Pop. 2,123.

HILLSDALE, p. o., Guilford co., N. C., 95 ms. N. w. of Raleigh; from W. 290 ms.

HILLSDALE, p. v., Fayette township, Hillsdale co., Mich., 98 ms. s. w. of Detroit; from W. 534 ms. Watered by St. Joseph or Baubese outlet.

HILL'S GROVE, p. o., Sullivan co., Pa., 100 ms. N. E. of Harrisburgh; from W. 211 ms.

HILL'S GROVE, p. o., McDonough co., Ill., 98 ms. N. w. of Springfield; from W. 871 ms.

HILL SIDE, p. o., Oneida co., N. Y.

HILL'S STORE, p. o., Randolph co., N. C., 84 ms. w. of Raleigh; from W. 390 ms.

HILL'S VALLEY, p. o., Williamson co., Tenn.

HILLSVIEW, p. o., Westmoreland co., Pa., 154 ms. w. of Harrisburgh; from W. 180 ms.

HILLSVILLE, p. o., Carroll co., Va., 245 ms. s. w. of Richmond; from W. 320 ms.

HILLSVILLE, p. v., Lawrence co., Pa., 245 ms. w. of Harrisburgh; from W. 283 ms.

HILL TOP, p. o., Wayne co., Pa., 181 ms. N. E. of Harrisburgh; from W. 278 ms.

HILLTOWN, p. t., Bucks co., Pa., 100 ms. E. of Harris-

burgh; from W. 169 ms. Watered by tributaries of Neshaminy creek. Pop. 2,101.

HILOCHEE, p. o., Washington co., Ark.

HILTON, p. o., Monroe co., Ky.

HILTON'S, p. o., Sullivan co., Tenn.

HINCKLEY. p., Medina co., O., 132 ms. N. E. of Columbus; from W. 352 ms. Watered by a tributary of Rocky river.

HINDMAN'S HILL, p. o., Coffee co., Tenn.

HINDS COUNTY, situated toward the westerly part of Mississippi, with Pearl river on the east, and Big Black river on the west. Area, 875 square miles. Seat of justice, Raymond. Pop. in 1830, 8,645; in 1840, 19,098; in 1850, 25,340.

HIND'S, p. o., Brazoria co., Tex.

HINDSBURGH, p. o., Murray township, Orleans co., N. Y., 245 ms. N. w. of Albany; from W. 394 ms.

HINESBURGH, p. t., Chittenden co., Vt., 42 ms. w. of Montpelier; from W. 506 ms. Watered by Platte river and Lewis creek. Pop. 1,834.

HINES' MILLS, p. o., Ohio co., Ky.

HINESTON, p. o., Rapides parish, La.

HINESVILLE, c. h.. p. v., seat of justice of Liberty co., Ga., 196 ms. s. E. of Milledgeville; from W. 700 ms.

HINGHAM, p. t., Plymouth co., Mass., 15 ms. s. E. of Boston; from W. 455 ms. Watered by Boston bay. Pop. 3,980.

HINGHAM, p. o., Sheboygan co., Wis.

HINKLETOWN, p. v., Lancaster co., Pa., 42 ms. s. E. of Harrisburgh; from W. 130 ms. Watered by Conestoga creek.

HINMANSVILLE, p. v., Oswego co., N. Y.

HINSDALE, p. t., Cheshire co., N. H., 71 ms. from Concord; from W. 419 ms. Watered by Ashuelot and Connecticut rivers. Pop. 1,903.

HINSDALE, p. t., Berkshire co., Mass., 121 ms. w. of Boston; from W. 385 ms. Pop. 1,253.

HINSDALE, p. t., Cattaraugus co., N. Y., 287 ms. s. w. of Albany; from W. 313 ms. Situated on the Genesee valley canal. Pop. 1,302.

HINTON'S GROVE, p. o., Pickens co., Ala.

HIRAM, p. t., Oxford co., Me., 79 ms. s. w. of Augusta; from W. 555 ms. Watered by Saco river. Pop. 863.

HIRAM, p. t., Portage co., O., 154 ms. N. E. of Columbus; from W. 323 ms. Pop. 1,106.

HIRAMSBURGH, p. o., Morgan co., O., 99 ms. s. E. of Columbus; from W. 308 ms.

HITCHCOCKVILLE. p. v., Bark Hamsead township, Litchfield co. Ct 26 ms N w of Hartford; from W. 350 ms. Watered by Farmington river.

HITESVILLE, p. v., Coles co., Ill., 105 ms. s. E. of Springfield. from W. 681 ms. Pop. 909.

HIX's FERRY, p. v., Randolph co., Ark., 170 ms. N. E. of Little Rock; from W. 967 ms. Watered by Currant river.

HIZERVILLE, p. o., Oneida co., N. Y.

HOADLIN, t., Van Wert co., O. Pop. 125.

HOAG's CORNERS, p. o., Nassau township, Rennselaer co., N. Y., 22 ms. E. of Albany; from W. 378 ms.

HOBART, p. o., Stamford township, Delaware co., N. Y., 65 ms. s. w. of Albany; from W. 353 ms. Watered by branches of Delaware river.

HOBART, p. o., Lake co., Ind.

HOBBIEVILLE, p. o., Greene co., Ind., 88 ms. s. w. of Indianapolis; from W. 638 ms.

HOBBYVILLE, p. o., Spartanburgh district, S. C.

HOBOKEN, p. v., Bergen township, Hudson co., N. J., 60 ms. N. E. of Trenton; from W. 226 ms. Watered by Hudson river. Pop. 2,668.

HOCKANUM, p. o., Hartford co., Ct.

HOCKING COUNTY, situated toward the southern part of Ohio, and traversed by Hocking river. Area, 432 square miles. Face of the country hilly and broken; soil in many parts fertile. Seat of justice, Logan. Pop. in 1820, 2,130; in 1830, 4,008; in 1840, 9,741; in 1850, 14,119.

HOCKING PORT, p. v., Athens co., O., 104 ms. s. E. of Columbus; from W 393 ms.

HODGEDON, p. t., Aroostook co., Me., 202 ms. N. E. of Augusta; from W. 797 ms. Pop. 862.

HODGEDON'S MILLS, p. o., Lincoln co., Me., 43 ms. s. of Augusta; from W. 604 ms.

HODGENSVILLE, p. v., La Rue co., Ky., 89 ms. s. w. of Frankfort; from W. 631 ms.

HODGE'S BEND, p. o., Fort Bend co., Tex.

HOFFMAN'S FERRY, p. o., Glenville township, Schenectady co., N. Y., 26 ms. N. w. of Albany; from W 394 ms.

HOFFMAN'S GATE, p. o., Claverack township, Columbia co., N. Y., 41 ms. s. of Albany; from W. 353 ms.

HOGANSBURGH, p. v.. Bombay township, Franklin co., N. Y., 234 ms. N. of Albany; from W. 538 ms. Watered by St. Regis river.

HOGANSVILLE, p. o., Dubuque co., Iowa.

HOGANSVILLE, p. o., Troup co., Ga.

HOG CREEK, p. o., Allen co., O.

HOGESTOWN, p. v., Cumberland co., Pa., 9 ms. s. w. of Harrisburgh; from W. 108 ms.

HOGLE'S CREEK, p. o., St. Clair co., Mo.

HOG MOUNTAIN, p. o., Hall co., Ga.

HOHENLINDEN, p. o., Chickasaw co., Miss.

HOLCOMB, p. o., Burke co., Ga., 58 ms. s. E. of Milledgeville; from W. 647 ms.

HOLDEN, p. t., Worcester co., Mass., 48 ms. w. of Boston; from W. 405 ms. Watered by tributaries of Blackstone and Nashua rivers.

HOLDERMAN'S GROVE, p. o., Kendall co., Ill.

HOLDERNESS, p. t., Grafton co., N. H., 38 ms. N. of Concord; from W. 519 ms. Watered by Squam lake and Pemigewasset river. Pop. 1,744.

HOLLAND, p. v., Hampden co., Mass., 67 ms. s. w. of Boston; from W. 373 ms. Watered by Quinnebaug river. Pop. 449.

HOLLAND, p. t., Erie co., N. Y., 284 ms. w. of Albany; from W. 351 ms. Watered by Seneca and Cazenove creeks. Pop. 1 315.

HOLLAND, p. t., Orleans co., Vt., 56 ms. N. E. of Montpelier; from W. 578 ms. Pop. 669.

HOLLAND, p. o., Venango co., Pa., 220 ms. N. w. of Harrisburgh; from W. 309 ms.

HOLLAND, p. o., Ottawa co., Mich.

HOLLAND PATENT, p. v., Trenton township. Oneida co., N. Y., 100 ms. N. w. of Albany; from W. 402 ms,

HOLLAND'S, p. o., Laurens district, S. C., 61 ms. N. w. of Columbia; from W. 505 ms.

HOLLEY, p. v., Murray township, Orleans co. N. Y., 240 ms. N. w. of Albany; from W. 389 ms. Watered by Sandy creek and Erie canal.

HOLLIDAYSBURGH, p. b., Frankstown township, Blair co., Pa., 118 ms. N. w. of Harrisburgh; from W. 161 ms. Watered by Beaver Dam creek. Pop. 2,430.

HOLLIDAY'S COVE, p. o., Hancock co., Va., 354 ms. N. w. of Richmond; from W. 265 ms.

HOLLIDAYSVILLE, p. o., Dooly co., Ga.

HOLLINGSWORTH, p. b., Habersham co., Ga., 132 ms. N. of Milledgeville; from W. 613 ms.

HOLLIS, p. t., York co., Me., 66 ms. s. w. of Augusta; from W. 531 ms. Watered by Saco river. Pop. 2,683.

HOLLIS, p. t., Hillsborough co., N. H., 44 ms. s. of Concord; from W. 439 ms. Watered by Nashua river. Pop. 1,293.

HOLLIS, p. o., Peoria co., Ill.

HOLLIS CENTRE, p. o., Hollis township, York co., Me.

HOLLISTER'S MILLS, p. o., Holt co., Mo.

HOLLISTON, p. t., Middlesex co., Mass., 24 ms. s. w. of Boston; from W. 415 ms. Watered by a branch of Charles river. Pop. 2,428.

HOLLOW CREEK, p. o., Lexington district, S. C., 26 ms. w. of Columbia; from W. 532 ms.

HOLLOW SQUARE, p. o., Greene co., Ala.

HOLLY, t., Oakland co., Mich. Pop. 941.

HOLLY CREEK, p. o., Murray co., Ga.

HOLLY GROVE, p. o., Walker co., Ala.

HOLLY GROVE, p. o., Stewart co., Ga.

HOLLY HILL, p. o., Charleston district, S. C.

HOLLY MILLS, p. o., Oakland co., Mich.

HOLLY POINT, p. o., Drew co., Ark.

HOLLY RETREAT, p. o., Wilkinson co., Miss.

HOLLY SPRING, p. v., Wake co., N. C., 16 ms. from Raleigh; from W. 304 ms.

HOLLY SPRING, p. o., Dallas co., Ark.

HOLLY SPRINGS, c. h., p. v., seat of justice of Marshall co., Miss., 193 ms. N. of Jackson; from W. 893 ms.

HOLMDEL, p. v., Middletown township, Monmouth co., N. J., 45 ms. E. of Trenton; from W. 211 ms.

HOLMES COUNTY, situated toward the northeastern part of Ohio. Area, 422 square miles. Soil, generally productive. Seat of justice, Millersburgh. Pop. in 1830, 9,133; in 1840, 18,088; in 1850, 20,452.

HOLMES COUNTY, situated toward the western part of Mississippi, with Big Black river on the east, and the Yazoo on the west. Area, 600 square miles. Seat of justice, Lexington. Pop. in 1840, 9,452; in 1850, 13,928.

HOLMES COUNTY, situated on the northern boundary of Florida, and traversed by Choctawhatchee river. Area, —— square miles. Seat of justice, Cerro Gordo Pop. in 1850, 1,644.

HOLMES, t., Crawford co., O., 74 ms. N. of Columbus; from W. 414 ms. Pop. 1,238.

HOLMES' BAY, p. o., Washington co., Me.

HOLMES, p. v., Lower Dublin township, Philadelphia co., Pa., 107 ms. E. of Harrisburgh; from W. 147 ms. Watered by Pennypack creek.

HOLMES' HOLE, p. v., Tisbury township, Dukes co., Martha's Vineyard, Mass., 89 ms. s. E. of Boston; from W. 471 ms. Watered by Vineyard sound.

HOLMES VALLEY, p. o., Washington co., Flor.

HOLMESVILLE, p. v., Holmes co., O., 93 ms. N. E. of Columbus; from W. 349 ms.

HOLMESVILLE, c. h., p. v., seat of justice of Appling co., Ga., 177 ms. s. E. of Milledgeville; from W. 788 ms.

HOLMESVILLE. c. h., p. v., seat of justice of Pike co., Miss., 87 ms. s. of Jackson; from W. 1,095 ms. Watered by Bogue Chitto river.

HOLMESVILLE, p. v., Avoyelles parish, La.

HOLSTON, p. o., Washington co., Va., 312 ms. s. w. of Richmond; from W. 380 ms.

HOLSTON VALLEY, p. o., Sullivan co., Tenn.

HOLT COUNTY, situated on the westerly boundary of Missouri, with Missouri river on the southwest. Area, —— square miles. Seat of justice, Oregon. Pop. in 1850, 3,957.

HOLT'S STORE, p. o., Orange co., N. C., 64 ms. N. w. of Raleigh; from W. 307 ms.

HOLY NECK, p. o., Nansemond co., Va.

HOLYOKE, p. o., Hampden co., Mass.

HOMASASSA, p. o., Benton co., Flor.

HOME, p. o., Indiana co., Pa., 165 ms. N. w. of Harrisburgh; from W. 218 ms.

HOME, p. v., Jefferson co., Ind., 98 ms. s. E. of Indianapolis; from W. 550 ms.

HOME, p. v., Van Buren co., Iowa.

HOME CITY, p. o., Hamilton co., O.

HOMER, p. t., Cortland co., N. Y., 141 ms. w. of Albany; from W. 317 ms. Watered by Toughnioga creek, and tributaries. Pop. 3,816.

HOMER, t., Medina co., O. Pop. 1,102.

HOMER, p. v., Burlington township, Licking co., O., 46 ms. N. E. of Columbus; from W. 385 ms. Watered by north fork of Licking river.

HOMER, t., Athens co., O., 80 ms. s. E. of Columbus; from W. 342 ms. Watered by Federal creek.

HOMER, p. o., Champaign co., Ill.

HOMER, p. t., Colhoun co., Mich. Pop. 929.

HOMER, p. o., Potter co., Pa.

HOMER, c. h., p. v., seat of justice of Claiborne parish, La.

HOMERVILLE, p. v., Homer township, Medina co., O.

HOME SPRING, p. o., Holmes co., Flor.

HOMEWOOD, p. o., Scott co., Miss.

HOMMONY CREEK, p. o., Buncombe co., N. C.

HOMOCHITTO, p. o., Franklin co., Miss.

HONEOYE, p. v., Richmond township, Ontario co., N. Y., 214 ms. w. of Albany; from W. 338 ms. Watered by Honeoye lake.

HONEOYE FALLS, p. v., Mendon township, Monroe co., N. Y., 214 ms. w. of Albany; from W. 360 ms. Watered by Honeoye creek.

HONESDALE, p. b., Texas township, Wayne co., Pa., 172 ms. N. E. of Harrisburgh; from W. 269 ms. Watered by Dyberry and Lackawaxen creeks. Pop. 2,263.

HONEY BROOK, p. t., Chester co., Pa., 55 ms. E. of Harrisburgh; from W. 133 ms. Watered by branches of Brandywine river. Pop. 1,937.

HONEY CREEK, p. o., McDonald co., Mo.

HONEY CREEK, p. o., Walworth co., Wis.

HONEY CUT, p. o., Baldwin co., Ala.

HONEY GROVE, p. o., Fannin co., Tex.

HONEY POINT, p. o., Macoupin co., Ill.

HONEY TOWN, p. o., Dale co., Ala.

HONEYVILLE, p. v., Page co., Va., 125 ms. N. w. of Richmond; from W. 108 ms. Watered by Shenandoah river.

HOOD'S MILLS, p. o., Carroll co., Md., 56 ms. N. w. of Annapolis; from W. 61 ms.

HOODSVILLE, p. o., Marion co., Va.

HOOKERSTOWN, p. o., Greene co., N. C., 94 ms. E. of Raleigh; from W. 304 ms.

HOOKER, p. o., Hunt co., Tex.

HOOKSETT, p. t., Merrimack co., N. H., 9 ms. s. E. of

Concord; from W. 472 ms. Watered by Merrimack river. Pop. 1,503.

HOOKSTOWN, p. v., Greene township, Beaver co., Pa., 242 ms. w. of Harrisburgh; from W. 264 ms. Watered by a branch of Mill creek.

HOOKSTOWN, p. o., Baltimore co., Md.

HOOSICK, p. t., Rensselaer co., N. Y., 32 ms. N. E. of Albany; from W. 400 ms. Watered by Hoosick river. Pop. 3,724.

HOOSICK, p. o., Greene co., Wis.

HOOSICK FALLS, p. v., Hoosick township, Rensselaer co., N. Y., 35 ms. N. E. of Albany; from W. 403 ms. Watered by Hoosick river.

HOOSIER GROVE, p. o., Linn co., Iowa.

HOOSIER GROVE, p. o., Greene co., Wis.

HOOTENSVILLE, p. o., Upson co., Ga., 71 ms. w. of Milledgeville; from W. 727 ms. Watered by Flint river.

HOOVER HILL, p. o., Randolph co., N. C.

HOOVER'S POINT, p. o., Macoupin co., Ill.

HOPAHKA, p. o., Leake co., Miss., 55 ms. N. E. of Jackson; from W. 955 ms.

HOPE, p. t., Waldo co., Me., 36 ms. s. E. of Augusta; from W. 623 ms. Watered by St. George's river. Pop. 1,108.

HOPE, p, t., Hamilton co., N. Y., 58 ms. N. w. of Albany; from W. 427 ms. Watered by Sacandaga river. Pop. 789.

HOPE, p. t., Warren co., N. J., 66 ms. N. of Trenton; from W. 221 ms. Watered by a branch of Beaver brook. Pop. 1,755.

HOPE, p. o., Franklin co., O., 24 ms. N. of Columbus; from W. 395 ms.

HOPE, p. o., Pickens co., Ala.; from W. 873 ms.

HOPE, p. o., Bartholomew co., Ind., 55 ms. s. E. of Indianapolis; from W. 575 ms.

HOPE, p. o., Stewart co., Tenn.

HOPE CENTRE, p. o., Hope township, Hamilton co., N. Y., 63 ms. N. w. of Albany; from W. 432 ms.

HOPEDALE, p. o., Harrison co., O.

HOPE FALLS, p. o., Hamilton co., N. Y.

HOPE FARM, p. o., Louisa co., Iowa.

HOPE HILL, p. o., Pike co., Miss.

HOPE HILL, p. o., Gibson co., Tenn.

HOPE MILL, p. o., Maury co., Tenn.

HOPE MILLS, p. o., Page co., Va., 134 ms. N. w. of Richmond; from W. 100 ms.

HOPE STATION, p. o., Lexington district, S. C.

HOPEWELL, p. o., Mahaska co., Iowa.

HOPEWELL, p. t., Ontario co., N. Y., 187 ms. w. of Albany; from W. 349 ms. Watered by Canandaigua lake outlet. Pop. 1,923.

HOPEWELL, p. t., Mercer co., N. J., 17 ms. N. of Trenton; from W. 183 ms. Pop. 3,696.

HOPEWELL, t., Cumberland co., N. J., 66 ms. s. of Trenton; from W. 173 ms. Watered by Cohansey, Mount's, and Mill creeks. Pop. 1,480.

HOPEWELL, p. t., Huntingdon co., Pa., 94 ms. w. of Harrisburgh; from W. 133 ms. Pop. 788.

HOPEWELL, p. t., Beaver co., Pa., 217 ms. w. of Harrisburgh; from W. 239 ms. Pop. 1,025.

HOPEWELL, p. t., York co., Pa., 36 ms. s. E. of Harrisburgh; from W. 73 ms. Watered by sources of Deer creek. Pop. 3,432.

HOPEWELL, p. t., Washington co., Pa., 225 ms. w. of Harrisburgh; from W. 243 ms. Pop. 1,748.

HOPEWELL, p. t., Bedford co., Pa., 104 ms. w. of Harrisburgh; from W. 130 ms. Watered by Raystown branch of Juniata river. Pop. 840.

HOPEWELL, t., Cumberland co., Pa., 38 ms. w. of Harrisburgh; from W. 107 ms. Pop. 1,053.

HOPEWELL, p. v., Mecklenburgh co., N. C., 170 ms. s. w. of Raleigh; from W. 410 ms.

HOPEWELL, p. v., York district, S. C., 92 ms. N. of Columbia; from W. 443 ms.

HOPEWELL, p. o., Crawford co., Ga., 60 ms. s. w. of Milledgeville; from W. 716 ms.

HOPEWELL, p. t., Muskingum co., O., 40 ms. N. E. of Columbus; from W. 347 ms. Pop. 2,378.

HOPEWELL, t., Licking co., O., 46 ms. E. of Columbus; from W. 349 ms. Pop. 1,227.

HOPEWELL, t., Perry co., O., 44 ms. s. E. of Columbus; from W. 356 ms. Watered by Jonathan's creek.

HOPEWELL, t., Seneca co., O., 87 ms. N. of Columbus; from W. 434 ms. Watered by Sandusky river.

HOPEWELL, p. o., Greene co., Ala.; from W. 871 ms.

HOPEWELL, p. o., Chickasaw co., Miss.

HOPEWELL, p. o., Macon co., Ill.

HOPEWELL, p. o., Jennings co., Ind.

HOPEWELL, p. o., Upshur co., Tex.

HOPEWELL CENTRE, p. o., York co., Pa.

HOPEWELL COTTON WORKS, p. o., Chester co., Pa., 67 ms. s. E. of Harrisburgh; from W. 96 ms.

HOPEWELL CROSS-ROADS, p. o., Harford co., Md.

HOPKINS COUNTY, situated in the westerly part of Kentucky, with Green river on the northeast. Area, 750 square miles. Seat of justice, Madisonville. Pop. in 1810, 2,964; in 1820, 5,322; in 1830, 6,763; in 1840, 9,171; in 1850, 12.441.

HOPKINS COUNTY, situated in the northern part of Texas. Area, —— square miles. Seat of justice, Tarrant. Pop. in 1850, 2,623.

HOPKINS' GROVE, p. o., Polk co., Iowa.

HOPKINS' TURNOUT, p. o., Richland district, S. C.

HOPKINSVILLE, p. t., Hamilton township, Warren co., O., 96 ms. s. w. of Columbus; from W. 469 ms.

HOPKINSVILLE, c. h., p. v., seat of justice of Christian co., Ky., 204 ms. s. w. of Frankfort; from W. 731 ms. Watered by Little river.

HOPKINSVILLE, c. h., v., seat of justice of Adair co., Mo.

HOPKINTON, p. t., Merrimack co., N. H., 7 ms. w. of Concord; from W. 475 ms. Watered by Contoocook Warner, and Blackwater rivers. Pop. 2,169.

HOPKINTON, p. t., Middlesex co., Mass., 29 ms. s. w. of Boston; from W. 416 ms. Watered by tributaries of Charles and Mill rivers. Pop. 2,189.

HOPKINTON, p. t., Washington co., R. I., 34 ms. s. w. of Providence; from W. 374 ms. Watered by Wood and Pawcatuck rivers. Pop. 2,477.

HOPKINTON, p. t., St. Lawrence co., N. Y., 215 ms. N. w. of Albany; from W. 512 ms. Watered by Racket and St. Regis rivers. Pop. 1,476.

HOPPER'S MILLS, p. o., Henderson co., Ill., 116 ms. N. w. of Springfield; from W. 862 ms.

HORACE, t., Tioga co., Pa.

HORICON, p. t., Warren co., N. Y., 90 ms. N. of Albany; from W. 460 ms. Watered by Brant and Schroon lakes, and Hudson river. Pop. 1,152.

HORICON, p. o., Dodge co., Wis.

HORNBROOK, p. o., Bradford co., Pa., 141 ms. N. of Harrisburgh; from W. 254 ms.

HORNBY, p. t., Steuben co., N. Y., 205 ms. w. of Albany; from W. 294 ms. Watered by Mead's creek. Pop. 1,314.

HORNELLSVILLE, p. t., Steuben co., N. Y., 241 ms. w. of Albany; from W. 316 ms. Watered by Canisteo river. Pop. 2,637.

HORNERSTOWN, p. o., Ocean co., N. J.

HORNET'S NEST, p. o., Mecklenburgh co., N. C.

HORNSBOROUGH, p. o., Chesterfield district, S C.

HORNTOWN, p. v., Accomac co., Va., 219 ms. E. of Richmond; from W. 171 ms.

HORSE BRANCH, p. o., Tuolumne co., Cal.

HORRY DISTRICT, situated on the northeastern boundary of South Carolina, with the Atlantic on the southeast, and Little Pedee river on the west. Area, 1,000 square miles. Face of the country, level; soil, sterile. Seat of justice, Conwayborough. Pop. in 1810, 4,349; in 1820, 5,025; in 1830, 5,323; in 1840, 5,755; in 1850, 7,646.

HORSE CREEK, p. o., Lexington district, S. C.

HORSE CREEK, p. o., Greene co., Tenn.

HORSE CREEK, p. o., Will co., Ill.

HORSE CREEK, p. o., Rutherford co., N. C.

HORSE HEAD, p. o., Prince George's co., Md., 45 ms. s. w. of Annapolis; from W. 39 ms.

HORSE HEAD, p. o., Johnson co., Ark., 109 ms. N. w. of Little Rock; from W. 1,174 ms.

HORSE HEAD, p. o., Macon co., Ga.

HORSE PASTURE, p. o., Henry co., Va., 205 ms. s. w. of Richmond; from W. 280 ms.

HORSE PEN, p. o., Choctaw co., Miss.

HORSE SHOE, p. o., Pickens district, S. C., 164 ms. N. w. of Columbia; from W. 566 ms.

HORSESHOE BEND, p. o., Tallapoosa co., Ala.; from W. 784 ms.

HORSESHOE BOTTOM, p. o., Russell co., Ky., 103 ms. s. of Frankfort; from W. 617 ms. Watered by Cumberland river.

HORSEY'S CROSS-ROADS, p. o., Sussex co., Del., 43 ms. s. of Dover; from W. 110 ms.

HORSEHAM, p. o., Montgomery co., Pa.

HORTONVILLE, p. o., Brown co., Wis.

HOSENSACK, p. o., Lehigh co., Pa.

HOSKINVILLE, p. v., Brookfield township, Morgan co., O., 90 ms. E. of Columbus ; from W. 318 ms.

HOTCHKISSVILLE, p. o., Litchfield co., Ct.

HOTEL, p. o.. Bertie co., N. C., 141 ms. E. of Raleigh ; from W. 200 ms.

HOT HOUSE. p. o.. Gilmer co., Ga.

HOT SPRINGS COUNTY, situated near the central part of Arkansas, with Saline river on the east, and traversed by Wachita river. Area, 1,980 square miles. Seat of justice, Hot Springs. Pop. in 1830, 6,116 ; in 1840, 1.907 ; in 1850, 3,609.

HOT SPRINGS, p. o., Bath co., Va., 169 ms. N. w. of Richmond ; from W. — ms.

HOT SPRINGS, p. v., seat of justice of Hot Springs co., Ark., 53 ms. w. of Little Rock ; from W. 1,118 ms.

HOUCK'S STORE, p. o., Carroll co., Md.

HOUGH'S STORE, p. o., Jasper co., Miss.

HOUGHTON COUNTY, situated in the northwestern part of Michigan on Lake Superior. Seat of justice, Eagle Harbor. Pop. in 1850, 708.

HOUGHTON, p. o., Houghton co., Mich.

HOUGHTONVILLE, p. o., Windham co., Vt., 109 ms. s. of Montpelier ; from W. 457 ms.

HOULKA, p. o., Chickasaw co., Miss.

HOULTON, c. h., p. t., seat of justice of Aroostook co., Me., 196 ms. N. of Augusta ; from W. 791 ms. Watered by Meduxnekeag river. Pop, 1,453.

HOUMA, c. h., p. v., seat of justice of Terre Bonne parish, La., 132 ms. s. w. of New Orleans ; from W. 1,294 ms. Watered by Bayou Terre Bonne.

HOUNDSFIELD, t. Jefferson co., N. Y., 161 ms. N. w. of Albany ; from W. 207 ms. Watered by Black river, and Black River and Hungry bays. Pop. 4,136.

HOUSATONIC, p. o., Berkshire co., Mass.

HOUSE CREEK, p. o., Irwin co., Ga., 104 ms. s. of Milledgeville ; from W. 751 ms.

HOUSE'S SPRINGS, p. o., Jefferson co., Mo., 125 ms. E. of Jefferson city ; from W. 838 ms.

HOUSEVILLE, p. o., Turin township, Lewis co., N. Y., 130 ms. N. w. of Albany ; from W. 429 ms.

HOUSTON COUNTY, situated toward the southern part of Georgia, with Ocmulgee river on the northeast. Area, 510 square miles. Seat of justice, Perry. Pop. in 1830, 7,369 ; in 1840. 9,711 ; in 1850, 16,450.

HOUSTON COUNTY, situated toward the eastern part of Texas, with Trinity river on the southwest, and the Neches on the northeast. Seat of justice, Crockett. Pop. in 1850, 2,721.

HOUSTON, p. o., Heard co., Ga.

HOUSTON, p. o., Jackson co., Ind.

HOUSTON, p. o., Adams co., Ill., 100 ms. w. of Springfield ; from W. 877 ms.

HOUSTON, t., Clearfield co., Pa. Pop. 230.

HOUSTON, p. o. on Alleghany co., Pa., 211 ms. w. of Harrisburgh ; from W. 237 ms.

HOUSTON, p. o., Shelby co., O., 82 ms. N. w. of Columbus ; from W. 476 ms.

HOUSTON. p. v., Wayne co., Tenn., 111 ms. s. w. of Nashville ; from W. 788 ms.

HOUSTON, p. o., Marion co., Mo.

HOUSTON, c. h., p, v., seat of justice of Chickasaw co., Miss., 145 ms. N. E. of Jackson ; from W. 910 ms. Watered by source of Oktibbeha creek.

HOUSTON, p. o., Harris co., Tex.

HOUSTON, c. h., p. v., seat of justice of Texas co., Mo.

HOUSTON, p. o., Bourbon co., Ky.

HOUSTON'S STORE, p. o., Morgan co., Ala. ; from W. 754 ms.

HOUSTONVILLE, p. o., Iredell co., N. C., 154 ms. w. of Raleigh ; from W. 365 ms.

HOWARD COUNTY, situated toward the northern part of Missouri, with Missouri river on the south and west. Area, 398 square miles. Soil fertile. Seat of justice, Fayette. Pop. in 1830, 10,844 ; in 1840, 13,108 ; in 1850, 13,969.

HOWARD COUNTY, Indiana. Area. —— square miles. Seat of justice, Kokomo. Pop. in 1850, 6,657.

HOWARD, p. t., Steuben co., N. Y., 231 ms. w. of Albany ; from W. 311 ms. Watered by tributaries of Canisteo creek and Conhocton river. Pop. 3,244.

HOWARD, p. t., Centre co., Pa., 97 ms. N. w. of Harrisburgh ; from W. 189 ms. Watered by Bald Eagle, Marsh, and Beech creeks. Pop. 1,292.

HOWARD, t., Knox co., O. Watered by Vernon and Jelloway rivers.

HOWARD, t., Cass co., Mich. Watered by Putnam's creek. Pop. 766.

HOWARD, p. o., Warren co., N. J.

HOWARD, p. o., Parke co., Ind.

HOWARD, p. o., Winnebago co.. Ill.

HOWARD'S, p. o., Waukesha co., Wis.

HOWARD'S GROVE, p. o., Sheboygan co., Wis.

HOWARD'S MILLS, p. o., Montgomery co., Ky.

HOWARD'S POINT, p. o., Fayette co., Ill., 94 ms. s. E. of Springfield ; from W. 728 ms.

HOWARD'S VALLEY, p. o. Windham co., Ct., 38 ms. E. of Hartford ; from W, 365 ms.

HOWARDSVILLE, p o., Albemarle co., Va., 85 ms. N.W. of Richmond ; from W. 151 ms.

HOWARDSVILLE, p. o., Stephenson co., Ill.

HOWELL, t., Monmouth co., N. J., 44 ms. E. of Trenton ; from W. 209 ms. Watered by Shark, Manasquan, and Mettekunk rivers. Pop. 4,058.

HOWELL, c. h., p. t., seat of justice of Livingston co., Mich., 51 ms. N. w. of Detroit ; from W. 554. Pop. 1,155.

HOWELL'S DEPOT. p. o., Orange co., N. Y.

HOWELL'S SPRINGS, p. o., Hardin co., Ky., 90 ms. s. w. of Frankfort ; from W. 632 ms.

HOWELLSVILLE, p. v., Delaware co., Pa., 90 ms. s. E. of Harrisburgh ; from W. 124 ms.

HOWELLSVILLE, v., Warren co., Va., 146 ms. N. w. of Richmond ; from W. 77 ms. Watered by Shenandoah river.

HOWELLSVILLE. p. o., Robeson co., N. C.

HOWELL WORKS, p. o., Monmouth co., N. J., 47 ms. E. of Trenton ; from W. 213 ms. Watered by Manasquan river.

HOWLAND, p. t., Penobscot co., Me., 106 ms. N. E. of Augusta ; from W. 701 ms. Watered by Piscataquis river. Pop. 214.

HOWLAND, p. t., Trumbull co., O.

HOWLET HILL, p. o., Onondaga township, Onondaga co., N. Y.

HOYSVILLE, p. v., Loudoun co., Va., 166 ms. N. of Richmond ; from W. 43 ms. Watered by Kittoctan creek.

HUBBARD, p. t., Trumbull co., O., 183 ms. N. E. of Columbus ; from W. 296 ms. Pop. 1,272.

HUBBARD'S CORNERS. p. o., Madison co., N. Y.

HUBBARDSTON, p. t., Worcester co., Mass., 54 ms. w. of Boston ; from W. 412 ms. Watered by tributaries of Ware river. Pop. 825.

HUBBARDTON, p. t., Rutland co., Vt., 81 ms. s. w. of Montpelier ; from W. 450 ms. Watered by Hubbardton river. Pop.701.

HUBBLETON, p. o., Jefferson co., Wis.

HUBBLERSBURGH, p. v., Walker township, Centre co., Pa.. 88 ms. N. w. of Harrisburgh ; from W. 180 ms.

HUDDLESTON, p. o., Rapides parish, La.

HUDDLESTON, p. o., Pike co., Ark.

HUDDLESTON'S CROSS ROADS, p. o., Wilson co., Tenn., 22 ms. E. of Nashville ; from W. 659 ms.

HUDSON COUNTY, situated in the eastern part of New Jersey, with Hudson river on the east. Area, 75 square miles. Face of the country hilly ; soil generally productive. Seat of justice, Bergen. Pop. in 1840, 9,483 ; in 1850, 21,819.

HUDSON, p. t., Hillsborough co., N. H., 68 ms. s. of Concord ; from W. 446 ms. Watered by Merrimack river. Pop. 1,312.

HUDSON, c. h., city, seat of justice of Columbia co., N. Y., 29 ms. s. of Albany ; from W. 335 ms. Watered by Hudson river. Pop. in 1820, 2,900 ; in 1830, 5,392 ; in 1840, 5,672 ; in 1850, 6,286.

HUDSON, p. t., Summit co., O., 137 ms. N. E. of Columbus ; from W. 335 ms. Seat of Western Reserve college. Pop. 1,457.

HUDSON, p. t., Lenawee co., Mich., 84 ms. s. w. of Detroit ; from W. 516 ms. Watered by Bean or Tiffin creek. Pop. 1,544.

HUDSON, p. t., Hudson co., N. J., incorporated since 1850.

HUDSON, p. v., McLean co., Ill., 94 ms. N. E. of Springfield ; from W. 754 ms.

HUDSON, p. o., La Porte co., Ind.

HUDSON, p. o., Franklin, co., Ga.

HUDSONVILLE, p. v., Breckenridge co., Ky., 121 ms. s. w. of Frankfort ; from W. 663 ms.

HUDSONVILLE, p. v.. Marshall co., Miss., 201 ms. N. of Jackson ; from W. 885 ms.

HUFF'S CREEK, p. o., Logan co., Va.

HUGGIN'S CREEK, p. o., McNairy co., Tenn.

HUGHESVILLE. p. v., Muncy Creek township. Lycoming co., Pa., 90 ms. N. of Harrisburgh ; from W. 200 ms.

HUGHESVILLE, p. o., Loudoun co., Va., 149 ms. N. of Richmond ; from W. 40 ms.

HUGHSONVILLE, p. v., Fishkill township, Dutchess co., N. Y.

HUGUENOT, p. o., Deer Park township, Orange co., N. Y.. 113 ms. s. w. of Albany ; from W. 268 ms.

HULBURTON, p. v., Murray township, Orleans co., N. Y. Situated on Erie canal.

HULL, p. t., Plymouth co., Mass., 9 ms. s. E. of Boston ; from W. 442 ms. Watered by Boston harbor.

HULL'S, p. o., Athens co., O.

HULL'S CORNERS, p. o., Hannibal township, Oswego co., N. Y.

HULL'S MILLS, p. o., Stanford township, Dutchess co., N. Y., 63 ms. s. of Albany ; from W. 329 ms.

HULLMESVILLE, p. v., Middletown township, Bucks co., Pa., 118 ms. E. of Harrisburgh ; from W. 160 ms.

HUMANSVILLE, p. o., Polk co., Mo., 147 ms. s. w. of Jefferson city ; from W. 1,083.

HUME, p. t., Alleghany co., N. Y., 263 ms. w. of Albany : from W. 345 ms. Watered by Genesee river and tributaries. Pop. 2,159.

HUMILITY, p. o., Pulaski co., Va.

HUMMELSTOWN, p. b., Derry township, Dauphin co., Pa., 9 ms. E. of Harrisburgh ; from W. 119 ms. Pop. 619.

HUMPHREY, t., Cattaraugus co., N. Y., 300 ms. w. of Albany ; from W. —— ms. Watered by Great Valley creek and Five Mile run. Pop. 824.

HUMPRHEYS COUNTY, situated toward the western part of Tennessee, with Tennessee river on the west. Area, 475 square miles. Face of the country diversified ; soil generally productive. Seat of justice, Waverly. Pop. in 1820, 4,057 ; in 1830, 6,189 ; in 1840, 5,195 ; in 1850, 6,422.

HUMPHREYEVILLE, p. v., Derby township, New Haven co., Ct., 51 ms. s. w. of Hartford ; from W. 305 ms. Watered by Naugatuck river.

HUMPHREY'S VILLA, p. o., Holmes co., O., 72 ms. N. E. of Columbus ; from W. 358 ms.

HUNLOCK'S CREEK, p. o., Luzerne co., Pa.

HUNTER, p. t., Greene co., N. Y., 54 ms. s. w. of Albany ; from W. 377 ms. Watered by sources of Schoharie creek. Pop. 1,841.

HUNTER, p. o., Belmont co., O.

HUNTER, p., Boone co., Ill.

HUNT COUNTY, situated in the northern part of Texas, with Sabine river on the south. Area, —— square miles. Seat of justice, Greenville. Pop. in 1850, 1,520.

HUNTERDON COUNTY, situated on the western boundary of New Jersey, with Delaware river on the southwest. Area, 345 square miles. Face of the country mountainous and hilly ; soil generally productive. Seat of justice, Flemington. Pop. in 1810, 24,553 ; in 1820, 28,604 ; in 1830, 31,066 ; in 1840, 24,789 ; in 1850, 28,981.

HUNTER'S CAVE, p. o., Greene co., Pa.

HUNTER'S LAND, p. o., Middleburgh township, Schoharie co., N. Y., 34 ms. w. of Albany ; from W. 377 ms.

HUNTERTOWN, p. v., Strabane township, Adams co., Pa., 35 ms. s. w. of Harrisburgh ; from W. 85 ms. Pop. 158.

HUNTERSVILLE, p. o., Lycoming co., Pa.

HUNTERSVILLE, c. h., p. v., seat of justice of Pocahontas co., Va., 190 ms. N. w. of Richmond ; from W. 235 ms. Watered by Knpp's creek.

HUNTERVILLE, p. v., Hardin co., O., 81 ms. N. w. of Columbus ; from W. 452 ms.

HUNTINGSBURGH, p. o., Dubois co., Ind.

HUNTING CREEK, p. o., Accomac co., Va., 199 ms. E. of Richmond ; from W. 196 ms.

HUNTINGDON COUNTY, situated toward the southern part of Pennsylvania, and traversed by Juniata river. Area, 1,276 square miles. Face of the country mountainous ; soil barren, except on the streams. Seat of justice, Huntingdon. Pop. in 1810, 14,778 ; in 1820. 20,142 ; in 1830, 27,159 ; in 1840, 35,484 ; in 1850. 24,786.

HUNTINGDON, c. h., p. b., seat of justice of Huntingdon co., Pa., 92 ms. N. w. of Harrisburgh ; from W. 151 ms. Watered by Juniata river and Frankstown branch of the same. Pop. 1,470.

HUNTINGDON, t., Luzerne co., Pa., 92 ms. N. E. of Harrisburgh ; from W. 202 ms. Pop. 1747.

HUNTINGDON, t., Adams co., Pa., 21 ms. s. of Harrisburgh ; from W. 76 ms. Watered by Bermudian creek. Pop. 1,764.

HUNTINGDON, c. h., p. v., seat of justice of Carroll

co., Tenn., 98 ms. w. of Nashville ; from W. 783 ms. Watered by south fork of Obion river.

HUNTINGTON VALLEY, p. o., Montgomery co., Pa.

HUNTINGTON COUNTY, situated in the northeasterly part of Indiana, and traversed by Wabash river. Area. 384 square miles. Seat of justice, Huntington. Pop. in 1840, 1,579 ; in 1850, 7,850.

HUNTINGTON, p. t., Chittenden co., Vt., 20 ms. w. of Montpelier ; from W. 511 ms. Watered by Huntington river. Pop. 885.

HUNTINGTON, p. t., Fairfield co., Ct., 49 ms. s. w. of Hartford ; from W. 298 ms. Watered by Housatonic river. Pop. 1,301.

HUNTINGTON, p. t., Suffolk co., Long Island, N. Y., 189 ms. s. of Albany ; from W. 269 ms. Watered by Great South bay. Pop. 7,481.

HUNTINGTON, p. t., Lorain co., O., 95 ms. N. E. of Columbus ; from W. 376 ms. Watered by west branch of Black river. Pop. 1,173.

HUNTINGTON, t., Brown co., O., 118 s. w. of Columbus ; from W. 479 ms. Watered by Ohio river. Pop. 1,876.

HUNTINGTON, t., Gallia co., O., 90 ms. from Columbus ; from W. 372 ms. Watered by Raccoon creek. Pop. 1,308.

HUNTINGTON, t., Ross co., O. Pop. 1,658.

HUNTINGTON, p. v., Laurens district, S. C., 82 ms. N. w. of Columbia ; from W. 484 ms.

HUNTINGTON, c. h., p. v., seat of justice of Huntington co., Ind., 105 ms. N. E. of Indianapolis ; from W. 570 ms. Watered by Wabash river. Pop. 594.

HUNTINGTON, p. v., Calvert co., Md., 42 ms. s. w. of Annapolis ; from W. 72 ms.

HUNTLEY GROVE, p. o., McHenry co., Ill.

HUNTSBURGH, p. t., Geauga co., O., 175 ms. N. E. of Columbus ; from W. 334 ms. Pop. 1,007.

HUNT'S HOLLOW, p. v., Portage township, Livingston co., N. Y., 258 ms. w. of Albany ; from W. 353 ms.

HUNT'S STORE, p. o., Guilford co., N. C., 98 ms. N. w. of Raleigh ; from W. 319 ms.

HUNTSVILLE, p. o., Litchfield co., Ct.,

HUNTSVILLE, p. o., Luzerne co., Pa., 126 ms. N. E. of Harrisburgh ; from W. 237 ms.

HUNTSVILLE, v., Liberty township, Butler co., O., 95 ms. s. w. of Columbus ; from W. 479 ms.

HUNTSVILLE, p. v., Surry co., N. C., 138 ms. N. w. of Raleigh ; from W. 339 ms. Watered by Yadkin river.

HUNTSVILLE, p. v., Laurens district, S. C., 56 ms. N. W. of Columbia ; from W. 510 ms.

HUNTSVILLE, c. h., p. v., seat of justice of Madison co., Ala. ; from W. 708 ms. Pop. 2,863.

HUNTSVILLE, p. v., Schuyler co., Ill., 80 ms. N. w. of Springfield ; from W. 858 ms. Pop. 513.

HUNTSVILLE, c. h., p. v., seat of justice of Randolph co., Mo., 78 ms. N. w. of Jefferson City ; from W. 961 ms. Watered by East Charlton river.

HUNTSVILLE, p. v., Paulding co., Ga., 136 ms. N. w. of Milledgeville ; from W. 661 ms.

HUNTSVILLE, c. h., p. v., seat of justice of Madison co., Ark., 175 ms. N. w. of Little Rock ; from W. 1,183 ms. Watered by War Eagle branch of White river Pop. 255.

HUNTSVILLE, p. o., Choctaw co., Miss.

HUNTSVILLE, p. o., Walker co., Tex.

HUNTSVILLE, p. o., Madison co., Ind.

HUNTSVILLE, p. o., Logan co., O.

HUNTSVILLE, p. o., Scott co., Tex.,

HURDTOWN, p. o., Morris co., N. J.

HURLEY, p. t., Ulster co., N. Y., 60 ms. s. w. of Albany ; from W. 319 ms. Watered by Esopus creek. Pop. 2,003.

HURON COUNTY, situated in the northern part of Ohio. Area, 800 square miles. Face of the country generally even ; soil fertile. Seat of justice, Norwalk. Pop. in 1820, 6,676 ; in 1830, 13,485 ; in 1840, 23,933 ; in 1850, 26,203.

HURON COUNTY, situated on the eastern boundary of Michigan, with Lake Michigan on the east, and Saginaw bay on the north. Area, —— square miles. Seat of justice, ——. Pop. in 1850. 210.

HURON, p. t., Wayne co., N. Y., 183 ms. w. of Albany ; from W. 363 ms. Watered by Lake Ontario and East Port and Sodus bays. Pop. 1,966.

HURON, p. t., Erie co., O., 111 ms. N. of Columbus ; from W. 399 ms. Watered by Huron river and Lake Erie. Pop. 1,397.

HURON, p. t., Wayne co., Mich., 29 ms. s. w. of Detroit ; from W. 509 ms. Pop. 504.

HURON, p. o., Des Moines co., Iowa. Pop. 597.

HURRICANE, p. o., Conway co., Ark.

HURRICANE, p. o.. Montgomery co., Ill., 69 ms. s. of Springfield ; from W. 753 ms.

HURRICANE, p. o., Franklin parish, La.

HURRICANE, p. t., Lincoln co., Mo.

HURRICANE, p. o., Spartanburgh 'district, S. C., 105 ms. N. W. of Columbia ; from W. 464 ms.

HURRICANE BRIDGE, p. o., Putnam co., Va.

HURRICANE CREEK, p. o., Lauderdale co., Miss.

HURRICANE CREEK, p. o., Saline co., Ark.

HURRICANE CREEK, p. o., Henderson co., Tenn.

HURRICANE GROVE, p. o., Grant co., Wis., 127 ms. w. of Madison ; from W. 917 ms.

HURRICANE HILL, p. o., Lafayette co., Ark.

HURT'S CROSS-ROADS, p. o., Maury co., Tenn., 34 ms. s. of Nashville ; from W. 711 ms.

HURT'S MILLS, p. o., Harrison co., Ind.

HURUM'S CITY, p. o., El Dorado co., Cal.

HUSSAW, p. o., Carroll co., Ark.

HUSTISFORD, p. o., Dodge co., Wis.

HUSTON, t., Centre co., Pa. Pop. 375.

HUSTONVILLE, p. v., Lincoln co., Ky., 53 ms. s. E. of Frankfort ; from W. 567 ms.

HUTSONVILLE, p. v., Crawford co., Ill., 147 ms. s. E. of Springfield ; from W. 681 ms.

HUTTONSVILLE, p. v., Randolph co., Va., 195 ms. N. w. of Richmond ; from W. 222 ms.

HYANNIS, p. v., Barnstable township, Barnstable co., Mass., 77 ms. s. E. of Boston ; from W. 478 ms.

HYANNIS PORT, p. o., Barnstable township, Barnstable co., 79 ms. s. E. of Boston ; from W. 480 ms. Watered by Hyannis bay.

HYATTSTOWN, p. v., Montgomery co., Md., 72 ms. w. of Annapolis ; from W. 32 ms.

HYATTSVILLE, p. v., Monroe township, Miami co., O., 82 ms. w. of Columbus ; from W. 475 ms. Situated near the Miami canal. Pop. 235.

HYCO, p. o., Halifax co., Va.

HYCO FALLS, p. o., Halifax co., Va.

HYDE COUNTY, situated in the eastern part of North Carolina, on Pamlico sound. Area, 800 square miles. Face of the country low, flat, and marshy ; soil generally unproductive. Seat of justice, Swan Quarter. Pop. in 1810, 6,029 ; in 1820, 4,967 ; in 1830, 6,177 ; in 1840, 6,458 ; in 1850, 7,636.

HYDE, p. o., Warren co., N. C.

HYDE PARK, c. h., p. t., seat of justice of Lamoille co., Vt., 31 ms. N. of Montpelier ; from W. 545 ms. Watered by Lamoille river. Pop. 1,107.

HYDE PARK, p. t., Dutchess co., N. Y., 66 ms. s. of Albany ; from W. 305 ms. Watered by Hudson river and Crum Elbow creek. Pop. 2,425.

HYDE PARK, p. o., Luzerne co., Pa., 144 ms. N. E. of Harrisburgh ; from W. 248 ms.

HYDE PARK, p. o., Grundy co., Ill.

HYDESBURGH, p. v., Ralls co., Mo., 108 ms. N. E. of Jefferson City ; from W. 919 ms.

HYDE SETTLEMENT, p. o., Barker township, Broome co., N. Y., 134 ms. s. w. of Albany ; from W. 310 ms.

HYDEVILLE, p. o., Rutland co., Vt.

HYDRAULIC MILLS, p. o., Albemarle co., Va., 90 ms. N. w. of Richmond ; from W. 126 ms.

HYGEIA, p. o., Hamilton co., O.

HYNDSVILLE, p. o., Seward township, Schoharie co., N. Y., 44 ms. w. of Albany ; from W. 491 ms.

I.

IBERIA, p. v., Washington township, Morrow co., O., 54 ms. N. of Columbus ; from W. 399 ms.

IBERIA, p. v., Miller co., Mo., 50 ms. s. w. of Jefferson city ; from W. 986 ms.

IBERVILLE PARISH, situated toward the south-eastern part of Louisiana, and traversed by Mississippi river. Area, 350 square miles. Face of the country flat ; soil rich, but generally subject to inundation. Seat of justice, Plaquemine. Pop. in 1810, 2,679 ; in 1820, 4,414 ; in 1830, 7,049 ; in 1840, 8,495 ; in 1850, 12,216.

IBERVILLE, c. h., p. v., seat of justice of Iberville parish, La., 92 ms. N. w. of New Orleans ; from W. 1,192 ms.

ICE'S FERRY, p. o., Monongalia co., Va.

ICHEPUCKESASSA, p. o., Hillsborough co., Flor.

ICKESBURGH, p. v., Perry co., Pa., 40 ms. N.w. of Harrisburgh ; from W. 128 ms.

IDA, p. t., Monroe co., Mich. Pop. 345.

IJAMSVILLE, p. v., Frederick co., Md., 71 ms. N. w. of Annapolis ; from W. 51 ms.

ILCHESTER MILLS, p. o., Anne Arundel co., Md.

ILION, p. o., Herkimer co., N. Y.

ILLINOIS, sometimes called the " Prairie state," is situated between 37° and 42° 30' north latitude, and 87° 49' and 91° 30' longitude west from Greenwich ; it is bounded north by Wisconsin, east by Lake Michigan and Indiana, south by the Ohio river, which separates it from Kentucky, and west by the Mississippi river, which separates it from Missouri and Iowa. Its superficial area is 55,400 square miles.

Physical Aspect.—The general surface of this state may be regarded as a gentle plain, more or less rolling inclined in the direction of its rivers. The northern and southern sections, however, are somewhat broken, but no portion of the territory is traversed by ranges of mountains, or hills. It is estimated that Illinois contains more arable land than any other state in the Union. In that portion north of Kaskasia river the prairie country predominates ; and it is computed that two thirds of the state are covered with this class of lands. Many

portions of them are undulating, entirely dry, and abound in wholesome springs ; but as a general rule, they consist of plains ; and in the true meaning of the term, in French, they are " meadows," presenting every degree of fertility, down to extreme barrenness. Many of them exhibit alluvial deposites, which prove that they have once been morasses, and perhaps lakes. In numerous instances, there are thickets, or groves of timber, amid these prairies, containing from 100 to 2,000 acres each, which resemble oases in the desert, or islands in the sea. Along the borders of many of the streams are rich "bottoms," or alluvial deposites. The "American bottom" commences at the confluence of the Mississippi and Kaskaskia rivers, extending northward to the mouth of the Missouri, a distance of about eighty miles, and comprises an area of 288,000 acres. It is bounded on the east by a chain of " bluffs," some of which occur in parallel ridges, while others are of a conical shape, formed of lime-rock, from 50 to 200 feet in height.

Rivers and Lakes.—The principal rivers are, the Mississippi, which bounds the state on the west, the Ohio, which bounds it on the south, Kankokee, Kaskaskia, Sangamon, Little Wabash, Muddy, Saline, Rock, Embarras, Fox, the Wabash, the principal river in the state, which forms a portion of the eastern boundary, Des Plaines, and Vermilion. Besides Lake Michigan, which lies on the northeast corner, this state contains Peoria lake, an expansion of Illinois river.

Climate.—The climate of this state is generally healthy, and the air pure and serene, except in the vicinity of wet, low lands, or stagnant pools. The winters, which are cold, are somewhat milder than those of the Atlantic states in the same latitude. Snow seldom falls to the depth of six inches, and it as rarely remains on the ground more than ten or twelve days. The Mississippi is sometimes frozen over as far down as St. Louis, sufficiently strong to be crossed on the ice. The summers are warm, particularly in the southern part, but the intensity of the heat is modified by the breeze.

Productive Resources.—The staple products are, horses, mules, neat cattle, sheep, swine, poultry, butter, cheese, wool, cotton, hemp, flax, hops, hay, wine, wheat, barley, buckwheat, potatoes, and Indian corn. Among the mineral resources are, zinc, copper, iron, and lime. Bituminous coal may be found in nearly every county in the state. Common salt is procured by evaporating the water of salt springs. The lead mines in the vicinity of Galena are very extensive, and of great value to the state. The mineral has been found in every portion

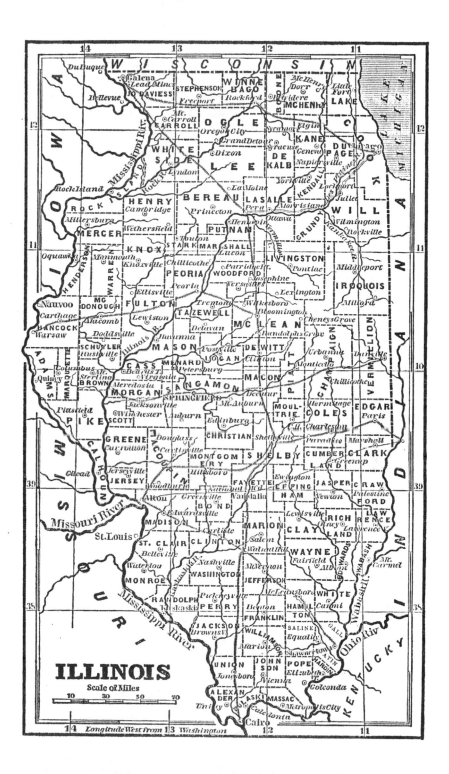

ILLINOIS

Scale of Miles

of a tract of more than fifty miles in extent. The ore lies in beds, or horizontal strata, varying in thickness from one inch to several feet.

Manufactures.—In 1850 there were, in Illinois, 3,099 manufacturing establishments, producing each $500 and upward annually. The manufactures consist mostly of woollen fabrics, machinery, saddlery, agricultural implements, &c.

Railroads and Canals.—There are about 1,200 miles of railroad completed and in course of construction in this state; some of them, particularly the Central railroad, are very important. The Illinois and Michigan canal, connecting the waters of Lake Erie, at Chicago, with those of the Illinois river at Peru, is one of the most important works of internal improvement in the country. It is the connecting link of an unbroken internal water communication from the Atlantic, off Sandy Hook, New York, by the way of the lakes, the Illinois and Mississippi rivers, to the gulf of Mexico. The canal is 113 miles long, 60 feet wide, and 6 feet deep, and designed for boats of 120 tons. It cost over $8,000,000.

Commerce.—The direct foreign commerce of Illinois is, of course, from its insular position, very small; but its coasting and lake trade is important, amounting, in 1850, to over $10,000,000.

Education.—The principal collegiate institutions in Illinois are, the Illinois college, at Jacksonville, founded in 1829; the M'Kendree college, at Lebanon, in 1834; the Shurtleff college, at Upper Alton, in 1835; the Knox Manual Labor college, at Galesburg, in 1837; and the College of St. Mary of the Lakes, at Chicago, in 1846. There are about 100 academies, and 2,000 common schools in the state.

Government.—The legislative authority is vested in a senate, the members of which, 25 in number, are elected for four years, one half every two years; and a house of representatives, 75 in number, elected for two years. Senators must be thirty years of age, and five years inhabitants of the state. Representatives must be twenty-five years of age, citizens of the United States, and three years inhabitants of the state. The executive power is vested in a governor and lieutenant-governor, chosen by a plurality of votes, once in four years, on the Tuesday after the first Monday in November, who must be thirty-five years of age, citizens of the United States for fourteen years, and residents of the state for ten years. The governor is not eligible for two consecutive terms. A majority of members elected to both houses may defeat the governor's veto. A majority of the members elected to each house is required for the passage of any law. The legislature meets biennially at Springfield, on the first Monday in January. The judicial power is vested in a supreme court, of three judges, elected by the people, for a term of nine years, one being chosen triennially; also in circuit courts, of one judge each, elected by the people in nine judicial circuits, into which the state is divided, for six years; and county courts, of one judge each, elected by the people for four years. All white male citizens, 21 years of age, resident in the state for one year, may vote at elections. No state bank can be created or revived. Acts creating banks must be submitted to the people. Stockholders are individually liable to the amount of their shares.

Population.—In 1810, 12,282; in 1820, 55,211; in 1830, 157,455; in 1840, 476,183; in 1850, 851,470.

History.—This state embraces a part of Upper Louisiana, as held by the French prior to 1763, when it was ceded to England, together with Canada and Acadia. The first permanent settlement was made at Kaskaskia, in 1685, although La Salle had built a fort, called Crevecœur, on Illinois river, five years before. At the close of the revolutionary war. in 1783, this country was claimed under the charter of Virginia, and held by that state until ceded to the United States, in 1787. It was then made a part of the territory northwest of Ohio river. When Ohio was made a separate territory, in 1800, Illinois and Indiana were formed into another territory, and remained as such until 1809, when they were divided into two. In 1812, a territorial government was formed, with a legislature and one delegate to Congress. In 1818 a state constitution was formed, and Illinois admitted into the Union as an independent state. The present constitution of the state was adopted by a state convention in August, 1847, and accepted by the people in March, 1848. Motto of the seal, "State Sovereignty; National Union."

ILLINOIS, t., Pope co., Ark.

ILLINOIS, t., Washington co., Ark. Pop. 714.
ILLINOIS, t., Calhoun co., Ill.
ILLINOISTOWN, p. o., St. Clair co., Ill.
ILLYRIA, p. o., Fayette co., Iowa.
INCLAYSTOWN, p. v., Upper Freehold township, Monmouth co., N. J., 16 ms. E. of Trenton; from W. 182 ms.
INCREASE, p. o., Early co., Ga.
INDEPENDENCE COUNTY, situated toward the northeastern part of Arkansas, with Big Black river on the east, and traversed by White river. Area, 1.250 square miles. Seat of justice, Batesville. Pop. in 1830, 2,032; in 1840, 3,669; in 1850, 7,767.
INDEPENDENCE, p. t., Alleghany co., N. Y., 261 ms. w. of Albany; from W. 300 ms. Watered by Cryder's and Independence creeks. Pop. 1,701.
INDEPENDENCE, p. t., Warren co., N. J., 59 ms. N. of Trenton; from W. 215 ms. Watered by Pequest and Bacon creeks, and Musconecong rivers. Pop. 2,621.
INDEPENDENCE, p. v., Washington co., Pa., 227 ms. w. of Harrisburgh; from W. 254 ms.
INDEPENDENCE, p. v., Autauga co., Ala.; from W. 834 ms.
INDEPENDENCE, p. t., Cuyahoga co., O., 145 ms. N. E. of Columbus; from 358 ms. Watered by Cuyahoga river and Ohio canal. Pop. 1,485.
INDEPENDENCE, c. h., p. v., seat of justice of Kenton co., Ky., 82 ms. N. E. of Frankfort; from W. 505 ms.
INDEPENDENCE, t., Oakland co., Mich. Pop. 1,279.
INDEPENDENCE, p. v., Warren co., Ind., 85 ms. N. w. of Indianapolis; from W. 643 ms.
INDEPENDENCE, t., Macon co., Mo.
INDEPENDENCE, t., Washington co., O. Pop. 728.
INDEPENDENCE, c. h., p. v., seat of justice of Jackson co., Mo., 146 ms. N. w. of Jefferson City; from W. 1,072 ms.
INDEPENDENCE, c. h., p. v., seat of justice of Grayson co., Va.
INDEPENDENCE, p. o., Washington co., Tex.
INDEPENDENCE, p. o., McLean co., Ill.
INDEPENDENCE, p. t., Appanoose co., Iowa. Pop. 176.
INDEPENDENCE HILL, p. o., Prince William co., Va., 94 ms. N. of Richmond; from W. 41 ms.
INDESVILLE, p. o., Surry co., N. C.

INDIANA, one of the United States, situated between 37° 45' and 41° 52' north latitude, and 84° 42' and 88° 12' longitude west from Greenwich; and is bounded north by Michigan lake and state, east by a small portion of Michigan, Ohio, and a small part of Kentucky, southeast by the Ohio river, which separates it from Kentucky. and west by Illinois, from which it is separated in part by Wabash river. Its superficial area is 34,000 square miles.

Physical Aspect.—In features, soil, and climate, Indiana forms a connecting link between Ohio and Illinois. It is more hilly than the latter, but contains no mountains. A range of high land. called the "Knobs," extends from the falls of the Ohio to the Wabash, which in many places produces a broken surface. Bordering on all the principal streams, except the Ohio, are belts of "bottom" and prairie. Between the Wabash and Lake Michigan the country is generally level, abounding alternately in woodlands, prairies, lakes, and swamps. A range of hills runs parallel with the Ohio, from the mouth of the Great Miami to Blue river, alternately approaching to within a few rods, and receding to the distance of two miles. Immediately below Blue river the hills disappear, and the country immediately becomes level. The prairies of this state are of two kinds, the "river," and the "upland." The former are bottoms, destitute of timber; the latter are from 30 to 100 feet or more in elevation, and are far more numerous and extensive. The soil of these plains, or table-lands, are often as deep and fertile as the best bottoms. The prairies bordering on the Wabash are particularly rich, varying from two to twenty feet in depth. In truth, no state in the Union can show a greater extent of fertile land, in one body, than Indiana.

Rivers and Lakes.—The principal rivers are, the

INDIANA

Scale of Miles
10   20   30   40   50

Ohio, which flows along the entire southern boundary; the Wabash, which bounds the state partly on the west; the Patoka, Tippecanoe, Eel, Salamanic, Plein, Theakiki, St. Mary's, St. Joseph's, White, Whitewater, and Kankakee, a branch of the Illinois. Besides Lake Michigan, there are English and Beaver lakes, all of which lie at the northwestern part of the state.

Climate.—The climate is generally healthy, and resembles that of Ohio and Illinois. In all places situated near stagnant waters or sluggish streams, fevers and bilious attacks prevail during the hotter months of the year. The Wabash is generally closed in the winter, and may be safely crossed on the ice. In the central and southern parts of the state snow seldom falls to a greater depth than six inches; but in the northern parts it is sometimes from a foot to eighteen inches deep.

Productive Resources.—The staple productions of this state are, horses, mules, neat cattle, sheep, swine, poultry, butter, cheese, wax, furs, skins, wool, sugar, wine, hops, hay, hemp, flax, tobacco, wheat, barley, rye, buckwheat, oats, potatoes, and Indian corn. Among the mineral resources may be mentioned, iron, coal, and Epsom salts.

Manufactures.—In 1850 there were in Indiana, 4,326 manufacturing establishments, which produced $500 and upward each annually. The total amount of manufacturing capital in the state was over $7,000,000, having more than doubled since 1840.

Railroads and Canals.—Indiana has about 1,000 miles of railroad already completed, and in successful operation, and new lines projected. The principal canal in Indiana is the Wabash and Erie, 459 miles long, connecting the waters of Lake Erie with those of the Ohio river; next in importance is the Whitewater canal, extending from Lawrenceburg to Cambridge, 76 miles.

Commerce.—Indiana has no direct foreign commerce, its exports being shipped at the ports of other states. Its river and lake trade is considerable, and increasing.

Education.—The collegiate institutions of Indiana are, the State University, at Bloomington, founded in 1827; Hanover College, at South Hanover, in 1829; Wabash College, at Crawfordsville, in 1833; Franklin College, at Franklin, in 1837; Indiana Asbury University, in 1839; St. Gabriel's College, at Vincennes, in 1843. A law school is attached to the state university, and medical schools at Laporte and Indianapolis. There are about 100 academies and high schools in the state. The common school fund is nearly a million of dollars.

Population.—In 1800, 2,640; in 1810, 24,520, exclusive of Indians; in 1820, 147,178, in 1830, 343,031; in 1840, 685,866; in 1850, 988,416.

Government.—The legislative authority is vested in a senate and house of representatives; the senate is not to exceed 50 members, elected for four years; the representatives, not to exceed 100 in number, are chosen for two years. The executive power is vested in a governor, elected by the people for four years, but not eligible the next four years. A lieutenant-governor is also chosen in the same manner, and for the same term. The elections are held once in two years, on the second Tuesday in October. All elections by the people are by ballot, and decided by a plurality of votes; all elections by the legislature are *viva voce.* The legislature meets biennially, at Indianapolis, the first Monday in January. The judicial power is vested in a supreme court of not less than three, nor more than five judges, elected by the people at large, for a term of six years; in circuit courts, the judges of which (one in each) are elected by the people in each judicial circuit for a term of six years; and in such inferior courts as the legislature may establish. The right of suffrage extends to every white male citizen of the United States, of the age of 21 years and upward, who shall have resided in the state during the six months immediately preceding an election.

History.—This state embraces a part of the ancient territory of Upper Louisiana, as held by the French prior to 1763, when it was ceded to England, together with Canada and Acadia. The first permanent settlement was made at Vincennes, in about the year 1690. At the close of the revolutionary war, and by the treaty of 1783, the country was claimed under the charter of Virginia, and held by that state until ceded to the United States, in 1787. It was then made a part of the territory northwest of Ohio river. When Ohio was made a separate territory, in 1800, Indiana and Illinois remained united, and continued under one government until 1809, when each became a distinct territory. In 1816 Indiana was admitted into the Union as an independent state. A new constitution was adopted in 1851.

INDIANA COUNTY, situated toward the westerly part of Pennsylvania, with Kiskiminitas river on the southwest. Area, 770 square miles. Face of the country, hilly; soil, mostly sterile. Seat of justice, Indiana. Pop. in 1810, 6,214; in 1820, 8,882; in 1830, 14,251; in 1840, 20,782; in 1850, 27,070.

INDIANA, c. h., p. b., seat of justice of Indiana co., Pa., 155 ms. N. w. of Harrisburgh; from W. 208 ms. Pop. 963.

INDIANA, p. t., Alleghany co., Pa., 200 ms. N. w. of Harrisburgh; from W. 222 ms. Watered by Deer, Long, Pine, and Squaw creeks.

INDIANAPOLIS, city, seat of justice of Marion co., and capital of Indiana, situated in the centre of the state, and on the east side of White river, in the midst of a rich and rapidly populating country, 108 miles northwest of Cincinnati, and 573 miles from Washington. Thirty years ago, a dense forest occupied the site of this city. In 1821, it became the seat of the state government, and has since continued to increase in population and prosperity. It is laid out with ingenuity and beauty. A circular street surrounds an open space, with the governor's mansion in the middle. From this diverge several streets, intersecting, diagonally, the others, which are rectangular. Besides a number of churches, mills, and factories, the city contains a splendid statehouse, 180 feet long, 85 wide, and 45 feet high, adorned by Ionic porticoes and columns, and surmounted by a dome. The courthouse is also a conspicuous edifice. White river is here spanned by an elegant bridge. The whole is an interesting specimen of industry, enterprise, and thrift, and bids fair to become one of the principal cities in the west. When high, the river is navigable to this point for steamboats. Indianapolis is connected by railroad with Madison, on the Ohio, 86 miles distant, and railways also extend toward Peru, as well as toward Bellefontaine, in Logan county, Ohio. Pop. in 1830, was about 1,200; in 1840, 2,692; in 1850, 8,090.

INDIANAPOLIS, p. o., Mahaska co., Iowa.

INDIAN CREEK, p. o., Monroe co., Va., 241 ms. w. of Richmond; from W. 278 ms.

INDIAN CREEK, p. o., Monroe co., Mo., 91 ms. N. of Jefferson city; from W. 931 ms.

INDIAN CREEK, p. t. Monroe co., Ind. Pop. 1,202.

INDIAN CREEK, p. o., Newbury co., S. C.

INDIAN CREEK, p. o., Jackson co., Ga.

INDIAN CREEK, p. o., Washington co., Tex.

INDIAN CREEK, p. o., Pike co., Ala.

INDIAN FIELDS, p. o., Albany co., N. Y.

INDIAN GROVE, p. o., Livingston co., Ill.

INDIAN HILLS, p. o., Abbeville district, S. C.

INDIAN KEY, p. v., Dade co., on a small key, or island, in southern Florida, 75 ms. N. E. of Key West. Watered by Barnes sound, and the straits of Florida.

INDIAN MOUND, p. o., Stewart co., Tenn.

INDIANOLA, c. h., p. v., seat of justice of Warren co., Iowa.

INDIANOLA, p. o., Vermillion co., Ill.

INDIANOLA, p. o., Calhoun co., Tex.

INDIAN PRAIRIE, p. o., Van Buren co.. Iowa.

INDIAN RIVER HUNDRED, Sussex co., Del. Pop. 1,683.

INDIAN RIVER, p. o., Watson township, Lewis co., N. Y., 155 ms. N. w. of Albany; from W. 454 ms.

INDIAN RIVER, p. o., St. Lucie co., Flor.

INDIAN RIVER, p. o., Washington co., Me.

INDIAN SPRINGS, p. v., Butts co., Ga., 52 ms. w. of Milledgeville; from W. 659 ms. Watered by tributaries of Ocmulgee river.

INDIAN STREAM, t., Coos co., N. H.

INDIAN TERRITORY, a vast region set apart by the United States as the permanent home of certain Indian tribes who have been removed thither, and natives of the soil, lies between 34° and 40° north latitude, and 94° 20′ and 100° longitude west from Greenwich. It is bounded north by the Northwestern Territory, east by Missouri and Arkansas, south by Texas and New Mexico, and west by Texas, New Mexico, and Utah. Its superficial area is about 200,000 square miles.

Physical Aspect.—The Ozark range of mountains traverse the southwestern corner of this tract. From this point eastward the country presents a series of slightly undulating plains, gradually ascending toward the Rocky mountains, where they have an elevation of 4,000 or 5,000 feet. These mountains, forming the western boundary, rise to the elevation of 12,000 feet. The Great American desert stretches along the eastern part of the Rocky mountains, from the Northwestern territory through the Indian territory into Texas, a length of nearly 600 miles. Its width varies from 100 to 200 miles. The soil of this is arid, sterile, and almost destitute of trees, and even of shrubs. There are occasional plains and prairies, which afford subsistence to herds of bison, wild horses, and other animals. A belt of about 200 miles wide, adjoining Arkansas and Missouri, is favorable to settlement. Its soil is fertile, and it is watered by numerous rivers, none of which, however, are adapted to navigation.

Rivers.—The principal rivers are, Red river, Canadian, Arkansas, Neosho, Kansas, and Platte rivers, with their tributaries. The largest of these rivers rise in the Rocky mountains, and flow east into the Missouri and Mississippi. Red river and the Arkansas are navigable at certain seasons to within the Indian territory by steamboats, and the Kansas by boats.

Climate.—The atmosphere is salubrious, and in the southern portion the climate is so mild, that domestic animals find support through the winter without the care of their owners.

Resources.—Iron, lead, and coal, are abundant. The Indians have, in many instances, converted their settlements into well-cultivated farms, and the various grains, vegetables, and other agricultural products of corresponding latitudes east of the Mississippi, are raised in abundance.

Population.—The inhabitants of the Indian territory consist of tribes indigenous to the country, and the tribes transported thither under the authority of the United States. The numbers belonging to each class and tribe, in 1841, were as follows :—*Indigenous Tribes.*—Pawnees, 12,500 ; Osages, 4,102 ; Kansas, 1,700 ; Omahas, 1,301 ; Otoes and Missouris, 931 ; Puncahs, 777 ; Quapaws, 400. *Immigrant Tribes.*—Cherokees, 25,911 ; Creeks, 24,594 ; Choctaws, 12.410 ; Seminoles, 3,136 ; Chippewas, Ottawas, &c., 2,028 ; Chickasaws, 4,111 ; Delawares, 1,059 ; Kickapoos, 505 ; Peorias and Kaskaskias, 150 ; Piankeshaws, 98 ; Senecas from Sandusky, 125 ; Senecas and Shawnees, 211 ; Shawnees, 887 ; Stockbridges, Munsees, &c., 278 ; Swan Creek, &c., 62 ; Weas, 176 ; Winnebagoes, 2,182 ; Wyandots of Ohio, 385. Total, 96,020.

Government.—The Cherokees, Creeks, and Choctaws, are the most advanced toward civilization of any of the foregoing tribes. They have good houses, well-fenced and well-tilled fields, and own horses and cattle to a considerable extent. They have also native mechanics and merchants. They have adopted an improved system of government. The Choctaws and Creeks have a written constitution ; and the former have introduced trial by jury. The other transported tribes are said to have improved in their condition since their removal from the east. But the indigenous tribes have not, as a general thing, improved in the same degree as their brethren from the east. They still cling to their wild pleasures, and prefer the excitement of the hunt, and of war, to the peaceful monotony of civilization.

INDIANTOWN, p. v., Currituck co., N. C., 232 ms. N.E. of Raleigh ; from W. 280 ms. Watered by North river.

INDIANTOWN, p. v., Williamsburgh district, S. C., 118 ms. S. E. of Columbia ; from W. 480 ms. Watered by Cedar creek.

INDIANTOWN, p. o., Bureau co., Ill.

INDIANTOWN, p. o., Vermillion co,, Ill.

INDIAN VALLEY, p. o., Floyd co., Va.

INDIAN VILLAGE, p. o., Wachita parish, La.

INDIGO HEAD, p. o., Coffee co., Ala.

INDUSTRY, p. t., Franklin co., Me., 34 ms. N. w. of Augusta ; from W. 627 ms. Watered by Sandy river. Pop. 1,041.

INDUSTRY, p. v., Beaver co., Pa., 234 ms. w. of Harrisburgh.

INDUSTRY, p. o., Austin co., Tex.

INDUSTRY. p. o., Hamilton co., O.

INEABAR, t., Lafayette co., Mo.

INGHAM COUNTY, situated toward the southerly part of Michigan. Area, 560 square miles. Seat of justice, Lansing, which is also the state capital. Pop. in 1840. 2,498 ; in 1850, 8,631.

INGHAM, p. t., Ingham co., Mich., 77 ms. w. of Detroit ; from W. 563 ms. Pop. 744.

INGLE's FERRY, v., Monterey co., Va., 215 ms. w. of Richmond ; from W. 283 ms.

INGRAM's CROSS-ROADS, p. o., Lauderdale co., Ala.

INLAND, p. o., Summit co., O., 126 ms. N. E. of Columbus ; from W. 326 ms.

INMANSVILLE, p. o., Rock co., Wis.

INSTITUTE, p. o., Randolph co., N. C.

INTERCOURSE, p. v., Leacock township, Lancaster co., Pa., 48 ms. E. of Harrisburgh ; from W. 123 ms.

INTERCOURSE, p. o., Sumter co., Ala. ; from W. 901 ms.

INVERNESS, p. o., Columbiana co., O., 146 ms. N. E. of Columbus ; from W. 278 ms.

IOLA, v., Calhoun co., Flor., 58 ms. s. w. of Tallahassee. Watered by Appalachicola river.

IONI, p. o,, Anderson co., Tex.

IONIA COUNTY, situated toward the westerly part of Michigan, and traversed by Grand river. Area, 576 square miles. Soil generally productive. Seat of justice, Ionia. Pop. in 1840, 1,923 ; in 1850, 7,597.

IONIA, c. h., p. t., seat of justice of Ionia co., Mich., 136 ms. w. of Detroit ; from W. 623 ms. Watered by Grand river. Pop. 774.

IONIA, v., Morgan co., Mo. Watered by Moreau creek.

IOSCO, t., Livingston co., Mich. Pop. 645.

IOWA, one of the United States, formerly a portion of the Louisiana territory, situated between 40° 30′ and 43° 30′ north latitude, and 90° 20′ and 96° 50′ west longitude from Greenwich, and is bounded north by Minnesota, east by Mississippi river, which separates it from Wisconsin and Illinois, south by Missouri, and west by the Indian territory. Its superficial area is 50,000 square miles.

Physical Aspect.—The general surface of this state is moderately undulating, without mountains or high hills, except in the northern part, where the hills are of considerable height. Along the margins of the rivers there are frequent ranges of bluffs, which vary in height from 40 to 130 feet. In other instances, the streams are skirted by rich "bottoms," covered with trees. A large proportion of the territory consists of prairies, some of which have a level, others a rolling surface. The soil on the bottoms, as well as on the prairies, is generally good, the former consisting of a deep, rich, black mould, and the latter of a sandy loam, sometimes intermingled with gravel, or red clay.

Rivers and Lakes.—The principal rivers are the Mississippi, Des Moines, Iowa, Keosauque, Little Iowa, Turkey, Shunk, Red, Cedar, Maquoketa, and Wabsipinecon. At the north part of the state there are numerous small lakes.

Climate.—The climate is pleasant, and generally healthy, except near the borders of stagnant waters, or sluggish streams, where, during the summer, bilious complaints, fevers, and agues, usually prevail. Snow rarely falls to exceed eight or ten inches in depth ; and the Mississippi, at Prairie du Chien, is not frozen sufficiently strong to be crossed more than five or six weeks in the year. The summers are warm, but not oppressively so, and are refreshed by frequent showers.

Productive Resources.—The staple products of this state are, horses, mules, neat cattle, sheep, swine, poultry, butter, cheese, wax, wool, hay, hemp, flax, skins, furs, sugar, tobacco, wheat, barley, rye, oats, buckwheat, potatoes, and Indian corn. Among the mineral resources are found lead, iron, copper, zinc, and coal ; but lead is the most abundant, and the mines are extensively worked in the vicinity of Dubuque.

Manufactures.—The manufacturing and mechanic arts have as yet but a slight foothold in Iowa ; but with its abundant water power and other resources, it undoubtedly will not remain long as now almost entirely an agricultural state.

Commerce.—From its position, lying upon the Mississippi river, with numerous navigable streams traversing its interior, Iowa possesses commercial advantages equal to those of any other western state. It contributes largely to the valuable cargoes that are floated down the Mississippi to New Orleans.

Education.—There are two collegiate institutions in

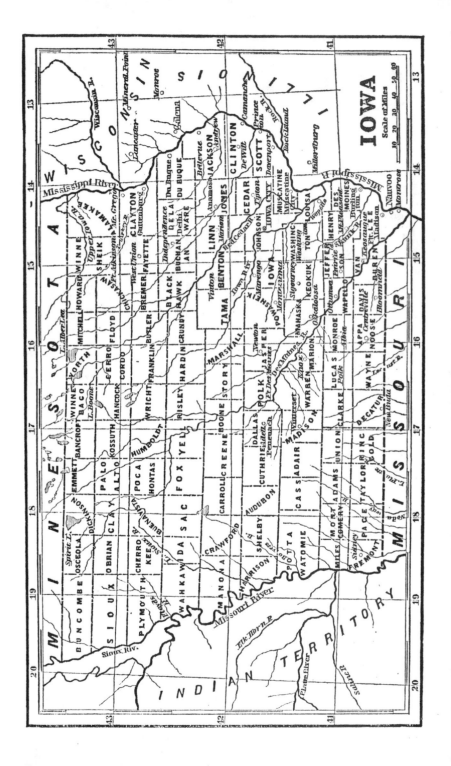

IOWA

Scale or Miles
10   20   30   40   50   60

this state ; the Iowa university, at Iowa City, and the Franklin college, at Franklin. The constitution makes it imperative that a school shall be established in each district. All lands granted by Congress, and other specified avails, constitute a fund to be applied to education. A special fund is also provided for the support of the state university.

Population.—In 1840, 43,111 ; in 1850, 192,214.

Government.—The legislative power is vested in a senate consisting of not more than one half, nor less than one third, of the number of representatives, and who àre chosen for four years, one half biennially; and in a house of representatives, not less than thirty-nine, nor more than seventy-two in number, chosen for two years. The executive power is vested in a governor, chosen for four years. The judicial power is vested in a supreme court, consisting of a chief justice and two associates, elected by the legislature for six years ; in district courts, the judges of which are elected by the people for five years; and in justices of the peace. Every white male citizen, twenty-one years old (idiots, insane, or infamous persons excepted), having resided in the state six months, and in the county twenty days, has the right of suffrage. State elections first Monday in August ; the legislature meets biennially, first Monday in December.

History.—Iowa embraces a portion of the ancient territory of Upper Louisiana, the eastern border of which was explored by Marquette and Jolyet, in 1673. It remained under the jurisdiction of France until 1763, when it was ceded to Spain. In 1800 it was retroceded to France, who formally took possession of the country, and sold the whole to the United States in 1803. Subsequently to this, Iowa constituted a part of the territory of Louisiana, and afterward of that of Missouri. Until as late as the year 1832, the whole of this territory north of Missouri, which was admitted into the Union as a state in 1821, was in undisputed possession of the Indians. By a treaty made in 1830, the Sacs and Foxes, then the principal tribes, had ceded to the United States the last of their lands east of the Mississippi. In consequence of not leaving the territory, in compliance with the treaty, arose the " Black Hawk war," which resulted in the total defeat of the Indians at the battle of Bad Ax, in Wisconsin, in 1832. In the autumn of that year a belt of country along the west side of the Mississippi, extending northward from Missouri for nearly 300 miles, and 50 miles in width, commonly known as the " Black Hawk purchase," was ceded by the Indians to the United States. In 1836–'37 further purchases were made, and in 1838 Iowa was erected into a territory. By another treaty in 1842, a tract of some 15,000,000 acres more were purchased of the Sacs and Foxes for $1,000,000. From that time the Indian title became extinct in the whole country lying within this state, which was admitted into the Union in 1846. This state is being rapidly settled, and the tide of emigration now flowing westward will, at no distant day, make this one of the most populous states in the Union.

IOWA COUNTY, situated toward the southwesterly part of Wisconsin, with Wisconsin river on the north. Area, 1,300 square miles. Seat of justice, Mineral Point. Pop. in 1830, 1,576 ; in 1840, 3,978 ; in 1850, 5,672.

IOWA COUNTY, situated in Iowa. Area, —— square miles. Seat of justice, ——. Pop. in 1850, 822.

IOWA, p. o., Perry co.. Ill., 149 ms. s. of Springfield ; from W. 824 ms.

IOWA CITY, seat of justice of Johnson co., and capital of the state of Iowa, situated on the east bank of Iowa river, about 50 miles from its entrance into the Mississippi. and 75 miles northwest of Burlington. For romantic and agreeable scenery, as well as in some measure for commercial advantages, it is eminently worthy to be the seat of government of so flourishing a state. It is built on successive elevations, rising, like terraces, one above the other. The ground, near the river, is level and open. Above and beyond, upon two heights, run broad and beautiful avenues, and, at right angles to this, is " Iowa avenue," a magnificent street, at the head of which stands the statehouse, a splendid edifice of richly-variegated stone, called " bird's-eye marble." It is in the Grecian-Doric architecture, 60 feet wide, and 100 feet long, surmounted by a beautiful dome. There are churches, schools, stores, and all the accompaniments of civilization and prosperity in the west. The river is navigable to Iowa city for steamboats and vessels of ordinary draught, and navigation will doubtless be speedily improved by canals and other channels of intercommunication. The population in 1840, was 800 ; in 1850. 1,250.

IOWAVILLE, p. o., Van Buren co., Iowa.

IPSWICH, c. h., p. t., seat of justice, together with Salem and Newburyport of Essex co., Mass., 26 ms. N. E. of Boston ; from W. 466 ms. Watered by Ipswich river. Pop. 3.349.

IRA, p. t., St. Clair co., Mich. Pop. 596.

IRA, p. o., Cayuga co., N. Y.

IRA, p. o., Rutland co., Vt.

IRASBURGH, c. h., p. t., seat of justice of Orleans co., Vt., 45 ms. N. of Montpelier ; from W. 561 ms. Watered by Black and Barton rivers. Pop. 1,034.

IREDELL COUNTY, situated toward the westerly part of North Carolina, with Catawba river on the southwest. Area, 800 square miles. Face of the country, hilly and mountainous ; soil, fertile. Seat of justice, Statesville. Pop. in 1810, 10,972, in 1820, 13,071 ; in 1830, 15,262 ; in 1840, 15,685; in 1850, 14,719.

IRELAND, p. o., Hampden co., Mass., 101 ms. s. w. of Boston ; from W. 371 ms.

IRELAND, p. o., Lewis co., Va.

IRELAND CORNERS, p. o., Albany co., N. Y.

IRISH CREEK, p. o., De Witt co., Tex.

IRISH GROVE, p. o., Atchison co., Mo.

IRISH RIPPLE, p. o., Lawrence co., Pa., 241 ms. w. of Harrisburgh ; from W. 267 ms.

IRISHTOWN, p. o., Mercer co., Pa.

IRON COUNTY, Utah. Area, —— square miles. Seat of justice, Centre Creek. Pop. 1850, ——.

IRON CREEK, p. o., Washtenaw co., Mich., 57 ms. w. of Detroit ; from W. 521 ms.

IRONDEQUOIT, p. t., Monroe co., N. Y., 223 ms. w. of Albany ; from W. 373 ms. Watered by Genesee river and Irondequoit bay and Lake Ontario. Pop. 2,297.

IRON FURNACE, p. o., Scioto co., O., 105 ms. s. of Columbus.

IRON HILLS, p. o., Jackson co., Iowa.

IRON MOUNTAIN, p. o., St. Francis co.. Mo.

IRON RIDGE, p. o., Dodge co., Wis.

IRONTON, p. o., Lawrence co., O.

IRONWOOD BLUFF, p. o., Itawamba co., Miss.

IROQUOIS COUNTY, situated on the east boundary of Illinois, and traversed by Iroquois river. Area, 1,108 square miles. Seat of justice, Middleport. Pop. in 1840, 1,695 ; in 1850, 4,149.

IROQUOIS, p. v., Iroquois co., Ill., 180 ms. N. E. of Springfield ; from W. 682 ms. Watered by Iroquois river.

IRVILLE, p. o., Licking township, Muskingum co., O., 56 ms. E. of Columbus ; from W. 349 ms.

IRVINE, c. h., p. v., seat of justice of Estill co., Ky., 68 ms. s. E. of Frankfort ; from W. 534 ms. Watered by Kentucky river.

IRVINE, p. o., Broken Straw township, Warren co., Pa., 215 ms. N. w. of Harrisburgh ; from W. 307 ms.

IRVINE'S STORE, p. o., Weakly co., Tenn., 114 ms. w. of Nashville ; from W. 800 ms.

IRVING, p. v., Hanover township, Chautauque co., N. Y., 315 ms. w. of Albany ; from W. 353 ms. Watered by Cattaraugus creek, and Lake Erie.

IRVING, v., Greenburgh township, Westchester co., N. Y. Watered by Tappan bay of Hudson river.

IRVING, p. o., Noble co., Ind.

IRVING, p. o., Barry co., Mich.

IRVING COLLEGE. p. o., Warren co., Tenn.

IRWIN COUNTY, situated in the southerly part of Georgia, with Ocmulgee river on the northeast. Area, 2,079 square miles. Face of the country, generally level. Seat of justice, Irwinville. Pop. in 1820, 411 ; in 1830, 1,180 ; in 1840, 2,038 ; in 1850, 3,334.

IRWIN, t., Venango co., Pa., 186 ms. N. w. of Harrisburgh ; from W. 226 ms. Watered by Scrub Grass creek. Pop. 1,504.

IRWIN'S CROSS-ROADS, p. o., Washington co., Ga.

IRWINSVILLE, p. o., Nicholas co., Ky.

IRWINSVILLE, c. h., p. v., seat of justice of Irwin co., Ga., 105 ms. s. of Milledgeville ; from W. 763 ms. Watered by Alapahaw river.

IRWINTON, c. h., p. v., seat of justice of Wilkinson co., Ga., 20 ms. s. of Milledgeville ; from W. 668 ms.

ISABELLA COUNTY, situated in the central part of Michigan, and traversed by Chippewa river. Area, 579 square miles. Seat of justice, ——.

ISLAND CREEK, p. t., Jefferson co., O., 145 ms. E. of Columbus ; from W. 271 ms. Pop. 1,981.

ISLAND FORD, p. o., Rutherford co., N. C., 231 ms. w. of Raleigh ; from W. 468 ms.

ISLEBOROUGH, p. t., Waldo co., Me., 54 ms. E. of Augusta ; from W. 643 ms. Watered by Penobscot river, consisting of several islands. Pop. 984.

ISLE BREVILLE, p. o., Natchitoches parish, La.

ISLE LA MOTT, v., Grand Isle co., Vt. Pop. 476.

ISLE OF WIGHT COUNTY, situated in the southeast of Virginia, with James river on the northeast, and the Blackwater on the southwest. Area, 400 square miles. Face of the country level ; soil, of middling quality. Seat of justice, Isle of Wight C. H. Pop. in 1810, 9,186 ; in 1820, 10,139 ; in 1830, 10,517 ; in 1840, 9,972, in 1850, 8,015.

ISLIP, p. t., Suffolk co., Long Island, N. Y., 191 ms. s. E. of Albany ; from W. 271 ms. Watered by Atlantic Ocean.

ISNEY, p. o., Choctaw co., Ala. ; from W. 971 ms.

ISOR'S STORE, p. o., Maury co., Tenn.

ISRAEL, t., Preble co., O., 106 ms. w. of Columbus ; from W. 502 ms. Pop. 1,641.

ISSAQUENA COUNTY, situated on the west boundary of Mississippi, with Mississippi river on the west, and the Yazoo on the southeast. Area, —— square miles. Seat of justice, Tallulah. Pop. in 1850, 4,478.

ITALY, t., Yates co., N. Y., 198 ms. w. of Albany ; from W. 319 ms. Watered by Flint creek, and Canandaigua lake. Pop. 1,627.

ITALY HILL, p. o., Italy township, Yates co., N. Y.

ITALY HOLLOW, p. o., Italy township, Yates co., N. Y.

ITAWAMBA COUNTY, situated on the east boundary of Mississippi, and traversed by Little Tombigbee

river. Area, 900 square miles. Seat of justice, Fulton Pop. in 1840, 5,375 ; in 1850, 13,528.

ITHACA, c. h., p. t., seat of justice of Tompkins co., N. Y., 162 ms. w. of Albany ; from W. 295 ms. Watered by Cayuga lake inlet, Fall, Cascadilla, and Six Mile creeks, and Seneca canal. Pop. in 1830, 3,324 ; in 1840, 5,650; in 1850, 6,909.

ITHACA, p. o., Darke co., O., 104 ms. w. of Columbus ; from W. 497 ms.

IVERSON, p. o., Bienville parish, La.

IVES' GROVE, p. o., Racine co., Wis., 101 ms. s. E. of Madison ; from W. 791 ms.

IVES' STORE, p. o., Princess Ann co., Va., 133 ms. s. E. of Richmond ; from W. 258 ms.

IVY, p. o. Miami co., Ind.

IVY, p. o., Yancy co., N. C., 262 ms. w. of Raleigh , from W. 492 ms.

IVY BEND, p. o., Madison co., N. C.

IVY ISLAND, p. o., Edgefield district, S. C.

IVY LOG, p. o., Union co., Va.

IVY MILLS, p. v., Delaware co., Pa., 88 ms. E. of Harrisburgh ; from W. 119 ms.

IXONIA, p. o., Jefferson co., Wis.

IZARD COUNTY, situated in the north part of Arkansas, and traversed by White river. Area, 1,600 square miles. Seat of justice, Izard. Pop. in 1830, 1,266 ; in 1840, 2,240 ; in 1850, 3,213.

IZARD, c. h., p. v., seat of justice of Izard co., Ark., 150 ms. N. of Little Rock ; from W. 1,076 ms. Watered by White river.

J.

JACINTO, c, h., p. v., seat of justice of Tishemingo co., Miss., 233 ms. N. E. of Jackson ; from W. 830 ms. Watered by sources of Tuscumbia creek.

JACKSONBOROUGH, c. h., p. v., seat of justice of Campbell co., Tenn.

JACK'S CREEK, p. o., Henderson co., Tenn., 133 ms. s. w. of Nashville ; from W. 817 ms.

JACK'S FORKS, p. o., Texas co., Mo.

JACKSON COUNTY, situated on the northwest boundary of Virginia, with Ohio river on the northwest. Area, 480 square miles. Seat of justice, Jackson C. H. Pop. in 1840, 4,890 ; in 1850, 6,554.

JACKSON COUNTY, situated toward the northeasterly part of Georgia. Area, 432 square miles. Seat of justice, Jefferson. Pop. in 1810, 10,569 ; in 1820, 8,355 ; in 1830, 9,004 ; in 1840, 8,522 ; in 1850, 9,768.

JACKSON COUNTY, situated on the north boundary of Florida, with Chattahoochee and Appalachicola rivers on the east. Area, 1,500 square miles. Seat of justice, Mariana. Pop. in 1840, 4,681 ; in 1850, 6,639.

JACKSON COUNTY, situated on the north boundary of Alabama, and traversed by Tennessee river. Area, 975 square miles. Seat of justice, Bellefonte. Pop. in 1840, 15,715 ; in 1850, 14,088.

JACKSON COUNTY, situated at the southeast corner of Mississippi, on the gulf of Mexico, and traversed by Pascagoula river. Area, 1,175 square miles. Face of the county varied ; soil, sterile. Seat of justice, Jackson C. H. Pop. in 1840, 1,965 ; in 1850, 3,196.

JACKSON COUNTY, situated on the north boundary of Tennessee, and traversed by Cumberland river. Area, 625 square miles. Face of the country, undulating. Soil, productive. Seat of justice, Gainesborough. Pop. in 1820, 7,593 ; in 1830, 9,698 ; in 1840, 12,872 ; in 1850, 15,673.

JACKSON COUNTY, situated toward the northeasterly part of Arkansas, with Big Black and White rivers on the west, and the Cache on the east. Area, 800 square miles. Seat of justice, Elizabeth. Pop. in 1830, 333 ; in 1840, 1,540 ; in 1850, 3,086.

JACKSON PARISH, situated toward the north part of Louisiana. Area, —— square miles. Seat of justice, ——. Pop. in 1850, 5,566.

JACKSON COUNTY, situated in the southerly part of Ohio. Area, 400 square miles. Face of the country uneven ; soil. productive. Seat of justice, Jackson. Pop. in 1820, 3,746 ; in 1830, 5,974 ; in 1840, 9,744 ; in 1850, 12,621.

JACKSON COUNTY, situated toward the south part of Indiana, and traversed by east fork of White river. Area, 500 square miles. Face of the country, even ; soil, fertile ; seat of justice, Brownstown. Pop. in

1820, 4,010; in 1830, 4,894 ; in 1840, 8,961; in 1850, 11,048.

JACKSON COUNTY, situated on the southwest boundary of Illinois, on Mississippi river. Area, 576 square miles. Face of the country, even. Seat of justice, Brownsville. Pop. in 1820, 1,542 ; in 1830, 1,827 ; in 1840, 3,566 ; in 1850, 5,862.

JACKSON COUNTY, situated in the southerly part of Michigan. Area, 720 square miles. Face of the country, even ; soil, rich. Seat of justice, Jackson. Pop. in 1840, 13,130 ; in 1850, 19,431.

JACKSON COUNTY, situated on the northeasterly boundary of Iowa, on Mississippi river. Area, 628 square miles. Seat of justice, Bellevue. Pop. in 1840, 1,411 ; in 1850, 7,210.

JACKSON COUNTY, situated on the west boundary of Missouri, with Missouri river on the north. Area, 525 square miles. Soil, fertile. Seat of justice, Independence. Pop. in 1840, 7,612 ; in 1850, 14,000.

JACKSON COUNTY, situated in the southern part of Texas. Area, —— square miles. Seat of justice, Texana. Pop. in 1850, 997.

JACKSON, p. t., Waldo co., Me., 47 ms. N. E. of Augusta ; from W. 642 ms. Watered by tributaries of Marsh river. Pop. 833.

JACKSON, p. t., Coos co., N. H., 79 ms. N. of Concord ; from W. 565 ms. Watered by tributaries of Ellis' river. Pop. 589.

JACKSON, p. t., Washington co., N. Y., 40 ms. N. E. of Albany ; from W. 410 ms. Pop. 2,129.

JACKSON, t., Northumberland co., Pa. Pop. 1,935.

JACKSON, t., Dauphin co., Pa., 22 ms. N. of Harrisburgh ; from W. 136 ms. Watered by Armstrong's and Powell's creeks.

JACKSON, t., Lycoming co., Pa. Pop. 407.

JACKSON, p. t., Susquehanna co., Pa., 181 ms. N. E. of Harrisburgh ; from W. 285 ms. Watered by Lackawannock and Tunkhannock creeks. Pop. 978.

JACKSON, t., Columbia co., Pa. Watered by tributaries of Fishery creek. Pop. 374.

JACKSON, t., Greene co., Pa. Pop. 1,252.

JACKSON, t., Lebanon co., Pa., 31 ms. E. of Harrisburgh ; from W. 141 ms. Watered by Tulpehocken and Swatara creeks, and Union canal. Pop. 2,857.

JACKSON, t., Tioga co., Pa., 149 ms. N. of Harrisburgh ; from W. 255 ms. Watered by Mill and Seely's creeks.

JACKSON, t., Cambria co., Pa., 138 ms. w. of Harrisburgh ; from W. 185 ms. Pop. 832.

JACKSON, c. h., p. v., Lick township, seat of justice of Jackson co., O., 63 ms. s. E. of Columbus ; from W. 377 ms. Pop. 482.

JACKSON, p. t., Preble co., O. Pop. 1,406.

JACKSON, t., Montgomery co., O., 79 ms. s. w. of Columbus ; from W. 475 ms. Pop. 2,012.

JACKSON, p. t., Monroe co., O. Pop. 1,163.

JACKSON, t., Wayne co., O., 98 ms. N. E. of Columbus ; from W. 356 ms.

JACKSON, p. t., Sandusky co., O. Pop. 1,092.

JACKSON, t., Muskingum co., O., 81 ms. E. of Columbus ; from W. 358 ms. Pop. 1,233.

JACKSON, t., Union co., O., 38 ms. N. w. of Columbus ; from W. 434 ms. Pop. 436.

JACKSON, t., Starke co., O., 112 ms. N. E. of Columbus ; from W. 324 ms. Pop. 1,517.

JACKSON, t., Wood co., O. Pop. 74.

JACKSON, t., Trumbull co., O., 152 ms. N. E. of Columbus ; from W. 298 ms. Pop. 1,079.

JACKSON, t., Allen co., O. Pop. 1,175.

JACKSON, t., Shelby co., O. Pop. 705.

JACKSON, t., Brown co., O.

JACKSON, t., Champaign co., O., 63 ms. w. of Columbus ; from W. 460 ms. Pop. 1,735.

JACKSON, t., Clermont co., O. Pop. 1,241.

JACKSON, t., Seneca co., O. Pop. 995.

JACKSON, t., Coshocton co., O., 80 ms. N. E. of Columbus ; from W. 340 ms. Watered by Muskingum river. Pop. 829.

JACKSON, t., Crawford co., O. Pop. 1,711.

JACKSON, t., Franklin co., O., 5 ms. from Columbus ; from W. 395 ms. Watered by Scioto river. Pop. 1,550.

JACKSON, t., Darke co., O. Pop. 565.

JACKSON, t., Guernsey co., O., 81 ms. E. of Columbus ; from W, 316 ms. Pop. 1,192.

JACKSON, t., Hancock co., O., 109 ms. N. w. of Columbus ; from W. 497 ms. Pop. 830.

JACKSON, t., Hardin co., O. Pop. 530.

JACKSON, t., Highland co., O., 92 ms. s. w. of Columbus; from W. 451 ms. Pop. 1,449.

JACKSON t., Hocking co., O.

JACKSON. t., Jackson co., O., 70 ms. s. E. of Columbus ; from W. 389 ms. Pop. 1,195.

JACKSON, t., Knox co., O., 60 ms. N. E. of Columbus ; from W, 382 ms. Watered by Wakatomica creek. Pop. 1,080.

JACKSON, t., Morgan co., O. Pop. 1,249.

JACKSON, p. t., Perry co., O., 49 ms. s. E. of Columbus ; from W. 351 ms. Pop. 1,740.

JACKSON, t., Pickaway co., O., 21 ms. s. of Columbus ; from W. 394 ms. Pop. 1,042.

JACKSON, t., Pike co., O., 58 ms. s. of Columbus ; from W. 391 ms.

JACKSON, p. v., Elkhart co., Ind., 146 ms. N. of Indianapolis ; from W. 610 ms. Pop. 991.

JACKSON, t., Brown co., Ind. Pop. 1,098.

JACKSON. t., Clay co., Ind., 64 ms. s. w. of Indianapolis ; from W. 640 ms. Pop. 735.

JACKSON, t., Dearborn co., Ind., 91 ms. s. E. of Indianapolis ; from W. 532 ms. Pop. 916.

JACKSON. t., Fayette co., Ind., 71 ms, E. of Indianapolis ; from W. 530 ms. Pop. 1,283.

JACKSON, t., Fountain co., Ind., 55 ms. N. w. of Indianapolis ; from W. 628 ms. Pop. 1,170.

JACKSON, t., Hamilton co., Ind. Pop. 1,800.

JACKSON, t., Hancock co., Ind., 28 ms. from Indianapolis ; from W. 559 ms. Pop. 677.

JACKSON, t., Orange co., Ind., 102 ms. s. of Indianapolis ; from W. 640 ms. Pop. 687.

JACKSON, t., Owen co., Ind. Pop. 981.

JACKSON, t., Putnam co., Ind., 30 ms. w. of Indianapolis ; from W. 603 ms.

JACKSON, t., Randolph co., Ind.

JACKSON. t., Ripley co., Ind., 67 ms. s. E. of Indianapolis ; from W. 563 ms. Pop. 887.

JACKSON, t., Rush co., Ind., 35 ms. E. of Indianapolis ; from W. 558 ms. Pop. 887.

JACKSON, t., Shelby co., Ind., 29 ms. s. E. of Indianapolis ; from W. 583 ms. Pop. 1,181.

JACKSON, t., Tippecanoe co., Ind., 59 ms. N. w. of Indianapolis ; from W. 633 ms. Pop. 966.

JACKSON, t., Steuben co., Ind. Pop. 594.

JACKSON, t., Washington co., Ind., 97 ms. s. of Indianapolis ; from W. 613 ms. Pop. 2,806.

JACKSON, v., Wayne co., Ind., 69 ms. E. of Indianapolis ; from W. 517 ms. Pop. 752.

JACKSON, c. h., p. t., seat of justice of Jackson co., Mich., 79 ms. w. of Detroit ; from W. 549 ms. Watered by Grand river. Pop. 4,147.

JACKSON, p. o., Louisa co., Va. 41 ms. N. w. of Richmond ; from W 97 ms.

JACKSON, c. h., p. v., seat of justice of Jackson co., Va., 336 ms. N. w. of Richmond ; from W. 335 ms.

JACKSON, p. v., Northampton co., N. C., 108 ms. N. E. of Raleigh ; from W. 211 ms.

JACKSON, c. h., p. v., seat of justice of Butts co., Ga., 67 ms. w. of Milledgeville; from W. 664 ms. Watered by Ocmulgee river.

JACKSON, p. v., Clark co., Ala. ; from W. 959 ms.

JACKSON, c. h., p. v., seat of justice of Jackson co., Miss., 235 ms. s. E. of Jackson ; from W. 1,053 ms.

JACKSON, seat of justice of Hinds co., and capital of Mississippi, is situated at the head of boat navigation, on the west bank of Pearl river. It is built on a beautiful level ground, half a mile square. It contains a magnificent statehouse, governor's house, a penitentiary, and other elegant public buildings. It is connected with Jackson by a railroad 45 miles long. It lies 1,015 miles southwest of Washington. Pop. in 1840, 2,126 ; in 1850,

----

JACKSON, c. h., p, v., seat of justice of East Feliciana parish, La., 124 ms. N. w. of New Orleans ; from W. 1,142 ms. Watered by Thompson's creek. Seat of Louisiana college.

JACKSON, c. h., p. v., seat of justice of Madison co., Tenn., 134 ms. s. w. of Nashville ; from W. 819 ms. Watered by Forked Deer river.

JACKSON, c. h., p. v., seat of justice of Cape Girardeau co., Mo., 196 ms. s. E. of Jefferson city ; from W. 866 ms. Watered by White Water river.

JACKSON, t., Johnson co., Mo. Pop. 2,256.

JACKSON, t., Livingston co., Mo.

JACKSON, t., Adair co., Mo. Pop. 1,502.

JACKSON, t., Buchanan co., Mo. Pop. 584.

JACKSON, p. t., Greene co., Mo. Pop. 1,972.

JACKSON, t., St. Genevieve co., Mo. Pop. 546.

JACKSON, t., Osage co., Mo. Pop. 943.

JACKSON, t., Clarke co., Mo.

JACKSON. v., Lawrence co., Ark., 140 ms. N. E. of Little Rock ; from W. 997 ms.

JACKSON, t., Dallas co., Ark. Pop. 910.

JACKSON, t., Sevier co., Ark. Pop. 856.

JACKSON, t., Union co., Ark. Pop. 796.

JACKSON, p. o., Stephenson co., Ill.

JACKSON, c. h., p. v., seat of justice of Breathitt co., Ky.

JACKSON, c. h., p. v., seat of justice of Calaveras co., Cal.

JACKSONBOROUGH, v., Maryland township, Otsego co., N. Y., 162 ms. w of Albany ; from W, 366 ms.

JACKSONBOROUGH, p. v., Wayne township, Butler co., O., 91 ms. s. w. of Columbus ; from W, 484 ms.

JACKSONBOROUGH, c. h., p. v., seat of justice of Scriven co., Ga., 116 ms. s. E. of Milledgeville ; from W. 637 ms. Watered by Brier creek.

JACKSON BROOK, p. o., Washington co,, Me., 241 ms. N. E. of Augusta ; from W. 829 ms.

JACKSONBURGH, p. o., Herkimer co., N. Y., 73 ms. N. w. of Albany ; from W. 390 ms.

JACKSONBURGH, p. v., Wayne co., Ind., 57 ms. E. of Indianapolis ; from W. 516 ms. Pop. 752.

JACKSON CORNERS, p. o., Milan township, Dutchess co., N. Y., 49 ms. s. of Albany ; from W. 327 ms.

JACKSON CREEK, p. o., Will co., Ill.

JACKSON FURNACE, p. o., Jackson co., O.

JACKSON HALL, p. o., Franklin co., Pa., 51 ms. s. w. of Harrisburgh ; from W. 89 ms.

JACKSONHAM, p. v., Lancaster district, S. C., 80 ms. N. E. of Columbia ; from W. 427 ms.

JACKSON HILL, p. o., Spartanburgh district, S. C.

JACKSON POINT, p. o., Holt co., Mo.

JACKSONPORT, p. o., Jackson co., Ark.

JACKSON'S CAMP, p. o., Tallapoosa co., Ala.

JACKSON'S FERRY, p. o., Wythe co., Va., 244 ms. w. of Richmond ; from W. 312 ms.

JACKSON'S MILLS, p. o., Ocean co., N. J., 31 ms. E. of Trenton ; from W. 497 ms.

JACKSON'S MILLS, p. o., Lenawee co., Mich.

JACKSONTOWN, p. v., Licking township, Licking co., O., 31 ms. N. E. of Columbus ; from W. 362 ms.

JACKSON VALLEY, p. o., Susquehanna co., Pa.

JACKSONVILLE, p. v., Windham co., Vt., 142 ms. s. of Montpelier ; from W. 423 ms.

JACKSONVILLE, p. v., Ulysses township, Tompkins co., N. Y., 170 ms. w. of Albany ; from W. 303 ms.

JACKSONVILLE, p. o., Burlington co., N. J., 15 ms. n. of Trenton ; from W. 160 ms.

JACKSONVILLE, p. v., Lehigh co., Pa., 89 ms. N. E. of Harrisburgh ; from W. 183 ms.

JACKSONVILLE, c. h., p. v., seat of justice of Telfair co., Ga., 115 ms. s. of Milledgeville; from W. 762 ms. Watered by Ocmulgee river. Pop. 119.

JACKSONVILLE, c. h., p. v., seat of justice of Duvall co., Flor., 252 ms. E. of Tallahassee; from W. 801 ms. Watered by St. John's river. Pop. 1,045.

JACKSONVILLE, c. h., p. v., seat of justice of Benton co., Ala.: from W. 717 ms. Pop. 716.

JACKSONVILLE, p. v., Wayne township, Darke co., O., 94 ms. w. of Columbus; from W. 485 ms. Pop. 565.

JACKSONVILLE, p. v., Switzerland co, Ind., 111 ms. s. E. of Indianapolis; from W. 550 ms.

JACKSONVILLE, c. h., p. v., seat of justice of Morgan co., Ill., 33 ms. w. of Springfield; from W. 813 ms. Seat of Illinois college. Pop. 2,745,

JACKSONVILLE, p. o., Cherokee co., Tex.

JACKSONVILLE, p. o., Bourbon co., Ky.

JACKSONVILLE, p. o., Tuolumne co., Cal.

JACK'S REEF, p. o., Elbridge township, Onondaga co., N. Y., 150 ms. w. of Albany; from W. 354 ms.

JACKSVILLE, p. o., Butler co., Pa.

JACOBSBURGH, p. v., Bushkill township, Northampton co., Pa., 106 ms. N. E. of Harrisburgh; from W. 119 ms.

JACOBSBURGH, p. v., Smith township, Belmont co., O., 126 ms. E. of Columbus; from W. 287 ms.

JACOB'S FORK, p. o., Catawba co., N. C.

JACOBSTOWN, p. o., Burlington co., N. J.

JADDEN, p. o., Grant co., Ind.

JAFFREY, p. t., Cheshire co., N. H., 48 ms. s. w. of Concord; from W. 449 ms. Watered by tributaries of Contoocook and Ashuelot rivers. Pop. 1,497.

JAILES, t., Van Buren co., Ark.

JAKE'S PRAIRIE, p. o., Gasconade co., Mo., 61 ms. s. E. of Jefferson city; from W. 925 ms.

JAKE'S RUN, p. o., Monongalia co.. Va.

JALAPA, p. o., Grant co., Ind.

JALAPA, p. o., McMinn co., Tenn.

JALAPA, p. o., Greene co., Ill.

JALAPA, p. o., Dooly co., Ga.

JAMAICA, p. t., Windham co., Vt., 127 ms. s. of Montpelier; from W. 449 ms. Watered by West river and Bald Mountain brook. Pop. 1,606.

JAMAICA, p. t., Queen's co., Long Island, N. Y., 158 ms. s. of Albany; from W. 238 ms. Watered by Jamaica bay. Pop. 4,247.

JAMAICA, p. o., Middlesex co., Va., 74 ms. E. of Richmond; from W. 136 ms.

JAMAICA PLAIN, p. v., Roxbury township, Norfolk co., Mass., 6 ms. s. w. of Boston; from W. 438 ms. Watered by Jamaica pond.

JAMES, t., Steuben co., Ind. Pop. 415.

JAMES, t., Taney co., Mo.

JAMES' BAYOU, t., Scott co.. Mo.

JAMESBURGH. p. o., Middlesex co., N. J.

JAMES CITY COUNTY, situated in the easterly part of Virginia, with York river on the northeast, and James and Chickahominy rivers on the southwest. Area, 150 square miles. Face of the country undulating; soil generally barren. Seat of justice, Williamsburgh. Pop. in 1810, 4,094; in 1820, 3,161; in 1830, 3,838; in 1840, 3,779; in 1850, 4,020.

JAMES' CREEK. p. o., Huntingdon co., Pa., 106 ms. w. of Harrisburgh; from W. 152 ms.

JAMES' CROSS-ROADS, p. o., Washington co., Tenn.

JAMES' FORK. p. o., Crawford co., Ark.

JAMES' MILL, p. o., Monroe co., Ill., 122 ms. s. of Springfield; from W. 835 ms.

JAMESON'S, p. o., Owen co., Ky.

JAMESPORT, p. o., Suffolk co., Long Island, N. Y.

JAMESTOWN. t., Newport co., R. I., 3 ms. w. of Newport; from W. 411 ms.: including Canonicut island, in Narraganset bay. Pop. 358.

JAMESTOWN, p. v., Ellicott township, Chautauque co., N. Y. 331 ms. w. of Albany; from W. 318 ms. Watered by Chautauque lake outlet.

JAMESTOWN, p. v., Mercer co., Pa, 251 ms. N. w. of Harrisburgh; from W. 298 ms.

JAMESTOWN, v., Prince Edward co., Va., 69 s. w. of Richmond; from W. 167 ms. Watered by Appomatox river.

JAMESTOWN, p., James City co., Va., 44 ms. s. E. of Richmond; from W. 114 ms. Watered by James river. The first English settlement in America, and founded by Captain John Smith, in 1607. It is now in ruins, and nearly depopulated.

JAMESTOWN, p. v., Guilford co., N. C., 93 ms. w. of Raleigh; from W. 314 ms. Watered by Deep river.

JAMESTOWN, p. v., seat of justice of Fentress co., Tenn., 124 ms. E. of Nashville; from W. 580 ms.

JAMESTOWN, p. v., seat of justice of Russell co., Ky., 99 ms. s. of Frankfort; from W. 613 ms.

JAMESTOWN, p. v., Silver Creek township, Greene co., O., 64 ms. s. w. of Columbus; from W. 449 ms.

JAMESTOWN, p. v., Boone co., Ind., 28 ms. N. w. of Indianapolis; from W. 599 ms.

JAMESTOWN, p. v., Grant co., Wis., 108 ms. w. of Madison; from W. 898 ms.

JAMESTOWN, p. v., Andrew co., Mo.

JAMESTOWN, p. o., Moniteau co., Mo.

JAMESTOWN, p. o., Muscogee co., Ga.

JAMESTOWN, p. o., Winneshiek co., Iowa.

JAMESTOWN, p. o., Clinton co., Ill.

JAMESVILLE, p. v., De Witt township, Onondaga co., N. Y., 127 ms. w. of Albany; from W. 348 ms.

JAMESVILLE, v., Cherokee co. N. C., 351 ms. w. of Raleigh; from W. 581 ms. Watered by Valley river.

JANELAW, p. o., Lewis co., Va.

JANESVILLE, p. v., Rock co., Wis., 41 ms. s. E. of Madison; from W. 806 ms.

JARRATT'S, p. o., Sussex co., Va., 52 ms. s. of Richmond; from W. 171 ms.

JARRETT'S FORD, p. o., Kanawha co., Va., 323 N. w. of Richmond; from W. 348 ms.

JARRETTSVILLE, p. o., Harford co., Md., 63 ms. N. of Annapolis; from W. 73 ms.

JARVIS GORE, t., Penobscot co., Me.

JASPER COUNTY, situated in the central part of Georgia, with Ocmulgee river on the southwest. Area, 480 square miles. Seat of justice, Monticello. Pop. in 1810, 7,573; in 1820, 13,614; in 1830, 13,131; in 1840, 11,111; in 1850, 11,486.

JASPER COUNTY, situated toward the southeasterly part of Mississippi. Area, 650 square miles. Seat of justice, Paulding. Pop. in 1840, 2,958; in 1850, 6,184.

JASPER COUNTY, situated on the west boundary of Indiana, and traversed by Iroquois river. Area, 980 square miles. Seat of justice, Rensselaer. Pop. in 1840, 1,267; in 1850. 3,540.

JASPER COUNTY, situated in the southeasterly part of Illinois. Area, 475 square miles. Soil poor. Seat of justice, Newton. Pop. in 1840, 1,472; in 1850. 3,220.

JASPER COUNTY, situated in the southeasterly part of Texas, with Neches river on the west. Area, —— square miles. Seat of justice, Jasper. Pop. in 1850, 3,546.

JASPER COUNTY, situated in the central part of Iowa. Area, —— square miles. Seat of justice, Newton. Pop. in 1850, 1,280.

JASPER COUNTY, situated on the west boundary of Missouri. Area, 980 square miles. Seat of justice, Jasper. Pop. in 1850, 4,223.

JASPER, p. t., Steuben co., N. Y., 239 ms. w. of Albany; from W. 289 ms. Watered by Bennett's and Tuscarora creeks. Pop. 1,749.

JASPER, c. h., p. v., seat of justice of Walker co., Ala.

JASPER, p. v., Sunfish township, Pike co., O., 66 ms. s. of Columbus; from W. 401 ms. Situated on the Ohio canal.

JASPER, c. h., p. v., seat of justice of Marion co., Tenn., 114 ms. s. E. of Nashville; from W. 634 ms. Watered by Sequatchy river.

JASPER, p. v., seat of justice of Hamilton co., Flor., 90 ms. E. of Tallahassee.

JASPER, t., Polk co., Mo.

JASPER, c. h., p. v., seat of justice of Jasper co., Mo., 163 ms. s. w. of Jefferson city; from W. 1,109 ms. Watered by a tributary of Neosho river.

JASPER, c. h., p. v., seat of justice of Dubois co., Ind., 124 ms. s. w. of Indianapolis; from W. 655 ms. Watered by Patoka creek.

JASPER, t., Ralls co., Mo.

JASPER, t., Newton co., Mo.

JASPER, p. o., Jasper co., Tex.

JATT, p. o., Rapides parish, La.

JAVA, p. t., Wyoming co., N. Y., 267 ms. w. of Albany; from W. 352 ms. Watered by Seneca creek and the sources of Cattaraugus creek. Pop. 2,245.

JAVA, p. o., Lucas co., O.

JAVA VILLAGE, p. o., Java township, Wyoming co., N. Y., 271 ms. w. of Albany; from W. 356 ms.

JAY COUNTY, situated on the east boundary of Indiana. Area, 370 square miles. Seat of justice, Jay Pop. in 1840, 3,863; in 1850, 7,065.

JAY, p. t., Franklin co., Me., 29 ms. N. w. of Augusta;

from W. 607 ms. Watered by Androscoggin river. Pop. 1,733.

JAY, p. t., Orleans co., Vt., 58 ms. N. of Montpelier; from W. 574 ms. Watered by tributaries of Missisque river. Pop. 371.

JAY. p. t., Essex co., N. Y., 148 ms. N. of Albany; from W. 528 ms. Watered by a tributary of Au Sable river. Pop. 2,688.

JAY, c. h., p. v., seat of justice of Jay co., Ind., 100 ms. N. E. of Indianapolis; from W. 523 ms. Watered by Salamanic river.

JAY BRIDGE, p. o., Franklin co., Me.

JAYNESVILLE, p. o., Covington co.,,Miss., 69 ms. s. E. of Jackson; from W. 1,038 ms. Watered by a branch of Leaf river.

JEANCRETTS, p. o., St. Mary's parish, La., 162 ms. w. of New Orleans; from W. 1,297 ms.

JEANSVILLE, p. o., Luzerne co., Pa.

JEDDO, p. o., Orleans co., N. Y.

JEDDO, p. o., Jefferson co., O.

JEFFERSON COUNTY, situated in the northerly part of New York, with Lake Ontario on the west, and St. Lawrence river on the northwest. Area, 1.125 square miles. Face of the country, broken, in the interior, but even toward Lake Ontario and St. Lawrence river; soil fertile. Seat of justice, Watertown. Pop. in 1810, 15,140; in 1820, 32,952; in 1830, 48,515; in 1840, 60,984; in 1850, 68,153.

JEFFERSON COUNTY, situated toward the westerly part of Pennsylvania. Area, 1,200 square miles. Face of the country hilly; soil of middling quality. Seat of justice, Brookville. Pop. in 1810, 161; in 1820, 561; in 1830, 2,225; in 1840, 7,253; in 1850, 13,518.

JEFFERSON COUNTY, situated on the northeasterly boundary of Virginia, with Potomac river on the northeast, and traversed by the Shenandoah. Area, 225 square miles. Face of the country pleasantly di, versified with hills and valleys; soil rich and well cultivated. Seat of justice, Charleston. Pop. in 1810, 11,851; in 1820, 13,087; in 1830, 12,927; in 1840, 14,082; in 1850, 15.357.

JEFFERSON COUNTY, situated in the easterly part of Georgia, and traversed by Ogeechee river. Area, 660 square miles. Face of the country undulating; soil sandy. Seat of justice, Louisville. Pop. in 1810, 6,111; in 1820, 7,058; in 1830, 7,309; in 1840, 7,254; in 1850, 9,131.

JEFFERSON COUNTY, situated on the north boundary of Florida, with the gulf of Mexico on the south Area, 702 square miles. Seat of justice, Monticello. Pop. in 1830, 3,317; in 1840, 5,713; in 1850, 7,718.

JEFFERSON COUNTY, situated toward the northerly part of Alabama. Area, 1.040 square miles. Seat of justice, Elyton. Pop. in 1830, 6,865; in 1840, 7,131; in 1850, 8,989.

JEFFERSON COUNTY, situated on the westerly boundary of Mississippi, on the easterly side of Mississippi river. Area, 630 square miles. Face of the country uneven; soil generally fertile. Seat of justice, Fayette. Pop. in 1810, 4,001; in 1820, 6,822; in 1830, 9,755; in 1840, 11,650; in 1850, 13,193.

JEFFERSON COUNTY, situated toward the southeasterly part of Arkansas, and traversed by Arkansas river. Area, 1,180 square miles. Seat of justice, Pine Bluffs. Pop. in 1830, 772; in 1840, 2,566; in 1850, 5,834.

JEFFERSON COUNTY, situated toward the northeasterly part of Tennessee. with Holston river on the northwest, and traversed by the Nolichucky river. Area, 356 square miles. Soil pleasantly fertile. Seat of justice, Danbridge. Pop. in 1820, 8,953; in 1830, 11,801; in 1840, 12,076; in 1850, 13,204.

JEFFERSON COUNTY, situated in the northerly part of Kentucky, on Ohio river. Area 504 square miles. Face of the country undulating; soil rich. Seat of justice, Louisville. Pop. in 1810, 13,399; in 1820, 20,768; in 1830, 23,979; in 1840, 36,346; in 1850, 59,829.

JEFFERSON COUNTY, situated on the easterly boundary of Ohio, on the Ohio river. Area, 396 square miles. Soil fertile. Seat of justice, Steubenville. Pop. in 1810, 17,260; in 1820, 18,531; in 1830, 22,489; in 1840, 25,030; in 1850, 29,f32.

JEFFERSON COUNTY, situated toward the southeast part of Wisconsin, and traversed by Rock river. Area, 576 square miles. Seat of justice, Jefferson. Pop. in 1840, 914; in 1850, 6,955.

JEFFERSON COUNTY, situated in the southeast part of Iowa. Area, 380 square miles. Seat of justice, Fairfield. Pop. in 1840, 2,773; in 1850, 8,890.

JEFFERSON COUNTY, situated on the southerly boundary of Indiana, on Ohio river. Area, 360 square miles. Face of the country hilly; soil fertile. Seat of justice, Madison. Pop. in 1820, 8,030; in 1830, 11,465; in 1840, 16,614; in 1850, 23,914.

JEFFERSON COUNTY, situated toward the south part of Illinois. Area, 576 square miles. Face of the country level. Seat of justice, Mount Vernon. Pop. in 1820, 691; in 1830, 2,555; in 1840, 5,762; in 1850, 8,109.

JEFFERSON COUNTY, situated on the easterly boundary of Missouri, with Mississippi river on the east. Area, 500 square miles. Face of the country broken; soil generally sterile. Seat of justice, Hillsborough. Pop. in 1820, 1,835; in 1830, 2,586; in 1840, 4,296; in 1850, 6,928.

JEFFERSON COUNTY, situated at the southeast corner of Texas, on the gulf of Mexico, lake and river Sabine on the east, and traversed by Neches river Area, —— square miles. Seat of justice, Beaumont. Pop. in 1850, 1,836.

JEFFERSON PARISH, situated in the southeasterly part of Louisiana, traversed by the Mississippi, and bounded by bayous and inlets of the gulf of Mexico. Area, 720 square miles. Face of the country low and level; soil generally unproductive. Seat of justice, La Fayette. Pop. in 1830, 6,846; in 1840, 10,470; in 1850, 25,091.

JEFFERSON, p. t. Lincoln co., Me., 21 ms. s. E. of Augusta; from W. 613 ms. Watered by Damariscotta pond and river. Pop. 2,225.

JEFFERSON, p. t., Coos co., N. H., 108 ms. N. of Concord; from W. 569 ms. Watered by Israel's river. Pop. 629.

JEFFERSON, p. t., Schoharie co., N. Y., 56 ms. w. of Albany; from W. 375 ms. Watered by tributaries of Delaware river and Schoharie creek. Pop. 1,748.

JEFFERSON, v., Dix township, Chemung co., N. Y. Watered by Seneca lake and Chemung canal.

JEFFERSON, t., Morris co., N. J. Watered by Rockaway river, Hurd's pond, and Hopatcong lake. Pop. 1,358.

JEFFERSON, t., Greene co., Pa., 204 ms. w. of Harrisburgh; from W. 220 ms. Watered by Monongahela river, and Ten-Mile creek. Pop 1,435.

JEFFERSON, t., Alleghany co., Pa. Pop. 1,138.

JEFFERSON, t., Cambria co., Pa.

JEFFERSON, t., Fayette co., Pa. Pop. 1,435,

JEFFERSON, t., Luzerne co., Pa. Pop. 414.

JEFFERSON, c. h., p. t., seat of justice of Ashtabula co., O., 204 ms. N. E. of Columbus; from W. 338 ms. Watered by Mills creek. Pop. 1,064.

JEFFERSON, t., Adams co., O.

JEFFERSON, t., Clinton co., O. Pop. 810.

JEFFERSON, t., Coshocton co., O. Pop. 929.

JEFFERSON, t., Franklin co., O. Watered by Black Lick, and Rocky fork of Big Walnut creek. Pop. 1,236.

JEFFERSON, t., Guernsey co., O. Pop. 857.

JEFFERSON, t., Jackson co., O. Pop. 1,036.

JEFFERSON, t., Fayette co., O.

JEFFERSON, t., Logan co., O. Pop. 2,042.

JEFFERSON, t., Knox co., O. Pop. 1,484.

JEFFERSON, t., Montgomery co., O. Pop. 1,808.

JEFFERSON, t., Madison co., O. Watered by Little Darby creek. Pop. 634.

JEFFERSON, t., Mercer co., O. Pop. 271.

JEFFERSON, t., Muskingum co., O. Pop. 2,822.

JEFFERSON, t., Preble co., O. Pop. 2,258.

JEFFERSON, t., Ross co., O. Watered by Scioto river and Walnut and Salt creeks.

JEFFERSON, t., Richland co., O. Pop. 2,564.

JEFFERSON, t., Scioto co., O. Watered by Scioto river. Pop. 840.

JEFFERSON, t., Tuscarawas co., O. Pop. 1,063.

JEFFERSON, t., Williams co., O. Pop. 1,015.

JEFFERSON, t., Allen co., Ind. Pop. 563.

JEFFERSON, p. v., Clinton co., Ind., 46 ms. N. of Indianapolis; from W. 604 ms. Pop. 254.

JEFFERSON, t., Grant co., Ind. Pop. 1,029.

JEFFERSON, t., Miami co., Ind. Pop. 1,138.

JEFFERSON, t., Hamilton co., Ind.

JEFFERSON, t., Noble co., Ind. Pop. 722.

JEFFERSON, t., Putnam co., Ind. Pop. 1,046.

JEFFERSON, t., Switzerland co., Ind. Pop 3,082.

JEFFERSON, t., Wayne co., Ind. Pop. 1,117.

JEFFERSON, t., Adair co., Mo. Pop. 1,502.

JEFFERSON, t., Johnson co., Mo. Pop. 1,003.

JEFFERSON, t., Scotland co., Mo. Pop. 1,024.

JEFFERSON, t., Jefferson co., Wis.

JEFFERSON, t., Sevier co., Ark. Pop. 489.

JEFFERSON, p. v., Frederick co., Md., 83 ms. N. w. of Annapolis; from W. 51 ms.

JEFFERSON, p. o., Powhatan co., Va., 34 ms. w. of Richmond; from W. 136 ms.

JEFFERSON, c. h., p. v., seat of justice of Ashe co., N. C., 202 ms. N. w. of Raleigh; from W. 366 ms. Watered by New river.

JEFFERSON, c. h., p. v., seat of justice of Jackson co., Ga., 95 ms. N. of Milledgeville; from W. 630 ms. Watered by Oconee river.

JEFFERSON, p. v., Rutherford co.. Tenn., 22 ms. s. E. of Nashville; from W. 677 ms. Watered by Stone's river, and west fork of Cumberland river.

JEFFERSON, t., Cass co., Mich. Pop. 887.

JEFFERSON, c. h., p. t., seat of justice of Jefferson co., Wis., 36 ms. E. of Madison; from W. 834 ms.

JEFFERSON, p. o., Cass co., Tex.

JEFFERSON, p. o., Marengo co., Ala.

JEFFERSON, t., Cole co., Mo.; from W. 980 ms.

JEFFERSON, t., Osage co., Mo. Pop. 492.

JEFFERSON, t., Johnson co., Mo.

JEFFERSON, t., Livingston co., Mo.

JEFFERSON, t., Monroe co., Mo.

JEFFERSON, t. Sevier co., Ark. Pop. 489.

JEFFERSON BARRACKS, p. v., St. Louis co., Mo., 142 ms. E. of Jefferson City; from W. 822 ms. Military station of the U.-S.

JEFFERSON CITY, seat of justice of Cole co., and capital of Missouri, is situated near the central part of the state, on the south bank of the Missouri, nine miles from the mouth of Osage river, 134 miles west of St. Louis, and 936 miles from Washington. Its site is elevated, and it contains the statehouse, governor's mansion, penitentiary, and other public buildings, and is gradually and substantially rising in wealth and intelligence. The population in 1830, was 1,200; in 1840, 1,174; in 1850, 3,721.

JEFFERSON FURNACE, p. o., Clarion co., Pa.

JEFFERSON MILLS, p. o., Coos co., N. H.

JEFFERSON MILLS, p. o., Jefferson co., Mo.

JEFFERSONTON, p. v., Culpeper co., Va., 112 ms. N. w. of Richmond; from W. 61 ms. Watered by Rappahannock river.

JEFFERSONTON, c. h., p. v., seat of justice of Camden co., Ga., 270 ms. s. E. of Milledgeville; from W. 779 ms. Watered by St. Illa river

JEFFERSONTOWN, p. v., Jefferson co., Ky., 66 ms. w. of Frankfort; from W. 608 ms.

JEFFERSONVILLE, p. v., Lamoille co., Vt., 45 ms. N. of Montpelier; from W. 545 ms.

JEFFERSON VALLEY, p. o., Westchester co., N. Y.

JEFFERSONVILLE, p. o., Sullivan co., N. Y.

JEFFERSONVILLE, p. v., Clark co., Ind., 117 ms. s. E. of Indianapolis: from W. 597 ms. Watered by Ohio river. Pop. 1,725.

JEFFERSONVILLE, p. v., Morristown township, Montgomery co., Pa., 101 ms. E. of Harrisburgh; from W. 159 ms.

JEFFERSONVILLE, p. v., Fayette co., Ohio., 60 ms. s. w. of Columbus; from W. 453 ms. Pop. 1,872.

JEFFERSONVILLE, p. o., Twiggs co., Ga.

JEFFREYS' STORE, p. o., Nottoway co., Va., 74 ms. s. w. of Richmond; from W. 193 ms.

JEFFREY'S CREEK, p. o., Marion district, S. C., 129 ms. E. of Columbia; from W. 470 ms.

JEFFRIES, p. o., Clearfield co., Pa.

JELLOWAY, p. o.. Knox co., O.

JENA, t., Livingston co., Mich.

JENA, p. o., Tuscaloosa co., Ala.; from W. 839 ms.

JENKS, t., Jefferson co., Pa. Pop. 88.

JENKINS' BRIDGE, p. o., St. Clair co., Mo.

JENKINS' CREEK, p. o., Jasper co., Mo.

JENKINS' STORE, p. o., Union co., N. C., 168 ms. s. w. of Raleigh; from W. 413 ms.

JENKINTOWN, p. v., Montgomery co., Pa., 107 ms. E. of Harrisburgh; from W. 148 ms.

JENNER, p. t., Somerset co., Pa., 142 ms. from Harrisburgh; from W. 162 ms. Watered by Beaver Dam run.

JENNER'S CROSS-ROADS, p. o., Jenner township, Somerset co., Pa.

JENNERSVILLE, p. v., Chester co., Pa., 69 ms. E. of Harrisburgh; from W. 98 ms.

JENNINGS COUNTY, situated in the southeast part of Indiana. Area, 380 square miles. Face of the coun-

try, undulating; soil, productive. Seat of justice, Vernon. Pop. in 1820, 2,000; in 1830, 3,950; in 1840, 8,829; in 1850, 3,422.

JENNINGS, t., Van Wert co., O. Pop. 201.

JENNINGS, t., Putnam co., O., 145 ms. from Columbus: from W. 481 ms. Pop. 336.

JENNINGS, t., Fayette co , Ind. Pop. 893.

JENNINGS, p. o., Franklin co., Ind., 79 ms. s. E. of Indianapolis.

JENNINGS, p. o., Hamilton co., Flor.

JENNINGS GAP, p. o., Augusta co., Va., 129 ms. N. w. of Richmond; from W. 156 ms.

JENNINGS ORDINARY, p. o., Nottoway co., Va., 75 ms. s. w. of Richmond; from W. 182 ms.

JENNY LIND, p. o., Sebastian co., Ark.

JENNY LIND, p. o., Chatham co., N. C.

JERICHO, p. o., Perry co., Ala.; from W. 821 ms.

JERICHO, p. t., Chittenden co., Vt., 52 ms. N. w. of Montpelier; from W. 528 ms. Watered by Brown's, Onion, and other rivers. Pop. 1,837.

JERICHO, p. v., Oyster bay township, Queens co., Long Island, N. Y., 173 ms. s. of Albany; from W. 253 ms.

JERICHO, p. v., Wayne co., N. C., 71 ms. s. w. of Raleigh; from W. 301 ms.

JERICHO, p. o., Kane co., Ill.

JERICHO CENTRE, p. v., Jericho township, Chittenden co., Vt., 32 ms. N. w. of Montpelier; from W. 518 ms.

JERNIGAN, p. o., Orange co., Flor.

JEROME, p. t., Union co., O. Pop. 881.

JEROME, p. o., Howard co., Ind.

JEROMESVILLE, p. v., Mohican township, Ashland co., O., 82 ms. N. E. of Columbus; from W. 359 ms.

JERSEY, v., Bradford township, Steuben co., N Y., 205 ms. of Albany; from W. 317 ms. Watered by Mead creek.

JERSEY, p. o., Licking co., O., 35 ms. N. E. of Columbus; from W. 384 ms.

JERSEY, p. o., Oakland co., Mich.

JERSEY CITY, Hudson co., N. J., is situated upon a peninsula, on the west bank of the Hudson, opposite the lower extremity of New York. In the days of the Revolution it was known as Paulus Hook, and was the scene of several events interwoven in American history. Upon the neck of the peninsula, a little in advance of Bergen hill, was quite a strong fortification, which was occupied as a British outpost during a long period of the war. It was surprised, and its force made prisoners, in July, 1779, by Major Henry Lee, and a part of his legion. Here the Paterson railway, connected with the Erie; the Morris and Essex railway; the Central railway, reaching toward Easton, on the Delaware; the New Jersey railway, extending to Trenton, and connecting with routes to Philadelphia; all have a terminus. Here, also, the Morris canal terminates, after pursuing a circuitous route of 100 miles from the Delaware river. Here the Cunard British Steam Navigation Company have an extensive wharf, from which their magnificent ocean-steamers sail for Europe at regular intervals. Manufactories of various kinds are giving to Jersey city the most active prosperity, and its population, like that of all the towns near New York, is rapidly increasing. Several ferries communicate with New York. Pop. in 1830, about 1,500; in 1840, 3,072; in 1850, 6,856.

JERSEY SETTLEMENT, p. o., Davidson co., N. C.

JERSEY SHORE, p. b.. Mifflin township, Lycoming co., Pa., 99 ms. N. w. of Harrisburgh; from W. 209 ms. Watered by west branch of Susquehanna river, and Pennsylvania canal. Pop. 632.

JERSEYTOWN, p. v., Madison township, Montour co., Pa., 84 ms. N. of Harrisburgh; from W. 194 ms.

JERSEYVILLE, c. h., p. v., seat of justice of Jersey co., Ill., 71 ms. s. w. of Springfield; from W. 821 ms.

JERUSALEM, p. t., Yates co., N. Y., 199 ms. w. of Albany; from W. 325 ms. Watered by west branch of Crooked lake. Pop. 2,912.

JERUSALEM, p. v., seat of justice of Southampton co., Va., 70 ms. s. E. of Richmond; from W. 189 ms.

JERUSALEM, p. o., Davie co., N. C.

JERUSALEM, p. o., Monroe co., O.

JERUSALEM MILLS, p. o., Harford co., Md.

JERUSALEM SOUTH, p. v., Hempstead township, Queen's co., Long Island, N. Y.

JESSE'S STORE, p. o., Shelby co., Ky.

JESSAMINE COUNTY, situated in the central part of Kentucky, with Kentucky river on the southwest. Area, 256 square miles. Face of the country level; soil fertile. Seat of justice, Nicholasville. Pop. in 1820, 9,297 ; in 1830, 9,960 ; in 1840, 9,396 ; in 1850, 10,249.

JESSAMINE, t., Clark co., Mo.

JESSUP's LANDING, v., Corinth township, Saratoga co., N. Y. Watered by Hudson river.

JETERSVILLE, p. o., Amelia co., Va., 53 ms. s. w. of Richmond ; from W. 170 ms.

JEWELL HILL, p. o., Madison co., N. C.

JEWETT, p. t., Greene co., N. Y. Pop. 1,452.

JEWETT CENTRE, p. o., Greene co., N. Y.

JEWETT CITY, p. v., Griswold township, New London co., Ct., 47 ms. E. of Hartford ; from W. 365 ms. Watered by Quinnebaug and Patchaug rivers.

JIM TOWN, p. o., Monongalia co., Va.

JOANNA FURNACE, p. o., Berks co., Pa., 59 ms. E. of Harrisburgh ; from W. 140 ms.

JOACHIM, t., Jefferson co., Mo.

JOBE, p. o., Oregon co., Mo.

JOBSTOWN, p. v., Springfield township, Burlington co., N. J., 26 ms. s. of Trenton ; from W. 166 ms.

JO-DAVIESS COUNTY, situated at the northwest corner of Illinois, on the Mississippi river. Area, 724 square miles. Soil rich. Seat of justice, Galena, Pop. in 1830, 2,111 ; in 1840, 6,180 ; in 1850, 18,604.

JOHN's. p. o., Liberty co., Tex.

JOHNSBURGH, p. t., Warren co., N. Y., 88 ms. N. of Albany ; from W. 457 ms. Watered by Hudson river and tributaries. Pop. 1,824.

JOHNSON COUNTY, situated toward the east part of North Carolina, and traversed by Neuse river. Area, 660 square miles. Face of the country undulating. Seat of justice, Smithfield. Pop. in 1810, 6,867 ; in 1830, 9,607 ; in 1830, 10,938 ; in 1840, 10,600 ; in 1850, 13,726.

JOHNSON COUNTY, situated at the northeast corner of Tennessee. Area, 300 square miles. Seat of justice, Taylorsville. Pop. in 1840, 2,658 ; in 1850, 3,499.

JOHNSON COUNTY, situated toward the south part of Indiana. Area, 320 square miles. Seat of justice, Franklin. Pop. in 1830, 4,019 ; in 1840, 9,352 ; in 1850, 12,101.

JOHNSON COUNTY, situated in the easterly part of Kentucky. Area, —— square miles. Seat of justice, Paintsville. Pop. in 1850, 3,873.

JOHNSON COUNTY, situated in the south part of Illinois. Area, 486 square miles. Face of the country uneven ; soil fertile. Seat of justice, Vienna. Pop. in 1820, 843 ; in 1830, 1,596 ; in 1840, 3,626 ; in 1850, 4,113.

JOHNSON COUNTY, situated in the easterly part of Iowa, and traversed by Iowa river. Area, 610 square miles. Seat of justice, Iowa city, which is also the state capital. Pop. in 1840, 1,491 ; in 1850, 4,472.

JOHNSON COUNTY, situated in the westerly part of Missouri. Area, 785 square miles, Seat of justice, Warrensburgh. Pop. in 1840, 4,471 ; in 1850, 7,464.

JOHNSON COUNTY, situated toward the northwest part of Arkansas, and traversed by Arkansas river. Area, 900 square miles. Seat of justice, Clarksville. Pop. in 1840, 3,433 ; in 1850, 5,227.

JOHNSON, p. t., Lamoille co., Vt., 36 ms. N. w. of Montpelier ; from W. 550 ms. Watered by Lamoille river.

JOHNSON, b., Cambria co., Pa. Pop. 1,269.

JOHNSON, t., Champaign co., O., 64 ms. w. of Columbus ; from W. 461 ms. Pop. 1,553.

JOHNSON, t., Brown co., Ind. Pop. 418.

JOHNSON, p. t., Gibson co., Ind. Pop. 1,568.

JOHNSON, t., Barry co., Mich. Pop. 451.

JOHNSON, t., Union co., Ark. Pop. 1,625.

JOHNSON, t., Licking co., O.

JOHNSON, p. t., Trumbull co., O. Pop. 1,099.

JOHNSON, t., La Grange co., Ind. Pop. 878.

JOHNSON, t., Scotland co., Mo. Pop. 538

JOHNSON, t., Washington co., Mo. Pop. 462.

JOHNSON, t., Crawford co., Mo.

JOHNSON, p. o., Floyd co., Ga.

JOHNSON, p. o., McDonough co., Ill.

JOHNSON, p. o., Washington co., Mo.

JOHNSONBURGH, p. v., Hardwick township, Warren co., N. J., 70 ms. N. of Trenton ; from W. 227 ms. Watered by Bear branch of Pequest creek.

JOHNSONSBURGH, p. o., Orangeville township, Wyoming co., N. Y., 261 ms. w. of Albany ; from W. 367 ms.

JOHNSON'S, p. o., Montgomery co., Tenn., 61 ms. N.W. of Nashville ; from W. 750 ms.

JOHNSON's CORNERS, p. o., Summit co., O.

JOHNSON's CREEK, p. o., Niagara co., N. Y

JOHNSON's FORKS, p. o., Morgan co., Ky.

JOHNSON's MILLS, p. o., Clark co., Ill.

JOHNSON's MILLS, p. o., Pitt co., N. C., 114 ms. E. of Raleigh , from W. 308 ms.

JOHNSON'S SPRINGS, p. o., Goochland co., Va., 27 ms. N. w. of Richmond ; from W. 144 ms.

JOHNSON STATION, p. o., Tarrant co., Tex.

JOHNSONTOWN, p. o., Northampton co., Va.

JOHNSONVILLE, p. v., Cumberland co., N. C., 65 ms. s. of Raleigh ; from W. 353 ms.

JOHNSONVILLE, p. o., Johnson township, Trumbull co., O., 154 ms. N. E. of Columbus ; from W. 308 ms.

JOHNSONVILLE, p. o., Williamsburgh district, S. C.

JOHNSTON, t., Providence co., R. I., 5 ms. w. of Providence. Watered by Powchasset and Wanasquattuck rivers, and Cedar brook.

JOHNSTON, p. o., Poinsett co., Ark.

JOHNSTONVILLE, p. o., Monroe co., Ga., 64 ms. w. of Milledgeville ; from W. 680 ms.

JOHNSTOWN, c. h. p. t., Fulton co., N. Y., 46 ms. N. w. of Albany ; from W. 410 ms. Watered by Garoga and Cuyadutta creeks. Pop. in 1840, 5,409 ; in 1850, 6,131.

JOHNSTOWN, p. b., Connemaugh township, Cambria co., Pa., 150 ms. w. of Harrisburgh ; from W. 176 ms. Watered by Stony creek and Little Connemaugh river. Pop. 1,269.

JOHNSTOWN, p. v., Monroe township, Licking co., O., 36 ms. N. E. of Columbus ; from W. 384 ms.

JOHNSTOWN, p. t., Barry co., Mich., 128 ms. w. of Detroit ; from W. 593 ms. Pop. 451.

JOHNSTOWN, p. t., Rock co., Wis., 53 ms. s. E. of Madison ; from W. 818 ms.

JOHNSTOWN CENTRE, p. o., Rock co., Wis.

JOHNSVILLE, p. v., Frederick co., Md., 74 ms. N. W. of Annapolis ; from W. 59 ms.

JOHNSVILLE, p. o., Montgomery co., O.

JOLIET, p. t., seat of justice of Will co., Ill., 165 ms. N. E. of Springfield ; from W. 742 ms. Watered by Des Plaines river, and the Illinois and Michigan canal. Pop. 2,659.

JOLLY, p. t., Washington co., O. Pop. 1,014.

JOLLYTOWN, p. o., Greene co., Pa.

JONATHAN's CREEK, p. o., Haywood co., N. C.

JONES COUNTY, situated in the southeasterly part of North Carolina. Area, 380 square miles. Face of the country, level ; soil, sandy or marshy. Seat of justice, Trenton. Pop. in 1810, 4,968 ; in 1820, 5,216 ; in 1830, 5,628 ; in 1840, 4,945 ; in 1850, 5,083.

JONES COUNTY, situated in the central part of Georgia, with Ocmulgee river on the west. Area, 360 square miles. Seat of justice, Clinton. Pop. in 1810, 8,597 ; in 1820, 17,411 ; in 1830, 13,342 ; in 1840, 10,065 ; in 1850, 10,224.

JONES COUNTY, situated in the southeasterly part of Mississippi. Area, 672 square miles. Seat of justice, Ellisville. Pop. in 1830, 1,471 ; in 1840, 1,258 ; in 1850, 2,164.

JONES COUNTY, situated in the easterly part of Iowa, and traversed by Wapsipinecon river. Area, 576 square miles. Seat of justice, Anamosa. Pop. in 1840, 471 ; in 1850, 3,007.

JONES, t., Hancock co., Ind.

JONES, p. o., Panola co., Tex.

JONES' BLUFF, p. o., Sumter co., Ala.

JONESBOROUGH, p. t., Washington co., Me., 143 ms. N. E. of Augusta ; from W. 725 ms. Watered by Englishman's bay and Chandler's river. Pop. 466.

JONESBOROUGH, p. o., Brunswick co., Va., 99 ms. s. of Richmond ; from W. 215 ms.

JONESBOROUGH, p. o., Jefferson co., Ala.; from W. 773 ms.

JONESBOROUGH, c. h. p. v., seat of justice of Union co., Ill., 154 ms. s. of Springfield ; from W. 834 ms. Pop. 230.

JONESBOROUGH, p. o., Grant co., Ind.

JONESBOROUGH, p. o., Fayette co., Ga.

JONESBOROUGH, p. o., Saline co., Mo.

JONESBOROUGH, c. h., p. v., seat of justice of Washington co., Tenn., 283 ms. E. of Nashville ; from W. 412 ms. Watered by Little Limestone creek.

JONES' CREEK, p. o., Randolph co., Ill., 157 ms. s. of Springfield ; from W. 849 ms.

JONES' CREEK, p. o., Liberty co., Ga.

JONES' MILLS, p. o., Yallabusha co., Miss.

JONES' MILLS, p. o., McNairy co., Tenn.

JONES' MILLS, p. o., Meriwether co., Ga.

JONES' MILLS, p. o., Westmoreland co., Pa.

JONES' NURSERY, p. o., Clark co., Ky.

JONES' SPRING, p. o., Berkley co., Va.

JONESPORT, t., Washington co., Me., 147 ms. E. of

Augusta; fi om W. 730 ms. Watered by Englishman's and Addison bays. Pop. 826.

JONES' TAN-YARD, p. o., Callaway co., Mo., 30 ms. N. E. of Jefferson City; from W. 909 ms.

JONESTOWN, p. v., Lebanon co,, Pa., 29 ms. E. of Harrisburgh; from W. 139 ms. Watered by Great and Little Swatara creeks.

JONESVILLE, p. v., Clifton Park township, Saratoga co., N. Y., 21 ms. N. of Albany; from W. 391 ms. Watered by Hudson river, and the Erie canal.

JONESVILLE. c. h., p. v., seat of justice of Lee co., Va., 384 ms. w. of Richmond; from W. 452 ms. Watered by a tributary of Powell's river.

JONESVILLE. p. v., Surry co., N. C., 160 ms. N. w. of Raleigh; from W. 364 ms.

JONESVILLE, p. v., Ninon district, S. C., 81 ms. N. w. of Columbia; from W. 475 ms.

JONESVILLE, p. v., Salem township, Monroe co, O., 129 ms. E. of Columbia; from W. 285 ms.

JONESVILLE, p. v., seat of justice of Hillsdale co., Mich,. 92 ms. s. w. of Detroit; from W. 540 ms. Watered by St. Joseph river. Pop. 565.

JONESVILLE, p. o., Harrison co., Tex.

JONESVILLE, p. o., Chittenden co., Vt.

JORDAN, p. v., Elldridge township, Onondaga co., N. Y., 152 ms. w. of Albany; from W. 350 ms. Situated on the Erie canal.

JORDAN, p. o., Greene co., Wis.

JORDAN'S MILLS, p. o., Orangeburgh district, S. C., 113 ms. s. of Columbia; from W. 618 ms.

JORDAN'S PRAIRIE, p. o., Jefferson co., Ill., 122 ms. s. E. of Springfield; from W. 784 ms.

JORDAN'S SALINE, c. h., p. v., seat of justice of Van Zant co,. Tex.

JORDAN'S STORE, p. o., Williamson co., Tex.

JORDAN'S VALLEY, p. o., Rutherford co., Tenn.

JORDANSVILLE, p. o., Herkimer co., N. Y.

JORDON, t., Clearfield co., Pa. Pop. 612.

JASCO, p. o.. Livingston co., Mich., 61 ms. w. of Detroit; from W. 564 ms.

JOSEPHINE, p. o.. Woodford co., Ill., 93 ms. N. E. of Springfield; from W. 762 ms.

JOY, p. o., Wayne co., N. Y.

JOYNER'S DEPOT. p. o., Edgecombe co., N. C.

JOY'S MILLS, p. o., Burke co., Ga.

JUDA, p. o., Greene co., Wis.

JULIA DEAN, p. o., Davidson co., Tenn.

JULIANN FURNACE, p. o., Centre co., Pa.

JULIAN'S GAP, p. o., Hamilton co., Tenn.

JULIUSTOWN. p. v., Springfield township, Burlington co., N. J., 24 ms. s. of Trenton; from W. 164 ms.

JUNCTION, p. o., Hanover co., Va., 24 ms. N. of Richmond; from W. 93 ms.

JUNCTION, p. o., Dupage co., Ill.

JUNCTION. p. o., Schagticoke township, Rensselaer co., N. Y., 16 ms. E. of Albany; from W. 386 ms.

JUNCTION, p. o, Yuba co., Cal.

JUNCTION, p. o., Paulding co., O.

JUNCTION STORE, p. o., Botetourt co., Va.

JUNEAN, p. o., Dodge co., Wis.

JUNIATA COUNTY, situated toward the southerly part of Pennsylvania, and traversed by Juniata river. Area, 360 square miles. Face of the country, hilly; soil, productive. Seat of justice, Mifflintown. Pop. in 1830, 7,672; in 1840, 11,080; in 1850, 13,029.

JUNIATA, p. t., Perry co., Pa., 39 ms. N. w. of Harrisburgh; from W. 131 ms. Watered by Raccoon, Buffalo, and Little Buffalo creeks. Pop. 1,435.

JUNIATA CROSSINGS, p. o., Bedford co., Pa.

JUNIOR, p. o., Scioto co., O.

JUNIUS, p. t., Seneca co., N. Y., 182 ms. w. of Albany; from W. 352 ms. Pop. 1,516.

JUNO, p. o., Lumpkin co., Ga.

JUNO, p o., Henderson co., Tenn.

JUSTUS' MILLS, p. o., Hempstead, Ark.

K.

KABLETOWN. p. o., Jefferson co.. Va.

KALAMAZOO COUNTY, situated toward the southwest part of Michigan. Area, 576 square miles. Face of the country, generally even; soil. rich. Seat of justice, Kalamazoo. Pop. in 1840, 7,380; in 1850, 13,179.

KALAMAZOO, c. h., p. t., seat of justice of Kalamazoo co., Mich,. 141 ms. w. of Detroit; from W. 605 ms. Watered by Kalamazoo river. Pop. 3,284.

KALAMO, p. t., Eaton co., Mich.

KALIDA. c. h., p. v., seat of justice of Putnam co., O., 114 ms. N. w. of Columbus; from W. 479 ms. Watered by Ottowa river.

KANAKANIC. t., Milwaukie co,, Wis.

KANAWHA COUNTY, situated in the westerly part of Virginia, and traversed by Great Kanawha river. Area, 2,000 square miles. Face of the country, broken and mountainous. Soil, generally sterile, though in some parts rich. Seat of justice, Charleston. Pop. in 1810 3,866; in 1820, 7,000; in 1830, 9,261; in 1840, 13,567; in 1850, 15,353.

KANAWHA, c. h., p. v., Seat of justice of Kanawha co., Va., 313 ms. N. w. of Richmond; from W. 350 ms. Watered by Great Kanawha and Elk rivers.

KANAWHA SALINE, p. v., Kanawha co., Va., 307 ms. N. w of Richmond; from W. 344 ms. Watered by Kanawha river.

KANE COUNTY, situated in the northeast part of Illinois, and traversed by Fox river. Area. 1,296 square miles. Seat of justice, Geneva. Pop. in 1840, 6,501; in 1850, 16,703.

KANE, p. o., Greene co., Ill., 76 ms. s. w. of Springfield; from W. 826 ms.

KANE, p. o., Pottawatamie co.. Iowa.

KANENILLE, p. o., Kane co., Ill.

KANZAS. p. o., Jackson co., Mo.

KARTHAUS. p. v., Covington township, Clearfield co., Pa., 114 ms. N. w. of Harrisburgh; from W. 206 ms. Watered by west branch of Susquehanna river. Pop. 316.

KASEY'S, p. o., Bedford co., Va., 154 ms. w. of Richmond; from W. 229 ms.

KASKASKIA, c. h., p. v., seat of justice of Randolph co., Ill., 142 ms. s. of Springfield; from W. 834 ms. Watered by Kaskaskia river.

KASOAG, p. o., Oswego co., N. Y.

KATAHDIN IRON WORKS, p. o., Piscataquis co., Me.

KATTELVILLE, p. o., Broome co., N. Y.

KAUFMAN COUNTY, situated in the northerly part of Texas. Area, —— square miles. Seat of justice, Kaufman. Pop. in 1850, 1,047.

KAUFMAN, p. t., seat of justice of Kaufman co., Tex.

KAUKAUNA, p. o., Brown co., Wis., 148 ms. N. E. of Madison; from W. 958 ms. Watered by Kaukauna rapids of Fox river.

KEARSLEY, p. t., Genesee co., Mich.

KEAS' BRIDGE, p. o., Chickasaw co., Miss.

KEATCHIE, p. o., De Soto parish, La.

KEATING, t., McKean co., Pa., 188 ms. N. w. of Harrisburgh; from W. 285 ms. Watered by Alleghany river and Potato creek. Pop. 1,181.

KEATON'S SHOALS, p. o., Baker co., Ga.

KECK'S CHURCH, p. o., Martin co., Ind.

KEEDYSVILLE, p. o., Washington co., Md.

KEEFER'S STORE, p, o., Franklin co., Pa.

KEELERSBURGH, p. v., Wyoming co., Pa.

KEELERSVILLE, p. v., Van Buren co., Mich., 175 ms. w. of Detroit; from W. 636 ms. Pop. 443.

KEENE, c. h., p. t., seat of justice, together with Charleston, of Cheshire co., N. H., 48 ms. s. w. of Concord; from W. 424 ms. Watered by Ashuelot river. Pop. 3,392.

KEENE. p. t., Essex co., N. Y., 136 ms. N. of Albany; from W. 513 miles. Watered by tributaries of Au Sable river.

KEENE, p. v., Jessamine co., Ky.,. 33 ms. s. E. of Frankfort; from W. 531 ms.

KEENE, p. t., Coshocton co., O., 99 ms. N. E. of Columbus; from W. 344 ms.

KEENEVILLE, p. o., Wayne co., Ill.

KEENEY'S SETTLEMENT, p. o., Cortland co., N. Y., 134 ms. w. of Albany; from W. 333 ms.

KEENSVILLE, p. o., Union co., Pa.

KEESEVILLE, p. v., Chesterfield township, Essex co., N. Y. Watered by Au Sable river.

KEEZLETOWN, p. o., Rockingham co., Va.

KEITH'S, p. o., Morgan co., O., 88 ms. E. of Columbus; from W. 318 ms.

KEITHSBURGH, p. o., Mercer co., Ill.

KELLERSVILLE, p. o., Monroe co., Pa.

KELLERTOWN, v.. Wilkinson co., Miss., 118 ms. s. w. of Jackson ; from W. 1,128 ms.

KELLEY'S MILLS, p. o.. Lawrence co., O., 109 ms. s. e. of Columbus ; from W, 405 ms.

KELLOGSVILLE, p. v., Niles township, Cayuga co., N. Y., 158 ms. w. of Albany ; from W. 329 ms.

KELLOGVILLE. p. o., Monroe township, Ashtabula co., O., 222 ms. N. E. of Columbus ; from W. 337 ms.

KELLY, t., Union co., Pa., 66 ms. N. of Harrisburgh ; from W. 175 ms. Watered by Buffalo creek. Pop. 834.

KELLY, t., Ottawa co., O., including Cunningham's island in Lake Erie.

KELLY'S CREEK, p. o., St. Clair co., Ala., 101 ms. from Tuscaloosa ; from W. 753 ms.

KELLY'S FERRY, p. o., Meigs co., Tenn., 137 ms. s. e. of Nashville ; from W. 569 ms. Watered by Tennessee river.

KELLY'S SPRINGS, p. o., Talladega co., Ala. ; from W. 757 ms.

KELLYSVILLE, p. o., Delaware co., Pa.

KELLYSVILLE. p. o., Culpeper co., Va.

KELSO, p. t., Dearborn co., Ind., 84 ms. s. e. of Indianapolis ; from W. 531 ms. Pop. 1,593.

KELSO, t., Scott co., Mo.

KELVIN GROVE, p. o., Wake co., N. C., 16 ms. N. of Raleigh ; from W. 294 ms.

KEMBLESVILLE, p. o., Chester co., Pa., 76 ms. s. e. of Harrisburgh ; from W. 99 ms.

KEMP'S CREEK, p. o., Benton co., Ala. ; from W. 744 ms.

KEMP, p. o., Kaufman co., Tex.

KEMPER COUNTY, situated on the east boundary of Mississippi. Area, 750 square miles. Seat of justice, De Kalb. Pop. in 1840, 7,663 ; in 1850, 12,517.

KEMPSVILLE, p. o., Princess Ann co., Va., 116 ms. s. e. of Richmond ; from W. 240 ms. Watered by east branch of Elizabeth river.

KENANSVILLE, c. h., p. v.. seat of justice of Duplin co., N. C., 89 ms. s. e. of Raleigh ; from W. 319 ms. Watered by Grove creek.

KENDALL COUNTY, situated on the northeasterly part of Illinois, and traversed by Fox river. Area, 324 square miles. Seat of justice, Yorkville. Pop, in 1850, 7,730.

KENDALL, p. t., Orleans co., N. Y., 249 ms. w. of Albany ; from W. 398 ms. Watered by Lake Ontario. Pop. 2,289.

KENDALL, p. o., Beaver co., Pa., 238 ms. w. of Harrisburgh ; from W. 260 ms.

KENDALL, p. o., Kendall co , Ill.

KENDALL CREEK, p. o., McKean co., Pa.

KENDALL MILLS, p. o., Orleans co., N. Y.

KENDALL'S MILLS, p. o., Somerset co., Me.

KENDALL'S STORE, p. o., Stanley co., N. C., 143 ms. s. w. of Raleigh ; from W. 380 ms.

KENDALLSVILLE, p. v.. Noble co., Ind., 159 ms. N. E. of Indianapolis ; from W. 581 ms.

KENDRICK'S SPUR, p. o., Patrick co., Va.

KENNEMER, p. o., Marshall co., Ala.

KENNEBEC COUNTY, situated in the southerly part of Maine, and traversed by Kennebec river. Area, 1.050 square miles. Face of the country hilly ; soil productive. Seat of justice, Augusta, which is also the state capital. Pop. in 1810, 32,564 ; in 1820, 42,623 ; in 1830, 52.491 ; in 1840, 56,823 ; in 1850, 62,520.

KENNEBUNK, p. t., York co., Me., 75 ms. s. w. of Augusta ; from W. 517 ms. Watered by Kennebunk river and the Atlantic ocean. Pop. 2,659.

KENNEBUNK DEPOT, p. o., York co., Me.

KENNEBUNKPORT, p. t., York co., Me., 78 ms. s. w. of Augusta ; from W. 520 ms. Watered by Kennebunk river. Pop. 2,706.

KENNEDY'S, p. o., Brunswick co., Va., 91 ms. s. of Richmond ; from W. 207 ms.

KENNEDYSVILLE, p. v., Bath township, Steuben co., N. Y., 223 ms. w. of Albany ; from W. 303 ms.

KENNET, t., Chester co., Pa. Watered by Red Clay creek. Pop. 1,706.

KENNET'S SQUARE. p. v., Kennet township, Chester co., Pa., 74 ms. s. e. of Harrisburgh ; from W. 105 ms.

KENNON, p. o., Belmont co., O.

KENNONSBURGH, p. o., Guernsey co., O.

KENOZHA COUNTY, situated at the southeast corner of Wisconsin, on Lake Michigan. Area, —— square miles. Seat of justice, Kenozha. Pop. in 1850, 10,734.

KENOZHA, p. t., seat of justice of Kenozha co., Wis.

KENSICO, p. o., Westchester co., N. Y.

KENSINGTON, p. v., Berlin township. Hartford co., Ct., 13 ms. s. w. of Hartford ; from W. 321 ms.

KENSINGTON. p. t., Rockingham co., N. H., 41 ms. s. e. of Concord ; from W. 478 ms. Pop. 700.

KENSINGTON, p. t., Philadelphia co., Pa., 100 ms. e. of Harrisburgh ; from W. 140 ms. Watered by Delaware river. Pop. 46,774.

KENSINGTON, p. v., Lyon township, Oakland co., Mich., 35 ms. w. of Detroit ; from W. 544 ms.

KENT COUNTY, situated in the central part of Rhode Island, on Narraganset bay. Area, 186 square miles. Face of the country undulating ; soil productive. Seat of justice, East Greenwich. Pop. in 1810, 9,834 ; in 1820. 10,228 ; in 1830, 12,784 ; in 1840, 13,083 ; in 1850, 15,068.

KENT COUNTY, situated in the central part of Delaware, on Delaware bay. Area, 640 square miles. Face of the country generally level ; soil of middling quality. Seat of justice, Dover, which is also the state capital. Pop. in 1810, 20,495 ; in 1820, 20,793 ; in 1830, 19,911 ; in 1840, 19,872 ; in 1850, 22,816.

KENT COUNTY, situated on the east boundary of Maryland, with Chesapeake bay on the northwest. Area, 240 square miles. Face of the country undulating or level ; soil of middling quality. Seat of justice, Chester. Pop. in 1810, 11,450 ; in 1820, 12,453 ; in 1830, 10.502 ; in 1840. 10,842 ; in 1850, 11,386.

KENT COUNTY, situated in the westerly part of Michigan, and traversed by Grand river. Area, 576 square miles. Seat of justice, Kent or Grand Rapids. Pop. in 1840, 2,587 ; in 1850, 12,016.

KENT, p. t., Litchfield co., Ct., 51 ms. w. of Hartford ; from W. 322 ms. Watered by Housatonic river and tributaries. Pop. 1,848.

KENT, p. t., Putnam co., N. Y., 99 ms. s. of Albany ; from W. 292 ms. Watered by head waters of Croton river. Pop. 1,557.

KENT, p. o., Indiana co., Pa., 165 ms. w. of Harrisburgh ; from W. 218 ms.

KENT, t., Kent co., Mich., 168 ms. N. w. of Detroit ; from W. 649 ms.

KENT, p. o., Stephenson co., Ill.

KENT, p. o., Jefferson co., Ind.

KENTON COUNTY, situated on the northerly boundary of Kentucky, on Ohio river. Area, 150 square miles. Seat of justice, Independence. Pop. in 1840, 7,816 ; in 1850, 17,038.

KENTON, c h. p t, seat of justice of Hardin co., O., 71 ms. N. w. of Columbus ; from W. 442 ms. Watered by Scioto river.

KENTONTOWN, p. v., Harrison co., Ky., 53 ms. N. E. of Frankfort ; from W. 489 ms.

KENT'S HILL, p. o., Kennebec co., Me., 14 ms. from Augusta ; from W. 604 ms.

KENTUCKY, one of the United States, formerly a district of Virginia lies between 36° 30' and 39° 10' north latitude, and 80° 35' and 82° west longitude f'm Greenwich ; and is bounded north by Ohio river, which separates it from Illinois, Indiana, and Ohio, east by Virginia, south by Tennessee, and west by Missouri. Its superficial area is 40,500 square miles.

Physical Aspect.—Kentucky lies entirely in the valley of the Ohio, and is a part of an immense inclined plain, more or less broken in its surface, descending from Cumberland mountain to the river Ohio. The Cumberland range divides this state from Virginia on the southeast. Descending from the foot of this mountain toward the northwest, to the distance of 100 miles, the country is hilly and rather mountainous. This broken section includes at least one third part of the state, and extends from Tennessee line to the river Ohio. A tract along this river, from five to twenty miles wide, is also broken and hilly, stretching through the whole length of the state. But these hills are gently rounded, and are fertile quite to their tops, having narrow valleys between them of great fertility. Along the margin of this stream there are rich alluvial bottoms, of an average width of a mile, subject to periodical inundation.

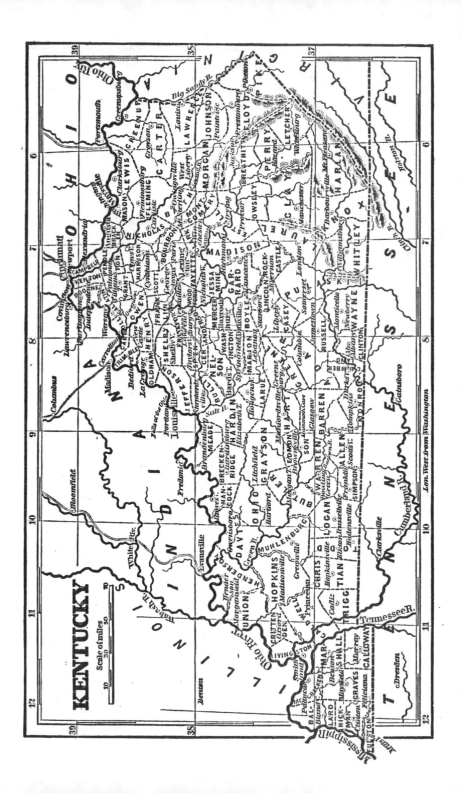

tween the hilly tract on the Ohio and the mountainous country on the Virginia line and Green river there is a tract, 100 miles long and 50 miles broad, beautifully undulating, with a black and rich soil, which has been denominated the "garden of Kentucky." The whole state below the mountains rests on a bed of limestone, in general about eight feet below the surface. The rivers have worn deep channels into this calcareous bed, forming stupendous precipices, particularly on Kentucky river, where the banks in many places are 300 feet high.

Mammoth Cave.—In the southwest part of the state, between Green and Cumberland rivers, are several wonderful caverns. The "Mammoth Cave," in Edmondson county, 130 miles from Lexington, near the road leading to Nashville, is some nine or ten miles in extent, with a great number of avenues and intricate windings. Most of those caves yield an inexhaustible supply of nitrate of lime. During the late war with Great Britain, fifty men were constantly employed in lixiviating the earth of the Mammoth cave, to obtain the saltpetre it contained; and in about three years after the washed earth is said to have become as strongly impregnated with nitric acid as at first.

Mountains.—The Cumberland range, before referred to, forms the southeast boundary of this state.

Rivers.—The principal rivers are, the Ohio, Mississippi, Tennessee, Cumberland, Kentucky (Kutawa), Green, Licking, Salt, Rolling, and Big Sandy.

Climate.—The climate through most of the state is generally healthy. The winters are mild, and usually of only two or three months' duration. Spring and autumn are delightfully pleasant. The extremes of season, however, are widened by the peculiar features of the country. The rivers in their descent have abraded the plains, and flow in deep chasms or vales, which receive the rays of the sun in various inclinations. In these situations the summers are hot, and the winters mild.

Productive Resources.—The staple products of this state are, horses, mules, neat cattle, sheep, swine, poultry, eggs, butter, cheese, wine, wax, sugar, tobacco, wool, cotton, hemp, flax, hay, lumber, wheat, barley, rye, oats, buckwheat, rice, potatoes, and Indian corn. Tobacco and hemp are the great staples of the state. Among the mineral resources are, iron, coal, salt, and lime. The salt springs are numerous, and not only supply this state, but a great part of Ohio and Tennessee, as well as other parts.

Manufactures.—About half a million of dollars is invested in cotton and woollen manufactures in Kentucky, and about $900,000 in the manufacture of iron. Other principal manufactures are, cordage, cotton-bagging, hardware, tobacco, spirits, &c. In 1850, the number of manufacturing establishments in the state, producing $500 and over, each, annually, was 3,471.

Railroads and Canals.—The principal railroads at present in operation in Kentucky are, the Louisville and Frankfort, 65 miles, and the Frankfort and Lexington, 29 miles. Several important railroads are projected, which, when completed, will render easily accessible all the important points in the state.

Commerce.—In common with other inland states, Kentucky has no direct foreign commerce, but ships mostly at New Orleans. The river trade of this state is considerable. About 15,000 tons of shipping is owned in the state.

Education.—There are several collegiate institutions in Kentucky; St. Joseph's, Centre, Augusta, Georgetown, and Bacon colleges; and Louisville and Transylvania universities, to both of which law and medical schools are attached. There are also a theological institution at Covington, and the Western Military college, at Blue-Lick Springs. There are also, asylums for the blind, the deaf and dumb, and the insane. The state has a school fund of $1,300,000.

Government.—The legislative power is vested in a senate and house of representatives, which together are styled the general assembly. The senators are 38 in number, chosen by the people, from single districts, for four years. Representatives, 100 in number, are chosen by the people for two years. A governor and lieutenant-governor are elected by the people for a term of four years. The governor is ineligible the immediately succeeding term. He may return a bill passed by the legislature, but a majority of the members elected to each house may pass the bill afterward, and it then becomes a law notwithstanding his objections. The gen-

eral election first Monday in August biennially. The state officers are elected by the people for a term of four years. The judicial power is vested in a court of appeals, circuit, and county courts; the judges of each are elected by the people. Every free, white, male citizen, 21 years of age or over, resident in the state two years, and in the county where he offers to vote one year, next preceding an election, may vote at such election. Elections by the people are *viva voce.*

Population.—In 1790, 73.077; in 1800, 220,955; in 1810, 406,511; in 1820, 564,317; in 1830, 687,917; in 1840, 779,828; in 1850, 982,405. Number of slaves in 1790, 11,830; in 1800, 40,343; in 1810, 80,561; in 1820, 126,372; in 1830, 165,213; in 1840, 182,258; in 1850, 210,981.

History.—The first permanent settlement in Kentucky was made by Daniel Boone, in 1775, though the country had been visited by John Finley, and others, as early as 1769. In 1777, the legislature of Virginia made it a county, and in 1782 a supreme court was established. In about the year 1776, the region south of Kentucky river was purchased of the Cherokees, who called their domain "Transylvania" (beyond the woods). In 1786, an act was passed by Congress, erecting the district of Kentucky into a new territory; but the separation from Virginia did not take place before 1792, when it was admitted into the Union as an independent state. The first constitution was adopted in 1790, which was superseded by a new one in 1799, and that by the present one in 1850. Motto of its seal, "United we stand, divided we fall."

KENTUCKY GROVE, p. o., Paisley co., Iowa.

KENTUCKYVILLE, p. o., Susquehanna co., Pa., 174 ms. N. E. of Harrisburgh; from W. 278 ms.

KENYON, p. o., Jackson co., Ark.

KEOKUK COUNTY, situated toward the southeast part of Iowa. Area, —— square miles. Seat of justice, Lancaster. Pop. in 1850, 4,822.

KEOKUK, p. v., Lee co., Iowa. Watered by Mississippi river.

KEOSAUQUA, c. h., p. t., seat of justice of Van Buren co., Iowa. Pop. 705.

KEPNER'S, p. o., Schuylkill co., Pa., 73 ms. N. E. of Harrisburgh; from W. 183 ms.

KERNERSVILLE, p. o., Forsyth co., N. C., 98 ms. N.W. of Raleigh; from W. 309 ms.

KERNEYSVILLE, p. o., Jefferson co., Va.

KERR'S CREEK, p. o., Rockbridge co., Va.

KERR'S STORE, p. o., Clarion co., Pa.

KERSEY'S, p. o., Elk co., Pa., 150 ms. N. W. of Harrisburgh; from W. 242 ms.

KERSHAW DISTRICT, situated toward the north part of South Carolina, and traversed by Wateree river. Area, 792 square miles. Face of the country pleasantly diversified; soil fertile. Seat of justice, Camden. Pop. in 1830, 13,545; in 1840, 12,181; in 1850, 14,473.

KESNICK DEPOT, p. o., Albemarle co., Va.

KESSLER'S, p. o., Northampton co., Pa.

KETCHUM'S CORNERS, p. o., Stillwater township, Saratoga co., N. Y.

KETCHUMVILLE, p. o., Tioga co., N. Y.

KETTLE CREEK, p. o., Potter co., Pa.

KETTLE CREEK, p. o., Monmouth co., N. J.

KEWANNA, p. v., Fulton co., Ind. Pop. 308.

KEWASKUM, p. o., Washington co., Wis.

KEWENAW BAY, p. o., Houghton co., Mich.

KEYPORT, p. v., Middletown township, Monmouth co., N. J., 46 ms. E. of Trenton; from W. 213 ms. Watered by New York bay.

KEYSBURGH, p. v., Logan co., Ky., 194 ms. s. w. of Frankfort; from W. 721 ms.

KEYSBURGH, p. v., Pike co., Ill., 77 ms. w. of Springfield; from W. 857 ms.

KEYSER'S RIDGE, p. o., Alleghany co., Md.

KEYSPORT, p. o., Clinton co., Ill.

KEY STONE, p. o., Perry co., Pa.

KEY STONE, p. o., Jackson co., O.

KEYSVILLE, p. v., Charlotte co., Va., 93 ms. s. w. of Richmond; from W. 183 ms.

KEYTESVILLE, c. h., p. v., seat of justice of Chariton co., Mo., 91 ms. w. of Jefferson city; from W. 985 ms. Pop. 954.

KEY WEST, p. v., seat of justice of Monroe co., Flor., situated on one of the most southerly keys of that state, formerly known as Thompson's island, and containing a military station of the United States. Watered by the straits of Florida. Pop. 1,943.

KEZAR FALLS. p. o., York co., Me., 80 ms. s. w. of Augusta; from W. 547 ms.

KICKAPOO, p. o., Peoria co., Ill.

KICKAPOO, p. o., Anderson co., Tex.

KIDDVILLE, p. o., Clarke co., Ky.

KIDRON, p. v., Cherokee Nation. Ark.

KIDRON, p. o., Coweta co., Ga., 96 ms. w. of Milledgeville; from W. 700 ms.

KILGORE, p. o., Carroll co., O., 118 ms. N. E. of Columbus; from W. 289 ms.

KILKENNY, t., Coos co., N. H., 106 ms. N. of Concord; from W. 575 ms.

KILBOURN, p. o., Delaware co., O., 29 ms. N. of Columbus; from W. 289 ms.

KILLBUCK, p. o., Cattaraugus co., N. Y.

KILLBUCK. p. t., Holmes co., O., 80 ms. N. E. of Columbus; from W. 350 ms. Watered by Killbuck creek. Pop. 1,244.

KILLUCK, p. o., Ogle co., Ill.

KILLIAN'S MILLS, p. o., Lincoln co., N. C., 177 ms. w. of Raleigh; from W. 414 ms.

KILLINGLY, p. t., Windham co., Ct., 47 ms. E. of Hartford; from W. 378 ms. Watered by Quinnebaug river. Pop. 4,543.

KILLINGWORTH, p. t., Middlesex co., Ct., 49 ms. s. of Hartford; from W. 326 ms. Watered by Long Island sound, and Hammonasset and Menuketesurk rivers. Pop. 1,107.

KILMARNOCK, p. t., Piscataquis co., Me., 104 ms. N. E. of Augusta; from W. 701 ms. Watered by Piscataquis river, and a tributary, the outlet of Otter pond. Pop. 322.

KILMARNOCK, p. v., Lancaster co., Va., 90 ms. E. of Richmond; from W. 150 ms. Watered by Chesapeake bay.

KILMORE, p. o., Clinton co., Ind.

KILMICHAEL, p. o., Choctaw co., Miss.

KIMBERLIN, p. o., Giles co., Va.

KIMBERTON, p. v., East Pikeland township, Chester co., Pa., 75 ms. s. E. of Harrisburgh; from W. 153 ms.

KIMBLE, t., Athens co., O.

KIMBOLTON, p. v., Guernsey co., O., 88 ms. E. of Columbus; from W. 327 ms.

KIMULGA, p. o., Talladega co., Ala.; from W. 769 ms.

KINCANNON'S FERRY, p. o., Meigs co., Tenn.

KINDER, p. o., Hancock co., Ind.

KINDERHOOK, p. t., Columbia co., N. Y., 19 ms. s. of Albany; from W. 351 ms. Watered by Kinderhook creek. Pop. 3,978.

KINDERHOOK, p. o., Pike co., Ill., 84 ms. w. of Springfield; from W. 864 ms.

KINDERHOOK, p. o., Van Buren co., Ark., 120 ms. N. of Little Rock; from W. 1,096 ms.

KINDERHOOK, p. o., Branch co., Mich. Pop. 356.

KINDERHOOK, p. o., Lincoln co., Tenn.

KINDERHOOK. p. o., Washington co., Va.

KING AND QUEEN COUNTY, situated in the easterly part of Virginia. Area, 335 square miles. Face of the country, undulating; soil of middling quality. Seat of justice, King and Queen c. h. Pop. in 1810, 10,988; in 1820, 11,798; in 1830, 11,644; in 1840, 10,862; in 1850, 10,319.

KING AND QUEEN, p. v., seat of justice of King and Queen co., Va., 53 ms. N. E. of Richmond; from W. 141 ms.

KING CREEK, p. o., Barnwell district, S. C., 147 ms. s. w. of Columbia; from W. 643 ms.

KINGFIELD, p. t., Franklin co., Me., 59 ms. N. w. of Augusta; from W. 648 ms. Watered by Seven-mile river. Pop. 662.

KING GEORGE COUNTY, situated in the easterly part of Virginia, with Potomac river on the northeast, and the Rappahannock on the southwest. Area, 254 square miles. Face of the country hilly; soil of middling quality. Seat of justice, King George C. H. Pop. in 1810, 6,454; in 1820, 6,116; in 1830, 3,397; in 1840, 5,927; in 1850, 5,971.

KING GEORGE, c. h., p. v., seat of justice of King George co., 82 ms. N. E. of Richmond; from W. 76 ms.

KING OF PRUSSIA, p. o., Montgomery co., Pa.

KING'S COUNTY, situated in the southeast part of New York, at the west end of Long Island. Area, 76 square miles. Face of the country diversified; soil productive, and well cultivated. Seat of justice, Brooklyn. Pop. in 1810, 8,303; in 1820, 11,187; in 1830, 20,537; in 1840, 47,613; in 1850, 218,881.

KING'S, p. o., Barbour co., Ala.

KING'S BENCH, p. o., Franklin co., Ga.

KINGSBOROUGH, p. v., Johnstown township, Fulton co., N. Y., 50 ms. N. w. of Albany; from W. 414 ms.

KING'S BRIDGE, p. v., city and co. of New York. Watered by Harlem river.

KINGSBURY, p. t., Piscataquis co., Me. Pop. 181.

KINGSBURY, p. t., Washington co., N. Y., 58 ms. N, of Albany; from W. 428 ms. Watered by Hudson river. Pop. 3,032.

KINGSBURY, p. o., La Porte co., Ind., 145 ms. N. of Indianapolis; from W. 660 ms.

KINGSBURY, p. o., Whitesides co., Ill.

KINGSBURY. p. o., Cumberland co., N. C.

KING'S CREEK, p. o., Caldwell co., N. C.

KINGSESSING, p. t., Philadelphia co., Pa., 98 ms. s. E. of Harrisburgh; from W. 134 ms. Watered by Delaware and Schuylkill rivers, and Darby creek. Site of the ancient Bartram botanical garden. Pop. 1,775.

KING'S FERRY, p. o., Genoa township, Cayuga co., N. Y., 173 ms. w. of Albany; from W. 315 ms.

KING'S GAP, p. o., Harris co., Ga., 118 ms. w. of Milledgeville; from W. 756 ms.

KINGSLEY'S, p. o., Crawford co., Pa., 243 ms. N. w. of Harrisburgh; from W. 324 ms.

KING'S MILLS, p. o., Montgomery co., Mo., 62 ms. N. w. of Jefferson City; from W. 877 ms.

KING'S MILLS, p. o., Kane co., Ill.

KING'S MOUNTAIN, p. o., Lincoln co., N. C.

KING'S POINT, p. o., Dade co., Mo.

KINGSPORT, p. v., Sullivan co., Tenn., 273 ms. from Nashville; from W. 409 ms. Watered by Holston river.

KING'S RIVER, p. t., Carroll co., Ark., 190 ms. N. w. of Little Rock; from W. 1,168 ms.

KING'S SETTLEMENT, p. o., Norwich township, Chenango co., N. Y., 106 ms. w. of Albany; from W. 342 ms.

KINGSTON, c. h., v., seat of justice of Autauga co., Ala.; from W. 826 ms. Watered by Autauga creek.

KINGSTON, p. t., Rockingham co., N. H., 33 ms. s. E. of Concord; from W. 471 ms. Watered by Great and Little ponds, the former the source of Powow river, and the latter that of a branch of Exeter river. Pop. 1,192.

KINGSTON, p. t., Plymouth co., Mass., 34 ms. s. E. of Boston; from W. 443 ms. Watered by Jones river, and Plymouth harbor. Pop. 1,591.

KINGSTON, c. h., p. v., South Kingston township, seat of justice of Washington co., R. I., 32 ms. s. of Providence; from W. 391 ms.

KINGSTON, c. h., p. t., seat of justice of Ulster co., N. Y., 57 ms. s. of Albany; from W. 316 ms. Watered by Esopus and Rondout creeks, and Hudson river. Pop. in 1840, 5,824; in 1850, 10,232.

KINGSTON, p. v., Middlesex co., N. J., 14 ms. N. E. of Trenton; from W. 180 ms. Watered by Middletown river, and Delaware and Raritan canal.

KINGSTON, p. t., Luzerne co., Pa., 127 ms. N. E. of Harrisburgh; from W. 232 ms. Watered by Susquehanna river. Pop. 2,454.

KINGSTON, p. v., Somerset co., Md., 118 ms. s. E. of Annapolis; from W. 158 ms.

KINGSTON, p. v., Greene township, Ross co., O., 55 ms. s. of Columbus; from W. 400 ms. Pop. 336.

KINGSTON, c. h., p. v., seat of justice of Roane co., Tenn., 143 ms. E. of Nashville; from W. 538 ms. Watered by Clinch and Tennessee rivers.

KINGSTON, p. v., De Kalb co., Ill., 218 ms. N. E. of Springfield; from W. 789 ms.

KINGSTON, p. o., Marquette co., Wis.

KINGSTON, p. o., Decatur co., Ind.

KINGSTON, p. v., Adams co., Miss., 119 ms. s. w. of Jackson; from W. 1,129 ms.

KINGSTON, p. o., Cumberland co., N. C.

KINGSTON, c. h., p. v., seat of justice of Caldwell co., Mo.

KINGSTON, p. o., Cass co., Ga.

KINGSTON, p. o., Madison co., Ky.

KINGSTON CENTRE, p. o., Kingston township, Delaware co., O.

KINGSTON MINES, p. o., Peoria co., Ill.

KINGSTREE, c. h., p. v., seat of justice of Williamsburgh district, S. C., 105 ms. s. E. of Columbia; from W. 439 ms. Watered by Black river.

KINGSVILLE, p. o., Clarion co., Pa.

KINGSVILLE, p. t., Ashtabuia co., O., 213 ms. N. E. of Columbus; from W. 348 ms. Pop. 1,494.

KINGVILLE, p. o., Talladega co., Ala.

KING WILLIAM COUNTY, situated in the easterly part of Virginia, between Pamunky and Matapony rivers. Area, 270 square miles. Face of the country, uneven; soil, generally poor. Seat of justice, King William C H. Pop. in 1810, 9,285; in 1820, 9,697; in 1830, 9,812; in 1840, 9,258; in 1850, 8,779.

KING WILLIAM, c. h., p. v., seat of justice of King William co., Va., 38 ms. N. E. of Richmond; from W. 126 ms.

KINGWOOD, p. t., Hunterdon co., N. J., 29 ms. N. w. of Trenton; from W. 186 ms. Watered by Loakatong creek. Pop. 1,799.

KINGWOOD, p. v., seat of justice of Preston co., Va., 284 ms. N. w. of Richmond; from W. 207 ms.

KINFAD, p. o., St. Francois co., Mo.

KINLOCK, p. o., Lawrence co., Ala.

KINLOCK, p. o., Panola co., Tex.

KINNARD, p. o., Hancock co., Ind.

KINNARD's STORE. p. o., Maury co., Tenn.

KINNEY's FOUR CORNERS, p. o., Hannibal township, Oswego co., N. Y., 174 ms. N. w. of Albany; from W. 365 ms.

KINNICONICK, p. o., Lewis co., Ky., 121 ms. N. E. of Frankfort; from W. 455 ms.

KINSALE, p. o., Westmoreland co., Va., 83 ms. N. E. of Richmond; from W. 142 ms.

KINSMAN, p. t., Trumbull co., O., 193 ms. N. E. of Columbus; from W 309 ms. Pop. 1.005.

KINSTON, c. h., p. v., seat of justice of Lenoir co., N. C., 80 ms. s. E. of Raleigh; from W. 308 ms. Watered by Neuse river.

KLINTERBISH, p. o., Sumter co., Ala.

KINZER's. p. o., Lancaster co., Pa.

KINZUA, p. v., Warren co., Pa., 223 ms. N. w. of Harrisburgh; from W. 307 ms. Pop. 232.

KIOMATIA, p. o., Red River, co., Tex.

KIRBY, t., Caledonia co., Vt., 36 ms. N. E. of Montpelier; from W. 552 ms. Watered by Moose river. Pop. 509.

KIRBY. p. o., Greene co., Pa., 231 ms. w. of Harrisburgh; from W. 234 ms.

KIRKERSVILLE, p. v., Harrison township, Licking co., O., 22 ms. E. of Columbus; from W. 371 ms.

KIRKLAND, p. t., Penobscot co., Me., 84 ms. N. E. of Augusta; from W. 679 ms. Watered by streams flowing into Pushan lake. Pop. 2,108.

KIRKLAND, p. t., Oneida co., N. Y., 100 ms. N. w. of Albany; from W. 380 ms. Watered by Oriskang creek. Pop. 3,421.

KIRKLAND, p. o., Cabarras co., N. C., 147 ms. N. of Raleigh; from W. 904 ms.

KIRKS' CROSS-ROADS, p. o., Clinton co., Ind., 32 ms. N. w. of Indianapolis; from W. 590 ms.

KIRKSEY's CROSS-ROADS, Edgefield district, S. C., 72 ms. w. of Columbia; from W. 535 ms.

KIRK's FERRY, p. o., Tensas parish, La.

KIRK's MILLS, p. o., Lancaster co., Pa., 61 ms. E. of Harrisburgh; from W. 90 ms.

KIRKSVILLE, p. o., Madison co., Ky.

KIRKSVILLE, c. h., p. v., seat of justice of Adair co., Mo.

KIRKVILLE, p. v., Butler co., Ala.; from W. 872 ms.

KIRKVILLE, p. v., Manlius township, Onondaga co., N. Y., 130 ms. w. of Albany; from W. 353 ms.

KIRKVILLE, p. o., Wapello co., Iowa.

KIRKWOOD, t., Belmont co., O., 108 ms. E. of Columbus; from W. 291 ms.

KIRKWOOD, p. o., Broome co., N. Y.

KIRTLAND, p. t., Lake co., O., 167 ms. N. E. of Columbus; from W. 353 ms. Pop. 1,598.

KISHACOQUILLAS, p. o., Mifflin co., Pa., 67 ms. N. w. of Harrisburgh; from W. 159 ms.

KISHWAUKIE, p. v., Winnebago co., Ill., 197 ms. N. of Springfield; from W. 810 ms.

KISKATOM. p. o., Greene co., N. Y.

KISKIMINITAS. p. t., Armstrong co., Pa., 187 ms. w. of Harrisburgh; from W. 211 ms. Watered by Connemaugh river. and Pennsylvania canal. Pop. 2,430.

KITCHING's MILLS, p. o., Orangeburgh district, S. C.

KITNANING, c. h., p. b., seat of justice of Armstrong co., Pa., 182 ms. w. N. w. of Harrisburgh; from W. 236 ms. Watered by Alleghany river.

KITTANING, p. t., Armstrong co., Pa., 180 ms. w. of Harrisburgh; from W. 234 ms. Pop. 1.175.

KITTERY, p. t., York co., Me., 100 ms. s. w. of Augusta; from W. 497 ms. Watered by Piscataqua river, and the Atlantic ocean. Pop. 2,706.

KLECKNERSVILLE, p. o., Notrhampton co., Pa., 104 ms. N. E. of Harrisburgh; from W. 197 ms.

KLINESVILLE, p. o., Berks co., Pa., 73 ms. E. of Harrisburgh; from W. 165 ms.

KLINESVILLE, p. o., Hunterdon co., N. J.

KLINGERSTOWN, p. o., Schuylkill co., Pa.

KLUTT's TAN YARD, p. o., Catarras co., N. C.

KNIGHT's FERRY, p. o., San Joaquin co., Cal.

KNAP OF REEDS, p. o., Granville co., N. C.

KNAP's, p. o., Carter co., Ky.

KNIGHTSTOWN, p. v., Henry co., Ind., 33 ms. E. of Indianapolis; from W. 543 ms. Watered by Blue river.

KNIGHTSVILLE, p. o., Providence co., R. I.

KNOB, p. o., Tazewell co., Va.

KNOB CREEK, p. o., Harrison co., Ind.

KNOB FORK, p. o., Wetzel co., Va.

KNOBNOSTER, p. o., Johnson co., Mo.

KNOTTSVILLE, p. o., Daviess co., Ky., 149 ms. s. w. of Frankfort; from W. 691 ms.

KNOWERSVILLE, p. o., Albany co., N. Y., 16 ms. w. of Albany; from W. 386 ms.

KNOWLESVILLE, p. v., Ridgeway township, Orleans co., N. Y., 256 ms. w. of Albany; from W. 398 ms. Situated on the Erie canal.

KNOWLTON, p. t., Warren co., N. J., 66 ms. N. of Trenton; from W. 224 ms. Watered by Shawpocussing creek, Paulin's kill, and Beaver brook. Pop. 1,356.

KNOX COUNTY, situated in the easterly part of Tennessee, and traversed by Tennessee river. Area, 864 square miles. Face of the country mountainous; soil fertile. Seat of justice, Knoxville. Pop. in 1810, 10,171; in 1820, 13,034; in 1830, 14,498; in 1840, 15,485; in 1850, 18,775.

KNOX COUNTY, situated in the southeast part of Kentucky, and traversed by Cumberland river. Area, 495 square miles. Face of the country hilly and mountainous. Seat of justice, Barboursville. Pop. in 1810, 5,875; in 1820, 3,661; in 1830, 4,321; in 1840, 5,722; in 1850, 7,050.

KNOX COUNTY, situated in the central part of Ohio. Area, 618 square miles. Face of the country generally level; soil productive. Seat of justice, Mount Vernon. Pop. in 1810, 2,149; in 1820, 8,326; in 1830, 17,124; in 1840, 29,579; in 1850, 28,773.

KNOX COUNTY, situated on the westerly boundary of Indiana, with the Wabash on the west, and White river on the southeast. Area, 540 square miles. Face of the country, toward the Wabash, even; in the interior, hilly; soil generally fertile. Seat of justice, Vincennes. Pop. in 1810, 7,945; in 1820, 5,437; in 1830, 6,557; in 1840, 10,657; in 1850, 11,084.

KNOX COUNTY, situated toward the west part of Illinois. Area, 792 square miles. Seat of justice, Knoxville. Pop. in 1830, 274; in 1840, 7,060; in 1850, 13,279.

KNOX COUNTY, situated in the northeasterly part of Missouri. Area, —— square miles. Seat of justice, Edina. Pop. in 1850, 2,894.

KNOX, p. t., Waldo co., Me., 35 ms. N. E. of Augusta; from W. 630 ms.

KNOX, p. t., Albany co., N. Y., 21 ms. w. of Albany; from W. 391 ms. Watered by Bozrah kill. Pop. 2,021.

KNOX, p. o., Middlebury township, Knox co, O., 62 ms. N. E. of Columbus; from W. 387 ms.

KNOX, t., Columbiana co., O., 136 ms. N. E. of Columbus; from W. 297 ms. Watered by Mahoning creek. Pop. 2,155.

KNOX, t., Guernsey co., O. Pop. 755.

KNOX, t., Holmes co., O., 70 ms. N. E. of Columbus; from W. 351 ms. Pop. 1,210.

KNOX, t., Jefferson co., O., 141 ms. E. of Columbus; from W. 275 ms. Pop. 1,902.

KNOX, p. o., Stark co., Ind.

KNOX CENTRE, p. o., Knox township, Waldo co., Me.

KNOX CORNERS, p. o., Oneida co., N. Y.

KNOXVILLE, p. o., Greene co., Ala.; from W. 844 ms.

KNOXVILLE, city, c. h., seat of justice of Knox co., Tenn., 183 ms. E. of Nashville; from W. 498 ms. Watered by Holston river. Seat of East Tennessee college. Pop. 2,076.

KNOXVILLE, p. o., Tioga co., Pa., 162 ms. N. of Harrisburgh; from W. 276 ms.

KNOXVILLE, v., Frederick co., Md., 91 ms. N. w. of Annapolis; from W. 59 ms.

KNOXVILLE, p. v., Knox township, Jefferson co., O., 141 ms. E. of Columbus; from W. 275 ms.

KNOXVILLE, p. v., seat of justice of Crawford co., Ga., 55 ms. s. w. of Milledgeville; from W. 711 ms.

KNOXVILLE, c. h., p. v., seat of justice of Knox co., Ill., 100 ms. N. w. of Springfield; from W. 829 ms.

KNOXVILLE, p. o., Franklin co., Miss.

KNOXVILLE, p. o., Marion co.. Iowa.

KNOXVILLE, p. v., Ray co., Mo., 156 ms. N. w. of Jefferson city; from W. 1,059 ms.

KOKOMO, p. o., Howard co., Ind.

KORO, p. o., Winnebago co., Wis.

KORTRIGHT. p. t., Delaware co., N. Y., 69 ms. s. w. of Albany; from W. 365 ms. Watered by Delaware river and tributaries. Pop. 2,181.

KOSCIUSKO COUNTY, situated in the northerly part of Indiana. Area, 567 square miles. Seat of justice, Warsaw. Pop. in 1840, 4,170: in 1850, 10,243.

KOSCIUSKO, c. h., p. v., seat of justice of Attala co., Miss., 67 ms. N. E. of Jackson; from W. 958 ms. Watered by Yockonockony river.

KOSKONONG, p. o., Jefferson co., Wis., 48 ms. E. of Madison; from W. 822 ms.

KOSSUTH, p. o., Des Moines co., Iowa.

KOSSUTH, p. o., Racine co., Wis.

KOSSUTH, p. o., Boone co., Ill.

KOSSUTH, p. o., Auglaize co., O.

KOSSUTH, p. o., Washington co., Ind.

KOSSUTH, p. o., Washington co.,' Me.

KOSSUTH, p. o., Cherokee co., Ga.

KOSSUTH, p. o., Clarion co., Pa.

KOWALIGA, p. o., Tallapoosa co., Ala.

KRATZERSVILLE, p. o., Union co., Pa.

KREIDERSVILLE, p. b., Northampton co., Pa., 103 ms. N. E. of Harrisburgh; from W. 196 ms. Watered by Hockendocque creek.

KRESGEVILLE, p. o., Monroe co., Pa.

KROH'S MILLS, p. o., Carroll co., Md.

KULER, t., Van Buren co., Mich. Pop. 443.

KULPSVILLE, p. o., Montgomery co., Pa.

KUNKLETOWN, p. o., Monroe co., Pa.

KUTZTOWN, p. b., Maxatawny township, Berks co., Pa., 69 ms. E. of Harrisburgh; from W. 162 ms. Watered by a branch of Maiden creek. Pop. 640.

KYGER, p. o., Gallia co., O., 98 ms. s. E. of Columbus; from W. 353 ms.

KYSERIKE, p. o., Rochester township, Ulster co., N. Y., 71 ms. s. E. of Albany; from W. 311 ms.

KEYSERVILLE, p. o., Livingston co., N. Y.

KYTE RIVER, p. o., Ogle co., Ill.

L.

LABANUS, p. o., Robertson co., Tenn.

LACEY, p. o., De Kalb co., Ill.

LACEY SPRING, p. o., Rockingham co., Va.

LACEY'S SPRING, p. o., Morgan co., Ala; from W. 722 ms.

LACEYVILLE, p. o., Wyoming co., Pa.

LACEYVILLE, p. o., Harrison co.. O.

LACKAWACK, p. o., Wawarsing township, Ulster co., N. Y., 91 ms. s. w. of Albany; from W. 307 ms.

LACKAWANNA, p. t. Luzerne co., Pa. Pop. 389.

LACKAWANNOCK, t., Mercer co., Pa., 235 ms. N. w. of Harrisburgh; from W. 267 ms. Watered by Little Neseannock creek.

LACKAWAXEN, p. t., Pike co., Pa., 182 ms. N. E. of Harrisburgh; from W. 279 ms. Watered by Delaware river and Lackawaxen creek. Pop. 1,419.

LACKEMUTE, p. o., Polk co., Oregon.

LA CLAIR, p. o., De Kalb co.. Ill.

LACLEDE COUNTY, situated in the south part of Missouri. Area, —— square miles. Seat of justice, Cave Spring. Pop. in 1850. 2,498.

LACON, c. h., p. v., seat of justice of Marshall co., Ill., 99 ms. N. of Springfield; from W. 816 ms. Watered by Illinois river.

LACONA, p. o., Jefferson co., Ky.

LACONIA, p. o., Desha co., Ark.

LACONIA, p. v., Harrison co., Ind., 147 ms. s. of Indianapolis; from W. 643 ms.

LAC QUI PARLE, p. o., Dahkotah co., Minn.

LA CROSS, p. o., Crawford co., Wis.

LACY, p. o., Drew co., Ark.

LACY'S HILL, p. o., Pickens co., Ala.

LADDSBURGH. p. o., Bradford co., Pa.

LADIESBURGH, p. v., Frederick co., Md., 81 ms. N. W. of Annapolis; from W. 58 ms.

LADIGA, p. o., Benton co., Ala.; from W. 708 ms.

LADOGA, p. o., Montgomery co., Ind., 38 ms. N. w. of Indianapolis; from W. 609 ms.

LADOGO, p. o., Fond du Lac co., Wis.

LA FARGEVILLE, p. o., Orleans township, Jefferson co., N. Y., 182 ms. N. w. of Albany; from W. 432 ms.

LAFAYETTE COUNTY, situated in the northerly part of Mississippi. Area, 790 square miles. Seat of justice, Oxford. Pop. in 1840, 6,531; in 1850, 14,069.

LAFAYETTE COUNTY, situated in the westerly part of Missouri, with Missouri river on the north. Area, 450 square miles. Seat of justice, Lexington. Pop. in 1840, 6,815; in 1850, 13,690.

LAFAYETTE COUNTY, situated at the southwest corner of Arkansas, and traversed by Red river. Area, 1,260 square miles. Seat of justice, Lewisville. Pop. in 1830. 748; in 1840, 2,200; in 1850, 5,220.

LAFAYETTE COUNTY, situated on the south boundary of Wisconsin. Area, —— square miles. Seat of justice, ——. Pop. in 1850, 11,531.

LAFAYETTE PARISH, situated in the southerly part of Louisiana, and traversed by Vermillion river. Area, —— square miles. Seat of justice, Vermillion-

ville. Pop. in 1830, 5,653; in 1840, 7,841; in 1850, 6,720.

LAFAYETTE, p. t., Onondaga co., N. Y., 130 ms. w. of Albany; from W. 330 ms. Watered by Onondaga creek. Pop. 2,533.

LAFAYETTE, p. o., Stark co., Ill.

LAFAYETTE, c. h., p. v., Newton township, Sussex co., N. J., 75 ms. N. of Trenton; from W. 243 ms. Watered by Paulinskill river. Pop. 928.

LAFAYETTE, p. o., McKean co., Pa., 208 ms. N. w. of Harrisburgh; from W. 291 ms.

LAFAYETTE, p. v., Deer creek township, Madison co., O.. 22 ms. w. of Columbus; from W. 415 ms. Pop. 147.

LAFAYETTE, t., Coshocton co., O. Pop. 1,040.

LAFAYETTE, t., Medina co., O. Pop. 1,532.

LAFAYETTE, p. v., Christian co., Ky., 221 ms. s. w. of Frankfort; from W. 738 ms.

LAFAYETTE, p. v., Montgomery co., Va., 188 ms. w. of Richmond; from W. 256 ms.

LAFAYETTE, p. v., seat of justice of Walker co., Ga., 199 ms. N. w. of Milledgeville; from W 634 ms. Watered by Chattooga river. Pop. 588.

LAFAYETTE, t., Floyd co., Ind. Pop. 1,215.

LAFAYETTE, c. h., p. v., seat of justice of Tippecanoe co., Ind., 70 ms. N. w. of Indianapolis; from W. 628 ms. Situated on Wabash river, at the head of steamboat navigation. Pop. 6,129.

LAFAYETTE, t., Owen co., Ind. Pop. 754.

LAFAYETTE, city, c. h., seat of justice of Jefferson parish, La., 2 ms. w. of New Orleans; from W. 1,174 ms. Watered by Mississippi river. Pop. 14,190.

LAFAYETTE, t., Van Buren co., Mich. Pop. 1,143.

LAFAYETTE, t., Wachita co., Ark. Pop. 1,181.

LAFAYETTE, t., Livingston co., Mo.

LAFAYETTE, p. o., Linn co., Iowa.

LAFAYETTE, p. o., Grafton co., N. H.

LAFAYETTE, p. o., Macon co., Tenn.

LAFAYETTE, p. o., Walworth co., Wis.

LAFAYETTE, p. o., Yum Hill co., Oregon.

LAFAYETTE HILL, p. o., Fluvanna co., Va.

LAFAYETTE SPRINGS, p. o., Lafayette co., Miss.

LAFAYETTEVILLE, p. o., Dutchess co., N. Y.

LAFFING GALL, p. o., Cherokee co., Ga.

LA FONTAINE, p. o., Harlan co., Ky.

LA FONTAINE, p. o., Wabash co., Ind.

LA FOURCHE INTERIOR PARISH, situated in the southeast part of Louisiana, with the gulf of Mexico on the south. Area, 1,100 square miles. Face of the country low and flat; soil marshy, except along the streams. Seat of justice, Thibodeauxville. Pop. in 1810, 4,467; in 1820, 3,755; in 1830, 5,503; in 1840, 7,303; in 1850, 9,533.

LAGADO, p. v., Wilson co., Tenn., 30 ms. E. of Nashville; from W. 673 ms.

LA GRANGE COUNTY, situated on the north boundary of Indiana. Area, 380 square miles. Watered by Fawn, Pigeon, and Little Elkhart rivers. Seat of justice, La Grange. Pop. in 1840, 3,364; 1850, 8,537.

LA GRANGE, p. t., Penobscot co., Me., 97 ms. N. E. of Augusta ; from W. 693 ms. Watered by tributaries of Penobscot river. Pop. 482.

LA GRANGE, t., Dutchess co., N. Y.. 92 ms. s. of Albany ; from W. 322 ms. Watered by Sprout and Wappinger's creeks. Pop. 1,941.

LA GRANGE, p. o., Covington township. Wyoming co., N. Y., 224 ms. w. of Albany ; from W. 366 ms.

LA GRANGE, p. o., Wyoming co., Pa., 158 ms. N. E. of Harrisburgh ; from W. 203 ms.

LA GRANGE, p. t., Lorain co., O., 111 ms. N. E. of Columbus ; from W. 370 ms. Watered by the tributaries of Black river. Pop. 1,402.

LA GRANGE. c. h., p. v., seat of justice of Oldham co., Ky., 35 ms. N. w. of Frankfort ; from W. 577 ms. Watered by Ohio river.

LA GRANGE, p. v.. Randolph co., N. C., 92 ms. w. of Raleigh ; from W. 331 ms.

LA GRANGE, c. h., p. v., seat of justice of Troup co., Ga., 121 ms. w. of Milledgeville ; from W. 739 ms. Pop. 1,614.

LA GRANGE, p. v., Franklin co., Ala. ; from W. 776 ms. Seat of La Grange college.

LA GRANGE, p. v.. Fayette co., Tenn., 184 ms. s. w. of Nashville ; from W. 869 ms.

LA GRANGE, p. t., Cass co., Mich., 171 ms. w. of Detroit ; from W. 616 ms. Watered by a tributary of Dowagiake river, and Putnam's creek. Pop. 1,327.

LA GRANGE, t., Fayette co.. Ark.

LA GRANGE, p. v., Lewis co., Mo., 129 ms. N. E. of Jefferson city ; from W. 898 ms. Watered by Mississippi river.

LA GRANGE, c. h.. p. v., seat of justice of La Grange co., Ind.

LA GRANGE, p. o., Fayette co., Tex.

LA GRANGE, p. o., Walworth co., Wis.

LA GRANGE, p. o., Monroe co., Iowa.

LA GRANGE BLUFF. p. o., Brown co., Ill., 66 ms. w. of Springfield ; from W. 816 ms.

LA GREW SPRINGS, p. o., Arkansas co., Ark.

LAGRO, p. t., Wabash co., Ind.. 94 ms. N. of Indianapolis ; from W. 581 ms. Pop. 2,515.

LA HARPE, p. o.. Hancock co., Ill., 104 ms. N. w. of Springfield ; from W. 865 ms.

LAHASKA, p. o., Bucks co., Pa.

LAING'S, p. o., Greene township, Monroe co., O., 120 ms. E. of Columbus ; from W. 287 ms.

LAINGSBURGH, p. v., Shiawassee co., Mich., 93 ms. N. w. of Detroit ; from W. 596 ms.

LAIRDSVILLE, p. a., Woodmoreland township, Oneida co., N. Y., 102 ms. N. w. of Albany ; from W 384 ms.

LAIRDSVILLE, p. o., Lycoming co., Pa., 98 ms. N. of Harrisburgh ; from W. 208 ms.

LAKE COUNTY, situated on the north boundary of Ohio, on Lake Erie. Area, 820 square miles. Seat of justice, Painesville. Pop. in 1840, 13,719 ; in 1850, 14,650.

LAKE COUNTY, situated at the northwest corner of Indiana, on Lake Michigan. Area, 468 square miles. Seat of justice, Lake c. h., Crown Point. Pop. in 1840, 1,468 ; in 1850, 3,991.

LAKE COUNTY, situated at the northeast corner of Illinois, on Lake Michigan. Area, 425 square miles. Seat of justice, Waukegan. Pop. in 1840, 2,634 ; in 1850, 14,226.

LAKE, p. o., Greenwich township. Washington co., N. Y., 44 ms. N. w. of Albany ; from W. 414 ms.

LAKE, p, t., Wood co., O. Pop. 152.

LAKE, p. o., Luzerne co., Pa.

LAKE, t., Logan co., O., 62 ms. N. w. of Columbus ; from W. 458 ms. Pop. 1.767.

LAKE, t., Wayne co., O., 71 ms. N. E. of Columbus ; from W. 359 ms. Watered by east fork of Mohican river.

LAKE, t., Allen co., Ind. Pop. 578.

LAKE, c. h., Crown Point township, seat of justice of Lake co., Ind., 158 ms. N. w. of Indianapolis ; from W. 703 ms.

LAKE, t., Milwaukee co., Wis.

LAKE CARRAWAY, p. o., Carroll parish, La.

LAKE CHARLES, p. o., Calcasieu parish, La.

LAKE COMFORT, p. o.. Hyde co., N. C.

LAKE CREEK, p. o., Lamar co., Tex.

LAKE DRUMMOND. p. o., Norfolk co., Va., 123 ms. s. E. of Richmond ; from W. 253 ms.

LAKE GRIFFIN, p. o., Marion co., Flor.

LAKELAND, p. o., Brookhaven township, Suffolk co., Long Island, N. Y. Situated near Ronkonkoma lake.

LAKE LANDING, c. h., p. v., seat of justice of Hyde co., N. C., 215 ms. E. of Raleigh ; from W. 400 ms. Watered by Mattimuskett lake.

LAKE MARIA, p. o., Marquette co., Wis.

LAKE MILLS, p. o., Jefferson co.. Wis.

LAKE PLEASANT, p. t., Hamilton co., N. Y., 81 ms. N. w. of Albany ; from W. 450 ms. Watered by Sacandaga and Indian rivers, and Lake Pleasant. Pop. 505.

LAKE PROVIDENCE, c. h., p. v.. seat of justice of Carroll parish, La.. 366 ms. N. w. of New Orleans ; from W. 1,154 ms. Watered by Lake Providence and Tensas river.

LAKEFORT, p. o., Madison co., N. Y.

LAKE RIDGE, p. o.. Tompkins co., N. Y., 177 ms. w. of Albany ; from W. 311 ms.

LAKESVILLE, p. o., Dorchester co., Md.

LAKE SWAMP, p. o.. Horry district. S. C.

LAKETON, p. v.. Wabash co., Ind., 104 ms. N. of Indianapolis ; from W. 594 ms. Watered by Eel river.

LAKE VIEW, p. o., Dane co., Wis.

LAKE VILLAGE, p. v., Gilford township, Belknap co., N. H., 35 ms. N. of Concord ; from W. 506 ms. Watered by Lake Winnipiseogee.

LAKEVILLE, p. o., Livonia township, Livingston co., N. Y., 228 ms. w. of Albany ; from W. 353 ms.

LAKEVILLE, v., North Hempstead township. Queen's co., Long Island, N. Y., 20 ms. E. of New York. Watered by Success pond.

LAKEVILLE, p. v.. Oakland co., Mich., 40 ms. N.w. of Detroit ; from W. 568 ms.

LAKEVILLE, p. o., Litchfield co.. Ct.

LAKEVILLE, p. o., St. Joseph co.. Ind.

LAKE ZURICH. p. o., Lake co., Ill.

LAMAR COUNTY, situated on the northerly boundary of Texas, with Red river on the north. Area, —— square miles. Seat of justice, Paris. Pop. in 1850, 3,978.

LAMAR, p. t., Clinton co., Pa., 101 ms. N. w. of Harrisburgh ; from W. 209 ms. Watered by Cedar and Big Fishing creeks. Pop. 1,182.

LAMAR. p. o., Marshall co., Miss., 207 ms. N. of Jackson ; from W. 879 ms.

LAMAR, p. o., Randolph co., Ala.

LAMAR, p. o., Refugio co., Tex.

LAMAR, p. o., Lake co., Ill.

LAMARTINE, p. o., Giles co., Tenn.

LAMARTINE, p. o., Carroll co., O.

LAMARTINE, p. o., Benton co., Ala.

LAMARTINE, p. o., Fond du Lac co., Wis.

LAMARTINE, p. o., Clarion co., O.

LAMARTINE, p. o., Wachita co., Ark.

LAMBERTSVILLE, p. v., Amwell township, Hunterdon co., N. J., 15 ms. N. w. of Trenton ; from W. 173 ms. Pop. 1,417.

LAMBERTVILLE. p. v., Monroe co., Mich., 70 ms. N.w. of Detroit ; from W. 475 ms.

LAMB'S POINT, p. o., Madison co., Ill.

LAMBURGH, p. o., Iroquois co.. Ill.

LA MINE, p. o., Cooper co., Mo., 60 ms. N. w. of Jefferson City ; from W. 974 ms.

LAMINGTON, p. o., Russell co.. Ala.

LA MIRA, p. o., Belmont co., O.

LAMOILLE COUNTY, situated in the northerly part of Vermont. Area, 420 square miles. Face of the country, mountainous. Seat of justice, Hyde Park. Pop. in 1840, 10,475 ; in 1850, 10,872.

LAMOILLE, p. o., Bureau co., Ill.

LA MOTT, p. o., Jackson co., Iowa.

LAMPETER. p. t., Lancaster co., Pa., 40 ms. s. E. of Harrisburgh ; from W. 114 ms. Watered by Mill and Pecquea creeks, and Conestoga river. Pop. 1,918.

LAMPSVILLE, p. o., Belmont co., O.

LAMSON'S. p. o., Onondaga co., N. Y.

LANARK, p. o., Bradley co., Ark.

LANCASTER COUNTY, situated on the south boundary of Pennsylvania, with Susquehanna river on the southwest. Area, 928 square miles. Face of the country, diversified with mountains, hills, and valleys ; soil, generally productive. Seat of justice, Lancaster. Pop. in 1810, 53,927 ; in 1820, 68,336 ; in 1830, 76,558 ; in 1840, 84.203 ; in 1850, 98.944.

LANCASTER COUNTY, situated in the easterly part of Virginia, on the west shore of Chesapeake bay, with Rappahannock river on the southwest. Area, 161 square miles. Seat of justice, Lancaster C. H. Pop. in 1810, 5,592 ; in 1820, 5,517 ; in 1830, 4,800 ; in 1840, 4,628 ; in 1850, 4,708.

LANCASTER DISTRICT, situated on the northerly boundary of South Carolina, with Catawba river on the west. Area, 524 square miles. Seat of justice, Lancaster. Pop. in 1810, 6,318 ; in 1820, 8,716 ; in 1830, 10,361 ; in 1840, 9,907 ; in 1850, 10,986.

LANCASTER, c. h., p. t., seat of justice of Coos co., N. H., 101 ms. N. of Concord ; from W. 562 ms. Watered by Connecticut and Israel's rivers. Pop. 1,559.

LANCASTER, p. t., Worcester co., Mass., 36 ms. w. of Boston ; from W. 416 ms. Watered by Nashua river. Pop. 1,688.

LANCASTER, p. t., Erie co., N. Y., 280 ms. w. of Albany ; from W. 387 ms. Watered by Ellicott, Cayuga, and Seneca creeks. Pop. 3,794.

LANCASTER, city, seat of justice of Lancaster co., Pa., is situated 36 miles southeast of Harrisburgh, and 62 miles west of Philadelphia. In 1812, the state government was transferred from this place to Harrisburgh. In the midst of the beautiful and fertile valley of Conestoga creek, it constitutes the centre of an extensive trade with the surrounding region, and a thoroughfare between Philadelphia and the west. This is one of those towns which are interesting for both age and prosperity. Some of its buildings are antiquated ; others are modern ; but generally all are neat and pleasant. By a series of dams and locks, forming the Conestoga canal, the navigation of the creek has been improved to the Susquehanna, a distance of 18 miles.

The manufacturing establishments are various and flourishing.

The Columbia and Philadelphia railroad communicates with Lancaster, and leads toward Harrisburgh ; and here, the Westchester branch diverges toward York.

The population in 1810 was 5,405 ; in 1820, 6,633 ; in 1830, 7,704 ; in 1840, 8,417 ; in 1850, 8,811.

LANCASTER, c. h., p. v., seat of justice of Hocking township, Fairfield co., O., 30 ms. s. E. of Columbia ; from W. 375 ms. Pop. 3,483.

LANCASTER, c. h., p. v., seat of justice of Garrard co., Ky., 57 ms. s. of Frankfort ; from W. 555 ms.

LANCASTER, p. v., Smith co., Tenn., 61 ms. s. E. of Nashville ; from W. 644 ms. Watered by Cany fork of Cumberland river.

LANCASTER, p. t., Jefferson co., Ind., 74 ms. s. E. of Indianapolis ; from W. 574 ms. Pop. 1,381.

LANCASTER, p. v., Cass co., Ill., 24 ms. s. w. of Springfield ; from W. 804 ms.

LANCASTER, c. h., p. v., seat of justice of Grant co., Wis., 96 ms. s. w. of Madison ; from W. 928 ms.

LANCASTER, c. h., p. v., seat of justice of Lancaster co., Va. 83 ms. E. of Richmond ; from W. 144 ms.

LANCASTER, p. v., Lancaster district, S. C., 72 ms. N. E. of Columbia ; from W. 434. Watered by a tributary of Catawba river.

LANCASTER, c. h., p. v., seat of justice of Schuyler co., Mo.

LANCASTER, c. h., p. v., seat of justice of Keokuk co., Iowa. Pop. 444.

LANDAFF, p. t., Grafton co., N. H., 84 ms. N. w. of Concord ; from W. 532 ms. Watered by Great and Wild Ammonoosuck rivers. Pop. 948.

LANDERSVILLE, p. o., Lawrence co., Ala.

LANDGROVE, p. t., Bennington co., Vt., 98 ms. s. w. of Montpelier ; from W. 442 ms. Watered by tributaries of West river. Pop. 337.

LANDISBURGH. p. v., Perry co., Pa., 29 ms. w. of Harrisburgh ; from W. 117 ms. Pop. 416.

LANDISVILLE, p. o., Lancaster co., Pa., 31 ms. s. E. of Harrisburgh ; from W. 117 ms.

LAND OF PROMISE, p. o., Princess Ann co., Va.

LANDSDOWN, p. o., Prince William co., Va.

LANDSFORD, p. o., Chester district, S. C.

LANE, p. o., Elkhart co., Ind.

LANEFIELD, p. o., Haywood co., Tenn.

LANESBOROUGH. p. t., Berkshire co., Mass., 135 ms. N. w. of Boston ; from W. 382 ms. Watered by head branches of Hoosick and Housatonic rivers. Pop. 1,229.

LANESBOROUGH, p. o., Susquehanna co., Pa., 190 ms. N. E. of Harrisburgh ; from W. 290 ms.

LANESBOROUGH, p. v., Anson co., N. C., 155 ms. s. w. of Raleigh ; from W. 424 ms.

LANE's CREEK. p. o., Union co., N. C., 158 ms. s. w. of Raleigh ; from W. 427 ms.

LANE's PRAIRIE, p. o., Osage co., Mo.

LANESVILLE, p. v., Harrison co., Ind., 135 ms. s. of ndianapolis ; from W. 614 ms.

LANESVILLE, p. o., Floyd co., Ky.

LANESVILLE, p. o., King William co., Va.

LANGDON, p. t., Sullivan co., N. H., 59 ms. s. w. of Concord ; from W. 456 ms. Watered by a tributary of Cold river. Pop. 575.

LANGDON, p. o., Du Page co., Ill.

LANGLEY, p. o., Fairfax co., Va.

LANGSBURY, p. o., Camden co., Ga., 257 ms. s. E. of Milledgeville ; from W. 766 ms.

LANGSTON, p. o., Jackson co., Ala. ; from W. 683 ms.

LANGSVILLE, p. o., Meigs co., O.

LANGUELLE, p. t., St. Francis co., Ark., 132 ms. N. of Little Rock ; from W. 977 ms. Watered by Languelle river.

LANIER, c. h., p. v., seat of justice of Macon co., Ga., 76 ms. s. w. of Milledgeville ; from W. 732 ms. Watered by Flint river.

LANNAHASSE, p. o., Stewart co., Ga., 118 ms. s. w. of Milledgeville ; from W. 774 ms.

LANQUILLE, t., Poinsett co., Ark.

LANSING, p. t., Tompkins co., N. Y., 170 ms. w. of Albany ; from W. 313 ms. Pop. 3,318.

LANSING, p. o., Brown co., Wis.

LANSING, p. o., Potter co., Ind.

LANSING, p. v., Ingham co., Mich., situated on the east side of Grand river, succeeded Detroit as the capital of the state, in December, 1847. It is 95 miles northwest of Detroit, and 80 miles east of Lake Michigan. The state and public buildings are projected, and finishing on a scale creditable to this great state. Pop. in 1850, 1,229.

LANSING, p. o., Allemakee co., Iowa.

LANSINGBURGH, p. t., Rensselaer co., N. Y., 10 ms. N. E. of Albany ; from W. 380 ms. Situated on Hudson river, at the head of boat navigation. Pop. 5,752.

LANSINGVILLE, p. v., Lansing township. Tompkins co., N Y., 175 ms. w. of Albany ; from W. 308 ms.

LAONA, p. o., Chautauque co., N. Y.

LAONA, p. o., Winnebago co., Ill.

LAPEER COUNTY, situated on the easterly part of Michigan. Area, 828 square miles. Seat of justice, Lapeer. Pop. in 1840, 4,265 ; in 1850, 7,029.

LAPEER, c. h., p. t., seat of justice of Lapeer co., Mich., 61 ms. N. of Detroit ; from W. 584 ms. Watered by Flint river and Farmer's creek. Pop. 1,468.

LAPEER, p. o., Cortland co., N. Y.

LAPHAMSVILLE, p. o., Kent co., Mich.

LAPLAND, p. v., Buncombe co., N. C., 275 ms. w. of Raleigh ; from W. 478 ms.

LA POINTE, p. o., St. Croix co., Wis.

LAPOMBA, p. o., Lafayette co., Miss.

LA PORTE COUNTY, situated on the north boundary of Indiana, with Lake Michigan on the northwest. Area, 460 square miles. Seat of justice, La Porte. Pop. in 1840, 8,184 ; in 1850, 12,145.

LA PORTE, c. h., p. v., seat of justice of La Porte co., Ind., 145 ms. N. of Indianapolis ; from W. 660 ms. Pop. 1,821.

LA PORTE, p. o., Lorain co., O., 119 ms. N. E. of Columbus ; from W. 371 ms.

LAPPON'S CROSS-ROADS, p. o., Washington co., Md.

LAPUTA, v., Franklin co., Ky., 10 ms. w. of Frankfort ; from W. 552 ms. Watered by Kentucky river.

LAREDO, p. o., Webb co., Tex.

LARESSA, p. o., Cherokee co., Tex.

LARKINSBURGH, p. o., Clay co., Ill.

LARKIN's FORK, p. o., Jackson co., Ala. ; from W. 688 ms.

LARKINSVILLE. p. v., at the Blue Springs, Jackson co., Ala. ; from W. 700 ms.

LARNED's CORNERS, p. o., Hopewell township, Ontario co., N. Y., 200 ms. w. of Albany ; from W. 346 ms.

LARNER, p. t., Preble co., O. Pop. 1,694.

LARONE, p. o., Somerset co., Me.

LARRABEE's POINT, p. o., Addison co., Vt.

LARRY's CREEK, p. o., Lycoming co., Pa.

LA RUE COUNTY, situated in Kentucky. Area, —— square miles. Seat of justice, ———. Pop. in 1850, 5,859.

LA SALLE COUNTY, situated in the northerly part of Illinois, and traversed by Illinois river. Area, 1,864 square miles. Seat of justice, Ottawa. Pop. in 1840, 9,348 ; in 1850, 17,815.

LA SALLE, p. o., Monroe co., Mich., 42 ms. s. w. of Detroit ; from W. 481 ms. Pop. 1,100.

LA SALLE, p. v., La Salle co., Ill., 133 ms. N. E. of Springfield ; from W. 788 ms.

LA SALLE, p. o., Calhoun co., Tex.

LA SALLE, p. o., Niagara co., N. Y.

Las Casas, p. o., Rutherford co., Tenn., 43 ms. s. e. of Nashville ; from W. 662 ms.

Lassellville, p. o., Euphrata township, Fulton co., N. Y., 58 ms. n. w. of Albany ; from W. 408 ms.

Lassen's, p. o., Butte co., N. C.

Lassiter's Mills, p. o., Randolph co., N. C.

Las Vegas, p. o., New Mexico.

Lathrop, p. o., Susquehanna co., Pa.

Latimore. t., Adams co., Pa., 38 ms. s. of Harrisburgh ; from W. 75 ms. Watered by Bermudian creek. Pop. 1,138.

Lattas, p. o., Ross co., O., 63 ms. s. of Columbus ; from W. 418 ms.

Laubach, p. o., Northampton co., Pa.

LAUDERDALE COUNTY, situated at the northwest corner of Alabama, with Tennessee river on the south. Area, 672 square miles. Face of the country, hilly ; soil, productive. Pop. in 1820, 4,963 ; in 1830, 11,782 ; in 1840. 14,485 ; in 1850, 17,172.

LAUDERDALE COUNTY, situated on the east boundary of Mississippi. Area, 700 square miles. Seat of justice. Marion. Pop. in 1840, 5,358 ; in 1850, 8,708.

LAUDERDALE COUNTY, situated on the westerly boundary of Tennessee, with Mississippi river on the west. Area, 375 square miles. Seat of justice, Ripley. Pop. in 1840, 3,435 ; 1850, 5,169.

Lauderdale Factory, p. o., Lauderdale co., Ala.

Lauderdale Springs, p. o., Lauderdale co., Miss.

Laughery, t., Dearborn co., Ind., 102 ms. s. e. of Indianapolis ; from W. 527 ms. Pop. 1,092.

Laughery, v.. Ripley co.. Ind., 69 ms. s. e. of Indianapolis ; from W. 532 ms. Watered by Laughery creek.

Laughlintown, p. v., Ligonier township, Westmoreland co., Pa., 140 ms. w. of Harrisburgh ; from W. 172 ms.

Laura, p. o., Miami co., Ind.

Lauramie, p. o., Tippecanoe co., Ind.

Lauraville, p. o., Baltimore co., Md.

LAUREL COUNTY, situated toward the southeast part of Kentucky. Area, 400 square miles. Seat of justice, London. Pop. in 1830, 2,206 ; in 1840, 3,079 ; in 1850, 4,145.

Laurel, p. v., Sussex co., Del., 52 ms. s. of Dover ; from W. 129 ms.

Laurel, p. o., Washington co., Va , 296 ms. w. of Richmond.

Laurel, p. v., Franklin co., Ind., 57 ms. s. e. of Indianapolis ; from W. 531 ms. Watered by Whitewater river, and Whitewater canal. Pop. 11,845.

Laurel, p. o., Clermont co., O.

Laurel, p. t., Hocking co., O. Pop. 1,126.

Laurel Creek, p. o., Floyd co., Va.

Laurel Creek, p. o., Fayette co., Tenn., 190 ms. s. w. of Nashville ; from W. 879 ms.

Laurel Factory, p. o., Prince George's co., Md.

Laurel Fork, p. o., Carroll co., Va.

Laurel Fork, p. o., Bath co., Ky.

Laurel Gap, p. o., Greene co., Tenn., 255 ms. e. of Nashville ; from W 431 ms.

Laurel Grove, p. o., Pittsylvania co., Va., 149 ms. s. w. of Richmond ; from W. 236 ms.

Laurel Hill, p. o., Marengo co., Ala. ; from W. 904 ms.

Laurel Hill, p. o., Carroll co., Ga., 133 ms. n. w. of Milledgeville ; from W. 729 ms.

Laurel Hill, p. o., Richmond co., N. C., 99 ms. s.w. of Raleigh ; from W. 387 ms.

Laurel Hill, p. o., Lunenburgh co., Va., 80 ms. s. w. of Richmond ; from W. 199 ms.

Laurel Mills, p. o., Rappahannock co., Va.

Laurel Point, p. o., Monongalia co., Va.

Laurel Spring, p. o., Ashe co., N. C., 202 ms. w. of Raleigh ; from W. 374 ms.

Laurelville, p. o , Westmoreland co., Pa.

LAURENS COUNTY, situated toward the southeasterly part of Georgia, and traversed by Oconee river. Area, 780 square miles. Seat of justice, Dublin. Pop. in 1810, 2,210 ; in 1820, 5,436 ; in 1830, 5,589 ; in 1840, 5,585 ; in 1850, 6,422.

LAURENS DISTRICT, situated toward the northwesterly part of South Carolina. Area, 920 square miles. Face of the country uneven ; soil productive. Seat of justice, Laurenceville. Pop. in 1810, 14,982 ; in 1820, 17,682 ; in 1830, 20,263 ; in 1840, 21,584 ; in 1850, 23,407.

Laurens, p. t., Otsego co., N. Y., 83 ms. w. of Albany ; from W. 358 ms. Watered by Otsego creek. Pop. 2,168.

Laurens, c. h., p. v., seat of justice of Laurence district, S. C., 70 ms. n. w. of Columbia ; from W. 496 ms.

Laurens Hill. p. o., Laurens co., Ga., 63 ms. s. e. of Milledgeville ; from W. 706 ms.

Laurensville, p. v., Laurens township, Otsego co., N. Y.

Lausanne, p. t., Carbon co., Pa., 100 ms. n. e. of Harrisburgh ; from W. 208 ms. Watered by Lehigh river and Laurel run.

LA VACA COUNTY, situated in the southerly part of Texas. Area, —— square miles. Seat of justice, Peterburgh. Pop. in 1850, 2,608.

Lavansville, p. o., Somerset co., Pa., 144 ms. w. of Harrisburgh ; from W. 170 ms.

Lavona, p. o., Lucas co., O.

Lawn Ridge, p. o.. Marshall co., Ill.

LAWRENCE COUNTY, situated in the northerly part of Alabama, with Tennessee river on the north. Area, 725 square miles. Seat of justice, Moulton. Pop. in 1840, 13.313 ; in 1850, 15,258.

LAWRENCE COUNTY, situated in the southerly part of Mississippi, and traversed by Pearl river. Area, 790 square miles. Face of the country hilly ; soil generally sterile. Seat of justice, Monticello. Pop. in 1820, 4,916 ; in 1830, 5,321 ; in 1840, 5,920 ; in 1850, 6,478.

LAWRENCE COUNTY, situated on the north boundary of Arkansas, and traversed by Big Black river. Area, 1,300 square miles. Seat of justice, Smithville. Pop. in 1820, 5,602 ; in 1830, 2,806 ; in 1840, 2,835 ; in 1850, 5,271.

LAWRENCE COUNTY, situated on the south boundary of Tennessee. Area, 680 square miles. Seat of justice, Lawrenceburgh. Pop. in 1820, 3,271 ; in 1830, 5,411 ; in 1840. 7,121 ; in 1850, 9,280.

LAWRENCE COUNTY, situated on the easterly boundary of Kentucky, with Big Sandy river on the east. Area, 650 square miles. Seat of justice, ——. Pop. in 1830. 3,900 ; in 1840, 4,730 ; in 1850, 6,281.

LAWRENCE COUNTY, situated on the southerly boundary of Ohio, with Ohio river on the south. Area, 430 square miles. Face of the country hilly ; soil generally unproductive. Seat of justice, Burlington. Pop. in 1820, 3,499 ; in 1830, 5,367 ; in 1840, 9,738 ; in 1850, 15,726.

LAWRENCE COUNTY, situated on the west boundary of Pennsylvania. Area, —— square miles. Seat of justice, New Castle. Pop. in 1850, 21,079.

LAWRENCE COUNTY, situated toward the southerly part of Indiana, and traversed by east fork of White river. Area, 438 square miles. Seat of justice, Bedford. Pop. in 1820, 4,116 ; in 1830, 9,237 ; in 1840, 11,782 ; in 1850, 12,097.

LAWRENCE COUNTY, situated on the southeasterly boundary of Illinois, with Wabash river on the southeast. Area, 560 square miles. Seat of justice, Lawrenceville. Pop. in 1830, 3,668 ; in 1840, 7,092 ; in 1850, 6,122.

LAWRENCE COUNTY, situated in the southwesterly part of Missouri. Area, —— square miles. Seat of justice, Mount Vernon. Pop. in 1850, 4,859.

Lawrence, p. t., Van Buren co., Mich. Pop. 510.

Lawrence, t., St. Lawrence co., N. Y., 230 ms. n. w. of Albany ; from W. 505 ms. Watered by St. Regis and Deer rivers. Pop. 2,214.

Lawrence, p. t., Washington co., O., 114 ms. s. e. of Columbus ; from W. 305 ms. Watered by Little Muskingum river. Pop. 814.

Lawrence, t., Mercer co., N. J., 6 ms. n. e. of Trenton ; from W. 172 ms. Watered by Assunpink creek and Stony brook. Pop. 1,835.

Lawrence, p. t., Clearfield co., Pa. Pop. 1,173.

Lawrence, t., Tioga co.. Pa., 153 ms. n. of Harrisburgh ; from W. 259 ms. Pop. 1,029.

Lawrence, t., Lawrence co.. O., 124 ms. s. e. of Columbus ; from W. 406 ms. Pop. 534.

Lawrence, t., Stark co.. O., 116 ms. n. e. of Columbus ; from W. 335 ms. Situated on the Ohio canal. Pop. 2,287.

Lawrence, t.. Tuscarawas co., O., 111 ms. from Columbus ; from W. 321 ms. Pop. 1,468.

Lawrence, p. v., Essex co., Mass., 25 ms. n. of Boston ; from W. 453 ms. Watered by Merrimack river. Pop. 8.282.

Lawrence, p. o., Monroe co., Miss.

Lawrence, p. o., Marion co., Ind.

Lawrenceburgh, p. v., Perry township, Armstrong co., Pa., 200 ms. n. w. of Harrisburgh ; from W. 266 ms. Watered by Alleghany river.

LAWRENCE, c. h., p. v., seat of justice of Lawrence co., Tenn., 75 ms. s. w. of Nashville; from W. 752 ms. Watered by Shoal creek.

LAWRENCEBURGH, c. h., p. v., seat of justice of Anderson co., Ky., 12 ms. s. of Frankfort; from W. 554 ms. Watered by Kentucky river.

LAWRENCEBURGH, c. h., p. v., seat of justice of Dearborn co., Ind., 86 ms. s. E. of Indianapolis; from W. 514 ms. Watered by Ohio river. Terminus of Whitewater canal. Pop. 3,487.

LAWRENCEPORT, p. o., Lawrence co., Ind.

LAWRENCEVILLE, p. v., Lawrence township, St. Lawrence co., N. Y., 231 ms. N. w. of Albany; from W. 513 ms.

LAWRENCEVILLE, p. v., Lawrence township, Mercer co., N. J., 6 ms. N. of Trenton; from W. 172 ms.

LAWRENCEVILLE, p. v., Lawrence township, Tioga co., Pa., 158 ms. N. of Harrisburgh; from W. 268 ms. Watered by Tioga river and tributaries. Pop. 494.

LAWRENCEVILLE, b., Pitt township, Alleghany co., Pa. Watered by Alleghany river. Site of the Alleghany U. S. Arsenal. Pop. 1,746.

LAWRENCEVILLE, c. h., p. v., seat of justice of Brunswick co., Va., 73 ms. s. w. of Richmond; from W. 189 ms. Watered by a tributary of Meherrin river.

LAWRENCEVILLE, c. h., p. v., seat of justice of Gwinnett co., Ga., 84 ms. N. w. of Milledgeville; from W. 655 ms. Watered by Chattahoochee river.

LAWRENCEVILLE, c. h., p. v., seat of justice of Lawrence co., Ill., 159 ms. s. E. of Springfield; from W. 697 ms. Watered by Embarrass river.

LAWRENCEVILLE, p. v., seat of justice of Monroe co., Ark., 75 ms. E. of Little Rock; from W. 1,015 ms.

LAWRENCEVILLE, p. o., Dearborn co., Ind.

LAWRENCEVILLE, p. o., Henry co., Ala.

LAWSONVILLE, p. o., Rockingham co., N. C., 102 ms. N. w. of Raleigh; from W. 278 ms.

LAWSVILLE, p. t., Susquehanna co., Pa., 171 ms. from Harrisburgh; from W. 279 ms. Watered by Snake creek.

LAWSVILLE CENTRE, p. o., Lawsville township, Susquehanna co., Pa., 187 ms. N. E. of Harrisburgh; from W. 297 ms.

LAWTON, p. o., Van Buren co., Mich.

LAWTONVILLE, p. v., Beaufort district, S. C., 121 ms. s. of Columbia; from W. 627 ms.

LAWYERSVILLE, p. v., Cobbleskill township, Scoharie co., N. Y., 44 ms. w. of Albany; from W. 388 ms.

LAYSVILLE, p. o., New London co., Ct.

LAYTONSVILLE, p. o., Montgomery co., Md.

LEACHMAN, p. o., Buchanan co., Mo.

LEACOCK. p. t., Lancaster co., Pa., 44 ms. s. E. of Harrisburgh: from W. 118 ms. Watered by Conestoga river and Mill and Pecquea creeks. Pop. 1,943.

LEADING CREEK, p. v., Lewis co., Va., 301 ms. N. w. of Richmond; from W. 269 ms. Watered by Leading creek.

LEADSVILLE, p. o., Randolph co., Va.

LEADVALE, p. o., Jefferson co., Tenn.

LEAKE COUNTY, situated in the central part of Mississippi. Area, 576 square miles. Seat of justice, Carthage. Pop. in 1840, 2 162; in 1850, 5.533.

LEAKE'S STORE, p. o., Wachita co., Ark.

LEAKESVILLE, p. v., Rockingham co., N. C., 124 ms. N. w. of Raleigh; from W. 283 ms. Watered by Dan river.

LEAKESVILLE, p. v., Newton co., Ga., 49 ms. N. w. of Milledgeville; from W. 656 ms.

LEAKESVILLE, p. v., seat of justice of Greene co., Miss., 190 ms. s. E. of Jackson; from W. 1,022 ms. Watered by Chickasawha river.

LEANDER, p. o., Graves co., Ky.

LEASBURGH, p. v., Caswell co., N. C., 64 ms. N. w. of Raleigh; from W. 260 ms.

LEATHERWOOD, p. o., Clarion co., Pa., 195 ms. N. w. of Harrisburgh; from W. 258 ms.

LEATHERWOOD, p. o., Guernsey co., O., 109 ms. E. of Columbus; from W. 312 ms.

LEATHERWOOD'S STORE, p. o., Henry co. Va., 192 ms. s. w. of Richmond; from W. 275 ms.

LEAVENSWORTH, p. o., Darlington district, S. C.

LEAVENWORTH, p. v., Crawford co., Ind., 124 ms. s. of Indianapolis; from W. 637 ms. Watered by Ohio river.

LEAVITT, p. o., Carroll co., O., 130 ms. N. E. of Columbus, from W. 304 ms.

LEBANON COUNTY, situated toward the southeast part of Pennsylvania. Area, 348 square miles. Face

of the country diversified; soil productive. Seat of justice, Lebanon. Pop. in 1820, 16,988; in 1830, 20,546 in 1840, 21,872; in 1850, 26,071.

LEBANON, p. t., York co., Me., 88 ms. s. w. of Augusta; from W. 510 ms. Watered by Salmon Fall river. Pop. 2,208.

LEBANON, p. t., Grafton co., N. H., 50 ms. N. w. of Concord; from W. 484 ms. Watered by Connecticut and Masconey rivers. Pop. 2,136.

LEBANON, p. t., New London co., Ct., 31 ms. s. E. of Hartford; from W. 352 ms. Watered by Yantic river and tributaries. Pop. 1,901.

LEBANON, p. t., Madison co., N. Y., 107 ms. w. of Albany; from W. 353 ms. Watered by Chenango river and tributaries. Pop. 1,709.

LEBANON, p. t., Hunterdon co., N. J., 40 ms. N. of Trenton; from W. 200 ms. Watered by Spruce run and south branch of Raritan river. Pop. 2,127.

LEBANON, p. t., Wayne co., Pa., 168 ms. N. E. of Harrisburgh; from W. 271 ms. Watered by tributaries of Dyberry creek. Pop. 426.

LEBANON, c. h., p. b., seat of justice of Lebanon co., Pa., 24 ms. E. of Harrisburgh; from W. 134 ms. Situated on the Union canal.

LEBANON, c. h., p. v., Turtle creek township, seat of justice of Warren co., O., 85 ms. s. w. of Columbus; from W. 469 ms. Watered by tributaries of Turtle creek. Pop. 2,088.

LEBANON, c. h., p. v., seat of justice of Russell co., Va., 325 ms. w. of Richmond; from W. 384 ms. Watered by a tributary of Clinch river.

LEBANON, t., Meigs co., O., 103 ms. s. E. of Columbus; from W. 334 ms. Watered by Ohio river. Pop. 1,008.

LEBANON, p. v., Abbeville district, S. C.

LEBANON, p. v., Cobb co., Ga., 106 ms. N. w. of Milledgeville; from W. 662 ms. Watered by Chattahoochee river.

LEBANON, c. h., p. v., seat of justice of Marion co., Ky., 59 ms. s. w. of Frankfort; from W. 581 ms. Watered by Salt river.

LEBANON, c. h., p. v., seat of justice of Wilson co., Tenn., 32 ms. E. of Nashville; from W. 652 ms. Watered by a tributary of Cumberland river. Seat of the Southern University.

LEBANON, c. h., p. v., seat of justice of Boone co., Ind., 25 ms. N. w. of Indianapolis; from W. 599 ms.

LEBANON, t., Lawrence co., Ark. Pop. 182.

LEBANON, c. h., p. v., seat of justice of Searcy co., Ark., 95 ms. N. of Little Rock. Watered by Buffalo fork of White river.

LEBANON, c. h., p. v., seat of justice of De Kalb co., Ala.; from W. 675 ms. Watered by Big Wills creek.

LEBANON, c. h., p. v., seat of justice of St. Clair co., Ill., 71 ms. s. of Springfield; from W. 797 ms. Seat of McKendree college. Pop. 607.

LEBANON, t., Cooper co., Mo.

LEBANON, p. o., Laclede co., Mo.

LEBANON SPRINGS, p. v., Columbia co., N. Y.

LEBANON WHITE SULPHUR SPRINGS, p. o., Augusta co., Va.

LE BOEUF, t., Erie co., Pa.

LE CLAIRE, p. o., Scott co., Iowa.

LEDLIES, p. o., Meigs co., O., 91 ms. s. E. of Columbus; from W. 352 ms.

LEDYARD. p. t., New London, Ct., 47 ms. s. E. of Hartford; from W. 365 ms. Watered by Thames river. Pop. 1,558.

LEDYARD, p. o., Cayuga co., N. Y., 171 ms. w. of Albany; from W. 317 ms. Watered by Cayuga lake.

LEE COUNTY, situated at the southwest corner of Virginia. Area, 512 square miles. Face of the country mountainous; soil barren. Seat of justice, Jonesville. Pop. in 1810, 4,694; in 1820, 4,256; in 1830, 6,461; in 1840, 8,441; in 1850, 10,267.

LEE COUNTY, situated toward the southwest part of Georgia, with Flint river on the east. Area, 600 square miles. Seat of justice, Starkville. Pop. in 1830, 1,680; in 1840, 4.520; in 1850, 6,660.

LEE COUNTY, situated in the north part of Illinois, and traversed by Rock river. Area, 720 square miles. Seat of justice, Dixon. Pop. in 1840, 2,035; in 1850, 5,292.

LEE COUNTY, situated at the southeast corner of Iowa, with Des Moines river on the southwest, and the Mississippi on the southeast. Area, 600 square miles. Seat of justice, Fort Madison. Pop. in 1840, 6,093; in 1850, 18,860.

LEE, p. t., Penobscot co., Me., 125 ms. N. E. of Augusta. Watered by a tributary of Mattawamkeag river. Pop. 917.

LEE, p. t., Strafford co., N. H., 38 ms. E. of Concord; from W. 485 ms. Watered by Lamprey, North Little, and Oyster rivers. Pop. 832.

LEE, p. t., Berkshire co., Mass., 128 ms. w. of Boston; from W. 368 ms. Watered by Housatonic river. Pop. 3,220.

LEE, p. t., Oneida co., N. Y., 114 ms. N. w. of Albany; from W. 398 ms. Watered by Canada and Fish creeks. Pop. 3,033.

LEE, p. t., Athens co., O., 81 ms. s. E. of Columbus; from W. 348 ms. Pop. 961.

LEE, p. o., Warrick co., Ind.

LEE, t., Calhoun co., Mich. Pop. 381.

LEE, p. o., Ogle co., Ill.

LEE CENTRE, p. o., Lee co., Ill.

LEE CENTRE, p. o., Oneida co., N. Y.

LEECHBURG, p. o., Armstrong co. Pa., 190 ms. N. W. of Harrisburgh; from W. 223 ms.

LEECHVILLE, p. v., Beaufort district, S. C., 165 ms. s. of Columbia; from W. 351 ms.

LEEDS, p. t., Kennebec co., Me., 21 ms. w. of Augusta; from W. 587 ms. Watered by Androscoggin river. Pop. 1,652.

LEEDS, p. o., Hampshire co., Mass.

LEEDS, p. t., Catskill township. Greene co., N. Y., 38 ms. s. w. of Albany; from W. 340 ms. Watered by Catskill creek.

LEEDS MANOR, p. o., Fauquier co., Va., 127 ms. N. of Richmond; from W. 70 ms.

LEEDS POINT, p. v., Galloway township, Atlantic co., N. J., 86 ms. s. E. of Trenton; from W. 196 ms.

LEEDS STATION, p. o., Kennebec co., Me.

LEEDSVILLE, p. v., Monmouth co., N. J., 48 ms. E. of Trenton; from W. 214 ms.

LEEDSVILLE, p. o., Amenia township, Dutchess co., N. Y., 68 ms. s. of Albany; from W. 327 ms.

LEEDSVILLE, p. v., Randolph co., Va., 213 ms. N. W. of Richmond; from W. 240 ms.

LEEPERTOWN, p. o., Bureau co., Ill.

LEESBURGH, v., Maurice River township, Cumberland co., N. J., 78 ms. s. of Trenton; from W. 189 ms. Watered by Maurice river.

LEESBURGH, c. h., p. v., seat of justice of Loudoun co., Va., 153 ms. N. of Richmond; from W. 34 ms. Pop. 1,691.

LEESBURGH, p. v., Washington co., Tenn., 278 ms. W. of Nashville; from W. 417 ms.

LEESBURGH, p. v., Harrison co., Ky., 97 ms. N. E. of Frankfort; from W. 515 ms.

LEESBURGH, p. v., Fairfield township, Highland co., O., 64 ms. s. w. of Columbus; from W. 436 ms.

LEESBURGH, t., Union co., O.

LEESBURGH, p. v., Kosciusko co., Ind., 133 ms. N. of Indianapolis; from W. 603 ms. Pop. 217.

LEESBURGH, p. v., Cherokee co., Ala.; from W. 089 ms.

LEESBURGH, p. o., Mercer co., Pa.

LEE'S COVE, p. o., Shelby co., Ala.

LEE'S CREEK, t., Crawford co., Ark.

LEE'S CREEK, p. o., Clinton co., O.

LEE'S CROSS-ROADS, p. o., Cumberland co., Pa., 30 ms. s. w. of Harrisburgh; from W. 105 ms.

LEE'S MILLS, p. o., Owen co., Ky.

LEESPORT, p. o., Berks co., Pa.

LEE'S RIDGE, p. o., Randolph co., Ala.

LEESVILLE, p. v., Sharon township, Schoharie co., N. Y.

LEESVILLE, p. v., Campbell co., Va., 147 ms. w. of Richmond; from W. 222 ms. Watered by Stanton river and Goose creek.

LEESVILLE, p. v., Robeson co., N. C., 102 ms. s. w. of Raleigh; from W. 390 ms.

LEESVILLE, p. v., Lexington district, S. C., 30 ms. w. of Columbia; from W. 536 ms.

LEESVILLE, p. v., Orange township, Carroll co., O., 115 ms. N. E. of Columbus; from W. 301 ms. Pop. 124.

LEESVILLE, p. v., Hart co., Ky., 101 ms. s. w. of Frankfort; from W. 643 ms.

LEESVILLE, p. v., Lawrence co., Ind., 78 ms. s. of Indianapolis; from W. 609 ms. Watered by Guthrie's creek.

LEESVILLE, p. o., Middlesex co., Ct.

LEESVILLE CROSS-ROADS, p. v., Sandusky township, Crawford co., O., 74 ms. N. of Columbus; from W. 412 ms.

LEETOWN, p. v., Jefferson co., Va., 177 ms. N. of Richmond; from W. 70 ms.

LEE VALLEY, p. v., Hawkins co., Tenn., 256 ms. E. of Nashville; from W. 449 ms.

LEFEVRE, p. o., Bartholomew co., Ind.

LEFLORE, p. o., Carroll co., Miss.

LEGAL LAW, p. o., York district, S. C.

LEHI, p. o., Jefferson co., Ark.

LEHIGH COUNTY, situated in the east part of Pennsylvania, with Lehigh river on the northeast. Area, 389 square miles. Face of the country diversified and picturesque; soil fertile. Seat of justice, Allentown. Pop. in 1820, 18,895; in 1830, 22,256; in 1840, 25,787; in 1850, 32,479.

LEHIGH, t., Northampton co., Pa., 104 ms. N. E. of Harrisburgh; from W. 198 ms. Watered by Lehigh river and Indian creek. Pop. 2,343.

LEHIGH GAP, p. o., Lehigh township, Northampton co., Pa. Watered by Lehigh river.

LEHIGHTON, p. v., Penn township, Carbon co., Pa., 96 ms. N. E. of Harrisburgh; from W. 196 ms. Watered by Lehigh river.

LEHMAN, p. t., Luzerne co., Pa., 121 ms. N. w. of Harrisburgh; from W. 232 ms. Watered by Lehman's lake, and Lehman's, Harvey's, Bowman's, and Mahoopeny creeks. Pop. 960.

LEHMAN, t., Pike co., Pa. Watered by Delaware river. Pop. 869.

LEICESTER, p. t., Addison co., Vt., 73 ms. s. w. of Montpelier; from W. 477 ms. Watered by Otter creek and Leicester river. Pop. 596.

LEICESTER, p. t., Worcester co., Mass., 48 ms. w. of Boston; from W. 400 ms. Watered by tributaries of French and Blackstone rivers. Pop. 2,269.

LEICESTER, t., Livingston co., N. Y., 232 ms. w. of Albany; from W. 351 ms. Watered by Genesee river. Pop. 2,142.

LEIGHTON, p. o., Lawrence co., Ala.; from W. 772 ms.

LEIGHTON'S, p. o., Yallabusha co., Miss.

LEIGHTON'S CORNERS, p. o., Carroll co., N. H., 55 ms. N. of Concord; from W. 536 ms.

LEIPER'S FORK, p. o., Williamson co., Tenn., 26 ms. s. of Nashville; from W. 703 ms.

LEIPERSVILLE, p. v., Ridley township, Delaware co., Pa., 97 ms. s. E. of Harrisburgh; from W. 124 ms.

LEIPSIC, p. v., Kent co., Del.

LEIPSIC, p. o., Putnam co., O.

LEITERSBURGH, p. o., Washington co., Md., 107 ms. N. w. of Annapolis; from W. 75 ms.

LELAND'S MILL, p. o., Sauk co., Wis.

LEMINGTON, p. t., Essex co., Vt., 94 ms. N. E. of Montpelier; from W. 591 ms. Watered by Connecticut river. Pop. 187.

LEMON, t., Butler co., O., 90 ms. s. w. of Columbus; from W. 487 ms. Pop. 1,728.

LEMONT, p. o., Cook co., Ill.

LEMPSTER, p. t., Sullivan co., N. H., 40 ms. w. of Concord; from W. 466 ms. Watered by branches of Sugar and Cold rivers. Pop. 906.

LENAWEE COUNTY, situated on the south boundary of Michigan. Area, 735 square miles. Seat of justice, Adrian. Pop. in 1830, 1,491; in 1840, 17,889; in 1850, 24,572.

LENOIR COUNTY, situated toward the southeast part of North Carolina, and traversed by Neuse river. Area, 390 square miles. Face of the country level; soil moderately productive. Seat of justice, Kingston. Pop. in 1810, 5,572; in 1820, 6,800; in 1830, 7,723; in 1840, 7,605; in 1850, 7,828.

LENOIR, c. h., p. v., seat of justice of Caldwell co., N. C. Watered by Yadkin river.

LENOIR'S, p. o., Roane co., Tenn.

LENOX, c. h., p. t., seat of justice of Berkshire co., Mass., 132 ms. w. of Boston; from W. 370 ms. Watered by Housatonic river. Pop. 1,599.

LENOX, p. t., Madison co., N. Y., 121 ms. N. w. of Albany; from W. 358 ms. Watered by Cowasalon and Oneida creeks, and Oneida lake. Pop. 1,669.

LENOX, p. o., Susquehanna co., Pa., 170 ms. N. w. of Harrisburgh; from W. 274 ms. Watered by Tunkhannock creek.

LENOX, p. t., Ashtabula co., O., 201 ms. N. E. of Columbus; from W. 335 ms. Pop. 731.

LENOX, p. t., Macomb co., Mich. Pop. 652.

LENOX CASTLE, p. o., Rockingham co., N. C.

LENOX FURNACE, p. o., Berkshire co., Mass.

LENOXVILLE, p. o., Susquehanna co., Pa.

LEO, p. o., Allen co., Ind.

LEO, p. o., Habersham co., Ga.

LEO, p. o., Washington co., N. C.

LEOMINSTER, p. t., Worcester co., Mass., 44 ms. N.W. of Boston; from W. 417 ms. Watered by a tributary of Nashua river. Pop. 3,121.

LEON COUNTY, situated in the central part of Texas. Area, —— square miles. Seat of justice, Leona. Pop. in 1850, 1,946.

LEON COUNTY, situated on the north boundary of Florida, with Ocklockony river on the west. Area, 1,224 square miles. Seat of justice, Tallahassee, which is also the state capital. Pop. in 1840, 10,713; in 1850, 11,442.

LEON, p. t., Cattaraugus co., N. Y., 311 ms. w. of Albany; from W. 343 ms. Watered by Conewango creek and tributaries. Pop. 1,340.

LEON, p. v., Madison co., Va., 165 ms. N. w. of Richmond; from W. 89 ms. Watered by Crooked run.

LEON, p. o., Richmond township, Ashtabula co., O., 208 ms. N. E. of Columbus; from W. 324 ms.

LEONA, p. t., seat of justice of Leon co., Tex.

LEONARDTOWN, c. h., p. v., seat of justice of St. Mary's co., Md., 87 ms. s. of Annapolis; from W. 64 ms. Watered by Britton's river.

LEONARDSVILLE, p. v., Brookfield township, Madison co., N. Y., 86 ms. N. w. of Albany; from W. 364 ms. Watered by Unadilla river.

LEONI, p. t., Jackson co., Mich., 71 ms. w. of Detroit; from W. 546 ms. Pop. 1,290.

LEONIDAS, p. t., St. Joseph co., Mich. Pop. 857.

LEOPOLD, p. o., Perry co., Ind.

LE RAY, p. t., Jefferson co., N. Y. Watered by Black and Indian rivers. Pop. 3,654.

LE RAYSVILLE, p. v., Le Ray township, Jefferson co., N. Y., 162 ms. N. w. of Albany; from W. 428 ms.

LE RAYSVILLE, p. v., Pike township, Bradford co., Pa., 152 ms. N. of Harrisburgh; from W. 262 ms. Pop. 102.

LE ROY, p. t., Genesee co., N. Y., 236 ms. w. of Albany; from W. 370 ms. Watered by Allen's creek. Pop. 3,473.

LE ROY, v., Exeter township, Otsego co., N. Y. Watered by Canandaigua lake outlet.

LE ROY, p. t., Bradford co., Pa., 143 ms. N. of Harrisburgh; from W. 253 ms, Pop. 916.

LE ROY, p. t., Lake co., O., 185 ms. N. E. of Columbus. Pop. 1,128.

LE ROY, p. o., Westfield township, Medina co., O., 113 ms. N. E. of Columbus; from W. 356 ms.

LE ROY, p. o., McLean co., Ill., 94 ms. N. E. of Springfield; from W. 729 ms.

LE ROY, t., Calhoun co., Mich. Pop. 878.

LE ROY, t., Ingham co., Mich. Pop. 254.

LE ROY, p. o., Dodge co., Wis.

LESKAR, t., New Madrid co., Mo.

LESLIE, p. t., Ingham co., Mich., 89 ms. w. of Detroit; from W. 575 ms. Pop. 673.

LE SOURDSVILLE, p. o., Butler co., O.

LESSER CROSS-ROADS, p. o., Somerset co., N. J., 42 ms. N. of Trenton; from W. 216 ms.

LESSLEY, p. o., Benton co., Mo.

LESTERVILLE, p. o., Reynolds co., Mo.

LESTER's DISTRICT, p. o., Burke co., Ga.

LETART, t., Meigs co., O., 108 ms. s. w. of Columbus; from W. 343 ms., opposite Letart's rapids of Ohio river. Pop. 966.

LETART FALLS, p. o., Letart township, Meigs co., O.

LETCHER COUNTY, situated on the southeast boundary of Kentucky. Area, 200 square miles. Seat of justice, Whitesburgh. Pop. in 1850, 2,512.

LETCHER, p. o., Harlan co., Ky., 147 ms. s. E. of Frankfort; from W. 491 m.

LETCHERVILLE, p. o., Greene co., Ill.

LETIMBERVILLE, p. v., Scott township, Marion co., O., 56 ms. N. of Columbus; from W. 412 ms.

LETTER A, t., Aroostook co., Me.

LETTER A, p. o., Oxford co., Me.

LETTER A, No. 2, p. o., Oxford co., Me.

LETTER B, p. t., Oxford co., Me., 77 ms. N. w. of Augusta; from W. 628 ms. Watered by Umbagog lake.

LETTERKENNY, t., Franklin co., Pa., 47 ms. s. w. of Harrisburgh; from W. 99 ms. Watered by Conedogwinit and Raccoon creeks. Pop. 2,048.

LEVANNA, p. v., Ledyard township, Cayuga co., N. Y., 172 ms. w. of Albany; from W. 325 ms. Watered by Cayuga lake.

LEVANT, p. t., Penobscot co., Me., 80 ms. N. E. of Au-

gusta; from W. 675 ms. Watered by Kenduskeag stream. Pop. 1,841.

LEVANT, p. o., Chautauque co., N. Y., 326 ms. w. of Albany; from W. 323 ms.

LEVEE, p. o., Montgomery co., Ky.

LEVEL, p. o., Richland district, S. C.

LEVEL, p. o., Warren co., O., 81 ms. s. w. of Columbus; from W. 464 ms.

LEVEL GREEN, p. o., Giles co., Va., 221 ms. w. of Richmond; from W. 261 ms.

LEVERETT, p. t., Franklin co., Mass., 83 ms. w. of Boston; from W. 393 ms. Watered by tributaries of Connecticut river. Pop. 948.

LEVERING, p. o., Knox co., O.

LEVERINGTON, p. o., Philadelphia co., Pa., 98 ms. E. of Harrisburgh; from W. 147 ms.

LEVI, p. o., Jackson co., O.

LEVY COUNTY, toward the westerly part of Florida, on the Gulf of Mexico. Area, —— square miles. Seat of justice, ——————. Pop. in 1850, 465.

LEWES, p. v., Sussex co., Del., 45 ms. s. of Dover; from W. 153 ms.

LEWIS COUNTY, situated toward the north part of New York. Area, 1,122 square miles. Face of the country, hilly; soil productive. Seat of justice, Martinsburgh. Pop. in 1810, 6,438; in 1820, 9,227; in 1830, 14,958; in 1840, 17,830; in 1850, 24,464.

LEWIS COUNTY, situated toward the northwest part of Virginia. Area, 1,600 square miles. Face of the country, hilly; soil barren. Seat of justice, Weston. Pop. in 1820, 4,247; in 1830, 6,241; in 1840, 8,151; in 1850, 10,031.

LEWIS COUNTY, situated on the northerly boundary of Kentucky, with Ohio river on the north. Area, 375 square miles. Face of the country, hilly; soil productive. Seat of justice, Clarksburgh. Pop. in 1830, 5,206; in 1840, 6,303; in 1850, 7,202.

LEWIS COUNTY, situated toward the south part of Tennessee. Area, —— square miles. Seat of justice, Newburgh. Pop. in 1850, 4,438.

LEWIS COUNTY, situated on the easterly boundary of Missouri, with Mississippi river on the east. Area, 500 square miles. Face of the country, even; soil, fertile. Seat of justice, Monticello. Pop. in 1840, 6,040; in 1850, 6,578.

LEWIS, p. o., Vigo co., Ind., 78 ms. s. w. of Indianapolis; from W. 649 ms.

LEWIS, p. t., Essex co., N. Y., 131 ms. N. of Albany; from W. 506 ms. Watered by Boquet creek and tributaries. Pop. 2,058.

LEWIS, t., Lycoming co., Pa. Pop. 596.

LEWIS, t., Brown co., O., 121 ms. s. w. of Columbus; from W. 483 ms. Watered by Whiteoak, Eagle, and Bullskin creeks. Pop. 2,720.

LEWIS, t., Clay co., Ind., Pop. 574.

LEWIS AND REHOBOTH, hundred, Sussex co., Del.

LEWISBERRY, p. v., York co., Pa., 17 ms. s. of Harrisburgh; from W. 109 ms. Pop. 245.

LEWISBOROUGH, p. t., Westchester co., N. Y., 130 ms. s. of Albany; from W. 286 ms. Watered by Croton river. Pop. 1,608.

LEWISBURGH, p. b., Buffalo township, Union co., Pa., 67 ms. N. of Harrisburgh; from W. 177 ms. Watered by Susquehanna river. Pop. 2,012.

LEWISBURGH, c. h., p. v., seat of justice of Greenbrier co., Va., 214 ms. w. of Richmond; from W. 251 ms.

LEWISBURGH, p. v., Harrison township, Preble co., O., 97 ms. w. of Columbus; from W. 490 ms.

LEWISBURGH, c. h., p. v., seat of justice of Marshall co., Tenn., 54 ms. s. of Nashville; from W. 703 ms.

LEWISBURGH, p. v., Cass co., Ind., 81 ms. N. of Indianapolis; from W. 601 ms. Watered by Wabash river, and Wabash and Erie canal.

LEWISBURGH, c. h., p. v., seat of justice of Conway co., Ark., 45 ms. N. w. of Little Rock; from W. 1,110 ms. Watered by Arkansas river.

LEWIS' FORK, p. o., Wilkes co., N. C.

LEWISPORT, p. o., Hancock co., Ky.

LEWIS' STORE, p. o., Spottsylvania co., Va., 99 ms. N. of Richmond; from W. 90 ms.

LEWISTON, p. t., Niagara co., N. Y., 297 ms. w. of Albany; from 410 ms. Watered by Niagara river. Pop. 2,924.

LEWISTON, p. t., Lincoln co., Me., 31 ms. s. w. of Augusta; from W. 577 ms. Watered by Androscoggin river. Pop. 3,584.

LEWISTOWN, c. h., p. b., seat of justice of Mifflin co.,

Pa., 57 ms. N. w. of Harrisburgh ; from W. 148 ms. Watered by Juniata river and Kishcoquillas creek, and Pennsylvania canal. Pop. 2,735.

LEWISTOWN, p. o., Frederick co., Md.

LEWISTOWN, p. v., Bloomfield township, Logan co., O., 77 ms. N w. of Columbus; from W. 464 ms. Watered by Miami river.

LEWISTOWN, c. h., p. v., seat of justice of Fulton co., Ill., 55 ms. N. w. of Springfield ; from W. 833 ms. Pop. 1,515.

LEWISTOWN, v., Columbiana co., O.

LEWISTOWN. p. v., Logan co., O.

LEWISVILLE. p. v., Brunswick co., Va., 82 ms. s. of Richmond ; from W. 198 ms.

LEWISVILLE, p. v.. Chester district, S. C., 64 ms. N. of Columbia ; from W. 450 ms.

LEWISVILLE, c. h., p. v., seat of justice of Lafayette co., Ark., 162 ms. s. w. of Little Rock ; from W. 1,237 ms.

LEWISVILLE, t., Coshocton co., O.

LEWISVILLE, p. v., Monroe co., O. Pop. 96.

LEWISVILLE, p. v., Henry co., Ind., 42 ms. E. of Indianapolls ; from W. 529 ms. Watered by Flat Rock creek.

LEWISVILLE, p. o., Chester co., Pa.

LEXINGTON DISTRICT, situated in the central part of South Carolina, with Broad river on the northeast. Area, 900 square miles. Seat of justice, Lexington C. H. Pop. in 1810, 6,641 ; in 1820, 8,083 ; in 1830, 9,076 ; in 1840, 12,111 ; in 1850, 12,930.

LEXINGTON, p. t.. Somerset co., Me., 63 ms. N. of Augusta ; from W. 657 ms. Watered by a tributary of Kennebec river. Pop. 538.

LEXINGTON, p. t.. Middlesex co., Mass., 11 ms. N. w. of Boston ; from W. 451 ms. Watered by tributaries of Shawsheen river. Pop. 1,893.

LEXINGTON, p t., Greene co., N. Y., 55 ms. s. w. of Albany ; from W. 365 ms. Watered by Schoharie creek. Pop 2,263.

LEXINGTON, c. h., p. v., seat of justice of Rockbridge co., Va., 146 ms. w. of Richmond ; from W. 188 ms. Watered by North river. Seat of Washington college. Pop. 1,733.

LEXINGTON, c. h., p. v., seat of justice of Davidson co., N. C., 117 ms. w. of Raleigh ; from W. 338 ms. Watered by Abbott's creek.

LEXINGTON, c. h., p. v., seat of justice of Oglethorpe co., Ga., 70 ms. N. of Milledgeville ; from W. 594 ms.

LEXINGTON, p. v., Lauderdale co., Ala. ; from W, 761 ms

LEXINGTON, c. h., p. v., seat of justice of Holmes co., Miss., 62 ms. N. of Jackson ; from W. 997 ms.

LEXINGTON, c. h., p. v., seat of justice of Henderson co., Tenn., 117 ms. s. w. of Nashville ; from W. 801 ms. Watered by Beech river.

LEXINGTON, city, seat of justice of Fayette co., Ky., 24 ms. s. E. of Frankfort, situated on a branch of Elkhorn river, 70 miles from Louisville, and 515 from Washington. It is the oldest town in the state, and was formerly the capital. It has many handsome, paved streets, Main street being 75 feet wide, and 1½ miles in length. The noble shade-trees that border the streets, give it a pleasing appearance. A large public square adorns the centre of the place, which is surrounded by stately private mansions. The public buildings are, a courthouse, Masonic hall, jail, state lunatic asylum, and the halls of the Transylvania university, together with several churches and academies, and the hospitality and intelligence of its citizens, and render it a desirable southern residence. The population in 1820, was 5,283 ; in 1830, 6,408 ; in 1840, 6,984 ; in 1850, ——.

LEXINGTON, p. t., St. Clair co., Mich.

LEXINGTON, t., Stark co., O., 132 ms. N. E. of Columbus ; from W. 303 ms. Pop. 1,996.

LEXINGTON. p. v., Troy township, Richland co., O., 56 ms. N. E. of Columbus ; from W. 385 ms. Watered by Clear fork of Mohiccan creek.

LEXINGTON, c. h., p. v., seat of justice of Scott co., Ind., 89 ms. s. of Indianapolis ; from W. 577 ms. Watered by Muscatatack fork of White river. Pop. 2,202.

LEXINGTON, p. v., McLean co., Ill., 90 ms. N. E. of Indianapolis ; from W. 757 ms.

LEXINGTON, c. h., p. v., seat of justice of Lafayette co., Mo., 132 ms. N. w. of Jefferson city ; from W. 1,046 ms. Pop. 4,877.

LEXINGTON, p. o., Clatsop co., Oregon.

LEXINGTON, c. h., p. v., seat of justice of Lexington district, S. C., 12 ms. w. of Columbia ; from W. 518 ms. Watered by a tributary of Saluda river.

LEYDEN, p. t.. Franklin co., Mass., 102 ms. N. w. of Boston ; from W. 412 ms. Watered by Greene river. Pop. 716.

LEYDEN, p. t., Lewis co.. N. Y.. 120 ms. N. w. of Albany ; from W. 425 ms. Watered by Moose and Black rivers. Pop. 2,253.

LEYDEN, p. o., Cook co., Ill.

LEYDEN, p. o.. Rock co., Wis.

LIBERTY COUNTY, situated on the southeast boundary of Georgia, with Altamaha river on the southwest, and the Atlantic on the southeast. Area, 660 square miles. Seat of justice, Hinesville. Pop. in 1810, 6,228 ; in 1820, 6,695 ; in 1830, 7,233 ; in 1840, 7,241 ; in 1850, 7,926.

LIBERTY COUNTY, situated in the south part of Texas, with Galveston bay on the south, and traversed by Trinity river. Area, —— square miles. Seat of justice, Liberty. Pop. in 1850, 2,522.

LIBERTY. p. t., Waldo co., Me., 20 ms. E. of Augusta ; from W. 616 ms. Watered by a tributary of St. George's river. Pop. 1,116.

LIBERTY. p. t., Sullivan co., N. Y., 119 ms. s. w. of Albany ; from W. 304 ms. Watered by Collikoon creek. Pop. 2,612.

LIBERTY, v., Conhocton township, Steuben co., N. Y.

LIBERTY, p. t., Tioga co., Pa., 123 ms. N. of Harrisburgh ; from W. 233 ms. Pop. 1,472.

LIBERTY, t., Adams co., Pa., 40 ms. s. w. of Harrisburgh ; from W. 70 ms. Pop. 722.

LIBERTY, t., Montour co., Pa. Pop. 1,233.

LIBERTY, t., Bedford co., Pa. Pop. 522.

LIBERTY, t., Columbia co., Pa., 60 ms. N. of Harrisburgh ; from W. 170 ms. Watered by Chilisquaque and Mahoning creeks.

LIBERTY, t., McKean co., Pa. Pop. 612.

LIBERTY, t., Susquehanna co., Pa. Pop. 833.

LIBERTY, c. h., p. v., seat of justice of Bedford co., Va., 142 ms. w. of Richmond ; from W. 217 ms. Watered by Otter river.

LIBERTY, p. v., DeKalb co., Tenn., 50 ms. E. of Nashville ; from W. 631 ms. Watered by a tributary of Cumberland river.

LIBERTY, c. h., p. v., seat of justice of Casey co., Ky., 69 ms. s. of Frankfort ; from W. 583 ms. Watered by Green river.

LIBERTY, p. v., Jefferson township, seat of justice of Montgomery co., O., 75 ms. w. of Columbus ; from W. 468 ms.

LIBERTY, t., Adams co., O., 107 ms. s. of Columbus ; from W. 466 ms. Pop. 1,498.

LIBERTY, t., Butler co., O., 96 ms. s. w. of Columbus; from W. 503 ms. Pop. 1,501.

LIBERTY, t., Clinton co., O., 60 ms. s. w. of Columbus ; from W. 449 ms. Pop. 1,232.

LIBERTY, t., Crawford co., O., 74 ms. N. of Columbus; from W. 474 ms. Pop. 1,782.

LIBERTY, t., Delaware co., O., 15 ms. N. of Columbus ; from W. 411 ms. Pop. 1,051.

LIBERTY, t., Fairfield co., O., 30 ms.s. E. of Columbus; from W. 374 ms. Situated on the Ohio canal. Pop. 2,209.

LIBERTY, t., Guernsey co., O., 85 ms. E. of Columbus ; from W. 313 ms. Pop. 1,001.

LIBERTY, t., Hancock co., O. Pop. 874.

LIBERTY, t., Hardin co., O. Pop. 422.

LIBERTY, t., Highland co., O., 74 ms. s. w. of Columbus ; from W. 441 ms. Pop. 2,683.

LIBERTY, t., Jackson co., O. Pop. 1,017.

LIBERTY, t., Knox co., O., 39 ms. N. E. of Columbus ; from W. 375 ms. Pop. 1,320.

LIBERTY, t., Licking co., O., 26 ms. N. E. of Columbus ; from W. 372 ms. Pop. 1,190.

LIBERTY, t., Logan co., O., 60 ms. N. w. of Columbus; from W. 457 ms. Pop. 619.

LIBERTY, t., Putnam co.; O., Pop. 322.

LIBERTY, p. t., Ross co., O. Pop. 967.

LIBERTY, p. t., Trumbull co., O. Pop. 1,329.

LIBERTY, t., Seneca co., O. Pop. 1,400.

LIBERTY, t., Union co., O.

LIBERTY, t., Van Wert co., O. Pop. 427.

LIBERTY, t., Washington co., O. Pop. 1,223.

LIBERTY, t., Wood co., O. Pop. 236.

LIBERTY, p. t., Jackson co., Mich., 79 ms. w. of Detroit ; from W. 539 ms. Pop. 891.

LIBERTY, c. h., p. v., seat of justice of Union co., Ind., 72 ms. E. of Indianapolis ; from W. 515 ms. Watered by Silver creek. Pop. 979.

LIBERTY, t., Grant co., Ind. Pop. 797.

LIBERTY, t., Henry co., Ind., 57 ms, N. E. of Indianapolis; from W. 544 ms. Pop. 1,766.

LIBERTY, t., Shelby co., Ind., 36 ms. s. E. of Indianapolis; from W. 569 ms. Pop. 1,113.

LIBERTY, p. t., Wabash co., Ind. Pop. 1,425.

LIBERTY, c. h., p. v., seat of justice of Adams co., Ill., 90 ms. w. of Springfield; from W. 870 ms. Pop. 1,077.

LIBERTY, c. h., p. v., seat of justice of Clay co., Mo., 159 ms. N. w. of Jefferson City; from W. 1,072 ms.

LIBERTY, c. h., p. v., seat of justice of Amite co., Miss., 101 ms. s. w. of Jackson; from W. 1,101 ms. Watered by West fork of Amite river.

LIBERTY, t., Callaway co., Mo.

LIBERTY, t., Crawford co., Mo.

LIBERTY, t., Macon co., Mo.

LIBERTY, t., Madison co., Mo.

LIBERTY/ t., Marion co., Mo. Pop. 1,064.

LIBERTY, t., St. Francis co., Mo.

LIBERTY, t., Washington co., Mo. Pop. 1,044.

LIBERTY, t., Jackson co., Mich. Pop. 891.

LIBERTY. p. t., Pope co., Ark., 93 ms. N. w. of Little Rock; from W. 1,158 ms.

LIBERTY, p. o., Liberty co., Tex.

LIBERTY, p. o., Racine co., Wis.

LIBERTY, p. t., Wachita co., Ark. Pop. 824.

LIBERTY CORNER, p. o., Somerset co., N. J., 40 ms. N. of Trenton; from W. 211 ms.

LIBERTY CORNERS, p. o., Crawford co., O.

LIBERTY FALLS, p. o., Sullivan co., N. Y.

LIBERTY HALL, p. o., Washington co., Va., 291 ms. w. of Richmond; from W. 356 ms.

LIBERTY HALL, p. o., Newberry district, S. C., 57 ms. N. w. of Columbia; from W. 491 ms.

LIBERTY HILL, p. o., Dallas co., Ala.; from W. 869 ms.

LIBERTY HILL, p. o., New London co., Ct.

LIBERTY HILL, p. o., Iredell co., N. C., 175 ms. w. of Raleigh; from W. 383 ms.

LIBERTY HILL, p. o., Kershaw district, S. C., 55 ms. N. E. of Columbia; from W. 482 ms.

LIBERTY HILL, p. o., Pike co., Ga.

LIBERTY HILL, p. o., Lafayette co., Miss.

LIBERTY MILLS, p. o., Orange co., Va., 79 ms. N. w. of Richmond; from W. 100 ms.

LIBERTY MILLS, p. o., Wabash co., Ind., 115 ms. N.E. of Indianapolis; from W. 604 ms.

LIBERTY SQUARE, p. o., Lancaster co., Pa.

LIBERTY TOWN, p. v., Frederick co., Md., 70 ms. N. w. of Annapolis; from W. 55 ms.

LIBERTYVILLE. p. o., New Paltz township, Ulster co., N. Y., 78 ms. s. of Albany; from W. 308 ms. Watered by Wallkill creek.

LIBERTYVILLE. p. v., Sussex co., N. J., 90 ms. N. of Trenton; from W. 259 ms.

LIBERTYVILLE, p. o., Lake co., Ill., 239 ms. N. E. of Springfield; from W. 745 ms.

LIBERTYVILLE, p. o., Jefferson co., Iowa.

LIBRARY, p. o., Alleghany co., Pa.

LICK, t., Jackson co., O. Pop. 1,021.

LICK BRANCH, p. o., Parke co., Ind.

LICK CREEK, p. o., Hickman co., Tenn., 40 ms. s. w. of Nashville; from W. 724 ms.

LICK CREEK, p. o., Sangamon co., Ill.

LICK CREEK, p. o., Ralls co., Mo.

LICK CREEK, p. o. Van Buren co., Iowa.

LICKE, p. o., Fannin co., Tex.

LICK FORK, p. o., Davies co., Mo.

LICKING COUNTY, situated in the central part of Ohio. Area, 666 square miles. Face of the country pleasantly diversified with hills and valleys; soil rich. Seat of justice, Newark. Pop. in 1820, 11,861; in 1830, 20,868; in 1840, 35.096; in 1850, 38,852.

LICKING, t., Licking co., O. Pop. 1,371.

LICKING, t., Muskingum co., O. Pop. 1,434.

LICKING, t., Blackford co., Ind. Pop. 975.

LICKING, p. o., Texas co., Mo.

LICKING CREEK, t., Bedford co., Pa.,

LICK MOUNTAIN, t., Conway co., Ark.

LICKVILLE, p. v., Greenville district, S. C., 106 ms. N. w. of Columbia; from W. 519 ms.

LIGHT'S CORNERS, p. o., Waldo co., Me., 25 ms. E. of Augusta; from W. 621 ms.

LIGHT STREET, p. o., Columbia co., Pa.

LIGONIER, p. t., Westmoreland co., Pa., 149 ms. w. of Harrisburgh; from W. 175 ms. Pop. 2,582.

LIGONIER, p. o., Noble co., Ind.

LIKINS, p. o., Crawford co., O.

LILESVILLE, p. v., Anson co., N. C., 141 ms. s. w. of Raleigh; from W. 417 ms.

LILLECASH, p. o., Will co., Ill.

LIMA, p. t., Livingston co., N. Y., 213 ms. w. of Albany; from W. 399 ms. Watered by Honeoye creek and branches. Pop. 2,433.

LIMA, p. v., Delaware co., Pa., 88 ms. s. E. of Harrisburgh; from W. 122 ms.

LIMA, c. h., p. v., seat of justice of Allen co., O., 101 ms. N. w. of Columbus; from W. 472 ms. Watered by Ottawa river. Pop. 757.

LIMA, t., Licking co., O. Pop. 973.

LIMA, p. t., Washtenaw co., Mich., 51 ms. w. of Detroit; from W. 539 ms. Watered by a branch of Mill creek. Pop. 912.

LIMA, p. t., Adams co., Ill., 122 ms. w. of Springfield; from W. 902 ms. Pop. 920.

LIMA, p. v., seat of justice of La Grange co., Ind., 175 ms. N. E. of Indianapolis; from W. 578 ms. Watered by Pigeon river.

LIMA, p. o., St., Tammany parish, La.

LIMA, p. o., Rock co., Wis.

LIMAVILLE, p. v., Stark co., O., 144 ms. N. E. of Columbus; from W. 307 ms.

LIMBER LOST, p. o., Adams co., Ind.

LIME HILL, p. o., Bradford co., Pa.

LIMERICK, p. t., York co., Me., 76 ms. s. w. of Augusta; from W. 535 ms. Watered by Little Ossipee river. Pop. 1,473.

LIMERICK, p. v., Brownville township, Jefferson co., N. Y., 172 ms. N. w. of Albany; from W. 424 ms. Watered by Perch river.

LIMERICK, p. t., Montgomery co., Pa., 78 ms. E. of Harrisburgh; from W. 167 ms. Watered by Schuylkill river. Pop. 2,165.

LIMERICK BRIDGE, p. o., Limerick township, Montgomery co., Pa.

LIME BRIDGE, p. o., Columbia co., Pa.

LIME ROCK, p. o., Littlefield co., Ct., 47 ms. w. of Hartford; from W. 339 ms.

LIME ROCK, p. v., Providence co., R. I., 10 ms. N. of Providence; from W. 410 ms.

LIMESTONE COUNTY, situated on the north boundary of Alabama, with Tennessee river on the, south. Area, 575 square miles. Face of the country undulating; soil generally productive. Seat of justice, Athens. Pop. in 1820, 9,871; in 1830, 14,843; in 1840, 14,374; in 1850, 16,483.

LIMESTONE COUNTY, situated in the central part of Texas. Area, —— square miles. Seat of justice, Springfield. Pop. in 1850, 2,520.

LIMESTONE, t., Clinton co., Pa.

LIMESTONE. t., Columbia co., Pa., 68 ms. N. of Harrisburgh; from W. 178 ms. Watered by Chilisquaque creek and Limestone run.

LIMESTONE, t., Warren co., Pa., 240 ms. N. w. of Harrisburgh; from W. 313 ms. Pop. 248.

LIMESTONE, t., Lycoming co., Pa. Pop. 983.

LIMESTONE, p. t., Clarion co., Pa., 154 ms. N. w. of Harrisburgh; from W. 263 ms. Pop. 1,461.

LIMESTONE, p. o., Buncombe co., N. C., 266 ms. w. of Raleigh; from W. 496 ms.

LIMESTONE, p. o., Hamilton co., Tenn., 144 ms. s. E of Nashville; from W. 581 ms.

LIMESTONE, p. o., Cattaraugus co., N. Y.

LIMESTONE, p. o., Iroquois co., Ill.

LIMESTONE RIVER, p. o., Aroostook co., Me.

LIMESTONE SPRINGS, p. o., Spartanburgh district, S. C., 93 ms. N. w. of Columbia; from W. 450 ms.

LIMESTONE SPRINGS, p. o., Greene co., Tenn.

LIMESTONE WELL, p. t., Forsyth co., N. C., 103 ms. N. w. of Raleigh; from W. 314 ms.

LIMETOWN, p. o., Washington co., Pa.

LIMINGTON, p. t., York co., Me., 70 ms. s. w. of Augusta; from W. 541 ms. Watered by Saco and Little Ossipee rivers. Pop. 2,116.

LINCOLN COUNTY, situated on the southerly boundary of Maine, on the Atlantic ocean, and traversed by Kennebec river. Face of the country diversified; soil productive. Area, 950 square miles. Seat of justice, Wiscasset. Pop. in 1810, 42,992; in 1820, 53,189; in 1830, 57,181; in 1840, 63,517; in 1850, 74,878.

LINCOLN COUNTY, situated on the south boundary of North Carolina, with Catawba river on the east. Area, 1,200 square miles. Face of the country hilly; soil productive, especially on the streams. Seat of justice, Lincolnton. Pop. in 1810, 16,359; in 1820, 18,147; in 1830, 22,625; in 1840, 25,160; in 1850, 7,746.

LINCOLN COUNTY, situated on the northeasterly boundary of Georgia, with Savannah river on the northeast. Area, 220 square miles. Seat of justice, Lincolnton. Pop. in 1810, 4,555 ; in 1820, 6,458 ; in 1830, 6,145 ; in 1840, 5,895 ; in 1850, 5,998.

LINCOLN COUNTY, situated on the south boundary of Tennessee. Area, 650 square miles. Face of the country diversified ; soil productive. Seat of justice, Fayetteville. Pop. in 1810, 6,104 ; in 1820, 14,761 ; in 1830, 22,086 ; in 1840, 21,493 ; in 1850, 23,492.

LINCOLN COUNTY, situated in the central part of Kentucky. Area, 432 square miles. Face of the country hilly ; soil fertile. Seat of justice, Stanford. Pop. in 1810, 8,676 ; in 1820, 9,979 ; in 1830, 11,602 ; in 1840, 10,187 ; in 1850, 10,093.

LINCOLN COUNTY, situated on the easterly boundary of Missouri, with the Mississippi river on the east. Area, 576 square miles. Seat of justice, Troy. Pop. in 1830, 4,060 ; in 1840, 7,449 ; in 1850, 9,421.

LINCOLN, p. t., Penobscot co., Me., 117 ms. N. E. of Augusta ; from W. 712 ms. Watered by Penobscot and Mattanaucook rivers. Pop. 1,356.

LINCOLN, p. t., Grafton co., N. H., 62 ms. N. of Concord ; from W. 543 ms. Watered by Pemigewasset river. Pop. 57.

LINCOLN, p. t., Addison co., Vt., 55 ms. s. w. of Montpelier ; from W. 495 ms. Watered by New Haven river. Pop. 1,057.

LINCOLN, p. t., Middlesex co., Mass., 16 ms. w. of Boston ; from W. 434 ms. Watered by Sudbury river and a tributary of the Charles river. Pop. 719.

LINCOLN, p. t., Delaware co., O., 44 ms. N. of Columbus ; from W. 405 ms.

LINCOLN, p. v., Yazoo county, Miss., 40 ms. N. w. of Jackson ; from W. 1,029 ms. Watered by Yazoo river.

LINCOLN, p. t., Morrow co., O. Pop. 891.

LINCOLN, p. o., Waushara co., Wis.

LINCOLN CENTRE, p. o., Lincoln township, Penobscot co., Me., 119 ms. N. E. of Augusta ; from W. 714 ms.

LINCOLNTON, c. h., p. v. seat of justice of Lincoln co., N. C., 172 ms. w. of Raleigh ; from W. 409 ms. Watered by Little Catawba river.

LINCOLNTON, c. h., p. v., seat of justice of Lincoln co., Ga., 98 ms. N. E. of Milledgeville ; from W. 566 ms.

LINCOLNVILLE, p. t., Waldo co., Me., 49 ms. E. of Augusta ; from W. 638 ms. Watered by Penobscot river. Pop. 2,174.

LIND, p. o., Winnebago co., Wis.

LINDEN, p. o., Genesee co., N. Y., 250 ms. w. of Albany ; from W. 768 ms.

LINDEN, c. h., p. v., seat of justice of Marengo co., Ala. ; from W. 892 ms. Watered by Chickasaw bogue creek.

LINDEN, p. o., Copiah co., Miss.

LINDEN, p. o., Atchison co., Mo.

LINDEN, p. o., Lycoming co., Pa.

LINDEN, p. o., Montgomery co., Ind.

LINDEN, p. o., Iowa co., Wis.

LINDEN, p. o., Perry co., Tenn.

LINDEN, p. o., Union co., La.

LINDENVILLE, p. o., Ashtabula co., O.

LINDENWOOD, p. o., Ogle co., Ill.

LINDLEY, t., Steuben co., N. Y., 221 ms. s. w. of Albany ; from W. 262 ms. Watered by Tioga river. Pop. 686.

LINDLEY'S, p. o., Ohio co., Ky., 166 ms. s. w. of Frankfort ; from W. 708 ms.

LINDLEYTOWN, p. o., Lindley township, Steuben co., N. Y., 229 ms. s. w. of Albany ; from W. 270 ms.

LINDLEY'S STORE, p. o., Orange co., N. C., 47 ms. N. w. of Raleigh ; from W. 305 ms.

LINDLEY'S MILLS, p. o., Washington co., Pa., 233 ms. w. of Harrisburgh ; from W. 247 ms.

LINDSAY'S MILL, p. o., Trigg co., Ky.

LINDSEY, t., Benton co., Mo.

LINDSEY'S CREEK, p. o., Choctaw co., Miss.

LINDVILLE, p. o., Genesee co., Mich.

LINE, p. o., De Kalb co., Ill.

LINE, p. o., Fulton co., Ky.

LIME CREEK, p. o., Laurens district, S. C., 100 ms. N. w. of Columbia ; from W. 525.

LINE CREEK, p. o., Montgomery co., Ala. ; from W. 839 ms.

LINE CREEK, p o., Oktibbeha co., Miss.

LINE LEXINGTON, p. v., Bucks co., Pa., 93 ms. E. of Harrisburgh ; from W. 162 ms.

LINE MILLS, p. o., Crawford co., Pa., 249 ms. N. w. of Harrisburgh ; from W. 315 ms.

LINE MOUNTAIN, p. o., Northumberland co., Pa.

LINE PORT, p. o., Stewart co., Tenn.

LINE STORE, p. o., Hinds co., Miss., 22 ms. s. of Jackson ; from W. 1,032 ms.

LINGLESTOWN, p. v., Lower Paxton township, Dauphin co., Pa., 8 ms. N. E. of Harrisburgh ; from W. 118 ms.

LINKLAEN, p. t., Chenango co., N. Y., 122 ms. w. of Albany ; from W. 336 ms. Watered by tributaries of Ostelic river. Pop. 1,196.

LINN COUNTY, situated on the northerly part of Missouri. Area. 588 square miles. Seat of justice, Linneus. Pop. in 1840, 2,245 ; in 1850, 4,058.

LINN COUNTY, situated toward the east part of Iowa. Area, 720 square miles. Seat of justice, Marion. Pop. in 1840. 1,373 ; in 1850, 5,444.

LINN COUNTY, situated in Oregon Territory. Area, —— square miles. Seat of justice, ——. Pop. in 1850, 994.

LINN, c. h., p. v., seat of justice of Osage co., Mo. Pop. 1,213.

LINN CITY, p. o., Washington co., Oregon.

LINNEUS, p. t., Aroostook co., Me., 190 ms. N. E. of Augusta ; from W. 785 ms. Watered by a tributary of Matawamkeag river. Pop. 561.

LINNEUS, p. v., seat of justice of Linn co., Mo., 136 ms. N. w. of Jefferson city ; from W. 1,030 ms.

LINN FLAT, p. o., Nacogdoches co., Tex.

LINN GROVE, p. o., Adams co., Ind.

LINNVILLE, p. v. Bowling Green township, Licking co., O., 35 ms. E. of Columbus ; from W. 358 ms.

LINNVILLE CREEK, p. o., Rockingham co., Va., 136 ms. N. w. of Richmond ; from W. 135 ms.

LINNVILLE RIVER, p. o., Burke co., N. C., 209 ms. w. of Raleigh ; from W. 439 ms.

LINTON, t., Coshocton co., O., 87 ms. N. E. of Columbus ; from W. 331 ms. Pop. 1,373.

LINTON, p. o., Greene co., Ind., 87 ms. s. w. of Indianapolis ; from W. 654 ms.

LINTON, p. o., Des Moines co., Iowa.

LINWOOD, p. o., Cherokee co., Tex.

LION'S BEARD, p. o., Sevier co., Ark.

LIONVILLE, p. v., Chester co., Pa., 71 ms. E. of Harrisburgh ; from W. 127 ms.

LISBON, p. t., Lincoln co., Me., 33 ms. s. w. of Augusta ; from W. 572 ms. Watered by Androscoggin river. Pop. 1,495.

LISBON, p. t., Grafton co., N. H., 89 ms. N. w. of Concord ; from W. 534 ms. Watered by Great Ammonoosuck river and tributaries. Pop. 1,881.

LISBON, p. t., New London co., Ct., 43 ms. s. E. of Hartford ; from W. 361 ms. Watered by Quinnebaug and Shetucket rivers. Pop. 938.

LISBON, p. t., St. Lawrence co., N. Y., 218 ms. N. w. of Albany ; from W. 485 ms. Watered by Grass and St. Lawrence rivers. Pop. 5,295.

LISBON, p. v., Anne Arundel co., Md., 56 ms. N. w. of Annapolis ; from W. 60 ms.

LISBON, p. v., Bedford co., Va., 150 ms. w. of Richmond ; from W. 225 ms.

LISBON, p. o., Claiborne parish, La.

LISBON, p. v., Kendall co., Ill., 154 ms. N. E. of Springfield ; from W. 772 ms. Pop. 519.

LISBON, p. t., Waukesha co., Wis.

LISBON, p. o., Union co., Ark.

LISBON, c. h., p. v., seat of justice of Calcasieu parish, La. Watered by Calcasieu river.

LISBON, p. o., Noble co., Ind.

LISBON, p. o., Linn co., Iowa.

LISBON CENTRE, p. o., Lisbon township, St. Lawrence co., N. Y.

LISBURN, p. v., Cumberland co., Pa., 9 ms. s. w. of Harrisburgh ; from W. 107 ms. Watered by Yellow Breeches creek.

LISBURN, p. v., Sampson co., N. C., 113 ms. s. E. of Raleigh ; from W. 343 ms.

LISHA'S KILL, p. o., Albany co., N. Y.

LISLE, p. t., Broome co., N. Y., 133 ms. s. w. of Albany ; from W. 310 ms. Watered by Toughnioga river and tributaries. Pop. 1,680.

LISLE, p. v., Osage co., Mo., 10 ms. s. E. of Jefferson city ; from W. 926 ms.

LITCHFIELD COUNTY, situated at the northwest corner of Connecticut. Area, 885 square miles. Face of the country hilly ; soil generally productive. Seat of justice, Litchfield. Pop. in 1810, 41,375 ; in 1820, 41,266 ; in 1830, 42,855 ; in 1840, 40,448 ; in 1850, 42,253.

LITCHFIELD, p. t., Kennebec co., Me., 11 ms. s. w. of

Augusta; from W. 584 ms. Watered by tributaries of Cobbeseconte river. Pop. 2,100.

LITCHFIELD, t., Hillsborough co.. N. H., 26 ms. s. of Concord; from W. 454 ms. Watered by Merrimac river. Pop. 447.

LITCHFIELD, c. h., p. t., seat of justice of Litchfield co.. Ct., 32 ms. w. of Hartford; from W. 326 ms. Watered by Naugatuck, Shepang, and Bantam rivers, and Bantam lake, or Great pond. Pop. in 1840, 4,038; in 1850, 3,953.

LITCHFIELD, p. t., Herkimer co., N. Y., 83 ms. N. w. of Albany; from W. 387 ms. Watered by tributaries of Mohawk river. Pop. 1,481.

LITCHFIELD, p. t., Bradford co., Pa., 156 ms. N. of Harrisburgh; from W. 266 ms. Watered by tributaries of Wepassining creek. Pop. 1.112.

LITCHFIELD, p. t.. Medina co., O., 113 ms. N. E. of Columbus; from W. 360 me. Pop. 1.312.

LITCHFIELD, p. t., Hillsdale co., Mich. Pop. 1,362.

LITCHFIELD, c. h., p. v., seat of justice of Grayson co., Ky., 109 ms. s. w. of Frankfort; from W. 651 ms.

LITCHFIELD CORNERS, p. o., Kennebec co., Me., 15 ms. s. w. of Augusta; from W. 580 ms.

LITHGOW, p. o., Washington township, Dutchess co., N. Y., 75 ms. s. of Albany; from W. 319 ms.

LITHOPOLIS, p. v., Bloom township, Fairfield co., O., 17 ms. s. E. of Columbus; from W. 388 ms. Pop. 386.

LITIZ, p. v., Warwick township, Lancaster co., Pa., 45 ms. E. of Harrisburgh; from W. 119 ms.

LITTLE BEAVER, p. t., Beaver co., Pa., 241 ms. w. of Harrisburgh; from W. 263 ms. Watered by Little Beaver creek.

LITTLE BEAVER BRIDGE, p. o., Columbiana co., O., 161 ms. N. E. of Columbus; from W. 268 ms.

LITTLE BLACK, t., Randolph co., Ark.

LITTLE BRITAIN, p. o., Hamptonburgh township, Orange co., N. Y., 98 ms. s. of Albany; from W. 286 ms.

LITTLE BRITAIN, t., Lancaster co., Pa., 58 ms. s. E. of Harrisburgh; from W. 81 ms. Watered by Octarara and Conewingo creeks. Pop. 1,794.

LITTLE CHUCKY, p. o., Greene co., Tenn.

LITTLE CHUTE, p. o., Brown co., Wis.

LITTLE COMPTON, p. t.. Newport co., R. I., 38 ms. s. E. of Providence; from W. 425 ms. Watered by Narraganset bay and Atlantic ocean. Pop. 1,462.

LITTLE COMPTON, p. o., Carroll co., Mo.

LITTLE CREEK, hundred, p. o., Kent co , Del.

LITTLE CREEK, hundred, Sussex co., Del., 58 ms. s. of Dover; from W. 108 ms. Pop. 2,315.

LITTLE CREEK LANDING, p. o., Kent co., Del.

LITTLE DETROIT, p. o., Tazewell co., Ill.

LITTLE EAGLE, p. o., Scott co., Ky.

LITTLE ELKHART, p. o , Elkhart co., Ind.

LITTLE FALLS, p. t., Herkimer co., N. Y., 91 ms. N. w. of Albany; from W. 390 ms. Watered by Mohawk river, and the Erie canal. Pop. 4,855.

LITTLE FALLS, p. v., Passaic co., N. J., 79 ms. N. E. of Trenton; from W. 245 ms. Watered by Passaic river and Morris canal.

LITTLE FLAT, p. o., Bath co., Ky.

LITTLE GAP, p. o., Carbon co., Pa.

LITTLE GENESEE, p. o., Genesee township, Alleghany co., N. Y., 288 ms. w. of Albany; from W. 309 ms.

LITTLE GROVE. p. o., Montgomery co., Tenn.

LITTLE GUNPOWDER, p. o., Baltimore co., Md., 46 N. of Annapolis; from W. 56 ms.

LITTLE HOCKHOCKING, p. o., Decatur township, Washington co., O., 107 ms. s. E. of Columbus; from W. 314 ms.

LITTLE LEVEL, p. o., Pocahontas co., Va., 217 ms. N. w. of Richmond; from W. 252 ms.

LITTLE MAHANOY, p. o., Northumberland co., Pa. Pop. 1,474.

LITTLE MARSH, p. o., Tioga co., Pa., 160 ms. N. of Harrisburgh; from W. 274 ms.

LITTLE MEADOWS, p. o., Susquehanna co., Pa., 199 ms. N. E. of Harrisburgh; from W. 289 ms.

LITTLE MILL CREEK, p. o.. Delaware co., O., 36 ms. N. of Columbus; from W. 420 ms.

LITTLE MILLS, p. o., Richmond co., N. C.

LITTLE MUDDY, p. o., Franklin co., Ill., 154 ms. s. E. of Springfield; from W. 826 ms.

LITTLE NORTH FORK, t., Marion co., Ark.

LITTLE OSAGE, p. o., Bates co., Mo., 158 ms. s. w. of Jefferson City; from W. 1,094 ms. Watered by Little Osage and Marmetou rivers.

LITTLE PINE CREEK. p. o., Lycoming co., Pa.

LITTLE PINEY, p. o., Pulaski co.. Mo., 90 ms. s. of Jefferson City; from W. 965 ms. Watered by Little Piney and Gasconade rivers.

LITTLE PLYMOUTH, p. v., King and Queen co., Va., 60 ms. E. of Richmond; from W. 148 ms.

LITTLE PRAIRIE, p. o., Crawford co., Mo., 73 ms. s. E of Jefferson City; from W. 945 ms.

LITTLE PRAIRIE, t., New Madrid co., Mo.

LITTLE PRAIRIE, p. o., Cass co., Ga.

LITTLE PRAIRIE. p. o., Catahoola parish. La.

LITTLE PRAIRIE, p. o., Walworth co., Wis.

LITTLE PRAIRIE RONDE, p. o., Cass co., Mich., 166 ms. w. of Detroit; from W. 623 ms.

LITTLE RED RIVER, t., Van Buren co., Ark.

LITTLE REST, p. o., Dutchess co., N. Y.

LITTLE RIVER, p. o., Caldwell co., N. C., 172 ms. w. of Raleigh; from W. 410 ms.

LITTLE RIVER, p. o.. Horry district, S. C., 224 ms. E. of Columbia; from W. 440 ms.

LITTLE RIVER, p. o., Columbia co.. Flor.

LITTLE RIVER, p. o., Blount co., Tenn.

LITTLE RIVER, p. o., Floyd co.. Va.

LITTLE RIVER VILLAGE, p. o., Lincoln co., Me., 25 ms. s. E. of Augusta; from W. 570 ms.

LITTLE ROCK, city, seat of justice of Pulaski co., and capital of the state of Arkansas, is situated on a rock, or bluff, on the south side of Arkansas river, at the head of steamboat navigation, except during high water, when Fort Gibson, 1,100 miles further up, may be reached. It is 300 miles by the river from the Mississippi, and 1,065 miles from W. The town is well laid out, and has the usual number of churches and other public buildings, among which may be mentioned the statehouse, courthouse, and penitentiary. The population in 1840, was 3,000; in 1850, 4,138.

LITTLE ROCK, p. o., Kendall co., Ill., 192 ms. N. E. of Springfield; from W. 769 ms.

LITTLE ROCKFISH, p. o., Cumberland co., N. C.

LITTLE SANDUSKY, p. v., Pitt township, Wyandott co., O., 56 ms. N. of Columbus; from W. 419 ms. Watered by Little Sandusky creek.

LITTLE SANDY, p. o., Morgan co., Ky.

LITTLE SCIOTA, p. o., Marion co.. O.

LITTLE SKIN CREEK, p. o., Lewis co.. Va.

LITTLE SODUS, p. o., Sterling township, Cayuga co., N. Y., 181 ms. w. of Albany; from W. 364 ms.

LITTLESTOWN, p. v., Adams co., Pa., 42 ms. s. w. of Harrisburgh; from W. 77 ms.

LITTLETON, p. o., Grafton co., N. H., 83 ms. N. w. of Concord; from W. 544 ms. Watered by Connecticut and Ammonoosuck rivers.

LITTLETON, p. t., Middlesex co., Mass., 26 ms. N. w. of Boston; from W. 426 ms. Watered by Stony river. and Beaver branch of Concord river. Pop. 987.

LITTLETON, p. o., Sussex co., Va., 53 ms. s. of Richmond; from W. 172 ms.

LITTLETON, p. v., Halifax co., N. C., 78 ms. N. E. of Raleigh; from W. 210 ms.

LITTLETON, p. o., Richland district, S. C.

LITTLETON, p. o., Schuyler co., Ill.

LITTLETON, p. o., Morris co., N. J.

LITTLE UTICA. p. o., Onondaga co., N. Y.

LITTLE VALLEY, p. t., Cattaraugus co., N. Y., 300 ms. w. of Albany; from W. 342 ms. Watered by Alleghany river and tributaries. Pop. 1,383.

LITTLEVILLE, v., Avon township, Livingston co., N. Y.

LITTLE WOODS, p. o., Kane co., Ill.

LITTLE YADKIN, p. o.. Stokes co., N. C., 137 ms. N. w. of Raleigh; from W 330 ms.

LITTLE YORK, p. o., Homer township, Cortland co., N. Y., 134 ms. w. of Albany; from W. 321 ms.

LITTLE YORK, p. o., Hunterdon co., N. J.

LITTLE YORK, p. o., Butler township, Montgomery co., O., 75 ms. w. of Columbus; from W. 468 ms.

LITTLE YORK, p. o., Warren co., Ill., 131 ms. N. w. of Springfield; from W. 861 ms.

LITTLE YORK, p. o., Washington co., Ind., 89 ms. s. of Indianapolis; from. 594 ms.

LITWALTON, p. o., Lancaster co., Va.

LIVELY, p. o., St. Clair co., Ill., 113 ms. s. of Springfield; from W. 822 ms.

LIVELY OAK, p. o., Lancaster co., Va.

LIVE OAK, p. o., Ascension parish, La.

LIVE OAK, p. o., De Witt co., Tex.

LIVERMORE, p. o., Westmoreland co., Pa., 176 ms. w. of Harrisburgh; from W. 204 ms.

LIVERMORE, p. t., Oxford co., Me., 30 ms. w. of Augusta; from W. 596 ms. Watered by Androscoggin river. Pop. 1,764.

LIVERMORE, p. o., Ohio co., Ky., 169 ms. s. w. of Frankfort; from W. 711 ms.

LIVERMORE RANCHO, p. o., Contra Costa co., Cal.

LIVERMORE CENTRE, p. o., Livermore township, Oxford co., Me., 24 ms. w. of Augusta; from W. 600 ms.

LIVERMORE FALLS, p. o., Livermore township, Oxford co., Me., 26 ms. w. of Augusta; from W. 604 ms.

LIVERPOOL, p. v., Salina township, Onondaga co., N. Y., 136 ms. w. of Albany; from W. 353 ms. Watered by Onondaga lake, Oswego canal. Noted for Saline springs belonging to the state of New York.

LIVERPOOL, p. b., and t., Perry co., Pa., 29 ms. N. of Harrisburgh; from W. 139 ms. Watered by Susquehanna river. Pop. 1,562.

LIVERPOOL, t., Columbiana co., O., 170 ms. N. E. of Columbus; from W. 280 ms. Pop. 729.

LIVERPOOL, p. t., Medina co., O., 125 ms. N. E. of Columbus; from W. 356 ms. Watered by Rocky river and tributaries. Pop. 2,203.

LIVERPOOL, p. o., Brazoria co., Tex.

LIVERPOOL, p. o., Fulton co., Ill.

LIVINGSTON COUNTY, situated toward west part of New York, and traversed by Genesee river. Area, 509 square miles. Face of the country, diversified; soil, generally fertile. Seat of justice, Genesee. Pop. in 1820, 19,196; in 1830, 27,709; in 1840, 35,140; in 1850, 40,875.

LIVINGSTON COUNTY, situated on the westerly boundary of Kentucky, and traversed by Cumberland river, and bounded by the Mississippi on the west, and the Tennessee on the south. Area, 330 square miles. Face of the country, generally level; soil fertile. Seat of justice, Salem. Pop. in 1810, 3,474; in 1820, 5,824; in 1830, 6,007; in 1840, 9,025; in 1850, 6,578.

LIVINGSTON COUNTY, situated toward the northwest part of Missouri, and traversed by Grand river. Area, 510 square miles. Seat of justice, Chillicothe. Pop. in 1840, 4,325; in 1850, 4,247.

LIVINGSTON COUNTY, situated toward the northeast part of Illinois. Area, 1,026 square miles. Seat of justice, Pontiac. Pop. in 1840, 759; in 1850, 1,552.

LIVINGSTON COUNTY, situated toward the east part of Michigan. Area, 576 miles. Seat of justice, Howell. Pop. in 1840, 7,430; in 1850, 13,485.

LIVINGSTON PARISH, situated toward the southeast part of Louisiana. Area, 730 square miles. Seat of justice, Springfield. Pop. in 1840, 2,315; in 1850, 3,385.

LIVINGSTON, p. t., Columbia co., N. Y., 37 ms. s. of Albany; from W. 334 ms. Watered by Ancram creek and Hudson river. Pop. 2,020.

LIVINGSTON, p. t., Essex co., N. J., 58 ms. N. E. of Trenton; from W. 224 ms. Watered by Passaic river. Pop. 1,151.

LIVINGSTON, p. v. Livingston co., Mich.. 46 ms. N. w. of Detroit; from W. 539 ms. Watered by Woodruff creek.

LIVINGSTON, c. h., p. v., seat of justice of Sumter co., A.a; from W. 886 ms. Watered by Sucarnochee river.

LIVINGSTON, p. o., Clark co., Ill., 127 ms. s. E. of Springfield; from W. 657 ms.

LIVINGSTON, p. v., Madison co., Miss., 22 ms. N. of Jackson; from W. 1,026 ms.

LIVINGSTON, p. o., Polk co., Tex.

LIVINGSTON, c. h., p. v.; seat of justice of Overton co., Tenn., 96 ms. E. of Nashville; from W. 608 ms.

LIVINGSTON, Crawford co., O.

LIVINGSTONVILLE, p. v., Broome township, Schoharie co., N. Y., 42 ms. w. of Albany; from W. 369 ms.

LIVONIA, p. t., Livingston co., N. Y., 224 ms. w. of Albany; from W. 353 ms. Watered by Hemlock lake. Pop. 2,527.

LIVONIA, p. v., Washington co., Ind., 104 ms. s. of Indianapolis; from W. 615 ms.

LIVONIA, p. o., Point Coupee parish, La.

LIVONIA, p. t., Wayne co., Mich. (Now Plank Road.) Pop. 1,375.

LLEWELLYN, p. o., Schuylkill co., Pa.

LLOYD'S, p. o., Essex co., Va.

LOACHAPOKA, p. o., Macon co., Ala.

LOAG, p. o., Chester co., Pa.

LOBACHSVILLE, p. o., Berks co., Pa., 66 ms. E. of Harrisburgh; from W. 159 ms.

LOBDELL'S STORE, p. o., West Baton Rouge parish, La.

LOCATION, p. o., Coweta co., Ga., 97 ms. w. of Milledgeville; from W. 719 ms.

LOCH LEVEN, p. o., Lunenburgh co., Va.

LOCH LOMOND, p. o., Goochland co., Va.

LOCK, p. o., Knox co., O., 56 ms. N. E. of Columbus; from W. 395 ms.

LOCK BERLIN, p. o., Galen township, Wayne co., N. Y., 180 ms. w. of Albany; from W. —— ms.

LOCKBOURNE, p. v., Hamilton township, Franklin co., O., 11 ms. s. of Columbus; from W. 404 ms.

LOCKE, p. t., Cayuga co., N. Y., 155 ms. w. of Albany; from W. 319 ms. Watered by Oswego inlet. Pop. 1,478.

LOCKE, p. o., Elkhart co., Ind.

LOCK'S MILLS, p. o., Oxford co., Me., 60 ms. w. of Augusta; from W. 604 ms.

LOCKE'S MILLS, p. o., Mifflin co., Pa.

LOCKHART, p. o., Caldwell co., Tex.

LOCKHART'S STORE, p. o., Holmes co., Miss., 71 ms. N. of Jackson; from W. 988 ms.

LOCK HAVEN, c. h., p. v., seat of justice of Clinton co., Pa., 107 ms. N. w. of Harrisburgh; from W. 199 ms. Watered by Susquehanna river. Pop. 830.

LOCKINGTON, p. o., Shelby co., O.

LOCKLAND, p. o., Macon co., Ala.

LOCKPORT, c. h., p. t., seat of justice of Niagara co., N. Y., 277 ms. w. of Albany; from W. 402 ms. Watered by Niagara river, Lake Ontario, and Tonawanda and Eighteen-Mile creeks, and the Erie canal. Pop. in 1823, 500; in 1830, 3,823; in 1840, 9,125; in 1850, 12,323.

LOCKPORT, p. v., Williams co., O., 170 ms. N. w of Columbus; from W. 501 ms. Watered by Tiffin's river.

LOCKPORT, p. v., Carroll co., Ind., 80 ms. N w. of Indianapolis; from W. 622 ms. Watered by Wabash river.

LOCKPORT, p. t., Will co., Ill., 170 ms. N. E. of Springfield; from W. 747 ms. Situated on the Illinois and Michigan canal, which afford extensive water power at this place. Pop. 1,657

LOCKPORT, p. o., Henry co., Ky.

LOCKRIDGE, p. o., Jefferson co., Iowa.

LOCK'S VILLAGE, p. v., Franklin co., Mass., 79 ms. w. of Boston; from W. 402 ms.

LOCKVILLE, p. o., Fairfield co., O.

LOCKWOOD, p. v., Byram township, Sussex co., N. J., 62 ms. N. of Trenton; from W. 232 ms. Watered by Lubber run.

LOCO PRAIRIE, p. o., Mc Henry co., Ill.

LOCUST BAYOU, p. o., Washita co., Ark.

LOCUST CORNER, p. o., Clermont co., O.

LOCUST CREEK, p. o., Louisa co., Va., 38 ms. N w. of Richmond; from W. 97 ms.

LOCUST CREEK, t., Linn co., Mo.

LOCUST DALE, p. o., Madison co., Va., 92 ms. N. w. of Richmond; from W. 94 ms.

LOCUST GROVE, p. o., Orange co., Va., 82 ms. N. w. of Richmond; from W. 76 ms.

LOCUST GROVE, p. o., Henry co., Ga., 65 ms. N. w. of Milledgeville; from W. 670 ms.

LOCUST GROVE, p. o., Galloway co., Ky.

LOCUST GROVE, p. o., Weakly co., Tenn., 132 ms. w. of Nashville; from W. 818 ms.

LOCUST GROVE, p. o., Adams co., O., 90 ms. s. w. of Columbus; from W. 427 ms.

LOCUST GROVE, p. o., Searcy co., Ark.

LOCUST GROVE, p. o., Williamson co., Ill.

LOCUST GROVE, p. o., Montgomery co., Ind.

LOCUST GROVE, p. o., Henry co., Mo.

LOCUST HILL, p. o., Washington co., Pa., 214 ms. w. of Harrisburgh; from W. 241 ms.

LOCUST HILL, p. o., Caswell co., N. C.

LOCUST HILL, p. o., Anderson district, S. C.

LOCUST LANE, p. o., Fayette co., Va., 253 ms. w. of Richmond; from W. 290 ms.

LOCUST MILL, p. o., Bracken co., Ky, 79 ms. N. n. of Frankfort; from W. 493 ms.

LOCUST MOUNT, p. o., Accomac co., Va.

LOCUST MOUNT, p. o., Washington co., Tenn., 279 ms. E. of Nashville; from W. 419 ms.

LOCUST SHADE, p. o., Overton co., Tenn., 104 ms. E. of Nashville; from W. 617 ms.

LOCUST SPRING, p. o., Macoupin co., Ill.

LOCUST TREE, p. o., Niagara co., N. Y., 281 ms. w. of Albany; from W. 399 ms.

LOCUSTVILLE, p. o., Accomac co., Va.

LODDY, p. o., Hamilton co., Tenn.

LODERSVILLE, p. o., Susquehanna co., Pa.

LODI, p. t., Seneca co., N. Y., 185 ms. w. of Albany; from W. 318 ms. Watered by Seneca lake. Pop. 2,269.

LODI, v., Persia township, Cattaraugus co., N. Y., 302 ms. w. of Albany; from W. 354 ms. Watered by tributaries of Cattaraugus creek.

LODI, p. t., Bergen co., N. J., 53 ms. N. E. of Trenton; from W. 219 ms. Watered by Hackensack and Passaic rivers. Pop. 1,113.

LODI, p. v., Harrisville township, Medina co., O., 114 ms. N. E. of Columbus; from W. 359 ms.

LODI, t., Athens co., O., 82 ms. N. E. of Columbus; from W. 342 ms. Watered by Shade river. Pop. 1,336.

LODI, p. t., Washtenaw co., Mich., 43 ms. w. of Detroit; from W. 520 ms. Pop. 1,234.

LODI, p. v., Abbeville district, S. C., 74 ms. w. of Columbia; from W. 520 ms.

LODI, p. o., Coweta co., Ga., 114 ms. w. of Milledgeville; from W. 718 ms.

LODI, p. v., Jackson co., Tenn., 99 ms. N. E. of Nashville; from W. 638 ms.

LODI, p. o., Choctaw co., Miss.

LODI, p. o., Wabash co., Ind.

LODI, p. o., Clark co., Ill.

LODI, p. o., Columbia co., Wis.

LODI BAR, p. o., Sumter district, S. C.

LODI CENTRE, p. o., Lodi township, Seneca co., N. Y.

LODIVILLE, p. o., Parke co., Ind.

LODORE, p. o., Amelia co., Va.

LOGAN COUNTY, situated on the western boundary of Virginia. Area, 2,930 square miles. Seat of justice, Logan, C. H. Pop. in 1830, 3,680; in 1840, 4,309; in 1850, 3,620.

LOGAN COUNTY, situated on the south boundary of Kentucky. Area, 600 square miles. Face of the country, undulating; soil, rich. Seat of justice, Russelville. Pop. in 1810, 12,123; in 1820, 14,423; in 1830, 13,002; in 1840. 12,615; in 1850, 16,581.

LOGAN COUNTY, situated toward the west part of Ohio. Area, 425 square miles. Face of the country, level; soil generally productive. Seat of justice, Bellefontaine. Pop. in 1820, 3,181; in 1830, 6,442; in 1840, 14,015; in 1850, 19.162.

LOGAN COUNTY, situated in the central part of Illinois. Area, 529 square miles. Seat of justice, Postville. Pop. in 1840, 2,333; in 1850, 5,128.

LOGAN, t., Clinton co., Pa. Watered by Big Fishing creek. Pop. 263.

LOGAN, p. o., Hector township. Tompkins co., N. Y., 181 ms. w. of Albany; from W. 314 ms.

LOGAN, c. h., p. v., seat of justice of Hocking co., O., 47 ms. S. E. of Columbus; from W. 365 ms. Watered by Hockhocking river. Pop. 1.066.

LOGAN, p. t., Dearborn co., Ind., 87 ms. S. E. of Indianapolis; from W. 528 ms. Pop. 753.

LOGAN, p. t., Fountain co., Ind. Pop. 1,717.

LOGAN, c. h., p. v., seat of justice of Logan co., Va., 351 ms. w. of Richmond; from W. 388 ms. Watered by Guyandotte river.

LOGAN, t., Wayne co., Mo.

LOGAN MILLS, p. o., Clinton co., Pa.

LOGAN'S CREEK, p. o., Reynolds co., Mo.

LOGAN'S FERRY, p. o., Alleghany co., Pa.

LOGANSPORT, c. h., p. v., seat of justice of Cass co., Ind., 72 ms. N. of Indianapolis; from W. 610 ms. Watered by Wabash and Eel rivers, and the Wabash and Erie canal.

LOGANSPORT, p. o., De Soto parish, La.

LOGAN'S STORE, p. o., Rutherford co., N. C.

LOGANVILLE, p. v., York co., Pa., 31 ms. S. of Harrisburgh; from W. 83 ms.

LOGANVILLE, p. v., Miami township, Logan co., O., 73 ms. N. w. of Columbus; from W. 465 ms. Watered by Miami river.

LOGANVILLE, p. o., Walton co., Ga.

LOG CABIN, p. o., Morgan co., O.

LOG LICK, p. o., Switzerland co., Ind.

LOGTOWN, p. o., Wachita parish, La.

LOMBARDVILLE, p. o., Cecil co., Md.

LOMBARDY, p. o., Columbia co., Ga., 66 ms. N. E. of Milledgeville; from W. —— ms.

LOMBARDY GROVE, p. o., Mecklenburgh co., Va., 97 ms. s. w. of Richmond; from W. 213 ms.

LOMIRA, p. o., Dodge co., Wis.

LONACONING, p. o., Alleghany co., Md., 184 ms. N. w. of Annapolis; from W. 152 ms.

LONDON, c. h., p. v., seat of justice of Madison co., O., 27 ms. w. of Columbus; from W. 420 ms. Pop. 513.

LONDON, t., Seneca co., O. Pop. 1,781.

LONDON, c. h., p. v., seat of justice of Laurel co., Ky., 94 ms. s. w. of Frankfort; from W. 544 ms. Watered by a tributary of Laurel river.

LONDON, p. t., Monroe co., Mich., 45 ms. s. w. of Detroit; from W. 502 ms. Pop. 626.

LONDON BRIDGE, p. v., Princess Ann co., Va., 124 ms. s. E. of Richmond; from W. 248 ms.

LONDON BRITAIN, t., Chester co., Pa. Watered by White Clay creek. Pop. 680.

LONDON CITY, p. o., Fayette co., Ill.

LONDONDERRY, p. t., Rockingham co., N. H., 34 ms. S. E. of Concord; from W. 454 ms. Watered by Beaver river. Pop. 1,731.

LONDONDERRY, p. t., Windham co., Vt., 96 ms. s. of Montpelier; from W. 444 ms. Watered by West and Windhall rivers and Utly brook. Pop. 1,274.

LONDONDERRY, p. t., Chester co., Pa., 62 ms. s. E. of Harrisburgh; from W. 102 ms. Watered by Doe run. Pop. 643.

LONDONDERRY, t., Bedford co., Pa., 115 ms. s. w. of Harrisburgh; from W. 131 ms. Watered by Will's creek. Pop. 823.

LONDONDERRY, t., Dauphin co., Pa., 14 ms. s. E. of Harrisburgh; from W. 121 ms. Watered by Spring and Conewago creeks. Pop. 1,587.

LONDONDERRY, t., Lebanon co., Pa., 15 ms. E. of Harrisburgh; from W. 120 ms. Watered by Conewaga, Swatara, and Quitapahilla creeks, and Klinger's run. Pop. 1,563.

LONDONDERRY, p. t., Guernsey co., O., 95 ms. E. of Columbus; from W. 303 ms.

LONDON GROVE, p. t., Chester co., Pa., 71 ms. s. of Harrisburgh; from W. 105 ms. Watered by White Clay creek and tributaries. Pop. 1,425.

LONE JACK, p. o., Jackson co., Mo., 128 ms. w. of Jefferson city; from W. 1,054 ms.

LONE STAR, p. o., Titus co., Tex.

LONE TREE, p. o., Bureau co., Ill.

LONG-A-COMING, p. v., Gloucester and Waterford townships, Gloucester co., N. J., 44 ms. s. w. of Trenton; from W. 154 ms.

LONG BOTTOM, p. o., Olive township, Meigs co., O., 105 ms. s. E. of Columbus; from W. 323 ms.

LONG BOTTOM, p. o., Marshall co., Va.

LONG BRANCH, p. o., Franklin co., Va., 209 ms. w. of Richmond; from W. 286 ms.

LONG BRANCH, p. v., Shrewsbury township, Monmouth co., N. J., 50 ms. E. of Trenton; from W. 216 ms.

LONG BRANCH, p. o., Monroe co., Mo., 62 ms. N. of Jefferson City; from W. 937 ms.

LONG CANE, p. o., Troup co., Ga., 131 ms. w. of Milledgeville; from W. 749 ms.

LONG CANE, p. o., Abbeville district, S. C.

LONG CREEK, p. o., New Hanover co., N. C., 139 ms. s. E. of Raleigh; from W. 369 ms.

LONG CREEK, p. o., Louisa co., Va., 45 ms. N. w. of Richmond; from W. 94 ms.

LONG CREEK, p. o., Panola co., Miss.

LONG FALLS CREEK, p. o., Daviess co., Ky., 181 ms. s. w. of Frankfort; from W. 708 ms.

LONG GLADE, p. o., Augusta co., 123 ms. N. w. of Richmond; from W. 163 ms.

LONG GREEN ACADEMY, p. o., Baltimore co., Md., 52 ms. N. of Annapolis; from W. 62 ms.

LONG GROVE, p. o., Lake co., Ill.

LONG HALL, p. o., Caldwell co., Ky.

LONG HILL, p. o., Morris co., N. J., 51 ms. N. of Trenton; from W. 221 ms.

LONG ISLAND, p. o., Hancock co., Me.

LONG JOHN, p. o., Will co., Ill.

LONG LAKE, p. o., Manitowoc co., Wis.

LONG LAKE, p. o., Marquette co., Wis.

LONG LAKE, p. o., Genesee co., Mich.

LONG LANE, p. o., Dallas co., Mo.

LONG MARSH, p. o., Queen Anne co., Md., 46 ms. E. of Annapolis; from W. 56 ms.

LONG MEADOW, p. t., Hampden co., Mass., 95 ms. s. w. of Boston; from W. 359 ms. Watered by Connecticut river. Pop. 1,253.

LONG MEADOW, p. o., Page co., Va., 130 ms. N. w. of Richmond; from W. 103 ms.

LONGMIRE, p. o., Washington co., Tenn., 297 ms. E. of Nashville ; from W. 426 ms.

LONGMIRE'S STORE, p. o., Edgefield district, S. C., 74 ms. w. of Columbia ; from W. 552 ms.

LONG OLD FIELDS, p. o., Prince George co., Md., 31 ms. w. of Annapolis ; from W. 9 ms.

LONG PINE, p. o., Bedford co., Va.

· LONG PLAIN. p, o., Bristol co., Mass., 50 ms. s. of Boston : from W. 437 ms.

,LONG POINT, p. o., Livingston co., Ill.

LONG POINT, p. o., Washington co., Tex.

LONG POND, p. o., Caldwell co., Ky.

LONG PRAIRIE, p. o., Wahnahta co., Minnesota.

LONG RIDGE, p. o., Fairfield co., Ct.

LONG RUN, p. o., Jefferson co., Ky., 36 ms. w. of Frankfort; from W. 578 ms.

LONG SAVANNAH, p. o., Hamilton co., Tenn., 139 ms. E. of Nashville ; from W. 586 ms.

LONG'S BRIDGE, p. o., Hancock co., Ga., 36 ms. N. E. of Milledgeville ; from W. 661 ms.

LONG'S MILLS, p. o., Randolph co., N. C., 62 ms. w. of Raleigh ; from W. 313 ms.

LONG STREET, p. o., Moore co., N. C., 43 ms. s. w. of Raleigh ; from W. 331 ms.

LONG STREET, p. o., Lancaster district, S. C., 68 ms. N. w. of Columbia ; from W. 462 ms.

LONG STREET, p. o., Pulaski co., Ga.

LONG SWAMP, p. t., Berks co., Pa., 72 ms. E. of Harrisburgh ; from W. 165 ms. Watered by Little Lehigh river. Pop. 1,868.

LONG SWAMP, p. o., Marion co., Flor.

LONGTOWN, p. o., Fairfield district, S. C.

LONGTOWN. p. o., Panola co., Miss.

LONG VALLEY, p. o., Monroe co., Pa.

LONG VIEW, p. o., Morgan co., Tenn.

LONG VIEW, p. o., Bradley co., Ark.

LONG VIEW, p. o., Christian co., Ky.

LONGWOOD, p. o., Union co., Ky., 226 ms. s. w. of Frankfort ; from W. 753 ms.

LONGWOOD, p. o., Fayette co., Ind.

LONGWOOD, p. o., Sabine co., Tex.

LONSDALE, p. o., Providence co., R. I., 10 ms. w. of Providence ; from W. 410 ms.

LONSVILLE. p. o., Pike co., Ky.

LOOKING-GLASS, p. o., Clinton co., Ill.

LOOK-OUT, p. o., Cole co., Mo.

LOOMISVILLE. p. o., Kent co., Mich.

LOONEY'S CREEK, p. o., Marion co., Tenn.

LOONIESVILLE, p. o., Seneca co., Mo.

LOOSE CREEK, p. o., Osage co., Mo.

LOOXAHOMA, p. o., De Soto co., Miss.

LORADO, p. o., Greene co., Ark.

LORAMIE'S, p. t., Shelby co., O., 86 ms. N. w. of Columbus ; from W. 483 ms.

LORAN, p. o., Whitley co., Ind.

LORAIN COUNTY, situated on the north boundary of Ohio, on Lake Erie. Area, 540 square miles. Seat of justice, Elyria. Pop. in 1830, 5,696 ; in 1840, 18,467 ; in 1850, 26,086.

LORAIN, t., Shelby co., O. Pop. 1,049.

LORAIN, p. t., Tippecanoe co., Ind. Pop. 1,611.

LORANCE, t., Cape Girardeau co., Mo.

LORDSTOWN, p. t., Trumbull co., O. Pop. 1,329.

LORENTZ STORE, p. o., Lewis co., Va., 292 ms. N. w. of Richmond ; from W. 260 ms.

LORENZOVILLE FOUNDRY, p. o., Shenandoah co., Va.

LORETTO, p. v., Alleghany township, Cambria co., Pa., 145 ms. w. of Harrisburgh ; from W. 188 ms. Pop. 193.

LORETTO, p. o., Essex co., Va., 62 ms. N. E. of Richmond ; from W. 90 ms.

LORETTO, p. o., Marion co., Ky., 67 ms. s. w. of Frankfort ; from W. 593 ms.

LORRAINE, p. t., Jefferson co., N. Y., 157 ms. N. w. of Albany ; from W. 408 ms. Watered by Sandy creek and tributaries. Pop. 1 511.

LOS ANGELOS COUNTY, situated on the southeasterly boundary of California, on the Pacific ocean. Area, —— square miles. Seat of justice, Los Angelos. Pop. in 1850. 3,530.

LOS ANGELOS, c. h., p. v., seat of justice of Los Angelos co., Cal.

LOSS CREEK, p. o., Crawford co., O., 70 ms. N. of Columbus ; from W. 414 ms.

LOST CREEK, p. o., Harrison co., Va., 269 ms. N. w. of Richmond ; from W. 237 ms.

LOST CREEK, p. o., Campbell co., Tenn., 201 ms. E. of Nashville ; from W. 493 ms.

LOST CREEK, t., Miami co., O., 63 ms. w. of Columbus ; from W. 457 ms. Pop. 1,064.

LOST CREEK, p. o., Lincoln co., Mo., 102 ms. N. E. of Jefferson city ; from W. 875 ms.

LOST GROVE, p. o., De Kalb co., Ill.

LOST MOUNTAIN, p. o., Cobb co., Ga.

LOST RIVER, p. o., Orange co., Ind.

LOST RIVER, p. o., Hardy co., Va., 173 ms. N. w. of Richmond ; from W. 123 ms.

LOST VILLAGE, p. o., New Madrid co., Mo.

LOTTRIDGE, p. o., Athens co., O.

LOTT'S, p. o., Edgefield district, S. C., 47 ms. w. of Columbia ; from W. 545 ms.

LOTTSVILLE, p. v., Warren co., Pa.. 233 ms. N. w. of Harrisburgh ; from W. 325 ms. Watered by Little Broken Straw creek.

LOUDON (or LOUDOUN) COUNTY, situated in the northeasterly boundary of Virginia. with Potomac river on the northeast. Area, 460 square miles. Face of the country pleasantly diversified ; soil fertile. Seat of justice, Leesburgh. Pop. in 1810, 21,338 ; in 1820, 22,702 ; in 1830, 21,938 ; in 1840, 20,431 ; in 1850, 22,089.

LOUDON, p. t., Merrimac co., N. H., 8 ms. N. E. of Concord ; from W. 489 ms. Watered by Soucook river. Pop. 1,552.

LOUDON, p. t., Peters township. Franklin co., Pa., 59 ms. s. w. of Harrisburgh ; from W. 103 ms. Watered by west branch of Connecocheague creek. Pop. 1,228.

LOUDON, p. t., Seneca co., O., 88 ms. N. of Columbus ; from W. 433 ms. Pop. 1,781.

LOUDON, t., Carroll co., O. Pop. 840.

LOUDON, t., Monroe co., Mich. Pop. 626.

LOUDON CENTRE, p. o., Loudon township, Merrimac co., N. H., 14 ms. N. E. of Concord ; from W. 495 ms.

LOUDON RIDGE, p. o., Loudon township, Merrimac co., N. H., 15 ms. N. E. of Concord ; from W. 496 ms.

LOUDONVILLE, p. v., Hanover township, Ashland co., O., 73 ms. N. E. of Columbus ; from W. 363 ms. Watered by Black fork of Mohican creek.

LOUDSVILLE, p. v., Habersham co., Ga., 159 ms. N. of Milledgeville ; from W. 615 ms. Watered by sources of Chestatee river in the gold region.

LOUINA, p. o., Randolph co., Ala.

LOUISA COUNTY, situated toward the east part of Virginia. Area, 570 square miles. Face of the country uneven ; soil generally productive. Seat of justice, Louisa c. h. Pop. in 1810, 11,900 ; in 1820, 13 746 ; in 1830, 16,131 ; in 1840, 15,433 ; in 1850, 16,691.

LOUISA COUNTY, situated on the easterly boundary of Iowa, and traversed by Iowa river, with the Mississippi on the east. Area, 442 square miles. Seat of justice, Wapello. Pop. in 1840, 1,927 ; in 1850, 4,939.

LOUISA, p. o., Stephenson co., Ill.

LOUISA. c. h., p. v., seat of justice of Lawrence co., Ky., 158 ms. E. of Frankfort ; from W. 436 ms. Watered by Big Sandy river.

LOUISA, c. h., p. v., seat of justice of Louisa co., Va., 60 ms. N. w. of Richmond ; from W. 103 ms.

LOUISBURGH. c. h., p. v., seat of justice of Franklin co., N. C., 36 ms. N. E. of Raleigh ; from W. 262 ms. Watered by Tar river.

LOUISIANA, one of the United States, so called by La Salle, in 1682, in honor of his royal patron, Louis XIV., of France. It is situated between 29° and 33° north latitude, and 88° 40' and 94° 25' west longitude from Greenwich ; and is bounded north by Arkansas and Mississippi, east by Mississippi, from which it is separated by Mississippi and Pearl rivers, southeast and south by the gulf of Mexico, and west by Texas, from which it is separated in part by Sabine river. Its superficial area is 46,341 square miles.

Physical Aspect.—The entire border of the state, from Pearl river to the Sabine, presents itself in a vast tract of irreclaimable sea-marsh, from 20 to 30 miles in width, extending farthest inland in the regions between the streams ; for it is a singular feature, in all the rivers which flow into this part of the Mississippi, that narrow

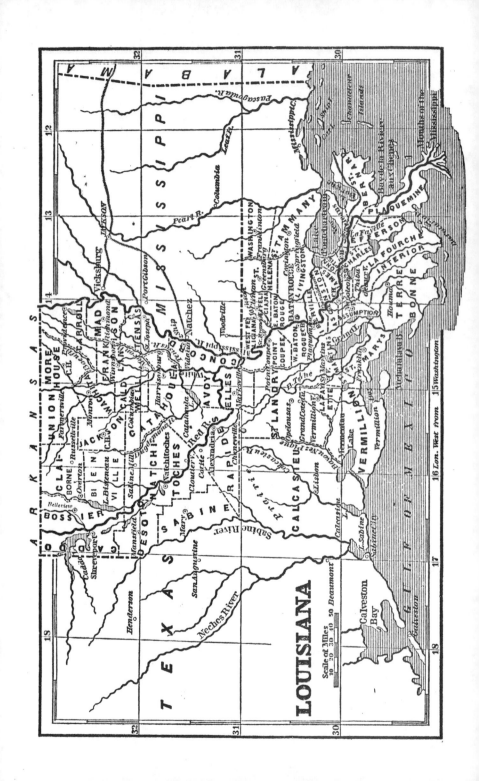

LOUISIANA

Scale of Miles
10 20 30 40 50

strips of arable land, of greater or less width, occur on their banks, extending far beyond the interior limits of the sea-marsh; none, however, retain these elevated borders to the Mexican gulf. Contiguous to the sea-marsh are vast prairies, with which the former has often been confounded, in consequence of their similarity in appearance. On the waters of the Sabine, Calcasieu, and Mermentau, the prairies have generally a thin, sterile soil, while on the Vermilion, Teche, and Cortableau, they are almost uniformly good. The alluvial banks of the rivers of Louisiana, in their natural state, are more or less subject to inundation; but in many cases, where valuable tracts are situated in the rear of the elevated strips on their borders, in order to prevent them from being overflowed, artificial embankments, or dikes, called "levees," are raised, on the margins of the streams. These arable river-borders are usually composed of a fine, loose, rich soil; but the interior plains are hard, stiff, and less fertile. In some instances, when these plains are laid dry, the soil becomes almost as hard as stone. Taken as a whole, Louisiana consists of inundated and non-inundated lands. Above the mouth of Red river, the tract liable to periodical inundation is narrow; but below that stream it widens and expands like a fan, and finally embraces the whole gulf border. All of the soil, sufficiently elevated for cultivation within the inundated region, is of superior quality. The northern part of the state has an undulating surface. Northward from the prairies of Opelousas, and westward of the inundated border near the Mississippi, lies what has been denominated the "pine region." The surface has been somewhat broken into hills, though of moderate elevation, and within the tract some snow, and even waterfalls appear. The banks of the Vermilion, which are generally fertile, are high, broken, and diversified, above the termination of the timber near the sea marsh. The country between the Mississippi, Iberville, and Pearl rivers, is an important part of the state. The southern or level portion is highly productive of the staple crops, and the northern portion, which is undulating, has been considered as the "garden of Louisiana."

Rivers, Lakes, and Bays.—Louisiana is intersected by numerous, creeks (bayous), and lakes, dividing the state into a great number of islands, or "deltas," similar in some respects to those at the mouths of the Ganges, the Nile, and the Parana. The principal rivers are, the Mississippi, Pearl, Bogue Chitto, Chifuncte, Tangipao, Tickfoha, Lafourche, Teche, Vermilion, Tensas, Red, Mermentau, Atchafalaya, Amite, New, Calcasieu, Black, Bodcau, Dacheet, Saline, Wachita, Plaquemine, and the Cabine. The principal lakes are, Ponchartrain, Maurepas, Brogne, Chetimaches, Mermentau, Calcasieu, and Sabine. The chief bays are, Vermilion, Cote, Blanche, Atchafalaya, Timbalier, West, and Chandeleur.

Climate.—In the southern part of the state the climate, in summer, is hot, sultry, and unhealthy; in the northern part it is more temperate and salubrious. The winters are usually mild, though snow sometimes falls at Opelousas, from ten to twelve inches deep: such instances, however, are rare. The creeks and ponds at New Orleans are sometimes closed with ice, and snow has been known to fall sufficiently deep for sleighing.

Productive Resources.—The staple products are, cotton, sugar, molasses, tobacco and rice. This state also produces to some extent, horses, mules, neat cattle, sheep, swine, poultry, wool, hay, lumber, tar, turpentine, wheat, rye, oats, potatoes, Indian corn, wine, oranges, and figs.

Manufactures.—The manufactures of Louisiana are confined chiefly to the eastern portion of the state. In 1850 there were 1,021 manufacturing establishments producing $500 and upward annually. The articles manufactured are principally to supply the immediate wants of the community.

Railroads and Canals.—Louisiana is so well provided with navigable channels, that little attention has been given to artificial means of internal communication. The public mind, however, has recently been awakened to the subject, and we may confidently predict that this state will ere long be traversed by iron bands, connecting New Orleans with important points within her own borders, and extending to other states. At present there are but about 50 miles of railroad and 100 miles of canal in the state.

Commerce.—The exports and imports of Louisiana are about $50,000,000 annually. Its coasting and river trade amounts to about double that sum. Shipping owned within the state is about 250,000 tons.

Education.—The principal collegiate institutions in Louisiana are, the St. Charles college, at Grande Coteau, founded in 1833, the Baton Rouge college, in 1838, the Franklin college, at Opelousas, in 1839, the Centenary college of Louisiana, at Jackson, in 1841, and the University of Louisiana, at New Orleans. There are about 100 academies and 300 common schools in the state.

Population.—In 1732, about 7,500; in 1810, 76,556; in 1820, 153,407; in 1830, 215,739; in 1840, 352,411; in 1850, 517,739. Number of slaves in 1800, 3,489; in 1810, 34,660; in 1820, 69,064; in 1830, 109,588; in 1840, 168,452; in 1850, 244,786.

Government.—The legislative power is vested in a senate and house of representatives. The senators, 32 in number, are elected by the people, by districts, for the term of four years, one half being chosen every two years; the representatives are elected by the people, by parishes, for a term of two years. The number of representatives can not be more than 100, nor less than 70, divided among the parishes, according to their total population, but each parish is entitled to a representative. The executive power is vested in a governor, who is elected by the people, for a term of four years, and is ineligible for the next four years. The elections are held in November, and the legislature meets biennially at Baton Rouge the third Monday in January. The judicial power is vested in a supreme court of five judges, which has appellate jurisdiction only, and such inferior courts as the legislature may establish. The chief justice is elected for ten years, and the associate judges for eight years. The right of suffrage is extended to all white males, above 21 years of age, who have resided in the state one year, and in the parish six months, next preceding the election. All citizens are disfranchized, both as to voting and holding office, who may fight, or in any way be connected with fighting, a duel, with a citizen of the state, either in or out of it. The constitution provides for the establishment of free public schools throughout the state.

History.—Louisiana embraces a part of the ancient territory bearing this name, once so comprehensive, including the entire valley of the Mississippi and its tributary streams, consisting of all the present states of Texas, Louisiana, Alabama, Mississippi, Tennessee, Kentucky, Ohio, Indiana, Michigan, Wisconsin, Minnesota, Illinois, Iowa, Missouri, Arkansas, and California, a portion of Mexico, North Carolina, Virginia, and Pennsylvania, and all the undefined regions between the Rio del Norte and the northern sources of the Mississippi, extending westward to the Pacific. It also constitutes a portion of Florida, as named by Ponce de Leon, in 1512. The first permanent settlement in the present Louisiana was made at New Orleans, in 1718, by the emigrants of the "Mississippi Company," under the auspices of John Law, who received a royal grant the year before of a complete monopoly of the trade and mines of the territory of twenty-seven years. In 1732, for the want of success, this company surrendered its chartered rights to Louisiana, and the control of its commerce reverted to the king. In 1763, France was compelled to cede to England, not only Canada and Acadia, but all of Louisiana east of the Mississippi, as far south as the river D'Iberville, and thence all their territory north and east of a line running along that stream and Amite river, through Lakes Maurepas and Ponchartrain, to the Mexican gulf. The same year she formed a treaty with Spain, surrendering the remaining portion of Louisiana, not ceded to England, and thus deprived herself of all her possessions on the continent of North America. In 1800, it was retroceded to France by a secret treaty, who formally took possession of the country, in 1803, and immediately sold it to the United States for $15,000,000. In the meantime the Revolution had occurred, and all the former territory of Louisiana, lying east of the Mississippi, which had been ceded to England in 1763, had also become a part of the Union. By an act of Congress, in 1804, Louisiana was definitely subdivided; the northern part, above latitude 31°, was called "The Territory of Mississippi," and the lower division, "The Territory of Orleans." In 1811, the latter was authorized to form a constitution of government, which, together with that portion of West Florida west of Pearl river, was formally received into the Union, in 1812, under the name of Louisiana, as a sovereign state. Subsequently to this other lands were annexed to this state, until it received its present bounds. The original constitution was revised in 1845, and a new one adopted in 1852. Motto of the seal. "Union and Confidence."

LOUISIANA, p. v., Pike co., Mo., 88 ms. N. E. of Jefferson City; from W. 868 ms. Watered by Mississippi river.

LOUISIANA, p. t., Chicot co., Ark. Pop. 1,613.

LOUISVILLE, p. t., St. Lawrence co., N. Y., 253 ms. N. w. of Albany; from W. 523 ms. Watered by Grass and St. Lawrence rivers. Pop. 2,054.

LOUISVILLE, c. h., p. v., seat of justice of Jefferson co., Ga., 53 ms. E. of Milledgeville; from W. 634 ms. Watered by Rocky Comfort creek.

LOUISVILLE, p. v., Barbour co., Ala., from W. 836 ms.

LOUISVILLE, c. h., p. v., Winston co., Miss., 92 ms. N. E. of Jackson; from W. 918 ms. Watered by head branches of Pearl river.

LOUISVILLE, p. v., Blount co., Tenn., 158 ms. E. of Nashville; from W. 436 ms. Watered by Tennessee river.

LOUISVILLE, city, the seat of justice of Jefferson co., Ky., the commercial metropolis of the western states is situated on the Ohio river, at the head of uninterrupted steamboat navigation, except when the river is high. Here the Ohio descends by rapids over a limestone ledge, forming a barrier to navigation, which is now surmounted by a canal from below the city to a point above the falls. From the water, the ground rises gently and with undulations, affording a fine site, and a magnificent and varied prospect of the river and its islands, forming rapids, pleasant villages, and fertile shores. The city is intersected by broad and pleasant streets, parallel with the river, crossed at right angles by other streets and alleys. Beargrass creek, passing through the upper part of the town, falls into the Ohio, above the rapids, and is spanned by bridges. The public buildings are numerous, and commensurate with the importance and prosperity of Louisville, including banks, churches, hospitals, jails, a city-hall, and court-house, medical institute, and other benevolent, scientific, and educational establishments.

The Medical Institute at Louisville, is a very important institution, founded in 1837, with six professors, and about two hundred and fifty students. The Kentucky Historical Society, has a considerable library with numerous manuscripts.

This city may be regarded as one of the great magazines for provisions in the west. It is the market of a vast agricultural region, extending through Kentucky, Ohio, Indiana, and Illinois, and trades extensively with the whole valleys of the Mississippi and the Ohio. Manufactures of numerous kinds are also prosecuted with great enterprise and success. It is supplied by an aqueduct with pure and abundant water, and is brilliantly illuminated with gas.

Louisville is the terminus of the Lexington and Ohio railroad, and the port of a large number of steamboats from New Orleans, St. Louis, and other places in the great valley of the west.

The population 1778, was 30; in 1800, 600; in 1810, 1,357; in 1820, 4,012; in 1830, 10,352; in 1840, 21,210; in 1850, 43,194.

LOUISVILLE, p. v., Stark co., O., 131 ms. N. E. of Columbus; from W. 313 ms.

LOUISVILLE, p. v., Clay co., Ill., 112 ms. s. E. of Springfield; from W. 741 ms.

LOUISVILLE, p. v., Lincoln co., Mo., 74 ms. N. E. of Jefferson City; from W. 882 ms.

LOUISVILLE, p. o., El Dorado co., Cal.

LOUISVILLE LANDING, p. o., St. Lawrence co,, N. Y.

LOUNDE's FERRY, p. o., Williamsburgh co., S. C.

LOUTRE, t., Audrain co., Mo.

LOUTRE ISLAND, p. o., Montgomery co., Mo., 43 ms. N. E. of Jefferson City; from W. 903 ms.

LOVELACE, p. o., Wilkes co., N. C.

LOVELACEVILLE, p. o., Ballard co., Ky., 296 ms. s. w. of Frankfort; from W. 823 ms.

LOVELADY, p. o., Caldwell co., N. C., 182 ms. w. of Raleigh; from W. 419 ms.

LOVELAND, p. o., Clinton co., Pa.

LOVELAND, p. o., Clermont co., O.

LOVELIA, p. o., Monroe co., Iowa.

LOVELL, p. t., Oxford co., Me., 63 ms. s. w. of Augusta; from W. 578 ms. Pop. 1,193.

LOVELY MOUNT, p. o., Montgomery co., Va.

LOVE's MILLS, p. o., Washington co., Va., 285 ms. w. of Richmond.

LOVETT's, p. o., Adams co., O.

LOVETTSVILLE, p. v.. Loudoun co., Va., 166 ms. N. of Richmond; from W. 46 ms.

LOVEVILLE, p. v., Newcastle co., Del., 54 ms. N. of Dover; from W. 103 ms.

LOVINGSTON, c. h., p. v., seat of justice of Nelson co., Va., 105 ms. w. of Richmond; from W. 157 ms.

LOVINGTON, p. o., Moultrie co., Ill., 61 ms. E. of Springfield; from W. 718 ms.

LOWELL, p. t., Penobscot co., Me. Pop. 378.

LOWELL, p. t., Orleans co., Vt., 45 ms. N. of Montpelier; from W. 568 ms. Watered by Missisque river. Pop. 637..

LOWELL, city, the seat of justice, together with Cambridge and Concord, of Middlesex co., Mass., is situated at the confluence of Concord and Merrimac rivers, 25 miles northwest of Boston. From an insignificant village, in 1822, it has sprung up into a wealthy and populous city, celebrated over the world for its unrivalled manufactories of cotton and woollen fabrics, by which it has gained the title of the "Manchester of America." The secret of its prosperity lies in the vast water-power, which enterprise and skill have turned into available channels. By a canal which connects the Merrimac below Pawtucket falls, with Concord river, water is conveyed to the town, and distributed to the various factories. About thirty are employed in the manufacture of cotton; a number of others produce woollen fabrics of various kinds, as carpets, broadcloths, cassimeres, calicoes, machinery for railroads, &c. About $20,000,000 are invested in these operations. Lowell is pleasantly situated, and is laid out with broad streets, and the inhabitants are distinguished for industry and good morals. The operatives in the factories, are far above the ignorance and degradation which belong to those similarly employed in other countries. The "Lowell Offering," a periodical composed of communications from the young women of the "mills," is an instance of the truth of this remark. The principal public buildings are the court-house, city-hall, mechanics' hall (the latter of which is devoted to literary and scientific intelligence, and furnished with a museum and/library), and the public schools, which receive a very liberal support. Lowell is connected with Boston by the Middlesex canal, and by railroad; there is also railroad communication with all the principal towns of the surrounding country. The population in 1822, 100 or less; in 1830, 6,474; in 1840, 20,796; in 1850, 27,436.

LOWELL, p. o., Washington co., O., 96 ms. s. E. of Columbus; from W. 312 ms.

LOWELL, p. o., Randolph co., Ga.

LOWELL, p. o., Henry co., Iowa.

LOWELL, p. o., Johnson co., N. C.

LOWELL, p. o., Dodge co., Wis.

LOWELL, p. o., Kent co., Mich.

LOWELL, p. o., Oneida co., N. Y.

LOWELL, p. o., La Salle co., Ill.

LOWELLVILLE, p. o., Mahoning co., O., 184 ms. N. E. of Columbus; from W. 297 ms.

LOWER, t., Cape May co., N. J., 112 ms. s. of Trenton; from W. 114 ms. Watered by Delaware bay, Atlantic ocean, and Pond, New England, and Cox Hall creeks. Pop. 604.

LOWER BARTLETT, p. o., Coos co., N. H., 74 ms. N.E. of Concord; from W. 560 ms.

LOWER ALLOWAY'S CREEK, t., Salem co., N. J.,74 ms. s. of Trenton; from W. 180 ms. Watered by Hope, Deep, and Muddy creeks. Pop. 1,423.

LOWER BERN, p. o., Bern township, Berks co., Pa., 60 ms. E. of Harrisburgh; from W. 153 ms.

LOWER CHANCEFORD, p. t., York co., Pa., 51 ms. s.E. of Harrisburgh; from W. 91 ms. Watered by Susquehanna river, Tom's and Muddy creeks, and Orson's run.

LOWER CHICHESTER, p. t., Delaware co., Pa., 92 ms. s. E. of Harrisburgh; from W. 116 ms. Watered by Hook creek. Pop. 1,552.

LOWER COLUMBIA, p. o., Coos co., N. H.

LOWER DUBLIN, t., Philadelphia co., Pa., 110 ms from Harrisburgh; from W. 148 ms. Watered by Pennypack creek, and Saw-Mill river. Pop. 2.294.

LOWER GILMANTON, p. o., Gilmanton township Belknap co., N. H., 18 ms. N. of Concord; from W. 499 ms.

LOWER LAWRENCE, p. o., Washington co.. O.

LOWER LOUTRE, t., Montgomery co., Mo.

LOWER MACUNGIE, t., Lehigh co., Pa. Pop. 2.353.

LOWER MAHANOY, t,. Northumberland co.. Pa., 37 ms. N. of Harrisburgh; from W. 147 ms. Pop. 1,474.

LOWER MAHANTANGO, p. t., Schuylkill co., Pa., 55 ms. N. E. of Harrisburgh; from W. 165 ms. Watered by Deep and Swatara creeks. Pop. 1,505.

LOWER WAKEFIELD, t., Bucks co., Pa., 110 ms. E. of Harrisburgh. Pop. 1,746.

LOWER MARLBOROUGH, p. v., Calvert co., Md., 41 ms. s. w. of Annapolis; from W. 68 ms.

LOWER MERION, p. t., Montgomery co., Pa., 93 ms. E. of Harrisburgh; from W. 150 ms. Watered by Schuylkill river, and Mill and Cobb creeks. Pop. 3,517.

LOWER MIDDLETON, b., Swatara township, Dauphin co., Pa. Watered by Swatara and Susquehanna rivers, and Pennsylvania and Union canals.

LOWER MOUNT BETHEL, t., Northampton co., Pa., 112 ms. from Harrisburgh; from W. 199 ms. Pop. 3,117.

LOWER NAZARETH, t., Northampton co., Pa. Watered by Manookisy creek. Pop. 1.297.

LOWER NEWPORT, p. o., Washington co., O.

LOWER OXFORD, p. t., Chester co., Pa., 64 ms. s. E. of Harrisburgh; from W. 94 ms. Watered by tributaries of Octarara and Elk creeks. Pop. 1,341.

LOWER PEACH TREE, p. o., Wilcox co., Ala.; from W. 907 ms.

LOWER PAXTON, t., Dauphin co., Pa., 6 ms. N. E. of Harrisburgh; from W. 114 ms. Watered by Beaver and Paxton's creeks. Pop. 1.572.

LOWER PENN'S NECK, t., Salem co., N. J., 60 ms. s. of Trenton; from W. 171 ms. Watered by Salem river. Pop. 1,429.

LOWER PROVIDENCE, t., Montgomery co., Pa., 84 ms. E. of Harrisburgh; from W. 141 ms. Watered by Perkiomen and Shippack creeks. Pop. 1,961.

LOWER SALEM, p. o., Salem township. Washington co., O., 114 ms. s. E. of Columbus; from W. 302 ms.

LOWER SALFORD, t., Montgomery co., Pa., 94 ms. E. of Harrisburgh; from W. 157 ms. Watered by tributaries of Perkiomen and Shippack creeks.

LOWER SANDUSKY, c. h., v., Sandusky township, seat of justice of Sandusky co., O., 105 ms. N. of Columbus; from W. 423 ms. Watered by Sandusky river.

LOWER SAUCON, p. o., Northampton co., Pa., 99 ms. N. E. of Harrisburgh; from W. 192 ms. Watered by Lehigh river and Saucon creek.

LOWER SQUANKUM, p. o., Monmouth co., N. J.

LOWER SMITHFIELD, t., Monroe co., Pa.

LOWER SWATARA, t., Dauphin co., Pa., 5 ms. s. E. of Harrisburgh. Watered by Susquehanna river and Spring creek. Pop. 750.

LOWER THREE RUNS, p. o., Barnwell district, S. C., 128 ms. s. of Columbia; from W. 624 ms.

LOWER ST. CLAIR, t., Alleghany co., Pa. Watered by Monongahela and Ohio rivers. Pop. 5,930.

LOWER WATERFORD, p. o., Caledonia co., Vt., 53 ms. N. E. of Montpelier; from W. 543 ms.

LOWER WINDSOR, t., York co., Pa. Pop. 1,923.

LOWERY, p. o., Barnwell district, S. C.

LOWEVILLE, p. o., Meriwether co., Ga.

LOW HAMPTON, p. o., Hampton township, Washington co., N. Y., 78 ms. N. E. of Albany; from W. 448 ms.

LOWHILL, p. t., Lehigh co., Pa., 88 ms. N. E. of Harrisburgh; from W. 181 ms. Pop. 1,021.

LOWNDES COUNTY, situated on the south boundary of Georgia. Area, 2,080 square miles. Seat of justice, Troupsville. Pop. in 1830, 2,453; in 1840, 5,574; in 1850, 8,351.

LOWNDES COUNTY, situated toward the south part of Alabama, with Alabama river on the north. Area 1,600 square miles. Seat of justice, Lowndesborough. Pop. in 1830, 9,410; in 1840, 19,539; in 1850, 21,915.

LOWNDES COUNTY, situated on the east boundary of Mississippi, and traversed by Tombigbee river. Area, 324 square miles. Seat of justice, Columbus. Pop. in 1830, 3,169; in 1840, 14,513; in 1850, 19,544.

LOWNDES, p. o., Wayne co., Mo., 209 ms. s. E. of Jefferson City; from W. 920 ms.

LOWNDESBOROUGH, p. v., Lowndes co., Ala.; from W. 858 ms.

LOWNDESVILLE, p. v., Abbeville district, S. C., 113 ms. w. of Columbia; from W. 550 ms.

LOW POINT, p. o., Woodford co., Ill.

LOWRANCE'S MILL, p. o., Lincoln co., N. C., 166 ms. w. of Raleigh; from W. 403 ms.

LOWRY, p. o., Athens co., O.

LOWRYVILLE, p. o., Hardin co., Tenn.

LOW'S CORNER, p. o., Sullivan co., N. Y.

LOWVILLE, p. t., Lewis co., N. Y., 137 ms. N. w. of Albany; from W. 436 ms. Watered by Black river. Pop. 2,377.

LOWVILLE, p. o., Columbia co., Wis.

LOYD, p. o., Ulster co., N. Y.

LOYDSVILLE, p. o., Benton co., Ala.

LOYALHANNAH, p. t., Westmoreland co., Pa. Pop. 1,258.

LOYALSOCK, t., Lycoming co., Pa., 94 ms. N. of Harrisburgh; from W. 203 ms. Pop. 1,581.

LOYDSVILLE, p. o., Belmont co., O., 109 ms. E. of Columbus; from W. 284 ms.

LOY'S CROSS-ROADS, p. o., Anderson co., Tenn., 194 ms. E. of Nashville; from W. 500 ms.

LUBEC, p. t., Washington co., Me., 180 ms. N. E. of Augusta; from W. 766 ms. Watered by Passamaquoddy bay. Pop. 2,814.

LUBEC MILLS, p. o., Lubec township, Washington co., Me.

LUCAS COUNTY, situated on the north boundary of Ohio, with Maumee river on the southeast. Area, 600 square miles. Seat of justice, Maumee City. Pop. in 1840, 9,382; in 1850, 12,263.

LUCAS COUNTY, situated in the southerly part of Iowa. Area, —— square miles. Seat of justice, Chariton. Pop. in 1850, 471.

LUCAS, p. o., Richland co., O.

LUCASVILLE, p. v., Jefferson township, Scioto co., O., 78 ms. s. of Columbus; from W. 412 ms.

LUCERNE, p. o., Washtenaw co., Mich., 38 ms. w. of Detroit; from W. 542 ms.

LUCERNE, p. o., Knox co., O.

LUCINDA FURNACE, p. o., Clarion co., Pa.

LUCKY HIT, p. o., Limestone co., Ala.

LUDA, p. o., Wachita co., Ark.

LUDLOW, p. t., Windsor co., Vt., 80 ms. s. of Montpelier, from W. 472 ms. Watered by Black river. Pop. 1,619.

LUDLOW, p. t., Hampden co., Mass., 82 ms. w. of Boston; from W. 373 ms. Watered by Chickapee river. Pop. 1,186.

LUDLOW, p. o., Scott co., Miss.

LUDLOW, t., Washington co., O. Pop. 1,051.

LUDLOW, p. o., Dubois co., Ind.

LUDLOWVILLE, p. v., Lansing t., Tompkins co., N. Y., 172 ms. w. of Albany; from W. 305 ms. Watered by Salmon creek.

LUMBER CITY, p. v., Telfair co., Ga., 138 ms. s. E. of Milledgeville; from W. 750 ms.

LUMBER, t., Clinton co., Pa. Pop. 1,182.

LUMBERLAND, p. t., Sullivan co., N. Y., 199 s. w. of Albany; from W. 287 ms. Watered by Mongoup river. Pop. 2.635.

LUMBERPORT, p. v., Harrison co., Va., 261 ms. N. w. of Richmond; from W. 221 ms.

LUMBERTON, p. v., Clinton co., O., 74 ms. s. w. of Columbus; from W. 453 ms.

LUMBERTON, c. h., p. v., seat of justice of Robeson co., N. C., 91 ms. s. of Raleigh; from W. 379 ms. Watered by Lumber river.

LUMBERTON, p. o., Burlington co., N. J.

LUMBERVILLE, p. v. Solebury township, Bucks co., Pa., 117 ms. E. of Harrisburgh; from W. 179 ms. Watered by Delaware river.

LUMPKIN COUNTY, situated in the northern part of Georgia. Area, 700 square miles. Face of the country hilly. Seat of justice, Dahlonega. Pop. in 1840, 5,671; in 1850, 8,954.

LUMPKIN, p. v., seat of justice of Stewart co., Ga., 137 ms. s. w. of Milledgeville; from W. 793 ms. Watered by Hannahatchie creek.

LUNENBURGH COUNTY, situated in the south part of Virginia. Area, 400 square miles. Face of the country diversified; soil productive. Seat of justice, Lewiston. Pop. in 1810, 12,265; in 1820, 10,662; in 1830, 11,957; in 1840, 11,055; in 1850, 11.692.

LUNENBURGH, p. t., Essex co., Vt., 58 ms. N. E. of Montpelier; from W. 567 ms. Watered by Connecticut river. Pop. 1,123.

LUNENBURGH, p. t., Worcester co., Mass., 46 ms. N. w. of Boston; from W. 428 ms. Watered by tributaries of Nashua river. Pop. 1,249.

LUNENBURGH, c. h., p. v., seat of justice of Lunenburgh co., Va., 78 ms. s. w. of Richmond; from W. 197 ms.

LUNEY'S CREEK, p. o., Hardy co., Va., 190 ms. N. w. of Richmond; from W. 142 ms.

LURAY, c. h., p. v., seat of justice of Page co., Va., 130

ms. N. w. of Richmond ; from W. 96 ms. Watered by Hawkskill creek.

LURAY, p. v., Henry co., Ind., 57 ms. E. of Indianapolis ; from W. 538 ms.

LURGAN, t., Franklin co., Pa. Watered by branches of Conedogwinnet creek. Pop. 1,228.

LUTHERSBURGH, p. v., Clearfield co., Pa., 145 ms. N. w. of Harrisburgh ; from W. 237 ms.

LUTHERSVILLE, p. v., Meriwether co., Ga., 108 ms. w. of Milledgeville ; from W. 727 ms.

LUZERNE COUNTY, situated toward the northeasterly part of Pennsylvania, and traversed by Susquehanna river. Area, 1,350 square miles. Face of the country hilly and mountainous ; soil varied ; in the valleys, generally rich. Seat of justice, Wilkesbarre. Pop. in 1810, 18,109 ; in 1820, 20,027 ; in 1830, 27,304 ; in 1840, 44,006 ; in 1850, 56,072.

LUZERNE, p. t., Fayette co., Pa. Watered by Dunlap's creek. Pop. 1.869.

LUZERNE, p. t., Warren co., N. Y., 55 ms. of Albany ; from W. 432 ms. Watered by Hudson river. Pop. 1,300.

LUZERNE. p. o., Fond du Lac co., Wis.

LYCOMING COUNTY, situated toward the north part of Pennsylvania, and traversed by West branch of Susquehanna river. Area, 1,600 square miles. Face of the country hilly and broken ; soil, in the valleys, fertile. Seat of justice, Williamsport. Pop. in 1810, 11,006 ; in 1820, 13,517 ; in 1830, 17,637 ; in 1840, 22,649 ; in 1850, 26,257.

LYCOMING, t., Lycoming co., Pa. Watered by Lycoming creek. Pop. 1,275.

LYCOMING CREEK, p. o., Lycoming co., Pa.

LYCURGUS, p. o., Allamakee co., Iowa.

LYELL'S STORE, p. o., Richmond co., Va.

LYKENS, t., Dauphin co., Pa., 26 ms. N. of Harrisburgh ; from W. — ms. Watered by Wisconisco river and Little Mahantango creek. Pop. 1,371.

LYKINS, t., Crawford co., O. Pop. 1.185.

LYMAN, p. t., York co., Me., 72 ms. s. w. of Augusta ; from W. 523 ms. Watered by tributaries of Saco and Kennebunk rivers. Pop. 1,376.

LYMAN, p. t., Grafton co., N. H., 90 ms. N. w. of Concord ; from W. 533 ms. Watered by Connecticut, Burnham's, and Ammonoosuck rivers. Pop. 1,442.

LYMAN CENTRE, p. o., Lyman township, York co., Me., 74 ms. s. w. of Augusta ; from W. 522 ms.

LYMANSVILLE, p. v., Potter, Pa., 167 ms. N. w. of Harrisburgh ; from W. 277 ms.

LYME, p. t., Grfaton co., N. H., 53 ms. N. w. of Concord ; from W. 498 ms. Watered by Connecticut river. Pop. 1,617.

LYME, p. t., New London co., Ct., 45 ms. s. of Hartford from W. 338 ms. Watered by Connecticut river. Pop. 2,668.

LYME, t., Jefferson co., N. Y., 172 ms. N. w. of Albany ; from W. 425 ms. Watered by Chaumont and St. Lawrence rivers and Lake Ontario. Pop. 2,119.

LYME, p. t., Huron co., O., 99 ms. N. of Columbus ; from W. 402 ms.

LYNCHBURGH, p. v., Campbell co., Va., 116 ms. w. of Richmond ; from W. 191 ms. Watered by James river. Pop. 8,071.

LYNCHBURGH, p. v., Lincoln co., Tenn., 78 ms. s. of Nashville ; from W. 701 ms. Watered by a tributary of Elk river.

LYNCHBURGH, p. v., Dodson township, Highland co., O, 88 ms. s. w. of Columbus ; from W. 451 ms. Watered by East fork of Little Miami river.

LYNCHBURGH, p. o., Sumter district, S. C.

LYNCHBURGH, p. o., Coosa co., Ala.

LYNCH'S CREEK, p. v., Marion district, S. C., 151 ms. F of Columbia ; from W. 448 ms. Watered by Lynch's creek.

LYNCH'S LAKE, p. o., Williamsburgh district, S. C.

LYNCHWOOD, p. v., Kershaw district, S. C., 51 ms. N. E. of Columbus ; from W. 365 ms.

LYNDEBOROUGH, p. t., Hillsbourgh co., N. H., 33 ms. s. w. of Concord ; from W. 461 ms. Watered by tributaries of Souhegan river. Pop. 968.

LYNDON, p. v., Whitesides co., Ill., 180 ms. N. of Springfield : from W- 855 ms.

LYNDON, p. t., Caledonia co.,Vt., 44 ms. N. E. of Montpelier ; from W. 554 ms. Watered by Pasumpsic river. Pop. 1,752.

LYNDON, t., Cattaraugus co., N. Y., 274 ms. w. of Albany ; from W. 319 ms. Watered by Ischua and Oil creeks. Pop. 1,092.

LYNDON, v., Yates township, Orleans co., N. Y., 270 ms. w. of Albany ; from W. 416 ms.

LYNDON CENTRE, p. o., Lyndon township, Caledonia co., Vt., 46 ms. N. E. of Montpelier ; from W. 556 ms.

LYNDONVILLE, p. o., Lyndon township, Orleans co., N. Y.

LYNESVILLE, p. v., Granville co., N. C., 54 ms. N. of Raleigh ; from W. 241 ms.

LYNN, p. t., Essex co., Mass., 9 ms. N. E. of Boston ; from W. 449 ms. Watered by Saugus river, Lynn bay. and the Atlantic ocean, embracing the romantic and rocky peninsula of Nahant. Pop. in 1830, 6,138 ; in 1840, 9,367 ; in 1850, 14,257.

LYNN, p. o., Susquehanna co., Pa., 169 ms. N. E. of Harrisburgh ; from W. 276 ms.

LYNN, t., Lehigh co., Pa. Pop. 1,997.

LYNN, p. o., Posey co., Ind., 169 ms. s. w. of Indianapolis ; from W. 745 ms. Pop. 1,227.

LYNN, p. o., Randolph co., Ind.

LYNN, p. o., Calumet co., Wis.

LYNN CAMP, p. o., Knox co., Ky., 107 ms. s. E. of Frankfort ; from W. 531 ms.

LYNNFIELD, p. t., Essex co., Mass., 20 ms. N. of Boston ; from W. 460 ms. Watered by Ipswich river and several ponds. Pop. 1,723.

LYNNFIELD CENTRE, p. o., Lynnfield township, Essex co., Mass.

LYNNVILLE, p. v., Lynn township, Lehigh co., Pa., 83 ms. N. E. of Harrisburgh ; from W. 175 ms.

LYNNVILLE, p. v., Warrick co., Ind., 162 ms. s. w. of Indianapolis ; from W. 700 ms. Watered by head branches of Great Pigeon creek.

LYNNVILLE, p. v., Giles co., Tenn., 60 ms. s. of Nashville ; from W. 724 ms. Watered by Richland creek.

LYNNVILLE, p. v., Morgan co., Ill., 41 ms. w. of Springfield ; from W. 821 ms.

LYNNVILLE, p. v., Jasper co., Iowa.

LYON, t., Oakland co., Mich.

LYONS, c. h., p. t., seat of justice of Wayne co., N. Y., 180 ms. w. of Albany ; from W. 357 ms. Watered by Clyde river, at the confluence of Mud creek and Canandagua outlet, and the Erie canal. Pop. 4,925.

LYONS, p. o., Fulton co., O., 165 ms. N. w. of Columbus ; from W. 496 ms.

LYONS, p. t., Ionia co., Mich., 134 ms. N. w. of Detroit ; from W. 628 ms., at the head of steamboat navigation. Watered by Grand river. Pop. 850.

LYONS, p. o., Clinton co., Iowa.

LYONS, p. o., Cook co., Ill.

LYONS, p. o., Walworth co., Wis.

LYONS, p. o., Fayette co., Tex.

LYONSDALE, p. o., Greig township, Lewis co., N. Y., 122 ms. N. w. of Albany ; from W. 426 ms.

LYON'S HOLLOW, p. o., Steuben co., N. Y.

LYON'S LANDING, p. o., Bladen co., N. C.

LYON'S STORE, p. o., Hawkins co., Tenn., 257 ms. E. of Nashville ; from W. 425 ms.

LYRA, p. o., Scioto co., O.

LYSANDER, p. t., Onondaga co., N. Y., 144 ms. w. of Albany ; from W. 364 ms. Watered by Seneca riv. Pop. 5,833

LYTHONIA, p. o., De Kalb co., Ga.

LYTLESVILLE, p. o., McLean co., Ill.

M.

MABBETTSVILLE, p. o., Washington township, Dutchess co., N. Y., 78 ms. s. of Albany ; from W. 316 ms.

MABEE'S, p. o., Jackson co., O.

MACEDON, p. o., Mercer co., O.

MACEDON, p. t., Wayne co., N. Y., 199 ms. w. of Albany ; from W. 356 ms. Watered by Mud creek. Pop. 2,384.

MACEDON CENTRE, p. o., Macedon township, Wayne co., N. Y., 202 ms. w. of Albany ; from W. 359 ms.

MACEDONIA. p. v., Carroll co., Tenn., 108 ms. w. of Nashville ; from W. 793 ms.

MACEDONIA, p. o. Montgomery co., N. C.

MACEDONIA, p. o., Potawatamie co., Iowa.

MACHIAS, c. h., p. t., seat of justice of Washington co., Me., 151 ms. E. of Augusta ; from W. 773 ms. Watered by west branch of Machias river. Pop. 1,590.

MACHIAS, p. t., Cattaraugus co., N. Y., 286 ms. w. of Albany ; from W. 333 ms. Watered by Ischua creek, and Lime lake outlet. Pop. 1,242.

MACHIAS PORT, p. o., Washington co., Me., 155 ms. E. of Augusta ; from W. 777 ms. Watered by Machias river.

MACKEREL CORNER, p. o., Carroll co., N. H.

MACKESVILLE, p. o., Clark co., Miss.

MACKINAC, c. h., p. v., seat of justice of Michilimackinac co., Mich., 300 ms. N. w. of Detroit ; from W. 821 ms. Situated on an island of the same name, near the straits of Mackinaw.

MACKINAW, p. o., Tazewell co., Ill., 64 ms. N. of Springfield ; from W. 764 ms.

MACKSBURGH, p. o., Giles co., Va.

MACK'S PLACE, p. o., St. Clair co., Mich.

MACKSVILLE, p. v., Randolph co., Ind., 75 ms. N. E. of Indianapolis ; from W. 512 ms.

MACKVILLE, p., v., Washington co., Ky., 45 ms. s. w. of Frankfort ; from W. 567 ms.

MACOMB COUNTY, situated in the east part of Michigan, on Lake St. Clair. Area, 485 square miles. Face of the country, undulating ; soil, fertile. Seat of justice, Mount Clemens. Pop. in 1830, 2,413 ; in 1840, 9,716 ; in 1850, 15,530.

MACOMB. c. h., p. v., seat of justice of McDonough co., Ill., 86 ms. N. w. of Springfield : from W. 859 ms.

MACOMB. p. t., Macomb co., Mich., 35 ms. N. E. of Detroit, from W. 569 ms. Watered by Clinton river. Pop. 757.

MACOMB, p. o., St. Lawrence co., N. Y.

MACON COUNTY, situated in the central part of Illinois. Area, 1,400 square miles. Seat of justice, Decatur. Pop. in 1830, 1,122; in 1840, 3,039, in 1850, 3,988.

MACON COUNTY, situated on the south boundary of North Carolina. Area, 900 square miles. Face of the country, elevated and mountainous. Seat of justice, Franklin. Pop. in 1830, 5,333 ; in 1840, 4,869 ; in 1850. 6,389.

MACON COUNTY, situated toward the south west part of Georgia, and traversed by Flint river. Area, 420 square miles. Seat of justice, Lanier. Pop. in 1840, 5,045 ; in 1850, 7,052.

MACON COUNTY, situated toward the southeast part of Alabama, with Tallapoosa river on the northwest. Area, 970 square miles. Seat of justice, Tuskegee. Pop. in 1840, 11,247 ; in 1850, 26,898.

MACON COUNTY, situated in the northerly part of Missouri, and traversed by Chariton river. Area, 846 square miles. Seat of justice, Bloomington. Pop. in 1840, 6,034 ; in 1850, 6,565.

MACON COUNTY, situated on the north boundary of Tennessee. Area, —— square miles. Seat of justice, Lafayette. Pop. in 1850, 6,948.

MACON, p. o., Powhattan co., Va., 40 ms. w. of Richmond ; from W. 157 ms.

MACON, city, seat of justice of Bibb co., Ga., 30 ms. s. w. of Milledgeville ; from W. 686 ms. Watered by Ocmulgee river, at the head of steam navigation.

MACON, p. v., Marengo co., Ala. ; from W. 868 ms.

MACON, c. h., p. v., seat of justice of Noxubee co., Miss., 125 ms. N. E. of Jackson ; from W. 885 ms. Watered by Noxubee river.

MACON, p. t., Lenawee co., Mich., 66 ms. s. w. of Detroit ; from W. 520 ms. Watered by south branch of Raisin river. Pop. 1,030.

MACON, p. v., Fayette co., Tenn., 196 ms. s. w. of Nashville ; from W. 881 ms.

MADON DEPOT, p. o., Warren co., N. C., 67 ms. N. E. of Raleigh ; from W. 221 ms.

MACOPIN, p. o., Passaic co., N. J.

MACOUPIN COUNTY, situated toward the western boundary of Illinois. Area, 800 square miles. Face of the country level, and soil productive. Watered by Macoupin river. Seat of justice, Carlinville. Pop. in 1835, 5,554 ; in 1840, 7,826 ; in 1850. 12,355.

MACUNGIE, p. t., Lehigh co., Pa., 83 ms. N. E. of Harrisburgh ; from W. 176 ms. Watered by Jordan and Little Lehigh creeks.

MADAWASKA, t., Aroostook co., Me. Watered by St. John's river. Pop. 1.276.

MADBURY, t., Strafford co., N. H., 36 ms. E. of Concord ; from W. 494 ms. Watered by Bellamy river. Pop. 483.

MADDENVILLE, p. o., Huntingdon co., Pa.

MADDOX, p. o., Hanover co., Va.

MADISON COUNTY, situated in the central part of New York. Area, 582 square miles. Face of the country hilly ; soil fertile. Seat of justice, Morrisville. Pop. in 1810, 25,144 ; in 1820, 32,208 ; in 1830, 39,039 ; in 1840. 40.098 ; in 1850, 43,072.

MADISON COUNTY, situated toward the northeast part of Virginia. Area. 330 square miles. Face of the country uneven ; soil of middling quality. Seat of justice, Madison. Pop. in 1810. 8,381 ; in 1820, 8,490 ; in 1830, 9,236 ; in 1840, 8,107 ; in 1850. 9,331.

MADISON COUNTY, situated in the northeasterly part of Georgia. Area, 250 square miles. Face of the country hilly ; soil productive. Seat of justice, Danielsville. Pop. in 1820, 3,745 ; in 1830, 4,626 ; in 1840, 4,510 ; in 1850, 5.703.

MADISON COUNTY, situated on the north bound ary of Florida, with the gulf of Mexico on the southwest, and Suwanee river on the east. Area, —— square miles. Seat of justice, Madison. Pop. in 1840, 2,644 ; in 1850. 5,490.

MADISON COUNTY, situated on the north boundary of Alabama, with Tennessee river on the south. Area, 760 square miles. Face of the country diversified ; soil fertile. Seat of justice, Huntsville. Pop. in 1820, 17,481 ; in 1830, 27,990 ; in 1840, 25,706 ; in 1850, 26,397.

MADISON COUNTY, situated in the central part of Mississippi, with Big Black river on the northwest, and the Pearl river on the southwest. Area, 548 square miles. Seat of justice. Canton. Pop. in 1830, 4,973 ; in 1840, 15,530 ; in 1850, 18,173.

MADISON COUNTY, situated in the west part of Tennessee. Area, 670 square miles. Seat of justice, Jackson. Pop. in 1830, 11,549 ; in 1840, 16,530 ; in 1850, 21,470.

MADISON COUNTY, situated toward the east part of Kentucky, with Kentucky river on the north. Area, 520 square miles. Seat of justice, Richmond. Pop. in 1820, 15,954 ; in 1830, 18,751 ; in 1840, 16,355 ; in 1850, 15,727.

MADISON COUNTY, situated in the central part of Ohio. Area, 400 square miles. Soil productive. Seat of justice, London. Pop. in 1810. 1,603 ; in 1820, 4,799 ; in 1830, 6,190 ; in 1840, 9,025 ; in 1850, 10,046.

MADISON COUNTY, situated toward the east part of Indiana. Area, 390 square miles. Seat of justice, Andersontown. Pop. in 1830, 2,238 ; in 1840, 8,874 ; in 1850, 12,369.

MADISON COUNTY, situated on the westerly boundary of Illinois, on the Mississippi river. Area, 760 square miles. Face of the country level ; soil fertile. Seat of justice, Edwardsville. Pop. in 1830, 6,229 ; in 1840, 14,433 ; in 1850, 20,436.

MADISON COUNTY, situated in the southeasterly part of Missouri. Area, 780 square miles. Seat of justice, Fredericktown. Pop. in 1830, 2,371 ; in 1840, 3,395 ; in 1850, 6,003.

MADISON COUNTY, situated on the north boundary of Arkansas. Area, 1,050 square miles. Seat of justice, Huntsville. Pop. in 1840, 2,775 ; in 1850, 4,823.

MADISON COUNTY, situated toward the southwest part of Iowa. Area, —— square miles. Seat of justice, ——. Pop. in 1850, 1,179.

MADISON PARISH. situated on the east boundary

of Louisiana, with Mississippi river on the east. Area, 800 square miles. Seat of justice, Richmond. Pop. in 1840, 5,142 ; in 1850. 7,863.

MADISON, p. v., Morris co., N. J., 58 ms. N. of Trenton ; from 223 ms.

MADISON, p. t., Somerset co., Me., 40 ms. N. of Augusta ; from W. 635 ms. Watered by Kennebec river. Pop. 1,769.

MADISON, p. t., New Haven co., Ct., 56 ms. s. of Hartford ; from W. 320 ms. Watered by Long Island sound. Pop. 1,729.

MADISON, p. t., Madison co., N. Y., 95 ms. w. of Albany ; from W. 365 ms. Watered by head branches of Chenango river, Oriskany creek, and Chenango canal. Pop. 2.405.

MADISON, p. o., Westmoreland co., Pa., 179 ms. w. of Harrisburgh ; from W. 205 ms.

MADISON, t., Columbia co.. Pa., 89 ms. N. of Harrisburgh ; from W. 198 ms. Watered by Little Fishing and Mahoning creeks. Pop. 712.

MADISON, t., Armstrong co., Pa. Pop. 1,151.

MADISON, t., Perry co., Pa. Pop. 1,292.

MADISON. p. t., Lake co., O., 190 ms. N. E. of Columbus ; from W. 349 ms. Watered by Grand river. Pop. 2,986.

MADISON, t., Clark co., O., 40 ms. w. of Columbus ; from W. 436 ms. Pop. 949.

MADISON, p. t., Columbiana co., O., 164 ms. N. E. of Columbus ; from W. 286 ms. Pop. 1,406.

MADISON, t., Butler co., O., 93 ms. s. w. of Columbus ; from W. 490 ms. Pop. 2,242.

MADISON, t., Fayette co., O., 35 ms. s. w. of Columbus ; from W. 412 ms. Pop. 865.

MADISON, t., Franklin co., O., 6 ms. from Columbus ; from W. 386 ms. Watered by Alum, Big Walnut, and Black Lick creeks. Pop. 2.480.

MADISON, t., Fairfield co., O., 31 ms. s. E. of Columbus ; from W. 369 ms. Pop. 1.164.

MADISON, t., Guernsey co., O., 93 ms. from Columbus ; from W. 304 ms. Pop. 1,519.

MADISON, t., Jackson co., O., 84 ms. s. E. of Columbus ; from W. 380 ms. Watered by Symmes' creek. Pop. 1,515.

MADISON, t., Licking co., O., 35 ms. N. E. of Columbus ; from W. 359 ms. Watered by Licking river, and the Ohio canal. Pop. 1.027.

MADISON, t., Highland co., O., 68 ms. s. w. of Columbus ; from W. 427 ms. Pop. 1,163.

MADISON, p. t., Montgomery co., O. Pop. 1,668.

MADISON, p. t., Muskingum co., O. Pop. 1,047.

MADISON. t., Pickaway co., O., 12 ms. s. of Columbus , from W. 360 ms. Pop 885.

MADISON, t., Perry co., O., 47 ms. s. E. of Columbus ; from W. 353 ms. Pop. 988.

MADISON, p. t., Richland co.. O. Pop. 1.732.

MADISON, t., Sandusky co., O. Pop. 389.

MADISON, t., Scioto co., O. Pop. 1,367.

MADISON, p. v., Rockingham co., N. C., 116 ms. N. W. of Raleigh ; from W. 296 ms.

MADISON, c. h., p. v.. seat of justice of Morgan co., Ga., 41 ms. N. w. of Milledgeville ; from W, 625 ms.

MADISON, city, p. v.. seat of justice of Jefferson co., Ind., 88 ms. s. E. of Indianapolis ; from W. 560 ms. Watered by Ohio river. Pop. 7,908.

MADISON, p. t.. Jefferson co., Ind. Pop. 3,193.

MADISON, t., Montgomery co., Ind., 49 ms. N. w. of Indianapolis ; from W. 622 ms. Pop. 651.

MADISON, t., Putnam co., Ind., 47 ms. from Indianapolis ; from W. 619 ms. Pop. 1,199.

MADISON, t., Lenawee co., Mich. Pop. 2,404.

MADISON, t., Sevier co., Ark. Pop. 350.

MADISON, t., Clarke co., Mo.

MADISON, t., Polk co., Mo.

MADISON, t., Livingston co., Mo.

MADISON, t., Johnson co., Mo. Pop. 668.

MADISON, p. v., Monroe co., Mo., 83 ms. N. of Jefferson city ; from W. 943 ms.

MADISON, c. h., p. v., seat of justice of Madison co., Va.. 97 ms. N. w. of Richmond ; from W. 98 ms.

MADISON, c. h., p. v., seat of justice of Madison co., Flor.

MADISON, c. h., p. v., seat of justice of Dane co., and capital of Wis. It occupies a delightful position on a strip of land between Third and Fourth lakes, two of a chain of four beautiful sheets of water, not far apart, and connected by streams. It is 90 miles w. of Milwaukie ; from W. 847 ms. From the former lake, the shore rises abruptly 50 feet, and, gradually, 20 feet

higher. Upon this elevation stands the statehouse, a prominent structure of stone, in the centre of a large park, which overlooks an enchanting panorama of lakes, lawns, groves, hills, vales, and winding streams. Toward Fourth lake, the ground again descends with different degrees of steepness, the whole distance from one shore to the other being about three fourths of a mile. The university of Wisconsin is delightfully situated upon an eminence, 125 feet above the lakes. The beauty and healthfulness of location, central position, business, and political advantages of Madison, are elements of permanent prosperity, if not of rapid progress, and it bids fair to become one of the largest towns in the state. Pop. in 1840, 376 ; in 1850, 1,871.

MADISON, p. v., Livingston co., Mich.

MADISONBURGH, p. o., Wayne co., O.

MADISONBOROUGH, p. o., Alachua co., Flor.

MADISON CENTRE, p. o., Madison township, Somerset co., Me., 43 ms. N. of Augusta ; from W. 638 ms.

MADISON CROSS-ROADS, p. o., Madison co., Ala ; from W. 723 ms.

MADISON MILLS, p. o., Madison co., Va.

MADISON SPRINGS, p. v., Madison co., Ga., 99 ms. N. of Milledgeville ; from W. 597 ms. Site of a salubrious mineral spring.

MADISONVILLE, p. v., Columbia township, Hamilton co., O., 120 ms. s. w. of Columbus ; from W. 492 ms.

MADISONVILLE, c. h., p. v., seat of justice of Hopkins co., Ky., 127 ms. s. w. of Frankfort ; from W. 729 ms.

MADISONVILLE, p. v., seat of justice of Monroe co., Tenn., 172 ms. s. E. of Nashville ; from W. 540 ms.

MADISONVILLE, p. v., Ralls co., Mo., 96 ms. N. E. of Jefferson city ; from W. 900 ms.

MADISONVILLE, p. v., St. Tammany parish, La., 35 ms. N. w. of New Orleans ; from W. 1,137 ms. Watered by Chefonte river.

MADISONVILLE, p. v.. Madison co., Miss., 20 ms. N.E. of Jackson ; from W. 990 ms.

MADRID, p. t., Franklin co., Me., 105 ms. N. w. of Augusta. Watered by head branches of Sandy river. Pop. 404.

MADRID, p. t., St. Lawrence co., N. Y., 235 ms. N. w. of Albany ; from W. 505 ms. Watered by Grass and St. Lawrence rivers. Pop. 4,856.

MAD RIVER, t., Champaign co., O., 54 ms. w. of Columbus ; from W. 450 ms. Watered by head branches of Mad river. Pop. 1,907.

MAD RIVER, t., Clark co., O., 47 ms. w. of Columbus ; from W. 444 ms. Pop 1,496.

MAGAZINE, t., Yell co., Ark. Pop. 571.

MAGNOLIA, p. o., Chautauque township, Chautauque co.. N. Y., 346 ms. w. of Albany ; from W. 333 ms.

MAGNOLIA, p. o., Harford co., Md.

MAGNOLIA, p. o., Washington co., Va.

MAGNOLIA, p. o., Stark co., O., 128 ms. N. E. of Columbus ; from W. 311 ms.

MAGNOLIA, p. o., Putnam co., Ill., 103 ms. N. of Springfield ; from W. 796 ms.

MAGNOLIA, p. o., Rock co., Wis.

MAGNOLIA, p. o., Crawford co., Ind.

MAGNOLIA, p. o., Anderson co., Tex.

MAGNOLIA, p. o., La Rue co., Ky.

MAGNOLIA SPRINGS, p. o., Jasper co., Tex.

MAHALA, p. o., Adams co., O.

MAHANOY, p. o., Northumberland co., Pa., 48 ms. N. of Harrisburg ; from W. 155 ms.

MAHASKA COUNTY, situated toward the south part of Iowa, and traversed by Des Moines river. Area, —— square miles. Seat of justice, Oskaloosa. Pop. in 1850, 5,989.

MAHOMET, p. o.. Champaign co., Ill., 87 ms. E. of Springfield ; from W. 704 ms.

MAHONING COUNTY, situated on the east boundary of Ohio. Area, —— square miles. Seat of justice, Canfield. Pop. in 1850, 23,735.

MAHONING, t., Montour co., Pa., from W. 275 ms. Pop. 867.

MAHONING. t., Carbon co., Pa. ; from W. 175 ms. Watered by Susquehanna river, and Mahoning creek. Pop. 1,521.

MAHONING, p. t., Lawrence co., Pa., 65 ms. N. of Harrisburgh ; from W. 226 ms. Watered by Great and Little Mahoning creeks. Pop. 1,841.

MAHONING, p. o., Stark co., O., 142 ms. N. E. of Columbus ; from W. 305 ms.

MAHOPAC, p. o., Oakland co.. Mich.

MAHOPAK, p. o., Carmel township, Putnam co., N. Y., near Mahopak lake.

MAIDEN CREEK, p. t., Berks co., Pa., 60 ms. E. of Harrisburgh; from W. 153 ms. Watered by Schuylkill river, and Maiden creek.

MAIDEN SPRING, p. o., Tazewell co., Va., 295 ms. w. of Richmond; from W. 350 ms.

MAIDSTON, p. t., Essex co., Vt., 54 ms. N. E. of Montpelier; from W. 570 ms. Pop. 237.

MAINE, one of the United States, lying on its northeastern border, so called ed from *Maine*, a department of France, of which Henrietta Maria, queen of England, was proprietor. It lies between 43° 5′ and 47° 20′ north latitude, and 66° 49′ and 71° 4′ west longitude from Greenwich, and is bounded north by Canada East, from which it is separated by the river St. John's, east by New Brunswick, from which it is separated in part by the St. Croix, south by the Atlantic, west by New Hampshire, from which it is separated in part by Piscataqua and Salmon Falls rivers, and northwest by Canada East. Superficial area, 32,628 square miles.

Physical Aspect.—On the seaboard the surface is generally level, though not very fertile. Some ten or twenty miles back the soil is sandy, gravelly, clayey, or loamy, seldom very rich, but tolerably fertile in some places, though oftener poor. In the tract lying north of this, extending from fifty to ninety miles from the sea, the same kinds of soil are found, but generally more fertile. The surface rises into large swells of generally good soil, between which, along the margins of the streams, are frequently rich "intervale," or alluvial lands; while in other places sandy or gravelly pine plains occur, or spruce or cedar swamps. In the central parts of the state, the surface is more broken; and in many of the river valleys the soil is not exceeded in fertility in any of the other New England states. At the extreme north the country is less hilly, and is but little settled.

Mountains.—On the western side of the state, a little to the eastward of the White mountains, in New Hampshire, an irregular chain of high lands commences and extends northeastwardly, more or less interrupted, to the easterly boundary of the state, terminating at an isolated peak, 1,683 feet in height, called Mars hill. Katahdin mountain, which may be considered as a part of the above-named range, is much the highest land in the state, being 5,335 feet above the level of the sea. Agamenticus, which is of considerable elevation, is in York, near the southwest corner of the state.

Rivers, Lakes, and Bays.—The principal rivers are the Penobscot, Kennebec, Androscoggin, Saco, Sheepscot, Damariscotta, Machias, Salmon Falls, Piscataqua, St. Croix, and the St. John's. The lakes, or ponds, are rather numerous, the most noted of which are Moosehead, Umbagog, Sebago, Schoodic, Chesuncook, Pemadumcook, and Mooselogmaguntic. The principal bays are Casco, Penobscot, Frenchman's, Englishman's, Machias, and Passamaquoddy.

Islands.—The chief islands are Mount Desert, Deer, Long, Boon, Fox, and Cranberry.

Climate.—Although the climate is subject to great extremes of heat and cold, the air in all parts of the state is salubrious and pure. Near the ocean and bays, the heats of summer are greatly tempered by the breezes; and the rigors of winter, though severe, are more uniform and less trying to health than in many situations farther south. The range of the temperature varies from 100° Fahrenheit to 27° below zero. Snow often lies upon the ground from four to five months in the year.

Productive Resources.—The principal products of the state are horses, neat cattle, sheep, swine, poultry, wool, butter, cheese, sugar, hay, wheat, rye, barley, oats, potatoes, and Indian corn. Among the other resources are lime, lumber, ice, and fish.

Manufactures.—There are about twenty cotton, and double that number of woollen factories in the state. Ship-building is also extensively carried on.

Railroads and Canals.—The railroads already com-

pleted in Maine are of essential value to the interests of the state. They extend about 500 miles, and connect Portland, the commercial capital, with important points in Maine, and with Boston and Montreal. The only canal in this state is the Cumberland and Oxford canal, connecting Portland with Sebago pond, 20 miles, and by a lock in Sago river, navigation is extended to Long pond, 31 miles farther. It cost about $250,000.

Commerce.—The commerce and navigation of this state are mostly confined to coasting and fishing. Its principal exports are lumber, stone, lime, fish, prepared meats, &c. Its commerce with foreign states, in 1850, amounted to about two and a half millions of dollars; and the shipping owned within the state to somewhat over half a million of tons.

Education.—The common schools in Maine are supported by the districts in which they are located. They number over 5,000. The principal collegiate institutions are Bowdoin college, at Brunswick, to which is attached a medical school, and Waterville college, at Waterville. There are theological seminaries at Bangor and Redfield, and upward of 100 academies in various parts of the state.

Population.—In 1790, 96,540; in 1800, 151,719; in 1810, 228,705; in 1820, 298,335; in 1830, 399,955; in 1840, 501,796; in 1850, 583,188.

Government is vested in a governor, senate, and house of representatives, who are elected annually on the 2d Monday in September. The senate can not be less than 20, nor exceed 31 members; the house of representatives can not be less than 100, nor exceed 200 members. Seven councillors are elected by the legislature, to advise the governor in his executive duties. The judicial power is vested in a supreme judicial court, and such other courts as the legislature may establish. Judges are appointed by the governor, and hold their offices during good behavior, or until seventy years of age. The right of suffrage is vested in every male citizen, 21 years of age (except paupers, persons under guardian ship, and Indians not taxed), who shall have resided three months in the state next preceding an election.

History.—This state embraces a part of New France, as named by Verrazanni, in 1524; or a portion of Acadia, as granted to De Monts in 1603; or a part of North Virginia, or the Plymouth Company, as claimed by the English in 1606; or, more recently, a part of the territory of the "Council of Plymouth," chartered in 1620. In 1622, a grant was made to Ferdinand Gorges and John Mason, of all the country between Merrimack and Kennebec rivers, extending interior to the lakes and rivers of New France, or Canadas, which they called "Laconia." In 1629, that portion of this tract lying between the Merrimack and Piscataqua, extending sixty miles from the sea, was conveyed to Mason alone, and then first received the name of "New Hampshire." In 1633, Gorges obtained a royal charter, constituting him lord proprietor of the province; but, from his stately scheme of government, the people became dissatisfied, and sought protection of Massachusetts, who took them under her jurisdiction in 1652, and called it the county of Yorkshire. In 1677 she purchased the claims of the heirs of Gorges, as to both jurisdiction and soil. In 1686 Sir Edmund Andros was appointed royal governor over all New England. Plymouth, Massachusetts, New Hampshire, and Rhode Island, immediately submitted to his jurisdiction. A few months after Connecticut was added, and in 1688 his power was further extended over New York, and New Jersey. In 1691, Plymouth, Massachusetts, Maine, Acadia, or Nova Scotia, were formed into one royal colony, under Governor Phipps, upon which Plymouth lost her separate government, contrary to her wishes; while New Hampshire, then under the protection of Massachusetts, was forcibly severed from her. Massachusetts obtained a confirmation of her charter, and, through long disputes with the Indians and the French, those additions to her territory were maintained under her jurisdiction until she became an independent state. The first settlement made in Maine was by the "Sagahahock colony," which consisted of one hundred planters, under the command of George Popham. They landed at the mouth of the Kennebec, in 1607 (thirteen years before the settlement of Plymouth), at the place now called Hill's Point, Phippsburg, and erected a few cabins, a storehouse, and some slight fortifications, naming their plantation "St. George." Seventy-five of the number were left to pass the winter, who lost their storehouse by fire, and their president by death; and the year following they

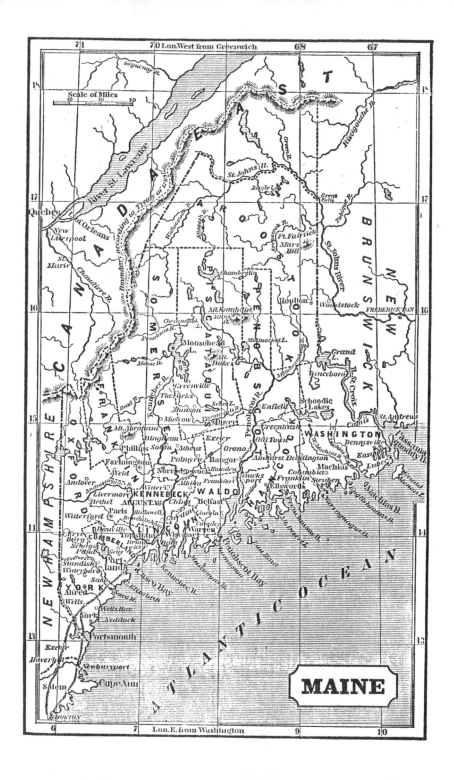

MAINE

abandoned the enterprise, and returned to England. The first permanent settlement was in Bristol, as early as 1620, Maine, from its first corporation, was a district of Plymouth, or Massachusetts, and was usually called the "province or district of Maine." Although it had long been sufficiently populous to become a state, and efforts had been made for that purpose, in 1785–'86, and in 1802, it was not admitted into the Union before 1820, when it became a sovereign state. The motto of its seal is *Dirigo*, "I direct," having reference to the north star on the crest of the coat-of-arms, which is a directing point to the mariner; it also implies that this state was the northernmost member of the confederation at the time of its admission.

MAINE, p. v., Union township, Broome co., N. Y., 107 ms. s. w. of Albany; from W. 296 ms.

MAINE, p. o., Cook co., Ill,

MAINESBURGH, p. o., Tioga co., Pa., 142 ms. N. of Harrisburgh; from W. 252 ms.

MAINEVILLE, p. o., Columbia co., Pa.

MALAGA, p. t., Monroe co., O., 110 ms. E. of Columbus; from W. 290 ms. Pop. 1,561.

MALAGA, p. v., Gloucester co., N. J., 55 ms. s. of Trenton; from W. 166 ms. Watered by a branch of Maurice river.

MALCOLM, p. o., Jefferson co., Miss., 70 ms. sl w. of Jackson; from W. 1,080 ms.

MALDEN, p. t., Middlesex co., Mass., 5 ms. N. of Boston; from W. 445 ms. Watered by Mystic river. Pop. 3,520.

MALDEN, p. v., Saugerties township, Ulster co., N. Y., 43 ms. s. of Albany; from W. 333 ms. Watered by Hudson river.

MALDEN BRIDGE, p. v., Chatham township, Columbia co., N. Y., 16 ms. s. E. of Albany; from W. 361 ms. Watered by Kinderhook creek.

MALLET CREEK, p. o.. Medina co., O., 117 ms. N. E. of Columbus; from W. 356 ms.

MALLORYSVILLE, p. v., Wilkes co., Ga., 91 ms. N. E. of Milledgeville; from W. 583 ms.

MALONE, c. h., p. t., seat of justice of Franklin co., N. Y., 214 ms. N. w. of Albany; from W. 509 ms. Watered by Salmon and Trout rivers. Pop. 4,550.

MALTA, p. t., Saratoga co., N. Y., 29 ms. N. of Albany; from W. 400 ms. Watered by Anthony's kill. Pop. 1,349.

MALTA, p. v., Morgan co., O., 72 ms. E. of Columbus; from W. 331 ms. Watered by Muskingum river. Pop. 2,308.

MALTAVILLE, p. v., Malta township, Saratoga co., N. Y. Situated near Round lake.

MALUGIN GROVE, p. o., Lee co., Ill.

MALVERN, p. o., Carroll co., O., 137 ms. N. E. of Columbus; from W. 306 ms.

MAMAKATING, p. t., Sullivan co., N. Y., l01 s. w. of Albany; from W. —— ms. Watered by Bushe's kill and Delaware and Hudson canal. Pop. 4,107.

MAMARONECK, p. t., Westchester co., N. Y., 143 ms. s. of Albany; from W. 248 ms. Watered by Mamaroneck creek and Long Island sound. Pop. 928.

MAMMELLE, t., Poinsett co., Ark.

MAMMOTH CAVE, p. o., Edmonson co., near Green river, Ky., at the great cavern of the same name, celebrated for its extent and depth, and as affording a healthy subterranean climate for invalids.

MANACK, p. o., Lowndes co., Ala.

MANAHAWKIN, p. v., Stafford township, Ocean co., N. J., 61 ms. E of Trenton; from W. 200 ms. Watered by Manahawkin creek.

MANALAPAN, p. o., Monmouth co., N. J., 26 ms. N. E., of Trenton; from W. 192 ms.

MANASQUAM, p. v., Howell township, Monmouth co., N. J.. 51 ms. s, E. of Trenton; from W. 217 ms. Watered by Manasquam river.

MANATAWNY, p. o., Berks co., Pa.

MANATEE, p. o., Hillsborough co., Flor.

MANAYUNK, p. v., Roxborough township, Philadelphia co., Pa., 99 ms. E. of Harrisburgh; from W. 144 ms. Watered by Schuylkill river and Flat Rock canal. Pop. 6,158.

MANCHAC, p. v., East Baton Rouge parish, La. Watered by Mississippi river.

MANCHAC HOUSE, p. o., Travis co., Tex.

MANCHAUG, p. o., Worcester co., Mass., 43 ms. w. of Boston; from W. 400 ms.

MANCHESTER, city and p. t., Hillsborough co., N. H., celebrated for its immense water power, and extensive manufactures, 21 ms. s. E. of Concord, from W. 461

ms., situated on the east bank of Merrimack river, which affords extensive water-power for propelling the machinery. The great chain of railroads leading from Boston and Lowell through Concord, toward Montreal and Vermont, pass through this city, and Amoskeag Falls canal here facilitates navigation between Boston and Concord. Before the year 1810, this place constituted a part of the town of Derryfield. The population in 1810, was 615; in 1820, 761; in 1830. 877; in 1840, 3,235; in 1850, 13,932.

MANCHESTER, c. h., p. v., seat of justice, together with Bennington, of Bennington co., Vt., 95 ms. s. w. of Montpelier; from W. 428 ms. Watered by Battenkill river and tributaries. Pop. 1,782.

MANCHESTER, p. t., Essex co., Mass., 23 ms. N. E. of Boston; from W. 463 ms. Watered by Massachusetts bay. Pop. 1,638.

MANCHESTER, p. t., Hartford co., Ct., 10 ms. E. of Hartford; from W. 346 ms. Watered by Hockanum river. Pop. 2,546.

MANCHESTER, p. t., Ontario co., N. Y., 202 ms. w. of Albany; from W. 348 ms. Watered by Canandaigua outlet. Pop. 2,940.

MANCHESTER, v., Kirtland, township, Oneida co., N. Y. Watered by Oriskany creek.

MANCHESTER, t., Wayne co., Pa. Pop. 749.

MANCHESTER, p. o., Ocean co., N. J.

MANCHESTER, t., Passaic co., N. J. Watered by Ramapo, Pompton, and Passaic rivers. Pop. 2,781.

MANCHESTER, p. t., York co., Pa., 18 ms. s. of Harrisburgh; from W. 96 ms. Pop. 2,603.

MANCHESTER, p. v., Carroll co., Md., 60 ms. N. w. of Annapolis; from W. 70 ms. Pop. 507.

MANCHESTER, p. v., Sprigg township, Adams co., O., 114 ms. s. of Columbus; from W. 451 ms. Watered by Ohio river.

MANCHESTER, t., Morgan co., O., 78 ms. s. E. of Columbus; from W. 332 ms. Pop. 1,337.

MANCHESTER, v. Franklin township, Summit co., O., 121 ms. N. E. of Columbus; from W. 327 ms.

MANCHESTER, p. v., Chesterfield co., Va., 2 ms. s. of Richmond; from W. 119 ms. Watered by James river.

MANCHESTER, c. h., p. v., seat of justice of Clay co., Ky., 119 ms. s. E. of Frankfort; from W. 540 ms. Watered by Goose creek.

MANCHESTER, p. t., Washtenaw co., Mich., 55 ms. w. of Detroit; from W. 523 ms. Pop. 1,275.

MANCHESTER, t., Clark co., Ark.

MANCHESTER, p. t., Dearborn co., Ind., 70 ms. s. E. of Indianapolis; from W. 524 ms. Pop. 2,748.

MANCHESTER, p. v., Scott co., Ill., 51 ms. w. of Springfield; from W. 831 ms.

MANCHESTER, p. v., St. Louis co., Mo., 108 ms. E. of Jefferson city; from W. 828 ms.

MANCHESTER. c. h., p. v., seat of justice of Coffee co., Tenn., 68 ms. s. E. of Nashville; from W. 652 ms. Watered by head branches of Duck river.

MANCHESTER, p. v., Sumter co., S. C.

MANCHESTER BRIDGE, p. o., Poughkeepsie township, Dutchess co., N. Y. Watered by Wappinger's creek.

MANCHESTER CENTRE, p. o., Manchester township, Ontario co., N. Y., 205 ms. w. of Albany; from W. 315 ms.

MANCHESTER STATION, p. o., Hartford co., Ct.

MANDANO, p. o., Skeneateles township, Onondaga co., N. Y.

MANDARIN, p. o., Duval co., Flor. Watered by St. John's river.

MANDEVILLE, p. o., St. Tammany parish, La. Watered by Lake Pontchartrain.

MANGOHICK, p. o., King William co., Va.

MANHASSET, p. v., North Hempstead township, Queen's co., Long Island, N. Y., 137 ms. s. of Albany; from W. 247 ms. Watered by Long Island sound.

MANHATTAN, p. v, Port Lawrence township, Lucas co., O., 137 ms. N. of Columbus; from W. 467 ms. Watered by Maumee river, and Lake Erie, at the terminus of Wabash and Erie canal. Pop. 541.

MANHATTAN, p. v., Putnam co., Ind., 46 ms. w. of Indianapolis; from W. 617 ms. Watered by Eel river.

MANHATTANVILLE, p. v., city and county of New York. Watered by Hudson river.

MANHEIM, p. t., Herkimer co., N. Y., 64 ms. N. w. of Albany; from W. 397 ms. Watered by East Canada creek and Mohawk river. Pop. 1,902.

MANHEIM, p. t., Lancaster co., Pa.; 33 ms. s. E. of Harrisburgh, from W. 123 ms. Watered by Moravia, and Great and Little Conestoga creeks. Pop. 2,087.

MANHEIM, t., Schuylkill co., Pa., 55 ms. N. E. of Harrisburgh ; from W. 171 ms. Watered by Schuylkill river.

MANHEIM, t., York co., Pa., 21 ms. s. of Harrisburgh ; from W. 88 ms. Watered by Hammer creek. Pop. 1,806.

MANHEIM CENTRE, p. o., Manheim township, Herkimer co., N. Y., 72 ms. N. W. of Albany ; from W. 394 ms.

MANILLA, p. o., Rush co., Ind., 42 ms. s. E. of Indianapolis ; from W. 548 ms.

MANISTEE COUNTY, situated on the west boundary of Michigan, on Lake Michigan, and traversed by Manistee river. Area, —— square miles. Seat of justice, Manistee. Pop. in 1850, 65.

MANITOOWOC COUNTY, situated on the east boundary of Wisconsin, on Lake Michigan. Area, 468 square miles. Seat of justice, Manitowoc. Pop. in 1840, 235 ; in 1850, 3,702.

MANITOOWOC, c. h., p. v., seat of justice of Manitoowoc co., Wis., 178 ms. N. E. of Madison ; from W. 900 ms. Watered by Manitoowoc river and Lake Michigan.

MANITOOWOC RAPIDS, p. o., Manitoowoc co., Wis.

MANLIUS, p. t., Onondaga co., N. Y., 121 ms. w. of Albany ; from W. 346 ms. Watered by Limestone and Chittenango creeks. Pop. 6,289.

MANLIUS, p. t., Allegan co., Mich. Pop. 82.

MANLIUS CENTRE, p. v., Manlius township, Onondaga co., N. Y., 135 ms. w. of Albany ; from W. 350 ms. Situated on the Erie canal.

MANLY, p. o., Ashe co., N. C.

MANLYVILLE, p. o., Henry co., Tenn.

MANNBOROUGH, p. v., Amelia co., Va., 46 ms. s. w. of Richmond ; from W. 165 ms.

MANNINGHAM, p. v., Butler co., Ala. ; from W. 889 ms.

MANNINGTON, p. o., Leon co., Flor.

MANINGTON, t., Salem co., N. J., 58 ms. s. of Trenton ; from W. 164 ms. Watered by Salem river and Mannington creek. Pop. 2,187.

MANN'S CHOICE, p. o., Bedford co., Pa.

MANNSVILLE, p. v., Ellisburgh township, Jefferson co., N. Y., 166 ms. N. w. of Albany ; from W. 396 ms.

MANNY, c. h., p. v., seat of justice of Sabine parish, La.

MANOR, p. t., Lancaster co., Pa., 33 ms. s. E. of Harrisburgh ; from W. 105 ms. Watered by Conestoga river and tributaries. Pop. 3,135.

MANOR HILL, p. o., Schoharie co., N. Y.

MANOR HILL, p. o., Huntingdon co., Pa., 83 ms. w. of Harrisburgh ; from W, —— ms.

MANORVILLE, p. o., Suffolk co., Long Island, N. Y.

MANSFIELD, t., Lamoille co., Vt., 20 ms. N. w. of Montpelier ; from W. —— ms. Watered by Waterbury and Brown's rivers. Pop. 1,016.

MANSFIELD, p. t., Bristol co., Mass., 29 ms. s. w. of Boston ; from W. 421 ms. Watered by tributaries of Taunton river. Pop. 1,789.

MANSFIELD, p. t., Tolland co., Ct., 24 ms. E. of Hartford ; from W. 360 ms. Watered by Willimantic and Natchaug rivers. Pop. 2,517.

MANSFIELD, t., Cattaraugus co., N. Y., 300 ms. w. of Albany ; from W. 342 ms. Watered by Cattaraugus creek and tributaries of Alleghany river. Pop. 1,057.

MANSFIELD, p. t., Warren co., N. J., 48 ms. N. w. of Trenton ; from W. 207 ms. Watered by Musconetcong and Pohatcong creeks. Pop. 1,617.

MANSFIELD, t., Burlington co., N. J., 8 ms. from Trenton ; from W. 163 ms. Watered by Black's, Craft's, and Assiscunk creeks. Pop. 2,953.

MANSFIELD, p. o., Tioga co., Pa., 143 ms. N. of Harrisburgh ; from W. 253 ms.

MANSFIELD, c. h., p. v., seat of justice of Richland co., O., 63 ms. N. E. of Columbus ; from W. 378 ms. Pop. 3,557.

MANSFIELD, p. o., Louisa co., Va., 61 ms. N. w. of Richmond ; from W. 104 ms.

MANSFIELD, c. h., p. v., seat of justice of De Soto parish, La.

MANSFIELD, p. o., Henry co., Tenn.

MANSFIELD, p. o., Kendall co., Ill.

MANSFIELD CENTRE, p. o., Mansfield township, Tolland co., Ct. 29 ms. E. of Hartford ; from W. 363 ms.

MANSFIELD DEPOT, p. o., Tolland co., Ct.

MANSKER'S CREEK, p. o., Davidson co., Tenn., 13 ms. N. E. of Nashville ; from W. 692 ms.

MANSURA, p. o., Avoyelles parish, La., 249 ms. N. w. of New Orleans from W. 1,206 ms.

MANTI, p. o., San Pete co., Utah.

MANTON, p. o., Providence co., R. I.

MANTON, p. o., Marion co., Ky.

MANTUA, p. t., Portage co., O. 150 ms. N. E. of Columbus ; from W. 327 ms. Watered by Cayahoga river and tributaries. Pop. 11,69.

MANTUA, p. v., McMinn co., Tenn., 164 ms. s. E. of Nashville ; from W. 564 ms.

MANTUA, p. o., Pickens co., Ala.

MANTUA CENTRE, p. o., Mantua township, Portage co., O.

MANVILLE, p. o., Providence co., R. I.

MANWARING'S, p. o., Shelby co., Ind., 23 ms. s. E. of Indianapolis ; from W. 573 ms.

MAON, p. o., Panola co., Miss.

MAPLE, p. t., Ionia co., Mich., 129 ms. N. w. of Detroit ; from W. 623 ms.

MAPLE, p. o., Brown co., O.

MAPLE CREEK, p. o., Washington co., Pa.

MAPLE FURNACE, p. o., Butler co., Pa.

MAPLE GROVE, p. o., Butternuts township, Otsego co., N. Y., 90 ms. w. of Albany ; from W. 340 ms.

MAPLE GROVE, p. o., Barry co., Mich.

MAPLE GROVE, p. o., Aroostook co., Me.

MAPLE GROVE, p. o., Knox co., O., 90 ms. w. of Albany ; from W. 340 ms.

MAPLE HILL, p. o., Davidson co., N. C.

MAPLE SPRINGS, p. o., Red River co., Tex.

MAPLESVILLE, p. v., Bibb co., Ala. ; from W. 809 ms.

MAPLETON, p. v., Abbeville district, S. C., 110 ms. w. of Columbia ; from W. 558 ms.

MAPLETON, p. v., Stark co., O., 132 ms. N. E. of Columbus ; from W. 308 ms.

MAPLETON, p. o., Niagara co., N. Y.

MAPLETON, p. o., Waukesha co., Wis.

MAPLETOWN, p. t., Greene co., Pa., 201 ms. s. w. of Harrisburgh ; from W. 219 ms. Pop. 864.

MAPLEVILLE, p. o., Providence co., R. I.

MAQUOKETA, p. o., Jackson co., Iowa.

MAQUON, p. o., Knox co., Ill., 89 ms. N. w. of Springfield ; from W. 819 ms.

MARADOSIA, p. o., Morgan co., Ill.

MARAMEC, p. o., Crawford co., Mo., 63 ms. s. w. of Jefferson city ; from W. 935 ms. At Big Spring of Maramec river.

MARATHON, p. t., Cortland co., N. Y., 141 ms. w. of Albany ; from W. 318 ms. Watered by Toughnioga river and tributaries. Pop. 1,149.

MARATHON, t., Lapeer co., Mich. Pop. 205.

MARATHON, p. o., Clermont co., O.

MARBLE, t., Hot Springs co., Ark.

MARBLE CREEK, p. o., Jessamine co., Ky.

MARBLE DALE, p. o., Litchfield co., Ct.

MARBLE FURNACE, p. o., Adams co., O.

MARBLE HALL, p. o., Hawkins co., Tenn.

MARBLEHEAD, p. t., Essex co., Mass., 18 ms. N. E. of Boston ; from W. 458 ms. Watered by Massachusetts bay. Pop. in 1830, 5,150 ; in 1840, 5,575 ; in 1850, 6,107.

MARBLEHEAD, p. o., Ottawa co., O.

MARBLEHEAD, p. o., Gilmer co., Ga.

MARBLE HILL, p. o., Prince Edward co., Va., 85 ms. s. w. of Richmond ; from W. 175 ms.

MARBLE HILL, p. o., Franklin co., Tenn.

MARBLETOWN, p. t., Ulster co., N. Y., 64 ms. s. w. of Albany ; from W. 318 ms. Watered by Esopus and Rondout creeks, and Delaware and Hudson canal. Pop. 3,839.

MARBURYVILLE, v., St. Tammany parish, La., 70 ms. N. w. of New Orleans ; from W. 1,172 ms.

MARCELLINE, p. o., Adams co., Ill.

MARCELLON, p. o., Columbia co., Wis.

MARCELLUS, p. o., Washington co., Iowa.

MARCELLUS, p. t., Onondaga co., N. Y., 141 ms. w. of Albany ; from W. 343 ms. Watered by Nine-Mile creek. Pop. 2,759.

MARCELLUS FALLS, p. v., Marcellus township, Onondaga co., N. Y., 143 ms. w. of Albany ; from W. 345 ms. Watered by Nine-Mile creek.

MARCHAND, p. o., Indiana co., Pa.

MARCUS, p. o., Jackson co., Ga.

MARCUS HOOK, p. v., Lower Chichester township, Delaware co., Pa., 94 ms. s. E. of Harrisburgh ; from W. 119 ms. Watered by Delaware river. Pop. 492.

MARCY, p. t., Oneida co., N. Y., 98 ms. N. w. of Albany ; from W. 394 ms. Watered by Nine-mile creek, and Mohawk river. Pop. 1,857.

MARCY, p. o., La Grange co., Ind.

MARCY, p. o., Waukesha co., Wis.

MARDISVILLE, p. v., Talladega co., Ala. ; from W. 762 ms. Watered by Talladega creek.

MARENGO COUNTY, situated in the westerly part of Alabama, with Tombigbee river on the west. Area, 975 square miles. Face of the country hilly ; soil generally barren. Seat of justice, Linden. Pop. in 1820, 3,933 ; in 1830, 7,742 ; in 1840, 17,264 ; in 1850, 27,831.

MARENGO, p. t., Calhoun co., Mich., 100 ms. w. of Detroit ; from W. 572 ms. Pop. 1,014.

MARENGO, p. o., Galen township, Wayne co., N. Y., 179 ms. w. of Albany ; from W. 355 ms.

MARENGO, p. t., McHenry co., Ill., 226 ms. N. E. of Springfield ; from W. 778 ms. Watered by Kishawaukie river. Pop. 1,030.

MARENGO, p. o., Iowa co., Iowa.

MARENGO, p. o., Morrow co., O.

MARENGO, p. o., Laurens district, S. C.

MARGARETTA, p. t., Erie co., O., 100 ms. N.w. of Columbus ; from W. 414 ms. Pop. 1,537.

MARGARETTA FURNACE, p. o., York co., Pa., 36 ms. S. E. of Harrisburgh ; from W. 104 ms.

MARIA CREEK, p. o., Knox co., Ind., 111 ms. S. w. of Indianapolis ; from W. 678 ms.

MARIA FORGE, p. o., Talladega co., Ala.

MARIANA, c. h., p. v., seat of justice of Jackson co., Flor., 77 ms. N. w. of Tallahasse ; from W. 927 ms. Watered by Chipola river.

MARIA STEIN, p. o., Mercer co., O.

MARIAVILLE (now called Tilden), p. t., Hancock co., Me., 103 ms. N. E. of Augusta ; from W. 685 ms. Watered by Union river and tributaries. Pop. 374.

MARIAVILLE, p. o., Duanesburgh township, Schenectady co., N. Y.

MARIES, t., Gasconade co., Mo.

MARIETTA, p. o., Marcellus township, Onondaga co., N. Y., 145 ms. w. of Albany ; from W. 338 ms.

MARIETTA, p. h., East Donegal township, Lancaster co., Pa., 27 ms. S. E. of Harrisburgh. Watered by Susquehanna river and Chiques creek. Pop. 2,099.

MARIETTA, c. h., p. t., seat of justice of Washington co., O., 104 ms. S. E. of Columbus ; from W. 300 ms. Watered by Muskingum and Ohio rivers. Seat of Marietta Collegiate Institute. Pop. in 1830, 1,207 ; in 1840, 1,814 ; in 1850, 4,244.

MARIETTA, p. o., Fulton co., Ill.

MARIETTA, c. h., p. v., seat of justice of Cobb co., Ga., 113 ms. N. w. of Milledgeville ; from W. 676 ms.

MARIETTA, p. v., Shelby co., Ind.

MARIETTA, p. o., Itawamba co., Miss.

MARIN COUNTY, lying on the coast, north of San Francisco bay, Cal. Seat of justice, San Rafael. Pop. in 1852, 1,036.

MARINE, p. o., Madison co., Ill., 90 ms. s. of Springfield ; from W. 784 ms.

MARINE MILLS, p. o., St. Croix co., Wis.

MARION COUNTY, situated in the northern part of Virginia. Area, —— square miles. Seat of justice, ——. Pop. 10,551.

MARION COUNTY, situated in the west part of Georgia. Area, 330 square miles. Seat of justice, Tazewell. Pop. in 1830, 1,436 ; in 1840, 4,812 ; in 1850, 10,280.

MARION COUNTY, situated on the west boundary of Alabama. Area, 1,144 square miles. Seat of justice, Pikeville. Pop. in 1830, 4,058 ; in 1840, 5,847 ; in 1850, 7,833.

MARION COUNTY, situated in the central part of Kentucky. Area, 276 square miles. Seat of justice, Lebanon. Pop. in 1840, 11,032 ; in 1850, 11,765.

MARION COUNTY, situated toward the north part of Ohio. Area, 460 square miles. Face of the country even ; soil rich. Seat of justice, Marion. Pop. in 1830, 6,558 ; in 1840, 14.765 ; in 1850, 12.618.

MARION COUNTY, situated in the centre of Indiana, and traversed by West Fork of White river. Area, 400 square miles. Seat of justice, Indianapolis, which is also the state capital. Pop in 1830, 7,192 ; in 1840, 16.080 ; in 1850. 24,100.

MARION COUNTY, situated toward the south part of Illinois. Area, 576 square miles. Seat of justice, Salem. Pop. in 1830, 2,125 ; in 1840, 4,742 ; in 1850, 6,720.

MARION COUNTY, situated in the central part of Iowa, and traversed by Des Moines river. Area, —— square miles. Seat of justice, Knoxville. Pop. in 1850, 5,482.

MARION COUNTY, situated in Oregon. Area, —— square miles. Seat of justice, ——. Pop. in 1850, 2,749.

MARION COUNTY, situated on the south boundary of Mississippi, and traversed by Pearl river. Area, 1,476 square miles. Face of the country hilly ; soil mostly barren. Seat of justice, Columbia. Pop. in 1820, 3,116 ; in 1830, 3,701 ; in 1840, 3,830 ; in 1850, 4,410.

MARION COUNTY, situated on the south boundary of Tennessee, and traversed by Tennessee river. Area, 600 square miles. Face of the country hilly and mountainous. Seat of justice, Jasper. Pop. in 1820, 3,888 ; in 1830, 5,516 ; in 1840, 6,070 ; in 1850, 6,314.

MARION COUNTY, situated on the easterly boundary of Missouri, with Mississippi river on the east. Area, 425 square miles. Seat of justice, Palmyra. Pop. in 1830, 4.837 ; in 1840, 9,623 ; in 1850, 12,230.

MARION COUNTY, situated on the north boundary of Arkansas, and traversed by White river. Area, 800 square miles. Seat of justice, Yellville. Pop. in 1840, 1,325 ; in 1850. 2,302.

MARION COUNTY, situated in the central part of Florida, and traversed by Ocklawaha river. Area, —— square miles. Seat of justice, ——. Pop. in 1850, 3.338.

MARION DISTRICT, situated on the northeast boundary of South Carolina, and traversed by Great Pedee river. Area, 1,200 square miles. Face of the country generally level ; soil sandy. Seat of justice, Marion. Pop. in 1810, 8,884 ; in 1820, 10,201 ; in 1830, 11,208 ; in 1840, 13,932 ; in 1850, 17,407.

MARION, t., Greene co., Pa.

MARION, p. t., Washington co., Me., 170 ms. N. E. of Augusta ; from W. 756 ms. Pop. 270.

MARION, p. t., Wayne co., N. Y., 201 ms. w. of Albany ; from W. 358 ms. Watered by a tributary of Mud creek. Pop. 1,839.

MARION, p. o., Franklin co., Pa., 51 ms. S. w. of Harrisburgh ; from W. 84 ms.

MARION, t., Centre co., Pa. Pop. 595.

MARION, c. h., p. t., seat of justice of Marion co., O. 44 ms. N. of Columbus ; from W. 416 ms. Pop. 2,291.

MARION, t., Athens co., O. Watered by Federal and Wolf creeks.

MARION, t., Allen co., O. Pop. 1,046.

MARION, t., Clinton co., O., 76 ms. s. w. of Columbus; from W. 453 ms. Pop. 468.

MARION, t., Fayette co., O. Pop. 841.

MARION, t, Hancock co., O. Pop. 904.

MARION, t., Hardin co., O. Pop. 452.

MARION, p. t., Hocklug co., O. Pop. 1,140.

MARION, p. t., Mercer co., O. Pop. 1,428.

MARION, p. t., Shelby co., O.

MARION, t., Putnam co., Ind. Pop. 1,320.

MARION, t., Shelby co., Ind., 25 ms. s. E. of Indianapolis ; from W. 579 ms. Pop. 786.

MARION, p. t., Livingston co., Mich., 56 ms. N. w. of Detroit ; from W. 459 ms. Pop. 883.

MARION, v., Scott co., Ky., 22 ms. N. E. of Frankfort; from W. 530 ms.

MARION, p. o., Crittenden co., Ky.

MARION, c. h., p. v., seat of justice of Smyth co., Va., 275 ms. w. of Richmond ; from W. 343 ms. Watered by Middle fork of Holston river.

MARION, p. v., McDowell co., N. C.

MARION, c. h., p. v., seat of justice of Twiggs co., Ga., 41 ms. s. w. of Milledgeville ; from W. 689 ms.

MARION, c. h., p. v., seat of justice of Grant co., Ind., 73 ms. N. E. of Indianapolis ; from W. 560 ms. Watered by Missisinewa river. Pop. 703.

MARION, c. h., p. v., seat of justice of Williamson co., Ill., 172 ms. s. E. of Springfield ; from W. 823 ms.

MARION, c. h., p. v., seat of justice of Perry co., Ala., from W. 834 ms. Pop. 1.544.

MARION, c. h., p. v., Lauderdale co., Miss., 110 ms. E. of Jackson ; from W. 921 ms. Watered by head branches of Oktibbeha creek.

MARION, p. v., Cole co., Mo., 15 ms. N. w. of Jefferson City ; from W. 951 ms. Watered by Missouri river.

MARION, t., Buchanan co., Mo. Pop. 796.

MARION, c. h., p. v., seat of justice of Linn co., Iowa.

MARION, c. h., p. v., seat of justice of Crittenden co., Ark., 140 ms. N. E. of Little Rock ; from W. 925 ms.

MARION, t., Union co., Ark. Pop. 169.

MARION, t., White co., Ark. Pop. 404.

MARION, t., Newton co., Mo.

MARION, t., Livingston co., Mo.

MARION, t., Polk co., Mo.

MARION, t., Monroe co., Mo.

MARION, t., Ray co., Mo.

MARION, t., St. Francis co., Mo.

MARION, t., Saline co., Mo.

MARION, t., Taney co., Mo.

MARION, p. o., Union parish, La.

MARION, p. o., Angelina co., Tex.

MARION, c. h., p. v., seat of justice of Marion co., S. C., 146 ms. E. of Columbia ; from W. 423 ms. Watered by Catfish creek.

MARION. p. o., Hartford co., Ct.

MARION. p. o., Kenozha co., Wis.

MARION CITY, p. v., Marion co., Mo. Watered by Mississippi river.

MARION COLLEGE, v., Marion co., Mo., 134 ms. N. W. of Jefferson city; from W. 938 ms. Seat of Marion college.

MARIONSVILLE, p. o., Forest co., Pa.

MARIPOSA COUNTY, Cal., situated on the east side of the Sierra Nevada mountains, with the parallel of 38° for its northern boundary. Face of the country mountainous, and rich in auriferous deposite. Seat of justice, Aqua Fria. Pop. in 1852, 8,969.

MARIPOSA, p. o., Mariposa co., Cal.

MARISSA, p. o., St. Clair co., Ill.

MARITS, p. o., Morrow co., O., 47 ms. N. of Columbus ; from W. 406 ms.

MARKESAN, p. o., Marquette co., Wis.

MARKSBOROUGH, p. v., Warren co., N. J., 73 ms. N. of Trenton ; from W. 230 ms.

MARKSVILLE, p. v., Page co., Va., 120 ms. N. W. of Richmond ; from W. 106 ms.

MARKSVILLE, c. h., p. v., seat of justice of Avoyelles parish, La., 255 ms. N. W. of New Orleans ; from W. 1,218 ms.

MARLBOROUGH DISTRICT, situated at the northeast corner of South Carolina, with Great Pedee river on the southwest. Area, 480 square miles. Soil, sandy, and in many places productive. Seat of justice, Bennettsville. Pop. in 1810, 4,966 ; in 1820, 6,425 ; in 1830, 8,578 ; in 1840, 8,408 ; in 1850, 10,789.

MARLBOROUGH, p. t., Cheshire co., N. H., 53 ms. s. w. of Concord ; from W. 439 ms. Watered by tributaries of Ashuelot river. Pop. 887.

MARLBOROUGH, p. t., Windham co., Vt., 130 ms. s. of Montpelier ; from W. 431 ms. Watered by west branch of West river, Green river, and Whetstone brook. Pop. 896.

MARLBOROUGH, p. t., Middlesex co., Mass., 27 ms. w. of Boston ; from W. 414 ms. Watered by a tributary of Concord river. Pop. 2,941.

MARLBOROUGH, p. t., Hartford co., Ct., 16 ms. s. E. of Hartford ; from W. 340 ms. Pop. 832.

MARLBOROUGH, p. t., Ulster co., N. Y., 84 ms. s. w. of Albany ; from W. 294 ms. Watered by Hudson river. Pop. 2,869.

MARLBOROUGH, p. o., Monmouth co., N. J., 40 ms. E. of Trenton : from W. 206.

MARLBOROUGH, p. t., Montgomery co., Pa., 83 ms. E. of Harrisburgh ; from W. 166 ms. Watered by Perkiomen and Swamp creeks. Pop. 1,174.

MARLBOROUGH, p. t., Stark co., O., 135 ms. N. E. of Columbus ; from W. 312 ms. Pop. 2,133.

MARLBOROUGH, t., Delaware co., O., 33 ms. N. of Columbus ; from W. 429 ms. Pop. 587.

MARLBOROUGH, p. o., Chester co., Pa.

MARLBROOK, p. o., Hempstead co., Ark.

MARLEY'S MILLS, p. o., Randolph co., N. C., 56 ms. w. of Raleigh ; from W. 344 ms.

MARLIN BOTTOM, p. o., Pocahontas co., Va.

MARLOW, p. t., Cheshire co., N. H., 39 ms. s. w. of Concord ; from W. 450 ms. Watered by Ashuelot river and tributaries. Pop. 708.

MARLTON, p. o., Burlington co., N. J.

MARPLE, p. o., Delaware co., Pa., 88 ms. s. E. of Harrisburgh ; from W. 126 ms. Pop. 876.

MARQUETTE COUNTY, situated in the central part of Wisconsin. Area, —— square miles. Seat of justice, Marquette. Pop. in 1840, 18 ; in 1850, 8,642.

MARQUETTE COUNTY, situated in the northwest part of the northerly peninsula of Michigan, on Lake Superior. Area, —— square miles. Seat of justice, ——. Pop. in 1850, 136.

MARQUETTE. c. h., p. v., seat of justice of Marquette co., Wis. Watered by Neenah river.

MARQUETTE, p. o., Marquette co., Mich.

MARRIOTTSVILLE, p. o., Anne Arundel co., Md.

MARROWBONE, p. o., Cumberland co., Ky.

MARS, p. o., Bibb co., Ala. ; from W. 820 ms.

MARS, t., Posey co., Ind., 181 ms. s. w. of Indianapolis , from W. 742 ms. Pop. 1,319.

MARS BLUFF, p. o., Marion district, S. C., 122 ms. E. of Columbia ; from W. 466 ms.

MARSEILLES, p. v., Noble co., Ind., 164 ms. N. E. of Indianapolis ; from W. 576 ms.

MARSEILLES, p. v., La Salle co., Ill., 141 ms. N. E. of Springfield ; from W. 776 ms. Situated on the Grand Rapids of Illinois river, and the Illinois and Michigan canal.

MARSEILLES, p. o., Wyandott co., O.

MARSH, p. o., Chester co., Pa., 61 ms. E. of Harrisburgh ; from W. 189 ms.

MARSHALL COUNTY, situated on the north boundary of western Virginia, on the Ohio river. Area, 350 square miles. Seat of justice, Elizabethtown. Pop. in 1840, 6.937 ; in 1850, 10,138.

MARSHALL COUNTY, situated in the northeasterly part of Alabama, and traversed by Tennessee river. Area, 600 square miles. Seat of justice, Warrenton. Pop. in 1840, 7,553 ; in 1850, 8,846.

MARSHALL COUNTY, situated on the north boundary of Mississippi. Area, 800 square miles. Seat of justice, Holly Springs. Pop. in 1840, 17,526 ; in 1850, 29,689.

MARSHALL COUNTY, situated toward the south part of Tennessee. Area, 200 square miles. Seat of justice, Lewisburgh. Pop. in 1840, 14,555 ; in 1850, 15,616.

MARSHALL COUNTY, situated in the west part of Kentucky, with Tennessee river on the northeast. Seat of justice, Benton. Pop. in 1850, 5,269.

MARSHALL COUNTY, situated in the northeasterly part of Indiana. Area, 440 square miles. Seat of justice, Plymouth. Pop. in 1840, 1,651 ; in 1850, 5,348.

MARSHALL COUNTY, situated toward the north part of Illinois, and traversed by Illinois river. Area, 384 square miles. Seat of justice, Lacon. Pop. in 1840, 1,849 ; in 1850, 5,180.

MARSHALL COUNTY, situated in the central part of Iowa, and traversed by Iowa river. Area, —— square miles. Seat of justice, ——. Pop. in 1850, 338.

MARSHALL, p. t., Oneida co., N. Y., 93 ms. N. W. of Albany ; from W. 379 ms. Watered by Oriskany creek and Chenango canal. Pop. 2,115.

MARSHALL, c. h., p. t., seat of justice of Calhoun co., Mich., 105 ms. w. of Detroit ; from W. 570 ms. Situated at the confluence of Kalamazoo river and Rice creek. Pop. 2,822.

MARSHALL, c. h. p. t., seat of justice of Clark co., Ill., 123 ms. s. E. of Springfield ; from W. 661 ms. Pop. 1,341.

MARSHALL, p. o., Henry co., Iowa.

MARSHALL, c. h., p. v., Saline co., Mo., 87 ms. N. W. of Jefferson City ; from W. 1,001 ms.

MARSHALL, p. v., Marshall co., Ind.

MARSHALL, p. o., Highland co., O.

MARSHALL, p. o., Bath co., Ky.

MARSHALL, p. o., Harrison co., Tex.

MARSHALL'S CREEK, p. o., Monroe co., Pa.

MARSHALL'S FERRY, p. o., Grainger co., Tenn., 232 ms. E. of Nashville ; from W. 456 ms.

MARSHALLVILLE, p. v., Baughman's township, Wayne co., O., 107 ms. N. E. of Columbus ; from W. 342 ms.

MARSHALLVILLE, p. v., Macon co., Ga., 70 ms. s. w. of Milledgeville ; from W. 726 ms.

MARSHALLTON, p. v., Chester co., Pa., 73 ms. s. E. of Harrisburgh ; from W. 122 ms.

MARSHFIELD, p. t., Washington co., Vt. 15 ms. N. E. of Montpelier ; from W. 528 ms. Watered by· Onion river. Pop. 1,102.

MARSHFIELD, p. t., Plymouth co., Mass., 31 ms. s. E. of Boston ; from W. 453 ms. Watered by Massachusetts bay, and North and South rivers. Pop. 1,837.

MARSHFIELD, p. o., Erie co., Pa.

MARSTON'S MILLS, p. o., Barnstable co., Mass., 70 ms. s. E. of Boston ; from W. 47 ms.

MARTHA FURNACE, p. o., Centre co., Pa., 101 ms. N. w. of Harrisburgh ; from W. 193 ms.

MARTHA FURNACE, p. o., Hardin co., Ill.

MARTHA MILLS, p. o., Fleming co., Ky., 90 ms. E. of Frankfort ; from W. 493 ms.

MARTHASVILLE, p. v., Warren co., Mo., 73 ms. E. of Jefferson City ; from W. 873 ms.

MARTHASVILLE, p. o., Macon co., Ga.

MARTHA'S VINEYARD, p. o., Chatham co., N. C., 38 ms. w. of Raleigh ; from W. 326 ms.

MARTICKVILLE, p. v., Martick township, Lancaster co., Pa., 48 ms. s. E. of Harrisburgh ; from W. 122 ms.

MARTICK, p. t., Lancaster co., Pa. Watered by Beaver, Muddy, and Pecquea creeks, and Susquehanna river. Pop. 3,099.

MARTIN COUNTY, situated in the easterly part of North Carolina, on Roanoke river. Area, 481 square miles. Face of the country level ; soil sandy. Seat of justice, Williamston. Pop. in 1820, 6,320 ; in 1830, 8,539 ; in 1840, 7,637 ; in 1850, 8,307.

MARTIN COUNTY, situated in the southerly part of Indiana, and traversed by east fork of White river. Area, 300 square miles. Face of the country diversified ; soil good. Seat of justice, Mount Pleasant. Pop. in 1820, 1,032 ; in 1830, 2,010 ; in 1840, 3,875 ; in 1850, 5,941.

MARTIN, t., Pope co., Ark.

MARTIN, p. t., Allegan co., Mich. Pop. 329.

MARTINDALE, p. o., Mecklenburgh co., N. C., 164 ms. s. w. of Raleigh ; from W. 403 ms.

MARTINEZ, p. o., Contra Costa co., Cal.

MARTINSBURGH, c. h., p. t., seat of justice of Lewis co., N. Y., 134 ms. N. w. of Albany ; from W. 433 ms. Watered by Martin's creek and Black river. Pop. 2,677.

MARTINSBURGH, p. v., Woodberry township. Blair co., Pa., 112 ms. w. of Harrisburgh ; from W. 145 ms. Watered by tributaries of Frankstown branch of Juniata river. Pop. 442.

MARTINSBURGH, c. h., p. v., seat of justice of Berkley co., Va. 169 ms. N. of Richmond ; from W. 77 ms. Pop. 1,930.

MARTINSBURGH, v., Monroe co. Ky., 149 ms. s. w. of Frankfort ; from W. 638 ms.

MARTINSBURGH, p. v., Clay township, Knox co., O., 57 ms. N. E. of Columbus ; from W. 366 ms.

MARTINBURGH, p. v., Washington co., Ind., 105 ms. s. of Indianapolis ; from W 616 ms.

MARTINSBURGH, p. o., Pike co., Ill.

MARTINSBURGH, p. o, Ripley co., Mo.

MARTIN'S CREEK, p. o., Northampton co., Pa., 114 ms. N. E. of Harrisburgh ; from W. 207 ms.

MARTIN'S CREEK, p. o., Carroll co., Tenn.

MARTIN'S CREEK, p. o., Pickens district, S. C., 154 ms. N. w. of Columbia ; from W. 560 ms.

MARTIN'S FERRY, p. o., Belmont co., O., 127 ms. E. of Columbus ; from W. 287 ms.

MARTIN'S HILL, p. o., Catlin township, Chemung co., N. Y., 207 ms. w. of Albany ; from W. 291 ms.

MARTIN'S LANDING, p. o., Perry co., Ind.

MARTIN'S LIME-KILNS, p. o., Stokes co., N. C.

MARTIN'S STORE, p. o., Macon co., Ga.

MARTINSVILLE, p. o., Somerset co., N. J., 35 ms. N. of Trenton ; from W. 206 ms.

MARTINSVILLE, c. h., p. v., seat of justice of Henry co., Va., 194 ms. s. w. of Richmond ; from W. 269 ms. Watered by Smith's river.

MARTINSVILLE, p. v., Clinton co., O., 82 ms. s. w. of Columbus ; from W. 455 ms.

MARTINSVILLE, c. h., p. v., seat of justice of Morgan co., Ind., 28 ms. s. w. of Indianapolis ; from W. 599 ms.

MARTINSVILLE, p. v., Clark co., Ill., 127 ms, s. E. of Springfield ; from W. 673 ms. Watered by north fork of Embarrass river. Pop. 1,131.

MARTINSVILLE, p. o., Lancaster co., Pa.

MARTINSVILLE, p. o., Niagara co., N. Y.

MARTVILLE, p. v., Sterling township, Cayuga co., N. Y., 175 ms. w. of Albany ; from W. 358 ms. Watered by Sodus creek.

MARVEL, p. o., Bates co., Mo.

MARVIN, p. o., Chautauque co., N. Y.

MARY, p. o., Pulaski co., Ark.

MARY ANN, t., Licking co., O., 39 ms. E. of Columbus ; from W. 358 ms. Pop. 999.

MARYLAND, one of the United States. named in honor of Henrietta Maria, queen of Charles I., and daughter of Henry IV., of France. It is situated between 38° and 39° 43′ north latitude and 75° 10′ and 79° 20′ west longitude, from Greenwich, and is bounded north by Pennsylvania and Delaware ; east by Delaware and the Atlantic ; south by Virginia and Chesapeake bay, and southwest and west by Virginia, from which it is separated in part by the Potomac. Its superficial area is 13,959 square miles.

Physical Aspect.—This state may be said to embrace the three great zones of soil, alluvial, hilly, and mountainous. In the counties on the eastern side of the Chesapeake, with the exception of a small part of the northern extremity, is an extensive plain, low and sandy, and much intersected by rivers and creeks, having but few springs, and abounding, in many places, with stagnant pools. The land in this portion of the peninsula is of much better quality than in the Delaware part. The country, on the western shore of the Chesapeake, below the falls of the rivers, is similar to that on the eastern side. Above the falls the surface becomes gradually uneven and hilly, and in the western part of the state it is mountainous. There is much good soil existing in every section of the state ; but the most productive in grain and fruits are some of the limestone tracts in the western counties.

Mountains.—Several branches of the Alleghany chain cross the state from Pennsylvania to Virginia, the principal of which are, North mountain, South mountain, Warrior's, Sugar-loaf, Savage, Will's mountains, and Sidling hill.

Rivers and Bays.—The principal rivers are, the Potomac, Susquehannah, Patapsco, Patuxent, Elk, Sassafras, Chester, Choptank, Nanticoke, Pokomoke, St. Mary's, and the Severn. Chesapeake bay runs through the state from north to south, dividing it into two parts. The part east of the bay is called the "Eastern Shore," and the portion adjoining the bay on the west is called the "Western Shore." Sinepuxent bay lies near the Atlantic coast, and is connected to the ocean by an inlet of the same name.

Climate.—In the eastern part of the state the climate in summer is moist, sultry, and disagreeable, and the inhabitants are subject to agues, intermittents, and bilious attacks ; but in the western regions, toward Virginia, where the land is more elevated, the climate is agreeable and highly salubrious.

Productive Resources.—The chief products are, horses, mules, neat cattle, sheep, swine, poultry, butter, cheese, sugar, wax, hops, tobacco, wool, cotton, silk, hemp, flax, hay, wheat, rye, oats, barley, buckwheat, potatoes, and Indian corn. Among the mineral resources are, bog iron ore, bituminous coal, porcelain and other clays, red and yellow ochre, chrome ores, alum earth, and copperas.

Manufactures.—In manufactures, Maryland occupies a respectable position. Numerous woollen and cotton mills, copper and iron-rolling mills, are established near Baltimore, and also scattered over other parts of the state. Silk, flax, and mixed goods, are also manufactured to a considerable extent. Tanneries are numerous, and ship-building is carried on extensively. The flour of Maryland is considered second to none in the market. The capital invested in manufactures is about $12,000,000.

Railroads and Canals.—The great chain of southern railroads traverses this state. The Baltimore and Ohio railroad, extending from Baltimore to Wheeling, 178 miles, is a magnificent work. Other lines intersect the state in different directions. The Chesapeake and Ohio canal, from Georgetown, D. C., to Cumberland, 184 miles long, lies mostly in this state. It is intended to continue it to Pittsburgh, Pa., 340 miles.

Commerce.—The imports and exports of Maryland are about $14,000,000 annually. The shipping owned within the state is about 2,000,000 tons, about one half of which is engaged in the coasting trade.

Education.—There are several colleges in Maryland. Washington college. at Chestertown, founded in 1783, is the oldest ; St. John's college, at Annapolis, founded in 1784, is next. Besides these are, the University of Maryland, and the St. Mary's, both of Baltimore ; Mount St. Mary's, at Emmitsburg, and St. James, near Hagerstown. There are two medical schools at Baltimore. There are besides, in the state, about 200 academies and grammar-schools, and 800 common schools.

Population.—In 1790, 319,728 ; in 1800, 341,548 ; in 1810, 380,546 ; in 1820, 407,350 ; in 1830, 447,040 ; in 1840, 469,232 ; in 1850, 583,035. Number of slaves in 1790, 103,036 ; in 1800, 105,635 ; in 1810, 111,502 ; in 1820, 107,398 ; in 1830, 102,294 ; in 1840, 89,737 ; in 1850, 90,368.

Government—The legislative power is vested in a

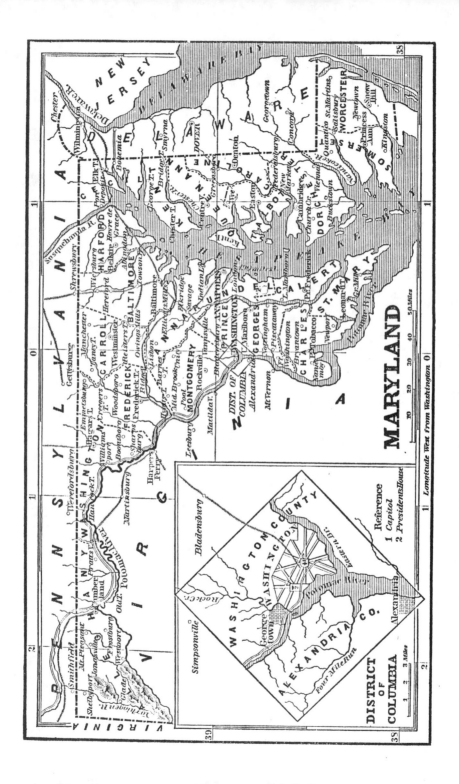

senate, and a house of delegates. The senators are elected by the people for a term of four years, one half of them being chosen biennially. One senator is chosen from each county, and one from the city of Baltimore; making the present number of senators twenty-two. The members of the house of delegates are elected by the people once in two years, and until the apportionment to be made under the census of 1860, are seventy-two in number. The executive power is vested in a governor, who is chosen by the people, for a term of four years. The state is divided into three districts, and the governor is taken from each of the three districts alternately. The judicial power is vested in a court of appeals, in circuit courts, courts for the city of Baltimore, and in justices of the peace, all elected by the people. The judges of the court of appeals, four in number, and the circuit judges, eight in number, are chosen for ten years. The general election is held on the first Wednesday in November, biennially. The constitution conveys the right of suffrage on every free white male citizen, of 21 years of age, having resided one year in the state, and six months in the county in which he offers to vote. Imprisonment for debt, and lotteries, are now prohibited.

History.—In 1632, Charles I. granted to Sir George Calvert (Lord Baltimore) the whole territory extending from the Potomac to the fortieth degree of north latitude, comprising not only all the present states of Maryland and Delaware, but a part of Pennsylvania and New Jersey. Though involved in a controversy for many years, respecting their common boundaries, Maryland and Pennsylvania did not fix upon their existing limits before the year 1762, when they were determined by actual survey by two eminent English engineers, Charles Mason and Jeremiah Dixon, and hence the present boundary between these two states is called "Mason and Dixon's line." The first permanent settlement within the limits of Maryland was made on the island of Kent, by William Claiborne, in 1632. A few months later, the grant was made to Lord Baltimore, and his brother, Leonard Calvert, proceeded to the Potomac, in 1634, with one hundred emigrants, mostly catholics, and formed a settlement at St. Mary's, where the first legislative assembly convened, in 1635. In 1774, a provincial Congress took the government into its own hands. It joined the confederacy in 1776, and adopted the federal constitution in 1788. In 1790, that portion of the state now constituting the District of Columbia, was ceded to the general government. Maryland formed her constitution in 1776, which was subjected to numerous amendments till 1851, when a new one was framed by a state convention, and adopted by the people. The motto of the state seal is, "Industry the means, and plenty the result."

MARYLAND, p. t., Otsego co., N. Y., 66 ms. w. of Albany; from W. 362 ms. Watered by Scheneva's creek. Pop. 2,152.

MARYLAND LINE, p. o., Baltimore co., Md., 62 ms. N. of Annapolis; from W. 72 ms.

MARYSVILLE, c. h., p. v., seat of justice of Union co., O., 41 ms. N. W. of Columbus; from W. 431 ms. Watered by Mill creek. Pop. 605.

MARYSVILLE, p. v., Campbell co., Va., 137 ms. s.w. of Richmond; from W. 218 ms. Watered by Stanton river

MARYSVILLE. p.v., seat of justice of Blount co., Tenn., 183 ms. s. E of Nashville; from W. 523 ms. Watered by a tributary of Pistol creek.

MARYSVILLE, p. o., Paulding co., Ga.

MARYSVILLE, p. o., Benton co., Oregon.

MARYSVILLE, p. o., Benton co., Iowa.

MARYSVILLE, p. o., Yuba co., Cal.

MARYSVILLE, p. o., Noddaway co., Mo.

MASARDIS, p. o., Aroostook co., Me.

MASCOUTAH, p. v., St. Clair co., Ill., 110 ms. s. of Springfield; from W. 819 ms.

MASHAPANG, p. o., Tolland co., Ct.

MASKEGON, t., Ottawa co., Mich., 227 ms. N. w. of Detroit; from W. 708 ms. Watered by Maskegon lake. Pop. 484.

MASON COUNTY, situated on the northwesterly boundary of Virginia, with Ohio river on the northwest, and traversed by Great Kanawha river. Area, 875 square miles. Face of the country hilly; soil near the rivers fertile. Seat of justice Point Pleasant. Pop. in 1810, 1,991; in 1820, 4,868; in 1830, 6,534; in 1840, 6,777; in 1850, 7,539.

MASON COUNTY, situated on the northerly boundary of Kentucky, with Ohio river on the north. Area,

260 square miles. Face of the country hilly; soil near the streams fertile. Seat of justice, Washington. Pop. in 1810, 12,459; in 1820, 13,588; in 1830, 16,203; in 1840 15,719; in 1850, 18,344.

MASON COUNTY, situated in the central part of Illinois, with Illinois river on the northwest, and the Sangamon on the south. Area, —— square miles. Seat of justice, Bath. Pop. in 1850, 5,921.

MASON, p. t., Hillsborough co., N. H., 44 ms. s. w. of Concord; from W. 450 ms. Watered by Souhegan river, and tributaries of the Nashua. Pop. 1,626.

MASON, p. o., Warren co., O., 93 ms. s. w. of Columbus; from W. 477 ms.

MASON, t., Lawrence co., O., 120 ms. s. E. of Columbus; from W. 309 ms. Watered by Symmes creek. Pop. 1,132.

MASON, t., Cass co., Mich. Pop. 1,259.

MASON, t., Ingham co., Mich. Pop. 462.

MASON, p. t., Marion co., Mo.

MASON CENTRE, p. v., Ingham co., Mich., 85 ms. w. of Detroit; fm.W. 571 ms. Watered by Sycamore creek.

MASON HALL, p. o., Orange co., N. C., 49 ms. N. w. of Raleigh; from W. 283 ms.

MASON'S GROVE, p. o., Madison co., Tenn., 149 ms. s. w. of Nashville; from W. 834 ms.

MASONTOWN, p. o., Fayette co., Pa., 190 ms. s. w. of Harrisburgh; from W. 198 ms.

MASON VILLAGE, p. v., Mason township, Hillsborough co., N. H., 44 ms. s. w. of Concord; from W. 450 ms.

MASONVILLE, p. t., Delaware co., N. Y., 111 ms. s. w. of Albany; from W. 313 ms. Watered by tributaries of Susquehanna and Delaware rivers. Pop. 1,550.

MASONVILLE, p. v., Lauderdale co., Ala.; from W. 770 ms,

MAGPETH, p. o., Queen's co, Long Island, N. Y.

MASSAC COUNTY, situated on the southerly boundary of Illinois, with Ohio river on the south. Area, —— square miles. Seat of justice, Metropolis. Pop. in 1850, 4,092.

MASSACHUSETTS, one of the United States, so-called from a tribe of Indians, formerly at Barnstable, or from *Moswetuset*, the aboriginal name of Blue Hill, a few miles s. of Boston. It lies between 41° 23' and 42° 52' north latitude, and 69° 50' and 73° 30' west longitude from Greenwich; and is bounded north by Vermont and New Hampshire; east by the Atlantic; south by Rhode Island and Connecticut; and west by New York. Its superficial area is 7,500 square miles.

Physical Aspect.—The surface of this state is greatly diversified, and the soil may be divided into three distinct zones—mountainous in the western, hilly in the central and northern, and level in the southeastern sections. Salt marshes are numerous on most of the maritime border. The soil is exceedingly varied. In the southeastern part it is mostly light and sandy; interspersed, however, with numerous spots that are fertile. In the middle and northern sections, particularly toward the seaboard, it is of much better quality, but distinguished more for its superior cultivation, than its natural fertility. The more western parts, especially in the valley of the Connecticut river, have generally a strong, rich soil, excellent for grazing, and suited to most of the purposes of farming.

Mountains.—The Green mountain range passes through the western part of the state, from north to south. The principal chain takes the name of Hoosac mountains, the highest summits of which are the Saddle and Taghkanic. The other elevations, noted for their size and height, are Wachusett, Mount Tom, Mount Holyoke, Mount Toby, Blue and Pow-Wow hills.

Rivers and Bays.—The principal rivers are the Connecticut, Merrimack, Concord, Nashua, Pow-Wow, Ipswich, North, Saugus, Charles, Mystic, Neponset, Taunton, Chickapee, Deerfield, Westfield, French, Miller's, and the Housatonic. Massachusetts bay lies on the easterly side of the state, between Capes Cod and Ann.

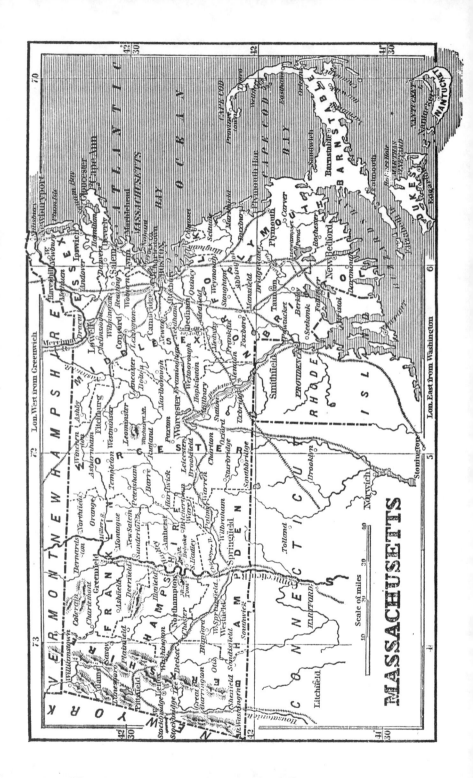

MASSACHUSETTS

Numerous other bays indent the coast, the principal of which are, Buzzard's, Barnstable, Plymouth, and Cape Cod.

Islands.—The most noted of these are, Nantucket, Martha's Vineyard, the Elizabeth islands (sixteen in number), Plum island, and those in Massachusetts bay.

Climate.—The climate is generally favorable to health, though persons with feeble lungs, living near the seaboard, are liable to suffer from the ocean winds. The air from the interior is generally dry, serene, and salubrious. The summers are pleasant, but subject to excessive heat, often followed by a depression of temperature, of 50° Fahrenheit in a few hours. The winters are generally rigorous, the thermometer often standing below zero.

Productive Resources.—The principal products are horses, mules, neat cattle, sheep, swine, poultry, eggs, butter, cheese, silk, wool, hay, fish, spermaceti, whale and other fish oil, wheat, rye, barley, oats, buckwheat, potatoes, orchard and garden fruits, and Indian corn. Among the fossil resources are marble, granite, freestone, slate, flagstone, and various kinds of ochre and clay. This state abounds in mines of iron ore, and has also some coal.

Manufactures.—Massachusetts is distinguished as a manufacturing state. Water-power for the supply of machinery is abundant in nearly every section of the state. There are five or six hundred cotton and woollen factories. Calico-printing and carpet-weaving are also largely carried on. Boots and shoes, leather, wrought and cast iron, straw hats, cabinet-work, paper, and oil, are extensively manufactured. Fire-arms are also manufactured at the national armory at Springfield.

Railroads and Canals.—Massachusetts has a greater number of railroads, in proportion to its area, than any other state in the Union. There are, within the limits of the state, about forty different roads, exclusive of their various branches, with a total length of over 1,200 miles, and built at an aggregate cost of rising $50,000,000. Their principal centres are Boston, Worcester, Springfield, Lowell, and Fitchburgh. The principal canals of Massachusetts are, the Middlesex, 27 miles long, connecting the Merrimack river at Lowell with Boston harbor; the Blackstone, 45 miles long, from Worcester to Providence; and the Hampshire and Hampden, 22 miles long, from the Farmington canal (now disused), on the Connecticut line, to Northampton.

Commerce.—The commerce of Massachusetts centres chiefly at Boston, and is inferior only to that of two other states (New York and Louisiana) in the Union. Its exports and imports in 1850 were over forty millions of dollars. Amount of shipping owned within the state, 685,442 tons.

Education.—The university of Cambridge is the oldest and best-endowed school in the United States; attached to it are schools of law, medicine, divinity, and science. Williams' college, at Williamstown, and Amherst college, are also flourishing institutions. At Andover, Newton, and Worcester, theological seminaries are established. Academies and common schools exist throughout the state.

Population.—In 1790, 378,717; in 1800, 423,245; in 1810, 472,040; in 1820, 523,287; in 1830, 610,408; in 1840, 737,699; in 1850, 994,499. Number of slaves in 1778, 18,000. Slavery was abolished in 1781.

Government.—The executive power is vested in a governor, lieutenant-governor, and council; and the legislative power, in a senate of forty members, and a house of representatives; all elected annually, by the people, on the second Monday in November, excepting the council, which is chosen by the legislature. The judiciary is vested in a supreme court, court of common pleas, and such other courts as the legislature may establish. The judges are appointed by the governor, and hold their offices during good behavior. The right of suffrage is enjoyed by every male citizen, twenty-one years of age (excepting paupers, and persons under guardianship), who has resided in the state one year, and in the election district six months, and shall have paid a state or county tax (or been exempted therefrom) two years next preceding any election.

History.—The coasts of Massachusetts, after Cabot and Cartier's voyages, were annually visited for trade with the natives, and for fishing, yet little was known of the interior, until Captain Smith, the hero of Virginia, explored its shores from the Penobscot to Cape Cod, and penetrated its interminable forests. It was Smith who gave that whole country the name of New England. That region was not permanently settled until 1620, when a party of 101 Independents, who had fled from England to Holland, in 1608, in consequence of persecutions, obtained a grant of land from the Virginia Company, intending to settle within their jurisdiction. But through accident or treachery, they reached the coast within the jurisdiction of the Plymouth Company,* from whom they subsequently obtained a patent. The great moral spectacle which this little company of emigrants presented, can not be passed unnoticed. Deprived of the privilege of worshipping God according to the dictates of their own consciences and judgments, they left England, with their pastor, John Robinson, and became voluntary exiles in Holland. They cherished the sentiment, however, "England, with all thy faults, I love thee still," and they felt a yearning to live where they might retain their language and laws in their purity and strength. They therefore turned their thoughts toward the wilds of America, where no restraining power should interfere with their religious privileges; and obtaining a grant from the London or Virginia Company, they left Delft Haven, in Holland, in August 1, 1620, in the Speedwell. They were joined at Southampton, England, by the May-Flower. bearing a number of business men of London, who had formed a partnership with those from Holland. The Speedwell, however, proved unseaworthy, and the whole company, numbering in men, women, and children, as before remarked, 101 souls, sailed from Plymouth in the May-Flower on the 16th of September. They reached the American coast, and descried the bleak hills of Cape Cod, on the 19th of November. For a month they laid at anchor, and in the meanwhile they entered into a solemn political compact, and chose John Carver their governor for the first year. Exploring parties were sent ashore to find a good place for settlement; and on the 21st of December the harbor of Plymouth was sounded, and found fit for shipping, and the shore well-watered and wooded, and there they landed, and commenced a settlement. They named the place New Plymouth, and soon afterward obtained a charter. In 1628, the Plymouth council granted to a number of nonconformists, of Devonshire, the territory of New England, lying between the Merrimack and Charles rivers, and three miles beyond, and extending to the South sea. A company of planters, with their families, were sent out, and founded the town of Salem. In 1629, the patentees obtained a charter from Charles I, confirming the grant of the council, and incorporating them under the name of the Governor and Company of Massachusetts Bay. Subsequently to this period, other grants and accessions were made, and the colony of Massachusetts extended its jurisdiction over the present state of Rhode Island, a part of Connecticut, New Hampshire, Maine, and Acadia. In 1641, the settlements of New Hampshire were incorporated with Massachusetts. In 1643, the four colonies, Massachusetts, Plymouth, Connecticut, and New Haven, entered into articles of confederation, under the title of the "United Colonies of New England." In 1652, Maine placed itself under the protection of Massachusetts, called the county of "Yorkshire," and remained a part of her territory, with some modifications, until it became a sovereign state. In 1686, the charter government of Massachusetts Bay was taken from her, and a president placed over the dominion from Narraganset bay to Nova Scotia. The same year, Sir Edmund Andros arrived at Boston, with a commission as royal governor of all New England. Plymouth, Massachusetts, New Hampshire, and Rhode Island, immediately submitted to his jurisdiction. A few months after, Connecticut was added, and in 1688, his power was further extended over New Jersey and New York. In 1689, Plymouth was united to Massachusetts by royal order, and its old charter confirmed. In 1691, Plymouth, Massachusetts, Maine, and Acadia, were formed into one royal colony, under the name of "Massachusetts." In 1699, New Hampshire and Maa

* In 1606, James the First of England, claiming all the territory lying between the latitude of Cape Fear on the south, and of Halifax on the north, divided it into two nearly equal districts. One, extending from the 41st to the 45th degree, he called North Virginia; the other, extending from the 34th to the 38th degree, he called South Virginia. On the 20th day of April, 1606, he issued a charter to a "company of knights, gentlemen, and merchants," of the west of England, called the Plymouth Company, granting to them the right of settlement of the territory of North Virginia. At the same time a similar charter was granted to like persons residing in London, and called the London Company for the settlement of South Virginia. It was stipulated that neither should form a settlement within a hundred miles of the other.

sachusetts were placed under the jurisdiction of New York, but were again reunited in 1702. and thus continued until 1741, when a final separation took place. In conformity to the original grant of the Plymouth Company, Massachusetts claimed an indefinite extent of country westward, which was adjusted with New York, by ceding all her territory west of a line, running north and south, one mile east of Geneva, and was known as the "Genesee Country." In 1776, on the declaration of independence, Massachusetts formed a state constitution, which went into operation in 1780, and, with the exception of the amendment in 1820, is the same as the one of the present day. In 1778, it ratified the constitution of the United States. The motto of the seal is, *Ense petit placidam sub libertate quietem*— "By his sword he seeks the calm repose of liberty."

MASSACK, p. o., McCraken co., Ky.

MASSAMUTTON, p. o., Page co., Va., 138 ms. N. w. of Richmond; from W. 106 ms.

MASSENA, p. t., St. Lawrence co., N. Y., 247 ms. N. w. of Albany; from W. 524 ms. Watered by Racket, Grass, and St. Lawrence rivers. Pop. 2,870.

MASSENA CENTRE, p. o., Massena township, St. Lawrence co., N. Y.

MASSEY'S CROSS-ROADS, p. o., Kent co., Md.

MASSILLON, p. v., Perry township, Stark co., O., 116 ms. N. E. of Columbus; from W. 321 ms., on the Ohio canal.

MASILLON, p. o., Allen co., Ind.

MASILLON, p. o., Clinton co., Iowa.

MASTEN'S CORNER, p. o., Kent co., Del.

MASTERSONVILLE, p. o., Lancaster co., Pa.

MASTERTON, p. o., Monroe co., O.

MAST-YARD, p. o, Merrimack co., N. H.

MATAGORDA COUNTY, situated in the south part of Texas, with Matagorda bay and the Gulf of Mexico on the south, and traversed by Colorado river. Area, —— square miles. Seat of justice, Matagorda. Pop. in 1850, 2,124.

MATAGORDA, p. v., Matagorda co., Tex.

MATAMORA, p. o., Hardeman co., Tenn., 173 ms. S. w. of Nashville; from W. 849 ms.

MATAMORAS, p. o., Montgomery co., N. C.

MATHERTON, p. o., Iowa co., Mich.

MATILDAVILLE, p. o., Clarion co., Pa.

MATILDAVILLE, p. o., Parishville township, St. Lawrence co., N. Y.

MATTAPOISET, p. v., Rochester township, Plymouth co., Mass., 60 ms. S. E. of Boston; from W. 441 ms. Watered by an outlet from Buzzard's bay.

MATTAWAMKEAG, p. o., Penobscot co., Me., 130 ms. N. E. of Augusta; from W. 725 ms.

MATTAWAN, p. v., Van Buren co., Mich.

MATTAWAN, p. v., Fishkill township, Dutchess co. N. Y. Watered by Fishkill creek.

MATTHEWS COUNTY, situated in the southeast part of Virginia, and bounded on the north, east, and south, by Chesapeake bay. Area, 80 square miles. Seat of justice, Matthews c. h. Pop. in 1810, 4,227; in 1820, 6,920; in 1830, 7,663; in 1840, 7,442; in 1850, 6.714.

MATTHEWS. c. h., p. v., seat of justice of Matthews co., Va., 102 ms. E. of Richmond; from W. 187 ms.

MATTHEWS' MILLS, p. o., Richland co., Ill.

MATTHEWS' STORE, p. o., Anne Arundel co., Md.

MATTISON, p. t., Branch co., Mich. Pop. 475.

MATTITUCK, p. v., Southold township, Suffolk co., Long Island, N. Y., 233 ms. S. E. of Albany; from W. 313 ms.

MAUCH CHUNK, p. t., Carbon co., Pa., 92 ms. N. E. of Harrisburgh; from W. 200 ms. Watered by Lehigh river, Beaver, Mauch Chunk, Nesquihoning, and Kettle creeks, and Room run. Pop. 3,727.

MAUCKPORT, p. v., Harrison co., Ind., 141 ms. s. of Indianapolis; from W. 635 ms.

MAULDING'S MILLS, p. o., Wayne co., Ill., 147 ms. s. E. of Springfield; from W. 766 ms.

MAUMEE, t., Allen co., Ind.

MAUMEE CITY, c. h., p. v., seat of justice of Lucas co., O., 124 ms. N. w. of Columbus; from W. 445 ms. Watered by Maumee river.

MAUMELLE, p. o., Pulaski co., Ark.

MAURICE RIVER, t., Cumberland co., N. J., 85 ms. s. of Trenton; from W. 182 ms. Watered by Delaware bay, and Tuckahoe, Tarkill, and Maurice rivers. Pop. 2,245.

MAURICETOWN, p. v., Downe township, Cumberland co., N. J., 75 ms. s. of Trenton; from W. 187 ms. Watered by Maurice river.

MAURIUS, p. o., Viogo co., Ind.

MAURY COUNTY, situated in the central part of Tennessee. Area, 750 square miles. Face of the country, hilly; soil fertile. Seat of justice, Columbia. Pop. in 1810, 10.359; in 1820, 22,141; in 1830, 28,153; in 1840, 28,186; in 1850, 29,520.

MAVAIS, p. o., Osage co., Mo., 28 ms. E. of Jefferson city; from W. 964 ms.

MAXATAWNY, t., Berks co., Pa., 74 ms. N. E. of Harrisburgh; from W. 165 ms. Watered by Maiden and Sacony creeks. Pop. 1,740.

MAXEY, p. o., Oglethorpe co., Ga.

MAXFIELD, p. t., Penobscot co., Me., 112 ms. N. E. of Augusta; from W. 707 ms. Watered by Piscataquis river, and Sebais stream. Pop. 186.

MAXWELL, p. o., Delaware co., O

MAY, p. o., Lancaster co., Pa.

MAYBERRY, p. o., Lewis co., Mo.

MAYBINTON, p. v., Newberry district, S. C., 45 ms. w. of Columbia; from W. 488 ms.

MAYFIELD. t., Somerset co., Me., 52 ms. N. of Augusta; from W. 657 ms. Pop. 1,682.

MAYFIELD, p. t., Fulton co., N. Y., 58 ms. N. w. of Albany; from W. 422 ms. Watered by tributaries of Sacondaga river. Pop. 2,429.

MAYFIELD, p. o., Isle of Wight co., Va., 81 ms. S. E. of Richmond; from W. 197 ms.

MAYFIELD, c. h., p. v., seat of justice of Graves co., Ky., 275 ms. s. w. of Frankfort; from W. 802 ms. Watered by a tributary of Mayfield river.

MARYFIELD, p. t., Cuyahoga co., O., 161 ms. N. E. of Columbus; from W. 349 ms. Watered by Chagrin river. Pop. 1,117.

MAYFIELD. p. o., Warren co., Ga., 35 ms. N. E. of Milledgeville; from W. 636 ms. Watered by Ogeechee river.

MAY-FLOWER, p. o., Otsego co., N. Y.

MAY HILL, p. o., Lee co., Ill.

MAYO. p. o., Halifax co., Va., 143 ms. s. w. of Richmond; from W. 230 ms.

MAYONING, p. v., Patrick co., Va., 217 ms. s. w. of Richmond; from W. 292 ms. Watered by a tributary of North Mayo river.

MAYPORT MILLS, p. o., Duval co., Flo.

MAY'S LANDING, c. h., p. v., Hamilton township, seat of justice of Atlantic co., N. J., 73 ms. s. of Trenton; from W. 183 ms. Watered by Great Egg Harbor river, at the head of sloop navigation.

MAY'S LICK, p. o., Mason co., Ky., 70 ms. N. E. of Frankfort; from W. 473 ms.

MAYSVILLE. c. h., p. v., seat of justice of Buckingham co., Va., 79 ms. w. of Richmond; from W. 158 ms. Watered by Slate river.

MAYSVILLE, p. v., Greenbrier co., Va., 232 ms. w. of Richmond; from W. 269 ms.

MAYSVILLE, t., Morgan co., O. Pop. 1,512.

MAYSVILLE, city, Mason co., Ky., 81 ms. N. E. of Frankfort; from W. 461 ms. Watered by Ohio river. Pop. 3.840.

MAYSVILLE, v., Fountain co., Ind., 84 ms. N. w. of Indianapolis; from W. 642 ms.

MAYSVILLE, p. o., Huntington co., Ind.

MAYSVILLE, c. h., p. v., seat of justice of Clay co., Ill., 122 ms. s. E. of Springfield; from W. 733 ms.

MAYSVILLE, p. o., Madison co., Ala.

MAYSVILLE, c. h., p. v., seat of justice of De Kalb co., Mo.

MAYSVILLE, p. o., Benton co., Ark.

MAYSVILLE, p. o., Yuba co., Cal.

MAYTOWN, p. v., Donegal township, Lancaster co., Pa., 30 ms. s. E. of Harrisburgh; from W. 108 ms. Pop. 634.

MAYVILLE, c. h., p. v., seat of justice of Chautauque co., N. Y., 344 ms. w. of Albany; from W. 339 ms.

MAYVILLE, p. o., Dodge co., Wis.

MAZON, p. o., Grundy co., Ill.

MCAFEE, p. o., Mercer co., Ky.

MCALEVY'S FORT, p. o., Huntingdon co., Pa.

MCALLISTER'S CROSS-ROADS, p. o., Montgomery co., Tenn., 53 ms. N. w. of Nashville; from W. 737 ms.

MCALLISTERVILLE, p. v., Juniata co., Pa., 55 ms. N.W. of Harrisburgh; from W. 149 ms.

MCARTHUR. c. h., p. v., seat of justice of Vinton co., O., 71 ms. s. E. of Columbus; from W. 365 ms. Watered by a branch of Raccoon creek. Pop. 424.

MCBEEN, p. o., Richmond co., Ga.

MCBRIDESVILLE, p. v., Union district, S. C., 80 ms. N. w. of Columbia; from W. 474 ms.

McCALL'S CREEK, p. o., Franklin co., Miss., 70 ms. s. w. of Jackson; from W. 1,080 ms.

McCALLUM'S STORE, p. o., Montgomery co., N. C.

McCLELLANDTOWN, p. v., German township, Fayette co., Pa, 107 ms. w. of Harrisburgh; from W. 204 ms.

McCOMB, p. o., Hancock co., O.

McCONNELLSBURGH, p. v., Air township, Fulton co., Pa., 67 ms. s. w. of Harrisburgh; from W. 95 ms. Watered by Big Cove creek. Pop. 477.

McCONNELL'S GROVE, p. o., Stephenson co., Ill.

McCONNELLSTOWN, p. o., Huntingdon co., Pa.

McCONNELLSVILLE, p. o., Vienna township, Oneida co., N. Y., 121 ms. N. w. of Albany; from W. 391 ms.

McCONNELLSVILLE, c.h., p. v., Morgan township, and seat of justice of Morgan co., O., 73 ms. E. of Columbus; from W. 330 ms. Watered by Muskingum river.

McCOYSVILLE, p. o., Juniata co., Pa.

McCRACKEN COUNTY, situated on the northwesterly boundary of Kentucky, with Ohio river on the north, and the Tennessee river on the northeast. Area, 200 square miles. Seat of justice, Paducah. Pop. in 1830, 1,297; in 1840, 4,745; in 1850, 6,067.

McCULLOCH'S MILLS, p. o., Juniata co., Pa.

McCUTCHANVILLE, p. o., Vanderburgh co., Ind.

McCUTCHENVILLE, p. o., Wyandott co., O., 70 ms. N. of Columbus; from W. 425 ms.

McCUTCHON'S, p. o., St. Charles parish, La.

McDANIEL'S, p. o., Orange co., N. C., 61 ms. N. w. of Raleigh; from W. 296 ms.

McDANIELSVILLE, v., Spartanburgh district, S. C., 92 ms. N. w. of Columbia; from W. 481 ms.

McDONALD COUNTY, situated at the southwest corner of Missouri. Area, —— square miles. Seat of justice, Rutledge. Pop. in 1850, 2,236.

McDONALD, p. o., Wilkinson co., Ga.

McDONALD, t., Hardin co., O. Pop. 582.

McDONALD, c. h., v., seat of justice of Randolph co., Ala.; from W. 757 ms.

McDONALD, c. h., v., seat of justice of Barry co., Mo., 200 ms. s. w. of Jefferson city; from W. 1,115 ms. Watered by a branch of White river.

McDONALD'S MILL, p. o., Montgomery co., Va.

McDONOUGH COUNTY, situated in the west part of Illinois. Area, 576 square miles. Seat of justice, Macomb. Pop. in 1840, 5,308; in 1850, 7,615.

McDONOUGH, p. t., Chenango co., N. Y., 119 ms. w. of Albany; from W. 326 ms. Watered by Bowman's and Canasawlotte creeks. Pop. 1,522.

McDONOUGH, c. h., p. v., seat of justice of Henry co., Ga., 65 ms. N. w. of Milledgeville; from W. 669 ms. Situated between Towelagga and South Ocmulgee rivers.

McDONOUGH, p. o., Newcastle co., Del.

McDOWELL COUNTY, situated in the westerly part of North Carolina. Area, —— square miles. Seat of justice, Marion. Pop. in 1850, 6,246.

McDOWELL, p. o., Highland co., Va.

McELROY, p. o., Doddridge co., Va.

McEWEN'S CROSS-ROADS. p. o., Troy township, Morrow co., O., 57 ms. N. E. of Columbus; from W. 388 ms.

McEWINGSVILLE, p. o., Northumberland co., Pa., 75 ms. N. of Harrisburgh; from W. 185 ms.

McFARLAND'S, p. o., Lunenburgh co., Va., 70 ms. s. w. of Richmond; from W. 189 ms.

McGAHEYSVILLE, p. o., Rockingham co., Va., 116 ms. N. w. of Richmond; from W. 131 ms.

McGARY, p. o., Hancock co., Ill.

McGEE'S, p. o., Polk co., Tex.

McGEE'S BRIDGE, p. o., Yallabusha co., Miss.

McGHEE'S STORE, p. o., Jackson co., O.

McGRAWVILLE. p. v., Cortlandville township, Cortland co., N. Y., 142 ms. w. of Albany; from W. 318 ms.

McGREGOR'S LANDING, p. o., Clayton co., Iowa.

McHARGUE'S MILLS, p. o., Knox co., Ky.

McHENRY COUNTY, situated on the north boundary of Illinois. Area, 960 square miles. Seat of justice, Dorr. Pop. in 1840, 2,578; in 1850, 14,979.

McHENRY, c. h., p. v., seat of justice of McHenry co., Ill., 223 ms. N. E. of Springfield; from W. 758 ms. Watered by Fox river.

McINDOE'S FALLS, p. v., Barnet township, Caledonia co., Vt., 46 ms. E. of Montpelier; from W. 532 ms. Watered by Connecticut river at the head of navigation.

McINTOSH COUNTY. situated on the southeast boundary of Georgia, with the Atlantic on the south-

east, and Altamaha river on the southwest. Area, 600 square miles. Face of the country level; soil sandy. Seat of justice, Darien. Pop. in 1810, 3,730; in 1820, 5,129; in 1830, 4,998; in 1840, 5,360; in 1850, 6,028.

McKAIG'S MILLS. p. o., Columbiana co., O., 145 ms. N. E. of Columbus; from W. 284 ms.

McKAY, p. o., Ashland co., O.

McKAY, p. o., Dallas co., Iowa.

McKEAN COUNTY, situated on the north boundary of Pennsylvania. Area, 1,470 square miles. Face of the country hilly; soil of middling quality. Seat of justice, Smithport. Pop. in 1810, 144; in 1820, 728; in 1830, 1,439; in 1840, 2,975; in 1850, 5,254.

McKEAN, p. t., Erie co., Pa., 265 ms. N. w. of Harrisburgh; from W. 338 ms. Watered by Elk and Walnut creeks. Pop. 1,916.

McKEAN, t., Licking co., O., 32 ms. N. E. of Columbus; from W. 372 ms. Pop. 1,378.

McKEANSBURGH, p. v., Brunswick township, Schuylkill co., Pa., 67 ms. N. E. of Harrisburgh; from W. 177 ms.

McKINNEY, p. o., Collin co., Tex.

McKEAN'S OLD STAND, p. o., Westmoreland co., Pa., 175 ms. w. of Harrisburgh; from W. 201 ms.

McKEE'S HALF FALLS, p. o., Union co., Pa., 40 ms. N. of Harrisburgh; from W. 150 ms.

McKEE'S PORT, p. v., Versailles township, Alleghany co., Pa., 199 ms. w. of Harrisburgh; from W. 212 ms. Pop. 1,392.

McKINLEY, p. o., Marengo co., Ala.; from W. 890 ms.

McKINSTRY'S MILLS, p. o., Carroll co., Md., 66 ms. N. w. of Annapolis; from W. 69 ms.

McKISSACK'S GROVE, p. o., Fremont co.. Iowa.

McLAIN'S MILLS, p. o., Waldo co., Me., 33 ms. E. of Augusta; from W. 622 ms.

McLEAN COUNTY, situated in the central part of Illinois. Area, 1,296 square miles. Seat of justice, Bloomington. Pop. in 1840, 6,565; in 1850, 10,163.

McLEAN, p. v., Groton township, Tompkins co., N. Y., 149 ms. w. of Albany; from W. 311 ms. Watered by Fall creek.

McLEAN, t., Shelby co., O.

McLEANSBURGH, c. h., p.v., seat of justice of Hamilton co., Ill., 156 ms. s. E. of Springfield; from W. 776 ms. Watered by a tributary of Saline creek.

McLEAN'S STORE, p. o., Tippah co., Miss.

McLEMORESVILLE, p. v., Carroll co., Tenn., 107 ms. from Nashville; from W. 790 ms.

McLEOD'S, p. o., Greene co., Miss., 195 ms. s. E. of Jackson; from W. 1,073 ms.

McMANUS, p. o., Greene co., Miss., 210 ms. s. E. of Jackson; from W. 1,042 ms.

McMATH'S, p. o., Tuscaloosa co., Ala.; from W. 786 ms.

McMEEKINS, p. o., Fairfield district, S. C., 28 ms. N. of Columbia; from W. 502 ms.

McMILLAN'S, p. o., Panola co., Tex.

McMINN COUNTY, situated in the southeast part of Tennessee. Area, 608 square miles. Face of the country hilly; soil varied. Seat of justice, Athens. Pop. in 1820, 1,623; in 1830, 14,497; in 1840, 12,719; in 1850, 13,906.

McMINNVILLE, c. h., p. v., seat of justice of Warren co., Tenn., 75 ms. s. E. of Nashville; from W. 624 ms. Watered by Barren fork.

McNUTT, p. o., Sun-Flower co., Miss.

McRAE'S MILLS, p. o., Montgomery co., N. C.

McRAE'S STORE, p. o., Telfair co., Ga.

McSHERRYSTOWN, p. o., Adams co., Pa.

McVEYTOWN, p. b., Mifflin co., Pa., 68 ms. N. w. of Harrisburgh; from W. 154 ms. Pop. 580.

McWILLIAMSTOWN, p. v., Chester co., Pa., 65 ms. s. E. of Harrisburgh; from W. 154 ms.

McELROY, p. o., Doddridge co., Va.

McNAIRY COUNTY, situated on the south boundary of Tennessee. Area, 960 square miles. Seat of justice, Purdy. Pop. in 1830, 5,697; in 1840, 9,385; in 1850, 12,864.

MEAD COUNTY, situated on the northerly boundary of Kentucky, with Ohio river on the north. Area, 360 square miles. Seat of justice, Brandenburgh. Pop. in 1840, 5,780; in 1850, 7,393.

MEAD, t., Crawford co., Pa., 236 ms. N. w. of Harrisburgh; from W. 297 ms. Pop. 1,810.

MEAD, t., Belmont co., O., 134 ms. E. of Columbus; from W. 285 ms. Watered by Ohio river and Pipe creek. Pop. 1,626.

MEADORVILLE, p. o., Macon co., Tenn.

MEADOW BLUFF, p. o., Greenbrier co., Va.

MEADOW BRANCH, p. o., Jackson co., O.

MEADOW CREEK, p. o., Orange co., N. C.

MEADOW CREEK, p. o., Whitley co., Ky.

MEADOW DALE, p. o., Highland co., Va.

MEADOW DAM, p. o., Patrick co., Va.

MEADOW FARM, p. o., Muskingum co., O

MEADOW'S, p. o., Van Buren co., Ark.

MEAD'S BASIN, p. o., Passaic co., N. J., 73 ms. N. E. of Trenton ; from W. 244 ms.

MEAD'S CORNERS, p. o., Crawford co., Pa.

MEADVILLE, c. h., p. b., seat of justice of Crawford co., Pa., 234 ms. N. W. of Harrisburgh ; from W. 307 ms. Watered by French creek. Seat of Alleghany college. Pop. 2,578.

MEAD'S MILL, p. o., Wayne co., Mich.

MEADVILLE, p. o., Jackson co., Ala.

MEADVILLE, c.*h., p. v., seat of justice of Franklin co., Miss., 80 ms. s. w. of Jackson ; from W. 1,090 ms. Watered by Homochitto river.

MEADVILLE, p. v., Halifax co., Va., 136 ms. s. w. of Richmond , from W. 223 ms.

MEADVILLE, p. o., Mead co., Ky.

MEADSVILLE, p. v., Union district, S. C., 81 ms. N. W. of Columbia ; from W. 475 ms.

MECCA, p. t., Trumbull co., O., 180 ms. N. E. of Columbus ; from W. 314 ms. Pop. 872.

MECHANIC, t., Holmes co., O., 80 ms. N. E. of Columbus ; from W. 335 ms. Pop. 1,647.

MECHANICSBURGH, p. o., Lehigh co., Pa.

MECHANICSBURGH, p. v., Sangamon co., Ill., 15 ms. E. of Springfield ; from W. 765 ms.

MECHANICSBURGH, p. v., Goshen township, Champaign co., O., 36 ms. w. of Columbus ; from W. 429 ms. Watered by Little Darby creek. Pop. 682.

MECHANICSBURGH, p. v., Giles co., Va., 248 ms. w. of Richmond ; from W. 308 ms.

MECHANICSBURGH, p. o., Henry co., Ind.

MECHANICSBURGH, p. b.. Cumberland co., Pa., 6 ms. s. w. of Harrisburgh : from W. 105 ms.

MECHANIC'S FALLS, p. v., Cumberland co., Me.

MECHANIC'S GROVE, p. o.. Lancaster co., Pa.

MECHANICSTOWN, p. v., Frederick co., Md., 89 ms. N. w. of Annapolis ; from W. 60 ms.

MECHANICSTOWN, p. v., Fox township, Carroll co., O., 135 ms. N. E. of Columbus ; from W. 285 ms.

MECHANICSVILLE, p. v., Rutland co., Vt., 82 ms. s. w. of Montpelier ; from W. 465 ms.

MECHANICSVILLE, p. v., Stillwater township, Saratoga co., N. Y., 29 ms. N. of Albany ; from W. 389 ms. Watered by Hudson river.

MECHANICSVILLE, p. o., Bucks co., Pa., 104 ms. E. of Harrisburgh ; from W. 166 ms.

MECHANICSVILLE, p. v., Louisa co., Va., 70 ms. N. w. of Richmond ; from W. 114 ms.

MECHANICSVILLE. v., Sumter district, S. C., 78 ms. E. of Columbia ; from W. 504 ms.

MECHANICSVILLE, p. v., Jasper co., Ga., 45 ms. w. of Milledgeville ; from W. 652 ms.

MECHANICSVILLE, p. v., Cannon co., Tenn., 30 ms. s. E. of Nashville ; from W. 680 ms.

MECHANICSVILLE, p. o., Russell co., Ala.

MECHISSES, t., Washington co., Me., 157 ms. E. of Augusta ; from W. 743 ms. Watered by East Machias river. Pop. 1,590.

MECHUM'S RIVER, p. o., Albemarle co., Va.

MECKLENBBURGH COUNTY, situated on the south boundary of Virginia, and traversed by Roanoke river. Area, 640 square miles. Face of the country undulating ; soil productive. Seat of justice, Boydton. Pop. in 1810, 18,443 ; in 1820, 19,786 ; in 1830, 20,366 ; in 1840, 20,724 ; in 1850, 20,630.

MECKLENBURGH COUNTY, situated on the southerly boundary of North Carolina, with Catawba river on the west. Area, 900 square miles. Face of the country undulating ; soil, near the streams, fertile. Seat of justice, Charlotte. Pop. in 1810, 14,272 ; in 1820, 16,895 ; in 1830, 20,076 ; in 1840, 18,273 ; in 1850, 13,914.

MECKLENBURGH, p. v., Hector township, Tompkins co., N. Y., 174 ms. w. of Albany ; from W. 307 ms.

MECKLENBURGH, p. v., Knox co., Tenn., 188 ms. E. of Nashville ; from W. 503 ms. Watered by Holston river.

MEDARY, p. o., Putnam co., O.

MEDFIELD, p. t. Norfolk co., Mass., 21 ms. s. w. of Boston ; from W. 425 ms. Watered by Charles and Stop rivers. Pop. 966.

MEDFORD, p. t., Middlesex co., Mass., 5 ms. N. w. of

Boston ; from W. 445 ms. Watered by Mystic river, at the head of navigation. Pop. in 1840, 2,478 ; in 1850, 3,749.

MEDFORD, p. v., Evesham township. Burlington co., N. J., 31 ms. s. E. of Trenton ; from W. 155 ms. Pop. 3,022.

MEDINA COUNTY, situated in the north part of Ohio. Area, 450 square miles. Seat of justice, Medina. Pop. in 1820, 3,082 ; in 1830, 7,560 ; in 1840, 18,352 ; in 1850. 24,441.

MEDINA COUNTY, situated in Texas. Area, —— square miles. Seat of justice, Castroville. Pop. in 1850, 909.

MEDINA, p. v., Ridgeway township, Orleans co., N. Y., 262 ms. w. of Albany ; from W. 397 ms. Watered by Oak Orchard creek and Erie canal.

MEDINA, c. h.. p. t., seat of justice of Medina co., O., 117 ms. N. E. of Columbus ; from W. 351 ms. Pop. 2,291.

MEDINA, p. t., Lenawee co., Mich., 81 ms. s. w. of Detroit ; from W. 510 ms. Pop. 1,600.

MEDINA, p. o., Winnebago co., Ill.

MEDON, p. o., Madison co., Tenn., 146 ms. s. w. of Nashville ; from W. 831 ms.

MEDUSA, p. o., Albany co., N. Y.

MEDWAY, p. t., Norfolk co., Mass., 28 ms. s. w. of Boston ; from W. 418 ms. Watered by Charles river Pop. 2,778.

MEDWAY, v., Liberty co., Ga.

MEDWAY, p. o., Clark co., O.

MEDWAY, p. o., Green co., N. Y.

MEDYBEMPS, p. o., Washington co., Me.

MEEK'S HILL, p. o., York district, S. C., 86 ms. N. o' Columbia ; from W. 437 ms.

MEEME, p. o., Manitoowoc co,. Wis.

MEETING STREET, p. o., Edgefield district, S. C.

MEEHOOPANY, p. o., Luzerne co., Pa., 160 ms. N. w of Harrisburgh.

MEIGS COUNTY, situated on the southeasterly boundary of Ohio, on Ohio river. Area, 425 square miles. Face of the country, broken ; soil, generally productive. Seat of justice, Pomeroy. Pop. in 1820, 4,480 ; in 1830, 6,159 ; in 1840, 11,452 ; in 1850, 17,969.

MEIGS COUNTY, situated in the southeast part of Tennessee, with Tennessee river on the northwest. Area, 215 square miles. Seat of justice, Decatur. Pop. in 1840, 4,794 ; in 1850, 4,879.

MEIGS, t., Adams co., O., 96 ms. s. of Columbus ; from W. 455 ms. Pop. 1,438.

MEIGS, t., Muskingum co., O. Pop. 1,680.

MEIGS CREEK. p. o., Morgan co., O., 78 ms. E. of Columbus ; from W. 338 ms.

MEIGSVILLE, p. t., Morgan co., O. Pop. 1,512.

MEIGSVILLE, p. v., Jackson co., Tenn., 82 ms. E. of Nashville ; from W. 639 ms. Watered by Cumberland river.

MELENDEZ MILLS, c. h., p. v., seat of justice of Benton co., Flor.

MELLONVILLE, p. v., Claverack township, Columbia co., N. Y., 37 ms. s. of Albany ; from W. 349 ms.

MELLONVILLE, c. h., p. v., seat of justice of Orange co., Flor.

MELMORE, p. v., Eden township, Seneca co., O., 82 ms. N. of Columbus ; from W. 416 ms. Watered by Honey creek.

MELON, p. o., Harrison co., Va.

MELPINE, p. o., Muscatine co., Iowa.

MELROSE, p. v., Clarke co., Ill., 152 ms. s. E. of Springfield ; from W. 686 ms. Pop. 672.

MELROSE, v., Westfarms t., Westchester co., N. Y.

MELROSE, p. o., Rockingham co., Va.

MELROSE, p. o., Middlesex co., Mass.

MELROSE, p. o., Rush co., Ind.

MELROSE, p. o., Nacogdoches co., Tex

MELTON'S, p. o., Navarro co., Tex.

MELTONSVILLE, p, v., Anson co., N. C., 160 ms. s. w. of Raleigh ; from W. 454 ms.

MELTONSVILLE, p. v., Marshall co., Ala. ; from W. 687 ms.

MELVILLE, p. o., Orange co., N. C.

MELVILLE, p. o., Chattooga co., Ga.

MELVIN, p. o., Ballard co., Ky.

MELVIN VILLAGE, p. v., Carroll co., N. H., 49 ms. E. of Concord ; from 530 ms.

MEMPHIS, c. h., p. v., seat of justice of Shelby co., Tenn., 230 ms. s. w. of Nashville ; from W. 915 ms Watered by Mississippi river. Pop. 8,841.

MEMPHIS, p. v., Scotland co., Mo., 184 ms. N. of Jefferson city ; from W. 951 ms.

MEMPHIS, p. o., Pickens co., Ala., from W. 951 ms.

MEMPHIS, p. o., St. Clair co., Mich.

MENALLEN, p. t., Adams co., Pa., 48 ms. s. w. of Harrisburgh; from W. 89 ms. Pop. 1,455.

MENALLAN. t., Fayette co., Pa. Pop. 1,411.

MENARD COUNTY, situated in the central part of Illinois. and traversed by Sangamon river. Area, 260 square miles. Seat of justice, Petersburgh. Pop. in 1840, 4,431 ; in 1850, 6,349.

MENASHA, p. o., Winnebago co., Wis.

MENASSES' GAP, p. o., Warren co., Va., 136 ms. N. of Richmond ; from W. 79 ms.

MENDHAM, p. t., Morris co., N. J., 56 ms. E. of Trenton , from W. 230 ms. Watered by tributaries of Raritan, and Whippany rivers. Pop. 1,720.

MENDON, p. t., Rutland co., Vt., 47 ms. s. of Montpelier ; from W. —— ms. Watered by tributaries of Otter creek. Pop. 504.

MENDON, p. t., Worcester co., Mass., 33 ms. s. w. of Boston ; from W. 406 ms. Watered by Mill and Blackstone rivers. Pop. 1,300.

MENDON, p. t., Monroe co., N. Y., 210 ms. w. of Albany ; from W. 356 ms. Watered by Honeyoye and Irondequoit creeks. Pop. 3,351.

MENDON, p. o., Mercer co., O., 123 ms. N. w. of Columbus ; from W. 495 ms.

MENDON, p. o., Lenawee co., Mich., 75 ms. s. w. of Detroit ; from W. 515 ms.

MENDON, p. v.. Adams co., Ill., 116 ms. w. of Springfield ; from W. 894 ms.

MENDON, p. o., Madison co., Ind.

MENELOS, p. o., Madison co., Ky.

MENOMINEE, t., Waukesha co., Wis.

MENOMINEE FALLS, p. o., Waukesha co., Wis.

MENTER, p. o., Sheboygan co., Wis.

MENTOR, p. t.. Lake co., O., 169 ms. N. E. of Columbus ; from W. 355 ms. Watered by Lake Erie. Pop. 1,571.

MENTZ, t., Cayuga co., N. Y., 156 ms. w. of Albany ; from W. 345 ms. Watered by Seneca river, Owasco inlet, and Erie canal. Pop. 5,239.

MEQUON RIVER, p. o., Washington co., Wis., 97 ms. E. of Madison ; from W. 819 ms.

MEQUANEGO, t., Waukesha co., Wis.

MERATA, p. o.. Jefferson co., Pa.

MERCER COUNTY, situated on the westerly boundary of New Jersey, with Delaware river on the west. Area, 260 square miles, Seat of justice, Trenton, which is also the capital of the state. Pop. in 1840, 21,502 ; in 1850, 27,986.

MERCER COUNTY, situated on the west boundary of Pennsylvania. Area, 850 square miles. Face of the country, uneven ; soil, productive. Seat of justice, Mercer. Pop. in 1810, 8,277 ; in 1820, 11,681 ; in 1830, 19,731 ; in 1840, 32.873 ; in 1850, 33.172.

MERCER COUNTY, situated in the southwesterly part of Virginia, with Great Kanawha river on the northeast. Area, 540 square miles. Seat of justice, Princeton. Pop. in 1840, 2,233 ; in 1850, 4,222.

MERCER COUNTY, situated in the central part of Kentucky, with Kentucky river on the northeast. Area, 350 square miles. Seat of justice, Harrisburgh. Pop. in 1810, 12,430 ; in 1820, 15,587 ; in 1830, 17,706 ; in 1840, 18,720 ; in 1850, 17,067.

MERCER COUNTY, situated on the west boundary of Ohio. Area, 576 square miles. Face of the country, level ; soil, productive where not marshy. Seat of justice, Celina. Pop. in 1830, 1,110 ; in 1840, 8,277 ; in 1950, 7,712.

MERCER COUNTY, situated on the west boundary of Illinois, with the Mississippi river on the west. Area, 550 square miles. Seat of justice, Millersburgh. Pop. in 1840, 2.352 ; in 1850, 5,246.

MERCER COUNTY, situated on the north boundary of Missouri. Area, —— square miles. Seat of justice, Princeton. Pop. in 1850, 2,691.

MERCER, p. t., Somerset co., Me., 34 ms. N. w. of Augusta ; from W. 627 ms. Watered by Sandy river. Pop. 1,186.

MERCER. p. o., Mercer co., O., 119 ms. N. w. of Columbus ; from W. 499 ms.

MERCER, c. h., p. b.. seat of justice of Mercer co., Pa., 234 ms. N. w. of Harrisburgh ; from W. 277 ms. Pop. 1.004.

MERCER, t.. Butler co., Pa., 187 ms. w. of Harrisburgh ; from W. 219 ms. Pop. 1.296.

MERCER SALT WORKS, p. o., Mercer co., Va.

MERCERSBURGH, p. b., Montgomery township, Frank-

lin co., Pa., 62 ms. s. w. of Harrisburgh ; from W. 85 ms. Watered by a tributary of Conecocheague creek. Seat of Marshall college.

MERCHANT'S BLUFF, p. o.. Darlington district, S. C.

MEREDITH, t., Belknap co., N. H., 29 ms. N. of Concord ; from W. 504 ms. Watered by Winnipiseogee lake, and Winnipiseogee river. Pop. 3,521.

MEREDITH, p. t., Delaware co., N. Y., 79 ms. s. w. of Albany ; from W. 345 ms. Watered by Oleout creek, and Susquehanna river. Pop. 1,634.

MEREDITH CENTRE, p. o., Meredith township, Belknap co., N. H., 34 ms. N. of Concord ; from W. 509 ms.

MEREDITH MILLS, p. o., Fulton co., Ind.

MEREDITH'S TAVERN, p. o., Monongalia co.. Va.

MEREDITH VILLAGE, p. v., Belknap co., N. H., 37 ms. N. of Concord ; from W. 512 ms. Watered by Winnipiseogee lake.

MEREDOSIA, v., Morgan co., Ill., 53 ms. w. of Springfield ; from W. 833 ms. Watered by Illinois river.

MERIDEN, p. v.. Sullivan co., N. H., 57 ms. s. w. of Concord ; from W. 478 ms.

MERIDEN, p. t., New Haven co., Ct., 16 ms. s. of Hartford. Watered by Quinnipiac river. Pop. 3,559.

MERIDIAN, p. v., Mercer co., Ill., 130 ms. N. w. of Springfield ; from W. 859 ms.

MERIDIAN, p. o., Cayuga co., N. Y.

MERIDIAN SPRINGS, p. v., Hinds co., Miss., 9 ms. N. of Jackson ; from W. 1,019 ms. Watered by Bogue Chitto creek.

MERIDIANVILLE, p. v., Madison co., Ala. ; from W. 716 ms. Watered by Flint river.

MERIVALE, p. o., Montgomery co., Tenn.

MERMAID, p. o., Newcastle co., Del.

MEROM, p. v., Sullivan co., Ind., 103 ms. s. w. of Indianapolis ; from W. 688 ms. Watered by Wabash river.

MERONA, p. o., McHenry co., Ill.

MERRELL, p. o., Greene co., Ga

MERRICK, p. o., Queens co., N. Y.

MERRILLSVILLE, p. o.. Franklin township, Franklin co., N. Y., 174 ms. N. of Albany ; from W. 549 ms.

MERRILLTOWN, p. o., Travis co., Tex.

MERRILLVILLE, p. o., Lake co., Ind.

MERRIMACK COUNTY, situated toward the south part of New Hampshire, and traversed by Merrimack river. Area, 816 square miles. Face of the country, undulating and hilly ; soil, fertile. Seat of justice, Concord, which is also the state capital. Pop. in 1830, 34.619 ; in 1840, 36,253 ; in 1850, 40,377.

MERRIMACK, t., Hillsborough co., N. H., 29 ms. s. of Concord ; from W. 452 ms. Watered by Merrimack and Souhegan rivers. Pop. 1,250.

MERRIMACK, t., Franklin co., Mo.

MERRIMACK, t., Jefferson co., Mo.

MERRIMACK, t., St. Louis co., Mo.

MERRIMAN, t., Crawford co., Mo.

MERRIMAN'S SHOP, p. o., Prince Edward co., Va.

MERRITT, p. o., Barry co., Mich.

MERRITT'S BRIDGE, p. o. Lexington district, S. C.

MERRITTSTOWN, p. v.. Luzerne township. Fayette co., Pa., 191 ms. w. of Harrisburgh ; from W. 207 ms. Watered by Dunlap's creek.

MERRITTSVILLE, p. v., Greenville district, S. C., 130 ms. N. w. of Columbia ; from W. 523 ms.

MERRIWETHER COUNTY, situated in the westerly part of Georgia. Area, 400 square miles. Seat of justice, Greenville. Pop. in 1830, 4,422 ; in 1840, 14,132 ; in 1850, 16.476.

MERRYALL, p. o., Bradford co., Pa.

MERRY HILL, p. o., Bertie co., N. C., 173 ms. E. of Raleigh ; from W. 264 ms.

MERRY MOUNT, p. o., Warren co., N. C.

MERRY OAKS, p. o., Barren co., Ky., 135 ms. s. w. of Frankfort ; from W. 656 ms.

MERRY OAKS, p. o., Hamilton co,, Tenn.

MERSHON'S CROSS-ROADS, p. o., Laurel co., Ky., 86 ms. s. E. of Frankfort ; from W. 555 ms.

MESOPOTAMIA, p. t., Trumbull co., O., 171 ms. N. E. of Columbus ; from W. 322 ms. Pop. 959.

MERTON, p. o., Waukesha co., Wis.

MERIOMSBURGH, p. o., Monroe co., Pa.

MESSINA SPRINGS, p. o., Onondaga co., N. Y.

MESSONGO, p. o., Accomac co., Va., 213 ms. E. of Richmond ; from W. 182 ms.

METAL, t., Franklin co., Pa., 54 ms. s. of Harrisburgh ; from W. 106 ms. Pop. 1,221.

METAMORA, p. o., Fulton co., O., 160 ms. N. w. of Columbus ; from W. 491 ms.

METAMORA, p. o., Franklin co., Ind., 62 ms. S. E. of Indianapolis; from W. 526 ms.

METAMORA, p. t., Lapeer co., Mich. Pop. 821.

METAMORA, p. o., Woodford co., Ill.

METAMORA, p. o., Pike co., Ill.

META. p. v., Cass co., Ind., 84 ms. N. of Indianapolis; from W. 622 ms.

METRDECONK, p. o., Ocean co., N. J., 48 ms. E. of Trenton; from W. 209 ms.

METHUEN, p. t., Essex co., Mass., 26 ms. N. of Boston; from W. 454 ms. Watered by Merrimack and Spicket rivers. Pop. 2,538.

METOMEN, p. o., Fond du Lac co., Wis.

METOMPKIN, p. o., Accomac co., Va.

METROPOLIS CITY, p. v., Johnson co., Ill., 225 ms. S. E. of Springfield; from W. 830 ms. Pop. 1,215.

METS. p. o., Steuben co., Ind.

METUCHEN, p. v., Middlesex co., N. J., 32 ms. N. E. of Trenton; from W. 198 ms.

MEXICO, p. t., Oxford co., Me., 42 ms. N. w. of Augusta; from W. 614 ms. Watered by Androscoggin river and tributaries. Pop. 482.

MEXICO, p. t., Oswego co., N. Y., 156 ms. N. w. of Albany; from W. 381 ms. Watered by Salmon creek and Lake Ontario. Pop. 4,221.

MEXICO. p. v., Juniata co., Pa., 42 ms. N. w. of Harrisburgh; from W. 139 ms.

MEXICO, p. o., Tymochtee township, Wyandott co., O., 79 ms. N. of Columbus; from W. 424 ms.

MEXICO, c. h., p. v., seat of justice of Audrain co., Mo., 47 ms. N. of Jefferson city; from W. 922 ms. Watered by Salt river.

MEXICO, p. o., Miami co., Ind.

MEXICO, p o., Jefferson co., Ala.

MEYER'S MILLS, p. o., Somerset co., Pa., 151 ms. w. of Harrisburgh; from W. 168 ms.

MEYERSTOWN, p. v., Jackson township, Lebanon co., Pa., 31 ms. E. of Harrisburgh; from W. 144 ms. Pop. 877.

MIAMI COUNTY. situated in the westerly part of Ohio, and traversed by Miami river. Area, 410 square miles. Seat of justice, Troy. Pop. in 1830. 12,806; in 1840, 19.688: in 1850, 24,996.

MIAMI COUNTY, situated in the northerly part of Indiana, and traversed by Wabash river. Area, 380 square miles. Seat of justice, Peru. Pop. in 1840, 3,048; in 1850, 11,304.

MIAMI, p. t., Hamilton co., O. Watered by Ohio and Wabash rivers. Pop. 1.305.

MIAMI, p. v., Whitewater township, Hamilton co., O., 119 ms. s. w. of Columbus; from W. 562 ms. Watered by Miami river.

MIAMI. t., Clermont co., O., 96 ms. s. w. of Columbus; from W. 478 ms. Pop. 2.690.

MIAMI, t., Greene co., O., 52 ms. s. w. of Columbus; from W. 448 ms. Watered by Little Miami river and tributaries. Pop. 1,865.

MIAMI, t., Logan co., O., 70 ms. N. w. of Columbus; from W. 464 ms. Pop. 775.

MIAMI, t., Montgomery co., O., 71 ms. s. w. of Columbus; from W. 367 ms. Pop. 3,456,

MIAMI. p. o., Dade co., Flor.

MIAMI, p. o., Saline co., Mo., 99 ms. N. w. of Jefferson city; from W. 1,004 ms.

MIAMI, p. o., Miami co., Ind.

MIAMISBURGH, p. v., Miami township, Montgomery co., O., 78 ms. w. of Columbus; from W. 473 ms. Watered by Miami river and Miami canal.

MIAMISVILLE, p. o., Clermont co., O.

MIANUS, p. o., Fairfield co., Ct.

MIATT, p. t., Lawrence co., O.

MICANOPY. p. o., Alachua co., Flor.

MICHIGAN, one of the United States, consisting of two distinct peninsulas, and is situated between 41° 48′ and 47° 30′ north latitude, and 82° 20′ and 90° 10′ longitude west from Greenwich. Michigan proper, or the lower peninsula, is bounded north by the straits of Mackinaw, which separate it from the upper peninsula, northeast by Lake Huron, which separates it from Canada West, east by Lake Huron, the river St. Clair, Lake St. Clair, the river Detroit and Lake Erie, which separate it from Canada West, south by Ohio and Indiana, and west by Lake Michigan, and contains 39,856 square miles. The upper peninsula, which is annexed to Michigan proper, merely for the temporary purposes of civil government, is bounded north by Lake Superior; easterly by St. Mary's river, which separates it from Canada West, southerly by Wisconsin, Lakes Michigan and Huron, and Mackinaw straits, and contains 20,664 square miles; making the total superficial area 60,520 square miles.

Physical Aspect.—The surface of Michigan proper is less varied than any other section of equal extent in the United States. The dividing ridge, or table land, which separates the sources of the Great Miami and Maumee from those of the Wabash, is continued in a northerly direction across the lower peninsula, dividing it into two inclined plains, more or less rolling, one sloping toward Lake Michigan on the west, and the other toward Lakes Huron, St. Clair, and Erie, on the east. This table-land is interspersed with marshes and small lakes, from which issue the head branches of the principal streams. Small prairies occur from the banks of the St. Joseph's to Lake St. Clair, the soil of some of which is excellent, while that of others is sandy, sterile, or wet; but a greater portion of the country is covered with dense forests, the soil of which is well adapted to the production of most kinds of northern farm-crops. The trans-peninsula, or northern division, is diversified by mountains, hills, valleys, and plains. A range of high lands runs nearly throughout the length of the peninsula, rising gradually from the shores of Lakes Michigan and Superior toward its summit. The surface in the region of Keweenaw point is broken and rolling, and some of the hills are elevated nearly 900 feet above the level of the lake. From its high latitude and sterile character, this division of the state does not promise much to agriculture; though there are many fertile tracts, particularly in the prairies on the eastern part of this peninsula, as well as in the valleys, which are highly productive, when cultivated with appropriate crops. Isle Royale presents a broken and rugged outline on its coast, and is deeply indented by long and narrow inlets and bays. About one fourth of this island is sandstone and conglomerate rock. The remainder consists of trap-rock, which lies in ridges from 300 to 500 feet in height above the lake, and extending in a broken line throughout the isle.

Mountains.—Porcupine mountains, which form the dividing ridge between Lakes Superior and Michigan, toward the western boundary of the state, are represented to be elevated from 1,800 to 2,000 feet above the lake.

Rivers, Lakes, and Bays.—The principal rivers of the lower peninsula are, the Raisin, Rouge, Detroit, Clinton, Black, or Delude, St. Clair, Saginaw, Thunder Bay, Sheboygan, St. Joseph's, Kalamazoo, Grand, Marame, Barbice. White, Rocky, Beauvais, St. Nicholas, Marguerite, Manistee, Au Sable, or Sandy, Aux Betises, Belle, Tittibawasse, Grand Traverse, Aux Carpe, Maskegon, Flint, and the Pentwater. The chief rivers of the upper peninsula are, the Ontonagon, Huron, Monomonee, Dead, Montreal, St. Mary's, Eagle, Cedar, White Fish, Black, Sturgeon, Rapid, and the Manistic. The principal lakes are, Superior, Michigan, Erie, Huron, St. Clair, Long, Houghton, and Michigamme. The chief bays are, Green, Saginaw, Thunder, Great and Little Traverse, Tah-qua-me-naw, and Keewaiwona.

Islands.—Grand, Isle Royale, Sugar, Drummond's, Cockburn, Mackinaw, Boisblanc, Great and Little Beaver, Garden, and Hog.

Climate.—The climate of Michigan is generally regarded as healthy, though near the lakes, swamps, and turbid streams, intermittents prevail to some extent in summer and fall. The seasons of the lower peninsula somewhat resemble those of western Pennsylvania, Wisconsin, and Canada West. In the northern peninsula the climate is colder and more severe. Lake St. Clair is usually frozen from December till March.

Productive Resources.—The chief productions are, horses, mules, neat cattle, sheep, swine, poultry, eggs, butter, cheese, fish, sugar, wax, hops, hay, tobacco, wool, hemp, wheat, rye, barley, oats, buckwheat, potatoes, Indian corn, and lumber. Among the mineral resources are rich veins of iron ore, in inexhaustible quantities, in the district of country extending from Dead river to the Menomonee. But what is more val-

uable, and of great importance to this country, are the rich veins of copper. blended more or less with silver, which occur at Keweenaw Point, Eagle River, Isle Royale, and other parts of the upper peninsula. Many of these mines have been opened to a considerable extent, and have been sufficiently proved to show that they may be advantageously wrought for centuries to come. From one of the veins of the Copper Falls mines a single mass of native copper has been taken, which weighed 30 tons. It was perfectly pure, and as dense as the best hammered copper of commerce, showing its perfect fineness. These ores frequently contain a sufficient quantity of silver to be of commercial value. To show the extent to which these veins are susceptible of being wrought, it may be stated that a single mine annually sends to market nearly 1,000 tons of ore, that will contain 60 per cent. of pure copper. In another instance masses of pure copper, of large size, weighing some thousands of pounds, have been obtained from an ancient ravine, that had been gullied out by the floods. In the same ravine large pieces of silver also were found.

Manufactures.—The manufactures of Michigan are confined mostly to supplying the immediate wants of the people. Saw, planing, and grist mills are numerous, as also tanneries, &c. The number of manufacturing establishments in the state, in 1850, whose annual product amounted in value to $500 and upward, was 1,979.

Railroads.—Michigan has several important railroads, which traverse the state. Among them are, the Central railroad, from Detroit to Chicago, 281 miles long, and the Southern, from Monroe to Chicago, 247 miles. The aggregate length of railroads in operation in the state is about 500 miles.

Commerce.—Situated as Michigan is, on the four great lakes of Huron, Superior, Michigan, and Erie (furnishing a continuous water communication of nearly 1,000 miles, navigable for vessels, and the opening of a canal around the falls of St. Mary, will add about 400 miles to this, through Lake Superior), it possesses superior advantages for an extensive commerce. Its foreign trade is confined to the British provinces. But its coasting trade is large—its exports from the single port of Detroit, amounting to over $4,000.000 in value annually. An immense traffic is carried on in lumber, consisting of pine, walnut, maple, and white-wood, with the eastern and southern states.

Education.—The University of Michigan, at Ann Arbor, founded in 1837, and the St. Philip's college, near Detroit, founded in 1839, are the principal collegiate institutions in Michigan. There are about 3,000 common schools throughout the state.

Population.—In 1810, within the four districts of Detroit, Erie, Huron, and Mackinaw, was 4,762; in 1820, 8,896. In 1830, the whole population of the territory was 31,639; in 1840, 212,276; in 1850, 397,654.

Government.—The legislative power is vested in a senate of 32 members, and a house of representatives, of not less than 64, nor more than 100 members, elected by the people, for two years, by single districts. The executive power is vested in a governor, and lieutenant-governor, elected by the people, for a term of two years. The general election is held on the Tuesday succeeding the first Monday in November, biennially. At each general election a secretary of state, superintendent of public instruction, treasurer, commissioner of the land-office, an auditor-general, and an attorney-general, are chosen by the people at large, for a term of two years. The county officers are also chosen every two years. The judicial power is vested in a supreme court, circuit courts, probate courts, and in justices of the peace. The judges of the several circuit courts are to be judges of the supreme court, for the term of six years, thereafter, and until the legislature otherwise provide. The right of suffrage is held by every white male citizen above the age of twenty-one years, every white male inhabitant residing in the state on the first of January, 1850, who has declared his intention to become a citizen of the United States six months preceding an election, or who has resided in the state two years and six months, and declared his intention as aforesaid, who has resided in the state two months, and in the township or ward in which he offers to vote ten days next preceding such election. Slavery and imprisonment for debt are prohibited. The personal property of debtors, under $500, and every homestead not exceeding forty acres of land, and occupied dwelling, not exceeding $1,500, are ex-

empt from sale on execution, or any other final process from a court, for any debt contracted after the adoption of this constitution.

History—Among the earlier settlements of this state were Fort Ponchartrain, at Detroit, in about the year 1600: the Jesuit mission on the island of Mackinaw, by Marquette, in 1665; and Fort Miami, at the mouth of St. Joseph's river, by La Salle, in 1678. Michigan remained as a portion of the British possessions in North America until the treaty of Grenville, in 1795. The year following it was ceded to the United States; and in 1800 it was annexed to the "Territory Northwest of the River Ohio." In 1802, Ohio was detached and formed into an independent state; but a territorial government was not established in Michigan before the year 1805. In 1812 it was invaded by the British, but was retaken by the Americans the next year. In 1835 a constitution was formed, and in 1837 it was admitted into the Union as an independent state. The present constitution of the state was adopted by a convention at Lansing, August 15, 1850, and ratified by the people in November of that year. Mottoes of the seal, *E pluribus unum:* "Many in one." *Tuebor:* "I will defend." *Si quæris peninsulam amænam circumspice:* "If thou seekest a beautiful peninsula, behold it here."

MICCOSUKEE, p. o., Leon co., Flor.

MICHAELSVILLE, p. v., Harford co., Md., 62 ms. N. of Annapolis; from W. 70 ms.

MICHIGAN CITY, p. v., La Porte co., Ind., 157 N. W. of Indianapolis; from W. 666 ms. Watered by Lake Michigan and Trail creek. Pop. 1,002.

MICHIGANTOWN, p. v., Clinton co., Ind., 42 ms. N. of Indianapolis; from W. 600 ms.

MICHILIMACKINAC COUNTY, situated in the north peninsula of Michigan, with the straits of Mackinaw on the south. Area, —— square miles. Seat of justice, Mackinaw. Pop. in 1840, 923; in 1850, 3.598.

MIDDLE, t., Cape May co., N. J., 102 ms. s. of Trenton; from W. 104 ms. Watered by Delaware bay, Atlantic ocean, and several creeks. Pop. 1,884.

MIDDLEBOROUGH, p. t., Plymouth co., Mass., 40 ms. s. of Boston; from W. 433 ms. Watered by Taunton river. Pop. 5,336.

MIDDLEBOURNE, p. o., Oxford township, Guernsey co., O., 92 ms. E. of Columbus; from W. 301 ms.

MIDDLEBOURNE, c. h., p. v., seat of justice of Tyler co., Va., 307 ms. N. w. of Richmond; from W. 275 ms. Watered by Middle Island creek.

MIDDLE BRANCH, p. o., Stark co., O.,

MIDDLEBROOK, p. v., Augusta co., Va., 129 ms. N. w. of Richmond; from W. 170 ms.

MIDDLEBROOK MILLS. p. o., Montgomery co., Md.

MIDDLEBURGH, p. t. Schoharie co., N. Y., 37 ms. w. of Albany; from W. 378 ms. Watered by Schoharie kill. Pop. 2,967.

MIDDLEBURGH, p. v., Centre township, Union co., Pa., 77 ms. N. of Harrisburgh; from W. 182 ms.

MIDDLEBURGH, p. v., Carroll co., Md., 78 ms. N. W. of Annapolis; from W. 61 ms.

MIDDLEBURGH, p. v., Loudon co., Va., 134 ms. N. of Richmond; from W. 47 ms.

MIDDLEBURGH, p. v., Hardeman co., Tenn., 169 ms. s. w. of Nashville; from W. 854 ms.

MIDDLEBURGH, p. v., Casey co., Ky., 61 ms. s. of Frankfort; from W. 575 ms.

MIDDLEBURGH, p. t., Cuyahoga co., O., 128 ms. N. E. of Columbus; from W. 366 ms. Watered by east branch of Rocky river, Baldwin's creek, and Lake Abraham outlet. Pop. 1,490.

MIDDLEBURGH, p. v., Lane township, Logan co., O.

MIDDLEBURGH, p. t., Shiawassee co., Mich. Pop. 132.

MIDDLEURGH, p. o., Boone co., Mo.

MIDDLEBURGH, p. o., Duval co., Flor.

MIDDLEBURY, c. h., p. t., seat of justice, of Addison co., Vt., 59 ms. s. w. of Montpelier; from W. 481 ms. Watered by Otter creek. Seat of Middlebury college. Pop. 3,517.

MIDDLEBURY, p. t., New Haven co., Ct., 52 ms. s. w. of Hartford; from W. 310 ms, Watered by Quassepang pond, and tributaries of Naugatuck river. Pop. 763.

MIDDLEBURY, p. t., Wyoming co., N. Y., 247 ms. w. of Albany; from W. 365 ms. Watered by Allen's creek, and a tributary of Tonawanda creek. Pop. 1,749.

MIDDLEBURY, t., Tioga co., Pa., 154 N. of Harrisburgh: from W. 260 ms. Pop. 1,096.

MIDDLEBURY, p. v., Talmadge township, Summit co.,

O., 125 ms. N. E. of Columbus ; from W. 320 ms. Watered by Little Cuyahoga river.

MIDDLEBURY, p. v., Elkhart co., Ind., 162 ms. N. of Indianapolis ; from W. 593 ms. Pop. 1,155.

MIDDLEBURY, p. o., Mercer co., Mo.

MIDDLEBURY, t., Knox co., O., 52 ms. N. E. of Columbus ; from W. 384 ms. Pop. 1,092.

MIDDLE BUSH, p. o., Somerset co., N. J.

MIDDLE CREEK, p. t., Union co., Pa. Pop. 614.

MIDDLE CREEK, p. o., Monroe co., O., 113 ms. E. of Columbus ; from W. 302 ms.

MIDDLE CREEK, p. o., Wake co., N. C.

MIDDLE CREEK MILLS, p. o., Boone co., Ky.

MIDDLE FABIES, p. o., Scotland co., Mo.

MIDDLEFIELD, p. t., Hampshire co., Mass., 124 ms. w. of Boston ; from W. 388 ms. Watered by a tributary of Westfield river. Pop. 737.

MIDDLEFIELD, p. t., Otsego co., N. Y., 64 ms. w. of Albany ; from W. 387 ms. Watered by Otsego lake and outlet, and Cherry Valley creek. Pop. 3,131.

MIDDLEFIELD, p. o., Batavia township, Geauga co., O., 169 ms. N. E. of Columbus ; from W. 328 ms.

MIDDLEFIELD CENTRE, p. o., Middlefield township, Otsego co., N. Y., 62 ms. w. of Albany ; from W. 373 ms.

MIDDLEFORD, p. v., Sussex co., Del., 43 ms. s. of Dover ; from W. 120 ms. Pop. 368.

MIDDLE FORK, p. o., Clinton co., Ind., 48 ms. N. w. of Indianapolis ; from W. 606 ms.

MIDDLE FORK, p. t., Macon co., Mo., 92 ms. N. of Jefferson City ; from W. —— ms.

MIDDLE FORK, p. o., Henderson co., Tenn.

MIDDLE GRANVILLE, p. v., Granville township, Washington co., N. Y., 65 ms. N. E. of Albany ; from W. 435 ms.

MIDDLE GROVE, p. o., Fulton co., Ill., 53 ms. N. w. of Springfield ; from W. 813 ms.

MIDDLE GROVE, p. o., Monroe co., Mo., 84 ms. N. of Jefferson city ; from W. 947 ms.

MIDDLE GROVE, p. o., Saratoga co., N. Y.

MIDDLE HADDAM, p. v., Chatham township, Middlesex co., Ct., 21 ms. s. E. of Hartford ; from W. 333 ms. Watered by Connecticut river.

MIDDLE HOPE, p. o., Newburgh township, Orange co., N. Y., 88 ms. s. of Albany ; from W. 290 ms.

MIDDLE ISLAND, p. v., Brookhaven township, Suffolk co., Long Island, N. Y., 211 ms. s. E. of Albany ; from W. 285 ms.

MIDDLE LANCASTER, p. o., Butler co., Pa.

MIDDLE MILLS, p. o., Chippewa co., Wis.

MIDDLE MOUNTAIN, p. o., Botetourt co., Va., 192 ms. w. of Richmond ; from W. 242 ms.

MIDDLEPORT, p. v., Royalton township, Niagara co., N. Y., 285 ms. w. of Albany ; from W. 400 ms. Situated on the Erie canal.

MIDDLEPORT, p. v., Schuylkill co., Pa., 71 ms. E. of Harrisburgh ; from W. 181 ms.

MIDDLEPORT, c. h., p. v., seat of justice of Iroquois co., Ill., 192 ms. N. E. of Springfield ; from W. 694 ms.

MIDDLE RIDGE, p. o., Newton co., Ga.

MIDDLE RIVER, p. o., Franklin co., Ga., 120 ms. w. of Milledgeville ; from W. 606 ms.

MIDDLE RIVER, p. o., Allen co., O.

MIDDLESEX COUNTY, situated in the east part of Massachusetts, with Massachusetts bay on the east, and traversed by Merrimack river. Area, 800 square miles. Face of the country diversified ; soil generally stony or sandy, but productive from cultivation. Seats of justice. Cambridge, Lowell, and Concord. Pop. in 1810, 52,789 ; in 1820, 61,476 ; in 1830, 77,968 ; in 1840, 106,611; in 1850, 161,383.

MIDDLESEX COUNTY, situated on the south boundary of Connecticut, with Long Island sound on the south, and traversed by Connecticut river. Area, 342 square miles. Face of the country hilly ; soil varied, but generally productive. Seat of justice, Middletown. Pop. in 1810. 20,723 ; in 1820, 22,408 ; in 1830, 24,845 ; in 1840, 24,879 ; in 1850, 27,216.

MIDDLESEX COUNTY, situated in the central part of New Jersey. Area, 339 square miles. Face of the country uneven ; soil generally productive. Seat of justice, New Brunswick. Pop. in 1810, 20,381 ; in 1820, 21,470 ; in 1830, 23,157 ; in 1840, 21,893 ; in 1850, 28,624.

MIDDLESEX COUNTY, situated in the east part of Virginia, with Rappahannock river on the northeast. Area, 170 square miles. Soil sandy and barren. Seat of justice, Urbana. Pop. in 1810, 4.414 ; in 1820, 4.057 ; in 1830, 4,122 ; in 1840, 4,392 ; in 1850, 4,394.

MIDDLESEX, p. t., Washington co., Vt., 6 ms. N. E. of Montpelier ; from W. 523 ms. Watered by Onion river Pop. 1,365.

MIDDLESEX, p. o., Yates co., N. Y., 194 ms. w. of Albany ; from W. 323 ms. Watered by West creek and Canandaigua lake.

MIDDLESEX, t., Butler co., Pa., 204 ms. N. w. of Harrisburgh ; from W. 229 ms. Pop. 2,262.

MIDDLESEX VILLAGE, p. v., Middlesex co., Mass., 23 ms. N. w. of Boston ; from W. 441 ms.

MIDDLE SMITHFIELD, t., Monroe co. Pa. Pop. 1,678.

MIDDLETON, p. t., Essex co., Mass., 22 ms. N. of Boston ; from W. 462 ms. Watered by Ipswich river. Pop. 832.

MIDDLETON, p. t., Strafford co., N. H., 38 ms. N. E. of Concord ; from W. 519 ms. Pop. 1,724.

MIDDLETON, t., Wood co., O. Pop. 331.

MIDDLETON, p. v., Carroll co., Miss., 102 ms. N. of Jackson ; from W. 987 ms.

MIDDLETON, p. o., Dane co., Wis.

MIDDLETOWN, p. t., Rutland co., Vt., 77 ms. s. w. of Montpelier ; from W. 441 ms. Watered by Poultney river. Pop. 875.

MIDDLETOWN, t., Newport co., R. I., 28 ms. s. of Providence ; from W. 404 ms. Watered by Narraganset bay. Pop. 830.

MIDDLETOWN, city, p. t., seat of justice, together with Haddam, of Middlesex co., Ct., 14 ms. s. of Hartford ; from W. 326 ms. Watered by Connecticut river. Seat of the Wesleyan university. Pop. 4,211.

MIDDLETOWN, p. t., Delaware co., N. Y., 79 ms. s. w. of Albany : from W. 335 ms. Watered by Papacton branch of Delaware river. Pop. 2,689.

MIDDLETOWN, p. v., Orange co., N. Y., 109 ms. s. of Albany ; from W. 276 ms.

MIDDLETOWN, p. t., Monmouth co., N. J., 51 ms. N. E. of Trenton ; from W. 220 ms. Watered by Sandy Hook bay, and Navesink and Swimming rivers. Pop. 3,245.

MIDDLETOWN, p. o., Swatara township, Dauphin co., Pa., 10 ms. s. E. of Harrisburgh ; from W. 120 ms. Watered by Swatara and Susquehanna rivers, and the Union and Pennsylvania canals.

MIDDLETOWN, t., Bucks co., Pa., 125 ms. E. of Harrisburgh ; from W. 163 ms. Watered by Neshaminy and Bristol creeks. Pop. 2,223.

MIDDLETOWN, t., Delaware co., Pa., 93 ms. s. E. of Harrisburgh ; from W. 119 ms. Watered by Chester and Ridley creeks. Pop. 1,972.

MIDDLETOWN, t., Susquehanna co., Pa., 109 ms. N. Harrisburgh ; from W. 277 ms. Watered by Wyalusing creek and tributaries. Pop. 1,140.

MIDDLETOWN, p. v., New Castle co., Del., 47 ms. N. of Dover ; from W. 121 ms. Watered by Appoquinimink creek. Pop. 368.

MIDDLETOWN, p. v., Frederick co., Md., 83 ms. N. w. of Annapolis ; from W. 51 ms. Watered by Middle creek.

MIDDLETOWN, p. v., Frederick co., Va., 158 ms. N. w. of Richmond ; from W. 87 ms. Watered by Meadow run.

MIDDLETOWN, p. v., Hyde co., N. C., 219 ms. E. of Raleigh ; from W. 404 ms.

MIDDLETOWN, p. v., Lemon township, Butler co., O., 90 ms. s. w. of Columbus ; from W. 480 ms. Watered by Miami river, and Miami canal. Pop. 1,087.

MIDDLETOWN, t., Columbiana co., O. Pop. 1,479.

MIDDLETOWN, p. v., Jefferson co., Ky., 42 ms. w. of Frankfort ; from W. 584 ms.

MIDDLETOWN, p. v., Henry co., Ind., 44 ms. E. of Indianapolis ; from W. 546 ms. Watered by Fall creek. Pop. 198.

MIDDLETOWN, t., Shelby co., Ind.

MIDDLETOWN, p. v., Montgomery co., Mo., 57 ms. N. E. of Jefferson city ; from W. 899 ms.

MIDDLETOWN, p. o., Livingston co., Mich.

MIDDLETOWN, p. v., Logan co., Ill., 20 ms. N. E. of Springfield ; from W. 792 ms.

MIDDLETOWN, p. o., Des Moines co., Iowa.

MIDDLETOWN CENTRE, p. o., Delaware co., N. Y.

MIDDLETOWN POINT, p. v., Middletown township, Monmouth co., N. J., 43 ms. E. of Trenton ; from W. 209 ms. Watered by Middletown creek.

MIDDLE VILLAGE, p. v., Queen's co., N. Y.

MIDDLEVILLE, p. v., Fairfield township, Herkimer co., N. Y., 82 ms. N. w. of Albany ; from W. 401 ms. Watered by West Canada creek.

MIDDLEVILLE, p. o., Sussex co., N. J.

MIDDLEWAY, p. v., Jefferson co., Va., 162 ms. N. of Richmond; from W. 72 ms.

MIDLAND COUNTY, situated in the east part of Michigan, on Saginaw bay, and traversed by Titibawassee river. Area, —— square miles. Seat of justice, Midland. Pop. in 1850, 95.

MIDLAND, p. o., Charlotte co., Va.

MIDVIEW, p. o., Henry co., Ky.

MIDVILLE, p. o., Burke co., Ga.

MIDWAY, p. o., Davidson co., N. C., 119 ms. w. of Raleigh; from W. 330 ms.

MIDWAY, p. v., Barnwell district, S. C., 72 ms. s. w. of Columbia; from W. 578 ms.

MIDWAY, p. o., Monroe co., Tenn., 164 ms. s. E. of Nashville; from W. 544 ms.

MIDWAY, p. v., Woodford co., Ky., 20 ms. s. E. of Frankfort; from W. 542 ms.

MIDWAY. p. o., Spencer co., Ind., 172 ms. s. w. of Indianapolis; from W. 699 ms.

MIDWAY, p. v., Barbour co., Ala.; from W. 807 ms.

MIDWAY, p. o., Fulton co., Ill.

MIDWAY, p. o., Cooper co., Mo.

MIDWAY, p. o., Newton co., Tex.

MIDWAY, p. o., Hot Springs co., Ark.

MIDWAY INN, p. o., Prince Edward; 85 ms. s. w. of Richmond; from W. 175 ms.

MIER, p. o., Grant co., Ind.

MIER, p. o., Wabash co., Ill.

MIER, p. o., Madison co., Mo.

MIFFLIN COUNTY, situated in the central part of Pennsylvania, and traversed by Juniata river. Area, 900 square miles. Face of the country, broken and mountainous; soil, varied, but fertile in the valleys. Seat of justice, Lewiston. Pop. in 1810, 12,132; in 1820, 16,618; in 1830, 14,323; in 1840, 13,092; in 1850, 14.980.

MIFFLIN, t., Lycoming co., Pa., 102 ms. N. of Harrisburgh; from W. 211 ms. Pop. 1,186.

MIFFLIN, t., Alleghany co., Pa., 218 ms. w. of Harrisburgh; from W. 242 ms. Watered by Thompson's and Strut's runs, and Peter's creek. Pop. 2,693.

MIFFLIN, t., Cumberland co., Pa., 33 ms. w. of Harrisburgh; from W. 119 ms. Watered by Conedogwinit creek. Pop. 1,574.

MIFFLIN. t., Columbia co., Pa., 76 ms. N. E. of Harrisburgh; from W. 186 ms. Pop. 1,024.

MIFFLIN, t., Dauphin co., Pa., 23 ms. N. E. of Harrisburgh; from W. 140 ms. Watered by Wiconisco creek. Pop. 1,302.

MIFFLIN. p. t., Ashland co., O. 72 ms. N. of Columbus; from W. 369 ms. Pop. 891.

MIFFLIN. t., Franklin co., O., 5 ms. from Columbus; from W. 391 ms. Pop. 1,095.

MIFFLIN, t., Crawford co., O.

MIFFLIN. t.. Pike co., O., 65 ms. s. of Columbus; from W. 424 ms. Pop. 546.

MIFFLIN, p. v., Henderson co., Tenn., 133 ms. s. w. of Nashville; from W. 817 ms.

MIFFLIN, p. o., Iowa co., Wis.

MIFFLIN, p. o., Crawford co., Ind.

MIFFLINBURGH, p. b., Buffalo township. Union co., Pa., 76 ms. N. of Harrisburgh; from W. 186 ms. Watered by Buffalo creek. Pop. 783.

MIFFLINTOWN, c. h., p. b., Fermaugh township, seat of justice of Juniata co., Pa.. 45 ms. N. w. of Harrisburgh; from W. 136 ms. Watered by Juniata river, and Pennsylvania canal. Pop. 485.

MIFFLINVILLE, p. v., Columbia co., Pa., 103 ms. N. E. of Harrisburgh; from W. 213 ms. Watered by Susquehanna river.

MILAM, p. o., Sabine co., Tex.

MILAN COUNTY, situated in the central part of Texas. with Brazos river on the northeast. Area, —— square miles. Seat of justice, Cameron. Pop. in 1850, 2,907.

MILAN, p. t., Coos co., N. H., 118 ms. N. of Concord; from W. 587 ms. Watered by Androscoggin river, and a tributary of Upper Ammonoosuc river. Pop. 493.

MILAN, p. t., Dutchess co., N. Y.. 62 ms. s. of Albany; from W. 322 ms. Watered by Sawkill creek, and a tributary of Roeliff Jansen's creek. Pop. 1,764.

MILAN, p. o.. Bradford co., Pa., 149 ms. N. of Harrisburgh; from W. 259 ms.

MILAN. p. t., Erie co., O., 103 ms. N. of Columbus; from W. 396 ms. Watered by Huron river. Pop. 2,697.

MILAN, p. t., Monroe co., Mich., 50 ms. s. w. of Detroit; from W. 507 ms. Watered by Saline and Macon rivers. Pop. 442.

MILAN, t., Allen co., Ind. Pop. 361.

MILAN, t., Calhoun co., Ill., 94 ms. s. w. of Springfield; from W. 835 ms.

MILAN, p. o., Sullivan co., Mo.

MILBURGH, p. o., Greenville district, S. C.

MILBURY, p. t., Worcester co., Mass., 43 ms. w. of Boston; from W. 403 ms. Watered by Blackstone river, and Blackstone canal.

MILES, p. t., Centre co., Pa., 93 ms. N. w. of Harrisburgh; from W. 201 ms. Pop. 1,306.

MILESBURGH, p. v., Centre co., Pa.

MILESTOWN, p. v., Bristol township. Philadelphia co., Pa., 104 ms. E. of Harrisburgh; from W. 144 ms.

MILESTOWN, p. o., St. Mary's co., Md.

MILFORD, p. t.. Penobscot co., Me., 82 ms. N. E. of Augusta; from W. 677 ms. Watered by Penobscot and Sunkhaze rivers. Pop. 687.

MILFORD, p. t., Hillsborough co., N. H., 33 ms. s. of Concord; from W. 458 ms. Watered by Souhegan river. Pop. 2,159.

MILFORD, p. t., Worcester co., Mass., 30 ms. s. w. of Boston; from W. 409 ms. Watered by Charles and Mill rivers. Pop. 4.819.

MILFORD, p. t., New Haven co., Ct., 45 ms. s. w. of Hartford; from W. 291 ms. Watered by Wepawaug and Housatonic rivers. Pop. 2,465.

MILFORD, p. t., Otsego co., N. Y., 77 ms. w. of Albany; from W. 365 ms. Watered by Susquehanna river. Pop. 2,227.

MILFORD, p. v., Alexandria township, Hunterdon co., N. J., 39 ms. N. w. of Trenton; from W. 196 ms. Watered by Delaware rivers.

MILFORD, c. h.. p. t., seat of justice of Pike co.. Pa., 162 ms. N. E. of Harrisburgh; from W. 256 ms. Watered by Delaware river. Pop. 830.

MILFORD, p. t., Bucks co., Pa., 84 ms. from Harrisburgh; from W. 172 m. Watered by Swamp river. Pop. 2,527.

MILFORD, t., Juniata co., Pa., 43 ms. from Harrisburgh; from W. 150 ms. Watered by Juniata river. Pop. 1,094.

MILFORD, p. t. Somerset co., Pa. Watered by Castleman's river, and Laurel Hill creek. Pop. 2,070.

MILFORD, p. o., Caroline co., Pa.

MILFORD, p. o.. Pike co., Pa.

MILFORD. hundred, p. v., Kent co., Del., 21 ms. s. of Dover; from W. 129 ms. Watered by Mispillon creek.

MILFORD. p. v., Greenville district, S. C., 119 ms. N. w. of Columbia; from W. 491 ms.

MILFORD, p. v., Bracken co., Ky., 54 ms. N. E. of Frankfort; from W. 499 ms. Watered by a branch of Licking river.

MILFORD, p. v., Miami township, Clermont co., O., 112 ms. s. w. of Columbus; from W. 484 ms. Watered by Little Miami river.

MILFORD, t., Butler co.. O. Pop. 2,068.

MILFORD, p. t. Knox co., O. Pop. 1,349.

MILFORD, p. t., Oakland co., Mich., 41 ms. N. w. of Detroit; from W. 565 ms. Pop. 1,470.

MILFORD, t., Williams co., O. Pop. 1,282.

MILFORD, p. o., Kosciusko co., Ind., 139 ms. N. of Indianapolis; from W. 616 ms.

MILFORD, t., La Grange co., Ind. Pop. 806.

MILFORD, p. o., Iroquois co., Ill., 168 ms. N. E. of Springfield; from W. 694 ms.

MILFORD, p. o., Jefferson co., Wis.

MILFORD, p. o., Hunterdon co., N. J.

MILFORD CENTRE, p. o., Union township, Union co., O., 32 ms. N. w. of Columbus; from W. 425 ms.

MILFORDTON, p. o., Knox co., O.

MILITARY GROVE, p. o., McDowell co., N. C., 220 ms. N. w. of Raleigh; from W. 440 ms.

MILITARY INSTITUTE, p. o., Franklin co., Ky.

MILITARY ROAD, p. o., Theresa township, Jefferson co., N. Y., 179 ms. N. w. of Albany; from W. 431 ms.

MILITARY SPRINGS, p. o., Fayette co., Ala.

MILL, t., Tuscarawas co., O. Pop.1,510.

MILLAN, p. o., Pike co., Miss.

MILLARD, p. o., Jackson co.. Va.

MILLARD, p. o., Walworth co., Wis.

MILLARD, p. o., Jefferson co., Ind.

MILLARDSVILLE, p. v., Susquehanna co., Pa., 162 ms N. E. of Harrisburgh

MILL ARK, p. o., Fulton co., Ind.

MILLBACH, p. o., Lebanon co., Pa.

MILL BEND, p. o., Hawkins co., Tenn.

MILLBOROUGH SPRINGS. p. o., Bath co., Va.

MILLBRIDGE, p. o., Washington co., Me.

MILL BROOK, p. o., Litchfield co., Ct., 31 ms. w. of Hartford ; from W. 349 ms.

MILL BROOK, p. o., Warren co., N. J.

MILL BROOK, p. v., Clinton township, Wayne co., O., 98 ms. N. E. of Columbus ; from W. 350 ms.

MILLBURN, p. o., Ballard co., Ky.

MILLBURN, p. o., Lake co., Ill.

MILLBURNE, p. o., Columbia co., N. Y.

MILLBURY, p. t., Worcester co., Mass., 43 ms. s. w. of Boston. Watered by tributaries of Blackstone river, and Blackstone canal. Pop. 2,617.

MILL CREEK, p. o., Huntington co., Pa., 87 ms. w. of Harrisburgh ; from W. 146 ms.

MILL CREEK HUNDRED, p. t., Newcastle co., Del. Pop. 3,317.

MILL CREEK, t., Erie co., Pa. Pop. 2,064.

MILL CREEK, p. o., Berkeley co., Va., 159 ms. N. of Richmond ; from W. 83 ms.

MILL CREEK, t., Coshocton co., O., 93 ms. N. E. of Columbus ; from W. 348 ms. Pop. 872.

MILL CREEK, t., Hamilton co., O. Pop. 6,287.

MILL CREEK, t., Union co., O. Pop. 726.

MILL CREEK, t., Williams co., O. Pop. 408.

MILL CREEK, p. o., Pulaski co., Ill., 207 ms. s. of Springfield ; from W. 841 ms.

MILL CREEK. p. o., Ripley co., Mo.

MILL CREEK, p. o., Fulton co., O.

MILL CREEK, p. o., Sabine parish, La.

MILL CREEK, p. o., Bowie co., Tex.

MILLDALE, p. o.. Defiance co., O.,157 ms. N. w. of Columbus ; from W. 499 ms.

MILLDALE, p. v., Warren co., Miss., 151 ms. w. of Jackson : from W. 1,061 ms.

MILLDALE, p. o., Warren co., Va.

MILL DAM, p. o., Madison co., Mo.

MILLEDGEVILLE, p. v., Montgomery co., N. C., 133 ms. s. w. of Raleigh ; from W. 389 ms.

MILLEDGEVILLE, city, seat of justice of Baldwin co., and capital of the state of Georgia, situated at the head of steamboat navigation on Oconee river, and is 300 miles from the sea ; from W. 648 ms. The city is built on elevated and somewhat uneven ground, in the midst of a rich and populous cotton-producing region, and is laid out with broad streets and pleasant squares. The statehouse is a fine edifice of Gothic architecture, surmounted by a cupola, and containing in its halls portraits of General Oglethorpe and other eminent men of early times. Among the other prominent buildings, are banks, a market house, governor's house, state arsenal, and churches. A bridge extends to the west bank of the river. Pop. in 1810, 1,256 ; in 1820, —— in 1830, 1,599 ; in 1840, 2,095 ; in 1850, 2,216.

MILLEDGEVILLE, p. o., Carroll co., Ill.

MILLEDGEVILLE, p. o., Lincoln co., Ky.

MILLEN'S BAY, p. o., Jefferson co., N. Y.

MILLER COUNTY, situated in the central part of Missouri, and traversed by Osage river. Area, 555 square miles. Seat of justice, Tuscumbia. Pop. in 1840, 2,282 ; in 1850, 3,834.

MILLER, t., Dearborn co., Ind.

MILLER, t., Scotland co., Mo. Pop. 666.

MILLER, t., Polk co., Mo.

MILLER, t., Knox co., O. Pop. 1,064.

MILLER'S, p. o., Lawrence co., O., 131 ms. s. of Columbus ; from W. 393 ms.

MILLER'S, p. o., Fayette co., Tex.

MILLERSBURGH, p. v., Upper Paxton township, Dauphin co., Pa., 31 ms. N. of Harrisburgh ; from W. 141 ms. Watered by Susquehanna river, at the confluence of Wiconisco creek.

MILLERSBURGH. p. v., Bourbon co., Ky., 44 ms. E. of Frankfort ; from W. 499 ms.

MILLERSBURGH, p. v., Rutherford co., Tenn., 44 ms. s. E. of Nashville ; from W. 675 ms.

MILLERSBURGH, c. h., p. v., Hardy township, seat of justice of Holmes co., O., 87 ms. N. E. of Columbus ; from W. 313 ms. Watered by Killbuck creek.

MILLERSBURGH, c. h., p. v., seat of justice of Mercer co., Ill.

MILLERSBURGH, p. v., Callaway co., Mo., 34 ms. N. E. of Jefferson city ; from W. 929 ms.

MILLER'S CREEK, p. o., Estill co., Ky.

MILLER'S CREEK, p. o., Davis co., Utah.

MILLER'S MILL, p. o., Christian co., Ky.

MILLER'S MILL, p. o., Bath co., Va.

MILLER'S PLACE, p. v., Brookhaven township, Suffolk co.. Long Island, N. Y., 207 ms. s. E. of Albany ; from W. 257 ms.

MILLERSPORT, p. v., Walnut township, Fairfield co., O.. 30 ms. s. E. of Columbus ; from W. 373 ms.

MILLER'S TAVERN, p. o., Essex co., Va., 40 ms. N. E. of Richmond ; from W. 122 ms.

MILLERSTOWN, p. v., Greenwood township, Perry co., Pa., 30 ms. N. w. of Harrisburgh ; from W. 140 ms. Pop. 389.

MILLERSTOWN, p. v., Champaign co., O., 55 ms. w. of Columbus ; from W. 449 ms.

MILLERSTOWN, p. v., Grayson co., Ky., 125 ms. s. w. of Frankfort, from W. 650 ms.

MILLERSVILLE, p. v., Lancaster co., Pa., 39 ms. s. E. of Harrisburgh ; from W. 111 ms. Pop. 498.

MILLERSVILLE, p. v., Marion co., Ind., 7 ms. from Indianapolis ; from W. 578 ms.

MILLERSVILLE, p. o., Anne Arundel co., Md.

MILLERSVILLE, p. o., Adair co., Ky.

MILLERSVILLE, p. o., Barnwell district, S. C.

MILLFIELD, p. v., Dover township, Athens co., O., 73 ms. s. E. of Columbus ; from W. 348 ms. Watered by Sunday creek.

MILLFORD MILLS, p. o., Prince William co., Va., 41 ms. s. w. of Richmond ; from W. 105 ms.

MILL GREEN, p. o., Harford co., Md.

MILL GROVE, p. o., Sumter district, S. C., 81 ms. E. of Columbia ; from W. 501 ms.

MILL GROVE, p. o., Cobb co., Ga., 114 ms. N. w. of Milledgeville ; from W. 685 ms.

MILL GROVE, p. o., Owen co., Ind., 50 ms. s. w. of Indianapolis ; from W. 619 ms.

MILL GROVE, t., Steuben co., Ind. Pop. 523.

MILL GROVE, p. o., Erie co., N. Y.

MILL HALL, p. o., Clinton co., Pa., 104 ms. N. w. of Harrisburgh ; from W. 196 ms.

MILL HAVEN, p. v., Scriven co., Ga., 106 ms. E. of Milledgeville ; from W. 629 ms.

MILLHEIM, p. v., Hains township, Centre co., Pa., 88 ms. N. w. of Harrisburgh ; from W. 180 ms.

MILL HILL, p. o., Cabarras co., N. C., 148 ms. w. of Raleigh ; from W. 385 ms.

MILL HOUGEN, p. o., Decatur co., Ind.

MILLICAN, p. o., Brazos co., Tex.

MILLIKEN'S BEND, p. o., Madison parish, La.

MILLIN, p. o., Burke co., Ga.

MILLINGTON, p. v., East Haddam township, Middlesex co., Ct., 36 ms. E. of Hartford ; from W. 350 ms.

MILLINGTON, p. o., Somerset co., N. J., 43 ms. N. of Trenton ; from W. 213 ms

MILLINGTON, p. v., Kent co., Md., 61 ms. N. E. of Annapolis ; from W. 101 ms. Watered by Chester river.

MILLINGTON, p. o., Albermarle co., Va., 103 ms. N. w. of Richmond ; from W. 139 ms.

MILL PLAIN, p. v., Fairfield co., Ct., 72 ms. s. w. of Hartford ; from W. 296 ms.

MILL POINT, p. o., Sullivan co., Tenn.

MILL POINT, p. v., Pocahontas co., Va., 210 ms. N. w. of Richmond ; from W. 245 ms.

MILL POINT, p. o., Ottawa co., Mich.

MILLPORT, p. v., Veteran township, Chemung co., N. Y., 199 ms. s. w. of Albany ; from W. 292 ms. Watered by Catharine's creek.

MILLPORT, p. v., Potter co., Pa., 185 ms. N. w. of Harrisburgh ; from W. 296 ms.

MILLPORT, p. o., Fayette co., Ala. ; from W. 867 ms.

MILLPORT, p. o., Washington co., Ind., 80 ms. s. of Indianapolis ; from W. 605 ms.

MILL RAY, p. o., Bullock co., Ga.

MILL RIDGE, p. o., St. Francis co., Ark.

MILL RIVER, p. o., Berkshire co., Mass., 133 ms. w. of Boston ; from W. 354 ms.

MILL RIVER, p. o., Henderson co., N. C., 272 ms. w. of Raleigh ; from W. 502 ms.

MILLSBOROUGH, p.o., Washington co., Pa.

MILLSBOROUGH, p. v., Sussex co., Del., 49 ms. s. of Dover ; from W. 143 ms.

MILLS BRIDGE, p. o., Pike co., Ala.

MILLS' CORNERS, p. o., Broadalbin township, Fulton co., Pa., 43 ms. N. w. of Albany ; from W. 411 ms.

MILLSFIELD, t., Coos co., N. H. Pop. 682.

MILLSFIELD, t., Ashtabula co., O.

MILLSFORD, t., Steuben co., Ind.

MILLS' GAP, p. o., Rutherford co., N. C.

MILLS' MILLS, p. o., Alleghany co., N. Y.

MILLS' POINT, p. v., Hickman co., Ky., 310 ms. s. w. of Frankfort ; from W. 337 ms. Watered by Mississippi river.

MILLS' PRAIRIE, p. o., Edwards co., Ill., 150 ms. s. E. of Springfield ; from W. 730 ms.

MILL SPRING, p. o., Jefferson co., Tenn.

MILL SPRING, p. o., Wayne co., Ky., 101 ms. s. of Frankfort; from W. 607 ms.

MILLSTADT, p. o., St. Clair co., Ill.

MILLSTONE, p. v., Hillsborough township. Somerset co., N. J., 27 ms. N. of Trenton; from W. 201 ms. Watered by Millstone river.

MILLSTONE, p. o., Oglethorpe co., Ga.

MILLTOWN, p. o., Washington co., Me., 198 ms. E. of Augusta; from W. 784 ms.

MILLTOWN, p. v., Kent township, Putnam co., N. Y., 100 ms. s. of Albany; from W. 297 ms.

MILLTOWN, p. v., Crawford co., Ind., 113 ms. s. of Indianapolis; from W. 627 ms.

MILLTOWN, p. o., Chester co., Pa.

MILLVIEW. p. v., Fauquier co., Va., 103 ms. N. of Richmond; from W. 86 ms.

MILLVIEW, p. o., Sullivan co., Pa.

MILLVILLE, p. v., Worcester co., Mass., 43 ms. w. of Boston; from W. 408 ms.

MILLVILLE, p. v., Shelby township, Orleans co., N. Y., 257 ms. N. w. of Albany; from W. 397 ms.

MILLVILLE, p. t., Cumberland co., N. J., 67 ms. s. of Trenton; from W. —— ms. Watered by Maurice river and tributaries. Pop. 2,332.

MILLVILLE, p. o., Columbia co., Pa., 89 ms. N. E. of Harrisburgh; from W. 199 ms.

MILLVILLE, p. o., King George co., Va., 89 ms. N. E. of Richmond; from W. 86 ms.

MILLVILLE, p. v., Spartanburgh district, S. C., 101 ms. N. w. of Columbia; from W. 486 ms.

MILLVILLE, p. o., Lincoln co., Tenn., 97 ms. s. of Nashville; from W. 732 ms.

MILLVILLE, p. v., Ross township, Butler co., O., 108 ms. s. w. of Columbus; from W. 496 ms. Watered by Indian creek.

MILLVILLE, p. v., Butler co., Ala.; from W. 890 ms.

MILLVILLE, p. o., Jo-Daviess co., Ill.

MILLVILLE, p. o., Clayton co., Iowa.

MILLVILLE, p. o., Cherokee co., Ga.

MILLVILLE, p. o., Ray co., Mo.

MILLWEES, p. o., Anderson district, S. C.

MILLWOOD, p. o., Dooly co., Ga., 86 ms. s. w. of Milledgeville; from W. 733 ms.

MILLWOOD, p. v., Clarke co., Va., 135 ms. N. of Richmond; from W. 66 ms.

MILLWOOD, p. o., Knox co., O., 69 ms. N. E. of Columbus; from W. 369 ms.

MILLWOOD, t., Guernsey co., O. Pop. 1,624.

MILLWOOD, p. o., Lincoln co., Mo.

MILLWOOD, p. o., Jackson co., Flor.

MILLWOOD, p. o., Collin co., Tex.

MILNER, p. o., Pike co., Ga.

MILNERSVILLE, p. o., Monroe township, Guernsey co., O., 89 ms. E. of Columbus; from W. 314 ms.

MILO, p. t., Piscataquis co., Me., 98 ms. N. E. of Augusta; from W. 695 ms. Watered by Piscataquis and Pleasant river. Pop. 932.

MILO, p. t., Yates co., N. Y., 193 ms. w. of Albany; from W. 370 ms. Watered by Crooked lake outlet. Pop. 4,791.

MILO, p. o., Brown co., Ind.

MILO, p. o., Bureau co., Ill.

MILO, p. o., Bradley co., Ark.

MILO, p. o., Defiance co., O.

MILO CENTRE. p. v., Milo township, Yates co., N. Y., 196 ms. w. of Albany; from W. 325 ms.

MILROY, p. v., Rush co., Ind., 48 ms. s. E. of Indianapolis; from W. 546 ms.

MILROY, p. o., Mifflin co., Pa.

MILTON, p., Piscataquis co., Me. Pop. 932.

MILTON, p. t., Strafford co., N. H., 47 ms. N. E. of Concord; from W. 515 ms. Watered by Salmon Fall river and tributaries. Pop. 1,629.

MILTON, p. t., Chittenden co., Vt., 55 ms. N. w. of Montpelier; from W. 528 ms. Watered by Lamoille river, and Lake Champlain. Pop. 2,451.

MILTON, p. t., Norfolk co., Mass., 7 ms. s. of Boston; from W. 435 ms. Watered by Neponset river. Pop. 2,241.

MILTON, p. v., Litchfield township, Litchfield co., Ct., 36 ms. w. of Hartford; from W. 330 ms. Watered by Shepaug river.

MILTON, t., Saratoga co., N. Y., 30 ms. N. of Albany; from W. —— ms. Watered by Kayaderosseras creek and tributaries. Pop. 4,220.

MILTON, p. v., Marlborough township, Ulster co., N. Y., 79 ms. s. of Albany; from W. 299 ms. Watered by Hudson river.

MILTON, p. v., Morris co., N. J., 75 ms. N. of Trenton; from W. 246 ms.

MILTON. p. b., Turbot township, Northumberland co., Pa., 71 ms. N. of Harrisburgh; from W. 181 ms. Watered by west branch of Susquehanna river, and Limestone run. Pop. 1,649.

MILTON, p. v., Sussex co., Del., 33 ms. s. of Dover; from W. 141 ms.

MILTON. p. v. Caswell co., N. C., 74 ms. N. w. of Raleigh; from W. 250 ms.

MILTON, p. v., Laurens district, S. C., 60 ms. N. w. of Columbia; from W. 516 ms.

MILTON, p. v., Outauga co., Ala.; from W. 841 ms.

MILTON, p. v., seat of justice of Santa Rosa co., Flor.; from W. —— ms. Watered by Blackwater river.

MILTON, p. v. Rutherford co., Tenn., 37 ms. s. E. of Nashville; from W. 656 ms.

MILTON, p. v., Trimble co., Ky., 52 ms. N. w. of Frankfort; from W. 561 ms. Watered by Ohio river.

MILTON, p. t., Mahoning co., O., 157 ms. N. E. of Columbus; from W. 316 ms. Watered by Mahoning river. Pop. 1,123.

MILTON, t., Jackson co., O. Pop. 1,472.

MILTON, t., Miami co., O. Pop. 398.

MILTON, t., Richland co., O. Pop. 1,106.

MILTON, t., Wayne co., O. Pop. 1,360.

MILTON, t., Wood co., O. Pop. 244.

MILTON, p. t., Jefferson co., Ind. Pop. 1,544.

MILTON, p. t., Wayne co., Ind., 54 ms. E. of Indianapolis; from W. 521 ms. Pop. 765.

MILTON, p. o., Pike co., Ill., 64 ms. w. of Springfield; from W. 844 ms.

MILTON, p. o., Rock co., Wis., 49 ms. s. E. of Madison; from W. 814 ms.

MILTON, p. o., Lafayette co., Miss., 178 ms. N. w. of Jackson; from W. 905 ms.

MILTON, p. o., Randolph co., Mo., 80 ms. N. w. of Jefferson city; from W. 949 ms.

MILTON, t., Cass co., Mich. Pop. 611.

MILTON, p. o., Wilkinson co., Ga.

MILTON MILLS, p. o., Milton township, Strafford co., N. H., 43 ms. N. E. of Concord; from W. 524 ms.

MILTONSBURGH, p. o., Monroe co., O.

MILTONVILLE. p. v., Middletown township, Wood co., O., 123 ms. N. w. of Columbus; from W. 461 ms.

MILTONVILLE, v., Madison township, Butler co., O.

MILVILLE, p. o., Rusk co., Tex.

MILWAUKEE COUNTY, situated on the east boundary of Wisconsin, on Lake Michigan, and traversed by Milwaukee river. Area, —— square miles. Seat of justice, Milwaukee. Pop. in 1840, 5,605; in 1850, 31,010.

MILWAUKEE, the chief city of Wisconsin, and next to Chicago, the largest on Lake Michigan, is situated in Milwaukee co., finely located for commerce, on both sides of Milwaukee river, at its entrance into the lake, 90 miles north of Chicago, 90 miles east of Madison, and 805 miles from Washington. It is the market of a large part of the productions of the state. Steamboats and other vessels, navigating Lake Michigan, touch here, on their way to and from Detroit and points on Lake Erie, and the St. Lawrence, Erie, and Welland canals. The surrounding region is rich, and rapidly increasing in an industrious and enterprising population, of which Milwaukee is the nucleus and the centre of trade. This city is remarkable for the peculiarly bright straw-color and excellent quality of its bricks, for which the rich clay-beds along the lake afford abundant material. Besides the large quantities of these which are exported, they are used for the majority of the buildings, some of which, in large and uniform rows of dwellings or stores, present a beautiful and splendid effect. Here are churches, a jail, courthouse, and other prominent edifices.

The Milwaukee and Mississippi railroad is completed to Palmyra, 43 miles westward.

The population in 1840, was 1,700; in 1850, 20,026.

MILWAUKEE, p. o., Clackamas co., Oregon.

MINA. p. t., Chautauque co., N. Y., 363 ms. w. of Albany; from W. 347 ms. Watered by French creek and Finley's lake. Pop. 996.

MINAVILLE, p. o., Florida township, Montgomery co., N. Y., 37 ms. N. w. of Albany; from W. 405 ms.

MINDEN, p. t., Montgomery co., N. Y., 61 ms. N. w. of Albany; from W. 396 ms. Watered by Mohawk river and Otsquake creek. Pop. 4,633.

MINDEN, c. h., p. v., seat of justice of Claiborne par

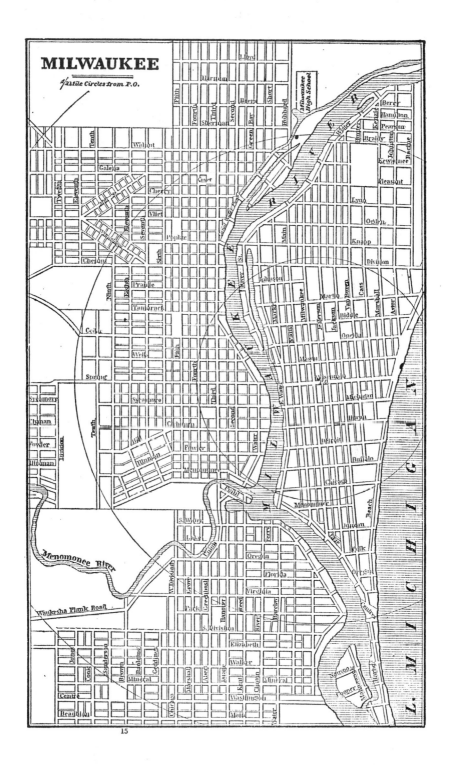

MILWAUKEE

½ mile Circles from P.O.

15

ish, La., 404 ms. N. w. of New Orleans; from W. 1,274 ms.

MINDENVILLE, p. o., Minden township, Montgomery co., N. Y.

MINDORA. p. o., La Cross co., Wis.

MINE-A-BRETON, p. t., Washington co., Mo.

MINE CREEK. p. t., Hempstead co., Ark. Pop. 1,185.

MINE KILL FALLS, p. o., Schoharie co., N. Y.

MINE LA MOTTE, p. o., Madison co., Mo., 154 ms. s. e. of Jefferson city; from W. 886 ms.

MINERAL POINT, c. h., p. v.. seat of justice of Iowa co., Wis., 52 ms. s. w. of Madison; from W. 884 ms. Watered by Pickatonokee river.

MINERAL SPRINGS, p. o., Columbia co., Flor., 84 ms. e. of Tallahassee.

MINERAL SPRING, p. o., Anderson district, S. C.

MINERAL SPRINGS, p. o., Lowndes co., Ga.

MINERSVILLE, p. v., McDowell co., N. C., 223 ms. w. of Raleigh; from W. 461 ms.

MINERSVILLE, p. v., Norwegian township, Schuylkill co., Pa., 66 ms. N. E. of Harrisburgh; from W. 176 ms. Pop. 2,951.

MINERSVILLE, v., Alleghany co., Pa.

MINERSVILLE, p. v., Meigs co., O.

MINERVA, p. t., Essex co., N. Y., 94 ms. N. of Albany; from W. 469 ms. Watered by Hudson river and tributaries. Pop. 586.

MINERVA, p. v.. Mason co., Ky., 75 ms. N. E. of Frankfort; from W. 475 ms.

MINERVA, p. v., Paris township, Stark co., O., 139 ms. N. E. of Columbus; from W. 303 ms. Situated on the Sandy and Beaver canal.

MINERVA, p. o., Houston co., Ga.

MINETTO, p. o., Oswego co., N. Y.

MINGO FLAT, p. o., Randolph co., Va.

MINISINK, p. t., Orange co., N. Y., 120 ms. s. w. of Albany; from W. 270 ms. Watered by the Wall Kill. Pop. 4,972.

MINNESOTA TERRITORY, so-called from the Indian name of the St. Peter's river, the principal local stream of the country. The Indians living on its banks called it thus on account of the different appearance of the waters from those of the Mississippi. At the junction of the two streams, the waters of the last-named river may be observed generally tinged of a chocolate color, derived from the extensive tamarac and pine swamps toward the north, in which it partly has its head-springs; while the waters of the Minnesota are entirely different in appearance, being light-colored and clear. The name is compounded of two words, minne, "water," sotah, "sky-colored." This poetical designation. "The territory of the sky-colored water," receives additional ornament in the Dakotah name, bestowed on the junction of the river with the Mississippi, that of Mendota, or "Mingling of the waters." This is also the appellation of the Indian trading town at the mouth.

This territory lies between 43° 30' and 49° north latitude, and 89° 30' and 102° 12' longitude west from Greenwich; and is bounded north by the British possessions, east by Lake Superior and Wisconsin, from which it is separated in part by the Mississippi, south by the Iowa, and west by Nebraska, from which it is separated in part by the Missouri. Its superficial area is 93,000 square miles.

Physical Aspect.—One of the most remarkable features in the face of this country is its general monotony. It contains no mountains nor mountain chains, nor any very lofty hills; but presents a dreary void of extensive prairies, interspersed by innumerable lakes, which give rise to various streams. Some elevations indeed there are, toward the sources of the larger rivers, and even there are a few hills that might be dignified, by way of contrast, with the title of mountains, sometimes rising abruptly amidst the prairies like an island in the sea. At many points along the Mississippi the banks are high, broken, and precipitous, yet there are many cases where they gradually slope to the water. In general the prairie region is less hilly and rocky than that of the forest; and in situations where they are not too wet, they appear to be adapted for similar agricultural purposes as those in the same latitudes in Wisconsin and Michigan. The lands about Lake Pepin, in their general aspect, are suited for general crops, and for dairies, stock-raising, &c., they are seldom surpassed.

Rivers, Lakes, and Bay.—The chief rivers are, the Mississippi, Missouri, St. Peter's or Minnesota, James or Jacques, Wasses or Vermilion, Tchankasudata or

Sioux, Hokah or Root, Crow, Crow-Wing, North Red, White Earth, East Swan, St. Louis. Turtle, Elk, Sac and Pine. The lakes are numerous, among the largest, of which are, Minsi Saigaigoning or Mille Lac. Winibigoshish, Leech, Kadikomeg, Gayaskh, Morrah Tanka, Pepin, and Superior. Fond du Lac bay, at the southwest corner of Lake Superior, borders on this territory.

Climate.—The climate of this territory, notwithstanding its northern position, is more favorable than the northern portions of New England and New York. Its winters, it is true, are severe and long, with continued deep snows for several months, and the lakes and streams strongly bound in ice: but during the growing season vegetation springs up like magic, and puts forward with astonishing rapidity and luxuriance. The spring and autumn are usually mild, and are less liable to destructive frosts, than those of the more eastern or northern states.

Productive Resources.—The agricultural products of this territory are similar to those of Wisconsin. At present the chief resources are, furs, lumber, and fish. Population.—The population in 1850 was 6,077.

Government.—The government of Minnesota is that usually applied to territories of the United States. All citizens of adult age are voters, and elect a territorial legislature. The governor, secretary of state, and judges of the supreme and other courts, are appointed by the president of the United States. Among the important acts of the first territorial legislature, are those establishing a judiciary, a school system, dividing the territory into suitable civil districts, and appointing officers to enforce the laws, and relative to the improvement of roads. All these will have a paramount influence over the future destiny of the country. Perhaps one of the most humane and politic acts of the legislature is, the admission to citizenship of "all persons of a mixture of white and Indian blood, who shall have adopted the habits and customs of civilized men;" and not less politic is that law which requires the establishment of schools throughout the territory. The act of the general government organizing the territory, appropriates two sections of land in every township for the support of common schools. No other territory or state in the Union has received more than one section in each township for such purpose. The capital of Minnesota is St. Paul's.

History.—The territory of Minnesota embraces a portion of Upper Louisiana, as held by the French, prior to the year 1762, when it was ceded to Spain, together with the remainder of her possessions in North America. It was first explored by Hennipen, in 1680, who ascended the Mississippi beyond the Falls of St. Anthony. In 1800, it was receded to France by a secret treaty, who formally took possession of the country in 1803, and immediately after it was sold to the United States. Subsequent to this Minnesota constituted a part of the Missouri territory, which was supposed to contain all the Mississippi to the "South sea," except a portion of the present state of Louisiana. Still later, Wisconsin and Iowa territories were erected, from portions of which this new territory was organized by act of Congress, in 1849. Earl Selkirk commenced a settlement on Red river, near the mouth of the Pembina, in 1812.

MINO, t., Mifflin co., Pa. Pop. 1,020.

MINOT, p. t., Cumberland co., Me., 46 ms. s. w. of Augusta; from W. 576 ms. Watered by Androscoggin and Little Androscoggin rivers. Pop. 1,734.

MINSTER, p. o., Mercer co., O., 94 ms. N. w. of Columbus; from W. 488 ms.

MINTONSVILLE, p. v., Gates co., N. C., 106 ms. N. E. of Raleigh; from W. 261 ms.

MINTONVILLE, p. o., Casey co., Ky.

MINT SPRING, p. o., Augusta co., Va.

MIRABILLE, p. o.. Caldwell co., Mo.

MIRANDA, p. v.. Rowan co., N. C., 132 ms w. of Raleigh; from W. 369 ms.

MIRICKVILLE, p. o., Bristol co., Mass.

MISHAWAKA. p. v., St Joseph co., Ind., 143 ms. N. of Indianapolis; from W. 620 ms.

MISPILLON, hundred, Kent co., Del.

MISSIONARY STATION, p. o., Floyd co., Ga., 173 ms N. w. of Milledgeville; from W. 674 ms. Watered by Coosa river.

MISSION POINT, p. o., La Salle co., Ill.

MISSION SAN JOSE, p. o., Contra Costa co., Cal.

MISSISSINAWA, p. t., Darke co., O. Pop. 378.

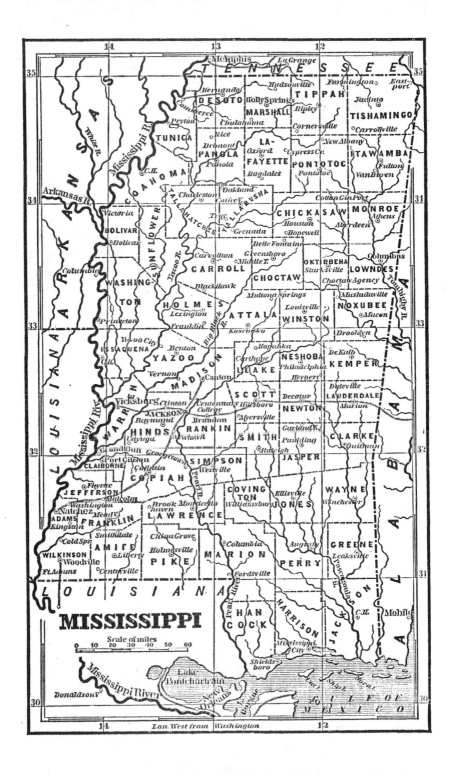

MISSISSIPPI, one of the United States, situated between 30° 10' and 35° north latitude, and 88° 10' and 91° 35' west longitude from Greenwich; and is bounded north by Tennessee, east by Alabama, south by the gulf of Mexico and Louisiana, and west by Pearl and Mississippi rivers, the latter of which separates this state from Louisiana and Arkansas, and the former separates it from Louisiana. Its superficial area is 47,157 square miles.

Physical Aspect.—The surface of the southern portions of this state, for 100 miles inland from the Mexican gulf, is even, with occasional hills of moderate elevation, interspersed with prairies, inundated marshes, and cypress swamps. The soil is generally sandy and gravelly, mingled more or less with clay, and is capable of producing all the crops peculiar to the south. The central and northern parts of the state are more elevated, and the face of the country agreeably diversified by hills and dales. The soil is exceedingly fertile, producing abundant crops.

Rivers and Bays.—The principal rivers are,' the Mississippi, Pearl, Pascagoula, Yazoo, Tombigbee, and the Big Black. The only bays are, the Pascagoula, Biloxi, and St. Louis, which lie contiguous to the Mexican gulf.

Climate.—The winters of Mississippi, as compared with the winters at the north, may be regarded as mild; but, like those of the adjoining states, they vary from each other, and not unfrequently are quite severe. No winter passes without more or less frost, and few, in some parts of the state, without snow. Neither the sugar-cane nor the orange will grow, unprotected, north of latitude 31°. In general the winters along the Mississippi are two or three degrees colder than in corresponding parallels on the Atlantic. The summers are usually very hot, subject to long droughts, and not unfrequently to excessive and protracted rains. Like most other southern countries, this state is generally healthy, except in the vicinity of swamps, and sluggish streams, where in summer and autumn, fevers and bilious complaints frequently prevail.

Productive Resources.—The products of this state are, horses, mules, neat cattle, sheep, swine, poultry, wax, wool, lumber, tar, pitch, turpentine, cotton, tobacco, rice, wheat, rye, barley, oats, potatoes, and Indian corn. Cotton is the great staple, little regard being had to other crops.

Manufactures.—But little attention is paid in this state to manufactures, beyond supplying some of the more immediate wants of the people. In 1850 there were 866 manufacturing establishments, whose annual products amounted to $500 and upward.

Railroads.—There are about 200 miles of railroad completed in Mississippi, and others are projected. The Vicksburg, Jackson, and Brandon road, 60 miles long, is the most important road as yet built. Another road, from Natchez to Jackson, the capital of the state, is in progress.

Commerce.—Mississippi has no direct foreign commerce, its shipping to foreign countries being made through the ports of neighboring states.

Education.—The principal collegiate institutions of Mississippi are, the Oakland college, founded in 1830; the Centenary college, in 1841; and the Mississippi university, at Oxford, founded in 1846. There are also about 100 academies and 500 common schools in the state.

Population.—In 1800, 8,850; in 1810, 40,352; in 1820, 75,448; in 1830, 136,621; in 1840, 375,651; in 1850, 606,555. Number of slaves in 1800, 3,489; in 1810, 17,088; in 1820, 32,814; in 1830, 65,659; in 1840, 195,211; in 1850, 309,898.

Government.—The governor is elected by the people for a term of two years, and can not hold office more than four years out of six; and in case of his death, resignation, or other inability, it is provided, that the president of the senate shall perform the duties of governor, until another shall be duly qualified. The senate is composed of 32 members, elected for four years, half of the number being chosen biennially. The represen-

tatives are elected biennially, on the first Monday in November; the present number is 98, and can not exceed 100 members. The legislature meets biennially at Jackson, on the first Monday in January. The judicial power is vested in a high court of errors and appeals, consisting of three judges, chosen by the people for six years, one being chosen biennially; in a circuit court, held in each county, the judges chosen by the people for four years; in a superior court of chancery, the chancellor chosen by the people of the whole state for six years; in a court of probate, the judge elected by the people of each county for two years. Every free white male citizen of the United States, 21 years of age, and who has resided in the state one year next preceding the election, and four months in the county, city, or town, in which he offers his vote, is deemed a qualified voter.

History.—De Soto traversed the Mississippi region in 1542, but made no settlement. La Salle visited it in 1681, having proceeded down the great valley from the lakes of the north. In 1698, D'Iberville, who was appointed governor of Louisiana, arrived with a colony, chiefly Canadians, and settled on Ship island. The next year he built Fort Biloxi, on the eastern side of Biloxi bay, which became the headquarters of the province. D'Iberville gave the name of Rosalie to the spot now called Natchez. That settlement was surprised and destroyed by the Natchez Indians, in 1729. The French were avenged, and destroyed or dispersed the whole tribe. The northern part of Mississippi was ceded to England by France, in 1763. The southern portion was ceded to England by Spain, and attached to Florida. A portion was retroceded to Spain in 1783. A large portion of the present state was erected into a territory in 1798. The Alabama territory was separated from it in 1817, and toward the close of that year Mississippi was admitted into the Union. The first constitution was adopted in 1817, and revised in 1832.

MISSISSIPPI COUNTY, situated on the easterly boundary of Arkansas, with Mississippi river on the east, and the St. Francis on the west, and traversed by Whitewater river. Area, 1,000 square miles. Seat of justice, Osceola. Pop. in 1840, 1,410; in 1850, 2,368.

MISSISSIPPI COUNTY, situated on the southeasterly part of Missouri, with Mississippi river on the east. Area, —— square miles. Seat of justice, Charleston. Pop. in 1850, 3,123.

MISSISSIPPI CITY, p. v., seat of justice of Harrison co., Miss., 265 ms. s. E. of Jackson; from W. 1,143 ms. Watered by the Gulf of Mexico.

MISSISSIPPI, t., Scott co., Mo.

MISSOURI, one of the U. States, which embraces a part of Upper Louisiana, as held by the French prior to 1763, when it was ceded to Spain, together with all her North American territory. It is situated between 36° 30' and 40° 30' north latitude, 89° 20' and 96° west longitude from Greenwich; and is bounded north by Iowa, east by Illinois and Kentucky, from which it is separated by the Mississippi, and south by Arkansas, and west by Arkansas, the Indian Territory, and Nebraska, from a part of the latter of which it is separated by the river Missouri, whence it derives its name. Its superficial area is 67,380 square miles.

Physical Aspect.—This state presents a great variety of soil, as well as of surface; but, taking it as a whole, it is hilly, and in many parts broken and even mountainous. Starting from a point opposite the mouth of the Kaskaskias, and extending southwesterly, there is a vast ridge, rising into rocky elevations, which divides the country into two unequal slopes. The southeastern angle of the state is level, a large portion of which is annually inundated. The western counties are divided into prairies and forests, and much of the soil is good. North of the Missouri the surface is somewhat diversified, presenting a fair proportion of woodlands, prairies, and other arable soil. The lands bordering on the Missouri are exceedingly rich and fertile, often consisting of strata of dark-colored alluvion, of un-

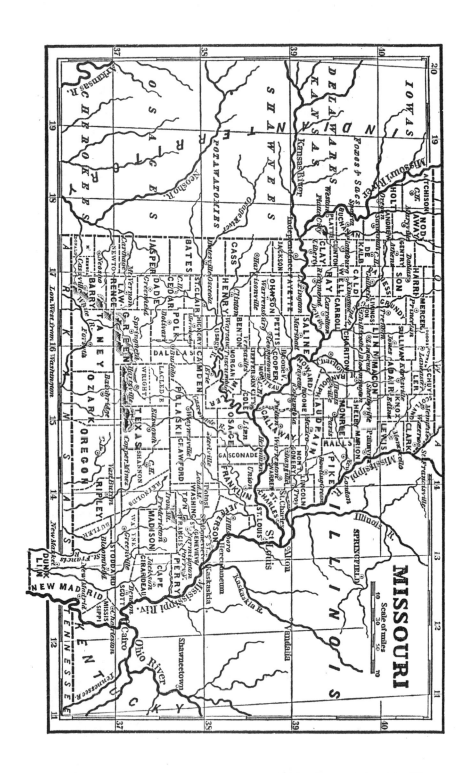

MISSOURI

Scale of miles

known depth. but more frequently mixed with sand. In receding from the river, the land in general is gradual in its ascent, but sometimes rises abruptly into elevated barrens, flinty ridges, and limestone cliffs. The land of this state may be regarded either as fertile or very poor, there being but little soil of an intermediate quality ; it is either bottom land, or cliff ; prairie, or barren ; sterile ridges, or sloping woodlands.

Mountains.—The state is traversed by many ridges of the Ozark mountains, which have a breadth of from 100 to 150 miles ; but although they often shoot up into precipitous peaks, it is believed they rarely exceed 2,000 feet in height. In St. François county exists the celebrated Iron mountain, which has an elevation of 350 feet above the level of the surrounding plain, is a mile and a half across its summit, and yields 80 per cent. of pure metal. Five miles south is another pyramidal mountain of oxyde of iron. known as the Pilot Knob, 300 feet high, with a base of a mile and a half in circumference. This pyramid also yields 80 per cent. of pure metal.

Rivers and Lakes.—The principal rivers are, the Mississippi, Missouri, Osage, Salt, Gasconade, Chariton, Maramec, St. Francis, Whitewater, Wachita, Big Black, and Des Moines. In the southeast part of the state are several lakes, the most noted of which are Pemiçco, St. Mary's, and Nic Carny.

Climate.—The climate is remarkably dry, pure, and serene ; and remote from the streams and inundated lands it is healthy, but is subject to great extremes of heat and cold. The Mississippi is usually frozen, and passable on the ice, by the first of January. The extremes of temperature vary from 100° Fahrenheit to 8° below zero.

Productive Resources.—The principal products of this state are horses, mules, neat cattle, sheep, swine, poultry, sugar, wax, wool, hay, tobacco, cotton, hemp, flax, lumber, wheat, rye, barley, buckwheat, potatoes, oats, and Indian corn. The mineral wealth of Missouri, particularly lead, iron, and bituminous coal, may be regarded as inexhaustible. The counties of Washington, Madison, St. François, Jefferson, and St. Genevieve, embrace what is called the "mineral tract." The lead mines have been worked from the time of the first settlement of the country, and produce ores of the richest kind, yielding, in some instances, more than 80 per cent. of pure metal. In addition to the above-named substances, there is found in this state zinc, copper, manganese, antimony, calamine, cobalt, ochres, common salt, nitre, plumbago, burr-stone, free-stone, gypsum, and marble.

Manufactures.—The manufactures of Missouri are comparatively of small account. The number of establishments in 1850, in which goods were manufactured to the annual amount of $500 worth or upward each, were 3,030, and of these nearly one half were located in the city and county of St. Louis.

Commerce.—The commerce of Missouri consists mostly of its river-trade, its foreign commerce being of very trifling account. The shipping owned within the state (being mostly steamboats) amounts to about 30,000 tons.

Education.—There are several collegiate institutions in Missouri : the Masonic college, in Marion county, founded in 1831 ; University of St. Louis, in 1832 ; St. Charles college, in 1837 ; Missouri university, at Columbia, in 1840 ; St. Vincent's college, at Cape Girardeau, in 1843 ; and Fayette college, in 1846. Medical schools are attached to the two universities. There are nearly 2,000 common schools, and about 100 academies in the state.

Population.—In 1810, 19.833 ; in 1820. 66,586 ; in 1830, 140,074 ; in 1840. 383,702 ; in 1850. 682,044. Number of slaves in 1810. 3,011 ; in 1820, 10,222 ; in 1830, 24,990 ; in 1840, 58.240 ; in 1850. 87,422.

Government.—The governor is elected by the people for four years, but is ineligible for the succeeding four years. A lieutenant-governor is chosen at the same time, and for the same term, who is president of the senate. Every county is entitled to send one representative, but the whole number can never exceed 100, and are elected for two years. The senators are elected every four years, one half retiring every second year; and their number can never be less than 14, nor more than 33, chosen by districts, and apportioned according to the number of free white inhabitants. The elections are held biennially, in August. The legislature meets once in two years, the last Monday in December, at Jefferson city. Every white male citizen, over 21 years of age, who has resided one year in the state, and three months in the county in which he offers his vote, has the right of suffrage. The judges of the various courts are elected by the people for the term of six years. One bank only, with not more than five branches, may be established in the state.

History.—Father Marquette, a Jesuit missionary, and Jolyet, a citizen of Quebec, visited the territory of the present state of Missouri in 1673, and soon afterward the Canadian trappers and Jesuit missionaries penetrated the country in every direction. The lead mines of Missouri were worked by the French as early as 1720. The first permanent European settlement was made at St. Genevieve, in 1763, by a lead mining company, under the name of "Laclede, Maxam, & Co." St. Louis was founded the next year. In 1800, Spain retroceded all her claims to Louisiana to France, who formally took possession of the country, and sold it to the United States in 1803. In 1805, that portion of Louisiana lying east of the Mississippi, and all of the country bearing that name west of that river, was erected into a territorial government, under the name of the "Territory of Louisiana." In 1812, a part of the present state of Louisiana was separated from the rest of the territory, and admitted into the Union as an independant state, and the remainder was reorganized under the name of the "Territory of Missouri," which was supposed to contain all the lands west of the Mississippi to the "South sea," except a part of the state of Louisiana. In 1821, a part of this territory was admitted into the Union as the present state of Missouri. On the subject of its admission a long debate ensued in Congress, it having been proposed to prohibit slavery in the new state. It was finally admitted by what is called the Missouri compromise, which tolerated slavery in the state, but prohibited it in the territory north of it. Mottoes of the seal, *Salus populi suprema lex esto* : "The welfare of the people is the first great law." "United we stand, divided we fall. '

MISSOURI, t., Boone co., Mo.
MISSOURI, t., Scott co., Mo.
MISSOURI. p. v., Pike co., Ala. ; from W. 873 ms.
MISSOURI, t., Wachita co., Ark. Pop. 730.
MISSOURI, t., Hempstead co., Ark. Pop. 513.
MISSOURITON, p. v., St. Charles co., Mo., 92 ms. E. of Jefferson city ; from W. 854 ms. Watered by Missouri river.
MITCHELL, t., Poinsett co., Ark. Pop. 760.
MITCHELL, p. o., Sheboygan co.. Wis.
MITCHELL, p. o., Walker co., Tex.
MITCHELL'S MILLS, p. o., Indiana co., Pa., 166 ms. w. of Harrisburgh ; from W. 219 ms.
MITCHELL'S SALT WORKS, p. o., Jefferson co., O.
MITCHELLSVILLE, p. v., Robertson co., Tenn., 34 ms. N. of Nashville ; from W. 686 ms.
MITCHELLSVILLE, p. o.. Boone co., Ky.
MITTINEAGUE, p. o., Hampden co., Mass.
MIXERVILLE, p. o.. Franklin co., Ind.
MIXTOWN, p. o., Tioga co., Pa.
MIXVILLE, p. v., Haine township, Alleghany co., N. Y., 267 ms. w. of Albany ; from W. 349 ms. Watered by West Kog creek.
MOBILE COUNTY, situated at the southwest corner of Alabama, with the gulf of Mexico on the south, Mobile bay and Texas river on the east, and traversed by Mobile river. Area, 2,250 square miles. Face of the country level; soil generally barren. Seat of justice, Mobile. Pop. in 1816, 1,300 ; in 1820, 2,672 ; in 1840, 3,071 ; in 1840, 18,741 ; in 1850, 27,600.
MOBILE, city, seat of justice of Mobile co., Ala., situated 30 miles N. of the gulf of Mexico, on Mobile bay, 160 miles E. of New Orleans, and 1,013 miles from W., and is the principal city and only port of entry of Alabama. It occupies an elevated plain, overlooking the pleasant bay, and is fanned by its breezes. Fires have several times injured the city, but it has been rebuilt with improved appearance and solidity. From its position in the state, it is the receptacle of the commerce of Alabama. Vast quantities of cotton are annually exported. The harbor is difficult of access, being obstructed by marshy islands and shoals, but within, deep and spacious enough for large vessels. These, by a circuit around an island, in front of the city, anchor at its wharves. The entrance to the bay is defended by a fortification, and marked by a lighthouse. Good water, from a neighboring source, is distributed over the city by iron-pipes. Railroads are in process of construction

to connect the city with the Ohio river, and also with the Atlantic states through Georgia. It has daily communication, by steamboat, to Proctorsville, and thence, by railroad, with New Orleans. There are a customhouse, courthouse, hospitals, banks, and churches. In 1813, the period when Mobile passed from the hands of Spain into possession of the United States, it contained about 100 buildings. In 1830, the population was 3,194 ; in 1840, 12,672 ; in 1850, 20,515.

MOBLEY POND, p. o., Scriven co., Ga.

MOCKVILLE, p. v., seat of justice of Davie co., N. C., 141 ms. w. of Raleigh ; from W. 369 ms.

MODENA, p. o., Plattekill township, Ulster co., N. Y., 80 ms. s. w. of Albany ; from W. 300 ms.

MODEST TOWN, p. v., Accomac co., Va., 228 ms.. E. of Richmond ; from W. 192 ms.

MODRELL'S POINT, p. o., Coles co., Ill.

MOFFETT'S STORE, p. o., New Lebanon township, Columbia co., N. Y., 19 ms. s. of Albany ; from W. 372 ms.

MOFFETTSVILLE, p. v., Anderson district, S. C., 117 ms. N. w. of Columbia ; from W. 549 ms.

MOFFITT'S MILL, p. o., Randolph co., N. C., 67 ms. w. of Raleigh ; from W. 341 ms.

MOGADORE, p. o., Summit co., O.

MOHAWK, p. v., German Flats township, Herkimer co., N. Y., 79 ms. N. w. of Albany. Watered by Mohawk river and Erie canal.

MOHAWK, t., Montgomery co., N. Y. Watered by Mohawk river. Pop. 3,095.

MOHAWK VALLEY, p. o., Coshocton co., O.

MOHICAN, p. t., Ashland co., O., 88 ms. N. E. of Columbus ; from W. 359 ms. Pop. 1,774.

MOHRSVILLE, p. o., Berks co., Pa., 62 ms. E. of Harrisburgh ; from W. 155 ms.

MOIRA, p. t., Franklin co., N. Y., 227 ms. N. of Albany ; from W. 518 ms. Watered by Little Salmon river. Pop. 1,340.

MOKELUMNE HILL, p. o., Calaveras co., Cal.

MOLINE, p. o., Rock Island co., Ill.

MOLINO, p. o., Tippah co., Miss.

MOLINO, p. o., Lincoln co., Tenn.

MOLINO, p. o., Randolph co., Ala.

MOLLIHORN, p. o., Newberry district, S. C.

MOLLTOWN, p. v., Berks co., Pa., 64 ms. E. of Harrisburgh ; from W. 156 ms.

MOMENCE, p. o., Will co., Ill.

MONAGAN, p. t., St. Clair co., Mo.

MONCHES, p. o., Waukesha co., Wis.

MONCLOVA, p. o., Lucas co., O.

MONEEK, p. o., Winneshiek co., Iowa.

MONDAY CREEK, t., Perry co., O. Pop. 1,124.

MONEY CREEK, p. o., McLean co., Ill.

MONGAUGON, t., Wayne co., Mich. Pop. 984.

MONGAUP, p. o., Sullivan co., N. Y.

MONGAUP VALLEY, p. o., Sullivan co., N. Y.

MONGOQUINONG, p. o., La Grange co., Ind.

MONITEAU COUNTY, situated in the central part of Missouri, with Missouri river on the northeast. Area, —— square miles. Seat of justice, Jamestown. Pop. in 1850, 6,004.

MONITEAU, t., Cole co., Mo., 20 ms. N. w. of Jefferson city ; from W. 956 ms.

MONITEAU, t., Cooper co., Mo.

MONITEAU, t., Howard co., Mo.

MONK'S CORNERS, p. o., Charleston district, S. C., 149 ms. s. E. of Columbia ; from W. 956 ms.

MONK'S STORE, p. o., Sampson co.. N. C.

MONKTON, p. t., Addison co., Vt., 50 ms. w. of Montpelier ; from W. 500 ms. Watered by tributaries of Lewis creek. Pop. 1,246.

MONKTON MILLS, p. o., Baltimore co., Md.

MONMOUTH COUNTY, situated on the east boundary of New Jersey, on the Atlantic ocean. Area, 1,030 square miles. Face of the country undulating ; soil of middling quality,—here and there rich. Seat of justice, Freehold. Pop. in 1810, 22,150 ; in 1820, 25,038 ; in 1830, 29,233 ; in 1840, 32,909 ; in 1850, 30,238.

MONMOUTH, p. t., Kennebec co., Me., 16 ms. s. w. of Augusta ; from W. 592 ms. Watered by head waters of Cobesseconte river. Pop. 1,925.

MONMOUTH, p. v., Adams co., Ind., 135 ms. N. E. of Indianapolis ; from W. 525 ms. Watered by St. Mary's river.

MONMOUTH, c. h., p. v., seat of justice of Warren co., Ill., 120 ms. N. w. of Springfield ; from W. 850 ms.

MONOHAN, t., York co., Pa. Pop. 880.

MONON, p. o., White co., Ind.

MONONA, p. o., Clayton co., Iowa.

MONONGAHELA. t., Greene co., Pa. Watered by Whitley creek. Pop. 1,153.

MONONGAHELA, city, p. o., Fallowfield township, Washington co., Pa., 189 ms. w. of Harrisburgh ; from W. 216 ms. Pop. 977.

MONONGALIA COUNTY, situated on the north boundary of Virginia, and traversed by Monongahela river. Area, 560 square miles. Face of the country hilly and mountainous ; soil generally fertile. Seat of justice, Morgantown. Pop. in 1810, 12,793 ; in 1820, 11,060 ; in 1830, 14.056 ; in 1840, 17,368 ; in 1850, 12,387.

MONOQUET, p., Kosciusko co., Ind.

MONREATH, p. o.. Shelby co,, Tenn.

MONROE COUNTY, situated on the north boundary of New York, on Lake Ontario, and traversed by Genesee river. Area, 607 square miles. Face of the country hilly ; soil fertile. Seat of justice, Rochester. Pop. in 1830, 49.862 ; in 1840, 64,902 ; in 1850, 87.649.

MONROE COUNTY, situated on the easterly boundary of Pennsylvania, with Delaware river on the southeast. Area, 750 square miles. Face of the country mountainous. Seat of justice, Stroudsburgh. Pop. in 1840, 9.879 ; in 1850, 13,270.

MONROE COUNTY, situated in the westerly part of Virginia, with Great Kanawha river on the west. Area, 750 square miles. Face of the country mountainous ; soil rocky, but along the streams good. Seat of justice, Union. Pop. in 1810, 5,444 ; in 1820, 6,620 ; in 1830, 7,798 ; in 1840, 8,422 ; in 1850, 9,827.

MONROE COUNTY, situated in the central part of Georgia, with Ocmulgee river on the east. Area, 370 square miles. Seat of justice, Forsyth. Pop. in 1830, 16,202 ; in 1840, 16,275 ; in 1850, 16.985.

MONROE COUNTY, situated in the south part of Alabama, with Alabama river on the west. Area, 980 square miles. Face of the country even ; soil sterile. Seat of justice, Monroeville. Pop. in 1820, 8,838 ; in 1830, 8,784 ; in 1840, 10,680 ; in 1850, 12,013.

MONROE COUNTY, situated on the south part of Florida, with the gulf of Mexico on the southwest. Area, —— square miles. Face of the country level ; soil generally sandy and swampy. Seat of justice. Key West. Pop. in 1840, 688 ; in 1850, 2,643.

MONROE COUNTY, situated on the east boundary of the Mississippi, and traversed by Little Tombigbee river. Area, 650 square miles. Seat of justice, Athens. Pop. in 1820, 2,721 ; in 1830, 3,861 ; in 1840, 9,250 ; in 1860, 21,172.

MONROE COUNTY, situated on the southeast boundary of Tennessee, near Tennessee river. Area, 750 square miles. Face of the country broken and mountainous. Seat of justice, Madisonville. Pop. in 1820, 2,539 ; in 1830, 13.709 ; in 1840, 12,056 ; in 1850, 11,717.

MONROE COUNTY, situated on the south boundary of Kentucky, and traversed by Cumberland river. Area, 375 square miles. Seat of justice, Tompkinsville. Pop. in 1820, 4,956 ; in 1830, 5,340 ; in 1840, 6.526 ; in 1850. 7.756.

MONROE COUNTY, situated on the southeasterly boundary of Ohio, with Ohio river on the southeast. Area, 520 square miles. Face of the country broken and hilly ; soil productive. Seat of justice, Woodsfield. Pop. in 1820, 4,641 ; in 1830, 8,768 ; in 1840, 18,521 ; in 1850. 28.151.

MONROE COUNTY, situated toward the south part of Indiana. Area, 390 square miles. Seat of justice, Bloomington. Pop. in 1820, 4,641 ; in 1830, 8,768 ; in 1840, 10,143 ; in 1850, 11,285.

MONROE COUNTY, situated on the southwest boundary of Illinois, with the Mississippi river on the west, and the Kaskaskia river on the east. Area. 360 square miles. Seat of justice, Waterloo. Pop. in 1830, 2,000 ; in 1840, 4.481 ; in 1850, 7,679.

MONROE COUNTY, situated on the northeasterly part of Missouri. Area, 744 square miles. Seat of justice. Paris. Pop. in 1840, 9,505 ; in 1850, 10.541.

MONROE COUNTY, situated in the south part of Iowa. Area, —— square miles. Seat of justice, Albia. Pop. in 1850, 2.884.

MONROE COUNTY, situated at the southeast corner of Michigan, on Lake Erie. Area, 540 square miles. Seat of justice, Monroe. Pop. in 1820, 1,831 ; in 1830, 3,187 ; in 1840, 9.922 ; in 1850. 14,698.

MONROE COUNTY, situated in the easterly part of Arkansas, and traversed by White river. Area, 1,150 square miles. Seat of justice, Lawrenceville. Pop. in 1840, 936 ; in 1850, 2,049.

MONROE, p. t., Waldo county. Me., 54 ms. N. E. of Augusta; from W. 649 ms. Watered by Marsh river. Pop. 1,606.

MONROE, t., Washington co., Vt., 15 ms. N. E. of Montpelier. Watered by tributaries of Onion or Winooski, and Lamoille rivers. Pop. 1,335.

MONROE, p. t., Franklin co., Mass.. 120 ms. w. of Boston; from W. 407 ms. Watered by Deerfield river. Pop. 654.

MONROE, p. t., Franklin co., Ct., 54 ms. s. w. of Hartford; from W. 293 ms. Pop. 1,319.

MONROE, p. t., Orange co., N. Y., 117 ms. s. of Albany; from W. 279 ms. Watered by Ramapo river. Pop. 4,280.

MONROE, p. v., Hardiston township. Sussex co., N. J., 80 ms. N. of Trenton; from W. 248 ms.

MONROE, t., Middlesex co., N. J. Pop. 3,001.

MONROE, t., Bradford co., Pa. Pop. 1,436.

MONROE. v., Durham township, Bucks co., Pa., 116 ms. E. of Harrisburgh; from W. 181 ms.

MONROE, t., Cumberland co., Pa. Watered by Yellow Breeches creek. Pop. 1,772.

MONROE, t., Luzerne co., Pa. Pop. 681.

MONROE, t., Armstrong co., Pa. Pop. 775.

MONROE, c. h., p. v., seat of justice of Walton co., Ga., 61 ms. N. W. of Milledgeville; from W. 635 ms. Watered by Ocmulgee river.

MONROE, p. v., Wachita parish, La., 300 ms. N. w. of New Orleans; from W. 1,190 ms. Watered by Wachita river, at the head of steam navigation.

MONROE, p. v., Overton co., Tenn., 102 ms. E. of Nashville; from W. 602 ms. Watered by a tributary of Obie's river.

MONROE. p. v., Hart co., Ky., 100 ms. s. w. of Frankfort; from W. 623 ms. Watered by Little Barren river.

MONROE, p. v., Lemon township, Butler co., O., 95 ms. s. w. of Columbus; from W. 479 ms. Pop. 206.

MONROE, t., Adams co., O. Watered by Ohio river. Pop. 1,191.

MONROE, t., Ashtabula co., O. Pop. 1,587.

MONROE, p. t., Butler co., O.

MONROE, t., Carroll co., O. Pop. 1,117.

MONROE, t., Clermont co., O. Pop. 1,897.

MONROE, t., Coshocton co., O. Pop. 760.

MONROE, t., Darke co., O. Pop. 918.

MONROE, t., Guernsey co., O. Pop. 1,076.

MONROE, t., Harrison co., O. Pop. 1,154.

MONROE, t., Holmes co., O. Pop. 966.

MONROE, t., Knox co., O. Watered by Schenck's creek. Pop. 1,324.

MONROE, t., Licking co., O. Pop. 1,089.

MONROE, t., Logan co., O. Pop. 1,435.

MONROE, t., Madison co., O. Pop. 403.

MONROE, t., Miami co., O. Pop. 2,035.

MONROE, t., Muskingum co., O. Pop. 977.

MONROE, t., Perry co., O. Pop. 1,429.

MONROE, t., Preble co., O. Pop. 1,343.

MONROE, t., Pickaway co., O. Pop. 1,637.

MONROE, t., Richland co., O. Watered by Mohiccan creek. Pop. 1,719.

MONROE, t., Putnam co., O.

MONROE, t., Grant co., Ind. Pop. 777.

MONROE, t., Putnam co., Ind. Pop. 1,089.

MONROE, t., Washington co., Ind. Pop. 1,476.

MONROE, city, seat of justice of Monroe co., Mich., 37 ms. s. w. of Detroit; from W. 486 ms. Watered by Rai-in river. Pop. 2,813.

MONROE, c. h., p. v., seat of justice of Greene co., Wis., 81 ms. s. of Madison; from W. 846 ms. Watered by a tributary of Pickatonokee river.

MONROE, t., Ogle co., Ill. Pop. 413.

MONROE, t., Lincoln co., Mo.

MONROE, t., Livingston co., Mo.

MONROE, t., Mississippi co., Ark. Pop. 652.

MONROE, t., Sevier co., Ark. Pop. 335.

MONROE, p. o., Perry co., Miss.

MONROE, p. o., Tippecanoe co., Ind.

MONROE, p. o., Bedford co., Pa.

MONROE, c. h., p. v., seat of justice of Union co., N. C.

MONROE CENTRE, p. o., Monroe township, Waldo co., Me.

MONROE CENTRE, p. o., Monroe township, Ashtabula co., O.

MONROE MILLS, p. o., Knox co., O.

MONROETON. p. v., Monroe township, Bradford co., Pa., 130 ms. N. of Harrisburgh; from W. 240 ms.

MONROETON, p. v., Rockingham co., N. C., 100 ms. N. w. of Raleigh; from W. 285 ms.

MONROEVILLE, c. h.. p. v., seat of justice of Monroe co., Ala.; from W. 943 ms. Watered by a tributary of Limestone creek.

MONROEVILLE, p. v. Ridefield township, Huron co., O., 97 ms. N. of Columbus; from W. 396 ms. Watered by Huron river.

MONROEVILLE, p. o., Alleghany co., Pa.

MONROEVILLE, c. h., p. v., seat of justice of Colosi co., Cal.

MONROE WORKS, p. v., Monroe township, Orange co., N. Y.. 105 ms. s. of Albany; from W. —— ms.

MONROVIA, p. v., Morgan co., Ind., 23 ms. s. w. of Indianapolis; from W. 594 ms.

MONROVIA, c. h., Frederick co., Md., 68 ms. N. w. of Annapolis: from W. 48 ms.

MONSEY. p. o., Rockland co., N. Y.

MONSON, p. t., Piscataquis co., Me., 77 ms. N. of Augusta; from W. 672 ms. Watered by Piscataquis river and Sebec pond. Pop. 654.

MONSON, p. t., Hampden co., Mass., 75 ms. s. w. of Boston; from W. 380 ms. Watered by Chickopee river and tributaries. Pop. 2,831.

MONTACUTE, p. o., Polk co., Iowa.

MONTAGUE. p. t., Franklin co., Mass., 85 ms. w. of Boston; from W. 396 ms. Watered by Connecticut and Sawmill rivers. Pop. 1,518.

MONTAGUE, p. t., Sussex co., N. J., 91 ms. N. of Trenton; from W. 245 ms. Watered by Delaware river and tributaries. Pop. 1,009.

MONTAGUE, p. v., Essex co., Va., 68 ms. N. E. of Richmond; from W. 130 ms.

MONTAGUE CANAL, p. v., Montague township, Franklin co., Mass., 88 ms. of Boston; from W. 399 ms. Watered by Connecticut river.

MONT ALTO, p. v., Franklin co., Pa.

MONTAUK, p. o., Crawford co., Mo.

MONTCALM COUNTY, situated toward the west part of Michigan. Area, —— square miles. Seat of justice, Montcalm. Pop. in 1850, 891.

MONTCALM, p. o., Montcalm co., Mich.

MONTEBELLO, p. o., Hancock co., Ill.

MONTEITHVILLE, p. o., Stafford co., Va.

MONTELLO, p. o., Marquette co., Wis.

MONTEREY COUNTY, in the west part of California, on the Pacific ocean. Area, —— square miles. Seat of justice, Monterey. Pop. in 1852, 2,728.

MONTEREY, c. h., p. v., seat of justice of Monterey co., Cal.

MONTEREY, p. o., Berkshire co., Mass.

MONTEREY, p. o., Dutchess co., N. Y.

MONTEREY, p. o., Berks co., Pa.

MONTEREY, p. o., Clermont co., O.

MONTEREY, p. o., Highland co., Va.

MONTEREY, p. o., Abbeville district, S. C.

MONTEREY, p. o., McNairy co., Tenn.

MONTEREY, p. o., Butler co., Ala.

MONTEREY, p. o., Owen co., Ky.

MONTEREY, p. o., Calhoun co., Il .

MONTEREY, p. o., Davis co., Iowa.

MONTEREY, p. o., Waukesha co., Wis.

MONTEREY, p. o., Rankin co., Miss.

MONTEREY, p. o., Red River co., Tex.

MONTEREY, p. o., Pulaski co., Ind.

MONTEREY LANDING, p. o , Concordia parish, La.

MONTEVALLO, p.v., Shelby co., Ala.; from W. 786 ms

MONTEVIDEO, p. o.. Elbert co., Ga., 125 ms. N. E. of Milledgeville; from W. 565 ms.

MONTEZUMA, p. v., Mentz township, Cayuga co., N. Y., 162 ms. w. of Albany; from W. 342 ms. Situated at the junction of Cayuga and Seneca canal with the Erie canal, and watered by Seneca river and Cayuga lake outlet.

MONTEZUMA, p. o., Pike co., Ill., 60 ms. w. of Springfield; from W, 840 ms. Watered by Illinois river.

MONTEZUMA, p. v., Parke co., Ind., 72 ms. w. of Indianapolis; from W. 644 ms. Watered by Wabash river.

MONTEZUMA, p. o., Mercer co., O,

MONTEZUMA, p. o., Union co., Ky., 219 ms. w. of Frankfort; from W. 760 ms.

MONTEZUMA, p. v., McNairy co., Tenn., 155 ms. s. w. of Nashville; from W. 840 ms.

MONTEZUMA, p. o., Green co., Wis.

MONTEZUMA, p. o., Poweshiek co., Iowa.

MONTFORT, p. o., Grant co., Wis.

MONTGOMERY COUNTY, situated toward the

east part of New York, and traversed by Mohawk river and the Erie canal. Area, 356 square miles. Face of the country diversified ; soil rich, except where rocky. Seat of justice, Fonda. Pop. in 1810, 41,214 ; in 1820, 37,569 ; in 1830, 43,595 ; in 1840, 35,818 ; in 1850, 31,992.

MONTGOMERY COUNTY, situated in the southeast part of Pennsylvania, with Schuylkill river on the southwest. Area, 425 square miles. Face of the country pleasantly diversified ; soil productive. Seat of justice, Norristown. Pop. in 1810, 29,703 ; in 1820, 35,793 ; in 1830, 39,404 ; in 1840, 47,241 ; in 1850, 58,291.

MONTGOMERY COUNTY, situated on the southwest boundary of Maryland, with Potomac river on the southwest. Area, 576 square miles. Face of the country uneven ; soil generally poor. Seat of justice, Rockville. Pop. in 1810, 17,980 ; in 1820, 16,400 ; in 1830, 19,816 ; in 1840, 14,669 ; in 1850, 15,860.

MONTGOMERY COUNTY, situated in the southwesterly part of Virginia, with Great Kanawha river on the west. Area, 600 square miles. Face of the country hilly and mountainous ; soil mostly unproductive. Seat of justice, Christiansburgh. Pop. in 1810, 8,409; in 1820, 8,733 ; in 1830, 12,304 ; in 1840, 7,405 ; in 1850, 8,559.

MONTGOMERY COUNTY, situated in the southerly part of North Carolina, with Yadkin river on the southwest. Area, 500 square miles. Face of the country uneven ; soil, near the streams, fertile. Seat of justice, Lawrenceville. Pop. in 1810, 8,430 ; in 1820, 8,693 ; in 1830, 10.918 ; in 1840, 10.780 ; in 1850, 6,872.

MONTGOMERY COUNTY, situated toward the southeast part of Georgia, traversed by Oconee river. Area, 1,100 square miles. Face of the country even ; soil sterile. Seat of justice, Mount Vernon. Pop. in 1820, 1,869 ; in 1830, 1,269 ; in 1840, 1.616 ; in 1850, 2,154.

MONTGOMERY COUNTY, situated toward the southeast part of Alabama, with Alabama river on the northwest, and traversed by the Tallapoosa. Area, 900 square miles. Face of the country hilly ; soil generally sterile. Seat of justice, Montgomery. Pop. in 1820, 6,604 ; in 1830, 12,694 ; in 1840, 24,574 ; in 1850, 29,711.

MONTGOMERY COUNTY, situated on the north boundary of Tennessee, and traversed by Cumberland river. Area, 500 square miles. Face of the country uneven : soil generally not productive. Seat of justice, Clarksville. Pop. in 1810, 8,020 ; in 1820, 12,219 ; in 1830, 14,365 ; in 1840, 16.927 ; in 1850, 21,045.

MONTGOMERY COUNTY, situated toward the northeast part of Kentucky. Area, 260 square miles. Face of the country uneven ; soil productive. Seat of justice, Mount Sterling. Pop. in 1810, 12,975 ; in 1820, 9,587 ; in 1830, 10,221 ; in 1840, 9,332 ; in 1850, 9,903.

MONTGOMERY COUNTY, situated in the southwesterly part of Ohio, and traversed by Miami river. Area, 480 square miles. Face of the country undulating ; soil fertile, and well cultivated. Seat of justice, Dayton. Pop. in 1810, 7,722; in 1820, 15,999 ; in 1830, 24,252; in 1840, 31,938 ; in 1850, 38.219.

MONTGOMERY COUNTY, situated in the westerly part of Indiana. Area, 504 square miles. Seat of justice, Crawfordsville. Pop. in 1830, 7,317 ; in 1840, 14,348 ; in 1850, 18,094.

MONTGOMERY COUNTY, situated toward the south part of Illinois. Area, 684 square miles. Face of the country even ; soil fertile. Seat of justice, Hillsborough. Pop. in 1830, 2,953 ; in 1840, 4,490 ; in 1850, 6,276.

MONTGOMERY COUNTY, situated in the easterly part of Missouri, with Missouri river on the south. Area, 576 square miles. Seat of justice, Danville. Pop. in 1820, 3,074 ; in 1830, 3,902 ; in 1840, 4,371 ; in 1850, 5,849.

MONTGOMERY COUNTY, situated in the westerly part of Arkansas. Area, —— square miles. Seat of justice, Montgomery. Pop. in 1850, 1,958.

MONTGOMERY COUNTY, situated in the southerly part of Texas. Area, —— square miles. Seat of justice, Montgomery. Pop. in 1850, 2,384.

MONTGOMERY, p. t., Franklin co., Vt., 61 ms. N. of Montpelier ; from 568 ms. Watered by Trout river. Pop. 1,001.

MONTGOMERY, p. t., Hampden co., Mass., 108 ms. w. of Boston ; from W. 372 ms. Watered by Westfield river. Pop. 393.

MONTGOMERY, p. t., Orange co., N. Y., 95 ms. s. w. of Albany ; from W. 288 ms. Watered by Wall kill. Pop. 3,933.

MONTGOMERY, t., Somerset co., N. J. Watered by Beden's and Stony brooks. Pop, 1,763.

MONTGOMERY, t., Franklin co., Pa. Watered by Conecocheague creek and tributaries. Pop. 3,235.

MONTGOMERY, t., Montgomery co., Pa. Watered by Wissahickon creek and west branch of Neshaminy creek. Pop. 971.

MONTGOMERY, t., Indiana co., Pa. Pop. 751.

MONTGOMERY, p. v., Sycamore township, Hamilton co., O., 107 ms. w. of Columbus ; from W. 480 ms.

MONTGOMERY, t., Franklin co., O. Pop. 1,331.

MONTGOMERY, t., Marion co., O. Pop. 643.

MONTGOMERY, p. t., Richland co., O. Pop. 986.

MONTGOMERY, t., Wood co., O. Pop. 922.

MONTGOMERY, t., Monroe co., Ark. Pop. 317.

MONTGOMERY, t., Benton co., Mo.

MONTGOMERY, p. o., Sumner co., Tenn., 21 ms. N. of Nashville ; from W. 682 ms.

MONTGOMERY, city, seat of justice of Montgomery co., and the capital of the state of Alabama, having succeeded Tuscaloosa, as the seat of government, in 1847, has a central situation in Montgomery county, 220 miles northeast of Mobile, and 809 miles from Washington. It is the centre of an extensive trade in cotton, which is brought from the surrounding country to this point, the head of steamboat navigation on Alabama river. It contains the usual number of public buildings. The Montgomery and West Point and the Lagrange railroads, unite the city to Atlanta, on the route of the Georgia railroad, and to the intermediate points. The population in 1840, was 2.179 ; in 1850, 11,937.

MONTGOMERY, p. o., Montgomery co., Tex.

MONTGOMERY, p. o., Jennings co., Ind.

MONTGOMERY, p. t., Owen co., Ind.

MONTGOMERY CENTRE, p. o., Montgomery township, Franklin co., Vt.

MONTGOMERY CROSS-ROADS, p. o., Montgomery township, Wood co., O., 103 ms., N. w. of Columbus ; from W. 448 ms.

MONTGOMERY'S FERRY, p. o., Perry co., Pa., 19 ms. N. w. of Harrisburgh ; from W, 134 ms. Situated on Susquehanna river.

MONTGOMERYVILLE, p. v., Montgomery co., Pa., 101 ms. E. of Harrisburgh ; from W, 159 ms. Pop. 971.

MONTHALIA, p. o., Panola co., Miss.

MONTICELLO, p. t., Aroostook co., Me. Pop. 227.

MONTICELLO, c. h., p. v., Thompson township, seat of justice of Sullivan co., N. Y., 110 ms. s. w. of Albany ; from W 994 ms.

MONTICELLO, p. v., seat of justice of Fairfield district, S. C., 31 ms. N. of Columbia ; from W. 499 ms.

MONTICELLO, c. h., p. v., seat of justice of Jasper co., Ga., 35 ms. N. w. of Milledgeville ; from W. 649 ms.

MONTICELLO, c. h., p. v., seat of justice of Jefferson co., Flor., 29 ms. N. E. of Tallahassee ; from W. 925 ms. Pop. 329 ms.

MONTICELLO, p. v., Pike co., Ala. ; from W. 849 ms. Watered by a tributary of Pea river.

MONTICELLO, c. h., p. v., seat of justice of Lawrence co., Miss., 85 ms. s. of Jackson ; from W. 1,064 ms. Watered by Pearl river.

MONTICELLO, c. h., p. v., seat of justice of Wayne co., Ky., 110 ms. s. of Frankfort ; from W. 599 ms. Watered by Beaver creek.

MONTICELLO, c. h., p. v., seat of justice of White co., Ind., 73 ms. N. w. of Indianapolis ; from W. 632 ms. Watered by Tippecanoe river.

MONTICELLO, c. h., p. v., seat of justice of Piatt co., Ill. ; from W. —— ms. Watered by Sangamon river.

MONTICELLO, c. h., p. v., seat of justice of Lewis co., Mo., 145 ms. N. of Jefferson city ; from W. 912 ms. Watered by North Fabias river.

MONTICELLO, p. o., Drew co., Ark.

MONTICELLO, p. o., Jones co., Iowa.

MONTICELLO, p. o., Guilford co., N. C.

MONTICELLO, p. o., Green co., Wis.

MONTICELLO, p. o., Lewis co., Oregon.

MONTICELLO, p. o., Carroll parish, La.

MONTOUR COUNTY, situated in the easterly part of Pennsylvania. Area, —— square miles. Seat of justice, Danville. Pop. in 1850, 13,239.

MONTOUR, t., Columbia co., Pa. Pop. 409.

MONTOURS, p. o., Alleghany co., Pa.

MONTPELIER, p. t., seat of justice of Washington co., and capital of the state of Vt., is pleasantly situated amid rugged hills. 160 miles northwest of Boston, and 516 miles from Washington. Watered by Onion river and tributaries. It is the thoroughfare and centre of an extensive trade from Boston and other points. The dwellings are neat and handsome, and the architecture of the state capitol is admired for its purity and beauty. The edifice is built of dark granite, in the form of a cross, and is of the Doric order. The centre is 72 feet wide, and 100 feet deep; the two wings are each 39 feet wide and 50 feet deep; the top of the dome is 36 feet above the ridge, and 100 feet from the ground.

Montpelier is connected by railway with Burlington and Boston, and the intermediate places. The population in 1810, was 1,877 in 1820, ——; in 1830, 1,792; in 1840, 3,725; in 1850, 3,210.

MONTPELIER, p. o., Hanover co., Va., 23 ms. N. of Richmond; from W. 112 ms.

MONTPELIER, p. v., Richmond co., N. C., 91 ms. s. w. of Raleigh; from W. 379 ms.

MONTPELIER, p. v., Marengo co., Ala.

MONTPELIER, p. v., Blackford co., Ind., 81 ms. N. E. of Indianapolis; from W. 552 ms. Watered by Salamanic river.

MONTPELIER, p. o., Adair co., Ky.

MONT PETREA, p. o., De Witt co., Tex.

MONTRA, p. o., Shelby co., O.

MONTROSE, c. h., p. b., Bridgewater township, seat of justice of Susquehanna co., Pa., 175 ms. N. E. of Harrisburgh; from W. 285 ms. Pop. 917.

MONTROSE, p. t., Lee co., Iowa. Pop. 1,722

MONTROSE, p. o., Jasper co., Miss.

MONTROSE, p. o., Smith co., Tenn.

MONTROSE, p. o., Summit co., O.

MONTURESVILE, p. v., Lycoming co., Pa., 95 ms. N. of Harrisburgh; from W. 205 ms. Pop. 228.

MONTVILLE, p. t., Waldo co., Me., 26 ms. N. E. of Augusta; from W. 622 ms. Watered by tributaries of Sheepscot river. Pop. 1,881.

MONTVILLE, t., New London co., Ct., 36 ms. s. E. of Hartford; from W. 360 ms. Watered by Thames and Yantic rivers. Pop. 1,848.

MONTVILLE, p v., Pequannock township, Morris co., N. J., 67 ms. N. of Trenton; from W. 238 ms. Situated on the Morris canal.

MONTVILLE, p. t., Geauga co., O., 180 ms. N. E. of Columbus; from W. 339 ms. Pop. 702.

MONTVILLE, t., Medina co., O. Pop. 1,077.

MONUMENT, p. v., Sandwich township, Barnstable co., Mass., 60 ms. s. of Boston; from W. 461 ms. Watered by Buzzard's bay.

MONUMENT ISLAND, p. o., Delaware co., N. Y.

MOODUS, p. o., East Haddam township, Middlesex co., Ct., 27 ms. s. of Hartford; from W. 339 ms.

MOODY'S MILL, p. o., Morgan co., O.

MOOERS, p. t., Clinton co., N. Y., 198 ms. N. of Albany; from W. 573 ms. Watered by Chazy river. Pop. 3,355.

MOON, t., Beaver co., Pa. Pop. 916.

MOON, p. t., Alleghany co., Pa. Watered by Ohio river. Pop. 1,383.

MOONEY, t., Polk co., Mo.

MOONEY, p. t., Phillips co., Ark. Pop. 335.

MOONEY, p. o., Jackson co., Ind.

MOON'S, p. t., Fayette co., O., 58 ms. s. w. of Columbus; from W. 431 ms.

MOON'S PRAIRIE, p. o., Jefferson co., Ill.

MOON'S RANCHO, p. o., Colusi co., Cal.

MOORE COUNTY. situated in the central part of North Carolina. Area, 740 square miles. Face of the country, hilly; soil, generally sterile. Seat of justice, Carthage. Pop. in 1810, 6 367; in 1820, 7,128; in 1830, 7,753; in 1840, 7,988; in 1850, 9,342.

MOORE, t., Northampton co., Pa. Pop. 2,615.

MOOREFIELD, c. h., p. v., seat of justice of Hardy co., Va., 178 ms. N. w. of Richmond; from W. 130 ms. Watered by Potomac river and a branch of the same.

MOOREFIELD, p. v., Nicholas co., Ky., 58 ms. E. of Frankfort; from W. 501 ms. Watered by a branch of Licking river.

MOOREFIELD, p. t., Harrison co., O., 102 ms. E. of Columbus; from W. 295 ms. Pop. 1,265.

MOOREFIELD. p. v., Switzerland co., Ind., 95 ms. s. E. of Indianapolis; from W. 546 ms.

MOORE'S, p. o., Bowie co., Tex.

MOORESBOROUGH, p. v., Cleveland co., N. C. Watered by Sandy run.

MOORESBURGH, p. v., Liberty township, Montour co., Pa., 77 ms. N. of Harrisburgh; from W. 187 ms.

MOORESBURGH, p. o., Pulaski co., Ind.

MOORESBURGH, p. o., Hawkins co., Tenn.

MOORE'S CREEK, p. o., New Hanover co., N. C.

MOORE'S CROSS-ROADS, p. o., Hardeman co., Tenn., 194 ms. s. w. of Nashville; from W. 879 ms.

MOORE'S FORKS, p. o., Clinton co., N. Y.

MOORE'S HILL, p. o., Dearborn co., Ind., 74 ms. s. E. of Indianapolis; from W. 530 ms.

MOORE'S MILLS, p. o., Jackson co., Va.

MOORE'S ORDINARY, p. o., Prince Edward co., Va.

MOORE'S PRAIRIE, p. o., Jefferson co., Ill., 143 ms. s. w. of Springfield; from W. 789 ms.

MOORE'S SALT WORKS, p. o., Ross township. Jefferson co., O., 133 ms. E. of Columbus; from W. 286 ms.

MOORE'S STORE, p. o., Shenandoah co., Va., 158 ms. N. w. of Richmond; from W. 125 ms.

MOORE'S VINEYARD, p. o., Bartholomew co., Ind.

MOOREHEADVILLE, Erie co., Pa.

MOORLAND, p. o., Morefield township, Wayne co., O., 95 ms. N. E. of Columbus; from W. 353 ms.

MOORVILLE, p. o., Itawamba co., Miss.

MOOSE MEADOW, p. o., Tolland co., Ct.

MOOSE RIVER, p. o., Somerset co., Me., 113 ms. N. of Augusta; from W. 708 ms.

MOOSOP, p. o., Windham co., Ct., 45 ms. E. of Hartford; from W. 376 ms.

MORAL, t., Shelby co.. Ind. Pop. 1,192.

MORALS DE LA VACA, p. o., Jackson co., Tex.

MORAVIA, p. t., Cayuga co., N. Y., 158 ms. w. of Albany; from W. 322 ms. Watered by Owasco lake and inlet. Pop. 1,876.

MORAVIA, p. o., Appanoose co., Iowa.

MORDANSVILLE, p. v., Columbia co., Pa.

MOREAU, p. t., Saratoga co., N. Y., 50 ms. N. of Albany; from W. 421 ms. Watered by Hudson river. Pop. 1,834.

MOREAU, t., Morgan co., Mo.

MOREAU, p. t., Cole co., Mo., 18 ms. s. w. of Jefferson city; from W. 954 ms.

MOREAU STATION, p. o., Saratoga co., N. Y.

MOREFIELD, t., Clark co., O. Pop. 1,214.

MOREFIELD, t., Harrison co., O. Pop. 1,265.

MOREHOUSE PARISH, situated on the north boundary of Louisiana, with Wachita river on the west. Area, —— square miles. Seat of justice, Bastrop. Pop. in 1850, 3,913.

MOREHOUSE, t., Hamilton co., N. Y., 82 ms. N. w. of Albany. Pop. 242.

MOREHOUSEVILLE, c. h., p. v., seat of justice of Hamilton co., N. Y., 117 ms. N. w. of Albany; from W. 432 ms. Watered by Canada creek.

MORELAND, p. o., Dix township, Chemung co., N. Y., 198 ms. w. of Albany; from W. 301 ms.

MORELAND, t., Montgomery co., Pa. Watered by Pennypack creek and tributaries. Pop. 2,348.

MORELAND, p. t., Lycoming co., Pa., 94 ms. N. of Harrisburgh; from W. 204 ms. Watered by Little Muncy creek.

MORELAND, t., Philadelphia co., Pa. Pop. 714.

MORELAND, p. o., Bourbon co., Ky., 32 ms. E. of Frankfort; from W. 514 ms.

MORELAND, t., Scott co., Mo.

MORELAND, p. o., Fauquier co., Va.

MOREMAN'S RIVER, p. o., Albemarle co., Va., 106 ms. N. w. of Richmond; from W. 142 ms.

MORENCI, p. o., Lenawee co., Mich., 99 ms. s. w. of Detroit; from W. 507 ms.

MORESVILLE, p. v., Roxbury township, Delaware co., N. Y., 58 ms. s. w. of Albany; from W. 359 ms.

MORETOWN, p. t., Washington co., Vt., 13 ms. s. w. of Montpelier; from W. 512 ms. Watered by Mad and Winooski rivers. Pop. 1,335.

MORETZ MILL, p. o., Ashe co., N. C.

MORGAN COUNTY, situated on the northeasterly boundary of Virginia, with Potomac river on the north. Area, 350 square miles. Face of the country broken and mountainous; soil fertile on the streams. Seat of justice, Bath. Pop. in 1820, 2,500; in 1830, 2,692; in 1840, 4,253; in 1850, 3,557.

MORGAN COUNTY, situated in the central part of Georgia, with Altamaha river on the east. Area, 320 square miles. Seat of justice, Madison. Pop. in 1810, 8,369 ; in 1820, 13,520 ; in 1830, 12,023 ; in 1840, 9,121 ; in 1850, 10,774.

MORGAN COUNTY, situated in the easterly part of Kentucky, and traversed by Licking river. Area, 890 square miles. Seat of justice, West Liberty. Pop. in 1840, 4,603 ; in 1850, 7,620.

MORGAN COUNTY, situated toward the northeast part of Tennessee. Area, 640 square miles. Face of the country elevated and broken. Seat of justice, Morgan. Pop. in 1830, 2,582; in 1840, 2,660 ; in 1850, 3,430.

MORGAN COUNTY, situated in the northerly part of Alabama, with Tennessee river on the north. Area, 720 square miles. Seat of justice, Somerville. Pop. in 1830, 9,062 ; in 1840, 9,841 ; in 1850, 10,125.

MORGAN COUNTY, situated in the southeasterly part of Ohio, and traversed by Muskingum river. Area, 500 square miles. Face of the country broken and hilly ; soil generally good. Seat of justice, M'Connelsville. Pop. in 1820, 5,297 ; in 1830, 11,796 ; in 1840, 20,852 ; in 1850, 28,585.

MORGAN COUNTY, situated in the central part of Indiana, and traversed by west fork of White river. Area, 453 square miles. Pop. in 1830, 5,593 ; in 1840, 10,741 ; in 1850, 14,579.

MORGAN COUNTY, situated in the westerly part of Illinois, with Illinois river on the west. Area, 510 square miles. Seat of justice, Jacksonville. Pop. in 1830, 12,714 ; in 1840, 19,547; in 1850, 16,064.

MORGAN COUNTY, situated in the central part of Missouri, with Osage river on the south. Area, 792 square miles. Seat of justice, Versailles. Pop. in 1840, 4,407 ; in 1850, 4,650.

MORGAN, p. t., Orleans co., Vt., 50 ms. N. E. of Montpelier. Watered by a tributary of Clyde river, and Seymour's lake. Pop. 486.

MORGAN, t., Greene co., Pa. Pop. 1,157.

MORGAN, p. t., Ashtabula co., O., 195 ms. N. E. of Columbus ; from W. 355 ms. Watered by Grand river. Pop. 888.

MORGAN, t., Butler co., O. Pop. 1,706.

MORGAN, t., Gallia co., O. Pop. 1,128.

MORGAN, p. t., Harrison co., O.

MORGAN, t., Knox co., O. Pop. 823.

MORGAN, p. t., Morgan co., O. Pop. 2,308.

MORGAN, t., Scioto co., O. Watered by Scioto river and Ohio canal. Pap. 900.

MORGAN, t., Owen co., Ind. Pop. 951.

MORGAN, t., Livingston co., Mo.

MORGAN, p. t., Polk co., Mo.

MORGAN, c. h., p. v. seat of justice of Morgan co., Tenn., 156 ms. E. of Nashville ; from W. 548 ms. Watered by Emery's river.

MORGANFIELD, c. h., p. v., seat of justice of Union co., Ky., 221 ms. s. w. of Frankfort; from W. 748 ms.

MORGANSBURGH, p. v., Fauquier co., Va., 108 ms. N. of Richmond ; from W. 81 ms.

MORGAN'S CREEK, p. o., Benton co., Tenn., 99 ms. s. w. of Nashville ; from W. 783.

MORGAN'S CREEK, p. o., Orange co., N. C.

MORGAN'S FORK, p. o., Pike co., O., 74 ms. s. of Columbus ; from W. 409 ms.

MORGAN'S MILLS, p. o., Union co., N. C.

MORGAN'S RIDGE, p. o., Marion co., Va.

MORGANSVILLE, p. o., Morgan co., O.

MORGANSVILLE, p. o., Genesee co., N. Y.

MORGANTOWN, p. v., Morgan co., Ind., 39 ms. s. of Indianapolis ; from W. 598 ms. Watered by Big Indian creek.

MORGANTOWN, c. h., p. v., seat of justice of Monongalia co., Va., 295 ms. N. w. of Richmond ; from W. 218 ms. Watered by Monongahela river, at the head of steam navigation.

MORGANTOWN, p. v., Caernarvon township, Berks co., Pa., 56 ms. E. of Harrisburgh ; from W. 134 ms.

MORGANTOWN, c. h., p. v., seat of justice of Burke co., N. C., 197 ms. w. of Raleigh ; from W. 427 ms. Watered by Catawba river.

MORGANTOWN, p. v., Blount co., Tenn., 178 ms. E. of Nashville ; from W. 534 ms.

MORGANTOWN, c. h., p. v., seat of justice of Butler co., Ky., 143 ms. s. w. of Frankfort. Watered by Green river.

MORGANVILLE, p. o., Nottoway co., Va., 55 ms. s. w. of Richmond ; from W. 175 ms.

MORGANVILLE, p. o., Hillsdale co., Mich.

MORIAH, p. t., Essex co., N. Y., 115 ms. N. of Albany from W. 486 ms. Watered by Lake Champlain and Schroon branch of Hudson river. Pop. 3,065.

MORICHES, p. v., Brookhaven township, Suffolk co., Long Island, N. Y., 218 ms. s. E. of Albany ; from W 298 ms.

MORINGVILLE. p. v., Chatham co., N. C., 20 ms. N. of Raleigh ; from W. 294 ms.

MORINGVILLE, p. o., Westchester co., N. Y.

MORLEY, p. o., Canton township, St. Lawrence co. N. Y.

MORMON HILL, p. o., Marshall co., Iowa.

MORMON ISLAND, p. o., Sacramento co.. Cal.

MORNING SUN, p. v., Israel township, Preble co., O., 111 ms. w. of Columbus ; from W. 508 ms.

MORNING SUN, p. o., Shelby co., Tenn., 207 ms. s. w. of Nashville ; from W. 892 ms.

MORNING SUN, p. o., Louisa co., Iowa.

MORO. p. o., Dallas co., Ark.

MORRIS COUNTY, situated in the northerly part of New Jersey. Area, 500 square miles. Face of the country pleasantly diversified with hills and vales ; soil productive. Seat of justice, Morristown. Pop. in 1810, 21,828 ; in 1820, 21,368 ; in 1830, 23,580 ; in 1840, 28,844 ; in 1850, 30,139.

MORRIS, t., Morris co., N. J. Watered by Whippany river, and Passaic river and tributaries. Pop. 4,492.

MORRIS, t., Clearfield co., Pa. Pop. 639.

MORRIS, p. t., Tioga co., Pa., 133 ms. N. of Harrisburgh ; from W. 247 ms. Pop. 278.

MORRIS, t., Greene co., Pa. Pop. 1,250.

MORRIS, t., Huntingdon co., Pa. Pop. 787.

MORRIS, t., Washington co., Pa. Pop. 1,688.

MORRIS, p. o., Otsego co., N. Y.

MORRIS, t., Knox co., O. Watered by Vernon river and tributaries. Pop. 1,028.

MORRISANIA, p. v., West-Farms township, Westchester co., N. Y. Watered by Harlem river.

MORRIS' CHURCH, p. o., Campbell co., Va.

MORRIS CROSS. p. o., Fayette co., Pa.

MORRISDALE, p. o., Clearfield co., Pa.

MORRIS' HILL. p. o., Alleghany co., Pa.

MORRISON'S BLUFF, p. o., Johnson co., Ark., 101 ms N. w. of Little Rock ; from W. 1,169 ms.

MORRISON'S TAN-YARD, p. o., Mecklenburgh co., N. C., 158 ms. s. w. of Raleigh ; from W. 395 ms.

MORRISONVILLE, p. o., Clinton co., N. Y.

MORRISTOWN, p t, Lamoille co., Vt., 20 ms. N. of Montpelier ; from W. 544 ms. Watered by Lamoille river. Pop. 1,141.

MORRISTOWN, p. t., St. Lawrence co., N. Y., 199 ms N. w. of Albany ; from W. 466 ms. Watered by St. Lawrence river, and Black lake. Pop. 2,274.

MORRISTOWN, c. h., p. v., seat of justice of Morris co, N. J., 53 ms. N. of Trenton ; from W. 224 ms. Pop. 4,492.

MORRISTOWN, p. v., Union township, Belmont co., O., 105 ms. E. of Columbus ; from W. 288 ms. Pop. 456.

MORRISTOWN, p. v., Shelby co., Ind., 26 ms. E. of Indianapolis ; from W. 552 ms. Watered by Blue river.

MORRISTOWN, c. h., p. v., seat of justice of Henry co., Ill., 141 ms. N. w. of Springfield ; from W. 870 ms.

MORRISTOWN, p. v., Grainger co., Tenn., 226 ms. E. of Nashville ; from W. 458 ms.

MORRISTOWN, p. o., Cass co., Mo.

MORRISVILLE, p. v., Morristown township, Lamoille co.. Vt., 26 ms. N. of Montpelier ; from W. 542 ms.

MORRISVILLE, c. h., p. v., Eaton township, seat of justice of Madison co., N. Y., 102 ms. w. of Albany ; from W. 359 ms.

MORRISVILLE, p. b., Bucks co., Pa., 125 ms. E. of Harrisburgh ; from W. 165 ms. Watered by Delaware river. Pop. 565.

MORRISVILLE, p. o., Fauquier co., Va., 88 ms. N. of Richmond ; from W. 75 ms.

MORROW COUNTY, situated in the central part of Ohio. Area, —— square miles. Seat of justice, Mount Gilead. Pop. in 1850, 20,280.

MORROW, p. o., Warren co., O.

MORSE CREEK, p. o., McNairy co., Tenn., 158 ms. s. w. of Nashville ; from W. 834 ms.

MORSEVILLE, p. o., Schoharie co., N. Y., 56 ms. w. of Albany ; from W. 379 ms.

MORTON, p. o., Tazewell co., Ill.

MORTONVILLE, p. o., Woodford co., Ky., 19 ms. s. ≪ of Frankfort ; from W. 541 ms.

MORTONVILLE, p. o., Orange co., N. Y.

MORVEN, t., Marion co., O. Pop. 1,311.

MORVEN, p. v., Anson co., N. C., 141 ms. s. w. of Raleigh ; from W. 422 ms.

MORVIN, p. o., Clark co., Ala.

MOSALEM, p. o., Du Buque co., Iowa.

MOSCOW, t., Somerset co., Me., 58 ms. N. of Augusta. Watered by Kennebec river. Pop. 577.

MOSCOW, p. v., Leicester township, Livingston co., N. Y., 236 ms. w. of Albany ; from W. 353 ms.

MOSCOW, p. o., Luzerne co., Pa.

MOSCOW, p. v., Washington township, Clermont co., O., 129 ms. s. w. of Columbus ; from W. 490 ms. Watered by Ohio river.

MOSCOW, p. t., Hillsdale co., Mich., 80 ms. s. w. of Detroit. Pop. 942.

MOSCOW, p. v., Hickman co., Ky., 309 ms. s. w. of Frankfort ; from W. 835 ms. Watered by a branch of Bayou Deshe.

MOSCOW, p. v., Fayette co., Tenn., 194 ms. s. w. of Nashville ; from W. 879 ms. Watered by Wolf creek.

MOSCOW. p. t., Muscatine co., Iowa. Watered by Red Cedar creek. Pop. 566.

MOSCOW, p v., Rush co., Ind., 54 ms. s. E. of Indianapolis ; from W. 552 ms. Watered by Flat Rock creek.

MOSCOW. p. o., Marion co., Ala. ; from W. 858 ms.

MOSCOW MILLS, p. o., Morgan co., O.

MOSELEM, p. o., Berks co., Pa.

MOSELEY HALL, p. o., Lenoir co., N. C., 66 ms. w. of Raleigh ; from W. 294 ms.

MOSELEY'S GROVE, p. o., Dallas co., Ala.

MOSELLE, p. o., Jo-Daviess co., Ill.

MOSELY HALL, p. o., Madison co., Flor.

MOSELEY'S STORE, p. o.. Franklin co., Ga.

MOSS, p. o., Lafayette co., Mo.

MOSS SIDE, p. o., Alleghany co., Pa.

MOSSY CREEK, p. o., Jefferson co., Tenn., 212 ms. E. of Nashville ; from W. 472 ms.

MOTIER, p. o., Pendleton co., Ky., 87 ms. N. E. of Frankfort ; from W. 500 ms.

MOTT HAVEN, p. v., Westchester co., N. Y.

MOTT'S CORNERS, p. v., Caroline township. Tompkins co., N. Y., 168 ms. w. of Albany ; from W. 298 ms.

MOTTVILLE, p. t., St. Joseph co., Mich., 154 ms. s. w. of Detroit ; from W. 599 ms. Watered by St. Joseph river. Pop. 611.

MOTTVILLE, p. v., Skeneateles township, Onondaga co., N. Y., 149 ms. w. of Albany ; from W. 343 ms. Watered by Skeneateles Lake outlet.

MOULTON, c. h.. p. v.. seat of justice of Lawrence co., Ala. ; from W. 768 ms. Watered by Big Nance creek.

MOULTONBOROUGH. p. t., Carroll co.. N. H., 46 ms. N. of Concord ; from W. 527 ms. Watered by Winnipiseogee and Squam lakes, embracing Long and Low islands in Lake Winnipiseogee. Pop. 1,748.

MOULTONVILLE, p. o.. Madison co., Ill.

MOULTRIE COUNTY. situated in the central part of Illinois. Watered by Kaskaskia river. Pop. in 1850, 3,234.

MOULTRIE, p. o., Spartanburgh district, S. C.

MOUND BAYOU. p. o., Tensas parish. La.

MOUNDVILLE, p. o.. Marquette co., Wis.

MOUNTAIN, t.. Hot Spring co., Ark.

MOUNTAIN, t., Newton co., Mo.

MOUNTAIN, t., Washington co., Ark. Pop. 909.

MOUNTAIN COVE, p. o., Fayette co., Va., 262 ms. w. of Richmond ; from W. 299 ms.

MOUNTAIN CREEK. p. o.. Catawba co., N. C., 169 ms. w. of Raleigh ; from W. 406 ms.

MOUNTAIN FALLS, p. o., Frederick co., Va.

MOUNTAIN GROVE, p. o., Bath co., Va.

MOUNTAIN HOME, p. o., McDowell co., N. C.

MOUNTAIN HOME, p. o., Lawrence co., Ala.

MOUNTAIN INN, p. o., Tuolumne co., Cal.

MOUNTAIN SHOALS, .p. o., Spartanburgh district, S. C., 82 ms. N. w. of Columbia ; from W. 505 ms.

MOUNTAIN SPRING, p. o., Martin co., Ind.

MOUNTAIN STAND, p. o., Marshall co., Ala.

MOUNTAIN VIEW, p. o., Abbeville district, S. C., 107 ms. w. of Columbia ; from W. 539 ms.

MOUNT AIRY, p. v., Berks co., Pa., 62 ms. E. of Harrisburgh ; from W. 155 ms.

MOUNT AIRY, p. o., Pittsylvania co., Va., 145 ms. s.w. of Richmond ; from W. 232 ms.

MOUNT AIRY, p. v., Surry co., N. C., 150 ms. N. w. of Raleigh ; from W. 331 ms.

MOUNT AIRY, p. o., Bledsoe co., Tenn., 113 ms. s. E. of Nashville ; from W. 602 ms.

MOUNT AIRY. p. o., Randolph co., Mo., 80 ms. N. of Jefferson city ; from W 967 ms.

MOUNT ANDREW, p. o., Barbour co., Ala.

MOUNT AUBURN, p. o., Christian co., Ill., 22 ms. s. x of Springfield ; from W. 772 ms.

MOUNT AUBURN, p. o., Shelby co., Ind.

MOUNT BETHEL, p. t., Northampton co., Pa., 123 ms. N. E. of Harrisburgh ; from W. 216 ms.

MOUNT BETHEL, p. o., Newberry district, S. C., 50 ms. N. w. of Columbia ; from W. 494 ms.

MOUNT BLANCHARD, p. v., Delaware township. Hancock co., O., 76 ms. N. w. of Columbus ; from W. 447 ms.

MOUNT CAMBRIA, p. o., Cambria township, Niagara co., N. Y., 283 ms. w. of Albany ; from W. — ms.

MOUNT CARMEL, p. o., Union township, Clermont co., O., 113 ms. s. w. of Columbus ; from W. 484 ms.

MOUNT CARMEL, p. o., Fleming co., Ky., 96 ms. E. of Frankfort ; from W. 481 ms. Watered by Fleming creek.

MOUNT CARMEL, p. o., Franklin co., Ind., 78 ms. s. E. of Indianapolis ; from W. 508 ms.

MOUNT CARMEL, c. h., p. v., seat of justice of Wabash co., Ill., 166 ms. s. E. of Springfield ; from W. 714 ms. Watered by Illinois river. Pop. 935.

MOUNT CARMEL, p. o., Cooper co., Mo., 48 ms. w. of Jefferson city ; from W. 984 ms.

MOUNT CARMEL, p. v., Covington co., Miss., 94 ms. s. E. of Jackson : from W. 1,044 ms. Watered by White Sand creek.

MOUNT CARMEL, p. o., Wilson co., Tenn.

MOUNT CARMEL, p. o., Northumberland co., Pa.

MOUNT CARROLL, c. h., p. v., seat of justice of Carroll co., Ill. Pop. 462.

MOUNT CHESTNUT, p. o., Butler co., Pa.

MOUNT CLEMEL, p. v., seat of justice of Macomb co., Mich., 18 ms. N. E. of Detroit ; from W. 542 ms. Watered by Clinton river.

MOUNT CLIFTON, p. o., Shenandoah co., Va.

MOUNT CLINTON, p. o., Rockingham co., Pa.

MOUNT CLIO, p. o., Sumter district, S. C., 76 ms. E. of Columbia ; from W. 486 ms.

MOUNT COMFORT, p. o., Fayette co., Tenn., 180 ms. s. w. of Nashville ; from W. 865 ms.

MOUNT COMFORT, p. o., Hancock co., Ind.

MOUNT CRAWFORD, p. o., Rockingham co., Va., 131 ms. N. w. of Richmond ; from W. 139 ms. Watered by North river.

MOUNT CROGHAN, p. o., Chesterfield district, S. C., 113 ms. N. E. of Columbia ; from W. 444 ms.

MOUNT DESERT. p. t., Hancock co., Me., 146 ms. E. of Augusta ; from W. 688 ms. Situated on Mount Desert island. Pop. 777.

MOUNT EATON, p. v., Paint township, Wayne co., O., 104 ms. N. E. of Columbus ; from W. 332 ms.

MOUNT EDEN, p. o., Spencer co., Ky., 44 ms. s. w. of Frankfort , from W. 562 ms. Watered by Big Beech creek.

MOUNT ELBA, p. o., Bradley co., Ark.

MOUNT ELON, p. o., Darlington district, S. C., 110 ms. E. of Columbia ; from W. 472 ms.

MOUNT EMINENCE, p. o., Orange co., Va.

MOUNT ENTERPRISE, p. o., Rusk co., Tex.

MOUNT EOLIA, p. o., Union co., Ga.

MOUNT EPHRAIM, p. o., Guernsey co., O.

MOUNT ETNA, p. o., Huntington co., N. C.

MOUNT FREEDOM, p. o., Jessamine co., Ky.

MOUNT FREEDOM, p. o., Pendleton co., Va.

MOUNT GALLAGHER, p. v., Laurens district, S. C., 89 ms. N. w. of Columbia ; from W. 517 ms.

• MOUNT GILEAD. p. t., Loudoun co., Va., 144 ms. N. of Richmond ; from W. 45 ms.

MOUNT GILEAD, p. v., Mason co., Ky., 91 ms. N. E. of Frankfort ; from W. 476 ms.

MOUNT GILEAD, p. v., Gilead township, Morrow co., O.. 41 ms. N. of Columbus ; from W. 400 ms. Pop. 646.

MOUNT GILEAD, p. o., Montgomery co., N. C., 123 ms. s. w. of Raleigh ; from W. 397 ms.

MOUNT HAWKINS, p. o., Perry co., Ill., 142 ms. s. of Springfield ; from W. 817 ms.

MOUNT HAWLEY, p. o., Peoria co., Ill., 80 ms. N. of Springfield ; from W. 794 ms.

MOUNT HEALTHY, p. v., Springfield township, Hamilton co., O., 118 ms. s. w. of Columbus ; from W. 502 ms.

MOUNT HEALTHY, p. o., Bartholomew co., Ind.

MOUNT HEBRON, p. o., Greene co., Ala. ; from W. 866 ms.

MOUNT HICKORY, p. o., Chambers co., Ala. ; from W. 775 ms.

MOUNT HICKORY, p. o., Chattooga co., Ga.
MOUNT HILL, p. o., Abbeville district, S. C., 99 ms.
w. of Columbia ; from W. 529 ms.
MOUNT HILL, p. o., Morgan co., Ala.
MOUNT HILLIARD, p. o., Pike co., Ala.
MOUNT HOLLY, p. t., Rutland co., Vt., 79 ms. s. of Montpelier ; from W. 468 ms. Watered by Mill river, a tributary of Otter creek. Pop. 1,534.
MOUNT HOLLY, c. h., p. v., Northampton township, seat of justice of Burlington co., N. J., 18 ms. s. of Trenton ; from W. 156 ms. Watered by Rancocus creek, at the head of navigation.
MOUNT HOLLY, p. o., Randolph co., Ind.. 97 ms. N. E. of Indianapolis ; from W. 502 ms.
MOUNT HOLLY, p. o., Warren co., O.
MOUNT HOLYOKE, p. o., Henry co., Tenn., 106 ms. w. of Nashville ; from W. 792 ms.
MOUNT HOPE, p. t., Orange co., N. Y., 112 ms. s. w. of Albany , from W. 276 ms. Watered by Shawangunk creek. Pop. 1,512.
MOUNT HOPE, p. o., Lancaster co., Pa., 26 ms. E. of Harrisburgh ; from W. 130 ms.
MOUNT HOPE, p. o., Lawrence co., Ala. ; from W. 780 ms. Watered by Town creek.
MOUNT HOPE, p.o., Saltcreek township, Holmes co., O.
MOUNT HOPE, p. o., Lafayette co., Mo.. 113 ms. N. w. of Jefferson city ; from W. 1 027 ms.
MOUNT HOPE, p. o., McLean co , Ill.
MOUNT HOPE, p. o., De Kalb co., Ind.
MOUNT HOPE, p. o.. Delaware co., Iowa.
MOUNT HOPE, p. o., Tyler co., Tex.
MOUNT HOREB, p. o., Nelson co., Va., 113 ms. w. of Richmond ; from W. 150 ms.
MOUNT IDA, p. o., Montgomery co., Ark.
MOUNT IDA, p. o., Montgomery co., Ky.
MOUNT ISABEL, p. o., De Soto co., Miss.
MOUNT ISRAEL, p. o.. Albemarle co., Va., 93 ms. N. w. of Richmond ; from W. 143 ms.
MOUNT JACKSON, p. v., Shenandoah co., Va.. 146 ms. N. w. of Richmond ; from W. 117 ms.
MOUNT JACKSON, p. v., Lawrence co., Pa., 239 ms. w. of Harrisburgh ; from W. 277 ms. Watered by Hickory creek.
MOUNT JEFFERSON, p. o., Chambers co., Ala. ; from W. 774 ms.
MOUNT JEFFERSON, p. o.. Carroll co., Ind., 68 ms. N. w. of Indianapolis ; from W. 632 ms.
MOUNT JOY, t., Adams co., Pa. Watered by Rock and Willoway's creeks.
MOUNT JOY, p. t., Lancaster co., Pa., 25 ms. s. E. of Harrisburgh ; from W. 123 ms. Watered by Little Chicques and Conewago creeks. Pop. 2,626.
MOUNT KINGSTON, p. o., Montgomery co., Ill., 60 ms. s. of Springfield ; from W. 777 ms.
MOUNT KISTO, p. o., Westchester co., N. Y.
MOUNT LANGUM, p. o., Iroquois co., Ill.
MOUNT LAUREL, p. o., Halifax co., Va., 115 ms. s. w. of Richmond ; from W. 202 ms.
MOUNT LAUREL, p. o., Burlington co., N. J.
MOUNT LEBANON, p. o., Claiborne parish, La., 300 ms. N. w. of New Orleans ; from W. 1,270 ms.
MOUNT LEBANON, p. o., Spartanburgh district, S. C., 112 ms. N. w. of Columbia ; from W. 485 ms.
MOUNT LEVEL, p. o., Dinwiddie co., Va.
MOUNT LIBERTY, p. v., Liberty township, Knox co., O., 41 ms. N. E. of Columbus ; from W. 386 ms.
MOUNT LIBERTY, p. o.. Marion co., Ill.
MOUNT MEIGS, p. v., Montgomery co., Ala. ; from W. 826 ms.
MOUNT MERIDIAN, p. o., Pulaski co., Ky.
MOUNT MERIDIAN, p. v., Putnam co., Ind., 36 ms. w. of Indianapolis ; from W. 607 ms.
MOUNT MERIDIAN, p. v., Augusta co., Va., 125 ms. N. w. of Richmond ; from W. 144 ms.
MOUNT MERIDIAN, p. o., Pulaski co., Mo.
MOUNT MORIA, p. o., Hempstead co., Ark.
MOUNT MORIAH, p. o., Mecklenburgh co., N. C.
MOUNT MORIAH, p. o., Brown co., Ind.
MOUNT MORRIS, p. t., Livingston co., N. Y., 242 ms. w. of Albany ; from W. 353 ms. Watered by Genesee river and Genesee Valley canal. Pop. 4,531.
MOUNT MORRIS, p. v., Whately township, Greene co., Pa., 228 ms. w. of Harrisburgh ; from W. 227 ms. Watered by Dunkard's creek.
MOUNT MORRIS, p. o., Ogle co., Ill., 177 ms. N. of Springfield ; from W. 837 ms.
MOUNT MOURNE, p. o., Iredell co., N. C., 146 ms. w. of Raleigh ; from W. 383 ms.

MOUNT NEBO, p. o., Lancaster co., Pa.
MOUNT NEBO, p. o., Surry co., N. C
MOUNT NEBO, p. o., Williamson co., Tenn.
MOUNT NILES, p. o., St. Clair co., Ala. ; from W. 727 ms.
MOUNT OLIVE, p. o., Clermont co., O.
MOUNT OLIVE, p. o., St. Mary's co., Md.
MOUNT OLIVE, p. o., Izard co., Ark.
MOUNT OLIVET, p. o., Bracken co., Ky.
MOUNT PALATINE, p. o., Putnam co., Ill.
MOUNT PARTHENON, p. o., Newton co., Ark.
MOUNT PERRY, p. o., Perry co., O.
MOUNT PELIA, p. o., Weakly co., Tenn.
MOUNT PINSON, p. o., Jefferson co., Ala. ; from W. 766 ms.
MOUNT PINSON, p. o., Jackson co., Ark.
MOUNT PINSON, p. o., Madison co., Tenn.
MOUNT PISGAH, p. o., Alexander co., N. C., 168 ms. w. of Raleigh ; from W. 379 ms.
MOUNT PISGAH, p. o., La Grange co., Ind.
MOUNT PISGAH, p. o., Clermont co., O.
MOUNT PLEASANT. t., Westchester co., N. Y., 125 ms. s. of Albany ; from W. —— ms. Pop. 3,223.
MOUNT PLEASANT, p. v., Alexandria township, Hunterdon co., N. J., 38 ms. N. of Trenton ; from W. 195 ms. Watered by Hakehokakee creek.
MOUNT PLEASANT, b., Tioga co., Pa.
MOUNT PLEASANT, t., Adams co., Pa. Watered by Conewago creek and tributaries. Pop. 1,614.
MOUNT PLEASANT, p. t., Westmoreland co., Pa., 170 ms. w. of Harrisburgh ; from W. 196 ms. Watered by Big Sewickly and Jacobs creeks. Pop. 3,110.
MOUNT PLEASANT, t., Columbia co., Pa. Pop. 708.
MOUNT PLEASANT, t., Wayne co., Pa. Watered by head waters of Lackawaxen, Dyberry and Great Equimink creeks. Pop. 1,551.
MOUNT PLEASANT, t., Washington co., Pa. Pop. 1,254.
MOUNT PLEASANT, p. v.. Frederick co., Md., 81 ms. N. w. of Annapolis ; from W. 49 ms.
MOUNT PLEASANT, p. v.. Spottsylvania co., Va., 64 ms. N. of Richmond ; from W. 73 ms.
MOUNT PLEASANT, p. o., Monroe co., Ala. ; from W. 948 ms.
MOUNT PLEASANT, p. t. Jefferson co., O., 131 ms. E. of Columbus ; from W. 277 ms. Pop. 1,847.
MOUNT PLEASANT, p. v., Oakland co., Mich., 41 ms. N. w. of Detroit ; from W. 565 ms.
MOUNT PLEASANT, p. v., Claburree co., N. C.
MOUNT PLEASANT, p. v., Maury co., Tenn., 53 ms. s. w. of Nashville ; from W. 790 ms.
MOUNT PLEASANT, c. h., p. v., seat of justice of Martin co., Ind., 106 ms. s. w. of Indianapolis ; from W. 653 ms. Watered by east fork of White river.
MOUNT PLEASANT. p. o., Union co., Ill., 209 ms. s. of Springfield ; from W. 819 ms.
MOUNT PLEASANT, t., Scotland co., Mo. Pop. 801.
MOUNT PLEASANT, t., Barry co., Mo., 212 ms. s. w. of Jefferson city ; from W. 1,123 ms.
MOUNT PLEASANT, c. h., p. v., seat of justice of Henry co., Iowa. Watered by Big creek. Pop. 758.
MOUNT PLEASANT, p. o., Titus co., Tex.
MOUNT PLEASANT, p. o., Talbot co., Ga.
MOUNT PLEASANT, p. o., Lawrence co., Mo.
MOUNT PLEASANT, p. o., Saratoga co., N. Y.
MOUNT PLEASANT, p. o., Racine co., Wis., 106 ms. s. E. of Madison ; from W. 786 ms.
MOUNT PLEASANT, p. o., Greene co., Wis.
MOUNT PLEASANT MILLS, p. o., Perry township, Union co., Pa., 61 ms. N. of Harrisburgh ; from W. 164 ms.
MOUNT POLK, p. o., Benton co., Ala.
MOUNT PROSPECT, p. o., Crawford co., Ind., 106 ms. s. of Indianapolis ; from W. 637 ms.
MOUNT PROSPECT, p. o., Whitesides co., Ill.
MOUNT PULASKI, p. o., Sangamon co., Ill., 27 ms. E. of Springfield ; from W. 787 ms.
MOUNT ROCK, p. o., Cumberland co., Pa., 22 ms. s. w. of Harrisburgh ; from W. 110 ms.
MOUNT ROSE, p. o., Mercer co., N. J.
MOUNT SALEM, p. o., Kanawha co., Va.
MOUNT SALEM, p. o., Sussex co., N. J.
MOUNT SAVAGE, p. o., Alleghany co., Md.
MOUNT SAVAGE, p. o., Carter co., Ky.
MOUNT SERRENE, p. o., Barbour co., Ala.
MOUNT SIDNEY, p. o., Augusta co., Va., 127 ms. N. w of Richmond ; from W. 145 ms.
MOUNT SINAI, p. o., Suffolk co.. Long Island, N. Y 205 ms. s. E. of Albany ; from W. 285 ms.

MOUNT SOLON, p. o., Augusta co., Va., 139 ms. N. .w of Richmond ; from W. 146 ms.

MOUNT STERLING, p. v., Pleasant township, Madison co., O., 32 ms. w. of Columbus ; from W. 421 ms.

MOUNT STERLING, p. t., Muskingum co., O.

MOUNT STERLING. c. h., p. v., seat of justice of Montgomery co., Ky., 59 ms. E. of Frankfort ; from W. 514 ms. Watered by a tributary of the south fork of Licking river.

MOUNT STERLING. c. h., p. v., seat of justice of Brown co., Ill., 77 ms. w. of Springfield ; from W. 854 ms. Watered by a tributary of Crooked creek.

MOUNT STERLING, t., Pettis co., Mo.

MOUNT STERLING. p. v., Choctaw co., Ala. ; from W. 927 ms. Watered by Shuckeba creek.

MOUNT STERLING, p. o., Crawford co. Wis.

MOUNT STERLING, p. o., Switzerland co., Ind.

MOUNT SUMNER, p. o., Jo-Daviess co., Ill.

MOUNT SURPRISE, p. o., Luzerne co., Pa.

MOUNT SYLVAN, p. o., Lafayette co., Miss.

MOUNT TABOR, t., Rutland co., Vt. Watered by headwaters of Otter creek. Pop. 308.

MOUNT TABOR, p. v., Union district, S. C., 76 ms. n. w. of Columbia ; from W. 452 ms.

MOUNT TABOR, p. v., Monroe co., Ind., 45 ms. s. w. of Indianapolis ; from W. 616 ms. Watered by Bean Blossom creek.

MOUNT TIRZAH. p. o., Person co., N. C., 44 ms. N. w. of Raleigh ; from W. 260 ms.

ᴵ MOUNT ULLA, p. o., Rowan co., N. C.

MOUNT UNION, p. o., Huntington co., Pa.

MOUNT UNION, p. v., Stark co., O., 138 ms. N. E. of Columbus ; from W. 304 ms.

MOUNT UPTON, p. v., Guilford township, Chenango co., N. Y., 99 ms. N. w. of Albany ; from W. 331 ms. Watered by Unadilla river.

MOUNT VALE SPRINGS. p. o., Blount co., Tenn.

MOUNT VERNON, p. t., Kennebec co., Me., 15 ms. N. w. of Augusta ; from W. 609 ms. Pop. 1,479.

MOUNT VERNON, p. t., Hillsborough co., N. H., 32 ms. s. w. of Concord ; from W. 366 ms. Watered by a tributary of Souhegan river. Pop. 722.

MOUNT VERNON, p. v., Chester co., Pa., 72 ms. s. E. of Harrisburgh ; from W. 101 ms.

MOUNT VERNON, Fairfax co., Va., the former residence and last resting-place of Washington. Watered by Potomac river.

MOUNT VERNON, c. h., p. v., seat of justice of Montgomery co., Ga., 112 ms. s. E. of Milledgeville ; from W. 723 ms.

MOUNT VERNON, p. v., Mobile co., Ala. ; from W. 996 ms.

MOUNT VERNON, c. h., p. v., seat of justice of St. Francis co., Ark.

MOUNT VERNON, p. o., Monroe co., Tenn., 170 ms. s. E. of Nashville ; from W. 547 ms.

MOUNT VERNON, c. h., p. v.. seat of justice of Rock Castle co., Ky., 75 ms. s. E. of Frankfort ; from W. 563 ms.

MOUNT VERNON, c. h., p. v., seat of justice of Knox co.. O., 51 ms. N. E. of Columbus ; from W. 376 ms. Watered by Vernon river, or Owl creek. Pop. 3,711.

MOUNT VERNON, p. v., Macomb co., Mich., 32 ms. N. of Detroit ; from W. 554 ms.

MOUNT VERNON, c. h., p. v., seat of justice of Posey co., Ind., 188 ms. s. w. of Indianapolis ; from W. 749 ms. Watered by Ohio river.

MOUNT VERNON. c. h., p. v., seat of Jefferson co., Ill., 129 ms. s. E. of Springfield ; from W. 794 ms.

MOUNT VERNON, p. v., Lawrence co., Mo. Pop. 1,579.

MOUNT VERNON, p. o., Rowan co., N. C., 132 ms. w. of Raleigh ; from W. 366 ms.

MOUNT VERNON, p. o., Linn co., Iowa.

MOUNT VIEW, p. o., Davidson co.. Tenn.

MOUNT VIEW, p. o., Benton co., Mo.

MOUNTVILLE. p. v., Loudoun co., Va., 139 ms. N. of Richmond ; from W. 50 ms.

MOUNTVILLE. p. v., Laurens district, S. C., 74 ms. N. w. of Columbia ; from W. 512 ms.

MOUNTVILLE. p. v., Troup co., Ga., 112 ms. w. of Milledgeville . from W. 731 ms.

MOUNTVILLE. p. v., Lancaster co., Pa.

MOUNT VINCO. p. o., Buckingham co., Va.

MOUNT VISION, p. v., Laurens township, Otsego co., N. Y., 79 ms. w. of Albany ; from W. 362 ms.

MOUNT WARREN, p. o., Weakly co., Tenn.

MOUNT WASHINGTON, t., Berkshire co., Mass. Watered by a branch of Ancram creek. Pop. 357.

MOUNT WASHINGTON, p. o., Urbanna township, Steuben co., N. Y., 212 ms. w. of Albany ; from W. 312 ms.

MOUNT WASHINGTON, p. v., Bullitt co., Ky.

MOUNT WASHINGTON, p. o., Hamilton co., O.

MOUNT WELCOME, p. o., Clay co., Ky.

MOUNT WILLING, p. o., Orange co., N. C., 53 ms. N. w. of Raleigh ; from W. 287 ms.

MOUNT WILLING, p. v., Edgefield district, S. C., 41 ms. w. of Columbia ; from W. 527 ms. Watered by a tributary of Little Saluda river.

MOUNT WILLING, p. v., Lowndes co., Ala. ; from W. 869 ms. Watered by Cedar creek.

MOUNT WILLING, p. o., East Feliciana parish, La.

MOUNT YONAH, p. o., Habersham co., Ga., 154 ms. N. of Milledgeville ; from W. 620 ms.

MOUNT ZION, p. o., Lebanon co., Pa., 30 ms. E. of Harrisburgh ; from W. 140 ms.

MOUNT ZION, p. o., Spartanburgh district, S. C., 106 ms. N. w. of Columbia ; from W. 480 ms.

MOUNT ZION, p. v., Hancock co., Ga., 30 ms. N. E. of Milledgeville ; from W. 654 ms.

MOUNT ZION, p. o., Campbell co., Va., 118 ms. w. of Richmond ; from W. 208 ms.

MOUTH OF HEWASEE, p. o., Meigs co., Tenn.

MOUTH OF INDIAN, p. o., Monroe co., Va.

MOUTH OF LITTLE RIVER, p. o., Blount co., Tenn.

MOUTH OF POCA, p. o., Putnam co., Va., 329 ms. N. w. of Richmond ; from W. 366 ms.

MOUTH OF SANDY, p. o., Henry co., Tenn., 91 ms. w. of Nashville ; from W. 769 ms.

MOUTH OF SENECA, p. o., Pendleton co., Va.

MOUTH OF WILLAMETTE, p. o., Elk co., Oregon.

MOUTH OF WILSON, p. o., Grayson co., Va., 291 ms. s. w. of Richmond ; from W. 356 ms.

MOUTH OF YELLOW CREEK, p. o., Jefferson co., O., 149 ms. E. of Columbus ; from W. 275 ms.

MOWRYSTOWN, p. o., Highland co., O.

MOYAMENSING, t., Philadelphia co., Pa. A suburban district of Philadelphia, having an independent incorporation. Pop. in 1840, 14,573 ; in 1850, 26,979.

MUCHINIPPE, p. o., Logan co., O., 84 ms. N. w. of Columbus ; from W. 469 ms.

MUCKALUSHY, p. o., Neoshoba co., Miss.

MUD BRIDGE, p. o., Cabell co., Va.

MUD CREEK, p. o., St. Clair co., Ill.

MUD CREEK, p. o., McNairy co., Tenn.

MUD CREEK, p. o., Henderson co., N. C.

MUD CREEK, p. o., Eaton co., Mich.

MUDDY CREEK, t., Butler co., Pa. Pop. 1,142.

MUDDY CREEK, p. o., Preston co., Va., 275 ms. N. w of Richmond ; from W. 197 ms.

MUDDY CREEK, p. o., Forsyth co., N. C.

MUDDY CREEK FORKS, p. o., York co., Pa

MUDDY FORKS, p. o., Cleveland co., N. C., 194 ms. w. of Nashville ; from W. 439 ms.

MUDDY LANE, p. o., McDonough co., Ill., 98 ms. N. w. of Springfield ; from W. — ms.

MUD LICK, p. o., Chatham co., N. C., 60 ms. w. of Raleigh ; from W. 314 ms.

MUD SPRING, p. o., El Dorado co., Cal.

MUHLENBURGH COUNTY, situated in the westerly part of Kentucky, with Green river on the northeast. Area, 490 square miles. Seat of justice, Greenville. Pop. in 1820, 4,979 ; in 1830, 5,341 ; in 1840, 6,964 ; in 1850, 9,809.

MUHLENBURGH, p. o., Luzerne co., Pa., 112 ms. N. E. of Harrisburgh ; from W. 223 ms.

MUHLENBURGH, t., Pickaway co., O. Pop. 585.

MUKER, p. o., Washington co., Wis.

MUCKWA, p. o., Brown co., Wis.

MUKWANAGO, p. o., Waukesha co., Wis.

MULBERRY, p. o., Miami township. Clermont co., O., 108 ms. s. w. of Columbus ; from W. 480 ms.

MULBERRY, p. o., Wilkes co., N. C., 193 ms. w. of Raleigh ; from W. 383 ms.

MULBERRY, p. o., Jackson co., Ga., 164 ms. N. of Milledgeville ; from W. 645 ms.

MULBERRY, t., Franklin co., Ark. Pop. 532.

MULBERRY, t., Johnson co., Ark. Pop. 339.

MULBERRY, p. o., Lincoln co., Tenn., 86 ms. s. of Nashville ; from W. 709 ms.

MULBERRY GAP, p. o., Hancock co., Tenn.

MULBERRY GROVE, p. o., Harris co., Ga., 139 ms. w. of Milledgeville ; from W. 778 ms.

MULBERRY GROVE, p. o., Hopkins co., Ky., 206 ms. s. w. of Frankfort; from W. 748 ms.

MULBERRY GROVE, p. o., Bond co., Ill., 82 ms. s. of Springfield ; from W. 750 ms.

MULL GROVE, p. o., Lincoln co., N. C., 188 ms. w. of Raleigh ; from W. 425 ms.

MULLICO HILL, p. v., Gloucester co., N. J., 45 ms. s. of Trenton ; from W. 156 ms. Watered by Raccoon creek.

MULLICA, t., Atlantic co., N. J. Pop. 918.

MULLLINGAR, p. o., Warren co., Pa.

MULLOYS, p., Robertson co., Tenn.

MUMFORD, p. o., Monroe co., N. Y.

MUNCIETOWN, c. h., p. v., seat of justice of Delaware co., Ind., 58 ms. N. E. of Indianapolis ; from W. 529 ms. Watered by White river.

MUNCY, p. b., Muncy Creek township, Lycoming co., Pa., 85 ms. N. of Harrisburgh; from W. 195 ms. Pop. 901.

MUNCY, t., Lycoming co., Pa. Watered by Muncy and Loyalsock creeks. Pop. 1,879.

MUNCY CREEK, t., Lycoming co., Pa. Watered by Big and Little Muncy creeks. Pop. 1,250.

MUNDY, t., Genesee co., Mich. Pop. 786.

MUMFORDSVILLE, c. h., p. v., seat of justice of Hart co., Ky., 111 ms. s. w. of Frankfort; from W. 635 ms. Watered by Green river.

MUNGER'S MILLS, p. o., Shannon co., Mo., 129 ms. s. E. of Jefferson city ; from W. 903 ms,

MUNGO PARK, p. o., Washington co., Pa.

MUNNTOWN, p. o., Washington co., Pa.

MUNNSVILLE, p. o., Madison co., N. Y.

MUNNVILLE, p. o., Coshocton co., O.

MUNSON, t., Geauga co., O., 166 ms. N. E. of Columbus ; from W. 340 ms. Pop. 1,193.

MUNSONVILLE, p. o., Cheshire co., N. H.

MUNSTER, p. v., Alleghany township, Cambria co., Pa., 133 ms. w. of Harrisburgh ; from W. 177 ms.

MURDER KILL, hundred. Kent co,, Del.

MURDOCKSVILLE, p. v., Washington co., Pa., 230 ms. w. of Harrisburgh ; from W. 255 ms.

MURFREESBOROUGH, p. v., Hertford co., N. C., 142 ms. N. E. of Raleigh ; from W. 214 ms. Watered by Chowan river.

MURFREESBOROUGH, c. h., p. v., seat of justice of Rutherford co., Tenn., 34 ms. s. E. of Nashville ; from W. 665 ms. Watered by a tributary of Stone creek.

MURFREESBOROUGH, p. o., Pike co., Ala.

MURPHY, c. h., p. v., seat of justice of Cherokee co., N. C., 367 ms. w. of Raleigh ; from W. 597 ms. Situated at the confluence of Hiawassee and Valley rivers.

MURPHREE'S VALLEY, p. o., Blount co., Ala. ; from W. 738 ms.

MURPHY'S, p. o., Calaveras co., Cal.

MURPHYSBOROUGH, p. o., Jackson co., Ill.

MURPHYSVILLE, p. o., Mason co., Ky., 73 ms. N. E. of Frankfort; from W. 469 ms.

MURRAY COUNTY, situated on the north boundary of Georgia. Area, 650 square miles. Seat of justice, Spring Place. Pop. in 1840, 4,695 ; in 1850, 14,133.

MURRAY, p. v., Wells co., Ind., 111 ms. N. E. of Indianapolis ; from W. 553 ms.

MURRAY, p. t., Orleans co., N. Y., 243 ms. w. of Albany ; from W. 392 ms. Watered by Sandy creek. Pop. 2,520.

MURRAY, p. o., Callaway co., Ky.

MURRAY'S FERRY, p. o., Williamsburgh district, S. C.

MURRAYSVILLE. p. o., Jackson co., Va.

MURRILL'S SHOP, p. o., Nelson co., Va., 97 ms. w. of Richmond ; from W. 152 ms.

MURRINSVILLE, p. o., Butler co., Pa., 210 ms. w. of Harrisburgh ; from W. 265 ms.

MURRYSVILLE, p. o., Franklin township, Westmoreland co., Pa., 181 ms. w. of Harrisburgh ; from W. 207 ms.

MUSCATINE COUNTY, situated on the easterly boundary of Iowa, with Mississippi river on the east. Area, 440 square miles. Seat of justice, Muscatine. Pop. in 1840, 1,942 ; in 1850, 5,731.

MUSCATINE, p. t., seat of justice of Muscatine co., Iowa. Watered by Muscatine slue. Pop. 2,539.

MUSCODA, p. o., Grant co., Wis.

MUSCOGEE COUNTY, situated on the west boundary of Georgia. Area, 410 square miles. Seat of justice, Columbus. Pop. in 1840, 11,699 ; in 1850, 18,578.

MUSH CREEK, p. o., Greenville district, S. C. 133 ms. N. W. of Columbia ; from W. 578 ms.

MUSHULAVILLE, p. o., Noxubee co., Miss.

MUSKEEGO, p. t., Milwaukee co., Wis.

MUSKEEGO CENTRE, p. o., Waukesha co., Wis.

MUSKEGON, p. o., Ottawa co., Mich.

MUSKET, p. o., Navarro co., Tex.

MUSKINGUM COUNTY, situated toward the south east part of Ohio, and traversed by Muskingum river. Area, 665 square miles. Seat of justice, Zanesville. Pop. in 1810, 10,036 ; in 1820, 17,824 ; in 1830, 29,325 ; in 1840, 38,749 ; in 1850, 45,037.

MUSKINGUM, p. t., Muskingum co., O., 61 ms. E. of Columbus ; from W. 346 ms. Pop. 1,509

MUSTANG, p. o., La Vaca co., Tex.

MUTUAL, p. o., Champaign co., O.

MYERSBURGH, p. o., Bradford co., Pa.

MYATTE, p. o., Fulton co., Ark.

MYERSVILLE, p. o. Frederick co., Md.

MYER'S MILLS, p. o., Vermillion co., Ill.

MYRTLE SPRINGS, p. o., Bowie co., Tex.

MYSTIC, p. v., Stonington township, New London co., Ct., 52 ms. s. E. of Hartford ; from W. 362 ms. Watered by Mystic river. Pop. 89.

MYSTIC BRIDGE, p. o., Groton township, New London co., Ct.

MYSTIC RIVER, p. o., New London co., Ct.

N.

NAAMAN'S CREEK, p. o., New Castle co., Del.

NAAUSAY, p. o., Kendall co., Ill.

NACOGDOCHES COUNTY, situated in the easterly part of Texas. Area, —— square miles. Seat of justice, Nacogdoches. Pop. in 1850, 5,192.

NACOGDOCHES, c. h., p. v., seat of justice of Nacogdoches co., Tex.

NACOOCHE, p. o., Habersham co., Ga., 155 ms. N. of Milledgeville ; from W. 611 ms.

NAGLESVILLE, p. o., Monroe co., Pa.

NAHANT, p. v., a favorite summer resort and residence, in Lynn township, Essex co., Mass., 14 ms. N. E. of Boston. It is a rock-bound peninsula, stretching several miles into Massachusetts bay, and joined to the main land by a smooth beach of compact sand.

NAHUNTA, p. o., Wayne co., N. C., 61 ms. s. E. of Raleigh ; from W. 271 ms.

NAIL FACTORY, p. o. Gaston co., N. C.

NAIRN, p. o., Scioto co., O.

NAMAHKUM, p. o., Marquette co., Wis.

NAMOZINE, p. o., Amelia co., Va., 41 ms. s. w. of Richmond ; from W. 160 ms.

MANAFALIA, p. o., Marengo co., Ala. ; from W. 912 ms. Watered by Tombigbee river.

NANCEMONT, p. o., Cass co., Ill.

NANJEMOY, p. v Charles co,, Md., 88 ms. s. w. of Annapolis ; from W. 48 ms. Watered by Nanjemoy bay.

NANKIN. p. v., Orange township, Ashland co., O., 83 ms. N. of Columbus ; from W. 372 ms.

NANKIN, p. t., Wayne co., Mich., 20 ms. w. of Detroit ; from W. 534 ms. Watered by tributaries of Rouge river. Pop. 1.617.

NANSEMOND COUNTY, situated on the south boundary of Virginia, with James river on the northeast. Area, 444 square miles. Face of the country, low and marshy, the Dismal Swamp covering the eastern part. Seat of justice, Suffolk. Pop. in 1810, 10,324 ; in 1820, 10,494 ; in 1830, 11,784 ; in 1840, 10,795 ; in 1850, 12,283.

NANTICOKE, p. o., Luzerne co., Pa., 120 ms. N. E. of Harrisburgh ; from W. 224 ms.

NANTICOKE, p. t., Broome co., N. Y. Watered by Nanticoke creek. Pop. 576.

NANTICOKE, hundred, Sussex co., Del. Pop. 1,546.

NANTICOKE SPRINGS, p. v., Nanticoke township, Broome co., N. Y., 142 ms. s. w. of Albany ; from W. 301 ms. Site of a salubrious sulphur spring.

NANTUCKET COUNTY, an island, situated off the southeast part of Massachusetts, in the Atlantic ocean. Area, 50 square miles. Face of the country, level ; soil sandy, and generally poor. Seat of justice, Nantucket.

Pop. in 1810, 6,807; in 1820, 7,266; in 1830, 7,202; in 1840, 9,012; in 1850, 8,454.

NANTUCKET, c. h., p. v., seat of justice of Nantucket co., Mass., 119 ms. s. e. of Boston; from W. 500 ms. Watered by Nantucket bay. Pop. 8,454.

NANUET, p. o., Rockland co., N. Y.

NAPA COUNTY, situated in the westerly part of California. Area, —— square miles. Seat of justice, Napa. Pop. in 1852, 2,116.

NAPA, c. h., p. t., seat of justice of Napa co., Cal.

NAPANOCK, p. o., Ulster co., N. Y.

NAPIER, t., Bedford co., Pa. Pop. 2,051.

NAPIERVILLE, p. v., Du Page co., Ill., 176 ms. n. e. of Springfield; from W. 745 ms. Watered by west fork of Du Page river.

NAPLES, p. t., Cumberland co., Me., 66 ms. s. w. of Augusta; from W. 569 ms. Watered by Crooked and Saugo rivers. Pop. 1,025.

NAPLES, p. t., Ontario co., N. Y., 220 ms. w. of Albany; from W. 325 ms. Watered by inlets of Canandaigua and Honeoye lakes. Pop. 2,376.

NAPLES, p. v., Scott co., Ill., 56 ms. w. of Springfield; from W. 834 ms. Watered by Illinois river.

NAPOLEON, p. t., Jackson co., Mich., 66 ms. w. of Detroit; from W. 542 ms. Pop. 1,208.

NAPOLEON, p. v., Gallatin co., Ky., 51 ms. n. of Frankfort; from W. 528 ms.

NAPOLEON, p. v., Ripley co., Ind., 59 ms. s. e. of Indiana; from W. 542 ms.*

NAPOLEON, p. v., Desha co., Ark., 148 ms. s. e. of Little Rock; from W. 1,087 ms. Situated at the confluence of the Arkansas and Mississippi rivers. Pop. 243.

NAPOLEON, c. h., p. t., seat of justice of Henry co., O., 154 ms. n. w. of Columbus; from W. 485 ms. Watered by Maumee river. Pop. 566.

NAPOLI, p. t., Cattaraugus co., N. Y., 308 ms. w. of Albany; from W. 341 ms. Watered by Coldspring creek. Pop. 1,233.

NAPONOCH, v., Wawarsing township, Ulster co., N. Y. Watered by Rondout creek.

NARRAGANSET, p. o., Washington co., R. I.

NARRAGUAGUS, p. v., Washington co., Me., 124 ms. e. of Augusta; from W. 706 ms. Watered by Narragaugus bay.

NARROWS, p. o., Jefferson co., N. Y.

NARROWS, p. o., Daviess co., Ky.

NARROWS, p. o., Pike co., Pa.

NARROWS, t., Macon co., Mo.

NARROWS, p. o., Noddaway co., Mo.

NARROWSBURGH, p. o., Lumberland township, Sullivan co., N. Y., 141 ms. s. w. of Albany; from W. 283 ms.

NARROW VALLEY, p. o., Benton co., Ala.

NASH COUNTY, situated toward the northwest part of North Carolina, and traversed by Tar river. Area, 640 square miles. Face of the country uneven; soil productive. Seat of justice, Nashville. Pop. in 1810, 7,268; in 1820, 8,185; in 1830, 8,492; in 1840, 9,047; in 1850, 10,657.

NASHPORT, p. v., Licking township, Muskingum co., O., 54 ms. e. of Columbus; from W. 351 ms. Situated on Ohio and Erie canal.

NASH'S FORD, p. o., Russell co., Va.

NASHUA, p. t., Hillsborough co., N. H., 36 ms. s. of Concord; from W. 447 ms. Watered by Merrimac and Nashua rivers. Celebrated for its manufactures of cotton. Pop. 1840, 6,054; in 1850, 5,820.

NASHVILLE, city, seat of justice of Davidson co., and capital of Tennessee, situated on the south bank of Cumberland river, at the head of steamboat navigation, 120 miles from its entrance into the Mississippi, and 648 miles from Washington. Built upon an uneven surface, amid the picturesque scenery of a fertile and populous region, few southern cities combine a pleasant situation with more attractive hospitality and refinement, or display, in proportion to their population, a greater number of elegant public structures. Of these, a new statehouse is the most magnificent. The courthouse is a spacious and convenient edifice; the churches are beautiful and costly; and the schools are excellent. The medical department of Nashville university is in a prosperous condition, with commodious buildings, well supplied with apparatus and other means of instruction. The other public buildings are, the jail, the penitentiary, and an asylum for the insane.

Large steamboats navigate Cumberland river to Nashville, during the greater part of the year. When the water is low, the stream admits vessels only of 30 or 40 tons burden. These carry on an extensive trade with New Orleans and intermediate places.

Water is elevated from the river into a reservoir, and thence distributed over the city.

The population in 1830, was 5,566; in 1840, 6,929; in 1850, 9,125.

NASHVILLE, p. o., Hanover township, Chautauque co., N. Y., 310 ms. w. of Albany; from W. 358 ms.

NASHVILLE, p. v., Washington township, Holmes co., O., 82 ms. n. e. of Columbus; from W. 354 ms.

NASHVILLE, c. h., p. v., seat of justice of Nash co., N. C., 44 ms. e. of Raleigh; from W. 254 ms. Watered by Peach-Tree creek.

NASHVILLE, p. v., Lowndes co., Miss., 155 ms. n. e. of Jackson; from W. 871 ms. Watered by Tombigbee river.

NASHVILLE, c. h., p. v., seat of justice of Brown co., Ind., 54 ms. s. of Indianapolis; from W. 599 ms. Watered by Salt creek.

NASHVILLE, c. h., p. v., seat of justice of Washington co., Ill., 118 ms. s. of Springfield; from W. 793 ms. Watered by Little Crooked creek.

NASHVILLE, p. v., Boone co., Mo., 24 ms. n. w. of Jefferson city; from W. 953 ms. Watered by Missouri river.

NASHVILLE, p. o., Milan co., Tex.

NASONVILLE, p. o., Providence co., R. I.

NASSAU COUNTY, situated at the northeast corner of Florida, with St. Mary's river on the west, and the Atlantic on the east. Area, 576 square miles. Seat of justice, Nassau c. h. Pop. in 1830, 1,511; in 1840, 1,892; in 1850, 2,164.

NASSAU, p. t., Rensselaer co., N. Y., 12 ms. s. e. of Albany; from W. 365 ms. Watered by Kinderhook creek and tributaries. Pop. 3,261.

NATCHEZ, city, seat of justice of Adams co., Miss., situated on the east bank of Mississippi river, 292 ms. from New Orleans and, 1,110 ms. from Washington. Along the river, at the foot of the bluff, which rises 200 feet from the water, there are stores, warehouses, and other buildings, but the more respectable part of the city occupies the top of the elevation, which affords fine sites for residences, and from its heights a beautiful view of the river and its banks. Broad streets divide pleasant mansions; which indicate the wealth and taste of their owners. Rich and varied trees lend their charms to the other attractions of the city. Natchez is the mart of the interior of Mississippi, receiving the vast quantities of cotton and other staples, which are conveyed by numerous steamboats to New Orleans and other towns on the river. There is a railroad, 30 miles long, from Natchez to Malcom.

The population in 1810, was 1,511; in 1820, 2,184; in 1830, 2,789; in 1840, 4,800; in 1850, 4,434.

NATCHITOCHES PARISH, situated in the westerly part of Louisiana, and traversed by Red river. Area, 4000 square miles. Face of the country generally hilly; soil barren, except along Red river. Seat of justice, Natchitoches. Pop. in 1810, 2,870; in 1820, 7,486; in 1830, 7,905; in 1840, 14,350; in 1850, 14,201.

NATCHITOCHES, c. h., p. v., seat of justice of Natchitoches parish, La., 368 ms. n. w. of New Orleans; from W. 1,287 ms. Watered by Red river.

NATHAN'S CREEK, p. o., Ashe co., N. C.

NATHANSVILLE, p. v., Conecuh co., Ala.; from W. 950 ms.

NATICK, p. t., Middlesex co., Mass., 17 ms. s. w. of Boston; from W. 423 ms. Watered by Charles river Pop. 2,744.

NATICK, p. v., Warwick township, Kent co., R. I., 9 ms. s. e. of Providence; from W. 399 ms. Watered by Patuxet river.

NATION FORD, p. o., York district, S. C., 81 ms. n. of Columbia; from W. 426 ms.

NATURAL BRIDGE, p. v., Wilna township, Jefferson co., N. Y., 153 ms. n. w. of Albany; from W. 452 ms. Watered by Indian river, over which is a natural bridge.

NATURAL BRIDGE, p. o., Rockbridge co., Va., 156 ms. w. of Richmond; from W. —— ms. Situated on Cedar creek, over which is the celebrated natural bridge, 215 feet above the water.

NATURAL DAM, p. o., Crawford co., Ark., 174 ms. n. w. of Little Rock; from W. 1,230.

NATURAL GROVE, p. o., Williamsburgh district, S. C.

NAUGATUCK, p. v., Waterbury township, New Haven co., Ct., 53 ms. s. w. of Hartford; from W. 317 ms. Watered by Naugatuck river

NAUVOO, p. o., Tioga co., Pa.

NAUVOO, p. o., Hancock co., Ill., 124 ms. N. w. of Springfield ; from W. 891 ms. Watered by Mississippi river ; formerly site of the Nauvoo Temple of the Mormon sect.

NAVARINO, p. o., Onondaga township, Onondaga co., N. Y., 148 ms. w. of Albany ; from W. —— ms.

NAVARRE, p. o., Starke co., O.

NAVARRO COUNTY, situated in the central part of Texas, between Trinity river on the east, and the Brazos on the west. Area, —— square miles. Seat of justice, Corsicana. Pop. in 1850, 3,843.

NAVARRO, p. o., Leon co., Tex.

NAYLOR'S STORE, p. o., St. Charles co., Mo.

NAZARETH, p. o., Northampton co., Va.

NEASHOE, c. h., p. v., seat of justice of Newton co., Mo.

NEATSVILLE, p. v., Adair co., Ky., 84 ms. s. of Frankfort ; from W. 598 ms.

NEAVES, t., Darke co., O. Pop. 888.

NEBO, p. o., Hopkins co., Ky., 206 ms. s. w. of Frankfort ; from W. 748 ms.

NEBO, p. o., Jefferson co., O.

NEBRASKA TERRITORY lies, between the summit of the Rocky mountains on the west, and the states of Missouri and Iowa on the east, the parallel of 43° north latitude on the north, and the territory of New Mexico and the parallel of 36° 30' north latitude on the south. An act for the organization of this territory passed the house of representatives, in February, 1853, but failed to be acted on in the senate. It includes a part of the land set apart for the Indians, and the act provides that their rights shall not be affected by the organization, without their consent.

NEBRASKA, p. o., Crawford co., Ind.

NECOT, p. o., Linn co., Iowa.

NEEDHAM, p. t., Norfolk co., Mass., 12 ms. s. w. of Boston ; from W. 427 ms. Watered by Charles river. Pop. 1,944.

NEEL'S CREEK, p. o., Jefferson co., Ind.

NEELYSVILLE, p. o., Morgan co., O.

NEENAH, p. o., Winnebago co., Wis.

NEERSVILLE, p. o., Loudoun co., Va., 168 ms. N. of Richmond ; from W. 52 ms.

NEFFSVILLE, p. v., Mankeim township, Lancaster co., Pa., 41 ms. s. E. of Harrisburgh ; from W. 115 ms.

NEGRO FOOT, p. o., Hanover co., Va.

NEHAMICO, p. o., Russell co., Ala.

NEILL'S CREEK, p. o., Cumberland co., N. C.

NEKRAMA, p. o., Winnebago co., Wis.

NELSON COUNTY, situated in the central part of Virginia, with James river on the southeast. Area, 490 square miles. Face of the country pleasantly diversified. Seat of justice, Livingston. Pop. in 1810, 9,684 ; in 1820, 10,137 ; in 1830, 11,251 ; in 1840, 12,287 ; in 1850, 12,598.

NELSON COUNTY, situated toward the north part of Kentucky. Area, 460 square miles. Soil productive. Seat of justice, Bardstown. Pop. in 1810,.14,078 ; in 1820, 16,273 ; in 1830, 14,916 ; in 1840, 13,637 ; in 1850, 14,789.

NELSON, p. t., Cheshire co., N. H., 44 ms. s. w. of Concord ; from W. 444 ms. Watered by Connecticut and Merrimac rivers. Pop. 750.

NELSON, p. t., Madison co., N. Y., 109 ms. w. of Albany ; from W. —— ms. Watered by Chittenango creek. Pop. 1,965.

NELSON, p. o., Tioga co., Pa., 165 ms. N. of Harrisburgh ; from W. 275 ms.

NELSON, p. t., Portage co., O., 164 ms. N. E. of Columbus ; from W. 320 ms. Pop. 1,383.

NELSONPORT, p. o., Potter co., Pa.

NELSON'S LANDING, p. o., Chippewa co., Wis.

NELSONVILLE, p. v., York township, Athens co., O., 59 ms. s. E. of Columbus ; from W. 353 ms. Watered by Hockhocking river.

NEOSHO, p. o., Dodge co., Wis.

NEOSHO, c. h., p. v., seat of justice of Newton co., Mo., 175 ms. N. w. of Jefferson city ; from W. —— ms. Watered by Spring creek.

NEPERAN, p. o., Westchester co., N. Y.

NEPEUSKUN, p. o., Winnebago co., Wis.

NEPONSET VILLAGE, p. v., Dorchester township, Norfolk co., Mass., 7 ms. s. of Boston ; from W. 445 ms. Watered by Neponset river.

NEPTUNE, p. o., Mercer co., O., 112 ms. N. w. of Columbus ; from W. 505 ms.

NERO, p. o., Henderson co., Tenn.

NESHANOCK, t., Mercer co., Pa.

NESHCOPECK, p. t., Luzerne co., Pa., 98 ms. N. E. of Harrisburgh ; from W. 208 ms. Watered by Big and Little Wapwallopen and Nescopeck creeks. Pop. 920.

NESHKORO, p. o., Marquette co., Wis.

NESHOBA COUNTY, situated in the easterly part of Mississippi. Area, 600 square miles. Seat of justice, Philadelphia. Pop. in 1840, 2,437 ; in 1850, 4,728.

NESMITH'S, p. o., Polk co., Oregon.

NESQUEHONING, p. o., Carbon co., Pa.

NESTORVILLE, p. o., Barbour co., Va.

NETHERLAND, p. o., Overton co., Tenn.

NETHER PROVIDENCE, p. t., Delaware co., Pa., 90 ms. s. E. of Harrisburgh ; from W. 124 ms. Watered by Ridley and Crum creeks. Pop. 1,494.

NETTLE CARIER, p. o., Overton co., Tenn.

NETTLE CREEK, t., Randolph co., Ind. Pop. 468.

NETTLE LAKE, p. o., Williams co., O.

NEVADA COUNTY, situated toward the northeastern part of California, on the western slope of the Sierra Nevada. It is the great centre of gold-quartz mining. Area, —— square miles. Seat of justice, Nevada city. Pop. in 1852, 21,365.

NEVADA CITY, p. t., seat of justice of Nevada co., Cal.

NEVERSINK, p. t., Sullivan co., N. Y., 99 ms. s. w. of Albany ; from W. 312 ms. Watered by Neversink river and Rondout creek. Pop. 2,281.

NEVILLE, p. v., Washington township, Clermont co., O., 126 ms. s. E. of Columbus ; from W. 486 ms. Watered by Ohio river.

NEVIN, p. o., Highland co., O., 82 ms. s. w. of Columbus ; from W. 449 ms.

NEW ALBANY, p. v., Albany township, Bradford co., Pa., 136 ms. N. of Harrisburgh ; from W. 247 ms.

NEW ALBANY, city and p. t., seat of justice of Floyd co., Ind., located on the north bank of the Ohio, 4 miles below Louisville, and 2 miles below the falls, 121 miles southerly from Indianapolis, and 600 miles from Washington. Like most other favorably-situated western towns, its population has rapidly increased within. In ten years, and exhibits all the signs of enterprise and prosperity. Here steamboats and other vessels are extensively built, and carry on a brisk trade with the valleys of the Ohio and Mississippi. The population in 1830, was about 1,900 ; in 1840, 4,226 ; in 1850, 6,418.

NEW ALBANY, p. v., Pontotoc co., Miss.

NEW ALBANY, v., Green township, Columbiana co., O.

NEW ALBANY, p. o., Mahoning co., O.

NEW ALBANY, p. o., Linn co., Oregon.

NEW ALBION, p. t., Cattaraugus co., N. Y., 307 ms. w. of Albany ; from W. 347 ms. Watered by Cattaraugus creek and Alleghany river. Pop. 1,633.

NEW ALEXANDER, p. v., West township, Columbiana co., O., 146 ms. N. E. of Columbus ; from W. 292 ms.

NEW ALEXANDRIA, p. v., Westmoreland co., Pa., 171 ms. w. of Harrisburgh ; from W. 197 ms. Watered by Loyalhanna river.

NEW ALEXANDRIA, p. o., Jefferson co., O.

NEW ALSACE, p. o., Dearborn co., Ind.

NEW ALSTEAD, p. v., Alstead township, Cheshire co., N. H., 54 ms. s. w. of Concord ; from W. 458 ms. Watered by Cold river.

NEW AMSTERDAM, p. v., Harrison co., Ind. 140 ms. s. of Indianapolis ; from W. 637 ms. Watered by Ohio river.

NEW ANTIOCH, p. o., Clinton co., O.

NEWARK, p. t., Caledonia co., Vt., 57 ms. N. E. of Montpelier ; from W. 567 ms. Watered by head waters of Pasumpsic river. Pop. 434.

NEWARK, t., Tioga co., N. Y., 161 ms. s. w. of Albany ; from W. —— ms. Watered by East and West Oswego creeks. Pop. 1,983.

NEWARK, p. v., Arcadia township, Wayne co., N. Y., 186 ms. w. of Albany ; from W. 357 ms. Situated on the Erie canal.

NEWARK, city, seat of justice of Essex co., N. J., 49 N. E. of Trenton, is situated on the west side of Passaic river, 3 miles from its entrance into Newark bay, 9 miles west of New York, and 215 miles from Washington. It has a pleasant location on level ground, somewhat elevated above the river. The streets are broad and straight, lighted with gas, and supplied through iron-pipes with pure water from a neighboring spring. Two spacious public parks, shaded by lofty trees, add much to the beauty of the place. The houses are generally of wood, or brick, the former white and neat, the latter substantial and elegant. Toward the west, the elevated ground affords a commanding site for residences ; and the courthouse, which is a large structure of brown freestone, in the Egyptian style of architecture. The materials for this, were wrought from the neighboring quarries, which furnish large quantities of material for buildings in New York and elsewhere. The New Jersey railroad, connecting New York with Newark, Trenton, and Philadelphia, here enters a splendid depot, which is one of the most prominent buildings in the city. The Morris and Essex railroad also terminates here. Newark has also a number of churches, of which some are elegant and beautiful; also several banks, literary institutions, and libraries.

In proportion to its population, few cities are more extensively engaged in manufactures. Whalebone, oil, carriages, varnish, leather, shoes, candles, soap, harness, machinery, castings, zinc, paint, and glass, are among the articles most largely produced.

Steamboats ply several times a-day to New York ; and the Morris canal, traversing the fruitful county from which it is named, has contributed much to the trade and prosperity of the place.

The population in 1810, was 5.000 (in whole township, 8,008): in 1820, 6,507 ; in 1830, 10,953 ; in 1840, 17,290 ; in 1850, 38,893.

NEWARK, p. v., New Castle co., Del., 59 ms. N. of Dover ; from W. 99 ms.

NEWARK, p. v., Worcester co., Md., 123 ms. s. E. of Annapolis ; from W. 163 ms. Pop. 395.

NEWARK, c. h., p. v., seat of justice of Licking co., O., 39 ms. N. E. of Columbus ; from W. 366 ms. Watered by Licking river at the confluence of its three principal tributaries, and Ohio and Erie canal. Pop. 3,654.

NEWARK, t., Allegan co., Mich., 180 ms. w. of Detroit ; from W. —— ms. Watered by Kalamazoo river. Pop. 246.

NEWARK, p. v., La Salle co., Ill., 153 ms. N. E. of Springfield ; from W. 776 ms.

NEWARK, p. v., Knox co., Mo., 44 ms. N. of Jefferson city ; from W. 958 ms. Watered by South Fabius river.

NEWARK, p. o., Kendall co., Ill.

NEWARK, p. o., Rock co., Wis.

NEWARK, p. o., White co., Tenn.

NEWARK, p. o. Wirt co., Va.

NEWARK VALLEY, p. v., Newark township, Tioga co., N. Y., 154 ms. s. w. of Albany ; from W. 285 ms. Watered by East Owego creek.

NEW ASHFORD. p. t., Berkshire co., Mass., 130 ms. w. of Boston ; from W. —— ms. Watered by head waters of Green and Housatonic rivers. Pop. 186.

NEW ATHENS, p. v., Athens township, Harrison co., O., 115 ms. E. of Columbus ; from W. 291 ms. Seat of Franklin college. Pop. 331.

NEW ATHENS, p. o., Clarion co., Pa.

NEW BABYLON. p. o., Paulding co., Ga.

NEW BALTIMORE, p. t., Greene co., N. Y., 15 ms. s. of Albany ; from W. 354 ms. Watered by Dieppe and Haivrakraus creeks, and Hudson river. Pop. 2,381.

NEW BALTIMORE, p. v., Fauquier co., Va., 108 ms. N. of Richmond ; from W. 45 ms.

NEW BALTIMORE, p. v., Marlborough township, Stark co., O., 138 ms. N. E. of Columbus ; from W. 315 ms.

NEW BARBADOES, t., Bergen co., N. J. Watered by Hackensack river. Pop. 2,258.

NEW BAVARIA. p. o., Henry co., O.

NEW BEDFORD, c. h. sp. t., seat of justice together with Taunton of Bristol co., Mass., 58 ms. s. of Boston ; from W. 434 ms. The town is built on a bold elevation, contains many fine buildings, and appears with advantage from the harbor. A bridge across the Acushnet leads to Fairhaven, on the opposite side. No other place in the country is engaged so exclusively and extensively in the whaling business as this. About $5,000,000 of capital, and two hundred vessels are employed.

The New Bedford and Taunton railroad joins the Boston and Providence railroad at Mansfield, and communicates with this place.

The population in 1810, was 5,651 ; in 1820, 3,947 ; in 1830, 7,592 ; in 1840, 12,087 ; in 1850, 16,443.

NEW BEDFORD. p. v., Mahoning township, Lawrence co., Pa., 244 ms. N. w. of Columbus ; from W. 285 ms.

NEW BEDFORD, p. v., Crawford township, Coshoc-

ton co. O., 99 ms. N. E. of Columbus ; from W. 333 ms.

NEWBERG. p. t., Cass co., Mich., 157 ms. w. of Detroit ; from W. 605 ms. Pop. 388.

NEW BERLIN, p. t., Chenango co., N. Y., 104 ms. w. of Albany ; from W. 345 ms. Watered by Unadilla river. Pop. 2,562.

NEW BERLIN, c. h., p. b., seat of justice of Union co., Pa., 69 ms. N. of Harrisburgh ; from W. 179 ms. Watered by Penn's creek. Pop. 741.

NEW BERLIN, p. v., Blair township, Stark co., O., 129 ms. N. E. of Columbus ; from W. 318 ms.

NEW BERLIN, p. v., Milwaukee co., Wis., 91 ms. E. of Madison ; from W. 818 ms.

NEW BERLIN CENTRE, p. o., New Berlin township, Chenango co., N. Y., 102 ms. w. of Albany ; from W. 343 ms.

NEWBERN, p. v., Greene co., Ala.

NEWBERN, p. v., Bartholomew co., Ind., 50 ms. s. of Indianapolis ; from W. 570 ms. Watered by Clifty creek.

NEWBERN, p. v., Jersey co., Ill., 83 ms. s. w. of Springfield ; from W. 820 ms.

NEWBERN, c. h., p. v., seat of justice of Craven co., N. C., 120 ms. s. E. of Raleigh ; from W. 348 ms. Situated at the confluence of Neuse and Trent rivers. Pop. in 1830, 3,776 ; in 1840, 3,690.

NEWBERN, p. o., Pulaski co., Va.

NEWBERRY DISTRICT, situated in the westerly part of South Carolina, with Broad river on the east, and the Saluda, on the south. Area, 540 square miles. Face of the country, undulating ; soil, productive. Seat of justice, Newberry. Pop. in 1820, 16,104 ; in 1830, 17,441 ; in 1840, 18,350 ; in 1850. 20,143.

NEWBERRY, p. v., Wayne co., Ky., 119 ms. s. of Frankfort ; from W. 608 ms. Watered by Otter creek.

NEWBERRY, p. v., Lycoming co., Pa., 95 ms. N. of Harrisburgh ; from W. 205 ms.

NEWBERRY, c. h., p. v., seat of justice of Newberry district. S. C., 40 ms. N. w. of Columbus ; from W. 504 ms.

NEWBERRY, p. o., Greene co., Ind.

NEWBERRYTOWN, p. t., York co., Pa., 19 ms. s. of Harrisburgh ; from W. 105 ms. Pop. 1,936.

NEW BETHEL, p. v., Marion co., Ind., 8 ms. s. E. of Indianapolis ; from W. 579 ms.

NEW BETHLEHEM, p. o., Clarion co., Pa.

NEW BLOOMFIELD, p. v., Callaway co., Mo., 11 ms. N. of Jefferson city ; from W. 928 ms.

NEW BLOOMFIELD, c. h., p. v., seat of justice of Juniata township, Perry co., Pa., 34 ms. w. of Harrisburgh ; from W. 126 ms. Pop. 517.

NEWBORN, p. v., Newton co., Ga., 55 ms. N. w. of Milledgeville ; from W. 654 ms.

NEW BOSTON, p t., Hillsborough co., N. H., 22 ms. s. of Concord ; from W. 467 ms. Watered by a tributary of Piscataquog river. Pop. 1,447.

NEW BOSTON, p. v., Sandisfield township. Berkshire co., Mass., 122 ms. w. of Boston : from W. 360 ms.

NEW BOSTON, p. v., Thompson township, Windham co., Ct., 48 ms. N. E. of Hartford ; from W. 384 ms. Watered by Quinnebaug river.

NEW BOSTON, p. o., Mercer co., Ill.

NEW BOSTON, p. o., Lewis co., N. Y.

NEW BOSTON, p. o., Henry co., Tenn.

NEW BRAINTREE, p. t., Worcester co., Mass., 66 ms. w. of Boston ; from W. 399 ms. Watered by Ware river. Pop. 852.

NEW BRAUMFELS, p. o., Comal co., Tex.

NEW BREMEN, p. v., German township, Auglaize co., O., 97 ms. N. w. of Columbus ; from W. 491 ms.

NEW BREMEN, p. o., Cook co., Ill.

NEW BREMEN, p. o., Lewis co., N. Y.

NEW BRIDGE, p. v., Lumpkin co., Ga., 136 ms. N. w. of Milledgeville ; from W. 630 ms. Watered by Chestatee river.

NEW BRIDGEVILLE, p. o., York co., Pa., 39 ms. s. of Harrisburgh ; from W. 101 ms.

NEW BRIGHTON, p. v., Castleton township, Richmond co., Staten Island, N. Y. Watered by New York bay.

NEW BRIGHTON, p. v., Beaver co., Pa. Watered by Beaver river, and Pennsylvania and Ohio canal. Pop. 1.443.

NEW BRITAIN, p. v., Berlin township, Hartford co., Ct., 10 ms. s. w. of Hartford ; from W. 326 ms. Pop 3,029.

NEW BRITAIN, p. o., New Lebanon township, Columbia co., N. Y., 24 ms. s. E. of Albany ; from W. 368 ms.

NEW BRITAIN. p. t., Bucks co., Pa., 96 ms. E. of Harrisburgh ; from W. 165 ms. Watered by tributaries of Neshaminy river. Pop. 1,313.

NEW BRUNSWICK. city. seat of justice of Middlesex co.. N. J., 27 ms. N. E. of Trenton ; from W. 193 ms. Watered by Raritan river and Delaware and Raritan canal. Seat of Rutger's college. Pop. in 1830, 7,831 ; in 1840, 8,693 ; in 1850, 10,008.

NEW BUDA, p. o., Decatur co., Iowa.

NEW BUFFALO, p. o., Buffalo township, Perry co., Pa., 19 ms. N. of Harrisburgh ; from W. 129 ms. Watered by Susquehanna river.

NEW BUFFALO, p. t., Berrien co., Mich,, 225 ms. w. of Detroit ; from W. 678 ms. Watered by Galien river and Lake Michigan.

NEWBURGH, p. t., Penobscot co., Me., 51 ms. N. E. of Augusta ; from W. 646 ms. Pop. 1,399.

NEWBURGH, c. h., p. t., and city, seat of justice, together with Goshen, of Orange co., N. Y., 84 ms. s. of Albany ; from W. 286 ms. Watered by Hudson river. Pop. in 1830, 6,424 ; in 1840, 8,933 ; in 1850, 11,415.

NEWBURGH, p. v., Hopewell township, Cumberland co.. Pa., 41 ms. w. of Harrisburgh ; from W. 109 ms. Pop. 715.

NEWBURGH, p. v., Cuyahoga co., O., 150 ms. N. E. of Columbus ; from W. 353 ms. Watered by Mill creek. Pop. 1.542.

NEWBURGH, t., Geauga co., O. Pop. 1,253.

NEWBURGH, t., Miami co., O. Pop. 1,690.

NEWBURGH, p. v., Warrick co.. Ind., 183 ms. s. w. of Indianapolis ; from W. 717 ms. Watered by Ohio river. Pop. 526.

NEWBURGH, p. v., Franklin co.. Ala. ; from W. 786 ms.

NEWBURGH, v., Pittsylvania co., Va., 138 ms. s. w. of Richmond ; from W. 225 ms.

NEWBURGH, v., Pike co., Ill.. 65 ms. w. of Springfield ; from W. 845 ms.

NEWBURGH, p. o., Washington co., Wis.

NEWBURGH, p. o., Macon co., Mo.

NEWBURGH, c. h., p. v., seat of justice of Lewis co., Tenn.

NEW BURLINGTON, p. v., Clinton co., O., 69 ms. s.w. of Columbus ; from W. 458 ms.

NEW BURLINGTON, p. v., Delaware co., Ind., 66 ms. N. E. of Indianapolis ; from W. 536 ms.

NEWBURY, p. t., Merrimack co., N. H., 30 ms. N. w. of Concord ; from W. 477 ms. Watered by Sunapee lake, and a tributary of Warner river. Pop. 738.

NEWBURY, p. t., Orange co., Vt.. 36 ms. s. E. of Montpelier ; from W. 518 ms. Watered by Wells and Connecticut rivers. Pop. 2,984.

NEWBURY, p. t., Essex co., Mass., 31 ms. N. of Boston ; from W. 480 ms. Watered by Parker and Merrimack rivers. Pop. 4.426.

NEWBURY, t., York co., Pa. Watered by Stony run, and Beaver, Conewago, and Fishing creeks. Pop. 1,936.

NEWBURY, t., La Grange co., Ind. Pop. 503.

NEWBURY, t., Geauga co. O., 159 ms. N. w. of Columbus ; from W. 333 ms. Pop. 1,253.

NEWBURYPORT, city, seat of justice, together with Salem and Ipswich, of Essex co., Mass., situated on the south bank of Merrimack river, three miles from its entrance into the ocean, and 30 miles north of Boston. It embraces about one mile square with regular streets, those parallel with the river rising one above the other, after the manner of terraces. That nearest the water is occupied by stores and warehouses, and the higher ones by neat and commodious dwellings, which command a beautiful prospect of the harbor and ocean. A road and bridge lead to Plumb island, at the mouth of the river, which is a pleasant summer resort. A suspension bridge and a railroad bridge extend across the Merrimack to Salisbury. The harbor is ample, and is protected by a breakwater, but is obstructed by a sand-bar at its entrance. Newburyport has been and is still extensively engaged in commerce and fisheries ; and although of late its maritime trade has diminished, its population and general prosperity has' increased. The town contains a customhouse, of rough granite, with a Grecian Doric portico, churches, a courthouse, jail, market, and other public buildings. The Eastern railroad from Boston and Salem, enters the place, and unites it to the Portsmouth, Portland, and Saco railroads.

The pop. in 1810, was 7,634 ; in 1820, 6,852 ; in 1830, 6,375 ; in 1840, 7,161 ; in 1850, 9.532.

NEWBY'S BRIDGE, p. o., Perquimans co., N. C., 199 ms. E. of Raleigh ; from W. 291 ms

NEW CALIFORNIA, p. o., Grant co., Wis.

NEW CALIFORNIA, p. o., Union co.. O.

NEW CANAAN. p. t.. Fairfield co., Ct., 74 ms. s. w. of Hartford ; from W. 273 ms. Watered by Long Island sound. Pop. 2,600.

NEW CANANDAIGUA. p. o., Oakland co., Mich.

NEW CANTON, p. v., Hawkins co., Tenn., 264 ms. E. of Nashville ; from W. 418 ms.

NEW CANTON, p. v.. Buckingham co., Va., 64 ms. w. of Richmond ; from W. 134 ms. Watered by Slate creek.

NEW CARLISLE, p. v., Bethel township, Clark co.. O., 102 ms. w. of Columbus ; from W. 496 ms. Pop. 634.

NEW CARLISLE, p. v., St. Joseph co., Ind., 166 ms. N. of Indianapolis ; from W. 652 ms.

NEW CARTHAGE. p. v., Madison parish, La., 284 ms. N. w. of New Orleans ; from 1,075 ms.

NEW CASTLE COUNTY, situated in the north part of Delaware, with Delaware bay and river on the east. Area, 456 square miles. Face of the country hilly and broken ; soil, which is a strong clay, generally productive. Seats of justice, Wilmington and New Castle. Pop. in 1820, 27,899 ; in 1830, 29,710 ; in 1840, 33,120 ; in 1850, 42,390.

NEW CASTLE, p. t., Lincoln co., Me., 35 ms. s. E. of Augusta ; from W. 603 ms. Watered by Sheepscot and Damariscotta rivers. Pop. 2,012.

NEW CASTLE. p. t. Westchester co., N. Y., 128 ms. s. of Albany ; from W. 270 ms. Watered by Croton and Saw-Mill rivers. Pop. 1,800.

NEW CASTLE, p. t., Rockingham co. N. H. Watered by Portsmouth harbor, in which it constitutes an island. Pop. 891.

NEW CASTLE, p. b., Neshannock township, Mercer co., Pa., 234 ms. N. w. of Harrisburgh ; from W. 275 ms. Situated at the confluence of Shenango and Neshannock creeks.

NEW CASTLE, c. h., p. v., seat of justice of New Castle co., Del., 42 ms. N. of Dover ; from W. 115 ms. Watered by Delaware river. Pop. 1,202.

NEW CASTLE, p. v., Bottetourt co., Va., 192 ms. w. of Richmond ; from W. 232 ms. Watered by Craig's creek, at the confluence of its two tributaries.

NEW CASTLE. p. v., Wilkes co., N. C., 157 ms. w. of Raleigh ; from W. 361 ms.

NEW CASTLE, p. v., Hardeman co., Tenn., 174 ms. s. w. of Nashville ; from W. 859 ms.

NEW CASTLE, c. h., p. v., seat of justice of Henry co., Ky., 25 ms. N. w. of Frankfort ; from W. 567 ms.

NEW CASTLE, p. t., Coshocton co., O., 71 ms. N. E. of Columbus ; from W. 360 ms. Pop. 1,229.

NEW CASTLE, c. h.. p. v., seat of justice of Henry co., Ind., 47 ms. E. of Indianapolis ; from W. 534 ms. Watered by Blue river. Pop. 666.

NEW CASTLE, p. o., Gentry co., Mo.

NEW CASTLE, p. o., Logan co., Ill.

NEW CASTLE, p. o., Hampshire co.. Va.

NEW CENTRE, p. o., York district, S. C.

NEW CENTREVILLE, p. o., Jennings co., Ind.

NEW CHAMBERSBURGH, p. o., Columbiana co., O.

NEW CHESTER, p. v., Strabane township, Adams co., Pa., 31 ms. s. w. of Harrisburgh ; from W. —— ms. Pop. 87.

NEW CHURCH, p. o., Accomac co., Va., 219 ms. E. of Richmond ; from W. 176 ms.

NEW COLUMBIA, p. v., Union co., Pa., 72 ms. N. of Harrisburgh ; from W.,182 ms. Watered by the west branch of Susquehanna river.

NEW COLUMBUS, p. o., Jackson co., Tenn.

NEW COMERSTOWN, p. v., Oxford township, Tuscarawas co., O., 93 ms. N. E. of Columbus ; from W. 324 ms. Watered by Tuscarawas river, and the Ohio and Erie canal.

NEWCOMB, t., Essex co., N. Y., 92 ms. N. of Albany ; from W. 462 ms. Watered by the head waters of Hudson river. Pop. 277.

NEW CONCORD, p. o., Calloway co., Ky.

NEW CONCORD, p. v., Union township, Muskingum co.. O., 68 ms. ms. E. of Columbus ; from W. 325 ms.

NEW CORWIN, p. o., Highland co., O.

NEW CORYDON, p. o., Jay co., Ind.

NEW CREEK, p. o., Hampshire co., Va.

NEW Cumberland, p. o., Warren township, Tuscarawas co., O., 123 ms. N. E. of Columbus ; from W. 309 ms. Watered by Conoten creek and Ohio canal.

NEW 'CUMBERLAND, p. b., Allen township, Cumberland co., Pa., 4 ms. s. w. of Harrisburgh ; from W. 111 ms. Watered by Susquehanna river, at the confluence of Yellow Breeches creek.

NEW CUMBERLAND, p. o., Brooke co., Va.

NEW DANVILLE, p. o., Rusk co., Tex.

NEW DERRY, p. v., Westmoreland co., Va.

NEW DIGGINS, p. o.. Lafayette co., Wis.

NEW DURHAM, p. t., Strafford co., N. H., 33 ms. N. E. of Concord ; from W. 514 ms. Watered by Merrymeeting pond. Pop. 1,049.

NEW DURHAM, v., Hudson co., N. J.

NEW DURHAM, p. o., La Porte co., Ind.

NEW EGYPT, p. v., Upper Freehold township, Monmouth co., N. J., 18 ms. s. E. of Trenton ; from W. 179 ms. Watered by Crosswick's creek.

NEWELL, p. o., Anderson district, S. C.

NEW ENGLAND VILLAGE, p. v., Worcester co., Mass., 38 ms. w. of Boston ; from W. 404 ms.

NEW FAIRFIELD, p. t., Fairfield co., Ct., 74 ms. s. w. of Hartford ; from W. 298 ms. Pop. 927.

NEWFANE, c. h., p. t., seat of justice of Windham co., Vt., 100 ms. s. of Montpelier ; from W. — ms. Watered by West river and tributaries. Pop. 1,304.

NEWFERNE, p. t., Niagara co., N. Y., 279 ms. w. of Albany ; from W. 416 ms. Watered by Lake Ontario and Eighteen Mile creek. Pop. 3,255.

NEWFIELD, p. t., York co., Me., 80 ms. s. w. of Augusta ; from W. 531 ms. Watered by Little Ossipee river. Pop. 1,418.

NEWFIELD, p. t., Tompkins co., N. Y., 283 ms. w. of Albany ; from W. 410 ms. Watered by Cayuga creek. Pop. 3, 816.

NEW FLORENCE, p. o., Westmoreland co., Pa.

NEWFOUNDLAND, p. o., Morris co., N. J., 93 ms. N. of Trenton ; from W. 259 ms.

NEW FRANKFORT, p, v., Scott co., Ind., 81 ms. s. of Indianapolis ; from W. 585 ms. Pop. 223.

NEW FRANKLIN, p. v., Paris township, Stark co., O.. 140 ms. N. E. of Columbus ; from W. 298 ms.

NEW FRANKLIN, p. o., Wayne co., Ill.

NEW FREEDOM, p. o., York co., Pa.

NEW GARDEN, p. t., Chester co., Pa., 74 ms. s. E. of Harrisburgh ; from W. 104 ms. Watered by Red-Clay and White-Clay creeks. Pop. 1,391.

NEW GARDEN, p. o., Russell co., Va.

NEW GARDEN, p. v., Guildford co., N. C., 98 ms. N. W. of Raleigh ; from W. 319 ms.

NEW GARDEN, p. o., Hanover township, Columbiana O., 150 ms. N. E. of Columbus ; from W. 288 ms.

NEW GARDEN, p. t., Wayne co., Ind., 78 ms. E. of Indianapolis ; from W. 507 ms. Pop. 1,609.

NEW GARDEN. p. o., Chester co., Pa.

NEW GARDEN, p. o., Ray co., Mo.

NEW GASCONY, p. o., Jefferson co., Ark.

NEW GENEVA, p. v., Springfield township, Fayette co., Pa., 196 ms. w. of Harrisburgh ; from W. 242 ms. Watered by Monongahela river and George creek.

NEW GEORGETOWN, v., Columbiana co., O.

NEW GERMANTOWN, p v., Toboyne township, Perry co., Pa., 46 ms. w. of Harrisburgh ; from W. 134 ms.

NEW GERMANTOWN, p. o., Tewksbury township, Hunterdon co., N. J.

NEW GILEAD, p. v., Moore co., N. C., 101 ms. s. w. of Raleigh ; from W. 388 ms.

NEW GLARUS, p. o., Green co., Wis.

NEW GLASGOW, p. v., Amherst co., Va., 119 m. w. of Richmond ; from W. 171 ms.

NEW GLOUCESTER, p. o., Cumberland co., Me., 41 ms. s. w. of Augusta ; from W. 567 ms. Watered by Royal's river.

NEW GOSHEN, p. o., Vigo co., Ind.

NEW GOTTINGEN, p. o., Guernsey co., O.

NEW GRÆFENBERG, p. o., Herkimer co., N. Y.

NEW GRANADA, p. o., Fulton co., Pa.

NEW GRETNA, p. o., Burlington co., N. J,

NEW GUILFORD, p. v. Perry township, Coshocton co., O., 67 ms. N. E. of Columbus ; from W. 356 ms.

New Guilford, p. o., Franklin co., Pa.

New Hackensack, p. o., Fishkill township, Dutchess co., N. Y. 79 ms. s. of Albany ; from W. 306 ms.

NEW HAGERSTOWN, p. v., Orange township. Carroll co., O.. 114 ms. N. E. of Columbus ; from W. 300 ms.

NEW HAMBURGH, p. v., Poughkeepsie township, Dutchess co., N. Y. Watered by Hudson river and Wappinger's creek

NEW HAMPSHIRE, one of the United States, so named by John Mason, to whom a portion of its territory was granted, in 1629, after Hampshire in England, the county from which he emigrated. It lies between 42° 41' and 45° 11' north latitude, and 70° 40' and 72° 28' west longitude from Greenwich, and is bounded north by Canada East, east by Maine, from which it is separated in part by Salmon Fall river ; southeast by the Atlantic ; south by Massachusetts ; and west by Connecticut river, which separ ates it from Vermont. Superficial area, 9,411 square miles.

Physical Aspect.—Taking into consideration the small extent of surface in this state, it is more varied in its natural features than any other in the Union. Commencing at the seashore, we find a sandy beach, bordered by extensive salt marshes, which are intersected by numerous creeks. In the midst of this beach there is a bold promontory, called the "Boar's Head." For the first twenty or thirty miles from the sea, the country is either level, or variegated by rolling swells, fertile valleys, and small conical hills. The remainder of the state is greatly diversified by sloping woodlands, rich intervales, rugged mountains, fruitful valleys, foaming cascades, crystal rivers, and silvery lakes, which, from their wild and picturesque effect, have distinguished this country as the "Switzerland of America." The soil is as varied in its character as the surface ; a considerable portion is fertile, and it is generally better adapted to grazing than tillage. The "intervale lands," on the borders of the large rivers, are esteemed as the most valuable, particularly if they are enriched by annual floods. The uplands, of an uneven surface, and of a warm, moist, stony soil, are regarded as the best for grazing. The sandy, pine plains are the poorest, and often are of little or no use, except for growing wood.

Mountains.—The most considerable of these are the White mountains, the Monadnock, Moosehillock, Ossipee, Sunipee, Patuckoway, and Kearsarge.

Rivers, Lakes, and Bays.—The principal rivers are, the Connecticut, Merrimack, Androscoggin, Salmon Fall, Piscataqua, Exeter, or Swamscot, Saco, Upper and Lower Ammonoosuc, Sugar, Ashuelet, Winnipiseogee, Contoocook, Lamprey, Nashua, Margallaway, and Piscataquog. The chief lakes are the Winnipiseogee, Umbagog, Ossipee, Massabesick, Sunipee, Newfound, and Squam. There are two "Great bays" in this state ; the largest situated at the confluence of Swamscot, Winnicut, and Lamprey rivers ; the other at the southwest corner of Lake Winnipiseogee. Merrymeeting bay is situated at the easterly end of the same lake.

Islands.—The only islands worthy of note are the Isles of Shoals, seven in number, off Portsmouth harbor, and numerous islets in Winnipiseogee lake. Of the latter, Long Cow, and Davis's, are the largest, and are in a high state of cultivation.

Climate.—The climate, like that of the states adjacent, is subject to the extremes of heat and cold, but the air is generally salubrious and pure. Along the seaboard, invalids subject to complaints of the lungs generally suffer from the ocean winds. Morning and evening fires become necessary from September till May. The streams are generally locked up in ice, and in the open country the snow often abides on the earth from November till April, and in the woods till May or June.

Productive Resources.—The chief products of this state are, horses, mules, horned cattle, sheep, swine, poultry, eggs, sugar, butter, cheese, hay, wood, lumber, wheat, rye, barley, oats, buckwheat, potatoes, and Indian corn. Of the mineral resources there are iron, lead, silver, tin, zinc, magnesia, soap-stone, granite, feldspar, and mica.

Manufactures.—The principal manufactures, of this state are cotton and woollen goods, cast-iron, paper, leather, boots and shoes, carriages, furniture, hats, pottery-ware, mechanical and agricultural instruments, &c.

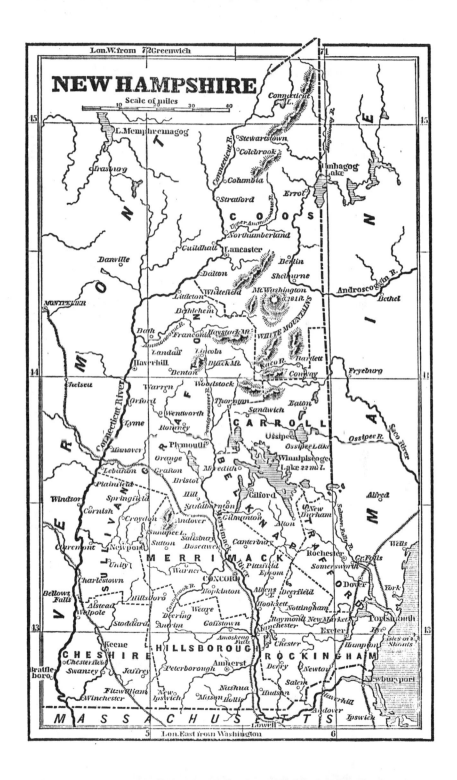

NEW 246 NEW

Railroads and Canals.—There are about 600 miles of railroads in New Hampshire, a large proportion of them radiating from Concord, the political capital of the state, to almost every point of the compass. The only canals in the state are those for facilitating the navigation of the Merrimack river.

Commerce.—New Hampshire has but the single port of Portsmouth on the Atlantic, and its direct foreign commerce heretofore has been extremely small, amounting in the aggregate to less than $60,000 in 1851; but the increased facilities afforded by the opening of railroad communication between Portsmouth and the interior of the state will materially enlarge its foreign trade. The shipping owned within the state amounts to about 23,000 tons.

Education.—The principal literary institutions of the state are, Dartmouth college, at Hanover, attached to which is the New Hampshire medical school; and theological seminaries at Gilmanton, Concord, and New Hampton. There are also 70 or 80 academies, and about 3,000 common schools throughout the state.

Population.—In 1790, 141,899; in 1800, 183,762; in 1810, 214,360; in 1820, 244,161; in 1830, 269,328; in 1840, 284,574; in 1850, 317,964. Number of slaves in 1790, 158; in 1800, 8; in 1840, 1.

Government.—The legislative power is vested in a senate, of 12 members, and house of representatives, of about 300 members, and the executive power in a governor and five councillors, all elected by the people, the second Tuesday in March. The right of suffrage is vested in every male inhabitant, of twenty-one years, excepting paupers and persons not taxed. The judiciary power is vested in a superior court, and court of common pleas. Judges are appointed by the governor and council during good behavior, or until seventy years of age.

History.—The first permanent settlements in New Hampshire were made at Little Harbor, Portsmouth, and Dover, in 1623. In 1641, all the colonists of this state placed themselves under the protection of Massachusetts, and formed a part of the county of Norfolk. In 1679, it was again constituted a separate province by Charles II., and in 1680, the first assembly convened. In 1690 it reunited with Massachusetts, from which, two years after, it was again separated, against the wishes of the people. In 1695, the two provinces were placed under the jurisdiction of New York, but were reunited in 1702, and thus continued until 1741, when a separate governor was appointed over each, and New Hampshire ever after constituted a distinct government. During the war of independence the government was conducted by a temporary administration. The state constitution was established in 1784, which, with the amendments of 1792, forms the one at present in force. In 1788, this state, in convention, adopted the constitution of the United States.

NEW HAMPTON, p. t., Belknap co., N. H., 29 ms. N. of Concord; from W. 510 ms. Watered by Pemigewasset river. Pop. 1,612.

NEW HAMPTON, p. v., Lebanon township, Hunterdon co., N. J., 47 ms. N. of Trenton; from W. 204 ms. Watered by Musconetcong creek.

NEW HAMPTON, p. o., Orange co., N. Y.

NEW HANOVER COUNTY, situated in the south part of North Carolina, with Cape Fear river on the southwest, and the Atlantic on the southeast. Area, 995 square miles. Face of the country, level, and along the coast marshy. Seat of justice, Wilmington. Pop. in 1810, 11,465; in 1820, 10,866; in 1830, 10,759, in 1840, 13,312; in 1850, 17,668.

NEW HANOVER, p. t., Burlington co., N. J. Pop. 2,245.

NEW HANOVER, p. t., Montgomery co., Pa., 74 ms. E. of Harrisburgh; from W. 150 ms. Watered by Swamp creek.

NEW HARMONY, p. v., Posey co., Ind., 172 ms. s. w. of Indianapolis; from W. 742 ms.

NEW HARMONY, p. o., Brown co., O.

NEW HARRISBURGH, p. v., Carroll co., O., 130 ms. N. E. of Columbus; from W. 301 ms.

NEW HARTFORD, p. t., Litchfield co., Ct., 20 ms. w. of Hartford; from W. 344 ms. Watered by Farmington river. Pop. 2,643.

NEW HARTFORD, p. t., Oneida co., N. Y., 95 ms. N. w. of Albany; from W. 384 ms. Watered by Sadaquada creek. Pop. 4,147.

NEW HARTFORD, p. v., Pike co., Ill., 76 ms. w. of Springfield; from W. 856 ms.

NEW HARTFORD CENTRE, p. v., New Hartford township, Litchfield co., Ct., 18 ms. w. of Hartford; from W. 341 ms.

NEW HAVEN COUNTY, situated in the south part of Connecticut, on Long Island sound. Area 540 square miles. Face of the country, undulating and hilly; soil productive. Seat of justice, New Haven. Pop. in 1810, 37,064; in 1820, 39,616; in 1830, 43,848; in 1840, 48,619; in 1850, 65,580.

NEW HAVEN, p. t., Addison co., Vt., 60 ms. w. of Montpelier; from W. 489 ms. Watered by Otter and Little Otter Creeks, and Middlebury river. Pop. 1,663.

NEW HAVEN, city, seat of justice of New Haven co., and capital, together with Hartford, of Connecticut, situated on a bay of Long Island sound, which is here about twenty miles broad. It is 76 miles northeast of New York, and 300 miles from Washington. The city is built on a plain, or gentle slope, at the foot of two bold spurs from the Green Mountain range, which here terminate in two abrupt cliffs, called "East Rock" and "West Rock," rising like sentinels on either side. From the top of these, the eye beholds a wide and enchanting prospect. Below the feet, New Haven lies in quiet beauty, with its white mansions and steeples embowered amid clusters of rich foliage. Far around stretch hills, slopes, and valleys, rich with the colors of nature and cultivation; away to the south and east, like an ocean, spreads the sound, sprinkled here and there by a mote-like sail, and dimly bounded by the cloud-like shores of Long Island. New Haven is one of the most beautiful of cities. Its streets are broad and regular; tasteful, chaste, and splendid buildings are surrounded by pleasant gardens, parks, and trees. Many of these are elms, stately and venerable, planted by the fathers of the town, and cherished, with commendable pride and care, by their descendants. This profusion of foliage and freedom from contracted and uncleanly streets, combine for New Haven the advantages of the city and the country. The "Green" is a pleasant spot of ground, shaded by rows of lofty elms; in the centre, stand the three oldest churches in the city. Toward the west is the statehouse, a large and imposing structure; still further to the west, are the buildings of Yale College, one of the oldest, most flourishing, and respectable institutions of America. Hillhouse avenue, bordered by sides of undulating green, from which spring rows of stately trees, runs between splendid mansions and gardens, that rival Italian villas in loveliness. Northwest of the city, is the cemetery, beautifully laid out, and adorned with an imposing entrance in Egyptian architecture.

The harbor is spacious, but so shallow that large vessels are obliged to anchor at Long wharf, which, from time to time, has been extended to a length of 3,943 feet. New Haven prosecutes an extensive coasting-trade with New York and the towns along the sound. Several ships from foreign shores also make this city their port. The New York and New Haven railroad has largely increased the communication between the two cities, and the New Haven and Hartford railroad joins the lines at Springfield, which traverse the valley of Connecticut river, and other parts of Massachusetts. The population in 1810, was 5,772; in 1820, 7,147; in 1830, 10,180; in 1840, 14,890; in 1850, 20,345.

NEW HAVEN, p. t., Oswego co., N. Y., 161 ms. N. w, of Albany; from W. 383 ms. Watered by Catfish creek and Lake Ontario. Pop. 4,221.

NEW HAVEN, p. t., Nelson co., Ky., 68 ms. s. w. of Frankfort; from W. 610 ms.

NEW HAVEN, p. t., Huron co., O., 82 ms. N. of Columbus; from W. 394 ms. Pop. 1,398.

NEW HAVEN, p. o., Macomb co., Mich., 25 ms. N. E. of Detroit; from W. 549.

NEW Haven, p. v., Gallatin co., Ill., 197 ms. s. E. of Springfield; from W. 765 ms. Watered by Little Wabash river.

NEW HAVEN, p. o., Allen co., Ind.

NEW HAVEN, p. t., Portage co., Wis.

NEW HAVEN MILLS, p. v., New Haven township, Addison co., Vt., 54 ms. s. w. of Montpelier; from W. 486 ms.

NEW HEBRON, p. o., Crawford co., Ill.

NEW HILL, p. o., Wake co., N. C.

NEW HOLLAND, p. v., Earl township, Lancaster co., Pa., 49 ms. E. of Harrisburgh; from W. 123 ms. Pop. 2,702.

NEW Holland, p. v., Perry township, Pickaway co., O., 43 ms. s. of Columbus; from W. 413 ms.

NEW HOLLAND, p. o., Wabash co., Ind.

NEW HOLSTEIN, p. o., Calumet co., Wis.

NEW HOPE, p. v., Solesbury township, Bucks co., Pa., 110 ms. E. of Harrisburgh; from W. —— ms. Watered by Delaware river. Pop. 1,144.

NEW HOPE, p. v., Augusta co., Va., 130 ms. N. w. of Richmond; from W. 149 ms.

NEW HOPE, p. v., Iredell co., N. C., 163 ms. w. of Raleigh; from W, 374 ms.

NEW HOPE, p. v., Spartanburgh district, S. C., 110 ms. N. w. of Columbia; from W. 483 ms.

NEW HOPE, p. v., Madison co., Ala.; from W. 713 ms.

NEW HOPE, p. v., Scott township, Brown co., O., 99 ms. s. w. of Columbus; from W. 466 ms. Watered by White Oak creek. Pop. 106.

NEW HOPE, p. v., Lincoln co., Mo.

NEW HOPE, p. o., Nelson co., Ky.

NEW HOPE, p. o., Spencer co., Ind.

NEW HOPE, p. o., Tishamingo co., Miss.

NEW HOPE, p. o., Caroline co., Md.

NEW HOPE, p. o., Marshal co., Tenn.

NEW HOUSE, p. o., York district, S. C.

NEW HUDSON, p. t., Alleghany co., N. Y., 270 ms. s. w. of Albany; from W. —— ms. Watered by Black creek. Pop. 1,433.

NEW HURLEY, p. v., Shawangunk township, Ulster co., N. Y., 83 ms. s. w. of Albany; from W. 300 ms.

NEW IBERIA, p. v., St. Martin's parish, La., 170 ms. w. of New Orleans; from W. 1,289 ms. Watered by Teche river.

NEWINGTON, p. t., Rockingham co., N. H., 40 ms. s. E. of Concord; from W. 496 ms. Watered by Piscataqua river, and Great Bay. Pop. 472.

NEWINGTOW, p. v., Wethersfield township, Hartford co., Ct., 6 ms. s. of Hartford; from W. 330 ms.

NEW IPSWICH, p. t., Hillsborough co., N. H., 47 ms. s. w. of Concord; from W. 447 ms. Watered by Souhegan river, and tributaries. Pop. 1,877.

NEW JASPER, p. o., Greene co., O.

NEW JERSEY, one of the U. States, so named after the island of Jersey, on the coast of France, of which Sir George Carteret, to whom New Jersey was conveyed, in 1664, was formerly governor. It lies between 90° 57' and 41° 22' north latitude, and 73° 58' and 75° 29' west longitude from Greenwich, and is bounded north by New York, east by the Hudson river, Staten island sound, and the Atlantic, southeast by Delaware bay, which separates it from Delaware, and west by Delaware river, which separates it from Pennsylvania. It has a superficial area of 8,320 square miles.

Physical Aspect.—The state presents a great diversity of surface, as well as of soil. The northern portions are mountainous, interspersed with rich valleys, and extensive tracts, well adapted for grazing, and for the plough. An elevated range, called the "Palisades," commences near Hoboken, and extends along the Hudson for miles, forming a perpendicular wall of stone, which at some points is 500 feet high. The middle portions are less hilly than the northern, and much of the soil is fertile, and well tilled. The southern counties are principally composed of a long range of level country, commencing near Sandy Hook, and lines the whole coast of the middle states. Much of this range is sandy, and nearly barren, producing little else than small oaks and yellow pine; in other cases, swamps of white cedar occur. In the southern section along the Atlantic and Delaware bay, there are extensive marshes, which are monthly inundated by the tides. A stratum of greensand marl, in some places thirty feet thick, underlies the surface throughout the length of this tract, which has been extensively used as a fertilizer in reclaiming the land.

Mountains.—In the northwesterly part of the state there are two ranges, subordinate to the Alleganies, one called South mountain, and the other, Blue mountain, or Kittatinny ridge. The more prominent points of the former are designated by the names of Mosconetcong, Schooley's, Hamburg, Wawayanda, and Bear

Mountains. The other elevations worthy of note are Mine, Trowbridge, Second, and Ramapo mountains.

Rivers and Bays.—The principal rivers are the Hudson, and Delaware, its eastern and western boundaries; the Raritan, the Passaic (the great falls of which, above Paterson, have a perpendicular descent of seventy feet), Hackensack, Egg Harbor, Great Egg Harbor, Shrewsbury, Toms, Maurice, Delaware, and Mosconetong. The chief bays are the Delaware, Newark, New York, Raritan, Sandy Hook, Barnegat, Little and Great Egg Harbors, and Grassy.

Climate.—The climate along the seaboard, and in the valleys of the interior may be regarded as mild, though the former is often rendered disagreeable by ocean winds. In the mountainous region, at the north, the winters are cold, and often severe. The range of temperature varies from a few degrees below zero to 90° above. The air is remarkably pure, and usually salubrious, except in summer and autumn, near marshes and streams.

Productive Resources.—The chief products are horses, mules, neat cattle, sheep, swine, poultry, eggs, butter, shad, oysters, cheese, fruit, cider, wine, flax-seed, wax, pitch, tar, resin, turpentine, silk, wool, lumber, hay, wheat, rye, barley, buckwheat, oats, potatoes, and Indian corn. Of the mineral and fossil resources of this state, iron and zinc are the most abundant, and their ores are extensively wrought. An extensive bed of phosphorite, a native phosphate of lime, has been opened in Morris county, which promises to add much to the agricultural wealth of the state.

Manufactures.—The manufactures of New Jersey are numerous, embracing almost every variety of goods. Cotton and woollen mills are established in many parts of the state; silk and linen goods are manufactured to a considerable extent; also, machinery, hardware, railroad-cars, carriages, fire-arms, jewelry, glass, earthen-ware, fire-brick, &c. There are also extensive tanneries, and other manufactories of leather. Whole villages are employed in boot and shoe making.

Railroads and Canals.—The great lines of railroad between New York and Pennsylvania traverse this state. Branch roads are also constructed from the central roads to the more important towns; making, in the aggregate, about 200 miles of railway in the state. The Delaware and Raritan, 42 miles, and Morris, 102 miles long, are the most important canals in this state.

Commerce.—The foreign commerce of New Jersey is small, on account of its proximity to New York; its coasting trade, however, is considerable. The shipping owned within the state amounts to about 80,000 tons.

Education.—The principal literary institutions are, the college of New Jersey, at Princeton, founded in 1738, and Rutgers college, at New Brunswick, founded in 1770, to both of which are attached theological seminaries, and to the former a law-school; and Burlington college, founded in 1846. There are about 100 academies, and 1,500 common schools in New Jersey.

Population.—In 1790, 184,139; in 1800, 211,949; in 1810, 249,555; in 1820, 277,575; in 1830, 320,823; in 1840, 373,306: in 1850, 489,555. Number of slaves in 1790, 11,423; in 1800, 12,422; in 1810, 10,851; in 1820, 7,557; in 1830, 2,254; in 1840, 674; in 1850, 222.

Government.—The legislative power is vested in a senate, elected for three years, one third renewed each year, and a general assembly, chosen annually, on the second Tuesday of October; the executive power in a governor, elected by the people, once in three years, at the general election, and is ineligible for the next term. The judiciary power is vested in a court of errors and appeals, composed of the chancellor, supreme court, and six other judges; a court for trial of impeachments; a court of chancery; a supreme court of five judges, and courts of common pleas. The chancellor and supreme court judges hold their offices for seven years; the six judges of the court of errors and appeals for six years, one judge vacating his seat each year in rotation; and the judges of the courts of common pleas for five years. The latter are chosen by the legislature; the others receive their appointment from the governor. The right of suffrage is vested in every white male citizen, who shall have resided in the state one year, and in the county where he votes, five months, paupers, idiots, insane persons, and criminals, excepted.

History.—The territory of the present state of New Jersey was formally included, in part, in New Swedeland, which lay on the west side of the Delaware, as far

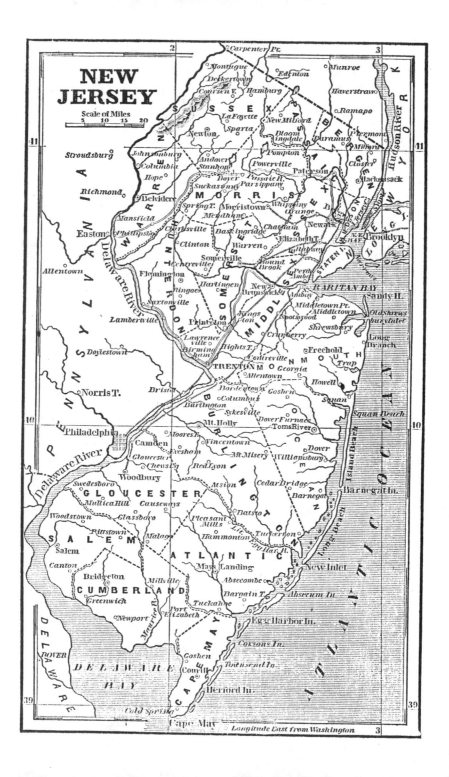

up as Trenton falls, and was purchased of the Indians, and settled by the Swedes, in 1638. It also formed a part of the Dutch province of New Netherlands, and was included within the jurisdiction of Governor Stuyvesant, in 1655. The first permanent settlement within the present limits of this state was made at Bergen, in 1623, by the Danes. In 1664, Charles II., of England, having granted to his brother James. the duke of York, the whole territory from Connecticut river to the shores of the Delaware, the latter immediately compelled the Dutch and Swedes to surrender, and took possession of the province, with its subordinate settlements west of the river, except the present state of New Jersey, which he conveyed to Sir George Carteret, and Lord Berkeley, who were already proprietors of Carolina. In 1673, the Dutch regained all their former possessions, including New Jersey, but relinquished them to the English again, in 1674. After this event, the duke of York obtained a second charter, confirming the former grant, and restored to Berkeley and Carteret their former rights. Berkeley sold his share of the territory. which two years afterward, fell into the hands of William Penn and two other quakers, and the province was divided into "East Jersey," and "West Jersey." The former was governed by Carteret, and the latter by the quakers. In 1682, after the death of Carteret, East Jersey was sold to Penn, and eleven other individuals of the same order and faith, who were joined by twelve partners, and were known as the "twenty-four proprietors." The celebrated Robert Barclay was appointed governor for life. In 1688, the whole province was placed under the jurisdiction of Andros, who had already become royal governor over New England and New York. From this time, up to 1702, the country remained in an unsettled condition; the people surrendered their powers of government to the crown, making New Jersey a royal province, and uniting it to New York. From this period, up to 1738, the province remained under the jurisdiction of New York, but had a distinct legislative assembly, and a separate government was instituted, which continued in force until the American Revolution. The state constitution was formed in 1776, and the constitution of the United States adopted in 1787. Motto of the seal, "Liberty and Independence."

NEW JERUSALEM. p. o., Berks co., Pa., 66 ms. E. of Harrisburgh; from W. 159 ms.

NEW KENT COUNTY, situated in the east part of Virginia, with York and Pamunky rivers on the northeast, and the Chickahoning on the southwest. Area, 225 square miles. Face of the country, uneven; soil, of middling quality. Seat of justice, New Kent c. h. Pop. in 1810, 6,478; in 1820, 6,630; in 1830, 6,457; in 1840, 6,230; in 1850, 6,064.

NEW KENT, c. h., p. v., seat of justice of New Kent co., Va., 30 ms. E. of Richmond; from W. 147 ms.

NEW KINGSTON, p. o., Cumberland co. Pa.

NEWKIRK'S MILLS, p. o., Bleecker township, Fulton co., N. Y., 59 ms. N. w. of Albany; from W. 411 ms.

NEW LANCASTER, p. v., Warren co., Ill., 102 ms. N. w. of Springfield; from W. 848 ms.

NEW LANCASTER, p. o., Tipton co., Ind.

NEW LA PORTE, p. o., Sullivan co., Pa.

New LEBANON. p. t.. Columbia co., N. Y., 23 ms. S. E. of Albany; from W. 368 ms. Pop. 2,300.

NEW LEBANON, p. v., Sullivan co., Ind., 103 ms. s. w. of Indianapolis; from W. 670 ms.

NEW LEBANON, p. o., De Kalb co., Ill.

NEW LEBANON, p. o., Mercer co., Pa.

NEW LEBANON, p. o., Montgomery co., O.

NEW LEBANON CENTRE, p. o., New Lebanon township, Columbia, N. Y.

NEW LEBANON SHAKER SETTLEMENT, v., New Lebanon township, Columbia co., N. Y.

NEW LEBANON SPRINGS, p. v., New Lebanon township, Columbia, N. Y., 25 ms. s. E. of Albany; from W. 367 ms.

NEW LENNOX, p. o., Will co., Ill.

NEW LEXINGTON, p. v., Pike township, Perry co., O., 52 ms. E. of Columbus; from W. 351 ms. Watered by Big Rush creek.

NEW LEXINGTON, p. v., Tuscaloosa co., Ala.; from W. 826 ms. Watered by North river.

NEW LEXINGTON, p. o., Somerset co., Pa.

NEW LIBERTY, p. v., Owen co., Ky., 36 ms. N. of Frankfort; from W. 543 ms. Watered by Eagle creek.

NEW LIBERTY, p. o., Pope co., Ill.

NEW LIGHT, p. o., Wake co., N. C., 25 ms. from Raleigh; from W. 279 ms.

NEW LIMA, t., Columbiana co., O.

NEW LIMERICK, t., Aroostook co., Me. Pop. 160.

NEWLIN, t., Chester co., Pa. Watered by west branch of Brandywine creek. Pop. 738.

NEW LISBON, p. t., Otsego co., N. Y., 90 ms. w. of Albany; from W. 345 ms. Watered by Butternut and Otego creeks. Pop. 1,773.

NEW LISBON, c. h., p. v., Centre township, seat of justice of Columbiana co., 150 ms. N E. of Columbus; from W. 280 ms. Watered by middle fork of Little Beaver river, and Sandy and Beaver canal.

NEW LISBON, p. v., Henry co., Ind., 55 ms. E. of Indianapolis; from W. 526 ms.

NEW LISBON. p. o., Burlington co., N. J.

NEW LONDON COUNTY, situated at the southeast corner of Connecticut, and traversed by Thames river, with the Connecticut on the west. Area 600 square miles. Face of the country, hilly; soil, productive. Seats of justice, Norwich and New London. Pop. in 1810. 34.707; in 1820, 35,943; in 1830, 42,295; in 1840, 44 463; in 1850, 51,822.

NEW LONDON, city, seat of justice, together with Norwich, of New London co., Ct., 44 ms. s. E. of Hartford; from W. 353 ms. occupies a gentle elevation facing the southeast, on the west bank of the Thames river, three miles from its entrance into Long Island sound. The ground on which it stands is rocky and rough, and seems to have discouraged the builders from attempting to construct it with regularity. The houses erected within a few years, however, are superior to the rest, and the appearance of the town is much improved.

New London harbor is deep and convenient, although its entrance is narrow, and might be easily blockaded, if it were not defended by two fortifications. Fort Griswold, in Groton, opposite the city, and Fort Trumbull, one mile below, shared severely the struggles of the Revolution, and the former, especially, was the scene of bloody barbarities under Benedict Arnold, who, in 1781, entered the harbor, took Fort Griswold, and burned the town. An obelisk of granite, 125 feet high, preserves the memory of the patriots who here suffered and died.

The business of the city is chiefly whale-fishing and commerce; its tonnage is larger than that of any other town in the state.

The Worcester and Norwich railroad unites with the Thames at Allyn's Point, a few miles above.

The population in 1810. was 3,238; in 1820, 3,330; in 1830, 4,356; in 1840, 5,519; in 1850. 8,994.

NEW LONDON, p. t. Merrimack co., N. H., 30 ms. N. w. of Concord; from W. 484 ms. Watered by Sunapee lake. Pop. 945.

NEW LONDON, p. v., Verona township, Oneida co., N. Y.. 117 ms. N. w. of Albany; from W. 388 ms. Situated on the Erie canal.

NEW LONDON, p. t., Chester co., Pa. Watered by Elk and Clay creeks. Pop. 2,042.

NEW LONDON, p. v., Frederick co., Md., 70 ms. N. w. of Annapolis; from W. 52 ms.

NEW LONDON, p. v.. Campbell co., Va., 127 ms. w. of Richmond; from W. 202 ms. Watered by a tributary of Staunton river.

NEW LONDON. p. t., Huron co., O., 96 ms. N. of Columbus; from W. 385 ms. Pop. 1.329.

NEW LONDON, p. t., Henry co., Iowa. Pop. 1,358.

NEW LONDON, c. h., p. v., seat of justice of Ralls co., Mo., 98 ms. N. E. of Jefferson city; from W. 902 ms. Watered by Salt river.

NEW LONDON, p. o., Howard co., Ind.

NEW LYME, p. t., Ashtabula co., O., 195 ms. N. E. of Columbus; from W. 329 ms. Pop. 628. Its original name was New Lebanon.

NEW MADISON. p. v., Harrison township, Darke co., O., 100 ms. w. of Columbus; from W. 494 ms.

NEW MADRID COUNTY, situated in the southeast part of Missouri, with the Mississippi river on the southeast, and Lake St. Mary's in the north. Area, 1,625 square miles. Face of the country, level, and subject to inundation; soil productive where arable. Seat of justice, New Madrid. Pop. in 1820, 2,296; in 1830, 2,351; in 1840, 4,554; in 1850, 5,541.

NEW MADRID, c. h., p. v.. seat of justice of New Madrid co., Mo., 271 ms. s.E. of Jefferson city; from W. 911 ms. Watered by Mississippi river.

NEW MAHONING, p. o., Carbon co., Pa.

NEWMAN'S MILLS, p. o., Indiana co., Pa.

NEWMANSVILLE, p. o., Greene co., Tenn., 268 ms. E. of Nashville; from W. 430 ms.

NEW MARION, p. v., Ripley co., Ind., 73 ms. S. E. of Indianapolis; from W. 553 ms.

NEW MARKET, p. t., Rockingham co., N. H., 38 ms. s. E. of Concord; from W. 488 ms. Watered by Lamprey and Exeter rivers, and Great bay. Pop. 1,937.

NEW MARKET, p. v., Piscataway township, Middlesex co., N. J., 36 ms. N. E. of Trenton; from W. 203 ms. Watered by Cedar creek.

NEW MARKET, p. v., Frederick co., Md., 67 ms. N. w. of Annapolis; from W. 49 ms. Watered by north branch of Bush creek.

NEW MARKET, p. v., Shenandoah co., Va., 139 ms. N. w. of Richmond; from W. 112 ms. Watered by north fork of Shenandoah river.

NEW MARKET, p. v., Randolph co., N. C., 85 ms. w. of Raleigh; from W. 324 ms.

NEW MARKET, p. v., Abbeville district, S. C., 90 ms. w. of Columbia; from W. 528 m.

NEW MARKET, p. v., Madison co., Ala.; from W. 691 ms.

NEW MARKET, p. v., Jefferson co., Tenn., 208 ms. E. of Nashville; from W. 476 ms. Watered by head waters of Loss creek.

NEW MARKET, p. v., Marion co., Ky., 65 ms. s. w. of Frankfort; from W. 587 ms. Watered by Rolling fork of Salt river.

NEW MARKET, p. t., Highland co., O., 81 ms. s. w. of Columbus; from W. 448 ms. Pop. 1,528.

NEW MARKET, p. v., Vigo co., Ind., 82 ms. w. of Indianapolis; from W. 654 ms.

NEW MARKET, p. v., Platte co., Mo.

NEW MARKET, p. o., Van Buren co., Iowa.

NEW MARKET, p. o., Monroe co., Ga.

NEW MARLBOROUGH, p. t., Berkshire co., Mass., 131 ms. s. w. of Boston; from W. 364 ms. Watered by Konkapot river, and tributaries. Pop. 1,847.

NEW MARTINSVILLE, p. o., Wetzel co., Va.

NEW MAYSVILLE, p. v., Putnam co., Ind., 32 ms. w. of Indianapolis; from W. 603 ms.

NEW MAYSVILLE, p. o., Pike co., Ill.

NEW MEXICO TERRITORY, situated between 38° and 32° north latitude, and 103° and 116° longitude west from Greenwich; and is bounded north by Utah and Nebraska territories, east by Nebraska territory and Texas, south by Mexico, and west by California and Utah. Its superficial area is about 211,000 square miles.

Physical Aspect.—The general appearance of the country is mountainous with a large valley in the middle running north and south, formed by the Rio Grande del Norte. This valley is generally about twenty miles wide, bordered on the east and west by mountain chains. There are some valleys of less extent along the borders of smaller streams, and a few spaces of elevated table-land. East of the Rocky mountains there are prairies and plains, and a portion of the great American desert. The soil in the valley of the Rio Grande in New Mexico is generally sandy, and looks poor, but by irrigation it produces abundant crops. The most fertile part of the valley begins below Santa Fe, along the river, where it is not uncommon to raise two crops within one year. The dryness of the soil makes it necessary to employ irrigation.

Mountains.—The Rocky mountain range traverses the eastern part of New Mexico, bearing different names at different points. South of Santa Fe it rises to 6,000 or 8,000 feet, while to the north some snow-capped peaks are seen which rise to from 10,000 to 12,000 feet above the sea-level. The Sierra Madre or Anahuac range stretches northward from the Mexican Cordilleras through the centre of the territory, and the Wahsatch mountains lie near the western boundary.

Rivers and Lakes.—The principal river of New Mexico is the Rio Grande del Norte. Its head waters are found in the Rocky mountains, and flowing south it enters the gulf of Mexico, forming, in the lower part of its course, the boundary line between Mexico and the United States. Its length is about 2,000 miles, and it is navigable for steamboats, about 700 miles from its mouth. Its principal tributaries are, the Chames, Pecos, Conchos, Salado, Alamo, and San Juan. The Colorado, which empties into the gulf of California, forms part of the western boundary, until it extends into the territory. The Gila, which flows westward, extends along the southern boundary until reaching its source

in the Sierra Madre range; its principal branches are San Francisco and Salt rivers. About 100 miles southeast of Santa Fe, on the high table-land east of the Rio Grande, are several salt lakes, which furnish the country with salt.

Climate.—The climate is generally temperate, constant, and healthy. Considerable atmospheric differences, however, are experienced in the mountain districts, and in the low valley of the rivers. In the latter the summer heat sometimes rises to 100° Fahrenheit, but the nights are always cool and pleasant. The winters are comparatively of long duration, and frequently severe. The sky is generally clear, and the atmosphere dry, except during the rainy season, from July to October. Disease is little known, except some inflammations and typhoid fevers in the winter season.

Productive Resources.—Indian corn, wheat, beans, onions, and fruits, are raised in large quantities, and the grape-vine is extensively cultivated. The inhabitants pay considerable attention to cattle-raising, and are possessed of large flocks and herds. The country is rich in gold, silver, copper, iron, coal, gypsum, and salt. None but the silver mines, however, have been much wrought. There are considerable domestic manufactures.

Population.—The whole population of New Mexico, according to the census of 1793, was 30,953; in 1833, it was estimated at 52,360, composed of one twentieth Spaniards, one fifth Creoles, one fourth Mestizos of all grades, and one half Pueblo Indians. In 1842, the population was 57,026; and according to the census of 1850, 61,547. This is exclusive of the independent tribes of Indians which still exist in the country.

Government.—The government of New Mexico is similar to that of Utah, and that generally applied to territories of the United States. All citizens of adult ages are voters, and elect a territorial legislature. The governor and judges are appointed by the president of the United States.

History.—The history of New Mexico lies very much in the dark. The Spaniards, it seems, received the first information about it in 1581, from a party of adventurers under Captain Francisco de Leyva Bonillo, who, upon finding the aboriginal inhabitants and the mineral wealth of the country to be similar to those of Mexico, called it New Mexico. In 1594, the then viceroy of Mexico, Count de Monterey, sent the gallant Juan de Oñate, of Zacatecas, to New Mexico, to take formal possession of the country in the name of Spain, and to establish colonies, missions, and presidios (forts). They found a great many Indian tribes and settlements, which they succeeded in Christianizing in the usual Spanish way, with sword in hand, and made them slaves. The villages of the Christianized Indians were called Pueblos, in opposition to the wild and roving tribes that refused such favors. Many towns, of which only ruins exist now, were established at that time; many mines were worked, and the occupation of the country seemed to be secured, when, quite unexpectedly, in 1680, a general insurrection of all the Indian tribes broke out against the Spanish yoke. The Spaniards were either massacred or driven southward, where they founded Paso del Norte. The country was not recovered for ten or twelve years. Several insurrections have since occurred, but none so universal or disastrous as this one. This country followed the fate of Mexico after the revolution that overthrew the Spanish power. The history of New Mexico previous to the invasion by the Americans, has little to arrest attention. It is a continuous record of barbarism and tyranny. On the 8th of September, 1846, Santa Fe was captured by the Americans under General Kearney, and soon after several of the river towns were visited on his route to California. A civil government was now established. On the 19th of January, 1847, an insurrection broke out against the Americans, and in several pueblos many Americans were murdered. Taos, Arroya-Hondo, and Rio Colorado, were the chief scenes of strife. The battles of La Canada and El Embudo also occurred in this month, and in February the battle of Taos; in all of which the Mexicans were completely vanquished. Some few skirmishes occurred after these, but none of importance. From this period the United States authorities exercised exclusive power. On the 2d of February, 1848, a treaty of peace and cession was signed at Guadalupe Hidalgo, by which New Mexico was assigned to the Union. On the 9th of Sep-

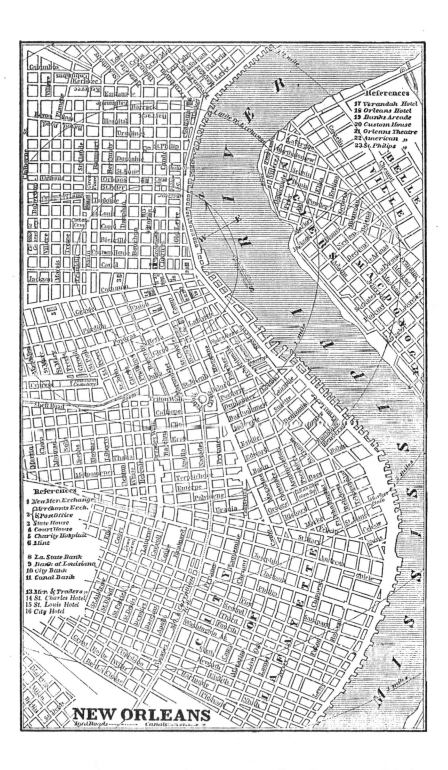

NEW ORLEANS

References
17 Verandah Hotel
18 Orleans Hotel
19 Banks Arcade
20 Custom House
21 Orleans Theatre
22 American "
23 St. Philips "

References
1 New Mer. Exchange
Merchants Exch.
2 & Post Office
3 State House
4 Court House
5 Charity Hospital
6 Mint

8 La. State Bank
9 Bank of Louisiana
10 City Bank
11 Canal Bank

13 Mer. & Traders "
14 St. Charles Hotel
15 St. Louis Hotel
16 City Hotel

Rail Roads   Canals

tember, 1850, it was erected into a territory, the United States paying Texas ten millions of dollars as an equivalent for the claim she preferred to that portion of the territory of New Mexico which lies east of the Rio Grande.

NEW MICHIGAN, p. o., Livingston co., Ill.

NEW MIDDLETOWN, p. o., Mahoning co., O.

NEW MILFORD, p. t. Litchfield co., Ct., 51 ms. s. w. of Hartford ; from W. 308 miles. Watered by Housatonic river. Pop. 4,508.

NEW MILFORD, p. o., Warwick township, Orange co., N. Y., 120 ms. s. of Albany ; from W. 264 ms.

NEW MILFORD, p. t., Susquehanna co., Pa., 185 ms. N. of Harrisburgh ; from W. 289 ms. Watered by Mitchell's and Salt Lick creeks. Pop. 1,433.

NEW MILFORD, p. o., Winnebago co., Ill.

NEW MILLS, p. o., Essex co., Mass.

NEW MILLTOWN, p. o., Lancaster co., Pa.

NEW MILTON, p. o., Doddridge co., Va.

NEW MOSCOW, p. o., Coshocton co., O.

NEW MOUNT PLEASANT, p. v., Jay co., Ind., 97 ms. N. E. of Indianapolis ; from W. 520 ms.

NEW MOUNT PLEASANT, p. o., Monroe co., Pa.

NEWNAN, c. h., p. v., seat of justice of Coweta co., Ga., 106 ms. w. of Milledgeville ; from W. 710 ms.

NEWNANSVILLE, c. h., p. v., seat of justice of Alachua co., Flor., 120 ms. s. e. of Tallahassee ; from W. 1,016 ms.

NEW METAMORA, p. o., Washington co., O.

NEW OHIO, p. o., Colesville township, Broome co., N. Y., 127 ms. s. w. of Albany ; from W. 310 ms.

NEW ORLEANS, city, seat of justice of Orleans parish, and commercial metropolis of Louisiana, situated on the north bank of Mississippi river, 100 miles from its entrance into the gulf of Mexico, 1,185 miles below the mouth of the Missouri, and 1,172 miles from Washington. Its position and appearance are both singularly different from those of other American cities. The ground, as it recedes from the river, descends by a gentle inclination, causing the houses, when viewed from a point not much above the level of high water, to seem to rise immediately from it. A "levee," or dike, forms a margin between the city and the river, and protects the former from inundation by the latter. It is built of wood, 200 feet wide, and extends for four miles, presenting a most animated scene of commercial prosperity. Within, not only the houses, but the inhabitants, are of many descriptions. Except New York, no city includes Americans from so many different states, while the number of blacks, with the French and Spanish Creoles, and the foreigners, is still greater. These representatives of many nations are drawn to New Orleans by its geographical and commercial relations to the West Indies, South America, Mexico, and the southern parts of North America. The Creole citizens are descendants of the French, Spanish, and Germans, who originally founded and peopled the city, and constitute a large portion of the population. The position of New Orleans, with regard to the interior of the United States, is still more important. Situated near the mouth of the great river of the American continent, the Mississippi, with its immense confluents the Ohio and the Missouri, almost the whole trade of those streams, and of their thousand tributaries, flows toward this point, as to a vast receiving and distributing reservoir. Hence the exports of New Orleans are exceeded by those of no other American city, New York excepted. The great staples of the southern and western states, sugar, cotton, tobacco, wheat, flour, and corn, are the articles chiefly shipped from this port. The harbor is, excellent, deep, and spacious. Ships, and vessels of every description, from the flatboat of the Mississippi to the magnificent ocean-steamer, here congregate, or enliven the scene, as they move from point to point. From the city to the bar, near the gulf, 100 miles below, the river has an average depth of 100 feet, affording anchorage for several miles along the wharves. The bed of the river, and its banks toward the mouth, are gradually rising. In 1722 there were 25 feet of water on the bar. In 1767 there were but 20, and now there are but 9 feet. The present mouth of the river is three miles beyond the mouth of 1724.

The city is gradually extending toward Lake Ponchartrain on the north, which communicates with the Mississippi by a canal, the Bayou St. John, and a railroad six miles long, and with the gulf of Mexico by Lake Borgne and intermediate passages. The Mexican Gulf railroad communicates with Proctorville, 27 miles

distant. From the nature of the commercial advantages which New Orleans possesses, it is apparent that its prosperity is almost unlimited, and is the necessary result of the settlement of the vast region of the valley of the Mississippi. It is now the sixth city in population, and the third in commerce. in the Union, and perhaps would already have held a higher rank, but from the check it receives from the prevalence of yellow fever, and other maladies, consequent upon its situation. There were formerly three municipalities and the city of Lafayette, with distinct councils for the management of internal affairs, in. the geographical limits of the city ; these were consolidated in 1852, under one municipal government. This city was also the capital of Louisiana until 1849, when the seat of government was removed to Baton Rouge. It contains churches of various ages and styles of architecture ; hospitals, charitable institutions, theatres, banks, warehouses, hotels, and the United States branch mint, a large building, 108 feet deep, 282 feet long, and three stories high ; also the University of Louisiana, and many excellent schools. The city is supplied with water, elevated by steam from the Mississippi into a reservoir, and thence distributed through iron pipes.

The population in 1763, was 3,190 ; in 1785, 4,980 ; in 1810, 17,242 ; in 1820, 27,176 ; in 1830, 46,310 ; in 1840, 102,193 ; in 1850, 115,625.

NEW OXFORD, p. v., Berwick township, Adams co., Pa., 33 ms. s. of Harrisburgh ; from W. 85 ms.

NEW PALESTINE, p. o., Clermont co., O.

NEW PALTZ, p. o., Ulster co., N. Y., 74 ms. s. of Albany ; from W. 306 ms. Watered by Hudson river and Wall kill. Pop. 2,729.

NEW PALTZ LANDING, p. v., New Paltz township, Ulster co., N. Y., 73 ms. s. of Albany ; from W. 300 ms. Watered by Hudson river.

NEW PARIS, p. v., Jefferson township, Preble co., O., 106 ms. w. of Columbus ; from W. 499 ms. Watered by Whitewater river.

NEW PETERSBURGH, p. v., Paint township, Highland co., O., 79 ms. s. w. of Columbus ; from W. 434 ms.

NEW PHILADELPHIA, p. v., Goshen township, seat of justice of Tuscarawas co., O., 115 ms. N. E. of Columbus ; from W. 313 ms. Watered by Tuscarawas river.

NEW PHILADELPHIA, p. v., Washington co., Ind., 96 ms. s. of Indianapolis ; from W. 596 ms.

NEW PHILADELPHIA, p. o., Pike co., Ill.

NEW PITTSBURGH, p. v., Chester township, Wayne co., O., 92 ms. N. E. of Columbus ; from W. 355 ms.

NEW PLYMOUTH, p. o., Vinton co., O.

NEWPORT COUNTY, Rhode Island, comprising several islands in Narraganset bay and a portion of the mainland. Area, 136 square miles. Surface gently undulating ; soil fertile. Seat of justice, Newport. Pop. in 1840, 16,874 ; in 1850, 20,007.

NEWPORT, p. t., Penobscot co., Me., 54 ms. N. E. of Augusta ; from W. 649 ms. Watered by head waters of Sebasticook river. Pop. 1,210.

NEWPORT, c. h., p. t., seat of justice of Sullivan co., N. H., 39 ms. w. of Concord ; from W. 474 ms. Watered by Sugar river, at the confluence of its three tributaries. Pop. 2,020.

NEWPORT, p. t., Orleans co., Vt., 64 ms. N. of Montpelier ; from W. 580 ms. Watered by Lake Memphramagog and head waters of Mississippi river. Pop. 748.

NEWPORT, p. t., seat of justice of Newport co., and capital, together with Providence, of Rhode Island, situated on the southwest side of the isle of Rhode Island, at the main entrance to Narraganset bay, 30 miles south of Providence. It occupies a gentle eminence fronting the harbor, from which it presents a fine appearance. Its pleasant scenery, embracing many spacious views of the ocean and its rocky shores, its healthful climate, abundance and variety of fish in its waters, and its interesting historic associations and relics of early times, render Newport one of the most attractive places of summer resort in the country. Not far from the town stands a curious monument of antiquity—the Old Tower. Its age and origin are unknown, and have been the subject of much learned but fruitless disquisition.

Newport harbor is one of the most accessible, safe, and capacious in America. Long before the Revolution, it gave to the town a rapid growth and prosperity, which, at one time, seemed likely to outstrip that of New York. Here, at different periods, anchored the

British fleet, and occupied the town as well as the surrounding country. Here, also, the French fleets entered, under Count D'Estaing and Admiral de Ternay. From these naval operations Newport suffered greatly, but soon recovered its former vigor, and continued to be one of the chief commercial ports in the Union, until the manufacturing success of Providence diverted the tide of enterprise into other channels. Manufactures and commerce are still extensively prosecuted.

The population in 1810, was 7,907 ; in 1820, 7,319 ; in 1830, 8,010 ; in 1840, 8,333 ; in 1850, 9,563.

NEWPORT, p. t., Herkimer co., N. Y., 86 ms. N. w. of Albany ; from W. 405 ms. Watered by West Canada creek. Pop. 2,125.

NEWPORT, p. v., Dover township, Cumberland co., N. J., 79 ms. s. of Trenton ; from W. 190 ms. Watered by Nautuxet creek.

NEWPORT, p. v., Juniata township, Perry co., Pa., 28 ms. N. w. of Harrisburgh ; from W. 132 ms. Watered by Juniata creek. Pop. 517.

NEWPORT, t., Luzerne co., Pa. Watered by Nanticoke river. Pop. 868.

NEWPORT, p. v., New Castle co., Del., 49 ms. N. of Dover ; from W. 108 ms.

NEWPORT, p. v., Charles co., Md., 83 ms. s. w. of Annapolis ; from W. 44 ms.

NEWPORT, p. o., Giles co., Va., 222 ms. w. of Richmond ; from W. 268 ms.

NEWPORT, c. h., p. v., seat of justice of Cocke co., Tenn., 232 ms. E. of Nashville ; from W. 465 ms. Watered by French Broad river.

NEWPORT, c. h., p. v., seat of justice of Campbell co., Ky., 86 ms. N. E. of Frankfort ; from W. 493 ms. Watered by Ohio river. Pop. 5,895.

NEWPORT, p. t., Washington co., O., 118 ms. s. E. of Columbus ; from W. 293 ms. Watered by Ohio river. Pop. 1,425.

NEWPORT, c. h., p. v., seat of justice of Vermilion co., Ind., 78 ms. w. of Indianapolis ; from W. 650 ms. Watered by Vermilion river. Pop. 328.

NEWPORT, c. h., p. v., seat of justice of Franklin co., Mo., 70 ms. E. of Jefferson City ; from W. 877 ms.

NEWPORT, p. o., Wakulla co., Flor.

NEWPORT, p. o., Monroe co., Mich.

NEWPORT, p. o., Lake co., Ill.

NEWPORT CENTRE, p. o., Newport township, Luzerne co., Pa.

NEW PORTAGE, p. v., Norton township, Medina co., O., 119 ms. N. E. of Columbus ; from W. 334 ms.

NEW PORTLAND, p. t., Somerset co., Me., 56 ms. N. w. of Augusta ; from W. 650 ms. Watered by Seven-Mile brook. Pop. 1,460.

NEW PORTLAND, p. o., Ralla co., Mo.

NEW PORTLAND, p. o., Stewart co., Tenn.

NEWPORT NEWS, p. o., Warwick co., Va.

NEWPORTVILLE, p. v., Bristol township, Bucks co., Pa., 116 ms. E. of Harrisburgh ; from W. 158 ms. Watered by Neshaminy creek at the head of navigation.

NEW PRESTON, p. v., Washington township, Litchfield co., Ct., 43 ms. w. of Hartford ; from W. 320 ms. Watered by Aspetuck river.

NEW PRINCETON, p. o., Coshocton co., O.

NEW PROSPECT, p. v., Franklin township, Bergen co., N. J., 87 ms. N. E. of Trenton ; from W. 253 ms. Watered by Hokokus creek.

NEW PROSPECT, p. v., Spartanburgh district, S. C., 117 ms. N. w. of Columbia ; from W. 483 ms.

NEW PROSPECT, p. v., Greene co., Ala. ; from W. 874 ms.

NEW PROSPECT, p. o., Milton township, Wayne co., O., 110 ms. N. E. of Columbus ; from W. 341 ms.

NEW PROSPECT, p. o., Winston co., Miss.

NEW PROSPECT, p. o., Orange co., Ind.

NEW PROVIDENCE, p. t., Essex co., N. J., 56 ms. N. E. of Trenton ; from W. 222 ms. Pop. 1,216.

NEW PROVIDENCE, p. o., Lancaster co., Pa., 46 ms, E. of Harrisburgh ; from W. 121 ms.

NEW PROVIDENCE, p. o., Pike co., Ala.

NEW PROVIDENCE, p. v., Montgomery co., Tenn., 47 ms. N. w. of Nashville ; from W. 732 ms.

NEW PROVIDENCE, p. v., Clarke co., Ind., 107 ms. s. of Indianapolis ; from W. 618 ms.

NEW READING, t., Perry co., O., Pop. 1.689.

NEW RETREAT, p. o., Washington co., Ind.

NEW RICHLAND, p. o., Logan co., O.

NEW RICHMOND, p. o., Crawford co., Pa., 246 ms. N. w. of Harrisburgh ; from W. — ms.

NEW RICHMOND, p. v., Ohio township, Clermont co., O., 116 ms. s. w. of Columbus ; from W. 487 ms. Watered by Ohio river.

NEW RICHMOND, p. o., Montgomery co., Ind.

NEW RIVER. p. o., Ascension parish, La., 83 ms. N. w. of New Orleans ; from W. 1,200 ms.

NEW RIVER. p. o., Columbia co., Flor.

NEW ROAD, p. o., Sidney township, Delaware co., N. Y., 102 ms. s. w. of Albany ; from W. 329 ms.

NEW ROCHELLE, p. t., Westchester co., N. Y., 145 ms. s. of Albany ; from W. 244 ms. Watered by Long Island sound. Pop. 2,458.

NEW ROCHESTER, p. v., Freedom township, Wood co., O., 108 ms. N. w. of Columbus ; from W. 453 ms.

NEW ROE, p. o., Allen co., Ky.

NEW ROSS, p. v., Montgomery co., Ind.. 35 ms. N. w. of Indianapolis ; from W. 606 ms.

NEW RUMLEY, p. v., Rumley township. Harrison co., O.. 116 ms. E. of Columbus ; from W. 290 ms.

NEW RUSSIA, p. o., Essex co., N. Y.

NEWRY, p. t., Oxford co., Me., 64 ms. w. of Augusta ; from W. 611 ms. Watered by Bear river. Pop. 459.

NEWRY, p. v., Frankstown township, Blair co., Pa., 122 ms. w. of Harrisburgh ; from W. 157 ms. Watered by Poplar river.

NEWRY, p. o., Jackson co., Ind.

NEWS, p. o., Calhoun co., Ill.

NEW SALEM, p. t., Franklin co., Mass., 73 ms. N. w. of Boston ; from W. 403 ms. Watered by Miller's river and tributaries. Pop. 1,253.

NEW SALEM, p. v., New Scotland township, Albany co.. N. Y., 12 ms. w. of Albany ; from W. 382 ms.

NEW SALEM, p. v., Salem township, Fayette co., Pa., 187 ms. w. of Harrisburgh ; from W. 203 ms.

NEW SALEM. p. o., Harrison co., Va., 267 ms. N. w. of Richmond ; from W. 235 ms.

NEW SALEM, p. v., Randolph co., N. C., 81 ms. w. of Raleigh ; from. W. 319 ms.

NEW SALEM, p. v., Walnut township, Fairfield co., O., 40 ms. s. E. of Columbus ; from W. 371 ms.

NEW SALEM, p. v., Rush co., Ind., 47 ms. s. E. of Indianapolis ; from W. 541 ms.

NEW SALEM, p. o., Rusk co., Tex.

NEW SALEM, p. o., Pike co., Ill.

NEW SALISBURY, p. v., Harrison co., Ind. 124 ms s. of Indianapolis ; from W. 616 ms.

NEW SCOTLAND, p. t., Albany co., N. Y., 9 ms. w. of Albany ; from W. 379 ms. Watered by Coeman's creek, and a tributary of Norman's kill. Pop. 3.459.

NEW SEWICKLY, t., Beaver co., Pa. Watered by Big Beaver river. Pop. 2,131.

NEW SHARON, p. t., Franklin co., Me., 28 ms. N. w. of Augusta ; from W. 621 ms. Watered by Sandy river. Pop. 1,732.

NEW SHARON, p. o., Monmouth co., N. J.

NEW SHEFFIELD, p. o., Beaver co., Pa.

NEW SHOREHAM, p. t., Block Island, Newport co., R. I. Watered by Long Island sound, and the Atlantic ocean. Pop. 1,262.

NEW SMYRNA, p. v., Orange co., Flor. Settled by a colony of 1,500 Greeks and Minorcans, in 1769. Watered by Mosquito river.

NEW SOMERSET, p. o., Jefferson co., O.

NEWSON'S Depot, p. v., Southampton co., Va., 78 ms. s. E. of Richmond ; from W. 197 ms.

NEWSON, p. o., Bibb co., Ga.

NEW SPRINGFIELD, p. v., Mahoning co., O,, 167 ms. N. E. of Columbus ; from W. 289 ms.

NEW STANTON, p. v., Westmoreland co., Va.

NEWSTEAD, p. t., Erie co., N. Y., 266 ms. w. of Albany ; from W. 386 ms. Watered by Ellicott creek and other tributaries of Tonawanda creek. Pop. 2,899.

NEWSTEAD, p. o., Christian co., Ky.

NEW STORE, p. o., Buckingham co., Va., 75 ms. w. of Richmond ; from W. 165 ms.

NEW SWEDEN, p. v., Au Sable township, Clinton co., N. Y., 155 ms. N. of Albany ; from W. 530 ms. Watered by Au Sable river.

NEWTON COUNTY, situated in the central part of Georgia. Area, 460 square miles. Seat of justice, Covington. Pop. in 1840, 11,628 ; in 1850, 13,296.

NEWTON COUNTY, situated toward the easterly part of Mississippi. Area, 540 square miles. Seat of justice, Decatur. Pop. in 1840, 2,527 ; in 1850, 4,465.

NEWTON COUNTY, situated on the west boundary of Missouri. Area (in 1840), 1,150 square miles. Seat of justice, Neosho. Pop. in 1840, 3,790 ; in 1850, 4,268.

NEWTON COUNTY, situated toward the northwesterly part of Arkansas. Area, —— square miles. Seat of justice, —— Pop. in 1850, 1,758.

NEWTON COUNTY, situated on the east boundary of Texas, with Sabine river on the east. Area, —— square miles. Seat of justice, Burkville. Pop. in 1850, 1,681.

NEWTON, p. t., Middlesex co., Mass., 7 ms. w. of Boston; from W. 433 ms. Watered by Charles river. Pop. 5,258.

NEWTON, c. h., p. t., seat of justice of Sussex co., N. J., 70 ms. N. of Trenton; from W. 238 ms. Watered by Paulin's kill. Pop. 3,279.

NEWTON, t. Gloucester co., N. J. Watered by Cooper's and Newton creeks.

NEWTON, t., Cumberland co., Pa. Watered by Yellow Breeches creek. Pop. 715.

NEWTON, t., Miami co., O. Pop. 1,447.

NEWTON, p. t., Muskingum co., O., 60 ms., E. of Columbus; from W. 345 ms. Pop. 2,356.

NEWTON, t., Licking co., O. Pop. 1,363.

NEWTON, t., Pike co., O. Pop. 461.

NEWTON, p. t., Trumbull co., O. Pop. 1,678.

NEWTON, p. t., Calhoun co., Mich., 114 ms. w. of Detroit; from W. 579 ms. Pop. 569.

NEWTON, c. h., p. v., seat of justice of Jasper co., Ill., 130 ms. s. E. of Springfield; from W. 707 ms.

NEWTON, c. h., p. v., seat of justice of Dale co., Ala.

NEWTON, c. h., p. o., seat of justice of Baker co., Ga.

NEWTON, p. o., Jasper co., Iowa.

NEWTON, c. h., p. v., seat of justice of Catawba co., N. C.

NEWTON CENTRE, p. v., Newton township, Middlesex co., Mass., 9 ms. w. of Boston; from W. 431 ms.

NEWTON CORNERS, p. o., Jefferson co., Wis.

NEWTON FACTORY, p. o., Newton co., Ga.

NEWTON FALLS, p. v., Newton township, Trumbull co., O., 162 ms. N. E., of Columbus; from W. 311 ms. Situated on the Pennsylvania and Ohio canal, at the confluence of the two tributaries of Mahoning river.

NEWTON GROVE, p. o., Sampson co., N. C.

NEWTON LOWER FALLS, p. v., Newton township, Middlesex. co., Mass., 11 ms. w. of Boston; from W. 429 ms. Watered by Charles river.

NEWTON STEWART, p. o., Orange co., Ind.

NEWTONSVILLE, p. o., Clermont co., O.

NEWTONSVILLE, p. o., Attala co., Miss.

NEWTON UPPER FALLS, p. v., Newton township, Middlesex co., Mass., 9 ms. w. of Boston; from W. 431 ms. Watered by Charles river.

NEWTONVILLE, p. o., Albany co., N. Y.

NEWTONVILLE, p. o., Fayette co., Ala.

NEWTOWN, t., Rockingham co., N. H., 30 ms. s. E. of Concord; from W. 474 ms. Pop. 685.

NEWTOWN, p. t., Fairfield co., Ct., 62 ms. s. w. of Hartford; from W. 293 ms. Watered by Potatuck river. Pop. 3,338.

NEWTOWN, p. t., Queen's co., Long Island, N. Y., 152 ms. s. of Albany; from W. 232 ms. Watered by Newtown creek, East river, and Long Island sound. Pop. 7,208.

NEWTOWN, p. t., Bucks co., Pa., 118 ms. E. of Harrisburgh; from W. 160 ms. Watered by Newtown creek. Pop. 841.

NEWTOWN, t., Delaware co., Pa. Watered by Crum and Darby creeks. Pop. 823.

NEWTOWN, p. v., Worcester co., Md., 126 ms. s. E. of Annapolis; from W. 166 ms. Pop. 395.

NEWTOWN, p. v., King and Queen co., Va., 38 ms. N. E. of Richmond; from W. 106 ms. Watered by Mattapony river.

NEWTOWN, p. v., Scott co., Ky., 25 ms. E. of Frankfort; from W. 513 ms.

NEWTOWN, p. v., Anderson township, Hamilton co., O., 119 ms. s. w. of Columbus; from W. 490 ms. Watered by Little Miami river.

NEWTOWN, p. v., Fountain co., Ind., 63 ms. N. w. of Indianapolis; from W. 634 ms.

NEWTOWN, p. v., Hinds co., Miss., 10 ms. s. of Jackson; from W. 1,020 ms.

NEWTOWN ACADEMY, p. o., Monroe co., Ala.

NEWTOWN HAMILTON, p. v., Mifflin co., Pa. Watered by Juniata river.

NEWTOWN SQUARE, p. v., Delaware co., Pa., 90 ms. s. E. of Harrisburgh; from W. 132 ms.

NEWTOWN STEPHENSBURGH, p. o., Frederick co., Va., 154 ms. N. w. of Richmond; from W. 82 ms.

NEW TRENTON, p. v., Whitewater township, Franklin co., Ind., 81 ms. s. E. of Indianapolis; from W. 516 ms.

NEW TRIER, p. o., Cook co., Ill.

NEW TRIPOLI. p. v., Linn township, Lehigh co., Pa., 86 ms. N. E. of Harrisburgh; from W. 178 ms. Watered by a tributary of Maiden creek.

NEW UPTON, p. o., Gloucester co., Va.

NEW UTRECHT, p. t., King's co., Long Island, N. Y., 151 ms. s. of Albany; from W. 231 ms. Watered by the Narrows and New York bay. Pop. 2,129

NEW VERNON, p. o., Mount Hope township. Orange co., N. Y., 105 ms. s. w. of Albany; from W. 280 ms.

NEW VERNON, p. v., Morris co., N. J., 49 ms. N. of Trenton; from W. 220 ms.

NEW VERNON, p. t., Mercer co., Pa., 228 ms. N. w. of Harrisburgh; from W. 302 ms.

NEW VIENNA, p. o., Clinton co., O.

NEW VILLAGE, p. v., Brookhaven township, Suffolk co., N. Y., 198 ms. s. E. of Albany; from W. 278 ms.

NEW VILLAGE, p. v., Greenwich township, Warren co., N. J., 54 ms. N. w. of Trenton; from W. 205 ms.

NEWVILLE, p. v., Danube township, Herkimer co., N. Y., 66 ms. N. w. of Albany; from W. 389 ms.

NEWVILLE, p. b., Newton township, Cumberland co., Pa., 30 ms. s. w. of Harrisburgh; from W. 113 ms. Watered by Big Spring creek. Pop. 715.

NEWVILLE, p. o., Sussex co., Va., 46 ms. s. E. of Richmond; from W. 165 ms.

NEWVILLE, p. v., Worthington township, Richland co., O., 74 ms. N. E. of Columbus; from W. 372 ms. Watered by Clear fork of Mohiccan creek.

NEWVILLE, p. v., De Kalb co., Ind., 156 ms. N. E. of Indianapolis; from W. 538 ms.

NEW VINE, p. o., Du Buque co., Iowa.

NEW VINEYARD, t., Franklin co., Me., 48 ms. N. w. of Augusta; from W. 635 ms. Watered by tributaries of Seven-Mile and Sandy rivers. Pop. 635.

NEW WAKEFIELD, p. v., Washington co., Ala.; from W. 976 ms.

NEW WASHINGTON, p. v.. Clarke co., Ind., 97 ms. s. of Indianapolis; from W. 578 ms.

NEW WASHINGTON, p. o., Clearfield co., Pa.

NEW WASHINGTON, p. o., Crawford co., O.

NEW WAY, p. o., Licking co., O.

NEW WESTVILLE. p. o., Preble co., O., 104 ms. w. of Columbus; from W. 497 ms.

NEW WILMINGTON, p. v., Lackawannock township, Mercer co., Pa., 241 ms. N. w. of Harrisburgh; from W. 284 ms.

NEW WINCHESTER, p. v., Crawford co., O., 62 ms. N. of Columbus; from W. 407 ms.

NEW WINCHESTER, p. v., Hendricks co., Ind., 27 ms. w. of Indianapolis; from W. 598 ms.

NEW WINDSOR, p. t., Orange co., N. Y., 86 ms. s. of Albany; from W. 288 ms. Watered by Murderer's creek and Hudson river. Pop. 11,415.

NEW WINDSOR, p. v., Carroll co., Md., 65 ms. N. w. of Annapolis; from W. 66 ms.

NEW WOODSTOCK, p. v., Cazenovia township, Madison co., N. Y., 115 ms. w. of Albany; from W. 347 ms.

NEW YORK, one of the United States, the wealthiest and the most populous in the Union, is situated between 40° 30' and 45° N. latitude, and 71° 56' and 79° 56' w. longitude from Greenwich, and is bounded N. by Canada, which is separated in part by Lake Ontario and the river St. Lawrence; E. by Vermont, Massachusetts, and Connecticut; s. by the Atlantic, New Jersey, and Pennsylvania; and w. by Pennsylvania, Lake Erie, and the Niagara river; the two latter separating it, in part from Canada West. It has a superficial area of about 46,000 square miles, or 30,000,000 acres.

Physical Aspect.—The natural features of this state are greatly diversified, but in general may be regarded as an elevated tract, with numerous indentations and depressions, which form the basins of the lakes and the valleys of fertilizing streams. The surface of the eastern division is more varied in its character than the western. There are some level tracts, the principal of which embrace the prairies and larger plains of Long Island; but the greater portion is mountainous and

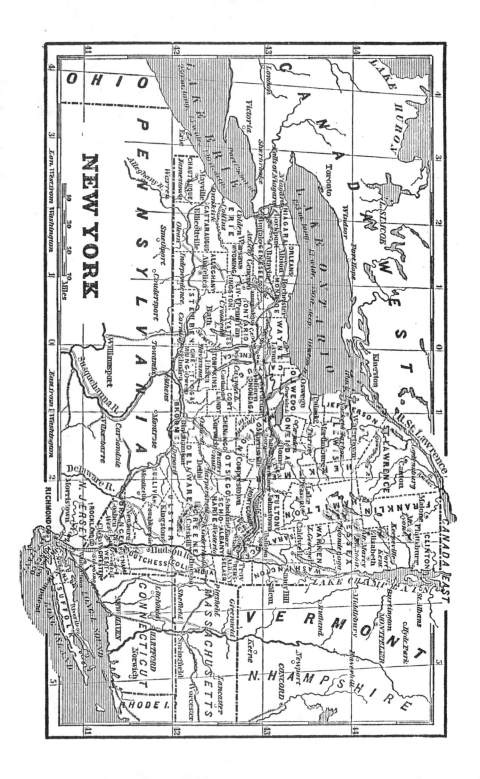

billy. The central and western divisions are mostly level, or moderately undulating, except near the Pennsylvania line, where it becomes broken and hilly. The soil of this state is generally good, except on the more sterile parts of the Hudson highlands, and other mountainous tracts, and many parts are celebrated for their extraordinary fertility. The valleys of the Mohawk and the Genesee, in particular, have long been proverbial for their productiveness, and are regarded as inexhaustible in their yield. The extensive plains in the central part of Long island, heretofore used as woodlands, producing large quantities of fuel for the New York market, are now being converted into farms and gardens, and the soil, with a moderate outlay for amendments, is found to produce, when properly cultivated, as well as any other land on the island.

Mountains.—There are several ridges of mountains in this state, which are generally considered as extensions of the Allegany or Appalachian chain. Two of these cross the eastern division, one of which extends from New Jersey to West Point, forming the Hudson highlands ; thence in a northerly direction to the Taghkannic mountains, constituting the dividing ridge between the Housatonic and Hudson rivers. The same range continues to Vermont, and is there known as the Green mountains. The other range, from New Jersey, terminates at the Shawangunk mountains, on the west side of the Hudson. Another range still more prominent, also extends from New Jersey, as a continuation of the Kittatinny ridge, to the Kaatsbergs (Catskill), near the Hudson, whence it continues in a northwesterly direction, through the counties of Albany and Schoharie, forming the Helderberg ; thence to the Little Falls, through Herkimer, where it is known by the name of Sacondaga mountain ; thence along to the westward of Lake Champlain to the river St. Lawrence, forming the Adirondack mountains, Mount Marcy being the most lofty pinnacle of the range.

Rivers, Creeks, Lakes, and Bays.—The principal rivers are, the St. Lawrence, Niagara, Hudson, Delaware, Susquehannah, Genesee, Oswego, Oswegatchie, Black, St. Regis, Mohawk, Saranac, Salmon, Chenango, Tioga, Seneca, Canisteo, Allegany, Croton, Harlem, and East. The most noted creeks are, the Tonawanda, Ellicott, Eighteen-Mile, Oak-Orchard, Oriskany, East and West Canada, Schoharie, Sacondaga, Rondout, and the Wall Kill. Lakes Erie, Ontario, and Champlain, lie partly in this state. The other chief lakes are George, Cayuga, Seneca, Oneida, Oswegatchie, Canandaigua, Chautauque, Skaneateles, and Crooked. The principal bays are, New York, Jamaica, Great South, Shinnecock, Gardiner's, Peconic, Oyster, and Flushing.

Cataracts.—New York is noted for a number of magnificent waterfalls. The falls of Niagara form the most stupendous cataract in the world. The water accumulated from the great upper lakes, forming a river about three quarters of a mile wide, and from forty to sixty feet deep, flows with a current of seven miles an hour. As it proceeds the river widens, and embosoms Grand and Navy islands, and again contracts to its former width. Below the islands are rapids, which extend a mile, to the precipice, in which space the river descends fifty-seven feet. Here Goat island divides the river into two channels. Over the precipice the river falls perpendicularly about 160 feet. Much the greater part of the water passes in the channel between Goat island and the Canada shore, and this fall is called, from its shape, the Horseshoe. Between Goat island and the small island in the eastern channel the stream is only eight or ten yards wide, forming a beautiful cascade. Between this small island and the American shore the sheet of water is broad, and the descent greater by a few feet than at the Horsehoe fall, but the stream is comparatively shallow. The best single view of the falls is from Table-Rock, on the Canada shore, and the best view of the rapids is from Goat island. Trenton falls, twelve miles north of Utica, are a succession of magnificent cascades. The Cohoes falls are formed by the passage of the Mohawk over a wall of rock, in one sheet, sixty-two feet high. At Rochester, the Genesee has a fall of ninety-six feet. At Ithaca, Fall creek has a descent of 438 feet in the space of a mile. The Cauterskill falls are a beautiful cascade, of great elevation, in the Highlands.

Mineral Springs.—The Saratoga and Ballston mineral springs are the resort of invalids at all seasons, and of the fashionable world during summer. The salt springs, near Syracuse, annually yield four million bushels of salt. The sulphur Springs, at Sharon, in Schoharie county, and at Avon, in Livingston county, are efficacious in the treatment of chronic complaints.

Islands.—The chief islands, surrounded by tide water, are Long, Staten, Manhattan, Blackwell's, Gardiner's, Shelter, and Plum. Those of the inland waters are, Grand and Tonawanda islands, in the Niagara river, and several others in the St. Lawrence.

Climate.—The climate is more varied, perhaps, than in any other state. In the easterly section, below the Hudson highlands, the winters, are comparatively mild, but changeable, and frequently are rendered disagreeable by the ocean winds. In the northeastern and central divisions they are more uniform, but severe. In the western division they are also mild, and are subject to less variation than either of the other divisions, except near the lakes, where they are often rendered unpleasant by tempestuous winds. The extremes of temperature near the city of New York vary from 4° below zero Fahrenheit to 90° above ; at Albany, from 16° below to 93° above ; at Canandaigua, from 8° below to 87° above ; and at Buffalo, from zero to 80° above. The climate of the state is generally regarded as healthy, with the exception of a few months in summer and autumn, in the vicinity of stagnant marshes and sluggish streams. Here, as in most other parts of the country, situated in similar circumstances, intermittents and bilious disorders more or less prevail.

Productive Resources.—The chief products are horses, mules, neat cattle, sheep, swine, poultry, eggs, beef, pork, fish, butter, cheese, silk, hay, wool, sugar, wine, hops, tobacco, flax, hemp, lumber, pot and pearl ashes, pitch, tar, turpentine, wheat, flour, rye, barley, oats, peas, beans, flax-seed, buckwheat, potatoes, Indian corn, apples, cider, pears, plums, peaches, grapes, and other fruits peculiar to the latitude. Of the mineral and fossil resources, iron, salt, marble, hydraulic cement, gypsum, super-phosphate of lime, flagstone and lime, are the most important, all of which are extensively and profitably wrought.

Manufactures.—The manufactures of New York are extensive. Every section of the state abounds in excellent water-power, which is generally improved for manufactories, flour-mills, saw-mills, &c. Cotton, woollens, iron, paper, leather, glass, oil, silk, cutlery, hardware, firearms, carriages, &c., are the more important articles of manufacture.

Railroads and Canals.—New York has about 2,000 miles of railroads in successful operation. The most important are, the New York and Erie, extending from the Hudson river to Lake Erie, a distance of 450 miles ; and the Hudson river, and the New York, Harlem, and Albany railroads, extending from New York city to Albany. From Albany railroads extend eastward to Boston, northward to Canada, and westward to Buffalo. From all these roads branches extend to various important points in the state. The New Haven connects New York city with the eastern states. The principal canal in New York is the Erie, extending from Albany to Buffalo, 364 miles. From the Erie lateral canals diverge north and south, traversing many important sections of country. The canals are, with a single exception, the property of the state. They have an aggregate length of about 1,000 miles, and have been principally built for the purpose of uniting the navigation of the lakes with the Hudson river.

Commerce.—The foreign commerce of New York is nearly equal to that of all the rest of the Union combined. Her lake and interior commerce is equally immense. In 1850, its imports and exports amounted to $163,836,313. The shipping owned within the state is over one million of tons, of which about one half is employed in the coasting trade and on the lakes.

Education.—Among the literary institutions of New York are, Columbia, Union, Hamilton, and Geneva colleges ; and the New York, Madison, and Rochester universities. There are seven theological seminaries, and five medical schools. There are, also, about 250 academies, and 12,000 common schools in the state. The money appropriated for the support of common schools amounts to over a million of dollars annually.

Population.—In 1790, 340,120 ; in 1800 ; 586,756 ; in 1810, 959,949 ; in 1820, 1,372,812; in 1830, 1,918,608 ; in 1840, 2,428,957 ; in 1850, 3,097,394. Number of slaves in 1790, 21,324 ; in 1800, 20,343 ; in 1810, 15,017 ; in 1820, 10,088 ; in 1830, 75 ; in 1840, 4. .

Government.—The executive power is vested in a governor, and lieutenant-governor, who must be native-

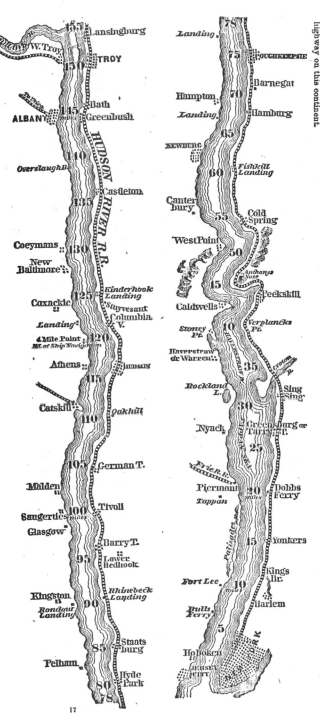

MAP OF HUDSON RIVER and Hudson River Railroad.

The Hudson river proper rises by two branches, in the mountainous regions of Hamilton and Essex counties, New York. The Eastern branch is composed of two streams, which unite in Warren county. Fifteen miles below this, the Sacandaga unites with the Hudson at Jessup's falls; eighteen miles below this, it passes Hadley's falls; and twenty miles further is Glen's falls. The only considerable tributary below this, is the Mohawk, ten miles above Albany. Its whole course, from its source to its entrance into New York bay, is 320 miles. The tide flows as far as Albany. The city of New York owes much of its prosperity to this river, connected as it is with the Erie and Champlain canals. The Hudson River railroad, which connects Albany with New York, together with the river travel, are greater thoroughfares than any other highway on this continent.

17

born citizens of the United States, and have resided in the state five years, and who are elected biennially ; and the legislative power in a senate, of 32 members, elected biennially, and a house of assembly, of 128 members, elected annually, on the Tuesday succeeding the first Monday in November. The secretary of state, comptroller, treasurer, canal commissioners, attorney-general, engineer, and surveyor, are elected biennially by the people. Judges are elected by the people, and hold their office eight years. Every white male citizen, 21 years of age, who has resided in the state one year, and in the county where he offers his vote four months next preceding the election, enjoys the right of suffrage. Persons of color who have resided three years in the state, and have possessed a freehold of $250, one year previous to the election, are allowed the right of suffrage.

History.—In the year 1609, Henry Hudson, a navigator (who had previously made two voyages to the American continent, in the service of a company of London merchants), in the employ of the Dutch East India Company, while exploring the coasts of what are now Virginia, Delaware, and New Jersey, in search of a passage to the Pacific ocean, passed through the Narrows, entered the magnificent bay of New York, and discovered the mouth of the Manhattan (now Hudson) river. For ten days he continued his voyage cautiously up this river, confidently hoping it would open through to the great ocean, and it was not until he reached the head of tide-water, in fact until he was at the mouth of the Mohawk, that he relinquished this idea. He reached England in the autumn of that year. During the same year, Champlain, having fortified Quebec, passed through the lake which bears his name, and descended Lake George. The two navigators came very near meeting each other from different points, in the interior of New York. The Dutch commenced a regular trade with the Indians upon the Hudson in 1610, which was continued several years before a permanent settlement was commenced. They began a settlement at Albany in 1615, built a fort, and called the country upon the river *New Netherlands.* About the same time, a small settlement was made upon Manhattan island, but actual colonization did not take place until after 1621, when the Dutch West India Company was formed. In 1629, this company issued patroon privileges, for the purpose of encouraging settlements, and emigration rapidly increased. In 1633, the Dutch erected a fort on the Connecticut river, upon the present site of Hartford, but soon after abandoned the place. The Dutch at this time claimed Long Island, yet the English commenced settlements upon the eastern end of it. They also claimed jurisdiction over the whole country bordering the Delaware and its bay, but there a colony of Swedes, which had been projected by and planted under the auspices of Gustavus Adolphus, disputed their authority, and they built a fort upon the island of Tinicum, in the Delaware, a few miles below Philadelphia. In 1643–'44, the Dutch waged a war against the neighboring Indian tribes upon Long Island, and in New Jersey, who showed signs of disaffection, having been badly treated by the whites. The Indians were subdued and dispersed. In 1647, Peter Stuyvesant, the most celebrated of the Dutch governors, arrived, and by order of the home government, he set about reducing the Swedish colony to submission. This was accomplished in 1655, and *New Sweden* upon the Delaware became a part of the New Netherlands. In 1664, Charles II. granted the country between the Connecticut and the Delaware to his brother, the Duke of York, who sent an armed force to take possession. This they accomplished in the autumn of that year, and the name of the settlement and province was changed to New York. When, in 1689, Governor Andros was imprisoned, the people of New York, under Leisler, took possession of the fort there. Leisler continued at the head of affairs until 1691, when he was arrested by Slaughter, a newly-appointed royal governor, and executed on a charge of high treason. From the year 1700 until 1744, the province of New York was quiet, except the excitement produced by a pretended negro plot. It was then that the "five years' war" with France took place, and then northern New York became the theatre of hostilities. Hoosick and Schenectady were burnt. From 1755 to 1763 occurred the French and Indian wars, and New York was the chief field of operations within the English colonies. Fort Oswego was captured by Montcalm, August 13, 1756, and the next year, on August

9, he stormed and took Port William Henry, on Lake George. The English also made conquests of fortresses in the possession of the French ; Ticonderoga, Frontenac, and Niagara. The congress of the colonies, which the stamp-act gave birth to, was held in the city of New York, in 1765, and about the same time the association called the Sons of Liberty was organized in this province. In 1767, the powers of the colonial legislature were annulled by parliament, because the assembly refused to grant supplies to troops. In 1773, the people of New York, like those of Boston, successfully resisted the landing of tea. In 1775, after hearing of the battle of Lexington, a provincial congress was assembled, and thus the colony was governed until 1777, when a constitution was adopted. On August, 27, 1776, occurred the battle on Long Island, between the Americans and British and Hessians. The city was evacuated by the Americans on the 23d of September. From that time until the close of the Revolution, this state was the scene of some of the most exciting and important events of the war. But our limits forbid a detail of them. On the 25th of November, 1783, the British evacuated New York. It was there that Washington, the first president of the United States, was inaugurated, on the 30th of April, 1789. New York ratified the Constitution of the United States July 26, 1788.

NEW YORK COUNTY, is situated at the southeast part of the state, between Hudson and East rivers, and includes Manhattan, Blackwell's, Ward's, and Randall's islands. Area, 20 square miles. Face of the country, undulating ; soil, fertile. Seat of justice, New York city. Pop. in 1653, 1,120 ; in 1661, 1,743 ; in 1675, 2,580 ; in 1696, 4,455 ; in 1730, 8,256 ; in 1756, 10,530 ; in 1774, 22,861 ; in 1786, 23,688; in 1790, 33,131 ; in 1800, 60,489 ; in 1810, 96,373 ; in 1820, 123,706 ; in 1830, 202,589 ; in 1840, 312,710 ; in 1850, 515, 507.

NEW YORK, city, the great commercial metropolis of the United States, and in population, commerce, and wealth, one of the first cities of the globe, is situated in latitude 40° 42' 40" north, and in longitude 74° 1' 8" west from Greenwich, and 3° 0' 22" east from Washington, 216 miles southwest of Boston, and 86 miles northeast of Philadelphia.

The city is located on Manhattan island, between Hudson and East rivers, which unite at its southern extremity, forming one of the most admirable harbors for beauty and convenience in the world. The island is 13½ miles long, bounded on the north by Harlem river, formerly Spuytendevil creek, and embraces an area of about 20 square miles. On the south part of this, the compact part of the city is built, extending northward about four miles from river to river, and spreading by a rate of progress which will soon cover the whole island. Its admirable position for foreign commerce, with its noble bay, and its remarkable facilities of internal communication with every portion of the Union, have been the unfailing sources of its extraordinary growth and prosperity. Here the noble Hudson, after a course of more than 200 miles, through a rich and populous region, sweeps majestically along, bearing on its bosom the vast commerce of the Erie canal and the west, expands into the upper bay, and passes through the "Narrows" into the ocean. Here, too, on the opposite side, courses the strong tide of East river, which, winding between Long Island and the main land, forms the rocky pass of "Hell-Gate," and several islands. This stream, which averages about three fourths of a mile in width, and thirty feet in depth, affords a passage for vessels of a large class into Long Island sound and the Atlantic ; while those engaged in foreign commerce, as well as in the southern coasting-trade, usually enter and leave the harbor through the Narrows, between Staten and Long islands. The best anchorage for these is at the wharves along the East river, which is more secure from ice than the Hudson. British packets, coasting vessels, and canal-boats generally, lie along the former river ; some at Brooklyn, and the Atlantic dock, on the opposite bank ; while the Hudson is thickly lined with steamboats and ships from England, France, Spain, Portugal, Holland, Sweden, and other foreign countries. On this river, also, at the foot of Canal street, is the wharf of the Collins' line of steamers, between Liverpool and New York. The Cunard steamers land at Jersey city, on the opposite side of the river. Other splendid lines run between the city and Southampton, Bremen, and Havre, in Europe, Charleston, Savannah, New Orleans, Havana, Chagres, Nicaragua, and Panama. Steamboats of dif-

BIRD'S-EYE VIEW OF NEW YORK,

SHOWING THE CITIES OF NEW YORK, BROOKLYN, AND WILLIAMSBURGH, WITH THE HARBOR AND RIVERS.

ferent grades, from the magnificent floating palaces of the Hudson, to the lesser propeller and steam-ferry boats, are constantly leaving or approaching the city, and animate its waters with the most varied prospect of life and activity. For pleasant, salubrious position, and beauty of surrounding country, New York is as conspicuous as it is for commercial advantages. Entering the outer bay, from the Atlantic, the traveller sees on the left of the broad expanse of water, the blue hills of New Jersey, formerly known as the highlands of Navesink. Toward the north, the romantic heights of Staten island rise to view, and on the east, the shores of Long island. Following the Narrows, between the two islands, which are defended by strong fortifications, the upper or inner part of the bay opens an enchanting scene. Staten island recedes, and the shores of New Jersey reappear. Long island continues on the right, and after passing Governor's island, with its fortifications, the great city displays its forest of masts and spires, its domes, and its houses, relieved by the green foliage of the "Battery," set, like an emerald, in some darker stone. The ground rises from the Battery, and from both rivers, by a gradual ascent, of which Broadway is the ridge, or summit. This surface, with the outline of the city, which rapidly widens from its southern point to a breadth of two miles, at Corlear's Hook, on the East river, gives an imposing effect, unequalled by almost any in the world. At the lower and ancient part of the city, the streets are somewhat irregular, but not unpleasant, being lined with rows of warehouses and stores of the most splendid and solid construction. Many of these are brick, some of freestone, and others of white marble. This is the business part of the city, and embraces comparatively few residences. Wall street is the principal theatre of financial and mercantile operations, and is a broad, straight avenue, leading from East river to Broadway. On either side of this are numerous splendid banking-houses, and other public buildings, among which is the Merchants' Exchange, of blue granite, or sienite, 200 feet long, 171 feet wide, and 124 feet high to the top of the dome, with a portico supported by massive solid pillars. Within, the most remarkable apartment is the exchange, a rotunda, 80 feet in diameter, and 80 feet high, lighted from above by the dome, and resting upon eight Corinthian columns of Italian marble. The whole building is of fire-proof materials, and is a splendid ornament to the city. The customhouse, on the same street, is a beautiful structure of white marble, in Doric architecture, surrounded by rows of Corinthian columns, with a portico extending across the entire front on Wall street. It is 200 feet long, 90 feet wide, and 80 feet high, and contains numerous apartments for the different offices, the principal of which is of circular form, 80 feet in diameter, surrounded by columns, and lighted by a beautiful dome. This structure occupies the site of where once stood Federal Hall, where Washington was inaugurated first president of the United States, April 30, 1789. At the head of Wall street, fronting on Broadway, stands Trinity church, the most costly and magnificent structure of the kind in America. It is of light-brown freestone, in purely Gothic architecture, and is 192 feet deep, 84 feet wide, the walls 60 feet high, and the spire reaching 284 feet above the ground. From the battlements, at the base of the spire, appears a magnificent panorama of New York bay, its islands, New Jersey, and Long island, with Brooklyn, Williamsburgh, and other populous towns; while below the feet the giant city spreads east, west, north, and south, on each side of Broadway, for which for three miles bisects it in nearly a straight direction. This splendid street, which is 80 feet wide, is lined with large and magnificent stores, warehouses, and hotels, built of white marble, freestone, and other durable materials. Below Trinity church, besides a number of fine hotels, there is the United States bonded warehouse. Proceeding northward, successively appear the American Museum, the Astor house, occupying an entire square, built of blue granite, the city-hall, the Irving house, opposite to which is Stuart's dry-goods palace, a massive structure of white marble, the Society library, City hospital, American institute, St. Nicholas hotel, Academy of Design, Metropolitan hotel, and Grace church, of pure white marble, elaborately sculptured. At Tenth street, Broadway makes a small angle, and, after passing Union and Madison squares, proceeds nearly northward to the upper end of the island. Among the public buildings in the lower part of the city

is the city-hall, in the "Park," a pleasant triangular enclosure, of ten acres. This edifice is of white marble, except the back, which is of brown freestone. Its architecture is a combination of the Ionic, Corinthian, and Composite orders. It is 216 feet long, 105 feet deep, and 65 feet high. Upon the roof is a cupola, with a clock, illuminated at night, and an enormous bell, the powerful tones of which send the alarm of fire over an area of many miles. Within are well-furnished apartments for different offices of the city government; and in the second story the governor's room, which is decorated with portraits of the presidents, governors of the state, mayors of the city, and many American heroes and statesmen. In front of this edifice a splendid fountain rises, from the middle of a circular basin, surrounded by flowers and shrubs. The park also contains the new city-hall, the hall of records, and several other public buildings, for the accommodation of the courts, and city business. The hall of justice, often called, from its architecture, the "Egyptian Tombs," is a massive and large building, on Centre street, of light-colored granite, 253 feet long, and 200 feet wide. It contains the city prison, and other departments of justice. Columbia college is pleasantly situated westward of the park, fronting a beautiful green, the west side of which once overlooked the Hudson, but it is now at a distance of about a fourth of a mile. This institution was founded under George II., in 1754, and has educated some of the most distinguished men of the country. The New York postoffice occupies the old Middle Dutch church on Nassau, Cedar, and Liberty streets. Other prominent buildings worthy of note are Clinton hall, occupied by the Mercantile library; Odd-Fellows hall, an imposing structure of freestone; the New York university, an elegant white marble Gothic structure; the university medical college, on Fourteenth street; the New York college of physicians and surgeons, on Crosby street; the New York medical college; the general theological seminary of the protestant episcopal church; the Union theological seminary; the free academy; the Astor library; the institution for the blind; the deaf and dumb asylum; the New York orphan asylum, upon an attractive slope overlooking the Hudson; the colored orphan asylum for friendless boys; the sailors' home; the colored home, and many other noble, charitable institutions, which form a most enviable ornament of pride and honor for the metropolis of America.

New York is well furnished with educational and literary privileges, and manifests its high interest in mental culture, by the number and excellence of its libraries, schools, colleges, lectures, and journals, the latter of which are, in general, superior to those of any other city in the Union, for intrinsic merits, despatch, and for every requisite of newspaper literature.

The public grounds of New York are numerous, but scarcely commensurate with its greatness and wealth. The "Battery," at the south extremity, is an airy and delightful resort in summer, carpeted with greensward, shaded with large trees, and fanned by the breezes of the bay. At the southwest side, built up from the water, is Castle-Garden, once a fortification, but now used for public gatherings, and for the magnificent annual fairs of the American Institute. Its vast amphitheatre will contain 10,000 persons. Not far from the battery, at the foot of Broadway, is the "Bowling-Green," a small elliptical enclosure, containing a fountain and lofty trees. Here, before the Revolution, stood a gilded leaden statue of George III., which was converted by the patriots into bullets, to be fired at the troops of the king, whom it represented. The park has been already noticed. Union square is a pleasant oval ground, adorned with flowers, grass, trees, and a fountain. Washington square, formerly a potter's field, lies westward of Broadway, and affords a pleasant promenade. Tompkins, Stuyvesant, and Madison squares, are the other public grounds, none of which are sufficiently ample for the wants of the city. St. John's, and Grammercy, are beautiful private parks.

It remains to notice a work which, in grandeur of design, and magnificent execution, is truly worthy of the commercial metropolis of America: the Croton waterworks, the most extensive and costly structure of the kind in the country, and probably in the world, if we except those at Marseilles, in France. A dam across Croton river, 40 miles north of the city-hall, creates an exhaustless and beautiful lake, of about 400 acres in area, five miles in circumference, and capable of containing

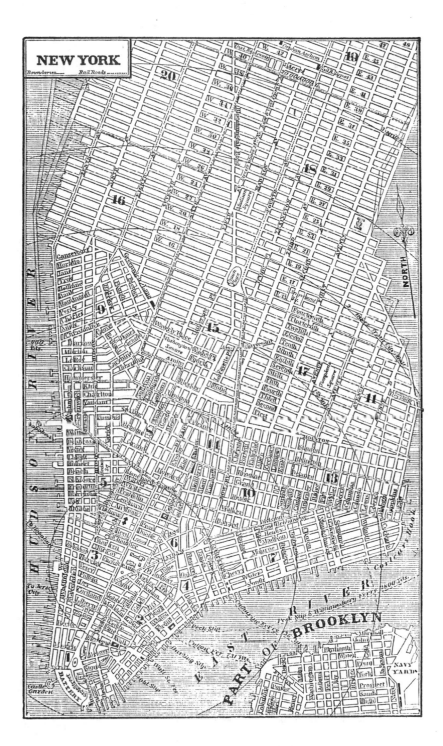

NEW YORK

Boundaries———— Rail Roads———————

550,000,000 gallons of water. The aqueduct extends from this point to Harlem river, without interruption, conveying the water through a conduit of masonwork, which has a descent of about one foot, to a mile, is six feet three inches wide at the bottom, seven feet eight inches at the top, and eight feet five inches high. It passes Harlem river upon the "High Bridge, which has been pronounced equal to the most magnificent structures, of a similar kind in ancient Rome. Fourteen piers of solid masonry support arches, upon which rests the bridge, 1,450 feet long, and 114 feet above tide-water. After crossing the river, the aqueduct conveys the water to the receiving reservoir, 836 feet wide, 1,825 feet long, and containing 150,000,000 gallons. The water is separated by a partition of masonry, forming two divisions, which may be alternately full and empty, or both full at the same time. The whole area of the surface of the water is equal to 35 acres. From this basin the water is conveyed through iron pipes to the distributing reservoir, two miles southward, whence it is distributed through iron pipes under ground, enters the houses, and cleanses the streets, administering comfort, beauty, and health, to the city and its denizens. The area of the latter reservoir is equal to four acres; its capacity is 20,000,000 gallons. The water-works can supply 60,000,000 gallons daily; the average quantity is 30,000,000. The cost of the aqueduct and reservoirs was over $12,000,000.

The manufactures of New York, like its commerce, are more extensive than those of any other American city. Ship-building and machinery, are among the branches most largely carried on. Here are built the magnificent ocean steamers, packets, and steamboats, that are the glory of New York.

The principal streets are traversed in various directions by omnibus lines, connecting the important points. Ferries communicate with Hoboken, Jersey city, Staten Island, Brooklyn, Williamsburgh, and Astoria.

The railroads diverging from New York are, the Harlem; Hudson River, to Albany; the New York and New Haven; the Camden and Amboy; the Philadelphia; the New Jersey Central; the Morris and Essex; the Paterson and Ramapo; the Erie; and the Long Island. Not all of these enter the city; many communicate by steamboats from different distances.

The population in 1653. was 1,120; in 1661, 1,743; in 1675. 2,580; in 1696, 4,455; in 1730. 8,256; in 1756, 10,530; in 1774, 22,861; in 1786, 23,688; in 1790, 33,131; in 1800, 60,489; in 1810, 96,373; in 1820,123,706; in 1825, 166,136; in 1830, 202,589; in 1835, 270,089; in 1840, 312,710; in 1845, 371,280; in 1850, 515,507.

NEW YORK, p. o., Sumter co., Ala.

NEW YORK, p. o., Montgomery co., Tenn.

NEW YORK MILLS, p. v., Whitestown township, Oneida co., N. Y., 96 ms. N. w. of Albany; from W. 392. ms. Watered by Sadaquada creek.

NEY, p. o., Defiance co., O.

NEY, p. o., De Kalb co., Ill.

NIAGARA COUNTY, situated at the northwest corner of New York, with Lake Ontario on the north, Niagara river on the west, and Tonawanda creek on the south. Area, 660 square miles. Face of the country, undulating and hilly; soil, productive. Seat of justice, Lockport. Pop. in 1810, 8.971; in 1820, 22,990; in 1830, 18,485; in 1840, 31,132; in 1850, 42,260.

NIAGARA, p. t., Niagara co., N. Y., 298 ms. w. of Albany Situated on Niagara river, and Niagara falls. Pop. 1,951.

NIAGARA FALLS, p. v., Niagara township, Niagara co., N. Y., 297 ms. w. of Albany; from W. 403 ms. Watered by Niagara river at Niagara falls.

NIANGUA, t., Benton co., Mo.

NICCOTTOO, p. o., Arkansas co., Ark.

NICHOLAS COUNTY, situated in the west part of Virginia, with Great Kanawha river on the southwest, and traversed by Gauley river. Area, 1,430 square miles. Face of the country hilly and mountainous. Seat of justice, Summersville. Pop. in 1820, 1,853; in 1830, 3,346; in 1840, 2,515; in 1850, 3,963.

NICHOLAS COUNTY, situated in the northeast part of Kentucky, and traversed by Licking river. Area, 350 square miles. Seat of justice, Carlisle. Pop. in 1810, 4,898; in 1820, 7,973; in 1830, 8,832; in 1840, 8,745; in 1850, 10,361.

NICHOLAS, c. h., p. t., seat of justice of Nicholas co., Va., 310 ms. w. of Richmond; from W. 322 ms.

NICHOLASVILLE, c. h., p. v., seat of justice of Jessa-

mine co., Ky., 36 ms. S. E. of Frankfort; from W. 534 ms. Watered by a tributary of Kentucky river.

NICHOLS, p. t., Tioga co., N. Y., 170 ms. s. w. of Albany; from W. 268 ms. Watered by Susquehanna river. Pop. 1,905.

NICHOLSON, p. t., Wyoming co., Pa., 161 ms. N. E. of Harrisburgh; from W. 268 ms. Pop. 727.

NICHOLSON'S STORE, p. o., Choctaw co., Ala.

NICHOLSONVILLE, p. o., Putnam co., Ind.

NICHOLSVILLE, p. o., Clermont co., O.

NICHOLVILLE, p. v., Hopkinton township, St. Lawrence co., N. Y., 213 ms. N. w. of Albany; from W. — ms., Watered by east branch of St. Regis river.

NICKELSVILLE, p. o., Scott co., Va.

NICKELL'S MILLS, p. o., Monroe co., Va.

NICOLANS. p. o., Sutter co., Cal.

NICONZA, p. o., Miami co., Ind., 108 ms. N. of Indianapolis; from W. 601 ms.

NIGHT'S PRAIRIE, p. o., Hamilton co., Ill.

NILE, p. o., Alleghany co., N. Y.

NILES, p. t., Cayuga co., N. Y., 169 ms. w. of Albany; from W. 339 ms. Watered by Owasco and Skeneateles lakes. Pop. 2,053.

NILES, p. t., Berrien co., Mich., 182 ms. s. w. of Detroit; from W. 627 ms. Watered by St. Joseph's river.

NILES, p. o., Cook co., Ill.

NILES, p. o., Appanoose co., Iowa.

NILES. p. o., Trumbull co., O.

NIMISHILLEN, t., Stark co., O. Watered by Nimishillen creek. Pop. 2,587.

NIMISILLA, p. v., Franklin township, Summit co., O., 121 ms. N. E. of Columbus; from W. 327 ms.

NIMMON'S CROSS-ROADS, p. o., Delaware co., 36 ms. N. of Columbus; from W. 406 ms.

NINE CORNERS, p. o., Cayuga co., N. Y.

NINE EAGLES, p. o., Decatur co., Iowa.

NINE MILE, p. o., Bledsoe co., Tenn.

NINE MILE PRAIRIE, p. t, Callaway co., Mo.

NINE MILE PRAIRIE. p. o., Perry co., Ill., 156 ms. s. of Springfield; from W. 831 ms.

NINE POINTS, p. o., Lancaster co.. Pa.

NINEVAH, p. v., Colesville township, Broome co., N. Y., 116 ms. s. w. of Albany; from W. 310 ms. Watered by Susquehanna river.

NINEVEH, p. o., Warren co., Va., 146 ms. N. w. of Richmond; from W. 77 ms.

NINEVEH, p. t., Bartholomew co., Ind. Pop. 720.

NINEVEH, p. o., Johnson co., Ind., 28 ms. s. of Indianapolis; from W. 587 ms.

NIPPENOSE, p. t., Lycoming co., Pa., 96 ms. N. of Harrisburgh; from W. 206 ms. Watered by Nippenose creek, and north branch of Susquehanna river. Pop. 351.

NISKAYUNA, p. t., Schenectady co., N. Y., 12 ms. N. w. of Albany; from W. — ms. Watered by Mohawk river. Pop. 783.

NITTANY, p. o., Centre co., Pa., 93 ms. N. w. of Harrisburgh; from W. 185 ms.

NIVERVILLE, p. o., Columbia co., N. Y.

NIXBURGH, p. v., Coosa co., Ala.; from W. 812 ms.

NOAH, p. o., Shelby co., Ind., 31 ms. s. E. of Indianapolis; from W. 559 ms.

NOANK, p. o., New London co., Ct., 52 ms. s. E. of Hartford; from W. 361 ms.

NOBLE COUNTY, situated in the northeast part of Indiana. Area, 432 square miles. Seats of justice Noble and Albion. Pop. in 1840, 2,702; in 1850, 7,946.

NOBLE COUNTY, situated in the southeastern corner of Ohio. Watered by branches of Will's creek, and Muskingum and Ohio rivers. Area, 450 square miles. Face of the country hilly; Soil moderately good. Seat of justice, Sarahsville. Organized since 1850.

NOBLE, c. h., p. v., seat of justice of Noble co., Ind., 159 ms. N. E. of Indianapolis; from W. 578 ms. Watered by Elkhart river. Pop. 595.

NOBLE, t., Cass co., Ind. Pop. 743.

NOBLE, t., Wabash co., Ind. Pop. 3,489.

NOBLE, t., Noble co., O. Pop. 1,702.

NOBLE, t., Defiance co., O. Pop. 389.

NOBLE CENTRE, p. o., Branch co., Mich.

NOBLE IRON WORKS, p. o., Noble co., Ind.

NOBLESBURGH, p. t., Lincoln co., Me., 32 ms. s. E. of Augusta; from W. 600 ms. Watered by Damariscotta pond and river. Pop.

NOBLETOWN, p. v., Fayette township, Allegheny co., Pa., 214 ms. w. of Harrisburgh; from W. 238 ms. Watered by a tributary of Chartier's creek.

NOBLESVILLE, c. h., p. v., seat of justice of Hamilton co., Ind.. 20 ms. N. E. of Indianapolis ; from W. 574 ms. Watered by west fork of White river. Pop. 1,643.

NOBLEVILLE, p. o,, Noble co., O.

NOCHWAY, p. o., Randolph co., Ga.

NOCKAMIXON, t., Bucks co., Pa. Watered by Delaware river and Gallows run. Pop. 2,445.

NODAWAY COUNTY, situated on the north boundary of Missouri. Area, —— square miles. Seat of justice, Marysville. Pop. in 1850, 2,118.

NODAWAY, p. o., Page co., Iowa.

NODAWAY, p. t., Andrews co., Mo. Pop. 2,667.

NOLAND'S FERRY, p. o., Loudoun co.. Va., 161 ms. N. of Richmond ; from W. 42 ms. Watered by Monocacy river.

NOLANSVILLE, p. o., Bell co., Tex.

NOLENSVILLE, p. v., Williamson co., Tenn., 17 ms. s. of Nashville ; from W. 693 ms.

NOLIN, p. o., Hardin co., Ky.

NOMING GROVE, p. o., Westmoreland co., Va.

NONCONNER, p. o., Fayette co., Tenn.

NONPARIEL, p. o., Knox co., O.

NORFOLK COUNTY, situated in the southeasterly part of Massachusetts, with Massachusetts bay on the east. Area, 400 square miles. Face of the country uneven ; soil productive. Seat of justice, Dedham. Pop. in 1810, 31,245 ; in 1820, 36,452 ; in 1830, 41,993 ; in 1840, 53,140 ; in 1850, 57,983.

NORFOLK COUNTY, situated on the south boundary of Virginia. Area, 544 square miles. Face of the country, flat and marshy, being princiipally covered with the Dismal swamp ; soil sterile. Seat of justice, Norfolk. Pop. in 1810, 13,679 ; in 1820, 15,465 ; in 1830, 14,998 ; in 1840, 27,569 ; in 1850, 25,115.

NORFOLK, p. t., Litchfield, co., Ct., 36 ms. N. w. of Hartford ; from W. 344 ms. Watered by Blackberry river, Pop. 1,643.

NORFOLK, p. t., St. Lawrence co., 234 ms. N. w. of Albany ; from W. 513 ms. Watered by Racket river and tributaries. Pop. 1,753.

NORFOLK, city, seat of justice of Norfolk co., Va. Situated on Elizabeth river, opposite Portsmouth, 32 miles from its entrance through Hampton Roads into the ocean, 106 miles southeast of Richmond, and 230 miles from Washington. This town is more remarkable for its deep and spacious harbor, than for its appearance. The ground is low and marshy, the Great Dismal swamp covering a large portion of Norfolk county. The streets are generally irregular, and the houses not splendid, though some of the principal avenues are wide, straight, and neat. Hampton Roads are the basin formed by James and Elizabeth rivers before passing into the Atlantic. The entrance to these from the ocean, is defended by strong fortifications. At Gosport, near Portsmouth, on the west side of Elizabeth river, is a navy-yard, with a dry-dock built of hewn granite.

The Seaboard and Roanoke railroad connects Portsmouth with Weldon, on the route of the Washington and Wilmington line.

The commerce of Norfolk exceeds that of any other place in Virginia, and several hundred thousand dollars are invested in manufactures.

The population in 1810, was 9,193 ; in 1820, 8,478 ; in 1830, 9,816 ; in 1840, 10,920 ; in 1850, 14,326.

NORFOLK. p. o., Mississippi co., Mo.

NORRIDGEWOCK. c. h., p. t., seat of justice of Somerset co., Me., 32 ms. N. of Augusta ; from W. 627 ms. Watered by Kennebec river. Pop. 1,848.

NORRIS CREEK, p. o., Lincoln co., Tenn.

NORRISTOWN, c. h., p. b., seat of justice of Montgomery co., Pa., 91 ms. E. of Harrisburgh ; from W. 154 ms. Watered by Schuylkill river. Pop. 6,024.

NORRISTOWN, p. v., Carroll co., O., 130 ms. N. E. of Columbus ; from W. 299 ms.

NORRISTOWN, c. h., p. v., seat of justice of Pope co., Ark., 71 ms. N. w. of Little Rock ; from W. 1,136 ms.

NORRITONVILLE, p. v., Montgomery co., Pa., 93 ms. E. of Harrisburgh ; from W. 158 ms.

NORRITON. t., Montgomery co., Pa. Watered by Schuylkill river and tributaries. Pop. 1,594.

NORTH ACTON, p. o., York co., Me.

NORTH, p. t., Harrison co., O. Pop. 1,123.

NORTH ADAMS, p. v., Adams township, Berkshire co., Mass., 126 ms. N. w. of Boston ; from W. 398 ms.

NORTH ADAMS, p. o., Adams township, Jefferson co.. N. Y 169 ms. N. w. of Albany from W. 410 ms.

NORTH ADAMS, p. o., Hillsdale co., Mich.

NORTH ADRIAN, p. o., Adrian township, Lenawee co., Mich.

NORTH ALBANY, p. o., Albany township, Oxford co.. Me.

NORTH ALMOND, p. o., Almond township, Alleghany co.. N. Y., 250 ms. w. of Albany ; from W. 335 ms.

NORTH AMHERST, p. v., Amherst township, Hampshire co., Mass., 88 ms. w. of Boston ; from W. 389 ms.

NORTHAMPTON COUNTY, situated on the easterly boundary of Pennsylvania, with Delaware river on the east, and traversed by Lehigh river. Area, 600 square miles. Face of the country hilly ; soil productive. Seat of justice, Easton. Pop. in 1810, 38,145 ; in 1820, 31,765 ; in 1830, 39,267 ; in 1840, 40,996 ; in 1850, 40,235.

NORTHAMPTON COUNTY, situated on the east shore of Virginia, with the Atlantic ocean on the east, and Chesapeake bay on the west. Area, 320 square miles. Face of the country level ; soil sandy. Seat of justice, Eastville. Pop. in 1810, 7,474 ; in 1820, 7,705 ; in 1830, 8,644 ; in 1840, 7,715 ; in 1850, 7,498.

NORTHAMPTON COUNTY, situated on the north boundary of North Carolina, with Roanoke river on the southwest. Area, 546 square miles. Face of the country even ; soil good. Seat of justice, Jackson. Pop. in 1810, 13,087 ; in 1820, 13,242 ; in 1830, 13,103 ; in 1840, 13,369 ; in 1850, 13,335.

NORTHAMPTON. c. h., p. t., seat of justice of Hampshire co., Mass., 93 ms. w. of Boston ; from W. 280 ms. Watered by Connecticut river. Pop. in 1810, 2,631 ; in 1820, 2,854 ; in 1830, 3,613 ; in 1840, 3,750 ; in 1850, 5,278.

NORTHAMPTON, p. t., Fulton co., N. Y., 47 ms. N. w. of Albany ; from W. 415 ms. Watered by Sacandaga river and tributaries. Pop. 1,701.

NORTHAMPTON, t., Burlington co., N. J. Watered by Rancocus creek, and tributaries of Little Egg Harbor river. Pop. 3,035.

NORTHAMPTON, t., Bucks co., Pa. Watered by tributaries of Neshaming creek. Pop. 1,843.

NORTHAMPTON, t., Lehigh co., Pa. Pop. 332.

NORTHAMPTON, p. t., Summit co., O. Pop. 1,147.

NORTHAMPTON, t., Peoria co., Ill.

NORTHAMPTON, p. o., Saganaw co., Mich.

NORTH ANDOVER, v., Andover township, Oxford co., Me

NORTH ANDOVER, p. v., Andover township, Essex co., Mass., 23 ms. N. of Boston ; from W. 456 ms.

NORTH AND SOUTH AKRON, p. t., Summit co., O.

NORTH ANSEN, p. o., Somerset co., Me.

NORTH APPLETON, p. o., Waldo co., Me.

NORTH ARGYLE, p. o., Argyle township, Washington co., N. Y., 50 ms. N. of Albany ; from W. 420 ms.

NORTH ASHFORD, p. v., Ashford township, Windham co.. Ct., 35 ms. N. E. of Hartford ; from W. 371 ms.

NORTH ATTLEBOROUGH, p. v., Attleborough township, Bristol co., Mass., 38 ms. s. of Boston ; from W. 412 ms.

NORTH AUBURN, p. o., Cumberland co., Me.

NORTH BANGOR, p. v., Bangor township, Penobscot co., Me., 71 ms. N. E. of Augusta ; from W. 667 ms.

NORTH BANGOR, p. o., Franklin co., N. Y.

NORTH BARNSTEAD, p. o., Barnstead township, Belknap co., N. H.

NORTH BAG, p. o., Oneida co., N. Y.

NORTH BEAVER, t., Beaver co., Pa. Watered by Hickory creek.

NORTH BECKET, p. v., Becket township, Berkshire co., Mass., 128 ms. w. of Boston ; from W. 392 ms.

NORTH BELGRADE, p. o., Belgrade township, Kennebec co., Me., 17 ms. N. E. of Augusta ; from W. 613 ms.

NORTH BELLINGHAM, p. o., Norfolk co., Mass.

NORTH BELMONT, p. o., Belmont township, Waldo co.. Me., 35 ms. E. of Augusta ; from W. 631 ms.

NORTH BEND, p. o., Piatt co., Ill., 78 ms. E. of Springfield ; from W. 705 ms.

NORTH BEND, p. o., De Kalb co., Ala.

NORTH BEND, p. o., Stark co., Ind.

NORTH BENNINGTON, p. o., Bennington township, Bennington co., Vt., 121 ms. s. w. of Montpelier ; from W. 411 ms.

NORTH BENTON, p. o., Mahoning co., O., 147 ms. N. E. of Columbus ; from W. 300 ms.

NORTH BERGEN, p. o., Bergen township, Genesee co.. N. Y., 240 ms. w. of Albany ; from W. 381 ms.

NORTH BERNARDSTON, p. o., Franklin co., Mass.

North Berwick, p. t., York co. Me., 89 ms. s. w. of Augusta; from W. 506 ms. Pop. 1,593.

North Bethel, p. o., Oxford co., Me., 55 ms. w. of Augusta; from W. 611 ms.

North Blackstone, p. o., Worcester co., Mass.

North Blanford, p. o., Blanford township, Hampden co., Mass., 114 ms. w. of Boston; from W. 374 ms.

North Blenheim, p. o., Blenheim township, Schoharie co., N. Y., 47 ms. w. of Albany; from W. 375 ms.

North Bloomfield, p. v., West Bloomfield township, Ontario co,, N. Y., 212 ms. w. of Albany; from W. 358 ms. Watered by Honeoye creek.

North Bloomfield, p. o., Bloomfield township, Trumbull co., O., 178 ms. N. E., of Columbus; from W. 319 ms.

North Blue Hill, p. o., Blue Hill township, Hancock co., Me., 69 ms. E. of Augusta; from W. 666 ms.

North Boothbay, p. v., Boothbay township, Lincoln co., Me., 35 ms. s. E. of Augusta; from W. 596 ms.

Northborough, p. t., Worcester co., Mass., 33 ms. w. of Boston; from W. 408 ms. Watered by Assabet river. Pop. 1,535.

North Boston, p. o., Boston township, Erie co., N. Y., 303 ms. w. of Albany; from W. 366 ms.

North Branch, p. o., Hillsborough co., N. H., 26 ms. s. of Concord; from W. 456 ms.

North Branch, p. o., Somerset co., N. J., 35 ms. N. of Trenton; from W. 206 ms.

North Branch, p. o., Baltimore co., Md.

North Branch, p. o., Sullivan co., N. Y.

North Branford, p. t., New Haven co., Ct. Pop. 998.

Northbridge, p. t., Worcester co., Mass., 39 ms. s. w. of Boston; from W. 406 ms. Watered by Blackstone and Mumford rivers. Pop. 2,230.

Northbridge Centre, p. o., Worcester co., Mass.

North Bridgeton, p. o., Bridgeton township, Cumberland co., Me., 60 ms. s. w. of Augusta; from W. 581 ms.

North Bridgewater, p. t., Plymouth co., Mass., 22 ms. s. of Boston; from W. 438 ms. Pop. 3,939.

North Brighton, p. o., Livingston co., Mich.

North Broadalbin, p. o. Fulton co., N. Y.

North Brookfield, p. t., Worcester co., Mass., 60 ms. w. of Boston; from W. 392 ms. Pop. 1,939.

North Brookfield, p. o., Brookfield township, Madison co. N. Y., 84 ms. w. of Albany; from W. 366 ms.

North Brownsville, p. o., Piscataquis co., Me.

North Brunswick, t., Middlesex co., N. J. Watered by Raritan and South rivers. Pop. 10,008.

North Bucksport, p. v., Bucksport township, Hancock co., Me., 62 ms. N. E. of Augusta; from W. 658 ms.

North Cambridge, p. o., Lamoille co., Vt.

North Cambridge, p. o., Washington co., N. Y.

North Camden, p. o., Lorain co., O., 111 ms. N. E. of Columbus; from W. 380 ms.

North Cameron, p. o., Steuben co., N. Y.

North Cannon, p. o., Kent co., Mich.

North Canton, p. v., Canton township, Hartford co.. Ct., 19 ms. N. w. of Hartford; from W. 355 ms.

NORTH CAROLINA, one of the United States, situated between 33° 53' and 36° 33' north latitude, and 75°, 45' and 84° west longitude from Greenwich, and is bounded north by Virginia, east and southeast by the Atlantic, south by South Carolina and Georgia, and west and northwest by Tennessee. Superficial area 43,800 sq. miles.

Physical Aspect.—This state, like South Carolina and Georgia, presents a variety of surface, soil, and climate. It may be physically divided into three zones; first, the flat sea border, including numerous small islands; second, the sand hill zone, spreading by an indefinite outline between the sea border, and the third, a hilly and partly mountainous tract, beyond the lower falls of the rivers. The maritime section, which extends from 80 to 100 miles inland, is nearly a dead level, varied only by deeply-indented, though shallow sounds, and occasional openings, in the immense forests of pine, with which it is covered, and extensive glades, marshes,

or swamps. In the northeastern part, extending into Virginia, lies the Great Dismal swamp, thirty miles long, and ten broad, thickly wooded with pine, juniper, cypress, and in the drier portions with red and white oak. Between Albemarle and Pamlico sounds is the Alligator, or Little Dismal swamp, which contains a lake. Here the soil is generally sandy and poor, though on the banks of some of the streams, particularly those of the Roanoke, it is remarkably fertile. In other instances, there are ridges of oak land, of a dark-colored and fruitful soil. After traversing this tedious plain, we are relieved by the appearance of the sand-hills, in the middle section, which, in general, presents an indifferent soil. But the third, the hilly and mountainous section, abounds in excellent soil, pure fountain water, and salubrious air. Those portions of the state lying west of the mountains are also exuberantly fertile, and will richly reward the planter's toil.

Mountains.—The Blue ridge constitutes the main range through the western part of the state; but on most maps is made to represent the outer chain of the Appalachian system, as in the contiguous states. Strictly speaking, there are two other chains, between the Blue ridge and the ocean. Black mountain, in Yancey county, is the highest land in the United States, east of the Rocky mountains, being 6,476 feet above the level of the sea. Roan mountain is 6,038 feet high, and Great Father mountain 5,556 feet. The chain in the extreme western part of the state, in which Roan mountain is situated, is known by different names, as Smoky, Unica, Bald, Yellow Iron, and Stone mountains.

Rivers, Lakes, Bays, and Sounds.—The principal rivers are, the Chowan, Roanoke, Tar, Neuse, Cape Fear, Waccamaw, Lumber, Catawba, Broad, Yadkin, North, Pungo, Hiwassee, Pamlico, and the Little Tennessee. Lake Phelps, Alligator, Mattimuskeet, and Waccamaw, are situated in this state. The principal sounds and bays are, Pamlico and Albemarle sounds, and Onslow and Raleigh bays.

Islands and Capes.—The chief islands are, Roanoke, Smith's, Brodie's, Currituck, Hatteras, and Cove. Capes Lookout and Fear are much dreaded by mariners; and Hatteras is considered the most dangerous headland on the American coast.

Climate.—Like most of the other southern states, North Carolina is somewhat varied in its climate, occasioned by physical peculiarities of its different parts. In the lower districts, intermittents are frequent during the summer and autumn, and the countenances of the inhabitants often have a pale yellowish hue, occasioned by the prevalence of bilious disease. In winter, pleurisies are frequent, as well as inflammation of the lungs. In the western and hilly parts of the state the air is elastic, salubrious and pure, which renders the country as healthy as any part of the United States. The summers are hot, though the evenings are refreshing and cool. Autumn is temperate and serene; and in some years the winters are so mild, that autumn may be said to continue till spring. The winters in the mountains, however, are visited by frost and snow, and the rigors of the climate are nearly as severe as at the north.

Productive Resources.—The great staples of the south, tobacco, cotton, and rice, are extensively cultivated. Other products are, silk, wool, lumber, turpentine, spirits of turpentine, resin, pitch, tar, hay, hemp, flax, wine, sugar, wheat, rye, barley, oats, buckwheat, potatoes, and Indian corn; also, horses, mules, neat cattle, swine, and poultry. Of the mineral resources, gold, coal, and iron, are the most important. The gold region lies on both sides of the Blue ridge, and extends to the eastward of the river Yadkin. It occurs in fine grains, in small masses, or lumps, weighing from one to two pounds, and in veins.

Manufactures.—North Carolina being an agricultural state, but little attention has been paid to manufactures. There are, however, about thirty cotton factories in the state, which consume about 5,000,000 pounds of cotton annually. There are also a few woollen factories. Other manufactures are, paper, leather, furniture, cutlery, carriages, &c., though none of them are carried on to any great extent.

Railroads and Canals.—There are some 600 miles of railroads in operation and under construction, in North Carolina. The principal roads completed at present are, the Raleigh and Gaston, 87 miles, and the Wilmington and Weldon, 167 miles, which connect the towns indicated by their titles. The only canals wholly within the state are, the Weldon, extending around the

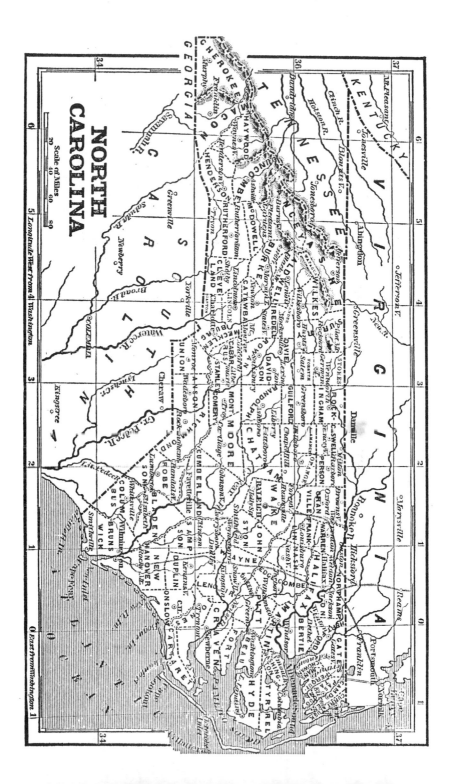

falls of the Roanoke, 12 miles, and a short one connecting Harlow and Clubfoot creeks.

Population.—In 1790, 393.751; in 1800, 478,103; in 1810, 555.500; in 1820, 638,829; in 1830, 737,987; in 1840, 753,419; in 1850, 868,903.

Number of slaves in 1790, 100.572; in 1800, 133,296; in 1810. 168,824; in 1820, 295,017; in 1830, 235,601; in 1840, 245,817; in 1850, 288,412.

Commerce.—North Carolina has but a limited foreign commerce, its imports and exports being less than a million annually. Its coasting trade, however, is considerable. The shipping owned within the state is about 50,000 tons.

Education.—The literary institutions are, a university at Chapel Hill, Davidson college, in Mecklenburgh county, and Wake Forest college. There are about 200 academies, and 1.500 common schools in the state.

History.—North Carolina embraces a portion of the ancient territory of Florida, as named by Ponce de Leon, in 1512, and was, more recently, a portion of South Virginia, as granted by James I. of England, in 1606. It was within the limits of this state that Sir Walter Raleigh's unsuccessful attempts at settlement were made, in 1584 to 1590. In about the year 1630, another grant was made to Sir Robert Heath, of the tract lying between the thirtieth and thirty-sixth degrees of north latitude, which was erected into a province, under the name of "Carolina." No settlements were made under this grant, however, and consequently it was declared void. The first permanent settlement in the region now called North Carolina was made on the east bank of the river Chowan, near the present village of Edenton, in about the year 1650, by a company of emigrants from Virginia, who fled from religious persecution. In 1661, a small English colony, from Massachusetts, purchased a tract of land, on Cape Fear river, from the Indians, and formed a settlement on Old Town creek, a few miles below Wilmington; but the enterprise was abandoned from the hostility of the Indians. Two years later the province was granted, by Charles II., to Lord Clarendon and seven others, and a government was established over the infant settlement on the Chowan, which was called the "Albemarle County Colony," in compliment to one of the proprietors, the duke of Albemarle. In 1665, their grant was enlarged, embracing the territory between 31° and 36½° north latitude, extending westward to the South sea. In 1667, a new settlement was established on Cape Fear river, near the abandoned site of the New England colony, called "Clarendon county," which was again surrendered to the Indians before the year 1690. In 1707, a company of French protestants, who had previously settled in Virginia, removed to Carolina, and two years later were followed by 100 German protestant families, who were driven from their homes by religious persecution. In 1729, the crown of England purchased the whole of Carolina, which had hitherto been under the superintendence of the same board, for £17,500; and the king divided it into two provinces, "North" and "South," which have ever since been continued separate. A convention, or a kind of Congress, composed of military officers, assembled at Charlotte, in the county of Mecklenburgh, in 1775, and declared the people independent of British rule. In 1776, this state formed a constitution, which, with subsequent modifications, continues to the present time. In 1789, it ratified the constitution of the United States, and was admitted into the Union as an independent state.

Government.—The legislative power is vested in a senate of 50, and a house of commons of 120 members, both elected biennially, on the first Thursday in August, by the people. The executive power is vested in a governor, elected biennially by the people, who is not eligible for more than two terms in succession. The judicial power is vested in a supreme court, of three judges, and a superior, or circuit court, of seven judges, besides inferior courts. The judges of the supreme and superior courts are elected by the legislature, and hold office during good behavior. All free white males, of 21 years of age, who have resided in the state one year, are entitled to vote for governor, and members of the lower house; to qualify to vote for senators, a freehold of fifty acres, of six months' possession, is also required.

NORTH CARVER, p. o., Plymouth co., Mass.

NORTH CASTINE, p. o., Castine township, Hancock co., Me. 72 ms. E. of Augusta; from W. 668 ms.

NORTH CASTLE, p. t., Westchester co., N. Y., 132 ms.

s. of A.bany; from W. 263 ms. Watered by Byram river. Pop. 1,800.

NORTH CHARLESTOWN, p. v., Charlestown township, Sullivan co., N. H., 54 ms. w. of Concord; from W. 459 ms.

NORTH CHATHAM, p. v., Chatham township, Columbia co., N. Y., 15 ms. s. of Albany; from W. 363 ms.

NORTH CHATHAM, p. o., Clinton co., Pa.

NORTH CHATHAM, p. v., Chatham township, Barnstable co., Mass., 98 ms. s. E. of Boston; from W. 499 ms

NORTH CHELMSFORD, p. o., Chelmsford township, Middlesex co., Mass., 25 ms. N. w. of Boston.

NORTH CHELSEA, p. o., Suffolk co., Mass.

NORTH CHEMUNG, p. o., Chemung co., N. Y.

NORTH CHENANGO, t., Crawford co., Pa. Pop. 825.

NORTH CHESTER, p. o., Chester township, Hampden co., Mass.

NORTH CHESTER, p. o., Windsor co., Vt.

NORTH CHESTERFIELD, p. o., Franklin co., Me.

NORTH CHICHESTER, p. v., Chichester township, Merrimack co., N. H., 11 ms. E. of Concord; from W. 492 ms.

NORTH CHILI, p. o., Chili township, Monroe co., N. Y., 230 ms. w. of Albany; from W. 377 ms.

NORTH CLARENCE, p. o., Clarence township, Kennebec co., Me., 28 ms. N. of Augusta; from 623 ms.

NORTH CLARENDON, p. o., Rutland co., Vt.

NORTH CLARKSON, p. o., Monroe co., N. Y.

NORTH CLYMER, p. o., Clymer township, Chautauque co., N. Y., 356 ms. w. of Albany; from W. 377 ms.

NORTH CODORUS, t., York co., Pa. Pop. 2,126.

NORTH COHASSETT, p. o., Norfolk co., Mass.

NORTH CONHOCTON, p. o., Conhocton township, Steuben co., N. Y., 225 ms. w. of Albany; from W. —— ms.

NORTH COLEBROOK, p. o., Litchfield co., Ct.

NORTH COVE, p. o., McDowell co., N. C., 219 ms. w. of Raleigh; from W. 449 ms.

NORTH CREEK, p. o., Beaufort co., N. C.

NORTH CREEK, p. o., Laurens district, S. C.

NORTH CREEK, p. o., Philips co., Ark.

NORTH DANVERS, p. v., Danvers township, Essex co., Mass., 20 ms. N. E. of Boston; from W. 461 ms.

NORTH DANVILLE, p. o., Caledonia co., Vt., 34 ms. N. E. of Montpelier; from W. 547 ms.

NORTH DARTMOUTH, p. v., Dartmouth township, Bristol co., Mass., 61 ms. s. of Boston; from W. 430 ms.

NORTH DIGHTON, p. o., Bristol co., Mass., 37 ms. s. of Boston; from W. 424 ms.

NORTH DIXMONT, p. o., Dixmont township, Penobscot co., Me., 44 ms. N. E. of Augusta; from W. 639 ms.

NORTH DORSET, p. o., Dorset township, Bennington co., Vt., 84 ms. s. w. of Montpelier; from W. 439 ms.

NORTH DOVER, p. o., Dover township, Cuyahoga co., O., 129 ms. N. E. of Columbus; from W. 371 ms.

NORTH DUANESBURGH, p. o., Schenectady co., N. Y.

NORTH DUNBARTON, p. v., Dunbarton township, Merrimack co., N. H., 7 ms. s. of Concord; from W. 477 ms.

NORTH EAST, p. t., Dutchess co., N. Y., 53 ms. s. E. of Albany; from W. 332 ms. Watered by Ten-Mile creek and tributaries. Pop. 1,555.

NORTH EAST, p. t., Erie co., Pa., 281 ms. N. w. of Harrisburgh; from W. 358 ms. Watered by Sixteen and Twenty-Mile creeks, and Lake Erie. Pop. 2,379.

NORTH EAST, p. v., Cecil co., Md., 74 ms. N. E. of Annapolis; from W. 84 ms. Pop. 340.

NORTH EAST, p. t., Orange co., Ind.

NORTH EAST CENTRE, p. o., North East township, Dutchess co., N. Y., 56 ms. s. E. of Albany, from W. 329 ms.

NORTH EASTHAM, p. o., Barnstable co., Mass.

NORTH EASTON, p. o., Easton township, Bristol co., Mass.

NORTH EASTON, p. o., Easton township, Washington co., N. Y., 30 ms. N. E. of Albany; from W. 400 ms.

NORTH EAST PASS, or Balize, v., Plaquemine parish, La. Watered by North East Pass of Mississippi river, 100 ms. below New Orleans.

NORTH EATON, p. o., Eaton township, Lorain co., O., 121 ms. N. E. of Columbus; from W. 379 ms.

NORTH EDGECOMB, Edgecomb township, Lincoln co., Me., 121 ms. N. E. of Columbus; from W. 590 ms.

NORTH EGREMONT, p. v., Egremont township, Berkshire co., Mass., 142 ms. w. of Boston; from W. 358 ms.

NORTH ELBA, p. o., Essex co., N. Y.

NORTH ELIZABETHAN, p. o., Hendricks co., Ind.

NORTH ELLSWORTH, p. o., Ellsworth township, Hancock co., Me., 85 ms. E. of Augusta ; from W. 680 ms.

NORTH END, p. o., Matthews co., Va., 93 ms. E. of Richmond ; from W. 178 ms.

NORTH ENFIELD, p. o., Enfield township, Grafton co., N. H., 47 ms. N. of Concord ; from W. 490 ms.

NORTHERN LIBERTIES, Philadelphia co., Pa., a suburban district of Philadelphia, having an independent corporation. Pop. in 1840 ———— ; in 1850, 47,223.

NORTH EVANS, p. o., Erie co., N. Y.

NORTH FAIRFAX, p. o., Fairfax township, Franklin co., Vt., 64 ms. N. w. of Montpelier ; from W. 542 ms.

NORTH FAIRFIELD, p. o., Fairfield township. Somerset co., Me., 28 ms. N. of Augusta; from W. 623 ms.

NORTH FAIRFIELD, p. o., Huron co., O., 92 ms. N. of Columbus ; from W. 395 ms.

NORTH FAIRHAVEN, p. v., Fairhaven township, Bristol co., Mass., 55 ms. s. of Boston ; from W. 438 ms.

NORTH FALMOUTH, p. v., Falmouth township. Barnstable co., Mass., 67 ms. s. E. of Boston ; from W. 468 ms.

NORTH FARMINGTON, p. o., Oakland co., Miss.

NORTH FAYETTE, p. o., Kennebec co., Me.

NORTH FERRISBURGH, p. o., Ferrisburgh township, Addison co., Vt., 60 ms. w. of Montpelier ; from W. 495 ms.

NORTHFIELD, p. t., Washington co., Me., 159 ms. N. E. of Augusta ; from W. 741 ms. Pop. 246.

NORTHFIELD, t., Merrimack co., N. H., 15 ms. N. of Concord ; from W. 406 ms. Watered by Winnipisogee river. Pop. 1,332.

NORTHFIELD, p. t., Franklin co., Mass., 92 ms. N. w. of Boston ; from W. 412 ms. Watered by Connecticut river. Pop. 1,772.

NORTHFIELD, p. v., Litchfield township, Litchfield co., Ct., 28 ms. w. of Hartford ; from W. 334 ms.

NORTHFIELD, p. t., Washington co., Vt., 10 ms. s. of Montpelier ; from W. 506 ms. Watered by Dog river. Pop. 2,922.

NORTHFIELD, t., Richmond co., Staten Island, N. Y., 156 ms. s. of Albany ; from W. ———— ms. Watered by Staten Island sound. Pop 4,020.

NORTHFIELD, p. t., Summit co., O., 143 ms. N. E. of Columbus ; from W. 342 ms. Watered by Cuyahoga river and Ohio canal. Pop. 1,147.

NORTHFIELD, p. t., Washtenaw co., Mich., 43 ms. w. of Detroit ; from W, 536 ms. Pop 1 116

NORTHFIELD, p. o , Boone co., Ind., 20 ms. N. w. of Indianapolis ; from W. 580 ms.

NORTHFIELD, p. o., Cook co., Ill.

NORTH FLAT, p. o., Wyoming co., Pa.

NORTHFORD, p. v., North Brantford township, New Haven co., Ct., 28 ms. s. of Hartford ; from W. 312 ms.

NORTH FORK, p. t., Izard co., Ark. Pop. 378.

NORTH FORK, p. o., Ashe co., N. C., 214 ms. w. of Raleigh ; from W. 378 ms.

NORTH FORK, p. o., Mason co., Ky., 83 ms. N. E. of Frankfort ; from W. 471 ms.

NORTH FORK. p. o. Vermilion co., Ill., 146 ms. E. of Springfield ; from W. 673 ms.

NORTH FORK, t., Newton co., Mo.

NORTH FORK, p. o., Washington co., Va.

NORTH FRANKFORT, p. o., Frankfort township, Waldo co., Me., 66 ms. N. E. of Augusta ; from W. 660 ms.

NORTH FRANKLIN, p. o., Franklin township, Delaware co., N. Y., 79 ms. s. w. of Albany ; from W. 349 ms.

NORTH FRANKLIN, p. o., New London co., Ct.

NORTH FRYEBURGH, p. o., Fryeburgh township, Oxford co., Me., 71 ms. s. w. of Augusta ; from W. 578 ms.

NORTH GAGE, p. o., Deerfield township, Oneida co., N. Y., 92 ms. N. w. of Albany ; from W. 412 ms.

NORTH GALWAY, p. o., Galway township, Saratoga co., N. Y., 39 ms. N. of Albany ; from W. 407 ms.

NORTH GARDEN, p. o., Albermarle co., Va., 89 ms. N. w. of Richmond ; from W. 139 ms.

NORTH GEORGETOWN, p. v., Knox township, Columbiana co., O., 146 ms. N. E. of Columbus ; from W. 298 ms.

NORTH GOSHEN, p. v., Goshen township. Litchfield co., Ct., 34 ms. w. of Hartford ; from W. 336 ms. Watered by a branch of Naugatuck river.

NORTH GRANBY, p. v., Granby township, Hartford co., Ct., 20 ms. N. of Hartford ; from W. 356 ms.

NORTH GRANVILLE, p. v., Greenville township, Washington co., N. Y., 66 ms. N. E. of Albany ; from W. 436 ms.

NORTH GREECE, p. o., Monroe co. N. Y.

NORTH GREENWICH, p. o., Fairfield co., Ct.

NORTH GREENWICH, p. o., Greenwich township, Washington co., N. Y., 40 ms. N. E. of Albany ; from W. 410 ms.

NORTH GROTON, p. o., Grafton co., N. H.

NORTH GUILFORD, p. v., Guilford township, New Haven co., Ct., 28 ms. s. of Hartford ; from W. 320 ms.

NORTH GUILFORD, p. o., Chenango co,, N. Y.

NORTH HADLEY, p. v., Hadley township. Hampshire co., Mass., 94 ms. w. of Boston : from W. 387 ms.

NORTH HAMDEN, p. o., Hamden township, Delaware co., N. Y.

NORTH HAMPDEN, p. o., Penobscot co., Me.

NORTH HAMPTON, p. t., Rockingham co., N. H., 50 ms. s. E. of Concord ; from W. 487 ms. Watered by the Atlantic ocean on the east. Pop. 822

NORTH HAMPTON, p. o., Clarke co., O., 52 ms. w. of Columbus ; from W. 445 ms.

NORTH HAMPTON, p. o., Peoria co., Ill., 90 ms. N. of Springfield : from W. 804 ms.

NORTH HANCOCK, p. o., Hancock co., Me.

NORTH HARPERSFIELD, p. o., Harpersfield township, Delaware co., N. Y., 61 ms. s. w. of Albany ; from W. 370 ms.

NORTH HARTLAND, p. o., Hartland township, Windsor co., Vt., 57 ms. s. of Montpelier ; from W. 482 ms.

NORTH HAVEN, p. o., Hancock co., Me.

NORTH HAVEN, p. t., New Haven co. Ct., 30 ms. s. w. of Hartford ; from W. 306 ms. Watered by Quinnipiac river. Pop. 1,325.

NORTH HAVERHILL, p. v., Haverhill township, Grafton co., N. H., 74 ms. N. w. of Concord ; from W. 519 ms.

NORTH HAVERSTRAW, p. o., Rockland co., N. Y.

NORTH HEBRON, p. o., Hebron township, Washington co., N. Y., 60 ms. N. E. of Albany ; from W. 430 ms.

NORTH HECTOR, p. o., Hector township, Tompkins co., N. Y., 184 ms. w. of Albany ; from W. 314 ms.

NORTH HEMPSTEAD, c. h., p. t., seat of justice of Queens co., Long Island, N. Y., 168 ms. s. of Albany ; from W. 248 ms. Watered by Long Island sound and Success pond. Pop. 4,291.

NORTH HENDERSON, p. o., Mercer co., Ill

NORTH HERMON, p. o., Penobscot co., Me.

NORTH HERO, c. h., p. t., seat of justice of Grand Isle co., Vt., 71 ms. N. w. of Montpelier ; from W. 544 ms. Watered by Lake Champlain. Pop. 730.

NORTH HOGAN, p. o., Ripley co., Ind.

NORTH HOLLIS, p. o., Hollis township, York co., Me., 67 ms. s. w. of Augusta ; from W. 533 ms.

NORTH HOOSICK, p. o., Rensselaer co., N. Y.

NORTH HOPE, p. o , Butler co., Pa.

NORTH HUDSON, p. o , Essex co., N. Y.

NORTH HUNDINGDON, t., Westmoreland co., Pa. Pop. 2,570.

NORTH HYDEPARK, p. o., Hydepark township, Lamoille co., Vt., 41 ms. N. of Montpelier ; from W. 555 ms.

NORTH INDUSTRY, p. o., Lawrence co., Pa.

NORTH INDUSTRY, p. v., Canton township, Stark co., O., 128 ms. N. E. of Columbus ; from W. 317 ms.

NORTH INDUSTRY, p. o., Franklin co., Me.

NORTHINGTON, p. v., Cumberland co., N. C., 51 ms s. of Raleigh ; from W. 339 ms.

NORTH JACKSON, p. o., Mahoning co., O., 160 ms. N E. of Columbus ; from W. 311 ms.

NORTH JANESVILLE, p. o., Rock co., Wis.

NORTH JAVA, p. o., Wyoming co., N. Y.

NORTH JAY, p. o., Franklin co., Me.

NORTH KENNEBUNK PORT, p. o., York co., Me., 69 ms. s. w. of Augusta ; from W. 528 ms.

NORTH KILLINGLY, p. v., Killingly township, Windham co., Ct., 51 ms. E. of Hartford ; from W. 382 ms. Watered by Quinnebaug river.

NORTH KINGSTON, t., Washington co., R. I., 21 ms. s. of Providence ; from W, ———— ms. Watered by Narraganset bay. Pop. 2,971.

NORTH KORTRIGHT, p. o., Kortright township, Delaware co., N. Y., 66 ms. s. w. of Albany ; from W. 365 ms.

NORTH LANSING, p. o., Lansing township, Tompkins co., N. Y., 175 ms. w. of Albany ; from W. 308 ms.

NORTH LAWRENCE, p. o., St. Lawrence co., N. Y.

NORTH LEEDS, p. o., Leeds township, Kennebec co., Me., 19 ms. s. w. of Augusta; from W. 598 ms.

NORTH LEOMINSTER, p. v., Worcester co., Mass.

NORTH LEVERETT, p. v., Leverett township, Franklin co., Mass., 82 ms. n. w. of Boston; from W. 399 ms.

NORTH LEWISBURGH, p. o., Champaigne co., O.

NORTH LIBERTY, p. o., Mercer co., Pa., 224 ms. n. w. of Harrisburgh; from W. 266 ms.

NORTH LIBERTY, p. o., Knox co., O.

NORTH LIBERTY, p. o., St. Joseph co., Ind.

NORTH LIMA, p. v., Beaver township, Mahoning co., O., 172 ms. n. e. of Columbus; from W. 284 ms.

NORTH LINCOLN, p. o., Lincoln township, Penobscot co., Me., 122 ms. n. e. of Augusta; from W. 717 ms.

NORTH LINKLEAN, p. o., Chenango co., N. Y.

NORTH LITTLETON, p. o., Grafton co., N. H.

NORTH LIVERMORE, p. o., Livermore township, Oxford co., Me., 26 ms. w. of Augusta; from W. 602 ms.

NORTH LOVELL, p. o., Yell co., Ark.,

NORTH LONDONDERRY, p. o., Londonderry township, Rockingham co., N. H., 28 ms. s. e. of Concord; from W. 460 ms.

NORTH LYMAN, p. o., Lyman township, Grafton co., N. H., 90 ms. n. w. of Concord; from W. 538 ms.

NORTH LYME, p. v., Lyme township, New London co.. Ct., 37 ms. s. e. of Hartford; from W. 340 ms.

NORTH MADISON, p. v., Madison township, New Haven co., Ct. Watered by Hamonnasset river.

NORTH MADISON, p. o., Jefferson co., Ind.

NORTH MANCHESTER, p. v., Wabash co., Ind., 109 ms. n. of Indianapolis; from W. 589 ms.

NORTH MARLOW, p. o., Marlow township, Cheshire co., N. H., 50 ms. w. of Concord; from W. 454 ms.

NORTH MARSHALL, p. o., Marshall township, Calhoun co., Mich., 109 ms. w. of Detroit; from W. 574 ms.

NORTH MARSHFIELD, p. v., Marshfield township, Plymouth co., Mass., 26 ms. s. e. of Boston; from W. 450 ms. Watered by North river.

NORTH MIDDLEBOROUGH, p. v., Middleborough township, Plymouth co., Mass., 35 ms. s. of Boston; from W. 428 ms.

NORTH MIDDLESEX, p. o., Middlesex township, Yates co., N. Y., 210 ms. w. of Albany from W. 331 ms.

NORTH MIDDLETON, t., Cumberland co., Pa. Watered by Conadogwinit creek and tributaries, Pop. 2,235.

NORTH MIDDLETOWN, p. v., Bourbon co., Ky., 49 ms. e. of Frankfort; from W. 517 ms.

NORTH MONMOUTH, p. o., Kennebec co., Me.

NORTH MONTPELIER, p. o., Montpelier township, Washington co., Vt., 8 ms. n. of Montpelier; from W. 524 ms.

NORTH MORELAND, t., Luzerne co., Pa., 146 ms. n. e. of Harrisburgh; from W. 251 ms. Pop. 2,109.

NORTH MOUNTAIN, p. o., Berkeley co., Va.

NORTH MOUNT PLEASANT, p. o., Marshall co., Miss., 208 ms. n. of Jackson; from W. 908 ms.

NORTH NEWBURGH, p. o., Newburgh township, Penobscot co., Me., 52 ms. n. e. of Augusta; from W. 647 ms.

NORTH NEWBURY, p. o., Geauga co., O.

NORTH NEWPORT, p. o., Newport township, Penobscot co., Me., 67 ms. n. e. of Augusta; from W. 662 ms.

NORTH NEW PORTLAND, p. o., New Portland township, Somerset co., Me., 56 ms. n. w. of Augusta; from W. 650 ms.

NORTH NEW SALEM, p. o., New Salem township, Franklin co., Mass., 78 ms. w. of Boston; from W. 408 ms.

NORTH NORWAY, p. o., Norway township, Oxford co., Me., 50 ms. w. of Augusta; from W. 594 ms.

NORTH NORWICH, p. o., Norwich township, Chenango co., N. Y., 108 ms. w. of Albany; from W. 342 ms.

NORTH NORWICH, p. o., Norwich township, Huron co., O., 90 ms. n. of Columbus; from W. 404 ms.

NORTH Orange, p. o., Franklin co., Mass.

NORTH ORWELL, p. o., Bradford co., Pa., 147 ms. n. e. of Harrisburgh; from W. — ms.

NORTH OXFORD, p. v., Oxford township, Worcester co., Mass., 51 ms. w. of Boston; from W. 391 ms.

NORTH PALERMO, p. o., Palermo township, Waldo co., Me., 23 ms. n. e. of Augusta; from W. 618 ms.

NORTH PARIS, p. o., Paris township, Oxford co., Me., 45 ms. w. of Augusta; from W. 599 ms.

NORTH PARMA, p. o., Monroe co., N. Y.

NORTH PARSONSFIELD, p. o., Parsonsfield township, York co., Me., 85 ms. s. w. of Augusta; from W. 540 ms.

NORTH PERRY, p. o., Perry township, Lake co., O., 182 ms. n. e. of Columbus; from W. 356 ms.

NORTH PERRYSBURGH, p. o., Perrysburgh township, Cattaraugus co., N. Y., 302 ms. w. of Albany; from W. 358 ms.

NORTH PINE GROVE, p. o., Clarion co., Pa.

NORTH Pittston, p. o., Kennebec co., Me.

NORTH PLAINS, p. o., Ionia co. Mich.

NORTH PLYMPTON, p. o., Plympton township, Plymouth co., Mass., 38 ms. s. e. of Boston; from W. 439 ms.

NORTH POINT, p. o., Pulaski co., Ark.

NORTH PORT, p. v., Huntington township, Suffolk co., Long Island, N. Y.. 195 ms. s. e. of Albany; from W. 275 ms.

NORTHPORT, p. t., Waldo co., Me., 50 ms. e. of Augusta; from W. 643 ms. Watered by Penobscot river Belfast bay. Pop. 1,260.

NORTHPORT, p. v., Tuscaloosa co., Ala. From W. 819 ms. Watered by Black Warrior river.

NORTHPORT, p. o., Noble co., Ind.

NORTH POTSDAM, p. o.. St. Lawrence co., N. Y.

NORTH POWNAL, p. o., Pownal township, Cumberland co., Me., 45 ms. s. w. of Augusta; from W. 566 ms.

NORTH POWNAL, p. o., Pownal township, Bennington co., Vt.

NORTH PRAIRIE, p. o., Knox co., Ill.

NORTH PRESCOTT, p. o., Hampshire co., Mass.

NORTH PROSPECT, p. o., Prospect township, Waldo co., Me., 56 ms. n. e. of Augusta; from W. 650 ms.

NORTH PROVIDENCE, p. t., Providence co., R. I. Watered by Sekonk, Wanasquatucket, and Mashasuck rivers. Pop. 7,680.

NORTH RAISINVILLE, p. o., Monroe co., Mich., 47 ms. s, w. of Detroit; from W. 496 ms.

NORTH RAYMOND, p. o., Raymond township, Cumberland co., Me., 66 ms. s. w. of Augusta; from W. 569 ms.

NORTH READING, p. v., Reading township, Middlesex co., Mass.. 15 ms. n. of Boston; from W. 455 ms. Watered by Ipswich river.

NORTH READING, p. v., Reading township, Steuben co., N. Y., 195 ms. w. of Albany; from W. 314 ms.

NORTH REHOBOTH, Bristol co., Mass.

NORTH RIDGE, p. o., Niagara co., N. Y.

NORTH RIDGEVILLE, p. o., Ridgeville township, Lorain co., O., 120 ms. n. e. of Columbus; from W. 378 ms.

NORTH RIDGEWAY, p. o., Ridgeway township, Orleans co., N. Y.

NORTH RIVER, p. o., Tuscaloosa co., Ala.

NORTH RIVER MEETING HOUSE, p. o., Hampshire co., Va., 183 ms. n. w. of Richmond; from W. 111 ms.

NORTH RIVER MILLS, p. o., Hampshire co.. Va., 172 ms. n. w. of Richmond; from W. 100 ms.

NORTH ROCHESTER, p. v., Rochester township, Plymouth co., Mass., 48 ms. s. e. of Boston; from W. 435 ms.

NORTH ROCHESTER, p. o., Lorain co., O., 101 ms. n. e. of Columbus; from W. 396 ms.

NORTH ROME, p. o., Bradford co., Pa.

NORTH ROYALTON, p. o.. Royalton township, Cuyahoga co., O., 136 ms. n. e. of Columbus; from W. 396 ms.

NORTH RUSSEL, p. o., St. Lawrence co., N. Y.

NORTH SALEM, p. o., Salem township, Rockingham co., N. H., 45 ms. s. e. of Concord; from W. 462 ms.

NORTH SALEM, p. t., Westchester co., N. Y., 113 ms. s. of Albany; from W. 281 ms. Watered by Titicus creek, and Croton river. Pop. 1,335.

NORTH SALEM, p. o., Hendricks co., Ind., 30 ms. w. of Indianapolis; from W. 601 ms.

NORTH Saluda, p. o., Greenwich district, S. C.

NORTH SANBORNTON, p. o., Sanbornton township, Belknap co., N. H.

NORTH SANDWICH, p. v., Sandwich township, Carroll co., N. H., 56 ms. n. of Concord; from W. 537 ms.

NORTH SANDWICH, p. v., Sandwich township, Barnstable co., Mass., 60 ms. s. of Boston; from W. 453 ms.

NORTH SCITUATE, p. v., Scituate township, Plymouth co., Mass., 25 ms. s. e. of Boston; from W. 456 ms.

NORTH SCITUATE, p. v., Scituate township, Providence co., R. I., 10 ms. w. of Providence; from W. 392 ms.

NORTH SEARSMONT, p. o., Searsmont township, Waldo co., Me., 39 ms. e. of Augusta; from W. 625 ms.

NORTH SEDGWICK, p. o., Hancock co. Me.

NORTH SEWICKLY, p. t., Beaver co., P., 233 ms. w. of

Harrisburgh ; from W. 263 ms. Watered by Slippery Rock and Conequenessing creeks. Pop. 2,131.

NORTH SEARSPORT, p. o., Waldo co.. Me.

NORTH SHAPLEIGH, p. o., York co., Me.

NORTH SHEFFIELD, p. o. Ashtabula co., O.

NORTH SHELDON, p. o., Sheldon township, Wyoming co., N. Y., 267 ms. w. of Albany ; from W. 365 ms.

NORTH SHENANGO, p. t., Crawford co., Pa. Pop. 825.

NORTH SHERBURN, p. o., Rutland co., Vt.

NORTH SHORE, p. o., Castleton township, Richmond co.. N. Y., 153 ms. s. of Albany ; from W. 231 ms.

NORTH SMITHFIELD, p. v., Bradford co.. Pa., 153 ms. N. of Harrisburgh ; from W. 263 ms.

NORTH SOMERS, p. o., Somers township, Tolland co., Ct., 25 ms. N. E., of Hartford ; from W. 361 ms.

NORTH SPARTA, p. o., Livingston co., N. Y., 238 ms. w. of Albany ; from W. 339 ms.

NORTH SPENCER, p. v., Spencer township, Worcester co.. Mass., 53 ms. w. of Boston ; from W. 408 ms.

NORTH SPRING, p. o., Jackson co., Tenn.

NORTH SPRINGFIELD, p. o., Springfield township, Windsor co.. Vt., 74 ms. s. of Montpelier ; from W. 462 ms.

NORTH SPRINGFIELD, p. o., Springfield township, Summit co., O., 130 ms. N. E. of Columbus ; from W. 324 ms.

NORTH STAMFORD, p. v., Stamford township, Fairfield, co., Ct., 78 ms. s. w. of Hartford ; from W. 269 ms. Watered by Mill river.

NORTH STAR, p. o., Washington co., Pa.

NORTH STAR, p. o., Darke co., O.

NORTH STARKEY, p. o., Yates co., N. Y.

NORTH STEPHENTOWN, p. o., Stephentown township, Rensselaer co., N. Y., 35 ms. s. E. of Albany ; from W. 380 ms.

NORTH STERLING, p. o., Sterling township, Cayuga co., N. Y., 174 ms. N. w. of Albany ; from W. 367 ms.

NORTH STOCKHOLM, p. o., St. Lawrence co., N. Y.

NORTH STONINGTON, p. t., New London co., Ct., 53 N. E. of Hartford ; from W. 368 ms. Watered by Pawcatuck river. Pop. 1,936.

NORTH STRABANE, t., Washington co., Pa. Watered by Chartier's and Little Chartier's creeks. Pop. 1,210.

NORTH STRAFFORD, p. o., Strafford co., N. H.

NORTH STRAFFORD, p. o., Coos co., N. H.

NORTH SUDBURY, p. v., Sudbury township, Middlesex co.. Mass., 20 ms. w. of Boston ; from W. 439 ms.

NORTH SWANSEA, p. v., Swansea township, Bristol co. Mass., 51 ms. s. of Boston ; from W. 409 ms.

NORTH TARRYTOWN, p. o., Westchester co., N. Y.

NORTH TEWKSBURY, p. o., Tewksbury township, Middlesex co.. Mass.

NORTH THETFORD, p. o., Orange co., Vt.

NORTH TOWANDA, p. o., Bradford co., Pa.

NORTH TROY, p. o., Troy township, Orleans co., Vt., 60 ms. N. of Montpelier ; from W. 576 ms.

NORTH TRURO, p. v., Truro township, Barnstable co., Mass., 116 ms. s. E. of Boston ; from W. 517 ms. Watered by Cape Cod bay.

NORTH TURNER, p. o., Turner township, Oxford co., Me., 25 ms. s. w. of Augusta ; from W. 591 ms.

NORTH TURNER BRIDGE, p. o., Turner township, Oxford co., Me., 21 ms. s. w. of Augusta ; from W. 596 ms.

NORTHUMBERLAND COUNTY, situated toward the east part of Pennsylvania, with Susquehanna river on the west, and traversed by its east branch. Area, 440 square miles. Face of the country, mountainous ; soil, productive. Seat of justice. Sunbury. Pop. in 1810, 36,327 ; in 1820. 15,424 ; in 1830, 18,168 ; in 1840, 20,027 ; in 1850, 23,272.

NORTHUMBERLAND COUNTY, situated in the east part of Virginia, with Potomac river and Chesapeake bay on the east. Area, 240 square miles. Face of the country, undulating ; soil, of middling quality. Seat of justice, Heathsville. Pop. in 1810, 8,308, in 1820, 8,016; in 1830. 7,953 ; in 1840, 7,924 : in 1850, 7,346.

NORTHUMBERLAND, p. t., Coos co., N. H., 107 ms. N. of Concord ; from W. 568 ms. Watered by Connecticut and Upper Ammonoosuck rivers and tributaries. Pop. 429.

NORTHUMBERLAND, p. t., Saratoga co., N. Y., 38 ms. N. of Albany ; from W. 408 ms. Watered by Hudson river. Pop. 1,775.

NORTHUMBERLAND, p. b., Northumberland co., Pa., 59 ms. N. of Harrisburgh ; from W. 169 ms. Watered by Susquehanna river at the confluence of its east and west branches, and of the Susquehanna and North and West branch canals. Pop. 1,044.

NORTH UNION, p. o., Washington co., O.

NORTH UNION, p. o., Lincoln co., Me.

NORTH UNIONTOWN, p. o., Highland co., O.

NORTH URBANA, p. o., Steuben co., N. Y.

NORTH UXBRIDGE, p. o., Worcester co., Mass.

NORTH VASSALBOROUGH, p. o., Vassalborough township, Kennebec co., Me., 18 ms. N. of Augusta ; from W. 613 ms.

NORTH VERNON, p. o., Shiawassee co.. Mich.

NORTHVILLE, p. v., New Milford township, Litchfield co., Ct., 47 ms. w. of Hartford ; from W. 312 ms.

NORTHVILLE, p. v., Northampton township, Fulton co., N. Y., 55 ms. N. w. of Albany ; from W. 424 ms.

NORTHVILLE, p. v., Erie co., Pa., 285 ms. N. w. of Harrisburgh ; from W. 358 ms.

NORTHVILLE, p. v., Wayne co., Mich., 28 ms. w. of Detroit ; from W. 534 ms. Watered by west branch of Rouge river at the confluence of Walled lake outlet.

NORTHVILLE, p. v., La Salle co., Ill, 152 ms. N. E. of Springfield ; from W. 781 ms.

NORTH WAKEFIELD, p. o., Carroll co., N. H.

NORTH WALDOBOROUGH, p. o., Lincoln co., Me.

NORTH WARDSBOROUGH, p. o., Wardsborough township, Windham co., Vt., 117 ms. s. of Montpelier ; from W. 444 ms.

NORTH WASHINGTON, p. o., Lincoln co., Me.

NORTH WASHINGTON, p. v., Washington township, Westmoreland co., Pa., 189 ms. w. of Harrisburgh : from W. 214 ms.

NORTH WATERFORD, p. o., Oxford co., Me.

NORTH WAYNE, p. o., Kennebec co., Me.

NORTH WEARE, p. o., Hillsborough co., N. H.

NORTH WEST, p. o., Williams co., O.

NORTH WEST, p. t., Orange co., Ind. Pop. 1,245.

NORTH WEST BRIDGEWATER, p. o., Plymouth co., Mass., 19 ms. s. of Boston ; from W. 432 ms.

NORTH WESTERN, p. o., Oneida co., N. Y.

NORTHWESTERN TERRITORY, a vast unorganized territory, the greater portion of which has never been explored, except by the Indians. It lies between 43° and 49° north latitude, and 99° and 114° longitude west from Greenwich : and is bounded north by the British possessions, east by Minnesota, south by Nebraska territory, and west by the Rocky mountains, which divide it from Oregon Territory. Its superficial area is about 200,000 square miles.

Physical Aspect.—The greater part of this immense territory is watered by the Missouri river and its numerous tributaries. The Yellow Stone, the largest tributary, extends its branches to the very base of the Rocky mountains, and to near the sources of the Nebraska. A mountain ridge, which branches from the great Rocky mountains, in about 42° north latitude, traverses the country in a northeasterly direction toward Lake Winnipeg. In the eastern portion of the territory the country is partly covered with forests, but beyond this commences a vast ocean of prairie, almost level, and clothed in grass and flowers.

Climate.—In a country of such extent, generally level, naked, and open, the climate must in a great measure correspond to the latitude. Immediately on the borders of the settled states it is mild and temperate ; beyond, it gradually becomes more extreme ; and toward the mountains, cold, bleak, and polar. Travellers speak of encountering storms of hail and sleet in the summer. When the winds blow from the west, over the mountain summits, the cold is intense.

History.—This territory is a part of the Louisiana purchase. That portion of the country lying in the valley of the Platte is generally termed "Nebraska Territory," and as such it has been proposed to organize it. A bill for the purpose passed the house of representatives in February, 1853, but it failed to be acted on in the senate. The section of country north of this valley still retains the name of "Northwestern Territory," it being a part of the former extensive territory under that name, from which several states have been set off. As yet the whole territory is inhabited by Indians, but the time is not far distant when the pioneer will penetrate its forests and prairies, and bring under cultivation the soil that from its creation has not been turned by the labor of man.

NORTH WEST MINE, p. o., Houghton co,. Mich.

NORTH WEST RIVER BRIDGE, p. o., Norfolk co., Va., 130 ms. s. E. of Richmond ; from W. 255 ms.

NORTH WETHERSFIELD, p. o., Wethersfield township. Wyoming co., N. Y., 256 ms. w. of Albany; from W. 371 ms.

NORTH WEST FORK, hundred, Sussex co., Del.

NORTH WEYMOUTH. p. v., Norfolk co., Mass., 12 ms. s. e. of Boston; from W. 452 ms.

NORTH WHARTON, p. o., Potter co., Pa.

NORTH WHITE CREEK, p. v., White Creek township, Washington co., N. Y., 36 ms. N. E. of Albany; from W. 406 ms.

NORTH WHITEFIELD, p. o., Whitefield township, Lincoln co., Me., 16 ms. s. e. of Augusta; from W. 604 ms.

NORTH WHITEHALL, p. t., Lehigh co., Pa., 95 ms. N. E. of Harrisburgh; from W. 188 ms. Watered by Coply and Jordan creeks. Pop. 2,955.

NORTH WILNA, p. o., Wilna township, Jefferson co., N. Y.

NORTH WILTON, p. o., Wilton township, Franklin co., Me.. 38 ms. N. w. of Augusta; from W. 616 ms.

NORTH WILTON, p. o., Fairfield co., Ct.

NORTH WINDHAM, p. v., Windham township, Cumberland co., Me., 53 ms. s. w. of Augusta; from W. 556 ms.

NORTH WINDHAM, p. v., Windham township, Windham co., Ct., 36 ms. e. of Hartford; from W. 363 ms.

NORTH WINDFIELD, p. o., Herkimer co., N. Y.

NORTH WOLFBOROUGH, p. o., Wolfborough township. Carroll co., N. H., 42 ms. N. E. of Concord; from W. 523 ms.

NORTH WOODBURY, p. t., Blair co., Pa. Pop. 1,836.

NORTH WOODSTOCK, p. v., Woodstock township, Windham co., Ct., 42 ms. N. E. of Hartford; from W. 378 ms. Watered by a tributary of Quinnebaug river.

NORTH WOODSTOCK, p. o., Woodstock township, Oxford co., Me.

NORTHWOOD, t., Rockingham co.. N. H. Watered by head waters of Lamprey, Isinglass and Suncook rivers. Pop. 1,308.

NORTH WRENTHAM, p. o., Wrentham township, Norfolk co., Mass., 28 ms. s. of Boston; from W. 425 ms.

NORTH YAM HILL, p. o., Yam Hill co., Oregon.

NORTH YARMOUTH, p. t., Cumberland co., Me., 40 ms. s. w. of Augusta; from W. 555 ms. Watered by Casco bay. Pop. 1,121.

NORTH YARMOUTH CENTRE, p. o., North Yarmouth township, Cumberland co., Me., 48 ms. s. w. of Augusta; from W. 557 ms.

NORTON. p. t., Bristol co.. Mass., 33 ms. s. of Boston; from W. 428 ms. Watered by Rumford, Cocasset, and Canoe rivers. Pop. 1,966.

NORTON, p. v., Marlborough township, Delaware co., O., 34 ms. N. of Columbus; from W. 418 ms. Watered by Olentaugy river.

NORTON, p. t., Summit co., O. Watered by Hudson's run, Wolf creek, and Tuscarawas rivers. Pop. 1,346.

NORTON CENTRE, p. o., Norton township, Summit co., O.

NORTON. t., Ottawa co., Mich.

NORTON HILL, p. o., Greene co., N. Y.

NORTON's MILLS, p. o., Ontario co., N. Y.

NORTONSVILLE, p. o., Albermarle co., Va., 105 ms. N. w. of Richmond; from W. 124 ms.

NORTONSVILLE, p. o., Ottawa co., Mich.

NORVELL. p. o., Jackson co., Mich.

NORWALK, p. t., Fairfield co., Ct., 68 ms. s. w. of Hartford; from W. 269 ms. Watered by Long Island sound and Norwalk river. Pop. 4,651.

NORWALK, c. h., p. t., seat of justice of Huron co., O., 99 ms. N. of Columbus; from W. 392 ms. Pop. 3,159.

NORWAY, p. t., Oxford co., Me., 44 ms. w. of Augusta; from W. 588 ms. Watered by a pond discharging into Little Androscoggin river. Pop. 1,963.

NORWAY. p. t., Herkimer co., N. Y., 86 ms. N. w. of Albany; from W. 411 ms. Watered by a tributary of West Canada creek. Pop. 1,052.

NORWAY, p. o., Racine co., Wis.

NORWAY, p. o., Miller co., Mo.

NORWEGIAN, t., Schuylkill co., Pa. Watered by Schuylkill river and tributaries. Pop. 2,642.

NORWICH, p. t., Windsor co., Vt., 46 ms. s. e. of Montpelier; from W. 490 ms. Watered by Connecticut and Ompompanoosuc river and tributaries. Pop. 1,978.

NORWICH, p. t., Hampshire co., Mass., 104 ms. w. of Boston; from W. 381 ms. Pop. 756.

NORWICH, city, and t., seat of justice, together with New London. of New London co., Ct., 39 ms. s. e.,of Hartford; from W. 357 ms. Situated at the head of navigation of Thames river, at the junction of the Shetucket and Yantic rivers, 14 miles from Long Island sound. The main part of the city is situated on a steep acclivity, the houses being built in tiers rising one above another, present a beautiful appearance -when approached from the south. Here are extensive manufactories of cotton and woollen goods, paper, hardware, pottery, &c. This location was the scene of severe contests between the Mohegan and Narraganset Indians. It was the stronghold of the latter, and here the burial-place of their kings is still to be seen. Near the city there are several picturesque falls or cataracts, and from a high rock which overhangs these water-falls, the Mohegan Indians plunged and perished, rather than fall into the hands of the Narragansets, who were pursuing them.

The population in 1840, 7,239; in 1850, 10,265.

NORWICH, c. h., p. t., seat of justice of Chenango co., N. Y., 112 ms. w. of Albany; from W. 336 ms. Watered by Chenango river. Pop. 3,615.

NORWICH, v., Oyster Bay township, Queen's co., Long Island, N. Y.

NORWICH, p. t., McKean co., Pa., 190 ms. N. w. of Harrisburgh: from W. 272 ms. Watered by Potatoe creek. Pop. 265.

NORWICH, p. v., Union township, Muskingum co., O., 65 ms. e. of Columbus; from W. 328 ms. Pop. 224.

NORWICH, t., Franklin co., O. Pop. 1,053.

NORWICH, t., Huron co., O., 90 ms. N. E. of Columbus; from W. — ms. Pop. 1,021.

NORWICHTOWN, p. v., Norwich township, New London co., Ct., 37 ms. s. e. of Hartford; from, W. 355 ms.

NORWOOD, p. v., Stanley co., N. C., 158 s. w. of Raleigh; from W. 395 ms.

NORWOOD, p. o., Bedford co., Va.

NOTASULGA, p. o., Macon co., Ala.

NOTRE DAME, p. o., St. Joseph co., Ind.

NOTTINGHAM, p. t., Rockingham co., N. H., 25 ms. s. E. of Concord; from W. 482 ms. Watered by Little and North rivers. Pop. 1,268.

NOTTINGHAM, t., Mercer co., N. J. Watered by Assunpink and Crosswick's creeks. Pop. 4,489.

NOTTINGHAM. t., Washington co., Pa. Watered by Peter's, Mingo, and Little Mingo creeks. Pop. 1,008.

NOTTINGHAM, p. v., Prince George's co., Md., 32 ms. s. w. of Annapolis; from W. 26 ms.

NOTTINGHAM, p. t., Harrison co., O. Pop. 1,236.

NOTTINGHAM, p. o., Davis co., Iowa.

NOTTINGHAM, p. o., Wells co., Ind.

NOTTINGHAM TURNPIKE, p. o., Rockingham N. H., 25 ms. s. e. of Concord; from W. 486 ms.

NOTLA, p. o. Cherokee co., N. C.

NOTTOWAY COUNTY, situated in the southeasterly part of Virginia. Area, 290 square miles. Seat of justice. Nottoway c. h. Pop. in 1810, 9,279; in 1820, 9,658; in 1830, 10.141; in 1840, 9,719; in 1850, 8,437.

NOTTOWAY, c. h., p. v., seat of justice of Nottoway co., Va., 67 ms.. s. w. of Richmond; from W. 186 ms. Watered by Nottoway river.

NOTTOWAY, t., St. Joseph co., Mich., 137 ms. s. w. of Detroit; from W. 592 ms. Pop. 1,165.

NOVI, p. t., Oakland co., Mich., 25 ms. N. w. of Detroit; from W. 547 ms. Watered by west branch of Rouge river. Pop. 1,428.

NOXAPATER, p. o., Winston co., Miss.

NOXUBEE COUNTY, situated on the east boundary of Mississippi. Area, 680 square miles. Seat of justice, Macon. Pop. in 1840, 6,975; in 1850, 16,299.

NOYSVILLE, p. o., Cook co., Ill.

NOYSVILLE, p. o., Dodge co., Wis.

NUBBIN RIDGE, p. o., Hardman co., Tenn., 179 ms. s. w. of Nashville; from W. — ms.

NUECES COUNTY, situated in the southerly part of Texas. Area, — square miles. Seat of justice, Corpus Christi. Pop. in 1850, 698.

NULL's MILLS, p. o., Fayette co., Ind.

NUMA, p. o., Parker co., Ind.

NUMBER ONE, p. o., Wayne co., O.

NUMBER TWO, p. o., Marion co., Flor.

NUMBER THREE, p. o., Aroostook co., Me., 154 ms. N. e. of Augusta; from W. 749 ms.

NUNDA, p. t., Livingston co., N. Y., 253 ms. w. of Albany; from W. 352 ms. Watered by Canaseraga and Cashaqua creeks. Pop. 2,138.

NUNDA VALLEY, v., Nunda township, Livingston co., N. Y., 253 ms. w. of Albany; from W. 352 ms. Watered by Cashaqua creek.

NUTBUSH, p. o., Warren co., N. C.

NYACK, p. v., Orangetown township, Rockland co., N. Y., 128 ms. s. of Albany; from W. 262 ms. Watered by Hudson river.

NYACK TURNPIKE, p. o., Clarkstown township, Rockland co., N. Y., 128 ms. s. of Albany; from W. 264 ms.

O.

OAKACHICKAMA, p. o., Yallabusha co., Miss., 126 ms. N. E. of Jackson; from W. 945 ms.

OAK, p. o., Williams co., O.

OAK BLUFFS, p. o., Greene co., Ark.

OAK BOWERY, p. o., Chambers co., Ala.; from W. 773 ms.

OAK CREEK, p. o., Milwaukee co., Wis., 93 ms. E. of Madison; from W. 795 ms.

OAKDALE, c. h., p. v., seat of justice of Shelby co., Mo., 94 ms. N. of Jefferson city; from W. 951 ms.

OAKDAM, p. o., Vanderburgh co., Ind.

OAKDALE, p. o., Worcester co., Mass.

OAKFIELD, p. o., Genesee co., N. Y., 257 ms. w. of Albany; from W. 382 ms.

OAKFIELD, p. o., Fond du Lac co., Wis.

OAKFIELD, p. o., Perry co., O.

OAKFIELD, p. o., Kent co., Mich.

OAKFIELD, p. o., Franklin co., Mo.

OAK FLAT, p. o., Pendleton co., Va., 161 ms. N. w. of Richmond; from W. 161 ms.

OAK FOREST, p. o., Cumberland co., Va., 57 ms. w. of Richmond; from W. 137 ms.

OAK FOREST, p. o., Iredell co., N. C., 152 ms. w. of Raleigh; from W. 370 ms.

OAK FOREST, p. o., Wayne co., Ky.

OAK FOREST, p. o., Franklin co., Ind.

OAKFUSKY, p. o., Randolph co., Ala.; from W. 747 ms.

OAK GROVE, p. o., Westmoreland co., Va., 82 ms. N. E. of Richmond; from W. 93 ms.

OAK GROVE, p. o., Livingston co., Mich., 57 ms. N. w. of Detroit; from W. 560 ms.

OAK GROVE, p. o., Washington parish, La., 80 ms. N. of New Orleans; from W. 1,117 ms.

OAK GROVE, p. o., Christian co., Ky., 218 ms. s. w. of Frankfort; from W. 742 ms.

OAK GROVE, p. o., Jackson co., Mo., 128 ms. s. E. of Jefferson city; from W. 1,054 ms.

OAK GROVE, p. o., Union co., N. C.

OAK GROVE, p. o., Montgomery co., Ala.

OAK GROVE, p. o., Chickasaw co., Miss.

OAK GROVE, p. o., Titus co., Tex.

OAK GROVE, p. o., Jefferson co., Tenn.

OAK GROVE, p. o., Linn co., Iowa.

OAK GROVE, p. o., Dodge co., Wis.

OAKHAM, p. t., Worcester co., Mass., 64 ms. w. of Boston; from W. 416 ms. Watered by Five-Mile and Ware rivers.

OAK HILL, p. o., Cumberland co., Me., 56 ms. s. w. of Augusta; from W. 539 ms.

OAK HILL, p. o., Lancaster co., Pa., 64 ms. s. E. of Harrisburgh; from W. 94 ms.

OAK HILL, p. o., Durham township, Greene co., N. Y., 34 ms. s. w. of Albany; from W. 361 ms.

OAK HILL, p. v., Madison township, Jackson co., O., 80 ms. s. E. of Columbus; from W. 391 ms.

OAK HILL, p. o., Fauquier co., Va., 119 ms. N. of Richmond; from W. 62 ms.

OAK HILL, p. o., Granville co., N. C., 71 ms. N. of Raleigh; from W. 256 ms.

OAK HILL, p. o., Newton co., Ga., 72 ms. N. w. of Milledgeville; from W. 659 ms.

OAK HILL, p. o., Overton co., Tenn., 104 ms. E. of Nashville; from W. 616 ms.

OAK HILL, p. o., Franklin co., Ala.

OAK HILL, p. o., Hardie co., Ky.

OAK HILL, p. o., De Kalb co., Ind.

OAK HILL, p. o., Lake co., Ill.

OAK HILL, p. o., Jefferson co., Wis.

OAK HILL. p. o., Panola co., Miss.

OAKLAND COUNTY, situated in the easterly part of Michigan. Area, 900 square miles. Soil rich. Seat of justice, Pontiac. Pop. in 1830, 4,911; in 1840, 23,646; in 1850, 31,270.

OAKLAND, p. v., Portage township, Livingston co., N. Y., 254 ms. w. of Albany; from W. 357 ms. Watered by Cashaqua creek.

OAKLAND, p. o., Armstrong co., Pa.

OAKLAND, p. o., Morgan co., Va., 170 ms. N. of Richmond; from W. 98 ms.

OAKLAND, p. o., Clinton co., O., 77 ms. s. w. of Columbus; from W. 450 ms.

OAKLAND, p. v., Fayette co., Tenn., 195 ms. s. w. of Nashville; from W. 880 ms.

OAKLAND, p. o., Coles co., Ill., 97 ms. s. E. of Springfield; from W. 682 ms.

OAKLAND, p. o., Yallabusha co., Miss., 139 ms. N. of Jackson; from W. 984 ms.

OAKLAND, p. o., Oakland co., Mich., 58 ms. from Detroit; from W. — ms. Watered by Paint creek, and a branch of Stony creek. Pop. 978.

OAKLAND, p. o., La Clede co., Mo. Situated on the Osage fork of Gasconade river.

OAKLAND, p. o., St. Francis co., Ark.

OAKLAND, p. o., Christian co., Ky.

OAKLAND, p. o., Chatham co., N. C.

OAKLAND, p. o., Spencer co., Ind.

OAKLAND, p. o., La Vaca co., Tex.

OAKLAND, p. o., Armstrong co., Pa.

OAKLAND, p. o., Edgefield district, S. C.

OAKLAND, p. o., Jefferson co., Wis.

OAKLAND, p. o., Lauderdale co., Ala.

OAKLAND CITY, p. t., Contra Costa co., Cal.

OAKLAND COLLEGE, p. v., Claiborne co., Miss., 87 ms. s. w. of Jackson; from W. 1,097 ms. Seat of Oakland college.

OAKLAND GROVE, p. o., Prairie co., Ark.

OAKLAND MILLS, p. v., Juniata co., Pa., 50 ms. N. of Harrisburgh; from W. 144 ms.

OAK LAWN, p. o., Baker co., Ga., 138 ms. s. w. of Milledgeville; from W. 795 ms.

OAK LAWN, p. o., Cabarras co., N. C.

OAK LEVEL, p. o., Benton co., Ala.

OAK LEVEL, p. o., Henry co., Va., 196 ms. s. w. of Richmond; from W. 271 ms.

OAKLEY, p. o., Mecklenburgh co., Va., 120 ms. s. w. of Richmond; from W. 218 ms.

OAKLEY, p. o., Overton co., Tenn.

OAKLEY, p. o., Macon co., Ill.

OAKLEY, p. o., Lewis co., Mo.

OAKLY, p. o., Franklin parish, La.

OAKMULGEE, p. o., Bedford co., Va.

OAKOHAY, p. o., Covington co., Miss.

OAK ORCHARD, p. o., Ridgeway township, Orleans co., N. Y., 259 ms. w. of Albany; from W. 403 ms.

OAK PLAINS, p. o., Livingston co., Mich.

OAK POINT, p. o., St. Lawrence co., N. Y.

OAK POINT, p. o., Louis co., Oregon.

OAK POINT, p. o., Van Buren co., Iowa.

OAK RIDGE, p. o., Guilford co., N. C., 104 ms. N. w. of Raleigh; from W. 289 ms.

OAK RIDGE, p. o., Hancock co., O.

OAK RIDGE, p. o., Green co., Ark.

OAK RIDGE, p. o., Graves co., Ky.

OAK RIDGE, p. o., Meriwether co., Ga.

OAK'S CORNERS, p. o., Phelps township, Ontario co., N. Y., 181 ms. w. of Albany; from W. 346 ms.

OAK SHADE, p. o., Culpeper co., Va.

OAK SPRING, p. o., Ballard co., Ky.

OAK SPRING, p. o., Davis co., Iowa.

OAK SPRINGS, p. o., Tuolumne co. Cal.

OAK'S SHOP, p. o., Pittsylvania co., Va.

OAKSVILLE, p. v., Otsego township, Otsego co., N. Y., 73 ms. w. of Albany; from W. 362 ms. Watered by Oak creek.

OAKTIBBEHA, p. o., Kemper co., Miss.

OAKVILLE, p. v., Buckingham co., Va., 102 ms. w. of Richmond; from W. 188 ms.

OAKVILLE, p. v., Mecklenburgh co., N. C., 183 ms, s. w. of Raleigh; from W. 420 ms.

OAKVILLE, p. o., Lexington district, S. C., 13 ms. s. w. of Columbia; from W. 519 ms.

OAKVILLE, p. o., Lawrence co., Ala., from W. 759 ms.

OAKVILLE, p. v., London township, Monroe co., Mich.
OAKVILLE, p. v., St. Louis co., Mo.
OAKVILLE, p. o., Madison co., Tenn.
OAKVILLE, p. o., St. Mary's co., Md.
OAKVILLE, p. o., Union co., N. C.
OAKVILLE, p. o., Cumberland co., Pa.
OAKVILLE, p. o., Appomatox co., Va.
OAK WOODS, p. o., Fleming co., Ky.
OAK WOODS, p. o., Grant co., Ind.
OASIS, p. o., Marquette co., Wis.
OATLANDS, p. o., Loudon co., Va.
OBERLIN, p. v., Russia township, Lorain co., O., 110 ms. N. E. of Columbus; from W. 379 ms. Seat of Oberlin Collegiate Institute.
OBION COUNTY, situated at the northwest corner of Tennessee, with the Mississippi river for its western boundary. Area, 700 square miles. Seat of justice, Troy. Pop., in 1840, 4,814; in 1850, 7,633.
OBION, p. o., Hickman co., Ky.
OBISPO, p. o., San Louis Obispo co., Cal.
OCCOQUAN, p. v., Prince William co., Va., 96 ms. N. of Richmond; from W. 23 ms.
OCCUPACIA, p. o., Essex co., Va.
OCEAN COUNTY, situated on the east coast of New Jersey, on the Atlantic. Area, —— square miles. Face of the country, level; soil, of middling quality. Seat of justice, Tom's River. Pop. in 1850, 10,032.
OCEANA COUNTY, situated on the west boundary of Michigan, with Lake Michigan on the west. Area, —— square miles. Seat of justice, ——. Pop. in 1840, 208; in 1850, 300.
OCEAN PORT, p. o., Monmouth co., N. J.
OCEOLA, p. o., Cherokee co., Ala.
OCEOLA, p. t., Livingston co,, Mich.
OCEOLA, p. o., Crawford co., O., 68 ms. N. of Columbus; from W. 412 ms.
OCEOLA, c. h., p. v., seat of justice of Mississippi co., Ark., 130 ms. N. E. of Little Rock; from W. —— ms. Watered by Mississippi river.
OCEOLA CENTRE, p. v., Oceola township, Livingston co., Mich. 57 N. w. Detroit; from W. 560 ms.
OCHESSEE, p. o., Calhoun co., Flor.
OCKLOCKNEY, p. o., Thomas co., Ga.
OCMULGEE, p. o., Perry co., Ala.
OCMULGEEVILLE, p. v., Telfair co., Ga., 148 ms. s. of Milledgeville; from W. 759 ms.
OCOA, p. o., Polk co., Tenn.
OCOLA, p. o., Marion co., Flor.
OCONA LUFTY, p. o., Haywood co., N. C.
OCONEE, p. o, Washington co., Ga.
OCONEE STATION, p. o,, Pickens district, S. C.
OCONOMOWOCK, p. o., Waukesha co., Wis.
OCRACOKE, p. v., Hyde co., N. C. Watered by Ocracoke inlet.
OCTORARO, p. o., Lancaster co., Pa.
ODDVILLE, p. o., Harrison co., Ky.
OENCA, p. o., Jefferson co., Wis.
OGALLA, p. o., Chippewa co., Wis.
OGDEN COUNTY, situated in Utah territory. Area, —— square miles. Seat of justice, Brownsville.
OGDEN, p. t., Monroe co., N. Y., 227 ms. w. of Albany; from W. —— ms. Watered by tributaries of Salmon and Rush creeks, and the Erie canal. Pop. 2,598.
OGDEN,'p. v., Henry co., Ind., 36 ms. E. of Indianapolis; from W. 535 ms.
OGDEN, t., Lenawee co., Mich. Pop. 579.
OGDEN, p. o., New Madrid co., Mo., 248 ms. s. E. of Jefferson City; from W. 888 ms.
OGDENSBURGH, p. v., Oswegatchie township, St. Lawrence co., N. Y., 210 ms. N. w. of Albany; from W. 477 ms. Watered by St. Lawrence river at the confluence of the Oswegatchie.
OGDENSBURGH, p. o., Union co., Pa.
OGEECHEE, p. o., Scriven co., Ga.
OGLE COUNTY, situated in the north part of Illinois, and traversed by Rock river. Area, 625 square miles. Seat of justice, Oregon city. Pop. in 1840, 3,497; in 1850, 10,020.
OGLE, p. o., Butler co., Pa.
OGLE, p. o., Ogle co., Ill.
OGLETHORPE COUNTY, situated in the northeasterly part of Georgia. Area, 490 square miles. Face of the country uneven; soil productive. Seat of justice, Lexington. Pop. in 1810, 12,297; in 1820. 14,046; in 1830, 13,558; in 1840, 10, 10.868; in 1850, 12,259.
OGLETHORPE, p. o., Macon co., Ga.
OGUNQUIT, p. o., York co., Me., 82 ms. s. w. of Augusta; from W. 510 ms.

OHIO, one of the United States, situated between 38° 34' and 42° north latitude, and 80° 35' and 84° 57' west longitude from Greenwich; and is bounded north by Michigan and Lake Erie, and east by Pennsylvania, southeast by Virginia, from which it is separated by Ohio river, south by Kentucky, from which it is also separated by the same river, and west by Indiana. Its superficial area is 40,000 square miles.

Physical Aspect.—This state presents a considerable diversity of surface, as well as of climate. A range of comparatively high land divides the waters which flow into Lake Erie from those which descend into the Ohio, forming two inclined plains of unequal areas. The northern, or Erie plain, does not exceed 25 miles in width at the northeast extremity, but expands to 80 miles in width along the east boundary of Indiana. The mean elevation of the apex of this range is estimated to be 1,000 feet above the ocean tides; so that, from its proximity to the lake, the descent of the streams, flowing in this direction, is somewhat precipitate, and all roll over direct cascades, or falls. On the other hand, the plain inclined toward the Ohio is very gradual in its descent, and falls of any kind are rarely to be found. The central portion of the state occupies an immense plateau, or table-land, comparatively level, and in part marshy, which consists of a diversity of soil, from rich alluvion and prairie, to wild oak "barrens." Along the Ohio river, for fifty or sixty miles back, the country is hilly, and in some parts quite rugged, caused by the abrasion of the streams; but the chief part of the central table-land remains unchannelled, presenting a series of broad prairies and other plains. A similar feature is observable along the Ohio shores of Lake Erie, but the surface is less broken, and the hills are more moderate in their height.

Rivers, Lakes, and Bays.—The principal rivers of this state are, the Ohio, Muskingum, Hockhocking, Scioto, Great and Little Miami, Maumee, Sandusky, Huron, Vermilion, Black, Cuyahoga, Grand, Ashtabula, Auglaize, Tuscarawas, Walhonding, Olentangy or Whetstone, and St. Mary's. Lake Erie lies partly in Ohio, in the western part of which are Maumee and Sandusky bays; there is also a good harbor at Cleveland.

Climate.—The climate, in general, may be regarded as healthy, except in the vicinity of stagnant marshes and sluggish streams, where, in summer and autumn, intermittents usually prevail. Spring and autumn are pleasant; but the winters, though comparatively mild, are subject to great fluctuations of temperature, varying from temperate to 16° Fahrenheit below zero.

Productive Resources.—The chief products are, horses, mules, neat cattle, sheep, swine, poultry, eggs, butter, cheese, beef, pork, wax, silk, wool, wine, sugar, hops, tobacco, madder, hay, flax, hemp,, lumber, pot and pearl ashes, wheat, rye, barley, oats, buckwheat, potatoes, and Indian corn. Of the mineral resources, coal, iron, and salt, are the principal, the latter of which is extensively manufactured from salt creeks and springs.

Manufactures.—The manufactures of Ohio are already of considerable importance, and are rapidly increasing, in both variety and extent. The abundance of waterpower, and the cheapness of coal, will make this section of the Ohio valley the seat of vast manufacturing industry. The more important articles of manufacture are, machinery, cotton, woollen, silk, and mixed goods, leather, paper, ironware, agricultural and mechanical implements, cabinetware, hats, steamboats, &c. The number of manufacturing establishments in the state in 1850, producing each $500 worth or more annually, was 10,550.

Railroads and Canals.—Ohio has an extensive system of railroads and canals, communicating with every important point. There are about 2,000 miles already in operation, or in rapid process of construction. The principal of them are, the Cleveland, Columbus, and Cincinnati, 255 miles; the Cincinnati and Sandusky, 218 miles; Cleveland and Pittsburgh, 100 miles; the

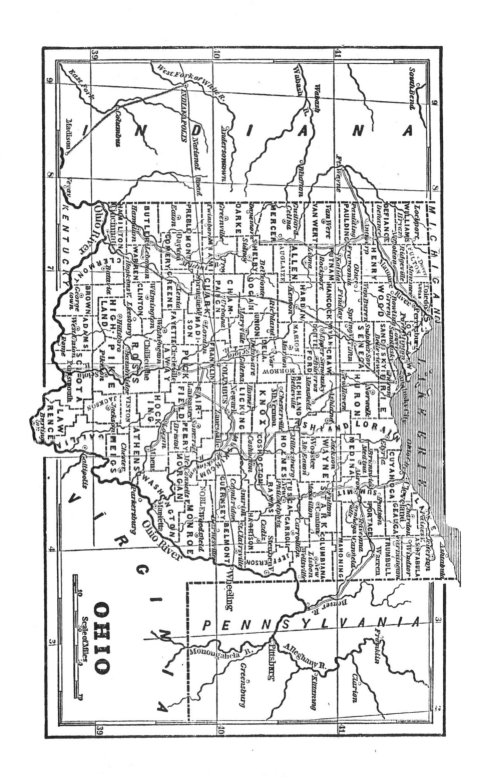

Ohio and Pennsylvania, running through the centre of the state, and connecting the Indiana with the Pennsylvania roads ; and the Lake-Shore road, uniting Illinois and Michigan with New York and the eastern states. The most important of the canals in the state is the Ohio canal, 309 miles long, connecting the waters of Lake Erie at Cleveland with those of the Ohio river at Portsmouth. The agregate length of the canals is about 850 miles. The tolls collected are about $800,000 annually.

Commerce.—With the exception of the trade with Canada, the direct foreign commerce of Ohio is trifling, the exports and imports of 1850 amounting to only $800,000. But the coasting and river trade is immense. Amount of shipping enrolled in the state about 65,000 tons.

Population.—In 1790, about 3,000; in 1800, 45,365 ; in 1810, 230,760 ; in 1820, 581,434 ; in 1830, 937,903 ; in 1840, 1,519,467 ; in 1850, 1,980,408.

Education.—The facilities of education in Ohio are ample. The permanent school fund amounts to rising $600,000. The principal literary institutions are, the University of Ohio, at Athens, founded in 1804 ; the Miami university, in 1809 ; Cincinnati college, in 1819 ; Franklin college, at New Athens, in 1825 ; Western Reserve college, at Hudson, in 1826 ; the Kenyon college, at Gambia, in 1827 ; the Granville college, at Granville, and Woodward college, at Cincinnati, in 1831 ; the Oberlin college, in 1834 ; the Marietta college, in 1835 ; the St. Xavier college, at Cincinnati, in 1840 ; the Ohio Wesleyan university, at Delaware, in 1842 ; and the Wittenberg college, at Springfield, in 1845. Law, medical, and theological schools are attached to many of the above. There are near 200 academies, and over 5,000 free common schools established throughout the state. The state has also provided liberally for the education and support of the deaf and dumb, blind, and lunatic. The buildings, with spacious grounds for each class, are situated at Columbus.

Government.—The legislative power is vested in a general assembly, consisting of a senate and house of representatives, elected biennially, on the second Tuesday in October. The senate consists of 35 members, and the house of representatives of 100 members. The legislature meets biennially at Columbus, the first Monday in January. The executive department consists of a governor, lieutenant-governor (who is president of the senate), secretary of state, auditor, treasurer, and an attorney-general, who are chosen by the people at the biennial election. They hold their offices for two years, except the auditor, whose term is four years. The board of public works, consisting of three members, is elected by the people, one annually, for the term of three years. The judicial power is vested in a supreme court, in district courts, courts of common pleas, courts of probate, justices of the peace, and in such other courts, inferior to the supreme court, as the general assembly may establish ; the five supreme court judges hold their office five years, the term of one of the judges expiring annually. There are nine judges of the common pleas, elected by district for five years. All judges are elected by the people. The elective franchise is enjoyed by every white male citizen of the United States, of the age of 21 years, a resident of the state one year next preceding the election.

History.—The French explored the region, and erected forts along the banks of the Ohio river, as far up as Pittsburgh, Penn., as early as 1754. In 1786, what now constitutes the state of Ohio, was erected, by act of Congress, into the " Western Territory," the name of which was afterward changed to the "Territory Northwest of the River Ohio." The first permanent settlement was made at Marietta, in 1788, by a small colony from Massachusetts, and the year following a settlement was made near Cincinnati ; this was followed by another at Cleveland, in 1796, the emigrants being mostly from New England. Soon after the treaty of Greenville, in 1795, Michigan was surrendered by Great Britain to the United States, and was annexed to the territory northwest of the river Ohio in 1800. The same year Connecticut relinquished her jurisdiction over the " Western Reserve." In 1799, the first territorial legislature met at Cincinnati, and organized the government. In 1802, Ohio was detached from Michigan, and admitted into the Union as an independent state. Her constitution was framed the same year, at Chillicothe (the capital of the state until it was removed to Columbus, in 1812), and continued in operation till 1851, when

a new constitution was framed at Columbus, by a convention of delegates, and adopted by the people.

OHIO COUNTY, situated in the northwest corner of Virginia, with Ohio river on the northwest. Area, 125 square miles. Face of the country broken ; soil productive. Seat of justice, Wheeling. Pop. in 1810, 8,175 ; in 1820, 9,182 ; in 1830, 15,590 ; in 1840, 13,357 ; in 1850. 18,006.

OHIO COUNTY, situated in the westerly part of Kentucky, with Green river on the southwest. Area, 576 squares. Seat of justice, Hartford. Pop. in 1810, 3,792 ; in 1820, 3,879 ; in 1830, 4,913 ; in 1840, 6,592 ; in 1850, 9,479.

OHIO COUNTY, situated in Indiana. Area, —— square miles. Seat of justice, Hartford. Pop. in 1850, 5,308.

OHIO, p. t., Herkimer co., N. Y., 108 ms. N. w. of Albany ; from W. 423 ms. Watered by West Camden creek and tributaries. Pop. 1,051.

OHIO, t., Alleghany co., Pa. Watered by Ohio river, Great and Little Sewickly creeks, and Jones' and Hawser's runs. Pop. 2,329.

OHIO, t., Beaver co., Pa. Watered by Little Beaver creek and Ohio river. Pop. 1,660.

OHIO, t., Clermont co., O. Pop. 4,479.

OHIO, t., Gallia co., O. Watered by Ohio river. Pop. 504.

OHIO, p. t., Monroe co., O. Pop. 1,444.

OHIO, t., Warwick co., Ind. Pop. 924.

OHIO, t., Boones co., Ill.

OHIO, p. o., Andrew co., Mo.

OHIO CITY, p. v., Brooklyn township, Cuyahoga co., O., 145 ms. N. E. of Columbus ; from W. 360 ms. Watered by Lake Erie, at the mouth of Cuyahoga river.

OHIO CITY, p. o., Mississippi co., Mo.

OHIO FARM, p. o., Kendall co., Ill.

OHIO GROVE, p. o., De Kalb co., Ill.

OHIOVILLE, p. v., Ohio township, Beaver co., Pa., 243 ms. w. of Harrisburgh ; from W. 269 ms.

OHLSTOWN, p. o., Trumbull co., O.

OIL CREEK, p. t., Crawford co., Pa., 227 ms. N. w. of Harrisburgh ; from W. 308 ms. Watered by Oil creek and tributaries. Pop. 811.

OIL MILLS, p. o., Clarke co., Ky.

OIL MILL VILLAGE, p. o., Hillsborough co., N. H.

OIL TROUGH, p. o., Independence co., Ark.

OKAHUMKA, p. o., Marion co., Flor.

OKAUCHEE, p. o., Waukesha co., Wis.

OKAPILCO, p. o., Lowndes co., Ga.

OKAW, p. o., Washington co., Ill.

OKOLONA, p. o., Chickasaw co., Miss.

OKTIBBEHA COUNTY, situated in the easterly part of Mississippi. Area, 625 square miles. Seat of justice, Starkeville. Pop. in 1840, 4,276 in 1850, 9,171.

OLAMON, p. o., Penobscot co., Me.

OLCOTT, p. v., Newfane township, Niagara co., N. Y., 284 ms. w. of Albany ; from W. 414 ms. Watered by Lake Ontario and Eighteen-Mile creek.

OLD BRIDGE, p. v., North Berwick township, Middlesex co., N. J., 24 ms. N. E. of Trenton ; from W. 200 ms.

OLD CEDAR SPRINGS, p.o., Spartanburgh district, S.C.

OLD CHURCH. p. o., Hanover co., Va., 15 ms. N. of Richmond ; from W. 129 ms.

OLD COURT HOUSE, p. o., Bryan co., Ga., 125 ms. s. E. of Milledgeville ; from W. 679 ms.

OLD CODORUS, t., York co., Pa. Watered by Codorus creek and tributaries.

OLDENBURGH, p. o., Franklin co., Ind.

OLDENBURGH, p. o., Smith co., Tex.

OLD FARM, p. o., Lawrence co., Ill.

OLDFIELD FORK OF ELK, p. o., Pocahontas co., Va.

OLD FORGE, p. o., Luzerne co., Pa.

OLD FORT, p. o., Centre co., Pa., 77 ms. N. w. of Harrisburgh ; from W. 169 ms.

OLD FORT, p. o., McDowell co., N. C., 232 ms. w. of Raleigh ; from W. 462 ms.

OLD FRANKLIN, p. o., Howard co., Mo.

OLD FURNACE, p. o., Gaston co., N. C.

OLDHAM COUNTY, situated on the northerly boundary of Kentucky, with Ohio river on the northwest. Area, 220 square miles. Seat of justice, Westport. Pop. in 1830, 9,563 ; in 1840, 7,380 ; in 1850, 7,629.

OLDHAM, p. o., Crittenden co., Ark., 148 ms. N. E. of Little Rock ; from W. 872 ms.

OLDHAM CROSS-ROADS, p. o., Westmoreland co., Va.

OLD HICKORY, p. o., Bradford co., Pa., 163 ms. N. of Harrisburgh ; from W. 272 ms.
OLD HICKORY, p o., Wayne co., O., 104 ms. N. E. of Columbus ; from W. 347 ms.
OLD HICKORY, p. o., Simpson co., Miss.
OLD HICKORY, p. o., Botetourt co., Va.
OLD HICKORY, p. o., Weakly co,, Tenn.
OLD MINES, p. v., Washington co., Mo., 112 ms. s. E. of Jefferson city ; from W. 872 ms.
OLD MISSION, p. o., Winneshiek, Iowa.
OLD POINT COMFORT, p. o., Elizabeth City co., Va., 97 ms. s. E. of Richmond ; from W. 212 ms. Situated on James river.
OLD RIVER, t., Arkansas co., Ark.
OLD RIVER, t., Chicot co., Ark. Pop. 867.
OLD TOWN, p. t., Penobscot co., Me., 80 ms. N. E. of Augusta ; from W. 675 ms. Watered by Penobscot river. Pop. 3,087.
OLD TOWN, p. v., Alleghany co., Md., 191 ms. N. w. of Annapolis ; from W. 124 ms. Watered by Potomac river.
OLD TOWN, p. v.. Forsyth co., N. C., 115 ms. N. w. of Raleigh ; from W. 326 ms.
OLD TOWN, p. v., Philips co., Ark. Watered by Mississippi river.
OLD TOWN, p. v., Claiborne co., Tenn., 224 ms. E. of Nashville ; from W. 496 ms.
OLD TOWN, p. o., Greenup, co., Ky., 137 ms. E. of Frankfort ; from W. 431 ms.
OLD TOWN, p. o., Coffee co., Ala.
OLD WASHINGTON, c. h., p. v., seat of justice of Washington co., Ala.
OLEAN, p. t.. Cattaraugus co., N. Y., 293 ms. w. of Albany ; from W. 307 ms. Watered by Alleghany river and Genesee River canal. Pop. 899.
OLEAN, p. o., Ripley co., Ind.
OLEANDER, p. o., Marshall co., Ala.; from W. 719 ms.
OLENA, p. o., Henderson co., Ill., 112 ms. N. w. .of Springfield ; from W. 858 ms.
OLENA, p. o., Huron co., O.
OLENTANGY, p. o., Crawford co., O.
OLEY, p. t., Berks co., Pa., 62 ms. E. of Harrisburgh ; from W. 155 ms. Watered by head waters of Mannatawny and Manooktsy creeks.
OLINDA, p. o., Fayette co., Ala.
OLIO, p. o., Hamilton co., Ind.
OLIO, p. o., Stoddard co., Mo.
OLIVE, p. t., Ulster co., N. Y., 79 ms. s. w. of Albany; from W. 326 ms. Watered by Esopus creek. Pop 2,710.
OLIVE, p. v., Morgan co., O., 96 ms. E. of Columbus ; from W. 310 ms. Pop. 2,013.
OLIVE, t., Meigs co., O. Watered by Shade river and tributaries. Pop. 924.
OLIVE, p. o., Clinton co.,Mich.
OLIVE, p. o., Marion co., Ind.
OLIVE BRANCH, p. o., De Soto co., Miss.
OLIVE BRANCH, p. o., Clermont co., O.
OLIVE BRANCH, p. o., Holt co., Mo.
OLIVE BRIDGE, p. o., Ulster co., N. Y.
OLIVE GROVE, p. o., Decatur co., Ga.
OLIVE HILL, p. o., Carter co., Ky., 116 ms. E. of Frankfort ; from W. 444 ms.
OLIVE HILL, p. o., Person co., N. C.
OLIVER, p. t., Mifflin co., Pa. Pop. 1,688.
OLIVER, t., PERRY co., Pa.
OLIVER's, p. o., Anderson co., Tenn.,162 ms. E. of Nashville ; from W. 527 ms.
OLIVER's PRAIRIE, p. o., Newton co., Mo.
OLIVESBURGH, p. v., Milton township, Richland co., O., 73 ms. N. of Columbus ; from W. 374 ms. Watered by Whetstone river.
OLIVET, p. o., Eaton co., Mich.
OLIVET, p. o., Armstrong co., Pa.
OLIVET, p. o., Russell co. Ala.
OLMSTEAD, p. t., Cuyahoga co., O. Pop. 1,216.
OLNEY, p. o., Montgomery co., Md.
OLNEY, c. h., p. v., seat of justice of Richland co., Ill. Watered by Little Wabash river.
OLNEY, p. o., Pickens co., Ala.
OLNEY, p. o., Philadelphia co., Pa.
OLNEYVILLE, p. v., Providence co., R. I
OLUSTEE, p. o., Columbia co., Flor.
OLUSTEE CREEK, p. o., Pike co., Ala.
OLYMPIA, p. o., Louis co., Oregon.
OLYMPIAN SPRINGS, p. o., Bath co., Ky
OLYMPUS, t., Muskingum co., O.

OLYMPUS, p. o., Overton co., Tenn.
OMAR, p. v., Villenova township, Jefferson co., N. Y., 187 ms. N. of Albany ; from W. 437 ms. Watered by west branch of Conewango creek.
OMEGA, p. o., Pike co., O., 64 ms. s. of Columbus ; from W. 411 ms.
OMRO, p. o., Winnebago co., Wis.
ONANCOCK, p. v., Accomac co., Va., 185 ms. E. of Richmond ; from W. 205 ms. Watered by Chesapeake bay.
O'NEAL's MILLS, p. o., Troup co., Ga.
ONECHO, p. o., Montgomery co., Tenn., 30 ms. N. w. of Nashville ; from W. 714 ms.
ONECO, p. o., Stephenson co., Ill., 222 ms. N. of Springfield ; from W. 842 ms.
ONEIDA COUNTY, situated in the central part of New York, with Oneida lake on the southwest, and traversed by Mohawk river and the Erie canal. Area, 1,101 square miles. Face of the country, diversified , soil. productive. Seats of justice, Rome, Utica, and Whittlesborough. Pop. in 1810, 33,792 ; in 1820, 50,997 in 1830, 71,326 ; in 1840, 85,310 ; in 1850, 99,568.
ONEIDA, p. t., Eaton co., Mich., 130 ms. w. of Detroit; from W. 600 ms. Pop. 492.
ONEIDA, p. o., Brown co., Wis.
ONEIDA CASTLE, p. v., Vernon township, Oneida co., N. Y., 113 ms. N. w. of Albany ; from W. 366 ms. Watered by Oneida creek.
ONEIDA DEPOT, p. o., Verona township, Madison co., N. Y.
ONEIDA LAKE, p. o., Lenox township, Madison co., N. Y., 123 ms. N. w. of Albany ; from W. 372 ms.
ONEIDA MILLS, p. o., Carroll co., O.
ONEIDA VALLEY, p. o., Madison co., N. Y.
ONEONTA, p. t., Otsego co., N. Y., 79 ms. w. of Albany ; from W. 349 ms. Watered by Susquehanna river and tributaries. Pop. 1,903.
ONION RIVER, p. o., Sheboygan co., Wis.
ONONDAGA COUNTY, situated in the central part of New York, with Oneida lake on the northeast, and Skeneatelos lake on the southwest, and traversed by Oswego river and the Erie canal. Area, 711 square miles. Face of the country, uneven ; soil productive. This county contains the celebrated salt springs of New York, which yield the state an annual revenue of about $171,000. Seat of justice, Syracuse. Pop. in 1810, 25,987 ; in 1820, 41,467 ; in 1830, 58,974 ; in 1840, 67,911 ; in 1850, 85,891
UNONDAGA, p. t., Onondaga co., N. Y., 133 ms. w. of Albany ; from W. 940 ms. Watered by Onondaga creek. Pop. 5,094.
ONONDAGA, p. o., Ingham co., Mich., 96 ms. w. of Detroit ; from W. 582 ms.
ONONDAGA, p. o., Marshall co., Ind., 122 ms. N. of Indianapolis ; from W. 641 ms.
ONONDAGA CASTLE, p. o., Onondaga co., N. Y.
ONONDAGA HOLLOW, v., Onondaga township, Onondaga co., N. Y., 131 ms. w. of Albany ; from W. 344 ms.
ONONDAGA VALLEY, p. o., Onondaga co., N. Y.
ONOVILLE, p. o., Cattaraugus co., N. Y.
ONSLOW COUNTY, situated on the southeast boundary of North Carolina, with the Atlantic Ocean on the southeast. Area, 720 square miles. Face of the country, flat ; soil, sterile. Seat of justice, Onslow c. h. Pop. in 1810, 6,669 ; in 1820, 7,018 ; in 1830, 7,814 ; in 1840 7,527 ; in 1850, 8,283.
ONSLOW, c. h., p. v., seat of justice of Onslow co., N. C., 145 ms. s. E. of Raleigh ; from W. 372 ms. Watered by New river.
ONTARIO COUNTY, situated toward the west part of New York, with Seneca lake on the east, and Canandaigua lake in the south. Area, 617 square miles. Face of the country uneven ; soil fertile and well cultivated. Seat of justice, Canandaigua. Pop. in 1810, 42,032 ; in 1820, 35,312 ; in 1830, 40,167 ; in 1840, 43,500 ; in 1850, 43,925.
ONTARIO, p. t., Wayne co., N. Y., 205 ms. w. of Albany ; from W. 362 ms. Watered by Lake Ontario. Pop. 2,246.
ONTARIO, p. o., Richland co., O., 60 ms. N. of Columbus ; from W. 385 ms.
ONTARIO. p. o., La Grange co., Ind.
ONTARIO, p. o., Knox co., Ill.
ONTONAGON, p. o., Ontonagon co., Mich.
ONTWA. t., Cass co., Mich. Pop. 780.
ONWARD, p. o., Stewart co., Tenn., 88 ms. N. w. of Nashville , from W. 769 ms.

OOSOOLA, p. o., Somerset co., Me.

OOTHCALOGA, p. o., Cass co., Ga.

OPALIKA, p. o., Walker co., Ga.

OPELIKA, p. o., Russell co., Ala.; from W. 784 ms.

OPELOUSAS, c. h., p. v., seat of justice of St. Landry parish, La., 217 ms. N. w. of New Orleans; from W. 1,242 ms. Watered by Vermilion river. Seat of Franklin college.

OPEN POND, p. o., Henry co., Ala.

OPHIR, p. o., La Salle co., Ill.

OPORTO, p. v., St. Joseph co., Mich., 135 ms. s. w. of Detroit; from W. 583 ms.

OPPENHEIM, p. t., Fulton co., N. Y., 64 ms. N. w. of Albany; from W. 402 ms. Watered by East Canada creek. Pop. 2,315.

OQUAWKA, p. v., seat of justice of Henderson co., Ill., 138 ms. N. w. of Springfield; from W. 868 ms. Watered by Mississippi river.

ORAN, p. v., Pompey township, Onondaga co., N. Y., 119 ms. w. of Albany; from W. 348 ms.

ORAN. p. o., Kosciusko co., Ind.

ORANGE COUNTY, situated on the east boundary of Vermont, with Connecticut river on the east. Area, 650 square miles. Face of the country, uneven and mountainous; soil, productive. Seat of justice, Chelsea. Pop. in 1810, 25,247; in 1820, 24,681; in 1830, 27,285; in 1840, 27,873; in 1850, 27,296.

ORANGE COUNTY, situated in the southeast part of New York, with Hudson river on the east, and traversed by the Delaware and Hudson canal. Area, 760 square miles. Face of the country, diversified; soil, productive, and especially adapted to grazing. Seat of justice, Goshen and Newburgh. Pop. in 1810, 24,347; in 1820, 41,213; in 1830, 45,372; in 1840, 50,739; in 1850, 57,145.

ORANGE COUNTY, situated in the easterly part of Virginia, with Rappahannock river on the north. Area, 380 square miles. Face of the country, hilly and mountainous; soil varied. Seat of justice, Orange c. h., Pop. in 1810. 12,323; in 1820, 12,913; in 1830, 14,637; in 1840, 9,125; in 1850. 10,067.

ORANGE COUNTY, situated in the north part of North Carolina. Area, 1,300 square miles. Seat of justice, Hillsborough. Pop. in 1810, 20,135; in 1820, 23,492; in 1830, 23,875; in 1840, 24,356; in 1850, 17.055.

ORANGE COUNTY, situated on the east boundary of Florida, with the Atlantic ocean on the east. Area, —— square miles. Seat of justice, Melonville. Pop. in 1850. 466.

ORANGE COUNTY, situated in the southerly part of Indiana. Area, 378 square miles. Seat of justice, Paoli. Pop. in 1820, 5,368; in 1830, 7,909; in 1840, 9,602; in 1850, 10,809.

ORANGE. p. t., Orange co., Vt., 14 ms. s. E. of Montpelier; from W. 527 ms. Watered by Jail branch of Onion river. Pop. 1,007.

ORANGE, t., Grafton co., N. H., 40 ms. N. w. of Concord; from W. —— ms. Pop. 451.

ORANGE. p. t., Franklin co., Mass., 74 ms. w. of Boston; from W. 415 ms. Watered by Miller's river. Pop. 1,701.

ORANGE, t., New Haven co., Ct. Watered by Wopewaug river. Pop. 1,476.

ORANGE, p. t., Steuben co., N. Y., 201 ms. w. of Albany; from W. 313 ms. Watered by Mead's creek. Pop. 2,055.

ORANGE, p. t., Essex co., N. J., 53 ms. N. E. of Trenton; from W. 219 ms. Watered by Second river and tributaries of the Rahway. Pop. 4,385.

ORANGE, p. t., Columbia co., Pa.

ORANGE t., Cuyahoga co., O. Watered by Chagrin river. Pop. 1,063.

ORANGE, t., Delaware co., O. Pop. 1,150.

ORANGE, t., Hancock co., O. Pop. 704.

ORANGE, p. t., Meigs co., O. Pop. 948.

ORANGE, t., Richland co., O.

ORANGE, t., Shelby co., O. Pop. 922.

ORANGE. p. o., Austintown township, Mahoning co., O., 169 ms. N. E. of Columbus; from W. 298 ms.

ORANGE, t., Noble co., Ind. Pop. 607.

ORANGE, t., Rush co., Ind.

ORANGE, t., Ionia co., Mich. Pop. 378.

ORANGE. p. v., Cherokee co., Ga., 129 ms. N. w. of Milledgeville; from W. 660 ms.

ORANGE, p. t., Fayette co., Ind., 49 ms. E. of Indianapolis; from W. 535 ms. Pop. 1,129.

ORANGE p. o., Luzerne co., Pa.

ORANGE, p. t., Columbia co., Pa. Pop. 1,077.

ORANGE, c. h., p. v., seat of justice of Orange co., Va., 84 ms. N. w. of Richmond; from W. 94 miles.

ORANGEBURGH DISTRICT, situated in the central part of South Carolina, with Congaree and Santee rivers on the northeast, and the South Edisto on the southwest. Area, 1,824 square miles. Face of the country, level; soil, sterile. Seat of justice, Orangeburgh c. h. Pop. 1810, 13,229; in 1820, 15,653; in 1830, 18,455; in 1840, 18,519; in 1850, 23,582.

ORANGEBURGH, c. h., seat of justice of Orangeburgh district, S. C., 43 ms. s. of Columbia; from W. 549 ms. Watered by North Edisto river.

ORANGEBURGH, p. o., Mason co., Ky.

ORANGE HILL, p. o., Washington co., Flor.

ORANGE LAKE, p. o., Marion co., Flor.

ORANGE PORT, p. o., Niagara co., N. Y.

ORANGE SPRINGS, p. v., Orange co., Va., 76 ms. N. w. of Richmond; from W. 98 ms.

ORANGE SPRINGS, p. o., Marion co., Flor.

ORANGETOWN. t., Rockland co., N. Y., 123 ms. s. of Albany; from W. —— ms. Watered by Hudson and Hackensack rivers. Pop. 4.769.

ORANGEVILLE, p. t., Wyoming co., N. Y., 257 ms. w. of Albany; from W. 369 ms. Watered by Tonawanda creek and tributaries. Pop. 1,438.

ORANGEVILLE, p. v., Bloom township, Columbia co., Pa., 81 ms. N. of Harrisburgh; from W. 191 ms. Watered by Fishing creek.

ORANGEVILLE, p. o., Trumbull co., O., 194 ms. N. E. of Columbus; from W. 300 ms.

ORBISONIA, p. o., Huntingdon co., Pa., 81 ms. w. of Harrisburgh; from W. 125 ms.

ORCUTT CREEK, p. o., Bradford co., Pa.

OREFIELD, p. o., Lehigh co., Pa.

OREGON TERRITORY, situated between 42° and 46° north latitude, and 109° and 124° longitude west from Greenwich; and is bounded on the north by Washington Territory, from which it is separated in part by the Columbia river, east by the Rocky mountains, which separate it from the Northwest or Nebraska territory, south by Utah and California, and west by the Pacific. Its superficial area is about 200,000 square miles.

Physical Aspect.—Most of the surface of this territory is mountainous and broken. Westward of the Rocky mountains the country is divided into three sections, separated from each other by ranges, running nearly parallel with the shores of the Pacific, each of which have a distinction of soil, climate, and productions. The region between the Rocky and Blue mountains is rocky and sterile, traversed in various directions by stupendous spurs, and affords but little level ground. The middle section generally consists of a light sandy soil, though in the valleys it is of rich alluvion, and barren on the hills. The soil along the coast is less broken, and for the most part is well adapted for agricultural purposes, wherever it can properly be irrigated.

Mountains.—Along the easterly boundary lie the Oregon or Rocky mountains, several of the spurs of which traverse the upper region of this territory, and are of stupendous height. About 250 miles at the westward is the Blue mountain range, which is irregular in its course, and occasionally interrupted, but generally extends from a point east of north to the south of west. About 80 to 110 miles from the coast, and about 200 miles at the westward of the Blue mountains, is the Cascade or President range, the highest peaks of which are called Mount Jefferson, Mount Rainier, Mount Baker, Mount St. Helen's (an extinct volcano), Mount Pitt, and Mount Hood. Some of these are elevated from 12,000 to 17,000 feet above the level of the sea, and are perpetually crowned with snow. In the south part of the territory is the Klamath range, which forms the northern boundary of California.

Rivers and Harbors.—The chief river is the Columbia, which takes its rise near the sources of the Missouri, along the western dividing ridges of the Rocky mountains. Its principal tributaries are the Lewis or Saptin, Flathead or Clark's, Kootanie or Flatbow, Chute or Falls, John Day's, Willamette, and Okonagon. The Klamath and Umpqua are considerable rivers, which empty into the Pacific. The Columbia river and Puget's sound afford the only good harbors at present on the coast of Oregon. The trade of that territory is principally through the former. Puget's sound is one of the best harbors on the Pacific coast. It has numerous narrow bays or inlets, all of them capable of floating the

.argest vessels, extending back into the surrounding country in every direction, and is accessible at all seasons of the year.

Climate.—The climate of the region between the coast and the first range of mountains though not regarded as unhealthy, is temperate during the year, and is not subject to the extremes of heat and cold that are experienced in corresponding parallels on the eastern coast. The mean annual temperature is about 54° Fahrenheit. The rain begins to fall in November, and usually continues at frequent intervals till March. Snow sometimes falls, but rarely endures more than two or three days. From the proximity to the mountain winds frosts sometimes occur in August. The climate of the middle region, though colder than that along the coast, is favorable to the growth of the small grains and grass. In the higher mountain regions the climate is severe, the temperature often varying 40° between sunrise and noon. Here it seldom rains, and dews are rarely known. On the most elevated parts deep snows occur, and abide during the year.

Productive Resources.—The chief products are, horses, mules, neat cattle, sheep, swine, furs, wool, lumber, wheat, rye, oats, barley, potatoes, and Indian corn. Oregon is peculiarly adapted to grazing, butter and cheesemaking, for the cattle range all winter, and feed upon the grass, which is never entirely killed by frost, nor covered with snow. The mineral resources of the country are as yet unknown.

Commerce.—Since the discovery of gold in California. a great demand has arisen for the agricultural productions and lumber (which can be furnished to an almost unlimited extent) of Oregon, and, as a consequence, a commercial trade has sprung up. Commercial intercourse is also maintained with the Sandwich islands, and the Russian settlements on the north.

Education.—A female seminary is established at Portland, and three academies at Oregon City, and well-regulated schools in all the principal settlements.

Population.—In 1850, 13,293.

History.—Oregon embraces Oregon as claimed by Spain, prior to 1820, or a part of the territory claimed by Russia, prior to 1824, or a portion of the country claimed by Great Britain prior to 1846. Although this coast was explored by the Spaniards, in about the year 1542, and by Sir Francis Drake, in 1578, it would appear that no one penetrated far into the interior before 1792, when Captain Robert Gray, of Boston, Massachusetts, entered Oregon, or Columbia river, in the ship "Columbia Rediviva," and gave to this river the present name it bears, after that of his vessel. In 1805, Lewis and Clarke were sent out by the United States government, with the express object of exploring the sources of the Missouri, and the region beyond the Rocky mountains, and descended the river Columbia to the Pacific, and returned the following year by the same streams. In 1808, a trading-house was established by the "Missouri Fur Company" on Lewis river, the first white settlement of any kind ever made on the waters of the Columbia. In 1810, a private expedition, called the "Pacific Fur Company," was undertaken, at the expense and under the direction of John Jacob Astor, of New York, who, in 1811, established a colony of one hundred and twenty men, near the mouth of the latter, and called the principal depot "Astoria," after his own name. Two years after, settlements were made on the Willamette and Lewis rivers, and other places in the interior. Soon after the commencement of the war between Great Britain and the United States, in 1813, Astoria was sold to the Hudson Bay Company, but was restored to the original proprietors in 1818, agreeably to the first articles of the treaty of Ghent. The sovereignty of Oregon was for a long time subject to a tedious and vexatious controversy by France, Spain, Great Britain, and Russia, with our government. In the convention of 1818, between the United States and Great Britain, the right of both parties to the country was mutually conceded. After much controversy the northern boundary was finally established at 49° in 1846, and a territorial government was organized, under an act of Congress, in 1848. In March, 1853, the territory was divided, the southern portion retaining the original name, and the northern part was organized as Washington territory.

OREGON COUNTY, situated on the south boundary of Missouri. Area, — square miles. Seat of justice, Thomasville. Pop. in 1850, 1,432.

OREGON, p. o., Jefferson co., Ala.

OREGON, p. o., Lancaster co., Pa.

OREGON, c. h., v., seat of justice of Holt co., Mo. Watered by Missouri river.

OREGON, t., Lucas co., O. Pop. 436.

OREGON, p. o., Clark co., Ind.

OREGON, p. o., Stocton township, Chautauque co., N. Y., 333 ms. w. of Albany; from W. 334 ms.

OREGON, p. o., Dane co., Wis.

OREGON, p. v., Ogle co., Ill., 176 ms. N. of Springfield; from W. 818 ms. Watered by Rock river. Pop. 540.

OREGON, p. o., Lincoln co., Tenn.

OREGON CITY, p. v., Clackamas co., Oregon, The principal settlement in the territory, and from its favorable position in the fertile valley of Willamette, or Multnomah river, 30 miles from its entrance into the Columbia, will probably become the business and political metropolis of the territory. It is in latitude 45° 20′ north, and longitude 45° 45′ west of Washington, at the head of navigation, below the falls of the Willamette, which furnish a most valuable water power. From Fort Vancouver, on the Columbia, it is 20 miles south; from Astoria, 100 miles southeast; and 2,171 miles northwest of independence, on Missouri river, which is 1,072 miles west of Washington. Most of the settlers are Americans, and the swift tide of migration toward California, has contributed considerably to its growth. There are a number of stores, dwellings, mills, schools, &c., which are receiving accessions. The pop. in 1848, was from 200 to 300; in 1850, 702.

OREGONIA, p. o., Tuscaloosa co., Ala.

ORE HILL, p. o., Litchfield co., Ct.

ORFORD, p. t., Grafton co., N. H., 60 N. w. of Concord; from W. 505 ms. Watered by Connecticut river and tributaries. Pop. 1,406.

ORFORDVILLE, p. v., Orford township, Grafton co., N. H., 62 ms. N. w. of Concord; from W. 507 ms.

ORGAN CHURCH, p. o., Rowan co., N. C.

ORIENT, p. t., Aroostook co., Me., 222 ms. N. E. of Augusta; from W. 817 ms. Pop. 205.

ORIENT. p. v., Southold township, Suffolk co., Long Island, N. Y., 232 ms. S. E. of Albany; from W. 332 ms. Watered by Oyster Pond harbor.

ORION, t., Oakland co., Michigan, 35 ms. N. of Detroit; from W. 558 ms. Watered by Paint creek. Pop. 1,119.

ORION, p. o., Pike co., Ala.

ORION, p. o., Richland co., Wis.

ORION, p. o., Henry co., Ill.

ORISKANY, p. o., Whitestown township, Oneida co., N. Y., 99 ms. N. w. of Albany; from W. 307 ms.

ORISKANY FALLS, p v., Augusta township, Oneida co., N. Y. Watered by Oriskany creek and Chenango canal.

ORIZABA, p. o., Tippah co., Miss.

ORLAND, p. t., Hancock co., Me., 61 ms. E. of Augusta; from W. 657 ms. Watered by Penobscot river. Pop. 1,579.

ORLAND, p. t., Steuben co., Ind., 190 ms. N. E. of Indianapolis; from W. 562 ms.

ORLAND, p. o., Cook co., Ill.

ORLEAN, p. o., Fauquier co., Va., 114 ms. N. of Richmond; from W. 63 ms.

ORLEANS COUNTY, situated on the north boundary of Vermont, with Lake Memphremagog on the north. Area, 700 square miles. Face of the country broken and mountainous. Soil rocky and sterile. Seat of justice, Irasburgh. Pop. in 1810, 5,838; in 1820, 6,976; in 1830, 13,980; in 1840, 13,634; in 1850, 15,707.

ORLEANS COUNTY, situated on the northerly boundary of New York, with Lake Ontario on the north, and traversed by the Erie canal. Area, 372 square miles. Face of the country undulating; soil fertile. Seat of justice, Albion. Pop. in 1820, 7,625; in 1830, 17,732; in 1840, 25,127; in 1850, 28,501.

ORLEANS PARISH, situated in the southeast part of Louisiana, with Lake Pontchartrain on the northwest, Lake Borgne on the southeast, and Mississippi river on the southwest. Area, 100 square miles. Face of the country flat and marshy. Seat of justice, New Orleans. Pop. in 1810, 24,552; in 1820, 41,351; in 1830, 49,826; in 1840, 102, 193; in 1850, 119,461.

ORLEANS, p. t., Barnstable co., Mass., 95 ms. S. E. of Boston; from W. 496 ms. Watered by Cape Cod bay and the Atlantic ocean. Pop. 1,848.

ORLEANS, t., Jefferson co., N. Y., 172 ms. N. w. of Albany; from W. — ms. Watered by Chaumont and Perch rivers. Pop. 3,265.

ORLEANS, p. v., Phelps township, Ontario co., N. Y.,

190 ms. w. of Albany; from W. 355 ms. Watered by Flint creek.

ORLEANS, p. o., Polk co., Mo.

ORLEANS, p. o., Alleghany co., Md.

ORLEANS, p. v., Orange co., Ind., 86 ms. s. of Indianapolis; from W. 625 ms.

ORLEANS FOUR CORNERS, p. o., Jefferson co., N. Y.

ORME'S STORE, p. o., Bledsoe co., Tenn., 125 ms. s. E. of Nashville; from W. 584 ms.

ORNEVILLE, p. o., Piscataquis co., Me.

ORONO, p. t., Penobscot co., Me., 75 ms. N. E. of Augusta; from W. 670 ms. Watered by Penobscot and Pushaw rivers. Pop. 2,785.

ORONOCO, p. o., Amherst co., Va.

ORONOKO, t., Berrien co., Mich.

ORRIN GLEN, p. o., Delaware co., Iowa.

ORRINGTON, p. t., Penobscot co., Me., 70 ms. N. E. of Augusta; from W. 666 ms. Watered by Penobscot river. Pop. 1,852.

ORRSTOWN, p. o., Franklin co., Pa., 39 ms. s. w. of Harrisburgh; from W. 106 ms.

ORRSVILLE, p. v., Pine township, Armstrong co., Pa., 192 ms. N. w. of Harrisburgh; from W. 246 ms.

ORRVILLE, p. o., Mecklenburgh co., N. C., 170 ms. s. w. of Raleigh; from W. 409 ms.

ORRVILLE, p. o., Dallas co., Ala.

ORWELL, p. t., Oswego co., N. Y., 148 ms. N. w. of Albany; from W. 393 ms. Watered by Salmon river. Pop. 1,106.

ORWELL, p. t., Rutland co., Vt., 79 ms. s. w. of Montpelier; from W. 463 ms. Watered by Lake Champlain, East creek, and Lenonfair river. Pop. 1,682.

ORWELL, p. t., Bradford co., Pa., 146 ms. N. of Harrisburgh; from W. 256 ms. Watered by Wysox creek. Pop. 1,241.

ORWELL, p. t., Ashtabula co., O., 185 ms. N. E. of Columbus; from W. 325 ms. Pop. 825.

ORWIGSBURGH, c. h., p. b., seat of justice of Schuylkill co., Pa., 62 ms. N. E. of Harrisburgh; from W. 172 ms. Watered by a tributary of Schuylkill river. Pop. 909.

OSAGE COUNTY, situated in the central part of Missouri, with Missouri and Osage rivers on the northwest, and traversed by the Gasconade river. Area, —— square miles. Seat of justice, Linn. Pop. in 1850, 6,704.

OSAGE, p. o., Crawford co., Mo., 87 ms. s. E. of Jefferson city; from W. 911 ms.

OSAGE, t., Miller co., Mo.

OSAGE, t., Morgan co., Mo.

OSAGE, t., Van Buren co., Mo.

OSAGE, p. t., Carroll co., Ark.

OSAGE, p. o., Fremont co., Iowa.

OSANIPPA, p. o., Chambers co., Ala.

OSBORN, p. o., Rock co., Wis.

OSBORN HOLLOW, p. o., Chenango township, Broome co., N. Y., 130 ms. s. w. of Albany; from W. 306 ms.

OSBORN'S BRIDGE, p. o., Northampton township, Fulton co., N. Y., 58 ms. N. w. of Albany; from W. 421 ms.

OSBORN'S FORD, p. o., Scott co., Va., 350 ms. w. of Richmond; from W. 410 ms.

OSCEOLA, p. o., Lewis co., N. Y.

OSELICHA, p. o., Chambers co., Ala.

OSEOLA, c. h., p. v., seat of justice of St. Clair co., Mo., 132 ms. w. of Jefferson city; from W. 1,068 ms. Watered by Osage river.

OSHAUKUTA, p. o., Columbia co., Wis.

OSHKOSH, p. o., Winnebago co., Wis., 118 ms. N. E. of Madison; from W. 965 ms.

OSHTOME, t., Kalamazoo co., Mich. Pop. 587.

OSKALOOSA. c. h., p. v., seat of justice of Mahaska co., Iowa. Pop. 625.

OSNABURGH, p. t., Stark co., O., 129 ms. N. E. of Columbus; from W. 308 ms. Pop. 2,225.

OSSAWA, p. o., Clinton co., Mich.

OSSIAN, p. t., Alleghany co., N. Y., 244 ms. w. of Albany; from W. 334 ms. Watered by Canaseraga creek. Pop. 1,283.

OSSIAN. p. o., Wells co., Ind.

OSSIPEE, c. h., p. t., seat of justice of Carroll co., N. H., 52 ms. N. E. of Concord; from W. 533 ms. Watered by Ossipee lake and Bearcamp river. Pop. 2,123.

OSTEND, p. o., McHenry co., Ill.

OSTEND, p. o., Washington co., O.

OSTERVILLE, p. v., Barnstable township, Barnstable co., Mass., 72 ms. s. E. of Boston; from W. 477 ms. Watered by Oyster bay.

OSWAYO, p. o., Potter co., Pa.

OSWEGATCHIE, p. t., St. Lawrence co., N. Y., 200 ms. N. w. of Albany; from W. —— ms. Watered by Black lake and Oswegatchie and St. Lawrence rivers. Pop. 7,756.

OSWEGO COUNTY, situated on the northwesterly boundary of New York, with Lake Ontario on the northwest, Oneida lake on the south, and traversed by Oswego river. Area, 923 square miles. Face of the country hilly; soil of middling quality. Seats of justice, Oswego and Pulaski. Pop. in 1820, 12,374; in 1830, 27,104; in 1840, 43.619; in 1850, 62,198.

OSWEGO, c. h., p. v., seat of justice, together with Pulaski, of Oswego co., N. Y., 160 ms. N. w. of Albany; from W. 373 ms. Watered by Oswego river, Lake Ontario, and Oswego canal. Pop. in 1830, 2,703; in 1840, 4,665; in 1850, 12.205.

OSWEGO, t., Potter co., Pa.

OSWEGO, p. v., Kosciusko co., Ind., 133 ms. N. of Indianapolis; from W. 603 ms. Pop. 137.

OSWEGO, p. t., Kendall co., Ill., 171 ms. N. E. of Springfield; from W. 760 ms. Pop. 1,599.

OSWEGO FALLS, p. o., Oswego co., N. Y.

OSWEGO VILLAGE, p. o., Dutchess co., N. Y.

OSWICCHEE, p. o., Russell co., Ala.

OTEGO, p. t., Otsego co., N. Y., 86 ms. w. of Albany; from W. 340 ms. Watered by Otsdawa creek and Susquehanna river. Pop. 1,792.

OTIS, p. t., Berkshire co., Mass., 119 ms. w. of Boston; from W. 368 ms. Watered by head waters of Farmington and Westfield rivers. Pop. 1,224.

OTIS, t., Hancock co., Me. Pop. 124.

OTISCO, p. t., Onondaga co., N. Y., 138 ms. w. of Albany; from W. 335 ms. Watered by Otisco lake and Nine-Mile creek. Pop. 1,804.

OTISCO, p. t., Ionia co.. Mich. Pop. 1,018.

OTISFIELD. p. t., Cumberland co., Me., 71 ms. s. w. of Augusta; from W. 578 ms. Watered by Crooked river. Pop. 1,171.

OTISVILLE, p. o., Mount Hope township, Orange co., N. Y., 110 ms. s. w. of Albany; from W. 275 ms.

OTSDAWA. p. v., Otsego township, Otsego co., N. Y., 86 ms. w. of Albany; from W. 344 ms.

OTSEGO COUNTY, situated in the central part of New York, with Otsego and Canaderaga lakes in the north. Area, 892 square miles. Face of the country, hilly; soil, productive. Seat of justice, Cooperstown. Pop. in 1810, 38,802; in 1820, 44,856; in 1830, 51,372; in 1840, 49,628; in 1850, 48,639.

OTSEGO, p. t., Otsego co., N. Y., 66 ms. w. of Albany; from W. —— ms. Watered by Otsego and Canaderaga lakes and Oak creek. Pop. 3,901.

OTSEGO, p. o., Muskingum co., O., 73 ms. E. of Columbus; from W. 337 ms.

OTSEGO, p. o. Ray co., Mo.

OTSEGO, p. t., Allegan co., Mich., 149 ms. w. of Detroit; from W. 614 ms. Watered by Kalamazoo river. Pop. 818.

OTSEGO, p. t., Lake co., Ill., 250 ms. N. E. of Springfield; from W. 756 ms.

OTSEGO, p. o., Columbia co., Wis.

OTSELIC, p. t., Chenango co., N. Y., 86 ms. w. of Albany; from W. 344 ms. Watered by Otselic creek. Pop. 1,800.

OTTAWA COUNTY, situated on the west boundary of Michigan, with Lake Michigan on the west, and traversed by Grand river. Area, —— square miles. Seat of justice, Grand Haven. Pop. in 1840, 208; in in 1850, 5,587.

OTTAWA COUNTY, situated on the northerly boundary of Ohio, with Lake Erie on the north, and Sandusky bay on the southeast. Area, 350 square miles. Seat of justice, Port Clinton. Pop. in 1840, 2,248; in 1850, 3,308.

OTTAWA, c. h., p. v., seat of justice of La Salle co., Ill., 133 ms. N. E. of Springfield; from W. 773 ms. Watered by Illinois and Fox rivers.

OTTAWA, p. t., Ottawa co., O., 132 ms. N. of Columbus; from W. 450 ms.

OTTAWA, t., Ottawa co., Mich. Pop. 430.

OTTAWA, t., Putnam co., O. Pop. 1,166.

OTTAWA LAKE, p. o., Monroe co., Mich.

OTTER BRIDGE, p. o., Bedford co., Va.

OTTER CREEK, t., Ripley co., Ind. Pop. 741.

OTTER CREEK, p. o., Jersey co., Ill., 80 ms. s. w. of Springfield; from W. 830 ms.

OTTER CREEK, p. o., Addison co., Vt.

OTTER CREEK, p. o., Jackson co., Mich.

OTTER CREEK, t., Wayne co., Mo.
OTTER DALE, p. o., Chesterfield co., Va.
OTTER VILLAGE, p. v., Ripley co., Ind., 67 ms. s. E. of Indianapolis ; from W. —— ms.
OTTO, p. o., Fulton co., Ill.
OTTERVILLE, p. o., Cooper co., Mo.
OTTO, p. t., Cattaraugus co., N. Y., 306 ms. w. of Albany. Watered by Cattaraugus creek. Pop. 2,267.
OTTOHEE, p. v., Fulton co., O.
OTTOBINE, p. o., Rockingham co., Va., 144 ms. w. of Richmond ; from W. 144 ms.
OTTSVILLE, p. o., Nockamixon township, Bucks co., Pa., 112 ms. E. of Harrisburgh : from W. 174 ms.
OTTUMWA, c. h., p. v., seat of justice of Wapello co., Iowa.
OUELOUT, p. o., Delaware co., N. Y.
OURY'S, p. o., Hamilton co., C., 124 ms. s. w. of Columbus ; from W. 508 ms.
OUTLET, p. o., Lake co., Ind.
OVERALLS, p. o., Warren co., Va.
OVERFIELD, p. o., Barbour co., Va.
OVERMAN'S FERRY, p. o., Muscatine co., Iowa.
OVERTON COUNTY, situated on the north boundary of Tennessee. Area, 625 square miles. Seat of justice, Monroe. Pop. in 1810, 5,643 ; in 1820, 7,128 ; in 1830, 7,188 ; in 1840, 9,279 ; in 1850, 11,211.
OVID, p. t., Branch co., Mich. Pop. 710.
OVID, c. h., p. t., seat of justice together with Waterloo of Seneca co., N. Y., 189 ms. w. of Albany ; from W. 323 ms. Watered by Cayuga and Seneca lakes. Pop. 2,258.
OVID, p. o., Jefferson township, Franklin co., O., 17 ms. E. of Columbus ; from W. 388 ms.
OVID, p. v., Madison co., Ind., 36 ms. N. E. of Indianapolis ; from W. 554 ms.
OVID, p. o., Lee co., Ill.
OWASCO, p. t., Cayuga co., N. Y., 162 ms. w. of Albany ; from W. 334 ms. Watered by Owasco lake. Pop. 1,254.
OWASCO LAKE, p. o., Cayuga co., N. Y.
OWASCUS, p. o., Fond du Lac co., Wis.
OWASSO, p. t., Shiawassee co., Mich., 82 ms. N. w. of Detroit ; from W. 585 ms. Watered by Shiawassee river. Pop. 392.
OWEGO, c. h., p. t., seat of justice of Tioga co., N. Y., 161 ms. s. w. of Albany; from W. 275 ms. Watered by Owego creek and Susquehanna river. Pop. 7,159.
OWEN COUNTY, situated in the north part of Kentucky with Kentucky river on the southwest. Area, 320 square miles. Seat of justice, Owenton. Pop in 1820, 2,031 ; in 1830, 5,793 ; in 1840, 8,232 ; in 1850, 10,444.
OWEN COUNTY, situated toward the westerly part of Indiana, and traversed by west fork of White river. Area, 380 square miles. Face of the country, undulating ; soil productive. Seat of justice, Spencer. Pop. in 1820, 838 ; in 1830, 4,060 ; in 1840, 8,359 ; in 1850, 12,118.
OWEN, t., Dallas co., Ark. Pop. 366.
OWENSBOROUGH, c. h., p. v., seat of justice of Daviess co., Ky., 166 ms. s. w. of Frankfort; from W. 693 ms. Watered by Ohio river. Pop. 1,215.
OWENSBURGH, p. o., Green co., Ind.
OWENSVILLE, v., Somers township, Westchester co., N. Y., 115 ms. s. of Albany ; from W. 283 ms. Watered by Croton river.
OWENSVILLE, p. o., Stonelick township, Clermont co., O., 100 ms. s. w. of Columbus ; from W. 471 ms.
OWENSVILLE, p. v., Gibson co., Ind., 152 ms. s. w. of Indianapolis ; from W. 722 ms.
OWENSVILLE, p. v., Saline co., Ark., 33 ms. s. w. of Little Rock ; from W. 1,098 ms.
OWENTON, c. h., p. v., seat of justice of Owen co., Ky., 48 ms. N. of Frankfort; from W. 551 ms.
OWENVILLE, p. v., Sampson co., N. C., 84 ms. s. E. of Raleigh ; from W. 336 ms.
OWING'S MILLS, p. o., Baltimore co., Md., 42 m. N. of Annapolis ; from W. 52 ms.
OWINGSVILLE, p. o., Anne Arundel co., Md.
OWINGSVILLE, c. h., p. v., seat of justice of Bath co., Ky., 73 ms. E. of Frankfort; from W. 499 ms. Watered by Slate creek.
OWL PRAIRIE, p. o., Daviess co., Ind., 90 ms. s. w. of Indianapolis ; from W. 657 ms.
OWSLEY COUNTY, situated in the easterly part of Kentucky, and traversed by Kentucky river. Area,

—— square miles. Seat of justice, Booneville. Pop. in 1850, 3,774.
OXBOW, p. v., Antwerp township, Jefferson co., N. Y., 176 ms. N. w. of Albany ; from W. 445 ms. Watered by Oswegatchie river.
OXBOW, p. o., Wyoming co., Pa.
OXBOW, p. o., Putnam co., Ill.
OXFORD COUNTY, situated on the west boundary of Maine, and traversed by the Androscoggin and Oxford and Cumberland canal. Area, 1,600 square miles. Face of the country, hilly ; soil, of middling quality. Seat of justice, Paris. Pop. in 1810, 17,630 ; in 1820, 27,104; in 1830, 35,217 ; in 1840, 38,351 ; in 1850, 39,763.
OXFORD, p. t., Oxford co., Me., 50 ms. s. w. of Augusta ; from W. 582 ms. Watered by Little Androscoggin river. Pop. 1,233.
OXFORD, p. t., Worcester co., Mass., 52 ms. w. of Boston ; from W. 394 ms. Watered by French river. Pop. 2,380.
OXFORD, p. t., Chenango co., N. Y., 109 ms. w. of Albany ; from W. 328 ms. Watered by Chenango river and Chenango canal. Pop. 3,227.
OXFORD, t., Warren co., N. J. Watered by Pequest creek and Beaver brook. Pop. 1,718.
OXFORD, p. v., Chester co., Pa., 69 ms. s. E. of Harrisburgh ; from W. 98 ms. Pop. 106.
OXFORD, p. t., Philadelphia co., Pa. Watered by Delaware river, and Tacony and Sissiocksink creeks. Pop. 1,787.
OXFORD, p. t., Butler co., O., 105 ms. s. w. of Columbus ; from W. 502 ms. Seat of Miami university. Pop. 3,139.
OXFORD, t., Coshocton co., O. Pop. 1,112.
OXFORD, t., Delaware co., O. Pop. 828.
OXFORD, t., Guernsey co., O. Pop. 2,209.
OXFORD, t., Tuscarawas co., O. Pop. 1,436.
OXFORD, p. t., Oakland co., Mich., 42 ms. N. w. of Detroit ; from W. 565 ms. Pop. 1, 019.
OXFORD, c. h., p. v., seat of justice of Granville co., N. C., 45 ms. N. of Raleigh ; from W. 256 ms. Watered by Fishing creek.
OXFORD, p. v., Henry co., Ill., 122 ms. N. w. of Springfield ; from W. 851 ms.
OXFORD, c. h., p. v., seat of justice of Lafayette co., Miss. 160 ms. N. E. of Jackson ; from W. 911 ms.
OXFORD, p. o., Newton co., Ga.
OXFORD, p. t., New Haven co., Ct., 55 ms. s. w. of Hartford ; from W. 309 ms. Watered by Housatonic and Naugatuck rivers. Pop. 1,564.
OXFORD, c. h., p. v., seat of justice of Benton co., Ind.
OXFORD, p. o., Scott co., Ky.
OXFORD, t., Erie co., O. Pop. 984.
OXFORD, p. o., Talbot co., Md.
OXFORD, p. o., Grafton co., N. H. Pop. 1,406.
OXFORD, p. o., Benton co., Ala.
OXFORD, p. o., Chester co., Pa.
OXFORD, p. o., McMinn co., Tenn.
OXFORD, p. o., Ritchie co., Va.
OXFORD DEPOT, Orange co., N. Y.
OXFORD FURNACE, p. v., Oxford township, Warren co., N. J., 52 ms. N. of Trenton ; from W. 210 ms. Watered by a tributary of Pequest creek.
OXFORD VALLEY, p. o., Bucks co., Pa.
OYSTER BAY, p. t., Queen's co., Long Island, N. Y., 182 ms. s. of Albany ; from W. 262 ms. Watered by Oyster bay of Long Island sound, and Great South bay of Atlantic ocean. Pop. 6,900.
OYSTER BAY SOUTH, p. v., Oyster Bay township, Queen's co., Long Island, N. Y., 179 ms. s. of Albany ; from W. 259 ms.
OYSTER POND, p. v., Southold township, Suffolk co., Long Island, N. Y. Watered by Oyster Pond harbor.
OZAN, t., Hempstead co., Ark. Pop. 1,547.
OZARK COUNTY, situated on the south boundary of Missouri. Area, —— square miles. Seat of justice, Rockbridge. Pop. in 1850, 2,294.
OZARK, c. h., p. v., seat of justice of Franklin co., Ark., 121 ms. N. w. of Little Rock ; from W. 1,186 ms. Watered by Arkansas river.
OZARK, p. v., Greene co., Mo., 172 ms. s. w. of Jefferson city ; from W. 1,089 ms. Pop. 569.
OZARK, c. h., v., Ozark co., Mo., 140 ms. s. of Jefferson city ; from W. —— ms. Watered by north fork of White river.
OZAUKEE, p. o., Washington co., Wis.

P.

PACES, p. o., Barren co., Ky., 124 ms. s. w. of Frankfort; from W. 660 ms.

PACHITTA, p. o., Early co., Ga., 166 ms. s. w. of Milledgeville; from W. 823 ms.

PACIFIC, p. o., Franklin co., N. C.

PACIFIC CITY, p. o., Lewis co., Oregon.

PACK'S FERRY, p. o., Monroe co., Va.

PACSKVILLE, p. o., Sumter district, S. C.

PACOLETT MILLS, p. o., Union district, S. C.

PACTOLUS, p. o., Pitt co., N. C., 114 ms. E. of Raleigh; from W. 300 ms.

PADDOCK'S GROVE, p. o., Madison co., Ill., 67 ms. s. of Springfield; from W. 801 ms.

PADDY MILLS, p. o., Shenandoah co., Va.

PADDY'S RUN, p. o., Morgan township, Butler co., O., 114 ms. s. w. of Columbus; from W. 502 ms.

PADUCAH, c. h., p. v., seat of justice of McCracken co., Ky., 284 ms. s. w. of Frankfort; from W. 816 ms. Watered by Ohio river at the confluence of the Tennessee. Pop. 2,428.

PAGE COUNTY, situated toward the northeast part of Virginia, with south fork of Shenandoah river on the northwest. Area. 160 square miles. Seat of justice, Luray. Pop. in 1840, 6,194; in 1850, 7,600.

PAGE COUNTY, situated on the south boundary of Iowa. Area. —— square miles. Seat of justice, Nodaway. Pop. in 1850, 551.

PAGE'S CORNERS, Herkimer co., N. Y.

PAGESVILLE, p. v., Newberry district, S. C., 49 ms. N. w. of Columbia; from W. 514 ms.

PAGEVILLE, p. o., Barren co., co., Ky.

PAINCOURTVILLE, p. v., Assumption parish, La., 81 ms. w. of New Orleans; from W. 1,218 ms.

PAINE'S HOLLOW, p. o., German Flats township, Herkimer co., N. Y., 74 ms. N. w. of Albany; from W. 385 ms.

PAINE'S POINT, p. o., Ogle co., Ill.

PAINESVILLE, p. v., Amelia co., Va., 49 ms. s. w. of Richmond; from W. 166 ms.

PAINESVILLE, c. h., p. v. seat of justice of Lake co., O., 179 ms. N. E. of Columbus; from W. 349 ms. Watered by Grand river and Lake Erie. Pop. 3,128.

PAINESVILLE, p. o., Chittenden co., Vt.

PAINT, t., Fayette co., O. Pop. 1,253.

PAINT, p. v., Clarion co., Pa, Pop. 610.

PAINT, t., Somerset co., Pa. Pop. 878.

PAINT, t., Holmes co., O. Watered by a tributary of Sugar creek. Pop. 1.618.

PAINT, t., Highland co., O. Pop. 2,678.

PAINT, t,, Ross co., O. Watered by Paint and Buckskin creeks. Pop. 1,123.

PAINT, t., Wayne co., O., 95 ms. N. E. of Columbus; from W. —— ms. Pop. 1,627.

PAINT CREEK, p. o., Kanawha co., Va.

PAINT CREEK, p. o., Washtenaw co., Mich., 36 ms. w. of Detroit; from W. 511 ms.

PAINTED POST, p. t., Steuben co., N. Y., 210 s. w. of Albany; from W. —— ms. Pop. 4,372.

PAINTED POST, p. v., Erwin township, Steuben co., N. Y., 212 ms. w. of Albany; from W. 286 ms. Watered by Chemung river at the confluence of Conhocton and Tioga rivers.

PAINTERSVILLE, p. o., Greene co., O.

PAINT LICK, p. o., Garrard co., Ky., 62 ms. s. E. of Frankfort; from W. 560 ms.

PAINT ROCK, p. o., Allamachee co., Iowa.

PAINT ROCK, p. o., Cocke co., Tenn.

PAINTSVILLE, c. h., p. v., seat of justice of Johnson co., Ky.

PAKWAUKEE, p. o.. Marquette co., Wis.

PALATINE, p. t., Montgomery co.. N. Y., 56 ms. N. w. of Albany; from W. 390 ms. Watered by Garoga creek and Mohawk river. Pop. 2,856.

PALATINE, p. o., Marion co., Va.

PALATINE, p. o., Cook co., Ill.

PALATINE BRIDGE, p. v., Palatine township, Montgomery co., N. Y., 51 ms. N. w. of Albany; from W. 394 ms. Watered by Mohawk river.

PALENVILLE, p. o., Greene co., N. Y., 54 ms. s. w. of Albany; from W. 360 ms.

PALERMO, p. t., Waldo co., Me., 19 ms. N. E. of Augusta; from W. 614 ms. Pop. 1,659.

PALERMO, p. t., Oswego co., N. Y., 157 ms N. w. of Albany; from W. 380 ms. Watered by Catfish creek. Pop. 2,053.

PALESTINE, p. o., Greenbrier co., Va.

PALESTINE, p. o., Hickman co., Tenn., 68 ms. s. w of Nashville; from W. 745 ms.

PALESTINE, p. o., Benton co., Ala.

PALESTINE, p. o., Washington parish, La., 65 ms. N. of New Orleans; from W. 1,132 ms.

PALESTINE, p. v., Darby township, Pickaway co., O., 29 ms. s. of Columbus; from W. 422 ms. Watered by Deer creek.

PALESTINE, p. v., Kosciusko co., Ind., 119 ms. N, of Indianapolis; from W. 610 ms.

PALESTINE, c. h., p. v., seat of justice of Crawford co., Ill., 153 ms. s. E. of Springfield; from W. 689 ms.

PALESTINE, p. o., Adams co.. Miss.

PALESTINE, v., Cooper co., Mo.

PALESTINE, p. o., Anderson co., Tex.

PALL MALL, p. o., Fentress co., Tenn. 120 ms. E. of Nashville; from W. 592 ms.

PALMER, p. t., Hampden co., Mass., 81 ms. w. of Boston; from W. 391 ms. Watered by Ware and Swift rivers. Pop. 3974.

PALMER'S, p. o., Polk co., Tex.

PALMER'S SPRINGS, p. o., Mecklenburgh co., Va., 102 ms. s. w. of Richmond; from W. 218 ms.

PALMER'S STORE, p. o., Weakly co., Tenn.

PALMER'S TAVERN, p. o., Prince George's co., Md., 50 ms. s. w. of Annapolis; from W. 10 ms.

PALMETTO, p. o., Pontotoc co., Miss.

PALMETTO, p. o., Coweta co., Ga.

PALMETTO, p. o., Lawrence district, S. C.

PALMYRA, p. t., Somerset co., Me., 49 ms. N. E. of Augusta; from W. 644 ms. Watered by Sebasticook river. Pop. 1,625.

PALMYRA, p. t., Wayne co., N. Y., 195 ms. w. of Albany; from W. 352 ms. Watered by Mud creek and Erie canal. Pop. 3,893.

PALMYRA, p. o., Burlington co., N. J.

PALMYRA, p. v., Londonderry township, Lebanon co., Pa., 14 ms. E. of Harrisburgh; from W. 124 ms. Pop. 286.

PALMYRA, c. h., p. v., seat of justice of Fluvanna co., Va., 62 ms. N. w. of Richmond; from W. 136 ms. Watered by Rivanna river.

PALMYRA, t., Pike co., Pa. Pop. 447.

PALMYRA, p. v., Halifax co., N. C., 115 ms. N. E. of Raleigh; from W. 239 ms. Watered by Roanoke river.

PALMYRA, p. v., Lee co., Ga., 128 ms. s. w. of Milledgeville; from W. 785 ms.

PALMYRA, p. v., Montgomery co., Tenn., 37 ms. N. w. of Nashville; faom W. 744 ms.

PALMYRA, t., Wayne co., Pa. Pop, 2,015.

PALMYRA, p. t., Portage co., O., 152 ms. N. of Columbus; from W. 310 ms. Pop. 1,093.

PALMYRA, p. v., Harrison co., Ind., 116 ms. s. of Indianapolis; from W. 620 ms.

PALMYRA, p. t., Lenawee co., Mich., 75 ms. s. w. of Detroit; from W. 493 ms. Watered by Raisin river and Bear creek. Pop. 1,098.

PALMYRA, c. h., p. v., seat of justice of Marion co., Mo., 111 ms. N. w. of Jefferson city; from W. 925 ms. Pop. 1,284.

PALMYRA, p. o., Warren co., Miss.

PALMYRA, p. o., Jefferson co., Wis.

PALMYRA, p. o., Simpson co., Ky.

PALO, p. o., Linn co., Iowa.

PALO, p. o.. Fayette co., Ala.

PALO ALTO, p. o., Jasper co., Ga.

PALO ALTO, p. o., Highland co., Va.

PALO ALTO, p. o., Lawrence co., Tenn.

PALO ALTO, p. o., Louisa co., Iowa.

PALO ALTO, p. o., Hamilton co., Ill.

PALO ALTO, p. o., Onslow co., N. C.

PALO ALTO, p. o., Chickasaw co., Miss.

PALONA. p. o., Greenville district, S. C.

PALOS, p. o., Miami co., Ind.

PALOS, p. o., Cook co., Ill.

PAMELIA, p. t., Jefferson co., N. Y., 168 ms. N. w. of Albany; from W. 420 ms. Watered by Perch and Black river. Pop. 2,528.

PAMELIA FOUR CORNERS, p. o., Pamelia township, Jefferson co., N. Y.

PANAMA, p. v., Harmony township, Chautauque co., N. Y., 345 ms. w. of Albany ; from W. 324 ms.

PANAMA, p. o., Defiance co., O.

PANCOASTBURGH. p. o., Fayette co., O.

PANDORA. p. o., Johnson co., Tenn.

PANOLA COUNTY, situated in the northwesterly part of Mississippi, and traversed by Tallahatchie river. Area, 760 square miles. Seat of justice, Panola. Pop. in 1840, 4,657 ; in 1850, 11,444.

PANOLA COUNTY, situated on the east boundary of Texas, and traversed by Sabine river. Area, —— square miles. Seat of justice, Carthage. Pop. in 1850, 3,871.

PANOLA, c. h.. p. v., seat of justice of Panola co., Miss., 161 ms. N. of Jackson ; from W. 939 ms. Watered by Tallahatchee river.

PANTEGO. p. o., Beaufort co., N. C., 186 ms. E of Raleigh ; from W. 342 ms.

PANTHER, p. o., Polk co., Ark.

PANTHER CREEK, p. o., Surry co., N. C., 125 ms. N. w. of Raleigh ; from W. 336 ms.

PANTHER CREEK. p. o., Cass co., Ill., 125 ms. w. of Springfield ; from W. 905 ms.

PANTHER CREEK, p. o., Clayton co., Iowa.

PANTHER FORK, p. o., Greenville district, S. C.

PANTHER'S GAP, p. o., Rockbridge co., Va., 170 ms. w. of Richmond ; from W. 212 ms.

PANTHER SPRINGS, p. o., Jefferson co., Tenn., 220 ms. E. of Nashville ; from W. 464 ms.

PANTHERVILLE, p. o., De Kalb co., Ga., 87 ms. N. w. of Milledgeville ; from W. 682 ms.

PANTON, p. t., Addison co., Vt., 71 ms. s. w. of Montpelier ; from W. 494 ms. Watered by Lake Champlain. Pop. 559.

PAN YAN. p. o., Racine co., Wis.

PAOLI, c. h., p. v., seat of justice of Orange co., Ind., 94 ms. s. of Indianapolis ; from W. 625 ms. Watered by Lick creek. Pop 461.

PAOLI, p. v., Fredypain township, Chester co., Pa., 78 ms. s. E. of Harrisburgh ; from W. 128 ms.

PAPAW GROVE, p. o., Lee co., Ill., 165 ms. N. of Springfield ; from W. 792 ms.

PAPER MILL VILLAGE, p. v., Cheshire co., N. H., 57 ms. s. w. of Concord ; from W. 454 ms.

PAPER MILLS, p. o., Baltimore co., Md.

PAPERTOWN, p. o., Cumberland co., Pa.

PAPERVILLE, p. v., Sullivan co., Tenn., 309 ms. E. of Nashville ; from W. 384 ms. Watered by a tributary of Holston river.

PAPINSVILLE, p. o., Bates co., Mo.

PARACLIFTA, c. h., p. v., seat of justice of Sevier co., Ark., 142 ms. s. w. of Little Rock ; from W. 1,207 ms. Watered by Little river.

PARADISE, p. t., Strasburgh township, Lancaster co., Pa., 46 ms. s. E. of Harrisburgh ; from W. 119 ms. Pop. 1,828.

PARADISE, t., York co., Pa.

PARADISE, p. o., Rockingham co., Va.

PARADISE FURNACE, p. o., Huntingdon co., Pa.

PARADISE VALLEY, p. o., Monroe co., Pa.

PARAN CITY, p. o. Marion co., Iowa.

PARCHER'S CORNERS, p. o., Fulton co., O.

PARDEEVILLE, p. o., Columbia co., Wis.

PARHAM'S LANDING. p. o., Catahoola parish, La.

PARHAM'S STORE. p. o., Sussex co., Va., 45 ms. s. E. of Richmond ; from W. —— ms.

PARIS, c. h., p. t., seat of justice of Oxford co., Me., 39 ms. w. of Augusta ; from W. 593 ms. Watered by Little Androscoggin river. Pop. 682.

PARIS, p. t., Oneida co., N. Y., 96 ms. N. w. of Albany ; from W. 378 ms. Watered by Sadaquada creek. Pop. 4,283.

PARIS, p. o., Washington co., Pa., 232 ms. w. of Harrisburgh ; from W. 257 ms.

PARIS, p. v. Fauquier co., Va., 129 ms. N. of Richmond ; from W. 59 ms.

PARIS, c. h.. p. v., seat of justice of Henry co., Tenn., 98 ms. w. of Nashville ; from W. 784 ms. Watered by a tributary of Little Sandy river.

PARIS, c. h., p. v., seat of justice of Bourbon co., Ky., 36 ms. E. of Frankfort ; from W. 507 ms. Watered by south fork of Licking river. Pop. 384.

PARIS, p. t., Stark co., O., 135 ms. N. E. of Columbus ; from W. 302 ms. Watered by Sandy creek. Pop. 2,135.

PARIS, p. t., Portage co., O. Pop. 1,018.

PARIS, t., Union co., O. Pop. 982.

PARIS, p. v., Jennings co. Ind., 77 ms. s. E. of In-

dianopolis ; from W. 578 ms. Watered by south fork of Muscatatack creek.

PARIS, c. h., p. v., seat of justice of Edgar co., Ill., 114 ms. E. of Springfield ; from W. 665 ms.

PARIS, c. h., p. v., seat of justice of Monroe co., Mo., 71 ms. N. of Jefferson city ; from W. —— ms. Watered by Middle fork of Salt river.

PARIS, p. o., Kent co., Mich.

PARIS, p. o., Coweta co., Ga.

PARIS, p. o., Lafayette co., Miss.

PARIS, p. o., Lamar co., Tex.

PARIS, p. o., Kenozha co., Wis.

PARISH, p. t., Otsego co., N. Y., 147 ms. N. w. of Albany ; from W. 376 ms. Watered by Salmon creek. Pop. 1,799.

PARISHVILLE, p. t., St. Lawrence co.. N. Y., 221 ms. N. w. of Albany ; from W. 505 ms. Watered by St. Regis, Racket, Grass, and Oswegatchie rivers. Pop. 2,132.

PARISVILLE, p o., Paris township, Portage co., O., 150 ms. N. E. of Columbus ; from W. 313 ms.

PARK, p. t., St. Joseph co., Mich. Pop. 805.

PARKE COUNTY, situated in the westerly part of Indiana, with Wabash river on the west. Area, 450 square miles. Seat of justice, Rockville. Pop. in 1830, 7,535 ; in 1840, 13,449; in 1850, 14,966.

PARKER, p. t., Butler co., O.

PARKERSBURGH, p. v., Washington township, Morris co., N. J., 56 ms. N. of Trenton ; from W. 218 ms. Site of a mineral spring.

PARKERSBURGH. c. h., p. v., seat of justice of Wood co., Va., 335 ms. N. w. of Richmond ; from W. 303 ms. Watered by Little Kanawha river, at its confluence with the Ohio. Pop. 1,218.

PARKERSBURGH. p. v., Montgomery co., Ind., 44 ms. N. w. of Indianapolis ; from W. 615 ms.

PARKERSBURGH, p v., Richland co., Ill., 140 ms. s. E. of Springfield : from W. 740 ms.

PARKER'S HEAD, p. o., Lincoln co., Me.

PARKER'S SETTLEMENT, p. o., Posey co., Ind.

PARKER'S STORE, p. o., Franklin co., Ga.

PARKERSVILLE, p. o., Chester co., Pa., 79 ms. s. E. of Harrisburgh ; from W. —— ms.

PARKERSVILLE, p. o., St. Tammany parish, La.

PARKESBURGH, p. v., Chester co., Pa., 57 ms. s. E. of Harrisburgh ; from W. 117 ms.

PARKVILLE, p. o., Noxubee co., Miss.

PARKHEAD, p. o., Washington co., Md.

PARKISON, p. o., Beaver co., Pa.

PARK HALL, p. o., St. Mary's co., Md.

PARKMAN, p. t., Piscataquis co., Me., 71 ms. N. of Augusta ; from W. 666 ms. Watered by a tributary of Piscataquis river. Pop. 1,243.

PARKMAN, p. t., Geauga co., O., 162 ms. N. E. of Columbus ; from W. 321 ms. Watered by head waters of Grand river, and a tributary of Cuyahoga river. Pop. 1,383.

PARKS, p. o., Edgefield district, S. C., 108 ms. w. of Columbia ; from W. 570 ms.

PARKS', p. o., Scott co., Ark.

PARKS' BAR, p. o., Yuba co., Cal.

PARKS' CORNERS, p. o., Boone co., Ill.

PARKS' MILLS, p. o., Franklin co., O.

PARKS' STORE, p. o., Cabarras co., N. C.

PARKS' STORE, p. o., Jackson co., Ala.

PARKSVILLE, p. v., Sullivan co., N. Y., 116 ms. s. w. of Albany ; from W. 308 ms.

PARKVILLE, p. v., Platte co., Mo. Pop. 309.

PARMA, p. t., Monroe co., N. Y., 231 ms. w. of Albany ; from W. 380 ms. Watered by Salmon and Little Salmon creeks, and Lake Ontario. Pop. 2,946.

PARMA, p. t., Cuyahoga co., O., 137 ms. N. E. of Columbus ; from W. 367 ms. Watered by a tributary of Cuyahoga river. Pop. 1,329.

PARMA, p. o., Jackson co., Mich. Pop. 1,081.

PARMA, p. o., Shelby co., Ind.

PARMA CENTRE, p. o., Parma township, Monroe co., N. Y., 234 ms. w. of Albany ; from W. 383 ms.

PARNASSUS, p. o., Augusta co., Va., 133 ms. N. w. of Richmond ; from W. 152 ms.

PARNASSUS, p. o., Wilcox co., Ala.

PARRISH. p. o., Des Moines co., Iowa.

PARRIZADE, p. o., Wayne co., Va.

PARROTTSVILLE, p. v., Cocke co., Tenn., 237 ms. E. of Nashville ; from W. 460 ms.

PARRYSVILLE, p. v., Carbon co., Pa., 99 ms. N. E. of Harrisburgh ; from W. 199 ms.

PARSIPPANY, p. v., Hanover township, Morris co., N.

J., 60 ms. N. of Trenton ; from W. 231 ms. Watered by Parsippany river.

PARSONAGE, p. o., Williamsburgh district, S. C.

PARSONSFIELD, p. t., York co., Me., 86 ms. s. w. of Augusta ; from 538 ms. Watered by Ossipee river. Pop. 2,322.

PARSON'S MILLS, p. o., Guilford co., N. C.

PARTLOW'S, p. o., Spottsylvania co., Va., 92 ms. N. of Richmond ; from W. 83 ms.

PARTNERSHIP, p. o., Charles co., Md.

PARTRIDGE ISLAND, p. o., Hancock township, Delaware co., N. Y., 116 ms. s. w. of Albany ; from W. 298 ms.

PASCAGOULA, p. o., Jackson co., Miss. Watered by Pascagoula river and Pascagoula bay.

PASCO, p. o., Dallas co., Mo.

PASCOAG, p. o., Providence co., R. I.

PASHAWN, p. o., La Grange co., Ind.

PASKACK, p. v., Washington township, Passaic co., N. J., 88 ms. N. E. of Trenton ; from W. 254 ms. Watered by Hackensack river.

PASQUOTANK COUNTY, situated in the northeast part of North Carolina, with Albemarle sound on the south. Area, 300 square miles. Face of the country level ; soil of middling quality. Seat of justice, Elizabeth City. Pop. in 1810, 7,674 ; in 1820, 8,008 ; in 1830, 8,616 ; in 1840. 8.514 ; in 1850. 8,950.

PASSADUMKEAG, p. t., Penobscot co., Me., 100 ms. N. E. of Augusta ; from W. 695 ms. Watered by Penobscot and Passadumkeag rivers. Pop. 295.

PASSAIC COUNTY, situated in the northeast part of New Jersey. Area. 180 square miles. Watered by Passaic river and its tributaries. Seat of justice, Paterson. Pop. in 1840, 16,734 ; in 1850, 22,575.

PASS CHRISTIAN, p. v., Harrison co., Miss. Watered by Bay of St. Louis.

PASSUMPSIC, p. v., Caledonia co., Vt., 41 ms. E. of Montpelier ; from W. 542 ms.

PASSYUNK, t., Philadelphia co., Pa. Watered by Delaware and Schuylkill rivers. Pop. 1,607.

PATCHIN, p. o., Erie co., N. Y.

PATCHIN'S MILLS, p. o., Conhocton township, Steuben co., N. Y., 238 ms. w. of Albany ; from W. 323 ms.

PATCHOGUE, p. v., Brookhaven township, Suffolk co., N. Y., 204 ms. s. E. of Albany ; from W. 284 ms. Watered by Great South bay.

PATERSON, city, seat of justice of Passaic co., N. J., situated on both sides of the Passaic river, 17 miles northwest of New York. It owes its existence and prosperity to the great water-power furnished by the Passaic. A large number of cotton factories, as well as other establishments for making machinery, firearms, and paper, are here in successful operation. The genius of Alexander Hamilton first perceived these natural advantages, and devised the means for their application. Difficulties at first prevented the success of his plans, but time has proved their practicability and sagacity. The beauty of Passaic falls, which are near this place, is not less admirable than their utility. Hither many resort in the summer, to enjoy the picturesque scenery and healthful air.

Paterson contains several churches and institutions for improvement in knowledge. The Morris canal passes near the south part of the city ; the Paterson railroad connects it with Jersey City and New York, and the Ramapo and Paterson railroad communicates with the Erie railroad at Ramapo.

The population in 1810, was 292 ; in 1820, 1,578 ; in 1830, 7,731 ; in 1840, 7,596 ; in 1850, 11,138.

PATMOS, p. o., Mahoning co., O.

PATOKA. p. t., Gibson co., Ind., 138 ms. s. w. of Indianapolis ; from W. 708 ms. Pop. 2,579.

PATON, p. o., Cape Girardeau co., Mo.

PATRICK COUNTY, situated on the south boundary of Virginia. Area, 541 square miles. Face of the country, pleasantly diversified ; soil of middling quality. Seat of justice, Taylorsville. Pop. in 1810, 4,695 ; in 1820, 5,089 ; in 1830, 7,393 ; in 1840, 8,032, in 1850, 9,609.

PATRICK, c. h., p. v., seat of justice of Patrick co., Va., 226 ms. s. w. of Richmond ; from W. 301 ms.

PATRICKTOWN. p. t., Lincoln co., Me., 15 ms. E. of Augusta ; from W. 611 ms. Watered by head waters of Sheepscot and Damariscotta rivers. Pop. 552.

PATRIOT, p. v., Switzerland co.. Ind., 105 ms. s. E. of Indianapolis ; from W. 536 ms. Watered by Ohio river.

PATRIOT, p. v., Perry township, Gallia co., O., 97 ms. s. E. of Columbus ; from W. 381 ms.

PATTEN, t., Penobscot co., Me. Pop. 470.

PATTEN, p. t., Centre co., Pa. Pop. 2,206.

PATTEN'S HOME, p. o., Rutherford co., N. C.

PATTEN'S MILLS, p. o., Fort Ann township, Washington co., N. Y., 59 ms. N. of Albany ; from W. 431 ms.

PATTERSON, p. o.. Putnam co.. N. Y., 92 ms. s. of Albany ; from W. 295 ms. Watered by Croton river.

PATTERSON, p. o., Thompson township, Delaware co., O., 40 ms. N. of Columbus ; from W. 424 ms.

PATTERSON, v., Wayne co., Mo., 176 ms. s. E. of Jefferson City ; from W. 864 ms.

PATTERSON'S DEPOT, p. o., Hampshire co., Va.

PATTERSON'S MILLS, p. o., Washington co., Pa., 223 ms. w. of Harrisburgh ; from W. 252 ms.

PATTERSON'S STORE, p. o., Allemance co., N. C., 59 ms. N. w. of Raleigh ; from W. 310 ms.

PATTERSONVILLE, p. o., St. Mary's parish, La.

PATTILLOS, p. o., Jefferson co., Tex.

PATTONSBURGH, p. v., Bottetourt co., Va., 166 ms. w. of Richmond ; from W. 213 ms. Watered by James river.

PATTONSBURGH, p. o., Daviess co., Mo.

PATTONSVILLE, p. o., Scott co., Va.

PATTONVILLE, p. o., Bedford co., Pa.

PATUXENT, p. o., Anne Arundel co., Md., 25 ms. N. w. of Annapolis ; from W. 28 ms.

PAULDING COUNTY, situated on the west boundary of Georgia. Area, 600 square miles. Seat of justice, Van Wert. Pop. in 1840, 2.556 ; in 1850. 7.039.

PAULDING COUNTY, situated on the west boundary of Ohio, with Maumee river on the north. Area, 432 square miles. Seat of justice, Charloe. Pop. in 1830, 160 ; in 1840, 1,034 ; in 1850, 1,766.

PAULDING, p. o., Paulding co., O.

PAULDING. c. h.. p. v., Jasper co., Miss., 109 ms. s. E. of Jackson ; from W. 987 ms. Watered by head waters of Leaf river.

PAULINA, p. o., Warren co., N. J.

PAULINA, v.. Hancock township, Delaware co., N. Y.

PAVILION, Kendall co., Ill.

PAVILION, p. t., Genesee co., N. Y., 243 ms. w. of Albany ; from W. 361 ms. Watered by Allen's creek. Pop. 1,640.

PAVILION, p. t., Kalamazoo co., Mich., 138 ms. w. of Detroit ; from W. 600 ms. Watered by the Sandy lakes and tributaries of St. Joseph's river. Pop. 495.

PAVILION CENTRE, p. o., Pavilion township, Genesee co., N. Y.

PAWLET, p. t., Rutland co., Vt., 87 ms. s. w. of Montpelier ; from W. 431 ms. Watered by Pawlet river and Indian stream. Pop. 1,843.

PAWLINGS, p. t., Dutchess co., N. Y., 89 ms. s. of Albany ; from W. 298 ms. *Watered by Croton river. Pop. 1,720.

PAWLINGSVILLE, p. o., Pawlings township, Dutchess co., N. Y., 86 ms. s. of Albany ; from W. 301 ms.

PAW PAW, c. h., p. v., seat of justice of Van Buren co., Mich., 159 ms. w. of Detroit ; from W. 623 ms. Watered by head waters of Papaw river.

PAW PAW, p. o., Miami co., Ind.

PAW PAW, p. o., Morgan co., Va.

PAW PAW GROVE, (See Papaw Grove.)

PAWTUCKET, p. v., partly in Pawtucket township, Mass., and North Providence township, Providence co., R. I. 4 ms. N. of Providence ; from W. 404 ms. Watered by Pawtucket river at the head of navigation.

PAWTUCKET. p. t., Bristol co., Mass., 36 ms. s. of Boston ; from W. —— ms. Watered by Pawtucket river. Pop. 2,987.

PAWTUXET, p. v., Warwick and Cranston townships, Kent co., R. I., 5. ms. s. of Providence ; from W. 405 ms. Watered by Pawtuxet river.

PAWTUXET, p. o., Wakulla co., Flor.

PAXINOS, p. o., Northumberland co., Pa.

PAXTON, p. t., Worcester co., Mass., 50 ms. w. of Boston ; from W. 405 ms.

PAXTON, t., Ross co., O. Pop. 930.

PAY DOWN, p. o., Osage co., Mo.

PAYNESVILLE, p. v.. Pike co., Mo., 92 ms. N. E. of Jefferson City ; from W. 880 ms.

PAYNEVILLE, p. o., Sumter co., Ala, from W. 896 ms. Watered by Sucarnockie creek.

PAYNTERSVILLE, p. o., Jackson co., Ind.

PAYSON, p. o., Adams co., Ill., 92 ms. w. of Springfield ; from W. 872 ms.

PEACE DALE, p. v., Washington co., R. I.

PEACHAM, p. t., Caledonia co., Vt., 36 ms. E. of Montpelier ; from W. 538 ms. Watered by Onion River pond. Pop. 1,377.

PEACH BOTTOM, p. t., York co., Pa., 62 ms., s. E. of Harrisburgh : from W. 81 ms. Watered by Fishing creek, Neal's Hole run and Susquehanna river. Pop. 2,409.

PEACH BOTTOM, p. o., Grayson co., Va.

PEACH CREEK, p. o., Panola co., Miss.

PEACH GROVE, p. o., Fairfax co., Va.

PEACH ORCHARD, p. o., Lawrence co., Ky.

PEACH TREE, p. o., Cherokee co., N. C.

PEACH TREE GROVE, p. o., Nash co., N. C.

PEAKSVILLE, p. o., Bedford co., Va.

PEALER'S, p. o., Columbia co., Pa., 93 ms. N. E. of Harrisburgh ; from W. 204 ms.

PEAPACK, p. o., Somerset co., N. J., 45 ms. N. of Trenton : from W. 220 ms.

PEAR GROVE, p. o., Prince Edward co., Va.

PEA RIDGE, p. o., Union district, S. C.

PEA RIDGE, p. o., Montgomery co., Tenn.

PEA RIDGE, p. o., Benton co., Ark.

PEA RIVER, p. o., Pike co., Ala., from W. 861 ms.

PEARLINGTON, p. v., Hancock co., Miss., 191 ms. s. of Jackson ; from W. 1,141 ms. Watered by Pearl river.

PEARL RIVER, p. o., Copiah co., Miss.

PEARL VALLEY, p. o., Neshoba co., Miss.

PEASE, t., Belmont co., O. Watered by Indian Wheeling creek. Pop. 3,515.

PEA VINE, p. o., Walker co., Ga.

PECAN GROVE, p. o., Carroll parish, La.

PECAN POINT, p. o., Mississippi co., Ark.

PECK'S RUN, p. o., Barbour co., Va.

PECKSVILLE, p. o., Fishkill township, Dutchess co., N. Y., 106 ms. s. of Albany ; from W. 269 ms.

PEDEE, p. o., Cedar co., Iowa.

PEDENSVILLE, p. v., Chester district, S. C.

PEDLAR'S HILL, p. o., Chatham co., N. C., 44 ms. w. of Raleigh ; from W. — ms.

PEDLAR'S MILLS, p. o., Amherst co., Va.

PEDRICKTOWN, p. v., Upper Penn's Creek township, Salem co., N. J., 55 ms. s. of Trenton ; from W. 166 ms. Watered by Oldman's creek.

PEEBLES, p. t., Alleghany co., Pa. Pop. 2,168.

PEEDEE, p. o., Anson co., N. C., 135 ms. s. w. of Raleigh ; from W. 409 ms.

PEEKSKILL, p. v., Cortland township, Westchester co., N. Y., 106 ms. s. of Albany ; from W. 269 ms. Watered by Hudson river.

PEELED OAK, p. o., Bath co., Ky., 71 ms. E. of Frankfort ; from W. 595 ms

PEEL TREE. p. o., Harrison co., Va.

PEE PEE, t., Pike co., O. Pop. 1,321.

PEERY'S STORE, p., Tazewell co., Va.

PEIRCERVILLE, p. o., Dane co., Wis.

PEKIN, p. o., Lewiston township, Niagara co., N. Y., 289 ms. w. of Albany ; from W. — ms.

PEKIN, p. o., Brown township, Carroll co., O., 138 ms. s. w. of Columbus ; from W. 304 ms.

PEKIN, p. o., Jackson co., Tenn., 67 ms. E. of Nashville ; from W. 627 ms.

PEKIN, p. o., Washington co., Ind.

PEKIN, p. v., Tazewell co., Ill., 62 ms. N. of Springfield ; from W. 779 ms. Watered by Illinois river.

PEKIN. p. o., Jessamine co., Ky.

PELHAM, p. t., Hampshire co., Mass., 81 ms. w. of Boston ; from W. 391 ms. Watered by Swift and Fort rivers. Pop. 3,186.

PELHAM, p. t., Hillsborough co., N. H., 37 ms. s. of Concord ; from W. — ms. Watered by Beaver river. Pop. 1,071.

PELHAM, p. t., Westchester co., N. Y., including several islands in East river, 140 ms. s. of Albany ; from W. — ms. Pop. 577.

PELHAM, p. v., Grundy co., Tenn., 85 ms. s. E. of Nashville ; from W. 651 ms.

PELLA, p. o., Marion co., Iowa.

PELTONVILLE, p. o., Pultney township, Steuben co., N. Y., 208 ms. w. of Albany ; from W. 331 ms.

PEMAQUID, p. o., Bremen township, Lincoln co., Mo. 46 ms s. of Augusta ; from W. 614 ms.

PEMBERTON, p. v., Burlington co., N. J., 22 ms. s. of Trenton ; from W. 162 ms. Watered by north branch of Rancocus creek. Pop. 2,866.

PEMBERTON. p. o., Goochland co., Va.

PEMBINA COUNTY, situated in Minnesota. Area, —— square miles. Seat of justice, Pembina. Pop. in 1850, 1,134.

PEMBINA, c. h., p. v., seat of justice of Pembina co., Minn.

PEMBROKE, p. t., Washington co., Me., 180 ms. N. E. of Augusta ; from W. 766 ms. Watered by Cobscook bay. Pop. 1,712.

PEMBROKE, p. t., Merrimack co., N. H., 5 ms. s. E. of Concord ; from W. 480 ms. Watered by Merrimack and Suncook rivers. Pop. 1,733.

PEMBROKE, p. t., Plymouth co., Mass., 26 ms. s. E. of Boston ; from W. 445 ms. Watered by North river Pop. 1,388.

PEMBROKE, p. t., Genesee co., N. Y., 262 ms. w. of Albany ; from W. 387 ms. Watered by Tonawanda creek. Pop. 2,279.

PEMBROKE, p. o., Giles co., Va., 230 ms. w. of Richmond ; from W. 276 ms.

PEMBROKE, p. v., Christian co., Ky., 197 ms. s. w. of Frankfort ; from W. 721 ms.

PEMISCO, t., New Madrid co., Mo.

PENATAQUIT, p. o., Suffolk co., Long Island, N. Y.

PENDARVIS' STORE. p. o., Wayne co., Ga.

PENDLETON COUNTY, situated toward the north part of Virginia. Area, 999 square miles. Face of the country, mountainous ; soil, rocky and barren. Seat of justice, Franklin. Pop. in 1810, 4,239 ; in 1820, 4,836 ; in 1830, 6,271 ; in 1840, 6,490 ; in 1850, 5,795.

PENDLETON COUNTY, situated on the northeasterly boundary of Kentucky, with Ohio river on the northeast, and traversed by Licking river. Area, 450 square miles. Face of the country, broken : soil, sterile. Seat of justice, Falmouth. Pop. in 1810, 3,061 ; in 1820, 3,086 ; in 1830, 3,866 ; in 1840, 4,455 ; in 1850, 6,774.

PENDLETON, p. t., Niagara co., N. Y., 284 ms. w. of Albany ; from W. 406 ms. Watered by Tonawanda creek and Erie canal. Pop. 2,166.

PENDLETON, p. v., Anderson district, S. C., 136 ms. N. w. of Columbia ; from W. 531 ms. Watered by a tributary of Savannah river.

PENDLETON, p. o., Putnam co., O., 110 ms. N. w. of Columbus ; from W. 475 ms.

PENDLETON, p. v., Madison co., Ind., 31 ms. N. E. of Indianapolis ; from W. 558 ms. Watered by Fall Creek falls.

PENDLETON, t., St. Francis co., Mo.

PENDLETON, p. o., Sabine co., Tex.

PENDLETON CENTRE, p. o., Niagara co., N. Y.

PENDLETON HILL, p. o., New London co., Ct.

PENFIELD, p. t., Monroe co., N. Y., 222 ms. w. of Albany ; from W. 371 ms. Watered by Irondequoit creek. Pop. 3,185.

PENFIELD, p. t., Lorain co., O., 106 ms. N. E. of Columbus ; from W. 305 ms. Watered by a branch of Black river. Pop. 672.

PENFIELD, p. v., Greene co., Ga., 51 ms. N. of Milledgeville ; from W. 610 ms.

PENFIELD, p. o., Kane co., Ill., 162 ms. N. E. of Springfield ; from W. 771 ms.

PENFIELD, t., Calhoun co., Mich. Pop. 598.

PENFIELD, p. o., Hamilton co., Ind.

PENFIELD, (see Pennfield).

PENINSULA, p. o., Boston township, Summit co. O., 136 ms. N. E. of Columbus ; from W. 345 ms. Situated on the Ohio canal.

PENN, t., Morgan co., O. Pop. 1,370.

PENN, t., Chester co., Pa. Watered by tributaries of Elk and White Clay creeks. Pop. 738.

PENN, t., Clearfield co., Pa. Pop. 528.

PENN, t., Lycoming co., Pa. Pop. 578.

PENN, p. o., Lancaster co., Pa.

PENN, t., Perry co., Pa.

PENN, t., Union co., Pa. Pop. 2,736.

PENN, t., Cass co., Mich. Pop. 698.

PENN, t., Philadelphia co., Pa. Watered by Schuylkill river. Seat of Girard college. Pop. 8,939.

PENNEY'S, p. o., Randolph co., Mo.

PENNELLVILLE, p. o., Oswego co., N. Y.

PENNFIELD, p. o., Davidson co., N. C.

PENNFIELD, p. o., Calhoun co., Mich.

PENNFIELD, (see Penfield).

PENNINGTON, p. v., Hopewell township, Mercer co., N. J., 8 ms. N. of Trenton ; from W. 177 ms.

PENNINGTON, t., Licking co., O.

PENNINGTON, t., Union co., Ark.

PENNINGTONVILLE, p. o., Chester co., Pa.

PENN LINE, p. o., Crawford co., Pa., 256 ms. N. w. of Harrisburgh ; from W. 322 ms.

PENN RUN, p. o., Indiana co., Pa., 161 ms. N. w of Harrisburgh ; from W. 214 ms.

PENNSBOROUGH, p. o., Irwin co., Ga.

PENNSBOROUGH. p. o., Ritchie co., Va., 295 ms. N. w. of Richmond; from W. 263 ms.

PENNSBURGH, p. v., Montgomery co., Pa.

PENNSBURY, t., Chester co., Pa. Watered by Brandywine creek. Pop. 761.

PENN'S CREEK, p. o., Union co., Pa.

PENN'S GROVE, p. o., Delaware co., Pa., 97 ms. S. E. of Harrisburgh; from W. 127 ms.

PENN'S GROVE, p. o., Salem co., N. J.

PENN'S NECK (Lower), t., Salem co., N. J. Watered by Delaware river. Pop. 1,429.

PENN'S NECK (Upper), t., Salem co., N. J. Pop. 2,422.

PENN'S SQUARE, p. o., Montgomery co., Pa.

PENN'S STORE, p. o., Patrick co., Va., 210 ms. s. w. of Richmond; from W. 285 ms.

PENNSVILLE. p. v., Fayette co., Pa.

PENNSVILLE, p. v., Penn township, Morgan co., O., 77 ms. E. of Columbus; from W. 331 ms.

PENNSYLVANIA, one of the United States, so called in honor of the father of its illustrious founder, lies between 74° 44' and 80° 34' west longitude from Greenwich, and 39° 43' and 42° 17' north latitude, and is bounded north by Lake Erie and New York; east by New York and New Jersey, from which it is separated by Delaware river; south by Delaware, Maryland, and Virginia; and west by Virginia and Ohio. Its superficial area is 46,000 square miles.

Physical Aspect.—The surface of this state is greatly diversified by mountains, hills, and dales. It contains but a few large tracts of level land, and these generally occur along the borders of streams. With one or two partial exceptions, it is composed of two great plains, declining from the dividing ridge of its waters. The eastern declivity, drained by the Delaware and Susquehanna, and their tributaries, gradually descends to the level of the tide; the western in like manner, drains the numerous confluents of the Ohio. The southeastern counties may be regarded as undulating, rather than hilly, and are under a high state of cultivation, particularly along the Susquehanna. Most of the central part of this state is mountainous, often interspersed with high and sterile ridges, occurring in close succession, interlocking each other, and enclosing long and pointed valleys between. It is within this region, too, that the fertile valley of Wyoming occurs, surrounded by a lofty chain, known at different points by as many local names. Most of the country west of the Alleganies is hilly, with numerous irregular and abrupt elevations, not disposed in regular chains. In this part of the state, particularly along the streams, the soil is highly fertile; and between the Allegany river and Lake Erie, as well as on the western border, the soil is good.

Mountains.—The structure and position of the mountains in this state have given it an aspect peculiar to itself, and constitute its most prominent features. South mountain extends from New Jersey, interrupted by the Delaware, below Easton, in a southwesterly direction across the state to Adams county, on the borders of Maryland. Next to this, the Blue mountain, or Kittatinny range, extends from the western part of New Jersey, also interrupted by the Delaware, to Parnell's Knob, near the south border of this state. Next come Second, Sharp, and Broad mountains, the latter of which is an irregular elevation, with a broad and barren table-land at its top. Between the Kittatinny and Allegany ranges is what is called the Appalachian chain, which consists of elevated and nearly parallel ridges, in some instances twenty miles apart, and frequently divided by subordinate ridges. The great Allegany ridge extends nearly across the state, presenting on its southeasterly side an abrupt ascent, but a gentle descent on the northwesterly slope, consisting of an elevated and undulating table-land. Westward of this range are Laurel ridge, and Chestnut ridge, running parallel therewith.

Rivers and Lake.—The principal rivers are the Dela-

ware, Schuylkill, Lehigh, Susquehanna, Juniata, Genesee, Allegany, Monongahela, Ohio, Clarion, and Youhioghany. Lake Erie bounds this state on the northwest.

Islands.—Tinicum island, in the Delaware, and Presque isle, on the south side of Lake Erie, are those most worthy of note.

Climate.—The climate, though generally healthy and temperate, is fluctuating and varied. The extremes of temperature are from 20° below zero to 98° Fahrenheit above. On both inclined plains, it is a rare occurrence that the rivers in winter are not more or less frozen, and rendered unnavigable. Receding to the more elevated tracts and high mountain valleys, summer is visited by occasional frosts, which, in some situations, appear in every month of the year. In all the higher regions, abiding snows usually appear in December, and remain until March. Spring and autumn are usually delightful seasons in all parts of the state.

Productive Resources.-The principal products are horses, mules, neat cattle, sheep, swine, poultry, eggs, butter, cheese, wax, peaches, sugar, wine, hops, tobacco, silk, wool, hemp, flax, hay, lumber, wheat, rye, barley, oats, buckwheat, potatoes, and Indian corn. The mineral wealth of this state is immense, consisting principally of coal, iron, and salt. The coal is of two kinds, "bituminous," which occurs in great abundance on the western side of the Alleganies, and "anthracite," which is found only on the easterly side of the mountains. The iron, which is of superior quality, is extensively wrought, and is inexhaustible in its supply. Toward the southwest part of the state salt springs abound, from which is manufactured large quantities of salt.

Manufactures.—The manufactures of Pennsylvania are varied and extensive. The number of iron-works in the state are rising 500, and the capital invested over $20,000,000, employing over 40,000 men. Next in importance are cotton and woollen fabrics, in which a capital of $8.000,000 is invested, employing 15,000 men, and the annual products amount to about $10,000,000. Leather, paper, and glass, are among the minor manufactures.

Railroads and Canals.—Pennsylvania has greatly extended and facilitated her trade by her internal improvements. The great central line of railroad communication extends from Philadelphia to Lancaster, 70 miles, thence to Hollidaysburgh, 175 miles, thence to Johnstown, 36 miles, and thence to Pittsburgh. From Pittsburgh it continues west to connect with the railroads in Ohio. The principal roads beside the line above-named, are, the Reading, 92 miles; Philadelphia and Baltimore, 98 miles; and the Cumberland Valley, 77 miles. There are about 50 railroads in the state, of an aggregate length of 1,500 miles. The railroads of Pennsylvania have been built at a cost of $45,000,000. Among the canals of Pennsylvania are, the Eastern and Juniata sections of the Pennsylvania canal, extending from the Susquehanna to Hollidaysburgh, 172 miles; and the western division, extending from Johnstown to Pittsburgh. From Pittsburgh the Beaver canal runs into Ohio, 31 miles, and the Erie Extension canal will continue the line to Erie, on the lake, 105 miles. The whole length of canals in the state is 1,280 miles, 848 miles of which are owned by the state, and 432 miles by companies. The total cost of the canals of Pennsylvania is $35,000,000.

Commerce.—The exports of Pennsylvania, to foreign ports, in 1850, amounted to $4,501,606; the imports to $12,066,154. The total shipping of the state amounts to 260,000 tons, of which about 65,000 tons are engaged in foreign trade.

Education.—The colleges of Pennsylvania are numerous. The principal are, the university, at Philadelphia, founded in 1755, with a medical school attached; Dickinson college, at Carlisle, founded in 1783, to which is attached a law school; Jefferson college, at Canonsburgh, founded in 1802; Washington college, founded in 1006; Alleghany college, at Meadville; Pennsylvania college, at Gettysburgh; Lafayette college, at Easton; Marshall college, at Mercersburgh; and the Western university, at Pittsburgh. Jefferson and Philadelphia medical colleges are located at Philadelphia. There are theological schools at Gettysburgh, Mercersburgh, Alleghany, Canonsburgh, Pittsburgh, Meadville, and Philadelphia. There are in the state about 500 academies, and 10,000 common schools.

Population.—In 1790, 434.373; in 1800, 602,365; in 1810, 810,091; in 1820, 1,049,458; in 1830, 1,348,233; in

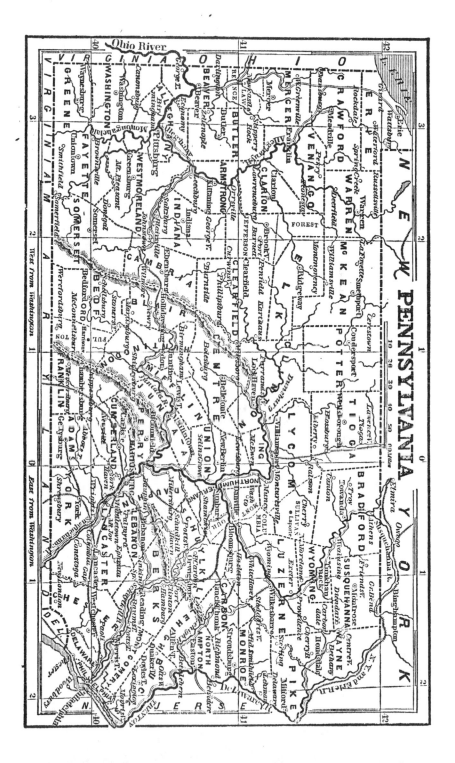

1840, 1,724,031 ; in 1850, 2,311,786. Number of slaves in 1790, 3,737 ; in 1800, 1,706 ; in 1810, 795 ; in 1820, 211 ; in 1830, 403 ; in 1840, 64.

Government.—The government is vested in a governor, senate, and house of representatives. The governor is elected for three years, and is ineligible for the next three years ; the senate for three years, one third, annually, in districts ; and the representatives annually, at the state election, second Tuesday in October. The judicial power is vested in a supreme court, courts of oyer and terminer, common pleas, and other inferior courts. The judiciary is elected by the people. The right of suffrage is vested in every white freeman for twenty-two years of age, who has resided in the state one year, and paid a tax. White freemen, between twenty-one and twenty-two years of age, having resided in the state a year, may vote without having paid a tax.

History.—The Dutch, from their first settlement upon Manhattan island, carried on trade upon the banks of the Delaware ; but there seems not to have been a permanent settlement in Pennsylvania until about the year 1640, when a fort was erected upon the island of Tinicum by the Swedes, and a number of settlements were soon after made. In 1681, William Penn obtained a grant from Charles II., of the lands northward of Maryland, and westward of Delaware, which was called "Pennsylvania." In 1682, the territories (the present state of "Delaware") were annexed to his grant, and thus remained until 1691, when they withdrew from the Union. The year following, Penn's provincial government was taken from him, and Delaware was reunited to Pennsylvania. In 1694, Penn was restored to his proprietary right, and the two colonies continued their union until 1703, when they agreed on separation, and never after united in legislation, although the governor of Pennsylvania continued to preside over both, until the three lower counties on the Delaware, as such, were represented in the first Congress in New York, in 1775. The first permanent settlement in Pennsylvania was made on Tinicum island, just below the mouth of the Schuylkill, in 1640. The first deliberate assembly was convened at New Castle, in 1682. The second assembly was held at Philadelphia, in 1683 Penn died in 1718, leaving his interest in Pennsylvania, as an inheritance to his children, in whose possession it remained until the Revolution, when their claim was purchased by the commonwealth for £130,000. In consequence of a controversy between Maryland and Pennsylvania, respecting their common boundaries, a line was finally fixed in 1762, by actual survey, by two eminent English engineers, Charles Mason and Jeremiah Dixon, and since that time the boundary between these states has been known by the name of "Mason and Dixon's Line." The last remaining portion of Pennsylvania, lying in the northwest portion of the state, not previously purchased, was bought of the Indians, in 1784. In 1776, a state constitution was framed, which continued until 1790, when it was changed, and remained in force until 1838, at which time the present one was adopted. The constitution of the United States was ratified by this state in 1787. Motto of the seal, "Virtue, Liberty, and Independence."

PENNVILLE, p. o., Jay co., Ind.

PENN YAN. c. h., p. v., Milo township, seat of justice of Yates co., N. Y., 192 ms. w. of Albany ; from W. 320 ms. Watered by Crooked Lake outlet, and Crooked Lake canal.

PENNY'S FERRY, p. o., Henry co., Ill.

PENOBSCOT COUNTY, situated in the central part of Maine, and traversed by Penobscot river. Area, 3,282 square miles, Face of the country, undulating and hilly ; soil, fertile. Seat of justice, Bangor. Pop. in 1810, 7,471 ; in 1820, 13,870 ; in 1840, 45,705 ; in 1850, 64,089.

PENOBSCOT, p. t., Hancock co., Me., 78 ms. E. of Augusta ; from W. 674 ms. Watered by Penobscot river.

PENOLA, p. o., Sumter co., Ala.

PENSACOLA, city, and seat of justice of Escambia county, Flor., situated on the bay of the same name, in Escambia county, about 16 miles from the gulf of Mexico, 242 miles west of Tallahassee, and 1,042 miles from Washington, is the principal port of entry and city in Florida. The site is a low sandy plain, extending into the harbor, making it too shallow near the town for large vessels, which are obliged to anchor at a distance. The entrance to the port is deeper than any other on the north coast of the gulf. Five miles above the mouth, is one of the United States navy-yards. The

city is a parallelogram, with regular streets and public squares. It was among the earliest settlements in Florida, having been founded in 1699, by a Spanish officer.

The population in 1830, was about 2,000 ; in 1840, about 2,000 ; in 1850, 3,164.

PENSACOLA, p. o., Lake co., Miss.

PENTRESS, p. o., Monongalia co., Va.

PEOLA MILLS, p. o., Madison co., Va.

PEOLI, p. o., Tuscarawas co., O.

PEORIA COUNTY, situated toward the west part of Illinois, with Illinois river on the southeast. Area, 648 square miles. Seat of justice, Peoria. Pop. in 1840, 6,153 ; in 1850, 17,547.

PEORIA, c. h., p. v., seat of justice of Peoria co., Ill., 70 ms. N. of Springfield ; from W. 784 ms. Watered by Illinois river. Pop. 5,562.

PEORIA, p. o., Wyoming co., N. Y., 238 ms. w. of Albany ; from W. 356 ms.

PEORIA, p. o., Franklin co., Ind.

PEORIAVILLE, p. o., Peoria co., Ill.

PEPACTON, p. o., Colchester township, Delaware co., N. Y., 93 ms. s. w. of Albany ; from W. 321 ms.

PEPOKATING, p. o., Sussex co., N. J.

PEPPERELL, p. t., Middlesex co., Mass., 38 ms. N. w. of Boston ; from W. 434 ms. Watered by Nassau and Nisitissit rivers. Pop. 1,754.

PEPPER'S FERRY, p. o., Pulaski co., Va.

PEQUOT, p. o., Calumet co., Wis., 114 ms. N. E. of Madison ; from W. 962 ms.

PERCH RIVER, p. o., Brownville township, Jefferson co., N. Y., 175 ms. N. w. of Albany ; from W. 427 ms.

PERCY'S CREEK, p. o., Wilkinson co., Miss.

PERIN'S MILLS, p. o., Miami township, Clermont co., O., 109 ms. s. w. of Columbus ; from W. 480 ms.

PERKINS, t., Erie co., O., 115 ms. N. of Columbus : from W. 419 ms. Pop. 1,207.

PERKINS' CREEK, p. o., Bullinger co., Mo.

PERKINS GROVE, p. o., Bureau co., Ill.

PERKINSVILLE, p. v., Wethersfield township, Windsor co., Vt., 71 ms. s. of Montpelier ; from W. 465 ms.

PERKINSVILLE, p. v., Burke co., N. C., 270 ms. w. of Raleigh ; from W. 425 ms.

PERKINSVILLE, p. o., Madison co., Ind.

PERKINSVILLE, p. o., Goochland co., Va.

PERKIOMEN BRIDGE, p. o., Montgomery co., Pa.

PEROTE, p. o., Ashland co., O.

PERQUIMANS COUNTY, situated in the northeast part of North Carolina, with Albemarle Sound on the southeast, and traversed by Perquimans river. Area, 175 square miles. Face of the country, level and marshy ; soil, generally productive. Seat of justice, Hertford. Pop. in 1810, 6,052 ; in 1820, 6,859 ; in 1830, 7,417 ; in 1840, 7,346 ; in 1850, 7,332.

PERRINE, p. o., Mercer co., Pa., 224 ms. N. w. of Harrisburgh ; from W. 277 ms.

PERRINEVILLE, p. v., Monmouth co., N. J., 24 ms. E. of Trenton ; from W. 190 ms.

PERRINTON, p. t., Monroe co., N. Y. Pop. 2,891.

PERRY COUNTY, situated in the central part of Pennsylvania, with Susquehanna river on the east, and traversed by the Juniata. Area, 540 square miles. Face of the country, generally hilly ; soil, productice. Seat of justice, New Bloomfield. Pop. in 1820, 11,342 ; in 1830, 14,361 ; in 1840, 17,096 ; in 1850, 20,088.

PERRY COUNTY, situated in the central part of Alabama, and traversed by Cahawba river. Area, 936 square miles. Seat of justice, Marion. Pop. in 1830, 11,509 ; in 1840, 19,086 ; in 1850, 22,285.

PERRY COUNTY, situated in the southeast part of Mississippi, and traversed by Leaf river. Area, 1,044 square miles. Face of the country, hilly ; soil, generally sterile. Seat of justice, Augusta. Pop. in 1830, 2,037 ; in 1830, 2,300 ; in 1840, 1,889 ; in 1850, 2,438.

PERRY COUNTY, situated in the westerly part of Tennessee, and traversed by Tennessee river. Area, 780 square miles. Seat of justice, Perryville. Pop. in 1820, 2,384 ; in 1830, 7,038 ; in 1840, 7,419 ; in 1850. 5,822.

PERRY COUNTY, situated in the southeast part of Kentucky. Area, 760 square miles. Face of the country, broken. Seat of justice, Perry. Pop. in 1830, 3,331 ; in 1840, 3,089 ; in 1850, 3,092.

PERRY COUNTY, situated in the central part of Ohio. Area, 400 square miles. Face of the country, hilly ; soil, productive. Seat of justice, Somerset. Pop. in 1820, 8,429 ; in 1830, 14,018 ; in 1840, 19,244 ; in 1850, 20,775.

PERRY COUNTY, situated on the southerly boundary of Indiana, with Ohio river on the south. Area, 400 square miles. Face of the country, broken; soil, fertile. Seat of justice. Troy. Pop. in 1820, 2,330; in 1830, 3,378; in 1840, 4,655; in 1850, 7,268.

PERRY COUNTY, situated in the south part of Illinois. Area, 432 square miles. Seat of justice, Pinckeyville. Pop. in 1830, 1,215; in 1840, 3,222; in 1850, 5,278.

PERRY COUNTY, situated on the easterly boundary of Missouri, with Mississippi river on the northeast. Area, 400 square miles. Seat of justice, Perryville. Pop. in 1830, 3,349; in 1840, 5,760; in 1850, 2,438.

PERRY COUNTY, situated in the central part of Arkansas, with Arkansas river on the northeast. Area, —— square miles. Seat of justice, Perryville. Pop. in 1850, 978.

PERRY, p. t., Washington co., Me., 191 ms. N. E. of Augusta; from W. 777 ms. Watered by St. Croix river, and Passamaquoddy and Cobscook bays. Pop. 1,324.

PERRY, p. t., Wyoming co., N. Y., 243 ms. w. of Albany; from W. 360 ms. Watered by Silver lake and its outlet. Pop. 2,832.

PERRY, p. o., Venango co., Pa., 216 ms. N. w. of Harrisburgh; from W. 305 ms.

PERRY, t., Union co., Pa. Pop. 1,341.

PERRY, t., Armstrong co., Pa. Watered by Allegany and Clarion rivers. Pop. 799.

PERRY, t. Jefferson co., Pa. Watered by Little Sandy Lick and Mahoning river.

PERRY, t., Fayette co., Pa. Pop. 1,272.

PERRY, p. t., Lake co., O., 182 ms. N. E. of Columbus; from W. 356 ms. Watered by Lake Erie. Pop. 1,131.

PERRY, t., Allen co., O. Pop. 923.

PERRY, t., Brown co., O. Pop. 2,464.

PERRY, t., Coshocton co., O. Pop. 1,340.

PERRY, t., Carroll co., O. Pop. 1,277.

PERRY, t., Columbiana co., O. Pop. 2,371.

PERRY, t., Pike co., O. Pop. 653.

PERRY, t., Franklin co., O. Watered by Scioto river. Pop. 1,169.

PERRY, t., Fairfield co., O.

PERRY, t., Gallia co., O. Watered by Raccoon and Symme's creeks. Pop. 1,208.

PERRY, t., Lawrence co., O. Pop. 924.

PERRY, t., Licking co., O. Pop. 1,250.

PERRY, t., Wayne co., O.

PERRY, t., Shelby co., O. Pop. 899.

PERRY, p. t., Logan co., O. Watered by Rush creek. Pop. 1,230.

PERRY, p. t., Stark co., O. Pop. 4,669.

PERRY, p. t., Montgomery co., O. Pop. 1,906.

PERRY, p. t., Monroe co., O. Pop. 1,459.

PERRY, t., Muskingum co., O. Pop. 1,016.

PERRY, t., Pickaway co., O. Pop. 1,120.

PERRY, t., Putnam co., O. Pop. 262.

PERRY, t., Richland co., O. Pop. 924.

PERRY, t., Tuscarawas co., O. Pop. 1,396.

PERRY, t., Wood co., O. Pop. 1,779.

PERRY, t., Marion co., Ind. Pop. 1,803.

PERRY, t., Miami co., Ind. Pop. 1,980.

PERRY, t., Tippecanoe co., Ind. Pop. 1,036.

PERRY, t., Wayne co., Ind. Pop. 710.

PERRY, t., Johnson co., Ark. Pop. 603.

PERRY, p. t., Allen co., Ind., 143 ms. N. E. of Indianapolis; from W. 566 ms. Pop. 842.

PERRY, t., Clay co., Ind. Pop. 691.

PERRY, t., Noble co., Ind. Pop. 1,104.

PERRY, p. v., Pike co., Ill., 66 ms. w. of Springfield; from W. 846 ms.

PERRY, c. h., p. v., seat of justice of Houston co., Ga., 59 ms. s. w. of Milledgeville; from W. 715 ms. Watered by Indian creek.

PERRY, c. h., p. v., seat of justice of Perry co., Ky., 151 ms. s. E. of Frankfort. Watered by Kentucky river.

PERRY, p. t., St. Francis co., Mo.

PERRY, p. o., Shiawassee co., Mich.

PERRY CENTRE, p. v., Perry township, Wyoming co., N. Y., 245 ms. w. of Albany; from W. 362 ms.

PERRYMANSVILLE, p. v., Hartford co., Md.

PERRYOPOLIS, p. v., Fayette co., Pa., 192 ms. w. of Harrisburgh; from W. 217 ms. Watered by Youghiogeny river.

PERRY'S BRIDGE, p. v., Vermilion parish, La., 218 ms. w. of New Orleans; from W. —— ms. Watered by Vermilion river.

PERRYSBURGH, p. t., Cattaraugus co., N. Y., 306 ms. w. of Albany; from W. 358 ms. Watered by Cattaraugus creek. Pop. 1,861.

PERRYSBURGH, c. h., p. v., seat of justice of Wood co., O., 123 ms. N. w. of Columbus; from W. 454 ms. Watered by Maumee river at the head of steam navigation. Pop. 1,199.

PERRYSBURGH, p. v., Miami co., Ind., 101 ms. N. of Indianapolis; from W. 610 ms. Pop. 1,266.

PERRY'S CORNER. p. o., Dutchess co., N. Y.

PERRY'S CROSS ROADS, p. o., Edgefield district, S. C., 52 ms. w. of Columbia; from W. 516 ms.

PERRY'S MILLS, c. h., p. v., seat of justice of Tatnall co., Ga., 144 ms. s. E. of Milledgeville; from W. 755 ms.

PERRY'S MILLS, p. v., Champlain township, Clinton co., N. Y., 193 ms. N. of Albany; from W. 568 ms. Watered by Chazy river.

PERRYSVILLE, p. v., South Kingston township, Washington co., R. I., 41 ms. s. of Providence; from W. 389 ms.

PERRYSVILLE, p. v., Ross township, Alleghany co., Pa., 208 ms. w. of Harrisburgh; from W. 234 ms.

PERRYVILLE, p. t., Vermilion co., Ind., 81 ms. w. of Indianapolis; from W. 652 ms. Watered by Wabash river. Pop. 742.

PERRYTON, p. v., Perry township, Licking co., O., 61 ms. N. E. of Columbus; from W. 358 ms.

PERRYTON, p. o., Mercer co., Ill.

PERRYVILLE, p. v., Cecil co., Md., 65 ms. N. E. of Annapolis; from W. 75 ms.

PERRYVILLE, p. v., Perry co., Ala.

PERRYVILLE, p. v., Decatur co., Tenn.

PERRYVILLE, p. v., Boyle co., Ky., 41 ms. s. of Frankfort; from W. 563 ms.

PERRYVILLE, c. h., p. v., seat of justice of Perry co., Mo., 214 ms. s. E. of Jefferson city; from W. 868 ms. Watered by Saline creek.

PERRYVILLE, c. h., p. v., seat of justice of Perry co., Ark., 55 ms. N. w. of Little Rock; from W. 1,110 ms. Watered by La Fêve river.

PERRYVILLE, p. o., Ashland co., O.

PERRYVILLE, p. v., Bethlehem township, Hunterdon co., N. J., 36 ms. N. w. of Trenton; from W. 196 ms.

PERSIA, t., Cattaraugus co., N. Y., 302 ms. w. of Albany; from W. 354 ms. Watered by Cattaraugus creek. Pop. 1,953.

PERSIA, p. o., Boone co., Mo.

PERSIFER, p. o., Knox co., Ill.

PERSIMON CREEK, p. o., Cherokee co., N. C.

PERSON COUNTY, situated on the north boundary of North Carolina. Area, 440 square miles. Seat of justice, Roxborough. Pop. in 1820, 9,029; in 1830, 10,027; in 1840, 9,790; in 1850, 10,781.

PERTH, p. t., Fulton co., N. Y., 46 ms. N. w. of Albany; from W. 419 ms. Watered by Chucktenunda creek. Pop. 1,440.

PERTH AMBOY, city, Middlesex co., N. J., 46 ms. N. E. of Trenton; from W. 212 ms. Watered by Raritan bay and Raritan river. Pop. 1,865.

PERU, p. t., Oxford co., Me., 40 ms. w. of Augusta; from W. 612 ms. Watered by Androscoggin river. Pop. 1,298.

PERU, p. t., Bennington co., Vt., 100 ms. s. w. of Montpelier; from W. 439 ms. Watered by head waters of West river. Pop. 567.

PERU, p. t., Berkshire co., Mass., 118 ms. w. of Boston; from W. 388 ms. Pop. 519.

PERU, p. t., Clinton co., N. Y., 153 ms. N. of Albany; from W. 528 ms. Watered by Little Au Sable river and Lake Champlain. Pop. 3,640.

PERU, p. t., Huron co., O., 93 ms. N. of Columbus; from W. 398 ms. Watered by the east branch of Huron river. Pop. 1,632.

PERU, t., Delaware co., O., 36 ms. N. of Columbus; from W. —— ms.

PERU, p. o., La Salle co., Ill.

PERU, c. h., p. v., seat of justice of Miami co., Ind., 90 ms. N. of Indianapolis; from W. 562 ms. Watered by Wabash river and Wabash and Erie canal.

PERU, p. t., Pike co., Mo.

PERU MILLS, p. o., Juniata co., Pa.

PERU, p. t., Groton township, Tompkins co., N. Y., 165 ms. w. of Albany; from W. 309 ms.

PETAWLA, p. o., Randolph co., Ga.

PETERBOROUGH, p. v., Smithfield township, Madison co., N. Y., 108 ms. w. of Albany; from W. 364 ms.

PETERBOROUGH, p. t., Hillsborough co., N. H. 41 ms.

s. w. of Concord ; from W. 447 ms. Watered by a branch of Contoocook river. Pop. 2,222.

PETERS, t., Franklin co., Pa. Watered by the west branch of Conecocheague creek. Pop. 2,310.

PETERS, t., Washington co., Pa. Watered by Chartier's and Peter's creeks. Pop. 924.

PETERSBURGH. p. t., Rensselaer co., N. Y., 26 ms. E. of Albany ; from W. 392 ms. Watered by Little Hoosick creek. Pop. 1,908.

PETERSBURGH, t., Huntingdon co., Pa. Pop. 264.

PETERSBURGH, p. b., Dinwiddie co., Va., a port of entry, on the south bank of Appomattox river, 12 miles from its entrance into the James, 23 miles south of Richmond, and 140 miles from Washington. The houses, which are principally of brick, have risen on the ruins of about 400 less elegant ones that were destroyed by fire, in 1815. Like Richmond it is situated at the foot of falls in the river, which afford valuable water-power; while the barrier that they present to navigation has been surmounted by a canal, passing around the falls, and admitting boats to navigate the river 80 miles above. Vessels of 100 tons anchor at Petersburgh ; those of larger burden come to the City Point, at the confluence of the Appomattox with the James. A railroad connects the two points ; and the Washington and Wilmington railroad line communicates with the place.
The population in 1810, was 5,668 ; in 1820, ——— ; in 1830, 8,322 ; in 1840, 11,136 ; in 1850, 14,010.

PETERSBURGH, p. v., Elbert co., Ga., 96 ms. N. E. of Milledgeville ; from W. 552 ms. Watered by Savannah and Broad rivers.

PETERSBURGH, p. v., Lincoln co., Tenn., 72 ms. s. of Nashville ; from W. 718 ms.

PETERSBURGH, p. v., Boone co., Ky., 91 ms. N. of Frankfort ; from W. 516 ms.

PETERSBURGH, p. v., Springfield township, Mahoning co., O., 181 ms. N. E. of Columbus; from W. 275 ms.

PETERSBURGH. p. v., seat of justice of Pike co., Ind., 138 ms. s. w. of Indianapolis ; from W. 677 ms. Watered by White river.

PETERSBURGH, c. h., p. v., seat of justice of Menard co., Ill., 21 ms. N. w. of Springfield ; from W. 801 ms. Watered by Sangamon river.

PETERSBURGH, p. o., La Vaca co., Tex.

PETERSBURGH, p. o., Cape May co., N. J.

PETERSBURGH FOUR CORNERS, p. o., Petersburgh township, Rensselaer co., N. Y., 31 ms. E. of Albany ; from W. 397 ms.

PETER'S CREEK, p. o., Bladen co., N. C.

PETER'S CREEK, p. o., Barren co., Ky., 143 ms. s. w. of Frankfort; from W. 664 ms.

PETERSHAM, p. t., Worcester co., Mass., 64 ms. w. of Boston ; from W. 462 ms. Watered by Swift river. Pop. 1,527.

PETERSTOWN, p. v., Monroe co., Va., 247 ms. w. of Richmond ; from W. 293 ms. Watered by Rich creek.

PETERSVILLE, p. v., Northampton co., Pa., 105 ms. N. E. of Harrisburgh ; from W. 198 ms.

PETERSVILLE, p. v., Frederick co., Md., 89 ms. N. w. of Annapolis ; from W. 57 ms. Pop. 2,351.

PETIT JEAN, p. t., Yell co., Ark.

PETTIS COUNTY, situated toward the west part of Missouri. Area, 600 square miles. Seat of justice, Georgetown. Pop. in 1840, 2,930 ; in 1850, 5,150.

PETTIS, t., Platte co., Mo. Pop. 2,954.

PETRA, t., Saline co., Mo.

PETTYS, p. o., Lawrence co., Ill.

PEWAUKEE, p. t., Waukesha co., Wis.

PEYTONA, p. o., Boone co., Va.

PEYTONSBURGH, p. v., Pittsylvania co., Va., 145 ms. s. w. of Richmond ; from W. 232 ms.

PEYTON'S CREEK, p. o., Smith co., Tenn.

PEYTONSVILLE, p. v., Williamson co., Tenn., 27 ms. s. of Nashville ; from W. 693 ms.

PHARISBURGH, p. v., Union co., O., 49 ms. N. w. of Columbus ; from W. 439 ms.

PHARR'S MILLS, p. o., Moore co., N. C.

PHARSALIA, p. t., Chenango co., N. Y., 127 ms. w. of Albany ; from W. 336 ms. Watered by Geneganslette creek and Ostelic river. Pop. 1,185.

PHEASANT BRANCH, p. o., Dane co., Wis.

PHELPS, p. t., Ontario co., N. Y., 185 ms. w. of Albany ; from W. 350 ms. Watered by Canandaigua outlet and Flint creek. Pop. 5,542.

PHELPS, p. t., Ashtabula co., O., 190 ms. N. E. of Columbus ; from W. 324 ms. Watered by Rock and Musquito creek.

PHELPSTOWN, p. t., Ingham co., Mich., 71 ms. w. of Detroit ; from W. 574 ms. Pop. 393.

PHENIX (see Phœnix), p. o., Kent co., R. I.

PHILADELPHIA COUNTY, situated in the southeast part of Pennsylvania, with Delaware river on the southeast, and traversed by the Schuylkill. Area, 120 square miles. Face of the country, undulating ; soil, good. Seat of justice, Philadelphia. Pop. in 1810, 111.210 ; in 1820, 137.097 ; in 1830, 188,777 ; in 1840, 258,037; in 1850, 408,762.

PHILADELPHIA, p. t., Jefferson co., N. Y., 172 ms. N. w. of Albany ; from W. 432 ms. Watered by Indian river and tributaries.

PHILADELPHIA, the first city of Pennsylvania, in population, wealth, and manufactures, and the second in the United States, is situated on a peninsula, formed by the confluence of Delaware and Schuylkill rivers. The city was laid out with beautiful regularity, in 1683, by its illustrious founder, William Penn, who gave it its name, signifying "brotherly love." Many of the noble trees which grew on the site, are now commemorated by the names of the streets running east and west, as Chestnut, Walnut, Pine, &c., while those crossing them are designated by numerals.
The ground on which Philadelphia is built is even, rising gently from each river, along which it extends for several miles. On the Delaware, the scenery is monotonous, but the water being deeper than that of the other river, the commerce and business of the city tends to this side ; while the Schuylkill affords pleasing landscapes and agreeable places of residence. Many of the smaller vessels, sloops, and boats, here congregate, laden with coal, and other products of the valley of the Schuylkill : this part of the city is now rapidly increasing in wealth and business. No feature of Philadelphia is more striking than the regularity and neatness of its streets. The latter peculiarity is chiefly owing to the convenient grade, which allows the water to descend and find its way through sewers and other channels, into the Delaware. The houses, also, are more remarkable for neatness and solidity, than for splendor and show ; they are mostly of brick, adorned with steps and basements of white marble, which the neighboring quarries furnish in abundance, and of fine quality. Of this material, a number of the public buildings are constructed, among which are the United States Marine hospital, the Pennsylvania bank, the Girard bank, the building formerly occupied by the United States bank, and the Girard college, which deserves more than a passing mention. A bequest of $2,000,000, with grounds beautifully situated on an elevation near the city, was made in 1831, by Stephen Girard, an eccentric, though wealthy citizen of Philadelphia, for the purpose of founding a college for orphans. With part of these funds, has been erected one of the most magnificent structures in the United States. The college consists of five buildings, the main edifice in the centre is devoted to the education of pupils and students of various ages and acquirements ; the other four, two on each side, are residences for the instructors and students. The whole is of richly-wrought white marble. The central structure is 218 feet long, and 160 feet wide, surrounded by 34 Corinthian columns, 55 feet high, and six feet in diameter. The interior is in a corresponding style of splendor. The four other buildings are each 125 feet long, and 52 feet wide.
Another building of Philadelphia, of less magnificence, probably excites greater interest. This is the old statehouse, or Independence hall, where the Declaration of American Independence was decreed and signed by the first continental congress. The bell which announced to the anxious people the adoption of this great instrument, is carefully preserved in the cupola ; it bears the prophetic inscription : "Proclaim Liberty throughout this land unto all the inhabitants thereof." These words were imprinted on the bell long before the use which was afterward made of it could have been known. In this building are a statue of Washington, in wood, and many other relics of the Revolution.
Philadelphia contains a large number of important public buildings and institutions. Among them are the Pennsylvania hospital, which owes its origin to Doctors Franklin and Bond ; the Insane asylum, outside of the city ; the Almshouse, fronting Schuylkill river on its west side ; institutions for the deaf and for the blind, and several other charitable establishments. Besides these, there are the American Philosophical Society, founded in 1743, by the exertions of Dr. Franklin, and

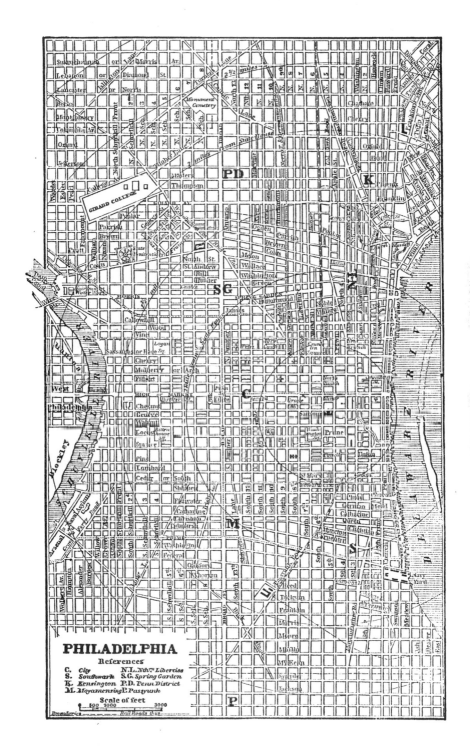

PHILADELPHIA

References

C. City
S. Southwark
K. Kensington
M. Moyamensing

N.L. Nth'n Liberties
S.G. Spring Garden
P.D. Penn District
P. Passyunk

Scale of feet
500 1000 3000

Boundaries ____ Rail Roads thus ____

possessing a large and valuable library and cabinet; the Philadelphia library, also established under the auspices of Franklin; the Franklin Institute; the Academy of Natural Sciences; the Pennsylvania Academy of Fine Arts; and numerous other flourishing institutions for improvement in knowledge and art.

Another great structure is the United States Mint, built of white marble, with two porticoes, resting on Ionic columns, one fronting Chestnut, the other Olive street. Here a vast amount of bullion, from California and other parts of the Union is coined.

The markets of Philadelphia are among the most convenient, well-supplied, and well-conducted, in the country. To these come vast quantities of provisions from the surrounding region, with the rich and varied fruits of New Jersey and Delaware.

By the water-works on the Schuylkill, at Fairmount, a large body of water is raised into elevated reservoirs, whence it is distributed over the city by iron-pipes. A beautiful suspension bridge spans the Schuylkill at Fairmount, and several railroad bridges also lead to the city.

There are in Philadelphia a number of public parks, laid out with taste and beauty, shaded by trees, and adorned with walks, fountains, and other appropriate ornaments. In the rear of Independence hall, is Independence square, a favorite and agreeable public resort. Other public grounds are Franklin, Washington, Logan, and Rittenhouse squares.

Outside of the city are Pratt's gardens, on the Schuylkill, near the water-works, and below, Barton's gardens, both of which are interesting spots. These, with the beautiful villas, and soft but rich scenery of the river, render Philadelphia as agreeable a place of residence as any large city in the country.

Properly forming a part of the city, but having distinct municipal incorporations, are the five districts, Southwark, Moyamensing, Northern Liberties, Kensington, and Spring Garden. These with several adjacent villages, though for convenience of government and for local causes, separated from the city, in nature, connection, and interest, and for all practical purposes, may be identified with it, except perhaps in the crookedness of their streets, which form one distinctive feature from the city itself.

The manufactures of Philadelphia are varied and important, embracing nearly all the articles produced by American industry.

The railroads diverging from Philadelphia, are the Philadelphia, Wilmington, and Baltimore; the Philadelphia, Harrisburgh, and Pittsburgh: the Philadelphia, Reading, and Pottsville; the Philadelphia, Germantown, and Norristown; the Camden and Amboy; the Columbia and Philadelphia; the Philadelphia and Westchester; the Philadelphia and Trenton Branch; the Philadelphia and Germantown Branch; and the New York and Philadelphia steamer line.

The canals, communicating directly, or through rivers, with Philadelphia, are the Schuylkill Navigation, which extends to Port Carbon; the Pennsylvania; the Morris, which enters the Delaware at Easton; and the Delaware and Raritan, between Bordentown and New Brunswick on the Raritan river, which is navigable for steamboats from New York.

The population in 1685 was 2,500; in 1790, 42,520; in 1800. 70,287; in 1810, 96,664; in 1820, 108,116; in 1830, 167,188; in 1840, 258,037; in 1850, 409,353; city proper, 121,376.

PHILADELPHIA, p. v., seat of justice of Neshoba co., Miss., 83 ms. N. E. of Jackson; from W. 951 ms. Watered by Kentokey creek.

PHILADELPHIA, p. o., Darlington district, S. C.

PHILADELPHIA, p. v., Monroe co., Tenn., 160 ms. s. E. of Nashville; from W. 533 ms.

PHILADELPHIA, p. v., Hancock co., Ind., 15 ms. E. of Indianapolis; from W. 556 ms.

PHILADELPHIA, p. v., Van Buren co., Iowa. Watered by Des Moines river and Lick creek.

PHILADELPHIA, p. o., Marion co., Mo.

PHILADELPHUS, p. v., Robeson co., N. C., 106 ms. s. of Raleigh; from W. 394 ms.

PHILANTHROPY, p. o., Reily township, Butler co., O., 120 ms. s. w. of Columbus; from W. 508 ms.

PHILIPS COUNTY, situated on the eastern boundary of Arkansas, with the Mississippi river on the east, and traversed by the St. Francis. Area, 730 square miles. Seat of justice, Helena. Pop. in 1820, 1,201; in 1830, 1,152; in 1840, 3,547; in 1850, 6,935.

PHILIPSBURGH, p. v., Rush township, Centre co., Pa., 119 ms. N. w. of Harrisburgh; from W. 211 ms. Watered by Mushannon creek.

PHILIPSBURGH, p. v., Wells township, Jefferson co., O., 137 ms. E. of Columbus; from W. 262 ms. Watered by Ohio river.

PHILIPSPORT, p. v., Mamakating township, Sullivan co., N. Y., 92 ms. s. w. of Albany; from W. 287 ms. Situated on the Delaware and Hudson canal.

PHILIPSTOWN, p. v., White co., Ill., 190 ms. s. E. of Springfield; from W. 742 ms.

PHILIPSVILLE, p. v., Amity township, Alleghany co., N. Y. Watered by Genesee river.

PHILIPSVILLE, p. o., Weakly co., Tenn.

PHILLIPPA, p. o., Barbour co., Va.

PHILLIPS, p. t., Franklin co., Me., 55 ms. N. w. of Augusta; from W. 636 miles. Watered by Sandy river. Pop. 1,173.

PHILLIPSBURGH, t., Beaver co., Pa.

PHILLIPSBURGH, p. b., New Sewickly township, Beaver co., Pa. Watered by Ohio river.

PHILLIPS' CREEK, p. o., Alleghany co., N. Y.

PHILLIPSTON, p. t., Worcester co., Mass., 65 ms. N. w. of Boston, from W. 414 ms. Pop. 809.

PHILLIPSTOWN, t., Putnam co., N. Y., 96 ms. s. of Albany. Watered by Hudson river. Pop., 5,063.

PHILLIPSVILLE, v., Granby township, Oswego co., N. Y. Watered by Oswego river.

PHILLIPSVILLE, p. o., Erie co., Pa.

PHILO, p. o., Muskingum co., O.

PHILOMATH, p. o., Union co., Ind., 69 ms. E. of Indianapolis; from W. 508 ms.

PHILOMATH, p. o., Oglethorpe co., Ga.

PHILOMONT, p. v., Loudoun co., Va., 141 ms. N. of Richmond; from W. 48 ms.

PHILOPOLIS, p. o., Baltimore co., Md.

PHIPPSBURGH, p. t., Lincoln co., Me., 44 ms. s. of Augusta; from W. 584 ms. Watered by Kennebec river and Atlantic ocean. Pop. 1,805.

PHIPP'S MILLS, p. o., Venango co., Pa., 215 ms. N. w. of Harrisburgh; from W. 273 ms.

PHŒNIX, R. I., (See Phenix).

PHŒNIX, p. v., Schrœppel township, Oswego co., N. Y., 148 ms. N. w. of Albany; from W. 365 ms. Watered by Oswego river and Oswego canal. Pop. 872.

PHŒNIX, p. o., Edgefield district, S. C., 77 ms. w. of Columbia; from W. 541 ms.

PHŒNIX, p. o., Armstrong co., Pa.

PHŒNIXVILLE, p. v., Schuylkill township, Chester co., Pa., 79 ms. s. E. of Harrisburgh; from W. 156 ms. Watered by French creek at its confluence with Schuylkill river. Pop. 2,670.

PHŒNIXVILLE, p. o., Windham co., Ct.

PIASA, p. o., Macoupin co., Ill.

PIATT COUNTY, situated toward the east part of Illinois. Area, 440 square miles. Seat of justice, Monticello. Pop. in 1850, 1.606.

PICKAWAY COUNTY, situated in the central part of Ohio, and traversed by Scioto river. Area, 470 square miles. Face of the country even; soil, generally productive. Seat of justice, Circleville. Pop. in 1810, 7,124; in 1820, 13,149; in 1830, 15,935; in 1840, 19,725; in 1850, 21,008.

PICKAWAY, t., Pickaway co., O. Pop. 1,425.

PICKAWAY PLAINS, p. o., Monroe co., Va.

PICKAYUNE, p. o., Henderson co., Ill.

PICKENS COUNTY, situated on the west boundary of Alabama, and traversed by Tombigbee river. Area, 720 square miles. Seat of justice, Carrollton. Pop. in 1830, 6,622; in 1840, 17,118; in 1850, 21,512.

PICKENS DISTRICT, situated in the northwest corner of South Carolina, with Savannah river on the southwest. Area, 1,050 square miles. Face of the country hilly. Seat of justice, Pickens c. h. Pop. in 1830, 14,473; in 1840, 14,356; in 1850, 16,904.

PICKENS, c. h., p. v., Pickens district, S. C., 130 ms. N. w. of Columbia; from W. — ms.

PICKENSVILLE, p. v., Pickens district, S. C., 120 ms. N. w. of Columbia; from W. 515 ms.

PICKENSVILLE, p. v., Pickens co., Ala., — ms. w. of Montgomery; from W. 861 ms. Watered by Tombigbee river. Pop. 276.

PICKERELTOWN, p. o., Logan co., O.

PICKERINGTON, p. v., Violet township, Fairfield co., O., 17 ms. s. E. of Columbus; from W. 388 ms. Pop. 849.

PICOLATA, p. o., St. Johns co., Flor.

PIEDMONT, p. v., Harris co., Ga., 135 ms. s. w. of Milledgeville; from W. 768 ms.

PIEDMONT, p. o., Nelson co., Va.
PIERMONT, p. t., Grafton co., N. H., 65 ms. N. w. of Concord ; from W. 510 ms. Watered by Connecticut river and Eastman's brook. Pop. 948.
PIERMONT, p. v., Orangetown township, Rockland co., N. Y., 135 s. of Albany ; from W. 258 ms. Watered by Hudson river and Sparkhill creek.
PIERPONT, p. t., St. Lawrence co., N. Y., 202 ms. N. w. of Albany ; from W. 486 ms. Watered by Oswegatchie, Grass, and Racket rivers. Pop. 1,459.
PIERPONT, p. t., Ashtabula co., O., 213 ms. N. E. of Columbus ; from W. 330 ms. Pop. 999.
PIERREPONT MANOR, p. o., Jefferson co., N. Y.
PIFFARD, p. o., Livingston co., N. Y.
PIGEON, t., Vanderburgh co., Ind. Pop. 5,205.
PIGEON CREEK, p. o. Ralls co., Mo., 104 ms. N. E. of Jefferson city ; from W. 919 ms.
PIGEON FORGE, p. o., Sevier co., Tenn.
PIGEON GROVE, p. o., Columbia co., Wis.
PIGEON RIVER, p. o., Haywood co., N. C., 284 ms. w. of Raleigh ; from W. 514 ms.
PIGEON ROOST, p. o., Choctaw co., Miss.
PIGEON RUN, p. o., Campbell co., Va., 133 ms. s. w. of Richmond ; from W. 211 ms.
PIKE COUNTY, situated on the easterly boundary of Pennsylvania, with Delaware river on the southeast and northeast. Area, 729 square miles. Face of the country, mountainous ; soil, rocky and barren. Seat of justice, Milford. Pop. in 1820, 2,894 ; in 1830, 4,843 ; in 1840, 3,832 ; in 1850, 5,881.
PIKE COUNTY, situated toward the west part of Georgia. Area, 470 square miles. Seat of justice, Zebulon. Pop. in 1830, 6,149 ; in 1840, 9,176 ; in 1850, 14,306.
PIKE COUNTY, situated in the southeasterly part of Alabama. Area, 1,100 square miles. Seat of justice, Troy. Pop. in 1830, 7,108 ; in 1840, 10,108 ; in 1850, 15,926.
PIKE COUNTY, situated on the south boundary of Mississippi. Area, 804 square miles. Face of the country, uneven ; soil sterile, except near the streams. Seat of justice, Holmesville. Pop. in 1820, 4,438 ; in 1830, 5,402 ; in 1840, 6,151 ; in 1850, 13,609.
PIKE COUNTY, situated in the east part of Kentucky, with Big Sandy river on the northeast. Area, 400 square miles. Face of the country, hilly. Seat of justice, Piketon. Pop. in 1830, 2,677 ; in 1840, 3,567 ; in 1850, 5,365.
PIKE COUNTY, situated in the south part of Ohio, and traversed by Scioto river. Area, 421 square miles. Face of the country, rough and hilly ; soil varied but mostly of middling quality. Seat of justice, Piketon. Pop. in 1820, 4,253 ; in 1830, 6,024 ; in 1840, 7,626 ; in 1850, 10,953.
PIKE COUNTY, situated in the southwest part of Indiana, with White river on the north. Area, 325 square miles. Seat of justice, Petersburgh. Pop. in 1820, 1,472 ; in 1830, 2,464 ; in 1840, 4,760 ; in 1850, 7,720.
PIKE COUNTY, situated on the southwesterly boundary of Illinois, with Mississippi river on the southwest and the Illinois on the east. Area, 800 square miles. Seat of justice, Pittsfield. Pop. in 1830, 2,396 ; in 1840, 11,728 ; in 1850, 9,095.
PIKE COUNTY, situated on the northeasterly boundary of Missouri, with Mississippi river on the northeast. Area, 720 square miles. Seat of justice, Bowling Green. Pop. in 1820, 3,747 ; in 1830, 6,122 ; in 1840, 10,646 ; in 1850, 13,609.
PIKE COUNTY, situated in the southwesterly part of Arkansas. Area, 500 square miles. Seat of justice. Murfreesborough. Pop. in 1840, 969 ; in 1850, 1,861.
PIKE, p. t., Wyoming co., N. Y., 257 ms. w. of Albany ; from W. 350 ms. Watered by East and West Koy creeks. Pop. 2,003.
PIKE, p. t., Potter co., Pa.
PIKE, p. t., Berks co., Pa. Watered by the headwaters of Nanatawny creek. Pop. 883.
PIKE, p. t., Bradford co., Pa., 158 ms. N. of Harrisburgh ; from W. 268 ms. Watered by Wyalusing creek. Pop. 1,747.
PIKE, t., Clearfield co., Pa. Pop. 1,249.
PIKE, p. o.,, Muscatine co., Iowa.
PIKE, t., Brown co., O. Pop. 1,022.
PIKE, t., Perry co., O. Pop. 2,147.
PIKE, t., Clarke co., O. Pop. 1,315.
PIKE, t., Coshocton co., O. Pop. 1,081.
PIKE, t., Knox co., O. Pop. 1,720.
PIKE, t., Madison co., O. Pop. 423.

PIKE, t., Stark co., O. Pop. 1,447.
PIKE, p. o., Washington co., Me.
PIKE, p. t., Jay co., Ind. Pop. 786.
PIKE CREEK, p. o., Ripley co., Mo.
PIKE MILLS, p. o., Potter co., Pa.
PIKE POND, p. o., Sullivan co, N. Y.
PIKE RUN, p. t., Washington co., Pa., 194 ms. w. of Harrisburgh ; from W. 210 miles. Watered by Pike and Little Pike runs.
PIKETON, c. h., p. v., seat of justice of Pike co., O., 64 ms. s. of Columbus ; from W. 398 ms. Watered by Scioto river. Pop. 690.
PIKETON, c. h., p. v., seat of justice of Pike co., Ky., 173 ms. s. E. of Frankfort ; from W. 438 ms. Watered by the west fork of Sandy river.
PIKETON, p. v., Marion co., Ind., 9 ms. N. w. of Indianapolis ; from W. 580 ms.
PIKE TOWNSHIP, p. o., Berks co., Pa., 68 ms. E. of Harrisburgh ; from W. 161 ms.
PIKE VALLEY, p. o., Potter co., Pa.
PIKESVILLE. p. v., Baltimore co., Md., 38 ms. N. of Annapolis ; from W. 48 ms. Watered by Patapsco river. Pop. ——.
PIKEVILLE, c. h., p. v., seat of justice of Marion co., Ala. ; from W. 839 ms.
PIKEVILLE, c. h., p. v., seat of justice of Bledsoe co., Tenn., 112 ms. s. E. of Nashville ; from W. 588 ms.
PIKEVILLE, p. o., Chickasaw co., Miss.
PILAHATCHEE, p. o., Rankin co., Mo.
PILATKA, p. v., Putnam co., Flor. Watered by St. John's river.
PILCHER, p. o., Belmont co., O., 126 ms. E. of Columbus ; from W. 293 ms.
PILE's GROVE. t., Salem co., N. J. Watered by Salem creek. Pop. 2,962.
PILLAR POINT, p. o., Brownville township, Jefferson co., N. Y.
PILLOW, p. o., Dauphin co., Pa.
PILLOWVILLE, p. o., Weakly co., Tenn.
PILOT, p. o., Vermilion co., Ill.
PILOT GROVE, p. o., Cooper co., Mo., 62 ms. w. of Jefferson City ; from W. 976 ms.
PILOT GROVE, p. o., Lee co., Iowa.
PILOT GROVE, p. o., Hancock co., Ill.
PILOT GROVE, p. o., Grayson co., Tex.
PILOT HILL, c. h., p. v., seat of justice of Fulton co., Ark.
PILOT HILL, p. o., Mason co. Ill.
PILOT KNOB, p. o., Crawford co., Ill.
PILOT KNOB, p. o., Todd co., Ky.
PINCHECO, p. o., Ohio co., Ky.
PINCKNEY, t., Lewis co., N. Y., 156 ms. N. of Albany ; from W. 526 ms. Watered by Deer river and Sandy creek. Pop. 1.208.
PINCKNEY, v., Rutherford co., N. C., 226 ms. w. of Raleigh ; from W. 457 ms.
PINCKNEY, p v., Williamson co., Tenn. 28 ms. s. of Nashville ; from W. 705 ms. Watered by Harpeth river.
PINCKNEY, p. v., Warren co., Mo., 61 ms. N. E. of Jefferson City ; from W. 885 ms. Watered by Missouri river.
PINCKNEY, p. o., Livingston co., Mich., 54 ms. w. of Detroit ; from W. 547 ms.
FINCKNEY (See Pinkney).
PINCKNEYVILLE, p. v., Union district, S. C., 79 ms. N. w. of Columbia ; from W. 449 ms. Watered by Broad river.
PINCKNEYVILLE, p. v., Gwinnett co., Ga., 96 ms. N. w. of Milledgeville ; from W. 667 ms. Situated near Chattahoochie river.
PINCKNEYVILLE, p. v. Tallapoosa co., Ala.
PINCKNEYVILLE, c. h., p. v., seat of justice of Perry co., Ill., 134 ms. s. of Springfield ; from W. 839 ms. Watered by Big Beaucoup creek.
PINE, p. o., Vienna township, Oneida co., N. Y., 117 ms. N. w. of Albany ; from W. 387 ms.
PINE, t., Alleghany co., Pa. Watered by branches of Alleghany river. Pop. 2,109.
PINE, t., Armstrong co., Pa. Watered by Alleghany river and branches. Pop. 2,288.
PINE BLUFF, p. o., Copiah co., Miss., 49 ms. s. w. of Jackson ; from W. 1,064 ms.
PINE BLUFF, p. o., Pulaski co., Mo., 82 ms. s. of Jefferson city ; from W. 973 ms.
PINE BLUFF, p. v., seat of justice of Jefferson co., Ark., 28 ms. s. E. of Little Rock ; from W. 1,113 ms. Watered by Arkansas river. Pop. 460.
PINE BLUFF, p. o., Callaway co., Ky.

PINE BLUFF, p. o., Dane co., Wis.
PINE BLUFF, p. o., Red River co., Tex.
PINEBOROUGH, Marion co., Flor.
PINE BROOK, p. v., Hanover township, Morris co., N. J., 63 ms. N. of Trenton ; from W. 234 ms.
PINE BUSH, p. o., Ulster co., N. Y.
PINE CREEK, t., Clinton co., Pa.
PINE CREEK, p. o., Tioga co., Pa., 157 ms. N. of Harrisburgh ; from W. 271 ms.
PINE CREEK, t., Jefferson co., Pa.
PINE CREEK, p. o., Calhoun co., Mich.
PINE CREEK, p. o., Ogle co., Ill.
PINE FLAT, p. o., Bossier parish, La.
PINE GROVE, p. o., Tyrone township, Steuben co., N. Y., 198 ms. w. of Albany ; from W. 306 ms.
PINE GROVE, t., Venango co., Pa.
PINE GROVE, p. t., Schuylkill co., Pa., 43 ms. N. E. of Harrisburgh ; from W. 153 ms. Watered by Swatara creek. Pop. 1,967.
PINE GROVE, p. t., Warren co., Pa. Pop. 1,531.
PINE GROVE, p. o., Wetzel co., Va., 328 ms. N. w. of Richmond ; from W. 296 ms.
PINE GROVE, p. o., St. Tammany parish, La., 51 ms. N. of New Orleans ; from W. 1,153 ms.
PINE GROVE, p. o., Springfield township, Gallia co., O., 97 ms. s. E. of Columbus ; from W. 369 ms.
PINE GROVE, p. o., Clarke co., Ky.
PINE GROVE MILLS, p. o., Centre co., Pa., 90 ms. N. w. of Harrisburgh ; from W. 181 ms.
PINE HILL, p. o., Washington co., R. I., 22 ms. s. of Providence ; from W. 386 ms.
PINE HILL, p. o., Shandaken township, Ulster co., N. Y., 75 ms. s. w. of Albany ; from W. 349 ms.
PINE HILL, v., Elba township, Genesee co., N. Y.
PINE HILL, p. o., Wilcox co., Ala., from W. 894 ms.
PINE HILL, p. o., York co., Pa.
PINE HILL, p. o., Talbot co., Ga.
PINE HILL, p. o., Wachita parish, La.
PINE HILL, p. o., Rusk co., Tex.
PINE ISLAND, p. o., Jefferson co., Tex.
PINE LAKE, p. o., Oakland co., Mich.
PINE LAND, p. o., Meigs co., Tenn.
PINE LEVEL, p. o., Montgomery co., Ala., from W. 852 ms.
PINE LICK, p. o., Clarke co., Ind., 94 ms. s. E. of Indianapolis ; from W. 594 ms.
PINE LOG, p. o., Cass co., Ga., 156 ms. N. w. of Milledgeville ; from W. 647 ms.
PINE MEADOW, p. o., Litchfield co., Ct.
PINE PLAIN, p. o., Montcalm co., Mich.
PINE PLAINS, p. t., Dutchess co., N. Y., 62 ms. s. of Albany ; from W, 327 ms. Watered by Chicomico creek. Pop. 1,416.
PINE PLAINS, p. o., Ocean co., N. J.
PINE RIVER, p. o., Marquette co., Wis.
PINE RUN, p. o., Genesee co., Mich., 72 ms. N. w. of Detroit ; from W. 596 ms.
PINER'S CROSS ROADS, p. o., Kenton co., Ky.
PINE'S BRIDGE, p. o., Yorktown township, Westchester co., N. Y., 123 ms. s. of Albany : from W. 265 ms.
PINE STREET, p. o., Elk co., Pa., 159 ms. N. w. of Harrisburgh ; from W. 242 ms.
PINE TOWN, p. o., Cherokee co., Tex.
PINE TREE, p. o., Upshur co., Tex.
PINE VALLEY. p. o., Chemung co., N. Y.
PINE VALLEY, p. o., Warren co., Pa.
PINE VALLEY, p. o., Yallabusha co., Miss.
PINE VIEW, p. o., Fauquier co., Va.
PINEVILLE, p. o., Bucks co., Pa., 108 ms. E. of Harrisburgh ; from W. 163 ms.
PINEVILLE, p. v., Charleston district, S. C., 130 ms. s. E., of Columbia ; from W. 518 ms. Watered by Santee river.
PINEVILLE, p. v., Marengo co., Ala.; from W. 922 ms. Watered by Tombigbee river.
PINEVILLE, p. o., Marion co., Ga.
PINEVILLE, p. o., Gloucester co., N. J.
PINEVILLE, p. o., Bossier parish, La.
PINEVILLE, p. o., Smith co., Miss.
PINE WOODS, p. o., Madison co., Ill.
PINEY, p. o., Johnson co., Ark.
PINEY CREEK, p. o., Carroll co., Md.
PINEY GROVE, p. o., Sampson co., N. C.
PINEY GROVE, p. o., Hardeman co., Tenn.
PINEY HEAD, p. o., Appling district, S. C.
PINGREE GROVE, Kane co., Ill.
PINK, p. t., Wayne co., Pa.

PINKHAM'S GRANT, t., Coos co., N. H., 92 ms. N. of Concord : from W. 578 ms.
PINK HILL, p. o., Marshall co., Miss.
PINK HILL, p. o., Lenoir co., N. C.
PINKNEY, (see Pinckney).
PINKNEY, p. o., Lewis co., N. Y.
PINKNEY, t., Calhoun co., Mich.
PINNELLVILLE, p. o., Jones co., Miss.
PIN OAK, p. o., Du Buque co., Iowa.
PINTLALA, p. o., Montgomery co., Ala. ; from W. 852 ms. Watered by Pintlala river.
PINTLEE'S CORNERS, p. o., Ottawa co., Mich.
PINY, p. o., Clarion co., Pa.
PINY GREEN, p. o., Onslow co., N. C.
PIONEER, p. o., Greene co., Ill.
PIONEER, p. o., Williams co., O.
PIONEER GROVE, p. o., Cedar co., Wis.
PIONEER MILLS, p. o., Cabarras co., N. C., 155 ms. w. of Raleigh; from W. 392 ms.
PIPE CREEK, p. o., Madison co., Ind., 41 ms. N. E. of Indianapolis ; from W. 563 ms.
PIPERSVILLE, p. o., Bucks co., Pa.
PIPE STEM, p. o., Mercer co., Va.
PIPE STONE, p. o., Berrien co., Mich.
PIQUA, p. v., Miami co., O., 73 ms. w. of Columbus ; from W. 467 ms. Watered by Miami river and Miami canal. Pop. 3,277.
PIQUEA, p. o., Lancaster co., Pa., 54 ms. s. E. of Harrisburgh ; from W. 129 ms.
PISCATAQUIS COUNTY, situated in the central part of Maine, with Moosehead lake on the west. Area, —— square miles. Seat of justice, Dover. Pop. in 1840, 13,138 ; in 1850, 14,735.
PISCATAWAY, t., Middlesex co., N. J. Watered by Amherst and Cedar brooks. Pop. 2,975.
PISCATAWAY, p. v., Prince George's co., Md., 56 ms. s. w. of Annapolis ; from W. 16 ms. Watered by Piscataway river.
PISCOLA, p. o., Lowndes co., Ga.
PISGAH, p. o., Cole co., Mo., 33 ms. N. w. of Jefferson city ; from W. 969 ms.
PISGAH, p. o., Butler co., O.
PISGAH, p. o., Union co., Iowa.
PISHON'S FERRY, p. o., Kennebec co., Me.
PISTOL CREEK, p. o., Wilkes co., Ga.
PITCAIRN, p. t., St. Lawrence co., N. Y., 171 ms. N. w. of Albany ; from W. 470 ms. Watered by south west branch of Oswegatchie river. Pop. 503.
PITCHER, p. t., Chenango co., N. Y., 127 ms. s. w. of Albany. Watered by Ostelic river. Pop. 1,503.
PITCHER SPRINGS, p. v., Pitcher township, Chenango co., N. Y., 126 ms. s. w. of Albany ; from W. 332 ms. Near the village are three sulphur springs of some celebrity.
PITCH LANDING, p. v., Hertford co., N. C., 165 ms. N. E. of Raleigh ; from W. 237 ms. Watered by Piney creek.
PITMAN, p. o., Schuylkill co., Pa.
PITT COUNTY, situated in the easterly part of North Carolina, with Muse river at the south, and traversed by Tar river. Area, 800 square miles. Seat of justice, Greenville. Pop. in 1810, 9,169 ; in 1820, 10,001 ; in 1830, 12,174 ; in 1840, 11,806 ; in 1850, 13,397.
PITT, t., Alleghany co., Pa. Watered by Alleghany and Monongahela rivers. Pop. 2,033.
PITT, t., Crawford co., O.
PITTSBOROUGH, c. h., p. v., seat of justice of Chatham co., N. C., 34 ms. w. of Raleigh ; from W. 322 ms. Watered by Robinson creek.
PITTSBOROUGH, p. o., Marion co., Ind.
PITTSBURGH, city, Alleghany co., Pa., is situated at the head of Ohio river, which is here formed by the confluence of the Alleghany and Monongahela rivers. It is 297 miles westerly from Philadelphia, and 226 miles from Washington.
The city is built on a broad level point of land, between the two rivers, and is enclosed by hills, which are filled with bituminous coal. This constitutes the fuel for the vast number of factories, the tall chimneys of which bristle the town, belching black clouds of smoke, that darken the air and stain the houses a dusky hue. In point of beauty, therefore, Pittsburgh has little that is attractive ; yet there is something interesting in the concentration of industry and enterprise which this dark city exhibits. Here, before the settlement of the town, in 1790, stood Fort du Quesne, for a long time one of the most important posts in the hands of the French, who abandoned it in 1758, when it was

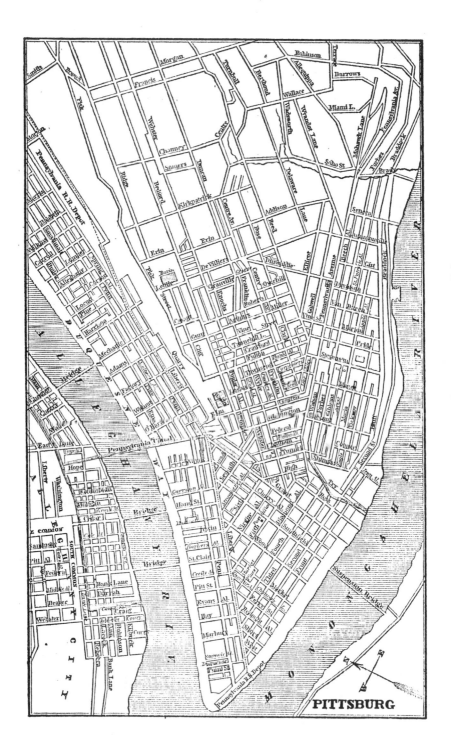

PITTSBURG

named by the British Fort Pitt. The dwellings are mostly of brick, many of them elegant and substantial, though dingy with smoke. The flourishing towns and villages which surround the city, afford pleasant sites for residence. Of these places, which are virtual suburbs of Pittsburgh, Alleghany city, on the opposite bank of the Alleghany, is the most important. The river is here spanned by a fine bridge 1,122 feet long, resting upon five stone piers; two bridges cross it at other points, and the Pennsylvania canal has a splendid aqueduct, 1,200 feet long, over the same stream. On the Monongahela are Birmingham and other settlements, which are connected by a bridge 1,500 feet long, and several ferries.

From its position, Pittsburgh is a great commercial as well as manufacturing emporium. It holds to Pennsylvania the same relation as Buffalo does to New York, being the gate of commerce between the east and the west. Hither come a large number of steamboats, during the season of navigation, from New Orleans and the valley of the Mississippi and Ohio rivers. The Pennsylvania canal, after traversing the whole state, and crossing the Alleghany on its great aqueduct, passes by a great tunnel under a hill near the city, and enters the Monongahela. Pittsburgh is connected with Lake Erie by the Ohio and Pennsylvania and the Cleveland and Pittsburgh railroads, and with Philadelphia by the Grand Trunk railroad.

The city contains an elegant courthouse, 165 feet long, 100 feet wide, and 148 feet from the ground to the top of the dome, which affords a delightful view of the populous neighborhood and rich picturesque surrounding region; also a prison, the Western University of Pennsylvania, finely seated on an adjacent elevation, and numerous churches, banks, hotels, and other prominent buildings. The Alleghany river affords a plentiful supply of water, which is distributed over the city by expensive and convenient water-works: and the bituminous coal of the adjoining hills yields gas for illuminating the town.

The manufactures embrace almost every article of domestic necessity and convenience. Machinery, cutlery, glass, cotton, cloth, pottery, paints, and drugs, are a few of the vast and innumerable variety produced.

The population in 1800, was 1,565; in 1810, 4,768; in 1820, 7,248; in 1830, 12,542; in 1840, 21,115; in 1850, 46,601.

PITTSBURGH, p. t., Coos co., N. H. Watered by Connecticut lake and other head waters of Connecticut river. Pop. 425.

PITTSBURGH, p. v., Carroll co., Ind., 68 ms. N. w. of Indianapolis; from W. 626 ms. Pop. 336.

PITTSBURGH, v., Henry co., Ga., 75 ms. N. w. of Milledgeville; from W. 679 ms.

PITTSBURGH, p. v., Johnson co., Ark., 91 ms. N. w. of Little Rock; from W. 756 ms. Watered by Arkansas river. Pop. 680.

PITTSBURGH, p. o., Darke co., O.

PITTSBURGH, p. o., Van Buren co., Iowa.

PITTSBURGH, p. o., Hickory co., Mo.

PITTSFIELD, p. t., Somerset co., Me., 43 ms. N. of Augusta; from W. 638 ms. Watered by a tributary of Sebasticook river. Pop. 1,176.

PITTSFIELD, p. t., Rutland co., Vt., 70 ms. s. w. of Montpelier; from W. 464 ms. Watered by Tweed river. Pop. 512.

PITTSFIELD, p. t., Merrimack co., N. H., 15 ms. N. E. of Concord; from W. 496 ms. Watered by Suncook river. Pop. 1,828.

PITTSFIELD, p. t., Berkshire co., Mass., 131 ms. w. of Boston; from W. 376 ms. Watered by tributaries of Housatonic river. Pop. 5,872.

PITTSFIELD, p. t., Otsego co., N. Y., 95 ms. w. of Albany; from W. 352 ms. Watered by Unadilla river and tributaries. Pop. 1,591.

PITTSFIELD, p. o., Warren co., Pa.

PITTSFIELD, p. t., Lorain co., O., 106 ms. N. E. of Columbus; from W. 375 ms. Pop. 1,088.

PITTSFIELD, p. t., Washtenaw co., Mich., 35 ms. w. of Detroit; from W. 522 ms. Pop. 1,234.

PITTSFIELD, c. h., p. v., seat of justice of Pike co., Ill., 70 ms. s. w. of Springfield; from W. 850 ms.

PITTSFORD, p. t., Rutland co., 70 ms. s. w. of Montpelier; from W. 464 ms. Watered by Otter creek and Furnace river. Pop. 2,026.

PITTSFORD, p. t., Monroe co., N. Y., 213 ms. w. of Albany; from W. 362 ms. Watered by Irondiquoit creek and tributaries. Pop. 2,061.

PITTSFORD, p. t., Hillsdale co., Mich., 89 ms. s. w. of Detroit; from W. 521 ms. Pop. 1,223.

PITTS' GROVE, p. t., Salem co., N. J. Watered by tributaries of Maurice run. Pop. 1,151.

PITTS' POINT, p. o., Bullitt co., Ky.

PITTSTON, p. t., Kennebec co., Me., 7 ms. s. of Augusta; from W. 595 ms. Watered by Kennebec river. Pop. 1,967.

PITTSTON FERRY, p. o., Luzerne co., Pa., 136 ms. N. E. of Harrisburgh; from W. 240 ms.

PITTSTOWN, p. t., Luzerne co., Pa. Pop. 4,049.

PITTSTOWN, p. t., Rensselaer co., N. Y., 25 ms. N. F. of Albany; from W. 393 ms. Watered by Tomhannock creek and Hoosick river. Pop. 3,732.

PITTSTOWN, p. v., Alexander township, Hunterdon co., N. J., 33 ms. N. w. of Trenton; from W. 193 ms. Watered by a tributary of Raritan river.

PITTSYLVANIA COUNTY, situated on the south boundary of Virginia, with Dan river on the south. Area, 891 square miles. Face of the country, uneven; soil, productive near the streams. Seat of justice, Pittsylvania c. h. Pop. in 1810, 17,172; in 1820, 21,313; in 1830, 20,063; in 1840, 26,398; in 1850, 28,786.

PITTSYLVANIA, c. h., p. v., seat of justice of Pittsylvania co., Va., 162 ms. s. w. of Richmond; from W. 245 ms. Watered by a branch of Banister river.

PLACERVILLE, p. o., El Dorado co., California.

PLAIN, t., Stark co., O. Pop. 2,211.

PLAIN, t., Franklin co., O. Pop. 1,561.

PLAIN, t., Wood co., O. Pop. 492.

PLAIN, t., St. Francis co., Ark.

PLAIN, p. t., Wayne co., O., 92 ms. N. E. of Columbus; from W. 349 ms. Pop. 2,375.

PLAIN. p. o., Greenville district, S. C., 95 ms. N. w. of Columbia; from W. 514 ms.

PLAINFIELD, p. t. Sullivan co., N. H., 62 ms. N. w. of Concord; from W. 478 ms. Watered by Connecticut river. Pop. 1,392.

PLAINFIELD, p. t., Washington co., Vt., 9 ms. E. of Montpelier; from W. 525 ms. Watered by Onion river and Great brook. Pop. 808.

PLAINFIELD, p. t., Hampshire co., Mass., 115 ms. w. of Boston; from W. 402 ms. Watered by head waters of Westfield river and North pond. Pop. 814.

PLAINFIELD, p. t., Windham co., Ct., 45 ms. E. of Hartford; from W. 372 ms. Watered by Quinnebaug and Moosup rivers. Pop. 2,732.

PLAINFIELD, p. t., Otsego co., N. Y., 84 ms. w. of Albany; from W. 373 ms. Watered by Unadilla river and tributaries. Pop. 1,450.

PLAINFIELD, p. t., Westfield township, Essex co., N. J., 39 ms. N. E. of Trenton; from W. 206 ms. Watered by Green brook. Pop. 2,446.

PLAINFIELD, p. t., Northampton co., Pa. Watered by east branch of Bushkill creek. Pop. 1,753.

PLAINFIELD, p. v.. Linton township, Coshocton co., O., 81 ms. N. E. of Columbus; from W. 329 ms. Watered by Wills creek.

PLAINFIELD, t., Allegan co., Mich.

PLAINFIELD, p. o., Livingston co., Mich., 71 ms. N. w. of Detroit; from W. 557 ms.

PLAINFIELD, p. t., Hendricks co., Ind., 15 ms. s. w. of Indianapolis; from W. 586 ms.

PLAINFIELD, p. t., Will co., Ill., 173 ms. N. E. of Springfield; from W. 750 ms. Pop. 1.093.

PLAINFIELD, p. o., Cumberland co., Pa.

PLAIN GROVE, p. o., Lawrence co., Pa.

PLAINSBOROUGH, p. o., Middlesex co., N. J.

PLAINS OF DURA, p. o., Sumter co., Ga., 113 ms. s. w. of Milledgeville; from W. 769 ms.

PLAINSVILLE, p. o., Exeter township. Luzerne co., Pa. 119 ms. N. E. of Harrisburgh; from W. 227 ms

PLAIN VIEW, p. o., Macoupin co., Ill.

PLAIN VIEW, p. o., King and Queen co., Va.

PLAINVILLE, p. o., Farmington township, Hartford co., Ct., 13 ms. w. of Hartford; from W. 326 ms.

PLAINVILLE, p. v., Lysander township, Onondaga co., N. Y., 155 ms. w. of Albany; from W. 360 ms.

PLAINVILLE, p. o., Hamilton co., O., 117 ms. s. w. of Columbus; from W. 489 ms.

PLAINWELL, p. o., Allegan co., Mich.

PLAISTOW, p. t., Rockingham co., N. H., 37 ms. s. E of Concord; from W. 465 ms. Pop. 748.

PLANK ROAD, p. o., Onondaga co., N. Y.

PLANK ROAD, p. t., Wayne co., Mich., 16 ms. s. w. of Detroit; from W. 510 ms.

PLANTERS. p. o., Attala co., Miss., 80 ms. N. E. of Jackson; from W. 975 ms.

PLANTERS, p. t. Philips co., Ark. Pop. 687.
PLANTERS' Hall, p. o., Breckenridge co., Ky., 122 ms.
s. w. of Frankfort; from W. 664 ms.
PLANTERS' STAND, p. o., Madison co., Ga.
PLANTERSVILLE, p. v., Perry co., Ala.
PLAQUEMINE PARISH, situated at the southeast extremity of Louisiana, on the Gulf of Mexico, including the main embouchure of the Mississippi. Area, 2,500 square miles. Face of the country low and level; soil, where arable, fertile. Seat of justice, Fort Jackson. Pop. in 1810, 1,549; in 1820, 2,354; in 1830, 4,489; in 1840, 5,060; in 1850, 7,390.
PLAQUEMINE, c. h., p. v., seat of justice of Iberville parish, La., 112 ms. N. w. of New Orleans; from W. 1,192 ms. Watered by Mississippi river.
PLAQUEMINE BRULEE, p. o., St. Landry parish, La.
PLATEA, p. o., Erie co., Pa.
PLATEAU, t., Jefferson co., Mo.
PLATO, p. o. Amherst township, Lorain co., O., 123 ms. N. E. of Columbus; from W. 381 ms.
PLATO, p. o., Cattaraugus co., N. Y.
PLATO, p. o., Iroquois co., Ill.
PLATTE COUNTY, situated on the westerly boundary of Missouri, with Missouri river on the southwest. Area, —— square miles. Seat of justice, Platte city. Pop. in 1850, 16,845.
PLATTE, t., Buchanan co., Mo.
PLATTE CITY, c. h., p. v., seat of justice of Platte co., Mo. Watered by Little Platte river. Pop. 881.
PLATTEKILL, p. t., Ulster co., N. Y., 85 ms. s. w. of Albany; from W. 295 ms. Watered by Old Man's kill and tributaries of Wall kill. Pop. 1,998.
PLATTE RIVER, p. o., Buchanan co., Mo.
PLATTEVILLE, p. v., Grant co., Wis., 78 ms. s. w. of Madison; from W. 910 ms.
PLATTSBURGH, c. h., p. t., seat of justice of Clinton co., N. Y., 163 ms. N. of Albany; from W. 538 ms. Watered by Saranac river and Lake Champlain. Pop. in 1830, 4,913; in 1840, 6,416; in 1850, 5,618.
PLATTSBURGH, c. h., p. v., seat of justice of Clinton co., Mo., 180 ms. N. w. of Jefferson city; from W. 1,092 ms. Watered by Smith's fork of Little Platte river.
PLATTVILLE, p. o., Kendall co., Ill.
PLEASANT, t., Warren co., Pa.
PLEASANT, t., Hardin co., O. Pop. 1,059.
PLEASANT, t., Franklin co., O. Watered by Big and Little Darby creeks. Pop. 1,071.
PLEASANT, t., Knox co., O. Watered by Vernon river. Seat of Kenyon college Pop. 900.
PLEASANT, p. t., Putnam co., O. Pop. 714.
PLEASANT, t., Seneca co., O. Pop. 1,592.
PLEASANT, Van Wert co., O. Pop. 619.
PLEASANT, t., Fairfield co., O.
PLEASANT, t., Madison co., O.
PLEASANT, t., Clark co. O. Pop. 1,188.
PLEASANT, t., Brown co., O. Pop. 1,456.
PLEASANT, t., Hancock co., O. Pop. 522.
PLEASANT, t., Grant co., Ind. Pop. 1,082.
PLEASANT, t., Steuben co., Ind. Pop. 739,
PLEASANT, p. t., Switzerland co., Ind., 82 ms. s. E. of Indianapolis; from W. 549 ms. Pop. 2,211.
PLEASANT, t., Wabash co., Ind. Pop. 1,312.
PLEASANT, p. o., Kent co., Mich.
PLEASANT, p. t.. Marion co., Mo.
PLEASANT, p. o., Otsego co., N. Y.
PLEASANT CREEK, p. o.. Taylor co., Va.
PLEASANT DALE, p. o., Hampshire co., Va.
PLEASANT EXCHANGE, p. o., Henderson co., Tenn., 108 ms. s. w. of Nashville; from W. 792 ms.
PLEASANT FLAT, p. o., Mason co., Va., 358 ms. N. w. of Richmond; from W. 372 ms.
PLEASANT GAP, p. o., Bates co., Mo., 133 ms. s. w. of Jefferson city; from W. 1,062 ms.
PLEASANT GAP, p. o., Centre co., Pa.
PLEASANT GAP, p. o., Cherokee co., Ala.
PLEASANT GREEN, p. o., Cooper co., Mo.
PLEASANT GROVE, p. v., Washington township, Morris co., N. J., 40 ms. N. of Trenton; from W. 215 ms.
PLEASANT GROVE, p. o., Lancaster co., Pa., 60 ms. E. of Harrisburgh; from W. 89 ms.
PLEASANT GROVE, p. o., Lunenburgh co., Va., 88 ms. s. w. of Richmond; from W. 190 ms.
PLEASANT GROVE, p. o., Orange co., N. C., 64 ms. N. w. of Raleigh; from W. 296 ms.
PLEASANT GROVE, p. o., Greenville district, S. C., 116 ms. N. w. of Columbia; from W. 489 ms.
PLEASANT GROVE, p. o., Pickens co., Ala., from W. 846 ms.

PLEASANT GROVE, p. o., Maury co., Tenn., 66 ms. s. w. of Nashville; from W. 726 ms.
PLEASANT GROVE, p. o., Ohio co., Ky., 156 ms. s. w. of Frankfort; from W. 698 ms.
PLEASANT GROVE, p. o., Des Moines co., Iowa.
PLEASANT GROVE, p. o., Jasper co., Ind.
PLEASANT GROVE, p. o., Effingham co., Ga.
PLEASANT GROVE, p. o., Clermont co., O.
PLEASANT GROVE, p. o., Macoupin co., Ill.
PLEASANT GROVE, p. o., Alleghany co., Md.
PLEASANT GROVE, p. o., Kenosha co., Wis.
PLEASANT GROVE, p. o., De Soto parish, La.
PLEASANT GROVE, p. o., Jefferson co., Tex.
PLEASANT GROVE MILLS, p. o., Fleming co., Ky.
PLEASANT HALL, p. o., Franklin co., Pa.
PLEASANT HILL, p. o., New Castle co., Del., 54 ms. N. of Dover; from W. 117 ms.
PLEASANT HILL, p. o., Miami co., O., 84 ms. w. of Columbus; from W. 476 ms.
PLEASANT HILL, p. o., Northampton co., N. C., 101 ms. N. E. of Raleigh; from W. 208 ms.
PLEASANT HILL, p. o., Lancaster district, S. C., 61 ms. N. E. of Columbia; from W. 445 ms.
PLEASANT HILL, p. o., Talbot co., Ga., 92 ms, s. w. of Milledgeville; from W. 714 ms.
PLEASANT HILL, p. o., Dallas co., Ala., from W. 867 ms.
PLEASANT HILL, p. o., Franklin co., Ark., 133 ms. N. w. of Little Rock; from W. 1,198 ms.
PLEASANT HILL, p. o., Van Buren co., Iowa.
PLEASANT HILL, p. o., Montgomery co., Ind., 58 ms. N. w. of Indianapolis; from W. 629 ms.
PLEASANT HILL, p. o., Cass co., Mo., 135 ms. w. of Jefferson city; from W. 1,061 ms.
PLEASANT HILL, p. o., Pike co., Ill., 83 ms. s. w. of Springfield; from W. 863 ms.
PLEASANT HILL, p. o., Benton co., Oregon.
PLEASANT HILL, p. o., Mercer co., Ky.
PLEASANT HILL, p. o., De Soto co., Miss.
PLEASANT HILL, p. o., De Soto parish, La.
PLEASANT HILL, p. o., Fayette co., Va.
PLEASANT HILL, p. o., Hopkins co., Tex.
PLEASANT LAKE, p. o., Steuben co., Ind., 170 ms. N. E. of Indianapolis; from W. 545 ms.
PLEASANT LANE, p. o., Edgefield district, S. C.
PLEASANT MILLS, p. o., Galloway township, Atlantic co., N. J., 67 ms. s. of Trenton; from W. 177 ms.
PLEASANT MILLS, p. o. Adams co., Ind.
PLEASANT MOUNT, p. o.. Wayne co., Pa., 179 ms. N. E. of Harrisburgh; from W. 273 ms.
PLEASANT MOUNT, p. o., Panola co., Miss.
PLEASANT MOUNT, p. o., Harrison co., O.
PLEASANT MOUNT, p. o.. Miller co., Mo.
PLEASANT OAKS, p. o., Brunswick co., Va.
PLEASANT OAKS, p. o., Mecklenburgh co. N. C.
PLEASANTON, p. o., Athens co., O.
PLEASANTON, p. o., Itawamba co., Miss.
PLEASANT PARK, p. o., Carroll co., Mo., 112 ms. N. w. of Jefferson city; from W. 1,000 ms.
PLEASANT PLAIN, p. o., Jefferson co., Iowa.
PLEASANT PLAIN, p. o., Clermont co., O.
PLEASANT PLAINS, p. o., Clinton township, Dutchess co., N. Y., 67 ms. s. of Albany; from W. 312 ms.
PLEASANT PLAINS, p. o., Scott co., Mo., 240 ms. s. E. of Jefferson city; from W. 880 ms.
PLEASANT PLAINS, p. o., Sangamon co., Ill.
PLEASANT PLAINS, p. o., Lincoln co., Tenn.
PLEASANT PLAINS, p. o., Cumberland co., N. C.
PLEASANT PRAIRIE, p. o., Greene co., Mo., 137 ms. s. w. of Jefferson city; from W. 1,052 ms.
PLEASANT RETREAT, p. o., Lumpkin co., Ga.
PLEASANT RETREAT, p. o., Scotland co., Mo.
PLEASANT RIDGE, p. o., Hamilton co., O., 112 ms. s. w. of Columbus; from W. 485 ms.
PLEASANT RIDGE, p. o., Greene co., Ala.; from W. 860 ms.
PLEASANT RIDGE, p. o., Bracken co., Ky., 66 ms. N. E. of Frankfort; from W. 496 ms.
PLEASANT RIDGE, p. o., Princess Ann co., Va.
PLEASANT RIDGE, Tippah co., Miss.
PLEASANT RIDGE, p. o., Greene co., Ind.
PLEASANT RIDGE, p. o., Rock Island co., O.
PLEASANT RUN, p. o., Hamilton co., O.
PLEASANT RUN, p. o., Dallas co., Tex.
PLEASANT SHADE, p. o., Smith co., Tenn.
PLEASANT SHADE, p. o., Perry co., Ill.
PLEASANT SITE, p. o., Franklin co., Ala.
PLEASANT SPRINGS, p. o., Lexington district, S C

PLEASANT SPRING, p. o., Kemper cc., Miss.

PLEASANT SPRING, p. o., Howard co., Ind.

PLEASANT UNITY, p. v., Unity township, Westmoreland co., Pa., 164 ms. w. of Harrisburgh ; from W. 190 ms. Watered by Big Sewickly creek.

PLEASANT VALE, p. v., Pike co., Ill., 90 ms. s. w. of Springfield ; from W. 873 ms.

PLEASANT VALLEY, p. v., Litchfield co., Ct., 22 ms. w. of Hartford ; from W. 346 ms.

PLEASANT VALLEY, p. t., Dutchess co., N. Y., 79 ms. s. of Albany ; from W. 306 ms. Watered by Wappinger's creek. Pop. 2,226.

PLEASANT VALLEY, p. v., Springfield township, Bucks co., Pa., 103 ms. E. of Harrisburgh ; from W. 182 ms.

PLEASANT VALLEY, p. o., Livingston co., Mich.

PLEASANT VALLEY, p. o., Fairfax co., Va., 131 ms. N. of Richmond ; from W. 31 ms.

PLEASANT VALLEY, p. o., Lancaster district, S. C., 94 ms. N. E. of Columbia ; from W. 412 ms.

PLEASANT VALLEY, p. o., Murray co., Ga., 191 ms. N. W. of Milledgeville ; from W. 599 ms.

PLEASANT VALLEY, p. o., Washington co., Ala. ; from W. 968 ms.

PLEASANT VALLEY, p. o., Yell co., Ark.

PLEASANT VALLEY, p. o., Scott co., Iowa.

PLEASANT VALLEY, p. o., Jo-Daviess co., Ill.

PLEASANT VALLEY, p. o., Sussex co., N. J.

PLEASANT VALLEY, p. o., Morgan co., O.

PLEASANT VALLEY, p. o., Wayne co., Tenn., 119 ms. s. w. of Nashville ; from W. 796 ms.

PLEASANT VALLEY, p. o., Wright co., Mo.

PLEASANT VALLEY, p. o., Chittenden co., Vt.

PLEASANT VALLEY MILLS, p. o., Nicholas co., Ky.

PLEASANT VIEW, p. o., Shelby co., Ind.

PLEASANT VIEW, p. o., Darlington district, S. C., 95 ms. N. E. of Columbia ; from W. 467 ms.

PLEASANT VIEW, p. o., Jackson co., Va.

PLEASANT VIEW, p. o., Juniata co., Pa.

PLEASANT VIEW, p. o., Schuyler co., Ill.

PLEASANTVILLE, p. v., Mount Pleasant township, Westchester co., N. Y., 122 ms. s. of Albany ; from W. 264 ms.

PLEASANTVILLE, p. v., Montgomery township, Montgomery co., Pa., 105 ms. E. of Harrisburgh ; from W. 163 ms.

PLEASANTVILLE, p. v., Rockingham co., N. C., 112 ms. N. w. of Raleigh ; from W. 300 ms.

PLEASANTVILLE, p. v., Hickman co., Tenn., 73 ms. s. w. of Nashville ; from W. 757 ms.

PLEASANTVILLE, p. v., Pleasant township, Fairfield co., O., 39 ms. s. E. of Columbus ; from W. 375 ms.

PLEASANTVILLE, p. o., Fulton co., Ill.

PLEASANTVILLE, p. o., Marion co., Iowa.

PLEASANTVILLE, p. o., Bucks co., Pa.

PLEASANTVILLE, p. o., Harford co., Md.

PLEASANT WOODS, p. o., Delaware co., Ind.

PLEASUREVILLE, p. v., Henry co., Ky., 19 ms. N. w. of Frankfort ; from W. 561 ms.

PLENITUDE, p. o., Anderson co., Tex.

PLESIS. p. v., Alexander township, Jefferson co., N. Y., 189 ms. N. w. of Albany ; from W. 441 ms.

PLINY, p. o., Greenville district, S. C.

PLINY, p. o., Putnam co., Va.

PLOVER. p. o., Portage co., Wis.

PLOWDEN'S MILLS, p. v., Sumter district, S. C., 66 ms. s. E. of Columbia ; from W. 502 ms.

PLUCKEMIN. p. v., Bedminster township, Somerset co., N. J., 37 ms. N. of Trenton ; from W. 212 ms.

PLUM, p. t., Venango co., Pa. Pop. 835.

PLUM, p. o., Cook co., Ill.

PLUMB, t., Alleghany co., Pa. Watered by Alleghany river, Plumb and Turtle creeks ; and Thompson's run. Pop. 1,241.

PLUMB BAYOU, p. o., Jefferson co., Ark.

PLUMB BROOK, p. o., Macomb co., Mich., 25 ms. N. E. of Detroit ; from W. 550 ms.

PLUMB CREEK, t., Armstrong co., Pa.

PLUMB CREEK, p. o., Caldwell co., Tex.

PLUMB CREEK, p. o., Clinton co., Mo.

PLUMER, p. o., Venango co., Pa., 223 ms. N. w. of Harrisburgh ; from W. 297 ms.

PLUM GROVE, p. o., Bloomer co., Tenn.

PLUM GROVE, p. o., Fayette co., Tex.

PLUM HILL, p. o., Washington co., Ill.

PLUMMER'S MILL, p. o., Fleming co., Ky.

PLUM RIVER, p. o., Jo-Daviess co., Ill.

PLUMSTEAD, p. t., Bucks co., Pa., 106 ms. E. of Harrisburgh ; from W. 168 ms. Watered by Tohickon and Neshaminy creeks. Pop. 2,298.

PLUMSTEADVILLE, p. o., Bucks co., Pa.

PLUNGE CREEK, p. o., Clay co., Ind.

PLUNKET'S CREEK, t., Lycoming co., Pa.

PLYMOUTH COUNTY, situated in the southeast part of Massachusetts, with Cape Cod bay on the east. Area, 600 square miles. Face of the country, generally level ; soil, sandy and thin. Seat of justice, Plymouth. Pop. in 1810, 35,169 ; in 1820, 38,136 ; in 1830, 42,993 : in 1840, 47,373 ; in 1850, 55,697.

PLYMOUTH, p. t., Penobscot co., Me., 59 ms. N. E. of Augusta ; from W. 654 ms. Watered by a tributary of Sebasticook river.

PLYMOUTH, c. h., p. o., seat of justice, together with Haverhill, of Grafton co., N. H., 40 ms. N. of Concord ; from W. 521 ms. Watered by Pemigewasset and Baker's rivers.

PLYMOUTH, p. t., Windsor co., Vt., 73 ms. s. of Montpelier ; from W. 475 ms. Watered by Black river.

PLYMOUTH, p. t., p. t., seat of justice of Plymouth co., Mass., 38 ms. s. E. of Boston ; from W. 447 ms. Watered by Eel and Wonkinqua rivers, numerous brooks and ponds, and Cape Cod bay. Celebrated as the first landing-place of the Pilgrims, in 1620, and the earliest built town in New England. The rock on which they first landed consists of the larger part of a boulder, and was conveyed, in 1774, to the centre of the town, where it is now protected by a strong iron fence. Pop. in 1820, 4,348 ; in 1830, 4,751 ; in 1840, 5,281 ; in 1850, 6,026.

PLYMOUTH, p. t., Litchfield co., Ct., 23 ms. w. of Hartford ; from W. 339 ms. Watered by Naugatuck river. Pop. 2,568.

PLYMOUTH, p. t., Chenango co., N. Y., 120 ms. w. of Albany ; from W. 344 ms. Watered by Canasawacta creek. Pop. 1,551.

PLYMOUTH, p. t., Luzerne co., Pa., 124 ms. N. E. of Harrisburgh ; from W. 228 ms. Watered by Harvey's and Toby's creeks. Pop. 1,473.

PLYMOUTH, p. t., Montgomery co., Pa. Pop. 1,383.

PLYMOUTH, c. h., p. v., seat of justice of Washington co., N. C., 162 ms. E. of Raleigh ; from W. 286 ms. Watered by Roanoke river. Pop. 951.

PLYMOUTH, c. h., p. v. seat of justice of Marshall co., Ind., 113 ms. N. of Indianapolis ; from W. 634 ms.

PLYMOUTH, t., Ashtabula co., O. Pop. 752.

PLYMOUTH, p. v.. Hancock co., Ill., 92 ms. N. w. of Springfield ; from W. 870 ms.

PLYMOUTH, p. t., Richmond co., O., 77 ms. N. E. of Columbus ; from W. 389 ms. Pop. 1,663.

PLYMOUTH, p. t., Wayne co., Mich., 25 ms. s. w. of Detroit ; from W. 529 ms. Watered by the west branch of Rouge river. Pop. 2,431.

PLYMOUTH, p. v.. Lowndes co., Miss., 147 ms. N. E. of Jackson ; from W. 890 ms.

PLYMOUTH, p. o., Sheboygan co., Wis.

PLYMOUTH GRANT, t., Aropstook co., Me.

PLYMOUTH HOLLOW, p. v., Plymouth township, Litchfield co., Ct., 25 ms. w. of Hartford ; from W. 337 ms.

PLYMOUTH MEETING, p. o., Montgomery co., Pa.

PLYMPTON, p. t., Plymouth co., Mass., 41 ms, s. E. of Boston ; from W. 439 ms. Watered by a tributary of Taunton river. Pop. 927.

POAST TOWN, p. o., Butler co., O.

POCAHONTAS COUNTY, situated toward the west part of Virginia. Area, 710 square miles. Face of the country, mountainous ; soil, not fertile. Seat of justice, Huntersville, Pop. in 1830, 2,542 ; in 1840, 2,922 ; in 1850, 3,598.

POCAHONTAS, c. h., p. v., seat of justice of Randolph co., Ark., 152 ms. N. E. of Little Rock ; from W. 1,009 ms. Watered by Black river.

POCAHONTAS, p. o., Bond co., Ill.

POCAHONTAS, p. o., Somerset co., Pa.

POCASSET, p. v., Barnstable co., Mass., 63 ms. s. E. of Boston ; from W. 464 miles. Watered by Buzzard's bay.

POCKET, p. o., Moore co., N. C., 51 ms. s. w. of Raleigh ; from W. 339 ms.

POCONA, t., Monroe co., Pa. Pop. 925.

POCOTALIGO, p. o., Kanawha co., Va., 321 ms. N. w. of Richmond ; from W. 358 ms. Situated on Pocotaligo river.

POCOTALIGO, p. v., Beaufort district, S. C., 125 ms. s. of Columbia ; from W. 614 ms. Watered by Combahee river.

POESTENKILL, p. v., Sand Lake township, Rensselaer co., N Y., 13 ms. E. of Albany ; from W. 383 ms.
POINDEXTER, p. o., Marion co., Ga.
POINDEXTER'S STORE, p. o., Louisa co., Va., 59 ms. N. w. of Richmond ; from W. 138 ms.
POINSETT COUNTY, situated in the northeasterly part of Arkansas, with St. Francis river on the east. Area. — square miles. Seat of justice, Bolivar. Pop. in 1850. 2.308.
POINT, t., Northumberland co., Pa. Pop. 876.
POINT, p. o., Perry co., Ind.
POINT COMMERCE, p. o., Greene co., Ind. Situated at the confluence of Eel and White rivers.
POINT COUPEE PARISH, situated in the central part of Louisiana, with Mississippi river on the northeast and the Atchafalaya on the west. Area, 600 square miles. Face of the country, flat; soil rich where capable of cultivation. Seat of justice, Point Coupée. Pop. in 1810, 4,539 ; in 1820, 4,912 ; in 1830, 5,936 ; in 1840, 7,898 ; in 1850, 11,339.
POINT COUPEE, c. h., p. v., seat of justice of Point Coupée parish, La., 140 ms. N. w. of New Orleans ; from W. 1,174 ms. Watered by Mississippi river.
POINT DOUGLASS, p. o., Washington co., Minn.
POINT ISABEL, p. o., Clermont co., O.
POINT JEFFERSON, p. o., Morehouse parish, La.
POINT MAGREL, p. o., Avoyelles parish, La.
POINT MEERS, p. o., Johnson co., Ark.
POINT MONTEREY, p. o., Cass co., Tex.
POINT OF ROCKS, p. v., Frederick co., Md., 92 ms. N. w. of Annapolis ; from W. 60 ms.
POINT PENINSULA, p. o., Brownsville township, Jefferson co., N. Y.
POINT PETER, p. o., Searcy co., Ark.
POINT PETER, p. o., Oglethorpe co., Ga.
POINT PLEASANT, p. o., Ocean co., N. J., 53 ms. E. of Trenton ; from W. 219 ms.
POINT PLEASANT, p. v., Tinicum township, Bucks co., Pa , 119 ms. E. of Harrisburgh; from W. 181 ms. Watered by Delaware river.
POINT PLEASANT, c. h., p. v., seat of justice of Mason co., Va., 370 ms. N. w. of Richmond ; from W. 361 ms. Watered by Ohio river at the confluence of the Great Kanawha.
POINT PLEASANT, p. v., Monroe township, Clermont co., O., 120 ms. s. w. of Columbus ; from W. 495 ms. Watered by Ohio river.
POINT PLEASANT, p. o., New Madrid co., Mo.
POINT PLEASANT, p. o., Jasper co., Iowa.
POINT PRAIRIE, p. o., Franklin co., Ark., 130 ms N. w. of Little Rock ; from W. 1,195 ms.
POINT REMOVE, t., Conway co., Ark.
POINT REPUBLIC, p. o., La Salle co., Ill., 116 ms. N E. of Springfield ; from W. 790 ms.
POINT WORTHINGTON, Washington co., Miss.
POKEGON, t., Cass co., Mich. Pop. 994.
POKE BAYOU, p. o., Independence co., Ark.
POKE RUN, p. o., Westmoreland co., Pa., 185 ms. w. of Harrisburgh; from W. 210 ms.
POLAND, p. t., Cumberland co., Me., 51 ms. s. w. of Augusta ; from W. 574 ms. Watered by Little Androscoggin river. Pop. 1,379.
POLAND, p. v., Russia township, Herkimer co., N. Y., 89 ms. N. w. of Albany ; from W. 406 ms. Watered by West Canada creek.
POLAND, p. t., Chautauque co., N. Y., 317 ms. w. of Albany ; from W. — ms. Watered by Connewango creek and Chautauque outlet. Pop. 1.174.
POLAND, p. o., Mahoning co., O., 73 ms. N. E. of Columbus ; from W. 284 ms. Watered by Mahoning river.
POLAND, p. o., Clay co., Ind.
POLAND CENTRE, p. o., Poland township, Chautauque co., N. Y.
POLK COUNTY, situated on the south boundary of North Carolina. Area, — square miles. Seat of justice, Horse Creek. Pop. in 1850, ——.
POLK COUNTY, situated in the southeast corner of Tennessee. Area, 330 square miles. Seat of justice, Bentonville. Pop. in 1840, 3,570; in 1850, 6,388.
POLK COUNTY, situated in the southwesterly part of Missouri. Area, 760 square miles. Seat of justice, Bolivar. Pop. in 1840, 8,449 ; in 1850, 6,186.
POLK COUNTY, situated on the west boundary of Arkansas. Area, — square miles. Seat of justice, Liberty. Pop. in 1850, 1,263.
POLK COUNTY, situated in the southeasterly part of Texas, and traversed by Trinity river. Area, — square miles. Seat of justice, Livingston. Pop. 2,106.

POLK COUNTY, situated in the central part of Iowa, and traversed by Des Moines river. Area, — square miles. Seat of justice, Des Moines. Pop. in 1850, 4.515.
POLK COUNTY, situated in Oregon. Area, — square miles. Seat of justice, Lackemute. Pop. in 1850, 1,051.
POLK, p. o., Monroe co., Ala.
POLK, p. o., Ashland co., O.
POLK, p. o., Venango co., Pa.
POLK, p. o., Clinch co., Ga.
POLK RUN, p. o., Clarke co., Ind.
POLKTON, p. o., Ottawa co., Mich.
POLKVILLE, p. o., Benton co., Ala.
POLKVILLE, p. o., Cleveland co., N. C.
POLKVILLE, p. o., Smith co., Miss.
POLKVILLE, p. o., Warren co., N. J.
POLKVILLE, p. o., Columbia co., Pa.
POLLARD'S MILLS, p. o., Greenup co., Ky.
POLLOCK'S, p. o., Randolph co., Ill., 131 ms. s. of Springfield ; from W. 841 ms.
POLLOCKSVILLE, p. v., Jones co., N. C.
POMARIA, p. o., Newberry district, S. C., 26 ms. N. w. of Columbia ; from W. 507 ms.
POMEROY, p. t., Meigs co., O., 101 ms. s. E. of Columbus ; from W. 340 ms. Pop. 1.638.
POMFRET, p. t., Windsor co., Vt., 49 ms. s. of Montpelier ; from W. 490 ms. Watered by Queechee and White rivers. Pop. 1.546.
POMFRET, p. t., Windham co., Ct., 41 ms. E. of Hartford ; from W. 377 ms. Watered by Quinnebaug river. Pop. 1,848.
POMFRET, p. t., Chautauque co., N. Y., 315 ms. w. of Albany ; from W. — ms. Watered by Lake Erie and Cassadaga creek. Pop 4,493.
POMFRET LANDING, p. o., Pomfret township, Windham co., Ct., 43 ms. E. of Hartford ; from W. 376 ms.
POMONA, p. o., St. Charles co., Mo.
POMONKEY, p. o., Charles co., Md., 67 ms. s. w. of Annapolis ; from W. 27 ms.
POMPANOOSUC, p. o., Windsor co., Vt.
POMPEY, p. t., Onondaga co., N. Y., 125 ms. w. of Albany ; from W. 337 ms. Watered by Limestone creek and Toughnioga river. Pop. 4,006.
POMPEY CENTRE, p. o., Pompey township, Onondaga co., N. Y.
POMPTON, p. t., Passaic co., N. J. Watered by Ringwood river. Pop. 1 790.
POMPTON PLAINS, p. v., Pequannoc township, Morris co., N. J., 84 ms. N. E. of Trenton ; from W. 250 ms.
POND CREEK, p. o., Greene co., Mo.
POND CREEK MILLS, p. o., Knox co., Ind.
POND EDDY, p. o., Sullivan co., N. Y.
POND FORK, p. o., Jackson co., Ga.
POND HILL, p. o., Gibson co., Tenn.
POND SETTLEMENT, p. o., Steuben co, N. Y.
POND SPRING, p. o., Walker co., Ga.
PONDTOWN, p. o., Sumter co., Ga., 102 ms. s. w. of Milledgeville ; from W. 758 ms.
PONTIAC, c. h., p. t., seat of justice of Oakland co., Mich., 25 ms. N. w. of Detroit ; from W. 549 ms. Watered by Clinton river. Pop. 2,820.
PONTIAC, c. h., p. v., seat of justice of Livingston co., Ill., 110 ms. N. E. of Springfield ; from W. 737.
PONTIAC, p. o., Erie co., N. Y.
PONTIAC, p. o., Huron co., O.
PONTICO, p. o., Cayuga co., N. Y.
PONTOOSAC, p. o., Hancock co., Ill.
PONTOTOC COUNTY, situated in the northeast part of Mississippi. Area, 900 square miles. Seat of justice, Pontotoc. Pop. in 1840, 4.491 ; in 1850, 17,112.
PONTOTOC, c. h., p. v., seat of justice of Pontotoc co., Miss., 175 ms. N. E. of Jackson ; from W. 888 ms.
PONTOTOC, p. o., Fulton co., Ky.
POOLESVILLE, p. v., Montgomery co., Md., 73 ms. N. w. of Annapolis ; from W. 33 ms.
POOL'S MILLS, p. o., Jones co., Miss.
POOLSVILLE, p. v., Spartanburgh district, S. C., 107 ms. N. w. of Columbia ; from W. 480 ms.
POOLSVILLE, p. v., Warren co., Ind., 83 ms. N. w. of Indianapolis ; from W. 641 ms.
POORVILLE, p. v., Hamilton township, Madison co., N. Y., 95 ms. w. of Albany ; from W. 355 ms.
POOR FORK, p. o., Harlan co., Ky.
POOR HILL, p. o., Sullivan co., Tenn.
POPE COUNTY, situated toward the northwest part of Arkansas, with Arkansas river on the south. Area, 720 square miles. Face of the country, diversi-

fied. Seat of justice, Narristown. Pop. 1830, 1,483; in 1840, 2.850; in 1850, 4,710.

POPE COUNTY, situated on the southerly boundary of Illinois, with Ohio river on the southeast. Area, 576 square miles. Seat of justice. Golconda. Pop. in 1820, 2,610; in 1830, 3,323; in 1840, 4,094; in 1850, 3,975.

POPE CREEK, p. o., Mercer co., Ill., 140 ms. N. w. of Springfield; from W. 870 ms.

POPE'S CORNERS, p. o., Saratoga co., N. Y.

POPE'S MILLS, p. o., St. Lawrence co., N. Y.

POPE'S MILLS, p. o., Mercer co., Ill., 142 ms. N. w. of Springfield; from W. 872 ms.

POPE'S STORE, p. o., Southampton co., Va.

POPLAR, p. o., Crawford co., O., 75 ms. N. of Columbus; from W. 419 ms.

POPLAR, p. o., Orangeburgh district, S. C.

POPLAR BLUFF, p. o., Butler co., Mo.

POPLAR BRANCH, p. o., Currituck co., N. C., 242 ms. N. E. of Raleigh; from W. 290 ms.

POPLAR CORNER, p. o., Madison co., Tenn.

POPLAR CREEK, p. o., Choctaw co., Miss.

POPLAR FLAT, p. o., Lewis co., Ky., 97 ms. N. E. of Frankfort; from W. 476 ms.

POPLAR GROVE, p. o., Iredell co., N. C., 154 ms. w. of Raleigh; from W. 391 ms.

POPLAR GROVE, p. o., Owen co., Ky., 42 ms. N. of Frankfort; from W. 537 ms.

POPLAR GROVE, p. o., Gibson co., Tenn., 144 ms. w. of Nashville; from W. 827 ms.

POPLAR GROVE, p. o., Boone co., Ill.

POPLAR HILL, p. o., Giles co., Va., 234 ms. w. of Richmond; from W. 294 ms.

POPLAR HILL, p. o., Vigo co., Ind.

POPLAR HILL, p. o., Anson co., N. C., 151 ms. s. w. of Raleigh; from W. 420 ms.

POPLAR MOUNT, p. o., Greenville co., Va., 63 ms. s. of Richmond; from W. 182 ms. Situated on Nottaway river.

POPLAR PLAINS, p. v., Fleming co., Ky., 96 ms. E. of Frankfort; from W. 493 ms.

POPLAR RIDGE, p. o., Venice township, Cayuga co., N. Y., 168 ms. w. of Albany; from W. 324 ms.

POPLAR RIDGE, p. o., Darke co., O.

POPLAR RIDGE, p. o., Maury co., Tenn.

POPLAR SPRING, p. o., Fairfield district, S. C.

POPLAR SPRING, p. o., Marshall co., Va.

POPLAR SPRING, p. o., Pontotoc co., Miss.

POPLAR SPRINGS, p. o., Howard co., Md., 57 ms. N. w. of Annapolis; from W. 62 ms.

POPLAR SPRINGS, p. o., Hall co., Ga.

POPLIN, p. t., Rockingham co., N. H., 29 ms. s. E. of Concord; from W. 477 ms. Watered by Swamscot, or Exeter river, Red and Watchie brooks, and Loon pond. Pop. 509.

POQUANOC BRIDGE, p. o., New London co., Ct.

POQUEBANUCK, p. v., New London co., Ct., 43 ms. s. E. of Hartford; from W. 361 ms. Watered by a cove of Thames river.

POQUONOCK, p. v., Windsor township, Hartford co., Ct., 10 ms. N. of Hartford; from W. 346 ms. Watered by Farmington river.

PORTAGE COUNTY, situated in the northeasterly part of Ohio, and traversed by Cuyahoga and Tuscarawas rivers, which are separated by a portage of one mile. Area, 500 square miles. Face of the country, elevated and broken. Seat of justice, Ravenna. Pop. in 1810, 2,995; in 1820, 10,095; in 1830, 18,827; in 1840, 22,965; in 1850, 24,419.

PORTAGE COUNTY, situated in the central part of Wisconsin, and traversed by Wisconsin river. Area, 800 square miles. Seat of justice, Fort Winnebago. Pop. in 1840, 1,623; in 1850, 1,250.

PORTAGE, p. t., Wyoming co., N. Y., 247 ms. w. of Albany; from W. —— ms. Watered by Genesee river and Genesee Falls, and Genesee Valley canal.

PORTAGE, p. t., Wood co., O., 111 ms. N. w. of Columbus; from W. 647 ms. Pop. 403.

PORTAGE, t., Ottawa co., O. Pop. 377.

PORTAGE, t., Hancock co., O. Pop. 614.

PORTAGE, p. t., Summit co., O. Pop. 1,160.

PORTAGE, p. t., Kalamazoo co., Mich., 147 ms. w. of Detroit; from W. 611 ms. Pop. 726.

PORTAGE, p. o., Cambria co., Pa.

PORTAGE CITY, p. o., Columbia co., Wis.

PORTAGE DES SIEUR, p. v., St. Charles co., Mo., 122 ms. N. E. of Jefferson city; from W. 381 ms. Watered by Mississippi river.

PORTAGE ENTRY, p. o., Houghton co., Mich.

PORTAGE LAKE, p. o., Jackson co., Mich.

PORTAGEVILLE, p. v., Portage township, Wyoming co., N. Y., 262 ms. w. of Albany; from W. 357 ms. Watered by Genesee river, and Genesee Valley canal.

PORT ALLEGHANY, p. v., McKean co., Pa., 192 ms. N. w. of Harrisburgh; from W. 275 ms. Watered by Alleghany river.

PORT ALLEN, p. o., Louisa co., Iowa.

PORT BLANCHARD, p. o., Luzerne co., Pa.

PORT BYRON, p. v., Mentz township. Cayuga co., N. Y., 158 ms. w. of Albany; from W. 341 ms. Situated on the Erie canal.

PORT BYRON, p. o., Rock Island co., Ill., 160 ms. N. w. of Springfield; from W. 890 ms. Watered by Mississippi river.

PORT CADDO, p. o., Harrison co., Tex.

PORT CARBON, p. o., Branch township, Schuylkill co Pa., 65 ms. N. E. of Harrisburgh; from W. 175 ms. Watered by Mill creek and Schuylkill river.

PORT CHESTER, p. v., Rye township, Westchester co., N. Y., 136 ms. s. of Albany; from W. 255 ms. Watered by Byram river.

PORT CLINTON, p. v., Brunswick township, Schuylkill co.. Pa., 69 ms. N. E. of Harrisburgh; from W. 167 ms. Watered by Schuylkill river at its confluence with the Little Schuylkill.

PORT CLINTON, p. v., seat of justice of Ottawa co., O., 120 ms. N. of Columbus; from W. 428 ms. Watered by Portage river, and Lake Erie. Pop. 249.

PORT CLINTON, p. o., Lake co., Ill.

PORT CONWAY, p. o., King George co., Va., 84 ms. N. E. of Richmond; from W. 78 ms.

PORT CRANE, p. o., Broome co., N. Y.

PORT DEPOSIT, p. v., Cecil co., Md., 68 ms. N. E. of Annapolis; from W. 78 ms. Watered by Susquehanna river.

PORT ELIZABETH, p. v., Maurice River township, Cumberland co., N. J., 73 ms. s. of Trenton; from W. 184 ms. Watered by Manamuskin creek.

PORTER COUNTY, situated on the northerly boundary of Indiana, with Lake Michigan on the north and Kankakee river on the south. Seat of justice, Valparaiso. Pop. in 1840, 2,162; in 1850, 5,234.

PORTER, p. t., Oxford co., Me., 86 ms. s. w. of Augusta; from W. 543 ms. Watered by Ossipee river. Pop. 1,208.

PORTER, p. t., Niagara co., N. Y., 300 ms. w. of Albany; from W. —— ms. Watered by Tuscarora creek, Niagara river and Lake Ontario. Pop. 2,455.

PORTER, p. t., Huntingdon co., Pa. Pop. 1,050.

PORTER, p. t., Delaware co., O. Watered by Walnut creek. Pop. 1,087.

PORTER, t., Scioto co., O. Pop. 1,674.

PORTER, p. t., Jefferson co., Pa.

PORTER, p. t., Cass co., Mich. Pop. 1,259.

PORTERFIELD, p. o., Venango co., Pa., 206 ms. N. w. of Harrisburgh; from W. 278 ms.

PORTER RIDGE, p. o., Susquehanna co., Pa.

PORTER's, p. o., Carroll co., Md., 53 ms. N. w. of Annapolis; from W. 63 ms.

PORTER's CORNERS, p. o., Greenfield township, Saratoga co., N. Y., 43 ms. N. w. of Albany; from W. 413 ms.

PORTER's CROSS ROADS, p. o., Porter co., Ind.

PORTER's FALLS, p. o., Wetzel co., Va.

PORTER's PRECINCT, p. o., Albemarle co., Va.

PORTERSVILLE, p. v., Muddy Creek township, Butler co., Pa., 218 ms. N. w. of Harrisburgh; from W. 260 ms. Pop. 240.

PORTERSVILLE, p. v., Tipton co., Tenn., 214 ms. s. w. of Nashville; from W. 894 ms.

PORTERSVILLE, v., Dubois co., Ind., 124 ms. s. w. of India napolis; from W. 664 ms. Watered by east fork of White river.

PORTERSVILLE, p. o., Perry co., O.

PORT GIBSON, p. v., Manchester township, Ontario co., N. Y., 189 ms. w. of Albany; from W. 337 ms. Watered by Erie canal.

PORT GIBSON, c. h., p. v., seat of justice of Claiborne co., Miss., 72 ms. s. w. of Jackson; from W. 1,082 ms. Watered by Pierre Bayou.

PORT GLASGOW, p. o.. Huron township. Wayne co., N. Y., 186 ms. N. w. of Albany; from W. 366 ms.

PORT HENRY, p. v., Moriah township. Essex co., N. Y., 118 ms. N. of Albany; from W. 489 ms. Watered by Lake Champlain.

PORT HOMER, p. v., Jefferson co., O.

PORT HUDSON, p. v., East Feliciana parish, La., 146 ms. N. w. of New Orleans; from W. 1,080 ms.

PORT HURON, p. t., St. Clair co., Mich., 59 ms. N. E. of Detroit; from W. 583 ms. Watered by Black and St. Clair rivers. Pop. 2,302.

PORT JACKSON, p. v., Florida township, Montgomery co., N. Y., 33 ms. N. w. of Albany; from W. 400 ms. Watered by Mohawk river and Erie canal.

PORT JEFFERSON, p. v., Brookhaven township, Suffolk co., Long Island, N. Y., 202 ms. s. E. of Albany; from W. 282 ms. Watered by Drowned Meadow harbor.

PORT JERVIS, p. v., Deerpark township, Orange co., N. Y., 117 ms. s. w. of Albany; from W. 264 ms. Watered by Delaware river and Delaware and Hudson canal.

PORT KENNEDY, p. o., Montgomery co., Pa.

PORT KENT, p. v., Chesterfield township, Essex co., N. Y., 151 ms. N. of Albany; from W. 526 ms. Watered by Lake Champlain.

PORTLAND, city, seat of justice of Cumberland co., Me., situated on a peninsula, at the southwest extremity of Casco bay, facing the Atlantic, from which it presents a beautiful view. It is 50 miles southwest of Augusta, 110 northeast of Boston, and 545 miles from Washington. The harbor is one of the best in the United States, being capacious and protected by the islands at its entrance, from the severity of the northeast storms, which prevail on this coast. A lighthouse, 72 feet high, built in 1790, still in good preservation, stands on Portland Head. On an eminence, in the northeast part of the city, is an observatory, 70 feet high, which affords a fine view of the neighboring harbor and islands, and the surrounding country, to the White mountains in New Hampshire. Railroads extend from this city to Vermont, via the valley of the Androscoggin. Augusta, Portsmouth, Boston, &c., and steamboats and packets ply to Boston and other ports, during the season of navigation. Cumberland and Oxford canal communicates with Sebago and Long ponds in the interior of the county. Portland has an extensive inland and coasting-trade, and exports large quantities of lumber, ice, and provisions, to the West Indies and elsewhere. The city is regularly laid out with wide streets, some of which are lined with beautiful shade trees and handsome dwellings. The hospitality and intelligence of the citizens, and the sea-breezes by which the city is fanned, render it a pleasant resort in the warm season. The population in 1790, was 2,240; in 1800, 3,677; in 1810, 7,169; in 1820, 8,581; in 1830, 12,601; in 1840, 15,218; in 1850, 20,815.

PORTLAND, p. t., Middlesex co., Ct., 15 ms. s. of Hartford; from W. 327 ms. Watered by Connecticut river. Pop. 2,836.

PORTLAND, p. v., Dallas co., Ala.; from W. 869 ms. Watered by Alabama river.

PORTLAND, t., Erie co., O. Watered by Sandusky bay.

PORTLAND, t., Ionia co., Mich., 123 ms. N. w. of Detroit; from W. 617 ms. Pop. 763.

PORTLAND, p. v., Jefferson co., Ky., 52 ms. w. of Frankfort; from W. 598 ms. Watered by Ohio river.

PORTLAND, p. v., Fountain co., Ind., 74 ms. N. w. of Indianapolis; from W. 645 ms. Watered by Wabash river.

PORTLAND, p. v., Whitesides co., Ill., 177 ms. N. of Springfield; from W. 869 ms.

PORTLAND, p. v., Van Buren co., Iowa.

PORTLAND, p. v., Callaway co., Mo., 31 ms. N. E. of Jefferson city; from W. 915 ms.

PORTLAND, p. o., Washington co., Oregon.

PORTLAND, p. t., Chautauque co., N. Y., 332 ms. w. of Albany; from W. 352 ms. Watered by Lake Erie. Pop. 1,905.

PORTLAND MILLS, p. o., Putnam co., Ind., 51 ms. w. of Indianapolis; from W. 623 ms.

PORTLANDVILLE, p. o., Otsego co., N. Y.

PORT LA VACA, p. o., Calhoun co., Tex.

PORT LEYDEN, p. o., Lewis co., N. Y.

PORT LOUISA, p. o., Louisa co., Iowa.

PORT MERCER, p. o., Mercer co., N. J.

PORT ONTARIO, p. v., Kirkland township, Oswego co., N. Y., 170 ms. N. w. of Albany; from W. 392 ms. Watered by Salmon river at its entrance into Lake Ontario.

PORT PENN, p. v., New Castle co., Del., 39 ms. N. of Dover; from W. 134 ms. Watered by Delaware river.

PORT PERRY, p. o., Alleghany co., Pa.

PORT PERRY, p. o., Perry co., Mo.

PORT PROVIDENCE, p. o., Montgomery co., Pa.

PORT REPUBLIC, p. v., Atlantic co., N. J., 81 ms. s. of Trenton; from W. 191 ms.

PORT REPUBLIC, p. v., Calvert co., Md., 51 ms. s. of Annapolis; from W. 81 ms.

PORT REPUBLIC, p. v., Rockingham co., Va., 121 ms. N. w. of Richmond; from W. 140 ms.

PORT RICHMOND, p. o., Philadelphia co., Pa.

PORT RICHMOND, p. v., Richmond co., Staten Island, N. Y., 155 ms. s. of Albany; from W. 219 ms. Watered by Kill Van Kull.

PORT ROYAL, p. v., Juniata co., Pa., 46 ms. w. of Harrisburgh; from W. 134 ms.

PORT ROYAL, p. v., Henry co., Ky.

PORT ROYAL, p. v., Montgomery co., Tenn., 43 ms. N. w. of Nashville; from W. 725 ms.

PORT ROYAL, p. v., Caroline co., Va., 84 ms. N. of Richmond; from W. 78 ms. Pop. 470.

PORTSMOUTH, city, seat of justice, together with Exeter, of Rockingham co., N. H., occupies a peninsula on the south side of Piscataqua river, three miles from the Atlantic. It has one of the finest harbors in the world, being completely land-locked, defended by several forts, and having from 45 to 53 feet of water at low-tide. The town is built on ground gradually sloping toward the river, presenting a beautiful aspect from the ocean. It is well built. and possesses much wealth, many of the houses being spacious and elegant. Its public buildings are an ornament to the city, consisting of the court-house, churches, banking houses, markets, and Athenæum. A United States navy-yard, is situated on Continental, or Navy island, on the east side of the river, opposite the town. Ship-building and cotton-manufactures employ a large amount of capital. The Eastern railroad connects the place with Boston and Portland. Another railroad extends to Concord. The population in 1810, was 6,934; in 1820, 7,327; in 1830, 8,082; in 1840, 7,887; in 1850, 9,738.

PORTSMOUTH, c. h., p. v., seat of justice, together with Norfolk, of Norfolk co., Va., 105 ms. s. E. of Richmond; from W. 213 ms. Watered by Elizabeth river.

PORTSMOUTH, c. h., p. v., seat of justice of Scioto co., O., 90 ms. s. of Columbus; from W. 424 ms. Watered by Scioto river at its confluence with the Ohio, and situated at the terminus of the Ohio canal. Pop. 4,001.

PORTSMOUTH, p. v., Carteret co., N. C.

PORTSMOUTH, p. v., Newport co., R. I., 24 ms. s. E. of Providence; from W. 417 ms. Watered by Narragan-set bay. Pop. 1,833.

PORTSMOUTH, p. o., Dauphin co., Pa.

PORT TOBACCO, c. h., p. v., seat of justice of Charles co., Md., 72 ms. s. w. of Annapolis; from W. 32 ms. Watered by a cove of Potomac river.

PORT UNION, p. o., Butler co., O.

PORTVILLE, p. t., Cattaraugus co., N. Y., 296 ms. s. w. of Albany; from W. — ms. Watered by Alleghany river. Pop. 746.

PORT WASHINGTON, p. v., Salem township, Tuscarawas co., O., 99 ms. N. E. of Columbus; from W. 318 ms. Situated on Ohio canal and Tuscarawas river.

PORT WILLIAM, p. o., Franklin co., Mo.

PORT WILLIAM, p. o., Clinton co., O.

POSEY COUNTY, situated at the southwest corner of Indiana, with Ohio river on the south, and the Wabash on the west. Area, 450 square miles. Seat of justice, Mount Vernon. Pop. in 1820, 4,061; in 1830, 6,546; in 1840, 9,683; in 1850, 12,550.

POSEY, t., Clay co., Ind. Pop. 1,220.

POSEY, t., Harrison co., Ind.

POSEY, t., Fayette co., Ind. Pop. 1,184.

POSEY, t., Rush co., Ind. Pop. 870.

POSEY, t., Washington co., Ind. Pop. 1,877.

POSEY, p. t., Switzerland co., Ind. Pop. 2,395.

POSEY, p. o., Madison co., Ky.

POSEYVILLE, p. o., Posey co., Ind.

POST CREEK, p. o., Chemung co., N. Y.

POST MILLS VILLAGE, p. v., Orange co., Vt., 38 ms. s. of Montpelier; from W. 503 ms.

POST OAK, p. o., Yallabusha co., Miss.

POST OAK, p. o., Johnson co., Mo.

POST OAK, p. o., Iredell co., N. C.

POST OAK SPRINGS, p. o., Roane co., Tenn., 136 ms. E. of Nashville; from W. 545 ms.

POSTVILLE, p. v., Russia township, Herkimer co., N. Y., 98 ms. N. w. of Albany; from W. 413 ms.

POSTVILLE, p. v., seat of justice of Logan co., Ill., 39 ms. N. E. of Springfield; from W. — ms. Watered by Salt creek.

POSTVILLE, p. o., Allamakee co., Iowa.

POTATO CREEK, p. o., Ashe co., N. C.

POTATO HILL, p. o., Benton co., Iowa.

POTECASI, p. o., Northampton co., N. C., 155 ms. N. E. of Raleigh; from W. 224 ms.

POTOSI, c. h., p. v., seat of justice of Washington co., Mo., 111 ms. S. E. of Jefferson city; from W. 879 ms.

POTOSI, p. v., Grant co., Wis.

POTSDAM, p. t., St. Lawrence co., N. Y., 212 ms. N. w. of Albany; from W. 496 ms. Watered by Racket and Grass rivers. Pop. 5,349.

POTTAWATAMIE COUNTY, situated on the west boundary of Iowa, with Missouri river on the west. Area, —— square miles. Seat of justice, ——. Pop. in 1850, 7,828.

POTTER COUNTY, situated on the north boundary of Pennsylvania. Area, 1,110 square miles. Face of the country, an elevated table-land. Seat of justice, Coudersport. Pop. in 1810, 1,584; in 1820, 4,836; in 1830, 1,265; in 1840, 3,371; in 1850, 6,048.

POTTER, p. t., Yates co., N. Y., 201 ms. w. of Albany; from W. 326 ms. Watered by Flint creek. Pop. 2,394.

POTTER, t., Centre co., Pa., 71 ms. N. w. of Harrisburgh; from W. 170 ms. Pop. 2,216.

POTTER'S CREEK, p. o., Ocean co., N. J.

POTTER'S HILL, p. o., Washington co., R. I.

POTTER'S HILL, p. o., Rensselaer co., N. Y.

POTTER'S HOLLOW, p. v., Rensselaerville township, Albany co., N. Y.

POTTER'S MILLS, p. v., Potter township, Centre co., Pa., 73 ms. N. w. of Harrisburgh; from W. 165 ms.

POTTERSVILLE, p. o., Chester township, Warren co., N. Y., 87 ms. N. of Albany; from W. 462 ms.

POTTERSVILLE, p. v., Hunterdon co., N. J., 48 ms. N. w. of Trenton; from W. 222 ms.

POTTERSVILLE, p. o., Mahoning co., O., 143 ms. N. E. of Columbus; from W. 299 ms.

POTTERSVILLE, p. o., Cheshire co., N. H.

POTTIESVILLE, p. v., Louisa co., Va., 47 ms. N. w. of Richmond; from W. 89 ms.

POTT'S CREEK, p. o., Alleghany co., Va.

POTT'S GROVE, p. t., Montgomery co., Pa. Watered by Schuylkill river and Manatawny creek. Pop. 1,689.

POTT'S GROVE, p. o., Northumberland co., Pa.

POTT'S MILLS, p. o., Jessamine co., Ky.

POTTSTOWN, p. b., Pott's Grove township, Montgomery co., Pa., 71 ms. E. of Harrisburgh; from W. 164 ms. Watered by Schuylkill river and Manatawny creek. Pop. 1,664.

POTTSVILLE, p. b., Norwegian township, Schuylkill co., Pa., 62 ms. E. of Harrisburgh; from W. 172 ms. Situated at the termination of the Schuylkill canal. Pop. 7,515.

POTTSVILLE, p. o., Washington co., Iowa.

POUCH CREEK, p. o., Campbell co., Tenn.

POUGHKEEPSIE, c. h., p. t., seat of justice of Dutchess co., N. Y., situated on the Hudson, at the head of ship-navigation. It lies on the east side of the river, 75 ms. N. of New York, 71 ms. s. of Albany; from W. 301 ms. Wappinger's creek bounds the town on the east, the Hudson on the west. From the latter river the village is concealed, being delightfully seated on an elevated plain, one mile eastward. At the landing there are a number of wharves, where steamboats and other vessels stop on their way between Albany and New York. Ascending by the road the steep bank, the village bursts upon the sight, presenting an interesting spectacle of industry and prosperity. It has the appearance of a city, with its compact buildings, regular streets, stores, churches, banks, and manufactories. Upon a neighboring elevation stands the Poughkeepsie collegiate school, a fine building in Grecian architecture; besides this there are an academy and other schools. Formerly whaling-vessels were owned in Poughkeepsie, and returned hither from their voyages. An expensive aqueduct supplies the village with water from neighboring springs. The Hudson River railroad passes through the place. The population, in 1810, was 4,670; in 1820, 5,726; in 1830, 7,222; in 1840, 10,006; in 1850, 13,944.

POUGHKEEPSIE, p. v., Allen co., Ind., 126 ms. N. E. of Indianapolis; from W. 534 ms.

POUGHQUAG, p. o., Beekman township, Dutchess co., N. Y.

POUND, p. o., Russell co., Va.

POULTNEY p. t., Rutland co., 60 ms. s. w. of Montpelier; from W. 440 ms. Watered by Poultney river. Pop. 2,329.

POULTNEY, p. t., Steuben co., N. Y. Pop. 1,815.

POUNDRIDGE, p. t., Westchester co., N. Y., 121 ms. s. of Albany; from W. 274 ms. Watered by Mill river. Pop. 3,837.

POVERTY HILL, p. o., Edgefield district, S. C., 87 ms. w. of Columbia; from W. 581 ms.

POWDER SPRING GAP, p. o., Grainger co., Tenn.

POWDER SPRINGS, p. o., Cobb co., Ga., 112 ms. N. w. of Milledgeville; from W. 690 ms.

POWELL'S MOUNTAIN, p. o., Lee co., Va., 378 ms. w. of Richmond; from W. 446 ms.

POWELL'S POINT, p. o., Currituck co., N. C., 257 ms. N. E. of Raleigh; from W. 305 ms.

POWELL'S TAVERN, Goochland co., Va., 14 ms. N. w. of Richmond; from W. 131 ms.

POWELLTON, p. o., Brunswick co., Va., 91 ms. s. w. of Richmond; from W. 207 ms.

POWELLTON, p. o., Harrison co., Tex.

POWELTON, p. v., Richmond co., N. C., 118 ms. s. w. of Raleigh; from W. 392 ms.

POWELTON, p. v., Hancock co., Ga., 36 ms. N. E. of Milledgeville; from W. 626 ms. Watered by Great Ogeechee river.

POWERS' MILL, p. o., Waukesha co., Wis.

POWERSVILLE, p. v., Bracken co., Ky., 61 ms. N. E. of Frankfort; from W. 489 ms.

POWESHIEK COUNTY, situated in the central part of Iowa. Area, —— square miles. Seat of justice, Montezuma. Pop. in 1850, 615.

POWHATAN COUNTY, situated toward the east part of Virginia, with James river on the north, and the Appomattox on the south. Area, 300 square miles. Seat of justice, Scottsville. Pop. in 1810, 8,073; in 1820, 8,292; in 1830, 8,517; in 1840, 7,924; in 1850, 8,778.

POWHATAN, p. o., Lawrence co., Ark.

POWHATAN, c. h., p. v., seat of justice of Powhatan co., Va.

POWHATAN POINT, p. o., Mead township, Belmont co., O., 138 ms. E. of Columbus; from W. 275 ms.

POWL'S VALLEY, p. o., Dauphin co., Pa.

POWNAL, p. t., Cumberland co., Me., 42 ms. s. w. of Augusta; from W. 563 ms.

POWNAL, p. t., Bennington co., Vt., 126 ms. s. of Montpelier; from W. 398 ms. Watered by Hoosick river. Pop. 1,742.

POYNETT, p. o., Columbia co., Wis.

POY SIPPI, p. o., Marquette co., Wis.

PRAIRIE COUNTY, situated in the central part of Arkansas. Area, —— square miles. Seat of justice, Brownsville. Pop. in 1850, 2,097.

PRAIRIE, t., Franklin co., O. Watered by Darby creek. Pop. 1,043.

PRAIRIE, t., Arkansas co., Ark.

PRAIRIE, t., Holmes co., O. Pop. 1,451.

PRAIRIE, t., Chariton co., Mo. Pop. 936.

PRAIRIE, p. t., Henry co., Ind. Pop. 1,340.

PRAIRIE, t., Howard co., Ill.

PRAIRIE, t., Carroll co., Ark.

PRAIRIE, t., Washington co., Ark. Pop. 1,830.

PRAIRIE, t., Franklin co., Ark. Pop, 497.

PRAIRIE, p. t., Madison co., Ark. Pop. 784.

PRAIRIE, t., Montgomery co., Mo.

PRAIRIE, p. t., Lewis co., Mo.

PRAIRIE BIRD, p. o., Shelby co., Ill.

PRAIRIE BLUFF, p. o., Wilcox co., Ala.; from W. 877 ms.

PRAIRIE CREEK, p. o., Vigo co., Ind., 88 ms. s. w. of Indianapolis; from W. 659 ms.

PRAIRIE CREEK, p. o., Logan co., Ill.

PRAIRIE CREEK, p. o., Yell co., Ark.

PRAIRIE DE LONG, p. o., St. Clair co., Ill., 116 ms. s. of Springfield; from W. 826 ms. Situated on Prairie de Long creek.

PRAIRIE DU CHIEN, c. h., p. v., seat of justice of Crawford co., Wis., 125 ms. w. of Madison; from W. 957 ms. Watered by Mississippi river.

PRAIRIE DU ROCHE, (Prairie du Rocher), p. v., Randolph co., Ill., 137 ms. s. of Springfield; from W. 848 ms. Watered by Mississippi river.

PRAIRIE DU SAUK, p. v., c. h., seat of justice of Sauk co., Wis. Watered by Wisconsin river.

PRAIRIE LEA, p. o., Caldwell co., Tex.

PRAIRIE MER ROUGE, p. o., Morehouse parish, La.

PRAIRIE MOUNT, p. o., Chickasaw co., Miss.

PRAIRIE PLAINS, p. o., Grimes co., Tex.

PRAIRIE POINT, p. o., Noxubee co., Miss., 137 ms. N. E. of Jackson; from W. 873 ms.

PRAIRIE RIDGE, p. o., White co., Ind.

PRAIRIE RIVER, p. o., Branch co., Mich., 122 ms. s. w. of Detroit; from W. 575 ms.

PRAIRIE RONDE, p. t., Kalamazoo co., Mich. Pop. 690.

PRAIRIETON, p. v., Prairie township, Vigo co., Ind., 80 ms. s. w. of Indianapolis; from W. 651 ms. Watered by Prairie creek.

PRAIRIETON, v., Lawrence co., Ill., 147 ms. s. E. of Springfield; from W. 709 ms. Pop. 875.

PRAIRIEVILLE, t., Milwaukie co., Wis.

PRAIRIEVILLE, p. v., Clinton co., Ind., 52 ms. N. w. of Indianapolis; from W. 610 ms.

PRAIRIEVILLE, p. o., Pike co., Mo.

PRAIRIEVILLE, p. o., Barry co., Mich.

PRALLSVILLE, p. v., Amwell township, Hunterdon co., N. J., 20 ms. N. w. of Trenton; from W. 177 ms. Watered by Delaware river and Wickhecheeoke creek.

PRATT, p. o., Shelby co., O., 74 ms. N. w. of Columbus; from W. 468 ms.

PRATTSBURGH, p. t., Steuben co., N. Y., 209 ms. w. of Albany; from W. 315 ms. Watered by Conhocton river. Pop. 2,786.

PRATTSBURGH, p. v., Orange co., N. C., 34 ms. N. w. of Raleigh; from W. 294 ms.

PRATTSBURGH, p. v., Talbot co., Ga., 80 ms. s. w. of Milledgeville; from W. 736 ms.

PRATTSBURGH, p. o., Ripley co., Ind.

PRATT'S HOLLOW, p. o., Eaton township, Madison co., N. Y., 106 ms. w. of Albany; from W. 363 ms.

PRATTSVILLE, p. t., Greene co., N. Y., 54 ms. s. w. of Albany; from W. 360 ms. Watered by Schoharie creek. Pop. 1,989.

PRATTSVILLE, p. o., Vinton co., O.

PRATTSVILLE, p. o., Autauga co., Ala.

PREBLE COUNTY, situated on the west boundary of Ohio. Area, 432 square miles. Face of the country, even, or gently undulating; soil, productive. Seat of justice, Eaton. Pop. in 1810, 3,304; in 1820, 10,237; in 1830, 16,291; in 1840, 19,482; in 1850, 21,736.

PREBLE, p. t., Cortland co., N. Y., 131 ms. w. of Albany; from W. 324 ms. Watered by Toughnioga river. Pop. 1,312.

PREBLE, t., Pike co., O. Pop. 914.

PREBLE, t., Adams co., Ind. Pop. 547.

PRECINCT, p. o., Boone co., Ill.

PRE-EMPTION, p. o., Mercer co., Ill.

PRENTISS VALE, p. o., McKean co., Pa.

PRESCOTT, p. t., Hampshire co., Mass., 77 ms. w. of Boston; from W. 395 ms. Watered by tributaries of Swift river.

PRESCOTT, t., Washington co., Me.

PRESIDENT FURNACE, p. o., Venango co., Pa.

PRESQUE ISLE, p. o., Aroostook co., Me.

PRESTON COUNTY, situated on the north boundary of Virginia, and traversed by Cheat river. Area, 501 square miles. Face of the country, hilly and mountainous. Seat of justice, Kingwood. Pop. in 1820, 3,498; in 1830, 5,099; in 1840, 8,866; in 1850, 11,708.

PRESTON, p. t., New London co., Ct., 45 ms. s. E. of Hartford; from W. 363 ms. Watered by Thames and Quinnebaug rivers. Pop. 1,841.

PRESTON, p. t., Chenango co., N. Y., 118 ms. w. of Albany; from W. 342 ms. Watered by tributaries of Chenango river. Pop. 1,082.

PRESTON, p. t., Wayne co., Pa., 184 ms. N. E. of Harrisburgh; from W. 280 ms. Pop. 875.

PRESTON, p. o., Crosby township, Hamilton co., O., 122 ms. s. w. of Columbus; from W. 510 ms.

PRESTON, p. o., Yallabusha co., Miss., 129 ms. N. of Jackson; from W. 974 ms.

PRESTON, p. o., Wharton co., Tex.

PRESTONBURGH, c. h., p. v., seat of justice of Floyd co., Ky., 120 ms. s. E. of Frankfort; from W. 461 ms. Watered by west fork of Sandy river.

PRESTON HOLLOW, p. v., Rensselaerville township, Albany co., N. Y., 38 ms. w. of Albany; from W. 365 ms.

PRESTONVILLE, p. v., Carroll co., Ky.

PREWETT'S KNOB, p. o., Barrien co., Ky., 119 ms. s. w. of Frankfort; from W. 642 ms.

PRICE, p. o., Huntington co., Ind.

PRICEBURGH, p. o., Monroe co., Pa.

PRICETOWN, p. v., Ruscomb Manor township, Berks co., 62 ms. E. of Harrisburgh; from W. 155 ms.

PRICETOWN, p. o., Highland co., O.

PRICEVILLE, p. v., Price township, Wayne co., Pa., 199 ms. N. E. of Harrisburgh; from W. 295 ms.

PRILLAMAN'S, p. o., Franklin co., Va., 203 ms. s. w. of Richmond; from W. 278 ms.

PRIMEROSE, p. o., Lee co., Iowa.

PRIMEROSE, p. o., Dane co., Wis.

PRINCE EDWARD COUNTY, situated in the southerly part of Virginia. Area, 375 square miles. Seat of justice, Prince Edward c. h. Pop. in 1810, 12,409; in 1820, 12,557; in 1830, 14,107; in 1840, 14,069; in 1850, 11,857.

PRINCE EDWARD, c. h., p. v., seat of justice of Prince Edward co., Va., 77 ms. s. w. of Richmond; from W. 167 ms.

PRINCE EDWARD, p. o., Gilmer co., Ga., 165 ms. N. w. of Milledgeville; from W. 645 ms.

PRINCE FREDERICKTOWN, c. h., p. v., seat of justice of Calvert co., Md., 46 ms. s. of Annapolis; from W. 76 ms. Watered by Parker's creek.

PRINCE GEORGE COUNTY, situated in the southeasterly part of Virginia, with James river on the north. Area, 305 square miles. Face of the country, uneven; soil, tolerably productive. Seat of justice, Prince George, c. h. Pop. in 1810, 8,050; in 1820, 8,030; in 1830, 8,367; in 1840, 7,175; in 1850, 7,596.

PRINCE GEORGE'S COUNTY, situated on the southwesterly boundary of Maryland, with Potomac river on the southwest, and the Patuxent on the east. Area, 575 square miles. Face of the country, uneven; soil of middling quality. Seat of justice, Upper Marlborough. Pop. in 1810, 20,569; in 1820, 20,216; in 1830, 20, 473; in 1840, 19,539; in 1850, 21,550.

PRINCE GEORGE, c. h., p. v., seat of justice of Prince George co., V., 28 ms. s. E. of Richmond; from W. 147 ms.

PRINCESS ANN COUNTY, situated at the southeast corner of Virginia, with the Atlantic on the east. Area, 374 square miles. Seat of justice, Princess Ann, c. h. Pop. in 1810, 4,699; in 1820, 8,767; in 1830, 9,102; in 1840, 7,285; in 1850, 7,669.

PRINCESS ANN, c. h., p. v., seat of justice of Somerset co., Md., 110 ms. s. E. of Annapolis; from W. 150 ms. Watered by Manokin river.

PRINCESS ANN, c. h., p. v., seat of justice of Princess Ann co., Va., 132 ms. s. E. of Richmond; from W. 256 ms.

PRINCETON, p. v., Washington co., Me., 219 ms. N. E. of Augusta; from W. 805 ms. Watered by Schoodic lake. Pop. 280.

PRINCETON, p. t., Worcester co., Mass., 47 ms. w. of Boston; from W. 417 ms. Watered by tributaries of Nashau and Wave rivers. Pop. 1,318.

PRINCETON, p. t., Schenectady co., N. Y., 19 ms. N. w. of Albany; from W. 390 ms. Watered by Norman's kill. Pop. 1,031.

PRINCETON, p. v., Mercer co., N. J., 11 ms. N. E. of Trenton; from W. 177 ms. Situated on the Delaware and Raritan canal. Seat of the college of New Jersey. Pop. in 1840, 3,055; in 1850, 3,021.

PRINCETON, c. h., p. v., seat of justice of Washington co., Miss., 119 ms. w. of Jackson; from W. 1,154 ms. Watered by Mississippi river.

PRINCETON, c. h., p. v., seat of justice of Caldwell co., Ky., 225 ms. s. w. of Frankfort; from W. 757 ms.

PRINCETON, c. h., p. v., Liberty township, Butler co.; O., 102 ms. s. w. of Columbus; from W. 486 ms.

PRINCETON, p. v., seat of justice of Bureau co., Ill., 135 ms. N. of Springfield; from W. 808 ms.

PRINCETON, p. v., Scott co., Iowa. Watered by Mississippi river.

PRINCETON, c. h., p. v., seat of justice of Gibson co., Ind., 142 ms. s. w. of Indianapolis; from W. 712 ms. Pop. 806.

PRINCETON, c. h., p. t., seat of justice of Dallas co., Ark. Pop. 1,163.

PRINCETON, p. o., Jackson co., Ala.

PRINCETON, p. o., Mercer co., Mo.

PRINCETON, p. o., Marquette co., Wis.

PRINCETON, p. o., Mercer co., Va.

PRINCEVILLE, p. v., Peoria co., Ill., 92 ms. N. of Springfield; from W. 806 ms.

PRINCE WILLIAM COUNTY, situated on the easterly boundary of Virginia, with Potomac river on the east. Area, 370 square miles. Face of the country, uneven; soil, sandy. Seat of justice, Brentsville. Pop. in 1810, 11,311; in 1820, 9,419; in 1830, 9,330; in 1840, 8,144; in 1850, 8,129.

PRINCE WILLIAM, p. o., Carroll co., Ind., 56 ms. N. w. of Indianapolis; from W. 614 ms.

PRINCIPIO FURNACE, p. o., Cecil co., Md.

PRIVATEER, p. o., Sumter co., S. C.

PROCTOR, p. o., Owsley co., Ky.

PROCTOR. p. o., Allegan co., Mich.

PROCTOR. p. o., Wetzel co., Va.

PROCTOR'S CREEK, p. o., Chesterfield Va.

PROCTORSVILLE, p. v., Crawford co., Ind., 109 ms. S. of Indianapolis ; from W. 631 ms. Watered by Great Blue river.

PROCTORSVILLE, p. o., Windsor co., Vt., 73 ms. E. of Montpelier ; from W. 468 ms.

PROMPTON, p. o., Wayne co., Pa., 169 ms. N. E. of Harrisburgh ; from W. 260 ms.

PROPHETSTOWN, p. o., Whitesides co., Ill.

PROSPECT. p. t., Waldo co., Me., 53 ms. E. of Augusta ; from W. 649 ms. Watered by Penobscot river and Penobscot bay. Pop. 2,467.

PROSPECT. p. t., New Haven co., Ct., 54 ms. s. of Hartford ; from W. 320 ms. Pop. 666.

PROSPECT, p. o., Remsen township, Oneida co., N. Y., 103 ms., N. w. of Albany ; from W. 408 ms.

PROSPECT, p. v., Muddy Creek township, Butler co., Pa., 212 ms. N. w. of Harrisburgh ; from W. 254 ms. Pop. 254.

PROSPECT, p. o., Prince Edward co., Va., 80 ms. s. w. of Richmond ; from W. 170 ms.

PROSPECT, p. o., Marion co., O.

PROSPECT. p. o., Giles co., Tenn., 97 ms. s. of Nashville ; from W. 746 ms.

PROSPECT, p. o., Burleson co., Tex.

PROSPECT FERRY, p. o., Waldo co., Me.

PROSPECT GROVE, p. o., Scotland co., Mo.

PROSPECT HALL, p. o., Bladen co. N. C., 82 ms. s. of Raleigh ; from W. 370 ms.

PROSPECT HARBOR, p. o., Prospect township, Hancock co., Me., 119 ms. E. of Augusta ; from W. 701 ms.

PROSPECT HILL, p. o., Pittstown township, Rensselaer co., N. Y., 24 ms. N. E. of Albany ; from W. 394 ms.

PROSPECT HILL, p. o., Fairfax co., Va., 131 ms. N. of Richmond ; from W. 12 ms.

PROSPECT HILL, p. o., Caswell co., N. C., 60 ms. N. w. of Raleigh ; from W. 372 ms.

PROSPECT HILL, p. o., Lincoln co., Tenn.

PROSPECT HILL, p. o., Ray co., Mo.

PROSPECT HILL, p. o., Waukesha co., Wis.

PROSPECT LAKE, p. o., Van Buren co., Mich.

PROSPECT MILLS, p. o., Lycoming co., Pa.

PROSPERITY, p. o., Moore co., N. C., 68 ms. s. w. of Raleigh ; from W. 356 ms.

PROSPERITY, p. o., Newberry district. S. C.

PROSPERITY, p. o., Washington co., Pa.

PROSPERITY, p. o., Van Buren co., Mich.

PROVIDENCE COUNTY, situated in the north part of Rhode Island. Area, 380 square miles. Face of the country, hilly ; soil, of middling quality. Seat of justice, Providence. Pop. in 1810, 30,769 ; in 1820, 35,726 ; in 1830, 47,014 ; in 1840, 50,073 ; in 1850, 87,986.

PROVIDENCE, city, the seat of justice of Providence co., and capital, with Newport, of the state of Rhode Island ; the second city in population of New England. is situated at the head of Narraganset bay, on the Providence river, 42 miles southwest of Boston, and 173 miles northeast of New York. The older part of the city lies on the east side of the river, and though many of the streets partake of that irregularity, which seems peculiar to olden times, they contain many splendid stores, warehouses, dwellings, and public buildings. Ascending by an abrupt acclivity from the river, the streets and houses become more regular, many of the residences being of a superior style of elegance and structure, and affording delightful views of the harbor and the surrounding country. Crowning the elevation, are the buildings of Brown university, a flourishing institution. Crossing the river by one of the bridges, the west part of the city is laid out with more regularity upon ground less uneven. Here is the " Arcade," the largest and most important edifice in the city, built of granite, and adorned with a Grecian-Doric portico and columns. It is 225 feet long, 80 feet deep, and 72 feet high.

The name of the city, which it received from the Rev. Roger Williams, its founder, may serve to indicate its prosperity. Its location upon a spacious and convenient harbor, sufficient for a great number of the largest vessels, the manufacturing facilities of the surrounding districts, their facility of access to the city, and the enterprising spirit which has improved and adapted these advantages, are the sources of its increasing wealth and population. The Blackstone canal, beginning at Worcester, and winding through the productive regions and manufacturing towns of Massachusetts, brings large stores to its market. On Pawtucket river, and other streams of Providence county, are extensive factories of cotton, wool, machinery, calico printing, and dyeing ; and within the city are also various similar establishments. These are chiefly kept in operation by capitalists of Providence, and employ more than $3,000,000 of capital. This city communicates by railroad with Boston, Worcester, and Stonington, and, in a great measure, has dispensed with the steamboat lines which traversed Long Island sound and the Atlantic to New York, Boston, and other places.

The population in 1810, was 10,071. in 1820, 11,767 ; in 1830, 16,833 ; in 1840, 23,171 ; in 1850, 44,512.

PROVIDENCE, p. t., Saratoga co., N. Y., 41 ms. N. w. of Albany ; from W. 409 ms. Watered by Sacandaga river. Pop. 1,458.

PROVIDENCE. p. t., Luzerne co., Pa., 146 ms. N. E. of Harrisburgh ; from W. 250 ms. Watered by Lackawannock creek and Roaring brook. Pop. 4,467.

PROVIDENCE, p. t., Bedford co., Pa.

PROVIDENCE, p. v., Fairfax co., Va., 120 ms. N. of Richmond ; from W. 207 ms.

PROVIDENCE, p. v., Mechlenburgh co., N. C., 173 ms. s. w. of Raleigh ; from W. 412 ms.

PROVIDENCE, p. v., Pickens co., Ala. ; from W. 873 ms.

PROVIDENCE, p. v., Hopkins co., Ky., 214 ms. s. w. of Frankfort ; from W. 655 ms.

PROVIDENCE, p. v., Bureau co., Ill., 114 ms. N. of Springfield ; from W. 819 ms.

PROVIDENCE, p. v., Lucas co., O., 140 ms. N. w. of Columbus ; from W. 471 ms. Pop. 467.

PROVIDENCE, p. o., Sumter district, S. C.

PROVIDENCE, p. o., Sumter co., Ga.

PROVIDENCE, p. o., Carroll co., Miss.

PROVIDENCE HILL, p. o., Tyler co., Tex.

PROVINCETOWN, p. b., Barnstable co., Mass., 123 ms. s. E. of Boston ; from 524 ms. Watered by Cape Cod bay. Pop. 3,157.

PROVISO, p. o., Cook co., Ill.

PRUNE HILL, p. o., Montgomery co., Ala.

PRUNTYS, p. o., Patrick co., Va.

PRUNTYTOWN, c. h., p. v., seat of justice of Taylor co., Va., 267 ms. N. w. of Richmond ; from W. 205 ms. Watered by Tygart's Valley river.

PRYOR'S VALE, p. o., Amherst co., Va.

PUBLIC SQUARE, p. o., Greene co., Ga., 58 ms. N. of Milledgeville ; from W. 590 ms.

PUCKETAS, p. o., Westmoreland co., Pa.

PUEBLA, p. o., Westmoreland co., Pa.

PUEBLA. p. o., Brown co., O.

PUGH'S HILL, p. o., Franklin co., N. C.

PUGHTOWN, p. v., Coventry township, Chester co., Pa., 68 ms. s. E. of Harrisburgh ; from W. 146 ms. Watered by French creek.

PUGSLEY'S DEPOT, p. o., Tompkins co., N. Y.

PULASKI COUNTY, situated in the southwesterly part of Virginia, and traversed by New river. Area, 350 square miles. Seat of justice, Newbern. Pop. in 1840, 3,739 : in 1850, 5,118.

PULASKI COUNTY, situated toward the south part of Georgia, and traversed by Ocmulgee river. Area, 680 square miles. Seat of justice, Hawkinsville. Pop. in 1810, 2,098 ; in 1820, 5,223 ; in 1830, 4,899 ; in 1840, 5,389 ; in 1850, 6,627.

PULASKI COUNTY, situated in the northwesterly part of Indiana, and traversed by Tippecanoe river. Area, 342 square miles. Seat of justice, Winamac. Pop. in 1840, 561 ; in 1850, 2,595.

PULASKI COUNTY, situated in the southeast part of Kentucky, and traversed by Cumberland river. Area, 800 square miles. Seat of justice, Somerset. Pop. in 1810, 6,897 ; in 1820, 7,597 ; in 1830, 9,522 ; in 1840, 9,620 ; in 1850, 14,195.

PULASKI COUNTY, situated toward the south part of Missouri. Area, 1,332 square miles. Seat of justice, Waynesville. Pop. in 1840, 6,529 ; in 1850, 3,998.

PULASKI COUNTY, situated in the central part of Arkansas, and traversed by Arkansas river. Area, 2,050 square miles. Seat of justice, Little Rock, which is also the state capital. Pop. in 1830, 2,395 ; in 1840, 5,350 ; in 1850, 5,658.

PULASKI, c. h., v., Richland township, together with Oswego seat of justice of Oswego co., N. Y., 155 ms. N. w. of Albany ; from W. 385 ms. Watered by Salmon river.

PULASKI, p. v., Lawrence co., Pa., 248 ms. N. w. of Harrisburgh ; from W. 289 ms.

PULASKI, c. h., p. v., seat of justice of Giles co., Tenn.,

74 ms. s. of Nashville ; from W. 734 ms. Watered by Richland creek.

PULASKI, p. t., Jackson co., Mich., 89 ms. w. of Detroit ; from W. 561 ms. Watered by south branch of Kalamazoo river. Pop. 760.

PULASKI, p. v., Hancock co., Ill., 85 ms. N. w. of Springfield ; from W. 863 ms.

PULASKI, p. o., Panola co., Tex.

PULASKI, p. o., Scott co., Miss.

PULASKI, p. o., Williams co., O.

PULASKIVILLE, p. v., Morrow co., O., 52 ms. N. E. of Columbus ; from W. 393 ms.

PULTNEY, p. t., Steuben co., N. Y., 213 ms. w. of Albany ; from W. 316 ms. Watered by west branch of Crooked lake. Pop. 1,815.

PULTNEY, t., Belmont co., O.

PULTNEYVILLE, p. v., Williamson township, Wayne co., N. Y., 204 ms. w. of Albany ; from W. 368 ms. Watered by Lake Ontario.

PULVER'S CORNERS, p. o., Pine Plains township, Dutchess co., N. Y., 58 s. of Albany ; from W. 331 ms.

PUMPKIN, p. o., Southampton co., Va.

PUMPKIN PILE, p. o., Paulding co., Ga.

PUMPKINTOWN, p. v., Pickens district, S. C., 135 ms. N. w. of Columbia ; from W. 530 ms.

PUMPKINTOWN, p. o., Randolph co., Ga.

PUMPKIN VINE, p. o., Paulding co., Ga., 127 ms. N. w. of Milledgeville ; from W. 670 ms.

PUNCHEON, p. o., Allen co., Ky.

PUNGO CREEK, p. o., Beaufort co., N. C.

PUNGOTEAGUE, p. v., Accomac co., Va., 181 ms. E. of Richmond ; from W. 209 ms.

PUNXETAWNY, p. v., Young township, Jefferson co., Pa., 183 N. w. of Harrisburgh ; from W. 236 ms. Watered by a tributary of Mahoning creek.

PURCEL'S STORE, p. o., Loudoun co., Va., 163 ms. N. of Richmond ; from W. 44 ms.

PURDY, c. h., p. v., seat of justice of McNairy co., Tenn., 148 ms. s. w. of Nashville ; from W. 821 ms. Watered by a tributary of Hatchy river.

PURDY CREEK, p. o., Hornellsville township, Steuben co., N. Y., 247 ms. w. of Albany ; from W. 315 ms.

PURDY'S STATION, p. o., Westchester co., N. Y.

PURGITSVILLE, p. o., Hampshire co., Va.

PURVIS, p. o., Rockland township, Sullivan co., N. Y., 109 ms. s. w. of Albany ; from W. 314 ms.

PUSEYVILLE, D. o., Lancaster co., Pa.

PUSHMATAHA, p. o., Choctaw co., Ala.

PUSHUTA. t., Allen co., O.

PUTNAM COUNTY, situated on the east boundary

of New York, with Hudson river on the west. Area, 216 square miles. Face of the country, hilly ; soil, productive. Seat of justice. Carmel. Pop. in 1810. 10.293; in 1820, 11,268 ; in 1830, 12,701 ; in 1840, 12,825 ; in 1850, 14,138.

PUTNAM COUNTY, situated in the west part of Virginia, and traversed by Great Kanawha river. Area, —— square miles. Seat of justice, ——. Pop. in 1850. 5,335.

PUTNAM COUNTY, situated in the central part of Georgia, with Oconee river on the east. Area, 340 square miles. Seat of justice, Eatonton. Pop. in 1810, 10,029 ; in 1820, 15,475 ; in 1830, 13,656 ; in 1840, 10,260 ; in 1850, 10,794.

PUTNAM COUNTY, situated on the north boundary of Missouri, with Chariton river on the east. Area, —— square miles. Seat of justice, Putnamville. Pop. in 1850, 1,657.

PUTNAM COUNTY, situated toward the west part of Indiana. Area, 486 square miles. Seat of justice, Green Castle. Pop. in 1830, 8,262 ; in 1840, 16,842 ; in 1850, 20,614.

PUTNAM COUNTY, situated toward the north part of Illinois, and traversed by Illinois river. Area, 325 square miles. Seat of justice, Hennepin. Pop. in 1840, 2,131 ; in 1850, 3,924.

PUTNAM COUNTY, situated in the northwest part of Ohio, and traversed by Auglaize river. Area, 376 square smiles. Face of the country, even ; soil productive where not marshy. Seat of justice, Kalida. Pop. in 1830, 230 ; in 1840, 5,189 ; in 1850, 7,221.

PUTNAM. p. t., Washington co., N. Y., 90 ms. N. of Albany ; from W. 460 ms. Watered by Lake Champlain and Lake George. Pop. 753.

PUTNAM, p. t., Muskingum co., O., 55 ms. E. of Columbus ; from W. 340 ms. Watered by Muskingum river. Pop. 1,363.

PUTNAM, t., Livingston co., Mich. Pop. 977.

PUTNAM VALLEY. p. t., Putnam co., N. Y., 100 ms. s. of Albany ; from W. 275 ms. Watered by Peekskill creek and several lakes. Pop. 1,626.

PUTNAMVILLE, p. v., Putnam co., Ind., 42 ms. w. of Indianapolis ; from W. 613 ms.

PUTNEY, p. t., Windham co., Vt., 111 ms. s. of Montpelier ; from W. 432 ms. Watered by Connecticut river at the falls of Sacket's brooks. Pop. 1,425.

PUTNEYVILLE, p. o., Armetrong co., Pa.

PYLESVILLE, p. o., Harford co., Md.

PYMATUNING. p. t., Mercer co., Pa. Pop. 2,161.

PYRMONT, p. o., Montgomery co., O.

Q.

QUAHAW COUNTY, situated in Missouri. Area, —— square miles. Seat of justice, Crawford Seminary.

QUAKER BOTTOM, p. o., Lawrence co., O., 123 ms. s. of Columbus ; from W. 400 ms.

QUAKER HILL, p. o., Pawling's township, Dutchess co., N. Y., 92 ms. s. of Albany ; from W. 304 ms.

QUAKER SPRINGS, p. o., Saratoga township, Saratoga co., N. Y., 32 ms. N. of Albany ; from W. 402 ms.

QUAKER STREET. p. o., Duanesburgh township, Schenectady co., N. Y.

QUAKERTOWN, p. v., Kingwood township, Hunterdon co., N. J., 31 ms. N. w. of Trenton ; from W. 191 ms.

QUAKERTOWN. p. v., Richland township. Bucks co., Pa., 101 ms. E. of Harrisburgh ; from W. 174 ms.

QUALLATOWN, p. v., Haywood co., N. C., 326 ms. w. of Raleigh ; from W. 556 ms.

QUANTICO, p. v., Somerset co., Md., 93 ms. s. E. of Annapolis ; from W. 133 ms.

QUARRYVILLE, p. o., Lancaster co., Pa.

QUARRYVILLE, p. o., Tolland co., Ct.

QUARTYBURGH. p. o., Mariposa co., Cal.

QUASQUETON, p. o., Buchanan co., Iowa.

QUAY, p. o., Claiborne parish, La., 367 ms. N. w. of New Orleans ; from W. 1,237 ms.

QUEECHY VILLAGE, p. v., Hartford township, Windsor co., Vt., 57 ms. s. of Montpelier ; from W. 487 ms. Situated at the falls of Queechy river.

QUEEN ANNE COUNTY, situated on the east boundary of Maryland, with Chester river and Chesapeake bay on the northwest. Area, 400 square miles. Seat of justice, Centreville. Pop. in 1810, 16,648 ; in

1820, 14,952 ; in 1830, 14,396 ; in 1840, 12,633 ; in 1850, 14,414.

QUEEN ANNE. p. o., Prince George's co., Md.

QUEEN'S COUNTY, situated in the southeast part of New York, on Long Island, with the Atlantic ocean on the south, Long Island sound on the north, and East river on the northwest. Area, 396 square miles. Face of the country, undulating and hilly, and on the north toward the Atlantic, level ; soil, productive. Seat of justice, North Hempstead. Pop. in 1810, 19,336 ; in 1820, 21,519 ; in 1830, 22,276 ; in 1840, 30,324 ; in 1850, 36,853.

QUEENSBOROUGH, p. v., Anderson district, S. C., 113 ms. N. w. of Columbia ; from W. 529 ms.

QUEENSBURY. p. t., Warren co., N. Y., 57 ms. N. of Albany ; from W. 429 ms. Watered by Wood creek and Hudson river.

QUEENSDALE, p. v., Robeson co., N. C., 110 ms. s. w. of Raleigh ; from W. 406 ms.

QUEENSTOWN, p. v., Queen Anne co., Md., 26 ms. E. of Annapolis ; from W. 66 ms. Watered by Chester bay.

QUEENSVILLE, p. o., Jennings co., Ind.

QUEMAHONING, t., Somerset co., Pa.

QUERCUS GROVE, p. o., Switzerland co., Ind., 102 ms. s. E. of Indianapolis ; from W. 538 ms.

QUIET DELL, p. o., Harrison co., Va.

QUILLINSVILLE. p. o., Scott co., Va., 351 ms. w. of Richmond ; from W. 419 ms.

QUINCY, p. t., Norfolk co., Mass., 9 ms. s. of Boston ; from W. 449 ms. Watered by Neponset river, and Boston bay. Celebrated for its extensive quarries of sienite, as the birth-place of the Presidents Adams, and for the first railroad constructed in the United States. At the north part of the town is a bold promontory called Quantum, a pleasant summer resort. Pop. in 1830, 2,192 ; in 1840, 3,486 ; in 1850, 5,017.

QUINCY, p. t., Franklin co., Pa., 57 ms. s. w. of Harrisburgh ; from W. 83 ms.

QUINCY, p. v., Miami township, Logan co., O., 68 ms. N. w. of Columbus ; from W. 462 ms.

QUINCY, p. t., Branch co., Mich., 104 ms. s. w. of Detroit ; from W. 552 ms. Pop. 1,111.

QUINCY, c. h., p. v., seat of justice of Gadsden co., Flor., 23 ms. N. of Tallahassee ; from W. 873 ms. Watered by Attapulgus creek.

QUINCY, p. v., Monroe co., Miss., 181 ms. N. E. of Jackson ; from W. 912 ms.

QUINCY, p. o., Wachita co., Ark.

QUINCY, c. h., p v., seat of justice of Adams co., Ill., 104 ms. w. of Springfield ; from W. 884 ms. Watered by Mississippi river. Pop. 6,911.

QUINCY, p. v., Gibson co., Tenn., 144 ms. w. of Nashville ; from W. 827 ms.

QUINCY, p. o., Hickory co., Mo.

QUITO, p. o., Polk co., Ill.

QUINEBAUGH, p. o., Windham co., Ct.

QUINFIELD. p. o., Muscogee co., Ga.

QUINN's MILLS, p. o., Clinton co., O.

QUITMAN, p. v., seat of justice of Clarke co., Miss., 140 ms. E. of Jackson ; from W. 951 ms. Watered by Chickasawha river.

QUITMAN, p. o., Benton co., Ala.

QUITMAN, p. o., Van Buren co., Ark.

QUITMAN, p. o., Wood co., Tex.

QUITO, p. o., Talbot co., Ga.

QUIVER, p. o., Mason co., Ill.

QUOGUE. p. v., Southampton township, Suffolk co., Long Island, N. Y., 235 ms. s. E. of Albany ; from W. 335 ms. Watered by Shinnecock bay.

QUONOCHONTAUG, p. o., Washington co., R. I.

R.

RABBIT CREEK, p. o., Rush co., Tex.

RABBIT RIVER. p. o., Allegan co., Mich.

RABBITSVILLE, p. o., Logan co., Ky.

RABBIT TOWN, p. o., Benton co., Ala.

RABUN COUNTY, situated on the north boundary of Georgia. Area, 330 square miles. Face of the country. mountainous. Seat of justice, Clayton. Pop. in 1820, 524 ; in 1830, 2,176 ; in 1840, 1,912 ; in 1850, 2,448.

RACCOON, p. t., Beaver co., Pa. Pop. 1,023.

RACCOON, p. o., Marion co., Ill.

RACCOON, p. o., Gallia co., O., 94 ms. s. E. of Columbus ; from W. —— ms. Watered by Raccoon creek. Pop. 1,473.

RACCOON, p. o., Preston co., Va.

RACCOON FORD, p. o., Culpeper co., Va., 98 ms. N. W. of Richmond ; from W. 89 ms. Watered by Rapidan river.

RACCOON ISLAND, p. o., Gallia co., O.

RACCOON VALLEY, p. o., Knox co., Tenn.

RACINE COUNTY, situated on the east boundary of Wisconsin, with Lake Michigan on the east. Area, 610 square miles. Face of the country, undulating ; soil, fertile. Seat of justice, Racine. Pop. 1840, 3,475 ; in 1850, 10,833.

RACINE, p. t., seat of justice of Racine co., Wis., 112 ms. E. of Madison ; from W. 780 ms. Watered by Root river and Lake Michigan.

RACKET RIVER, p. o., St. Lawrence co., N. Y.

RADFORDSFILLE, p. o., Perry co., Ala.

RADNOR, p. t., Delaware co., O., 32 ms. N. of Columbus ; from W. 416 ms. Pop. 864.

RADNOR, p. t., Delaware co., Pa. Watered by Darby creek.

RAGLESVILLE, p. o., Daviess co., Ind.

RAHWAY, p. t., Middlesex co., N. J., 39 ms. N. E. of Trenton ; from W. 205 ms. Watered by Rahway river. Pop. 3,306.

RAIBORN's CREEK. p. o., Laurens district, S. C., 78 ms. N. w. of Columbus ; from W. —— ms.

RAINBOW, p. o., Hartford co., Ct.

RAINESBOROUGH, p. v., Paint township, Highland co., O., 77 ms. s. w. of Columbus ; from W. 432 ms.

RAINE's TAVERN, p. o., Cumberland co., Va., 65 ms. w. of Richmond ; from W. 155 ms.

RAINESVILLE, p. v., Warren co., Ind., 90 ms. N. w. of Indianapolis ; from W. 651 ms.

RAINSBURGH, p. v., Bedford co., Pa., 113 ms. w. of Harrisburgh ; from W. 129 ms.

RAISIN, p. t., Lenawee co., Mich. Watered by Raisin river. Pop. 1,267.

RAISINVILLE, t., Monroe co., Mich. Watered by Raisin river. Pop. 967.

RALEIGH COUNTY, situated in the westerly part of Virginia. Area, —— square miles. Face of the country, mountainous. Seat of justice, Raleigh. Pop. in 1850, 1,765.

RALEIGH, city, seat of justice of Wake co., and the capital of North Carolina, situated about six miles west of Neuse river, which is not generally navigable for ordinary vessels above Smithfield, 27 miles southeast of this place. Four broad avenues divide the town into as many squares, which are each again subdivided into four squares by streets of less width. At the junction of the main avenues, in the midst of an open park of 10 acres, stands the statehouse, a chaste and elegant structure of granite, 166 feet long, and 90 feet wide, surrounded by massy columns, and crowned by a beautiful dome. In 1831, the statehouse upon the same site was destroyed by fire, with a marble statue of Washington, by Canova. The Gaston and Raleigh railroad extends to the former place, 85 miles distant, where the Greenville and Roanoke connects it with Petersburgh. In 1810, the population was about 1,000 ; in 1820, 2,674 ; in 1830, 1,700 ; in 1840, 2,224 ; in 1850. 4,518.

RALEIGH, c. h., p. v., seat of justice of Shelby co., Tenn., 220 ms. s. w. of Nashville ; from W. 905 ms. Watered by Wolf river.

RALEIGH, p. v., seat of justice of Smith co., Miss., 87 ms. s. E. of Jackson ; from W. 992 ms. Watered by a tributary of Leaf river.

RALEIGH, c. h., p. v., seat of justice of Raleigh co., Va.

RALEIGH, c. h., p. v., seat of justice of Saline co., Ill.

RALEIGH, p. o., Rush co., Ind.

RALEIGH, p. o.. Union co., Ky.

RALLS COUNTY, situated on the easterly boundary of Missouri, with Mississippi, river on the east, and traversed by Salt river. Area, 470 square miles. Face of the country, uneven ; soil, productive. Seat of justice, New London. Pop. in 1830, 4,375 ; in 1840, 5,670 ; in 1850, 6,151.

RALLY HILL, p. o., Maury co., Tenn.

RALPHTON, p. o., Fulton co., Ky.

RALSTON, p. o., Lycoming co., Pa., 115 ms. N. of Harrisburgh ; from W. 225 ms.

RAMAPO, p. t., Rockland co., N. Y., 132 ms. s. of Albany : from W. —— ms. Watered by Ramapo and Saddle rivers. Pop. 3,197.

RAMAPO WORKS, p. v., Ramapo township, Rockland co., N. Y., 113 ms. s. of Albany ; from W. 265 ms. Watered by Ramapo river.

RAMER, p. o., Montgomery co., Ala.

RAMSAY COUNTY, situated in the easterly part of Minnesota, with Lake Minsi Sagaigoning, or Mille Lac, in the north, and Mississippi river on the southwest. Area, —— square miles. Seat of justice, St. Paul's. Pop. in 1850, 2,227.

RAMSAYSBURGH, p. v., Knowlton township, Warren co., N. J., 61 ms. N. of Trenton ; from W. 216 ms. Watered by Delaware river.

RANALEBURGH, p. v., Mecklenburgh co., N. C., 174 ms. s. w. of Raleigh ; from W. 413 ms.

RANCOCUS, p. o., Burlington co., N. J.

RANDALLSVILLE, p. v., Robeson co., N. C., 85 ms. s. w. of Raleigh ; from W. 373 ms. Watered by a tributary of Lumber river.

RANDOLPH COUNTY, situated in the northerly part of Virginia, and traversed by Cheat river. Area, 2,060 square miles. Face of the country, mountainous and hilly. Seat of justice, Beverly. Pop. in 1810, 2,854 ; in 1820, 3,350 ; in 1830, 5,000 ; in 1840, 6,208 ; in 1860. 5,248.

RANDOLPH COUNTY, situated in the central part of North Carolina. Area, 900 square miles. Face of country, hilly ; soil fertile. Seat of justice, Ashborough. Pop. in 1810. 10,112 ; in 1820. 11,325 ; in 1830, 12,400 ; in 1840, 12,875 ; in 1850, 15,832.

RANDOLPH COUNTY, situated on the west boundary of Georgia, with Chattahoochee river on the west. Area, 620 square miles. Seat of justice, Cuthbert. Pop. in 1830. 2,191 ; in 1840, 8.276 ; in 1850, 12,868.

RANDOLPH COUNTY, situated on the east boundary of Alabama, and traversed by Tallapoosa river. Area, 875 square miles. Seat of justice, McDonald. Pop. in 1840. 4,973 ; in 1850, 11,581.

RANDOLPH COUNTY, situated on the north boundary of Arkansas, and traversed by Big Black river. Area, 820 square miles. Seat of justice, Pocahontas. Pop. in 1840. 2,196 ; in 1850, 3,275.

RANDOLPH COUNTY, situated toward the northeast part of Missouri.' Area, 450 square miles. Seat of justice, Huntsville. Pop. in 1830, 2,942 ; in 1840, 7,198 ; in 1850, 9,439.

RANDOLPH COUNTY, situate on the southwesterly boundary of Illinois, with Mississippi river on the southwest, and traversed by the Kaskaskia. Area, 540 square miles. Seat of justice, Kaskaskia. Pop. in 1810, 7,275 ; in 1820, 3,492 ; in 1830, 4,436 ; in 1840, 7,944 ; in 1850, 11,079.

RANDOLPH COUNTY, situated on the east boundary of Indiana. Area, 440 squre miles. Face of the country, level ; soil, fertile. Seat of justice, Winchester. Pop. in 1820, 1,808 ; in 1830, 3,912 ; in 1840, 10,684; in 1850, 14,725.

RANDOLPH, p. t., Coos co., N. H., 99 ms. N. of Concord ; from W. 582 ms. Watered by tributaries of Ammonoosuc and Israel's rivers. Pop. 113.

RANDOLPH. p. t., Orange co., Vt., 23 ms. s. of Montpelier ; from W. 498 ms. Watered by tributaries of White river. Pop. 2,666.

RANDOLPH, p. t., Norfolk co., Mass., 16 ms. s. of Boston ; from W. 444 ms. Watered by Mantiquot river. Pop. 4,741.

RANDOLPH, p. t., Cattaraugus co., N. Y., 313 ms. w. of Albany ; from W. 336 ms. Watered by Alleghany river. Pop. 1,606.

RANDOLPH, p. t., Crawford co., Pa. Pop. 1,260.

RANDOLPH, p. t., Morris co., N. J. Watered by Den's branch of Rockaway river. Pop. 2,632.

RANDOLPH, p. v., Tipton co., Tenn.

RANDOLPH, p. t., Portage co., O., 139 ms. N. E. of Columbus ; from W. 315 ms. Pop. 1,732.

RANDOLPH, p. t., Montgomery co., O. Pop. 1,883.

RANDOLPH, p. o., Bibb co., Ala. ; from W. 819 ms.

RANDOLPH, p. v., Randolph co., Ind., 88 ms. N. E. of Indianapolis ; from W. 499 ms.

RANDOLPH, p. o., Barren co., Ky.

RANDOLPH, p. o., Clay co., Mo.

RANDOLPH Centre, p. o., Columbia co., Wis.

RANDOLPH, p. t., Tippecanoe co., Ind. Pop. 1,105.

RANDOLPH MACON COLLEGE, p. o., Mecklenburgh co., Va.

RANDOLPH'S GROVE, p. o., McLean co., Ill.

RANEYSBURGH, p. o., Washington co., Ill.

RANGE, t., Madison co., O. Pop. 988.

RANGELEY, p. o., Franklin co., Me.

RANKIN COUNTY, situated in the central part of Mississippi, with Pearl river on the northwest. Area, 800 square miles. Seat of justice, Brandon. Pop. in 1830, 2,083 ; in 1840, 4,631 ; in 1850, 7,227.

RANSOM, p. o., Hillsdale co., Mich.

RANSOM, p. o., Luzerne co., Pa.

RANSOM'S BRIDGE, p. o., Nash co., N. C , 56 ms. E. of Raleigh ; from W. 282 ms.

RANSOMVILLE, p. o., Porter township, Niagara co., N. Y., 290 ms. w. of Albany ; from W. 416 ms.

RANTOWLE'S, p. o., Colleton district co., S. C.

RAPHO, p. t., Lancaster co., Pa. Watered by Great and Little Chiques creeks. Pop. 3,160.

RAPIDAN, p. o., Madison co., Va., 104 ms. N. w. of Richmond ; from W. 105 ms.

RAPIDES PARISH, situatad toward the west part of Louisiana, and traversed by Red river. Area, 600 square miles. Face of the country, in the north and south, hilly, subsiding into an alluvial plain which skirts Red river. Seat of justice, Alexandria. Pop. in 1810, 2,200 ; in 1820, 6,065 ; in 1830, 7,559 ; in 1840, 14,132 ; in 1850, 16,561.

RAPIDS, p. o., Portage co., O., 157 ms. N. E. of Columbus ; from W. 320 ms.

RAPIDS, p. o., Whitesides co., Ill.

RAPIDS, p. o., Boone co.. Iowa.

RAPIDS, p. o., Niagara co., N. Y.

RAPPAHANNOCK COUNTY, situated toward the northeast part of Virginia. Area, 100 square miles. Face of the country, uneven and mountainous. Seat

of justice, Washington. Pop. in 1840, 9,257 ; in 1850, 9,782.

RAPPAHANNOCK ACADEMY, p. o.. Caroline co., Va., 79 ms. N. of Richmond ; from W. 73 ms.

RAPP'S BARRENS, p. o., Fulton co., Ark.

RARITAN, t., Hunterdon co., N. J., 20 ms. N. of Trenton ; from W. ____ ms. Watered by tributaries of Raritan river. Pop. 3,066.

RATCLIFF'S, p. o., Tyler co., Tex.

RATCLIFFSBURGH, p. o., Vinton co., O.

RATHBONEVILLE, p. o., Addison township, Steuben co., N. Y., 233 ms. w. of Albany ; from W. 298 ms.

RATHBUN, p. o., Sheboygan co., Wis.

RAULERSON'S FERRY, p. o., Columbia co., Flor.

RAVEN CREEK, p. o., Harrison co., Ky.

RAVENNA, p. o. Ottawa co., Mich.

RAVENNA, c. h., p. v., seat of justice of Portage co., O., 140 ms. N. E. of Columbus ; from W. 319 ms. Watered by tributaries of Beaver creek and Cuyahoga river, and by the Pennsylvania and Ohio canal. Pop. 2,240.

RAVEN'S NEST, p. o., Washington co., Va.

RAVENSWOOD, p. o., Jackson co., Va., 367 ms. N. w. of Richmond ; from W. 339 ms.

RAVENSWOOD, v., Newtown township, Queens co., N. Y. Watered by East river.

RAWLINGSBURGH, p. v.. Rockingham co., N. C., 103 ms. N. w. of Raleigh ; from W. 268 ms.

RAWLINGSVILLE, c. h., p. v., seat of justice of De Kalb co., Ala. ; from W. 664 ms.

RAWLINGSVILLE, p. o., Lancaster co., Pa.

RAWSON, p. o., Cattaraugus co., N. Y.

RAWSONVILLE, p. o., Wayne co., Mich., 36 ms. w. of Detroit ; from W. 522 ms.

RAY COUNTY, situated in the westerly part of Missouri, with Missouri river on the south. Area, 570 square miles. Seat of justice, Richmond. Pop. in 1830, 2,657 ; in 1840, 6,553 ; in 1850, 10,373.

RAY, p. t., Macomb co., Mich., 37 ms. N. E. of Detroit ; from W. 562 ms, Pop. 1.232.

RAY CENTRE, p. o., Ray township, Macomb co., Mich.

RAYMERTOWN, p. o., Pittstown township, Rensselaer co., N. Y., 21 ms. N. E. of Albany ; from W. 389 ms.

RAYMOND, p. t., Cumberland co., Me., 58 ms. s. w. of Augusta ; from W. 501 ms. Watered by Sebago and other ponds. Pop. 1,142.

RAYMOND, p. t., Rockingham co., N. H., 24 ms. s. E. of Concord ; from W. 472 ms. Watered by Lamprey river, and a tributary of Exeter river. Pop. 1,200.

RAYMOND, p. v., Hinds co., Miss., 18 ms. W. of Jackson ; from W. 1,028 ms. Watered by a branch of Pearl river.

RAYMOND, p. v., Clark co., Ark., 66 ms. s. w. of Little Rock ; from W. 1,131 ms.

RAYMOND, p. o., Racine co., Wis.

RAYMOND'S, p. o., Union co., O.. 66 ms. N. w. of Columbus ; from W. 456 ms.

RAYMONDVILLE, p. o., St. Lawrence co., N. Y., 246 ms. N. w. of Albany ; from W. 516 ms.

RAYNHAM, p. t., Bristol co., Mass. Watered by Taunton river. Pop. 1,541.

RAYNORTOWN, v., Hempstead township, Queens co., Long Island, N. Y. Watered by Hempstead bay.

RAY'S FORK, p. o., Scott co., Ky.

RAY'S HILL, p. o., Bedford co., Pa., 86 ms. w. of Harrisburgh ; from W. 112 ms.

RAYSVILLE, p. v., Henry co., Ind.

RAYSVILLE, p. o., Columbia co., Ga.

RAYTOWN, p. v., Taliaferro co., Ga., 61 ms. N. E. of Milledgeville ; from W. 612 ms.

RAYVILLE, p. o., Lawrence co., Miss.

RAYWICK, p. o., Marion co., Ky.

READFIELD, p. t., Kennebec co., Me., 12 ms. w. of Augusta ; from W. 604 ms. Watered by head waters of Cobbesseconte river. Pop. 1,985.

READFIELD DEPOT, p. o., Kennebec co., Me.

READFIELD, t., Oswego co., N. Y., 131 ms. N. w. of Albany ; from W. ____ ms. Watered by Salmon river Pop. 752.

READING, p. t., Windsor co., Vt., 61 ms. s. of Montpelier ; from W. 478 ms. Watered by tributaries of Queechee and Black rivers. Pop. 1,171.

READING, p. t., Middlesex co., Mass., 12 ms. N. of Boston ; from W. 452 ms. Watered by Ipswich river Pop. 3,108.

READING, Fairfield co., Ct., (See Redding).

READING, p. t., Steuben co., N. Y., 194 ms. w. of

20

Albany; from W. 305 ms. Watered by Seneca lake. Pop. 1,434.

READING, c. h., p. b., seat of justice of Berks co., Pa., 52 ms. E. of Harrisburgh; from W. 145 ms., situated on the east side of Schuylkill river, 57 miles northwest of Philadelphia, and 52 miles east of Harrisburgh, and has a delightful situation amid picturesque vales, hills, and streams. In the regularity of its streets, the neatness of its houses, and the industry and good order of its inhabitants, it still retains the character stamped upon it by its founders, Thomas and Richard Penn, the sons of William Penn.

Reading is a town of considerable trade and manufactures, for which it has great natural and improved advantages. Tulpehocken creek and the Schuylkill furnish excellent water-power, by which numerous manufactories are kept in successful operation. Hats are the fabrics most extensively made.

Reading contains an imposing courthouse, several elegant churches, and market-houses, banks, an academy, and other public buildings. A neighboring spring supplies the town with an abundant supply of pure water, which is distributed by means of a reservoir and iron-pipes. Here the Schuylkill Navigation canal meets the Union canal, which terminates at Middletown, on the Susquehannah, and the Philadelphia and Reading railroad communicates with this town.

The population in 1810, was 3,463; in 1820, 4,332; in 1830, 5,850; in 1840, 8,410; in 1850, 15,790.

READING, t., Adams co., Pa. Watered by Conewago creek and Muddy run. Pop. 1,252.

READING, p. v.. Sycamore township, Hamilton co., O., 105 ms. s. w. of Columbus; from W. 489 ms.

READING, t., Perry co., O. Pop. 2,744.

READING, p. t., Hillsdale co., Mich., 108 ms. s w. of Detroit; from W. 544 ms. Watered by Little St. Joseph's river. Pop. 956.

READING, p. o., Livingston co., Ill.

READING CENTRE, p. o., Steuben co., N. Y.

READINGTON, p. t., Hunterdon co., N. Y. Watered by Rockaway creek and south branch of Raritan river. Pop. 2,836.

READSBOROUGH, p. t, Bennington co., Vt. Watered by Deerfield river. Pop. 857.

READYVILLE, p. v., Rutherford co., Tenn., 47 ms. s. E. of Nashville; from W. 652 ms. Watered by a tributary of Cumberland river.

REAMSTOWN, p. v., Cocalico township, Lancaster co.. Pa., 42 ms. s. E. of Harrisburgh; from W. 131 ms.

REAVILLE, p. o., Hunterdon co., N. J.

REBERSBURGH, p. v., Miles township, Centre co., Pa., 93 ms. N. w. of Harrisburgh; from W. 184 ms.

RECKLESSTOWN, p. v., Chesterfield township, Burlington co., N. J., 10 ms. s. of Trenton; from W. 171 ms.

RECOVERY, t., Mercer co., O. Pop. 596.

RECTOR'S CROSS ROADS, p. o., Fauquier co., Va., 130 ms. N. of Richmond; from W. 51 ms.

RECTORTOWN, p. v., Fauquier co., Va., 122 ms. N. of Richmond; from W. 59 ms.

RED BANK, p. v., Shrewsbury township. Monmouth co., N. J., 46 ms. E. of Trenton; from W. —— ms. Watered by Neversink river. A pleasant and popular resort during the summer season.

RED BANK, p. t., Clarion co.. Pa., 190 ms. N. w. of Harrisburgh; from W. 256 ms. Watered by Red Bank, Mahoning and Beaver creeks.

RED BANK, p. o., Lawrence co., Ark.

RED BANK FURNACE, p. o., Armstrong co., Pa.

RED BANKS, p. o., Marshall co., Miss.

RED BEACH, p. o., Washington co., Me.

RED BLUFF, p. o., Wythe co., Va., 255 ms. w. of Richmond; from W. 323 ms.

RED BLUFF. p. o., Marion district, S. C.

RED BOILING SPRINGS, p. o., Macon co., Tenn.

RED BRIDGE, p. o., Ulster co., N. Y.

RED BUD, p. o., Randolph co., Ill.

RED BUD, p. o., Ozark co., Mo.

RED CLAY, p. o., Murray co., Ga.

RED CREEK, p. o., Wayne co., N. Y.

REDDING, p. t., Fairfield co., Ct., 59 ms. s. w. of Hartford; from W. 284 ms. Watered by Saugatuck and Norwalk rivers. Pop. 1,734.

REDDING RIDGE, p. v., Redding township, Fairfield co., Ct., 66 ms. s. w. of Hartford; from W. 286 ms.

REDDINGTON, p. v., Jackson co., Ind., 55 ms. s. of Indianapolis; from W. 591 ms. Pop. 1,325.

RED FALLS, p. o., Greene co., N. Y.

REDFIELD, p. t., Oswego co., N. Y., 139 ms. N. w. of Albany; from W. 402 ms. Watered by Salmon river. Pop. 752.

REDFORD, p. t., Wayne co., Mich., 13 ms. N. w. of Detroit; from W. 537 ms. Watered by Powers' creek and north branch of Rouge river. Pop. 1,645.

REDFORD, p. v., Saranac township, Clinton co., N. Y., 185 ms. N. of Albany; from W. 560 ms.

RED HILL, p. o., Kershaw district, S. C., 49 ms. N. E. of Columbia; from W. 488 ms.

RED HILL, p. o., Murray co., Ga., 198 ms. N. w. of Milledgeville; from W. 623 ms.

RED HILL, p. o., Marshall co., Ala.; from W. 718 ms.

RED HILL, p. o., Wayne co., Miss.

RED HILL, p. o., Grainger co., Tenn., 218 ms. E. of Nashville; from W. 488 ms.

RED HILL, p. o., Hardin co., Ky.

RED HOOK, p. t., Dutchess co., N. Y., 49 ms. s. of Albany; from W. 321 ms. Watered by Hudson river. Pop. 3,264.

RET HOUSE, p. o., Charlotte co., Va., 103 ms. s. w. of Richmond; from W. 193 ms.

RED HOUSE SHOALS, p. o., Mason co., Va., 377 ms. N. w. of Richmond; from W. 374 ms.

RED JACKET, p. o., Erie co., N. Y.

RED LAND, p. o., Pontotoc co., Miss.

RED LAND, p. o., Bossier parish, La.

RED LEVEL SPRINGS, p. o., Alleghany co., Pa.

RED LION, p. v., and hundred, New Castle co., Del., 35 ms. N. of Dover; from W. 122 ms. Watered by Red Lion creek. Pop. 1,153.

RED LION, p. o., Clear Creek township, Warren co., O., 90 ms. s. w. of Columbus; from W. 474 ms.

RED MAN, p. o., Jackson co., Ala.

RED MILLS, p. o., Carmel township, Putnam co., N. Y., 107 ms. s. of Albany; from W. 280 ms.

RED MOUND, p. o., Henderson co., Tenn., 114 ms. s. w. of Nashville; from W. 799 ms.

RED MOUNTAIN, p. o., Orange co., N. C., 39 ms. N. w. of Raleigh; from W. 265 ms.

RED OAK, p. o., Fayette co., Ga.

RED OAK, p. o., Navarro co., Tex.

RED OAK GROVE, p. o., Barnwell district, S. C.

RED OAK GROVE, p. o., Charlotte co., Va., 112 ms. s. w. of Richmond; from W. 210 ms.

RED OAK GROVE, p. o., Burlington co., N. J.

RED PLAINS, p. o., Surry co., N. C., 128 ms. N. w. of Raleigh; from W. 336 ms.

RED RIVER COUNTY, situated on the north boundary of Texas, with Red river on the northeast. Area, —— square miles. Seat of justice, Clarkesville. Pop. in 1850, 3,906.

RED RIVER, t., Lafayette co., Ark.

RED RIVER, t., White co., Ark.

RED RIVER, p. o., Robertson co., Tenn., 36 ms. N. of Nashville; from W. 718 ms.

RED RIVER IRON WORKS, p. v., Estill co., Ky., 74 ms. s. E. of Frankfort; from W. 718 ms. Watered by Red river.

RED RIVER LANDING, p. o., Point Coupée parish, La.

RED ROCK, p. o., Marion co., Iowa.

RED ROCK, p. o., Upshur co., Tex.

RED ROCK, p. o., Ramsay co., Minn.

RED SHOALS, p. o., Stokes co., N. C., 135 ms. N. w. of Raleigh; from W. 323 ms.

RED SPRING, p. o., Polk co., Tenn.

RED STONE, p. t., Fayette co., Pa. Pop. 1,287.

RED SULPHUR SPRINGS, p. v., Monroe co., Va., 249 ms. w. of Richmond; from W. 286 ms. Watered by Indian creek.

RED SULPHUR SPRINGS, p. o., Hardin co., Tenn.

RED WING, p. o., Wabashaw co., Minn.

REDWOOD, p. v., Alexandria township, Jefferson co., N. Y., 188 ms. N. w. of Albany; from W. 440 ms. Watered by Butterfield lake.

REDWOOD, p. o., Grainger co., Tenn.

REED, p. t., Seneca co., O. Pop. 1,494.

REED CREEK, p. o., Randolph co., N. C.

REED ISLAND, Pulaski co., Va.

REEDSBURGH, p. o., Plain township, Wayne co., O., 86 ms. N. E. of Columbus; from W. 355 ms.

REEDSBURGH, p. o., Sauk co., Wis.

REED'S CORNERS, p. o., Canandaigua township, Ontario co., N. Y.

REED'S CREEK, p. o., Lawrence co., Ark., 110 ms. N. E. of Little Rock; from W. 1,027 ms.

REED'S FERRY, p. o., Hillsborough co., N. H.

REED'S GROVE p. o., Will co., Ill.

REED'S LANDING, p. o., Wabashaw co., Minn.
REED'S MILLS, p. o., Vinton co., O., 77 ms. s. E. of Columbus; from W. 373 ms.
REED'S SETTLEMENT, p. o., Panola co., Tex.
REEDSVILLE, p. o., Mifflin co., Pa.
REEDTOWN, p. o., Reed township, Seneca co., O., 86 ms. N. of Columbus; from W. 408 ms.
REEDY BRANCH, p. o., Moore co., N. C.
REEDY CREEK, p. o., Jefferson co., Ga.
REEDY CREEK, p. o., Marion district, S. C.
REEDY RIPPLE, p. o., Wirt co., Va.
REEDYVILLE, p. o., Wirt co., Va.
REEDYVILLE, p. o., Cameron co., Tex.
REELFOOT, p. o., Obion co., Tenn.
REELSVILLE, p. o., Putnam co., Ind.
REEM'S CREEK, p. o., Buncombe co., N. C.
REESE'S MILL, p. o., Boone co., Ind.
REFORM, p. o., Pickens co., Ala.
REFORM, p. o., Union co., Ark.
REFUGIO COUNTY, situated in Texas. Area, —— square miles. Seat of justice, Refugio. Pop. in 1850, 288.
REFUGIO, p. o., Refugio co., Tex.
REGNIER'S MILLS, p. o., Aurelius township, Washington co., O., 106 ms. s. E. of Columbus; from W. 307 ms.
REHOBOTH. p. t., Bristol co., Mass., 40 ms. s. of Boston; from W. 413 ms. Watered by Palmer's river. Pop. 2,104.
REHOBOTH, p. v., Lunenburgh co., Va., 85 ms. s. w. of Richmond; from W. 204 ms.
REHOBOTH, p. v., Edgefield district, S. C., 80 ms. w. of Columbia; from W. 558 ms.
REHOBOTH, p. v., Wilkes co., Ga., 88 ms. N. E. of Milledgeville; from W. 576 ms.
REHOBOTH, p. v., Perry co., O., 51 ms. E. of Columbus; from W. 358 ms.
REHRERSBURGH, p. v., Tulpehocken township, Berks co., Pa., 55 ms. E. of Harrisburgh; from W. 165 ms.
REIDSBURGH, p. v., Clarion co., Pa., 187 ms. N. w. of Harrisburgh; from W. 264 ms.
REIDSVILLE, c. h., p. v., seat of justice of Tatnall co., Ga., 162 miles s. E. of Milledgeville; from W. 773 ms. Watered by Great Ohoopee river.
REIDSVILLE, p. v., Bern township, Albany co., N. Y., 18 ms. w. of Albany; from W. 372 ms.
REIDSVILLE, p. v., Rockingham co., N. C., 108 ms. N. w of Raleigh; from W. 277 ms.
REILY, p. o., Butler co., O., 111 ms. s. w. of Columbus; from W. 508 ms.
REINDEER, p. o., Nodaway co., Mo.
REINHOLDSVILLE, p. v., Lancaster co., Pa., 41 ms. s. E. of Harrisburgh; from W. 139 ms.
REISTERTOWN, p. v., Baltimore co., Md., 46 ms. N. of Annapolis; from W. 56 ms.
RELFE, p. o., Pulaski co., Mo.
RELF'S BLUFF, p. o., Drew co., Ark.
REMINGTON, p. o., Alleghany co., Pa.
REMSEN, p. t., Oneida co., N. Y., 100 ms. N. w. of Albany; from W. 405 ms. Watered by Black river. Pop. 2,407.
RENICK'S MILLS, p. o., Lafayette co., Mo.
RENROCK, p. o., Morgan co., O.
RENSSELAER COUNTY, situated on the east boundary of New York, with Hudson river on the west. Area, 626 square miles. Face of the country, hilly; soil, productive. Seat of justice, Troy. Pop. in 1810, 36,309; in 1820, 40,153; in 1830, 49,472; in 1840, 60,259; in 1850, 73,361.
RENSSELAER, v., Sand Lake township, Rensselaer co. N. Y.
RENSSELAER, c. h., p. v., seat of justice of Jasper co., Ind. Watered by Iroquois river.
RENSSELAER, t., Wayne co., Mich.
RENSSELAERVILLE, p. t., Albany co., N. Y., 26 ms. w. of Albany; from W. 369 ms. Watered by Catskill and Foxes creeks. Pop. 3,929.
REPTON, p. o., Clarke co., Ind.
REPUBLIC, p. o., Scipio township, Seneca co., O.
REPUBLIC, p. o., Surry co., N. C.
REPUBLICAN, p. o., German township, Darke co., O., 91 ms. w. of Columbus; from W. 417 ms.
REPUBLICAN, p. t., Jefferson co., Ind. Pop. 1,528.
REPUBLICAN, p. o., Columbia co., Ga., 73 ms. N. E. of Milledgeville; from W. 612 ms.
REPUBLICAN GROVE, p. o., Halifax co., Va., 140 ms. s. w. of Richmond; from W. 227 ms.
REPUBLICAN GROVE, p. o., De Kalb co., Tenn.

REPUBLICAN MILLS, p. o., Fairfax co., Va.
RESACA, p. o., Murray co., Ga.
RESERVE, t., Alleghany co., Pa. Pop. 1,160.
RESERVE, p. o., Miami co., Ind.
RESERVE. p. o., St. Joseph co., Mich.
RETREAT, p. o., Franklin co., Va., 189 ms. s. w. of Richmond; from W. 264 ms.
RETREAT, p. o., Grimes co., Tex.
REVILEE, p. o., Scott co., Ark.
REXFORD FLATS, p. o., Clifton Park township, Saratoga co., N. Y., 21 ms. N. w. of Albany; from W. 389 ms.
REYNALE'S BASIN, p. o., Niagara co., N. Y.
REYNOLDS COUNTY, situated toward the southeast part of Missouri. Area, —— square miles. Seat of justice, Alamode. Pop. in 1850, 1,849.
REYNOLDS, p. o., Houston co., Ga.
REYNOLDSBURGH, p. v., Truro township, Franklin co., O., 11 ms. E. of Columbus; from W. 382 ms. Watered by Black Lick creek.
REYNOLDSBURGH, v., Humphrey co., Tenn., 69 ms. w. of Nashville; from W. 753 ms. Watered by Tennessee river.
REYNOLDSVILLE, p. v., Hector township, Tompkins co., N. Y., 178 ms. w. of Albany; from W. 311 ms.
REYNOLDSVILLE, p. o., Jefferson co., Pa.
REYNOSA, p. o., Laurens district, S. C.
RHEA COUNTY, situated in the easterly part of Tennessee, with Tennessee river on the southeast. Area, 440 square miles. Face of the country, hilly and mountainous. Seat of justice, Washington. Pop. in 1810, 2,504; in 1820, 4,215; in 1830, 8,182; in 1840, 3,985; in 1850, 4,415.
RHEATOWN, p. v., Greene co., Tenn., 268 ms. E. of Nashville; from W. 427 ms.
RHINEBECK, p. t., Dutchess co., N. Y., 55 ms. s. of Albany; from W. 315 ms. Watered by Hudson river and Landtman's creek. Pop. 2,816.
RHINEBECK LANDING, v., Rhinebeck township, Dutchess co., N. Y. Situated on Hudson river opposite Kingston Point.
RHOADS POINT, p. o., Macoupin co., Ill., 59 ms. s. w. of Springfield; from W. 826 ms.

RHODE ISLAND, one of the United States, so called from its island of the same name, which was supposed to bear a resemblance to the isle of Rhodes, in the Mediterranean. It is the smallest state, as regards its territory, in the Union, and lies between 41° 22′ and 42° 3′ north latitude, and 71° 6′ and 71° 38′ west longitude from Greenwich, and is bounded on the north and east by Massachusetts; south by the Atlantic; and west by Connecticut. Its superficial area is 1,340 square miles.

Physical Aspect.—The surface of this state is generally level, except in the northwest part, where it is rocky and hilly. There are many hills, however, as Mount Hope, in Bristol, Hopkins' hill, in West Greenwich, and Woonsocket hill, in Smithfield. The soil on the continental part is tolerably fertile, though thin and lean, and requires much labor to be tilled. But the lands near Narragansett bay, as well as those on the islands, have great fertility, and are in a high state of cultivation. The soil of this state is generally regarded as better adapted to grazing than tillage.

Rivers and Bays.—The principal rivers are the Pawtucket or Blackstone, Providence, Pawtuxet, Wood, and Pawcatuck. Narragansett is the only bay worthy of note, and nearly divides the state in two.

Islands.—Besides the isle from which this state takes its name, Block, Canonicut, Prudence, Patience, Hope, Dyer's, and Hog islands, are included within its territory.

Climate.—The climate is proverbially healthy; and on the islands, where the sea breezes have the effect, not only to mitigate the heat in summer, but to moderate the winter's cold, it is more temperate than in any of the other New England states. Newport has long been celebrated as a delightful summer residence, and is much resorted to by people from the south.

Productive Resources.—The principal products are

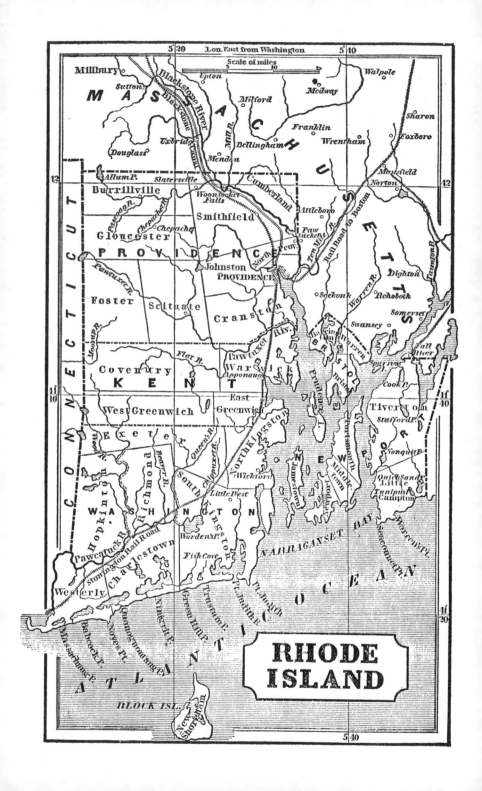

RHODE ISLAND

crses, mules, neat cattle, sheep, swine, poultry, eggs, butter, cheese, wool, hemp, flax, hay, lumber, wheat, rye, barley, oats, potatoes, and Indian corn. Anthracite coal is found and wrought to a small extent in this state.

Manufactures.—A greater proportion of the people of Rhode Island are employed in manufacturing than in any other state of the Union. The state abounds in excellent water-power, affording sites for manufactories, which are extensively improved. The principal manufactures are woollen and cotton; but it has several furnaces, tanneries, paper-mills, and other establishments.

Railroads and Canals.—The railroads are principally connecting links in the great line of travel from New England to the south. The three principal roads extend from Providence to Boston, Worcester, Mass., and Stonington, Conn., respectively, and have an aggregate length of about 150 miles. The Blackstone canal, from Providence to Worcester, lies partly within this state.

Commerce.—The direct foreign commerce of Rhode Island (owing to the greater eligibility of the ports of neighboring states) is small, compared with its population and industry. Its exports and imports in 1850 amounted to $474,568. Shipping owned in the state amounts to about 28,000 tons.

Education.—Brown university, at Providence, is the only college in the state. There is an atheneum also at Providence, and academies and common schools are numerous. Provision is also made for the insane and blind.

Population.—In 1790, 69,110; in 1800, 69,122; in 1810, 77,031; in 1820, 83,059; in 1830, 97,199; in 1840, 108,830; in 1850, 147,544. Number of slaves in 1720, 952; in 1800, 381; in 1810, 103; in 1820, 48; in 1830, 17; in 1840, 5.

Government.—The legislative power is vested in a senate, and house of representatives; and the executive power in a governor, and lieutenant-governor; all chosen annually by the people, on the first Wednesday of April. The judicial powers are vested in a supreme court, consisting of a chief justice and three associates, who hold their offices at the discretion of the legislature; and in a court of common pleas for each county, consisting of a justice of the supreme court and two associates. The right of suffrage is vested in all male native citizens, who have resided in the state two years, and in the town where they propose to vote, six months; who have been registered seven days in the town clerk's office; have paid a tax, or done military duty, within the preceding year; and in all other male citizens (naturalized foreigners) who, in addition to the preceding qualifications, possess real estate in the town or city where offering to vote worth $134 over all incumbrances, or which rents for $7 per annum.

History.—The first permanent settlement by Europeans, within the present limits of Rhode Island, was made at Providence, in 1636, by Rev. Roger Williams, who had been banished from the Massachusetts colony for his peculiar religious opinions. This settlement was called the "Providence Plantation." The next settlement was made at Portsmouth, in the northern part of Rhode Island, in 1638, which, the year following, received the name of the "Rhode Island Plantation." In 1643, when the four colonies of Massachusetts entered into articles of confederation, under the title of the "United Colonies of New England," under the pretence that the Providence and Rhode Island plantations had no charter, and that their territory was claimed by Plymouth and Massachusetts, they were excluded from the confederacy. The year following, Roger Williams obtained a free charter from the British parliament, and incorporated the two plantations under one government, which continued in force till 1663, when a new charter was granted by Charles II. The latter is the venerable charter under which the people lived and prospered, until its constitution was amended, in 1842. The first general assembly was held at Portsmouth, in 1647, when the executive power was confided to a president and four assistants. The constitution of the United States was not adopted in Rhode Island until 1790, after it had received the assent of all the other states.

RIBLET'S, p. o., Richland co., O.

RICE, p. o., Cattaraugus co., N. Y.

RICE, t., Sandusky co., O. Pop. 483.

RICEBOROUGH, c. h., p. v., seat of justice of Liberty co., Ga., 194 ms. s. E. of Milledgeville; from W. 696 ms. Watered by Newport river.

RICE CITY, p. v., Coventry township, Kent co., R. I., 19 ms. w. of Providence; from W. 381 ms.

RICE CREEK, p. o., Calhoun co., Mich., 112 ms. w. of Detroit; from W. 577 ms.

RICE'S LANDING, p. o., Greene co., Pa., 200 ms. w. of Harrisburgh; from W. 218 ms.

RICE'S STORE, p. o., Westmoreland co., Va., 70 ms. N. E. of Richmond; from W. 129 ms.

RICEVILLE, p. o., Hancock co., Miss.

RICEVILLE, p. o., Monmouth co., N. J

RICEVILLE, p. o., Crawford co., Pa.

RICEVILLE, p. o., Pittsylvania co., Va.

RICHARDSON, p. o., Vermillion co., Ill.

RICHARDSON'S, p. o., Montgomery co., Tenn.

RICHARDSON'S CREEK, p. o., Union co., N. C., 167 ms. s. w. of Raleigh; from W. 436 ms.

RICHARDSONVILLE, p. v., Edgefield district, S. C., 75 ms. w. of Columbia; from W. 539 ms.

RICHARDSVILLE, p. v., Culpeper co., Va., 79 ms. N. w. of Richmond; from W. 70 ms.

RICHARDSVILLE, p. o., Jefferson co., Pa.

RICHBOROUGH, p. v., Bucks co., Pa., 114 ms. E. of Harrisburgh; from W. 159 ms.

RICHBURGH, p. o., Wirt township, Alleghany co., N. Y., 282 ms. w. of Albany; from W. 315 ms.

RICH CREEK, p. o., Logan co., Va.

RICHFIELD, p. t. Otsego co., N. Y., 72 ms. w. of Albany; from W. 376 ms. Watered by Canaderaga lake. Pop. 1,502.

RICHFIELD, p. o., Juniata co., Pa., 65 ms. N. w. of Harrisburgh; from W. 159 ms.

RICHFIELD, p. o., Adams co., Ill.

RICHFIELD, p. t., Summit co., O., 134 ms. N. E. of Columbus; from W. 347 ms. Pop. 1,268.

RICHFIELD, t., Henry co., O. Pop. 136

RICHFIELD, t., Huron co., O. Pop. 1,944.

RICHFIELD, t., Lucas co., O. Pop. 399.

RICHFIELD, p. o., Adams co., Ill.

RICHFIELD, t., Genesee co., Mich. Pop. 482.

RICHFIELD SPRINGS, p. v., Richfield township, Otsego co., N. Y. Situated near a celebrated sulphur spring.

RICHFORD, p. t., Franklin co., Vt., 66 ms. N. of Montpelier; from W. 567 ms. Watered by Missisque river and tributaries. Pop. 1,074.

RICHFORD, p. t., Tioga co., N. Y., 144 ms. s. w. of Albany; from W. 295 ms. Watered by East and West Oswego creeks. Pop. 1,208

RICH FORK, p. o., Davidson co., N. C., 109 ms. w. of Raleigh; from W. 330 ms.

RICH HILL, p. t., Greene co., Pa.

RICH HILL, p. t., Muskingum co., O. Pop. 1,495.

RICH HILL, p. o., Maury co., Tenn.

RICHLAND DISTRICT, situated in the central part of South Carolina, with Congaree river on the southwest, and the Wateree on the east. Area, 630 square miles. Face of the country, uneven; soil, productive. Seat of justice, Columbia. Pop. in 1810, 9,027; in 1820, 12,321; in 1830, 14,772; in 1840, 16,397; in 1850, 20,243.

RICHLAND COUNTY, situated toward the north part of Ohio. Area, 900 square miles. Face of the country, even; soil, fertile. Seat of justice, Mansfield. Pop. in 1820, 9,169; in 1830, 24,007; in 1840, 44,532; in 1850, 30,879.

RICHLAND COUNTY, situated in the southeasterly part of Illinois. Area — square miles. Seat of justice, Olney. Pop. in 1850, 4,012.

RICHLAND COUNTY, situated in the westerly part of Wisconsin, with Wisconsin river on the south. Area, — square miles. Seat of justice, Richmond, Pop. in 1850, 903.

RICHLAND, p. t., seat of justice, together with Oswego, of Oswego co., N. Y., 155 ms. N. w. of Albany; from W. 385 ms. Watered by Salmon river and Lake Ontario. The county buildings are in the village of Pulaski. Pop. 4,079.

RICHLAND, t., Venango co., Pa. Pop. 1,008.

RICHLAND, t., Bucks co., Pa. Watered by Tohickon creek. Pop. 1,734.

RICHLAND, t., Cambria co., Pa. Pop. 1,942.

RICHLAND, p. v., Richland co., O., 82 ms. N. of Columbus; from W. 389 ms.

RICHLAND, t., Belmont co., O. Pop. 3,351.

RICHLAND, t., Clinton co., O. Pop. 1,975.

RICHLAND, t., Darke co., O. Pop. 798.

RICHLAND, t., Defiance co., O. Pop. 1,218.

RICHLAND, t., Guernsey co., O., 95 ms. E. of Columbus. Pop. 1,438.

RICHLAND, t., Hancock co., O.
RICHLAND, t., Henry co., O. Pop. 136.
RICHLAND, t., Holmes co., O. Pop. 1,349.
RICHLAND, t., Logan co., O. Pop. 1,169.
RICHLAND, p. t., Marion co., O. Pop. 1,229.
RICHLAND, t., Miami co., Ind.
RICHLAND, t., Allen co., O. Pop. 989.
RICHLAND, t., Madison co., Ark. Pop. 736.
RICHLAND, t., Phillips co., Ark. Pop. 851.
RICHLAND, t., Washington co., Ark. Pop. 489.
RICHLAND. p. v., Giles co., Tenn., 69 ms. s. of Nashville; from W. 719 ms.
RICHLAND, p. v., Holmes co., Miss.
RICHLAND, p. v., Stewart co., Ga., 127 ms. s. w. of Milledgeville; from W. 783 ms.
RICHLAND, p. t., Jefferson co., Ark., 70 ms. s. E. of Little Rock; from W. 1,124 ms, Pop. 1,124.
RICHLAND, p. t., Kalamazoo co., Mich., 135 ms. w. of Detroit; from W. 600 ms. Pop. 795.
RICHLAND, p. t., Fountain co., Ind. Pop. 1,725.
RICHLAND, p. v., Rush co., Ind., 51 ms. s. E. of Indianapolis; from W. 545 ms.
RICHLAND, t., Steuben co., Ind. Pop. 393.
RICHLAND, p. v., Sangamon co., Ill., 10 ms. N. of Springfield; from W. 790 ms.
RICHLAND, p, o., Greene co., Mo.
RICHLAND, p. t., Morgan co., Mo.
RICHLAND, t., Scott co., Mo.
RICHLAND, p. o., Keokuk co., Iowa.
RICHLAND. .p. o., Tazewell co., Va., 314 ms. w. of Richmond; from W. 369 ms.
RICHLAND CENTRE, p. o., De Kalb co., Ind.
RICHLAND, city, p. o., Richland co., Wis.
RICHLAND CROSSINGS, p o., Navarro co., Tex.
RICHLAND GROVE, p. o., Mercer co., Ill.
RICHLANDS, p. o., Onslow co., N. C., 128 ms. s. E. of Raleigh; from W. 358 ms.
RICHLANDTOWN, p. v., Bucks co., Pa., 105 ms. E. of Harrisburgh; from W. 178 ms.
RICHMOND COUNTY, situated in the southeast part of New York, consisting of Staten Island. Area 63 square miles. Face of the country, hilly; soil, fertile and well-cultivated. Seat of justice, Richmond. Pop. in 1810, 5,347; in 1820, 6,135; in 1830, 7,084; in 1840, 10,965; in 1850, 15,161.
RICHMOND COUNTY, situated in the easterly part of Virginia, with Rappahannock river on the southwest. Area, 200 square miles. Seat of justice, Warsaw. Pop. in 1810, 6,214; in 1820, 5,706; in 1830, 6,056; in 1840. 5.965; in 1850, 6,448.
RICHMOND COUNTY, situated on the southwesterly boundary of North Carolina, with Yadkin river on the west. Area, 540 square miles. Seat of justice, Rockingham. Pop. in 1810, 6,695; in 1820, 7,537; in 1830, 9,326; in 1840, 8,909; in 1850, 9,818.
RICHMOND COUNTY, situated on the northeasterly boundary of Georgia, with Savannah river on the northeast. Area, 384 square miles. Seat of justice, Augusta. Pop. in 1810, 6,189; in 1820, 8,608; in 1830, 11,644; in 1840, 11,932; in 1850, 16,246.
RICHMOND, p. t., Lincoln co., Me., 15 ms. s. of Augusta; from W. 585 ms. Watered by Kennebec river. Pop. 2,056.
RICHMOND, p. t., Cheshire co., N. H., 61 ms. s. w. of Concord; from W. 424 ms. Watered by tributaries of Ashuelot and Miller's rivers. Pop. 1,128.
RICHMOND, p. t., Chittenden co., Vt., 27 ms. N. w. of Montpelier; from W. 513 ms. Watered by Onion and Huntington rivers. Pop. 1,453.
RICHMOND, p. t., Berkshire co., Mass., 142 ms. w. of Boston; from W. 369. Watered by a tributary of Housatonic river. Pop. 907.
RICHMOND, p. t., Washington co., R. I., 30 ms. s. w. of Providence; from W. — ms. Watered by Wood and Charles rivers. Pop. 1,784.
RICHMOND, p. t., Ontario co., N. Y., 209 ms. w. of Albany; from W. — ms. Watered by Honeoye lake and its outlet. Pop. 1,852.
RICHMOND, c. h., p. v., seat of justice of Richmond co., Staten Island, N. Y., 159 ms. s. of Albany; from W. 237 ms.
RICHMOND, t., Crawford co., Pa. Pop. 1,139.
RICHMOND, t., Tioga co., Pa. Pop. 1,231.
RICHMOND, t., Berks co., Pa. Watered by Moslem creek. Pop. 2,056.
RICHMOND, p. v., Lower Mount Bethel township, Northampton co., Pa., 119 ms. N. E., of Harrisburgh; from W. 212 ms.

RICHMOND, city, seat of justice of Henrico co., and capital of Virginia, situated on the north side of James river, 150 miles from its entrance into Chesapeake bay, and 120 miles south of Washington. In trade, manufactures, and population, it is the principal city of the state. Directly above it, the river has a descent of about 80 feet in six miles, forming a natural barrier to navigation, which has been overcome by a canal around the falls, and extending 176 miles farther up the river. Through these channels, Richmond has become the entrepot of a fertile region, and receives large quantities of flour, tobacco, and coal. Vessels of 10 feet draught pass the bar, six miles below the city, and those of 14 feet navigate the river below this point. The location of the city is pleasant and healthful, and is situated on two hills, though not densely built, and in the valley between them runs Shockoe creek, a rapid stream. Many beautiful mansions are scattered on these elevations, and on the level top of the westerly one, stands the statehouse, a chaste and beautiful building, in the centre of an open square. Near this is the city-hall, a large and elegant edifice of Grecian architecture. In 1811, a theatre was burned on the site where an episcopal church now stands, and a large number of respectable citizens, including the governor of the state, perished. To commemorate this sad event, the Monumental church was erected on the spot where it took place. Near the city is a penitentiary, extending with its grounds over an area of several acres.

The manufactures of Richmond are varied and valuable, the neighboring streams affording fine water-power which has been extensively supplied. There are cotton factories, flouring mills, nail and iron works, and numerous other prosperous establishments.

Besides the canal before noticed, the city is connected with Norfolk, New York, and other points, by steamboats and sailing-packets. Two bridges extend over James river to Manchester, a flourishing suburb of Richmond, upon one of which the Washington and Wilmington railroad enters the city, whence it traverses Virginia and North Carolina. The Virginia Central railroad begins at Richmond, and penetrates the interior of the state.

The water-works, by which Richmond is supplied, raise the water, by hydraulic power, into three reservoirs, each containing a million of gallons, and from these lead off to all parts of the city.

The spot on which this large and fine city stands was first visited by white men in 1609, when "Master West" penetrated to the falls in search of provisions for the young colony at Jamestown, but found nothing edible except acorns. Richmond was founded in 1742, and made the capital of the state in 1780, since which it has been steadily increasing.

The population in 1800, was 5,537; in 1810. 9,735; in 1820. 12,046; in 1830, 16,060; in 1840, 20,153; in 1850, 35,482.

RICHMOND. p. v., Dallas co., Ala.; from W. 879 ms.
RICHMOND, c. h., p. v., seat of justice of Madison parish, La., 200 ms. N. w. of New Orleans; from W. — ms. Watered by Roundaway and Bruhy bayous.
RICHMOND, p. v., Bedford co., Tenn., 70 ms. s. of Nashville; from W. 694 ms.
RICHMOND, c. h., p. v., seat of justice of Madison co., Ky., 48 ms. s. E. of Frankfort; from W. 546 ms. Watered by a tributary of Kentucky river.
RICHMOND, t., Ashtabula co., O. Pop. 706.
RICHMOND, p. v., Salem township, Jefferson co., O., 134 ms. E. of Columbus; from W. 275 ms.
RICHMOND, p. t., Macomb co., Mich. Watered by Belle river and tributaries of Red and South rivers. Pop. 1,000.
RICHMOND, p. v., Wayne co., Ind, 68 ms. E. of Indianapolis; from W. 503 ms.
RICHMOND, t., Gasconade co., Mo. Pop. 238.
RICHMOND, c. h., p. v., seat of justice of Ray co., Mo., 142 ms. N. w. of Jefferson city; from W. 1,045 ms. Watered by Elkhorn creek.
RICHMOND, p. o., Washington co., Iowa.
RICHMOND, p. v., McHenry co., Ill.
RICHMOND, p. o., Itawamba co., Miss,
RICHMOND, p. o., Fort Bend co., Tex.
RICHMOND, c. h., p. v., seat of justice of Henrico co., Va.
RICHMOND, p. t., Huron co., O. Pop. 609.
RICHMOND, p. o., Walworth co., Wis.
RICHMOND CENTRE, p. o., Ashtabula co., O.
RICHMOND CITY, p. v., Lake co., O., 177 ms. N. E. of

Columbus; from W. 351 ms. Watered by Grand river.

RICHMOND CORNER, p. o., Richmond township, Lincoln co., Me.

RICHMOND DALE, p. o., Richmond township, Ross co., O., 51 ms. s. of Columbus ; from W. 392 ms.

RICHMOND FACTORY, p. o., Richmond co., Ga., 102 ms. E. of Milledgeville; from W. —— ms.

RICHMOND MILLS, p. o., Ontario co., N. Y.

RICHMOND VALLEY, p. o., Westfield township, Richmond co., Staten Island, N. Y., 167 ms. s. of Albany ; from W. 245 ms.

RICHMONDVILLE, p. v., Cobbleskill township, Scoharie co., N. Y., 47 ms. w. of Albany ; from W. 381 ms.

RICH PATCH, p. o., Alleghany co., Va.

RICH SQUARE, p. o., Northampton co., N. C., 124 ms. N. E. of Raleigh; from W. 227 ms.

RICH VALLEY, p. o., Bedford co., Tenn., 64 ms. s. of Nashville ; from W. 687 ms.

RICH VALLEY, p. o., Wythe co., Va.

RICHVIEW, p. o., Washington co., Ill.

RICHVILLE, p. o., De Kalb township, St. Lawrence co., N. Y.. 187 ms. N. w. of Albany ; from W. 456 ms.

RICHWOOD, p. o., Union co., O., 57 ms. N. w. of Columbus ; from W. 447 ms.

RICH WOODS, p. o.. Izard co., Ark., 120 ms. N. of Little Rock ; from W. 1,076 ms.

RICH WOODS, p. o., Delaware co., Ind.

RICH WOODS, p. t., Washington co., Me. Pop. 829.

RICH WOODS, t., Miller co., Mo.

RICKOE'S BLUFF, p. o., Gadsden co., Flor.

RICKREAL, p. o., Polk co., Oregon.

RIDDICKSVILLE, p. o., Hertford co., N. C.

RIDGE, p. o., St. Mary's co., Md., 110 ms. s. of Annapolis ; from W. 87 ms.

RIDGE, p. o., Mount Morris township, Livingston co., N. Y., 246 ms. w, of Albany ; from W. 357 ms.

RIDGE, p. o., Coshocton co., O.

RIDGE, t., Hancock co., O.

RIDGE, t., Van Wert co., O. Pop. 400.

RIDGE, p. o., Lenawee co., Mich.

RIDGE, p. o., Edgefield district, S. C., 40 ms. w. of Columbia ; from W. 538 ms.

RIDGEBURY, p. v., Ridgefield township, Fairfield co., Ct., 74 ms. s. w. of Hartford ; from W. 287 ms.

RIDGEBURY, p. v., Minisink township, Orange co., N. Y., 113 ms. s. of Albany ; from W. 270 ms.

RIDGEBURY, p. t., Bradford co., Pa. Watered by Bentley and South creeks. Pop. 1,616.

RIDGE FARM p o, Vermilion so.. Ill.

RIDGEFIELD, p. t., Fairfield co., Ct., 81 ms. s. w. of Hartford ; from W. 281 ms. Watered by Saugatuck and Norwalk rivers. Pop. 2,237.

RIDGE GROVE, p. o., Macon co., Ga.

RIDGE HALL, p. o., Baltimore co., Md.

RIDGELAND, p. o., Henry co., O.

RIDGELEY, p. o., Madison co., Ill.

RIDGELY, p. o., Macon co., Ala.

RIDGE POST, p. o., Davidson co., Tenn.

RIDGE PRAIRIE, p. o., Saline co., Mo.

RIDGE SPRING, p. o., Pitt co., N. C.

RIDGEVILLE, p. o., Carroll co., Md.

RIDGEVILLE, p. o., Hampshire co., Va., 203 ms. N. w. of Richmond ; from W. 131 ms.

RIDGEVILLE, p. o., Butler co., Ala.; from W. 894 ms.

RIDGEVILLE, p. v., Warren co., O., 79 ms. s. w. of Columbus ; from W. 465 ms.

RIDGEVILLE, p. t., Lorain co., O. Pop. 1,212.

RIDGEVILLE, p. o., Cook co.. Ill.

RIDGEVILLE, p. o., Colleton district, S. C.

RIDGEVILLE, p. o., Randolph co., Ind.

RIDGEVILLE CORNERS, p. o., Henry co., O.

RIDGEWAY, p. t., Orleans co., N. Y., 262 ms. w. of Albany ; from W. 400 ms. Watered by Oak Orchard creek. Pop. 4,591.

RIDGEWAY, t., Jefferson co., Pa.

RIDGEWAY, p. t., Bradford co., Pa. Watered by Toby's and Kersey's creek and Clarion river. Pop. 1,216.

RIDGEWAY, p. v., Lenawee co., Mich., 61 ms. s. w. of Detroit ; from W. 513 ms. Pop. 633.

RIDGEWAY, p. o., Warren co., N. C., 57 ms. N. E. of Raleigh ; from W. 231 ms.

RIDGEWAY, p. o.. Iowa co., Wis., 35 ms. w. of Madison ; from W. 882 ms.

RIDGEWAY, p. o., Muskingum co., O.

RIDGEWAY, p. o., Fairfield district, S. C.

RIDGEWAY, c. h., p. v., seat of justice of Elk co., Pa.

RIDGEWOOD, p. o., Fairfield district, S. C.

RIDGLEY, p. o., Platte co.. Mo.

RIDLEY, p. t., Delaware co., Pa.

RIDOTT'S. p. o., Stephenson co., Ill.

RIEGELSVILLE, p. o., Bucks co.. Pa.

RIENZI, p. o., Tishamingo co., Miss., 233 ms. N. w. of Jackson ; from W. 838 ms.

RIFLE POINT, p. o., Concordia parish, La.

RIGA, p. t., Monroe co., N. Y., 241 ms. w. of Albany ; from W. 382 ms. Watered by Black creek. Pop. 2,159.

RIGA, p. o., Lucas co., O., 152 ms. N w. of Columbus from W. 483 ms.

RIGA, p. o., Lenawee co., Mich.

RIGG'S CROSS-ROADS, p. o., Williamson co., Tenn., 31 ms. s. of Nashville ; from W. 694 ms.

RILEY, t., Oxford co., Me.

RILEY, p. o., Clinton co., Mich.

RILEY, t., St. Clair co., Mich.

RILEY, p. o., Vigo co., Ind., 83 ms. s. w. of Indianapolis ; from W. 654 ms.

RILEY, t., Sandusky co., O. Pop. 682.

RILEY, t., Putnam co., O. Pop. 849.

RILEY, t., Pope co., Ark.

RILEY, p. o., McHenry co., Ill.

RILEY CENTRE, p. o., Riley township, Sandusky co., O.

RILEYVILLE, p. v.. Wayne co., Pa., 191 ms. N. E. of Harrisburgh ; from W. 285 ms.

RIMERSBURGH, p. o., Clarion co., Pa.

RINDGE, p. t., Cheshire co., N. H., 67 ms. s. w. of Concord ; from W. 435 ms. Watered by numerous ponds, tributaries of Connecticut and Merrimack rivers. Pop. 1,274.

RINGGOLD, p. o., Cook co., Ill.

RINGGOLD, p. o., Jefferson co., Pa.

RINGGOLD, p. o., Morgan co., O.

RINGGOLD, p. o., Walker co., Ga.

RINGGOLD, p. o., Cherokee co., Ala.

RINGGOLD, p. o., Washington co., Md.

RINGGOLD, p. o., Bienville parish, La.

RINGGOLD, p. o., Platte co., Mo.

RINGGOLD, p. o., Montgomery co., Tenn.

RINGGOLD, p. o., Pittsylvania co., Va.

RINGGOLD, p. o., La Grange co., Ind.

RINGOES, p. v., Amwell township, Hunterdon co., N. J., 19 ms. N. w. of Trenton ; from W. 176 ms.

RINGVILLE, p. o., Hampshire co., Mass.

RINGWOOD, p. o., Halifax co., N C

RINGWOOD, p. o., McHenry co., Ill.

RINOBA, p. o., Iroquois co., Ill.

RIO, p. o., Coweta co., Ga.

RIO, p. o., Vermilion co., Ill.

RIO FRIO, p. o., Scott co., Va.

RIO GRANDE, p. o., Gallia co., O.

RIO GRANDE CITY, p. o., Starr co., Tex.

RIPLEY COUNTY, situated in the southeast part of Indiana. Area, 400 square miles. Face of the country, elevated and even; soil, sandy. Seat of justice, Versailles. Pop. in 1820, 1,822 ; in 1830, 3,957 ; in 1840, 10.392 ; in 1850, 7,198.

RIPLEY COUNTY, situated on the south boundary of Missouri. Area, 1 080 square miles. Seat of justice, Doniphan. Pop. in 1840, 2,856 ; in 1850, 2,830.

RIPLEY, p. t., Somerset co., Me., 66 ms. N. of Augusta ; from W. 661 ms. Watered by head-waters of Sebasticook river. Pop. 641.

RIPLEY, c. h., p. v., seat of justice of Tippah co., Miss., 207 ms. N. E. of Jackson ; from W. 864 ms.

RIPLEY, p. t., Montgomery co., Ind. Pop. 1,250.

RIPLEY, p. t., Rush co., Ind. Pop. 1,908.

RIPLEY, p. v., Brown co., Ill.

RIPLEY, p. t., Chautauque co., N. Y., 350 ms. w. of Albany ; from W. 358 ms. Watered by Twenty-Mile creek and Lake Erie. Pop. 1,732.

RIPLEY, p. v., Union township, Brown co., O., 115 ms. s. w. of Columbus ; from W. 474 ms. Watered by Ohio river at the confluence of Red Oak creek.

RIPLEY, t., Holmes co., O. Pop. 1,330.

RIPLEY, t., Huron co., O. Pop. 1,230.

RIPLEY, c. h., p. v., seat of justice of Lauderdale co., Tenn., 175 ms. w. of Nashville ; from W. 857 ms. Watered by Cane creek.

RIPLEY'S, p. o., Tyler co., Va., 300 ms. N. w. of Richmond ; from W. 268 ms.

RIPLEY, p. o., Ripley township, Huron co., O., 89 ms. N. of Columbus ; from W. 388 ms.

RIPTON, p. t., Addison co., Vt., 51 ms. s. w. of Montpelier; from W. 489 ms. Watered by Middlebury river. Pop. 567.

RISDON, t., Hancock co., O.

RISDON. p. o., Seneca co., O., 93 ms. N. of Columbus; from W. 438 ms.

RISDON, p. v., St. Clair co., Ill., 121 ms. s. of Springfield; from W. 831 ms.

RISING FAWN, p. o., Dade co., Ga., 252 ms. N. w. of Milledgeville; from W. 640 ms.

RISING SUN. p. v., Philadelphia co., Pa., 101 ms. s. E. of Harrisburgh; from W. 141 ms.

RISING SUN, p. o., Cecil co., Md., 82 ms. N. E. of Annapolis; from W. 92 ms.

RISING SUN, p. o., Montgomery co., Ind.

RISING SUN, p. v., Ohio co., Ind., 95 ms. s. E. of Indianapolis; from W. 526 ms. Watered by Ohio river.

RITCHIE COUNTY, situated in the northwest part of Virginia. Area, —— square miles. Seat of justice, Ritchie c. h. Pop. in 1850, 3,902.

RITCHIE, c. h., p. v., seat of justice of Ritchie co., Va.

RITCHIEVILLE, p. v., Dinwiddie co., Va., 41 ms. s. of Richmond; from W. 160 ms.

RITTERSVILLE, p. o., Lehigh co., Pa., 91 ms. N. E. of Harrisburgh; from W. 184 ms.

RIVER, p. o., Clarion co., Pa., 204 ms. N. w. of Harrisburgh; from W. 270 ms.

RIVER HEAD. c. h., p. t., seat of justice of Suffolk co., Long Island, N. Y., 226 ms. s. E. of Albany; from W. 306 ms. Watered by Peconic river, Little Peconic bay, and Long Island sound. Pop. 2,540.

RIVER HILL, p. o., White co., Tenn.

RIVER ROAD FORKS, p. o., Mount Morris township, Livingston co., N. Y., 247 ms. w. of Albany; from W. 358 ms.

RIVERS, t., Jackson co., Mich. Pop. 518.

RIVER'S BRIDGE, p. o., Barnwell district, S. C.

RIVER SIDE, p. o., Ulster co., N. Y.

RIVER SIDE, p. o., Cumberland co., N. C.

RIVER STYX, p. o., Guilford township, Medina co., O., 125 ms. N. E. of Columbus; from W. 346 ms.

RIVER TOWN, p. v., Campbell co., Ga., 108 ms. N. W. of Milledgeville; from W. 705 ms.

RIVES, p. v., Richland co., O., 79 ms. N. E. of Columbus; from W. 380 ms.

RIVES, c. h., v., seat of justice of Henry co., Mo., 107 ms. w. of Jefferson city; from W. 1,043 ms.

RIVESVILLE, p. v., Marion co., Va., 282 ms. N. w. of Richmond; from W. 215 ms.

RIX, p. o., Ionia co., Ind.

RIXEYVILLE, p. v., Culpeper co., Va., 107 ms. N. w. of Richmond; from W. 67 ms.

RIX'S MILLS, p. o., Muskingum co., O.

ROAD HALL, p. o., Lycoming co., Pa., 83 ms. N. of Harrisburgh; from W. 193 ms.

ROADSTOWN, p. v., Cumberland co., N. J., 68 ms. s. of Trenton; from W. 179 ms.

ROADVILLE, p. v., Charleston district, S. C., 110 ms. s. E. of Columbia; from W. 548 ms.

ROANE COUNTY, situated in the easterly part of Tennessee, and traversed by Tennessee and Clinch rivers. Area, 600 square miles. Face of the country, broken; soil, thin and sterile. Seat of justice, Kingston. Pop. in 1820, 7,895; in 1830, 11,340; in 1840, 10,948; in 1850, 12,185.

ROAN MOUNTAIN, p. o., Carter co., Tenn.

ROANOKE COUNTY, situated toward the southwest part of Virginia, and traversed by Roanoke river. Area, 370 square miles. Face of the country, uneven and mountainous. Seat of justice, Salem, or Roanoke c. h. Pop. in 1840, 5,499; in 1850, 8,447.

ROANOKE, p. v., Stafford township, Genesee co., N. Y. Watered by Allen's creek.

ROANOKE, p. v., Randolph co., Ala.; from W. 765 ms.

ROANOKE, t, Randolph co., Ark.

ROANOKE, p. v., Randolph co., Mo., 75 ms. N. w. of Jefferson city; from W. 972 ms.

ROANOKE, p. o., Huntington co., Ind.

ROANOKE BRIDGE, p. o., Charlotte co., Va., 89 ms. s. w. of Richmond; from W. 180 ms.

ROAN'S CREEK, p. o., Carroll co., Tenn.

ROARING CREEK, p. o., Montour co., Pa.

ROARING SPRING, p. o., Trigg co., Ky.

ROARK, t., Gasconade co., Mo. Pop. 1,007.

ROBB, p. t., Posey co., Ind.

ROBBINSTON, p. t., Washington co., Me., 193 ms. N. E. of Augusta; from W. 779 ms. Watered by Schoodic or St. Croix rivers. Pop. 1,028.

ROBERSON'S CROSS ROADS, p. o., Bledsoe co., Tenn.

ROBERTS' CORNERS, p. o., Jefferson co., N. Y.

ROBERTSON COUNTY, situated on the north boundary of Tennessee. Area, 350 square miles. Seat of justice, Springfield. Pop. in 1810, 7,270; in 1820, 9,938; in 1830, 13,302; in 1840, 13,801; in 1850, 16,145.

ROBERTSON'S STORE, p. o., Pittsylvania co., Va., 155 ms. s. w. of Richmond; from W. 238 ms.

ROBERTSONVILLE, p. o., Sullivan co., N. Y.

ROBERTSVILLE, p. v., Anderson co., Tenn., 166 ms. E. of Nashville; from W. 523 ms.

ROBESON COUNTY, situated on the southwesterly boundary of North Carolina. Area, 700 square miles. Seat of justice, Lumberton. Pop. in 1810, 7,528; in 1820, 8,204; in 1830, 9,355; in 1840, 10,370; in 1850, 15,826.

ROBESON, p. t., Berks co., Pa. Watered by Schuylkill river, and Alleghany and Hay creeks.

ROBESON, p. o., Brunswick co., N. C.

ROBINA, p. o., Panola co., Miss.

ROBIN'S NEST, p. o., Peoria co., Ill., 84 ms. N. of Springfield; from W. 798 ms.

ROBINSON, t., Posey co., Ind. Pop. 1,619.

ROBINSON CREEK. p. o., Pike co., Ky.

ROBINSON, p. t., Washington co., Pa. Pop. 843.

ROBINSON, p. t., Alleghany co., Pa. Watered by Ohio river, Chartier's creek, and Montour's run. Pop. 1,917.

ROBINSON'S, c. h., p. v., seat of justice of Crawford co., Ill.

ROBINSON'S CROSS ROADS, p. o., Benton co., Ark.

ROBINSON'S MILLS, p. o., Menard co., Ill.

ROBINSON'S SPRING, p. o., Autauga co., Ala.

ROBINSON'S STORE, p. o., Lincoln co., Tenn.

ROBISON'S, p. o., Darke co., O.

ROBISONVILLE, p. o., Bedford co., Pa.

ROB ROY, p. v., Fountain co., Ind., 49 ms. N. w. of Indianapolis; from W. 954 ms.

ROB ROY, p. o., Jefferson co., Ark.

ROCHEPORT, p. v., Boone co., Mo., 49 ms. N. w. of Jefferson city; from W. 954 ms. Watered by Missouri river.

ROCHESTER, c. h., p. t., seat of justice, together with Dover, of Strafford co., N. H., 46 ms. E. of Concord; from W. 505 ms. Watered by Salmon Fall and Cocheco rivers. Pop. 3,006.

ROCHESTER, p. t., Windsor co., Vt., 43 ms. s. w. of Montpelier; from W. 482 ms. Watered by White river. Pop. 1,493.

ROCHESTER, p. t., Plymouth co., Mass., 54 ms. s. E. of Boston; from W. 441 ms. Watered by Buzzard's bay, and Mattapoiset and Sipican rivers. Pop. 3,808.

ROCHESTER, city, seat of justice of Monroe co., N. Y., situated on both sides of Genesee river, 7 miles from its entrance into Lake Ontario, 73 miles northeasterly from Buffalo, and 220 miles northwest of Albany. Three bridges, and the magnificent aqueduct of the Erie canal, span the river from the west to the east part of the city. The public buildings are generally substantial and imposing; but the most interesting structures are the flour-mills along the rapids and falls of Genesee river, which here descend 270 feet. Here the vast stores of wheat produced in the Genesee valley and the surrounding country, as well as the western states, are ground and prepared for market. To its vast water-power and the Erie canal, Rochester owes its prosperity and surprising growth. Thirty years ago, the site of the city was a marshy, unhealthy wilderness; now, it is populous with men, and active with industry. The population in 1820 was 1,502; in 1830, 9,269; in 1840, 20,191; in 1850, 36,403.

ROCHESTER, p. t., Ulster co., N. Y., 74 ms. s. of Albany; from W. 300 ms. Watered by Rondout creek.

ROCHESTER, p. v., Salem township, Warren co., O. 75 ms. s. w. of Columbus; from W. 460 ms. Watered by Little Miami river.

ROCHESTER, t., Lorain co., O. Pop. 896.

ROCHESTER, v., Beaver co., Pa. Watered by Beaver river at its confluence with the Ohio. Pop. 993.

ROCHESTER, p. o., Avon township, Oakland co., Mich., 128 ms. N. w. of Detroit; from W. 551 ms. Watered by Paint creek and Clinton river.

ROCHESTER, p. v., Racine co., Wis., 87 ms. s. E. of Madison; from W. 796 ms. Watered by Fox river.

ROCHESTER, c. h., p. t., seat of justice of Fulton co., Ind., 95 ms. N. of Indianapolis; from W. 616 ms. Watered by Tippecanoe river. Pop. 1,401.

ROCHESTER, p. v., Sangamon co., Ill., 10 ms. E. of Springfield; from W. 772 ms. Watered by Sangamon river at the confluence of its north and south forks.

ROCHESTER, p. o., Butler co., Ky.
ROCHESTER, p. o., Andrew co., Mo
ROCHESTER, p. o., Jackson parish, La.
ROCHESTER DEPOT, p. o., Lorain co., O.
ROCHESTER MILLS, p. o., Wabash co., Ill.
ROCK COUNTY, situated on the south boundary of Wisconsin, and traversed by Rock river. Area, —— square miles. Face of the country, even; soil, rich. Seat of justice, Janesville. Pop. in 1840, 1,701; in 1850, 20,708.
ROCK. p. o,. Plymouth co., Mass.
ROCK, p. o., Lancaster co., Pa.
ROCK, t., Jefferson co., Mo.
ROCKAWAY, p. v., Hempstead township, Queens co., Long Island, N. Y., 168 ms. s. of Albany; from W. 248 ms. Watered by Rockaway bay.
ROCKAWAY, p. v., Morris co., N. J., 61 ms. N. of Trenton; from W. 234 ms. Watered by Rockaway river. Pop. 3,139.
ROCK BOTTOM, p. o., Middlesex co., Mass., 27 ms. N. w. of Boston; from W. 420 ms.
ROCKBRIDGE COUNTY, situated in the central part of Virginia, and traversed by James river. Area, 680 square miles. Face of the country, agreeably diversified; soil, of middling quality. Seat of justice, Lexington. Pop. in 1810. 10,318; in 1820, 11,945; in 1830. 14,244; in 1840, 14.284; in 1850, 16,055.
ROCKBRIDGE, p. v., Gwinnett co., Ga., 87 ms. N. w. of Milledgeville; from W. 661 ms.
ROCKBRIDGE, p. o., Greene co., Ill.
ROCKBRIDGE, c. h., p. v., seat of justice of Ozark co., Mo.
ROCK CAMP, p. o., Braxton co., Va.
ROCK CASTLE COUNTY, situated toward the southeast part of Kentucky. Area, 330 square miles. Face of the country, elevated and even. Seat of justice, Mount Vernon. Pop. in 1810, 1,731; in 1820, 2,249; in 1830, 2,875; in 1840, 3,409; in 1850. 4,697.
ROCK CASTLE, p. v., Patrick co., Va., 230 ms. s. w. of Richmond; from W. 305 ms
ROCK CITY, p. o., Milan township, Dutchess co., N. Y., 59 ms. s. of Albany; from W. 310 ms.
ROCK CITY MILLS, p. o., Saratoga co., N. Y.
ROCK CREEK, p. o., Orange co., N. C., 67 ms. N. w. of Raleigh; from W. 300 ms.
ROCK CREEK, p. o., Lewis co., Ky., 125 ms. N. E. of Frankfort; from W. 450 ms.
ROCK CREEK, p. o., Cedar co., Iowa.
ROCK CREEK, p. t., Bartholomew co., Ind. Pop. 820.
ROCK CREEK, p. o., Carroll co., Ill.
ROCK CREEK, p. o., Somerset co., Md.
ROCK CREEK, p. o., Franklin co, Ala.
ROCK CREEK, p. o., Yell co., Ark.
ROCKDALE, p. t., Crawford co., Pa., 246 ms. N. w. of Harrisburgh; from W. 319 ms. Pop. 1,086.
ROCKDALE, p. o., Chenango co., N. Y.
ROCKDALE, p. o., Randolph co., Ala.
ROCKFORD, c. h., p. v., seat of justice of Surry co, N. C., 145 ms. w. of Raleigh; from W. 351 ms. Watered by Yadkin river.
ROCKFORD, c. h., p. v., seat of justice of Coosa co., Ala.; from W. 803 ms.
ROCKFORD, t., Caldwell co., Mo.
ROCKFORD, p. v., Jackson co., Ind., 60 ms. s. of Indianapolis; from W. 586 ms.
ROCKFORD, c. h., p. t., seat of justice of Winnebago co., Ill., 203 ms. N. of Springfield; from W. 804 ms. Situated on the Rock river rapids. Pop. 2.093.
ROCK GROVE, p. o., Stephenson co., Ill., 230 ms. N. of Springfield; from W. 834 ms.
ROCK HALL, p. v., Kent co., Md., 68 ms. N. E. of Annapolis; from W. 108 ms.
ROCK HAVEN, p. o, Mead co., Ky.
ROCK HILL, t., Bucks co., Pa., 111 ms. E. of Harrisburgh; from W. 173 ms. Watered by tributaries of Tohickon and Perkiomen creeks. Pop. 2,448.
ROCK HILL, p. o., St. Louis co., Mo.
ROCK HILL, p. o., Marquette co., Wis.
ROCKHOLDS, p. o., Whitley co., Ky., 118 ms. s. E. of Frankfort; from W. 550 ms.
ROCKHOLDS, p. o., Sullivan co., Tenn.
ROCK HOUSE, p. o., Sumner co., Tenn.
ROCK HOUSE, p. o., Hocking co., O.
ROCKHOUSE PRAIRIE, p. o., Buchanan co., Mo.
ROCKINGHAM COUNTY, situated at the southeast corner of New Hampshire, with the Atlantic ocean on the southeast, and Piscataqua river on the northeast. Area, 695 square miles. Face of the country, diversi-

fied; soil, productive. Seats of justice, Portsmouth and Exeter. Pop. in 1810, 50,175; in 1820, 55,226; in 1830, 44,325; in 1840. 45,771: in 1850, 48.184.
ROCKINGHAM COUNTY, situated toward the northeast part of Virginia, and traversed by Shenandoah river. Area, 833 square miles. Face of the country, hilly and mountainous; soil, of middling quality. Seat of justice, Harrisonburgh. Pop. in 1810, 12.753; in 1820, 14,784; in 1830, 20,683; in 1840, 17,344; in 1850, 20,294.
ROCKINGHAM COUNTY, situated on the north boundary of North Carolina, and traversed by Dan river. Area. 475 square miles. Seat of justice, Wentworth. Pop. in 1810, 10,316: in 1820, 11,474; in 1830, 12,935; in 1840, 13,442; in 1850, 14,495.
ROCKINGHAM, p. t., Windham co., Vt., 93 ms. s. of Montpelier: from W. 450 ms. Watered by Connecticut. Williams', and Saxton's rivers. Pop. 2,837.
ROCKINGHAM, c. h., p. v., seat of justice of Richmond co., N. C., 135 ms. s. w. of Raleigh; from W. 409 ms. Watered by Hitchcock's creek.
ROCK ISLAND COUNTY, situated on the northwesterly boundary of Illinois, on the Mississippi, and traversed by Rock river. Area, —— square miles. Seat of justice, Rock Island. Pop. in 1850, 6,937.
ROCK ISLAND, p. o., Warren co., Tenn., 88 ms. s. E. of Nashville; from W. 611 ms.
ROCK ISLAND, p. o., Austin co., Tex.
ROCK ISLAND, c. h., p. v., seat of justice of Rock Island co., Ill.
ROCKLAND COUNTY, situated in the southeastern part of New York, with the Hudson river for its eastern boundary. Area, 172 square miles. Face of the country, mountainous and much broken; soil, productive; iron ore and variegated marble abound. Seat of justice, Clarkstown. Pop. in 1830, 9,388; in 1840, 11,975; in 1850, 16,962.
ROCKLAND, p. t., Sullivan co., N. Y., 102 ms. s. w. of Albany; from W. 321 ms. Watered by Big Beaver Kill and tributaries. Pop. 1,175.
ROCKLAND, p. t., Venango co., Pa., 212 ms. N. w. of Harrisburgh; from W. 284 ms. Pop. 1,409.
ROCKLAND, t., Bucks co., Pa. Watered by Maxatawny and Sacony creeks. Pop. 1,734.
ROCKLAND, p. v., East Thomaston township, Lincoln co., Me., 46 ms. s. E. of Augusta; from W. 623 ms. Pop. 5,052.
ROCKLAND LAKE, p. o., Clarkstown township, Rockland co., N, Y, Situated near Rockland lake.
ROCKLAND MILLS, p. o., Augusta co., Va., 129 ms. N. w. of Richmond; from W. 148 ms.
ROCK MILLS, p. o., Rappahannock co., Va.
ROCK MILLS, p. o., Anderson district, S, C,. 171 ms. N. w. of Columbia; from W. 440 ms.
ROCK MILLS, p. o., Hancock co., Ga., 39 ms. N. E. of Milledgeville; from W. 640 ms.
ROCK MILLS, p. o., Randolph co., Ala.
ROCK POINT, p. o., Independence co., Ark.
ROCKPORT, p. t., Essex co., Mass., 32 ms, N. E. of Boston; from W. 464 ms. Watered by the Atlantic ocean. Pop. 3,274.
ROCKPORT, p. o., Carbon co., Pa.
ROCKPORT, p. t., Cuyahoga co., O., 132 ms. N. E. of Columbus; from W. 367 ms. Watered by Lake Erie and Rocky river. Pop. 1,441.
ROCKPORT, c. h., p. v., seat of justice of Spencer co., Ind., 162 ms s. w. of Indianapolis; from W. 689 ms. Watered by Ohio river.
ROCKPORT, p. o., Hot Springs co., Ark., 46 ms. s. w. of Little Rock; from W. 1,111 ms. Watered by Wachita river.
ROCKPORT, p. o., Pike co., Ill.
ROCK PRAIRIE, p. o., Rock co., Wis.
ROCK PRAIRIE, p. o., Dade co., Mo.
ROCK QUARRY, p. o., Pope co., Ill.
ROCK RIFT, p. o., Delaware co., N. Y.
ROCK RIVER, p. o., Fond du Lac co., Wis.
ROCK RUN, p. o., Stephenson co., Ill., 229 ms. N. of Springfield; from W. 827 ms.
ROCK RUN, p. o., Harford co., Md., 67 ms. N. E. of Annapolis; from W. 77 ms.
ROCKSBURGH, p. o., Warren co., N. J.
ROCKSFORD, p. o., Tuscarawas co., O.
ROCK SPRING, p. o., Walker co., Ga.
ROCK SPRING, p. o., Orange co., N. C.
ROCK SPRINGS, p. o., Cecil co., Md.
ROCK STREAM, p. o., Starkey township, Yates co., N. Y., 198 ms. w. of Albany; from W. 213 ms.

ROCKTON, p. o., Winnebago co., Ill.
ROCKTON, p. o., Herkimer co., N. Y.
ROCKY VALLEY, p. o., Marshall co., Va.
ROCK VALLEY, p. o., Hampden co., Mass.
ROCKVILLE, p. v., Norfolk co., Mass., 26 ms. s. of Boston; from W. 420 ms.
ROCKVILLE, p. o., Belfast township, Alleghany co., N. Y., 269 ms. w. of Albany; from W. 331 ms.
ROCKVILLE, p. v., Chester co., Pa., 58 ms. s. E. of Harrisburgh; from W. 133 ms.
ROCKVILLE, c. h., p. v., seat of justice of Montgomery co., Md., 56 ms. w. of Annapolis; from W. 16 ms. Watered by head waters of Watt's branch of Potomac river.
ROCKVILLE, p. v., Adams co., O., 112 ms. s. of Columbus; from W. 446 ms.
ROCKVILLE, p. v., Rowan co., N. C., 133 ms. w. of Raleigh; from W. 370 ms.
ROCKVILLE, p. v., Putnam co., Ga., 32 ms. N. of Milledgeville; from W. 638 ms.
ROCKVILLE, c. h., p. v., seat of justice of Parke co.. Ind., 64 ms. w. of Indianapolis; from W. 636 ms.
ROCKVILLE, p. v., Will co., Ill., 162 ms. N. E. of Springfield; from W. 716 ms. Pop. 514.
ROCKVILLE, p. v., Monroe co., Tenn., 164 ms. s. E. of Nashville; from W. 537 ms.
ROCKVILLE, p. o., Tolland co., Ct.
ROCKVILLE, p, o., Washington co., R. I.
ROCKVILLE, p. o., Delaware co., Iowa.
ROCKVILLE, p. o., Hanover co., Va.
·ROCKVILLE, p. o., Lexington district, S. C.
ROCKVILLE CENTRE, p. o., Queens co., Long Island, N. Y.
ROCKWELL, p. o., Pickens district, S. C.
ROCKWELL, p. o., Bond co., Ill.
ROCKY BAYOU, p. o., Izard co,, Ark.
ROCKY BRANCH, p. o., Greenup co., Ky.
ROCKY COMFORT, p. o., Sevier, co., Ark.
ROCKY CREEK, p. o., Iredell co., N. C.
ROCKY FORD, p. o., Pontotoc co., Miss.
ROCKY FORK, p. t., Boone co., Mo.
ROCKY GAP, p. o., Tazewell co., Va.
ROCKY HILL, p. t., Hartford co., Ct., 7 ms. s. of Hartford; from W. 333 ms. Watered by Connecticut river.
ROCKY HILL, p. v., Montgomery township, Somerset co., N. J., 14 ms. N. of Trenton; from W. 185 ms. Watered by Millstone river.
ROCKY HILL, p. o., Jackson co., O., 77 ms. s. of Columbus; from W. 381 ms.
ROCKY HILL, p. o., Barren co., Ky., 129 ms. s. w. of Frankfort; from W. 652 ms.
ROCKY HILL, p. o., Fayette co., Va.
ROCKY MILLS, p. o., La Vaca co., Tex.
ROCKY MOUNT, c. h., p. v., seat of justice of Franklin co., Va., 179 ms. w. of Richmond; from W. 254 ms. Watered by a tributary of Roanoke river.
ROCKY MOUNT, p. v., Edgecombe co., N. C., 56 ms. E. of Raleigh; from W. 242 ms.
ROCKY MOUNT, p. v., Meriwether co., Ga., 102 ms. w. of Milledgeville; from W. 721 ms.
ROCKY MOUNT, p. o., Miller co., Mo., 50 ms. s. w. of Jefferson city; from W. 985 ms.
ROCKY MOUNT, p. o., Kemper co., Miss., 115 ms. N. E. of Jackson; from W. 912 ms.
ROCKY MOUNT, p. o., Fairfield district, S. C.
ROCKY NARROWS, p. o., Monroe co., O., 127 ms. E. of Columbus; from W. 280 ms.
ROCKY PLAINS, p. o., Newton co., Ga.
ROCKY POINT, p. o., Scott co., Va.
ROCKY POINT, p. o., Attala co., Miss.
ROCKY RIDGE, p. o., Anderson district, S. C.
ROCKY RIVER, p. o., Warren co,. Tenn.
ROCKY RUN, p. o,, Hancock co., Ill.
ROCKY RUN, p. o, Columbia co., Wis.
ROCKY SPRING, p. o., Jackson co., Ala.; from W. 645 ms.
ROCKY SPRING, p. o., Grainger co., Tenn., 229 ms. E. of Nashville; from W .453 ms.
ROCKY SPRING, p. v., Claiborne co., Miss., 45 ms. N. w. of Jackson; from W. 1,055 ms.
ROCKY WELL, p. o., Lexington district, S. C.
RODMAN, p. t., Jefferson co., N. Y., 163 ms. N. w. of Albany; from W. 408 ms. Watered by Sandy creek. Pop. 1,784.
RODNEY, p. v., Jefferson co., Miss., 92 ms. s. w. of Jackson; from W 1,192 ms. Watered by Mississippi river. Pop. 210.

RODNEY, p. o., Gallia co., O.
ROESFIELD, p. o., Catahoola parish, La.
ROGER'S BRIDGE, p. o., Spartanburgh district, S. C.
ROGER'S FARM, p. o., McLean co., Ill.
ROGERS' STORE, p. o., Wake co., N. C., 16 ms. from Raleigh; from W. 288 ms.
ROGERSVILLE, p. o., Lauderdale co., Ala.
ROGERSVILLE, c. h., p. v., seat of justice of Hawkins co., Tenn., 246 ms. E. of Nashville; from W. 436 ms.
ROGERSVILLE, p. o., Tuscarawas co., O.
ROGERSVILLE, p. o., Halifax co., Va.
ROGERSVILLE, p. o., Madison co., Ky.
ROGERSVILLE, p. o., Henry co., Ind.
ROGERSVILLE, p. o., Greene co., Pa.
ROHRERSVILLE, p. v., Washington co., Md.
ROHRSBURGH, p. v., Columbia co., Pa., 93 ms. N. E. of Harrisburgh; from W. 204 ms.
ROKEBY, p. o., Morgan co., O., 74 ms. E. of Columbus; from W. 337 ms.
ROLAND, p. o., Muscogee co., Ga.
ROLESVILLE, p. v., Wake co., N. C., 21 ms. N. E. of Raleigh; from W. 279 ms.
ROLLERSVILLE, p. v., Sandusky co., O., 42 ms. N of Columbus; from W. 437 ms.
ROLLIN, p. t., Lenawee co., Mich., 79 ms. s. w. of Detroit; from W. 519 ms. Watered by Tiffin's and Bean creeks.
ROLLING FORK, p. o., Nelson co., Ky., 77 ms. s. w. of Frankfort; from W. 599 ms.
ROLLING PRAIRIE, p. o., Marion co., Ark.
ROLLINS' STORE, p. o., Moore co., N. C.
ROMA, p. o., Starr co., Tex.
ROME, p. t., Kennebec co., Me., 20 ms. N. w. of Augusta; from W. 613 ms. Watered by tributaries of Kennebec river. Pop. 830.
ROME, c. h., p. t., seat of justice, together with Utica, of Oneida co., N. Y., 107 ms. N. w. of Albany; from W. 391 ms. Watered by Mohawk river, Wood creek, and Black river, and Erie canals. Pop. in 1830, 4,360; in 1840, 5,680; in 1850, 7,918.
ROME, p. t., Bradford co., Pa., 142 ms. N. of Harrisburgh; from W. 252 ms. Pop. 1,308.
ROME, t., Crawford co., Pa. Pop. 940.
ROME, c. h., p. v., seat of justice of Floyd co., Ga., 161 ms. N. w. of Milledgeville; from W. 672 ms. Watered by Etowah and Oostanaula rivers.
ROME, p. v., Smith co., Tenn., 45 ms. N. E. of Nashville; from W. 639 ms. Watered by Tennessee river.
ROME, p. t., Ashtabula co., O., 190 ms. N. E. of Columbus; from W. 330 ms. Pop. 744.
ROME, t., Athens co., O. Pop. 1,309.
ROME, t., Lawrence co., O.
ROME, p. v., Lenawee co. Mich., 70 ms. s. w. of Detroit; from W. 510 ms. Watered by head waters of Beaver creek. Pop. 1,525.
ROME, p. v., Perry co., Ind., 143 ms. s. of Indianapolis; from W. 653 ms. Watered by Ohio river.
ROME, v., Peoria co., Ill., 85 ms. N. of Springfield; from W. 799 ms. Watered by Peoria lake.
ROME, p. t., Jones co., Iowa. Pop. 584.
ROME, p. o., Clarke co., Ark.
ROME, p. o., Jefferson co., Wis.
ROME, p. o., Marion co., Oregon.
ROME, p. o., Tallapoosa co., Ala.
ROMEO, p. o., Greene co., Tenn., 250 ms. E. of Nashville; from W. 436 ms.
ROMEO, p. v., Washington township, Macomb co, Mich., 70 ms. N. of Detroit; from W. 510 ms.
ROMEO, p. o., McHenry co., Ill.
ROMINE's MILLS, p. o., Harrison co., Va., 243 ms. N. w. of Richmond; from W. 231 ms.
ROMNEY, c. h., p. v., seat of justice of Hampshire co., Va., 188 ms. N. w. of Richmond; from W. 116 ms. Watered by south branch of Potomac river.
ROMNEY, p. o., Tippecanoe co., Ind.
ROMULUS, p. t., Seneca co., N. Y., 183 ms. w. of Albany; from W. 329 ms. Watered by Cayuga and Seneca lakes. Pop. 2,040.
ROMULUS, p. t., Wayne co., Mich., 36 ms. s. w. of Detroit; from W. 516 ms. Pop. 621.
ROMULUS, p. o., Tuscaloosa co., Ala.; from W. 830 ms.
RONALD, p. o., Ionia co., Mich.
RONDOUT, p. v., Kingston township, Ulster co., N. Y., 59 ms. s. of Albany; from 314 ms. Watered by Rondout creek at the terminus of the Delaware and Hudson canal.
ROOK's CREEK, p. o., Livingston co., Ill.
ROOT, p. t., Montgomery co., N. Y., 43 ms. w. of Al-

bany ; from W. 402 ms. Watered by Mohawk river and tributaries. Pop. 2,736.

ROOT, p. t., Adams co., Ind. Pop. 1,099.

ROOT CREEK, p. o., Milwaukee co., Wis.

ROOTSTOWN, p. t., Portage co., O., 144 ms. N. E. of Columbus ; from W. 320 ms. Pop. 1,308.

ROSCOE, p. v., Coshocton co., O., 84 ms. E. N. E. of Columbus ; from W. 338 ms. Watered by Muskingum river at the confluence of Wahonding and Tuscarawas rivers, and situated on the Ohio canal.

ROSCOE, p. v., Henry co., Mo., 130 ms. w. of Jefferson city ; from W. 1,076 ms.

ROSCOE, p. v., Winnebago co., Ill., 216 ms. N. of Springfield ; from W. 817 ms. Pop. 1,050.

ROSCOE, p. o., Todd co., Ky.

ROSE, p. t., Wayne co., N. Y., 179 ms. w. of Albany ; from W. 359 ms. Pop. 2,264.

ROSE, t., Jefferson co., Pa.

ROSE, p. t., Carroll co., O., 128 ms. N. E. of Columbus ; from W. 308 ms. Pop. 1,537.

ROSE, p. t., Oakland co., Mich., 49 ms. N. w. of Detroit; from W. 571 ms. Pop. 886.

ROSEBOOM. p. o., Otsego co., N. Y., 59 ms. w. of Albany ; from W. 384 ms.

ROSEBOROUGH, p. o., Laurens district, S. C.

ROSEBURGH, p. v., Perry co., Pa., 38 ms. w. of Harrisburgh ; from W. 126 ms.

ᐟ ROSE CREEK, p. o., McNairy co., Tenn., 158 ms. s. w. of Nashville ; from W. 834 ms.

ROSEDALE, p. v., Madison co., O., 30 ms. w. of Columbus ; from W. 425 ms.

ROSE GROVE, p. o., Appomattox co., Va.

ROSE HILL, p. o., Seneca co., N. Y.

ROSE HILL, p. o., Mecklenburg co., N. C.

ROSE HILL, p. o., Jasper co., Ill.

ROSE HILL, p. o., Robertson co., Tenn.

ROSE HILL, p. o., Lee co., Va., 402 ms. w. of Richmond ; from W. 470 ms.

ROSE HILL. p. o., Amite co., Miss., 112 ms. s. of Jackson ; from W. 1,112 ms.

ROSE HILL, p. o., Mahaska co., Iowa.

ROSELAND, p. o., Cambria co., Pa., 126 ms. w. of Harrisburgh ; from W. 208 ms.

ROSELAND, p. o., Nelson co., Va., 114 ms. w. of Richmond ; from W. 166 ms.

ROSE MILLS, p. o., Amherst co., Va.

ROSENDALE, p. t., Hurley township, Ulster co., N. Y., 65 ms. s. of Albany ; from W. 315 ms. Watered by Rondout creek. Pop. 2,418.

ROSENDALE, p. o., Fond du Lac co., Wis.

ROSE TREE, p. o., Delaware co., Pa.

ROSEVILLE, p. v., Parke co., Ind., 74 ms. w. of Indianapolis ; from W. 646 ms. Watered by Big Raccoon creek.

ROSEVILLE, p. v., Bush creek township, Muskingum co., O., 65 ms. E. of Columbus ; from W. 349 ms. Watered by south fork of Jonathan's creek.

ROSEVILLE, p. o., Macomb co., Mich., 7 ms. N. E. of Detroit ; from W. 531 ms.

ROSEVILLE, p. o., Franklin co., Ark.

ROSICLARE, p. o., Hardin co., Ill.

ROSLIN, p. o., Marquette co., Wis.

ROSLYN. p. v., Queens co., Long Island, N. Y.

ROSS COUNTY, situated toward the south part of Ohio, and traversed by Scioto river. Area, 650 square miles. Face of the country, diversified with meadow and uplands ; soil, fertile. Seat of justice, Chillicothe. Pop. in 1810, 15.514 ; in 1820, 20,619 ; in 1830, 24,068 ; in 1840, 27,460 ; in 1850, 32,071.

ROSS, t., Monroe co., Pa. Pop. 1,373.

ROSS, t., Alleghany co., Pa. Watered by Alleghany and Ohio rivers and Pine creek. Pop. 1.442.

ROSS, t., Kalamazoo co., Mich. Pop. 680.

ROSS, p. t. Butler co., O.. 110 ms. s. w. of Columbus ; from W. 498 ms. Pop. 1,648.

ROSS, t., Greene co., O. Pop. 1,367.

ROSS, t., Jefferson co., O. Watered by Big Yellow creek. Pop. 1,144.

ROSS, p. o., Anderson co., Tenn., 82 ms. E. of Nashville ; from W. 521 ms.

ROSSBURGH, p. v., Decatur co., Ind.

ROSS CORNER. p. o., York co., Me., 85 ms. s. w. of Augusta ; from W. 527 ms.

ROSSEAU. p. o., Morgan co., O., 79 ms. E. of Columbus ; from W. 338 ms.

ROSS' FERRY, p. o., Livingston co., Ky.

ROSS' GROVE, p. o., De Kalb co., Ill.

ROSSIE, p. t., St. Lawrence co., N. Y., 183 ms. N. w.

of Albany ; from W. 452 ms. Watered by Oswegatchie and Indian rivers. Pop. 1,471.

ROSSTOWN, p. o., Shelby co., Tenn.

ROSSVILLE, p. v., Walker co., Ga., 221 ms. N. w. of Milledgeville ; from W. 615 ms.

ROSSVILLE, p. v., Westfield township, Richmond co. Staten Island, N. Y., 163 ms. s. of Albany ; from W. 241 ms. Watered by Staten Island sound.

ROSSVILLE, p. v., York co., Pa., 24 ms. s. of Harrisburgh ; from W. 103 ms.

ROSSVILLE, p. v., Baltimore co., Md.

ROSSVILLE, p. t., Butler co., O., 102 ms. s. w. of Columbus ; from W. 490 ms. Pop. 1,452.

ROSSVILLE, t., Muskingum co., O.

ROSSVILLE, p. v., Clinton co., Ind., 164 ms. N. of Indianapolis ; from W. 548 ms.

ROSSVILLE, p. o., Chester district, S. C.

ROSTRAVER, p. t., Westmoreland co., Pa., 191 ms. w. of Harrisburgh ; from W. 217 ms. Watered by Youghiogheny and Monongahela rivers. Pop. 2.087.

ROSWELL, p. o., Cobb co., Ga.

ROTHERWOOD, p. o., Carroll co., Ga., 119 ms. w. of Milledgeville ; from W. 726 ms.

ROTTERDAM, p. t., Schenectady co., N. Y., 22 ms. N. w. of Albany; from W. 390 ms. Watered by Mohawk river. Pop. 2,447.

ROUBIDOUX, p. o., Texas co., Mo.

ROUGH CREEK, p. o., Charlotte co., Va.

ROUGH CREEK, p. o., Grayson co., Ky., 107 ms. s. w. of Richmond ; from W. 194 ms.

ROUGH AND READY, p. o., Schuylkill co., Pa.

ROUGH AND READY, p. o., Anderson co., Ky.

ROUGH AND READY, p. o., Hancock co., Ill.

ROUGH AND READY, p. o., Chambers co., Ala.

ROUGH AND READY, p. o., Fayette co., Ga.

ROUGH AND READY, p. o., Steuben co., N. Y.

ROUGH AND READY, p. o., Monroe co., Ark.

ROUGH AND READY, p. o., Warren co., Tenn.

ROUGH AND READY, p. o., Nevada co., Cal.

ROUGH AND READY MILLS, p. o., Henry co., Va.

ROULETTE, p. t., Potter co., Pa., 179 ms. N. w. of Harrisburgh ; from W. 289 ms. Pop. 222.

ROUND BOTTOM, p. o., Izard co., Ark.

ROUND GROVE, p. t., Marion co., Mo. Pop. 1,107.

ROUND GROVE, p. o., Carroll co., Mo., 137 ms. N. w. of Jefferson city ; from W. 1,031 ms.

ROUND HEAD, p. t., Hardin co., O., 89 ms. N. w. of Columbus ; from W. 476 ms. Watered by head-waters of Scioto river Pop 665.

ROUND HILL, p. v., Greenwich township, Fairfield co., Ct., 85 ms. s. w. of Hartford ; from W. 261 ms.

ROUND HILL, p. o., Orange co., N. C., 34 ms. N. w. of Raleigh ; from W. 270 ms.

ROUND HILL, p. o., Lumpkin co., Ga.

ROUND HILL, p. o., Cooper co., Mo., 40 ms. w. of Jefferson city ; from W. 976 ms.

ROUND POND, p. o., Wayne co., Miss.

ROUND PRAIRIE, p. o., Dallas co., Mo.

ROUND PRAIRIE, p. t., Callaway co., Mo.

ROUND TOP, p. o., Fayette co., Tex.

ROUNSVILLE, p. o., Alleghany co., N. Y.

ROUSE'S POINT, p. v., Champlain township, Clinton co., N. Y., 185 ms. N. of Albany ; from W. 560 ms. Watered by Lake Champlain.

ROUTH'S POINT, p. o., Concordia parish, La.

ROVER, p. o., Bedford co., Tenn.

ROWAN COUNTY, situated in the central part of North Carolina, with Yadkin river on the northeast Area, 375 square miles. Seat of justice, Salisbury. Pop. in 1810, 21,543 ; in 1820, 26,009 ; in 1830, 20,786 ; in 1840, 12.109 ; in 1850, 13,870.

ROWE, p. t., Franklin co., Mass., 130 ms. N. w. of Boston ; from W. 420 ms. Watered by Pelham brook. Pop. 659.

ROWENA, p. o., Russell co., Ky.

ROWESVILLE, p. v., Bedford co., Tenn., 68 ms. s. of Nashville ; from W. 691 ms.

ROW's, p. o., Ashland co., O., 89 ms. N. E. of Columbus ; from W. 358 ms.

ROWLAND, t., Hillsdale co., Mich.

ROWLANDSVILLE, p. v., Cecil co., Md., 73 ms. N. E. of Annapolis ; from W. 83 ms.

ROWLANDSVILLE, p. o., Stanly co., N. C.

ROWLEY, p. t., Essex co., Mass., 30 ms. N. of Boston, from W. 470 ms. Watered by Rowley river. Pop. 1,075.

ROXANA, p. o., Eaton co., Mich.

ROXBOROUGH, p. t., Philadelphia co., Pa. Watered by Schuylkill river. Pop. 2,660.

ROXBOROUGH, c. h., p. v., seat of justice of Person co., N. C., 54 ms. N. W. of Raleigh ; from W. 250.

ROXBURY, p. t., Cheshire co., N. H., 49 ms. s. w. of Concord ; from W. 439 ms. Watered by tributaries of Ashuelot river. Pop. 260.

ROXBURY, p. t., Washington co., Vt., 16 ms. s. of Montpelier ; from W. 500 ms. Watered by tributaries of Onion and White rivers. Pop. 967.

ROXBURY, city, Norfolk co., Mass., 2 ms. s. w. of Boston, of which it is a suburb ; from W. 438 ms. Pop. in 1830, 5,249 ; in 1840, 9,089 ; in 1850, 18,364.

ROXBURY, p. t., Litchfield co., Ct., 53 ms. s. w. of Hartford ; from W. 314 ms. Watered by Shepaug river. Pop. 1,114.

ROXBURY, p. t., Delaware co., N. Y., 65 ms. s. w. of Albany ; from W. 352 ms. Watered by Papacton branch of Delaware river. Pop. 2,853.

ROXBURY, t., Morris co., N. J. Watered by Budd's pond and Black river. Pop. 2,269.

ROXBURY, p. v., Lurgan township, Franklin co., Pa., 47 ms. w. of Harrisburgh ; from W. 103 ms. Watered by Conedogwinit creek.

ROXBURY, p. o., Oxford co., Me.

ROXBURY, p. t., Washington co., O. Pop. 1,373.

ROXO, p. o., Marquette co., Wis.

ROXOBEL. p. o., Bertie co., N. C.

ROYAL CENTRE, p. o., Cass co., Ind.

ROYAL OAK, p. o., Talbot co., Md., 53 ms. E. of Annapolis ; from W. 93 ms.

ROYAL OAK, p t., Oakland co., Mich., 14 ms. N. of Detroit ; from W. 538 ms. Watered by Red river. Pop. 1,092.

ROYAL OAKS. p. o., Cumberland co., Va.

ROYALSTON, p. t., Worcester co., Mass., 74 ms. w. of Boston ; from W. 416 ms. Watered by Miller's river and tributaries. Pop. 1,546.

ROYALTON, p. t., Windsor co., Vt., 33 ms. s. of Montpelier ; from W. 488 ms. Watered by White river. Pop. 1,850.

ROYALTON, p. t., Niagara co., N. Y., 271 ms. w. of Albany ; from W. 394 ms Watered by Tonawanda creek and the Erie canal. Pop. 4,024.

ROYALTON, p. t., Cuyahoga co., O., 126 ms. N. E. of Columbus ; from W. — ms.

ROYALTON, p. t., Lucas co., O.

ROYALTON, p. v., Amanda township, Fairfield co., O., 40 ms. s. E. of Columbus ; from W. 385 ms.

ROYALTON, t., Berrien co., Mich., 198 ms. w. of Detroit ; from W. 640 ms.

ROYALTON, p. v., Boone co., Ind., 14 ms. N. w. of Indianapolis ; from W. 585 ms.

ROYALTON CENTRE, p. o., Royalton township, Niagara co., N. Y., 271 ms. w. of Albany ; from W. 396 ms.

ROYER'S FORD, p. o., Montgomery co., Pa.

ROYTON, p. o., Delaware co., Ind.

ROZELL'S FERRY, Mecklenburgh co., N. C.

RUARK, p. o., Lawrence co.. Ill. 171 ms. s. E. of Springfield ; from W. 709 ms.

RUCKERSVILLE, p. v., Greene co., Va.

RUCKERSVILLE. p. v., Elbert co., Ga., 118 ms. N. E. of Milledgeville ; from W. 561 ms. Watered by Van's creek.

RUCKERSVILLE, p. o., Greene co., Va.

RUCKERVILLE, p. o., Clarke co., Ky.

RUCKMANVILLE, p. o., Highland co., Va., 173 ms. N. w. of Richmond ; from W. 193 ms.

RUDDLE, t., Independence co., Ark.

RUDDLE'S MILLS, p. o., Bourbon co., Ky., 42 ms. E. of Frankfort ; from W. 513 ms.

RUDE'S MILLS, p. o., Lewis co., Va.

RUGGLES, p. t., Ashland co., O.. 91 ms. N. of Columbus ; from W. 380 ms. Pop. 1,168.

RUMA, p. o., Randolph co., Ill.

RUMFORD, p. t., Oxford co., Me., 52 ms. N. w. of Augusta ; from W. 614 ms. Watered by Androscoggin river. Pop. 1,375.

RUMFORD CENTRE, p. o., Rumford township, Oxford co., Me.

RUMFORD POINT, p. o., Oxford co., Me.

RUMMERFIELD CREEK, p. o., Wysox township, Bradford co., Pa., 143 ms. N. of Harrisburgh ; from W. 253 ms.

RUMLEY, p. t., Harrison co., O. Pop. 1,088.

RUMNEY, p. t., Grafton co., N. H., 47 ms. N. of Concord ; from W. 525 ms. Watered by Baker's river and tributaries. Pop. 1,109.

RUMSEY, p. v., Muhlenburgh co., Ky., 82 ms. s. w. of Frankfort ; from W. 714 ms.

RUNDELL'S, p. o., Crawford co., Pa.

RUNDLE, t., Cape Girardeau co., Mo.

RUPERT, p. t, Bennington co., Vt., 94 ms. s. w. of Montpelier ; from W. 424 ms. Watered by Pawlet river. Pop. 1,001.

RURAL, p. o., Clermont co., O.

RURAL, p. o., Jasper co., Mo.

RURAL HILL, p. o., Wilson co., Tenn., 16 ms. E. of Nashville ; from W. 668 ms.

RURAL HILL, p. o., Jefferson co., N. Y.

RURAL HILL, p. o., Conecuh co., Ala.

RURAL RETREAT, p. o., Wythe co., Va., 257 ms. w. of Richmond ; from W. 325 ms.

RURAL VALE, p. o., Lapeer co., Mich.

RURAL VALLEY, p. o., Armstrong co., Pa., 190 ms. N. w. of Harrisburgh ; from W. 224 ms.

RUSCUMB MANOR, t., Berks co., Pa. Watered by Maiden creek.

RUSH COUNTY, situated toward the east part of Indiana. Area, 400 square miles. Face of the country, undulating ; soil, moderately productive. Seat of justice, Rushville. Pop. in 1830, 9,707 ; in 1840, 16,454 ; in 1850, 16,466.

RUSH, p. t., Monroe co., N. Y., 218 ms. w. of Albany ; from W. 363 ms. Watered by Honeoye creek and Genesee river. Pop. 2,015.

RUSH, t., Centre co., Pa. Pop. 371.

RUSH, p. t., Susquehanna co., Pa. Watered by Wyalusing lake and Deer Lick creeks. Pop. 1,159.

RUSH, t., Northumberland co., Pa. Pop. 1,178.

RUSH, p. t., Dauphin co., Pa., 20 ms. N. E. of Harrisburgh ; from W. — ms.

RUSH, t., Schuylkill co., Pa.

RUSH, p. t., Tuscarawas co., O., 108 ms. N. E. of Columbus ; from W. 307 ms.

RUSH, t., Champaign co., O.

RUSH, p. o., Shiawassee co., Mich.

RUSH, p. o., Jo-Daviess co., Ill.

RUSH BOTTOM, p. o., Holt co., Mo.

RUSH CREEK, p. t., Fairfield co., O. Pop. 1,218.

RUSH CREEK, p. t., Logan co., O. Pop. 1,458.

RUSH CREEK, p. o., Union co, O.

RUSHFORD, p. t., Alleghany co., N. Y., 272 ms. w. of Albany ; from W. 331 ms. Watered by Cold creek. Pop. 1,816.

RUSHING CREEK, p. o., Benton co., Tenn.

RUSH LAKE, p. o., Fond du Lac co., Wis.

RUSH TOWER, p. o., Jefferson co., Mo.

RUSHTOWN, p. o., Northumberland co., Pa.

RUSHVILLE, p. v., Ontario co., N. Y., 205 ms. w. of Albany ; from W. 331 ms. Watered by West river.

RUSHVILLE, p. v., Rush township, Susquehanna co., Pa., 159 ms. N. E. of Harrisburgh ; from W. 269 ms.

RUSHVILLE, p. v., Richland township, Fairfield co., O., 39 ms. s. E. of Columbus ; from W. 366 ms.

RUSHVILLE, c. h., p. v., seat of justice of Rush co., Ind., 40 ms. s. E. of Indianapolis ; from W. 538 ms. Watered by Big Flat Rock creek.

RUSHVILLE, c. h., p v., seat of justice of Schuyler co., Ill., 60 ms. N. w. of Springfield ; from W. 838 ms. Pop. 2,609,

RUSHSYLVANIA, p. o., Logan co., O., 78 ms. N. w. of Columbus ; from W. 452 ms.

RUSK COUNTY, situated in the east part of Texas, with Sabine river on the north. Area, — square miles. Seat of justice, Henderson. Pop. in 1850, 8,148.

RUSK, p. o., Haywood co , Tenn.

RUSK, p. o., Cherokee co., Tex.

RUSK, p. o., Surry co., N. C.

RUSSELL COUNTY, situated in the southwest part of Virginia, and traversed by Clinch river. Area, 1,370 square miles. Face of the country, broken and mountainous ; soil, rocky and barren. Seat of justice, Lebanon. Pop. in 1810, 6,316 ; in 1820, 5,536 ; in 1830, 6,714 ; in 1840, 7,878 ; in 1850, 11,929.

RUSSELL COUNTY, situated on the east boundary of Alabama, with Chattahoochee river on the east. Area, 865 square miles. Seat of justice, Crawford. Pop. in 1840. 13,513 ; in 1850, 19,548.

RUSSELL COUNTY, situated in the south part of Kentucky, and traversed by Cumberland river. Area, 260 square miles. Seat of justice, Jamestown. Pop. in 1830, 3,879 ; in 1840, 4,238 ; in 1850, 5,349.

RUSSELL, p. t., Hampden co., Mass., 108 ms. w. of Boston ; from W. 392 ms. Watered by Westfield river.

RUSSELL, p. t., St. Lawrence co., N. Y., 192 ms. N. w. of Albany ; from W. 476 ms. Watered by West Canada creek. Pop. 1,808.

RUSSELL, p. t., Geauga co., O., 154 ms. N. E. of Columbus; from W. 340 ms. Pop. 1,083.

RUSSELL, p. t., Putnam co., Ind.

RUSSELL, p o., Atchison co., Mo.

RUSSELL HILL, p. o., Wyoming co., Pa., 160 ms. N. E. of Harrisburgh; from W. 265 ms.

RUSSELL PLACE, p. o., Kershaw district, S. C. 63 ms. N. E. of Columbia; from W. 474 ms.

RUSSELL'S CORNERS, p. o., Sauk co., Wis.

RUSSELL'S MILLS, p. o., Tyler co., Va.

RUSSELL'S MILLS, p. o., Parke co., Ind.

RUSSELL'S PLACE, p. o., Lawrence co., O.

RUSSELLSVILLE, c. h., p. v., seat of justice of Franklin co., Ala.; from W. 796 ms. Watered by Cedar creek.

RUSSELLVILLE, p. v., Chester co., Pa., 65 ms. S. E. of Harrisburgh; from W. 102 ms.

RUSSELLVILLE, p. v., Byrd township, Brown co., O., 103 ms. s. w. of Columbus: from W. 459 ms.

RUSSELLVILLE, p. v., Putnam co., Ind., 50 ms. w. of Indianapolis; from W. 621 ms.

RUSSELLVILLE, p. v., Lawrence co., Ill., 170 ms. S. E. of Springfield; from W. 698 ms. Watered by Wabash river.

RUSSELLVILLE, p. o., Monroe co., Ga.

RUSSELLVILLE, c. h., p. v., seat of justice of Logan co., Ky., 172 ms. s. w. of Frankfort; from W. 606 ms. Pop. 1,272.

RUSSELLVILLE, p. o., Cole co., Mo.

RUSSELLVILLE, p. o., Jefferson co., Tenn.

RUSSELSBURGH, p. v., Pine Grove township, Warren co., Pa., 212 ms. N. w. of Harrisburgh; from W. 304 ms. Watered by Conewango creek.

RUSSIA, p. t., Herkimer co., N. Y., 93 ms. N. w. of Albany; from W. 408 ms. Watered by West Canada creek. Pop. 2,349.

RUSSIA, p. t., Lorain co., O. Pop. 2,061.

RUSSIAVILLE, p. o., Clinton co., Ind.

RUTERSVILLE, p. o., Fayette co., Tex.

RUTHERFORD COUNTY, situated on the south boundary of North Carolina. Area, 1,025 square miles. Face of the country, hilly and mountainous; soil, generally poor. Seat of justice, Rutherfordtown. Pop. in 1810, 13,202; in 1820, 15,351; in 1830, 17,557; in 1840, 19,202; in 1850, 13,550.

RUTHERFORD COUNTY, situated in the central part of Tennessee. Area, 540 square miles. Seat of justice, Murfreesborough. Pop. in 1810, 10,265; in 1820, 19,552; in 1830, 26,133; in 1840, 24,280; in 1850, 29,122.

RUTHERFORDTOWN, c. h., p. v., seat of justice of Rutherford co., N. C., 216 ms. w. of Raleigh; from W. 453 ms. Watered by a tributary of Broad river.

RUTHER GLENN, p. o., Caroline co., Va., 37 ms. N. of Richmond; from W. 97 ms.

RUTLAND COUNTY, situated on the west boundary of Vermont, with Lake Champlain on the west. Area, 958 square miles. Face of the country diversified with plains, hills, and mountains; soil, productive. Seat of justice, Rutland. Pop. in 1810, 29,486; in 1820, 29,983; in 1830, 31,295; in 1840, 30,699; in 1850, 33,059.

RUTLAND, c. h., p. t., seat of justice of Rutland co.. Vt., 62 ms. s. w. of Montpelier; from W. 456 ms. Watered by Otter creek. Pop. 3,715.

RUTLAND, p. t., Worcester co., Mass., 55 ms. w. of Boston; from W. 412 ms. Watered by a tributary of Ware river. Pop. 1,223.

RUTLAND, p. t., Jefferson co. N. Y., 158 ms. N. w. of Albany; from W. — ms. Watered by Sandy creek and Black river. Pop. 2,265.

Rutland, p. t., Tioga co., Pa., 151 ms. N. of Harrisburgh; from W. 261 ms. Pop. 1,006.

RUTLAND, p. t., Meigs co., O., 92 ms. s. E. of Columbus; from W. 347 ms. Pop. 1,748.

RUTLAND, p. o., Dane co., Wis.

RUTLEDGE, v.. Conewango township, Cattaraugus co., N. Y.

RUTLEDGE, c. h., p. v., seat of justice of Grainger co., Tenn., 216 ms. E. of Nashville; from W. 466 ms.

RUTLEDGE, c. h., p. v., seat of justice of McDonald co., Mo.

RYAN'S MILLS, p. o., Washington co., Ky.

RYAN'S STORE, p. o., Montgomery co., Tenn.

RYAN'S WELL, p. o., Itawamba co., Miss.

RYE, p. t., Rockingham co. N. H., 42 ms. s. E. of Concord; from W. 479 ms. Watered by the Atlantic ocean. Pop. 1,295.

RYE, p. t., Westchester co., N. Y., 146 ms. s. of Albany; from W. 251 ms. Watered by Byram river. Pop. 2,584.

RYE, t., Perry co., Pa.

RYE COVE, p. o., Scott co., Va.

RYEGATE, p. t., Caledonia co., Vt., 43 ms. E. of Montpelier; from W. 529 ms. Watered by Connecticut and Wells rivers. Pop. 1,606.

RYERSON'S STATION, p. o., Greene co., Pa., 231 ms. w. of Harrisburgh; from W. 247 ms.

RYE VALLEY, p. o., Smyth co., Va., 280 ms. w of Richmond; from W. 346 ms.

RYLAND'S DEPOT, p. o., Greenville co., Va.

S.

SABATUS. p. o., Lincoln co., Me., 35 ms. s. of Augusta; from W. 578 ms.

SABILLISVILLE, p. t., Frederick co., Va., 95 ms. N. w. of Annapolis; from W. 66 ms.

SABINA, p. v., Richland township. Clinton co., O., 62 ms. s. w. of Columbus; from W. 435 ms.

SABINE COUNTY, situated on the east boundary of Texas, Sabine river on the east. Area — square miles. Seat of justice, Milan. Pop. in 1850, 2,498.

SABINE PARISH, situated on the westerly boundary of Louisiana, with Sabine river on the west. Area — square miles. Seat of justice, Manny. Pop. in 1850, 4,515.

SABINE, p. t., Sabine co., Ark.

SABINE CITY, p. o., Jefferson co., Tex.

SABINE TOWN, p. o., Sabine co., Tex.

SABINSVILLE, p. o., Tioga co., Pa.

SABOUGLY, p. o., Yallabusha co., Miss.

SABULA. p. o., Jackson co., Iowa.

SACARAPPA, p. v., Westbrook township, Cumberland co., Me., 56 ms. s. w. of Augusta; from W. 545 ms. Watered by Presumpscot river.

SACHEM'S HEAD, v., Guilford township, New Haven co., Ct.

SACKET'S, p o., Macomb co., Mich., 24 ms. N. of Detroit; from W. 548 ms.

SACKETT'S HARBOR, p. v., Houndsfield township, Jefferson co., N. Y., 174 ms. N. w. of Albany; from W. 415 ms. Watered by Black river bay.

SACO, p. t., York co., Me., 65 ms. s. w. of Augusta; from W. 530 ms. Watered by Saco river. Pop. 5,801.

SACRAMENTO COUNTY, situated in the central part of California, with Sacramento river on the west.

Area — square miles. Face of the country, level; soil rich. Seat of justice, Sacramento city. Pop. in 1852, 12,589.

SACRAMENTO, city, seat of justice of Sacramento co., Cal., 125 miles from San Francisco, on the east bank of Sacramento river, is the second city, in point of location and importance, in California. It is the principal depot for the greater part of the northern mining district. This city is destined to be of great importance, as it is the highest point to which steamers and other vessels can ascend at low water. A good and substantial levee has been constructed around the city, to protect it from the overflow of the river, during the annual and occasional freshets. The city is rapidly increasing, and must become a large commercial town, from the fact of its being a central point in the northern section of the state. The population in 1852, was about 8,000.

SACRAMENTO. p. o., Marquette co., Wis.

SACTON, p. o., Clark co., Ill.

SADDLE RIVER, t., Bergen co., N. J. Watered by Saddle and Passaic rivers, and Singac and other brooks. Pop. 823.

SADSBURY, t., Lancaster co., Pa. Watered by Octarara creek. Pop. 1,529.

SADSBURY, t. Crawford co., Pa. Pop. 982.

SADSBURY, t., Chester co., Pa., 59 ms. s. E. of Harrisburgh; from W. 129 ms. Watered by Octarara creek, and west branch of Brandywine river. Pop. 2,767.

SADSBURYVILLE, p. o., Sadsbury township, Chester co., Pa.

SAEGERSTOWN, p. o., Crawford co., Pa., 240 ms. N. w. of Harrisburgh; from W. 313 ms.

SAEGERSVILLE, p. o., Lehigh co., Pa., 91 ms. N. E. of Harrisburgh ; from W. 184 ms.

SAFE HARBOR, p. o., Lancaster co., Pa.

SAGE HILL, p. o., Graves co., Ky.

SAGE'S FERRY, p. o., Jackson co., Ind., 83 ms. s. of Indianapolis ; from W. 600 ms.

SAGEVILLE, p. o., Hamilton co., N. Y.

SAGEVILLE, p. o., Lauderdale co., Miss.

SAG HARBOR, p. v., East Hampton and South Hampton townships, Suffolk co., Long Island, N. Y., 260 ms. s. E. of Albany ; from W. 340 ms. Watered by Sag Harbor bay.

SAGG VILLAGE, v., South Hampton township, Suffolk co., Long Island, N. Y.

SAGINAW COUNTY, situated in the northeasterly part of Michigan, and traversed by Shiawassee, Saginaw, Flint, and Tittibawassee rivers. Area, —— square miles. Seat of justice, Saginaw. Pop. in 1840, 892 ; in 1850, 2,609.

SAGINAW, c. h., p. t., seat of justice of Saginaw co., Mich., 97 ms. N. of Detroit ; from W.621 ms. Watered by Saginaw river. Pop. 917.

SAGO. p. o., Lewis co., Va.

SAGON, p. o., Du Page co., Ill.

SAIL CREEK, p. o., Hamilton co., Tenn.

SAILOR'S REST, p. o., Montgomery co., Tenn., 60 ms. N. w. of Nashville ; from W. 744 ms.

SAINT ALBANS, p. t., Somerset co., Me., 50 ms. N. E. of Augusta ; from W. 645 ms. Watered by a tributary of Sebasticook river. Pop. 1,792.

SAINT ALBANS, c. h., p. t., seat of justice of Franklin co., Vt., 63 ms. N. w. of Montpelier ; from W. 537 ms. Watered by Lake Champlain, Pop. 3,567.

SAINT ALBANS, p. t., Licking co., O. Watered by Raccoon fork of Licking river. Pop. 1,429.

SAINT ALBANS, p. v., Hancock co., Ill., 99 ms. N. w. of Springfield ; from W. 877 ms.

SAINT ALBANS' BAY, p. o., Franklin co., Vt.

SAINT ANDREWS, p. o., Montgomery township, Orange co., N. Y., 94 ms. s. of Albany ; from W. 296 ms.

SAINT ANDREW'S BAY, p. o., Washington co., Flor.

SAINT ANTHONY'S FALLS, p. o., Ramsey co., Minn.

SAINT ARMAND, p. o., Essex co., N. Y.

SAINT AUBERT, p. o., Callaway co., Mo.

SAINT AUGUSTINE, city, seat of justice of St. John's co., Flor., 200 ms. E. of Tallahassee; from W. 880 ms. Watered by Matanzas sound. Pop. 1,934.

SAINT AUGUSTINE, p. o., Fulton co., Ill., 85 ms. N. w. of Springfield ; from W. 831 ms.

SAINT BERNARD PARISH, situated in the southeast part of Louisiana, with Mississippi river on the northwest, and surrounded by the gulf of Mexico, and its indentations. Area, 150 square miles. Face of the country, flat ; soil, marshy. Seat of justice, ————. Pop. in 1830, 3,356 ; in 1840, 3,237 ; in 1850, 3,802.

SAINT CHARLES COUNTY, situated on the easterly boundary of Missouri, with Mississippi river on the northeast, and the Missouri on the southeast. Area, 470 square miles. Seat of justice, St. Charles. Pop. in 1810, 3,505 ; in 1820, 3,970; in 1830, 4,322; in 1840, 7,911 ; in 1850, 11,454.

SAINT CHARLES PARISH, situated in the southeast part of Louisiana, with Lake Pontchartrain on the north, and traversed by Mississippi river. Area, 512 square miles. Seat of justice, Saint Charles c. h. Pop. in 1820, 3,862 ; in 1830, 5,107; in 1840, 4,700; in 1850, 5,120.

SAINT CHARLES, p. v., Kane co., Ill., 89 ms. N. E. of Springfield ; from W. 760 ms.

SAINT CHARLES, p. v., seat of justice of St. Charles co., Mo., 110 ms. E. of Jefferson city ; from W. 828 ms. Watered by Missouri river. Seat of St. Charles college.

SAINT CHARLES, p. o., Butler co., O.

SAINT CHARLES, p. o., Johnson co., N. C.

SAINT CHARLES, p. o., Arkansas co., Ark.

SAINT CLAIR COUNTY, situated toward the northeast part of Alabama, with Coosa river on the southeast. Area, 840 square miles. Face of the country, hilly and broken. Seat of justice, Ashville. Pop. in 1820, 4,166; in 1830, 5,975; in 1840, 5,638; in 1850, 6,829.

SAINT CLAIR COUNTY, situated on the southwesterly boundary of Illinois, with Mississippi river on the west, and traversed by the Kaskaskia. Area, 648 square miles. Face of the country, even ; soil, generally fertile. Seat of justice, Bellville. Pop. in 1820, 5,253 ; in 1830, 7,078; in 1840, 13,631 ; in 1850, 20,181.

SAINT CLAIR COUNTY, situated on the east boundary of Michigan with Lake Huron and St. Clair river on the east, and with Lake St. Clair on the south. Area, 930 square miles. Seat of justice, Saint Clair. Pop. in 1830, 1,114 ; in 1840, 4,606 ; in 1850, 10,420.

SAINT CLAIR COUNTY, situated toward the southwest part of Missouri, and traversed by Osage river. Area, 820 square miles. Seat of justice, Osceola. Pop. in 1850, 3,556.

SAINT CLAIR, c. h., p. t., seat of justice of St. Clair co., Mich., 48 ms. N. E. of Detroit ; from W. 572 ms. Watered by St. Clair strait. Pop. 1,729.

SAINT CLAIR, p. t., Bedford co., Pa., 113 ms. w. of Harrisburgh ; from W. 139 ms. Pop. 1,945.

SAINT CLAIR, t., Butler co., O. Watered by Great Miami river. Pop. 1,150.

SAINT CLAIR. p. t., Columbiana co., O. Watered by Little Beaver river, and the Sandy and Beaver canal. Pop. 1,153.

SAINT CLAIR, p. o., Schuylkill co., Pa.

SAINT CLAIR, p. o., Hawkins co., Tenn.

SAINT CLAIRSVILLE, c. h., p. v., seat of justice of Belmont co., O., 116 ms. E. of Columbus ; from W. 277 ms. Pop. 1,025.

SAINT CLEMENTS' BAY, p. o., St. Mary's co., Md., 81 ms. s. of Annapolis ; from W. 58 ms.

SAINT CLOUD, p. o., East Feliciana parish, La.

SAINT CROIX COUNTY, situated in the northwesterly part of Wisconsin, with Mississippi river on the southwest, and St. Croix river and lake on the west. Area, —— square miles. Seat of justice, St. Croix. Pop. in 1850, 624.

SAINT CROIX, c. h., v., seat of justice of St. Croix co., Wis. Watered by St. Croix lake.

SAINT DENNIS, p. o., Baltimore co., Md.

SAINT FERDINANT, p. t., St. Louis co., Mo.

SAINTFIELD, p. o., Muskingum co., O., 66 ms. E. of Columbus ; from W. 339 ms.

SAINT FRANCIS COUNTY, situated toward the southeast part of Missouri. Area, 425 square miles. Seat of justice, Farmington. Pop. in 1830, 2,366 ; in 1840, 3,211 ; in 1850, 4,964.

SAINT FRANCIS COUNTY, situated in the easterly part of Arkansas, with White river on the west, and the Saint Francis on the east. Area, 1,080 square miles. Seat of justice. Mount Vernon. Pop. in 1830, 1,505; in 1840, 2,499; in 1850, 4,479.

SAINT FRANCIS, p. v., St. Francis co., Ark., 110 ms. E. of Little Rock ; from W. —— ms.

SAINT FRANCIS, t., Phillips co., Ark. Pop. 1,276.

SAINT FRANCIS, t., Wayne co., Mo.

SAINT FRANCIS. p. t., St. Francis co., Mo

SAINT FRNCISVILLE. p. v., Lawrence co., Ill., 178 ms. s. E. of Springfield ; from W. 698 ms.

SAINT FRANCISVILLE, c. h., p. v., seat of justice of West Feliciana parish, La., 136 ms. N. w. of New Orleans ; from W. 1,170 ms. Watered by Mississippi river.

SAINT FRANCISVILLE, p. v., Clark co., Mo., 177 ms. N. of Jefferson city ; from W. 904 ms. Watered by Des Moines river.

SAINT GENEVIEVE COUNTY, situated on the easterly boundary of Missouri, with Mississippi river on the northeast. Area, 400 square miles. Seat of justice, Saint Genevieve. Pop. in 1810, 4,620 ; in 1820, 4,962 ; in 1830, 2,182 ; in 1840, 3,148 ; in 1850, 5,313.

SAINT GENEVIEVE, c. h., p. v., seat of justice of St. Genevieve co., Mo., 190 ms. s. E. of Jefferson city ; from W. 844 ms. Watered by the Mississippi river and Gabourie creek.

SAINT GEORGE. p. t., Lincoln co., Me., 48 ms. s. E. of Augusta ; from W. 625 ms. Watered by Muscongus bay, and the Atlantic ocean. Pop. 2,217.

SAINT GEORGE, t., Chittenden co., Vt., 28 ms. w. of Montpelier ; from W. —— ms. Pop. 127.

SAINT GEORGE'S, p. hundred, New Castle co., Del., 31 ms. N. of Dover ; irom W. 126 ms. Pop. 2,343.

SAINT GEORGE'S, p. o., Colleton district, S. C.

SAINT HELEN, p. o., Cedar co., Mo.

SAINT HELEN, p. o., Washington co., Oregon.

SAINT HELENA PARISH, situated on the north boundary of the southeast section of Louisiana. Area, 1,700 square miles. Soil, generally sterile. Seat of justice, Greensburgh. Pop. in 1800, 2,970 ; in 1820, 3,026 ; in 1830, 4,027 ; in 1840, 3,525 ; in 1850, 4,561.

SAINT HELENA. p. v., St. Helena parish, La., 85 ms. N. of New Orleans ; from W. 1,157 ms. Watered by Ticfah river.

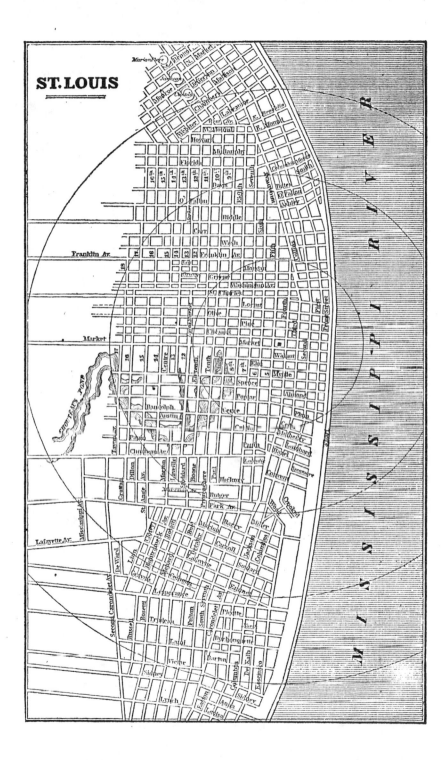

SAINT HENRY'S, p. o., Mercer co., O.

SAINT ILLA, p. o., Ware co., Ga.

SAINT INIGOES, v., St. Mary's co., Md., 105 ms. s. of Annapolis ; from W. 82 ms. Watered by Saint Inigoes river.

SAINT JACOB, p. o., Madison co., Ill.

SAINT JAMES' PARISH, situated in the southeast part of Louisiana, and traversed by Mississippi river. Area, 250 square miles. Seat of justice, Bringiers. Pop. in 1820, 5,660 ; in 1830, 7,646 ; in 1840, 8,548 ; in 1850, 11,098.

SAINT JAMES, t., Scott co., Mo.

SAINT JOHN, p. o., Lake co., Ind.

SAINT JOHN, p. o., Dodge co., Mo.

SAINT JOHN, p. o., Hertford co., N. C. 162 ms. E. of Raleigh ; from W. 291 ms.

SAINT JOHN BAPTIST PARISH, situated in the southeast part of Louisiana, with Lakes Maurepas and Ponchartrain on the northwest and east, Lake Allemande on the south, and traversed by Mississippi river. Area, 260 square miles. Seat of justice, St. John Baptist Parish c. h. Pop. in 1820, 3,854 ; in 1830, 5,700 ; in 1840, 5,776 ; in 1850, 7,317.

SAINT JOHN'S COUNTY, situated on the east boundary of Florida, with Atlantic ocean on the east, and traversed by Saint John's river. Area, 1,450 square miles. Face of the country, level, abounding in everglades. Seat of justice, Saint Augustine. Pop. in 1830, 2,538 ; in 1840, 2,694 ; in 1850. 2,525.

SAINT JOHN'S, p. o., Auglaize co., O., 95 ms. n. w. of Columbus ; from W. 480 ms.

SAINT JOHN'S, t., New Madrid co., Mo.

SAINT JOHNS, p. t., Franklin co., Mo.

SAINT JOHNSBURY, p. t., Caledonia co., Vt., 37 ms. n. e. of Montpelier ; from W. 546 ms. Watered by Pasumpsic river and tributaries. Pop. 2,758.

SAINT JOHNSBURY CENTRE, p. o., Saint Johnsbury township, Caledonia co., Vt., 40 ms. n. e. of Montpelier ; from W. 549 ms.

SAINT JOHNSBURY EAST, p. o., St. Johnsbury township, Caledonia co., Vt., 41 ms. n. e. of Montpelier ; from W. 550 ms.

SAINT JOHNSVILLE, p. t., Montgomery co., N. Y., 61 ms. n. w. of Albany ; from W, 394 ms. Watered by East Canada and Zimmerman's creeks, and Mohawk river. Pop. 1,629.

SAINT JOSEPH COUNTY, situated on the south boundary of Michigan, and traversed by St. Joseph's river. Area, 528 square miles. Face of the country, even ; soil, good. Seat of justice, Centreville. Pop. in 1830, 1,313 ; in 1840, 7,068 ; in 1850, 12,705.

SAINT JOSEPH COUNTY, situated on the north boundary of Indiana, and traversed by Saint Joseph's river. Area, 468 square miles. Face of the country, undulating ; soil, varied. Seat of justice, South Bend. Pop. in 1830, 287 ; in 1840, 6.425 ; in 1850, 10,954.

SAINT JOSEPH, p. t., Williams co., O., 180 ms. n. w. of Columbus ; from W. 524 ms. Pop. 589.

SAINT JOSEPH, p. t, Berrien co., Mich., 195 ms. w. of Detroit ; from W. 652 ms. Watered by St. Joseph and Papaw rivers, and Lake Michigan.

SAINT JOSEPH, p. o., Calhoun co., Flor.

SAINT JOSEPH, p. t., Allen co., Ind.

SAINT JOSEPH, c. h., p. o., seat of justice of Tensas parish, La.

SAINT JOSEPH'S, p. o., Champlain co., Ill.

SAINT JULIAN, p. o., Linn co., Iowa.

SAINT LANDRE PARISH, situated toward the south part of Louisiana, with Atchafalaya river on the east. Area, 2,000 square miles. Face of the country, uneven, subsiding toward the south into a plain ; soil, generally sterile. Seat of justice, Opelousas. Pop. in 1820, 10,085 ; in 1830, 12,591 ; in 1840, 15,233 ; in 1850, 22,353.

SAINT LAWRENCE COUNTY, situated on the northwest boundary of New York, with St. Lawrence river on the northwest. Area, 2,717 square miles. Face of the country, uneven ; soil, generally productive. Seat of justice, Canton. Pop. in 1810, 7,885 ; in 1820, 16,037 ; in 1830, 36,354 ; in 1840, 56,706 ; in 1850, 68,617.

SAINT LAWRENCE, p. o., Chatham co., N. C., 46 ms. west of Raleigh ; from W. 334 ms.

SAINT LAWRENCE, p. o., Jefferson co., N. Y.

SAINT LEGER, p. o., Ozark co., Mo.

SAINT LEONARD'S, p. v., Calvert co., Md., 56 ms. s. of Annapolis ; from W. 86 ms.

SAINT LOUIS COUNTY, situated on the easterly boundary of Missouri, with Mississippi river on the east, the Missouri on the northwest, and the Marameo on the south. Area, 550 square miles. Face of the country, even ; soil, fertile. Seat of justice, Saint Louis. Pop. in 1810, 6,567 ; in 1820, 10,049 ; in 1830, 14,125 ; in 1840, 35,079 ; in 1850. 104,978.

SAINT LOUIS, city, seat of justice of St. Louis county, Missouri, situated on the west bank of Mississippi river, 20 miles below the junction of the Missouri, 180 miles above the Ohio, 1,150 miles from New Orleans, and 856 miles from Washington. It is built upon two elevations, the lower twenty feet above the river, and the higher sixty feet. The terrace, as it may be styled, next the water, affords room for several business streets, some of which are lined with rows of spacious and imposing warehouses. Above, are many fine sites for residence and for public buildings, churches, asylums, schools, banks, and various other prominent edifices. The thickly-peopled part of the city extends several miles along the river, and about a mile westward. The whole area is much larger, including 36 square miles or more, and is filling up with unexampled rapidity.

The commercial position and advantages are remarkable, as its growing prosperity conclusively testifies. Few towns on the Mississippi have so favorable a position with respect to that river, while it is the entrepot of a vast trade from the valleys of Ohio and Missouri rivers. It is thus identified in progress with an extensive section of the west, to which it holds an important relation. The surrounding land is fertile, populous, and well cultivated, and of course contributes largely to the maintenance and trade of the city. The harbor is sufficient for steamboats of the largest class, many hundreds of which stop at this point every year. The manufactures of St. Louis are also extensive and varied, embracing articles of different descriptions, to the amount of many hundred thousand dollars. The city is lighted with gas, and supplied with water from the river, elevated into reservoirs by steam-engines, and thence distributed by iron pipes. It is the seat of St. Louis university, and contains other scientific and literary institutions of different grades. The population in 1810 was 1,600 ; in 1820, 4,598 ; in 1830, 5,852 ; in 1840, 16,469 ; in 1850, 77,864.

SAINT LOUISVILLE, p. o., Licking co., O.

SAINT MARIE, p. v., Jasper co., Ill., 139 ms. s. E. of Springfield ; from W. 716 ms. Pop. 420.

SAINT MARK'S, p. v., Leon co., Flor., 20 ms. s. of Tallahassee ; from W. 816 ms. Situated near the union of St. Mark's, Wakully, and Appalachee rivers.

SAINT MARTIN'S PARISH, situated toward the south part of Louisiana, with Chetimaches lake on the south. Area, 850 square miles. Face of the country, flat ; soil, where arable, rich. Seat of justice, St. Martinsville. Pop. in 1830, 7,204 ; in 1840, 8,674 ; in 1850, 11,765.

SAINT MARTIN'S, p. v., Worcester co., Md., 131 ms. s. E. of Annapolis ; from W. 171 ms.

SAINT MARTINSVILLE, c. h., p. v., seat of justice of St. Martin's parish, La., 178 ms. w. of New Orleans ; from W. 1,281 ms. Watered by Bayou Têche, at the head of steam-navigation.

SAINT MARY'S PARISH, situated on the south boundary of Louisiana, with the gulf of Mexico on the south, and Chetimaches lake on the northeast. Area, 870 square miles. Seat of justice, Franklin. Pop. in 1830, 6,442 ; in 1840, 8,950 ; in 1850, 13,700.

SAINT MARY'S COUNTY, situated in the south part of Maryland, with Chesapeake bay and Patuxent river on the northeast, and the Potomac on the southwest. Area, 200 square miles. Seat of justice, Leonardtown. Pop. in 1810, 12,794 ; in 1820, 12,974 ; in 1830, 13,459 ; in 1840, 13,224 ; in 1850, 13,698.

SAINT MARY'S, p. o., Chester co., Pa., 64 ms. s. E. of Harrisburgh ; from W. 139 ms.

SAINT MARY'S, c. h., p. v., seat of justice of Auglaize co., O., 105 ms. n. w. of Columbus ; from W. 498 ms. Watered by St. Mary's river, at the head of navigation. Pop. 873.

SAINT MARY'S, p. v., Camden co., Ga., 293 ms. s. E. of Milledgeville ; from W. 802 ms. Watered by St. Mary's river.

SAINT MARY'S, p. o., Hancock co., Ill., 95 ms. n. w. of Springfield ; from W. 873 ms.

SAINT MARY'S, p. o., Wood co., Va.

SAINT MARY'S, p. o., Linn co., Iowa.

SAINT MARY'S, p. o., Vigo co., Ind.

SAINT MARY'S, p. o., Lafayette co., Wis.

SAINT MARY'S LANDING, p. v., St. Genevieve co.,

Mo., 202 ms. s. E. of Jefferson city ; from W. 856 ms. Watered by Mississippi river.

SAINT MATTHEWS, p. o., Jefferson co., Ky.

SAINT MATTHEW'S, p. o., Orangeburgh district, S. C.

SAINT MICHAEL, p. t., Madison co., Mo.

SAINT MICHAEL'S, p. v., Talbot co., Md., 57 ms. E. of Annapolis; from W. 97 ms. Watered by St. Michael's river. Pop. 863.

SAINT OMER, p. v., Decatur co., Ind., 37 ms. s. E. of Indianapolis ; from W. 560 ms. Watered by Flat Rock creek.

SAINT PARIS, p. v., Johnston township, Champaign co., O., 57 ms. w. of Columbus ; from W. 451 ms.

SAINT PAUL, p. o., Madison co., Ark., 151 ms. N. w. of Little Rock ; from 1,207 ms.

SAINT PAUL, p. o., Greene co., Mo.

SAINT PAUL, p. v., seat of justice of Ramsey co., and capital of Minnesota, occupies a plateau, at the head of the bold bank of the Mississippi, on its north side, eight miles below the falls of St. Anthony, the head of navigation. The central position of the town is level, terminating on the bluff, eighty feet high, which recedes from the river at the upper and lower end of the village, forming two landings. Though yet in embryo, it bids fair to become an important point on the westward stream of civilization. Pop. in 1850, 1,135.

SAINT PAUL, p. o., Clarke co., Ala.

SAINT PAUL'S, p. o., Robeson co., N. C., 75 ms. s. w. of Raleigh ; from W. 363 ms.

SAINT PETER'S, p. o., Chester co., Pa.

SAINT PETER'S, p. o., Franklin co., Ind.

SAINT STEPHEN, p. o., Fauquier co., Va.

SAINT STEPHEN'S, p. v., Washington co., Ala. ; from W. 961 ms. Watered by Tombigbee river.

SAINT TAMMANY PARISH, situated on the east boundary of Louisiana, with Pearl river on the east, and Lake Ponchartrain on the south. Area, 972 square miles. Face of the country undulating, subsiding toward the south into a plain ; soil, generally sterile. Seat of justice, Covington. Pop. in 1820, 1,723 ; in 1830, 2,864 ; in 1840, 4,598 ; in 1850, 6,364.

SAINT TAMMANY'S, p. o., Mecklenburgh co,, Va., 97 ms. s. w. of Richmond ; from W. 213 ms.

SAINT THOMAS, p. t., Franklin co., Pa., 53 ms. s. w. of Harrisburgh ; from W. 98 ms. Watered by Back creek and tributaries. Pop. 1,957.

SALEM COUNTY, situated at the southwesterly corner of New Jersey, with Delaware bay and Delaware river on the southwest and northwest, Area, 320 square miles. Face of the country, level ; soil, sandy but productive. Seat of justice, Salem. Pop. in 1810, 19,761 ; in 1820, 14,022 ; in 1830, 14,155 ; in 1840, 16,024 ; in 1850, 19,467.

SALEM, city, seat of justice, together with Ipswich and Newburyport, of Essex co., Mass., 14 miles northeast of Boston, and 454 miles from Washington. The tongue of land on which it is situated is nearly surrounded by water, and comprises the oldest and most irregular part of the town. Two bridges over each inlet of the sea connect this with the more modern parts. The position of the city is low, and its harbor shallow ; but here, as elsewhere, obstacles seem to have stimulated rather than prevented effort. Next to Plymouth and Weymouth, Salem is the oldest town in Massachusetts, and from an early period it has been distinguished for the extent of its maritime operations. Its ships and sailors were active in the Revolution, and since that period it has been celebrated for its East India trade. At present, though other towns more favorably situated have outstripped it in commerce and population, its vessels are as numerous as ever, and visit every quarter of the globe. Several millions of dollars in capital are invested in the manufacture of machinery, useful and precious metals, &c. In the centre of the city is a park, or "Common," of about nine acres. The streets are not very regular, but some of the houses are handsome. The most noted public buildings are the Athenæum, East India museum, city-hall, courthouse, hospital, customhouse, jail, and about twenty churches of various denominations. The population in 1790 was 7,921 ; in 1800, 9,457 ; in 1810, 12,613 ; in 1820, 12,721 ; in 1830, 13,886; in 1840, 15,082 ; in 1850, 20,264.

SALEM, p. t., Franklin Co.. Me., 52 ms. N. w. of Augusta ; from W. 642 ms. Pop. 454.

SALEM, p. t., Rockingham co., N. H., 37 ms. s. E. of Concord ; from W. 458 ms. Watered by Spiggot river and tributaries. Pop. 1,555.

SALEM, p. t., Orleans co., Vt., 62 ms. N. E. of Mont-

pelier ; from W. 578 ms. Watered by Clyde river and Lake Memphremagog. Pop. 455.

SALEM, p. t., New London co., Ct., 30 ms. s. E. of Hartford ; from W. 354 ms. Watered by a tributary of Connecticut river. Pop. 764.

SALEM, c. h., p. t., seat of justice, together with Sandy Hill, of Washington co., N. Y., 46 ms. N. E. of Albany ; from W. 416 ms. Watered by Black and White creeks. Pop. 2,904.

SALEM, v., Portland township, Chautauque co., N. Y.

SALEM, c. h., p. t., seat of justice of Salem co,, N. J., 64 ms. s. of Trenton ; from W. 175 ms. Watered by Salem creek and tributaries. Pop. 3,052.

SALEM, p. t., Mercer co., Pa., 241 ms. N. w. of Harrisburgh ; from W. 296 ms. Watered by Little Chenango and Crooked creeks. Pop. 2,196.

SALEM, t., Wayne co., Pa. Watered by Waullenpapack creek. Pop. 1,454.

SALEM, t., Luzerne co., Pa.

SALEM, t., Westmoreland co., Pa. Watered by Beaver Dam river. Pop. 2,364.

SALEM, c. h., p. v., seat of justice of Roanoke co., Va., 178 ms. w. of Richmond ; from W. 246 ms. Watered by Roanoke river.

SALEM, p. v., Forsyth co., N. C., 109 ms. w. of Raleigh; from W. 320 ms. Watered by a tributary of Yadkin r.

SALEM, p. v., Sumter district, S. C., 91 ms. E. of Columbia ; from W. 507 ms. Watered by Black river.

SALEM, p. v., Clark co., Ga , 58 ms. N. of Milledgeville; from W. 615 ms. Pop. 323.

SALEM, p. v., Russell co., Ala. ; from W. 775 ms.

SALEM, p. v., Tippah co., Miss., 208 ms. N. E. of Jackson ; from W. 882 ms.

SALEM. p. v., Franklin co., Tenn., 104 ms. s. E. of Nashville ; from W. 674 ms.

SALEM, c. h., p. v , seat of justice of Livingston co., Ky., 249 ms. s. w. of Frankfort ; from W. 781 ms.

SALEM, p. t., Columbiana co., O., 167 ms. N. E. of Columbus ; from W. 289 ms. Pop. 1,960.

SALEM, v., Perry township, Columbiana co., O

SALEM, t., Mercer co., O.

SALEM, t., Munroe co., O. Pop. 1,111.

SALEM, t., Champaign co., O. Pop. 1,634.

SALEM, t., Highland co., O. Pop. 813.

SALEM, t., Jefferson co., O. Pop. 2,191.

SALEM, t., Meigs co., O. Pop. 1,405.

SALEM, t., Muskingum co., O. Pop. 111.

SALEM, t., Ottawa co., O. Pop. 187.

SALEM, t, Shelby co., O. Pop. 1,010.

SALEM, t., Tuscarawas co., O. Pop. 1,853.

SALEM, p. t., Warren co., O. Pop. 3,526.

SALEM, t., Washington co., O. Pop. 1,246.

SALEM, t., Washington co., Mich, Pop. 1,343.

SALEM, t., Steuben co., Ind. Pop. 550.

SALEM, t., Washington co., Ind.

SALEM, c. h., p. v., seat of justice of Washington co., Ind., 93 ms. s. of Indianapolis ; from W. 604 ms. Watered by head waters of Blue river.

SALEM, c. h., p. v., seat of justice of Marion co., Ill., 108 ms. s. E. of Springfield ; from W. 760 ms.

SALEM, p. v., Racine co., Wis., 90 ms. E. of Madison ; from W. 775 ms. Watered by Lake Michigan.

SALEM, p. t., Henry co., Iowa. Pop. 1,418.

SALEM, p. o., Newton co., Tex.

SALEM, p. o., Washtenaw co., Mich.

SALEM, p. o., Marion co., Oregon.

SALEM CENTRE, p. v., North Salem township, Westchester co., N. Y., 115 ms. s. of Albany ; from W. 279 ms.

SALEM CHURCH, p. v., Randolph co., N. C., 121 ms. w. of Raleigh; from W. 389 ms.

SALEM CROSS ROADS, p. o., Portland township, Chautauque co., N. Y., 330 ms. w. of Albany; from W. 352 ms.

SALEM CROSS ROADS, p. v., Salem township, Westmoreland co., Pa., 180 ms. w. of Harrisburgh ; from W. 205 ms. Watered by Beaver Dam creek.

SALEM FAUQUIER, p. v., Fauquier co., Va., 115 ms. N. of Richmond ; from W. 59 ms.

SALFORDVILLE, p. o., Montgomery co., Pa., 85 ms. E. of Harrisburgh ; from W. 170 ms.

SALINA, p. t., Onondaga co., N. Y., 133 ms. w. of Albany ; from W. 350 ms. Watered by Onondaga creek, and lake and celebrated for the most productive salt springs in the state. Pop. in 1830, 6,929 ; in 1840, 11,013 ; in 1850, 2,142.

SALINA, p. v., Jefferson co., Ky., 65 ms. w. of Frankfort ; from W. 605 ms.

SALINE COUNTY, situated toward the northwest part of Missouri, with Missouri river on the north and east. Area, 829 square miles. Seat of justice, Marshall. Pop. in 1830, 2,873; in 1840, 5,258; in 1850, 8,843.

SALINE COUNTY, situated in the central part of Arkansas. Area, 720 square miles. Seat of justice, Benton. Pop. in 1840, 2,061; in 1850, 3,901.

SALINE COUNTY, situated in the southerly part of Illinois. Area, —— square miles. Seat of justice, Raleigh. Pop. in 1850, 5,558.

SALINE, t., Hot Springs co., Ark.

SALINE, p. t., Jefferson co.. O. Pop. 1,090.

SALINE, p. t., Washtenaw co., Mich., 40 ms. w. of Detroit; from W. 517 ms. Pop. 1,631.

SALINE, p. t., Cooper co., Mo.

SALINE, p. o., Ralls co., Mo., 98 ms. N. E. of Jefferson city; from W. 929 ms.

SALINE, t., Miller co., Mo.

SALINE, t., St. Genevieve co., Mo. Pop. 858.

SALINE, p. t., Sevier co., Ark. Pop. 400.

SALINE, p. t., Dallas co., Ark. Pop. 335.

SALINE, p. o., Bienville parish. La.

SALINE MILLS, p. o., Natchitoches parish, La.

SALINE MILLS, p. o., Gallatin co., Ill.

SALINEVILLE, p. o., Columbiana co., O., 141 ms. N. E. of Columbus; from W. 283 ms.

SALING, p. t., Audrain co., Mo.

SALIQUOY, p. o., Cass co., Ga.

Salisbury, p. t., Merrimack co., N. H., 16 ms. N. w. of Concord; from W. 491 ms. Watered by Blackwater and Merrimack rivers. Pop. 1,288.

SALISBURY. p. t., Addison co., Vt., 69 ms. s. w. of Montpelier; from W. 481 ms. Watered by Middlebury river and Lake Dunmore. Pop. 1,027.

SALISBURY, p. t., Essex co., Mass., 42 ms. N. E. of Boston; from W. 477 ms. Watered by Merrimack and Powow rivers, and the Atlantic ocean. At the westerly end of this town is a small district cut off from the body of the town by Amesbury, called "Little Salisbury." The village of Amesbury and Salisbury Mills lies partly in this town. Pop. in 1830, 2,519; in 1840, 2,739; in 1850, 3,100.

SALISBURY. p. t., Litchfield co., Ct., 53 ms. w. of Hartford; from W. 337 ms. Watered by Housatonic and Salmon rivers. Pop. 3,103.

SALISBURY, p. t., Herkimer co., N. Y., 73 ms. N. w. of Albany; from W. 413 ms. Watered by East and West Canada and Spruce creeks. Pop. 2,035.

SALISBURY, p. t., Lancaster co., Pa., 51 ms. s. E. of Harrisburgh; from W. 121 ms. Watered by Picquea creek. Pop. 3,647.

SALISBURY, t., Lehigh co., Pa. Pop. 1,884.

SALISBURY, p. v., Somerset co., Md., 95 ms. s. E. of Annapolis; from W. 135 ms. Watered by Wicomico river.

SALISBURY, c. h., p. v., seat of justice of Rowan co., N. C., 118 ms. w. of Raleigh; from W. 355 ms. Watered by a tributary of Yadkin river.

SALISBURY, p. t., Meigs co., 98 ms. s. w. of Columbus; from W. 346 ms. Watered by Ohio river. Pop. 2,921.

SALISBURY, p. o., Greene co., Ind.

SALISBURY, p. v., Sangamon co., Ill., 10 ms. N. w. of Springfield; from W. 790 ms. Watered by a tributary of Sangamon river.

SALISBURY CENTRE, p. v., Salisbury township, Herkimer co., N. Y., 75 ms. N. w. of Albany; from W. 405 ms.

SALISBURY COVE, p. o., Hancock co.. Me.

SALISBURY MILLS, p. v., Blooming Grove township, Orange co., N. Y., 93 ms. s. of Albany; from W. 287 ms.

SALMAGUNDI, p. o., Wachita parish, La.

SALMON CREEK, p. o., Monroe co., N. Y.

SALMON FALLS, p. o., Strafford co., N. H.

SALMON FALLS, p. o., El Dorado co., Cal.

SALMON RIVER, p. o., Albion township, Oswego co., N. Y.

SALONA, p. o., Clinton co., Pa.

SALONIA, p. v., Greene co., Ky.

SAL SODA, p. o., Butler co., Ala.

SALT CREEK, p. t., Muskingum co., O., 65 ms. E. of Columbus; from W. 350 ms. Pop. 1,012.

SALT CREEK, t., Holmes co., O. Pop. 1,699.

SALT CREEK, t., Hocking co., O. Watered by a tributary of Scioto Salt creek. Pop. 1,094.

SALT CREEK, t., Marion co., O. Pop. 347.

SALT CREEK, t., Pickaway co., O. Pop. 1,846.

SALT CREEK, t., Wayne co., O. Pop. 1,669.

SALT CREEK, p. o., Davis co., Iowa.

SALTILLO, p. o., Itawamba co. Miss.

SALTILLO, p. o., Morgan co.. Ky.

SALTILLO, p. o., Hardin co.. Tenn.

SALTILLO, p. o., Jasper co., Ind.

SALTKETCHER BRIDGE, p. o., Colleton district, S. C.

SALT LAKE COUNTY, situated in the north part of Utah territory. Area, —— square miles. Seat of justice, Salt Lake city.

SALT LAKE CITY, p. t., Salt Lake co., Utah. Founded and inhabited principally by Mormons.

SALT LICK, p. t., Fayette co., Pa. Pop. 879.

SALT LICK, t., Perry co., O. Pop. 1,747.

SALTLICK FALLS, p. o., Preston, Va.

SALTPETRE, p. o., Washington co., O.

SALT POINT, p. o., Pleasant Valley township, Dutchess co., N. Y., 74 ms. s. of Albany; from W. 311 ms.

SALT POINT, p. o., St. Genevieve co., Mo.

SALT POND, t., Saline co., Mo.

SALT RIVER, p. o.. Audrain co., Mo., 58 ms. N. of Jefferson city; from W. 930 ms.

SALT RIVER, t., Knox co., Mo. Pop. 602.

SALT RIVER, p. t., Randolph co., Mo. Pop. 2,848.

SALTSBURGH, p. v., Conemaugh township, Indiana co., Pa., 179 ms. w. of Harrisburgh; from W. 205 ms. Watered by Conemaugh river. Pop. 623.

SALT SPRING, p. o., Campbell co., Ga.

SALT SPRING, p. o., Bienville parish, La.

SALT SPRINGVILLE, p. o., Otsego co., N. Y.

SALT SULPHUR SPRINGS. p. o., Monroe co., Va., 232 ms. w. of Richmond; from W. 269 ms.

SALTVILLE, p. v., Washington co., Va., 288 ms. w. of Richmond; from W. 356 ms. Watered by north fork of Holston river.

SALUBRIA, p. o., Dix township, Chemung co., N. Y., 191 ms. s. w. of Albany; from W. 302 ms.

SALUBRITY, p. o., Pickens district, S. C.

SALUDA, p. t., Jefferson co., Ind., 100 ms. s. E. of Indianapolis; from W. 572 ms. Pop. 1,344.

SALUDA, p. o., Coweta co., Ga.

SALUDA, p. o., Middlesex co., Va.

SALUDA MILLS, p. o., Newberry district, S. C.

SALUNGA, p. o., Lancaster co., Pa.

SALURIA, p. o., Calhoun co., Tex.

SALVISA, p. v., Mercer co., Ky., 21 ms. s. of Frankfort; from W. 563 ms. Pop. 154.

SAMANTHA, p. o., Highland co., O.

SAMMONSVILLE, p. o., Fulton co., N. Y.

SAMMON'S POINT, p. o., Iroquois co., Il.

SAMPSON COUNTY, situated in the southerly part of North Carolina. Area, 800 square miles. Seat of justice, Clinton. Pop. in 1810, 6,620; in 1820, 8,903; in 1830, 11,634; in 1840, 12,157; in 1850, 14,585.

SAMPSON, p. o., Darke co., O.

SAMPSONDALE, v., Haverstraw township, Rockland co., N. Y.

SAMPTOWN, v., Piscataway township, Middlesex co., N. J. Watered by Cedar creek.

SAM'S CREEK, p. o., Carroll co., Md., 62 ms. N. w. of Indianapolis; from W. 63 ms.

SAMPSONVILLE, p. o., Ulster co., N. Y.

SAN ANTONIO, p. o., Bexar co., Tex.

SAN AUGUSTINE COUNTY, situated in the east part of Texas. Area, —— square miles. Seat of justice, San Augustin. Pop. in 1850, 3,647.

SAN AUGUSTINE, c. h., p. v., seat of justice of San Augustine co., Tex.

SANBORNTON, p. t., Belknap co., N. H., 21 ms. N. of Concord; from W. 502 ms. Watered by Winnipiseogee and Pemigewasset rivers. Pop. 2,695.

SANBORNTON BRIDGE, p. v., Sanbornton township, Belknap co., N. H., 17 ms. N. of Concord; from W. 498 ms.

SAN COSME, p. o., Rusk co., Tex.

SAND BANK, p. o., Albion township, Oswego co., N. Y., 147 ms. N. w. of Albany; from W. 393 ms.

SANDBURGH, p. o., Fallsbury township, Sullivan co., N. Y., 98 ms. s. w. of Albany; from W. 303 ms.

SAND CREEK, p. t., Bartholomew co., Ind. Pop. 1,071.

SANDERSVILLE, p. v., Chester district, S. C., 66 ms. N. of Columbia; from W. 461 ms.

SANDERSVILLE, c. h., p. v., seat of justice of Washington co., Ga., 28 ms. s. E. of Milledgeville; from W. 658 ms.

SAND FORT, p. o., Russell co., Ala.

SANDGATE, p. t., Bennington co., Vt., 111 ms. s. of Montpelier; from W. 421 ms. Watered by tributaries of the Battenkill, and of White creek. Pop. 850.

SAND HILL, p. o., Scotland co., Mo., 171 ms. N. of Jefferson city ; from W. 938 ms.

SAN DIEGO COUNTY, situated at the southwest corner of California, with the Pacific on the west. Area, —— square miles. Seat of justice, San Diego. Pop. in 1850, 3,530.

SAN DIEGO, p. t., seat of justice of San Diego co., Cal.

SANDIGE'S, p. o., Amherst co., Va., 128 ms. w. of Richmond ; from W. 180 ms.

SANDIFER'S MILLS, p. o., Copiah co., Miss.

SANDFIER'S STORE, p. o., Carroll co., Ky.

SANDISFIELD, p. t., Berkshire co., Mass., 126 ms. w. of Boston ; from W. 361 ms. Watered by a tributary of Farmington river. Pop. 1,649.

SAND LAKE, p. t., Rensselaer co., N. Y., 17 ms. E. of Albany ; from W. 384 ms. Watered by Poesten and Wynants kills. Pop. 2,558.

SAND MOUNTAIN. p. o., De Kalb co., Ala.

SANDOVER, p. o., Abbeville district, S. C., 81 ms. w. of Columbus ; from W. 534 ms.

SANDOWN, p. t., Rockingham co., N. H., 26 ms. S. E. of Concord ; from W. 467 ms. Watered by Cub pond, the head water of Exeter river. Pop. 566.

SAND PRAIRIE, p. o., Richland co., Wis.

SANDS' MILLS, p. o., Westchester co., N. Y.

SANDSTONE, t., Jackson co., Mo.

SANDTOWN, p. v., Campbell co., Ga., 100 ms. N. w. of Milledgeville ; from W. 695 ms.

SANDUSKY COUNTY, situated in the north part of Ohio, with Sandusky bay on the northeast, and traversed by Sandusky river. Area, 320 square miles. Face of the country, low and level. Seat of justice, Fremont. Pop. in 1820, 852 ; in 1830, 2,851 ; in 1840, 10,182 ; in 1850, 14,305.

SANDUSKY, p. o., Freedom township, Cattaraugus co., N. Y., 272 ms. w. of Albany ; from W. 343 ms.

SANDUSKY, seat of justice of Erie co., O., an interesting, pleasant, and thriving village, and one of the principal ports of entry on Lake Erie, is finely located on the inner shore of Sandusky bay, 60 ms. w. of Cleveland, 110 miles north of Columbus, and 414 miles from Washington. Few western towns combine so pleasant a situation with so many sources of prosperity. On a beautiful site, overlooking the whole bay, its entrance, and lake beyond, the harbor, dotted with sails and steamboats, moving in different directions, the town and its environs form a pleasing picture of industry and comfort. A rich quarry of fine limestone, furnishes a foundation for the village and material for its buildings. Of these, a number are conspicuous for beauty and elegance. Besides the numerous steamboats and other vessels which visit Sandusky city from different points on the lake, it is the terminus of railroads from Cincinnati, Columbus, and intermediate towns. The population in 1830, was 593 ; in 1840, 1,200 ; in 1850, 5,087.

SANDUSKY, t., Crawford co., O. Pop. 822.

SANDUSKY, t., Richland co., O. Pop. 678.

SANDUSKY, t., Sandusky co., O. Pop. 782.

SANDWICH, p. t. Carroll co., N. H., 49 ms. N. of Concord ; from W. 530 ms. Watered by Squam lake and Bearcamp river. Pop. 2,577.

SANDWICH, p. t., Barnstable co., Mass., 58 ms. S. E. of Boston ; from W. 459 ms. Watered by Sandwich river and Cape Cod bay. Pop. in 1830, 3,367 ; in 1840, 3,625 ; in 1850, 4.368.

SANDY, t., Tuscarawas co., O. Pop. 1,227.

SANDY, t., Stark co., O. Pop. 1,270.

SANDY, p. o., Columbiana co., O., 141 ms. N. E. of Columbus ; from W. 298 ms.

SANDY, p. o., Jackson co., Va., 355 ms. N. w. of Richmond ; from W. 324 ms.

SANDY BAY, v., Gloucester township, Essex co., Mass. Watered by the Atlantic ocean.

SANDY BOTTOM, p. o., Middlesex co., Va., 103 ms. E. of Richmond ; from W. 165 ms.

SANDY BRIDGE, p. o., Carroll co., Tenn., 87 ms. w. of Nashville , from W. 771 ms.

SANDY CREEK, p. t., Oswego co., N. Y., 161 ms. N. w. of Albany ; from W. 391 ms. Watered by Little Sandy creek and Lake Ontario. Pop. 2,456.

SANDY CREEK, t., Venango co., Pa. Pop. 957.

SANDY CREEK, p. o., Randolph co., N. C., 71 ms. w. of Raleigh ; from W. 322 ms.

SANDY FLAT, p. o., Greenville district, S. C.

SANDY FOUNDATION, p. o., Lenoir co., N. C.

SANDY GROVE, p. o., Chatham co., N. C., 58 ms. w. of Raleigh ; from W. 309 ms.

SANDY HILL, c. h., p. v., seat of justice, together with Salem, of Washington co., N. Y., 53 ms. N. of Albany ; from W. 423 ms. Watered by Hudson river at Baker's Falls.

SANDY HILL, p. v., Worcester co., Md., 124 ms. s. E. of Annapolis ; from W. 164 ms.

SANDY HILL, p. o., Henry co., Tenn., 86 ms. w. of Nashville ; from W. 772 ms.

SANDY HOOK, p. o., Harford co., Md.

SANDY LAKE, p. t., Mercer co., Pa., 228 ms. N. w. of Harrisburgh ; from W. 283 ms. Watered by Sandy creek and Sandy lake. Pop. 1,100.

SANDY LEVEL, p. o., Pittsylvania co., Va.

SANDY MARSH, p. o., Buncombe co., N. C.

SANDY PLAINS, p. o., Rutherford co., N. C., 230 ms. w. of Raleigh ; from W. 467 ms.

SANDY RIDGE, p. o., Henry co., Ga., 59 ms. N. w. of Milledgeville ; from W. 667 ms.

SANDY RIDGE, p. o., Lowndes co., Ala. ; from W. 867 ms.

SANDY RIDGE, p. o., Steuben co., Ind.

SANDY RIVER, p. o., Pittsylvania co., Va., 184 ms. s. w. of Richmond ; from W. 267 ms.

SANDY RUN, p. o., Cleveland co., N. C.

SANDY RUN, p. o., Lexington district, S. C., 16 ms. w. of Columbia ; from W. 522 ms.

SANDY SPRING, p. o., Montgomery co., Md., 60 ms. s. w. of Annapolis ; from W. 20 ms.

SANDY SPRING, p. o., Fayette co., Tenn., 201 ms. s. w. of Nashville ; from W. 896 ms.

SANDYSTON, p. t., Sussex co., N. J., 87 ms. N. of Trenton ; from W. 256 ms. Watered by Delaware river and Big and Little Flat kills. Pop. 783.

SANDYVILLE, p. v., Sandy township, Tuscarawas co., O., 123 ms. N. E. of Columbus ; from W. 318 ms.

SAN ELIZARIO, p. o., Socorro co., New Mex.

SAN FELIPE, p. o., Austin co., Tex.

SANFORD, p. t., York co., Me., 83 ms. s. w. of Augusta ; from W. 512 ms. Watered by Mousum river. Pop. 2,330.

SANFORD, p. t., Broome co., N. Y., 120 ms. s. E. of Albany ; from W. 304 ms. Watered by Ocquaga creek. Pop. 2.508.

SANFORD, p. o., Ingham co., Mich., 100 ms. w. of Detroit ; from W. 586 ms.

SANFORD'S CORNERS, p. o., Le Ray township, Jefferson co., N. Y., 169 ms. N. w. of Albany.

SAN FRANCISCO COUNTY, situated on the westerly boundary of California, with the Pacific ocean on the west, and San Francisco bay on the northeast. Area, —— square miles. Seat of justice, San Francisco. Pop. in 1852, 36,151.

SAN FRANCISCO, the "Empire city" of the Pacific, and seat of justice of San Francisco co., Cal., stands on a narrow neck of land between the bay of San Francisco and the ocean, fronting eastward on the bay, and having the ocean five miles on the west. The bay is safe and commodious, being capable of holding the combined navies of the world. It extends southward some fifty miles, parallel with the sea, from which it is separated by a narrow strip of land, varying from five to twenty miles in width. The city of San Francisco is on the extreme point of this promontory. Its site is handsome and commanding, being on an inclined plane half a mile in extent from the water's edge to the hills in the rear. Two points of land—Clark's point on the north, and Rincon point on the south—one mile apart, project into the bay, forming a crescent between them, which is the water-front of the city, and which has already been filled in and covered with buildings to the extent of half a mile. Those points, and the lofty hills north and west, upon which the city is rapidly climbing, afford a most extensive and picturesque view of the surrounding country. There are scarcely to be found more charming and diversified prospects than are presented from these heights.

For growing importance, commercial advantages, and the enterprise of its citizens, San Francisco deserves the rank of one of the great cities of the Union. Although it has been repeatedly destroyed by fire, it has each time risen, phœnix-like, from its own ashes, with new beauty and with greater splendor than before. It contains a large number of elegant brick fire-proof stores and banking-houses, and the streets are paved with heavy timbers and planks, which will soon give place to more durable materials. There are several daily lines of steamers to Sacramento, Marysville, Stockton, San Joaquin city, and other points on the rivers,

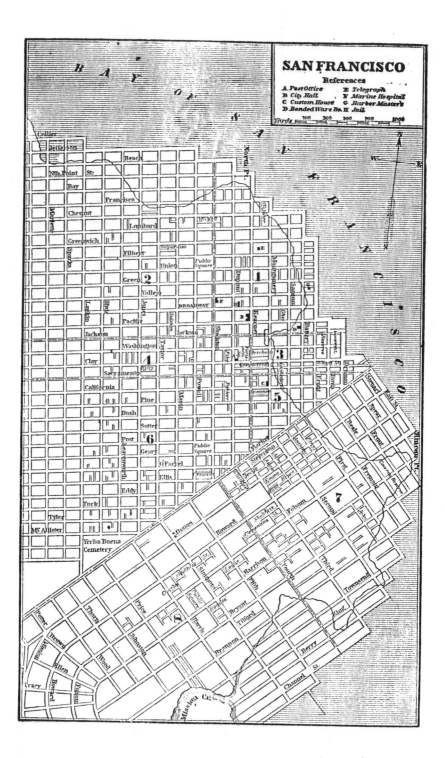

and in the northern and southern mines; while ocean-steamers ply from San Francisco to Panama and San Juan del Sur, the port of Nicaragua. Vessels from the Atlantic coast, and all parts of the world, constantly arrive or depart. The population in 1847 was 375; in 1852, 34,876.

SAN GABRIEL, p. o., Williamson co., Tex.

SANGAMON or SANGAMO COUNTY, situated in the central part of Illinois, and traversed by Sangamon river. Area, 900 square miles. Face of the country, even; soil, rich. Seat of justice, Springfield, which is also the state capital. Pop. in 1830, 12,960; in 1840, 14,716; in 1850, 19,228.

SANGERFIELD, p. t., Oneida co., N. Y., 88 ms. N. w. of Albany; from W. 372 ms. Watered by Chenango river and Oriskany creek. Pop. 2,371.

SANGERVILLE, p. t., Piscataquis co., Me., 77 ms. N. w. of Augusta; from W. 672 ms. Watered by Penobscot and Kennebec rivers. Pop. 1,267.

SANILAC COUNTY, situated on the east boundary of Michigan, with Lake Huron on the east. Area, 730 square miles. Seat of justice, Sanilac Mills. Pop. in 1850, 2,112.

SANILAC MILLS, p. t., seat of justice of Sanilac co., Mich.

SAN JACINTO, p. v., Harris co., Tex.

SAN JOAQUIN COUNTY, situated in the central part of California, and traversed by San Joaquin river. Area, —— square miles. Face of the country, level, bordered on the east and west by mountains; soil, fertile. Seat of justice, Stockton. Pop. in 1852, 5,929.

SAN JOAQUIN, p. o., San Joaquin co., Cal.

SAN JOSE, p. o., Santa Clara co.. Cal.

SAN JUAN, p. o., Monterey co., Cal.

SAN LOUIS, p. o., Brazoria co., Tex.

SAN LUIS OBISPO COUNTY, situated on the western boundary of California, extending from the summit of the coast range of mountains to the Pacific ocean. Traversed by Nacimiento and Monterey rivers. Area, —— square miles. Seat of justice, San Luis Obispo. Pop. in 1852, 984.

SAN LUIS OBISPO, c. h., p. v., seat of justice of San Luis Obispo co., Cal.

SAN MARCO, p. o., Travis co., Tex.

SAN MIGUEL COUNTY, situated in the central part of the territory of New Mexico. Area, —— square miles. Face of the country, mountainous; soil, sandy and sterile. Seat of justice, Las Vegas. Pop. in 1850, 7,074.

SAN MIGUEL, p. t., San Miguel co., New Mex. Pop. 700.

SAN PATRICIO COUNTY, situated in Texas. Area, —— square miles. Seat of justice, San Patricio. Pop. in 1850, 200.

SAN PATRICIO. p. o., San Patricio co., Tex.

SAN PEDRO, p. o., Houston co., Tex.

SAN PETE, p. o., Utah.

SAN RAFAEL. p. o., Marin co., Cal.

SANTA ANNA COUNTY, situated in the —— part of the territory of New Mexico. Pop. in 1850, 4,645.

SANTA ANNA, p. o., De Witt co., Ill., 84 ms. N. E. of Springfield; from W. 719 ms.

SANTA BARBARA COUNTY, situated on the southwest boundary of California, with the Pacific ocean on the west. Area, —— square miles. Face of the country. mountainous. Seat of justice, Santa Barbara. Pop. in 1852, 2,131.

SANTA BARBARA, p. t., seat of justice of Santa Barbara co.. Cal.

SANTA CLARA COUNTY, situated in the west part of California, with San Francisco bay on the northwest. Area, —— square miles. Face of the country, mountainous: soil, productive. Seat of justice, San José. Pop. in 1852, 6,664.

SANTA CLARA, p. o., Santa Clara co., Cal.

SANTA CRUZ COUNTY, situated in California. Area, —— square miles. Seat of justice, Santa Cruz. Pop. in 1852, 1,219.

SANTA CRUZ, p. t., seat of justice of Santa Cruz co., Cal.

SANTA FE COUNTY, situated in the northern part of the territory of New Mexico, on the western side of the Rocky mountains. Area, —— square miles. Watered by the Rio Grande del Norte. Seat of justice, city of Santa Fé. Pop. in 1850, 7,713.

SANTA FE, city, seat of justice of Santa Fé co.. New Mexico, is situated east of the Rio del Norte, about 600

miles from the gulf of Mexico. It has long been an important rendezvous of traders from other parts of the Union and from Mexico. Between 1834 and 1841. the annual value of the trade passing through this place was from $2,000.000 to $3,000,000. The hostilities be tween the United States and Mexico checked this prosperity; but the annexation of New Mexico, and the rapid settlement of California, are sources of permanent advantage, of which the influence has been already felt. The annoyances from hostile Indians, to which traders have always been more or less exposed, are the principal obstacles to its rapid increase. The population is about 5,000.

SANTA FE, p. o.. Alexander co., Ill., 228 ms. s. of Springfield; from W. 862 ms.

SANTA FE, p. o., Maury co., Tenn.

SANTA FE, p. o., Bracken co., Ky.

SANTA FE, p. o., Miami co., Ind.

SANTA FE, p. o., Poinsett co., Ark.

SANTEE, p. o.. Covington co., Miss.

SANTYAM, p. o., Linn co., Oregon.

SANTYAM FORKS, p. o., Linn co., Oregon

SAPLING GROVE. p. o., Washington co., Va., 317 ms. w. of Richmond; from W. 385 ms.

SAPPINGTON, p. v., St. Louis co., Mo., 140 ms. E. of Jefferson city; from W. 820 ms.

SAPP'S CROSS ROADS, p. o., Blount co., Ala.

SARAH, p. o.. Blair co., Pa., 122 ms. w. of Harrisburgh; from W. 148 ms.

SARAHSVILLE, p. o., Franklin co., Ill., 181 ms. s. of Springfield; from W. 830 ms.

SARAHSVILLE, p. v., Noble township, Morgan co., O., 99 ms. s. E. of Columbus; from W. 325 ms. Watered by Buffalo fork of Wills's creek.

SARANAC, p. t., Clinton co., N. Y., 181 ms. N. of Albany; from W. 551 ms. Watered by Saranac river. Pop. 2,582.

SARATOGA COUNTY, situated in the east part of New York, with Hudson river on the east, and the Mohawk on the south. Area, 800 square miles. Face of the country, varied with hills and valleys in the north, and alluvial plains toward the Mohawk; soil varied—along the streams, fertile. Seat of justice, Ballston Spa. Pop. in 1810, 33,147; in 1820, 36,052; in 1830, 38,679; in 1840, 40,533; in 1850, 45,646.

SARATOGA, p. t., Saratoga co., N. Y. Watered by Saratoga lake, and Kayaderosseras and Fish creeks, and Hudson river. Pop. in 1830, 2,204; in 1840, 3,384; in 1850. 0,142.

SARATOGA SPRINGS, p. v., Saratoga co., N. Y., 36 ms. N. of Albany; from W 406 ms. The most celebrated watering-place in the United States, containing numerous salubrious mineral springs. Pop. in 1840, 2,500; in 1850, 4,650.

SARCOXIE, p. t., Jasper co., Mo. Pop. 1,009.

SARDINIA, p. t., Erie co., N. Y., 276 ms. w. of Albany; from W. 343 ms. Watered by Cattaraugus creek. Pop. 1,761.

SARDINIA, p. o., Decatur co., Ind.

SARDINIA, p. v., Washington township, Brown co., O., 92 ms. s. w. of Columbus; from W. 459 ms. Pop. 198.

SARDIS, p. o., Burke co., Ga., 97 ms. E. of Milledgeville; from W. 620 ms.

SARDIS, p. o., Mason co., Ky.

SARDIS, p. o., Monroe co., O.

SARECTA, p. o., Duplin co., N. C.

SAREPTA, p. o., Lafayette co., Miss., 160 ms. N. E. of Jackson; from W. 913 ms.

SARGENT, p. o., Waushara co., Wis.

SARIETTA, p. o., Marion co., Va.

SARVERSVILLE, p. o., Butler co., Pa.

SASSAFRAS HILL, p. o., Washington co., Ill.

SATARTIA, p. v., Yazoo co., Miss., 52 ms. N. w. of Jackson; from W. 1,041 ms. Watered by Yazoo river.

SAUCON VALLEY, p. o., Lehigh co., Pa.

SAUGATUCK, p. o., Allegan co., Mich., 183 ms. w. of Detroit; from W. 648 ms.

SAUGERTIES, p. t., Ulster co., N. Y., 45 ms. s. of Albany; from W. 331 ms. Watered by Hudson river, Platte kill, and Esopus creek. Pop. 8,041.

SAUGUS, p. t., Essex co., Mass., 11 ms. N. of Boston; from W. 451 ms. Watered by Saugus river. Pop. 1,552.

SAUK COUNTY, situated in the central part of Wisconsin, with Wisconsin river on the south, which also traverses it in the northeast. Area, —— square miles. Seat of justice, Adams. Pop. in 1850, 4,371.

SAUK RAPIDS, p. o., Benton co., Minn.

SAUK VILLAGE, p. o., La Porte co., Ind.

SAUKVILLE, p. o., Washington co., Wis.

SAULT DE STE. MARIE, p. v., seat of justice of Chippewa co., Mich., 400 ms. N. of Detroit; from W. 921 ms. Watered by the rapids of St. Mary's strait (Sault de Ste. Marie).

SAUNDERSVILLE, p. v., Vanderburgh co., Ind., 162 ms. s. w. of Indianapolis; from W. 732 ms.

SAUNDERSVILLE, p. o., Worcester co., Mass.

SAUQUOIT, p. v., Oneida co., N. Y., 90 ms. N. w. of Albany; from W. 379 ms. Watered by Sadaquada creek.

SAUTA, p. o., Jackson co., Ala.

SAVAGE, p. o., Anne Arundel co., Md., 20 ms. N. w. of Annapolis; from W. 20 ms.

SAVAGE GRANT, p. o., Wayne co., Va.

SAVANNAH. p. t., Wayne co., N. Y., 168 ms. w. of Albany; from W. 348 ms. Watered by Crusoe lake. Pop. 1,700.

SAVANNAH, p. o., Macon co., N. C.

SAVANNAH, p. o., Ashland co., O., 86 ms. N. of Columbus; from W. 375 ms.

SAVANNAH, city, the seat of justice of Chatham co., Ga., situated on the south side of the river from which it is named, 17 miles from the sea, and 158 miles southeast of Milledgeville, the state capital, is the principal city of Georgia, and one of the most favorably-located ports in the southern states. It is 90 miles southwest of Charleston, and 662 miles from Washington. Near the river, the bank is about forty feet high. Along the foot of this bluff are stores and warehouses, while the streets of the city extend over the level at the top of this eminence. They are rendered remarkably pleasant by lines of trees along their sides and through their middle, shading the traveller from the southern sun, and affording delightful walks at all times of the day. In 1820, a conflagration destroyed a great portion of the city, but it has been rebuilt with increased solidity and beauty. Formerly, the rice-swamps in the vicinity, and other circumstances, contributed to render Savannah as unhealthy as it is now salubrious. This change is owing to the improvements in the culture of rice, and in the condition of the city. The exchange, courthouse, hospital, arsenal, guardhouse, jail, together with numerous churches and banks, display the characteristic enterprise and liberality of the citizens; while airy, verdant, and shady parks, are interspersed more frequently in this than in most other American cities. Among other splendid trees, the "Pride of China" (azederach) holds a conspicuous rank.

Savannah has an excellent harbor, with a safe and easy entrance from the ocean. Several islands are formed by the embouchures of the river, affording both protection and ornament. Upon Tybee island, a lighthouse marks the entrance to the port, while two forts protect the city from outward assault. Vessels of 13 feet draught anchor at the wharves of the city, those of larger size at a point several miles below. Above Savannah, the river is navigable for steamboats of 150 tons to Augusta, 150 miles. By this and other channels, most of the cotton, tobacco, sugar, lumber, and other staples of Georgia, are conveyed to Savannah, where they find a market, or are exported. This city, from its favorable commercial situation, on a coast not well supplied with good harbors, is the receptable of productions from an extensive region. Late improvements in railroads and other channels of communication have added largely to its growth and prosperity. A canal connects Ogeechee river with the Savannah. Steamboats navigate the principal rivers of the state, and sail to Charleston and other cities on the coast, and regular steam and sailing packets communicate with New York.

The Central railroad extends 191 miles to Macon, whence the Macon and Western railroad proceeds 101 miles, in a northwesterly direction, to Atlanta. Through this place passes the Georgia and Western and Atlantic railroad, from Augusta to Chattanooga, on Tennessee river, in Hamilton county. Tennessee. The population in 1810 was 5,595; in 1820, 7,523; in 1830, 9,748; in 1840, 11,214; in 1850, 16,060.

SAVANNAH. c. h., p. v., seat of justice of Hardin co., Tenn., 131 ms. s. w. of Nashville; from W. 807 ms. Watered by Tennessee river. Pop. 502.

SAVANNAH, c. h., p. v., seat of justice of Carroll co., Ill., 202 ms. N. of Springfield; from W. 872 ms. Watered by Mississippi river. Pop. 546.

SAVANNAH, c. h., p. v., seat of justice of Andrew co., Mo.

SAVANNAH, p. o., Red River co., Tex.

SAVERN, p. o., Owen co., Ky.

SAVERTON, v., Ralls co., Mo.. 107 ms. N. E. of Jefferson city; from W. 911 ms. Watered by Mississippi river.

SAVILLE, t., Perry co., Pa. Pop. 1,501.

SAVONA, p. o., Steuben co., N. Y.

SAVOY, p. t., Berkshire co., Mass., 122 ms. N. w. of Boston; from W. 395 ms. Watered by tributaries of Hoosic, Deerfield, and Westfield rivers. Pop. 955.

SAW MILL, p. o., Dale co., Ala.

SAWYER'S MILLS, p. o., Lexington district, S. C.

SAWYERSVILLE, p. o., Randolph co., N. C.

SAXENBURGH, p. v., Butler co., Pa., 205 ms. w. of Harrisburgh; from W. 236 ms.

SAXE'S MILLS, p. o., Franklin co., Vt., 76 ms. N. of Montpelier; from W. 550 ms.

SAXONVILLE, p. v., Middlesex co., Mass., 22 ms. N. w. of Boston; from W. 428 ms.

SAXTON'S RIVER, p. o., Windham co., Vt.

SAYBROOK, p. t., Middlesex co., Ct., 42 ms. s. E. of Hartford; from W. 334 ms. Watered by Connecticut river and Long Island sound. Pop. 2,904.

SAYBROOK, p. t., Ashtabula co., O., 200 ms. N. E. of Columbus; from W. 347 ms. Watered by Lake Erie.

SAYLERSBURGH, p. v., Monroe co., Pa., 112 ms. N. E. of Harrisburgh; from W. 205 ms.

SAYLORVILLE, p. o., Polk co., Iowa.

SAYVILLE, p. o., Islip township, Suffolk co., Long Island, 199 ms. s. E. of Albany; from W. 279 ms.

SCALP LEVEL, p. o., Cambria co., Pa.

SCARBOROUGH, p. t., Cumberland co., Me., 59 ms. s. w. of Augusta; from W. 536 ms. Watered by the Atlantic ocean. Pop. 1,827.

SCARBOROUGH, p. o., Scriven co., Ga., 68 ms. E. of Milledgeville; from W. 637 ms.

SCARSDALE, p. t., Westchester co., N. Y., 135 ms. s of Albany; from W. 240 ms. Watered by Bronx river Pop. 342.

SCHAGHTICOKE, p. t., Rensselaer co., N. Y., 20 ms. N. of Albany; from W. 390 ms. Watered by Hudson and Hoosic rivers and Tompanio creek. Pop. 3,290.

SCHELLSBURGH, p. o., Bedford co., Pa., 112 ms. w. of Harrisburgh; from W. 138 ms.

SCHENECTADY COUNTY, situated in the east part of New York, and traversed by Mohawk river, and the Erie canal. Area, 200 square miles. Face of the country, hilly and broken; soil, near the Mohawk, alluvial and rich. Seat of justice, Schenectady. Pop. in 1810, 10,201; in 1820, 13,081; in 1830, 12,347, in 1840, 17,387; in 1850, 20,054.

SCHENECTADY, city, p. t., seat of justice of Schenectady co., N. Y., 16 ms. N. w. of Albany; from W. 384 miles. Watered by the Mohawk river, which forms its northern boundary. It is one of the oldest towns in the state, having been settled by the Dutch as a trading post in 1620, and was, for a long period, important as a frontier position, nothing but a wilderness being found between it and Canada. In the year 1769, while a mere village, garrisoned by a few troops, Schenectady was the victim of the jealousies and contentions of those sent for its protection; for the soldiers having deserted their posts, one of those secret predatory bands of savages, which were long the scourge of our frontier settlements, led on by Frenchmen from Canada, fell upon it in the dead of night, massacred almost every man, woman, and child, and burnt their dwellings. A few fugitives escaped, and carried the shocking tale to Albany. Schenectady was chartered as a city in 1798. For a number of years it has been distinguished as the seat of one of the most flourishing literary institutions in the state, Union college, the edifices of which occupy a pleasant and commanding position, overlooking the extensive meadows of the Mohawk, surrounded by a succession of undulated and hilly country, and enlivened by the Erie canal and the lines of railroads which here meet by various routes from Albany, and proceed on in company, with occasional separations, to Rochester, and finally terminate together at Buffalo. Pop. in 1830, 4,268; in 1840. 6,784; in 1850, 8,921.

SCHENEVUS, p. o., Otsego co., N. Y.

SCHLEISINGERVILLE, p. o., Washington co., Wis.

SCHNECKSVILLE, p. o., Lehigh co., Pa.

SCHODACK, p. t., Rensselaer co., N. Y., 7 ms. s. of Albany; 372 ms. Watered by Hudson river. Pop. 3,509.

SCHODACK CENTRE, p. o., Schodack township, Rensselaer co., N. Y., 6 ms. s. of Albany ; from W. 371 ms.

SCHODACK DEPOT, p. o., Schodack township, Rensselaer co., N. Y.

SCHODACK LANDING, p. v., Schodack township, Rensselaer co., N. Y., 12 ms. s. of Albany ; from W. 358 ms. Watered by Hudson river.

SCHOENECK, p. o., Lancaster co., Pa., 45 ms. E. of Harrisburgh ; from W. 135 ms.

SCHOHARIE COUNTY, situated in the easterly part of New York. Area, 621 square miles. Face of the country, mountainous and hilly ; soil, productive. Seat of justice, Schoharie. Pop. in 1810, 18,945 ; in 1820, 23,154 ; in 1830, 27,902; in 1840, 32,358 ; in 1850, 33,548.

SCHOHARIE, c. h., p. t., seat of justice of Schoharie co., N. Y., 32 ms. w. of Albany ; from W. 383 ms. Watered by Schoharie and Fox creeks. Pop. 2,588.

SCHOOLCRAFT, p. v., Kalamazoo co., Mich., 149 ms. w. of Detroit ; from W. 608 ms. Pop. 1,101.

SCHRAALENBURGH, p. o., Bergen co., N. J.

SCHREPPEL, t., Oswego co., N. Y., 150 ms. N. w. of Albany. Watered by Oneida and Oswego rivers. Pop. 2,586.

SCHROON, p. t., Essex co., N. Y., 95 ms. N. of Albany ; from W. —— ms. Watered by head waters of Schroon river and by Schroon lake. Pop. 2,031.

SCHROON LAKE, p o., Schroon township, Essex co., N. Y., 95 ms. N. of Albany ; from W. 470 ms.

SCHROON RIVER, p. o., Essex co., N. Y.

SCHULTZSVILLE, p. o., Clinton township, Dutchess co., N. Y.

SCHUMLA, p. o., Ritchie co., Va.

SCHUYLER COUNTY, situated in the westerly part of Illinois, with Illinois river on the southeast. Area, 360 square miles. Face of the country, flat ; soil, generally fertile, Seat of justice, Rushville. Pop. in 1840, 6,972 ; in 1850, 10,573.

SCHUYLER COUNTY, situated on the north boundary of Missouri, with Chariton river on the west. Area, —— square miles. Seat of justice, Lancaster. Pop. in 1850, 3,287.

SCHUYLER, p. t., Herkimer co., N. Y., 87 ms. N. w. of Albany ; from W. —— ms. Watered by Mohawk river. Pop. 1,696.

SCHUYLER'S FALLS, p. o., Plattsburgh township. Clinton co., N. Y., 157 ms. N. of Albany ; from W. 532 ms.

SCHUYLER'S LAKE, p. o., Exeter township, Otsego co., N. Y., 75 ms. w. of Albany ; from W. 365 ms.

SCHUYLERSVILLE, p. v., Saratoga township, Saratoga co., N. Y. 34 ms. N. of Albany ; from W. 400 ms. Watered by Hudson river.

SCHUYLKILL COUNTY, situated in the easterly part of Pennsylvania, and traversed by Schuylkill river. Area, 660 square miles. Face of the country, hilly and mountainous ; soil, generally rocky and barren. Seat of justice, Orwigsburgh. Pop. in 1820, 11,339 ; in 1830, 20,744 ; in 1840, 29,053 ; in 1850, 60,713.

SCHUYLKILL. p. t., Chester co., Pa., 78 ms. s. E. of Harrisburgh ; from W. 157 ms. Watered by Schuylkill river. Pop. 1,403.

SCHUYLKILL, t., Schuylkill co., Pa. Pop. 1,742.

SCHUYLKILL BEND, p. o., Berks co., Pa., 57 ms. E. of Harrisburgh ; from W. 150 ms.

SCHUYLKILL HAVEN, p. v., Manheim township, Schuylkill co., Pa., 58 ms. N. E. of Harrisburgh ; from W. 168 ms. Watered by West Branch and Schuylkill rivers, and Schuylkill canal.

SCHWENKS' STORE, p. o., Montgomery co., Pa., 83 ms. E. of Harrisburgh ; from W. 169 ms.

SCIENCEVILLE, p. v., Windham township, Greene co., N. Y., 48 ms. s. w. of Albany ; from W. 365 ms.

SCIENCEVILLE, p. o., Stewart co., Ga.

SCIO. p. t., Alleghany co., N. Y., 266 ms. w. of Albany ; from W. 320 ms. Watered by Genesee river. Pop. 1,922.

SCIO, p. o., Harrison co., O.

SCIO, p. t., Washtenaw co., Mich., 56 ms. w. of Detroit ; from W. 542 ms. Watered by Huron river and Honey Mill creeks. Pop. 1,106.

SCIOTA, p. o., Clinton co., N. Y.

SCIOTO COUNTY, situated on the southerly boundary of Ohio, with Ohio river on the south, and traversed by the Scioto. Area, 600 square miles. Face of the country, broken ; soil, of middling quality. Seat of justice, Portsmouth. Pop. in 1810, 3,399 ; in 1820, 5,749 ; in 1830, 8,740 ; in 1840, 11,192 ; in 1850, 18,438.

SCIOTO, p. o., Scioto co., O., 195 ms. s. of Columbus ; from W. 439 ms.

SCIOTO, p. t., Delaware co., O. Watered by Scioto river. Pop. 1,126.

SCIOTO, t., Pickaway co., O. Pop. 1,347.

SCIOTO, t., Ross co., O. Pop. 1,596.

SCIOTO, t., Jackson co., O. Pop. 1,347.

SCIOTO BRIDGE, p. o., Scioto township, Delaware co., O.

SCIOTOVILLE, p. o., Scioto co.,O.

SCIPIO, p. t., Cayuga co., N. Y., 164 ms. w. of Albany ; from W. 329 ms. Watered by Owasco lake and Salmon creek. Pop. 2,137.

SCIPIO, t., Meigs co., O. Pop. 1,405.

SCIPIO, p. t., Hillsdale co., Mich. Pop. 864.

SCIPIO, t., Seneca co., O. Pop. 2,322.

SCIPIO, p. v., Jennings co., Ind., 56 ms. s. E. of Indianapolis ; from W. 578 ms.

SCIPIO CENTRE, p. o., Hillsdale co., Mich.

SCIPIOVILLE, p. o., Scipio township, Cayuga co., N. Y., 164 ms. w. of Albany ; from W. 323 ms.

SCITICO, p. o., Hartford co., Ct., 20 ms. N. E. of Hartford ; from W. 356 ms.

SCITUATE, p. t., Plymouth co., Mass., 26 ms. s. E. of Boston ; from W. 454 ms. Watered by North river and the Atlantic ocean. Pop. 2,149.

SCITUATE, p. t., Providence co., R. I. Watered by north branch of Pawtuxet river. Pop. 4,582.

SCONONDOAH, p. v., Verona township, Oneida co., N. Y., 115 ms. N. w. of Albany ; from W. 378 ms. Watered by Sconondoah creek.

SCOOBER, p. o,, Kemper co., Miss.

SCOTCH GROVE, p. o., Jones co., Iowa.

SCOTCH HILL, p. o., Clarion co., Pa.

SCOTCH PLAINS, p. v., Westfield township, Essex co., N. J., 42 ms. N. E. of Trenton ; from W. 209 ms. Watered by Green brook.

SCOTCH RIDGE, p. o., Wood co., O.

SCOTCHTOWN, p. v., Wallkill township, Orange co., N. Y., 107 ms. s. w. of Albany ; from W. 284 ms.

SCOTIA, p. v,, Glenville township, Schenectady co., N. Y., 18 ms. N. w. of Albany ; from W. 386 ms. Watered by Mohawk river.

SCOTIA, p. v., Pope co., Ark., 83 ms. N. w. of Little Rock ; from W. 1,148 ms. Watered by Arkansas river.

SCOTLAND COUNTY, situated on the north boundary of Missouri. Area, —— square miles. Seat of justice, Memphis. Pop. in 1850, 3,782.

SCOTLAND, p. o., York co., Me., 96 ms. s. w. of Augusta ; from W. 506 ms.

SCOTLAND, p. o., Plymouth co., Mass., 35 ms. s. of Boston ; from W. 427 ms.

SCOTLAND, p. v., Windham co., Ct., 35 ms. E. of Hartford ; from W. 362 ms.

SCOTLAND, p. o., Franklin co., Pa.

SCOTLAND, p. o., Jefferson co., Miss.

SCOTLAND, p. o., Greene co., Ind.

SCOTLAND NECK, p. o., Halifax co., N. C., 108 ms. N. E. of Raleigh ; from W. 232 ms.

SCOTT COUNTY, situated on the south boundary of Virginia, and traversed by Clinch river. Area, 624 square miles. Face of the country, hilly and mountainous. Seat of justice, Estillville. Pop. in 1830, 4,263; in 1830, 5,724 ; in 1840, 7,303 ; in 1850, 9,829.

SCOTT COUNTY, situated in the central part of Mississippi. Area, 576 square miles. Seat of justice, Hillsborough. Pop. in 1840, 1,653 ; in 1850, 3,961.

SCOTT COUNTY, situated in the northerly part of Kentucky. Area, 252 square miles. Seat of justice, Georgetown. Soil, productive. Pop. in 1810, 12,419 ; in 1820,12,219; in 1830, 14,677; in 1840, 13,668; in 1850, 14,946.

SCOTT COUNTY, situated in the southeast part of Indiana. Area, 200 square miles. Seat of justice, Lexington. Pop. in 1820, 2,334 ; in 1830, 3,092 ; in 1840, 4,242; in 1850, 5,855.

SCOTT COUNTY, situated in the westerly part of Illinois, with Illinois river on the west. Area, 240 square miles. Seat of justice, Winchester. Pop. in 1840, 6,125 ; in 1850, 7,914.

SCOTT COUNTY, situated on the easterly boundary of Missouri, with Mississippi river on the northeast. Area, 936 square miles. Face of the country, even ; soil, fertile. Seat of justice, Benton. Pop. in 1830. 2,136 ; in 1840, 5,974 ; in 1850, 7,914.

SCOTT COUNTY, situated on the west boundary of Arkansas. Area, 950 square miles. Seat of justice, Booneville. Pop. in 1840, 1,694 ; in 1850, 3,083.

SCOTT COUNTY, situated in Tennessee. Area, —— square miles. Seat of justice, Huntsville. Pop. in 1850, 1,905.

SCOTT COUNTY, situated on the southeasterly boundary of Iowa, with Mississippi river on the southeast. Area, 540 square miles. Seat of justice, Davenport. Pop. in 1840, 2,140 : in 1850. 5 986.

SCOTT, p. t., Cortland co., N. Y., 149 ms. w. of Albany; from W. 325 ms. Watered by headwaters of Toughnioga river and Skaneateles lake inlet. Pop. 1,290.

SCOTT, p. t., Wayne co., Pa., 199 ms. N. E. of Harrisburgh; from W. 293 ms. Watered by Susquehanna river and tributaries. Pop. 617.

SCOTT, p. t., Adams co., O., 95 ms. s. of Columbus; from W. 460 ms. Pop. 1,270.

SCOTT, p. t., Brown co., O. Pop. 930.

SCOTT. t, Marion co., O. Pop. 717.

SCOTT, t., Sandusky co., O. Pop. 792.

SCOTT, p. t., La Grange co., Ind., 183 ms. N. E. of Indianapolis; from W. 586 ms.

SCOTT, t., Montgomery co., Ind. Pop. 1,209.

SCOTT, p. t., Vanderburgh co., Ind.

SCOTT, p. o., Sheboygan co., Wis.

SCOTT, p. o., La Salle co., Ill.

SCOTT, p. o., Mahaska co., Iowa.

SCOTT HILL, p. o., New Hanover co., S. C.

SCOTTSBURGH, p. v., Halifax co., Va., 119 ms. s. w. of Richmond; from W. 217 ms.

SCOTTSBURGH, p. o., Livingston co., N. Y.

SCOTTSBURGH, p. o., Benton co., Oregon.

SCOTT's CREEK. p. o., Haywood co., N. C., 312 ms. w. of Raleigh; from W. 542 ms.

SCOTT's HILL, p. o., Henderson co., Tenn.

SCOTTSVILLE, p. v., Bibb co., Ala.; from W. 814 ms.

SCOTTSVILLE, p. v., Wheatland township, Monroe co., N. Y., 232 ms. w. of Albany; from W. 372 ms. Watered by Allen's creek.

SCOTTSVILLE, p. o., Wyoming co., Pa.

SCOTTSVILLE, c. h., p. v., seat of justice of Allen co., Ky., 148 ms. s. w. of Frankfort; from W. 671 ms. Watered by a tributary of Green river. Pop. 400.

SCOTTSVILLE, p. o., Claiborne parish, La.

SCOTT-VILLE, p. o., Sullivan co., Mo.

SCOTTSVILLE, p. o., Albermarle co., Va.

SCOTTVILLE, p. o., Macoupin co., Ill.

SCRABBLE, p. o., Berkeley co., Va.

SCRANTON. p. o., Luzerne co., Pa.

SCREAMERSVILLE, p. o., Maury co., Tenn.

SCRIBA, p. t., Oswego co., N. Y., 167 ms. N. w. of Albany; from W. 377 ms. Watered by Oswego river and Lake Ontario. Pop. 2,738.

SCRIVEN COUNTY, situated on the northeasterly boundary of Georgia, with Savannah river on the northeast. Area, 748 square miles. Seats of justice, Jacksonborough, and Sylvania. Pop. in 1810, 4,477; in 1820, 3,941; in 1830, 4,776; in 1840, 2,794; in 1850, 6,847.

SCROGGINS' Mills, p. o., Dale co., Ala.

SCROGGSFIELD, p. v., Fox township, Carroll co., O., 132 ms. N. E. of Columbus; from W. 291 ms.

SCRUB GRASS, p. t., Armstrong co., Pa. Pop. 1,702.

SCUFFLETOWN, p. v., Laurens district, S. C., 78 ms. N. w. of Columbus; from W. 504 ms. Watered by Saluda river.

SCULL CAMP, p. o., Surry co., N. C., 167 ms. w. of Raleigh; from W. 348 ms.

SCULL SHOALS, p. o., Greene co., Ga., 65 ms. N. of Milledgeville; from W. 608 ms. Situated on Oconee river.

SCULLTOWN, p. v., Upper Penn's Neck township, Salem co., N. J., 51 ms. s. of Trenton; from W. 162 ms. Watered by Old Man's creek.

SCUPPERNONG, p. o., Washington co., N. C.

SEABROOK, p. t., Rockingham co., N. H., 47 ms. s. E. of Concord; from W. 480 ms. Watered by Black, Brown's, and Walton rivers, and the Atlantic ocean. Pop. 1.296.

SEAFORD, p. v., Sussex co., Del., 46 ms. s. of Dover; from W. 121 ms. Watered by Nanticoke river.

SEAL, p. t., Pike co., O. Pop. 1,520.

SEAL, p. o., Wyandott co., O.

SEAL Cove, p. o., Hancock co., Me., 113 ms. E. of Augusta; from W. —— ms.

SEARCY COUNTY, situated in the north part of Arkansas, with White river on the northeast. Area, 850 square miles. Seat of justice, Lebanon. Pop. in 1840, 936; in 1850, 1,979.

SEARCY, c. h., p. v., seat of justice of White co., Ark., 50 ms. N. E. of Little Rock; from W. 1,076. Watered by Little Red river.

SEARIGHTS, p. o., Fayette co., Pa.

SEARSBURGH, p. t., Bennington co., Vt. Watered by Deerfield river Pop. 201.

SEARSBURGH, p. o., Hector township, Tompkins co., N. Y.

SEARSMONT, p. t., Waldo co., Me., 38 ms. E. of Augusta; from W. 627 ms. Watered by St. George's river. Pop. 1,693.

SEARSPORT, Waldo co., Me.

SEARSVILLE, p. o., Stewart co., Ga., 128 ms. s. w. of Milledgeville ; from W. 784 ms.

SEARSVILLE, p. o., Orange co., N. Y.

SEATUCK, p. o., Suffolk co., Long Island, N. Y.

SEA VIEW, p. o., Northampton co., Va., 163 ms. E. of Richmond ; from W. 239 ms.

SEAVILLE, p. o., Cape May co., N. J.

SEAVILLE, t., Hancock co., Me. Pop. 139.

SEBAGO, p. t., Cumberland co., Me., 76 ms. s. w. of Augusta ; from W. 562 ms. Watered by Sebago lake. Pop. 850.

SEBASTIAN COUNTY, situated in Arkansas. Area, —— square miles. Seat of justice, ——. Pop. about 4,000.

SEBASTICOOK, p. o., Kennebec co., Me.

SEBEC, p. t., Piscataquis co.. Me., 96 ms. N. E. of Augusta ; from W. 693 ms. Watered by Sebec lake and Piscataquis river. Pop. 1,223.

SEBEWA, p. o., Iowa co., Mich.

SECLUDA, p. o., Gadsden co., Flor.

SECOND CREEK, p. o., Greenbrier co., Va., 220 ms. w. of Richmond ; from W. 257 ms.

SECOND FORK, p. v., Elk co., Pa., 157 ms. N. w. of Harrisburgh ; from W. 249 ms.

SECOND TURN OUT, p. o., Louisa co., Va.

SECTION, p. o., Preston co., Va.

SEDGWICK, p. t., Hancock co., Me., 85 ms. E. of Augusta ; from W. 681 ms. Watered by the Atlantic ocean. Pop. 1,235.

SEEKONK, p. t., Bristol co., Mass., 46 ms. s. w. of Boston ; from W. 404 ms. Watered by Seekonk, or Providence, and Ten-Mile rivers. Pop. 2,243.

SEELY CREEK, p. o., Southport township, Chemung co., N. Y., 203 ms. s. w. of Albany ; from W. 271 ms.

SEELYSBURGH, p. o., Napoli township, Cattaraugus co., N. Y.

SEGO, p. o., Perry co., O.

SEGUIN, c. h., p. v., seat of justice of Guadalupe co., Tex.

SEIBERLINGVILLE, p. o., Lehigh co., Pa., 88 ms. s. E. of Harrisburgh ; from W. 178 ms.

SEISHOLTZVILLE, p. o., Berks co., Pa.

SELBY, p. o., Bureau co., Ill.

SELARVILLE, p. o., Sussex co., Del.

SELBYSPORT. p. v., Alleghany co., Md., 214 ms. N. w. of Annapolis ; from W. 172 ms.

SELIN's GROVE, p. v., Penn township, Union co., Pa., 51 ms. N. of Harrisburgh : from W. 161 ms. Watered by Susquehanna, at the confluence of Penn's creek.

SELKIRK, p. o., Marion co., S. C.

SELLER'S TAVERN, p. o., Bucks co., Pa., 49 ms. E. of Harrisburgh ; from W. 168 ms.

SELMA, p. v., Dallas co., Ala. Watered by Alabama river.

SELMA, p. v., Jefferson co., Mo., 168 ms. E. of Jefferson city ; from W. 818 ms. Watered by Mississippi river.

SELMA, p. o., McLean co., Ill.

SELMA, p. o., Clark co., O.

SELTZERVILLE, p. o., Lebanon co., Pa.

SEMINARY, p. o., Wachita co., Ark.

SEMPRONIUS, p. t., Cayuga co., N. Y., 164 ms. w. of Albany ; from W. 328 ms. Watered by Skaneateles lake. Pop. 1,266.

SEMPRONIUS, p. o., Austin co., Tex.

SENATOBIA, p. o., De Soto co., Miss.

SENECA COUNTY, situated toward the west part of New York, with Cayuga lake on the east, and Seneca lake on the west. Area, 308 square miles. Face of the country, diversified ; soil, rich and well cultivated. Seats of justice, Ovid and Waterloo. Pop. in 1810, 16,609 ; in 1820, 23,619 ; in 1830, 21,041 ; in 1840, 24,874 ; in 1850, 25,441.

SENECA COUNTY, situated in the north part of Ohio, and traversed by Sandusky river. Area, 540 square miles. Soil, productive. Seat of justice, Tiffin. Pop. in 1830, 5,159 ; in 1840, 18,128 ; in 1850, 37,105.

SENECA, p. t., Ontario co., N. Y., 179 ms. w. of Albany ; from W. —— ms. Watered by Seneca lake and Flint creek. Pop. 8,505.

SENECA, p. t., Guernsey co., O. Pop. 1,411.

SENECA, p. t., Monroe co., O. Pop. 1,803.

SENECA, p. t., Seneca co., O. Pop. 1,662.
SENECA, p. t., Lenawee co., Mich. Pop. 1,092.
SENECA. p. o., Anderson district, S. C.
SENECA, p. o., Tompkins co., N. Y.
SENECA. p. o., Whitesides co., Ill.
SENECA CASTLE, p. o., Seneca township, Ontario co., N. Y.. 186 ms. w. of Albany ; from W. 351 ms.
SENECA FALLS, p. t., Seneca co., N. Y., 166 ms. w. of Albany ; from W. 342 ms. Watered by Seneca river, Cayuga lake, and the Cayuga and Seneca canal. Pop. 4,296.
SENECA MILLS, p. o., Montgomery co., Md.
SENECA RIVER, p. o.. Cayuga co., N. Y.
SENECAVILLE, p. v., Seneca township, Guernsey co., O., 90 ms. E. of Columbus ; from W. 316 ms.
SENEX, p. o., McLean co., Ill., 98 ms. N. E. of Springfield ; from W. 758 ms.
SENNET, p. t., Cayuga co., N. Y., 158 ms. N. of Albany ; from W. 338 ms. Watered by tributaries of Seneca river. Pop. 2,347.
SENETELL'S STORE, p. o., Bossier parish, La.
SEPULGA.p. o., Conecuh co., Ala.
SEQUATCHEE, p. o., Marion co., Tenn.
SERENA, p. o., La Salle co., Ill.
SERGEANT. t., McKean co., Pa. Pop. 172.
SEARGEANTSVILLE. p. o., Hunterdon co., N. J.
SERRYSE, p. o., Lake co., Ill.
SERVICE, p. o., Beaver co., Pa.
SETAUKET, p. v., Brookhaven township, Suffolk co., N. Y., 200 ms. S. E. of Albany ; from W. 280 ms. Watered by Long Island sound.
SETZLER'S STORE, p. o., Chester co., Pa., 74 ms. S. E. of Harrisburgh : from W. 162 ms.
SEVEN ISLANDS. p. o., Fluvanna co., Va.
SEVEN ISLANDS, p. o., Butts co., Ga.
SEVEN LEAGUES, p. o., Smith co., Tex.
SEVEN-MILE, p. o., Butler co., O.
SEVEN-MILE CREEK, p. o., Eault co., Wis.
SEVEN-MILE FORD, p. o., Smyth co., Va., 281 ms. w. of Richmond ; from W. 349 ms.
SEVEN-MILE PRAIRIE, p. o., Darke co., O.
SEVENTY-SEVEN, p. o., Johnson co., Iowa.
SEVENTY-SIX, p. o., Clinton co., Ky., 120 ms. s. of Frankfort; from W. 626 ms.
SEVENTY-SIX, p. o., Beaver co., Pa., 232 ms. w. of Harrisburgh ; from W. 257 ms.
SEVEN VALLEYS, p. o., York co., Pa.
SEVIER COUNTY, situated on the southeasterly boundary of Tennessee, and traversed by Hollehucky river. Area, 600 square miles. Face of the country, hilly and mountainous ; soil, generally sterile. Seat of justice, Sevier. Pop. in 1810, 4,495 ; in 1820, 4,772 ; in 1830, 5.717 ; in 1840, 6,442 ; in 1850, 6,920.
SEVIER COUNTY, situated on the west boundary of Arkansas, with Red river on the south. Area, about 1,000 square miles. Seat of justice, Paraclifta. Pop. in 1830, 634 ; in 1840, 2,810 ; in 1850, 3,453.
SEVIER, c. h., p. v., seat of justice of Sevier co., Tenn., 213 ms. E. of Nashville; from W. 494 ms.
SEVILLE, t., Medina co., O.
SEVILLE, p. o., Madison co., Va.
SEWARD, p. t., Schoharie co., N. Y., 47 ms. w. of Albany ; from W. —— ms. Watered by Cobbles kill. Pop. 2,203.
SEWARD'S POINT, p. o., Montgomery co., Ill.
SEWEE, p. o., Meigs co., Tenn.
SEWELL MOUNTAIN, p. o., Fayette co., Va., 243 ms. w. of Richmond ; from W. 280 ms.
SEWELLSVILLE, p. o., Kirkwood township, Belmont co., O., 99 ms. E. of Columbus ; from W. 302 ms.
SEWICKLY, p. t., Westmoreland co., Pa. Watered by Sewickly creek. Pop, 1,918.
SEWICKLY BOTTOM, p. o., Alleghany co., Pa., 214 ms. w. of Harrisburgh ; from W. 240 ms.
SEWICKLYVILLE, p. o , Alleghany co., Pa., 214 ms. w. of Harrisburgh ; from W. 240 ms.
SEXTON's, p. o., Boone co., Mo., 45 ms. N. of Jefferson city ; from W. 950 ms.
SEXTON's CREEK, p. o., Clay co., Ky.
SEXTONVILLE, p. o., Richland co., Wis.
SHABBONAS' GROVE, p. o., De Kalb co., Ill.
SHADE, p. o., Athens co., O., 180 ms. s. E. of Columbus ; from W. 347 ms.
SHADE, p. t., Somerset co., Pa. Pop. 1,266.
SHADE FURNACE, p. o., Somerset co., Pa.
SHADE GAP, p. o., Huntingdon co., Pa., 73 ms. w. of Harrisburgh ; from W. 119 ms.
SHADE MILLS, p. o., Alleghany co,, Md.

SHADEWELL, p. o. Albemarle co., Va.
SHADY, p. o., Johnson co., Tenn.
SHADY DALE, p. o., Jasper co., Ga., 41 ms. s. w. of Milledgeville ; from W. 634 ms.
SHADY GROVE, p. o., Franklin co., Va., 184 ms. s. w. of Richmond ; from W. 259 ms.
SHADY GROVE, p. o., Union district, S. C., 68 ms. N. w. of Columbia ; from W. 476 ms.
SHADY GROVE, p. o.. Union co., Ga., 170 ms. N. w. of Milledgeville ; from W. 611 ms.
SHADY GROVE, p. o., Gibson co., Tenn., 115 ms. w. of Nashville ; from W. 798 ms.
SHADY GROVE, p. o., Washington parish, La., 84 ms N. of New Orleans ; from W. 1,008 ms.
SHADY GROVE, p. o., Dallas co., Mo.
SHADY GROVE, p. o., Dallas co., Mo.
SHADY HILL. p. o., Henderson co., Tenn.
SHADY SPRING, p. o., Raleigh co., Va.
SHAEFFERSTOWN, p. v., Heidelberg township, Lebanon co., Pa., 32 ms. E. of Harrisburgh ; from W. 130 ms. Pop. 616.
SHAFERS, p. o., Monroe co., Pa., 116 ms. N. E. of Harrisburgh ; from W. 212 ms.
SHAFTSBURY, p. t., Bennington co., Vt., 110 ms. s. of Montpelier ; from W. 414 ms. Watered by tributaries of Walloomsack river and the Battenkill. Pop. 1,896.
SHAKER VILLAGE, p. v., Canterbury township, Merrimack co., N. H., 14 ms. N. of Concord ; from W. 495 ms.
SHAKELFORD's, p. o., King and Queen co., Va.
SHALER'S MILLS, p. o., Knox co., O.
SHALEKSVILLE, p. t., Portage co., O., 145 ms. N. E. of Columbus ; from W. 330 ms. Watered by Cuyahoga river. Pop. 1,190.
SHALLOTTE, p. o., Brunswick co., N. C., 167 ms. s. of Raleigh ; from W. 420 ms.
SHALLOW FORD, p. o., Orange co , N. C.
SHAMOKIN, p. t., Northumberland co., Pa., 76 ms. N. of Harrisburgh ; from W. 186 ms. Watered by Shamokin creek. Pop. 2.191.
SHAMONY, p. o., Burlington co., N. J.
SHAMROCK. p. o., Callaway co., Mo., 39 ms. N. E. of Jefferson city ; from W. 913 ms.
SHAMROCK MILLS, p. o.. Washington co., R. I.
SHANANDOAH, p. o., Richland co., O.
SHANDAKEN, p. t., Ulster co., N. Y., 83 ms. s. w. of Albany ; from W. 342 ms. Watered by Esopus creek and Neversink river. Pop. 2,307.
SHANE'S CROSSINGS, p. o., Dublin township, Mercer co., O., 124 ms. N. W. of Columbus ; from W. 501 ms.
SHANESVILLE, p. v., Sugar creek township, Tuscarawas co., O., 107 ms. N. E. of Columbus ; from W. 325 ms. Watered by Sugar creek.
SHANESVILLE, p. o., Berks co., Pa.
SHANKSVILLE, p. o., Somerset co., Pa.
SHANNON COUNTY, situated in the south part of Missouri. Area, about 1,300 square miles. Seat of justice. Eminence. Pop. in 1850, 1,199.
SHANNON, p. o., Steuben co., N. Y.
SHANNON, p. o., Muskingum co., O.
SHANNON HILL, p. o., Goochland co., Va., 48 ms. s. w. of Richmond ; from W. 149 ms.
SHANNON's, p. o., Montgomery co., Tex.
SHANNONVILLE, p. v., Montgomery co., Pa., 84 ms, E. of Harrisburgh ; from W. 160 ms.
SHAPLEIGH, p. t., York co., Me., 89 ms. s. w. of Augusta ; from W. 522 ms. Pop. 1,348.
SHARK RIVER, p. o., Ocean co., N. J.
SHARON, t., Hillsborough co., N. H.
SHARON, p. t., Windsor co., Vt., 40 ms. s. of Montpelier ; from W. 495 ms. Watered by White river. Pop. 1,240.
SHARON, p. t., Norfolk co., Mass., 17 ms. s. E. of Boston ; from W. 425 ms. Watered by Mashapoag pond. Pop. 1,128.
SHARON, p. t.. Litchfield co., Ct., 48 ms. w. of Hartford ; from W. 332 ms. Watered by Housatonic river. Pop. 2,507.
SHARON, p. t., Schoharie co., N. Y., 43 ms. w. of Albany ; from W. 392 ms. Site of a celebrated salubrious mineral Spring. Pop. 2,632.
SHARON, p. v., Pymatuning township, Mercer co., Pa., 249 ms. N. w. of Harrisburgh ; from W. 292 ms. Watered by Shenango creek. Pop. 541.
SHARON, t., Potter co., Pa. Pop. 501.
SHARON, p. v., Wythe co., Va., 265 ms. s. w. of Raleigh ; from W. 333 ms.
SHARON, p. o., Mecklenburgh co., N. C., 165 ms. s. w. of Raleigh ; from W. 404 ms.
SHARON, p. t., Franklin co., O. Pop. 1,509.

SHARON, p. o., Olive township, Morgan co., O., 93 ms.
E. of Columbus ; from W. 315 ms.
SHARON, p. t., Medina co., O. Pop. 1,519.
SHARON, p. t., Richmond co., O. Pop. 1,959.
SHARON. p. t.. Washtenaw co., Mich., 56 ms. **w.** of Detroit ; from W. 532 ms. Pop. 868.
SHARON, p. o., Chambers co., Ala.
SHARON, p. v., Whitesides co., Ill., 174 ms. **N.** of Springfield ; from W. 869 ms.
SHARON, p. v., Madison co., Miss., 30 ms. **N.** of Jackson ; from W. 1,005 ms.
SHARON, p. o., Appanoose co., Iowa.
SHARON, p. o., Walworth co., Wis.
SHARON CENTRE, p. o., Sharon township, Schoharie co., N. Y., 46 ms. **w.** of Albany ; from W. 388 ms.
SHARON CENTRE, p. v., Potter co., Pa., 192 ms. **N. W.** of Harrisburgh ; from W. 308 ms.
SHARON CENTRE, p. v., Sharon township, Medina co., O.. 126 ms. **N. E,** of Columbus ; from W. 342 ms.
SHARON SPRINGS, p. o., Schoharie co., N. Y.
SHARONVILLE, p. o., King William co., Va.
SHARONVILLE. p. v., Hamilton co., O., 102 ms. **s. w.** of Columbus ; from W. 485 ms.
SHARPE'S STORE, p. o., Lowndes co., Ga., 256 ms. **s.** of Milledgeville ; from W. 900 ms.
SHARPESVILLE, p. v., Montgomery co., Ala. ; from W. 855 ms.
SHARPSBURGH, p. v., Bath co., Ky., 62 ms. **E.** of Frankfort ; from W. 508 ms.
SHARPSBURGH, p. v., Alleghany co., Pa., 206 ms. **w.** of Harrisburgh ; from W. 233 ms.
SHARPSBURGH, p. v., Washington co.. Md., 97 ms. **N. w.** of Annapolis ; from W. 65 ms. Watered by Potomac river.
SHARPSBURGH, p. o., Marion co., Mo.
SHARP'S FORK, p. o., Athens co., O.
SHARP'S MILLS, p. o., Harrison co., Ind.
SHARPSVILLE, p. o., Tipton co., Ind.
SHARP TOP, p. o., Cherokee co., Ga.
SHARPTOWN, p. v., Pilesgrove township, Salem co., **N. J.,** 55 ms. **s.** of Trenton ; from W. 166 ms. Watered by Salem creek.
SHARTLESVILLE, p. v., Berks co., Pa., 65 ms. **E.** of Harrisburgh ; from W. 175 ms.
SHASTA COUNTY, situated in the northeast corner of California, and traversed by tributaries of the Sacramento river. Area, —— square miles. Face of the country, mountainous. Seat of justice, Reading's Ranch. Pop. in 1852, 4,050.
SHASTA, p. o., Shasta co., Cal.
SHAUCKS. p. o., Morrow co., O.
SHAUMBURGH, p. o., Cook co., Ill.
SHAVER'S CREEK, p. o., Huntington co., Pa., 95 ms. **w.** of Harrisburgh ; from W. 160 ms.
SHAVER'S CREEK, p. o., Lee co., Va.
SHAVERTOWN, p o., Andes township, Delaware co., **N. Y.,** 89 ms. **s. w.** of Albany ; from W. 325 ms.
SHAWANGUNK, p. t., Ulster co., N. Y., 87 ms. **s.** of Albany ; from W. 296 ms. Watered by Shawangunk creek and Wall kill. Pop. 4,036.
SHAWNEE, p. o., Kheatfield township, Niagara co., **N. Y.,** 285 ms. **w.** of Albany ; from W. 410 ms.
SHAWNEE, p. o., Monroe co., Pa.
SHAWNEE, t., Allen co., O. Pop. 716.
SHAWNEE, p. t., Fountain co., Ind. Pop. 1,103.
SHAWNEE MOUND, p. o., Tippecanoe co., Ind.
SHAWNEE PRAIRIE, p. o., Fountain co., Ind., 78 ms. **w.** of Indianapolis ; from W. 644 ms.
SHAWNEETOWN, p. v., Gallatin co., Ill., 195 ms. **s. E.** of Springfield : from W. 762 ms. Watered by Ohio river. Pop. 1,764.
SHAW'S MILLS, p. o., Guilford co., N. C., 73 ms. **w.** of Raleigh ; from W. 313 ms.
SHAWSVILLE, p. o., Harford co., Md.
SHAWSVILLE, p. o., Montgomery co., Va.
SHAWSVILLE, p. o., Broome co., N. Y.
SHEARER'S CROSS ROADS, p. o., Westmoreland co., Pa.
SHEBOYGAN COUNTY, situated on the east boundary of Wisconsin, with Lake Michigan on the east. Area, 500 square miles. Seat of justice, Sheboygan. Pop. in 1840, 133 ; in 1850, 8,378.
SHEBOYGAN, c. h., p. v., seat of justice of Sheboygan co., Wis., 146 ms. **N. E.** of Madison ; from W. 868 ms. Watered by Sheboygan river and Lake Michigan.
SHEBOYGAN FALLS. p. o., Sheboygan co., Wis.
SHEEPSCOT BRIDGE, p, v., Lincoln co., Me., 25 ms. **s.** of Augusta ; from W. 593 ms.

SHEETZ' MILLS, p. o., Hampshire co., Va., 204 ms. **N. w.** of Richmond ; from W. 132 ms.
SHEFFIELD. p. t.. Caledonia co., Vt., 45 ms. **N. E.** of Montpelier ; from W. 558 ms. Watered by head-waters of Passumpsic and Barton rivers. Pop. 797.
SHEFFIELD, p. t., Berkshire co., Mass., 138 ms. **s. w.** of Boston ; from W. 349 ms. Watered by Housatonic and Konkopot rivers. Pop. 2,769.
SHEFFIELD, p. t., Warren co., Pa., 91 ms. **N. w.** of Harrisburgh ; from W. 283 ms. Pop. 317.
SHEFFIELD, p. v., Newton co., Ga., 71 ms. **N. w.** of Milledgeville ; from W. 658 ms.
SHEFFIELD, p. t , Lorain co., O., 137 ms. **N. E.** of Columbus ; from W. 382 ms. Watered by Lake Erie and Black river. Pop. 906.
SHEFFIELD, t., Ashtabula co., O. Pop. 845.
SHEFFIELD, p. o., Fayette co., Ala.
SHEFFIELD, p. t., Tippecanoe co., Ind.
SHEFFIELD LAKE, p. o., Lorain co., O.
SHEKOLA. p. o., Pike co., Pa.
SHEILVILLE, p. o., Hamilton co., Ind.
SHELBURNE, p. t., Coos co., N. H., 111 ms. **N.** of Concord ; from W. 594 ms. Watered by Androscoggin river and tributaries. Pop. 480.
SHELBURNE, p. t., Chittenden co., Vt., 48 ms. **w.** of Montpelier ; from W. 505 ms. Watered by Lake Champlain and La Platte river. Pop. 1,257.
SHELBURNE, p. t.. Franklin co., Mass., 96 ms. **w.** of Boston ; from W. 406 ms. Watered by Deerfield river. Pop. 1,239.
SHELBURNE FALLS, p. v., Shelburne township, Franklin co., Mass., 101 ms. **w.** of Boston ; from W. 411 ms. Watered by Deerfield river.
SHELBY COUNTY, situated in the central part of Alabama, with Coosa river on the east, and the Catawba on the west. Area, 950 square miles. Seat of justice, Columbiana. Pop. in 1820, 2,416 ; in 1830, 5,704 ; in 1840, 6.112 ; in 1850, 9,536.
SHELBY COUNTY, situated at the southwest corner of Tennessee, with Mississippi river on the west. Area, 600 square miles. Face of the country, hilly ; soil, of good quality. Seat of justice, Raleigh. Pop. in 1820, 354 ; in 1830, 5,648 ; in 1840, 14,721 ; in 1850, 31,157.
SHELBY COUNTY, situated in the northerly part of Kentucky. Area, 442 square miles. Face of the country, uneven ; soil, rich. Seat of justice, Shelbyville. Pop. in 1810. 14,778 ; in 1820, 21,047 ; in 1830, 19,030 ; in 1840, 17,768 ; in 1850, 17,095.
SHELBY COUNTY, situated in the west part of Ohio, and traversed by Miami river. Area, 418 square miles. Face of the country, even ; soil, fertile. Seat of justice, Sidney. Pop. in 1820, 2,106 ; in 1830, 3,671 ; in 1840, 12,154 ; in 1850, 13 958.
SHELBY COUNTY, situated toward the southeast part of Indiana. Area, 432 square miles. Face of the country, even ; soil, productive. Seat of justice, Shelbyville. Pop. in 1830, 6,294 ; in 1840, 12,005 ; in 1850, 15,502.
SHELBY COUNTY, situated in the central part of Illinois, and traversed by Kaskaskia river. Area, 1,080 square miles. Soil, in many parts, fertile. Seat of justice, Shelbyville. Pop. in 1830, 2,972 ; in 1840, 6,659 ; in 1850. 7,807.
SHELBY COUNTY, situated in the northeast part of Missouri. Area, 432 square miles. Seat of justice, Shelbyville. Pop. in 1840, 3,056 ; in 1850, 4,253.
SHELBY COUNTY, situated on the east boundary of Texas, with Sabine river on the east. Area, —— square miles. Seat of justice, Shelbyville. Pop. in 1850, 4,239.
SHELBY, p. t., Orleans co., N. Y., 262 ms. **w.** of Albany ; from W. 395 ms. Watered by Oak-Orchard creek and Erie canal. Pop. 3,082.
SHELBY, p. v., Sharon township, Richland co., O., 69 ms. **N.** of Columbus ; from W. 394 ms. Watered by head-waters of Black fork of Mohiccan creek.
SHELBY, c. h., p. v.. seat of justice of Cleveland co., N. C. Watered by First Broad river.
SHELBY, t., Jefferson co., Ind. Pop. 1,772.
SHELBY, p. t., Macomb co., Mich. Pop. 1,482.
SHELBY, t., Polk co., Mo.
SHELBY BASIN, p. v.. Shelby township, Orleans co., N. Y., 265 ms. **w.** of Albany ; from W. 400 ms. Situated on the Erie canal.
SHELBY'S CREEK. p. o., Tippah co., Miss.
SHELBY SPRINGS. p. o., Shelby co., Ala.
SHELBYVILLE, c. h., p. v., seat of justice of Bedford

co., Tenn., 59 ms. s. of Nashville ; from W. 682 ms. Watered by Duck creek.

SHELBYVILLE, c. h., p. v., seat of justice of Shelby co., Ky. ; 23 ms. w. of Frankfort ; from W. 565 ms. Watered by Brashear's creek.

SHELBYVILLE, c. h., p. t., seat of justice of Shelby co., Ind., 26 ms. s. E. of Indianapolis ; from W. 564 ms. Watered by Blue river. Pop. 995.

SHELBYVILLE, c. h., p. v., seat of justice of Shelby co., Ill., 60 ms. s. E. of Springfield ; from W. 724 ms. Watered by Kaskaskia river.

SHELBYVILLE, c. h., p. v., seat of justice of Shelby co., Mo., 101 ms. N. of Jefferson city ; from W. 958 ms. Pop. 359.

SHELBYVILLE, c. h., p. v., seat of justice of Shelby co., Tex.

SHELDON, p. t., Franklin co., Vt., 62 ms. N. of Montpelier ; from W. 546 ms. Watered by Missisque and Black rivers. Pop. 1,814.

SHELDON, p. t., Wyoming co., N. Y., 265 ms. w. of Albany ; from W. 363 ms. Watered by Tonawanda and Seneca creeks. Pop. 2,527.

SHELDONVILLE, p. o., Norfolk co., Mass.

SHELDRAKE, p. o., Seneca co., N. Y.

SHELEMIAH, p. o., Cecil co., Md.

SHELL POINT, p. o., Wakulla co., Flor.

SHELLTOWN. p. o., Ocean co., N. J.

SHELOCTA, p. v., Armstrong township, Indiana co., Pa., 164 ms. w. of Harrisburgh ; from W. 217 ms.

SHELTER ISLAND, p. o., Suffolk co., N. Y., 245 ms. s. E. of Albany ; from W. 4— ms. Situated between Gardener's and Great Peconic bays.

SHELTONVILLE. p. o., Forsyth co., Ga.

SHENANDOAH COUNTY, situated toward the northeast part of Virginia. Area, 410 square miles. Face of the country, hilly and mountainous ; soil, productive. Seat of justice, Woodstock. Pop. in 1810, 13,646 ; in 1820, 18,926 ; in 1830, 19,750 ; in 1840, 11,618 ; in 1850, 13,768.

SHENANDOAH, p. o., Fishkill township, Dutchess co., N. Y., 93 ms. s. of Albany ; from W. 294 ms.

SHENANDOAH IRON WORKS, p. o., Page co., Va., 113 ms. N. w. of Richmond ; from W. 118 ms.

SHENANDOAH SPRINGS, p. o., Shenandoah co., Va.

SHENANGO, p. t., Beaver co., Pa.

SHENANGO. p. t., Mercer co., Pa. Watered by Shenango creek. Pop. 1,574.

SHEPHERD'S GROVE, p. o., Culpeper co., Va.

SHEPHERDSTOWN, p. v. Cumberland co., Pa., 19 ms. w. of Harrisburgh ; from W. 102 ms.

SHEPHERDSTOWN, p. v., Jefferson co., Va., 179 ms. N. of Richmond ; from W. 67 ms. Watered by Potomac river.

SHEPHERDSTOWN, p. v., Wheeling township, Belmont co., O. Pop. 90.

SHEPHERDSVILLE, c. h., p. v., seat of justice of Bullitt co., Ky., 72 ms. s. w. of Frankfort ; from W. 616 ms. Watered by Salt river.

SHERBURNE, p. t., Rutland co., Vt., 68 ms. s. of Montpelier ; from W. 468 ms. Watered by Queechee river and Thundering brook. Pop. 578.

SHERBURNE, p. t., Middlesex co., Mass., 19 ms. s. w. of Boston ; from W. 420 ms. Watered by Charles and Sudbury rivers. Pop. 1,043.

SHERBURNE, p. t., Chenango co., N. Y., 103 ms. w. of Albany ; from W. 347 ms. Watered by Chenango river and Chenango canal. Pop. 2,623.

SHERBURNE MILLS, p. v., Fleming co., Ky., 83 ms. E. of Frankfort ; from W. 500 ms. Watered by Licking river.

SHERBURNVILLE, p. o., Will co., Ill.

SHERIDAN, p t., Chautauque co., N. Y., 324 ms. w. of Albany ; from W. 351 ms. Watered by Lake Erie, and Scott's, Walnut, and other creeks. Pop. 2,173.

SHERIDAN, t., Calhoun co., Mich. Pop. 972.

SHERMAN, p. t., Fairfield co., Ct., 57 ms. s. w. of Hartford ; from W. 308 ms. Watered by Rocky river. Pop. 984.

SHERMAN, p. t., Chautauque co., N. Y., 357 ms. w. of Albany ; from W. 346 ms. Watered by French creek. Pop. 1,292.

SHERMAN, p. t., Huron co., O., 90 ms. N. of Columbus ; from W. 412 ms.

SHERMAN, p. t., St. Joseph co., Mich., 135 ms. w. of Detroit ; from W. 584 ms. Watered by Prairie creek. Pop. 364.

SHERMAN. p. o., Cook co., Ill.

SHERMAN, p. o., Grayson co., Tex.

SHERMAN'S DALE, p. o., Perry co., Pa.

SHERMAN'S HOLLOW, p. o., Yates co., N. Y.

SHERODSVILLE, p. o., Carroll co., O., 118 ms. N. E. of Columbus ; from W. 304 ms.

SHERRILL'S FORD, p. o., Lincoln co., N. C., 159 ms. w. of Raleigh ; from W. 396 ms.

SHERRARD'S STORE, p. o,, Hampshire co.. Va., 173 ms N. w. of Richmond ; from W. 101 ms.

SHERWOOD, p. t., Branch co., Mich., 125 ms. s. w. of Detroit ; from W. 583 ms. Pop. 686.

SHERWOOD'S, p. o., Scipio township, Cayuga co., N. Y., 156 ms. w. of Albany ; from W. 321 ms.

SHESHEQUIN, p. t., Bradford co., Pa., 144 ms. N. of Harrisburgh ; from W. 254 ms. Watered by tributaries of Susquehanna river. Pop. 1,455.

SHIAWASSEE COUNTY, situated in the central part of Michigan, and traversed by Shiawassee river. Area, 544 square miles. Seat of justice, Corunna. Pop. in 1840, 2,103 ; in 1850, 5,230.

SHIAWASSEE, p. t., Shiawassee co., Mich., 76 ms. N. w. of Detroit ; from W. 579 ms. Watered by Shiawassee river.

SHICKSHINNY, p. o., Luzerne co., Pa., 114 ms. N. E. of Harrisburgh ; from W. 218 ms.

SHIELDSBOROUGH, c. h., p. o., seat of justice of Hancock co., Miss., 212 ms. s. of Jackson ; from W. 1,162 ms. Watered by the bay of St. Louis.

SHILOAH, p. v., Camden co., N. C., 226 ms. N. E. of Raleigh ; from W. 286 ms.

SHILOH, p. o., Marengo co., Ala. ; from W. 909 ms.

SHILOH, p. o,, Gibson co., Tenn., 149 ms. w. of Nashville ; from W. 823 ms.

SHILOH, p. o., Cumberland co., N. J.

SHILOH, p. o., St. Clair co., Ill.

SHILOH, p. o., Callaway co., Ky.

SHILOH, p. o., King George co., Va.

SHILOH, p. o., Sumter district, S. C.

SHILOH, p. o., Union parish, La.

SHIN CREEK, p. o., Ulster co., N. Y.

SHINGLE CREEK. p. o., St, Lawrence co., N Y.

SHINNSTON, p. v., Harrison co., Va., 265 ms. N. w. of Richmond ; from W. 233 ms.

SHIPPEN, p. t., McKean co., Pa., 171 ms. N. w. of Harrisburgh ; from W. 254 ms. Watered by Driftwood creek. Pop. 369.

SHIPPEN, t., Cumberland co., Pa. Pop. 1,786.

SHIPPEN. t., Tioga co., Pa. Pop. 298.

SHIPPENSBURGH, p. b., Cumberland co., Pa., 34 ms. s. w. of Harrisburgh ; from W. 101 ms. Watered by Meau's run. Pop. 1,568.

SHIPPENSVILLE, p. v., Clarion co., Pa., 188 ms. s. w. of Harrisburgh ; from W. 277 ms.

SHIPPINGPORT, v., a suburb of Louisville, Jefferson co., Ky.

SHIREMANTOWN, p. v., Cumberland co., Pa., 4 ms. w. of Harrisburgh ; from W. 108 ms.

SHIRLAND, p. o., Alleghany co., Pa.

SHIRLEY, p. t., Piscataquis co., Me., 84 ms. N. of Augusta ; from W. 679 ms. Watered by head-waters of Piscataquis river. Pop. 250.

SHIRLEY, p. t., Middlesex co., Mass., 40 ms. N. w. of Boston ; from W. 423 ms. Pop. 1,158.

SHIRLEY, p. o., Erie co., N. Y.

SHIRLEY, p. t., Huntingdon co., Pa. Pop. 1,615.

SHIRLEY, p. o., Tyler co., Va.

SHIRLEY MILLS, p. o., Piscataquis co., Me.

SHIRLEYSBURGH, p. b., Shirley township, Huntingdon co., Pa., 85 ms. s. w. of Harrisburgh ; from W. 130 ms. Pop. 361.

SHIRLEY VILLAGE, p. v., Shirley township, Middlesex co., Mass., 41 ms. N. w. of Boston ; from W. 423 ms. Watered by Nashua river.

SHIRLEYVILLE, p. o., Abbeville district, S. C.

SHOAL CREEK, p. o., Johnson co., Ark., 100 ms. N. w. of Little Rock ; from W. 1,165 ms.

SHOAL CREEK, p. o., Clinton co., Ill., 105 ms. s. of Springfield ; from W. 780 ms.

SHOAL CREEK, p. o., Newton co., Mo.

SHOAL CREEK, p. o., Lauderdale co., Miss.

SHOAL FORD, p. o., Limestone co.. Ala. ; from W. 721 ms.

SHOALS OF OGECHEE, p. o., Hancock co., Ga., 45 ms. N. E. of Milledgeville ; from W. 646 ms.

SHOAL SPRINGS, p. o., Giles co., Tenn.

SHOBER'S MILLS, p. o., Carroll co., O., 122 ms. N. E. of Columbus ; from W. 285 ms.

SHOCCO SPRINGS, p. o., Warren co., N. C.

SHOCKEY'S PRAIRIE, p. o., Lamar co., Tex.
SHOKAN, p. o., Ulster co., N. Y.
SHOKOKON, p. o., Henderson co., Il\., 217 ms. N. w. of Springfield ; from W. 868 ms.
SHONGALO, p. o., Carroll co., Miss.
SHONGO, p. o., Alleghany co., N. Y.
SHOOBOTA, p. o., Clarke co., Miss.
SHOOLING CREEK, p. o., Cherokee co., N. C.
SHOPIERE, p. o.. Rock co., Wis.
SHOP SPRING, p. o., Newberry district, S. C., 46 ms. N. w. of Columbia ; from W. 510 ms.
SHOREHAM, p. t., Addison co., Vt., 73 ms. s. w. of Montpelier ; from W. 469 ms. Watered by Lake Champlain and Lemon Fair river. Pop. 1,601.
SHORT BEND, p. o., Crawford co., Mo.
SHORT CREEK, p. t., Harrison co.. O.. 120 ms. E. of Columbus ; from W. 281 ms. Pop. 1,490.
SHORT CREEK. p. o., Brooke co.. Va.
SHORT TRACT, p. o., Granger township, Alleghany co., N. Y., 266 ms. w. of Albany ; from W. 345 ms.
SHOUSTOWN, p. o., Alleghany co., Pa.
SHREVE, p. o., Wayne co., O., 90 ms. N. E. of Columbus ; from W. 358 ms.
SHREVEPORT, c. h., p. v., seat of justice of Caddo parish, La., 380 ms. N. w. of New Orleans ; from W. 1,260 ms. Watered by Red river. Pop. 1.133.
SHREWSBURY, p. t., Worcester co., Mass., 37 ms. w. of Boston ; from W. 404 ms. Watered by Long pond. Pop. 1,596.
SHREWSBURY, p. t., Rutland co., Vt., 72 ms. s. E. of Montpelier ; from W. 466 ms. Watered by Mill and Cold rivers. Pop. 1,268 ms.
SHREWSBURY, p. t., Monmouth co., N. J., 52 ms. E. of Trenton ; from W. 218 ms. Watered by Neversink, Shrewsbury, and Shark rivers, and the Atlantic ocean. Pop. 3,180.
SHREWSBURY, t., Lycoming co., Pa. Pop. 225.
SHREWSBURY, p. t., York co., Pa., 38 ms. s. of Harrisburgh ; from W. 76 ms. Watered by tributaries of Codorus creek. Pop. 472.
SHREWSBURY, p. o., Kanawha co., Va.
SHRUB OAK, p. v., Yorktown township, Westchester co., N. Y., 112 ms. s. of Albany ; from W. 275 ms.
SHULLSBURGH. p. o., Lafayette co., Wis.
SHUNK, p. o., Sullivan co., Pa.
SHUNK, p. o., Henry co., O.
SHUSHAN, p. v., Salem township, Washington co., N. Y., 47 ms. N. E. of Albany ; from W. 417 ms. Watered by Batten kill.
SHUTESBURY, p. t., Franklin co., Mass., 79 ms. w. of Boston ; from W. 397 ms. Watered by Swift river. Pop. 912.
SHY POST, p. o., Audrian co., Mo.
SIAM, p. o., Leon co., Tex.
SIASCONSET, v., Nantucket co., Mass. Situated on Nantucket island, and watered by the Atlantic ocean.
SIBILA, p. o., Washington parish, La., 94 ms. N. of New Orleans ; from W. 1,131 ms.
SIBLEY. p. o., Jackson co., Mo.
SIBLEY'S MILLS. p. o., Wilkinson co., Miss.
SICILY, p. o., Highland co., O.
SIDNEY, p. t., Kennebec co., Me.. 9 ms. N. of Augusta ; from W. 604 ms. Watered by Kennebec river. Pop. 1,955.
SIDNEY, p. t., Delaware co. N. Y., 93 ms. s. w. of Albany ; from W. 334 ms. Watered by Oleout creek. Pop. 1,807.
SIDNEY, p. o., Hunterdon co., N. J., 35 ms. N. of Trenton ; from W. 195 ms.
SIDNEY, c. h., p. t., seat of justice of Shelby co., O., 78 ms. w. of Columbus ; from W. 473 ms. Watered by west branch of Great Miami river. Pop. 1,302.
SIDNEY, p. v., Marshall co., Ind., 105 ms. N. of Indianapolis ; from W. 626 ms.
SIDNEY, p. o.. Fremont co., Iowa.
SIDNEY CENTRE, p. o., Sidney township, Delaware co., N. Y., 98 ms. s. w. of Albany ; from W. 333 ms.
SIDNEY PLAINS, p. v., Sidney township, Delaware co., N. Y., 99 ms. s. w. of Albany ; from W. 325 ms. Watered by Susquehanna river.
SIDON, p. o., Carroll co., Miss.
SIDONSBURGH, p. o., York co., Pa.
SIEGEL'S STORE. p. o., Lincoln co., N. C., 180 ms. w. of Raleigh ; from W. 418 ms.
SIERRA COUNTY, situated in the ———— part of California. Pop. in 1852, 4,855.
SIGOURNEY, c. h., p. v., seat of justice of Keokuk co., Iowa. Pop. 162.

SILOA. p. o., Sullivan co., Ind., 88 ms, s. w. of Indianapolis ; from W. 659 ms.
SILOAM, p. v., Smithfield township, Madison co., N Y., 110 ms. w. of Albany ; from W. 364 ms.
SILOAM, p. v., Surry co., N. C., 141 ms. N. w. of Raleigh ; from W. 344 ms.
SILVAN, t., Washtenaw co., Mich. Pop. 1,343.
SILVER CREEK, p. o., Hanover township, Chautauque co.. N. Y.
SILVER CREEK, p. t., Greene co., O. Pop. 2.565.
SILVER CREEK, p. o., Cass co., Mich., 181 ms. s. w. of Detroit ; from W. 629 ms. Watered by Dowagiake river.
SILVER CREEK, p. o., Madison co., Ky., 56 ms. s. E. of Frankfort ; from W. 554 ms.
SILVER CREEK. p. o., Maury co., Tenn., 54 ms. s. of Nashville ; from W. 712 ms.
SILVER CREEK, p. o., Stephenson co., Ill., 206 ms. N. of Springfield ; from W. 826 ms.
SILVER GLADE, p. o., Anderson district, S. C., 137 ms. N. w. of Columbia ; from W. 532 ms.
SILVER HILL, p. o., Davidson co., N. C.
SILVER LAKE, p. t., Susquehanna co., Pa., 184 ms. N. E. of Harrisburgh ; from W. 294 ms. Watered by Silver lake and Silver creek. Pop. 1,213.
SILVER LAKE, p. o., Washtenaw co., Mich.
SILVER LAKE, p. o., Waushara co., Wis.
SILVER RUN, p. o., Talladega co., Ala.
SILVER RUN, p. o., Meigs co., O.
SILVER SPRING, p. t., Cumberland co., Pa. Watered by Conedogwinit creek and tributaries. Pop 2,308.
SILVER SPRING, p. o., St. Francis co., Mo.
SILVERTON, p. v., Barnwell district, S. C., 9€ u▪ ▪ w. of Columbia ; from W. 591 ms. Watered by Savan nah river.
SILVER TOP, p. o., Obion co., Tenn.
SILVERVILLE, p. o., Lawrence co., Ind.
SIMMONS, p. o., Lawrence co., O.
SIMM'S PORT, p. v., Avoyelles parish, La., 237 ms ▪ w. of New Orleans ; from W. 1,194 ms.
SIMMONSVILLE, p. o., Giles co., Va.
SIMONSVILLE, p. v., Windsor co., Vt., 89 ms. s. ci Montpelier ; from W. 451 ms.
SIMPSON COUNTY, situated in the southerly part of Mississippi, with Pearl river on the west. Area, 550 square miles. Seat of justice, Westville. Pop. in 1830, 2,680 ; in 1840, 3,380 ; in 1850, 4,734.
SIMPSON COUNTY, situated on the south bound ary of Kentucky. Area, 288 square miles. Seat of justice, Franklin. Pop. in 1820, 4,852 ; in 1830, 5,815 ; in 1840 ; 6,537 ; in 1850, 7,733.
SIMPSON's, p. o., Floyd co., Va., 203 ms. w. of Richmond ; from W. 278 ms.
SIMPSON's MILL, p. o., Laurens district, S. C.
SIMPSON'S STORE, p. o., Washington co., Pa., 226 ms. w. of Harrisburgh ; from W. 242 ms.
SIMPSONVILLE, p. o., Shelby co., Ky., 31 ms. w. of Frankfort ; from W. 573 ms. Watered by Floyd's fork of Salt river.
SIMPSONVILLE, p. o., Anne Arundel co., Md.
SIMSRURY, p. t., Hartford co., Ct., 13 ms. N. of Hartford ; from W. 349 ms. Pop. 2,737.
SINA, p. t., Clinton co., Mich.
SINCLAIR'S BOTTOM, p. o., Smyth co., Va., 281 ms. w of Richmond ; from W. 346 ms.
SING SING, p. v., Mount Pleasant township, Westchester co., N. Y., 116 ms. s. of Albany ; from W. 258 ms. Watered by Hudson river. Site of a state-prison.
SINKING CREEK, p. o., Botetourt co., Va., 204 ms. w. of Richmond ; from W. 244 ms.
SINKING CREEK, p. o., Bedford co., Tenn., 65 ms. s. of Nashville ; from W. 699 ms.
SINKING SPRING, p. o., Berks co., Pa, 47 ms. E. of Harrisburgh ; from W. 151 ms.
SINKING SPRING, p. v., Brush Creek township, Highland co., O., 84 ms. s. w. of Columbus ; from -W. 421 ms.
SINKING SPRING, p. o., Lawrence co., Ind., 78 ms. s. w. of Indianapolis ; from W. 628 ms.
SINKING VALLEY MILLS, p. o., Blair co., Pa., 114 ms. w. of Harrisburgh ; from W. 173 ms.
SINNAMAHONING, p. o., Clinton co., Pa., 119 ms. N. of Harrisburgh ; from W. 251 ms.
SIPESVILLE, p. o., Somerset co., Pa.
SIPPICAN, p. v., Rochester township, Plymouth co., Mass., 59 ms, s. of Boston ; from W. 446 ms.
SIPSEY TURNPIKE, p, o., Tuscaloosa co., Ala.

SIR JOHN'S RUN, p. o., Morgan co., Va.

SISKIYOU COUNTY, situated in the ———— part of California. Pop. in 1852, 2,242.

SISSONVILLE, p. v., Kanawha co., Va., 333 ms. N. W. of Richmond; from W. 358 ms. Watered by Poco-talico river.

SISTERDALE, p. o., Comal co., Tex.

SISTERSVILLE, p. v., Tyler co., Va., 316 ms. N. W. of Richmond; from W. 272 ms. Watered by Ohio river.

SIX CORNERS, p. o., Richland co., O.

SIX-MILE, p. o., Jennings co., Ind., 70 ms. S. E. of Indianapolis; from W. 576 ms.

SIX-MILE. t., Madison co., Ill., 99 ms. s. of Springfield; from W. 814 ms.

SIX-MILE FALLS, p. o., Penobscot co., Me.

SIX-MILE RUN, p. o., Somerset co., N. J., 21 ms. N. of Trenton; from W. 187 ms.

SIX-MILE RUN, p. o., Bedford co., Pa.

SIX RUNS, p. o., Sampson co., N. C.

SKANEATELES, p. t., Onondaga co., N. Y., 147 ms. w. of Albany; from W. 340 ms. Watered by Skaneateles Lake outlet. Pop. 4.081.

SKEEL'S CROSS ROADS, p. o., Mercer co., O.

SKEGG'S CREEK. p. o., Barren co., Ky., 135 ms. s. w. of Frankfort; from W. 656 ms.

SKEINAH, p. o., Union co., Ga.

SKELTON, t., Warrick co., Ind. Pop. 532.

SKINNERS, p. o., Benton co., Oregon.

SKINNER'S EDDY, p. o., Wyoming co., Pa., 159 ms. N. E. of Harrisburgh; from W. 267 ms. Watered by Susquehanna river.

SKINQUARTER, p. o., Chesterfield co., Pa.

SKIPPACK, p. t., Montgomery co., Pa., 86 ms. E. of Harrisburgh; from W. 165 ms. Watered by Skippack creek.

SKITT'S MOUNTAIN, Hull co., Ga.

SKOWHEGAN, p. t., Somerset co., Me., 36 ms. N. of Augusta; from W. 631 ms. Watered by Kennebec river at Skowhegan falls. Pop. 1,756.

SLABTOWN, p. v., Anderson district, S. C., 130 ms. N. w. of Columbia; from W. 525 ms.

SLACK, p. o., Mason co., Ky.

SLADE, p. o., Lee co., Ga.,

SLADESVILLE, Hyde co., N C

SLASH COTTAGE, p. o., Hanover co., Va., 18 ms. N. of Richmond; from W. 117 ms.

SLATE, p. o., Bath co., Ky., 81 ms. E. of Frankfort; from W. 507 ms.

SLATE CREEK, p. o., Tazewell co., Va

SLATEFORD, p. o., Northampton co., Pa.

SLATE HILL, p. o., Minisink township, Orange co., N. Y., 113 ms. s. w. of Albany; from W. 276 ms.

SLATE HILL, p. o., York co., Pa.

SLATE LICK, p. o., Armstrong co., Pa., 190 ms. N. W. of Harrisburgh; from W. 234 ms.

SLATE MILLS, p. o., Rappahannock co., Va., 112 ms. N. w. of Richmond; from W. 91 ms.

SLATERVILLE, p. v., Smithfield township, Providence co., R. I., 19 ms. N. w. of Providence; from W. 410 ms. Watered by a tributary of Pawtucket river.

SLATERVILLE, p. v., Caroline township, Tompkins co., N. Y., 153 ms. w. of Albany; from W. 304 ms. Watered by Six-Mile creek.

SLATINGTON, p. o., Lehigh co., Pa.

SLEEPY CREEK, p. v., Wayne co., N. C., 63 ms. s. E. of Raleigh; from W. 293 ms.

SLEEPY CREEK, p. o., Edgefield district, S. C., 74 ms. w. of Columbia; from W. 584 ms.

SLEEPY CREEK BRIDGE, p. o., Morgan co., Va.

SLIGO, p. o., De Kalb co., Ala.

SLIGO, p. o., Henry co., Tenn.

SLIGO, p. o., Clinton co., O.

SLIPPERY ROCK, p. o., Butler co., Pa., 22 ms. N. w. of Harrisburgh; from W. 263 ms. Watered by Slippery Rock and Wolf creeks.

SLIPPERY ROCK, p. o., Beaver co., Pa.

SLIPPERY ROCK, p. t., Mercer co., Pa.

SLOANSVILLE, p. v., Schoharie township, Schoharie co., N. Y., 33 ms. w. of Albany; from W. 392 ms. Watered by Vly creek.

SLOATSBURGH, p. o., Rockland co., N. Y.

SLOUGH, p. o., Clackamas co., Oregon.

SLOYERSVILLE, p. o., Luzerne co., Pa.

SMELSER'S MILLS, p. o., Rush co., Ind., 45 ms. S. E. of Indianapolis; from W. 537 ms.

SMELTZER'S GROVE, p. o., Grant co., Wis.

SMICKSBURGH, p. o., Indiana co., Pa.

SMITH COUNTY, situated toward the southeast part of Mississippi. Area. 520 square miles. Seat of justice, Raleigh. Pop. in 1840 1,961; in 1850. 4,071.

SMITH COUNTY, situated in the north part of Tennessee, and traversed by Cumberland river. Area, 590 square miles. Face of the country, undulating; soil, productive. Seat of justice, Carthage. Pop. in 1810, 11,649; in 1820, 17,580; in 1830, 19,906; in 1840, 21,179; in 1850, 18,412.

SMITH COUNTY, situated in Texas. Area, ——— square miles. Seat of justice, ————. Pop. in 1850, 4,292.

SMITH, p. o., Belmont co., O. Watered by McMahon's creek.

SMITH, p. t., Washington co., Pa. Pop. 1,462.

SMITH, p. o., Columbiana co., O.

SMITH, t., Posey co., Ind. Pop. 765.

SMITH, p. o., Barry co., Mo.

SMITHDALE, p. v., Amite co., Miss., 92 ms. s. w., of Jackson; from W. 1,102 ms.

SMITHFIELD, p. t., Somerset co., Me. Pop. 873.

SMITHFIELD, p. t., Providence co., R. I., situated on Blackstone river, 16 miles north of Providence; from W. 413 ms. Its resources consist in a favorable position in a region naturally productive, and affording lime and several useful stones, and in the extensive water-power, which keep numerous manufactories in active operation. A number of these are congregated at Woonsocket falls, on the Blackstone, where there is a pleasant village of the same name. The population in 1810, was 3,828; in 1830, 6,857; in 1840, 9,534; in 1850, 11,504.

SMITHFIELD, p. t., Madison co., N. Y., 106 ms. w. of Albany; from W. ——— ms. Watered by Canaseraga and Corvasalon creeks. Pop. 1,669.

SMITHFIELD, p. t., Bradford co., Pa. Watered by Tom, Jack's, and Brown's creeks. Pop. 1.948.

SMITHFIELD, p. v., George township, Fayette co., Pa., 188 ms. s. w. of Harrisburgh; from W. 204 ms. Pop. 1,080.

SMITHFIELD, c. h., p. v., seat of justice of Isle of Wight co., Va., 65 ms. s. E. of Richmond; from W. 208 ms. Watered by an inlet of James river. Pop. 450.

SMITHFIELD, p. o., p. v., seat of justice of Johnson co., N. C., 27 ms. s. E. of Raleigh; from W. 305 ms. Watered by Neuse river.

SMITHFIELD, p. t., Jefferson co., O., 126 ms. E. of Columbus; from W. 273 ms. Pop. 1,882.

SMITHFIELD, p. o., Delaware co., Ind., 65 ms. N. E. of Indianapolis; from W. 522 ms. Watered by White river.

SMITHFIELD, p. o., Polk co., Tex.

SMITHFIELD, p. o., Henry co., Ky.

SMITH GROVE, p. o., Davies co., N. C.

SMITHLAND, p. v., Livingston co., Ky., 264 ms. s. w. of Frankfort; from W. 796 ms. Watered by Ohio river at the confluence of Cumberland river.

SMITHLAND, p. v., Randolph co., Mo., 71 ms. N. of Jefferson city; from W. 960 ms.

SMITHLAND, p. o., Cass co., Tex.

SMITHPORT, c. h., p. v., seat of justice of McKean co., Pa., 196 ms. N. w. of Harrisburgh; from W. 279 ms. situated at the confluence of Potatoe and Stanton creeks.

SMITH'S, p. o., Gallia co., O.

SMITH'S BASIN, p. o., Washington co., N. Y.

SMITHSBOROUGH, p. v., Tioga township, Tioga co., N. Y., 171 ms. s. w. of Albany; from W. 272 ms. Watered by Susquehanna river.

SMITH'S BRIDGE, p. o., Robeson co., N. C.

SMITHSBURGH, p. v., Washington co., Md., 106 ms. N. w. of Annapolis; from W. 77 ms. Pop. 386.

SMITH'S CREEK, p. o., Washington co., Va.

SMITH'S CROSS ROADS, p. o., Rhea co., Tenn., 127 ms. s. E. of Nashville; from W. 573 ms.

SMITH'S CROSS ROADS, p. o., Morgan co., Va.

SMITH'S FERRY, p. o., Beaver co., Pa., 240 ms. N. w. of Harrisburgh; from W. 266 ms.

SMITH'S FORD, p. o., York district, S. C., 94 ms. N. of Columbia; from W. 445 ms.

SMITH'S FORK, p. o., Hardin co., Tenn., 120 ms. s. w of Nashville; from 796 ms.

SMITH'S GAP, p. o., Hampshire co., Va.

SMITH'S GROVE, p. o., Warren co., Ky.

SMITH'S GROVE, p. o., Davies co., N. C.

SMITH'S LANDING, p. o., Atlantic co., N. J., 90 ms. s. of Trenton; from W. 200 ms.

SMITH'S MILLS, p. o., Hanover township, Chautauque co., N. Y., 313 ms. w. of Albany; from W. 360 ms.

SMITH'S MILLS, p. o., Clearfield co., Pa., 122 ms. N. w. of Harrisburgh; from W. 212 ms.

SMITH'S MILLS, p. o., Morrow co., O., 52 ms. N. of Columbus; from W. 399 ms.

SMITH'S MILLS, p. o., Henderson co., Ky., 209 ms. w. of Frankfort; from W. 736 ms.

SMITH'S MILLS, p. o., Carroll co., Miss., 105 ms. N. of Jackson; from W. 992 ms.

SMITH'S STORE, p. o., Spartanburgh district, S. C., 87 ms. N. w. of Columbia; from W. 481 ms.

SMITH'S BRIDGE, p. o., Robeson co., N. C.

SMITHSVILLE, p. v., Powhattan co., Va., 39 ms. w. of Richmond; from W. 156 ms.

SMITHTOWN, p. t., Suffolk co., Long Island, N. Y., 191 ms. s. E. of Albany; from W. 271 ms. Watered by Long Island sound and Nesaquake river. Pop. 1,972.

SMITHTOWN BRANCH, p. o., Suffolk co., Long Island, N. Y.

SMITHVILLE, p. t., Chenango co., N. Y., 131 ms. w. of Albany; from W. 325 ms. Watered by Geneganslette creek. Pop. 1,771.

SMITHVILLE, p. o., Adams township, Jefferson co., N. Y., 179 ms. N. w. of Albany; from W. 410 ms.

SMITHVILLE, p. v., Lancaster co., Pa., 46 ms. s. E. of Harrisburgh; from W. 103 ms.

SMITHVILLE, c. h., p. v., seat of justice of Brunswick co., N. C., 173 ms. s. of Raleigh; from W. 300 ms. Watered by Cape Fear river. Pop. 1,464.

SMITHVILLE, p. v., Wayne co., O., 101 ms. N. E. of Columbus; from W. 348 ms.

SMITHVILLE, c. h., p. v., seat of justice of De Kalb co., Tenn., 61 ms. E. of Nashville; from W. 620 ms.

SMITHVILLE, p. v., seat of justice of Lawrence co., Ark., 125 ms. N. E. of Little Rock; from W. 1,012 ms. Watered by Strawberry river.

SMITHVILLE, p. o., Monroe co., Miss.

SMITHVILLE, p. o., Peoria co., Ill.

SMITHVILLE, p. o., Clay co., Mo.

SMITHVILLE, p. v., Abbeville district S. C., 94 ms. w. of Columbia; from W. 520 ms.

SMITHVILLE FLATS, p. v., Smithville township, Chenango co., N. Y., 125 ms. w. of Albany; from W. 319 ms. Watered by Geneganslette creek.

SMOKY HOLLOW, p. v., Claverack township, Columbia co., N. Y., 37 ms. s. E. of Albany; from W. 349 ms.

SMOKY ORDINARY, p. o., Brunswick co., Va., 64 ms. s. w. of Richmond; from W. 117 ms.

SMUT EYE, p. o., Coffee co., Ala.

SMYRNA, p. t., Chenango co., N. Y., 103 ms. w. of Albany; from W. 351 ms. Watered by tributaries of Chenango river. Pop. 1,927.

SMYRNA, p. v., Kent co., Del., 12 ms. N. of Dover; from W. 132 ms. Watered by a tributary of Duck creek.

SMYRNA, p. v., Harrison co., O., 99 ms. N. E. of Columbus; from W. 299 ms. Pop. 93.

SMYRNA, p. o., Ionia co., Mich.

SMYRNA, p. o., Aroostook co., Me.

SMYRNA, p. o., Barnwell district, S. C.

SMYRNA, p. o., Rutherford co., Tenn., 20 ms. s. E. of Nashville; from W. 679 ms. Situated on Stone river.

SMYTH COUNTY, situated in the southwest part of Virginia. Area 480 square miles. Face of the country, uneven and mountainous. Seat of justice, Marion. Pop. in 1840, 6,522; in 1850, 8,161.

SNAPPING SHOALS, p. o., Newton co., Ga.

SNEAD'S FERRY, p. o., Onslow co., N. C.

SNEEDSVILLE, p. o., Hancock co., Tenn.

SNIBAR, p. o., Lafayette co., Mo.

SNICKERSVILLE, p. v., Loudoun co., Va., 168 ms. N. of Richmond; from W. 52 ms.

SNIDERS, p. o., Washington co., Ky.

SNODDYVILLE, v., Jefferson co., Tenn., 226 ms. E. of Nashville; from W. 470 ms.

SNOW CAMP, p. o., Orange co., N. C., 53 ms. N. w. of Raleigh; from W. 304 ms.

SNOW CREEK, p. o., Franklin co., Va., 177 ms. s. w. of Richmond; from W. 252 ms.

SNOW CREEK, p. o., Iredell co., N. C.

SNOW CREEK, p. o., Pickens district, S. C.

SNOW CREEK, p. o., Marshall co., Miss

SNOW FALLS, p. o., Oxford co., Me.

SNOW HILL, c. h., p. v., seat of justice of Worcester co., Md., 115 ms. s. E. of Annapolis; from W. 155 ms. Watered by Pokomoke river. Pop. 714.

SNOW HILL, c. h., p. v., seat of justice of Greene co., N. C., 89 ms. s. E. of Raleigh; from W. 299 ms. Watered by a tributary of Neuse river.

SNOW HILL, p. v., Clinton co., O., 74 ms. s. w. of Columbus; from W. 448 ms.

SNOW HILL, p. v., Walker co., Ga., 211 ms. N. w. of Milledgeville; from W. 625 ms.

SNOW HILL, p. v., Wilcox co., Ala.; from W. 887 ms.

SNOW HILL, p. o., Hamilton co., Tenn.

SNOW SHOE, p. t., Centre co., Pa., 101 ms. N. w. of Harrisburgh; from W. 193 ms. Pop. 432.

SNOW'S STORE, p. o., Windsor co., Vt., 46 ms. s. of Montpelier; from W. 492 ms.

SNOWSVILLE, p. v., Choctaw co., Miss., 110 ms. N. E. of Jackson; from W. 936 ms.

SNYDER, t., Jefferson co., Pa. Pop. 306.

SNYDERSVILLE, p. v., Monroe co., Pa., 116 ms. N. E. of Harrisburgh; from W. 209 ms.

SNYDERTOWN, p. o., Northumberland co., Pa.

SOAP CREEK, p. o., Davis co., Wis.

SOAPSTONE MOUNTAIN, p. o., Randolph co., N. C.

SOCCOPATOY, p. o., Coosa co., Ala.; from W. 799 ms.

SOCIAL CIRCLE, p. o., Walton co., Ga., 60 ms. N. w. of Milledgeville; from W. 642 ms.

SOCIALITY, p. o., Dayton township, Cattaraugus co., N. Y., 309 ms. w. of Albany; from W. 347 ms.

SOCIETY HILL, p. v., Macon co., Ala.; from W. 784 ms.

SOCIETY HILL, p. v., Darlington district, S. C., 108 ms. N. E. of Columbia; from W. 438 ms. Watered by Great Pedee river.

SOCORRO COUNTY, situated in the southern portion of the territory of New Mexico, and traversed by the Rio Grande del Norte. Area, —— square miles. Soil, productive. Seat of justice, Socorro. New co

SOCORRO, p. o., Socorro co., New Mex.

SODUS, p. t., Wayne co., N. Y., 195 ms. N. w. of Albany; from W. 371 ms. Watered by Lake Ontario. Pop. 4,598.

SODUS CENTRE, p. o., Sodus township, Wayne co., N. Y., 191 ms. N. w. of Albany; from W. 367 ms.

SODUS POINT, p. v., Sodus township, Wayne co., N. Y., 201 ms. N. w. of Albany; from W. 377 ms. Watered by Lake Ontario.

SOLANO COUNTY, situated in the west part of California, with Rio Sacramento on the south and east. Area, —— square miles. Face of the country, toward the west, hilly and mountainous—toward the southeast, level and swampy. Seat of justice, Benicia. Pop. in 1852, 2,835.

SOLEMN GROVE, p. o., Moore co., N. C., 90 ms. s. w. of Raleigh; from W. 377 ms.

SOLESBURY, p. t., Bucks co., Pa. Watered by Delaware river. Pop. 2,634.

SOLITUDE, p. o., Brazoria co., Tex.

SOLON, p. t., Somerset county, Me.. 52 ms. N. of Augusta; from W. 647 ms. Watered by Kennebec river. Pop. 1,415.

SOLON, p. t., Cortland co., N. Y., 138 ms. w. of Albany; from W. 323 ms. Watered by Ostelico river. Pop. 1,150.

SOLON, p. t., Cuyahoga co., O., 154 ms. N. E. of Columbus; from W. 344 ms. Watered by Chagrin river and Tinker's creek. Pop. 1,034.

SOLON, p. o., Johnson co., Iowa.

SOLON MILLS, p. o., McHenry co., Ill.

SOLSVILLE, p. o., Madison co., N. Y.

SOMERFIELD, p. o., Somerset co., Pa., 158 ms. w. of Harrisburgh; from W. 174 ms.

SOMERFORD, p. t., Madison co., O. Pop. 755.

SOMERS, p. t., Tolland co., Ct., 23 ms. N. E. of Hartford; from W. 359 ms. Pop. 1,508.

SOMERS, p. t., Westchester co., N. Y., 119 ms. s. of Albany; from W. 274 ms. Watered by Croton river. Pop. 1,722.

SOMERS CENTRE, p. o., Somers township, Westchester co., N. Y.

SOMERS, p. t., Preble co., O.

SOMERSET COUNTY, situated on the northwest boundary of Maine, and traversed by Kennebec river, with Moosehead or Umbagog lake on the east. Area, 3,600 square miles. Face of the country, hilly and mountainous. Seat of justice, Norridgewock. Pop. in 1810, 12,910; in 1820, 21,787; in 1830, 35,787; in 1840, 33,912; in 1850, 35,581.

SOMERSET COUNTY, situated in the central part of New Jersey. Area, 275 square miles. Face of the country, pleasantly diversified with hills and vales; soil, generally productive. Seat of justice, Somerville. Pop. in 1810, 14,728; in 1820, 16,506; in 1830, 17,689; in 1840, 17,455; in 1850, 19,661.

SOMERSET COUNTY, situated on the south boundary of Pennsylvania. Area, 1,000 square miles. Face of the country, mountainous on the east and west borders, with a valley between. Seat of justice, Somerset. Pop. in 1810, 11,284; in 1820, 13,374; in 1830, 17,762; in 1840, 19.650; in 1850, 24,416.

SOMERSET COUNTY, situated in the southeast part of Maryland, with Pocomoke bay and Tangier sound (indentations of Chesapeake bay) on the southwest. Area, 500 square miles. Face of the country, level; soil sandy, but generally productive. Seat of justice, Princess Anne. Pop. in 1810, 17,195; in 1820, 19,579 ; in 1830, 20,166; in 1840, 19,508 ; in 1850, 22,056.

SOMERSET, p. t., Bristol co., Mass., 44 ms. s. of Boston; from W. 418 ms. Watered by Taunton river. Pop. 1,166.

SOMERSET, t., Windham co., Vt. Watered by Deerfield and Moose rivers. Pop. 321.

SOMERSET, p. t., Niagara co., N. Y., 276 ms. w. of Albany; from W. 419 ms. Watered by Lake Ontario and Golden Hill creek. Pop. 2,154.

SOMERSET, p. t., Washington co., Pa. Pop. 1,512.

SOMERSET, c. h., p. b., Somerset township, seat of justice of Somerset co., Pa., 40 ms. w. of Harrisburgh; from W. 166 ms. Watered by Cox's creek. Pop. 866.

SOMERSET, t., Somerset co., Pa. Watered by Laurel Hill. Middle, and Cox's creeks. Pop. 2,554.

SOMERSET, c. h., p. t., seat of justice of Perry co., O., 47 ms. s. E. of Columbus ; from W. 358 ms. Pop. 1,240.

SOMERSET, p. t., Belmont co., O. Pop. 1,943.

SOMERSET, c. h., p. v., seat of justice of Pulaski co., Ky., 84 ms. s. E. of Frankfort; from W. 590 ms.

SOMERSET, p. t., Hillsdale co., Mich. Pop. 913.

SOMERSET. p. o., Monroe co., Mo., 83 ms. N. of Jefferson city ; from W. 943 ms.

SOMERORT, p. o., Wabash co., Ind.

SOMERS' POINT, p. v., Atlantic co., N. J., 91 ms. s. of Trenton ; from W. 201 ms. Watered by Great Egg Harbor bay.

SOMERSVILLE, p. o., Somers township, Tolland co.. Ct.

SOMERSWORTH, p. t., Strafford co., N. H., 45 ms E. of Concord; from W. 4— ms. Watered by Salmon Fall and Cocheco rivers.

SOMERTON, p. o., Moreland township, Philadelphia co., Pa., 113 ms. E. of Harrisburgh ; from W. 153 ms.

SOMERTON. p. v., Nansemond co., Va., 95 ms. s. E. of Richmond ; from W. 214 ms.

SOMERTON, p. v., Somerset township, Belmont co., O., 107 ms. m. of Columbus, from W. 293 ms. Watered by south fork of Captina creek.

SOMERVILLE, p. v., Rossie township, St. Lawrence co., N. Y., 176 ms. N. w. of Albany ; from W. 445 ms.

SOMERVILLE, c. h., p v, seat of justice of Somerset co., N. J., 31 ms. N. of Trenton ; from W. 202 ms.

SOMERVILLE, p. v., Fauquier co., Va., 83 ms. N. of Richmond ; from W. 70 ms.

SOMERVILLE, c. h., p. v., seat of justice of Morgan co., Ala. ; from W. 732 ms.

SOMERVILLE, c. h., p. v., seat of justice of Fayette co., Tenn., 185 ms. s. w. of Nashville ; from W. 871 ms.

SOMERVILLE, p. v., Milford township, Butler co., O., 101 ms. s. w. of Columbus ; from W. 494 ms.

SOMERVILLE, p. o., Middlesex co., Mass.

SOMONAUK, p. o., De Kalb co., Ill., 182 ms. N. E. of Springfield ; from W. 775 ms.

SONET, p. o., Natchitoches parish, La.

SONOMA COUNTY, situated in the westerly part of California, with San Pablo bay on the south. Area, —— square miles. Face of the country, uneven and mountainous. Seat of justice, Sonoma. Pop. in 1852, 2,337.

SONOMA, p. o., seat of justice of Sonoma co., Cal.

SONORA, p. o., Tuolumne co., Cal.

SOOKALENA, p. o., Benton co., Ala.

SOOKALENA, p. o., Lauderdale co., Ala.

SOOY'S INN, p. o., Burlington co., N. J., 55 ms. s. of Trenton ; from W. 179 ms.

SOPCHOPPY, p. o., Wakulla co., Flor.

SORBY, p. o., Wayne co., Tenn.

SORREL HORSE, p. o., Montgomery co., Pa., 113 ms. E. of Harrisburgh ; from W. 153 ms.

SOUCHAHATCHIE, p. o., Macon co.. Ala. ; from W. 796 ms.

SOUTH ABINGTON, p. o., Plymouth co.. Mass.

SOUTH ACWORTH, p. o., Sullivan co., N. H.

SOUTH ALABAMA. p. o., Genesee co., N. Y.

SOUTH ALBION, p. v., Albion township, Kennebec co., Me., 25 ms. N. E. of Augusta ; from W. 620 ms.

SOUTH ALBION, p. o., Calhoun co., Mich.

SOUTH ALBION, p. o., Oswego co., N. Y.

SOUTH ALDEN, p. o., Erie co., N. Y.

SOUTH ALTON, p. v., Alton township, Belknap co., N. H., 28 ms. N. E. of Concord ; from W. 509 ms.

SOUTH AMBOY, p. t., Middlesex co., N. J. Watered by Raritan, Millstone, and South rivers. Pop. 2,266.

SOUTH AMENIA, p. o., Amenia township, Dutchess co., N. Y., 68 ms. s. of Albany ; from W. 325 ms.

SOUTH AMHERST. p. o., Hampshire co., Mass.

SOUTHAMPTON COUNTY, situated on the south boundary of Virginia, and traversed by Nottoway river. Area, 648 square miles. Seat of justice, Jerusalem. Pop. in 1810, 13,497 ; in 1820, 14,170; in 1830, 16,073 ; in 1840, 14,525; in 1850, 13,521.

SOUTHAMPTON, p. t., Hampshire co., Mass., 102 ms. w. of Boston ; from W. 372 ms. Watered by Manhan river. Pop. 1,064.

SOUTHAMPTON, p. t., Somerset co., Pa. Pop. 1,326.

SOUTHAMPTON, p. t., Bucks co., Pa. Watered by Poquessing and Pennypack creeks. Pop. 1,416.

SOUTHAMPTON, p. t., Cumberland co., Pa. Pop. 1,651.

SOUTHAMPTON, p. t., Franklin co., Pa. Watered by Conedogwinit creek and Mean's run. Pop. 1,795.

SOUTHAMPTON, p. t., Bedford co., Pa. Pop. 1,347.

SOUTHAMPTON, t., Trumbull co., O. Pop. 1,013.

SOUTHAMPTON, p. o., Peoria co., Ill.

SOUTH ANDOVER, p. o., Oxford co., Me.

SOUTH ANNA, p. v., Louisa co., Va., 67 ms. N. w. of Richmond ; from W. 110 ms.

SOUTH ARGYLE, p. o., Argyle township, Washington co., N. Y., 42 ms. N. E. of Albany ; from W. 412 ms.

SOUTH ASSYRIA, p. o., Barry co., Mich.

SOUTH ATKINSON, p. o., Piscataquis co., Me.

SOUTH ATTLEBOROUGH, p. v., Attleborough township, Bristol co., Mass., 43 ms. s. w. of Boston ; from W. 407 ms.

SOUTH AUBURN, p. o., Susquehanna co., Pa., 179 ms. N. E. of Harrisburgh ; from W. 278 ms.

SOUTH AVON, p. o., Avon township, Livingston co., N. Y., 224 ms w. of Albany ; from W. 353 ms.

SOUTH BAINBRIDGE, p. v., Bainbridge township, Chenango co., N. Y., 110 ms. W. of Albany ; from W. 314 ms. Watered by Susquehanna river.

SOUTH BARRE, p. v., Barre township, Washington co., Vt., 8 ms. s. E. of Montpelier ; from W. 518 ms.

SOUTH BARRE, p. o., Barre township, Orleans co., N. Y., 256 ms. w. of Albany ; from W, 386 ms.

SOUTH BELLINGHAM, p. o., Norfolk co., Mass.

SOUTH BEND, c. h., p. v., seat of justice of St. Joseph co., Ind., 139 ms. N. of Indianapolis ; from W. 624 ms. Watered by St. Joseph's river.

SOUTH BEND, p. o., Arkansas co., Ark.

SOUTH BEND, p. o., Armstrong co., Pa.

SOUTH BEND, p. o., Lawrence co., Mo.

SOUTH BERNE, p. o., Albany co., N. Y.

SOUTH BERWICK, p t., York co., Me., 95 ms. a. w. of Augusta ; from W. 500 ms. Watered by Salmon Fall river at the Great Falls. Pop. 2,592.

SOUTH BLOOMFIELD, p. v., Harrison township, Pickaway co., O., 17 ms. s. of Columbus ; from W. 405 ms.

SOUTH BLOOMFIELD, p. o., Somerset co., Me.

SOUTHBOROUGH, p. t., Worcester co., Mass., 26 ms. w. of Boston ; from W. 414 ms. Watered by a tributary of Sudbury river. Pop. 1,347.

SOUTH BOSTON, p. o., Ionia co., Mich.

SOUTH BOSTON, p. o., Washington co., Ind.

SOUTH BRADFORD, p. o., Merrimack co., N. H.

SOUTH BRADFORD, p. o., Orange co., Vt.

SOUTH BRADFORD, p. o., Steuben co., N. Y.

SOUTH BRAINTREE, p. o., Norfolk co., Mass.

SOUTHBRIDGE, p. t., Worcester co., Mass., 61 ms. s. w. of Boston ; from W. 381 ms. Watered by Quinnebaug river. Pop. 2,824.

SOUTH BRIDGETON, p. o., Bridgeton township, Cumberland co., Me., 83 ms. s. w. of Augusta ; from W. 569 ms.

SOUTH BRISTOL, p. t., Ontario co., N. Y., 213 ms. w. of Albany ; from W. 349 ms. Watered by Mud creek and Canandaigua lake. Pop. 1,129.

SOUTH BRISTOL, p. o., Racine co., Wis.

SOUTH BRITAIN, p. v., Southbury township, New Haven co., Ct., 57 ms. s. of Hartford ; from W. 301 ms.

SOUTH BROOKFIELD, p. o., Madison co., N. Y.

SOUTH BROOKS, p. o., Waldo co., Me.

SOUTH BRUNSWICK, p. t., Middlesex co., N. J. Watered by Lawrence's brook and tributaries of Millstone river. Pop. 3,368.

SOUTHBURY, p. t., New Haven co., Ct., 54 ms. s. w. of Hartford ; from W. 304 ms. Watered by Pampe- raug river. Pop. 1,484.

SOUTH BUTLER, p. o., Butler township, Wayne co., N. Y., 174 ms. w. of Albany ; from W. 354 ms.

SOUTH BUTLER, p. o., Butler co., Ala.

SOUTH BYRON, p. o., Byron township, Genesee co., N. Y.

SOUTH CAIRO, p. o., Cairo township, Greene co., N. Y.

SOUTH CAMERON, p. o., Cameron township, Steuben co., N. Y., 230 ms. w. of Albany ; from W. 298 ms.

SOUTH CANAAN, p. o., Essex co., Vt.

SOUTH CANAAN, p. v., Canaan township, Litchfield co., Ct., 43 ms. n. w. of Hartford ; from W. 340 ms. Watered by Housatonic river.

SOUTH CAROLI- NA, one of the Uni- ted States, lies be- tween 32° 2' and 35° 10' north latitude, and 78° 24' and 83° 30' west longitude from Greenwich ; bound- ed N. by North Caro- lina, S. E. by the Atlan- tic, and westerly by Georgia, from which it is separated by Sa- vannah river. Its su- perficial area is 28,000 square miles.

Physical Aspect.—This state, like North Carolina and Georgia, presents a great diversity of surface, as well as of soil and climate, and may also be physically di- vided into three zones. The first bordering on the Atlan- tic, is that of sea-sand alluvion, below the lower falls of the rivers, about 60 miles wide, and in most places pen- etrated by the tide. The second commences along or near the lower falls and primitive ledge. The sea-sand zone is very nearly a dead plain, but at its interior mar- gin hills begin to appear, springs of water become plen- tiful, the soil meliorates, and the whole face of nature assumes an agreeable diversity of surface. The third, or what may be called the mountain zone, though but little of it is really mountainous, comprises the north- western part of the state, and lies based on the Blue Ridge chain. The first of these zones, which includes the " Sea islands," is covered with extensive tracts of pine " barrens," open plains without wood, savannas, swamps, and salt marsh, presenting the most fertile and the most sterile extremes of soil. The second zone displays, amid a series of hills, bold, swelling, and va- ried in their form, a rapid succession of rich cotton lands, meadows, orchards, and fields of small grain, in- terluded by extensive forests, barrens, and swamps. As we approach the mountainous zone, we are gratified by the pleasant alternation of hill and dale ; the lively verdure of the hills is contrasted with the deeper tints of the forests which decorates their sides ; and in the valleys, broad rivers roll their waters through the va- ried beauties of the luxuriant and cultivated fields. From these delightful regions the surface still continues to rise, till we reach the western limit of the state.

Mountains.—The Blue Ridge, or Appalachian chain, traverses this state in its northwest part, of which Table mountain is the most conspicuous. The other mountains are Olenoy, Oconee, Paris, Glassy's, Hog- Back, and King's.

Rivers, Bays, and Sounds.—The principal rivers are, the Savannah, Pedee, Black, Santee, Cooper, Ashley, Stono, Edisto, Ashepos, Combahee, Coosaw, Broad, and Waccamaw. Besides Bull's and Winyaw bays, this state contains numerous estuaries, and sounds, the principal of which are, Port Royal and Georgetown entrances, and Tyree and St. Helena sounds.

Islands.—The coast is bordered by a chain of fine islands, the most important of which are, Port Royal, St. Helena, Edisto, Ladu's, Trench's, Hunting, and Rac- coon keys.

Climate.—The climate along the seaboard is moist, very changeable, and, during summer and autumn, is extremely unhealthy. The middle region, particularly in winter and spring, is regarded as the most healthy part of the state. In short, all the districts of the up- per country enjoy as salubrious a climate as is found in the Union.

Productive Resources.—The principal products of

this state are, horses, mules, neat cattle, sheep, swine, poultry, sugar, wax, hay, lumber, pitch, tar, turpen- tine, cotton, wool, silk, tobacco, rice, wheat, rye, barley, oats, sweet potatoes, and Indian corn. Of the miner- al and fossil resources of the state, gold is found in con- siderable abundance, but the " diggings" are less nu- merous than in Georgia and North Carolina. Marble, limestone, granite, oil and soap-stone, iron and lead ores, talc, asbestos, plumbago, pyrites, ochres used for painting, potter's clay, and fullers' earth, also occur in greater or less abundance.

Manufactures.—The manufactures of South Carolina are limited in extent. There are about 20 cotton-mills, which consume about 4,000,000 pounds of cotton an- nually. There were, in 1850, over 1,400 manufactur- ing establishments of all kinds in the state.

Railroads and Canals.—The aggregate length of rail- roads in operation in the state is about 300 miles, and about the same amount in process of construction. The longest canal in the state is the Santee, from Charleston to Santee river, 22 miles. There are sev- eral other shorter ones, amounting in the aggregate to about 30 miles.

Commerce.—The foreign commerce of South Caro- lina is quite large, its exports and imports amounting to about $14,000,000 annually. The shipping owned in the state is about 40,000 tons. Charleston is the principal port, and enjoys about nine tenths of the commerce.

Education.—There are three colleges in South Caro- lina. The Charleston college, founded in 1785 ; the college of South Carolina, founded in 1804 ; and the Erskine college, in Abbeville district. There are three theological seminaries in the state. There is also a medical college at Charleston. There are about 1,000 public schools, and 200 academies, in various parts of the state.

Population.—In 1790, 249,073 ; in 1800, 345,591 ; in 1810, 415,715 ; in 1820, 502,741 ; in 1830, 581,185 ; in 1840, 594,398 ; in 1850, 668,507. Number of slaves in 1790, 107,094 ; in 1800, 146,151 ; in 1810, 196,365 ; in 1820, 258,475 ; in 1830, 315,401 ; in 1840, 327,038 ; in 1850, 384,984.

History.—The state of South Carolina embraces a portion of the ancient territory of Florida, as first dis- covered by Ponce de Leon, in 1512 ; as well as a part of Carolina, as colonized by Coligni with Huguenots, in 1562–'65 ; or a part of Virginia, as granted to Sir Wal- ter Raleigh, in 1584. In about the year 1630, another grant was made to Sir Robert Heath, of the tract lying between 30° and 36° north latitude, which was erected into a province, under the name of " Carolina." As no settlements were made under this grant, the charter was declared void. In 1663, the province of Carolina was granted, by Charles II. to Lord Clarendon and seven others. Two years later, the grant was enlarged, so as to comprise all the territory between 31° and 36½° north latitude, extending westward from sea to sea. In 1670, a small body of English emigrants, under Wil- liam Sayle, commenced the settlement of Old Charles- ton, on the south side of Ashley river, which they called " Carteret County Colony," in honor of one of the proprietors. From this place they removed, in 1679, to the present site of Charleston. In 1720, the proprie- tary government was thrown off, and that of the crown established. In 1729, after much controversy and diffi- culty between the proprietors and the crown, seven out of the eight sold all their claims to the soil and rents in both Carolinas to the king, for £17,500, and the provinces then became royal governments, entirely unconnected under which they remained until the Revolution. South Carolina early resisted British oppression, and was one of the confederacy in 1776. It ratified the constitution of the United States, and was admitted into the Union as a sovereign state, in 1788. Mottoes of the seal *Animis ophibusque parati:* " Ever ready in spirit and achieve- ments." Reverse—*Dum spiro spero:* " While I live I hope."

Government.—The governor is elected for two years, by a joint vote of both houses of the assembly. After having served one term, he is ineligible for the next four years. A lieutenant-governor is chosen in the same manner, and for the same period. The senate consists of 45 members, elected by districts for four years. The house of representatives consists of 124 members, apportioned among the several districts, ac- cording to the number of white inhabitants and taxa- tion, and are elected for two years. The representatives and half the senators are chosen every second year, in

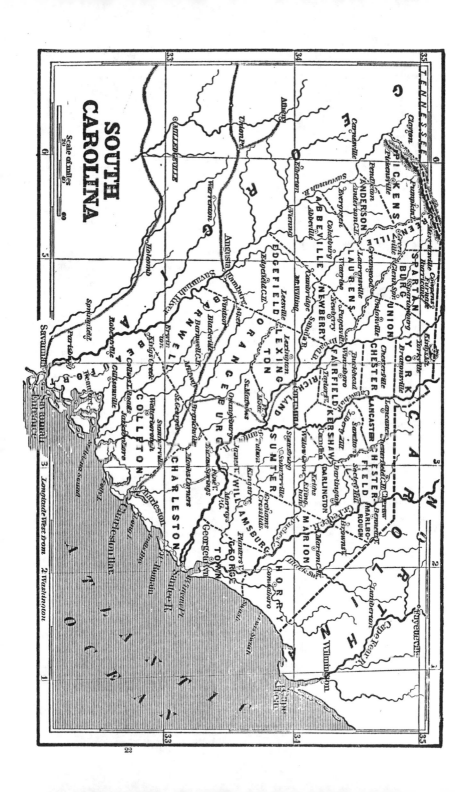

October. The chancellor and judges of the supreme court are chosen by the joint ballot of both houses of the assembly, and hold their offices during good behavior. Every free white male citizen, 21 years of age, who has resided in the state two years immediately preceding the election, and who is possessed of a freehold of 50 acres of land, or a town-lot, six months before the election ; or not possessing this freehold, who shall have resided in the election district in which he offers to vote six months before the election, and have paid a tax of three shillings sterling to the support of the government, has the right of suffrage.

SOUTH CARROLL, p. o., Carroll co., Tenn., 114 ms. w. of Nashville ; from W. 799 ms.

SOUTH CARROLLTON, p. o., Muhlenburgh co., Ky.

SOUTH CARTHAGE, p. o., Franklin co., Me.

SOUTH CARVER, p. o., Plymouth co., Mass.

SOUTH CASS, p. o., Cass township, Ionia co., Mich., 138 ms. N. w. of Detroit ; from W. 608 ms.

SOUTH CHARLESTON, p. v., Madison township, Clark co., O., 55 ms. w. of Columbus ; from W. 445 ms. Pop. 413.

SOUTH CHARLESTOWN, p. o., Sullivan co., N. H.

SOUTH CHESTERVILLE, p. o., Chesterville township, Franklin co., Me., 22 ms. N. w. of Augusta ; from W. 612 ms.

SOUTH CHINA, p. o., China township, Kennebec co., Me., 14 ms. N. E. of Augusta ; from W. 609 ms.

SOUTH COLUMBIA, p. o., Columbia township, Herkimer co., N. Y., 72 ms. N. w. of Albany ; from W. 376 ms.

SOUTH CORINTH, p. o., Corinth township, Saratoga co., N. Y., 47 ms. N. w. of Albany ; from W. 417 ms.

SOUTH CORTLAND, p. o., Cortlandville township, Cortland co., N. Y., 151 ms. w. of Albany ; from W. 313 ms.

SOUTH COVENTRY, p. o., Coventry township, Tolland co., Ct., 22 ms. N. E. of Hartford ; from W. 358 ms.

SOUTH CRAFTSBURY, p. o., Orleans co., Vt.

SOUTH CREEK, p. t., Bradford co., Pa., 163 ms. N. of Harrisburgh ; from W. 270 ms. Pop. 709.

SOUTH CREEK, p. o., Beaufort district, S. C.

SOUTH DANBY, p. o., Danby township, Tompkins co., N. Y., 171 ms. w. of Albany ; from W. 292 ms.

SOUTH DANSVILLE, p. o., Dansville township, Steuben co., N. Y.

SOUTH DARTMOUTH, p. o., Dartmouth township, Bristol co., Mass., 62 ms. s. of Boston ; from W. 438 ms.

SOUTH DEDHAM, p. o., Norfolk co., Mass.

SOUTH DEERFIELD, p. v., Deerfield township, Rockingham co., N. H., 18 ms. s. E. of Concord ; from W. 472 ms.

SOUTH DEERFIELD, p. v., Deerfield township, Franklin co., Mass., 91 ms. w. of Boston ; from W. 394 ms.

SOUTH DEER ISLE, p. o., Hancock co., Me., 97 ms. E. of Augusta ; from W. 693 ms.

SOUTH DENNIS, p. o., Dennis township, Barnstable co., Mass., 84 ms. s. E. of Boston ; from W. 485 ms.

SOUTH DICKINSON, p. o., Dickinson township, Franklin co., N. Y.

SOUTH DORSET, p. o., Bennington co., Vt.

SOUTH DOVER, p. o., Dover township, Piscataquis co., Me., 88 ms. N. E. of Augusta ; from W. 685 ms.

SOUTH DOVER, p. o., Dover township, Dutchess co., N. Y., 80 ms. s. of Albany ; from W. 307 ms.

SOUTH DRESDEN, p. o., Lincoln co., Me.

SOUTH DURHAM, p. o., Durham township, Greene co., N. Y., 50 ms. s. w. of Albany ; from W. 352 ms.

SOUTH DURHAM, p. o., Durham township, Cumberland co., Me., 28 ms. s. w. of Augusta ; from W. 567 ms.

SOUTH EAST, p. t., Putnam co., N. Y., 107 ms. s. of Albany ; from W. 291 ms. Watered by Croton river. Pop. 2,079.

SOUTH EAST, p. t., Orange co., Ind.

SOUTH EASTON, p. o., Easton township, Washington co., N. Y., 30 ms. N. of Albany ; from W. 400 ms.

SOUTH EASTON, b., Northampton co., Pa. Watered by Lehigh river. Pop. 1,511.

SOUTH EASTON, p. o., Bristol co., Mass.

SOUTH EDMESTON, p. o., Edmeston township, Otsego co., N. Y., 93 ms. w. of Albany ; from W. 351 ms.

SOUTH EDWARDS, p. o., Edwards township, St. Lawrence co., N. Y., 191 ms. N. w. of Albany ; from W. 460 ms.

SOUTH EGREMONT, p. v., Egremont township, Berkshire co., Mass.

SOUTH ENGLISH, p. o., Keokuk co., Iowa.

SOUTH ERIN, p. o., Chemung co., N. Y.

SOUTHERLAND, p. o., Jefferson co., Flor.

SOUTHERLAND SPRINGS, p. o., Bexar co., Tex.

SOUTH FARMS, p. v., Litchfield township, Litchfield co., Ct., 40 ms. w. of Hartford ; from W. 318 ms.

SOUTHFIELD, p. t., Richmond co., Staten Island, N Y., 155 ms. s. of Albany ; from W. —— ms. Watere by New York bay. Pop. 2,709.

SOUTHFIELD, p. t., Oakland co., Mich., 17 ms. N. of Detroit ; from W. 540 ms. Watered by north branch of Ronge river. Pop. 1,658.

SOUTHFIELD, p. o., Berkshire co., Mass.

SOUTH FLORENCE, p. v., Franklin co., Ala. Watered by Tennessee river.

SOUTHFORD, p. v., New Haven co., Ct.

SOUTH FORK, t., Izard co., Ark.

SOUTH FORK, p. o., Owsley co., Ky.

SOUTH FORK, p. o., Wayne co., Iowa.

SOUTH FORK, p. o., Ashe co., N. C.

SOUTH FORT, t., Monroe co., Mo.

SOUTH FOSTER, p. o., Foster township, Providence co., R. I., 16 ms. w. of Providence ; from W. 386 ms.

SOUTH FRAMINGHAM, p. o., Framingham township, Middlesex co., Mass.

SOUTH FRANKLIN, p. o., Franklin township, Delaware co., N. Y.

SOUTH FRANKLIN, p. o., Norfolk co., Mass.

SOUTH FREEDOM, p. o., Freedom township, Waldo co., Me., 28 ms. E. of Augusta ; from W. 623 ms.

SOUTH GALWAY, p. o., Saratoga co., N. Y.

SOUTH GARDNER, p. o., Gardner township, Worcester co., Mass., 56 ms. N. w. of Boston ; from W. 416 ms.

SOUTH GATE, p. o., Franklin co., Ind.

SOUTH GENESEE, p. o., Waukesha co., W.

SOUTH GIBSON, p. o., Gibson co., Tenn., 145 ms. w. of Nashville ; from W. 828 ms.

SOUTH GILBOA, p. o., Schoharie co., N. Y.

SOUTH GLASTONBURY, p. v., Glastonbury township, Hartford co., Ct., 9 ms. s. of Hartford ; from W. 335 ms. Watered by Connecticut river.

SOUTH GRANBY, p. o., Oswego co., N. Y.

SOUTH GRANVILLE, p. o., Granville township, Washington co., N. Y.

SOUTH GROTON, p. o., Middlesex co., Mass.

SOUTH GROVE, p. o., De Kalb co., Ill.

SOUTH GROVE, p. o., Walworth co., Wis.

SOUTH HADLEY, p. t., Hampshire co., Mass., 88 ms. w. of Boston ; from W. 377 ms. Watered by Muddy and Connecticut rivers. Pop. 2,495.

SOUTH HADLEY FALLS, p. v., South Hadley township, Hampshire co., Mass., 92 ms. w. of Boston ; from W. 372 ms. Watered by Connecticut river.

SOUTH HALIFAX, p. o., Halifax township, Windham co., Vt., 140 ms. s. of Montpelier ; from W. 416 ms.

SOUTH HAMMOND, p. o., Hammond township, St. Lawrence co., N. Y.

SOUTH HAMPTON, p. o., Suffolk co., N. Y., 250 ms. s. E. of Albany ; from W. 330 ms. Watered by Great and Little Peconic bays, and the Atlantic ocean. Pop. 6,501.

SOUTH HAMPTON, p. t., Rockingham co., N. H., 39 ms. s. of Concord ; from W. 474 ms. Watered by Powow river. Pop. 472.

SOUTH HANOVER, p. v., Jefferson co., Ind., 93 ms. s. E. of Indianapolis ; from W. 565 ms. Pop. 683.

SOUTH HANSON, p. o., Plymouth co., Mass.

SOUTH HARDWICK, p. o., Hardwick township, Caledonia co., Vt., 22 ms. N. E. of Montpelier ; from W. 538 ms.

SOUTH HARPETH, p. o., Davidson co., Tenn., 17 ms. s. of Nashville ; from W. 701 ms.

SOUTH HARRISBURGH, p. o., Lewis co., N. Y.

SOUTH HARTFORD, p. o., Hartford township, Oxford co., Me., 27 ms. w. of Augusta ; from W. 593 ms.

SOUTH HARTFORD, p. v., Hartford township, Washington co., N. Y., 55 ms. N. E. of Albany ; from W. 425 ms.

SOUTH HARTWICK, p. o., Otsego co., N. Y.

SOUTH HARWICH, p. v., Harwich township, Barnstable co., Mass., 91 ms. s. w. of Boston ; from W. 492 ms.

SOUTH HAVEN, t., Van Buren co., Mich. Pop. 220.

SOUTH HAWLEY, p. v., Hawley township, Franklin co., Mass., 114 ms. w. of Boston ; from W. 408 ms.

SOUTH HENRIETTA, p. o., Jackson co., Mich.

SOUTH HERMITAGE, p. o., Lancaster co., Pa.

SOUTH HERO, p. t., Grand Isle co., Vt., 58 ms. N. w of Montpelier ; from W. 531 ms. This town constitutes the south part of the largest island in Lake Champlain. Pop. 705.

SOUTH HILL, p. v., Bradford co., Pa., 150 ms. N. of Harrisburgh ; from W. 260 ms

SOUTH HILL, p. o., Mecklenburgh co., Va., 93 ms. s. w. of Richmond; from W. 299 ms.

SOUTH HILL, p. o., Steuben co., N. Y.

SOUTH HINGHAM, p. v., Hingham township, Plymouth co., Mass., 18 ms. s. E. of Boston; from W. 452 ms.

SOUTH HOLLOW, p. o., Jo-Daviess co., Ill.

SOUTH HOPE, p. o., Waldo co., Me.

SOUTH HUNTINGDON, p. t., Westmoreland co.. Pa.,

SOUTHINGTON, p. t., Hartford co., Ct., 18 ms. s. w. of Hartford; from W. 321 ms. Watered by Quinnipiack river. Pop. 2,135.

SOUTHINGTON, p. t., Trumbull co., O., 170 ms. N. E. of Columbus; from W. 313 ms. Pop. 1,013.

SOUTH JACKSON, p. v., Jackson township, Jackson co., Mich., 76 ms. w. of Detroit; from W. 544 ms.

SOUTH KENT. p. v., Kent township, Litchfield co., Ct., 55 ms. w. of Hartford; from W. 320 ms.

SOUTH KILLINGLY, p. v., Killingly township, Windham co., Ct., 51 ms. E. of Hartford; from W. 378 ms.

SOUTH KINGSTON, p. t., seat of justice of Washington co.. R. I., 30 ms. s. w. of Providence; from W. 389 ms. Watered by Long Island sound and Narraganset bay. Near the centre of this town is the village of North Kingston, containing the county buildings. Pop. in 1830. 3.663; in 1840, 3,717; in 1850, 3,807.

SOUTH KIRTLAND, p. o., Kirtland township, Lake co., O., 163 ms., N. E. of Columbus; from W. 349 ms.

SOUTH KORTRIGHT, p. o., Kortright township, Delaware co., N. Y., 69 ms. s. w. of Albany; from W. 349 ms.

SOUTH LANSING, p. o., Lansing township, Tompkins co., N. Y., 170 ms. w. of Albany; from W. 303 ms.

SOUTH LEE, p. v., Lee township, Berkshire co., Mass., 131 ms. w. of Boston; from W. 365 ms.

SOUTH LEEDS, p. o., Leeds township, Kennebec co., Me., 23 ms. s. w. of Augusta; from W. 587 ms.

SOUTH LEVANT, p. o., Levant township, Penobscot co., Me., 78 ms. N. E. of Augusta; from W. 673 ms.

SOUTH LINCOLN, p. v., Lincoln township, Penobscot co., Me., 111 ms. N. E. of Augusta; from W. 706 ms.

SOUTH LIVONIA, p. o., Livonia township, Livingston co., N. Y., 22 ms. w. of Albany; from W. 349 ms.

SOUTH LODI, p. o., Lodi township, Seneca co., N. Y., 188 ms. w. of Albany; from W. 319 ms.

SOUTH LOWELL MILLS, p. o., Orange co., N. C.

SOUTH LYME, p. v., Lyme township, New London co.. Ct., 50 ms. s. of Hartford; from W. 343 ms.

SOUTH LYMANSBOROUGH, p. o., Hillsborough co., N. H., 41 ms. s. w. of Concord; from W, 459 ms.

SOUTH LYON, p. o., Oakland co., Mich.

SOUTH MANCHESTER, p. o., Hartford co., Ct.

SOUTH MARCELLUS. p. o., Marcellus township, Onondaga co., N., 144 ms. w. of Albany; from W. 340 ms.

SOUTH MAXFIELD, p. o., Penobscot co., Me.

SOUTH MERRIMACK, p. o., Hillsborough co., N. H.,

SOUTH MIDDLEBOROUGH, p. o., Middleborough township, Plymouth co., Mass., 46 ms. s. of Boston; from W. 439 ms.

SOUTH MIDDLETOWN, p. t., Cumberland co., Pa. Watered by Yellow Breeches and Mountain creeks. Pop. 2,252.

SOUTH MIDDLETOWN, v., Wallkill township, Orange co., N. Y., 112 ms. s. w. of Albany; from W. 285 ms.

SOUTH MILFORD, p. o., Milford township, Worcester co., Mass., 35 ms. s. w. of Boston; from W. 411 ms.

SOUTH MILFORD, p. o., Cecil co., Md.

SOUTH MILFORD, p. o., La Grange co., Ind.

SOUTH MILFORD, p. o., Otsego co., N. Y.

SOUTH MILLS, p. o., Camden co., N. C., 232 ms. N. E. of Raleigh; from W. 266 ms.

SOUTH MOLUNCUS, p. o., Aroostook co., Me.

SOUTH MONTVILLE, p. o., Waldo co., Me.

SOUTH MOUNT VERNON, p. o., Kennebec co., Me.

SOUTH NANKIN, p. o., Nankin township, Wayne co., Mich., 15 ms. s. w. of Detroit; from W. 532 ms.

SOUTH NATICK, p. v., Natick township, Middlesex co., Mass.

SOUTH NASHVILLE, p. o., Davidson co., Tenn.

SOUTH NEW BERLIN, p. v., New Berlin township, Chenango co., N. Y., 106 ms. s. w. of Albany; from W. 339 ms.

SOUTH NEWBURGH, p. o., Newburgh township, Penobscot co., Me., 54 ms. N. E. of Augusta; from W. 649 ms.

SOUTH NEWBURY, p. o., Newbury township, Orange co., Vt.

SOUTH NEWBURY, p. o., Merrimack co., N. H.

SOUTH NEWCASTLE, p. v., Ohio township, Gallia co.,

O., 121 ms. s. E. of Columbus; from W. 379 ms. Watered by Ohio river.

SOUTH NEW MARKET, p. v., New Market township, Rockingham co., N. H., 41 ms. s. E. of Concord; from W. 488 ms. Watered by Lamprey river.

SOUTH NEWPORT, p. v., McIntosh co., Ga., 108 ms. s. E. of Milledgeville; from W. 710 ms.

SOUTH NEWRY, p. o., Newry township, Oxford co., Me., 68 ms. w. of Augusta; from W. 608 ms.

SOUTH NORWALK, p. v., Norwalk township, Fairfield co., Ct.

SOUTHOLD, p. t., Suffolk co., Long Island, N. Y., 241 ms. s. E. of Albany; from W. 321 ms. Watered by Long Island sound, and Great Peconic and Gardiner's bays. Pop. 4,723.

SOUTH OLIVE, p. o., Morgan co., O.

SOUTH ONONDAGA, p. o., Onondaga township, Onondago co., N. Y., 138 ms. w. of Albany; from W. 341 ms.

SOUTH ORANGE, p. o., Orange township, Franklin co., Mass., 74 ms. w. of Boston; from W. 412 ms.

SOUTH ORANGE, p. v., Essex co., N. J.

SOUTH ORLEANS, p. o., Orleans township, Barnstable co., Mass., 97 ms. s. E. of Boston; from W. 498 ms.

SOUTH ORRINGTON, p. o., Orrington township, Penobscot co., Me., 67 ms. N. E. of Augusta; from W. 663 ms.

SOUTH OTSELIC, p. o., Otselic township, Chenango co., N. Y., 119 ms. w. of Albany; from W. 339 ms.

SOUTH OWEGO, p. o., Owego township, Tioga co., N. Y., 169 ms. s. w. of Albany; from W. 283 ms.

SOUTH OXFORD, p. o., Oxford township, Chenango co., N. Y., 115 ms. w. of Albany; from W. 322 ms.

SOUTH OYSTER BAY, p. o., Oyster Bay township, Queens co., N. Y.

SOUTH PARIS, p. o., Paris township, Oxford co., Me., 42 ms. w. of Augusta; from W. 590 ms.

SOUTH PARSONSFIELD, p. o., Parsonsfield township, York co., Me., 84 ms. s. w. of Augusta; from W. 535 ms.

SOUTH PERRY, p. o., Fairfield co., O.

SOUTH PLYMOUTH, p. o., Wayne co., Mich., 23 ms. s. w. of Detroit; from W. 524 ms.

SOUTH PLYMOUTH, p. o., Chenango co., N. Y.

SOUTH POINT, p. o., Lincoln co., N. C., 177 ms. w. of Albany; from W. 416 ms.

SOUTH POMFRET, p. o., Windsor co., Vt.

SOUTHPORT, p. t., Chemung co. N. Y., 197 ms. s. w. of Albany; from W. 277 ms. Watered by Chemung river. Pop. 3,181.

SOUTHPORT, p. v., Fairfield township, Fairfield co., Ct., 60 ms. s. w. of Hartford; from W. 277 ms. Watered by Mill river and Long Island sound.

SOUTHPORT, v., Racine co., Wis., 110 ms. s. E. of Madison; from W. 769 ms.

SOUTHPORT, p. o., Marion co., Ind.

SOUTHPORT, p. o., Lincoln co., Me.

SOUTH PRAIRIE, p. o., Boone co., Ill.

SOUTH PROSPECT, p. o., Waldo co., Me.

SOUTH PULTNEY, p. o., Pultney township, Steuben co., N. Y., 216 ms. w. of Albany; from W. 312 ms.

SOUTH QUAY, p. o., Nansemond co., Va., 85 ms. s. E. of Richmond; from W. 204 ms.

SOUTH RAYMOND, p. o., Rockingham co., N. H.

SOUTH READING, p. o., Reading township, Windsor co., Vt., 64 ms. s. of Montpelier; from W. 475 ms.

SOUTH READING, p. t., Middlesex co., Mass., 11 ms. N. of Boston; from W. 451 ms. Watered by Reading pond. Pop. 2,407.

SOUTH RICHLAND, p. o., Oswego co., N. Y.

SOUTH RIDGE, p. o., Ashtabula co., O.

SOUTH RIVER, p. o., Middlesex co., N. J., 32 ms. s. E. of Trenton; from W. 198 ms.

SOUTH RIVER, p. o., Anne Arundel co., Md.

SOUTH RIVER, t., Marion co., Mo. Pop. 757.

SOUTH ROYALTON, p. o., Worcester co., Mass.

SOUTH ROYALTON, p. o., Royalton township, Niagara co., N. Y., 274 ms. w. of Albany; from W. 394 ms.

SOUTH ROYALTON, p. o., Windsor co., Vt.

SOUTH RUTLAND, p. o., Rutland township, Jefferson co., N. Y., 164 ms. N. w. of Albany; from W. 416 ms.

SOUTH RYEGATE, p. o., Caledonia co., Vt.

SOUTH SALUDA, p. o., Greenville district, S. C.

SOUTH ST. GEORGE, p. o., Lincoln co., Me., 57 ms. E. of Augusta; from W. 634 ms.

SOUTH SALEM, p. v., Lewisborough township, Westchester co., N. Y., 118 ms. s. of Albany; from W. 279 ms. Watered by a tributary of Croton river.

SOUTH SALEM, p. o., Ross co., O.

SOUTH SANDWICH, p. v., Sandwich township, Barnstable co., Mass., 64 ms. s. of Boston; from W. 465 ms.

SOUTH SANFORD, p. o., York co., Me.

SOUTH SANGERVILLE, p. o., Siscataquis co., Me.

SOUTH SCHODACK, p. o., Schodack township, Rensselaer co., N. Y., 13 ms. s. of Albany; from W. 364 ms.

SOUTH SCITUATE, p. o., Scituate township, Providence co., R. I., 11 ms. w. of Providence; from W. 389 ms.

SOUTH SCITUATE, p. o., Scituate township, Plymouth co., Mass., 24 ms. s. E. of Boston; from W. 448 ms.

SOUTH SEBEC, p. o., Sebec township, Piscataquis co., Me., 93 ms. N. E. of Augusta; from W. 690 ms.

SOUTH SEKONK, p. v., Bristol co., Mass., 48 ms. s. of Boston; from W. 406 ms.

SOUTH SHAFTSBURY, p. o., Shaftsbury township, Bennington co., Vt., 113 ms. s. w. of Montpelier; from W. 411 ms.

SOUTH SHENANGO, p. t., Crawford co., Pa., 252 ms. N. w. of Harrisburgh; from W. 302 ms. Pop. 1,664.

SOUTH SHREWSBURY, p. v., Shrewsbury township, Worcester co., Mass., 37 ms. w. of Boston; from W. 492 ms.

SOUTH SIDE, p. o., Richmond co., Staten Island, N. Y.

SOUTH SODUS, p. v., Sodus township, Wayne co., N. Y., 188 ms. w. of Albany; from W. 364 ms.

SOUTH SOLON, p. o., Solon township, Somerset co., Me., 46 ms. N. of Augusta; from W. 641 ms.

SOUTH SOLON, p. o., Stokes township, Madison co., O., 56 ms. w. of Columbus; from W. 411 ms.

SOUTH STEPHENTOWN, p. o., Stephentown township, Rensselaer co., N. Y., 28 ms. s. w. of Albany; from W. 373 ms.

SOUTH STERLING, p. o., Sterling township, Wayne co., Pa., 142 ms. N. E. of Harrisburgh; from W. 236 ms.

SOUTH STODDARD, p. o., Cheshire co., N. H.

SOUTH STRABANE, p. o., Washington co., Pa.

SOUTH STRAFFORD, p. o., Strafford township, Orange co., Vt., 36 ms. s. E. of Montpelier; from W. 500 ms.

SOUTH TAMWORTH, p. o., Tamworth township, Carroll co., N. H., 53 ms. N. of Concord; from W. 537 ms.

SOUTH THOMASTON, p. v., Lincoln co., Me.

SOUTH THOMPSON, p. o., Geauga co., O.

SOUTH THURSTON, p. o., Steuben co., N. Y.

SOUTH TRENTON, p. o., Trenton township, Oneida co., N. Y., 100 ms. N. w. of Albany; from W. 397 ms.

SOUTH UNION, p. v., Logan co., Ky., 158 ms. s. w. of Frankfort; from W. 682 ms.

SOUTH VALLEY. p. o., Cherry Valley township, Otsego co., N. Y., 63 ms. w. of Albany; from W. 385 ms.

SOUTH VASSALBOROUGH, p. o., Vassalborough township, Kennebec co., Me., 9 ms. N. of Augusta; from W. 604 ms.

SOUTH VENICE, v., Venice township, Cayuga co., N. Y., 163 ms. w. of Albany; from W. 321 ms.

SOUTHVILLE, p. o., Stockholm township, St. Lawrence co., N. Y., 223 ms. N. w. of Albany; from W. 507 ms.

SOUTHVILLE, p. v., Shelby co., Ky., 31 ms. N. w. of Frankfort; from W. 573 ms.

SOUTHVILLE, p. o., Litchfield co., Ct.

SOUTH WALDEN, p. o., Walden township, Caledonia co., Vt., 25 ms. N. E. of Montpelier; from W. 538 ms.

SOUTH WALES, p. o., Wales township, Erie co., N. Y., 285 ms. w. of Albany; from W. 356 ms.

SOUTH WALLINGFORD, p. o., Wallingford township, Rutland co., Vt., 71 ms. s. of Montpelier; from W. 452 ms.

SOUTH WALPOLE, p. o., Walpole township, Norfolk co., Mass., 20 ms. s. w. of Boston; from W. 4— ms.

SOUTH WARREN, p. o., Bradford co., Pa., 155 ms. N. of Harrisburgh; from W. 265 ms.

SOUTH WARSAW, p. o., Wyoming co., N. Y.

SOUTH WATERFORD, p. o., Waterford township, Oxford co., Me., 54 ms. w. of Augusta; from W. 587 ms.

SOUTH WEARE, p. o., Weare township, Hillsborough co., N. H., 17 ms. s. w. of Concord; from W. 472 ms.

SOUTH WELLFLEET, p. o., Wellfleet township, Barnstable co., Mass., 101 ms. s. E. of Boston; from W. 502 ms.

SOUTH WEST, p. t., Orange co., Ind.

SOUTH WEST, t., Warren co., Ind.

SOUTH WESTERLOO. p. v., Westerloo township, Albany co., N. Y., 27 ms. w. of Albany; from W. 363 ms.

SOUTHWEST HARBOR, p. v., Hancock co., Me., 114 ms. s. E. of Augusta; from W. 696 ms.

SOUTHWEST OSWEGO, p. o., Oswego co., N. Y.

SOUTH WESTPORT, p. v., Westport township, Bristol co., Mass., 72 ms. s. of Boston; from W. 436 ms.

SOUTH WEYMOUTH, p. o., Weymouth township, Norfolk co., Mass., 15 ms. s. of Boston; from W. 443 ms.

SOUTH WHITEHALL, p. t., Lehigh co., Pa., 87 ms. N. E. of Harrisburgh; from W. 180 ms. Watered by Jordan and Cedar creeks. Pop. 2,913.

SOUTH WHITLEY, p. t., Hampden co., Mass.

SOUTHWICK, p. t., Hampden co., Mass., 103 ms. w. of Boston; from W. 359 ms. Watered by a tributary of Westfield river. Pop. 1,120.

SOUTH WILBRAHAM, p. o., Wilbraham township, Hampden co., Mass., 82 ms. s. w. of Boston; from W. 373 ms.

SOUTH WILLIAMSTOWN, p. v., Williamstown township, Berkshire co., Mass., 135 ms. w. of Boston; from W. 389 ms.

SOUTH WILSON, p. o., Wilson township, Niagara co., N. Y.

SOUTH WINDHAM, p. o., Windham township, Cumberland co., Me., 60 ms. s. w. of Augusta; from W. 519 ms.

SOUTH WINDHAM, p. o., Windham township, Windham co., Vt.

SOUTH WINDHAM, p. o., Windham township, Windham co., Ct.

SOUTH WINDSOR, p. o., Windsor township, Kennebec co., Me., 10 ms. E. of Augusta; from W. 602 ms.

SOUTH WINDSOR, p. v., Windsor township, Broome co., N. Y., 131 ms. s. w. of Albany; from W. 295 ms.

SOUTH WINDSOR, p. o., Windsor township, Hartford co., Ct.

SOUTH WOLFBOROUGH, p. v., Wolfborough township, Carroll co., N. H., 37 ms. N. E. of Concord; from W. 518 ms.

SOUTH WOODBURY, p. t., Bedford co., Pa. Pop. 1,122.

SOUTH WOODSTOCK, p. v., Woodstock township, Windsor co., Vt., 55 ms. s. of Montpelier; from W. 484 ms.

SOUTH WORCESTER, p. v., Worcester township, Otsego co., N. Y., 62 ms. w. of Albany; from W. 368 ms. Watered by Charlotte river.

SOUTH WRENTHAM, p. o., Wrentham township, Norfolk co., Mass., 36 ms. s. of Boston; from W. 414 ms.

SOUTH YARMOUTH, p. v., Yarmouth township, Barnstable co., Mass., 82 ms. s. E. of Boston; from W. 483 ms.

SOUTH ZANESVILLE, v., Muskingum co., O.

SOWARDTOWN, p. v., Kent co., Del., 27 ms. s. of Dover; from W. 112 ms.

SOXVILLE, p. v., Monroe co., Pa., 131 ms. N. E. of Harrisburgh; from W. 228 ms.

SPADRA, p. t., Johnson co., Ark. Pop. 1,209.

SPAFFORD, p. t., Onondaga co., N. Y., 137 ms. w. of Albany; from W. 334 ms. Watered by Skaneateles and Otisco lakes. Pop. 1,903.

SPAFFORD HOLLOW, p. o., Spafford township, Onondaga co., N. Y., 137 w. of Albany; from W. 331 ms.

SPANISH PRAIRIE, p. o., Crawford co., Mo.

SPANGSVILLE, p. o., Berks co., Pa.

SPARTA, p. t., Livingston co., N. Y., 241 ms. w. of Albany; from W. 336 ms. Watered by Canaseraga creek. Pop. 1,372.

SPARTA, p. v., Hardiston township, Sussex co., N. J., 78 ms. N. of Trenton; from W. 246 ms. Pop. 1,919.

SPARTA, p. o., Morris township, Washington co., Pa., 219 ms. w. of Harrisburgh; from W. 246 ms.

SPARTA, t., Westmoreland co., Pa. Pop. 1,719.

SPARTA, p. v., Bloomfield township, Morrow co., O., 46 ms. N. E. of Columbus; from W. 391 ms. Pop. 127.

SPARTA, p. o., Caroline co., Va., 51 ms. N. of Richmond; from W. 91 ms.

SPARTA, p. v., Edgecombe co., N. C., 84 ms. E. of Raleigh; from W. 270 ms.

SPARTA, c. h., p. v., seat of justice of Hancock co., Ga., 23 ms. N. E. of Milledgeville; from W. 648 ms.

SPARTA, c. h., p. v., seat of justice of Conecuh co., Ala.; from W. 925 ms. Watered by Murder creek.

SPARTA, c. h., p. v., seat of justice of White co., Tenn., 83 ms. E. of Nashville; from W. 598 ms. Watered by a tributary of Caney fork of Cumberland river.

SPARTA, p. o., Randolph co., Ill., 141 ms. s. of Springfield; from W. 816 ms.

SPARTA, c. h., p. v., seat of justice of Buchanan co., Mo. Watered by head-waters of Bee creek

SPARTA, p. o., Chickasaw co., Miss.

SPARTA, p. o., Dearborn co., Ind.

SPARTA, t., Noble co., Ind.
SPARTA, p. o., Bienville parish, La.
SPARTA, p. o., Hillsdale co., Mich.
SPARTA CENTRE, p. o., Kent co., Mich.
SPARTANBURGH DISTRICT, situated on the north boundary of South Carolina, with Broad river on the northeast. Area, 1,050 square miles. Face of the country, hilly ; soil, fertile. Seat of justice, Spartanburgh. Pop. in 1810, 14,259 ; in 1820, 16,989 ; in 1830, 21,150 ; in 1840, 23,669 ; in 1850, 26,400.
SPARTANBURGH. c. h., p. v., seat of justice of Spartanburgh district, S. C. ; 98 ms. N. w. of Columbia ; from W. 471 ms.
SPARTANBURGH, p. v., Randolph co., Ind.
SPARTANSBURGH, p. o., Crawford co., Pa.
SPARTAPOLIS. p. v., Rockingham co., Va., 142 ms. N. w. of Richmond ; from W. 120 ms.
SPEAR'S STORE, p. o., Union parish, La.
SPEEDSVILLE, p. v., Caroline township. Tompkins co., N. Y., 177 ms. w. of Albany ; from W. 307 ms. Watered by West Owego creek.
SPEEDWELL, p. o., Wythe co., Va., 269 ms. w. of Richmond ; from W. 330 ms.
SPEEDWELL. p. v., Barnwell district, S. C., 114 ms. s. w. of Columbia ; from W. 610 ms. Watered by Savannah river.
SPEEDWELL, p. v., Claiborne co., Tenn., 212 ms. E. of Nashville ; from W. 508 ms.
SPEER'S LANDING, p. o., Shelby co., O.
SPEERSVILLE. p. o., Fulton co., Pa., 83 ms. w. of Harrisburgh ; from 109 ms.
SPEIGHT'S BRIDGE, p. v., Greene co., N. C., 79 s. E. of Raleigh ; from W. 289 ms. Watered by Mocassin creek.
SPEIR'S TURNOUT, p. o., Jefferson co., Ga.
SPENCER COUNTY, situated toward the north part of Kentucky. Area, 260 square miles. Seat of justice, Taylorsville. Pop. in 1830, 6,812 ; in 1840, 6,581 ; in 1850, 6,842.
SPENCER COUNTY, situated on the southerly boundary of Indiana, with Ohio river on the south. Area, 400 square miles. Face of the country, hilly and broken ; soil, fertile. Seat of justice, Rockport. Pop. in 1820, 1,882 ; in 1830, 3,196 ; in 1840, 6,305 ; in 1850, 8,620.
SPENCER, p. t., Worcester co., Mass., 53 ms. w. of Boston ; from W. 395 ms. Watered by Seven-Mile river. Pop. 2,244.
SPENCER, p. t., Tioga co., N. Y., 179 ms. s. w. of Albany ; from W. 280 ms. Watered by Cattotong creek and tributaries. Pop. 1,782.
SPENCER, p. v., Davidson co., N. C., 191 ms. w. of Raleigh ; from W. 348 ms.
SPENCER, p. t., Medina co., O., 111 ms. N. E. of Columbus ; from W. 366 ms. Pop. 1,336.
SPENCER, p. t., Guernsey co., O. Watered by headwaters of Wills creek. Pop. 1,847.
SPENCER, c. h., p. v., seat of justice of Van Buren co., Tenn., 90 ms. s. E. of Nashville ; from W. 641 ms.
SPENCER, c. h., p. v., seat of justice of Owen co., Ind., 58 ms. s. w. of Indianapolis ; from W. 621 ms. Watered by north fork of White river.
SPENCER, p. t., Pike co., Mo.
SPENCER, p. t., Ralls co., Mo.
SPENCERPORT. p. v., Ogden township. Monroe co., N. Y., 234 ms. w. of Albany ; from W. 380 ms. Situated on the Erie canal.
SPENCERSBURGH, p. v., Pike co., Mo., 88 ms. N. E. of Jefferson city ; from W. 892 ms.
SPENCERTOWN, p. v., Austerlitz township, Columbia co., N. Y., 29 ms. s. E. of Albany ; from W. 359 ms.
SPENCERVILLE. p. o., De Kalb co., Ind., 150 ms. N. E. of Indianopolis ; from W. 544 ms.
SPENCERVILLE, p. o., Marengo co., Ala.
SPEONK, p. o., South Hampton township, Suffolk co., Long Island, N. Y., 228 ms. s. E. of Albany ; from W. 308 ms.
SPERRYVILLE, p. v., Rappahannock co., Va., 123 ms. N. w. of Richmond ; from W. 80 ms,
SPICELAND, p. o., Henry co., Ind., 38 ms. N. E. of Indianapolis ; from W. 543 ms.
SPINNERSTOWN, p. v., Bucks co., Pa., 91 ms. E. of Harrisburgh ; from W. 178 ms.
SPLICE CREEK, p. o., Moniteau co., Mo.
SPLUNG, p. o., Monroe co., Miss.
SPORTING HILL, p. o., Lancaster co., Pa
SPOTTEDVILLE, p. v., Stafford co., Va., 76 ms. N. of Richmond ; from W. 67 ms.

SPOTTSWOOD, p. v., Amboy township, Middlesex co., N. J., 36 ms. N. E. of Trenton : from W. 202 ms.
SPOTTSYLVANIA COUNTY, situated in the easterly part of Virginia, with Rappahannock river on the northeast. Area. 408 square miles. Face of the country, pleasantly diversified ; soil, productive. Seat of justice, Spottsylvania c. h. Pop. in 1810, 13,296 ; in 1820, 14,254 ; in 1830, 15,134 ; in 1840, 15,161 ; in 1850, 14,911.
SPOTTSYLVANIA, c. h., p. v., seat of justice of Spottsylvania co., Va. 71 ms. N. of Richmond ; from W. 68 ms. Watered by Po river.
SPOUT SPRING, p. o., Appomattox co., Va., 99 ms. w. of Richmond ; from W. 185 ms.
SPRAGUE'S FALLS, p. o., Washington co., Me.
SPRAGUEVILLE, p. o., Jackson co., Iowa.
SPRAKER'S BASIN, p. v., Root township, Montgomery co., N. Y., 47 ms. N. w. of Albany ; from W. 398 ms. Situated on the Erie canal.
SPREAD EAGLE, p. v., Radnor township, Delaware co., Pa., 83 ms. s. E. of Harrisburgh ; from W. 133 ms.
SPREAD OAK, p. o., Jefferson co., Ga.
SPRIGG, p. t., Adams co., O. Pop. 3,118.
SPRING, p. t., Crawford co., Pa., 257 ms. N. w. of Harrisburgh ; from W. 330 ms. Pop. 1,836.
SPRING, p. t., Centre co., Pa. Pop. 2,280.
SPRING, p. o., Henry co., Ga.
SPRING ARBOR, p. t., Jackson co., Mich., 88 ms. w. of Detroit ; from W. 552 ms. Pop. 1,095.
SPRING BAY, p. o., Woodford co., Ill.
SPRINGBOROUGH, p. v., Clear Creek township, Warren co., O., 84 ms. s. w. of Columbus ; from W. 470 ms. Watered by Clear creek. Pop. 454.
SPRING BROOK, p. o., Erie co., N. Y.
SPRING BROOK, p. o., Jackson co., Iowa.
SPRING CHURCH, p. o., Armstrong co., Pa.
SPRING COTTAGE, p. o., Marion co., Miss.
SPRING CREEK, p. t., Warren co., Pa., 232 ms. N. w. of Harrisburgh ; from W. 324 ms. Watered by Broken Straw creek. Pop. 601.
SPRING CREEK, p. o., Greenbrier co., Va., 226 ms. w. of Richmond ; from W. 261 ms.
SPRING CREEK, p. t., Miami co., O. Pop. 1,249.
SPRING CREEK, p. o., Early co., Ga.
SPRING CREEK, p. o., Madison co., Tenn., 121 ms. s. w. of Nashville ; from W. 806 ms.
SPRING CREEK, p. o., Randolph co., Ark.
SPRING CREEK, p. o., McDonough co., Ill.
SPRING CREEK, p. o., Brunswick co., N. C.
SPRING CREEK, p o., Cass co., Ind.
SPRING CREEK, p. o., Harris co., Tex.
SPRING CREEK, p. o., Berrien co., Mich.
SPRING DALE, p. o., Springfield township, Hamilton co., O., 110 ms. s. o. of Columbus ; from W. 500 ms.
SPRING DALE, p. o., Lafayette co ; Miss.
SPRING DALE, p. o., Dane co., Wis.
SPRING DALE, p. o., Scott co., Ky.
SPRING DALE, p. o., Cedar co., Iowa.
SPRINGFIELD, p. t., Penobscot co., Me. Watered by tributaries of Mattawamkeag river. Pop. 583.
SPRINGFIELD, p. t., Sullivan co., N. H., 35 ms. N. w. of Concord ; from W. 492 ms. Watered by head-waters of Black and Sugar rivers. Pop. 1,270.
SPRINGFIELD, p. t., Windsor co., Vt., 77 ms. s. of Montpelier ; from W. 450 ms. Watered by Connecticut and Black rivers. Pop. 2.762.
SPRINGFIELD, city, p. t., and seat of justice of Hampden county, Mass., situated on the east side of Connecticut river, 91 miles southwest of Boston, and 363 miles from Washington. It principally occupies a single street, parallel with the river, and contains many handsome buildings. Pleasant alluvial meadows gradually rise from the river into a region of less fertility. A bridge here spans the river to West Springfield. Manufactures of various kinds are largely produced, and give to the place its prosperity. The most important establishment is the United States arsenal, which, built on an elevation above the village, presents within and without an imposing spectacle. Small-arms are made at the factory, one mile distant, on Mill river. The Western railroad, between Albany and Boston, and the chain of railways through Connecticut river valley to Hartford, New Haven, and New York, concentre at this point. The population in 1810 was 2,767 ; in 1820, 3,914 ; in 1830, 6,784 ; in 1840, 10,985 ; in 1850, 11,766.
SPRINGFIELD, p. t., Otsego co., N. Y., 61 ms. w. of Albany ; from W. 379 ms. Watered by Otsego lake Pop. 2,322.
SPRINGFIELD, p. t., Essex co., N. J., 52 ms. N. E. of

Trenton ; from W. 217 ms. Watered by Rahway river and tributaries. Pop. 1,945.

SPRINGFIELD, t., Burlington co., N. J. Watered by Assiscunk creek and tributaries. Pop. 1,827.

SPRINGFIELD, p. t., Bradford co., Pa., 154 ms. N. of Harrisburgh ; from W. 261 ms. Watered by Bentley's creek. Pop. 1,848.

SPRINGFIELD, t., Bucks co., Pa. Watered by Durham creek. Pop. 2,259.

SPRINGFIELD, t., Delaware co., Pa. Watered by Crum creek. Pop. 1,033.

SPRINGFIELD, t., Mercer co., Pa. Pop. 1,275.

SPRINGFIELD, t., Erie co., Pa. Watered by Crooked, Elk, and Raccoon creeks. Pop. 1,946.

SPRINGFIELD, t., Huntington co., Pa. Watered by Great Aughwick creek and its tributaries. Pop. 593.

SPRINGFIELD, t., Montgomery co., Pa. Watered by a tributary of Wissahickon creek. Pop. 743.

SPRINGFIELD, t., York co., Pa. Pop. 1,345.

SPRINGFIELD, p. v., Hampshire co., Va., 197 ms. N. w. of Richmond ; from W. 125 ms. Watered by a tributary of Potomac river.

SPRINGFIELD, c. h., p. v., seat of justice of Effingham co., Ga., 133 ms. S. E. of Milledgeville ; from W. 678 ms.

SPRINGFIELD, p. v., Greene co.. Ala. ; from W. 851 ms.

SPRINGFIELD, p. v., seat of justice of Livingston parish, La., 65 ms. N. w. of New Orleans ; from W. 1,152 ms. Watered by Notalbaney river.

SPRINGFIELD, c. h., p. v., seat of justice of Robertson co., Tenn., 26 ms. N. of Nashville ; from W. 708 ms. Watered by Sulphur fork of Red river.

SPRINGFIELD, c. h., p. v., seat of justice of Washington co., Ky., 68 ms. s. w. of Frankfort ; from W. 590 ms.

SPRINGFIELD, t., Muskingum co., O. Pop. 1,592.

SPRINGFIELD, c. h., p. v., seat of justice of Clark co., O., 43 ms. w. of Columbus ; from W. 436 ms. Watered by east fork of Mad river. Pop. 5,108.

SPRINGFIELD, t., Gallia co., O. Pop. 1,230.

SPRINGFIELD, t., Hamilton co., O. Pop. 3,632

SPRINGFIELD, t., Jefferson co., O. Pop. 1,298.

SPRINGFIELD, t., Lucas co., O. Pop. 728.

SPRINGFIELD, t., Richland co., O. Pop. 2,100.

SPRINGFIELD, t., Ross co., O. Pop. 1,162.

SPRINGFIELD, t., Summit co., O. Pop. 1,907.

SPRINGFIELD, t., Williams co., O. Pop. 782.

SPRINGFIELD, p. t., Oakland co., Mich., 37 ms. N. w. of Detroit ; from W. 561 ms. Pop. 956.

SPRINGFIELD, t., Allen co., Ind. Pop. 702.

SPRINGFIELD, p. v., Franklin co., Ind., 71 ms. S. E. of Indianapolis ; from W. 507 ms. Watered by a tributary of Whitewater river. Pop. 1,657.

SPRINGFIELD, t., La Grange co., Ind. Pop. 760.

SPRINGFIELD, p. v., seat of justice of Sangamon co., and capital of the state of Illinois ; from W. 780 ms. The town is situated four miles south of Sangamon river, and became the capital of the state in 1840. It is surrounded by a rich and populous region, picturesquely varied with prairies, forests, vales, and gentle elevations. The village is one of the most pleasant and beautiful in the west, situated on the border of extensive prairie, laid out with broad and shaded streets, interspersed with spacious lawns and squares, and indicating, in its neat and comfortable dwellings, prosperity and vigorous health. It contains a number of fine public schools, academies, churches, a jail, market-house, courthouse, and the statehouse, a costly and elegant structure. The Sangamon and Morgan railroad extends to Naples, on Illinois river, 54 miles distant. The population in 1840 was 2,579 ; in 1850, 4,533.

SPRINGFIELD, p. v., Keokuk co., Iowa.

SPRINGFIELD, c. h., p. v., seat of justice of Greene co., Mo., 158 ms. s. w. of Jefferson city ; from W. 1,073 ms. Watered by head-waters of James fork of White river. Pop. 415.

SPRINGFIELD, t., Rives co., Mo.

SPRINGFIELD, p. o., Richmond co., N. C.

SPRINGFIELD, p. o., Limestone co., Tex.

SPRINGFIELD CENTRE, p. o., Otsego co. N. Y.

SPRINGFIELD CROSS ROADS, p. o., Erie co., Pa., 270 ms. N. w. of Harrisburgh ; from W. 341 ms.

SPRINGFIELD FURNACE, p. o., Blair co., Pa., 115 ms. w. of Harrisburgh ; from W. 153 ms.

SPRINGFIELD MILLS, p. o., Noble co., Ind.

SPRING FORGE, p. o., York co., Pa., 31 ms. s. of Harrisburgh ; from W. 92 ms.

SPRING FORK, p. o., Pettis co., Mo.

SPRING GARDEN, p. t., York co., Pa. Pop. 2,435.

SPRING GARDEN, p. v., Philadelphia co., Pa., 100 ms. s. E. of Harrisburgh ; from W. 140 ms. A suburban district of Philadelphia, having an independent corporation ; site of the Fairmount water-works. Pop. 58,894.

SPRING GARDEN, p. v., Pittsylvania co., Va., 154 ms. s. w. of Richmond ; from W. 241 ms.

SPRING GARDEN, p. o., Jefferson co., Ill., 140 ms. s. w. of Springfield ; from W. 805 ms.

SPRING GARDEN, p. o., Cherokee co., Ala.

SPRING GROVE, p. o., Rowan co., N. C., 139 ms. w. of Raleigh ; from W. 376 ms.

SPRING GROVE, p. o., Laurens district, S. C., 66 ms. N. w. of Columbia ; from W. —— ms.

SPRING GROVE. p. o., Warren co., Ill., 128 ms. N. w. of Springfield ; from W. 858 ms.

SPRING GROVE, Greene co., Wis.

SPRING GROVE, p. o., Linn co.. Iowa.

SPRING HILL, p. v., Marengo co., Ala. ; from W. 883 ms. Watered by Tombigbee river.

SPRING HILL, p. o., Hernando co., Flor.

SPRING HILL, p. t., Fayette co., Pa. Pop. 1,080.

SPRING HILL, p. o., York district, S. C., 92 ms. N. of Columbia ; from W. 415 ms.

SPRING HILL, p. o., Tippah co., Miss., 214 ms. N. E. of Jackson ; from W. 879 ms.

SPRING HILL, p. t., Hempstead co., Ark., 136 ms. s. w. of Little Rock ; from W. 1,201 ms.

SPRING HILL, p. o., Maury co., Tenn., 30 ms. s. w. of Nashville ; from W. 707 ms.

SPRING HILL, p. o., Decatur co., Ind., 54 ms. s. E. of Indianapolis ; from W. 542 ms.

SPRING HILL, p. o., Whitesides co., Ill.

SPRING HILL, p. o., Livingston co., Mo.

SPRING HILL, p. o., Navarro co., Tex.

SPRING HILL FURNACE, p. o., Fayette co., Pa.

SPRING HILLS, p. o. Champaign co., O.

SPRING HOUSE, p. o., Montgomery co., Pa., 99 ms. E. of Harrisburgh ; from W. 154 ms.

SPRING HOUSE, p. o., Grainger co., Tenn.

SPRING LAKE, p. o., Williams co., O.

SPRING MILLS, p. o., Lawrence co., Ind., 81 ms. s. w. of Indianapolis ; from W. 626 ms.

SPRING MILLS, p. o., Centre co., Pa., 80 ms. N. w. of Harrisburgh ; from W. 174 ms.

SPRING MILLS, p. o., Independence township, Alleghany co., N. Y., 269 ms. w. of Albany ; from W. 297 ms.

SPRING MILLS, p. o., Crawford co., Mo.

SPRING PLACE, c. h., p. v., seat of justice of Murray co., Ga., 184 ms. N. w. of Milledgeville ; from W. 605 ms.

SPRING PLACE, v., Marshall co., Tenn., 66 ms. s. of Nashville ; from W. 712 ms.

SPRINGPORT, p. t., Cayuga co., N. Y., 165 ms. w. of Albany ; from W. —— ms. Watered by Cayuga lake. Pop. 2,041.

SPRINGPORT, p. t., Jackson co., Mich., 100 ms. w. of Detroit ; from W. 570 ms. Pop. 759.

SPRINGPORT, p. o., Panola co., Miss.

SPRING PRAIRIE, p. t., Walworth co., Wis.

SPRING RIDGE, p. o., Hinds co., Miss.

SPRING RIVER, p. t., Lawrence co., Ark. Pop. 976.

SPRING RIVER, p. o., Lawrence co., Mo.

SPRING ROCK, p. o., York district, S. C., 71 ms. N. of Columbia ; from W. 438 ms.

SPRING ROCK, p. o., Clinton co., Iowa.

SPRING RUN, p. o., Franklin co., Pa.

SPRINGS., p. o. Suffolk co., Long Island, N. Y.,

SPRINGTOWN, p. v., Springfield township. Bucks co., Pa., 106 ms. E. of Harrisburgh ; from W. 185 ms.

SPRINGTOWN, p. o., Hendricks co., Ind.

SPRINGTOWN, p. o., Polk co., Tenn.

SPRINGTOWN, p. o., Oxford co., Me.

SPRINGTOWN, p. o., York co., Me, 86 ms. s. w. of Augusta ; from W. 515 ms.

SPRINGVALE, p. o., Jefferson co., Tenn.

SPRINGVALE, p, o., Sampson co., N. C.

SPRINGVALE, p. o., Fairfax co., Va.

SPRINGVALE, p. o., Fond du Lac co., Wis.

SPRING VALLEY, p. o., Greene co., O.

SPRING VALLEY, p. o., Rockland co., N. Y.

SPRING VALLEY, p. o., Bergen co., N. J.

SPRING VALLEY, p. o., Marion co., Ind.

SPRING VALLEY, p. o., Rock co., Wis.

SPRINGVILLE, p. t., Susquehanna co., Pa., 173 ms. N. E. of Harrisburgh ; from W. 274 ms. Pop. 1,148.

SPRINGVILLE, p. v., Concord township. Erie co., N. Y., 287 ms. w. of Albany; from W. 353 ms. Watered by Spring creek.

SPRINGVILLE, p. v., Lenawee co., Mich., 68 ms. s. w. of Detroit; from W. 523 ms.

SPRINGVILLE, p. v., Greenup co., Ky., 134 ms. E. of Frankfort; from W. 441 ms. Watered by Ohio river.

SPRINGVILLE, p. v., St. Clair co., Ala.; from W. 734 ms.

SPRINGVILLE, p. v., Lawrence co., Ind., 81 ms. s. w. of Indianapolis; from W. 631 ms.

SPRINGVILLE, p. o., Coles co., Ill.

SPRINGVILLE, p. o., Crawford co., Wis.

SPRINGVILLE, p. o., Linn co., Iowa.

SPRING WATER, p. t., Livingston co., N. Y., 226 ms. w. of Albany; from W. 341 ms. Watered by Hemlock lake inlet. Pop. 2,670.

SPRING WELLS, p. t., Washtenaw co., Mich.

SPRING YARD, p. t., Barry co., Mo.

SPROUT CREEK, p. o., La Grange township, Dutchess co., N. Y., 80 ms. s. of Albany; from W. 307 ms.

SPROUT BROOK, p. o., Montgomery co., N. Y.

SPRUCE, p. o., Bates co., Mo.

SPRUCE GROVE, p. o., Monroe co., Pa.

SPRUCE HILL, p. o., Highland co., Va.

SPRUCE HILL, p. o., Juniata co., Pa.

SQUAM, v,, Gloucester township, Essex co., Mass. Watered by Atlantic ocean.

SQUAM VILLAGE, p. v., Ocean co., N. J.

SQUANKUM, p. v., Howell township, Ocean co., N. J., 43 ms. s. E. of Trenton; from W. 209 ms.

SQUARE POND, p. o., Tolland co., Ct., 26 ms. N. E. of Hartford; from W. 362 ms.

SQUAW BETTY, p. o., Bristol co., Mass.

STAATSBURGH, p. o., Hyde Park township, Dutchess co., N. Y., 61 ms. s. of Albany; from W. 309 ms.

STAFFORD COUNTY, situated on the easterly boundary of Virginia, with Potomac on the east, and the Rappahannock on the southwest. Area, 335 square miles. Face of the country, hilly; soil, sandy. Seat ot justice, Stafford, c. h. Pop. in 1810, 9,830; in 1820, 9,517; in 1830, 9,362; in 1840, 8,454; in 1850, 8,044.

STAFFORD, p. o,, Tolland co., Ct., 24 ms. N. E. of Hartford. Watered by Furnace and Willimantic rivers.

STAFFORD, p. t., Genesee co., N. Y., 243 ms. w. of Albany; trom W. 377 ms. Watered by Allen's and Black creeks. Pop. 1,195.

STAFFORD, p. t., Ocean co., N. J. Watered by Cedar and Manahawkin creeks. Pop. 1,384.

STAFFORD, p. o., Monroe co., O., 118 ms. B. of Columbus; from W. 287 ms.

STAFFORD, c. h., p. v., seat of justice of Stafford co., Va., 73 ms. N. of Richmond; from W. 46 ms. Watered by Rappahannock river.

STAFFORD SPRINGS, p. v., Stafford township, Tolland co., Ct., 28 ms. N. E. of Hartford; from W. 364 ms. Celebrated for its salubrious mineral springs.

STAFFORDVILLE, p. o., Stafford township, Tolland co., Ct.

STAGVILLE, p. v., Orange co., N. C., 31 ms. N. w. of Raleigh; from W. 273 ms.

STAHLSTOWN, p. o., Westmoreland co., Pa.

STAMFORD, p. t., Bennington co., Vt., 143 ms. s. w. of Montpelier; from W. 404 ms. Watered by tributaries of Hoosic and Deerfield rivers. Pop. 833.

STAMFORD, p. t., Fairfield co., Ct., 77 ms. s. w. of Hartford; from W. 263 ms. Watered by Long Island sound and Mill and Miannus rivers. Pop. 5,000.

STAMFORD, p. t., Delaware co., N. Y., 61 ms. s. w. of Albany; from W. 357 ms. Watered by head waters of Delaware river. Pop. 1,708.

STAMPER'S CREEK, t., Orange co., Ind. Pop. 777.

STAMPING GROUND, p. o., Scott co., Ky., 21 ms. N. E. of Frankfort; from W. 531 ms.

STANARDSVILLE, p. v., Orange co., Va., 95 ms. N. w. of Richmond; from W. 114 ms.

STANDARDVILLE, p. o., Carroll co., Tenn.

STANDING ROCK, p. o., Stewart co., Tenn., 84 ms. N. w. of Nashville; from W. 762 ms.

STANDING STONE, p. o., Bradford co., Pa., 140 ms. N. of Harrisburgh; from W. 250 ms.

STANDISH, p. t., Cumberland co., Me., 62 ms. s. w. of Augusta; from W. 538 ms. Watered by Sebago lake. Pop. 2,290.

STANFORD, p. t., Dutchess co., N. Y., 72 ms. s. of Albany; from W. —— ms. Watered by Wappinger's creek. Pop. 2,158.

STANFORD, c. h., p. v., seat of justice of Lincoln co., Ky., 52 ms. s. E. of Frankfort; from W. 563 ms. Watered by a tributary of Dick's river.

STANFORD, p. v., Monroe co., Ind., 59 ms. s. w. of Indianapolis; from W. 626 ms.

STANFORDVILLE, p. v., Stanford township, Dutchess co., N. Y., 67 ms. s. of Albany; from W. 318 ms. Watered by Wappinger's creek.

STANFORDVILLE, p. v., Putnam co., Ga., 21 ms. N. w. of Milledgeville; from W. 642 ms.

STANHOPE, p. v., Sussex co., N. J., 60 ms. N. of Trenton; from W. 230 ms. Watered by Musconetcong river, and the Morris canal.

STANHOPE, p. v., Monroe co., Pa., 128 ms. N. E. of Harrisburgh; from W. 222 ms.

STANHOPE, p. v., Nash co., N. C., 32 ms. E. of Raleigh; from W. 266 ms.

STANLEY COUNTY, situated in the southern part of North Carolina, with Yadkin river on the northeast. Area, —— square miles. Face of the country, hilly. Seat of justice, Albemarle. Pop. in 1850, 6,922.

STANLEY CORNERS, p. o., Ontario., N. Y.

STANTON, p. o., Hunterdon co., N. J.

STANTON, p. o., Bracken co., Ky.

STANTON, p. o., Newcastle co., Del.

STANTONSBURGH, p. v., Edgecombe co., N. C., 71 ms. E. of Raleigh; from W. 281 ms.

STANTONVILLE, p. v., Anderson district, S. C., 118 ms. N. w. of Columbia; from W. 522 ms.

STANTONVILLE, p. o., McNairy co., Tenn.

STANTONVILLE, p. o., Calumet co., Wis.

STANWICH, p. o., Fairfield co., Ct., 89 ms. s. w. of Hartford; from W. 265 ms.

STANWIX, p. o., Oneida co., N. Y.

STAPLES RANCHO, p. o., Calaveras co., Cal.

STAPLETON, p. v., Southfield township, Richmond co., Staten Island, N. Y. Watered by New York harbor.

STAPLETON, p. o., Amherst co., Va.

STAR, p. o., Assumption parish, La.

STAR, p. o., Walker co., Tex.

STARFIELD, p. o., Peoria co., Ill.

STAR FURNACE, p. o., Carter co., Ky.

STARK COUNTY, situated in the east part of Ohio, and traversed by Tuscarawas river. Area, 650 square miles. Seat of justice, Canton. Pop. in 1810, 2,734; in 1820, 14,506; in 1830, 26,588; in 1840, 34,603; in 1850, 39,878.

STARK COUNTY, situated in the northwesterly part of Indiana, and traversed by Kankakee river. Area, 432 square miles. Seat of justice, ——. Pop. in 1840, 149; in 1850, 557.

STARK COUNTY, situated toward the northwest part of Illinois, and traversed by Spoon river. Area, 288 square miles. Seat of justice, Toulon. Pop. in 1840, 1,573; in 1850, 3,710.

STARK, p. t., Somerset co., Me., 40 ms. N. w. of Augusta; from W. 633 ms. Watered by Sandy and Kennebec rivers. Pop. 1,446.

STARK, p. t., Coos co., N. H., 117 ms. N. of Concord; from W. 578 ms. Pop. 418.

STARK, p. t., Herkimer co., N. Y., 69 ms. N. w. of Albany; from W. —— ms. Watered by Otsquaga creek. Pop. 1,243.

STARKEY, p. t., Yates co., N. Y., 188 ms. w. of Albany; from W. 315 ms. Watered by Seneca lake. Pop. 2,675.

STARKSBOROUGH, p. t., Addison co., Vt., 42 ms. w. of Montpelier; from W. 498 ms. Watered by Huntingdon river and Lewis creek. Pop. 1,400.

STARK, p. t., Stark township, Herkimer co., N. Y., 62 ms. N. w. of Albany; from W. 385 ms.

STARKVILLE, v., Hoosick township, Rensselaer co., N. Y. Watered by Walloomsack creek.

STARKVILLE, c. h., p. v., seat of justice of Lee co., Ga., 133 ms. s. w. of Milledgeville; from W. 778 ms. Watered by a tributary of Flint river.

STARKVILLE, c. h., p. v., seat of justice of Oktibbeha co., Miss., 143 ms. N. E. of Jackson; from W. 912 ms.

STARLINGTON, p. o., Butler co., Ala.; from W. 903 ms.

STARR COUNTY, situated in the western part of Texas, on the Rio Grande del Norte. Area, —— square miles. Seat of justice, ——. Pop. about 2,000.

STARR, p t., Hocking co., O., 59 ms. s. E. of Columbus; from W. 377 ms. Watered by headwaters of Raccoon creek. Pop. 1,045.

STARRSVILLE, p. v., Newton co., Ga., 55 ms. N. W. of Milledgeville ; from W. 654 ms.

STARUCCA, p. v., Wayne co., Pa., 191 ms. N. E. of Harrisburgh ; from W. 285 ms.

STATE BRIDGE, p. o., Lenox township, Madison co., N Y., 119 ms. w. of Albany ; from W. 376 ms.

STATEBURGH, c. h., p. v., seat of justice of Sumter district, S. C.

STATE LINE, p. o., Franklin co., Pa., 61 ms. s. w. of Harrisburgh ; from W. 74 ms.

STATE LINE, p. o., Trumbull co., O., 197 ms. N. E. of Columbus ; from W. 306 ms.

STATE LINE, p. o., McHenry co., Ill.

STATE LINE, p. o., Walworth co., Wis.

STATE RIGHTS, p. o., Oglethorpe co., Ga., 70 ms. N. of Milledgeville ; from W. 589 ms.

STATE ROAD, p. o., Lycoming co., Pa.

STATESBOROUGH, c. h., p. v., seat of justice of Bullock co., Ga., 133 ms. s. E. of Milledgeville ; from W. 671 ms.

STATESVILLE, c. h., p. v., seat of justice of Iredell co., N. C., 145 ms. w. of Raleigh ; from W. 382 ms.

STATESVILLE, p. v., Wilson co., Tenn., 39 ms. E. of Nashville ; from W. 642 ms.

STATION, p. o., Thomas co., Ga.

STAUNTON, c. h., p. v., seat of justice of Augusta co., Va., 116 ms. N. w. of Richmond ; from W. 156 ms. Watered by Lewis creek.

STAUNTON, p. v., Granville co., N. C.

STAUNTON, p. t., Miami co., O. Pop. 1,475.

STAUNTON, p. v., Macoupin co., Ill., 69 ms. s. w. of Springfield ; from W. 789 ms. Watered by head waters of Silver creek.

STAUNTON, p. o., Fayette co., O.

STEADY RUN, p. o., Keokuk co., Iowa.

STEAM FACTORY, p. o., Muscogee co., Ga.

STEAM MILL, p. o., Warren co., Pa.

STEAMPORT, p. o., Henderson co., Ky.

STEEDMAN'S, p. o., Lexington district, S. C.

STEELE CREEK, p. o., Mecklenburgh co., N. C., 170 ms. s. w. of Raleigh ; from W. 409 ms.

STEELE'S, p. o., Anderson district, S. C., 135 ms. N. w. of Columbia ; from W. 538 ms.

STEELE'S, p. o., Rush co., Ind., 48 ms. s. E. of Indianapolis ; from W. 520 ms.

STEELE'S LANDING, p. o., Ottawa co., Mich.

STEELE'S MILLS, p. o., Randolph co., Ill., 159 ms. s. of Springfield ; from W. 851 ms.

STEELE'S TAVERN, p. o., Augusta co., Va., 129 ms. N. w. of Richmond ; from W. 171 ms.

STEELEVILLE, p. v., Chester co., Pa.

STEELSVILLE, c. h., p. v., seat of justice of Crawford co., Mo., 75 ms. s. E. of Jefferson city ; from W. 923 ms. Watered by Maramec river.

STEEN'S CREEK, p. o., Rankin co., Miss.

STEEP BOTTOM, p. o., Beaufort district, S. C.

STEEP'S FALLS, p. o., Cumberland co., Me.

STEER CREEK, p. o., Gilmer co., Va.

STEMBERSVILLE, p. o., Carbon co., Pa.

STEPHENSBURGH, p. o., Hardin co., Ky.

STEPHENS' CHALLENGE, p. o., Bledsoe co., Tenn.

STEPHENSON COUNTY, situated on the north boundary of Illinois, and traversed by Pekatonica river. Area, 500 square miles. Seat of justice, Freeport. Pop. in 1840, 2,800 ; in 1850, 11,666.

STEPHENSON'S DEPOT, p. o., Frederick co., Va.

STEPHENSPORT, p. v., Breckenridge co., Ky., 125 ms. s. w. of Frankfort ; from W. 667 ms.

STEPHENTOWN, p. t., Rensselaer co., N Y., 28 ms. s. E. of Albany ; from W. 376 ms. Watered by Kinderhook river. Pop. 2,622.

STEPHENSVILLE, p. o., Wilkinson co., Ga.

STEPNEY, p. v., Monroe township, Fairfield co., Ct., 58 ms. s. w. of Frankfort ; from W. 286 ms.

STEPNEY DEPOT, p. o., Fairfield co., Ct.

STERLING, t., Lamoille co , Vt., 24 ms. N. w. of Montpelier ; from W. —— ms. Watered by tributaries of Lamoille and Onion rivers. Pop. 233.

STERLING, p. t., Worcester co., Mass., 41 ms. w. of Boston ; from W. 411 ms. Watered by Still river. Pop. 1,805.

STERLING, p. t., Windham co., Ct., 49 ms. E. of Hartford ; from W. 376 ms. Watered by tributaries of Noosup river. Pop. 1,025.

STERLING. p. t., Cayuga co., N. Y., 179 ms. w. of Albany ; from W. 362 ms. Watered by Sodus creek and Lake Ontario. Pop. 2,808.

STERLING, t., Brown co., O. Pop. 981.

STERLING, t., Macomb co., Mich. Pop. 876.

STERLING, p. t., Wayne co., Pa., 146 ms. N. E. of Harrisburgh ; from W. 240 ms. Watered by Waullen paupack creek. and Lehigh river. Pop. 1,033.

STERLING, p. o., Montgomery co., Ga.

STERLING, p. o., Whitesides co., Ill.

STERLING, p. o., Philips co., Ark.

STERLING, p. o., Crawford co., Ind.

STERLING BOTTOM, p. o., Meigs co., O.

STERLING GROVE. p. o., Greenville district, S. C., 104 ms. N. w. of Columbia ; from W. 514 ms.

STERLING HILL, p. o., Windham co., Ct.

STERLINGTON, p. o., Crawford co., Pa.

STERLINGVILLE, p. o., Wyoming co., Pa.

STERLINGVILLE, p. v., Philadelphia township, Jefferson co., N. Y. Watered by a tributury of Indian river.

STERRETANIA, p. o., Erie co., Pa.

STETSON, p. t., Penobscot co., Me., 71 ms. N. E. of Augusta ; from W. 666 ms. Watered by tributaries of Sebasticook and Sowadabscook rivers. Pop. 885.

STEUBEN COUNTY, situated on the south boundary of New York, with Crooked lake in the northeast. Area, 1,400 square miles. Face of the country, hilly and broken ; soil, of middling quality. Seat of justice, Bath. Pop. in 1810, 7,246 ; in 1820, 21,989 ; in 1830, 33,851 ; in 1840, 46.138 ; in 1850, 63,771.

STEUBEN COUNTY, situated at the northeast corner of Indiana. Area, 225 square miles.' Seat of justice, Angola. Pop. in 1840, 2,578 ; in 1850, 6,104.

STEUBEN, p. t., Washington co., Me., 119 ms. E. of Augusta ; from W. 701 ms. Watered by Dyers, Pigeon Hill, and Narraguagus bays, Atlantic ocean, Goldsborough harbor, and Narraguagus river. Pop. 1,122.

STEUBEN, p. t., Oneida co., N. Y., 110 ms. N. w. of Albany ; from W. 407 ms.' Watered by Cincinnati creek, and tributaries of Mohawk river. Pop. 1,744.

STEUBEN, p. v., Greenfield township, Huron co., O., 87 ms. N. of Columbus ; from W. 399 ms.

STEUBEN, t., Steuben co., Ind. Pop. 645.

STEUBEN, p. o., Crawford co., Pa.

STEUBEN, p. o., Marshall co., Ill.

STEUBENVILLE, c. h., p. v., seat of justice of Jefferson co., O., 141 ms. N. E. of Columbus ; from W. 264 ms. Watered by Ohio river. Pop. 6,139.

STEUBENVILLE (now called Pleasant Lake), p. v., Steuben co., Ind., 170 ms. N. E. of Indianapolis ; from W. 545 ms.

STEVENSBURGH, p. o., Culpeper co., Va., 91 ms. N. w. of Richmond ; from W. 82 ms.

STEVENS' PLAINS, p. o., Cumberland co., Me., 53 ms. s. w. of Augusta ; from W. 548 ms.

STEVEN'S POINT, p. o., Portage co., Wis.

STEVENSVILLE, p. v., Bradford co., Pa., 159 ms. N. of Harrisburgh ; from W. 269 ms.

STEVENSVILLE, p. v., King and Queen co., Va., 48 ms. N. E. of Richmond ; from W. 136 ms.

STEVENSVILLE, p. o., Sullivan co., N. Y.

STEWART COUNTY, situated on the westerly boundary of Georgia, with Chattahoochee river on the west. Area, 682 square miles. Seat of justice, Lumpkin. Pop. in 1840, 12,933 ; in 1850, 16,027.

STEWART COUNTY. situated on the north boundary of Tennessee, with Tennessee river on the southwest, and traversed by the Cumberland. Seat of justice, Dover. Pop. in 1810, 4,262 ; in 1820, 8,388 ; in 1830, 6,968 ; in 1840, 8,587 ; in 1850,.9,719.

STEWART'S DRAFT, p. o., Augusta co., Va., 115 ms. N. w. of Richmond ; from W. 157 ms.

STEWART'S FERRY, p. o., Davidson co., Tenn., 10 ms. N. of Nashville ; from W. 674 ms.

STEWART'S RUN, p. o., Venango co., Pa.

STEWART'S SPRINGS, p. o., Polk co., Ark.

STEWARTSTOWN, p. t., Coos co., N. H., 108 ms. N. of Concord ; from W. 609 ms. Watered by Connecticut river, and Great and Little Diamond ponds. Pop. 747

STEWARTSTOWN, p. o., York co., Pa., 44 ms. s. of Harrisburgh ; from W. 82 ms.

STEWARTSTOWN, p. v., Richmond co., N. C., 137 ms. s. w. of Raleigh ; from W. 422 ms.

STEWARTSTOWN, p. o., Monongalia co., Va.

STEWARTSVILLE, p. v., Greenwich township, Warren co., N. J., 56 ms. N. w. of Trenton ; from W. 207 ms. Watered by Merritt's branch of Pohatcong creek.

STEWARTSVILLE, p. v., Richmond co., N. C., 107 ms. s. w. of Raleigh ; from W. 403 ms.

STEWARTSVILLE, p. o., Westmoreland co , Pa.

STICE'S SHOAL, p. o., Cleveland co., N. C.

STICKLEYVILLE, p. o., Lee co., Va.

STIKOIH, p. o., Cherokee co., N. C.

STILES, p. o., Davis co., Iowa.

STILESBOROUGH, p. o.. Cass. co., Ga.

STILESVILLE, p. v., Hendricks co., Ind., 28 ms. w. of Indianapolis ; from W. 599 ms.

STILL VALLEY, p. v., Greenwich township, Warren co., N J., 48 ms. N. w. of Trenton ; from W. 204 ms.

STILLWATER, p. t., Saratoga co., N. Y., 20 ms. N. of Albany ; from W. 392 ms. Watered by Anthony's kill and Hudson river. Pop. 2,967.

STILLWATER, p. t., Sussex co., N. J., 77 ms. N. of Trenton ; from W. 234 ms. Watered by Paulin's kill. Pop. 1,742.

STILLWATER, p. o., Tuscarawas co., O., 103 ms. N. E. of Columbus : from W. 302 ms.

STILLWATER, p. o., Columbia co., Pa.

STILLWATER, p. o., Washington co. Minn.

STILLWELL, p. o., Wood co., Va.

STILLWELL, p. o., Hanover township, Butler co., O., 111 ms. s. w. of Columbus ; from W. 501 ms.

STIP'S HILL, p. o., Franklin co., Ind., 64 ms. s. E. of Indianapolis ; from W. 530 ms.

STITTVILLE, p. o., Oneida co., N. Y.

STOCKBRIDGE, p. t., Windsor co., Vt., 42 ms. s. of Montpelier ; from W. 475 ms. Watered by White river and a tributary of the Tweed. Pop. 1,327.

STOCKBRIDGE, p. t., Berkshire co., Mass. 133 ms. w. of Boston ; from W. 363 ms. Watered by Housatonic river. Pop. 1,941.

STOCKBRIDGE, p. t., Madison co., N. Y., 113 ms. w. of Albany ; from W. 366 ms. Watered by Oneida creek. Pop. 2,081.

STOCKBRIDGE, p. t., Ingham co., Mich. Pop. 657.

STOCKBRIDGE, p. v., Calumet co., Wis., 121 ms. N. E. of Madison ; from W. 968 ms. Watered by Lake Winnebago.

STOCKBRIDGE, p. o., Henry co., Ga.

STOCK CREEK, p. o., Scott co., Va., 360 ms. s. w. of Richmond ; from W. 428 ms.

STOCKERTOWN, p. o., Northampton co., Pa.

STOCKHOLM, p. t., St. Lawrence co., N. Y., 223 ms. N. w. of Albany ; from W. 507 ms. Watered by St. Regis river. Pop. 3,661.

STOCKHOLM, p. v., Sussex co., N. J., 95 ms. N. E. of Trenton ; from W. 263 ms. Watered by Pequannock creek.

STOCKHOLM DEPOT, p. o., St Lawrence co., N. Y.

STOCKPORT, p. t., Columbia co., N. Y., 24 ms. s. of Albany ; from W. 346 ms. Watered by Kinderhook creek and Hudson river. Pop. 1,655.

STOCKPORT, p v , Buckingham township, Wayne co., Pa., 191 ms. N. E. of Harrisburgh ; from W. 287 ms. Watered by Delaware river.

STOCKPORT, p. o., Morgan co., O., 82 ms. E. of Columbus ; from W. 326 ms.

STOCKPORT STATION, p. o., Delaware co., N. Y.

STOCKSVILLE, p. o., Buncombe co., N. C.

STOCKTON, p. t., Chautauque co., N. Y., 331 ms. w. of Albany ; from W. 338 ms. Watered by Bear creek. Pop. 164.

STOCKTON, p. o., Baldwin co., Ala. ; from W. 984 ms.

STOCKTON, p. o., Madison co., Flor.

STOCKTON, p. o., San Joaquin co., Cal.

STOCK TOWNSHIP, t., Harrison co., O., 113 ms. N. E. of Columbus ; from W. 296 ms. Pop. 888.

STODDARD COUNTY, situated in the southeast part of Missouri, and interspersed with numerous lakes and their connecting streams. Area, 900 square miles. Seat of justice, Bloomfield. Pop. in 1840, 3,153 ; in 1850, 4,277.

STODDARD, p. t., Cheshire co., N. H., 44 ms. s. w. of Concord ; from W. 448 ms. Watered by tributaries of Connecticut and Merrimack rivers. Pop. 1,105.

STODDARTSVILLE, p. v., Covington township, Monroe co., Pa., 138 ms. N. E. of Harrisburgh ; from W. 235 ms.

STOKES COUNTY, situated on the north boundary of North Carolina, and traversed by Dan and Yadkin rivers. Area, 836 square miles. Face of the country, hilly. Seat of justice, Germantown. Pop. in 1810, 11,645 ; in 1820, 14,033 ; in 1830, 16,196 ; in 1840, 16,265 ; in 1850, 9,206.

STOKES, p. o., Lee township, Oneida co., N. Y., 115 ms. N. w. of Albany ; from W. 399 ms.

STOKES, t., Madison co., O. Pop. 591.

STONE, t., Hamilton co., O.

STONE ARABIA, p. v., Palatine township, Montgomery co., 57 ms. N. w. of Albany ; from W. 400 ms.

STONE CHURCH, p. o., Bergen township, Genesee co., N. Y., 240 ms. w. of Albany ; from W. 375 ms.

STONE CHURCH, p. o., Northampton co., Pa., 121 ms. N. E. of Harrisburgh ; from W. 214 ms.

STONE CREEK, p. o., Tuscarawas co., O.

STONEHAM, p. t., Middlesex co., Mass., 10 ms. N. of Boston ; from W. 450 ms. Watered by Spot pond. Pop. 2,085.

STONE LICK, p. t., Clermont co., O. Pop. 1,840.

STONE LICK, p. o., Randolph co., N. C.

STONE MILLS, p. o., Orleans township, Jefferson co., N. Y., 176 ms. N. w. of Albany ; from W. 426 ms.

STONE MOUNTAIN, p. o., De Kalb co., Ga., 94 ms. N. w. of Milledgeville ; from W. 668 ms.

STONE MOUNTAIN, p. o., McDowell co., N. C

STONER, p. o., Seneca co., O.

STONE RIDGE, p. v., Marbletown township, Ulster co., N. Y., 97 ms. s. w. of Albany ; from W. 315 ms.

STONER'S PRAIRIE, p. o., Dane co., Wis.

STONER'S STORE, p. o., Roanoke co., Va., 157 ms. w. of Richmond ; from W. 236 ms.

STONERSTOWN, p. v., Bedford co., Pa., 100 ms. w. of Harrisburgh ; from W. 126 ms.

STONERSVILLE, p. o., Berks co., Pa.

STONERSVILLE, p. o., Greenville district, S. C., 97 ms. N. w. of Columbia ; from W. 493 ms.

STONE WALL MILL, p. v., Appomattox co., Va., 110 ms. w. of Richmond ; from W. 196 ms. Watered by James river.

STONINGTON, p. t., New London co., Ct., 60 ms. s. E. of Hartford ; from W. 355 ms. Watered by Mystic and Pawcatuck rivers, and Long Island sound. Pop. in 1830, 3,401 ; in 1840, 3,898 ; in 1850, 5,431.

STONINGTON, p. o., Christian co., Ill.

STONY BROOK, p. v., Brookhaven township, Suffolk co., Long Island, N. Y., 197 ms. s. E. of Albany ; from W. 277 ms. Watered by an inlet of Long Island sound.

STONY CREEK, p t., Somerset co., Pa. Watered by Stony creek. Pop. 1,396.

STONY CREEK, p. o., Caswell co., N. C., 79 ms. N. w. of Raleigh ; from W. 281 ms.

STONY CREEK, p. t., Henry co., Ind. Pop. 1,029.

STONY CREEK, p. t., Randolph co., Ind. Pop. 1,153.

STONY CREEK, p. o., Warren co., N. Y.

STONY CREEK, p. o., Scott co., Va.

STONY CREEK WAREHOUSE, p. o., Sussex co., Va., 42 ms. s. E. of Richmond ; from W. 161 ms.

STONY FORK, p. o., Amherst co., Va.

STONY FORK, p. o., Watauga co., N. C.

STONY HILL, p. o., Richmond co., Va., 71 ms, N. E. of Richmond ; from W. 110 ms.

STONY MOUNT, p. o., Brunswick co., Va., 79 ms. s. w. of Richmond ; from W. 191 ms.

STONY POINT, p. o., Albemarle co., Va., 81 ms. N. w. of Richmond ; from W. 111 ms.

STONY POINT, p. o., Alexander co., N. C.

STONY POINT, p. o., Cobb co., Ga.

STONY POINT, p. o., East Baton Rouge parish, La., 100 ms. N. w. of New Orleans ; from W. 1,142 ms.

STONY POINT, p. o., Bradley co., Tenn.

STONY POINT, p. o., White co., Ark.

STONY POINT, p. o., Abbeville district, S. C.

STONY POINT, p. o., Jackson co., Mo.

STONY POINT MILLS, p. o., Cumberland co., Va., 58 ms. w. of Richmond ; from W. 148 ms.

STONY RIDGE, p. o., Wood co., O., 128 ms. N. w. of Columbus ; from W. 445 ms.

STONY RIDGE, p. o., Surry co., N. C.

STONY RUN, p. o., Genesee co., Mich., 49 ms. N. w. of Detroit ; from W. 573 ms.

STOREVILLE, p. v., Anderson district, S. C., 117 ms. N. w. of Columbia ; from W. 544 ms.

STORMVILLE, p. o., Fishkill township, Dutchess co., N. Y., 90 ms. s. of Albany ; from W. 301 ms.

STORRS, p. o., Hamilton co., O.

STORY, p. o., Ogle co., Ill.

STOUCHBURGH, p. o., Berks co., Pa., 34 ms. E. of Harrisburgh ; from W. 147 ms.

STOUGHSTOWN, p. v., Cumberland co., Pa., 29 ms. s. w. of Harrisburgh ; from W. 108 ms.

STOUGHTON, p. t., Norfolk co., Mass., 20 ms. s. of Boston ; from W. 428 ms. Watered by head waters of Neponset river. Pop. 3,494.

STOUGHTON, p. o., Dane co., Wis.

STOUTS, p. o., Northampton co., Pa., 102 ms. N. E. of Harrisburgh ; from W. 191 ms.

STOUTS, p. o., Adams co., O., 118 ms. s. of Columbus from W. 456 ms.

STOUTS' GROVE, p. o., McLean co., Ill.

STOVER, p. o., Dallas co., Ark.

STOVER'S PLACE, p. o., Centre co,, Pa.

STOVERTOWN, p. o., Muskingum co., O.

STOW, p. t., Oxford co., Me., 74 ms. w. of Augusta; from W. 581 ms. Watered by head waters of Saco river. Pop. 471.

STOW, p. t., Lamoille co., Vt., 22 ms. N. w. of Montpelier; from W. 535 ms. Watered by Waterbury river and tributaries. Pop. 1,771.

STOW, p. t., Middlesex co., Mass., 25 ms. w. of Boston; from W. 427 ms. Watered by Assabet river. Pop. 1,455.

STOW, p. t., Summit co., O., 131 ms. N. E. of Columbus; from W. 329 ms. Watered by Cuyahoga river. Pop. 1,701.

STOW CREEK, t., Cumberland co., N. J. Watered by Newport creek. Pop. 1,095.

STOWELL'S CORNERS, p. o., Jefferson co., N. Y.

STOWESVILLE, p. v., Gaston co., N. C., 180 ms. w. of Raleigh; from W. 419 ms.

STOW'S FERRY, p. o., Tallapoosa co., Ala.

STOW'S SQUARE, p. o., Lewis co., N. Y., 140 ms. N. w. of Albany; from W. 439 ms.

STOYSTOWN, p. b., Quemahoning township, Somerset co., Pa., 131 ms. w. of Harrisburgh; from W. 157 ms. Watered by Stony creek. Pop. 321.

STRABANE, p. t., Adams co., Pa. Watered by Conewaga creek and tributaries.

STRABANE, p. t., Washington co., Pa. Watered by Chartiers and Little Chartiers creeks.

STRABANE, p. v., Lenoir co., N. C., 78 ms. s. E. of Raleigh; from W. 308 ms.

STRAFFORD COUNTY, situated on the east boundary of New Hampshire. with Salmon Falls river on the northeast. Area, 500 square miles. Face of the country, hilly or undulating; soil, good. Seat of justice, Dover. Pop. in 1810, 41,594; in 1820, 51,117; in 1830, 58.910; in 1840, 61,127; in 1850, 29,314.

STRAFFORD, p. t., Strafford co., N. H., 25 ms. N. E. of Concord; from W. 506 ms. Watered by tributaries of Isinglass and Suncook rivers. Pop. 1,920.

STRAFFORD, p. o., Orange co., Vt., 34 ms. s. E. of Montpelier; from W. 502 ms. Watered by a tributary of Ompompanoosuc river. Pop. 1,540.

STRAFFORD CORNER, p. o., Strafford co., N. H.

STRAIGHT FORK, p. o., Campbell co., Tenn.

STRAIGHT NECK, p. o., Cherokee co., Ala.

STRAIT'S LAKE, p. o., Oakland co., Mich., 33 ms. N. w. of Detroit; from W. 557 ms.

STRAITSVILLE, p. o., New Haven co., Ct., 50 ms. s. of Hartford; from W. 314 ms.

STRAITSVILLE, p. o., Perry co., O.

STRASBURGH, p. o., Lancaster co., Pa., 46 ms. s. E. of Harrisburgh; from W. 120 ms. Watered by Pecquea and Little Beaver creeks.

STRASBURGH, p. v., Shenandoah co., Va., 153 ms. N. w. of Richmond; from W. 92 ms. Watered by north branch of Shenandoah river.

STRASBUSGH, p. v., Wayne township, Tuscarawas co., O., 115 ms. N. E. of Columbus; from W. 321 ms.

STRATA, p. o., Montgomery co., Ala.

STRATFORD, p. t., Fulton co., N. Y., 60 ms. N. w. of Albany; from W. 430 ms. Watered by East Canada creek. Pop. 801.

STRATFORD, p. t., Coos co., N. H., 116 ms. N. of Concord; from W. 577 ms. Watered by Connecticut river and tributaries. Pop. 352.

STRATFORD, p. t., Fairfield co., Ct., 50 ms. s. w. of Hartford; from W. 287 ms. Watered by Housatonic river. Pop. 2,040.

STRATFORD, p. o., Delaware co., O.

STRATHAM, p. t., Rockingham co., N. H. 41 ms. s. E. of Concord; from W. 484 ms. Watered by Exeter river. Pop. 840.

STRATTON, p. t., Windham co., Vt., 109 ms. s. of Montpelier; from W. 436 ms. Watered by sources of Deerfield and Windhall rivers. Pop. 286.

STRATTON'S FALL, p. o., Delaware co., N. Y., 68 ms. s. w. of Albany; from W. 349 ms.

STRATTONVILLE, p. v., Clarion co., Pa., 180 ms. N. w. of Harrisburgh; from W. 269 ms.

STRAUSTOWN, p. o., Berks co., Pa.

STRAWBERRY, t., Lawrence co., Ark. Pop. 701.

STRAWBERRY HILL, p. o., Muscatine co., Iowa.

STRAWBERRY PLAINS, p. o., Jefferson co., Tenn., 199 ms. E. of Nashville; from W. 483 ms.

STRAWBERRY POINT, p. o., Clayton co., Iowa.

STRAWBRIDGE, p. o., York co., Pa., 49 ms. s. E. of Harrisburgh; from W. 87 ms.

STRAWNTOWN, p. v., Haycock township, Bucks co., Pa., 108 ms. E. of Harrisburgh; from W. 177 ms.

STRAWTOWN, p. v., Hamilton co., Ind., 27 ms. N. of Indianapolis; from W. 565 ms. Watered by White river.

STREETSBOROUGH, p. t., Portage co., O., 139 ms. N. E. of Columbus; from W. 330 ms. Watered by Cuyahoga river and Tinker's creek. Pop. 1,108.

STREET'S RUN, p. t., Alleghany co., Pa., 204 ms. w. of Harrisburgh; from W. 203 ms.

STRICKERSVILLE, p. v., Chester co., Pa., 78 ms. E. of Harrisburgh; from W. 230 ms.

STRICKLAND'S, p. o., Ware co., Ga.

STRICKLAND'S DEPOT, p. o., Duplin co., N. C.

STRINESTOWN, p. o., York co., Pa.

STRING PRAIRIE, p. o., Lee co., Iowa.

STRING PRAIRIE, p. o., Burleson co., Tex.

STRINGTOWN, p. o., Ripley co., Ind.

STRINGTOWN, p. o., Richland co., Ill.

STRINGTOWN, p. o., Cole co., Mo.

STRODE, p. o., Culpeper co., Va.

STRODE'S MILLS, p. o., Mifflin co., Pa., 63 ms. N. w. of Harrisburgh; from W. 154 ms.

STRONG, p. t., Franklin co., Me., 43 ms. N. w. of Augusta; from W. 632 ms. Watered by Sandy river. Pop. 1,008.

STRONGSTOWN, p. v., Wheatley township, Indiana co., Pa., 141 ms. N. w. of Harrisburgh; from W. 194 ms.

STRONGSVILLE, p. v., Cuyahoga co., O., 131 ms. N. E. of Columbus; from W. 361 ms. Watered by east branch of Rocky river. Pop, 1,199.

STROUD, p. t., Monroe co., Pa. Watered by Smithfield and Cherry creeks. Pop. 1,419.

STROUDSBURGH, c. h., p. b., Stroud township, seat of justice of Monroe co., Pa., 124 ms. N. E. of Harrisburgh; from W. 217 ms. Watered by Smithfield creek. Pop. 811.

STRYKERSVILLE, p. v., Sheldon township. Wyoming co., N. Y., 270 ms. w. of Albany; from W. 358 ms. Watered by Buffalo creek.

STUMP BRIDGE, p. o., Madison co., Mo.

STUMP SOUND, p. o., Onslow co., N. C.

STURBRIDGE, p. t., Worcester co., Mass., 61 ms. s. w. of Boston; from W. 379 ms. Watered by Quinnebaug river. Pop. 2,119.

STURGEONVILLE, p. v., Brunswick co., Va., 83 ms. s. w. of Richmond; from W. 199 ms.

STURGIS, p. o., St. Joseph co., Mich.

STUYVESANT, p. t., Columbia co., N. Y., 17 ms. s. of Albany; from W. 350 ms. Watered by Hudson river. Pop. 1.766.

STUYVESANT FALLS, p. v., Stuyvesant township, Columbia co., N. Y., 17 ms. s. of Albany; from W. 350 ms. Watered by Kinderhook creek.

SUBLETT'S TAVERN, p. o., Powhatan co., Va., 22 ms. w. of Richmond; from W. 139 ms.

SUBLIGNA, p. o., Chattooga co., Ga.

SUCCESS, p. o., Riverhead township, Suffolk co., Long Island, N. Y.

SUCCESS, t., Coos co., N. H., 143 ms. N. of Concord; from W. 604 ms.

SUCKASUNNY, p. v., Morris co., N. J., 59 ms. N. of Trenton; from W. 229 ms.

SUDBURY, p. t., Rutland co., Vt., 75 ms. s. w. of Montpelier; from W. 465 ms. Watered by Otter creek. Pop. 794.

SUDBURY, p. t., Middlesex co., Mass., 20 ms. w. of Boston; from W. 421 ms. Watered by Sudbury river Pop. 1,578.

SUDLERSVILLE, p. v., Queen Anne co., Md., 55 ms. E. of Annapolis; from W. 95 ms.

SUFFERN, p. o., Rockland co., N. Y.

SUFFIELD, p. t., Hartford co., Ct., 17 ms. N. of Hartford; from W. 352 ms. Watered by Connecticut river. Pop. 2,962.

SUFFIELD, p. t., Portage co., O., 134 ms. N. E. of Columbus; from W. 320 ms. Pop. 1,281.

SUFFOLK COUNTY, situated in the east part of Massachusetts, at the head of Massachusetts bay, comprising Boston, Chelsea, and the adjacent islands. Area, 116 square miles. Seat of justice, Boston. Pop. in 1810, 34,381; in 1820, 43,940; in 1830, 62,163; in 1840, 95,773; in 1850, 144.507.

SUFFOLK COUNTY, situated in the southeast part of New York, occupying the eastern part of Long Island, with the Atlantic ocean on the south, and Long Island sound on the north. Area, 640 square miles. Face of the country, undulating on the north, level in the south;

soil, sterile. Seat of justice, Riverhead. Pop. in 1810, 21,113; in 1820, 24,272; in 1830, 26,780; in 1840, 32,469; in 1850, 36,922.

SUFFOLK, c. h., p. v., Riverhead township, Suffolk co., Long Island, N. Y., 226 ms. s. e. of Albany; from W. 306 ms.

SUFFOLK, c. h., p. v., seat of justice of Nansemond co., Va., 285 ms. s. e. of Richmond; from W. 218 ms. Watered by Nansemond river.

SUGAR CREEK, p. t., Armstrong co., Pa. Pop. 1,688.

SUGAR CREEK, p. o., Crawford co., Pa., 222 ms. N. w. of Harrisburgh; from W. 296 ms.

SUGAR CREEK, t., Venango co., Pa. Watered by Sugar creek. Pop. 875.

SUGAR CREEK, p. o., Hancock co., Ind., 15 ms. e. of Indianapolis; from W. 563 ms.

SUGAR CREEK, p. o., Lawrence co., Tenn., 91 ms. s. w. of Nashville; from W. 751 ms.

SUGAR CREEK, p. o., Telfair co., Ga.

SUGAR CREEK, p. t., Greene co., O. Pop. 3,082.

SUGAR CREEK, t., Putnam co., O. Pop. 550.

SUGAR CREEK, t., Stark co., O. Pop. 1,743.

SUGAR CREEK, t., Wayne co., O. Pop. 2,321.

SUGAR CREEK, t., Tuscarawas co., O. Pop. 1,400.

SUGAR CREEK, t., Montgomery co., Ind. Pop. 777.

SUGAR CREEK, p. t., Shelby co., Ind. Pop. 743.

SUGAR CREEK, p. t., Barry co., Mo.

SUGAR CREEK, t., Newton co., Mo.

SUGAR CREEK, t., Benton co., Ark. Pop. 580.

SUGAR CREEK, p. o., Walworth co., Wis., 65 ms. s. e. of Madison; from W. 814 ms.

SUGAR GROVE, p. t., Sugar Grove township, Warren co., Pa., 239 ms. N. w. of Harrisburgh; from W. 328 ms. Watered by Stillwater creek. Pop. 1,523.

SUGAR GROVE, p. o., Kane co., Ill., 182 ms. N. e. of Springfield; from W. 759 ms.

SUGAR GROVE, p. o., Tippecanoe co., Ind.

SUGAR GROVE, p. o., Fairfield co., O., 37 ms. s. e. of Columbus; from W. 375 ms.

SUGAR GROVE, p. o., Pendleton co., Va.

SUGAR GROVE, p. o., Poweshiek co., Iowa.

SUGAR GROVE, p. o., Butler co., Ky.

SUGAR GROVE, p. o., Ashe co., N. C., 232 ms. N. w. of Raleigh; from W. 398 ms.

SUGAR HILL, p. o., Grafton co., N. H., 78 ms. N. of Concord; from W. 538 ms.

SUGAR HILL, p. o., Orange township, Steuben co., N. Y., 198 ms. w. of Albany; from W. 310 ms.

SUGAR HILL, p. o., Panola co., Tan.

SUGAR HILL, p. o., McDowell co., N. C.

SUGAR HILL, p. o., Marion district, S. C.

SUGAR HILL, p. o., Hall co., Ga.

SUGAR LAKE, p. o., Crawford co., Pa., 243 ms. N. w. of Harrisburgh; from W. 316 ms.

SUGAR LAND, p. o., Matagorda co., Tex.

SUGAR LOAF, p. v., Goshen and Warwick township, Orange co., N. Y., 105 ms. s. w. of Albany; from W. 374 ms.

SUGAR LOAF, p. t., Columbia co., Pa., 112 ms. N. e. of Harrisburgh; from W. 221 ms. Watered by Fishing creek and tributaries. Pop 1,316.

SUGAR LOAF, t., Luzerne co., Pa. Watered by Necopoke and Black creeks. Pop. 1,023.

SUGAR LOAF, t., Carroll co., Ark.

SUGAR LOAF, t., Crawford co., Ark. Pop. 911.

SUGAR LOAF, t., Sebastian co., Ark.

SUGAR LOAF, t., Van Buren co., Ark.

SUGAR RUN, p. o., Bradford co., Pa.

SUGAR RUN, p. o., Wetzel co., Va.

SUGARTOWN, p. v., Chester co., Pa., 79 ms. s. e. of Harrisburgh; from W. 124 ms.

SUGAR TREE, p. o., Pittsylvania co., Va., 183 ms. s. w. of Richmond; from W. 266 ms.

SUGAR TREE BOTTOM, t., Carroll co., Mo.

SUGAR TREE RIDGE, p. o., Highland co., O., 86 ms. s. w. of Columbus; from W. 453 ms.

SUGAR VALLEY, p. o., Clinton co., Pa.

SUGAR VALLEY, p. o., Preble co., O., 100 ms. w. of Columbus; from W. 493 ms.

SUGAR VALLEY, p. o., Murray co., Ga.

SUGGSVILLE, p. v., Clarke co., Ala.; from W. 944 ms. Watered by Basset's creek.

SULLIVAN COUNTY, situated on the west boundary of New Hampshire, on the east bank of Connecticut river. Area, 530 square miles. Face of the country, hilly and mountainous; soil, fertile along the streams. Seat of justice, Newport. Pop. in 1830, 19,669; in 1840, 20,340; in 1850, 19,375.

SULLIVAN COUNTY, situated on the southwesterly boundary of New York, with Delaware river on the southwest. Area, 919 square miles. Face of the country, broken and mountainous; soil, of middling quality. Seat of justice, Monticello. Pop. in 1810, 6,108; in 1820, 8,900; in 1830, 12,364; in 1840, 15,629; in 1850, 25,088.

SULLIVAN COUNTY, situated on the north boundary of Tennessee, and traversed by Holston river. Area, 520 square miles. Face of the country, hilly and mountainous; soil, on the streams, fertile. Seat of justice, Blountsville. Pop. in 1810, 6,847; in 1820, 7,015; in 1830, 10,073; in 1840, 10,736; in 1850,11,742.

SULLIVAN COUNTY, situated on the west boundary of Indiana, with Wabash river on the west. Area, 430 square miles. Seat of justice, Sullivan c. h. Pop. in 1830, 4,690; in 1840, 8,315; in 1850, 10,143.

SULLIVAN COUNTY, situated in the northeasterly part of Pennsylvania. Area, —— square miles. Seat of justice, Laporte. Pop. in 1850, 3,694.

SULLIVAN COUNTY, situated in the north part of Missouri. Area, —— square miles. Seat of justice, Milan. Pop. in 1850, 2,983.

SULLIVAN, p. t., Hancock co., Me., 101 ms. e. of Augusta, from W. 683 ms. Watered by Frenchman's and Taunton bays. Pop. 810.

SULLIVAN, p. t., Cheshire co., N. H., 52 ms. s. w. of Concord; from W. 440 ms. Watered by a tributary of Ashuelot river. Pop. 468.

SULLIVAN, p. t., Madison co., N. Y., 122 ms. w. of Albany; from W. 345 ms. Watered by Oneida lake, and Canaseraga and Chittenango creeks. Pop. 4,764.

SULLIVAN, p. t., Tioga co., Pa., 146 ms. N. of Harrisburgh; from W. 256 ms. Watered by head-waters of Tioga river. Pop. 1,757.

SULLIVAN, p. t., Ashland co., O., 91 ms. N. e. of Columbus; from W. 386 ms. Watered by tributaries of Black river. Pop. 1,099.

SULLIVAN, p. o., Moultrie co., Ill.

SULLIVAN, c. h., p. v., seat of justice of Sullivan co., Ind.

SULLIVAN, p. o., Jackson co., Iowa.

SULLIVAN, p. o., Jefferson co., Wis.

SULLIVANSVILLE, p. o., Chemung co., N. Y.

SULLY, p. t., Marion co., O.

SULPHUR BLUFF, p. o., Hopkins co., Tex.

SULPHUR HILL, p. o., Shelby co., Ind., 67 ms. s. e. of Indianapolis; from W. 570 ms.

SULPHUR LICK, p. o., Lincoln co., Mo.

SULPHUR LICK, p. o., Monroe co., Ky.

SULPHUR ROCK, p. o., Independence co., Ark.

SULPHUR SPRING, p. o., Crawford co., O.

SULPHUR SPRING, t., Hot Springs co., Ark.

SULPHUR SPRINGS, p. o., Buncombe co., N. C., 260 ms. w. of Raleigh; from W. 490 ms.

SULPHUR SPRINGS, p. o., Rhea co., Tenn., 144 ms. s. e. of Nashville; from W. 563 ms.

SULPHUR SPRINGS, p. o., Jefferson co., Mo., 151 ms. e. of Jefferson city; from W. 831 ms.

SULPHUR SPRINGS, p. o., Williamson co., Ill.

SULPHUR SPRINGS, p. o., Madison co., Miss.

SULPHUR SPRINGS, p. o., Henry co., Ind.

SULPHUR SPRINGS, p. o., Cherokee co., Tex.

SULPHUR SPRINGS, p. o., St. Clair co., Ala.

SULPHUR WELL, p. o., Shelby co., Tenn.

SUMMERFIELD, p. v., Guilford co., N. C., 99 ms. N. w. of Raleigh; from W. 294 ms.

SUMMERFIELD, p. t., Seneca township, Monroe co., O., 112 ms. e. of Columbus; from W. 325 ms.

SUMMERFIELD, p. t., Monroe co., Mich., 60 ms. s. w. of Detroit; from W. 500 ms. Watered by Raisin river.

SUMMERFIELD, p. o., Dallas co., Ala.

SUMMERFORD, p. o., Madison co., O.

SUMMER GROVE, p. o., Smith co., Tex.

SUMMER HILL, p. t., Cayuga co., N. Y., 149 ms. w. of Albany; from W. 325 ms. Watered by head waters of Fall creek. Pop. 1,251.

SUMMER HILL, p. o., Crawford co., Pa.

SUMMER HILL, p. t., Cambria co., Pa., 150 ms. w. of Harrisburgh; from W. 187 ms. Pop. 1,497.

SUMMER HILL, p. o., Stoddard co., Mo.

SUMMERSET, p. o., Polk co., Iowa.

SUMMERSVILLE, p. o., Clarke co., Ky., 95 ms. s. w. of Frankfort; from W. 629 ms.

SUMMERVILLE, p. o., Jefferson co., Pa., 171 ms. N. w. of Harrisburgh; from W. 260 ms.

SUMMERVILLE, p. v., Charleston district, S. C.

SUMMERVILLE, p. v., p. v., seat of justice of Chattooga co., Ga., 181 ms. N. w. of Milledgeville; from W. 652 ms. Watered by Chattooga river.

SUMMERVILLE, p. o., Cumberland co., N. C.
SUMMERVILLE, p. o., Cass co., Mich., 177 ms. w. of Detroit; from W. 629 ms. Watered by Dowagiake river.
SUMMERVILLE, p. o., Rock co., Wis.
SUMMERVILLE, p. o., Boone co., Mo.
SUMMIT COUNTY, situated in the northeast part of Ohio, and traversed by Cuyahoga river. Area, 422 square miles. Seat of justice, Akron. Pop. in 1840, 22,650; in 1850, 27,485.
SUMMIT, p. o., Oakland co., Mich., 34 ms. N. w. of Detroit; from W. 540 ms.
SUMMIT, p. t., Schoharie co., N. Y., 52 ms. w. of Albany; from W. 378 ms. Watered by Charlotte river and tributaries of Schoharie creek. Pop. 1,800.
SUMMIT, p. v., Washington township, Cambria co., Pa., 129 ms. w. of Harrisburgh; from W. 172 ms. Watered by a tributary of Kiskiminetas river. Pop. 406.
SUMMIT. p. o., Northampton co., N. C.
SUMMIT, p. o., Summit co., O.
SUMMIT, p. t., Waukesha co., Wis., 50 ms. E. of Madison; from W. 835 ms.
SUMMIT, p. o., Blount co., Ala.
SUMMIT, p. o., Whitley co., Ind.
SUMMIT, p. o., Essex co., N. J.
SUMMIT BRIDGE, p. v., New Castle co., Del., 41 ms. N. of Dover; from W. 117 ms.
SUMMIT HILL, p. v., Carbon co., Pa., 84 ms. N. E. of Harrisburgh; from W. 194 ms.
SUMMIT MILLS, p. o., Somerset co., Pa.
SUMMIT POINT, p. o., Jefferson co., Va., 161 ms. N. of Richmond; from W. 71 ms.
SUMMITVILLE, p. o., Lee co., Iowa.
SUMMITVILLE, p. o., Madison co., Ind.
SUMMUM, p. o., Fulton co., Ill.
SUMNER COUNTY, situated on the north boundary of Tennessee, with Cumberland river on the south. Area, 625 square miles. Seat of justice, Gallatin. Pop. in 1810, 13,792; in 1820, 19,211; in 1830, 20,569; in 1840, 22,445; in 1850, 22,717.
SUMNER, p. t., Oxford co., Me., 40 ms. w. of Augusta; from W. 606 ms. Watered by tributaries of Androscoggin river. Pop. 1,151.
SUMNEYTOWN, p. v., Montgomery co., Pa., 182 ms. E. of Harrisburgh; from W. 173 ms.
SUMPTIONS PRAIRIE, p. o., St. Joseph's co., Ind.
SUMTER DISTRICT, situated in the central part of South Carolina, with Wateree and Santee rivers on the southwest. Area, 1,240 square miles. Face of the country, level; soil, sandy. Seat of justice, Statesburgh. Pop. in 1810, 19,054; in 1820, 25,369; in 1830, 28,277; in 1840, 27,892; in 1850, 33,220.
SUMTER COUNTY, situated in the southwesterly part of Georgia, with Flint river on the east. Area, 675 square miles. Seat of justice, Americus. Pop. in 1840, 5,759; in 1850, 10,322.
SUMTER COUNTY, situated on the west boundary of Alabama, with Tombigbee and Little Tombigbee rivers on the east and northeast. Area, 1,200 square miles. Seat of justice, Livingston. Pop. in 1840, 29,937; in 1850, 22,250.
SUMTER, t., Wayne co., Mich. Pop. 434.
SUMTER, p. o., Trinity co., Tex.
SUMTERVILLE, p. v., Sumter district, S. C., 63 ms. E. of Columbia; from W. 499 ms.
SUMTERVILLE, p. v., Lee co., Ga.
SUMTERVILLE, p. o., Sumter co., Ala.; from W. 882 ms. Watered by Tombigbee river.
SUN, p. o., St. Tammany parish, La.
SUNBURY, p. b., Augusta township, seat of justice of Northumberland co., Pa., 58 ms. N. of Harrisburgh; from W. 168 ms. Watered by Susquehanna river, and the Pennsylvania canal. Pop. 1,218.
SUNBURY, p. v., Gates co., N. C., 224 ms. N. E. of Raleigh; from W. 243 ms.
SUNBURY, p. v., Berkshire township, Delaware co., O., 25 ms. N. of Columbus; from W. 395 ms.
SUNBURY, p. t., Monroe co., O. Pop. 1,257.
SUNBURY, p. v., Livingston co., Ill., 121 ms. N. E. of Springfield; from W. 748 ms.
SUNBURY, v., Liberty co., Ga., 212 ms. s. E. of Milledgeville; from W. 702 ms. Watered by Medway river, and St. Catherine's sound.
SUNCOOK, p. v., Merrimack co., N. H., 7 ms. s. of Concord; from W. 478 ms.
SUNDAY CREEK CROSS ROADS, p. o., Perry co., O., 62 ms. E. of Columbus; from W. 361 ms.
SUNDERLAND, p. t., Bennington co., Vt., 98 ms. s. w.

of Montpelier; from W. 425 ms. Watered by Batten kill and Roaring brook. Pop. 479.
SUNDERLAND, p. t., Franklin co., Mass., 80 ms. w. of Boston; from W. 392 ms. Watered by Connecticut river. Pop. 792.
SUNFISH, p. o., Clarington village, Salem township, Monroe co., O., 131 ms. E. of Columbus; from W. 281 ms.
SUNFISH, t., Pike co., O. Pop. 371.
SUN FLOWER COUNTY, situated in the west part of Mississippi, with Yazoo river on the east, and traversed by Sun Flower river. Area, —— square miles. Seat of justice, ——. Pop. in 1850, 1,102.
SUNKHAZE, p. o., Penobscot co., Me., 85 ms. E. of Augusta; from W. 680 ms.
SUNNY SIDE, p. o., Lowndes co., Ala.
SUN PRAIRIE, p. o., Dane co., Wis.
SUNRISE, p. o., Bath co., Va.
SUNVILLE, p. o., Venango co., Pa.
SUPERIOR, t., Williams co., O. Pop. 723.
SUPERIOR, p. t., Washtenaw co., Mich., 31 ms. w. of Detroit; from W. 523 ms. Pop. 1,127.
SURGEON'S HALL. p. o., Alleghany co., Pa., 201 ms. w. of Harrisburgh; from W. 228 ms.
SURRENCY'S, p. o., Tatnall co., Ga., 162 ms. s. E. of Milledgeville; from W. 773 ms.
SURROUNDED HILLS, p. t., Monroe co., Ark.
SURRY COUNTY, situated in the southeast part of Virginia, with James river on the northeast. Area, 324 square miles. Seat of justice, Surry c. h. Pop. in 1810, 6,855; in 1820, 6,594; in 1830, 7,109; in 1840, 6,840; in 1850, 5,679.
SURRY COUNTY, situated on the north boundary of North Carolina, and traversed by Yadkin river. Area, 726 square miles. Face of the country, hilly and mountainous. Seat of justice, Rockford. Pop. in 1810, 10,366; in 1820, 12,320; in 1830, 14,504; in 1840, 15,079; in 1850, 18,443.
SURRY, p. t., Hancock co., Me., 83 ms. E. of Augusta; from W. 677 ms. Watered by Union river and Union bay. Pop. 1,189.
SURRY, p. t., Cheshire co., N. H., 55 ms. s. w. of Concord; from W. 441 ms. Watered by Ashuelot river. Pop. 556.
SURRY, c. h., p. v., seat of justice of Surry co., Va., 55 ms. s. E. of Richmond; from W. 178 ms.
SUSPENSION BRIDGE, p. o., Niagara co., N. Y.
SUSQUEHANNA COUNTY, situated on the north boundary of Pennsylvania, and traversed in the northeast by Susquehanna river. Area, 825 square miles. Face of the country, broken; soil, of middling quality. Seat of justice, Montrose. Pop. in 1820, 9,960; in 1830, 16,787; in 1840, 21,195; in 1850, 28,688.
SUSQUEHANNA, p. o., Colesville township, Broome co., N. Y., 122 ms. s. w. of Albany; from W. 304 ms.
SUSQUEHANNA, p. t., Dauphin co., Pa. Watered by Paxton creek. Pop. 1,535.
SUSQUEHANNA, t., Lycoming co., Pa. Pop. 406.
SUSQUEHANNA, Cambria co., Pa. Pop. 640.
SUSQUEHANNA DEPOT, p. o., Susquehanna co., Pa.
SUSSEX COUNTY, situated in the north part of New Jersey, with Delaware river on the northwest. Area, 415 square miles. Face of the country, diversified with hills, mountains, and marshy plains; soil, varied. Seat of justice, Newton. Pop. in 1810, 25,549; in 1820, 32,752; in 1830, 20,346; in 1840, 21,770; in 1850, 22,988.
SUSSEX COUNTY, situated in the south part of Delaware, with the Atlantic ocean and Delaware bay on the east. Area, 860 square miles. Face of the country, level and marshy; soil, sandy. Seat of justice, Georgetown. Pop. in 1810, 27,750; in 1820, 24,057; in 1830, 27,115; in 1840, 25,093; in 1850, 25,935.
SUSSEX COUNTY, situated in the southeast part of Virginia, and traversed by Nottoway river. Area, 465 square miles. Seat of justice, Sussex c. h. Pop. in 1810, 11,362; in 1820, 11,854; in 1830, 12,720; in 1840, 11,229; in 1850, 9,820.
SUSSEX, c. h., p. v., seat of justice of Sussex co., Va., 48 ms. s. E. of Richmond; from W. 167 ms.
SUSSEX, p. o., Waukesha co., Wis.
SUTTON, p. t., Merrimack co., N. H., 26 ms. N. w. of Concord; from W. 480 square miles. Watered by tributaries of Warner river. Pop. 1,387.
SUTTER COUNTY, situated in the northern part of California, and traversed by the Sacramento, American, and Feather rivers, and Honcut and Bear creeks. Area, —— square miles. Face of the country, undu-

lating. Soil, fertile. Seat of justice, Oro. Pop. in 1852, 1,207.

SUTTON, p. t., Caledonia co., Vt., 53 ms. N. E. of Montpelier ; from W. 564 ms. Watered by tributaries of Pasumpsic river. Pop. 1,001.

SUTTON, p. t., Worcester co., Mass., 46 ms. w. of Boston ; from W. 400 ms. Watered by Blackstone river. Pop. 1.816.

SUTTON, p. t., Meigs co., O. Pop. 1,596.

SUTTON'S, p. o., Williamsburgh co., S. C.

SUTTON'S MILLS, p. o., Essex co., Mass.

SUTTON'S POINT, p. o., Clay co., Ill.

SUWANEE, p. o., Gwinnett co., Ga., 90 ms. N. w. of Milledgeville ; from W. 654 ms.

SUWANEE SHOALS, p. o., Columbia co., Flor.

SWAINSBOROUGH, c. h., p. v., seat of justice of Emanuel co., Ga., 96 ms. E. of Milledgeville ; from W. 668 ms. Watered by Cannouchee river.

SWAMPSCOT, p. t., Essex co., Mass.

SWAN. p. t., Hocking co., O.

SWAN, p. t., Noble co., Ind. Pop. 568.

SWAN, t., Taney co., Mo.

SWAN CREEK, p. o., Gallia co., O., 27 ms. s. E. of Columbus ; from W. 385 ms.

SWAN CREEK, p. o., Warren co., Ill., 102 ms. N. w. of Springfield ; from W. 868 ms.

SWAN CREEK, t., Lucas co., O.

SWAN CREEK, p. o., Warren co., Ky.

SWAN LAKE, p. o., Arkansas co., Ark.

SWAN POND, p. o., Wilkes co., N. C.

SWANCY'S FERRY, p. o., Abbeville district, S. C.

SWANGSTOWN, p. v., Cleveland co., N. C., 197 ms. w. of Raleigh ; from W. 434 ms.

SWAN LAKE, p. o., Carroll parish, La.

SWANNANO, p. o., Buncombe co., N. C., 244 ms. w. of Raleigh ; from W. 474 ms.

SWAN POINT, p. o., Knox co., Ky.

SWAN QUARTER, c. h., seat of justice of Hyde co., N. C., 203 ms. E. of Raleigh ; from W. 400 ms.

SWAN RIVER, p. o, Benton co., Minn.

SWANSBOROUGH, p. v., Onslow co., N. C., 160 ms. s. E. of Raleigh ; from W. 400 ms. Watered by Whittock river. .

SWANSONVILLE, p. o., Pittsylvania co., Va.

SWANTON, p. t., Franklin co., Vt., 71 ms. N. w. of Montpelier ; from W. 545 ms. Watered by Lake Champlain and Missisque river. Pop. 2,824.

SWANTON, p. v., Lucas co., O., 139 ms. N. w. of Columbus ; from W. 470 ms.

SWANTON CENTRE, p. o., Swahton township, Franklin co., Vt., 67 ms. N, of Montpelier ; from W. 541 ms.

SWANVILLE, p. t., Waldo co., Me., 50 ms. E. ot Augusta ; from W. 644 ms. Pop. 944.

SWANVILLE, p. o., Jefferson co., Ind.

SWANZEY, p. t., Bristol co., Mass., 48 ms. s. of Boston ; from 414 ms. Watered by Mount Hope bay. Pop. 1,554.

SWANZEY, p. t., Cheshire co., N. H., 53 ms. s. w. of Concord ; from W. 429 ms. Watered by Ashuelot river. Pop. 2,106.

SWARTSWOOD, p. o., Sussex co., N. J.

SWARTWOUT, p. o., Liberty co., Tex.

SWARTZ CREEK, p. o., Genesee co., Mich.

SWATARA, p. t., Lebanon co., Pa. Watered by Swatara creek and tributaries. Pop. 1843.

SWEARINGENS, p. o., Austin co., Tex.

SWEDEN, p. t., Oxford co., Me., 59 ms. s. w. of Augusta ; from W. 582 ms. Pop. 696.

SWEDEN, p. b., Potter co., Pa., 171 ms. N. w. of Harrisburgh ; from W. 281 ms. Pop. 254.

SWEDEN, p. t., Monroe co., N. Y., 237 ms. w. of Albany ; from W. 386 ms. Watered by Salmon creek. Pop. 3,623.

SWEEDLIN HILL, p. o., Pendleton co., Va.

SWEEDSBOROUGH. p. v., Woolwich township, Gloucester co., Pa., 47 ms. s. w. of Harrisburgh ; from W. 158 ms. Watered by Raccoon creek.

SWEET AIR, p. o., Baltimore co., Md.

SWEET HOME, p. o., Nodaway co., Mo.

SWEET HOME. t., Clark co., Mo.

SWEETLAND, p. o., Muscatine co., Iowa.

SWEET SPRINGS, p. v., Monroe co., Va., 209 ms. w. of Richnomd ; from W. 256 ms.

SWEET VALLEY, p. o., Luzerne co., Pa.

SWEET WATER, p. o., Marengo co.. Ala.

SWEET WATER, p. o., Gwinnett co., Ga., 90 ms. N. w. of Milledgeville ; from W. 661 ms.

SWEET WATER, p. o., Monroe co., Tenn., 165 ms. s. E. of Nashville ; from W. 538 ms.

SWEET WATER, p. o., Watauga co.. N. C.

SWEET WATER, p. o., Menard co., Ill.

SWEET WATER FACTORY, p. o, Campbell co., Ga.

SWIFT CREEK, p. o., Darlington district, S. C.

SWIFT CREEK BRIDGE, p. o., Craven co., N. C., 137 ms. s. E. of Raleigh ; from W. 331 ms.

SWIFT ISLAND, p. o., Montgomery co., N. C.

SWINEYARDS, p. o., Charles City co., Va.

SWINTON, p. o., Kane co., Ill.

SWITZERLAND COUNTY, situated on the southcasterly boundary of Indiana, with Ohio river on the southeast. Area, 216 square miles. Face of the country, hilly ; soil, productive. Seat of justice, Vevay. Pop. in 1820, 3,934; in 1830, 7028 ; in 1840, 9,920 ; in 1850, 12,890.

SWITZERLAND, t., Monroe co., O. Pop. 1,216.

SYBERTSVILLE, p. o., Luzerne co., Pa.

SYCAMORE, p. t., Wyandott co., O., 75 ms. N. of Columbus ; from W. 423 ms. Pop. 1,109.

SYCAMORE, p. t., Hamilton co., O. Watered by Mill creek and tributaries. Pop. 3,731.

SYCAMORE, p. o., Claiborne co., Tenn., 226 ms. E. of Nashville ; from W. 468 ms.

SYCAMORE, c. h., p. v., seat of justice of De Kalb co., Ill., 208 ms. N. E. of Springfield ; from W. 779 ms.

SYCAMORE ALLEY, p. o., Halifax co., N. C., 85 ms. N. E. of Raleigh ; from W. 231 ms.

SYCAMORE GROVE, p. o., Overton co., Tenn.

SYCAMORE MILLS, p. o., Davidson co., Tenn.

SYDNORSVILLE, p. o., Franklin co., Va., 183 ms. w. of Richmond ; from W. 358 ms.

SYKESVILLE, p. v., Carroll co., Md., 61 ms. N. w. of Annapolis ; from W. 56 ms.

SYLACAUGA, p. o., Talladega co., Ala. ; from W. 780 ms,

SYLAMORE, p. o., Izard co., Ark.

SYLCO, p. o., Polk co., Tenn.

SYLVA, p. o., Washington co., Ark.

SYLVAN. p. o., Washtenaw co., Mich., 59 ms. w. of Detroit ; from W. 547 ms.

SYLVAN, p. o., Franklin co., Pa.

SYLVAN DALE, p, o., Hancock co., Ill.

SYLVAN GROVE, p. o., Jefferson co., Ga., 67 ms. E. of Milledgeville ; from W. 625 ms

SYLVAN GROVE, p. o., Clarke co., Ind.

SYLVANIA, p. o., Bradford co., Pa., 150 ms. N. of Harrisburgh ; from W. 260 ms.

SYLVANIA, p. o., Racine co., Wis.

SYLVANIA, c. h., p. v., seat of justice of Scriven co., Ga.

SYLVANIA, t., Lucas co., O. Pop. 751.

SYLVANIA, p. o., Licking co., O.

SYLVANIA, p. o., Parke co., Ind.

SYLVANUS, p. o., Hilledale co., Mich., 97 ms. s. w. of Detroit ; from W. 545 ms.

SYLVIA, p. o., Hardin co., O.

SYMMES, p. t., Hamilton co., O. Watered by Little Miami river. Pop. 1,115.

SYMMES, t., Lawrence co.. O. Watered by Symmes creek. Pop. 487.

SYMMES' CORNERS, p. o., Butler co., O.

SYMMES' CREEK, p. o., Muskingum co., O.

SYMSONIA, p. o., Graves co., Ky.

SYRACUSE, city, Salina township, seat of justice of Onondaga co.. N. Y., 131 ms. w. of Albany ; from W. 348 ms. Few inland towns have a more advantageous position ; in the midst of a region rich in exhaustless salt springs, it communicates with Lake Ontario by the Oswego canal, and the Oswego and Syracuse railroad, which here join respectively the Erie canal and the great central railroad of New York. The buildings of Syracuse are chiefly of brick ; it also contains an elegant hotel and several churches. A branch canal connects the place with Salina, about a mile distant, and between the two places, are extensive manufactories, yielding a vast quantity of salt, and a large annual revenue to the state. The population in 1830, was 2,565 ; in 1840, 6,502 ; in 1850, 25,251.

SYRACUSE, p. v., Kosciusko co., Ind., 141 ms. N. of Indianapolis ; from W. 596 ms.

SYRACUSE, p. o., Marion co Oregon

T.

TABB's CREEK, p. o., Granville co., N. C.

TABERG, p. v., Annsville township, Oneida co., N. Y., 118 ms. N. w. of Albany ; from W. 402 ms. Watered by Fish creek.

TABERNACLE, p. o., Marion district, S. C.

TABLE GROVE, p. o., Fulton co., Ill., 71 ms. N. w. of Springfield ; from W. 849 ms.

TABO, p. o., Lafayette co., Mo.

TABOR, p. o., Tuscarawas co., O.

TACALUCHE, p. o., Marshall co., Miss.

TACHORAH, p. o., Marquette co., Wis.

TACOAH, p. o., Gilmer co., Ga., 194 ms. N. w. of Milledgeville ; from W. 622 ms.

TACKETT's MILL, p, o., Stafford co., Va.

TAFTON, p. v., Pike co., Pa., 175 ms. N. E. of Harrisburgh ; from W. 269 ms.

TAFTSVILLE, p. v., Windsor co., Vt., 54 ms. s. of Montpelier ; from W. 488 ms.

TAGHKANICK, p. t,, Columbia co., N. Y., 41 ms. s. of Albany ; from W. 347 ms. Watered by Copake creek. Pop. 1,540.

TAHLEQUAH, p. o., Cherokee co., Ark.

TAILS CREEK, p. o., Gilmer co., Ga.

TALAHATAH, p. o., Newton co., Miss.

TALASHA, p o., Newton co., Miss.

TALBOT COUNTY, situated on the east shore of Maryland, on the east side of Chesapeake bay. Area, 250 square miles. Seat of justice, Easton, Pop. in 1810, 14,230 ; in 1820, 14,389 ; in 1830, 12,947 ; in 1840, 12,090 ; in 1850, 13,811.

TALBOT COUNTY, situated in the westerly part of Georgia, with Flint river on the northeast. Area, 400 square miles. Seat of justice, Talbotton. Pop. in 1830, 5,940 ; in 1840, 15,627 ; in 1850, 16,534.

TALBOTTON, c. h., p. v., seat of justice of Talbot co., Ga., 92 ms. s. w. of Milledgeville ; from W. 726 ms.

TALIAFERRO COUNTY, situated in the easterly part of Georgia. Area, 130 square miles. Seat of justice, Crawfordsville. Pop. in 1830, 4,934 ; in 1840, 5,190 ; in 1850, 5,146.

TALIBENELA, p. o., Pontotoc co., Miss.

TALKING ROCK, p. o., Gilmer co., Ga., 176 ms. N. w. of Milledgeville ; from W. 627 ms.

TALLADEGA COUNTY, situated in the easterly part of Alabama, with Coosa river on the west. Area, 1,230 square miles. Seat of justice, Talladega. Pop. in 1840, 12,587 ; in 1850, 18,624.

TALLADEGA, c. h., p. v., seat of justice of Talladega co., Ala. ; from W. 757 ms. Watered by a tributary of Coosa river.

TALLAHASSEE, city, seat of justice of Leon co., and capital of the state of Florida ; from W. 896 ms. Situated in the midst of a fertile and undulating region, upon elevated ground, from which several pure springs issue and unite in a good mill-stream. This city, like the state, is of recent growth. Thirty years ago, its site was a luxuriant but unpeopled wilderness. It is now an increasing town, laid out with streets and public squares, with respectable buildings. It has a statehouse, churches, jail, markethouse, bank, and other conspicuous edifices. Twenty miles south of Tallahassee is St. Marks, on the gulf of Mexico, where ships discharge their cargoes bound for the capital, to which a railroad conveys them. The population varies in winter and in summer. In the former season, many resort to this place from colder regions to enjoy the mild and salubrious climate. In 1826, there about 800 inhabitants ; in 1830, 1,500 ; in 1840, from 1,616 to 2,500 ; in 1850 ——.

TALLAHATCHEE COUNTY, situated in the northwesterly part of Mississippi, and traversed by Yazoo river. Area, 1,188 square miles. Seat of justice, Charleston. Pop. in 1840, 2,985 ; in 1850, 4,643.

TALLALOOSA, p. o., Marshall co., Miss.

TALLAPOOSA COUNTY, situated in the east part of Alabama, and traversed by Tallapoosa river. Area, 910 square miles. Seat of justice, Dadeville. Pop. in 1840, 6,444 ; in 1850, 15,584.

TALLAPOOSA, p. o., Carroll co., Ga., 153 ms. N.'w. of Milledgeville ; from W. 741 ms.

TALLASSEE, p. v., Tallapoosa co., Ala. ; from W. 814 ms. Watered by Tallapoosa river.

TALLEYVILLE, p. o., New Castle co., Del.

TALLMADGE, p. t., Summit co., O., 128 ms. N. E. of Columbus ; from W. 332 ms. Watered by Cuyahoga river, and the Pennsylvania and Ohio canal. Pop. 2,456.

TALLMADGE, p. t., Ottawa co., Mich., 181 ms. N. w. of Detroit ; from W. 662 ms. Pop. 534.

TALLMADGE. t., Oceana co., Mich.

TALLOKAS, p. o., Lowndes co., Ga.

TALLULAH, c. h., p. v., seat of justice of Issaquena co., Miss.

TALLY Ho, p. o., Granville co., N. C., 43 ms. N. of Raleigh ; from W. 266 ms.

TALOFA, p. o., Madison co., Flor.

TAMAQUA, p. b., Schuylkill co., Pa., 79 ms. N. E. of Harrisburgh ; from W. 189 ms. Watered by Tamaqua or Little Schuylkill river.

TAMARAWA. v., St. Clair co., Ill., 114 ms. s. of Springfield ; from W. 823 ms. Watered by Kaskaskia river.

TAMPA, p. v., seat of justice of Hillsborough co., Flor. Watered by Tampa bay.

TAMPICO, p. o., Oktibbeha co., Miss.

TAMPICO, p. o., Darke co., O.

TAMPICO, p. o., Grainger co., Tenn.

TAMPICO, p. o., Jackson co., Ind.

TAMWORTH. p. t., Carroll co., N. H., 55 ms. N. of Concord ; from W. 539 ms. Watered by Bear camp and Conway rivers. Pop. 1,766.

TAMWORTH IRON WORKS, p. o., Carroll co., N. Y.

TANEY COUNTY, situated on the south boundary of Missouri, and traversed by White river and many of its tributaries. Area, 1,426 square miles. Seat of justice, Forsyth. Pop. in 1840, 2,264 ; in 1850, 4,373.

TANEY, p. o., Washington co., Ark.

TANEYTOWN, p. v., Carroll co., Md., 71 ms. N. w. of Annapolis ; from W. 68 ms. Pop. 290.

TANGAPAHA, p. o., St. Helena parish, La.

TANNER's CROSS ROADS, p. o., Jefferson co., Va.

TANNER's FORD, p. o., Walton co., Ga.

TANNER's STORE, p. o., Mecklenburgh co., Va., 89 ms. s. w. of Richmond ; from W. 205 ms.

TANNERSVILLE, p. v., Hunter township, Greene co., N. Y., 50 ms. s. w. of Albany ; from W 352 ms.

TANNERSVILLE, p. v., Monroe co., Pa., 124 ms. N. E. of Harrisburgh ; from W. 218 ms.

TAOS, p. o., Cole co., Miss.

TAOS, p. o., Navarre co., Tex.

TAPLEYVILLE, p. o., Essex co., Mass.

TAPPAHANNOCK, c. h., p. v., seat of justice of Essex co., Va., 50 ms. N. E. of Richmond ; from W. 112 ms. Watered by Rappahannock river.

TAPPAN, p. o., Harrison co., O., 110 ms. N. E. of Columbus ; from W. 299 ms.

TAPPANTOWN, p. v., Orangetown township, Rockland co., N. Y., 134 ms. s. of Albany ; from W. 256 ms.

TARBOROUGH, c. h., p. v., seat of justice of Edgecombe co., N. C., 76 ms. E. of Raleigh ; from W. 262 ms. Watered by Tar river.

TARDYVILLE, p. o., Pontotoc co., Miss.

TARENTUM, p. v., Deer township, Alleghany co., Pa., 204 ms. w. of Harrisburgh ; from W. 235 ms. Watered by Alleghany river and Pennsylvania canal. Pop. 519.

TARIFF, p. o., Butler co., O., 117 ms. s. w. of Columbus ; from W. 505 ms.

TARIFFVILLE. p. v., Simsbury township, Hartford co., Ct, 12 ms. N. of Hartford ; from W. 348 ms. Watered by Farmington river.

TARKIO, p. o., Holt co., Mo.

TARLTON, p. v., Salt Creek township, Pickaway co., O., 46 ms. s. of Columbus ; from W. 391 ms.

TARRANT, p. o., Hopkins co., Tex.

TAR RIVER, p. o., Granville co., N. C.

TARRYTOWN, p. v., Greenburgh township, Westchester co., N. Y., 122 ms. s. of Albany ; from W. 252 ms. Watered by Hudson river.

TARVERSVILLE, p. v., Twiggs co., Ga., 50 ms. s. w of Milledgeville ; from W. 698 ms.

TASCINTO, p. o., Neshoba co., Miss.

TASSINONG GROVE, Porter co., Ind., 126 ms. N. w. of Indianapolis ; from W. 685 ms.

TATE, p. t., Clermont co., O. Pop. 2,901.

TATESVILLE, p. o., De Soto co., Miss.

TATESVILLE, p. o., McNairy co., Tenn.

TAUNTON, c. h., p. t., seat of justice, together with New Bedford, of Bristol co., Mass., 32 ms. s. of Boston; from W. 420 ms. Watered by Taunton river. Pop. in 1830, 6,042; in 1840, 7,645; in 1850, 10,441.

TAWAWA, p. o., Shelby co., O.

TAW TAW, p. o., Allen co., Ind.

TAYCHEEDA, p. v., Fond du Lac co., Wis., 92 ms. N. E. of Madison; from W. 949 ms.

TAYLOR COUNTY, situated in the northerly part of Virginia, and traversed by east fork of Monongahela river. Area, —— square miles. Face of the country, rugged and hilly; soil, generally barren. Seat of justice, Pruntytown. Pop. in 1850, 5,367.

TAYLOR COUNTY, situated in the central part of Kentucky. Area, —— square miles. Seat of justice, Campbellsville. Pop. in 1850, 7,250.

TAYLOR, p. o., Cortland co., N. Y.

TAYLOR, p. o., St. Charles parish, La.

TAYLOR, p. o., Harford co., Md.

TAYLOR, p. o., Ogle co., Ill.

TAYLOR, p. o., Davis co., Iowa.

TAYLOR, p. o., Posey co., Ind.

TAYLOR'S, p. o., Sumter district, S. C.

TAYLOR'S, p. o., Jefferson co., Ala.

TAYLOR'S BRIDGE, p. o., Sampson co., N. C., 106 ms. s. E. of Raleigh; from W. 336 ms.

TAYLORSBURGH, p. o., Bartholomew co., Ind.

TAYLOR'S CORNERS, c. h., De Kalb co., Ind.

TAYLOR'S CREEK, t., Hardin co., O. Pop. 531.

TAYLOR'S CREEK, p. o., Liberty co., Ga.

TAYLOR'S FALLS, p. o., Washington co., Minn.

TAYLOR'S ISLAND, p. o., Dorchester co., Ind.

TAYLOR'S STAND, p. o., Crawford co., Pa., 249 ms. N. w. of Harrisburgh; from W. 326 ms.

TAYLOR'S STORE, p. o., Franklin co., Va., 169 ms. w. of Richmond; from W. 244 ms.

TAYLOR'S STORE, p. o., Knox co., Mo.

TAYLORSTOWN, p. v., Washington co., Pa., 216 ms. w. of Harrisburgh; from W. 244 ms.

TAYLORSVILLE, p. v., Upper Makefield township, Bucks co., Pa., 116 ms. E. of Harrisburgh; from W. 166 ms. Watered by Delaware river.

TAYLORSVILLE, p. v., Hanover co., Va., 22 ms. N. of Richmond; from W. 95 ms. Watered by Newfound and South Anna rivers.

TAYLORSVILLE, c. h., p. v., seat of justice of Patrick co., Va. Watered by Mayo river.

TAYLORSVILLE, c. h., p. v., seat of justice of Johnson co., Tenn., 332 ms. E. of Nashville; from W 399 ms. Watered by Roan's creek.

TAYLORSVILLE, c. h., p t., seat of justice of Spencer co., Ky., 39 ms. s w. of Frankfort; from W. 581 ms. Watered by Salt river.

TAYLORSVILLE, p. t., Muskingum co., O.

TAYLORSVILLE, p. o., Montgomery co., O.

TAYLORSVILLE, c. h., p. v., seat of justice of Christian co., Ill., 26 ms. s. E. of Springfield; from W. 754 ms.

TAYLORSVILLE, p. o., Clinton co., Ind.

TAYLORSVILLE, p. o., Anne Arundel co., Md.

TAYLORSVILLE, p. o., Ontario co., N. Y.

TAYLORSVILLE, p. o., Oakland co., Mich.

TAYLORSVILLE, p. o, Smith co., Miss.

TAYLORSVILLE, p. o., Madison co., Ga.

TAYLORTON, p. o., Wayne co., Miss.

TAYLORVILLE, p. o., Alexander co., N. C.

TAYLORVILLE, p. o., Andrew co., Mo.

TAZEWELL COUNTY, situated in the southwest part of Virginia. Area, 1,000 square miles. Face of the country, hilly and mountainous. Seat of justice, Jeffersonville, or Tazewell c. h. Pop. in 1820, 3,916; in 1830, 5,749; in 1840, 6,290; in 1850, 9,942.

TAZEWELL COUNTY, situated in the central part of Illinois, with Illinois river on the northwest. Area, 1,130 square miles. Seat of justice, Tremont. Pop. in 1830, 4,716; in 1840, 7,221; in 1850, 12,052.

TAZEWELL, c. h., p. v., seat of justice of Marion co., Ga., 110 ms. s. w. of Milledgeville; from W. 764 ms. Watered by South Whitewater creek.

TAZEWELL, c. h., p. v., seat of justice of Claiborne co., Tenn., 221 ms. E. of Nashville; from W. 473 ms. Watered by Russell's creek.

TAZEWELL, c. h., p. v., seat of justice of Tazewell co., Va., 284 ms. w. of Richmond; from W. 339 ms. Watered by north fork of Clinch river.

TCHULA, p. v., Holmes co., Miss., 77 ms. N. of Jackson; from W. 1,012 ms. Watered by Yazoo river.

TEACHY'S, p. o., Duplin co., N. C., 98 ms. s. E. of Raleigh; from W. 328 ms.

TEAZE'S VALLEY, p. o., Kanawha co., Va., 334 ms. N. w. of Richmond; from W. 371 ms.

TEAVO, p. t., Rives co., Mo.

TEBO, p. o., Henry co., Mo.

TECOLITA, p. o., San Miguel co., New Mex.

TECUMSEH, c. h., p. t., seat of justice of Lenawee co., Mich., 57 ms. s. w. of Detroit; from W. 511 ms. Watered by Raisin river. Pop. 2,670.

TEDROW, p. o., Fulton co., O., 158 ms. N. w. of Columbus; from W. 489 ms.

TEE, p. t., Carroll co., O.

TEKONSHA, p. t., Calhoun co., Mich., 105 ms. w. of Detroit; from W 566 ms. Watered by St. Joseph river. Pop. 651.

TELFAIR COUNTY, situated in the southerly part of Georgia, and traversed by Ocmulgee river. Area, 950 square miles. Seat of justice, Jacksonville. Pop. in 1810, 744; in 1820, 2,104; in 1830, 2,136; in 1840, 2,763; in 1850, 3,026.

TELLICO PLAINS, p. o., Monroe co., Tenn., 178 ms. s. E. of Nashville; from W. 555 ms.

TELOGA SPRINGS, p. o., Chattooga co., Ga., 191 ms. N. w. of Milledgeville; from W. 645 ms.

TEMPERANCE, p. o., Telfair co., Ga., 104 ms. s. of Milledgeville; from, W. 751 ms.

TEMPERANCE, p. o., Amherst co., Va., 118 ms. w. of Richmond; from W. 170 ms.

TEMPERANCE HALL, p. o., De Kalb co., Tenn.

TEMPERANCEVILLE, p. o., Alleghany co., Pa.

TEMPERANCEVILLE, p. o., Belmont co., O.

TEMPLE, p. t., Hillsborough co., N. H., 44 ms. s. w. of Concord; from W. 455 ms. Watered by tributaries of Souhegan river. Pop. 579.

TEMPLE, p. t., Franklin co., Me., 40 ms. N. w. of Augusta; from W. 621 ms. Pop. 785.

TEMPLE MILLS, p. o., Temple township, Franklin co., Me., 38 ms. N. w. of Augusta; from W. 619 ms.

TEMPLE OF HEALTH, p. o., Abbeville district, S. C., 107 ms. w. of Columbia; from W. 530 ms.

TEMPLETON, p. t., Worcester co., Mass., 61 ms. N. w. of Boston; from W. 411 ms. Watered by tributaries of Miller's and Chicopee rivers. Pop. 2,173.

TEMPLETON, p. v., Prince George co., Va., 36 ms. s. E. of Richmond; from W. 156 ms.

TEMPLEVILLE, p. o., Queen Anne co., Md.

TEN-MILE, p. o., Washington co., Pa., 223 ms. w. of Harrisburgh; from W. 239 ms.

TEN-MILE, p. o., Macon co., Mo.

TEN MILE SPRING, p. o., Cattaraugus co., N. Y.

TEN-MILE STAND, p. o, Meigs co., Tenn., 152 ms. s. E. of Nashville; from W. 556 ms.

TENALLYTOWN, p. o., Washington co., D. C.

TENNESSEE, one of the United States, lies between 36° and 37° 42′ north latitude, and 81° 30′ and 90° 10′ w. longitude from Greenwich; and is bounded north by Kentucky and Virginia, southeast by North Carolina, from which it is separated by the Iron and Unaka mountains, south by Georgia, Alabama, and Mississippi, and west by Arkansas and Missouri, from which it is separated by the Mississippi river. Its superficial area is 45,600 square miles.

Physical Aspect.—This state is widely diversified in surface, soil, and climate. The eastern portion abounds in mountains and hills, some of them lofty, and presenting scenery peculiarly grand and picturesque. The middle section is less bold in its features, though hilly, and gradually becomes undulating, and even level, as we approach the Ohio. The geological formation is wholly secondary, except a small portion of the eastern part, which is transition, and numerous spots of alluvion on the banks of the streams. The soil of the western division is black and rich; in the middle there are large quantities of excellent land; and in the eastern or mountainous parts the soil is generally thin, except in the valleys, where it is exuberantly fertile.

Mountains.—Of these, the Cumberland, or Great Laurel ridge, is the most remarkable. Stone, Yellow-Iron, Smoky, and Unaka mountains, join each other, and

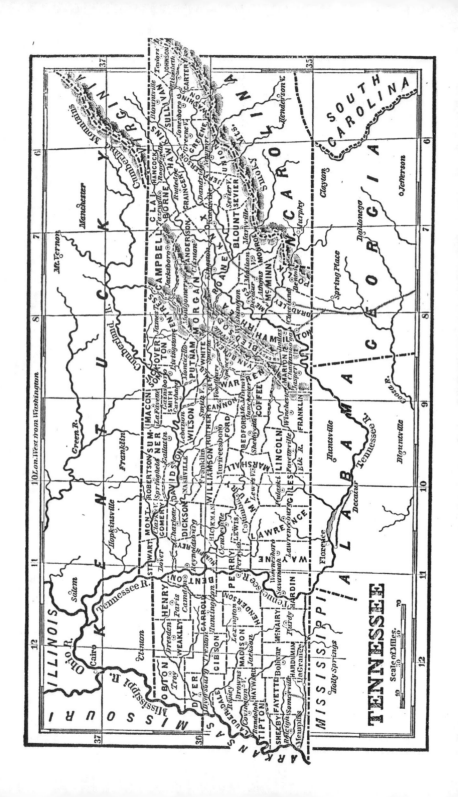

form (in a direction nearly northeast and southwest) the boundary between North Carolina and this state. Northwesterly of these, and separated from each other by valleys from five to fifteen miles wide, are Bay's, Clinch, and Powell's mountains, and Copper and Welling's ridges.

Rivers.—The principal rivers are, the Mississippi, Cumberland, Tennessee, Clinch, Holston, Duck, French, Broad, Hiwasse, Nolichucky, Reelfoot, Tellico, Obion, Elk, Forked Deer, and Wolf.

Climate.—The climate is comparatively mild, and generally healthy. On some low grounds, however, in the western part of the state, bilious attacks and agues prevail more or less during the summer and autumn months. In the eastern division, the temperature is so modified by the mountain air on one side, and the breezes from the Mexican gulf on the other, that its climate, perhaps, is as desirable as any in the Union. The winters are by no means severe, and snow seldom falls to a greater depth than ten inches, or lies upon the ground longer than ten days.

Productive Resources.—The chief products are, horses, mules, neat cattle, sheep, swine, poultry, sugar, wax, silk, wool, cotton, hemp, flax, hay, pitch, tar, tobacco, rice, wheat, rye, barley, buckwheat, oats, potatoes, and Indian corn. Of the mineral and fossil resources, iron, gold, bituminous coal, salt, marl, buhr-stone, and saltpetre, are the principal. Nitrous earth is obtained from the caverns, of which there are several in the state.

Manufactures.—In 1850, there were in Tennessee 2,789 manufacturing establishments, that produced goods to the value of $500 and upward each annually. The principal manufactures are, cotton and woollen goods, leather, pottery, machinery, carriages, cordage, &c.

Railroads.—The principal roads in Tennessee now in operation are, the Charleston and Memphis, and one from the Georgia state line to Chattanooga; but there are several other roads in rapid process of construction, and still others projected.

Commerce.—Tennessee has no direct foreign commerce, but its internal and river trade is large.

Education.—There are in Tennessee two universities, and six colleges, namely: East Tennessee college, founded in 1792; Greenville and Washington colleges, in 1794; Nashville university, in 1806; Jackson college, in 1833; Cumberland university, in 1844; Franklin college, in 1845; and Union college, in 1848. There are also two theological seminaries, a law and a medical school, about 200 academies and high schools, and 1,500 common schools in the state.

Population.—In 1790, 30,791; in 1800, 105,602; in 1810, 261,727; in 1820, 422,813; in 1830, 681,904; in 1840, 829,210; in 1850, 1,002,625. Number of slaves in 1790, 3,417; in 1800, 13,584; in 1810, 44,535; in 1820, 80,107; in 1830, 141,603; in 1840, 183,059; in 1850, 239,461.

Government.—The legislative power is vested in a general assembly, consisting of a senate of 25 members, and house of representatives, of 75 members, and the executive power in a governor (eligible six years out of eight); all chosen biennially (the odd year), the first Monday in October. The judicial power is vested in a supreme court, of three judges, elected by the legislature for twelve years, and inferior courts, whose judges are elected by the legislature for eight years. Every free white citizen of the United States, of the age of twenty-one years, and a citizen of the county wherein he may offer his vote six months next preceding the day of election, is entitled to vote for civil officers. Ministers of the gospel are not eligible to a seat in the legislature. No person who denies the being of a God, or a future state of rewards and punishments, can hold any civil office. Lotteries are prohibited; and persons who may be concerned in duels are disqualified for holding office in the state.

History.—Tennessee was originally a part of the province of Louisiana, as settled and claimed by the French, prior to the year 1763; or a part of Carolina, as granted by Charles II., of England, to Lord Clarendon and others, in 1663. The first settlement was made by Bienville, in 1740, who built Fort Assumption, on the site where Memphis now stands. The first permanent settlements, however, were not made before 1768-'69, and these were by emigrants from North Carolina and Virginia. The country was included within the jurisdiction of North Carolina from 1729 to 1790, when it was placed under a separate territorial government, by the name of the "Territory South of the River

Ohio." In 1784, North Carolina ceded this territory to the United States on condition that they should accept of it within two years from the passage of the act, retaining jurisdiction over it herself, until Congress should make provision for a territorial government. Upon this, the same year, the inhabitants resolved to organize a territorial government on their own responsibility; and accordingly a convention of deputies formed a constitution for a new state, to be denominated "Frankland," and announced to North Carolina, that they considered themselves independent of her. A portion of the people adhering to North Carolina, two conflicting legislatures, with their subordinate courts, were exercising authority in the territory. In 1789, the legislature of North Carolina authorized and instructed its members in Congress to execute deeds of conveyance for the territory of Tennessee, which they did the following year. In 1796 the inhabitants, by a convention at Nashville, formed a constitution, and Tennessee was, the same year, admitted into the Union as an independent state. The original constitution of Tennessee continued in force till 1835, when the present constitution was adopted by the people. Motto of the seal, "Agriculture," "Commerce."

TENNESSEE IRON WORKS, p. o., Montgomery co., Tenn.

TENNESSEE LANDING, p. o., Issaquena co., Miss.

TENNESSEE RIVER, p. o., Macon co., N. C., 341 ms. w. of Raleigh; from W. 571 ms.

TENNILLE, p. o., Washington co., Ga.

TENSAS PARISH, situated on the east boundary of Louisiana, with Mississippi river on the east, and the Tensas on the west. Area, —— square miles. Seat of justice, St. Joseph. Pop. in 1850, 8,940.

TENSAW, p. o., Baldwin co., Ala.; from W. 969 ms.

TENTOPOLIS, p. o., Effingham co., Ill.

TEOTSA, p. o., Rock co., Wis.

TEREBINTHE, p. o., Cumberland co., N. C.

TERRE BONNE PARISH, situated in the south part of Louisiana, on the gulf of Mexico. Area, 1,850 square miles. Face of the country, level; soil, good, where arable. Seat of justice, Houma. Pop. in 1830, 2,121; in 1840, 4,410; in 1850, 7,724.

TERRE COUPEE, p. v., St. Joseph co., Ind., 163 ms. N. of Indianapolis; from W. 645 ms.

TERRE HAUTE, p. v., seat of justice of Vigo co., Ind., 73 ms. w. of Indianapolis; from W. 644 ms. Watered by Wabash river.

TERRE HAUTE, p. o., Champaign co., O.

TERRE HILL, p. o., Lancaster co., Pa.

TERRYSVILLE, p. v., Plymouth township, Litchfield co., Ct., 21 ms. s. w. of Hartford; from W. 341 ms.

TERRYSVILLE, p. v., Abbeville district, S. C., 104 ms. w. of Columbia; from W. 551 ms.

TERRYTOWN, p. v., Bradford co., Pa., 149 ms. N. of Harrisburgh; from W. 260 ms.

TERRYVILLE, p. o., Carroll co., Tenn.

TETE DE MORT, p. o., Jackson co., Iowa.

TETERSBURGH, p. o., Tipton co., Ind.

TEWKESBURY, p. t., Middlesex co., Mass., 21 ms. N. w. of Boston; from W. 449 ms. Watered by Merrimack and Shawsheen rivers. Pop. 1,044.

TEWKESBURY, p. t., Hunterdon co., N. J. Watered by Rockaway creek and Lamington river. Pop. 2,300.

TEDANA, p. o., Jackson co., Tex.

TEXAS, one of the United States, so called, according to tradition, from the Camanches, who, on discovering the country, exclaimed, "Tehas! Tehas!" which, in their language, signified, "The happy hunting-ground." According to other authority, it was named Texas, by the Spanish commander, De Leon, to commemorate the kindness he received from the Asinais Indians of this region, on visiting them in 1689, the appellation, signifying, in their dialect, "friends." It lies between 26° and 36° 30' north latitude, and 93° 20' and 107° w. longitude from Greenwich. It is bounded north by New Mexico, and the Indian Territory, the latter of which is separated in part by Red river, east by Arkansas and Louisiana, the

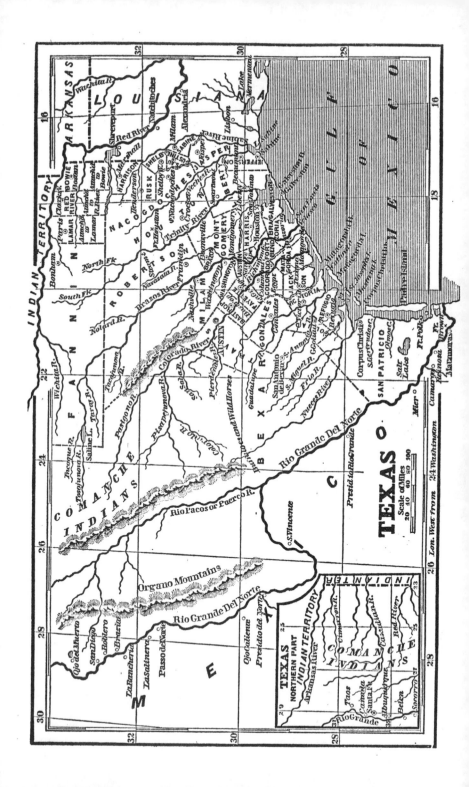

TEX 355 TEX

latter being separated in part by the Sabine, southeast by the gulf of Mexico, and southwest by Mexico, from which it is separated by the Rio Grande. Its superficial area is 225,000 square miles.

Physical Aspect.—The general aspect of this state is that of a vast inclined plain, gradually sloping eastward from the mountains on the westerly side to the coast. From the borders of the Mexican gulf, and ranging inland from 30 to 75 miles, the surface is even; but, unlike any of the other southern states, it is remarkably free from marshes, or swamps. The country between the Sabine and Galveston bay consists mostly of barren prairies, except along the streams, where it is woody and flat. The remaining portion of the coast, southwestward, is low and sandy, and, for some distance inland, the eye is relieved by beautiful prairies, insulated groves, and meandering streams. The soil of this region is mostly, if not wholly, made up of alluvion, which is often remarkably fertile, and of great depth. Next in order comes the "rolling country," which extends inland from 150 to 200 miles further, presenting a delightful country, diversified by fertile prairies, pleasant woodlands, and numerous rivulets, fed from the purest springs. Limestone and sandstone form the common sub-strata of this region, the surface soil being a rich, friable loam, mixed more or less with sand. The upper, or mountainous region, situated chiefly in the western section of the state, forms a part of the great Sierra Madre, or Mexican Alps, the remotest extremity of which consists of an elevated table-land, "where the prairies not unfrequently resemble the vast steppes of Asia, except in their superior fertility."

Mountains.—The chief mountains are, the Guadalupe and Oregon ranges, which lie in the western part of the state.

Rivers, Lakes, and Bays.—The principal rivers are, the Rio del Norte or Rio Grande, Neches, Trinity, Brazos Dios, Colorado, Guadalupe, La Vaca, San Antonio, Nueces, Salado, Sabine, Red, and San Jacinto. Sabine and Caddo lakes lie partly in this state. The chief bays are, the Galveston, Matagorda, Copano, Espiritu Santo, and Corpus Christi.

Islands.—The principal of these are, Galveston, Matagorda, St. Joseph, Mustang, and Padre.

Climate.—The climate is decidedly more healthy than that of Louisiana, or of any of the other gulf states; still, on the low, alluvial coast, intermittents are prevalent in summer and autumn, but the yellow-fever is rarely known. From March till October but little rain falls, though gusts of wind, with thunder, frequently occur. During the rest of the year wet weather generally prevails. The winters are warm and mild on the coast, and for some distance inland snow is seldom seen, except on the higher mountains, or table-lands. From April to September the thermometer near the coast ranges from 63° to 100° Fahrenheit. The greatest heats, however, are tempered by strong and constant breezes, which begin to blow soon after the rising of the sun, and continue until afternoon. The nights throughout the middle region are refreshing and cool during the year.

Productive Resources.—The chief products of this state are, horses, mules, neat cattle, sheep, swine, wool, cotton, tobacco, oranges, figs, wine, olives, dates, sugarcane, wheat, rye, barley, oats, rice, potatoes, and Indian corn. Cotton and sugar-cane are the agricultural staples. The mineral and fossil resources are, silver, iron, coal, bitumen, nitre, granite, limestone, slate, and gypsum. Salt may be manufactured from numerous lakes and springs. Buffalo and wild horses are found in vast numbers on the prairies.

Manufactures.—Texas at present is wholly an agricultural state: but it possesses all the pre-requisites for becoming eminently a manufacturing one. Its waterpower is abundant; its labor cheap; and in its cotton, wool, iron, &c., may be found material to supply the demand of a manufacturing industry to almost an unlimited extent.

Railroads and Canals.—Texas is as yet without these important aids to internal commerce. Several railroads have been projected; among them may be mentioned, one extending from Red river to the gulf of Mexico.

Commerce.—The direct foreign commerce of Texas is small, amounting, in 1850, to but about $50,000. Its coasting-trade, however, is of more importance. The shipping owned within the state amounts to about 50,000 tons.

Education.—The principal collegiate institutions in Texas are, the Baylor university, at Independence, founded in 1844; the University of San Augustine; Wesleyan college, at San Augustine; Rutersville college, and university of Nacogdoches. Its public school fund is derived principally from the school lands, and common schools are being established throughout the state.

Population.—In 1820, about 3,000; in 1850, 213,492 Number of slaves in 1850, 50,161.

Government.—The legislative power is vested in a senate and house of representatives. The senators are elected by the people, by districts, for the term of four years, one half being chosen biennially; their number is not to be less than nineteen, nor more than thirtyone. The representatives are elected for two years, by the people, by counties; the number is not to be less than forty-five, nor more than ninety. The executive power is vested in a governor, elected by the people, at the time and places of elections for members of the legislature; he holds his office for the term of two years, but is not eligible for more than four years in any term of six years. At the same time, a lieutenant-governor is chosen for the same term, who is president of the senate, and succeeds the governor in case of death, resignation, &c., of the latter. The judicial power is vested in a supreme court of three judges, in district courts, and in such inferior courts, as the legislature may, from time to time, establish. The judges of the supreme and district courts are appointed by the governor, and hold their offices for six years. The right of suffrage is granted to every free white male person over the age of 21 years, a citizen of the United States, who shall have resided in the state one year next preceding an election, and the last six months within the district in which he offers to vote. The creation, extension, or renewal of any banking or discounting company is prohibited. There is no imprisonment for debt.

History.—The present state of Texas embraces a part of the extensive country of Louisiana, as claimed by France, prior to the year 1763. It also comprised a province of Mexico, in the Provincias Internas, and remained as such, under Spanish, and subsequently under Mexican rule, until it declared its independence, in 1836. The first post in this country was established at Bexar, by the Spaniards, in 1681. In the year 1685, La Salle, in attempting to establish a colony at the mouth of the Mississippi, was deceived by his reckoning, and landed at the head of Matagorda bay, within the present limits of Texas, where the settlement of St. Louis was formed. Although this little colony was soon after broken up by the Indians, yet, as the standard of France had first been planted there, this region was thenceforth claimed as an appendage to Louisiana. With the exception of one or two unimportant missions, no other settlements were made in Texas until 1692, when a Spanish colony was planted at San Antonio de Bexar. Owing to various circumstances, it remained almost entirely unknown to the rest of the world, until the breaking out of the first Mexican revolution, in 1810. The only settlements of importance at that time were those of San Antonio de Bexar, Nacogdoches, and La Bahia, or Goliad. From the unsettled state of the country immigration was prevented, and it was not until after the second Mexican revolution, when she achieved her independence, in 1821, that any substantial advances were made toward further colonization. From this period emigrants in large numbers, mostly from the United States, continued to flow into Texas, under the encouragement of Mexico. When the federal constitution was overthrown, in 1834, the people of Texas refused to acknowledge the new government. They had sued for admission into the Mexican confederacy, as an independent state in 1832, but were refused, as Mexico was jealous of the growing power of the province. In 1835, a Mexican army was sent to reduce them to submission. In March, 1836, Texas declared itself an independent republic, and elected David G. Burnett president. A constitution was formed, having for its basis that of the United States. The battle of San Jacinto was fought on the 21st of April, between the Texan troops, under General Houston, and the Mexican army, under President Santa Aña, in which the latter was signally defeated. General Houston was elected president of the republic in September following. It sought for admission into the Union, which was granted by an act of Congress passed in February, 1845. On the 4th of July following the people of Texas, in convention, adopted a state constitution, and it became an independent state of the Union.

TEXAS COUNTY, situated in the southerly part of Missouri. Area, —— square miles. Seat of justice, Houston. Pop. in 1850, 2,312.

TEXAS, p. o., Mexico township, Oswego co., N. Y., 165 ms. N. w. of Albany; from W. 387 ms.

TEXAS, p. t., Wayne co., Pa. Watered by Lackawaxen creek. Pop. 2,550.

TEXAS, p. o., Washington co., Ind.

TEXAS, t., Kalamazoo co., Mich. Pop. 410.

TEXAS, p. o., Randolph co., Ill.

TEXAS, p. o., Lycoming co., Pa.

TEXAS, p. o., Henry co., O.

TEXAS HILL, p. o., Sacramento co., Cal.

TEXAS VALLEY, p. o., Cortland co., N. Y.

THEBES, p. o., Alexander co., Ill.

THE CORNER, p. o., Ulster co., N. Y., 77 ms. s. w. of Albany; from W. 336 ms.

THE FORKS, p. o., Somerset co., Me., 84 ms. N. w. of Augusta; from W. 679 ms.

THE GLEN, p. o., Warren co., N. Y.

THE GULF, p. o., Chatham co., N. C.

THE NARROWS, p. o., Crawford co., Ark.

THEOLOGICAL SEMINARY, p. o., Fairfax co., Va.

THE PLAINS, p. o., Fauquier co., Va., 119 ms. N. w. of Richmond; from W. 55 ms.

THE PURCHASE, p. o., Harrison township, Westchester co., N. Y., 133 ms. s. of Albany; from W. 288 ms.

THERESA, p. t., Jefferson co., N. Y., 183 ms. N. w. of Albany; from W. 435 ms. Watered by Indian river. Pop. 2,618.

THERESA, p. o., Dodge co., Wis.

THETFORD, p. o., Genesee co., Mich.

THE SQUARE, p. o., Cayuga co., N. Y.

THETFORD, p. o., Orange co., Vt., 43 ms. s. E. of Montpelier; from W. 498 ms. Watered by Connecticut and Ompompanoosuc rivers.

THE VILLAGE, c. h., Point Coupée parish, La.

THIBODEAUX, c. h., p. v., seat of justice of La Fourche parish, La., 106 ms. s. w. of New Orleans; from W. 1,243 ms. Watered by Bayou La Fourche.

THICKETY FORK, p. o., Spartanburgh district, S. C.

THIVENER, p. o., Gallia co., O.

THOMAS COUNTY, situated on the south boundary of Georgia. Area, 1,089 square miles. Seat of justice, Thomasville. Pop. in 1830, 3,299; in 1840, 6,766; in 1850, 10,103.

THOMASTON, p. t., Lincoln co., Me., 42 ms. s. E. of Augusta; from W. 619 ms. Watered by Penobscot bay and St. George's river. Celebrated for its extensive quarries of lime, netting a revenue of nearly one million of dollars per annum. Pop. in 1830, 4,221; in 1840, 6,227; in 1850, 6,723.

THOMASTON, c. h., p. v., seat of justice of Upson co., Ga., 81 ms. w. of Milledgeville; from W. 703 ms.

THOMASTOWN, p. v., Leake co., Miss., 52 ms. N. E. of Jackson; from W. 994 ms.

THOMASVILLE, c. h., p. v., seat of justice of Thomas co., Ga., 231 ms. w. of Milledgeville; from W. 888 ms.

THOMASVILLE, p. o., Oregon co., Mo.

THOMASVILLE, p. o., Robertson co., Tenn.

THOMPSON, p. t., Windnam co., Ct., 48 ms. N. E. of Hartford; from W. 384 ms. Watered by Quinnebaug, French, and Five-Mile rivers.

THOMPSON, p. t., Sullivan co., N. Y., 110 ms. s. w. of Albany; from W. 2— ms. Watered by Mongoup and Neversink rivers. Pop. 3,198.

THOMPSON, p. t., Susquehanna co., Pa., 184 ms. N. E. of Harrisburgh; from W. 284 ms. Pop. 509.

THOMPSON, p. t., Geauga co., O., 196 ms. N. E. of Columbus; from W. 349 ms.

THOMPSON, t., Seneca co., O. Pop. 1,669.

THOMPSON, t., Delaware co., O. Watered by Scioto river. Pop 732.

THOMPSON, t., Pike co., Ark.

THOMPSON, p. o., Columbia co., Ga.

THOMPSON'S, p. o.. Fairfield district, S. C., 24 ms. N. of Columbia; from W. 506 ms.

THOMPSON'S CROSS ROADS, p. o., Louisa co., Va., 53 ms. N. w. of Richmond; from W. 102 ms. Watered by South Anna river.

THOMPSON'S STATION, p. o., Suffolk co., Long Island, N. Y.

THOMPSON'S STORE, p. o., Guilford co.. N. C.

THOMPSONTOWN, p. v., Juniate co., Pa., 36 ms. N. w. of Harrisburgh; from W. 146 ms. Watered by Juniata river and Pennsylvania canal.

THOMPSONVILLE, p. v., Enfield township, Hartford co., Ct., 20 ms. N. of Hartford; from W. 355 ms. Watered by Freshwater river.

THOMPSONVILLE, p. o., Racine co., Wis.

THOMPSONVILLE, p. v., Thompson township, Sullivan co., N. Y., 105 ms. s. w. of Albany; from W. 299 ms.

THOMPSONVILLE, p. o., Culpeper co., Va., 108 ms. N. w. of Richmond; from W. 80 ms.

THOMPSONVILLE, p. o., Washington co., Ky.

THOMPSONVILLE, p. o., Rockingham co., N. C.

THOMPSONVILLE, p. o., Washington co., Pa.

THORNAPPLE, t., Barry co., Mich. Pop. :36.

THORNBURGH, p. v., Spottsylvania co., Va., 76 ms, N. w. of Richmond; from W. 70 ms.

THORN, t., Perry co., O. Pop. 1,847.

THORNBURY. p. t., Chester co., Pa., 76 ms. ms. s. E. of Harrisburgh; from W. 118 ms. Watered by Chester creek and Brandywine river. Pop. 233.

THORNBURY, t.. Delaware co., Pa., 87 ms. E. of Harrisburgh; from W. 1— ms. Watered by Chester creek.

THORNDIKE, p. t., Waldo co., Me., 42 ms. N. E. of Augusta; from W. 637 ms. Pop. 1,029.

THORNDIKE. p. o.. Hampden co., Mass.

THORN HILL, p. o., Walker co., Ala.; from W. 797 ms.

THORN HILL, p. o., Grainger co., Tenn.. 229 ms. E. of Nashville; from W. 461 ms.

THORN HILL, p. o., Orange co., Va., 71 ms. N. w. of Richmond; from W. 103 ms.

THORNLEYSVILLE, p. o., Boone co., Ind.

THORNTON, p. t., Grafton co., N. H., 52 ms. N. of Concord; from W. 533 ms. Watered by Pemigewasset and Mad rivers. Pop. 1,011.

THORNTON, p. v., Thornbury township, Delaware co., Pa., 87 ms. E. of Harrisburgh; from W. 121 ms.

THORNTON, p. t., Cook co., Ill., 192 ms. N. E. of Springfield; from W. 737 ms. Watered by Thorn creek.

THORNTON'S FERRY, p. o., Hillsborough co., N. H.

THORNTON'S MILLS. p. o., Rappahannock co., Va.

THORNTOWN, p. v., Boone co., Ind., 35 ms. N. E. of Indianapolis; from W. 606 ms. Watered by a tributary of Sugar creek.

THORNVILLE, p. v., Perry co., O., 35 ms. E. of Columbus; from W. 366 ms.

THOROUGHFARE, p. o., Prince William co., Va., 118 ms. N. of Richmond; from W. 50 ms. Watered by Broad run.

THREE-CREEK, p. o., Mississippi co., Ark.

THREE FORKS, p. o., Wilson co., Tenn., 45 ms. E. of Nashville; from W. 645 ms.

THREE FORKS, p. o., Barren co., Ky., 122 ms. s. w. of Frankfort; from W. 646 ms.

THREE-MILE BAY, p. o., Lyme township, Jefferson co.. N. Y., 182 ms. N. w. of Albany; from W. 434 ms.

THREE RIVERS, p. v., Palmer township, Hampton co., Mass., 76 ms. s. w. of Boston; from W. 376 ms. Watered by Chicopee river, at the confluence of Ware and Swift rivers.

THREE RIVERS, p. v., St. Josepn co.. Mich., 145 ms. s. w. of Detroit; from W. 593 ms. Watered by St. Joseph's and Portage rivers.

THREE RIVERS, p. o., Polk co., Iowa.

THREE ROADS, p. o., Cambria co., Pa.

THREE SPRINGS, p. o., Hart co., Ky., 106 ms. s. w. of Frankfort; from W. 629 ms.

THREE SPRINGS, p. o., Huntingdon co., Pa., 85 ms. s. w. of Harrisburgh; from W. 129 ms.

THREE SPRINGS, p. o., Washington co., Va.

THROOPSVILLE, p. v., Mentz township, Cayuga co., N. Y., 158 ms. w. of Albany; from W. 337 ms. Watered by Owasca outlet.

THURMAN, p. o., Gallia co., O.

THURSTON. p. o., Steuben co., N. Y.

TIARA, p. o., Montgomery co., Ala.; from W. 860 ms.

TIBBATT'S CROSS ROADS, p. o., Campbell co., Ky.

TICONDEROGA. p. t., Essex co., N. Y., 97 ms. N. of Albany; from W. 469 ms. Watered by Lake Champlain and Lake George outlet. Pop. 2,669.

TIDIONTE, p. o., Warren co., Pa.

TIFFIN. c. h., p. v., Clinton township, seat of justice of Seneca co., O., 86 ms. N. of Columbus; from W. 3— ms. Watered by Sandusky river.

TIFFIN, p. t. Adams co., O.

TIFFIN, t., Defiance co., O. Pop. 544.

TIGER, p. o., Rabun co., Ga.

TIGER CREEK, p. o., Claiborne parish, La.

TIGERVILLE, p. o., Terre Bonne parish, La.

TILDEN, p. o., Hancock co., Me.
TILLER'S FERRY, p. o., Kershaw district, S. C., 58 ms. N. E. of Columbia ; from W. 358 ms.
TILTON, p. o., Murray co., Ga.
TIMBER, p. o., Peoria co., Ill.
TIMBER CREEK, p. o., Marshall co., Iowa.
TIMBER CREEK, p. o., Hunt co., Tex.
TIMBER GROVE, p. o., Washington co., Va.
TIMBER RIDGE, p. o., Union district, S. C.
TIMBER RIDGE, p. o., Rockbridge co., Va., 140 ms. w. of Richmond ; from W. 182 ms.
TIMBER RIDGE, p. o., Greene co., Tenn.
TIMBERVILLE, p. v., Rockingham co., Va., 145 ms. N. w. of Richmond ; from W. 118 ms.
TINICUM, p. t., Bucks co., Pa. Watered by Tohickon and Tinicum creeks, and Delaware river. Pop. 2,047.
TINICUM. t., Delaware co., Pa., an island at the confluence of Darby and Bow creeks with Delaware river.
TINKER KNOB, p. o., Bottetourt co., Va.
TINKER RUN. p. o., Westmoreland co., Pa., 180 ms. w. of Harrisburgh ; from W. 206 ms.
TINKER'S CREEK, p. o., Barnwell district, S. C.
TINMOUTH, p. t., Rutland co., Vt., 76 ms. s. of Montpelier ; from W. 443 ms. Watered by Furnace brook and Poultney river. Pop. 717.
TINNEY'S GROVE, p. o., Ray co., Mo.
TINTON FALLS, p. o., Monmouth co., N. J.
TIOGA COUNTY, situated on the south boundary of New York, and traversed by Susquehanna river. Area, 490 square miles. Face of the country, hilly ; soil, fertile and well watered. Seat of justice, Owego. Pop. in 1810, 7,899 ; in 1820, 14,716 ; in 1830, 27,690 ; in 1840, 20,527 ; in 1850, 24,880.
TIOGA COUNTY, situated on the north boundary of Pennsylvania. Area, 1,200 square miles. Face of the country, broken ; soil, of middling quality. Seat of justice, Wellsborough. Pop. in 1810, 1,687 ; in 1820, 4,021 ; in 1830, 9,062 ; in 1840, 15,498 ; in 1850, 23,987.
TIOGA, p. t., Tioga co., N. Y., 170 ms. s. w. of Albany ; from W. 277 ms. Watered by Susquehanna river and tributaries. Pop. 2,839.
TIOGA, p. t., Tioga co., Pa., 151 ms. N. of Harrisburgh ; from W. 261 ms. Watered by Tioga river, and Mill and Crooked creeks. Pop 1,157.
TIOGA CENTRE, p. o., Tioga township, Tioga co., N. Y., 167 ms. s. w. of Albany ; from W. 276 ms.
TIONESTA, p. t., Venango co., Pa., 206 ms. N. w. of Harrisburgh ; from W. 295 ms. Watered by Susquehanna river. Pop. 1,185.
TIONESTA, t., Jefferson co., Pa. Pop. 106.
TIPPAH COUNTY, situated on the north boundary of Mississippi. Area, 1,000 square miles. Seat of justice, Ripley. Pop. in 1840, 9,444 ; in 1850, 20,741.
TIPPECANOE COUNTY, situated in the westerly part of Indiana, and traversed by Wabash river. Area, 504 square miles. Face of the country, level. Seat of justice, La Fayette. Pop. in 1830, 7,187 ; in 1840, 13,724 ; in 1850, 19,377.
TIPPECANOE, p. o., Harrison co., O.
TIPPECANOE, p. o., Henderson co., Tenn.
TIPPECANOE, p. t., Tippecanoe co.. Ind., 82 ms. N. w. of Indianapolis ; from W. 640 ms. Pop. 1,273.
TIPPECANOE, p. o., Fayette co., Pa.
TIPPO, p. o., Davis co., Iowa.
TIPTON COUNTY, situated on the westerly boundary of Tennessee, with Mississippi river on the west. Area, 415 square miles. Seat of justice, Covington. Pop. in 1830, 5,317 ; in 1840, 6,800 ; in 1850, 8,887.
TIPTON COUNTY, situated in the central part of Indiana. Area, —— square miles. Seat of justice, Tipton. Pop. in 1850, 3,532.
TIPTON, c. h., p. v., seat of justice of Tipton co., Ind. Pop. 197.
TIPTON, c. h., p. v., seat of justice of Cedar co., Iowa.
TIPTON, p. o., Lenawee co., Mich., 63 ms. s. w. of Detroit ; from W. 518 ms.
TIRO, p. o., Auburn township, Richland co., O., 84 ms. N. E. of Columbus ; from W. 402 ms.
TIRO, p. o., Marshall co., Miss.
TISHAMINGO COUNTY, situated in the northeast corner of Mississippi, with Tennessee river on the northeast. Area, 1,300 square miles. Seat of justice, Jacinto. Pop. in 1840, 6,681 ; in 1850, 15,490.
TISBURY, p. o., Dukes co., Martha's Vineyard, Mass., 85 ms. s. E. of Boston ; from W. 4— ms. Watered by the Atlantic ocean.
TITSWORTH. p. o., Madison co., Ark.
TITUROY, p. o., Greenville district, S. C

TITUS COUNTY, situated in Texas. Area, —— square miles. Seat of justice, ——. Pop. in 1850, 3,636.
TITUSVILLE, p. v., Mercer co., N. J., 8 ms. E. of Trenton ; from W. 167 ms.
TITUSVILLE, p. o.. Crawford co., Pa.
TIVERTON, p. t., Newport co., R. I., 24 ms. s. E. of Providence ; from W. 420 ms. Watered by Mount Hope and Narraganset bays. Pop. 4,699.
TIVERTON, p. t., Coshocton co., O. Pop. 842.
TIVERTON FOUR CORNERS, p. o., Newport co., R. I., 28 ms. s. E. of Providence ; from W. 424 ms.
TIVOLI, p. v., Redhook township, Dutchess co., N. Y., 51 ms. s. of Albany ; from W. 329 ms. Watered by Hudson river.
TIVOLI, p. o., Du Buque co., Iowa.
TIWOCKNY SPRINGS, p. o., Limestone co., Tex.
TOBACCO PORT, p. v., Stewart co., Tenn., 85 ms. N. w. of Nashville ; from W. 765 ms.
TOBACCO ROW, p. o., Amherst co., Va.
TOBACCO-STICK, p. o., Dorchester co., Md.
TOBOYNE, p. t., Perry co., Pa. Pop. 707.
TOBY, p. t., Clarion co., Pa., 190 ms. N. E. of Harrisburgh ; from W. 236 ms. Watered by Clarion and Alleghany rivers, Licking and other creeks. Pop. 2,234
TOCCOA FALLS, p. o., Habersham co., Ga.
TOCCOPOLA, p. o., Pontotoc co., Miss.
TODD COUNTY, situated on the southwest boundary of Kentucky. Area, 612 square miles. Seat of justice, Elkton. Pop. in 1820, 5,089 ; in 1830, 8,680 ; in 1840, 9,991 ; in 1850, 12,268.
TODD, p. t., Huntingdon co., Pa. Pop. 1,222.
TODDS, p. t., Spottsylvania co., Va., 79 ms. N. of Richmond ; from W. 78 ms.
TODDSVILLE, p. o., Otsego co., N. Y.
TOGUS SPRINGS, p. o., Kennebec co., Me.
TOLAND PRAIRIE, p. o., Washington co., Wis.
TOLEDO, p. o., Union co., Ill.
TOLEDO, c. h., p. v., Port Lawrence township, seat of justice of Lucas co., O., 134 ms. N. w. of Columbus ; from W. 464 ms. Watered by Maumee river. Pop. in 1840, 1,222 ; in 1850, 3,829.
TOLER'S, p. o., Amite co., Miss., 110 ms. s. w. of Jackson ; from W. 1,110 ms.
TOLERSVILLE, p. v., Louisa co., Va., 54 ms. N. w. of Richmond ; from W. 97 ms.
TOLESBOROUGH, p. o., Lewis co., Ky.,
TOLLAND COUNTY, situated on the north bound ary of Connecticut. Area, 337 square miles. Face of the country, hilly ; soil, of middling quality. Seat of justice, Tolland. Pop. in 1810, 13,779 ; in 1820, 14,330 ; in 1830, 18.702 ; in 1840, 17,980 ; in 1850, 20,091.
TOLLAND, p. t., Hampden co., Mass., 118 ms. w. of Boston ; from W. 364 ms. Watered by Farmington river. Pop. 594.
TOLLAND, c. h., p. t., seat of justice of Tolland co., Ct., 18 ms. N. E. of Hartford ; from W. 354 ms. Watered by Snipsic pond and Hockanum river. Pop. 1,406.
TOLL GATE, p. o., Marion co., Ala. ; from W. 829 ms.
TOMAHAWK, p. o., Searcy co., Ark.
TOMAHAWK SPRING, p. o., Berkeley co., Va.
TOM CORWIN, p. o., Allamakee co., Iowa.
TOMHANNOCK, p. o., Pittstown, township, Rensselaer co., N. Y., 20 ms. E. of Albany ; from W. 390 ms.
TOMPKINS COUNTY, situated in the south part of New York, with Cayuga and Seneca lakes at the northwest. Area, 580 square miles. Face of the country, hilly ; soil, productive. Seat of justice, Ithaca. Pop. in 1820, 26,178 ; in 1830, 36,545 ; in 1840, 37,948 ; in 1850, 38,748.
TOMPKINS, p. t., Jackson co., Mich., 91 ms. w. of Detroit ; from W. 561 ms. Watered by Grand and Sandstone rivers. Pop. 623.
TOMPKINS, p. t., Delaware co., N. Y., 100 ms. s. w. of Albany ; from W. —— ms. Watered by Mohawk branch of Delaware river. Pop. 3,022.
TOMPKINSVILLE, p. v., Castleton township, Staten Island, Richmond co., N. Y., 154 ms. s. of Albany ; from W. 234 ms. Watered by New York bay. Site of the United States Marine Hospital and Quarantine of the port of New York.
TOMPKINSVILLE, c. h., p. v., seat of justice of Monroe co., Ky., 153 ms. s. w. of Frankfort ; from W. 648 ms. Watered by a tributary of Big Barren river.
TOMPKINSVILLE, p. o., Choctaw co., Ala.
TOM'S BROOK, p. o., Shenandoah co., Va., 156 ms. N. w. of Richmond ; from W. 98 ms

TOM'S CREEK, p. o., Surry co., N. C., 139 ms. N. W. of Raleigh; from W. 332 ms.

TOM'S RIVER. p. v., Dover township, Ocean co., N. J., 38 ms. S. E. of Trenton; from W. 199 ms. Watered by Tom's river.

TOMSVILLE, p. v., Chester district, S. C., 74 ms. N. of Columbia; from W. 455 ms.

TONAWANDA or TONEWANTA, p. t., Erie co., N. Y., 298 ms. w. of Albany; from W. 392 ms. Watered by Niagara river, Tonawanda and Ellicot creeks, and the Erie canal. This township embraces Grand Island in the Niagara. Pop. in 1840, 1,261; in 1850, 2,072.

TONTINE, p. o., Steuben co., N. Y.

TOOLEY'S, p. o., Concordia parish, La.

TOOLSBOROUGH, p. o., Louisa co., Iowa.

TOOL'S POINT, p. o., Jasper co., Iowa.

TOOMBS, p. o., Richmond co., Ga.

TOOMSBOROUGH, p. o., Wilkinson co., Ga.

TOPSAIL SOUND, p. o., New Hanover co., N. C.

TOPSFIELD, p. t.. Washington co., Me., 235 ms. N. E. of Augusta; from W. 821 ms. Watered by the head waters of Mattawamkeag river. Pop. 268.

TOPSFIELD, p. t., Essex co., Mass., 25 ms. N. of Boston; from W. 465 ms. Watered by Ipswich river. Pop. 1.170.

TOPSHAM, c. h., p. t., seat of justice, together with Wiscasset and Warren, of Lincoln co., Me., 29 ms. s. of Augusta; from W. 571 ms. Watered by Androscoggin river. Pop. 2,723.

TOPSHAM, p. t., Orange co., Vt., 23 ms. s. E. of Montpelier; from W. 525 ms. Watered by head waters of Wait's river. Pop. 1,668.

TORAH, p. o., Linn co., Iowa.

TORBIT'S STORE, p. o., Chester district co., S. C., 65 ms. N. of Columbia; from W. 458 ms.

TORCH, p. o., Athens co., O.

TORO, p. o., Sabine parish, La.

TORONTO, p. o., Vermilion co., Ind., 81 ms. w. of Indianapolis; from W. 652 ms.

TORRINGFORD, p. v., Torrington township, Litchfield co., Ct., 24 ms. w. of Hartford; from W. 335 ms.

TORRINGTON, p. t., Litchfield co., Ct., 28 ms. w. of Hartford; from W. 335 ms. Watered by Naugatuck river and tributaries. Pop. 1,916.

TOTTEN'S WELLS, p. o., Obion co., Tenn., 140 ms. w. of Nashville; from W. 826 ms.

TOTTENVILLE, p. o., Richmond co., Staten Island, N. Y.

TOTTY'S BEND, p. o., Hickman co., Tenn.

TOULON, c. h., p. v., seat of justice of Stark co., Ill.

TOWALLIGA, p. o., Butts co., Ga.

TOWAMENSING, t., Montgomery co., Pa. Watered by Skippack and Towamensing creeks. Pop. 904.

TOWAMENSING, p. t., Northampton co., Pa., 87 ms. N. E. of Harrisburgh; from W. 194 ms. Watered by Lehigh river.

TOWANDA, c. h., p. t., seat of justice of Bradford co., Pa., 134 ms. N. of Harrisburgh; from W. 244 ms. Watered by Sugar creek and Susquehanna river. Pop. 2,309.

TOWEE FALLS, p. o., Monroe co., Tenn.

TOWER HILL, p. v., South Kingston township, Washington co., R. I., 37 ms. s. of Providence; from W. 396 ms.

TOWLESVILLE, p. o., Howard township, Steuben co., N. Y., 227 ms. w. of Albany; from W. 307 ms.

TOWN BLUFF, p. o., Tyler co., Tex.

TOWNERS, p. o., Patterson township, Putnam co., N. Y., 95 ms. s. of Albany; from W. 292 ms.

TOWN HILL, p. o., Luzerne co., Pa.

TOWN HOUSE, p. o., Smyth co., Va.

TOWN LINE, p. o., Lancaster township, Erie co., N. Y., 275 ms. w. of Albany; from W. 382 ms.

TOWNSBURY, p. o., Warren co., N. J., 65 ms. N. w. of Trenton; from W. 220 ms.

TOWNSEND, p. t., Windham co., Vt., 117 ms. s. of Montpelier; from W. 439 ms. Watered by West river. Pop. 1,354.

TOWNSEND, p. t., Middlesex co., Mass., 41 ms. N. w. of Boston; from W. 437 ms. Watered by Squanticook river and tributaries. Pop. 1,947.

TOWNSEND, p. o., Dix township, Chemung co., N. Y., 194 ms. s. w. of Albany; from W. 302 ms.

TOWNSEND, p. t., Sandusky co., O., 102 ms. N. of Columbus; from W. 417 ms.

TOWNSEND, p. t., Huron co., O. Watered by tributaries of Old Woman's creek. Pop. 1,332.

TOWNSEND HARBOR p. v., Townsend township,

Middlesex co., Mass., 39 ms. N. w. of Boston; from W. 435 ms.

TOWNSEND'S INLET, p. o., Cape May co., N. J.

TOWNSENDVILLE, p. o., Lodi township, Seneca co., N. Y:

TOWNSHEND, p. o., Windham co., Vt.

TOWNSHIP, p. o., Albany co., N. Y.

TOWNVILLE, p. o., Anderson district, S. C., 154 ms. N. w. of Columbia; from W. 559 ms.

TOWSONTOWN, p. v., Baltimore co., Md., 37 ms. N. of Annapolis; from W. 47 ms.

TRACY, p. o., Huntington co., Ind.

TRACY'S LANDING, p. o., Anne Arundel co., Md., 24 ms. N. of Annapolis; from W. 44 ms.

TRADERSVILLE, p. o., Madison co., O.

TRADE'S HILL, p. o., Chatham co., N. C.

TRANQUILLITY, p. o., Granville co., N. C., 29 ms. N. of Raleigh; from W. 276 ms.

TRANQUILLITY, p. o., Sussex co., N. J

TRANQUILLITY, p. o., Adams co., O.

TRANQUILLA. p. o., Jones co., Ga.

TRANSIT, p. o., Genesee co.. N. Y.

TRANSIT BRIDGE, p. o., Alleghany co., N. Y.

TRAP HILL, p. o.. Wilkes co.. N. C., 173 ms. w. of Raleigh; from W. 380 ms.

TRAPPE, p. v., Talbot co., Md., 54 ms. s. E. of Annapolis; from W. 94 ms.

TRAPPE, p. v., Upper Providence township, Montgomery co., Pa., 81 ms. E. of Harrisburgh; from W. 164 ms.

TRASK, p. o., Grant co., Ind.

TRAVELLER'S REPOSE, p. o., Pocahontas co., Va., 177 ms. N. w. of Richmond; from W. 204 ms.

TRAVELLER'S REPOSE, p. o.. Franklin co., Mo.

TRAVELLER'S REST, p. o., Greenville district, S. C., 117 ms. N. w. of Columbia; from W. 512 ms.

TRAVELLER'S REST, p. v., Dooly co., Ga., 87 ms. s. w. of Milledgeville; from W. 443 ms.

TRAVELLER'S REST, p. o., Coosa co., Ala.

TRAVIS COUNTY, situated in the central part of Texas, and traversed by Colorado river. Area, —— square miles. Seat of justice, Austin. Pop. in 1850, 3,138.

TRAVIS, p. o., Austin co., Tex.

TRAYLERSVILLE, p. o., Henry co., Va., 200 ms. s. w. of Richmond; from W. 275 ms.

TREADWAY, p. o., Barnwell district, S. C.

TREAT'S MILLS, p. o., Penobscot co., Me., 107 ms. from Augusta; from W. 700 ms.

TREDYFIN, p. t., Chester co., Pa. Watered by Valley creek. Pop. 1,727.

TREIBLEVILLE, p. o., Monroe co., Pa.

TREICHLERSVILLE, p. o., Lehigh co., Pa.

TREMAINVILLE, p. o., Lucas co., O., 137 ms. N. w. of Columbus; from W. 467 ms.

TREMONT, c. h., p. v., seat of justice of Tazewell co., Ill., 57 ms. N. of Springfield; from W. 771 ms.

TREMONT, t., Buchanan co., Mo.

TREMONT, p. o., Schuylkill co., Pa.

TREMONT, p. o., Clark co., O.

TRENTON, p. t., Hancock co., Me. Pop. 1,207.

TRENTON, p. o., Oneida co., N. Y., 96 ms. N. w. of Albany; from W. 401 ms. Watered by Nine-Mile and West Canada creeks. Contains a series of cascades, known as Trenton falls. Pop. 3,540.

TRENTON, city, seat of justice of Mercer co., and capital of the state of New Jersey, situated on the east side of Delaware river, at the head of sloop-navigation, 30 miles northeast of Philadelphia, 60 miles southwest of New York, and 166 miles from Washington. The city is pleasantly located on ground somewhat uneven, the streets regular, and many of the buildings are elegant and substantial. The statehouse, built of stone, and covered with stucco, in imitation of granite, is finely situated, and commands a delightful prospect of the Delaware and surrounding country. Above the city, the river descends by rapids, or falls; and at the foot of this descent it is spanned by a fine bridge, 1,100 feet long, with five arches, supported by stone piers. One side of this bridge is appropriated to the railroad from New York to Philadelphia. At Trenton, the Delaware and Raritan canal meets a feeder, which enters the river 23 miles above the city. The falls afford an extensive water-power for manufacturing purposes, which has been increased by means of a dam across the river, and a raceway along its bank. Trenton is united to New Brunswick and New York by the New Jersey railroad; and, by the Philadelphia and Trenton railroad, with the metropolis of Pennsylvania. The population in 1810 was 3,003; in 1820, 3,942; in 1830, 3,925 (township); in 1840, 4,035; in 1850, 6,466.

TRENTON, c. h., p. v., seat of justice of Jones co., N. C., 129 ms. s. e. of Raleigh; from W. 359 ms. Watered by Trent river.

TRENTON, p. v., seat of justice of Dade co., Ga. *

TRENTON, p. v., Jackson co., Ala.; from W. 704 ms.

TRENTON, p. t., Henry co., Iowa. Pop. 1,000.

TRENTON, p. v., Todd co., Ky., 197 ms. s. w. of Frankfort; from W. 721 ms.

TRENTON, p. v., Madison township, Butler co., O., 94 ms. s. w. of Columbus; from W. 484 ms.

TRENTON, p. t., Delaware co., O. Pop. 1,238.

TRENTON, c. h., p. v., seat of justice of Grundy co., Mo. Watered by east fork of Grand river. '

TRENTON, p. o., Wayne co., Mich.

TRENTON, p. o., Wachita parish, La.

TRENTON, p. o., Randolph co., Ind.

TRENTON, c. h., p. v., seat of justice of Gibson co., Tenn., 131 ms. w. of Nashville; from W. 814 ms. Watered by north fork of Forked Deer river.

TRENTON FALLS, p. v., Trenton township, Oneida co., N. Y., 93 ms. n. w. of Albany; from W. 403 ms. Watered by West Canada creek at Trenton falls.

TRENTON'S CORNERS, p. o., Dodge co., Wis.

TRESCOT, p. t., Washington co., Me. Watered by Cobscook bay and the Atlantic ocean. Pop. 782.

TREVILLIAN'S DEPOT, p. o., Louisa co., Va., 65 ms. n. w. of Richmond; from W. 107 ms.

TREVORTON, p. o., Northumberland co., Pa.

TREXLERTOWN, p. v., Makungy township, Lehigh co., Pa., 79 ms. n. e. of Harrisburgh; from W. 172 ms.

TRIADELPHIA, p. v., Montgomery co., Md., 50 ms. n. w. of Annapolis; from W. 29 ms. Watered by Patuxont river.

TRIADELPHIA, p. v., Ohio co., Va., 343 ms. n. w. of Richmond; from W. 256 ms. Pop. 248.

TRIADELPHIA, p. o., Morgan co., O.

TRIANA. p. v., Madison co., Ala.; from W. 723 ms. Watered by Tennessee river.

TRIANGLE, p. t., Broome co., N. Y., 126 ms. s. w. of Albany; from W. 317 ms. Watered by Ostelic and Toughnioga rivers. Pop. 1,728.

TRIBES HILL, p. o., Montgomery co., N. Y.

TRICE'S STORE, p. o., Orange co., N. C., 35 ms. n. w. of Raleigh; from W. 293 ms.

TRIER, p. o., Bexar co., Tex.

TRIGG COUNTY, situated on the south boundary of Kentucky, with Tennessee river on the west, and traversed by the Cumberland. Area, 510 square miles. Face of the country, flat. Seat of justice, Cadiz. Pop. in 1820, 3,874; in 1830, 5,196; in 1840, 7,716; in 1850, 10,129.

TRIMBLE COUNTY, situated on the northwesterly boundary of Kentucky, with Ohio river on the northwest. Area, 150 square miles. Seat of justice, Bedford. Pop. in 1840, 4,480; in 1850, 5,963.

TRIMBLE, p. t., Athens co., O., 71 ms. s. e. of Columbus; from W. 354 ms. Watered by Sunday creek.

TRINIDAD, p. o., Trinity co., Cal.

TRINITY COUNTY, situated in the northwest corner of California, with the Pacific ocean for its western and the summit of the Coast Range of mountains for its eastern boundary line; and is traversed by Smith's river and tributaries. Area, —— square miles. Seat of justice, ——. Pop. in 1852, 1,764.

TRINITY, p. o., Catahoola parish, La.

TRINITY, p. o., Morgan co., Ala.

TRINITY SPRINGS, p. o., Martin co., Ind.

TRION, p. o., Jefferson co., Tenn.

TRION, p. o., Tuscaloosa co., Ala.

TRION FACTORY. p. o., Chattooga co., Ga.

TRIPLET, p. o., Fleming co., Ky., 97 ms. e. of Frankfort; from W. 475 ms.

TRIPOLI, p. o., Tishamingo co., Miss.

TRIUNE, p. o., Williamson co., Tenn.

TRIVOLI, p. o., Peoria co., Ill., 86 ms. n. of Springfield; from W. 802 ms.

TROUBLE HILL, p. o., Scott co., Ark.

TROUBLESOME, p. v., Rockingham co., N. C., 104 ms. n. w. of Raleigh; from W. 281 ms. Watered by Troublesome creek.

TROUBLESOME, p. o., Clinch co., Ga.

TROUP COUNTY, situated on the west boundary of Georgia, and traversed by Chattahoochee river. Area, 430 square miles. Seat of justice, La Grange. Pop. in 1830, 5,799; in 1840, 15,733; in 1850, 16,879.

TROUPSBURGH, p. t., Steuben co., N. Y., 246 ms. w. of Albany; from W. 282 ms. Watered by Cowanesque creek. Pop. 1,754.

TROUPVILLE, c. h., p. v., seat of justice of Lowndes co., Ga., 271 ms. s. of Milledgeville; from W. 886 ms.

TROUSDALE, p. o., Warren co., Tenn.

TROUT CREEK, p. o., Delaware co., N. Y.

TROUT CREEK, p. o., St. Clair co., Ala.

TROUT RUN, p. o., Jackson township, Lycoming co., Pa., 108 ms. n. of Harrisburgh; from W. 218 ms.

TROY, p. t., Waldo co., Me., 39 ms. n. e. of Augusta; from W. 634 ms. Watered by tributaries of Sebasticook river. Pop. 1,484.

TROY, p. t., Cheshire co., N. H., 57 ms. s. w. of Concord; from W. 432 ms. Watered by tributaries of Ashuelot river. Pop. 759.

TROY, p. t. Orleans co., Vt., 53 ms. n. of Montpelier; from W. 569 ms. Watered by Missisque river and tributaries. Pop. 1,008.

TROY, city, seat of justice of Rensselaer co., N. Y., is situated on the east side of Hudson river, 6 miles north of Albany, and 151 miles north of New York. Formerly, this point was the head of sloop-navigation; but a dam across the river above, 1,100 feet long, and 9 feet high, with a lock, enables sloops to ascend to Lansingburgh, four miles higher up. The city is built on level ground, at the foot of steep hills, the two chief of which have the classic names "Mount Ida" and "Mount Olympus." From both of these eminences spreads a wide prospect of the Hudson and the towns along its valley. It is laid out with broad and pleasant streets, and the houses are neat and substantial. South of the city, the Poestenkill comes tumbling and foaming through a wild ravine, affording a fine water-power for several mills, which lie buried in the deep, dark gorge. A railroad-bridge spans the Hudson to West Troy, a flourishing village in Albany county, where there is a United States arsenal, an extensive bell-foundry, cotton factories, and other establishments. Among the public buildings of Troy, besides its churches, the Troy Female institute and the Troy academy deserve notice from the reputation which they enjoy. Water is conveyed to the city from a basin in Lansingburgh, elevated 72 feet above the level of the streets, through which it is distributed by iron pipes buried under ground. One and a half millions of gallons are thus supplied for daily consumption, or to extinguish fires.

Troy is united to Lake Champlain by railroad, via Saratoga and Whitehall, to Greenbush, opposite Albany; and to Schenectady, on the great central line, by one of two branch railroads—the other proceeding from Schenectady to Albany. There has been considerable rivalry in enterprise between Albany and Troy, which has probably injured neither city. The Erie canal passes through West Troy, and steamboats and numerous vessels communicate with New York and the other towns on the river. The population in 1810 was 3,885; in 1820, 5,264; in 1830, 11,401; in 1840, 19,334; in 1850, 28,785.

TROY, p. t., Bradford co., Pa., 149 ms. n. of Harrisburgh; from W. 256 ms. Watered by tributaries of Susquehanna river. Pop. 1,418.

TROY, p. t., Crawford co., Pa. Pop. 740.

TROY, c. h., p. v., seat of justice of Pike co., Ala.; from W. 863 ms.

TROY, p. v., Yallabusha co., Miss.; 119 ms. n. e. of Jackson; from W. 964 ms.

TROY, c. h., p. v., seat of justice of Obion co., Tenn., 164 ms. w. of Nashville; from W. 846 ms. Watered by a tributary of Obion river.

TROY, c. h., p. t., seat of justice of Miami co., O., 68 ms. w. of Columbus; from W. 460 ms. Watered by Great Miami river. Pop. 1,954.

TROY, p. t., Athens co., O. Pop. 1,421.

TROY, t., Delaware co., O. Pop. 976.

TROY, p. t., Geauga co., O. Pop. 1,164.

TROY, t., Lorain co., O.

TROY, t., Richland co., O. Pop. 1,544.

TROY, t., Wood co., O. Pop. 559.

TROY, c. h., p. v., seat of justice of Perry co., Ind., 168 ms. s. w. of Indianapolis; from W. 687 ms. Watered by Ohio river.

TROY, p. t., Fountain co., Ind. Pop. 1,139.

TROY, p. o., Oakland co., Mich., 22 ms. n. w. of Detroit; from W. 546 ms. Watered by head-waters of Red river. Pop. 1,427.

TROY, p. t., Walworth co., Wis.

TROY, c. h., p. v., seat of justice of Lincoln co., Mo., 129 ms. N. E. of Jefferson city; from W. 860 ms. Watered by Cuivre river.

TROY, p. o., Cherokee co., Ga.

TROY, p. o., Madison co., Ill.

TROY, p. o., Montgomery co., N. C.

TROY, p. o., Davis co., Iowa.

TROY, p. o., Freestone co., Tex.

TROY CENTRE, p. o.. Walworth co., Wis.

TROY GROVE, p. o., La Salle co., Ill.

TROY LAKE, p. o., Walworth co., Wis.

TROY MILLS, p. o., Fulton co., Ill., 80 ms. N. w. of Springfield; from W. 826 ms.

TROY'S STORE, p. o., Randolph co., N. C., 67 ms. w. of Raleigh; from W. 318 ms.

TRUCKSVILLE, p. o., Luzerne co., Pa., 129 ms. N. E. of Harrisburgh; from W. 236 ms.

TRUITTSVILLE, p. o., Greenup co., Ky.

TRUMANSBURGH, p. v., Ulysses township, Tompkins co., N. Y., 173 ms. w. of Albany; from W. 306 ms.

TRUMBAURSVILLE, p. o., Bucks co., Pa., 95 ms. E. of Harrisburgh; from W. 174 ms.

TRUMBULL COUNTY, situated on the east boundary of Ohio, and traversed by Mahoning river. Area, 875 square miles. Face of the country, hilly; soil, fertile. Seat of justice, Warren. Pop. in 1810, 8,671; in 1820. 15,546; in 1830, 26,154; in 1840, 38,107; in 1850, 30,491.

TRUMBULL, p. t., Fairfield co., Ct., 59 ms. s. w. of Hartford; from W. 288 ms. Watered by Pequannock river. Pop. 1,309.

TRUMBULL, p. t., Ashtabula co., O., 186 ms. N. E. of Columbus; from W. 337 ms. Pop. 805.

TRUMBULL CORNERS, p. o., Tompkins co., N. Y.

TRUMBULL LONG HILL, p. v., Trumbull township, Fairfield co., Ct., 62 ms. s. w. of Hartford; from W. 291 ms.

TRUNDLE'S CROSS ROADS, p. o., Sevier co., Tenn., 198 ms. E. of Nashville; from W. 509 ms.

TRURO, p. t., Barnstable co., Mass., 112 ms. s. E. of Boston; from W. 513 ms. Watered by Cape Cod bay and the Atlantic ocean. Pop. 2,051.

TRURO, p. t., Knox co., Ill.

TRURO, p. t., Franklin co., O. Watered by Gahannah and Blacklick creeks. Pop. 1,589.

TRUSS, p. o., Jefferson co., Ala.; from W. 747 ms.

TRUXTON. p. t., Cortland co., N Y., 130 ms. w. of Albany; from W. 327 ms. Watered by Toughnioga river. Pop. 3,623.

TRUXTON, p. o., Bureau co., Ill.

TYRON, p. o., Rutherford co., N. C., 237 ms. s. w. of Raleigh; from W. 479 ms.

TUCKAHOE, p. o., Jefferson co., Tenn., 203 ms. E. of Nashville; from W. 493 ms.

TUCKAHOE, p. v., Cape May co., N. J., 76 ms. s. of Trenton; from W. 186 ms. Watered by Tuckahoe creek.

TUCKAHOE, p. o., Westchester co., N. Y.

TUCKALEECHEE COVE, p. o., Blount co., Tenn.

TUCKASAGA, p. v.. Mecklenburgh co., N. C., 169 ms. s. w. of Raleigh; from W. 408 ms.

TUCKER'S CABIN, p. o., Henry co., Ga., 79 ms. N. w. of Milledgeville; from W. 683 ms.

TUCKERTON, p. v.. Little Egg Harbor township, Burlington co., N. J., 69 ms. s. of Trenton; from W. 192 ms. Watered by Shord's Mill Branch creek.

TUFTONBOROUGH, p. o., Carroll co., N. H., 44 ms. E. of Concord; from W. 525 ms. Watered by Winnipiseogee lake.

TUG RIVER, p. o., Tazewell co., Va.

TULARE COUNTY, situated toward the southern part of California, between the Coast Range and Sierra Nevada, and traversed by tributaries of the San Joaquin. Area, —— square miles. Face of the country, undulating. Soil, fertile. Seat of justice, ————. Pop. in 1852, 8,575.

TULATIN PLAINS, p. o., Washington co., Oregon.

TULIP, p. o., Dallas co., Ark.

TULLAHOMA, p. o., Franklin co., Tenn.

TULLY, p. t., Onondaga co., N. Y., 127 ms. w. of Albany; from W. 328 ms. Watered by Onondaga creek and Toughnioga river. Pop. 1,559.

TULLY, p. v., Lewis co., Mo., 136 ms. N. of Jefferson city; from W. 905 ms.

TULLY, p. t., Marion co., O. Pop. 736.

TULLY, p. o., Van Wert co., O.

TULLYTOWN, p. v., Falls township, Bucks co., Pa., 119 ms. E. of Harrisburgh; from W. 159 ms. Pop. 234.

TULLY VALLEY, p. o., Tully township, Onondaga co., N. Y., 131 ms. w. of Albany; from W. 332 ms.

TULLYVILLE, p. o., Monroe co., Ark.

TULPEHOCKEN, p. t., Berks co., Pa. Watered by North and Little North kills. Pop. 1,803.

TUMBLING CREEK, p. o., Tazewell co., Va.

TUMBLING SHOALS, p. o., Laurens district, S. C., 82 ms. N. w. of Columbia; from W. 508 ms.

TUMLINSONVILLE, p. o., Scott co., Ark.

TUNBRIDGE, p. o., Orange co., Vt., 32 ms. s. E. of Montpelier; from W. 495 ms. Watered by First branch of White river.

TUNA, p. o., Cattaraugus co., N. Y.

TUNICA COUNTY, situated on the westerly bound ary of Mississippi, with Mississippi river on the west. Area, 600 square miles. Seat of justice, Peyton. Pop. in 1840, 821; in 1850, 1,304.

TUNICA, p. o., West Feliciana parish, La.

TUNKHANNOCK, c. h., p. t., seat of justice of Wyoming co., Pa., 154 ms. N. E. of Harrisburgh; from W. 259 ms. Watered by Susquehanna river, and Tunkhannock and Meshoppen creeks. Pop. 1.312.

TUNNEL, p. o., Indiana co., Pa., 180 ms. N. w. of Harrisburgh; from W. 208 ms.

TUNNEL, p. o., Franklin co., Tenn.

TUNNEL, p. o., Augusta co., Va.

TUNNELL HILL, p. o., Murray co., Ga., 200 ms. N. w. of Milledgeville; from W. 621 ms.

TUNNELL'S STORE, p. o., Sussex co., Del., 74 ms. s. of Dover; from W. 161 ms.

TUOLUMNE COUNTY, situated in the central part of California, in the valley of the San Joaquin, between the Coast Range and Sierra Nevada, and traversed by the San Joaquin river and tributaries. Area, —— square miles. Face of the country, broken. Seat of justice, Sonora. Pop. in 1852, 17,657.

TUPPER'S PLAINS. p. o., Meigs co., O.

TURBOT, p. t. Northumberland co., Pa. Watered by tributaries of West branch of Susquehanna river. Pop. 1,047.

TURBOTVILLE, p. o., Turbot township, Northumberland co., Pa., 78 ms. N. of Harrisburgh; from W. 188 ms.

TURBUT, p. t., Juniata co., Pa. Pop. 1,399.

TURIN, p. t., Lewis co., N. Y., 126 ms. N. w. of Albany; from W. 435 ms. Watered by tributaries of Black river. Pop. 1,826.

TURKEY, p. o., Monmouth co., N. J., 39 ms. E. of Trenton; from W. 205 ms.

TUKKEY COVE, p. o., Lee co., Va.

TURKEY CREEK, p. o., Buncombe co., N. C., 271 ms. w. of Raleigh; from W. 501 ms.

TURKEY CREEK, p. o., Benton co., Mo.

TURKEY FOOT, p. t., Somerset co., Pa., 160 ms. w. of Harrisburgh; from W. 178 ms. Watered by Castleman's river, and Laurel Hill creek. Pop. 867.

TUKKEY GROVE, p. v., Dane co., Wis.

TURKEY TOWN, p. v., Cherokee co., Ala.; from W. 721 ms.

TURMAN'S CREEK, p. o., Sullivan co., Ind., 95 ms. s. w. of Indianapolis; from W. 666 ms.

TURMAN'S FERRY, p. o., Lawrence co., Ky., 164 ms. E. of Frankfort; from W. 424 ms.

TURNBACK, p. o., Dade co., Mo.

TURNBULL, p. v., Monroe co., Ala.; from W. 919 ms.

TURNER, p. t., Oxford co., Me., 30 ms. s. w. of Augusta; from W. 586 ms. Watered by Androscoggin river. Pop. 2,536.

TURNER CREEK, p. o., Potter co., Pa.

TURNER'S, p. o., Orange co., N. Y.

TURNER'S STORE, p. o., Caroline co., Va., 37 ms. N. of Richmond; from W. 88 ms.

TURNERSVILLE, p. o., Crawford co., Pa.

TURNERSVILLE, p. v., Robertson co., Tenn., 36 ms. N. w. of Nashville; from W. 718 ms. Watered by a tributary of Sulphur fork of Red river.

TURNERSVILLE, p. o., Lincoln co., Tenn.

TURNS, p. o., Monroe co., Pa.

TURTLE CREEK, p. o., Alleghany co., Pa., 187 ms. w. of Harrisburgh; from W. 213 ms.

TURTLE CREEK, p. t., Shelby co., O. Pop. 792.

TURTLE CREEK, p. t., Warren co., O.

TURTLETOWN, p. o., Cherokee co., N. C.

TURTLEVILLE, p. o., Union co., Pa.

TUSCAHOMA, p. v., Tallahatchee co., Miss. Watered by Yallabusha river.

TUSCALOOSA COUNTY, situated in the westerly

part of Alabama, and traversed by Black Warrior river. Area, 1,350 square miles. Seat of justice, Tuscaloosa, Pop. in 1820. 8,229 ; in 1830, 13,646 ; in 1840, 16,583 ; in 1850, 18.056.

TUSCALOOSA, city, Tuscaloosa co., Ala., 112 ms. N. W. of Montgomery ; from W. 818 ms. Watered by Tuscaloosa or Black Warrior river.

TUSCARAWAS COUNTY, situated in the easterly part of Ohio, and traversed by Tuscarawas river. Area, 655 square miles. Seat of justice, New Philadelphia. Pop. in 1810, 3,045 ; in 1820, 8.328 ; in 1830, 14,298 ; in 1840, 25,631 ; in 1850, 31,161.

TUSCARAWAS, p. v., Warwick township, Tuscarawas co., O.. 108 ms. E. of Columbus ; from W. 315 ms. Watered by Tuscarawas river and the Ohio canal.

TUSCARAWAS. t., Coshocton co., O. Pop. 743.

TUSCARAWAS, p. t., Stark co., O. Pop. 2.041.

TUSCARORA, p. o., Sparta township, Livingston co., N. Y., 249 ms. w. of Albany ; from W. 346 ms.

TUSCARORA. an Indian village, Lewiston township, Niagara co., N. Y.

TUSCARORA, p. t., Bradford co., Pa. Watered by Tuscarora creek.

TUSCARORA, p. t., Juniata co., Pa. Pop. 1,175.

TUSCARORA, p. v., Rush township, Schuylkill co., Pa., 75 ms. N. E. of Harrisburgh ; from W. 185 ms. Watered by a tributary of Juniata river.

TUSCARORA, p. o., Lee co., Iowa.

TUSCOLA. p. t., Livingston co., Mich. Pop. 544.

TUSCOLA, t., Saginaw co., Mich.

TUSCUMBIA, p. v., Franklin co., Ala. ; from W. 782 ms.

TUSCUMBIA, c. h., p. v., seat of justice of Miller co., Mo., 35 ms. s. w. of Jefferson city ; from W. 971 ms. Watered by Osage river.

TUSKEGEE, c. h., p. v., seat of justice of Macon co., Ala. ; from W. 799 ms. Watered by a tributary of Tallapoosa river.

TUSQUITEE, p. o., Cherokee co.; Ala.

TUTHILL, p. v., Shawangunk township, Ulster co., N. Y., 81 ms, s. w. of Albany ; from W. 305 ms.

TUTTLE'S CORNER, p. o., Sussex co., N. J.

TUTTLE'S CORNERS, p. o., Strafford co., N. H.

TWALITY PLAINS, p. o., Washington co., Oregon.

TWELVE-MILE. p. o., Pickens district, S. C., 135 ms. N. w. of Columbia; from W. 530 ms.

TWELVE-MILE, p. o., Cass co., Ind.

TWELVE-MILE, t.. Madison co., Mo.

TWELVE-MILE CREEK, p. o., Steuben co., N. Y.

TWELVE-MILE PRAIRIE, p. o , St. Clair co , Ill

TWENTY-MILE STAND, p. o., Deerfield township, Warren co., O., 100 ms. s. w. of Columbus ; from W. 473 ms.

TWIGGS COUNTY, situated in the central part of Georgia, with Ocmulgee river on the southwest. Area, 410 square miles. Seat of justice, Marion. Pop. in 1810, 3,405 ; in 1820, 10,447 ; in 1830, 8,031 ; in 1840, 8,422 ; in 1850, 8,179.

TWINSBURGH, p. t.. Summit co., O , 142 ms. N. E. of Columbus ; from W. 300 ms. Watered by Tinker's creek. Pop. 1,281.

TWIN, p. t., Darke co., O. Pop. 1,400.

TWIN, p. t., Ross co., O. Pop. 2,021.

TWIN, p. t., Preble co., O. Pop. 1,942.

TWO BAYOU, p. o., Wachita co., Ark.

TWO-MILE BRANCH, p. o., Smyth co., Va.

TWO-MILE PRAIRIE, p. o., Pulaski co., Ind.

TWO RIVERS, p. o., Pike co., Pa.

TWO RIVERS. p. o., Manitoowoc co., Wis.

TWO TAVERNS, p. o., Adams co., Pa., 40 ms. s. w. of Harrisburgh ; from W. 80 ms.

TWYMAN'S STORE, p. o., Spottsylvania co., Va., 81 ms. N. of Richmond ; from W. 93 ms.

TYE RIVER WAREHOUSE. p. o., Nelson co., Va., 100 ms. w. of Richmond ; from W. 166 ms.

TYGERT'S CREEK, p. o., Greenup co., Ky.

TYLER COUNTY, situated on the northwesterly boundary of Virginia, with Ohio river on the northwest. Area, 855 square miles. Face of the country, broken ; soil, fertile. Seat of justice, Middlebourne. Pop. in 1820, 2,314 ; in 1830, 4,104 ; in 1840, 6,954 ; in 1850, 5,498.

TYLER COUNTY, situated in the southeast part of Texas, with Neches river on the east. Area, —— square miles. Seat of justice, Woodville. Pop. in 1850, 1,894.

TYLER, p. o., Winnebago co., Ill.

TYLER, p. o., Smith co., Tex.

TYLER MOUNTAIN, p. o., Kanawha co., Va.

TYLERSBURGH, p. o., Clarion co., Pa.

TYLER'S PORT, p. o., Montgomery co., Pa.

TYLERSVILLE, p. o., Laurens district, S. C.

TYMOCHTEE, p. t., Wyandott co., O., 73 ms. N. of Columbus ; from W. 430 ms. Watered by tributaries of Sandusky river. Pop. 1.818.

TYNGSBOROUGH, p. t.. Middlesex co., Mass., 28 ms. N. w. of Boston ; from W. 440 ms. Watered by Merrimack river. Pop. 799.

TYRE, p. t., Seneca co., N. Y., 171 ms, w. of Albany ; from W. 347 ms. Watered by Clyde river. Pop. 1,356.

TYREE SPRINGS, p. o.. Sumner co., Tenn., 20 ms. N. E. of Nashville ; from W. 699 ms.

TYRINGHAM, p. t., Berkshire co., Mass., 130 ms. w. of Boston ; from W. 369 ms. Watered by tributaries of Housatonic river. Pop. 821.

TYRONE, p. t., Steuben co., N. Y., 202 ms. w. of Albany ; from W. 310 ms. Watered by Mud creek. Pop. 1,894.

TYRONE, p. t., Fayette co., Pa. Pop. 419.

TYRONE, p. t., Adams co., Pa. Watered by Bermudian and Conewago creeks. Pop. 789

TYRONE, p. t., Perry co., Pa. Watered by Sherman's creek and tributaries. Pop. 1,060.

TYRONE, p. t., Blair co.. Pa. Pop. 108.

TYRONE, p. t., Livingston co.. Mich., 61 ms. N. w. of Detroit ; from W. 583 ms. Watered by tributaries of Shiawassee river. Pop. 867.

TYRONE, p. o., Coshocton co., O.

TYRONE MILLS. p. o., Fayette co., Pa.

TYRELL COUNTY, situated on the east coast of North Carolina, with Albermarle sound on the north, and Atlantic ocean on the east. Area, 740 square miles. Face of the country, level ; soil, sandy and poor. Seat of justice, Columbia. Pop. in 1810, 3,364 ; in 1820, 4,319 ; in 1830, 4,732 ; in 1840, 4,657 ; in 1850, 5.133.

TYRRELL. p. o., Venango co., Pa.

TYSON FURNACE, p. o., Windsor co Vt

U.

UCHEE, p. v., Russel co., Ala. ; from W. 781 ms.

UCHEE ANNA, c. h., p. v., seat of justice of Walton co., Flor. Watered by a tributary of Choctawhatchie river.

UDINA, p. o., Kane co., Ill., 204 ms. N. E. of Springfield ; from W. 757 ms.

UFFINGTON, p. o., Monongalia co., Va.

UHLERSVILLE, p. o., Northampton co., Pa.

UHRICKSVILLE, p. o., Mill township, Tuscarawas co., O.. 110 ms. N, E. of Columbus ; from W. 309 ms.

ULAO. p. o., Washington co., Wis.

ULSTER COUNTY, situated in the southeast part of New York, with Hudson river on the east. Area, 1,096 square miles. Face of the country, diversified and picturesque ; soil productive. Seat of justice, Kingston. Pop. in 1810, 26,576 ; in 1820, 30,934 ; in 1830. 36,550 ; in 1840, 45.822 ; in 1850, 58,936.

USTER, v., Ulster co., N. Y. (See Saugerties).

ULSTER, p. t., Bradford co., Pa., 142 ms. N. of Harris-burgh ; from W. 252 ms. Watered by Susquehanna river. Pop. 1,082.

ULSTERVILLE, p. o., Shawangunk township, Ulster co., N. Y., 94 ms. s. w. of Albany ; from W. 292 ms.

ULTIMA THULE, p. o., Sevier co., Ark., 167 ms. s. w. of Little Rock ; from W. 1,232 ms. Watered by a tributary of Little river.

ULYSSES, p. t., Tompkins co., N. Y. Watered by Cayuga lake. Pop. 3,122.

ULYSSES, p. t., Potter co., Pa., 183 ms. N. w. of Harrisburgh ; from W. 293 ms. Pop. 699.

UMCOLCUS, p. o., Aroostook co., Me.

UMPQUA CITY, p. o., Umpqua co., Oregon.

UNADILLA, p. t., Otsego co., N. Y., 94 ms. w. of Albany ; from W. 334 ms. Watered by Unadilla and Susquehanna rivers. Pop. 2.463.

UNADILLA, p. t., Livingston co., Mich., 95 ms. N. w. of Detroit ; from W. 551 ms. Watered by Portage river. Pop. 1,027.

UNADILLA CENTRE, p. o., Unadilla township, Otsego co.. N. Y., 100 ms. w. of Albany; from W. 337 ms.

UNADILLA FORKS, p. v., Plainfield township, Otsego co., N. Y., 84 ms. w. of Albany; from W. 369 ms. Situated at the confluence of east and west branches of Unadilla river.

UNCASVILLE, p. v., Montville township, New London co., Ct., 45 ms. s. E. of Hartford; from W. 359 ms. Situated on the reservation of the Mohegan Indians.

UNDERHILL, p. t., Chittenden co., Vt., 56 ms. N. w. of Montpelier; from W. 532 ms. Watered by head waters of Brown river. Pop. 1,599.

UNDERHILL CENTRE, p. o., Chittenden co., Vt.

UNDERWOOD, p. o., Hopkins co., Ky.

UNDERWOOD's, p. o., Marion co., O.

UNION COUNTY, situated in the central part of Pennsylvania, with Susquehanna river on the east. Area, 520 square miles. Face of the country, mountainous and broken; soil, in the valleys productive. Seat of justice, New Berlin. Pop. in 1820, 18,619; in 1830, 20,656; in 1840, 22,787; in 1850, 26,083.

UNION COUNTY, situated on the south boundary of North Carolina. Area, —— square miles. Seat of justice, Monroe. Pop. in 1850, 9,854.

UNION DISTRICT, situated in the north part of South Carolina, with Broad river on the east. Area, 340 square miles. Seat of justice, Unionville. Pop. in 1810, 10,995; in 1820, 14,126; in 1830, 17,906; in 1840, 18,936; in 1850, 19,852.

UNION COUNTY, situated on the north boundary of Georgia. Area, 600 square miles. Face of the country, hilly and mountainous. Seat of justice, Blairsville. Pop. in 1840, 3,152; in 1850, 7,234.

UNION PARISH, situated on the north boundary of Louisiana, with Wachita river on the east. Area, 1,200 square miles. Seat of justice, Farmersville. Pop. in 1840, 1,838; in 1850, 8,203.

UNION COUNTY, situated on the south boundary of Arkansas, with Wachita river on the northeast. Area, 2,600 square miles. Seat of justice, El Dorado. Pop. in 1840, 2,889; in 1850, 10,298.

UNION COUNTY, situated on the northwesterly boundary of Kentucky, with Ohio river on the northwest. Area, 450 square miles. Seat of justice, Morganfield. Pop. in 1820, 3,470; in 1830, 4,764; in 1840, 6,673; in 1850, 9,012.

UNION COUNTY, situated toward the west part of Ohio. Area, 450 square miles. Face of the country, even; soil, fertile. Seat of justice, Marysville. Pop. in 1820, 1,996; in 1830, 3,192; in 1840, 8,422; in 1850, 12,204.

UNION COUNTY, situated on the east boundary of Indiana. Area, 224 square miles. Face of the country, undulating; soil, well-watered, and generally fertile. Seat of justice, Liberty. Pop. in 1830, 7,944; in 1840, 8,017; in 1850, 6,944.

UNION COUNTY, situated on the southwesterly boundary of Illinois, with Mississippi river on the southwest. Area, 380 square miles. Seat of justice, Jonesborough. Pop. in 1820, 2,362; in 1830, 3,239; in 1840, 5,524; in 1850, 7,615.

UNION, p. t., Lincoln co., Me., 31 ms. s. E. of Augusta; from W. 616 ms. Watered by St. George and Muscongus rivers. Pop. 1,972.

UNION, p. o., Carroll co., N. H., 41 ms. N. E. of Concord; from W. 522 ms.

UNION, p. t., Tolland co., Ct., 35 ms. N. E. of Hartford; from W. 371 ms. Watered by Quinnebaug river. Pop. 728.

UNION, p. t., Broome co., N. Y., 146 ms. s. w. of Albany; from W. 288 ms. Watered by Susquehanna river and tributaries. Pop. 2,143.

UNION, p. t., Essex co., N. J., 48 ms. N. E. of Trenton; from W. 214 ms. Watered by Elizabeth and Rahway rivers. Pop. 1,662.

UNION, p. t., Camden co., N. J. Pop. 1,095.

UNION, p. t., Berks co., Pa. Watered by Mill, French, and Sixpence creeks, and Schuylkill river. Pop. 1,665.

UNION, p. t., Erie co., Pa. Watered by south branch of French creek. Pop. 1,076.

UNION, p. t., Huntingdon co., Pa. Pop. 631.

UNION, p. t., Bedford co., Pa. Pop. 1,291.

UNION, p. t., Luzerne co., Pa. Watered by Susquehanna river and tributaries. Pop. 1,308.

UNION, p. t., Washington co., Pa. Pop. 1,192.

UNION, p. t. Mifflin co., Pa. Pop. 1,284.

UNION, p. t., Fayette co., Pa. Watered by Redstone creek and tributaries. Pop. 2,333.

UNION, p. t., Schuylkill co., Pa. Pop. 1,064.

UNION, t., Tioga co., Pa. Pop. 825.

UNION, p. t., Union co., Pa. Watered by Susque hanna river. Pop. 1,452.

UNION, p. o., York co., Pa.

UNION, c. h., p. v., seat of justice of Monroe co., Va., 229 ms. w. of Richmond; from W. 266 ms. Pop. 377.

UNION, p. v., Randolph township, Montgomery co., O., 75 ms. w. of Columbus; from W. 438 ms.

UNION, t., Auglaize co., O. Pop. 2,020.

UNION, p. t., Belmont co., O. Watered by Stillwater creek. Pop. 1,872.

UNION, t., Brown co., O. Watered by Ohio river, Red Oak and Eagle creeks. Pop. 4,379.

UNION, t., Carroll co., O. Pop. 804.

UNION, t., Butler co., O. Pop. 2,173.

UNION, t., Champaign co., O. Pop. 1,646.

UNION, t., Clermont co., O.

UNION, t., Clinton co., O. Pop. 2,320.

UNION, t., Hancock co., O. Pop. 1,150.

UNION, t., Highland co., O. Pop. 1,408.

UNION, t., Knox co., O. Watered by Mohiccan river Pop. 1,192.

UNION, t., Lafayette co., O.

UNION, t., Lawrence co. Pop. 1,318.

UNION, t., Licking co., Pop. 2,368.

UNION, t., Logan co., O. Pop. 804.

UNION, t., Madison co., O. Pop. 1,647.

UNION, t., Mercer co., O. Pop. 746.

UNION, t., Miami co., O. Pop. 2,227.

UNION, t., Monroe co., O. Pop. 1,930.

UNION, t., Morgan co., O. Pop. 1,795.

UNION, t., Muskingum co., O. Pop. 901.

UNION, t., Putnam co., O. Pop. 515.

UNION, t., Scioto co., O. Watered by Little Scioto river. Pop. 1,105.

UNION, t., Tuscarawas co., O. Pop. 994.

UNION, t., Ross co., O. Pop. 2,666.

UNION, t., Union co., O. Pop. 994.

UNION, t., Warren co., O. Pop. 722.

UNION, t., Washington co., O. Pop. 1,165.

UNION, v., Boone co., Ky., 73 ms. N. of Frankfort; from W. 507 ms.

UNION, t., Branch co., Mich. Pop. 1,271.

UNION, p. v., Cass co., Mich., 160 ms. s. w. of Detroit; from W. 605 ms.

UNION, p. o., Rock co., Wis., 20 ms. s. E. of Madison; from W. 827 ms.

UNION, t., Cape Girardeau co., Mo.

UNION, t., Washington co., Mo. Pop. 1,761.

UNION, t., Randolph co., Mo. Pop. 504.

UNION, t., Marion co., Mo. Pop. 1,107.

UNION, t., Monroe co., Mo.

UNION, t., St. Genevieve co., Mo. Pop. 898.

UNION, t., Saline co., Mo.

UNION, p. v., Greene co., Ala.; from W. 851 ms.

UNION, p. v., Newton co., Miss., 75 ms. E. of Jackson; from W. 942 ms.

UNION, t., Grant co., Ind. Pop. 544.

UNION, p. t., Hancock co., Ind. Pop. 522.

UNION, p. t., Miami co., Ind. Pop. 812.

UNION, p. t., Rush co., Ind.

UNION, p. t., Shelby co., Ind. Pop. 1,071.

UNION, p. t., Montgomery co., Ind. Pop. 5,627.

UNION, p. v., Franklin co., Mo., 73 ms. E. of Jefferson city; from W. 863 ms. Watered by Bourbeuse creek.

UNION, t., Johnson co., Ark.

UNION, t., Fulton co., Ark. Pop. 363.

UNION, t., Lawrence co., Ark. Pop. 530.

UNION, t., Izard co., Ark. Pop. 466.

UNION, t., Pope co., Ark.

UNION, t., St. Francis co., Ark.

UNION, t., Van Buren co., Ark.

UNION, p. o., Pike co., Ind.

UNION, p. o., Van Buren co.. Iowa.

UNION, p. o., Washington co., N. C.

UNION, p. o., Jasper co., Tex.

UNION, p. o., Santa Clara co., Cal.

UNION AND PERRY, p. t., Vanderburgh co., Ind.

UNION BRIDGE, p. o., Carroll co., Md., 67 ms. N. w. of Annapolis; from W. 68 ms.

UNION BRIDGE, p. o., Titus co., Tex.

UNION CENTRE, p. o., Union township, Broome co., N. Y.

UNION CENTRE, p. o., Miama co., Ind.

UNION CITY. p. o., Randolph co., Ind.

UNION CITY, p. v., Sherwood township, Branch co.,

Mich., 116 ms. s. w. of Detroit ; from W. 572 ms. Watered by St. Joseph's river, at the head of navigation.

Union Church, p. o., Jefferson co., Miss.

Union Corners, p. o., Sparta township, Livingston co., N. Y., 251 ms. w. of Albany : from W. 343 ms.

Union Corners, p. o., Van Buren co., Iowa.

Union District, p. o., Washtenaw co., Mich., 44 ms. w. of Detroit; from W. 520 ms.

Union Falls, p. v., Black Brook township, Clinton co., N. Y., 168 ms. N. of Albany ; from W. 543 ms. Watered by Saranac river.

Union Furnace, p. o., Huntingdon co., Pa.

Union Furnace, p. o., Patrick co., Va.

Union Grove, p. o., Prince George co., Va., 36 ms. s. E. of Richmond ; from W. 155 ms.

Union Grove, p. o., Whitesides co., Ill., 191 ms. N. of Springfield ; from W. 854 ms.

Union Grove, p. o,, Racine co., Wis.

Union Hall, p. o., Franklin co., Va., 164 ms. s. w. of Richmond ; from W. 239 ms. Watered by Pig river.

Union Level, p. o., Mecklenburgh co., Va., 103 ms. s. w. of Richmond ; from W. 217 ms.

Union Line, p. o., Spartansburgh district, S. C.

Union Meeting House, p. o., Baltimore co., Md., 61 ms. N. w. of Annapolis ; from W. 71 ms.

Union Mills, p. v., Broadalbin township, Fulton co., N. Y., 46 ms. N. w. of Albany ; from W. 420 ms.

Union Mills, p. v., Union township, Erie co., Pa., 249 ms. N. w. of Harrisburgh ; from W. 330 ms. Watered by a tributary of French creek.

Union Mills, p. v., Carroll co., Md., 65 ms. N. w. of Annapolis ; from W. 75 ms.

Union Mills, p. v., Fluvanna co., Va., 73 ms. N. w. of Richmond ; from W. 126 ms. Watered by Rivanna river.

Union Mills, p. o., Heard co., Ga.

Union Mills, p. o., La Porte co., Ind.

Union Mills, p. o., Mahaska co., Iowa.

Union Plain, p. o., Brown co., O.

Union Point, p. o., Greene co., Ga.

Union Point, p. o., Concordia parish, La.

Union Point, p. o., Union co., Ill.

Union Prairie, p. o., Allemakee co., Iowa.

Union Settlement, p. o., Oswego co., N. Y.

Union Society, p. o., Windham township, Greene co., N. Y., 51 ms. s. w. of Albany ; from W. 358 ms.

Union Springs, p. v., Springport township, Cayuga co., N. Y., 168 ms. w. of Albany ; from W. 329 ms. Watered by Cayuga lake.

Union Springs, p. v., Macon co., Ala. ; from W. 824 ms.

Union Springs, p. o., Harrison co., Tex.

Union Square, p. v., Montgomery co., Pa., 92 ms. E. of Harrisburgh ; from W. 162 ms.

Union Square, p. o., Mexico township, Oswego co., N. Y., 152 ms. N. w. of Albany ; from W. 377 ms.

Uniontown, c. h., p. b., Union township, seat of justice of Fayette co., Pa., 179 ms. w. of Harrisburgh ; from W. 195 ms. Watered by Redstone creek. Seat of Madison college. Pop. 2,333.

Uniontown, v., Lake township, Stark co., O., 128 ms. N. E. of Columbus ; from W. —— ms.

Uniontown, p. v., Carroll co., Md., 65 ms. N. w. of Annapolis ; from W. 72 ms.

Uniontown, p. v., Perry co , Ala. ; from W. 872 ms. Watered by head waters of Chilalopee creek. Pop. 290.

Uniontown, p. v., Wheeling township, Belmont co. O., 114 ms. E. of Columbus ; from W. 284 ms. Pop. 194.

Uniontown, p. o., Union co., Ky.

Uniontown, p. o., Knox co., Ill.

Uniontown, p. o., Wells co., Ind.

Uniontown, p. o., Indian territory.

Union Vale, p. t., Dutchess co., N. Y. Watered by Fishkill creek. Pop. 1,552.

Union Valley, p. o , Cortland co., N. Y.

Union Village, p. v., Orange co., Vt., 46 ms. s. E. of Montpelier; from W. 496 ms.

Union Village, v., Warren co., O. Pop. 722.

Union Village, v., Lisle township, Broome co., N. Y., 137 ms. s. w. of Albany ; from W. 314 ms.

Union Village, p. v., Northumberland co., Va., 88 ms. N. E. of Richmond ; from W. 147 ms.

Union Village, v., Greenwich township, Washington co., N. Y. Watered by Batten kill.

Unionville, p. v., Hartford co., Ct., 10 ms. w. of Hartford ; from W. 334 ms.

Unionville, p. v., Minisink township, Orange co. N. Y., 119 ms. s. w. of Albany ; from W. 264 ms.

Unionville, p. v., East Marlborough township, Ches ter co., Pa., 74 ms. s. E. of Harrisburgh ; from W. 118 ms.

Unionville, p. v., Frederick co., Md., 67 ms. N. w. of Annapolis ; from W. 58 ms.

Unionville, c. h., p. v., seat of justice of Union district, S. C., 70 ms. N. w. of Columbia ; from W. 464 ms. Watered by a tributary of Tyger river.

Unionville, p. v., Monroe co., Ga., 63 ms. w. of Milledgeville ; from W. 670 ms.

Unionville, p. v., Bedford co., Tenn., 46 ms. s. E. of Nashville ; from W. 695 ms.

Unionville, p. v., Madison township, Lake co., O., 192 ms. N. E. of Columbus ; from W. 347 ms.

Unionville, p. o., Monroe co., Ind.

Unionville, p. o., Appanoose co., Iowa.

Unionville, p. o., Cass co., Tex.

Unionville Centre, p. o., Union co., O.

Uniopolis, p. o., Auglaize co., O.

Unison, p. v., Loudoun co., Va., 137 ms. N. of Richmond ; from W. 52 ms.

Unionville, p. o., Delaware co., O., 34 ms. N. of Columbus; from W. 418 ms.

Unitaria, p. o., Broome co., N. Y.

Unitia, p. o., Blount co., Tenn., 178 ms. s. E. of Nashville ; from W. 523 ms.

Unity, p. t., Waldo co., Me., 34 ms. N. E. of Augusta ; from W. 629 ms. Watered by a tributary of Sebasticook river. Pop. 1,557.

Unity, p. t., Sullivan co., N. H., 45 ms. w. of Concord ; from W. 471 ms. Watered by Little Sugar and Beaver Meadow rivers, and Cold pond. Pop. 961.

Unity, p. t., Westmoreland co., Pa. Watered by Crabtree and Big Sewicklv creeks, and Nine Milo run. Pop. 4,152.

Unity, p. o., Crawford co., Pa., 254 ms. N. w. of Harrisburgh ; from W. 320 ms.

Unity, p. o., Montgomery co , Md., 58 ms. N. w. of Annapolis ; from W. 27 ms.

Unity, p. t., Columbiana co., O., 164 ms. N. E. of Columbus ; from W. 277 ms. Pop. 2,095.

Unity, c. h., p. v., seat of justice of Alexander co., Ill., 219 ms. s. of Springfield ; from W. 853 ms. Watered by Cash river.

University of Virginia, p. o., Albermarle co., Va., 07 ms. N. w. of Richmond ; from W. 122 ms.

Upatoie, p. v., Muscogee co., Ga., 138 ms. s. w. of Milledgeville ; from W. 774 ms. Watered by Upatoie creek.

Updegraff's, p. o., Smithfield township, Jefferson co., O., 131 ms. N. E. of Columbus ; from W. 278 ms.

Uphaupee, p. o., Macon co., Ala. ; from W. 869 ms.

Upland, p. o., Mason co., Va.

Upper, p. t., Cape May co., N. J. Watered by the Atlantic ocean. Pop. 1,341.

Upper, p. t., Lawrence co., O.

Upper. t., Carroll co., Ark.

Upper, p. t., Crawford co., Ark. Pop. 524.

Upper Alloway's Creek, p. o., Salem co., N. J. Watered by Alloway's and Stow creeks.

Upper Alton, p. v., Madison co., Ill., 79 ms. s. of Springfield ; from W. 806 ms.

Upper Aquebogue, p. v., River Head township, Suffolk co., N. Y., 226 ms.s. E. of Albany ; from W. 306 ms.

Upper Bern, p. t., Berks co., Pa. Watered by Schuylkill river. Pop. 1,746.

Upper Black Eddy, p. o., Bucks co., Pa., 121 ms. E. of Harrisburgh ; from W. 186 ms.

Upper Chichester, p. t., Delaware co., Pa. Watered by Hook and Naaman's creeks. Pop. 531.

Upperco, p. o., Baltimore co., Md., 51 ms. N. of Annapolis ; from W. 61 ms.

Upper Cross-Roads, p. o., Hartford co., Md.

Upper Darby, p. t., Delaware co., Pa. Watered by Darby and Cobb's creeks. Pop. 2,044.

Upper Dublin, p. t., Montgomery co., Pa., 106 ms. E. of Harrisburgh ; from W. 152 ms. Watered by tributaries of Wissahiccon creek. Pop. 1,330.

Upper Embarrass, p. o., Coles co., Ill.

Upper Falls, p. o., Windsor co., Vt.

Upper Freehold, p. t., Monmouth co., N. J. Pop. 2,556.

Upper Gilmanton, p. o., Gilmanton township, Belknap co., N. H., 22 ms. N. E. of Concord ; from W. 503 ms.

UPPER GLOUCESTER, New Gloucester township, Cumberland co., Me., 39 ms. s. w. of Augusta; from W. 596 ms.

UPPER HANOVER, p. t., Montgomery co., Pa., 82 ms. E. of Harrisburgh; from W. 178 ms. Watered by Perkiomen creek. Pop. 1,741.

UPPER HUNTING CREEK. p. v., Caroline co., Md., 57 ms. E. of Annapolis; from W. 97 ms.

UPPER JAY, p. o., Essex co., N. Y.

UPPER LISLE, p. o., Lisle township, Broome co., N. Y., 133 ms. s. w. of Albany; from W. 316 ms.

UPPER LOUTRE, t., Montgomery co., Mo.

UPPER MACUNGY, p. t., Lehigh co., Pa. Watered by Lehigh creek. Pop. 3,035.

UPPER MAHANTANGO, p. t., Schuylkill co., Pa., 65 ms. N. E. of Harrisburgh; from W. 175 ms. Watered by tributaries of Mahantango creek. Pop. 1,654.

UPPER MAHANOY, p. t., Northumberland co., Pa.

UPPER MAKEFIELD, p. t., Bucks co., Pa. Watered by Pidcock's creek. Pop. 1,701.

UPPER MARLBOROUGH, c. h., p. v., seat of justice of Prince George's co., Md., 23 ms. s. w. of Annapolis; from W. 17 ms. Watered by Patuxent river.

UPPER MIDDLETOWN (now called CROMWELL), p. t., Middlesex co., Ct., 12 ms. s. of Hartford; from W. 328 ms. Watered by Connecticut river.

UPPER MIDDLETOWN, p. v., Manallen township, Fayette co., Pa., 184 ms. w. of Harrisburgh; from W. 200 ms. Watered by Redstone creek.

UPPER MERION, p. t., Montgomery co., Pa. Watered by Valley and Gulf creeks.

UPPER MILFORD, p. t., Lehigh co., Pa. Watered by tributaries of Perkiomen and Upper Saucon creeks. Pop. 3,259.

UPPER NAZARETH, p. t., Northampton co., Pa. Watored by tributaries of Manooking creek. Pop. 708.

UPPER OXFORD, p. t., Chester co., Pa. Pop. 1,021.

UPPER PAXTON, p. t., Dauphin co., Pa., 22 ms. N. of Harrisburgh; from W. 1— ms. Watered by Mahantango and Great and Little Wiconisco creeks, and Susquehanna river. Pop. 1,690.

UPPER PEACH-TREE, p. o., Wilcox co., Ala.

UPPER PENN'S NECK, p. t., Salem co., N. J. Watered by Delaware river. Pop. 2,422.

UPPER PROVIDENCE, p. t., Delaware co., Pa. Watered by Crum and Ridley Creeks. Pop. 778.

UPPER PROVIDENCE, p. t., Montgomery co., Pa. Watered by Schuylkill river, and Perkiomen and Mingo creeks. Pop. 2,457.

UPPER RED HOOK, p. v., Red Hook township, Dutchess co., N. Y., 46 ms. s. of Albany; from W. 324 ms. Watered by Hudson river.

UPPER ST. CLAIR, p. t., Alleghany co., Pa. Watered by Chartier's creek. Pop. 1,626.

UPPER SALFORD, p. t., Montgomery co., Pa. Watered by Perkiomen and Rich Valley creeks. Pop. 1,440.

UPPER SANDUSKY, p. v., Crawford co., O., 63 ms. N. of Columbus; from W. 426 ms. Watered by Sandusky river.

UPPER SAUCON, p. t., Lehigh co., Pa. Watered by Saucon creek. Pop. 2,372.

UPPER STILLWATER, p. v., Orono township, Penobscot co., Me. Watered by Penobscot river, the falls of which here furnish a fine water-power.

UPPER STRASBURGH, p. v., Franklin co., Pa., 51 ms. s. w. of Harrisburgh; from W. 99 ms. Watered by a tributary of Conedogwinit creek.

UPPER SWATARA, p. t., Dauphin co., Pa. Watered by Swatara creek. Pop. 1,259.

UPPER TRACT, p. o., Pendleton co., Va., 182 ms. N. w. of Richmond; from W. 182 ms.

UPPER TRAPPE, p. o., Somerset co., Md.

UPPER TULPEHOCKEN, p. t., Berks co., Pa. Watered by North kill and Little North kill, and Union canal. Pop. 1,983.

UPPER TYGART, p. o., Carter co., Ky., 109 ms. E. of Frankfort; from W. 451 ms.

UPPERVILLE, p. v., Fauquier co., Va., 129 ms. N. of Richmond; from W. 55 ms.

UPPER YARMOUTH, p. v., North Yarmouth township, Cumberland co., Me.47 ms. s. w. of Augusta; from W. 562 ms.

UPSHUR COUNTY, situated in the northeast part of Texas, with Sabine river on the southwest. Area, —— square miles. Seat of justice, Gilmer. Pop. in 1850, 3,394.

UPSHUR, p. o., Preble co., O.

UPSON COUNTY, situated in the west part of Georgia, with Flint river on the southwest. Area, 225 square miles. Face of the country, mountainous. Seat of justice, Thomaston. Pop. in 1830, 7,013 ; in 1840, 9,408 ; in 1850. 9.424.

UPSONVILLE, p. v., Susquehanna co., Pa., 180 ms. N. E. of Harrisburgh; from W. 293 ms.

UPTON, p. t., Worcester co., Mass., 35 ms. s. w. of Boston; from W. 410 ms. Watered by West river. Pop. 2,023.

UPTON, p. o., Franklin co., Pa., 60 ms. s. w. of Harrisburgh; from W. 83 ms.

UPTON, p. o., Dodge co., Wis.

URBANA. p. t., Steuben co., N. Y., 211 ms. w. of Albany ; from W. 307 ms. Watered by Crooked lake. Pop. 2,079.

URBANA, p. v., Frederick co., Md., 76 ms. N. w. of Annapolis ; from W. 36 ms.

URBANA, c. h., p. t., seat of justice of Champaign co., O., 46 ms. w. of Columbus ; from W. 439 ms. Pop. 2,404.

URBANA, c. h., p. v., seat of justice of Champaign co., Ill., 92 ms. N. E. of Springfield ; from W. 691 ms. Watered by Salt fork of Vermilion river. Pop. 2,020.

URBANA, p. o., Hickory co., Mo.

URBANA, c. h., p. v., seat of justice of Middlesex co., Va., 84 ms. E. of Richmond; from W. 146 ms. Watered by Rappahannock river.

URBANE, p. o., Jackson co., Ill.

URIEVILLE, p. o., Kent co., Md.

URSA, p. o., Adams co., Ill., 114 ms. w. of Springfield ; from W. 894 ms.

URSINE, p. o., Grant co., Wis.

USQUEBAUGH, p. o., Washington co., R. I.

UTAH COUNTY, situated in Utah territory. Area, —— square miles. Seat of justice, Utah Lake.

UTAH LAKE, p. o., Utah co., Utah territory.

UTAH TERRITORY, formerly a part of California, and the "DESERET" of the Mormons, is situated between 37° and 42° north latitude, and 106° and 120° longitude west from Greenwich ; and is bounded on the north by the territory of Oregon, on the east by the Indian territory and New Mexico (from which it is separated by the crest of the Rocky mountains), on the south by New Mexico, and on the west by California. Its superficial area is 188,000 square miles.

Physical Aspect.—Utah is one of the most singular countries in the world. It occupies the northern portion of the great basin between the Sierra Nevada and the Rocky mountains. The basin is some 500 miles in diameter every way, and comprises an area of 393,601 square miles. It is between 4,000 and 5,000 feet above the level of the sea, shut in all around by mountains, with its own system of lakes and rivers, and without any direct connection with the ocean. Partly arid and thinly inhabited, its general character is that of a desert, but with great exceptions—there being many parts of it very fit for the residence of a civilized people ; and of these the Mormons have established themselves in one of the largest and best. Mountain is the predominating structure of the interior of the basin, with plains between ; the mountains wooded and watered—the plains arid and sterile.

Mountains.—As mentioned above, the Rocky mountains extend along the eastern border of this territory, and the Sierra Nevada along the west. Two other ranges cross the territory, one named the Wahsatch river mountains, and the other the Humboldt's River or Timpanogos mountains.

Rivers and Lakes.—The principal rivers in Utah are, the Colorado, which, rising among the Rocky mountains in Oregon, empties into the gulf of California ; and Humboldt's river, rising in the mountains to which it has given a name, and, after a long and solitary course, emptying into Humboldt lake. Other rivers are, Bear, Utah, Timpanogos, Nicollet, Salmon-Trout, Carson, Walker's, and Owen's rivers.—The most important lake in Utah is the Great Salt lake. The waters of this sheet are shallow, so far as explored, and are intensely salt, more so than those of the ocean—three gallons making one gallon of the purest, whitest, and finest salt. The shape of this lake is irregular, and it encloses numerous islands. It is supposed to be about 70 miles long. The lake has no known outlet. Utah lake is of fresh water, 35 miles long, and receives numerous fresh-water streams from the mountains. This lake abounds in fish. Utah lake is about 100 feet above the level of the Salt lake, and is connected with it by a strait, about 35 miles in length, called by the Mormons the river Jordan. There are several other smaller lakes in Utah, but little is known of them beyond their locality.

Climate.—The climate of Utah does not present the rigorous winter which its mountain structure would seem to call for. The temperature is little lower than that incident to the latitude, and summer is scarcely gone before November.

Productive Resources.—Wheat, oats, and barley, yield abundantly in the Great Valley. Melons and all the vines grow in perfection, as also do vegetables ; while hopeful efforts are making to raise the olive, orange, lemon, pineapple, tea, coffee, &c. The valley below produces tropical fruits, while the beech-land, or old lake-shore, at the altitude of three or four hundred feet, brings forth all the productions of the temperate zones ; and still higher up, the cedar, pine, juniper, and other evergreens of a northern clime, flourish. The pasturage on the plains, as well as on the beech-land and side-hills, is luxuriant (the verdure reaching to the mountain-tops), equal for fattening qualities to that of California. Utah abounds in minerals. A geographical survey has brought to light an inexhaustible bed of stone-coal, equalling that of Newcastle ; iron ore, with a vein of silver running through it, which latter alone would pay for working ; gold, in small quantities, and platina, are found ; and traces of copper and zinc have been discovered. Its mineral springs are famous, little as they have been tried, and their analysis shows them to be equal to those most resorted to at the east.

Population.—According to the census of 1850, there were 11,380 inhabitants in this territory.

Government.—Under the act of Congress organizing the territory of Utah, a legislative assembly is provided for, elected annually by the people, consisting of a council and house of representatives. All laws passed by the legislature require the approval of Congress to be valid. The governor and secretary of state are appointed by the president for four years. The judicial power is vested in a supreme court, district and probate courts, the judges of which are appointed by the president. The right of suffrage and eligibility to office are secured to every white male inhabitant, who was a resident of the territory at its organization, but the qualifications at subsequent elections are prescribed by the territorial legislature.

History.—That portion of Alta-California, now designated as the territory of Utah, was never settled by the Spaniards, nor was it ever more than a nominal dependency of that nation, or of the Mexican republic. Previous to the Mexican war, indeed, few white men, except those engaged in scientific explorations, had entered the country. About the period when that war broke out, the Mormons were driven from their city of Nauvoo, in Illinois, by mob-violence ; and shortly afterward, a portion of them, under the leadership of Strang, removed to Beaver island, in Lake Michigan ; while the main body of the sect, directed by Brigham Young (who was regarded as their true "prophet" after the death of their founder, Joseph Smith, and in opposition to the "infidel" leader Strang), migrated to the borders of the Great Salt lake. Their settlements became prosperous and populous, and within two years after the first pioneers had entered the country their

numbers had increased to about 10,000. After peace had been ratified, they found themselves without a civil government, and without protection for their persons or property. To remedy this anomalous condition of things, they organized a temporary government under the style of the "State of Deseret." Under its sanction they elected officers to manage the affairs of the commonwealth, and made application to Congress to be admitted into the Union as a sovereign state. But Congress did not deem that this new settlement had arrived at that state of maturity which would justify its erection into a state, and passed a law authorizing its organization as a territory. Congress reserved the right with Utah, as also with New Mexico, to divide it into two or more territories, or to attach portions of it to any state or territory in such manner and at such times as it may deem convenient and proper.

UTAH, p. o., Warren co., Ill.

UTAH, p. o., La Grange co., Ind.

UTAH, p. o., Lucas co., O.

UTICA, city, seat of justice of Oneida co., N. Y., situated south of Mohawk river, 92 miles northwest of Albany, 233 miles east of Buffalo, and 388 miles from Washington. The city is built on a pleasant slope, facing the river ; its streets are generally broad and regular, and its aspect exhibits the signs of prosperity, business activity, and successful industry. The Erie canal and the great central chain of railroads pass through Utica, and the former is here joined by the Chenango canal, which extends to Binghamton, on the Erie railroad, and furnishing an outlet for the agricultural products of the surrounding country. Manufactures of various kinds are extensively carried on. The population in 1820 was 2,972 ; in 1830, 8,323 ; in 1840, 12,782 ; in 1850, 17,565.

UTICA, p. o., Venango co., Pa., 218 ms. N. w. of Harrisburgh ; from W. 292 ms.

UTICA, p. v., Washington township, Licking co., O., 51 ms. E. of Columbus ; from W. 372 ms.

UTICA, p. v., Shelby township, Macomb co., Mich., 22 ms. N. E. of Detroit ; from W. 546 ms. Watered by Clinton river.

UTICA, p. t., Clark co., Ind., 109 ms. s. of Indianapolis ; from W. 597 ms. Watered by Ohio river. Pop. 5,138.

UTICA, p. o., La Salle co., Ill.

UTICA, p. v., Hinds co., Miss., 38 ms. w. of Jackson ; from W. 1,048 ms.

UTICA, p. v., Livingston co., Mo., 167 ms. N. w. of Jefferson city ; from W. 1,059 ms. Watered by Grand river.

UTICA, p. o., Dane co., Wis.

UTICA, p. o., Van Buren co., Iowa.

UTICA MILLS, p. o., Frederick co., Md., 84 ms. N. w. of Annapolis ; from W. 51 ms.

UTOY, p. o., De Kalb co., Ga., 103 ms. N. w. of Milledgeville ; from W. 689 ms.

UTTER'S CORNERS. p. o., Walworth co., Wis.

UWCHLAND, p. t., Chester co., Pa., 69 ms. s. E. of Harrisburgh ; from W. 129 ms. Watered by Brandywine creek. Pop. 982.

UXBRIDGE, p. t., Worcester co., Mass., 38 ms. s. w. of Boston ; from W 403 ms. Watered by Mumford, West, and Blackstone rivers, and Blackstone canal Pop. 2,457.

V.

VAIL'S CROSS ROADS, p. o., Morrow co., O.

VAIL'S MILLS, p. o., Fulton co., N. Y.

VALATIE. p. v., Kinderhook township, Columbia co., N. Y., 20 ms. s. of Albany ; from W. 352 ms. Watered by Valatie and Kinderhook creeks.

VALEENE, p. v., Orange co., Ind., 104 ms. s. of Indianapolis ; from W. 635 ms.

VALE MILLS, p. o., Giles co., Tenn.

VALENCIA, p. o., Shelby co., O.

VALLE CRUCIS, p. o., Ashe co., N. C.

VALLEE, t., Jefferson co., O.

VALLEJO, p. o., Sonoma co., Cal.

VALLEJO, p. o., Solano co., capital of the state of California.

VALLEY, p. t., Columbia co., Pa.

VALLEY, p. o., Tazewell co., Va.

VALLEY FALLS, Providence co., R. I.

VALLEY FALLS, p. o., Marion co., Va.

VALLEY FORGE, p. v., Schuylkill township, Chester co., Pa., 81 ms. E. of Harrisburgh ; from W. 159 ms. Watered by Valley creek and Schuylkill river.

VALLEY FORGE, p. o., Jasper co., Mo.

VALLEY GROVE, p. o., Monroe co., Ark.

VALLEY GROVE, p. o., De Soto co., Miss.

VALLEY HEAD, p. o., De Kalb co., Ala. ; from W. 656 ms.

VALLEY PRAIRIE, p. o., Barry co., Mo.

VALLEY TOWN, p. o., Cherokee co., N. C.

VALLONIA, p. v., Jackson co., Ind., 75 ms. s. of Indianapolis ; from W. 600 ms.

VALLONIA SPRINGS, p.v., Colesville township, Broome co., N. Y., 114 ms. s. w. of Albany ; from W. 310 ms.

VALPARAISO, c. h., p. v., seat of justice of Porter co., Ind., 138 ms. N. w. of Indianapolis ; from W. 682 ms. Watered by Salt creek.

VAN BUREN COUNTY, situated in the central part

of Tennessee. Area, —— square miles. Face of the country, hilly. Seat of justice, Spencer. Pop. in 1850, 2,674.

VAN BUREN COUNTY, situated on the west boundary of Michigan, with Lake Michigan on the west. Area, 633 square miles. Face of the country, level; soil, fertile. Seat of justice, Paw-Paw. Pop. in 1830, 5; in 1840, 1,910; in 1850, 5.800 ms.

VAN BUREN COUNTY, situated on the south boundary of Iowa, and traversed by Des Moines river. Area, 504 square miles. Seat of justice, Keosauque. Pop. in 1840, 6,146; in 1850, 12.270.

VAN BUREN COUNTY, situated toward the north part of Arkansas. Area, 1,350 square miles. Face of the country in the north part, hilly. Seat of justice, Clinton. Pop. in 1840, 1,518; in 1850, 2,864.

VAN BUREN, p. o., Aroostook co., Me.

VAN BUREN, p. t., Onondaga co., N. Y., 141 ms. w. of Albany; from W. 358 ms. Watered by Camp brook and Seneca river. Pop. 3,873.

VAN BUREN, p. o., Washington co., Pa., 216 ms. w. of Harrisburgh; from W. 243 ms.

VAN BUREN, p. t, Hancock co., O., 96 ms. N. w. of Columbus; from W. 452 ms. Pop. 658.

VAN BUREN, t., Darke co., O. Pop. 780.

VAN BUREN, t., Shelby co., O. Pop. 629.

VAN BUREN, p. t., Wayne co., Mich. Watered by Huron river.

VAN BUREN, t., Brown co., Ind. Pop. 717.

VAN BUREN, t., Kosciusko co., Ind. Pop. 822.

VAN BUREN, p. t., Clay co., Ind., 61 ms. s. w. of Indianapolis; from W. 632 ms. Pop. 866.

VAN BUREN, p. v., Hardeman co., Tenn., 172 ms. s. w. of Nashville; from W. 857 ms.

VAN BUREN, p. v., De Kalb co., Ala.; from W. 682 ms.

VAN BUREN, p. v., Itawamba co., Miss. Watered by Tombigbee river.

VAN BUREN, v., Ripley co., Mo. Watered by Current river.

VAN BUREN, t., Polk co., Mo.

VAN BUREN, c. h., p. v., seat of justice of Crawford co., Ark. Watered by Arkansas river. Pop. 549.

VAN BUREN, t., Crawford co., Ark. Pop. 1,382.

VAN BUREN, p. o., Anderson co., Ky.

VAN BUREN, t. Grant co., Ind.

VAN BUREN, p. o., De Kalb co., Ill.

VAN BUREN CENTRE, p. o., Van Buren township, Onondaga co., N. Y., 144 ms. w. of Albany; from W. 351 ms.

VAN BUREN FURNACE, p. o., Shenandoah co., Va.

VAN BUREN HARBOR, p. v., Pomfret township. Chautauque co., N. Y., 334 ms. w. of Albany; from W. 354 ms. Watered by Lake Erie.

VANCEBOROUGH, p. v., Winnebago co., Ill.

VANCEBURGH, p. v., Lewis co., Ky., 110 ms. N. E. of Frankfort; from W. 466 ms. Watered by Ohio river and Salt creek.

VANCE'S FERRY, p. o., Orangeburgh district, S. C., 97 ms. s. of Columbia; from W. 535 ms.

VANCEVILLE, p. o., Washington co., Pa.

VAN CLEVESVILLE, p. o., Berkeley co., Va.

VANDALIA. c. h., p. v., seat of justice of Fayette co., Ill. Watered by Kaskaskia river.

VANDALIA, p. o., Cass co., Mich.

VANDALIA, p. o., Owen co., Ind.

VANDALIA. p. o.. Montgomery co., O.

VANDERBURG COUNTY, situated on the southerly boundary of Indiana, with Ohio river on the southwest. Area, 225 square miles. Face of the country, undulating: seat of justice, Evansville. Pop. in 1820, 1,798; in 1830, 2,611; in 1840, 6,250; in 1850, 11,414.

VAN DEUSENVILLE, p. v., Berkshire co., Mass., 137 ms. w. of Boston; from W. 358 ms.

VAN DYKE'S MILL, p. o., Spencer co., Ky.

VAN ETTENVILLE, p. o., Cayuta township. Chemung co.. N. Y., 183 ms. w. of Albany; from W. 284 ms.

VAN HILL, p. o., Hawkins co., Tenn., 261 ms. E. of Nashville; from W. 451 ms.

VAN HISEVILLE, p. o., Mercer co., Pa.

VAN HOOK'S STORE, p. o., Person co., N. C., 52 ms. N. w. of Raleigh; from W. 265 ms.

VAN HORNESVILLE, p. o., Stark township, Herkimer co., N. Y., 64 ms. N. w. of Albany; from W. 382 ms.

VANLUE, p. o., Hancock co., O.

VANNOY'S MILL, p. o., Pike co., Mo.

VANN'S VALLEY, p. o., Floyd co., Ga., 173 ms. N. w. of Milledgeville; from W. 684 ms.

VANN'S VALLEY, p. o., Delaware co., O.

VAN RENSSELAER, t., Ottawa co., O. It consists of the Bass islands in Lake Erie. Pop. 186.

VAN WERT COUNTY, situated on the west boundary of Ohio. Area, 432 square miles. Seat of justice, Van Wert. Pop. in 1830, 49; in 1840, 1,577; in 1850, 4,816.

VAN WERT, c. h., p. o., seat of justice of Paulding co., Ga., 138 ms. N. w. of Milledgeville; from W. 681 ms.

VAN WERT, c. h., p. v., seat of justice of Van Wert co., O., 136 ms. N. w. of Columbus; from W. 510 ms. Watered by a tributary of Little Auglaize river.

VAN ZANT COUNTY, situated in Texas. Area, —— square miles. Seat of justice, Jordan's Saline. Pop. in 1850, 1,138.

VARRENNES, p. v., Anderson district, S. C., 122 ms. N. w. of Columbus; from W. 549 ms.

VARICK, p. t., Seneca co., N. Y., 186 ms. w. of Albany; from W. 332 ms. Watered by Cayuga and Seneca lakes. Pop. 1,872.

VARIETY MILLS, p. o.. Nelson co., Va., 105 ms. w. of Richmond; from W. 165 ms.

VARNA, p. v., Dryden township, Tompkins co., N. Y., 161 ms. w. of Albany; from W. 299 ms. Watered by Fall creek.

VARYSBURGH, p. v., Sheldon township, Wyoming co., N. Y., 264 ms. w. of Albany; from W. 369 ms. Watered by Tonawanda creek.

VASSALBOROUGH, p. t., Kennebec co., Me., 11 ms. N. of Augusta; from W. 606 ms. Watered by Kennebec river. Pop. 3,099.

VASSAR, p. o., Tuscola co., Mich.

VAUGHNSVILLE, p. o.. Putnam co., O.

VAUGHN VALLEY, p o., Rutherford co., Tenn.

VAUGINE, p. t., Jefferson co., Ark. Pop. 1,122.

VEGA, p. o., Henry co., Iowa.

VELASCO. p. o., Brazoria co., Tex.

VENANGO COUNTY, situated in the northwesterly part of Pennsylvania, and traversed by Alleghany river. Area, 1,120 square miles. Face of the country, broken; soil along the streams, fertile. Seat of justice, Franklin. Pop. in 1810, 3,060; in 1820, 4,915; in 1830, 9,470; in 1840, 17.900; in 1850, 18,310.

VELMONT, t., Arkansas co., Ark. Pop. 162.

VENANGO, t., Erie co., Pa. Pop. 1,019.

VENANGO, t., Butler co., Pa. Pop. 1.473.

VENANGO, p. t., Crawford co., Pa. Pop. 1,607.

VENICE, p. t., Cayuga co., N. Y., 164 ms. w. of Albany; from W. 325 ms. Watered by Salmon creek. Pop. 2,028.

VENICE, p. o., Washington co., Pa.

VENICE, p. v., Erie co., O., 103 ms. N. of Columbus; from W. 417 ms. Watered by Sandusky bay of Lake Erie, and Cold creek.

VENICE, p. t., Seneca co., O. Pop. 1,830.

VENICE, p. o., Shiawassee co., Mich.

VENICE. p. o., Madison co., Ill.

VERA CRUZ, p. o., Wells co., Ind.

VERBANK, p. o., Unionvale township, Dutchess co., N. Y., 82 ms. s. of Albany; from W. 309 ms.

VERDIERVILLE, p. o., Orange co., Va., 88 ms. N. w. of Richmond; from W. 82 ms.

VERDON, p. o., Hanover co., Va., 28 ms. N. of Richmond; from W. 97 ms.

VERGENNES, city, Addison co., Vt., 66 ms. w. of Montpelier; from W. 489 ms. Watered by Otter creek at the head of navigation. Pop. 1,378.

VERGENNES. p. o., Jackson co., Ill.

VERGENNES, p. o., Kent co., Mich.

VERMILION COUNTY, situated on the west boundary of Indiana, with Wabash river on the east. Area, 280 square miles. Face of the country, undulating; soil, fertile. Seat of justice, Newport. Pop. in 1830, 5,692; in 1840. 8,274; in 1850, 8.661.

VERMILION COUNTY, situated on the east boundary of Illinois. Area, 1.000 square miles. Face of the country, level; soil, rich. Seat of justice, Danville. Pop. in 1830, 5,836; in 1840, 9,303; in 1850, 11,492.

VERMILION. p. t., Erie co., O., 119 ms. N. of Columbus; from W. 389 ms. Watered by Lake Erie and Vermilion river.

VERMILION. p. t., Richland co., O.

VERMILION, p. t., Vermilion co., Ind. Pop. 1,679.

VERMILION, p. o., Oswego co., N. Y.

VERMILIONVILLE, c. h., p. v., seat of justice of Lafayette co.. parish. Watered by Vermilion river at the head of navigation.

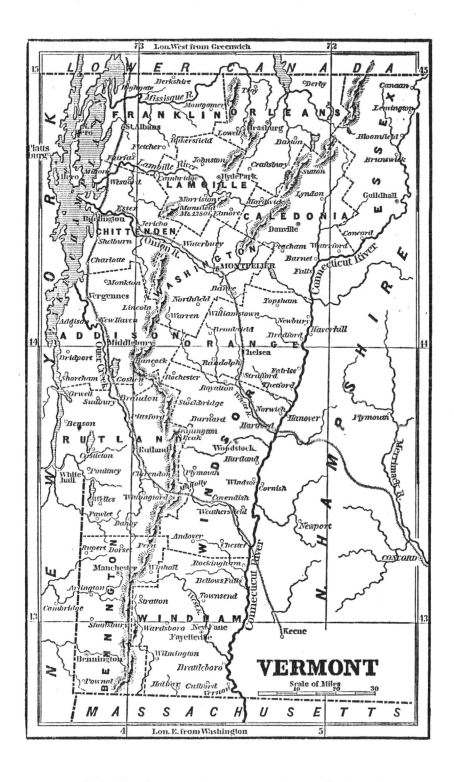

LOWER CANADA

15 45

NEW YORK

Platts burg

Highgate *Berkshire* *Troy* *Derby* *Canaan*
Montgomer *Lemington*

Missisque R.

FRANKLIN ORLEANS ESSEX

St.Albans *Lowell* *Irasburg* *Bloomfield*
Hero *Bakersfield* *Barton* *Brunswick*
Fletcher *Johnston* *Craftsbury* *Guildhall*
Fairfax *Milton* *HydePark* *Sutton*
Lamoille River *Cambridge* LAMOILLE *Lyndon*
Westford *Morriston* *Hardwick* *Concord*
Essex *Mansfield* *Elmore* CALEDONIA *Waterford*
Burlington *Mt.4280.* *Danville* *Connecticut River*
Jericho CHITTENDEN *Peacham*
Shelburn *Waterbury* WASHINGTON *Barnet*
Onion R. MONTPELIER *Falls*
Charlotte *Monkton* *Barre* *Topsham* *Newbury*
Vergennes *Northfield* *Haverhill*
Lincoln *Warren* *Williamstown* *Bradford*
Addison *NewHaven* *Brookfield* *Thelsea*
ADDISON *Middlebury* ORANGE NEW HAMPSHIRE
Bridport *Hancock* *Randolph* *Fairlee*
Shoreham *Goshen* *Rochester* *Strafford* *Thetford*
Orwell *Brandon* *Royalton* *Norwich* *Plymouth*
Sudbury *Stockbridge*
Benson *Pittsford* *Barnard* *Hartford* *Hanover*
RUTLAN *Killington* *Woodstock* Merrimack R.
Castleton *Rutland* Peak *Hartland*
Whitehall *Poultney* *Clarendon* *Plymouth* *Windsor* *Cornish*
Wells *Wallingford* *Mt Holly* *Cavendish*
Pawlet *Weathersfield*
Danby *Andover* *Newport*
Rupert Dorset *Peru* *Chester*
Manchester *Winhall* *Rockingham* CONCORD
Arlington *BellowsFalls*
Cambridge *Stratton* *Townsend*
BENNINGTON WINDHAM *Keene*
Shaftsbury *Wardsboro* *NewFane* *Fayetteville*
Bennington *Wilmington*
Pownal *Brattleboro* *West R.* *Connecticut River*
Halifax *Guilford* *Vernon*

WINDSOR

VERMONT

Scale of Miles
10 20 30

MASSACHUSETTS

14 14
13 13
43 43

VERMONT, one of the United States, signifying in French, "Green Mountains," was first so-called by the people, in their declaration of independence, in 1777. It lies between 42° 44' and 45° north latitude. and 71° 33' and 73° 25' west longitude from Greenwich, and is bounded north by Canada; east by New Hampshire, which is separated from it by Connecticut river; south by Massachusetts; and west by New York, from which it is separated, in part, by Lake Champlain, and contains 10,200 square miles.

Physical Aspect.—The surface of this state is generally uneven, and a great part of it mountainous. A large proportion of the soil is fertile, and adapted to the various purposes of northern agriculture. It is generally deep, of a dark color, rich, moist, warm, loamy, and seldom parched by drought. The "intervales" along the rivers and lakes are regarded as the best for tillage; and much of the land among the mountains is excellent for grazing, and here there are found many fine farms.

Mountains.—The Green mountains, so named on account of the evergreens with which they are covered, extend in a lofty, unbroken range, quite through the central part of the state, from north to south. In the southern part of Washington county they are separated into two ridges, the most westerly of which is much the highest. The highest elevations in this ridge are Killington peak, Camel's Hump, or "Camel's Rump," as it is commonly called, and the "Chin," in Mansfield mountains. Ascutney is another noted mountain of this state, lying at the southward of Windsor.

Rivers and Lakes.—The principal rivers are the Connecticut, Lamoille, Onion, Missisque, Winooski, White, Black, Passumpsic, Deerfield, West, and Otter Creek. Lakes Champlain and Memphremagog lie partly in this state. Among the smaller bodies of water are Lakes Dunmore and Bombazine.

Islands.—The principal of these are North and South Hero, and La Motte, all of which are in Lake Champlain.

Climate.—The climate is remarkably healthy, but is subject to great extremes of heat and cold, the range of temperature varying from 27° below zero Fahrenheit to 100° above. Winter usually commences in its greatest severity early in December, and often continues till April. During this season there is generally a prevalence of fair weather, and the cold is more uniform and steady than in other parts of New England near the coast.

Productive Resources.—The chief products are horses, mules, neat cattle, sheep, swine, poultry, butter, cheese, sugar, wax, silk, wool, lumber, pot and pearl ashes, hay, hops, hemp, flax, wheat, rye, barley, buckwheat, oats, potatoes, and Indian corn. Of the mineral or fossil resources, lead, iron, copperas, marble, limestone, and granite, form the principal.

Manufactures.—Leather, bar and cast iron, boots and shoes, linseed oil, nails, mechanical and agricultural implements, cotton and woollen goods, paper, &c., are among the products of manufacturing industry. Marble is quarried, sawn, and polished, in several places.

Railroads and Canals.—There are several long lines of railroads in Vermont, extending from the borders of Massachusetts and New Hampshire to Burlington and Canada, and from Rutland to Whitehall and Troy in New York. There are about 400 miles of railroad in the state. There are some short canals, designed to overcome obstructions in the navigation of the Connecticut and White rivers.

Commerce.—The foreign commerce of Vermont is mostly with Canada. Its principal port is Burlington, on Lake Champlain. Its domestic and foreign trade amounts in value to about three fourths of a million of dollars annually.

Education.—The oldest literary institution is the university at Burlington, founded in 1791. There are also, Middlebury college, Norwich university, and a medical school at Woodstock, all in a flourishing condi-

tion. Besides these, there are many academies, and some 3,000 common schools in the state.

Population.—In 1790 85,416; in 1800, 154,465; in 1810, 217,713; in 1820, 235,764; in 1830, 280,652; in 1840, 291,-948; in 1850, 314,120.

Government.—The legislative power is vested in a senate of thirty members, and a house of representatives, consisting of one member from each town; and the executive power in a governor, or, in his absence, a lieutenant-governor—all chosen annually by the people, on the first Tuesday in September. The judiciary powers are vested in a supreme court of five judges, and county courts (each composed of one judge of the supreme court and two assistant judges), all chosen annually by the legislature. A council of thirteen censors is chosen once in seven years, to supervise the legislative and executive branches of government. The right of suffrage vests in male citizens of twenty-one years of age, who have resided in the state one year, and are of quiet and peaceable behavior.

History.—The first permanent settlement in Vermont was made at Fort Dummer, in 1724, though the northwesterly part of this state was visited by Champlain and others as early as 1609. In the year 1739, New Hampshire claimed jurisdiction of the territory, and made many grants of land west of Connecticut river. The same territory was also claimed by New York, whose right was established by decision of the crown, in 1764. In the meantime, New York had also made grants to others of the same tracts, which caused continued disputes, and even resistance, for years, in 1774, New York passed severe enactments on the subject; but, at the commencement of the Revolution, the contest was suspended. In 1777, the people, preferring a government of their own, met in convention, and declared themselves a free and independent state. In consequence of these conflicting claims, Congress dared not admit Vermont into the Union at the commencement of the Revolutionary war, for fear of offending New Hampshire and New York, although she had expressed a readiness to throw off the British yoke. By another convention, held at Windsor, in 1777, a state constitution was adopted, but the government was not organized before 1778. In 1786, this constitution was modified, and was again revised in 1793. In 1790, the controversy with New York was ended by the payment of $30,000, and the year following Vermont was admitted into the Union as a sovereign state. Motto of the seal, "Freedom and Unity."

VERMONT, p. v., Fulton co., Ill.

VERMONT, p. o., Gerry township, Chautauque co., N. Y., 335 ms. w. of Albany; from W. 325 ms.

VERMONT, p. v., Cooper co., Mo.

VERMONT, p. o., Howard co., Ind.

VERMONT SETTLEMENT, p. o., Will co., Ill.

VERMONTVILLE, p. v., Eaton co., Mich. Watered by Thornapple river. Pop. 324.

VERNAL, p. o., Attica township, Wyoming co., N. Y., 252 ms. w. of Albany; from W. 370 ms.

VERNAL, p. o., Greene co., Miss.

VERNON, p. t., Windham co., Vt., 128 s. of Montpelier; from W. 418 ms. Watered by Connecticut river and White-Lily pond. Pop. 821.

VERNON, p. t., Tolland co., Ct., 12 ms. N. E. of Hartford; from W. 348 ms. Watered by Hockanum river and Snipsick pond. Pop. 2,900.

VERNON, p. t., Oneida co., N. Y., 108 ms. N. w. of Albany; from W. 371 ms. Watered by Oneida and Sconondoah creeks. Pop. 3,093.

VERNON, p. t., Sussex co., N. J., 92 ms. N. of Trenton; from W. 260 ms. Watered by Warwick, Pacack, and other creeks. Pop. 2,619.

VERNON, p. t., Crawford co., Pa. Pop. 1,299.

VERNON, p. v., Kent co., Del., 32 ms. s. w. of Dover; from W. 116 ms.

VERNON, p. v., Troup co., Ga., 129 ms. w. of Milledgeville; from W. 747 ms. Watered by Chattahoochee river.

VERNON, p. v., Autauga co., Ala.; from W. 852 ms. Watered by Alabama river and Swift creek.

VERNON, c. h., p. v., seat of justice of Hickman co., Tenn., 62 ms. s. w. of Nashville; from W. 746 ms. Watered by Pine creek.

VERNON, p. t., Trumbull co., O., 189 ms. N. E. of Columbus; from W. 304 ms. Pop. 828.

VERNON, t., Scioto co., O. Pop. 1,105.

VERNON, t., Clinton co., O. Pop. 1,468.

VERNON, t., Richland co., O

VERNON, c. h., p. v., seat of justice of Jennings co., Ind., 65 ms. s. E. of Indianapolis ; from W. 569 ms. Watered by Vernon fork of Muscatatack river.

VERNON, t., Hancock co., Ind. Pop. 908.

VERNON, t., Washington co., Ind. Pop. 1,796.

VERNON, p. t., Waukesha co., Wis.

VERNON, p. v., Madison co., Miss. Watered by Big Black river.

VERNON, p. o., Jackson parish, La.

VERNON, p. t., Shiawassee co., Mich. Pop. 674.

VERNON, p. v., seat of justice of Sutter co., Cal.

VERNON, p. o., Washington co., Flor.

VERNON CENTRE, p. v., Vernon township, Oneida co., N. Y., 105 ms. N. w. of Albany ; from W. 375 ms.

VERONA, p. v., Boone co., Ky., 53 ms. N. of Frankfort ; from W. 516 m.

VERONA, p. v., Dane co., Wis.

VERONA, p. t., Oneida co., N. Y., 116 ms. N. w. of Albany ; from W. 408 ms. Watered by Wood creek, Oneida lake, and Erie canal. Pop. 5,570.

VERONA MILLS, p. o., Oneida co., N. Y.

VERPLANCK, p. v., Cortland township, Westchester co., N. Y. Watered by Hudson river.

VERSAILLES, p. o., Perrysburgh township, Cattaraugus co., N. Y., 308 ms. w. of Albany ; from W. 361 ms.

VERSAILLES, p. t., Alleghany co., Pa.. Watered by Youghiogheny and Monongahela rivers.

VERSAILLES, p. v., Rutherford co., Tenn., 38 ms. s. of Nashville ; from W. 701 ms.

VERSAILLES, c. h., p. v., seat of justice of Woodford co., Ky., 12 ms. s. E. of Frankfort ; from W. 534 ms.

VERSAILLES, c. h., p. v., seat of justice of Ripley co., Ind., 69 ms. s. E. of Indianapolis ; from W. 545 ms. Watered by Laughery creek.

VERSAILLES, p. v., Brown co., Ill.

VERSAILLES, c. h., p. v., seat of justice of Morgan co., Mo., 36 ms. w. of Jefferson city ; from W. 1,020 ms.

VERSHIRE, p. t., Orange co., Vt., 31 ms. s. E. of Montpelier ; from W. 510 ms. Watered by Ompompanoosuc river. Pop. 1,071.

VESPER, p. o., Tully township. Onondaga co., N. Y., 135 ms. w. of Albany ; from W. 332 ms.

VESTAL, p. t., Broome co., N. Y., 147 ms. s. w. of Albany ; from W. 289 ms. Watered by Susquehanna river and Choconut creek. Pop. 2,054.

VESUVIUS FURNACE, p. o., Lincoln co., N. C., 162 ms. w. of Raleigh ; from W. 399 ms.

VETERAN, p. t., Chemung co., N. Y., 190 ms. s. w. of Albany ; from W. 290 ms. Watered by Seneca lake inlet. Pop. 2,698.

VETO, p. o., Washington co., O.

VEVAY, c. h., p. v., seat of justice of Switzerland co., Ind., 94 ms. s. E. of Indianapolis ; from W. 544 ms. Watered by Ohio river.

VEVAY, t., Ingham co., Mich. Pop. 781.

VICKER'S CREEK, p. o., Forsyth co., Ga.

VICKSBURGH, city, seat of justice of Warren co., Miss., 41 ms. w. of Jackson ; from W. 1,051 ms. It is situated on the east bank of the Mississippi river, and is quite a flourishing town. Considerable cotton is shipped at this port. Pop. 4,211.

VICKSVILLE, p. o., Southampton co., Va., 64 ms. s. of Richmond ; from W. 183 ms.

VICTOR, p. t., Ontario co., N. Y., 203 ms. w. of Albany ; from W. 353 ms. Watered by Mud creek. Pop. 2,230.

VICTOR, p. o., Clinton co., Mich.

VICTORIA COUNTY, situated in Texas. Area, —— square miles. Seat of justice, Victoria. Pop. in 1850, 1,448.

VICTORIA, p. v., Victoria co., Tex.

VICTORIA, p. o., Knox co., Ill.

VICTORIA, p. o., Daviess co., Mo.

VICTORIA, p. v., Bolivar co., Miss., 125 ms. N. of Jackson ; from W. 900 ms. Watered by Mississippi river.

VICTORY, t., Essex co., Vt. Watered by Moose river. Pop. 168.

VICTORY, p. t., Cayuga co., N. Y., 169 ms. w. of Albany ; from W. 352 ms. Watered by Sodus creek. Pop. 2,298.

VICTORY, p. o., Wayne co., Tenn.

VIDALIA, c. h., v., seat of justice of Concordia parish, La. Watered by Mississippi river.

VIENNA, p. t., Pickens co., Ala. ; from W. 868 ms. Watered by Tombigbee river.

VIENNA, p. t., Kennebec co., Me., 23 ms. N. w. of Augusta ; from W. 618 ms. Watered by a tributary of Sandy river. Pop. 851.

VIENNA, p. t., Oneida co., N. Y., 125 ms. w. of Albany ; from W. 391 ms. Watered by Fish creek and Oneida lake. Pop. 3,897.

VIENNA, v., Phelps township, Ontario co., N. Y. Watered by Canandaigua lake outlet and Flint creek.

VIENNA, p. v., Dorchester co., Md., 79 ms. s. E. of Annapolis ; from W. —— ms. Watered by Nanticoke river.

VIENNA, p. v., Dooly co., Ga., 85 ms. s. w. of Milledgeville ; from W. 742 ms. Watered by Indian creek.

VIENNA, p. t., Trumbull co., O., 178 ms. N. E. of Columbus ; from W. 298 ms. Pop. 1,007.

VIENNA, p. v., Macomb co., Mich.

VIENNA, t., Genesee co., Mich. Pop. 390.

VIENNA, p. t., Scott co., Ind., 85 ms. s. of Indianapolis : from W. 585 ms. Pop. 1,654.

VIENNA, c. h., p. v., seat of justice of Johnson co., Ill. Watered by east fork of Cash river.

VIENNA, p. o., Jackson parish, La.

VIENNA, p. o., Walworth co., Wis.

VIENNA CROSS ROADS, p. o., Harmony township, Clark co., O.

VIGO COUNTY, situated on the west boundary of Indiana river, with Wabash river on the west. Area, 400 square miles. Face of the country, diversified ; soil, fertile. Seat of justice, Terre Haute. Pop. in 1820, 3,390 ; in 1830, 5,766 ; in 1840, 12,076 ; in 1850, 15,283.

VILLAGE GREEN, p. v., Ashton township, Delaware co., Pa., 89 ms. E. of Harrisburgh ; from W. 123 ms.

VILLAGE SPRINGS, p. o., Blount co., Ala.

VILLANOVA, p. t., Chautauque co., N. Y., 323 ms. w. of Albany ; from W. 346 ms. Watered by Connewango creek. Pop. 1,536.

VILLANOW, p. o., Walker co., Ga.

VILLA RICA, p. o., Carroll co., Ga., 178 ms. N. w. of Milledgeville ; from W. 760 ms.

VILLE PLATTE, p. o., St. Landre parish, La.

VILULA, p. o., Russell co., Ala.

VINAL HAVEN, p. t., Waldo co., Me. It consists of Fox islands, in Penobscot bay. Pop. 1,252.

VINCENNES, c. h., p. v., seat of justice of Knox co., Ind., 118 ms. s. w. of Indianapolis ; from W. 688 ms. Watered by Wabash river. Pop. 2,070.

VINCENT, p. t., Chester co., Pa., 73 ms. s. E. of Harrisburgh ; from W. 153 ms. Watered by Stony, French, and Riding creeks, and Schuylkill river.

VINCENTOWN, p. v., Northampton township, Burlington co., N. J., 26 ms. s. of Trenton ; from W. 160 ms. Watered by south branch of Rancocus creek and by Stop the Jade creek.

VINEGAR HILL, p. o., Jo-Daviess co., Ill.

VINE GROVE, p. o., Washington co., Tex.

VINEYARD, p. t., Grand Isle co., Vt., 78 ms. N. w. of Montpelier ; from W. 551 ms. It consists of Vineyard island, in Lake Champlain.

VINEYARD, p. v., Irwin co., Ga.

VINEYARD, t., Washington co., Ark. Pop. 711.

VINEYARD, t., Lawrence co., Mo. Pop. 529.

VINEYARD MILLS, p. o., Huntingdon co., Pa., 87 ms. w. of Harrisburgh ; from W. 135 ms.

VINEY GROVE, p. o., Lincoln co., Tenn.

VINLAND, p. o., Winnebago co., Wis.

VINTON COUNTY, situated in the southerly part of Ohio. Area, —— square miles. Seat of justice, McArthur. Pop. in 1850, 9,353.

VINTON, p. t., Vinton co., O. Watered by Raccoon creek. Pop. 460.

VINTON, p. v., Huntingdon township, Gallia co., O., 92 ms. s. of Columbus ; fr. W. 367 ms. Watered by Big Raccoon creek. Pop. 460.

VINTON, c. h., p. v., seat of justice of Benton co., Iowa.

VIOLA, p. o., Delaware co., Iowa.

VIOLET, p. t., Fairfield co., O.

VIOLY, p. o., Blount co., Ala.

VIRDEN, p. o., Macoupin co., Ill.

VIRGIL, p. t., Cortland co., N. Y., 149 ms. w. of Albany ; from W. 308 ms. Watered by East Owego creek and Toughnioga river. Pop. 2,410.

VIRGIL, p. o., Fulton co., Ill.

VIRGINIA, c. h., p. v., seat of justice of Cass co., Ill., 36 ms. w. of Springfield ; from W. 800 ms.

VIRGINIA, p. t., Coshocton co., O. Pop. 1,226.

VIRGINIA GROVE, p. o., Louisa co., Iowa.

VIRGINIA MILLS, p. o., Buckingham co., Va., 69 ms. w. of Richmond ; from W. 143 ms.

VIRGINIA MINES, p. o., Franklin co., Mo.

VIRGINIA, one of the United States, popularly known as the "Old Dominion," is situated between 36° 33′ and 40° 43′ N. latitude, and 75° 25′ and 83° 40′ west longitude from Greenwich : and is bounded north by Ohio, Pennsylvania, and Maryland; northeast by Maryland, from which it is separated by the Potomac ; east by the Atlantic; south by North Carolina and Tennessee ; west by Kentucky, from which it is separated by the Cumberland mountains and Big Sandy river ; and northwest by Ohio, from which it is separated by the river Ohio. Its superficial area is 61,352 square miles.

Physical Aspect.—The face of the country of this state, though exhibiting but little grandeur, is greatly diversified, and in some parts is rich and pleasing, in the continued outline of hill, valley, river, and plain. The soil, too, is as varied as the surface, as every grade of fertility and sterility is to be met with, from the richest to the most barren. Virginia may be divided into four zones, essentially differing from each other. The first, which extends from the coast to the head of tidewater, at Fredericksburgh, Richmond, &c., over 100 miles, is low and flat, in some places fenny, in others sandy, and on the margin of rivers the soil is composed of a rich loam. The second division extends from the head of tide-water to the Blue ridge. Near the former the surface is level ; higher up the streams it becomes undulating and swelling ; and, as we approach the mountain, it is often broken and abrupt. The soil is divided into sections, unequal in quality, running parallel to each other, and extending quite across the state. The parallel of Chesterfield, Henrico, Hanover, &c., is thin and sandy, and, except on the borders of the rivers, is unproductive. That of Goochland, Cumberland, Prince Edward, Halifax, &c., is generally fertile. Fluvanna, Buckingham, Campbell, Pittsylvania, again, are poor ; and Culpeper, Orange, Albemarle, Bedford, &c., are rich, though frequently consisting of a stony, broken soil, reposing on a substratum of tenacious and red-colored clay. The third division embraces the valley between the Blue ridge and the great North Shenandoah and Branch mountain, and the Allegany chain, which, with little interruption, extends from the Potomac to Carolina and Tennessee. The surface of the valley in some instances is broken by sharp, solitary mountains, detached from the general chain, the flanks of which are nearly bare, or but thinly covered with stunted pines. The soil in the valley consists of a rich mould, formed on a bed of limestone. The fourth division extends from the Alleganies to the river Ohio, and is composed of a country wild and broken, in some parts fertile, but generally barren or poor. The surface is uneven and hilly, but the soil of a great proportion of Randolph and the adjacent counties, in the northwest part of the state, is excellent, and well adapted for grazing.

Mountains.—The Allegany range, including its numerous ridges, covers the whole middle sections of the state. Among the local names, besides the Blue ridge, may be mentioned the Cumberland, Great North Shenandoah, Branch, Great Flat Top, Iron, and Cacapon mountains.

Rivers, Lakes, and Bays.—The principal rivers are, the Potomac, James, Shenandoah, Rappahannock, Pamunky, Mattapony, York, Rivanna, Elizabeth, Appomattox, Nottoway, Staunton, Meherrin, Ohio, Great Kanawha, Sandy, Little Kanawha, Cheat, and Monongahela. Drummond lake lies in the Dismal swamp, which serves as a feeder to the main trunk of the Dismal-Swamp canal. The lower part of Chesapeake bay lies wholly in this state. Among the lesser bays are the Pokomoke, Sinepuxent, and Mob Jack.

Islands.—Along the coast there is a long chain of low, flat islands, the chief of which are, Wallop's, Matomkin, Cedar, Paramore's, Hog, Prout's, and Smith's.

Climate.—The climate of the tide-water region is generally healthy, except in the months of August, September, and October, during which it is hot and moist, and bilious complaints or intermittents prevail. As we approach the Blue ridge, the inhabitants are more robust and healthy than in any other part of the state. West of the mountains, the climate is salubrious and cool.

Productive Resources.—The principal products of this state are horses, mules, neat cattle, sheep, swine, poultry, butter, cheese, wine, sugar, wax, silk, cotton, wool, hemp, flax, tobacco, rice, wheat, rye, barley, oats, buckwheat, potatoes, and Indian corn. Of the fossil and mineral resources, gold, copper, iron, lead, coal, marble, limestone, and salt, are the most important. But the most valuable are iron, coal, and salt. The belt of country in which gold is found is in the county of Spottsylvania, and the regions adjacent. The coal-fields are very extensive, anthracite being found on the easterly side of the Alleganies, and bituminous on the western. Salt-springs occur on the banks of the Great Kanawha, where salt is manufactured in great abundance.

Manufactures.—Iron ranks first among the manufactures of Virginia, embracing machinery, firearms, hardware, cutlery, &c. Cotton and woollen manufactures rank next, in which about $2,500,000 is invested. In the manufacture of tobacco about $2,000,000 is invested.

Railroads and Canals.—There are about 700 miles of railroad in operation in Virginia, and more in process of construction. The most important canals in the state are, the James River and the Kanawha canal, reaching from Richmond to Lynchburg, 146 miles, and the Dismal-Swamp canal, 23 miles.

Commerce.—The foreign exports and imports of Virginia amount to about $5,000,000 annually. The domestic exports and imports amount to about $25,000,000 annually. The principal articles of domestic export are tobacco and flour. The shipping owned in the state is about 60,000 tons.

Population.—In 1790, 748,308 ; in 1800, 880,200 ; in 1810, 974,642 ; in 1820, 1,065,379 ; in 1830, 1,211,405 ; in 1840, 1,239,797 ; in 1850, 1,421,661. Number of slaves in 1790, 203,427 ; in 1800, 345,796 ; in 1810, 392,518 ; in 1820, 425,153 ; in 1830, 469,757 ; in 1840, 448,987 ; in 1850, 472,528.

Education.—The principal literary institutions of Virginia are, William and Mary college, at Williamsburg ; Hampden Sidney college, in Prince Edward county; Washington college, at Lexington ; the university, at Charlottesville ; Randolph college, at Boylstown; Emory and Henry college, at Glade Spring ; Rector college, in Taylor county ; Bethany college, at Bethany ; and Richmond college, at Richmond. There are also a military institute at Lexington ; medical schools at Richmond, Charlottesville (attached to the university), and Winchester; law schools, attached to the university and William and Mary college; and theological seminaries in Fairfax and Prince Edward counties, and at Richmond. There are also about 500 academies and 2,500 common schools in the state. The permanent literary fund of Virginia is over $1,500,000.

Government.—The legislative power is vested in a senate of 50 members, chosen for four years, one half biennially, and a house of delegates, of 152 members, chosen biennially. The executive power is vested in a governor, elected by the people, for four years, who is ineligible for the succeeding term ; and a lieutenant-governor, elected for a like term. The legislature meets biennially, at Richmond. A secretary of state, treasurer, and auditor, are elected by the assembly. The judiciary power is vested in a supreme court of appeals, district courts, and circuit courts, all the judges of which are elected by the people. The right of suffrage is extended to every white male citizen twenty-one years of age, who has resided two years in the state, and one year in the place where he offers to vote. Votes, in all elections, are *viva voce ;* dumb persons may vote by ballot.

History.—The present state of Virginia embraces but a portion of the ancient "Virginia," as granted to Sir Walter Raleigh, in 1584, which included all the lands he should discover between the thirty-third and fortieth degrees of north latitude, and which name became finally restricted to what now constitutes this state. Under this charter, Raleigh planted a colony on the island of Roanoke ; but, after repeated trials and disasters, the patent was vacated, and the country was again left to the quiet possession of the Indians. The first permanent settlement in America, by the English, was made at Jamestown, in 1607, by 105 adventurers. A second charter was granted to the London company, in 1609, radically changing the constitution, and enlarging the territory of the colony along the coast, within the limits

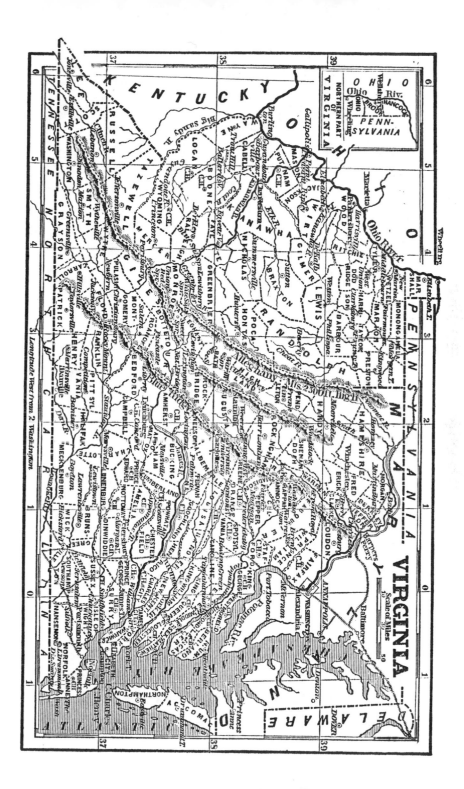

of 200 miles north and 200 miles south of Old Point Comfort; that is, from the southern limits of North Carolina to the northern boundary of Maryland, and extending westward from sea to sea. But so vague were the views of the company, or the adventurers, under this patent, that discord and wretchedness compelled the settlers to break up their establishment in 1610. The year following, Sir Thomas Gates arrived with 300 immigrants, and assumed the government of the colony, which then numbered 700 men. In 1612, a third charter was granted to the London company; but the colony remained under anarchy and tyranny until 1619, when martial law was abolished, and the first provincial assembly was convened at Jamestown. In 1621, the company granted to their colony a "written constitution," which, with singular liberality, ordained that a general assembly, chosen by the people, should be convened annually, its acts to be subject to the supervision of the company in England. The acts of the company, also, were not binding, till ratified by the assembly. It established the right of trial by jury. These rights and privileges were ever after claimed by Virginia, and formed the basis of her civil freedom. In 1622, a general massacre of the English was attempted by the Indians, and 347 of them perished. The rest were saved by the timely warning of Pocahontas, daughter of Powhatan, the Indian king. She was like a preserving angel to the feeble settlement. In 1624, the London company was dissolved, and the colony was again subject to the crown. In 1644, another general massacre of the whites was attempted, but without success, the blow having been fortunately averted by the skill, prudence, and courage, of Captain John Smith, one of the most efficient men in the colony. During the commonwealth, under Cromwell, to the restoration of Charles II., in 1660, Virginia was left almost entirely to her own independence. Her governors during this period were chosen by the burgesses, who were the representatives of the people. In 1673, Charles II. granted to Lord Culpeper, and the earl of Arlington, "all the dominion of land and water called Virginia," for thirty-one years. Within two years after this event the representative system was virtually abolished, and the liberties of the people were otherwise seriously abridged. This, together with the pressure of increasing grievances, resulted in open rebellion, followed by Indian aggressions, which continued for four years. In 1677, Culpeper, after purchasing the rights of Arlington, was appointed governor over the colony for life, and Virginia became a proprietary government, which remained in force until 1684, when the grant was recalled, and Culpeper expelled from office. The remaining portion of the history of this state is marked with few incidents of importance, down to the period of the Revolution, except those in the French and Indian war, between 1754 and 1763. In 1786, that part of Virginia now constituting the state of Ohio was erected by act of Congress into the "Western Territory," the name of which was afterward changed to the "Territory northwest of the river Ohio." The same year, the district of Kentucky was also set apart, by act of Congress, into a new territory, but the separation from the "Old Dominion" did not take place before 1792. The first constitution of Virginia was adopted in 1776, which was revised and amended in 1830, and continued in operation till October, 1851, when a new one was adopted. The constitution of the United States was ratified in 1788. Motto of the seal, *Sic semper tyrannis*—" So be it ever to tyrants"—in allusion to the emblem on the seal of an Amazon, resting on a spear with one hand, and holding a sword in the other, with her foot on Tyranny, which is represented by a prostrate man, with a crown fallen from his head, a broken chain in his left hand, and a scourge in his right.

VIRGINSVILLE, p. v., Berks co., Pa., 68 ms. E. of Harrisburgh; from W. 160 ms.

VISCHER'S FERRY, p. o., Clifton Park township, Saratoga co., N. Y., 17 ms. N. w. of Albany; from W. 387 ms.

VISTA, p. o., Lewisborough township, Westchester co., N. Y., 119 ms. s. of Albany; from W. 276 ms.

VOGANSVILLE, p. o., Lancaster co., Pa.

VOLCANO, p. o., Calaveras co., Cal.

VOLGA CITY, p. v., Clayton co., Iowa.

VOLINIA, p. t., Cass co., Mich. Pop. 607.

VOLNEY, p. t., Oswego co., N. Y., 152 ms. N. w. of Albany; from W. 375 ms. Watered by Big Black creek and Oswego river. Pop. 2,966.

VOLNEY, p. o., Logan co., Ky.

VOLUNTOWN, p. t., Windham co., Ct., 56 ms. N. E. of Hartford; from W. 374 ms. Watered by Pachaug river. Pop. 1,064.

VOLUSIA, p. o., Westfield township, Chautauque co., N. Y., 348 ms. w. of Albany; from W. 351 ms.

VOLUSIA, p. v., Marion co., Flor. Watered by St. John's river.

VUE DE L'EAU, p. o., Bristol co., Mass.

W.

WABASH COUNTY, situated toward the north part of Indiana, and traversed by Wabash river. Area, 415 square miles. Seat of justice, Wabash. Pop. in 1840, 2,756; in 1850, 12,138.

WABASH COUNTY, situated on the southeasterly boundary of Illinois, with Wabash river on the southwest. Area, 180 square miles. Seat of justice, Mount Carmel. Pop. in 1840, 4,240; in 1850, 4,690.

WABASH, c. h., p. v., seat of justice of Wabash co., Ind., 93 ms. N. of Indianapolis; from W. 582 ms. Watered by Wabash river.

WABASH, t., Adams co., Ind. Pop. 410.

WABASH, t., Fountain co., Ind. Pop. 1,300.

WABASH, t., Gibson co., Ind.

WABASH, t., Tippecanoe co., Ind. Pop. 1,196.

WABASH POINT, p. o., Coles co., Ill.

WABASHAW COUNTY, situated in Minnesota territory. Area, —— square miles. Seat of justice, Wabashaw. Pop. in 1850, 243.

WABASHAW, p. o., seat of justice of Wabashaw co., Minn.

WABLEAU, p. t., Henry co., Mo.

WACAHOOTIE. p. o., Marion co., Ind.

WACHITA COUNTY, situated in the south part of Arkansas, and traversed by Wachita river. Area, —— square miles. Seat of justice, Camden. Pop. in 1850, 3,304.

WACHITA PARISH, situated in the north part of Louisiana, and traversed by Wachita river. Area, 2,090 square miles. Soil unproductive, except along the river. Seat of justice, Monroe. Pop. in 1820, 2,896; in 1830. 5,140; in 1840, 4,640; in 1850, 5,308.

WACOOCHEE, p. v., Russell co., Ala.; from W. 774 ms.

WACONDA CREEK, p. t., Carroll co., Mo.

WACOOSTA, p. o., Fond du Lac co., Iowa.

WACOUSTA, p. v., Clinton co., Mich., 101 ms. N. w. of Detroit; from W. 604 ms.

WACO VILLAGE, p. o., Milan co., Tex.

WADDAM'S GROVE, p. t., Stephenson co., Ill., 212 ms. N. of Springfield; from W. 844 ms.

WADDINGTON, p. v., Madrid township, St. Lawrence co., N. Y., 228 ms. N. w. of Albany; from W. 495 ms. Watered by St. Lawrence river.

WADEBOROUGH, p. o., Livingston parish, La.

WADE'S, p. o.. Bedford co., Va., 137 ms. w. of Richmond; from W. 212 ms.

WADESBOROUGH, c. h., p. v., seat of justice of Anson co., N. C., 143 ms. s. E. of Raleigh; from W. 412 ms. Watered by Neuse river.

WADESBOROUGH, c. h., p. v., seat of justice of Callaway co., Ky., 255 ms. s. w. of Frankfort; from W. 782 ms.

WADESTOWN, p. o., Monongalia co., Va.

WADESVILLE, p. o., Clarke co., Va.

WADHAM'S MILLS, p. v., Westport township, Essex co., N. Y., 131 ms. N. of Albany; from W. 502 ms.

WADING RIVER, p. v., Riverhead township, Suffolk co., N. Y. 215 ms. s. E. of Albany; from W. 295 ms. Watered by Wading river.

WADSWORTH, p. t., Medina co., O., 127 ms. N. E. of Columbus; from W. 342 ms. Pop. 1,622.

WAGGONER'S RIPPLE, p. o., Adams co., O.

WAGGONTOWN, p. v., Chester co., Pa., 62 ms. s. E. of Harrisburgh; from W. 132 ms.

WAGRAM, p. o., Accomac co., Va.

WAHNATAH COUNTY, situated in Minnesota territory. Area, —— square miles. Seat of justice, ——. Pop. in 1850, 318.

WAHOLOCK, p. o.. Kemper co., Miss., 130 ms. N. E. of Jackson; from W. 891 ms.

WAHTAWAH, p. o., Adair co., Iowa.

WAITE. p. o., Washington co., Me.

WAITSFIELD, p. t., Washington co., Vt., 19 ms. s. w. of Montpelier ; from W. 506 ms. Watered by Mad river. Pop. 1,021.

WAKASASSA, p. o., Levy co., Flor.

WAKATOMIKA, p. o., Washington township, Coshocton co., O., 75 ms. N. E. of Columbus ; from W. 351 ms.

WAKE COUNTY, situated in the central part of North Carolina, and traversed by Neuse river. Area, 1,140 square miles. Seat of justice, Raleigh. Pop. in 1810, 17,585 ; in 1820, 20,102 ; in 1830, 20,398 ; in 1840, 21,118 ; in 1850, 24,888.

WAKEFIELD, p. t., Carroll co., N. H., 46 ms. N. E. of Concord ; from W. 527 ms. Watered by Saco river and Lovewell's pond. Pop. 1,405.

WAKEFIELD, p. v., Kingston township, Washington co., R. I., 37 ms. s. of Providence; from W. 393 ms.

WAKEFIELD, p. v., Carroll co., Md., 68 ms. N. w. of Annapolis ; from W. 69 ms.

WAKEFIELD, p. o., Wake co., N. C., 20 ms. N. of Raleigh ; from W. 278 ms.

WAKEMAN, p. t., Huron co., O., 107 ms. N. E. of Columbus ; from W. 385 ms. Pop. 704.

WAKULLA COUNTY, situated on the south boundary of Florida, with the gulf of Mexico on the south, and Ocklockony river on the west. Area, —— square miles. Seat of justice, ————. Pop. in 1850, ————.

WALCOTT, p. o., Greene co., Ark.

WALDEN, p. t., Caledonia co., Vt., 29 ms. N. E. of Montpelier ; from W. 544 ms. Watered by head-waters of Onion and Lamoille rivers. Pop. 910.

WALDEN, p. v., Montgomery township, Orange co., N. Y.. 90 ms. s. of Albany ; from W. 292 ms. Watered by Walkill river.

WALDEN'S CREEK, p o., Sevier co., Tenn.

WALDENSVILLE. p. o., Schoharie co., N. Y., 27 ms. w. of Albany ; from W. 391 ms.

WALDO COUNTY, situated in the south part of Maine, with Penobscot river and Penobscot bay on the southeast. Area, 812 square miles. Seat of justice, Belfast. Pop. in 1830, 29,788 ; in 1840, 41,509 ; in 1850, 47,129.

WALDO. p. t., Waldo co., Me., 47 ms. N. E. of Augusta ; from W. 641 ms. Watered by streams falling into Belfast bay. Pop. 812.

WALDO, p. v., Delaware co., O.

WALDO, p. o., Wright co., Mo.

WALDOBOROUGH, p. t., Lincoln co., Me., 00 ms. s. E. of Augusta ; from W. 606 ms. Watered by Muscongus river and Muscongus bay. Pop. 4,199.

WALDRON, p. o., Scott co., Ark.

WALES, p. t., Kennebec co., Me., 23 ms. s. w. of Augusta ; from W. 582 ms. Watered by a tributary of Androscoggin river. Pop. 612.

WALES, p. t., Hampden co., Mass.. 74 ms. s w. of Boston ; from W. 374 ms. Watered by a tributary of Quinnebaug river. Pop. 711.

WALES, p. t., Erie co., N. Y., 272 ms. w. of Albany ; from W. 369 ms. Watered by Seneca creek. Pop. 2,124.

WALES, p. o., Ogle co., Ill.

WALES, p. o., St. Clair co. Mich.

WALES CENTRE, p. o., Wales township, Erie co., N. Y.

WALESKA, p. o., Floyd co., Ga.

WALESVILLE, p. v., Whitestown township, Oneida co., N. Y.

WALHONDING. p. o., Coshocton co., O., 76 ms. N. E. of Columbus ; from W. 355 ms.

WALKER COUNTY, situated on the north and west boundary of Georgia. Area, 700 square miles. Face of the country, mountainous. Seat of justice, Lafayette. Pop. in 1840, 6,572 ; in 1850, 13,109.

WALKER COUNTY, situated toward the northwest part of Alabama. Area, 1,500 square miles. Seat of justice, Jasper. Pop. in 1830, 2,202 ; in 1840, 4,032 ; in 1850 5,124.

WALKER COUNTY, situated toward the east part of Texas, with Trinity river on the northeast. Area, —— square miles. Seat of justice, Huntsville. Pop. in 1850, 3,964.

WALKER, p. t., Centre co., Pa., 94 ms. N. w. of Harrisburgh ; from W. 186 ms. Watered by Little Fishing creek. Pop. 1,221.

WALKER, t., Huntingdon co., Pa. Watered by Raystown branch of Juniata river. Pop. 1,108.

WALKER t., Juniata co., Pa.

WALKER, p. t., Cole co., Mo.

WALKER. p. t., Rush co., Ind.

WALKER'S, p. o., Livingston co., Ky., 257 ms. s. w. of Frankfort ; from W. 789 ms.

WALKER'S, p. o., McDonough co., Ill.

WALKER'S, p. o., Colleton district, S. C.

WALKER'S CHURCH, p. o., Appomattox co., Va., 86 ms. s. w. of Richmond ; from W. 176 ms.

WALKER'S GROVE, p. o., Fulton co., Ill.

WALKER'S MILLS, p. o., Alleghany co., Pa., 208 ms. w. of Harrisburgh ; from W. 253 ms.

WALKER'S NECK, p. o., Brown co., Ill.

WALKERSVILLE. p. o., Frederick co., Md., 81 ms. N. w. of Annapolis ; from W. 49 ms.

WALKERSVILLE, p. o., Union co., N. C.

WALKERTON, p. v., King and Queen co.. Va., 40 ms. N. E. of Richmond ; from W. 128 ms. Watered by Mattapony river.

WALKERTOWN, p. o., Forsyth co., N. C.

WALKERVILLE, p. o., Lycoming co., Pa., 103 ms. N. of Harrisburgh ; from W. 213 ms.

WALLACE, p. v., Jones co., Ga., 13 ms. s. w. of Milledgeville ; from W. 661 ms.

WALLACE, p. v., Fountain co., Ind., 70 ms. N. w. of Indianapolis ; from W. 638 ms.

WALLACE, p. o., Iowa co., Wis.

WALLACE, p. o., Chester co., Pa.

WALLACE CREEK, p. o., Independence co., Ark.

WALLACE'S CROSS ROADS, p. o., Anderson co., Tenn.

WALLACEVILLE, p. o, Venango co., Pa.

WALLDEN'S RIDGE, p. o., Marion co., Tenn.

WALLED LAKE, p. o.. Novi township, Oakland co., Mich., 38 ms. N. w. of Detroit ; from W. 554 ms.

WALLER, p. o., Ross co., O.

WALLINGFORD, p. t., Rutland co., Vt., 71 ms. s. w. of Montpelier ; from W. 452 ms. Watered by Otter creek and Mill river. Pop. 1,688.

WALLINGFORD, p. t., New Haven co., Ct., 24 ms. s. of Hartford ; from W. 313 ms. Watered by Quinnipiac river. Pop. 2,595.

WALLINGFORD, p. o., Will co., Ill.

WALLING'S FERRY, p. o., Rusk co., Tex.

WALLKILL, p. t., Orange co., N. Y. Watered by Shawangunk creek and Wallkill river. Pop 4,942.

WALLONIA, p. v., Trigg co., Ky., 234 ms. s. w. of Frankfort ; from W. 761 ms. Watered by Muddy fork of Little river.

WALLSVILLE, p. o. Luzerne co., Pa., 154 ms. N. E. of Harrisburgh ; from W. 200 ms.

WALNFORD, p. o., Monmouth co., N. J.

WALNUT, p. o. Juniata co., Pa., 51 ms. N. w. of Harrisburgh ; from W. 142 ms.

WALNUT, t., Fairfield co., O. Situated on the Ohio canal. Pop. 2,130.

WALNUT, p. o., Gallia co., O. Pop. 905.

WALNUT, p. o., Holmes co., O. Watered by a tributary of Sugar creek. Pop. 1,452.

WALNUT, t., Pickaway co., O. Watered by Scioto river. Pop. 1,840.

WALNUT, t., Montgomery co., Ind. Pop. 1,059.

WALNUT, p. t., Phillips co., Ark. Pop. 288.

WALNUT, p. o., Jefferson co., Iowa.

WALNUT BEND, p. o., Phillips co., Ark.

WALNUT BOTTOM, p. o., Cumberland co., Pa.

WALNUT BOTTOM. p. o., Henderson co., Ky.

WALNUT CAMP, p. o., Poinsett co., Ark.

WALNUT COVE, p. o., Stokes co., N. C.

WALNUT CREEK, p. o., Claiborne parish, La.

WALNUT CREEK, p. o., Grant co., Ind.

WALNUT CREEK, p. o., Holmes co., O.

WALNUT CREEK, p. o., Buncombe co., N. C.

WALNUT FLAT, p. o., Lincoln co., Ky., 58 ms. s. E. of Frankfort ; from W. 571 ms.

WALNUT FOREST, p. o., Greene co., Mo., 150 ms. s. w. of Jefferson city ; from W. 1,065 ms.

WALNUT FORK, p. o., Jones co., Iowa.

WALNUT GROVE, p. o., Morris co., N. J., 58 ms. N. of Trenton ; from W. 230 ms.

WALNUT GROVE, p. o., Kanawha co., Va., 333 ms. N. w. of Richmond ; from W. 370 ms.

WALNUT GROVE, p. o., Orange co., N. C., 48 ms. N. w. of Raleigh ; from W. 266 ms.

WALNUT GROVE, p. o., Spartanburgh district, S. C., 106 ms. N. w. of Columbia ; from W. 481 ms.

WALNUT GROVE, p. o., Knox co., Ill.

WALNUT GROVE, p. o., Scott co., Iowa.

WALNUT GROVE, p. o., Overton co., Tenn.

WALNUT GROVE, p. o., Walker co., Ga.

WALNUT HILL, p. o., Lee co., Va., 410 ms. w. of Richmond ; from W. 478 ms.
WALNUT HILL, p. o., Franklin co., Ga.
WALNUT HILL, p. o., Hamilton co., O., 117 ms. s. w. of Columbus ; from W. 490 ms.
WALNUT HILL, p. o., Lafayette co., Ark.
WALNUT HILL, p. o., Panola co., Tex.
WALNUT HILL, p. o., Marion co., Ill., 114 ms. s. e. of Springfield ; from W. 775 ms.
WALNUT HILL, p. o., Buchanan co., Mo.
WALNUT HILL, p. o., Rapides parish, La.
WALNUT HILL, p. o., Fayette co., Ky.
WALNUT LANE, p. o., Surry co., N. C., 154 ms. s. w. of Raleigh ; from W. 360 ms.
WALNUT PEAK, p. o., Tishamingo co., Miss.
WALNUT POST, p. o., Lauderdale co., Tenn.
WALNUT RIDGE, p. o., Washington co., Ind., 86 ms. s. of Indianapolis ; from W. 607 ms.
WALNUT RIDGE, p. o., Phillips co., Ark.
WALNUT SPRINGS, p. o., Greene co., Wis.
WALNUT VALLEY, p. o., Madison co., Ky.
WALNUT VALLEY, p. o., Warren co., N. J., 70 ms. n. of Trenton ; from W. 225 ms.
WALNUT VALLEY, p. o., Rock Island co., Ill.
WALNUT VALLEY, p. o., Marion co., Tenn.
WALPACK, t., Sussex co., N. J., 91 ms. n. w. of Trenton ; from W. 248 ms. Watered by Flat kill. Pop. 783.
WALPOLE, p. t., Cheshire co., N. H., 63 ms. s. w. of Concord ; from W. 444 ms. Watered by Cold and Connecticut rivers. Pop. 2,034.
WALPOLE, p. t., Norfolk co., Mass., 21 ms. s. w. of Boston : from W. 427 ms. Watered by Neponset river. Pop. 1,929.
WALPOLE, p. o., Hancock co., Ind..
WALPOLE EAST, p. o., Walpole township, Norfolk co., Mass., 19 ms. s. w. of Boston ; from W. 426 ms.
WALSER'S MILLS, p. o., Davidson co., N. C.
WALTERBOROUGH, c. h., p. v., seat of justice of Colleton district, S. C., 99 ms. s. of Columbia ; from W. 605 ms. Watered by a tributary of Ashepoo river.
WALTHAM, t., Hancock co., Me. Pop. 394.
WALTHAM, t., Addison co., Vt. Watered by Otter creek. Pop. 270.
WALTHAM, p. t., Middlesex co., Mass., 10 ms. w. of Boston ; from W. 430 ms. Watered by Charles river. Pop. in 1830, 1,859 ; in 1840, 2,504 ; in 1850, 4,464.
WALTHOURVILLE, p. o., Liberty co., Ga.
WALTON COUNTY, situated toward the north part of Georgia. Area, 320 square miles. Seat of justice, Monroe. Pop. in 1810, 1,026 ; in 1820, 4,192 ; in 1830, 10,929 ; in 1840, 10.209 ; in 1850, 10,821.
WALTON COUNTY, situated on the north boundary of Florida, with Choctawhatchee bay on the south, and Choctawhatchee river on the east. Area. 1,584 square miles. Seat of justice, Euchee Anna. Pop. in 1840, 1,401 ; in 1850, 1,379.
WALTON, p. t., Delaware co., N. Y., 97 ms. s. w. of Albany ; from W. 321 ms. Watered by Delaware river and its west branch. Pop. 2,271.
WALTON, p. o., Boone co., Ky.
WALTON, p. o., Kanawha co., Va.
WALTON, t., Eaton co., Mich. Pop. 464.
WALTON, p. o., Newberry district, S. C.
WALTONHAM, p. v., St. Louis co., Mo., 121 ms. e. of Jefferson city ; from W. 817 ms.
WALTON'S FORD, p. o., Habersham co., Ga.
WALWORTH COUNTY, situated on the south boundary of Wisconsin, with Geneva lake at the north. Area, 675 square miles. Face of the country, undulating ; soil, rich. Seat of justice, Elkhorn. Pop. in 1840, 2,611 ; in 1850, 17,862.
WALWORTH, p. t., Wayne co., N. Y., 205 ms. w. of Albany ; from W. 362 ms. Watered by Lake Ontario. Pop. 1,981.
WALWORTH, p. t., Walworth co., Wis., 69 ms. s. e. of Madison ; from W. 778 ms.
WAMPSVILLE, p. v., Lenox township, Madison co., N. Y., 117 ms. w. of Albany ; from W. 362 ms. Watered by Cowassalon creek.
WANCONDA, p. o., Lake co., Ill.
WANTAGE, p. t., Sussex co., N. J. Watered by Deep Clove river and Papakating creek. Pop. 3,934.
WAPAUKONETTA, p. v., Allen co., O., 101 ms. n. w. of Columbus ; from W. 484 ms.
WAPELLO COUNTY, situated in the southeasterly part of Iowa, and traversed by Des Moines river. Area, —— square miles. Seat of justice, Ottumwa. Pop. in 1850, 8,471.

WAPELLO, c. h., p. v., seat of justice of Louisa co., Iowa. Pop. 937.
WAPPINGER'S FALLS, p. o., Fishkill township. Dutchess co., N. Y., 78 ms. s. of Albany ; from W. 294 ms.
WAQUOIT, p. o., Barnstable co., Mass.
WARD, t., Athens co., O.
WARD. p. t., Randolph co., Ind.
WARDBOROUGH, p. o., Warren co., N. Y.
WARDENSVILLE, p. o., Hardy co., Va., 177 ms. n. w. of Richmond ; from W. 105 ms.
WARDSBOROUGH, p. t., Windham co., Vt., 120 ms. s. of Montpelier ; from W. 447 ms. Watered by a tributary of West river. Pop. 1,125.
WARD'S GROVE, p. o., Jo-Daviess co., Ill.
WARE COUNTY, situated on the south boundary of Georgia, and traversed by Santilla river. Area, 3,440 square miles. Face of the country, level, being partly covered by Okefinoke swamp. Seat of justice, Waresborough. Pop. in 1830, 1,885 ; in 1840, 2,323 ; in 1850, 3,888.
WARE, p. t., Hampshire co., Mass., 68 ms. w. of Boston ; from W. 385 ms. Watered by Ware and Swift rivers. Pop. 3,785.
WAR EAGLE, p. t., Madison co., Ark.
WAREHAM, p. t., Plymouth co., Mass., 53 ms. s. e. of Boston ; from W. 446 ms. Watered by Agawam river and Buzzard's bay. Pop. 3,186.
WAREHOUSE POINT, p. v., East Windsor township, Hartford co.. Ct., 14 ms. n. of Hartford ; from W. 349 ms.
WARESBOROUGH, c. h., p. v., seat of justice of Ware co., Ga., 212 ms. s. e. of Milledgeville ; from W. 811 ms. Watered by Santilla river.
WARFIELDSBURGH. p. v., Carroll co., Md., 56 ms. n. w. of Annapolis ; from W. 61 ms.
WARFORDSBURGH, p. t., Fulton co., Pa., 85 ms. s. w. of Harrisburgh ; from W. 100 ms.
WAR GAP, p. o., Hawkins co., Tenn.
WAR HILL, p. o., Hall co., Ga.
WARM FORK, p. o., Oregon co., Mo.
WARMINSTER, p. t., Bucks co., Pa. Watered by tributaries of Pennypack creek. Pop. 1,007.
WARMINSTER, p. v., Nelson co., Va. Watered by James river.
WARM SPRINGS, p. v., Buncombe co., N. C., 291 ms. w. of Raleigh ; from W. 462 ms.
WARM SPRINGS, p. v., Meriwether co., Ga., 110 ms. w. of Milledgeville ; from W. 732 ms.
WARNER, p. t., Merrimack co., N. H., 17 ms. n. w. of Concord ; from W. 481 ms. Watered by Warner and Contoocook rivers. Pop. 2,038.
WARNER'S LANDING, p. o., Crawford co., Wis.
WARNERSVILLE, p. o., Schoharie co., N. Y.
WARNERSVILLE, p. o., Livingston co., Mich.
WARREN COUNTY, situated in the east part of New York, with Lake George on the east and Schroon lake at the north, and traversed by Hudson river. Area, 912 square miles. Face of the country, mountainous and hilly ; soil, rocky and barren. Seat of justice, Caldwell. Pop. in 1810, 7,565 ; in 1820, 9,453 ; in 1830, 11,795 ; in 1840, 13.422 ; in 1850, 12,425.
WARREN COUNTY, situated on the westerly boundary of New Jersey, with Delaware river on the west. Area, 350 square miles. Face of the country, uneven and mountainous ; soil, productive. Seat of justice, Belvidere. Pop. in 1830, 18,627 ; in 1840, 20,366 ; in 1850, 22.358.
WARREN COUNTY, situated on the north boundary of Pennsylvania, and traversed by Alleghany river. Area, 832 square miles. Face of the country, hilly ; soil, generally good. Seat of justice, Warren. Pop. in 1810. 827 ; in 1820, 1,976 ; in 1830, 4,706 ; in 1840, 9,278 ; in 1850, 13,671.
WARREN COUNTY, situated in the northeasterly part of Virginia, and traversed by Shenandoah river. Area, 200 square miles. Face of the country, mountainous and uneven. Seat of justice, Front Royal. Pop. in 1840. 5.627 ; in 1850, 6,608.
WARREN COUNTY, situated on the north boundary of North Carolina, and traversed by Roanoke river. Area, 391 square miles. Seat of justice, Warrenton. Pop. in 1820, 11,158 ; in 1830, 11,877 ; in 1840, 12,919 ; in 1850, 13,912.
WARREN COUNTY, situated in the east part of Georgia. Area, 560 square miles. Seat of justice, Warrenton. Pop. in 1810, 8,725 ; in 1820. 10,630 ; in 1830, 10.946 ; in 1840, 9,879 ; in 1850, 12,425.
WARREN COUNTY, situated on the west boundary of Mississippi, with Mississippi river on the west, the

Big Black on the southeast, and traversed by Yazoo river. Area, 600 square miles. Face of the country, uneven ; soil, generally fertile. Seat of justice, Vicksburgh. Pop. in 1810, 1,114 ; in 1820, 2,693 ; in 1830, 7,861 ; in 1840, 15,820 ; in 1850, 18,121.

WARREN COUNTY, situated in the central part of Tennessee. Area, 960 square miles. Seat of justice, McMinnville. Pop. in 1810. 5,725 ; in 1820. 10,348 ; in 1830. 15,210 ; in 1840. 10,803 ; in 1850, 10,179.

WARREN COUNTY, situated in the southerly part of Kentucky, and traversed by Big Barren river. Area, 612 square miles. Seat of justice, Bowling Green. Pop. in 1810, 11,937 ; in 1820, 11,776 ; in 1830, 10,949 ; in 1840, 15,446 ; in 1850, 15,123.

WARREN COUNTY, situated in the southwest part of Ohio, and traversed by Little Miami river. Area, 400 square miles. Face of the country, hilly ; soil, rich. Pop. in 1810, 9,925 ; in 1820, 17,837 ; in 1830, 21,468 ; in 1840, 23,141; in 1850, 25,571.

WARREN COUNTY, situated on the west boundary of Indiana, with Wabash river on the southeast. Area, 350 square miles. Face of the country, even ; soil, fertile. Seat of justice, Williamsport. Pop. in 1830, 2,862 ; in 1840. 5,656 ; in 1850. 7,387.

WARREN COUNTY, situated in the west part of Illinois. Area, 600 square miles. Seat of justice, Monmouth. Pop, in 1830, 308 ; in 1840, 6,739 ; in 1850, 8,176.

WARREN COUNTY, situated in the east part of Missouri, with Missouri river on the south. Area, 350 square miles. Seat of justice, Warrenton. Pop. in 1840, 4,253 ; in 1850, 5,860.

WARREN COUNTY, situated toward the south part of Iowa. Area, —— square miles. Seat of justice, Indianola. Pop. in 1850, 961.

WARREN, c. h., p. t., seat of justice, together with Wiscasset and Topsham, of Lincoln co., Me., 37 ms. s. E. of Augusta ; from W. 613 ms. Watered by St. George river. Pop. 2,428.

WARREN, p. t., Grafton co., N. H., 60 ms. N. w. of Concord ; from W. 522 ms. Watered by Baker's river. Pop. 872.

WARREN, p. t., Washington co., Vt., 25 ms. s. w. of Montpelier ; from W. 500 ms. Watered by Mud river. Pop. 962.

WARREN, p. t., Worcester co., Mass., 66 ms. s. w. of Boston ; from W. 385 ms. Watered by Chickopee river. Pop. 1,777.

WARREN, p. t., Litchfield co., Ct., 48 ms. w. of Hartford ; from W. 321 ms. Watered by Shepaug river and Raumaug pond. Pop. 830.

WARREN, p. t., Bristol co., R. I., 14 ms. s. E. of Providence ; from W. 414 ms. Watered by Narragansett bay. Pop. 3,103.

WARREN, p. t., Herkimer co., N. Y., 64 ms. N. w. of Albany ; from W. 375 ms. Watered by Nowadaga creek. Pop. 1,756.

WARREN, p. t., Somerset co., N. J. Watered by Middle brook. Pop. 2,148.

WARREN, c. h., p. b., seat of justice of Warren co., Pa., 205 ms. N. w. of Harrisburgh ; from W. 297 ms. Watered by Alleghany river and Connewango creek. Pop. 1,013.

WARREN, p. t., Franklin co., Pa. Watered by Little Cove creek. Pop. 616.

WARREN, t., Bradford co., Pa. Watered by Wepasening creek. Pop. 1,573.

WARREN, p. v., Baltimore co., Md., 45 ms. N. of Annapolis ; from W. 55 ms.

WARREN, p. v., Albemarle co., Va., 79 ms. N. w. of Richmond ; from W. 145 ms. Watered by James river at the confluence of Ballenger's creek.

WARREN, c. h., p. t., seat of justice of Trumbull co., O., 163 ms. N. E. of Columbus ; from W. 303 ms. Watered by Mahoning river, and the Pennsylvania and Ohio canal. Pop. 2,957.

WARREN, t., Belmont co., O. Watered by head-waters of Captina and Stillwater creeks. Pop. 1,917.

WARREN, t., Jefferson co., O. Pop. 1,918.

WARREN, t., Tuscarawas co., O. Pop. 1,140.

WARREN, t., Washington co., O. Watered by Ohio river. Pop. 1,461.

WARREN, p t., Macomb co., Mich.

WARREN, p. v., Huntington co., Ind., 123 ms. N. E. of Indianapolis ; from W. 588 ms. Pop. 169.

WARREN, t., Marion co., Ind. Pop. 1,733.

WARREN, t., Putnam co., Ind. Pop. 1,083.

WARREN, p. o., Jo-Daviess co., Ill.

WARREN, p. o., Lee co., Iowa.

WARREN, p. t., Marion co., Mo., 105 ms. N. E. of Jefferson city ; from W. 940 ms. Pop. 1,720.

WARREN, p. o., Marion co., Mo.

WARREN, c. h., p. v., seat of justice of Bradley co., Ark. Pop. 679.

WARREN, p. o., Fannin co., Tex.

WARRENHAM, p. o., Bradford co., Pa., 195 ms. N. of Harrisburgh ; from W. 285 ms.

WARRENSBURGH, p. t., Warren co., N. Y., 69 ms. N. of Albany ; from W. 444 ms. Watered by Hudson river and Schroon branch. Pop. 1,874.

WARRENSBURGH, p. v., Greene co., Tenn., 242 ms. E. of Nashville ; from W. 454 ms.

WARRENSBURGH, p. o., seat of justice of Johnson co., Mo., 98 ms. w. of Jefferson city ; from W. 1,034 ms. Watered by Blackwater river.

WARRENSVILLE, p. o., Mahaska co., Iowa.

WARRENSVILLE, p. v., Du Page co., Ill., 18? ms. N. E. of Springfield ; from W. 748 ms.

WARRENSVILLE, p. t., Cuyahoga co., O., 154 ms. N. E. of Columbus ; from W. 351 ms. Watered by a tributary of Cuyahoga river. Pop. 1,410.

WARRENSVILLE, p. o., Lycoming co., Pa.

WARREN TAVERN, p. o., Chester co., Pa., 76 ms. s. E. of Harrisburgh ; from W. 130 ms.

WARRENTON, p. v., Abbeville district, S. C., 103 ms. w. of Columbia ; from W. 535 ms.

WARRENTON, c. h., p. v., seat of justice of Warren co., Ga., 44 ms. N. E. of Milledgeville ; from W. 626 ms.

WARRENTON, c. h., p. v., seat of justice of Marshall co., Ala. ; from W. 707 ms.

WARRENTON, p. v., Warren township, Jefferson co., O., 136 ms. E. of Columbus ; from W 267 ms. Watered by Ohio river.

WARRENTON, p. v., Gibson co., Ind.

WARRENTON, p. v., Warren co., Miss., 50 ms. w. of Jackson ; from W. 1,060 ms. Watered by Mississippi river.

WARRENTON, c. h., p. v., seat of justice of Warren co., Mo., 71 ms. N. E. of Jefferson city ; from W. 868 ms.

WARRENTON, p. o., Warren co., Ky.

WARRENTON, c. h., p. v., seat of justice of Warren co., N. C., 62 ms. N. E. of Raleigh ; from W. 224 ms. Watered by head-waters of Fishing creek.

WARRENTON, c. h., p. v., seat of justice of Fauquier co., Va., 102 ms. N. of Richmond ; from W. 51 ms.

WARRENTON SPRINGS, p. o., Fauquier co., Va., 107 N. of Richmond ; from W. 56 ms.

WARRENVILLE, p o., Somerset co., N. J.

WARRICK COUNTY, situated on the southerly boundary of Indiana, with Ohio river on the south. Area, 360 square miles. Face of the country, undulating ; soil, a sandy loam. Seat of justice, Booneville. Pop. in 1830, 2,877 ; in 1840, 6,321 ; in 1850, 8,811.

WARRINGTON, p. t., Bucks co., Pa., 104 ms. E. of Harrisburgh ; from W. 158 ms. Pop. 761.

WARRINGTON, t., York co., Pa. Pop. 1,510.

WARRINGTON, p. o., Hancock co., Ind.

WARRINGTON, p. o., Escambia co., Flor.

WARRIOR CREEK, p. o., Wilkes co., N. C.

WARRIOR'S MARK, p. o., Huntington co., Pa., 108 ms. w. of Harrisburgh ; from W. 171 ms. Watered by Juniata and Bald Eagle creeks.

WARRIOR STAND, p. o., Macon co., Ala.

WARSAW, c. h., p. t., seat of justice of Wyoming co., N. Y., 251 ms. w. of Albany ; from W. 363 ms. Watered by Allen's creek. Pop. 2,624.

WARSAW, p. t., Jefferson co., Pa., 168 ms. N. w. of Harrisburgh ; from W. 260 ms. Watered by a tributary of Bank creek. Pop. 870.

WARSAW, p. v., Richmond co., Va., 58 ms. N. E. of Richmond ; from W. 117 ms.

WARSAW, p. v., Duplin co., N. C., 80 ms. s. E. of Raleigh ; from W. 310 ms.

WARSAW, p. v., Forsyth co., Ga., 97 ms. N. w. of Milledgeville ; from W. 668 ms. Watered by Chattahoochee river.

WARSAW, p. o., Coshocton co., O., 83 ms. N. E. of Columbus ; from W. 340 ms.

WARSAW, c. h., p. v., seat of justice of Gallatin co., Ky., 51 ms. N. w. of Frankfort ; from W. 535 ms. Watered by Ohio river.

WARSAW, c. h., p. v., seat of justice of Kosciusko co., Ind., 126 ms. N. of Indianapolis ; from W. 603 ms. Watered by Tippecanoe river. Pop. 304.

WARSAW, p. v., Hancock co., Ill., 114 ms. N. w. of

Springfield ; from W. 892 ms. Watered by Mississippi river at Des Moines rapids.

WARSAW, c. h., p. v., seat of justice of Benton co., Mo., 80 ms. s. w of Jefferson city ; from W. 1,016 ms. Watered by Osage river.

WARSAW PLAIRIE, p. o., Henderson co., Tex.

WARTHEN'S STORE, p. o., Washington co., Ga., 37 ms. s. E. of Milledgeville ; from W. 665 ms.

WARTRACE, p. o., Bedford co., Tenn., 51 ms. s. E. of Nashville ; from W. 682 ms.

WARWICK COUNTY, situated in the southeast part of Virginia, with James river on the southwest. Area, 95 square miles. Seat of justice, Warwick c. h. Pop. in 1810, 1,835 ; in 1820, 1,108; in 1830, 1,570 ; in 1840, 1,456 ; in 1850, 1,546.

WARWICK, p. t., Franklin co., Mass., 79 ms. N. W. of Boston ; from W. 420 ms. Watered by Miller's river. Pop. 1,021.

WARWICK, p. t., Kent co., R. I., 11 ms. s. w. of Providence ; from W. 401 ms. Watered by Pawtuxet river. Pop. 7,740.

WARWICK, p. t., Orange co., N. Y., 111 ms. s. w. of Albany ; from W. 268 ms. Watered by Wallkill river, and tributaries of the Passaic. Pop. 4,902.

WARWICK, p. t., Bucks co., Pa. Watered by Neshaminy creek. Pop. 1,234.

WARWICK, t., Lancaster co., Pa. Watered by Great Chiques, Hanmer, Cocalico, and Marovia creeks. Pop. 2,252.

WARWICK, p. v., Cecil co., Md., 73 ms. N. E. of Annapolis ; from W. 107 ms.

WARWICK, p. t., Tuscarawas co., O. Pop. 1,195.

WARWICK, c. h., p. v., seat of justice of Warwick co., Va., 79 ms. s. E. of Richmond ; from W. 194 ms.

WARWICK, p. o., Marquette co., Wis.

WARWICK NECK, p. o., Kent co., R. I.

WASHBOURN PRAIRIE. p. o.. Barry co., Mo., 220 ms. s. w. of Jefferson city ; from W. 1.135 ms.

WASHBURN, p. o., Marshall co., Ill.

WASHINGTON TERRITORY is situated north of Oregon territory, of which it formerly constituted a part, and consists of that portion of the latter territory lying south of 49° north latitude, and north of the middle of the main channel of the Columbia river from its mouth to where it is crossed by the forty-sixth parallel of north latitude, near Fort Walla-walla, and thence following that parallel to the summit of the Rocky mountains. Its superficial area is about 140,000 square miles. Its physical aspect, climate, resources, &c., are similar to those of Oregon territory, and are fully detailed under that head. It was erected into a separate territory by act of Congress, March 2, 1853. The law of Congress organizing the territory authorized the reservation of two sections of land in every township for the support of common schools. All laws, Congressional or territorial, in force in Oregon territory, are to remain in force in Washington territory until they shall be repealed or amended by future legislation.

WASHINGTON COUNTY, situated at the southeast corner of Maine, with the Atlantic ocean on the southeast, St. Croix river and Passamaquoddy bay on the northeast, and Schoodic lake toward the north. Area, 3,500 square miles. Face of the country, uneven ; soil, suitable for grazing. Seat of justice, Machias. Pop. in 1810, 7,870 ; in 1820, 12,744 ; in 1830, 21,295 ; in 1840, 28,327 ; in 1850, 38.113.

WASHINGTON COUNTY, situated toward the north part of Vermont. Area, 425 square miles. Face of the country, mountainous ; soil, generally good. Seat of justice, Montpelier. Pop. in 1820, 14,113 ; in 1830, 21,378 ; in 1840, 23,506; in 1850, 24,654.

WASHINGTON .COUNTY, situated on the south boundary of Rhode Island, with the Atlantic ocean on the south, and Narraganset bay on the east. Area, 367 square miles. Face of the country, uneven ; soil, of middling quality. Seat of justice, South Kingston. Pop. in 1810, 14,969 ; in 1820, 15,687 ; in 1830, 15,414 ; in 1840, 14,324 ; in 1850, 16,543.

WASHINGTON COUNTY, situated on the east boundary of New York, with Hudson river on the west, and Lake George on the northwest. Area, 807 square miles. Face of the country, diversified and picturesque ; soil, well watered and generally fertile. Seats of justice, Salem and Sandy Hill. Pop. in 1810, 36,724 ; in 1820, 38,831 ; in 1830, 42,635 ; in 1840, 41,080 ; in 1850, 44,750.

WASHINGTON COUNTY, situated on the west boundary of Pennsylvania, with Monongahela river on the east. Area, 1,000 square miles. Face of the country, hilly ; soil, productive. Seat of justice, Washington. Pop. in 1810, 36,289 ; in 1820, 40,038 ; in 1830, 42,680 ; in 1840, 41.279 ; in 1850, 44.939.

WASHINGTON COUNTY, situated on the north boundary of Maryland, with Potomac river on the southwest. Area, 440 square miles. Face of the country, broken and mountainous ; soil, where alluvial, fertile. Seat of justice, Hagerstown. Pop. in 1810, 18.730 ; in 1820, 23,075 ; in 1830, 25,268 ; in 1840, 28,850 ; in 1850, 30,848.

WASHINGTON COUNTY, situated in the District of Columbia, with Potomac river on the southwest. Area, 64 square miles. Face of the country, hilly ; soil, of middling quality. Seat of justice, Washington. Pop. in 1810, 15,471 ; in 1820, 23,336 ; in 1830, 30,858 ; in 1840. 33,735 : in 1850, 51.687.

WASHINGTON COUNTY, situated on the south boundary of Virginia. Area, 764 square miles. Face of the country, hilly ; soil, fertile. Seat of justice, Abington. Pop. in 1810, 12.136 ; in 1820, 12.444 ; in 1830, 15,614 ; in 1840, 13.001 ; in 1850. 14,612.

WASHINGTON COUNTY, situated in the east part of North Carolina, with Albemarle sound and Roanoke river on the north. Area, 360 square miles. Face of the country, level and marshy ; soil. thin and sterile. Seat of justice, Plymouth. Pop. in 1810, 3,464 ; in 1820, 3,986 ; in 1830, 4.552 ; in 1840. 4.525 ; in 1850. 5,664.

WASHINGTON COUNTY, situated toward the east part of Georgia, with Oconee river on the southwest. Area, 760 square miles. Seat of justice, Sandersville. Pop. in 1810, 9,940 ; in 1820, 10.627 ; in 1830, 9,820 ; in 1840. 10.565 ; in 1850. 11,766.

WASHINGTON COUNTY, situated on the south boundary of Florida, with the gulf of Mexico on the south, and Choctawhatchée river and bay on the west. Area, 1,500 square miles. Seat of justice, Roche's bluff. Pop. in 1840, 859 ; in 1850. 1,950.

WASHINGTON COUNTY, situated on the west boundary of Alabama, with Tombigbee river on the east. Area, 840 square miles. Face of the country, uneven ; soil, sterile. Seat of justice, Old Washington. Pop. in 1830, 3,478 ; in 1840, 5,300 ; in 1850, 2,713.

WASHINGTON COUNTY, situated on the west boundary of Mississippi, with Mississippi river on the west, and the Yazoo on the east. Area, 2,420 square miles. Seat of justice, Greenville. Pop. in 1840, 7,287 ; in 1850, 8,389.

WASHINGTON COUNTY, situated on the southeast boundary of Tennessee, and traversed by Nolichucky river. Area, 590 square miles. Face of the country, hilly and broken. Seat of justice, Jonesborough. Pop. in 1810, 7,740 ; in 1820, 9,557 ; in 1830, 10,995 ; in 1840, 11,751 ; in 1850, 13,861.

WASHINGTON COUNTY, situated in the central part of Kentucky. Area, 475 square miles. Seat of justice, Springfield. Pop. in 1810. 13.248 ; in 1820, 15,947 ; in 1830, 19.017 ; in 1840, 10.596 ; in 1850, 12,194.

WASHINGTON COUNTY, situated on the southeast boundary of Ohio, with Ohio river on the southeast, and traversed by Muskingum river. Area, 713 square miles. Face of the country, hilly ; soil, near the rivers, good ; elsewhere, unproductive. Seat of justice, Marietta. Pop. in 1820, 10,425 ; in 1830, 11,731 ; in 1840, 20,823 ; in 1850, 29,540.

WASHINGTON COUNTY, situated in the south part of Indiana. Area, 540 square miles. Seat of justice, Salem. Pop. in 1820, 9,039 ; in 1830, 13,064 ; in 1840, 15.269 ; in 1850, 17,040.

WASHINGTON COUNTY, situated toward the south part of Illinois, with Kaskaskia river on the northwest. Area, 656 square miles. Seat of justice, Nashville. Pop. in 1820, 1,517 ; in 1830, 1,674 ; in 1840, 4,810 ; in 1850, 6,953.

WASHINGTON COUNTY, situated in the east part of Missouri. Area, 820 square miles. Face of the country, mountainous ; soil, varied. Seat of justice, Potosi. Pop. in 1830, 6,784 ; in 1840, 7,231 ; in 1850, 8,811.

WASHINGTON COUNTY, situated on the east boundary of Wisconsin, with Lake Michigan on the east. Area, —— square miles. Seat of justice, Ozaukée. Pop. in 1840, 343 ; in 1850, 19,485.

WASHINGTON COUNTY, situated in the southeasterly part of Iowa, with Iowa river on the northeast. Area, 648 square miles. Seat of justice, Washington. Pop. in 1840, 1,594 ; in 1850. 4.957.

WASHINGTON COUNTY, situated on the east boundary of Minnesota, with St. Croix river on the east. Area, —— square miles. Seat of justice, ——. Pop. in 1850, 1.056.

WASHINGTON COUNTY, situated on the west boundary of Arkansas. Area, 900 square miles. Face of the country, hilly. Seat of justice, Fayetteville. Pop. in 1830, 2,122; in 1840, 7,148; in 1850, 9,567.

WASHINGTON COUNTY, situated in Oregon territory. Area, —— square miles. Seat of justice, ——. Pop. in 1850, 9,970.

WASHINGTON PARISH, situated on the north boundary of Louisiana, with Pearl river on the east. Area, 792 square miles. Face of the country, uneven; soil, sterile. Seat of justice, Franklinton. Pop. in 1820, 2,517; in 1830, 2,286; in 1840, 2,649; in 1850, 3,408.

WASHINGTON, p. t., Lincoln co., Mo., 31 ms. E. of Augusta; from W. 619 ms. Watered by tributaries of Damariscotta and Muscongus rivers. Pop. 1,756.

WASHINGTON, p. t., Sullivan co., N. H., 33 ms. w. of Concord; from W. 473 ms. Watered by head-waters of Ashuelot and Contoocook rivers. Pop. 1,053.

WASHINGTON, p. t., Orange co., Vt., 15 ms. s. E. of Montpelier; from W. 512 ms. Watered by Jail branch of Winooski river, and tributaries of Wait's and White rivers. Pop. 1,348.

WASHINGTON, p. t., Berkshire co., Mass., 128 ms. w. of Boston; from W. 392 ms. Watered by tributaries of Westfield and Housatonick rivers. Pop. 953.

WASHINGTON, p. t., Litchfield co., Ct., 47 ms. s. w. of Hartford; from W. 320 ms. Watered by Shepaug river. Pop. 1,802.

WASHINGTON, p. t., Dutchess co., N. Y., 79 ms. s. of Albany; from W. 314 ms. Watered by Wappinger's creek. Pop. 2,805.

WASHINGTON, t., Bergen co., N. J. Watered by Hackensack and Sadler rivers. Pop. 1,804

WASHINGTON, t., Burlington co., N. J. Watered by Little Egg Harbor river. Pop. 2,009.

WASHINGTON, p. t., Camden co., N. J. Pop. 2,114.

WASHINGTON, p. t., Morris co., N. J. Watered by south branch of Raritan river. Pop. 2,502.

WASHINGTON, c. h., p. b., seat of justice of Washington co., Pa., 209 ms. w. of Harrisburgh; from W. 236 ms. Seat of Washington college. Pop. 2,662.

WASHINGTON, t., Greene co., Pa. Pop. 914.

WASHINGTON, t., Lycoming co., Pa. Pop. 2,138.

WASHINGTON, t., Berks co., Pa. Pop. 1,154.

WASHINGTON, t., Franklin co., Pa. Watered by tributaries of Antictam creek. Pop. 2,471.

WASHINGTON, t., York co., Pa. Pop. 1,330.

WASHINGTON, t., Fayette co., Pa. Pop. 1,276.

WASHINGTON, t., Cambria co., Pa. Watered by a tributary of Kiskiminetas creek. Pop. 1,691.

WASHINGTON, t., Erie co., Pa. Watered by head-waters of French creek. Pop. 1.706.

WASHINGTON, t., Greene co., Pa. Watered by tributaries of Ten-Mile creek. Pop. 914.

WASHINGTON, t., Indiana co., Pa. Watered by Crooked and Plum creeks. Pop. 1,111.

WASHINGTON, t., Clarion co., Pa. Pop. 1,227.

WASHINGTON, t., Westmoreland co., Pa. Watered by White Deer Hole and Black Hole creeks. Pop. 2,076.

WASHINGTON, city, D. C., the capital of the United States, is pleasantly situated on the east bank of the Potomac river, in latitude 38° 53' 34" north, and longitude 77° 1' 30" west from Greenwich. It is 195 miles from the ocean, following the course of the river, 225 miles southwest of New York, and 1,203 miles northeast of New Orleans. The city is built on a point of land formed by the confluence of the Potomac and the Anacostia rivers, which afford a good harbor for vessels of the largest class. Commerce, however, flows naturally toward Baltimore, leaving to Washington perhaps a less rapid but more quiet growth. A more beautiful site for a city could hardly be obtained. It was selected by Washington as the fittest locality for the seat of the national government, and the city was laid out under his direction. It is said his attention was called to the advantages of this location as long previous as when he had been a youthful surveyor of the country around. Pleasant slopes, decked with elegant mansions, surrounded by hills and varied scenery, and the general aspect and airiness of the town, conduce to render Washington an agreeable place of residence. The city is planned on a grand scale, and, if ever built up as originally designed, would be one of the finest cities in the world. By this plan, seven spacious avenues were laid out, to diverge from the capitol as a centre, and five avenues form rays from the president's house, the latter building and the capitol being each situated on beautiful eminences, about one and a half miles apart, and connected by Pennsylvania avenue, now the principal street in the city. The avenues are named after different states, and are crossed diagonally by streets running east and west, named after the letters of the alphabet, and others running north and south, which are named after numbers. The avenues and streets leading to public places are from 120 to 160 feet wide, and the other streets are from 70 to 110 feet wide. Only a comparatively small part of its extensive site is yet covered by buildings, which, in connection with its spacious avenues, has given it the designation of the "city of magnificent distances." A bridge a mile long crosses the eastern branch of the Potomac, and two others, over Rock creek, connect Washington with Georgetown. On the Anacostia is a navy-yard, occupying an area of 27 acres.

The capitol is justly regarded as one of the finest national buildings in the world. It stands on a gentle eminence, in the midst of a beautiful space of 23 acres, highly ornamented with trees, shrubbery, &c. The dome, which is 120 feet from the ground, is the first object which strikes the eye from a distance. The edifice is of freestone, and, as originally built, consisted of a central part and two wings. The width of the whole building was 352 feet, and depth of the wings 121 feet, all occupying an area of one and a half acres. But, in the addition of new states to the Union, with the consequent numerical increase of congressional representation, the capitol, on its original plan, has become too limited, and an enlargement was commenced in 1851, and is being rapidly pressed to completion. These additions will consist of two wings at the ends of the buildings, with which they will be connected by corridors, or piazzas, 44 feet long and 50 feet wide. The wings will each be 143 feet by 238, exclusive of porticoes and steps; and the entire length of the building, when completed, will be 751 feet, and the area it covers 153,112 square feet, or over three and a half acres. Beneath the dome is the rotunda, a spacious apartment 96 feet high, and of the same diameter. On its walls the magnificent national paintings of Trumbull, Chapman, Wier, and Vanderlyn, are hung. The room is also adorned with basso-relievo groups, representing prominent events in American history. The senate-chamber is in the north wing, and the hall of the house of representatives in that of the south. Under the senate-chamber is the room where the supreme court sits. These apartments are all richly furnished, and ornamented with statuary and paintings.

The president's house is a noble and spacious edifice, also of freestone. It is 170 feet long, and 86 feet wide, with Ionic pilasters, comprehending two lofty stories, with a stone balustrade. The north front is ornamented with a portico, sustained by four Ionic columns, with three projecting columns, affording a shelter for carriages to drive under. The garden, or southern front, is embellished by a circular colonnade of six Ionic columns. The interior of the president's house possesses one superb reception-room, commonly known as the "East room," and two oval drawing-rooms, one in each story, of very beautiful proportions. The house stands in an enclosed area of some twenty acres, and commands from its balcony one of the loveliest prospects in the country.

Near the president's house are the buildings occupied by the state, treasury, war, and navy departments. The United States treasury is 300 feet long, with a wing in the rear of 100 feet. Along the front is a colonnade, composed of 23 columns, of massive proportions. The general postoffice is a splendid marble building, with two wings, and adorned with pilasters. The patent-office is a spacious and noble-looking building. The models of inventions are here placed on exhibition, and form an interesting development of the genius of our country.

The erection of the Washington monument is steadily progressing, and has reached a considerable altitude. The most prominent and imposing object of this colossal structure will be the obelisk shaft rising through the centre to the height of 600 feet, 70 feet square at the base, and 40 at the top. The several states of the Union, and many associations, have each prepared a stone, bearing an appropriate inscription, to be placed in the monument.

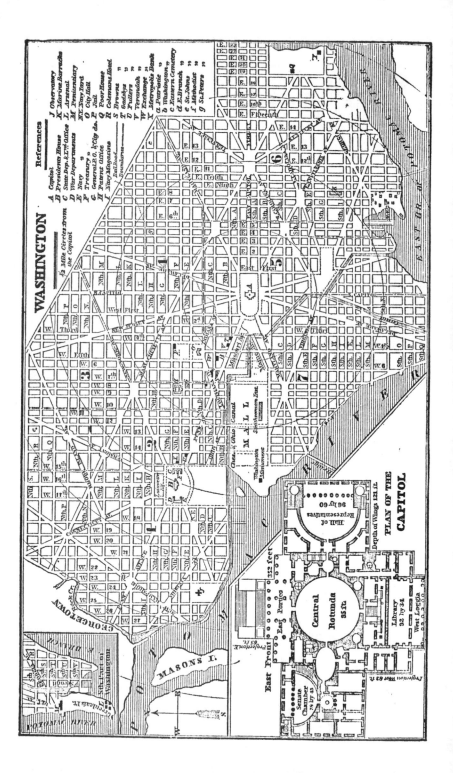

The Smithsonian Institute, founded by the munificent bequest of $500,000 made by an English gentleman (after whom it is named) to the American government, for the advancement of knowledge among men, is one of the purest specimens of architecture in the world.

The manufactures of Washington are by no means contemptible; and its trade with the surrounding country is facilitated by the Chesapeake and Ohio canal, which extends from Alexandria to Cumberland, Maryland, on the Potomac river.

The Washington Branch railroad connects the city with Baltimore; and the Washington and Wilmington line, through Virginia and North Carolina, diverges from this point.

The population in 1800 was 3,210; in 1810, 8.208; in 1820. 13.247; in 1830, 18.827; in 1840, 23,364; in 1850, 40,001.

WASHINGTON, p. v., Rappahannock co., Va., 123 ms. N. W. of Richmond; from W. 75 ms.

WASHINGTON, c. h., p. v., seat of justice of Beaufort co., N. C., 127 ms. E. of Raleigh; from W. 313 ms. Watered by Tar and Pamplico rivers.

WASHINGTON, c. h., p. v., seat of justice of Wilkes co., Ga, 78 ms. N. E. of Milledgeville; from W. 570 ms. Watered by Kettle creek.

WASHINGTON, c. h., p. v., seat of justice of Adams co., Miss., 84 ms. s. w. of Jackson; from W. 1,104 ms. Seat of Jefferson college.

WASHINGTON, p. v., St. Landre parish, La., 223 ms. N. W. of New Orleans; from W. 1,236 ms. Watered by Corteblenu bayou.

WASHINGTON, c. h., p. v., seat of justice of Rhea co., Tenn., 134 ms. s. E. of Nashville; from W. 566 ms. Watered by Tennessee river.

WASHINGTON, c. h., p. v., seat of justice of Mason co., Ky., 77 ms. s. E. of Frankfort; from W. 465 ms.

WASHINGTON, c. h., p. v., seat of justice of Fayette co., O., 50 ms. s. w. of Columbus; from W. 423 ms. Pop. 470.

WASHINGTON, p. t., Guernsey co., O., 85 ms. E. of Columbus; from W. 308 ms. Pop. 972

WASHINGTON, t., Auglaize co., O. Pop. 688.

WASHINGTON, t., Belmont co., O. Watered by Captina creek. Pop. 1,532.

WASHINGTON, t., Brown co., O. Pop. 987.

WASHINGTON, t., Carroll co., O. Pop. 1.020.

WASHINGTON, t., Clermont co., O. Watered by Ohio river. Pop. 2,540.

WASHINGTON, t., Clinton co., O. Pop. 1,216.

WASHINGTON, t., Coshocton co., O. Pop 998.

WASHINGTON, t., Columbiana co., O. Pop. 965.

WASHINGTON, t., Darke co., O. Pop. 1,250.

WASHINGTON, t., Franklin co., O. Watered by Selioto river. Pop. 1,270.

WASHINGTON, t., Hancock co., O. Pop. 1,222.

WASHINGTON, t., Hardin co., O. Pop. 391.

WASHINGTON, t., Harrison co., O. Pop 1,955.

WASHINGTON, t., Hocking co., O. Pop. 1,640.

WASHINGTON, t., Holmes co., O. Pop. 1,468.

WASHINGTON, t., Jackson co., O. Pop. 756.

WASHINGTON, t., Licking co., O. Pop. 1,361.

WASHINGTON, t., Logan co., O. Pop. 668.

WASHINGTON, t., Miami co., O. Pop. 981.

WASHINGTON, t., Mercer co., O. Pop. 456.

WASHINGTON, t., Monroe co., O. Pop. 865.

WASHINGTON, t., Montgomery co., O. Pop. 1.825.

WASHINGTON, t., Muskingum co., O. Pop. 1,335.

WASHINGTON, t., Pickaway co., O. Pop. 1,099.

WASHINGTON, t., Preble co., O. Pop. 714.

WASHINGTON, t., Richland co., O. Pop. 1,914.

WASHINGTON, t., Sandusky co., O. Pop. 1,499.

WASHINGTON, t., Scioto co., O. Watered by Ohio and Scioto rivers, and the Ohio canal. Pop. 706.

WASHINGTON, t., Shelby co., O. Watered by a tributary of Miami river. Pop. 1,261.

WASHINGTON, t., Stark co., O. Pop. 2,066.

WASHINGTON, t., Tuscarawas co., O. Pop. 1,091.

WASHINGTON, t., Union co., O. Pop. 333.

WASHINGTON, t., Van Wert co., O. Pop. 355.

WASHINGTON, t., Warren co., O. Pop. 1.566.

WASHINGTON, t., Williams co., O.

WASHINGTON, t., Wood co., O. Pop. 504.

WASHINGTON, t. Blackford co., Ind. Pop. 470.

WASHINGTON, Brown co., Ind. Pop. 1,249.

WASHINGTON, t., Clark co., Ind. Pop. 1,101.

WASHINGTON, c. h., p. t., seat of justice of Davies co., Ind., 106 ms. s. w. of Indianapolis; from W. 668 ms. Pop. 2,578.

WASHINGTON, t., Gibson co., Ind. Pop. 754.

WASHINGTON, t., Grant co., Ind. Pop. 1.007.

WASHINGTON, t., Hamilton co., Ind. Pop. 1,840.

WASHINGTON, t., Harrison co., Ind.

WASHINGTON, t., Marion co., Ind. Pop. 2,043.

WASHINGTON, t., Noble co., Ind. Pop. 645.

WASHINGTON, t., Putnam co., Ind. Pop. 2.129.

WASHINGTON, t., Randolph co., Ind.

WASHINGTON, t., Rush co., Ind. Pop. 1.075.

WASHINGTON, t., Tippecanoe co., Ind. Pop. 861.

WASHINGTON, t., Washington co., Ind. Pop. 3,322.

WASHINGTON, t., Wayne co., Ind. Pop. 1,540.

WASHINGTON, p. t., Macomb co., Mich., 29 ms. N. E. of Detroit; from W. 553 ms. Watered by Stony creek. Pop. 1,541.

WASHINGTON, p. v., Tazewell co., Ill., 71 ms. N. of Springfield; from W. 785 ms.

WASHINGTON, c. h., p. v., seat of justice of Washington co., Iowa. Pop. 327.

WASHINGTON, p. v., Franklin co., Mo., 76 ms. E. of Jefferson city; from W. 871 ms.

WASHINGTON, t., Buchanan co., Mo. Pop. 4,301.

WASHINGTON, t., Clark co., Mo.

WASHINGTON, t., Johnson co., Mo.

WASHINGTON, t., Lafayette co., Mo. Pop. 1,641.

WASHINGTON, t., Livingston co., Mo.

WASHINGTON, t., Osage co., Mo. Pop. 1,093.

WASHINGTON, t., Polk co., Mo.

WASHINGTON, t., Taney co., Mo.

WASHINGTON, c. h., p. v., seat of justice of Hempstead co., Ark., 111 ms. s. w. of Little Rock; from W. 1,176 ms. Watered by a tributary of Red river.

WASHINGTON, t., Independence co., Ark.

WASHINGTON, t., Sevier co., Ark.

WASHINGTON, p. o., Washington co., Tex.

WASHINGTON COLLEGE, p. o., Washington co., Tenn.

WASHINGTON HOLLOW, p. o., Washington township, Dutchess co., N. Y., 82 ms. s. of Albany; from W. 311 ms.

WASHINGTON MILLS, p. o., Oneida co., N. Y.

WASHINGTONVILLE, p. o., Sandy Creek township, Oswego co., N. Y.

WASHINGTONVILLE, v., Blooming Grove township, Orange co., N. Y.

WASHINGTONVILLE, p. v., Derry township, Montour co., Pa., 79 ms. N. E. of Harrisburgh; from W. 189 ms.

WASHINGTONVILLE, p. v., Greene township, Columbiana co., O., 162 ms. N. E. of Columbus; from W. 294 ms.

WASHINGTONVILLE, p. o., Baltimore co., Md.

WASHITA, p. o., Grayson co., Md.

WASHTENAW COUNTY, situated in the south part of Michigan. Area, 720 square miles. Seat of justice, Ann Arbor. Pop. in 1830, 4,042; in 1840, 23,571; in 1850, 28,568.

WASSAIC, p. o., Dutchess co., N. Y.

WASSONVILLE, p. o., Washington co., Iowa.

WATAUGA COUNTY, situated in North Carolina. Area, —— square miles. Seat of justice, ——. Pop. in 1850, 3,400.

WATAUGA BEND, p. o., Washington co., Tenn.

WATENSAW, p. o., Monroe co., Ark.

WATERBOROUGH, p. t., York co., Me., 76 ms. s. w. of Augusta; from W. 521 ms. Watered by Little Ossipee river. Pop. 1,985.

WATERBOROUGH CENTRE, p. o., Waterborough township, York co., Me., 75 ms. s. w. of Augusta; from W. 525 ms.

WATERBURG, p. o., Tompkins co., N. Y., 173 ms. w. of Albany; from W. 306 ms.

WATERBURY, p. t., Washington co., Vt., 12 ms. N. W. of Montpelier; from W. 525 ms. Watered by Onion and Waterbury rivers. Pop. 2,352.

WATERBURY, p. t., New Haven co., Ct., 52 ms. s. w. of Hartford; from W. 310 ms. Watered by Naugatuck river. Pop. 5,137.

WATERFORD, p. t., Oxford co., Me., 53 ms. w. of Augusta; from W. 588 ms. Watered by Crooked river. Pop. 1,448.

WATERFORD, p. t., Caledonia co., Vt., 49 ms. N. E. of Montpelier; from W. 547 ms. Watered by Connecticut, Passumpsic, and Moose rivers. Pop. 1,412.

WATERFORD, p. t., New London co., Ct., 46 ms. s. E. of Hartford; from W. 451 ms. Watered by Thames, Niantic, and Jordan rivers, and Long Island sound. Pop. 2,258.

WATERFORD, p. t., Saratoga co., N. Y., 10 ms. N. of

Albany ; from W. 380 ms. Watered by Mohawk and Hudson rivers, and the Champlain canal. Pop. 2,683.

WATERFORD, p. t., Camden co., N. J., 51 ms. s. w. of Trenton ; from W. 161 ms. Watered by Pensauken and Cooper's creeks. Pop. 1,638.

WATERFORD, p. t., Erie co., Pa., 256 ms. N. w. of Harrisburgh ; from W. 329 ms. Watered by Le Bœuf creek. Pop. 1,545.

WATERFORD, p. v., Loudoun co., Va., 159 ms. N. of Richmond ; from W. 40 ms. Watered by Kittoctan creek.

WATERFORD, p. v., Marshall co., Miss., 184 ms. N. of Jackson ; from W. 902 ms.

WATERFORD, p. v., Gibson co., Tenn., 121 ms. w. of Nashville ; from W. 804 ms.

WATERFORD, p. o., Spencer co., Ky.

WATERFORD, p. t., Washington co., O., 89 ms. s. E. of Columbus ; from W. 321 ms. Watered by Muskingum river. Pop. 1,373.

WATERFORD, p. t., Oakland co., Mich., 32 ms. N. w. of Detroit ; from W. 556 ms. Pop. 1,086.

WATERFORD, p. o., Laporte co., Ind.

WATERFORD, p. v., Fulton co., Ill., 50 ms. N. w. of Springfield ; from W. 830 ms.

WATERFORD, p. o., Racine co., Wis.

WATERFORD CENTRE, p. o., Waterford township, Oakland co., Mich.

WATERFORD WORKS, p. o., Waterford township, Camden co., N. J.

WATERLOO, c. h., p. t., seat of justice, together with Ovid, of Seneca co., N. Y., 17 ms. w. of Albany ; from W. 346 ms. Watered by Seneca river, and the Seneca and Cayuga canal. Pop. 3,795.

WATERLOO, p. o., Sussex co., N. J.

WATERLOO, p. v., Lock township, Juniata co., Pa., 69 ms. N. w. of Harrisburgh ; from W. 125 ms. Watered by Tuscarora creek.

WATERLOO, p. o., Fauquier co., Va.

WATERLOO, p. v., Granville co., N. C., 50 ms. N. of Raleigh ; from W. 266 ms.

WATERLOO, p. v., Laurens district, S. C., 79 ms. w. of Columbia : from W. 507 ms.

WATERLOO, p. o., Lauderdale co., Ala. ; from W. 805 ms. Watered by Tennessee river.

WATERLOO, p. v., Point Coupée parish, La. Watered by Mississippi river.

WATERLOO, p. o., Pulaski co., Ky.

WATERLOO, p. t., Athens co., O. Watered by Raccoon creek. Pop. 1,016.

WATERLOO, p. o., Lawrence co., O.

WATERLOO, p. o., Jackson co., Mich.

WATERLOO, p. t., Fayette co., Ind., 61 ms. E. of Indianapolis ; from W. 524 ms. Pop. 833.

WATERLOO, c. h., p. v., seat of justice of Monroe co., Ill., 115 ms. s. of Springfield ; from W. 828 ms.

WATERLOO, c. h., p. v., seat of justice of Clark co., Mo., 186 ms. N. of Jefferson city ; from W. 911 ms.

WATERLOO, p. o., Jefferson co., Wis.

WATERPORT, p. o., Orleans co., N. Y.

WATER-PROOF, p. o., Tensas parish, La.

WATER STREET, p. v., Morris township. Huntington co., Pa., 100 ms. w. of Harrisburgh ; from W. 159 ms. Watered by canal.

WATERTOWN, p. t., Middlesex co., Mass., 7 ms. w. of Boston ; from W. 433 ms. Watered by Charles river. Pop. 2,837.

WATERTOWN, p. t., Litchfield co., Ct., 42 ms. s. w. of Hartford ; from W. 320 ms. Watered by Steel's brook. Pop. 1,533.

WATERTOWN, c. h., p. t., seat of justice of Jefferson co., N. Y., 164 ms. N. w. of Albany ; from W. 416 ms. Watered by Stony and Sandy creeks, and Black river. Pop. 7,201.

WATERTOWN, p. t., Washington co., O., 92 ms. s. E. of Columbus ; from W. 312 ms. Watered by Wolf creek. Pop. 1,373.

WATERTOWN, p. t., Jefferson co., Wis., 39 ms. E. of Madison ; from W. 853 ms. Watered by Rock river.

WATERVALE, p. v., Pompey township. Onondaga co., N. Y., 125 ms. w. of Albany ; from W. 342 ms.

WATER VALLEY, p. o., Hamburgh township, Erie co., N. Y., 303 ms. w. of Albany ; from W. 375 ms.

WATER VALLEY, p. o., Yallabusha co., Miss.

WATER VILLAGE, p. v., Carroll co., N. H., 48 ms. N. E. of Concord ; from W. 529 ms.

WATERVILLE, p. t., Kennebec co., Me., 18 ms. N. of Augusta ; from W. 613 ms. Watered by Kennebec river. Seat of Waterville college. Pop. 3,966.

WATERVILLE, t., Grafton co., N. H. Pop. 42.

WATERVILLE, p. t., Lamoille co., Vt., 43 ms. N. w. of Montpelier ; from W. 553 ms. Watered by north branch of Lamoille river. Pop. 753.

WATERVILLE, p. v., Sangerfield township, Oneida co., N. Y., 90 ms. N. w. of Albany ; from W. 372 ms Watered by a tributary of Oriskany creek.

WATERVILLE, p. t., Lucas co., O. 130 ms. N. w. of Columbus ; from W. 461 ms. Watered by a tributary of Maumee river. Pop. 958.

WATERVILLE, p. o., New Haven co., Ct.

WATERVILLE, p. o., Lycoming co., Pa.

WATERVILLE, p. o., Waukesha co., Wis.

WATERVLIET, p. t., Albany co., N. Y., 5 ms. N. of Albany ; from W. 375 ms. Watered by Mohawk and Hudson rivers, and Erie and Champlain canal. Pop. 4,882.

WATERVLIET, p. o., Berrien co., Mich.

WATERVLIET CENTRE, p. o., Watervliet township, Albany co., N. Y.

WATKINS, p. o., Union co., O.

WATKINS, t., Crawford co., Mo.

WALKINSVILLE, p. v., Clark co., Ga., 68 ms. N. of Milledgeville ; from W. 617 ms. Watered by Beaver-Dam creek.

WATSON, p. t., Lewis co., N. Y., 140 ms. N. w. of Albany ; from W. 439 ms. Watered by Independence creek and Beaver river. Pop. 1,138.

WATSON'S BRIDGE, p. o., Moore co., N. C.

WATSONTOWN, p. v., Northumberland co., Pa., 77 ms N. of Harrisburgh ; from W. 187 ms.

WATTSBOROUGH, p. o., Lunenburgh co., Va., 116 ms. s. w. of Richmond ; from W. 232 ms.

WATTSBURGH, p. b., Erie co., Pa., 263 ms. N. w. of Harrisburgh ; from W. 344 ms. Watered by French creek. Pop. 227.

WATTS' MILLS, p. o., Westmoreland co., Pa.

WATTS' MILLS, p. o., Appanoose co., Iowa.

WAUHATCHEE, p. o., Dade co., Ga., 113 ms. N. w. of Milledgeville ; from W. 717 ms.

WAUCOUSTA, p. o., Fond du Lac co., Wis.

WAUHOO, or WAHOO, p. o., Vigo co., Ind.

WAUKAU, p. o., Winnebago co., Wis., 113 ms. N. w. of Madison ; from W. 717 ms.

WAUKEENAH, p. o., Jefferson co., Flor.

WAUKEGAN, p. o., Lake co., Ill.

WAUKESHA COUNTY, situated in the southeast part of Wisconsin. Area, —— square miles. Seat of justice, Waukesha. Pop. in 1850, 19,248.

WAUKESHA, c. h., p. v., seat of justice of Waukesha co., Wis.

WAUKSAIK, p. o., Cook co., Ill.

WAUPAKA, p. o., Marquette co., Wis.

WAUPUN, p. v., Fond du Lac co., Wis., 80 ms. N. E. of Madison ; from W. 927 ms.

WAUSAU, p. o., Marathon co., Wis.

WAUSHARA, p. o., Dodge co., Wis.

WAUTOMA, p. o., Marquette co., Wis.

WAUWATOSA, p. o., Milwaukie co., Wis.

WAVELAND, p. o., Montgomery co., Ind., 65 ms. N. w. of Indianapolis ; from W. 630 ms.

WAVERLY, p. o., Tioga co., N. Y.

WAVERLY, p. o., Luzerne co., Pa.

WAVERLY, p. o., Chambers co., Ala.

WAVERLY, p. o., Lowndes co., Miss., 147 ms. N. E. of Jackson ; from W. 892 ms.

WAVERLY, c. h., p. v., seat of justice of Humphreys co., Tenn., 60 ms. w. of Nashville ; from W. 744 ms.

WAVERLY, p. v., Pee-Pee township, Pike co., O., 60 ms. s. of Columbus ; from W. 407 ms. Situated on the Ohio canal.

WAVERLY, p. o., Henry co., Mo.

WAVERLY, p. t., Lincoln co., Mo.

WAVERLY HALL, p. o., Harris co., Ga., 111 ms. s. w of Milledgeville ; from W. 733 ms.

WAWARSING, p. t., Ulster co., N. Y., 82 ms. s. w. of Albany ; from W. 297 ms. Watered by Rondout creek Pop. 6,459.

WAWATOSA, t., Milwaukie co., Wis.

WAW-PE-CONG, p. o., Miami co., Ind.

WAXAHATCHIE, p. o., Ellis co., Tex.

WAY, p. o., Ripley co., Ind.

WAYLAND, p. t., Middlesex co., Mass., 17 ms. w. of Boston ; from W. 423 ms. Watered by Sudbury river. Pop. 1,115.

WAYLAND, p. o., Allegan co., Mich.

WAYLANDSBURGH, p. v., Culpeper co., Va., 104 ms. N. E. of Richmond ; from W. 90 ms.

WAYLAND'S SPRINGS, p. o., Lawrence co., Tenn.

WAYMART, p. v., Clinton township, Wayne co., Pa., 166 ms. N. E. of Harrisburgh; from W. 260 ms. Watered by a tributary of Lackawaxen creek.

WAYNE COUNTY, situated on the north boundary of New York, with Lake Ontario on the north. Area, 572 square miles. Face of the country, broken; soil, generally fertile. Seat of justice, Lyons. Pop. in 1820, 20,319; in 1830, 33,655; in 1840, 42,057; in 1850, 44,953.

WAYNE COUNTY, situated on the northwest boundary of Pennsylvania, with Delaware river on the northeast. Area, 648 square miles. Face of the country, broken; soil, poor. Seat of justice, Honesdale. Pop. in 1810, 4,125; in 1820, 4,127; in 1830, 7,663; in 1840, 11,848; in 1850, 21,890.

WAYNE COUNTY, situated on the western border of Virginia, with the Ohio river for its northern and Big Sandy river for its western boundary. Area, 350 square miles. Face of the country, broken; soil, moderately fertile. Seat of justice, Wayne c. h. Pop. in 1850, 4,738.

WAYNE COUNTY, situated toward the southeast part of North Carolina, and traversed by Neuse river. Area, 720 square miles. Seat of justice, Waynesborough. Pop. in 1810, 8,687; in 1820, 9,040; in 1830, 10,331; in 1840, 10,891; in 1850, 13,486.

WAYNE COUNTY, situated in the southeast part of Georgia, with Altamaha river on the north. Area, 900 square miles. Seat of justice, Wayne c. h. Pop. in 1810, 676; in 1820, 1,010; in 1830, 963; in 1840, 1,258; in 1850, 1,499.

WAYNE COUNTY, situated on the east boundary of Mississippi. Area, 790 square miles. Seat of justice, Winchester. Pop. in 1840, 2,120; in 1850, 2,892.

WAYNE COUNTY, situated on the south boundary of Tennessee. Area, 504 square miles. Seat of justice, Waynesborough. Pop. in 1820, 2,459; in 1830, 6,013; in 1840. 7.705; in 1850, 8,170.

WAYNE COUNTY, situated on the south boundary of Kentucky, with Cumberland river on the north. Area, 570 square miles. Seat of justice, Monticello. Pop. in 1810, 5,430; in 1820, 7,951; in 1830, 8,738; in 1840, 7,399; in 1850, 8,692.

WAYNE COUNTY, situated toward the northeast part of Ohio. Area, 660 square miles. Face of the country, level and elevated; soil, of middling quality. Seat of justice, Wooster. Pop. in 1820, 11,393; in 1830, 23,333; in 1840, 35,808; in 1850, 32,981.

WAYNE COUNTY, situated on the east boundary of Indiana. Area, 400 square miles. Face of the country, undulating; soil, fertile. Seat of justice, Centreville. Pop. in 1820, 7,951; in 1830, 18,571; in 1840, 23,292; in 1850, 25,321.

WAYNE COUNTY, situated in the southeast part of Illinois, with Little Wabash river on the east. Area, 720 square miles. Seat of justice, Fairfield. Pop. in 1820, 111; in 1830, 2,553; in 1840, 5,133; in 1850, 6,828.

WAYNE COUNTY, situated on the southeasterly boundary of Michigan, with St. Clair lake and St. Clair river on the east. Area, 600 square miles. Face of the country, even; soil, productive. Seat of justice, Detroit. Pop. in 1820, 3,574; in 1830, 6,781; in 1840, 24,173; in 1850, 32,756.

WAYNE COUNTY, situated on the south boundary of Iowa. Area, 375 square miles. Seat of justice, ———. Pop. in 1850, 340.

WAYNE COUNTY, situated in the southeast part of Missouri, with St. Francis river on the southeast, and traversed by the Big Black. Area, 1,200 square miles. Seat of justice, Greenville. Pop. in 1830, 3,264; in 1840, 3,403; in 1850, 4,518.

WAYNE, p. t., Kennebec co., Me., 15 ms. w. of Augusta; from W. 595 ms. Watered by Androscoggin river. Pop. 1,367.

WAYNE, p. t., Steuben co., N. Y., 198 ms. w. of Albany; from W. 316 ms. Watered by Crooked, Mud, and Little lakes. Pop. 1,347.

WAYNE, t., Armstrong co., Pa. Pop. 1,348.

WAYNE, t., Clinton co., Pa. Pop. 476.

WAYNE, t., Crawford co., Pa. Watered by Sugar river. Pop. 882.

WAYNE, p. t., Erie co., Pa., 250 ms. N. w. of Harrisburgh; from W. 335 ms. Watered by French creek. Pop. 1,122.

WAYNE, t., Greene co., Pa. Watered by Dunkard's creek. Pop. 1,258.

WAYNE, t., Mifflin co., Pa. Watered by Juniata river. Pop. 1,201.

WAYNE, t., Schuylkill co., Pa. Pop. 968.

WAYNE, c. h., p. v., seat of justice of Wayne co., Va.

WAYNE, t., Adams co., O. Watered by tributaries of west fork of Brush creek. Pop. 1,682.

WAYNE, t., Ashtabula co., O. Pop. 899.

WAYNE, t., Belmont co., O. Watered by Captina creek. Pop. 1,918.

WAYNE, t., Butler co., O. Watered by Elk creek, and tributaries of St. Clair creek. Pop. 1,502.

WAYNE, t., Champaign co., O. Watered by tributaries of Little Darby creek and of Mad river. Pop. 1,429.

WAYNE, t., Clermont co., O. Watered by Stone Lick fork of Little Miami river. Pop. 1,394.

WAYNE, t., Clinton co., O. Watered by Paint creek. Pop. 1,435.

WAYNE, t., Columbiana co., O. Watered by tributaries of Little Beaver river. Pop. 977.

WAYNE, t., Darke co., O. Watered by a tributary of Laramie creek.

WAYNE, t., Jefferson co., O. Watered by Cross creek. Pop. 1,801.

WAYNE, t., Knox co., O. Watered by Vernon river and tributaries. Pop. 1,152.

WAYNE, t., Lafayette co., O. Watered by Paint creek.

WAYNE, t., Mercer co., O.

WAYNE, t., Monroe co., O. Pop. 1,177.

WAYNE, t., Montgomery co., O. Watered by Miami river. Pop. 1,090.

WAYNE, t., Muskingum co., O. Pop. 1,244.

WAYNE, t., Pickaway co., O. Watered by Scioto river and the Ohio canal. Pop. 644.

WAYNE, t., Scioto co., O. Pop. 219.

WAYNE, t., Tuscarawas co., O. Pop. 2,342.

WAYNE, t., Warren co., O. Watered by Little Miami river. Pop. 2,995.

WAYNE, t., Wayne co., O.

WAYNE, t., Cass co., Mich. Pop. 682.

WAYNE, t., Allen co., Ind. Pop. 5,285.

WAYNE, t., Bartholomew co., Ind. Pop. 789.

WAYNE, t., Hamilton co., Ind. Pop. 955.

WAYNE, t., Henry co., Ind. Pop. 2,074.

WAYNE, t., Marion co., Ind. Pop. 2,323.

WAYNE, t., Montgomery co., Ind. Pop. 1,249.

WAYNE, t., Noble co., Ind. Pop. 624.

WAYNE, t., Owen co., Ind. Pop. 1,138.

WAYNE, t., Randolph co., Ind.

WAYNE, t., Tippecanoe co., Ind. Pop. 1,597.

WAYNE, t., Wayne co., Ind. Pop. 4,940.

WAYNE, p. o., Henry co., Iowa.

WAYNE CENTRE, p. o., Du Page co., Ill.

WAYNESBOROUGH, p. v., Augusta co., Va., 105 ms. N. w. of Richmond; from W. 147 ms. Watered by South river.

WAYNESBOROUGH, c. h., p. v., seat of justice of Wayne co., N. C., 51 ms. S. E. of Raleigh; from W. 281 ms. Watered by Neuse river.

WAYNESBOROUGH, c. h., p. v., seat of justice of Burke co., Ga., 82 ms. E. of Milledgeville; from W. 605 ms. Watered by a tributary of Brier creek.

WAYNESBOROUGH, c. h., p. v., seat of justice of Wayne co., Tenn., 99 ms. s. w. of Nashville; from W. 776 ms. Watered by Green river.

WAYNESBOROUGH, p. b., Washington township, Franklin co., Pa., 55 ms. s. w. of Harrisburgh; from W. 80 ms Pop. 1,019.

WAYNESBURGH, p. b., Franklin township, Greene co., Pa., 222 ms. w. of Harrisburgh; from W. 229 ms. Watered by Ten-Mile creek.

WAYNESBURGH, p. v., Sandy township, Stark co., O., 131 ms. N. E. of Columbus; from W. 308 ms. Watered by Sandy creek, and Sandy and Beaver canal.

WAYNESBURGH, p. o., Lincoln co., Ky., 67 ms. s. E. of Frankfort; from W. 578 ms. Watered by a tributary of Buck creek.

WAYNESVILLE, c. h., p. v., seat of justice of Haywood co., N. C., 29 ms. w. of Raleigh; from W. 524 ms. Watered by a tributary of Big Pigeon river.

WAYNESVILLE, p. v., Wayne co., Ga, 247 ms. s. E. of Milledgeville; from W. 756 ms.

WAYNESVILLE, p. v., Warren co., O. Watered by Little Miami river.

WAYNESVILLE, p. v., De Witt co., Ill., 55 ms. N. E. of Springfield; from W. 751 ms. Watered by Kickapoo creek.

WAYNESVILLE, p. v., Pulaski co., Mo., 70 ms. s. of Jefferson city; from W. 985 ms. Watered by Gasconade river.

WAYNETOWN, p. v., Montgomery co., Ind., 55 ms. N. w. of Indianapolis ; from W. 626 ms. Watered by Coal creek.

WAYNMANVILLE. p. o., Upson co., Ga.

WEAKLEY COUNTY, situated on the north boundary of Tennessee. Area, 680 square miles. Seat of justice, Dresden. Pop. in 1840, 9,870 ; in 1850, 14,608.

WEARE. p. t., Hillsborough co., N. H., 14 ms. s. w. of Concord ; from W. 475 ms. Watered by a tributary of Piscataquoag river. Pop. 2,435.

WEAR'S COVE. p. o., Sevier co., Tenn., 217 ms. E. of Nashville ; from W. 509 ms.

WEATHERLY, p. o., Carbon co., Pa.

WEATHERSFIELD, p. t., Windsor co., Vt., 74 ms. s. of Montpelier ; from W. 464 ms. Watered by Black and Connecticut rivers. Pop. 1,851.

WEATHERSFIELD, p. t., Trumbull co., O., 169 ms. N. E. of Columbus ; from W. 298 ms. Watered by Mahoning river, and the Pennsylvania and Ohio canal. Pop. 1,717.

WEATHERSFIELD CENTRE, p. o., Windsor co., Vt.

WEAVERSVILLE, p. v., Allen township, Northampton co., Pa., 100 ms. N. E. of Harrisburgh ; from W. 193 ms.

WEAVERSVILLE, p. o., Fauquier co., Va.

WEAVERSVILLE, p. v., seat of justice of Trinity co., Cal.

WEBB COUNTY, situated on the southwest boundary of Texas, on the Rio Grande. Area, —— square miles. Seat of justice, Laredo.

WEBBER'S PRAIRIE, p. o., Travis co., Tex.

WEBB'S FORD, p. o., Rutherford co., N. C., 215 ms. w. of Raleigh ; from W. 452 ms.

WEBB'S MILLS, p. o., Chemung co., N. Y.

WEBB'S MILLS, p. o., Ritchie co., Va., 214 ms. N. w. of Richmond ; from W. 283 ms.

WEBSTER, p. t., Lincoln co., Me., 31 ms. s. of Augusta ; from W. 574 ms. Pop. 1,110.

WEBSTER, p. t., Worcester co., Mass., 56 ms. s. w. of Boston ; from W. 394 ms. Watered by French river. Pop. 2,371.

WEBSTER, p. t., Monroe co., N. Y., 214 ms. w. of Albany ; from W. 371 ms. Watered by Lake Ontario. Pop. 2,446.

WEBSTER, p. t., Washtenaw co., Mich., 49 ms. w. of Detroit ; from W. 542 ms. Watered by Portage lake and Huron river. Pop. 924.

WEBSTER, p. o., Wayne co., Ind.

WEBSTER, p. o., Hancock co., Ill.

WEBSTER, p. o., Allamakee co., Iowa.

WEBSTER, p. o., Winston co., Miss.

WEBSTER'S MILLS, p. o., Fulton co., Pa.

WEEDOWEE, p. o., Randolph co., Ala.

WEEDSPORT, p. v., Brutus township, Cayuga co., N. Y., 155 ms. w. of Albany ; from W. 341 ms. Situated on the Erie canal.

WEHADKEE, p.o., Randolph co., Ala. ; from W. 755 ms.

WEEK'S MILLS, p. o., Kennebec co., Me., 13 ms. from Augusta ; from W. 608 ms.

WEELAUNEE, p. o., Winnebago co., Wis.

WEEWAKAVILLE, p. v., Talladega co., Ala. ; from W. 770 ms.

WEGATCHIE, p. o., St. Lawrence co., N. Y.

WEHOGA, p. o., Benton co., Ala.

WEIR'S BRIDGE, p. o., Belknap co., N. H.

WEISSENBURGH, p. t., Lehigh co., Pa., 72 ms. E. of Harrisburgh ; from W. 180 ms. Watered by Jordan creek and tributaries. Pop. 1,762.

WEISESBURGH, p. t., Baltimore co., Md., 55 ms. N. of Annapolis ; from W. 65 ms.

WEISPORT, p. o., Carbon co., Pa.

WELAKA, p. o., Putnam co., Flor.

WELBORN, t., Conway co., Ark.

WELB'S PRAIRIE, p. o., Franklin co., Ill.

WELCH'S MILLS, p. o., Cabarras co., N. C., 151 ms. w. of Raleigh ; from W. 388 ms.

WELCHVILLE, p. o., Oxford co., Me.

WELD, p. t., Franklin co., Me., 47 ms. N. w. of Augusta ; from W. 624 ms. Watered by tributaries of Androscoggin river. Pop. 995.

WELDON, p. v., Halifax co., N. C., 95 ms. N. E. of Raleigh ; from W. 204 ms. Watered by Roanoke river.

WELD'S LANDING, p. o., Dubuque co., Iowa.

WELLBORN, c. h., p. v., seat of justice of Coffee co., Ala.

WELLBORN'S MILLS, p. o., Houston co., Ga., 52 ms. s. w. of Milledgeville ; from W. 700 ms.

WELLERSBURGH, p. v., Somerset co., Pa., 128 ms. w. of Harrisburgh ; from W. 145 ms.

WELLERVILLE, p. o., Crawford co., O.

WELLFLEET. p. t., Barnstable co., Mass., 105 ms. s. E. of Boston ; from W. 506 ms. Watered by Atlantic ocean and Cape Cod bay. Pop. 2,411.

WELLINGTON. p. t., Piscataquis co., Me., 62 ms. N. of Augusta ; from W. 657 ms. Watered by a tributary of Sebasticook river. Pop. 600.

WELLINGTON, p. o., Camillus township, Onondaga co., N. Y., 144 ms. w. of Albany ; from W. 352 ms.

WELLINGTON, p. o., Morgan co., Ga.

WELLINGTON, p. t., Lorain co., O, 101 ms. N. E. of Columbus ; from W. 370 ms. Watered by tributaries of Black river. Pop. 1,556.

WELLINGTON. p. o., Lake co., Ill.

WELLINGTON, p. v., Lafayette co., Mo., 144 ms. N. w. of Jefferson city ; from W. 1,058 ms. Watered by Missouri river.

WELLS COUNTY, situated in the east part of Indiana. Area, 372 square miles. Seat of justice, Bluffton. Pop. in 1840, 1,822 ; in 1850, 6,152.

WELLS, p. t., York co., Me., 79 ms. s. w. of Augusta ; from W. 513 ms. Watered by Atlantic ocean. Pop. 2,945.

WELLS, p. t., Rutland co., Vt., 83 ms. s. w. of Montpelier ; from W. 438 ms. Watered by Lake Austin. Pop. 804.

WELLS, p. t., Hamilton co., N. Y., 69 ms. N. w. of Albany ; from W. 438 ms. Watered by Sacandaga creek. Pop. 486.

WELLS, p. t., Bradford co., Pa. Watered by South creek. Pop. 1,113.

WELLS, p. t., Jefferson co., O. Watered by Ohio river. Pop. 1,822.

WELLS, t., Macon co., Mo.

WELLSBOROUGH, c. h., p. v., seat of justice of Tioga co., Pa, 145 ms. N. of Harrisburgh ; from W. 259 ms. Watered by Crooked creek.

WELLSBURGH, p. o., Chemung co., N. Y.

WELLSBURGH, c. h., p. v., seat of justice of Brooke co., Va., 344 ms. N. w. of Richmond ; from W. 205 ms. Watered by Ohio river and Buffalo creek.

WELLSBURGH, p. o., St. Charles co., Mo.

WELLS' CORNER, p. o., Minisink township, Orange co., N. Y., 115 ms. s. w. of Albany ; from W. 275 ms.

WELLS' CORNERS, p. o., Erie co., Pa.

WELLSCOTT, p. o., Union co., Ga.

WELLS DEPOT, p. o., York co., Me.

WELLS' MILLS, p. o., Appanoose co., Iowa.

WELLS' RIVER, p. v., Orange co., Vt., 38 ms. s. E. of Montpelier ; from W. 524 ms. Situated at the confluence of Wells and Connecticut rivers.

WELLSVILLE, p. v., Scio township, Alleghany co., N. Y., 270 ms. w. of Albany ; from W. 316 ms. Watered by Genesee river.

WELLSVILLE, p. o., York co., Pa.

WELLSVILLE, p. v., Yellow Creek township, Columbiana co., O., 51 ms. N. E. of Columbus ; from W. 272 ms. Watered by Ohio river and Little Yellow creek. Pop. 1,505.

WELSHFIELD, p. o., Geauga co., O., 160 ms. N. E. of Columbus ; from W. 326 ms.

WELSH RUN, p. o., Montgomery township co., Pa., 67 ms. N. w. of Harrisburgh ; from W. 80 ms.

WELTON, p. o., Clinton co., Iowa.

WENDELL. p. t., Sullivan co., N. H., 44 ms. N. w. of Concord ; from W. 479 ms. Watered by Sunapee lake. Pop. 787.

WENDELL, p. t., Franklin co., Mass., 78 ms. w. of Boston ; from W. 408 ms. Watered by Miller's river.

WENDELL DEPOT, p. o., Wendell township, Franklin co., Mass.

WENHAM, p. t., Essex co., Mass., 20 ms. N. of Boston, from W. 460 ms. Watered by Wenham lake, the source of most of the ice exported from Boston. Pop. 977.

WENLOCK, t., Essex co., Vt., 53 ms. N. E. of Montpelier ; from W. 560 ms. Watered by Nulhegan river. Unorganized town. Pop. 26.

WENTWORTH, t., Grafton co., N. H., 56 ms. N. w. of Concord ; from W. 517 ms. Watered by Baker's river. Pop. 1,197.

WENTWORTH, c. h., p. v., seat of justice of Rockingham co., N. C., 116 ms. N. w. of Raleigh ; from W. 285 ms. Watered by a tributary of Dan river.

WENTWORTH, p. o., Lake co., Ill.

WENTWORTH'S LOCATION, p. o., Coos co., N. H.

WEQUIOC, p. o., Jasper co., Iowa.

WESAW, t., Berrien co., Mich.

WESCOSVILLE, p. o., Lehigh co., Pa.

WESLEY, p. t., Washington co., Me., 169 ms. E. of Augusta; from W. 751 ms. Pop. 329.

WESLEY, p. o., Venango co., Pa., 220 ms. N. W. of Harrisburgh; from W. 271 ms.

WESLEY, p. o., Monroe co., Miss.

WESLEY, p. v., Haywood co., Tenn., 174 ms. s. w. of Nashville; from W. 859 ms.

WESLEY, p. o., Hickman co., Ky.

WESLEY, p. t., Washington co., O., 94 ms. s. E. of Columbus; from W. 315 ms. Pop. 1,560.

WESLEY, p. v., Fulton co., Ind., 107 ms. N. of Indianapolis; from W. 610 ms.

WESLEY CHAPEL, p. o., Tippecanoe co., Ind.

WESLEY CITY, p. o., Tazewell co., Ill.

WESLEYVILLE, p. v., Mill Creek township, Erie co., Pa., 274 ms. N. w. of Harrisburgh; from W. 347 ms.

WESOBULGA, p. o., Randolph co., Ala.

WEST, p. t., Huntingdon co., Pa. Watered by Frankstown branch of Juniata river. Pop. 982.

WEST, p. t., Columbiana co., O. Watered by tributaries of Sandy creek, and Sandy and Beaver canal. Pop. 2.110.

WEST ACTON, p. o., Middlesex co., Mass.

WEST ADDISON, p. o., Addison township, Steuben co., N. Y., 233 ms. w. of Albany; from W. 298 ms.

WEST ALBURGH, p. o., Alburgh township, Grand Isle co., Vt., 91 ms. N. w. of Montpelier; from W. 565 ms.

WEST ALEXANDRIA, p. v., Donegal township, Washington co., Pa., 225 ms. w. of Harrisburgh; from W. 253 ms.

WEST ALEXANDRIA, p. v., Preble co., O., 188 ms. w. of Columbus; from W. 481 ms. Watered by Twin creek.

WEST ALMOND, p. t., Alleghany co., N. Y., 255 ms. w. of Albany; from W. 330 ms. Watered by Angelica creek.

WEST ALTON, p. v., Alton township, Belknap co., N. H., 36 ms. N. E. of Concord; from W. 517 ms.

WEST AMESBURY, p. o., Amesbury township, Essex co., Mass., 41 ms. N. E. of Boston; from W. 471 ms.

WEST ANDOVER, p. o., Andover township, Merrimack co., N. H.

WEST ANSON, p. o., Ashtabula co., O.

WEST ANSON, p. o., Somerset co., Me.

WEST ARLINGTON, p. v., Arlington township, Bennington co., Vt., 106 ms. s. w. of Montpelier; from W. 416 ms.

WEST ASHFORD, p. o., Ashford township, Windham co., Ct.

WEST AUBURN, p. o., Auburn township, Susquehanna co., Pa., 165 N. E. of Harrisburgh; from W. 276 ms.

WEST AURORA, p. o., Erie co., N. Y.

WEST AVON, p. o., Hartford co., Ct.

WEST BAINBRIDGE, p. o., Chenango co., N. Y.

WEST BALDWIN, p. o., Baldwin township, Cumberland co., Me., 76 ms. s. w. of Augusta; from W. 552 ms.

WEST BALTIMORE, p. o., Montgomery co., O.

WEST BARNSTABLE, p. v., Barnstable township, Barnstable co., Mass., 68 ms. s. E. of Boston; from W. 469 ms.

WEST BARRE, p. o., Barre township, Huntingdon co., Pa., 88 ms. w. of Harrisburgh; from W. 166 ms.

WEST BARRE, p. o., Fulton co., O.

WEST BATAVIA, p. o., Genesee co., N. Y.

WEST BATON ROUGE PARISH, situated in the central part of Louisiana, with Mississippi river on the east and the Red on the west. Area, 700 square miles. Face of the country, level; soil fertile, but mostly subject to inundation. Seat of justice, West Baton Rouge. Pop. in 1820, 2,335; in 1830, 3,084; in 1840, 4,638; in 1850, 6,270.

WEST BATON ROUGE, c. h., seat of justice of West Baton Rouge parish, La. Watered by Mississippi river.

WEST BEAVER, p. o., Columbiana co., O.

WEST BECKET, p. o., Becket township, Berkshire co., Mass., 121 ms. w. of Boston; from W. 373 ms.

WEST BEDFORD, p. v. Bedford township, Coshocton co., O., 73 ms. N. E. of Columbus; from W. 350 ms.

WEST BEND, p. o., Washington co., Wis.

WEST BERGEN, p. o., Bergen township, Genesee co., N. Y.

WEST BERKSHIRE, p. o., Berkshire township, Franklin co., Vt., 71 ms. N. w. of Montpelier; from W. 556 ms.

WEST BERLIN, p. o., Rensselaer co., N. Y.

WEST BERLIN, p. o., St. Clair co., Mich.

WEST BETHANY, p. o., Genesee co., N. Y.

WEST BETHEL, p. o., Bethel township, Oxford co., Me., 67 ms. w. of Augusta; from W. 606 ms.

WEST BETHLEHEM, p. t., Washington co., Pa.

WEST BLOOMFIELD, p. t., Ontario co., N. Y., 219 ms.

w. of Albany; from W. 355 ms. Watered by Honeoya creek. Pop. 1,698.

WEST BLOOMFIELD, p. v., Bloomfield township, Essex co., N. J., 56 ms. N. E. of Trenton; from W. 226 ms.

WEST BLOOMFIELD, p. t., Oakland co., Mich., 32 ms. N. w. of Detroit; from W. 556 ms. Pop. 1,086.

WEST BOLTON, p. o., Chittenden co., Vt.

WESTBOROUGH, p. t., Worcester co., Mass., 30 ms. w. of Boston; from W. 412 ms. Watered by tributaries of Concord and Sudbury rivers. Pop. 2,371.

WESTBOROUGH, p. o., Clinton co., O.

WEST BOSCAWEN, p. o., Boscawen township, Merrimack co., N. H., 19 ms. N. w. of Concord; from W. 484 ms.

WEST BOXFORD, p. o., Boxford township, Essex co., Mass., 27 ms. N. of Boston; from W. 460 ms.

WEST BOYLSTON, p. t., Worcester co., Mass., 42 ms. w. of Boston; from W. 405 ms. Pop. 1,749.

WEST BRADFORD, p. t., Chester co., Pa., 70 ms. s. E. of Harrisburgh; from W. 110 ms. Watered by Brandywine river. Pop. 1,585.

WEST BRAINTREE, p. o., Braintree township, Orange co., Vt., 32 ms. s. w. of Montpelier; from W. 495 ms.

WEST BRANCH, p. o., Western township, Oneida co., N. Y., 120 ms. N. w. of Albany; from W. 404 ms.

WEST BRATTLEBOROUGH, p. v., Windham co., Vt., 123 ms. s. of Montpelier; from W. 424 ms.

WEST BREWSTER, p. o., Brewster township, Barnstable co., Mass., 87 ms. s. E. of Boston; from W. 488 ms.

WEST BRIDGEWATER, p. t., Plymouth co., Mass., 25 ms. s. of Boston; from W. 431 ms. Watered by a tributary of Taunton river. Pop. 1,447.

WEST BROOK, p. t., Cumberland co., Me., 59 ms. s. w. of Augusta; from W. 550 ms. Watered by Presumpscot river. Pop. 4,852.

WEST BROOK, p. t., Middlesex co., Ct., 47 ms. s. of Hartford; from W. 229 ms. Watered by Pochaug river. Pop. 1,202.

WEST BROOK, p. o., Bladen co., N. C., 117 ms. s. of Raleigh; from W. 396 ms.

WEST BROOKFIELD, p. o., Brookfield township, Worcester co., Mass., 62 ms. w. of Boston; from W. 391 ms.

WEST BROOKFIELD, p. o., Stark co., O.

WEST BROOKVILLE, p. o., Mamakating township, Sullivan co., N. Y., 118 ms. s. w. of Albany; from W. 974 ms.

WEST BROOKVILLE, p. o., Brookville township, Hancock co., Me., 80 ms. E. of Augusta; from W. 676 ms.

WEST BROWNSVILLE, p. o., Washington co., Pa.

WEST BRUNSWICK, p. t., Schuylkill co., Pa. Pop. 1,604.

WEST BUFFALO, p. t., Union co., Pa. Watered by White Deer, Buffalo, and Penn's creek. Pop. 1,007.

WEST BUFFALO, p. o., Scott co., Iowa.

WEST BURLINGTON, p. o., Burlington township, Otsego co., N. Y., 86 ms. w. of Albany; from W. 358 ms.

WEST BURLINGTON, p. o., Burlington township. Bradford co., Pa., 148 ms. N. of Harrisburgh; from W. 258 ms.

WESTBURY, p. o., Wayne co., N. Y.

WEST BUTLER, p. o., Wayne co., N. Y.

WEST BUXTON, p. o., York co., Me.

WEST CALN, p. t., Chester co., Pa. Watered by west branch of Brandywine river. Pop. 1,508.

WEST CAMBRIDGE, p. t., Middlesex co., Mass., 6 ms. N. w. of Boston; from W. 446 ms. Watered by Alewife brook and Spy pond.

WEST CAMDEN, p. o., Camden township, Waldo co., Me., 48 ms. s. E. of Augusta; from W. 625 ms.

WEST CAMDEN, p. o., Camden township, Oneida co., N. Y.

WEST CAMERON, p. o., Cameron township, Steuben co., N. Y.

WEST CAMP, p. v., Saugerties township, Ulster co., N. Y., 42 ms. s. of Albany; from W. 334 ms. Watered by Hudson river.

WEST CAMPTON, p. o., Grafton co., N. H.

WEST CANAAN, p. v., Canaan township, Madison co., O., 22 ms. w. of Columbus; from W. 415 ms. Watered by Big Darby creek.

WEST CANAAN, p. o., Grafton co., N. H.

WEST CANDOR, p. o., Candor township, Tioga co., N. Y., 175 ms. s. w. of Albany; from W. 284 ms.

WEST CARLISLE, p. v., Pike township, Coshocton co., O., 72 ms. N. E. of Columbus; from W. 354 ms. Situated on the Ohio canal.

WEST CARLTON, p. o., Carlton township, Orleans co., N. Y., 262 ms. w. of Albany ; from W. 405 ms.

WEST CAYUTA, p. o., Cayuta township, Chemung co., N. Y., 195 ms. w. of Albany ; from W. 296 ms.

WEST CHARLESTON, p. v., Charleston township, Penobscot co., Me., 93 ms. N. E. of Augusta ; from W. 688 ms.

WEST CHARLESTON, p. v., Charleston township, Orleans co., Vt., 64 ms. N. E. of Montpelier ; from W. 580 ms. Watered by Clyde river.

WEST CHARLESTON, p. v., Bethel township, Miami co., O., 78 ms. w. of Columbus ; from W. 471 ms.

WEST CHARLTON, p. v., Charlton township, Saratoga co., N. Y., 33 ms. N. w. of Albany ; from W. 401 ms.

WEST CHAZY, p. v., Chazy township, Clinton co., N. Y., 173 ms. N. of Albany ; from W. 547 ms. Watered by Little Chazy river.

WEST CHELMSFORD, p. o., Chelmsford township, Middlesex co., Mass.

WESTCHESTER COUNTY, situated in the southeast part of New York, with Long Island sound on the southeast, and Hudson river on the west. Area, 470 square miles. Face of the country, rough and hilly ; soil, generally productive. Seats of justice, White Plains and Bedford. Pop. in 1810, 30,272 ; in 1820, 32,638 ; in 1830, 36,456 ; in 1840, 48 686 ; in 1850. 57,263.

WESTCHESTER, p. v., Colchester township, New London co., Ct., 29 ms. s. E. of Hartford ; from W. 343 ms.

WESTCHESTER, p. t., Westchester co., N. Y., 146 ms. s. of Albany ; from W. 237 ms. Watered by East and Bronx rivers. Pop. 2,492.

WEST CHESTER, c. h., p. b., seat of justice of Chester co., Pa., 73 s. E. of Harrisburgh ; from W. 118 ms. Pop. 3,172.

WEST CHESTER, p. v., Union township, Butler co., O., 106 ms. s. w. of Columbus ; from W. 490 ms.

WEST CHESTERFIELD, p. o., Chesterfield township, Hampshire co., Mass.

WEST CLAREMONT, p. o., Claremont township, Sullivan co., N. H., 53 ms. N. w. of Concord ; from W. 460 ms.

WEST CLAKSVILLE, p. o., Clarksville township, Alleghany co., N. Y., 289 ms. w. of Albany ; from W. 308 ms.

WEST CLIMAX, p. o., Kalamazoo co., Mich.

WEST COCALICO, p. t., Lancaster co., Pa. Watered by Cocalico creek.

WEST COLESVILLE, p. o., Broome co., N. Y.

WEST COLUMBIA, p. o., Mason co., Va.

WEST CONCORD, p. v., Merrimack co., N. H. Watered by Merrimack river.

WEST CONCORD, p. o., Essex co., Vt.

WEST CONCORD, p. o., Concord township, Erie co., N. Y.

WEST CONESUS, p. o., Conesus township, Livingston co., N. Y., 234 ms. w. of Albany ; from W. 343 ms.

WEST CONSTABLE, p. o., Westville township, Franklin co., N. Y., 221 ms. N. of Albany ; from 550 ms.

WEST CORNWALL, p. o., Addison co., Vt.

WEST CORNWALL, p. o., Cornwall township, Litchfield co., Ct., 41 ms. w. of Hartford ; from W. 331 ms. Watered by Housatonic river.

WEST CREEK, p. o., Ocean co., N. J., 66 ms. E. of Trenton ; from W. 195 ms.

WEST CREEK, p. o., Lake co., Ind., 179 ms. N. w. of Indianapolis ; from W. 714 ms.

WEST CUMBERLAND, p. o., Cumberland co., Me.

WEST DANBY, p. o., Tompkins co., N. Y.

WEST DANVILLE, p. o., Cumberland co., Me.

WEST DAVENPORT, p. o., Davenport township, Delaware co., N. Y., 77 ms. s. w. of Albany ; from W. 354 ms.

WEST DAY, p. o., Day township, Saratoga co., N. Y., 60 ms. N. of Albany ; from W. 428 ms.

WEST DEDHAM, p. v., Dedham township, Norfolk co., Mass., 16 ms. s. w. of Boston ; from W. 430 ms.

WEST DEER, p. t., Alleghany co., Pa. Watered by Deer creek. Pop. 1,716.

WEST DEERFIELD, p. o., Deerfield township, Rockingham co., N. H., 14 ms. s. E. of Concord ; from W. 476 ms.

WEST DENNIS, p. o., Dennis township, Barnstable co., Mass. 83 ms. s. E. of Boston ; from 484 ms.

WEST DERBY, p. o., Derby township, Orleans co., Vt., 61 ms. N. of Montpelier ; from W. 577 ms.

WEST DONEGAL, p. t., Lancaster co., Pa. Pop. 1,982.

WEST DOVER, p. o., Dover township, Windham co., Vt.

WEST DOVER, p. o., Dover township, Piscataquis co., Me.

WEST DRESDEN, p. o., Yates co., N. Y., 190 ms. w. of Albany ; from W. 327 ms.

WEST DRYDEN, p. v., Dryden township, Tompkins co., N. Y., 169 ms. w. of Albany ; from W. 305 ms.

WEST DUBLIN, p. o., Fulton co., Pa.

WEST DUMMERSTON, p. o., Dummerston township, Windham co., Vt., 119 ms. s. of Montpelier ; from W. 429 ms.

WEST DURHAM, p. o., Cumberland co., Me.

WEST DUXBURY, p. o, Plymouth co, Mass.

WEST EARL, p. t., Lancaster co., Pa. Watered by Conestoga creek.

WEST EATON, p. o., Madison co., N. Y.

WEST EDMESTON, p. o., Edmeston township, Otsego co., N. Y., 90 ms. w. of Albany ; from W. 360 ms.

WEST ELY, p. o., Marion co., Mo., 119 ms. N. E. of Jefferson city ; from W. 933 ms.

WEST ELLERY, p. o., Chautauque co., N. Y.

WEST ELIZABETH, p. o., Alleghany co., Pa.

WEST ELKTON, p. o., Preble co., O.

WEST EMBDEN, p. o., Embden township, Somerset co., Me., 48 ms. N. w. of Augusta ; from W. 643 ms.

WEST END. p. o., Bedford co., Pa.

WEST ENFIELD, p. o., Penobscot co., Me.

WEST ENFIELD, p. o., Grafton co., N. H.

WEST ENOSBURGH, p. o., Enosburgh township, Franklin co., Vt., 58 ms. N. w. of Montpelier ; from W. 555 ms.

WESTERLOO, p. t., Albany co., N. Y., 22 ms. s. w. of Albany ; from W. 368 ms. Watered by Provost creek. Pop. 2,860.

WESTERLY, p. t., Washington co., R. I., 42 ms. s. w. of Providence ; from W. 373 ms. Watered by Atlantic ocean and Pawcatuck river. Pop. 2,763.

WESTERMAN'S MILLS, p. o., Baltimore co., Md.

WESTERN, p. t., Oneida co., N. Y., 116 ms. N. w. of Albany ; from W. 406 ms. Watered by Mohawk river and tributaries. Pop. 2,516.

WESTERN, p. o., Poweshiek co., Iowa.

WESTERN FORD, p. o., Randolph co., Va., 240 ms. N. w. of Richmond ; from W. 266 ms.

WESTERNPORT, p. v., Alleghany co.. Md., 187 ms. N. w. of Annapolis ; from W. 147 ms. Watered by Potomac and Savage rivers.

WESTERN PRONG, p. o., Bladen co., N. C., 115 ms. s. w. of Raleigh ; from W. 403 ms.

WESTERN SARATOGA, p. o., Union co., Ill.

WESTERN STAR, p. o., Summit co., O., 122 ms. N. E. of Columbus ; from W. 337 ms.

WESTERNVILLE, p. v., Western township, Oneida co., N. Y., 109 ms. N. w. of Albany ; from W. 399 ms. Watered by Mohawk river.

WESTERNVILLE. p. o., Franklin co., O., 14 ms. from Columbus ; from W. 406 ms.

WEST EXETER, p. o., Exeter township, Otsego co., N. Y., 81 ms. w. of Albany ; from W. 371 ms.

WEST FAIRFIELD, p. v., Fairfield township, Westmoreland co., Pa., 160 ms. w. of Harrisburgh ; from W. 186 ms.

WEST FAIRLEE, p. t., Orange co., Vt., 36 ms. s. E. of Montpelier ; from W. 505 ms. Watered by Ompompanoosuc river. Pop. 696.

WEST FAIRVIEW, p. o., Cumberland co., Pa.

WEST FALMOUTH, p. o., Falmouth township, Cumberland co., Me., 56 ms. s. w. of Augusta ; from W. 552 ms.

WEST FALMOUTH, p. o., Falmouth township, Barnstable co., Mass., 71 ms. s. E. of Boston ; from W. 469 ms.

WESTFALL, p. t., Pike co., O. Pop. 567.

WEST FALLOWFIELD, p. t., Chester co., Pa., 65 ms. s. E. of Harrisburgh ; from W. 115 ms. Watered by Buck and Doe rivers, and Octara creek. Pop. 2,290.

WEST FALLS, p. o., Erie co., N. Y.

WEST FARMINGTON, p. o., Farmington township, Ontario co., N. Y., 201 ms. w. of Albany ; from W. 347 ms.

WEST FARMS, p. t., Westchester co., N. Y., 146 ms. s. of Albany ; from W. 237 ms. Watered by Bronx and Harlem rivers. Pop. 4,436.

WEST FAYETTE, p. o., Fayette township, Seneca co., N. Y., 182 ms. w. of Albany ; from W. 326 ms.

WEST FELICIANA PARISH, situated on the north boundary of Louisiana, with Mississippi river on the southwest. Area, 600 square miles. Face of the country, undulating, subsiding into a plain toward the Mis sissippi. Seat of justice, St. Francisville. Pop. in 1830, 8,629 ; in 1840, 10,910 ; in 1850, 13,245.

WESTFIELD, p. t., Orleans co., Vt., 51 ms. N. of Montpelier ; from W. 567 ms. Watered by Missisque river and tributaries. Pop. 502.

WESTFIELD, p. t., Hampden co., Mass., 100 ms. w. of Boston : from W. 364 ms. Watered by Westfield and Little rivers. Pop. 4,180.

WESTFIEI D, p. t., Richmond co., Staten Island, N. Y. Watered by New York bay and Staten Island sound. Pop. 2,943.

WESTFIELD, p. t., Chautauque co., N. Y., 342 ms. w. of Albany ; from W. 345 ms. Watered by Chautauque creek and Lake Erie. Pop. 3,100.

WESTFIELD, p. t., Essex co., N. J., 45 ms. N. E. of Trenton ; from W. 212 ms. Watered by Rahway river and Green brook. Pop. 1,575.

WESTFIELD, p t., Tioga co., Pa., 168 ms. N. of Harrisburgh ; from W. 282 ms. Watered by Cowanesque creek. Pop. 1,348.

WESTFIELD, p. t., Morrow co., O., 28 ms. N. of Columbus ; from W. 413 ms. Watered by east fork of Olentangy river. Pop. 1,414.

WESTFIELD, t., Medina co., O. Pop. 1,122.

WESTFIELD, p. o., Hamilton co., Ind., 27 ms. N. of Indianapolis ; from W. 581 ms.

WESTFIELD, p. o., Clark co., Ill. 106 ms. E. of Springfield ; from W. 678 ms.

WESTFIELD, p. o., Marquette co., Wis.

WESTFIELD, p. o., Fayette co., Iowa.

WEST FINLEY, p. t., Washington co., Pa., 231 ms. w. of Harrisburgh ; from W. 247 ms. Watered by tributaries of Wheeling creek. Pop. 1,213.

WEST FITCHBURGH, p. o., Worcester co., Mass.

WEST FLORENCE. p. v., Jackson township, Preble co., O., 101 ms. w. of Columbus ; from W. 494 ms.

WESTFORD, p. t., Chittenden co., Vt., 56 ms. N. w. of Montpelier ; from W. 531 ms. Watered by Brown's river. Pop. 1,458.

WESTFORD, p. t., Middlesex co., Mass., 32 ms. N. w. of Boston ; from W. 436 ms. Watered by Stony river. Pop. 1,473.

WESTFORD, p. v., Windham co., Ct., 30 ms. E. of Hartford ; from W. 366 ms. Watered by a tributary of Mount Hope river.

WESTFORD. p. t., Otsego co., N. Y., 65 ms. w. of Albany ; from W. 379 ms. Watered by Cherry Valley and Dlk creeks. Pop. 1,423.

WEST FORK p. o., Overton co., Tenn., 108 ms. E. of Nashville ; from W. 596 ms.

WEST FORK, p. t., Washington co., Ark. Pop. 605.

WEST FORT ANN, p. o., Washington co., N. Y.

WEST FOWLER, p. o., St. Lawrence co., N. Y.

WEST FOXBOROUGH, p. o., Foxborough township, Norfolk co., Mass., 27 ms. s. w. of Boston ; from W. 418 ms.

WEST FRANKLIN, p. o., Bradford co., Pa.

WEST FRANKLIN, p. v., Posey co., Ind., 182 ms. s. w. of Indianapolis ; from W. 737 ms.

WEST FREEDOM, p. o., Waldo co., Me.

WEST FREEMAN, p. o., Franklin co., Me.

WE-T FULTON, p. o., Schoharie co., N. Y.

WEST FULTON, p. o., Itawamba co., Miss.

WEST GAINES. p. o., Gaines township, Orleans co., N. Y., 256 ms. w. of Albany ; from W. 398 ms.

WEST GALWAY, p. o., Broadalbin township, Fulton co., N. Y., 39 ms. N. w. of Albany ; from W. 407 ms.

WEST GARLAND, p. o., Penobscot co., Me.

WEST GENESEE, p. o., Genesee township. Alleghany co., N. Y., 293 ms. w. of Albany ; from W. 304 ms.

WEST GILBOA, p. o., Schoharie co., N. Y.

WEST GLAZE, p. o., Camden co., Mo.

WEST GLENBURN, p. o., Glenburn township, Penobscot co., Me., 77 ms. N. E. of Augusta ; from W. 672 ms.

WEST GLOUCESTER, p. o., New Gloucester township, Cumberland co., Me., 54 ms. s. w. of Augusta ; from W. 568 ms.

WEST GORHAM, p. o., Cumberland co., Me., 63 ms. s. w. of Augusta ; from W. 542 ms.

WEST GOSHEN, p. o., Goshen township, Litchfield co., Ct.

WEST GOSHEN, p. t., Chester co., Pa. Watered by tributaries of Chester creek and Brandywine river.

WEST GOLDSBOROUGH, p. o., Goldsborough township, Hancock co., Me., 108 ms. E. of Augusta ; from W. 690 ms. Watered by Frenchman's bay.

WEST GRANBY, p. o., Granby township, Hartford

co., Ct., 19 ms. N. w. of Hartford ; from W. 355 ms. Watered by a tributary of Farmington river.

WEST GRANVILLE, p. v., Granville township. Hampden co., Mass., 114 ms. w. of Boston ; from W. 366 ms.

WEST GREAT WORKS, p. o., Penobscot co., Me.

WEST GREECE, p. o., Monroe co., N. Y.

WEST GREENFIELD, p. o., Greenfield township, Saratoga co., N. Y., 36 ms. N. of Albany ; from W. 406 ms.

WEST GREENVILLE, p. t., Mercer co., Pa., 245 ms. w. of Harrisburgh ; from W. 292 ms. Pop. 1,036.

WEST GREENWICH, p. t., Kent co , R. I., 18 ms. s. w. of Providence ; from W. 390 ms. Watered by Wood river, and the south branch of the Pawtuxet. Pop. 1,350.

WEST GREENWICH CENTRE, p. o., West Greenwich township, Kent co., R. I.

WEST GREENWOOD, p. o., Steuben co., N. Y.

WEST GROTON, p. o., Middlesex co., Mass.

WEST GROTON, p. o., Groton township, Tompkins co., N. Y., 170 ms. w. of Albany ; from W. 310 ms.

WEST GROVE, p. o., Chester co., Pa., 74 ms. s. E. of Harrisburgh ; from W. 98 ms.

WEST HADLEY, p. o., Hadley township, Saratoga co., N. Y.

WEST HALIFAX, p. o., Halifax township, Windham co., Vt., 138 ms. s. of Montpelier ; from W. 419 ms.

WEST HAMPDEN, p. o., Penobscot co., Me., 56 ms. N. E. of Augusta ; from W. 650 ms.

WEST HAMPTON, p. t., Hampshire co., Mass., 99 ms. w. of Boston ; from W. 386 ms. Watered by North river. Pop. 602.

WEST HANOVER, p. v., Dauphin co., Pa., 16 ms. s. w. of Harrisburgh ; from W. 126 ms.

WEST HARPETH, p. o., Williamson co., Tenn.

WEST HARPSWELL, p. o., Cumberland co., Me.

WEST HARTFORD, p. o., Hartford township, Windsor co., Vt., 43 ms. s. of Montpelier ; from W. 336 ms.

WEST HARTFORD, p. v., Hartford township, Hartford co., Ct., 4 ms. N. w. of Hartford ; from W. 493 ms.

WEST HARTLAND, p. v., Hartland township, Hartford co., Ct., 31 ms. N. w. of Hartford ; from W. 367 ms.

WEST HARWICK, p. o., Harwick township, Barnstable co., Mass., 87 ms. s. E. of Boston ; from W. 488 ms.

WEST HAVEN, p. t., Rutland co., Vt., 91 ms. s. w. of Montpelier ; from W. 451 ms. Watered by Lake Champlain, Poultney and Hubbardton rivers, and Coguian's creek. Pop, 718.

WEST HAVEN, p. v., New Haven co., Ct.

WEST HAVERFORD, p. o., Haverford township, Delaware co., Pa., 88 ms. s. E. of Harrisburgh ; from W. 138 ms.

WEST HAWLEY, p. o., Franklin co., Mass.

WEST HEBRON, p. o., Hebron township, Washington co., N. Y., 52 ms. N. of Albany ; from W. 423 ms.

WEST HEBRON, p. o., McHenry co., Ill.

WEST HEMPFIELD, p. t., Lancaster co., Pa. Watered by Susquehanna river, and Chicque's and Strickler's creeks. Pop. 1,618.

WEST HENRIETTA, p. o., Henrietta township, Monroe co., N. Y., 232 ms. w. of Albany ; from W. 381 ms.

WEST HILLS, p. o., Huntington township, Suffolk co., Long Island, N. Y., 180 ms. s. E. of Albany ; from W. 260 ms.

WEST HOWLAND, p. o., Penobscot co., Me.

WEST HURLEY, p. o., Hurley township, Ulster co., N. Y.

WEST JEFFERSON, p. v., Lincoln co., Me., 16 ms. s. E. of Augusta ; from W. 608 ms.

WEST JEFFERSON, p. v., Jefferson township, Madison co., O., 14 ms. w. of Columbus ; from W. 407 ms. Watered by Little Darby creek. Pop. 436.

WEST JERSEY, p. o., Stark co., Ill.

WEST JUNIUS, p. o., Seneca co., N. Y.

WEST KENDALL, p. o., Orleans co., N. Y.

WEST KILL, p. v., Lexington township, Greene co., N. Y., 59 ms. s. w. of Albany ; from W. 369 ms.

WEST KILLINGLY, p. v., Killingly township, Windham co., Ct., 48 ms. E. of Hartford ; from W. 375 ms.

WEST KINDERHOOK, p. o., Tipton co., Ind.

WEST LAFAYETTE, p. o., Lafayette township, Coshocton co., O., 89 ms. N. E. of Columbus ; from W. 333 ms.

WESTLAND, p. v., Halifax co., N. C., 86 ms. N. E. of Raleigh ; from W. 218 ms.

WESTLAND, p. t., Guernsey co., O., 70 ms. E. of Columbus ; from W. 310 ms. Watered by Crooked creek. Pop. 1,126.

WEST LAURENS, p. o., Otsego co., N. Y.

25

WEST LEBANON, p. t., Lebanon township, York co., Me.. 94 ms. s. w. of Augusta ; from W. 518 ms.

WEST LEBANON, p. o., Lebanon township, Grafton co., N. H., 54 ms. N. w. of Concord ; from W. 486 ms.

WEST LEBANON, p. o., Indiana co., Pa.

WEST LEBANON, p. v., Wayne co., O.

WEST LEBANON, p. v., Warren co., Ind., 84 ms. N. w. of Indianapolis ; from W. 651 ms.

WEST LEVANT, p. o., Penobscot co.. Me.

WEST LEXINGTON, p.o., Lexington township, Greene co., N. Y., 64 ms. s. w. of Albany ; from W. 350 ms.

WEST LEYDEN, p. o.. Leyden township, Lewis co., N. Y., 129 ms. N. w. of Albany ; from W. 413 ms.

WEST LIBERTY, p. v., Ohio co., Va., 357 ms. N. w. of Richmond ; from W. 264 ms.

WEST LIBERTY, c. h., p. v., seat of justice of Morgan co., Ky., 107 ms. E. of Frankfort : from W. 487 ms. Watered by Licking river.

WEST LIBERTY, p. v., Union township, Logan co., O., 57 ms. N. w. of Columbus ; from W. 450 ms. Watered by Mad river. Pop. 643.

WEST LIBERTY, p. o., Jay co., Ind., 106 ms. N. E. of Indianapolis ; from W. 529 ms.

WEST LIBERTY, p. o., Muscatine co., Iowa. Watered by Wapsinoenock river.

WEST LIBERTY, p. o., Liberty co., Tex.

WEST LINKLAEN, p. o., Linklaen township, Chenango co., N. Y., 128 ms. w. of Albany ; from W. 339 ms.

WEST LITTLETON, p. o., Middlesex co., Mass.

WEST LODI, p. o., Lodi township, Seneca co., O.

WEST LOWVILLE, p. o., Lowville township, Lewis co., N. Y., 141 ms. N. w. of Albany ; from W. 431 ms.

WEST LUBEC, p. o., Washington co., Me.

WEST MACEDON, p. o., Wayne co., N. Y.

WEST MADAWASKA, p. o., Aroostook co., Me.

WEST MANCHESTER. p. t., York co., Pa. Watered by Conewago and Codorus creeks. Pop. 1,361.

WEST MANCHESTER, p. o., Alleghany co., Pa.

WEST MARLBOROUGH, p. t., Chester co., Pa. Watered by Clay creek. Pop. 1,130.

WEST MARTINSBURGH. p. v., Martinsburgh township, Lewis co., N. Y., 137 ms. N. w. of Albany ; from W. 435 ms.

WEST MEDWAY, p. o., Medway township, Norfolk co., Mass., 30 ms. s. w. of Boston : from W. 416 ms.

WEST MERIDEN, p. o., Meriden township, New Haven co., Ct.

WEST MEREDITH, p. o., Meredith township, Delaware co., N. Y., 83 ms. s. w. of Albany ; from W. 344 ms.

WEST MIDDLEBURGH. p. v., Logan co., O., 56 ms. N. w. of Columbus ; from W. 446 ms.

WEST MIDDLESEX. p. o., Mercer co., Pa., 253 ms. N. w. of Harrisburgh ; from W. 294 ms.

WEST MIDDLETOWN, p. b., Washington co., Pa., 222 ms. w. of Harrisburgh ; from W. 249 ms. Pop. 326.

WEST MILFORD, p. t., Passaic co., N. J., 100 ms. N. E. of Trenton ; from W. 266 ms. Pop. 2,624.

WEST MILFORD, p. o., Harrison co., Va.

WEST MILLBURY, p. o., Millbury township, Worcester co., Mass., 46 ms. s. w. of Boston ; from W. 400 ms.

WEST MILL GROVE, p. o., Perry township, Wood co.. O., 99 ms. N. w. of Columbus ; from W. 444 ms.

WEST MILTON. p. o., Milton township, Chittenden co., Vt., 52 ms. N. w. of Montpelier ; from W. 525 ms.

WEST MILTON, p. v., Milton township, Saratoga co., N. Y., 31 ms. N. of Albany ; from W. 401 ms.

WEST MILTON, p. o., Milton township, Miami co., O., 85 ms. w. of Columbus ; from W. 478 ms.

WEST MINOT, p. o., Minot township, Cumberland co., Me., 41 ms. s. w. of Augusta ; from W. 582 ms.

WESTMINSTER, p. t., Windham co., Vt., 103 ms. s. of Montpelier ; from W. 440 ms. Watered by Connecticut river. Pop. 1,721.

WESTMINSTER, p. t., Worcester co., Mass., 53 ms. N. w. of Boston ; from W. 420 ms. Watered by tributaries of Nashua river. Pop. 1,914.

WESTMINSTER, p. v., Canterbury township, Windham co., Ct., 38 ms. E. of Hartford : from W. 365 ms.

WESTMINSTER, c. h., p. v., seat of justice of Carroll co., Md., 58 ms. N. w. of Annapolis ; from W. 68 ms. Watered by head-waters of Patapsco river. Pop. 845.

WESTMINSTER, p. o., Guilford co., N. C.

WESTMINSTER, p. o., Allen co., O., 102 ms. N. w. of Columbus ; from W. 479 ms.

WESTMINSTER. p. o., Shelby co.. Ill.

WESTMINSTER WEST, p. v., Westminster township, Windham co., Vt., 106 ms. s. of Montpelier ; from W. 443 ms.

WEST MONROE, p. t., Oswego co., N. Y., 140 ms. N w. of Albany ; from W. 368 ms. Watered by Bog creek and Oneida lake. Pop. 1,197.

WESTMORE, t., Orleans co.. Vt. Watered by Willoughby's lake. Pop. 152.

WESTMORELAND COUNTY, situated in the southwest part of Pennsylvania, with Kiskiminitas river on the northeast, the Alleghany on the northwest, and traversed by the Youghiogheny. Area, 1,050 square miles. Face of the country, hilly ; soil, generally productive. Seat of justice, Greensburgh. Pop. in 1810, 26,392 ; in 1820, 30,540 ; in 1830, 38,400 ; in 1840, 42,699 ; in 1850. 51,726.

WESTMORELAND COUNTY, situated on the northeast boundary of Virginia, with Potomac river on the northeast, and Rappahannock on the southwest. Area, 316 square miles. Seat of justice, Westmoreland c. h. Pop. in 1810, 8,102 ; in 1820, 6,901 ; in 1830, 8,411 ; in 1840, 8,019 ; in 1850, 8,080.

WESTMORELAND, p. t., Cheshire co., N. H., 65 ms. s. w..of Concord ; from W. 436 ms. Watered by Connecticut river. Pop. 1,678.

WESTMORELAND, p. t., Oneida co., N. Y., 103 ms. N. w. of Albany ; from W. 392 ms. Watered by Oriskany creek. Pop. 3,291.

WESTMORELAND, c. h., p. v., seat of justice of Westmoreland co., Va., 70 ms. N. E. of Richmond ; from W. 105 ms.

WESTMORELAND, p. o., Dallas co., Ala.

WESTMORELANDVILLE, p. o., Lauderdale co., Ala.

WEST NANTICOKE, p. o., Luzerne co., Pa.

WEST NECK, p. o., Kalamazoo co., Mich.

WEST NANTMEAL, p. t., Chester co., Pa. Watered by east branch of Brandywine river, and Indian and French creeks. Pop. 1,803.

WEST NEEDHAM, p. v., Needham township, Norfolk co., Mass., 14 ms. s. w. of Boston ; from W. 426 ms.

WEST NEWARK, p. o., Tioga co., N. Y.

WEST NEWBURY, p. t., Essex co., Mass., 39 ms. N. of Boston ; from W. 470 ms. Watered by Merrimack river. Pop. 1,746.

WEST NEWFIELD, p. o., Newfield township, York co., Me., 84 ms. s. w. of Augusta ; from W. 530 ms.

WEST NEWPORT, p. o., Orleans co., Vt.

WEST NEWSTEAD, p. o., Erie co., N. Y.

WEST NEWTON, p. o., Newton township, Middlesex co., Mass., 9 ms. w. of Boston ; from W. 431 ms.

WEST NEWTON, p. o., Westmoreland co., Pa., 182 ms. w. of Harrisburgh ; from W. 208 ms.

WEST NEWTON, p. o., Allen co., O.

WEST NILES, p. o., Niles township, Cayuga co., N. Y., 165 ms. w. of Albany ; from W. 329 ms.

WEST NORFOLK, p. o., Litchfield co., Ct.

WEST NORTHFIELD, p. o., Franklin co., Mass.

WEST NORTHWOOD, p. o., Northwood township, Rockingham co., N. H., 18 ms. E. of Concord ; from W. 488 ms.

WEST NOTTINGHAM, p. t., Chester co., Pa. Watered by Octara creek. Pop. 721.

WEST OGDEN, p. o., Lenawee co., Mich.

WESTON, p. t., Aroostook co., Me., 259 ms. N. E. of Augusta ; from W. 824 ms. Watered by tributaries of Mattawamkeag river. Pop. 293.

WESTON, p. t., Windsor co., Vt., 91 ms. s. of Montpelier ; from W. 456 ms. Watered by West river. Pop. 950.

WESTON, p. t., Middlesex co., Mass., 14 ms. w. of Boston ; from W. 426 ms. Watered by Stony brook. Pop. 1,205.

WESTON, p. t., Fairfield co., Ct., 63 ms. s. w. of Hartford ; from W 281 ms. Watered by Saugatuck and Mill rivers. Pop. 1,056.

WESTON, p. o., Steuben co., N. Y.

WESTON, p. v., Somerset co., N. J., 20 ms. N. of Trenton ; from W. 204 ms. Watered by Millstone river, and Delaware and Raritan canal.

WESTON, c. h., p. v., seat of justice of Lewis co., Va., 281 ms. N. w. of Richmond ; from W. 249 ms. Watered by west fork of Monongahela river.

WESTON, p. t., Wood co., O., 129 ms. N. w. of Columbus ; from W. 467 ms. Watered by Maumee river. Pop. 546.

WESTON, p. o., Jo-Daviess co., Ill.

WESTON, p. v., Platte co., Mo. Watered by Missouri river.

WEST ONEONTA, p. o., Oneonta township, Otsego co.. N. Y., 83 ms. w. of Albany ; from W. 353 ms.

WEST ONONDAGA, p. o., Onondaga co., N. Y.

WEST OSSIPEE, p. o., Ossipee township, Carroll co., N. H., 63 ms. N. E. of Concord ; from W. 544 ms.

WEST OTIS, p. o., Otis township, Berkshire co, Mass., 122 ms. w. of Boston ; from W. 367 ms.

WEST PARSONSFIELD, p. o., Parsonsfield township. York co., Me., 89 ms. s. w. of Augusta ; from W. 535 ms.

WEST PENN, p. t., Schuylkill co., Pa., 79 ms. N. E. of Harrisburgh ; from W. 189 ms. Watered by Little Schuylkill river, and Mahoning and Lizard creeks. Pop. 2,411.

WEST PENNSBOROUGH, p. t., Cumberland co., Pa. Watered by Conedogwinit creek. Pop. 2,040.

WEST PERRYSBURGH, p. o., Cattaraugus co., N. Y.

WEST PERTH, p. o., Fulton co., N. Y.

WEST PERU, p. o., Oxford co., Me.

WESTPHALIA, p. o., Clinton co., Mich.

WESTPHALIA, p. o., Osage co., Mo.

WEST PHILADELPHIA, p. v., Philadelphia co., Pa., 97 ms. E. of Harrisburgh ; from W. 137 ms. Watered by Schuylkill river.

WEST PIERPONT, p. o., Ashtabula co., O.

WEST PIKE, p. o., Potter co., Pa.

WEST PIKELAND, t., Chester co., Pa. Watered by tributaries of Schuylkill river. Pop. 881.

WEST PIKE RUN, p. t., Washington co., Pa. Pop. 1,166.

WEST PLAINS, p. o., Oregon co., Mo.

WEST PITTSFIELD, p. o., Pittsfield township, Berkshire co., Mass.

WEST PLATTSBURGH, p. o., Plattsburgh township, Clinton co., N. Y., 168 ms. N. of Albany ; from W. 543 ms.

WEST PLYMOUTH, p. o., Plymouth township, Grafton co., N. H., 43 ms. N. of Concord ; from W. 524 ms.

WEST POINT, p. v., Cornwall township, Orange co., N. Y., 92 ms. s. of Albany ; from W. 278 ms. Watered by Hudson river. Site of the United States military academy.

WEST POINT, p. v., Troup co., Ga., 136 ms. w. of Milledgeville ; from W. 751 ms.

WEST POINT, p. v., Hardin co., Ky., 75 ms. w. of Frankfort ; from W. 615 ms. Watered by Ohio river.

WEST POINT, p. o., Lawrence co., Tenn.

WEST POINT, p. v., Columbiana co., O., 158 ms. N. E. of Columbus ; from W. 280 ms.

WEST POINT, p. v., Tippecanoe co., Ind., 77 ms. N. W. of Indianapolis ; from W. 635 ms.

WEST POINT, p. o., Lee co., Iowa.

WEST POINT, p. o., Cass co., Mo.

WEST POINT, p. o., Hardin co., Ky.

WEST POINT, p. o., Lowndes co., Miss.

WEST POINT, p. v., Orange co., N. C., 29 ms. N. w. of Raleigh ; from W. 289 ms.

WEST POLAND, p. o., Poland township, Cumberland co., Me., 55 ms. s. w. of Augusta ; from W. 578 ms.

WESTPORT, p. t., Lincoln co., Me., 38 ms. s. of Augusta ; from W. 602 ms. Watered by Sheepscot river and Sheepscot bay. Pop. 761.

WESTPORT, p. v., Cheshire co., N. H., 59 ms. s. w. of Concord ; from W. 423 ms.

WESTPORT, p. t., Bristol co., Mass., 59 ms. s. of Boston ; from W. 426 ms. Watered by Atlantic ocean, Buzzard's bay, and Westport river. Pop. 1,473.

WESTPORT, p. t., Fairfield co., Ct., 64 ms. s. w. of Hartford ; from W. 273 ms. Watered by Long Island sound and Saugatuck river. Pop. 2,651.

WESTPORT, p. t., Essex co., N. Y., 125 ms. N. of Albany ; from W. 495 ms. Watered by Black creek. Pop. 2,352.

WESTPORT, p. v., Oldham co., Ky., 43 ms. N. w. of Frankfort ; from W. 584 ms.

WESTPORT, p. v., Decatur co., Ind., 70 ms. S. E. of Indianapolis ; from W. 564 ms. Watered by a tributary of east fork of White river.

WESTPORT, p. o., Clinton co., Pa.

WESTPORT, p. v., Jackson co., Mo., 158 ms. N. w. of Jefferson city ; from W. 1,084.

WESTPORT POINT, p. o., Bristol co., Mass.

WEST POTSDAM, p. o., St. Lawrence co., N. Y.

WEST POULTNEY, p. o., Poultney township, Rutland co., Vt., 83 ms. s. w. of Montpelier ; from W. 441 ms.

WEST PRAIRIE, p. o., Stoddard co., Mo.

WEST PROVIDENCE, p. t., Bedford co., Pa.

WEST RANDOLPH, p. o., Randolph township, Orange co., Vt., 27 ms. s. of Montpelier ; from W. 490 ms.

WEST RIPLEY, p. o., Somerset co., Me.

WEST RIVER, p. o., Anne Arundel co., Md., 17 ms. from Annapolis ; from W. 37 ms. Watered by an arm of Chesapeake bay.

WEST RIVER, p. t., Randolph co., Ind.

WEST RIVES, p. o., Jackson co., Mich., 86 ms. w. of Detroit ; from W. 556 ms.

WEST ROCHESTER, p. o., Windsor co., Vt.

WEST ROCKHILL, p. t., Bucks co., Pa., 92 ms. N. E. of Harrisburgh ; from W. 171 ms. Watered by Perkiomen creek.

WEST ROSENDALE, p. o., Fond du Lac co., Wis.

WEST ROXBURY, p. v., Roxbury township, Norfolk co., Mass., 10 ms. s. w. of Boston ; from W. 434 ms.

WEST RUMNEY, p. o., Rumney township, Grafton co., N. H., 51 ms. N. w. of Concord ; from W. 521 ms.

WEST RUPERT, p. o., Rupert township, Bennington co., Vt., 97 ms. s. of Montpelier ; from W. 421 ms.

WEST RUSH, p. o., Rush township, Monroe co., N. Y., 221 ms. w. of Albany ; from W. 360 ms.

WEST RUSHVILLE, p. o., Fairfield co., O.

WEST RUTLAND, p. v., Rutland township, Rutland co., Vt., 66 ms. s. w. of Montpelier ; from W. 452 ms.

WEST RUTLAND, p. o., Worcester co., Mass.

WEST SALEM, p. o., Morgan co., Ind.

WEST SALEM, p. t., Mercer co., Pa. Watered by Shenango creek. Pop. 2,571.

WEST SALEM, p. o., Wayne co., O.

WEST SALISBURY, p. o., Addison co., Vt.

WEST SAND LAKE, p. v., Sand Lake township, Rensselaer co., N. Y., 14 ms. E. of Albany ; from W. 384 ms.

WEST SANDWICH, p. v., Sandwich township, Barnstable co., Mass., 56 ms. s. w. of Boston ; from W. 457 ms.

WEST SCHUYLER, p. o., Schuyler township, Herkimer co., N. Y., 88 ms. N. w. of Albany ; from W. 392 ms.

WEST SCITUATE, p. v., Plymouth co., Mass., 20 ms. s. E. of Boston ; from W. 447 ms.

WEST SEDGWICK, p. o., Hancock co., Me.

WEST SHANDAKEN, p. o., Shandaken township, Ulster co., N. Y.

WEST SHONGO, p. o., Alleghany co., N. Y.

WEST SIDNEY, p. o., Sidney township, Kennebec co., Me., 106 ms. N. of Augusta ; from W. 601 ms.

WEST's MILLS, p. o., Franklin co., Me., 44 ms. N. w. of Augusta ; from W. 631 ms.

WEST SOMERS, p. v., Somers township, Westchester co., N. Y., 116 ms. s. of Albany ; from W. 278 ms.

WEST SOMERSET, p. o., Niagara co., N. Y.

WEST SOUTHOLD, p. o., Suffolk co., Long Island, N. Y.

WEST SPRING CREEK, p. o., Warren co., N. J.

WEST SPRINGFIELD, p. t., Hampden co., Mass., 93 ms. w. of Boston ; from W. 363 ms. Watered by Connecticut and Westfield rivers.

WEST SPRINGFIELD, p. o., Springfield township, Sullivan co., N. H., 38 ms. N. w. of Concord ; from W. 492 ms.

WEST SPRINGFIELD, p. o., Springfield township, Erie co., Pa., 269 ms. N. w. of Harrisburgh ; from W. 342 ms.

WEST SPRINGFIELD, p. o., Shelby co., Mo.

WEST STAFFORD, p. o., Stafford township, Tolland co., Ct., 29 ms. N. E. of Hartford ; from W. 365 ms.

WEST STEPHENTOWN, p. o., Stephentown township, Rensselaer co., N. Y.

WEST STERLING, p. o., Worcester co., Mass.

WEST STEWARTSTOWN, p. o., Stewartstown township, Coos co., N. H., 141 ms. N. of Concord ; from W. 602 ms.

WEST STOCKBRIDGE, p. t., Berkshire co., Mass., 138 ms. w. of Boston ; from W. 365 ms. Watered by Williams river. Pop. 1,713.

WEST STOCKBRIDGE CENTRE, p. o., Stockbridge township, Berkshire co., Mass., 141 ms. w. of Boston ; from W. 368 ms.

WEST STOCKHOLM, p. o., Stockholm township, St. Lawrence co., N. Y., 218 ms. N. w. of Albany ; from W. 502 ms.

WEST SUFFIELD, p. o., Suffield township, Hartford co., Ct., 20 ms. N. of Hartford ; from W. 356 ms.

WEST SULLIVAN, p. o., Hancock co., Me.

WEST SUTTON, p. v., Sutton township, Worcester co., Mass., 49 ms. s. w. of Boston ; from W. 397 ms.

WEST SUMNER, p. o., Sumner township, Oxford co., Me., 43 ms. w. of Augusta ; from W. 604 ms.

WEST SWANZEY, p. o., Cheshire co., N. H.

WEST TAGHKANIC, Taghkanic township, Columbia co., N. Y., 40 ms. s. of Albany ; from W. 345 ms

WEST THERESA, p. o., Jefferson co., N. Y.
WEST THORNTON, p. o., Thornton township. Grafton co., N. H., 53 ms. N. of Concord ; from W. 534 ms.
WEST TISBURY, p. v., Tisbury township. Dukes co., Mass., 96 ms. s. e. of Boston ; from W. 478 ms.
WEST TOPSHAM, p. o., Topsham township, Orange co., Vt., 19 ms. s. e. of Montpelier ; from W. 525 ms.
WEST TOWN, p. v., Minisink township, Orange co., N. Y., 116 ms. s. w. of Albany ; from W. 267 ms.
WEST TOWN, p. t., Chester co., Pa. Watered by Chester creek. Pop. 789.
WEST TOWNSEND, p. o., Middlesex co., Mass.
WEST TOWNSEND, p. o., Sandusky co., O.
WEST TOWNSHEND, p. o., Townshend township, Windham co., Vt., 122 ms. s. of Montpelier ; from W. 444 ms.
WEST TOWNSHIP, p. o., Albany co., N. Y.
WEST TRENTON, p. v., Trenton township, Hancock co., Me., 98 ms. e. of Augusta ; from W. 680 ms.
WEST TROUPSBURGH, p. o., Troupsburgh township, Steuben co., N. Y., 236 ms. w. of Albany ; from W. 295 ms.
WEST TROY, p. v., Watervliet township, Albany co., N. Y., a suburb of Troy. Watered by Hudson river and the south branch of the Mohawk. It contains a United States arsenal. Pop. in 1840, 5,000 ; in 1850, 7,564.
WEST TURIN, p. t., Lewis co., N. Y., 126 ms. N. w. of Albany ; from W. 425 ms. Watered by Salmon and Black rivers, and Fish creek. Pop. 3,793.
WEST UNION, v., Marshall co., Va., 347 ms. N. w. of Richmond ; from W. 254 ms. Watered by Wheeling river.
WEST UNION, c. h., p. v., seat of justice of Doddridge co., Va. Pop. 165.
WEST UNION, c. h., p. v., Tiffin township. seat of justice of Adams co., O., 106 ms. s. of Columbus ; from W. 443 ms. Pop. 444.
WEST UNION, p. v., Knox co., Ind., 108 ms. s. w. of Indianapolis ; from W. 679 ms.
WEST UNION, p. o., Fayette co., Iowa.
WEST UNION, p. o., Pickens district, S. C.
WEST UNION, p. o., Steuben co., N. Y.
WEST UNITY, p. o., Williams co., O.
WEST VAN BUREN, p. o.. Aroostook co., Me.
WEST VERMILION, p. o., Vermilion township. Huron co., O., 115 ms. N. of Columbus ; from W. 395 ms.
WEST VIENNA, p. o., Vienna township. Oneida co., N. Y., 125 ms. N. w. of Albany ; from W. 383 ms.
WEST VIEW, p. o., Augusta co., Va.
WEST VIEW, p. o., Hamilton co., O.
WESTVILLE, p. v., Hampden township, New Haven co., Ct., 39 ms. s. w. of Hartford ; from W. 303 ms. Watered by Wapowany river. Pop. 871.
WESTVILLE, p. v., Westford township. Otsego co., N. Y., 68 ms. w. of Albany ; from W. 383 ms.
WESTVILLE, p. t., Franklin co., N. Y., 220 ms. N. of Albany ; from W. 537 ms. Pop. 1,301.
WESTVILLE, p. v., Mad River township, Champaign co., O., 50 ms. w. of Columbus ; from W. 444 ms.
WESTVILLE, c. h., p. v., seat of justice of Simpson co., Miss., 55 ms. s. of Jackson ; from W. 1,024 ms.
WESTVILLE, v., Smith township, Columbiana co., O. Pop. 1,505.
WESTVILLE, v., Yellow Creek township, Columbiana co., O.
WESTVILLE, p. o., Gloucester co., N. J.
WEST VINCENT. p. t., Chester co., Pa. Watered by Stony French and Ring creeks. Pop. 1,350.
WEST WALWORTH, p. o., Walworth township, Wayne co., N. Y.
WEST WARDSBOROUGH, p. o., Windham co., Vt.
WEST WAREHAM, p. v., Wareham township, Plymouth co., Mass., 49 ms. s. e. of Boston ; from W. 442 ms.
WEST WASHINGTON, p. o., Lincoln co., Me.
WEST WATERVILLE, p. v., Waterville township, Kennebec co., Me., 19 ms. N. of Augusta ; from W. 613 ms. Watered by Emerson stream.
WEST WEBSTER, p. o., Monroe co., N. Y.
WEST WILLIAMSFIELD, p. o., Ashtabula co., O.
WEST WHITFLAND, p. t., Chester co., Pa., 72 ms. from Harrisburgh ; from W. 121 ms. Watered by Southern Valley creek. Pop. 1,141.
WEST WILLINGTON, p. o., Tolland co., Ct.
WEST WINCHESTER, p. v., Winchester township, Cheshire co., N. H., 67 ms. s. w. of Concord ; from W. 420 ms. Watered by Ashuelot river.

WEST WINDHAM, p. o., Bradford co.. Pa.
WEST WINDHAM, p. o., Rockingham co., N. H., 37 ms. s. e. of Concord ; from W. 457 ms.
WEST WINDSOR, p. o., Windsor township. Broome co., N. Y., 132 ms. s. w. of Albany ; from W. 304 ms.
WEST WINDSOR, p. t., Mercer co., N. J. Pop. 1,596.
WEST WINDSOR, p. o.. Richland co., O., 67 ms. N. E. of Columbus ; from W. 382 ms.
WEST WINDSOR, p. o., Eaton co., Mich.
WEST WINFIELD, p. o., Winfield township, Herkimer co., N. Y., 78 ms. N. w. of Albany ; from W. 373 ms.
WEST WINSTEAD, p. o., Litchfield co., Ct.
WESTWOOD. p. o.. Woodford co., Ill.
WEST WOODSTOCK, p. o., Woodstock township, Windham co., Ct., 39 ms. N. E. of Hartford ; from W. 375 ms.
WEST WOODVILLE, p. v., Clermont co., O., 89 ms. s. w. of Columbus ; from W. 462 ms.
WEST WORTHINGTON. p. o., Worthington township, Hampshire co. Mass., 115 ms. w. of Boston ; from W. 391 ms.
WEST WRENTHAM, p. o., Wrentham township, Norfolk co., Mass., 36 ms, s. w. of Boston ; from W. 424 ms.
WEST YARMOUTH, p. v.. Yarmouth township. Barnstable co., Mass., 80 ms. s. e. of Boston ; from W. 481 ms.
WEST YORKSHIRE, p. o., Cattaraugus co., N. Y.
WEST ZANESVILLE, v., Muskingum co., O. Pop. 524.
WETHERDVILLE. p. o., Baltimore co., Md.
WETHERSFIELD, p. t., Hartford co., Ct., 4 ms. s. of Hartford ; from W. 336 ms. Watered by Connecticut river. Pop. 2,523.
WETHERSFIELD. p. t.. Wyoming co.. N. Y., 258 ms. w. of Albany ; from W. 361 ms. Watered by Tonawanda and Wiskoy creeks. Pop. 1,489.
WETHERSFIELD, p. v., Henry co., Ill. Watered by a tributary of Spoon river.
WETHERSFIELD SPRINGS, p. v., Wethersfield township, Wyoming co., N. Y., 258 ms. w. of Albany ; from W. 363 ms.
WETUMPKA, city, Coosa co., Ala. Watered by Coosa river. Site of the Harrogate Springs.
WETZEL COUNTY, situated on the northwest boundary of Virginia. with Ohio river on the northwest Area, —— square miles. Seat of justice, New Martins ville. Pop. in 1850, 4,184.
WEVERTON, p. o., Frederick co., Md.
WEXFORD, p. o., Alleghany co., Pa., 215 ms. N. w. of Harrisburgh ; from W. 241 ms.
WEXFORD, p, o., Allamakee co., Iowa.
WEYAUWEYA, p. o., Winnebago co., Wis.
WEYBRIDGE, p. t., Addison co., Vt. Watered by Otter creek and Lemonfair river. Pop. 804.
WEYBRIDGE LOWER FALLS, p. o., Weybridge township. Addison co., Vt., 63 ms. s. w. of Montpelier ; from W. 486 ms.
WEYMOUTH, p. t., Norfolk co., Mass., 12 ms. s. e. of Boston ; from W. 446 ms. Watered by Weymouth, East, and West rivers. Pop. 5,369.
WEYMOUTH, p. t., Atlantic co., N. J. Pop. 1,032.
WEYMOUTH, p. o., Medina township, Medina co., O., 129 ms. N. E. of Columbus ; from W. 351 ms.
WHALEYSVILLE, p. v., Worcester co., Md., 115 ms. s. e. of Annapolis ; from W. 155 ms.
WHALLONSBURGH, p. o., Essex co., N. Y.
WHARTON COUNTY, situated in the south part of Texas, and traversed by the river Colorado. Area, —— square miles. Seat of justice, Wharton. Pop. in 1850, 1,752.
WHARTON, p. t., Fayette co., Pa. Watered by Youghiogeny river. Pop. 1,853.
WHARTON, t. Potter co., Pa., 179 ms. s. w. of Harrisburgh ; from W. 271 ms. Watered by a tributary of Sandy creek. Pop. 252.
WHARTON, c. h., p. v., seat of justice of Wharton co., Tex.
WHARTON'S, p. o., Brookfield township, Morgan co.. O., 99 ms. E. of Columbus ; from W. 318 ms.
WHATELY, p. t., Franklin co., Mass., 94 ms. w. of Boston ; from W. 389 ms. Watered by Connecticut and Mill rivers. Pop 1,101.
WHEATFIELD. p. t., Niagara co., N. Y., 289 ms. w. of Albany ; from W. 414 ms. Watered by Niagara river and Tonawanda creek. Pop. 2,659.
WHEATFIELD, t., Perry co., Pa. Pop. 678.

WHEATFIELD, p. o., Ingham co., Mich.
WHEATLAND. p. t., Monroe co., N. Y., 273 ms. w.
of Albany · from W. 368 ms. Watered by Allen's creek
and Genesee river. Pop. 2.916.
WHEATLAND, p. o., Loudoun co., Va., 163 ms. N. of
Richmond ; from W. 44 ms.
WHEATLAND, p. t., Hillsdale co., Mich., 88 ms. s. w.
of Detroit ; from W. 528 ms. Pop. 1,358.
WHEATLAND, p. o., Ionia co., Mich.
WHEATLAND, p. o., Racine co., Wis.
WHEATLAND CENTRE, p. o., Wheatland township,
Hillsdale co , Mich.
WHEATLEY. p. o., Fauquier co., Va., 99 ms. N. of
Richmond ; from W. 88 ms.
WHEAT RIDGE, p. o., Adams co , O.
WHEATVILLE. p. o., Genesee co., N. Y.
WHEELER. p. t., Steuben co., N. Y., 216 ms. w. of Al-
bany ; from W. 308 ms. Watered by Five-Mile creek.
Pop. 1,471.
WHEELERSBURGH, p. v., Porter township, Scioto co.,
O., 99 ms. s. of Columbus ; from W. 415 ms.
WHEELING, city, seat of justice of Ohio co., Va., 351
ms. N. W. of Richmond ; from W. 266 ms. Watered
by Ohio and Wheeling rivers. Pop. in 1810, 914 ; in
1820, 1,567 ; in 1830, 5,221 ; in 1840, 7,885 ; in 1850,
11,391.
WHEELING, p. v., Holmes co., Miss., 81 ms. N. of
Jackson ; from W. 978 ms. Watered by a tributary of
Big Black river.
WHEELING, p. t., Belmont co., O. Watered by In-
dian Wheeling creek. Pop. 1,218.
WHEELING. t., Guernsey co., O. Watered by Will's
creek. Pop. 1,159.
WHEELING, p. v., Delaware co., Ind., 71 ms. N. E. of
Indianapolis ; from W. 542 ms. Watered by Mississin-
ewa river.
WHEELING, p. o., Cook co., Ill., 227 ms. N. E. of
Springfield ; from W. 733 ms.
WHEELING VALLEY, p. o., Marshall co., Va.
WHEELOCK, p. t., Caledonia co , Vt., 43 ms N. E. of
Montpelier ; from W. 556 ms. Watered by Passump-
sic river. Pop 855.
WHEELOCK, p. o., Choctaw Nation, Ark.
WHEELOCK, p. o., Robertson co., Tex.
WHETSTONE, p. o., Pickens district, S. C.
WHETSTONE. p. t., Crawford co., O. Pop. 1,057.
WHIGVILLE, p. o., Noble co., O.
WHIGVILLE, p. o., Lapeer co., Mich.
WHIPPY SWAMP, p. o., Beaufort district, S. C.
WHITCOMB. p. o., Franklin co., Ind.
WHITE COUNTY, situated in the central part of
Tennessee. Area, 672 square miles. Seat of justice,
Sparta. Pop. in 1810, 4,028 ; in 1820, 8,701 ; in 1830,
9,967 ; in 1840, 10.747 ; in 1850, 11,444.
WHITE COUNTY, situated in the northwesterly
part of Indiana, and traversed by Tippecanoe river.
Area, 530 square miles. Seat of justice, Monticello.
Pop. in 1840, 1,832 ; in 1850, 4,761.
WHITE COUNTY, situated on the southeasterly
boundary of Illinois, with Wabash river on the east.
Area, 480 square miles. Face of the country, even ;
soil, fertile. Seat of justice, Carmi. Pop. in 1820,
4,828 ; in 1830. 6.091 ; in 1840, 7,919 ; in 1850, 8,925.
WHITE COUNTY, situated toward the northeast
part of Arkansas, with White river on the east. Area,
1,000 square miles. Seat of justice, Searcy. Pop. in
1840, 929 ; in 1850, 2,619.
WHITE, t., Cambria co., Pa. Pop. 667.
WHITE, t., Benton co., Mo.
WHITE, t., Ashley co., Ark. Pop. 648.
WHITE, t., Carroll co., Ark.
WHITE ASH, p. o., Alleghany co., Pa.
WHITE BREAST, p. o., Clark co., Iowa.
WHITE CHIMNEYS, p. o., Caroline co., Va., 30 ms. N.
of Richmond ; from W. 90 ms.
WHITE COTTAGE, p. o., Muskingum co., O., 60 ms.
from Columbus ; from W. 345 ms.
WHITE COTTAGE, p. o., Shelby co., Tex.
WHITE CREEK, p. t., Washington co., N. Y., 43 ms.
N. E. of Albany ; from W. 413 ms. Watered by Owl
and Little White creeks, and Hoosic river. Pop. 2,994.
WHITE CROSS, p. o., Orange co., N. C.
WHITE DAY, p. o., Monongahela co., Va., 284 ms. N.
w. of Richmond ; from W. 217 ms.
WHITE DEER, p. v., Lycoming co., Pa., 78 ms. N. of
Harrisburgh ; from W. 188 ms.
WHITE DEER, p. t., Union co., Pa. Watered by
White Deer creek. Pop. 1 452.

WHITE DEER MILLS, p. o., Union co., Pa., 75 ms. N
of Harrisburgh ; from W. 185 ms.
WHITE EYES, p. t., Coshocton co., O. Watered by
tributaries of Tuscarawas river. Pop. 1,132.
WHITE-EYES' PLAINS, p. v., Coshocton co., O., 88 ms.
N. E. of Columbus ; from W. 329 ms. Watered by
Tuscarawas river.
WHITEFIELD, or WHITFIELD, p. t , Lincoln co., Me.,
16 ms. s. E. of Augusta ; from W. 602 ms. Watered by
Sheepscot river. Pop. 2,158.
WHITEFIELD, p. t., Coos co., N. H., 93 ms. N. of Con-
cord ; from W. 554 ms. Watered by John's river.
Pop. 857.
WHITEFIELD, p. t., Indiana co., Pa. Pop. 2,387.
WHITEFIELD, p. o., Oktibbeha co., Miss.
WHITEFIELD, p. o., Marshall co., Ill.
WHITEFORD, p. o., Lucas co., O., 146 ms. N. w. of Co-
lumbus ; from W. 477 ms.
WHITE GATE, p. o., Giles co., Va.
WHITE HALL, p. t., Washington co., N. Y., 73 ms. N.
of Albany ; from W. 443 ms. Watered by Wood creek,
Pawlet and Poultney rivers, and Lake Champlain. Pop.
4,726.
WHITE HALL, p. o., Hunterdon co., N. J.
WHITE HALL, p. v., Madeira township, Montour co.,
Pa., 87 ms. N. of Harrisburgh ; from W. 197 ms.
WHITE HALL, p. o., Baltimore co., Md.
WHITE HALL, p. o., Frederick co., Va., 154 ms. N. w.
of Richmond ; from W. 82 ms.
WHITE HALL, p. v., Mecklenburgh co., N. C., 166 ms.
s. w. of Raleigh ; from W. 405 ms.
WHITE HALL, v., Fayette co., Tenn., 190 ms. s. w. of
Nashville ; from W. 875 ms.
WHITE HALL, p. o., Madison co., Ky.
WHITE HALL, p. o., Owen co., Ind.
WHITE HALL, p. v., Greene co., Ill., 59 ms. s. w. of
Springfield ; from W. 841 ms.
WHITEHALLVILLE, p. o., Bucks co., Pa.
WHITE HARE, p. o., Cedar co., Mo.
WHITE HAVEN, p. o., Luzerne co., Pa., 114 ms. N. E.
of Harrisburgh ; from W. 222 ms.
WHITE HAVEN, p. v., Somerset co., Md., 103 ms. s.
E. of Annapolis ; from W. 143 ms. Watered by Wi
comico river.
WHITE HILL, p. o., Cumberland co., Pa.
WHITE HILL, p. o., Giles co., Tenn.
WHITE HOUSE, p. o., Readington township, Hunter-
don co., N. J., 40 ms. N. w. of Trenton ; from W. 205
ms. Watered by Rockaway river.
WHITE HOUSE, p. o., Cumberland co., Pa., 21 ms. s.
w. of Harrisburgh ; from W. 110 ms.
WHITE HOUSE, p. o., Mecklenburgh co., Va., 129 ms
s. w. of Richmond ; from W. 234 ms.
WHITE HOUSE, p. o., Randolph co., N. C.
WHITE HOUSE, p. o., Henry co., Ga., 72 ms. N. w. of
Milledgeville ; from W. 676 ms.
WHITE HOUSE, p. o., Williamson co., Tenn.
WHITE LAKE, p. o., Bethel township, Sullivan co.,
N. Y., 118 ms. s. w. of Albany ; from W. 302 ms.
WHITE LAKE, p. t., Oakland co., Mich, 43 ms. N. w.
of Detroit ; from W. 567 ms. Pop. 904.
WHITELEY, p. t., Greene co., Pa. Watered by White-
ley creek. Pop. 992.
WHITELEYSBURGH, p. v., Kent co., Del., 20 ms. s. w.
of Dover ; from W. 103 ms.
WHITE MARSH, p. t., Montgomery co., Pa.. 104 ms.
E. of Harrisburgh ; from W. 150 ms. Watered by Wis-
sahickon creek. Pop. 2,408.
WHITE MARSH, p. o., Columbus co., N. C., 135 ms. s.
of Raleigh ; from W. 423 ms.
WHITE MILLS, p. o., Wayne co., Pa.
WHITE MOUNTAIN, p. o., Coos co., N. H., 101 ms. N.
of Concord ; from W. 562 ms.
WHITE OAK, p. o., Columbia co., Ga., 105 ms. N. E.
of Milledgeville ; from W. 597 ms.
WHITE OAK, p. o., Humphreys co., Tenn., 67 ms. w.
of Nashville ; from W. 751 ms.
WHITE OAK, p. t., Highland co., O. Watered by
tributaries of White Oak creek. Pop. 1,012.
WHITE OAK, p. t., Ingham co., Mich. Pop. 254.
WHITE OAK, p. o., Ritchie co., Va.
WHITE OAK, p. o., Hopkins co., Tex.
WHITE OAK, t., Franklin co., Ark. Pop. 1,052.
WHITE OAK, p. o., Jefferson co., Ark.
WHITE OAK GROVE, p. o., Greene co., Mo., 164 ms
s. w. of Jefferson city ; from W. 1,081 ms.
WHITE OAK GROVE, p. o., Dubois co., Ind.
WHITE OAK HILL, p. o., Fleming co., Ky

WHITE OAK SPRINGS. p. v., Iowa co., Wis., 92 ms. s. w. of Madison; from W. 876 ms.

WHITE OAK SPRINGS, p. o., Brown co., Ill.

WHITE PATH, p. o., Gilmer co., Ga.

WHITE PIGEON, p. t., St. Joseph co., Mich., 148 ms; s. w. of Detroit ; from W. 593 ms. Watered by White Pigeon creek. Pop. 795.

WHITE PLAINS, c. h., p. t., seat of justice, together with Bedford, of Westchester co., N. Y., 129 ms. s. of Albany ; from W. 254 ms. Watered by Bronx river and Mamaroneck creek. Pop. 1,414.

WHITE PLAINS, p. o., Brunswick co., Va., 90 ms. s. w. of Richmond ; from W. 206 ms.

WHITE PLAINS, p. o., Greene co., Ga., 56 ms. N. of Milledgeville ; from W. 616 ms.

WHITE PLAINS, p. o., Benton co., Ala. Pop. 724.

WHITE PLAINS, p. o., Jackson co., Tenn., 96 ms. N. E. of Nashville ; from W. 618 ms.

WHITE PLAINS, p. o., Cleveland co., N. C.

WHITE POND, p. o., Barnwell district, S. C.

WHITE POST, p. o., Pulaski co., Ind., 96 ms. N. w. of Indianapolis ; from W. 655 ms.

WHITE POST, p. v., Clarke co., Va., 140 ms. N. w. of Richmond ; from W. 71 ms.

WHITE RIVER, t., Gibson co., Ind. Pop. 731.

WHITE RIVER, p. t., Hamilton co., Ind. Pop. 1,493.

WHITE RIVER, p. t., Randolph co., Ind.

WHITE RIVER, p. o., Morgan co., Ind.

WHITE RIVER, p. t., Benton co., Ark. Pop. 385.

WHITE RIVER, p. o., Desha co., Ark., 139 ms. s. E. of Little Rock ; from W. 1,065 ms.

WHITE RIVER, t., Izard co., Ark.

WHITE RIVER, t., Independence co., Ark.

WHITE RIVER, t., Marion co., Ark.

WHITE RIVER, t., Washington co., Ark. Pop. 695.

WHITE RIVER JUNCTION, p. o., Windsor co., Vt.

WHITE ROAD, p. o., Forsyth co., N. C.

WHITE ROCK, p. o., Ogle co., Ill.

WHITE ROCK, p. o., Yancey co., N. C.

WHITESBOROUGH, c. h., p. v., Whitestown township, seat of justice, together with Rome and Utica, of Oneida co., N. Y., 96 ms. N. w. of Albany ; from W. 392 ms. Watered by Oriskany and Sadaquada creeks, and Mohawk river.

WHITESBURGH, p. v., Madison co., Ala., from W. 718 ms.

WHITESBURGH, c. h., p. v., seat of justice of Letcher co., Ky.

WHITE'S CORNERS, p. o., Erie co., N. Y.

WHITE'S CORNERS, p. o., Potter co., Pa.

WHITE'S CREEK. p. o., Bladen co., N. C.

WHITESIDES COUNTY, situated on the northwest boundary of Illinois, with Mississippi river on the west, and traversed by Rock river. Area, 770 square miles. Seat of justice, Lyndon. Pop. in 1840, 2,514; in 1850, 5,361.

WHITESIDES CORNERS, p. o., Saratoga co., N. Y.

WHITE SPRINGS, p. o., Hamilton co., Flor.

WHITE STONE, p. o., Lancaster co., Va., 95 ms. E. of Richmond ; from W. 156 ms.

WHITE'S STORE, p. o., Norwich township, Chenango co., N. Y., 102 ms. w. of Albany ; from W. 335 ms.

WHITE'S STORE, p. o., Anson co., N. C., 159 ms. s. w. of Raleigh ; from W. 428 ms.

WHITESTOWN, p. t., Oneida co., N. Y., 96 ms. N. w. of Albany ; from W. 392 ms. Watered by Mohawk river, and Oriskany and Sadaquada creeks. Pop. 6,810.

WHITESTOWN, p. o., Butler co., Pa., 211 ms. N. w. of Harrisburgh ; from W. 253 ms.

WHITESTOWN, p. o., Ottawa co., O., 125 ms. N. of Columbus ; from W. 443 ms.

WHITE SULPHUR, p. o., Scott co., Ky.

WHITE SULPHUR, p. o., Greene co., Tenn.

WHITE SULPHUR SPRINGS, p. v., Greenbrier co., Va., 205 ms. w. of Richmond ; from W. 242 ms. A celebrated resort for invalids.

WHITE SULPHUR SPRINGS, p. o., Meriwether co., Ga.

WHITE SULPHUR SPRINGS, p. o., Limestone co., Ala.

WHITE SULPHUR SPRINGS, p. o., Chattahoola parish, La.

WHITESVILLE, p. v., Harris co., Ga., 148 ms. s. w. of Milledgeville ; from W. 766 ms.

WHITESVILLE, p. v., Independence township, Alleghany co., N. Y., 265 ms. w. of Albany ; from W. 301 ms.

WHITESVILLE, p. o., Halifax co., Va.

WHITESVILLE, c. h., p. v., seat of justice of Columbus co., N. C., 125 ms. s. of Raleigh ; from W. 413 ms. Watered by Beaver Dam creek.

WHITESVILLE, p. v.. Wilkinson co., Miss., 136 ms. s. w. of Jackson ; from W. 1,136 ms.

WHITESVILLE, p. o., Andrew co., Mo.

WHITE TOP, p. o., Sullivan co., Tenn.

WHITEVILLE, p. o., Hardeman co., Tenn.

WHITEWATER, p. t., Hamilton co., O. Watered by Whitewater river. Pop. 1,567.

WHITEWATER, p. o., Wayne co., Ind., 83 ms. E. of Indianapolis ; from W. 502 ms.

WHITEWATER, p. o., Walworth co., Wis., 91 ms. s. E. of Madison ; from W. 824 ms.

WHITEWATER, p. o., Pike co., Ala.

WHITEWATER, p. o., Fayette co., Ga.

WHITFIELD, p. t., Indiana co., Pa. Pop. 2,387.

WHITFORD, p. t., Monroe co., Mich. Pop. 696.

WHITING, p. t., Washington co., Me., 169 ms. N. E. of Augusta ; from W. 755 ms. Watered by Machias bay. Pop. 470.

WHITING, p. t., Addison co., Vt., 69 ms. s. w. of Montpelier ; from W. 471 ms. Watered by Otter creek river. Pop. 629.

WHITTINGHAM, p. t., Windham co., Vt., 141 ms. s. of Montpelier ; from W. 422 ms. Watered by Deerfield river and tributaries. Pop. 1,380.

WHITINSVILLE, p. v., Worcester co., Mass., 39 ms. w. of Boston ; from W. 404 ms.

WHITLEY COUNTY, situated on the south boundary of Kentucky, and traversed by Cumberland river. Area, 600 square miles. Seat of justice, Whitley c. h. Pop. in 1820, 2,350 ; in 1830, 3,807 ; in 1840, 4,673 ; in 1850, 7,447.

WHITLEY COUNTY, situated in the northeast part of Indiana. Area, 324 square miles. Seat of justice, Whitley, c. h. Pop. in 1840, 1,237 ; in 1850, 5,190.

WHITLEY, c. h., p. v., seat of justice of Whitley co., Ky., 125 ms. s. E. of Frankfort ; from W. 543 ms. Watered by Cumberland river.

WHITLEY, c. h., p. v., seat of justice of Whitley co., Ind., 120 ms. N. E. of Indianapolis ; from W. 585 ms. Watered by Eel river.

WHITLEY'S POINT, p. o., Moultrie co., Ill.

WHITLEYVILLE, p. o., Jackson co., Tenn., 82 ms. E of Nashville ; from W. 640 ms.

WHITLOCKSVILLE, p. v., Bedford township, Westchester co., N. Y., 125 ms. s. of Albany ; from W. 268 ms. Watered by Croton and Cross rivers.

WHITNEY'S CORNERS, p. o., Jefferson co., N. Y.

WHITNEY'S POINT, p. o., Triangle township, Broome co., N. Y., 130 ms. s. w. of Albany ; from W. 313 ms.

WHITNEY'S VALLEY, p. v., Burns township, Alleghany co., N. Y., 248 ms. w. of Albany ; from W. 329 ms.

WHITNEYVILLE, p. o., Kent co., Mich.

WHITPAINE, p. t., Montgomery co., Pa. Pop. 1,351.

WHITTAKER'S BLUFF, p. o., Wayne co., Tenn.

WHITTLESEY, p. o., Medina co., O.

WHITTLE'S MILLS, p. o., Mecklenburgh co., Va., 99 ms. s. w. of Richmond ; from W. 215 ms.

WHORTON, p. o., Potter co., Pa.

WICK, p. o., Tyler co., Va.

WICKFORD, p. v., North Kingston township, Washington co., R. I., 22 ms. s. of Providence ; from W. 401 ms. Watered by Narraganset bay.

WICKLIFFE, p. o., Chambers co., Ala.

WICKLIFFE, p. o., Crawford co., Ind.

WICKLIFFE, p. o., Lake co., O.

WICKLIFFE, p. o., Jackson co., Iowa.

WICOMICO CHURCH, p. o., Northumberland co., Va., 99 ms. N. E. of Richmond ; from W. 160 ms.

WICONISCO, p. t., Dauphin co., Pa., 53 ms. N. of Harrisburgh ; from W. 163 ms. Watered by Wiconisco creek and Susquehanna river. Pop. 1,316.

WIDEMAN'S, p. o., Abbeville district, S. C., 87 ms. w. of Columbia ; from W. 548 ms.

WILBRAHAM, p. o., Hampden co., Mass., 83 ms. s. w. of Boston ; from W. 368 ms. Watered by Chickapee river.

WILCOX COUNTY, situated toward the southwest part of Alabama, and traversed by Alabama river. Area, 1,200 square miles. Seat of justice, Camden Pop. in 1820, 2,917 ; in 1830, 9,548; in 1840, 15,278 ; in 1850, 17,352.

WILCOX'S STORE, p. o., Casey co., Ky.

WILD CAT, p. o., Carroll co., Ind.

WILDERNESS, p. o., Spottsylvania co., Va., 77 ms. N w. of Richmond ; from W. 71 ms.

WILDERNESS, p. o., Clarke co., Ala.

WILD HAUS, p. o., Izard co., Ark.

WILEY'S COVE, p. o., Searcy co., Ark.

WILEYVILLE, p. o., Desha co., Ark.

WILKES COUNTY, situated in the northwest part of North Carolina, and traversed by Yadkin river. Area, 864 square miles. Face of the country, uneven and mountainous; soil, fertile. Seat of justice, Wilkesborough. Pop. in 1820, 9,967; in 1830, 11,942; in 1840, 12,577; in 1850, 12,099.

WILKES COUNTY, situated in the northeasterly part of Georgia. Area, 550 square miles. Seat of justice, Washington. Pop. in 1810, 14,887; in 1820, 16,912; in 1830, 14,237; in 1840, 10,148; in 1850. 12,107.

WILKESBARRE. c. h,. p. t., seat of justice of Luzerne co., Pa., 127 ms. N. E. of Harrisburgh; from W. 231 ms. Watered by Susquehanna river and tributaries.

WILKESBOROUGH, c. h., p. v.. seat of justice of Wilkes co., N. C., 172 ms. N. w. of Raleigh; from W. 379 ms. Watered by Yadkin river.

WILKESBOROUGH, p. v., McLean co., Ill., 74 ms. N. E. of Springfield; from W. 754 ms.

WILKESBURGH, p. o., Covington co., Miss.

WILKESVILLE, p. t, Vinton co., O., 84 ms. s. E. of Columbus; from W. 359 ms. Watered by Raccoon creek. Pop. 1,037.

WILKINS, p. t., Alleghany co., Pa., 195 ms. w. of Harrisburgh; from W. 221 ms. Watered by Plum creek and Thompson's run. Pop. 3,019.

WILKINS, p. o., Union co., O.

WILKINSBURGH, p. v., Wilkins township, Alleghany co., Pa., 192 ms. w. of Harrisburgh; from W. 221 ms. Watered by forks of Nine-Mile run.

WILKINSON COUNTY, situated in the central part of Georgia, with Oconee river on the northeast. Seat of justice, Irwinton. Pop. In 1810, 2,154; in 1820, 6,992; in 1830, 6,513; in 1840, 6,842; in 1850, 8,212.

WILKINSON COUNTY, situated at the southwest corner of Mississippi, with Mississippi river on the west. Area, 580 square miles. Seat of justice, Woodville. Pop. in 1810, 5,068; in 1820, 9,718; in 1830, 11,686; in 1840, 14,193; in 1850, 16,720.

WILKINSONVILLE, p. v., Worcester co., Mass., 39 ms. w. of Boston; from W. 404 ms.

WILKINSVILLE. p. v., Union district, S. C., 98 ms. N. w. of Columbia; from W. 447 ms.

WILL COUNTY, situated on the east boundary of Illinois, and traversed by Des Plaines river. Area, 504 square miles. Face of the country, even; soil, generally fertile. Seat of justice, Joliet. Pop in 1840, 10,167; in 1850, 16,703.

WILLAMETTE, p. o., Yam Hill, Oregon.

WILLAMETTE FORKS, p. o., Linn co., Oregon.

WILLARD'S, p. o., Wood co., Va.

WILLET, p. t., Cortland co., N. Y., 134 ms. w. of Albany; from W. 321 ms. Watered by Ostelic river. Pop 923.

WILLET, p. o., Greene co., Wis.

WILLETTVILLE. p. o., Highland co., O.

WILLIAMS COUNTY, situated at the northwest corner of Ohio. Area, 600 square miles. Seat of justice, Bryan. Pop. in 1830, 377; in 1840, 4,465; in 1850, 8.018.

WILLIAMS, p. t., Northampton co., Pa. Pop. 2,634.

WILLIAMS, p. o., Christian co., Ky.

WILLIAMS, t., Benton co., Mo.

WILLIAMS' BRIDGE, p. v., Westchester co., N. Y.

WILLIAMSBOROUGH, p. o., Granville co., N. C., 48 ms. N. of Raleigh; from W. 241 ms.

WILLIAMSBURGH DISTRICT, situated in the east part of South Carolina, with Santee river on the southwest. Area, 1,110 square miles. Seat of justice, Kingstree. Pop. in 1810, 6,871; in 1820, 8,716; in 1830, 9,018; in 1840, 10,327; in 1850, 12,447.

WILLIAMSBURGH, p. t., Piscataquis co., Me., 102 ms. N. E. of Augusta; from W. 699 ms. Watered by Pleasant river and tributaries. Pop. 124.

WILLIAMSBURGH, p. t., Hampshire co., Mass., 100 ms. w. of Boston; from W. 388 ms. Watered by Mill river. Pop. 1,537.

WILLIAMSBURGH, city, Kings co., N. Y., 147 ms. s. of Albany; from W. 227 ms. Watered by Bushwick creek and East river, the latter of which separates it from the city of New York. It is built on a slope, gently rising from the water for about a third of a mile, and then descending toward the east a distance of about a mile more. From the pleasant heights of North Brooklyn; at the south of this city, appears an interesting panorama of the towns which thickly cluster around this part of Long Island. Brooklyn, resting on somewhat

elevated ground, and bending around a wide circuit, is every day blending more closely with Williamsburgh. Far toward the east and north spreads the latter city, and north of this the pleasant villas of Greenpoint, Ravenswood, and Astoria; while the East river separates these from the great forest of masts and spires on the opposite shores. From the river, Williamsburgh presents a fine effect; its tall steeples, and a number of imposing manufactories along its water-front, add much to the picturesqueness of the place. Its streets are regular, generally well paved, lighted with gas, and ornamented with trees. Here a large number of persons who do business in New York reside, crossing daily by the four steam-ferries, the boats of which ply constantly between the two cities; other citizens are extensively engaged in ship-building, and in the manufacture of blocks, cordage, marble, glue, glass, chemicals, oil, castings, buttons, and lamps.

The progress of Williamsburgh is one of the phenomena of the age. Thirty years ago, a few insignificant buildings stood on the ground now covered by its northern part. After slowly increasing for about twenty years, it received a new impetus, and rose, in ten years, from a village of 5,000 souls, to the sixth city of the Empire state. It is destined to a still higher rank. Williamsburgh was formerly a part of the town of Bushwick, and was incorporated as a village in 1827; with extended powers in 1835, and as a city in 1851. The population of Bushwick, in 1820, was 930 : of Williamsburgh, in 1830, 1,620; in 1840, 5,680; in 1850, 30,780.

WILLIAMSBURGH, p. b., Blair co., Pa., 110 ms. w. of Harrisburgh; from W. 158 ms. Watered by Juniata river. Pop. 747.

WILLIAMSBURGH. c. h., p. v., seat of justice of James city co., Va., 58 ms. s. E. of Richmond; from W. 175 ms. Seat of William and Mary college. Pop. 877.

WILLIAMSBURGH, p. v., Iredell co , N. C., 157 ms. w. of Raleigh; from W. 368 ms.

WILLIAMSBURGH, p. v., Covington co., Miss., 82 ms. s. E. of Jackson; from W. 1,032 ms. Watered by headwaters of Leaf river.

WILLIAMSBURGH, p. t., Clermont co., O., 105 ms. s. w. of Columbus; from W. 472 ms. Watered by east branch of Little Miami river. Pop. 1,884.

WILLIAMSBURGH, p. v., Wayne co., Ind., 73 ms. E. of Indianapolis; from W. 512 ms. Watered by a tributary of Whitewater river. Pop. 219.

WILLIAMSBURGH, p. o., De Kalb co., Ill.

WILLIAMSBURGH, p. v., Calloway co., Mo., 37 ms. N. E. of Jefferson city; from W. 902 ms.

WILLIAMS' CENTRE, p. v., Williams co., O., 171 ms. N. w. of Columbus; from W. 523 ms.

WILLIAMS COLLEGE GRANT, t., Aroostook co.. Me.

WILLIAMS' CROSS ROADS, p. o., Choctaw co., Ala.

WILLIAMSFIELD, p. t., Ashtabula co., O., 200 ms. N. E. of Columbus; from W. 316 ms. Pop. 982.

WILLIAMSON COUNTY, situated in the central part of Tennessee. Area, 476 square miles. Seat of justice, Franklin. Pop. in 1810, 13,153; in 1820, 20,640; in 1830. 26,638; in 1840, 27,006; in 1850, 27,201.

WILLIAMSON COUNTY, situated in the south part of Illinois. Area, 432 square miles. Seat of justice, Marion. Pop. in 1840, 4,457; in 1850, 7,216.

WILLIAMSON, p. t., Wayne co., N. Y., 200 ms. w. of Albany; from W. 364 ms. Watered by Lake Ontario. Pop. 2,380.

WILLIAMSON, p. o., Jefferson co., Ky.

WILLIAMSON, p. o., Owen co., Ind.

WILLIAMSON'S MILLS, p. o., Lexington district, S. C.

WILLIAMSONVILLE, p. o., Macon co., Mo.

WILLIAMSPORT, c. h., p. b., seat of justice of Lycoming co., Pa., 93 ms. N. of Harrisburgh; from W. 203 ms. Watered by west branch of Susquehanna river and the Pennsylvania canal.

WILLIAMSPORT, p. v., Washington co., Md., 107 ms. N. w. of Annapolis; from W. 80 ms. Watered by Potomac river at the confluence of Conecocheague creek, and by the Chesapeake and Ohio canal. Pop. 1,060.

WILLIAMSPORT, p. v., Hardy co., Va., 180 ms. N. W. of Richmond; from W. 142 ms.

WILLIAMSPORT, p. o., Point Coupée parish, La.

WILLIAMSPORT, p. v., Maury co., Tenn., 45 ms. s. w. of Nashville; from W. 722 ms. Watered by Duck river.

WILLIAMSPORT, p. v., Duck Creek township, Pickaway co., O., 35 ms. s. of Columbus; from W. 405 ms.

WILLIAMSPORT, v., Madison township, Columbiana co., O.

WILLIAMSPORT, c. h., p. v., seat of justice of Warren co., Ind. 78 ms. N. W. of Indianapolis; from W. 645 ms. Watered by Wabash river.

WILLIAMS' STORE, p. o., Berks co., Pa.

WILLIAMS' STORE, p. o., Hardeman co., Tenn., 177 ms. s. w. of Nashville; from W. 862 ms.

WILLIAMSTON, c. h., p. v., seat of justice of Martin co., N. C., 140 ms. E. of Raleigh; from W. 264 ms. Watered by Roanoke river.

WILLIAMSTOWN, p. t., Orange co., Vt., 11 ms. s. E. of Montpelier; from W. 510 ms. Pop. 1,452.

WILLIAMSTOWN, p. t., Berkshire co., Mass., 131 ms. w. of Boston; from W. 393 ms. Watered by Hoosic and Green rivers. Seat of Williams college. Pop. 2,626.

WILLIAMSTOWN, p. t., Oswego co., N. Y., 139 ms. N. w. of Albany; from W. 388 ms. Watered by Salmon creek. Pop. 1.121.

WILLIAMSTOWN, p. o., Camden co., N. J.

WILLIAMSTOWN, c. h., p. v., seat of justice of Grant co., Ky., 49 ms. N. E. of Frankfort; from W. 529 ms. Watered by Eagle creek.

WILLIAMSTOWN, t, Hancock co., O. Pop. 1,126.

WILLIAMSTOWN, p. o., Montgomery co., O.

WILLIAMSTOWN, p. o., Ingham co., Mich.

WILLIAMSTOWN, p. v., Decatur co., Ind., 55 ms. s. E. of Indianapolis; from W. 558 ms.

WILLIAMSVILLE, p. v., Windham co., Vt., 119 ms. s. of Montpelier; from W. 438 ms.

WILLIAMSVILLE, p. v., Amherst township, Erie co., N. Y., 278 ms. w. of Albany; from W. 391 ms. Watered by Ellicott creek.

WILLIAMSVILLE, p. v., Elk co., Pa., 181 ms. N. w. of Harrisburgh; from W. 273 ms.

WILLIAMSVILLE, p. v., Kent co., Del., 22 ms. s. w. of Dover; from W. 126 ms.

WILLIAMSVILLE, p. o., Highland co., Va.

WILLIAMSVILLE, p. v., Person co., N. C., 61 ms. N. w. of Raleigh; from W. 257 ms.

WILLIAMSVILLE, p. o., Dixon co., Tenn.

WILLIAMSVILLE, p. o., Delaware co., O., 15 ms. N. of Columbus; from W. 408 ms.

WILLIMANSETT, p. v., Springfield township, Hampden co., Mass., 94 ms. w. of Boston; from W. 371 ms. Watered by Connecticut river.

WILLIMANTIC, p. v., Windham township, Windham co., Ct., 28 ms. E. of Hartford; from W. 364 ms. Watered by Willimantic river.

WILLING, p. o., Alleghany co., N. Y.

WILLINBOROUGH, p. t., Burlington co., N. J. Watered by Delaware river. Pop. 1,596.

WILLINGTON, t., Piscataquis co.. Me. Pop. 600.

WILLINGTON, p. t., Tolland co., Ct., 28 ms. w. of Hartford; from W. 264 ms. Watered by Willimantic river. Pop. 1,388.

WILLINGTON, p. v., Abbeville district, S. C., 100 ms. w. of Columbia; from W. 448 ms.

WILLISBURGH, p. o., Washington co., Ky.

WILLISTON, p. t., Chittenden co., Vt., 32 ms. N. w. of Montpelier; from W. 518 ms. Watered by Onion or Winooski river. Pop. 1,669.

WILLISTON, p. o., Potter co., Pa.

WILLISTON, p. v., Barnwell district, S. C., 98 ms. s. w. of Columbia; from W. 603 ms.

WILLISTOWN, p. t., Chester co., Pa. Watered by Ridley and Crum creeks. Pop. 1,463.

WILLOUGHBY, p. t., Lake co., O., 164 ms. N. E. of Columbus; from W. 358 ms. Seat of Willoughby university. Pop. 2,081.

WILLOW CREEK, p. o., Marion district, S. C.

WILLOW CREEK, p. o., Lee co., Ill.

WILLOW CREEK, p. o., Marquette co., Wis.

WILLOW DALE, p. o., Trumbull co., O.

WILLOW FORK, p. t., Morgan co., Mo.

WILLOW GROVE, p. v., Moreland township, Montgomery co., Pa., 111 ms. E. of Harrisburgh; from W. 151 ms.

WILLOW GROVE, p. o., Sumter district, S. C., 85 ms. E. of Columbia; from W. 477 ms.

WILLOW GROVE, p. o., Coweta co., Ga.

WILLOW GROVE, p. o., Sumner co., Tenn., 39 ms. N. E. of Nashville; from W. 678 ms.

WILLOW HILL, p. o., Jasper co., Ill.

WILLOW ISLAND, p. o., Wood co., Va.

WILLOW RIVER, p. o., St. Clair co., Wis.

WILLOW SPRING, p. o., Russell co., Va.

WILLOW SPRING, p. o., Claiborne co., Miss., 53 ms. s. w. of Jackson; from W. 1,063 ms.

WILLOW SPRINGS, p. o., Iowa co., Wis., 62 ms. s. w of Madison; from W. 874 ms.

WILLOW STREET, p. o., Lancaster co., Pa., 42 ms. s. E. of Harrisburgh; from W. 107 ms.

WILLSBOROUGH. p. t., Essex co., N. Y., 145 ms. N. of Albany; from W. 516 ms. Watered by Bouquet river and Lake Champlain. Pop. 1,932.

WILLSBOROUGH, t., Tioga co., Pa.

WILLS, p. t., Guernsey co., O. Pop. 2,216.

WILLS' CREEK, p. o., Coshocton co., O., 74 ms. N. E. of Columbus; from W. 347 ms.

WILLSEYVILLE, p. o., Candor township, Tioga co., N. Y., 176 ms. s. w. of Albany; from W. 290 ms.

WILLSHIRE, c. h., p. t., seat of justice of Van Wert co., O., 133 ms. N. w. of Columbus; from W. 513 ms. Watered by St. Mary's river. Pop. 1.073.

WILLS' POINT, p. o., Benton co., Tenn.

WILMINGTON, p. t., Windham co., Vt., 124 ms. s. of Montpelier; from W. 429 ms. Watered by Deerfield river, at the confluence of its east and west branches. Pop. 1,372.

WILMINGTON, p. t., Middlesex co., Mass., 16 ms. N. w. of Boston; from W. 454 ms. Watered by tributaries of Peabody's river. Pop. 874.

WILMINGTON. p. t., Essex co., N. Y., 153 ms. N. of Albany; from W. 528 ms. Watered by Saranac river and the west branch of the Au Sable. Pop. 1,216.

WILMINGTON, city, seat of justice, together with New Castle, of New Castle co., Del., situated between Christiana creek and Brandywine river, two miles from the entrance of the latter into the Delaware, 28 miles southwest of Philadelphia, and 70 miles northeast of Baltimore. The ground on which it is built rises from the river to an elevation of 112 feet, and offers a pleasant prospect of the neighboring scenery. The streets are broad and rectangular, and the houses, generally of brick, are many of them costly and beautiful. Wilmington has the usual number of public buildings, but the most interesting are the flour-mills, to which it owes its celebrity. These are situated near the falls of the Brandywine, not far from the town, and afford an ex tensive water-power. To this point, vessels ascend drawing eight feet of water, those of fourteen feet draught navigating both streams to the city. The Christiana admits vessels of eight feet draught, eight miles further up. A large number of ships anchor at Wilmington, receiving and exporting the produce of the mills and manufactories in its vicinity; others are employed in the whale-fishery. Each of the streams are crossed by bridges, and the Philadelphia, Wilmington, and Baltimore railroad communicates with this city. Five miles from Wilmington are the Brandywine chalybeate springs, the salubrious waters of which contribute much to the health and recreation of the visiters. The population in 1810, was 4.416; in 1820, 5,268; in 1830, 6,628; in 1840, 8,367; in 1850, 13,979.

WILMINGTON, p. o., Fluvanna co., Va., 58 ms. N. w. of Richmond; from W. 132 ms. Watered by Rivanna river.

WILMINGTON, p. v., seat of justice of New Hanover co.. N. C., situated on Cape Fear river, 35 miles from the sea, 148 miles southeasterly from Raleigh, and 365 miles from Washington. A large shoal at the mouth of the harbor, in a great measure destroys the effect of its other natural advantages. Two islands divide the river into three channels opposite the town. They afford the finest rice-fields in the state. The great body of the exports and imports of North Carolina pass through this port, and it is the terminus of the Washington and Wilmington chain of railroads. The population in 1810 was about 2,000; in 1830, 2,700; in 1840, 4,744; in 1850, 7.264.

WILMINGTON, c. h., p. v., seat of justice of Clinton co., O., 72 ms. s. w. of Columbus; from W. 445 ms. Watered by Todd's fork of Little Miami river. Pop. 1,238.

WILMINGTON, p. v., Dearborn co., Ind., 84 ms. s. E. of Indianapolis; from W. 520 ms. Pop. 287.

WILMINGTON, p. v., Will co., Ill., 152 ms. N. E. of Springfield; from W. 726 ms. Pop. 1,346.

WILMINGTON, p. o., Union co., Ark.

WILMORE, p. v., Cambria co., Pa.

WILMOT, p. t., Merrimack co., N. H., 27 ms. N. w. of Concord; from W. 302 ms. Watered by tributaries of Blackwater river. Pop. 1.272.

WILMOT, p. o., Boone co., Ill.

WILMOT, p. o., Kenosha co., Wis.

WILMOT, p. o., Noble co., Ind.

WILMOT FLAT, p. o., Merrimack co., N. H.

WILMURT, p. t.. Herkimer co., N. Y., 100 ms. N. w. of Albany ; from W. —— ms. Pop. 112.

WILNA, p. t., Jefferson co., N. Y., 157 ms. N. w. of Albany ; from W. 446 ms. Watered by Indian and Black rivers. Pop. 2,993.

WILNA, p. v., Houston co., Ga., 60 ms. s. w. of Milledgeville; from W. 708 ms.

WILSON COUNTY, situated in the northerly part of Tennessee, with Cumberland river on the north. Area, 625 square miles. Seat of justice, Lebanon. Pop. in 1810, 11,952 ; in 1820, 18,730 ; in 1830, 25,472 ; in 1840, 24,460 ; in 1850, 27,443.

WILSON, p. t., Piscataquis co., Me. Watered by a tributary of Piscataquis river, Pop. 813.

WILSON, p. t., Niagara co.. N. Y., 290 ms. w. of Albany ; from W. 420 ms. Watered by Howell's and Tuscarora creeks, and Lake Ontario. Pop. 2,955.

WILSON, t., Audrain co., Mo.

WILSON, p. o., Edgecomb co., N. C.

WILSON's, p. o.. Anderson co., Tenn., 181 ms. E. of Nashville ; from W. 508 ms.

WILSON's, p. o., Tyler co., Tex.

WILSON's CREEK, p. o., Graves co., Ky., 287 ms. s. w. of Frankfort ; from W. 814 ms.

WILSON's CREEK, p. o., Abbeville district, S. C., 112 ms. w. of Columbia ; from W. 544 ms.

WILSON's CREEK, p. o.. Knox co., Ind.

WILSON's MILLS, p. o., Oxford co., Me.

WILSON's MILLS, p. o., Venango co., Pa.

WILSON's STATION, p. o., Clinton co., O.

WILSONVILLE, p. v.. Highland co., Va., 198 ms. N. w. of Richmond ; from W. 178 ms.

WILSONVILLE, p. v., Shelby co., Ala. ; from W. 772 ms.

WILSONVILLE, p. v., Spencer co., Ky., 35 ms. s. w. of Frankfort ; from W. 577 ms.

WILSONVILLE, p. o., Cocke co., Tenn.

WILTON, p. t., Franklin co., Me., 38 ms. N. w. of Augusta; from W. 275 ms. Watered by tributaries of Sandy river. Pop. 1,909.

WILTON. p. t., Hillsborough co., N. H., 40 ms. s. of Concord ; from W. 454 ms. Watered by Souhegan river. Pop. 1,161.

WILTON, p. t., Fairfield co., Ct., 74 ms. s. w. of Hartford ; from W. 275 ms. Watered by Norwalk river. Pop. 2,066.

WILTON, p. t., Saratoga co., N. Y., 43 ms. N. of Albany ; from W. 413 ms. Watered by a tributary of Hudson river. Pop. 1,458.

WILTON, v., Granville co., N. C., 34 ms. N. of Raleigh ; from W. 270 ms.

WILTON. p. o., Pike co., Ark.

WILT's SPUR, p. o., Patrick co., Va.

WINABAGO, p. o., Bureau co., Ill.

WINCHENDON, p. t., Worcester co., Mass., 60 ms. N. w. of Boston ; from W. 419 ms. Watered by tributaries of Miller's river. Pop. 2,445.

WINCHESTER, p. t., Cheshire co., N. H., 64 ms. s. w. of Concord ; from W. 418 ms. Watered by Ashuelot river and tributaries. Pop. 3,296.

WINCHESTER, p. t., Litchfield co., Ct., 26 ms. N. w. of Hartford ; from W. 350 ms. Watered by Mad river. Pop. 2,179.

WINCHESTER, c. h., p. v., seat of justice of Frederick co., Va., 146 ms. N. w. of Richmond ; from W. 74 ms. Watered by Abraham's branch of Opequan creek.

WINCHESTER, p. o., Macon co., Ga.

WINCHESTER, p. t., Adams co., O. Watered by a tributary of Brush creek. Pop. 1,693.

WINCHESTER, p. v., Madison township, Guernsey co., O., 87 ms. E. of Columbus ; from W. 311 ms.

WINCHESTER, c. h., p. v., seat of justice of Clarke co., Ky., 44 ms. s. E. of Frankfort ; from W. 545 ms.

WINCHESTER, c. h., p. v., seat of justice of Franklin co., Tenn., 94 ms. s. E. of Nashville ; from W. 664 ms. Watered by a tributary of Elk river.

WINCHESTER, c. h., p. v., seat of justice of Randolph co., Ind., 81 ms. N. E. of Indianapolis ; from W. 506 ms. Pop. in 1850, 29.062.

WINCHESTER, p. v., Van Buren co., Iowa.

WINCHESTER, c. h., p. v., seat of justice of Wayne co., Miss., 151 ms. s. E. of Jackson ; from W. 982 ms. Watered by Chickasawha river.

WINCHESTER, p. v.. Clark co., Mo., 165 ms. N. of Jefferson City ; from W. 916 ms.

WINCHESTER, p. o., Middlesex co., Mass.

WINCHESTER, p. o., Union co., N. C.

WINCHESTER, p. o., Umpqua co., Oregon.

WINCHESTER CENTRE, p. v., Winchester township, Litchfield co., Ct., 31 ms. N. w. of Hartford ; from W 355 ms.

WINCHESTER SPRINGS, p. o., Franklin co., Tenn., 90 ms. s. E. of Nashville ; from W. 670 ms.

WINCHESTER, c. h., p. v., seat of justice of Scott co., Ill.. 50 ms. s. w. of Springfield ; from W. 830 ms.

WIND CREEK, p. o., Tallapoosa co., Ala.

WIND GAP, p. o., Northampton co., Pa., 110 ms. N. of Harrisburgh ; from W. 203 ms.

WINDHAM COUNTY, situated in the southeast corner of Vermont, with Connecticut river on the east. Area, 780 square miles. Face of the country, hilly and broken ; soil, generally good. Seat of justice, Fayetteville or Newfane. Pop. in 1810, 26,760 ; in 1820, 28,659 ; in 1830, 28,758 ; in 1840, 27,442 ; in 1850, 29.062.

WINDHAM COUNTY, situated at the northeast corner of Connecticut. Area, 620 square miles. Face of the country, diversified ; soil, good for grazing. Seat of justice, Brooklyn. Pop. in 1810, 28,611 ; in 1820. 25,331 ; in 1830, 27,077 ; in 1840, 28,080 ; in 1850, 31,079.

WINDHAM, p. t., Cumberland co., Me., 56 ms. s. E. of Augusta ; from W. 553 ms. Watered by Presumpscot river. Pop. 2,380.

WINDHAM, p. t., Rockingham co., N. H., 40 ms. s. E. of Concord ; from W. 457 ms. Watered by Beaver river. Pop. 818.

WINDHAM, p. t., Windham co., Vt., 104 ms. s. of Montpelier ; from W. 452 ms. Watered by tributaries of Williams, West, and Saxton's rivers, Pop. 763.

WINDHAM, p. t., Windham co., Ct., 31 ms. E. of Hartford ; from W. 358 ms. Watered by Shetucket river. Pop. 4,503.

WINDHAM, p. t, Greene co., N. Y., 45 ms. s. w. of Albany ; from W. 363 ms. Watered by Batavia Kill creek. Pop. 2,048.

WINDHAM, p. t., Bradford co., Pa., 169 ms. N. of Harrisburgh ; from W. 272 ms. Watered by Wepasening creek. Pop. 957.

WINDHAM, p. t., Luzerne co., Pa. Watered by Big and Little Mahoopeny creeks.

WINDHAM, p. t., Portage co., O., 159 ms. N. E. of Columbus ; from W. 315 ms. Pop. 808.

WINDHAM CENTRE, p. v., Windham township, Greene co., N. Y., 49 ms. s. w. of Albany ; from W. 360 ms.

WIND HILL, p. o., Montgomery co., N. C.

WINDRIDGE, p. o.. Greene co., Pa

WINDSOR COUNTY, situated on the east boundary of Vermont, with Connecticut river on the east. Area, 900 square miles. Face of the country, hilly ; soil, good for grazing. Seat of justice, Woodstock. Pop. in 1810. 34,877 ; in 1820, 38,233 ; in 1830, 40,623 , in 1840, 40,356 ; in 1850, 38,320.

WINDSOR, p. t. Kennebec co., Maine, 10 ms. E of Augusta ; from W. 605 ms. Watered by Sheepscot river. Pop. 1,793.

WINDSOR, p. t. Hillsborough co., N. H. Watered by tributaries of Contoocook river. Pop. 172.

WINDSOR, p. t., Windsor co., Vt., 65 ms. s. E. of Montpelier ; from W. 471 ms. Watered by Connecticut and Mill rivers. Pop. 1,928.

WINDSOR, p. t., Berkshire co., Mass., 123 ms. w. of Boston ; from W. 388 ms. Watered by tributaries of Westfield and Housatonic rivers. Pop. 897.

WINDSOR, p. t,. Hartford co., Ct., 7 ms. N. of Hartford : from W. 343 ms. Watered by Connecticut and Farmington rivers. Pop. 3,294.

WINDSOR, p. t., Broome co., N. Y., 126 ms. s. w. of Albany : from W. 300 ms. Watered by Susquehanna river. Pop. 2,645.

WINDSOR, p. o., Mercer co., N. J.

WINDSOR, p. t., York co., Pa., 42 ms. s. of Harrisburgh ; from W. 102 ms. Watered by Grist and Fish creeks, and Cabin's Branch and Beaver runs. Pop. 1,711.

WINDSOR, p. t., Berks co., Pa. Watered by Schuylkill river and Maiden creek, and Schuylkill canal. Pop. 1,115.

WINDSOR, c. h., p. v.. seat of justice of Bertie co., N. C., 157 ms. of Raleigh ; from W. 260 ms. Watered by Cashie river.

WINDSOR, p. v., Walton co., Ga., 71 ms. N. w. of Milledgeville ; from W. 645 ms. Watered by head-waters of Ocmulgee river.

WINDSOR, p. t., Ashtabula co., O., 126 ms. N. E. of Columbus ; from W. 327 ms. Watered by Grand river. Pop. 1,053.

WINDSOR, p. t., Lawrence co., O., 110 ms. s. e. of Columbus; from W. 410 ms. Watered by Symmes and Indian Guyandot creeks. Pop. 1,001.

WINDSOR, p. v., Randall co., Ind., 71 ms. n. e. of Indianapolis; from W. 516 ms. Watered by Stony creek.

WINDSOR, p. o., Eaton co., Mich.

WINDSOR, p. o., Dane co., Wis.

WINDSOR, p. o., Henry co., Mo.

WINDSOR LOCKS, p. v., Windsor township, Hartford co., Ct., 12 ms. n. of Hartford; from W. 348 ms.

WINDSORVILLE., p. o., Hartford co., Ct.

WINESBURGH, p. v., Paint township, Holmes co., O., 105 ms. n. e. of Columbus; from W. 331 ms.

WINFIELD, p. t., Herkimer co., N. Y., 76 ms. w. of Albany; from W. 375 ms. Watered by head-waters of Unadilla river. Pop. 1,481.

WINFIELD, p. o., Union co., Pa.,

WINFIELD, p. o., Carroll co., Md.

WINFIELD, p. o., Putnam co., Va.

WINFIELD, p. o., Columbia co., Ga.

WINFIELD, p. o., Tuscarawas co., O.

WINFIELD, p. o., Lake co., Ind.

WING, t., Lucas co., O. Pop. 261.

WINHALL, p. t., Bennington co., Vt., 97 ms. s. of Montpelier; from W. 434 ms. Watered by Winhall river. Pop. 762.

WINNAMAC, c. h., p. v., seat of justice of Pulaski co., Ind., 100 ms. n. of Indianapolis; from W. 638 ms.

WINNEBAGO COUNTY, situated on the north boundary of Illinois, and traversed by Rock river. Area, 504 square miles. Seat of justice, Rockford. Pop. in 1840, 4,609; in 1850, 11,773.

WINNEBAGO COUNTY, situated toward the east part of Wisconsin, with Winnebago lake on the east, and other bodies of water in the interior. Area, 500 square miles. Seat of justice, Oshkosh. Pop. in 1840, 135; in 1850, 10,167.

WINNEGANCE. p. o., Lincoln co., Me.

WINNESHIEK COUNTY, situated on the north boundary of Iowa, and traversed by Upper Iowa river. Area, —— square miles. Seat of justice, Fort Atkinson. Pop. in 1850, 546.

WINNESHIEK, p. o., Winneshiek co., Iowa.

WINNECOUNCE, p. o., Winnebago co., Wis.

WINNSBOROUGH, p. v., Fairfield district, S. C., 29 ms. n. w. of Columbia; from W. 480 ms.

WINNSBOROUGH, p. o., Franklin parish, La.

WINONA, p. o., Trimble co., Ky.

WINOOSKI FALLS, p. o., Chittenden co., Vt.

WINSLOW, p. t., Kennebec co., Me., 20 ms. n. of Augusta; from W. 615 ms. Watered by Kennebec and Sebasticook rivers. Pop. 1,796.

WINSLOW, p. t., Camden co., N. J., 54 ms. s. of Trenton; from W. 164 ms. Pop. 1,540.

WINSLOW, p. v., Pike co., Ind., 146 ms. s. w. of Indianapolis; from W. 685 ms.

WINSLOW, p. o., Stephenson co., Ill.

WINSTEAD, v., Litchfield co., Ct.

WINSTON COUNTY, situated in the easterly part of Mississippi. Area, 720 square miles. Seat of justice, Louisville. pop. in 1840, 4,650; in 1850, 7,956.

WINSTON, p. o., Allegany co., Md.

WINSTON, c. h., seat of justice of Forsyth co., N. C.

WINSTON, p. o., Randolph co., Ala.

WINSTON, p. o., Weakly co., Tenn., 127 ms. w. of Nashville; from W. 813 ms.

WINTER HARBOR, p. o., Hancock co., Me.

WINTERPOCK, p. o., Chesterfield co., Va.

WINTER SEAT, p. o., Abbeville district, S. C.

WINTERSET, p. o., Madison co., Iowa.

WINTERSVILLE, p. v., Cross Creek township. Jefferson co., O., 134 ms. e. of Columbus; from W. 269 ms.

WINTERSVILLE, p. o., Decatur co., Ind.

WINTHROP, p. t., Kennebec co., Me., 10 ms. w. of Augusta; from W. 598 ms. Watered by Cobbeseconte river. Pop. 2,154.

WINTHROP, p. o., Middlesex co., Ct.

WINTHROP, p. o., Kane co., Ill.

WINTON, c. h., p. v., seat of justice of Hertford co., N. C., 155 ms. n. e. of Raleigh; from W. 227 ms. Watered by Chowan river.

WINTON, p. o., Butler co., O.

WIOTA, p v., Lafayette co., Wis., 75 ms. n. of Madison; from W. 861 ms.

WIRETOWN, p. v., Ocean co., N. J., 51 ms. e. of Trenton; from W. 210 ms.

WIRT COUNTY, situated in the northwest part of Virginia, and traversed by Little Kanawha river. Area,

—— square miles. Seat of justice, Elizabethtown, or Wirt c. h. Pop. in 1850, 3,353.

WIRT, p. t., Alleghany co., N. Y. Watered by Little Genesee creek. Pop. 1,544.

WIRT, c. h., p. v., seat of justice of Wirt co., Va.

WIRT COLLEGE, p. v., Sumner co., Tenn., 38 ms. n. e. of Nashville; from W. 655 ms.

WISCASSET, c. h., p. t., seat of justice of Lincoln co., Me., 27 ms. s. e. of Augusta; from W. 588 ms. Watered by Sheepscot river and Atlantic ocean. Pop 2,332.

WISCONISCO. t., Dauphin co., Pa. (See Wiconisco.)

WISCONSIN, one of the United States, situated between 42° 30′ and 47° north latitude, and 87° and 92° 40′ w. longitude from Greenwich; — and is bounded on the north by Lake Superior; on the northeast by the peninsula of Michigan (from which it is separated in part by Menomonee river); east by Lake Michigan; south by Illinois; and west by Iowa and Minnesota (from which it is separated in part by the Mississippi river). Its superficial area is 53,924 square miles.

Physical Aspect.—The face of the country is rather undulating, than either hilly or flat, though both extremes exist. The highest lands in the state are those forming the dividing ridge between the Mississippi and Lake Superior. From this ridge, toward the south and southwest, the descent is gradual, until the inclination is interrupted by another ridge, in the region of the Wisconsin and Neenah rivers, which extends across the state. From the latter ridge proceeds another gentle inclined plain, down which flow the waters of Rock river and its branches into the Illinois. Along the Mississippi, Wisconsin, and Helena rivers, there are numerous hills and bluffs, varying from 300 to 1,000 feet in height above the surface of these streams. The country bordering directly on Superior has a very precipitous descent toward the lake. From the entrance of Green bay there is another ridge of broken land, running in a southwesterly direction, more or less uninterrupted, until it passes the confines of the state. The soil is generally of great fertility, and productive of all northern crops, in most situations that are not marshy or too wet. In Dane county, it is stated that the soil is composed, for the most part, of the black deposite of decayed vegetation, which for countless ages has flourished in wild luxuriance, and rotted upon the surface; of loam; and, in a few localities, of clay mixed with sand. The deposite of vegetable mould has uniformly several inches of thickness on the tops and sides of hills; in the valleys it is frequently a number of feet. A soil thus created, of impalpable powder, formed of the elements of organic matter—"the dust of death"—we need scarcely remark, is adapted to the highest and most profitable purposes of agriculture; yielding crop after crop, in rank abundance, without any artificial manuring.

Rivers, Lakes, and Bays.—The chief rivers are, the Mississippi, Wisconsin, Rock, St. Louis, Montreal, Baraboo, Wolf, Fox or Neenah, Black, Chippewa or Ojibwa, Catfish, and the Menomonee. The principal lakes, besides Superior and Michigan, are, Winnebago, Four Lakes, Wingra, Koshkonong, Packawa, Buffalo, Green, Little Green, Pewaugone, Great and Little Butte-des-Morts, Maquanago, Wissaua, Kanchee, La Belle, Nagowicka, Oconomewoc, Nashotah (Twin Lakes), Como, Delavan, Geneva, Deer, Sarah, Swan, Mud, Katakittekon, or Lac Vieux Desert. The chief bays are the Chegowawegon and Fond du Lac, in Lake Superior, and a part of Green bay in Lake Michigan.

Islands.—These are, Bartlett's, Apostles', Stocton's, and Madeline, in Lake Superior, and Doty's island, in Fox river.

Climate.—The climate of this state, notwithstanding its high northern latitude, is more favorable than that of corresponding parallels in New England and New York. Yet its winters are severe and long, with continued deep snows for several months, and the lakes and streams are strongly locked up in ice. The harbor

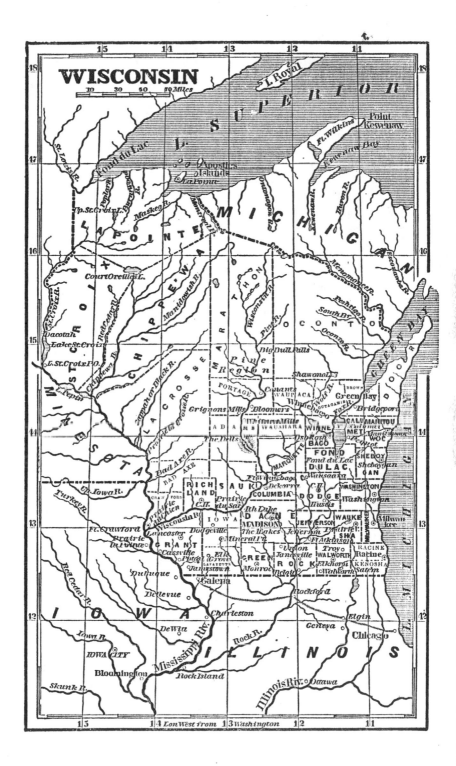

of Milwaukee is usually closed from the middle to the end of November, and is opened in the spring sometimes as early as the first week in March, while in other seasons it is closed as late as the middle of April. During the growing season, however, vegetation springs up as if by magic, and puts forward with astonishing rapidity and luxuriance. Spring and autumn are usually mild, and are less liable to destructive frosts than the more easterly states.

Productive Resources.—The chief products of this state are, horses, mules, neat cattle, sheep, swine, poultry, butter, cheese, wax, sugar, wool, hemp, flax, wheat, rye, barley, buckwheat, oats, potatoes, and Indian corn. Of the mineral wealth, lead, copper, and iron, are found in considerable abundance, but have not, as yet, been extensively wrought.

Manufactures.—This state is yet too young in years to have made much progress in manufactures. More than nine tenths of the people are engaged in agriculture, and a portion of the remaining tenth are engaged in mining. In 1850, there were in the state 1,273 manufacturing establishments, which produced $500 and upward each annually.

Railroads and Canals.—There are several railroads being constructed, or are already in operation, in Wisconsin. Among them are, one from Milwaukee to Galena, 70 miles long, forming a junction with the Chicago and Galena Union railroad; and the Rock River road, extending from Chicago, Illinois, to Fond du Lac, in this state. Plank-roads are also constructed here to a considerable extent, the abundance of lumber and the level surface of the country offering ready facilities for their construction. The Portage canal, connecting the Fox and Wisconsin rivers, and through them the great lakes with the Mississippi river, is an important internal improvement.

Commerce.—Lying, as this state does, with two of the great inland seas for its northern and eastern boundaries, and the Mississippi upon its western border, Wisconsin possesses commercial facilities not exceeded by those of any other of the western states.

Education.—The principal educational institutions of the higher class in this state are, the Wisconsin university, at Madison, founded in 1849, and the Beloit college, founded in 1847. There is also a theological seminary (Roman catholic) at Milwaukee. The educational resources of the state are extensive. The school-fund consists of the proceeds of about 2,000,000 of acres of land, five per cent. of the proceeds of all United States lands in the state, and moneys arising from several minor sources.

Population.—In 1840, 30,945; in 1850, 305,191.

Government.—The legislative power is vested in an assembly, of not fewer than 54 nor more than 100 members, chosen annually; and in a senate, numbering not less than a third nor more than one half the members of assembly, chosen for two years, one half each year. The executive power is vested in a governor and lieutenant-governor, who are chosen by a plurality vote for two years. The judicial power is vested in a supreme court, circuit courts, and probate courts, the judges of which are all chosen by the people—supreme and circuit judges for six years, and probate judges and justices of the peace for two years. State election the Tuesday succeeding the first Monday in November. All white male citizens of the United States, or white foreigners, who have declared their intentions to become citizens, who have resided in the state one year, have the right of suffrage.

History.—The first European settlement made within the limits of the present state of Wisconsin was by the French missionary Claude Allouez, and others, at La Pointe, on Madeline island, in the western end of Lake Superior, in 1665. This state embraces a part of the territory of Upper Louisiana, as claimed by the French, prior to 1763, when it was ceded to England, together with all their territory east of the Mississippi, under whose jurisdiction it remained until the treaty of Grenville, in 1795. The year following it was ceded to the United States, and in 1800 it was annexed to the "Territory northwest of the River Ohio." In 1802, Ohio was detached and formed into an independent state; and, in 1805, a territorial government was established in Michigan, under whose jurisdiction for civil purposes Wisconsin remained until 1836, when it was erected into a distinct territory. In 1847, Wisconsin, with its present boundaries, was formally admitted into the Union as a sovereign state. Motto of the seal, *Civilitas*

successit Barbarum: " Civilization has succeeded Barbarism."

WISCOY, p. o., Alleghany co., N. Y.

WISEMAN'S, p. o., Boone co., Mo.

WITCHER'S CROSS ROADS, p. o., Smith co., Tenn., 64 ms. E. of Nashville; from W. 650 ms.

WITHAMSVILLE. p. v., Union township, Clermont co., O., 128 ms. s. w. of Columbus; from W. 499 ms.

WITTENBERG'S, p. o., Caldwell co., N. C., 179 ms. w. of Raleigh; from W. 416 ms.

WITTEN'S, p. o., Jackson township, Monroe co., O., 136 ms. E. of Columbus; from W. 269 ms.

WITTSBURGH, p. o., St. Francis co., Ark.

WITTVILLE, p. o., Jefferson co., Tenn.

WOBURN, p. t., Middlesex co., Mass., 10 ms. N. W. of Boston; from W. 450 ms. Watered by Mystic river and Horn pond, and Middlesex canal. Pop. 3,956.

WOLCOTT, p. t., Lamoille co., Vt., 23 ms. N. of Montpelier; from W. 539 ms. Watered by Lamoille river. Pop. 983.

WOLCOTT, p. t., New Haven co., Ct., 54 ms. s. of Hartford; from W. 320 ms. Watered by Mad river. Pop. 603.

WOLCOTT, p. t., Wayne co., N. Y., 180 ms. w. of Albany; from W. 360 ms. Watered by Lake Ontario. Pop. 1,981.

WOLCOTT'S MILLS, p. o., La Grange co., Ind.

WOLCOTTVILLE, p. v., Torrington township, Litchfield co., Ct., 26 ms. w. of Hartford; from W. 333 ms. Watered by Naugatuck river.

WOLF, t., Lycoming co., Pa. Pop. 982.

WOLF, p. o., Knox co., O.

WOLFBOROUGH, p. t., Carroll co., N. H., 39 ms. N. E. of Concord; from W. 520 ms. Watered by Lake Winnipisiogee and Smith's river. Pop. 2,038.

WOLF BAYOU, p. o., Independence co., Ark.

WOLF CREEK, p. t., Mercer co., Pa. Watered by Wolf creek. Pop. 2,038.

WOLF CREEK, p. o., Pickens district, S. C., 159 ms. N. w. of Columbia; from W. 524 ms.

WOLF CREEK, p. o., Lenawee co., Mich. 67 ms. s. w. of Detroit; from W. 513 ms.

WOLF CREEK. p. o., Wilson co., Ala.

WOLF LAKE. p. o. Noble co., Ind., 160 ms. N. of Indianapolis; from W. 673 ms.

WOLF RIVER, p. o., Fayette co., Tenn., 186 ms. s. w. of Nashville; from W. 871 ms.

WOLF RUN, p. o., Lycoming co., Pa.

WOLFSVILLE, p. o., Frederick co., Md., 93 ms. N. w. of Annapolis; from W. 61 ms.

WOLFSVILLE, p. v., Union co., N. C., 178 ms. s. w. of Raleigh; from W. 417 ms.

WOMELSDORF, p. b., Berks co., Pa., 38 ms. E. of Harrisburgh; from W. 151 ms. Pop. 947.

WOOD COUNTY, situated in the north part of Ohio, with Maumee river on the northwest. Area, 590 square miles. Seat of justice, Perrysburgh. Pop. in 1820, 733; in 1830, 1,095; in 1840, 5,357; in 1850, 9,257.

WOOD COUNTY, situated on the northwesterly boundary of Virginia, with the Ohio river on the northwest, and traversed by the Little Kanawha. Area, 1,233 square miles. Seat of justice, Parkersburgh. Pop. in 1810, 3,036; in 1820, 5,860; in 1830, 6,429; in 1840, 7,923; in 1850, 9,450.

WOODBERRY, p. o., Butler co., Ky.

WOODBERRY, p. o., Merriwether co., Ga.

WOODBINE, p. o., Carroll co., Md., 60 ms. N. w. of Annapolis. Pop. 65 ms.

WOODBINE, p. o., Whitley co., Ky.

WOODBOURNE, p. v., Fallsburgh township, Sullivan co., N. Y., 103 ms. s. w. of Albany; from W. 308 ms.

WOODBOURNE, p. v., Knox co., Tenn., 202 ms. E. of Nashville; from W. 480 ms.

WOODBRIDGE, p. t., New Haven co., Ct., 6 ms. N. w. of New Haven; from W. 306 ms. Watered by West river. Pop. 912.

WOODBRIDGE, p. t., Middlesex co., N. J., 43 ms. N. E. of Trenton; from W. 209 ms. Watered by Rahway river. Pop. 5,141.

WOODBRIDGE, t., Hillsdale co., Mich. Pop. 404.

WOODBRIDGE, p. o., Cedar co., Iowa.

WOODBURN, p. o., Burke co., Ga.

WOODBURN, p. v., Macoupin co., Ill., 63 ms. s. of Springfield; from W. 803 ms.

WOODBURN, p. o., Warren co., Ky.

WOODBURY, p. t., Litchfield co., Ct., 50 ms. w. of Hartford; from W. 398 ms. Watered by Pomperaug river. Pop. 2,150.

WOODBURY, v., Oyster Bay township, Queens co., Long Island, N. Y.

WOODBURY, c. h., p. v., seat of justice of Gloucester co., N. J., 37 ms. s. w. of Trenton; from W. 148 ms. Watered by Woodbury creek.

WOODBURY, p. t., Huntingdon co., Pa.

WOODBURY, p. t., Bedford co., Pa., 113 ms. w. of Harrisburgh; from W. 139 ms. Watered by Yellow creek, and Frankstown branch of Juniata river.

WOODBURY, p. v., Wood co., O., 105 ms. N. w. of Columbus; from W. 461 ms.

WOODBURY, c. h., p. v., seat of justice of Cannon co., Tenn., 54 ms. from Nashville; from W. 645 ms. Watered by a tributary of Stone's creek, a branch of Cumberland river.

WOODBURY, p. o., Cumberland co., Ill.

WOODBURY, p. o., Hamilton co., Ind.

WOODBURY, p. o., Wright co., Mo.

WOODBURY, p. o., Washington co., Vt.

WOODCOCK. p. t., Crawford co., Pa., 213 ms. N. w. of Harrisburgh; from W. 315 ms. Watered by Woodcock creek. Pop. 2,073.

WOODFORD COUNTY, situated toward the north part of Kentucky, with Kentucky river on the southwest. Area, 154 square miles. Seat of justice, Versailles. Pop. in 1810, 9,659; in 1820, 12,207; in 1830, 12,273; in 1840. 11,740; in 1850, 12,423.

WOODFORD COUNTY, situated in the central part of Illinois, with Illinois river on the northwest. Area, 470 square miles. Seat of justice, Woodford. Pop. in 1850. 4,416.

WOODFORD, p. t., Bennington co., Vt., 121 ms. s. of Montpelier; from W. 411 ms. Watered by head waters of Walloomsac and Deerfield rivers. Pop. 423.

WOOD GROVE, p. o., Morgan co., O., 84 ms. E. of Columbus; from W. 319 ms.

WOODHULL, p. t., Steuben co., N. Y., 239 ms. w. of Albany; from W. 295 ms. Watered by Tuscarora creek. Pop. 1,769.

WOODHULL. p. t., Shiawassee co., Mich. Pop. 259.

WOODINGTON, p. t., Darke co., O.

WOODLAND, p. v., East Feliciana parish, La., 122 ms. N. w. of New Orleans; from W. 1,140 ms.

WOODLAND, p. o., Barry co., Mich.

WOODLAND, p. o., Barren co., Ky.

WOODLAND. p. o., Clearfield co., Pa.

WOODLANDS, p. o., Marshall co., Va., 340 ms. N. w. of Richmond; from W. 278 ms.

WOODLAWN, p. o., Dallas co., Ala.; from W. 831 ms.

WOODLAWN, p. o., Murray co., Ga.

WOODLAWN, p. o., Itawamba co., Miss.

WOODLAWN, p. o., Wachita co., Ark.

WOODLAWN, p. o., Cecil co., Md.

WOODLAWN, p. o., Monroe co., Mo.

WOODLAWN, p. o., Appomattox co., Va.

WOODLAWN, p. v., Lincoln co., N. C., 173 ms. w. of Raleigh; from W. 412 ms.

WOODLAWN, p. o., Jasper co., Tex.

WOODLAWN, p. o., Edgefield district, S. C., 98 ms. w. of Columbia; from W. 580 ms.

WOODPORT, p. o., Victoria co., Tex.

WOODRUFF'S. p. o., Spartanburgh district, S. C., 96 ms. N. w. of Columbia; from W. 491 ms.

WOOD'S, p. o., Perry co., Tenn.

WOOD-BOROUGH, p. o., Shelby co.; from W. 783 ms.

WOODSBOROUGH, p. o., Montgomery co., Ill.

WOODSBOROUGH, p. v., Frederick co., Md., 85 ms. N. w. of Annapolis; from W. 54 ms.

WOOD'S CORNERS, p. o., Hillsdale co., Mich.

WOOD'S CROSS ROADS, p. o., Gloucester co., Va.

WOODSDALE, p. o., Person co., N. C., 62 ms. N. of Raleigh; from W. 242 ms.

WOOD'S DIGGINGS, p. o., Tuolumne co., Cal.

WOODSFIELD, c. h., p. v., Centre township, seat of justice of Monroe co., O., 117 ms. E. of Columbus; from W. 283 ms. Pop. 393.

WOOD'S HILL, p. o., Roane co., Tenn., 162 ms. E. of Nashville; from W. 519 ms.

WOOD'S HOLE, p. v., Falmouth township, Barnstable co., Mass., 79 ms. s. of Boston; from W. 461 ms. Watered by Vineyard sound.

WOOD SHOP, p. o., Dale co., Ala.

WOOD'S MILLS, p. o., Ripley co., Mo.

WOODSONVILLE, p. v., Hart co., Ky. Watered by Green river.

WOOD'S STATION, p. o., Walker co., Ga., 214 ms., N. w. of Milledgeville; from W. 623 ms.

WOODSTOCK, p. t., Oxford co., Me., 49 ms. w. of

Augusta; from W. 603 ms. Watered by a tributary of Little Androscoggin river. Pop. 1,012.

WOODSTOCK, p. t., Grafton co., N. H., 57 ms. N. of Concord; from W. 532 ms. Watered by a tributary of Pemigewasset river.

WOODSTOCK, c. h., seat of justice of Windsor co., Vt., 51 ms. s. of Montpelier; from W. 485 ms. Watered by Ottaqueechee river and Beaver brook. Pop. 3,041.

WOODSTOCK. p. t., Windham co., Ct., 43 ms. N. E. of Hartford; from W. 379 ms. Watered by Muddy brook, and tributaries of Quinnebaug and Natchaug rivers. Pop. 3,380.

WOODSTOCK, p. t., Ulster co., N. Y., 69 ms. s. of Albany; from W. 328 ms. Watered by Saghkill and tributaries of Esopus creek. Pop. 1,650.

WOODSTOCK, p. v., Anne Arundel co., Md., 50 ms. N. w. of Annapolis; from W. 55 ms.

WOODSTOCK, c. h., p. v., seat of justice of Shenandoah co., Va., 150 ms. N. w. of Richmond; from W. 104 ms. Watered by north fork of Shenandoah river.

WOODSTOCK, p. v., Cherokee co,, Ga., 125 ms. N. w. of Milledgeville; from W. 683 ms. Watered by Little river.

WOODSTOCK, p. v., Rush township. Champaign co., O., 37 ms. N. w. of Columbus; from W. 430 ms. Pop. 205.

WOODSTOCK, p. t., Lenawee co., Miss., 73 ms. s. w. of Detroit; from W. 533 ms. Watered by head waters of Raisin river.

WOODSTOCK, p. o., Fulton co., Ill.

WOODSTOCK MILLS, p. o., Nassau co., Flor.

WOODSTOWN, p. v., Pitt's Grove township, Salem co., N. J., 53 ms. s. of Trenton; from W. 164 ms. Watered by north fork of Salem creek.

WOODSVILLE, p. v., Hopewell township, Mercer co., N. J., 13 ms. N. of Trenton; from W. 179 ms.

WOODVALE, p. o., Fayette co., Pa.

WOODVIEW, p. o., Morrow co., O.

WOODVILLE, c. h., p. v., seat of justice of Jackson co., Ala.; from W. 688 ms.

WOODVILLE, p. v., Litchfield co., Ct., 39 ms. w. of Hartford; from W. 320 ms.

WOODVILLE, p. v., Ellisburgh township, Jefferson co., 179 ms. N. w. of Albany; from W. 399 ms.

WOODVILLE, p. v., Rappahannock co., Va., 118 ms. N. w, of Richmond; from W. 85 ms.

WOODVILLE, p. v., Perquimans co., N. C., 205 ms. N. E. of Raleigh; from W. 293 ms.

WOODVILLE, p. t., Sandusky co., O., 120 ms. N. w. of Columbus; from W. 438 ms. Watered by Portage river. Pop. 1,237.

WOODVILLE, p. v., Jackson co., Ind., 74 ms. s. of Indianapolis; from W. 601 ms.

WOODVILLE, p. v., Hancock co., Ill., 106 ms. N. w. of Springfield; from W. 884 ms.

WOODVILLE, c. h., p. v., seat of justice of Wilkinson co., Miss., 135 ms. s. w. of Jackson; from W. 1,145 ms.

WOODVILLE. p. v., Macon co., Mo., 96 ms. N. of Jefferson city; from W. 979 ms.

WOODVILLE, p. o., Haywood co., Tenn.

WOODVILLE, p. v., Middlesex co., Mass.

WOODVILLE, c. h., p. v., seat of justice of Tyler co., Tex.

WOODVILLE, p. v., Greene co., Ga.

WOODWARD, p. o., Centre co., Pa.

WOODWARDSVILLE, p. o., Schroon township, Essex co., N. Y., 101 ms. N. of Albany; from W. 476 ms.

WOODWORTH'S, p. o., Granville co., N. C., 61 ms. N. of Raleigh; from W. 236 ms.

WOODYARDS, p. o., Athens co., O.

WOODRIDGE'S STORE, p. o., Christian co., Ky.

WOOLWICH, p. t., Lincoln co., Me., 35 ms. s. of Augusta; from W. 580 ms. Watered by Kennebec river. Pop. 1,420.

WOOLWICH, p. t., Gloucester co., N. J. Watered by Delaware river and tributaries. Pop. 3,265.

WOONSOCKET FALLS, p. v., Smithfield township, Providence co., R. I., 15 ms. N. w. of Providence; from W. 414 ms. Watered by Blackstone river and Blackstone canal.

WOOSTER, c. h., p. t., seat of justice of Wayne co., O., 93 ms. N. E. of Columbus; from W. 344 ms. Watered by forks of Killbuck and Apple creeks. Pop. 4,122.

WORCESTER COUNTY, situated in the central part of Massachusetts. Area, 1,500 square miles. Face of the country, hilly; soil, of middling quality. Seat of justice, Worcester. Pop. in 1810, 64,910; in 1820, 73,625; in 1830, 84,365; in 1840, 95,313; in 1850, 130,789.

WORCESTER COUNTY, situated on the southeast boundary of Maryland, with the Atlantic ocean on the east. Area, 700 square miles. Seat of justice, Snow Hill. Pop. in 1810, 16,971; in 1820, 17,521; in 1830, 18,271; in 1840, 18,377; in 1850. 18,979.

WORCESTER, p. t., Washington co., Vt., 8 ms. N. of Montpelier; from W. 524 ms. Watered by north branch of Onion river. Pop. 702.

WORCESTER, city, seat of justice of Worcester co., Mass., 42 ms. w. of Boston; from W. 425 ms. It is situated in a pleasant valley, surrounded by gentle hills, laid out with regularity and taste, its streets animated by industry, and beautified by nature with shady trees and pleasant gardens. It is, in fact, a New England village. Here, as veins at the heart, concentre railroads from Boston, Providence, Norwich, Springfield, Hartford and New Haven, New York, the valley of the Hudson, New Hampshire, and Vermont, which discharge their burdens, and bear away as swiftly the productions of Worcester and the fruitful region which surrounds it. The Blackstone canal, 45 miles long, forms another channel of communication with Providence. The state lunatic asylum, and the hall of the American Antiquarian Society, are the most prominent public buildings. The population in 1810 was 2,577; in 1820, 2,962; in 1830 4,172; in 1840, 7,497; in 1850, 17,049.

WORCESTER, p. t., Otsego co., N. Y., 57 ms. s. w. of Albany; from W. 371 ms. Watered by Charlotte river and tributaries. Pop. 2,047.

WORCESTER, p. t., Montgomery co., Pa., 89 ms. E. of Harrisburgh; from W. 162 ms. Pop. 1,453.

WORTH, p. o., Mercer co., Pa.

WORTH, p. o., De Kalb co., Ala.

WORTH, p. o., Perry co., O.

WORTH, p. o., Saginaw co., Mich.

WORTH, p. o., Dubois co., Ind.

WORTH, p. o., Cook co., Ill.

WORTH, p. o., Sheboygan co., Wis.

WORTH, p. o., Marion co., Ark.

WORTHINGTON, p. t., Hampshire co., Mass., 112 ms. w. of Boston; from W. 395 ms. Watered by Westfield river. Pop. 1,132.

WORTHINGTON, p. v., Armstrong co., Pa., 189 ms. w. of Harrisburgh; from W. 243 ms.

WORTHINGTON, p. o., Marion co., Va.

WORTHINGTON, p. o., Muhlenburgh co., Ky., 172 ms. s. w. of Frankfort; from W. 714 ms.

WORTHINGTON, p. v., Sharon township, Franklin co., O., 9 ms. N. of Columbus; from W. 402 ms. Watered by Olentangy or Whetstone river.

WORTHINGTON, p. t., Richland co., O. Pop. 2,003.

WORTHINGTON, p. o., Greene co., Ind.

WORTHVILLE, p. o., Jefferson co., N. Y.

WORTHVILLE, p. o., Butts co., Ga.

WORTHVILLE, p. o., Carroll co., Ky.

WORTHVILLE, p. o., Johnson co., Ind.

WRENTHAM, p. t., Norfolk co., Mass., 32 ms. s. w. of Boston; from W. 418 ms. Watered by tributaries of Charles, Taunton, and Neponset rivers. Pop. 3,037.

WRIGHT COUNTY, situated in the southerly part of Missouri. Area, —— square miles. Seat of justice, Hartsville. Pop. in 1850, 3,387.

WRIGHT, p. o., Ottawa co., Mich.

WRIGHT, p. o., Greene co., Ind.

WRIGHT'S BLUFF, p. o., Sumter district, S. C.

WRIGHTSBOROUGH, p. v., Columbia co., Ga., 95 ms. N. E. of Milledgeville; from W. 613 ms. Watered by a tributary of Little river.

WRIGHT'S CORNERS, p. o., Newfane township, Niagara co., N. Y., 279 ms. w. of Albany; from W. 406 ms.

WRIGHTSTOWN, p. v., Hanover township, Burlington co., N. J., 23 ms. s. of Trenton; from W. 171 ms.

WRIGHTSTOWN, p. t., Bucks co., Pa. Watered by Neshaminy creek.

WRIGHTSVILLE, p. o., Clinton co., N. Y.

WRIGHTSVILLE, p. b., York co., Pa., 31 ms. s. E. of Harrisburgh; from W. 101 ms. Watered by Susquehanna river. Pop. 1,310.

WRIGHTSVILLE, p. o., Pontotoc co., Miss.

WRIGHTSVILLE, p. v., Roane co., Tenn., 154 ms. E. of Nashville; from W. 539 ms.

WURTEMBURGH, p. o., Lawrence co., Pa.

WURTSBOROUGH, p. v., Mamakating township, Sullivan co., N. Y., 97 ms. s. w. of Albany; from W. 287 ms. Situated on the Delaware and Hudson canal.

WYACONDA, p. o., Scotland co., Mo.

WYALUSING, p. t., Bradford co., Pa., 149 ms. N. of Harrisburgh; from W. 259 ms. Watered by Wyalusing creek. Pop. 1,275.

WYALUSING, p. o., Grant co., Wis.

WYANDOTT COUNTY, situated toward the north part of Ohio. Area, —— square miles. Seat of justice, Upper Sandusky. Pop. in 1850, 11,292.

WYANDOTT, p. o., Wyandott co., O., 61 ms. N. of Columbus; from W. 416 ms.

WYANDOTTE, p. o., Tippecanoe co., Ind.

WYATT, p. v., Lafayette co., Miss., 174 ms. N. E. of Jackson; from W. 912 ms. Watered by Tallahatchie river.

WYE MILLS, p. v., Talbot co., Md., 31 ms. E. of Annapolis; from W. 71 ms. Watered by Wye river.

WYKERTOWN, p. o., Sussex co., N. J., 80 ms. N. of Trenton; from W. 249 ms.

WYLLIESBURGH, p. o., Charlotte co., Va., 106 ms. s. w. of Richmond; from W. 204 ms.

WYNANT, p. o., Shelby co., O.

WYNANT'S KILL, p. v., Greenbush township, Rensselaer co., N. Y., 10 ms. E. of Albany; from W. 380 ms.

WYNCOOP'S CREEK, p. v., Chemung co., N. Y.

WYNN, p. o., Franklin co., Ind.

WYOCENA, p. o., Columbia co., Wis.

WYOMING COUNTY, situated in the west part of New York. Area, 500 square miles. Seat of justice, Warsaw. Pop. in 1850, 31,981.

WYOMING COUNTY, situated in the northeast part of Pennsylvania, and traversed by Susquehanna river. Area, 480 square miles. Seat of justice, Tunkhannock. Pop. in 1850, 10,655.

WYOMING COUNTY, situated in Virginia. Area, —— square miles. Seat of justice, Ginseng. Pop. in 1850, 1,645.

WYOMING, p. v., Middlebury township, Wyoming co., N. Y., 248 ms. w. of Albany; from W. 366 ms. Watered by Allen's creek.

WYOMING, p. v., Luzerne co., Pa., 131 ms. N. E. of Harrisburgh; from W. 236 ms. Watered by Susquehanna river.

WYOMING, p. v., Dinwiddie co., Va., 59 ms. s. of Richmond; from W. 178 ms.

WYOMING, p. o., Jackson co., Mich., 85 ms. w. of Detroit; from W. 555 ms.

WYOMING, p. v., Stark co., Ill., 101 ms. N. of Springfield; from W. 815 ms. Watered by Spoon river.

WYOMING, p. o., Iowa co., Wis.

WYSOX, p. t., Bradford co., Pa., 136 ms. N. of Harrisburgh; from W. 246 ms. Watered by Rumfield and Wysox creeks. Pop. 1,167.

WYTHE COUNTY, situated in the southwest part of Virginia, and traversed by New river. Area, 700 square miles. Face of the country, mountainous. Seat of justice, Wytheville. Pop. in 1810, 8,356; in 1820, 9,692; in 1830, 12,163; in 1840, 9,375; in 1850, 12,024.

WYTHE, p. o., Hancock co., Ill.

WYTHEVILLE, c. h., p. v., seat of justice of Wythe co., Va., 248 ms. w. of Richmond; from W. 316 ms. Watered by a tributary of New river.

X.

XENIA, c. h., p. t., seat of justice of Greene co., O., 61 ms. s. w. of Columbus; from W. 454 ms. It is a large and rapidly-growing town, in the centre of a fertile and highly-cultivated country, and is watered by Little Miami river and Cæsar's and Shawnee creeks, on the latter of which, three miles from its entrance into Little Miami river (of which it is a chief tributary), the principal village is located. Its streets are handsomely and regularly laid out, and adorned with several churches and other public buildings, together with many elegant private residences. The population of the township in 1830 was 4,127; in 1840, 4,913; in 1850, 7,055.

XENIA, p. o., Clay co., Ill.

Y.

YALLABUSHA COUNTY, situated toward the north part of Mississippi, and traversed by Yallabusha river. Area, 720 square miles. Seat of justice, Coffeeville. Pop. in 1840, 12,248 ; in 1850, 17,258.

YAM HILL COUNTY, situated in Oregon. Area, —— square miles. Seat of justice, ———. Pop. in 1850, 1,512.

YAM HILL FALLS, p. o., Yam Hill co., Oregon.

YANCEY COUNTY, situated on the northwest boundary of North Carolina. Area, 1,760 square miles. Face of the country, mountainous. Seat of justice, Burnsville. Pop. in 1840, 5,962 ; in 1850, 8,205.

YANCEY'S MILLS, p. o., Albemarle co., Va., 101 ms. N. W. of Richmond ; from W. 136 ms.

YANCEYVILLE, c. h., p. v., seat of justice of Caswell co., N. C., 87 ms. N. W. of Raleigh ; from W. 263 ms.

YANHANNA, p. o., Georgetown district, S. C.

YANKEE HILL, p. o., Menard co., Ill.

YANKEE SETTLEMENT, p. o., Delaware co., Iowa.

YANKEE SPRING, p. t., Barry co., Mich., 150 ms. w. of Detroit ; from W. 615 ms. Pop. 292.

YAPHANK, p. o., Suffolk co., Long Island, N. Y.

YARBOROUGH, p. o., Bossier parish, La.

YARDLEYVILLE. p. v., Makefield township, Bucks co., Pa., 128 ms. E. of Harrisburgh ; from W. 168 ms. Watered by Delaware river.

YARDVILLE, p. o., Mercer co., N. J., 6 ms. E. of Trenton ; from W. 172 ms.

YARMOUTH, p. t., Barnstable co., Mass., 78 ms. s. E. of Boston ; from W. 479 ms. Watered by Cape Cod bay and Atlantic ocean. Pop. 2,595.

YARMOUTH PORT. p. v., Yarmouth township, Barnstable co., Mass., 77 ms. s. E. of Boston ; from W. 478 ms. Watered by an arm of Cape Cod bay.

YATES COUNTY, situated toward the westerly part of New York, with Seneca lake on the east, and Crooked lake on the south. Area, 320 square miles. Face of the country, hilly ; soil, fertile. Pop. in 1820, 11,025 ; in 1830, 19,019 ; in 1840, 20.444 ; in 1850. 20,590.

YATES, p. t., Orleans co., N. Y.. 266 ms. w. of Albany ; from W. 409 ms. Watered by Johnson's creek and Lake Ontario. Pop. 2,242.

YATESVILLE, p. o., Potter township, Yates co., N. Y., 197 ms. w. of Albany ; from W. 330 ms.

YATESVILLE, p. o., Lunenburgh co., Va., 80 ms. s. w. of Richmond ; from W. 208 ms.

YATTON, p. o., Washington co., Iowa.

YAZOO COUNTY, situated in the westerly part of Mississippi, with Yazoo river on the northwest, and the Big Black on the southeast. Area, 650 square miles. Seat of justice, Benton. Pop. in 1830, 6,550 ; in 1840, 10.480 ; in 1850, 14,118.

YAZOO CITY, p. v., Yazoo co., Miss., 60 ms. N. W. of Jackson ; from W. 1,029 ms. Watered by Yazoo river.

YELL COUNTY, situated in the westerly part of Arkansas, with Arkansas river on the northeast. Area, 936 square miles. Seat of justice, Danville. Pop. in 1850, 3.341.

YELLOW BRANCH. p. o., Campbell co., Va., 130 ms. w. of Richmond ; from W. 208 ms.

YELLOW BUD, p. o., Ross co., O.

YELLOW BUSH, p. o., Chickasaw co., Miss.

YELLOW CREEK, p. o., Lumpkin co., Ga.

YELLOW CREEK, p. o.. Tishamingo co., Flor.

YELLOW CREEK, p. o., Knox co., Ky., 146 ms. s. E. of Frankfort ; from W. 492 ms.

YELLOW CREEK, p. t., Columbiana co., O. Pop. 854.

YELLOW CREEK, p. o., Stephenson co., Ill.

YELLOW CREEK, p. t., Chariton co., Mo., 111 ms. N. W. of Jefferson city ; from W. 1.005 ms.

YELLOW CREEK. t., Linn co., Mo.

YELLOW CREEK FURNACE, p. o., Montgomery co., Tenn., 36 ms. N. W. of Nashville ; from W. 747 ms.

YELLOW MOUNTAIN, p. o., Yancey co., N. C.

YELLOW HEAD GROVE, p. o., Will co., Ill.

YELLOW RIVER, p. o., Gwinnett co., Ga.

YELLOW RIVER, p. o., Marshall co., Ind.

YELLOW SPRING, p. o., Blair co., Penn.

YELLOW SPRING, p. o., Hampshire co., Va., 169 ms. N. w of Richmond ; from W. 97 ms.

YELLOW SPRING, p. o., Johnson co., Ind., 16 ms. s. of Indianapolis ; from W. 580 ms.

YELLOW SPRING, p. o., Des Moines co , Iowa.

YELLOW SPRINGS, p. o., Claiborne co., Tenn., 233 ms. E. of Nashville ; from W. 472 ms.

YELLOW SPRINGS, p. v., Miami township, Greene co.. O., 52 ms. s. w. of Columbus ; from W. 445 ms.

YELLOW STONE, p. o., Paulding co., Ga.

YELLOW STONE, p. o., Lafayette co., Wis.

YELLOW STORE, p. o.. Hawkins co., Tenn., 254 ms. E. of Nashville ; from W. 428 ms.

YELLVILLE, c. h., p. v., seat of justice of Marion co., Ark., 180 ms. N. of Little Rock ; from W. 1,106 ms. Watered by a tributary of White river.

YELVINGTON, p. v., Daviess co., Ky., 156 ms. w. of Frankfort ; from W. 683 ms.

YNOOSKI, p. o., Kalamazoo co.. Mich.

YOCONY, p. o., Itawamba co., Miss.

YOCUMTOWN, p. v.. York co., Pa., 21 ms. s. of Harrisburgh ; from W. 113 ms.

YOCUM STATION, p. o., Lee co., Va.

YOHOGANY, p. o., Westmoreland co., Pa.

YOLO COUNTY, situated in the central part of California, extending from the summit of the Coast Range of mountains to the Sacramento river. Area, —— square miles. Seat of justice, Fremont. Pop. in 1852, 1,307.

YONCALLA, p. o., Benton co., Oregon.

YONGUESVILLE. p. v., Fairfield district, S. C., 41 ms. N. of Columbia ; from W. 468 ms. Watered by Little river.

YONKERS, p. t., formerly Philipsburgh, Westchester co., N. Y., 132 ms. s. of Albany ; from W. 242 ms. Watered by Bronx, Saw-Mill, and Hudson rivers. Pop. in 1810, 1,365 ; in 1820, 1,586 ; in 1830, 1,761 ; in 1840, 2.968 ; in 1850, 4,160.

YORK COUNTY, situated at the southwest corner of Maine, with the Atlantic ocean on the southeast, and Salmon Fall and Piscataqua rivers on the southwest. Area, 818 square miles. Seats of justice, Alfred and York. Pop. in 1810. 41,877 ; in 1820. 46,283 ; in 1830, 51,710 ; in 1840. 54,034 ; in 1850. 60.106.

YORK COUNTY, situated on the south boundary of Pennsylvania, with Susquehanna river on the northeast. Area, 864 square miles. Face of the country, hilly ; soil, varied. Seat of justice, York. Pop. in 1810, 31,958 ; in 1820, 38,759 ; in 1830, 42,658 ; in 1840, 47,010 ; in 1850. 57,450.

YORK COUNTY, situated on the southeast boundary of Virginia, with York river on the northeast, and Chesapeake bay on the east. Area, 150 square miles. Seat of justice, Yorktown. Pop. in 1810, 5,187 ; in 1820, 4,384 ; in 1830, 5,354 ; in 1840, 4,720 ; in 1850. 4,460.

YORK DISTRICT, situated on the north boundary of South Carolina, with Broad river on the west, and the Wateree on the east. Area, 700 square miles. Seat of justice, Yorkville. Pop. in 1810. 10,032 ; in 1820. 14,936 ; in 1830, 17,790 ; in 1840, 18,383 ; in 1850, 19,433.

YORK, c. h., p. t., seat of justice of York co., Me., 92 ms. s. w. of Augusta ; from W. 592 ms. Watered by York and Cape Neddock rivers. Pop. 2,980.

YORK, p. t., Livingston co., N. Y., 238 ms. w. of Albany ; from W. 354 ms. Watered by tributaries of Genesee river. Pop. 2,785.

YORK, p. t., York co., Pa. Pop. 1,960.

YORK, c. h., p. b., seat of justice of York co., Pa., 24 ms. s. of Harrisburgh ; from W. 90 ms. Watered by Codorus creek. Pop. 134.

YORK, p. v., Fayette co., Ga., 87 ms. N. w. of Milledgeville ; from W. 691 ms.

YORK, p. t., Athens co., O. Watered by Hockhocking river. Pop. 1,391.

YORK, t., Belmont co., O. Watered by Ohio river and Captina creek. Pop. 1,312.

YORK, t., Darke co., O. Pop. 499.

YORK, t., Lucas co., O.

YORK, t., Medina co., O. Pop. 1,211.

YORK, t., Morgan co., O. Pop. 1,207.

YORK, t., Sandusky co, O. Pop. 1,811.

YORK, t., Tuscarawas co., O. Pop. 1,303.

YORK, t., Union co., O. Pop. 831.

YORK, t, Van Wert co., O. Pop. 375.

YORK, p. t., Washtenaw co., Mich., 46 ms. w. of Detroit; from W. 511 ms. Pop. 1,360.

YORK, p. t., Switzerland co., Ind. Pop. 1,523.

YORK, t., Steuben co., Ind.

YORK. t., Noble co., Ind. Pop. 565.

YORK, p. o., Gibson co., Ind.

YORK, p. v., Crawford co., Ill., 142 ms. s. E. of Springfield: from W. 676 ms. Watered by Wabash river.

YORK. p. o., Walker co., Ala.

YORK, p. o., Dane co., Wis.

YORK CENTRE, p. o,, Du Page co., Ill., 151 ms. N. W. of Columbus; from W. 482 ms.

YORK HAVEN, v., Newberry township, York co., Pa., 14 ms. s. of Harrisburgh; from W. 100 ms. Watered by Susquehanna river. Pop. 131.

YORK NORTH RIDGE. p. o., Sandusky co., O., 99 ms. N. of Columbus; from W. 414 ms.

YORK-HIRE, p. t. Cattaraugus co., N. Y., 278 ms. w. of Albany; from W. 341 ms. Watered by Cattaraugus creek and tributaries. Pop. 2,010.

YORK SOUTH RIDGE, p. o.. Sandusky co., O.

YORK SULPHUR SPRINGS, p. v., Latimore township, Adams co. Pa., 21 ms. s. of Harrisburgh; from W. 89 ms.

YORKTOWN, p. t., Westchester co., N. Y., 112 ms. s. of Albany; from W. 275 ms. Pop. 2,273.

YORKTOWN, c. h., p. v., seat of justice of York co. Va., 70 ms. s. E. of Richmond; from W. 185 ms. Watered by York river.

YORKTOWN, p. v., Delaware co., Ind., 50 ms. N. E. of Indianapolis; from W. 537 ms.

YORKTOWN, p. o., Bureau co., Ill.

YORKTOWN, p. o., De Witt co., Tex.

YORKVILLE, p. v., city and county of New York. Site of the receiving reservoir of the Croton waterworks.

YORKVILLE. c. h., p. v., seat of justice of York district, S. C., 79 ms. N. of Columbia; from W. 480 ms. Watered by a tributary of Broad river. Pop. 983.

YORKVILLE, p. v., Pickens co., Ala.; from W. 876 ms.

YORKVILLE, p. v., Racine co., Wis., 96 ms. s. E. of Madison; from W. 796 ms.

YORKVILLE. p. v., Gibson co., Tenn., 143 ms. w. of Nashville; from W. 826 ms. Watered by a tributary of Obion river.

YORKVILLE, p. o., Dearborn co., Ind.

YORKVILLE, p. o., Kalamazoo co., Mich.

YOUGH GLADES, p. o.. Alleghany co., Md., 219 ms. N. w. of Annapolis; from W. 180 ms.

YOUNG, p. t., Indiana co., Pa. Pop. 1,513.

YOUNG, p. t., Jefferson co., Pa.

YOUNG, p. o., McDonough co., Ill., 95 ms. N. w. of Springfield; from W. 868 ms.

YOUNG CANE, p. o., Union co., Ga.

YOUNGERS, p. o., Boone co., Me., 45 ms. N. of Jefferson city; from W. 930 ms.

YOUNG HICKORY, p. o., Will co., Ill.

YOUNG HICKORY. p. o., Muskingum co., O.

YOUNG HICKORY. p. o.. Washington co., Wis.

YOUNG'S CROSS ROADS. p. o., Granville co., N. C., 68 ms. N. of Raleigh; from W. 263 ms.

YOUNG'S POINT, p. o., Madison parish, La.

YOUNG'S SETTLEMENT. p. o., Bastrop co., Tex.

YOUNG'S STORE, p. o., Laurens district, S. C.

YOUNG-TOWN, p. v., Porter township, Niagara co., N Y., 298 ms. w. of Albany; from W. 416 ms. Watered by Niagara river.

YOUNGSTOWN. p. b., Unity township, Westmoreland co., Pa., 158 ms. w. of Harrisburgh; from W. 184 ms.

YOUNGSTOWN, p. t.. Mahoning co., O., 177 ms. N. E. of Columbus; from W. 290 ms. Watered by Mahoning river and tributaries. Pop. 2,802.

YOUNGSVILLE, p. v., Warren co., Pa., 218 ms. N. w. of Harrisburgh: from W. 310 ms. Watered by Big Broken Straw creek.

YOUNGSVILLE, p. o., Sullivan co., N. Y.

YOUNGSVILLE, p. v., Tallapoosa co., Ala.; from W. 806 ms.

YOUNGSVILLE. p. o., Adams co., O.

YOUNG WOMANSTOWN, p. v., Clinton co., Pa., 134 ms. N. of Harrisburgh; from W. 226 ms. Watered by Susquehanna river.

YOUNTSVILLE, p. o., Montgomery co., Ind.

YPSILANTI, p. t., Washtenaw co., Mich., 30 ms. w. of Detroit; from W. 517 ms. Watered by Huron river and Stony creek. Pop. 3,051.

YUBA COUNTY, situated in the northeastern part of California, and traversed by Feather, Yuba, and American rivers. and Honcut and Bear creeks. Area, —— square miles. Seat of justice, Marysville. Pop. in 1852, 22,005.

YUBA CITY, p. o., Yuba co., Cal.

Z.

ZABRISKI, p. o., De Witt co., Ill.

ZACHARY, p. o., Marshall co., Ala.

ZACKVILLE, p. o., Wirt co., Va.

ZANE, p. t., Logan co., O. Pop. 1,090.

ZANESVILLE, p. v., Logan co., O., 64 ms. N. w. of Columbus; from W. 451 ms. Watered by head waters of Mad river.

ZANESVILLE, c. h., p. t., seat of justice of Muskingum co., O., situated on the east side of Muskingum river, opposite the mouth of the Licking, and one of the most enterprising and flourishing towns in the interior of the state. It is 54 miles east of Columbus, and 359 miles from Washington. The river is navigable to the falls near the town; and a canal, passing round this obstruction, enables boats to ascend to Coshocton, about 25 miles above, and furnishes a great water-power. A number of dams and locks in the vicinity, serve to keep in operation the various manufactories of woollen, cotton, and other fabrics, which contribute to Zanesville its prosperity and importance, as well as to afford means of communication with the Ohio canal and surrounding points. On the west bank of the Muskingum, are Putnam and West Zanesville, two flourishing villages, intimately connected with the town, not only by two bridges, but also by reciprocal interests and operations. Population in 1830, 3,216; in 1840. 4,766 or including the adjacent places, 7,000; in 1850, 7,929.

ZANESVILLE, p. v., Montgomery co., Ill., 38 ms. s. of Springfield; from W. 784 ms.

ZAVALLA, p. o., Jasper co., Tex.

ZEBULON, c. h., p. v., seat of justice of Pike co., Ga., 77 ms. w. of Milledgeville; from W. 696 ms.

ZEBULON, c. h., v., seat of justice of Pike co., Ark., 136 ms. s. w. of Little Rock; from W. 1,201 ms. Watered by a tributary of Washita river.

ZELIENOPLE, p. v., Conequenessing township, Butler co., Pa., 224 ms. w. of Harrisburgh; from W 252 ms. Watered by Conequenessing creek. Poop. 385.

ZENAS, p. v., Jennings co., Ind., 62 ms. s. of Indianapolis; from W. 565 ms.

ZENO, p. o., York district, S. C.

ZILWAUKIE, p. o., Saganaw co., Mich.

ZIMMERMAN. p. o., Greene co., O.

ZION. p. v., Iredell co., N. C., 155 ms. w. of Raleigh · from W. 366 ms.

ZION, p. o., Centre co., Pa.

ZION, p. o., Cecil co., Md.

ZION. p. o., Grant co., Ind.

ZION HILL, p. o., Hamilton co., Tenn.

ZION HILL, p. o., Amitie co., Miss.

ZION SEMINARY, p. v., Covington co., Miss.

ZIONSVILLE, p. o., Lehigh co., Pa.

ZOAR. p. o., Edentownship, Erie co., N. Y., 296 ms. w. of Albany; from W. 353 ms.

ZOAR, p. v., Lawrence township, Tuscarawas co., O., 120 ms. N. E. of Columbus; from W. 319 ms. Watered by Tuscarawas river.

ZOAR BRIDGE, p. v., New Haven co., Ct., 51 ms. s. E of Hartford; from W. 293 ms.

ZOLLERSVILLE, p. o., Washington co., Pa.

THE END.